Bethany's
Bible

My Very First
Holy Bible

ENGLISH STANDARD VERSION®

CONCORDIA PUBLISHING HOUSE • SAINT LOUIS

ESV Text Edition: 2007

Also published by Crossway as *The Seek and Find Bible.*

Shenzhen, China/055760/410405
Published by Concordia Publishing House
3558 S. Jefferson Avenue
St. Louis, Missouri 63118
www.cph.org

RRD 19 18 17 16 15
13 12 11 10 9 8 7 6 5 4 3 2

Contents

About My Very First Holy Bible

"Seek, and you will find"
Luke 11:9

A "Real" Bible for Kids

Even young children want to have a "real" Bible to call their own—the whole Bible, with kid-friendly features, that they can grow into over the years. The Bible you are holding is just that kind of Bible. Colorful and complete, it will help young readers explore, understand, and love God's Word—even at a very young age.

The ESV Bible

The ESV® Bible is a great choice for every age and stage of life—for personal reading by children and adults, for family devotions, for memorizing, and for teaching, preaching, and worship. A "word-for-word" Bible translation, the ESV Bible was created by more than 100 of the world's leading Bible scholars and teachers. The ESV Bible is trusted worldwide, and has become the fastest growing English Bible translation today.

130 Beautiful Paintings

With more than 130 beautiful, full-color paintings, *My Very First Holy Bible* is truly a remarkable Bible edition. Each painting illustrates an important story or event in the Bible, and is located right along with the text of the Bible. Pre-reading children will love to study the paintings on their own, while the story is being read to them. Early readers will continue to enjoy the colorful pictures, even as they are able to read the Bible text more and more by themselves. Children of all ages will love and appreciate these beautiful, realistic works of art.

Bible Stories

Each painting is also paired with a clear and simple retelling of that Bible story in child-friendly language. These stories summarize the longer Bible passages that surround them, and were carefully crafted for helping children understand the Bible. Rather than being a substitute for reading the Bible itself, these simplified stories are placed right within the Bible text where the stories occur, so that children will learn to love and discover the Bible text itself.

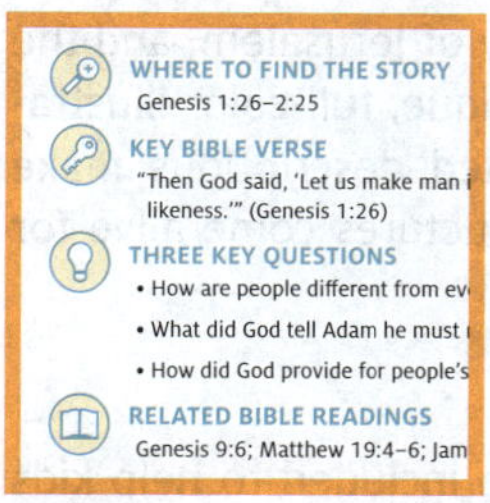

Seek and Find

At the end of each Bible story you'll find a "Seek and Find" section, to help children understand and apply Bible truths. This includes:

- **Where to Find the Story** makes it easy to locate where the story appears in the Bible text, so children may explore the full passage.
- **Key Bible Verse** identifies one important verse related to the main theme of the story, showing connections throughout the Bible.
- **Three Key Questions** encourage conversation and thinking about the story for children and adults, as well as understanding and personal application of its truths.
- **Related Bible Readings** lead readers to other parts of the Bible that are connected to the story by major themes, events, or characters.
- **Icons** for each of the features above make it easy and fun to locate and connect the Bible passages, stories, key verses, and paintings.

Book Introductions

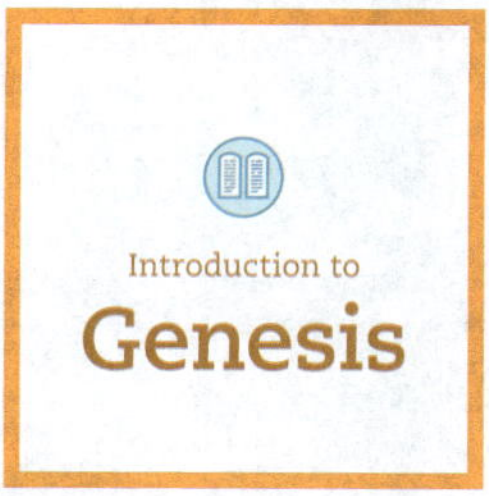

At the beginning of each book of the Bible is a brief, one-page introduction, with key information about each book including: author, date, key people, purpose, central themes, a timeline, and memory verses. Although some information will be too "old" for young children, this information will be a great resource for parents and for kids to discover for themselves as they grow older.

Character Profiles

More than 50 key people of the Bible are highlighted with a brief description and a full-color illustration—from Adam and Eve to Timothy—providing children with a quick understanding of who they are, what they did, and how they fit into the storyline of the Bible.

Bible Places, Structures, and Objects

More than 20 beautiful, full-color illustrations are also featured, including detailed drawings of the Tabernacle, Solomon's Temple, the Ark of the Covenant, the City of Jerusalem, and the Tomb of Jesus. These unique, full-color illustrations and short, fact-filled descriptions make these Bible sites and structures come alive for young readers.

Maps

Eight full-color maps are included to help kids locate Bible places as they read about them, and to trace the travels of Jesus, Paul, and other key people of the Bible.

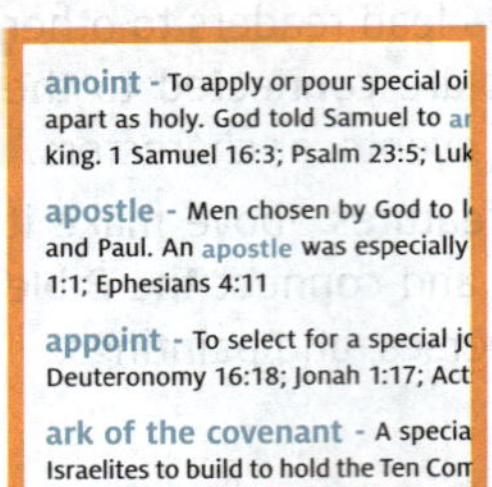

Dictionary/Concordance

A simple dictionary and concordance allows children to find out the meanings of important Biblical terms, and to find places throughout the Bible where those words are used.

A Treasure for Life

My Very First Holy Bible provides a great way for children and parents to explore the riches of God's Word together—and to treasure the Bible for all of life.

The Old Testament

Introduction to

Genesis

Author
Moses the prophet

Date
About 1446–1406 B.C.

Key People
Adam; Eve; Cain; Abel; Seth; Noah; Abraham; Sarah; Lot; Isaac; Rebekah; Jacob; Esau; Joseph

Purpose
The purpose of the book of Genesis is to show the beginnings of creation, of sin and death, of God's promise of a Savior to Israel and to all the nations.

Central Themes
Death and a curse come from sin and disobedience to God; God promises a Savior from sin; God chooses a people to be His people and makes a covenant with them; God faithfully preserves His people and works toward accomplishing His promise of a Savior.

Memory Verses
The image of God (Genesis 1:26–27); the trees of Eden (Genesis 2:16–17); the promised Deliverer (Genesis 3:15); man's heart is evil (Genesis 6:5; 8:21); all families blessed through Abraham (Genesis 12:3; 18:18; 26:4); righteousness through faith (Genesis 15:6); scepter of Judah (Genesis 49:10–12)

Introduction

The word "Genesis" means "beginning." The book of Genesis shows us the way many things began. The world around us began when God created it out of nothing, by His powerful word (Genesis 1–2). Marriage and families began when God created Eve from Adam's rib and brought her to him (Genesis 2:18–25). Sin began when Adam and Eve listened to the devil and ate fruit that God had told them not to eat. All the difficult and sad things in life, even death, began because of sin (Genesis 3). But God's wonderful promise of a Savior had its beginning in the Garden of Eden, when God promised that a child from the woman would crush the serpent's head (Genesis 3:15). God also promised Abraham that a great nation would come from him and be given its own land, and that all the families of the earth would be blessed through him (Genesis 12:1–3). This was the beginning of God's covenant with Abraham, and the beginning of God's covenant people, Israel. One thing we don't find in Genesis is how God began. That's because God has always been, and always will be. As the first words of the book say, "In the beginning, God."

?	About 2091 B.C.	1876 B.C.	1446 B.C.
Creation	Call of Abraham	Israel goes to Egypt	Exodus from Egypt

Genesis

The Creation of the World

1 In the beginning, God created
the heavens and the earth. **2** The
5 earth was without form and void,
and darkness was over the face of
the deep. And the Spirit of God was
5 hovering over the face of the waters.

3 And God said, "Let there be light," and there was light. **4** And God saw that the light was good. And God separated the light from the darkness. **5** God called the light Day, and the darkness he called Night. And there was evening and there was morning, the first day.

6 And God said, "Let there be an expanse[1] in the midst of the waters, and let it separate the waters from the waters." **7** And God made[2] the expanse and separated the waters that were under the expanse from the waters that were above the expanse. And it was so. **8** And God called the expanse Heaven.[3] And there was evening and there was morning, the second day.

9 And God said, "Let the waters under the heavens be gathered together into one place, and let the dry land appear." And it was so. **10** God called the dry land Earth,[4] and the waters that were gathered together he called Seas. And God saw that it was good.

11 And God said, "Let the earth sprout vegetation, plants[5] yielding seed, and fruit trees bearing fruit in which is their seed, each according to its kind, on the earth." And it was so. **12** The earth brought forth vegetation, plants yielding seed according to their own kinds, and trees bearing fruit in which is their seed, each according to its kind. And God saw that it was good. **13** And there was evening and there was morning, the third day.

14 And God said, "Let there be lights in the expanse of the heavens to separate the day from the night. And let them be for signs and for seasons,[6] and for days and years, **15** and let them be lights in the expanse of the heavens to give light upon the earth." And it was so. **16** And God made the two great lights—the greater light to rule the day and the lesser light to rule the night—and the stars. **17** And God set them in the expanse of the heavens to give light on the earth, **18** to rule over the day and over the night, and to separate the light from the darkness. And God saw that it was good. **19** And there was evening and there was morning, the fourth day.

20 And God said, "Let the waters swarm with swarms of living creatures, and let birds[7] fly above the earth across the expanse of the heavens." **21** So God created the great sea creatures and every living creature that moves, with which the waters swarm, according to their kinds, and every winged bird according to its kind. And God saw that it was good. **22** And God blessed them, saying, "Be fruitful and multiply and fill the waters in the seas, and let birds multiply on the earth." **23** And there was evening and there was morning, the fifth day.

24 And God said, "Let the earth bring forth living creatures according to their kinds—livestock and creeping things and beasts of the earth according to their kinds." And it was so. **25** And God made the beasts of the earth according to their kinds and the livestock according to their kinds, and everything that creeps on the ground according to its kind. And God saw that it was good.

[1] Or *a canopy*; also verses 7, 8, 14, 15, 17, 20 [2] Or *fashioned*; also verse 16 [3] Or *Sky*; also verses 9, 14, 15, 17, 20, 26, 28, 30; 2:1 [4] Or *Land*; also verses 11, 12, 22, 24, 25, 26, 28, 30; 2:1 [5] Or *small plants*; also verses 12, 29 [6] Or *appointed times* [7] Or *flying things*; see Leviticus 11:19-20

[26]Then God said, "Let us make
man[1] in our image, after our like-
9 ness. And let them have dominion
over the fish of the sea and over the
birds of the heavens and over the
9 livestock and over all the earth and
over every creeping thing that creeps on
the earth."

27 So God created man in his own
image,
in the image of God he created him;
male and female he created them.

[28]And God blessed them. And God said to them, "Be fruitful and multiply and fill the earth and subdue it and have dominion over the fish of the sea and over the birds of the heavens and over every living thing that moves on the earth." [29]And God said, "Behold, I have given you every plant yielding seed that is on the face of all the earth, and every tree with seed in its fruit. You shall have them for food. [30]And to every beast of the earth and to every bird of the heavens and to everything that creeps on the earth, everything that has the breath of life, I have given every green plant for food." And it was so. [31]And God saw everything that he had made, and behold, it was very good. And there was evening and there was morning, the sixth day.

The Seventh Day, God Rests

2 Thus the heavens and the earth were finished, and all the host of them. [2]And on the seventh day God finished his work that he had done, and he rested on the seventh day from all his work that he had done. [3]So God blessed the seventh day and made it holy, because on it God rested from all his work that he had done in creation.

The Creation of Man and Woman

4 These are the generations
of the heavens and the earth when
they were created,
in the day that the LORD God made
the earth and the heavens.

[5]When no bush of the field[2] was yet in the land[3] and no small plant of the field had yet sprung up—for the LORD God had not caused it to rain on the land, and there was no man to work the ground, [6]and a mist[4] was going up from the land and was watering the whole face of the ground— [7]then the LORD God formed the man of dust from the ground and breathed into his nostrils the breath of life, and the man became a living creature. [8]And the LORD God planted a garden in Eden, in the east,

CHARACTER PROFILE

ADAM AND EVE

Adam and Eve were the first two people. God created Adam and Eve in His own image. God told them to care for the garden, but not to eat from the tree of the knowledge of good and evil. When the serpent tempted Eve, she ate fruit from that tree, and gave some to Adam, who ate it also. This was how sin and death came into the world. But Adam and Eve also received good news: the first promise of the gospel (see Genesis 3:15).

[1] The Hebrew word for *man* (*adam*) is the generic term for mankind and becomes the proper name *Adam* [2] Or *open country* [3] Or *earth*; also verse 6 [4] Or *spring*

God Creates the World

Long, long ago there was no world. There were no birds and bees, no fields and flowers, no lakes and rivers, no sun, no moon, and no stars. There were no people either. There was only God.

Then God created the heavens and the earth in six days. He made all there is out of nothing with the power of His word. All He had to do was say the words and the entire earth and all the animals were created by God.

On the first day, God said, "Let there be light"—and there it was, brightly shining wherever God wanted the light to shine! So, the Bible says, "God separated the light from the darkness. God called the light Day, and the darkness He called Night. And there was evening and there was morning, the first day."

On the second day, God spoke again. On this day He made the sky above, which separates the waters above from the waters below. "And there was evening and there was morning, the second day."

On the third day, God said, "Let the waters under the heavens be gathered together into one place, and let the dry land appear." In this way, God made mountains and hills, valleys and plains, flatlands and islands. Here and there, all over the land, were lakes and rivers, and around it all, the great oceans.

God spoke again, and plants covered the land. Grass, flowers, bushes, and trees of every kind grew. Many of the bushes had berries, and many of the trees had fruit. God gave the plants seeds so that more plants could always grow. And God saw that what He had done was good. "And there was evening and there was morning, the third day."

On the fourth day, God spoke again and made still more. This time God spoke and at once the sky was filled with lights. He made the sun and the moon and all the stars that twinkle at night. And He made the lights "for signs and for seasons, and for days and years." God saw that His lights were good. "And there was evening and there was morning, the fourth day."

The earth was beautiful now, but God made it even better. On the fifth day, God spoke and made fish to fill the waters and birds to fly in the sky. God saw that all of His creatures were good. He blessed them and told them to have babies, so that the waters and the skies would be filled with more fish and more birds. "And there was evening and there was morning, the fifth day."

Once more, on the sixth day, God spoke and created land animals. Bees flew from flower to flower. Cats and dogs played in the fields. Horses and cows walked around looking for food. Last of all, God made the first people, Adam and Eve, in His image and His likeness. He told them to rule over all the living things that He had made. "And there was evening and there was morning, the sixth day." God looked at everything that He had made, and He saw that it was very good.

God made all there is out of nothing with just the power

of His word. He only had to say, "Let it be," and everything was made. Finally, on the seventh day, God rested. God blessed the seventh day, and set it apart for a special purpose—rest.

Right now God is in heaven making a new heavenly home for everyone who has faith in God and in what He has done for them. Because of Christ's work on the cross, one day God will graciously give this new heavenly home to all His children who have faith in Christ.

SEEK and FIND

WHERE TO FIND THE STORY

Genesis 1:1–2:3

KEY BIBLE VERSE

"In the beginning, God created the heavens and the earth." (Genesis 1:1)

THREE KEY QUESTIONS

- God made everything just by speaking. What does that tell us about God?
- Every bird, animal, plant, and fish was created exactly as it needs to be to live in the place where it lives. What does that tell us about God?
- Think of all the different kinds of food that God made—fruits and vegetables and animals. What does this tell us about God's care for us?

RELATED BIBLE READINGS

Psalm 19:1–6; 104:1–35; John 1:1–3; Romans 1:19–20; Colossians 1:15–17; Hebrews 11:3

God Creates Adam and Eve

A very, very long time ago, there was no earth or sky, no trees or plants, not even one animal and no people at all. Then, by the power of God's word, God made the world and everything in it out of nothing. Finally, on the sixth day of creation, after God had finished making everything else, He made people. The Lord God made people different from all other creatures, because He made them in His own image.

The Lord made the very first man out of the dust of the ground and called him Adam. He breathed into him the breath of life, and the man became a living creature.

Before God made Adam, He planted a beautiful garden in a place called Eden. God made all kinds of trees to grow in the garden—beautiful trees, full of delicious fruit. Two very special trees grew in the garden. One was called "the tree of life," and the other was called "the tree of the knowledge of good and evil." The Lord God placed Adam in the garden and gave him the job of working in the garden and taking care of all the trees and plants. Then God told Adam that he could eat the fruit of every tree in the garden, except the fruit of "the tree of the knowledge of good and evil, for in the day that you eat of it you shall surely die."

Then the Lord said, "It is not good that the man should be alone; I will make him a helper fit for him." So God brought every animal and every bird for Adam to give each one a name, but not one of the animals was found to be a good helper for Adam.

Then the Lord caused Adam to fall into a deep sleep. While he was asleep, the Lord took out one of Adam's ribs and then He closed up the opening. From the rib that the Lord had taken from Adam the Lord God made the first woman and brought her to Adam. Adam said, "This at last is bone of my bones and flesh of my flesh." The woman became Adam's wife, and Adam called her Eve.

God, our heavenly Father, took care of all their needs. God always takes care of the needs of His own people. He took care of our greatest need when He sent His one and only Son, Jesus, to suffer and die for the sins of His people. Through Jesus, God gives His people salvation and everlasting life.

SEEK and FIND

WHERE TO FIND THE STORY

Genesis 1:26–2:25

KEY BIBLE VERSE

"Then God said, 'Let us make man in our image, after our likeness.'" (Genesis 1:26)

THREE KEY QUESTIONS

- How are people different from everything else God made?
- What did God tell Adam he must not do?
- How did God provide for people's greatest need?

RELATED BIBLE READINGS

Genesis 9:6; Matthew 19:4–6; James 3:8–10

and there he put the man whom he had formed. **9** And out of the ground the LORD God made to spring up every tree that is pleasant to the sight and good for food. The tree of life was in the midst of the garden, and the tree of the knowledge of good and evil.

10 A river flowed out of Eden to water the garden, and there it divided and became four rivers. **11** The name of the first is the Pishon. It is the one that flowed around the whole land of Havilah, where there is gold. **12** And the gold of that land is good; bdellium and onyx stone are there. **13** The name of the second river is the Gihon. It is the one that flowed around the whole land of Cush. **14** And the name of the third river is the Tigris, which flows east of Assyria. And the fourth river is the Euphrates.

15 The LORD God took the man and put him in the garden of Eden to work it and keep it. **16** And the LORD God commanded the man, saying, "You may surely eat of every tree of the garden, **17** but of the tree of the knowledge of good and evil you shall not eat, for in the day that you eat[1] of it you shall surely die."

18 Then the LORD God said, "It is not good that the man should be alone; I will make him a helper fit for[2] him." **19** Now out of the ground the LORD God had formed[3] every beast of the field and every bird of the heavens and brought them to the man to see what he would call them. And whatever the man called every living creature, that was its name. **20** The man gave names to all livestock and to the birds of the heavens and to every beast of the field. But for Adam[4] there was not found a helper fit for him. **21** So the LORD God caused a deep sleep to fall upon the man, and while he slept took one of his ribs and closed up its place with flesh. **22** And the rib that the LORD God had taken from the man he made[5] into a woman and brought her to the man. **23** Then the man said,

"This at last is bone of my bones
  and flesh of my flesh;
she shall be called Woman,
  because she was taken out of
    Man."[6]

24 Therefore a man shall leave his father and his mother and hold fast to his wife, and they shall become one flesh. **25** And the man and his wife were both naked and were not ashamed.

The Fall

13

3 Now the serpent was more crafty than any other beast of the field that the LORD God had made.

He said to the woman, "Did God actually say, 'You[7] shall not eat of any tree in the garden'?" **2** And the woman said to the serpent, "We may eat of the fruit of the trees in the garden, **3** but God said, 'You shall not eat of the fruit of the tree that is in the midst of the garden, neither shall you touch it, lest you die.'" **4** But the serpent said to the woman, "You will not surely die. **5** For God knows that when you eat of it your eyes will be opened, and you will be like God, knowing good and evil." **6** So when the woman saw that the tree was good for food, and that it was a delight to the eyes, and that the tree was to be desired to make one wise,[8] she took of its fruit and ate, and she also gave some to her husband who was with her, and he ate. **7** Then the eyes of both were opened, and they knew that they were naked. And they sewed fig leaves together and made themselves loincloths.

8 And they heard the sound of the LORD God walking in the garden in the cool[9] of the day, and the man and his wife hid themselves from the presence of the LORD God among the trees of the garden. **9** But the LORD God called to the man and said to him, "Where are you?"[10] **10** And he said, "I heard the sound of you in the

[1] Or *when you eat* [2] Or *corresponding to*; also verse 20 [3] Or *And out of the ground the LORD God formed* [4] Or *the man* [5] Hebrew *built* [6] The Hebrew words for *woman* (*ishshah*) and *man* (*ish*) sound alike [7] In Hebrew *you* is plural in verses 1-5 [8] Or *to give insight* [9] Hebrew *wind* [10] In Hebrew *you* is singular in verses 9 and 11

Sin Enters the World

God had told Adam and Eve that they must not eat the fruit from the tree of the knowledge of good and evil, which was in the middle of the garden. But one day a serpent came into the garden and said to Eve, "Did God actually say, 'You shall not eat of any tree in the garden'?" This serpent was Satan, the enemy of God.

Eve told the serpent that they could eat fruit from any tree except the one in the middle of the garden. If they ate that fruit, God had said they would die. But the serpent lied to Eve: "You will not surely die," he said. "For God knows that when you eat of it your eyes will be opened, and you will be like God."

Eve listened to Satan's lie and was tempted. She took some fruit and ate it. Then she gave some to Adam, and he ate it, too.

Adam and Eve did not trust God. They did not obey Him. This was the first sin.

Adam and Eve knew right away that they had done wrong, and they tried to hide from God. God came into the garden and called out to Adam, "Where are you?" After Adam and Eve blamed others for their sin, God told them what would happen because of their sin. The snake would always crawl around on its belly all its days. Eve would have pain in childbirth. Adam would have trouble growing food to eat, because from now on working the ground would be hard. And Adam and Eve would not live forever—they would grow old and die.

But God also gave Adam and Eve a wonderful promise. He promised that a child would be born someday who would grow up to bruise the serpent's head, even though the serpent would bruise this man's heel. This was the first promise that God would send a Savior to save us from our sin.

Then God sent Adam and Eve out of the garden. They could never go back to the beautiful place that God had made for them, and they would have to find a new home.

Adam and Eve were the very first people to sin. They brought sin into the world. But God still loved them very much, and so He gave them the promise that one day a Savior would come. Many years later, God sent His Son, Jesus, to earth. Satan came to Jesus too, and tempted Him to disobey God, but Jesus did not listen to Satan. Jesus lived His whole life without sin. Then He suffered and died on the cross for the sins of the world and rose from the dead to give us eternal life.

SEEK and FIND

WHERE TO FIND THE STORY

Genesis 3

KEY BIBLE VERSE

"The Lord God said to the serpent . . . 'I will put enmity between you and the woman, and between your offspring and her offspring; he shall bruise your head, and you shall *bruise his heel.*'" (Genesis 3:14, 15)

THREE KEY QUESTIONS

- What was the first sin?
- Was there a time today when you did not trust and obey God?
- What did God promise Adam and Eve?

RELATED BIBLE READINGS

Matthew 1:20–21; 4:1–11; Romans 5:12; 1 Peter 5:8–9

garden, and I was afraid, because I was
naked, and I hid myself." 11 He said, "Who
told you that you were naked? Have you
eaten of the tree of which I commanded
you not to eat?" 12 The man said, "The
woman whom you gave to be with me,
she gave me fruit of the tree, and I ate."
13 Then the LORD God said to the woman,
"What is this that you have done?" The
woman said, "The serpent deceived me,
and I ate."

14 The LORD God said to the serpent,

13
"Because you have done this,
cursed are you above all
livestock
and above all beasts of the field;
on your belly you shall go,
and dust you shall eat
all the days of your life.
15 I will put enmity between you and
the woman,
and between your offspring[1] and
her offspring;
he shall bruise your head,
and you shall bruise his heel."

16 To the woman he said,

"I will surely multiply your pain in
childbearing;
in pain you shall bring forth
children.
Your desire shall be for[2] your
husband,
and he shall rule over you."

17 And to Adam he said,

"Because you have listened to the
voice of your wife
and have eaten of the tree
of which I commanded you,
'You shall not eat of it,'
cursed is the ground because of you;
in pain you shall eat of it all the
days of your life;
18 thorns and thistles it shall bring
forth for you;
and you shall eat the plants of the
field.
19 By the sweat of your face
you shall eat bread,
till you return to the ground,
for out of it you were taken;
for you are dust,
and to dust you shall return."

20 The man called his wife's name Eve,
because she was the mother of all liv-
ing.[3] 21 And the LORD God made for Adam
and for his wife garments of skins and
clothed them.
22 Then the LORD God said, "Behold, the
man has become like one of us in know-
ing good and evil. Now, lest he reach out

[1] Hebrew *seed*; so throughout Genesis [2] Or *against* [3] *Eve* sounds like the Hebrew for *life-giver* and resembles the word for *living*

his hand and take also of the tree of life and eat, and live forever—" 23 therefore the LORD God sent him out from the garden of Eden to work the ground from which he was taken. 24 He drove out the man, and at the east of the garden of Eden he placed the cherubim and a flaming sword that turned every way to guard the way to the tree of life.

Cain and Abel

19 **4** Now Adam knew Eve his wife, and she conceived and bore Cain, saying, "I have gotten[1] a man with the help of the LORD." 2 And again, she bore his brother Abel. Now Abel was a keeper of sheep, and Cain a worker of the ground. 3 In the course of time Cain brought to the LORD an offering of the fruit of the ground, 4 and Abel also brought of the firstborn of his flock and of their fat portions. And the LORD had regard for Abel and his offering, 5 but for Cain and his offering he had no regard. So Cain was very angry, and his face fell. 6 The LORD said to Cain, "Why are you angry, and why has your face fallen? 7 If you do well, will you not be accepted?[2] And if you do not do well, sin is crouching at the door. Its desire is for[3] you, but you must rule over it."

8 Cain spoke to Abel his brother.[4] And when they were in the field, Cain rose up against his brother Abel and killed him. 9 Then the LORD said to Cain, "Where is Abel your brother?" He said, "I do not know; am I my brother's keeper?" 10 And the LORD said, "What have you done? The voice of your brother's blood is crying to me from the ground. 11 And now you are cursed from the ground, which has opened its mouth to receive your brother's blood from your hand. 12 When you work the ground, it shall no longer yield to you its strength. You shall be a fugitive and a wanderer on the earth." 13 Cain said to the LORD, "My punishment is greater than I can bear.[5] 14 Behold, you have driven me today away from the ground, and from your face I shall be hidden. I shall be a fugitive and a wanderer on the earth, and whoever finds me will kill me." 15 Then the LORD said to him, "Not so! If anyone kills Cain, vengeance shall be taken on him sevenfold." And the LORD put a mark on Cain, lest any who found him should attack him. 16 Then Cain went away from the presence of the LORD and settled in the land of Nod,[6] east of Eden.

17 Cain knew his wife, and she conceived and bore Enoch. When he built a city, he called the name of the city after the name of his son, Enoch. 18 To Enoch was born Irad, and Irad fathered Mehujael, and Mehujael fathered Methushael, and

CHARACTER PROFILE

CAIN AND ABEL

Cain and Abel were the first two children. Cain grew up to be a farmer. Abel raised sheep. Cain brought God an offering of things he had grown, but God didn't accept it. Abel brought an offering from his flock, and God accepted it. The difference was that Abel offered his sacrifice with faith in God. Cain became angry and killed his brother Abel.

[1] *Cain* sounds like the Hebrew for *gotten* [2] Hebrew *will there not be a lifting up* [of your face]? [3] Or *against* [4] Hebrew; Samaritan, Septuagint, Syriac, Vulgate add *Let us go out to the field* [5] Or *My guilt is too great to bear* [6] *Nod* means *wandering*

Methushael fathered Lamech. 19 And
Lamech took two wives. The name of the
one was Adah, and the name of the other
Zillah. 20 Adah bore Jabal; he was the father
of those who dwell in tents and have live-
stock. 21 His brother's name was Jubal; he
was the father of all those who play the
lyre and pipe. 22 Zillah also bore Tubal-
cain; he was the forger of all instruments
of bronze and iron. The sister of Tubal-
cain was Naamah.

23 Lamech said to his wives:

"Adah and Zillah, hear my voice;
you wives of Lamech, listen to
what I say:
I have killed a man for wounding me,
a young man for striking me.
24 If Cain's revenge is sevenfold,
then Lamech's is
seventy-sevenfold."

25 And Adam knew his wife again, and
she bore a son and called his name Seth,
for she said, "God has appointed[1] for me
another offspring instead of Abel, for Cain
killed him." 26 To Seth also a son was born,
and he called his name Enosh. At that
time people began to call upon the name
of the LORD.

Adam's Descendants to Noah

5 This is the book of the generations
of Adam. When God created man, he
made him in the likeness of God. 2 Male
and female he created them, and he
blessed them and named them Man[2] when
they were created. 3 When Adam had lived
130 years, he fathered a son in his own like-
ness, after his image, and named him Seth.
4 The days of Adam after he fathered Seth
were 800 years; and he had other sons and
daughters. 5 Thus all the days that Adam
lived were 930 years, and he died.

6 When Seth had lived 105 years, he
fathered Enosh. 7 Seth lived after he
fathered Enosh 807 years and had other
sons and daughters. 8 Thus all the days of
Seth were 912 years, and he died.

9 When Enosh had lived 90 years, he
fathered Kenan. 10 Enosh lived after he
fathered Kenan 815 years and had other
sons and daughters. 11 Thus all the days of
Enosh were 905 years, and he died.

12 When Kenan had lived 70 years, he
fathered Mahalalel. 13 Kenan lived after
he fathered Mahalalel 840 years and had
other sons and daughters. 14 Thus all the
days of Kenan were 910 years, and he died.

15 When Mahalalel had lived 65 years,
he fathered Jared. 16 Mahalalel lived after
he fathered Jared 830 years and had other
sons and daughters. 17 Thus all the days
of Mahalalel were 895 years, and he died.

18 When Jared had lived 162 years he
fathered Enoch. 19 Jared lived after he
fathered Enoch 800 years and had other
sons and daughters. 20 Thus all the days of
Jared were 962 years, and he died.

21 When Enoch had lived 65 years, he
fathered Methuselah. 22 Enoch walked
with God[3] after he fathered Methuselah
300 years and had other sons and daugh-
ters. 23 Thus all the days of Enoch were 365
years. 24 Enoch walked with God, and he
was not,[4] for God took him.

25 When Methuselah had lived 187 years,
he fathered Lamech. 26 Methuselah lived
after he fathered Lamech 782 years and
had other sons and daughters. 27 Thus all
the days of Methuselah were 969 years,
and he died.

28 When Lamech had lived 182 years,
he fathered a son 29 and called his name
Noah, saying, "Out of the ground that the
LORD has cursed this one shall bring us
relief[5] from our work and from the pain-
ful toil of our hands." 30 Lamech lived after
he fathered Noah 595 years and had other
sons and daughters. 31 Thus all the days of
Lamech were 777 years, and he died.

32 After Noah was 500 years old, Noah
fathered Shem, Ham, and Japheth.

[1] *Seth* sounds like the Hebrew for *he appointed* [2] Hebrew *adam* [3] Septuagint *pleased God* [4] Septuagint *was not found* [5] *Noah* sounds like the Hebrew for *rest*

Cain and Abel

Adam and Eve were the first husband and wife, and they became the first mommy and daddy. They had two sons, Cain and Abel.

When Cain grew up, he became a farmer. When Abel grew up, he became a shepherd.

Cain and Abel both brought offerings to God. Cain brought an offering of things he had grown, "the fruit of the ground." Abel brought an offering of some of his sheep. The difference was that Abel offered his sacrifice with faith in God.

God was pleased with Abel's offering, but He was not pleased with Cain's. This made Cain very angry. The Lord warned Cain not to sin. But Cain didn't listen to God.

One day, when the two brothers were out in the field together, Cain killed his brother Abel.

God came to Cain again. "Where is Abel your brother?" God asked him.

Cain answered, "I do not know; am I my brother's keeper?"

But God knew what Cain had done. "The voice of your brother's blood is crying to Me from the ground," God said to Cain. God told him that he would be cursed because of what he had done. He would no longer find it easy to grow food in the ground. He would have to run away from people, and he would always have to wander throughout the earth.

"My punishment is greater than I can bear," Cain said. "Whoever finds me will kill me."

Even though Cain had sinned, God showed mercy to Cain. He put a mark on Cain to protect him. People who saw this mark would know they should not kill Cain. Cain went away from the presence of the Lord and from his mother and father, and he built a city in another place.

When God saw Abel's blood, He punished Cain for what he had done. Jesus was also killed by human hands, but He died willingly in the place of His people. When God sees the blood of Jesus, He forgives the sins of all who trust Him as their Savior.

SEEK and FIND

WHERE TO FIND THE STORY

Genesis 4:1–16

KEY BIBLE VERSE

"For this is the message that you have heard from the beginning, that we should love one another. We should not be like Cain, who was of the evil one and murdered his brother." (1 John 3:11–12)

THREE KEY QUESTIONS

- What did God do in this story that shows us He hates sin?
- What did God do in this story that shows us He is merciful?
- What should you do when you're tempted to be angry with your brother or sister?

RELATED BIBLE READINGS

Hebrews 11:4; 12:22–24; 1 John 3:11–15

Increasing Corruption on Earth

25

6 When man began to multiply on the face of the land and daughters were born to them, 2 the sons of God saw that the daughters of man were attractive. And they took as their wives any they chose. 3 Then the LORD said, "My Spirit shall not abide in[1] man forever, for he is flesh: his days shall be 120 years." 4 The Nephilim[2] were on the earth in those days, and also afterward, when the sons of God came in to the daughters of man and they bore children to them. These were the mighty men who were of old, the men of renown.

5 The LORD saw that the wickedness of man was great in the earth, and that every intention of the thoughts of his heart was only evil continually. 6 And the LORD was sorry that he had made man on the earth, and it grieved him to his heart. 7 So the LORD said, "I will blot out man whom I have created from the face of the land, man and animals and creeping things and birds of the heavens, for I am sorry that I have made them." 8 But Noah found favor in the eyes of the LORD.

25

Noah and the Flood

9 These are the generations of Noah. Noah was a righteous man, blameless in his generation. Noah walked with God. 10 And Noah had three sons, Shem, Ham, and Japheth.

11 Now the earth was corrupt in God's sight, and the earth was filled with violence. 12 And God saw the earth, and behold, it was corrupt, for all flesh had corrupted their way on the earth. 13 And God said to Noah, "I have determined to make an end of all flesh,[3] for the earth is filled with violence through them. Behold, I will destroy them with the earth. 14 Make yourself an ark of gopher wood.[4] Make rooms in the ark, and cover it inside and out with pitch. 15 This is how you are to make it: the length of the ark 300 cubits,[5] its breadth 50 cubits, and its height 30 cubits. 16 Make a roof[6] for the ark, and finish it to a cubit above, and set the door of the ark in its side. Make it with lower, second, and third decks. 17 For behold, I will bring a flood of waters upon the earth to destroy all flesh in which is the breath of life under heaven. Everything that is on the earth shall die. 18 But I will establish my covenant with you, and you shall come into the ark, you, your sons, your wife, and your sons' wives with you. 19 And of every living thing of all flesh, you shall bring two of every sort into the ark to keep them alive with you. They shall be male and female. 20 Of the

25

CHARACTER PROFILE

NOAH

Noah was a righteous man when everyone else had become more and more wicked. When God sent a flood to destroy the earth and everyone on it, He told Noah to build an ark for his family and for every kind of animal. God kept Noah and his family—and the animals—safe in the ark during the great flood. Through Noah and his family, God saved the whole human race from destruction.

25

[1] Or *My Spirit shall not contend with* [2] Or *giants* [3] Hebrew *The end of all flesh has come before me* [4] An unknown kind of tree; transliterated from Hebrew
[5] A *cubit* was about 18 inches or 45 centimeters [6] Or *skylight*

birds according to their kinds, and of the animals according to their kinds, of every creeping thing of the ground, according to its kind, two of every sort shall come in to you to keep them alive. 21 Also take with you every sort of food that is eaten, and store it up. It shall serve as food for you and for them." 22 Noah did this; he did all that God commanded him.

7 Then the LORD said to Noah, "Go into the ark, you and all your household, for I have seen that you are righteous before me in this generation. 2 Take with you seven pairs of all clean animals,[1] the male and his mate, and a pair of the animals that are not clean, the male and his mate, 3 and seven pairs[2] of the birds of the heavens also, male and female, to keep their offspring alive on the face of all the earth. 4 For in seven days I will send rain on the earth forty days and forty nights, and every living thing[3] that I have made I will blot out from the face of the ground." 5 And Noah did all that the LORD had commanded him.

6 Noah was six hundred years old when the flood of waters came upon the earth. 7 And Noah and his sons and his wife and his sons' wives with him went into the ark to escape the waters of the flood. 8 Of clean animals, and of animals that are not clean, and of birds, and of everything that creeps on the ground, 9 two and two, male and female, went into the ark with Noah, as God had commanded Noah. 10 And after seven days the waters of the flood came upon the earth.

11 In the six hundredth year of Noah's life, in the second month, on the seventeenth day of the month, on that day all the fountains of the great deep burst forth, and the windows of the heavens were opened. 12 And rain fell upon the earth forty days and forty nights. 13 On the very same day Noah and his sons, Shem and Ham and Japheth, and Noah's wife and the three wives of his sons with them entered the ark, 14 they and every beast, according to its kind, and all the livestock according to their kinds, and every creeping thing that creeps on the earth, according to its kind, and every bird, according to its kind, every winged creature. 15 They went into the ark with Noah, two and two of all flesh in which there was the breath of life. 16 And those that entered, male and female of all flesh, went in as God had commanded him. And the LORD shut him in.

17 The flood continued forty days on the earth. The waters increased and bore up the ark, and it rose high above the earth. 18 The waters prevailed and increased greatly on the earth, and the ark floated on the face of the waters. 19 And the waters prevailed so mightily on the earth that all the high mountains under the whole heaven were covered. 20 The waters prevailed above the mountains, covering them fifteen cubits[4] deep. 21 And all flesh died that moved on the earth, birds, livestock, beasts, all swarming creatures that swarm on the earth, and all mankind. 22 Everything on the dry land in whose nostrils was the breath of life died. 23 He blotted out every living thing that was on the face of the ground, man and animals and creeping things and birds of the heavens. They were blotted out from the earth. Only Noah was left, and those who were with him in the ark. 24 And the waters prevailed on the earth 150 days.

The Flood Subsides

8 But God remembered Noah and all the beasts and all the livestock that were with him in the ark. And God made a wind blow over the earth, and the waters subsided. 2 The fountains of the deep and the windows of the heavens were closed, the rain from the heavens was restrained, 3 and the waters receded from the earth continually. At the end of 150 days the waters had abated, 4 and in the seventh month, on the seventeenth day of the month, the ark

[1] Or *seven of each kind of clean animal* [2] Or *seven of each kind* [3] Hebrew *all existence*; also verse 23 [4] A *cubit* was about 18 inches or 45 centimeters

came to rest on the mountains of Ararat.
5 And the waters continued to abate until
the tenth month; in the tenth month, on
the first day of the month, the tops of the
mountains were seen.
6 At the end of forty days Noah opened
the window of the ark that he had made
7 and sent forth a raven. It went to and fro
until the waters were dried up from the
earth. 8 Then he sent forth a dove from
him, to see if the waters had subsided
from the face of the ground. 9 But the dove
found no place to set her foot, and she
returned to him to the ark, for the waters
were still on the face of the whole earth.
So he put out his hand and took her and
brought her into the ark with him. 10 He
waited another seven days, and again he
sent forth the dove out of the ark. 11 And
the dove came back to him in the evening,
and behold, in her mouth was a freshly
plucked olive leaf. So Noah knew that
the waters had subsided from the earth.
12 Then he waited another seven days and
sent forth the dove, and she did not return
to him anymore.
13 In the six hundred and first year, in
the first month, the first day of the month,
the waters were dried from off the earth.
And Noah removed the covering of the
ark and looked, and behold, the face of the
ground was dry. 14 In the second month,
on the twenty-seventh day of the month,
the earth had dried out. 15 Then God said
to Noah, 16 "Go out from the ark, you and
your wife, and your sons and your sons'
wives with you. 17 Bring out with you
every living thing that is with you of all
flesh—birds and animals and every creep-
ing thing that creeps on the earth—that
they may swarm on the earth, and be
fruitful and multiply on the earth." 18 So
Noah went out, and his sons and his wife
and his sons' wives with him. 19 Every
beast, every creeping thing, and every
bird, everything that moves on the earth,
went out by families from the ark.

God's Covenant with Noah

20 Then Noah built an altar to the LORD
and took some of every clean animal
and some of every clean bird and offered
burnt offerings on the altar. 21 And when
the LORD smelled the pleasing aroma,
the LORD said in his heart, "I will never
again curse[1] the ground because of man,
for the intention of man's heart is evil
from his youth. Neither will I ever again
strike down every living creature as I
have done. 22 While the earth remains,
seedtime and harvest, cold and heat,
summer and winter, day and night, shall
not cease."

9 And God blessed Noah and his sons
and said to them, "Be fruitful and
multiply and fill the earth. 2 The fear of
you and the dread of you shall be upon
every beast of the earth and upon every
bird of the heavens, upon everything that
creeps on the ground and all the fish of
the sea. Into your hand they are deliv-
ered. 3 Every moving thing that lives shall
be food for you. And as I gave you the
green plants, I give you everything. 4 But
you shall not eat flesh with its life, that
is, its blood. 5 And for your lifeblood I will
require a reckoning: from every beast I
will require it and from man. From his
fellow man I will require a reckoning for
the life of man.

6 "Whoever sheds the blood of man,
by man shall his blood be shed,
9 for God made man in his own
image.

7 And you,[2] be fruitful and multiply, teem
on the earth and multiply in it."
8 Then God said to Noah and to his
sons with him, 9 "Behold, I establish my
covenant with you and your offspring
after you, 10 and with every living crea-
ture that is with you, the birds, the live-
stock, and every beast of the earth with
you, as many as came out of the ark; it is
for every beast of the earth. 11 I establish

[1] Or *dishonor* [2] In Hebrew *you* is plural

Noah and the Flood

As time went on, more and more people were born, filling the earth that God had made. But because of Adam and Eve's sin, they were all born sinners. The Lord saw the great wickedness of the people and the evil in their hearts. This grieved God, and He said, "I will blot out man whom I have created from the face of the land."

But there was one man, named Noah, who found favor in the eyes of the Lord. "Noah was a righteous man," the Bible says. "Noah walked with God." God told Noah He would destroy the earth, and everyone and everything in it. He would do this because the wickedness of the people had grown so great. But because God is gracious, He wanted to save Noah and his family and make a covenant with him.

God told Noah exactly how to build an enormous boat called an "ark." He told him to put food in the ark and to fill it with two of every kind of animal and bird, and with seven of some kinds. Noah did exactly as God commanded.

When all of the animals and everyone in Noah's family were in the ark, God shut the door. Then it began to rain. It rained for forty days and nights. Every day the water outside the ark grew deeper and deeper. At last the water was so deep that it even covered the mountaintops. Everyone and everything on the earth was destroyed. But by God's grace, Noah and his family and all the animals in the ark were safe.

Once the rain stopped, it still took many days for all of the water to dry up. At last the ground was dry, and Noah and his family and all of the animals could leave the ark. Noah gave offerings to God and thanked Him for saving him and his family. God blessed Noah and his family, telling them to "be fruitful and multiply, and fill the earth."

God told Noah, "I establish My covenant with you," promising never again to send a great flood to destroy all of the people and animals, and the whole earth. Then God put a rainbow in the sky and said that it would be a sign of His covenant—a reminder of God's everlasting promise to every living creature that He would never again destroy the whole earth with a flood.

Many centuries later, God's own Son, Jesus, would be born from Noah's descendants. And because of God's great love, Jesus would suffer and die on the cross to pay for the sins of the world, so that all who trust in Jesus will be saved from God's righteous judgment and punishment for their sin.

SEEK and FIND

WHERE TO FIND THE STORY

Genesis 6:1–9:17

KEY BIBLE VERSE

"Noah found favor in the eyes of the LORD . . . 'Everything that is on the earth shall die. But I will establish my covenant with you.' " (Genesis 6:8, 17b–18a)

THREE KEY QUESTIONS

- How does God feel about sin?
- What did God provide so Noah's family and some of the animals could be protected from His judgment on the world?
- What has God provided so His people can safe from His judgment on sin?

RELATED BIBLE READINGS

Matthew 24:36–39; Hebrews 11:7; 2 Peter 2:5, 9

my covenant with you, that never again
shall all flesh be cut off by the waters of
the flood, and never again shall there be
a flood to destroy the earth." 12 And God
said, "This is the sign of the covenant that
I make between me and you and every liv-
ing creature that is with you, for all future
generations: 13 I have set my bow in the
cloud, and it shall be a sign of the cov-
enant between me and the earth. 14 When
I bring clouds over the earth and the bow
is seen in the clouds, 15 I will remember
my covenant that is between me and you
and every living creature of all flesh. And
the waters shall never again become a
flood to destroy all flesh. 16 When the bow
is in the clouds, I will see it and remem-
ber the everlasting covenant between God
and every living creature of all flesh that is
on the earth." 17 God said to Noah, "This is
the sign of the covenant that I have estab-
lished between me and all flesh that is
on the earth."

Noah's Descendants

18 The sons of Noah who went forth
from the ark were Shem, Ham, and
Japheth. (Ham was the father of Canaan.)
19 These three were the sons of Noah, and
from these the people of the whole earth
were dispersed.[1]

20 Noah began to be a man of the soil,
and he planted a vineyard.[2] 21 He drank
of the wine and became drunk and lay
uncovered in his tent. 22 And Ham, the
father of Canaan, saw the nakedness of his
father and told his two brothers outside.
23 Then Shem and Japheth took a garment,
laid it on both their shoulders, and walked
backward and covered the nakedness of
their father. Their faces were turned back-
ward, and they did not see their father's
nakedness. 24 When Noah awoke from
his wine and knew what his youngest son
had done to him, 25 he said,

"Cursed be Canaan;
 a servant of servants shall he be to
  his brothers."

26 He also said,

"Blessed be the LORD, the God of
  Shem;
 and let Canaan be his servant.
27 May God enlarge Japheth,[3]
 and let him dwell in the tents of
  Shem,
 and let Canaan be his servant."

28 After the flood Noah lived 350 years.
29 All the days of Noah were 950 years, and
he died.

[1] Or *from these the whole earth was populated* [2] Or *Noah, a man of the soil, was the first to plant a vineyard* [3] *Japheth* sounds like the Hebrew for *enlarge*

Nations Descended from Noah

10 These are the generations of the sons of Noah, Shem, Ham, and Japheth. Sons were born to them after the flood.

2 The sons of Japheth: Gomer, Magog, Madai, Javan, Tubal, Meshech, and Tiras. 3 The sons of Gomer: Ashkenaz, Riphath, and Togarmah. 4 The sons of Javan: Elishah, Tarshish, Kittim, and Dodanim. 5 From these the coastland peoples spread in their lands, each with his own language, by their clans, in their nations.

6 The sons of Ham: Cush, Egypt, Put, and Canaan. 7 The sons of Cush: Seba, Havilah, Sabtah, Raamah, and Sabteca. The sons of Raamah: Sheba and Dedan. 8 Cush fathered Nimrod; he was the first on earth to be a mighty man.[1] 9 He was a mighty hunter before the LORD. Therefore it is said, "Like Nimrod a mighty hunter before the LORD." 10 The beginning of his kingdom was Babel, Erech, Accad, and Calneh, in the land of Shinar. 11 From that land he went into Assyria and built Nineveh, Rehoboth-Ir, Calah, and 12 Resen between Nineveh and Calah; that is the great city. 13 Egypt fathered Ludim, Anamim, Lehabim, Naphtuhim, 14 Pathrusim, Casluhim (from whom[2] the Philistines came), and Caphtorim.

15 Canaan fathered Sidon his firstborn and Heth, 16 and the Jebusites, the Amorites, the Girgashites, 17 the Hivites, the Arkites, the Sinites, 18 the Arvadites, the Zemarites, and the Hamathites. Afterward the clans of the Canaanites dispersed. 19 And the territory of the Canaanites extended from Sidon in the direction of Gerar as far as Gaza, and in the direction of Sodom, Gomorrah, Admah, and Zeboiim, as far as Lasha. 20 These are the sons of Ham, by their clans, their languages, their lands, and their nations.

21 To Shem also, the father of all the children of Eber, the elder brother of Japheth, children were born. 22 The sons of Shem: Elam, Asshur, Arpachshad, Lud, and Aram. 23 The sons of Aram: Uz, Hul, Gether, and Mash. 24 Arpachshad fathered Shelah; and Shelah fathered Eber. 25 To Eber were born two sons: the name of the one was Peleg,[3] for in his days the earth was divided, and his brother's name was Joktan. 26 Joktan fathered Almodad, Sheleph, Hazarmaveth, Jerah, 27 Hadoram, Uzal, Diklah, 28 Obal, Abimael, Sheba, 29 Ophir, Havilah, and Jobab; all these were the sons of Joktan. 30 The territory in which they lived extended from Mesha in the direction of Sephar to the hill country of the east. 31 These are the sons of Shem, by their clans, their languages, their lands, and their nations.

32 These are the clans of the sons of Noah, according to their genealogies, in their nations, and from these the nations spread abroad on the earth after the flood.

The Tower of Babel

11 Now the whole earth had one language and the same words. 2 And as people migrated from the east, they found a plain in the land of Shinar and settled there. 3 And they said to one another, "Come, let us make bricks, and burn them thoroughly." And they had brick for stone, and bitumen for mortar. 4 Then they said, "Come, let us build ourselves a city and a tower with its top in the heavens, and let us make a name for ourselves, lest we be dispersed over the face of the whole earth." 5 And the LORD came down to see the city and the tower, which the children of man had built. 6 And the LORD said, "Behold, they are one people, and they have all one language, and this is only the beginning of what they will do. And nothing that they propose to do will now be impossible for them. 7 Come, let us go down and there confuse their language, so that they may not understand one another's speech." 8 So the LORD dispersed them from there over the face of all the earth, and they left off

[1] Or *he began to be a mighty man on the earth* [2] Or *from where* [3] *Peleg* means *division*

building the city. 9 Therefore its name was
called Babel, because the there the LORD con-
fused[1] the language of all the earth. And
from there the LORD dispersed them over
the face of all the earth.

Shem's Descendants

10 These are the generations of Shem.
When Shem was 100 years old, he
fathered Arpachshad two years after the
flood. 11 And Shem lived after he fathered
Arpachshad 500 years and had other sons
and daughters.
12 When Arpachshad had lived 35 years,
he fathered Shelah. 13 And Arpachshad
lived after he fathered Shelah 403 years
and had other sons and daughters.
14 When Shelah had lived 30 years, he
fathered Eber. 15 And Shelah lived after
he fathered Eber 403 years and had other
sons and daughters.
16 When Eber had lived 34 years, he
fathered Peleg. 17 And Eber lived after he
fathered Peleg 430 years and had other
sons and daughters.
18 When Peleg had lived 30 years, he
fathered Reu. 19 And Peleg lived after he
fathered Reu 209 years and had other sons
and daughters.
20 When Reu had lived 32 years, he
fathered Serug. 21 And Reu lived after he
fathered Serug 207 years and had other
sons and daughters.
22 When Serug had lived 30 years, he
fathered Nahor. 23 And Serug lived after he
fathered Nahor 200 years and had other
sons and daughters.
24 When Nahor had lived 29 years, he

[1] *Babel* sounds like the Hebrew for *confused*

Ziggurat

The Tower of Babel probably looked a lot like this tower, called a "ziggurat." A ziggurat was a large tower used to worship false gods in the ancient world of Mesopotamia. A stairway led to the top of the tower where there was a small temple. The bricks for building a ziggurat were made of straw and sun-dried mud. The Tower of Babel was probably about as tall as an eight-story building. (See Genesis 11:1–9.)

fathered Terah. 25 And Nahor lived after he fathered Terah 119 years and had other sons and daughters.

26 When Terah had lived 70 years, he fathered Abram, Nahor, and Haran.

Terah's Descendants

27 Now these are the generations of Terah. Terah fathered Abram, Nahor, and Haran; and Haran fathered Lot. 28 Haran died in the presence of his father Terah in the land of his kindred, in Ur of the Chaldeans. 29 And Abram and Nahor took wives. The name of Abram's wife was Sarai, and the name of Nahor's wife, Milcah, the daughter of Haran the father of Milcah and Iscah. 30 Now Sarai was barren; she had no child.

31 Terah took Abram his son and Lot the son of Haran, his grandson, and Sarai his daughter-in-law, his son Abram's wife, and they went forth together from Ur of the Chaldeans to go into the land of Canaan, but when they came to Haran, they settled there. 32 The days of Terah were 205 years, and Terah died in Haran.

The Call of Abram

12 Now the LORD said[1] to
Abram, "Go from your coun-
33 try and your kindred and your
father's house to the land that I will
show you. 2 And I will make of you a
1297 great nation, and I will bless you
and make your name great, so that you will
be a blessing. 3 I will bless those who bless
you, and him who dishonors you I
will curse, and in you all the fami-
1645 lies of the earth shall be blessed."[2]

4 So Abram went, as the LORD had told him, and Lot went with him. Abram was seventy-five years old when he departed from Haran. 5 And Abram took Sarai his wife, and Lot his brother's son, and all their possessions that they had gathered, and the people that they had acquired in Haran, and they set out to go to the land of Canaan. When they came to the land of Canaan, 6 Abram passed through the land to the place at Shechem, to the oak[3] of Moreh. At that time the Canaanites were in the land. 7 Then the LORD appeared to Abram and said, "To your offspring I will give this land." So he built there an altar to the LORD, who had appeared to him. 8 From there he moved to the hill country on the east of Bethel and pitched his tent, with Bethel on the west and Ai on the east. And there he built an altar to the LORD and called upon the name of the LORD. 9 And Abram journeyed on, still going toward the Negeb.

Abram and Sarai in Egypt

10 Now there was a famine in the land. So Abram went down to Egypt to sojourn

CHARACTER PROFILE

ABRAHAM

Abraham obeyed God's call to leave home and go where God would show him. God made a covenant with Abraham. He promised that a great nation would come from Abraham, that God would give that nation the Promised Land, and that all nations would be blessed through Abraham. Abraham was 100 years old when he finally had the son, Isaac, that God had promised. The Israelites came from Abraham, and Jesus was an Israelite.

33, 37, 43, 47, 53, 57

[1] Or *had said* [2] Or *by you all the families of the earth shall bless themselves* [3] Or *terebinth*

there, for the famine was severe in the land. 11 When he was about to enter Egypt, he said to Sarai his wife, "I know that you are a woman beautiful in appearance, 12 and when the Egyptians see you, they will say, 'This is his wife.' Then they will kill me, but they will let you live. 13 Say you are my sister, that it may go well with me because of you, and that my life may be spared for your sake." 14 When Abram entered Egypt, the Egyptians saw that the woman was very beautiful. 15 And when the princes of Pharaoh saw her, they praised her to Pharaoh. And the woman was taken into Pharaoh's house. 16 And for her sake he dealt well with Abram; and he had sheep, oxen, male donkeys, male servants, female servants, female donkeys, and camels.

17 But the LORD afflicted Pharaoh and his house with great plagues because of Sarai, Abram's wife. 18 So Pharaoh called Abram and said, "What is this you have done to me? Why did you not tell me that she was your wife? 19 Why did you say, 'She is my sister,' so that I took her for my wife? Now then, here is your wife; take her, and go." 20 And Pharaoh gave men orders concerning him, and they sent him away with his wife and all that he had.

Abram and Lot Separate

37

13 So Abram went up from Egypt, he and his wife and all that he had, and Lot with him, into the Negeb.

2 Now Abram was very rich in livestock, in silver, and in gold. 3 And he journeyed on from the Negeb as far as Bethel to the place where his tent had been at the beginning, between Bethel and Ai, 4 to the place where he had made an altar at the first. And there Abram called upon the name of the LORD. 5 And Lot, who went with Abram, also had flocks and herds and tents, 6 so that the land could not support both of them dwelling together; for their possessions were so great that they could not dwell together, 7 and there was strife between the herdsmen of Abram's livestock and the herdsmen of Lot's livestock. At that time the Canaanites and the Perizzites were dwelling in the land.

8 Then Abram said to Lot, "Let there be no strife between you and me, and between your herdsmen and my herdsmen, for we are kinsmen.[1] 9 Is not the whole land before you? Separate yourself from me. If you take the left hand, then I will go to the right, or if you take the right hand, then I will go to the left." 10 And Lot lifted up his eyes and saw that the Jordan Valley was well watered everywhere like the garden of the LORD, like the land of Egypt, in the direction of Zoar. (This was before the LORD destroyed Sodom and Gomorrah.) 11 So Lot chose for himself all the Jordan Valley, and Lot journeyed east. Thus they separated from each other. 12 Abram settled in the land of Canaan, while Lot settled among the cities of the valley and moved his tent as far as Sodom. 13 Now the men of Sodom were wicked, great sinners against the LORD.

14 The LORD said to Abram, after Lot had separated from him, "Lift up your eyes and look from the place where you are, northward and southward and eastward and westward, 15 for all the land that you see I will give to you and to your offspring forever. 16 I will make your offspring as the dust of the earth, so that if one can count the dust of the earth, your offspring also can be counted. 17 Arise, walk through the length and the breadth of the land, for I will give it to you." 18 So Abram moved his tent and came and settled by the oaks[2] of Mamre, which are at Hebron, and there he built an altar to the LORD.

Abram Rescues Lot

14 In the days of Amraphel king of Shinar, Arioch king of Ellasar, Chedorlaomer king of Elam, and Tidal king of Goiim, 2 these kings made war with Bera king of Sodom, Birsha king

[1] Hebrew *we are men, brothers* [2] Or *terebinths*

Gauthier

God Calls Abram

Abram lived in a far-away land called Ur. In the land of Ur, the people worshiped idols—false gods made out of metal, wood, or stone. One day, the Lord God spoke to Abram. God told him to leave his home and to travel to a land that God would show him. "I will make of you a great nation," God promised Abram, "and I will bless you and make your name great, so that you will be a blessing." God also promised him that "in you all the families of the earth shall be blessed."

So when Abram was 75 years old, he took Sarai, his wife, and Lot, his brother's son, and all their possessions to set out for the land of Canaan. After a long trip, Abram arrived in Canaan, where the Canaanite people lived. There in Canaan, at a place called Shechem, God appeared to Abram. God told Abram that He would give this land to the children, the grandchildren, and the great-grandchildren who would come from Abram. In thanks, Abram built an altar to God. Then Abram moved on to the hill country, where he set up his tent. Once again, he built an altar to God and called upon His name.

God kept His Word. It took a long time, but a great nation did come from Abram, and God did give the land of Canaan to them. Best of all, the Lord Jesus Christ, the promised Messiah, came from that nation to save us from our sin. And in Him all the families throughout the earth are being blessed.

SEEK and FIND

WHERE TO FIND THE STORY

Genesis 12:1–9

KEY BIBLE VERSE

"[God] preached the gospel beforehand to Abraham, saying, 'In you shall all the nations be blessed.'" (Galatians 3:8)

THREE KEY QUESTIONS

- Why was Abram willing to leave his comfortable home to go to a place he didn't know?
- What are the three special things that God promise to Abram?
- How are families all over the world blessed through Abram?

RELATED BIBLE READINGS

Joshua 24:2–3, 14–15; Acts 7:2–5; Galatians 3:7–9; Hebrews 11:8–10; 13:14

of Gomorrah, Shinab king of Admah,
Shemeber king of Zeboiim, and the king
of Bela (that is, Zoar). 3 And all these joined
forces in the Valley of Siddim (that is, the
Salt Sea). 4 Twelve years they had served
Chedorlaomer, but in the thirteenth year
they rebelled. 5 In the fourteenth year
Chedorlaomer and the kings who were
with him came and defeated the Rephaim
in Ashteroth-karnaim, the Zuzim in Ham,
the Emim in Shaveh-kiriathaim, 6 and the
Horites in their hill country of Seir as far
as El-paran on the border of the wilder-
ness. 7 Then they turned back and came to
En-mishpat (that is, Kadesh) and defeated
all the country of the Amalekites, and
also the Amorites who were dwelling in
Hazazon-tamar.

8 Then the king of Sodom, the king of
Gomorrah, the king of Admah, the king
of Zeboiim, and the king of Bela (that is,
Zoar) went out, and they joined battle in
the Valley of Siddim 9 with Chedorlaomer
king of Elam, Tidal king of Goiim,
Amraphel king of Shinar, and Arioch king
of Ellasar, four kings against five. 10 Now
the Valley of Siddim was full of bitu-
men pits, and as the kings of Sodom and
Gomorrah fled, some fell into them, and
the rest fled to the hill country. 11 So the
enemy took all the possessions of Sodom
and Gomorrah, and all their provisions,
and went their way. 12 They also took
Lot, the son of Abram's brother, who was
dwelling in Sodom, and his possessions,
and went their way.

13 Then one who had escaped came and
told Abram the Hebrew, who was living by
the oaks[1] of Mamre the Amorite, brother
of Eshcol and of Aner. These were allies
of Abram. 14 When Abram heard that his
kinsman had been taken captive, he led
forth his trained men, born in his house,
318 of them, and went in pursuit as far as
Dan. 15 And he divided his forces against
them by night, he and his servants, and

[1] Or *terebinths*

defeated them and pursued them to
Hobah, north of Damascus. 16 Then he
brought back all the possessions, and
also brought back his kinsman Lot with
his possessions, and the women and
the people.

Abram Blessed by Melchizedek

17 After his return from the defeat of
Chedorlaomer and the kings who were
with him, the king of Sodom went out
to meet him at the Valley of Shaveh (that
is, the King's Valley). 18 And Melchizedek
king of Salem brought out bread and wine.
(He was priest of God Most High.) 19 And
he blessed him and said,

> "Blessed be Abram by God Most High,
> Possessor[1] of heaven and earth;
> 20 and blessed be God Most High,
> who has delivered your enemies
> 37 into your hand!"

And Abram gave him a tenth of every-
thing. 21 And the king of Sodom said to
Abram, "Give me the persons, but take the
goods for yourself." 22 But Abram said to
the king of Sodom, "I have lifted my hand[2]
to the LORD, God Most High, Possessor of
heaven and earth, 23 that I would not take
a thread or a sandal strap or anything that
is yours, lest you should say, 'I have made
Abram rich.' 24 I will take nothing but what
the young men have eaten, and the share
of the men who went with me. Let Aner,
Eshcol, and Mamre take their share."

God's Covenant with Abram

15 After these things the word
of the LORD came to Abram
43 in a vision: "Fear not, Abram, I am
your shield; your reward shall be very
great." 2 But Abram said, "O Lord GOD, what
will you give me, for I continue[3] childless,
and the heir of my house is Eliezer of
Damascus?" 3 And Abram said, "Behold,
you have given me no offspring, and a
member of my household will be my heir."
4 And behold, the word of the LORD came
to him: "This man shall not be your heir;
your very own son[4] shall be your heir."
5 And he brought him outside and said,
"Look toward heaven, and number the
stars, if you are able to number them."
Then he said to him, "So shall your off-
spring be." 6 And he believed the LORD, and
he counted it to him as righteousness.

7 And he said to him, "I am the LORD who
brought you out from Ur of the Chaldeans
to give you this land to possess." 8 But he
said, "O Lord GOD, how am I to know that
I shall possess it?" 9 He said to him, "Bring
me a heifer three years old, a female goat
three years old, a ram three years old, a
turtledove, and a young pigeon." 10 And
he brought him all these, cut them in half,
and laid each half over against the other.
But he did not cut the birds in half. 11 And
when birds of prey came down on the car-
casses, Abram drove them away.

12 As the sun was going down, a deep
sleep fell on Abram. And behold, dreadful
and great darkness fell upon him. 13 Then
the LORD said to Abram, "Know for certain
that your offspring will be sojourners in a
land that is not theirs and will be servants
there, and they will be afflicted for four
hundred years. 14 But I will bring judgment
on the nation that they serve, and after-
ward they shall come out with great pos-
sessions. 15 As for yourself, you shall go to
your fathers in peace; you shall be buried in
a good old age. 16 And they shall come back
here in the fourth generation, for the iniq-
uity of the Amorites is not yet complete."

17 When the sun had gone down and
it was dark, behold, a smoking fire pot
and a flaming torch passed between
these pieces. 18 On that day the LORD
made a covenant with Abram, saying,
"To your offspring I give[5] this land, from
the river of Egypt to the great river, the
river Euphrates, 19 the land of the Kenites,
the Kenizzites, the Kadmonites, 20 the
Hittites, the Perizzites, the Rephaim, 21 the

[1] Or *Creator;* also verse 22 [2] Or *I have taken a solemn oath* [3] Or *I shall die* [4] Hebrew *what will come out of your own loins* [5] Or *have given*

Gauthier

Abram Rescues Lot

God had blessed Abram. He was rich in cattle and sheep, in silver, and in gold. His nephew Lot was also blessed with flocks and herds of animals. The land where they lived was not able to provide enough water and grass for so many animals. Soon the servants of Lot and Abram who took care of the animals began to argue and fight with each other.

Abram told Lot that they and their servants should not fight over the land. After all, Abram and Lot were family. Abram said they should separate and that Lot could have first choice of where he would like to go. “If you take the left hand,” Abram said, “then I will go to the right, or if you take the right hand, then I will go to the left.”

Lot looked and saw that the land by the Jordan River was good and well-watered. Lot chose that land, and he set up his tent near the city of Sodom. Abram lived in the land of Canaan.

God promised Abram that He would give him all the land, as far as Abram could see. God promised that so many people would come from Abram that trying to count them would be like trying to count the dust on the earth. In thanks, Abram built an altar to make offerings to the Lord.

One day, there was trouble in the place Lot had chosen,

near the city of Sodom. War broke out between the kings of five cities and the kings of four other cities. The side that Sodom's king was on lost the battle. The enemy soldiers carried away many of the possessions and people of Sodom. And they took Lot as a prisoner, along with all his people and possessions.

When Abram heard that Lot had been taken captive, he armed his 318 trained servants and pursued the enemy kings. In the night, Abram divided his forces and attacked the enemy's forces, chasing them a long way away. Abram rescued Lot, and the other prisoners with him, and took back all the things that belonged to them.

Abram would take no reward from the king of Sodom. Instead, Abram gave a gift of a tenth of all that he had to Melchizedek, a priest of God. This priest blessed Abram and praised God, saying: "Blessed be God Most High, who has delivered your enemies into your hand!"

God helped Abram rescue Lot from his enemies. God has also rescued sinners by sending His Son, Jesus, to defeat sin, death, and the devil. Through Jesus' victory on the cross, He won the forgiveness of sins and the riches of heaven for all who put their trust in Him.

SEEK and FIND

WHERE TO FIND THE STORY

Genesis 13:1–14:20

KEY BIBLE VERSE

"Blessed be God Most High, who has delivered your enemies into your hand!" (Genesis 14:20)

THREE KEY QUESTIONS

- Why did Lot choose the land near Sodom?
- Why was Abram willing to receive nothing from the king of Sodom?
- Why was Abram willing to give a tenth of all he had to the priest of God?

RELATED BIBLE READINGS

Psalm 73:25–28; Luke 16:13; Hebrews 6:19–7:19

Amorites, the Canaanites, the Girgashites
and the Jebusites."

Sarai and Hagar

16 Now Sarai, Abram's wife, had
borne him no children. She had
a female Egyptian servant whose name
was Hagar. 2 And Sarai said to Abram,
"Behold now, the LORD has prevented
me from bearing children. Go in to my
servant; it may be that I shall obtain chil-
dren[1] by her." And Abram listened to the
voice of Sarai. 3 So, after Abram had lived
ten years in the land of Canaan, Sarai,
Abram's wife, took Hagar the Egyptian,
her servant, and gave her to Abram her
husband as a wife. 4 And he went in to
Hagar, and she conceived. And when she
saw that she had conceived, she looked
with contempt on her mistress.[2] 5 And
Sarai said to Abram, "May the wrong done
to me be on you! I gave my servant to your
embrace, and when she saw that she had
conceived, she looked on me with con-
tempt. May the LORD judge between
you and me!" 6 But Abram said to Sarai,
"Behold, your servant is in your power;
do to her as you please." Then Sarai dealt
harshly with her, and she fled from her.
7 The angel of the LORD found her by
a spring of water in the wilderness, the
spring on the way to Shur. 8 And he said,
"Hagar, servant of Sarai, where have you
come from and where are you going?" She
said, "I am fleeing from my mistress Sarai."
9 The angel of the LORD said to her, "Return
to your mistress and submit to her." 10 The
angel of the LORD also said to her, "I will
surely multiply your offspring so that they
cannot be numbered for multitude." 11 And
the angel of the LORD said to her,

"Behold, you are pregnant
and shall bear a son.
You shall call his name Ishmael,[3]
because the LORD has listened to
your affliction.
12 He shall be a wild donkey of a man,
his hand against everyone
and everyone's hand against him,
and he shall dwell over against all
his kinsmen."

13 So she called the name of the LORD who
spoke to her, "You are a God of seeing,"[4]
for she said, "Truly here I have seen him
who looks after me."[5] 14 Therefore the well
was called Beer-lahai-roi;[6] it lies between
Kadesh and Bered.
15 And Hagar bore Abram a son, and

[1] Hebrew *be built up*, which sounds like the Hebrew for *children* [2] Hebrew *her mistress was dishonorable in her eyes*; similarly in verse 5 [3] *Ishmael* means *God hears* [4] Or *You are a God who sees me* [5] Hebrew *Have I really seen him here who sees me?* or *Would I have looked here for the one who sees me?* [6] *Beer-lahai-roi* means *the well of the Living One who sees me*

Abram called the name of his son, whom Hagar bore, Ishmael. **16** Abram was eighty-six years old when Hagar bore Ishmael to Abram.

Abraham and the Covenant of Circumcision

17 When Abram was ninety-nine years old the LORD
43 appeared to Abram and said to him,
"I am God Almighty;[1] walk before me, and be blameless, **2** that I may make my covenant between me and you, and may multiply you greatly." **3** Then Abram fell on his face. And God said to him, **4** "Behold, my covenant is with you, and you shall be the father of a multitude of nations. **5** No longer shall your name be called Abram,[2] but your name shall be Abraham,[3] for I have made you the father of a multitude of nations. **6** I will make you exceedingly fruitful, and I will make you into nations, and kings shall come from you. **7** And I will
establish my covenant between me
and you and your offspring after
43 you throughout their generations
for an everlasting covenant, to be God to you and to your offspring after you. **8** And I will give to you and to your offspring after you the land of your sojournings, all the land of Canaan, for an everlasting possession, and I will be their God."

9 And God said to Abraham, "As for you, you shall keep my covenant, you and your offspring after you throughout their generations. **10** This is my covenant, which you shall keep, between me and you and your offspring after you: Every male among you shall be circumcised. **11** You shall be circumcised in the flesh of your foreskins, and it shall be a sign of the covenant between me and you. **12** He who is eight days old among you shall be circumcised. Every male throughout your generations, whether born in your house or bought with your money from any foreigner who is not of your offspring, **13** both he who is born in your house and he who is bought with your money, shall surely be circumcised. So shall my covenant be in your flesh an everlasting covenant. **14** Any uncircumcised male who is not circumcised in the flesh of his foreskin shall be cut off from his people; he has broken my covenant."

Isaac's Birth Promised

15 And God said to Abraham, "As for Sarai your wife, you shall not call her name Sarai, but Sarah[4] shall be her name. **16** I will bless her, and moreover, I will give[5] you a son by her. I will bless her, and she shall become nations; kings of peoples shall come from her." **17** Then Abraham fell on his face and laughed and said to himself, "Shall a child be born to a man who is a hundred years old? Shall Sarah, who is ninety years old, bear a child?" **18** And Abraham said to God, "Oh that Ishmael might live before you!" **19** God said, "No, but Sarah your wife shall bear you a son, and you shall call his name Isaac.[6] I will establish my covenant with him as an everlasting covenant for his offspring after him. **20** As for Ishmael, I have heard you; behold, I have blessed him and will make him fruitful and multiply him greatly. He shall father twelve princes, and I will make him into a great nation. **21** But I will establish my covenant with Isaac, whom Sarah shall bear to you at this time next year."

22 When he had finished talking with him, God went up from Abraham. **23** Then Abraham took Ishmael his son and all those born in his house or bought with his money, every male among the men of Abraham's house, and he circumcised the flesh of their foreskins that very day, as God had said to him. **24** Abraham was ninety-nine years old when he was circumcised in the flesh of his foreskin. **25** And Ishmael his son was thirteen years old when he was circumcised in the flesh of his foreskin. **26** That very day Abraham and his son Ishmael were circumcised. **27** And all the men of his house, those born in the

[1] Hebrew *El Shaddai* [2] *Abram* means *exalted father* [3] *Abraham* means *father of a multitude* [4] *Sarai* and *Sarah* mean *princess* [5] Hebrew *have given* [6] *Isaac* means *he laughs*

house and those bought with money from a foreigner, were circumcised with him.

18 And the LORD appeared to
him by the oaks[1] of Mamre,
47 as he sat at the door of his tent in
the heat of the day. 2 He lifted up his eyes and looked, and behold, three men were standing in front of him. When he saw them, he ran from the tent door to meet them and bowed himself to the earth 3 and said, "O Lord,[2] if I have found favor in your sight, do not pass by your servant. 4 Let a little water be brought, and wash your feet, and rest yourselves under the tree, 5 while I bring a morsel of bread, that you may refresh yourselves, and after that you may pass on—since you have come to your servant." So they said, "Do as you have said." 6 And Abraham went quickly into the tent to Sarah and said, "Quick! Three seahs[3] of fine flour! Knead it, and make cakes." 7 And Abraham ran to the herd and took a calf, tender and good, and gave it to a young man, who prepared it quickly. 8 Then he took curds and milk and the calf that he had prepared, and set it before them. And he stood by them under the tree while they ate.

9 They said to him, "Where is Sarah your wife?" And he said, "She is in the tent." 10 The LORD said, "I will surely return to you about this time next year, and Sarah your wife shall have a son." And Sarah was listening at the tent door behind him. 11 Now Abraham and Sarah were old, advanced in years. The way of women had ceased to be with Sarah. 12 So Sarah laughed to herself, saying, "After I am worn out, and my lord is old, shall I have pleasure?" 13 The LORD said to Abraham, "Why did Sarah laugh and say, 'Shall I indeed bear a child, now that I am old?'
14 Is anything too hard[4] for the
LORD? At the appointed time I will
47 return to you, about this time next
year, and Sarah shall have a son." 15 But Sarah denied it,[5] saying, "I did not laugh," for she was afraid. He said, "No, but you did laugh."

16 Then the men set out from there, and they looked down toward Sodom. And Abraham went with them to set them on their way. 17 The LORD said, "Shall I hide from Abraham what I am about to do, 18 seeing that Abraham shall surely become a great and mighty nation, and all the nations of the earth shall be blessed in him? 19 For I have chosen[6] him, that he may command his children and his household after him to keep the way of the LORD by doing righteousness and justice, so that the LORD may bring to Abraham what he has promised him." 20 Then the LORD said, "Because the outcry against Sodom and Gomorrah is great and their sin is very grave, 21 I will go down to see whether they have done altogether[7] according to the outcry that has come to me. And if not, I will know."

Abraham Intercedes for Sodom

22 So the men turned from there and went toward Sodom, but Abraham still stood before the LORD. 23 Then Abraham drew near and said, "Will you indeed sweep away the righteous with the wicked? 24 Suppose there are fifty righteous within the city. Will you then sweep away the place and not spare it for the fifty righteous who are in it? 25 Far be it from you to do such a thing, to put the righteous to death with the wicked, so that the righteous fare as the wicked! Far be that from you! Shall not the Judge of all the earth do what is just?" 26 And the LORD said, "If I find at Sodom fifty righteous in the city, I will spare the whole place for their sake."

27 Abraham answered and said, "Behold, I have undertaken to speak to the Lord, I who am but dust and ashes. 28 Suppose five of the fifty righteous are lacking. Will you destroy the whole city for lack of five?" And he said, "I will not destroy it if I find forty-five there." 29 Again he spoke to him

[1] Or *terebinths* [2] Or *My lord* [3] A *seah* was about 7 quarts or 7.3 liters [4] Or *wonderful* [5] Or *acted falsely* [6] Hebrew *known* [7] Or *they deserve destruction;* Hebrew *they have made a complete end*

God's Covenant with Abram

One day, after Abram had rescued Lot, the Lord spoke to Abram in a vision, saying, "Fear not, Abram, I am your shield; your reward shall be very great."

Abram asked God what God would give him, since Abram still had no children.

God took Abram outside and told him to count the stars. Of course, there were too many to count. God told Abram that was how many children and grandchildren and great-grandchildren would come from him. Abram believed the Lord, and the Lord "counted it to him as righteousness."

God promised Abram again that the people who would come from Abram would own this land on which Abram lived in a tent. God made a covenant with Abram that day, a promise to do all He had said He would.

Later, when Abram was 99 years old, the Lord appeared to Abram again and changed Abram's name to "Abraham." "Abraham" means "father of a multitude (or a great crowd)" and that's what Abraham would be—the father of many nations! God said, "I will establish my covenant between Me and you and your offspring after you throughout your generations for an everlasting covenant, to be God to you and to your offspring after you." God told Abraham to circumcise every male as a sign of the covenant promise between them. Those who were not circumcised would break God's special covenant.

God changed Sarai's name, too. He changed it to "Sarah" (meaning "princess") and promised that kings would come from her. Soon, Abraham and Sarah would have a son, even though Abraham was 99 years old and Sarah was 90! God told Abraham to name his son "Isaac," which means "laughter."

God kept all His promises to Abraham and Sarah. Many years later, God's promised Savior would be one of Abraham and Sarah's descendants. He would become the King of kings and the Savior of all who put their faith in Him. This Savior, Jesus, would come to suffer and die on the cross for our sins. And He would rise from the dead three days later as our shield and great reward—victorious over sin, death, and the devil.

SEEK and FIND

WHERE TO FIND THE STORY

Genesis 15; 17:1–19

KEY BIBLE VERSE

"And I will establish my covenant between me and you and your offspring after you throughout their generations for an everlasting covenant, to be God to you and to your offspring after you." (Genesis 17:7)

THREE KEY QUESTIONS

- What do we call the special kind of promise that God made with Abraham?
- What special relationship would Abraham and his children have with God?
- Who is the greatest of all Abraham's descendants and why?

RELATED BIBLE READINGS

Deuteronomy 4:31; 7:6–9; 9:5; Psalm 25:10; Luke 1:46–55, 67–79; Romans 4:1–25

and said, "Suppose forty are found there." He answered, "For the sake of forty I will not do it." 30 Then he said, "Oh let not the Lord be angry, and I will speak. Suppose thirty are found there." He answered, "I will not do it, if I find thirty there." 31 He said, "Behold, I have undertaken to speak to the Lord. Suppose twenty are found there." He answered, "For the sake of twenty I will not destroy it." 32 Then he said, "Oh let not the Lord be angry, and I will speak again but this once. Suppose ten are found there." He answered, "For the sake of ten I will not destroy it." 33 And the LORD went his way, when he had finished speaking to Abraham, and Abraham returned to his place.

God Rescues Lot

19 The two angels came to Sodom in the evening, and Lot was sitting in the gate of Sodom. When Lot saw them, he rose to meet them and bowed himself with his face to the earth 2 and said, "My lords, please turn aside to your servant's house and spend the night and wash your feet. Then you may rise up early and go on your way." They said, "No; we will spend the night in the town square." 3 But he pressed them strongly; so they turned aside to him and entered his house. And he made them a feast and baked unleavened bread, and they ate.

4 But before they lay down, the men of the city, the men of Sodom, both young and old, all the people to the last man, surrounded the house. 5 And they called to Lot, "Where are the men who came to you tonight? Bring them out to us, that we may know them." 6 Lot went out to the men at the entrance, shut the door after him, 7 and said, "I beg you, my brothers, do not act so wickedly. 8 Behold, I have two daughters who have not known any man. Let me bring them out to you, and do to them as you please. Only do nothing to these men, for they have come under the shelter of my roof." 9 But they said, "Stand back!" And they said, "This fellow came to sojourn, and he has become the judge! Now we will deal worse with you than with them." Then they pressed hard against the man Lot, and drew near to break the door down. 10 But the men reached out their hands and brought Lot into the house with them and shut the door. 11 And they struck with blindness the men who were at the entrance of the house, both small and great, so that they wore themselves out groping for the door.

12 Then the men said to Lot, "Have you anyone else here? Sons-in-law, sons, daughters, or anyone you have in the city, bring them out of the place. 13 For we are about to destroy this place, because the outcry against its people has become great before the LORD, and the LORD has sent us to destroy it." 14 So Lot went out and said to his sons-in-law, who were to marry his daughters, "Up! Get out of this place, for the LORD is about to destroy the city." But he seemed to his sons-in-law to be jesting.

15 As morning dawned, the angels urged Lot, saying, "Up! Take your wife and your two daughters who are here, lest you be

Abraham's Visitors from Heaven

One hot day, as Abraham sat at the entrance to his tent, the Lord appeared to him. Abraham looked up and saw three men standing in front of him—and one of them was the Lord and the other two were angels.

Abraham ran to meet them. He invited them to stop, rest, and eat before going on.

Sarah, Abraham's wife, made bread. Abraham and his servant prepared meat, cheese, and milk. He served the food to his guests. They sat down under a big tree and ate.

While they ate, they said to Abraham, "Where is Sarah your wife?"

"She is in the tent," answered Abraham.

The one who was the Lord said that He would come again in about a year and Sarah would have a son.

Sarah heard this, but she did not believe the Lord, because she was so old. In fact, Sarah laughed at the Lord's words.

The Lord knew that Sarah had laughed and asked, "Why did Sarah laugh?" He asked why she didn't believe the Lord's promise that she would have a child, even in her old age. Then God asked, "Is anything too hard for the LORD?"

God's promise came true. About a year later, Abraham and Sarah's son was born.

Many years later, another Son would be born from Abraham and Sarah's family. That Baby would be God's Son, who would become a human baby to save God's people from their sin. A baby with a father 100 years old is amazing. But a baby whose Father is God is even more amazing. Through that Baby, Jesus, all the families of earth would be blessed, as God had promised Abraham.

SEEK and FIND

WHERE TO FIND THE STORY

Genesis 18:1–15

KEY BIBLE VERSE

"Is anything too hard for the LORD?" (Genesis 18:14a)

THREE KEY QUESTIONS

- How was one of the three visitors very different from the other two and who was He?
- What did Sarah do when the Lord said she would have a baby?
- Can you think of some other "impossible" things that God did in the Bible?

RELATED BIBLE READINGS

Jeremiah 32:17; Luke 1:30–37; Hebrews 11:11–12

swept away in the punishment of the city." 16 But he lingered. So the men seized him and his wife and his two daughters by the hand, the LORD being merciful to him, and they brought him out and *set him* outside the city. 17 And as they brought them out, one said, "Escape for your life. Do not look back or stop anywhere in the valley. Escape to the hills, lest you be swept away." 18 And Lot said to them, "Oh, no, my lords. 19 Behold, your servant has found favor in your sight, and you have shown me great kindness in saving my life. But I cannot escape to the hills, lest the disaster overtake me and I die. 20 Behold, this city is near enough to flee to, and it is a little one. Let me escape there—is it not a little one?—and my life will be saved!" 21 He said to him, "Behold, I grant you this favor also, that I will not overthrow the city of which you have spoken. 22 Escape there quickly, for I can do nothing till you arrive there." Therefore the name of the city was called Zoar.[1]

God Destroys Sodom

23 The sun had risen on the earth when Lot came to Zoar. 24 Then the LORD rained on Sodom and Gomorrah sulfur and fire from the LORD out of heaven. 25 And he overthrew those cities, and all the valley, and all the inhabitants of the cities, and what grew on the ground. 26 But Lot's wife, behind him, looked back, and she became a pillar of salt.

27 And Abraham went early in the morning to the place where he had stood before the LORD. 28 And he looked down toward Sodom and Gomorrah and toward all the land of the valley, and he looked and, behold, the smoke of the land went up like the smoke of a furnace.

29 So it was that, when God destroyed the cities of the valley, God remembered Abraham and sent Lot out of the midst of the overthrow when he overthrew the cities in which Lot had lived.

Lot and His Daughters

30 Now Lot went up out of Zoar and lived in the hills with his two daughters, for he was afraid to live in Zoar. So he lived in a cave with his two daughters. 31 And the firstborn said to the younger, "Our father is old, and there is not a man on earth to come in to us after the manner of all the earth. 32 Come, let us make our father drink wine, and we will lie with him, that we may preserve offspring from our father." 33 So they made their father drink wine that night. And the firstborn went in and lay with her father. He did not know when she lay down or when she arose.

34 The next day, the firstborn said to the younger, "Behold, I lay last night with my father. Let us make him drink wine tonight also. Then you go in and lie with him, that we may preserve offspring from our father." 35 So they made their father drink wine that night also. And the younger arose and lay with him, and he did not know when she lay down or when she arose. 36 Thus both the daughters of Lot became pregnant by their father. 37 The firstborn bore a son and called his name Moab.[2] He is the father of the Moabites to this day. 38 The younger also bore a son and called his name Ben-ammi.[3] He is the father of the Ammonites to this day.

Abraham and Abimelech

20 From there Abraham journeyed toward the territory of the Negeb and lived between Kadesh and Shur; and he sojourned in Gerar. 2 And Abraham said of Sarah his wife, "She is my sister." And Abimelech king of Gerar sent and took Sarah. 3 But God came to Abimelech in a dream by night and said to him, "Behold, you are a dead man because of the woman whom you have taken, for she is a man's wife." 4 Now Abimelech had not approached her. So he said, "Lord, will you kill an innocent people? 5 Did he not himself say to me, 'She is my sister'? And she herself said, 'He is my brother.' In the integrity of my heart and the innocence of my hands I have done this." 6 Then God said to him in the dream, "Yes, I know that you have done this in the integrity of your heart, and it was I who kept you from sinning against me. Therefore I did not let you touch her. 7 Now then, return the man's wife, for he is a prophet, so that he will pray for you, and you shall live. But if you do not return her, know that you shall surely die, you and all who are yours."

8 So Abimelech rose early in the morning and called all his servants and told them all these things. And the men were very much afraid. 9 Then Abimelech called Abraham and said to him, "What have you done to us? And how have I sinned against you, that you have brought on me and my kingdom a great sin? You have done to me things that

[1] *Zoar* means *little* [2] *Moab* sounds like the Hebrew for *from father* [3] *Ben-ammi* means *son of my people*

ought not to be done." 10 And Abimelech
said to Abraham, "What did you see, that
you did this thing?" 11 Abraham said, "I
did it because I thought, There is no fear
of God at all in this place, and they will
kill me because of my wife. 12 Besides,
she is indeed my sister, the daughter of
my father though not the daughter of my
mother, and she became my wife. 13 And
when God caused me to wander from my
father's house, I said to her, 'This is the
kindness you must do me: at every place
to which we come, say of me, He is my
brother.'"

14 Then Abimelech took sheep and
oxen, and male servants and female ser-
vants, and gave them to Abraham, and
returned Sarah his wife to him. 15 And
Abimelech said, "Behold, my land is
before you; dwell where it pleases you."
16 To Sarah he said, "Behold, I have given
your brother a thousand pieces of sil-
ver. It is a sign of your innocence in the
eyes of all[1] who are with you, and before
everyone you are vindicated." 17 Then
Abraham prayed to God, and God healed
Abimelech, and also healed his wife and
female slaves so that they bore children.
18 For the LORD had closed all the wombs
of the house of Abimelech because of
Sarah, Abraham's wife.

The Birth of Isaac

53

21 The LORD visited Sarah as
he had said, and the LORD
did to Sarah as he had promised.
2 And Sarah conceived and bore Abraham a
son in his old age at the time of which God
had spoken to him. 3 Abraham called the
name of his son who was born to him,
whom Sarah bore him, Isaac.[2] 4 And
Abraham circumcised his son Isaac when
he was eight days old, as God had com-
manded him. 5 Abraham was a hundred
years old when his son Isaac was born to
him. 6 And Sarah said, "God has made
laughter for me; everyone who hears will
laugh over me." 7 And she said, "Who would
have said to Abraham that Sarah would
nurse children? Yet I have borne him a son
in his old age."

God Protects Hagar and Ishmael

8 And the child grew and was weaned.
And Abraham made a great feast on the
day that Isaac was weaned. 9 But Sarah
saw the son of Hagar the Egyptian, whom
she had borne to Abraham, laughing.[3]
10 So she said to Abraham, "Cast out this
slave woman with her son, for the son of
this slave woman shall not be heir with
my son Isaac." 11 And the thing was very
displeasing to Abraham on account of his
son. 12 But God said to Abraham, "Be not
displeased because of the boy and
because of your slave woman. Whatever

CHARACTER PROFILE

SARAH

Sarah was Abraham's wife. After she moved to the Promised Land with Abraham, she grew very old without having any children. But God promised Abraham and Sarah that they would have a special baby. At first Sarah laughed at God, but later she believed. Her baby, Isaac, was born when she was 90 years old.

33, 43, 47, 53

[1] Hebrew *It is a covering of eyes for all* [2] Isaac means *he laughs* [3] Possibly *laughing in mockery*

Sarah says to you, do as she tells you, for
through Isaac shall your offspring
be named. 13 And I will make a
53 nation of the son of the slave
woman also, because he is your offspring." 14 So Abraham rose early in the morning and took bread and a skin of water and gave it to Hagar, putting it on her shoulder, along with the child, and sent her away. And she departed and wandered in the wilderness of Beersheba.

15 When the water in the skin was gone, she put the child under one of the bushes. 16 Then she went and sat down opposite him a good way off, about the distance of a bowshot, for she said, "Let me not look on the death of the child." And as she sat opposite him, she lifted up her voice and wept. 17 And God heard the voice of the boy, and the angel of God called to Hagar from heaven and said to her, "What troubles you, Hagar? Fear not, for God has heard the voice of the boy where he is. 18 Up! Lift up the boy, and hold him fast with your hand, for I will make him into a great nation." 19 Then God opened her eyes, and she saw a well of water. And she went and filled the skin with water and gave the boy a drink. 20 And God was with the boy, and he grew up. He lived in the wilderness and became an expert with the bow. 21 He lived in the wilderness of Paran, and his mother took a wife for him from the land of Egypt.

A Treaty with Abimelech

22 At that time Abimelech and Phicol the commander of his army said to Abraham, "God is with you in all that you do. 23 Now therefore swear to me here by God that you will not deal falsely with me or with my descendants or with my posterity, but as I have dealt kindly with you, so you will deal with me and with the land where you have sojourned." 24 And Abraham said, "I will swear."

25 When Abraham reproved Abimelech about a well of water that Abimelech's servants had seized, 26 Abimelech said, "I do not know who has done this thing; you did not tell me, and I have not heard of it until today." 27 So Abraham took sheep and oxen and gave them to Abimelech, and the two men made a covenant. 28 Abraham set seven ewe lambs of the flock apart. 29 And Abimelech said to Abraham, "What is the meaning of these seven ewe lambs that you have set apart?" 30 He said, "These seven ewe lambs you will take from my hand, that this[1] may be a witness for me that I dug this well." 31 Therefore that place was called Beersheba,[2] because there both of them swore an oath. 32 So they made a covenant at Beersheba. Then Abimelech and Phicol the commander of his army rose up and returned to the land of the Philistines. 33 Abraham planted a tamarisk tree in Beersheba and called there on the name of the LORD, the Everlasting God. 34 And Abraham sojourned many days in the land of the Philistines.

The Sacrifice of Isaac

22 After these things God
tested Abraham and said
57 to him, "Abraham!" And he said,
"Here am I." 2 He said, "Take your son, your only son Isaac, whom you love, and go to the land of Moriah, and offer him there as a burnt offering on one of the mountains of which I shall tell you." 3 So Abraham rose early in the morning, saddled his donkey, and took two of his young men with him, and his son Isaac. And he cut the wood for the burnt offering and arose and went to the place of which God had told him. 4 On the third day Abraham lifted up his eyes and saw the place from afar. 5 Then Abraham said to his young men, "Stay here with the donkey; I and the boy[3] will go over there and worship and come again to you." 6 And Abraham took the wood of the burnt offering and laid it on Isaac his son. And he took in his hand the fire and the knife. So they went both of

[1] Or *you* [2] *Beersheba* means *well of seven* or *well of the oath* [3] Or *young man*; also verse 12

Abraham and Sarah Isaac and Ishmael

Many years had passed after God first gave His promise that Abraham and Sarah would have a child. They had to wait a long, long time.

But, one day, God's promise finally came true. When Abraham was 100 years old, God gave Abraham and Sarah a baby boy. Abraham named this son "Isaac"—which means "laughter." Sarah said, "God has made laughter for me," because everyone who heard that she'd had a baby would laugh too.

When Isaac had grown a bit, Abraham gave a big feast for him. Hagar, Sarah's maid, and Hagar's son by Abraham, Ishmael, lived with Abraham and Sarah. On the day of the feast, Sarah saw Ishmael laughing at Isaac. Sarah became very upset and told Abraham to send Ishmael and his mother away. She did not want Ishmael to share in Abraham's inheritance—what he would pass on to Isaac when he died.

Abraham did not know what to do. God told Abraham not to be sad, but to do what Sarah asked. God said His promises to Abraham and His covenant with him would be passed on to Isaac, not to Ishmael. God also promised Abraham that Ishmael would one day have a great family, too. So Hagar and Ishmael went away to live in another land, and God provided what they needed.

Isaac was the child God had promised. Abraham and

Sarah had believed that God would keep His promises and give them this child. God's covenant with Abraham was passed on to Isaac. God's covenant today is with all who believe His promises and trust in His only Son that He promised and gave, Jesus our Lord.

SEEK and FIND

WHERE TO FIND THE STORY

Genesis 21:1–21

KEY BIBLE VERSE

"Through Isaac shall your offspring be named." (Genesis 21:12)

THREE KEY QUESTIONS

- What does Isaac's name mean, and why was this a good name for him?
- When Hagar and Ishmael were sent away, what did God do for them?
- God always keeps His promises, but do they always happen right away?

RELATED BIBLE READINGS

Romans 9:6–8; Galatians 4:21–31

them together. 7 And Isaac said to his
father Abraham, "My father!" And he said,
"Here am I, my son." He said, "Behold, the
fire and the wood, but where is the lamb
for a burnt offering?" 8 Abraham
said, "God will provide for himself
57 the lamb for a burnt offering, my
son." So they went both of them together.
9 When they came to the place of which
God had told him, Abraham built the
altar there and laid the wood in order and
bound Isaac his son and laid him on the
altar, on top of the wood. 10 Then Abraham
reached out his hand and took the knife
to slaughter his son. 11 But the angel of
the LORD called to him from heaven and
said, "Abraham, Abraham!" And he said,
"Here am I." 12 He said, "Do not lay your
hand on the boy or do anything to him,
for now I know that you fear God, seeing
you have not withheld your son, your only
son, from me." 13 And Abraham lifted up
his eyes and looked, and behold, behind
him was a ram, caught in a thicket by his

horns. And Abraham went and took the ram and offered it up as a burnt offering instead of his son. 14 So Abraham called the name of that place, "The LORD will provide";[1] as it is said to this day, "On the mount of the LORD it shall be provided."[2]

15 And the angel of the LORD called to Abraham a second time from heaven 16 and said, "By myself I have sworn, declares the LORD, because you have done this and have not withheld your son, your only son, 17 I will surely bless you, and I will surely multiply your offspring as the stars of heaven and as the sand that is on the seashore. And your offspring shall possess the gate of his[3] enemies, 18 and in your offspring shall all the nations of the earth be blessed, because you have obeyed my voice." 19 So Abraham returned to his young men, and they arose and went together to Beersheba. And Abraham lived at Beersheba.

20 Now after these things it was told to Abraham, "Behold, Milcah also has borne children to your brother Nahor: 21 Uz his firstborn, Buz his brother, Kemuel the father of Aram, 22 Chesed, Hazo, Pildash, Jidlaph, and Bethuel." 23 (Bethuel fathered Rebekah.) These eight Milcah bore to Nahor, Abraham's brother. 24 Moreover, his concubine, whose name was Reumah, bore Tebah, Gaham, Tahash, and Maacah.

Sarah's Death and Burial

23 Sarah lived 127 years; these were the years of the life of Sarah. 2 And Sarah died at Kiriath-arba (that is, Hebron) in the land of Canaan, and Abraham went in to mourn for Sarah and to weep for her. 3 And Abraham rose up from before his dead and said to the Hittites,[4] 4 "I am a sojourner and foreigner among you; give me property among you for a burying place, that I may bury my dead out of my sight." 5 The Hittites answered Abraham, 6 "Hear us, my lord; you are a prince of God[5] among us. Bury your dead in the choicest of our tombs. None of us will withhold from you his tomb to hinder you from burying your dead." 7 Abraham rose and bowed to the Hittites, the people of the land. 8 And he said to them, "If you are willing that I should bury my dead out of my sight, hear me and entreat for me Ephron the son of Zohar, 9 that he may give me the cave of Machpelah, which he owns; it is at the end of his field. For the full price let him give it to me in your presence as property for a burying place."

10 Now Ephron was sitting among the Hittites, and Ephron the Hittite answered Abraham in the hearing of the Hittites, of all who went in at the gate of his city, 11 "No, my lord, hear me: I give you the field, and I give you the cave that is in it. In the sight of the sons of my people I give it to you. Bury your dead." 12 Then Abraham bowed down before the people of the land. 13 And he said to Ephron in the hearing of the people of the land, "But if you will, hear me: I give the price of the field. Accept it from me, that I may bury my dead there." 14 Ephron answered Abraham, 15 "My lord, listen to me: a piece of land worth four hundred shekels[6] of silver, what is that between you and me? Bury your dead." 16 Abraham listened to Ephron, and Abraham weighed out for Ephron the silver that he had named in the hearing of the Hittites, four hundred shekels of silver, according to the weights current among the merchants.

17 So the field of Ephron in Machpelah, which was to the east of Mamre, the field with the cave that was in it and all the trees that were in the field, throughout its whole area, was made over 18 to Abraham as a possession in the presence of the Hittites, before all who went in at the gate of his city. 19 After this, Abraham buried Sarah his wife in the cave of the field of Machpelah east of Mamre (that is, Hebron) in the land of Canaan. 20 The field and the cave that is in it were made over to

[1] Or *will see* [2] Or *he will be seen* [3] Or *their* [4] Hebrew *sons of Heth*; also verses 5, 7, 10, 16, 18, 20 [5] Or *a mighty prince* [6] A *shekel* was about 2/5 ounce or 11 grams

Abraham and Isaac

The Lord kept the promise He had made to Abraham and Sarah, and Sarah had a son when she and Abraham were very old. They named their son "Isaac," and he grew up to be a fine boy. Isaac was their only child, and Sarah and Abraham loved him very much.

One day, God tested Abraham. God told Abraham to take Isaac, his only son whom he loved, and go to a mountain God would show them. There in the land of Moriah, God said, Abraham was to offer his son Isaac as a burnt offering.

Abraham got up early the next morning, saddled his donkey, and cut some wood—and together with Isaac, they started out for the place where Abraham was to offer his son.

It took three days, but finally, they were almost there. Abraham gave wood to Isaac to carry, while Abraham carried the fire and the knife. Isaac saw that there was fire and wood, "but," he asked, "where is the lamb for a burnt offering?"

Abraham said, "God will provide for Himself the lamb for a burnt offering, my son."

Abraham and Isaac continued walking, until they came to the place that God had said. There Abraham built an altar and put the wood on it. Then Abraham laid Isaac on the wood, and took out his knife.

Suddenly the angel of the Lord called out to Abraham from

heaven, telling him not to kill Isaac or do anything to harm him. "Now I know that you fear God," the Lord told Abraham, for "you have not withheld your son, your only son, from Me."

Just then, Abraham looked up and saw a ram caught in the bushes by his horns. Abraham offered the ram as a burnt offering instead of his son. So Abraham called the name of that place "The LORD will provide," because God had provided the ram for a sacrifice in Isaac's place.

Many years later, God's Temple would be built in exactly the same place, in the city of Jerusalem. Many sacrifices for sin would be offered in the Temple—until one day, God would send His own Son to be born from Abraham's family. God's very own Son, Jesus Christ, would be the perfect sacrifice for the sins of all who trust in Him.

SEEK and FIND

WHERE TO FIND THE STORY

Genesis 22:1–14

KEY BIBLE VERSE

"Abraham said, 'God will provide for himself the lamb for a burnt offering.'" (Genesis 22:8)

THREE KEY QUESTIONS

- Why did Abraham obey God when God told him to sacrifice his son?
- What did God provide instead of Isaac for a sacrifice?
- Who is the perfect sacrifice that God provided for our sins?

RELATED BIBLE READINGS

John 1:29; Hebrews 11:17–19; James 2:21–23; 1 John 4:9–10; Revelation 5:7–10

Abraham as property for a burying place by the Hittites.

Isaac and Rebekah

24 Now Abraham was old, well advanced in years. And the
61 LORD had blessed Abraham in all things. 2 And Abraham said to his servant, the oldest of his household, who had charge of all that he had, "Put your hand under my thigh, 3 that I may make you swear by the LORD, the God of heaven and God of the earth, that you will not take a wife for my son from the daughters of the Canaanites, among whom I dwell, 4 but will go to my country and to my kindred, and take a wife for my son Isaac." 5 The servant said to him, "Perhaps the woman may not be willing to follow me to this land. Must I then take your son back to the land from which you came?" 6 Abraham said to him, "See to it that you do not take my son back there. 7 The LORD, the God of heaven, who took me from my father's house and from the land of my kindred, and who spoke to me and swore to me, 'To your offspring I will give this land,' he will send his angel before you, and you shall take a wife for my son from there. 8 But if the woman is not willing to follow you, then you will be free from this oath of mine; only you must not take my son back there." 9 So the servant put his hand under the thigh of Abraham his master and swore to him concerning this matter.

10 Then the servant took ten of his master's camels and departed, taking all sorts of choice gifts from his master; and he arose and went to Mesopotamia[1] to the city of Nahor. 11 And he made the camels kneel down outside the city by the well of water at the time of evening, the time when women go out to draw water. 12 And he said, "O LORD, God of my master Abraham, please grant me success today and show steadfast love to my master Abraham. 13 Behold, I am standing by the spring of water, and the daughters of the men of the city are coming out to draw water. 14 Let the young woman to whom I shall say, 'Please let down your jar that I may drink,' and who shall say, 'Drink, and I will water your camels'—let her be the one whom you have appointed for your servant Isaac. By this[2] I shall know that you have shown steadfast love to my master."

15 Before he had finished speaking, behold, Rebekah, who was born to Bethuel the son of Milcah, the wife of Nahor, Abraham's brother, came out with her water jar on her shoulder. 16 The young woman was very attractive in appearance, a maiden[3] whom no man had known. She went down to the spring and filled her jar and came up. 17 Then the servant ran to meet her and said, "Please give me a little water to drink from your jar." 18 She said, "Drink, my lord." And she quickly let down her jar upon her hand and gave him a drink. 19 When she had finished giving him a drink, she said, "I will draw water for your camels also, until they have finished drinking." 20 So she quickly emptied her jar into the trough and ran again to the well to draw water, and she drew for all his camels. 21 The man gazed at her in silence to learn whether the LORD had prospered his journey or not.

22 When the camels had finished drinking, the man took a gold ring weighing a half shekel,[4] and two bracelets for her arms weighing ten gold shekels, 23 and said, "Please tell me whose daughter you are. Is there room in your father's house for us to spend the night?" 24 She said to him, "I am the daughter of Bethuel the son of Milcah, whom she bore to Nahor." 25 She added, "We have plenty of both straw and fodder, and room to spend the night." 26 The man bowed his head and worshiped the LORD 27 and said, "Blessed be the LORD, the God of my master Abraham, who has not forsaken his steadfast love and
61 his faithfulness toward my master.

[1] Hebrew *Aram-naharaim* [2] Or *By her* [3] Or *a woman of marriageable age* [4] A *shekel* was about 2/5 ounce or 11 grams

Isaac and Rebekah

Isaac grew up and Abraham became very old. Abraham knew that the time had come for Isaac to have a wife. So Abraham told his servant Eliezer to travel far away to the land where Abraham's relatives lived and to find a wife for Isaac.

The servant left with 10 of his master's camels loaded with gifts from Abraham. When Eliezer arrived at the city where Abraham's relatives lived, he went to the well with all the camels. It was time for the young women to come with their water jars to get water for their families. Eliezer prayed that God would show him the exact woman to be Isaac's wife—the woman would give a drink to Eliezer.

Before Eliezer had finished praying, a beautiful girl named Rebekah came to the well. Eliezer asked her for a drink from her pitcher of water, and immediately Rebekah gave him a drink. Then she said, "I will draw water for your camels also, until they have finished drinking." And she drew enough water from the well for all those thirsty camels!

Eliezer gave Rebekah a gold ring and two gold bracelets. "Please tell me whose daughter you are," he asked. "Is there room in your father's house for us to spend the night?"

There was more than enough room for Eliezer and all his camels. And when Eliezer found out that Rebekah's father was

Abraham's relative, Eliezer exclaimed, "Blessed be the LORD, the God of my master Abraham"!

Just then, Rebekah's brother Laban ran out to the well to meet Eliezer. Laban brought Eliezer to their home and helped unload and feed the camels.

When it was time for dinner, Eliezer said he would not eat until he had told them why he had come. When Abraham's servant told them his story, Rebekah's family saw that the Lord had caused all this to happen. When Eliezer heard their words, he bowed down and worshiped the Lord. When they asked Rebekah if she wanted to go with Eliezer to marry Isaac, Rebekah answered, "I will go." In the morning, they set off. When Isaac met Rebekah, he loved her and took her as his wife.

God continued to keep His promises through this special family. Then one day, when it was God's right time, he sent Jesus to suffer and die for the sins of the world and to rise triumphantly from the grave.

SEEK and FIND

WHERE TO FIND THE STORY

Genesis 24

KEY BIBLE VERSE

"Blessed be the LORD, the God of my master Abraham, who has not forsaken his steadfast love and his faithfulness toward my master." (Genesis 24:27)

THREE KEY QUESTIONS

- What did God do when Eliezer came to the well and prayed to God?
- Is there anything too small or too big to pray about?

- What is something you need that you can ask God to provide for you?

RELATED BIBLE READINGS

Psalm 103:17–18; Proverbs 3:5–6; 19:14

As for me, the LORD has led me in the way to the house of my master's kinsmen." 28 Then the young woman ran and told her mother's household about these things.

29 Rebekah had a brother whose name was Laban. Laban ran out toward the man, to the spring. 30 As soon as he saw the ring and the bracelets on his sister's arms, and heard the words of Rebekah his sister, "Thus the man spoke to me," he went to the man. And behold, he was standing by the camels at the spring. 31 He said, "Come in, O blessed of the LORD. Why do you stand outside? For I have prepared the house and a place for the camels." 32 So the man came to the house and unharnessed the camels, and gave straw and fodder to the camels, and there was water to wash his feet and the feet of the men who were with him. 33 Then food was set before him to eat. But he said, "I will not eat until I have said what I have to say." He said, "Speak on."

34 So he said, "I am Abraham's servant. 35 The LORD has greatly blessed my master, and he has become great. He has given him flocks and herds, silver and gold, male servants and female servants, camels and donkeys. 36 And Sarah my master's wife bore a son to my master when she was old, and to him he has given all that he has. 37 My master made me swear, saying, 'You shall not take a wife for my son from the daughters of the Canaanites, in whose land I dwell, 38 but you shall go to my father's house and to my clan and take a wife for my son.' 39 I said to my master, 'Perhaps the woman will not follow me.' 40 But he said to me, 'The LORD, before whom I have walked, will send his angel with you and prosper your way. You shall take a wife for my son from my clan and from my father's house. 41 Then you will be free from my oath, when you come to my clan. And if they will not give her to you, you will be free from my oath.'

42 "I came today to the spring and said, 'O LORD, the God of my master Abraham, if now you are prospering the way that I go, 43 behold, I am standing by the spring of water. Let the virgin who comes out to draw water, to whom I shall say, "Please give me a little water from your jar to drink," 44 and who will say to me, "Drink, and I will draw for your camels also," let her be the woman whom the LORD has appointed for my master's son.'

45 "Before I had finished speaking in my heart, behold, Rebekah came out with her water jar on her shoulder, and she went down to the spring and drew water. I said to her, 'Please let me drink.' 46 She quickly let down her jar from her shoulder and said, 'Drink, and I will give your camels drink also.' So I drank, and she gave the camels drink also. 47 Then I asked her, 'Whose daughter are you?' She said, 'The daughter of Bethuel, Nahor's son, whom Milcah bore to him.' So I put the ring on her nose and the bracelets on her arms. 48 Then I bowed my head and worshiped

the LORD and blessed the LORD, the God of my master Abraham, who had led me by the right way[1] to take the daughter of my master's kinsman for his son. 49 Now then, if you are going to show steadfast love and faithfulness to my master, tell me; and if not, tell me, that I may turn to the right hand or to the left."

50 Then Laban and Bethuel answered and said, "The thing has come from the LORD; we cannot speak to you bad or good. 51 Behold, Rebekah is before you; take her and go, and let her be the wife of your master's son, as the LORD has spoken."

52 When Abraham's servant heard their words, he bowed himself to the earth before the LORD. 53 And the servant brought out jewelry of silver and of gold, and garments, and gave them to Rebekah. He also gave to her brother and to her mother costly ornaments. 54 And he and the men who were with him ate and drank, and they spent the night there. When they arose in the morning, he said, "Send me away to my master." 55 Her brother and her mother said, "Let the young woman remain with us a while, at least ten days; after that she may go." 56 But he said to them, "Do not delay me, since the LORD has prospered my way. Send me away that I may go to my master." 57 They said, "Let us call the young woman and ask her." 58 And they called Rebekah and said to her, "Will you go with this man?" She said, "I will go." 59 So they sent away Rebekah their sister and her nurse, and Abraham's servant and his men. 60 And they blessed Rebekah and said to her,

"Our sister, may you become
  thousands of ten thousands,
and may your offspring possess
  the gate of those who hate him!"[2]

61 Then Rebekah and her young women arose and rode on the camels and followed the man. Thus the servant took Rebekah and went his way.

62 Now Isaac had returned from Beer-lahai-roi and was dwelling in the Negeb. 63 And Isaac went out to meditate in the field toward evening. And he lifted up his eyes and saw, and behold, there were camels coming. 64 And Rebekah lifted up her eyes, and when she saw Isaac, she dismounted from the camel 65 and said to the servant, "Who is that man, walking in the field to meet us?" The servant said, "It is my master." So she took her veil and covered herself. 66 And the servant told Isaac all the things that he had done. 67 Then Isaac brought her into the tent of Sarah his mother and took Rebekah, and she became his wife, and he loved her. So Isaac was comforted after his mother's death.

Abraham's Death and His Descendants

25 Abraham took another wife, whose name was Keturah. 2 She bore him Zimran, Jokshan, Medan, Midian, Ishbak, and Shuah. 3 Jokshan fathered Sheba and Dedan. The sons of Dedan were Asshurim, Letushim, and Leummim. 4 The sons of Midian were Ephah, Epher, Hanoch, Abida, and Eldaah. All these were the children of Keturah. 5 Abraham gave all he had to Isaac. 6 But to the sons of his concubines Abraham gave gifts, and while he was still living he sent them away from his son Isaac, eastward to the east country.

7 These are the days of the years of Abraham's life, 175 years. 8 Abraham breathed his last and died in a good old age, an old man and full of years, and was gathered to his people. 9 Isaac and Ishmael his sons buried him in the cave of Machpelah, in the field of Ephron the son of Zohar the Hittite, east of Mamre, 10 the field that Abraham purchased from the Hittites. There Abraham was buried, with Sarah his wife. 11 After the death of

[1] Or *faithfully* [2] Or *hate them*

Abraham, God blessed Isaac his son. And
Isaac settled at Beer-lahai-roi.
12 These are the generations of Ishmael,
Abraham's son, whom Hagar the Egyptian,
Sarah's servant, bore to Abraham.
13 These are the names of the sons of
Ishmael, named in the order of their
birth: Nebaioth, the firstborn of Ishmael;
and Kedar, Adbeel, Mibsam, 14 Mishma,
Dumah, Massa, 15 Hadad, Tema, Jetur,
Naphish, and Kedemah. 16 These are
the sons of Ishmael and these are their
names, by their villages and by their
encampments, twelve princes according
to their tribes. 17 (These are the years of
the life of Ishmael: 137 years. He breathed
his last and died, and was gathered to his
people.) 18 They settled from Havilah to
Shur, which is opposite Egypt in the direc-
tion of Assyria. He settled[1] over against all
his kinsmen.

The Birth of Esau and Jacob

69
19 These are the generations of
Isaac, Abraham's son: Abraham
fathered Isaac, 20 and Isaac was
forty years old when he took Rebekah, the
daughter of Bethuel the Aramean of
Paddan-aram, the sister of Laban the
Aramean, to be his wife. 21 And Isaac
prayed to the LORD for his wife, because
she was barren. And the LORD granted his
prayer, and Rebekah his wife conceived.
22 The children struggled together within
her, and she said, "If it is thus, why is this
happening to me?"[2] So she went to
inquire of the LORD. 23 And the LORD said
to her,

"Two nations are in your womb,
and two peoples from within you[3]
shall be divided;
the one shall be stronger than the
other,
the older shall serve the younger."

24 When her days to give birth were com-
pleted, behold, there were twins in her
womb. 25 The first came out red, all his
body like a hairy cloak, so they called his
name Esau. 26 Afterward his brother came
out with his hand holding Esau's heel, so
his name was called Jacob.[4] Isaac was sixty
years old when she bore them.
27 When the boys grew up, Esau was a
skillful hunter, a man of the field, while
Jacob was a quiet man, dwelling in tents.
28 Isaac loved Esau because he ate of his
game, but Rebekah loved Jacob.

Esau Sells His Birthright

29 Once when Jacob was cooking stew,
Esau came in from the field, and he was
exhausted. 30 And Esau said to Jacob, "Let

CHARACTER PROFILE

JACOB

Jacob cheated his twin brother Esau out of the blessing that should belong to the firstborn. Jacob had to run away from Esau to live in another land. Much later, as Jacob was on his way back home, Jacob wrestled with God in the form of a man. Jacob wouldn't let go until God blessed him. God changed Jacob's name to "Israel." Jacob's 12 sons became the 12 tribes of Israel.

69, 75, 79, 87

[1] Hebrew *fell* [2] Or *why do I live?* [3] Or *from birth* [4] *Jacob* means *He takes by the heel*, or *He cheats*

me eat some of that red stew, for I am exhausted!" (Therefore his name was called Edom.[1]) 31 Jacob said, "Sell me your birthright now." 32 Esau said, "I am about to die; of what use is a birthright to me?" 33 Jacob said, "Swear to me now." So he swore to him and sold his birthright to Jacob. 34 Then Jacob gave Esau bread and lentil stew, and he ate and drank and rose and went his way. Thus Esau despised his birthright.

God's Promise to Isaac

26 Now there was a famine in the land, besides the former famine that was in the days of Abraham. And Isaac went to Gerar to Abimelech king of the Philistines. 2 And the LORD appeared to him and said, "Do not go down to Egypt; dwell in the land of which I shall tell you. 3 Sojourn in this land, and I will be with you and will bless you, for to you and to your offspring I will give all these lands, and I will establish the oath that I swore to Abraham your father. 4 I will multiply your offspring as the stars of heaven and will give to your offspring all these lands. And in your offspring all the nations of the earth shall be blessed, 5 because Abraham obeyed my voice and kept my charge, my commandments, my statutes, and my laws."

Isaac and Abimelech

6 So Isaac settled in Gerar. 7 When the men of the place asked him about his wife, he said, "She is my sister," for he feared to say, "My wife," thinking, "lest the men of the place should kill me because of Rebekah," because she was attractive in appearance. 8 When he had been there a long time, Abimelech king of the Philistines looked out of a window and saw Isaac laughing with[2] Rebekah his wife. 9 So Abimelech called Isaac and said, "Behold, she is your wife. How then could you say, 'She is my sister'?" Isaac said to him, "Because I thought, 'Lest I die because of her.'" 10 Abimelech said, "What is this you have done to us? One of the people might easily have lain with your wife, and you would have brought guilt upon us." 11 So Abimelech warned all the people, saying, "Whoever touches this man or his wife shall surely be put to death."

12 And Isaac sowed in that land and reaped in the same year a hundredfold. The LORD blessed him, 13 and the man became rich, and gained more and more until he became very wealthy. 14 He had possessions of flocks and herds and many servants, so that the Philistines envied him. 15 (Now the Philistines had stopped and filled with earth all the wells that his father's servants had dug in the days of Abraham his father.) 16 And Abimelech said to Isaac, "Go away from us, for you are much mightier than we."

17 So Isaac departed from there and encamped in the Valley of Gerar and settled there. 18 And Isaac dug again the wells of water that had been dug in the days of Abraham his father, which the Philistines had stopped after the death of Abraham. And he gave them the names that his father had given them. 19 But when Isaac's servants dug in the valley and found there a well of spring water, 20 the herdsmen of Gerar quarreled with Isaac's herdsmen, saying, "The water is ours." So he called the name of the well Esek,[3] because they contended with him. 21 Then they dug another well, and they quarreled over that also, so he called its name Sitnah.[4] 22 And he moved from there and dug another well, and they did not quarrel over it. So he called its name Rehoboth,[5] saying, "For now the LORD has made room for us, and we shall be fruitful in the land."

23 From there he went up to Beersheba. 24 And the LORD appeared to him the same night and said, "I am the God of Abraham your father. Fear not, for I am with you and will bless you and multiply your offspring for my servant Abraham's sake." 25 So he

[1] *Edom* sounds like the Hebrew for *red* [2] Hebrew may suggest an intimate relationship [3] *Esek* means *contention* [4] *Sitnah* means *enmity* [5] *Rehoboth* means *broad places, or room*

built an altar there and called upon the name of the LORD and pitched his tent there. And there Isaac's servants dug a well.

26 When Abimelech went to him from Gerar with Ahuzzath his adviser and Phicol the commander of his army, 27 Isaac said to them, "Why have you come to me, seeing that you hate me and have sent me away from you?" 28 They said, "We see plainly that the LORD has been with you. So we said, let there be a sworn pact between us, between you and us, and let us make a covenant with you, 29 that you will do us no harm, just as we have not touched you and have done to you nothing but good and have sent you away in peace. You are now the blessed of the LORD." 30 So he made them a feast, and they ate and drank. 31 In the morning they rose early and exchanged oaths. And Isaac sent them on their way, and they departed from him in peace. 32 That same day Isaac's servants came and told him about the well that they had dug and said to him, "We have found water." 33 He called it Shibah;[1] therefore the name of the city is Beersheba to this day.

34 When Esau was forty years old, he took Judith the daughter of Beeri the Hittite to be his wife, and Basemath the daughter of Elon the Hittite, 35 and they made life bitter[2] for Isaac and Rebekah.

Isaac Blesses Jacob

69

27 When Isaac was old and his eyes were dim so that he could not see, he called Esau his older son and said to him, "My son"; and he answered, "Here I am." 2 He said, "Behold, I am old; I do not know the day of my death. 3 Now then, take your weapons, your quiver and your bow, and go out to the field and hunt game for me, 4 and prepare for me delicious food, such as I love, and bring it to me so that I may eat, that my soul may bless you before I die."

5 Now Rebekah was listening when Isaac spoke to his son Esau. So when Esau went to the field to hunt for game and bring it, 6 Rebekah said to her son Jacob, "I heard your father speak to your brother Esau, 7 'Bring me game and prepare for me delicious food, that I may eat it and bless you before the LORD before I die.' 8 Now therefore, my son, obey my voice as I command you. 9 Go to the flock and bring me two good young goats, so that I may prepare from them delicious food for your father, such as he loves. 10 And you shall bring it to your father to eat, so that he may bless you before he dies." 11 But Jacob said to Rebekah his mother, "Behold, my brother Esau is a hairy man, and I am a smooth man. 12 Perhaps my father will feel me, and I shall seem to be mocking him and bring a curse upon myself and not a blessing." 13 His mother said to him, "Let your curse be on me, my son; only obey my voice, and go, bring them to me."

14 So he went and took them and brought them to his mother, and his mother prepared delicious food, such as his father loved. 15 Then Rebekah took the best garments of Esau her older son, which were with her in the house, and put them on Jacob her younger son. 16 And the skins of the young goats she put on his hands and on the smooth part of his neck. 17 And she put the delicious food and the bread, which she had prepared, into the hand of her son Jacob.

18 So he went in to his father and said, "My father." And he said, "Here I am. Who are you, my son?" 19 Jacob said to his father, "I am Esau your firstborn. I have done as you told me; now sit up and eat of my game, that your soul may bless me." 20 But Isaac said to his son, "How is it that you have found it so quickly, my son?" He answered, "Because the LORD your God granted me success." 21 Then Isaac said to Jacob, "Please come near, that I may feel you, my son, to know whether you are really my son Esau or not." 22 So Jacob went near to Isaac his father, who felt him

[1] *Shibah* sounds like the Hebrew for *oath* [2] Hebrew *they were bitterness of spirit*

Jacob and Esau

Isaac and Rebekah knew they were going to have a baby. God told Rebekah that she would have not just one baby, but two babies—twins! God said that the older twin would serve the younger one.

The first twin born was named Esau. Esau had a lot of hair. The second twin was born right away, holding on to his brother's heel. He was named Jacob.

Esau grew up loving the outdoors. Jacob grew up loving to stay quietly at home. Isaac loved Esau since he brought home meat from hunting. But Rebekah loved Jacob.

One day, when the boys were older, Esau came in from the field very hungry, and he found his brother Jacob cooking stew. Esau asked for some stew, and Jacob said, "Sell me your birthright now." Because Esau was a little older, the birthright made Esau the head of the family, and he would receive more land and goods when Isaac died. And the birthright also included God's promises to Abraham.

But Esau was so hungry that he didn't care about the birthright just then. And so he sold his birthright to his brother Jacob for a bowl of stew.

Many years later, when Isaac was so old he could no longer see, he called Esau to him. Isaac asked Esau to go hunting, and then to prepare a delicious meal from what he caught. "Bring it to me so that I may eat," Isaac said, "that my soul may bless you before I die."

Rebekah heard what Isaac said. When Esau went to the field to hunt, Rebekah told Jacob to get two goats from the flock, so that she could cook them and make a delicious meal. Then Rebekah told Jacob, "You shall bring it to your father to eat, so that he may bless you before he dies."

Jacob said to his mother, "My brother Esau is a hairy man," but Jacob's skin was smooth. Jacob knew Isaac would be very angry if he discovered that Jacob was trying to trick him. But his mother had a plan. She told Jacob to bring her the goats. Jacob obeyed his mother, and she made a delicious meal. Then Rebekah took some of Esau's clothes and put them on Jacob. And she put the hairy skins from the goats on his hands and neck.

Jacob brought the food Rebekah had prepared to his father. "Who are you, my son?" Isaac asked.

Jacob lied and said he was Esau. Jacob didn't sound like Esau, so Isaac asked him to come near so he could touch him. When he felt the hair of the goat skins, Isaac was puzzled. This person sounded like Jacob, but he felt like Esau.

"Are you really my son Esau?" Isaac asked.

Jacob answered, "I am." Isaac ate the food Jacob had brought, and he blessed him with the blessing he had for his firstborn son.

As soon as Jacob left his father, Esau came in from hunting. He prepared a delicious meal and brought it to his father, asking for a blessing. But it was too late—the blessing for the firstborn son had already been given to Jacob!

Isaac, Rebekah, Esau, and Jacob all sinned – just like all of us sin. Yet God uses even human sin to carry out His plans. God was faithful and kept all of the promises that He first gave to Abraham. Jacob's family inherited the Promised Land. And one of Jacob's descendants was God's very own Son, Jesus Christ, the Savior promised long ago.

SEEK and FIND

WHERE TO FIND THE STORY

Genesis 25:19–34; 27:1–40

KEY BIBLE VERSE

"Though they were not yet born and had done nothing either good or bad—in order that God's purpose of election might continue, not because of works but because of him who calls—[Rebekah] was told, 'The older will serve the younger.' " (Romans 9:11–12)

THREE KEY QUESTIONS

- What made the birthright so wonderful?
- How much did Esau care about his birthright, and what did he sell it for?
- Does God still keep all His promises even when people sin?

RELATED BIBLE READINGS

Obadiah 17–18; Malachi 1:2–3; Romans 9:10–13; Hebrews 11:20; 12:15–17

and said, "The voice is Jacob's voice, but
the hands are the hands of Esau." 23 And
he did not recognize him, because his
hands were hairy like his brother Esau's
hands. So he blessed him. 24 He said, "Are
you really my son Esau?" He answered,
"I am." 25 Then he said, "Bring it near to
me, that I may eat of my son's game and
bless you." So he brought it near to him,
and he ate; and he brought him wine, and
he drank.

26 Then his father Isaac said to him,
"Come near and kiss me, my son." 27 So
he came near and kissed him. And Isaac
smelled the smell of his garments and
blessed him and said,

"See, the smell of my son
is as the smell of a field that the
LORD has blessed!
28 May God give you of the dew of
heaven
and of the fatness of the earth
and plenty of grain and wine.
29 Let peoples serve you,
and nations bow down to you.
Be lord over your brothers,
and may your mother's sons bow
down to you.
Cursed be everyone who curses you,
and blessed be everyone who
blesses you!"

30 As soon as Isaac had finished blessing
Jacob, when Jacob had scarcely gone out
from the presence of Isaac his father, Esau
his brother came in from his hunting. 31 He
also prepared delicious food and brought it
to his father. And he said to his father, "Let
my father arise and eat of his son's game,
that you may bless me." 32 His father Isaac
said to him, "Who are you?" He answered,
"I am your son, your firstborn, Esau."
33 Then Isaac trembled very violently and
said, "Who was it then that hunted game
and brought it to me, and I ate it all before
you came, and I have blessed him? Yes,
and he shall be blessed." 34 As soon as
Esau heard the words of his father, he
cried out with an exceedingly great and
bitter cry and said to his father, "Bless
me, even me also, O my father!" 35 But he
said, "Your brother came deceitfully, and
he has taken away your blessing." 36 Esau
said, "Is he not rightly named Jacob?[1] For
he has cheated me these two times. He
took away my birthright, and behold, now
he has taken away my blessing." Then he
said, "Have you not reserved a blessing for
me?" 37 Isaac answered and said to Esau,
"Behold, I have made him lord over you,
and all his brothers I have given to him for
servants, and with grain and wine I have
sustained him. What then can I do for you,
my son?" 38 Esau said to his father, "Have
you but one blessing, my father? Bless me,
even me also, O my father." And Esau lifted
up his voice and wept.

39 Then Isaac his father answered and
said to him:

"Behold, away from[2] the fatness of the
earth shall your dwelling be,
and away from[3] the dew of
heaven on high.
40 By your sword you shall live,
and you shall serve your brother;
but when you grow restless
you shall break his yoke from
your neck."

75

41 Now Esau hated Jacob because of
the blessing with which his father
had blessed him, and Esau said to
himself, "The days of mourning for my
father are approaching; then I will kill my
brother Jacob." 42 But the words of Esau her
older son were told to Rebekah. So she
sent and called Jacob her younger son and
said to him, "Behold, your brother Esau
comforts himself about you by planning
to kill you. 43 Now therefore, my son, obey
my voice. Arise, flee to Laban my brother
in Haran 44 and stay with him a while,
until your brother's fury turns away—
45 until your brother's anger turns away
from you, and he forgets what you have
done to him. Then I will send and bring
you from there. Why should I be bereft of
you both in one day?"

46 Then Rebekah said to Isaac, "I loathe
my life because of the Hittite women.[4] If
Jacob marries one of the Hittite women
like these, one of the women of the land,
what good will my life be to me?"

Jacob Sent to Laban

28 Then Isaac called Jacob and
blessed him and directed him,
"You must not take a wife from the
Canaanite women. 2 Arise, go to Paddan-
aram to the house of Bethuel your moth-

[1] *Jacob* means *He takes by the heel*, or *He cheats* [2] Or *Behold, of* [3] Or *and of* [4] Hebrew *daughters of Heth*

er's father, and take as your wife from there one of the daughters of Laban your mother's brother. 3 God Almighty[1] bless you and make you fruitful and multiply you, that you may become a company of peoples. 4 May he give the blessing of Abraham to you and to your offspring with you, that you may take possession of the land of your sojournings that God gave to Abraham!" 5 Thus Isaac sent Jacob away. And he went to Paddan-aram, to Laban, the son of Bethuel the Aramean, the brother of Rebekah, Jacob's and Esau's mother.

Esau Marries an Ishmaelite

6 Now Esau saw that Isaac had blessed Jacob and sent him away to Paddan-aram to take a wife from there, and that as he blessed him he directed him, "You must not take a wife from the Canaanite women," 7 and that Jacob had obeyed his father and his mother and gone to Paddan-aram. 8 So when Esau saw that the Canaanite women did not please Isaac his father, 9 Esau went to Ishmael and took as his wife, besides the wives he had, Mahalath the daughter of Ishmael, Abraham's son, the sister of Nebaioth.

Jacob's Dream

10 Jacob left Beersheba and went toward
Haran. 11 And he came to a certain place
and stayed there that night, because the
sun had set. Taking one of the stones of
the place, he put it under his head and lay
down in that place to sleep. 12 And he
dreamed, and behold, there was a
ladder[2] set up on the earth, and the
1537 top of it reached to heaven. And
behold, the angels of God were ascending
and descending on it! 13 And behold, the
LORD stood above it[3] and said, "I am the
LORD, the God of Abraham your father and
the God of Isaac. The land on which you
lie I will give to you and to your offspring.
14 Your offspring shall be like the dust of
the earth, and you shall spread abroad to
the west and to the east and to the north
and to the south, and in you and your off-
spring shall all the families of the earth be
blessed. 15 Behold, I am with you
and will keep you wherever you go,
75 and will bring you back to this
land. For I will not leave you until I have
done what I have promised you." 16 Then
Jacob awoke from his sleep and said,
"Surely the LORD is in this place, and I did
not know it." 17 And he was afraid and said,
"How awesome is this place! This is none
other than the house of God, and this is
the gate of heaven."

18 So early in the morning Jacob took the stone that he had put under his head and set it up for a pillar and poured oil on the top of it. 19 He called the name of that place Bethel,[4] but the name of the city was Luz at the first. 20 Then Jacob made a vow, saying, "If God will be with me and will keep me in this way that I go, and will give me bread to eat and clothing to wear, 21 so that I come again to my father's house in peace, then the LORD shall be my God, 22 and this stone, which I have set up for a pillar, shall be God's house. And of all that you give me I will give a full tenth to you."

Jacob Marries Leah and Rachel

29 Then Jacob went on his
journey and came to the
79 land of the people of the east. 2 As
he looked, he saw a well in the field, and
behold, three flocks of sheep lying beside
it, for out of that well the flocks were
watered. The stone on the well's mouth
was large, 3 and when all the flocks were
gathered there, the shepherds would roll
the stone from the mouth of the well and
water the sheep, and put the stone back in
its place over the mouth of the well.

4 Jacob said to them, "My brothers, where do you come from?" They said, "We are from Haran." 5 He said to them, "Do you know Laban the son of Nahor?" They said, "We know him." 6 He said to them, "Is it well with him?" They said, "It is well; and see, Rachel his daughter is coming with

[1] Hebrew *El Shaddai* [2] Or *a flight of steps* [3] Or *beside him* [4] *Bethel* means *the house of God*

Jacob's Dream

When Isaac was old, he blessed both of his sons. Jacob received the better blessing. This made Esau very angry. He said, "I will kill my brother Jacob."

Rebekah found out how angry Esau was. She told Jacob he must leave home for a while so Esau wouldn't hurt him. She told Jacob to go quickly to the home of her brother Laban and stay there until Esau was no longer angry.

Soon Jacob was on his way. When night came, there was no house nearby, so Jacob lay down on the ground to sleep. He put a stone under his head for a pillow.

During the night Jacob had a dream. In his dream he saw a ladder or stairway going up to heaven. The bottom step was on the ground, and the top reached all the way to heaven. Angels walked up and down the steps, and God was at the very top.

God spoke to Jacob in the dream. "I am the Lord, the God of Abraham your father and the God of Isaac," He said. God promised to give the land where he was sleeping to Jacob, and to the children who would come from him. God promised that there would be so many children and grandchildren and great-grandchildren from Jacob that they would be like the dust that covers the ground! Best of all, God promised Jacob, "I am with you and will keep you wherever you go."

Jacob woke up and said, "Surely the Lord is in this place,

and I did not know it. This is none other than the house of God. This is the gate of heaven."

Early in the morning, Jacob took the stone he had used for a pillow and set it up for a pillar to show that something very special had happened here. He poured oil on it. He named the place Bethel, which means "the house of God."

In Jacob's dream, he saw a ladder or stairway going from heaven to earth. Many years later the Savior would be born from Jacob's family. This Savior is God's very own Son—the one and the only way to heaven. Jesus suffered and died for our sins. And He rose victorious on Easter morning. Because of Jesus' work, through faith in Him, God grants His children a rich inheritance and the blessings of His victory—the forgiveness of sins and life forever with Him.

SEEK and FIND

WHERE TO FIND THE STORY

Genesis 27:41–28:22

KEY BIBLE VERSE

"I am with you and will keep you wherever you go" (Genesis 28:15).

THREE KEY QUESTIONS

- How do you think Jacob felt sleeping outside, away from home, all alone?
- Who spoke to Jacob from the top of the ladder in his dream? What did He say?
- What was the great promise that God made to Jacob?

RELATED BIBLE READINGS

Psalm 105:8–11; 139:7–12; John 1:49–51; Ephesians 2:4–6

the sheep!" 7 He said, "Behold, it is still high
day; it is not time for the livestock to be
gathered together. Water the sheep and go,
pasture them." 8 But they said, "We cannot
until all the flocks are gathered together
and the stone is rolled from the mouth of
the well; then we water the sheep."

9 While he was still speaking with them,
Rachel came with her father's sheep, for
she was a shepherdess. 10 Now as soon as
Jacob saw Rachel the daughter of Laban
his mother's brother, and the sheep of
Laban his mother's brother, Jacob came
near and rolled the stone from the well's
mouth and watered the flock of Laban
his mother's brother. 11 Then Jacob kissed
Rachel and wept aloud. 12 And Jacob told
Rachel that he was her father's kinsman,
and that he was Rebekah's son, and she
ran and told her father.

13 As soon as Laban heard the news
about Jacob, his sister's son, he ran to
meet him and embraced him and kissed
him and brought him to his house. Jacob
told Laban all these things, 14 and Laban
said to him, "Surely you are my bone
and my flesh!" And he stayed with him
a month.

15 Then Laban said to Jacob, "Because
you are my kinsman, should you there-
fore serve me for nothing? Tell me, what
shall your wages be?" 16 Now Laban had
two daughters. The name of the older
was Leah, and the name of the younger
was Rachel. 17 Leah's eyes were weak,[1] but
Rachel was beautiful in form and appear-
ance. 18 Jacob loved Rachel. And he said,
"I will serve you seven years for your
younger daughter Rachel." 19 Laban said,
"It is better that I give her to you than that
I should give her to any other man; stay
with me." 20 So Jacob served seven years for
Rachel, and they seemed to him but a few
days because of the love he had for her.

21 Then Jacob said to Laban, "Give me my
wife that I may go in to her, for my time is
completed." 22 So Laban gathered together
all the people of the place and made a
feast. 23 But in the evening he took his
daughter Leah and brought her to Jacob,
and he went in to her. 24 (Laban gave[2] his
female servant Zilpah to his daughter Leah
to be her servant.) 25 And in the morn-
ing, behold, it was Leah! And Jacob said
to Laban, "What is this you have done to
me? Did I not serve with you for Rachel?
Why then have you deceived me?" 26 Laban
said, "It is not so done in our country, to
give the younger before the firstborn.
27 Complete the week of this one, and we
will give you the other also in return for
serving me another seven years." 28 Jacob
did so, and completed her week. Then
Laban gave him his daughter Rachel to be
his wife. 29 (Laban gave his female servant
Bilhah to his daughter Rachel to be her ser-
vant.) 30 So Jacob went in to Rachel also,
and he loved Rachel more than Leah, and
served Laban for another seven years.

Jacob's Children

31 When the LORD saw that Leah was
hated, he opened her womb, but Rachel
was barren. 32 And Leah conceived and
bore a son, and she called his name
Reuben,[3] for she said, "Because the LORD
has looked upon my affliction; for now
my husband will love me." 33 She con-
ceived again and bore a son, and said,
"Because the LORD has heard that I am
hated, he has given me this son also." And
she called his name Simeon.[4] 34 Again she
conceived and bore a son, and said, "Now
this time my husband will be attached to
me, because I have borne him three sons."
Therefore his name was called Levi.[5]
35 And she conceived again and bore a
son, and said, "This time I will praise the
LORD." Therefore she called his name
Judah.[6] Then she ceased bearing.

30 When Rachel saw that she bore
Jacob no children, she envied her
sister. She said to Jacob, "Give me children,
or I shall die!" 2 Jacob's anger was kindled

[1] Or *soft* [2] Or *had given*; also verse 29 [3] *Reuben* means *See, a son* [4] *Simeon* sounds like the Hebrew for *heard* [5] *Levi* sounds like the Hebrew for *attached* [6] *Judah* sounds like the Hebrew for *praise*

Jacob's Family

Jacob had traveled far from home to escape from his angry twin brother, Esau. He was on his way to Haran to stay with his Uncle Laban. As he was traveling to the land in the east, he saw a well and shepherds tending sheep. Jacob said to the shepherds, "My brothers, where do you come from?"

The shepherds were from Haran—the very place where Jacob was going. He asked them if they knew Laban.

The shepherds did know who Laban was. In fact, they said, "See, Rachel his daughter is coming with the sheep." When Rachel arrived, Jacob was very happy to see Rachel. He kissed her and cried for joy. Now he was no longer alone. He had found his uncle's family! Rachel was happy, too. She ran to tell her father about Jacob. Uncle Laban came quickly and took Jacob to his house. Laban and his family were happy to have Jacob stay and work with them.

One day, Laban told Jacob that it was not right that Jacob should work for nothing. Laban asked Jacob what he would like to be paid for his work. Jacob told Laban that he would work for seven years if, at the end of the seven years, he could marry Rachel. Laban agreed. So Jacob worked seven years, but the time seemed like only a few days because he loved Rachel so much.

But Laban was tricky. Rachel had an older sister named Leah, who was not married, and Laban tricked Jacob into marrying Leah first.

At a wedding, the bride wore a veil that covered her face so no one could see her face. Laban tricked Jacob by bringing Leah to the wedding instead of Rachel. Because Leah was covered with the wedding veil, Jacob could not see her face. He married Leah, thinking he was marrying Rachel!

Of course, Jacob was very angry when he discovered the trick. Laban told him that the older sister must get married before the younger sister. Now that the older sister was married, Laban told Jacob he could marry Rachel too, as long as he would stay and work for Laban for seven more years. Jacob agreed. He stayed married to Leah, and he also married Rachel the next week. After that, he worked for Laban for seven more years.

God blessed Leah with children. For a long time, Rachel had no children and was jealous of her sister. Finally, after Jacob already had ten sons, God gave Rachel a baby of her own. The baby's name was Joseph.

God is good. Even though Jacob, his wives, and their relatives lied to one another, tricked each other, and were jealous of one another, God blessed Jacob with a large family.

God had plans for Jacob's family. Through them, God was keeping His promise to send a Savior. Our Savior Jesus came from the family of Judah, one of Jacob's many sons. Through Jacob's family, all families are blessed, even yours!

SEEK and FIND

WHERE TO FIND THE STORY

Genesis 29:1–30:24

KEY BIBLE VERSE

"A star shall come out of Jacob, and a scepter shall rise out of Israel" (Numbers 24:17).

THREE KEY QUESTIONS

- What was the "trick" that Laban played on Jacob?
- God was gracious to Jacob, even though he didn't deserve God's blessing. Is God good to us, too, even though we don't deserve His blessing? Can you think of some ways that God is good to you?
- How was God's promise to Abraham fulfilled through Jacob, Leah, and Rachel?

RELATED BIBLE READINGS

Genesis 49:1–28; Deuteronomy 33:1–29

against Rachel, and he said, "Am I in the
place of God, who has withheld from you
the fruit of the womb?" **3** Then she said,
"Here is my servant Bilhah; go in to her,
so that she may give birth on my behalf,[1]
that even I may have children[2] through
her." **4** So she gave him her servant Bilhah
as a wife, and Jacob went in to her. **5** And
Bilhah conceived and bore Jacob a son.
6 Then Rachel said, "God has judged me,
and has also heard my voice and given
me a son." Therefore she called his name
Dan.[3] **7** Rachel's servant Bilhah conceived
again and bore Jacob a second son. **8** Then
Rachel said, "With mighty wrestlings[4] I
have wrestled with my sister and have prevailed."
So she called his name Naphtali.[5]
9 When Leah saw that she had ceased
bearing children, she took her servant
Zilpah and gave her to Jacob as a wife.
10 Then Leah's servant Zilpah bore Jacob
a son. **11** And Leah said, "Good fortune
has come!" so she called his name Gad.[6]
12 Leah's servant Zilpah bore Jacob a second
son. **13** And Leah said, "Happy am I!
For women have called me happy." So she
called his name Asher.[7]
14 In the days of wheat harvest Reuben
went and found mandrakes in the field
and brought them to his mother Leah.
Then Rachel said to Leah, "Please give
me some of your son's mandrakes." **15** But
she said to her, "Is it a small matter that
you have taken away my husband? Would
you take away my son's mandrakes also?"
Rachel said, "Then he may lie with you
tonight in exchange for your son's mandrakes."
16 When Jacob came from the field
in the evening, Leah went out to meet him
and said, "You must come in to me, for I

[1] Hebrew *on my knees* [2] Hebrew *be built up*, which sounds like the Hebrew for *children* [3] *Dan* sounds like the Hebrew for *judged* [4] Hebrew *With wrestlings of God* [5] *Naphtali* sounds like the Hebrew for *wrestling* [6] *Gad* sounds like the Hebrew for *good fortune* [7] *Asher* sounds like the Hebrew for *happy*

have hired you with my son's mandrakes."
So he lay with her that night. 17 And God
listened to Leah, and she conceived and
bore Jacob a fifth son. 18 Leah said, "God
has given me my wages because I gave my
servant to my husband." So she called his
name Issachar.[1]

19 And Leah conceived again, and
she bore Jacob a sixth son. 20 Then Leah
said, "God has endowed me with a good
endowment; now my husband will
honor me, because I have borne him six
sons." So she called his name Zebulun.[2]
21 Afterward she bore a daughter and
called her name Dinah.

22 Then God remembered Rachel, and
God listened to her and opened her womb.
23 She conceived and bore a son and said,
"God has taken away my reproach." 24 And
she called his name Joseph,[3] saying, "May
the LORD add to me another son!"

Jacob's Prosperity

25 As soon as Rachel had borne Joseph,
Jacob said to Laban, "Send me away, that
I may go to my own home and country.
26 Give me my wives and my children for
whom I have served you, that I may go,
for you know the service that I have given
you." 27 But Laban said to him, "If I have
found favor in your sight, I have learned
by divination that[4] the LORD has blessed
me because of you. 28 Name your wages,
and I will give it." 29 Jacob said to him, "You
yourself know how I have served you, and
how your livestock has fared with me.
30 For you had little before I came, and it
has increased abundantly, and the LORD
has blessed you wherever I turned. But
now when shall I provide for my own
household also?" 31 He said, "What shall
I give you?" Jacob said, "You shall not give
me anything. If you will do this for me, I
will again pasture *your* flock and keep it:
32 let me pass through all your flock today,
removing from it every speckled and spot-
ted sheep and every black lamb, and the
spotted and speckled among the goats,
and they shall be my wages. 33 So my hon-
esty will answer for me later, when you
come to look into my wages with you.
Every one that is not speckled and spot-
ted among the goats and black among the
lambs, if found with me, shall be counted
stolen." 34 Laban said, "Good! Let it be
as you have said." 35 But that day Laban
removed the male goats that were striped
and spotted, and all the female goats that
were speckled and spotted, every one that
had white on it, and every lamb that was
black, and put them in the charge of his
sons. 36 And he set a distance of three days'
journey between himself and Jacob, and
Jacob pastured the rest of Laban's flock.

37 Then Jacob took fresh sticks of pop-
lar and almond and plane trees, and
peeled white streaks in them, exposing
the white of the sticks. 38 He set the sticks
that he had peeled in front of the flocks in
the troughs, that is, the watering places,
where the flocks came to drink. And since
they bred when they came to drink, 39 the
flocks bred in front of the sticks and so the
flocks brought forth striped, speckled, and
spotted. 40 And Jacob separated the lambs
and set the faces of the flocks toward
the striped and all the black in the flock
of Laban. He put his own droves apart
and did not put them with Laban's flock.
41 Whenever the stronger of the flock were
breeding, Jacob would lay the sticks in the
troughs before the eyes of the flock, that
they might breed among the sticks, 42 but
for the feebler of the flock he would not
lay them there. So the feebler would be
Laban's, and the stronger Jacob's. 43 Thus
the man increased greatly and had large
flocks, female servants and male servants,
and camels and donkeys.

Jacob Flees from Laban

31 Now Jacob heard that the sons of
Laban were saying, "Jacob has
taken all that was our father's, and from

[1] *Issachar* sounds like the Hebrew for *wages*, or *hire* [2] *Zebulun* sounds like the Hebrew for *honor* [3] *Joseph* means *May he add*, and sounds like the Hebrew for *taken away* [4] Or *have become rich and*

what was our father's he has gained all this wealth." 2 And Jacob saw that Laban did not regard him with favor as before.

3 Then the LORD said to Jacob,
"Return to the land of your fathers
87 and to your kindred, and I will be
with you."

4 So Jacob sent and called Rachel
87 and Leah into the field where his
flock was 5 and said to them, "I see that your father does not regard me with favor as he did before. But the God of my father has been with me. 6 You know that I have served your father with all my strength, 7 yet your father has cheated me and changed my wages ten times. But God did not permit him to harm me. 8 If he said, 'The spotted shall be your wages,' then all the flock bore spotted; and if he said, 'The striped shall be your wages,' then all the flock bore striped. 9 Thus God has taken away the livestock of your father and given them to me. 10 In the breeding season of the flock I lifted up my eyes and saw in a dream that the goats that mated with the flock were striped, spotted, and mottled. 11 Then the angel of God said to me in the dream, 'Jacob,' and I said, 'Here I am!' 12 And he said, 'Lift up your eyes and see, all the goats that mate with the flock are striped, spotted, and mottled, for I have seen all that Laban is doing to you. 13 I am the God of Bethel, where you anointed a pillar and made a vow to me. Now arise, go out from this land and return to the land of your kindred.'" 14 Then Rachel and Leah answered and said to him, "Is there any portion or inheritance left to us in our father's house? 15 Are we not regarded by him as foreigners? For he has sold us, and he has indeed devoured our money. 16 All the wealth that God has taken away from our father belongs to us and to our children. Now then, whatever God has said to you, do."

17 So Jacob arose and set his sons and his wives on camels. 18 He drove away all his livestock, all his property that he had gained, the livestock in his possession that he had acquired in Paddan-aram, to go to the land of Canaan to his father Isaac. 19 Laban had gone to shear his sheep, and Rachel stole her father's household gods. 20 And Jacob tricked[1] Laban the Aramean, by not telling him that he intended to flee. 21 He fled with all that he had and arose and crossed the Euphrates, and set his face toward the hill country of Gilead.

22 When it was told Laban on the third day that Jacob had fled, 23 he took his kinsmen with him and pursued him for seven days and followed close after him into the hill country of Gilead. 24 But God came to Laban the Aramean in a dream by night and said to him, "Be careful not to say anything to Jacob, either good or bad."

25 And Laban overtook Jacob. Now Jacob had pitched his tent in the hill country, and Laban with his kinsmen pitched tents in the hill country of Gilead. 26 And Laban said to Jacob, "What have you done, that you have tricked me and driven away my daughters like captives of the sword? 27 Why did you flee secretly and trick me, and did not tell me, so that I might have sent you away with mirth and songs, with tambourine and lyre? 28 And why did you not permit me to kiss my sons and my daughters farewell? Now you have done foolishly. 29 It is in my power to do you harm. But the God of your[2] father spoke to me last night, saying, 'Be careful not to say anything to Jacob, either good or bad.' 30 And now you have gone away because you longed greatly for your father's house, but why did you steal my gods?" 31 Jacob answered and said to Laban, "Because I was afraid, for I thought that you would take your daughters from me by force. 32 Anyone with whom you find your gods shall not live. In the presence of our kinsmen point out what I have that is yours, and take it." Now Jacob did not know that Rachel had stolen them.

[1] Hebrew *stole the heart of*; also verses 26, 27 [2] The Hebrew for *your* is plural here

33 So Laban went into Jacob's tent and into Leah's tent and into the tent of the two female servants, but he did not find them. And he went out of Leah's tent and entered Rachel's. 34 Now Rachel had taken the household gods and put them in the camel's saddle and sat on them. Laban felt all about the tent, but did not find them. 35 And she said to her father, "Let not my lord be angry that I cannot rise before you, for the way of women is upon me." So he searched but did not find the household gods.

36 Then Jacob became angry and berated Laban. Jacob said to Laban, "What is my offense? What is my sin, that you have hotly pursued me? 37 For you have felt through all my goods; what have you found of all your household goods? Set it here before my kinsmen and your kinsmen, that they may decide between us two. 38 These twenty years I have been with you. Your ewes and your female goats have not miscarried, and I have not eaten the rams of your flocks. 39 What was torn by wild beasts I did not bring to you. I bore the loss of it myself. From my hand you required it, whether stolen by day or stolen by night. 40 There I was: by day the heat consumed me, and the cold by night, and my sleep fled from my eyes. 41 These twenty years I have been in your house. I served you fourteen years for your two daughters, and six years for your flock, and you have changed my wages ten times. 42 If the God of my father, the God of Abraham and the Fear of Isaac, had not been on my side, surely now you would have sent me away empty-handed. God saw my affliction and the labor of my hands and rebuked you last night."

43 Then Laban answered and said to Jacob, "The daughters are my daughters, the children are my children, the flocks are my flocks, and all that you see is mine. But what can I do this day for these my daughters or for their children whom they have borne? 44 Come now, let us make a covenant, you and I. And let it be a witness between you and me." 45 So Jacob took a stone and set it up as a pillar. 46 And Jacob said to his kinsmen, "Gather stones." And they took stones and made a heap, and they ate there by the heap. 47 Laban called it Jegar-sahadutha,[1] but Jacob called it Galeed.[2] 48 Laban said, "This heap is a witness between you and me today." Therefore he named it Galeed, 49 and Mizpah,[3] for he said, "The LORD watch between you and me, when we are out of one another's sight. 50 If you oppress my daughters, or if you take wives besides my daughters, although no one is with us, see, God is witness between you and me."

51 Then Laban said to Jacob, "See this heap and the pillar, which I have set between you and me. 52 This heap is a witness, and the pillar is a witness, that I will not pass over this heap to you, and you will not pass over this heap and this pillar to me, to do harm. 53 The God of Abraham and the God of Nahor, the God of their father, judge between us." So Jacob swore by the Fear of his father Isaac, 54 and Jacob offered a sacrifice in the hill country and called his kinsmen to eat bread. They ate bread and spent the night in the hill country.

55 [4] Early in the morning Laban arose and kissed his grandchildren and his daughters and blessed them. Then Laban departed and returned home.

Jacob Fears Esau

87

32 Jacob went on his way, and the angels of God met him. 2 And when Jacob saw them he said, "This is God's camp!" So he called the name of that place Mahanaim.[5]

3 And Jacob sent[6] messengers before him to Esau his brother in the land of Seir, the country of Edom, 4 instructing them, "Thus you shall say to my lord Esau: Thus says your servant Jacob, 'I have sojourned with Laban and stayed until now. 5 I have oxen, donkeys, flocks, male servants, and female

[1] Aramaic *the heap of witness* [2] Hebrew *the heap of witness* [3] *Mizpah* means *watchpost* [4] Ch 32:1 in Hebrew [5] *Mahanaim* means *two camps* [6] Or *had sent*

servants. I have sent to tell my lord, in
order that I may find favor in your sight.'"
6 And the messengers returned to Jacob,
saying, "We came to your brother Esau,
and he is coming to meet you, and there
are four hundred men with him." 7 Then
Jacob was greatly afraid and distressed. He
divided the people who were with him,
and the flocks and herds and camels, into
two camps, 8 thinking, "If Esau comes
to the one camp and attacks it, then the
camp that is left will escape."
9 And Jacob said, "O God of my father
Abraham and God of my father Isaac, O
LORD who said to me, 'Return to your
country and to your kindred, that I may do
you good,' 10 I am not worthy of the least of
all the deeds of steadfast love and all the
faithfulness that you have shown to your
servant, for with only my staff I crossed
this Jordan, and now I have become two
camps. 11 Please deliver me from the hand
of my brother, from the hand of Esau, for I
fear him, that he may come and attack me,
the mothers with the children. 12 But you
said, 'I will surely do you good, and make
your offspring as the sand of the sea, which
cannot be numbered for multitude.'"
13 So he stayed there that night, and
from what he had with him he took a pres-
ent for his brother Esau, 14 two hundred
female goats and twenty male goats, two
hundred ewes and twenty rams, 15 thirty
milking camels and their calves, forty
cows and ten bulls, twenty female don-
keys and ten male donkeys. 16 These he
handed over to his servants, every drove
by itself, and said to his servants, "Pass
on ahead of me and put a space between
drove and drove." 17 He instructed the first,
"When Esau my brother meets you and
asks you, 'To whom do you belong? Where
are you going? And whose are these ahead
of you?' 18 then you shall say, 'They belong
to your servant Jacob. They are a present
sent to my lord Esau. And moreover, he
is behind us.'" 19 He likewise instructed
the second and the third and all who fol-
lowed the droves, "You shall say the same
thing to Esau when you find him, 20 and
you shall say, 'Moreover, your servant
Jacob is behind us.'" For he thought, "I
may appease him[1] with the present that
goes ahead of me, and afterward I shall see
his face. Perhaps he will accept me."[2] 21 So
the present passed on ahead of him, and
he himself stayed that night in the camp.

Jacob Wrestles with God

22 The same night he arose and took his
two wives, his two female servants, and
his eleven children,[3] and crossed the ford
of the Jabbok. 23 He took them and sent
them across the stream, and everything
else that he had. 24 And Jacob was left
alone. And a man wrestled with him until
the breaking of the day. 25 When the man
saw that he did not prevail against Jacob,
he touched his hip socket, and Jacob's hip
was put out of joint as he wrestled with
him. 26 Then he said, "Let me go, for the
day has broken." But Jacob said, "I will not
let you go unless you bless me." 27 And he
said to him, "What is your name?" And he
said, "Jacob." 28 Then he said, "Your name
shall no longer be called Jacob, but Israel,[4]
for you have striven with God and with
men, and have prevailed." 29 Then Jacob
asked him, "Please tell me your name."
But he said, "Why is it that you ask my
name?" And there he blessed him. 30 So
Jacob called the name of the place Peniel,[5]
saying, "For I have seen God face to face,
and yet my life has been delivered." 31 The
sun rose upon him as he passed Penuel,
limping because of his hip. 32 Therefore
to this day the people of Israel do not eat
the sinew of the thigh that is on the hip
socket, because he touched the socket of
Jacob's hip on the sinew of the thigh.

Jacob Meets Esau

33 And Jacob lifted up his eyes and
looked, and behold, Esau was
coming, and four hundred men with him.

[1] Hebrew *appease his face* [2] Hebrew *he will lift my face* [3] Or *sons* [4] *Israel* means *He strives with God*, or *God strives* [5] *Peniel* means *the face of God*

Jacob and Esau

While Jacob was living with his Uncle Laban, God blessed Jacob with many children, with large flocks, and with many servants. One day, the Lord told Jacob to return to the land where his father lived.

It wasn't easy for Jacob to go home. Many years before, Jacob had sinned against his twin brother Esau. This made Esau so angry that he had said he would kill Jacob. That was why Jacob had left home many years ago—he was afraid of Esau. Now God told Jacob to go home and promised to be with him. Still, Jacob wondered if Esau would ever forgive him.

When Jacob got near his homeland, he sent messengers to Esau. Jacob wanted Esau to know that he had been staying with their Uncle Laban. And now that Jacob was coming home, he wanted to be at peace with Esau. The messengers brought Jacob's message to Esau, but they came back with frightening news. Esau was coming to meet Jacob with 400 men!

When Jacob heard this, he was afraid that Esau was coming to attack him. Jacob made a plan to save his family. He divided his family and herds into two groups. He thought if Esau attacked one group, the other group could escape. Then Jacob prayed to God. Jacob thanked God that He had always been with him. He thanked God for all the blessings and the children He had given him. Jacob told God he did not deserve even the smallest of all the good things God had done for him. Then he asked God to protect him from his brother.

Then Jacob sent goats, sheep, camels, cows, and donkeys as a gift to Esau. Jacob hoped that all these gifts would make Esau so happy that he would forgive him. Next Jacob also sent his two wives, servants, children, and everything else that he had across the stream—so that Jacob was all alone.

That night God came to Jacob in the form of a man. Jacob wrestled with God all night long. Finally, in the early morning, God told Jacob to let Him go. Jacob answered, "I will not let You go unless You bless me." The Wrestler (who was God) agreed and blessed Jacob with a new name. Now Jacob would be called "Israel," which means that Jacob had struggled with God and with man. Jacob said, "I have seen God face to face, and yet my life has been delivered."

After the struggle, Jacob looked up and saw Esau coming with four hundred men. Jacob went ahead of his wives and children, bowing to the ground seven times until he came to his brother. Esau ran to meet Jacob, and hugged him. Esau was happy to see Jacob, and the two brothers cried for joy.

Then Esau wanted to know why Jacob had sent the herds and servants. Jacob told him they were gifts. If Esau was truly glad to see him, he should keep the animals. Jacob was so glad to be at peace with his brother again that he insisted that Esau should keep the gifts.

Esau accepted Jacob's gifts and left his brother to go to the land of Seir. But Jacob went to the land of Canaan, to begin a new life, with a new name, in a new place—and with all the blessings that God had given him.

SEEK and FIND

WHERE TO FIND THE STORY

Genesis 31:3; 32:1–33:20

KEY BIBLE VERSE

"Then the LORD said to Jacob, 'Return to the land of your fathers and to your kindred, and I will be with you.'" (Genesis 31:3)

THREE KEY QUESTIONS

- Did Jacob deserve God's blessing and all God's good gifts to him? Do we deserve God's good gifts to us?
- Why was Jacob so afraid to see his brother Esau?
- What did Esau do when he saw his brother Jacob? Was Esau still angry with Jacob?

RELATED BIBLE READINGS

2 Samuel 7:18; Hosea 12:2–5; Luke 18:1

So he divided the children among Leah and Rachel and the two female servants. 2 And he put the servants with their children in front, then Leah with her children, and Rachel and Joseph last of all. 3 He himself went on before them, bowing himself to the ground seven times, until he came near to his brother.

4 But Esau ran to meet him and embraced him and fell on his neck and kissed him, and they wept. 5 And when Esau lifted up his eyes and saw the women and children, he said, "Who are these with you?" Jacob said, "The children whom God has graciously given your servant." 6 Then the servants drew near, they and their children, and bowed down. 7 Leah likewise and her children drew near and bowed down. And last Joseph and Rachel drew near, and they bowed down. 8 Esau said, "What do you mean by all this company[1] that I met?" Jacob answered, "To find favor in the sight of my lord." 9 But Esau said, "I have enough, my brother; keep what you have for yourself." 10 Jacob said, "No, please, if I have found favor in your sight, then accept my present from my hand. For I have seen your face, which is like seeing the face of God, and you have accepted me. 11 Please accept my blessing that is brought to you, because God has dealt graciously with me, and because I have enough." Thus he urged him, and he took it.

12 Then Esau said, "Let us journey on our way, and I will go ahead of[2] you." 13 But Jacob said to him, "My lord knows that the children are frail, and that the nursing flocks and herds are a care to me. If they are driven hard for one day, all the flocks will die. 14 Let my lord pass on ahead of his servant, and I will lead on slowly, at the pace of the livestock that are ahead of me and at the pace of the children, until I come to my lord in Seir."

[1] Hebrew *camp* [2] Or *along with*

15 So Esau said, "Let me leave with you
some of the people who are with me." But
he said, "What need is there? Let me find
favor in the sight of my lord." 16 So Esau
returned that day on his way to Seir. 17 But
Jacob journeyed to Succoth, and built
himself a house and made booths for his
livestock. Therefore the name of the place
is called Succoth.[1]

18 And Jacob came safely[2] to the city of
Shechem, which is in the land of Canaan,
on his way from Paddan-aram, and he
camped before the city. 19 And from the
sons of Hamor, Shechem's father, he
bought for a hundred pieces of money[3]
the piece of land on which he had pitched
his tent. 20 There he erected an altar and
called it El-Elohe-Israel.[4]

The Defiling of Dinah

34 Now Dinah the daughter of Leah,
whom she had borne to Jacob,
went out to see the women of the land.
2 And when Shechem the son of Hamor
the Hivite, the prince of the land, saw her,
he seized her and lay with her and humil-
iated her. 3 And his soul was drawn to
Dinah the daughter of Jacob. He loved the
young woman and spoke tenderly to her.
4 So Shechem spoke to his father Hamor,
saying, "Get me this girl for my wife."

5 Now Jacob heard that he had defiled
his daughter Dinah. But his sons were
with his livestock in the field, so Jacob
held his peace until they came. 6 And
Hamor the father of Shechem went out
to Jacob to speak with him. 7 The sons of
Jacob had come in from the field as soon
as they heard of it, and the men were
indignant and very angry, because he
had done an outrageous thing in Israel
by lying with Jacob's daughter, for such a
thing must not be done.

8 But Hamor spoke with them, saying,
"The soul of my son Shechem longs for
your[5] daughter. Please give her to him to
be his wife. 9 Make marriages with us. Give
your daughters to us, and take our daugh-
ters for yourselves. 10 You shall dwell with
us, and the land shall be open to you.
Dwell and trade in it, and get property
in it." 11 Shechem also said to her father
and to her brothers, "Let me find favor in
your eyes, and whatever you say to me
I will give. 12 Ask me for as great a bride
price[6] and gift as you will, and I will give
whatever you say to me. Only give me the
young woman to be my wife."

13 The sons of Jacob answered Shechem
and his father Hamor deceitfully, because
he had defiled their sister Dinah. 14 They
said to them, "We cannot do this thing,
to give our sister to one who is uncircum-
cised, for that would be a disgrace to us.
15 Only on this condition will we agree
with you—that you will become as we are
by every male among you being circum-
cised. 16 Then we will give our daughters
to you, and we will take your daughters
to ourselves, and we will dwell with you
and become one people. 17 But if you will
not listen to us and be circumcised, then
we will take our daughter, and we will
be gone."

18 Their words pleased Hamor and
Hamor's son Shechem. 19 And the young
man did not delay to do the thing, because
he delighted in Jacob's daughter. Now he
was the most honored of all his father's
house. 20 So Hamor and his son Shechem
came to the gate of their city and spoke
to the men of their city, saying, 21 "These
men are at peace with us; let them dwell
in the land and trade in it, for behold, the
land is large enough for them. Let us take
their daughters as wives, and let us give
them our daughters. 22 Only on this con-
dition will the men agree to dwell with
us to become one people—when every
male among us is circumcised as they are
circumcised. 23 Will not their livestock,
their property and all their beasts be ours?
Only let us agree with them, and they will
dwell with us." 24 And all who went out

[1] *Succoth* means *booths* [2] Or *peacefully* [3] Hebrew *a hundred qesitah*; a unit of money of unknown value [4] *El-Elohe-Israel* means *God, the God of Israel*
[5] The Hebrew for *your* is plural here [6] Or *engagement present*

of the gate of his city listened to Hamor
and his son Shechem, and every male was
circumcised, all who went out of the gate
of his city.
25 On the third day, when they were sore,
two of the sons of Jacob, Simeon and Levi,
Dinah's brothers, took their swords and
came against the city while it felt secure
and killed all the males. 26 They killed
Hamor and his son Shechem with the
sword and took Dinah out of Shechem's
house and went away. 27 The sons of Jacob
came upon the slain and plundered the
city, because they had defiled their sister.
28 They took their flocks and their herds,
their donkeys, and whatever was in the city
and in the field. 29 All their wealth, all their
little ones and their wives, all that was in
the houses, they captured and plundered.
30 Then Jacob said to Simeon and Levi,
"You have brought trouble on me by mak-
ing me stink to the inhabitants of the
land, the Canaanites and the Perizzites.
My numbers are few, and if they gather
themselves against me and attack me, I
shall be destroyed, both I and my house-
hold." 31 But they said, "Should he treat our
sister like a prostitute?"

God Blesses and Renames Jacob

35 God said to Jacob, "Arise, go up to
Bethel and dwell there. Make an
altar there to the God who appeared to you
when you fled from your brother Esau."
2 So Jacob said to his household and to all
who were with him, "Put away the foreign
gods that are among you and purify your-
selves and change your garments. 3 Then
let us arise and go up to Bethel, so that I
may make there an altar to the God who
answers me in the day of my distress and
has been with me wherever I have gone."
4 So they gave to Jacob all the foreign gods
that they had, and the rings that were in
their ears. Jacob hid them under the ter-
ebinth tree that was near Shechem.
5 And as they journeyed, a terror from
God fell upon the cities that were around
them, so that they did not pursue the
sons of Jacob. 6 And Jacob came to Luz
(that is, Bethel), which is in the land of
Canaan, he and all the people who were
with him, 7 and there he built an altar and
called the place El-bethel,[1] because there
God had revealed himself to him when
he fled from his brother. 8 And Deborah,
Rebekah's nurse, died, and she was buried
under an oak below Bethel. So he called its
name Allon-bacuth.[2]
9 God appeared[3] to Jacob again, when
he came from Paddan-aram, and blessed
him. 10 And God said to him, "Your name is
Jacob; no longer shall your name be called
Jacob, but Israel shall be your name." So
he called his name Israel. 11 And God said
to him, "I am God Almighty:[4] be fruitful
and multiply. A nation and a company of
nations shall come from you, and kings
shall come from your own body.[5] 12 The
land that I gave to Abraham and Isaac I
will give to you, and I will give the land
to your offspring after you." 13 Then God
went up from him in the place where he
had spoken with him. 14 And Jacob set up
a pillar in the place where he had spoken
with him, a pillar of stone. He poured out
a drink offering on it and poured oil on
it. 15 So Jacob called the name of the place
where God had spoken with him Bethel.

The Deaths of Rachel and Isaac

16 Then they journeyed from Bethel.
When they were still some distance[6] from
Ephrath, Rachel went into labor, and she
had hard labor. 17 And when her labor was
at its hardest, the midwife said to her,
"Do not fear, for you have another son."
18 And as her soul was departing (for she
was dying), she called his name Ben-oni;[7]
but his father called him Benjamin.[8] 19 So
Rachel died, and she was buried on the
way to Ephrath (that is, Bethlehem), 20 and
Jacob set up a pillar over her tomb. It is the
pillar of Rachel's tomb, which is there to

[1] *El-bethel* means *God of Bethel* [2] *Allon-bacuth* means *oak of weeping* [3] Or *had appeared* [4] Hebrew *El Shaddai* [5] Hebrew *from your loins* [6] Or *about two hours' distance*
[7] *Ben-oni* could mean *son of my sorrow*, or *son of my strength* [8] *Benjamin* means *son of the right hand*

this day. 21 Israel journeyed on and pitched his tent beyond the tower of Eder.

22 While Israel lived in that land, Reuben went and lay with Bilhah his father's concubine. And Israel heard of it.

Now the sons of Jacob were twelve. 23 The sons of Leah: Reuben (Jacob's firstborn), Simeon, Levi, Judah, Issachar, and Zebulun. 24 The sons of Rachel: Joseph and Benjamin. 25 The sons of Bilhah, Rachel's servant: Dan and Naphtali. 26 The sons of Zilpah, Leah's servant: Gad and Asher. These were the sons of Jacob who were born to him in Paddan-aram.

27 And Jacob came to his father Isaac at Mamre, or Kiriath-arba (that is, Hebron), where Abraham and Isaac had sojourned. 28 Now the days of Isaac were 180 years. 29 And Isaac breathed his last, and he died and was gathered to his people, old and full of days. And his sons Esau and Jacob buried him.

Esau's Descendants

36 These are the generations of Esau (that is, Edom). 2 Esau took his wives from the Canaanites: Adah the daughter of Elon the Hittite, Oholibamah the daughter of Anah the daughter[1] of Zibeon the Hivite, 3 and Basemath, Ishmael's daughter, the sister of Nebaioth. 4 And Adah bore to Esau, Eliphaz; Basemath bore Reuel; 5 and Oholibamah bore Jeush, Jalam, and Korah. These are the sons of Esau who were born to him in the land of Canaan.

6 Then Esau took his wives, his sons, his daughters, and all the members of his household, his livestock, all his beasts, and all his property that he had acquired in the land of Canaan. He went into a land away from his brother Jacob. 7 For their possessions were too great for them to dwell together. The land of their sojournings could not support them because of their livestock. 8 So Esau settled in the hill country of Seir. (Esau is Edom.)

9 These are the generations of Esau the father of the Edomites in the hill country of Seir. 10 These are the names of Esau's sons: Eliphaz the son of Adah the wife of Esau, Reuel the son of Basemath the wife of Esau. 11 The sons of Eliphaz were Teman, Omar, Zepho, Gatam, and Kenaz. 12 (Timna was a concubine of Eliphaz, Esau's son; she bore Amalek to Eliphaz.) These are the sons of Adah, Esau's wife. 13 These are the sons of Reuel: Nahath, Zerah, Shammah, and Mizzah. These are the sons of Basemath, Esau's wife. 14 These are the sons of Oholibamah the daughter of Anah the daughter of Zibeon, Esau's wife: she bore to Esau Jeush, Jalam, and Korah.

15 These are the chiefs of the sons of Esau. The sons of Eliphaz the firstborn of Esau: the chiefs Teman, Omar, Zepho, Kenaz, 16 Korah, Gatam, and Amalek; these are the chiefs of Eliphaz in the land of Edom; these are the sons of Adah. 17 These are the sons of Reuel, Esau's son: the chiefs Nahath, Zerah, Shammah, and Mizzah; these are the chiefs of Reuel in the land of Edom; these are the sons of Basemath, Esau's wife. 18 These are the sons of Oholibamah, Esau's wife: the chiefs Jeush, Jalam, and Korah; these are the chiefs born of Oholibamah the daughter of Anah, Esau's wife. 19 These are the sons of Esau (that is, Edom), and these are their chiefs.

20 These are the sons of Seir the Horite, the inhabitants of the land: Lotan, Shobal, Zibeon, Anah, 21 Dishon, Ezer, and Dishan; these are the chiefs of the Horites, the sons of Seir in the land of Edom. 22 The sons of Lotan were Hori and Hemam; and Lotan's sister was Timna. 23 These are the sons of Shobal: Alvan, Manahath, Ebal, Shepho, and Onam. 24 These are the sons of Zibeon: Aiah and Anah; he is the Anah who found the hot springs in the wilderness, as he pastured the donkeys of Zibeon his father. 25 These are the children of Anah: Dishon

[1] Hebrew; Samaritan, Septuagint, Syriac *son*; also verse 14

and Oholibamah the daughter of Anah. 26 These are the sons of Dishon: Hemdan, Eshban, Ithran, and Cheran. 27 These are the sons of Ezer: Bilhan, Zaavan, and Akan. 28 These are the sons of Dishan: Uz and Aran. 29 These are the chiefs of the Horites: the chiefs Lotan, Shobal, Zibeon, Anah, 30 Dishon, Ezer, and Dishan; these are the chiefs of the Horites, chief by chief in the land of Seir.

31 These are the kings who reigned in the land of Edom, before any king reigned over the Israelites. 32 Bela the son of Beor reigned in Edom, the name of his city being Dinhabah. 33 Bela died, and Jobab the son of Zerah of Bozrah reigned in his place. 34 Jobab died, and Husham of the land of the Temanites reigned in his place. 35 Husham died, and Hadad the son of Bedad, who defeated Midian in the country of Moab, reigned in his place, the name of his city being Avith. 36 Hadad died, and Samlah of Masrekah reigned in his place. 37 Samlah died, and Shaul of Rehoboth on the Euphrates[1] reigned in his place. 38 Shaul died, and Baal-hanan the son of Achbor reigned in his place. 39 Baal-hanan the son of Achbor died, and Hadar reigned in his place, the name of his city being Pau; his wife's name was Mehetabel, the daughter of Matred, daughter of Mezahab.

40 These are the names of the chiefs of Esau, according to their clans and their dwelling places, by their names: the chiefs Timna, Alvah, Jetheth, 41 Oholibamah, Elah, Pinon, 42 Kenaz, Teman, Mibzar, 43 Magdiel, and Iram; these are the chiefs of Edom (that is, Esau, the father of Edom), according to their dwelling places in the land of their possession.

Joseph's Dreams

95

37 Jacob lived in the land of his father's sojournings, in the land of Canaan.

2 These are the generations of Jacob.

Joseph, being seventeen years old, was pasturing the flock with his brothers. He was a boy with the sons of Bilhah and Zilpah, his father's wives. And Joseph brought a bad report of them to their father. 3 Now Israel loved Joseph more than any other of his sons, because he was the son of his old age. And he made him a robe of many colors.[2] 4 But when his brothers saw that their father loved him more than all his brothers, they hated him and could not speak peacefully to him.

5 Now Joseph had a dream, and when he told it to his brothers they hated him

CHARACTER PROFILE

JOSEPH

Joseph was Jacob's favorite son. Joseph's 10 brothers were jealous of him and sold him to traders, who took Joseph to Egypt and sold him as a slave. Joseph spent several years in jail in Egypt for something he had not done. Jacob got out of prison because he was able to tell Pharaoh the meaning of his mysterious dream. Joseph finally became the second most powerful ruler in Egypt. God used Joseph to save many people, including his own family, from famine.

95, 101, 107, 117

[1] Hebrew *the River* [2] See Septuagint, Vulgate; or (with Syriac) *a robe with long sleeves*. The meaning of the Hebrew is uncertain; also verses 23, 32

Joseph and His Brothers

Jacob loved Joseph more than any of his other 11 sons. Jacob made a robe of many colors for Joseph. The other brothers saw that Joseph was their father's favorite, and they hated Joseph because of it. Joseph's brothers could not even talk to Joseph without getting angry.

Something else made the brothers hate Joseph, too. It was his dreams. Joseph told his brothers that, in his dream, they were all tying up bundles of grain in the field. Joseph's bundle stood up straight. And all the brothers' bundles gathered around Joseph's bundle and bowed down to it.

His brothers said, "Are you indeed to reign over us? Or are you indeed to rule over us?" And Joseph's brothers hated him even more.

Then Joseph had another dream. He told this one to his brothers and to his father. In this dream, Joseph said, "The sun, the moon, and eleven stars were bowing down to me." Even Joseph's father scolded Joseph for this dream.

A short time later, Jacob sent Joseph out to check on his brothers, who were taking care of their sheep far from home. Joseph's brothers saw him coming. "Here comes this dreamer," they said. "Come now, let us kill him and throw him into one of the pits. Then we will say that a fierce animal has devoured him, and we will see what will become of his dreams." When Joseph came to them, the brothers tore off his many-colored robe and threw him into a pit.

Later, the brothers saw Ishmaelites coming with their camels. The Ishmaelites were traders who bought and sold things. They were on their way to Egypt. Instead of killing Joseph, the brothers decided to sell Joseph to the Ishmaelite traders. The brothers pulled Joseph out of the pit and sold him for twenty pieces of silver. The Ishmaelites then took Joseph with them to Egypt.

To hide their sin, the brothers lied to their father about Joseph. They dipped Joseph's coat of many colors in some goat blood and brought the robe home to their father, Jacob. He knew it was Joseph's special coat. Seeing the blood, Jacob was sure a wild animal had killed Joseph.

The angry and jealous brothers kept their secret, and Jacob was sad for a long time. He did not know that Joseph was alive or that God would use Joseph in Egypt many years later to save people's lives.

Even though Joseph had many troubles, God was always with him, preparing him for the big job God wanted him to do. Joseph's dreams came true—he became a great ruler and a deliverer in the land of Egypt. Because Joseph trusted in God and His faithfulness, God used Joseph in a mighty way to save His people from famine and starving. One day, many, many years later Jesus was born, descended from the people of Israel that Joseph saved from starving.

SEEK and FIND

WHERE TO FIND THE STORY

Genesis 37

KEY BIBLE VERSE

[Joseph said to his brothers], "you meant evil against me, but God meant it for good . . . that many people should be kept alive, as they are today." (Genesis 50:20)

THREE KEY QUESTIONS

- Why were Joseph's big brothers angry with Joseph? Was it right for them to be angry?
- What was the really bad thing that Joseph's brothers did to him?
- When the Ishmaelites took Joseph away all alone, was he really all alone? Who was with him?

RELATED BIBLE READINGS

Psalm 25:1–22; 118:6–7; Acts 7:9–10

even more. 6 He said to them, "Hear this
dream that I have dreamed: 7 Behold,
we were binding sheaves in the field,
and behold, my sheaf arose and stood
upright. And behold, your sheaves gathered around it and bowed down to my
sheaf." 8 His brothers said to him, "Are
you indeed to reign over us? Or are you
indeed to rule over us?" So they hated
him even more for his dreams and for
his words.
9 Then he dreamed another dream and
told it to his brothers and said, "Behold,
I have dreamed another dream. Behold,
the sun, the moon, and eleven stars
were bowing down to me." 10 But when
he told it to his father and to his brothers, his father rebuked him and said to
him, "What is this dream that you have
dreamed? Shall I and your mother and
your brothers indeed come to bow ourselves to the ground before you?" 11 And
his brothers were jealous of him, but his
father kept the saying in mind.

Joseph Sold by His Brothers

12 Now his brothers went to pasture
their father's flock near Shechem. 13 And
Israel said to Joseph, "Are not your brothers pasturing the flock at Shechem? Come,
I will send you to them." And he said to
him, "Here I am." 14 So he said to him, "Go
now, see if it is well with your brothers and
with the flock, and bring me word." So he
sent him from the Valley of Hebron, and
he came to Shechem. 15 And a man found
him wandering in the fields. And the man
asked him, "What are you seeking?" 16 "I
am seeking my brothers," he said. "Tell
me, please, where they are pasturing the
flock." 17 And the man said, "They have
gone away, for I heard them say, 'Let us

go to Dothan.'" So Joseph went after his brothers and found them at Dothan.

18 They saw him from afar, and before he came near to them they conspired against him to kill him. 19 They said to one another, "Here comes this dreamer. 20 Come now, let us kill him and throw him into one of the pits.[1] Then we will say that a fierce animal has devoured him, and we will see what will become of his dreams." 21 But when Reuben heard it, he rescued him out of their hands, saying, "Let us not take his life." 22 And Reuben said to them, "Shed no blood; throw him into this pit here in the wilderness, but do not lay a hand on him"—that he might rescue him out of their hand to restore him to his father. 23 So when Joseph came to his brothers, they stripped him of his robe, the robe of many colors that he wore. 24 And they took him and threw him into a pit. The pit was empty; there was no water in it.

25 Then they sat down to eat. And looking up they saw a caravan of Ishmaelites coming from Gilead, with their camels bearing gum, balm, and myrrh, on their way to carry it down to Egypt. 26 Then Judah said to his brothers, "What profit is it if we kill our brother and conceal his blood? 27 Come, let us sell him to the Ishmaelites, and let not our hand be upon him, for he is our brother, our own flesh." And his brothers listened to him. 28 Then Midianite traders passed by. And they drew Joseph up and lifted him out of the pit, and sold him to the Ishmaelites for twenty shekels[2] of silver. They took Joseph to Egypt.

29 When Reuben returned to the pit and saw that Joseph was not in the pit, he tore his clothes 30 and returned to his brothers and said, "The boy is gone, and I, where shall I go?" 31 Then they took Joseph's robe and slaughtered a goat and dipped the robe in the blood. 32 And they sent the robe of many colors and brought it to their father and said, "This we have found; please identify whether it is your son's robe or not." 33 And he identified it and said, "It is my son's robe. A fierce animal has devoured him. Joseph is without doubt torn to pieces." 34 Then Jacob tore his garments and put sackcloth on his loins and mourned for his son many days. 35 All his sons and all his daughters rose up to comfort him, but he refused to be comforted and said, "No, I shall go down to Sheol to my son, mourning." Thus his father wept for him. 36 Meanwhile the Midianites had sold him in Egypt to Potiphar, an officer of Pharaoh, the captain of the guard.

Judah and Tamar

38 It happened at that time that Judah went down from his brothers and turned aside to a certain Adullamite, whose name was Hirah. 2 There Judah saw the daughter of a certain Canaanite whose name was Shua. He took her and went in to her, 3 and she conceived and bore a son, and he called his name Er. 4 She conceived again and bore a son, and she called his name Onan. 5 Yet again she bore a son, and she called his name Shelah. Judah[3] was in Chezib when she bore him.

6 And Judah took a wife for Er his firstborn, and her name was Tamar. 7 But Er, Judah's firstborn, was wicked in the sight of the LORD, and the LORD put him to death. 8 Then Judah said to Onan, "Go in to your brother's wife and perform the duty of a brother-in-law to her, and raise up offspring for your brother." 9 But Onan knew that the offspring would not be his. So whenever he went in to his brother's wife he would waste the semen on the ground, so as not to give offspring to his brother. 10 And what he did was wicked in the sight of the LORD, and he put him to death also. 11 Then Judah said to Tamar his daughter-in-law, "Remain a widow in your father's house, till Shelah my son grows up"—for he feared that he would

[1] Or *cisterns*; also verses 22, 24 [2] A *shekel* was about 2/5 ounce or 11 grams [3] Hebrew *He*

die, like his brothers. So Tamar went and remained in her father's house.

12 In the course of time the wife of Judah, Shua's daughter, died. When Judah was comforted, he went up to Timnah to his sheepshearers, he and his friend Hirah the Adullamite. 13 And when Tamar was told, "Your father-in-law is going up to Timnah to shear his sheep," 14 she took off her widow's garments and covered herself with a veil, wrapping herself up, and sat at the entrance to Enaim, which is on the road to Timnah. For she saw that Shelah was grown up, and she had not been given to him in marriage. 15 When Judah saw her, he thought she was a prostitute, for she had covered her face. 16 He turned to her at the roadside and said, "Come, let me come in to you," for he did not know that she was his daughter-in-law. She said, "What will you give me, that you may come in to me?" 17 He answered, "I will send you a young goat from the flock." And she said, "If you give me a pledge, until you send it—" 18 He said, "What pledge shall I give you?" She replied, "Your signet and your cord and your staff that is in your hand." So he gave them to her and went in to her, and she conceived by him. 19 Then she arose and went away, and taking off her veil she put on the garments of her widowhood.

20 When Judah sent the young goat by his friend the Adullamite to take back the pledge from the woman's hand, he did not find her. 21 And he asked the men of the place, "Where is the cult prostitute[1] who was at Enaim at the roadside?" And they said, "No cult prostitute has been here." 22 So he returned to Judah and said, "I have not found her. Also, the men of the place said, 'No cult prostitute has been here.'" 23 And Judah replied, "Let her keep the things as her own, or we shall be laughed at. You see, I sent this young goat, and you did not find her."

24 About three months later Judah was told, "Tamar your daughter-in-law has been immoral.[2] Moreover, she is pregnant by immorality."[3] And Judah said, "Bring her out, and let her be burned." 25 As she was being brought out, she sent word to her father-in-law, "By the man to whom these belong, I am pregnant." And she said, "Please identify whose these are, the signet and the cord and the staff." 26 Then Judah identified them and said, "She is more righteous than I, since I did not give her to my son Shelah." And he did not know her again.

27 When the time of her labor came, there were twins in her womb. 28 And when she was in labor, one put out a hand, and the midwife took and tied a scarlet thread on his hand, saying, "This one came out first." 29 But as he drew back his hand, behold, his brother came out. And she said, "What a breach you have made for yourself!" Therefore his name was called Perez.[4] 30 Afterward his brother came out with the scarlet thread on his hand, and his name was called Zerah.

Joseph and Potiphar's Wife

101

39 Now Joseph had been brought down to Egypt, and Potiphar, an officer of Pharaoh, the captain of the guard, an Egyptian, had bought him from the Ishmaelites who had brought him down there. 2 The LORD was with Joseph, and he became a successful man, and he was in the house of his Egyptian master. 3 His master saw that the LORD was with him and that the LORD caused all that he did to succeed in his hands. 4 So Joseph found favor in his sight and attended him, and he made him overseer of his house and put him in charge of all that he had. 5 From the time that he made him overseer in his house and over all that he had the LORD blessed the Egyptian's house for Joseph's sake; the blessing of the LORD was on all that he had, in house and field. 6 So he left all that he had in Joseph's charge, and because of

[1] Hebrew *sacred woman*; a woman who served a pagan deity by prostitution; also verse 22 [2] Or *has committed prostitution* [3] Or *by prostitution* [4] *Perez* means *a breach*

Joseph's Troubles

Joseph was one of Jacob's sons. His brothers were jealous of him because Jacob loved him best and because God gave him dreams. In his dreams, Joseph saw that some day he would be a great ruler. He didn't know when it would happen, but he knew God had plans for him.

One day, his brothers sold Joseph to some traders. The traders took Joseph to Egypt where they sold him as a slave. So Joseph now lived far away in Egypt, working as a slave for a rich army officer named Potiphar.

Joseph worked hard for Potiphar. The Lord was with Joseph, and everything Joseph did turned out well. Joseph's master, Potiphar, saw this. So Potiphar put Joseph in charge of his whole house, all of his workers, and all of his things. The Lord blessed Potiphar and all he had because of Joseph.

One day, Potiphar's wife tried to get Joseph to sin with her. Joseph knew that Potiphar would not want his wife to do this wicked sin with Joseph. Joseph told Potiphar's wife that her husband trusted him. "How then can I do this great wickedness and sin against God?" Joseph asked her.

Day after day, Potiphar's wife kept talking to Joseph, trying to get him to sin with her. Day after day, Joseph would not listen to her. One day, when her husband was away, Potiphar's wife grabbed Joseph by his clothing and asked him, once again, to sin with her.

Joseph refused to sin with her and ran away. But she hung on to his clothing and it came off in her hands. Potiphar's wife began to scream and cry. The servants came running. Potiphar's wife lied and said that Joseph had attacked her. She told them that when she had screamed he had run away, leaving his clothes there with her. When Potiphar came home, his wife told him the same false story.

When Potiphar heard his wife's story and saw Joseph's clothing in her hand, he was angry. Potiphar locked up Joseph in the king's prison.

When Joseph was in prison, just like when he was in Potiphar's house, the Lord was with Joseph and showed him steadfast love. The keeper of the prison also liked Joseph and put him in charge of all the prisoners. Just as God had done in Potiphar's house, the Lord now made everything that Joseph did in prison turn out well. Even though Joseph had many troubles, the Lord was always with him, caring for him and blessing him. Today, no matter how scary or hard life can be, we know that Jesus has promised that He will never leave us or forsake us.

SEEK and FIND

WHERE TO FIND THE STORY

Genesis 39

KEY BIBLE VERSE

"But the LORD was with Joseph and showed him steadfast love." (Genesis 39:21)

THREE KEY QUESTIONS

- What was the name of the far away land where the traders took Joseph? Whose house did Joseph oversee there in the far away land?
- What did Joseph do when Potiphar's wife wanted him to do a wicked sin? What should we do when someone tempts us to sin?
- Sometimes we have many troubles, like Joseph did. Is the Lord with us even in these troubles, like He was with Joseph?

RELATED BIBLE READINGS

Psalm 1:1–3; 37:5–7, 39–40; Acts 7:9–10

him he had no concern about anything but the food he ate.

Now Joseph was handsome in form and appearance. 7 And after a time his master's wife cast her eyes on Joseph and said, "Lie with me." 8 But he refused and said to his master's wife, "Behold, because of me my master has no concern about anything in the house, and he has put everything that he has in my charge. 9 He is not greater in this house than I am, nor has he kept back anything from me except yourself, because you are his wife. How then can I do this great wickedness and sin against God?" 10 And as she spoke to Joseph day after day, he would not listen to her, to lie beside her or to be with her.

11 But one day, when he went into the house to do his work and none of the men of the house was there in the house, 12 she caught him by his garment, saying, "Lie with me." But he left his garment in her hand and fled and got out of the house. 13 And as soon as she saw that he had left his garment in her hand and had fled out of the house, 14 she called to the men of her household and said to them, "See, he has brought among us a Hebrew to laugh at us. He came in to me to lie with me, and I cried out with a loud voice. 15 And as soon as he heard that I lifted up my voice and cried out, he left his garment beside me and fled and got out of the house." 16 Then she laid up his garment by her until his master came home, 17 and she told him the same story, saying, "The Hebrew servant, whom you have brought among us, came in to me to laugh at me. 18 But as soon as I lifted up my voice and cried, he left his garment beside me and fled out of the house."

19 As soon as his master heard the words that his wife spoke to him, "This is the way your servant treated me," his anger was kindled. 20 And Joseph's master took him and put him into the prison, the place where the king's prisoners were confined, and he was there in prison.

21 But the LORD was with Joseph
and showed him steadfast love
101 and gave him favor in the sight of
the keeper of the prison. 22 And the keeper of the prison put Joseph in charge of all the prisoners who were in the prison. Whatever was done there, he was the one

who did it. 23 The keeper of the prison paid
no attention to anything that was in
Joseph's charge, because the LORD was
with him. And whatever he did, the LORD
made it succeed.

Joseph Interprets Two Prisoners' Dreams

107

40 Some time after this, the
cupbearer of the king of
Egypt and his baker committed an
offense against their lord the king of Egypt.
2 And Pharaoh was angry with his two offi-
cers, the chief cupbearer and the chief
baker, 3 and he put them in custody in the
house of the captain of the guard, in the
prison where Joseph was confined. 4 The
captain of the guard appointed Joseph to
be with them, and he attended them. They
continued for some time in custody.

5 And one night they both dreamed—
the cupbearer and the baker of the king
of Egypt, who were confined in the
prison—each his own dream, and each
dream with its own interpretation. 6 When
Joseph came to them in the morning, he
saw that they were troubled. 7 So he asked
Pharaoh's officers who were with him in
custody in his master's house, "Why are
your faces downcast today?" 8 They said to
him, "We have had dreams, and there is
no one to interpret them." And Joseph said
to them, "Do not interpretations belong to
God? Please tell them to me."

9 So the chief cupbearer told his dream
to Joseph and said to him, "In my dream
there was a vine before me, 10 and on the
vine there were three branches. As soon as
it budded, its blossoms shot forth, and the
clusters ripened into grapes. 11 Pharaoh's
cup was in my hand, and I took the grapes
and pressed them into Pharaoh's cup and
placed the cup in Pharaoh's hand." 12 Then
Joseph said to him, "This is its interpre-
tation: the three branches are three days.
13 In three days Pharaoh will lift up your
head and restore you to your office, and
you shall place Pharaoh's cup in his hand
as formerly, when you were his cupbearer.
14 Only remember me, when it is well with
you, and please do me the kindness to
mention me to Pharaoh, and so get me out
of this house. 15 For I was indeed stolen
out of the land of the Hebrews, and here
also I have done nothing that they should
put me into the pit."

16 When the chief baker saw that the
interpretation was favorable, he said to
Joseph, "I also had a dream: there were
three cake baskets on my head, 17 and
in the uppermost basket there were all
sorts of baked food for Pharaoh, but the
birds were eating it out of the basket on
my head." 18 And Joseph answered and
said, "This is its interpretation: the three
baskets are three days. 19 In three days
Pharaoh will lift up your head—from
you!—and hang you on a tree. And the
birds will eat the flesh from you."

20 On the third day, which was Pharaoh's
birthday, he made a feast for all his ser-
vants and lifted up the head of the chief
cupbearer and the head of the chief baker
among his servants. 21 He restored the
chief cupbearer to his position, and he
placed the cup in Pharaoh's hand. 22 But
he hanged the chief baker, as Joseph had
interpreted to them. 23 Yet the chief cup-
bearer did not remember Joseph, but for-
got him.

Joseph Interprets Pharaoh's Dreams

41 After two whole years, Pharaoh
dreamed that he was standing
by the Nile, 2 and behold, there came up
out of the Nile seven cows attractive and
plump, and they fed in the reed grass.
3 And behold, seven other cows, ugly and
thin, came up out of the Nile after them,
and stood by the other cows on the bank
of the Nile. 4 And the ugly, thin cows ate
up the seven attractive, plump cows. And
Pharaoh awoke. 5 And he fell asleep and
dreamed a second time. And behold,
seven ears of grain, plump and good,

were growing on one stalk. 6 And behold, after them sprouted seven ears, thin and blighted by the east wind. 7 And the thin ears swallowed up the seven plump, full ears. And Pharaoh awoke, and behold, it was a dream. 8 So in the morning his spirit was troubled, and he sent and called for all the magicians of Egypt and all its wise men. Pharaoh told them his dreams, but there was none who could interpret them to Pharaoh.

9 Then the chief cupbearer said to Pharaoh, "I remember my offenses today. 10 When Pharaoh was angry with his servants and put me and the chief baker in custody in the house of the captain of the guard, 11 we dreamed on the same night, he and I, each having a dream with its own interpretation. 12 A young Hebrew was there with us, a servant of the captain of the guard. When we told him, he interpreted our dreams to us, giving an interpretation to each man according to his dream. 13 And as he interpreted to us, so it came about. I was restored to my office, and the baker was hanged."

14 Then Pharaoh sent and called Joseph, and they quickly brought him out of the pit. And when he had shaved himself and changed his clothes, he came in before Pharaoh. 15 And Pharaoh said to Joseph, "I have had a dream, and there is no one who can interpret it. I have heard it said of you that when you hear a dream you can interpret it." 16 Joseph answered Pharaoh, "It is not in me; God will give Pharaoh a favorable answer."[1] 17 Then Pharaoh said to Joseph, "Behold, in my dream I was standing on the banks of the Nile. 18 Seven cows, plump and attractive, came up out of the Nile and fed in the reed grass. 19 Seven other cows came up after them, poor and very ugly and thin, such as I had never seen in all the land of Egypt. 20 And the thin, ugly cows ate up the first seven plump cows, 21 but when they had eaten them no one would have known that they had eaten them, for they were still as ugly as at the beginning. Then I awoke. 22 I also saw in my dream seven ears growing on one stalk, full and good. 23 Seven ears, withered, thin, and blighted by the east wind, sprouted after them, 24 and the thin ears swallowed up the seven good ears. And I told it to the magicians, but there was no one who could explain it to me."

25 Then Joseph said to Pharaoh, "The dreams of Pharaoh are one; God has revealed to Pharaoh what he is about to do. 26 The seven good cows are seven years, and the seven good ears are seven years; the dreams are one. 27 The seven lean and ugly cows that came up after them are seven years, and the seven empty ears blighted by the east wind are also seven years of famine. 28 It is as I told Pharaoh; God has shown to Pharaoh what he is about to do. 29 There will come seven years of great plenty throughout all the land of Egypt, 30 but after them there will arise seven years of famine, and all the plenty will be forgotten in the land of Egypt. The famine will consume the land, 31 and the plenty will be unknown in the land by reason of the famine that will follow, for it will be very severe. 32 And the doubling of Pharaoh's dream means that the thing is fixed by God, and God will shortly bring it about. 33 Now therefore let Pharaoh select a discerning and wise man, and set him over the land of Egypt. 34 Let Pharaoh proceed to appoint overseers over the land and take one-fifth of the produce of the land[2] of Egypt during the seven plentiful years. 35 And let them gather all the food of these good years that are coming and store up grain under the authority of Pharaoh for food in the cities, and let them keep it. 36 That food shall be a reserve for the land against the seven years of famine that are to occur in the land of Egypt, so that the land may not perish through the famine."

[1] Or (compare Samaritan, Septuagint) *Without God it is not possible to give Pharaoh an answer about his welfare* [2] Or *over the land and organize the land*

Joseph Saves People from Famine

While Joseph was in prison, Pharaoh's cupbearer and his baker got in trouble and were sent to the same prison. One night, both of them had dreams that troubled them. When they told Joseph this, he told them that only God knows what dreams mean. "Please tell them to me," Joseph said. So the two men told Joseph their dreams.

In the cupbearer's dream, he saw a grapevine with three branches, which grew buds and then clusters of grapes. The cupbearer squeezed the grapes into Pharaoh's cup, making wine for him. Then in the dream the cupbearer gave the cup of wine to Pharaoh.

Joseph said that the three branches were three days. The dream meant that in three days Pharaoh would free the cupbearer from prison—he would give him back his job of serving Pharaoh. Joseph asked the cupbearer to tell Pharaoh about Joseph when the cupbearer got out of prison, so that Joseph could get out of prison, too.

Then Joseph listened to the baker's dream. The baker dreamed that he was carrying three baskets on his head. The top basket was full of all kinds of baked foods for Pharaoh, but birds were eating Pharaoh's food. Then Joseph explained to the baker what his dream meant—that in three days the baker would be hanged for what he had done wrong.

Three days later, on Pharaoh's birthday, the chief cupbearer got his job back, but the baker was hanged. All this happened just as Joseph had said.

For two years, no one came to get Joseph out of prison. But God did not forget about Joseph.

One night, Pharaoh had two mysterious dreams that puzzled him. Pharaoh wanted to know what his dreams meant. Finally, the cupbearer remembered that Joseph had explained his dream, and he told Pharaoh about Joseph.

Pharaoh sent for Joseph who was still in prison. Joseph came to Pharaoh's palace and told Pharaoh that God is the one who can tell what dreams mean. Then Joseph listened to Pharaoh tell his dreams.

In Pharaoh's first dream, seven plump, healthy cows came up out of the river. Seven ugly, thin cows came up after them. The seven thin cows ate the seven healthy cows. In Pharaoh's second dream, seven full ears of corn grew on one stalk. After them, seven thin and withered ears of corn grew. Then the thin ears of corn swallowed up the good ears of corn.

Joseph told Pharaoh that God was showing him what God was going to do. The seven good cows and the seven good ears of corn meant there would be seven good years for farming. Right after the good years, though, seven bad would come when nothing would grow—when there would be a great famine throughout all the land of Egypt. Joseph told Pharaoh that he should put someone wise in charge of saving up food during the seven good years, so that the people of Egypt would not starve to death during the seven years of famine.

Pharaoh chose Joseph to be in charge of saving Egypt. He made him the highest ruler in the land, second only to Pharaoh himself. He gave Joseph fine clothes, a golden ring, and a special chariot.

During the seven good years, Joseph worked hard at storing up grain. He stored so much grain that it could not even be measured. When the seven years of famine began, Joseph had plenty of food to sell to the people of Egypt. The famine was so bad that people even came from far away countries to buy grain from Joseph.

God used Joseph to keep people from starving in the famine—and to save his own family, the family from which God's only Son, Jesus, would someday be born. Jesus would be an even greater Savior, saving His people not just from famine, but giving them eternal life.

SEEK and FIND

WHERE TO FIND THE STORY

Genesis 40–41

KEY BIBLE VERSE

"All the earth came to Egypt to Joseph to buy grain, because the famine was severe over all the earth." (Genesis 41:57)

THREE KEY QUESTIONS

- How did God know the meaning of all the dreams in the story?
- Who really sent Joseph to Egypt? Why did He send him there?
- Why can we trust God when even when bad things happen to us?

RELATED BIBLE READINGS

Psalm 105:16–22; Acts 7:9–12; Romans 8:28

Joseph Rises to Power

37 This proposal pleased Pharaoh and
all his servants. 38 And Pharaoh said to
his servants, "Can we find a man like this,
in whom is the Spirit of God?"[1] 39 Then
Pharaoh said to Joseph, "Since God has
shown you all this, there is none so dis-
cerning and wise as you are. 40 You shall
be over my house, and all my people shall
order themselves as you command.[2] Only
as regards the throne will I be greater than
you." 41 And Pharaoh said to Joseph, "See,
I have set you over all the land of Egypt."
42 Then Pharaoh took his signet ring from
his hand and put it on Joseph's hand, and
clothed him in garments of fine linen and
put a gold chain about his neck. 43 And
he made him ride in his second chariot.
And they called out before him, "Bow the
knee!"[3] Thus he set him over all the land
of Egypt. 44 Moreover, Pharaoh said to
Joseph, "I am Pharaoh, and without your
consent no one shall lift up hand or foot
in all the land of Egypt." 45 And Pharaoh
called Joseph's name Zaphenath-paneah.
And he gave him in marriage Asenath,
the daughter of Potiphera priest of On. So
Joseph went out over the land of Egypt.

46 Joseph was thirty years old when he
entered the service of Pharaoh king of
Egypt. And Joseph went out from the pres-
ence of Pharaoh and went through all the
land of Egypt. 47 During the seven plenti-
ful years the earth produced abundantly,
48 and he gathered up all the food of these
seven years, which occurred in the land
of Egypt, and put the food in the cities. He
put in every city the food from the fields
around it. 49 And Joseph stored up grain in
great abundance, like the sand of the sea,
until he ceased to measure it, for it could
not be measured.

50 Before the year of famine came, two
sons were born to Joseph. Asenath, the
daughter of Potiphera priest of On, bore
them to him. 51 Joseph called the name
of the firstborn Manasseh. "For," he said,
"God has made me forget all my hardship
and all my father's house."[4] 52 The name
of the second he called Ephraim, "For God
has made me fruitful in the land of my
affliction."[5]

53 The seven years of plenty that oc-
curred in the land of Egypt came to an
end, 54 and the seven years of famine
began to come, as Joseph had said. There
was famine in all lands, but in all the land
of Egypt there was bread. 55 When all the
land of Egypt was famished, the people
cried to Pharaoh for bread. Pharaoh said
to all the Egyptians, "Go to Joseph. What
he says to you, do."

56 So when the famine had spread over
all the land, Joseph opened all the store-
houses[6] and sold to the Egyptians, for the
famine was severe in the land of Egypt.
57 Moreover, all the earth came to
Egypt to Joseph to buy grain, be-
107 cause the famine was severe over
all the earth.

Joseph's Brothers Go to Egypt

42 When Jacob learned that
there was grain for sale in
117 Egypt, he said to his sons, "Why do
you look at one another?" 2 And he said,
"Behold, I have heard that there is grain
for sale in Egypt. Go down and buy grain
for us there, that we may live and not die."
3 So ten of Joseph's brothers went down to
buy grain in Egypt. 4 But Jacob did not send
Benjamin, Joseph's brother, with his
brothers, for he feared that harm might
happen to him. 5 Thus the sons of Israel
came to buy among the others who came,
for the famine was in the land of Canaan.

6 Now Joseph was governor over the
land. He was the one who sold to all the
people of the land. And Joseph's brothers
came and bowed themselves before him
with their faces to the ground. 7 Joseph
saw his brothers and recognized them, but
he treated them like strangers and spoke

[1] Or *of the gods* [2] Hebrew *and according to your command all my people shall kiss the ground* [3] *Abrek*, probably an Egyptian word, similar in sound to the Hebrew word meaning *to kneel* [4] *Manasseh* sounds like the Hebrew for *making to forget* [5] *Ephraim* sounds like the Hebrew for *making fruitful* [6] Hebrew *all that was in them*

roughly to them. "Where do you come from?" he said. They said, "From the land of Canaan, to buy food." 8 And Joseph recognized his brothers, but they did not recognize him. 9 And Joseph remembered the dreams that he had dreamed of them. And he said to them, "You are spies; you have come to see the nakedness of the land." 10 They said to him, "No, my lord, your servants have come to buy food. 11 We are all sons of one man. We are honest men. Your servants have never been spies."

12 He said to them, "No, it is the nakedness of the land that you have come to see." 13 And they said, "We, your servants, are twelve brothers, the sons of one man in the land of Canaan, and behold, the youngest is this day with our father, and one is no more." 14 But Joseph said to them, "It is as I said to you. You are spies. 15 By this you shall be tested: by the life of Pharaoh, you shall not go from this place unless your youngest brother comes here. 16 Send one of you, and let him bring your brother, while you remain confined, that your words may be tested, whether there is truth in you. Or else, by the life of Pharaoh, surely you are spies." 17 And he put them all together in custody for three days.

18 On the third day Joseph said to them, "Do this and you will live, for I fear God: 19 if you are honest men, let one of your brothers remain confined where you are in custody, and let the rest go and carry grain for the famine of your households, 20 and bring your youngest brother to me. So your words will be verified, and you shall not die." And they did so. 21 Then they said to one another, "In truth we are guilty concerning our brother, in that we saw the distress of his soul, when he begged us and we did not listen. That is why this distress has come upon us." 22 And Reuben answered them, "Did I not tell you not to sin against the boy? But you did not listen. So now there comes a reckoning for his blood." 23 They did not know that Joseph understood them, for there was an interpreter between them. 24 Then he turned away from them and wept. And he returned to them and spoke to them. And he took Simeon from them and bound him before their eyes. 25 And Joseph gave orders to fill their bags with grain, and to replace every man's money in his sack, and to give them provisions for the journey. This was done for them.

26 Then they loaded their donkeys with their grain and departed. 27 And as one of them opened his sack to give his donkey fodder at the lodging place, he saw his money in the mouth of his sack. 28 He said to his brothers, "My money has been put back; here it is in the mouth of my sack!" At this their hearts failed them, and they turned trembling to one another, saying, "What is this that God has done to us?"

29 When they came to Jacob their father in the land of Canaan, they told him all that had happened to them, saying, 30 "The man, the lord of the land, spoke roughly to us and took us to be spies of the land. 31 But we said to him, 'We are honest men; we have never been spies. 32 We are twelve brothers, sons of our father. One is no more, and the youngest is this day with our father in the land of Canaan.' 33 Then the man, the lord of the land, said to us, 'By this I shall know that you are honest men: leave one of your brothers with me, and take grain for the famine of your households, and go your way. 34 Bring your youngest brother to me. Then I shall know that you are not spies but honest men, and I will deliver your brother to you, and you shall trade in the land.'"

35 As they emptied their sacks, behold, every man's bundle of money was in his sack. And when they and their father saw their bundles of money, they were afraid. 36 And Jacob their father said to them, "You have bereaved me of my children: Joseph is no more, and Simeon is no more, and now you would take

Benjamin. All this has come against me."
37 Then Reuben said to his father, "Kill
my two sons if I do not bring him back
to you. Put him in my hands, and I will
bring him back to you." 38 But he said,
"My son shall not go down with you, for
his brother is dead, and he is the only one
left. If harm should happen to him on the
journey that you are to make, you would
bring down my gray hairs with sorrow
to Sheol."

Joseph's Brothers Return to Egypt

43 Now the famine was severe in
the land. 2 And when they had
eaten the grain that they had brought
from Egypt, their father said to them,
"Go again, buy us a little food." 3 But
Judah said to him, "The man solemnly
warned us, saying, 'You shall not see my
face unless your brother is with you.' 4 If
you will send our brother with us, we will
go down and buy you food. 5 But if you
will not send him, we will not go down,
for the man said to us, 'You shall not
see my face, unless your brother is with
you.'" 6 Israel said, "Why did you treat me
so badly as to tell the man that you had
another brother?" 7 They replied, "The
man questioned us carefully about our-
selves and our kindred, saying, 'Is your
father still alive? Do you have another
brother?' What we told him was in
answer to these questions. Could we in
any way know that he would say, 'Bring
your brother down'?" 8 And Judah said to
Israel his father, "Send the boy with me,
and we will arise and go, that we may live
and not die, both we and you and also our
little ones. 9 I will be a pledge of his safety.
From my hand you shall require him. If I
do not bring him back to you and set him
before you, then let me bear the blame
forever. 10 If we had not delayed, we would
now have returned twice."
11 Then their father Israel said to them,
"If it must be so, then do this: take some
of the choice fruits of the land in your
bags, and carry a present down to the
man, a little balm and a little honey, gum,
myrrh, pistachio nuts, and almonds.
12 Take double the money with you.
Carry back with you the money that was
returned in the mouth of your sacks.
Perhaps it was an oversight. 13 Take also
your brother, and arise, go again to the
man. 14 May God Almighty[1] grant you
mercy before the man, and may he send
back your other brother and Benjamin.
And as for me, if I am bereaved of my chil-
dren, I am bereaved."
15 So the men took this present, and
they took double the money with them,
and Benjamin. They arose and went down
to Egypt and stood before Joseph.
16 When Joseph saw Benjamin with
them, he said to the steward of his house,
"Bring the men into the house, and
slaughter an animal and make ready, for
the men are to dine with me at noon."
17 The man did as Joseph told him and
brought the men to Joseph's house. 18 And
the men were afraid because they were
brought to Joseph's house, and they said,
"It is because of the money, which was
replaced in our sacks the first time, that
we are brought in, so that he may assault
us and fall upon us to make us servants
and seize our donkeys." 19 So they went
up to the steward of Joseph's house and
spoke with him at the door of the house,
20 and said, "Oh, my lord, we came down
the first time to buy food. 21 And when we
came to the lodging place we opened our
sacks, and there was each man's money
in the mouth of his sack, our money in
full weight. So we have brought it again
with us, 22 and we have brought other
money down with us to buy food. We
do not know who put our money in our
sacks." 23 He replied, "Peace to you, do
not be afraid. Your God and the God of
your father has put treasure in your sacks
for you. I received your money." Then

[1] Hebrew *El Shaddai*

he brought Simeon out to them. 24 And
when the man had brought the men into
Joseph's house and given them water, and
they had washed their feet, and when he
had given their donkeys fodder, 25 they
prepared the present for Joseph's coming
at noon, for they heard that they should
eat bread there.

26 When Joseph came home, they
brought into the house to him the pres-
ent that they had with them and bowed
down to him to the ground. 27 And he
inquired about their welfare and said, "Is
your father well, the old man of whom you
spoke? Is he still alive?" 28 They said, "Your
servant our father is well; he is still alive."
And they bowed their heads and prostrated
themselves. 29 And he lifted up his eyes
and saw his brother Benjamin, his moth-
er's son, and said, "Is this your young-
est brother, of whom you spoke to me?
God be gracious to you, my son!" 30 Then
Joseph hurried out, for his compassion
grew warm for his brother, and he sought
a place to weep. And he entered his cham-
ber and wept there. 31 Then he washed his
face and came out. And controlling him-
self he said, "Serve the food." 32 They served
him by himself, and them by themselves,
and the Egyptians who ate with him by
themselves, because the Egyptians could
not eat with the Hebrews, for that is an
abomination to the Egyptians. 33 And they
sat before him, the firstborn according to
his birthright and the youngest accord-
ing to his youth. And the men looked at
one another in amazement. 34 Portions
were taken to them from Joseph's table,
but Benjamin's portion was five times as
much as any of theirs. And they drank and
were merry[1] with him.

Joseph Tests His Brothers

44 Then he commanded the steward
of his house, "Fill the men's sacks
with food, as much as they can carry, and
put each man's money in the mouth of
his sack, 2 and put my cup, the silver cup,
in the mouth of the sack of the youngest,
with his money for the grain." And he did
as Joseph told him.

3 As soon as the morning was light, the
men were sent away with their donkeys.
4 They had gone only a short distance from
the city. Now Joseph said to his steward,
"Up, follow after the men, and when you
overtake them, say to them, 'Why have
you repaid evil for good?[2] 5 Is it not from
this that my lord drinks, and by this that
he practices divination? You have done
evil in doing this.'"

6 When he overtook them, he spoke
to them these words. 7 They said to him,
"Why does my lord speak such words as
these? Far be it from your servants to do
such a thing! 8 Behold, the money that
we found in the mouths of our sacks we
brought back to you from the land of
Canaan. How then could we steal silver or
gold from your lord's house? 9 Whichever
of your servants is found with it shall die,
and we also will be my lord's servants."
10 He said, "Let it be as you say: he who
is found with it shall be my servant, and
the rest of you shall be innocent." 11 Then
each man quickly lowered his sack to the
ground, and each man opened his sack.
12 And he searched, beginning with the
eldest and ending with the youngest. And
the cup was found in Benjamin's sack.
13 Then they tore their clothes, and every
man loaded his donkey, and they returned
to the city.

14 When Judah and his brothers came to
Joseph's house, he was still there. They fell
before him to the ground. 15 Joseph said
to them, "What deed is this that you have
done? Do you not know that a man like me
can indeed practice divination?" 16 And
Judah said, "What shall we say to my lord?
What shall we speak? Or how can we clear
ourselves? God has found out the guilt of
your servants; behold, we are my lord's
servants, both we and he also in whose

[1] Hebrew *and became intoxicated* [2] Septuagint (compare Vulgate) adds *Why have you stolen my silver cup?*

hand the cup has been found." [17]But he said, "Far be it from me that I should do so! Only the man in whose hand the cup was found shall be my servant. But as for you, go up in peace to your father."

[18]Then Judah went up to him and said, "Oh, my lord, please let your servant speak a word in my lord's ears, and let not your anger burn against your servant, for you are like Pharaoh himself. [19]My lord asked his servants, saying, 'Have you a father, or a brother?' [20]And we said to my lord, 'We have a father, an old man, and a young brother, the child of his old age. His brother is dead, and he alone is left of his mother's children, and his father loves him.' [21]Then you said to your servants, 'Bring him down to me, that I may set my eyes on him.' [22]We said to my lord, 'The boy cannot leave his father, for if he should leave his father, his father would die.' [23]Then you said to your servants, 'Unless your youngest brother comes down with you, you shall not see my face again.'

[24]"When we went back to your servant my father, we told him the words of my lord. [25]And when our father said, 'Go again, buy us a little food,' [26]we said, 'We cannot go down. If our youngest brother goes with us, then we will go down. For we cannot see the man's face unless our youngest brother is with us.' [27]Then your servant my father said to us, 'You know that my wife bore me two sons. [28]One left me, and I said, Surely he has been torn to pieces, and I have never seen him since. [29]If you take this one also from me, and harm happens to him, you will bring down my gray hairs in evil to Sheol.'

[30]"Now therefore, as soon as I come to your servant my father, and the boy is not with us, then, as his life is bound up in the boy's life, [31]as soon as he sees that the boy is not with us, he will die, and your servants will bring down the gray hairs of your servant our father with sorrow to Sheol. [32]For your servant became a pledge of safety for the boy to my father, saying, 'If I do not bring him back to you, then I shall bear the blame before my father all my life.' [33]Now therefore, please let your servant remain instead of the boy as a servant to my lord, and let the boy go back with his brothers. [34]For how can I go back to my father if the boy is not with me? I fear to see the evil that would find my father."

Joseph Provides for His Brothers and Family

45 Then Joseph could not control himself before all those who stood by him. He cried, "Make everyone go out from me." So no one stayed with him when Joseph made himself known to his brothers. [2]And he wept aloud, so that the Egyptians heard it, and the household of Pharaoh heard it. [3]And Joseph said to his brothers, "I am Joseph! Is my father still alive?" But his brothers could not answer him, for they were dismayed at his presence.

[4]So Joseph said to his brothers, "Come near to me, please." And they came near. And he said, "I am your brother, Joseph, whom you sold into Egypt. [5]And now do not be distressed or angry with yourselves because you sold me here, for God sent me before you to preserve life. [6]For the famine has been in the land these two years, and there are yet five years in which there will be neither plowing nor harvest. [7]And God sent me before you to preserve for you a remnant on earth, and to keep alive for you many survivors. [8]So it was not you who sent me here, but God. He has made me a father to Pharaoh, and lord of all his house and ruler over all the land of Egypt. [9]Hurry and go up to my father and say to him, 'Thus says your son Joseph, God has made me lord of all Egypt. Come down to me; do not tarry. [10]You shall dwell in the land of Goshen, and you shall be near me, you and your children and your children's

children, and your flocks, your herds, and all that you have. 11 There I will provide for you, for there are yet five years of famine to come, so that you and your household, and all that you have, do not come to poverty.' 12 And now your eyes see, and the eyes of my brother Benjamin see, that it is my mouth that speaks to you. 13 You must tell my father of all my honor in Egypt, and of all that you have seen. Hurry and bring my father down here." 14 Then he fell upon his brother Benjamin's neck and wept, and Benjamin wept upon his neck. 15 And he kissed all his brothers and wept upon them. After that his brothers talked with him.

16 When the report was heard in Pharaoh's house, "Joseph's brothers have come," it pleased Pharaoh and his servants. 17 And Pharaoh said to Joseph, "Say to your brothers, 'Do this: load your beasts and go back to the land of Canaan, 18 and take your father and your households, and come to me, and I will give you the best of the land of Egypt, and you shall eat the fat of the land.' 19 And you, Joseph, are commanded to say, 'Do this: take wagons from the land of Egypt for your little ones and for your wives, and bring your father, and come. 20 Have no concern for[1] your goods, for the best of all the land of Egypt is yours.'"

21 The sons of Israel did so: and Joseph gave them wagons, according to the command of Pharaoh, and gave them provisions for the journey. 22 To each and all of them he gave a change of clothes, but to Benjamin he gave three hundred shekels[2] of silver and five changes of clothes. 23 To his father he sent as follows: ten donkeys loaded with the good things of Egypt, and ten female donkeys loaded with grain, bread, and provision for his father on the journey. 24 Then he sent his brothers away, and as they departed, he said to them, "Do not quarrel on the way."

25 So they went up out of Egypt and came to the land of Canaan to their father Jacob. 26 And they told him, "Joseph is still alive, and he is ruler over all the land of Egypt." And his heart became numb, for he did not believe them. 27 But when they told him all the words of Joseph, which he had said to them, and when he saw the wagons that Joseph had sent to carry him, the spirit of their father Jacob revived. 28 And Israel said, "It is enough; Joseph my son is still alive. I will go and see him before I die."

Joseph Brings His Family to Egypt

46 So Israel took his journey with all that he had and came to Beersheba, and offered sacrifices to the God of his father Isaac. 2 And God spoke to Israel in visions of the night and said, "Jacob, Jacob." And he said, "Here am I." 3 Then he said, "I am God, the God of your father. Do not be afraid to go down to Egypt, for there I will make you into a great nation. 4 I myself will go down with you to Egypt, and I will also bring you up again, and Joseph's hand shall close your eyes."

5 Then Jacob set out from Beersheba. The sons of Israel carried Jacob their father, their little ones, and their wives, in the wagons that Pharaoh had sent to carry him. 6 They also took their livestock and their goods, which they had gained in the land of Canaan, and came into Egypt, Jacob and all his offspring with him, 7 his sons, and his sons' sons with him, his daughters, and his sons' daughters. All his offspring he brought with him into Egypt.

8 Now these are the names of the descendants of Israel, who came into Egypt, Jacob and his sons. Reuben, Jacob's firstborn, 9 and the sons of Reuben: Hanoch, Pallu, Hezron, and Carmi. 10 The sons of Simeon: Jemuel, Jamin, Ohad, Jachin, Zohar, and Shaul, the son of a Canaanite woman. 11 The sons of Levi: Gershon, Kohath, and Merari. 12 The sons of Judah: Er, Onan, Shelah, Perez, and Zerah (but Er and Onan

[1] Hebrew *Let your eye not pity* [2] A *shekel* was about 2/5 ounce or 11 grams

Joseph Forgives

Jacob's family had run out of food because of the great famine throughout the land. Jacob had heard that there was food in Egypt, so he sent ten of his sons on a long journey to Egypt to buy some. When the ten brothers arrived in Egypt, they bowed down to the ruler of Egypt, who was in charge of selling grain. They didn't realize that he was their own brother, Joseph, whom they had sold into slavery! But Joseph knew they were his brothers.

Joseph sold grain to the brothers, but he made one of them, Simeon, stay in prison while the rest of them went home. Joseph said that Simeon could go free if the brothers brought their youngest brother, Benjamin, back to Egypt with them.

When the brothers arrived at their home, they told their father Jacob about the ruler in Egypt. They said he had kept Simeon and that he wanted to see their youngest brother, Benjamin. Jacob said he would never let Benjamin go to Egypt.

But before long, Jacob's family ran out of food again. His sons were afraid to go back to Egypt for more food without Benjamin. Jacob did not want to let Benjamin go, but he had no choice. He also sent gifts for the ruler in Egypt.

When Joseph saw the brothers, he was especially happy to see his younger brother, Benjamin. Still he did not tell his brothers who he was. Instead, he had his servants prepare a great feast. Then, when it was time for the brothers to go home, Joseph had his servant secretly place Joseph's special silver cup in Benjamin's sack.

The next morning, the brothers started on their way home again. Soon, they saw Joseph's servant coming after them. When the servant caught up with them, he asked them why they had stolen his master's cup.

Of course, the brothers said they had not stolen it. They opened their sacks to show that they did not have it. But to their great surprise, the cup was in Benjamin's sack! The brothers went back to Joseph, and bowed before him.

Joseph said that the one whose sack had the cup inside would need to stay in Egypt and be his servant. The rest of them could go home in peace. One of the older brothers, Judah, stepped forward. He told Joseph that if they went home without Benjamin, their old father would die of sorrow. He asked Joseph to please let him stay and be a servant instead, so Benjamin could go home.

Then Joseph could no longer keep his secret. He told everyone except his brothers to leave the room. "I am your brother, Joseph," he said, "whom you sold into Egypt." He told them that it was God who had sent him here, to save lives during the famine. He told them to hurry home and get Jacob their father and the rest of the family, because the famine would continue for five more years.

All of Jacob's family, 70 people in all, went to live in Egypt. They had plenty to eat through the rest of the famine. But Joseph's brothers were still afraid of him. Joseph told them not to be afraid. "As for you, you meant evil against me," he told them, "but God meant it for good, [so] that many people should be kept alive, as they are today."

Joseph could forgive his brothers because he knew that God had used even the terribly wrong things that they did to bring about good. God had sent Joseph to Egypt to get ready for the famine. In this way, God kept alive the family from whom the Savior would come some day.

SEEK and FIND

WHERE TO FIND THE STORY

Genesis 42–46; 50:18–21

KEY BIBLE VERSE

"Therefore let those who suffer according to God's will entrust their souls to a faithful Creator while doing good." (1 Peter 4:19)

THREE KEY QUESTIONS

- Why were Joseph's brothers so afraid to go back to Egypt?
- What did Joseph tell his brothers so that they would not be afraid?
- Who is our great Savior who came from Joseph's family many years later?

RELATED BIBLE READINGS

1 Peter 2:19–23; 3:13–17

died in the land of Canaan); and the sons
of Perez were Hezron and Hamul. 13 The
sons of Issachar: Tola, Puvah, Yob, and
Shimron. 14 The sons of Zebulun: Sered,
Elon, and Jahleel. 15 These are the sons of
Leah, whom she bore to Jacob in Paddan-
aram, together with his daughter Dinah;
altogether his sons and his daughters
numbered thirty-three.

16 The sons of Gad: Ziphion, Haggi,
Shuni, Ezbon, Eri, Arodi, and Areli. 17 The
sons of Asher: Imnah, Ishvah, Ishvi, Beriah,
with Serah their sister. And the sons of
Beriah: Heber and Malchiel. 18 These are

the sons of Zilpah, whom Laban gave to
Leah his daughter; and these she bore to
Jacob—sixteen persons.

19 The sons of Rachel, Jacob's wife:
Joseph and Benjamin. 20 And to Joseph
in the land of Egypt were born Manasseh
and Ephraim, whom Asenath, the daugh-
ter of Potiphera the priest of On, bore to
him. 21 And the sons of Benjamin: Bela,
Becher, Ashbel, Gera, Naaman, Ehi, Rosh,
Muppim, Huppim, and Ard. 22 These are
the sons of Rachel, who were born to
Jacob—fourteen persons in all.

23 The sons of Dan: Hushim. 24 The
sons of Naphtali: Jahzeel, Guni, Jezer, and
Shillem. 25 These are the sons of Bilhah,
whom Laban gave to Rachel his daughter,
and these she bore to Jacob—seven per-
sons in all.

26 All the persons belonging to Jacob
who came into Egypt, who were his own
descendants, not including Jacob's sons'
wives, were sixty-six persons in all. 27 And
the sons of Joseph, who were born to him
in Egypt, were two. All the persons of the
house of Jacob who came into Egypt were
seventy.

Jacob and Joseph Reunited

28 He had sent Judah ahead of him to
Joseph to show the way before him in
Goshen, and they came into the land of
Goshen. 29 Then Joseph prepared his char-
iot and went up to meet Israel his father
in Goshen. He presented himself to him
and fell on his neck and wept on his neck
a good while. 30 Israel said to Joseph, "Now
let me die, since I have seen your face and
know that you are still alive." 31 Joseph
said to his brothers and to his father's
household, "I will go up and tell Pharaoh
and will say to him, 'My brothers and my
father's household, who were in the land of
Canaan, have come to me. 32 And the men
are shepherds, for they have been keepers
of livestock, and they have brought their
flocks and their herds and all that they
have.' 33 When Pharaoh calls you and says,
'What is your occupation?' 34 you shall say,
'Your servants have been keepers of live-
stock from our youth even until now, both
we and our fathers,' in order that you may
dwell in the land of Goshen, for every shep-
herd is an abomination to the Egyptians."

Jacob's Family Settles in Goshen

47 So Joseph went in and told
Pharaoh, "My father and my
brothers, with their flocks and herds and
all that they possess, have come from the
land of Canaan. They are now in the land
of Goshen." 2 And from among his broth-
ers he took five men and presented them
to Pharaoh. 3 Pharaoh said to his broth-
ers, "What is your occupation?" And they
said to Pharaoh, "Your servants are shep-
herds, as our fathers were." 4 They said to
Pharaoh, "We have come to sojourn in the
land, for there is no pasture for your ser-
vants' flocks, for the famine is severe in
the land of Canaan. And now, please let
your servants dwell in the land of Goshen."
5 Then Pharaoh said to Joseph, "Your father
and your brothers have come to you. 6 The
land of Egypt is before you. Settle your
father and your brothers in the best of the
land. Let them settle in the land of Goshen,
and if you know any able men among
them, put them in charge of my livestock."

7 Then Joseph brought in Jacob his
father and stood him before Pharaoh,
and Jacob blessed Pharaoh. 8 And Pharaoh
said to Jacob, "How many are the days of
the years of your life?" 9 And Jacob said
to Pharaoh, "The days of the years of my
sojourning are 130 years. Few and evil have
been the days of the years of my life, and
they have not attained to the days of the
years of the life of my fathers in the days
of their sojourning." 10 And Jacob blessed
Pharaoh and went out from the presence
of Pharaoh. 11 Then Joseph settled his
father and his brothers and gave them
a possession in the land of Egypt, in the

best of the land, in the land of Rameses, as Pharaoh had commanded. 12 And Joseph provided his father, his brothers, and all his father's household with food, according to the number of their dependents.

Joseph and the Famine

13 Now there was no food in all the land, for the famine was very severe, so that the land of Egypt and the land of Canaan languished by reason of the famine. 14 And Joseph gathered up all the money that was found in the land of Egypt and in the land of Canaan, in exchange for the grain that they bought. And Joseph brought the money into Pharaoh's house. 15 And when the money was all spent in the land of Egypt and in the land of Canaan, all the Egyptians came to Joseph and said, "Give us food. Why should we die before your eyes? For our money is gone." 16 And Joseph answered, "Give your livestock, and I will give you food in exchange for your livestock, if your money is gone." 17 So they brought their livestock to Joseph, and Joseph gave them food in exchange for the horses, the flocks, the herds, and the donkeys. He supplied them with food in exchange for all their livestock that year. 18 And when that year was ended, they came to him the following year and said to him, "We will not hide from my lord that our money is all spent. The herds of livestock are my lord's. There is nothing left in the sight of my lord but our bodies and our land. 19 Why should we die before your eyes, both we and our land? Buy us and our land for food, and we with our land will be servants to Pharaoh. And give us seed that we may live and not die, and that the land may not be desolate."

20 So Joseph bought all the land of Egypt for Pharaoh, for all the Egyptians sold their fields, because the famine was severe on them. The land became Pharaoh's. 21 As for the people, he made servants of them[1] from one end of Egypt to the other. 22 Only the land of the priests he did not buy, for the priests had a fixed allowance from Pharaoh and lived on the allowance that Pharaoh gave them; therefore they did not sell their land.

23 Then Joseph said to the people, "Behold, I have this day bought you and your land for Pharaoh. Now here is seed for you, and you shall sow the land. 24 And at the harvests you shall give a fifth to Pharaoh, and four fifths shall be your own, as seed for the field and as food for yourselves and your households, and as food for your little ones." 25 And they said, "You have saved our lives; may it please my lord, we will be servants to Pharaoh." 26 So Joseph made it a statute concerning the land of Egypt, and it stands to this day, that Pharaoh should have the fifth; the land of the priests alone did not become Pharaoh's.

27 Thus Israel settled in the land of Egypt, in the land of Goshen. And they gained possessions in it, and were fruitful and multiplied greatly. 28 And Jacob lived in the land of Egypt seventeen years. So the days of Jacob, the years of his life, were 147 years.

29 And when the time drew near that Israel must die, he called his son Joseph and said to him, "If now I have found favor in your sight, put your hand under my thigh and promise to deal kindly and truly with me. Do not bury me in Egypt, 30 but let me lie with my fathers. Carry me out of Egypt and bury me in their burying place." He answered, "I will do as you have said." 31 And he said, "Swear to me"; and he swore to him. Then Israel bowed himself upon the head of his bed.[2]

Jacob Blesses Ephraim and Manasseh

48 After this, Joseph was told, "Behold, your father is ill." So he took with him his two sons, Manasseh and Ephraim. 2 And it was told to Jacob, "Your son Joseph has come to you." Then Israel summoned his strength and sat up in bed. 3 And Jacob said to Joseph, "God

[1] Samaritan, Septuagint, Vulgate; Hebrew *he removed them to the cities* [2] Hebrew; Septuagint *staff*

Almighty[1] appeared to me at Luz in the land of Canaan and blessed me, 4 and said to me, 'Behold, I will make you fruitful and multiply you, and I will make of you a company of peoples and will give this land to your offspring after you for an everlasting possession.' 5 And now your two sons, who were born to you in the land of Egypt before I came to you in Egypt, are mine; Ephraim and Manasseh shall be mine, as Reuben and Simeon are. 6 And the children that you fathered after them shall be yours. They shall be called by the name of their brothers in their inheritance. 7 As for me, when I came from Paddan, to my sorrow Rachel died in the land of Canaan on the way, when there was still some distance[2] to go to Ephrath, and I buried her there on the way to Ephrath (that is, Bethlehem)."

8 When Israel saw Joseph's sons, he said, "Who are these?" 9 Joseph said to his father, "They are my sons, whom God has given me here." And he said, "Bring them to me, please, that I may bless them." 10 Now the eyes of Israel were dim with age, so that he could not see. So Joseph brought them near him, and he kissed them and embraced them. 11 And Israel said to Joseph, "I never expected to see your face; and behold, God has let me see your offspring also." 12 Then Joseph removed them from his knees, and he bowed himself with his face to the earth. 13 And Joseph took them both, Ephraim in his right hand toward Israel's left hand, and Manasseh in his left hand toward Israel's right hand, and brought them near him. 14 And Israel stretched out his right hand and laid it on the head of Ephraim, who was the younger, and his left hand on the head of Manasseh, crossing his hands (for Manasseh was the firstborn). 15 And he blessed Joseph and said,

"The God before whom my fathers
Abraham and Isaac walked,
the God who has been my shepherd
all my life long to this day,
16 the angel who has redeemed me
from all evil, bless the boys;
and in them let my name be
carried on, and the name of
my fathers Abraham and Isaac;
and let them grow into a multitude[3]
in the midst of the earth."

17 When Joseph saw that his father laid his right hand on the head of Ephraim, it displeased him, and he took his father's hand to move it from Ephraim's head to Manasseh's head. 18 And Joseph said to his father, "Not this way, my father; since this one is the firstborn, put your right hand on his head." 19 But his father refused and said, "I know, my son, I know. He also shall become a people, and he also shall be great. Nevertheless, his younger brother shall be greater than he, and his offspring shall become a multitude[4] of nations." 20 So he blessed them that day, saying,

"By you Israel will pronounce
blessings, saying,
'God make you as Ephraim and as
Manasseh.'"

Thus he put Ephraim before Manasseh. 21 Then Israel said to Joseph, "Behold, I am about to die, but God will be with you and will bring you again to the land of your fathers. 22 Moreover, I have given to you rather than to your brothers one mountain slope[5] that I took from the hand of the Amorites with my sword and with my bow."

Jacob Blesses His Sons

79

49 Then Jacob called his sons and said, "Gather yourselves together, that I may tell you what shall happen to you in days to come.

[1] Hebrew *El Shaddai* [2] Or *about two hours' distance* [3] Or *let them be like fish for multitude* [4] Hebrew *fullness* [5] Or *one portion of the land*; Hebrew *shekem*, which sounds like the town and district called *Shechem*

2 "Assemble and listen, O sons of Jacob,
listen to Israel your father.

3 "Reuben, you are my firstborn,
my might, and the firstfruits of my strength,
preeminent in dignity and preeminent in power.
4 Unstable as water, you shall not have preeminence,
because you went up to your father's bed;
then you defiled it—he went up to my couch!

5 "Simeon and Levi are brothers;
weapons of violence are their swords.
6 Let my soul come not into their council;
O my glory, be not joined to their company.
For in their anger they killed men,
and in their willfulness they hamstrung oxen.
7 Cursed be their anger, for it is fierce,
and their wrath, for it is cruel!
I will divide them in Jacob
and scatter them in Israel.

8 "Judah, your brothers shall praise you;
your hand shall be on the neck of your enemies;
your father's sons shall bow down before you.
9 Judah is a lion's cub;
from the prey, my son, you have gone up.
He stooped down; he crouched as a lion
and as a lioness; who dares rouse him?
10 The scepter shall not depart from Judah,
nor the ruler's staff from between his feet,
until tribute comes to him;[1]
and to him shall be the obedience of the peoples.
11 Binding his foal to the vine
and his donkey's colt to the choice vine,
he has washed his garments in wine
and his vesture in the blood of grapes.
12 His eyes are darker than wine,
and his teeth whiter than milk.

13 "Zebulun shall dwell at the shore of the sea;
he shall become a haven for ships,
and his border shall be at Sidon.

14 "Issachar is a strong donkey,
crouching between the sheepfolds.[2]
15 He saw that a resting place was good,
and that the land was pleasant,
so he bowed his shoulder to bear,
and became a servant at forced labor.

16 "Dan shall judge his people
as one of the tribes of Israel.
17 Dan shall be a serpent in the way,
a viper by the path,
that bites the horse's heels
so that his rider falls backward.
18 I wait for your salvation, O LORD.

19 "Raiders shall raid Gad,[3]
but he shall raid at their heels.

20 "Asher's food shall be rich,
and he shall yield royal delicacies.

21 "Naphtali is a doe let loose
that bears beautiful fawns.[4]

22 "Joseph is a fruitful bough,
a fruitful bough by a spring;
his branches run over the wall.[5]
23 The archers bitterly attacked him,

[1] By a slight revocalization; a slight emendation yields (compare Septuagint, Syriac, Targum) *until he comes to whom it belongs*; Hebrew *until Shiloh comes*, or *until he comes to Shiloh* [2] Or *between its saddlebags* [3] *Gad* sounds like the Hebrew for *raiders* and *raid* [4] Or *he gives beautiful words*, or *that bears fawns of the fold* [5] Or *Joseph is a wild donkey, a wild donkey beside a spring, his wild colts beside the wall*

shot at him, and harassed him
severely,
24 yet his bow remained unmoved;
his arms[1] were made agile
by the hands of the Mighty One of
Jacob
(from there is the Shepherd,[2] the
Stone of Israel),
25 by the God of your father who will
help you,
by the Almighty[3] who will bless
you
with blessings of heaven above,
blessings of the deep that crouches
beneath,
blessings of the breasts and of the
womb.
26 The blessings of your father
are mighty beyond the blessings
of my parents,
up to the bounties of the
everlasting hills.[4]
May they be on the head of Joseph,
and on the brow of him who was
set apart from his brothers.

27 "Benjamin is a ravenous wolf,
in the morning devouring the prey
and at evening dividing the spoil."

Jacob's Death and Burial

28 All these are the twelve tribes of
Israel. This is what their father said to
them as he blessed them, blessing each
with the blessing suitable to him. 29 Then
he commanded them and said to them,
"I am to be gathered to my people; bury
me with my fathers in the cave that is in
the field of Ephron the Hittite, 30 in the
cave that is in the field at Machpelah, to
the east of Mamre, in the land of Canaan,
which Abraham bought with the field
from Ephron the Hittite to possess as
a burying place. 31 There they buried
Abraham and Sarah his wife. There they
buried Isaac and Rebekah his wife, and
there I buried Leah— 32 the field and the
cave that is in it were bought from the
Hittites." 33 When Jacob finished com-
manding his sons, he drew up his feet
into the bed and breathed his last and was
gathered to his people.

50 Then Joseph fell on his father's
face and wept over him and kissed
him. 2 And Joseph commanded his ser-
vants the physicians to embalm his father.
So the physicians embalmed Israel. 3 Forty
days were required for it, for that is how
many are required for embalming. And
the Egyptians wept for him seventy days.

4 And when the days of weeping for
him were past, Joseph spoke to the
household of Pharaoh, saying, "If now
I have found favor in your eyes, please
speak in the ears of Pharaoh, saying,
5 My father made me swear, saying, 'I am
about to die: in my tomb that I hewed out
for myself in the land of Canaan, there
shall you bury me.' Now therefore, let me
please go up and bury my father. Then I
will return." 6 And Pharaoh answered, "Go
up, and bury your father, as he made you
swear." 7 So Joseph went up to bury his
father. With him went up all the servants
of Pharaoh, the elders of his household,
and all the elders of the land of Egypt,
8 as well as all the household of Joseph,
his brothers, and his father's house-
hold. Only their children, their flocks,
and their herds were left in the land of
Goshen. 9 And there went up with him
both chariots and horsemen. It was a
very great company. 10 When they came
to the threshing floor of Atad, which is
beyond the Jordan, they lamented there
with a very great and grievous lamenta-
tion, and he made a mourning for his
father seven days. 11 When the inhabi-
tants of the land, the Canaanites, saw the
mourning on the threshing floor of Atad,
they said, "This is a grievous mourning
by the Egyptians." Therefore the place
was named Abel-mizraim;[5] it is beyond
the Jordan. 12 Thus his sons did for him

[1] Hebrew *the arms of his hands* [2] Or *by the name of the Shepherd* [3] Hebrew *Shaddai* [4] A slight emendation yields (compare Septuagint) *the blessings of the eternal mountains, the bounties of the everlasting hills* [5] *Abel-mizraim* means *mourning* (or *meadow*) *of Egypt*

as he had commanded them, 13 for his
sons carried him to the land of Canaan
and buried him in the cave of the field at
Machpelah, to the east of Mamre, which
Abraham bought with the field from
Ephron the Hittite to possess as a burying
place. 14 After he had buried his father,
Joseph returned to Egypt with his broth-
ers and all who had gone up with him to
bury his father.

God's Good Purposes

15 When Joseph's brothers saw that their
father was dead, they said, "It may be that
Joseph will hate us and pay us back for all
the evil that we did to him." 16 So they sent
a message to Joseph, saying, "Your father
gave this command before he died, 17 'Say
to Joseph, Please forgive the transgression
of your brothers and their sin, because
they did evil to you.' And now, please for-
give the transgression of the servants of
the God of your father." Joseph wept when
they spoke to him. 18 His brothers
also came and fell down before
117 him and said, "Behold, we are your
servants." 19 But Joseph said to them, "Do
not fear, for am I in the place of God? 20 As
for you, you meant evil against me,
but God meant it for good, to bring
95 it about that many people[1] should
be kept alive, as they are today. 21 So do not
fear; I will provide for you and your little
ones." Thus he comforted them and spoke
kindly to them.

The Death of Joseph

22 So Joseph remained in Egypt, he and
his father's house. Joseph lived 110 years.
23 And Joseph saw Ephraim's children of
the third generation. The children also of
Machir the son of Manasseh were counted
as Joseph's own.[2] 24 And Joseph said to his
brothers, "I am about to die, but God will
visit you and bring you up out of this land
to the land that he swore to Abraham, to
Isaac, and to Jacob." 25 Then Joseph made
the sons of Israel swear, saying, "God will
surely visit you, and you shall carry up my
bones from here." 26 So Joseph died, being
110 years old. They embalmed him, and he
was put in a coffin in Egypt.

[1] Or *a numerous people* [2] Hebrew *were born on Joseph's knees*

Introduction to

Exodus

Author
Moses the prophet

Date
1446 B.C.

People
Pharaoh; Jochebed; Miriam; Pharaoh's daughter; Moses; Jethro (Reuel); Aaron; Joshua; Bezalel

Purpose
The purpose of Exodus is to tell how God delivered His people Israel from slavery in Egypt, to set forth the covenant He made with them, and to describe the tabernacle where He promised to dwell among them.

Central Themes
God remembers and fulfills His promises to Abraham; God reveals His name; God shows His power in the plagues against Egypt; God gives the Ten Commandments; God makes a covenant with His people; God lives among His people.

Memory Verses
The Ten Commandments (Exodus 20:1–17); the Lord's two ways (Exodus 34:6–7)

Introduction

An "exodus" occurs when a large number of people leave a place. The book of Exodus gets its name from the large number of Israelites whom God led out of Egypt, where they worked as slaves. Exodus describes God saving the baby Moses (Exodus 1–2), then calling him to lead His people out of Egypt (Exodus 3–4). When Pharaoh refuses to obey God's command to free His people, God sends 10 powerful plagues; Pharaoh eventually let the Israelites go (Exodus 5–12). As God provides protection, quail, bread from heaven, and water from rocks for the Israelites in the wilderness, He shows His power to care for His people (Exodus 14–17). God meets with the Israelites at Mount Sinai, where He gives them the Ten Commandments and makes a covenant with them (Exodus 19–24). God also gives Moses detailed directions for building a tabernacle where God will dwell in a special way and where His people can offer sacrifices for sin (Exodus 25–40). In Exodus, we see God beginning to fulfill His promises to Abraham to make a great nation from his children, to give them the land where Abraham had lived in a tent, and to make them a blessing to the nations.

1876 B.C.	1526 B.C.	1446 B.C.
Israel goes to Egypt	Moses born	Exodus from Egypt

Exodus

Israel Increases Greatly in Egypt

1 These are the names of the sons
of Israel who came to Egypt
131 with Jacob, each with his house-
hold: 2 Reuben, Simeon, Levi, and Judah,
3 Issachar, Zebulun, and Benjamin, 4 Dan
and Naphtali, Gad and Asher. 5 All the
descendants of Jacob were seventy per-
sons; Joseph was already in Egypt. 6 Then
Joseph died, and all his brothers and all
that generation. 7 But the people of Israel
were fruitful and increased greatly; they
multiplied and grew exceedingly strong,
so that the land was filled with them.

Pharaoh Oppresses Israel

8 Now there arose a new king over
Egypt, who did not know Joseph. 9 And he
said to his people, "Behold, the people of
Israel are too many and too mighty for us.
10 Come, let us deal shrewdly with them,
lest they multiply, and, if war breaks
out, they join our enemies and fight
against us and escape from the land."
11 Therefore they set taskmasters over
them to afflict them with heavy burdens.
They built for Pharaoh store cities, Pithom
and Raamses. 12 But the more they were
oppressed, the more they multiplied and
the more they spread abroad. And the
Egyptians were in dread of the people
of Israel. 13 So they ruthlessly made the
people of Israel work as slaves 14 and made
their lives bitter with hard service, in mor-
tar and brick, and in all kinds of work in
the field. In all their work they ruthlessly
made them work as slaves.
15 Then the king of Egypt said to the
Hebrew midwives, one of whom was
named Shiphrah and the other Puah,
16 "When you serve as midwife to the
Hebrew women and see them on the
birthstool, if it is a son, you shall kill him,
but if it is a daughter, she shall live." 17 But
the midwives feared God and did not do as
the king of Egypt commanded them, but
let the male children live. 18 So the king
of Egypt called the midwives and said to
them, "Why have you done this, and let
the male children live?" 19 The midwives
said to Pharaoh, "Because the Hebrew
women are not like the Egyptian women,
for they are vigorous and give birth before
the midwife comes to them." 20 So God
dealt well with the midwives. And the
people multiplied and grew very strong.
21 And because the midwives feared God,
he gave them families. 22 Then Pharaoh
commanded all his people, "Every son
that is born to the Hebrews[1] you shall
cast into the Nile, but you shall let every
daughter live."

The Birth of Moses

2 Now a man from the house of Levi
went and took as his wife a Levite
woman. 2 The woman conceived and bore
a son, and when she saw that he was a fine
child, she hid him three months. 3 When
she could hide him no longer, she took
for him a basket made of bulrushes[2] and
daubed it with bitumen and pitch. She
put the child in it and placed it among the
reeds by the river bank. 4 And his sister
stood at a distance to know what would
be done to him. 5 Now the daughter of
Pharaoh came down to bathe at the river,
while her young women walked beside
the river. She saw the basket among the
reeds and sent her servant woman, and
she took it. 6 When she opened it, she saw
the child, and behold, the baby was crying.
She took pity on him and said, "This is
one of the Hebrews' children." 7 Then his

[1] Samaritan, Septuagint, Targum; Hebrew lacks *to the Hebrews* [2] Hebrew *papyrus reeds*

sister said to Pharaoh's daughter, "Shall I go and call you a nurse from the Hebrew women to nurse the child for you?" 8 And Pharaoh's daughter said to her, "Go." So the girl went and called the child's mother. 9 And Pharaoh's daughter said to her, "Take this child away and nurse him for me, and I will give you your wages." So the woman took the child and nursed him. 10 When the child grew up, she brought him to Pharaoh's daughter, and he became her son. She named him Moses, "Because," she said, "I drew him out of the water."[1]

Moses Flees to Midian

137

11 One day, when Moses had grown up, he went out to his people and looked on their burdens, and he saw an Egyptian beating a Hebrew, one of his people.[2] 12 He looked this way and that, and seeing no one, he struck down the Egyptian and hid him in the sand. 13 When he went out the next day, behold, two Hebrews were struggling together. And he said to the man in the wrong, "Why do you strike your companion?" 14 He answered, "Who made you a prince and a judge over us? Do you mean to kill me as you killed the Egyptian?" Then Moses was afraid, and thought, "Surely the thing is known." 15 When Pharaoh heard of it, he sought to kill Moses. But Moses fled from Pharaoh and stayed in the land of Midian. And he sat down by a well.

16 Now the priest of Midian had seven daughters, and they came and drew water and filled the troughs to water their father's flock. 17 The shepherds came and drove them away, but Moses stood up and saved them, and watered their flock. 18 When they came home to their father Reuel, he said, "How is it that you have come home so soon today?" 19 They said, "An Egyptian delivered us out of the hand of the shepherds and even drew water for us and watered the flock." 20 He said to his daughters, "Then where is he? Why have you left the man? Call him, that he may eat bread." 21 And Moses was content to dwell with the man, and he gave Moses his daughter Zipporah. 22 She gave birth to a son, and he called his name Gershom, for he said, "I have been a sojourner[3] in a foreign land."

God Hears Israel's Groaning

23 During those many days the king of Egypt died, and the people of Israel groaned because of their slavery and cried out for help. Their cry for rescue from slavery came up to God. 24 And God heard their groaning, and God remembered his covenant with Abraham, with Isaac, and with Jacob. 25 God saw the people of Israel—and God knew.

The Burning Bush

3 Now Moses was keeping the flock of his father-in-law, Jethro, the priest of Midian, and he led his flock to the west side of the wilderness and came to Horeb, the mountain of God. 2 And the angel of the LORD appeared to him in a flame of fire out of the midst of a bush. He looked, and behold, the bush was burning, yet it was not consumed. 3 And Moses said, "I will turn aside to see this great sight, why the bush is not burned." 4 When the LORD saw that he turned aside to see, God called to him out of the bush, "Moses, Moses!" And he said, "Here I am." 5 Then he said, "Do not come near; take your sandals off your feet, for the place on which you are standing is holy ground." 6 And he said, "I am the God of your father, the God of Abraham, the God of Isaac, and the God of Jacob." And Moses hid his face, for he was afraid to look at God.

7 Then the LORD said, "I have surely seen the affliction of my people who are in Egypt and have heard their cry because of their taskmasters. I know their sufferings, 8 and I have come down to deliver them out of the hand of the Egyptians and to bring them up out of that land to

[1] *Moses* sounds like the Hebrew for *draw out* [2] Hebrew *brothers* [3] *Gershom* sounds like the Hebrew for *sojourner*

The Birth of Moses

Jacob's twelve sons and their descendants lived in Egypt for a long, long time—for more than 400 years! More and more children were born, and Jacob's family became a great nation, just like God had promised Abraham. They were called Hebrews, or Israelites.

Eventually a new Pharaoh became king in Egypt. The new Pharaoh did not remember that Joseph had saved the people of Egypt 400 years earlier, and he worried that there were too many Israelites. So the new Pharaoh made all the Israelites become slaves of the Egyptians.

But the Israelites kept having more babies, no matter how hard Pharaoh made life for them. Finally Pharaoh made a law requiring every Hebrew (Israelite) mother, who gave birth to a baby boy, to throw him in the Nile River, so that he would drown!

But there was one Israelite woman—who was expecting a baby—who thought that Pharaoh's law was wrong and against the law of God. When her baby was born, it turned out to be a boy! The mother loved her baby boy very much and hid him for three months from the Egyptian soldiers. When she could hide him no longer, she took some of the plants that grew along the river and she wove them into a basket. Then she covered the basket with pitch (something like black tar) to keep the water out of the basket.

When the basket was safe and waterproof, the baby's mother put her precious baby in the basket and placed the basket in the Nile River, right along the riverbank, among the reeds. The baby's big sister, Miriam, stayed by the basket to make sure her little brother would be safe and to see what would happen.

Then an amazing thing happened. The daughter of Pharaoh came down to the river to take a bath. When she got into the water, she saw a basket floating among the reeds, and she sent her maid to get it. When Pharaoh's daughter opened the basket, she found a crying baby boy. Pharaoh's daughter felt sorry for the little baby and wanted to help him.

Then Miriam, the baby's sister, came out of her hiding place. Miriam ran up to Pharaoh's daughter and asked her if she wanted her to find someone to take care of the baby. Pharaoh's daughter agreed, and Miriam ran and got her mother—the baby's very own mother!—and brought her to Pharaoh's daughter. Then Pharaoh's daughter asked her to take the baby home and take care of him until he was older.

When the baby grew older, his mother took him to live with Pharaoh's daughter. Pharaoh's daughter named him "Moses" because "Moses" sounded like the word for "draw out," and Pharaoh's daughter had drawn Moses out of the water.

When Moses grew up and became a man, God used him to lead His people out of slavery in Egypt. It was through Moses that God gave His law and made His covenant with His people. Many generations later, God would send His only

Son, Jesus—first to be born as a baby and then to grow up and set His people free from slavery to sin. Through Jesus, God would make a new and better covenant called the gospel, for the salvation of all who put their faith in Jesus as their Savior.

SEEK and FIND

WHERE TO FIND THE STORY

Exodus 1:1–2:10

KEY BIBLE VERSE

"By faith Moses, when he was born, was hidden for three months by his parents, because they saw that the child was beautiful, and they were not afraid of the king's edict." (Hebrews 11:23)

THREE KEY QUESTIONS

- What could have happened to Moses' mother for hiding her baby boy?
- Why was Moses' mother willing to hide baby Moses, in spite of the Pharaoh's law (edict)?
- What happened to Moses when he grew up and where did he live?

RELATED BIBLE READINGS

Micah 6:3–4; Acts 7:17–22; Hebrews 11:23

a good and broad land, a land flowing
with milk and honey, to the place of the
Canaanites, the Hittites, the Amorites, the
Perizzites, the Hivites, and the Jebusites.
9 And now, behold, the cry of the people
of Israel has come to me, and I have also
seen the oppression with which the
Egyptians oppress them. 10 Come, I will
send you to Pharaoh that you may bring
my people, the children of Israel, out of
Egypt." 11 But Moses said to God, "Who
am I that I should go to Pharaoh and bring
the children of Israel out of Egypt?" 12 He
said, "But I will be with you, and this
shall be the sign for you, that I have sent
you: when you have brought the people
out of Egypt, you shall serve God on this
mountain."

13 Then Moses said to God, "If I come to
the people of Israel and say to them, 'The
God of your fathers has sent me to you,'
and they ask me, 'What is his name?' what

shall I say to them?" 14 God said to Moses,
"I AM WHO I AM."[1] And he said, "Say this
to the people of Israel, 'I AM has sent me
to you.'" 15 God also said to Moses, "Say
this to the people of Israel, 'The LORD,[2] the
God of your fathers, the God of Abraham,
the God of Isaac, and the God of Jacob, has
sent me to you.' This is my name forever,
and thus I am to be remembered through-
out all generations. 16 Go and gather the
elders of Israel together and say to them,
'The LORD, the God of your fathers, the
God of Abraham, of Isaac, and of Jacob, has
appeared to me, saying, "I have observed
you and what has been done to you in
Egypt, 17 and I promise that I will bring
you up out of the affliction of Egypt to the
land of the Canaanites, the Hittites, the
Amorites, the Perizzites, the Hivites, and
the Jebusites, a land flowing with milk
and honey."' 18 And they will listen to your
voice, and you and the elders of Israel shall
go to the king of Egypt and say to him,
'The LORD, the God of the Hebrews, has
met with us; and now, please let us go a
three days' journey into the wilderness,
that we may sacrifice to the LORD our God.'
19 But I know that the king of Egypt will not
let you go unless compelled by a mighty
hand.[3] 20 So I will stretch out my hand and
strike Egypt with all the wonders that I will
do in it; after that he will let you go. 21 And
I will give this people favor in the sight of
the Egyptians; and when you go, you shall
not go empty, 22 but each woman shall ask
of her neighbor, and any woman who lives
in her house, for silver and gold jewelry,
and for clothing. You shall put them on
your sons and on your daughters. So you
shall plunder the Egyptians."

CHARACTER PROFILE

MOSES

Moses was born as a slave in Egypt, but was raised by Pharaoh's daughter. When Moses was grown, he led the Israelites out of slavery. God worked many miracles through Moses. On Mount Sinai, God gave Moses the law, including the Ten Commandments, to give to His people. Moses led the Israelite people for 40 years in the wilderness. He died just before the Israelites entered the Promised Land.

137, 145, 153, 161, 175, 279

Moses Given Powerful Signs

4 Then Moses answered, "But behold,
they will not believe me or listen
to my voice, for they will say, 'The LORD
did not appear to you.'" 2 The LORD said
to him, "What is that in your hand?" He
said, "A staff." 3 And he said, "Throw it on
the ground." So he threw it on the ground,
and it became a serpent, and Moses ran
from it. 4 But the LORD said to Moses, "Put
out your hand and catch it by the tail"—so
he put out his hand and caught it, and it
became a staff in his hand— 5 "that they
may believe that the LORD, the God of their
fathers, the God of Abraham, the God of
Isaac, and the God of Jacob, has appeared
to you." 6 Again, the LORD said to him, "Put
your hand inside your cloak."[4] And he put
his hand inside his cloak, and when he
took it out, behold, his hand was leprous[5]

[1] Or *I AM WHAT I AM*, or *I WILL BE WHAT I WILL BE* [2] The word *LORD*, when spelled with capital letters, stands for the divine name, *YHWH*, which is here connected with the verb *hayah*, "to be" in verse 14 [3] Septuagint, Vulgate; Hebrew *go, not by a mighty hand* [4] Hebrew *into your bosom*; also verse 7 [5] *Leprosy* was a term for several skin diseases; see Leviticus 13

like snow. 7 Then God said, "Put your hand back inside your cloak." So he put his hand back inside his cloak, and when he took it out, behold, it was restored like the rest of his flesh. 8 "If they will not believe you," God said, "or listen to the first sign, they may believe the latter sign. 9 If they will not believe even these two signs or listen to your voice, you shall take some water from the Nile and pour it on the dry ground, and the water that you shall take from the Nile will become blood on the dry ground."

10 But Moses said to the LORD, "Oh, my Lord, I am not eloquent, either in the past or since you have spoken to your servant, but I am slow of speech and of tongue." 11 Then the LORD said to him, "Who has made man's mouth? Who makes him mute, or deaf, or seeing, or blind? Is it not I, the LORD? 12 Now therefore go, and I will be with your mouth and teach you what you shall speak." 13 But he said, "Oh, my Lord, please send someone else." 14 Then the anger of the LORD was kindled against Moses and he said, "Is there not Aaron, your brother, the Levite? I know that he can speak well. Behold, he is coming out to meet you, and when he sees you, he will be glad in his heart. 15 You shall speak to him and put the words in his mouth, and I will be with your mouth and with his mouth and will teach you both what to do. 16 He shall speak for you to the people, and he shall be your mouth, and you shall be as God to him. 17 And take in your hand this staff, with which you shall do the signs."

Moses Returns to Egypt

18 Moses went back to Jethro his father-in-law and said to him, "Please let me go back to my brothers in Egypt to see whether they are still alive." And Jethro said to Moses, "Go in peace." 19 And the LORD said to Moses in Midian, "Go back to Egypt, for all the men who were seeking your life are dead." 20 So Moses took his wife and his sons and had them ride on a donkey, and went back to the land of Egypt. And Moses took the staff of God in his hand.

21 And the LORD said to Moses, "When you go back to Egypt, see that you do before Pharaoh all the miracles that I have put in your power. But I will harden his heart, so that he will not let the people go. 22 Then you shall say to Pharaoh, 'Thus says the LORD, Israel is my firstborn son, 23 and I say to you, "Let my son go that he may serve me." If you refuse to let him go, behold, I will kill your firstborn son.'"

24 At a lodging place on the way the LORD met him and sought to put him to death. 25 Then Zipporah took a flint and cut off her son's foreskin and touched Moses'[1] feet with it and said, "Surely you are a bridegroom of blood to me!" 26 So he let him alone. It was then that she said, "A bridegroom of blood," because of the circumcision.

27 The LORD said to Aaron, "Go into the wilderness to meet Moses." So he went and met him at the mountain of God and kissed him. 28 And Moses told Aaron all the words of the LORD with which he had sent him to speak, and all the signs that he had commanded him to do. 29 Then Moses and Aaron went and gathered together all the elders of the people of Israel. 30 Aaron spoke all the words that the LORD had spoken to Moses and did the signs in the sight of the people. 31 And the people believed; and when they heard that the LORD had visited the people of Israel and that he had seen their affliction, they bowed their heads and worshiped.

137

Making Bricks Without Straw

145

5 Afterward Moses and Aaron went and said to Pharaoh, "Thus says the LORD, the God of Israel, 'Let my people go, that they may hold a feast to me in the wilderness.'" 2 But Pharaoh said, "Who is the LORD, that I

[1] Hebrew *his*

Moses and the Burning Bush

When Moses had grown up, he saw how terribly the Hebrew people (the people of Israel) were being treated by the Egyptians. One day, Moses saw an Egyptian beating a Hebrew slave. Moses became so angry that he killed the cruel Egyptian and buried his body in the sand. But Pharaoh found out what Moses had done, and he tried to kill Moses. So Moses ran away to live in the land of Midian. He worked there as a shepherd, and he married a woman named Zipporah, the daughter of the priest of Midian. Moses lived in Midian many years.

One day, when Moses was keeping watch over the sheep, an angel of the Lord appeared to him in a flame of fire in the middle of a bush. Moses saw that the bush was on fire, but it wasn't burning up. Moses got closer so he could see why.

When the Lord saw that Moses was looking closely at the bush, God called to him out of the bush, "Moses, Moses!"

Moses answered, "Here I am."

Then God said, "Do not come near; take your sandals off your feet, for the place on which you are standing is holy ground."

God said, "I am the God of your father, the God of Abraham, the God of Isaac, and the God of Jacob." Moses hid his face, because he was afraid to look at God. Then the Lord told Moses that He had seen the suffering of His people in Egypt, and He had come to take them away from Egypt and into a land "flowing with milk and honey." God said to Moses, "Come, I will send you to Pharaoh that you may bring My people, the children of Israel, out of Egypt."

Moses did not think he could do this terribly difficult job. God promised that He would be with Moses, but Moses still didn't think he could lead the Israelite people. Moses said, "They will not believe me or listen to my voice, for they will say, 'The LORD did not appear to you.' "

Then God did two miracles (called signs), to prove that God had appeared to Moses and called him to lead the people of Israel out of Egypt. First, Moses was holding a staff, a long stick he used when he worked with the sheep. The Lord told Moses to throw his staff on the ground. Moses did what God said—and the staff became a snake! Moses ran away from it, afraid of his staff that had become a snake! Then the Lord told Moses to catch the snake by the tail. When Moses did this, the snake became a staff again.

Next the Lord told Moses to put his hand inside his robe, and pull it out again. When Moses obeyed and did this, his hand was completely white with a disease called leprosy. Again God told Moses to put his hand in his robe and pull it out; and this time, his hand came out completely healed. God told Moses, if the Israelites did not believe that Moses had come from God, he could do these two signs to prove it.

Still, Moses did not think he could do this very difficult job. Finally, God promised Moses that his brother, Aaron, would come to meet him, and that Aaron would help Moses confront Pharaoh and bring the Israelites out of Egypt.

Together, Moses and Aaron went to the people of Israel and told them all that had happened. They showed them God's signs. The people believed that God wanted to save them, and they bowed their heads and worshiped God.

God made Moses able to do many miracles (or signs) to show that Moses really was sent by God. Many years later, God would send His own Son, Jesus, to save His people from their sins. Because Jesus was God, He was able to do many more signs than Moses did. God wants us to see that Jesus is the only Son of God and to put our faith in Him alone.

SEEK and FIND

WHERE TO FIND THE STORY

Exodus 2:11–4:31

KEY BIBLE VERSE

"Aaron spoke all the words that the LORD had spoken to Moses and did the signs in the sight of the people. And the people believed; and . . . they bowed their heads and worshiped." (Exodus 4:30–31)

THREE KEY QUESTIONS

- Why was the ground by the burning bush holy?
- What were the two signs (or miracles) that God gave to Moses to prove that He had sent Moses to lead the people of Israel?
- What did the people do when they saw the two signs that Moses did? How is this like our response to Jesus?

RELATED BIBLE READINGS

Psalm 105:23–27; Acts 7:23–34; Hebrews 11:1–40

should obey his voice and let Israel go? I do
not know the LORD, and moreover, I will
not let Israel go." 3 Then they said, "The
God of the Hebrews has met with us.
Please let us go a three days' journey into
the wilderness that we may sacrifice to the
LORD our God, lest he fall upon us with
pestilence or with the sword." 4 But the
king of Egypt said to them, "Moses and
Aaron, why do you take the people away
from their work? Get back to your bur-
dens." 5 And Pharaoh said, "Behold, the
people of the land are now many,[1] and you
make them rest from their burdens!" 6 The
same day Pharaoh commanded the task-
masters of the people and their foremen,
7 "You shall no longer give the people straw
to make bricks, as in the past; let them go
and gather straw for themselves. 8 But the
number of bricks that they made in the
past you shall impose on them, you shall
by no means reduce it, for they are idle.
Therefore they cry, 'Let us go and offer sac-
rifice to our God.' 9 Let heavier work be laid
on the men that they may labor at it and
pay no regard to lying words."

10 So the taskmasters and the foremen
of the people went out and said to the peo-
ple, "Thus says Pharaoh, 'I will not give
you straw. 11 Go and get your straw your-
selves wherever you can find it, but your
work will not be reduced in the least.'"
12 So the people were scattered through-
out all the land of Egypt to gather stubble
for straw. 13 The taskmasters were urgent,
saying, "Complete your work, your daily
task each day, as when there was straw."
14 And the foremen of the people of Israel,
whom Pharaoh's taskmasters had set over
them, were beaten and were asked, "Why
have you not done all your task of making
bricks today and yesterday, as in the past?"

15 Then the foremen of the people of
Israel came and cried to Pharaoh, "Why
do you treat your servants like this? 16 No
straw is given to your servants, yet they
say to us, 'Make bricks!' And behold, your
servants are beaten; but the fault is in your
own people." 17 But he said, "You are idle,
you are idle; that is why you say, 'Let us
go and sacrifice to the LORD.' 18 Go now
and work. No straw will be given you, but
you must still deliver the same number
of bricks." 19 The foremen of the people
of Israel saw that they were in trouble
when they said, "You shall by no means
reduce your number of bricks, your daily
task each day." 20 They met Moses and
Aaron, who were waiting for them, as
they came out from Pharaoh; 21 and they
said to them, "The LORD look on you and
judge, because you have made us stink in
the sight of Pharaoh and his servants, and
have put a sword in their hand to kill us."

22 Then Moses turned to the LORD and
said, "O Lord, why have you done evil to
this people? Why did you ever send me?
23 For since I came to Pharaoh to speak
in your name, he has done evil to this
people, and you have not delivered your
people at all."

God Promises Deliverance

6 But the LORD said to Moses, "Now you
shall see what I will do to Pharaoh; for
with a strong hand he will send them out,
and with a strong hand he will drive them
out of his land."

2 God spoke to Moses and said to him,
"I am the LORD. 3 I appeared to Abraham,
to Isaac, and to Jacob, as God Almighty,[2]
but by my name the LORD I did not make
myself known to them. 4 I also established
my covenant with them to give them the
land of Canaan, the land in which they
lived as sojourners. 5 Moreover, I have
heard the groaning of the people of Israel
whom the Egyptians hold as slaves, and
I have remembered my covenant. 6 Say
therefore to the people of Israel, 'I am the
LORD, and I will bring you out from under
the burdens of the Egyptians, and I will
deliver you from slavery to them, and I
will redeem you with an outstretched

[1] Samaritan *they are now more numerous than the people of the land* [2] Hebrew *El Shaddai*

arm and with great acts of judgment. 7 I will take you to be my people, and I will be your God, and you shall know that I am the LORD your God, who has brought you out from under the burdens of the Egyptians. 8 I will bring you into the land that I swore to give to Abraham, to Isaac, and to Jacob. I will give it to you for a possession. I am the LORD.'" 9 Moses spoke thus to the people of Israel, but they did not listen to Moses, because of their broken spirit and harsh slavery.

10 So the LORD said to Moses, 11 "Go in, tell Pharaoh king of Egypt to let the people of Israel go out of his land." 12 But Moses said to the LORD, "Behold, the people of Israel have not listened to me. How then shall Pharaoh listen to me, for I am of uncircumcised lips?" 13 But the LORD spoke to Moses and Aaron and gave them a charge about the people of Israel and about Pharaoh king of Egypt: to bring the people of Israel out of the land of Egypt.

The Genealogy of Moses and Aaron

14 These are the heads of their fathers' houses: the sons of Reuben, the firstborn of Israel: Hanoch, Pallu, Hezron, and Carmi; these are the clans of Reuben. 15 The sons of Simeon: Jemuel, Jamin, Ohad, Jachin, Zohar, and Shaul, the son of a Canaanite woman; these are the clans of Simeon. 16 These are the names of the sons of Levi according to their generations: Gershon, Kohath, and Merari, the years of the life of Levi being 137 years. 17 The sons of Gershon: Libni and Shimei, by their clans. 18 The sons of Kohath: Amram, Izhar, Hebron, and Uzziel, the years of the life of Kohath being 133 years. 19 The sons of Merari: Mahli and Mushi. These are the clans of the Levites according to their generations. 20 Amram took as his wife Jochebed his father's sister, and she bore him Aaron and Moses, the years of the life of Amram being 137 years. 21 The sons of Izhar: Korah, Nepheg, and Zichri. 22 The sons of Uzziel: Mishael, Elzaphan, and Sithri. 23 Aaron took as his wife Elisheba, the daughter of Amminadab and the sister of Nahshon, and she bore him Nadab, Abihu, Eleazar, and Ithamar. 24 The sons of Korah: Assir, Elkanah, and Abiasaph; these are the clans of the Korahites. 25 Eleazar, Aaron's son, took as his wife one of the daughters of Putiel, and she bore him Phinehas. These are the heads of the fathers' houses of the Levites by their clans.

26 These are the Aaron and Moses to whom the LORD said: "Bring out the people of Israel from the land of Egypt by their hosts." 27 It was they who spoke to Pharaoh king of Egypt about bringing out the people of Israel from Egypt, this Moses and this Aaron.

28 On the day when the LORD spoke to Moses in the land of Egypt, 29 the LORD said to Moses, "I am the LORD; tell Pharaoh king of Egypt all that I say to you." 30 But Moses said to the LORD, "Behold, I am of uncircumcised lips. How will Pharaoh listen to me?"

Moses and Aaron Before Pharaoh

7 And the LORD said to Moses, "See, I have made you like God to Pharaoh, and your brother Aaron shall be your prophet. 2 You shall speak all that I command you, and your brother Aaron shall tell Pharaoh to let the people of Israel go out of his land. 3 But I will harden Pharaoh's heart, and though I multiply my signs and wonders in the land of Egypt, 4 Pharaoh will not listen to you. Then I will lay my hand on Egypt and bring my hosts, my people the children of Israel, out of the land of Egypt by great acts of judgment. 5 The Egyptians shall know that I am the LORD, when I stretch out my hand against Egypt and bring out the people of Israel from among them." 6 Moses and Aaron did so; they did just as the LORD commanded them. 7 Now Moses was eighty years old, and Aaron eighty-three years old, when they spoke to Pharaoh.

145

[8] Then the LORD said to Moses and Aaron, [9] "When Pharaoh says to you, 'Prove yourselves by working a miracle,' then you shall say to Aaron, 'Take your staff and cast it down before Pharaoh, that it may become a serpent.'" [10] So Moses and Aaron went to Pharaoh and did just as the LORD commanded. Aaron cast down his staff before Pharaoh and his servants, and it became a serpent. [11] Then Pharaoh summoned the wise men and the sorcerers, and they, the magicians of Egypt, also did the same by their secret arts. [12] For each man cast down his staff, and they became serpents. But Aaron's staff swallowed up their staffs. [13] Still Pharaoh's heart was hardened, and he would not listen to them, as the LORD had said.

CHARACTER PROFILE

AARON

Aaron was Moses' brother. Together, Moses and Aaron told Pharaoh to let God's people leave Egypt. God chose Aaron to be the first high priest. God said Aaron's sons would be priests after him. Aaron and Miriam spoke against Moses, and God rebuked them for it.

137, 145, 153

The First Plague: Water Turned to Blood

[14] Then the LORD said to Moses, "Pharaoh's heart is hardened; he refuses to let the people go. [15] Go to Pharaoh in the morning, as he is going out to the water. Stand on the bank of the Nile to meet him, and take in your hand the staff that turned into a serpent. [16] And you shall say to him, 'The LORD, the God of the Hebrews, sent me to you, saying, "Let my people go, that they may serve me in the wilderness. But so far, you have not obeyed." [17] Thus says the LORD, "By this you shall know that I am the LORD: behold, with the staff that is in my hand I will strike the water that is in the Nile, and it shall turn into blood. [18] The fish in the Nile shall die, and the Nile will stink, and the Egyptians will grow weary of drinking water from the Nile."'" [19] And the LORD said to Moses, "Say to Aaron, 'Take your staff and stretch out your hand over the waters of Egypt, over their rivers, their canals, and their ponds, and all their pools of water, so that they may become blood, and there shall be blood throughout all the land of Egypt, even in vessels of wood and in vessels of stone.'"

[20] Moses and Aaron did as the LORD commanded. In the sight of Pharaoh and in the sight of his servants he lifted up the staff and struck the water in the Nile, and all the water in the Nile turned into blood. [21] And the fish in the Nile died, and the Nile stank, so that the Egyptians could not drink water from the Nile. There was blood throughout all the land of Egypt. [22] But the magicians of Egypt did the same by their secret arts. So Pharaoh's heart remained hardened, and he would not listen to them, as the LORD had said. [23] Pharaoh turned and went into his house, and he did not take even this to heart. [24] And all the Egyptians dug along the Nile for water to drink, for they could not drink the water of the Nile.

[25] Seven full days passed after the LORD had struck the Nile.

The Second Plague: Frogs

8 [1]Then the LORD said to Moses, "Go in
to Pharaoh and say to him, 'Thus says
the LORD, "Let my people go, that they may
serve me. 2 But if you refuse to let them go,
behold, I will plague all your country with
frogs. 3 The Nile shall swarm with frogs
that shall come up into your house and
into your bedroom and on your bed and
into the houses of your servants and your
people,[2] and into your ovens and your
kneading bowls. 4 The frogs shall come up
on you and on your people and on all your
servants."'" 5 [3] And the LORD said to Moses,
"Say to Aaron, 'Stretch out your hand with
your staff over the rivers, over the canals
and over the pools, and make frogs come
up on the land of Egypt!'" 6 So Aaron
stretched out his hand over the waters of
Egypt, and the frogs came up and covered
the land of Egypt. 7 But the magicians did
the same by their secret arts and made
frogs come up on the land of Egypt.

8 Then Pharaoh called Moses and Aaron
and said, "Plead with the LORD to take
away the frogs from me and from my
people, and I will let the people go to sacri-
fice to the LORD." 9 Moses said to Pharaoh,
"Be pleased to command me when I am
to plead for you and for your servants and
for your people, that the frogs be cut off
from you and your houses and be left only
in the Nile." 10 And he said, "Tomorrow."
Moses said, "Be it as you say, so that you
may know that there is no one like the
LORD our God. 11 The frogs shall go away
from you and your houses and your ser-
vants and your people. They shall be left
only in the Nile." 12 So Moses and Aaron
went out from Pharaoh, and Moses cried
to the LORD about the frogs, as he had
agreed with Pharaoh.[4] 13 And the LORD did
according to the word of Moses. The frogs
died out in the houses, the courtyards,
and the fields. 14 And they gathered them
together in heaps, and the land stank.
15 But when Pharaoh saw that there was a
respite, he hardened his heart and would
not listen to them, as the LORD had said.

The Third Plague: Gnats

16 Then the LORD said to Moses, "Say
to Aaron, 'Stretch out your staff and
strike the dust of the earth, so that it may
become gnats in all the land of Egypt.'"
17 And they did so. Aaron stretched out his
hand with his staff and struck the dust of
the earth, and there were gnats on man
and beast. All the dust of the earth became
gnats in all the land of Egypt. 18 The magi-
cians tried by their secret arts to produce
gnats, but they could not. So there were
gnats on man and beast. 19 Then the magi-
cians said to Pharaoh, "This is the finger of
God." But Pharaoh's heart was hardened,
and he would not listen to them, as the
LORD had said.

The Fourth Plague: Flies

20 Then the LORD said to Moses, "Rise up
early in the morning and present yourself
to Pharaoh, as he goes out to the water,
and say to him, 'Thus says the LORD, "Let
my people go, that they may serve me.
21 Or else, if you will not let my people go,
behold, I will send swarms of flies on you
and your servants and your people, and
into your houses. And the houses of the
Egyptians shall be filled with swarms of
flies, and also the ground on which they
stand. 22 But on that day I will set apart the
land of Goshen, where my people dwell,
so that no swarms of flies shall be there,
that you may know that I am the LORD
in the midst of the earth.[5] 23 Thus I will
put a division[6] between my people and
your people. Tomorrow this sign shall
happen."'" 24 And the LORD did so. There
came great swarms of flies into the house
of Pharaoh and into his servants' houses.
Throughout all the land of Egypt the land
was ruined by the swarms of flies.

25 Then Pharaoh called Moses and

[1] Ch 7:26 in Hebrew [2] Or *among your people* [3] Ch 8:1 in Hebrew [4] Or *which he had brought upon Pharaoh* [5] Or *that I the LORD am in the land* [6] Septuagint, Vulgate; Hebrew *set redemption*

Moses and the Plagues

Moses went to Pharaoh as God had told him to do. God, through Moses, told Pharaoh that he must "let My people go." God's people, the Israelites, were Pharaoh's slaves, working hard day after day to build Pharaoh's great cities. Pharaoh and the Egyptians were cruel to the Israelites. Now, through Moses, God was working to set the people of Israel free.

When Moses told Pharaoh to let the people go, Pharaoh said, "Who is the LORD that I should obey His voice and let Israel go? I do not know the LORD, and moreover, I will not let Israel go." Then Pharaoh made the Israelites' work even harder.

The Lord told Moses to speak to Pharaoh all that God commanded. God told Moses that Pharaoh would not listen to him. Because of the hardness of Pharaoh's heart, God would use His great power to judge the Egyptians and to bring His people out of Egypt. And the Egyptians would know that God is the Lord.

So Moses and Aaron did as the Lord commanded. Aaron threw down his staff before Pharaoh, and it became a serpent. Even though Pharaoh saw this powerful sign, he did not obey God.

So God told Moses to say to Pharaoh, "By this you shall

know that I am the LORD: with the staff that is in my hand, I will strike the water that is in the Nile, and it shall turn into blood."

Moses and Aaron did as the Lord commanded, and all the water in the Nile—and everywhere else in Egypt—turned into blood. But Pharaoh still would not listen. So God sent thousands of frogs all over Egypt. They were even in people's beds and in the dishes with their food! Pharaoh begged Moses to ask the Lord to take away the frogs. But when the Lord took them away, Pharaoh changed his mind and would not let the people go.

Then God told Moses that Aaron should stretch out his staff and strike the dust so that the dust would become gnats. When Aaron obeyed, gnats appeared. They were over all the people and all the animals, but still, Pharaoh would not let the people go.

Next God sent swarms of flies. The flies were everywhere in Egypt, except in the places where the Israelites lived. At first, Pharaoh said the Israelites could leave his land for a few days, so the Lord removed the flies. But Pharaoh hardened his heart, and he did not let the people go.

Again God told Moses to tell Pharaoh to let His people go. If he would not, Moses told him, God would send another plague—a terrible sickness—on the animals of the Egyptians. But Pharaoh would not obey God—and the next day, all the horses, donkeys, camels, cows, and sheep belonging to the Egyptians died, while none of the animals belonging to the Israelites died. Still Pharaoh would not let the people go.

God kept telling Moses what to do next. God sent plague

after plague on Egypt. There were painful sores (boils) on the skin of the Egyptians and on their animals. A terrible hailstorm scared the Egyptians and ruined the crops in their fields. Then a plague of locusts ate the new little plants that had begun to grow. This made Pharaoh afraid. But as soon as the locusts were gone, Pharaoh hardened his heart again. So God told Moses to stretch his hand toward heaven, and a great darkness lasted for three days.

Each time, Pharaoh refused to let the people go. He refused to listen to God. Through all the dreadful plagues God was working to deliver the Israelite people from slavery. He punished Pharaoh and all the people of Egypt, for the sinful treatment of His people. But God kept His own people, Israel, safe from all the plagues.

SEEK and FIND

WHERE TO FIND THE STORY

Exodus 5–10

KEY BIBLE VERSE

"The Egyptians shall know that I am the LORD, when I stretch out my hand against Egypt and bring out the people of Israel from among them." (Exodus 7:5)

THREE KEY QUESTIONS

- What is a plague? What was the first plague that Moses and Aaron did?
- What did Pharaoh do after most of the plagues were over?
- What do the plagues show us about God?

RELATED BIBLE READINGS

Psalm 78:43–50; 105:28–36; Romans 9:17

Aaron and said, "Go, sacrifice to your God within the land." 26 But Moses said, "It would not be right to do so, for the offerings we shall sacrifice to the LORD our God are an abomination to the Egyptians. If we sacrifice offerings abominable to the Egyptians before their eyes, will they not stone us? 27 We must go three days' journey into the wilderness and sacrifice to the LORD our God as he tells us." 28 So Pharaoh said, "I will let you go to sacrifice to the LORD your God in the wilderness; only you must not go very far away. Plead for me." 29 Then Moses said, "Behold, I am going out from you and I will plead with the LORD that the swarms of flies may depart from Pharaoh, from his servants, and from his people, tomorrow. Only let not Pharaoh cheat again by not letting the people go to sacrifice to the LORD." 30 So Moses went out from Pharaoh and prayed to the LORD. 31 And the LORD did as Moses asked, and removed the swarms of flies from Pharaoh, from his servants, and from his people; not one remained. 32 But Pharaoh hardened his heart this time also, and did not let the people go.

The Fifth Plague: Egyptian Livestock Die

9 Then the LORD said to Moses, "Go in to Pharaoh and say to him, 'Thus says the LORD, the God of the Hebrews, "Let my people go, that they may serve me. 2 For if you refuse to let them go and still hold them, 3 behold, the hand of the LORD will fall with a very severe plague upon your livestock that are in the field, the horses, the donkeys, the camels, the herds, and the flocks. 4 But the LORD will make a distinction between the livestock of Israel and the livestock of Egypt, so that nothing of all that belongs to the people of Israel shall die."'" 5 And the LORD set a time, saying, "Tomorrow the LORD will do this thing in the land." 6 And the next day the LORD did this thing. All the livestock of the Egyptians died, but not one of the livestock of the people of Israel died. 7 And Pharaoh sent, and behold, not one of the livestock of Israel was dead. But the heart of Pharaoh was hardened, and he did not let the people go.

The Sixth Plague: Boils

8 And the LORD said to Moses and Aaron, "Take handfuls of soot from the kiln, and let Moses throw them in the air in the sight of Pharaoh. 9 It shall become fine dust over all the land of Egypt, and become boils breaking out in sores on man and beast throughout all the land of Egypt." 10 So they took soot from the kiln and stood before Pharaoh. And Moses threw it in the air, and it became boils breaking out in sores on man and beast. 11 And the magicians could not stand before Moses because of the boils, for the boils came upon the magicians and upon all the Egyptians. 12 But the LORD hardened the heart of Pharaoh, and he did not listen to them, as the LORD had spoken to Moses.

The Seventh Plague: Hail

13 Then the LORD said to Moses, "Rise up early in the morning and present yourself before Pharaoh and say to him, 'Thus says the LORD, the God of the Hebrews, "Let my people go, that they may serve me. 14 For this time I will send all my plagues on you yourself,[1] and on your servants and your people, so that you may know that there is none like me in all the earth. 15 For by now I could have put out my hand and struck you and your people with pestilence, and you would have been cut off from the earth. 16 But for this purpose I have raised you up, to show you my power, so that my name may be proclaimed in all the earth. 17 You are still exalting yourself against my people and will not let them go. 18 Behold, about this time tomorrow I will cause very heavy hail to fall, such as never has been in Egypt from the day it was founded until now. 19 Now therefore send, get your live-

[1] Hebrew *on your heart*

stock and all that you have in the field into safe shelter, for every man and beast that is in the field and is not brought home will die when the hail falls on them."'" 20 Then whoever feared the word of the LORD among the servants of Pharaoh hurried his slaves and his livestock into the houses, 21 but whoever did not pay attention to the word of the LORD left his slaves and his livestock in the field.

22 Then the LORD said to Moses, "Stretch out your hand toward heaven, so that there may be hail in all the land of Egypt, on man and beast and every plant of the field, in the land of Egypt." 23 Then Moses stretched out his staff toward heaven, and the LORD sent thunder and hail, and fire ran down to the earth. And the LORD rained hail upon the land of Egypt. 24 There was hail and fire flashing continually in the midst of the hail, very heavy hail, such as had never been in all the land of Egypt since it became a nation. 25 The hail struck down everything that was in the field in all the land of Egypt, both man and beast. And the hail struck down every plant of the field and broke every tree of the field. 26 Only in the land of Goshen, where the people of Israel were, was there no hail.

27 Then Pharaoh sent and called Moses and Aaron and said to them, "This time I have sinned; the LORD is in the right, and I and my people are in the wrong. 28 Plead with the LORD, for there has been enough of God's thunder and hail. I will let you go, and you shall stay no longer." 29 Moses said to him, "As soon as I have gone out of the city, I will stretch out my hands to the LORD. The thunder will cease, and there will be no more hail, so that you may know that the earth is the LORD's. 30 But as for you and your servants, I know that you do not yet fear the LORD God." 31 (The flax and the barley were struck down, for the barley was in the ear and the flax was in bud. 32 But the wheat and the emmer[1] were not struck down, for they are late in coming up.) 33 So Moses went out of the city from Pharaoh and stretched out his hands to the LORD, and the thunder and the hail ceased, and the rain no longer poured upon the earth. 34 But when Pharaoh saw that the rain and the hail and the thunder had ceased, he sinned yet again and hardened his heart, he and his servants. 35 So the heart of Pharaoh was hardened, and he did not let the people of Israel go, just as the LORD had spoken through Moses.

The Eighth Plague: Locusts

10 Then the LORD said to Moses, "Go in to Pharaoh, for I have hardened his heart and the heart of his servants, that I may show these signs of mine among them, 2 and that you may tell in the hearing of your son and of your grandson how I have dealt harshly with the Egyptians and what signs I have done among them, that you may know that I am the LORD."

3 So Moses and Aaron went in to Pharaoh and said to him, "Thus says the LORD, the God of the Hebrews, 'How long will you refuse to humble yourself before me? Let my people go, that they may serve me. 4 For if you refuse to let my people go, behold, tomorrow I will bring locusts into your country, 5 and they shall cover the face of the land, so that no one can see the land. And they shall eat what is left to you after the hail, and they shall eat every tree of yours that grows in the field, 6 and they shall fill your houses and the houses of all your servants and of all the Egyptians, as neither your fathers nor your grandfathers have seen, from the day they came on earth to this day.'" Then he turned and went out from Pharaoh.

7 Then Pharaoh's servants said to him, "How long shall this man be a snare to us? Let the men go, that they may serve the LORD their God. Do you not yet understand that Egypt is ruined?" 8 So Moses

[1] A type of wheat

and Aaron were brought back to Pharaoh. And he said to them, "Go, serve the LORD your God. But which ones are to go?" 9 Moses said, "We will go with our young and our old. We will go with our sons and daughters and with our flocks and herds, for we must hold a feast to the LORD." 10 But he said to them, "The LORD be with you, if ever I let you and your little ones go! Look, you have some evil purpose in mind.[1] 11 No! Go, the men among you, and serve the LORD, for that is what you are asking." And they were driven out from Pharaoh's presence.

12 Then the LORD said to Moses, "Stretch out your hand over the land of Egypt for the locusts, so that they may come upon the land of Egypt and eat every plant in the land, all that the hail has left." 13 So Moses stretched out his staff over the land of Egypt, and the LORD brought an east wind upon the land all that day and all that night. When it was morning, the east wind had brought the locusts. 14 The locusts came up over all the land of Egypt and settled on the whole country of Egypt, such a dense swarm of locusts as had never been before, nor ever will be again. 15 They covered the face of the whole land, so that the land was darkened, and they ate all the plants in the land and all the fruit of the trees that the hail had left. Not a green thing remained, neither tree nor plant of the field, through all the land of Egypt. 16 Then Pharaoh hastily called Moses and Aaron and said, "I have sinned against the LORD your God, and against you. 17 Now therefore, forgive my sin, please, only this once, and plead with the LORD your God only to remove this death from me." 18 So he went out from Pharaoh and pleaded with the LORD. 19 And the LORD turned the wind into a very strong west wind, which lifted the locusts and drove them into the Red Sea. Not a single locust was left in all the country of Egypt. 20 But the LORD hardened Pharaoh's heart, and he did not let the people of Israel go.

The Ninth Plague: Darkness

21 Then the LORD said to Moses, "Stretch out your hand toward heaven, that there may be darkness over the land of Egypt, a darkness to be felt." 22 So Moses stretched out his hand toward heaven, and there was pitch darkness in all the land of Egypt three days. 23 They did not see one another, nor did anyone rise from his place for three days, but all the people of Israel had light where they lived. 24 Then Pharaoh called Moses and said, "Go, serve the LORD; your little ones also may go with you; only let your flocks and your herds remain behind." 25 But Moses said, "You must also let us have sacrifices and burnt offerings, that we may sacrifice to the LORD our God. 26 Our livestock also must go with us; not a hoof shall be left behind, for we must take of them to serve the LORD our God, and we do not know with what we must serve the LORD until we arrive there." 27 But the LORD hardened Pharaoh's heart, and he would not let them go. 28 Then Pharaoh said to him, "Get away from me; take care never to see my face again, for on the day you see my face you shall die." 29 Moses said, "As you say! I will not see your face again."

A Final Plague Threatened

153

11 The LORD said to Moses, "Yet one plague more I will bring upon Pharaoh and upon Egypt. Afterward he will let you go from here. When he lets you go, he will drive you away completely. 2 Speak now in the hearing of the people, that they ask, every man of his neighbor and every woman of her neighbor, for silver and gold jewelry." 3 And the LORD gave the people favor in the sight of the Egyptians. Moreover, the man Moses was very great in the land of Egypt, in the sight of Pharaoh's servants and in the sight of the people.

[1] Hebrew *before your face*

The Passover

God was setting His people free from slavery in Egypt. He was going to take them to a new land. God had sent Moses and his brother Aaron to tell Pharaoh, the ruler of Egypt, that he must let the Israelites go. But because Pharaoh would not obey God, bad things happened to the people of Egypt.

These bad things were called plagues—and after nine plagues, the land of Egypt had been ruined. Still, Pharaoh would not let Moses and the Israelites leave Egypt. Finally, the Lord said to Moses, "Yet one plague more I will bring upon Pharaoh and upon Egypt. Afterward he will let you go from here."

So Moses went to Pharaoh and told him what God had said. About midnight, Moses said, God would go through the land of Egypt and the oldest son of every family would die. There would be a great cry throughout all the land of Egypt. The firstborn of every animal would die in Egypt, too. But no harm would come to the Israelites or to their animals. Pharaoh was not afraid of this news, and he did not let the people of Israel go.

Then Moses went to the Israelites and told them what God wanted the Israelites to do. Each family was to choose a lamb without blemish—a perfect lamb that had nothing wrong with it. They were to kill the lamb and put some of its blood on the doorposts of their houses—on the sides of the doors and the tops of the doors. "None of you shall go out of the door of his house until the morning," Moses warned the people. "For the LORD will pass through to strike the Egyptians, and when He sees the blood on the lintel and on the two doorposts, the LORD will pass over the door and will not allow the destroyer to enter your houses to strike you."

God gave Moses and the people of Israel other important instructions, too. They were to eat roasted lamb with flat bread and bitter herbs. He told them to dress in traveling clothes, with their belts fastened, sandals on, and a staff nearby.

God told Moses that His people must always celebrate this night—it was the night of the Lord's Passover—when the Lord "passed over" their house marked with blood and did not harm them. Every year, they must kill a Passover lamb and eat the Passover meal, to remember what God had done for them on this night.

It all happened just as God had said. At midnight, the oldest son in every family in the land of Egypt died. The people of Egypt cried bitter tears. Each family had lost someone. The Israelites stayed inside their houses, trusting God to see the blood of the lamb applied to their doorposts. And the people of Israel had faith in God, trusting that He would save them.

Finally, after the last terrible plague, Pharaoh let God's people go. He called Moses and Aaron and told them to get up and "go out from among my people." The Egyptians were terrified by this last plague. They gave the Israelites silver and gold, jewelry and clothes, and made the Israelites hurry away from their land. At last, God's people were free!

The Passover lamb was a picture of what Jesus would be for His people. All of us deserve God's judgment because of our sin. But the blood of Jesus cleanses the sins of all who have faith in Him, to save us from God's judgment.

SEEK and FIND

WHERE TO FIND THE STORY

Exodus 11–12

KEY BIBLE VERSES

"And when I see the blood, I will pass over you." (Exodus 12:13)

"For Christ, our Passover lamb, has been sacrificed." (1 Corinthians 5:7)

THREE KEY QUESTIONS

- In the last plague, why did God "pass over" the houses of the Israelites?
- What were God's people supposed to do every year, to remember what God had done for them on the night of the LORD's Passover?
- How is Jesus the Passover lamb for all who have faith in Him?

RELATED BIBLE READINGS

Exodus 13:1–16; Psalm 105:36–38; 135:8–9; Matthew 26:17–29; 1 Corinthians 5:7–8

the month at evening. 19 For seven days
no leaven is to be found in your houses. If
anyone eats what is leavened, that person
will be cut off from the congregation of
Israel, whether he is a sojourner or a native
of the land. 20 You shall eat nothing leav-
ened; in all your dwelling places you shall
eat unleavened bread."

21 Then Moses called all the elders of
Israel and said to them, "Go and select
lambs for yourselves according to your
clans, and kill the Passover lamb. 22 Take
a bunch of hyssop and dip it in the blood
that is in the basin, and touch the lintel
and the two doorposts with the blood that
is in the basin. None of you shall go out

of the door of his house until the morning. 23 For the LORD will pass through to strike the Egyptians, and when he sees the blood on the lintel and on the two doorposts, the LORD will pass over the door and will not allow the destroyer to enter your houses to strike you. 24 You shall observe this rite as a statute for you and for your sons forever. 25 And when you come to the land that the LORD will give you, as he has promised, you shall keep this service. 26 And when your children say to you, 'What do you mean by this service?' 27 you shall say, 'It is the sacrifice of the LORD's Passover, for he passed over the houses of the people of Israel in Egypt, when he struck the Egyptians but spared our houses.'" And the people bowed their heads and worshiped.

28 Then the people of Israel went and did so; as the LORD had commanded Moses and Aaron, so they did.

The Tenth Plague: Death of the Firstborn

29 At midnight the LORD struck down all the firstborn in the land of Egypt, from the firstborn of Pharaoh who sat on his throne to the firstborn of the captive who was in the dungeon, and all the firstborn of the livestock. 30 And Pharaoh rose up in the night, he and all his servants and all the Egyptians. And there was a great cry in Egypt, for there was not a house where someone was not dead. 31 Then he summoned Moses and Aaron by night and said, "Up, go out from among my people, both you and the people of Israel; and go, serve the LORD, as you have said. 32 Take your flocks and your herds, as you have said, and be gone, and bless me also!"

The Exodus

33 The Egyptians were urgent with the people to send them out of the land in haste. For they said, "We shall all be dead." 34 So the people took their dough before it was leavened, their kneading bowls being bound up in their cloaks on their shoulders. 35 The people of Israel had also done as Moses told them, for they had asked the Egyptians for silver and gold jewelry and for clothing. 36 And the LORD had given the people favor in the sight of the Egyptians, so that they let them have what they asked. Thus they plundered the Egyptians.

37 And the people of Israel journeyed from Rameses to Succoth, about six hundred thousand men on foot, besides women and children. 38 A mixed multitude also went up with them, and very much livestock, both flocks and herds. 39 And they baked unleavened cakes of the dough that they had brought out of Egypt, for it was not leavened, because they were thrust out of Egypt and could not wait, nor had they prepared any provisions for themselves.

40 The time that the people of Israel lived in Egypt was 430 years. 41 At the end of 430 years, on that very day, all the hosts of the LORD went out from the land of Egypt. 42 It was a night of watching by the LORD, to bring them out of the land of Egypt; so this same night is a night of watching kept to the LORD by all the people of Israel throughout their generations.

Institution of the Passover

43 And the LORD said to Moses and Aaron, "This is the statute of the Passover: no foreigner shall eat of it, 44 but every slave that is bought for money may eat of it after you have circumcised him. 45 No foreigner or hired servant may eat of it. 46 It shall be eaten in one house; you shall not take any of the flesh outside the house, and you shall not break any of its bones. 47 All the congregation of Israel shall keep it. 48 If a stranger shall sojourn with you and would keep the Passover to the LORD, let all his males be circumcised. Then he may come near and keep it; he shall be as a native of the land. But no uncircumcised person shall eat of it. 49 There shall be one

law for the native and for the stranger who
sojourns among you."
50 All the people of Israel did just as the
LORD commanded Moses and Aaron.
51 And on that very day the LORD brought
the people of Israel out of the land of
Egypt by their hosts.

Consecration of the Firstborn

13 The LORD said to Moses,
2 "Consecrate to me all the
153 firstborn. Whatever is the first to
open the womb among the people of
Israel, both of man and of beast, is mine."

The Feast of Unleavened Bread

3 Then Moses said to the people,
"Remember this day in which you came
out from Egypt, out of the house of
slavery, for by a strong hand the LORD
brought you out from this place. No leav-
ened bread shall be eaten. 4 Today, in the
month of Abib, you are going out. 5 And
when the LORD brings you into the land of
the Canaanites, the Hittites, the Amorites,
the Hivites, and the Jebusites, which he
swore to your fathers to give you, a land
flowing with milk and honey, you shall
keep this service in this month. 6 Seven
days you shall eat unleavened bread, and
on the seventh day there shall be a feast
to the LORD. 7 Unleavened bread shall be
eaten for seven days; no leavened bread
shall be seen with you, and no leaven
shall be seen with you in all your terri-
tory. 8 You shall tell your son on that day,
'It is because of what the LORD did for me
when I came out of Egypt.' 9 And it shall
be to you as a sign on your hand and as a
memorial between your eyes, that the law
of the LORD may be in your mouth. For
with a strong hand the LORD has brought
you out of Egypt. 10 You shall therefore
keep this statute at its appointed time
from year to year.
11 "When the LORD brings you into the
land of the Canaanites, as he swore to you
and your fathers, and shall give it to you,
12 you shall set apart to the LORD all that
first opens the womb. All the firstborn of
your animals that are males shall be the
LORD's. 13 Every firstborn of a donkey you
shall redeem with a lamb, or if you will
not redeem it you shall break its neck.
Every firstborn of man among your sons
you shall redeem. 14 And when in time to
come your son asks you, 'What does this
mean?' you shall say to him, 'By a strong
hand the LORD brought us out of Egypt,
from the house of slavery. 15 For when
Pharaoh stubbornly refused to let us go,
the LORD killed all the firstborn in the
land of Egypt, both the firstborn of man
and the firstborn of animals. Therefore
I sacrifice to the LORD all the males that
first open the womb, but all the firstborn
of my sons I redeem.' 16 It shall be as a
mark on your hand or frontlets between
your eyes, for by a strong hand the LORD
brought us out of Egypt."

Pillars of Cloud and Fire

17 When Pharaoh let the people go,
God did not lead them by way of the
161 land of the Philistines, although
that was near. For God said, "Lest the peo-
ple change their minds when they see war
and return to Egypt." 18 But God led the
people around by the way of the wilder-
ness toward the Red Sea. And the people of
Israel went up out of the land of Egypt
equipped for battle. 19 Moses took the
bones of Joseph with him, for Joseph[1] had
made the sons of Israel solemnly swear,
saying, "God will surely visit you, and you
shall carry up my bones with you from
here." 20 And they moved on from Succoth
and encamped at Etham, on the edge of the
wilderness. 21 And the LORD went before
them by day in a pillar of cloud to lead
them along the way, and by night in a pillar
of fire to give them light, that they might
travel by day and by night. 22 The pillar of
cloud by day and the pillar of fire by night
did not depart from before the people.

[1] Samaritan, Septuagint; Hebrew *he*

Crossing the Red Sea

14 Then the LORD said to Moses, 2 "Tell the people of Israel to turn back and encamp in front of Pi-hahiroth, between Migdol and the sea, in front of Baal-zephon; you shall encamp facing it, by the sea. 3 For Pharaoh will say of the people of Israel, 'They are wandering in the land; the wilderness has shut them in.' 4 And I will harden Pharaoh's heart, and he will pursue them, and I will get glory over Pharaoh and all his host, and the Egyptians shall know that I am the LORD." And they did so.

5 When the king of Egypt was told that the people had fled, the mind of Pharaoh and his servants was changed toward the people, and they said, "What is this we have done, that we have let Israel go from serving us?" 6 So he made ready his chariot and took his army with him, 7 and took six hundred chosen chariots and all the other chariots of Egypt with officers over all of them. 8 And the LORD hardened the heart of Pharaoh king of Egypt, and he pursued the people of Israel while the people of Israel were going out defiantly. 9 The Egyptians pursued them, all Pharaoh's horses and chariots and his horsemen and his army, and overtook them encamped at the sea, by Pi-hahiroth, in front of Baal-zephon.

10 When Pharaoh drew near, the people of Israel lifted up their eyes, and behold, the Egyptians were marching after them, and they feared greatly. And the people of Israel cried out to the LORD. 11 They said to Moses, "Is it because there are no graves in Egypt that you have taken us away to die in the wilderness? What have you done to us in bringing us out of Egypt? 12 Is not this what we said to you in Egypt: 'Leave us alone that we may serve the Egyptians'? For it would have been better for us to serve the Egyptians than to die in the wilderness." 13 And Moses said to the people, "Fear not, stand firm, and see the salvation of the LORD, which he will work for you today. For the Egyptians whom you see today, you shall never see again. 14 The LORD will fight for you, and you have only to be silent."

15 The LORD said to Moses, "Why do you cry to me? Tell the people of Israel to go forward. 16 Lift up your staff, and stretch out your hand over the sea and divide it, that the people of Israel may go through the sea on dry ground. 17 And I will harden the hearts of the Egyptians so that they shall go in after them, and I will get glory over Pharaoh and all his host, his chariots, and his horsemen. 18 And the Egyptians shall know that I am the LORD, when I have gotten glory over Pharaoh, his chariots, and his horsemen."

19 Then the angel of God who was going before the host of Israel moved and went behind them, and the pillar of cloud moved from before them and stood behind them, 20 coming between the host of Egypt and the host of Israel. And there was the cloud and the darkness. And it lit up the night[1] without one coming near the other all night.

21 Then Moses stretched out his hand over the sea, and the LORD drove the sea back by a strong east wind all night and made the sea dry land, and the waters were divided. 22 And the people of Israel went into the midst of the sea on dry ground, the waters being a wall to them on their right hand and on their left. 23 The Egyptians pursued and went in after them into the midst of the sea, all Pharaoh's horses, his chariots, and his horsemen. 24 And in the morning watch the LORD in the pillar of fire and of cloud looked down on the Egyptian forces and threw the Egyptian forces into a panic, 25 clogging[2] their chariot wheels so that they drove heavily. And the Egyptians said, "Let us flee from before Israel, for the LORD fights for them against the Egyptians."

26 Then the LORD said to Moses, "Stretch

[1] Septuagint *and the night passed* [2] Or *binding* (compare Samaritan, Septuagint, Syriac); Hebrew *removing*

out your hand over the sea, that the water
may come back upon the Egyptians, upon
their chariots, and upon their horsemen."
27 So Moses stretched out his hand over
the sea, and the sea returned to its nor-
mal course when the morning appeared.
And as the Egyptians fled into it, the LORD
threw[1] the Egyptians into the midst of the
sea. 28 The waters returned and covered
the chariots and the horsemen; of all the
host of Pharaoh that had followed them
into the sea, not one of them remained.
29 But the people of Israel walked on dry
ground through the sea, the waters being
a wall to them on their right hand and on
their left.

30 Thus the LORD saved Israel that day
from the hand of the Egyptians, and Israel
saw the Egyptians dead on the seashore.
31 Israel saw the great power that the LORD
used against the Egyptians, so the people
feared the LORD, and they believed in the
LORD and in his servant Moses.

The Song of Moses

15 Then Moses and the people of Israel sang this song to the LORD, saying,

"I will sing to the LORD, for he has
triumphed gloriously;
the horse and his rider[2] he has
thrown into the sea.

161

2 The LORD is my strength and my
song,
and he has become my salvation;
this is my God, and I will praise
him,
my father's God, and I will exalt
him.
3 The LORD is a man of war;
the LORD is his name.

4 "Pharaoh's chariots and his host he
cast into the sea,
and his chosen officers were sunk
in the Red Sea.
5 The floods covered them;
they went down into the depths
like a stone.
6 Your right hand, O LORD, glorious in
power,
your right hand, O LORD, shatters
the enemy.
7 In the greatness of your majesty you
overthrow your adversaries;
you send out your fury; it
consumes them like stubble.
8 At the blast of your nostrils the
waters piled up;
the floods stood up in a heap;
the deeps congealed in the heart
of the sea.
9 The enemy said, 'I will pursue, I will
overtake,
I will divide the spoil, my desire
shall have its fill of them.

CHARACTER PROFILE

MIRIAM

Miriam was Moses' big sister. When Moses was put in the river in a basket, Miriam stood nearby to watch. Miriam led the Israelite women in a song of praise after God led His people through the Red Sea. Miriam and Aaron spoke against Moses, and God struck Miriam with leprosy for a short time.

131, 161

[1] Hebrew *shook off* [2] Or *its chariot*; also verse 21

Crossing the Red Sea

After the tenth and worst plague Pharaoh finally let the Israelites go. God led them away from Egypt, toward the Red Sea. The Lord went before them in a pillar of cloud by day and in a pillar of fire by night. But right after the Israelites left Egypt, the Lord hardened Pharaoh's heart—and Pharaoh changed his mind again! "What is this we have done, that we have let Israel go?" Pharaoh said.

Quickly, Pharaoh got his chariot and army ready, taking more than 600 chariots with him. The Egyptians chased after the Israelites until they came near them while they were camped by the Red Sea. When the people of Israel saw the chariots coming after them, they were afraid. "What have you done to us in bringing us out of Egypt?" they complained to Moses. "It would have been better for us to serve the Egyptians than to die in the wilderness."

Moses believed that God would save the Israelites, and he wanted God's people to believe too. "Fear not," Moses said, "stand firm, and see the salvation of the LORD, which He will work for you today. The LORD will fight for you, and you have only to be silent."

The Lord told Moses to lift up his staff and to stretch out his hand over the sea and divide it, so that the people of Israel could to go through the sea on dry ground.

Moses stretched out his hand over the sea. The Lord pushed back the sea and divided the waters. The people of Israel walked through the water on dry ground, with a wall of water on their right and a wall of water on their left.

The mighty Egyptians chased the Israelites into the sea. But God made the Egyptians panic, causing their chariot wheels to get caught in the mud. "Let us flee from before Israel," the Egyptian soldiers said, "for the LORD fights for them against the Egyptians." But it was too late to flee. The Lord said to Moses, "Stretch out your hand over the sea, that the water may come back upon the Egyptians, upon their chariots, and upon their horsemen." Moses stretched out his hand. The waters rushed back to their normal place, drowning the Egyptians in the Red Sea. Not one of them was left.

God's people saw His great power, and they feared the Lord. They believed in the Lord, and in His servant Moses. Then Moses led the people of Israel in a song of praise and thanks to God.

The Israelites could never have fought Pharaoh's army on their own. God fought for them and destroyed their enemies. Likewise, sinful people cannot fight sin and death on their own. The Lord Jesus Christ fought for His people and defeated our terrible enemy, Satan, on the cross. Through faith in His death and resurrection, Jesus gives us the victory over our greatest enemy.

SEEK and FIND

WHERE TO FIND THE STORY
Exodus 13:17–15:21

KEY BIBLE VERSE
"I will sing to the LORD, for he has triumphed gloriously."
(Exodus 15:1)

THREE KEY QUESTIONS
- When the Israelites were afraid at the edge of the Red Sea, what did they forget?
- What happened to Pharaoh's army when they chased the Israelites into the Red Sea?
- God saved the Israelites from Egypt's army. What greater salvation does God provide for all who put their trust in Christ?

RELATED BIBLE READINGS
Nehemiah 9:9–11; Psalm 66:5–7; 77:16–20; 106:7–12; Isaiah 51:10; Hebrews 11:29

I will draw my sword; my hand
shall destroy them.'
10 You blew with your wind; the sea
covered them;
they sank like lead in the mighty
waters.

11 "Who is like you, O LORD, among the
gods?
Who is like you, majestic in
holiness,
awesome in glorious deeds, doing
wonders?
12 You stretched out your right hand;
the earth swallowed them.

13 "You have led in your steadfast love
the people whom you have
redeemed;
you have guided them by your
strength to your holy abode.
14 The peoples have heard; they
tremble;
pangs have seized the inhabitants
of Philistia.
15 Now are the chiefs of Edom
dismayed;
trembling seizes the leaders of
Moab;
all the inhabitants of Canaan have
melted away.
16 Terror and dread fall upon them;
because of the greatness of your
arm, they are still as a stone,
till your people, O LORD, pass by,
till the people pass by whom you
have purchased.
17 You will bring them in and plant
them on your own mountain,
the place, O LORD, which you have
made for your abode,

the sanctuary, O Lord, which your
hands have established.
18 The LORD will reign forever and
ever."

19 For when the horses of Pharaoh with
his chariots and his horsemen went into
the sea, the LORD brought back the waters
of the sea upon them, but the people of
Israel walked on dry ground in the midst
of the sea. 20 Then Miriam the prophetess,
the sister of Aaron, took a tambourine in
her hand, and all the women went out
after her with tambourines and dancing.
21 And Miriam sang to them:

"Sing to the LORD, for he has
triumphed gloriously;
the horse and his rider he has
thrown into the sea."

Bitter Water Made Sweet

22 Then Moses made Israel set out from
the Red Sea, and they went into the wil-
derness of Shur. They went three days
in the wilderness and found no water.
23 When they came to Marah, they could
not drink the water of Marah because
it was bitter; therefore it was named
Marah.[1] 24 And the people grumbled
against Moses, saying, "What shall we
drink?" 25 And he cried to the LORD, and
the LORD showed him a log,[2] and he
threw it into the water, and the water
became sweet.

There the LORD[3] made for them a stat-
ute and a rule, and there he tested them,
26 saying, "If you will diligently listen to
the voice of the LORD your God, and do
that which is right in his eyes, and give
ear to his commandments and keep all his
statutes, I will put none of the diseases on
you that I put on the Egyptians, for I am
the LORD, your healer."

27 Then they came to Elim, where there
were twelve springs of water and seventy
palm trees, and they encamped there by
the water.

Bread from Heaven

167

16 They set out from Elim, and
all the congregation of the
people of Israel came to the wilder-
ness of Sin, which is between Elim and
Sinai, on the fifteenth day of the second
month after they had departed from the
land of Egypt. 2 And the whole congrega-
tion of the people of Israel grumbled
against Moses and Aaron in the wilder-
ness, 3 and the people of Israel said to
them, "Would that we had died by the
hand of the LORD in the land of Egypt,
when we sat by the meat pots and ate
bread to the full, for you have brought us
out into this wilderness to kill this whole
assembly with hunger."

4 Then the LORD said to Moses, "Behold,
I am about to rain bread from heaven
for you, and the people shall go out and
gather a day's portion every day, that I
may test them, whether they will walk in
my law or not. 5 On the sixth day, when
they prepare what they bring in, it will be
twice as much as they gather daily." 6 So
Moses and Aaron said to all the people of
Israel, "At evening you shall know that it
was the LORD who brought you out of the
land of Egypt, 7 and in the morning you
shall see the glory of the LORD, because
he has heard your grumbling against the
LORD. For what are we, that you grumble
against us?" 8 And Moses said, "When
the LORD gives you in the evening meat
to eat and in the morning bread to the
full, because the LORD has heard your
grumbling that you grumble against
him—what are we? Your grumbling is not
against us but against the LORD."

9 Then Moses said to Aaron, "Say to
the whole congregation of the people of
Israel, 'Come near before the LORD, for he
has heard your grumbling.'" 10 And as soon
as Aaron spoke to the whole congregation
of the people of Israel, they looked toward
the wilderness, and behold, the glory of
the LORD appeared in the cloud. 11 And the

[1] *Marah* means *bitterness* [2] Or *tree* [3] Hebrew *he*

LORD said to Moses, 12 “I have heard the
grumbling of the people of Israel. Say to
them, ‘At twilight you shall eat meat, and
in the morning you shall be filled with
bread. Then you shall know that I am the
LORD your God.’ ”
13 In the evening quail came up and
covered the camp, and in the morning
dew lay around the camp. 14 And when
the dew had gone up, there was on the
face of the wilderness a fine, flake-like
thing, fine as frost on the ground. 15 When
the people of Israel saw it, they said to
one another, “What is it?”[1] For they did
not know what it was. And Moses said to
them, “It is the bread that the LORD has
given you to eat. 16 This is what the LORD
has commanded: ‘Gather of it, each one
of you, as much as he can eat. You shall
each take an omer,[2] according to the
number of the persons that each of you
has in his tent.’ ” 17 And the people of Israel
did so. They gathered, some more, some
less. 18 But when they measured it with
an omer, whoever gathered much had
nothing left over, and whoever gathered
little had no lack. Each of them gathered
as much as he could eat. 19 And Moses
said to them, “Let no one leave any of
it over till the morning.” 20 But they did
not listen to Moses. Some left part of it
till the morning, and it bred worms and
stank. And Moses was angry with them.
21 Morning by morning they gathered it,
each as much as he could eat; but when
the sun grew hot, it melted.
22 On the sixth day they gathered twice
as much bread, two omers each. And
when all the leaders of the congregation
came and told Moses, 23 he said to them,
“This is what the LORD has commanded:
‘Tomorrow is a day of solemn rest, a holy
Sabbath to the LORD; bake what you will
bake and boil what you will boil, and all
that is left over lay aside to be kept till the
morning.’ ” 24 So they laid it aside till the
morning, as Moses commanded them,
and it did not stink, and there were no
worms in it. 25 Moses said, “Eat it today,
for today is a Sabbath to the LORD; today
you will not find it in the field. 26 Six days
you shall gather it, but on the seventh day,
which is a Sabbath, there will be none.”
27 On the seventh day some of the people
went out to gather, but they found none.
28 And the LORD said to Moses, “How long
will you refuse to keep my command-
ments and my laws? 29 See! The LORD has
given you the Sabbath; therefore on the
sixth day he gives you bread for two days.
Remain each of you in his place; let no one
go out of his place on the seventh day.”
30 So the people rested on the seventh day.
31 Now the house of Israel called its
name manna. It was like coriander seed,
white, and the taste of it was like wafers
made with honey. 32 Moses said, “This is
what the LORD has commanded: ‘Let an
omer of it be kept throughout your gener-
ations, so that they may see the bread with
which I fed you in the wilderness, when
I brought you out of the land of Egypt.’ ”
33 And Moses said to Aaron, “Take a jar,
and put an omer of manna in it, and place
it before the LORD to be kept throughout
your generations.” 34 As the LORD com-
manded Moses, so Aaron placed it before
the testimony to be kept. 35 The people of
Israel ate the manna forty years, till they
came to a habitable land. They ate the
manna till they came to the border of the
land of Canaan. 36 (An omer is the tenth
part of an ephah.)[3]

Water from the Rock

17 All the congregation of the peo-
ple of Israel moved on from the
wilderness of Sin by stages, according
to the commandment of the LORD, and
camped at Rephidim, but there was no
water for the people to drink. 2 Therefore
the people quarreled with Moses and
said, “Give us water to drink.” And Moses
said to them, “Why do you quarrel with

[1] Or *“It is manna.”* Hebrew *man hu* [2] An *omer* was about 2 quarts or 2 liters [3] An *ephah* was about 3/5 bushel or 22 liters

God Provides Manna, Water, and Quail

As the Israelite people traveled through the desert on their way to the Promised Land, they camped in tent homes along the way, out in the wilderness. Living in the wilderness was not always easy. Such a large group of people—probably more than 3 million men, women, and children—required a great deal of food, and there were no stores in the wilderness! Soon, all the people were grumbling against Moses and Aaron. They said they had plenty of meat and bread in Egypt. They wondered why Moses had brought them out into the wilderness, if they were only going to die of hunger.

Moses asked the people why they were grumbling against him and against Aaron. "Your grumbling," Moses said, "is not against us but against the LORD."

The Lord said to Moses, "I have heard the grumbling of the people of Israel. Say to them, 'At twilight you shall eat meat, and in the morning you shall be filled with bread. Then you shall know that I am the LORD your God.'"

And it happened just as God promised. At twilight, quail covered the camp. The people were able to catch as many as they needed to cook for meat.

In the morning, small drops of water called dew lay on the ground all around the camp. When the sun dried up the dew, there on the ground was a fine flake-like bread that tasted like wafers made with honey. The Israelite people called this food manna. "It is the bread," Moses said, "that the LORD has given you to eat."

Every day, the Israelites gathered just enough food for their needs—but on the Sabbath day, God's day of rest, there was no manna. To provide for the Sabbath, God told the people to gather twice as much manna the day before. Because of this they could rest on the Sabbath. So God cared for the people of Israel and provided them with the food they needed.

But it was also hard to find water in the wilderness. As the Israelites traveled, they, and all their animals, became very thirsty. The people quarreled with Moses. They said, "Why did you bring us up out of Egypt, to kill us and our children and our livestock with thirst?" Again Moses asked, "Why do you quarrel with me? Why do you test the LORD?"

God heard their complaints. God told Moses that He would stand before Moses on a rock, and that Moses was to strike the rock with his staff. When Moses did this, water flowed from the rock. So God cared for the people of Israel and provided them with the water they needed.

God satisfied every need that the Israelites had as they traveled through the desert on their way to the Promised Land. He kept them alive with food and water even in the wilderness. God satisfies the needs of His people now through His Son, Jesus. Jesus said that He is living water. He also said that He is the Bread of Life. Those who believe in Jesus have eternal life that never ends.

SEEK and FIND

WHERE TO FIND THE STORY

Exodus 16:1–17:7

KEY BIBLE VERSE

"Jesus said to them, 'I am the bread of life; whoever comes to me shall not hunger, and whoever believes in me shall never thirst.'" (John 6:35)

THREE KEY QUESTIONS

- Who were the Israelites really grumbling against?
- What did God do to provide for the needs of the people of Israel in the wilderness?
- What did God do to provide for our needs forever?

RELATED BIBLE READINGS

Psalm 105:40–42; John 4:7–14; 6:25–59;
1 Corinthians 10:1–4

me? Why do you test the LORD?" 3 But the
people thirsted there for water, and the
people grumbled against Moses and said,
"Why did you bring us up out of Egypt, to
kill us and our children and our livestock
with thirst?" 4 So Moses cried to the LORD,
"What shall I do with this people? They
are almost ready to stone me." 5 And the
LORD said to Moses, "Pass on before the
people, taking with you some of the elders
of Israel, and take in your hand the staff
with which you struck the Nile, and go.
6 Behold, I will stand before you there on
the rock at Horeb, and you shall strike the
rock, and water shall come out of it, and
the people will drink." And Moses did so,
in the sight of the elders of Israel. 7 And he
called the name of the place Massah[1] and
Meribah,[2] because of the quarreling of the
people of Israel, and because they tested
the LORD by saying, "Is the LORD among
us or not?"

Israel Defeats Amalek

8 Then Amalek came and fought with
Israel at Rephidim. 9 So Moses said to
Joshua, "Choose for us men, and go out
and fight with Amalek. Tomorrow I will
stand on the top of the hill with the staff
of God in my hand." 10 So Joshua did as
Moses told him, and fought with Amalek,
while Moses, Aaron, and Hur went up
to the top of the hill. 11 Whenever Moses
held up his hand, Israel prevailed, and
whenever he lowered his hand, Amalek
prevailed. 12 But Moses' hands grew weary,
so they took a stone and put it under him,
and he sat on it, while Aaron and Hur held
up his hands, one on one side, and the
other on the other side. So his hands were
steady until the going down of the sun.
13 And Joshua overwhelmed Amalek and
his people with the sword.
14 Then the LORD said to Moses, "Write
this as a memorial in a book and recite

[1] *Massah* means *testing* [2] *Meribah* means *quarreling*

it in the ears of Joshua, that I will utterly
blot out the memory of Amalek from
under heaven." 15 And Moses built an
altar and called the name of it, The LORD
Is My Banner, 16 saying, "A hand upon the
throne[1] of the LORD! The LORD will have
war with Amalek from generation to
generation."

Jethro's Advice

18 Jethro, the priest of Midian,
Moses' father-in-law, heard of
all that God had done for Moses and
for Israel his people, how the LORD had
brought Israel out of Egypt. 2 Now Jethro,
Moses' father-in-law, had taken Zipporah,
Moses' wife, after he had sent her home,
3 along with her two sons. The name of
the one was Gershom (for he said, "I have
been a sojourner[2] in a foreign land"),
4 and the name of the other, Eliezer[3] (for
he said, "The God of my father was my
help, and delivered me from the sword
of Pharaoh"). 5 Jethro, Moses' father-in-
law, came with his sons and his wife to
Moses in the wilderness where he was
encamped at the mountain of God. 6 And
when he sent word to Moses, "I,[4] your
father-in-law Jethro, am coming to you
with your wife and her two sons with
her," 7 Moses went out to meet his father-
in-law and bowed down and kissed him.
And they asked each other of their welfare
and went into the tent. 8 Then Moses told
his father-in-law all that the LORD had
done to Pharaoh and to the Egyptians
for Israel's sake, all the hardship that had
come upon them in the way, and how the
LORD had delivered them. 9 And Jethro
rejoiced for all the good that the LORD had
done to Israel, in that he had delivered
them out of the hand of the Egyptians.

10 Jethro said, "Blessed be the LORD, who
has delivered you out of the hand of the
Egyptians and out of the hand of Pharaoh
and has delivered the people from under
the hand of the Egyptians. 11 Now I know
that the LORD is greater than all gods,
because in this affair they dealt arrogantly
with the people."[5] 12 And Jethro, Moses'
father-in-law, brought a burnt offering
and sacrifices to God; and Aaron came
with all the elders of Israel to eat bread
with Moses' father-in-law before God.

13 The next day Moses sat to judge the
people, and the people stood around
Moses from morning till evening. 14 When
Moses' father-in-law saw all that he was
doing for the people, he said, "What is this
that you are doing for the people? Why do
you sit alone, and all the people stand
around you from morning till evening?"
15 And Moses said to his father-in-law,
"Because the people come to me to inquire
of God; 16 when they have a dispute, they
come to me and I decide between one per-
son and another, and I make them know
the statutes of God and his laws." 17 Moses'
father-in-law said to him, "What you are
doing is not good. 18 You and the people
with you will certainly wear yourselves
out, for the thing is too heavy for you. You
are not able to do it alone. 19 Now obey my
voice; I will give you advice, and God be
with you! You shall represent the people
before God and bring their cases to God,
20 and you shall warn them about the stat-
utes and the laws, and make them know
the way in which they must walk and
what they must do. 21 Moreover, look for
able men from all the people, men who
fear God, who are trustworthy and hate a
bribe, and place such men over the people
as chiefs of thousands, of hundreds, of fif-
ties, and of tens. 22 And let them judge the
people at all times. Every great matter they
shall bring to you, but any small matter
they shall decide themselves. So it will be
easier for you, and they will bear the bur-
den with you. 23 If you do this, God will
direct you, you will be able to endure, and
all this people also will go to their place
in peace."

24 So Moses listened to the voice of his

[1] A slight change would yield *upon the banner* [2] *Gershom* sounds like the Hebrew word for *sojourner* [3] *Eliezer* means *My God is help* [4] Hebrew; Samaritan, Septuagint, Syriac *behold* [5] Hebrew *with them*

father-in-law and did all that he had said.
25 Moses chose able men out of all Israel
and made them heads over the people,
chiefs of thousands, of hundreds, of fif-
ties, and of tens. 26 And they judged the
people at all times. Any hard case they
brought to Moses, but any small matter
they decided themselves. 27 Then Moses
let his father-in-law depart, and he went
away to his own country.

Israel at Mount Sinai

19 On the third new moon
after the people of Israel
175 had gone out of the land of Egypt,
on that day they came into the wilderness
of Sinai. 2 They set out from Rephidim and
came into the wilderness of Sinai, and
they encamped in the wilderness. There
Israel encamped before the mountain,
3 while Moses went up to God. The LORD
called to him out of the mountain, saying,
"Thus you shall say to the house of Jacob,
and tell the people of Israel: 4 You your-
selves have seen what I did to the
Egyptians, and how I bore you on eagles'
wings and brought you to myself. 5 Now
therefore, if you will indeed obey my voice
and keep my covenant, you shall be my
treasured possession among all peoples,
for all the earth is mine; 6 and you shall be
to me a kingdom of priests and a holy
nation. These are the words that you shall
speak to the people of Israel."

7 So Moses came and called the elders of
the people and set before them all these
words that the LORD had commanded
him. 8 All the people answered together
and said, "All that the LORD has spoken we
will do." And Moses reported the words
of the people to the LORD. 9 And the LORD
said to Moses, "Behold, I am coming to
you in a thick cloud, that the people may
hear when I speak with you, and may also
believe you forever."

When Moses told the words of the peo-
ple to the LORD, 10 the LORD said to Moses,
"Go to the people and consecrate them
today and tomorrow, and let them wash
their garments 11 and be ready for the third
day. For on the third day the LORD will
come down on Mount Sinai in the sight
of all the people. 12 And you shall set lim-
its for the people all around, saying, 'Take
care not to go up into the mountain or
touch the edge of it. Whoever touches the
mountain shall be put to death. 13 No hand
shall touch him, but he shall be stoned or
shot;[1] whether beast or man, he shall not
live.' When the trumpet sounds a long
blast, they shall come up to the mountain."
14 So Moses went down from the moun-
tain to the people and consecrated the
people; and they washed their garments.
15 And he said to the people, "Be ready for
the third day; do not go near a woman."

16 On the morning of the third day there
were thunders and lightnings and a thick
cloud on the mountain and a very loud
trumpet blast, so that all the people in the
camp trembled. 17 Then Moses brought
the people out of the camp to meet God,
and they took their stand at the foot of
the mountain. 18 Now Mount Sinai was
wrapped in smoke because the LORD had
descended on it in fire. The smoke of it
went up like the smoke of a kiln, and the
whole mountain trembled greatly. 19 And as
the sound of the trumpet grew louder and
louder, Moses spoke, and God answered
him in thunder. 20 The LORD came down on
Mount Sinai, to the top of the mountain.
And the LORD called Moses to the top of the
mountain, and Moses went up.

21 And the LORD said to Moses, "Go
down and warn the people, lest they break
through to the LORD to look and many of
them perish. 22 Also let the priests who
come near to the LORD consecrate them-
selves, lest the LORD break out against
them." 23 And Moses said to the LORD, "The
people cannot come up to Mount Sinai, for
you yourself warned us, saying, 'Set limits
around the mountain and consecrate it.'"

[1] That is, shot with an arrow

24 And the LORD said to him, "Go down, and come up bringing Aaron with you. But do not let the priests and the people break through to come up to the LORD, lest he break out against them." 25 So Moses went down to the people and told them.

The Ten Commandments

20 And God spoke all these words, saying,

2 "I am the LORD your God, who brought you out of the land of Egypt, out of the house of slavery.

3 "You shall have no other gods before[1] me.

175 4 "You shall not make for yourself a carved image, or any likeness of anything that is in heaven above, or

1181 that is in the earth beneath, or that is in the water under the earth. 5 You shall not bow down to them or serve them, for I the LORD your God am a jealous God, visiting the iniquity of the fathers on the children to the third and the fourth generation of those who hate me, 6 but showing steadfast love to thousands[2] of those who love me and keep my commandments.

7 "You shall not take the name of the LORD your God in vain, for the LORD will not hold him guiltless who takes his name in vain.

8 "Remember the Sabbath day, to keep it holy. 9 Six days you shall labor, and do all your work, 10 but the seventh day is a Sabbath to the LORD your God. On it you shall not do any work, you, or your son, or your daughter, your male servant, or your female servant, or your livestock, or the sojourner who is within your gates. 11 For in six days the LORD made heaven and earth, the sea, and all that is in them, and rested on the seventh day. Therefore the LORD blessed the Sabbath day and made it holy.

12 "Honor your father and your mother, that your days may be long in the land that the LORD your God is giv-

1453 ing you.

13 "You shall not murder.[3]

14 "You shall not commit adultery.

15 "You shall not steal.

16 "You shall not bear false witness against your neighbor.

17 "You shall not covet your neighbor's house; you shall not covet your neighbor's wife, or his male servant, or his female servant, or his ox, or his donkey, or anything that is your neighbor's."

18 Now when all the people saw the thunder and the flashes of lightning and the sound of the trumpet and the mountain smoking, the people were afraid[4] and trembled, and they stood far off 19 and said to Moses, "You speak to us, and we will listen; but do not let God speak to us, lest we die." 20 Moses said to the people, "Do not fear, for God has come to test you, that the fear of him may be before you, that you may not sin." 21 The people stood far off, while Moses drew near to the thick darkness where God was.

Laws About Altars

22 And the LORD said to Moses, "Thus you shall say to the people of Israel: 'You have seen for yourselves that I have talked with you from heaven. 23 You shall not make gods of silver to be with me, nor shall you make for yourselves gods of gold. 24 An altar of earth you shall make for me and sacrifice on it your burnt offerings and your peace offerings, your sheep and your oxen. In every place where I cause my name to be remembered I will come to you and bless you. 25 If you make me an altar of stone, you shall not build it of hewn stones, for if you wield your tool on it you profane it. 26 And you shall not go up by steps to my altar, that your nakedness be not exposed on it.'

Laws About Slaves

21 "Now these are the rules that you shall set before them. 2 When you buy a Hebrew slave, he shall serve six

[1] Or *besides* [2] Or *to the thousandth generation* [3] The Hebrew word also covers causing human death through carelessness or negligence [4] Samaritan, Septuagint, Syriac, Vulgate; Masoretic Text *the people saw*

years, and in the seventh he shall go out free, for nothing. **3** If he comes in single, he shall go out single; if he comes in married, then his wife shall go out with him. **4** If his master gives him a wife and she bears him sons or daughters, the wife and her children shall be her master's, and he shall go out alone. **5** But if the slave plainly says, 'I love my master, my wife, and my children; I will not go out free,' **6** then his master shall bring him to God, and he shall bring him to the door or the doorpost. And his master shall bore his ear through with an awl, and he shall be his slave forever.

7 "When a man sells his daughter as a slave, she shall not go out as the male slaves do. **8** If she does not please her master, who has designated her[1] for himself, then he shall let her be redeemed. He shall have no right to sell her to a foreign people, since he has broken faith with her. **9** If he designates her for his son, he shall deal with her as with a daughter. **10** If he takes another wife to himself, he shall not diminish her food, her clothing, or her marital rights. **11** And if he does not do these three things for her, she shall go out for nothing, without payment of money.

12 "Whoever strikes a man so that he dies shall be put to death. **13** But if he did not lie in wait for him, but God let him fall into his hand, then I will appoint for you a place to which he may flee. **14** But if a man willfully attacks another to kill him by cunning, you shall take him from my altar, that he may die.

15 "Whoever strikes his father or his mother shall be put to death.

16 "Whoever steals a man and sells him, and anyone found in possession of him, shall be put to death.

17 "Whoever curses[2] his father or his mother shall be put to death.

18 "When men quarrel and one strikes the other with a stone or with his fist and the man does not die but takes to his bed, **19** then if the man rises again and walks outdoors with his staff, he who struck him shall be clear; only he shall pay for the loss of his time, and shall have him thoroughly healed.

20 "When a man strikes his slave, male or female, with a rod and the slave dies under his hand, he shall be avenged. **21** But if the slave survives a day or two, he is not to be avenged, for the slave is his money.

22 "When men strive together and hit a pregnant woman, so that her children come out, but there is no harm, the one who hit her shall surely be fined, as the woman's husband shall impose on him, and he shall pay as the judges determine. **23** But if there is harm,[3] then you shall pay life for life, **24** eye for eye, tooth for tooth, hand for hand, foot for foot, **25** burn for burn, wound for wound, stripe for stripe.

26 "When a man strikes the eye of his slave, male or female, and destroys it, he shall let the slave go free because of his eye. **27** If he knocks out the tooth of his slave, male or female, he shall let the slave go free because of his tooth.

28 "When an ox gores a man or a woman to death, the ox shall be stoned, and its flesh shall not be eaten, but the owner of the ox shall not be liable. **29** But if the ox has been accustomed to gore in the past, and its owner has been warned but has not kept it in, and it kills a man or a woman, the ox shall be stoned, and its owner also shall be put to death. **30** If a ransom is imposed on him, then he shall give for the redemption of his life whatever is imposed on him. **31** If it gores a man's son or daughter, he shall be dealt with according to this same rule. **32** If the ox gores a slave, male or female, the owner shall give to their master thirty shekels[4] of silver, and the ox shall be stoned.

Laws About Restitution

33 "When a man opens a pit, or when a man digs a pit and does not cover it, and an ox or a donkey falls into it, **34** the owner

[1] Or *so that he has not designated her* [2] Or *dishonors*; Septuagint *reviles* [3] Or *so that her children come out and it is clear who was to blame, he shall be fined as the woman's husband shall impose on him, and he alone shall pay. If it is unclear who was to blame . . .* [4] A *shekel* was about 2/5 ounce or 11 grams

The Ten Commandments

God led the Israelite people out of Egypt—the land where they had been slaves—toward the good land that God had promised to give them. God provided for all their needs each step of the way, telling them when they should set out and where they should stop and camp.

As they went on their way, God told Moses to stop and camp beneath Mount Sinai in the desert. God called to Moses from the mountain. God said, "Tell the people of Israel: You yourselves have seen what I did to the Egyptians, and how I brought you to Myself. Now, if you will indeed obey My voice and keep My covenant, you shall be My treasured possession among all peoples."

Moses told the people everything the Lord had told him. The Israelite people were happy to obey the Lord and to keep His covenant. They wanted to be God's treasured people. Together, they said, "All that the LORD has spoken we will do."

God told Moses, "Behold, I am coming to you in a thick cloud, that the people may hear when I speak with you." God said He would do this soon, but first the people must take this day and the next day to get ready. They needed to wash their clothing and prepare for the third day, which would be a very special day—when God would speak to them from the mountain.

On the morning of the third day, the people saw lightning and heard thunder. There was a thick cloud on the mountain, and a trumpet blast so loud that all the people trembled. Moses brought the people out of the camp to the foot of the mountain to meet God. But, as God had told Moses, no one, not even an animal, could touch the mountain.

Mount Sinai was wrapped in smoke because the Lord had come down on it in fire. The whole mountain trembled. There, God spoke all the words of the Ten Commandments. He said, "I am the LORD your God, who brought you out of the land of Egypt, out of the house of slavery." God commanded that they have no other gods before Him, and never to worship or serve idols. They could not use the name of the LORD their God in vain. God commanded them to keep the Sabbath day holy, and to honor their parents. He lovingly insisted that they not murder, live with another man's wife, steal, lie, or desire what belonged to others—whether his neighbor's wife or anything else that belonged to him.

When the people saw the lightning and the smoking mountain, and when they heard the thunder and the trumpet, they were afraid, and they asked Moses to go talk with God for them.

God wanted His treasured people to learn these Ten Commandments and to know them well. However, God knew that His people would not be able to keep His commands. He wanted them to look to Him for mercy and help. God promised to send a Savior, His Son, Jesus, to keep the commandments for us and to take the punishment we deserve for not keeping them.

SEEK and FIND

WHERE TO FIND THE STORY

Exodus 19:1–20:21

KEY BIBLE VERSE

"You shall have no other gods before me." (Exodus 20:3)

THREE KEY QUESTIONS

- What was the name of the mountain where Moses and the Israelites camped when God gave the Ten Commandments?
- What is the first commandment and why is it so important?
- What did Jesus do for all who put their faith in Him—even when they break one of the Ten Commandments?

RELATED BIBLE READINGS

Deuteronomy 5:1–6:25; Matthew 19:16–22; Mark 12:28–34; Romans 7:7–12; 13:8–10; James 2:8–12

of the pit shall make restoration. He shall
give money to its owner, and the dead
beast shall be his.
35 "When one man's ox butts another's,
so that it dies, then they shall sell the live
ox and share its price, and the dead beast
also they shall share. 36 Or if it is known
that the ox has been accustomed to gore
in the past, and its owner has not kept it
in, he shall repay ox for ox, and the dead
beast shall be his.

22 1[1] "If a man steals an ox or a sheep,
and kills it or sells it, he shall
repay five oxen for an ox, and four sheep
for a sheep. 2[2] If a thief is found breaking
in and is struck so that he dies, there shall
be no bloodguilt for him, 3 but if the sun
has risen on him, there shall be blood-
guilt for him. He shall surely pay. If he has
nothing, then he shall be sold for his theft.
4 If the stolen beast is found alive in his
possession, whether it is an ox or a donkey
or a sheep, he shall pay double.

5 "If a man causes a field or vineyard to
be grazed over, or lets his beast loose and
it feeds in another man's field, he shall
make restitution from the best in his own
field and in his own vineyard.
6 "If fire breaks out and catches in thorns
so that the stacked grain or the standing
grain or the field is consumed, he who
started the fire shall make full restitution.
7 "If a man gives to his neighbor money
or goods to keep safe, and it is stolen
from the man's house, then, if the thief
is found, he shall pay double. 8 If the thief
is not found, the owner of the house
shall come near to God to show whether
or not he has put his hand to his neigh-
bor's property. 9 For every breach of trust,
whether it is for an ox, for a donkey, for a
sheep, for a cloak, or for any kind of lost
thing, of which one says, 'This is it,' the
case of both parties shall come before
God. The one whom God condemns shall
pay double to his neighbor.

[1] Ch 21:37 in Hebrew [2] Ch 22:1 in Hebrew

10 "If a man gives to his neighbor a donkey or an ox or a sheep or any beast to keep safe, and it dies or is injured or is driven away, without anyone seeing it, 11 an oath by the LORD shall be between them both to see whether or not he has put his hand to his neighbor's property. The owner shall accept the oath, and he shall not make restitution. 12 But if it is stolen from him, he shall make restitution to its owner. 13 If it is torn by beasts, let him bring it as evidence. He shall not make restitution for what has been torn.

14 "If a man borrows anything of his neighbor, and it is injured or dies, the owner not being with it, he shall make full restitution. 15 If the owner was with it, he shall not make restitution; if it was hired, it came for its hiring fee.[1]

Laws About Social Justice

16 "If a man seduces a virgin[2] who is not betrothed and lies with her, he shall give the bride-price[3] for her and make her his wife. 17 If her father utterly refuses to give her to him, he shall pay money equal to the bride-price for virgins.

18 "You shall not permit a sorceress to live.

19 "Whoever lies with an animal shall be put to death.

20 "Whoever sacrifices to any god, other than the LORD alone, shall be devoted to destruction.[4]

21 "You shall not wrong a sojourner or oppress him, for you were sojourners in the land of Egypt. 22 You shall not mistreat any widow or fatherless child. 23 If you do mistreat them, and they cry out to me, I will surely hear their cry, 24 and my wrath will burn, and I will kill you with the sword, and your wives shall become widows and your children fatherless.

25 "If you lend money to any of my people with you who is poor, you shall not be like a moneylender to him, and you shall not exact interest from him. 26 If ever you take your neighbor's cloak in pledge, you shall return it to him before the sun goes down, 27 for that is his only covering, and it is his cloak for his body; in what else shall he sleep? And if he cries to me, I will hear, for I am compassionate.

28 "You shall not revile God, nor curse a ruler of your people.

29 "You shall not delay to offer from the fullness of your harvest and from the outflow of your presses. The firstborn of your sons you shall give to me. 30 You shall do the same with your oxen and with your sheep: seven days it shall be with its mother; on the eighth day you shall give it to me.

31 "You shall be consecrated to me. Therefore you shall not eat any flesh that is torn by beasts in the field; you shall throw it to the dogs.

23 "You shall not spread a false report. You shall not join hands with a wicked man to be a malicious witness. 2 You shall not fall in with the many to do evil, nor shall you bear witness in a lawsuit, siding with the many, so as to pervert justice, 3 nor shall you be partial to a poor man in his lawsuit.

4 "If you meet your enemy's ox or his donkey going astray, you shall bring it back to him. 5 If you see the donkey of one who hates you lying down under its burden, you shall refrain from leaving him with it; you shall rescue it with him.

6 "You shall not pervert the justice due to your poor in his lawsuit. 7 Keep far from a false charge, and do not kill the innocent and righteous, for I will not acquit the wicked. 8 And you shall take no bribe, for a bribe blinds the clear-sighted and subverts the cause of those who are in the right.

9 "You shall not oppress a sojourner. You know the heart of a sojourner, for you were sojourners in the land of Egypt.

Laws About the Sabbath and Festivals

10 "For six years you shall sow your land and gather in its yield, 11 but the seventh

[1] Or *it is reckoned in* (Hebrew *comes into*) *its hiring fee* [2] Or *a girl of marriageable age*; also verse 17 [3] Or *engagement present*; also verse 17 [4] That is, set apart (devoted) as an offering to the Lord (for destruction)

year you shall let it rest and lie fallow, that the poor of your people may eat; and what they leave the beasts of the field may eat. You shall do likewise with your vineyard, and with your olive orchard.

12 "Six days you shall do your work, but on the seventh day you shall rest; that your ox and your donkey may have rest, and the son of your servant woman, and the alien, may be refreshed.

13 "Pay attention to all that I have said to you, and make no mention of the names of other gods, nor let it be heard on your lips.

14 "Three times in the year you shall keep a feast to me. 15 You shall keep the Feast of Unleavened Bread. As I commanded you, you shall eat unleavened bread for seven days at the appointed time in the month of Abib, for in it you came out of Egypt. None shall appear before me empty-handed. 16 You shall keep the Feast of Harvest, of the firstfruits of your labor, of what you sow in the field. You shall keep the Feast of Ingathering at the end of the year, when you gather in from the field the fruit of your labor. 17 Three times in the year shall all your males appear before the Lord GOD.

18 "You shall not offer the blood of my sacrifice with anything leavened, or let the fat of my feast remain until the morning.

19 "The best of the firstfruits of your ground you shall bring into the house of the LORD your God.

"You shall not boil a young goat in its mother's milk.

Conquest of Canaan Promised

20 "Behold, I send an angel before you to guard you on the way and to bring you to the place that I have prepared. 21 Pay careful attention to him and obey his voice; do not rebel against him, for he will not pardon your transgression, for my name is in him.

22 "But if you carefully obey his voice and do all that I say, then I will be an enemy to your enemies and an adversary to your adversaries.

23 "When my angel goes before you and brings you to the Amorites and the Hittites and the Perizzites and the Canaanites, the Hivites and the Jebusites, and I blot them out, 24 you shall not bow down to their gods nor serve them, nor do as they do, but you shall utterly overthrow them and break their pillars in pieces. 25 You shall serve the LORD your God, and he[1] will bless your bread and your water, and I will take sickness away from among you. 26 None shall miscarry or be barren in your land; I will fulfill the number of your days. 27 I will send my terror before you and will throw into confusion all the people against whom you shall come, and I will make all your enemies turn their backs to you. 28 And I will send hornets before you, which shall drive out the Hivites, the Canaanites, and the Hittites from before you. 29 I will not drive them out from before you in one year, lest the land become desolate and the wild beasts multiply against you. 30 Little by little I will drive them out from before you, until you have increased and possess the land. 31 And I will set your border from the Red Sea to the Sea of the Philistines, and from the wilderness to the Euphrates, for I will give the inhabitants of the land into your hand, and you shall drive them out before you. 32 You shall make no covenant with them and their gods. 33 They shall not dwell in your land, lest they make you sin against me; for if you serve their gods, it will surely be a snare to you."

The Covenant Confirmed

24 Then he said to Moses, "Come up to the LORD, you and Aaron, Nadab, and Abihu, and seventy of the elders of Israel, and worship from afar. 2 Moses alone shall come near to the LORD,

[1] Septuagint, Vulgate *I*

but the others shall not come near, and the people shall not come up with him."

3 Moses came and told the people all the words of the LORD and all the rules.[1] And all the people answered with one voice and said, "All the words that the LORD has spoken we will do." 4 And Moses wrote down all the words of the LORD. He rose early in the morning and built an altar at the foot of the mountain, and twelve pillars, according to the twelve tribes of Israel. 5 And he sent young men of the people of Israel, who offered burnt offerings and sacrificed peace offerings of oxen to the LORD. 6 And Moses took half of the blood and put it in basins, and half of the blood he threw against the altar. 7 Then he took the Book of the Covenant and read it in the hearing of the people. And they said, "All that the LORD has spoken we will do, and we will be obedient." 8 And Moses took the blood and threw it on the people and said, "Behold the blood of the covenant that the LORD has made with you in accordance with all these words."

9 Then Moses and Aaron, Nadab, and Abihu, and seventy of the elders of Israel went up, 10 and they saw the God of Israel. There was under his feet as it were a pavement of sapphire stone, like the very heaven for clearness. 11 And he did not lay his hand on the chief men of the people of Israel; they beheld God, and ate and drank.

12 The LORD said to Moses, "Come up to me on the mountain and wait there, that I may give you the tablets of stone, with the law and the commandment, which I have written for their instruction." 13 So Moses rose with his assistant Joshua, and Moses went up into the mountain of God. 14 And he said to the elders, "Wait here for us until we return to you. And behold, Aaron and Hur are with you. Whoever has a dispute, let him go to them."

15 Then Moses went up on the mountain, and the cloud covered the mountain. 16 The glory of the LORD dwelt on Mount Sinai, and the cloud covered it six days. And on the seventh day he called to Moses out of the midst of the cloud. 17 Now the appearance of the glory of the LORD was like a devouring fire on the top of the mountain in the sight of the people of Israel. 18 Moses entered the cloud and went up on the mountain. And Moses was on the mountain forty days and forty nights.

Contributions for the Sanctuary

25 The LORD said to Moses, 2 "Speak to the people of
205 Israel, that they take for me a contribution. From every man whose heart moves him you shall receive the contribution for me. 3 And this is the contribution that you shall receive from them: gold, silver, and bronze, 4 blue and purple and scarlet yarns and fine twined linen, goats' hair, 5 tanned rams' skins, goatskins,[2] acacia wood, 6 oil for the lamps, spices for the anointing oil and for the fragrant incense, 7 onyx stones, and stones for setting, for the ephod and for the breastpiece. 8 And let them make me a sanctuary, that I may dwell in their midst. 9 Exactly
205 as I show you concerning the pattern of the tabernacle, and of all its furniture, so you shall make it.

The Ark of the Covenant

10 "They shall make an ark of acacia wood. Two cubits[3] and a half shall be its length, a cubit and a half its breadth, and a cubit and a half its height. 11 You shall overlay it with pure gold, inside and outside shall you overlay it, and you shall make on it a molding of gold around it. 12 You shall cast four rings of gold for it and put them on its four feet, two rings on the one side of it, and two rings on the other side of it. 13 You shall make poles of acacia wood and overlay them with gold. 14 And you shall put the poles into the rings on the sides of the ark to carry the ark by them. 15 The poles shall remain in the rings of the ark; they shall not be taken

[1] Or *all the just decrees* [2] Uncertain; possibly *dolphin skins*, or *dugong skins*; compare 26:14 [3] A *cubit* was about 18 inches or 45 centimeters

from it. **16** And you shall put into the ark the testimony that I shall give you.

17 "You shall make a mercy seat[1] of pure gold. Two cubits and a half shall be its length, and a cubit and a half its breadth. **18** And you shall make two cherubim of gold; of hammered work shall you make them, on the two ends of the mercy seat. **19** Make one cherub on the one end, and one cherub on the other end. Of one piece with the mercy seat shall you make the cherubim on its two ends. **20** The cherubim shall spread out their wings above, overshadowing the mercy seat with their wings, their faces one to another; toward the mercy seat shall the faces of the cherubim be. **21** And you shall put the mercy seat on the top of the ark, and in the ark you shall put the testimony that I shall give you. **22** There I will meet with you, and from above the mercy seat, from between the two cherubim that are on the ark of the testimony, I will speak with you about all that I will give you in commandment for the people of Israel.

The Table for Bread

23 "You shall make a table of acacia wood. Two cubits shall be its length, a cubit its breadth, and a cubit and a half its height. **24** You shall overlay it with pure gold and make a molding of gold around it. **25** And you shall make a rim around it a handbreadth[2] wide, and a molding of gold around the rim. **26** And you shall make for it four rings of gold, and fasten the rings to the four corners at its four legs. **27** Close

[1] Or *cover* [2] A *handbreadth* was about 3 inches or 7.5 centimeters

The Ark of the Covenant

The ark of the covenant (Exodus 25:10–22; 37:1–9) was a wooden chest covered completely with pure gold. Inside it were the two stone tablets with the Ten Commandments, a golden urn with some manna (the food God provided for the Israelites) in it, and Aaron's rod that budded. The lid of the chest was called the mercy seat. It was made of solid gold. On the mercy seat were two angels or cherubim, also made of solid gold. The cherubim faced each other. God told Moses He would speak with him from the mercy seat, from between the cherubim. The ark of the covenant was the only piece of furniture in the Most Holy Place. The ark had two wooden poles, also covered with pure gold. When the Israelites traveled, Levites used the poles to carry the ark.

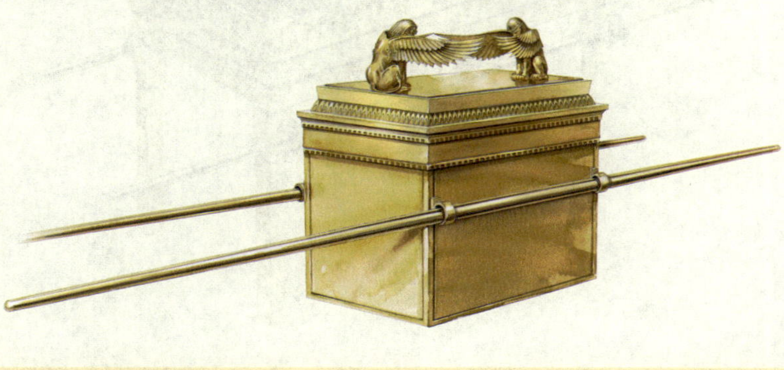

to the frame the rings shall lie, as holders
for the poles to carry the table. 28 You shall
make the poles of acacia wood, and overlay
them with gold, and the table shall be car-
ried with these. 29 And you shall make its
plates and dishes for incense, and its flag-
ons and bowls with which to pour drink
offerings; you shall make them of pure
gold. 30 And you shall set the bread of the
Presence on the table before me regularly.

The Golden Lampstand

31 "You shall make a lampstand of pure
gold. The lampstand shall be made of ham-
mered work: its base, its stem, its cups, its
calyxes, and its flowers shall be of one piece
with it. 32 And there shall be six branches
going out of its sides, three branches of the
lampstand out of one side of it and three
branches of the lampstand out of the other
side of it; 33 three cups made like almond
blossoms, each with calyx and flower,
on one branch, and three cups made like
almond blossoms, each with calyx and
flower, on the other branch—so for the
six branches going out of the lampstand.
34 And on the lampstand itself there shall
be four cups made like almond blossoms,
with their calyxes and flowers, 35 and a
calyx of one piece with it under each pair of
the six branches going out from the lamp-
stand. 36 Their calyxes and their branches
shall be of one piece with it, the whole of
it a single piece of hammered work of pure
gold. 37 You shall make seven lamps for
it. And the lamps shall be set up so as to
give light on the space in front of it. 38 Its
tongs and their trays shall be of pure gold.

The Table for the Bread of the Presence

This wooden table, overlaid with pure gold (Exodus 25:23–30; 37:10–16), held the 12 loaves of bread that were offered every Sabbath as a food offering to the Lord (Leviticus 24:5–9). Wooden poles, also covered with gold, were used to carry the table when the Israelites traveled. The table for the bread of the Presence stood in the Holy Place of the tabernacle.

39 It shall be made, with all these utensils,
out of a talent[1] of pure gold. 40 And see
that you make them after the pattern for
them, which is being shown you on the
mountain.

The Tabernacle

26 "Moreover, you shall make the
tabernacle with ten curtains of
fine twined linen and blue and purple
and scarlet yarns; you shall make them
with cherubim skillfully worked into
them. 2 The length of each curtain shall be
twenty-eight cubits,[2] and the breadth of
each curtain four cubits; all the curtains
shall be the same size. 3 Five curtains
shall be coupled to one another, and the
other five curtains shall be coupled to one
another. 4 And you shall make loops of blue
on the edge of the outermost curtain in the
first set. Likewise you shall make loops on
the edge of the outermost curtain in the
second set. 5 Fifty loops you shall make on
the one curtain, and fifty loops you shall
make on the edge of the curtain that is in
the second set; the loops shall be opposite
one another. 6 And you shall make fifty
clasps of gold, and couple the curtains
one to the other with the clasps, so that
the tabernacle may be a single whole.

7 "You shall also make curtains of goats'
hair for a tent over the tabernacle; eleven
curtains shall you make. 8 The length of
each curtain shall be thirty cubits, and
the breadth of each curtain four cubits.
The eleven curtains shall be the same size.
9 You shall couple five curtains by them-
selves, and six curtains by themselves,
and the sixth curtain you shall double
over at the front of the tent. 10 You shall
make fifty loops on the edge of the cur-
tain that is outermost in one set, and fifty
loops on the edge of the curtain that is
outermost in the second set.

11 "You shall make fifty clasps of
bronze, and put the clasps into the loops,
and couple the tent together that it may
be a single whole. 12 And the part that
remains of the curtains of the tent, the half
curtain that remains, shall hang over the
back of the tabernacle. 13 And the extra
that remains in the length of the curtains,
the cubit on the one side, and the cubit
on the other side, shall hang over the
sides of the tabernacle, on this side and
that side, to cover it. 14 And you shall make
for the tent a covering of tanned rams'
skins and a covering of goatskins on top.

15 "You shall make upright frames for
the tabernacle of acacia wood. 16 Ten
cubits shall be the length of a frame, and
a cubit and a half the breadth of each
frame. 17 There shall be two tenons in each
frame, for fitting together. So shall you do
for all the frames of the tabernacle. 18 You

The Golden Lampstand

The golden lampstand was made of pure gold, hammered out of one solid piece (Exodus 25:31–40). It had six branches, three on each side. The six branches, along with the stem in the middle, held seven lamps. The lampstand may have been 5 or 6 feet tall. The lampstand was in the Holy Place of the tabernacle.

[1] A *talent* was about 75 pounds or 34 kilograms [2] A *cubit* was about 18 inches or 45 centimeters

The Tabernacle Tent

The entire tent was 45 feet (13.7 m) long, 15 feet (4.6 m) wide, and 15 feet (4.6 m) high. It had a wooden frame overlaid with gold (Exodus 26:15–29). The frame could be taken apart so it could be easily carried as the Israelites traveled to the Promised Land.

The Most Holy Place was a 15-foot (4.6 m) cube. The only thing in it was the ark of the covenant (Exodus 25:10–22; 37:1–9). The Lord appeared in a cloud here, to meet with His people. The high priest could only go into the Most Holy Place once a year, on the Day of Atonement.

The veil, or curtain, separating the Most Holy Place from the Holy Place was blue, purple, and scarlet (red), and embroidered with cherubim or angels (Exodus 26:31–33). This veil hung on four golden pillars.

The golden lampstand (Exodus 25:31–40; 37:17–24)

The table for the bread of the Presence (Exodus 25:23–30)

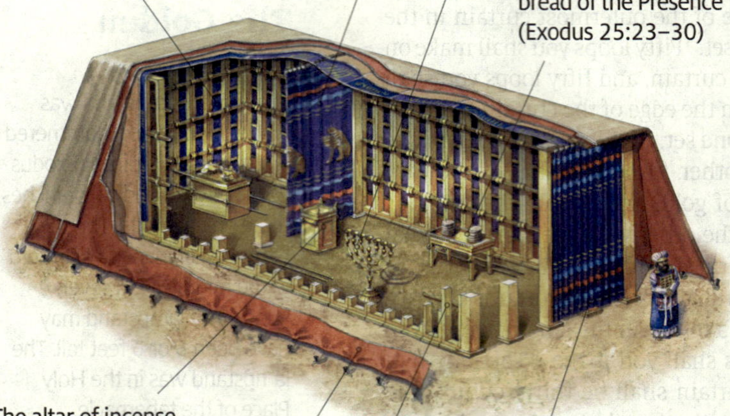

The altar of incense (Exodus 30:1–5; 37:25–29)

The frame was covered by four layers of cloth and animal skins (Exodus 26:1–14).

The Holy Place of the tabernacle tent was 30 feet (9.1 m) long, 15 feet (4.6 m) wide, and 15 feet (4.6 m) high.

The "door" into the tabernacle was a curtain, or veil. It was blue, purple, and scarlet (red). Unlike the veil into the Most Holy Place, it had no cherubim embroidered on it (Exodus 26:36–37).

shall make the frames for the tabernacle:
twenty frames for the south side; 19 and
forty bases of silver you shall make under
the twenty frames, two bases under one
frame for its two tenons, and two bases
under the next frame for its two tenons;
20 and for the second side of the taber-
nacle, on the north side twenty frames,
21 and their forty bases of silver, two bases
under one frame, and two bases under
the next frame. 22 And for the rear of the
tabernacle westward you shall make six
frames. 23 And you shall make two frames
for corners of the tabernacle in the rear;
24 they shall be separate beneath, but
joined at the top, at the first ring. Thus
shall it be with both of them; they shall
form the two corners. 25 And there shall
be eight frames, with their bases of silver,
sixteen bases; two bases under one frame,
and two bases under another frame.

26 “You shall make bars of acacia wood,
five for the frames of the one side of the
tabernacle, 27 and five bars for the frames
of the other side of the tabernacle, and five
bars for the frames of the side of the taber-
nacle at the rear westward. 28 The middle
bar, halfway up the frames, shall run from
end to end. 29 You shall overlay the frames
with gold and shall make their rings of
gold for holders for the bars, and you
shall overlay the bars with gold. 30 Then
you shall erect the tabernacle according
to the plan for it that you were shown on
the mountain.

31 “And you shall make a veil of blue and
purple and scarlet yarns and fine twined
linen. It shall be made with cherubim
skillfully worked into it. 32 And you shall
hang it on four pillars of acacia overlaid
with gold, with hooks of gold, on four
bases of silver. 33 And you shall hang the
veil from the clasps, and bring the ark of
the testimony in there within the veil.
And the veil shall separate for you the
Holy Place from the Most Holy. 34 You shall
put the mercy seat on the ark of the testi-
mony in the Most Holy Place. 35 And you
shall set the table outside the veil, and the
lampstand on the south side of the taber-
nacle opposite the table, and you shall put
the table on the north side.

36 “You shall make a screen for the
entrance of the tent, of blue and purple
and scarlet yarns and fine twined linen,
embroidered with needlework. 37 And you
shall make for the screen five pillars of
acacia, and overlay them with gold. Their
hooks shall be of gold, and you shall cast
five bases of bronze for them.

The Bronze Altar

27 “You shall make the altar of aca-
cia wood, five cubits[1] long and five
cubits broad. The altar shall be square,
and its height shall be three cubits. 2 And
you shall make horns for it on its four cor-
ners; its horns shall be of one piece with
it, and you shall overlay it with bronze.
3 You shall make pots for it to receive its
ashes, and shovels and basins and forks
and fire pans. You shall make all its uten-
sils of bronze. 4 You shall also make for
it a grating, a network of bronze, and on
the net you shall make four bronze rings
at its four corners. 5 And you shall set it
under the ledge of the altar so that the net
extends halfway down the altar. 6 And you
shall make poles for the altar, poles of aca-
cia wood, and overlay them with bronze.
7 And the poles shall be put through the
rings, so that the poles are on the two
sides of the altar when it is carried. 8 You
shall make it hollow, with boards. As it
has been shown you on the mountain, so
shall it be made.

The Court of the Tabernacle

9 “You shall make the court of the tab-
ernacle. On the south side the court shall
have hangings of fine twined linen a
hundred cubits long for one side. 10 Its
twenty pillars and their twenty bases
shall be of bronze, but the hooks of the
pillars and their fillets shall be of silver.

[1] A *cubit* was about 18 inches or 45 centimeters

[11] And likewise for its length on the north
side there shall be hangings a hundred
cubits long, its pillars twenty and their
bases twenty, of bronze, but the hooks of
the pillars and their fillets shall be of sil-
ver. [12] And for the breadth of the court on
the west side there shall be hangings for
fifty cubits, with ten pillars and ten bases.
[13] The breadth of the court on the front
to the east side shall be fifty cubits. [14] The
hangings for the one side of the gate
shall be fifteen cubits, with their three
pillars and three bases. [15] On the other
side the hangings shall be fifteen cubits,
with their three pillars and three bases.
[16] For the gate of the court there shall be
a screen twenty cubits long, of blue and
purple and scarlet yarns and fine twined
linen, embroidered with needlework.
It shall have four pillars and with them
four bases. [17] All the pillars around the
court shall be filleted with silver. Their
hooks shall be of silver, and their bases
of bronze. [18] The length of the court shall
be a hundred cubits, the breadth fifty, and
the height five cubits, with hangings of
fine twined linen and bases of bronze.
[19] All the utensils of the tabernacle for
every use, and all its pegs and all the pegs
of the court, shall be of bronze.

Oil for the Lamp

[20] "You shall command the people of
Israel that they bring to you pure beaten
olive oil for the light, that a lamp may
regularly be set up to burn. [21] In the tent
of meeting, outside the veil that is before
the testimony, Aaron and his sons shall
tend it from evening to morning before
the LORD. It shall be a statute forever to be
observed throughout their generations by
the people of Israel.

The Priests' Garments

28 "Then bring near to you Aaron
your brother, and his sons with
him, from among the people of Israel, to
serve me as priests—Aaron and Aaron's

The Bronze Altar

The bronze altar stood in the outer courtyard of the tabernacle. It was where the priests offered burnt offerings (Exodus 27:1–8; 38:1–7). It was made of wood overlaid with bronze. There was a bronze grating on the top and sides of the altar.

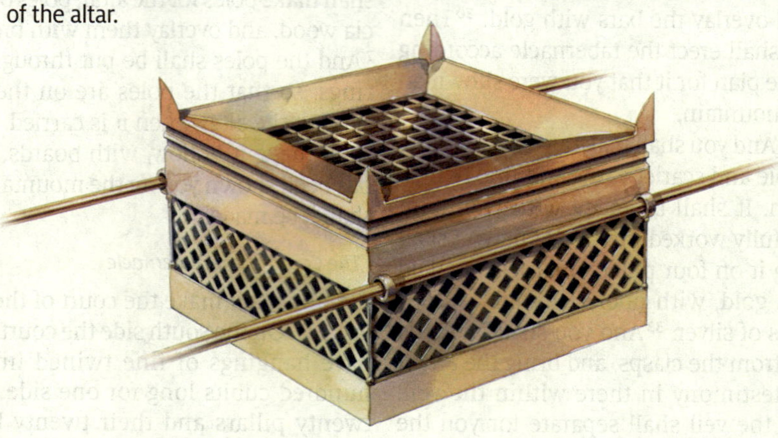

sons, Nadab and Abihu, Eleazar and Ithamar. 2 And you shall make holy garments for Aaron your brother, for glory and for beauty. 3 You shall speak to all the skillful, whom I have filled with a spirit of skill, that they make Aaron's garments to consecrate him for my priesthood. 4 These are the garments that they shall make: a breastpiece, an ephod, a robe, a coat of checker work, a turban, and a sash. They shall make holy garments for Aaron your brother and his sons to serve me as priests. 5 They shall receive gold, blue and purple and scarlet yarns, and fine twined linen.

6 "And they shall make the ephod of gold, of blue and purple and scarlet yarns, and of fine twined linen, skillfully worked. 7 It shall have two shoulder pieces attached to its two edges, so that it may be joined together. 8 And the skillfully woven band on it shall be made like it and be of one piece with it, of gold, blue and purple and scarlet yarns, and fine twined linen. 9 You shall take two onyx stones, and engrave on them the names of the sons of Israel, 10 six of their names on the one stone, and the names of the remaining six on the other stone, in the order of their birth. 11 As a jeweler engraves signets, so shall you engrave the two stones with the names of the sons of Israel. You shall enclose them in settings of gold filigree. 12 And you shall set the two stones on the shoulder pieces of the ephod, as stones of remembrance for the sons of Israel. And Aaron shall bear their names before the LORD on his two shoulders for remembrance. 13 You shall make settings of gold filigree, 14 and two chains of pure gold, twisted like cords; and you shall attach the corded chains to the settings.

15 "You shall make a breastpiece of judgment, in skilled work. In the style of the ephod you shall make it—of gold, blue and purple and scarlet yarns, and fine twined linen shall you make it. 16 It shall be square and doubled, a span[1] its length and a span its breadth. 17 You shall set in it four rows of stones. A row of sardius,[2] topaz, and carbuncle shall be the first row; 18 and the second row an emerald, a sapphire, and a diamond; 19 and the third row a jacinth, an agate, and an amethyst; 20 and the fourth row a beryl, an onyx, and a jasper. They shall be set in gold filigree. 21 There shall be twelve stones with their names according to the names of the sons of Israel. They shall be like signets, each engraved with its name, for the twelve tribes. 22 You shall make for the breastpiece twisted chains like cords, of pure gold. 23 And you shall make for the breastpiece two rings of gold, and put the two rings on the two edges of the breastpiece. 24 And you shall put the two cords of gold in the two rings at the edges of the breastpiece. 25 The two ends of the two cords you shall attach to the two settings of filigree, and so attach it in front to the shoulder pieces of the ephod. 26 You shall make two rings of gold, and put them at the two ends of the breastpiece, on its inside edge next to the ephod. 27 And you shall make two rings of gold, and attach them in front to the lower part of the two shoulder pieces of the ephod, at its seam above the skillfully woven band of the ephod. 28 And they shall bind the breastpiece by its rings to the rings of the ephod with a lace of blue, so that it may lie on the skillfully woven band of the ephod, so that the breastpiece shall not come loose from the ephod. 29 So Aaron shall bear the names of the sons of Israel in the breastpiece of judgment on his heart, when he goes into the Holy Place, to bring them to regular remembrance before the LORD. 30 And in the breastpiece of judgment you shall put the Urim and the Thummim, and they shall be on Aaron's heart, when he goes in before the LORD. Thus Aaron shall bear the judgment of the people of Israel on his heart before the LORD regularly.

[1] A *span* was about 9 inches or 22 centimeters [2] The identity of some of these stones is uncertain

The Tabernacle and Court

The tabernacle, also called "the tent of meeting," was a tent for worship that the Israelites could carry with them as they traveled through the wilderness. There was a fence around the tent, making a courtyard on the outside. The fence could also be taken down and carried. The Israelites built the tabernacle in the wilderness, on their way to the Promised Land. They made it and everything in it exactly as God had told Moses to make it.

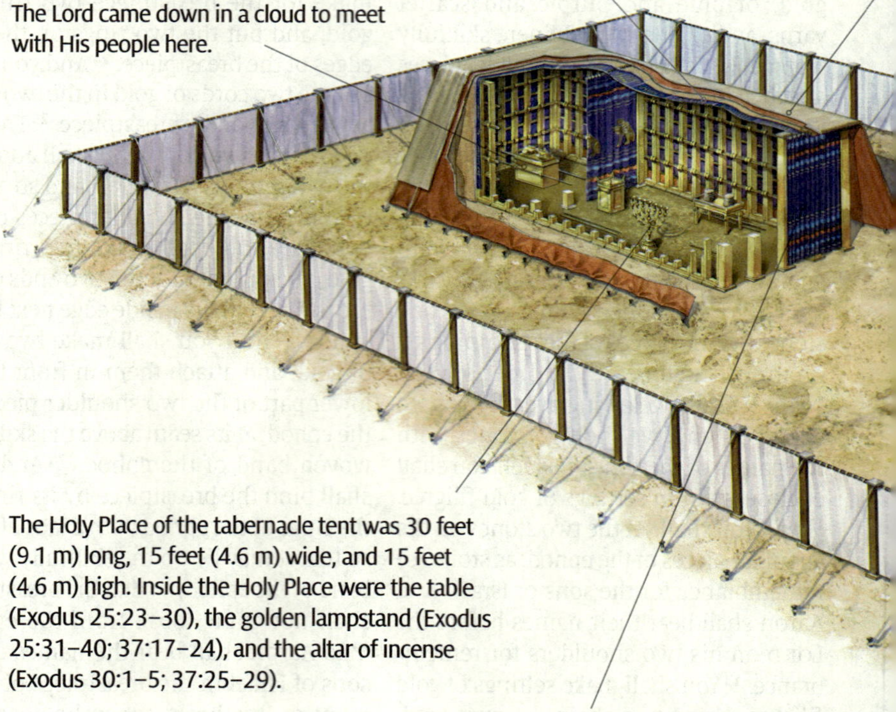

The Most Holy Place of the tabernacle tent was a 15-foot (4.6 m) cube. The only thing inside it was the ark of the covenant (Exodus 25:10–22; 37:1–9). The Lord came down in a cloud to meet with His people here.

The tabernacle's frame was covered by four layers of cloth and animal skin (Exodus 26:1–14).

The Holy Place of the tabernacle tent was 30 feet (9.1 m) long, 15 feet (4.6 m) wide, and 15 feet (4.6 m) high. Inside the Holy Place were the table (Exodus 25:23–30), the golden lampstand (Exodus 25:31–40; 37:17–24), and the altar of incense (Exodus 30:1–5; 37:25–29).

A curtain or veil separated the tabernacle from the courtyard outside. It was purple, blue, and red (scarlet), and hung on five golden pillars (Exodus 26:36–37).

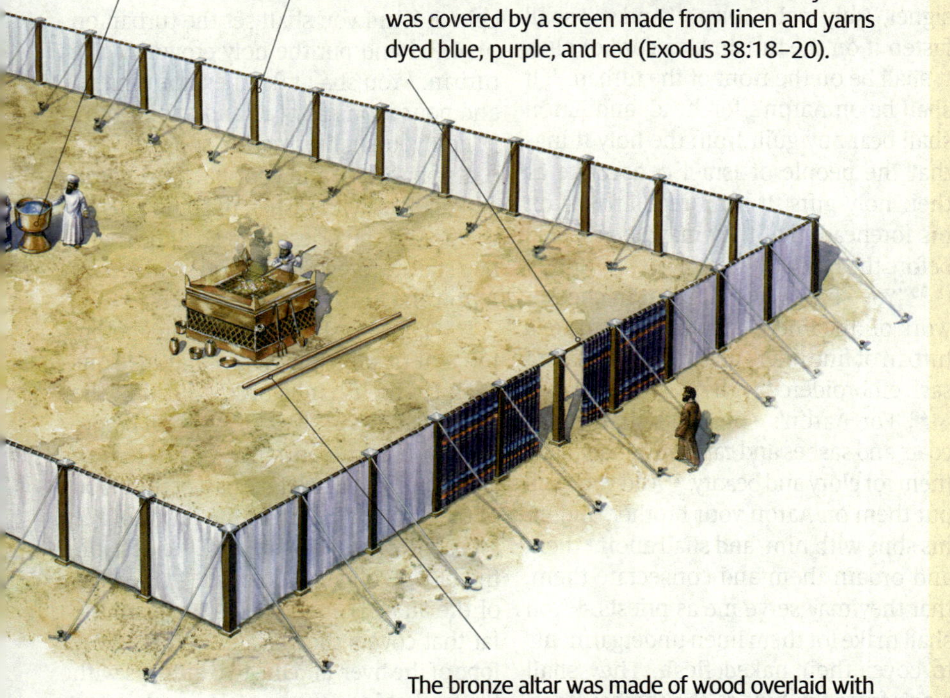
The tabernacle tent was 45 feet (14 m) long, 15 feet (4.6 m) wide, and 15 feet (4.6 m) high. The tent's frame was made of wood overlaid with gold (Exodus 26:15–29).
A large bronze basin where the priests could wash according to God's rules for priests stood in the courtyard (Exodus 30:17–21; 38:8).
All around the courtyard were 60 wooden pillars overlaid with bronze. They stood in copper sockets. There was silver on the tops of the pillars (Exodus 27:9–19; 38:9–17). The pillars held curtains that made a fence all the way around the courtyard. The curtains were held in place by ropes and pegs.
The wide entrance into the tabernacle's courtyard was covered by a screen made from linen and yarns dyed blue, purple, and red (Exodus 38:18–20).
The bronze altar was made of wood overlaid with bronze (Exodus 27:1–8; 38:1–7). This was where the priests offered burnt offerings. The altar had a horn at each corner. It had two poles that could be used to carry it as the Israelites traveled.

31 "You shall make the robe of the ephod all of blue. 32 It shall have an opening for the head in the middle of it, with a woven binding around the opening, like the opening in a garment,[1] so that it may not tear. 33 On its hem you shall make pomegranates of blue and purple and scarlet yarns, around its hem, with bells of gold between them, 34 a golden bell and a pomegranate, a golden bell and a pomegranate, around the hem of the robe. 35 And it shall be on Aaron when he ministers, and its sound shall be heard when he goes into the Holy Place before the LORD, and when he comes out, so that he does not die.

36 "You shall make a plate of pure gold and engrave on it, like the engraving of a signet, 'Holy to the LORD.' 37 And you shall fasten it on the turban by a cord of blue. It shall be on the front of the turban. 38 It shall be on Aaron's forehead, and Aaron shall bear any guilt from the holy things that the people of Israel consecrate as their holy gifts. It shall regularly be on his forehead, that they may be accepted before the LORD.

39 "You shall weave the coat in checker work of fine linen, and you shall make a turban of fine linen, and you shall make a sash embroidered with needlework.

40 "For Aaron's sons you shall make coats and sashes and caps. You shall make them for glory and beauty. 41 And you shall put them on Aaron your brother, and on his sons with him, and shall anoint them and ordain them and consecrate them, that they may serve me as priests. 42 You shall make for them linen undergarments to cover their naked flesh. They shall reach from the hips to the thighs; 43 and they shall be on Aaron and on his sons when they go into the tent of meeting or when they come near the altar to minister in the Holy Place, lest they bear guilt and die. This shall be a statute forever for him and for his offspring after him.

Consecration of the Priests

29 "Now this is what you shall do to them to consecrate them, that they may serve me as priests. Take one bull of the herd and two rams without blemish, 2 and unleavened bread, unleavened cakes mixed with oil, and unleavened wafers smeared with oil. You shall make them of fine wheat flour. 3 You shall put them in one basket and bring them in the basket, and bring the bull and the two rams. 4 You shall bring Aaron and his sons to the entrance of the tent of meeting and wash them with water. 5 Then you shall take the garments, and put on Aaron the coat and the robe of the ephod, and the ephod, and the breastpiece, and gird him with the skillfully woven band of the ephod. 6 And you shall set the turban on his head and put the holy crown on the turban. 7 You shall take the anointing oil and pour it on his head and anoint him. 8 Then you shall bring his sons and put coats on them, 9 and you shall gird Aaron and his sons with sashes and bind caps on them. And the priesthood shall be theirs by a statute forever. Thus you shall ordain Aaron and his sons.

10 "Then you shall bring the bull before the tent of meeting. Aaron and his sons shall lay their hands on the head of the bull. 11 Then you shall kill the bull before the LORD at the entrance of the tent of meeting, 12 and shall take part of the blood of the bull and put it on the horns of the altar with your finger, and the rest of[2] the blood you shall pour out at the base of the altar. 13 And you shall take all the fat that covers the entrails, and the long lobe of the liver, and the two kidneys with the fat that is on them, and burn them on the altar. 14 But the flesh of the bull and its skin and its dung you shall burn with fire outside the camp; it is a sin offering.

15 "Then you shall take one of the rams, and Aaron and his sons shall lay their hands on the head of the ram, 16 and you

[1] The meaning of the Hebrew word is uncertain; possibly *coat of mail* [2] Hebrew *all*

shall kill the ram and shall take its blood and throw it against the sides of the altar. 17 Then you shall cut the ram into pieces, and wash its entrails and its legs, and put them with its pieces and its head, 18 and burn the whole ram on the altar. It is a burnt offering to the LORD. It is a pleasing aroma, a food offering[1] to the LORD.

19 "You shall take the other ram, and Aaron and his sons shall lay their hands on the head of the ram, 20 and you shall kill the ram and take part of its blood and put it on the tip of the right ear of Aaron and on the tips of the right ears of his sons, and on the thumbs of their right hands and on the great toes of their right feet, and throw the rest of the blood against the sides of the altar. 21 Then you shall take part of the blood that is on the altar, and of the anointing oil, and sprinkle it on Aaron and his garments, and on his sons and his sons' garments with him. He and his garments shall be holy, and his sons and his sons' garments with him.

22 "You shall also take the fat from the ram and the fat tail and the fat that covers the entrails, and the long lobe of the liver and the two kidneys with the fat that is on them, and the right thigh (for it is a ram of ordination), 23 and one loaf of bread and one cake of bread made with oil, and one wafer out of the basket of unleavened bread that is before the LORD. 24 You shall put all these on the palms of Aaron and on the palms of his sons, and wave them for a wave offering before the LORD. 25 Then you shall take them from their hands and burn them on the altar on top of the burnt offering, as a pleasing aroma before the LORD. It is a food offering to the LORD.

26 "You shall take the breast of the ram of Aaron's ordination and wave it for a wave offering before the LORD, and it shall be your portion. 27 And you shall consecrate the breast of the wave offering that is waved and the thigh of the priests' portion that is contributed from the ram of ordination, from what was Aaron's and his sons'. 28 It shall be for Aaron and his sons as a perpetual due from the people of Israel, for it is a contribution. It shall be a contribution from the people of Israel from their peace offerings, their contribution to the LORD.

29 "The holy garments of Aaron shall be for his sons after him; they shall be anointed in them and ordained in them. 30 The son who succeeds him as priest, who comes into the tent of meeting to minister in the Holy Place, shall wear them seven days.

31 "You shall take the ram of ordination and boil its flesh in a holy place. 32 And Aaron and his sons shall eat the flesh of the ram and the bread that is in the basket in the entrance of the tent of meeting. 33 They shall eat those things with which atonement was made at their ordination and consecration, but an outsider shall not eat of them, because they are holy. 34 And if any of the flesh for the ordination or of the bread remain until the morning, then you shall burn the remainder with fire. It shall not be eaten, because it is holy.

35 "Thus you shall do to Aaron and to his sons, according to all that I have commanded you. Through seven days shall you ordain them, 36 and every day you shall offer a bull as a sin offering for atonement. Also you shall purify the altar, when you make atonement for it, and shall anoint it to consecrate it. 37 Seven days you shall make atonement for the altar and consecrate it, and the altar shall be most holy. Whatever touches the altar shall become holy.

38 "Now this is what you shall offer on the altar: two lambs a year old day by day regularly. 39 One lamb you shall offer in the morning, and the other lamb you shall offer at twilight. 40 And with the first lamb a tenth seah[2] of fine flour mingled with a fourth of a hin[3] of beaten oil, and a fourth of a hin of wine for a drink offering. 41 The

[1] Or *an offering by fire*; also verses 25, 41 [2] A *seah* was about 7 quarts or 7.3 liters [3] A *hin* was about 4 quarts or 3.5 liters

other lamb you shall offer at twilight, and
shall offer with it a grain offering and
its drink offering, as in the morning, for
a pleasing aroma, a food offering to the
LORD. 42 It shall be a regular burnt offer-
ing throughout your generations at the
entrance of the tent of meeting before the
LORD, where I will meet with you, to speak
to you there. 43 There I will meet with the
people of Israel, and it shall be sanctified
by my glory. 44 I will consecrate the tent
of meeting and the altar. Aaron also and
his sons I will consecrate to serve me as
priests. 45 I will dwell among the people
of Israel and will be their God. 46 And they
shall know that I am the LORD their God,
who brought them out of the land of Egypt
that I might dwell among them. I am the
LORD their God.

The Altar of Incense

30 "You shall make an altar on which
to burn incense; you shall make
it of acacia wood. 2 A cubit[1] shall be its
length, and a cubit its breadth. It shall be
square, and two cubits shall be its height.
Its horns shall be of one piece with it. 3 You
shall overlay it with pure gold, its top and
around its sides and its horns. And you
shall make a molding of gold around it.
4 And you shall make two golden rings
for it. Under its molding on two oppo-
site sides of it you shall make them, and
they shall be holders for poles with which
to carry it. 5 You shall make the poles of
acacia wood and overlay them with gold.
6 And you shall put it in front of the veil
that is above the ark of the testimony, in
front of the mercy seat that is above the
testimony, where I will meet with you.
7 And Aaron shall burn fragrant incense
on it. Every morning when he dresses the
lamps he shall burn it, 8 and when Aaron
sets up the lamps at twilight, he shall
burn it, a regular incense offering before
the LORD throughout your generations.
9 You shall not offer unauthorized incense
on it, or a burnt offering, or a grain offer-
ing, and you shall not pour a drink offer-
ing on it. 10 Aaron shall make atonement
on its horns once a year. With the blood
of the sin offering of atonement he shall
make atonement for it once in the year

[1] A *cubit* was about 18 inches or 45 centimeters

The Altar of Incense

Incense, something that smells good when it slowly burns, was burned for the Lord on this altar. The altar was made of wood, covered with pure gold (Exodus 30:1–10; 37:25–28). It was 3 feet high and 1.5 feet wide. The altar of incense was in the Holy Place of the tabernacle, in front of the veil that separated the Most Holy Place from the Holy Place. Wooden poles, also covered with gold, could be put through rings on the sides of the altar. The Levites used these poles to carry the altar of incense when the Israelites traveled.

throughout your generations. It is most holy to the LORD."

The Census Tax

11 The LORD said to Moses, 12 "When you take the census of the people of Israel, then each shall give a ransom for his life to the LORD when you number them, that there be no plague among them when you number them. 13 Each one who is numbered in the census shall give this: half a shekel[1] according to the shekel of the sanctuary (the shekel is twenty gerahs),[2] half a shekel as an offering to the LORD. 14 Everyone who is numbered in the census, from twenty years old and upward, shall give the LORD's offering. 15 The rich shall not give more, and the poor shall not give less, than the half shekel, when you give the LORD's offering to make atonement for your lives. 16 You shall take the atonement money from the people of Israel and shall give it for the service of the tent of meeting, that it may bring the people of Israel to remembrance before the LORD, so as to make atonement for your lives."

The Bronze Basin

17 The LORD said to Moses, 18 "You shall also make a basin of bronze, with its stand of bronze, for washing. You shall put it between the tent of meeting and the altar, and you shall put water in it, 19 with which Aaron and his sons shall wash their hands and their feet. 20 When they go into the tent of meeting, or when they come near the altar to minister, to burn a food offering[3] to the LORD, they shall wash with water, so that they may not die. 21 They shall wash their hands and their feet, so that they may not die. It shall be a statute forever to them, even to him and to his offspring throughout their generations."

The Anointing Oil and Incense

22 The LORD said to Moses, 23 "Take the finest spices: of liquid myrrh 500 shekels, and of sweet-smelling cinnamon half as much, that is, 250, and 250 of aromatic cane, 24 and 500 of cassia, according to the shekel of the sanctuary, and a hin[4] of olive oil. 25 And you shall make of these a sacred anointing oil blended as by the perfumer; it shall be a holy anointing oil. 26 With it you shall anoint the tent of meeting and the ark of the testimony, 27 and the table and all its utensils, and the lampstand and its utensils, and the altar of incense, 28 and the altar of burnt offering with all its utensils and the basin and its stand. 29 You shall consecrate them, that they may be most holy. Whatever touches them will become holy. 30 You shall anoint Aaron and his sons, and consecrate them, that they may serve me as priests. 31 And you shall say to the people of Israel, 'This shall be my holy anointing oil throughout your generations. 32 It shall not be poured on the body of an ordinary person, and you shall make no other like it in composition. It is holy, and it shall be holy to you. 33 Whoever compounds any like it or whoever puts any of it on an outsider shall be cut off from his people.'"

34 The LORD said to Moses, "Take sweet spices, stacte, and onycha, and galbanum, sweet spices with pure frankincense (of each shall there be an equal part), 35 and make an incense blended as by the perfumer, seasoned with salt, pure and holy. 36 You shall beat some of it very small, and put part of it before the testimony in the tent of meeting where I shall meet with you. It shall be most holy for you. 37 And the incense that you shall make according to its composition, you shall not make for yourselves. It shall be for you holy to the LORD. 38 Whoever makes any like it to use as perfume shall be cut off from his people."

Oholiab and Bezalel

31 The LORD said to Moses, 2 "See, I have called by name Bezalel the son of Uri, son of Hur, of the tribe of Judah, 3 and I have filled him with the Spirit of

[1] A *shekel* was about 2/5 ounce or 11 grams [2] A *gerah* was about 1/50 ounce or 0.6 gram [3] Or *an offering by fire* [4] A *hin* was about 4 quarts or 3.5 liters

God, with ability and intelligence, with knowledge and all craftsmanship, 4 to devise artistic designs, to work in gold, silver, and bronze, 5 in cutting stones for setting, and in carving wood, to work in every craft. 6 And behold, I have appointed with him Oholiab, the son of Ahisamach, of the tribe of Dan. And I have given to all able men ability, that they may make all that I have commanded you: 7 the tent of meeting, and the ark of the testimony, and the mercy seat that is on it, and all the furnishings of the tent, 8 the table and its utensils, and the pure lampstand with all its utensils, and the altar of incense, 9 and the altar of burnt offering with all its utensils, and the basin and its stand, 10 and the finely worked garments,[1] the holy garments for Aaron the priest and the garments of his sons, for their service as priests, 11 and the anointing oil and the fragrant incense for the Holy Place. According to all that I have commanded you, they shall do."

The Sabbath

12 And the LORD said to Moses, 13 "You are to speak to the people of Israel and say, 'Above all you shall keep my Sabbaths, for this is a sign between me and you throughout your generations, that you may know that I, the LORD, sanctify you. 14 You shall keep the Sabbath, because it is holy for you. Everyone who profanes it shall be put to death. Whoever does any work on it, that soul shall be cut off from among his people. 15 Six days shall work be done, but the seventh day is a Sabbath of solemn rest, holy to the LORD. Whoever does any work on the Sabbath day shall be put to death. 16 Therefore the people of Israel shall keep the Sabbath, observing the Sabbath throughout their generations, as a covenant forever. 17 It is a sign forever between me and the people of Israel that in six days the LORD made heaven and earth, and on the seventh day he rested and was refreshed.'"

18 And he gave to Moses, when he had finished speaking with him on Mount Sinai, the two tablets of the testimony, tablets of stone, written with the finger of God.

The Golden Calf

32 When the people saw that Moses delayed to come down from the mountain, the people gathered themselves together to Aaron and said to him, "Up, make us gods who shall go before us. As for this Moses, the man who brought us up out of the land of Egypt, we do not know what has become of him." 2 So Aaron said to them, "Take off the rings of gold that are in the ears of your wives, your sons, and your daughters, and bring them to me." 3 So all the people took off the rings of gold that were in their ears and brought them to Aaron. 4 And he received the gold from their hand and fashioned it with a graving tool and made a golden[2] calf. And they said, "These are your gods, O Israel, who brought you up out of the land of Egypt!" 5 When Aaron saw this, he built an altar before it. And Aaron made proclamation and said, "Tomorrow shall be a feast to the LORD." 6 And they rose up early the next day and offered burnt offerings and brought peace offerings. And the people sat down to eat and drink and rose up to play.

7 And the LORD said to Moses, "Go down, for your people, whom you brought up out of the land of Egypt, have corrupted themselves. 8 They have turned aside quickly out of the way that I commanded them. They have made for themselves a golden calf and have worshiped it and sacrificed to it and said, 'These are your gods, O Israel, who brought you up out of the land of Egypt!'" 9 And the LORD said to Moses, "I have seen this people, and behold, it is a stiff-necked people. 10 Now therefore let me alone, that my wrath may burn hot against them and I may consume them, in order that I may make a great nation of you."

[1] Or *garments for worship* [2] Hebrew *cast metal*; also verse 8

11 But Moses implored the LORD his God
and said, "O LORD, why does your wrath
burn hot against your people, whom you
have brought out of the land of Egypt with
great power and with a mighty hand?
12 Why should the Egyptians say, 'With evil
intent did he bring them out, to kill them
in the mountains and to consume them
from the face of the earth'? Turn from
your burning anger and relent from this
disaster against your people. 13 Remember
Abraham, Isaac, and Israel, your servants,
to whom you swore by your own self,
and said to them, 'I will multiply your
offspring as the stars of heaven, and all
this land that I have promised I will give
to your offspring, and they shall inherit
it forever.'" 14 And the LORD relented from
the disaster that he had spoken of bring-
ing on his people.

15 Then Moses turned and went down
from the mountain with the two tablets
of the testimony in his hand, tablets that
were written on both sides; on the front
and on the back they were written. 16 The
tablets were the work of God, and the
writing was the writing of God, engraved
on the tablets. 17 When Joshua heard the
noise of the people as they shouted, he
said to Moses, "There is a noise of war
in the camp." 18 But he said, "It is not
the sound of shouting for victory, or the
sound of the cry of defeat, but the sound
of singing that I hear." 19 And as soon as
he came near the camp and saw the calf
and the dancing, Moses' anger burned
hot, and he threw the tablets out of his
hands and broke them at the foot of the
mountain. 20 He took the calf that they had
made and burned it with fire and ground
it to powder and scattered it on the water
and made the people of Israel drink it.

21 And Moses said to Aaron, "What
did this people do to you that you have
brought such a great sin upon them?"
22 And Aaron said, "Let not the anger of
my lord burn hot. You know the people,
that they are set on evil. 23 For they said to
me, 'Make us gods who shall go before us.
As for this Moses, the man who brought
us up out of the land of Egypt, we do not
know what has become of him.' 24 So I said
to them, 'Let any who have gold take it off.'
So they gave it to me, and I threw it into
the fire, and out came this calf."

25 And when Moses saw that the peo-
ple had broken loose (for Aaron had let
them break loose, to the derision of their
enemies), 26 then Moses stood in the gate
of the camp and said, "Who is on the
LORD's side? Come to me." And all the
sons of Levi gathered around him. 27 And
he said to them, "Thus says the LORD God
of Israel, 'Put your sword on your side
each of you, and go to and fro from gate
to gate throughout the camp, and each of
you kill his brother and his companion
and his neighbor.'" 28 And the sons of Levi
did according to the word of Moses. And
that day about three thousand men of the
people fell. 29 And Moses said, "Today you
have been ordained for the service of the
LORD, each one at the cost of his son and
of his brother, so that he might bestow a
blessing upon you this day."

30 The next day Moses said to the people,
"You have sinned a great sin. And now I
will go up to the LORD; perhaps I can
make atonement for your sin." 31 So Moses
returned to the LORD and said, "Alas, this
people has sinned a great sin. They have
made for themselves gods of gold. 32 But
now, if you will forgive their sin—but if
not, please blot me out of your book that
you have written." 33 But the LORD said to
Moses, "Whoever has sinned against me, I
will blot out of my book. 34 But now go, lead
the people to the place about which I have
spoken to you; behold, my angel shall go
before you. Nevertheless, in the day when I
visit, I will visit their sin upon them."

35 Then the LORD sent a plague on the
people, because they made the calf, the
one that Aaron made.

The Command to Leave Sinai

33 The LORD said to Moses, "Depart; go up from here, you and the people whom you have brought up out of the land of Egypt, to the land of which I swore to Abraham, Isaac, and Jacob, saying, 'To your offspring I will give it.' 2 I will send an angel before you, and I will drive out the Canaanites, the Amorites, the Hittites, the Perizzites, the Hivites, and the Jebusites. 3 Go up to a land flowing with milk and honey; but I will not go up among you, lest I consume you on the way, for you are a stiff-necked people."

4 When the people heard this disastrous word, they mourned, and no one put on his ornaments. 5 For the LORD had said to Moses, "Say to the people of Israel, 'You are a stiff-necked people; if for a single moment I should go up among you, I would consume you. So now take off your ornaments, that I may know what to do with you.'" 6 Therefore the people of Israel stripped themselves of their ornaments, from Mount Horeb onward.

The Tent of Meeting

7 Now Moses used to take the tent and pitch it outside the camp, far off from the camp, and he called it the tent of meeting. And everyone who sought the LORD would go out to the tent of meeting, which was outside the camp. 8 Whenever Moses went out to the tent, all the people would rise up, and each would stand at his tent door, and watch Moses until he had gone into the tent. 9 When Moses entered the tent, the pillar of cloud would descend and stand at the entrance of the tent, and the LORD[1] would speak with Moses. 10 And when all the people saw the pillar of cloud standing at the entrance of the tent, all the people would rise up and worship, each at his tent door. 11 Thus the LORD used to speak to Moses face to face, as a man speaks to his friend. When Moses turned again into the camp, his assistant Joshua the son of Nun, a young man, would not depart from the tent.

Moses' Intercession

12 Moses said to the LORD, "See, you say to me, 'Bring up this people,' but you have not let me know whom you will send with me. Yet you have said, 'I know you by name, and you have also found favor in my sight.' 13 Now therefore, if I have found favor in your sight, please show me now your ways, that I may know you in order to find favor in your sight. Consider too that this nation is your people." 14 And he said, "My presence will go with you, and I will give you rest." 15 And he said to him, "If your presence will not go with me, do not bring us up from here. 16 For how shall it be known that I have found favor in your sight, I and your people? Is it not in your going with us, so that we are distinct, I and your people, from every other people on the face of the earth?"

17 And the LORD said to Moses, "This very thing that you have spoken I will do, for you have found favor in my sight, and I know you by name." 18 Moses said, "Please show me your glory." 19 And he said, "I will make all my goodness pass before you and will proclaim before you my name 'The LORD.' And I will be gracious to whom I will be gracious, and will show mercy on whom I will show mercy. 20 But," he said, "you cannot see my face, for man shall not see me and live." 21 And the LORD said, "Behold, there is a place by me where you shall stand on the rock, 22 and while my glory passes by I will put you in a cleft of the rock, and I will cover you with my hand until I have passed by. 23 Then I will take away my hand, and you shall see my back, but my face shall not be seen."

Moses Makes New Tablets

34 The LORD said to Moses, "Cut for yourself two tablets of stone like the first, and I will write on the tablets the words that were on the first tablets,

[1] Hebrew *he*

which you broke. 2 Be ready by the morn-
ing, and come up in the morning to Mount
Sinai, and present yourself there to me on
the top of the mountain. 3 No one shall
come up with you, and let no one be seen
throughout all the mountain. Let no flocks
or herds graze opposite that mountain."
4 So Moses cut two tablets of stone like the
first. And he rose early in the morning and
went up on Mount Sinai, as the LORD had
commanded him, and took in his hand
two tablets of stone. 5 The LORD descended
in the cloud and stood with him there, and
proclaimed the name of the LORD. 6 The
LORD passed before him and proclaimed,
"The LORD, the LORD, a God merciful and
gracious, slow to anger, and abounding in
steadfast love and faithfulness, 7 keeping
steadfast love for thousands,[1] forgiving
iniquity and transgression and sin, but
who will by no means clear the guilty,
visiting the iniquity of the fathers on the
children and the children's children, to
the third and the fourth generation." 8 And
Moses quickly bowed his head toward
the earth and worshiped. 9 And he said,
"If now I have found favor in your sight,
O Lord, please let the Lord go in the midst
of us, for it is a stiff-necked people, and
pardon our iniquity and our sin, and take
us for your inheritance."

The Covenant Renewed

10 And he said, "Behold, I am making a
covenant. Before all your people I will do
marvels, such as have not been created in
all the earth or in any nation. And all the
people among whom you are shall see
the work of the LORD, for it is an awesome
thing that I will do with you.

11 "Observe what I command you this
day. Behold, I will drive out before you the
Amorites, the Canaanites, the Hittites, the
Perizzites, the Hivites, and the Jebusites.
12 Take care, lest you make a covenant
with the inhabitants of the land to which
you go, lest it become a snare in your
midst. 13 You shall tear down their altars
and break their pillars and cut down their
Asherim 14 (for you shall worship no other
god, for the LORD, whose name is Jealous,
is a jealous God), 15 lest you make a cov-
enant with the inhabitants of the land,
and when they whore after their gods and
sacrifice to their gods and you are invited,
you eat of his sacrifice, 16 and you take of
their daughters for your sons, and their
daughters whore after their gods and
make your sons whore after their gods.

17 "You shall not make for yourself any
gods of cast metal.

18 "You shall keep the Feast of Unleav-
ened Bread. Seven days you shall eat
unleavened bread, as I commanded you,
at the time appointed in the month Abib,
for in the month Abib you came out from
Egypt. 19 All that open the womb are mine,
all your male[2] livestock, the firstborn of
cow and sheep. 20 The firstborn of a don-
key you shall redeem with a lamb, or if
you will not redeem it you shall break its
neck. All the firstborn of your sons you
shall redeem. And none shall appear
before me empty-handed.

21 "Six days you shall work, but on
the seventh day you shall rest. In plow-
ing time and in harvest you shall rest.
22 You shall observe the Feast of Weeks,
the firstfruits of wheat harvest, and the
Feast of Ingathering at the year's end.
23 Three times in the year shall all your
males appear before the LORD God, the
God of Israel. 24 For I will cast out nations
before you and enlarge your borders; no
one shall covet your land, when you go up
to appear before the LORD your God three
times in the year.

25 "You shall not offer the blood of my
sacrifice with anything leavened, or let
the sacrifice of the Feast of the Passover
remain until the morning. 26 The best of
the firstfruits of your ground you shall
bring to the house of the LORD your God.

[1] Or *to the thousandth generation* [2] Septuagint, Theodotion, Vulgate, Targum; the meaning of the Hebrew is uncertain

You shall not boil a young goat in its mother's milk."

27 And the LORD said to Moses, "Write these words, for in accordance with these words I have made a covenant with you and with Israel." 28 So he was there with the LORD forty days and forty nights. He neither ate bread nor drank water. And he wrote on the tablets the words of the covenant, the Ten Commandments.[1]

The Shining Face of Moses

29 When Moses came down from Mount Sinai, with the two tablets of the testimony in his hand as he came down from the mountain, Moses did not know that the skin of his face shone because he had been talking with God.[2] 30 Aaron and all the people of Israel saw Moses, and behold, the skin of his face shone, and they were afraid to come near him. 31 But Moses called to them, and Aaron and all the leaders of the congregation returned to him, and Moses talked with them. 32 Afterward all the people of Israel came near, and he commanded them all that the LORD had spoken with him in Mount Sinai. 33 And when Moses had finished speaking with them, he put a veil over his face.

34 Whenever Moses went in before the LORD to speak with him, he would remove the veil, until he came out. And when he came out and told the people of Israel what he was commanded, 35 the people of Israel would see the face of Moses, that the skin of Moses' face was shining. And Moses would put the veil over his face again, until he went in to speak with him.

Sabbath Regulations

205

35 Moses assembled all the congregation of the people of Israel and said to them, "These are the things that the LORD has commanded you to do. 2 Six days work shall be done, but on the seventh day you shall have a Sabbath of solemn rest, holy to the LORD. Whoever does any work on it shall be put to death. 3 You shall kindle no fire in all your dwelling places on the Sabbath day."

Contributions for the Tabernacle

4 Moses said to all the congregation of the people of Israel, "This is the thing that the LORD has commanded. 5 Take from among you a contribution to the LORD. Whoever is of a generous heart, let him bring the LORD's contribution: gold, silver, and bronze; 6 blue and purple and scarlet yarns and fine twined linen; goats' hair, 7 tanned rams' skins, and goatskins;[3] acacia wood, 8 oil for the light, spices for the anointing oil and for the fragrant incense, 9 and onyx stones and stones for setting, for the ephod and for the breastpiece.

10 "Let every skillful craftsman among you come and make all that the LORD has commanded: 11 the tabernacle, its tent and its covering, its hooks and its frames, its bars, its pillars, and its bases; 12 the ark with its poles, the mercy seat, and the veil of the screen; 13 the table with its poles and all its utensils, and the bread of the Presence; 14 the lampstand also for the light, with its utensils and its lamps, and the oil for the light; 15 and the altar of incense, with its poles, and the anointing oil and the fragrant incense, and the screen for the door, at the door of the tabernacle; 16 the altar of burnt offering, with its grating of bronze, its poles, and all its utensils, the basin and its stand; 17 the hangings of the court, its pillars and its bases, and the screen for the gate of the court; 18 the pegs of the tabernacle and the pegs of the court, and their cords; 19 the finely worked garments for ministering[4] in the Holy Place, the holy garments for Aaron the priest, and the garments of his sons, for their service as priests."

20 Then all the congregation of the people of Israel departed from the presence of Moses. 21 And they came, everyone whose heart stirred him, and everyone

[1] Hebrew *the ten words* [2] Hebrew *him* [3] The meaning of the Hebrew word is uncertain; also verse 23; compare 25:5 [4] Or *garments for worship*; see 31:10

whose spirit moved him, and brought the
LORD's contribution to be used for the tent
of meeting, and for all its service, and for
the holy garments. 22 So they came, both
men and women. All who were of a will-
ing heart brought brooches and earrings
and signet rings and armlets, all sorts of
gold objects, every man dedicating an
offering of gold to the LORD. 23 And every
one who possessed blue or purple or
scarlet yarns or fine linen or goats' hair or
tanned rams' skins or goatskins brought
them. 24 Everyone who could make a con-
tribution of silver or bronze brought it as
the LORD's contribution. And every one
who possessed acacia wood of any use in
the work brought it. 25 And every skillful
woman spun with her hands, and they
all brought what they had spun in blue
and purple and scarlet yarns and fine
twined linen. 26 All the women whose
hearts stirred them to use their skill spun
the goats' hair. 27 And the leaders brought
onyx stones and stones to be set, for the
ephod and for the breastpiece, 28 and
spices and oil for the light, and for the
anointing oil, and for the fragrant incense.
29 All the men and women, the people of
Israel, whose heart moved them to bring
anything for the work that the LORD had
commanded by Moses to be done brought
it as a freewill offering to the LORD.

Construction of the Tabernacle

30 Then Moses said to the people of
Israel, "See, the LORD has called by name
Bezalel the son of Uri, son of Hur, of the
tribe of Judah; 31 and he has filled him
with the Spirit of God, with skill, with
intelligence, with knowledge, and with
all craftsmanship, 32 to devise artistic
designs, to work in gold and silver and
bronze, 33 in cutting stones for setting,
and in carving wood, for work in every
skilled craft. 34 And he has inspired him
to teach, both him and Oholiab the son of
Ahisamach of the tribe of Dan. 35 He has
filled them with skill to do every sort of
work done by an engraver or by a designer
or by an embroiderer in blue and purple
and scarlet yarns and fine twined linen,
or by a weaver—by any sort of workman
or skilled designer.

36 "Bezalel and Oholiab and every
craftsman in whom the LORD has
put skill and intelligence to know how to
do any work in the construction of the
sanctuary shall work in accordance with
all that the LORD has commanded."

2 And Moses called Bezalel and Oholiab
and every craftsman in whose mind the
LORD had put skill, everyone whose heart
stirred him up to come to do the work.
3 And they received from Moses all the
contribution that the people of Israel had
brought for doing the work on the sanc-
tuary. They still kept bringing him free-
will offerings every morning, 4 so that
all the craftsmen who were doing every
sort of task on the sanctuary came, each
from the task that he was doing, 5 and
said to Moses, "The people bring much
more than enough for doing the work
that the LORD has commanded us to do."
6 So Moses gave command, and word was
proclaimed throughout the camp, "Let no
man or woman do anything more for the
contribution for the sanctuary." So the
people were restrained from bringing,
7 for the material they had was sufficient
to do all the work, and more.

8 And all the craftsmen among the
workmen made the tabernacle with ten
curtains. They were made of fine twined
linen and blue and purple and scarlet
yarns, with cherubim skillfully worked.
9 The length of each curtain was twenty-
eight cubits,[1] and the breadth of each cur-
tain four cubits. All the curtains were the
same size.

10 He coupled five curtains to one
another, and the other five curtains he cou-
pled to one another. 11 He made loops of
blue on the edge of the outermost curtain

[1] A *cubit* was about 18 inches or 45 centimeters

of the first set. Likewise he made them
on the edge of the outermost curtain of
the second set. 12 He made fifty loops on
the one curtain, and he made fifty loops
on the edge of the curtain that was in the
second set. The loops were opposite one
another. 13 And he made fifty clasps of
gold, and coupled the curtains one to the
other with clasps. So the tabernacle was a
single whole.

14 He also made curtains of goats' hair
for a tent over the tabernacle. He made
eleven curtains. 15 The length of each cur-
tain was thirty cubits, and the breadth
of each curtain four cubits. The eleven
curtains were the same size. 16 He cou-
pled five curtains by themselves, and six
curtains by themselves. 17 And he made
fifty loops on the edge of the outermost
curtain of the one set, and fifty loops on
the edge of the other connecting curtain.
18 And he made fifty clasps of bronze to
couple the tent together that it might be
a single whole. 19 And he made for the
tent a covering of tanned rams' skins and
goatskins.

20 Then he made the upright frames
for the tabernacle of acacia wood. 21 Ten
cubits was the length of a frame, and a
cubit and a half the breadth of each frame.
22 Each frame had two tenons for fitting
together. He did this for all the frames of
the tabernacle. 23 The frames for the tab-
ernacle he made thus: twenty frames for
the south side. 24 And he made forty bases
of silver under the twenty frames, two
bases under one frame for its two tenons,
and two bases under the next frame for
its two tenons. 25 For the second side of
the tabernacle, on the north side, he made
twenty frames 26 and their forty bases of
silver, two bases under one frame and two
bases under the next frame. 27 For the rear
of the tabernacle westward he made six
frames. 28 He made two frames for corners
of the tabernacle in the rear. 29 And they
were separate beneath but joined at the
top, at the first ring. He made two of them
this way for the two corners. 30 There were
eight frames with their bases of silver: six-
teen bases, under every frame two bases.

31 He made bars of acacia wood, five
for the frames of the one side of the tab-
ernacle, 32 and five bars for the frames of
the other side of the tabernacle, and five
bars for the frames of the tabernacle at the
rear westward. 33 And he made the middle
bar to run from end to end halfway up
the frames. 34 And he overlaid the frames
with gold, and made their rings of gold
for holders for the bars, and overlaid the
bars with gold.

35 He made the veil of blue and purple
and scarlet yarns and fine twined linen;
with cherubim skillfully worked into it
he made it. 36 And for it he made four pil-
lars of acacia and overlaid them with gold.
Their hooks were of gold, and he cast for
them four bases of silver. 37 He also made
a screen for the entrance of the tent, of
blue and purple and scarlet yarns and
fine twined linen, embroidered with nee-
dlework, 38 and its five pillars with their
hooks. He overlaid their capitals, and their
fillets were of gold, but their five bases
were of bronze.

Making the Ark

37 Bezalel made the ark of acacia
wood. Two cubits[1] and a half was
its length, a cubit and a half its breadth,
and a cubit and a half its height. 2 And he
overlaid it with pure gold inside and out-
side, and made a molding of gold around
it. 3 And he cast for it four rings of gold
for its four feet, two rings on its one side
and two rings on its other side. 4 And he
made poles of acacia wood and overlaid
them with gold 5 and put the poles into
the rings on the sides of the ark to carry
the ark. 6 And he made a mercy seat of
pure gold. Two cubits and a half was its
length, and a cubit and a half its breadth.
7 And he made two cherubim of gold. He

[1] A *cubit* was about 18 inches or 45 centimeters

made them of hammered work on the two ends of the mercy seat, 8 one cherub on the one end, and one cherub on the other end. Of one piece with the mercy seat he made the cherubim on its two ends. 9 The cherubim spread out their wings above, overshadowing the mercy seat with their wings, with their faces one to another; toward the mercy seat were the faces of the cherubim.

Making the Table

10 He also made the table of acacia wood. Two cubits was its length, a cubit its breadth, and a cubit and a half its height. 11 And he overlaid it with pure gold, and made a molding of gold around it. 12 And he made a rim around it a handbreadth[1] wide, and made a molding of gold around the rim. 13 He cast for it four rings of gold and fastened the rings to the four corners at its four legs. 14 Close to the frame were the rings, as holders for the poles to carry the table. 15 He made the poles of acacia wood to carry the table, and overlaid them with gold. 16 And he made the vessels of pure gold that were to be on the table, its plates and dishes for incense, and its bowls and flagons with which to pour drink offerings.

Making the Lampstand

17 He also made the lampstand of pure gold. He made the lampstand of hammered work. Its base, its stem, its cups, its calyxes, and its flowers were of one piece with it. 18 And there were six branches going out of its sides, three branches of the lampstand out of one side of it and three branches of the lampstand out of the other side of it; 19 three cups made like almond blossoms, each with calyx and flower, on one branch, and three cups made like almond blossoms, each with calyx and flower, on the other branch—so for the six branches going out of the lampstand. 20 And on the lampstand itself were four cups made like almond blossoms, with their calyxes and flowers, 21 and a calyx of one piece with it under each pair of the six branches going out of it. 22 Their calyxes and their branches were of one piece with it. The whole of it was a single piece of hammered work of pure gold. 23 And he made its seven lamps and its tongs and its trays of pure gold. 24 He made it and all its utensils out of a talent[2] of pure gold.

Making the Altar of Incense

25 He made the altar of incense of acacia wood. Its length was a cubit, and its breadth was a cubit. It was square, and two cubits was its height. Its horns were of one piece with it. 26 He overlaid it with pure gold, its top and around its sides and its horns. And he made a molding of gold around it, 27 and made two rings of gold on it under its molding, on two opposite sides of it, as holders for the poles with which to carry it. 28 And he made the poles of acacia wood and overlaid them with gold.

29 He made the holy anointing oil also, and the pure fragrant incense, blended as by the perfumer.

Making the Altar of Burnt Offering

38 He made the altar of burnt offering of acacia wood. Five cubits[3] was its length, and five cubits its breadth. It was square, and three cubits was its height. 2 He made horns for it on its four corners. Its horns were of one piece with it, and he overlaid it with bronze. 3 And he made all the utensils of the altar, the pots, the shovels, the basins, the forks, and the fire pans. He made all its utensils of bronze. 4 And he made for the altar a grating, a network of bronze, under its ledge, extending halfway down. 5 He cast four rings on the four corners of the bronze grating as holders for the poles. 6 He made the poles of acacia wood and overlaid them with bronze. 7 And he put the poles through the rings on the sides of the altar to carry it with them. He made it hollow, with boards.

[1] A *handbreadth* was about 3 inches or 7.5 centimeters [2] A *talent* was about 75 pounds or 34 kilograms [3] A *cubit* was about 18 inches or 45 centimeters

Making the Bronze Basin

8 He made the basin of bronze and its stand of bronze, from the mirrors of the ministering women who ministered in the entrance of the tent of meeting.

Making the Court

9 And he made the court. For the south side the hangings of the court were of fine twined linen, a hundred cubits; 10 their twenty pillars and their twenty bases were of bronze, but the hooks of the pillars and their fillets were of silver. 11 And for the north side there were hangings of a hundred cubits, their twenty pillars, their twenty bases were of bronze, but the hooks of the pillars and their fillets were of silver. 12 And for the west side were hangings of fifty cubits, their ten pillars, and their ten bases; the hooks of the pillars and their fillets were of silver. 13 And for the front to the east, fifty cubits. 14 The hangings for one side of the gate were fifteen cubits, with their three pillars and three bases. 15 And so for the other side. On both sides of the gate of the court were hangings of fifteen cubits, with their three pillars and their three bases. 16 All the hangings around the court were of fine twined linen. 17 And the bases for the pillars were of bronze, but the hooks of the pillars and their fillets were of silver. The overlaying of their capitals was also of silver, and all the pillars of the court were filleted with silver. 18 And the screen for the gate of the court was embroidered with needlework in blue and purple and scarlet yarns and fine twined linen. It was twenty cubits long and five cubits high in its breadth, corresponding to the hangings of the court. 19 And their pillars were four in number. Their four bases were of bronze, their hooks of silver, and the overlaying of their capitals and their fillets of silver. 20 And all the pegs for the tabernacle and for the court all around were of bronze.

Materials for the Tabernacle

21 These are the records of the tabernacle, the tabernacle of the testimony, as they were recorded at the commandment of Moses, the responsibility of the Levites under the direction of Ithamar the son of Aaron the priest. 22 Bezalel the son of Uri, son of Hur, of the tribe of Judah, made all that the LORD commanded Moses; 23 and with him was Oholiab the son of Ahisamach, of the tribe of Dan, an engraver and designer and embroiderer in blue and purple and scarlet yarns and fine twined linen.

24 All the gold that was used for the work, in all the construction of the sanctuary, the gold from the offering, was twenty-nine talents and 730 shekels,[1] by the shekel of the sanctuary. 25 The silver from those of the congregation who were recorded was a hundred talents and 1,775 shekels, by the shekel of the sanctuary: 26 a beka[2] a head (that is, half a shekel, by the shekel of the sanctuary), for everyone who was listed in the records, from twenty years old and upward, for 603,550 men. 27 The hundred talents of silver were for casting the bases of the sanctuary and the bases of the veil; a hundred bases for the hundred talents, a talent a base. 28 And of the 1,775 shekels he made hooks for the pillars and overlaid their capitals and made fillets for them. 29 The bronze that was offered was seventy talents and 2,400 shekels; 30 with it he made the bases for the entrance of the tent of meeting, the bronze altar and the bronze grating for it and all the utensils of the altar, 31 the bases around the court, and the bases of the gate of the court, all the pegs of the tabernacle, and all the pegs around the court.

Making the Priestly Garments

39 From the blue and purple and scarlet yarns they made finely woven garments,[3] for ministering in the

[1] A *talent* was about 75 pounds or 34 kilograms; a *shekel* was about 2/5 ounce or 11 grams [2] A *beka* was about 1/5 ounce or 5.5 grams [3] Or *garments for worship*

Holy Place. They made the holy garments
for Aaron, as the LORD had commanded
Moses.
2 He made the ephod of gold, blue and
purple and scarlet yarns, and fine twined
linen. 3 And they hammered out gold leaf,
and he cut it into threads to work into
the blue and purple and the scarlet yarns,
and into the fine twined linen, in skilled
design. 4 They made for the ephod attach-
ing shoulder pieces, joined to it at its two
edges. 5 And the skillfully woven band on
it was of one piece with it and made like it,
of gold, blue and purple and scarlet yarns,
and fine twined linen, as the LORD had
commanded Moses.
6 They made the onyx stones, enclosed
in settings of gold filigree, and engraved
like the engravings of a signet, according
to the names of the sons of Israel. 7 And
he set them on the shoulder pieces of the
ephod to be stones of remembrance for
the sons of Israel, as the LORD had com-
manded Moses.
8 He made the breastpiece, in skilled
work, in the style of the ephod, of gold,
blue and purple and scarlet yarns, and
fine twined linen. 9 It was square. They

The High Priest's Holy Garments

God told Moses exactly how the high priest's clothing should be made (Exodus 28; 39).

The turban was a kind of hat, made of fine linen. On it was a piece of pure shining gold where the words "Holy to the LORD" were engraved.

The priest wore a colorful ephod. A waistband held it around the middle. On each shoulder was a shoulder piece, holding a precious stone called an onyx. On one of these two stones, the names of six of the tribes of Israel were engraved. On the other stone, the names of the other six tribes were engraved. The breastpiece of the ephod had twelve precious stones on it. The name of a tribe of Israel was engraved on each stone. The breastpiece also had the Urim and the Thummim, attached to the ephod by gold chains and rings. Under the ephod was a blue robe. At the bottom of the robe, were imitation pomegranates and golden bells. Under the blue robe, the priest wore a white coat or tunic.

God's Presence in the Tabernacle

Long ago, God led the people of Israel from Egypt through the desert to the Promised Land. They would be God's people and He would be their God. God loved His people very much and wanted to dwell with them, living among them. So God gave Moses instructions about building a tabernacle—a large tent for worship—so that He could dwell in the midst of the people. God told Moses that he must be very careful to make the tabernacle and everything in it exactly the way God said it should be.

Moses told the people how to build the tabernacle and everything in it according to God's directions. To make the beautiful furnishings, the Israelites brought gifts of wood, gold, animal hides, and linen cloth.

Once the furnishings and curtains were made, God wanted them to be set apart, to be used only in a special way, for the worship of God. Because of this, everything in the Tabernacle had to be holy and all the priests who worked in the Tabernacle had to be holy. So God told Moses to anoint them with a special oil, to show that they had been set apart by God to be holy and to serve Him and to worship Him in a very special way.

Moses told the people how God wanted them to set up the tabernacle. In one special room—called the Most Holy Place—was a beautiful golden chest called the ark of the covenant.

Inside the chest were treasures, including the stone tablets on which God had written the Ten Commandments. Carved on the top of the ark were two golden angels, called cherubim. A beautiful curtain, or veil, divided the Most Holy Place from the next room. A golden lampstand was placed in the other room of the tabernacle.

Each day, morning and evening, the priests were to trim the wicks and make sure there was plenty of oil for the lamps. Moses also told the people to put a special table in this room. On this table, the priests would place twelve loaves of flat bread called the bread of the Presence. In this room was a golden altar on which sweet-smelling incense was to be burned.

On the outside of the tabernacle tent was a large area—a courtyard that was fenced around with walls of fabric. In the courtyard was a large container or basin. It would hold water that the priests would use for washing. At the entrance to the tabernacle was a special altar for sacrifices of grain and burnt offerings.

When everything had been done exactly as God had commanded, the glory of the Lord filled the tabernacle. God's cloud covered the tent of meeting and could be seen throughout the entire area where God's people were camped. During all their travels, the cloud of the Lord was on the tabernacle by day, and fire was in it by night.

God dwells with His people today through the gift of His Holy Spirit living in each one of His children. God is with us when we come together to worship Him. He tells us how He wants us to worship Him, and He gives us special ways to know His grace—through His Word, prayer, baptism, and the Lord's Supper. Through these gifts, God shows how much He loves His people. He forgives our sins for Jesus' sake and promises to take us to our new home in heaven.

SEEK and FIND

WHERE TO FIND THE STORY

Exodus 25–30; 35–40

KEY BIBLE VERSE

"And let them make me a sanctuary, that I may dwell in their midst. Exactly as I show you concerning the pattern of the tabernacle, and of all its furniture, so you shall make it." (Exodus 25:8–9)

THREE KEY QUESTIONS

- Why did God want Moses to make the tabernacle?
- When everything in the tabernacle was finished and set up exactly as God had said, what filled the temple?
- What are the special gifts that God gives to His people today?

RELATED BIBLE READINGS

1 Chronicles 17:1–27; John 1:14; Hebrews 8:1–6; 9:1–28; Revelation 21:1–3

made the breastpiece doubled, a span[1]
its length and a span its breadth when
doubled. 10 And they set in it four rows of
stones. A row of sardius, topaz, and car-
buncle was the first row; 11 and the sec-
ond row, an emerald, a sapphire, and a
diamond; 12 and the third row, a jacinth,
an agate, and an amethyst; 13 and the
fourth row, a beryl, an onyx, and a jas-
per. They were enclosed in settings of
gold filigree. 14 There were twelve stones
with their names according to the names
of the sons of Israel. They were like sig-
nets, each engraved with its name, for the
twelve tribes. 15 And they made on the
breastpiece twisted chains like cords, of
pure gold. 16 And they made two settings
of gold filigree and two gold rings, and
put the two rings on the two edges of the
breastpiece. 17 And they put the two cords
of gold in the two rings at the edges of
the breastpiece. 18 They attached the two
ends of the two cords to the two settings
of filigree. Thus they attached it in front to
the shoulder pieces of the ephod. 19 Then
they made two rings of gold, and put them

[1] A *span* was about 9 inches or 22 centimeters

at the two ends of the breastpiece, on its
inside edge next to the ephod. 20 And they
made two rings of gold, and attached
them in front to the lower part of the
two shoulder pieces of the ephod, at its
seam above the skillfully woven band of
the ephod. 21 And they bound the breast-
piece by its rings to the rings of the ephod
with a lace of blue, so that it should lie on
the skillfully woven band of the ephod,
and that the breastpiece should not come
loose from the ephod, as the LORD had
commanded Moses.

22 He also made the robe of the ephod
woven all of blue, 23 and the opening of
the robe in it was like the opening in a gar-
ment, with a binding around the open-
ing, so that it might not tear. 24 On the
hem of the robe they made pomegranates
of blue and purple and scarlet yarns and
fine twined linen. 25 They also made bells
of pure gold, and put the bells between
the pomegranates all around the hem of
the robe, between the pomegranates—
26 a bell and a pomegranate, a bell and a
pomegranate around the hem of the robe
for ministering, as the LORD had com-
manded Moses.

27 They also made the coats, woven of
fine linen, for Aaron and his sons, 28 and
the turban of fine linen, and the caps of
fine linen, and the linen undergarments
of fine twined linen, 29 and the sash of fine
twined linen and of blue and purple and
scarlet yarns, embroidered with needle-
work, as the LORD had commanded Moses.

30 They made the plate of the holy crown
of pure gold, and wrote on it an inscrip-
tion, like the engraving of a signet, "Holy
to the LORD." 31 And they tied to it a cord
of blue to fasten it on the turban above, as
the LORD had commanded Moses.

32 Thus all the work of the tabernacle of
the tent of meeting was finished, and the
people of Israel did according to all that
the LORD had commanded Moses; so they
did. 33 Then they brought the tabernacle
to Moses, the tent and all its utensils, its
hooks, its frames, its bars, its pillars, and
its bases; 34 the covering of tanned rams'
skins and goatskins, and the veil of the
screen; 35 the ark of the testimony with
its poles and the mercy seat; 36 the table
with all its utensils, and the bread of the
Presence; 37 the lampstand of pure gold
and its lamps with the lamps set and all
its utensils, and the oil for the light; 38 the
golden altar, the anointing oil and the fra-
grant incense, and the screen for the
entrance of the tent; 39 the bronze altar,
and its grating of bronze, its poles, and all
its utensils; the basin and its stand; 40 the
hangings of the court, its pillars, and its
bases, and the screen for the gate of the
court, its cords, and its pegs; and all the
utensils for the service of the taberna-
cle, for the tent of meeting; 41 the finely
worked garments for ministering in the
Holy Place, the holy garments for Aaron
the priest, and the garments of his sons
for their service as priests. 42 According to
all that the LORD had commanded Moses,
so the people of Israel had done all the
work. 43 And Moses saw all the work, and
behold, they had done it; as the LORD had
commanded, so had they done it. Then
Moses blessed them.

The Tabernacle Erected

40 The LORD spoke to Moses, say-
ing, 2 "On the first day of the first
month you shall erect the tabernacle of
the tent of meeting. 3 And you shall put in
it the ark of the testimony, and you shall
screen the ark with the veil. 4 And you shall
bring in the table and arrange it, and you
shall bring in the lampstand and set up
its lamps. 5 And you shall put the golden
altar for incense before the ark of the tes-
timony, and set up the screen for the door
of the tabernacle. 6 You shall set the altar of
burnt offering before the door of the taber-
nacle of the tent of meeting, 7 and place the
basin between the tent of meeting and the

altar, and put water in it. 8 And you shall set up the court all around, and hang up the screen for the gate of the court.

9 "Then you shall take the anointing oil and anoint the tabernacle and all that is in it, and consecrate it and all its furniture, so that it may become holy. 10 You shall also anoint the altar of burnt offering and all its utensils, and consecrate the altar, so that the altar may become most holy. 11 You shall also anoint the basin and its stand, and consecrate it. 12 Then you shall bring Aaron and his sons to the entrance of the tent of meeting and shall wash them with water 13 and put on Aaron the holy garments. And you shall anoint him and consecrate him, that he may serve me as priest. 14 You shall bring his sons also and put coats on them, 15 and anoint them, as you anointed their father, that they may serve me as priests. And their anointing shall admit them to a perpetual priesthood throughout their generations."

16 This Moses did; according to all that the LORD commanded him, so he did. 17 In the first month in the second year, on the first day of the month, the tabernacle was erected. 18 Moses erected the tabernacle. He laid its bases, and set up its frames, and put in its poles, and raised up its pillars. 19 And he spread the tent over the tabernacle and put the covering of the tent over it, as the LORD had commanded Moses. 20 He took the testimony and put it into the ark, and put the poles on the ark and set the mercy seat above on the ark. 21 And he brought the ark into the tabernacle and set up the veil of the screen, and screened the ark of the testimony, as the LORD had commanded Moses. 22 He put the table in the tent of meeting, on the north side of the tabernacle, outside the veil, 23 and arranged the bread on it before the LORD, as the LORD had commanded Moses. 24 He put the lampstand in the tent of meeting, opposite the table on the south side of the tabernacle, 25 and set up the lamps before the LORD, as the LORD had commanded Moses. 26 He put the golden altar in the tent of meeting before the veil, 27 and burned fragrant incense on it, as the LORD had commanded Moses. 28 He put in place the screen for the door of the tabernacle. 29 And he set the altar of burnt offering at the entrance of the tabernacle of the tent of meeting, and offered on it the burnt offering and the grain offering, as the LORD had commanded Moses. 30 He set the basin between the tent of meeting and the altar, and put water in it for washing, 31 with which Moses and Aaron and his sons washed their hands and their feet. 32 When they went into the tent of meeting, and when they approached the altar, they washed, as the LORD commanded Moses. 33 And he erected the court around the tabernacle and the altar, and set up the screen of the gate of the court. So Moses finished the work.

The Glory of the LORD

34 Then the cloud covered the tent of meeting, and the glory of the LORD filled the tabernacle. 35 And Moses was not able to enter the tent of meeting because the cloud settled on it, and the glory of the LORD filled the tabernacle. 36 Throughout all their journeys, whenever the cloud was taken up from over the tabernacle, the people of Israel would set out. 37 But if the cloud was not taken up, then they did not set out till the day that it was taken up. 38 For the cloud of the LORD was on the tabernacle by day, and fire was in it by night, in the sight of all the house of Israel throughout all their journeys.

Introduction to

Leviticus

Author
Moses the prophet

Date
1446 B.C.

People
Moses; Aaron; Nadab; Abihu

Purpose
The purpose of Leviticus is to teach God's old covenant people what to do about their sin so they could live with their holy God.

Central Themes
God is holy; sin needs to be atoned for; sacrifices were made for specific sins; God provided rules for "clean" and "unclean"; we need a mediator; God's people must be holy; Holy Days were to be observed.

Memory Verses
Teach the people (Leviticus 10:10–11); holy to the Lord (Leviticus 11:45; 20:26); atonement (Leviticus 16:30–34); sacrifice only to the Lord (Leviticus 17:1–5)

Introduction

The name "Leviticus" means "things concerning Levites." God had called priests from among the Levites, and much of Leviticus is about worship involving the priests. Leviticus gives God's instructions for how His sinful Old Testament people could live with their holy God. God required specific sacrifices for specific kinds of sin, with details on how to offer them (Leviticus 1–7). God explained who were to be priests and how they were to mediate between sinful people and a holy God (Leviticus 8–10). God also gave rules about what would make Israelites "clean" and "unclean" (Leviticus 11–15). God called for an annual Day of Atonement when the high priest would make atonement for the people's sin so that God could accept their worship (Leviticus 16). In Leviticus, God established Holy Days, when His people would set aside special times of worship (Leviticus 23–25). In addition, the book provided rules for daily life, some specifically for Israel in Old Testament times, some that still apply to us today. The overall emphasis of the book is summed up in the statement we find in Leviticus 19:2: "You shall be holy, for I the LORD your God am holy."

1876 B.C.	1526 B.C.	1446 B.C.
Israel goes to Egypt	Moses born	Exodus/events of Leviticus

Leviticus

Laws for Burnt Offerings

1 The LORD called Moses and spoke to him from the tent of meeting, saying, 2 "Speak to the people of Israel and say to them, When any one of you brings an offering to the LORD, you shall bring your offering of livestock from the herd or from the flock.

3 "If his offering is a burnt offering from the herd, he shall offer a male without blemish. He shall bring it to the entrance of the tent of meeting, that he may be accepted before the LORD. 4 He shall lay his hand on the head of the burnt offering, and it shall be accepted for him to make atonement for him. 5 Then he shall kill the bull before the LORD, and Aaron's sons the priests shall bring the blood and throw the blood against the sides of the altar that is at the entrance of the tent of meeting. 6 Then he shall flay the burnt offering and cut it into pieces, 7 and the sons of Aaron the priest shall put fire on the altar and arrange wood on the fire. 8 And Aaron's sons the priests shall arrange the pieces, the head, and the fat, on the wood that is on the fire on the altar; 9 but its entrails and its legs he shall wash with water. And the priest shall burn all of it on the altar, as a burnt offering, a food offering[1] with a pleasing aroma to the LORD.

10 "If his gift for a burnt offering is from the flock, from the sheep or goats, he shall bring a male without blemish, 11 and he shall kill it on the north side of the altar before the LORD, and Aaron's sons the priests shall throw its blood against the sides of the altar. 12 And he shall cut it into pieces, with its head and its fat, and the priest shall arrange them on the wood that is on the fire on the altar, 13 but the entrails and the legs he shall wash with water. And the priest shall offer all of it and burn it on the altar; it is a burnt offering, a food offering with a pleasing aroma to the LORD.

14 "If his offering to the LORD is a burnt offering of birds, then he shall bring his offering of turtledoves or pigeons. 15 And the priest shall bring it to the altar and wring off its head and burn it on the altar. Its blood shall be drained out on the side of the altar. 16 He shall remove its crop with its contents[2] and cast it beside the altar on the east side, in the place for ashes. 17 He shall tear it open by its wings, but shall not sever it completely. And the priest shall burn it on the altar, on the wood that is on the fire. It is a burnt offering, a food offering with a pleasing aroma to the LORD.

Laws for Grain Offerings

2 "When anyone brings a grain offering as an offering to the LORD, his offering shall be of fine flour. He shall pour oil on it and put frankincense on it 2 and bring it to Aaron's sons the priests. And he shall take from it a handful of the fine flour and oil, with all of its frankincense, and the priest shall burn this as its memorial portion on the altar, a food offering with a pleasing aroma to the LORD. 3 But the rest of the grain offering shall be for Aaron and his sons; it is a most holy part of the LORD's food offerings.

4 "When you bring a grain offering baked in the oven as an offering, it shall be unleavened loaves of fine flour mixed with oil or unleavened wafers smeared with oil. 5 And if your offering is a grain offering baked on a griddle, it shall be of fine flour unleavened, mixed with oil. 6 You shall break it in pieces and pour oil

[1] Or *an offering by fire*; so throughout Leviticus [2] Or *feathers*

on it; it is a grain offering. 7 And if your
offering is a grain offering cooked in a
pan, it shall be made of fine flour with
oil. 8 And you shall bring the grain offer-
ing that is made of these things to the
LORD, and when it is presented to the
priest, he shall bring it to the altar. 9 And
the priest shall take from the grain offer-
ing its memorial portion and burn this on
the altar, a food offering with a pleasing
aroma to the LORD. 10 But the rest of the
grain offering shall be for Aaron and his
sons; it is a most holy part of the LORD's
food offerings.

11 "No grain offering that you bring to
the LORD shall be made with leaven, for
you shall burn no leaven nor any honey as
a food offering to the LORD. 12 As an offer-
ing of firstfruits you may bring them to
the LORD, but they shall not be offered on
the altar for a pleasing aroma. 13 You shall
season all your grain offerings with salt.
You shall not let the salt of the covenant
with your God be missing from your grain
offering; with all your offerings you shall
offer salt.

14 "If you offer a grain offering of first-
fruits to the LORD, you shall offer for the
grain offering of your firstfruits fresh
ears, roasted with fire, crushed new grain.
15 And you shall put oil on it and lay frank-
incense on it; it is a grain offering. 16 And
the priest shall burn as its memorial por-
tion some of the crushed grain and some
of the oil with all of its frankincense; it is
a food offering to the LORD.

Laws for Peace Offerings

3 "If his offering is a sacrifice of peace
offering, if he offers an animal from
the herd, male or female, he shall offer it
without blemish before the LORD. 2 And he
shall lay his hand on the head of his offer-
ing and kill it at the entrance of the tent of
meeting, and Aaron's sons the priests shall
throw the blood against the sides of the
altar. 3 And from the sacrifice of the peace
offering, as a food offering to the LORD,
he shall offer the fat covering the entrails
and all the fat that is on the entrails, 4 and
the two kidneys with the fat that is on
them at the loins, and the long lobe of
the liver that he shall remove with the
kidneys. 5 Then Aaron's sons shall burn
it on the altar on top of the burnt offer-
ing, which is on the wood on the fire; it
is a food offering with a pleasing aroma
to the LORD.

6 "If his offering for a sacrifice of peace
offering to the LORD is an animal from
the flock, male or female, he shall offer it
without blemish. 7 If he offers a lamb for
his offering, then he shall offer it before
the LORD, 8 lay his hand on the head of his
offering, and kill it in front of the tent of
meeting; and Aaron's sons shall throw its
blood against the sides of the altar. 9 Then
from the sacrifice of the peace offering he
shall offer as a food offering to the LORD
its fat; he shall remove the whole fat tail,
cut off close to the backbone, and the fat
that covers the entrails and all the fat that
is on the entrails 10 and the two kidneys
with the fat that is on them at the loins
and the long lobe of the liver that he shall
remove with the kidneys. 11 And the priest
shall burn it on the altar as a food offering
to the LORD.

12 "If his offering is a goat, then he shall
offer it before the LORD 13 and lay his hand
on its head and kill it in front of the tent
of meeting, and the sons of Aaron shall
throw its blood against the sides of the
altar. 14 Then he shall offer from it, as his
offering for a food offering to the LORD,
the fat covering the entrails and all the fat
that is on the entrails 15 and the two kid-
neys with the fat that is on them at the
loins and the long lobe of the liver that
he shall remove with the kidneys. 16 And
the priest shall burn them on the altar as
a food offering with a pleasing aroma. All
fat is the LORD's. 17 It shall be a statute for-
ever throughout your generations, in all

your dwelling places, that you eat neither
fat nor blood.”

Laws for Sin Offerings

4 And the LORD spoke to Moses, saying,
2 “Speak to the people of Israel, saying,
If anyone sins unintentionally[1] in any of
the LORD’s commandments about things
not to be done, and does any one of them,
3 if it is the anointed priest who sins, thus
bringing guilt on the people, then he shall
offer for the sin that he has committed a
bull from the herd without blemish to the
LORD for a sin offering. 4 He shall bring the
bull to the entrance of the tent of meeting
before the LORD and lay his hand on the
head of the bull and kill the bull before
the LORD. 5 And the anointed priest shall
take some of the blood of the bull and
bring it into the tent of meeting, 6 and the
priest shall dip his finger in the blood and
sprinkle part of the blood seven times
before the LORD in front of the veil of the
sanctuary. 7 And the priest shall put some
of the blood on the horns of the altar of
fragrant incense before the LORD that is in
the tent of meeting, and all the rest of the
blood of the bull he shall pour out at the
base of the altar of burnt offering that is at
the entrance of the tent of meeting. 8 And
all the fat of the bull of the sin offering he
shall remove from it, the fat that covers
the entrails and all the fat that is on the
entrails 9 and the two kidneys with the fat
that is on them at the loins and the long
lobe of the liver that he shall remove with
the kidneys 10 (just as these are taken from
the ox of the sacrifice of the peace offer-
ings); and the priest shall burn them on
the altar of burnt offering. 11 But the skin
of the bull and all its flesh, with its head,
its legs, its entrails, and its dung— 12 all
the rest of the bull—he shall carry outside
the camp to a clean place, to the ash heap,
and shall burn it up on a fire of wood. On
the ash heap it shall be burned up.

13 “If the whole congregation of Israel
sins unintentionally[2] and the thing is
hidden from the eyes of the assembly,
and they do any one of the things that by
the LORD’s commandments ought not
to be done, and they realize their guilt,[3]
14 when the sin which they have commit-
ted becomes known, the assembly shall
offer a bull from the herd for a sin offering
and bring it in front of the tent of meet-
ing. 15 And the elders of the congregation
shall lay their hands on the head of the
bull before the LORD, and the bull shall
be killed before the LORD. 16 Then the
anointed priest shall bring some of the
blood of the bull into the tent of meeting,
17 and the priest shall dip his finger in the
blood and sprinkle it seven times before
the LORD in front of the veil. 18 And he
shall put some of the blood on the horns
of the altar that is in the tent of meeting
before the LORD, and the rest of the blood
he shall pour out at the base of the altar of
burnt offering that is at the entrance of the
tent of meeting. 19 And all its fat he shall
take from it and burn on the altar. 20 Thus
shall he do with the bull. As he did with
the bull of the sin offering, so shall he do
with this. And the priest shall make atone-
ment for them, and they shall be forgiven.
21 And he shall carry the bull outside the
camp and burn it up as he burned the first
bull; it is the sin offering for the assembly.

22 “When a leader sins, doing uninten-
tionally any one of all the things that by
the commandments of the LORD his God
ought not to be done, and realizes his
guilt, 23 or the sin which he has committed
is made known to him, he shall bring as
his offering a goat, a male without blem-
ish, 24 and shall lay his hand on the head of
the goat and kill it in the place where they
kill the burnt offering before the LORD; it
is a sin offering. 25 Then the priest shall
take some of the blood of the sin offering
with his finger and put it on the horns of
the altar of burnt offering and pour out
the rest of its blood at the base of the altar

[1] Or *by mistake*; so throughout Leviticus [2] Or *makes a mistake* [3] Or *suffer for their guilt*, or *are guilty*; also verses 22, 27, and chapter 5

of burnt offering. 26 And all its fat he shall burn on the altar, like the fat of the sacrifice of peace offerings. So the priest shall make atonement for him for his sin, and he shall be forgiven.

27 "If anyone of the common people sins unintentionally in doing any one of the things that by the LORD's commandments ought not to be done, and realizes his guilt, 28 or the sin which he has committed is made known to him, he shall bring for his offering a goat, a female without blemish, for his sin which he has committed. 29 And he shall lay his hand on the head of the sin offering and kill the sin offering in the place of burnt offering. 30 And the priest shall take some of its blood with his finger and put it on the horns of the altar of burnt offering and pour out all the rest of its blood at the base of the altar. 31 And all its fat he shall remove, as the fat is removed from the peace offerings, and the priest shall burn it on the altar for a pleasing aroma to the LORD. And the priest shall make atonement for him, and he shall be forgiven.

32 "If he brings a lamb as his offering for a sin offering, he shall bring a female without blemish 33 and lay his hand on the head of the sin offering and kill it for a sin offering in the place where they kill the burnt offering. 34 Then the priest shall take some of the blood of the sin offering with his finger and put it on the horns of the altar of burnt offering and pour out all the rest of its blood at the base of the altar. 35 And all its fat he shall remove as the fat of the lamb is removed from the sacrifice of peace offerings, and the priest shall burn it on the altar, on top of the LORD's food offerings. And the priest shall make atonement for him for the sin which he has committed, and he shall be forgiven.

5 "If anyone sins in that he hears a public adjuration to testify, and though he is a witness, whether he has seen or come to know the matter, yet does not speak, he shall bear his iniquity; 2 or if anyone touches an unclean thing, whether a carcass of an unclean wild animal or a carcass of unclean livestock or a carcass of unclean swarming things, and it is hidden from him and he has become unclean, and he realizes his guilt; 3 or if he touches human uncleanness, of whatever sort the uncleanness may be with which one becomes unclean, and it is hidden from him, when he comes to know it, and realizes his guilt; 4 or if anyone utters with his lips a rash oath to do evil or to do good, any sort of rash oath that people swear, and it is hidden from him, when he comes to know it, and he realizes his guilt in any of these; 5 when he realizes his guilt in any of these and confesses the sin he has committed, 6 he shall bring to the LORD as his compensation[1] for the sin that he has committed, a female from the flock, a lamb or a goat, for a sin offering. And the priest shall make atonement for him for his sin.

7 "But if he cannot afford a lamb, then he shall bring to the LORD as his compensation for the sin that he has committed two turtledoves or two pigeons,[2] one for a sin offering and the other for a burnt offering. 8 He shall bring them to the priest, who shall offer first the one for the sin offering. He shall wring its head from its neck but shall not sever it completely, 9 and he shall sprinkle some of the blood of the sin offering on the side of the altar, while the rest of the blood shall be drained out at the base of the altar; it is a sin offering. 10 Then he shall offer the second for a burnt offering according to the rule. And the priest shall make atonement for him for the sin that he has committed, and he shall be forgiven.

11 "But if he cannot afford two turtledoves or two pigeons, then he shall bring as his offering for the sin that he has committed a tenth of an ephah[3] of fine flour for a sin offering. He shall put no oil on

[1] Hebrew *his guilt penalty*; so throughout Leviticus [2] Septuagint *two young pigeons*; also verse 11 [3] An *ephah* was about 3/5 bushel or 22 liters

it and shall put no frankincense on it, for it is a sin offering. **12** And he shall bring it to the priest, and the priest shall take a handful of it as its memorial portion and burn this on the altar, on the LORD's food offerings; it is a sin offering. **13** Thus the priest shall make atonement for him for the sin which he has committed in any one of these things, and he shall be forgiven. And the remainder[1] shall be for the priest, as in the grain offering."

Laws for Guilt Offerings

14 The LORD spoke to Moses, saying, **15** "If anyone commits a breach of faith and sins unintentionally in any of the holy things of the LORD, he shall bring to the LORD as his compensation, a ram without blemish out of the flock, valued[2] in silver shekels,[3] according to the shekel of the sanctuary, for a guilt offering. **16** He shall also make restitution for what he has done amiss in the holy thing and shall add a fifth to it and give it to the priest. And the priest shall make atonement for him with the ram of the guilt offering, and he shall be forgiven.

17 "If anyone sins, doing any of the things that by the LORD's commandments ought not to be done, though he did not know it, then realizes his guilt, he shall bear his iniquity. **18** He shall bring to the priest a ram without blemish out of the flock, or its equivalent for a guilt offering, and the priest shall make atonement for him for the mistake that he made unintentionally, and he shall be forgiven. **19** It is a guilt offering; he has indeed incurred guilt before[4] the LORD."

6 [5] The LORD spoke to Moses, saying, **2** "If anyone sins and commits a breach of faith against the LORD by deceiving his neighbor in a matter of deposit or security, or through robbery, or if he has oppressed his neighbor **3** or has found something lost and lied about it, swearing falsely—in any of all the things that people do and sin thereby— **4** if he has sinned and has realized his guilt and will restore what he took by robbery or what he got by oppression or the deposit that was committed to him or the lost thing that he found **5** or anything about which he has sworn falsely, he shall restore it in full and shall add a fifth to it, and give it to him to whom it belongs on the day he realizes his guilt. **6** And he shall bring to the priest as his compensation to the LORD a ram without blemish out of the flock, or its equivalent for a guilt offering. **7** And the priest shall make atonement for him before the LORD, and he shall be forgiven for any of the things that one may do and thereby become guilty."

The Priests and the Offerings

8 [6] The LORD spoke to Moses, saying, **9** "Command Aaron and his sons, saying, This is the law of the burnt offering. The burnt offering shall be on the hearth on the altar all night until the morning, and the fire of the altar shall be kept burning on it. **10** And the priest shall put on his linen garment and put his linen undergarment on his body, and he shall take up the ashes to which the fire has reduced the burnt offering on the altar and put them beside the altar. **11** Then he shall take off his garments and put on other garments and carry the ashes outside the camp to a clean place. **12** The fire on the altar shall be kept burning on it; it shall not go out. The priest shall burn wood on it every morning, and he shall arrange the burnt offering on it and shall burn on it the fat of the peace offerings. **13** Fire shall be kept burning on the altar continually; it shall not go out.

14 "And this is the law of the grain offering. The sons of Aaron shall offer it before the LORD in front of the altar. **15** And one shall take from it a handful of the fine flour of the grain offering and its oil and all the frankincense that is on the grain

[1] Septuagint; Hebrew *it* [2] Or *flock, or its equivalent* [3] A *shekel* was about 2/5 ounce or 11 grams [4] Or *he has paid full compensation to* [5] Ch 5:20 in Hebrew
[6] Ch 6:1 in Hebrew

offering and burn this as its memorial portion on the altar, a pleasing aroma to the LORD. 16 And the rest of it Aaron and his sons shall eat. It shall be eaten unleavened in a holy place. In the court of the tent of meeting they shall eat it. 17 It shall not be baked with leaven. I have given it as their portion of my food offerings. It is a thing most holy, like the sin offering and the guilt offering. 18 Every male among the children of Aaron may eat of it, as decreed forever throughout your generations, from the LORD's food offerings. Whatever touches them shall become holy."

19 The LORD spoke to Moses, saying, 20 "This is the offering that Aaron and his sons shall offer to the LORD on the day when he is anointed: a tenth of an ephah[1] of fine flour as a regular grain offering, half of it in the morning and half in the evening. 21 It shall be made with oil on a griddle. You shall bring it well mixed, in baked[2] pieces like a grain offering, and offer it for a pleasing aroma to the LORD. 22 The priest from among Aaron's sons, who is anointed to succeed him, shall offer it to the LORD as decreed forever. The whole of it shall be burned. 23 Every grain offering of a priest shall be wholly burned. It shall not be eaten."

24 The LORD spoke to Moses, saying, 25 "Speak to Aaron and his sons, saying, This is the law of the sin offering. In the place where the burnt offering is killed shall the sin offering be killed before the LORD; it is most holy. 26 The priest who offers it for sin shall eat it. In a holy place it shall be eaten, in the court of the tent of meeting. 27 Whatever touches its flesh shall be holy, and when any of its blood is splashed on a garment, you shall wash that on which it was splashed in a holy place. 28 And the earthenware vessel in which it is boiled shall be broken. But if it is boiled in a bronze vessel, that shall be scoured and rinsed in water. 29 Every male among the priests may eat of it; it is most holy. 30 But no sin offering shall be eaten from which any blood is brought into the tent of meeting to make atonement in the Holy Place; it shall be burned up with fire.

7 "This is the law of the guilt offering. It is most holy. 2 In the place where they kill the burnt offering they shall kill the guilt offering, and its blood shall be thrown against the sides of the altar. 3 And all its fat shall be offered, the fat tail, the fat that covers the entrails, 4 the two kidneys with the fat that is on them at the loins, and the long lobe of the liver that he shall remove with the kidneys. 5 The priest shall burn them on the altar as a food offering to the LORD; it is a guilt offering. 6 Every male among the priests may eat of it. It shall be eaten in a holy place. It is most holy. 7 The guilt offering is just like the sin offering; there is one law for them. The priest who makes atonement with it shall have it. 8 And the priest who offers any man's burnt offering shall have for himself the skin of the burnt offering that he has offered. 9 And every grain offering baked in the oven and all that is prepared on a pan or a griddle shall belong to the priest who offers it. 10 And every grain offering, mixed with oil or dry, shall be shared equally among all the sons of Aaron.

11 "And this is the law of the sacrifice of peace offerings that one may offer to the LORD. 12 If he offers it for a thanksgiving, then he shall offer with the thanksgiving sacrifice unleavened loaves mixed with oil, unleavened wafers smeared with oil, and loaves of fine flour well mixed with oil. 13 With the sacrifice of his peace offerings for thanksgiving he shall bring his offering with loaves of leavened bread. 14 And from it he shall offer one loaf from each offering, as a gift to the LORD. It shall belong to the priest who throws the blood of the peace offerings. 15 And the flesh of the sacrifice of his peace offerings for thanksgiving shall be eaten on the day of

[1] An *ephah* was about 3/5 bushel or 22 liters [2] The meaning of the Hebrew is uncertain

his offering. He shall not leave any of it
until the morning. 16 But if the sacrifice of
his offering is a vow offering or a freewill
offering, it shall be eaten on the day that
he offers his sacrifice, and on the next day
what remains of it shall be eaten. 17 But
what remains of the flesh of the sacrifice
on the third day shall be burned up with
fire. 18 If any of the flesh of the sacrifice
of his peace offering is eaten on the third
day, he who offers it shall not be accepted,
neither shall it be credited to him. It is
tainted, and he who eats of it shall bear
his iniquity.

19 "Flesh that touches any unclean thing
shall not be eaten. It shall be burned up
with fire. All who are clean may eat flesh,
20 but the person who eats of the flesh of
the sacrifice of the LORD's peace offer-
ings while an uncleanness is on him, that
person shall be cut off from his people.
21 And if anyone touches an unclean
thing, whether human uncleanness or an
unclean beast or any unclean detestable
creature, and then eats some flesh from
the sacrifice of the LORD's peace offer-
ings, that person shall be cut off from his
people."

22 The LORD spoke to Moses, saying,
23 "Speak to the people of Israel, saying,
You shall eat no fat, of ox or sheep or goat.
24 The fat of an animal that dies of itself
and the fat of one that is torn by beasts
may be put to any other use, but on no
account shall you eat it. 25 For every per-
son who eats of the fat of an animal of
which a food offering may be made to
the LORD shall be cut off from his people.
26 Moreover, you shall eat no blood what-
ever, whether of fowl or of animal, in any
of your dwelling places. 27 Whoever eats
any blood, that person shall be cut off
from his people."

28 The LORD spoke to Moses, saying,
29 "Speak to the people of Israel, saying,
Whoever offers the sacrifice of his peace
offerings to the LORD shall bring his offer-
ing to the LORD from the sacrifice of his
peace offerings. 30 His own hands shall
bring the LORD's food offerings. He shall
bring the fat with the breast, that the
breast may be waved as a wave offering
before the LORD. 31 The priest shall burn
the fat on the altar, but the breast shall be
for Aaron and his sons. 32 And the right
thigh you shall give to the priest as a con-
tribution from the sacrifice of your peace
offerings. 33 Whoever among the sons
of Aaron offers the blood of the peace
offerings and the fat shall have the right
thigh for a portion. 34 For the breast that is
waved and the thigh that is contributed I
have taken from the people of Israel, out
of the sacrifices of their peace offerings,
and have given them to Aaron the priest
and to his sons, as a perpetual due from
the people of Israel. 35 This is the portion
of Aaron and of his sons from the LORD's
food offerings, from the day they were
presented to serve as priests of the LORD.
36 The LORD commanded this to be given
them by the people of Israel, from the day
that he anointed them. It is a perpetual
due throughout their generations."

37 This is the law of the burnt offering,
of the grain offering, of the sin offering, of
the guilt offering, of the ordination offer-
ing, and of the peace offering, 38 which
the LORD commanded Moses on Mount
Sinai, on the day that he commanded the
people of Israel to bring their offerings to
the LORD, in the wilderness of Sinai.

Consecration of Aaron and His Sons

8 The LORD spoke to Moses, saying,
2 "Take Aaron and his sons with him,
and the garments and the anointing oil
and the bull of the sin offering and the
two rams and the basket of unleavened
bread. 3 And assemble all the congregation
at the entrance of the tent of meeting."
4 And Moses did as the LORD commanded
him, and the congregation was assembled
at the entrance of the tent of meeting.

5 And Moses said to the congregation,
"This is the thing that the LORD has com-
manded to be done." 6 And Moses brought
Aaron and his sons and washed them with
water. 7 And he put the coat on him and
tied the sash around his waist and clothed
him with the robe and put the ephod on
him and tied the skillfully woven band of
the ephod around him, binding it to him
with the band.[1] 8 And he placed the breast-
piece on him, and in the breastpiece he
put the Urim and the Thummim. 9 And
he set the turban on his head, and on the
turban, in front, he set the golden plate,
the holy crown, as the LORD commanded
Moses.

10 Then Moses took the anointing oil
and anointed the tabernacle and all that
was in it, and consecrated them. 11 And
he sprinkled some of it on the altar seven
times, and anointed the altar and all its
utensils and the basin and its stand, to
consecrate them. 12 And he poured some
of the anointing oil on Aaron's head and
anointed him to consecrate him. 13 And
Moses brought Aaron's sons and clothed
them with coats and tied sashes around
their waists and bound caps on them, as
the LORD commanded Moses.

14 Then he brought the bull of the sin
offering, and Aaron and his sons laid their
hands on the head of the bull of the sin
offering. 15 And he[2] killed it, and Moses
took the blood, and with his finger put
it on the horns of the altar around it and
purified the altar and poured out the
blood at the base of the altar and conse-
crated it to make atonement for it. 16 And
he took all the fat that was on the entrails
and the long lobe of the liver and the two
kidneys with their fat, and Moses burned
them on the altar. 17 But the bull and its
skin and its flesh and its dung he burned
up with fire outside the camp, as the LORD
commanded Moses.

18 Then he presented the ram of the
burnt offering, and Aaron and his sons
laid their hands on the head of the ram.
19 And he killed it, and Moses threw the
blood against the sides of the altar. 20 He
cut the ram into pieces, and Moses burned
the head and the pieces and the fat. 21 He
washed the entrails and the legs with
water, and Moses burned the whole ram
on the altar. It was a burnt offering with
a pleasing aroma, a food offering for the
LORD, as the LORD commanded Moses.

22 Then he presented the other ram,
the ram of ordination, and Aaron and his
sons laid their hands on the head of the
ram. 23 And he killed it, and Moses took
some of its blood and put it on the lobe of
Aaron's right ear and on the thumb of his
right hand and on the big toe of his right
foot. 24 Then he presented Aaron's sons,
and Moses put some of the blood on the
lobes of their right ears and on the thumbs
of their right hands and on the big toes
of their right feet. And Moses threw the
blood against the sides of the altar. 25 Then
he took the fat and the fat tail and all the
fat that was on the entrails and the long
lobe of the liver and the two kidneys with
their fat and the right thigh, 26 and out of
the basket of unleavened bread that was
before the LORD he took one unleavened
loaf and one loaf of bread with oil and one
wafer and placed them on the pieces of
fat and on the right thigh. 27 And he put
all these in the hands of Aaron and in the
hands of his sons and waved them as a
wave offering before the LORD. 28 Then
Moses took them from their hands and
burned them on the altar with the burnt
offering. This was an ordination offering
with a pleasing aroma, a food offering to
the LORD. 29 And Moses took the breast
and waved it for a wave offering before
the LORD. It was Moses' portion of the ram
of ordination, as the LORD commanded
Moses.

30 Then Moses took some of the anoint-
ing oil and of the blood that was on the
altar and sprinkled it on Aaron and his

[1] Hebrew *with it* [2] Probably Aaron or his representative; possibly Moses; also verses 16-23

garments, and also on his sons and his
sons' garments. So he consecrated Aaron
and his garments, and his sons and his
sons' garments with him.
31 And Moses said to Aaron and his
sons, "Boil the flesh at the entrance of
the tent of meeting, and there eat it and
the bread that is in the basket of ordina-
tion offerings, as I commanded, saying,
'Aaron and his sons shall eat it.' 32 And
what remains of the flesh and the bread
you shall burn up with fire. 33 And you
shall not go outside the entrance of the
tent of meeting for seven days, until the
days of your ordination are completed, for
it will take seven days to ordain you. 34 As
has been done today, the LORD has com-
manded to be done to make atonement
for you. 35 At the entrance of the tent of
meeting you shall remain day and night
for seven days, performing what the LORD
has charged, so that you do not die, for so I
have been commanded." 36 And Aaron and
his sons did all the things that the LORD
commanded by Moses.

The LORD Accepts Aaron's Offering

9 On the eighth day Moses called Aaron
and his sons and the elders of Israel,
2 and he said to Aaron, "Take for yourself a
bull calf for a sin offering and a ram for a
burnt offering, both without blemish, and
offer them before the LORD. 3 And say to
the people of Israel, 'Take a male goat for
a sin offering, and a calf and a lamb, both
a year old without blemish, for a burnt
offering, 4 and an ox and a ram for peace
offerings, to sacrifice before the LORD,
and a grain offering mixed with oil, for
today the LORD will appear to you.'" 5 And
they brought what Moses commanded in
front of the tent of meeting, and all the
congregation drew near and stood before
the LORD. 6 And Moses said, "This is the
thing that the LORD commanded you to
do, that the glory of the LORD may appear
to you." 7 Then Moses said to Aaron, "Draw
near to the altar and offer your sin offering
and your burnt offering and make atone-
ment for yourself and for the people, and
bring the offering of the people and make
atonement for them, as the LORD has
commanded."
8 So Aaron drew near to the altar and
killed the calf of the sin offering, which
was for himself. 9 And the sons of Aaron
presented the blood to him, and he dipped
his finger in the blood and put it on the
horns of the altar and poured out the
blood at the base of the altar. 10 But the fat
and the kidneys and the long lobe of the
liver from the sin offering he burned on
the altar, as the LORD commanded Moses.
11 The flesh and the skin he burned up
with fire outside the camp.
12 Then he killed the burnt offering,
and Aaron's sons handed him the blood,
and he threw it against the sides of the
altar. 13 And they handed the burnt offer-
ing to him, piece by piece, and the head,
and he burned them on the altar. 14 And
he washed the entrails and the legs and
burned them with the burnt offering on
the altar.
15 Then he presented the people's offer-
ing and took the goat of the sin offering
that was for the people and killed it and
offered it as a sin offering, like the first
one. 16 And he presented the burnt offer-
ing and offered it according to the rule.
17 And he presented the grain offering,
took a handful of it, and burned it on the
altar, besides the burnt offering of the
morning.
18 Then he killed the ox and the ram,
the sacrifice of peace offerings for the
people. And Aaron's sons handed him the
blood, and he threw it against the sides of
the altar. 19 But the fat pieces of the ox and
of the ram, the fat tail and that which cov-
ers the entrails and the kidneys and the
long lobe of the liver— 20 they put the fat
pieces on the breasts, and he burned the
fat pieces on the altar, 21 but the breasts

and the right thigh Aaron waved for a wave offering before the LORD, as Moses commanded.

22 Then Aaron lifted up his hands toward the people and blessed them, and he came down from offering the sin offering and the burnt offering and the peace offerings. 23 And Moses and Aaron went into the tent of meeting, and when they came out they blessed the people, and the glory of the LORD appeared to all the people. 24 And fire came out from before the LORD and consumed the burnt offering and the pieces of fat on the altar, and when all the people saw it, they shouted and fell on their faces.

The Death of Nadab and Abihu

10 Now Nadab and Abihu, the sons of Aaron, each took his censer and put fire in it and laid incense on it and offered unauthorized[1] fire before the LORD, which he had not commanded them. 2 And fire came out from before the LORD and consumed them, and they died before the LORD. 3 Then Moses said to Aaron, "This is what the LORD has said, 'Among those who are near me I will be sanctified, and before all the people I will be glorified.'" And Aaron held his peace.

4 And Moses called Mishael and Elzaphan, the sons of Uzziel the uncle of Aaron, and said to them, "Come near; carry your brothers away from the front of the sanctuary and out of the camp." 5 So they came near and carried them in their coats out of the camp, as Moses had said. 6 And Moses said to Aaron and to Eleazar and Ithamar his sons, "Do not let the hair of your heads hang loose, and do not tear your clothes, lest you die, and wrath come upon all the congregation; but let your brothers, the whole house of Israel, bewail the burning that the LORD has kindled. 7 And do not go outside the entrance of the tent of meeting, lest you die, for the anointing oil of the LORD is upon you." And they did according to the word of Moses.

8 And the LORD spoke to Aaron, saying, 9 "Drink no wine or strong drink, you or your sons with you, when you go into the tent of meeting, lest you die. It shall be a statute forever throughout your generations. 10 You are to distinguish between the holy and the common, and between the unclean and the clean, 11 and you are to teach the people of Israel all the statutes that the LORD has spoken to them by Moses."

12 Moses spoke to Aaron and to Eleazar and Ithamar, his surviving sons: "Take the grain offering that is left of the LORD's food offerings, and eat it unleavened beside the altar, for it is most holy. 13 You shall eat it in a holy place, because it is your due and your sons' due, from the LORD's food offerings, for so I am commanded. 14 But the breast that is waved and the thigh that is contributed you shall eat in a clean place, you and your sons and your daughters with you, for they are given as your due and your sons' due from the sacrifices of the peace offerings of the people of Israel. 15 The thigh that is contributed and the breast that is waved they shall bring with the food offerings of the fat pieces to wave for a wave offering before the LORD, and it shall be yours and your sons' with you as a due forever, as the LORD has commanded."

16 Now Moses diligently inquired about the goat of the sin offering, and behold, it was burned up! And he was angry with Eleazar and Ithamar, the surviving sons of Aaron, saying, 17 "Why have you not eaten the sin offering in the place of the sanctuary, since it is a thing most holy and has been given to you that you may bear the iniquity of the congregation, to make atonement for them before the LORD? 18 Behold, its blood was not brought into the inner part of the sanctuary. You certainly ought to have eaten it

[1] Or *strange*

in the sanctuary, as I commanded." 19 And Aaron said to Moses, "Behold, today they have offered their sin offering and their burnt offering before the LORD, and yet such things as these have happened to me! If I had eaten the sin offering today, would the LORD have approved?" 20 And when Moses heard that, he approved.

Clean and Unclean Animals

11 And the LORD spoke to Moses and Aaron, saying to them, 2 "Speak to the people of Israel, saying, These are the living things that you may eat among all the animals that are on the earth. 3 Whatever parts the hoof and is cloven-footed and chews the cud, among the animals, you may eat. 4 Nevertheless, among those that chew the cud or part the hoof, you shall not eat these: The camel, because it chews the cud but does not part the hoof, is unclean to you. 5 And the rock badger, because it chews the cud but does not part the hoof, is unclean to you. 6 And the hare, because it chews the cud but does not part the hoof, is unclean to you. 7 And the pig, because it parts the hoof and is cloven-footed but does not chew the cud, is unclean to you. 8 You shall not eat any of their flesh, and you shall not touch their carcasses; they are unclean to you.

9 "These you may eat, of all that are in the waters. Everything in the waters that has fins and scales, whether in the seas or in the rivers, you may eat. 10 But anything in the seas or the rivers that has not fins and scales, of the swarming creatures in the waters and of the living creatures that are in the waters, is detestable to you. 11 You shall regard them as detestable; you shall not eat any of their flesh, and you shall detest their carcasses. 12 Everything in the waters that has not fins and scales is detestable to you.

13 "And these you shall detest among the birds;[1] they shall not be eaten; they are detestable: the eagle,[2] the bearded vulture, the black vulture, 14 the kite, the falcon of any kind, 15 every raven of any kind, 16 the ostrich, the nighthawk, the sea gull, the hawk of any kind, 17 the little owl, the cormorant, the short-eared owl, 18 the barn owl, the tawny owl, the carrion vulture, 19 the stork, the heron of any kind, the hoopoe, and the bat.

20 "All winged insects that go on all fours are detestable to you. 21 Yet among the winged insects that go on all fours you may eat those that have jointed legs above their feet, with which to hop on the ground. 22 Of them you may eat: the locust of any kind, the bald locust of any kind, the cricket of any kind, and the grasshopper of any kind. 23 But all other winged insects that have four feet are detestable to you.

24 "And by these you shall become unclean. Whoever touches their carcass shall be unclean until the evening, 25 and whoever carries any part of their carcass shall wash his clothes and be unclean until the evening. 26 Every animal that parts the hoof but is not cloven-footed or does not chew the cud is unclean to you. Everyone who touches them shall be unclean. 27 And all that walk on their paws, among the animals that go on all fours, are unclean to you. Whoever touches their carcass shall be unclean until the evening, 28 and he who carries their carcass shall wash his clothes and be unclean until the evening; they are unclean to you.

29 "And these are unclean to you among the swarming things that swarm on the ground: the mole rat, the mouse, the great lizard of any kind, 30 the gecko, the monitor lizard, the lizard, the sand lizard, and the chameleon. 31 These are unclean to you among all that swarm. Whoever touches them when they are dead shall be unclean until the evening. 32 And anything on which any of them falls when they are dead shall be unclean, whether it is an article of wood or a garment or a skin

[1] Or *things that fly*; compare Genesis 1:20 [2] The identity of many of these birds is uncertain

or a sack, any article that is used for any purpose. It must be put into water, and it shall be unclean until the evening; then it shall be clean. 33 And if any of them falls into any earthenware vessel, all that is in it shall be unclean, and you shall break it. 34 Any food in it that could be eaten, on which water comes, shall be unclean. And all drink that could be drunk from every such vessel shall be unclean. 35 And everything on which any part of their carcass falls shall be unclean. Whether oven or stove, it shall be broken in pieces. They are unclean and shall remain unclean for you. 36 Nevertheless, a spring or a cistern holding water shall be clean, but whoever touches a carcass in them shall be unclean. 37 And if any part of their carcass falls upon any seed grain that is to be sown, it is clean, 38 but if water is put on the seed and any part of their carcass falls on it, it is unclean to you.

39 "And if any animal which you may eat dies, whoever touches its carcass shall be unclean until the evening, 40 and whoever eats of its carcass shall wash his clothes and be unclean until the evening. And whoever carries the carcass shall wash his clothes and be unclean until the evening.

41 "Every swarming thing that swarms on the ground is detestable; it shall not be eaten. 42 Whatever goes on its belly, and whatever goes on all fours, or whatever has many feet, any swarming thing that swarms on the ground, you shall not eat, for they are detestable. 43 You shall not make yourselves detestable with any swarming thing that swarms, and you shall not defile yourselves with them, and become unclean through them. 44 For I am the LORD your God. Consecrate yourselves therefore, and be holy, for I am holy. You shall not defile yourselves with any swarming thing that crawls on the ground. 45 For I am the LORD who brought you up out of the land of Egypt to be your God. You shall therefore be holy, for I am holy."

46 This is the law about beast and bird and every living creature that moves through the waters and every creature that swarms on the ground, 47 to make a distinction between the unclean and the clean and between the living creature that may be eaten and the living creature that may not be eaten.

Purification After Childbirth

12 The LORD spoke to Moses, saying, 2 "Speak to the people of Israel, saying, 'If a woman conceives and bears a male child, then she shall be unclean seven days. As at the time of her menstruation, she shall be unclean. 3 And on the eighth day the flesh of his foreskin shall be circumcised. 4 Then she shall continue for thirty-three days in the blood of her purifying. She shall not touch anything holy, nor come into the sanctuary, until the days of her purifying are completed. 5 But if she bears a female child, then she shall be unclean two weeks, as in her menstruation. And she shall continue in the blood of her purifying for sixty-six days.

6 "'And when the days of her purifying are completed, whether for a son or for a daughter, she shall bring to the priest at the entrance of the tent of meeting a lamb a year old for a burnt offering, and a pigeon or a turtledove for a sin offering, 7 and he shall offer it before the LORD and make atonement for her. Then she shall be clean from the flow of her blood. This is the law for her who bears a child, either male or female. 8 And if she cannot afford a lamb, then she shall take two turtledoves or two pigeons,[1] one for a burnt offering and the other for a sin offering. And the priest shall make atonement for her, and she shall be clean.'"

Laws About Leprosy

13 The LORD spoke to Moses and Aaron, saying, 2 "When a person has on the skin of his body a swelling or an eruption or a spot, and it turns into

[1] Septuagint *two young pigeons*

a case of leprous[1] disease on the skin of his body, then he shall be brought to Aaron the priest or to one of his sons the priests, 3 and the priest shall examine the diseased area on the skin of his body. And if the hair in the diseased area has turned white and the disease appears to be deeper than the skin of his body, it is a case of leprous disease. When the priest has examined him, he shall pronounce him unclean. 4 But if the spot is white in the skin of his body and appears no deeper than the skin, and the hair in it has not turned white, the priest shall shut up the diseased person for seven days. 5 And the priest shall examine him on the seventh day, and if in his eyes the disease is checked and the disease has not spread in the skin, then the priest shall shut him up for another seven days. 6 And the priest shall examine him again on the seventh day, and if the diseased area has faded and the disease has not spread in the skin, then the priest shall pronounce him clean; it is only an eruption. And he shall wash his clothes and be clean. 7 But if the eruption spreads in the skin, after he has shown himself to the priest for his cleansing, he shall appear again before the priest. 8 And the priest shall look, and if the eruption has spread in the skin, then the priest shall pronounce him unclean; it is a leprous disease.

9 "When a man is afflicted with a leprous disease, he shall be brought to the priest, 10 and the priest shall look. And if there is a white swelling in the skin that has turned the hair white, and there is raw flesh in the swelling, 11 it is a chronic leprous disease in the skin of his body, and the priest shall pronounce him unclean. He shall not shut him up, for he is unclean. 12 And if the leprous disease breaks out in the skin, so that the leprous disease covers all the skin of the diseased person from head to foot, so far as the priest can see, 13 then the priest shall look, and if the leprous disease has covered all his body, he shall pronounce him clean of the disease; it has all turned white, and he is clean. 14 But when raw flesh appears on him, he shall be unclean. 15 And the priest
shall examine the raw flesh and
pronounce him unclean. Raw flesh
1507 is unclean, for it is a leprous dis-
ease. 16 But if the raw flesh recovers and turns white again, then he shall come to the priest, 17 and the priest shall examine him, and if the disease has turned white, then the priest shall pronounce the diseased person clean; he is clean.

18 "If there is in the skin of one's body a boil and it heals, 19 and in the place of the boil there comes a white swelling or a reddish-white spot, then it shall be shown to the priest. 20 And the priest shall look, and if it appears deeper than the skin and its hair has turned white, then the priest shall pronounce him unclean. It is a case of leprous disease that has broken out in the boil. 21 But if the priest examines it and there is no white hair in it and it is not deeper than the skin, but has faded, then the priest shall shut him up seven days. 22 And if it spreads in the skin, then the priest shall pronounce him unclean; it is a disease. 23 But if the spot remains in one place and does not spread, it is the scar of the boil, and the priest shall pronounce him clean.

24 "Or, when the body has a burn on its skin and the raw flesh of the burn becomes a spot, reddish-white or white, 25 the priest shall examine it, and if the hair in the spot has turned white and it appears deeper than the skin, then it is a leprous disease. It has broken out in the burn, and the priest shall pronounce him unclean; it is a case of leprous disease. 26 But if the priest examines it and there is no white hair in the spot and it is no deeper than the skin, but has faded, the priest shall shut him up seven days, 27 and the priest shall examine him the seventh day. If it is spreading in

[1] *Leprosy* was a term for several skin diseases

the skin, then the priest shall pronounce him unclean; it is a case of leprous disease. 28 But if the spot remains in one place and does not spread in the skin, but has faded, it is a swelling from the burn, and the priest shall pronounce him clean, for it is the scar of the burn.

29 "When a man or woman has a disease on the head or the beard, 30 the priest shall examine the disease. And if it appears deeper than the skin, and the hair in it is yellow and thin, then the priest shall pronounce him unclean. It is an itch, a leprous disease of the head or the beard. 31 And if the priest examines the itching disease and it appears no deeper than the skin and there is no black hair in it, then the priest shall shut up the person with the itching disease for seven days, 32 and on the seventh day the priest shall examine the disease. If the itch has not spread, and there is in it no yellow hair, and the itch appears to be no deeper than the skin, 33 then he shall shave himself, but the itch he shall not shave; and the priest shall shut up the person with the itching disease for another seven days. 34 And on the seventh day the priest shall examine the itch, and if the itch has not spread in the skin and it appears to be no deeper than the skin, then the priest shall pronounce him clean. And he shall wash his clothes and be clean. 35 But if the itch spreads in the skin after his cleansing, 36 then the priest shall examine him, and if the itch has spread in the skin, the priest need not seek for the yellow hair; he is unclean. 37 But if in his eyes the itch is unchanged and black hair has grown in it, the itch is healed and he is clean, and the priest shall pronounce him clean.

38 "When a man or a woman has spots on the skin of the body, white spots, 39 the priest shall look, and if the spots on the skin of the body are of a dull white, it is leukoderma that has broken out in the skin; he is clean.

40 "If a man's hair falls out from his head, he is bald; he is clean. 41 And if a man's hair falls out from his forehead, he has baldness of the forehead; he is clean. 42 But if there is on the bald head or the bald forehead a reddish-white diseased area, it is a leprous disease breaking out on his bald head or his bald forehead. 43 Then the priest shall examine him, and if the diseased swelling is reddish-white on his bald head or on his bald forehead, like the appearance of leprous disease in the skin of the body, 44 he is a leprous man, he is unclean. The priest must pronounce him unclean; his disease is on his head.

1507 45 "The leprous person who has the disease shall wear torn clothes and let the hair of his head hang loose, and he shall cover his upper lip[1] and cry out, 'Unclean, unclean.' 46 He shall remain unclean as long as he has the disease. He is unclean. He shall live alone. His dwelling shall be outside the camp.

47 "When there is a case of leprous disease in a garment, whether a woolen or a linen garment, 48 in warp or woof of linen or wool, or in a skin or in anything made of skin, 49 if the disease is greenish or reddish in the garment, or in the skin or in the warp or the woof or in any article made of skin, it is a case of leprous disease, and it shall be shown to the priest. 50 And the priest shall examine the disease and shut up that which has the disease for seven days. 51 Then he shall examine the disease on the seventh day. If the disease has spread in the garment, in the warp or the woof, or in the skin, whatever be the use of the skin, the disease is a persistent leprous disease; it is unclean. 52 And he shall burn the garment, or the warp or the woof, the wool or the linen, or any article made of skin that is diseased, for it is a persistent leprous disease. It shall be burned in the fire.

53 "And if the priest examines, and if the disease has not spread in the garment,

[1] Or *mustache*

in the warp or the woof or in any article made of skin, 54 then the priest shall command that they wash the thing in which is the disease, and he shall shut it up for another seven days. 55 And the priest shall examine the diseased thing after it has been washed. And if the appearance of the diseased area has not changed, though the disease has not spread, it is unclean. You shall burn it in the fire, whether the rot is on the back or on the front.

56 "But if the priest examines, and if the diseased area has faded after it has been washed, he shall tear it out of the garment or the skin or the warp or the woof. 57 Then if it appears again in the garment, in the warp or the woof, or in any article made of skin, it is spreading. You shall burn with fire whatever has the disease. 58 But the garment, or the warp or the woof, or any article made of skin from which the disease departs when you have washed it, shall then be washed a second time, and be clean."

59 This is the law for a case of leprous disease in a garment of wool or linen, either in the warp or the woof, or in any article made of skin, to determine whether it is clean or unclean.

Laws for Cleansing Lepers

14 The LORD spoke to Moses, saying, 2 "This shall be the law of the leprous person for the day of his cleansing. He shall be brought to the priest, 3 and the priest shall go out of the camp, and the priest shall look. Then, if the case of leprous disease is healed in the leprous person, 4 the priest shall command them to take for him who is to be cleansed two live[1] clean birds and cedarwood and scarlet yarn and hyssop. 5 And the priest shall command them to kill one of the birds in an earthenware vessel over fresh[2] water. 6 He shall take the live bird with the cedarwood and the scarlet yarn and the hyssop, and dip them and the live bird in the blood of the bird that was killed over the fresh water. 7 And he shall sprinkle it seven times on him who is to be cleansed of the leprous disease. Then he shall pronounce him clean and shall let the living bird go into the open field. 8 And he who is to be cleansed shall wash his clothes and shave off all his hair and bathe himself in water, and he shall be clean. And after that he may come into the camp, but live outside his tent seven days. 9 And on the seventh day he shall shave off all his hair from his head, his beard, and his eyebrows. He shall shave off all his hair, and then he shall wash his clothes and bathe his body in water, and he shall be clean.

10 "And on the eighth day he shall take two male lambs without blemish, and one ewe lamb a year old without blemish, and a grain offering of three tenths of an ephah[3] of fine flour mixed with oil, and one log[4] of oil. 11 And the priest who cleanses him shall set the man who is to be cleansed and these things before the LORD, at the entrance of the tent of meeting. 12 And the priest shall take one of the male lambs and offer it for a guilt offering, along with the log of oil, and wave them for a wave offering before the LORD. 13 And he shall kill the lamb in the place where they kill the sin offering and the burnt offering, in the place of the sanctuary. For the guilt offering, like the sin offering, belongs to the priest; it is most holy. 14 The priest shall take some of the blood of the guilt offering, and the priest shall put it on the lobe of the right ear of him who is to be cleansed and on the thumb of his right hand and on the big toe of his right foot. 15 Then the priest shall take some of the log of oil and pour it into the palm of his own left hand 16 and dip his right finger in the oil that is in his left hand and sprinkle some oil with his finger seven times before the LORD. 17 And some of the oil that remains in his

[1] Or *wild* [2] Or *running;* Hebrew *living;* also verses 6, 50, 51, 52 [3] An *ephah* was about 3/5 bushel or 22 liters [4] A *log* was about 1/3 quart or 0.3 liter

hand the priest shall put on the lobe of
the right ear of him who is to be cleansed
and on the thumb of his right hand and
on the big toe of his right foot, on top of
the blood of the guilt offering. 18 And the
rest of the oil that is in the priest's hand
he shall put on the head of him who is to
be cleansed. Then the priest shall make
atonement for him before the LORD.
19 The priest shall offer the sin offering,
to make atonement for him who is to
be cleansed from his uncleanness. And
afterward he shall kill the burnt offer-
ing. 20 And the priest shall offer the burnt
offering and the grain offering on the
altar. Thus the priest shall make atone-
ment for him, and he shall be clean.

21 "But if he is poor and cannot afford
so much, then he shall take one male
lamb for a guilt offering to be waved, to
make atonement for him, and a tenth of
an ephah of fine flour mixed with oil for a
grain offering, and a log of oil; 22 also two
turtledoves or two pigeons, whichever he
can afford. The one shall be a sin offering
and the other a burnt offering. 23 And on
the eighth day he shall bring them for his
cleansing to the priest, to the entrance
of the tent of meeting, before the LORD.
24 And the priest shall take the lamb of the
guilt offering and the log of oil, and the
priest shall wave them for a wave offering
before the LORD. 25 And he shall kill the
lamb of the guilt offering. And the priest
shall take some of the blood of the guilt
offering and put it on the lobe of the
right ear of him who is to be cleansed,
and on the thumb of his right hand and
on the big toe of his right foot. 26 And the
priest shall pour some of the oil into the
palm of his own left hand, 27 and shall
sprinkle with his right finger some of
the oil that is in his left hand seven times
before the LORD. 28 And the priest shall
put some of the oil that is in his hand
on the lobe of the right ear of him who
is to be cleansed and on the thumb of
his right hand and on the big toe of his
right foot, in the place where the blood
of the guilt offering was put. 29 And the
rest of the oil that is in the priest's hand
he shall put on the head of him who is
to be cleansed, to make atonement for
him before the LORD. 30 And he shall offer,
of the turtledoves or pigeons, whichever
he can afford, 31 one[1] for a sin offering
and the other for a burnt offering, along
with a grain offering. And the priest shall
make atonement before the LORD for him
who is being cleansed. 32 This is the law
for him in whom is a case of leprous dis-
ease, who cannot afford the offerings for
his cleansing."

Laws for Cleansing Houses

33 The LORD spoke to Moses and Aaron,
saying, 34 "When you come into the land
of Canaan, which I give you for a posses-
sion, and I put a case of leprous disease
in a house in the land of your possession,
35 then he who owns the house shall come
and tell the priest, 'There seems to me to
be some case of disease in my house.'
36 Then the priest shall command that
they empty the house before the priest
goes to examine the disease, lest all that
is in the house be declared unclean. And
afterward the priest shall go in to see the
house. 37 And he shall examine the dis-
ease. And if the disease is in the walls of
the house with greenish or reddish spots,
and if it appears to be deeper than the
surface, 38 then the priest shall go out of
the house to the door of the house and
shut up the house seven days. 39 And the
priest shall come again on the seventh
day, and look. If the disease has spread in
the walls of the house, 40 then the priest
shall command that they take out the
stones in which is the disease and throw
them into an unclean place outside the
city. 41 And he shall have the inside of the
house scraped all around, and the plaster
that they scrape off they shall pour out in

[1] Septuagint, Syriac; Hebrew *afford,* [31]*such as he can afford, one*

an unclean place outside the city. 42 Then they shall take other stones and put them in the place of those stones, and he shall take other plaster and plaster the house.

43 "If the disease breaks out again in the house, after he has taken out the stones and scraped the house and plastered it, 44 then the priest shall go and look. And if the disease has spread in the house, it is a persistent leprous disease in the house; it is unclean. 45 And he shall break down the house, its stones and timber and all the plaster of the house, and he shall carry them out of the city to an unclean place. 46 Moreover, whoever enters the house while it is shut up shall be unclean until the evening, 47 and whoever sleeps in the house shall wash his clothes, and whoever eats in the house shall wash his clothes.

48 "But if the priest comes and looks, and if the disease has not spread in the house after the house was plastered, then the priest shall pronounce the house clean, for the disease is healed. 49 And for the cleansing of the house he shall take two small birds, with cedarwood and scarlet yarn and hyssop, 50 and shall kill one of the birds in an earthenware vessel over fresh water 51 and shall take the cedarwood and the hyssop and the scarlet yarn, along with the live bird, and dip them in the blood of the bird that was killed and in the fresh water and sprinkle the house seven times. 52 Thus he shall cleanse the house with the blood of the bird and with the fresh water and with the live bird and with the cedarwood and hyssop and scarlet yarn. 53 And he shall let the live bird go out of the city into the open country. So he shall make atonement for the house, and it shall be clean."

54 This is the law for any case of leprous disease: for an itch, 55 for leprous disease in a garment or in a house, 56 and for a swelling or an eruption or a spot, 57 to show when it is unclean and when it is clean. This is the law for leprous disease.

Laws About Bodily Discharges

15 The LORD spoke to Moses and Aaron, saying, 2 "Speak to the people of Israel and say to them, When any man has a discharge from his body,[1] his discharge is unclean. 3 And this is the law of his uncleanness for a discharge: whether his body runs with his discharge, or his body is blocked up by his discharge, it is his uncleanness. 4 Every bed on which the one with the discharge lies shall be unclean, and everything on which he sits shall be unclean. 5 And anyone who touches his bed shall wash his clothes and bathe himself in water and be unclean until the evening. 6 And whoever sits on anything on which the one with the discharge has sat shall wash his clothes and bathe himself in water and be unclean until the evening. 7 And whoever touches the body of the one with the discharge shall wash his clothes and bathe himself in water and be unclean until the evening. 8 And if the one with the discharge spits on someone who is clean, then he shall wash his clothes and bathe himself in water and be unclean until the evening. 9 And any saddle on which the one with the discharge rides shall be unclean. 10 And whoever touches anything that was under him shall be unclean until the evening. And whoever carries such things shall wash his clothes and bathe himself in water and be unclean until the evening. 11 Anyone whom the one with the discharge touches without having rinsed his hands in water shall wash his clothes and bathe himself in water and be unclean until the evening. 12 And an earthenware vessel that the one with the discharge touches shall be broken, and every vessel of wood shall be rinsed in water.

13 "And when the one with a discharge is cleansed of his discharge, then he shall count for himself seven days for his cleansing, and wash his clothes. And he shall bathe his body in fresh water and

[1] Hebrew *flesh*; also verse 3

shall be clean. 14 And on the eighth day he shall take two turtledoves or two pigeons and come before the LORD to the entrance of the tent of meeting and give them to the priest. 15 And the priest shall use them, one for a sin offering and the other for a burnt offering. And the priest shall make atonement for him before the LORD for his discharge.

16 "If a man has an emission of semen, he shall bathe his whole body in water and be unclean until the evening. 17 And every garment and every skin on which the semen comes shall be washed with water and be unclean until the evening. 18 If a man lies with a woman and has an emission of semen, both of them shall bathe themselves in water and be unclean until the evening.

19 "When a woman has a discharge, and the discharge in her body is blood, she shall be in her menstrual impurity for seven days, and whoever touches her shall be unclean until the evening. 20 And everything on which she lies during her menstrual impurity shall be unclean. Everything also on which she sits shall be unclean. 21 And whoever touches her bed shall wash his clothes and bathe himself in water and be unclean until the evening. 22 And whoever touches anything on which she sits shall wash his clothes and bathe himself in water and be unclean until the evening. 23 Whether it is the bed or anything on which she sits, when he touches it he shall be unclean until the evening. 24 And if any man lies with her and her menstrual impurity comes upon him, he shall be unclean seven days, and every bed on which he lies shall be unclean.

25 "If a woman has a discharge of blood for many days, not at the time of her menstrual impurity, or if she has a discharge beyond the time of her impurity, all the days of the discharge she shall continue in uncleanness. As in the days of her impurity, she shall be unclean. 26 Every bed on which she lies, all the days of her discharge, shall be to her as the bed of her impurity. And everything on which she sits shall be unclean, as in the uncleanness of her menstrual impurity. 27 And whoever touches these things shall be unclean, and shall wash his clothes and bathe himself in water and be unclean until the evening. 28 But if she is cleansed of her discharge, she shall count for herself seven days, and after that she shall be clean. 29 And on the eighth day she shall take two turtledoves or two pigeons and bring them to the priest, to the entrance of the tent of meeting. 30 And the priest shall use one for a sin offering and the other for a burnt offering. And the priest shall make atonement for her before the LORD for her unclean discharge.

31 "Thus you shall keep the people of Israel separate from their uncleanness, lest they die in their uncleanness by defiling my tabernacle that is in their midst."

32 This is the law for him who has a discharge and for him who has an emission of semen, becoming unclean thereby; 33 also for her who is unwell with her menstrual impurity, that is, for anyone, male or female, who has a discharge, and for the man who lies with a woman who is unclean.

The Day of Atonement

16 The LORD spoke to Moses after the death of the two sons of Aaron, when they drew near before the LORD and died, 2 and the LORD said to Moses, "Tell Aaron your brother not to come at any time into the Holy Place inside the veil, before the mercy seat that is on the ark, so that he may not die. For I will appear in the cloud over the mercy seat. 3 But in this way Aaron shall come into the Holy Place: with a bull from the herd for a sin offering and a ram for a burnt offering. 4 He shall put on the holy linen coat and shall

have the linen undergarment on his body,
and he shall tie the linen sash around his
waist, and wear the linen turban; these
are the holy garments. He shall bathe his
body in water and then put them on. 5And
he shall take from the congregation of the
people of Israel two male goats for a sin
offering, and one ram for a burnt offering.

6"Aaron shall offer the bull as a sin
offering for himself and shall make atone-
ment for himself and for his house. 7Then
he shall take the two goats and set them
before the LORD at the entrance of the tent
of meeting. 8And Aaron shall cast lots over
the two goats, one lot for the LORD and
the other lot for Azazel.[1] 9And Aaron shall
present the goat on which the lot fell for
the LORD and use it as a sin offering, 10but
the goat on which the lot fell for Azazel
shall be presented alive before the LORD
to make atonement over it, that it may be
sent away into the wilderness to Azazel.

11"Aaron shall present the bull as a
sin offering for himself, and shall make
atonement for himself and for his house.
He shall kill the bull as a sin offering for
himself. 12And he shall take a censer full
of coals of fire from the altar before the
LORD, and two handfuls of sweet incense
beaten small, and he shall bring it inside
the veil 13and put the incense on the fire
before the LORD, that the cloud of the
incense may cover the mercy seat that is
over the testimony, so that he does not
die. 14And he shall take some of the blood
of the bull and sprinkle it with his finger
on the front of the mercy seat on the east
side, and in front of the mercy seat he
shall sprinkle some of the blood with his
finger seven times.

15"Then he shall kill the goat of the sin
offering that is for the people and bring its
blood inside the veil and do with its blood
as he did with the blood of the bull, sprin-
kling it over the mercy seat and in front
of the mercy seat. 16Thus he shall make
atonement for the Holy Place, because of
the uncleannesses of the people of Israel
and because of their transgressions, all
their sins. And so he shall do for the tent
of meeting, which dwells with them in
the midst of their uncleannesses. 17No
one may be in the tent of meeting from
the time he enters to make atonement in
the Holy Place until he comes out and has
made atonement for himself and for his
house and for all the assembly of Israel.
18Then he shall go out to the altar that is
before the LORD and make atonement for
it, and shall take some of the blood of the
bull and some of the blood of the goat, and
put it on the horns of the altar all around.
19And he shall sprinkle some of the
blood on it with his finger seven times,
and cleanse it and consecrate it from the
uncleannesses of the people of Israel.

20"And when he has made an end of
atoning for the Holy Place and the tent of
meeting and the altar, he shall present the
live goat. 21And Aaron shall lay both his
hands on the head of the live goat, and
confess over it all the iniquities of the
people of Israel, and all their transgres-
sions, all their sins. And he shall put them
on the head of the goat and send it away
into the wilderness by the hand of a man
who is in readiness. 22The goat shall bear
all their iniquities on itself to a remote
area, and he shall let the goat go free in
the wilderness.

23"Then Aaron shall come into the tent
of meeting and shall take off the linen gar-
ments that he put on when he went into
the Holy Place and shall leave them there.
24And he shall bathe his body in water
in a holy place and put on his garments
and come out and offer his burnt offering
and the burnt offering of the people and
make atonement for himself and for the
people. 25And the fat of the sin offering
he shall burn on the altar. 26And he who
lets the goat go to Azazel shall wash his
clothes and bathe his body in water, and
afterward he may come into the camp.

[1] The meaning of *Azazel* is uncertain; possibly the name of a place or a demon, traditionally a scapegoat; also verses 10, 26

27 And the bull for the sin offering and the goat for the sin offering, whose blood was brought in to make atonement in the Holy Place, shall be carried outside the camp. Their skin and their flesh and their dung shall be burned up with fire. 28 And he who burns them shall wash his clothes and bathe his body in water, and afterward he may come into the camp.

29 "And it shall be a statute to you forever that in the seventh month, on the tenth day of the month, you shall afflict yourselves[1] and shall do no work, either the native or the stranger who sojourns among you. 30 For on this day shall atonement be made for you to cleanse you. You shall be clean before the LORD from all your sins. 31 It is a Sabbath of solemn rest to you, and you shall afflict yourselves; it is a statute forever. 32 And the priest who is anointed and consecrated as priest in his father's place shall make atonement, wearing the holy linen garments. 33 He shall make atonement for the holy sanctuary, and he shall make atonement for the tent of meeting and for the altar, and he shall make atonement for the priests and for all the people of the assembly. 34 And this shall be a statute forever for you, that atonement may be made for the people of Israel once in the year because of all their sins." And Moses did as the LORD commanded him.

The Place of Sacrifice

17 And the LORD spoke to Moses, saying, 2 "Speak to Aaron and his sons and to all the people of Israel and say to them, This is the thing that the LORD has commanded. 3 If any one of the house of Israel kills an ox or a lamb or a goat in the camp, or kills it outside the camp, 4 and does not bring it to the entrance of the tent of meeting to offer it as a gift to the LORD in front of the tabernacle of the LORD, bloodguilt shall be imputed to that man. He has shed blood, and that man shall be cut off from among his people. 5 This is to the end that the people of Israel may bring their sacrifices that they sacrifice in the open field, that they may bring them to the LORD, to the priest at the entrance of the tent of meeting, and sacrifice them as sacrifices of peace offerings to the LORD. 6 And the priest shall throw the blood on the altar of the LORD at the entrance of the tent of meeting and burn the fat for a pleasing aroma to the LORD. 7 So they shall no more sacrifice their sacrifices to goat demons, after whom they whore. This shall be a statute forever for them throughout their generations.

8 "And you shall say to them, Any one of the house of Israel, or of the strangers who sojourn among them, who offers a burnt offering or sacrifice 9 and does not bring it to the entrance of the tent of meeting to offer it to the LORD, that man shall be cut off from his people.

Laws Against Eating Blood

10 "If any one of the house of Israel or of the strangers who sojourn among them eats any blood, I will set my face against that person who eats blood and will cut him off from among his people. 11 For the life of the flesh is in the blood, and I have given it for you on the altar to make atonement for your souls, for it is the blood that makes atonement by the life. 12 Therefore I have said to the people of Israel, No person among you shall eat blood, neither shall any stranger who sojourns among you eat blood.

13 "Any one also of the people of Israel, or of the strangers who sojourn among them, who takes in hunting any beast or bird that may be eaten shall pour out its blood and cover it with earth. 14 For the life of every creature[2] is its blood: its blood is its life.[3] Therefore I have said to the people of Israel, You shall not eat the blood of any creature, for the life of every creature is its blood. Whoever eats it shall be cut off.

1 Or *shall fast*; also verse 31 2 Hebrew *all flesh* 3 Hebrew *it is in its life*

15 And every person who eats what dies of
itself or what is torn by beasts, whether
he is a native or a sojourner, shall wash
his clothes and bathe himself in water
and be unclean until the evening; then he
shall be clean. 16 But if he does not wash
them or bathe his flesh, he shall bear his
iniquity."

Unlawful Sexual Relations

18 And the LORD spoke to Moses, say-
ing, 2 "Speak to the people of Israel
and say to them, I am the LORD your God.
3 You shall not do as they do in the land
of Egypt, where you lived, and you shall
not do as they do in the land of Canaan,
to which I am bringing you. You shall not
walk in their statutes. 4 You shall follow
my rules[1] and keep my statutes and walk
in them. I am the LORD your God. 5 You
shall therefore keep my statutes and my
rules; if a person does them, he shall live
by them: I am the LORD.

6 "None of you shall approach any one
of his close relatives to uncover naked-
ness. I am the LORD. 7 You shall not
uncover the nakedness of your father,
which is the nakedness of your mother;
she is your mother, you shall not uncover
her nakedness. 8 You shall not uncover
the nakedness of your father's wife; it is
your father's nakedness. 9 You shall not
uncover the nakedness of your sister, your
father's daughter or your mother's daugh-
ter, whether brought up in the family or
in another home. 10 You shall not uncover
the nakedness of your son's daughter
or of your daughter's daughter, for their
nakedness is your own nakedness. 11 You
shall not uncover the nakedness of your
father's wife's daughter, brought up in
your father's family, since she is your sis-
ter. 12 You shall not uncover the nakedness
of your father's sister; she is your father's
relative. 13 You shall not uncover the
nakedness of your mother's sister, for she
is your mother's relative. 14 You shall not
uncover the nakedness of your father's
brother, that is, you shall not approach
his wife; she is your aunt. 15 You shall not
uncover the nakedness of your daughter-
in-law; she is your son's wife, you shall
not uncover her nakedness. 16 You shall
not uncover the nakedness of your broth-
er's wife; it is your brother's nakedness.
17 You shall not uncover the nakedness
of a woman and of her daughter, and
you shall not take her son's daughter or
her daughter's daughter to uncover her
nakedness; they are relatives; it is deprav-
ity. 18 And you shall not take a woman as
a rival wife to her sister, uncovering her
nakedness while her sister is still alive.

19 "You shall not approach a woman to
uncover her nakedness while she is in her
menstrual uncleanness. 20 And you shall
not lie sexually with your neighbor's wife
and so make yourself unclean with her.
21 You shall not give any of your children
to offer them[2] to Molech, and so profane
the name of your God: I am the LORD.
22 You shall not lie with a male as with a
woman; it is an abomination. 23 And you
shall not lie with any animal and so make
yourself unclean with it, neither shall any
woman give herself to an animal to lie
with it: it is perversion.

24 "Do not make yourselves unclean by
any of these things, for by all these the
nations I am driving out before you have
become unclean, 25 and the land became
unclean, so that I punished its iniquity,
and the land vomited out its inhabitants.
26 But you shall keep my statutes and my
rules and do none of these abominations,
either the native or the stranger who
sojourns among you 27 (for the people
of the land, who were before you, did all
of these abominations, so that the land
became unclean), 28 lest the land vomit
you out when you make it unclean, as it
vomited out the nation that was before
you. 29 For everyone who does any of these
abominations, the persons who do them

[1] Or *my just decrees*; also verse 5 [2] Hebrew *to make them pass through* [the fire]

shall be cut off from among their people. 30 So keep my charge never to practice any of these abominable customs that were practiced before you, and never to make yourselves unclean by them: I am the LORD your God."

The LORD Is Holy

19 And the LORD spoke to Moses, saying, 2 "Speak to all the congregation of the people of Israel and say to them, You shall be holy, for I the LORD your God am holy. 3 Every one of you shall revere his mother and his father, and you shall keep my Sabbaths: I am the LORD your God. 4 Do not turn to idols or make for yourselves any gods of cast metal: I am the LORD your God.

5 "When you offer a sacrifice of peace offerings to the LORD, you shall offer it so that you may be accepted. 6 It shall be eaten the same day you offer it or on the day after, and anything left over until the third day shall be burned up with fire. 7 If it is eaten at all on the third day, it is tainted; it will not be accepted, 8 and everyone who eats it shall bear his iniquity, because he has profaned what is holy to the LORD, and that person shall be cut off from his people.

Love Your Neighbor as Yourself

9 "When you reap the harvest of your land, you shall not reap your field right up to its edge, neither shall you gather the gleanings after your harvest. 10 And you shall not strip your vineyard bare, neither shall you gather the fallen grapes of your vineyard. You shall leave them for the poor and for the sojourner: I am the LORD your God.

11 "You shall not steal; you shall not deal falsely; you shall not lie to one another. 12 You shall not swear by my name falsely, and so profane the name of your God: I am the LORD.

13 "You shall not oppress your neighbor or rob him. The wages of a hired servant shall not remain with you all night until the morning. 14 You shall not curse the deaf or put a stumbling block before the blind, but you shall fear your God: I am the LORD.

15 "You shall do no injustice in court. You shall not be partial to the poor or defer to the great, but in righteousness shall you judge your neighbor. 16 You shall not go around as a slanderer among your people, and you shall not stand up against the life[1] of your neighbor: I am the LORD.

17 "You shall not hate your brother in your heart, but you shall reason frankly with your neighbor, lest you incur sin because of him. 18 You shall not take vengeance or bear a grudge against the sons of your own people, but you shall love your neighbor as yourself: I am the LORD.

You Shall Keep My Statutes

19 "You shall keep my statutes. You shall not let your cattle breed with a different kind. You shall not sow your field with two kinds of seed, nor shall you wear a garment of cloth made of two kinds of material.

20 "If a man lies sexually with a woman who is a slave, assigned to another man and not yet ransomed or given her freedom, a distinction shall be made. They shall not be put to death, because she was not free; 21 but he shall bring his compensation to the LORD, to the entrance of the tent of meeting, a ram for a guilt offering. 22 And the priest shall make atonement for him with the ram of the guilt offering before the LORD for his sin that he has committed, and he shall be forgiven for the sin that he has committed.

23 "When you come into the land and plant any kind of tree for food, then you shall regard its fruit as forbidden.[2] Three years it shall be forbidden to you; it must not be eaten. 24 And in the fourth year all its fruit shall be holy, an offering of praise to the LORD. 25 But in the fifth year you

[1] Hebrew *blood* [2] Hebrew *as its uncircumcision*

may eat of its fruit, to increase its yield for you: I am the LORD your God.

26 "You shall not eat any flesh with the blood in it. You shall not interpret omens or tell fortunes. 27 You shall not round off the hair on your temples or mar the edges of your beard. 28 You shall not make any cuts on your body for the dead or tattoo yourselves: I am the LORD.

29 "Do not profane your daughter by making her a prostitute, lest the land fall into prostitution and the land become full of depravity. 30 You shall keep my Sabbaths and reverence my sanctuary: I am the LORD.

31 "Do not turn to mediums or necromancers; do not seek them out, and so make yourselves unclean by them: I am the LORD your God.

32 "You shall stand up before the gray head and honor the face of an old man, and you shall fear your God: I am the LORD.

33 "When a stranger sojourns with you in your land, you shall not do him wrong. 34 You shall treat the stranger who sojourns with you as the native among you, and you shall love him as yourself, for you were strangers in the land of Egypt: I am the LORD your God.

35 "You shall do no wrong in judgment, in measures of length or weight or quantity. 36 You shall have just balances, just weights, a just ephah, and a just hin:[1] I am the LORD your God, who brought you out of the land of Egypt. 37 And you shall observe all my statutes and all my rules, and do them: I am the LORD."

Punishment for Child Sacrifice

20 The LORD spoke to Moses, saying, 2 "Say to the people of Israel, Any one of the people of Israel or of the strangers who sojourn in Israel who gives any of his children to Molech shall surely be put to death. The people of the land shall stone him with stones. 3 I myself will set my face against that man and will cut him off from among his people, because he has given one of his children to Molech, to make my sanctuary unclean and to profane my holy name. 4 And if the people of the land do at all close their eyes to that man when he gives one of his children to Molech, and do not put him to death, 5 then I will set my face against that man and against his clan and will cut them off from among their people, him and all who follow him in whoring after Molech.

6 "If a person turns to mediums and necromancers, whoring after them, I will set my face against that person and will cut him off from among his people. 7 Consecrate yourselves, therefore, and be holy, for I am the LORD your God. 8 Keep my statutes and do them; I am the LORD who sanctifies you. 9 For anyone who curses his father or his mother shall surely be put to death; he has cursed his father or his mother; his blood is upon him.

Punishments for Sexual Immorality

10 "If a man commits adultery with the wife of[2] his neighbor, both the adulterer and the adulteress shall surely be put to death. 11 If a man lies with his father's wife, he has uncovered his father's nakedness; both of them shall surely be put to death; their blood is upon them. 12 If a man lies with his daughter-in-law, both of them shall surely be put to death; they have committed perversion; their blood is upon them. 13 If a man lies with a male as with a woman, both of them have committed an abomination; they shall surely be put to death; their blood is upon them. 14 If a man takes a woman and her mother also, it is depravity; he and they shall be burned with fire, that there may be no depravity among you. 15 If a man lies with an animal, he shall surely be put to death, and you shall kill the animal. 16 If a woman approaches any animal and lies with it, you shall kill the woman and the

[1] An *ephah* was about 3/5 bushel or 22 liters; a *hin* was about 4 quarts or 3.5 liters [2] Hebrew repeats *if a man commits adultery with the wife of*

animal; they shall surely be put to death; their blood is upon them.

17 "If a man takes his sister, a daughter of his father or a daughter of his mother, and sees her nakedness, and she sees his nakedness, it is a disgrace, and they shall be cut off in the sight of the children of their people. He has uncovered his sister's nakedness, and he shall bear his iniquity. 18 If a man lies with a woman during her menstrual period and uncovers her nakedness, he has made naked her fountain, and she has uncovered the fountain of her blood. Both of them shall be cut off from among their people. 19 You shall not uncover the nakedness of your mother's sister or of your father's sister, for that is to make naked one's relative; they shall bear their iniquity. 20 If a man lies with his uncle's wife, he has uncovered his uncle's nakedness; they shall bear their sin; they shall die childless. 21 If a man takes his brother's wife, it is impurity.[1] He has uncovered his brother's nakedness; they shall be childless.

You Shall Be Holy

22 "You shall therefore keep all my statutes and all my rules and do them, that the land where I am bringing you to live may not vomit you out. 23 And you shall not walk in the customs of the nation that I am driving out before you, for they did all these things, and therefore I detested them. 24 But I have said to you, 'You shall inherit their land, and I will give it to you to possess, a land flowing with milk and honey.' I am the LORD your God, who has separated you from the peoples. 25 You shall therefore separate the clean beast from the unclean, and the unclean bird from the clean. You shall not make yourselves detestable by beast or by bird or by anything with which the ground crawls, which I have set apart for you to hold unclean. 26 You shall be holy to me, for I the LORD am holy and have separated you from the peoples, that you should be mine.

27 "A man or a woman who is a medium or a necromancer shall surely be put to death. They shall be stoned with stones; their blood shall be upon them."

Holiness and the Priests

21 And the LORD said to Moses, "Speak to the priests, the sons of Aaron, and say to them: No one shall make himself unclean for the dead among his people, 2 except for his closest relatives, his mother, his father, his son, his daughter, his brother, 3 or his virgin sister (who is near to him because she has had no husband; for her he may make himself unclean). 4 He shall not make himself unclean as a husband among his people and so profane himself. 5 They shall not make bald patches on their heads, nor shave off the edges of their beards, nor make any cuts on their body. 6 They shall be holy to their God and not profane the name of their God. For they offer the LORD's food offerings, the bread of their God; therefore they shall be holy. 7 They shall not marry a prostitute or a woman who has been defiled, neither shall they marry a woman divorced from her husband, for the priest is holy to his God. 8 You shall sanctify him, for he offers the bread of your God. He shall be holy to you, for I, the LORD, who sanctify you, am holy. 9 And the daughter of any priest, if she profanes herself by whoring, profanes her father; she shall be burned with fire.

10 "The priest who is chief among his brothers, on whose head the anointing oil is poured and who has been consecrated to wear the garments, shall not let the hair of his head hang loose nor tear his clothes. 11 He shall not go in to any dead bodies nor make himself unclean, even for his father or for his mother. 12 He shall not go out of the sanctuary, lest he profane the sanctuary of his God, for the consecration of the

[1] Literally *menstrual impurity*

anointing oil of his God is on him: I am the LORD. 13 And he shall take a wife in her virginity.[1] 14 A widow, or a divorced woman, or a woman who has been defiled, or a prostitute, these he shall not marry. But he shall take as his wife a virgin[2] of his own people, 15 that he may not profane his offspring among his people, for I am the LORD who sanctifies him."

16 And the LORD spoke to Moses, saying, 17 "Speak to Aaron, saying, None of your offspring throughout their generations who has a blemish may approach to offer the bread of his God. 18 For no one who has a blemish shall draw near, a man blind or lame, or one who has a mutilated face or a limb too long, 19 or a man who has an injured foot or an injured hand, 20 or a hunchback or a dwarf or a man with a defect in his sight or an itching disease or scabs or crushed testicles. 21 No man of the offspring of Aaron the priest who has a blemish shall come near to offer the LORD's food offerings; since he has a blemish, he shall not come near to offer the bread of his God. 22 He may eat the bread of his God, both of the most holy and of the holy things, 23 but he shall not go through the veil or approach the altar, because he has a blemish, that he may not profane my sanctuaries, for I am the LORD who sanctifies them." 24 So Moses spoke to Aaron and to his sons and to all the people of Israel.

22 And the LORD spoke to Moses, saying, 2 "Speak to Aaron and his sons so that they abstain from the holy things of the people of Israel, which they dedicate to me, so that they do not profane my holy name: I am the LORD. 3 Say to them, 'If any one of all your offspring throughout your generations approaches the holy things that the people of Israel dedicate to the LORD, while he has an uncleanness, that person shall be cut off from my presence: I am the LORD. 4 None of the offspring of Aaron who has a leprous disease or a discharge may eat of the holy things until he is clean. Whoever touches anything that is unclean through contact with the dead or a man who has had an emission of semen, 5 and whoever touches a swarming thing by which he may be made unclean or a person from whom he may take uncleanness, whatever his uncleanness may be— 6 the person who touches such a thing shall be unclean until the evening and shall not eat of the holy things unless he has bathed his body in water. 7 When the sun goes down he shall be clean, and afterward he may eat of the holy things, because they are his food. 8 He shall not eat what dies of itself or is torn by beasts, and so make himself unclean by it: I am the LORD.' 9 They shall therefore keep my charge, lest they bear sin for it and die thereby when they profane it: I am the LORD who sanctifies them.

10 "A lay person shall not eat of a holy thing; no foreign guest of the priest or hired servant shall eat of a holy thing, 11 but if a priest buys a slave as his property for money, the slave[3] may eat of it, and anyone born in his house may eat of his food. 12 If a priest's daughter marries a layman, she shall not eat of the contribution of the holy things. 13 But if a priest's daughter is widowed or divorced and has no child and returns to her father's house, as in her youth, she may eat of her father's food; yet no lay person shall eat of it. 14 And if anyone eats of a holy thing unintentionally, he shall add the fifth of its value to it and give the holy thing to the priest. 15 They shall not profane the holy things of the people of Israel, which they contribute to the LORD, 16 and so cause them to bear iniquity and guilt, by eating their holy things: for I am the LORD who sanctifies them."

Acceptable Offerings

17 And the LORD spoke to Moses, saying, 18 "Speak to Aaron and his sons and all the people of Israel and say to them, When any one of the house of Israel or of

[1] *Or a young wife* [2] Hebrew *young woman* [3] Hebrew *he*

the sojourners in Israel presents a burnt offering as his offering, for any of their vows or freewill offerings that they offer to the LORD, 19 if it is to be accepted for you it shall be a male without blemish, of the bulls or the sheep or the goats. 20 You shall not offer anything that has a blemish, for it will not be acceptable for you. 21 And when anyone offers a sacrifice of peace offerings to the LORD to fulfill a vow or as a freewill offering from the herd or from the flock, to be accepted it must be perfect; there shall be no blemish in it. 22 Animals blind or disabled or mutilated or having a discharge or an itch or scabs you shall not offer to the LORD or give them to the LORD as a food offering on the altar. 23 You may present a bull or a lamb that has a part too long or too short for a freewill offering, but for a vow offering it cannot be accepted. 24 Any animal that has its testicles bruised or crushed or torn or cut you shall not offer to the LORD; you shall not do it within your land, 25 neither shall you offer as the bread of your God any such animals gotten from a foreigner. Since there is a blemish in them, because of their mutilation, they will not be accepted for you."

26 And the LORD spoke to Moses, saying, 27 "When an ox or sheep or goat is born, it shall remain seven days with its mother, and from the eighth day on it shall be acceptable as a food offering to the LORD. 28 But you shall not kill an ox or a sheep and her young in one day. 29 And when you sacrifice a sacrifice of thanksgiving to the LORD, you shall sacrifice it so that you may be accepted. 30 It shall be eaten on the same day; you shall leave none of it until morning: I am the LORD.

31 "So you shall keep my commandments and do them: I am the LORD. 32 And you shall not profane my holy name, that I may be sanctified among the people of Israel. I am the LORD who sanctifies you, 33 who brought you out of the land of Egypt to be your God: I am the LORD."

Feasts of the LORD

23 The LORD spoke to Moses, saying, 2 "Speak to the people of Israel and say to them, These are the appointed feasts of the LORD that you shall proclaim as holy convocations; they are my appointed feasts.

The Sabbath

3 "Six days shall work be done, but on the seventh day is a Sabbath of solemn rest, a holy convocation. You shall do no work. It is a Sabbath to the LORD in all your dwelling places.

The Passover

4 "These are the appointed feasts of the LORD, the holy convocations, which you shall proclaim at the time appointed for them. 5 In the first month, on the fourteenth day of the month at twilight,[1] is the LORD's Passover. 6 And on the fifteenth day of the same month is the Feast of Unleavened Bread to the LORD; for seven days you shall eat unleavened bread. 7 On the first day you shall have a holy convocation; you shall not do any ordinary work. 8 But you shall present a food offering to the LORD for seven days. On the seventh day is a holy convocation; you shall not do any ordinary work."

The Feast of Firstfruits

9 And the LORD spoke to Moses, saying, 10 "Speak to the people of Israel and say to them, When you come into the land that I give you and reap its harvest, you shall bring the sheaf of the firstfruits of your harvest to the priest, 11 and he shall wave the sheaf before the LORD, so that you may be accepted. On the day after the Sabbath the priest shall wave it. 12 And on the day when you wave the sheaf, you shall offer a male lamb a year old without blemish as a burnt offering to the LORD. 13 And the grain offering with it shall be two tenths of an ephah[2] of fine flour mixed with oil, a food offering to the LORD with a pleasing

[1] Hebrew *between the two evenings* [2] An *ephah* was about 3/5 bushel or 22 liters

aroma, and the drink offering with it shall
be of wine, a fourth of a hin.[1] 14 And you
shall eat neither bread nor grain parched
or fresh until this same day, until you have
brought the offering of your God: it is a
statute forever throughout your genera-
tions in all your dwellings.

The Feast of Weeks

15 "You shall count seven full weeks
from the day after the Sabbath, from the
day that you brought the sheaf of the
wave offering. 16 You shall count fifty
days to the day after the seventh Sabbath.
Then you shall present a grain offering of
new grain to the LORD. 17 You shall bring
from your dwelling places two loaves of
bread to be waved, made of two tenths of
an ephah. They shall be of fine flour, and
they shall be baked with leaven, as first-
fruits to the LORD. 18 And you shall pre-
sent with the bread seven lambs a year
old without blemish, and one bull from
the herd and two rams. They shall be a
burnt offering to the LORD, with their
grain offering and their drink offerings,
a food offering with a pleasing aroma
to the LORD. 19 And you shall offer one
male goat for a sin offering, and two male
lambs a year old as a sacrifice of peace
offerings. 20 And the priest shall wave
them with the bread of the firstfruits as
a wave offering before the LORD, with
the two lambs. They shall be holy to the
LORD for the priest. 21 And you shall make
proclamation on the same day. You shall
hold a holy convocation. You shall not do
any ordinary work. It is a statute forever
in all your dwelling places throughout
your generations.

22 "And when you reap the harvest of
your land, you shall not reap your field
right up to its edge, nor shall you gather
the gleanings after your harvest. You
shall leave them for the poor and for the
sojourner: I am the LORD your God."

The Feast of Trumpets

23 And the LORD spoke to Moses, saying,
24 "Speak to the people of Israel, saying, In
the seventh month, on the first day of the
month, you shall observe a day of solemn
rest, a memorial proclaimed with blast of
trumpets, a holy convocation. 25 You shall
not do any ordinary work, and you shall
present a food offering to the LORD."

The Day of Atonement

26 And the LORD spoke to Moses, saying,
27 "Now on the tenth day of this seventh
month is the Day of Atonement. It shall
be for you a time of holy convocation, and
you shall afflict yourselves and present a
food offering to the LORD. 28 And you shall
not do any work on that very day, for it is a
Day of Atonement, to make atonement for
you before the LORD your God. 29 For who-
ever is not afflicted on that very day shall
be cut off from his people. 30 And whoever
does any work on that very day, that per-
son I will destroy from among his people.
31 You shall not do any work. It is a statute
forever throughout your generations in all
your dwelling places. 32 It shall be to you
a Sabbath of solemn rest, and you shall
afflict yourselves. On the ninth day of the
month beginning at evening, from evening
to evening shall you keep your Sabbath."

The Feast of Booths

33 And the LORD spoke to Moses, saying,
34 "Speak to the people of Israel, saying, On
the fifteenth day of this seventh month
and for seven days is the Feast of Booths[2]
to the LORD. 35 On the first day shall be a
holy convocation; you shall not do any
ordinary work. 36 For seven days you shall
present food offerings to the LORD. On the
eighth day you shall hold a holy convo-
cation and present a food offering to the
LORD. It is a solemn assembly; you shall
not do any ordinary work.

37 "These are the appointed feasts of the
LORD, which you shall proclaim as times

[1] A *hin* was about 4 quarts or 3.5 liters [2] Or *tabernacles*

of holy convocation, for presenting to the LORD food offerings, burnt offerings and grain offerings, sacrifices and drink offerings, each on its proper day, 38 besides the LORD's Sabbaths and besides your gifts and besides all your vow offerings and besides all your freewill offerings, which you give to the LORD.

39 "On the fifteenth day of the seventh month, when you have gathered in the produce of the land, you shall celebrate the feast of the LORD seven days. On the first day shall be a solemn rest, and on the eighth day shall be a solemn rest. 40 And you shall take on the first day the fruit of splendid trees, branches of palm trees and boughs of leafy trees and willows of the brook, and you shall rejoice before the LORD your God seven days. 41 You shall celebrate it as a feast to the LORD for seven days in the year. It is a statute forever throughout your generations; you shall celebrate it in the seventh month. 42 You shall dwell in booths for seven days. All native Israelites shall dwell in booths, 43 that your generations may know that I made the people of Israel dwell in booths when I brought them out of the land of Egypt: I am the LORD your God."

44 Thus Moses declared to the people of Israel the appointed feasts of the LORD.

The Lamps

24 The LORD spoke to Moses, saying, 2 "Command the people of Israel to bring you pure oil from beaten olives for the lamp, that a light may be kept burning regularly. 3 Outside the veil of the testimony, in the tent of meeting, Aaron shall arrange it from evening to morning before the LORD regularly. It shall be a statute forever throughout your generations. 4 He shall arrange the lamps on the lampstand of pure gold[1] before the LORD regularly.

Bread for the Tabernacle

5 "You shall take fine flour and bake twelve loaves from it; two tenths of an ephah[2] shall be in each loaf. 6 And you shall set them in two piles, six in a pile, on the table of pure gold[3] before the LORD. 7 And you shall put pure frankincense on each pile, that it may go with the bread as a memorial portion as a food offering to the LORD. 8 Every Sabbath day Aaron shall arrange it before the LORD regularly; it is from the people of Israel as a covenant forever. 9 And it shall be for Aaron and his sons, and they shall eat it in a holy place, since it is for him a most holy portion out of the LORD's food offerings, a perpetual due."

Punishment for Blasphemy

10 Now an Israelite woman's son, whose father was an Egyptian, went out among the people of Israel. And the Israelite woman's son and a man of Israel fought in the camp, 11 and the Israelite woman's son blasphemed the Name, and cursed. Then they brought him to Moses. His mother's name was Shelomith, the daughter of Dibri, of the tribe of Dan. 12 And they put him in custody, till the will of the LORD should be clear to them.

13 Then the LORD spoke to Moses, saying, 14 "Bring out of the camp the one who cursed, and let all who heard him lay their hands on his head, and let all the congregation stone him. 15 And speak to the people of Israel, saying, Whoever curses his God shall bear his sin. 16 Whoever blasphemes the name of the LORD shall surely be put to death. All the congregation shall stone him. The sojourner as well as the native, when he blasphemes the Name, shall be put to death.

An Eye for an Eye

17 "Whoever takes a human life shall surely be put to death. 18 Whoever takes an animal's life shall make it good, life for life. 19 If anyone injures his neighbor, as he has done it shall be done to him, 20 fracture for fracture, eye for eye, tooth for tooth; whatever injury he has given a person

[1] Hebrew *the pure lampstand* [2] An *ephah* was about 3/5 bushel or 22 liters [3] Hebrew *the pure table*

shall be given to him. 21 Whoever kills an animal shall make it good, and whoever kills a person shall be put to death. 22 You shall have the same rule for the sojourner and for the native, for I am the LORD your God." 23 So Moses spoke to the people of Israel, and they brought out of the camp the one who had cursed and stoned him with stones. Thus the people of Israel did as the LORD commanded Moses.

The Sabbath Year

25 The LORD spoke to Moses on Mount Sinai, saying, 2 "Speak to the people of Israel and say to them, When you come into the land that I give you, the land shall keep a Sabbath to the LORD. 3 For six years you shall sow your field, and for six years you shall prune your vineyard and gather in its fruits, 4 but in the seventh year there shall be a Sabbath of solemn rest for the land, a Sabbath to the LORD. You shall not sow your field or prune your vineyard. 5 You shall not reap what grows of itself in your harvest, or gather the grapes of your undressed vine. It shall be a year of solemn rest for the land. 6 The Sabbath of the land shall provide food for you, for yourself and for your male and female slaves and for your hired servant and the sojourner who lives with you, 7 and for your cattle and for the wild animals that are in your land: all its yield shall be for food.

The Year of Jubilee

8 "You shall count seven weeks[1] of years, seven times seven years, so that the time of the seven weeks of years shall give you forty-nine years. 9 Then you shall sound the loud trumpet on the tenth day of the seventh month. On the Day of Atonement you shall sound the trumpet throughout all your land. 10 And you shall consecrate the fiftieth year, and proclaim liberty throughout the land to all its inhabitants. It shall be a jubilee for you, when each of you shall return to his property and each of you shall return to his clan. 11 That fiftieth year shall be a jubilee for you; in it you shall neither sow nor reap what grows of itself nor gather the grapes from the undressed vines. 12 For it is a jubilee. It shall be holy to you. You may eat the produce of the field.[2]

13 "In this year of jubilee each of you shall return to his property. 14 And if you make a sale to your neighbor or buy from your neighbor, you shall not wrong one another. 15 You shall pay your neighbor according to the number of years after the jubilee, and he shall sell to you according to the number of years for crops. 16 If the years are many, you shall increase the price, and if the years are few, you shall reduce the price, for it is the number of the crops that he is selling to you. 17 You shall not wrong one another, but you shall fear your God, for I am the LORD your God.

18 "Therefore you shall do my statutes and keep my rules and perform them, and then you will dwell in the land securely. 19 The land will yield its fruit, and you will eat your fill and dwell in it securely. 20 And if you say, 'What shall we eat in the seventh year, if we may not sow or gather in our crop?' 21 I will command my blessing on you in the sixth year, so that it will produce a crop sufficient for three years. 22 When you sow in the eighth year, you will be eating some of the old crop; you shall eat the old until the ninth year, when its crop arrives.

Redemption of Property

23 "The land shall not be sold in perpetuity, for the land is mine. For you are strangers and sojourners with me. 24 And in all the country you possess, you shall allow a redemption of the land.

25 "If your brother becomes poor and sells part of his property, then his nearest redeemer shall come and redeem what his brother has sold. 26 If a man has no one to redeem it and then himself becomes prosperous and finds sufficient means

[1] Or *Sabbaths* [2] Or *countryside*

to redeem it, 27 let him calculate the years since he sold it and pay back the balance to the man to whom he sold it, and then return to his property. 28 But if he has not sufficient means to recover it, then what he sold shall remain in the hand of the buyer until the year of jubilee. In the jubilee it shall be released, and he shall return to his property.

29 "If a man sells a dwelling house in a walled city, he may redeem it within a year of its sale. For a full year he shall have the right of redemption. 30 If it is not redeemed within a full year, then the house in the walled city shall belong in perpetuity to the buyer, throughout his generations; it shall not be released in the jubilee. 31 But the houses of the villages that have no wall around them shall be classified with the fields of the land. They may be redeemed, and they shall be released in the jubilee. 32 As for the cities of the Levites, the Levites may redeem at any time the houses in the cities they possess. 33 And if one of the Levites exercises his right of redemption, then the house that was sold in a city they possess shall be released in the jubilee. For the houses in the cities of the Levites are their possession among the people of Israel. 34 But the fields of pastureland belonging to their cities may not be sold, for that is their possession forever.

Kindness for Poor Brothers

35 "If your brother becomes poor and cannot maintain himself with you, you shall support him as though he were a stranger and a sojourner, and he shall live with you. 36 Take no interest from him or profit, but fear your God, that your brother may live beside you. 37 You shall not lend him your money at interest, nor give him your food for profit. 38 I am the LORD your God, who brought you out of the land of Egypt to give you the land of Canaan, and to be your God.

39 "If your brother becomes poor beside you and sells himself to you, you shall not make him serve as a slave: 40 he shall be with you as a hired servant and as a sojourner. He shall serve with you until the year of the jubilee. 41 Then he shall go out from you, he and his children with him, and go back to his own clan and return to the possession of his fathers. 42 For they are my servants,[1] whom I brought out of the land of Egypt; they shall not be sold as slaves. 43 You shall not rule over him ruthlessly but shall fear your God. 44 As for your male and female slaves whom you may have: you may buy male and female slaves from among the nations that are around you. 45 You may also buy from among the strangers who sojourn with you and their clans that are with you, who have been born in your land, and they may be your property. 46 You may bequeath them to your sons after you to inherit as a possession forever. You may make slaves of them, but over your brothers the people of Israel you shall not rule, one over another ruthlessly.

Redeeming a Poor Man

47 "If a stranger or sojourner with you becomes rich, and your brother beside him becomes poor and sells himself to the stranger or sojourner with you or to a member of the stranger's clan, 48 then after he is sold he may be redeemed. One of his brothers may redeem him, 49 or his uncle or his cousin may redeem him, or a close relative from his clan may redeem him. Or if he grows rich he may redeem himself. 50 He shall calculate with his buyer from the year when he sold himself to him until the year of jubilee, and the price of his sale shall vary with the number of years. The time he was with his owner shall be rated as the time of a hired servant. 51 If there are still many years left, he shall pay proportionately for his redemption some of his sale price. 52 If there remain but a few years until the year

[1] Hebrew *slaves*

of jubilee, he shall calculate and pay for
his redemption in proportion to his years
of service. 53 He shall treat him as a servant
hired year by year. He shall not rule ruth-
lessly over him in your sight. 54 And if he is
not redeemed by these means, then he and
his children with him shall be released in
the year of jubilee. 55 For it is to me that the
people of Israel are servants.[1] They are my
servants whom I brought out of the land of
Egypt: I am the LORD your God.

Blessings for Obedience

26 "You shall not make idols for
yourselves or erect an image or
pillar, and you shall not set up a figured
stone in your land to bow down to it, for
I am the LORD your God. 2 You shall keep
my Sabbaths and reverence my sanctuary:
I am the LORD.

3 "If you walk in my statutes and observe
my commandments and do them, 4 then I
will give you your rains in their season,
and the land shall yield its increase, and
the trees of the field shall yield their fruit.
5 Your threshing shall last to the time of
the grape harvest, and the grape harvest
shall last to the time for sowing. And you
shall eat your bread to the full and dwell
in your land securely. 6 I will give peace
in the land, and you shall lie down, and
none shall make you afraid. And I will
remove harmful beasts from the land, and
the sword shall not go through your land.
7 You shall chase your enemies, and they
shall fall before you by the sword. 8 Five
of you shall chase a hundred, and a hun-
dred of you shall chase ten thousand, and
your enemies shall fall before you by the
sword. 9 I will turn to you and make you
fruitful and multiply you and will confirm
my covenant with you. 10 You shall eat old
store long kept, and you shall clear out
the old to make way for the new. 11 I will
make my dwelling[2] among you, and my
soul shall not abhor you. 12 And I will walk
among you and will be your God, and you
shall be my people. 13 I am the LORD your
God, who brought you out of the land of
Egypt, that you should not be their slaves.
And I have broken the bars of your yoke
and made you walk erect.

Punishment for Disobedience

14 "But if you will not listen to me and
will not do all these commandments, 15 if
you spurn my statutes, and if your soul
abhors my rules, so that you will not do
all my commandments, but break my
covenant, 16 then I will do this to you: I
will visit you with panic, with wasting
disease and fever that consume the eyes
and make the heart ache. And you shall
sow your seed in vain, for your enemies
shall eat it. 17 I will set my face against you,
and you shall be struck down before your
enemies. Those who hate you shall rule
over you, and you shall flee when none
pursues you. 18 And if in spite of this you
will not listen to me, then I will discipline
you again sevenfold for your sins, 19 and I
will break the pride of your power, and I
will make your heavens like iron and your
earth like bronze. 20 And your strength
shall be spent in vain, for your land shall
not yield its increase, and the trees of the
land shall not yield their fruit.

21 "Then if you walk contrary to me and
will not listen to me, I will continue strik-
ing you, sevenfold for your sins. 22 And I
will let loose the wild beasts against you,
which shall bereave you of your children
and destroy your livestock and make you
few in number, so that your roads shall
be deserted.

23 "And if by this discipline you are not
turned to me but walk contrary to me,
24 then I also will walk contrary to you,
and I myself will strike you sevenfold for
your sins. 25 And I will bring a sword upon
you, that shall execute vengeance for the
covenant. And if you gather within your
cities, I will send pestilence among you,
and you shall be delivered into the hand

[1] Or *slaves* [2] Hebrew *tabernacle*

of the enemy. 26 When I break your supply[1] of bread, ten women shall bake your bread in a single oven and shall dole out your bread again by weight, and you shall eat and not be satisfied.

27 "But if in spite of this you will not listen to me, but walk contrary to me, 28 then I will walk contrary to you in fury, and I myself will discipline you sevenfold for your sins. 29 You shall eat the flesh of your sons, and you shall eat the flesh of your daughters. 30 And I will destroy your high places and cut down your incense altars and cast your dead bodies upon the dead bodies of your idols, and my soul will abhor you. 31 And I will lay your cities waste and will make your sanctuaries desolate, and I will not smell your pleasing aromas. 32 And I myself will devastate the land, so that your enemies who settle in it shall be appalled at it. 33 And I will scatter you among the nations, and I will unsheathe the sword after you, and your land shall be a desolation, and your cities shall be a waste.

34 "Then the land shall enjoy[2] its Sabbaths as long as it lies desolate, while you are in your enemies' land; then the land shall rest, and enjoy its Sabbaths. 35 As long as it lies desolate it shall have rest, the rest that it did not have on your Sabbaths when you were dwelling in it. 36 And as for those of you who are left, I will send faintness into their hearts in the lands of their enemies. The sound of a driven leaf shall put them to flight, and they shall flee as one flees from the sword, and they shall fall when none pursues. 37 They shall stumble over one another, as if to escape a sword, though none pursues. And you shall have no power to stand before your enemies. 38 And you shall perish among the nations, and the land of your enemies shall eat you up. 39 And those of you who are left shall rot away in your enemies' lands because of their iniquity, and also because of the iniquities of their fathers they shall rot away like them.

40 "But if they confess their iniquity and the iniquity of their fathers in their treachery that they committed against me, and also in walking contrary to me, 41 so that I walked contrary to them and brought them into the land of their enemies—if then their uncircumcised heart is humbled and they make amends for their iniquity, 42 then I will remember my covenant with Jacob, and I will remember my covenant with Isaac and my covenant with Abraham, and I will remember the land. 43 But the land shall be abandoned by them and enjoy its Sabbaths while it lies desolate without them, and they shall make amends for their iniquity, because they spurned my rules and their soul abhorred my statutes. 44 Yet for all that, when they are in the land of their enemies, I will not spurn them, neither will I abhor them so as to destroy them utterly and break my covenant with them, for I am the LORD their God. 45 But I will for their sake remember the covenant with their forefathers, whom I brought out of the land of Egypt in the sight of the nations, that I might be their God: I am the LORD."

46 These are the statutes and rules and laws that the LORD made between himself and the people of Israel through Moses on Mount Sinai.

Laws About Vows

27 The LORD spoke to Moses, saying, 2 "Speak to the people of Israel and say to them, If anyone makes a special vow to the LORD involving the valuation of persons, 3 then the valuation of a male from twenty years old up to sixty years old shall be fifty shekels[3] of silver, according to the shekel of the sanctuary. 4 If the person is a female, the valuation shall be thirty shekels. 5 If the person is from five years old up to twenty years old, the valuation shall be for a male twenty shekels, and for a female ten shekels. 6 If the person is from a month old up to five

[1] Hebrew *staff* [2] Or *pay for*; twice in this verse; also verse 43 [3] A *shekel* was about 2/5 ounce or 11 grams

years old, the valuation shall be for a male five shekels of silver, and for a female the valuation shall be three shekels of silver. 7 And if the person is sixty years old or over, then the valuation for a male shall be fifteen shekels, and for a female ten shekels. 8 And if someone is too poor to pay the valuation, then he shall be made to stand before the priest, and the priest shall value him; the priest shall value him according to what the vower can afford.

9 "If the vow[1] is an animal that may be offered as an offering to the LORD, all of it that he gives to the LORD is holy. 10 He shall not exchange it or make a substitute for it, good for bad, or bad for good; and if he does in fact substitute one animal for another, then both it and the substitute shall be holy. 11 And if it is any unclean animal that may not be offered as an offering to the LORD, then he shall stand the animal before the priest, 12 and the priest shall value it as either good or bad; as the priest values it, so it shall be. 13 But if he wishes to redeem it, he shall add a fifth to the valuation.

14 "When a man dedicates his house as a holy gift to the LORD, the priest shall value it as either good or bad; as the priest values it, so it shall stand. 15 And if the donor wishes to redeem his house, he shall add a fifth to the valuation price, and it shall be his.

16 "If a man dedicates to the LORD part of the land that is his possession, then the valuation shall be in proportion to its seed. A homer[2] of barley seed shall be valued at fifty shekels of silver. 17 If he dedicates his field from the year of jubilee, the valuation shall stand, 18 but if he dedicates his field after the jubilee, then the priest shall calculate the price according to the years that remain until the year of jubilee, and a deduction shall be made from the valuation. 19 And if he who dedicates the field wishes to redeem it, then he shall add a fifth to its valuation price, and it shall remain his. 20 But if he does not wish to redeem the field, or if he has sold the field to another man, it shall not be redeemed anymore. 21 But the field, when it is released in the jubilee, shall be a holy gift to the LORD, like a field that has been devoted. The priest shall be in possession of it. 22 If he dedicates to the LORD a field that he has bought, which is not a part of his possession, 23 then the priest shall calculate the amount of the valuation for it up to the year of jubilee, and the man shall give the valuation on that day as a holy gift to the LORD. 24 In the year of jubilee the field shall return to him from whom it was bought, to whom the land belongs as a possession. 25 Every valuation shall be according to the shekel of the sanctuary: twenty gerahs[3] shall make a shekel.

26 "But a firstborn of animals, which as a firstborn belongs to the LORD, no man may dedicate; whether ox or sheep, it is the LORD's. 27 And if it is an unclean animal, then he shall buy it back at the valuation, and add a fifth to it; or, if it is not redeemed, it shall be sold at the valuation.

28 "But no devoted thing that a man devotes to the LORD, of anything that he has, whether man or beast, or of his inherited field, shall be sold or redeemed; every devoted thing is most holy to the LORD. 29 No one devoted, who is to be devoted for destruction[4] from mankind, shall be ransomed; he shall surely be put to death.

30 "Every tithe of the land, whether of the seed of the land or of the fruit of the trees, is the LORD's; it is holy to the LORD. 31 If a man wishes to redeem some of his tithe, he shall add a fifth to it. 32 And every tithe of herds and flocks, every tenth animal of all that pass under the herdsman's staff, shall be holy to the LORD. 33 One shall not differentiate between good or bad, neither shall he make a substitute for it; and if he does substitute for it, then both it and the substitute shall be holy; it shall not be redeemed."

34 These are the commandments that the LORD commanded Moses for the people of Israel on Mount Sinai.

[1] Hebrew *it* [2] A *homer* was about 6 bushels or 220 liters [3] A *gerah* was about 1/50 ounce or 0.6 gram [4] That is, set apart (devoted) as an offering to the Lord (for destruction)

Introduction to

Numbers

Author
Moses the prophet

Date
1445–1406 B.C.

People
Moses; Aaron; Miriam; Joshua; Caleb; Korah; Dathan; Abiram; Balak; Balaam

Purpose
The purpose of Numbers is to explain and describe the 40-year delay between the time God's people arrived at the Promised Land and the time they entered it. We see in this God's amazing grace and faithfulness in spite of the sin of His people.

Central Themes
God's people are sinful; God faithfully keeps His promises; God graciously provides for the sin of His people; God justly punishes sin.

Memory Verses
Aaron's benediction (Numbers 6:24–27); God's Word is true (Numbers 23:19); star of Jacob (Numbers 24:17)

Introduction

The book of Numbers gets its name from chapters where people are counted (Numbers 1, 3–4, 26), resulting in lists of numbers. Scattered throughout Numbers are additional rules for Israel's life and worship. The story of God keeping His promises to Abraham continues in this book. Numbers begins with Israel leaving Mount Sinai to go to the Promised Land, and gives several instances of rebellion on the way (Numbers 10–12). Upon arriving at the border of Canaan, the people are too afraid of the Canaanites to obey God and enter the land (Numbers 13–14). Because of this rebellion, God leads them away from the land to spend 40 years in the wilderness, where the rebels will die, leaving their grown children and descendants to enter the land. Even during the 40 years, God must put up with complaining and rebellion, but He continues to lead and provide for His people (Numbers 16–17; 21:4–9; 25). When Numbers ends, the 40 years are over, and God's people are once more at the edge of the Promised Land, ready to enter. One of the final chapters gives the boundaries of the Promised Land and appoints men who will divide it among the 12 tribes (Numbers 34).

1526 B.C.	1446 B.C.	1406 B.C.
Moses born	Exodus from Egypt	Israel enters Promised Land

Numbers

A Census of Israel's Warriors

1 The LORD spoke to Moses in the wil-
derness of Sinai, in the tent of meet-
ing, on the first day of the second month,
in the second year after they had come
out of the land of Egypt, saying, 2 "Take a
census of all the congregation of the peo-
ple of Israel, by clans, by fathers' houses,
according to the number of names, every
male, head by head. 3 From twenty years
old and upward, all in Israel who are able
to go to war, you and Aaron shall list them,
company by company. 4 And there shall
be with you a man from each tribe, each
man being the head of the house of his
fathers. 5 And these are the names of the
men who shall assist you. From Reuben,
Elizur the son of Shedeur; 6 from Simeon,
Shelumiel the son of Zurishaddai; 7 from
Judah, Nahshon the son of Amminadab;
8 from Issachar, Nethanel the son of
Zuar; 9 from Zebulun, Eliab the son of
Helon; 10 from the sons of Joseph, from
Ephraim, Elishama the son of Ammihud,
and from Manasseh, Gamaliel the son
of Pedahzur; 11 from Benjamin, Abidan
the son of Gideoni; 12 from Dan, Ahiezer
the son of Ammishaddai; 13 from Asher,
Pagiel the son of Ochran; 14 from Gad, Elia-
saph the son of Deuel; 15 from Naphtali,
Ahira the son of Enan." 16 These were the
ones chosen from the congregation, the
chiefs of their ancestral tribes, the heads
of the clans of Israel.

17 Moses and Aaron took these men
who had been named, 18 and on the first
day of the second month, they assem-
bled the whole congregation together,
who registered themselves by clans, by
fathers' houses, according to the num-
ber of names from twenty years old and
upward, head by head, 19 as the LORD com-
manded Moses. So he listed them in the
wilderness of Sinai.

20 The people of Reuben, Israel's first-
born, their generations, by their clans,
by their fathers' houses, according to the
number of names, head by head, every
male from twenty years old and upward,
all who were able to go to war: 21 those
listed of the tribe of Reuben were 46,500.

22 Of the people of Simeon, their gen-
erations, by their clans, by their fathers'
houses, those of them who were listed,
according to the number of names, head
by head, every male from twenty years
old and upward, all who were able to go to
war: 23 those listed of the tribe of Simeon
were 59,300.

24 Of the people of Gad, their gen-
erations, by their clans, by their fathers'
houses, according to the number of the
names, from twenty years old and upward,
all who were able to go to war: 25 those
listed of the tribe of Gad were 45,650.

26 Of the people of Judah, their gen-
erations, by their clans, by their fathers'
houses, according to the number of
names, from twenty years old and upward,
every man able to go to war: 27 those listed
of the tribe of Judah were 74,600.

28 Of the people of Issachar, their gen-
erations, by their clans, by their fathers'
houses, according to the number of
names, from twenty years old and upward,
every man able to go to war: 29 those listed
of the tribe of Issachar were 54,400.

30 Of the people of Zebulun, their gen-
erations, by their clans, by their fathers'
houses, according to the number of
names, from twenty years old and upward,
every man able to go to war: 31 those listed
of the tribe of Zebulun were 57,400.

32 Of the people of Joseph, namely, of the people of Ephraim, their generations, by their clans, by their fathers' houses, according to the number of names, from twenty years old and upward, every man able to go to war: 33 those listed of the tribe of Ephraim were 40,500.

34 Of the people of Manasseh, their generations, by their clans, by their fathers' houses, according to the number of names, from twenty years old and upward, every man able to go to war: 35 those listed of the tribe of Manasseh were 32,200.

36 Of the people of Benjamin, their generations, by their clans, by their fathers' houses, according to the number of names, from twenty years old and upward, every man able to go to war: 37 those listed of the tribe of Benjamin were 35,400.

38 Of the people of Dan, their generations, by their clans, by their fathers' houses, according to the number of names, from twenty years old and upward, every man able to go to war: 39 those listed of the tribe of Dan were 62,700.

40 Of the people of Asher, their generations, by their clans, by their fathers' houses, according to the number of names, from twenty years old and upward, every man able to go to war: 41 those listed of the tribe of Asher were 41,500.

42 Of the people of Naphtali, their generations, by their clans, by their fathers' houses, according to the number of names, from twenty years old and upward, every man able to go to war: 43 those listed of the tribe of Naphtali were 53,400.

44 These are those who were listed, whom Moses and Aaron listed with the help of the chiefs of Israel, twelve men, each representing his fathers' house. 45 So all those listed of the people of Israel, by their fathers' houses, from twenty years old and upward, every man able to go to war in Israel— 46 all those listed were 603,550.

Levites Exempted

47 But the Levites were not listed along with them by their ancestral tribe. 48 For the LORD spoke to Moses, saying, 49 "Only the tribe of Levi you shall not list, and you shall not take a census of them among the people of Israel. 50 But appoint the Levites over the tabernacle of the testimony, and over all its furnishings, and over all that belongs to it. They are to carry the tabernacle and all its furnishings, and they shall take care of it and shall camp around the tabernacle. 51 When the tabernacle is to set out, the Levites shall take it down, and when the tabernacle is to be pitched, the Levites shall set it up. And if any outsider comes near, he shall be put to death. 52 The people of Israel shall pitch their tents by their companies, each man in his own camp and each man by his own standard. 53 But the Levites shall camp around the tabernacle of the testimony, so that there may be no wrath on the congregation of the people of Israel. And the Levites shall keep guard over the tabernacle of the testimony." 54 Thus did the people of Israel; they did according to all that the LORD commanded Moses.

Arrangement of the Camp

2 The LORD spoke to Moses and Aaron, saying, 2 "The people of Israel shall camp each by his own standard, with the banners of their fathers' houses. They shall camp facing the tent of meeting on every side. 3 Those to camp on the east side toward the sunrise shall be of the standard of the camp of Judah by their companies, the chief of the people of Judah being Nahshon the son of Amminadab, 4 his company as listed being 74,600. 5 Those to camp next to him shall be the tribe of Issachar, the chief of the people of Issachar being Nethanel the son of Zuar, 6 his company as listed being 54,400. 7 Then the tribe of Zebulun, the chief of the people of Zebulun being Eliab the son

of Helon, 8 his company as listed being 57,400. 9 All those listed of the camp of Judah, by their companies, were 186,400. They shall set out first on the march.

10 "On the south side shall be the standard of the camp of Reuben by their companies, the chief of the people of Reuben being Elizur the son of Shedeur, 11 his company as listed being 46,500. 12 And those to camp next to him shall be the tribe of Simeon, the chief of the people of Simeon being Shelumiel the son of Zurishaddai, 13 his company as listed being 59,300. 14 Then the tribe of Gad, the chief of the people of Gad being Eliasaph the son of Reuel, 15 his company as listed being 45,650. 16 All those listed of the camp of Reuben, by their companies, were 151,450. They shall set out second.

17 "Then the tent of meeting shall set out, with the camp of the Levites in the midst of the camps; as they camp, so shall they set out, each in position, standard by standard.

18 "On the west side shall be the standard of the camp of Ephraim by their companies, the chief of the people of Ephraim being Elishama the son of Ammihud, 19 his company as listed being 40,500. 20 And next to him shall be the tribe of Manasseh, the chief of the people of Manasseh being Gamaliel the son of Pedahzur, 21 his company as listed being 32,200. 22 Then the tribe of Benjamin, the chief of the people of Benjamin being Abidan the son of Gideoni, 23 his company as listed being 35,400. 24 All those listed of the camp of Ephraim, by their companies, were 108,100. They shall set out third on the march.

25 "On the north side shall be the standard of the camp of Dan by their companies, the chief of the people of Dan being Ahiezer the son of Ammishaddai, 26 his company as listed being 62,700. 27 And those to camp next to him shall be the tribe of Asher, the chief of the people of Asher being Pagiel the son of Ochran, 28 his company as listed being 41,500. 29 Then the tribe of Naphtali, the chief of the people of Naphtali being Ahira the son of Enan, 30 his company as listed being 53,400. 31 All those listed of the camp of Dan were 157,600. They shall set out last, standard by standard."

32 These are the people of Israel as listed by their fathers' houses. All those listed in the camps by their companies were 603,550. 33 But the Levites were not listed among the people of Israel, as the LORD commanded Moses.

34 Thus did the people of Israel. According to all that the LORD commanded Moses, so they camped by their standards, and so they set out, each one in his clan, according to his fathers' house.

The Sons of Aaron

3 These are the generations of Aaron and Moses at the time when the LORD spoke with Moses on Mount Sinai. 2 These are the names of the sons of Aaron: Nadab the firstborn, and Abihu, Eleazar, and Ithamar. 3 These are the names of the sons of Aaron, the anointed priests, whom he ordained to serve as priests. 4 But Nadab and Abihu died before the LORD when they offered unauthorized fire before the LORD in the wilderness of Sinai, and they had no children. So Eleazar and Ithamar served as priests in the lifetime of Aaron their father.

Duties of the Levites

5 And the LORD spoke to Moses, saying, 6 "Bring the tribe of Levi near, and set them before Aaron the priest, that they may minister to him. 7 They shall keep guard over him and over the whole congregation before the tent of meeting, as they minister at the tabernacle. 8 They shall guard all the furnishings of the tent of meeting, and keep guard over the people of Israel as they minister at the tabernacle. 9 And you shall give the Levites to Aaron and

his sons; they are wholly given to him from among the people of Israel. 10 And you shall appoint Aaron and his sons, and they shall guard their priesthood. But if any outsider comes near, he shall be put to death."

11 And the LORD spoke to Moses, saying, 12 "Behold, I have taken the Levites from among the people of Israel instead of every firstborn who opens the womb among the people of Israel. The Levites shall be mine, 13 for all the firstborn are mine. On the day that I struck down all the firstborn in the land of Egypt, I consecrated for my own all the firstborn in Israel, both of man and of beast. They shall be mine: I am the LORD."

14 And the LORD spoke to Moses in the wilderness of Sinai, saying, 15 "List the sons of Levi, by fathers' houses and by clans; every male from a month old and upward you shall list." 16 So Moses listed them according to the word of the LORD, as he was commanded. 17 And these were the sons of Levi by their names: Gershon and Kohath and Merari. 18 And these are the names of the sons of Gershon by their clans: Libni and Shimei. 19 And the sons of Kohath by their clans: Amram, Izhar, Hebron, and Uzziel. 20 And the sons of Merari by their clans: Mahli and Mushi. These are the clans of the Levites, by their fathers' houses.

21 To Gershon belonged the clan of the Libnites and the clan of the Shimeites; these were the clans of the Gershonites. 22 Their listing according to the number of all the males from a month old and upward was[1] 7,500. 23 The clans of the Gershonites were to camp behind the tabernacle on the west, 24 with Eliasaph, the son of Lael as chief of the fathers' house of the Gershonites. 25 And the guard duty of the sons of Gershon in the tent of meeting involved the tabernacle, the tent with its covering, the screen for the entrance of the tent of meeting, 26 the hangings of the court, the screen for the door of the court that is around the tabernacle and the altar, and its cords—all the service connected with these.

27 To Kohath belonged the clan of the Amramites and the clan of the Izharites and the clan of the Hebronites and the clan of the Uzzielites; these are the clans of the Kohathites. 28 According to the number of all the males, from a month old and upward, there were 8,600, keeping guard over the sanctuary. 29 The clans of the sons of Kohath were to camp on the south side of the tabernacle, 30 with Elizaphan the son of Uzziel as chief of the fathers' house of the clans of the Kohathites. 31 And their guard duty involved the ark, the table, the lampstand, the altars, the vessels of the sanctuary with which the priests minister, and the screen; all the service connected with these. 32 And Eleazar the son of Aaron the priest was to be chief over the chiefs of the Levites, and to have oversight of those who kept guard over the sanctuary.

33 To Merari belonged the clan of the Mahlites and the clan of the Mushites: these are the clans of Merari. 34 Their listing according to the number of all the males from a month old and upward was 6,200. 35 And the chief of the fathers' house of the clans of Merari was Zuriel the son of Abihail. They were to camp on the north side of the tabernacle. 36 And the appointed guard duty of the sons of Merari involved the frames of the tabernacle, the bars, the pillars, the bases, and all their accessories; all the service connected with these; 37 also the pillars around the court, with their bases and pegs and cords.

38 Those who were to camp before the tabernacle on the east, before the tent of meeting toward the sunrise, were Moses and Aaron and his sons, guarding the sanctuary itself, to protect[2] the people of Israel. And any outsider who came near was to be put to death. 39 All those listed among the Levites, whom Moses and

[1] Hebrew *their listing was* [2] Hebrew *guard*

Aaron listed at the commandment of
the LORD, by clans, all the males from a
month old and upward, were 22,000.

Redemption of the Firstborn

40 And the LORD said to Moses, "List all
the firstborn males of the people of Israel,
from a month old and upward, taking the
number of their names. 41 And you shall
take the Levites for me—I am the LORD—
instead of all the firstborn among the peo-
ple of Israel, and the cattle of the Levites
instead of all the firstborn among the
cattle of the people of Israel." 42 So Moses
listed all the firstborn among the people
of Israel, as the LORD commanded him.
43 And all the firstborn males, according to
the number of names, from a month old
and upward as listed were 22,273.

44 And the LORD spoke to Moses, say-
ing, 45 "Take the Levites instead of all the
firstborn among the people of Israel, and
the cattle of the Levites instead of their
cattle. The Levites shall be mine: I am the
LORD. 46 And as the redemption price for
the 273 of the firstborn of the people of
Israel, over and above the number of the
male Levites, 47 you shall take five shekels[1]
per head; you shall take them according
to the shekel of the sanctuary (the shekel
of twenty gerahs[2]), 48 and give the money
to Aaron and his sons as the redemption
price for those who are over." 49 So Moses
took the redemption money from those
who were over and above those redeemed
by the Levites. 50 From the firstborn of
the people of Israel he took the money,
1,365 shekels, by the shekel of the sanc-
tuary. 51 And Moses gave the redemption
money to Aaron and his sons, according
to the word of the LORD, as the LORD com-
manded Moses.

Duties of the Kohathites

4 The LORD spoke to Moses and Aaron,
saying, 2 "Take a census of the sons
of Kohath from among the sons of Levi,
by their clans and their fathers' houses,
3 from thirty years old up to fifty years
old, all who can come on duty, to do the
work in the tent of meeting. 4 This is the
service of the sons of Kohath in the tent of
meeting: the most holy things. 5 When the
camp is to set out, Aaron and his sons shall
go in and take down the veil of the screen
and cover the ark of the testimony with
it. 6 Then they shall put on it a covering of
goatskin[3] and spread on top of that a cloth
all of blue, and shall put in its poles. 7 And
over the table of the bread of the Presence
they shall spread a cloth of blue and put
on it the plates, the dishes for incense, the
bowls, and the flagons for the drink offer-
ing; the regular showbread also shall be
on it. 8 Then they shall spread over them
a cloth of scarlet and cover the same with
a covering of goatskin, and shall put in its
poles. 9 And they shall take a cloth of blue
and cover the lampstand for the light, with
its lamps, its tongs, its trays, and all the
vessels for oil with which it is supplied.
10 And they shall put it with all its utensils
in a covering of goatskin and put it on the
carrying frame. 11 And over the golden altar
they shall spread a cloth of blue and cover
it with a covering of goatskin, and shall put
in its poles. 12 And they shall take all the
vessels of the service that are used in the
sanctuary and put them in a cloth of blue
and cover them with a covering of goat-
skin and put them on the carrying frame.
13 And they shall take away the ashes from
the altar and spread a purple cloth over it.
14 And they shall put on it all the utensils
of the altar, which are used for the service
there, the fire pans, the forks, the shovels,
and the basins, all the utensils of the altar;
and they shall spread on it a covering of
goatskin, and shall put in its poles. 15 And
when Aaron and his sons have finished
covering the sanctuary and all the furnish-
ings of the sanctuary, as the camp sets out,
after that the sons of Kohath shall come to
carry these, but they must not touch the
holy things, lest they die. These are the

[1] A *shekel* was about 2/5 ounce or 11 grams [2] A *gerah* was about 1/50 ounce or 0.6 gram [3] The meaning of the Hebrew word is uncertain; compare Exodus 25:5

things of the tent of meeting that the sons of Kohath are to carry.

16 "And Eleazar the son of Aaron the priest shall have charge of the oil for the light, the fragrant incense, the regular grain offering, and the anointing oil, with the oversight of the whole tabernacle and all that is in it, of the sanctuary and its vessels."

17 The LORD spoke to Moses and Aaron, saying, 18 "Let not the tribe of the clans of the Kohathites be destroyed from among the Levites, 19 but deal thus with them, that they may live and not die when they come near to the most holy things: Aaron and his sons shall go in and appoint them each to his task and to his burden, 20 but they shall not go in to look on the holy things even for a moment, lest they die."

21 The LORD spoke to Moses, saying, 22 "Take a census of the sons of Gershon also, by their fathers' houses and by their clans. 23 From thirty years old up to fifty years old, you shall list them, all who can come to do duty, to do service in the tent of meeting. 24 This is the service of the clans of the Gershonites, in serving and bearing burdens: 25 they shall carry the curtains of the tabernacle and the tent of meeting with its covering and the covering of goatskin that is on top of it and the screen for the entrance of the tent of meeting 26 and the hangings of the court and the screen for the entrance of the gate of the court that is around the tabernacle and the altar, and their cords and all the equipment for their service. And they shall do all that needs to be done with regard to them. 27 All the service of the sons of the Gershonites shall be at the command of Aaron and his sons, in all that they are to carry and in all that they have to do. And you shall assign to their charge all that they are to carry. 28 This is the service of the clans of the sons of the Gershonites in the tent of meeting, and their guard duty is to be under the direction of Ithamar the son of Aaron the priest.

29 "As for the sons of Merari, you shall list them by their clans and their fathers' houses. 30 From thirty years old up to fifty years old, you shall list them, everyone who can come on duty, to do the service of the tent of meeting. 31 And this is what they are charged to carry, as the whole of their service in the tent of meeting: the frames of the tabernacle, with its bars, pillars, and bases, 32 and the pillars around the court with their bases, pegs, and cords, with all their equipment and all their accessories. And you shall list by name the objects that they are required to carry. 33 This is the service of the clans of the sons of Merari, the whole of their service in the tent of meeting, under the direction of Ithamar the son of Aaron the priest."

34 And Moses and Aaron and the chiefs of the congregation listed the sons of the Kohathites, by their clans and their fathers' houses, 35 from thirty years old up to fifty years old, everyone who could come on duty, for service in the tent of meeting; 36 and those listed by clans were 2,750. 37 This was the list of the clans of the Kohathites, all who served in the tent of meeting, whom Moses and Aaron listed according to the commandment of the LORD by Moses.

38 Those listed of the sons of Gershon, by their clans and their fathers' houses, 39 from thirty years old up to fifty years old, everyone who could come on duty for service in the tent of meeting— 40 those listed by their clans and their fathers' houses were 2,630. 41 This was the list of the clans of the sons of Gershon, all who served in the tent of meeting, whom Moses and Aaron listed according to the commandment of the LORD.

42 Those listed of the clans of the sons of Merari, by their clans and their fathers' houses, 43 from thirty years old up to fifty years old, everyone who could come on duty, for service in the tent of meeting— 44 those listed by clans were 3,200.

45 This was the list of the clans of the sons of Merari, whom Moses and Aaron listed according to the commandment of the LORD by Moses.

46 All those who were listed of the Levites, whom Moses and Aaron and the chiefs of Israel listed, by their clans and their fathers' houses, 47 from thirty years old up to fifty years old, everyone who could come to do the service of ministry and the service of bearing burdens in the tent of meeting, 48 those listed were 8,580. 49 According to the commandment of the LORD through Moses they were listed, each one with his task of serving or carrying. Thus they were listed by him, as the LORD commanded Moses.

Unclean People

5 The LORD spoke to Moses, saying, 2 "Command the people of Israel that they put out of the camp everyone who is leprous[1] or has a discharge and everyone who is unclean through contact with the dead. 3 You shall put out both male and female, putting them outside the camp, that they may not defile their camp, in the midst of which I dwell." 4 And the people of Israel did so, and put them outside the camp; as the LORD said to Moses, so the people of Israel did.

Confession and Restitution

5 And the LORD spoke to Moses, saying, 6 "Speak to the people of Israel, When a man or woman commits any of the sins that people commit by breaking faith with the LORD, and that person realizes his guilt, 7 he shall confess his sin that he has committed.[2] And he shall make full restitution for his wrong, adding a fifth to it and giving it to him to whom he did the wrong. 8 But if the man has no next of kin to whom restitution may be made for the wrong, the restitution for wrong shall go to the LORD for the priest, in addition to the ram of atonement with which atonement is made for him. 9 And every contribution, all the holy donations of the people of Israel, which they bring to the priest, shall be his. 10 Each one shall keep his holy donations: whatever anyone gives to the priest shall be his."

A Test for Adultery

11 And the LORD spoke to Moses, saying, 12 "Speak to the people of Israel, If any man's wife goes astray and breaks faith with him, 13 if a man lies with her sexually, and it is hidden from the eyes of her husband, and she is undetected though she has defiled herself, and there is no witness against her, since she was not taken in the act, 14 and if the spirit of jealousy comes over him and he is jealous of his wife who has defiled herself, or if the spirit of jealousy comes over him and he is jealous of his wife, though she has not defiled herself, 15 then the man shall bring his wife to the priest and bring the offering required of her, a tenth of an ephah[3] of barley flour. He shall pour no oil on it and put no frankincense on it, for it is a grain offering of jealousy, a grain offering of remembrance, bringing iniquity to remembrance.

16 "And the priest shall bring her near and set her before the LORD. 17 And the priest shall take holy water in an earthenware vessel and take some of the dust that is on the floor of the tabernacle and put it into the water. 18 And the priest shall set the woman before the LORD and unbind the hair of the woman's head and place in her hands the grain offering of remembrance, which is the grain offering of jealousy. And in his hand the priest shall have the water of bitterness that brings the curse. 19 Then the priest shall make her take an oath, saying, 'If no man has lain with you, and if you have not turned aside to uncleanness while you were under your husband's authority, be free from this water of bitterness that brings

[1] *Leprosy* was a term for several skin diseases; see Leviticus 13 [2] Hebrew *they shall confess their sin that they have committed* [3] An *ephah* was about 3/5 bushel or 22 liters

the curse. 20 But if you have gone astray, though you are under your husband's authority, and if you have defiled yourself, and some man other than your husband has lain with you, 21 then' (let the priest make the woman take the oath of the curse, and say to the woman) 'the LORD make you a curse and an oath among your people, when the LORD makes your thigh fall away and your body swell. 22 May this water that brings the curse pass into your bowels and make your womb swell and your thigh fall away.' And the woman shall say, 'Amen, Amen.'

23 "Then the priest shall write these curses in a book and wash them off into the water of bitterness. 24 And he shall make the woman drink the water of bitterness that brings the curse, and the water that brings the curse shall enter into her and cause bitter pain. 25 And the priest shall take the grain offering of jealousy out of the woman's hand and shall wave the grain offering before the LORD and bring it to the altar. 26 And the priest shall take a handful of the grain offering, as its memorial portion, and burn it on the altar, and afterward shall make the woman drink the water. 27 And when he has made her drink the water, then, if she has defiled herself and has broken faith with her husband, the water that brings the curse shall enter into her and cause bitter pain, and her womb shall swell, and her thigh shall fall away, and the woman shall become a curse among her people. 28 But if the woman has not defiled herself and is clean, then she shall be free and shall conceive children.

29 "This is the law in cases of jealousy, when a wife, though under her husband's authority, goes astray and defiles herself, 30 or when the spirit of jealousy comes over a man and he is jealous of his wife. Then he shall set the woman before the LORD, and the priest shall carry out for her all this law. 31 The man shall be free from iniquity, but the woman shall bear her iniquity."

The Nazirite Vow

6 And the LORD spoke to Moses, saying, 2 "Speak to the people of Israel and say to them, When either a man or a woman makes a special vow, the vow of a Nazirite,[1] to separate himself to the LORD, 3 he shall separate himself from wine and strong drink. He shall drink no vinegar made from wine or strong drink and shall not drink any juice of grapes or eat grapes, fresh or dried. 4 All the days of his separation[2] he shall eat nothing that is produced by the grapevine, not even the seeds or the skins.

5 "All the days of his vow of separation, no razor shall touch his head. Until the time is completed for which he separates himself to the LORD, he shall be holy. He shall let the locks of hair of his head grow long.

6 "All the days that he separates himself to the LORD he shall not go near a dead body. 7 Not even for his father or for his mother, for brother or sister, if they die, shall he make himself unclean, because his separation to God is on his head. 8 All the days of his separation he is holy to the LORD.

9 "And if any man dies very suddenly beside him and he defiles his consecrated head, then he shall shave his head on the day of his cleansing; on the seventh day he shall shave it. 10 On the eighth day he shall bring two turtledoves or two pigeons to the priest to the entrance of the tent of meeting, 11 and the priest shall offer one for a sin offering and the other for a burnt offering, and make atonement for him, because he sinned by reason of the dead body. And he shall consecrate his head that same day 12 and separate himself to the LORD for the days of his separation and bring a male lamb a year old for a guilt offering. But the previous period shall be void, because his separation was defiled.

[1] *Nazirite* means *one separated*, or *one consecrated* [2] Or *Naziriteship*

13 “And this is the law for the Nazirite,
when the time of his separation has been
completed: he shall be brought to the
entrance of the tent of meeting, 14 and he
shall bring his gift to the LORD, one male
lamb a year old without blemish for a
burnt offering, and one ewe lamb a year
old without blemish as a sin offering,
and one ram without blemish as a peace
offering, 15 and a basket of unleavened
bread, loaves of fine flour mixed with oil,
and unleavened wafers smeared with oil,
and their grain offering and their drink
offerings. 16 And the priest shall bring
them before the LORD and offer his sin
offering and his burnt offering, 17 and he
shall offer the ram as a sacrifice of peace
offering to the LORD, with the basket of
unleavened bread. The priest shall offer
also its grain offering and its drink offer-
ing. 18 And the Nazirite shall shave his
consecrated head at the entrance of the
tent of meeting and shall take the hair
from his consecrated head and put it on
the fire that is under the sacrifice of the
peace offering. 19 And the priest shall take
the shoulder of the ram, when it is boiled,
and one unleavened loaf out of the basket
and one unleavened wafer, and shall put
them on the hands of the Nazirite, after
he has shaved the hair of his consecra-
tion, 20 and the priest shall wave them for
a wave offering before the LORD. They are
a holy portion for the priest, together with
the breast that is waved and the thigh that
is contributed. And after that the Nazirite
may drink wine.

21 “This is the law of the Nazirite. But
if he vows an offering to the LORD above
his Nazirite vow, as he can afford, in exact
accordance with the vow that he takes,
then he shall do in addition to the law of
the Nazirite.”

Aaron's Blessing

22 The LORD spoke to Moses, saying,
23 “Speak to Aaron and his sons, saying,
Thus you shall bless the people of Israel:
you shall say to them,

24 The LORD bless you and keep you;
25 the LORD make his face to shine upon
you and be gracious to you;
26 the LORD lift up his countenance[1]
upon you and give you peace.

27 “So shall they put my name upon the
people of Israel, and I will bless them.”

Offerings at the Tabernacle's Consecration

7 On the day when Moses had finished
setting up the tabernacle and had
anointed and consecrated it with all its
furnishings and had anointed and con-
secrated the altar with all its utensils, 2 the
chiefs of Israel, heads of their fathers'
houses, who were the chiefs of the tribes,
who were over those who were listed,
approached 3 and brought their offerings
before the LORD, six wagons and twelve
oxen, a wagon for every two of the chiefs,
and for each one an ox. They brought them
before the tabernacle. 4 Then the LORD said
to Moses, 5 “Accept these from them, that
they may be used in the service of the tent
of meeting, and give them to the Levites,
to each man according to his service.”
6 So Moses took the wagons and the oxen
and gave them to the Levites. 7 Two wag-
ons and four oxen he gave to the sons of
Gershon, according to their service. 8 And
four wagons and eight oxen he gave to
the sons of Merari, according to their ser-
vice, under the direction of Ithamar the
son of Aaron the priest. 9 But to the sons
of Kohath he gave none, because they
were charged with the service of the holy
things that had to be carried on the shoul-
der. 10 And the chiefs offered offerings for
the dedication of the altar on the day it
was anointed; and the chiefs offered their
offering before the altar. 11 And the LORD
said to Moses, “They shall offer their offer-
ings, one chief each day, for the dedication
of the altar.”

[1] Or *face*

12 He who offered his offering the first day was Nahshon the son of Amminadab, of the tribe of Judah. 13 And his offering was one silver plate whose weight was 130 shekels,[1] one silver basin of 70 shekels, according to the shekel of the sanctuary, both of them full of fine flour mixed with oil for a grain offering; 14 one golden dish of 10 shekels, full of incense; 15 one bull from the herd, one ram, one male lamb a year old, for a burnt offering; 16 one male goat for a sin offering; 17 and for the sacrifice of peace offerings, two oxen, five rams, five male goats, and five male lambs a year old. This was the offering of Nahshon the son of Amminadab.

18 On the second day Nethanel the son of Zuar, the chief of Issachar, made an offering. 19 He offered for his offering one silver plate whose weight was 130 shekels, one silver basin of 70 shekels, according to the shekel of the sanctuary, both of them full of fine flour mixed with oil for a grain offering; 20 one golden dish of 10 shekels, full of incense; 21 one bull from the herd, one ram, one male lamb a year old, for a burnt offering; 22 one male goat for a sin offering; 23 and for the sacrifice of peace offerings, two oxen, five rams, five male goats, and five male lambs a year old. This was the offering of Nethanel the son of Zuar.

24 On the third day Eliab the son of Helon, the chief of the people of Zebulun: 25 his offering was one silver plate whose weight was 130 shekels, one silver basin of 70 shekels, according to the shekel of the sanctuary, both of them full of fine flour mixed with oil for a grain offering; 26 one golden dish of 10 shekels, full of incense; 27 one bull from the herd, one ram, one male lamb a year old, for a burnt offering; 28 one male goat for a sin offering; 29 and for the sacrifice of peace offerings, two oxen, five rams, five male goats, and five male lambs a year old. This was the offering of Eliab the son of Helon.

30 On the fourth day Elizur the son of Shedeur, the chief of the people of Reuben: 31 his offering was one silver plate whose weight was 130 shekels, one silver basin of 70 shekels, according to the shekel of the sanctuary, both of them full of fine flour mixed with oil for a grain offering; 32 one golden dish of 10 shekels, full of incense; 33 one bull from the herd, one ram, one male lamb a year old, for a burnt offering; 34 one male goat for a sin offering; 35 and for the sacrifice of peace offerings, two oxen, five rams, five male goats, and five male lambs a year old. This was the offering of Elizur the son of Shedeur.

36 On the fifth day Shelumiel the son of Zurishaddai, the chief of the people of Simeon: 37 his offering was one silver plate whose weight was 130 shekels, one silver basin of 70 shekels, according to the shekel of the sanctuary, both of them full of fine flour mixed with oil for a grain offering; 38 one golden dish of 10 shekels, full of incense; 39 one bull from the herd, one ram, one male lamb a year old, for a burnt offering; 40 one male goat for a sin offering; 41 and for the sacrifice of peace offerings, two oxen, five rams, five male goats, and five male lambs a year old. This was the offering of Shelumiel the son of Zurishaddai.

42 On the sixth day Eliasaph the son of Deuel, the chief of the people of Gad: 43 his offering was one silver plate whose weight was 130 shekels, one silver basin of 70 shekels, according to the shekel of the sanctuary, both of them full of fine flour mixed with oil for a grain offering; 44 one golden dish of 10 shekels, full of incense; 45 one bull from the herd, one ram, one male lamb a year old, for a burnt offering; 46 one male goat for a sin offering; 47 and for the sacrifice of peace offerings, two oxen, five rams, five male goats, and five male lambs a year old. This was the offering of Eliasaph the son of Deuel.

[1] A *shekel* was about 2/5 ounce or 11 grams

48 On the seventh day Elishama the son
of Ammihud, the chief of the people of
Ephraim: 49 his offering was one silver
plate whose weight was 130 shekels, one
silver basin of 70 shekels, according to
the shekel of the sanctuary, both of them
full of fine flour mixed with oil for a grain
offering; 50 one golden dish of 10 shekels,
full of incense; 51 one bull from the herd,
one ram, one male lamb a year old, for a
burnt offering; 52 one male goat for a sin
offering; 53 and for the sacrifice of peace
offerings, two oxen, five rams, five male
goats, and five male lambs a year old. This
was the offering of Elishama the son of
Ammihud.

54 On the eighth day Gamaliel the son
of Pedahzur, the chief of the people of
Manasseh: 55 his offering was one silver
plate whose weight was 130 shekels, one
silver basin of 70 shekels, according to
the shekel of the sanctuary, both of them
full of fine flour mixed with oil for a grain
offering; 56 one golden dish of 10 shekels,
full of incense; 57 one bull from the herd,
one ram, one male lamb a year old, for a
burnt offering; 58 one male goat for a sin
offering; 59 and for the sacrifice of peace
offerings, two oxen, five rams, five male
goats, and five male lambs a year old. This
was the offering of Gamaliel the son of
Pedahzur.

60 On the ninth day Abidan the son
of Gideoni, the chief of the people of
Benjamin: 61 his offering was one silver
plate whose weight was 130 shekels, one
silver basin of 70 shekels, according to the
shekel of the sanctuary, both of them full of
fine flour mixed with oil for a grain offer-
ing; 62 one golden dish of 10 shekels, full
of incense; 63 one bull from the herd, one
ram, one male lamb a year old, for a burnt
offering; 64 one male goat for a sin offering;
65 and for the sacrifice of peace offerings,
two oxen, five rams, five male goats, and
five male lambs a year old. This was the
offering of Abidan the son of Gideoni.

66 On the tenth day Ahiezer the son of
Ammishaddai, the chief of the people of
Dan: 67 his offering was one silver plate
whose weight was 130 shekels, one sil-
ver basin of 70 shekels, according to the
shekel of the sanctuary, both of them full
of fine flour mixed with oil for a grain
offering; 68 one golden dish of 10 shekels,
full of incense; 69 one bull from the herd,
one ram, one male lamb a year old, for a
burnt offering; 70 one male goat for a sin
offering; 71 and for the sacrifice of peace
offerings, two oxen, five rams, five male
goats, and five male lambs a year old.
This was the offering of Ahiezer the son
of Ammishaddai.

72 On the eleventh day Pagiel the son of
Ochran, the chief of the people of Asher:
73 his offering was one silver plate whose
weight was 130 shekels, one silver basin of
70 shekels, according to the shekel of the
sanctuary, both of them full of fine flour
mixed with oil for a grain offering; 74 one
golden dish of 10 shekels, full of incense;
75 one bull from the herd, one ram, one
male lamb a year old, for a burnt offering;
76 one male goat for a sin offering; 77 and
for the sacrifice of peace offerings, two
oxen, five rams, five male goats, and five
male lambs a year old. This was the offer-
ing of Pagiel the son of Ochran.

78 On the twelfth day Ahira the son of
Enan, the chief of the people of Naphtali:
79 his offering was one silver plate whose
weight was 130 shekels, one silver basin of
70 shekels, according to the shekel of the
sanctuary, both of them full of fine flour
mixed with oil for a grain offering; 80 one
golden dish of 10 shekels, full of incense;
81 one bull from the herd, one ram, one
male lamb a year old, for a burnt offering;
82 one male goat for a sin offering; 83 and
for the sacrifice of peace offerings, two
oxen, five rams, five male goats, and five
male lambs a year old. This was the offer-
ing of Ahira the son of Enan.

84 This was the dedication offering for

the altar on the day when it was anointed, from the chiefs of Israel: twelve silver plates, twelve silver basins, twelve golden dishes, 85 each silver plate weighing 130 shekels and each basin 70, all the silver of the vessels 2,400 shekels according to the shekel of the sanctuary, 86 the twelve golden dishes, full of incense, weighing 10 shekels apiece according to the shekel of the sanctuary, all the gold of the dishes being 120 shekels; 87 all the cattle for the burnt offering twelve bulls, twelve rams, twelve male lambs a year old, with their grain offering; and twelve male goats for a sin offering; 88 and all the cattle for the sacrifice of peace offerings twenty-four bulls, the rams sixty, the male goats sixty, the male lambs a year old sixty. This was the dedication offering for the altar after it was anointed.

89 And when Moses went into the tent of meeting to speak with the LORD, he heard the voice speaking to him from above the mercy seat that was on the ark of the testimony, from between the two cherubim; and it spoke to him.

The Seven Lamps

8 Now the LORD spoke to Moses, saying, 2 "Speak to Aaron and say to him, When you set up the lamps, the seven lamps shall give light in front of the lampstand." 3 And Aaron did so: he set up its lamps in front of the lampstand, as the LORD commanded Moses. 4 And this was the workmanship of the lampstand, hammered work of gold. From its base to its flowers, it was hammered work; according to the pattern that the LORD had shown Moses, so he made the lampstand.

Cleansing of the Levites

5 And the LORD spoke to Moses, saying, 6 "Take the Levites from among the people of Israel and cleanse them. 7 Thus you shall do to them to cleanse them: sprinkle the water of purification upon them, and let them go with a razor over all their body, and wash their clothes and cleanse themselves. 8 Then let them take a bull from the herd and its grain offering of fine flour mixed with oil, and you shall take another bull from the herd for a sin offering. 9 And you shall bring the Levites before the tent of meeting and assemble the whole congregation of the people of Israel. 10 When you bring the Levites before the LORD, the people of Israel shall lay their hands on the Levites, 11 and Aaron shall offer the Levites before the LORD as a wave offering from the people of Israel, that they may do the service of the LORD. 12 Then the Levites shall lay their hands on the heads of the bulls, and you shall offer the one for a sin offering and the other for a burnt offering to the LORD to make atonement for the Levites. 13 And you shall set the Levites before Aaron and his sons, and shall offer them as a wave offering to the LORD.

14 "Thus you shall separate the Levites from among the people of Israel, and the Levites shall be mine. 15 And after that the Levites shall go in to serve at the tent of meeting, when you have cleansed them and offered them as a wave offering. 16 For they are wholly given to me from among the people of Israel. Instead of all who open the womb, the firstborn of all the people of Israel, I have taken them for myself. 17 For all the firstborn among the people of Israel are mine, both of man and of beast. On the day that I struck down all the firstborn in the land of Egypt I consecrated them for myself, 18 and I have taken the Levites instead of all the firstborn among the people of Israel. 19 And I have given the Levites as a gift to Aaron and his sons from among the people of Israel, to do the service for the people of Israel at the tent of meeting and to make atonement for the people of Israel, that there may be no plague among the people of Israel when the people of Israel come near the sanctuary."

20 Thus did Moses and Aaron and all

the congregation of the people of Israel to the Levites. According to all that the LORD commanded Moses concerning the Levites, the people of Israel did to them. 21 And the Levites purified themselves from sin and washed their clothes, and Aaron offered them as a wave offering before the LORD, and Aaron made atonement for them to cleanse them. 22 And after that the Levites went in to do their service in the tent of meeting before Aaron and his sons; as the LORD had commanded Moses concerning the Levites, so they did to them.

Retirement of the Levites

23 And the LORD spoke to Moses, saying, 24 "This applies to the Levites: from twenty-five years old and upward they[1] shall come to do duty in the service of the tent of meeting. 25 And from the age of fifty years they shall withdraw from the duty of the service and serve no more. 26 They minister[2] to their brothers in the tent of meeting by keeping guard, but they shall do no service. Thus shall you do to the Levites in assigning their duties."

The Passover Celebrated

9 And the LORD spoke to Moses in the wilderness of Sinai, in the first month of the second year after they had come out of the land of Egypt, saying, 2 "Let the people of Israel keep the Passover at its appointed time. 3 On the fourteenth day of this month, at twilight, you shall keep it at its appointed time; according to all its statutes and all its rules you shall keep it." 4 So Moses told the people of Israel that they should keep the Passover. 5 And they kept the Passover in the first month, on the fourteenth day of the month, at twilight, in the wilderness of Sinai; according to all that the LORD commanded Moses, so the people of Israel did. 6 And there were certain men who were unclean through touching a dead body, so that they could not keep the Passover on that day, and they came before Moses and Aaron on that day. 7 And those men said to him, "We are unclean through touching a dead body. Why are we kept from bringing the LORD's offering at its appointed time among the people of Israel?" 8 And Moses said to them, "Wait, that I may hear what the LORD will command concerning you."

9 The LORD spoke to Moses, saying, 10 "Speak to the people of Israel, saying, If any one of you or of your descendants is unclean through touching a dead body, or is on a long journey, he shall still keep the Passover to the LORD. 11 In the second month on the fourteenth day at twilight they shall keep it. They shall eat it with unleavened bread and bitter herbs. 12 They shall leave none of it until the morning, nor break any of its bones; according to all the statute for the Passover they shall keep it. 13 But if anyone who is clean and is not on a journey fails to keep the Passover, that person shall be cut off from his people because he did not bring the LORD's offering at its appointed time; that man shall bear his sin. 14 And if a stranger sojourns among you and would keep the Passover to the LORD, according to the statute of the Passover and according to its rule, so shall he do. You shall have one statute, both for the sojourner and for the native."

The Cloud Covering the Tabernacle

15 On the day that the tabernacle was set up, the cloud covered the tabernacle, the tent of the testimony. And at evening it was over the tabernacle like the appearance of fire until morning. 16 So it was always: the cloud covered it by day[3] and the appearance of fire by night. 17 And whenever the cloud lifted from over the tent, after that the people of Israel set out, and in the place where the cloud settled down, there the people of Israel camped. 18 At the command of the LORD the people of Israel set out, and at the command of the LORD they camped. As long as the

[1] Hebrew *he*; also verses 25, 26 [2] Hebrew *He ministers* [3] Septuagint, Syriac, Vulgate; Hebrew lacks *by day*

cloud rested over the tabernacle, they remained in camp. 19 Even when the cloud continued over the tabernacle many days, the people of Israel kept the charge of the LORD and did not set out. 20 Sometimes the cloud was a few days over the tabernacle, and according to the command of the LORD they remained in camp; then according to the command of the LORD they set out. 21 And sometimes the cloud remained from evening until morning. And when the cloud lifted in the morning, they set out, or if it continued for a day and a night, when the cloud lifted they set out. 22 Whether it was two days, or a month, or a longer time, that the cloud continued over the tabernacle, abiding there, the people of Israel remained in camp and did not set out, but when it lifted they set out. 23 At the command of the LORD they camped, and at the command of the LORD they set out. They kept the charge of the LORD, at the command of the LORD by Moses.

The Silver Trumpets

10 The LORD spoke to Moses, saying, 2 "Make two silver trumpets. Of hammered work you shall make them, and you shall use them for summoning the congregation and for breaking camp. 3 And when both are blown, all the congregation shall gather themselves to you at the entrance of the tent of meeting. 4 But if they blow only one, then the chiefs, the heads of the tribes of Israel, shall gather themselves to you. 5 When you blow an alarm, the camps that are on the east side shall set out. 6 And when you blow an alarm the second time, the camps that are on the south side shall set out. An alarm is to be blown whenever they are to set out. 7 But when the assembly is to be gathered together, you shall blow a long blast, but you shall not sound an alarm. 8 And the sons of Aaron, the priests, shall blow the trumpets. The trumpets shall be to you for a perpetual statute throughout your generations. 9 And when you go to war in your land against the adversary who oppresses you, then you shall sound an alarm with the trumpets, that you may be remembered before the LORD your God, and you shall be saved from your enemies. 10 On the day of your gladness also, and at your appointed feasts and at the beginnings of your months, you shall blow the trumpets over your burnt offerings and over the sacrifices of your peace offerings. They shall be a reminder of you before your God: I am the LORD your God."

Israel Leaves Sinai

11 In the second year, in the second month, on the twentieth day of the month, the cloud lifted from over the tabernacle of the testimony, 12 and the people of Israel set out by stages from the wilderness of Sinai. And the cloud settled down in the wilderness of Paran. 13 They set out for the first time at the command of the LORD by Moses. 14 The standard of the camp of the people of Judah set out first by their companies, and over their company was Nahshon the son of Amminadab. 15 And over the company of the tribe of the people of Issachar was Nethanel the son of Zuar. 16 And over the company of the tribe of the people of Zebulun was Eliab the son of Helon.

17 And when the tabernacle was taken down, the sons of Gershon and the sons of Merari, who carried the tabernacle, set out. 18 And the standard of the camp of Reuben set out by their companies, and over their company was Elizur the son of Shedeur. 19 And over the company of the tribe of the people of Simeon was Shelumiel the son of Zurishaddai. 20 And over the company of the tribe of the people of Gad was Eliasaph the son of Deuel.

21 Then the Kohathites set out, carrying the holy things, and the tabernacle was set up before their arrival. 22 And the

standard of the camp of the people of Ephraim set out by their companies, and over their company was Elishama the son of Ammihud. 23 And over the company of the tribe of the people of Manasseh was Gamaliel the son of Pedahzur. 24 And over the company of the tribe of the people of Benjamin was Abidan the son of Gideoni.

25 Then the standard of the camp of the people of Dan, acting as the rear guard of all the camps, set out by their companies, and over their company was Ahiezer the son of Ammishaddai. 26 And over the company of the tribe of the people of Asher was Pagiel the son of Ochran. 27 And over the company of the tribe of the people of Naphtali was Ahira the son of Enan. 28 This was the order of march of the people of Israel by their companies, when they set out.

29 And Moses said to Hobab the son of Reuel the Midianite, Moses' father-in-law, "We are setting out for the place of which the LORD said, 'I will give it to you.' Come with us, and we will do good to you, for the LORD has promised good to Israel." 30 But he said to him, "I will not go. I will depart to my own land and to my kindred." 31 And he said, "Please do not leave us, for you know where we should camp in the wilderness, and you will serve as eyes for us. 32 And if you do go with us, whatever good the LORD will do to us, the same will we do to you."

33 So they set out from the mount of the LORD three days' journey. And the ark of the covenant of the LORD went before them three days' journey, to seek out a resting place for them. 34 And the cloud of the LORD was over them by day, whenever they set out from the camp.

35 And whenever the ark set out, Moses said, "Arise, O LORD, and let your enemies be scattered, and let those who hate you flee before you." 36 And when it rested, he said, "Return, O LORD, to the ten thousand thousands of Israel."

The People Complain

11 And the people complained in the hearing of the LORD about their misfortunes, and when the LORD heard it, his anger was kindled, and the fire of the LORD burned among them and consumed some outlying parts of the camp. 2 Then the people cried out to Moses, and Moses prayed to the LORD, and the fire died down. 3 So the name of that place was called Taberah,[1] because the fire of the LORD burned among them.

4 Now the rabble that was among them had a strong craving. And the people of Israel also wept again and said, "Oh that we had meat to eat! 5 We remember the fish we ate in Egypt that cost nothing, the cucumbers, the melons, the leeks, the onions, and the garlic. 6 But now our strength is dried up, and there is nothing at all but this manna to look at."

7 Now the manna was like coriander seed, and its appearance like that of bdellium. 8 The people went about and gathered it and ground it in handmills or beat it in mortars and boiled it in pots and made cakes of it. And the taste of it was like the taste of cakes baked with oil. 9 When the dew fell upon the camp in the night, the manna fell with it.

10 Moses heard the people weeping throughout their clans, everyone at the door of his tent. And the anger of the LORD blazed hotly, and Moses was displeased. 11 Moses said to the LORD, "Why have you dealt ill with your servant? And why have I not found favor in your sight, that you lay the burden of all this people on me? 12 Did I conceive all this people? Did I give them birth, that you should say to me, 'Carry them in your bosom, as a nurse carries a nursing child,' to the land that you swore to give their fathers? 13 Where am I to get meat to give to all this people? For they weep before me and say, 'Give us meat, that we may eat.' 14 I am not able to carry all this people alone; the burden is too heavy

[1] *Taberah means burning*

for me. 15 If you will treat me like this, kill
me at once, if I find favor in your sight,
that I may not see my wretchedness."

Elders Appointed to Aid Moses

16 Then the LORD said to Moses, "Gather
for me seventy men of the elders of Israel,
whom you know to be the elders of the
people and officers over them, and bring
them to the tent of meeting, and let them
take their stand there with you. 17 And I
will come down and talk with you there.
And I will take some of the Spirit that
is on you and put it on them, and they
shall bear the burden of the people with
you, so that you may not bear it yourself
alone. 18 And say to the people, 'Consecrate
yourselves for tomorrow, and you shall
eat meat, for you have wept in the hear-
ing of the LORD, saying, "Who will give
us meat to eat? For it was better for us in
Egypt." Therefore the LORD will give you
meat, and you shall eat. 19 You shall not
eat just one day, or two days, or five days,
or ten days, or twenty days, 20 but a whole
month, until it comes out at your nostrils
and becomes loathsome to you, because
you have rejected the LORD who is among
you and have wept before him, saying,
"Why did we come out of Egypt?"'" 21 But
Moses said, "The people among whom
I am number six hundred thousand on
foot, and you have said, 'I will give them
meat, that they may eat a whole month!'
22 Shall flocks and herds be slaughtered for
them, and be enough for them? Or shall all
the fish of the sea be gathered together for
them, and be enough for them?" 23 And the
LORD said to Moses, "Is the LORD's hand
shortened? Now you shall see whether my
word will come true for you or not."

24 So Moses went out and told the peo-
ple the words of the LORD. And he gath-
ered seventy men of the elders of the
people and placed them around the tent.
25 Then the LORD came down in the cloud
and spoke to him, and took some of the
Spirit that was on him and put it on the
seventy elders. And as soon as the Spirit
rested on them, they prophesied. But they
did not continue doing it.

26 Now two men remained in the camp,
one named Eldad, and the other named
Medad, and the Spirit rested on them.
They were among those registered, but
they had not gone out to the tent, and
so they prophesied in the camp. 27 And
a young man ran and told Moses, "Eldad
and Medad are prophesying in the camp."
28 And Joshua the son of Nun, the assistant
of Moses from his youth, said, "My lord
Moses, stop them." 29 But Moses said to
him, "Are you jealous for my sake? Would
that all the LORD's people were proph-
ets, that the LORD would put his Spirit
on them!" 30 And Moses and the elders of
Israel returned to the camp.

Quail and a Plague

31 Then a wind from the LORD sprang
up, and it brought quail from the sea and
let them fall beside the camp, about a
day's journey on this side and a day's jour-
ney on the other side, around the camp,
and about two cubits[1] above the ground.
32 And the people rose all that day and all
night and all the next day, and gathered
the quail. Those who gathered least gath-
ered ten homers.[2] And they spread them
out for themselves all around the camp.
33 While the meat was yet between their
teeth, before it was consumed, the anger
of the LORD was kindled against the peo-
ple, and the LORD struck down the people
with a very great plague. 34 Therefore the
name of that place was called Kibroth-
hattaavah,[3] because there they buried
the people who had the craving. 35 From
Kibroth-hattaavah the people journeyed to
Hazeroth, and they remained at Hazeroth.

Miriam and Aaron Oppose Moses

12 Miriam and Aaron spoke against
Moses because of the Cushite
woman whom he had married, for he

[1] A *cubit* was about 18 inches or 45 centimeters [2] A *homer* was about 6 bushels or 220 liters [3] *Kibroth-hattaavah* means *graves of craving*

had married a Cushite woman. 2 And they said, "Has the LORD indeed spoken only through Moses? Has he not spoken through us also?" And the LORD heard it. 3 Now the man Moses was very meek, more than all people who were on the face of the earth. 4 And suddenly the LORD said to Moses and to Aaron and Miriam, "Come out, you three, to the tent of meeting." And the three of them came out. 5 And the LORD came down in a pillar of cloud and stood at the entrance of the tent and called Aaron and Miriam, and they both came forward. 6 And he said, "Hear my words: If there is a prophet among you, I the LORD make myself known to him in a vision; I speak with him in a dream. 7 Not so with my servant Moses. He is faithful in all my house. 8 With him I speak mouth to mouth, clearly, and not in riddles, and he beholds the form of the LORD. Why then were you not afraid to speak against my servant Moses?" 9 And the anger of the LORD was kindled against them, and he departed.

10 When the cloud removed from over the tent, behold, Miriam was leprous,[1] like snow. And Aaron turned toward Miriam, and behold, she was leprous. 11 And Aaron said to Moses, "Oh, my lord, do not punish us[2] because we have done foolishly and have sinned. 12 Let her not be as one dead, whose flesh is half eaten away when he comes out of his mother's womb." 13 And Moses cried to the LORD, "O God, please heal her—please." 14 But the LORD said to Moses, "If her father had but spit in her face, should she not be shamed seven days? Let her be shut outside the camp seven days, and after that she may be brought in again." 15 So Miriam was shut outside the camp seven days, and the people did not set out on the march till Miriam was brought in again. 16 After that the people set out from Hazeroth, and camped in the wilderness of Paran.

Spies Sent into Canaan

265

13 The LORD spoke to Moses, saying, 2 "Send men to spy out the land of Canaan, which I am giving to the people of Israel. From each tribe of their fathers you shall send a man, every one a chief among them." 3 So Moses sent them from the wilderness of Paran, according to the command of the LORD, all of them men who were heads of the people of Israel. 4 And these were their names: From the tribe of Reuben, Shammua the son of Zaccur; 5 from the tribe of Simeon, Shaphat the son of Hori; 6 from the tribe of Judah, Caleb the son of Jephunneh; 7 from the tribe of Issachar, Igal the son of Joseph; 8 from the tribe of Ephraim, Hoshea the son of Nun; 9 from the tribe of Benjamin, Palti the son of Raphu; 10 from the tribe of Zebulun, Gaddiel the son of Sodi; 11 from the tribe of Joseph (that is, from the tribe of Manasseh), Gaddi the son of Susi; 12 from the tribe of Dan, Ammiel the son of Gemalli; 13 from the tribe of Asher, Sethur the son of Michael; 14 from the tribe of Naphtali, Nahbi the son of Vophsi; 15 from the tribe of Gad, Geuel the son of Machi. 16 These were the names of the men whom Moses sent to spy out the land. And Moses called Hoshea the son of Nun Joshua.

17 Moses sent them to spy out the land of Canaan and said to them, "Go up into the Negeb and go up into the hill country, 18 and see what the land is, and whether the people who dwell in it are strong or weak, whether they are few or many, 19 and whether the land that they dwell in is good or bad, and whether the cities that they dwell in are camps or strongholds, 20 and whether the land is rich or poor, and whether there are trees in it or not. Be of good courage and bring some of the fruit of the land." Now the time was the season of the first ripe grapes.

21 So they went up and spied out the land from the wilderness of Zin to Rehob,

[1] *Leprosy* was a term for several skin diseases; see Leviticus 13 [2] Hebrew *do not lay sin upon us*

near Lebo-hamath. 22 They went up into the Negeb and came to Hebron. Ahiman, Sheshai, and Talmai, the descendants of Anak, were there. (Hebron was built seven years before Zoan in Egypt.) 23 And they came to the Valley of Eshcol and cut down from there a branch with a single cluster of grapes, and they carried it on a pole between two of them; they also brought some pomegranates and figs. 24 That place was called the Valley of Eshcol,[1] because of the cluster that the people of Israel cut down from there.

Report of the Spies

25 At the end of forty days they returned from spying out the land. 26 And they came to Moses and Aaron and to all the congregation of the people of Israel in the wilderness of Paran, at Kadesh. They brought back word to them and to all the congregation, and showed them the fruit of the land. 27 And they told him, "We came to the land to which you sent us. It flows with milk and honey, and this is its fruit. 28 However, the people who dwell in the land are strong, and the cities are fortified and very large. And besides, we saw the descendants of Anak there. 29 The Amalekites dwell in the land of the Negeb. The Hittites, the Jebusites, and the Amorites dwell in the hill country. And the Canaanites dwell by the sea, and along the Jordan."

30 But Caleb quieted the people before Moses and said, "Let us go up at once and occupy it, for we are well able to overcome it." 31 Then the men who had gone up with him said, "We are not able to go up against the people, for they are stronger than we are." 32 So they brought to the people of Israel a bad report of the land that they had spied out, saying, "The land, through which we have gone to spy it out, is a land that devours its inhabitants, and all the people that we saw in it are of great height. 33 And there we saw the Nephilim (the sons of Anak, who come from the Nephilim), and we seemed to ourselves like grasshoppers, and so we seemed to them."

The People Rebel

14 Then all the congregation raised a loud cry, and the people wept that night. 2 And all the people of Israel grumbled against Moses and Aaron. The whole congregation said to them, "Would that we had died in the land of Egypt! Or would that we had died in this wilderness! 3 Why is the LORD bringing us into this land, to fall by the sword? Our wives and our little ones will become a prey. Would it not be better for us to go back to Egypt?" 4 And they said to one another, "Let us choose a leader and go back to Egypt."

5 Then Moses and Aaron fell on their faces before all the assembly of the congregation of the people of Israel. 6 And Joshua the son of Nun and Caleb the son of Jephunneh, who were among those who had spied out the land, tore their clothes 7 and said to all the congregation of the people of Israel, "The land, which we passed through to spy it out, is an exceedingly good land. 8 If the LORD delights in us, he will bring us into this land and give it to us, a land that flows with milk and honey. 9 Only do not rebel against the LORD. And do not fear the people of the land, for they are bread for us. Their protection is removed from them, and the LORD is with us; do not fear them." 10 Then all the congregation said to stone them with stones. But the glory of the LORD appeared at the tent of meeting to all the people of Israel.

11 And the LORD said to Moses, "How long will this people despise me? And how long will they not believe in me, in spite of all the signs that I have done among them? 12 I will strike them with the pestilence and disinherit them, and I will make of you a nation greater and mightier than they."

[1] *Eshcol* means *cluster*

The Twelve Spies and the Promised Land

Finally the people of Israel had reached the land of Canaan—the land that God had promised to give to them. God told Moses to choose 12 men, leaders from each of the 12 tribes, who would go into the Promised Land first, to spy out the land and the people who lived there. Moses told the men to find out if the people living there were strong or weak, many or few. They were to find out if the land was good for growing crops, and what the cities were like.

For 40 days the 12 spies walked through valleys, hills, and deserts in the Promised Land. They spied on the people in their cities. They saw what crops grew in the hills and valleys. On their way back, they picked fruit—grapes, pomegranates, and figs. The grape cluster they picked was so large, in fact, that it took two men to carry just one cluster on a pole between them.

The spies came back to camp and gave a report to Moses and the people. They showed them the fruit they had brought. The spies said that the Promised Land "flows with milk and honey," and they showed the people the enormous fruit they had found. Then the spies told about the cities they had seen. They were large, with strong walls all around them, to keep people out. They told about all the people they had seen in the land. They said that some of them were very big, like giants.

Caleb, one of the spies, said they should go in at once and take the land. But 10 of the other spies gave a bad report, saying that they would not be able to, because the people who lived in the land were too strong. The Israelites agreed with the spies who gave the bad report and they began to grumble against Moses and Aaron. They thought they would get them all killed by the sword. They wanted to choose a leader to take them back to Egypt. And worst of all, they did not trust God.

Joshua and Caleb told the people that God would give them the land. "The LORD is with us," they said "do not fear them." But the people only became more angry at Joshua and Caleb, and wanted to throw stones at them.

Then the glory of the LORD appeared at the tent of meeting. God was angry at the people. "How long," He said, "will they not believe in Me, in spite of all the signs that I have done among them?" God was so angry that He would have destroyed all the people of Israel, if Moses had not prayed for them. Still, God said that the 10 spies and all the people who grumbled could never go into the Promised Land. Instead, they would have to live in the desert for 40 years. Only after the 40 years, when those who had not trusted God had died, Caleb and Joshua and the people's children were allowed to enter the land of Canaan.

The people of Israel did not trust God or His promises. But God forgave their sin and took care of them throughout all the 40 years they lived in the desert. At the end of the 40 years, God kept His promise—He let Caleb and Joshua and the people's children go to the promised land of Canaan to live, just as He had promised.

Even though we sometimes doubt God's goodness to us, God is still always faithful. He gave His only Son, Jesus, to be our Savior. God forgives our sins if we trust in Jesus, and He gives us life eternal in the promised land of heaven.

SEEK and FIND

WHERE TO FIND THE STORY

Numbers 13:1–14:35

KEY BIBLE VERSE

"The LORD is slow to anger and abounding in steadfast love, forgiving iniquity and transgression, but he will by no means clear the guilty." (Numbers 14:18)

THREE KEY QUESTIONS

- What were the ten spies and the Israelites so afraid of?
- Why were Caleb and Joshua not afraid?
- What does God do if we sometimes doubt His goodness?

RELATED BIBLE READINGS

Deuteronomy 1:19–40; Psalm 78:37–41; 106:24–27; 1 Corinthians 10:1–5; Hebrews 3:12–19

Moses Intercedes for the People

13 But Moses said to the LORD, "Then
the Egyptians will hear of it, for you
brought up this people in your might
from among them, 14 and they will tell
the inhabitants of this land. They have
heard that you, O LORD, are in the midst
of this people. For you, O LORD, are seen
face to face, and your cloud stands over
them and you go before them, in a pillar
of cloud by day and in a pillar of fire by
night. 15 Now if you kill this people as
one man, then the nations who have
heard your fame will say, 16 'It is because
the LORD was not able to bring this people
into the land that he swore to give to them
that he has killed them in the wilderness.'
17 And now, please let the power of the
Lord be great as you have promised, say-
ing, 18 'The LORD is slow to anger
and abounding in steadfast love,
265
forgiving iniquity and transgres-
sion, but he will by no means clear the
guilty, visiting the iniquity of the fathers

on the children, to the third and the fourth generation.' 19 Please pardon the iniquity of this people, according to the greatness of your steadfast love, just as you have forgiven this people, from Egypt until now."

God Promises Judgment

20 Then the LORD said, "I have pardoned, according to your word. 21 But truly, as I live, and as all the earth shall be filled with the glory of the LORD, 22 none of the men who have seen my glory and my signs that I did in Egypt and in the wilderness, and yet have put me to the test these ten times and have not obeyed my voice, 23 shall see the land that I swore to give to their fathers. And none of those who despised me shall see it. 24 But my servant Caleb, because he has a different spirit and has followed me fully, I will bring into the land into which he went, and his descendants shall possess it. 25 Now, since the Amalekites and the Canaanites dwell in the valleys, turn tomorrow and set out for the wilderness by the way to the Red Sea."

26 And the LORD spoke to Moses and to Aaron, saying, 27 "How long shall this wicked congregation grumble against me? I have heard the grumblings of the people of Israel, which they grumble against me. 28 Say to them, 'As I live, declares the LORD, what you have said in my hearing I will do to you: 29 your dead bodies shall fall in this wilderness, and of all your number, listed in the census from twenty years old and upward, who have grumbled against me, 30 not one shall come into the land where I swore that I would make you dwell, except Caleb the son of Jephunneh and Joshua the son of Nun. 31 But your little ones, who you said would become a prey, I will bring in, and they shall know the land that you have rejected. 32 But as for you, your dead bodies shall fall in this wilderness. 33 And your children shall be shepherds in the wilderness forty years and shall suffer for your faithlessness, until the last of your dead bodies lies in the wilderness. 34 According to the number of the days in which you spied out the land, forty days, a year for each day, you shall bear your iniquity forty years, and you shall know my displeasure.' 35 I, the LORD, have spoken. Surely this will I do to all this wicked congregation who are gathered together against me: in this wilderness they shall come to a full end, and there they shall die."

36 And the men whom Moses sent to spy out the land, who returned and made all the congregation grumble against him by bringing up a bad report about the land— 37 the men who brought up a bad report of the land—died by plague before the LORD. 38 Of those men who went to spy out the land, only Joshua the son of Nun and Caleb the son of Jephunneh remained alive.

Israel Defeated in Battle

39 When Moses told these words to all the people of Israel, the people mourned greatly. 40 And they rose early in the morning and went up to the heights of the hill country, saying, "Here we are. We will go up to the place that the LORD has promised, for we have sinned." 41 But Moses said, "Why now are you transgressing the command of the LORD, when that will not succeed? 42 Do not go up, for the Lord is not among you, lest you be struck down before your enemies. 43 For there the Amalekites and the Canaanites are facing you, and you shall fall by the sword. Because you have turned back from following the LORD, the LORD will not be with you." 44 But they presumed to go up to the heights of the hill country, although neither the ark of the covenant of the LORD nor Moses departed out of the camp. 45 Then the Amalekites and the Canaanites who lived in that hill country came down and defeated them and pursued them, even to Hormah.

Laws About Sacrifices

15 The LORD spoke to Moses, saying, 2 "Speak to the people of Israel and say to them, When you come into the land you are to inhabit, which I am giving you, 3 and you offer to the LORD from the herd or from the flock a food offering[1] or a burnt offering or a sacrifice, to fulfill a vow or as a freewill offering or at your appointed feasts, to make a pleasing aroma to the LORD, 4 then he who brings his offering shall offer to the LORD a grain offering of a tenth of an ephah[2] of fine flour, mixed with a quarter of a hin[3] of oil; 5 and you shall offer with the burnt offering, or for the sacrifice, a quarter of a hin of wine for the drink offering for each lamb. 6 Or for a ram, you shall offer for a grain offering two tenths of an ephah of fine flour mixed with a third of a hin of oil. 7 And for the drink offering you shall offer a third of a hin of wine, a pleasing aroma to the LORD. 8 And when you offer a bull as a burnt offering or sacrifice, to fulfill a vow or for peace offerings to the LORD, 9 then one shall offer with the bull a grain offering of three tenths of an ephah of fine flour, mixed with half a hin of oil. 10 And you shall offer for the drink offering half a hin of wine, as a food offering, a pleasing aroma to the LORD.

11 "Thus it shall be done for each bull or ram, or for each lamb or young goat. 12 As many as you offer, so shall you do with each one, as many as there are. 13 Every native Israelite shall do these things in this way, in offering a food offering, with a pleasing aroma to the LORD. 14 And if a stranger is sojourning with you, or anyone is living permanently among you, and he wishes to offer a food offering, with a pleasing aroma to the LORD, he shall do as you do. 15 For the assembly, there shall be one statute for you and for the stranger who sojourns with you, a statute forever throughout your generations. You and the sojourner shall be alike before the LORD. 16 One law and one rule shall be for you and for the stranger who sojourns with you."

17 The LORD spoke to Moses, saying, 18 "Speak to the people of Israel and say to them, When you come into the land to which I bring you 19 and when you eat of the bread of the land, you shall present a contribution to the LORD. 20 Of the first of your dough you shall present a loaf as a contribution; like a contribution from the threshing floor, so shall you present it. 21 Some of the first of your dough you shall give to the LORD as a contribution throughout your generations.

Laws About Unintentional Sins

22 "But if you sin unintentionally,[4] and do not observe all these commandments that the LORD has spoken to Moses, 23 all that the LORD has commanded you by Moses, from the day that the LORD gave commandment, and onward throughout your generations, 24 then if it was done unintentionally without the knowledge of the congregation, all the congregation shall offer one bull from the herd for a burnt offering, a pleasing aroma to the LORD, with its grain offering and its drink offering, according to the rule, and one male goat for a sin offering. 25 And the priest shall make atonement for all the congregation of the people of Israel, and they shall be forgiven, because it was a mistake, and they have brought their offering, a food offering to the LORD, and their sin offering before the LORD for their mistake. 26 And all the congregation of the people of Israel shall be forgiven, and the stranger who sojourns among them, because the whole population was involved in the mistake.

27 "If one person sins unintentionally, he shall offer a female goat a year old for a sin offering. 28 And the priest shall make atonement before the LORD for the person

[1] Or *an offering by fire*; so throughout Numbers [2] An *ephah* was about 3/5 bushel or 22 liters [3] A *hin* was about 4 quarts or 3.5 liters [4] Or *by mistake*; also verses 24, 27, 28, 29

who makes a mistake, when he sins unin-
tentionally, to make atonement for him,
and he shall be forgiven. 29 You shall have
one law for him who does anything unin-
tentionally, for him who is native among
the people of Israel and for the stranger
who sojourns among them. 30 But the per-
son who does anything with a high hand,
whether he is native or a sojourner, reviles
the LORD, and that person shall be cut off
from among his people. 31 Because he has
despised the word of the LORD and has
broken his commandment, that person
shall be utterly cut off; his iniquity shall
be on him."

A Sabbathbreaker Executed

32 While the people of Israel were in the
wilderness, they found a man gathering
sticks on the Sabbath day. 33 And those
who found him gathering sticks brought
him to Moses and Aaron and to all the
congregation. 34 They put him in custody,
because it had not been made clear what
should be done to him. 35 And the LORD
said to Moses, "The man shall be put to
death; all the congregation shall stone
him with stones outside the camp." 36 And
all the congregation brought him outside
the camp and stoned him to death with
stones, as the LORD commanded Moses.

Tassels on Garments

37 The LORD said to Moses, 38 "Speak to
the people of Israel, and tell them to make
tassels on the corners of their garments
throughout their generations, and to put
a cord of blue on the tassel of each corner.
39 And it shall be a tassel for you to look at
and remember all the commandments of
the LORD, to do them, not to follow[1] after
your own heart and your own eyes, which
you are inclined to whore after. 40 So you
shall remember and do all my command-
ments, and be holy to your God. 41 I am the
LORD your God, who brought you out of
the land of Egypt to be your God: I am the
LORD your God."

Korah's Rebellion

16 Now Korah the son of Izhar, son
of Kohath, son of Levi, and Dathan
and Abiram the sons of Eliab, and On the
son of Peleth, sons of Reuben, took men.
2 And they rose up before Moses, with a
number of the people of Israel, 250 chiefs
of the congregation, chosen from the
assembly, well-known men. 3 They assem-
bled themselves together against Moses
and against Aaron and said to them, "You
have gone too far! For all in the congrega-
tion are holy, every one of them, and the
LORD is among them. Why then do you
exalt yourselves above the assembly of the
LORD?" 4 When Moses heard it, he fell on
his face, 5 and he said to Korah and all his
company, "In the morning the LORD will
show who is his,[2] and who is holy, and will
bring him near to him. The one whom he
chooses he will bring near to him. 6 Do
this: take censers, Korah and all his com-
pany; 7 put fire in them and put incense
on them before the LORD tomorrow, and
the man whom the LORD chooses shall be
the holy one. You have gone too far, sons
of Levi!" 8 And Moses said to Korah, "Hear
now, you sons of Levi: 9 is it too small a
thing for you that the God of Israel has
separated you from the congregation of
Israel, to bring you near to himself, to do
service in the tabernacle of the LORD and
to stand before the congregation to minis-
ter to them, 10 and that he has brought you
near him, and all your brothers the sons
of Levi with you? And would you seek the
priesthood also? 11 Therefore it is against
the LORD that you and all your company
have gathered together. What is Aaron
that you grumble against him?"

12 And Moses sent to call Dathan and
Abiram the sons of Eliab, and they said,
"We will not come up. 13 Is it a small thing
that you have brought us up out of a land
flowing with milk and honey, to kill us in
the wilderness, that you must also make
yourself a prince over us? 14 Moreover,

[1] Hebrew *to spy out* [2] Septuagint *The LORD knows those who are his*

you have not brought us into a land flowing with milk and honey, nor given us inheritance of fields and vineyards. Will you put out the eyes of these men? We will not come up." 15 And Moses was very angry and said to the LORD, "Do not respect their offering. I have not taken one donkey from them, and I have not harmed one of them."

16 And Moses said to Korah, "Be present, you and all your company, before the LORD, you and they, and Aaron, tomorrow. 17 And let every one of you take his censer and put incense on it, and every one of you bring before the LORD his censer, 250 censers; you also, and Aaron, each his censer." 18 So every man took his censer and put fire in them and laid incense on them and stood at the entrance of the tent of meeting with Moses and Aaron. 19 Then Korah assembled all the congregation against them at the entrance of the tent of meeting. And the glory of the LORD appeared to all the congregation.

20 And the LORD spoke to Moses and to Aaron, saying, 21 "Separate yourselves from among this congregation, that I may consume them in a moment." 22 And they fell on their faces and said, "O God, the God of the spirits of all flesh, shall one man sin, and will you be angry with all the congregation?" 23 And the LORD spoke to Moses, saying, 24 "Say to the congregation, Get away from the dwelling of Korah, Dathan, and Abiram."

25 Then Moses rose and went to Dathan and Abiram, and the elders of Israel followed him. 26 And he spoke to the congregation, saying, "Depart, please, from the tents of these wicked men, and touch nothing of theirs, lest you be swept away with all their sins." 27 So they got away from the dwelling of Korah, Dathan, and Abiram. And Dathan and Abiram came out and stood at the door of their tents, together with their wives, their sons, and their little ones. 28 And Moses said, "Hereby you shall know that the LORD has sent me to do all these works, and that it has not been of my own accord. 29 If these men die as all men die, or if they are visited by the fate of all mankind, then the LORD has not sent me. 30 But if the LORD creates something new, and the ground opens its mouth and swallows them up with all that belongs to them, and they go down alive into Sheol, then you shall know that these men have despised the LORD."

31 And as soon as he had finished speaking all these words, the ground under them split apart. 32 And the earth opened its mouth and swallowed them up, with their households and all the people who belonged to Korah and all their goods. 33 So they and all that belonged to them went down alive into Sheol, and the earth closed over them, and they perished from the midst of the assembly. 34 And all Israel who were around them fled at their cry, for they said, "Lest the earth swallow us up!" 35 And fire came out from the LORD and consumed the 250 men offering the incense.

36 [1] Then the LORD spoke to Moses, saying, 37 "Tell Eleazar the son of Aaron the priest to take up the censers out of the blaze. Then scatter the fire far and wide, for they have become holy. 38 As for the censers of these men who have sinned at the cost of their lives, let them be made into hammered plates as a covering for the altar, for they offered them before the LORD, and they became holy. Thus they shall be a sign to the people of Israel." 39 So Eleazar the priest took the bronze censers, which those who were burned had offered, and they were hammered out as a covering for the altar, 40 to be a reminder to the people of Israel, so that no outsider, who is not of the descendants of Aaron, should draw near to burn incense before the LORD, lest he become like Korah and his company—as the LORD said to him through Moses.

[1] Ch 17:1 in Hebrew

41 But on the next day all the congregation of the people of Israel grumbled against Moses and against Aaron, saying, "You have killed the people of the LORD." 42 And when the congregation had assembled against Moses and against Aaron, they turned toward the tent of meeting. And behold, the cloud covered it, and the glory of the LORD appeared. 43 And Moses and Aaron came to the front of the tent of meeting, 44 and the LORD spoke to Moses, saying, 45 "Get away from the midst of this congregation, that I may consume them in a moment." And they fell on their faces. 46 And Moses said to Aaron, "Take your censer, and put fire on it from off the altar and lay incense on it and carry it quickly to the congregation and make atonement for them, for wrath has gone out from the LORD; the plague has begun." 47 So Aaron took it as Moses said and ran into the midst of the assembly. And behold, the plague had already begun among the people. And he put on the incense and made atonement for the people. 48 And he stood between the dead and the living, and the plague was stopped. 49 Now those who died in the plague were 14,700, besides those who died in the affair of Korah. 50 And Aaron returned to Moses at the entrance of the tent of meeting, when the plague was stopped.

Aaron's Staff Buds

17 [1] The LORD spoke to Moses, saying, 2 "Speak to the people of Israel, and get from them staffs, one for each fathers' house, from all their chiefs according to their fathers' houses, twelve staffs. Write each man's name on his staff, 3 and write Aaron's name on the staff of Levi. For there shall be one staff for the head of each fathers' house. 4 Then you shall deposit them in the tent of meeting before the testimony, where I meet with you. 5 And the staff of the man whom I choose shall sprout. Thus I will make to cease from me the grumblings of the people of Israel, which they grumble against you." 6 Moses spoke to the people of Israel. And all their chiefs gave him staffs, one for each chief, according to their fathers' houses, twelve staffs. And the staff of Aaron was among their staffs. 7 And Moses deposited the staffs before the LORD in the tent of the testimony.

8 On the next day Moses went into the tent of the testimony, and behold, the staff of Aaron for the house of Levi had sprouted and put forth buds and produced blossoms, and it bore ripe almonds. 9 Then Moses brought out all the staffs from before the LORD to all the people of Israel. And they looked, and each man took his staff. 10 And the LORD said to Moses, "Put back the staff of Aaron before the testimony, to be kept as a sign for the rebels, that you may make an end of their grumblings against me, lest they die." 11 Thus did Moses; as the LORD commanded him, so he did.

12 And the people of Israel said to Moses, "Behold, we perish, we are undone, we are all undone. 13 Everyone who comes near, who comes near to the tabernacle of the LORD, shall die. Are we all to perish?"

Duties of Priests and Levites

18 So the LORD said to Aaron, "You and your sons and your father's house with you shall bear iniquity connected with the sanctuary, and you and your sons with you shall bear iniquity connected with your priesthood. 2 And with you bring your brothers also, the tribe of Levi, the tribe of your father, that they may join you and minister to you while you and your sons with you are before the tent of the testimony. 3 They shall keep guard over you and over the whole tent, but shall not come near to the vessels of the sanctuary or to the altar lest they, and you, die. 4 They shall join you and keep guard over the tent of meet-

[1] Ch 17:16 in Hebrew

ing for all the service of the tent, and no
outsider shall come near you. 5 And you
shall keep guard over the sanctuary and
over the altar, that there may never again
be wrath on the people of Israel. 6 And
behold, I have taken your brothers the
Levites from among the people of Israel.
They are a gift to you, given to the LORD, to
do the service of the tent of meeting. 7 And
you and your sons with you shall guard
your priesthood for all that concerns the
altar and that is within the veil; and you
shall serve. I give your priesthood as a
gift,[1] and any outsider who comes near
shall be put to death."

8 Then the LORD spoke to Aaron,
"Behold, I have given you charge of the
contributions made to me, all the con-
secrated things of the people of Israel. I
have given them to you as a portion and
to your sons as a perpetual due. 9 This
shall be yours of the most holy things,
reserved from the fire: every offering of
theirs, every grain offering of theirs and
every sin offering of theirs and every guilt
offering of theirs, which they render to
me, shall be most holy to you and to your
sons. 10 In a most holy place shall you eat
it. Every male may eat it; it is holy to you.
11 This also is yours: the contribution of
their gift, all the wave offerings of the
people of Israel. I have given them to you,
and to your sons and daughters with you,
as a perpetual due. Everyone who is clean
in your house may eat it. 12 All the best of
the oil and all the best of the wine and of
the grain, the firstfruits of what they give
to the LORD, I give to you. 13 The first ripe
fruits of all that is in their land, which
they bring to the LORD, shall be yours.
Everyone who is clean in your house
may eat it. 14 Every devoted thing in Israel
shall be yours. 15 Everything that opens
the womb of all flesh, whether man or
beast, which they offer to the LORD, shall
be yours. Nevertheless, the firstborn of
man you shall redeem, and the firstborn
of unclean animals you shall redeem.
16 And their redemption price (at a month
old you shall redeem them) you shall fix
at five shekels[2] in silver, according to the
shekel of the sanctuary, which is twenty
gerahs. 17 But the firstborn of a cow, or the
firstborn of a sheep, or the firstborn of a
goat, you shall not redeem; they are holy.
You shall sprinkle their blood on the altar
and shall burn their fat as a food offering,
with a pleasing aroma to the LORD. 18 But
their flesh shall be yours, as the breast that
is waved and as the right thigh are yours.
19 All the holy contributions that the peo-
ple of Israel present to the LORD I give to
you, and to your sons and daughters with
you, as a perpetual due. It is a covenant
of salt forever before the LORD for you
and for your offspring with you." 20 And
the LORD said to Aaron, "You shall have
no inheritance in their land, neither shall
you have any portion among them. I am
your portion and your inheritance among
the people of Israel.

21 "To the Levites I have given every tithe
in Israel for an inheritance, in return for
their service that they do, their service in
the tent of meeting, 22 so that the people of
Israel do not come near the tent of meet-
ing, lest they bear sin and die. 23 But the
Levites shall do the service of the tent of
meeting, and they shall bear their iniquity.
It shall be a perpetual statute throughout
your generations, and among the people
of Israel they shall have no inheritance.
24 For the tithe of the people of Israel,
which they present as a contribution to
the LORD, I have given to the Levites for an
inheritance. Therefore I have said of them
that they shall have no inheritance among
the people of Israel."

25 And the LORD spoke to Moses, say-
ing, 26 "Moreover, you shall speak and say
to the Levites, 'When you take from the
people of Israel the tithe that I have given
you from them for your inheritance, then
you shall present a contribution from it to

[1] Hebrew *service of gift* [2] A *shekel* was about 2/5 ounce or 11 grams

the LORD, a tithe of the tithe. 27 And your
contribution shall be counted to you as
though it were the grain of the threshing
floor, and as the fullness of the winepress.
28 So you shall also present a contribution
to the LORD from all your tithes, which
you receive from the people of Israel. And
from it you shall give the LORD's contribu-
tion to Aaron the priest. 29 Out of all the
gifts to you, you shall present every con-
tribution due to the LORD; from each its
best part is to be dedicated.' 30 Therefore
you shall say to them, 'When you have
offered from it the best of it, then the rest
shall be counted to the Levites as produce
of the threshing floor, and as produce of
the winepress. 31 And you may eat it in any
place, you and your households, for it is
your reward in return for your service in
the tent of meeting. 32 And you shall bear
no sin by reason of it, when you have con-
tributed the best of it. But you shall not
profane the holy things of the people of
Israel, lest you die.'"

Laws for Purification

19 Now the LORD spoke to Moses
and to Aaron, saying, 2 "This is
the statute of the law that the LORD has
commanded: Tell the people of Israel to
bring you a red heifer without defect, in
which there is no blemish, and on which
a yoke has never come. 3 And you shall
give it to Eleazar the priest, and it shall be
taken outside the camp and slaughtered
before him. 4 And Eleazar the priest shall
take some of its blood with his finger, and
sprinkle some of its blood toward the front
of the tent of meeting seven times. 5 And
the heifer shall be burned in his sight. Its
skin, its flesh, and its blood, with its dung,
shall be burned. 6 And the priest shall take
cedarwood and hyssop and scarlet yarn,
and throw them into the fire burning the
heifer. 7 Then the priest shall wash his
clothes and bathe his body in water, and
afterward he may come into the camp. But
the priest shall be unclean until evening.
8 The one who burns the heifer shall wash
his clothes in water and bathe his body in
water and shall be unclean until evening.
9 And a man who is clean shall gather up
the ashes of the heifer and deposit them
outside the camp in a clean place. And
they shall be kept for the water for impu-
rity for the congregation of the people of
Israel; it is a sin offering. 10 And the one
who gathers the ashes of the heifer shall
wash his clothes and be unclean until
evening. And this shall be a perpetual
statute for the people of Israel, and for the
stranger who sojourns among them.

11 "Whoever touches the dead body of
any person shall be unclean seven days.
12 He shall cleanse himself with the water
on the third day and on the seventh day,
and so be clean. But if he does not cleanse
himself on the third day and on the
seventh day, he will not become clean.
13 Whoever touches a dead person, the
body of anyone who has died, and does
not cleanse himself, defiles the taber-
nacle of the LORD, and that person shall
be cut off from Israel; because the water
for impurity was not thrown on him, he
shall be unclean. His uncleanness is still
on him.

14 "This is the law when someone dies
in a tent: everyone who comes into the
tent and everyone who is in the tent shall
be unclean seven days. 15 And every open
vessel that has no cover fastened on it
is unclean. 16 Whoever in the open field
touches someone who was killed with a
sword or who died naturally, or touches a
human bone or a grave, shall be unclean
seven days. 17 For the unclean they shall
take some ashes of the burnt sin offering,
and fresh[1] water shall be added in a ves-
sel. 18 Then a clean person shall take hys-
sop and dip it in the water and sprinkle
it on the tent and on all the furnishings
and on the persons who were there and
on whoever touched the bone, or the slain

1 Hebrew *living*

or the dead or the grave. 19 And the clean
person shall sprinkle it on the unclean on
the third day and on the seventh day. Thus
on the seventh day he shall cleanse him,
and he shall wash his clothes and bathe
himself in water, and at evening he shall
be clean.

20 "If the man who is unclean does not
cleanse himself, that person shall be cut
off from the midst of the assembly, since
he has defiled the sanctuary of the LORD.
Because the water for impurity has not
been thrown on him, he is unclean. 21 And
it shall be a statute forever for them. The
one who sprinkles the water for impu-
rity shall wash his clothes, and the one
who touches the water for impurity shall
be unclean until evening. 22 And what-
ever the unclean person touches shall be
unclean, and anyone who touches it shall
be unclean until evening."

The Death of Miriam

20 And the people of Israel, the whole
congregation, came into the wil-
derness of Zin in the first month, and the
people stayed in Kadesh. And Miriam died
there and was buried there.

The Waters of Meribah

2 Now there was no water for the con-
gregation. And they assembled them-
selves together against Moses and against
Aaron. 3 And the people quarreled with
Moses and said, "Would that we had per-
ished when our brothers perished before
the LORD! 4 Why have you brought the
assembly of the LORD into this wilder-
ness, that we should die here, both we and
our cattle? 5 And why have you made us
come up out of Egypt to bring us to this
evil place? It is no place for grain or figs
or vines or pomegranates, and there is no
water to drink." 6 Then Moses and Aaron
went from the presence of the assembly to
the entrance of the tent of meeting and fell
on their faces. And the glory of the LORD
appeared to them, 7 and the LORD spoke
to Moses, saying, 8 "Take the staff, and
assemble the congregation, you and Aaron
your brother, and tell the rock before their
eyes to yield its water. So you shall bring
water out of the rock for them and give
drink to the congregation and their cattle."
9 And Moses took the staff from before the
LORD, as he commanded him.

Moses Strikes the Rock

10 Then Moses and Aaron gathered the
assembly together before the rock, and he
said to them, "Hear now, you rebels: shall
we bring water for you out of this rock?"
11 And Moses lifted up his hand and struck
the rock with his staff twice, and water
came out abundantly, and the congrega-
tion drank, and their livestock. 12 And the
LORD said to Moses and Aaron, "Because
you did not believe in me, to uphold
me as holy in the eyes of the people of
Israel, therefore you shall not bring this
assembly into the land that I have given
them." 13 These are the waters of Meribah,[1]
where the people of Israel quarreled with
the LORD, and through them he showed
himself holy.

Edom Refuses Passage

14 Moses sent messengers from Kadesh
to the king of Edom: "Thus says your
brother Israel: You know all the hardship
that we have met: 15 how our fathers went
down to Egypt, and we lived in Egypt a
long time. And the Egyptians dealt harshly
with us and our fathers. 16 And when we
cried to the LORD, he heard our voice
and sent an angel and brought us out of
Egypt. And here we are in Kadesh, a city
on the edge of your territory. 17 Please let
us pass through your land. We will not
pass through field or vineyard, or drink
water from a well. We will go along the
King's Highway. We will not turn aside
to the right hand or to the left until we
have passed through your territory." 18 But
Edom said to him, "You shall not pass
through, lest I come out with the sword

[1] *Meribah* means *quarreling*

against you." 19 And the people of Israel said to him, "We will go up by the highway, and if we drink of your water, I and my livestock, then I will pay for it. Let me only pass through on foot, nothing more." 20 But he said, "You shall not pass through." And Edom came out against them with a large army and with a strong force. 21 Thus Edom refused to give Israel passage through his territory, so Israel turned away from him.

The Death of Aaron

22 And they journeyed from Kadesh, and the people of Israel, the whole congregation, came to Mount Hor. 23 And the LORD said to Moses and Aaron at Mount Hor, on the border of the land of Edom, 24 "Let Aaron be gathered to his people, for he shall not enter the land that I have given to the people of Israel, because you rebelled against my command at the waters of Meribah. 25 Take Aaron and Eleazar his son and bring them up to Mount Hor. 26 And strip Aaron of his garments and put them on Eleazar his son. And Aaron shall be gathered to his people and shall die there." 27 Moses did as the LORD commanded. And they went up Mount Hor in the sight of all the congregation. 28 And Moses stripped Aaron of his garments and put them on Eleazar his son. And Aaron died there on the top of the mountain. Then Moses and Eleazar came down from the mountain. 29 And when all the congregation saw that Aaron had perished, all the house of Israel wept for Aaron thirty days.

Arad Destroyed

21 When the Canaanite, the king of Arad, who lived in the Negeb, heard that Israel was coming by the way of Atharim, he fought against Israel, and took some of them captive. 2 And Israel vowed a vow to the LORD and said, "If you will indeed give this people into my hand, then I will devote their cities to destruction."[1] 3 And the LORD heeded the voice of Israel and gave over the Canaanites, and they devoted them and their cities to destruction. So the name of the place was called Hormah.[2]

The Bronze Serpent

4 From Mount Hor they set out by
the way to the Red Sea, to go around
279 the land of Edom. And the people
became impatient on the way. 5 And the people spoke against God and against Moses, "Why have you brought us up out of Egypt to die in the wilderness? For there is no food and no water, and we loathe this worthless food." 6 Then the LORD sent fiery
serpents among the people, and
they bit the people, so that many
1549 people of Israel died. 7 And the peo-
ple came to Moses and said, "We have sinned, for we have spoken against the LORD and against you. Pray to the LORD, that he take away the serpents from us." So Moses prayed for the people. 8 And the LORD said to Moses, "Make a fiery serpent and set it on a pole, and everyone who is bitten, when he sees it, shall live." 9 So Moses made a bronze[3] serpent and set it on a pole. And if a serpent bit anyone, he would look at the bronze serpent and live.

The Song of the Well

10 And the people of Israel set out and camped in Oboth. 11 And they set out from Oboth and camped at Iye-abarim, in the wilderness that is opposite Moab, toward the sunrise. 12 From there they set out and camped in the Valley of Zered. 13 From there they set out and camped on the other side of the Arnon, which is in the wilderness that extends from the border of the Amorites, for the Arnon is the border of Moab, between Moab and the Amorites. 14 Therefore it is said in the Book of the Wars of the LORD,

"Waheb in Suphah, and the valleys of
 the Arnon,
15 and the slope of the valleys

[1] That is, set apart (devote) as an offering to the Lord (for destruction); also verse 3 [2] *Hormah* means *destruction* [3] Or *copper*

that extends to the seat of Ar,
and leans to the border of Moab."

16 And from there they continued
to Beer;[1] that is the well of which the
LORD said to Moses, "Gather the people
together, so that I may give them water."
17 Then Israel sang this song:

"Spring up, O well!—Sing to it!—
18 the well that the princes made,
that the nobles of the people dug,
with the scepter and with their staffs."

And from the wilderness they went on
to Mattanah, 19 and from Mattanah to
Nahaliel, and from Nahaliel to Bamoth,
20 and from Bamoth to the valley lying in
the region of Moab by the top of Pisgah
that looks down on the desert.[2]

King Sihon Defeated

21 Then Israel sent messengers to Sihon
king of the Amorites, saying, 22 "Let me
pass through your land. We will not turn
aside into field or vineyard. We will not
drink the water of a well. We will go by
the King's Highway until we have passed
through your territory." 23 But Sihon would
not allow Israel to pass through his terri-
tory. He gathered all his people together
and went out against Israel to the wilder-
ness and came to Jahaz and fought against
Israel. 24 And Israel defeated him with the
edge of the sword and took possession of
his land from the Arnon to the Jabbok, as
far as to the Ammonites, for the border of
the Ammonites was strong. 25 And Israel
took all these cities, and Israel settled in
all the cities of the Amorites, in Heshbon,
and in all its villages. 26 For Heshbon was
the city of Sihon the king of the Amorites,
who had fought against the former king
of Moab and taken all his land out of his
hand, as far as the Arnon. 27 Therefore the
ballad singers say,

"Come to Heshbon, let it be built;
let the city of Sihon be established.
28 For fire came out from Heshbon,
flame from the city of Sihon.
It devoured Ar of Moab,
and swallowed[3] the heights of the
Arnon.
29 Woe to you, O Moab!
You are undone, O people of
Chemosh!
He has made his sons fugitives,
and his daughters captives,
to an Amorite king, Sihon.
30 So we overthrew them;
Heshbon, as far as Dibon, perished;
and we laid waste as far as Nophah;
fire spread as far as Medeba."[4]

King Og Defeated

31 Thus Israel lived in the land of the
Amorites. 32 And Moses sent to spy out
Jazer, and they captured its villages and
dispossessed the Amorites who were
there. 33 Then they turned and went up
by the way to Bashan. And Og the king of
Bashan came out against them, he and
all his people, to battle at Edrei. 34 But the
LORD said to Moses, "Do not fear him, for
I have given him into your hand, and all
his people, and his land. And you shall
do to him as you did to Sihon king of the
Amorites, who lived at Heshbon." 35 So
they defeated him and his sons and all his
people, until he had no survivor left. And
they possessed his land.

Balak Summons Balaam

22 Then the people of Israel set out
and camped in the plains of Moab
beyond the Jordan at Jericho. 2 And Balak
the son of Zippor saw all that Israel had
done to the Amorites. 3 And Moab was in
great dread of the people, because they
were many. Moab was overcome with
fear of the people of Israel. 4 And Moab
said to the elders of Midian, "This horde
will now lick up all that is around us, as
the ox licks up the grass of the field." So
Balak the son of Zippor, who was king of

[1] Beer means *well* [2] Or *Jeshimon* [3] Septuagint; Hebrew *the lords of* [4] Compare Samaritan and Septuagint; Hebrew *and we laid waste as far as Nophah, which is as far as Medeba*

The Bronze Serpent

The people of Israel were tired of living in the desert. They were tired of all their wandering. And they complained and grumbled against God. They said they should never have left Egypt. They complained that there was no food and no water. They said they were sick of eating manna—even though it was special food that God sent from heaven just for them!

Because the Israelites were so ungrateful for God's care for them and for all His blessings, God became very angry. Then the Lord sent deadly snakes to their camp. The snakes bit the people, and the people became very sick and many died.

The people came to Moses. They said, "We have sinned, for we have spoken against the LORD and against you. Pray to the LORD, that He take away the serpents from us." So Moses prayed to God, asking Him to save His people from the snakes.

God told Moses to make a snake out of bronze and put it up on a high pole, so everyone could see it. Anyone who would look at it would be healed of the snake bites. So Moses made the snake and hung it on the pole. Everyone who looked at the bronze snake hanging on the pole was healed. This is how God saved His people from the snakes when His people had sinned against Him.

God has given us something much better than a bronze

snake on a pole. God has given us His only Son, Jesus, to save us from our sins. When Jesus was here on earth long ago, Jesus said that He would be lifted up, like the snake on the pole. And so Jesus was lifted up—to hang on the cross and to suffer and die for us; to save everyone who believes in Him from sin and death and the devil; and to give us eternal life.

SEEK and FIND

WHERE TO FIND THE STORY

Numbers 21:4–9

KEY BIBLE VERSE

"And as Moses lifted up the serpent in the wilderness, so must the Son of Man be lifted up, that whoever believes in him may have eternal life." (John 3:14–15)

THREE KEY QUESTIONS

- Why was it sinful for the Israelites to complain against God about the manna?
- What did God do to save the people from the deadly snakes?
- What has God provided to save us from our sins, so that we can have eternal life?

RELATED BIBLE READINGS

Deuteronomy 8:11–16; John 3:14–16

Moab at that time, 5 sent messengers to
Balaam the son of Beor at Pethor, which
is near the River in the land of the people
of Amaw,[1] to call him, saying, "Behold, a
people has come out of Egypt. They cover
the face of the earth, and they are dwelling
opposite me. 6 Come now, curse this
people for me, since they are too mighty
for me. Perhaps I shall be able to defeat
them and drive them from the land, for I
know that he whom you bless is blessed,
and he whom you curse is cursed."

7 So the elders of Moab and the elders
of Midian departed with the fees for
divination in their hand. And they came
to Balaam and gave him Balak's message.
8 And he said to them, "Lodge here
tonight, and I will bring back word to you,

[1] Or *his kindred*

as the LORD speaks to me." So the princes of Moab stayed with Balaam. 9 And God came to Balaam and said, "Who are these men with you?" 10 And Balaam said to God, "Balak the son of Zippor, king of Moab, has sent to me, saying, 11 'Behold, a people has come out of Egypt, and it covers the face of the earth. Now come, curse them for me. Perhaps I shall be able to fight against them and drive them out.'" 12 God said to Balaam, "You shall not go with them. You shall not curse the people, for they are blessed." 13 So Balaam rose in the morning and said to the princes of Balak, "Go to your own land, for the LORD has refused to let me go with you." 14 So the princes of Moab rose and went to Balak and said, "Balaam refuses to come with us."

15 Once again Balak sent princes, more in number and more honorable than these. 16 And they came to Balaam and said to him, "Thus says Balak the son of Zippor: 'Let nothing hinder you from coming to me, 17 for I will surely do you great honor, and whatever you say to me I will do. Come, curse this people for me.'" 18 But Balaam answered and said to the servants of Balak, "Though Balak were to give me his house full of silver and gold, I could not go beyond the command of the LORD my God to do less or more. 19 So you, too, please stay here tonight, that I may know what more the LORD will say to me." 20 And God came to Balaam at night and said to him, "If the men have come to call you, rise, go with them; but only do what I tell you." 21 So Balaam rose in the morning and saddled his donkey and went with the princes of Moab.

Balaam's Donkey and the Angel

22 But God's anger was kindled because he went, and the angel of the LORD took his stand in the way as his adversary. Now he was riding on the donkey, and his two servants were with him. 23 And the donkey saw the angel of the LORD standing in the road, with a drawn sword in his hand. And the donkey turned aside out of the road and went into the field. And Balaam struck the donkey, to turn her into the road. 24 Then the angel of the LORD stood in a narrow path between the vineyards, with a wall on either side. 25 And when the donkey saw the angel of the LORD, she pushed against the wall and pressed Balaam's foot against the wall. So he struck her again. 26 Then the angel of the LORD went ahead and stood in a narrow place, where there was no way to turn either to the right or to the left. 27 When the donkey saw the angel of the LORD, she lay down under Balaam. And Balaam's anger was kindled, and he struck the donkey with his staff. 28 Then the LORD opened the mouth of the donkey, and she said to Balaam, "What have I done to you, that you have struck me these three times?" 29 And Balaam said to the donkey, "Because you have made a fool of me. I wish I had a sword in my hand, for then I would kill you." 30 And the donkey said to Balaam, "Am I not your donkey, on which you have ridden all your life long to this day? Is it my habit to treat you this way?" And he said, "No."

31 Then the LORD opened the eyes of Balaam, and he saw the angel of the LORD standing in the way, with his drawn sword in his hand. And he bowed down and fell on his face. 32 And the angel of the LORD said to him, "Why have you struck your donkey these three times? Behold, I have come out to oppose you because your way is perverse[1] before me. 33 The donkey saw me and turned aside before me these three times. If she had not turned aside from me, surely just now I would have killed you and let her live." 34 Then Balaam said to the angel of the LORD, "I have sinned, for I did not know that you stood in the road against me. Now therefore, if it is evil in your

[1] Or *reckless*

sight, I will turn back." 35 And the angel
of the LORD said to Balaam, "Go with the
men, but speak only the word that I tell
you." So Balaam went on with the princes
of Balak.
36 When Balak heard that Balaam had
come, he went out to meet him at the
city of Moab, on the border formed by
the Arnon, at the extremity of the bor-
der. 37 And Balak said to Balaam, "Did I
not send to you to call you? Why did you
not come to me? Am I not able to honor
you?" 38 Balaam said to Balak, "Behold, I
have come to you! Have I now any power
of my own to speak anything? The word
that God puts in my mouth, that must I
speak." 39 Then Balaam went with Balak,
and they came to Kiriath-huzoth. 40 And
Balak sacrificed oxen and sheep, and sent
for Balaam and for the princes who were
with him.
41 And in the morning Balak took
Balaam and brought him up to Bamoth-
baal, and from there he saw a fraction of
the people.

Balaam's First Oracle

23 And Balaam said to Balak, "Build
for me here seven altars, and pre-
pare for me here seven bulls and seven
rams." 2 Balak did as Balaam had said. And
Balak and Balaam offered on each altar
a bull and a ram. 3 And Balaam said to
Balak, "Stand beside your burnt offering,
and I will go. Perhaps the LORD will come
to meet me, and whatever he shows me I
will tell you." And he went to a bare height,
4 and God met Balaam. And Balaam said
to him, "I have arranged the seven altars
and I have offered on each altar a bull
and a ram." 5 And the LORD put a word
in Balaam's mouth and said, "Return to
Balak, and thus you shall speak." 6 And he
returned to him, and behold, he and all
the princes of Moab were standing beside
his burnt offering. 7 And Balaam took up
his discourse and said,

"From Aram Balak has brought me,
the king of Moab from the eastern
mountains:
'Come, curse Jacob for me,
and come, denounce Israel!'
8 How can I curse whom God has not
cursed?
How can I denounce whom the
LORD has not denounced?
9 For from the top of the crags I see
him,
from the hills I behold him;
behold, a people dwelling alone,
and not counting itself among the
nations!
10 Who can count the dust of Jacob
or number the fourth part[1] of
Israel?
Let me die the death of the upright,
and let my end be like his!"

11 And Balak said to Balaam, "What have
you done to me? I took you to curse my
enemies, and behold, you have done noth-
ing but bless them." 12 And he answered
and said, "Must I not take care to speak
what the LORD puts in my mouth?"

Balaam's Second Oracle

13 And Balak said to him, "Please come
with me to another place, from which
you may see them. You shall see only a
fraction of them and shall not see them
all. Then curse them for me from there."
14 And he took him to the field of Zophim,
to the top of Pisgah, and built seven altars
and offered a bull and a ram on each
altar. 15 Balaam said to Balak, "Stand here
beside your burnt offering, while I meet
the LORD over there." 16 And the LORD
met Balaam and put a word in his mouth
and said, "Return to Balak, and thus shall
you speak." 17 And he came to him, and
behold, he was standing beside his burnt
offering, and the princes of Moab with
him. And Balak said to him, "What has the
LORD spoken?" 18 And Balaam took up his
discourse and said,

[1] Or *dust clouds*

"Rise, Balak, and hear;
give ear to me, O son of Zippor:
19 God is not man, that he should lie,
or a son of man, that he should change his mind.
Has he said, and will he not do it?
Or has he spoken, and will he not fulfill it?
20 Behold, I received a command to bless:
he has blessed, and I cannot revoke it.
21 He has not beheld misfortune in Jacob,
nor has he seen trouble in Israel.
The LORD their God is with them,
and the shout of a king is among them.
22 God brings them out of Egypt
and is for them like the horns of the wild ox.
23 For there is no enchantment against Jacob,
no divination against Israel;
now it shall be said of Jacob and Israel,
'What has God wrought!'
24 Behold, a people! As a lioness it rises up
and as a lion it lifts itself;
it does not lie down until it has devoured the prey
and drunk the blood of the slain."

25 And Balak said to Balaam, "Do not
curse them at all, and do not bless them
at all." 26 But Balaam answered Balak,
"Did I not tell you, 'All that the LORD
says, that I must do'?" 27 And Balak said
to Balaam, "Come now, I will take you to
another place. Perhaps it will please God
that you may curse them for me from
there." 28 So Balak took Balaam to the
top of Peor, which overlooks the desert.[1]
29 And Balaam said to Balak, "Build for me
here seven altars and prepare for me here
seven bulls and seven rams." 30 And Balak
did as Balaam had said, and offered a bull
and a ram on each altar.

Balaam's Third Oracle

24 When Balaam saw that it pleased
the LORD to bless Israel, he did not
go, as at other times, to look for omens,
but set his face toward the wilderness.
2 And Balaam lifted up his eyes and saw
Israel camping tribe by tribe. And the
Spirit of God came upon him, 3 and he
took up his discourse and said,

"The oracle of Balaam the son of Beor,
the oracle of the man whose eye is opened,[2]
4 the oracle of him who hears the words of God,
who sees the vision of the Almighty,
falling down with his eyes uncovered:
5 How lovely are your tents, O Jacob,
your encampments, O Israel!
6 Like palm groves[3] that stretch afar,
like gardens beside a river,
like aloes that the LORD has planted,
like cedar trees beside the waters.
7 Water shall flow from his buckets,
and his seed shall be in many waters;
his king shall be higher than Agag,
and his kingdom shall be exalted.
8 God brings him out of Egypt
and is for him like the horns of the wild ox;
he shall eat up the nations, his adversaries,
and shall break their bones in pieces
and pierce them through with his arrows.
9 He crouched, he lay down like a lion
and like a lioness; who will rouse him up?
Blessed are those who bless you,
and cursed are those who curse you."

[1] Or *Jeshimon* [2] Or *closed, or perfect*; also verse 15 [3] Or *valleys*

10 And Balak's anger was kindled against
Balaam, and he struck his hands together.
And Balak said to Balaam, "I called you
to curse my enemies, and behold, you
have blessed them these three times.
11 Therefore now flee to your own place.
I said, 'I will certainly honor you,' but the
LORD has held you back from honor."
12 And Balaam said to Balak, "Did I not
tell your messengers whom you sent to
me, 13 'If Balak should give me his house
full of silver and gold, I would not be able
to go beyond the word of the LORD, to do
either good or bad of my own will. What
the LORD speaks, that will I speak'? 14 And
now, behold, I am going to my people.
Come, I will let you know what this people
will do to your people in the latter days."

Balaam's Final Oracle

15 And he took up his discourse and
said,

"The oracle of Balaam the son of Beor,
the oracle of the man whose eye is opened,
16 the oracle of him who hears the words of God,
and knows the knowledge of the Most High,
who sees the vision of the Almighty,
falling down with his eyes uncovered:
17 I see him, but not now;
I behold him, but not near:
a star shall come out of Jacob,
and a scepter shall rise out of Israel;
79
it shall crush the forehead[1] of Moab
and break down all the sons of Sheth.
18 Edom shall be dispossessed;
Seir also, his enemies, shall be dispossessed.
Israel is doing valiantly.
19 And one from Jacob shall exercise dominion
and destroy the survivors of cities!"

20 Then he looked on Amalek and took
up his discourse and said,

"Amalek was the first among the nations,
but its end is utter destruction."

21 And he looked on the Kenite, and took
up his discourse and said,

"Enduring is your dwelling place,
and your nest is set in the rock.
22 Nevertheless, Kain shall be burned
when Asshur takes you away captive."

23 And he took up his discourse and
said,

"Alas, who shall live when God does this?
24 But ships shall come from Kittim
and shall afflict Asshur and Eber;
and he too shall come to utter destruction."

25 Then Balaam rose and went back to
his place. And Balak also went his way.

Baal Worship at Peor

25 While Israel lived in Shittim,
the people began to whore with
the daughters of Moab. 2 These invited
the people to the sacrifices of their gods,
and the people ate and bowed down to
their gods. 3 So Israel yoked himself to
Baal of Peor. And the anger of the LORD
was kindled against Israel. 4 And the LORD
said to Moses, "Take all the chiefs of the
people and hang[2] them in the sun before
the LORD, that the fierce anger of the LORD
may turn away from Israel." 5 And Moses
said to the judges of Israel, "Each of you
kill those of his men who have yoked
themselves to Baal of Peor."
6 And behold, one of the people of Israel
came and brought a Midianite woman
to his family, in the sight of Moses and
in the sight of the whole congregation
of the people of Israel, while they were

[1] Hebrew *corners* [of the head] [2] Or *impale*

weeping in the entrance of the tent of
meeting. 7 When Phinehas the son of
Eleazar, son of Aaron the priest, saw it,
he rose and left the congregation and
took a spear in his hand 8 and went after
the man of Israel into the chamber and
pierced both of them, the man of Israel
and the woman through her belly. Thus
the plague on the people of Israel was
stopped. 9 Nevertheless, those who died
by the plague were twenty-four thousand.

The Zeal of Phinehas

10 And the LORD said to Moses,
11 "Phinehas the son of Eleazar, son of
Aaron the priest, has turned back my
wrath from the people of Israel, in that
he was jealous with my jealousy among
them, so that I did not consume the peo-
ple of Israel in my jealousy. 12 Therefore
say, 'Behold, I give to him my covenant
of peace, 13 and it shall be to him and to
his descendants after him the covenant
of a perpetual priesthood, because he was
jealous for his God and made atonement
for the people of Israel.'"

14 The name of the slain man of Israel,
who was killed with the Midianite wom-
an, was Zimri the son of Salu, chief
of a father's house belonging to the
Simeonites. 15 And the name of the Mid-
ianite woman who was killed was Cozbi
the daughter of Zur, who was the tribal
head of a father's house in Midian.

16 And the LORD spoke to Moses, saying,
17 "Harass the Midianites and strike them
down, 18 for they have harassed you with
their wiles, with which they beguiled you
in the matter of Peor, and in the matter of
Cozbi, the daughter of the chief of Midian,
their sister, who was killed on the day of
the plague on account of Peor."

Census of the New Generation

26 After the plague, the LORD said to
Moses and to Eleazar the son of
Aaron, the priest, 2 "Take a census of all
the congregation of the people of Israel,
from twenty years old and upward, by
their fathers' houses, all in Israel who are
able to go to war." 3 And Moses and Eleazar
the priest spoke with them in the plains
of Moab by the Jordan at Jericho, say-
ing, 4 "Take a census of the people,[1] from
twenty years old and upward," as the LORD
commanded Moses. The people of Israel
who came out of the land of Egypt were:

5 Reuben, the firstborn of Israel; the
sons of Reuben: of Hanoch, the clan of
the Hanochites; of Pallu, the clan of the
Palluites; 6 of Hezron, the clan of the Hez-
ronites; of Carmi, the clan of the Carmites.
7 These are the clans of the Reubenites,
and those listed were 43,730. 8 And the
sons of Pallu: Eliab. 9 The sons of Eliab:
Nemuel, Dathan, and Abiram. These are
the Dathan and Abiram, chosen from the
congregation, who contended against
Moses and Aaron in the company of
Korah, when they contended against the
LORD 10 and the earth opened its mouth
and swallowed them up together with
Korah, when that company died, when
the fire devoured 250 men, and they
became a warning. 11 But the sons of
Korah did not die.

12 The sons of Simeon according to
their clans: of Nemuel, the clan of the
Nemuelites; of Jamin, the clan of the Ja-
minites; of Jachin, the clan of the Jachinites;
13 of Zerah, the clan of the Zerahites; of
Shaul, the clan of the Shaulites. 14 These
are the clans of the Simeonites, 22,200.

15 The sons of Gad according to
their clans: of Zephon, the clan of the
Zephonites; of Haggi, the clan of the Hag-
gites; of Shuni, the clan of the Shunites;
16 of Ozni, the clan of the Oznites; of Eri,
the clan of the Erites; 17 of Arod, the clan
of the Arodites; of Areli, the clan of the
Arelites. 18 These are the clans of the sons
of Gad as they were listed, 40,500.

19 The sons of Judah were Er and
Onan; and Er and Onan died in the land
of Canaan. 20 And the sons of Judah

[1] *Take a census of the people* is implied (compare verse 2)

according to their clans were: of Shelah, the clan of the Shelanites; of Perez, the clan of the Perezites; of Zerah, the clan of the Zerahites. 21 And the sons of Perez were: of Hezron, the clan of the Hezronites; of Hamul, the clan of the Hamulites. 22 These are the clans of Judah as they were listed, 76,500.

23 The sons of Issachar according to their clans: of Tola, the clan of the Tolaites; of Puvah, the clan of the Punites; 24 of Jashub, the clan of the Jashubites; of Shimron, the clan of the Shimronites. 25 These are the clans of Issachar as they were listed, 64,300.

26 The sons of Zebulun, according to their clans: of Sered, the clan of the Seredites; of Elon, the clan of the Elonites; of Jahleel, the clan of the Jahleelites. 27 These are the clans of the Zebulunites as they were listed, 60,500.

28 The sons of Joseph according to their clans: Manasseh and Ephraim. 29 The sons of Manasseh: of Machir, the clan of the Machirites; and Machir was the father of Gilead; of Gilead, the clan of the Gileadites. 30 These are the sons of Gilead: of Iezer, the clan of the Iezerites; of Helek, the clan of the Helekites; 31 and of Asriel, the clan of the Asrielites; and of Shechem, the clan of the Shechemites; 32 and of Shemida, the clan of the Shemidaites; and of Hepher, the clan of the Hepherites. 33 Now Zelophehad the son of Hepher had no sons, but daughters. And the names of the daughters of Zelophehad were Mahlah, Noah, Hoglah, Milcah, and Tirzah. 34 These are the clans of Manasseh, and those listed were 52,700.

35 These are the sons of Ephraim according to their clans: of Shuthelah, the clan of the Shuthelahites; of Becher, the clan of the Becherites; of Tahan, the clan of the Tahanites. 36 And these are the sons of Shuthelah: of Eran, the clan of the Eranites. 37 These are the clans of the sons of Ephraim as they were listed, 32,500. These are the sons of Joseph according to their clans.

38 The sons of Benjamin according to their clans: of Bela, the clan of the Belaites; of Ashbel, the clan of the Ashbelites; of Ahiram, the clan of the Ahiramites; 39 of Shephupham, the clan of the Shuphamites; of Hupham, the clan of the Huphamites. 40 And the sons of Bela were Ard and Naaman: of Ard, the clan of the Ardites; of Naaman, the clan of the Naamites. 41 These are the sons of Benjamin according to their clans, and those listed were 45,600.

42 These are the sons of Dan according to their clans: of Shuham, the clan of the Shuhamites. These are the clans of Dan according to their clans. 43 All the clans of the Shuhamites, as they were listed, were 64,400.

44 The sons of Asher according to their clans: of Imnah, the clan of the Imnites; of Ishvi, the clan of the Ishvites; of Beriah, the clan of the Beriites. 45 Of the sons of Beriah: of Heber, the clan of the Heberites; of Malchiel, the clan of the Malchielites. 46 And the name of the daughter of Asher was Serah. 47 These are the clans of the sons of Asher as they were listed, 53,400.

48 The sons of Naphtali according to their clans: of Jahzeel, the clan of the Jahzeelites; of Guni, the clan of the Gunites; 49 of Jezer, the clan of the Jezerites; of Shillem, the clan of the Shillemites. 50 These are the clans of Naphtali according to their clans, and those listed were 45,400.

51 This was the list of the people of Israel, 601,730.

52 The LORD spoke to Moses, saying, 53 "Among these the land shall be divided for inheritance according to the number of names. 54 To a large tribe you shall give a large inheritance, and to a small tribe you shall give a small inheritance; every tribe shall be given its inheritance in proportion to its list. 55 But the land

shall be divided by lot. According to the names of the tribes of their fathers they shall inherit. 56 Their inheritance shall be divided according to lot between the larger and the smaller."

57 This was the list of the Levites according to their clans: of Gershon, the clan of the Gershonites; of Kohath, the clan of the Kohathites; of Merari, the clan of the Merarites. 58 These are the clans of Levi: the clan of the Libnites, the clan of the Hebronites, the clan of the Mahlites, the clan of the Mushites, the clan of the Korahites. And Kohath was the father of Amram. 59 The name of Amram's wife was Jochebed the daughter of Levi, who was born to Levi in Egypt. And she bore to Amram Aaron and Moses and Miriam their sister. 60 And to Aaron were born Nadab, Abihu, Eleazar, and Ithamar. 61 But Nadab and Abihu died when they offered unauthorized fire before the LORD. 62 And those listed were 23,000, every male from a month old and upward. For they were not listed among the people of Israel, because there was no inheritance given to them among the people of Israel.

63 These were those listed by Moses and Eleazar the priest, who listed the people of Israel in the plains of Moab by the Jordan at Jericho. 64 But among these there was not one of those listed by Moses and Aaron the priest, who had listed the people of Israel in the wilderness of Sinai. 65 For the LORD had said of them, "They shall die in the wilderness." Not one of them was left, except Caleb the son of Jephunneh and Joshua the son of Nun.

The Daughters of Zelophehad

27 Then drew near the daughters of Zelophehad the son of Hepher, son of Gilead, son of Machir, son of Manasseh, from the clans of Manasseh the son of Joseph. The names of his daughters were: Mahlah, Noah, Hoglah, Milcah, and Tirzah. 2 And they stood before Moses and before Eleazar the priest and before the chiefs and all the congregation, at the entrance of the tent of meeting, saying, 3 "Our father died in the wilderness. He was not among the company of those who gathered themselves together against the LORD in the company of Korah, but died for his own sin. And he had no sons. 4 Why should the name of our father be taken away from his clan because he had no son? Give to us a possession among our father's brothers."

5 Moses brought their case before the LORD. 6 And the LORD said to Moses, 7 "The daughters of Zelophehad are right. You shall give them possession of an inheritance among their father's brothers and transfer the inheritance of their father to them. 8 And you shall speak to the people of Israel, saying, 'If a man dies and has no son, then you shall transfer his inheritance to his daughter. 9 And if he has no daughter, then you shall give his inheritance to his brothers. 10 And if he has no brothers, then you shall give his inheritance to his father's brothers. 11 And if his father has no brothers, then you shall give his inheritance to the nearest kinsman of his clan, and he shall possess it. And it shall be for the people of Israel a statute and rule, as the LORD commanded Moses.'"

Joshua to Succeed Moses

12 The LORD said to Moses, "Go up into this mountain of Abarim and see the land that I have given to the people of Israel. 13 When you have seen it, you also shall be gathered to your people, as your brother Aaron was, 14 because you rebelled against my word in the wilderness of Zin when the congregation quarreled, failing to uphold me as holy at the waters before their eyes." (These are the waters of Meribah of Kadesh in the wilderness of Zin.) 15 Moses spoke to the LORD, saying, 16 "Let the LORD, the God of the spirits of all flesh, appoint a man over the congregation 17 who shall go out

before them and come in before them, who shall lead them out and bring them in, that the congregation of the LORD may not be as sheep that have no shepherd." 18 So the LORD said to Moses, "Take Joshua the son of Nun, a man in whom is the Spirit, and lay your hand on him. 19 Make him stand before Eleazar the priest and all the congregation, and you shall commission him in their sight. 20 You shall invest him with some of your authority, that all the congregation of the people of Israel may obey. 21 And he shall stand before Eleazar the priest, who shall inquire for him by the judgment of the Urim before the LORD. At his word they shall go out, and at his word they shall come in, both he and all the people of Israel with him, the whole congregation." 22 And Moses did as the LORD commanded him. He took Joshua and made him stand before Eleazar the priest and the whole congregation, 23 and he laid his hands on him and commissioned him as the LORD directed through Moses.

Daily Offerings

28 The LORD spoke to Moses, saying, 2 "Command the people of Israel and say to them, 'My offering, my food for my food offerings, my pleasing aroma, you shall be careful to offer to me at its appointed time.' 3 And you shall say to them, This is the food offering that you shall offer to the LORD: two male lambs a year old without blemish, day by day, as a regular offering. 4 The one lamb you shall offer in the morning, and the other lamb you shall offer at twilight; 5 also a tenth of an ephah[1] of fine flour for a grain offering, mixed with a quarter of a hin[2] of beaten oil. 6 It is a regular burnt offering, which was ordained at Mount Sinai for a pleasing aroma, a food offering to the LORD. 7 Its drink offering shall be a quarter of a hin for each lamb. In the Holy Place you shall pour out a drink offering of strong drink to the LORD. 8 The other lamb you shall offer at twilight. Like the grain offering of the morning, and like its drink offering, you shall offer it as a food offering, with a pleasing aroma to the LORD.

Sabbath Offerings

9 "On the Sabbath day, two male lambs a year old without blemish, and two tenths of an ephah of fine flour for a grain offering, mixed with oil, and its drink offering: 10 this is the burnt offering of every Sabbath, besides the regular burnt offering and its drink offering.

Monthly Offerings

11 "At the beginnings of your months, you shall offer a burnt offering to the LORD: two bulls from the herd, one ram, seven male lambs a year old without blemish; 12 also three tenths of an ephah of fine flour for a grain offering, mixed with oil, for each bull, and two tenths of fine flour for a grain offering, mixed with oil, for the one ram; 13 and a tenth of fine flour mixed with oil as a grain offering for every lamb; for a burnt offering with a pleasing aroma, a food offering to the LORD. 14 Their drink offerings shall be half a hin of wine for a bull, a third of a hin for a ram, and a quarter of a hin for a lamb. This is the burnt offering of each month throughout the months of the year. 15 Also one male goat for a sin offering to the LORD; it shall be offered besides the regular burnt offering and its drink offering.

Passover Offerings

16 "On the fourteenth day of the first month is the LORD's Passover, 17 and on the fifteenth day of this month is a feast. Seven days shall unleavened bread be eaten. 18 On the first day there shall be a holy convocation. You shall not do any ordinary work, 19 but offer a food offering, a burnt offering to the LORD: two bulls from the herd, one ram, and seven male lambs a year old; see that they are with-

[1] An *ephah* was about 3/5 bushel or 22 liters [2] A *hin* was about 4 quarts or 3.5 liters

out blemish; 20 also their grain offering
of fine flour mixed with oil; three tenths
of an ephah shall you offer for a bull, and
two tenths for a ram; 21 a tenth shall you
offer for each of the seven lambs; 22 also
one male goat for a sin offering, to make
atonement for you. 23 You shall offer these
besides the burnt offering of the morn-
ing, which is for a regular burnt offering.
24 In the same way you shall offer daily,
for seven days, the food of a food offering,
with a pleasing aroma to the LORD. It shall
be offered besides the regular burnt offer-
ing and its drink offering. 25 And on the
seventh day you shall have a holy convoca-
tion. You shall not do any ordinary work.

Offerings for the Feast of Weeks

26 "On the day of the firstfruits, when
you offer a grain offering of new grain to
the LORD at your Feast of Weeks, you shall
have a holy convocation. You shall not
do any ordinary work, 27 but offer a burnt
offering, with a pleasing aroma to the
LORD: two bulls from the herd, one ram,
seven male lambs a year old; 28 also their
grain offering of fine flour mixed with oil,
three tenths of an ephah for each bull, two
tenths for one ram, 29 a tenth for each of
the seven lambs; 30 with one male goat, to
make atonement for you. 31 Besides the
regular burnt offering and its grain offer-
ing, you shall offer them and their drink
offering. See that they are without blemish.

Offerings for the Feast of Trumpets

29 "On the first day of the seventh
month you shall have a holy con-
vocation. You shall not do any ordinary
work. It is a day for you to blow the trum-
pets, 2 and you shall offer a burnt offering,
for a pleasing aroma to the LORD: one bull
from the herd, one ram, seven male lambs
a year old without blemish; 3 also their
grain offering of fine flour mixed with
oil, three tenths of an ephah[1] for the bull,
two tenths for the ram, 4 and one tenth for
each of the seven lambs; 5 with one male
goat for a sin offering, to make atonement
for you; 6 besides the burnt offering of the
new moon, and its grain offering, and the
regular burnt offering and its grain offer-
ing, and their drink offering, according to
the rule for them, for a pleasing aroma, a
food offering to the LORD.

Offerings for the Day of Atonement

7 "On the tenth day of this seventh
month you shall have a holy convocation
and afflict yourselves. You shall do no
work, 8 but you shall offer a burnt offering
to the LORD, a pleasing aroma: one bull
from the herd, one ram, seven male lambs
a year old: see that they are without blem-
ish. 9 And their grain offering shall be of
fine flour mixed with oil, three tenths of
an ephah for the bull, two tenths for the
one ram, 10 a tenth for each of the seven
lambs: 11 also one male goat for a sin offer-
ing, besides the sin offering of atonement,
and the regular burnt offering and its
grain offering, and their drink offerings.

Offerings for the Feast of Booths

12 "On the fifteenth day of the seventh
month you shall have a holy convocation.
You shall not do any ordinary work, and
you shall keep a feast to the LORD seven
days. 13 And you shall offer a burnt offering,
a food offering, with a pleasing aroma to
the LORD, thirteen bulls from the herd, two
rams, fourteen male lambs a year old; they
shall be without blemish; 14 and their grain
offering of fine flour mixed with oil, three
tenths of an ephah for each of the thir-
teen bulls, two tenths for each of the two
rams, 15 and a tenth for each of the fourteen
lambs; 16 also one male goat for a sin offer-
ing, besides the regular burnt offering, its
grain offering and its drink offering.

17 "On the second day twelve bulls from
the herd, two rams, fourteen male lambs a
year old without blemish, 18 with the grain
offering and the drink offerings for the
bulls, for the rams, and for the lambs, in
the prescribed quantities; 19 also one male

[1] An *ephah* was about 3/5 bushel or 22 liters

goat for a sin offering, besides the regular burnt offering and its grain offering, and their drink offerings.

20 “On the third day eleven bulls, two rams, fourteen male lambs a year old without blemish, 21 with the grain offering and the drink offerings for the bulls, for the rams, and for the lambs, in the prescribed quantities; 22 also one male goat for a sin offering, besides the regular burnt offering and its grain offering and its drink offering.

23 “On the fourth day ten bulls, two rams, fourteen male lambs a year old without blemish, 24 with the grain offering and the drink offerings for the bulls, for the rams, and for the lambs, in the prescribed quantities; 25 also one male goat for a sin offering, besides the regular burnt offering, its grain offering and its drink offering.

26 “On the fifth day nine bulls, two rams, fourteen male lambs a year old without blemish, 27 with the grain offering and the drink offerings for the bulls, for the rams, and for the lambs, in the prescribed quantities; 28 also one male goat for a sin offering; besides the regular burnt offering and its grain offering and its drink offering.

29 “On the sixth day eight bulls, two rams, fourteen male lambs a year old without blemish, 30 with the grain offering and the drink offerings for the bulls, for the rams, and for the lambs, in the prescribed quantities; 31 also one male goat for a sin offering; besides the regular burnt offering, its grain offering, and its drink offerings.

32 “On the seventh day seven bulls, two rams, fourteen male lambs a year old without blemish, 33 with the grain offering and the drink offerings for the bulls, for the rams, and for the lambs, in the prescribed quantities; 34 also one male goat for a sin offering; besides the regular burnt offering, its grain offering, and its drink offering.

35 “On the eighth day you shall have a solemn assembly. You shall not do any ordinary work, 36 but you shall offer a burnt offering, a food offering, with a pleasing aroma to the LORD: one bull, one ram, seven male lambs a year old without blemish, 37 and the grain offering and the drink offerings for the bull, for the ram, and for the lambs, in the prescribed quantities; 38 also one male goat for a sin offering; besides the regular burnt offering and its grain offering and its drink offering.

39 “These you shall offer to the LORD at your appointed feasts, in addition to your vow offerings and your freewill offerings, for your burnt offerings, and for your grain offerings, and for your drink offerings, and for your peace offerings.”

40[1] So Moses told the people of Israel everything just as the LORD had commanded Moses.

Men and Vows

30 Moses spoke to the heads of the tribes of the people of Israel, saying, “This is what the LORD has commanded. 2 If a man vows a vow to the LORD, or swears an oath to bind himself by a pledge, he shall not break his word. He shall do according to all that proceeds out of his mouth.

Women and Vows

3 “If a woman vows a vow to the LORD and binds herself by a pledge, while within her father’s house in her youth, 4 and her father hears of her vow and of her pledge by which she has bound herself and says nothing to her, then all her vows shall stand, and every pledge by which she has bound herself shall stand. 5 But if her father opposes her on the day that he hears of it, no vow of hers, no pledge by which she has bound herself shall stand. And the LORD will forgive her, because her father opposed her.

6 “If she marries a husband, while under her vows or any thoughtless utterance of

[1] Ch 30:1 in Hebrew

her lips by which she has bound herself, 7 and her husband hears of it and says nothing to her on the day that he hears, then her vows shall stand, and her pledges by which she has bound herself shall stand. 8 But if, on the day that her husband comes to hear of it, he opposes her, then he makes void her vow that was on her, and the thoughtless utterance of her lips by which she bound herself. And the LORD will forgive her. 9 (But any vow of a widow or of a divorced woman, anything by which she has bound herself, shall stand against her.) 10 And if she vowed in her husband's house or bound herself by a pledge with an oath, 11 and her husband heard of it and said nothing to her and did not oppose her, then all her vows shall stand, and every pledge by which she bound herself shall stand. 12 But if her husband makes them null and void on the day that he hears them, then whatever proceeds out of her lips concerning her vows or concerning her pledge of herself shall not stand. Her husband has made them void, and the LORD will forgive her. 13 Any vow and any binding oath to afflict herself, her husband may establish,[1] or her husband may make void. 14 But if her husband says nothing to her from day to day, then he establishes all her vows or all her pledges that are upon her. He has established them, because he said nothing to her on the day that he heard of them. 15 But if he makes them null and void after he has heard of them, then he shall bear her iniquity."

16 These are the statutes that the LORD commanded Moses about a man and his wife and about a father and his daughter while she is in her youth within her father's house.

Vengeance on Midian

31 The LORD spoke to Moses, saying, 2 "Avenge the people of Israel on the Midianites. Afterward you shall be gathered to your people." 3 So Moses spoke to the people, saying, "Arm men from among you for the war, that they may go against Midian to execute the LORD's vengeance on Midian. 4 You shall send a thousand from each of the tribes of Israel to the war." 5 So there were provided, out of the thousands of Israel, a thousand from each tribe, twelve thousand armed for war. 6 And Moses sent them to the war, a thousand from each tribe, together with Phinehas the son of Eleazar the priest, with the vessels of the sanctuary and the trumpets for the alarm in his hand. 7 They warred against Midian, as the LORD commanded Moses, and killed every male. 8 They killed the kings of Midian with the rest of their slain, Evi, Rekem, Zur, Hur, and Reba, the five kings of Midian. And they also killed Balaam the son of Beor with the sword. 9 And the people of Israel took captive the women of Midian and their little ones, and they took as plunder all their cattle, their flocks, and all their goods. 10 All their cities in the places where they lived, and all their encampments, they burned with fire, 11 and took all the spoil and all the plunder, both of man and of beast. 12 Then they brought the captives and the plunder and the spoil to Moses, and to Eleazar the priest, and to the congregation of the people of Israel, at the camp on the plains of Moab by the Jordan at Jericho.

13 Moses and Eleazar the priest and all the chiefs of the congregation went to meet them outside the camp. 14 And Moses was angry with the officers of the army, the commanders of thousands and the commanders of hundreds, who had come from service in the war. 15 Moses said to them, "Have you let all the women live? 16 Behold, these, on Balaam's advice, caused the people of Israel to act treacherously against the LORD in the incident of Peor, and so the plague came among the congregation of the LORD. 17 Now therefore, kill every male among the little ones,

[1] Or *may allow to stand*

and kill every woman who has known man by lying with him. 18 But all the young girls who have not known man by lying with him keep alive for yourselves. 19 Encamp outside the camp seven days. Whoever of you has killed any person and whoever has touched any slain, purify yourselves and your captives on the third day and on the seventh day. 20 You shall purify every garment, every article of skin, all work of goats' hair, and every article of wood."

21 Then Eleazar the priest said to the men in the army who had gone to battle: "This is the statute of the law that the LORD has commanded Moses: 22 only the gold, the silver, the bronze, the iron, the tin, and the lead, 23 everything that can stand the fire, you shall pass through the fire, and it shall be clean. Nevertheless, it shall also be purified with the water for impurity. And whatever cannot stand the fire, you shall pass through the water. 24 You must wash your clothes on the seventh day, and you shall be clean. And afterward you may come into the camp."

25 The LORD said to Moses, 26 "Take the count of the plunder that was taken, both of man and of beast, you and Eleazar the priest and the heads of the fathers' houses of the congregation, 27 and divide the plunder into two parts between the warriors who went out to battle and all the congregation. 28 And levy for the LORD a tribute from the men of war who went out to battle, one out of five hundred, of the people and of the oxen and of the donkeys and of the flocks. 29 Take it from their half and give it to Eleazar the priest as a contribution to the LORD. 30 And from the people of Israel's half you shall take one drawn out of every fifty, of the people, of the oxen, of the donkeys, and of the flocks, of all the cattle, and give them to the Levites who keep guard over the tabernacle of the LORD." 31 And Moses and Eleazar the priest did as the LORD commanded Moses.

32 Now the plunder remaining of the spoil that the army took was 675,000 sheep, 33 72,000 cattle, 34 61,000 donkeys, 35 and 32,000 persons in all, women who had not known man by lying with him. 36 And the half, the portion of those who had gone out in the army, numbered 337,500 sheep, 37 and the LORD's tribute of sheep was 675. 38 The cattle were 36,000, of which the LORD's tribute was 72. 39 The donkeys were 30,500, of which the LORD's tribute was 61. 40 The persons were 16,000, of which the LORD's tribute was 32 persons. 41 And Moses gave the tribute, which was the contribution for the LORD, to Eleazar the priest, as the LORD commanded Moses.

42 From the people of Israel's half, which Moses separated from that of the men who had served in the army— 43 now the congregation's half was 337,500 sheep, 44 36,000 cattle, 45 and 30,500 donkeys, 46 and 16,000 persons— 47 from the people of Israel's half Moses took one of every 50, both of persons and of beasts, and gave them to the Levites who kept guard over the tabernacle of the LORD, as the LORD commanded Moses.

48 Then the officers who were over the thousands of the army, the commanders of thousands and the commanders of hundreds, came near to Moses 49 and said to Moses, "Your servants have counted the men of war who are under our command, and there is not a man missing from us. 50 And we have brought the LORD's offering, what each man found, articles of gold, armlets and bracelets, signet rings, earrings, and beads, to make atonement for ourselves before the LORD." 51 And Moses and Eleazar the priest received from them the gold, all crafted articles. 52 And all the gold of the contribution that they presented to the LORD, from the commanders of thousands and the commanders of hundreds, was 16,750 shekels.[1] 53 (The men in the army had each taken plunder

[1] A *shekel* was about 2/5 ounce or 11 grams

for himself.) 54 And Moses and Eleazar the priest received the gold from the commanders of thousands and of hundreds, and brought it into the tent of meeting, as a memorial for the people of Israel before the LORD.

Reuben and Gad Settle in Gilead

32 Now the people of Reuben and the people of Gad had a very great number of livestock. And they saw the land of Jazer and the land of Gilead, and behold, the place was a place for livestock. 2 So the people of Gad and the people of Reuben came and said to Moses and to Eleazar the priest and to the chiefs of the congregation, 3 "Ataroth, Dibon, Jazer, Nimrah, Heshbon, Elealeh, Sebam, Nebo, and Beon, 4 the land that the LORD struck down before the congregation of Israel, is a land for livestock, and your servants have livestock." 5 And they said, "If we have found favor in your sight, let this land be given to your servants for a possession. Do not take us across the Jordan."

6 But Moses said to the people of Gad and to the people of Reuben, "Shall your brothers go to the war while you sit here? 7 Why will you discourage the heart of the people of Israel from going over into the land that the LORD has given them? 8 Your fathers did this, when I sent them from Kadesh-barnea to see the land. 9 For when they went up to the Valley of Eshcol and saw the land, they discouraged the heart of the people of Israel from going into the land that the LORD had given them. 10 And the LORD's anger was kindled on that day, and he swore, saying, 11 'Surely none of the men who came up out of Egypt, from twenty years old and upward, shall see the land that I swore to give to Abraham, to Isaac, and to Jacob, because they have not wholly followed me, 12 none except Caleb the son of Jephunneh the Kenizzite and Joshua the son of Nun, for they have wholly followed the LORD.' 13 And the LORD's anger was kindled against Israel, and he made them wander in the wilderness forty years, until all the generation that had done evil in the sight of the LORD was gone. 14 And behold, you have risen in your fathers' place, a brood of sinful men, to increase still more the fierce anger of the LORD against Israel! 15 For if you turn away from following him, he will again abandon them in the wilderness, and you will destroy all this people."

16 Then they came near to him and said, "We will build sheepfolds here for our livestock, and cities for our little ones, 17 but we will take up arms, ready to go before the people of Israel, until we have brought them to their place. And our little ones shall live in the fortified cities because of the inhabitants of the land. 18 We will not return to our homes until each of the people of Israel has gained his inheritance. 19 For we will not inherit with them on the other side of the Jordan and beyond, because our inheritance has come to us on this side of the Jordan to the east." 20 So Moses said to them, "If you will do this, if you will take up arms to go before the LORD for the war, 21 and every armed man of you will pass over the Jordan before the LORD, until he has driven out his enemies from before him 22 and the land is subdued before the LORD; then after that you shall return and be free of obligation to the LORD and to Israel, and this land shall be your possession before the LORD. 23 But if you will not do so, behold, you have sinned against the LORD, and be sure your sin will find you out. 24 Build cities for your little ones and folds for your sheep, and do what you have promised." 25 And the people of Gad and the people of Reuben said to Moses, "Your servants will do as my lord commands. 26 Our little ones, our wives, our livestock, and all our cattle shall remain there in the cities of Gilead, 27 but your servants will pass over, every man who is

armed for war, before the LORD to battle,
as my lord orders."
28 So Moses gave command concern-
ing them to Eleazar the priest and to
Joshua the son of Nun and to the heads
of the fathers' houses of the tribes of the
people of Israel. 29 And Moses said to
them, "If the people of Gad and the peo-
ple of Reuben, every man who is armed
to battle before the LORD, will pass with
you over the Jordan and the land shall
be subdued before you, then you shall
give them the land of Gilead for a posses-
sion. 30 However, if they will not pass over
with you armed, they shall have posses-
sions among you in the land of Canaan."
31 And the people of Gad and the people
of Reuben answered, "What the LORD has
said to your servants, we will do. 32 We will
pass over armed before the LORD into the
land of Canaan, and the possession of our
inheritance shall remain with us beyond
the Jordan."
33 And Moses gave to them, to the peo-
ple of Gad and to the people of Reuben
and to the half-tribe of Manasseh the son
of Joseph, the kingdom of Sihon king of
the Amorites and the kingdom of Og king
of Bashan, the land and its cities with their
territories, the cities of the land through-
out the country. 34 And the people of Gad
built Dibon, Ataroth, Aroer, 35 Atroth-
shophan, Jazer, Jogbehah, 36 Beth-nimrah
and Beth-haran, fortified cities, and folds
for sheep. 37 And the people of Reuben
built Heshbon, Elealeh, Kiriathaim,
38 Nebo, and Baal-meon (their names
were changed), and Sibmah. And they
gave other names to the cities that they
built. 39 And the sons of Machir the son of
Manasseh went to Gilead and captured it,
and dispossessed the Amorites who were
in it. 40 And Moses gave Gilead to Machir
the son of Manasseh, and he settled in it.
41 And Jair the son of Manasseh went and
captured their villages, and called them
Havvoth-jair.[1] 42 And Nobah went and cap-
tured Kenath and its villages, and called it
Nobah, after his own name.

Recounting Israel's Journey

33 These are the stages of the peo-
ple of Israel, when they went
out of the land of Egypt by their compa-
nies under the leadership of Moses and
Aaron. 2 Moses wrote down their starting
places, stage by stage, by command of the
LORD, and these are their stages accord-
ing to their starting places. 3 They set
out from Rameses in the first month, on
the fifteenth day of the first month. On
the day after the Passover, the people of
Israel went out triumphantly in the sight
of all the Egyptians, 4 while the Egyptians
were burying all their firstborn, whom
the LORD had struck down among them.
On their gods also the LORD executed
judgments.
5 So the people of Israel set out from
Rameses and camped at Succoth. 6 And
they set out from Succoth and camped at
Etham, which is on the edge of the wil-
derness. 7 And they set out from Etham
and turned back to Pi-hahiroth, which
is east of Baal-zephon, and they camped
before Migdol. 8 And they set out from
before Hahiroth[2] and passed through
the midst of the sea into the wilderness,
and they went a three days' journey in
the wilderness of Etham and camped at
Marah. 9 And they set out from Marah and
came to Elim; at Elim there were twelve
springs of water and seventy palm trees,
and they camped there. 10 And they set
out from Elim and camped by the Red
Sea. 11 And they set out from the Red Sea
and camped in the wilderness of Sin.
12 And they set out from the wilderness
of Sin and camped at Dophkah. 13 And
they set out from Dophkah and camped
at Alush. 14 And they set out from Alush
and camped at Rephidim, where there
was no water for the people to drink.
15 And they set out from Rephidim and

[1] *Havvoth-jair* means *the villages of Jair* [2] Some manuscripts and versions *Pi-hahiroth*

camped in the wilderness of Sinai. 16 And they set out from the wilderness of Sinai and camped at Kibroth-hattaavah. 17 And they set out from Kibroth-hattaavah and camped at Hazeroth. 18 And they set out from Hazeroth and camped at Rithmah. 19 And they set out from Rithmah and camped at Rimmon-perez. 20 And they set out from Rimmon-perez and camped at Libnah. 21 And they set out from Libnah and camped at Rissah. 22 And they set out from Rissah and camped at Kehelathah. 23 And they set out from Kehelathah and camped at Mount Shepher. 24 And they set out from Mount Shepher and camped at Haradah. 25 And they set out from Haradah and camped at Makheloth. 26 And they set out from Makheloth and camped at Tahath. 27 And they set out from Tahath and camped at Terah. 28 And they set out from Terah and camped at Mithkah. 29 And they set out from Mithkah and camped at Hashmonah. 30 And they set out from Hashmonah and camped at Moseroth. 31 And they set out from Moseroth and camped at Bene-jaakan. 32 And they set out from Bene-jaakan and camped at Hor-haggidgad. 33 And they set out from Hor-haggidgad and camped at Jotbathah. 34 And they set out from Jotbathah and camped at Abronah. 35 And they set out from Abronah and camped at Ezion-geber. 36 And they set out from Ezion-geber and camped in the wilderness of Zin (that is, Kadesh). 37 And they set out from Kadesh and camped at Mount Hor, on the edge of the land of Edom.

38 And Aaron the priest went up Mount Hor at the command of the LORD and died there, in the fortieth year after the people of Israel had come out of the land of Egypt, on the first day of the fifth month. 39 And Aaron was 123 years old when he died on Mount Hor.

40 And the Canaanite, the king of Arad, who lived in the Negeb in the land of Canaan, heard of the coming of the people of Israel.

41 And they set out from Mount Hor and camped at Zalmonah. 42 And they set out from Zalmonah and camped at Punon. 43 And they set out from Punon and camped at Oboth. 44 And they set out from Oboth and camped at Iye-abarim, in the territory of Moab. 45 And they set out from Iyim and camped at Dibon-gad. 46 And they set out from Dibon-gad and camped at Almon-diblathaim. 47 And they set out from Almon-diblathaim and camped in the mountains of Abarim, before Nebo. 48 And they set out from the mountains of Abarim and camped in the plains of Moab by the Jordan at Jericho; 49 they camped by the Jordan from Beth-jeshimoth as far as Abel-shittim in the plains of Moab.

Drive Out the Inhabitants

50 And the LORD spoke to Moses in the plains of Moab by the Jordan at Jericho, saying, 51 "Speak to the people of Israel and say to them, When you pass over the Jordan into the land of Canaan, 52 then you shall drive out all the inhabitants of the land from before you and destroy all their figured stones and destroy all their metal images and demolish all their high places. 53 And you shall take possession of the land and settle in it, for I have given the land to you to possess it. 54 You shall inherit the land by lot according to your clans. To a large tribe you shall give a large inheritance, and to a small tribe you shall give a small inheritance. Wherever the lot falls for anyone, that shall be his. According to the tribes of your fathers you shall inherit. 55 But if you do not drive out the inhabitants of the land from before you, then those of them whom you let remain shall be as barbs in your eyes and thorns in your sides, and they shall trouble you in the land where you dwell. 56 And I will do to you as I thought to do to them."

Boundaries of the Land

34 The LORD spoke to Moses, saying, 2 "Command the people of Israel, and say to them, When you enter the land of Canaan (this is the land that shall fall to you for an inheritance, the land of Canaan as defined by its borders), 3 your south side shall be from the wilderness of Zin alongside Edom, and your southern border shall run from the end of the Salt Sea on the east. 4 And your border shall turn south of the ascent of Akrabbim, and cross to Zin, and its limit shall be south of Kadesh-barnea. Then it shall go on to Hazar-addar, and pass along to Azmon. 5 And the border shall turn from Azmon to the Brook of Egypt, and its limit shall be at the sea.

6 "For the western border, you shall have the Great Sea and its[1] coast. This shall be your western border.

7 "This shall be your northern border: from the Great Sea you shall draw a line to Mount Hor. 8 From Mount Hor you shall draw a line to Lebo-hamath, and the limit of the border shall be at Zedad. 9 Then the border shall extend to Ziphron, and its limit shall be at Hazar-enan. This shall be your northern border.

10 "You shall draw a line for your eastern border from Hazar-enan to Shepham. 11 And the border shall go down from Shepham to Riblah on the east side of Ain. And the border shall go down and reach to the shoulder of the Sea of Chinnereth on the east. 12 And the border shall go down to the Jordan, and its limit shall be at the Salt Sea. This shall be your land as defined by its borders all around."

13 Moses commanded the people of Israel, saying, "This is the land that you shall inherit by lot, which the LORD has commanded to give to the nine tribes and to the half-tribe. 14 For the tribe of the people of Reuben by fathers' houses and the tribe of the people of Gad by their fathers' houses have received their inheritance, and also the half-tribe of Manasseh. 15 The two tribes and the half-tribe have received their inheritance beyond the Jordan east of Jericho, toward the sunrise."

List of Tribal Chiefs

16 The LORD spoke to Moses, saying, 17 "These are the names of the men who shall divide the land to you for inheritance: Eleazar the priest and Joshua the son of Nun. 18 You shall take one chief from every tribe to divide the land for inheritance. 19 These are the names of the men: Of the tribe of Judah, Caleb the son of Jephunneh. 20 Of the tribe of the people of Simeon, Shemuel the son of Ammihud. 21 Of the tribe of Benjamin, Elidad the son of Chislon. 22 Of the tribe of the people of Dan a chief, Bukki the son of Jogli. 23 Of the people of Joseph: of the tribe of the people of Manasseh a chief, Hanniel the son of Ephod. 24 And of the tribe of the people of Ephraim a chief, Kemuel the son of Shiphtan. 25 Of the tribe of the people of Zebulun a chief, Elizaphan the son of Parnach. 26 Of the tribe of the people of Issachar a chief, Paltiel the son of Azzan. 27 And of the tribe of the people of Asher a chief, Ahihud the son of Shelomi. 28 Of the tribe of the people of Naphtali a chief, Pedahel the son of Ammihud. 29 These are the men whom the LORD commanded to divide the inheritance for the people of Israel in the land of Canaan."

Cities for the Levites

35 The LORD spoke to Moses in the plains of Moab by the Jordan at Jericho, saying, 2 "Command the people of Israel to give to the Levites some of the inheritance of their possession as cities for them to dwell in. And you shall give to the Levites pasturelands around the cities. 3 The cities shall be theirs to dwell in, and their pasturelands shall be for their cattle and for their livestock and for all their beasts. 4 The pasturelands of the cities, which you shall give to the Levites, shall reach from the wall of the city out-

[1] Syriac; Hebrew lacks *its*

ward a thousand cubits[1] all around. 5 And you shall measure, outside the city, on the east side two thousand cubits, and on the south side two thousand cubits, and on the west side two thousand cubits, and on the north side two thousand cubits, the city being in the middle. This shall belong to them as pastureland for their cities.

6 "The cities that you give to the Levites shall be the six cities of refuge, where you shall permit the manslayer to flee, and in addition to them you shall give forty-two cities. 7 All the cities that you give to the Levites shall be forty-eight, with their pasturelands. 8 And as for the cities that you shall give from the possession of the people of Israel, from the larger tribes you shall take many, and from the smaller tribes you shall take few; each, in proportion to the inheritance that it inherits, shall give of its cities to the Levites."

Cities of Refuge

9 And the LORD spoke to Moses, saying, 10 "Speak to the people of Israel and say to them, When you cross the Jordan into the land of Canaan, 11 then you shall select cities to be cities of refuge for you, that the manslayer who kills any person without intent may flee there. 12 The cities shall be for you a refuge from the avenger, that the manslayer may not die until he stands before the congregation for judgment. 13 And the cities that you give shall be your six cities of refuge. 14 You shall give three cities beyond the Jordan, and three cities in the land of Canaan, to be cities of refuge. 15 These six cities shall be for refuge for the people of Israel, and for the stranger and for the sojourner among them, that anyone who kills any person without intent may flee there.

16 "But if he struck him down with an iron object, so that he died, he is a murderer. The murderer shall be put to death. 17 And if he struck him down with a stone tool that could cause death, and he died, he is a murderer. The murderer shall be put to death. 18 Or if he struck him down with a wooden tool that could cause death, and he died, he is a murderer. The murderer shall be put to death. 19 The avenger of blood shall himself put the murderer to death; when he meets him, he shall put him to death. 20 And if he pushed him out of hatred or hurled something at him, lying in wait, so that he died, 21 or in enmity struck him down with his hand, so that he died, then he who struck the blow shall be put to death. He is a murderer. The avenger of blood shall put the murderer to death when he meets him.

22 "But if he pushed him suddenly without enmity, or hurled anything on him without lying in wait 23 or used a stone that could cause death, and without seeing him dropped it on him, so that he died, though he was not his enemy and did not seek his harm, 24 then the congregation shall judge between the manslayer and the avenger of blood, in accordance with these rules. 25 And the congregation shall rescue the manslayer from the hand of the avenger of blood, and the congregation shall restore him to his city of refuge to which he had fled, and he shall live in it until the death of the high priest who was anointed with the holy oil. 26 But if the manslayer shall at any time go beyond the boundaries of his city of refuge to which he fled, 27 and the avenger of blood finds him outside the boundaries of his city of refuge, and the avenger of blood kills the manslayer, he shall not be guilty of blood. 28 For he must remain in his city of refuge until the death of the high priest, but after the death of the high priest the manslayer may return to the land of his possession. 29 And these things shall be for a statute and rule for you throughout your generations in all your dwelling places.

30 "If anyone kills a person, the murderer shall be put to death on the evidence of

[1] A *cubit* was about 18 inches or 45 centimeters

witnesses. But no person shall be put to
death on the testimony of one witness.
31 Moreover, you shall accept no ransom
for the life of a murderer, who is guilty
of death, but he shall be put to death.
32 And you shall accept no ransom for
him who has fled to his city of refuge,
that he may return to dwell in the land
before the death of the high priest. 33 You
shall not pollute the land in which you
live, for blood pollutes the land, and no
atonement can be made for the land for
the blood that is shed in it, except by the
blood of the one who shed it. 34 You shall
not defile the land in which you live, in
the midst of which I dwell, for I the LORD
dwell in the midst of the people of Israel."

Marriage of Female Heirs

36 The heads of the fathers' houses
of the clan of the people of Gilead
the son of Machir, son of Manasseh,
from the clans of the people of Joseph,
came near and spoke before Moses and
before the chiefs, the heads of the fathers'
houses of the people of Israel. 2 They said,
"The LORD commanded my lord to give
the land for inheritance by lot to the
people of Israel, and my lord was com-
manded by the LORD to give the inheri-
tance of Zelophehad our brother to his
daughters. 3 But if they are married to any
of the sons of the other tribes of the peo-
ple of Israel, then their inheritance will be
taken from the inheritance of our fathers
and added to the inheritance of the tribe
into which they marry. So it will be taken
away from the lot of our inheritance.
4 And when the jubilee of the people of
Israel comes, then their inheritance will
be added to the inheritance of the tribe
into which they marry, and their inheri-
tance will be taken from the inheritance
of the tribe of our fathers."
5 And Moses commanded the people
of Israel according to the word of the
LORD, saying, "The tribe of the people of
Joseph is right. 6 This is what the LORD
commands concerning the daughters
of Zelophehad, 'Let them marry whom
they think best, only they shall marry
within the clan of the tribe of their father.
7 The inheritance of the people of Israel
shall not be transferred from one tribe
to another, for every one of the people of
Israel shall hold on to the inheritance of
the tribe of his fathers. 8 And every daugh-
ter who possesses an inheritance in any
tribe of the people of Israel shall be wife to
one of the clan of the tribe of her father, so
that every one of the people of Israel may
possess the inheritance of his fathers. 9 So
no inheritance shall be transferred from
one tribe to another, for each of the tribes
of the people of Israel shall hold on to its
own inheritance.'"
10 The daughters of Zelophehad did
as the LORD commanded Moses, 11 for
Mahlah, Tirzah, Hoglah, Milcah, and
Noah, the daughters of Zelophehad, were
married to sons of their father's brothers.
12 They were married into the clans of the
people of Manasseh the son of Joseph, and
their inheritance remained in the tribe of
their father's clan.
13 These are the commandments and
the rules that the LORD commanded
through Moses to the people of Israel
in the plains of Moab by the Jordan at
Jericho.

Introduction to

Deuteronomy

Author
Moses the prophet

Date
1407/1406 B.C.

People
Moses; Joshua

Purpose
The purpose of Deuteronomy is to remind God's people, the Israelites, of the covenant He made with them and to renew that covenant before the Israelites entered the Promised Land.

Central Themes
There is only one true God; Israel should remember the history between herself and God, the covenant He made, and the Law He provided; God gives blessings for obedience and curses for disobedience; God's power can defeat Israel's enemies in the land; God's people are called to love, serve, obey, and fear Him.

Memory Verses
Fair judgment (Deuteronomy 1:17); God's unchanging Word (Deuteronomy 4:2); the Lord is one (Deuteronomy 6:4–7); false prophets and the new prophet (Deuteronomy 18:15–22); God wounds and heals (Deuteronomy 32:39)

Introduction

Forty years have passed, and the Israelites who had rebelled against God by refusing to enter the Promised Land have died. Their grown children and their descendants are gathered at the edge of Canaan. Moses will soon die too. Before he dies and before the Israelites enter the land, Moses calls God's people to renew the covenant God had made with them. He reminds them of how God had led and provided for them, especially during the 40 years in the wilderness (Deuteronomy 1–3). In Deuteronomy, Moses reviews the Law God has given, including the Ten Commandments. He calls on the people to love and serve God with all their hearts (Deuteronomy 5–6). He reminds the Israelites of their failures to trust and obey God in the past, but also that God forgives (Deuteronomy 8–9). Moses tells of God's blessings for the people if they keep God's covenant, and of His curses if they fail to keep it (Deuteronomy 27–28). Near the end of the book Moses sings a song of praise to God and blesses each of the 12 tribes (Deuteronomy 32–33). The last chapter tells of Joshua's choice as Israel's next leader and of Moses' death (Deuteronomy 34).

1446 B.C.	1408 B.C.	1406 B.C.
Exodus from Egypt	Moses addresses Israel in Moab	Israel enters Promised Land

Deuteronomy

The Command to Leave Horeb

1 These are the words that Moses
spoke to all Israel beyond the Jordan
in the wilderness, in the Arabah oppo-
site Suph, between Paran and Tophel,
Laban, Hazeroth, and Dizahab. 2 It is
eleven days' journey from Horeb by the
way of Mount Seir to Kadesh-barnea.
3 In the fortieth year, on the first day of
the eleventh month, Moses spoke to the
people of Israel according to all that the
LORD had given him in commandment
to them, 4 after he had defeated Sihon
the king of the Amorites, who lived in
Heshbon, and Og the king of Bashan, who
lived in Ashtaroth and in Edrei. 5 Beyond
the Jordan, in the land of Moab, Moses
undertook to explain this law, saying,
6 "The LORD our God said to us in Horeb,
'You have stayed long enough at this
mountain. 7 Turn and take your journey,
and go to the hill country of the Amorites
and to all their neighbors in the Arabah,
in the hill country and in the lowland
and in the Negeb and by the seacoast, the
land of the Canaanites, and Lebanon, as
far as the great river, the river Euphrates.
8 See, I have set the land before you. Go in
and take possession of the land that the
LORD swore to your fathers, to Abraham,
to Isaac, and to Jacob, to give to them and
to their offspring after them.'

Leaders Appointed

9 "At that time I said to you, 'I am not
able to bear you by myself. 10 The LORD
your God has multiplied you, and behold,
you are today as numerous as the stars
of heaven. 11 May the LORD, the God of
your fathers, make you a thousand times
as many as you are and bless you, as he
has promised you! 12 How can I bear by
myself the weight and burden of you and
your strife? 13 Choose for your tribes wise,
understanding, and experienced men,
and I will appoint them as your heads.'
14 And you answered me, 'The thing that
you have spoken is good for us to do.'
15 So I took the heads of your tribes, wise
and experienced men, and set them as
heads over you, commanders of thou-
sands, commanders of hundreds, com-
manders of fifties, commanders of tens,
and officers, throughout your tribes.
16 And I charged your judges at that time,
'Hear the cases between your brothers,
and judge righteously between a man
and his brother or the alien who is with
him. 17 You shall not be partial in judg-
ment. You shall hear the small and the
great alike. You shall not be intimidated
by anyone, for the judgment is God's.
And the case that is too hard for you, you
shall bring to me, and I will hear it.' 18 And
I commanded you at that time all the
things that you should do.

Israel's Refusal to Enter the Land

19 "Then we set out from Horeb and
went through all that great and
265 terrifying wilderness that you saw,
on the way to the hill country of the
Amorites, as the LORD our God com-
manded us. And we came to Kadesh-
barnea. 20 And I said to you, 'You have
come to the hill country of the Amorites,
which the LORD our God is giving us.
21 See, the LORD your God has set the land
before you. Go up, take possession, as the
LORD, the God of your fathers, has told
you. Do not fear or be dismayed.' 22 Then
all of you came near me and said, 'Let us
send men before us, that they may explore
the land for us and bring us word again of

the way by which we must go up and the cities into which we shall come.' 23 The thing seemed good to me, and I took twelve men from you, one man from each tribe. 24 And they turned and went up into the hill country, and came to the Valley of Eshcol and spied it out. 25 And they took in their hands some of the fruit of the land and brought it down to us, and brought us word again and said, 'It is a good land that the LORD our God is giving us.'

26 "Yet you would not go up, but rebelled against the command of the LORD your God. 27 And you murmured in your tents and said, 'Because the LORD hated us he has brought us out of the land of Egypt, to give us into the hand of the Amorites, to destroy us. 28 Where are we going up? Our brothers have made our hearts melt, saying, "The people are greater and taller than we. The cities are great and fortified up to heaven. And besides, we have seen the sons of the Anakim there."' 29 Then I said to you, 'Do not be in dread or afraid of them. 30 The LORD your God who goes before you will himself fight for you, just as he did for you in Egypt before your eyes, 31 and in the wilderness, where you have seen how the LORD your God carried you, as a man carries his son, all the way that you went until you came to this place.' 32 Yet in spite of this word you did not believe the LORD your God, 33 who went before you in the way to seek you out a place to pitch your tents, in fire by night and in the cloud by day, to show you by what way you should go.

The Penalty for Israel's Rebellion

34 "And the LORD heard your words and was angered, and he swore, 35 'Not one of these men of this evil generation shall see the good land that I swore to give to your fathers, 36 except Caleb the son of Jephunneh. He shall see it, and to him and to his children I will give the land on which he has trodden, because he has wholly followed the LORD!' 37 Even with me the LORD was angry on your account and said, 'You also shall not go in there. 38 Joshua the son of Nun, who stands before you, he shall enter. Encourage him, for he shall cause Israel to inherit it. 39 And as for your little ones, who you said would become a prey, and your children, who today have no knowledge of good or evil, they shall go in there. And to them I will give it, and they shall possess it. 40 But as for you, turn, and journey into the wilderness in the direction of the Red Sea.'

41 "Then you answered me, 'We have sinned against the LORD. We ourselves will go up and fight, just as the LORD our God commanded us.' And every one of you fastened on his weapons of war and thought it easy to go up into the hill country. 42 And the LORD said to me, 'Say to them, Do not go up or fight, for I am not in your midst, lest you be defeated before your enemies.' 43 So I spoke to you, and you would not listen; but you rebelled against the command of the LORD and presumptuously went up into the hill country. 44 Then the Amorites who lived in that hill country came out against you and chased you as bees do and beat you down in Seir as far as Hormah. 45 And you returned and wept before the LORD, but the LORD did not listen to your voice or give ear to you. 46 So you remained at Kadesh many days, the days that you remained there.

The Wilderness Years

2 "Then we turned and journeyed into the wilderness in the direction of the Red Sea, as the LORD told me. And for many days we traveled around Mount Seir. 2 Then the LORD said to me, 3 'You have been traveling around this mountain country long enough. Turn northward 4 and command the people, "You are about to pass through the territory of your brothers, the people of Esau, who live in Seir; and they will be afraid of you. So be very

careful. [5]Do not contend with them, for I
will not give you any of their land, no, not
so much as for the sole of the foot to tread
on, because I have given Mount Seir to
Esau as a possession. [6]You shall purchase
food from them for money, that you may
eat, and you shall also buy water of them
for money, that you may drink. [7]For the
LORD your God has blessed you in all the
work of your hands. He knows your going
through this great wilderness. These forty
years the LORD your God has been with
you. You have lacked nothing."' [8]So we
went on, away from our brothers, the peo-
ple of Esau, who live in Seir, away from the
Arabah road from Elath and Ezion-geber.

"And we turned and went in the direc-
tion of the wilderness of Moab. [9]And the
LORD said to me, 'Do not harass Moab or
contend with them in battle, for I will
not give you any of their land for a pos-
session, because I have given Ar to the
people of Lot for a possession.' [10](The
Emim formerly lived there, a people
great and many, and tall as the Anakim.
[11]Like the Anakim they are also counted
as Rephaim, but the Moabites call them
Emim. [12]The Horites also lived in Seir
formerly, but the people of Esau dispos-
sessed them and destroyed them from
before them and settled in their place, as
Israel did to the land of their possession,
which the LORD gave to them.) [13]'Now
rise up and go over the brook Zered.' So
we went over the brook Zered. [14]And the
time from our leaving Kadesh-barnea
until we crossed the brook Zered was
thirty-eight years, until the entire genera-
tion, that is, the men of war, had perished
from the camp, as the LORD had sworn to
them. [15]For indeed the hand of the LORD
was against them, to destroy them from
the camp, until they had perished.

[16]"So as soon as all the men of war had
perished and were dead from among the
people, [17]the LORD said to me, [18]'Today
you are to cross the border of Moab at Ar.
[19]And when you approach the territory
of the people of Ammon, do not harass
them or contend with them, for I will not
give you any of the land of the people of
Ammon as a possession, because I have
given it to the sons of Lot for a possession.'
[20](It is also counted as a land of Rephaim.
Rephaim formerly lived there—but the
Ammonites call them Zamzummim—
[21]a people great and many, and tall as the
Anakim; but the LORD destroyed them
before the Ammonites,[1] and they dispos-
sessed them and settled in their place,
[22]as he did for the people of Esau, who
live in Seir, when he destroyed the Horites
before them and they dispossessed them
and settled in their place even to this
day. [23]As for the Avvim, who lived in vil-
lages as far as Gaza, the Caphtorim, who
came from Caphtor, destroyed them and
settled in their place.) [24]'Rise up, set out
on your journey and go over the Valley
of the Arnon. Behold, I have given into
your hand Sihon the Amorite, king of
Heshbon, and his land. Begin to take pos-
session, and contend with him in battle.
[25]This day I will begin to put the dread
and fear of you on the peoples who are
under the whole heaven, who shall hear
the report of you and shall tremble and be
in anguish because of you.'

The Defeat of King Sihon

[26]"So I sent messengers from the wil-
derness of Kedemoth to Sihon the king
of Heshbon, with words of peace, saying,
[27]'Let me pass through your land. I will go
only by the road; I will turn aside neither
to the right nor to the left. [28]You shall sell
me food for money, that I may eat, and
give me water for money, that I may drink.
Only let me pass through on foot, [29]as
the sons of Esau who live in Seir and the
Moabites who live in Ar did for me, until
I go over the Jordan into the land that the
LORD our God is giving to us.' [30]But Sihon
the king of Heshbon would not let us pass

[1] Hebrew *them*

by him, for the LORD your God hardened
his spirit and made his heart obstinate,
that he might give him into your hand, as
he is this day. 31 And the LORD said to me,
'Behold, I have begun to give Sihon and
his land over to you. Begin to take pos-
session, that you may occupy his land.'
32 Then Sihon came out against us, he and
all his people, to battle at Jahaz. 33 And the
LORD our God gave him over to us, and
we defeated him and his sons and all his
people. 34 And we captured all his cities
at that time and devoted to destruction[1]
every city, men, women, and children. We
left no survivors. 35 Only the livestock we
took as spoil for ourselves, with the plun-
der of the cities that we captured. 36 From
Aroer, which is on the edge of the Valley of
the Arnon, and from the city that is in the
valley, as far as Gilead, there was not a city
too high for us. The LORD our God gave all
into our hands. 37 Only to the land of the
sons of Ammon you did not draw near,
that is, to all the banks of the river Jabbok
and the cities of the hill country, whatever
the LORD our God had forbidden us.

The Defeat of King Og

3 "Then we turned and went up the way
to Bashan. And Og the king of Bashan
came out against us, he and all his people,
to battle at Edrei. 2 But the LORD said to
me, 'Do not fear him, for I have given him
and all his people and his land into your
hand. And you shall do to him as you did
to Sihon the king of the Amorites, who
lived at Heshbon.' 3 So the LORD our God
gave into our hand Og also, the king of
Bashan, and all his people, and we struck
him down until he had no survivor left.
4 And we took all his cities at that time—
there was not a city that we did not take
from them—sixty cities, the whole region
of Argob, the kingdom of Og in Bashan.
5 All these were cities fortified with high
walls, gates, and bars, besides very many
unwalled villages. 6 And we devoted them
to destruction,[2] as we did to Sihon the
king of Heshbon, devoting to destruction
every city, men, women, and children.
7 But all the livestock and the spoil of the
cities we took as our plunder. 8 So we took
the land at that time out of the hand of
the two kings of the Amorites who were
beyond the Jordan, from the Valley of the
Arnon to Mount Hermon 9 (the Sidonians
call Hermon Sirion, while the Amorites
call it Senir), 10 all the cities of the table-
land and all Gilead and all Bashan, as far
as Salecah and Edrei, cities of the king-
dom of Og in Bashan. 11 (For only Og the
king of Bashan was left of the remnant
of the Rephaim. Behold, his bed was a
bed of iron. Is it not in Rabbah of the
Ammonites? Nine cubits[3] was its length,
and four cubits its breadth, according to
the common cubit.[4])

12 "When we took possession of this
land at that time, I gave to the Reubenites
and the Gadites the territory beginning at
Aroer, which is on the edge of the Valley
of the Arnon, and half the hill country of
Gilead with its cities. 13 The rest of Gilead,
and all Bashan, the kingdom of Og, that
is, all the region of Argob, I gave to the
half-tribe of Manasseh. (All that portion of
Bashan is called the land of Rephaim. 14 Jair
the Manassite took all the region of Argob,
that is, Bashan, as far as the border of the
Geshurites and the Maacathites, and called
the villages after his own name, Havvoth-
jair, as it is to this day.) 15 To Machir I gave
Gilead, 16 and to the Reubenites and the
Gadites I gave the territory from Gilead
as far as the Valley of the Arnon, with the
middle of the valley as a border, as far
over as the river Jabbok, the border of the
Ammonites; 17 the Arabah also, with the
Jordan as the border, from Chinnereth as
far as the Sea of the Arabah, the Salt Sea,
under the slopes of Pisgah on the east.

18 "And I commanded you at that time,
saying, 'The LORD your God has given
you this land to possess. All your men of

[1] That is, set apart (devoted) as an offering to the Lord (for destruction) [2] That is, set apart (devoted) as an offering to the Lord (for destruction); twice in this verse
[3] A *cubit* was about 18 inches or 45 centimeters [4] Hebrew *cubit of a man*

valor shall cross over armed before your
brothers, the people of Israel. 19 Only your
wives, your little ones, and your livestock
(I know that you have much livestock)
shall remain in the cities that I have given
you, 20 until the LORD gives rest to your
brothers, as to you, and they also occupy
the land that the LORD your God gives
them beyond the Jordan. Then each of you
may return to his possession which I have
given you.’ 21 And I commanded Joshua
at that time, ‘Your eyes have seen all that
the LORD your God has done to these two
kings. So will the LORD do to all the king-
doms into which you are crossing. 22 You
shall not fear them, for it is the LORD your
God who fights for you.’

Moses Forbidden to Enter the Land

23 “And I pleaded with the LORD at that
time, saying, 24 ‘O Lord GOD, you have only
begun to show your servant your great-
ness and your mighty hand. For what god
is there in heaven or on earth who can
do such works and mighty acts as yours?
25 Please let me go over and see the good
land beyond the Jordan, that good hill
country and Lebanon.’ 26 But the LORD was
angry with me because of you and would
not listen to me. And the LORD said to me,
‘Enough from you; do not speak to me
of this matter again. 27 Go up to the top
of Pisgah and lift up your eyes westward
and northward and southward and east-
ward, and look at it with your eyes, for you
shall not go over this Jordan. 28 But charge
Joshua, and encourage and strengthen
him, for he shall go over at the head of
this people, and he shall put them in pos-
session of the land that you shall see.’
29 So we remained in the valley opposite
Beth-peor.

Moses Commands Obedience

4 “And now, O Israel, listen to the stat-
utes and the rules[1] that I am teaching
you, and do them, that you may live, and
go in and take possession of the land that
the LORD, the God of your fathers, is giv-
ing you. 2 You shall not add to the word
that I command you, nor take from it,
that you may keep the commandments
of the LORD your God that I command
you. 3 Your eyes have seen what the LORD
did at Baal-peor, for the LORD your God
destroyed from among you all the men
who followed the Baal of Peor. 4 But you
who held fast to the LORD your God are
all alive today. 5 See, I have taught you
statutes and rules, as the LORD my God
commanded me, that you should do
them in the land that you are entering to
take possession of it. 6 Keep them and do
them, for that will be your wisdom and
your understanding in the sight of the
peoples, who, when they hear all these
statutes, will say, ‘Surely this great nation
is a wise and understanding people.’ 7 For
what great nation is there that has a god
so near to it as the LORD our God is to us,
whenever we call upon him? 8 And what
great nation is there, that has statutes and
rules so righteous as all this law that I set
before you today?

9 “Only take care, and keep your soul
diligently, lest you forget the things that
your eyes have seen, and lest they depart
from your heart all the days of your life.
Make them known to your children and
your children’s children— 10 how on the
day that you stood before the LORD your
God at Horeb, the LORD said to me, ‘Gather
the people to me, that I may let them hear
my words, so that they may learn to fear
me all the days that they live on the earth,
and that they may teach their children
so.’ 11 And you came near and stood at the
foot of the mountain, while the mountain
burned with fire to the heart of heaven,
wrapped in darkness, cloud, and gloom.
12 Then the LORD spoke to you out of the
midst of the fire. You heard the sound of
words, but saw no form; there was only a
voice. 13 And he declared to you his cov-
enant, which he commanded you to per-

[1] Or *just decrees*; also verses 5, 8, 14, 45

form, that is, the Ten Commandments,[1] and he wrote them on two tablets of stone. 14 And the LORD commanded me at that time to teach you statutes and rules, that you might do them in the land that you are going over to possess.

Idolatry Forbidden

15 "Therefore watch yourselves very carefully. Since you saw no form on the day that the LORD spoke to you at Horeb out of the midst of the fire, 16 beware lest you act corruptly by making a carved image for yourselves, in the form of any figure, the likeness of male or female, 17 the likeness of any animal that is on the earth, the likeness of any winged bird that flies in the air, 18 the likeness of anything that creeps on the ground, the likeness of any fish that is in the water under the earth. 19 And beware lest you raise your eyes to heaven, and when you see the sun and the moon and the stars, all the host of heaven, you be drawn away and bow down to them and serve them, things that the LORD your God has allotted to all the peoples under the whole heaven. 20 But the LORD has taken you and brought you out of the iron furnace, out of Egypt, to be a people of his own inheritance, as you are this day. 21 Furthermore, the LORD was angry with me because of you, and he swore that I should not cross the Jordan, and that I should not enter the good land that the LORD your God is giving you for an inheritance. 22 For I must die in this land; I must not go over the Jordan. But you shall go over and take possession of that good land. 23 Take care, lest you forget the covenant of the LORD your God, which he made with you, and make a carved image, the form of anything that the LORD your God has forbidden you. 24 For the LORD your God is a consuming fire, a jealous God.

25 "When you father children and children's children, and have grown old in the land, if you act corruptly by making a carved image in the form of anything, and by doing what is evil in the sight of the LORD your God, so as to provoke him to anger, 26 I call heaven and earth to witness against you today, that you will soon utterly perish from the land that you are going over the Jordan to possess. You will not live long in it, but will be utterly destroyed. 27 And the LORD will scatter you among the peoples, and you will be left few in number among the nations where the LORD will drive you. 28 And there you will serve gods of wood and stone, the work of human hands, that neither see, nor hear, nor eat, nor smell. 29 But from there you will seek the LORD your God and you will find him, if you search after him with all your heart and with all your soul. 30 When you are in tribulation, and all these things come upon you in the latter days, you will return to the LORD your God and obey his voice.

43

31 For the LORD your God is a merciful God. He will not leave you or destroy you or forget the covenant with your fathers that he swore to them.

The LORD Alone Is God

32 "For ask now of the days that are past, which were before you, since the day that God created man on the earth, and ask from one end of heaven to the other, whether such a great thing as this has ever happened or was ever heard of. 33 Did any people ever hear the voice of a god speaking out of the midst of the fire, as you have heard, and still live? 34 Or has any god ever attempted to go and take a nation for himself from the midst of another nation, by trials, by signs, by wonders, and by war, by a mighty hand and an outstretched arm, and by great deeds of terror, all of which the LORD your God did for you in Egypt before your eyes? 35 To you it was shown, that you might know that the LORD is God; there is no other besides him. 36 Out of heaven he let you hear his voice, that he

[1] Hebrew *words*

might discipline you. And on earth he let you see his great fire, and you heard his words out of the midst of the fire. **37** And because he loved your fathers and chose their offspring after them[1] and brought you out of Egypt with his own presence, by his great power, **38** driving out before you nations greater and mightier than yourselves, to bring you in, to give you their land for an inheritance, as it is this day, **39** know therefore today, and lay it to your heart, that the LORD is God in heaven above and on the earth beneath; there is no other. **40** Therefore you shall keep his statutes and his commandments, which I command you today, that it may go well with you and with your children after you, and that you may prolong your days in the land that the LORD your God is giving you for all time."

Cities of Refuge

41 Then Moses set apart three cities in the east beyond the Jordan, **42** that the manslayer might flee there, anyone who kills his neighbor unintentionally, without being at enmity with him in time past; he may flee to one of these cities and save his life: **43** Bezer in the wilderness on the tableland for the Reubenites, Ramoth in Gilead for the Gadites, and Golan in Bashan for the Manassites.

Introduction to the Law

44 This is the law that Moses set before the people of Israel. **45** These are the testimonies, the statutes, and the rules, which Moses spoke to the people of Israel when they came out of Egypt, **46** beyond the Jordan in the valley opposite Beth-peor, in the land of Sihon the king of the Amorites, who lived at Heshbon, whom Moses and the people of Israel defeated when they came out of Egypt. **47** And they took possession of his land and the land of Og, the king of Bashan, the two kings of the Amorites, who lived to the east beyond the Jordan; **48** from Aroer, which is on the edge of the Valley of the Arnon, as far as Mount Sirion[2] (that is, Hermon), **49** together with all the Arabah on the east side of the Jordan as far as the Sea of the Arabah, under the slopes of Pisgah.

The Ten Commandments

175 **5** And Moses summoned all Israel and said to them, "Hear, O Israel, the statutes and the rules that I speak in your hearing today, and you shall learn them and be careful to do them. **2** The LORD our God made a covenant with us in Horeb. **3** Not with our fathers did the LORD make this covenant, but with us, who are all of us here alive today. **4** The LORD spoke with you face to face at the mountain, out of the midst of the fire, **5** while I stood between the LORD and you at that time, to declare to you the word of the LORD. For you were afraid because of the fire, and you did not go up into the mountain. He said:

6 "'I am the LORD your God, who brought you out of the land of Egypt, out of the house of slavery.

7 "'You shall have no other gods before[3] me.

8 "'You shall not make for yourself a carved image, or any likeness of anything that is in heaven above, or that is on the earth beneath, or that is in the water under the earth. **9** You shall not bow down to them or serve them; for I the LORD your God am a jealous God, visiting the iniquity of the fathers on the children to the third and fourth generation of those who hate me, **10** but showing steadfast love to thousands[4] of those who love me and keep my commandments.

11 "'You shall not take the name of the LORD your God in vain, for the LORD will not hold him guiltless who takes his name in vain.

12 "'Observe the Sabbath day, to keep it holy, as the LORD your God commanded you. **13** Six days you shall labor and do

[1] Hebrew *his offspring after him* [2] Syriac; Hebrew *Sion* [3] Or *besides* [4] Or *to the thousandth generation*

all your work, 14 but the seventh day is a Sabbath to the LORD your God. On it you shall not do any work, you or your son or your daughter or your male servant or your female servant, or your ox or your donkey or any of your livestock, or the sojourner who is within your gates, that your male servant and your female servant may rest as well as you. 15 You shall remember that you were a slave[1] in the land of Egypt, and the LORD your God brought you out from there with a mighty hand and an outstretched arm. Therefore the LORD your God commanded you to keep the Sabbath day.

16 "'Honor your father and your mother, as the LORD your God commanded you, that your days may be long, and that it may go well with you in the land that the LORD your God is giving you.

17 "'You shall not murder.[2]

18 "'And you shall not commit adultery.

19 "'And you shall not steal.

20 "'And you shall not bear false witness against your neighbor.

21 "'And you shall not covet your neighbor's wife. And you shall not desire your neighbor's house, his field, or his male servant, or his female servant, his ox, or his donkey, or anything that is your neighbor's.'

22 "These words the LORD spoke to all your assembly at the mountain out of the midst of the fire, the cloud, and the thick darkness, with a loud voice; and he added no more. And he wrote them on two tablets of stone and gave them to me. 23 And as soon as you heard the voice out of the midst of the darkness, while the mountain was burning with fire, you came near to me, all the heads of your tribes, and your elders. 24 And you said, 'Behold, the LORD our God has shown us his glory and greatness, and we have heard his voice out of the midst of the fire. This day we have seen God speak with man, and man still live. 25 Now therefore why should we die? For this great fire will consume us. If we hear the voice of the LORD our God any more, we shall die. 26 For who is there of all flesh, that has heard the voice of the living God speaking out of the midst of fire as we have, and has still lived? 27 Go near and hear all that the LORD our God will say and speak to us all that the LORD our God will speak to you, and we will hear and do it.'

28 "And the LORD heard your words, when you spoke to me. And the LORD said to me, 'I have heard the words of this people, which they have spoken to you. They are right in all that they have spoken. 29 Oh that they had such a mind as this always, to fear me and to keep all my commandments, that it might go well with them and with their descendants[3] forever! 30 Go and say to them, "Return to your tents." 31 But you, stand here by me, and I will tell you the whole commandment and the statutes and the rules that you shall teach them, that they may do them in the land that I am giving them to possess.' 32 You shall be careful therefore to do as the LORD your God has commanded you. You shall not turn aside to the right hand or to the left. 33 You shall walk in all the way that the LORD your God has commanded you, that you may live, and that it may go well with you, and that you may live long in the land that you shall possess.

The Greatest Commandment

6 "Now this is the commandment, the statutes and the rules[4] that the LORD your God commanded me to teach you, that you may do them in the land to which you are going over, to possess it, 2 that you may fear the LORD your God, you and your son and your son's son, by keeping all his statutes and his commandments, which I command you, all the days of your life, and that your days may be long. 3 Hear therefore, O Israel, and be careful to do them, that it may go well with you, and that you may multiply greatly, as the LORD,

[1] Or *servant* [2] The Hebrew word also covers causing human death through carelessness or negligence [3] Or *sons* [4] Or *just decrees*; also verse 20

the God of your fathers, has promised you, in a land flowing with milk and honey.

4 "Hear, O Israel: The LORD our God, the LORD is one.[1] 5 You shall love the LORD your God with all your heart and with all your soul and with all your might. 6 And these words that I command you today shall be on your heart. 7 You shall teach them diligently to your children, and shall talk of them when you sit in your house, and when you walk by the way, and when you lie down, and when you rise. 8 You shall bind them as a sign on your hand, and they shall be as frontlets between your eyes. 9 You shall write them on the doorposts of your house and on your gates.

10 "And when the LORD your God brings you into the land that he swore to your fathers, to Abraham, to Isaac, and to Jacob, to give you—with great and good cities that you did not build, 11 and houses full of all good things that you did not fill, and cisterns that you did not dig, and vineyards and olive trees that you did not plant—and when you eat and are full, 12 then take care lest you forget the LORD, who brought you out of the land of Egypt, out of the house of slavery. 13 It is the LORD your God you shall fear. Him you shall serve and by his name you shall swear. 14 You shall not go after other gods, the gods of the peoples who are around you— 15 for the LORD your God in your midst is a jealous God—lest the anger of the LORD your God be kindled against you, and he destroy you from off the face of the earth.

16 "You shall not put the LORD your God to the test, as you tested him at Massah. 17 You shall diligently keep the commandments of the LORD your God, and his testimonies and his statutes, which he has commanded you. 18 And you shall do what is right and good in the sight of the LORD, that it may go well with you, and that you may go in and take possession of the good land that the LORD swore to give to your fathers 19 by thrusting out all your enemies from before you, as the LORD has promised.

20 "When your son asks you in time to come, 'What is the meaning of the testimonies and the statutes and the rules that the LORD our God has commanded you?' 21 then you shall say to your son, 'We were Pharaoh's slaves in Egypt. And the LORD brought us out of Egypt with a mighty hand. 22 And the LORD showed signs and wonders, great and grievous, against Egypt and against Pharaoh and all his household, before our eyes. 23 And he brought us out from there, that he might bring us in and give us the land that he swore to give to our fathers. 24 And the LORD commanded us to do all these statutes, to fear the LORD our God, for our good always, that he might preserve us alive, as we are this day. 25 And it will be righteousness for us, if we are careful to do all this commandment before the LORD our God, as he has commanded us.'

A Chosen People

7 "When the LORD your God brings you into the land that you are entering to take possession of it, and clears away many nations before you, the Hittites, the Girgashites, the Amorites, the Canaanites, the Perizzites, the Hivites, and the Jebusites, seven nations more numerous and mightier than yourselves, 2 and when the LORD your God gives them over to you, and you defeat them, then you must devote them to complete destruction.[2] You shall make no covenant with them and show no mercy to them. 3 You shall not intermarry with them, giving your daughters to their sons or taking their daughters for your sons, 4 for they would turn away your sons from following me, to serve other gods. Then the anger of the LORD would be kindled against you, and he would destroy you quickly. 5 But thus shall you deal with them: you shall break down their altars and dash in pieces their

[1] Or *The LORD our God is one LORD*; or *The LORD is our God, the LORD is one*; or *The LORD is our God, the LORD alone* [2] That is, set apart (devote) as an offering to the Lord (for destruction)

pillars and chop down their Asherim and burn their carved images with fire.

6 "For you are a people holy to the Lord your God. The Lord your
43 God has chosen you to be a people for his treasured possession, out of all the peoples who are on the face of the earth. 7 It was not because you were more in number than any other people that the Lord set his love on you and chose you, for you were the fewest of all peoples, 8 but it is because the Lord loves you and is keeping the oath that he swore to your fathers, that the Lord has brought you out with a mighty hand and redeemed you from the house of slavery, from the hand of Pharaoh king of Egypt. 9 Know therefore that the Lord your God is God, the faithful God who keeps covenant and steadfast love with those who love him and keep his commandments, to a thousand generations, 10 and repays to their face those who hate him, by destroying them. He will not be slack with one who hates him. He will repay him to his face. 11 You shall therefore be careful to do the commandment and the statutes and the rules that I command you today.

12 "And because you listen to these rules and keep and do them, the Lord your God will keep with you the covenant and the steadfast love that he swore to your fathers. 13 He will love you, bless you, and multiply you. He will also bless the fruit of your womb and the fruit of your ground, your grain and your wine and your oil, the increase of your herds and the young of your flock, in the land that he swore to your fathers to give you. 14 You shall be blessed above all peoples. There shall not be male or female barren among you or among your livestock. 15 And the Lord will take away from you all sickness, and none of the evil diseases of Egypt, which you knew, will he inflict on you, but he will lay them on all who hate you. 16 And you shall consume all the peoples that the Lord your God will give over to you. Your eye shall not pity them, neither shall you serve their gods, for that would be a snare to you.

17 "If you say in your heart, 'These nations are greater than I. How can I dispossess them?' 18 you shall not be afraid of them but you shall remember what the Lord your God did to Pharaoh and to all Egypt, 19 the great trials that your eyes saw, the signs, the wonders, the mighty hand, and the outstretched arm, by which the Lord your God brought you out. So will the Lord your God do to all the peoples of whom you are afraid. 20 Moreover, the Lord your God will send hornets among them, until those who are left and hide themselves from you are destroyed. 21 You shall not be in dread of them, for the Lord your God is in your midst, a great and awesome God. 22 The Lord your God will clear away these nations before you little by little. You may not make an end of them at once,[1] lest the wild beasts grow too numerous for you. 23 But the Lord your God will give them over to you and throw them into great confusion, until they are destroyed. 24 And he will give their kings into your hand, and you shall make their name perish from under heaven. No one shall be able to stand against you until you have destroyed them. 25 The carved images of their gods you shall burn with fire. You shall not covet the silver or the gold that is on them or take it for yourselves, lest you be ensnared by it, for it is an abomination to the Lord your God. 26 And you shall not bring an abominable thing into your house and become devoted to destruction[2] like it. You shall utterly detest and abhor it, for it is devoted to destruction.

Remember the Lord Your God

8 "The whole commandment that I command you today you shall be careful to do, that you may live and multiply, and go in and possess the land that

[1] Or *quickly* [2] That is, set apart (devoted) as an offering to the Lord (for destruction); twice in this verse

the LORD swore to give to your fathers.
[2] And you shall remember the whole way
that the LORD your God has led you these
forty years in the wilderness, that he
might humble you, testing you to know
what was in your heart, whether you
would keep his commandments or not.
[3] And he humbled you and let you hunger
and fed you with manna, which you did
not know, nor did your fathers know, that
he might make you know that man does
not live by bread alone, but man lives by
every word[1] that comes from the mouth
of the LORD. [4] Your clothing did not wear
out on you and your foot did not swell
these forty years. [5] Know then in your
heart that, as a man disciplines his son,
the LORD your God disciplines you. [6] So
you shall keep the commandments of the
LORD your God by walking in his ways and
by fearing him. [7] For the LORD your God is
bringing you into a good land, a land of
brooks of water, of fountains and springs,
flowing out in the valleys and hills, [8] a
land of wheat and barley, of vines and fig
trees and pomegranates, a land of olive
trees and honey, [9] a land in which you will
eat bread without scarcity, in which you
will lack nothing, a land whose stones are
iron, and out of whose hills you can dig
copper. [10] And you shall eat and be full,
and you shall bless the LORD your God for
the good land he has given you.
[11] "Take care lest you forget the
LORD your God by not keeping his
279 commandments and his rules and
his statutes, which I command you today,
[12] lest, when you have eaten and are full
and have built good houses and live in
them, [13] and when your herds and flocks
multiply and your silver and gold is multi-
plied and all that you have is multiplied,
[14] then your heart be lifted up, and you for-
get the LORD your God, who brought you
out of the land of Egypt, out of the house of
slavery, [15] who led you through the great
and terrifying wilderness, with its fiery
serpents and scorpions and thirsty ground
where there was no water, who brought
you water out of the flinty rock, [16] who
fed you in the wilderness with manna that
your fathers did not know, that he might
humble you and test you, to do you good in
the end. [17] Beware lest you say in your
heart, 'My power and the might of my hand
have gotten me this wealth.' [18] You shall
remember the LORD your God, for it is he
who gives you power to get wealth, that he
may confirm his covenant that he swore to
your fathers, as it is this day. [19] And if you
forget the LORD your God and go after
other gods and serve them and worship
them, I solemnly warn you today that you
shall surely perish. [20] Like the nations that
the LORD makes to perish before you, so
shall you perish, because you would not
obey the voice of the LORD your God.

Not Because of Righteousness

9 "Hear, O Israel: you are to cross over
the Jordan today, to go in to dispos-
sess nations greater and mightier than
yourselves, cities great and fortified up to
heaven, [2] a people great and tall, the sons
of the Anakim, whom you know, and of
whom you have heard it said, 'Who can
stand before the sons of Anak?' [3] Know
therefore today that he who goes over
before you as a consuming fire is the LORD
your God. He will destroy them and sub-
due them before you. So you shall drive
them out and make them perish quickly,
as the LORD has promised you.
[4] "Do not say in your heart, after the
LORD your God has thrust them out before
you, 'It is because of my righteousness that
the LORD has brought me in to possess this
land,' whereas it is because of the wicked-
ness of these nations that the LORD is
driving them out before you. [5] Not
because of your righteousness or
43 the uprightness of your heart are
you going in to possess their land, but
because of the wickedness of these

[1] Hebrew *by all*

nations the LORD your God is driving them out from before you, and that he may confirm the word that the LORD swore to your fathers, to Abraham, to Isaac, and to Jacob.

6 "Know, therefore, that the LORD your God is not giving you this good land to possess because of your righteousness, for you are a stubborn people. 7 Remember and do not forget how you provoked the LORD your God to wrath in the wilderness. From the day you came out of the land of Egypt until you came to this place, you have been rebellious against the LORD. 8 Even at Horeb you provoked the LORD to wrath, and the LORD was so angry with you that he was ready to destroy you. 9 When I went up the mountain to receive the tablets of stone, the tablets of the covenant that the LORD made with you, I remained on the mountain forty days and forty nights. I neither ate bread nor drank water. 10 And the LORD gave me the two tablets of stone written with the finger of God, and on them were all the words that the LORD had spoken with you on the mountain out of the midst of the fire on the day of the assembly. 11 And at the end of forty days and forty nights the LORD gave me the two tablets of stone, the tablets of the covenant. 12 Then the LORD said to me, 'Arise, go down quickly from here, for your people whom you have brought from Egypt have acted corruptly. They have turned aside quickly out of the way that I commanded them; they have made themselves a metal image.'

The Golden Calf

13 "Furthermore, the LORD said to me, 'I have seen this people, and behold, it is a stubborn people. 14 Let me alone, that I may destroy them and blot out their name from under heaven. And I will make of you a nation mightier and greater than they.' 15 So I turned and came down from the mountain, and the mountain was burning with fire. And the two tablets of the covenant were in my two hands. 16 And I looked, and behold, you had sinned against the LORD your God. You had made yourselves a golden[1] calf. You had turned aside quickly from the way that the LORD had commanded you. 17 So I took hold of the two tablets and threw them out of my two hands and broke them before your eyes. 18 Then I lay prostrate before the LORD as before, forty days and forty nights. I neither ate bread nor drank water, because of all the sin that you had committed, in doing what was evil in the sight of the LORD to provoke him to anger. 19 For I was afraid of the anger and hot displeasure that the LORD bore against you, so that he was ready to destroy you. But the LORD listened to me that time also. 20 And the LORD was so angry with Aaron that he was ready to destroy him. And I prayed for Aaron also at the same time. 21 Then I took the sinful thing, the calf that you had made, and burned it with fire and crushed it, grinding it very small, until it was as fine as dust. And I threw the dust of it into the brook that ran down from the mountain.

22 "At Taberah also, and at Massah and at Kibroth-hattaavah you provoked the LORD to wrath. 23 And when the LORD sent you from Kadesh-barnea, saying, 'Go up and take possession of the land that I have given you,' then you rebelled against the commandment of the LORD your God and did not believe him or obey his voice. 24 You have been rebellious against the LORD from the day that I knew you.

25 "So I lay prostrate before the LORD for these forty days and forty nights, because the LORD had said he would destroy you. 26 And I prayed to the LORD, 'O Lord GOD, do not destroy your people and your heritage, whom you have redeemed through your greatness, whom you have brought out of Egypt with a mighty hand. 27 Remember your servants, Abraham, Isaac, and Jacob. Do not regard the stubbornness of this

[1] Hebrew *cast-metal*

people, or their wickedness or their sin, 28 lest the land from which you brought us say, "Because the LORD was not able to bring them into the land that he promised them, and because he hated them, he has brought them out to put them to death in the wilderness." 29 For they are your people and your heritage, whom you brought out by your great power and by your outstretched arm.'

New Tablets of Stone

10 "At that time the LORD said to me, 'Cut for yourself two tablets of stone like the first, and come up to me on the mountain and make an ark of wood. 2 And I will write on the tablets the words that were on the first tablets that you broke, and you shall put them in the ark.' 3 So I made an ark of acacia wood, and cut two tablets of stone like the first, and went up the mountain with the two tablets in my hand. 4 And he wrote on the tablets, in the same writing as before, the Ten Commandments[1] that the LORD had spoken to you on the mountain out of the midst of the fire on the day of the assembly. And the LORD gave them to me. 5 Then I turned and came down from the mountain and put the tablets in the ark that I had made. And there they are, as the LORD commanded me."

6 (The people of Israel journeyed from Beeroth Bene-jaakan[2] to Moserah. There Aaron died, and there he was buried. And his son Eleazar ministered as priest in his place. 7 From there they journeyed to Gudgodah, and from Gudgodah to Jotbathah, a land with brooks of water. 8 At that time the LORD set apart the tribe of Levi to carry the ark of the covenant of the LORD to stand before the LORD to minister to him and to bless in his name, to this day. 9 Therefore Levi has no portion or inheritance with his brothers. The LORD is his inheritance, as the LORD your God said to him.)

10 "I myself stayed on the mountain, as at the first time, forty days and forty nights, and the LORD listened to me that time also. The LORD was unwilling to destroy you. 11 And the LORD said to me, 'Arise, go on your journey at the head of the people, so that they may go in and possess the land, which I swore to their fathers to give them.'

Circumcise Your Heart

12 "And now, Israel, what does the LORD your God require of you, but to fear the LORD your God, to walk in all his ways, to love him, to serve the LORD your God with all your heart and with all your soul, 13 and to keep the commandments and statutes of the LORD, which I am commanding you today for your good? 14 Behold, to the LORD your God belong heaven and the heaven of heavens, the earth with all that is in it. 15 Yet the LORD set his heart in love on your fathers and chose their offspring after them, you above all peoples, as you are this day. 16 Circumcise therefore the foreskin of your heart, and be no longer stubborn. 17 For the LORD your God is God of gods and Lord of lords, the great, the mighty, and the awesome God, who is not partial and takes no bribe. 18 He executes justice for the fatherless and the widow, and loves the sojourner, giving him food and clothing. 19 Love the sojourner, therefore, for you were sojourners in the land of Egypt. 20 You shall fear the LORD your God. You shall serve him and hold fast to him, and by his name you shall swear. 21 He is your praise. He is your God, who has done for you these great and terrifying things that your eyes have seen. 22 Your fathers went down to Egypt seventy persons, and now the LORD your God has made you as numerous as the stars of heaven.

Love and Serve the LORD

11 "You shall therefore love the LORD your God and keep his charge, his statutes, his rules, and his command-

[1] *Hebrew words* [2] *Or the wells of the Bene-jaakan*

ments always. 2 And consider today (since I am not speaking to your children who have not known or seen it), consider the discipline[1] of the LORD your God, his greatness, his mighty hand and his outstretched arm, 3 his signs and his deeds that he did in Egypt to Pharaoh the king of Egypt and to all his land, 4 and what he did to the army of Egypt, to their horses and to their chariots, how he made the water of the Red Sea flow over them as they pursued after you, and how the LORD has destroyed them to this day, 5 and what he did to you in the wilderness, until you came to this place, 6 and what he did to Dathan and Abiram the sons of Eliab, son of Reuben, how the earth opened its mouth and swallowed them up, with their households, their tents, and every living thing that followed them, in the midst of all Israel. 7 For your eyes have seen all the great work of the LORD that he did.

8 "You shall therefore keep the whole commandment that I command you today, that you may be strong, and go in and take possession of the land that you are going over to possess, 9 and that you may live long in the land that the LORD swore to your fathers to give to them and to their offspring, a land flowing with milk and honey. 10 For the land that you are entering to take possession of it is not like the land of Egypt, from which you have come, where you sowed your seed and irrigated it,[2] like a garden of vegetables. 11 But the land that you are going over to possess is a land of hills and valleys, which drinks water by the rain from heaven, 12 a land that the LORD your God cares for. The eyes of the LORD your God are always upon it, from the beginning of the year to the end of the year.

13 "And if you will indeed obey my commandments that I command you today, to love the LORD your God, and to serve him with all your heart and with all your soul, 14 he[3] will give the rain for your land in its season, the early rain and the later rain, that you may gather in your grain and your wine and your oil. 15 And he will give grass in your fields for your livestock, and you shall eat and be full. 16 Take care lest your heart be deceived, and you turn aside and serve other gods and worship them; 17 then the anger of the LORD will be kindled against you, and he will shut up the heavens, so that there will be no rain, and the land will yield no fruit, and you will perish quickly off the good land that the LORD is giving you.

18 "You shall therefore lay up these words of mine in your heart and in your soul, and you shall bind them as a sign on your hand, and they shall be as frontlets between your eyes. 19 You shall teach them to your children, talking of them when you are sitting in your house, and when you are walking by the way, and when you lie down, and when you rise. 20 You shall write them on the doorposts of your house and on your gates, 21 that your days and the days of your children may be multiplied in the land that the LORD swore to your fathers to give them, as long as the heavens are above the earth. 22 For if you will be careful to do all this commandment that I command you to do, loving the LORD your God, walking in all his ways, and holding fast to him, 23 then the LORD will drive out all these nations before you, and you will dispossess nations greater and mightier than yourselves. 24 Every place on which the sole of your foot treads shall be yours. Your territory shall be from the wilderness to[4] the Lebanon and from the River, the river Euphrates, to the western sea. 25 No one shall be able to stand against you. The LORD your God will lay the fear of you and the dread of you on all the land that you shall tread, as he promised you.

26 "See, I am setting before you today a blessing and a curse: 27 the blessing, if

[1] Or *instruction* [2] Hebrew *watered it with your feet* [3] Samaritan, Septuagint, Vulgate; Hebrew *I*; also verse 15 [4] Hebrew *and*

you obey the commandments of the LORD your God, which I command you today, 28 and the curse, if you do not obey the commandments of the LORD your God, but turn aside from the way that I am commanding you today, to go after other gods that you have not known. 29 And when the LORD your God brings you into the land that you are entering to take possession of it, you shall set the blessing on Mount Gerizim and the curse on Mount Ebal. 30 Are they not beyond the Jordan, west of the road, toward the going down of the sun, in the land of the Canaanites who live in the Arabah, opposite Gilgal, beside the oak[1] of Moreh? 31 For you are to cross over the Jordan to go in to take possession of the land that the LORD your God is giving you. And when you possess it and live in it, 32 you shall be careful to do all the statutes and the rules that I am setting before you today.

The LORD's Chosen Place of Worship

12 "These are the statutes and rules that you shall be careful to do in the land that the LORD, the God of your fathers, has given you to possess, all the days that you live on the earth. 2 You shall surely destroy all the places where the nations whom you shall dispossess served their gods, on the high mountains and on the hills and under every green tree. 3 You shall tear down their altars and dash in pieces their pillars and burn their Asherim with fire. You shall chop down the carved images of their gods and destroy their name out of that place. 4 You shall not worship the LORD your God in that way. 5 But you shall seek the place that the LORD your God will choose out of all your tribes to put his name and make his habitation[2] there. There you shall go, 6 and there you shall bring your burnt offerings and your sacrifices, your tithes and the contribution that you present, your vow offerings, your freewill offerings, and the firstborn of your herd and of your flock. 7 And there you shall eat before the LORD your God, and you shall rejoice, you and your households, in all that you undertake, in which the LORD your God has blessed you.

8 "You shall not do according to all that we are doing here today, everyone doing whatever is right in his own eyes, 9 for you have not as yet come to the rest and to the inheritance that the LORD your God is giving you. 10 But when you go over the Jordan and live in the land that the LORD your God is giving you to inherit, and when he gives you rest from all your enemies around, so that you live in safety, 11 then to the place that the LORD your God will choose, to make his name dwell there, there you shall bring all that I command you: your burnt offerings and your sacrifices, your tithes and the contribution that you present, and all your finest vow offerings that you vow to the LORD. 12 And you shall rejoice before the LORD your God, you and your sons and your daughters, your male servants and your female servants, and the Levite that is within your towns, since he has no portion or inheritance with you. 13 Take care that you do not offer your burnt offerings at any place that you see, 14 but at the place that the LORD will choose in one of your tribes, there you shall offer your burnt offerings, and there you shall do all that I am commanding you.

15 "However, you may slaughter and eat meat within any of your towns, as much as you desire, according to the blessing of the LORD your God that he has given you. The unclean and the clean may eat of it, as of the gazelle and as of the deer. 16 Only you shall not eat the blood; you shall pour it out on the earth like water. 17 You may not eat within your towns the tithe of your grain or of your wine or of your oil, or the firstborn of your herd or of your flock, or any of your vow offerings

[1] Septuagint, Syriac; see Genesis 12:6. Hebrew *oaks*, or *terebinths* [2] Or *name as its habitation*

that you vow, or your freewill offerings or the contribution that you present, 18 but you shall eat them before the LORD your God in the place that the LORD your God will choose, you and your son and your daughter, your male servant and your female servant, and the Levite who is within your towns. And you shall rejoice before the LORD your God in all that you undertake. 19 Take care that you do not neglect the Levite as long as you live in your land.

20 "When the LORD your God enlarges your territory, as he has promised you, and you say, 'I will eat meat,' because you crave meat, you may eat meat whenever you desire. 21 If the place that the LORD your God will choose to put his name there is too far from you, then you may kill any of your herd or your flock, which the LORD has given you, as I have commanded you, and you may eat within your towns whenever you desire. 22 Just as the gazelle or the deer is eaten, so you may eat of it. The unclean and the clean alike may eat of it. 23 Only be sure that you do not eat the blood, for the blood is the life, and you shall not eat the life with the flesh. 24 You shall not eat it; you shall pour it out on the earth like water. 25 You shall not eat it, that all may go well with you and with your children after you, when you do what is right in the sight of the LORD. 26 But the holy things that are due from you, and your vow offerings, you shall take, and you shall go to the place that the LORD will choose, 27 and offer your burnt offerings, the flesh and the blood, on the altar of the LORD your God. The blood of your sacrifices shall be poured out on the altar of the LORD your God, but the flesh you may eat. 28 Be careful to obey all these words that I command you, that it may go well with you and with your children after you forever, when you do what is good and right in the sight of the LORD your God.

Warning Against Idolatry

29 "When the LORD your God cuts off before you the nations whom you go in to dispossess, and you dispossess them and dwell in their land, 30 take care that you be not ensnared to follow them, after they have been destroyed before you, and that you do not inquire about their gods, saying, 'How did these nations serve their gods?—that I also may do the same.' 31 You shall not worship the LORD your God in that way, for every abominable thing that the LORD hates they have done for their gods, for they even burn their sons and their daughters in the fire to their gods.

32 [1] "Everything that I command you, you shall be careful to do. You shall not add to it or take from it.

13 "If a prophet or a dreamer of dreams arises among you and gives you a sign or a wonder, 2 and the sign or wonder that he tells you comes to pass, and if he says, 'Let us go after other gods,' which you have not known, 'and let us serve them,' 3 you shall not listen to the words of that prophet or that dreamer of dreams. For the LORD your God is testing you, to know whether you love the LORD your God with all your heart and with all your soul. 4 You shall walk after the LORD your God and fear him and keep his commandments and obey his voice, and you shall serve him and hold fast to him. 5 But that prophet or that dreamer of dreams shall be put to death, because he has taught rebellion against the LORD your God, who brought you out of the land of Egypt and redeemed you out of the house of slavery, to make you leave the way in which the LORD your God commanded you to walk. So you shall purge the evil[2] from your midst.

6 "If your brother, the son of your mother, or your son or your daughter or the wife you embrace[3] or your friend who is as your own soul entices you secretly, saying, 'Let us go and serve other gods,'

[1] Ch 13:1 in Hebrew [2] Or *evil person* [3] Hebrew *the wife of your bosom*

which neither you nor your fathers have known, 7 some of the gods of the peoples who are around you, whether near you or far off from you, from the one end of the earth to the other, 8 you shall not yield to him or listen to him, nor shall your eye pity him, nor shall you spare him, nor shall you conceal him. 9 But you shall kill him. Your hand shall be first against him to put him to death, and afterward the hand of all the people. 10 You shall stone him to death with stones, because he sought to draw you away from the LORD your God, who brought you out of the land of Egypt, out of the house of slavery. 11 And all Israel shall hear and fear and never again do any such wickedness as this among you.

12 "If you hear in one of your cities, which the LORD your God is giving you to dwell there, 13 that certain worthless fellows have gone out among you and have drawn away the inhabitants of their city, saying, 'Let us go and serve other gods,' which you have not known, 14 then you shall inquire and make search and ask diligently. And behold, if it be true and certain that such an abomination has been done among you, 15 you shall surely put the inhabitants of that city to the sword, devoting it to destruction,[1] all who are in it and its cattle, with the edge of the sword. 16 You shall gather all its spoil into the midst of its open square and burn the city and all its spoil with fire, as a whole burnt offering to the LORD your God. It shall be a heap forever. It shall not be built again. 17 None of the devoted things shall stick to your hand, that the LORD may turn from the fierceness of his anger and show you mercy and have compassion on you and multiply you, as he swore to your fathers, 18 if you obey the voice of the LORD your God, keeping all his commandments that I am commanding you today, and doing what is right in the sight of the LORD your God.

Clean and Unclean Food

14 "You are the sons of the LORD your God. You shall not cut yourselves or make any baldness on your foreheads for the dead. 2 For you are a people holy to the LORD your God, and the LORD has chosen you to be a people for his treasured possession, out of all the peoples who are on the face of the earth.

3 "You shall not eat any abomination. 4 These are the animals you may eat: the ox, the sheep, the goat, 5 the deer, the gazelle, the roebuck, the wild goat, the ibex,[2] the antelope, and the mountain sheep. 6 Every animal that parts the hoof and has the hoof cloven in two and chews the cud, among the animals, you may eat. 7 Yet of those that chew the cud or have the hoof cloven you shall not eat these: the camel, the hare, and the rock badger, because they chew the cud but do not part the hoof, are unclean for you. 8 And the pig, because it parts the hoof but does not chew the cud, is unclean for you. Their flesh you shall not eat, and their carcasses you shall not touch.

9 "Of all that are in the waters you may eat these: whatever has fins and scales you may eat. 10 And whatever does not have fins and scales you shall not eat; it is unclean for you.

11 "You may eat all clean birds. 12 But these are the ones that you shall not eat: the eagle,[3] the bearded vulture, the black vulture, 13 the kite, the falcon of any kind; 14 every raven of any kind; 15 the ostrich, the nighthawk, the sea gull, the hawk of any kind; 16 the little owl and the short-eared owl, the barn owl 17 and the tawny owl, the carrion vulture and the cormorant, 18 the stork, the heron of any kind; the hoopoe and the bat. 19 And all winged insects are unclean for you; they shall not be eaten. 20 All clean winged things you may eat.

21 "You shall not eat anything that has died naturally. You may give it to the

[1] That is, setting apart (devoting) as an offering to the Lord (for destruction) [2] Or *addax* [3] The identity of many of these birds is uncertain

sojourner who is within your towns, that he may eat it, or you may sell it to a foreigner. For you are a people holy to the LORD your God.

"You shall not boil a young goat in its mother's milk.

Tithes

22 "You shall tithe all the yield of your seed that comes from the field year by year. 23 And before the LORD your God, in the place that he will choose, to make his name dwell there, you shall eat the tithe of your grain, of your wine, and of your oil, and the firstborn of your herd and flock, that you may learn to fear the LORD your God always. 24 And if the way is too long for you, so that you are not able to carry the tithe, when the LORD your God blesses you, because the place is too far from you, which the LORD your God chooses, to set his name there, 25 then you shall turn it into money and bind up the money in your hand and go to the place that the LORD your God chooses 26 and spend the money for whatever you desire—oxen or sheep or wine or strong drink, whatever your appetite craves. And you shall eat there before the LORD your God and rejoice, you and your household. 27 And you shall not neglect the Levite who is within your towns, for he has no portion or inheritance with you.

28 "At the end of every three years you shall bring out all the tithe of your produce in the same year and lay it up within your towns. 29 And the Levite, because he has no portion or inheritance with you, and the sojourner, the fatherless, and the widow, who are within your towns, shall come and eat and be filled, that the LORD your God may bless you in all the work of your hands that you do.

The Sabbatical Year

15 "At the end of every seven years you shall grant a release. 2 And this is the manner of the release: every creditor shall release what he has lent to his neighbor. He shall not exact it of his neighbor, his brother, because the LORD's release has been proclaimed. 3 Of a foreigner you may exact it, but whatever of yours is with your brother your hand shall release. 4 But there will be no poor among you; for the LORD will bless you in the land that the LORD your God is giving you for an inheritance to possess— 5 if only you will strictly obey the voice of the LORD your God, being careful to do all this commandment that I command you today. 6 For the LORD your God will bless you, as he promised you, and you shall lend to many nations, but you shall not borrow, and you shall rule over many nations, but they shall not rule over you.

7 "If among you, one of your brothers should become poor, in any of your towns within your land that the LORD your God is giving you, you shall not harden your heart or shut your hand against your poor brother, 8 but you shall open your hand to him and lend him sufficient for his need, whatever it may be. 9 Take care lest there be an unworthy thought in your heart and you say, 'The seventh year, the year of release is near,' and your eye look grudgingly[1] on your poor brother, and you give him nothing, and he cry to the LORD against you, and you be guilty of sin. 10 You shall give to him freely, and your heart shall not be grudging when you give to him, because for this the LORD your God will bless you in all your work and in all that you undertake. 11 For there will never cease to be poor in the land. Therefore I command you, 'You shall open wide your hand to your brother, to the needy and to the poor, in your land.'

12 "If your brother, a Hebrew man or a Hebrew woman, is sold[2] to you, he shall serve you six years, and in the seventh year you shall let him go free from you. 13 And when you let him go free from you, you shall not let him go empty-handed.

[1] Or *be evil*; also verse 10 [2] Or *sells himself*

14 You shall furnish him liberally out of
your flock, out of your threshing floor,
and out of your winepress. As the LORD
your God has blessed you, you shall give
to him. 15 You shall remember that you
were a slave in the land of Egypt, and the
LORD your God redeemed you; therefore
I command you this today. 16 But if he
says to you, 'I will not go out from you,'
because he loves you and your household,
since he is well-off with you, 17 then you
shall take an awl, and put it through his
ear into the door, and he shall be your
slave forever. And to your female slave
you shall do the same. 18 It shall not seem
hard to you when you let him go free from
you, for at half the cost of a hired servant
he has served you six years. So the LORD
your God will bless you in all that you do.

19 "All the firstborn males that are born
of your herd and flock you shall dedicate
to the LORD your God. You shall do no
work with the firstborn of your herd, nor
shear the firstborn of your flock. 20 You
shall eat it, you and your household,
before the LORD your God year by year at
the place that the LORD will choose. 21 But
if it has any blemish, if it is lame or blind
or has any serious blemish whatever, you
shall not sacrifice it to the LORD your God.
22 You shall eat it within your towns. The
unclean and the clean alike may eat it, as
though it were a gazelle or a deer. 23 Only
you shall not eat its blood; you shall pour
it out on the ground like water.

Passover

16 "Observe the month of Abib and
keep the Passover to the LORD
your God, for in the month of Abib the
LORD your God brought you out of Egypt
by night. 2 And you shall offer the Passover
sacrifice to the LORD your God, from the
flock or the herd, at the place that the
LORD will choose, to make his name
dwell there. 3 You shall eat no leavened
bread with it. Seven days you shall eat
it with unleavened bread, the bread of
affliction—for you came out of the land
of Egypt in haste—that all the days of your
life you may remember the day when you
came out of the land of Egypt. 4 No leaven
shall be seen with you in all your terri-
tory for seven days, nor shall any of the
flesh that you sacrifice on the evening of
the first day remain all night until morn-
ing. 5 You may not offer the Passover sac-
rifice within any of your towns that the
LORD your God is giving you, 6 but at the
place that the LORD your God will choose,
to make his name dwell in it, there you
shall offer the Passover sacrifice, in the
evening at sunset, at the time you came
out of Egypt. 7 And you shall cook it and
eat it at the place that the LORD your God
will choose. And in the morning you shall
turn and go to your tents. 8 For six days
you shall eat unleavened bread, and on
the seventh day there shall be a solemn
assembly to the LORD your God. You shall
do no work on it.

The Feast of Weeks

9 "You shall count seven weeks. Begin
to count the seven weeks from the time
the sickle is first put to the standing grain.
10 Then you shall keep the Feast of Weeks
to the LORD your God with the tribute
of a freewill offering from your hand,
which you shall give as the LORD your
God blesses you. 11 And you shall rejoice
before the LORD your God, you and your
son and your daughter, your male servant
and your female servant, the Levite who
is within your towns, the sojourner, the
fatherless, and the widow who are among
you, at the place that the LORD your God
will choose, to make his name dwell there.
12 You shall remember that you were a
slave in Egypt; and you shall be careful to
observe these statutes.

The Feast of Booths

13 "You shall keep the Feast of Booths
seven days, when you have gathered in

the produce from your threshing floor
and your winepress. 14 You shall rejoice
in your feast, you and your son and your
daughter, your male servant and your
female servant, the Levite, the sojourner,
the fatherless, and the widow who are
within your towns. 15 For seven days you
shall keep the feast to the LORD your God
at the place that the LORD will choose,
because the LORD your God will bless you
in all your produce and in all the work of
your hands, so that you will be altogether
joyful.

16 "Three times a year all your males
shall appear before the LORD your God
at the place that he will choose: at the
Feast of Unleavened Bread, at the Feast of
Weeks, and at the Feast of Booths. They
shall not appear before the LORD empty-
handed. 17 Every man shall give as he is
able, according to the blessing of the LORD
your God that he has given you.

Justice

18 "You shall appoint judges and officers
in all your towns that the LORD your God
is giving you, according to your tribes, and
they shall judge the people with righteous
judgment. 19 You shall not pervert justice.
You shall not show partiality, and you
shall not accept a bribe, for a bribe blinds
the eyes of the wise and subverts the
cause of the righteous. 20 Justice, and only
justice, you shall follow, that you may live
and inherit the land that the LORD your
God is giving you.

Forbidden Forms of Worship

21 "You shall not plant any tree as an
Asherah beside the altar of the LORD your
God that you shall make. 22 And you shall
not set up a pillar, which the LORD your
God hates.

17 "You shall not sacrifice to the LORD
your God an ox or a sheep in which
is a blemish, any defect whatever, for that
is an abomination to the LORD your God.

2 "If there is found among you, within
any of your towns that the LORD your God
is giving you, a man or woman who does
what is evil in the sight of the LORD your
God, in transgressing his covenant, 3 and
has gone and served other gods and wor-
shiped them, or the sun or the moon or
any of the host of heaven, which I have
forbidden, 4 and it is told you and you hear
of it, then you shall inquire diligently, and
if it is true and certain that such an abomi-
nation has been done in Israel, 5 then you
shall bring out to your gates that man
or woman who has done this evil thing,
and you shall stone that man or woman
to death with stones. 6 On the evidence of
two witnesses or of three witnesses the
one who is to die shall be put to death; a
person shall not be put to death on the
evidence of one witness. 7 The hand of the
witnesses shall be first against him to put
him to death, and afterward the hand of
all the people. So you shall purge[1] the evil[2]
from your midst.

Legal Decisions by Priests and Judges

8 "If any case arises requiring decision be-
tween one kind of homicide and another,
one kind of legal right and another, or
one kind of assault and another, any case
within your towns that is too difficult for
you, then you shall arise and go up to the
place that the LORD your God will choose.
9 And you shall come to the Levitical priests
and to the judge who is in office in those
days, and you shall consult them, and
they shall declare to you the decision.
10 Then you shall do according to what
they declare to you from that place that the
LORD will choose. And you shall be careful
to do according to all that they direct you.
11 According to the instructions that they
give you, and according to the decision
which they pronounce to you, you shall do.
You shall not turn aside from the verdict
that they declare to you, either to the right
hand or to the left. 12 The man who acts
presumptuously by not obeying the priest

[1] Septuagint *drive out*; also verse 12 [2] Or *evil person*; also verse 12

who stands to minister there before the LORD your God, or the judge, that man shall die. So you shall purge the evil from Israel. 13 And all the people shall hear and fear and not act presumptuously again.

Laws Concerning Israel's Kings

14 "When you come to the land that the
LORD your God is giving you, and
you possess it and dwell in it and
697 then say, 'I will set a king over me,
like all the nations that are around me,'
15 you may indeed set a king over you whom the LORD your God will choose. One from among your brothers you shall set as king over you. You may not put a foreigner over you, who is not your brother. 16 Only he must not acquire many horses for himself or cause the people to return to Egypt in order to acquire many horses, since the LORD has said to you, 'You shall never return that way again.' 17 And he shall not acquire many wives for himself, lest his heart turn away, nor shall he acquire for himself excessive silver and gold.

18 "And when he sits on the throne of his
kingdom, he shall write for himself
in a book a copy of this law,
697 approved by[1] the Levitical priests.
19 And it shall be with him, and he shall read in it all the days of his life, that he may learn to fear the LORD his God by keeping all the words of this law and these statutes, and doing them, 20 that his heart may not be lifted up above his brothers, and that he may not turn aside from the commandment, either to the right hand or to the left, so that he may continue long in his kingdom, he and his children, in Israel.

Provision for Priests and Levites

18 "The Levitical priests, all the tribe of Levi, shall have no portion or inheritance with Israel. They shall eat the LORD's food offerings[2] as their[3] inheritance. 2 They shall have no inheritance among their brothers; the LORD is their inheritance, as he promised them. 3 And this shall be the priests' due from the people, from those offering a sacrifice, whether an ox or a sheep: they shall give to the priest the shoulder and the two cheeks and the stomach. 4 The firstfruits of your grain, of your wine and of your oil, and the first fleece of your sheep, you shall give him. 5 For the LORD your God has chosen him out of all your tribes to stand and minister in the name of the LORD, him and his sons for all time.

6 "And if a Levite comes from any of your towns out of all Israel, where he lives—and he may come when he desires[4]—to the place that the LORD will choose, 7 and ministers in the name of the LORD his God, like all his fellow Levites who stand to minister there before the LORD, 8 then he may have equal portions to eat, besides what he receives from the sale of his patrimony.[5]

Abominable Practices

9 "When you come into the land that the LORD your God is giving you, you shall not learn to follow the abominable practices of those nations. 10 There shall not be found among you anyone who burns his son or his daughter as an offering,[6] anyone who practices divination or tells fortunes or interprets omens, or a sorcerer 11 or a charmer or a medium or a necromancer or one who inquires of the dead, 12 for whoever does these things is an abomination to the LORD. And because of these abominations the LORD your God is driving them out before you. 13 You shall be blameless before the LORD your God, 14 for these nations, which you are about to dispossess, listen to fortune-tellers and to diviners. But as for you, the LORD your God has not allowed you to do this.

A New Prophet like Moses

15 "The LORD your God will raise up for you a prophet like me from among

[1] Hebrew *from before* [2] *Or the offerings by fire to the LORD* [3] Hebrew *his* [4] *Or lives—if he comes enthusiastically* [5] The meaning of the Hebrew is uncertain [6] Hebrew *makes his son or his daughter pass through the fire*

you, from your brothers—it is to him
you shall listen— 16 just as you desired of
the LORD your God at Horeb on the day
of the assembly, when you said, 'Let me
not hear again the voice of the LORD my
God or see this great fire any more, lest I
die.' 17 And the LORD said to me, 'They are
right in what they have spoken. 18 I will
raise up for them a prophet like you from
among their brothers. And I will put my
words in his mouth, and he shall speak
to them all that I command him. 19 And
whoever will not listen to my words that
he shall speak in my name, I myself will
require it of him. 20 But the prophet who
presumes to speak a word in my name
that I have not commanded him to speak,
or[1] who speaks in the name of other gods,
that same prophet shall die.' 21 And if you
say in your heart, 'How may we know the
word that the LORD has not spoken?'—
22 when a prophet speaks in the name of
the LORD, if the word does not come to
pass or come true, that is a word that the
LORD has not spoken; the prophet has
spoken it presumptuously. You need not
be afraid of him.

Laws Concerning Cities of Refuge

19 "When the LORD your God cuts
off the nations whose land the
LORD your God is giving you, and you
dispossess them and dwell in their cities
and in their houses, 2 you shall set apart
three cities for yourselves in the land that
the LORD your God is giving you to pos-
sess. 3 You shall measure the distances[2]
and divide into three parts the area of the
land that the LORD your God gives you as
a possession, so that any manslayer can
flee to them.

4 "This is the provision for the man-
slayer, who by fleeing there may save his
life. If anyone kills his neighbor uninten-
tionally without having hated him in the
past— 5 as when someone goes into the
forest with his neighbor to cut wood, and
his hand swings the axe to cut down a
tree, and the head slips from the handle
and strikes his neighbor so that he dies—
he may flee to one of these cities and live,
6 lest the avenger of blood in hot anger
pursue the manslayer and overtake him,
because the way is long, and strike him
fatally, though the man did not deserve
to die, since he had not hated his neigh-
bor in the past. 7 Therefore I command
you, You shall set apart three cities. 8 And
if the LORD your God enlarges your terri-
tory, as he has sworn to your fathers, and
gives you all the land that he promised to
give to your fathers— 9 provided you are
careful to keep all this commandment,
which I command you today, by loving
the LORD your God and by walking ever
in his ways—then you shall add three
other cities to these three, 10 lest inno-
cent blood be shed in your land that the
LORD your God is giving you for an inher-
itance, and so the guilt of bloodshed be
upon you.

11 "But if anyone hates his neighbor
and lies in wait for him and attacks him
and strikes him fatally so that he dies, and
he flees into one of these cities, 12 then
the elders of his city shall send and take
him from there, and hand him over to
the avenger of blood, so that he may die.
13 Your eye shall not pity him, but you shall
purge the guilt of innocent blood[3] from
Israel, so that it may be well with you.

Property Boundaries

14 "You shall not move your neighbor's
landmark, which the men of old have set,
in the inheritance that you will hold in the
land that the LORD your God is giving you
to possess.

Laws Concerning Witnesses

15 "A single witness shall not suffice
against a person for any crime or for any
wrong in connection with any offense that
he has committed. Only on the evidence
of two witnesses or of three witnesses

[1] Or *and* [2] Hebrew *road* [3] Or *the blood of the innocent*

shall a charge be established. 16 If a mali-
cious witness arises to accuse a person
of wrongdoing, 17 then both parties to
the dispute shall appear before the LORD,
before the priests and the judges who are
in office in those days. 18 The judges shall
inquire diligently, and if the witness is a
false witness and has accused his brother
falsely, 19 then you shall do to him as he
had meant to do to his brother. So you
shall purge the evil[1] from your midst.
20 And the rest shall hear and fear, and
shall never again commit any such evil
among you. 21 Your eye shall not pity. It
shall be life for life, eye for eye, tooth for
tooth, hand for hand, foot for foot.

Laws Concerning Warfare

20 "When you go out to war against
your enemies, and see horses and
chariots and an army larger than your
own, you shall not be afraid of them,
for the LORD your God is with you, who
brought you up out of the land of Egypt.
2 And when you draw near to the battle,
the priest shall come forward and speak
to the people 3 and shall say to them, 'Hear,
O Israel, today you are drawing near for
battle against your enemies: let not your
heart faint. Do not fear or panic or be in
dread of them, 4 for the LORD your God
is he who goes with you to fight for you
against your enemies, to give you the vic-
tory.' 5 Then the officers shall speak to the
people, saying, 'Is there any man who has
built a new house and has not dedicated
it? Let him go back to his house, lest he
die in the battle and another man dedi-
cate it. 6 And is there any man who has
planted a vineyard and has not enjoyed
its fruit? Let him go back to his house, lest
he die in the battle and another man enjoy
its fruit. 7 And is there any man who has
betrothed a wife and has not taken her?
Let him go back to his house, lest he die
in the battle and another man take her.'
8 And the officers shall speak further to
the people, and say, 'Is there any man who
is fearful and fainthearted? Let him go
back to his house, lest he make the heart
of his fellows melt like his own.' 9 And
when the officers have finished speaking
to the people, then commanders shall be
appointed at the head of the people.

10 "When you draw near to a city to
fight against it, offer terms of peace to
it. 11 And if it responds to you peaceably
and it opens to you, then all the people
who are found in it shall do forced labor
for you and shall serve you. 12 But if it
makes no peace with you, but makes war
against you, then you shall besiege it.
13 And when the LORD your God gives it
into your hand, you shall put all its males
to the sword, 14 but the women and the
little ones, the livestock, and everything
else in the city, all its spoil, you shall take
as plunder for yourselves. And you shall
enjoy the spoil of your enemies, which
the LORD your God has given you. 15 Thus
you shall do to all the cities that are very
far from you, which are not cities of the
nations here. 16 But in the cities of these
peoples that the LORD your God is giv-
ing you for an inheritance, you shall save
alive nothing that breathes, 17 but you
shall devote them to complete destruc-
tion,[2] the Hittites and the Amorites, the
Canaanites and the Perizzites, the Hivites
and the Jebusites, as the LORD your God
has commanded, 18 that they may not
teach you to do according to all their
abominable practices that they have done
for their gods, and so you sin against the
LORD your God.

19 "When you besiege a city for a long
time, making war against it in order to
take it, you shall not destroy its trees by
wielding an axe against them. You may
eat from them, but you shall not cut them
down. Are the trees in the field human,
that they should be besieged by you?
20 Only the trees that you know are not
trees for food you may destroy and cut

[1] Or *evil person* [2] That is, set apart (devote) as an offering to the Lord (for destruction)

down, that you may build siegeworks
against the city that makes war with you,
until it falls.

Atonement for Unsolved Murders

21 "If in the land that the LORD your
God is giving you to possess
someone is found slain, lying in the open
country, and it is not known who killed
him, 2 then your elders and your judges
shall come out, and they shall measure
the distance to the surrounding cities.
3 And the elders of the city that is nearest
to the slain man shall take a heifer that
has never been worked and that has not
pulled in a yoke. 4 And the elders of that
city shall bring the heifer down to a val-
ley with running water, which is neither
plowed nor sown, and shall break the
heifer's neck there in the valley. 5 Then the
priests, the sons of Levi, shall come for-
ward, for the LORD your God has chosen
them to minister to him and to bless in
the name of the LORD, and by their word
every dispute and every assault shall be
settled. 6 And all the elders of that city
nearest to the slain man shall wash their
hands over the heifer whose neck was bro-
ken in the valley, 7 and they shall testify,
'Our hands did not shed this blood, nor
did our eyes see it shed. 8 Accept atone-
ment, O LORD, for your people Israel,
whom you have redeemed, and do not set
the guilt of innocent blood in the midst
of your people Israel, so that their blood
guilt be atoned for.' 9 So you shall purge
the guilt of innocent blood from your
midst, when you do what is right in the
sight of the LORD.

Marrying Female Captives

10 "When you go out to war against your
enemies, and the LORD your God gives
them into your hand and you take them
captive, 11 and you see among the cap-
tives a beautiful woman, and you desire to
take her to be your wife, 12 and you bring
her home to your house, she shall shave
her head and pare her nails. 13 And she
shall take off the clothes in which she
was captured and shall remain in your
house and lament her father and her
mother a full month. After that you may
go in to her and be her husband, and she
shall be your wife. 14 But if you no longer
delight in her, you shall let her go where
she wants. But you shall not sell her for
money, nor shall you treat her as a slave,
since you have humiliated her.

Inheritance Rights of the Firstborn

15 "If a man has two wives, the one loved
and the other unloved, and both the loved
and the unloved have borne him chil-
dren, and if the firstborn son belongs to
the unloved,[1] 16 then on the day when he
assigns his possessions as an inheritance
to his sons, he may not treat the son of the
loved as the firstborn in preference to the
son of the unloved, who is the firstborn,
17 but he shall acknowledge the firstborn,
the son of the unloved, by giving him a
double portion of all that he has, for he is
the firstfruits of his strength. The right of
the firstborn is his.

A Rebellious Son

18 "If a man has a stubborn and rebel-
lious son who will not obey the voice of
his father or the voice of his mother, and,
though they discipline him, will not listen
to them, 19 then his father and his mother
shall take hold of him and bring him out
to the elders of his city at the gate of the
place where he lives, 20 and they shall say
to the elders of his city, 'This our son is
stubborn and rebellious; he will not obey
our voice; he is a glutton and a drunkard.'
21 Then all the men of the city shall stone
him to death with stones. So you shall
purge the evil from your midst, and all
Israel shall hear, and fear.

A Man Hanged on a Tree Is Cursed

22 "And if a man has committed a crime
punishable by death and he is put to

[1] Or *hated*; also verses 16, 17

death, and you hang him on a tree, 23 his
body shall not remain all night on the tree,
but you shall bury him the same day, for a
hanged man is cursed by God. You shall
not defile your land that the LORD your
God is giving you for an inheritance.

Various Laws

22 "You shall not see your brother's
ox or his sheep going astray and
ignore them. You shall take them back
to your brother. 2 And if he does not live
near you and you do not know who he is,
you shall bring it home to your house, and
it shall stay with you until your brother
seeks it. Then you shall restore it to him.
3 And you shall do the same with his don-
key or with his garment, or with any lost
thing of your brother's, which he loses and
you find; you may not ignore it. 4 You shall
not see your brother's donkey or his ox
fallen down by the way and ignore them.
You shall help him to lift them up again.

5 "A woman shall not wear a man's gar-
ment, nor shall a man put on a woman's
cloak, for whoever does these things is an
abomination to the LORD your God.

6 "If you come across a bird's nest in any
tree or on the ground, with young ones or
eggs and the mother sitting on the young
or on the eggs, you shall not take the
mother with the young. 7 You shall let the
mother go, but the young you may take for
yourself, that it may go well with you, and
that you may live long.

8 "When you build a new house, you
shall make a parapet for your roof, that
you may not bring the guilt of blood upon
your house, if anyone should fall from it.

9 "You shall not sow your vineyard
with two kinds of seed, lest the whole
yield be forfeited,[1] the crop that you have
sown and the yield of the vineyard. 10 You
shall not plow with an ox and a donkey
together. 11 You shall not wear cloth of
wool and linen mixed together.

12 "You shall make yourself tassels on
the four corners of the garment with
which you cover yourself.

Laws Concerning Sexual Immorality

13 "If any man takes a wife and goes in
to her and then hates her 14 and accuses
her of misconduct and brings a bad name
upon her, saying, 'I took this woman, and
when I came near her, I did not find in her
evidence of virginity,' 15 then the father of
the young woman and her mother shall
take and bring out the evidence of her vir-
ginity to the elders of the city in the gate.
16 And the father of the young woman
shall say to the elders, 'I gave my daugh-
ter to this man to marry, and he hates
her; 17 and behold, he has accused her
of misconduct, saying, "I did not find in
your daughter evidence of virginity." And
yet this is the evidence of my daughter's
virginity.' And they shall spread the cloak
before the elders of the city. 18 Then the
elders of that city shall take the man and
whip[2] him, 19 and they shall fine him a
hundred shekels[3] of silver and give them
to the father of the young woman, because
he has brought a bad name upon a virgin[4]
of Israel. And she shall be his wife. He
may not divorce her all his days. 20 But if
the thing is true, that evidence of virgin-
ity was not found in the young woman,
21 then they shall bring out the young
woman to the door of her father's house,
and the men of her city shall stone her to
death with stones, because she has done
an outrageous thing in Israel by whoring
in her father's house. So you shall purge
the evil from your midst.

22 "If a man is found lying with the wife
of another man, both of them shall die,
the man who lay with the woman, and
the woman. So you shall purge the evil
from Israel.

23 "If there is a betrothed virgin, and a
man meets her in the city and lies with
her, 24 then you shall bring them both out
to the gate of that city, and you shall stone

[1] Hebrew *become holy* [2] Or *discipline* [3] A *shekel* was about 2/5 ounce or 11 grams [4] Or *girl of marriageable age*

them to death with stones, the young
woman because she did not cry for help
though she was in the city, and the man
because he violated his neighbor's wife. So
you shall purge the evil from your midst.
25 "But if in the open country a man
meets a young woman who is betrothed,
and the man seizes her and lies with
her, then only the man who lay with her
shall die. 26 But you shall do nothing to
the young woman; she has committed
no offense punishable by death. For this
case is like that of a man attacking and
murdering his neighbor, 27 because he
met her in the open country, and though
the betrothed young woman cried for help
there was no one to rescue her.
28 "If a man meets a virgin who is not
betrothed, and seizes her and lies with
her, and they are found, 29 then the man
who lay with her shall give to the father of
the young woman fifty shekels of silver,
and she shall be his wife, because he has
violated her. He may not divorce her all
his days.
30 [1] "A man shall not take his father's
wife, so that he does not uncover his
father's nakedness.[2]

Those Excluded from the Assembly

23 "No one whose testicles are
crushed or whose male organ is
cut off shall enter the assembly of the LORD.
2 "No one born of a forbidden union
may enter the assembly of the LORD.
Even to the tenth generation, none of his
descendants may enter the assembly of
the LORD.
3 "No Ammonite or Moabite may enter
the assembly of the LORD. Even to the
tenth generation, none of them may
enter the assembly of the LORD forever,
4 because they did not meet you with
bread and with water on the way, when
you came out of Egypt, and because they
hired against you Balaam the son of Beor
from Pethor of Mesopotamia, to curse
you. 5 But the LORD your God would not
listen to Balaam; instead the LORD your
God turned the curse into a blessing for
you, because the LORD your God loved
you. 6 You shall not seek their peace or
their prosperity all your days forever.
7 "You shall not abhor an Edomite, for
he is your brother. You shall not abhor an
Egyptian, because you were a sojourner
in his land. 8 Children born to them in the
third generation may enter the assembly
of the LORD.

Uncleanness in the Camp

9 "When you are encamped against your
enemies, then you shall keep yourself
from every evil thing.
10 "If any man among you becomes
unclean because of a nocturnal emis-
sion, then he shall go outside the camp.
He shall not come inside the camp, 11 but
when evening comes, he shall bathe him-
self in water, and as the sun sets, he may
come inside the camp.
12 "You shall have a place outside the
camp, and you shall go out to it. 13 And
you shall have a trowel with your tools,
and when you sit down outside, you
shall dig a hole with it and turn back and
cover up your excrement. 14 Because the
LORD your God walks in the midst of your
camp, to deliver you and to give up your
enemies before you, therefore your camp
must be holy, so that he may not see any-
thing indecent among you and turn away
from you.

Miscellaneous Laws

15 "You shall not give up to his master
a slave who has escaped from his master
to you. 16 He shall dwell with you, in your
midst, in the place that he shall choose
within one of your towns, wherever it
suits him. You shall not wrong him.
17 "None of the daughters of Israel shall
be a cult prostitute, and none of the sons
of Israel shall be a cult prostitute. 18 You
shall not bring the fee of a prostitute or

[1] Ch 23:1 in Hebrew [2] Hebrew *uncover his father's skirt*

the wages of a dog[1] into the house of the
LORD your God in payment for any vow,
for both of these are an abomination to
the LORD your God.

19 “You shall not charge interest on
loans to your brother, interest on money,
interest on food, interest on anything that
is lent for interest. 20 You may charge a for-
eigner interest, but you may not charge
your brother interest, that the LORD your
God may bless you in all that you under-
take in the land that you are entering to
take possession of it.

21 “If you make a vow to the LORD your
God, you shall not delay fulfilling it, for
the LORD your God will surely require it
of you, and you will be guilty of sin. 22 But
if you refrain from vowing, you will not
be guilty of sin. 23 You shall be careful to
do what has passed your lips, for you have
voluntarily vowed to the LORD your God
what you have promised with your mouth.

24 “If you go into your neighbor’s vine-
yard, you may eat your fill of grapes, as
many as you wish, but you shall not put
any in your bag. 25 If you go into your
neighbor’s standing grain, you may pluck
the ears with your hand, but you shall
not put a sickle to your neighbor’s stand-
ing grain.

Laws Concerning Divorce

24 “When a man takes a wife and
marries her, if then she finds no
favor in his eyes because he has found
some indecency in her, and he writes her
a certificate of divorce and puts it in her
hand and sends her out of his house, and
she departs out of his house, 2 and if she
goes and becomes another man’s wife,
3 and the latter man hates her and writes
her a certificate of divorce and puts it in
her hand and sends her out of his house,
or if the latter man dies, who took her to
be his wife, 4 then her former husband,
who sent her away, may not take her again
to be his wife, after she has been defiled,
for that is an abomination before the
LORD. And you shall not bring sin upon
the land that the LORD your God is giving
you for an inheritance.

Miscellaneous Laws

5 “When a man is newly married, he
shall not go out with the army or be liable
for any other public duty. He shall be free
at home one year to be happy with his
wife whom he has taken.

6 “No one shall take a mill or an upper
millstone in pledge, for that would be tak-
ing a life in pledge.

7 “If a man is found stealing one of his
brothers of the people of Israel, and if he
treats him as a slave or sells him, then that
thief shall die. So you shall purge the evil
from your midst.

8 “Take care, in a case of leprous[2] dis-
ease, to be very careful to do according to
all that the Levitical priests shall direct
you. As I commanded them, so you shall
be careful to do. 9 Remember what the
LORD your God did to Miriam on the way
as you came out of Egypt.

10 “When you make your neighbor a
loan of any sort, you shall not go into his
house to collect his pledge. 11 You shall
stand outside, and the man to whom you
make the loan shall bring the pledge out
to you. 12 And if he is a poor man, you
shall not sleep in his pledge. 13 You shall
restore to him the pledge as the sun sets,
that he may sleep in his cloak and bless
you. And it shall be righteousness for you
before the LORD your God.

14 “You shall not oppress a hired servant
who is poor and needy, whether he is one
of your brothers or one of the sojourners
who are in your land within your towns.
15 You shall give him his wages on the
same day, before the sun sets (for he is
poor and counts on it), lest he cry against
you to the LORD, and you be guilty of sin.

16 “Fathers shall not be put to death
because of their children, nor shall chil-

[1] Or *male prostitute* [2] *Leprosy* was a term for several skin diseases; see Leviticus 13

dren be put to death because of their
fathers. Each one shall be put to death for
his own sin.

17 "You shall not pervert the justice due
to the sojourner or to the fatherless, or
take a widow's garment in pledge, 18 but
you shall remember that you were a slave
in Egypt and the LORD your God redeemed
you from there; therefore I command you
to do this.

19 "When you reap your harvest in your
field and forget a sheaf in the field, you
shall not go back to get it. It shall be for the
sojourner, the fatherless, and the widow,
that the LORD your God may bless you in
all the work of your hands. 20 When you
beat your olive trees, you shall not go over
them again. It shall be for the sojourner,
the fatherless, and the widow. 21 When
you gather the grapes of your vineyard,
you shall not strip it afterward. It shall be
for the sojourner, the fatherless, and the
widow. 22 You shall remember that you
were a slave in the land of Egypt; therefore
I command you to do this.

25 "If there is a dispute between men
and they come into court and the
judges decide between them, acquitting
the innocent and condemning the guilty,
2 then if the guilty man deserves to be
beaten, the judge shall cause him to lie
down and be beaten in his presence with
a number of stripes in proportion to his
offense. 3 Forty stripes may be given him,
but not more, lest, if one should go on to
beat him with more stripes than these,
your brother be degraded in your sight.

4 "You shall not muzzle an ox when it is
treading out the grain.

Laws Concerning Levirate Marriage

5 "If brothers dwell together, and one of
them dies and has no son, the wife of the
dead man shall not be married outside
the family to a stranger. Her husband's
brother shall go in to her and take her
as his wife and perform the duty of a
husband's brother to her. 6 And the first
son whom she bears shall succeed to the
name of his dead brother, that his name
may not be blotted out of Israel. 7 And if
the man does not wish to take his broth-
er's wife, then his brother's wife shall go
up to the gate to the elders and say, 'My
husband's brother refuses to perpetuate
his brother's name in Israel; he will not
perform the duty of a husband's brother
to me.' 8 Then the elders of his city shall
call him and speak to him, and if he per-
sists, saying, 'I do not wish to take her,'
9 then his brother's wife shall go up to
him in the presence of the elders and pull
his sandal off his foot and spit in his face.
And she shall answer and say, 'So shall it
be done to the man who does not build
up his brother's house.' 10 And the name
of his house[1] shall be called in Israel,
'The house of him who had his sandal
pulled off.'

Miscellaneous Laws

11 "When men fight with one another
and the wife of the one draws near to res-
cue her husband from the hand of him
who is beating him and puts out her hand
and seizes him by the private parts, 12 then
you shall cut off her hand. Your eye shall
have no pity.

13 "You shall not have in your bag two
kinds of weights, a large and a small.
14 You shall not have in your house two
kinds of measures, a large and a small. 15 A
full and fair[2] weight you shall have, a full
and fair measure you shall have, that your
days may be long in the land that the LORD
your God is giving you. 16 For all who do
such things, all who act dishonestly, are
an abomination to the LORD your God.

17 "Remember what Amalek did to you
on the way as you came out of Egypt,
18 how he attacked you on the way when
you were faint and weary, and cut off
your tail, those who were lagging behind
you, and he did not fear God. 19 Therefore

[1] Hebrew *its name* [2] Or *just*, or *righteous*; twice in this verse

when the LORD your God has given you rest from all your enemies around you, in the land that the LORD your God is giving you for an inheritance to possess, you shall blot out the memory of Amalek from under heaven; you shall not forget.

Offerings of Firstfruits and Tithes

26 "When you come into the land that the LORD your God is giving you for an inheritance and have taken possession of it and live in it, 2 you shall take some of the first of all the fruit of the ground, which you harvest from your land that the LORD your God is giving you, and you shall put it in a basket, and you shall go to the place that the LORD your God will choose, to make his name to dwell there. 3 And you shall go to the priest who is in office at that time and say to him, 'I declare today to the LORD your God that I have come into the land that the LORD swore to our fathers to give us.' 4 Then the priest shall take the basket from your hand and set it down before the altar of the LORD your God.

5 "And you shall make response before the LORD your God, 'A wandering Aramean was my father. And he went down into Egypt and sojourned there, few in number, and there he became a nation, great, mighty, and populous. 6 And the Egyptians treated us harshly and humiliated us and laid on us hard labor. 7 Then we cried to the LORD, the God of our fathers, and the LORD heard our voice and saw our affliction, our toil, and our oppression. 8 And the LORD brought us out of Egypt with a mighty hand and an outstretched arm, with great deeds of terror,[1] with signs and wonders. 9 And he brought us into this place and gave us this land, a land flowing with milk and honey. 10 And behold, now I bring the first of the fruit of the ground, which you, O LORD, have given me.' And you shall set it down before the LORD your God and worship before the LORD your God. 11 And you shall rejoice in all the good that the LORD your God has given to you and to your house, you, and the Levite, and the sojourner who is among you.

12 "When you have finished paying all the tithe of your produce in the third year, which is the year of tithing, giving it to the Levite, the sojourner, the fatherless, and the widow, so that they may eat within your towns and be filled, 13 then you shall say before the LORD your God, 'I have removed the sacred portion out of my house, and moreover, I have given it to the Levite, the sojourner, the fatherless, and the widow, according to all your commandment that you have commanded me. I have not transgressed any of your commandments, nor have I forgotten them. 14 I have not eaten of the tithe while I was mourning, or removed any of it while I was unclean, or offered any of it to the dead. I have obeyed the voice of the LORD my God. I have done according to all that you have commanded me. 15 Look down from your holy habitation, from heaven, and bless your people Israel and the ground that you have given us, as you swore to our fathers, a land flowing with milk and honey.'

16 "This day the LORD your God commands you to do these statutes and rules. You shall therefore be careful to do them with all your heart and with all your soul. 17 You have declared today that the LORD is your God, and that you will walk in his ways, and keep his statutes and his commandments and his rules, and will obey his voice. 18 And the LORD has declared today that you are a people for his treasured possession, as he has promised you, and that you are to keep all his commandments, 19 and that he will set you in praise and in fame and in honor high above all nations that he has made, and that you shall be a people holy to the LORD your God, as he promised."

[1] Hebrew *with great terror*

The Altar on Mount Ebal

27 Now Moses and the elders of Israel
commanded the people, saying,
"Keep the whole commandment that I
command you today. 2 And on the day you
cross over the Jordan to the land that the
LORD your God is giving you, you shall
set up large stones and plaster them with
plaster. 3 And you shall write on them all
the words of this law, when you cross over
to enter the land that the LORD your God
is giving you, a land flowing with milk
and honey, as the LORD, the God of your
fathers, has promised you. 4 And when you
have crossed over the Jordan, you shall set
up these stones, concerning which I com-
mand you today, on Mount Ebal, and you
shall plaster them with plaster. 5 And there
you shall build an altar to the LORD your
God, an altar of stones. You shall wield no
iron tool on them; 6 you shall build an altar
to the LORD your God of uncut[1] stones.
And you shall offer burnt offerings on it
to the LORD your God, 7 and you shall sac-
rifice peace offerings and shall eat there,
and you shall rejoice before the LORD your
God. 8 And you shall write on the stones all
the words of this law very plainly."

Curses from Mount Ebal

9 Then Moses and the Levitical priests
said to all Israel, "Keep silence and hear,
O Israel: this day you have become the
people of the LORD your God. 10 You shall
therefore obey the voice of the LORD your
God, keeping his commandments and his
statutes, which I command you today."

11 That day Moses charged the people,
saying, 12 "When you have crossed over
the Jordan, these shall stand on Mount
Gerizim to bless the people: Simeon, Levi,
Judah, Issachar, Joseph, and Benjamin.
13 And these shall stand on Mount
Ebal for the curse: Reuben, Gad, Asher,
Zebulun, Dan, and Naphtali. 14 And the
Levites shall declare to all the men of
Israel in a loud voice:

15 "'Cursed be the man who makes a
carved or cast metal image, an abomi-
nation to the LORD, a thing made by the
hands of a craftsman, and sets it up in
secret.' And all the people shall answer
and say, 'Amen.'

16 "'Cursed be anyone who dishonors
his father or his mother.' And all the peo-
ple shall say, 'Amen.'

17 "'Cursed be anyone who moves his
neighbor's landmark.' And all the people
shall say, 'Amen.'

18 "'Cursed be anyone who misleads a
blind man on the road.' And all the people
shall say, 'Amen.'

19 "'Cursed be anyone who perverts the
justice due to the sojourner, the fatherless,
and the widow.' And all the people shall
say, 'Amen.'

20 "'Cursed be anyone who lies with his
father's wife, because he has uncovered
his father's nakedness.'[2] And all the people
shall say, 'Amen.'

21 "'Cursed be anyone who lies with any
kind of animal.' And all the people shall
say, 'Amen.'

22 "'Cursed be anyone who lies with his
sister, whether the daughter of his father
or the daughter of his mother.' And all the
people shall say, 'Amen.'

23 "'Cursed be anyone who lies with his
mother-in-law.' And all the people shall
say, 'Amen.'

24 "'Cursed be anyone who strikes down
his neighbor in secret.' And all the people
shall say, 'Amen.'

25 "'Cursed be anyone who takes a bribe
to shed innocent blood.' And all the peo-
ple shall say, 'Amen.'

26 "'Cursed be anyone who does not
confirm the words of this law by doing
them.' And all the people shall say, 'Amen.'

Blessings for Obedience

28 "And if you faithfully obey the
voice of the LORD your God, being
careful to do all his commandments that

[1] Hebrew *whole* [2] Hebrew *uncovered his father's skirt*

I command you today, the LORD your God
will set you high above all the nations of
the earth. 2 And all these blessings shall
come upon you and overtake you, if you
obey the voice of the LORD your God.
3 Blessed shall you be in the city, and
blessed shall you be in the field. 4 Blessed
shall be the fruit of your womb and the
fruit of your ground and the fruit of your
cattle, the increase of your herds and
the young of your flock. 5 Blessed shall
be your basket and your kneading bowl.
6 Blessed shall you be when you come in,
and blessed shall you be when you go out.
7 "The LORD will cause your enemies
who rise against you to be defeated before
you. They shall come out against you one
way and flee before you seven ways. 8 The
LORD will command the blessing on you in
your barns and in all that you undertake.
And he will bless you in the land that the
LORD your God is giving you. 9 The LORD
will establish you as a people holy to him-
self, as he has sworn to you, if you keep the
commandments of the LORD your God and
walk in his ways. 10 And all the peoples of
the earth shall see that you are called by the
name of the LORD, and they shall be afraid
of you. 11 And the LORD will make you
abound in prosperity, in the fruit of your
womb and in the fruit of your livestock
and in the fruit of your ground, within the
land that the LORD swore to your fathers to
give you. 12 The LORD will open to you his
good treasury, the heavens, to give the rain
to your land in its season and to bless all
the work of your hands. And you shall lend
to many nations, but you shall not borrow.
13 And the LORD will make you the head
and not the tail, and you shall only go up
and not down, if you obey the command-
ments of the LORD your God, which I com-
mand you today, being careful to do them,
14 and if you do not turn aside from any
of the words that I command you today,
to the right hand or to the left, to go after
other gods to serve them.

Curses for Disobedience

15 "But if you will not obey the voice
of the LORD your God or be careful to do
all his commandments and his statutes
that I command you today, then all these
curses shall come upon you and overtake
you. 16 Cursed shall you be in the city, and
cursed shall you be in the field. 17 Cursed
shall be your basket and your kneading
bowl. 18 Cursed shall be the fruit of your
womb and the fruit of your ground, the
increase of your herds and the young of
your flock. 19 Cursed shall you be when
you come in, and cursed shall you be
when you go out.
20 "The LORD will send on you curses,
confusion, and frustration in all that you
undertake to do, until you are destroyed
and perish quickly on account of the evil
of your deeds, because you have forsaken
me. 21 The LORD will make the pestilence
stick to you until he has consumed you
off the land that you are entering to take
possession of it. 22 The LORD will strike
you with wasting disease and with fever,
inflammation and fiery heat, and with
drought[1] and with blight and with mil-
dew. They shall pursue you until you per-
ish. 23 And the heavens over your head
shall be bronze, and the earth under you
shall be iron. 24 The LORD will make the
rain of your land powder. From heaven
dust shall come down on you until you
are destroyed.
25 "The LORD will cause you to be
defeated before your enemies. You shall
go out one way against them and flee
seven ways before them. And you shall be
a horror to all the kingdoms of the earth.
26 And your dead body shall be food for all
birds of the air and for the beasts of the
earth, and there shall be no one to frighten
them away. 27 The LORD will strike you
with the boils of Egypt, and with tumors
and scabs and itch, of which you cannot
be healed. 28 The LORD will strike you with
madness and blindness and confusion

[1] *Or sword*

of mind, 29 and you shall grope at noonday, as the blind grope in darkness, and you shall not prosper in your ways.[1] And you shall be only oppressed and robbed continually, and there shall be no one to help you. 30 You shall betroth a wife, but another man shall ravish her. You shall build a house, but you shall not dwell in it. You shall plant a vineyard, but you shall not enjoy its fruit. 31 Your ox shall be slaughtered before your eyes, but you shall not eat any of it. Your donkey shall be seized before your face, but shall not be restored to you. Your sheep shall be given to your enemies, but there shall be no one to help you. 32 Your sons and your daughters shall be given to another people, while your eyes look on and fail with longing for them all day long, but you shall be helpless. 33 A nation that you have not known shall eat up the fruit of your ground and of all your labors, and you shall be only oppressed and crushed continually, 34 so that you are driven mad by the sights that your eyes see. 35 The LORD will strike you on the knees and on the legs with grievous boils of which you cannot be healed, from the sole of your foot to the crown of your head.

36 "The LORD will bring you and your king whom you set over you to a nation that neither you nor your fathers have known. And there you shall serve other gods of wood and stone. 37 And you shall become a horror, a proverb, and a byword among all the peoples where the LORD will lead you away. 38 You shall carry much seed into the field and shall gather in little, for the locust shall consume it. 39 You shall plant vineyards and dress them, but you shall neither drink of the wine nor gather the grapes, for the worm shall eat them. 40 You shall have olive trees throughout all your territory, but you shall not anoint yourself with the oil, for your olives shall drop off. 41 You shall father sons and daughters, but they shall not be yours, for they shall go into captivity. 42 The cricket[2] shall possess all your trees and the fruit of your ground. 43 The sojourner who is among you shall rise higher and higher above you, and you shall come down lower and lower. 44 He shall lend to you, and you shall not lend to him. He shall be the head, and you shall be the tail.

45 "All these curses shall come upon you and pursue you and overtake you till you are destroyed, because you did not obey the voice of the LORD your God, to keep his commandments and his statutes that he commanded you. 46 They shall be a sign and a wonder against you and your offspring forever. 47 Because you did not serve the LORD your God with joyfulness and gladness of heart, because of the abundance of all things, 48 therefore you shall serve your enemies whom the LORD will send against you, in hunger and thirst, in nakedness, and lacking everything. And he will put a yoke of iron on your neck until he has destroyed you. 49 The LORD will bring a nation against you from far away, from the end of the earth, swooping down like the eagle, a nation whose language you do not understand, 50 a hard-faced nation who shall not respect the old or show mercy to the young. 51 It shall eat the offspring of your cattle and the fruit of your ground, until you are destroyed; it also shall not leave you grain, wine, or oil, the increase of your herds or the young of your flock, until they have caused you to perish.

52 "They shall besiege you in all your towns, until your high and fortified walls, in which you trusted, come down throughout all your land. And they shall besiege you in all your towns throughout all your land, which the LORD your God has given you. 53 And you shall eat the fruit of your womb, the flesh of your sons and daughters, whom the LORD your God has given you, in the siege and in the distress

[1] Or *shall not succeed in finding your ways* [2] Identity uncertain

with which your enemies shall distress
you. 54 The man who is the most tender
and refined among you will begrudge food
to his brother, to the wife he embraces,[1]
and to the last of the children whom he
has left, 55 so that he will not give to any
of them any of the flesh of his children
whom he is eating, because he has noth-
ing else left, in the siege and in the distress
with which your enemy shall distress you
in all your towns. 56 The most tender and
refined woman among you, who would
not venture to set the sole of her foot on
the ground because she is so delicate and
tender, will begrudge to the husband she
embraces,[2] to her son and to her daugh-
ter, 57 her afterbirth that comes out from
between her feet and her children whom
she bears, because lacking everything she
will eat them secretly, in the siege and in
the distress with which your enemy shall
distress you in your towns.

58 "If you are not careful to do all the
words of this law that are written in this
book, that you may fear this glorious
and awesome name, the LORD your God,
59 then the LORD will bring on you and
your offspring extraordinary afflictions,
afflictions severe and lasting, and sick-
nesses grievous and lasting. 60 And he will
bring upon you again all the diseases of
Egypt, of which you were afraid, and they
shall cling to you. 61 Every sickness also
and every affliction that is not recorded
in the book of this law, the LORD will
bring upon you, until you are destroyed.
62 Whereas you were as numerous as the
stars of heaven, you shall be left few in
number, because you did not obey the
voice of the LORD your God. 63 And as the
LORD took delight in doing you good and
multiplying you, so the LORD will take
delight in bringing ruin upon you and
destroying you. And you shall be plucked
off the land that you are entering to take
possession of it.

64 "And the LORD will scatter you among
all peoples, from one end of the earth to
the other, and there you shall serve other
gods of wood and stone, which neither
you nor your fathers have known. 65 And
among these nations you shall find no
respite, and there shall be no resting place
for the sole of your foot, but the LORD will
give you there a trembling heart and fail-
ing eyes and a languishing soul. 66 Your
life shall hang in doubt before you. Night
and day you shall be in dread and have no
assurance of your life. 67 In the morning
you shall say, 'If only it were evening!' and
at evening you shall say, 'If only it were
morning!' because of the dread that your
heart shall feel, and the sights that your
eyes shall see. 68 And the LORD will bring
you back in ships to Egypt, a journey that
I promised that you should never make
again; and there you shall offer yourselves
for sale to your enemies as male and
female slaves, but there will be no buyer."

The Covenant Renewed in Moab

29 [3] These are the words of the cov-
enant that the LORD commanded
Moses to make with the people of Israel
in the land of Moab, besides the covenant
that he had made with them at Horeb.

2 [4] And Moses summoned all Israel and
said to them: "You have seen all that the
LORD did before your eyes in the land of
Egypt, to Pharaoh and to all his servants
and to all his land, 3 the great trials that
your eyes saw, the signs, and those great
wonders. 4 But to this day the LORD has
not given you a heart to understand or
eyes to see or ears to hear. 5 I have led
you forty years in the wilderness. Your
clothes have not worn out on you, and
your sandals have not worn off your feet.
6 You have not eaten bread, and you have
not drunk wine or strong drink, that you
may know that I am the LORD your God.
7 And when you came to this place, Sihon
the king of Heshbon and Og the king of
Bashan came out against us to battle,

[1] Hebrew *the wife of his bosom* [2] Hebrew *the husband of her bosom* [3] Ch 28:69 in Hebrew [4] Ch 29:1 in Hebrew

but we defeated them. 8 We took their
land and gave it for an inheritance to the
Reubenites, the Gadites, and the half-tribe
of the Manassites. 9 Therefore keep the
words of this covenant and do them, that
you may prosper[1] in all that you do.

10 "You are standing today all of you
before the LORD your God: the heads of
your tribes,[2] your elders, and your officers,
all the men of Israel, 11 your little ones,
your wives, and the sojourner who is in
your camp, from the one who chops your
wood to the one who draws your water,
12 so that you may enter into the sworn
covenant of the LORD your God, which the
LORD your God is making with you today,
13 that he may establish you today as his
people, and that he may be your God, as
he promised you, and as he swore to your
fathers, to Abraham, to Isaac, and to Jacob.
14 It is not with you alone that I am making
this sworn covenant, 15 but with whoever
is standing here with us today before the
LORD our God, and with whoever is not
here with us today.

16 "You know how we lived in the land
of Egypt, and how we came through the
midst of the nations through which you
passed. 17 And you have seen their detest-
able things, their idols of wood and stone,
of silver and gold, which were among
them. 18 Beware lest there be among you
a man or woman or clan or tribe whose
heart is turning away today from the LORD
our God to go and serve the gods of those
nations. Beware lest there be among you
a root bearing poisonous and bitter fruit,
19 one who, when he hears the words of
this sworn covenant, blesses himself in
his heart, saying, 'I shall be safe, though
I walk in the stubbornness of my heart.'
This will lead to the sweeping away of
moist and dry alike. 20 The LORD will not be
willing to forgive him, but rather the anger
of the LORD and his jealousy will smoke
against that man, and the curses written
in this book will settle upon him, and the
LORD will blot out his name from under
heaven. 21 And the LORD will single him
out from all the tribes of Israel for calam-
ity, in accordance with all the curses of the
covenant written in this Book of the Law.
22 And the next generation, your children
who rise up after you, and the foreigner
who comes from a far land, will say, when
they see the afflictions of that land and the
sicknesses with which the LORD has made
it sick— 23 the whole land burned out with
brimstone and salt, nothing sown and
nothing growing, where no plant can
sprout, an overthrow like that of Sodom
and Gomorrah, Admah, and Zeboiim,
which the LORD overthrew in his anger
and wrath— 24 all the nations will say,
'Why has the LORD done thus to this land?
What caused the heat of this great anger?'
25 Then people will say, 'It is because they
abandoned the covenant of the LORD, the
God of their fathers, which he made with
them when he brought them out of the
land of Egypt, 26 and went and served other
gods and worshiped them, gods whom
they had not known and whom he had not
allotted to them. 27 Therefore the anger of
the LORD was kindled against this land,
bringing upon it all the curses written in
this book, 28 and the LORD uprooted them
from their land in anger and fury and great
wrath, and cast them into another land, as
they are this day.'

29 "The secret things belong to the LORD
our God, but the things that are revealed
belong to us and to our children forever,
that we may do all the words of this law.

Repentance and Forgiveness

30 "And when all these things come
upon you, the blessing and the
curse, which I have set before you, and
you call them to mind among all the
nations where the LORD your God has
driven you, 2 and return to the LORD your
God, you and your children, and obey his
voice in all that I command you today,

[1] Or *deal wisely* [2] Septuagint, Syriac; Hebrew *your heads, your tribes*

with all your heart and with all your soul,
3 then the LORD your God will restore
your fortunes and have compassion on
you, and he will gather you again from all
the peoples where the LORD your God has
scattered you. 4 If your outcasts are in the
uttermost parts of heaven, from there the
LORD your God will gather you, and from
there he will take you. 5 And the LORD your
God will bring you into the land that your
fathers possessed, that you may possess
it. And he will make you more prosperous
and numerous than your fathers. 6 And
the LORD your God will circumcise your
heart and the heart of your offspring, so
that you will love the LORD your God with
all your heart and with all your soul, that
you may live. 7 And the LORD your God
will put all these curses on your foes and
enemies who persecuted you. 8 And you
shall again obey the voice of the LORD and
keep all his commandments that I com-
mand you today. 9 The LORD your God will
make you abundantly prosperous in all
the work of your hand, in the fruit of your
womb and in the fruit of your cattle and
in the fruit of your ground. For the LORD
will again take delight in prospering you,
as he took delight in your fathers, 10 when
you obey the voice of the LORD your God,
to keep his commandments and his stat-
utes that are written in this Book of the
Law, when you turn to the LORD your God
with all your heart and with all your soul.

The Choice of Life and Death

11 "For this commandment that I com-
mand you today is not too hard for you,
neither is it far off. 12 It is not in heaven,
that you should say, 'Who will ascend
to heaven for us and bring it to us, that
we may hear it and do it?' 13 Neither is it
beyond the sea, that you should say, 'Who
will go over the sea for us and bring it to
us, that we may hear it and do it?' 14 But the
word is very near you. It is in your mouth
and in your heart, so that you can do it.

15 "See, I have set before you today life
and good, death and evil. 16 If you obey the
commandments of the LORD your God[1]
that I command you today, by loving the
LORD your God, by walking in his ways,
and by keeping his commandments and
his statutes and his rules,[2] then you shall
live and multiply, and the LORD your God
will bless you in the land that you are
entering to take possession of it. 17 But if
your heart turns away, and you will not
hear, but are drawn away to worship other
gods and serve them, 18 I declare to you
today, that you shall surely perish. You
shall not live long in the land that you are
going over the Jordan to enter and pos-
sess. 19 I call heaven and earth to witness
against you today, that I have set before
you life and death, blessing and curse.
Therefore choose life, that you and your
offspring may live, 20 loving the LORD your
God, obeying his voice and holding fast to
him, for he is your life and length of days,
that you may dwell in the land that the
LORD swore to your fathers, to Abraham,
to Isaac, and to Jacob, to give them."

Joshua to Succeed Moses

31 So Moses continued to speak
these words to all Israel. 2 And he
said to them, "I am 120 years old today.
I am no longer able to go out and come
in. The LORD has said to me, 'You shall
not go over this Jordan.' 3 The LORD your
God himself will go over before you. He
will destroy these nations before you,
so that you shall dispossess them, and
Joshua will go over at your head, as the
LORD has spoken. 4 And the LORD will do
to them as he did to Sihon and Og, the
kings of the Amorites, and to their land,
when he destroyed them. 5 And the LORD
will give them over to you, and you shall
do to them according to the whole com-
mandment that I have commanded you.
6 Be strong and courageous. Do not fear or
be in dread of them, for it is the LORD your

[1] Septuagint; Hebrew lacks *If you obey the commandments of the LORD your God* [2] Or *his just decrees*

God who goes with you. He will not leave you or forsake you."

7 Then Moses summoned Joshua and said to him in the sight of all Israel, "Be strong and courageous, for you shall go with this people into the land that the LORD has sworn to their fathers to give them, and you shall put them in possession of it. 8 It is the LORD who goes before you. He will be with you; he will not leave you or forsake you. Do not fear or be dismayed."

The Reading of the Law

9 Then Moses wrote this law and gave it to the priests, the sons of Levi, who carried the ark of the covenant of the LORD, and to all the elders of Israel. 10 And Moses commanded them, "At the end of every seven years, at the set time in the year of release, at the Feast of Booths, 11 when all Israel comes to appear before the LORD your God at the place that he will choose, you shall read this law before all Israel in their hearing. 12 Assemble the people, men, women, and little ones, and the sojourner within your towns, that they may hear and learn to fear the LORD your God, and be careful to do all the words of this law, 13 and that their children, who have not known it, may hear and learn to fear the LORD your God, as long as you live in the land that you are going over the Jordan to possess."

Joshua Commissioned to Lead Israel

14 And the LORD said to Moses, "Behold, the days approach when you must die. Call Joshua and present yourselves in the tent of meeting, that I may commission him." And Moses and Joshua went and presented themselves in the tent of meeting. 15 And the LORD appeared in the tent in a pillar of cloud. And the pillar of cloud stood over the entrance of the tent.

16 And the LORD said to Moses, "Behold, you are about to lie down with your fathers. Then this people will rise and whore after the foreign gods among them in the land that they are entering, and they will forsake me and break my covenant that I have made with them. 17 Then my anger will be kindled against them in that day, and I will forsake them and hide my face from them, and they will be devoured. And many evils and troubles will come upon them, so that they will say in that day, 'Have not these evils come upon us because our God is not among us?' 18 And I will surely hide my face in that day because of all the evil that they have done, because they have turned to other gods.

19 "Now therefore write this song and teach it to the people of Israel. Put it in their mouths, that this song may be a witness for me against the people of Israel. 20 For when I have brought them into the land flowing with milk and honey, which I swore to give to their fathers, and they have eaten and are full and grown fat, they will turn to other gods and serve them, and despise me and break my covenant. 21 And when many evils and troubles have come upon them, this song shall confront them as a witness (for it will live unforgotten in the mouths of their offspring). For I know what they are inclined to do even today, before I have brought them into the land that I swore to give." 22 So Moses wrote this song the same day and taught it to the people of Israel.

23 And the LORD commissioned Joshua the son of Nun and said, "Be strong and courageous, for you shall bring the people of Israel into the land that I swore to give them. I will be with you."

24 When Moses had finished writing the words of this law in a book to the very end, 25 Moses commanded the Levites who carried the ark of the covenant of the LORD, 26 "Take this Book of the Law and put it by the side of the ark of the covenant of the LORD your God, that it may be there for a witness against you. 27 For I know how rebellious and stubborn you are. Behold, even today while I am yet alive with you,

you have been rebellious against the
LORD. How much more after my death!
28 Assemble to me all the elders of your
tribes and your officers, that I may speak
these words in their ears and call heaven
and earth to witness against them. 29 For I
know that after my death you will surely
act corruptly and turn aside from the way
that I have commanded you. And in the
days to come evil will befall you, because
you will do what is evil in the sight of the
LORD, provoking him to anger through the
work of your hands."

The Song of Moses

30 Then Moses spoke the words of this
song until they were finished, in the ears
of all the assembly of Israel:

32 "Give ear, O heavens, and I will speak,
and let the earth hear the words of my mouth.
2 May my teaching drop as the rain,
my speech distill as the dew,
like gentle rain upon the tender grass,
and like showers upon the herb.
3 For I will proclaim the name of the LORD;
ascribe greatness to our God!

4 "The Rock, his work is perfect,
for all his ways are justice.
A God of faithfulness and without iniquity,
just and upright is he.
5 They have dealt corruptly with him;
they are no longer his children because they are blemished;
they are a crooked and twisted generation.
6 Do you thus repay the LORD,
you foolish and senseless people?
Is not he your father, who created you,
who made you and established you?
7 Remember the days of old;
consider the years of many generations;
ask your father, and he will show you,
your elders, and they will tell you.
8 When the Most High gave to the nations their inheritance,
when he divided mankind,
he fixed the borders[1] of the peoples
according to the number of the sons of God.[2]
9 But the LORD's portion is his people,
Jacob his allotted heritage.

10 "He found him in a desert land,
and in the howling waste of the wilderness;
he encircled him, he cared for him,
he kept him as the apple of his eye.
11 Like an eagle that stirs up its nest,
that flutters over its young,
spreading out its wings, catching them,
bearing them on its pinions,
12 the LORD alone guided him,
no foreign god was with him.
13 He made him ride on the high places of the land,
and he ate the produce of the field,
and he suckled him with honey out of the rock,
and oil out of the flinty rock.
14 Curds from the herd, and milk from the flock,
with fat[3] of lambs,
rams of Bashan and goats,
with the very finest[4] of the wheat—
and you drank foaming wine made from the blood of the grape.

15 "But Jeshurun grew fat, and kicked;
you grew fat, stout, and sleek;
then he forsook God who made him
and scoffed at the Rock of his salvation.
16 They stirred him to jealousy with strange gods;
with abominations they provoked him to anger.

[1] Or *territories* [2] Compare Dead Sea Scroll, Septuagint; Masoretic Text *Israel* [3] That is, with the best [4] Hebrew *with the kidney fat*

17 They sacrificed to demons that were
no gods,
to gods they had never known,
to new gods that had come recently,
whom your fathers had never
dreaded.
18 You were unmindful of the Rock
that bore[1] you,
and you forgot the God who gave
you birth.

19 "The LORD saw it and spurned them,
because of the provocation of his
sons and his daughters.
20 And he said, 'I will hide my face
from them;
I will see what their end will be,
For they are a perverse generation,
children in whom is no
faithfulness.
21 They have made me jealous with
what is no god;
they have provoked me to anger
with their idols.
So I will make them jealous with
those who are no people;
I will provoke them to anger with
a foolish nation.
22 For a fire is kindled by my anger,
and it burns to the depths of Sheol,
devours the earth and its increase,
and sets on fire the foundations
of the mountains.

23 "'And I will heap disasters upon them;
I will spend my arrows on them;
24 they shall be wasted with hunger,
and devoured by plague
and poisonous pestilence;
I will send the teeth of beasts
against them,
with the venom of things that
crawl in the dust.
25 Outdoors the sword shall bereave,
and indoors terror,
for young man and woman alike,
the nursing child with the man of
gray hairs.
26 I would have said, "I will cut them
to pieces;
I will wipe them from human
memory,"
27 had I not feared provocation by the
enemy,
lest their adversaries should
misunderstand,
lest they should say, "Our hand is
triumphant,
it was not the LORD who did all
this."'

28 "For they are a nation void of counsel,
and there is no understanding in
them.
29 If they were wise, they would
understand this;
they would discern their latter end!
30 How could one have chased a
thousand,
and two have put ten thousand to
flight,
unless their Rock had sold them,
and the LORD had given them up?
31 For their rock is not as our Rock;
our enemies are by themselves.
32 For their vine comes from the vine
of Sodom
and from the fields of Gomorrah;
their grapes are grapes of poison;
their clusters are bitter;
33 their wine is the poison of serpents
and the cruel venom of asps.

34 "'Is not this laid up in store with me,
sealed up in my treasuries?
35 Vengeance is mine, and
recompense,[2]
for the time when their foot shall
slip;
for the day of their calamity is at
hand,
and their doom comes swiftly.'
36 For the LORD will vindicate[3] his
people
and have compassion on his
servants,

[1] Or *fathered* [2] Septuagint *and I will repay* [3] Septuagint *judge*

when he sees that their power is gone
and there is none remaining,
bond or free.
37 Then he will say, 'Where are their
gods,
the rock in which they took refuge,
38 who ate the fat of their sacrifices
and drank the wine of their drink
offering?
Let them rise up and help you;
let them be your protection!

39 "'See now that I, even I, am he,
and there is no god beside me;
I kill and I make alive;
I wound and I heal;
and there is none that can deliver
out of my hand.
40 For I lift up my hand to heaven
and swear, As I live forever,
41 if I sharpen my flashing sword[1]
and my hand takes hold on
judgment,
I will take vengeance on my
adversaries
and will repay those who hate me.
42 I will make my arrows drunk with
blood,
and my sword shall devour flesh—
with the blood of the slain and the
captives,
from the long-haired heads of the
enemy.'

43 "Rejoice with him, O heavens;
bow down to him, all gods,[2]
for he avenges the blood of his
children[3]
and takes vengeance on his
adversaries.
He repays those who hate him[4]
and cleanses[5] his people's land."[6]

44 Moses came and recited all the words
of this song in the hearing of the people,
he and Joshua[7] the son of Nun. 45 And
when Moses had finished speaking all
these words to all Israel, 46 he said to them,
"Take to heart all the words by which I am
warning you today, that you may com-
mand them to your children, that they
may be careful to do all the words of this
law. 47 For it is no empty word for you, but
your very life, and by this word you shall
live long in the land that you are going
over the Jordan to possess."

Moses' Death Foretold

48 That very day the LORD spoke to Moses,
49 "Go up this mountain of the Abarim,
Mount Nebo, which is in the land of Moab,
opposite Jericho, and view the land of
Canaan, which I am giving to the people
of Israel for a possession. 50 And die on the
mountain which you go up, and be gath-
ered to your people, as Aaron your brother
died in Mount Hor and was gathered to his
people, 51 because you broke faith with me
in the midst of the people of Israel at the
waters of Meribah-kadesh, in the wilder-
ness of Zin, and because you did not treat
me as holy in the midst of the people of
Israel. 52 For you shall see the land before
you, but you shall not go there, into the
land that I am giving to the people of Israel."

Moses' Final Blessing on Israel

33 This is the blessing with
which Moses the man of
79 God blessed the people of Israel
before his death. 2 He said,

"The LORD came from Sinai
and dawned from Seir upon us;[8]
he shone forth from Mount Paran;
he came from the ten thousands of
holy ones,
with flaming fire[9] at his right hand.
3 Yes, he loved his people,[10]
all his holy ones were in his[11] hand;
so they followed[12] in your steps,
receiving direction from you,
4 when Moses commanded us a law,

[1] Hebrew *the lightning of my sword* [2] Dead Sea Scroll, Septuagint; Masoretic Text *Rejoice his people, O nations* [3] Dead Sea Scroll, Septuagint; Masoretic Text *servants* [4] Dead Sea Scroll, Septuagint; Masoretic Text lacks *He repays those who hate him* [5] Or *atones for* [6] Septuagint, Vulgate; Hebrew *his land his people* [7] Septuagint, Syriac, Vulgate; Hebrew *Hoshea* [8] Septuagint, Syriac, Vulgate; Hebrew *them* [9] The meaning of the Hebrew word is uncertain [10] Septuagint; Hebrew *peoples* [11] Hebrew *your* [12] The meaning of the Hebrew word is uncertain

as a possession for the assembly
of Jacob.
5 Thus the LORD became king in
Jeshurun,
when the heads of the people
were gathered,
all the tribes of Israel together.
6 "Let Reuben live, and not die,
but let his men be few."

7 And this he said of Judah:

"Hear, O LORD, the voice of Judah,
and bring him in to his people.
With your hands contend[1] for him,
and be a help against his
adversaries."

8 And of Levi he said,

"Give to Levi[2] your Thummim,
and your Urim to your godly one,
whom you tested at Massah,
with whom you quarreled at the
waters of Meribah;
9 who said of his father and mother,
'I regard them not';
he disowned his brothers
and ignored his children.
For they observed your word
and kept your covenant.
10 They shall teach Jacob your rules
and Israel your law;
they shall put incense before you
and whole burnt offerings on
your altar.
11 Bless, O LORD, his substance,
and accept the work of his hands;
crush the loins of his adversaries,
of those who hate him, that they
rise not again."

12 Of Benjamin he said,

"The beloved of the LORD dwells in
safety.
The High God[3] surrounds him all
day long,
and dwells between his shoulders."

13 And of Joseph he said,

"Blessed by the LORD be his land,
with the choicest gifts of heaven
above,[4]
and of the deep that crouches
beneath,
14 with the choicest fruits of the sun
and the rich yield of the months,
15 with the finest produce of the
ancient mountains
and the abundance of the
everlasting hills,
16 with the best gifts of the earth and
its fullness
and the favor of him who dwells
in the bush.
May these rest on the head of Joseph,
on the pate of him who is prince
among his brothers.
17 A firstborn bull[5]—he has majesty,
and his horns are the horns of a
wild ox;
with them he shall gore the peoples,
all of them, to the ends of the earth;
they are the ten thousands of
Ephraim,
and they are the thousands of
Manasseh."

18 And of Zebulun he said,

"Rejoice, Zebulun, in your going out,
and Issachar, in your tents.
19 They shall call peoples to their
mountain;
there they offer right sacrifices;
for they draw from the abundance
of the seas
and the hidden treasures of the
sand."

20 And of Gad he said,

"Blessed be he who enlarges Gad!
Gad crouches like a lion;
he tears off arm and scalp.
21 He chose the best of the land for
himself,

[1] Probable reading; Hebrew *With his hands he contended* [2] Dead Sea Scroll, Septuagint; Masoretic Text lacks *Give to Levi* [3] Septuagint; Hebrew *dwells in safety by him. He*
[4] Two Hebrew manuscripts and Targum; Hebrew *with the dew* [5] Dead Sea Scroll, Septuagint, Samaritan; Masoretic Text *His firstborn bull*

for there a commander's portion
was reserved;
and he came with the heads of the
people,
with Israel he executed the justice
of the LORD,
and his judgments for Israel."

22 And of Dan he said,

"Dan is a lion's cub
that leaps from Bashan."

23 And of Naphtali he said,

"O Naphtali, sated with favor,
and full of the blessing of the LORD,
possess the lake[1] and the south."

24 And of Asher he said,

"Most blessed of sons be Asher;
let him be the favorite of his
brothers,
and let him dip his foot in oil.
25 Your bars shall be iron and bronze,
and as your days, so shall your
strength be.

26 "There is none like God, O Jeshurun,
who rides through the heavens to
your help,
through the skies in his majesty.
27 The eternal God is your dwelling
place,[2]
and underneath are the
everlasting arms.[3]
And he thrust out the enemy before
you
and said, Destroy.
28 So Israel lived in safety,
Jacob lived alone,[4]
in a land of grain and wine,
whose heavens drop down dew.
29 Happy are you, O Israel! Who is like
you,
a people saved by the LORD,
the shield of your help,
and the sword of your triumph!
Your enemies shall come fawning
to you,
and you shall tread upon their
backs."

The Death of Moses

34 Then Moses went up from the
plains of Moab to Mount Nebo,
to the top of Pisgah, which is opposite
Jericho. And the LORD showed him all the
land, Gilead as far as Dan, 2 all Naphtali,
the land of Ephraim and Manasseh,
all the land of Judah as far as the west-
ern sea, 3 the Negeb, and the Plain, that
is, the Valley of Jericho the city of palm
trees, as far as Zoar. 4 And the LORD said
to him, "This is the land of which I swore
to Abraham, to Isaac, and to Jacob, 'I will
give it to your offspring.' I have let you see
it with your eyes, but you shall not go over
there." 5 So Moses the servant of the LORD
died there in the land of Moab, according
to the word of the LORD, 6 and he buried
him in the valley in the land of Moab
opposite Beth-peor; but no one knows
the place of his burial to this day. 7 Moses
was 120 years old when he died. His eye
was undimmed, and his vigor unabated.
8 And the people of Israel wept for Moses
in the plains of Moab thirty days. Then the
days of weeping and mourning for Moses
were ended.

9 And Joshua the son of Nun was full
of the spirit of wisdom, for Moses had
laid his hands on him. So the people of
Israel obeyed him and did as the LORD
had commanded Moses. 10 And there has
not arisen a prophet since in Israel like
Moses, whom the LORD knew face to face,
11 none like him for all the signs and the
wonders that the LORD sent him to do
in the land of Egypt, to Pharaoh and to
all his servants and to all his land, 12 and
for all the mighty power and all the great
deeds of terror that Moses did in the sight
of all Israel.

[1] Or *west* [2] Or *a dwelling place* [3] Revocalization of verse 27 yields *He subdues the ancient gods, and shatters the forces of old* [4] Hebrew *the abode of Jacob was alone*

Introduction to

Joshua

Author(s)
Joshua; an unknown writer

Date
1406–1375 B.C.

People
Joshua; Caleb; Rahab; Achan

Purpose
The purpose of Joshua is to show the faithfulness of God in giving the Israelites the land of Canaan, as He had promised Abraham He would.

Central Themes
God is faithful; God judges sin; God's people need to trust and obey Him; God's Word is essential; God's power gives victory to His people.

Memory Verses
Meditate on the Word (Joshua 1:7–8); my house will serve the Lord (Joshua 24:14–15)

Introduction

The book of Joshua tells the story of how God brought the Israelites into the land of Canaan and gave it to them as He had promised. This was God's gracious gift to His people. It was also God's judgment against the Canaanites who had lived in the land, worshiping false gods for centuries. The book begins with God's call to Joshua to be strong and courageous as Israel's new leader, and to know, meditate on, and obey God's Word (Joshua 1:1–9). The book ends with Joshua's charge to the Israelites to worship and serve God alone (Joshua 24:1–28). In between is the story of Israel's conquest of the land. God parts the waters of the Jordan River so the people can enter the land (Joshua 3–4). The first city, Jericho, falls because of God's power (Joshua 6). Rahab's family is spared because Rahab had hidden Israel's spies earlier and had come to trust in Israel's God (Joshua 2). Israel loses its second battle because of the sin and disobedience of Achan (Joshua 7). Once that sin is dealt with, Israel went on to victory after victory in Canaan (Joshua 8–12) and the land is divided up among the 12 tribes (Joshua 13–19).

1446 B.C.	**1406–1400** B.C.	**About 1375** B.C.
Exodus from Egypt	Conquest of Canaan	Period of judges begins

Joshua

God Commissions Joshua

1 After the death of Moses the servant of the LORD, the LORD said to Joshua the son of Nun, Moses' assistant, 2 "Moses my servant is dead. Now therefore arise, go over this Jordan, you and all this people, into the land that I am giving to them, to the people of Israel. 3 Every place that the sole of your foot will tread upon I have given to you, just as I promised to Moses. 4 From the wilderness and this Lebanon as far as the great river, the river Euphrates, all the land of the Hittites to the Great Sea toward the going down of the sun shall be your territory. 5 No man shall be able to stand before you all the days of your life. Just as I was with Moses, so I will be with you. I will not leave you or forsake you. 6 Be strong and courageous, for you shall cause this people to inherit the land that I swore to their fathers to give them. 7 Only be strong and very courageous, being careful to do according to all the law that Moses my servant commanded you. Do not turn from it to the right hand or to the left, that you may have good success[1] wherever you go. 8 This Book of the Law shall not depart from your mouth, but you shall meditate on it day and night, so that you may be careful to do according to all that is written in it. For then you will make your way prosperous, and then you will have good success. 9 Have I not commanded you? Be strong and courageous. Do not be frightened, and do not be dismayed, for the LORD your God is with you wherever you go."

Joshua Assumes Command

351

10 And Joshua commanded the officers of the people, 11 "Pass through the midst of the camp and command the people, 'Prepare your provisions, for within three days you are to pass over this Jordan to go in to take possession of the land that the LORD your God is giving you to possess.'"

12 And to the Reubenites, the Gadites, and the half-tribe of Manasseh Joshua said, 13 "Remember the word that Moses the servant of the LORD commanded you, saying, 'The LORD your God is providing

CHARACTER PROFILE

JOSHUA

Joshua and Caleb were the only two Israelite spies who believed that God could give the Israelites the Promised Land. Joshua served as Moses' assistant. When Moses died, God chose Joshua to lead the Israelites into the Promised Land. Joshua led the Israelites in all their battles with the Canaanites, until all the land was conquered. Then Joshua divided up the land among the 12 Israelite tribes as God had commanded him.

265, 345, 351, 357

[1] Or *may act wisely*

you a place of rest and will give you this
land.' 14 Your wives, your little ones, and
your livestock shall remain in the land
that Moses gave you beyond the Jordan,
but all the men of valor among you shall
pass over armed before your brothers and
shall help them, 15 until the LORD gives
rest to your brothers as he has to you, and
they also take possession of the land that
the LORD your God is giving them. Then
you shall return to the land of your pos-
session and shall possess it, the land that
Moses the servant of the LORD gave you
beyond the Jordan toward the sunrise."

16 And they answered Joshua, "All that
you have commanded us we will do, and
wherever you send us we will go. 17 Just
as we obeyed Moses in all things, so we
will obey you. Only may the LORD your
God be with you, as he was with Moses!
18 Whoever rebels against your command-
ment and disobeys your words, whatever
you command him, shall be put to death.
Only be strong and courageous."

Rahab Hides the Spies

345

2 And Joshua the son of Nun
sent[1] two men secretly from
Shittim as spies, saying, "Go, view
the land, especially Jericho." And they went
and came into the house of a prostitute
whose name was Rahab and lodged there.
2 And it was told to the king of Jericho,
"Behold, men of Israel have come here
tonight to search out the land." 3 Then the
king of Jericho sent to Rahab, saying,
"Bring out the men who have come to you,
who entered your house, for they have
come to search out all the land." 4 But the
woman had taken the two men and hidden
them. And she said, "True, the men came
to me, but I did not know where they were
from. 5 And when the gate was about to be
closed at dark, the men went out. I do not
know where the men went. Pursue them
quickly, for you will overtake them." 6 But
she had brought them up to the roof and
hid them with the stalks of flax that she
had laid in order on the roof. 7 So the men
pursued after them on the way to the
Jordan as far as the fords. And the gate was
shut as soon as the pursuers had gone out.

8 Before the men[2] lay down, she came up
to them on the roof 9 and said to the men,
"I know that the LORD has given you the
land, and that the fear of you has fallen
upon us, and that all the inhabitants of the
land melt away before you. 10 For we have
heard how the LORD dried up the water of
the Red Sea before you when you came out
of Egypt, and what you did to the two kings
of the Amorites who were beyond the
Jordan, to Sihon and Og, whom you
devoted to destruction.[3] 11 And as soon as
we heard it, our hearts melted, and there

CHARACTER PROFILE

RAHAB

Rahab lived in Jericho. She was a Canaanite woman, but she had heard about God and how He cared for His people. Rahab helped two Israelite spies by hiding them from Jericho's king. Later, when the Israelites destroyed Jericho, these two spies saved Rahab and her family, and she became one of God's people.

345, 357

[1] Or *had sent* [2] Hebrew *they* [3] That is, set apart (devoted) as an offering to the Lord (for destruction)

Rahab Trusts in God

After Moses died, Joshua became the leader of God's people. When it was time, Joshua sent two men to spy on the Promised Land. He told them to go look at the land, especially the city of Jericho. The two spies went to Jericho and hid in the house of a woman named Rahab.

But the king of Jericho found out about the spies. He heard that they had gone to Rahab's house, and he sent her a message, saying, "Bring out the men who have come to you."

But Rahab hid the two men. She took them up to the flat roof of her house, where she had laid out large flax plants to dry. There Rahab hid the men, buried under the piles of flax plants. When the king's messengers arrived at her house, she told them that the spies had left. But if the king's messengers hurried, she said, maybe they could catch the spies before they got too far away.

After the king's messengers had gone, Rahab went to the spies, who were still on the roof hidden under the flax. She said, "I know that the Lord has given you the land, and that the fear of you has fallen upon us. For we have heard how the Lord dried up the water of the Red Sea before you when you came out of Egypt."

Rahab and the people of Jericho had heard how God had helped the Israelites defeat all their enemies on their way to the Promised Land. "The LORD your God," Rahab said, "He is God in the heavens above and on the earth beneath."

Then Rahab asked the spies to promise her something. Since she had been kind to the spies, Rahab asked the spies to be kind to her and to all her family when the people of Israel came back to defeat the city of Jericho. So the men promised Rahab that they would protect her and her family.

The spies did not want anyone to see them leaving Rahab's house, so she took a rope and let them down through the window. She told them to hide in the hills for three days, until the people had stopped looking for them. Then they could go back to the Israelite camp.

The men said, "When we come into the land, you shall tie this scarlet cord in the window through which you let us down." This would be the signal to all the Israelites that they must not harm the people in this house. The men told Rahab to be sure to have all her family there in the house with her, and they would all be safe from the Israelites.

Rahab sent the men away and tied the scarlet cord in the window as a sign that her home was not to be attacked.

After hiding for three days, the two men returned to Joshua. They said, "Truly the LORD has given all the land into our hands." They told Joshua what Rahab had said—that all the people of Jericho were afraid because of all that God had done for the people of Israel.

Rahab was not afraid, though, because she trusted in the one true God. Even though Rahab was not an Israelite, she *put her trust* in the Lord, and God welcomed her as one of

His own people. Rahab became a great-great-grandmother of King David. And, much, much later, the Lord Jesus Himself was born in their family line!

SEEK and FIND

WHERE TO FIND THE STORY

Joshua 2

KEY BIBLE VERSE

"The LORD your God, he is God in the heavens above and on the earth beneath." (Joshua 2:11b)

THREE KEY QUESTIONS

- Why were the people of Jericho so afraid of the people of Israel?
- What did Rahab ask the spies to do for her and her family?
- Rahab was the great-great-grandmother of what king?

RELATED BIBLE READINGS

Joshua 6:16–17, 22–25; Matthew 1:5; Hebrews 11:31; James 2:25

was no spirit left in any man because of
you, for the LORD your God, he is
God in the heavens above and on
345 the earth beneath. [12]Now then,
please swear to me by the LORD that, as I
have dealt kindly with you, you also will
deal kindly with my father's house, and
give me a sure sign [13]that you will save
alive my father and mother, my brothers
and sisters, and all who belong to them,
and deliver our lives from death." [14]And the
men said to her, "Our life for yours even to
death! If you do not tell this business of
ours, then when the LORD gives us the land
we will deal kindly and faithfully with you."
[15]Then she let them down by a rope
through the window, for her house was
built into the city wall, so that she lived in
the wall. [16]And she said[1] to them, "Go into
the hills, or the pursuers will encounter
you, and hide there three days until the
pursuers have returned. Then afterward
you may go your way." [17]The men said to
her, "We will be guiltless with respect to
this oath of yours that you have made us
swear. [18]Behold, when we come into the
land, you shall tie this scarlet cord in the
window through which you let us down,
and you shall gather into your house your
father and mother, your brothers, and all

[1] Or *had said*

your father's household. 19 Then if anyone goes out of the doors of your house into the street, his blood shall be on his own head, and we shall be guiltless. But if a hand is laid on anyone who is with you in the house, his blood shall be on our head. 20 But if you tell this business of ours, then we shall be guiltless with respect to your oath that you have made us swear." 21 And she said, "According to your words, so be it." Then she sent them away, and they departed. And she tied the scarlet cord in the window.

22 They departed and went into the hills and remained there three days until the pursuers returned, and the pursuers searched all along the way and found nothing. 23 Then the two men returned. They came down from the hills and passed over and came to Joshua the son of Nun, and they told him all that had happened to them. 24 And they said to Joshua, "Truly the LORD has given all the land into our hands. And also, all the inhabitants of the land melt away because of us."

Israel Crosses the Jordan

351

3 Then Joshua rose early in the morning and they set out from Shittim. And they came to the Jordan, he and all the people of Israel, and lodged there before they passed over. 2 At the end of three days the officers went through the camp 3 and commanded the people, "As soon as you see the ark of the covenant of the LORD your God being carried by the Levitical priests, then you shall set out from your place and follow it. 4 Yet there shall be a distance between you and it, about 2,000 cubits[1] in length. Do not come near it, in order that you may know the way you shall go, for you have not passed this way before." 5 Then Joshua said to the people, "Consecrate yourselves, for tomorrow the LORD will do wonders among you." 6 And Joshua said to the priests, "Take up the ark of the covenant and pass on before the people." So they took up the ark of the covenant and went before the people.

7 The LORD said to Joshua, "Today I will begin to exalt you in the sight of all Israel, that they may know that, as I was with Moses, so I will be with you. 8 And as for you, command the priests who bear the ark of the covenant, 'When you come to the brink of the waters of the Jordan, you shall stand still in the Jordan.'" 9 And Joshua said to the people of Israel, "Come here and listen to the words of the LORD your God." 10 And Joshua said, "Here is how you shall know that the living God is among you and that he will without fail drive out from before you the Canaanites, the Hittites, the Hivites, the Perizzites, the Girgashites, the Amorites, and the Jebusites. 11 Behold, the ark of the covenant of the Lord of all the earth[2] is passing over before you into the Jordan. 12 Now therefore take twelve men from the tribes of Israel, from each tribe a man. 13 And when the soles of the feet of the priests bearing the ark of the LORD, the Lord of all the earth, shall rest in the waters of the Jordan, the waters of the Jordan shall be cut off from flowing, and the waters coming down from above shall stand in one heap."

14 So when the people set out from their tents to pass over the Jordan with the priests bearing the ark of the covenant before the people, 15 and as soon as those bearing the ark had come as far as the Jordan, and the feet of the priests bearing the ark were dipped in the brink of the water (now the Jordan overflows all its banks throughout the time of harvest), 16 the waters coming down from above stood and rose up in a heap very far away, at Adam, the city that is beside Zarethan, and those flowing down toward the Sea of the Arabah, the Salt Sea, were completely cut off. And the people passed over opposite Jericho. 17 Now the priests bearing the ark of the covenant of the LORD stood

[1] A *cubit* was about 18 inches or 45 centimeters [2] Hebrew *the ark of the covenant, the Lord of all the earth*

firmly on dry ground in the midst of the
Jordan, and all Israel was passing over on
dry ground until all the nation finished
passing over the Jordan.

Twelve Memorial Stones from the Jordan

4 When all the nation had finished
passing over the Jordan, the LORD said
to Joshua, 2 "Take twelve men from the
people, from each tribe a man, 3 and com-
mand them, saying, 'Take twelve stones
from here out of the midst of the Jordan,
from the very place where the priests' feet
stood firmly, and bring them over with
you and lay them down in the place where
you lodge tonight.'" 4 Then Joshua called
the twelve men from the people of Israel,
whom he had appointed, a man from each
tribe. 5 And Joshua said to them, "Pass on
before the ark of the LORD your God into
the midst of the Jordan, and take up each
of you a stone upon his shoulder, accord-
ing to the number of the tribes of the
people of Israel, 6 that this may be a sign
among you. When your children ask in
time to come, 'What do those stones mean
to you?' 7 then you shall tell them that the
waters of the Jordan were cut off before
the ark of the covenant of the LORD. When
it passed over the Jordan, the waters of
the Jordan were cut off. So these stones
shall be to the people of Israel a memorial
forever."

8 And the people of Israel did just as
Joshua commanded and took up twelve
stones out of the midst of the Jordan,
according to the number of the tribes
of the people of Israel, just as the LORD
told Joshua. And they carried them over
with them to the place where they lodged
and laid them down[1] there. 9 And Joshua
set up twelve stones in the midst of the
Jordan, in the place where the feet of the
priests bearing the ark of the covenant
had stood; and they are there to this day.
10 For the priests bearing the ark stood in
the midst of the Jordan until everything
was finished that the LORD commanded
Joshua to tell the people, according to all
that Moses had commanded Joshua.

The people passed over in haste. 11 And
when all the people had finished passing
over, the ark of the LORD and the priests
passed over before the people. 12 The sons
of Reuben and the sons of Gad and the
half-tribe of Manasseh passed over armed
before the people of Israel, as Moses had
told them. 13 About 40,000 ready for war
passed over before the LORD for battle,
to the plains of Jericho. 14 On that day the
LORD exalted Joshua in the sight of all
Israel, and they stood in awe of him just
as they had stood in awe of Moses, all the
days of his life.

15 And the LORD said to Joshua, 16 "Com-
mand the priests bearing the ark of the tes-
timony to come up out of the Jordan." 17 So
Joshua commanded the priests, "Come up
out of the Jordan." 18 And when the priests
bearing the ark of the covenant of the LORD
came up from the midst of the Jordan, and
the soles of the priests' feet were lifted up
on dry ground, the waters of the Jordan
returned to their place and overflowed all
its banks, as before.

19 The people came up out of the Jordan
on the tenth day of the first month, and
they encamped at Gilgal on the east bor-
der of Jericho. 20 And those twelve stones,
which they took out of the Jordan, Joshua
set up at Gilgal. 21 And he said to the peo-
ple of Israel, "When your children ask
their fathers in times to come, 'What do
these stones mean?' 22 then you shall let
your children know, 'Israel passed over
this Jordan on dry ground.' 23 For the LORD
your God dried up the waters of the Jordan
for you until you passed over, as the LORD
your God did to the Red Sea, which he
dried up for us until we passed over,
24 so that all the peoples of the
earth may know that the hand of
351 the LORD is mighty, that you may
fear the LORD your God forever."[2]

[1] Or *to rest* [2] Or *all the days*

The Promised Land

The people of Israel had been wandering in the desert for a long time. At last God wanted them to go into the new land He had promised them. God told Joshua, their new leader, to tell the people to get ready to go into the Promised Land. Joshua and the leaders of Israel went through the camp and told the people, "As soon as you see the ark of the covenant of the LORD your God you shall set out and follow it," wherever the Lord would lead them.

So the people followed the ark and walked to the Jordan River, where they camped for three days. There God told the people to prepare themselves for the wonders He was going to do among them. God would lead the people of Israel through the deep and wide Jordan River to the other side.

Then the Lord God told Joshua that he should tell the priests to carry the ark of the covenant into the Jordan River with strong poles. As soon as their feet touched the edge of the river, God said that the priests should stop and stand still. Immediately, God would make the waters of the Jordan stop flowing and rise up in a heap, very far away—and the people could walk across the river on dry land!

The priests did exactly what God said. As soon as their feet touched the river's edge, God dried up the water. Then all the people with all their belongings and animals walked across on dry ground.

When everyone reached the other side, God told Joshua to have one man from each of the 12 tribes pick up a large stone from the river. They carried the stones to the place where they had set up their tents, and there they laid down their stones. Then Joshua set up the 12 stones as a memorial forever, as a reminder of God's love and mercy.

Many years later, when the people of Israel walked by the memorial, God wanted them to tell their children how God had kept all His promises—how He had brought them across the Jordan River and given them the beautiful Promised Land.

God did many wonders for His people long ago in Israel. And God does many wonders for us too. The greatest wonder of all is that God sent Jesus to be the Savior of the world. He forgives the sins of all who trust in Him. Jesus is a much greater leader than Joshua ever could be, because Jesus leads His people into the very presence of God. He saves us from our sins and He promises to give us a new home in heaven forever with Him.

SEEK and FIND

WHERE TO FIND THE STORY

Joshua 1:10–11; Joshua 3–4

KEY BIBLE VERSE

"So that all the peoples of the earth may know that the hand of the LORD is mighty, that you may fear the LORD your God forever." (Joshua 4:24)

THREE KEY QUESTIONS

- What happened when the priests, carrying the ark of the *covenant*, stepped into the Jordan River?

- What was the reason for the pile of stones the Israelites built after they had crossed the river?
- What leader did God give us who is even greater than Joshua?

RELATED BIBLE READINGS

Psalm 77:16; 114:1–8; Hebrews 4:8–10

The New Generation Circumcised

5 As soon as all the kings of the Amorites who were beyond the Jordan to the west, and all the kings of the Canaanites who were by the sea, heard that the LORD had dried up the waters of the Jordan for the people of Israel until they had crossed over, their hearts melted and there was no longer any spirit in them because of the people of Israel.

2 At that time the LORD said to Joshua, "Make flint knives and circumcise the sons of Israel a second time." 3 So Joshua made flint knives and circumcised the sons of Israel at Gibeath-haaraloth.[1] 4 And this is the reason why Joshua circumcised them: all the males of the people who came out of Egypt, all the men of war, had died in the wilderness on the way after they had come out of Egypt. 5 Though all the people who came out had been circumcised, yet all the people who were born on the way in the wilderness after they had come out of Egypt had not been circumcised. 6 For the people of Israel walked forty years in the wilderness, until all the nation, the men of war who came out of Egypt, perished, because they did not obey the voice of the LORD; the LORD swore to them that he would not let them see the land that the LORD had sworn to their fathers to give to us, a land flowing with milk and honey. 7 So it was their children, whom he raised up in their place, that Joshua circumcised. For they were uncircumcised, because they had not been circumcised on the way.

8 When the circumcising of the whole nation was finished, they remained in their places in the camp until they were healed. 9 And the LORD said to Joshua, "Today I have rolled away the reproach of Egypt from you." And so the name of that place is called Gilgal[2] to this day.

First Passover in Canaan

10 While the people of Israel were encamped at Gilgal, they kept the Passover on the fourteenth day of the month in the evening on the plains of Jericho. 11 And the day after the Passover, on that very day, they ate of the produce of the land, unleavened cakes and parched grain. 12 And the manna ceased the day after they ate of the produce of the land. And there was no longer manna for the people of Israel, but they ate of the fruit of the land of Canaan that year.

The Commander of the LORD's Army

13 When Joshua was by Jericho, he lifted up his eyes and looked, and behold, a man was standing before him with his drawn sword in his hand. And Joshua went to him and said to him, "Are you for us, or for our adversaries?" 14 And he said, "No; but I am the commander of the army of the LORD. Now I have come." And Joshua fell on his face to the earth and worshiped

[1] *Gibeath-haaraloth* means *the hill of the foreskins* [2] *Gilgal* sounds like the Hebrew for *to roll*

and said to him, "What does my lord say to his servant?" 15 And the commander of the LORD's army said to Joshua, "Take off your sandals from your feet, for the place where you are standing is holy." And Joshua did so.

The Fall of Jericho

6 Now Jericho was shut up inside and outside because of
357 the people of Israel. None went
out, and none came in. 2 And the LORD said to Joshua, "See, I have given Jericho into your hand, with its king and mighty men of valor. 3 You shall march around the city, all the men of war going around the city once. Thus shall you do for six days. 4 Seven priests shall bear seven trumpets of rams' horns before the ark. On the seventh day you shall march around the city seven times, and the priests shall blow the trumpets. 5 And when they make a long blast with the ram's horn, when you hear the sound of the trumpet, then all the people shall shout with a great shout, and the wall of the city will fall down flat,[1] and the people shall go up, everyone straight before him." 6 So Joshua the son of Nun called the priests and said to them, "Take up the ark of the covenant and let seven priests bear seven trumpets of rams' horns before the ark of the LORD." 7 And he said to the people, "Go forward. March around the city and let the armed men pass on before the ark of the LORD."

8 And just as Joshua had commanded the people, the seven priests bearing the seven trumpets of rams' horns before the LORD went forward, blowing the trumpets, with the ark of the covenant of the LORD following them. 9 The armed men were walking before the priests who were blowing the trumpets, and the rear guard was walking after the ark, while the trumpets blew continually. 10 But Joshua commanded the people, "You shall not shout or make your voice heard, neither shall any word go out of your mouth, until the day I tell you to shout. Then you shall shout." 11 So he caused the ark of the LORD to circle the city, going about it once. And they came into the camp and spent the night in the camp.

12 Then Joshua rose early in the morning, and the priests took up the ark of the LORD. 13 And the seven priests bearing the seven trumpets of rams' horns before the ark of the LORD walked on, and they blew the trumpets continually. And the armed men were walking before them, and the rear guard was walking after the ark of the LORD, while the trumpets blew continually. 14 And the second day they marched around the city once, and returned into the camp. So they did for six days.

15 On the seventh day they rose early, at the dawn of day, and marched around the city in the same manner seven times. It was only on that day that they marched around the city seven times. 16 And at the seventh time, when the priests had blown the trumpets, Joshua said to
345 the people, "Shout, for the LORD
has given you the city. 17 And the city and all that is within it shall be devoted to the LORD for destruction.[2] Only Rahab the prostitute and all who are with her in her house shall live, because she hid the messengers whom we sent. 18 But you, keep yourselves from the things devoted to destruction, lest when you have devoted them you take any of the devoted things and make the camp of Israel a thing for destruction and bring trouble upon it. 19 But all silver and gold, and every vessel of bronze and iron, are holy to the LORD; they shall go into the treasury of the LORD." 20 So the people shouted, and the trumpets were blown. As soon as the people heard the sound of the trumpet, the people shouted a great shout, and the wall fell down flat, so that the people went up into the city, every man straight before him, and they captured the city. 21 Then

[1] Hebrew *under itself*; also verse 20 [2] That is, set apart (devoted) as an offering to the Lord (for destruction); also verses 18, 21

they devoted all in the city to destruction, both men and women, young and old, oxen, sheep, and donkeys, with the edge of the sword.

22 But to the two men who had spied out the land, Joshua said,
345 "Go into the prostitute's house and bring out from there the woman and all who belong to her, as you swore to her." 23 So the young men who had been spies went in and brought out Rahab and her father and mother and brothers and all who belonged to her. And they brought all her relatives and put them outside the camp of Israel. 24 And they burned the city with fire, and everything in it. Only the silver and gold, and the vessels of bronze and of iron, they put into the treasury of the house of the LORD. 25 But Rahab the prostitute and her father's household and all who belonged to her, Joshua saved alive. And she has lived in Israel to this day, because she hid the messengers whom Joshua sent to spy out Jericho.

26 Joshua laid an oath on them at that time, saying, "Cursed before the LORD be the man who rises up and rebuilds this city, Jericho.

"At the cost of his firstborn shall he
lay its foundation,
and at the cost of his youngest son
shall he set up its gates."

27 So the LORD was with Joshua, and his fame was in all the land.

Israel Defeated at Ai

7 But the people of Israel broke faith in regard to the devoted things, for Achan the son of Carmi, son of Zabdi, son of Zerah, of the tribe of Judah, took some of the devoted things. And the anger of the LORD burned against the people of Israel.

2 Joshua sent men from Jericho to Ai, which is near Beth-aven, east of Bethel, and said to them, "Go up and spy out the land." And the men went up and spied out Ai. 3 And they returned to Joshua and said to him, "Do not have all the people go up, but let about two or three thousand men go up and attack Ai. Do not make the whole people toil up there, for they are few." 4 So about 3,000 men went up there from the people. And they fled before the men of Ai, 5 and the men of Ai killed about thirty-six of their men and chased them before the gate as far as Shebarim and struck them at the descent. And the hearts of the people melted and became as water.

6 Then Joshua tore his clothes and fell to the earth on his face before the ark of the LORD until the evening, he and the elders of Israel. And they put dust on their heads. 7 And Joshua said, "Alas, O Lord GOD, why have you brought this people over the Jordan at all, to give us into the hands of the Amorites, to destroy us? Would that we had been content to dwell beyond the Jordan! 8 O Lord, what can I say, when Israel has turned their backs before their enemies! 9 For the Canaanites and all the inhabitants of the land will hear of it and will surround us and cut off our name from the earth. And what will you do for your great name?"

The Sin of Achan

10 The LORD said to Joshua, "Get up! Why have you fallen on your face? 11 Israel has sinned; they have transgressed my covenant that I commanded them; they have taken some of the devoted things; they have stolen and lied and put them among their own belongings. 12 Therefore the people of Israel cannot stand before their enemies. They turn their backs before their enemies, because they have become devoted for destruction.[1] I will be with you no more, unless you destroy the devoted things from among you. 13 Get up! Consecrate the people and say, 'Consecrate yourselves for tomorrow; for thus says the LORD, God of Israel, "There are devoted things in your midst, O Israel. You cannot stand before your enemies until you

[1] That is, set apart (devoted) as an offering to the Lord (for destruction)

The Walls Come Crashing Down

God led the people of Israel safely across the Jordan River into the land that He had promised to give to them. They were camped near the city of Jericho, where the two Israelite spies had searched and Rahab had hidden them. The people who lived in Jericho did not love or serve God, and God wanted to give the city of Jericho to Joshua and the people of Israel.

All around the city of Jericho were high walls in order to keep the people of Israel out and the people of Jericho safely inside. Even though the walls were strong and tall they could not keep God out. God told Joshua how to defeat the people of Jericho, and Joshua followed God's plan exactly.

Joshua told the people to march around the city for seven days. First in line were some soldiers. Next came some priests, carrying the ark of the covenant and blowing trumpets made from ram's horns. Last came more soldiers.

Each day, they all marched around the city one time. The soldiers kept quiet, but the priests blew their trumpets. Then, on the seventh day, God told the people to walk around the wall seven times. After the seventh time, when the priests blew their trumpets, Joshua called out, "Shout, for the LORD has given you the city!" As soon as the people shouted, the great walls of Jericho came crashing down to the ground!

The soldiers rushed in, taking the city. They burned the

city and everything in it just as God had told them to do. But they didn't destroy everything. God told them to keep all the gold and silver, and bronze and iron—because all of these were "holy to the LORD"—and to put these in a treasury for God's house. Everyone in the city was destroyed, except for the woman named Rahab and her family. Joshua saved her life because she had helped the spies of Israel.

God gave the people of Israel faith to trust His plan and to do exactly what He said. God gave them a mighty victory over the evil people of Jericho. God gives us faith to trust in Jesus and to live our lives in a way that pleases Him. Through faith in Jesus, God gives us His mighty victory over sin, death, and the devil—so we can shout for joy!

SEEK and FIND

WHERE TO FIND THE STORY

Joshua 6

KEY BIBLE VERSE

"For it is the LORD your God who has fought for you." (Joshua 23:3b)

THREE KEY QUESTIONS

- What really made the walls come crashing down—the trumpets and shouting, or something else?
- What would have happened if Joshua and the people tried to attack the walls on their own, instead of doing what God said?
- How did God defeat our fearful enemies of sin, death, and Satan?

RELATED BIBLE READINGS

Joshua 24:1–14; Psalm 78:54–55; 105:43–45; Acts 7:44–45; Hebrews 4:8–11; 11:30

take away the devoted things from among you.' 14 In the morning therefore you shall be brought near by your tribes. And the tribe that the LORD takes by lot shall come near by clans. And the clan that the LORD takes shall come near by households. And the household that the LORD takes shall come near man by man. 15 And he who is taken with the devoted things shall be burned with fire, he and all that he has, because he has transgressed the covenant of the LORD, and because he has done an outrageous thing in Israel.'"

16 So Joshua rose early in the morning and brought Israel near tribe by tribe, and the tribe of Judah was taken. 17 And he brought near the clans of Judah, and the clan of the Zerahites was taken. And he brought near the clan of the Zerahites man by man, and Zabdi was taken. 18 And he brought near his household man by man, and Achan the son of Carmi, son of Zabdi, son of Zerah, of the tribe of Judah, was taken. 19 Then Joshua said to Achan, "My son, give glory to the LORD God of Israel and give praise[1] to him. And tell me now what you have done; do not hide it from me." 20 And Achan answered Joshua, "Truly I have sinned against the LORD God of Israel, and this is what I did: 21 when I saw among the spoil a beautiful cloak from Shinar, and 200 shekels of silver, and a bar of gold weighing 50 shekels,[2] then I coveted them and took them. And see, they are hidden in the earth inside my tent, with the silver underneath."

22 So Joshua sent messengers, and they ran to the tent; and behold, it was hidden in his tent with the silver underneath. 23 And they took them out of the tent and brought them to Joshua and to all the people of Israel. And they laid them down before the LORD. 24 And Joshua and all Israel with him took Achan the son of Zerah, and the silver and the cloak and the bar of gold, and his sons and daughters and his oxen and donkeys and sheep and his tent and all that he had. And they brought them up to the Valley of Achor. 25 And Joshua said, "Why did you bring trouble on us? The LORD brings trouble on you today." And all Israel stoned him with stones. They burned them with fire and stoned them with stones. 26 And they raised over him a great heap of stones that remains to this day. Then the LORD turned from his burning anger. Therefore, to this day the name of that place is called the Valley of Achor.[3]

The Fall of Ai

8 And the LORD said to Joshua, "Do not fear and do not be dismayed. Take all the fighting men with you, and arise, go up to Ai. See, I have given into your hand the king of Ai, and his people, his city, and his land. 2 And you shall do to Ai and its king as you did to Jericho and its king. Only its spoil and its livestock you shall take as plunder for yourselves. Lay an ambush against the city, behind it."

3 So Joshua and all the fighting men arose to go up to Ai. And Joshua chose 30,000 mighty men of valor and sent them out by night. 4 And he commanded them, "Behold, you shall lie in ambush against the city, behind it. Do not go very far from the city, but all of you remain ready. 5 And I and all the people who are with me will approach the city. And when they come out against us just as before, we shall flee before them. 6 And they will come out after us, until we have drawn them away from the city. For they will say, 'They are fleeing from us, just as before.' So we will flee before them. 7 Then you shall rise up from the ambush and seize the city, for the LORD your God will give it into your hand. 8 And as soon as you have taken the city, you shall set the city on fire. You shall do according to the word of the LORD. See, I have commanded you." 9 So Joshua sent them out. And they went to the place of ambush and lay between Bethel and Ai, to

[1] Or *and make confession* [2] A *shekel* was about 2/5 ounce or 11 grams [3] *Achor* means *trouble*

the west of Ai, but Joshua spent that night among the people.

10 Joshua arose early in the morning and mustered the people and went up, he and the elders of Israel, before the people to Ai. 11 And all the fighting men who were with him went up and drew near before the city and encamped on the north side of Ai, with a ravine between them and Ai. 12 He took about 5,000 men and set them in ambush between Bethel and Ai, to the west of the city. 13 So they stationed the forces, the main encampment that was north of the city and its rear guard west of the city. But Joshua spent that night in the valley. 14 And as soon as the king of Ai saw this, he and all his people, the men of the city, hurried and went out early to the appointed place[1] toward the Arabah to meet Israel in battle. But he did not know that there was an ambush against him behind the city. 15 And Joshua and all Israel pretended to be beaten before them and fled in the direction of the wilderness. 16 So all the people who were in the city were called together to pursue them, and as they pursued Joshua they were drawn away from the city. 17 Not a man was left in Ai or Bethel who did not go out after Israel. They left the city open and pursued Israel.

18 Then the LORD said to Joshua, "Stretch out the javelin that is in your hand toward Ai, for I will give it into your hand." And Joshua stretched out the javelin that was in his hand toward the city. 19 And the men in the ambush rose quickly out of their place, and as soon as he had stretched out his hand, they ran and entered the city and captured it. And they hurried to set the city on fire. 20 So when the men of Ai looked back, behold, the smoke of the city went up to heaven, and they had no power to flee this way or that, for the people who *fled to the* wilderness turned back against the pursuers. 21 And when Joshua and all Israel saw that the ambush had captured the city, and that the smoke of the city went up, then they turned back and struck down the men of Ai. 22 And the others came out from the city against them, so they were in the midst of Israel, some on this side, and some on that side. And Israel struck them down, until there was left none that survived or escaped. 23 But the king of Ai they took alive, and brought him near to Joshua.

24 When Israel had finished killing all the inhabitants of Ai in the open wilderness where they pursued them, and all of them to the very last had fallen by the edge of the sword, all Israel returned to Ai and struck it down with the edge of the sword. 25 And all who fell that day, both men and women, were 12,000, all the people of Ai. 26 But Joshua did not draw back his hand with which he stretched out the javelin until he had devoted all the inhabitants of Ai to destruction.[2] 27 Only the livestock and the spoil of that city Israel took as their plunder, according to the word of the LORD that he commanded Joshua. 28 So Joshua burned Ai and made it forever a heap of ruins, as it is to this day. 29 And he hanged the king of Ai on a tree until evening. And at sunset Joshua commanded, and they took his body down from the tree and threw it at the entrance of the gate of the city and raised over it a great heap of stones, which stands there to this day.

Joshua Renews the Covenant

30 At that time Joshua built an altar to the LORD, the God of Israel, on Mount Ebal, 31 just as Moses the servant of the LORD had commanded the people of Israel, as it is written in the Book of the Law of Moses, "an altar of uncut stones, upon which no man has wielded an iron tool." And they offered on it burnt offerings to the LORD and sacrificed peace offerings. 32 And there, in the presence of the people of Israel, he wrote on the stones a copy of the law of Moses, which he had written. 33 And all Israel, sojourner

[1] Hebrew *appointed time* [2] That is, set apart (devoted) as an offering to the Lord (for destruction)

as well as native born, with their elders
and officers and their judges, stood
on opposite sides of the ark before the
Levitical priests who carried the ark of
the covenant of the LORD, half of them in
front of Mount Gerizim and half of them
in front of Mount Ebal, just as Moses the
servant of the LORD had commanded
at the first, to bless the people of Israel.
34 And afterward he read all the words
of the law, the blessing and the curse,
according to all that is written in the Book
of the Law. 35 There was not a word of all
that Moses commanded that Joshua did
not read before all the assembly of Israel,
and the women, and the little ones, and
the sojourners who lived[1] among them.

The Gibeonite Deception

9 As soon as all the kings who were
beyond the Jordan in the hill coun-
try and in the lowland all along the coast
of the Great Sea toward Lebanon, the
Hittites, the Amorites, the Canaanites, the
Perizzites, the Hivites, and the Jebusites,
heard of this, 2 they gathered together as
one to fight against Joshua and Israel.
3 But when the inhabitants of Gibeon
heard what Joshua had done to Jericho
and to Ai, 4 they on their part acted with
cunning and went and made ready pro-
visions and took worn-out sacks for
their donkeys, and wineskins, worn-out
and torn and mended, 5 with worn-out,
patched sandals on their feet, and worn-
out clothes. And all their provisions
were dry and crumbly. 6 And they went to
Joshua in the camp at Gilgal and said to
him and to the men of Israel, "We have
come from a distant country, so now
make a covenant with us." 7 But the men
of Israel said to the Hivites, "Perhaps you
live among us; then how can we make a
covenant with you?" 8 They said to Joshua,
"We are your servants." And Joshua said to
them, "Who are you? And where do you
come from?" 9 They said to him, "From a
very distant country your servants have
come, because of the name of the LORD
your God. For we have heard a report of
him, and all that he did in Egypt, 10 and
all that he did to the two kings of the
Amorites who were beyond the Jordan,
to Sihon the king of Heshbon, and to Og
king of Bashan, who lived in Ashtaroth.
11 So our elders and all the inhabitants of
our country said to us, 'Take provisions in
your hand for the journey and go to meet
them and say to them, "We are your ser-
vants. Come now, make a covenant with
us."' 12 Here is our bread. It was still warm
when we took it from our houses as our
food for the journey on the day we set out
to come to you, but now, behold, it is dry
and crumbly. 13 These wineskins were
new when we filled them, and behold,
they have burst. And these garments and
sandals of ours are worn out from the very
long journey." 14 So the men took some of
their provisions, but did not ask counsel
from the LORD. 15 And Joshua made peace
with them and made a covenant with
them, to let them live, and the leaders of
the congregation swore to them.
16 At the end of three days after they had
made a covenant with them, they heard
that they were their neighbors and that
they lived among them. 17 And the people
of Israel set out and reached their cities
on the third day. Now their cities were
Gibeon, Chephirah, Beeroth, and Kiriath-
jearim. 18 But the people of Israel did not
attack them, because the leaders of the
congregation had sworn to them by the
LORD, the God of Israel. Then all the con-
gregation murmured against the leaders.
19 But all the leaders said to all the con-
gregation, "We have sworn to them by
the LORD, the God of Israel, and now we
may not touch them. 20 This we will do
to them: let them live, lest wrath be upon
us, because of the oath that we swore to
them." 21 And the leaders said to them,
"Let them live." So they became cutters

[1] Or *traveled*

of wood and drawers of water for all the congregation, just as the leaders had said of them.

22 Joshua summoned them, and he said to them, "Why did you deceive us, saying, 'We are very far from you,' when you dwell among us? 23 Now therefore you are cursed, and some of you shall never be anything but servants, cutters of wood and drawers of water for the house of my God." 24 They answered Joshua, "Because it was told to your servants for a certainty that the LORD your God had commanded his servant Moses to give you all the land and to destroy all the inhabitants of the land from before you—so we feared greatly for our lives because of you and did this thing. 25 And now, behold, we are in your hand. Whatever seems good and right in your sight to do to us, do it." 26 So he did this to them and delivered them out of the hand of the people of Israel, and they did not kill them. 27 But Joshua made them that day cutters of wood and drawers of water for the congregation and for the altar of the LORD, to this day, in the place that he should choose.

The Sun Stands Still

10 As soon as Adoni-zedek, king of Jerusalem, heard how Joshua had captured Ai and had devoted it to destruction,[1] doing to Ai and its king as he had done to Jericho and its king, and how the inhabitants of Gibeon had made peace with Israel and were among them, 2 he[2] feared greatly, because Gibeon was a great city, like one of the royal cities, and because it was greater than Ai, and all its men were warriors. 3 So Adoni-zedek king of Jerusalem sent to Hoham king of Hebron, to Piram king of Jarmuth, to Japhia king of Lachish, and to Debir king of Eglon, saying, 4 "Come up to me and help me, and let us strike Gibeon. For it has made peace with Joshua and with the people of Israel." 5 Then the five kings of the Amorites, the king of Jerusalem, the king of Hebron, the king of Jarmuth, the king of Lachish, and the king of Eglon, gathered their forces and went up with all their armies and encamped against Gibeon and made war against it.

6 And the men of Gibeon sent to Joshua at the camp in Gilgal, saying, "Do not relax your hand from your servants. Come up to us quickly and save us and help us, for all the kings of the Amorites who dwell in the hill country are gathered against us." 7 So Joshua went up from Gilgal, he and all the people of war with him, and all the mighty men of valor. 8 And the LORD said to Joshua, "Do not fear them, for I have given them into your hands. Not a man of them shall stand before you." 9 So Joshua came upon them suddenly, having marched up all night from Gilgal. 10 And the LORD threw them into a panic before Israel, who[3] struck them with a great blow at Gibeon and chased them by the way of the ascent of Beth-horon and struck them as far as Azekah and Makkedah. 11 And as they fled before Israel, while they were going down the ascent of Beth-horon, the LORD threw down large stones from heaven on them as far as Azekah, and they died. There were more who died because of the hailstones than the sons of Israel killed with the sword.

12 At that time Joshua spoke to the LORD in the day when the LORD gave the Amorites over to the sons of Israel, and he said in the sight of Israel,

"Sun, stand still at Gibeon,
and moon, in the Valley of Aijalon."
13 And the sun stood still, and the
moon stopped,
until the nation took vengeance
on their enemies.

Is this not written in the Book of Jashar? The sun stopped in the midst of heaven and did not hurry to set for about a whole

[1] That is, set apart (devoted) as an offering to the Lord (for destruction); also verses 28, 35, 37, 39, 40 [2] One Hebrew manuscript, Vulgate (compare Syriac); most Hebrew manuscripts *they* [3] Or *and he*

day. 14 There has been no day like it before or since, when the LORD heeded the voice of a man, for the LORD fought for Israel.

15 So Joshua returned, and all Israel with him, to the camp at Gilgal.

Five Amorite Kings Executed

16 These five kings fled and hid themselves in the cave at Makkedah. 17 And it was told to Joshua, "The five kings have been found, hidden in the cave at Makkedah." 18 And Joshua said, "Roll large stones against the mouth of the cave and set men by it to guard them, 19 but do not stay there yourselves. Pursue your enemies; attack their rear guard. Do not let them enter their cities, for the LORD your God has given them into your hand." 20 When Joshua and the sons of Israel had finished striking them with a great blow until they were wiped out, and when the remnant that remained of them had entered into the fortified cities, 21 then all the people returned safe to Joshua in the camp at Makkedah. Not a man moved his tongue against any of the people of Israel.

22 Then Joshua said, "Open the mouth of the cave and bring those five kings out to me from the cave." 23 And they did so, and brought those five kings out to him from the cave, the king of Jerusalem, the king of Hebron, the king of Jarmuth, the king of Lachish, and the king of Eglon. 24 And when they brought those kings out to Joshua, Joshua summoned all the men of Israel and said to the chiefs of the men of war who had gone with him, "Come near; put your feet on the necks of these kings." Then they came near and put their feet on their necks. 25 And Joshua said to them, "Do not be afraid or dismayed; be strong and courageous. For thus the LORD will do to all your enemies against whom you fight." 26 And afterward Joshua struck them and put them to death, and he hanged them on five trees. And they hung on the trees until evening. 27 But at the time of the going down of the sun, Joshua commanded, and they took them down from the trees and threw them into the cave where they had hidden themselves, and they set large stones against the mouth of the cave, which remain to this very day.

28 As for Makkedah, Joshua captured it on that day and struck it, and its king, with the edge of the sword. He devoted to destruction every person in it; he left none remaining. And he did to the king of Makkedah just as he had done to the king of Jericho.

Conquest of Southern Canaan

29 Then Joshua and all Israel with him passed on from Makkedah to Libnah and fought against Libnah. 30 And the LORD gave it also and its king into the hand of Israel. And he struck it with the edge of the sword, and every person in it; he left none remaining in it. And he did to its king as he had done to the king of Jericho.

31 Then Joshua and all Israel with him passed on from Libnah to Lachish and laid siege to it and fought against it. 32 And the LORD gave Lachish into the hand of Israel, and he captured it on the second day and struck it with the edge of the sword, and every person in it, as he had done to Libnah.

33 Then Horam king of Gezer came up to help Lachish. And Joshua struck him and his people, until he left none remaining.

34 Then Joshua and all Israel with him passed on from Lachish to Eglon. And they laid siege to it and fought against it. 35 And they captured it on that day, and struck it with the edge of the sword. And he devoted every person in it to destruction that day, as he had done to Lachish.

36 Then Joshua and all Israel with him went up from Eglon to Hebron. And they fought against it 37 and captured it and struck it with the edge of the sword, and its king and its towns, and every person in

it. He left none remaining, as he had done to Eglon, and devoted it to destruction and every person in it.

38 Then Joshua and all Israel with him turned back to Debir and fought against it 39 and he captured it with its king and all its towns. And they struck them with the edge of the sword and devoted to destruction every person in it; he left none remaining. Just as he had done to Hebron and to Libnah and its king, so he did to Debir and to its king.

40 So Joshua struck the whole land, the hill country and the Negeb and the lowland and the slopes, and all their kings. He left none remaining, but devoted to destruction all that breathed, just as the LORD God of Israel commanded. 41 And Joshua struck them from Kadesh-barnea as far as Gaza, and all the country of Goshen, as far as Gibeon. 42 And Joshua captured all these kings and their land at one time, because the LORD God of Israel fought for Israel. 43 Then Joshua returned, and all Israel with him, to the camp at Gilgal.

Conquests in Northern Canaan

11 When Jabin, king of Hazor, heard of this, he sent to Jobab king of Madon, and to the king of Shimron, and to the king of Achshaph, 2 and to the kings who were in the northern hill country, and in the Arabah south of Chinneroth, and in the lowland, and in Naphoth-dor on the west, 3 to the Canaanites in the east and the west, the Amorites, the Hittites, the Perizzites, and the Jebusites in the hill country, and the Hivites under Hermon in the land of Mizpah. 4 And they came out with all their troops, a great horde, in number like the sand that is on the seashore, with very many horses and chariots. 5 And all these kings joined their forces and came and encamped together at the waters of Merom to fight against Israel.

6 And the LORD said to Joshua, "Do not be afraid of them, for tomorrow at this time I will give over all of them, slain, to Israel. You shall hamstring their horses and burn their chariots with fire." 7 So Joshua and all his warriors came suddenly against them by the waters of Merom and fell upon them. 8 And the LORD gave them into the hand of Israel, who struck them and chased them as far as Great Sidon and Misrephoth-maim, and eastward as far as the Valley of Mizpeh. And they struck them until he left none remaining. 9 And Joshua did to them just as the LORD said to him: he hamstrung their horses and burned their chariots with fire.

10 And Joshua turned back at that time and captured Hazor and struck its king with the sword, for Hazor formerly was the head of all those kingdoms. 11 And they struck with the sword all who were in it, devoting them to destruction;[1] there was none left that breathed. And he burned Hazor with fire. 12 And all the cities of those kings, and all their kings, Joshua captured, and struck them with the edge of the sword, devoting them to destruction, just as Moses the servant of the LORD had commanded. 13 But none of the cities that stood on mounds did Israel burn, except Hazor alone; that Joshua burned. 14 And all the spoil of these cities and the livestock, the people of Israel took for their plunder. But every man they struck with the edge of the sword until they had destroyed them, and they did not leave any who breathed. 15 Just as the LORD had commanded Moses his servant, so Moses commanded Joshua, and so Joshua did. He left nothing undone of all that the LORD had commanded Moses.

16 So Joshua took all that land, the hill country and all the Negeb and all the land of Goshen and the lowland and the Arabah and the hill country of Israel and its lowland 17 from Mount Halak, which rises toward Seir, as far as Baal-gad in the Valley of Lebanon below Mount Hermon. And he captured all their kings and struck

[1] That is, setting apart (devoting) as an offering to the Lord (for destruction); also verses 12, 20, 21

them and put them to death. 18 Joshua made war a long time with all those kings. 19 There was not a city that made peace with the people of Israel except the Hivites, the inhabitants of Gibeon. They took them all in battle. 20 For it was the LORD's doing to harden their hearts that they should come against Israel in battle, in order that they should be devoted to destruction and should receive no mercy but be destroyed, just as the LORD commanded Moses.

21 And Joshua came at that time and cut off the Anakim from the hill country, from Hebron, from Debir, from Anab, and from all the hill country of Judah, and from all the hill country of Israel. Joshua devoted them to destruction with their cities. 22 There was none of the Anakim left in the land of the people of Israel. Only in Gaza, in Gath, and in Ashdod did some remain. 23 So Joshua took the whole land, according to all that the LORD had spoken to Moses. And Joshua gave it for an inheritance to Israel according to their tribal allotments. And the land had rest from war.

Kings Defeated by Moses

12 Now these are the kings of the land whom the people of Israel defeated and took possession of their land beyond the Jordan toward the sunrise, from the Valley of the Arnon to Mount Hermon, with all the Arabah eastward: 2 Sihon king of the Amorites who lived at Heshbon and ruled from Aroer, which is on the edge of the Valley of the Arnon, and from the middle of the valley as far as the river Jabbok, the boundary of the Ammonites, that is, half of Gilead, 3 and the Arabah to the Sea of Chinneroth eastward, and in the direction of Beth-jeshimoth, to the Sea of the Arabah, the Salt Sea, southward to the foot of the slopes of Pisgah; 4 and Og[1] king of Bashan, one of the remnant of the Rephaim, who lived at Ashtaroth and at Edrei 5 and ruled over Mount Hermon and Salecah and all Bashan to the boundary of the Geshurites and the Maacathites, and over half of Gilead to the boundary of Sihon king of Heshbon. 6 Moses, the servant of the LORD, and the people of Israel defeated them. And Moses the servant of the LORD gave their land for a possession to the Reubenites and the Gadites and the half-tribe of Manasseh.

Kings Defeated by Joshua

7 And these are the kings of the land whom Joshua and the people of Israel defeated on the west side of the Jordan, from Baal-gad in the Valley of Lebanon to Mount Halak, that rises toward Seir (and Joshua gave their land to the tribes of Israel as a possession according to their allotments, 8 in the hill country, in the lowland, in the Arabah, in the slopes, in the wilderness, and in the Negeb, the land of the Hittites, the Amorites, the Canaanites, the Perizzites, the Hivites, and the Jebusites): 9 the king of Jericho, one; the king of Ai, which is beside Bethel, one; 10 the king of Jerusalem, one; the king of Hebron, one; 11 the king of Jarmuth, one; the king of Lachish, one; 12 the king of Eglon, one; the king of Gezer, one; 13 the king of Debir, one; the king of Geder, one; 14 the king of Hormah, one; the king of Arad, one; 15 the king of Libnah, one; the king of Adullam, one; 16 the king of Makkedah, one; the king of Bethel, one; 17 the king of Tappuah, one; the king of Hepher, one; 18 the king of Aphek, one; the king of Lasharon, one; 19 the king of Madon, one; the king of Hazor, one; 20 the king of Shimron-meron, one; the king of Achshaph, one; 21 the king of Taanach, one; the king of Megiddo, one; 22 the king of Kedesh, one; the king of Jokneam in Carmel, one; 23 the king of Dor in Naphath-dor, one; the king of Goiim in Galilee,[2] one; 24 the king of Tirzah, one: in all, thirty-one kings.

[1] Septuagint; Hebrew *the boundary of Og* [2] Septuagint; Hebrew *Gilgal*

Land Still to Be Conquered

13 Now Joshua was old and advanced
in years, and the LORD said to
him, "You are old and advanced in years,
and there remains yet very much land
to possess. 2 This is the land that yet
remains: all the regions of the Philistines,
and all those of the Geshurites 3 (from the
Shihor, which is east of Egypt, northward
to the boundary of Ekron, it is counted
as Canaanite; there are five rulers of
the Philistines, those of Gaza, Ashdod,
Ashkelon, Gath, and Ekron), and those of
the Avvim, 4 in the south, all the land of
the Canaanites, and Mearah that belongs
to the Sidonians, to Aphek, to the bound-
ary of the Amorites, 5 and the land of
the Gebalites, and all Lebanon, toward
the sunrise, from Baal-gad below Mount
Hermon to Lebo-hamath, 6 all the inhabit-
ants of the hill country from Lebanon to
Misrephoth-maim, even all the Sidonians.
I myself will drive them out from before
the people of Israel. Only allot the land to
Israel for an inheritance, as I have com-
manded you. 7 Now therefore divide this
land for an inheritance to the nine tribes
and half the tribe of Manasseh."

The Inheritance East of the Jordan

8 With the other half of the tribe of
Manasseh[1] the Reubenites and the Gadites
received their inheritance, which Moses
gave them, beyond the Jordan eastward,
as Moses the servant of the LORD gave
them: 9 from Aroer, which is on the edge
of the Valley of the Arnon, and the city
that is in the middle of the valley, and all
the tableland of Medeba as far as Dibon;
10 and all the cities of Sihon king of the
Amorites, who reigned in Heshbon, as far
as the boundary of the Ammonites; 11 and
Gilead, and the region of the Geshurites
and Maacathites, and all Mount Hermon,
and all Bashan to Salecah; 12 all the king-
dom of Og in Bashan, who reigned in
Ashtaroth and in Edrei (he alone was left
of the remnant of the Rephaim); these
Moses had struck and driven out. 13 Yet
the people of Israel did not drive out the
Geshurites or the Maacathites, but Geshur
and Maacath dwell in the midst of Israel
to this day.

14 To the tribe of Levi alone Moses gave
no inheritance. The offerings by fire to the
LORD God of Israel are their inheritance, as
he said to him.

15 And Moses gave an inheritance to
the tribe of the people of Reuben accord-
ing to their clans. 16 So their territory
was from Aroer, which is on the edge of
the Valley of the Arnon, and the city that
is in the middle of the valley, and all the
tableland by Medeba; 17 with Heshbon,
and all its cities that are in the tableland;
Dibon, and Bamoth-baal, and Beth-baal-
meon, 18 and Jahaz, and Kedemoth, and
Mephaath, 19 and Kiriathaim, and Sibmah,
and Zereth-shahar on the hill of the valley,
20 and Beth-peor, and the slopes of Pisgah,
and Beth-jeshimoth, 21 that is, all the cities
of the tableland, and all the kingdom of
Sihon king of the Amorites, who reigned
in Heshbon, whom Moses defeated with
the leaders of Midian, Evi and Rekem
and Zur and Hur and Reba, the princes
of Sihon, who lived in the land. 22 Balaam
also, the son of Beor, the one who prac-
ticed divination, was killed with the sword
by the people of Israel among the rest of
their slain. 23 And the border of the people
of Reuben was the Jordan as a boundary.
This was the inheritance of the people
of Reuben, according to their clans with
their cities and villages.

24 Moses gave an inheritance also to
the tribe of Gad, to the people of Gad,
according to their clans. 25 Their terri-
tory was Jazer, and all the cities of Gilead,
and half the land of the Ammonites, to
Aroer, which is east of Rabbah, 26 and
from Heshbon to Ramath-mizpeh and
Betonim, and from Mahanaim to the
territory of Debir,[2] 27 and in the valley

[1] Hebrew *With it* [2] Septuagint, Syriac, Vulgate; Hebrew *Lidebir*

Beth-haram, Beth-nimrah, Succoth, and
Zaphon, the rest of the kingdom of Sihon
king of Heshbon, having the Jordan as a
boundary, to the lower end of the Sea of
Chinnereth, eastward beyond the Jordan.
28 This is the inheritance of the people of
Gad according to their clans, with their
cities and villages.

29 And Moses gave an inheritance to the
half-tribe of Manasseh. It was allotted to
the half-tribe of the people of Manasseh
according to their clans. 30 Their region
extended from Mahanaim, through all
Bashan, the whole kingdom of Og king of
Bashan, and all the towns of Jair, which
are in Bashan, sixty cities, 31 and half
Gilead, and Ashtaroth, and Edrei, the cit-
ies of the kingdom of Og in Bashan. These
were allotted to the people of Machir the
son of Manasseh for the half of the people
of Machir according to their clans.

32 These are the inheritances that Moses
distributed in the plains of Moab, beyond
the Jordan east of Jericho. 33 But to the
tribe of Levi Moses gave no inheritance;
the LORD God of Israel is their inheritance,
just as he said to them.

The Inheritance West of the Jordan

14 These are the inheritances that
the people of Israel received in the
land of Canaan, which Eleazar the priest
and Joshua the son of Nun and the heads
of the fathers' houses of the tribes of the
people of Israel gave them to inherit.
2 Their inheritance was by lot, just as the
LORD had commanded by the hand of
Moses for the nine and one-half tribes.
3 For Moses had given an inheritance to
the two and one-half tribes beyond the
Jordan, but to the Levites he gave no
inheritance among them. 4 For the people
of Joseph were two tribes, Manasseh and
Ephraim. And no portion was given to the
Levites in the land, but only cities to dwell
in, with their pasturelands for their live-
stock and their substance. 5 The people of
Israel did as the LORD commanded Moses;
they allotted the land.

Caleb's Request and Inheritance

6 Then the people of Judah came to
Joshua at Gilgal. And Caleb the son of
Jephunneh the Kenizzite said to him,
"You know what the LORD said to Moses
the man of God in Kadesh-barnea con-
cerning you and me. 7 I was forty years
old when Moses the servant of the LORD
sent me from Kadesh-barnea to spy out
the land, and I brought him word again
as it was in my heart. 8 But my brothers
who went up with me made the heart of
the people melt; yet I wholly followed
the LORD my God. 9 And Moses swore on
that day, saying, 'Surely the land on which
your foot has trodden shall be an inheri-
tance for you and your children forever,
because you have wholly followed the
LORD my God.' 10 And now, behold, the
LORD has kept me alive, just as he said,
these forty-five years since the time that
the LORD spoke this word to Moses, while
Israel walked in the wilderness. And now,
behold, I am this day eighty-five years old.
11 I am still as strong today as I was in the
day that Moses sent me; my strength now
is as my strength was then, for war and
for going and coming. 12 So now give me
this hill country of which the LORD spoke
on that day, for you heard on that day how
the Anakim were there, with great forti-
fied cities. It may be that the LORD will be
with me, and I shall drive them out just as
the LORD said."

13 Then Joshua blessed him, and he gave
Hebron to Caleb the son of Jephunneh
for an inheritance. 14 Therefore Hebron
became the inheritance of Caleb the son
of Jephunneh the Kenizzite to this day,
because he wholly followed the LORD, the
God of Israel. 15 Now the name of Hebron
formerly was Kiriath-arba.[1] (Arba[2] was the
greatest man among the Anakim.) And the
land had rest from war.

[1] *Kiriath-arba* means *the city of Arba* [2] Hebrew *He*

The Allotment for Judah

15 The allotment for the tribe of the
people of Judah according to their
clans reached southward to the bound-
ary of Edom, to the wilderness of Zin
at the farthest south. 2 And their south
boundary ran from the end of the Salt
Sea, from the bay that faces southward.
3 It goes out southward of the ascent
of Akrabbim, passes along to Zin, and
goes up south of Kadesh-barnea, along
by Hezron, up to Addar, turns about to
Karka, 4 passes along to Azmon, goes out
by the Brook of Egypt, and comes to its
end at the sea. This shall be your south
boundary. 5 And the east boundary is
the Salt Sea, to the mouth of the Jordan.
And the boundary on the north side runs
from the bay of the sea at the mouth of
the Jordan. 6 And the boundary goes up
to Beth-hoglah and passes along north of
Beth-arabah. And the boundary goes up
to the stone of Bohan the son of Reuben.
7 And the boundary goes up to Debir from
the Valley of Achor, and so northward,
turning toward Gilgal, which is oppo-
site the ascent of Adummim, which is
on the south side of the valley. And the
boundary passes along to the waters of
En-shemesh and ends at En-rogel. 8 Then
the boundary goes up by the Valley of the
Son of Hinnom at the southern shoulder
of the Jebusite (that is, Jerusalem). And
the boundary goes up to the top of the
mountain that lies over against the Valley
of Hinnom, on the west, at the northern
end of the Valley of Rephaim. 9 Then the
boundary extends from the top of the
mountain to the spring of the waters of
Nephtoah, and from there to the cities
of Mount Ephron. Then the boundary
bends around to Baalah (that is, Kiriath-
jearim). 10 And the boundary circles west
of Baalah to Mount Seir, passes along to
the northern shoulder of Mount Jearim
(that is, Chesalon), and goes down to Beth-
shemesh and passes along by Timnah.
11 The boundary goes out to the shoulder
of the hill north of Ekron, then the bound-
ary bends around to Shikkeron and passes
along to Mount Baalah and goes out to
Jabneel. Then the boundary comes to an
end at the sea. 12 And the west boundary
was the Great Sea with its coastline. This
is the boundary around the people of
Judah according to their clans.

13 According to the commandment
of the LORD to Joshua, he gave to Caleb
the son of Jephunneh a portion among
the people of Judah, Kiriath-arba, that is,
Hebron (Arba was the father of Anak).
14 And Caleb drove out from there the
three sons of Anak, Sheshai and Ahiman
and Talmai, the descendants of Anak.
15 And he went up from there against the
inhabitants of Debir. Now the name of
Debir formerly was Kiriath-sepher. 16 And
Caleb said, "Whoever strikes Kiriath-
sepher and captures it, to him will I give
Achsah my daughter as wife." 17 And
Othniel the son of Kenaz, the brother
of Caleb, captured it. And he gave him
Achsah his daughter as wife. 18 When
she came to him, she urged him to ask
her father for a field. And she got off her
donkey, and Caleb said to her, "What do
you want?" 19 She said to him, "Give me
a blessing. Since you have given me the
land of the Negeb, give me also springs of
water." And he gave her the upper springs
and the lower springs.

20 This is the inheritance of the tribe
of the people of Judah according to their
clans. 21 The cities belonging to the tribe
of the people of Judah in the extreme
south, toward the boundary of Edom, were
Kabzeel, Eder, Jagur, 22 Kinah, Dimonah,
Adadah, 23 Kedesh, Hazor, Ithnan, 24 Ziph,
Telem, Bealoth, 25 Hazor-hadattah, Kerioth-
hezron (that is, Hazor), 26 Amam, Shema,
Moladah, 27 Hazar-gaddah, Heshmon,
Beth-pelet, 28 Hazar-shual, Beersheba,
Biziothiah, 29 Baalah, Iim, Ezem, 30 Eltolad,
Chesil, Hormah, 31 Ziklag, Madmannah,

Sansannah, 32 Lebaoth, Shilhim, Ain, and
Rimmon: in all, twenty-nine cities with
their villages.
33 And in the lowland, Eshtaol, Zorah,
Ashnah, 34 Zanoah, En-gannim, Tappuah,
Enam, 35 Jarmuth, Adullam, Socoh,
Azekah, 36 Shaaraim, Adithaim, Gederah,
Gederothaim: fourteen cities with their
villages.
37 Zenan, Hadashah, Migdal-gad, 38 Dil-
ean, Mizpeh, Joktheel, 39 Lachish, Bozkath,
Eglon, 40 Cabbon, Lahmam, Chitlish, 41 Ge-
deroth, Beth-dagon, Naamah, and Mak-
kedah: sixteen cities with their villages.
42 Libnah, Ether, Ashan, 43 Iphtah,
Ashnah, Nezib, 44 Keilah, Achzib, and Ma-
reshah: nine cities with their villages.
45 Ekron, with its towns and its villages;
46 from Ekron to the sea, all that were by
the side of Ashdod, with their villages.
47 Ashdod, its towns and its villages;
Gaza, its towns and its villages; to the
Brook of Egypt, and the Great Sea with its
coastline.
48 And in the hill country, Shamir, Jat-
tir, Socoh, 49 Dannah, Kiriath-sannah
(that is, Debir), 50 Anab, Eshtemoh, Anim,
51 Goshen, Holon, and Giloh: eleven cities
with their villages.
52 Arab, Dumah, Eshan, 53 Janim, Beth-
tappuah, Aphekah, 54 Humtah, Kiriath-
arba (that is, Hebron), and Zior: nine cities
with their villages.
55 Maon, Carmel, Ziph, Juttah, 56 Jezreel,
Jokdeam, Zanoah, 57 Kain, Gibeah, and
Timnah: ten cities with their villages.
58 Halhul, Beth-zur, Gedor, 59 Maarath,
Beth-anoth, and Eltekon: six cities with
their villages.
60 Kiriath-baal (that is, Kiriath-jearim),
and Rabbah: two cities with their villages.
61 In the wilderness, Beth-arabah, Mid-
din, Secacah, 62 Nibshan, the City of Salt,
and Engedi: six cities with their villages.
63 But the Jebusites, the inhabitants of
Jerusalem, the people of Judah could not
drive out, so the Jebusites dwell with the
people of Judah at Jerusalem to this day.

The Allotment for Ephraim and Manasseh

16 The allotment of the people of
Joseph went from the Jordan by
Jericho, east of the waters of Jericho, into
the wilderness, going up from Jericho
into the hill country to Bethel. 2 Then
going from Bethel to Luz, it passes along
to Ataroth, the territory of the Archites.
3 Then it goes down westward to the ter-
ritory of the Japhletites, as far as the terri-
tory of Lower Beth-horon, then to Gezer,
and it ends at the sea.
4 The people of Joseph, Manasseh and
Ephraim, received their inheritance.
5 The territory of the people of Ephraim
by their clans was as follows: the bound-
ary of their inheritance on the east was
Ataroth-addar as far as Upper Beth-horon,
6 and the boundary goes from there to the
sea. On the north is Michmethath. Then
on the east the boundary turns around
toward Taanath-shiloh and passes along
beyond it on the east to Janoah, 7 then it
goes down from Janoah to Ataroth and to
Naarah, and touches Jericho, ending at the
Jordan. 8 From Tappuah the boundary goes
westward to the brook Kanah and ends at
the sea. Such is the inheritance of the tribe
of the people of Ephraim by their clans,
9 together with the towns that were set
apart for the people of Ephraim within the
inheritance of the Manassites, all those
towns with their villages. 10 However, they
did not drive out the Canaanites who lived
in Gezer, so the Canaanites have lived in
the midst of Ephraim to this day but have
been made to do forced labor.

17 Then allotment was made to the
people of Manasseh, for he was the
firstborn of Joseph. To Machir the first-
born of Manasseh, the father of Gilead,
were allotted Gilead and Bashan, because
he was a man of war. 2 And allotments
were made to the rest of the people of

Manasseh by their clans, Abiezer, Helek,
Asriel, Shechem, Hepher, and Shemida.
These were the male descendants of
Manasseh the son of Joseph, by their clans.
3 Now Zelophehad the son of Hepher,
son of Gilead, son of Machir, son of
Manasseh, had no sons, but only
daughters, and these are the names of
his daughters: Mahlah, Noah, Hoglah,
Milcah, and Tirzah. 4 They approached
Eleazar the priest and Joshua the son
of Nun and the leaders and said, "The
LORD commanded Moses to give us an
inheritance along with our brothers."
So according to the mouth of the LORD
he gave them an inheritance among the
brothers of their father. 5 Thus there fell
to Manasseh ten portions, besides the
land of Gilead and Bashan, which is on
the other side of the Jordan, 6 because
the daughters of Manasseh received an
inheritance along with his sons. The land
of Gilead was allotted to the rest of the
people of Manasseh.

7 The territory of Manasseh reached
from Asher to Michmethath, which is
east of Shechem. Then the boundary
goes along southward to the inhabitants
of En-tappuah. 8 The land of Tappuah
belonged to Manasseh, but the town of
Tappuah on the boundary of Manasseh
belonged to the people of Ephraim. 9 Then
the boundary went down to the brook
Kanah. These cities, to the south of the
brook, among the cities of Manasseh,
belong to Ephraim. Then the boundary
of Manasseh goes on the north side of
the brook and ends at the sea, 10 the land
to the south being Ephraim's and that to
the north being Manasseh's, with the sea
forming its boundary. On the north Asher
is reached, and on the east Issachar. 11 Also
in Issachar and in Asher Manasseh had
Beth-shean and its villages, and Ibleam
and its villages, and the inhabitants of
Dor and its villages, and the inhabitants
of En-dor and its villages, and the inhab-
itants of Taanach and its villages, and the
inhabitants of Megiddo and its villages;
the third is Naphath.[1] 12 Yet the people of
Manasseh could not take possession of
those cities, but the Canaanites persisted
in dwelling in that land. 13 Now when the
people of Israel grew strong, they put the
Canaanites to forced labor, but did not
utterly drive them out.

14 Then the people of Joseph spoke to
Joshua, saying, "Why have you given me
but one lot and one portion as an inheri-
tance, although I am a numerous people,
since all along the LORD has blessed me?"
15 And Joshua said to them, "If you are a
numerous people, go up by yourselves
to the forest, and there clear ground for
yourselves in the land of the Perizzites
and the Rephaim, since the hill country
of Ephraim is too narrow for you." 16 The
people of Joseph said, "The hill country is
not enough for us. Yet all the Canaanites
who dwell in the plain have chariots of
iron, both those in Beth-shean and its vil-
lages and those in the Valley of Jezreel."
17 Then Joshua said to the house of Joseph,
to Ephraim and Manasseh, "You are a
numerous people and have great power.
You shall not have one allotment only,
18 but the hill country shall be yours, for
though it is a forest, you shall clear it and
possess it to its farthest borders. For you
shall drive out the Canaanites, though
they have chariots of iron, and though
they are strong."

Allotment of the Remaining Land

18 Then the whole congregation of
the people of Israel assembled
at Shiloh and set up the tent of meeting
there. The land lay subdued before them.

2 There remained among the people
of Israel seven tribes whose inheritance
had not yet been apportioned. 3 So Joshua
said to the people of Israel, "How long
will you put off going in to take posses-
sion of the land, which the LORD, the God

[1] The meaning of the Hebrew is uncertain

of your fathers, has given you? 4 Provide three men from each tribe, and I will send them out that they may set out and go up and down the land. They shall write a description of it with a view to their inheritances, and then come to me. 5 They shall divide it into seven portions. Judah shall continue in his territory on the south, and the house of Joseph shall continue in their territory on the north. 6 And you shall describe the land in seven divisions and bring the description here to me. And I will cast lots for you here before the LORD our God. 7 The Levites have no portion among you, for the priesthood of the LORD is their heritage. And Gad and Reuben and half the tribe of Manasseh have received their inheritance beyond the Jordan eastward, which Moses the servant of the LORD gave them."

8 So the men arose and went, and Joshua charged those who went to write the description of the land, saying, "Go up and down in the land and write a description and return to me. And I will cast lots for you here before the LORD in Shiloh." 9 So the men went and passed up and down in the land and wrote in a book a description of it by towns in seven divisions. Then they came to Joshua to the camp at Shiloh, 10 and Joshua cast lots for them in Shiloh before the LORD. And there Joshua apportioned the land to the people of Israel, to each his portion.

The Inheritance for Benjamin

11 The lot of the tribe of the people of Benjamin according to its clans came up, and the territory allotted to it fell between the people of Judah and the people of Joseph. 12 On the north side their boundary began at the Jordan. Then the boundary goes up to the shoulder north of Jericho, then up through the hill country westward, and it ends at the wilderness of Beth-aven. 13 From there the boundary passes along southward in the direction of Luz, to the shoulder of Luz (that is, Bethel), then the boundary goes down to Ataroth-addar, on the mountain that lies south of Lower Beth-horon. 14 Then the boundary goes in another direction, turning on the western side southward from the mountain that lies to the south, opposite Beth-horon, and it ends at Kiriath-baal (that is, Kiriath-jearim), a city belonging to the people of Judah. This forms the western side. 15 And the southern side begins at the outskirts of Kiriath-jearim. And the boundary goes from there to Ephron,[1] to the spring of the waters of Nephtoah. 16 Then the boundary goes down to the border of the mountain that overlooks the Valley of the Son of Hinnom, which is at the north end of the Valley of Rephaim. And it then goes down the Valley of Hinnom, south of the shoulder of the Jebusites, and downward to En-rogel. 17 Then it bends in a northerly direction going on to En-shemesh, and from there goes to Geliloth, which is opposite the ascent of Adummim. Then it goes down to the stone of Bohan the son of Reuben, 18 and passing on to the north of the shoulder of Beth-arabah[2] it goes down to the Arabah. 19 Then the boundary passes on to the north of the shoulder of Beth-hoglah. And the boundary ends at the northern bay of the Salt Sea, at the south end of the Jordan: this is the southern border. 20 The Jordan forms its boundary on the eastern side. This is the inheritance of the people of Benjamin, according to their clans, boundary by boundary all around.

21 Now the cities of the tribe of the people of Benjamin according to their clans were Jericho, Beth-hoglah, Emek-keziz, 22 Beth-arabah, Zemaraim, Bethel, 23 Avvim, Parah, Ophrah, 24 Chephar-ammoni, Ophni, Geba—twelve cities with their villages: 25 Gibeon, Ramah, Beeroth, 26 Mizpeh, Chephirah, Mozah, 27 Rekem, Irpeel, Taralah, 28 Zela, Haeleph, Jebus[3]

[1] See 15:9; Hebrew *westward* [2] Septuagint; Hebrew *to the shoulder over against the Arabah* [3] Septuagint, Syriac, Vulgate; Hebrew *the Jebusite*

(that is, Jerusalem), Gibeah[1] and Kiriath-jearim[2]—fourteen cities with their villages. This is the inheritance of the people of Benjamin according to its clans.

The Inheritance for Simeon

19 The second lot came out for Simeon, for the tribe of the people of Simeon, according to their clans, and their inheritance was in the midst of the inheritance of the people of Judah. 2 And they had for their inheritance Beersheba, Sheba, Moladah, 3 Hazar-shual, Balah, Ezem, 4 Eltolad, Bethul, Hormah, 5 Ziklag, Beth-marcaboth, Hazar-susah, 6 Beth-lebaoth, and Sharuhen—thirteen cities with their villages; 7 Ain, Rimmon, Ether, and Ashan—four cities with their villages, 8 together with all the villages around these cities as far as Baalath-beer, Ramah of the Negeb. This was the inheritance of the tribe of the people of Simeon according to their clans. 9 The inheritance of the people of Simeon formed part of the territory of the people of Judah. Because the portion of the people of Judah was too large for them, the people of Simeon obtained an inheritance in the midst of their inheritance.

The Inheritance for Zebulun

10 The third lot came up for the people of Zebulun, according to their clans. And the territory of their inheritance reached as far as Sarid. 11 Then their boundary goes up westward and on to Mareal and touches Dabbesheth, then the brook that is east of Jokneam. 12 From Sarid it goes in the other direction eastward toward the sunrise to the boundary of Chisloth-tabor. From there it goes to Daberath, then up to Japhia. 13 From there it passes along on the east toward the sunrise to Gath-hepher, to Eth-kazin, and going on to Rimmon it bends toward Neah, 14 then on the north the boundary turns about to Hannathon, and it ends at the Valley of Iphtahel; 15 and Kattath, Nahalal, Shimron, Idalah, and Bethlehem—twelve cities with their villages. 16 This is the inheritance of the people of Zebulun, according to their clans—these cities with their villages.

The Inheritance for Issachar

17 The fourth lot came out for Issachar, for the people of Issachar, according to their clans. 18 Their territory included Jezreel, Chesulloth, Shunem, 19 Hapharaim, Shion, Anaharath, 20 Rabbith, Kishion, Ebez, 21 Remeth, En-gannim, En-haddah, Beth-pazzez. 22 The boundary also touches Tabor, Shahazumah, and Beth-shemesh, and its boundary ends at the Jordan—sixteen cities with their villages. 23 This is the inheritance of the tribe of the people of Issachar, according to their clans—the cities with their villages.

The Inheritance for Asher

24 The fifth lot came out for the tribe of the people of Asher according to their clans. 25 Their territory included Helkath, Hali, Beten, Achshaph, 26 Allammelech, Amad, and Mishal. On the west it touches Carmel and Shihor-libnath, 27 then it turns eastward, it goes to Beth-dagon, and touches Zebulun and the Valley of Iphtahel northward to Beth-emek and Neiel. Then it continues in the north to Cabul, 28 Ebron, Rehob, Hammon, Kanah, as far as Sidon the Great. 29 Then the boundary turns to Ramah, reaching to the fortified city of Tyre. Then the boundary turns to Hosah, and it ends at the sea; Mahalab,[3] Achzib, 30 Ummah, Aphek and Rehob—twenty-two cities with their villages. 31 This is the inheritance of the tribe of the people of Asher according to their clans—these cities with their villages.

The Inheritance for Naphtali

32 The sixth lot came out for the people of Naphtali, for the people of Naphtali, according to their clans. 33 And their boundary ran from Heleph, from the oak in Zaanannim, and Adami-nekeb, and

[1] Hebrew *Gibeath* [2] Septuagint; Hebrew *Kiriath* [3] Compare Septuagint; Hebrew *Mehebel*

Jabneel, as far as Lakkum, and it ended at the Jordan. 34 Then the boundary turns westward to Aznoth-tabor and goes from there to Hukkok, touching Zebulun at the south and Asher on the west and Judah on the east at the Jordan. 35 The fortified cities are Ziddim, Zer, Hammath, Rakkath, Chinnereth, 36 Adamah, Ramah, Hazor, 37 Kedesh, Edrei, En-hazor, 38 Yiron, Migdal-el, Horem, Beth-anath, and Beth-shemesh—nineteen cities with their villages. 39 This is the inheritance of the tribe of the people of Naphtali according to their clans—the cities with their villages.

The Inheritance for Dan

40 The seventh lot came out for the tribe of the people of Dan, according to their clans. 41 And the territory of its inheritance included Zorah, Eshtaol, Ir-shemesh, 42 Shaalabbin, Aijalon, Ithlah, 43 Elon, Timnah, Ekron, 44 Eltekeh, Gibbethon, Baalath, 45 Jehud, Bene-berak, Gath-rimmon, 46 and Me-jarkon and Rakkon with the territory over against Joppa. 47 When the territory of the people of Dan was lost to them, the people of Dan went up and fought against Leshem, and after capturing it and striking it with the sword they took possession of it and settled in it, calling Leshem, Dan, after the name of Dan their ancestor. 48 This is the inheritance of the tribe of the people of Dan, according to their clans—these cities with their villages.

The Inheritance for Joshua

49 When they had finished distributing the several territories of the land as inheritances, the people of Israel gave an inheritance among them to Joshua the son of Nun. 50 By command of the LORD they gave him the city that he asked, Timnath-serah in the hill country of Ephraim. And he rebuilt the city and settled in it.

51 These are the inheritances that Eleazar the priest and Joshua the son of Nun and the heads of the fathers' houses of the tribes of the people of Israel distributed by lot at Shiloh before the LORD, at the entrance of the tent of meeting. So they finished dividing the land.

The Cities of Refuge

20 Then the LORD said to Joshua, 2 "Say to the people of Israel, 'Appoint the cities of refuge, of which I spoke to you through Moses, 3 that the manslayer who strikes any person without intent or unknowingly may flee there. They shall be for you a refuge from the avenger of blood. 4 He shall flee to one of these cities and shall stand at the entrance of the gate of the city and explain his case to the elders of that city. Then they shall take him into the city and give him a place, and he shall remain with them. 5 And if the avenger of blood pursues him, they shall not give up the manslayer into his hand, because he struck his neighbor unknowingly, and did not hate him in the past. 6 And he shall remain in that city until he has stood before the congregation for judgment, until the death of him who is high priest at the time. Then the manslayer may return to his own town and his own home, to the town from which he fled.'"

7 So they set apart Kedesh in Galilee in the hill country of Naphtali, and Shechem in the hill country of Ephraim, and Kiriath-arba (that is, Hebron) in the hill country of Judah. 8 And beyond the Jordan east of Jericho, they appointed Bezer in the wilderness on the tableland, from the tribe of Reuben, and Ramoth in Gilead, from the tribe of Gad, and Golan in Bashan, from the tribe of Manasseh. 9 These were the cities designated for all the people of Israel and for the stranger sojourning among them, that anyone who killed a person without intent could flee there, so that he might not die by the hand of the avenger of blood, till he stood before the congregation.

Cities and Pasturelands Allotted to Levi

21 Then the heads of the fathers' houses of the Levites came to Eleazar the priest and to Joshua the son of Nun and to the heads of the fathers' houses of the tribes of the people of Israel. 2 And they said to them at Shiloh in the land of Canaan, "The LORD commanded through Moses that we be given cities to dwell in, along with their pasturelands for our livestock." 3 So by command of the LORD the people of Israel gave to the Levites the following cities and pasturelands out of their inheritance.

4 The lot came out for the clans of the Kohathites. So those Levites who were descendants of Aaron the priest received by lot from the tribes of Judah, Simeon, and Benjamin, thirteen cities.

5 And the rest of the Kohathites received by lot from the clans of the tribe of Ephraim, from the tribe of Dan and the half-tribe of Manasseh, ten cities.

6 The Gershonites received by lot from the clans of the tribe of Issachar, from the tribe of Asher, from the tribe of Naphtali, and from the half-tribe of Manasseh in Bashan, thirteen cities.

7 The Merarites according to their clans received from the tribe of Reuben, the tribe of Gad, and the tribe of Zebulun, twelve cities.

8 These cities and their pasturelands the people of Israel gave by lot to the Levites, as the LORD had commanded through Moses.

9 Out of the tribe of the people of Judah and the tribe of the people of Simeon they gave the following cities mentioned by name, 10 which went to the descendants of Aaron, one of the clans of the Kohathites who belonged to the people of Levi; since the lot fell to them first. 11 They gave them Kiriath-arba (Arba being the father of Anak), that is Hebron, in the hill country of Judah, along with the pasturelands around it. 12 But the fields of the city and its villages had been given to Caleb the son of Jephunneh as his possession.

13 And to the descendants of Aaron the priest they gave Hebron, the city of refuge for the manslayer, with its pasturelands, Libnah with its pasturelands, 14 Jattir with its pasturelands, Eshtemoa with its pasturelands, 15 Holon with its pasturelands, Debir with its pasturelands, 16 Ain with its pasturelands, Juttah with its pasturelands, Beth-shemesh with its pasturelands—nine cities out of these two tribes; 17 then out of the tribe of Benjamin, Gibeon with its pasturelands, Geba with its pasturelands, 18 Anathoth with its pasturelands, and Almon with its pasturelands—four cities. 19 The cities of the descendants of Aaron, the priests, were in all thirteen cities with their pasturelands.

20 As to the rest of the Kohathites belonging to the Kohathite clans of the Levites, the cities allotted to them were out of the tribe of Ephraim. 21 To them were given Shechem, the city of refuge for the manslayer, with its pasturelands in the hill country of Ephraim, Gezer with its pasturelands, 22 Kibzaim with its pasturelands, Beth-horon with its pasturelands—four cities; 23 and out of the tribe of Dan, Elteke with its pasturelands, Gibbethon with its pasturelands, 24 Aijalon with its pasturelands, Gath-rimmon with its pasturelands—four cities; 25 and out of the half-tribe of Manasseh, Taanach with its pasturelands, and Gath-rimmon with its pasturelands—two cities. 26 The cities of the clans of the rest of the Kohathites were ten in all with their pasturelands.

27 And to the Gershonites, one of the clans of the Levites, were given out of the half-tribe of Manasseh, Golan in Bashan with its pasturelands, the city of refuge for the manslayer, and Beeshterah with its pasturelands—two cities; 28 and out of the tribe of Issachar, Kishion with its pasturelands, Daberath with its pasturelands, 29 Jarmuth with its pasturelands,

En-gannim with its pasturelands—four
cities; 30 and out of the tribe of Asher,
Mishal with its pasturelands, Abdon with
its pasturelands, 31 Helkath with its pas-
turelands, and Rehob with its pasture-
lands—four cities; 32 and out of the tribe
of Naphtali, Kedesh in Galilee with its
pasturelands, the city of refuge for the
manslayer, Hammoth-dor with its pas-
turelands, and Kartan with its pasture-
lands—three cities. 33 The cities of the
several clans of the Gershonites were in
all thirteen cities with their pasturelands.

34 And to the rest of the Levites, the
Merarite clans, were given out of the
tribe of Zebulun, Jokneam with its pas-
turelands, Kartah with its pasturelands,
35 Dimnah with its pasturelands, Nahalal
with its pasturelands—four cities; 36 and
out of the tribe of Reuben, Bezer with its
pasturelands, Jahaz with its pasturelands,
37 Kedemoth with its pasturelands, and
Mephaath with its pasturelands—four cit-
ies; 38 and out of the tribe of Gad, Ramoth
in Gilead with its pasturelands, the city of
refuge for the manslayer, Mahanaim with
its pasturelands, 39 Heshbon with its pas-
turelands, Jazer with its pasturelands—
four cities in all. 40 As for the cities of the
several Merarite clans, that is, the remain-
der of the clans of the Levites, those allot-
ted to them were in all twelve cities.

41 The cities of the Levites in the midst
of the possession of the people of Israel
were in all forty-eight cities with their
pasturelands. 42 These cities each had its
pasturelands around it. So it was with all
these cities.

43 Thus the LORD gave to Israel all the
land that he swore to give to their fathers.
And they took possession of it, and they
settled there. 44 And the LORD gave them
rest on every side just as he had sworn to
their fathers. Not one of all their enemies
had withstood them, for the LORD had
given all their enemies into their hands.
45 Not one word of all the good promises
that the LORD had made to the house of
Israel had failed; all came to pass.

The Eastern Tribes Return Home

22 At that time Joshua summoned
the Reubenites and the Gadites
and the half-tribe of Manasseh, 2 and said
to them, "You have kept all that Moses the
servant of the LORD commanded you and
have obeyed my voice in all that I have
commanded you. 3 You have not forsaken
your brothers these many days, down to
this day, but have been careful to keep the
charge of the LORD your God. 4 And now the
LORD your God has given rest to your broth-
ers, as he promised them. Therefore turn
and go to your tents in the land where your
possession lies, which Moses the servant of
the LORD gave you on the other side of the
Jordan. 5 Only be very careful to observe the
commandment and the law that Moses
the servant of the LORD commanded you,
to love the LORD your God, and to walk in
all his ways and to keep his command-
ments and to cling to him and to serve him
with all your heart and with all your soul."
6 So Joshua blessed them and sent them
away, and they went to their tents.

7 Now to the one half of the tribe of
Manasseh Moses had given a possession
in Bashan, but to the other half Joshua had
given a possession beside their brothers
in the land west of the Jordan. And when
Joshua sent them away to their homes and
blessed them, 8 he said to them, "Go back
to your tents with much wealth and with
very much livestock, with silver, gold,
bronze, and iron, and with much cloth-
ing. Divide the spoil of your enemies with
your brothers." 9 So the people of Reuben
and the people of Gad and the half-tribe
of Manasseh returned home, parting from
the people of Israel at Shiloh, which is in
the land of Canaan, to go to the land of
Gilead, their own land of which they had
possessed themselves by command of the
LORD through Moses.

The Eastern Tribes' Altar of Witness

[10]And when they came to the region of
the Jordan that is in the land of Canaan, the
people of Reuben and the people of Gad
and the half-tribe of Manasseh built there
an altar by the Jordan, an altar of impos-
ing size. [11]And the people of Israel heard
it said, "Behold, the people of Reuben and
the people of Gad and the half-tribe of
Manasseh have built the altar at the fron-
tier of the land of Canaan, in the region
about the Jordan, on the side that belongs
to the people of Israel." [12]And when the
people of Israel heard of it, the whole
assembly of the people of Israel gathered
at Shiloh to make war against them.

[13]Then the people of Israel sent to the
people of Reuben and the people of Gad
and the half-tribe of Manasseh, in the
land of Gilead, Phinehas the son of Eleazar
the priest, [14]and with him ten chiefs, one
from each of the tribal families of Israel,
every one of them the head of a family
among the clans of Israel. [15]And they
came to the people of Reuben, the people
of Gad, and the half-tribe of Manasseh, in
the land of Gilead, and they said to them,
[16]"Thus says the whole congregation of
the LORD, 'What is this breach of faith that
you have committed against the God of
Israel in turning away this day from fol-
lowing the LORD by building yourselves
an altar this day in rebellion against the
LORD? [17]Have we not had enough of the
sin at Peor from which even yet we have
not cleansed ourselves, and for which
there came a plague upon the congrega-
tion of the LORD, [18]that you too must turn
away this day from following the LORD?
And if you too rebel against the LORD
today then tomorrow he will be angry
with the whole congregation of Israel.
[19]But now, if the land of your possession
is unclean, pass over into the LORD's land
where the LORD's tabernacle stands, and
take for yourselves a possession among
us. Only do not rebel against the LORD or
make us as rebels by building for your-
selves an altar other than the altar of the
LORD our God. [20]Did not Achan the son
of Zerah break faith in the matter of the
devoted things, and wrath fell upon all the
congregation of Israel? And he did not per-
ish alone for his iniquity.'"

[21]Then the people of Reuben, the peo-
ple of Gad, and the half-tribe of Manasseh
said in answer to the heads of the fami-
lies of Israel, [22]"The Mighty One, God, the
LORD! The Mighty One, God, the LORD! He
knows; and let Israel itself know! If it was
in rebellion or in breach of faith against
the LORD, do not spare us today [23]for
building an altar to turn away from fol-
lowing the LORD. Or if we did so to offer
burnt offerings or grain offerings or peace
offerings on it, may the LORD himself take
vengeance. [24]No, but we did it from fear
that in time to come your children might
say to our children, 'What have you to do
with the LORD, the God of Israel? [25]For
the LORD has made the Jordan a bound-
ary between us and you, you people of
Reuben and people of Gad. You have no
portion in the LORD.' So your children
might make our children cease to wor-
ship the LORD. [26]Therefore we said, 'Let
us now build an altar, not for burnt offer-
ing, nor for sacrifice, [27]but to be a witness
between us and you, and between our
generations after us, that we do perform
the service of the LORD in his presence
with our burnt offerings and sacrifices
and peace offerings, so your children will
not say to our children in time to come,
"You have no portion in the LORD."' [28]And
we thought, If this should be said to us or
to our descendants in time to come, we
should say, 'Behold, the copy of the altar
of the LORD, which our fathers made, not
for burnt offerings, nor for sacrifice, but
to be a witness between us and you.' [29]Far
be it from us that we should rebel against
the LORD and turn away this day from fol-
lowing the LORD by building an altar for

burnt offering, grain offering, or sacrifice, other than the altar of the LORD our God that stands before his tabernacle!"

30 When Phinehas the priest and the chiefs of the congregation, the heads of the families of Israel who were with him, heard the words that the people of Reuben and the people of Gad and the people of Manasseh spoke, it was good in their eyes. 31 And Phinehas the son of Eleazar the priest said to the people of Reuben and the people of Gad and the people of Manasseh, "Today we know that the LORD is in our midst, because you have not committed this breach of faith against the LORD. Now you have delivered the people of Israel from the hand of the LORD."

32 Then Phinehas the son of Eleazar the priest, and the chiefs, returned from the people of Reuben and the people of Gad in the land of Gilead to the land of Canaan, to the people of Israel, and brought back word to them. 33 And the report was good in the eyes of the people of Israel. And the people of Israel blessed God and spoke no more of making war against them to destroy the land where the people of Reuben and the people of Gad were settled. 34 The people of Reuben and the people of Gad called the altar Witness, "For," they said, "it is a witness between us that the LORD is God."

Joshua's Charge to Israel's Leaders

23 A long time afterward, when the LORD had given rest to Israel from all their surrounding enemies, and Joshua was old and well advanced in years, 2 Joshua summoned all Israel, its elders and heads, its judges and officers, and said to them, "I am now old and well advanced in years. 3 And you have seen all that the LORD your God has done to all these nations for your sake, for it is the LORD your God who has fought for you. 4 Behold, I have allotted to you as an inheritance for your tribes those nations that remain, along with all the nations that I have already cut off, from the Jordan to the Great Sea in the west. 5 The LORD your God will push them back before you and drive them out of your sight. And you shall possess their land, just as the LORD your God promised you. 6 Therefore, be very strong to keep and to do all that is written in the Book of the Law of Moses, turning aside from it neither to the right hand nor to the left, 7 that you may not mix with these nations remaining among you or make mention of the names of their gods or swear by them or serve them or bow down to them, 8 but you shall cling to the LORD your God just as you have done to this day. 9 For the LORD has driven out before you great and strong nations. And as for you, no man has been able to stand before you to this day. 10 One man of you puts to flight a thousand, since it is the LORD your God who fights for you, just as he promised you. 11 Be very careful, therefore, to love the LORD your God. 12 For if you turn back and cling to the remnant of these nations remaining among you and make marriages with them, so that you associate with them and they with you, 13 know for certain that the LORD your God will no longer drive out these nations before you, but they shall be a snare and a trap for you, a whip on your sides and thorns in your eyes, until you perish from off this good ground that the LORD your God has given you.

357

14 "And now I am about to go the way of all the earth, and you know in your hearts and souls, all of you, that not one word has failed of all the good things[1] that the LORD your God promised concerning you. All have come to pass for you; not one of them has failed. 15 But just as all the good things that the LORD your God promised concerning you have been fulfilled for you, so the LORD will bring upon you all the evil things, until he has destroyed you

[1] Or *words*; also twice in verse 15

from off this good land that the LORD your
God has given you, [16] if you transgress the
covenant of the LORD your God, which he
commanded you, and go and serve other
gods and bow down to them. Then the
anger of the LORD will be kindled against
you, and you shall perish quickly from off
the good land that he has given to you."

The Covenant Renewal at Shechem

24 Joshua gathered all the tribes of
Israel to Shechem and summoned
the elders, the heads, the judges,
and the officers of Israel. And they
33, presented themselves before God.
357 [2] And Joshua said to all the people,
"Thus says the LORD, the God of Israel,
'Long ago, your fathers lived beyond the
Euphrates, Terah, the father of Abraham
and of Nahor; and they served other gods.
[3] Then I took your father Abraham from
beyond the River and led him through all
the land of Canaan, and made his off-
spring many. I gave him Isaac. [4] And to
Isaac I gave Jacob and Esau. And I gave
Esau the hill country of Seir to possess,
but Jacob and his children went down to
Egypt. [5] And I sent Moses and Aaron, and I
plagued Egypt with what I did in the midst
of it, and afterward I brought you out.
[6] "'Then I brought your fathers out of
Egypt, and you came to the sea. And the
Egyptians pursued your fathers with
chariots and horsemen to the Red Sea.
[7] And when they cried to the LORD, he put
darkness between you and the Egyptians
and made the sea come upon them and
cover them; and your eyes saw what I did
in Egypt. And you lived in the wilderness
a long time. [8] Then I brought you to the
land of the Amorites, who lived on the
other side of the Jordan. They fought with
you, and I gave them into your hand, and
you took possession of their land, and I
destroyed them before you. [9] Then Balak
the son of Zippor, king of Moab, arose and
fought against Israel. And he sent and
invited Balaam the son of Beor to curse
you, [10] but I would not listen to Balaam.
Indeed, he blessed you. So I delivered you
out of his hand. [11] And you went over the
Jordan and came to Jericho, and the leaders
of Jericho fought against you, and also the
Amorites, the Perizzites, the Canaanites,
the Hittites, the Girgashites, the Hivites,
and the Jebusites. And I gave them into
your hand. [12] And I sent the hornet before
you, which drove them out before you, the
two kings of the Amorites; it was not by
your sword or by your bow. [13] I gave you
a land on which you had not labored and
cities that you had not built, and you dwell
in them. You eat the fruit of vineyards and
olive orchards that you did not plant.'

Choose Whom You Will Serve

[14] "Now therefore fear the LORD and
serve him in sincerity and in faith-
fulness. Put away the gods that
33, your fathers served beyond the
573 River and in Egypt, and serve the
LORD. [15] And if it is evil in your eyes to
serve the LORD, choose this day whom you
will serve, whether the gods your fathers
served in the region beyond the River, or
the gods of the Amorites in whose
land you dwell. But as for me and
573 my house, we will serve the LORD."
[16] Then the people answered, "Far be it
from us that we should forsake the LORD
to serve other gods, [17] for it is the LORD
our God who brought us and our fathers
up from the land of Egypt, out of the
house of slavery, and who did those great
signs in our sight and preserved us in all
the way that we went, and among all the
peoples through whom we passed. [18] And
the LORD drove out before us all the peo-
ples, the Amorites who lived in the land.
Therefore we also will serve the LORD, for
he is our God."

[19] But Joshua said to the people, "You are
not able to serve the LORD, for he is a holy
God. He is a jealous God; he will not for-

give your transgressions or your sins. 20 If
you forsake the LORD and serve foreign
gods, then he will turn and do you harm
and consume you, after having done you
good." 21 And the people said to Joshua,
"No, but we will serve the LORD." 22 Then
Joshua said to the people, "You are wit-
nesses against yourselves that you have
chosen the LORD, to serve him." And they
said, "We are witnesses." 23 He said, "Then
put away the foreign gods that are among
you, and incline your heart to the LORD,
the God of Israel." 24 And the people said to
Joshua, "The LORD our God we will serve,
and his voice we will obey." 25 So Joshua
made a covenant with the people that
day, and put in place statutes and rules
for them at Shechem. 26 And Joshua wrote
these words in the Book of the Law of God.
And he took a large stone and set it up
there under the terebinth that was by the
sanctuary of the LORD. 27 And Joshua said
to all the people, "Behold, this stone shall
be a witness against us, for it has heard all
the words of the LORD that he spoke to us.
Therefore it shall be a witness against you,
lest you deal falsely with your God." 28 So
Joshua sent the people away, every man to
his inheritance.

Joshua's Death and Burial

29 After these things Joshua the son of
Nun, the servant of the LORD, died, being
110 years old. 30 And they buried him in his
own inheritance at Timnath-serah, which
is in the hill country of Ephraim, north of
the mountain of Gaash.

31 Israel served the LORD all the days of
Joshua, and all the days of the elders who
outlived Joshua and had known all the
work that the LORD did for Israel.

32 As for the bones of Joseph, which the
people of Israel brought up from Egypt,
they buried them at Shechem, in the piece
of land that Jacob bought from the sons
of Hamor the father of Shechem for a
hundred pieces of money.[1] It became an
inheritance of the descendants of Joseph.

33 And Eleazar the son of Aaron died,
and they buried him at Gibeah, the town
of Phinehas his son, which had been
given him in the hill country of Ephraim.

[1] Hebrew *for a hundred qesitah*; a unit of money of unknown value

Introduction to

Judges

Author
Unknown

Date
About 1000 B.C.

People
Deborah; Gideon; Jephthah; Samson; Delilah

Purpose
The purpose of Judges is to demonstrate the sinfulness of the people of God, showing their need for a godly king to lead them, and to show the grace and mercy of God in spite of His people's sin.

Central Themes
There are cycles of sin, oppression, crying out to God, deliverance, and sin again; God raises up judges or leaders; God can use unlikely means to save His people; the leaders are ungodly and the people need a godly king.

Memory Verses
The Lord's enemies and friends (Judges 5:31); 11 tribes repent (Judges 20:26); wayward Israel (Judges 21:25)

Introduction

The opening chapters of Judges show Israel's failure to obey God by conquering all the land and driving out all the Canaanites. They also describe the pattern seen over and over in the rest of the book: Israelites turning from God to idols, enemy neighbors raiding Israel, Israel crying to God for help, God raising up judges to save the people, and Israelites turning from God to idols (Judges 1–2). Most of the rest of the book tells the stories of the different judges God raises up and the victories God gives them. Some of the more famous judges are Deborah, the only woman judge listed (Judges 4–5); timid Gideon, to whom God gives a great victory by means of a very small army (Judges 6–8); Jephthah, who makes a foolish vow ending in the sacrifice of his own daughter (Judges 11–12); and Samson, whose great strength God uses repeatedly in spite of his life of disobedience (Judges 13–16). The final chapters tell two unpleasant stories describing how evil God's people had become (Judges 17–21). The book ends by restating what it has said several times before: "In those days there was no king in Israel. Everyone did what was right in his own eyes" (Judges 21:25).

About 1375 B.C.	**1209 B.C.**	**About 1162 B.C.**	**About 1100 B.C.**
Period of the judges begins	Deborah, Barak defeat Canaanites	Gideon defeats Midianites	Birth of Samuel

Judges

The Continuing Conquest of Canaan

1 After the death of Joshua, the people of Israel inquired of the LORD, "Who shall go up first for us against the Canaanites, to fight against them?" 2 The LORD said, "Judah shall go up; behold, I have given the land into his hand." 3 And Judah said to Simeon his brother, "Come up with me into the territory allotted to me, that we may fight against the Canaanites. And I likewise will go with you into the territory allotted to you." So Simeon went with him. 4 Then Judah went up and the LORD gave the Canaanites and the Perizzites into their hand, and they defeated 10,000 of them at Bezek. 5 They found Adoni-bezek at Bezek and fought against him and defeated the Canaanites and the Perizzites. 6 Adoni-bezek fled, but they pursued him and caught him and cut off his thumbs and his big toes. 7 And Adoni-bezek said, "Seventy kings with their thumbs and their big toes cut off used to pick up scraps under my table. As I have done, so God has repaid me." And they brought him to Jerusalem, and he died there.

8 And the men of Judah fought against Jerusalem and captured it and struck it with the edge of the sword and set the city on fire. 9 And afterward the men of Judah went down to fight against the Canaanites who lived in the hill country, in the Negeb, and in the lowland. 10 And Judah went against the Canaanites who lived in Hebron (now the name of Hebron was formerly Kiriath-arba), and they defeated Sheshai and Ahiman and Talmai.

11 From there they went against the inhabitants of Debir. The name of Debir was formerly Kiriath-sepher. 12 And Caleb said, "He who attacks Kiriath-sepher and captures it, I will give him Achsah my daughter for a wife." 13 And Othniel the son of Kenaz, Caleb's younger brother, captured it. And he gave him Achsah his daughter for a wife. 14 When she came to him, she urged him to ask her father for a field. And she dismounted from her donkey, and Caleb said to her, "What do you want?" 15 She said to him, "Give me a blessing. Since you have set me in the land of the Negeb, give me also springs of water." And Caleb gave her the upper springs and the lower springs.

16 And the descendants of the Kenite, Moses' father-in-law, went up with the people of Judah from the city of palms into the wilderness of Judah, which lies in the Negeb near Arad, and they went and settled with the people. 17 And Judah went with Simeon his brother, and they defeated the Canaanites who inhabited Zephath and devoted it to destruction. So the name of the city was called Hormah.[1] 18 Judah also captured Gaza with its territory, and Ashkelon with its territory, and Ekron with its territory. 19 And the LORD was with Judah, and he took possession of the hill country, but he could not drive out the inhabitants of the plain because they had chariots of iron. 20 And Hebron was given to Caleb, as Moses had said. And he drove out from it the three sons of Anak. 21 But the people of Benjamin did not drive out the Jebusites who lived in Jerusalem, so the Jebusites have lived with the people of Benjamin in Jerusalem to this day.

22 The house of Joseph also went up against Bethel, and the LORD was with them. 23 And the house of Joseph scouted out Bethel. (Now the name of the city was formerly Luz.) 24 And the spies saw a man coming out of the city, and they said to

[1] *Hormah means utter destruction*

him, "Please show us the way into the city,
and we will deal kindly with you." 25 And
he showed them the way into the city. And
they struck the city with the edge of the
sword, but they let the man and all his
family go. 26 And the man went to the land
of the Hittites and built a city and called
its name Luz. That is its name to this day.

Failure to Complete the Conquest

27 Manasseh did not drive out the
inhabitants of Beth-shean and its villages,
or Taanach and its villages, or the inhabi-
tants of Dor and its villages, or the inhab-
itants of Ibleam and its villages, or the
inhabitants of Megiddo and its villages,
for the Canaanites persisted in dwelling in
that land. 28 When Israel grew strong, they
put the Canaanites to forced labor, but did
not drive them out completely.

29 And Ephraim did not drive out the
Canaanites who lived in Gezer, so the
Canaanites lived in Gezer among them.

30 Zebulun did not drive out the inhab-
itants of Kitron, or the inhabitants of
Nahalol, so the Canaanites lived among
them, but became subject to forced labor.

31 Asher did not drive out the inhabi-
tants of Acco, or the inhabitants of Sidon
or of Ahlab or of Achzib or of Helbah or of
Aphik or of Rehob, 32 so the Asherites lived
among the Canaanites, the inhabitants of
the land, for they did not drive them out.

33 Naphtali did not drive out the inhab-
itants of Beth-shemesh, or the inhabitants
of Beth-anath, so they lived among the
Canaanites, the inhabitants of the land.
Nevertheless, the inhabitants of Beth-
shemesh and of Beth-anath became sub-
ject to forced labor for them.

34 The Amorites pressed the people of
Dan back into the hill country, for they did
not allow them to come down to the plain.
35 The Amorites persisted in dwelling in
Mount Heres, in Aijalon, and in Shaalbim,
but the hand of the house of Joseph rested
heavily on them, and they became sub-
ject to forced labor. 36 And the border
of the Amorites ran from the ascent of
Akrabbim, from Sela and upward.

Israel's Disobedience

2 Now the angel of the LORD went up
from Gilgal to Bochim. And he said, "I
brought you up from Egypt and brought
you into the land that I swore to give to
your fathers. I said, 'I will never break my
covenant with you, 2 and you shall make
no covenant with the inhabitants of this
land; you shall break down their altars.'
But you have not obeyed my voice. What
is this you have done? 3 So now I say, I will
not drive them out before you, but they
shall become thorns in your sides,[1] and
their gods shall be a snare to you." 4 As
soon as the angel of the LORD spoke these
words to all the people of Israel, the people
lifted up their voices and wept. 5 And they
called the name of that place Bochim.[2]
And they sacrificed there to the LORD.

The Death of Joshua

6 When Joshua dismissed the people,
the people of Israel went each to his inher-
itance to take possession of the land. 7 And
the people served the LORD all the days of
Joshua, and all the days of the elders who
outlived Joshua, who had seen all the great
work that the LORD had done for Israel.
8 And Joshua the son of Nun, the servant
of the LORD, died at the age of 110 years.
9 And they buried him within the bound-
aries of his inheritance in Timnath-heres,
in the hill country of Ephraim, north of
the mountain of Gaash. 10 And all that gen-
eration also were gathered to their fathers.
And there arose another generation after
them who did not know the LORD or the
work that he had done for Israel.

Israel's Unfaithfulness

11 And the people of Israel did what was
evil in the sight of the LORD and served
the Baals. 12 And they abandoned the
LORD, the God of their fathers, who had

[1] Vulgate, Old Latin (compare Septuagint); Hebrew *sides* [2] *Bochim* means *weepers*

brought them out of the land of Egypt. They went after other gods, from among the gods of the peoples who were around them, and bowed down to them. And they provoked the LORD to anger. 13 They abandoned the LORD and served the Baals and the Ashtaroth. 14 So the anger of the LORD was kindled against Israel, and he gave them over to plunderers, who plundered them. And he sold them into the hand of their surrounding enemies, so that they could no longer withstand their enemies. 15 Whenever they marched out, the hand of the LORD was against them for harm, as the LORD had warned, and as the LORD had sworn to them. And they were in terrible distress.

The LORD Raises Up Judges

16 Then the LORD raised up judges, who saved them out of the hand of those who plundered them. 17 Yet they did not listen to their judges, for they whored after other gods and bowed down to them. They soon turned aside from the way in which their fathers had walked, who had obeyed the commandments of the LORD, and they did not do so. 18 Whenever the LORD raised up judges for them, the LORD was with the judge, and he saved them from the hand of their enemies all the days of the judge. For the LORD was moved to pity by their groaning because of those who afflicted and oppressed them. 19 But whenever the judge died, they turned back and were more corrupt than their fathers, going after other gods, serving them and bowing down to them. They did not drop any of their practices or their stubborn ways. 20 So the anger of the LORD was kindled against Israel, and he said, "Because this people has transgressed my covenant that I commanded their fathers and have not obeyed my voice, 21 I will no longer drive out before them any of the nations that Joshua left when he died, 22 in order to test Israel by them, whether they will take care to walk in the way of the LORD as their fathers did, or not." 23 So the LORD left those nations, not driving them out quickly, and he did not give them into the hand of Joshua.

3 Now these are the nations that the LORD left, to test Israel by them, that is, all in Israel who had not experienced all the wars in Canaan. 2 It was only in order that the generations of the people of Israel might know war, to teach war to those who had not known it before. 3 These are the nations: the five lords of the Philistines and all the Canaanites and the Sidonians and the Hivites who lived on Mount Lebanon, from Mount Baal-hermon as far as Lebo-hamath. 4 They were for the testing of Israel, to know whether Israel would obey the commandments of the LORD, which he commanded their fathers by the hand of Moses. 5 So the people of Israel lived among the Canaanites, the Hittites, the Amorites, the Perizzites, the Hivites, and the Jebusites. 6 And their daughters they took to themselves for wives, and their own daughters they gave to their sons, and they served their gods.

Othniel

7 And the people of Israel did what was evil in the sight of the LORD. They forgot the LORD their God and served the Baals and the Asheroth. 8 Therefore the anger of the LORD was kindled against Israel, and he sold them into the hand of Cushan-rishathaim king of Mesopotamia. And the people of Israel served Cushan-rishathaim eight years. 9 But when the people of Israel cried out to the LORD, the LORD raised up a deliverer for the people of Israel, who saved them, Othniel the son of Kenaz, Caleb's younger brother. 10 The Spirit of the LORD was upon him, and he judged Israel. He went out to war, and the LORD gave Cushan-rishathaim king of Mesopotamia into his hand. And his hand prevailed over Cushan-rishathaim. 11 So the land had rest forty years. Then Othniel the son of Kenaz died.

Ehud

12 And the people of Israel again did what was evil in the sight of the LORD, and the LORD strengthened Eglon the king of Moab against Israel, because they had done what was evil in the sight of the LORD. 13 He gathered to himself the Ammonites and the Amalekites, and went and defeated Israel. And they took possession of the city of palms. 14 And the people of Israel served Eglon the king of Moab eighteen years.

15 Then the people of Israel cried out to the LORD, and the LORD raised up for them a deliverer, Ehud, the son of Gera, the Benjaminite, a left-handed man. The people of Israel sent tribute by him to Eglon the king of Moab. 16 And Ehud made for himself a sword with two edges, a cubit[1] in length, and he bound it on his right thigh under his clothes. 17 And he presented the tribute to Eglon king of Moab. Now Eglon was a very fat man. 18 And when Ehud had finished presenting the tribute, he sent away the people who carried the tribute. 19 But he himself turned back at the idols near Gilgal and said, "I have a secret message for you, O king." And he commanded, "Silence." And all his attendants went out from his presence. 20 And Ehud came to him as he was sitting alone in his cool roof chamber. And Ehud said, "I have a message from God for you." And he arose from his seat. 21 And Ehud reached with his left hand, took the sword from his right thigh, and thrust it into his belly. 22 And the hilt also went in after the blade, and the fat closed over the blade, for he did not pull the sword out of his belly; and the dung came out. 23 Then Ehud went out into the porch[2] and closed the doors of the roof chamber behind him and locked them.

24 When he had gone, the servants came, and when they saw that the doors of the roof chamber were locked, they thought, "Surely he is relieving himself in the closet of the cool chamber." 25 And they waited till they were embarrassed. But when he still did not open the doors of the roof chamber, they took the key and opened them, and there lay their lord dead on the floor.

26 Ehud escaped while they delayed, and he passed beyond the idols and escaped to Seirah. 27 When he arrived, he sounded the trumpet in the hill country of Ephraim. Then the people of Israel went down with him from the hill country, and he was their leader. 28 And he said to them, "Follow after me, for the LORD has given your enemies the Moabites into your hand." So they went down after him and seized the fords of the Jordan against the Moabites and did not allow anyone to pass over. 29 And they killed at that time about 10,000 of the Moabites, all strong, able-bodied men; not a man escaped. 30 So Moab was subdued that day under the hand of Israel. And the land had rest for eighty years.

Shamgar

31 After him was Shamgar the son of Anath, who killed 600 of the Philistines with an oxgoad, and he also saved Israel.

Deborah and Barak

389

4 And the people of Israel again did what was evil in the sight of the LORD after Ehud died. 2 And the LORD sold them into the hand of Jabin king of Canaan, who reigned in Hazor. The commander of his army was Sisera, who lived in Harosheth-hagoyim. 3 Then the people of Israel cried out to the LORD for help, for he had 900 chariots of iron and he oppressed the people of Israel cruelly for twenty years.

4 Now Deborah, a prophetess, the wife of Lappidoth, was judging Israel at that time. 5 She used to sit under the palm of Deborah between Ramah and Bethel in the hill country of Ephraim, and the people of Israel came up to her for judgment. 6 She sent and summoned Barak the son of Abinoam from Kedesh-naphtali and said to

[1] A *cubit* was about 18 inches or 45 centimeters [2] The meaning of the Hebrew word is uncertain

him, "Has not the LORD, the God of Israel,
commanded you, 'Go, gather your men at
Mount Tabor, taking 10,000 from the peo-
ple of Naphtali and the people of Zebulun.
7 And I will draw out Sisera, the general
of Jabin's army, to meet you by the river
Kishon with his chariots and his troops,
and I will give him into your hand'?" 8 Barak
said to her, "If you will go with me, I will
go, but if you will not go with me, I will not
go." 9 And she said, "I will surely go with
you. Nevertheless, the road on which you
are going will not lead to your glory, for
the LORD will sell Sisera into the hand of
a woman." Then Deborah arose and went
with Barak to Kedesh. 10 And Barak called
out Zebulun and Naphtali to Kedesh. And
10,000 men went up at his heels, and
Deborah went up with him.

11 Now Heber the Kenite had separated
from the Kenites, the descendants of
Hobab the father-in-law of Moses, and
had pitched his tent as far away as the oak
in Zaanannim, which is near Kedesh.

12 When Sisera was told that Barak the
son of Abinoam had gone up to Mount
Tabor, 13 Sisera called out all his chariots,
900 chariots of iron, and all the men who
were with him, from Harosheth-hagoyim
to the river Kishon. 14 And Deborah said
to Barak, "Up! For this is the day in which
the LORD has given Sisera into your hand.
Does not the LORD go out before you?" So
Barak went down from Mount Tabor with
10,000 men following him. 15 And the
LORD routed Sisera and all his chariots
and all his army before Barak by the edge
of the sword. And Sisera got down from
his chariot and fled away on foot. 16 And
Barak pursued the chariots and the army
to Harosheth-hagoyim, and all the army
of Sisera fell by the edge of the sword; not
a man was left.

17 But Sisera fled away on foot to the tent
of Jael, the wife of Heber the Kenite, for
there was peace between Jabin the king of
Hazor and the house of Heber the Kenite.
18 And Jael came out to meet Sisera and said
to him, "Turn aside, my lord; turn aside to
me; do not be afraid." So he turned aside to
her into the tent, and she covered him with
a rug. 19 And he said to her, "Please give me
a little water to drink, for I am thirsty." So
she opened a skin of milk and gave him a
drink and covered him. 20 And he said to
her, "Stand at the opening of the tent, and
if any man comes and asks you, 'Is any-
one here?' say, 'No.'" 21 But Jael the wife of
Heber took a tent peg, and took a hammer
in her hand. Then she went softly to him
and drove the peg into his temple until it
went down into the ground while he was
lying fast asleep from weariness. So he

CHARACTER PROFILE

DEBORAH

Deborah was a judge in Israel. Israelites came to her with their problems and she helped them know what to do. God gave Deborah a message for a man named Barak. God wanted Barak to go fight the soldiers of the king who had been troubling the Israelites. Deborah and Barak went together, and God gave them victory. Then Deborah and Barak sang a song praising God for the victory.

389

died. 22 And behold, as Barak was pursuing
Sisera, Jael went out to meet him and said
to him, "Come, and I will show you the
man whom you are seeking." So he went
in to her tent, and there lay Sisera dead,
with the tent peg in his temple.

23 So on that day God subdued Jabin the
king of Canaan before the people of Israel.
24 And the hand of the people of Israel
pressed harder and harder against Jabin
the king of Canaan, until they destroyed
Jabin king of Canaan.

The Song of Deborah and Barak

5 Then sang Deborah and Barak the son
of Abinoam on that day:

2 "That the leaders took the lead in
Israel,
that the people offered
themselves willingly,
bless the LORD!

3 "Hear, O kings; give ear, O princes;
to the LORD I will sing;
I will make melody to the LORD,
the God of Israel.

4 "LORD, when you went out from Seir,
when you marched from the
region of Edom,
the earth trembled
and the heavens dropped,
yes, the clouds dropped water.
5 The mountains quaked before the
LORD,
even Sinai before the LORD, the
God of Israel.

6 "In the days of Shamgar, son of Anath,
in the days of Jael, the highways
were abandoned,
and travelers kept to the byways.
7 The villagers ceased in Israel;
they ceased to be until I arose;
I, Deborah, arose as a mother in
Israel.
8 When new gods were chosen,
then war was in the gates.
Was shield or spear to be seen
among forty thousand in Israel?
9 My heart goes out to the
commanders of Israel
who offered themselves willingly
among the people.
Bless the LORD.

10 "Tell of it, you who ride on white
donkeys,
you who sit on rich carpets[1]
and you who walk by the way.
11 To the sound of musicians[2] at the
watering places,
there they repeat the righteous
triumphs of the LORD,
the righteous triumphs of his
villagers in Israel.

"Then down to the gates marched
the people of the LORD.

12 "Awake, awake, Deborah!
Awake, awake, break out in a song!
Arise, Barak, lead away your captives,
O son of Abinoam.
13 Then down marched the remnant
of the noble;
the people of the LORD marched
down for me against the
mighty.
14 From Ephraim their root they
marched down into the valley,[3]
following you, Benjamin, with
your kinsmen;
from Machir marched down the
commanders,
and from Zebulun those who bear
the lieutenant's[4] staff;
15 the princes of Issachar came with
Deborah,
and Issachar faithful to Barak;
into the valley they rushed at his
heels.
Among the clans of Reuben
there were great searchings of heart.
16 Why did you sit still among the
sheepfolds,

[1] The meaning of the Hebrew word is uncertain; it may connote *saddle blankets* [2] Or *archers*; the meaning of the Hebrew word is uncertain [3] Septuagint; Hebrew *in Amalek* [4] Hebrew *commander's*

Deborah's Message From God

After many years of living in the Promised Land, the people of Israel forgot about God. They stopped loving Him and didn't follow His commandments. And they did evil in the sight of the Lord. So God allowed an enemy king named Jabin to have power over His people. Jabin would not allow the Israelites to live in peace. Instead he bullied them and caused them great trouble.

After 20 years of living under the mean King Jabin, the people of Israel cried out to God for help. God listened to their prayers and sent them help through a judge named Deborah. Every day Deborah sat near a palm tree in the desert and helped the people of Israel with their problems.

God told Deborah exactly what to do. So Deborah went to a man named Barak and gave him the message she had received from God. She told him that God was commanding him to gather an army of fighting men from Israel and to fight against Sisera, the leader of Jabin's army. Deborah told Barak that God promised him the victory.

"If you will go with me, I will go," Barak told Deborah, "but if you will not go with me, I will not go." Deborah agreed, and together, they went to Mount Tabor with 10,000 men. When Sisera, the leader of Jabin's army, discovered where the Israelites were going, he gathered his army together and went out to battle Barak and the Israelite army. Compared to the Israelites, Jabin's army was a great and powerful army, with 900 iron chariots!

Deborah saw Sisera's powerful army with all his chariots, but Deborah trusted God. She said, "Up! For this is the day in which the LORD has given Sisera into your hand. Does not the LORD go out before you?"

Barak and his men charged down the mountain. The Lord caused Jabin's army to run away in panic—and Barak's army won a great victory. The Israelites rejoiced! No more trouble from King Jabin! Deborah and Barak sang a song to praise God for helping them.

God saved His people from the enemy king. God sent Jesus to save us from our enemies too. Jesus won the battle for us over our greatest enemies—sin, death, and the devil—when He died on the cross for us and rose again. We sing God's praises, too, for His great victory, and for His love and forgiveness!

SEEK and FIND

WHERE TO FIND THE STORY

Judges 4–5

KEY BIBLE VERSE

"Blessed be the Lord God of Israel,
for he has visited and redeemed his people
. . . that we should be saved from our enemies
and from the hand of all who hate us. . . ."
(Luke 1:68, 71)

THREE KEY QUESTIONS

- Why was Barak afraid to go fight Jabin's army and to save

the people of Israel?

- What happened when Barak's army came charging down the mountain to attack Jabin's powerful army with its 900 iron chariots? How did they do this?
- What are the great enemies that Jesus defeated for us on the cross? How should we respond to God's great victory for us?

RELATED BIBLE READINGS

Psalm 83:9–12; Hebrews 11:32–34

to hear the whistling for the flocks?
Among the clans of Reuben
there were great searchings of heart.
17 Gilead stayed beyond the Jordan;
and Dan, why did he stay with the ships?
Asher sat still at the coast of the sea,
staying by his landings.
18 Zebulun is a people who risked their lives to the death;
Naphtali, too, on the heights of the field.
19 "The kings came, they fought;
then fought the kings of Canaan,
at Taanach, by the waters of Megiddo;
they got no spoils of silver.
20 From heaven the stars fought,
from their courses they fought against Sisera.
21 The torrent Kishon swept them away,
the ancient torrent, the torrent Kishon.
March on, my soul, with might!
22 "Then loud beat the horses' hoofs
with the galloping, galloping of his steeds.
23 "Curse Meroz, says the angel of the LORD,
curse its inhabitants thoroughly,
because they did not come to the help of the LORD,
to the help of the LORD against the mighty.
24 "Most blessed of women be Jael,
the wife of Heber the Kenite,
of tent-dwelling women most blessed.
25 He asked water and she gave him milk;
she brought him curds in a noble's bowl.
26 She sent her hand to the tent peg
and her right hand to the workmen's mallet;
she struck Sisera;
she crushed his head;
she shattered and pierced his temple.
27 Between her feet
he sank, he fell, he lay still;
between her feet
he sank, he fell;
where he sank,
there he fell—dead.
28 "Out of the window she peered,
the mother of Sisera wailed through the lattice:
'Why is his chariot so long in coming?

Why tarry the hoofbeats of his
chariots?'
29 Her wisest princesses answer,
indeed, she answers herself,
30 'Have they not found and divided
the spoil?—
A womb or two for every man;
spoil of dyed materials for Sisera,
spoil of dyed materials
embroidered,
two pieces of dyed work
embroidered for the neck as
spoil?'

31 "So may all your enemies perish,
O LORD!
But your friends be like the sun as
he rises in his might."

And the land had rest for forty years.

Midian Oppresses Israel

397
6 The people of Israel did what
was evil in the sight of the
LORD, and the LORD gave them into
the hand of Midian seven years. 2 And the
hand of Midian overpowered Israel, and
because of Midian the people of Israel
made for themselves the dens that are in
the mountains and the caves and the
strongholds. 3 For whenever the Israelites
planted crops, the Midianites and the
Amalekites and the people of the East
would come up against them. 4 They
would encamp against them and devour
the produce of the land, as far as Gaza, and
leave no sustenance in Israel and no sheep
or ox or donkey. 5 For they would come up
with their livestock and their tents; they
would come like locusts in number—both
they and their camels could not be
counted—so that they laid waste the land
as they came in. 6 And Israel was brought
very low because of Midian. And the peo-
ple of Israel cried out for help to the LORD.

7 When the people of Israel cried out to
the LORD on account of the Midianites,
8 the LORD sent a prophet to the people of
Israel. And he said to them, "Thus says the
LORD, the God of Israel: I led you up from
Egypt and brought you out of the house
of bondage. 9 And I delivered you from the
hand of the Egyptians and from the hand
of all who oppressed you, and drove them
out before you and gave you their land.
10 And I said to you, 'I am the LORD your
God; you shall not fear the gods of the
Amorites in whose land you dwell.' But
you have not obeyed my voice."

The Call of Gideon

11 Now the angel of the LORD came and
sat under the terebinth at Ophrah, which
belonged to Joash the Abiezrite, while his
son Gideon was beating out wheat in the
winepress to hide it from the Midianites.
12 And the angel of the LORD appeared to
him and said to him, "The LORD is with
you, O mighty man of valor." 13 And Gideon
said to him, "Please, sir,[1] if the LORD is
with us, why then has all this happened to
us? And where are all his wonderful deeds
that our fathers recounted to us, saying,
'Did not the LORD bring us up from Egypt?'
But now the LORD has forsaken us and
given us into the hand of Midian." 14 And
the LORD[2] turned to him and said, "Go in
this might of yours and save Israel from
the hand of Midian; do not I send you?"
15 And he said to him, "Please, Lord, how
can I save Israel? Behold, my clan is the
weakest in Manasseh, and I am the least in
my father's house." 16 And the LORD said to
him, "But I will be with you, and you shall
strike the Midianites as one man." 17 And
he said to him, "If now I have found favor
in your eyes, then show me a sign that it
is you who speak with me. 18 Please do not
depart from here until I come to you and
bring out my present and set it before you."
And he said, "I will stay till you return."

19 So Gideon went into his house and
prepared a young goat and unleavened
cakes from an ephah[3] of flour. The meat
he put in a basket, and the broth he put

[1] Or *Please, my Lord* [2] Septuagint *the angel of the LORD*; also verse 16 [3] An *ephah* was about 3/5 bushel or 22 liters

in a pot, and brought them to him under
the terebinth and presented them. 20 And
the angel of God said to him, "Take the
meat and the unleavened cakes, and put
them on this rock, and pour the broth over
them." And he did so. 21 Then the angel of
the LORD reached out the tip of the staff
that was in his hand and touched the meat
and the unleavened cakes. And fire sprang
up from the rock and consumed the meat
and the unleavened cakes. And the angel
of the LORD vanished from his sight.
22 Then Gideon perceived that he was the
angel of the LORD. And Gideon said, "Alas,
O Lord GOD! For now I have seen the angel
of the LORD face to face." 23 But the LORD
said to him, "Peace be to you. Do not fear;
you shall not die." 24 Then Gideon built an
altar there to the LORD and called it, The
LORD Is Peace. To this day it still stands at
Ophrah, which belongs to the Abiezrites.
25 That night the LORD said to him,
"Take your father's bull, and the second
bull seven years old, and pull down the
altar of Baal that your father has, and cut
down the Asherah that is beside it 26 and
build an altar to the LORD your God on the
top of the stronghold here, with stones
laid in due order. Then take the second
bull and offer it as a burnt offering with
the wood of the Asherah that you shall
cut down." 27 So Gideon took ten men of
his servants and did as the LORD had told
him. But because he was too afraid of his
family and the men of the town to do it by
day, he did it by night.

Gideon Destroys the Altar of Baal

28 When the men of the town rose early
in the morning, behold, the altar of Baal
was broken down, and the Asherah beside
it was cut down, and the second bull was
offered on the altar that had been built.
29 And they said to one another, "Who
has done this thing?" And after they had
searched and inquired, they said, "Gideon
the son of Joash has done this thing."
30 Then the men of the town said to Joash,
"Bring out your son, that he may die, for
he has broken down the altar of Baal and
cut down the Asherah beside it." 31 But
Joash said to all who stood against him,
"Will you contend for Baal? Or will you
save him? Whoever contends for him shall
be put to death by morning. If he is a god,
let him contend for himself, because his
altar has been broken down." 32 Therefore
on that day Gideon[1] was called Jerubbaal,
that is to say, "Let Baal contend against
him," because he broke down his altar.
33 Now all the Midianites and the
Amalekites and the people of the East

CHARACTER PROFILE

GIDEON

Gideon was afraid of the powerful and cruel raiders from Midian, who stole crops and food from the Israelites. God chose Gideon to fight the Midianites. Gideon had to see God do several miracles first. Finally, Gideon believed God and obeyed Him. God told Gideon that he must only have a very small army. But God gave Gideon and his small army a great victory over thousands of Midianite soldiers.

397

[1] Hebrew *he*

came together, and they crossed the
Jordan and encamped in the Valley of
Jezreel. 34 But the Spirit of the LORD
clothed Gideon, and he sounded the
trumpet, and the Abiezrites were called
out to follow him. 35 And he sent messen-
gers throughout all Manasseh, and they
too were called out to follow him. And he
sent messengers to Asher, Zebulun, and
Naphtali, and they went up to meet them.

The Sign of the Fleece

36 Then Gideon said to God, "If you will
save Israel by my hand, as you have said,
37 behold, I am laying a fleece of wool on
the threshing floor. If there is dew on the
fleece alone, and it is dry on all the ground,
then I shall know that you will save Israel
by my hand, as you have said." 38 And it
was so. When he rose early next morning
and squeezed the fleece, he wrung enough
dew from the fleece to fill a bowl with
water. 39 Then Gideon said to God, "Let not
your anger burn against me; let me speak
just once more. Please let me test just once
more with the fleece. Please let it be dry on
the fleece only, and on all the ground let
there be dew." 40 And God did so that night;
and it was dry on the fleece only, and on
all the ground there was dew.

Gideon's Three Hundred Men

7 Then Jerubbaal (that is, Gideon) and
all the people who were with him rose
early and encamped beside the spring of
Harod. And the camp of Midian was north
of them, by the hill of Moreh, in the valley.

2 The LORD said to Gideon, "The peo-
ple with you are too many for me to
give the Midianites into their hand, lest
Israel boast over me, saying, 'My own
hand has saved me.' 3 Now therefore pro-
claim in the ears of the people, saying,
'Whoever is fearful and trembling, let
him return home and hurry away from
Mount Gilead.'" Then 22,000 of the people
returned, and 10,000 remained.

4 And the LORD said to Gideon, "The
people are still too many. Take them down
to the water, and I will test them for you
there, and anyone of whom I say to you,
'This one shall go with you,' shall go with
you, and anyone of whom I say to you,
'This one shall not go with you,' shall not
go." 5 So he brought the people down to
the water. And the LORD said to Gideon,
"Every one who laps the water with his
tongue, as a dog laps, you shall set by
himself. Likewise, every one who kneels
down to drink." 6 And the number of those
who lapped, putting their hands to their
mouths, was 300 men, but all the rest of
the people knelt down to drink water.
7 And the LORD said to Gideon, "With the
300 men who lapped I will save you and
give the Midianites into your hand, and let
all the others go every man to his home."
8 So the people took provisions in their
hands, and their trumpets. And he sent
all the rest of Israel every man to his tent,
but retained the 300 men. And the camp
of Midian was below him in the valley.

9 That same night the LORD said to him,
"Arise, go down against the camp, for I
have given it into your hand. 10 But if you
are afraid to go down, go down to the camp
with Purah your servant. 11 And you shall
hear what they say, and afterward your
hands shall be strengthened to go down
against the camp." Then he went down
with Purah his servant to the outposts of
the armed men who were in the camp.
12 And the Midianites and the Amalekites
and all the people of the East lay along
the valley like locusts in abundance, and
their camels were without number, as
the sand that is on the seashore in abun-
dance. 13 When Gideon came, behold, a
man was telling a dream to his comrade.
And he said, "Behold, I dreamed a dream,
and behold, a cake of barley bread tumbled
into the camp of Midian and came to the
tent and struck it so that it fell and turned
it upside down, so that the tent lay flat."
14 And his comrade answered, "This is no

other than the sword of Gideon the son of Joash, a man of Israel; God has given into his hand Midian and all the camp."

15 As soon as Gideon heard the telling of the dream and its interpretation, he worshiped. And he returned to the camp of Israel and said, "Arise, for the LORD has given the host of Midian into your hand." 16 And he divided the 300 men into three companies and put trumpets into the hands of all of them and empty jars, with torches inside the jars. 17 And he said to them, "Look at me, and do likewise. When I come to the outskirts of the camp, do as I do. 18 When I blow the trumpet, I and all who are with me, then blow the trumpets also on every side of all the camp and shout, 'For the LORD and for Gideon.'"

Gideon Defeats Midian

19 So Gideon and the hundred men who were with him came to the outskirts of the camp at the beginning of the middle watch, when they had just set the watch. And they blew the trumpets and smashed the jars that were in their hands. 20 Then the three companies blew the trumpets and broke the jars. They held in their left hands the torches, and in their right hands the trumpets to blow. And they cried out, "A sword for the LORD and for Gideon!" 21 Every man stood in his place around the camp, and all the army ran. They cried out and fled. 22 When they blew the 300 trumpets, the LORD set every man's sword against his comrade and against all the army. And the army fled as far as Beth-shittah toward Zererah,[1] as far as the border of Abel-meholah, by Tabbath. 23 And the men of Israel were called out from Naphtali and from Asher and from all Manasseh, and they pursued after Midian.

24 Gideon sent messengers throughout all the hill country of Ephraim, saying, "Come down against the Midianites and capture the waters against them, as far as Beth-barah, and also the Jordan." So all the men of Ephraim were called out, and they captured the waters as far as Beth-barah, and also the Jordan. 25 And they captured the two princes of Midian, Oreb and Zeeb. They killed Oreb at the rock of Oreb, and Zeeb they killed at the winepress of Zeeb. Then they pursued Midian, and they brought the heads of Oreb and Zeeb to Gideon across the Jordan.

Gideon Defeats Zebah and Zalmunna

8 Then the men of Ephraim said to him, "What is this that you have done to us, not to call us when you went to fight against Midian?" And they accused him fiercely. 2 And he said to them, "What have I done now in comparison with you? Is not the gleaning of the grapes of Ephraim better than the grape harvest of Abiezer? 3 God has given into your hands the princes of Midian, Oreb and Zeeb. What have I been able to do in comparison with you?" Then their anger[2] against him subsided when he said this.

4 And Gideon came to the Jordan and crossed over, he and the 300 men who were with him, exhausted yet pursuing. 5 So he said to the men of Succoth, "Please give loaves of bread to the people who follow me, for they are exhausted, and I am pursuing after Zebah and Zalmunna, the kings of Midian." 6 And the officials of Succoth said, "Are the hands of Zebah and Zalmunna already in your hand, that we should give bread to your army?" 7 So Gideon said, "Well then, when the LORD has given Zebah and Zalmunna into my hand, I will flail your flesh with the thorns of the wilderness and with briers." 8 And from there he went up to Penuel, and spoke to them in the same way, and the men of Penuel answered him as the men of Succoth had answered. 9 And he said to the men of Penuel, "When I come again in peace, I will break down this tower."

10 Now Zebah and Zalmunna were in Karkor with their army, about 15,000

[1] Some Hebrew manuscripts *Zeredah* [2] Hebrew *their spirit*

Gideon's Amazing Little Army

While the people of Israel were living in the Promised Land, they again forgot about God and His love for them. They began to worship false gods and idols, instead of the one true God. So the Lord made their enemies, the Midianites, stronger than the Israelites. The Midianites came often into Israel, and stole the crops the Israelites had planted. They stole their sheep, cows, and donkeys. The people of Israel were so afraid of their enemies that they hid in caves. Then they remembered God and cried out to Him for help.

God answered their prayers. He sent an angel to tell a man named Gideon that God was with His people and that He had chosen Gideon to lead an army to fight the Midianites. At first, Gideon was afraid. But God gave him special miraculous signs, making it clear to Gideon that God could do anything. God could even use Gideon to fight the Midianites. Then Gideon trusted God.

The Midianites had many more soldiers than Gideon had. But God said to Gideon, "The people with you are too many." When God defeated the Midianites for Israel, He did not want the Israelites to think they had won their own battle with their great army. So God told Gideon that everyone who was afraid of fighting should go home. More men went home than stayed to fight!

Then God said to Gideon, "The people are still too many. Take them down to the water, and I will test them for you there." So Gideon brought the Israelite army down to the water, so that each of the men could get a drink. Along the edge of the river, God said to Gideon, "Every one who laps the water with his tongue, as a dog laps, you shall set by himself. Likewise, every one who kneels down to drink." The number of men who lapped their water like a dog was 300. And the Lord said to Gideon, "With the 300 men who lapped I will save you and give the Midianites into your hand, and let all the others go every man to his home."

In the middle of the night, Gideon gave each of his 300 soldiers a trumpet to hold in one hand and a clay pot with a torch inside to hold in the other hand. Gideon and his army took their position around the enemy's camp. At just the right time, Gideon gave the signal. The men blew the trumpets. They smashed the pots. The torches blazed. The army of Israel cried out, "A sword for the LORD and for Gideon!"

The Midianite army was so afraid and so surprised that they began to fight each other instead of fighting the army of Israel. Many Midianites died fighting each other, and the rest ran far away as fast as they could.

God did not forget His people Israel, even though they had sinned greatly against God. When they cried out for help to the Lord, God chose Gideon and used him to save His people from their enemies. God loves us and saves us too. He sent Jesus for us even though we have sinned against Him. Jesus fought the devil for us and took away our sins on the cross, so that we can have peace with God—and one day live with Him forever in heaven.

SEEK and FIND

WHERE THE STORY IS FOUND

Judges 6:1–8:21

KEY BIBLE VERSE

"But God shows his love for us in that while we were still sinners, Christ died for us." (Romans 5:8)

THREE KEY QUESTIONS

- Why did God allow the Midianites to steal the Israelites' food and animals?
- Why did God want Gideon to have a very small army?
- What did the Israelites do when they were in great trouble with the Midianites? What should we do when we are in trouble?

RELATED BIBLE READINGS

Psalm 83:9–12; Hebrews 11:32–34

men, all who were left of all the army of
the people of the East, for there had fallen
120,000 men who drew the sword. 11 And
Gideon went up by the way of the tent
dwellers east of Nobah and Jogbehah and
attacked the army, for the army felt secure.
12 And Zebah and Zalmunna fled, and he
pursued them and captured the two kings
of Midian, Zebah and Zalmunna, and he
threw all the army into a panic.
13 Then Gideon the son of Joash
returned from the battle by the ascent of
Heres. 14 And he captured a young man
of Succoth and questioned him. And he
wrote down for him the officials and
elders of Succoth, seventy-seven men.
15 And he came to the men of Succoth
and said, "Behold Zebah and Zalmunna,
about whom you taunted me, saying, 'Are
the hands of Zebah and Zalmunna already
in your hand, that we should give bread
to your men who are exhausted?'" 16 And
he took the elders of the city, and he took
thorns of the wilderness and briers and
with them taught the men of Succoth a
lesson. 17 And he broke down the tower of
Penuel and killed the men of the city.
18 Then he said to Zebah and Zalmunna,
"Where are the men whom you killed at
Tabor?" They answered, "As you are, so
were they. Every one of them resembled
the son of a king." 19 And he said, "They
were my brothers, the sons of my mother.
As the LORD lives, if you had saved them
alive, I would not kill you." 20 So he said to
Jether his firstborn, "Rise and kill them!"
But the young man did not draw his sword,
for he was afraid, because he was still a
young man. 21 Then Zebah and Zalmunna
said, "Rise yourself and fall upon us, for as
the man is, so is his strength." And Gideon
arose and killed Zebah and Zalmunna, and
he took the crescent ornaments that were
on the necks of their camels.

Gideon's Ephod

22 Then the men of Israel said to Gideon, "Rule over us, you and your son and your grandson also, for you have saved us from the hand of Midian." 23 Gideon said to them, "I will not rule over you, and my son will not rule over you; the LORD will rule over you." 24 And Gideon said to them, "Let me make a request of you: every one of you give me the earrings from his spoil." (For they had golden earrings, because they were Ishmaelites.) 25 And they answered, "We will willingly give them." And they spread a cloak, and every man threw in it the earrings of his spoil. 26 And the weight of the golden earrings that he requested was 1,700 shekels[1] of gold, besides the crescent ornaments and the pendants and the purple garments worn by the kings of Midian, and besides the collars that were around the necks of their camels. 27 And Gideon made an ephod of it and put it in his city, in Ophrah. And all Israel whored after it there, and it became a snare to Gideon and to his family. 28 So Midian was subdued before the people of Israel, and they raised their heads no more. And the land had rest forty years in the days of Gideon.

The Death of Gideon

29 Jerubbaal the son of Joash went and lived in his own house. 30 Now Gideon had seventy sons, his own offspring,[2] for he had many wives. 31 And his concubine who was in Shechem also bore him a son, and he called his name Abimelech. 32 And Gideon the son of Joash died in a good old age and was buried in the tomb of Joash his father, at Ophrah of the Abiezrites.

33 As soon as Gideon died, the people of Israel turned again and whored after the Baals and made Baal-berith their god. 34 And the people of Israel did not remember the LORD their God, who had delivered them from the hand of all their enemies on every side, 35 and they did not show steadfast love to the family of Jerubbaal (that is, Gideon) in return for all the good that he had done to Israel.

Abimelech's Conspiracy

9 Now Abimelech the son of Jerubbaal went to Shechem to his mother's relatives and said to them and to the whole clan of his mother's family, 2 "Say in the ears of all the leaders of Shechem, 'Which is better for you, that all seventy of the sons of Jerubbaal rule over you, or that one rule over you?' Remember also that I am your bone and your flesh."

3 And his mother's relatives spoke all these words on his behalf in the ears of all the leaders of Shechem, and their hearts inclined to follow Abimelech, for they said, "He is our brother." 4 And they gave him seventy pieces of silver out of the house of Baal-berith with which Abimelech hired worthless and reckless fellows, who followed him. 5 And he went to his father's house at Ophrah and killed his brothers the sons of Jerubbaal, seventy men, on one stone. But Jotham the youngest son of Jerubbaal was left, for he hid himself. 6 And all the leaders of Shechem came together, and all Beth-millo, and they went and made Abimelech king, by the oak of the pillar at Shechem.

7 When it was told to Jotham, he went and stood on top of Mount Gerizim and cried aloud and said to them, "Listen to me, you leaders of Shechem, that God may listen to you. 8 The trees once went out to anoint a king over them, and they said to the olive tree, 'Reign over us.' 9 But the olive tree said to them, 'Shall I leave my abundance, by which gods and men are honored, and go hold sway over the trees?' 10 And the trees said to the fig tree, 'You come and reign over us.' 11 But the fig tree said to them, 'Shall I leave my sweetness and my good fruit and go hold sway over the trees?' 12 And the trees said to the vine, 'You come and reign over us.' 13 But

[1] A *shekel* was about 2/5 ounce or 11 grams [2] Hebrew *who came from his own loins*

the vine said to them, 'Shall I leave my wine
that cheers God and men and go hold sway
over the trees?' 14 Then all the trees said
to the bramble, 'You come and reign over
us.' 15 And the bramble said to the trees, 'If
in good faith you are anointing me king
over you, then come and take refuge in my
shade, but if not, let fire come out of the
bramble and devour the cedars of Lebanon.'

16 "Now therefore, if you acted in
good faith and integrity when you made
Abimelech king, and if you have dealt well
with Jerubbaal and his house and have
done to him as his deeds deserved— 17 for
my father fought for you and risked his
life and delivered you from the hand of
Midian, 18 and you have risen up against
my father's house this day and have killed
his sons, seventy men on one stone, and
have made Abimelech, the son of his
female servant, king over the leaders of
Shechem, because he is your relative—
19 if you then have acted in good faith
and integrity with Jerubbaal and with his
house this day, then rejoice in Abimelech,
and let him also rejoice in you. 20 But if
not, let fire come out from Abimelech
and devour the leaders of Shechem and
Beth-millo; and let fire come out from the
leaders of Shechem and from Beth-millo
and devour Abimelech." 21 And Jotham ran
away and fled and went to Beer and lived
there, because of Abimelech his brother.

The Downfall of Abimelech

22 Abimelech ruled over Israel three
years. 23 And God sent an evil spirit
between Abimelech and the leaders of
Shechem, and the leaders of Shechem
dealt treacherously with Abimelech,
24 that the violence done to the seventy
sons of Jerubbaal might come, and their
blood be laid on Abimelech their brother,
who killed them, and on the men of
Shechem, who strengthened his hands
to kill his brothers. 25 And the leaders of
Shechem put men in ambush against him
on the mountaintops, and they robbed all
who passed by them along that way. And
it was told to Abimelech.

26 And Gaal the son of Ebed moved
into Shechem with his relatives, and the
leaders of Shechem put confidence in
him. 27 And they went out into the field
and gathered the grapes from their vine-
yards and trod them and held a festival;
and they went into the house of their god
and ate and drank and reviled Abimelech.
28 And Gaal the son of Ebed said, "Who is
Abimelech, and who are we of Shechem,
that we should serve him? Is he not the
son of Jerubbaal, and is not Zebul his offi-
cer? Serve the men of Hamor the father of
Shechem; but why should we serve him?
29 Would that this people were under my
hand! Then I would remove Abimelech.
I would say[1] to Abimelech, 'Increase your
army, and come out.'"

30 When Zebul the ruler of the city heard
the words of Gaal the son of Ebed, his
anger was kindled. 31 And he sent mes-
sengers to Abimelech secretly,[2] saying,
"Behold, Gaal the son of Ebed and his rela-
tives have come to Shechem, and they are
stirring up[3] the city against you. 32 Now
therefore, go by night, you and the people
who are with you, and set an ambush in
the field. 33 Then in the morning, as soon
as the sun is up, rise early and rush upon
the city. And when he and the people who
are with him come out against you, you
may do to them as your hand finds to do."
34 So Abimelech and all the men who
were with him rose up by night and set an
ambush against Shechem in four compa-
nies. 35 And Gaal the son of Ebed went out
and stood in the entrance of the gate of the
city, and Abimelech and the people who
were with him rose from the ambush.
36 And when Gaal saw the people, he said
to Zebul, "Look, people are coming down
from the mountaintops!" And Zebul said
to him, "You mistake[4] the shadow of the
mountains for men." 37 Gaal spoke again

[1] Septuagint; Hebrew *and he said* [2] Or *at Tormah* [3] Hebrew *besieging, or closing up* [4] Hebrew *You see*

and said, "Look, people are coming down
from the center of the land, and one com-
pany is coming from the direction of the
Diviners' Oak." 38 Then Zebul said to him,
"Where is your mouth now, you who said,
'Who is Abimelech, that we should serve
him?' Are not these the people whom
you despised? Go out now and fight with
them." 39 And Gaal went out at the head of
the leaders of Shechem and fought with
Abimelech. 40 And Abimelech chased
him, and he fled before him. And many
fell wounded, up to the entrance of the
gate. 41 And Abimelech lived at Arumah,
and Zebul drove out Gaal and his relatives,
so that they could not dwell at Shechem.

42 On the following day, the people went
out into the field, and Abimelech was
told. 43 He took his people and divided
them into three companies and set an
ambush in the fields. And he looked and
saw the people coming out of the city. So
he rose against them and killed them.
44 Abimelech and the company that was
with him rushed forward and stood at
the entrance of the gate of the city, while
the two companies rushed upon all who
were in the field and killed them. 45 And
Abimelech fought against the city all that
day. He captured the city and killed the
people who were in it, and he razed the
city and sowed it with salt.

46 When all the leaders of the Tower
of Shechem heard of it, they entered the
stronghold of the house of El-berith.
47 Abimelech was told that all the leaders
of the Tower of Shechem were gathered
together. 48 And Abimelech went up to
Mount Zalmon, he and all the people who
were with him. And Abimelech took an
axe in his hand and cut down a bundle
of brushwood and took it up and laid it
on his shoulder. And he said to the men
who were with him, "What you have seen
me do, hurry and do as I have done." 49 So
every one of the people cut down his
bundle and following Abimelech put it
against the stronghold, and they set the
stronghold on fire over them, so that all
the people of the Tower of Shechem also
died, about 1,000 men and women.

50 Then Abimelech went to Thebez and
encamped against Thebez and captured
it. 51 But there was a strong tower within
the city, and all the men and women and
all the leaders of the city fled to it and shut
themselves in, and they went up to the
roof of the tower. 52 And Abimelech came
to the tower and fought against it and drew
near to the door of the tower to burn it
with fire. 53 And a certain woman threw an
upper millstone on Abimelech's head and
crushed his skull. 54 Then he called quickly
to the young man his armor-bearer and
said to him, "Draw your sword and kill me,
lest they say of me, 'A woman killed him.'"
And his young man thrust him through,
and he died. 55 And when the men of Israel
saw that Abimelech was dead, every-
one departed to his home. 56 Thus God
returned the evil of Abimelech, which he
committed against his father in killing his
seventy brothers. 57 And God also made
all the evil of the men of Shechem return
on their heads, and upon them came the
curse of Jotham the son of Jerubbaal.

Tola and Jair

10 After Abimelech there arose to save
Israel Tola the son of Puah, son of
Dodo, a man of Issachar, and he lived at
Shamir in the hill country of Ephraim.
2 And he judged Israel twenty-three years.
Then he died and was buried at Shamir.

3 After him arose Jair the Gileadite, who
judged Israel twenty-two years. 4 And he
had thirty sons who rode on thirty don-
keys, and they had thirty cities, called
Havvoth-jair to this day, which are in the
land of Gilead. 5 And Jair died and was bur-
ied in Kamon.

Further Disobedience and Oppression

6 The people of Israel again did what was
evil in the sight of the LORD and served the

Baals and the Ashtaroth, the gods of Syria,
the gods of Sidon, the gods of Moab, the
gods of the Ammonites, and the gods of
the Philistines. And they forsook the LORD
and did not serve him. 7 So the anger of the
LORD was kindled against Israel, and he
sold them into the hand of the Philistines
and into the hand of the Ammonites, 8 and
they crushed and oppressed the people of
Israel that year. For eighteen years they
oppressed all the people of Israel who
were beyond the Jordan in the land of the
Amorites, which is in Gilead. 9 And the
Ammonites crossed the Jordan to fight
also against Judah and against Benjamin
and against the house of Ephraim, so that
Israel was severely distressed.

10 And the people of Israel cried out to
the LORD, saying, "We have sinned against
you, because we have forsaken our God
and have served the Baals." 11 And the
LORD said to the people of Israel, "Did I
not save you from the Egyptians and from
the Amorites, from the Ammonites and
from the Philistines? 12 The Sidonians
also, and the Amalekites and the Maonites
oppressed you, and you cried out to me,
and I saved you out of their hand. 13 Yet
you have forsaken me and served other
gods; therefore I will save you no more.
14 Go and cry out to the gods whom you
have chosen; let them save you in the
time of your distress." 15 And the people of
Israel said to the LORD, "We have sinned;
do to us whatever seems good to you.
Only please deliver us this day." 16 So they
put away the foreign gods from among
them and served the LORD, and he became
impatient over the misery of Israel.

17 Then the Ammonites were called
to arms, and they encamped in Gilead.
And the people of Israel came together,
and they encamped at Mizpah. 18 And the
people, the leaders of Gilead, said one to
another, "Who is the man who will begin
to fight against the Ammonites? He shall
be head over all the inhabitants of Gilead."

Jephthah Delivers Israel

11 Now Jephthah the Gileadite was
a mighty warrior, but he was the
son of a prostitute. Gilead was the father
of Jephthah. 2 And Gilead's wife also bore
him sons. And when his wife's sons grew
up, they drove Jephthah out and said to
him, "You shall not have an inheritance
in our father's house, for you are the son
of another woman." 3 Then Jephthah fled
from his brothers and lived in the land
of Tob, and worthless fellows collected
around Jephthah and went out with him.

4 After a time the Ammonites made
war against Israel. 5 And when the Am-
monites made war against Israel, the
elders of Gilead went to bring Jephthah
from the land of Tob. 6 And they said to
Jephthah, "Come and be our leader, that
we may fight against the Ammonites."
7 But Jephthah said to the elders of Gilead,
"Did you not hate me and drive me out of
my father's house? Why have you come to
me now when you are in distress?" 8 And
the elders of Gilead said to Jephthah, "That
is why we have turned to you now, that
you may go with us and fight against the
Ammonites and be our head over all the
inhabitants of Gilead." 9 Jephthah said to
the elders of Gilead, "If you bring me home
again to fight against the Ammonites, and
the LORD gives them over to me, I will be
your head." 10 And the elders of Gilead
said to Jephthah, "The LORD will be wit-
ness between us, if we do not do as you
say." 11 So Jephthah went with the elders
of Gilead, and the people made him head
and leader over them. And Jephthah spoke
all his words before the LORD at Mizpah.

12 Then Jephthah sent messengers to the
king of the Ammonites and said, "What do
you have against me, that you have come
to me to fight against my land?" 13 And
the king of the Ammonites answered the
messengers of Jephthah, "Because Israel
on coming up from Egypt took away my
land, from the Arnon to the Jabbok and to

the Jordan; now therefore restore it peaceably." 14 Jephthah again sent messengers to the king of the Ammonites 15 and said to him, "Thus says Jephthah: Israel did not take away the land of Moab or the land of the Ammonites, 16 but when they came up from Egypt, Israel went through the wilderness to the Red Sea and came to Kadesh. 17 Israel then sent messengers to the king of Edom, saying, 'Please let us pass through your land,' but the king of Edom would not listen. And they sent also to the king of Moab, but he would not consent. So Israel remained at Kadesh.

18 "Then they journeyed through the wilderness and went around the land of Edom and the land of Moab and arrived on the east side of the land of Moab and camped on the other side of the Arnon. But they did not enter the territory of Moab, for the Arnon was the boundary of Moab. 19 Israel then sent messengers to Sihon king of the Amorites, king of Heshbon, and Israel said to him, 'Please let us pass through your land to our country,' 20 but Sihon did not trust Israel to pass through his territory, so Sihon gathered all his people together and encamped at Jahaz and fought with Israel. 21 And the LORD, the God of Israel, gave Sihon and all his people into the hand of Israel, and they defeated them. So Israel took possession of all the land of the Amorites, who inhabited that country. 22 And they took possession of all the territory of the Amorites from the Arnon to the Jabbok and from the wilderness to the Jordan. 23 So then the LORD, the God of Israel, dispossessed the Amorites from before his people Israel; and are you to take possession of them? 24 Will you not possess what Chemosh your god gives you to possess? And all that the LORD our God has dispossessed before us, we will possess. 25 Now are you any better than Balak the son of Zippor, king of Moab? Did he ever contend against Israel, or did he ever go to war with them? 26 While Israel lived in Heshbon and its villages, and in Aroer and its villages, and in all the cities that are on the banks of the Arnon, 300 years, why did you not deliver them within that time? 27 I therefore have not sinned against you, and you do me wrong by making war on me. The LORD, the Judge, decide this day between the people of Israel and the people of Ammon." 28 But the king of the Ammonites did not listen to the words of Jephthah that he sent to him.

Jephthah's Tragic Vow

29 Then the Spirit of the LORD was upon Jephthah, and he passed through Gilead and Manasseh and passed on to Mizpah of Gilead, and from Mizpah of Gilead he passed on to the Ammonites. 30 And Jephthah made a vow to the LORD and said, "If you will give the Ammonites into my hand, 31 then whatever[1] comes out from the doors of my house to meet me when I return in peace from the Ammonites shall be the LORD's, and I will offer it[2] up for a burnt offering." 32 So Jephthah crossed over to the Ammonites to fight against them, and the LORD gave them into his hand. 33 And he struck them from Aroer to the neighborhood of Minnith, twenty cities, and as far as Abel-keramim, with a great blow. So the Ammonites were subdued before the people of Israel.

34 Then Jephthah came to his home at Mizpah. And behold, his daughter came out to meet him with tambourines and with dances. She was his only child; besides her he had neither son nor daughter. 35 And as soon as he saw her, he tore his clothes and said, "Alas, my daughter! You have brought me very low, and you have become the cause of great trouble to me. For I have opened my mouth to the LORD, and I cannot take back my vow." 36 And she said to him, "My father, you have opened your mouth to the LORD; do to me according to what has gone out of your mouth, now that the LORD has

[1] Or *whoever* [2] Or *him*

avenged you on your enemies, on the
Ammonites." 37 So she said to her father,
"Let this thing be done for me: leave me
alone two months, that I may go up and
down on the mountains and weep for my
virginity, I and my companions." 38 So he
said, "Go." Then he sent her away for two
months, and she departed, she and her
companions, and wept for her virginity
on the mountains. 39 And at the end of two
months, she returned to her father, who
did with her according to his vow that he
had made. She had never known a man,
and it became a custom in Israel 40 that
the daughters of Israel went year by year
to lament the daughter of Jephthah the
Gileadite four days in the year.

Jephthah's Conflict with Ephraim

12 The men of Ephraim were called to
arms, and they crossed to Zaphon
and said to Jephthah, "Why did you cross
over to fight against the Ammonites and
did not call us to go with you? We will
burn your house over you with fire." 2 And
Jephthah said to them, "I and my people
had a great dispute with the Ammonites,
and when I called you, you did not save
me from their hand. 3 And when I saw
that you would not save me, I took my
life in my hand and crossed over against
the Ammonites, and the LORD gave them
into my hand. Why then have you come
up to me this day to fight against me?"
4 Then Jephthah gathered all the men of
Gilead and fought with Ephraim. And the
men of Gilead struck Ephraim, because
they said, "You are fugitives of Ephraim,
you Gileadites, in the midst of Ephraim
and Manasseh." 5 And the Gileadites cap-
tured the fords of the Jordan against the
Ephraimites. And when any of the fugi-
tives of Ephraim said, "Let me go over,"
the men of Gilead said to him, "Are you an
Ephraimite?" When he said, "No," 6 they
said to him, "Then say Shibboleth," and
he said, "Sibboleth," for he could not pro-
nounce it right. Then they seized him and
slaughtered him at the fords of the Jordan.
At that time 42,000 of the Ephraimites fell.
7 Jephthah judged Israel six years. Then
Jephthah the Gileadite died and was bur-
ied in his city in Gilead.[1]

Ibzan, Elon, and Abdon

8 After him Ibzan of Bethlehem judged
Israel. 9 He had thirty sons, and thirty
daughters he gave in marriage outside his
clan, and thirty daughters he brought in
from outside for his sons. And he judged
Israel seven years. 10 Then Ibzan died and
was buried at Bethlehem.
11 After him Elon the Zebulunite judged
Israel, and he judged Israel ten years.
12 Then Elon the Zebulunite died and was
buried at Aijalon in the land of Zebulun.
13 After him Abdon the son of Hillel the
Pirathonite judged Israel. 14 He had forty
sons and thirty grandsons, who rode on
seventy donkeys, and he judged Israel
eight years. 15 Then Abdon the son of
Hillel the Pirathonite died and was buried
at Pirathon in the land of Ephraim, in the
hill country of the Amalekites.

The Birth of Samson

411
13 And the people of Israel
again did what was evil in
the sight of the LORD, so the LORD
gave them into the hand of the Philistines
for forty years.
2 There was a certain man of Zorah, of
the tribe of the Danites, whose name was
Manoah. And his wife was barren and had
no children. 3 And the angel of the LORD
appeared to the woman and said to her,
"Behold, you are barren and have not
borne children, but you shall conceive
and bear a son. 4 Therefore be careful and
drink no wine or strong drink, and eat
nothing unclean, 5 for behold, you shall
conceive and bear a son. No razor shall
come upon his head, for the child shall be
a Nazirite to God from the womb, and he
shall begin to save Israel from the hand of

[1] Septuagint; Hebrew *in the cities of Gilead*

the Philistines." 6 Then the woman came and told her husband, "A man of God came to me, and his appearance was like the appearance of the angel of God, very awesome. I did not ask him where he was from, and he did not tell me his name, 7 but he said to me, 'Behold, you shall conceive and bear a son. So then drink no wine or strong drink, and eat nothing unclean, for the child shall be a Nazirite to God from the womb to the day of his death.'"

8 Then Manoah prayed to the LORD and said, "O Lord, please let the man of God whom you sent come again to us and teach us what we are to do with the child who will be born." 9 And God listened to the voice of Manoah, and the angel of God came again to the woman as she sat in the field. But Manoah her husband was not with her. 10 So the woman ran quickly and told her husband, "Behold, the man who came to me the other day has appeared to me." 11 And Manoah arose and went after his wife and came to the man and said to him, "Are you the man who spoke to this woman?" And he said, "I am." 12 And Manoah said, "Now when your words come true, what is to be the child's manner of life, and what is his mission?" 13 And the angel of the LORD said to Manoah, "Of all that I said to the woman let her be careful. 14 She may not eat of anything that comes from the vine, neither let her drink wine or strong drink, or eat any unclean thing. All that I commanded her let her observe."

15 Manoah said to the angel of the LORD, "Please let us detain you and prepare a young goat for you." 16 And the angel of the LORD said to Manoah, "If you detain me, I will not eat of your food. But if you prepare a burnt offering, then offer it to the LORD." (For Manoah did not know that he was the angel of the LORD.) 17 And Manoah said to the angel of the LORD, "What is your name, so that, when your words come true, we may honor you?" 18 And the angel of the LORD said to him, "Why do you ask my name, seeing it is wonderful?" 19 So Manoah took the young goat with the grain offering, and offered it on the rock to the LORD, to the one who works[1] wonders, and Manoah and his wife were watching. 20 And when the flame went up toward heaven from the altar, the angel of the LORD went up in the flame of the altar. Now Manoah and his wife were watching, and they fell on their faces to the ground.

21 The angel of the LORD appeared no more to Manoah and to his wife. Then Manoah knew that he was the angel of the LORD. 22 And Manoah said to his wife, "We shall surely die, for we have seen God." 23 But his wife said to him, "If the LORD had meant to kill us, he would not have accepted a burnt offering and a grain offering at our hands, or shown us all these things, or now announced to us such things as these." 24 And the woman bore a son and called his name Samson. And the young man grew, and the LORD blessed him. 25 And the Spirit of the LORD began to stir him in Mahaneh-dan, between Zorah and Eshtaol.

Samson's Marriage

14 Samson went down to Timnah, and at Timnah he saw one of the daughters of the Philistines. 2 Then he came up and told his father and mother, "I saw one of the daughters of the Philistines at Timnah. Now get her for me as my wife." 3 But his father and mother said to him, "Is there not a woman among the daughters of your relatives, or among all our people, that you must go to take a wife from the uncircumcised Philistines?" But Samson said to his father, "Get her for me, for she is right in my eyes."

4 His father and mother did not know that it was from the LORD, for he was seeking an opportunity against the Philistines. At that time the Philistines ruled over Israel.

[1] Septuagint, Vulgate; Hebrew *LORD, and working*

5 Then Samson went down with his
father and mother to Timnah, and they
came to the vineyards of Timnah. And
behold, a young lion came toward him
roaring. 6 Then the Spirit of the LORD
rushed upon him, and although he had
nothing in his hand, he tore the lion in
pieces as one tears a young goat. But he
did not tell his father or his mother what
he had done. 7 Then he went down and
talked with the woman, and she was right
in Samson's eyes.

8 After some days he returned to take
her. And he turned aside to see the car-
cass of the lion, and behold, there was a
swarm of bees in the body of the lion, and
honey. 9 He scraped it out into his hands
and went on, eating as he went. And he
came to his father and mother and gave
some to them, and they ate. But he did not
tell them that he had scraped the honey
from the carcass of the lion.

10 His father went down to the woman,
and Samson prepared a feast there, for
so the young men used to do. 11 As soon
as the people saw him, they brought
thirty companions to be with him. 12 And
Samson said to them, "Let me now put a
riddle to you. If you can tell me what it
is, within the seven days of the feast, and
find it out, then I will give you thirty linen
garments and thirty changes of clothes,
13 but if you cannot tell me what it is, then
you shall give me thirty linen garments
and thirty changes of clothes." And they
said to him, "Put your riddle, that we may
hear it." 14 And he said to them,

> "Out of the eater came something to
> eat.
> Out of the strong came something
> sweet."

And in three days they could not solve the
riddle.

15 On the fourth[1] day they said to
Samson's wife, "Entice your husband to
tell us what the riddle is, lest we burn you
and your father's house with fire. Have
you invited us here to impoverish us?"
16 And Samson's wife wept over him and
said, "You only hate me; you do not love
me. You have put a riddle to my people,
and you have not told me what it is." And
he said to her, "Behold, I have not told
my father nor my mother, and shall I tell
you?" 17 She wept before him the seven
days that their feast lasted, and on the sev-
enth day he told her, because she pressed
him hard. Then she told the riddle to her
people. 18 And the men of the city said to
him on the seventh day before the sun
went down,

> "What is sweeter than honey?
> What is stronger than a lion?"

And he said to them,

> "If you had not plowed with my
> heifer,
> you would not have found out my
> riddle."

19 And the Spirit of the LORD rushed upon
him, and he went down to Ashkelon and
struck down thirty men of the town and
took their spoil and gave the garments to
those who had told the riddle. In hot anger
he went back to his father's house. 20 And
Samson's wife was given to his compan-
ion, who had been his best man.

Samson Defeats the Philistines

15 After some days, at the time of
wheat harvest, Samson went to
visit his wife with a young goat. And he
said, "I will go in to my wife in the cham-
ber." But her father would not allow him
to go in. 2 And her father said, "I really
thought that you utterly hated her, so I
gave her to your companion. Is not her
younger sister more beautiful than she?
Please take her instead." 3 And Samson
said to them, "This time I shall be inno-
cent in regard to the Philistines, when I do
them harm." 4 So Samson went and caught

[1] Septuagint, Syriac; Hebrew *seventh*

300 foxes and took torches. And he turned
them tail to tail and put a torch between
each pair of tails. 5 And when he had set
fire to the torches, he let the foxes go into
the standing grain of the Philistines and
set fire to the stacked grain and the standing grain, as well as the olive orchards.
6 Then the Philistines said, "Who has
done this?" And they said, "Samson, the
son-in-law of the Timnite, because he has
taken his wife and given her to his companion." And the Philistines came up and
burned her and her father with fire. 7 And
Samson said to them, "If this is what you
do, I swear I will be avenged on you, and
after that I will quit." 8 And he struck them
hip and thigh with a great blow, and he
went down and stayed in the cleft of the
rock of Etam.

9 Then the Philistines came up and
encamped in Judah and made a raid on
Lehi. 10 And the men of Judah said, "Why
have you come up against us?" They said,
"We have come up to bind Samson, to do
to him as he did to us." 11 Then 3,000 men
of Judah went down to the cleft of the rock
of Etam, and said to Samson, "Do you not
know that the Philistines are rulers over
us? What then is this that you have done
to us?" And he said to them, "As they did
to me, so have I done to them." 12 And
they said to him, "We have come down to
bind you, that we may give you into the
hands of the Philistines." And Samson
said to them, "Swear to me that you will
not attack me yourselves." 13 They said to
him, "No; we will only bind you and give
you into their hands. We will surely not
kill you." So they bound him with two new
ropes and brought him up from the rock.

14 When he came to Lehi, the Philistines
came shouting to meet him. Then the
Spirit of the LORD rushed upon him, and
the ropes that were on his arms became
as flax that has caught fire, and his bonds
melted off his hands. 15 And he found a
fresh jawbone of a donkey, and put out
his hand and took it, and with it he struck
1,000 men. 16 And Samson said,

"With the jawbone of a donkey,
heaps upon heaps,
with the jawbone of a donkey
have I struck down a thousand
men."

17 As soon as he had finished speaking, he
threw away the jawbone out of his hand.
And that place was called Ramath-lehi.[1]

18 And he was very thirsty, and he
called upon the LORD and said, "You have

CHARACTER PROFILE

SAMSON

Samson was born after an angel spoke with his mother. The angel told her that Samson must never cut his hair. Samson was very strong, and he fought the Philistine enemies many times. But he was not always obedient to God. While Samson slept, Delilah cut his hair, and he lost his strength—and the Philistines took him and put him in prison. When his hair grew back, Samson prayed that God would give him strength again—to defeat the Philistines one more time.

411

[1] *Ramath-lehi* means *the hill of the jawbone*

granted this great salvation by the hand of
your servant, and shall I now die of thirst
and fall into the hands of the uncircum-
cised?" 19 And God split open the hollow
place that is at Lehi, and water came out
from it. And when he drank, his spirit
returned, and he revived. Therefore the
name of it was called En-hakkore;[1] it is at
Lehi to this day. 20 And he judged Israel in
the days of the Philistines twenty years.

Samson and Delilah

16 Samson went to Gaza, and there
he saw a prostitute, and he went
in to her. 2 The Gazites were told, "Samson
has come here." And they surrounded the
place and set an ambush for him all night
at the gate of the city. They kept quiet all
night, saying, "Let us wait till the light of
the morning; then we will kill him." 3 But
Samson lay till midnight, and at midnight
he arose and took hold of the doors of the
gate of the city and the two posts, and
pulled them up, bar and all, and put them
on his shoulders and carried them to the
top of the hill that is in front of Hebron.

4 After this he loved a woman in the
Valley of Sorek, whose name was Delilah.
5 And the lords of the Philistines came up
to her and said to her, "Seduce him, and
see where his great strength lies, and by
what means we may overpower him, that
we may bind him to humble him. And we
will each give you 1,100 pieces of silver."
6 So Delilah said to Samson, "Please tell
me where your great strength lies, and
how you might be bound, that one could
subdue you."

7 Samson said to her, "If they bind me
with seven fresh bowstrings that have
not been dried, then I shall become weak
and be like any other man." 8 Then the
lords of the Philistines brought up to her
seven fresh bowstrings that had not been
dried, and she bound him with them.
9 Now she had men lying in ambush in an
inner chamber. And she said to him, "The
Philistines are upon you, Samson!" But
he snapped the bowstrings, as a thread of
flax snaps when it touches the fire. So the
secret of his strength was not known.

10 Then Delilah said to Samson, "Behold,
you have mocked me and told me lies.
Please tell me how you might be bound."
11 And he said to her, "If they bind me with
new ropes that have not been used, then I
shall become weak and be like any other
man." 12 So Delilah took new ropes and
bound him with them and said to him,
"The Philistines are upon you, Samson!"
And the men lying in ambush were in an
inner chamber. But he snapped the ropes
off his arms like a thread.

13 Then Delilah said to Samson, "Until
now you have mocked me and told me
lies. Tell me how you might be bound."
And he said to her, "If you weave the seven
locks of my head with the web and fasten
it tight with the pin, then I shall become
weak and be like any other man." 14 So
while he slept, Delilah took the seven
locks of his head and wove them into the
web.[2] And she made them tight with the
pin and said to him, "The Philistines are
upon you, Samson!" But he awoke from
his sleep and pulled away the pin, the
loom, and the web.

15 And she said to him, "How can you
say, 'I love you,' when your heart is not
with me? You have mocked me these three
times, and you have not told me where
your great strength lies." 16 And when she
pressed him hard with her words day after
day, and urged him, his soul was vexed to
death. 17 And he told her all his heart, and
said to her, "A razor has never come upon
my head, for I have been a Nazirite to God
from my mother's womb. If my head is
shaved, then my strength will leave me,
and I shall become weak and be like any
other man."

18 When Delilah saw that he had told her
all his heart, she sent and called the lords
of the Philistines, saying, "Come up again,

[1] *En-hakkore* means *the spring of him who called* [2] Compare Septuagint; Hebrew lacks *and fasten it tight . . . into the web*

Samson the Strongest Man

Before Samson was born, an angel told his mother that he would begin to save the people of Israel from their Philistine enemies. The angel told Samson's mother that Samson must keep certain rules. One of these rules was that Samson was never supposed to cut his hair. As long as Samson did this, God would make Samson very strong.

The rulers of the Philistines were afraid of Samson, because he was so strong. They knew that Samson loved a Philistine woman named Delilah, so they secretly asked her to help them capture Samson. The rulers offered Delilah a large amount of silver if she would help them and find out the secret of Samson's strength.

So Delilah agreed to help the Philistine leaders. She begged Samson to tell her how he could be so strong. Samson said to her, "If they bind me with seven fresh bowstrings that have not been dried, then I shall become weak." When Samson was asleep, Delilah tied him up with seven fresh bowstrings. Then she told him that the Philistines were attacking! But Samson jumped up and snapped the bowstrings!

But Delilah kept trying. Again she asked Samson how he could be tied up. This time Samson said, "If they bind me with new ropes that have not been used, then I shall become weak." When Samson was asleep, Delilah wrapped Samson with new ropes and told him that the Philistines were attacking. But Samson had lied, and now he snapped off the new ropes like little threads.

Still Delilah didn't give up. She said to Samson, "Until now you have told me lies. Tell me how you might be bound." So this time Samson said that if she were to weave his hair into a loom and fasten the loom with a pin, he would become weak. Delilah tried this too. But Samson was lying again, and he easily got free once more.

Day after day Delilah asked Samson what gave him his great strength. Finally, he told her the truth. The secret, Samson told Delilah, is that his hair had never been cut. "If my head is shaved," he said, "then my strength will leave, and I shall become weak and be like any other man."

This time, Delilah was sure that Samson was telling the truth. She secretly called the Philistine leaders. While Samson slept, Delilah had someone cut off Samson's hair. Then she called out to Samson that the Philistines were attacking. When Samson awoke, he tried to get free like he had always done before. Samson did not know that the Lord had left him. But now he was too weak to get free.

The Philistines tied him up and blinded his eyes—and they took him away to prison. But while Samson was in prison, his hair began to grow out again.

Many days later, thousands of Philistines gathered at their temple to offer a sacrifice to Dagon, their idol god. They said, "Our god has given Samson our enemy into our hand." Then they sent for Samson to entertain them.

As Samson stood between the pillars of their temple, he

asked the young man who held his hand to let him feel the pillars of the temple. Samson called, "O LORD God, please remember me and please strengthen me only this once." With that prayer, Samson pushed the pillars with all his strength, and the temple fell, killing many of the Philistine people. God had strengthened Samson one last time to win a mighty victory over the Philistines.

God made Samson into a champion for the Israelites. God made him strong so he could defeat the Philistine enemies. But Samson also did many other things that did not follow God's commands. God gave us the greatest Champion ever in the Lord Jesus Christ. Jesus is stronger than all our enemies, and He always obeyed God the Father. When Jesus died on the cross, He defeated sin, death, and the devil! Because of Jesus, our sins are forgiven.

SEEK and FIND

WHERE THE STORY IS FOUND

Judges 13–16

KEY BIBLE VERSE

"But thanks be to God, who gives us the victory through our Lord Jesus Christ." (1 Corinthians 15:57)

THREE KEY QUESTIONS

- How did Samson get to be so strong?
- Who are the enemies that Samson conquered during his life and when he died?
- What enemies did Jesus conquer when He died on the cross?

RELATED BIBLE READINGS

Psalm 118:5–7; 1 Corinthians 15:24–26; Colossians 2:15; Hebrews 11:32

for he has told me all his heart." Then the
lords of the Philistines came up to her
and brought the money in their hands.
19 She made him sleep on her knees. And
she called a man and had him shave off
the seven locks of his head. Then she
began to torment him, and his strength
left him. 20 And she said, "The Philistines
are upon you, Samson!" And he awoke
from his sleep and said, "I will go out as
at other times and shake myself free." But
he did not know that the LORD had left
him. 21 And the Philistines seized him
and gouged out his eyes and brought him
down to Gaza and bound him with bronze
shackles. And he ground at the mill in the
prison. 22 But the hair of his head began to
grow again after it had been shaved.

The Death of Samson

23 Now the lords of the Philistines gath-
ered to offer a great sacrifice to Dagon
their god and to rejoice, and they said,
"Our god has given Samson our enemy
into our hand." 24 And when the people
saw him, they praised their god. For they
said, "Our god has given our enemy into
our hand, the ravager of our country,
who has killed many of us."[1] 25 And when
their hearts were merry, they said, "Call
Samson, that he may entertain us." So they
called Samson out of the prison, and he
entertained them. They made him stand
between the pillars. 26 And Samson said
to the young man who held him by the
hand, "Let me feel the pillars on which the
house rests, that I may lean against them."
27 Now the house was full of men and
women. All the lords of the Philistines
were there, and on the roof there were
about 3,000 men and women, who looked
on while Samson entertained.

28 Then Samson called to the LORD
and said, "O Lord GOD, please remember
me and please strengthen me only this
once, O God, that I may be avenged on the
Philistines for my two eyes." 29 And Samson
grasped the two middle pillars on which
the house rested, and he leaned his weight
against them, his right hand on the one and
his left hand on the other. 30 And Samson
said, "Let me die with the Philistines." Then
he bowed with all his strength, and the
house fell upon the lords and upon all the
people who were in it. So the dead whom
he killed at his death were more than those
whom he had killed during his life. 31 Then
his brothers and all his family came down
and took him and brought him up and bur-
ied him between Zorah and Eshtaol in the
tomb of Manoah his father. He had judged
Israel twenty years.

Micah and the Levite

17 There was a man of the hill coun-
try of Ephraim, whose name was
Micah. 2 And he said to his mother, "The
1,100 pieces of silver that were taken from
you, about which you uttered a curse, and
also spoke it in my ears, behold, the silver
is with me; I took it." And his mother said,
"Blessed be my son by the LORD." 3 And he
restored the 1,100 pieces of silver to his
mother. And his mother said, "I dedicate
the silver to the LORD from my hand for
my son, to make a carved image and a
metal image. Now therefore I will restore
it to you." 4 So when he restored the money
to his mother, his mother took 200 pieces
of silver and gave it to the silversmith, who
made it into a carved image and a metal
image. And it was in the house of Micah.
5 And the man Micah had a shrine, and he
made an ephod and household gods, and
ordained[2] one of his sons, who became
his priest. 6 In those days there was no
king in Israel. Everyone did what was
right in his own eyes.

7 Now there was a young man of
Bethlehem in Judah, of the family of
Judah, who was a Levite, and he sojourned
there. 8 And the man departed from the
town of Bethlehem in Judah to sojourn
where he could find a place. And as he

[1] Or *who has multiplied our slain* [2] Hebrew *filled the hand of*; also verse 12

journeyed, he came to the hill country
of Ephraim to the house of Micah. 9 And
Micah said to him, "Where do you come
from?" And he said to him, "I am a Levite
of Bethlehem in Judah, and I am going to
sojourn where I may find a place." 10 And
Micah said to him, "Stay with me, and
be to me a father and a priest, and I will
give you ten pieces of silver a year and a
suit of clothes and your living." And the
Levite went in. 11 And the Levite was con-
tent to dwell with the man, and the young
man became to him like one of his sons.
12 And Micah ordained the Levite, and the
young man became his priest, and was in
the house of Micah. 13 Then Micah said,
"Now I know that the LORD will prosper
me, because I have a Levite as priest."

Danites Take the Levite and the Idol

18 In those days there was no king in
Israel. And in those days the tribe
of the people of Dan was seeking for itself
an inheritance to dwell in, for until then
no inheritance among the tribes of Israel
had fallen to them. 2 So the people of Dan
sent five able men from the whole num-
ber of their tribe, from Zorah and from
Eshtaol, to spy out the land and to explore
it. And they said to them, "Go and explore
the land." And they came to the hill coun-
try of Ephraim, to the house of Micah,
and lodged there. 3 When they were by the
house of Micah, they recognized the voice
of the young Levite. And they turned aside
and said to him, "Who brought you here?
What are you doing in this place? What
is your business here?" 4 And he said to
them, "This is how Micah dealt with me:
he has hired me, and I have become his
priest." 5 And they said to him, "Inquire of
God, please, that we may know whether
the journey on which we are setting out
will succeed." 6 And the priest said to
them, "Go in peace. The journey on which
you go is under the eye of the LORD."

7 Then the five men departed and came
to Laish and saw the people who were
there, how they lived in security, after
the manner of the Sidonians, quiet and
unsuspecting, lacking[1] nothing that is
in the earth and possessing wealth, and
how they were far from the Sidonians
and had no dealings with anyone. 8 And
when they came to their brothers at Zorah
and Eshtaol, their brothers said to them,
"What do you report?" 9 They said, "Arise,
and let us go up against them, for we
have seen the land, and behold, it is very
good. And will you do nothing? Do not
be slow to go, to enter in and possess the
land. 10 As soon as you go, you will come
to an unsuspecting people. The land is
spacious, for God has given it into your
hands, a place where there is no lack of
anything that is in the earth."

11 So 600 men of the tribe of Dan,
armed with weapons of war, set out from
Zorah and Eshtaol, 12 and went up and
encamped at Kiriath-jearim in Judah. On
this account that place is called Mahaneh-
dan[2] to this day; behold, it is west of
Kiriath-jearim. 13 And they passed on from
there to the hill country of Ephraim, and
came to the house of Micah.

14 Then the five men who had gone
to scout out the country of Laish said to
their brothers, "Do you know that in these
houses there are an ephod, household
gods, a carved image, and a metal image?
Now therefore consider what you will do."
15 And they turned aside there and came to
the house of the young Levite, at the home
of Micah, and asked him about his wel-
fare. 16 Now the 600 men of the Danites,
armed with their weapons of war, stood
by the entrance of the gate. 17 And the five
men who had gone to scout out the land
went up and entered and took the carved
image, the ephod, the household gods,
and the metal image, while the priest
stood by the entrance of the gate with
the 600 men armed with weapons of
war. 18 And when these went into Micah's

[1] Compare 18:10; the meaning of the Hebrew word is uncertain [2] *Mahaneh-dan* means *camp of Dan*

house and took the carved image, the
ephod, the household gods, and the metal
image, the priest said to them, "What are
you doing?" 19 And they said to him, "Keep
quiet; put your hand on your mouth and
come with us and be to us a father and a
priest. Is it better for you to be priest to
the house of one man, or to be priest to a
tribe and clan in Israel?" 20 And the priest's
heart was glad. He took the ephod and the
household gods and the carved image and
went along with the people.

21 So they turned and departed, put-
ting the little ones and the livestock and
the goods in front of them. 22 When they
had gone a distance from the home of
Micah, the men who were in the houses
near Micah's house were called out, and
they overtook the people of Dan. 23 And
they shouted to the people of Dan, who
turned around and said to Micah, "What
is the matter with you, that you come with
such a company?" 24 And he said, "You
take my gods that I made and the priest,
and go away, and what have I left? How
then do you ask me, 'What is the matter
with you?'" 25 And the people of Dan said
to him, "Do not let your voice be heard
among us, lest angry fellows fall upon
you, and you lose your life with the lives
of your household." 26 Then the people
of Dan went their way. And when Micah
saw that they were too strong for him, he
turned and went back to his home.

27 But the people of Dan took what
Micah had made, and the priest who
belonged to him, and they came to Laish,
to a people quiet and unsuspecting, and
struck them with the edge of the sword
and burned the city with fire. 28 And there
was no deliverer because it was far from
Sidon, and they had no dealings with any-
one. It was in the valley that belongs to
Beth-rehob. Then they rebuilt the city and
lived in it. 29 And they named the city Dan,
after the name of Dan their ancestor, who
was born to Israel; but the name of the city
was Laish at the first. 30 And the people of
Dan set up the carved image for them-
selves, and Jonathan the son of Gershom,
son of Moses,[1] and his sons were priests
to the tribe of the Danites until the day
of the captivity of the land. 31 So they set
up Micah's carved image that he made, as
long as the house of God was at Shiloh.

A Levite and His Concubine

19 In those days, when there was
no king in Israel, a certain Levite
was sojourning in the remote parts of
the hill country of Ephraim, who took to
himself a concubine from Bethlehem in
Judah. 2 And his concubine was unfaithful
to[2] him, and she went away from him to
her father's house at Bethlehem in Judah,
and was there some four months. 3 Then
her husband arose and went after her, to
speak kindly to her and bring her back. He
had with him his servant and a couple of
donkeys. And she brought him into her
father's house. And when the girl's father
saw him, he came with joy to meet him.
4 And his father-in-law, the girl's father,
made him stay, and he remained with
him three days. So they ate and drank and
spent the night there. 5 And on the fourth
day they arose early in the morning, and
he prepared to go, but the girl's father said
to his son-in-law, "Strengthen your heart
with a morsel of bread, and after that you
may go." 6 So the two of them sat and ate
and drank together. And the girl's father
said to the man, "Be pleased to spend the
night, and let your heart be merry." 7 And
when the man rose up to go, his father-in-
law pressed him, till he spent the night
there again. 8 And on the fifth day he arose
early in the morning to depart. And the
girl's father said, "Strengthen your heart
and wait until the day declines." So they
ate, both of them. 9 And when the man and
his concubine and his servant rose up to
depart, his father-in-law, the girl's father,
said to him, "Behold, now the day has

[1] Or *Manasseh* [2] Septuagint, Old Latin *became angry with*

waned toward evening. Please, spend the night. Behold, the day draws to its close. Lodge here and let your heart be merry, and tomorrow you shall arise early in the morning for your journey, and go home."

10 But the man would not spend the night. He rose up and departed and arrived opposite Jebus (that is, Jerusalem). He had with him a couple of saddled donkeys, and his concubine was with him. 11 When they were near Jebus, the day was nearly over, and the servant said to his master, "Come now, let us turn aside to this city of the Jebusites and spend the night in it." 12 And his master said to him, "We will not turn aside into the city of foreigners, who do not belong to the people of Israel, but we will pass on to Gibeah." 13 And he said to his young man, "Come and let us draw near to one of these places and spend the night at Gibeah or at Ramah." 14 So they passed on and went their way. And the sun went down on them near Gibeah, which belongs to Benjamin, 15 and they turned aside there, to go in and spend the night at Gibeah. And he went in and sat down in the open square of the city, for no one took them into his house to spend the night.

16 And behold, an old man was coming from his work in the field at evening. The man was from the hill country of Ephraim, and he was sojourning in Gibeah. The men of the place were Benjaminites. 17 And he lifted up his eyes and saw the traveler in the open square of the city. And the old man said, "Where are you going? And where do you come from?" 18 And he said to him, "We are passing from Bethlehem in Judah to the remote parts of the hill country of Ephraim, from which I come. I went to Bethlehem in Judah, and I am going to the house of the Lord,[1] but no one has taken me into his house. 19 We have straw and feed for our donkeys, with bread and wine for me and your female servant and the young man with your servants. There is no lack of anything." 20 And the old man said, "Peace be to you; I will care for all your wants. Only, do not spend the night in the square." 21 So he brought him into his house and gave the donkeys feed. And they washed their feet, and ate and drank.

Gibeah's Crime

22 As they were making their hearts merry, behold, the men of the city, worthless fellows, surrounded the house, beating on the door. And they said to the old man, the master of the house, "Bring out the man who came into your house, that we may know him." 23 And the man, the master of the house, went out to them and said to them, "No, my brothers, do not act so wickedly; since this man has come into my house, do not do this vile thing. 24 Behold, here are my virgin daughter and his concubine. Let me bring them out now. Violate them and do with them what seems good to you, but against this man do not do this outrageous thing." 25 But the men would not listen to him. So the man seized his concubine and made her go out to them. And they knew her and abused her all night until the morning. And as the dawn began to break, they let her go. 26 And as morning appeared, the woman came and fell down at the door of the man's house where her master was, until it was light.

27 And her master rose up in the morning, and when he opened the doors of the house and went out to go on his way, behold, there was his concubine lying at the door of the house, with her hands on the threshold. 28 He said to her, "Get up, let us be going." But there was no answer. Then he put her on the donkey, and the man rose up and went away to his home. 29 And when he entered his house, he took a knife, and taking hold of his concubine he divided her, limb by limb, into twelve pieces, and sent her throughout all the territory of Israel. 30 And all who saw it said, "Such a thing has never happened or been

[1] Septuagint *my home*; compare verse 29

seen from the day that the people of Israel came up out of the land of Egypt until this day; consider it, take counsel, and speak."

Israel's War with the Tribe of Benjamin

20 Then all the people of Israel came out, from Dan to Beersheba, including the land of Gilead, and the congregation assembled as one man to the LORD at Mizpah. 2 And the chiefs of all the people, of all the tribes of Israel, presented themselves in the assembly of the people of God, 400,000 men on foot that drew the sword. 3 (Now the people of Benjamin heard that the people of Israel had gone up to Mizpah.) And the people of Israel said, "Tell us, how did this evil happen?" 4 And the Levite, the husband of the woman who was murdered, answered and said, "I came to Gibeah that belongs to Benjamin, I and my concubine, to spend the night. 5 And the leaders of Gibeah rose against me and surrounded the house against me by night. They meant to kill me, and they violated my concubine, and she is dead. 6 So I took hold of my concubine and cut her in pieces and sent her throughout all the country of the inheritance of Israel, for they have committed abomination and outrage in Israel. 7 Behold, you people of Israel, all of you, give your advice and counsel here."

8 And all the people arose as one man, saying, "None of us will go to his tent, and none of us will return to his house. 9 But now this is what we will do to Gibeah: we will go up against it by lot, 10 and we will take ten men of a hundred throughout all the tribes of Israel, and a hundred of a thousand, and a thousand of ten thousand, to bring provisions for the people, that when they come they may repay Gibeah of Benjamin, for all the outrage that they have committed in Israel." 11 So all the men of Israel gathered against the city, united as one man.

12 And the tribes of Israel sent men through all the tribe of Benjamin, saying, "What evil is this that has taken place among you? 13 Now therefore give up the men, the worthless fellows in Gibeah, that we may put them to death and purge evil from Israel." But the Benjaminites would not listen to the voice of their brothers, the people of Israel. 14 Then the people of Benjamin came together out of the cities to Gibeah to go out to battle against the people of Israel. 15 And the people of Benjamin mustered out of their cities on that day 26,000 men who drew the sword, besides the inhabitants of Gibeah, who mustered 700 chosen men. 16 Among all these were 700 chosen men who were left-handed; every one could sling a stone at a hair and not miss. 17 And the men of Israel, apart from Benjamin, mustered 400,000 men who drew the sword; all these were men of war.

18 The people of Israel arose and went up to Bethel and inquired of God, "Who shall go up first for us to fight against the people of Benjamin?" And the LORD said, "Judah shall go up first."

19 Then the people of Israel rose in the morning and encamped against Gibeah. 20 And the men of Israel went out to fight against Benjamin, and the men of Israel drew up the battle line against them at Gibeah. 21 The people of Benjamin came out of Gibeah and destroyed on that day 22,000 men of the Israelites. 22 But the people, the men of Israel, took courage, and again formed the battle line in the same place where they had formed it on the first day. 23 And the people of Israel went up and wept before the LORD until the evening. And they inquired of the LORD, "Shall we again draw near to fight against our brothers, the people of Benjamin?" And the LORD said, "Go up against them."

24 So the people of Israel came near against the people of Benjamin the second day. 25 And Benjamin went against them out of Gibeah the second day, and destroyed 18,000 men of the people of

Israel. All these were men who drew the
sword. 26 Then all the people of Israel, the
whole army, went up and came to Bethel
and wept. They sat there before the LORD
and fasted that day until evening, and
offered burnt offerings and peace offer-
ings before the LORD. 27 And the people
of Israel inquired of the LORD (for the ark
of the covenant of God was there in those
days, 28 and Phinehas the son of Eleazar,
son of Aaron, ministered before it in those
days), saying, "Shall we go out once more
to battle against our brothers, the people
of Benjamin, or shall we cease?" And the
LORD said, "Go up, for tomorrow I will give
them into your hand."

29 So Israel set men in ambush around
Gibeah. 30 And the people of Israel went
up against the people of Benjamin on
the third day and set themselves in array
against Gibeah, as at other times. 31 And
the people of Benjamin went out against
the people and were drawn away from the
city. And as at other times they began to
strike and kill some of the people in the
highways, one of which goes up to Bethel
and the other to Gibeah, and in the open
country, about thirty men of Israel. 32 And
the people of Benjamin said, "They are
routed before us, as at the first." But the
people of Israel said, "Let us flee and draw
them away from the city to the highways."
33 And all the men of Israel rose up out of
their place and set themselves in array at
Baal-tamar, and the men of Israel who
were in ambush rushed out of their place
from Maareh-geba.[1] 34 And there came
against Gibeah 10,000 chosen men out of
all Israel, and the battle was hard, but the
Benjaminites did not know that disaster
was close upon them. 35 And the LORD
defeated Benjamin before Israel, and the
people of Israel destroyed 25,100 men of
Benjamin that day. All these were men
who drew the sword. 36 So the people of
Benjamin saw that they were defeated.

The men of Israel gave ground to
Benjamin, because they trusted the men
in ambush whom they had set against
Gibeah. 37 Then the men in ambush hur-
ried and rushed against Gibeah; the men
in ambush moved out and struck all the
city with the edge of the sword. 38 Now
the appointed signal between the men of
Israel and the men in the main ambush
was that when they made a great cloud of
smoke rise up out of the city 39 the men of
Israel should turn in battle. Now Benjamin
had begun to strike and kill about thirty
men of Israel. They said, "Surely they are
defeated before us, as in the first battle."
40 But when the signal began to rise out
of the city in a column of smoke, the
Benjaminites looked behind them, and
behold, the whole of the city went up in
smoke to heaven. 41 Then the men of Israel
turned, and the men of Benjamin were
dismayed, for they saw that disaster was
close upon them. 42 Therefore they turned
their backs before the men of Israel in the
direction of the wilderness, but the battle
overtook them. And those who came out
of the cities were destroying them in their
midst. 43 Surrounding the Benjaminites,
they pursued them and trod them down
from Nohah[2] as far as opposite Gibeah
on the east. 44 Eighteen thousand men of
Benjamin fell, all of them men of valor.
45 And they turned and fled toward the
wilderness to the rock of Rimmon. Five
thousand men of them were cut down in
the highways. And they were pursued hard
to Gidom, and 2,000 men of them were
struck down. 46 So all who fell that day of
Benjamin were 25,000 men who drew the
sword, all of them men of valor. 47 But 600
men turned and fled toward the wilder-
ness to the rock of Rimmon and remained
at the rock of Rimmon four months. 48 And
the men of Israel turned back against the
people of Benjamin and struck them with
the edge of the sword, the city, men and
beasts and all that they found. And all the
towns that they found they set on fire.

[1] Some Septuagint manuscripts *place west of Geba* [2] Septuagint; Hebrew [at their] *resting place*

Wives Provided for the Tribe of Benjamin

21 Now the men of Israel had sworn
at Mizpah, "No one of us shall give
his daughter in marriage to Benjamin."
2 And the people came to Bethel and sat
there till evening before God, and they
lifted up their voices and wept bitterly.
3 And they said, "O LORD, the God of Israel,
why has this happened in Israel, that today
there should be one tribe lacking in Israel?"
4 And the next day the people rose early and
built there an altar and offered burnt offer-
ings and peace offerings. 5 And the people
of Israel said, "Which of all the tribes of
Israel did not come up in the assembly
to the LORD?" For they had taken a great
oath concerning him who did not come
up to the LORD to Mizpah, saying, "He shall
surely be put to death." 6 And the people of
Israel had compassion for Benjamin their
brother and said, "One tribe is cut off from
Israel this day. 7 What shall we do for wives
for those who are left, since we have sworn
by the LORD that we will not give them any
of our daughters for wives?"

8 And they said, "What one is there of the
tribes of Israel that did not come up to the
LORD to Mizpah?" And behold, no one had
come to the camp from Jabesh-gilead, to
the assembly. 9 For when the people were
mustered, behold, not one of the inhabi-
tants of Jabesh-gilead was there. 10 So the
congregation sent 12,000 of their bravest
men there and commanded them, "Go and
strike the inhabitants of Jabesh-gilead with
the edge of the sword; also the women and
the little ones. 11 This is what you shall do:
every male and every woman that has lain
with a male you shall devote to destruc-
tion." 12 And they found among the inhab-
itants of Jabesh-gilead 400 young virgins
who had not known a man by lying with
him, and they brought them to the camp
at Shiloh, which is in the land of Canaan.

13 Then the whole congregation sent
word to the people of Benjamin who were
at the rock of Rimmon and proclaimed
peace to them. 14 And Benjamin returned at
that time. And they gave them the women
whom they had saved alive of the women
of Jabesh-gilead, but they were not enough
for them. 15 And the people had compas-
sion on Benjamin because the LORD had
made a breach in the tribes of Israel.

16 Then the elders of the congrega-
tion said, "What shall we do for wives for
those who are left, since the women are
destroyed out of Benjamin?" 17 And they
said, "There must be an inheritance for
the survivors of Benjamin, that a tribe not
be blotted out from Israel. 18 Yet we can-
not give them wives from our daughters."
For the people of Israel had sworn, "Cursed
be he who gives a wife to Benjamin." 19 So
they said, "Behold, there is the yearly feast
of the LORD at Shiloh, which is north of
Bethel, on the east of the highway that goes
up from Bethel to Shechem, and south of
Lebonah." 20 And they commanded the
people of Benjamin, saying, "Go and lie in
ambush in the vineyards 21 and watch. If
the daughters of Shiloh come out to dance
in the dances, then come out of the vine-
yards and snatch each man his wife from
the daughters of Shiloh, and go to the land
of Benjamin. 22 And when their fathers or
their brothers come to complain to us, we
will say to them, 'Grant them graciously to
us, because we did not take for each man
of them his wife in battle, neither did you
give them to them, else you would now be
guilty.'" 23 And the people of Benjamin did
so and took their wives, according to their
number, from the dancers whom they car-
ried off. Then they went and returned to
their inheritance and rebuilt the towns
and lived in them. 24 And the people of
Israel departed from there at that time,
every man to his tribe and family, and
they went out from there every man to his
inheritance.

25 In those days there was no king in
Israel. Everyone did what was right in his
own eyes.

Introduction to

Ruth

Author
Unknown

Date
About 1000 B.C.

People
Ruth; Naomi; Boaz; Obed; Jesse; David

Purpose
The purpose of Ruth is to show how God works in everyday circumstances to care for His people, to bring people to Himself, and to work out His purposes.

Central Themes
God is in control; God provides a redeemer; God honors human faithfulness and kindness; God accepts Gentiles among His people; God guided and protected the ancestors of King David and the Lord Jesus.

Memory Verses
Ruth's faithfulness (Ruth 1:16–17); Boaz's blessing (Ruth 2:11–12); the women's blessing (Ruth 4:14–15)

Introduction

The book of Ruth describes God's work in the lives of its three main characters: Naomi, Ruth, and Boaz. Naomi and her family had left Israel and the people of God because of a famine (Ruth 1:1). The story describes how God brings Naomi back to His people and their land and provides for her needs. Ruth is a Moabite woman, a Gentile, whom God brings to faith in Him. Ruth had married Naomi's son, who is now dead. Ruth leaves her people and her gods to go with Naomi to Israel, promising to make the God of Israel her God (Ruth 1:16–17). Back in Israel, she provides for Naomi by working in a field (Ruth 2:1–7). The field belongs to Boaz, a godly man who is impressed by Ruth's good character (Ruth 2:8–13). Boaz provides for the two women by buying a piece of land that had belonged to Naomi's husband, redeeming it for Naomi, and by marrying Ruth (Ruth 4). Ruth and Boaz's son, Obed, is the grandfather of King David (Ruth 4:17), making Ruth an ancestor of the Lord Jesus Christ.

About 1375 B.C.	?	About 1040 B.C.
Period of the judges begins	Events of Ruth	Birth of David, descendant of Ruth

Ruth

Naomi Widowed

425 **1** In the days when the judges
ruled there was a famine in the
land, and a man of Bethlehem in
Judah went to sojourn in the country of
Moab, he and his wife and his two sons.
2 The name of the man was Elimelech and
the name of his wife Naomi, and the
names of his two sons were Mahlon and
Chilion. They were Ephrathites from
Bethlehem in Judah. They went into the
country of Moab and remained there.
3 But Elimelech, the husband of Naomi,
died, and she was left with her two sons.
4 These took Moabite wives; the name of
the one was Orpah and the name of the
other Ruth. They lived there about ten
years, 5 and both Mahlon and Chilion
died, so that the woman was left without
her two sons and her husband.

Ruth's Loyalty to Naomi

6 Then she arose with her daughters-in-
law to return from the country of Moab,
for she had heard in the fields of Moab that
the LORD had visited his people and given
them food. 7 So she set out from the place
where she was with her two daughters-in-
law, and they went on the way to return to
the land of Judah. 8 But Naomi said to her
two daughters-in-law, "Go, return each of
you to her mother's house. May the LORD
deal kindly with you, as you have dealt
with the dead and with me. 9 The LORD
grant that you may find rest, each of you
in the house of her husband!" Then she
kissed them, and they lifted up their voices
and wept. 10 And they said to her, "No, we
will *return* with you to your people." 11 But
Naomi said, "Turn back, my daughters;
why will you go with me? Have I yet sons in
my womb that they may become your hus-
bands? 12 Turn back, my daughters; go your
way, for I am too old to have a husband. If
I should say I have hope, even if I should
have a husband this night and should bear
sons, 13 would you therefore wait till they
were grown? Would you therefore refrain
from marrying? No, my daughters, for it is
exceedingly bitter to me for your sake that
the hand of the LORD has gone out against
me." 14 Then they lifted up their voices and

CHARACTER PROFILE

RUTH

Ruth was a Moabite woman who married an Israelite man. When Ruth's husband died, she chose to stay with her mother-in-law Naomi, and to be one of the people of God. She worked hard in the fields to gather grain for herself and Naomi. The man who owned the field, Boaz, was a relative and wanted to care for Ruth and Naomi. He married Ruth. Their baby, Obed, was King David's grandfather.

425

wept again. And Orpah kissed her mother-
in-law, but Ruth clung to her.
15 And she said, "See, your sister-in-law
has gone back to her people and to her
gods; return after your sister-in-law." 16 But
Ruth said, "Do not urge me to leave you or
to return from following you. For where
you go I will go, and where you lodge I will
lodge. Your people shall be my people, and
your God my God. 17 Where you die I will
die, and there will I be buried. May the
LORD do so to me and more also if any-
thing but death parts me from you." 18 And
when Naomi saw that she was determined
to go with her, she said no more.

Naomi and Ruth Return

19 So the two of them went on until
they came to Bethlehem. And when they
came to Bethlehem, the whole town was
stirred because of them. And the women
said, "Is this Naomi?" 20 She said to them,
"Do not call me Naomi;[1] call me Mara,[2]
for the Almighty has dealt very bitterly
with me. 21 I went away full, and the LORD
has brought me back empty. Why call
me Naomi, when the LORD has testified
against me and the Almighty has brought
calamity upon me?"
22 So Naomi returned, and Ruth the
Moabite her daughter-in-law with her,
who returned from the country of Moab.
And they came to Bethlehem at the begin-
ning of barley harvest.

Ruth Meets Boaz

2 Now Naomi had a relative of her hus-
band's, a worthy man of the clan of
Elimelech, whose name was Boaz. 2 And
Ruth the Moabite said to Naomi, "Let me
go to the field and glean among the ears
of grain after him in whose sight I shall
find favor." And she said to her, "Go, my
daughter." 3 So she set out and went and
gleaned in the field after the reapers, and
she happened to come to the part of the
field belonging to Boaz, who was of the
clan of Elimelech. 4 And behold, Boaz
came from Bethlehem. And he said to the
reapers, "The LORD be with you!" And they
answered, "The LORD bless you." 5 Then
Boaz said to his young man who was in
charge of the reapers, "Whose young
woman is this?" 6 And the servant who
was in charge of the reapers answered,
"She is the young Moabite woman, who
came back with Naomi from the country
of Moab. 7 She said, 'Please let me glean
and gather among the sheaves after the
reapers.' So she came, and she has contin-
ued from early morning until now, except
for a short rest."[3]
8 Then Boaz said to Ruth, "Now, listen,
my daughter, do not go to glean in another
field or leave this one, but keep close to

CHARACTER PROFILE

BOAZ

Boaz was the redeemer of Naomi and Ruth. Both their husbands had died and they were very poor. As their relative and redeemer, Boaz was able to help Naomi and Ruth. Boaz owned the field where Ruth worked. When he saw how much Ruth loved God, Boaz did everything necessary to redeem her, so that he could marry her. Their son, Obed, was the grandfather of King David.

425

[1] *Naomi* means *pleasant* [2] *Mara* means *bitter* [3] Compare Septuagint, Vulgate; the meaning of the Hebrew phrase is uncertain

Ruth and Her Redeemer

A long time ago, a woman named Naomi, along with her husband and her two sons, lived in the land of Israel, in the town of Bethlehem. When a great famine came to Israel, they went to live in the land of Moab. While they were there, Naomi's husband died.

Naomi's two sons grew up and married women from Moab—one was named Ruth and the other Orpah. These two women were Naomi's daughters-in-law. Then after 10 years, Naomi's two sons also died. Now Naomi was all alone.

Now Naomi had no one in Moab to help her or to care for her, so she decided to move back to Bethlehem. One daughter-in-law, the one named Orpah, stayed in Moab. But the other daughter-in-law, Ruth, loved Naomi very much. Ruth told Naomi, "Where you go I will go. Your people shall be my people, and your God my God."

Ruth and Naomi walked for many days back to Bethlehem together. Life in Bethlehem was hard for Naomi—she was poor and had no way to earn money. To get enough food for them to eat, Ruth followed the workers in the field, picking up the pieces of grain they dropped when they cut grain in the field.

One day Ruth went to work in the field of a man named Boaz. Boaz was a close relative of Naomi's husband, and he was very kind to Ruth. He told his workers to leave some of the grain behind in the field, so that Ruth could pick it up and take it home to Naomi for their food.

When Boaz saw how Ruth cared so much for Naomi, and how Ruth trusted in God, Boaz wanted to marry Ruth. But in those days, the only way that Boaz could marry Ruth was to buy the land that Naomi was selling. Boaz bought the land and married Ruth, so that he could love and care for Ruth and Naomi as well—and so Boaz became their "redeemer."

God blessed Ruth and Boaz with a baby boy. They named him Obed. Little Obed made his grandmother, Naomi, very happy! Obed grew up to become the father of Jesse, and Jesse became the father of King David. Many years later, from King David's family, a baby named Jesus would be born in Bethlehem.

God had not forgotten about Naomi or Ruth. He blessed Naomi and Ruth by sending them Boaz as their "redeemer." God blesses us too, by sending His Son Jesus. By paying the penalty for our sins on the cross, Jesus becomes our Redeemer, blessing us forever as His own children.

SEEK and FIND

WHERE THE STORY IS FOUND

Ruth 1–4

KEY BIBLE VERSE

"Then the women said to Naomi, 'Blessed be the Lord, who has not left you this day without a redeemer, and may his name be renowned in Israel!'" (Ruth 4:14)

THREE KEY QUESTIONS

- Why was Ruth willing to go with Naomi to live in Bethlehem, far from her own home in Moab?

- How was Ruth able to get food in the fields in Bethlehem?
- How was Boaz the redeemer of Ruth and Naomi? How is Jesus our redeemer?

RELATED BIBLE READINGS

1 Samuel 16:1, 12–13; Matthew 1:1, 5–6; Luke 1:68–70; 3:23, 31–32

my young women. 9 Let your eyes be on the field that they are reaping, and go after them. Have I not charged the young men not to touch you? And when you are thirsty, go to the vessels and drink what the young men have drawn." 10 Then she fell on her face, bowing to the ground, and said to him, "Why have I found favor in your eyes, that you should take notice of me, since I am a foreigner?" 11 But Boaz answered her, "All that you have done for your mother-in-law since the death of your husband has been fully told to me, and how you left your father and mother and your native land and came to a people that you did not know before. 12 The LORD repay you for what you have done, and a full reward be given you by the LORD, the God of Israel, under whose wings you have come to take refuge!" 13 Then she said, "I have found favor in your eyes, my lord, for you have comforted me and spoken kindly to your servant, though I am not one of your servants."

14 And at mealtime Boaz said to her, "Come here and eat some bread and dip your morsel in the wine." So she sat beside the reapers, and he passed to her roasted grain. And she ate until she was satisfied, and she had some left over. 15 When she rose to glean, Boaz instructed his young men, saying, "Let her glean even among the sheaves, and do not reproach her. 16 And also pull out some from the bundles for her and leave it for her to glean, and do not rebuke her."

17 So she gleaned in the field until evening. Then she beat out what she had gleaned, and it was about an ephah[1] of barley. 18 And she took it up and went into the city. Her mother-in-law saw what she had gleaned. She also brought out and gave her what food she had left over after being satisfied. 19 And her mother-in-law said to her, "Where did you glean today? And where have you worked? Blessed be the man who took notice of you." So she told her mother-in-law with whom she had worked and said, "The man's name with whom I worked today is Boaz." 20 And Naomi said to her daughter-in-law, "May he be blessed by the LORD, whose kindness has not forsaken the living or the dead!" Naomi also said to her, "The man is a close relative of ours, one of our redeemers." 21 And Ruth the Moabite said, "Besides, he said to me, 'You shall keep close by my young men until they have finished all my harvest.'" 22 And Naomi said to Ruth, her daughter-in-law, "It is good, my daughter, that you go out with his young women, lest in another field you be assaulted." 23 So she kept close to the young women of Boaz, gleaning until the end of the barley and wheat harvests. And she lived with her mother-in-law.

[1] An *ephah* was about 3/5 bushel or 22 liters

Ruth and Boaz at the Threshing Floor

3 Then Naomi her mother-in-law said
to her, "My daughter, should I not
seek rest for you, that it may be well with
you? 2 Is not Boaz our relative, with whose
young women you were? See, he is win-
nowing barley tonight at the threshing
floor. 3 Wash therefore and anoint yourself,
and put on your cloak and go down to the
threshing floor, but do not make yourself
known to the man until he has finished
eating and drinking. 4 But when he lies
down, observe the place where he lies.
Then go and uncover his feet and lie down,
and he will tell you what to do." 5 And she
replied, "All that you say I will do."

6 So she went down to the threshing
floor and did just as her mother-in-law
had commanded her. 7 And when Boaz
had eaten and drunk, and his heart was
merry, he went to lie down at the end of
the heap of grain. Then she came softly
and uncovered his feet and lay down.
8 At midnight the man was startled and
turned over, and behold, a woman lay at
his feet! 9 He said, "Who are you?" And
she answered, "I am Ruth, your servant.
Spread your wings[1] over your servant, for
you are a redeemer." 10 And he said, "May
you be blessed by the LORD, my daughter.
You have made this last kindness greater
than the first in that you have not gone
after young men, whether poor or rich.
11 And now, my daughter, do not fear.
I will do for you all that you ask, for all
my fellow townsmen know that you are a
worthy woman. 12 And now it is true that
I am a redeemer. Yet there is a redeemer
nearer than I. 13 Remain tonight, and in
the morning, if he will redeem you, good;
let him do it. But if he is not willing to
redeem you, then, as the LORD lives, I will
redeem you. Lie down until the morning."

14 So she lay at his feet until the morn-
ing, but arose before one could recognize
another. And he said, "Let it not be known
that the woman came to the threshing
floor." 15 And he said, "Bring the garment
you are wearing and hold it out." So she
held it, and he measured out six measures
of barley and put it on her. Then she went
into the city. 16 And when she came to her
mother-in-law, she said, "How did you
fare, my daughter?" Then she told her all
that the man had done for her, 17 saying,
"These six measures of barley he gave to
me, for he said to me, 'You must not go
back empty-handed to your mother-in-
law.'" 18 She replied, "Wait, my daughter,
until you learn how the matter turns out,
for the man will not rest but will settle the
matter today."

Boaz Redeems Ruth

4 Now Boaz had gone up to the gate
and sat down there. And behold, the
redeemer, of whom Boaz had spoken,
came by. So Boaz said, "Turn aside, friend;
sit down here." And he turned aside and
sat down. 2 And he took ten men of the
elders of the city and said, "Sit down here."
So they sat down. 3 Then he said to the
redeemer, "Naomi, who has come back
from the country of Moab, is selling the
parcel of land that belonged to our rela-
tive Elimelech. 4 So I thought I would tell
you of it and say, 'Buy it in the presence
of those sitting here and in the presence
of the elders of my people.' If you will
redeem it, redeem it. But if you[2] will not,
tell me, that I may know, for there is no
one besides you to redeem it, and I come
after you." And he said, "I will redeem it."
5 Then Boaz said, "The day you buy the
field from the hand of Naomi, you also
acquire Ruth[3] the Moabite, the widow of
the dead, in order to perpetuate the name
of the dead in his inheritance." 6 Then the
redeemer said, "I cannot redeem it for
myself, lest I impair my own inheritance.
Take my right of redemption yourself, for
I cannot redeem it."

7 Now this was the custom in former
times in Israel concerning redeeming and

[1] Compare 2:12; the word for *wings* can also mean *corners of a garment* [2] Hebrew *he* [3] Masoretic Text *you also buy it from Ruth*

exchanging: to confirm a transaction, the
one drew off his sandal and gave it to the
other, and this was the manner of attest-
ing in Israel. 8 So when the redeemer said
to Boaz, "Buy it for yourself," he drew off
his sandal. 9 Then Boaz said to the elders
and all the people, "You are witnesses
this day that I have bought from the hand
of Naomi all that belonged to Elimelech
and all that belonged to Chilion and to
Mahlon. 10 Also Ruth the Moabite, the
widow of Mahlon, I have bought to be my
wife, to perpetuate the name of the dead
in his inheritance, that the name of the
dead may not be cut off from among his
brothers and from the gate of his native
place. You are witnesses this day." 11 Then
all the people who were at the gate and
the elders said, "We are witnesses. May
the LORD make the woman, who is com-
ing into your house, like Rachel and Leah,
who together built up the house of Israel.
May you act worthily in Ephrathah and be
renowned in Bethlehem, 12 and may your
house be like the house of Perez, whom
Tamar bore to Judah, because of the off-
spring that the LORD will give you by this
young woman."

Ruth and Boaz Marry

13 So Boaz took Ruth, and she became his
wife. And he went in to her, and the LORD
gave her conception, and she bore a son.
14 Then the women said to Naomi,
"Blessed be the LORD, who has not
425 left you this day without a redeem-
er, and may his name be renowned in
Israel! 15 He shall be to you a restorer of life
and a nourisher of your old age, for your
daughter-in-law who loves you, who is
more to you than seven sons, has given
birth to him." 16 Then Naomi took the
child and laid him on her lap and became
his nurse. 17 And the women of the neigh-
borhood gave him a name, saying, "A son
has been born to Naomi." They named
him Obed. He was the father of Jesse, the
father of David.

The Genealogy of David

18 Now these are the generations of
Perez: Perez fathered Hezron, 19 Hezron
fathered Ram, Ram fathered Amminadab,
20 Amminadab fathered Nahshon,
Nahshon fathered Salmon, 21 Salmon
fathered Boaz, Boaz fathered Obed, 22 Obed
fathered Jesse, and Jesse fathered David.

Introduction to

1–2 Samuel

Author and Date

Author unknown. Written about 970 B.C.

People

Hannah; the priest Eli; the prophet Samuel; King Saul and Jonathan; King David; Goliath; Abigail; Mephibosheth; Bathsheba; the prophet Nathan; Joab; Absalom

Purpose

These books show God's faithfulness in providing a king for His people and in establishing His covenant with that king.

Central Themes

God raises up and brings down kings; God provides and preserves a faithful king for His people; a king's obedience results in good for God's people while a king's disobedience harms them; God makes a covenant with David, promising a king from his family who will reign forever; God establishes Jerusalem as the place for His temple.

Memory Verses

Hannah's prayer (1 Samuel 2:1–10); a new priesthood (1 Samuel 2:30–31, 35); the Lord calls Samuel (1 Samuel 3:10–11); obedience better than sacrifice (1 Samuel 15:22–23); the battle is the Lord's (1 Samuel 17:45–47); an eternal king (2 Samuel 7:16).

Introduction

First and Second Samuel tell of three leaders in Israel: Samuel, Saul, and David. Samuel is born when his mother prays earnestly for a child. He serves the Lord from a young age and becomes a prophet and judge in Israel (1 Samuel 1–3). As Samuel grows old, the Israelites ask for a king so they can be "like all the nations" (1 Samuel 8). God gives them Saul, who begins well, but after he starts disobeying God's commands (1 Samuel 13; 15) God rejects him as king. God sends Samuel to anoint David, a shepherd boy, as the next king (1 Samuel 16). David serves Saul as a faithful soldier, but Saul grows jealous and tries to kill him. For years, David runs from Saul, but, finally, Saul dies and David becomes king (2 Samuel 5:1–5). God makes a covenant with David, promising that a descendant of his will be king forever (2 Samuel 7). When King David sins with Bathsheba and then repents, God forgives him (2 Samuel 11:1–12:23). The sin causes troubles in David's family, though. His own son, Absalom, tries to take over his father's throne and is killed (2 Samuel 15–18).

About 1100 B.C.	1050/1030 B.C. ?	1010 B.C.
Birth of Samuel	Reign of Saul begins	Reign of David begins

1 Samuel

The Birth of Samuel

435

1 There was a certain man of Ramathaim-zophim of the hill country of Ephraim whose name was Elkanah the son of Jeroham, son of Elihu, son of Tohu, son of Zuph, an Ephrathite. 2 He had two wives. The name of the one was Hannah, and the name of the other, Peninnah. And Peninnah had children, but Hannah had no children.

3 Now this man used to go up year by year from his city to worship and to sacrifice to the LORD of hosts at Shiloh, where the two sons of Eli, Hophni and Phinehas, were priests of the LORD. 4 On the day when Elkanah sacrificed, he would give portions to Peninnah his wife and to all her sons and daughters. 5 But to Hannah he gave a double portion, because he loved her, though the LORD had closed her womb.[1] 6 And her rival used to provoke her grievously to irritate her, because the LORD had closed her womb. 7 So it went on year by year. As often as she went up to the house of the LORD, she used to provoke her. Therefore Hannah wept and would not eat. 8 And Elkanah, her husband, said to her, "Hannah, why do you weep? And why do you not eat? And why is your heart sad? Am I not more to you than ten sons?"

9 After they had eaten and drunk in Shiloh, Hannah rose. Now Eli the priest was sitting on the seat beside the doorpost of the temple of the LORD. 10 She was deeply distressed and prayed to the LORD and wept bitterly. 11 And she vowed a vow and said, "O LORD of hosts, if you will indeed look on the affliction of your servant and remember me and not forget your servant, but will give to your servant a son, then I will give him to the LORD all the days of his life, and no razor shall touch his head."

12 As she continued praying before the LORD, Eli observed her mouth. 13 Hannah was speaking in her heart; only her lips moved, and her voice was not heard. Therefore Eli took her to be a drunken woman. 14 And Eli said to her, "How long will you go on being drunk? Put your wine away from you." 15 But Hannah answered, "No, my lord, I am a woman troubled in spirit. I have drunk neither wine nor strong drink, but I have been pouring out my soul before the LORD. 16 Do not regard your servant as a worthless woman, for all along I have been speaking out of my great anxiety and vexation." 17 Then Eli answered, "Go in peace, and the God of Israel grant your petition that you have made to him." 18 And she said, "Let your servant find favor in your eyes." Then the woman went her way and ate, and her face was no longer sad.

19 They rose early in the morning and worshiped before the LORD; then they went back to their house at Ramah. And Elkanah knew Hannah his wife, and the LORD remembered her. 20 And in due time Hannah conceived and bore a son, and she called his name Samuel, for she said, "I have asked for him from the LORD."[2]

Samuel Given to the LORD

441

21 The man Elkanah and all his house went up to offer to the LORD the yearly sacrifice and to pay his vow. 22 But Hannah did not go up, for she said to her husband, "As soon as the child is weaned, I will bring him, so that he may appear in the presence of the LORD and dwell there forever." 23 Elkanah her

[1] Syriac; the meaning of the Hebrew is uncertain. Septuagint *And, although he loved Hannah, he would give Hannah only one portion, because the LORD had closed her womb* [2] *Samuel* sounds like the Hebrew for *heard of God*

husband said to her, "Do what seems best
to you; wait until you have weaned him;
only, may the LORD establish his word."
So the woman remained and nursed her
son until she weaned him. **24** And when
she had weaned him, she took him up
with her, along with a three-year-old
bull,[1] an ephah[2] of flour, and a skin of
wine, and she brought him to the house
of the LORD at Shiloh. And the child was
young. **25** Then they slaughtered the bull,
and they brought the child to Eli. **26** And
she said, "Oh, my lord! As you live, my
lord, I am the woman who was standing
here in your presence, praying to the
LORD. **27** For this child I prayed, and the
LORD has granted me my petition that I
made to him. **28** Therefore I have lent him
to the LORD. As long as he lives, he is
lent to the LORD."
And he worshiped the LORD there.

CHARACTER PROFILE

HANNAH

Hannah had no children. She prayed, asking God that He would give her a child. God answered Hannah's prayer and gave her a baby boy. She named the baby Samuel. When Samuel was old enough, Hannah took him to stay with Eli the priest, to help Eli with his work in the Lord's house, the Tabernacle tent.

435

Hannah's Prayer

1437

2 And Hannah prayed and said,

"My heart exults in the LORD;
 my strength[3] is exalted in the LORD.
My mouth derides my enemies,
 because I rejoice in your salvation.

2 "There is none holy like the LORD;
 there is none besides you;
 there is no rock like our God.
3 Talk no more so very proudly,
 let not arrogance come from your mouth;
for the LORD is a God of knowledge,
 and by him actions are weighed.
4 The bows of the mighty are broken,
 but the feeble bind on strength.
5 Those who were full have hired themselves out for bread,
 but those who were hungry have ceased to hunger.
The barren has borne seven,
 but she who has many children is forlorn.
6 The LORD kills and brings to life;
 he brings down to Sheol and raises up.
7 The LORD makes poor and makes rich;
 he brings low and he exalts.
8 He raises up the poor from the dust;
 he lifts the needy from the ash heap
to make them sit with princes
 and inherit a seat of honor.
For the pillars of the earth are the LORD's,
 and on them he has set the world.

9 "He will guard the feet of his faithful ones,
 but the wicked shall be cut off in darkness,

[1] Septuagint, Syriac; Hebrew *three bulls* [2] An *ephah* was about 3/5 bushel or 22 liters [3] Hebrew *horn*

God Answers Hannah's Prayer

Year after year Elkanah went to Shiloh to worship and sacrifice at the tabernacle, the tent of worship for the people of Israel. Elkanah's wife, Hannah, went too. Each year, she was very sad because she had no children and was teased about it.

One day, while they were at the tabernacle, Hannah prayed to the LORD. She asked God to remember her and give her a son. She promised, "Then I will give him to the LORD all the days of his life."

As she prayed, Eli the priest saw her. Hannah was speaking in her heart and quietly moving her lips. Eli thought Hannah was a drunken woman.

But Hannah answered, "No. I have drunk neither wine nor strong drink, but I have been pouring out my soul before the LORD."

Then Eli answered, "Go in peace, and the God of Israel grant your petition that you have made to Him." Hannah went on her way, no longer sad, and trusting the Lord that He would answer her prayer.

In time, Hannah found out she was going to have a baby. When the baby was born, she called him Samuel.

When Samuel grew up to be a young boy, Hannah kept her promise. She took Samuel to Eli the priest, to serve the Lord all his life in the Lord's house. Hannah said, "For this child I prayed, and the LORD has granted me my petition that I made to Him." God had answered Hannah's prayer. So Hannah gave Samuel to the Lord, to help Eli the priest serve in the house of the Lord.

Then Hannah prayed a beautiful prayer of thanks to God—because He "raises up the poor" and He "lifts the needy," and because He "will judge the ends of the earth" and "will give strength to His king."

Many years later, another woman—Mary the mother of Jesus—learned she was going to have a baby. Her baby would be the most special baby ever born, because He would be the Son of God. Mary sang a beautiful song of praise, much like Hannah's prayer. Mary praised God for the wonderful things God would do through her Son Jesus, to save us from our sins.

SEEK and FIND

WHERE TO FIND THE STORY

1 Samuel 1:1–2:11

KEY BIBLE VERSE

"In everything by prayer and supplication with thanksgiving let your requests be made known to God. And the peace of God, which surpasses all understanding, will guard your hearts and your minds in Christ Jesus." (Philippians 4:6–7)

THREE KEY QUESTIONS

- What did Hannah do when she was so sad?
- How did God answer Hannah's prayer?
- What did Samuel do, even when he was a little boy?

RELATED BIBLE READINGS
Luke 1:39–55; James 5:13–16; 1 Peter 5:6–7; 1 John 5:14–15

for not by might shall a man
prevail.
10 The adversaries of the LORD shall be
broken to pieces;
against them he will thunder in
heaven.
The LORD will judge the ends of the
earth;
he will give strength to his king
and exalt the power[1] of his
anointed."

11 Then Elkanah went home to Ramah.
And the boy ministered to the LORD in the
presence of Eli the priest.

Eli's Worthless Sons

12 Now the sons of Eli were worthless
men. They did not know the LORD. 13 The
custom of the priests with the people was
that when any man offered sacrifice, the
priest's servant[2] would come, while the
meat was boiling, with a three-pronged
fork in his hand, 14 and he would thrust
it into the pan or kettle or cauldron or
pot. All that the fork brought up the priest
would take for himself. This is what they
did at Shiloh to all the Israelites who came
there. 15 Moreover, before the fat was
burned, the priest's servant would come
and say to the man who was sacrificing,
"Give meat for the priest to roast, for he
will not accept boiled meat from you but
only raw." 16 And if the man said to him,
"Let them burn the fat first, and then take
as much as you wish," he would say, "No,
you must give it now, and if not, I will take
it by force." 17 Thus the sin of the young
men was very great in the sight of the
LORD, for the men treated the offering of
the LORD with contempt.

18 Samuel was ministering before the
LORD, a boy clothed with a linen ephod.
19 And his mother used to make for him
a little robe and take it to him each year
when she went up with her husband
to offer the yearly sacrifice. 20 Then Eli
would bless Elkanah and his wife, and
say, "May the LORD give you children by
this woman for the petition she asked of
the LORD." So then they would return to
their home.

21 Indeed the LORD visited Hannah,
and she conceived and bore three sons
and two daughters. And the young man
Samuel grew in the presence of the LORD.

Eli Rebukes His Sons

22 Now Eli was very old, and he kept
hearing all that his sons were doing to all
Israel, and how they lay with the women
who were serving at the entrance to the
tent of meeting. 23 And he said to them,
"Why do you do such things? For I hear
of your evil dealings from all the people.
24 No, my sons; it is no good report that
I hear the people of the LORD spreading
abroad. 25 If someone sins against a man,
God will mediate for him, but if someone
sins against the LORD, who can intercede
for him?" But they would not listen to the
voice of their father, for it was the will of
the LORD to put them to death.

26 Now the young man Samuel contin-
ued to grow both in stature and in favor
with the LORD and also with man.

[1] Hebrew *horn* [2] Hebrew *young man*; also verse 15

The LORD Rejects Eli's Household

27 And there came a man of God to Eli
and said to him, "Thus the LORD has said,
'Did I indeed reveal myself to the house of
your father when they were in Egypt sub-
ject to the house of Pharaoh? 28 Did I choose
him out of all the tribes of Israel to be my
priest, to go up to my altar, to burn incense,
to wear an ephod before me? I gave to the
house of your father all my offerings by fire
from the people of Israel. 29 Why then do
you scorn[1] my sacrifices and my offerings
that I commanded, and honor your sons
above me by fattening yourselves on the
choicest parts of every offering of my peo-
ple Israel?' 30 Therefore the LORD, the God of
Israel, declares: 'I promised that your house
and the house of your father should go in
and out before me forever,' but now the
LORD declares: 'Far be it from me, for those
who honor me I will honor, and those
who despise me shall be lightly esteemed.
31 Behold, the days are coming when I will
cut off your strength and the strength of
your father's house, so that there will not
be an old man in your house. 32 Then in
distress you will look with envious eye on
all the prosperity that shall be bestowed on
Israel, and there shall not be an old man
in your house forever. 33 The only one of
you whom I shall not cut off from my altar
shall be spared to weep his[2] eyes out to
grieve his heart, and all the descendants[3] of
your house shall die by the sword of men.[4]
34 And this that shall come upon your two
sons, Hophni and Phinehas, shall be the
sign to you: both of them shall die on the
same day. 35 And I will raise up for myself
a faithful priest, who shall do according to
what is in my heart and in my mind. And
I will build him a sure house, and he shall
go in and out before my anointed forever.
36 And everyone who is left in your house
shall come to implore him for a piece of sil-
ver or a loaf of bread and shall say, "Please
put me in one of the priests' places, that I
may eat a morsel of bread."'"

The LORD Calls Samuel

3 Now the young man Samuel
was ministering to the LORD
441 under Eli. And the word of the
LORD was rare in those days; there was no
frequent vision.

2 At that time Eli, whose eyesight had
begun to grow dim so that he could not
see, was lying down in his own place.
3 The lamp of God had not yet gone out,
and Samuel was lying down in the temple
of the LORD, where the ark of God was.

4 Then the LORD called Samuel, and he
said, "Here I am!" 5 and ran to Eli and said,
"Here I am, for you called me." But he said,
"I did not call; lie down again." So he went
and lay down.

6 And the LORD called again, "Samuel!"
and Samuel arose and went to Eli and
said, "Here I am, for you called me." But
he said, "I did not call, my son; lie down
again." 7 Now Samuel did not yet know the
LORD, and the word of the LORD had not
yet been revealed to him.

8 And the LORD called Samuel again the
third time. And he arose and went to Eli
and said, "Here I am, for you called me."
Then Eli perceived that the LORD was call-
ing the young man. 9 Therefore Eli said to
Samuel, "Go, lie down, and if he calls you,
you shall say, 'Speak, LORD, for your ser-
vant hears.'" So Samuel went and lay down
in his place.

10 And the LORD came and stood,
calling as at other times, "Samuel!
441 Samuel!" And Samuel said, "Speak,
for your servant hears." 11 Then the LORD
said to Samuel, "Behold, I am about to do
a thing in Israel at which the two ears of
everyone who hears it will tingle. 12 On
that day I will fulfill against Eli all that I
have spoken concerning his house, from
beginning to end. 13 And I declare to him
that I am about to punish his house for-
ever, for the iniquity that he knew,
because his sons were blaspheming God,[5]
and he did not restrain them. 14 Therefore

[1] Septuagint; Hebrew *kick at* [2] Septuagint; Hebrew *your;* twice in this verse [3] Hebrew *increase* [4] Septuagint; Hebrew *die as men* [5] Or *blaspheming for themselves*

I swear to the house of Eli that the iniquity
of Eli's house shall not be atoned for by
sacrifice or offering forever."
15 Samuel lay until morning; then he
opened the doors of the house of the
LORD. And Samuel was afraid to tell the
vision to Eli. 16 But Eli called Samuel and
said, "Samuel, my son." And he said, "Here
I am." 17 And Eli said, "What was it that he
told you? Do not hide it from me. May God
do so to you and more also if you hide any-
thing from me of all that he told you." 18 So
Samuel told him everything and hid noth-
ing from him. And he said, "It is the LORD.
Let him do what seems good to him."
19 And Samuel grew, and the LORD was
with him and let none of his words fall to
the ground. 20 And all Israel from Dan to
Beersheba knew that Samuel was estab-
lished as a prophet of the LORD. 21 And the
LORD appeared again at Shiloh, for the
LORD revealed himself to Samuel at Shiloh
by the word of the LORD.

CHARACTER PROFILE

SAMUEL

Samuel, as a young boy, helped Eli the priest. While he was still a child, God called and spoke to him in the night. God gave Samuel a message to give to Eli about his sons, who were sinning against God. Samuel grew up to be a prophet, speaking God's messages to God's people. Samuel anointed both Saul and then David as kings over Israel.

435, 441, 449, 463

The Philistines Capture the Ark

4 And the word of Samuel came to all
Israel.
Now Israel went out to battle against the
Philistines. They encamped at Ebenezer,
and the Philistines encamped at Aphek.
2 The Philistines drew up in line against
Israel, and when the battle spread, Israel
was defeated by the Philistines, who killed
about four thousand men on the field of
battle. 3 And when the troops came to the
camp, the elders of Israel said, "Why has
the LORD defeated us today before the
Philistines? Let us bring the ark of the cov-
enant of the LORD here from Shiloh, that it
may come among us and save us from the
power of our enemies." 4 So the people sent
to Shiloh and brought from there the ark of
the covenant of the LORD of hosts, who is
enthroned on the cherubim. And the two
sons of Eli, Hophni and Phinehas, were
there with the ark of the covenant of God.
5 As soon as the ark of the covenant of the
LORD came into the camp, all Israel gave a
mighty shout, so that the earth resounded.
6 And when the Philistines heard the noise
of the shouting, they said, "What does this
great shouting in the camp of the Hebrews
mean?" And when they learned that the ark
of the LORD had come to the camp, 7 the
Philistines were afraid, for they said, "A god
has come into the camp." And they said,
"Woe to us! For nothing like this has hap-
pened before. 8 Woe to us! Who can deliver
us from the power of these mighty gods?
These are the gods who struck the Egyptians
with every sort of plague in the wilderness.
9 Take courage, and be men, O Philistines,
lest you become slaves to the Hebrews as
they have been to you; be men and fight."

Samuel Hears God Speak to Him

God had answered Hannah's prayer, so she had given her son Samuel to the Lord. When Samuel grew up to be a young boy, he was old enough to serve in the tabernacle, God's tent of worship for the people of Israel. He would be a helper to Eli, the high priest. Every year, when Hannah and her husband came to the tabernacle to offer their sacrifices to God, Hannah would bring new clothes that she had made for Samuel.

One night, when Eli the priest and Samuel were in their beds, Samuel heard someone calling him. He thought it was Eli, so he got up and went to Eli. Samuel said, "Here I am, for you called me."

Eli said, "I did not call; lie down again."

Samuel went back to bed, but again he heard a voice say, "Samuel!"

Samuel returned to Eli. "Here I am, for you called me," he said.

But again, Eli said, "I did not call, my son; lie down again."

Samuel went back to bed and the voice called once more. Samuel went to Eli, again saying, "Here I am, for you called me."

Finally, Eli understood that it was God who was calling Samuel. He told Samuel, "Go, lie down, and if He calls you, you shall say, 'Speak, LORD, for your servant hears.'"

Samuel went back to bed. And the LORD called again, "Samuel! Samuel!"

Samuel said, "Speak, for your servant hears." Then God talked to Samuel and told him what He was going to do.

As Samuel grew, the Lord came and talked to him at other times too. All his life, Samuel served the Lord in the tabernacle. He told the people about God, and he taught God's Word to them. When God had a message for His people, He gave it to Samuel to tell them. God was with Samuel and blessed him.

Years later, God sent the Lord Jesus Christ to serve His Father and to be our Savior. Jesus taught God's Word perfectly. And He showed us perfectly what God is like. Jesus still speaks to us through His Word today. He gives us pastors who teach us about Him. They tell us about God's holiness and love, and how God sent Jesus to save us from our sins. And they teach us how we should live to please the Lord and serve Him.

SEEK and FIND

WHERE TO FIND THE STORY

1 Samuel 1:21–28; 3:1–21

KEY BIBLE VERSE

"And the LORD came and stood, calling as at other times, 'Samuel! Samuel!' And Samuel said, 'Speak, for your servant hears.'" (1 Samuel 3:10)

THREE KEY QUESTIONS

- Who spoke to Samuel in the middle of the night?
- What did God have Samuel do all his life?

- Who does God give to us to help teach us God's Word today?

RELATED BIBLE READINGS

1 Samuel 7:1–13:23; 15:1–16:13; Hebrews 1:1–3; 11:32–34

10 So the Philistines fought, and Israel
was defeated, and they fled, every man
to his home. And there was a very great
slaughter, for there fell of Israel thirty
thousand foot soldiers. 11 And the ark of
God was captured, and the two sons of Eli,
Hophni and Phinehas, died.

The Death of Eli

12 A man of Benjamin ran from the
battle line and came to Shiloh the same
day, with his clothes torn and with dirt
on his head. 13 When he arrived, Eli was
sitting on his seat by the road watching,
for his heart trembled for the ark of God.
And when the man came into the city
and told the news, all the city cried out.
14 When Eli heard the sound of the out-
cry, he said, "What is this uproar?" Then
the man hurried and came and told Eli.
15 Now Eli was ninety-eight years old and
his eyes were set so that he could not see.
16 And the man said to Eli, "I am he who
has come from the battle; I fled from the
battle today." And he said, "How did it go,
my son?" 17 He who brought the news
answered and said, "Israel has fled before
the Philistines, and there has also been a
great defeat among the people. Your two
sons also, Hophni and Phinehas, are dead,
and the ark of God has been captured."
18 As soon as he mentioned the ark of God,
Eli fell over backward from his seat by the
side of the gate, and his neck was broken
and he died, for the man was old and
heavy. He had judged Israel forty years.

19 Now his daughter-in-law, the wife
of Phinehas, was pregnant, about to give
birth. And when she heard the news that
the ark of God was captured, and that her
father-in-law and her husband were dead,
she bowed and gave birth, for her pains
came upon her. 20 And about the time of
her death the women attending her said
to her, "Do not be afraid, for you have
borne a son." But she did not answer or
pay attention. 21 And she named the child
Ichabod, saying, "The glory has departed[1]
from Israel!" because the ark of God had
been captured and because of her father-
in-law and her husband. 22 And she said,
"The glory has departed from Israel, for
the ark of God has been captured."

The Philistines and the Ark

5 When the Philistines captured the ark
of God, they brought it from Ebenezer
to Ashdod. 2 Then the Philistines took the
ark of God and brought it into the house
of Dagon and set it up beside Dagon. 3 And
when the people of Ashdod rose early the
next day, behold, Dagon had fallen face
downward on the ground before the ark
of the LORD. So they took Dagon and put
him back in his place. 4 But when they
rose early on the next morning, behold,
Dagon had fallen face downward on the
ground before the ark of the LORD, and the
head of Dagon and both his hands were
lying cut off on the threshold. Only the
trunk of Dagon was left to him. 5 This is
why the priests of Dagon and all who enter
the house of Dagon do not tread on the
threshold of Dagon in Ashdod to this day.

[1] Or *gone into exile*; also verse 22

[6] The hand of the LORD was heavy
against the people of Ashdod, and he ter-
rified and afflicted them with tumors,
both Ashdod and its territory. [7] And when
the men of Ashdod saw how things were,
they said, "The ark of the God of Israel
must not remain with us, for his hand
is hard against us and against Dagon our
god." [8] So they sent and gathered together
all the lords of the Philistines and said,
"What shall we do with the ark of the God
of Israel?" They answered, "Let the ark
of the God of Israel be brought around
to Gath." So they brought the ark of the
God of Israel there. [9] But after they had
brought it around, the hand of the LORD
was against the city, causing a very great
panic, and he afflicted the men of the
city, both young and old, so that tumors
broke out on them. [10] So they sent the ark
of God to Ekron. But as soon as the ark of
God came to Ekron, the people of Ekron
cried out, "They have brought around to
us the ark of the God of Israel to kill us
and our people." [11] They sent therefore
and gathered together all the lords of the
Philistines and said, "Send away the ark
of the God of Israel, and let it return to
its own place, that it may not kill us and
our people." For there was a deathly panic
throughout the whole city. The hand of
God was very heavy there. [12] The men who
did not die were struck with tumors, and
the cry of the city went up to heaven.

The Ark Returned to Israel

6 The ark of the LORD was in the country
of the Philistines seven months. [2] And
the Philistines called for the priests and the
diviners and said, "What shall we do with
the ark of the LORD? Tell us with what we
shall send it to its place." [3] They said, "If you
send away the ark of the God of Israel, do
not send it empty, but by all means return
him a guilt offering. Then you will be
healed, and it will be known to you why his
hand does not turn away from you." [4] And
they said, "What is the guilt offering that
we shall return to him?" They answered,
"Five golden tumors and five golden mice,
according to the number of the lords of
the Philistines, for the same plague was
on all of you and on your lords. [5] So you
must make images of your tumors and
images of your mice that ravage the land,
and give glory to the God of Israel. Perhaps
he will lighten his hand from off you and
your gods and your land. [6] Why should you
harden your hearts as the Egyptians and
Pharaoh hardened their hearts? After he
had dealt severely with them, did they not
send the people away, and they departed?
[7] Now then, take and prepare a new cart
and two milk cows on which there has
never come a yoke, and yoke the cows to
the cart, but take their calves home, away
from them. [8] And take the ark of the LORD
and place it on the cart and put in a box at
its side the figures of gold, which you are
returning to him as a guilt offering. Then
send it off and let it go its way [9] and watch.
If it goes up on the way to its own land, to
Beth-shemesh, then it is he who has done
us this great harm, but if not, then we shall
know that it is not his hand that struck us;
it happened to us by coincidence."

[10] The men did so, and took two milk
cows and yoked them to the cart and shut
up their calves at home. [11] And they put
the ark of the LORD on the cart and the
box with the golden mice and the images
of their tumors. [12] And the cows went
straight in the direction of Beth-shemesh
along one highway, lowing as they went.
They turned neither to the right nor to
the left, and the lords of the Philistines
went after them as far as the border of
Beth-shemesh. [13] Now the people of Beth-
shemesh were reaping their wheat harvest
in the valley. And when they lifted up their
eyes and saw the ark, they rejoiced to see
it. [14] The cart came into the field of Joshua
of Beth-shemesh and stopped there. A
great stone was there. And they split up

the wood of the cart and offered the cows as a burnt offering to the LORD. 15 And the Levites took down the ark of the LORD and the box that was beside it, in which were the golden figures, and set them upon the great stone. And the men of Beth-shemesh offered burnt offerings and sacrificed sacrifices on that day to the LORD. 16 And when the five lords of the Philistines saw it, they returned that day to Ekron.

17 These are the golden tumors that the Philistines returned as a guilt offering to the LORD: one for Ashdod, one for Gaza, one for Ashkelon, one for Gath, one for Ekron, 18 and the golden mice, according to the number of all the cities of the Philistines belonging to the five lords, both fortified cities and unwalled villages. The great stone beside which they set down the ark of the LORD is a witness to this day in the field of Joshua of Beth-shemesh.

19 And he struck some of the men of Beth-shemesh, because they looked upon the ark of the LORD. He struck seventy men of them,[1] and the people mourned because the LORD had struck the people with a great blow. 20 Then the men of Beth-shemesh said, "Who is able to stand before the LORD, this holy God? And to whom shall he go up away from us?" 21 So they sent messengers to the inhabitants of Kiriath-jearim, saying, "The Philistines have returned the ark of the LORD. Come down and take it up to you."

7 And the men of Kiriath-jearim
came and took up the ark of the
441 LORD and brought it to the house
of Abinadab on the hill. And they consecrated his son Eleazar to have charge of the ark of the LORD. 2 From the day that the ark was lodged at Kiriath-jearim, a long time passed, some twenty years, and all the house of Israel lamented after the LORD.

Samuel Judges Israel

3 And Samuel said to all the house of Israel, "If you are returning to the LORD with all your heart, then put away the foreign gods and the Ashtaroth from among you and direct your heart to the LORD and serve him only, and he will deliver you out of the hand of the Philistines." 4 So the people of Israel put away the Baals and the Ashtaroth, and they served the LORD only.

5 Then Samuel said, "Gather all Israel at Mizpah, and I will pray to the LORD for you." 6 So they gathered at Mizpah and drew water and poured it out before the LORD and fasted on that day and said there, "We have sinned against the LORD." And Samuel judged the people of Israel at Mizpah. 7 Now when the Philistines heard that the people of Israel had gathered at Mizpah, the lords of the Philistines went up against Israel. And when the people of Israel heard of it, they were afraid of the Philistines. 8 And the people of Israel said to Samuel, "Do not cease to cry out to the LORD our God for us, that he may save us from the hand of the Philistines." 9 So Samuel took a nursing lamb and offered it as a whole burnt offering to the LORD. And Samuel cried out to the LORD for Israel, and the LORD answered him. 10 As Samuel was offering up the burnt offering, the Philistines drew near to attack Israel. But the LORD thundered with a mighty sound that day against the Philistines and threw them into confusion, and they were routed before Israel. 11 And the men of Israel went out from Mizpah and pursued the Philistines and struck them, as far as below Beth-car.

12 Then Samuel took a stone and set it up between Mizpah and Shen[2] and called its name Ebenezer;[3] for he said, "Till now the LORD has helped us." 13 So the Philistines were subdued and did not again enter the territory of Israel. And the hand of the LORD was against the Philistines all the days of Samuel. 14 The cities that the Philistines had taken from Israel were restored to Israel, from Ekron

[1] Hebrew *of the people seventy men, fifty thousand men* [2] Hebrew; Septuagint, Syriac *Jeshanah* [3] *Ebenezer* means *stone of help*

to Gath, and Israel delivered their territory from the hand of the Philistines. There was peace also between Israel and the Amorites.

15 Samuel judged Israel all the days of his life. 16 And he went on a circuit year by year to Bethel, Gilgal, and Mizpah. And he judged Israel in all these places. 17 Then he would return to Ramah, for his home was there, and there also he judged Israel. And he built there an altar to the LORD.

Israel Demands a King

449

8 When Samuel became old, he made his sons judges over Israel. 2 The name of his firstborn son was Joel, and the name of his second, Abijah; they were judges in Beersheba. 3 Yet his sons did not walk in his ways but turned aside after gain. They took bribes and perverted justice.

4 Then all the elders of Israel gathered together and came to Samuel at Ramah 5 and said to him, "Behold, you are old and your sons do not walk in your ways. Now appoint for us a king to judge us like all the nations." 6 But the thing displeased Samuel when they said, "Give us a king to judge us." And Samuel prayed to the LORD. 7 And the LORD said to Samuel, "Obey the voice of the people in all that they say to you, for they have not rejected you, but they have rejected me from being king over them. 8 According to all the deeds that they have done, from the day I brought them up out of Egypt even to this day, forsaking me and serving other gods, so they are also doing to you. 9 Now then, obey their voice; only you shall solemnly warn them and show them the ways of the king who shall reign over them."

Samuel's Warning Against Kings

10 So Samuel told all the words of the LORD to the people who were asking for a king from him. 11 He said, "These will be the ways of the king who will reign over you: he will take your sons and appoint them to his chariots and to be his horsemen and to run before his chariots. 12 And he will appoint for himself commanders of thousands and commanders of fifties, and some to plow his ground and to reap his harvest, and to make his implements of war and the equipment of his chariots. 13 He will take your daughters to be perfumers and cooks and bakers. 14 He will take the best of your fields and vineyards and olive orchards and give them to his servants. 15 He will take the tenth of your grain and of your vineyards and give it to his officers and to his servants. 16 He will take your male servants and female servants and the best of your young men[1] and your donkeys, and put them to his work. 17 He will take the tenth of your flocks, and you shall be his slaves. 18 And in that day you will cry out because of your king, whom you have chosen for yourselves, but the LORD will not answer you in that day."

The LORD Grants Israel's Request

19 But the people refused to obey the voice of Samuel. And they said, "No! But there shall be a king over us, 20 that we also may be like all the nations, and that our king may judge us and go out before us and fight our battles." 21 And when Samuel had heard all the words of the people, he repeated them in the ears of the LORD. 22 And the LORD said to Samuel, "Obey their voice and make them a king." Samuel then said to the men of Israel, "Go every man to his city."

Saul Chosen to Be King

9 There was a man of Benjamin whose name was Kish, the son of Abiel, son of Zeror, son of Becorath, son of Aphiah, a Benjaminite, a man of wealth. 2 And he had a son whose name was Saul, a handsome young man. There was not a man among the people of Israel more handsome than he. From his shoulders upward he was taller than any of the people.

[1] Septuagint *cattle*

3 Now the donkeys of Kish, Saul's father,
were lost. So Kish said to Saul his son,
"Take one of the young men with you,
and arise, go and look for the donkeys."
4 And he passed through the hill coun-
try of Ephraim and passed through the
land of Shalishah, but they did not find
them. And they passed through the land
of Shaalim, but they were not there. Then
they passed through the land of Benjamin,
but did not find them.

5 When they came to the land of Zuph,
Saul said to his servant[1] who was with him,
"Come, let us go back, lest my father cease
to care about the donkeys and become
anxious about us." 6 But he said to him,
"Behold, there is a man of God in this city,
and he is a man who is held in honor; all
that he says comes true. So now let us go
there. Perhaps he can tell us the way we
should go." 7 Then Saul said to his servant,
"But if we go, what can we bring the man?
For the bread in our sacks is gone, and
there is no present to bring to the man
of God. What do we have?" 8 The servant
answered Saul again, "Here, I have with
me a quarter of a shekel[2] of silver, and I
will give it to the man of God to tell us our
way." 9 (Formerly in Israel, when a man
went to inquire of God, he said, "Come,
let us go to the seer," for today's "prophet"
was formerly called a seer.) 10 And Saul
said to his servant, "Well said; come, let
us go." So they went to the city where the
man of God was.

11 As they went up the hill to the city,
they met young women coming out to
draw water and said to them, "Is the seer
here?" 12 They answered, "He is; behold, he
is just ahead of you. Hurry. He has come
just now to the city, because the people
have a sacrifice today on the high place.
13 As soon as you enter the city you will
find him, before he goes up to the high
place to eat. For the people will not eat till
he comes, since he must bless the sacri-
fice; afterward those who are invited will
eat. Now go up, for you will meet him
immediately." 14 So they went up to the
city. As they were entering the city, they
saw Samuel coming out toward them on
his way up to the high place.

15 Now the day before Saul came, the
LORD had revealed to Samuel: 16 "To-
morrow about this time I will send to
you a man from the land of Benjamin,
and you shall anoint him to be prince
over my people Israel. He shall save my
people from the hand of the Philistines.
For I have seen[3] my people, because their
cry has come to me." 17 When Samuel
saw Saul, the LORD told him, "Here is
the man of whom I spoke to you! He it
is who shall restrain my people." 18 Then
Saul approached Samuel in the gate and
said, "Tell me where is the house of the
seer?" 19 Samuel answered Saul, "I am the
seer. Go up before me to the high place,
for today you shall eat with me, and in
the morning I will let you go and will tell
you all that is on your mind. 20 As for your
donkeys that were lost three days ago, do
not set your mind on them, for they have
been found. And for whom is all that is
desirable in Israel? Is it not for you and for
all your father's house?" 21 Saul answered,
"Am I not a Benjaminite, from the least of
the tribes of Israel? And is not my clan the
humblest of all the clans of the tribe of
Benjamin? Why then have you spoken to
me in this way?"

22 Then Samuel took Saul and his young
man and brought them into the hall and
gave them a place at the head of those
who had been invited, who were about
thirty persons. 23 And Samuel said to the
cook, "Bring the portion I gave you, of
which I said to you, 'Put it aside.'" 24 So
the cook took up the leg and what was on
it and set them before Saul. And Samuel
said, "See, what was kept is set before you.
Eat, because it was kept for you until the
hour appointed, that you might eat with
the guests."[4]

[1] Hebrew *young man*; also verses 7, 8, 10, 27 [2] A *shekel* was about 2/5 ounce or 11 grams [3] Septuagint adds *the affliction of* [4] Hebrew *appointed, saying, 'I have invited the people'*

Saul and the True King

As the years went by, Samuel grew from a little boy to become a great prophet, judge, and priest for the people of Israel. Then, many years later when Samuel was old, he made his sons judges over the people of Israel. But Samuel's son did not follow God's ways as their father had done.

The people of Israel did not want Samuel's sons to rule over them. So they told Samuel, "Appoint for us a king to judge us like all the nations." This news made Samuel sad. He didn't think it was a good idea for the people to have a king—after all, God was their true King.

Samuel prayed and asked God what to do. God told Samuel to do as the people had said, and to appoint a king over the people. "They have not rejected you," God told Samuel, "but they have rejected Me from being King over them." God told Samuel to be sure to warn the people about all the bad things that would happen if they had a king to rule over them.

So Samuel told the people what God had said. He warned them what it would be like to have a king rule over them. He told them a king would take the best of their fields, some of all the crops they grew, and some of all their animals. A king would make their sons and daughters work for him. He would make them pay him money and serve in his army. If they had a king, the Israelites would have to obey him in everything.

But the people didn't care. They said, "No! But there shall be a king over us, that we also may be like all the nations, and that our king may judge us and go out before us and fight our battles."

Then God told Samuel that He would send a man to him, and that Samuel was to anoint this man as king over Israel. The next day, a man named Saul came to Samuel with a question. When Samuel saw Saul, God told Samuel, "Here is the man!"

Samuel invited Saul to eat a special meal and to stay overnight at his house that night. Early the next morning, Samuel called for Saul to get up and come with him outside the city. There, Samuel told Saul that God had chosen him to be the king over God's people Israel. Samuel poured oil on Saul's head to anoint him as king. "You shall reign over the people of the LORD," Samuel told Saul, "and you will save them from the hand of their surrounding enemies."

Later, Samuel gathered the people of Israel together. He told them how God had rescued them from their enemies and how He had taken care of them. He reminded them that they had rejected God as their true King, and that they wanted a human king instead. Even though the people of Israel were often unfaithful to God, He still loved them. He answered their prayers, and He gave them Saul to be their king.

At first, Saul was a good king, but later he sinned and did many wrong things. But God continued to be the true King of the people of Israel. Many years later, God sent the perfect King for His people, His own Son, Jesus Christ.

Even though we have a perfect King, we don't always

obey Him as we should. God still loves us. When we are truly His people, He always leads us to be sorry for our sins and He forgives us—because of our perfect King's death on the cross in our place.

SEEK and FIND

WHERE TO FIND THE STORY

1 Samuel 8–10

KEY BIBLE VERSE

"Let the children of Zion rejoice in their King!" (Psalm 149:2)

THREE KEY QUESTIONS

- Why did the people of Israel want to have a king?
- What are some of the bad things that God said would happen if a human king ruled over them?
- Who is the perfect King that God has given to His people?

RELATED BIBLE READINGS

1 Samuel 11:1–15; 13:1–23; 15:1–35; 31:1–13;
1 Chronicles 10:1–14; Isaiah 9:6–7; Matthew 21:1–5

So Saul ate with Samuel that day. 25 And
when they came down from the high
place into the city, a bed was spread
for Saul[1] on the roof, and he lay down
to sleep. 26 Then at the break of dawn[2]
Samuel called to Saul on the roof, "Up,
that I may send you on your way." So Saul
arose, and both he and Samuel went out
into the street.

27 As they were going down to the out-
skirts of the city, Samuel said to Saul, "Tell
the servant to pass on before us, and when
he has passed on, stop here yourself for a
while, that I may make known to you the
word of God."

Saul Anointed King

10 Then Samuel took a flask of oil
and poured it on his head and
kissed him and said, "Has not the LORD
anointed you to be prince over his peo-
ple Israel? And you shall reign over the
people of the LORD and you will save
them from the hand of their surround-
ing enemies. And this shall be the sign
to you that the LORD has anointed you to
be prince[3] over his heritage. 2 When you
depart from me today, you will meet two
men by Rachel's tomb in the territory of
Benjamin at Zelzah, and they will say
to you, 'The donkeys that you went to

[1] Septuagint; Hebrew *and he spoke with Saul* [2] Septuagint; Hebrew *And they arose early and at the break of dawn* [3] Septuagint; Hebrew lacks *over his people Israel? And you shall. . . . to be prince*

seek are found, and now your father has
ceased to care about the donkeys and is
anxious about you, saying, "What shall I
do about my son?"' 3 Then you shall go on
from there farther and come to the oak
of Tabor. Three men going up to God at
Bethel will meet you there, one carrying
three young goats, another carrying three
loaves of bread, and another carrying a
skin of wine. 4 And they will greet you and
give you two loaves of bread, which you
shall accept from their hand. 5 After that
you shall come to Gibeath-elohim,[1] where
there is a garrison of the Philistines. And
there, as soon as you come to the city,
you will meet a group of prophets com-
ing down from the high place with harp,
tambourine, flute, and lyre before them,
prophesying. 6 Then the Spirit of the LORD
will rush upon you, and you will proph-
esy with them and be turned into another
man. 7 Now when these signs meet you,
do what your hand finds to do, for God
is with you. 8 Then go down before me to
Gilgal. And behold, I am coming to you to
offer burnt offerings and to sacrifice peace
offerings. Seven days you shall wait, until
I come to you and show you what you
shall do."

9 When he turned his back to leave
Samuel, God gave him another heart.
And all these signs came to pass that day.
10 When they came to Gibeah,[2] behold, a
group of prophets met him, and the Spirit
of God rushed upon him, and he proph-
esied among them. 11 And when all who
knew him previously saw how he proph-
esied with the prophets, the people said to
one another, "What has come over the son
of Kish? Is Saul also among the prophets?"
12 And a man of the place answered, "And
who is their father?" Therefore it became
a proverb, "Is Saul also among the proph-
ets?" 13 When he had finished prophesy-
ing, he came to the high place.

14 Saul's uncle said to him and to his ser-
vant, "Where did you go?" And he said, "To
seek the donkeys. And when we saw they
were not to be found, we went to Samuel."
15 And Saul's uncle said, "Please tell me
what Samuel said to you." 16 And Saul said
to his uncle, "He told us plainly that the
donkeys had been found." But about the
matter of the kingdom, of which Samuel
had spoken, he did not tell him anything.

Saul Proclaimed King

17 Now Samuel called the people together
to the LORD at Mizpah. 18 And he said to the
people of Israel, "Thus says the LORD, the
God of Israel, 'I brought up Israel out of
Egypt, and I delivered you from the hand
of the Egyptians and from the hand of all
the kingdoms that were oppressing you.'
19 But today you have rejected your God,
who saves you from all your calamities
and your distresses, and you have said to
him, 'Set a king over us.' Now therefore
present yourselves before the LORD by
your tribes and by your thousands."

20 Then Samuel brought all the tribes
of Israel near, and the tribe of Benjamin
was taken by lot. 21 He brought the tribe of
Benjamin near by its clans, and the clan
of the Matrites was taken by lot;[3] and Saul
the son of Kish was taken by lot. But when
they sought him, he could not be found.
22 So they inquired again of the LORD, "Is
there a man still to come?" and the LORD
said, "Behold, he has hidden himself
among the baggage." 23 Then they ran and
took him from there. And when he stood
among the people, he was taller than any
of the people from his shoulders upward.
24 And Samuel said to all the people, "Do
you see him whom the LORD has cho-
sen? There is none like him among all the
people." And all the people shouted, "Long
live the king!"

25 Then Samuel told the people the rights
and duties of the kingship, and he wrote
them in a book and laid it up before the
LORD. Then Samuel sent all the people
away, each one to his home. 26 Saul also

[1] *Gibeath-elohim* means *the hill of God* [2] *Gibeah* means *the hill* [3] Septuagint adds *finally he brought the family of the Matrites near, man by man*

went to his home at Gibeah, and with him went men of valor whose hearts God had touched. 27 But some worthless fellows said, "How can this man save us?" And they despised him and brought him no present. But he held his peace.

Saul Defeats the Ammonites

449

11 Then Nahash the Ammonite went up and besieged Jabesh-gilead, and all the men of Jabesh said to Nahash, "Make a treaty with us, and we will serve you." 2 But Nahash the Ammonite said to them, "On this condition I will make a treaty with you, that I gouge out all your right eyes, and thus bring disgrace on all Israel." 3 The elders of Jabesh said to him, "Give us seven days' respite that we may send messengers through all the territory of Israel. Then, if there is no one to save us, we will give ourselves up to you." 4 When the messengers came to Gibeah of Saul, they reported the matter in the ears of the people, and all the people wept aloud.

5 Now, behold, Saul was coming from the field behind the oxen. And Saul said, "What is wrong with the people, that they are weeping?" So they told him the news of the men of Jabesh. 6 And the Spirit of God rushed upon Saul when he heard these words, and his anger was greatly kindled. 7 He took a yoke of oxen and cut them in pieces and sent them throughout all the territory of Israel by the hand of messengers, saying, "Whoever does not come out after Saul and Samuel, so shall it be done to his oxen!" Then the dread of the LORD fell upon the people, and they came out as one man. 8 When he mustered them at Bezek, the people of Israel were three hundred thousand, and the men of Judah thirty thousand. 9 And they said to the messengers who had come, "Thus shall you say to the men of Jabesh-gilead: 'Tomorrow, by the time the sun is hot, you shall have deliverance.'" When the messengers came and told the men of Jabesh, they were glad. 10 Therefore the men of Jabesh said, "Tomorrow we will give ourselves up to you, and you may do to us whatever seems good to you." 11 And the next day Saul put the people in three companies. And they came into the midst of the camp in the morning watch and struck down the Ammonites until the heat of the day. And those who survived were scattered, so that no two of them were left together.

The Kingdom Is Renewed

12 Then the people said to Samuel, "Who is it that said, 'Shall Saul reign over us?' Bring the men, that we may put them to death." 13 But Saul said, "Not a man shall be put to death this day, for today the LORD has worked salvation in Israel." 14 Then Samuel said to the people, "Come, let us go to Gilgal and there renew the kingdom." 15 So all the people went to Gilgal, and there they made Saul king before the LORD in Gilgal. There they sacrificed peace offerings before the LORD, and there Saul and all the men of Israel rejoiced greatly.

Samuel's Farewell Address

12 And Samuel said to all Israel, "Behold, I have obeyed your voice in all that you have said to me and have made a king over you. 2 And now, behold, the king walks before you, and I am old and gray; and behold, my sons are with you. I have walked before you from my youth until this day. 3 Here I am; testify against me before the LORD and before his anointed. Whose ox have I taken? Or whose donkey have I taken? Or whom have I defrauded? Whom have I oppressed? Or from whose hand have I taken a bribe to blind my eyes with it? Testify against me[1] and I will restore it to you." 4 They said, "You have not defrauded us or oppressed us or taken anything from any man's hand." 5 And he said to them, "The LORD is witness against you, and his anointed is witness this day, that you have

[1] Septuagint; Hebrew lacks *Testify against me*

not found anything in my hand." And they said, "He is witness."

[6] And Samuel said to the people, "The LORD is witness,[1] who appointed Moses and Aaron and brought your fathers up out of the land of Egypt. [7] Now therefore stand still that I may plead with you before the LORD concerning all the righteous deeds of the LORD that he performed for you and for your fathers. [8] When Jacob went into Egypt, and the Egyptians oppressed them,[2] then your fathers cried out to the LORD and the LORD sent Moses and Aaron, who brought your fathers out of Egypt and made them dwell in this place. [9] But they forgot the LORD their God.

CHARACTER PROFILE

SAUL

Saul was Israel's first king. He helped the Israelites defeat their enemies the Philistines. But Saul failed to obey God's commands, so God said He would choose someone else to be king. Saul became very jealous of David, who was God's choice for his replacement, and tried to kill him. Some years later Saul died in battle against the Philistines and David became king over Israel.

449, 463, 467

And he sold them into the hand of Sisera, commander of the army of Hazor,[3] and into the hand of the Philistines, and into the hand of the king of Moab. And they fought against them. [10] And they cried out to the LORD and said, 'We have sinned, because we have forsaken the LORD and have served the Baals and the Ashtaroth. But now deliver us out of the hand of our enemies, that we may serve you.' [11] And the LORD sent Jerubbaal and Barak[4] and Jephthah and Samuel and delivered you out of the hand of your enemies on every side, and you lived in safety. [12] And when you saw that Nahash the king of the Ammonites came against you, you said to me, 'No, but a king shall reign over us,' when the LORD your God was your king. [13] And now behold the king whom you have chosen, for whom you have asked; behold, the LORD has set a king over you. [14] If you will fear the LORD and serve him and obey his voice and not rebel against the commandment of the LORD, and if both you and the king who reigns over you will follow the LORD your God, it will be well. [15] But if you will not obey the voice of the LORD, but rebel against the commandment of the LORD, then the hand of the LORD will be against you and your king.[5] [16] Now therefore stand still and see this great thing that the LORD will do before your eyes. [17] Is it not wheat harvest today? I will call upon the LORD, that he may send thunder and rain. And you shall know and see that your wickedness is great, which you have done in the sight of the LORD, in asking for yourselves a king." [18] So Samuel called upon the LORD, and the LORD sent thunder and rain that day, and all the people greatly feared the LORD and Samuel.

[19] And all the people said to Samuel, "Pray for your servants to the LORD your God, that we may not die, for we have added to all our sins this evil, to ask for ourselves a king." [20] And Samuel said to the people, "Do not be afraid; you have

[1] Septuagint; Hebrew lacks *is witness* [2] Septuagint; Hebrew lacks *and the Egyptians oppressed them* [3] Septuagint *the army of Jabin king of Hazor* [4] Septuagint, Syriac; Hebrew *Bedan* [5] Septuagint; Hebrew *fathers*

done all this evil. Yet do not turn aside from following the LORD, but serve the LORD with all your heart. 21 And do not turn aside after empty things that cannot profit or deliver, for they are empty. 22 For the LORD will not forsake his people, for his great name's sake, because it has pleased the LORD to make you a people for himself. 23 Moreover, as for me, far be it from me that I should sin against the LORD by ceasing to pray for you, and I will instruct you in the good and the right way. 24 Only fear the LORD and serve him faithfully with all your heart. For consider what great things he has done for you. 25 But if you still do wickedly, you shall be swept away, both you and your king."

Saul Fights the Philistines

13 Saul was . . .[1] years old when he began to reign, and he reigned . . . and two[2] years over Israel.

449

2 Saul chose three thousand men of Israel. Two thousand were with Saul in Michmash and the hill country of Bethel, and a thousand were with Jonathan in Gibeah of Benjamin. The rest of the people he sent home, every man to his tent. 3 Jonathan defeated the garrison of the Philistines that was at Geba, and the Philistines heard of it. And Saul blew the trumpet throughout all the land, saying, "Let the Hebrews hear." 4 And all Israel heard it said that Saul had defeated the garrison of the Philistines, and also that Israel had become a stench to the Philistines. And the people were called out to join Saul at Gilgal.

5 And the Philistines mustered to fight with Israel, thirty thousand chariots and six thousand horsemen and troops like the sand on the seashore in multitude. They came up and encamped in Michmash, to the east of Beth-aven. 6 When the men of Israel saw that they were in trouble (for the people were hard pressed), the people hid themselves in caves and in holes and in rocks and in tombs and in cisterns, 7 and some Hebrews crossed the fords of the Jordan to the land of Gad and Gilead. Saul was still at Gilgal, and all the people followed him trembling.

Saul's Unlawful Sacrifice

8 He waited seven days, the time appointed by Samuel. But Samuel did not come to Gilgal, and the people were scattering from him. 9 So Saul said, "Bring the burnt offering here to me, and the peace offerings." And he offered the burnt offering. 10 As soon as he had finished offering the burnt offering, behold, Samuel came. And Saul went out to meet him and greet him. 11 Samuel said, "What have you done?" And Saul said, "When I saw that the people were scattering from me, and that you did not come within the days appointed, and that the Philistines had mustered at Michmash, 12 I said, 'Now the Philistines will come down against me at Gilgal, and I have not sought the favor of the LORD.' So I forced myself, and offered the burnt offering." 13 And Samuel said to Saul, "You have done foolishly. You have not kept the command of the LORD your God, with which he commanded you. For then the LORD would have established your kingdom over Israel forever. 14 But now your kingdom shall not continue. The LORD has sought out a man after his own heart, and the LORD has commanded him to be prince over his people, because you have not kept what the LORD commanded you." 15 And Samuel arose and went up from Gilgal. The rest of the people went up after Saul to meet the army; they went up from Gilgal[3] to Gibeah of Benjamin.

463

And Saul numbered the people who were present with him, about six hundred men. 16 And Saul and Jonathan his son and the people who were present with them stayed in Geba of Benjamin, but the Philistines encamped in Michmash.

[1] The number is lacking in Hebrew and Septuagint [2] *Two* may not be the entire number; something may have dropped out [3] Septuagint; Hebrew lacks *The rest of the people . . . from Gilgal*

17 And raiders came out of the camp of the
Philistines in three companies. One com-
pany turned toward Ophrah, to the land of
Shual; 18 another company turned toward
Beth-horon; and another company turned
toward the border that looks down on the
Valley of Zeboim toward the wilderness.

19 Now there was no blacksmith to be
found throughout all the land of Israel,
for the Philistines said, "Lest the Hebrews
make themselves swords or spears." 20 But
every one of the Israelites went down to
the Philistines to sharpen his plowshare,
his mattock, his axe, or his sickle,[1] 21 and
the charge was two-thirds of a shekel[2] for
the plowshares and for the mattocks, and
a third of a shekel[3] for sharpening the axes
and for setting the goads.[4] 22 So on the
day of the battle there was neither sword
nor spear found in the hand of any of the
people with Saul and Jonathan, but Saul
and Jonathan his son had them. 23 And the
garrison of the Philistines went out to the
pass of Michmash.

Jonathan Defeats the Philistines

14 One day Jonathan the son of Saul
said to the young man who car-
ried his armor, "Come, let us go over to the
Philistine garrison on the other side." But
he did not tell his father. 2 Saul was staying
in the outskirts of Gibeah in the pome-
granate cave[5] at Migron. The people who
were with him were about six hundred
men, 3 including Ahijah the son of Ahitub,
Ichabod's brother, son of Phinehas, son of
Eli, the priest of the LORD in Shiloh, wear-
ing an ephod. And the people did not
know that Jonathan had gone. 4 Within
the passes, by which Jonathan sought to
go over to the Philistine garrison, there
was a rocky crag on the one side and a
rocky crag on the other side. The name of
the one was Bozez, and the name of the
other Seneh. 5 The one crag rose on the
north in front of Michmash, and the other
on the south in front of Geba.

6 Jonathan said to the young man who
carried his armor, "Come, let us go over
to the garrison of these uncircumcised. It
may be that the LORD will work for us, for
nothing can hinder the LORD from sav-
ing by many or by few." 7 And his armor-
bearer said to him, "Do all that is in your
heart. Do as you wish.[6] Behold, I am with
you heart and soul." 8 Then Jonathan said,
"Behold, we will cross over to the men,
and we will show ourselves to them. 9 If
they say to us, 'Wait until we come to you,'
then we will stand still in our place, and
we will not go up to them. 10 But if they
say, 'Come up to us,' then we will go up, for
the LORD has given them into our hand.
And this shall be the sign to us." 11 So both
of them showed themselves to the garri-
son of the Philistines. And the Philistines
said, "Look, Hebrews are coming out of
the holes where they have hidden them-
selves." 12 And the men of the garrison
hailed Jonathan and his armor-bearer
and said, "Come up to us, and we will
show you a thing." And Jonathan said to
his armor-bearer, "Come up after me, for
the LORD has given them into the hand of
Israel." 13 Then Jonathan climbed up on
his hands and feet, and his armor-bearer
after him. And they fell before Jonathan,
and his armor-bearer killed them after
him. 14 And that first strike, which
Jonathan and his armor-bearer made,
killed about twenty men within as it were
half a furrow's length in an acre[7] of land.
15 And there was a panic in the camp, in
the field, and among all the people. The
garrison and even the raiders trembled,
the earth quaked, and it became a very
great panic.

16 And the watchmen of Saul in Gibeah
of Benjamin looked, and behold, the mul-
titude was dispersing here and there.[8]
17 Then Saul said to the people who were
with him, "Count and see who has gone
from us." And when they had counted,
behold, Jonathan and his armor-bearer

[1] Septuagint; Hebrew *plowshare* [2] Hebrew *was a pim* [3] A *shekel* was about 2/5 ounce or 11 grams [4] The meaning of the Hebrew verse is uncertain [5] Or *under the pomegranate* [tree] [6] Septuagint *Do all that your mind inclines to* [7] Hebrew *a yoke* [8] Septuagint; Hebrew *they went here and there*

were not there. 18 So Saul said to Ahijah,
"Bring the ark of God here." For the
ark of God went at that time with the
people[1] of Israel. 19 Now while Saul was
talking to the priest, the tumult in the
camp of the Philistines increased more
and more. So Saul said to the priest,
"Withdraw your hand." 20 Then Saul and
all the people who were with him rallied
and went into the battle. And behold,
every Philistine's sword was against his
fellow, and there was very great confu-
sion. 21 Now the Hebrews who had been
with the Philistines before that time and
who had gone up with them into the
camp, even they also turned to be with
the Israelites who were with Saul and
Jonathan. 22 Likewise, when all the men
of Israel who had hidden themselves in
the hill country of Ephraim heard that
the Philistines were fleeing, they too fol-
lowed hard after them in the battle. 23 So
the LORD saved Israel that day. And the
battle passed beyond Beth-aven.

Saul's Rash Vow

24 And the men of Israel had been hard
pressed that day, so Saul had laid an oath
on the people, saying, "Cursed be the man
who eats food until it is evening and I
am avenged on my enemies." So none
of the people had tasted food. 25 Now
when all the people[2] came to the forest,
behold, there was honey on the ground.
26 And when the people entered the for-
est, behold, the honey was dropping, but
no one put his hand to his mouth, for the
people feared the oath. 27 But Jonathan
had not heard his father charge the people
with the oath, so he put out the tip of the
staff that was in his hand and dipped it
in the honeycomb and put his hand to
his mouth, and his eyes became bright.
28 Then one of the people said, "Your father
strictly charged the people with an oath,
saying, 'Cursed be the man who eats food
this day.'" And the people were faint.
29 Then Jonathan said, "My father has
troubled the land. See how my eyes have
become bright because I tasted a little
of this honey. 30 How much better if the
people had eaten freely today of the spoil
of their enemies that they found. For now
the defeat among the Philistines has not
been great."

31 They struck down the Philistines
that day from Michmash to Aijalon. And
the people were very faint. 32 The people
pounced on the spoil and took sheep and
oxen and calves and slaughtered them
on the ground. And the people ate them
with the blood. 33 Then they told Saul,
"Behold, the people are sinning against
the LORD by eating with the blood." And
he said, "You have dealt treacherously; roll
a great stone to me here."[3] 34 And Saul said,
"Disperse yourselves among the people
and say to them, 'Let every man bring his
ox or his sheep and slaughter them here
and eat, and do not sin against the LORD
by eating with the blood.'" So every one of
the people brought his ox with him that
night and they slaughtered them there.
35 And Saul built an altar to the LORD; it
was the first altar that he built to the LORD.

36 Then Saul said, "Let us go down
after the Philistines by night and plun-
der them until the morning light; let us
not leave a man of them." And they said,
"Do whatever seems good to you." But the
priest said, "Let us draw near to God here."
37 And Saul inquired of God, "Shall I go
down after the Philistines? Will you give
them into the hand of Israel?" But he did
not answer him that day. 38 And Saul said,
"Come here, all you leaders of the people,
and know and see how this sin has arisen
today. 39 For as the LORD lives who saves
Israel, though it be in Jonathan my son,
he shall surely die." But there was not a
man among all the people who answered
him. 40 Then he said to all Israel, "You
shall be on one side, and I and Jonathan
my son will be on the other side." And the

[1] Hebrew; Septuagint *"Bring the ephod." For at that time he wore the ephod before the people* [2] Hebrew *land* [3] Septuagint; Hebrew *this day*

people said to Saul, "Do what seems good to you." 41 Therefore Saul said, "O LORD God of Israel, why[1] have you not answered your servant this day? If this guilt is in me or in Jonathan my son, O LORD, God of Israel, give Urim. But if this guilt is in your people Israel, give Thummim." And Jonathan and Saul were taken, but the people escaped. 42 Then Saul said, "Cast the lot between me and my son Jonathan." And Jonathan was taken.

43 Then Saul said to Jonathan, "Tell me what you have done." And Jonathan told him, "I tasted a little honey with the tip of the staff that was in my hand. Here I am; I will die." 44 And Saul said, "God do so to me and more also; you shall surely die, Jonathan." 45 Then the people said to Saul, "Shall Jonathan die, who has worked this great salvation in Israel? Far from it! As the LORD lives, there shall not one hair of his head fall to the ground, for he has worked with God this day." So the people ransomed Jonathan, so that he did not die. 46 Then Saul went up from pursuing the Philistines, and the Philistines went to their own place.

Saul Fights Israel's Enemies

47 When Saul had taken the kingship over Israel, he fought against all his enemies on every side, against Moab, against the Ammonites, against Edom, against the kings of Zobah, and against the Philistines. Wherever he turned he routed them. 48 And he did valiantly and struck the Amalekites and delivered Israel out of the hands of those who plundered them.

49 Now the sons of Saul were Jonathan, Ishvi, and Malchi-shua. And the names of his two daughters were these: the name of the firstborn was Merab, and the name of the younger Michal. 50 And the name of Saul's wife was Ahinoam the daughter of Ahimaaz. And the name of the commander of his army was Abner the son of Ner, Saul's uncle. 51 Kish was the father of Saul, and Ner the father of Abner was the son of Abiel.

52 There was hard fighting against the Philistines all the days of Saul. And when Saul saw any strong man, or any valiant man, he attached him to himself.

The LORD Rejects Saul

441, 449

15 And Samuel said to Saul, "The LORD sent me to anoint you king over his people Israel; now therefore listen to the words of the LORD. 2 Thus says the LORD of hosts, 'I have noted what Amalek did to Israel in opposing them on the way when they came up out of Egypt. 3 Now go and strike Amalek and devote to destruction[2] all that they have. Do not spare them, but kill both man and woman, child and infant, ox and sheep, camel and donkey.'"

4 So Saul summoned the people and numbered them in Telaim, two hundred thousand men on foot, and ten thousand men of Judah. 5 And Saul came to the city of Amalek and lay in wait in the valley. 6 Then Saul said to the Kenites, "Go, depart; go down from among the Amalekites, lest I destroy you with them. For you showed kindness to all the people of Israel when they came up out of Egypt." So the Kenites departed from among the Amalekites. 7 And Saul defeated the Amalekites from Havilah as far as Shur, which is east of Egypt. 8 And he took Agag the king of the Amalekites alive and devoted to destruction all the people with the edge of the sword. 9 But Saul and the people spared Agag and the best of the sheep and of the oxen and of the fattened calves[3] and the lambs, and all that was good, and would not utterly destroy them. All that was despised and worthless they devoted to destruction.

10 The word of the LORD came to Samuel: 11 "I regret that I have made Saul king, for he has turned back from following me and has not performed my commandments."

[1] Vulgate (compare Septuagint); Hebrew *Saul said to the LORD, the God of Israel, "Why . . .* [2] That is, set apart (devote) as an offering to the Lord (for destruction); also verses 8, 9, 15, 18, 20, 21 [3] The meaning of the Hebrew term is uncertain

And Samuel was angry, and he cried to the
LORD all night. 12 And Samuel rose early
to meet Saul in the morning. And it was
told Samuel, "Saul came to Carmel, and
behold, he set up a monument for himself
and turned and passed on and went down
to Gilgal." 13 And Samuel came to Saul, and
Saul said to him, "Blessed be you to the
LORD. I have performed the command-
ment of the LORD." 14 And Samuel said,
"What then is this bleating of the sheep
in my ears and the lowing of the oxen that
I hear?" 15 Saul said, "They have brought
them from the Amalekites, for the people
spared the best of the sheep and of the
oxen to sacrifice to the LORD your God,
and the rest we have devoted to destruc-
tion." 16 Then Samuel said to Saul, "Stop! I
will tell you what the LORD said to me this
night." And he said to him, "Speak."

17 And Samuel said, "Though you are
little in your own eyes, are you not the
head of the tribes of Israel? The LORD
anointed you king over Israel. 18 And the
LORD sent you on a mission and said, 'Go,
devote to destruction the sinners, the
Amalekites, and fight against them until
they are consumed.' 19 Why then did you
not obey the voice of the LORD? Why did
you pounce on the spoil and do what was
evil in the sight of the LORD?" 20 And Saul
said to Samuel, "I have obeyed the voice of
the LORD. I have gone on the mission on
which the LORD sent me. I have brought
Agag the king of Amalek, and I have
devoted the Amalekites to destruction.
21 But the people took of the spoil, sheep
and oxen, the best of the things devoted to
destruction, to sacrifice to the LORD your
God in Gilgal." 22 And Samuel said,

"Has the LORD as great delight in
burnt offerings and sacrifices,
as in obeying the voice of the
LORD?
Behold, to obey is better than
sacrifice,
and to listen than the fat of rams.

23 For rebellion is as the sin of
divination,
and presumption is as iniquity
and idolatry.
Because you have rejected the word
of the LORD,
he has also rejected you from
being king."

24 Saul said to Samuel, "I have sinned,
for I have transgressed the commandment
of the LORD and your words, because I
feared the people and obeyed their voice.
25 Now therefore, please pardon my sin
and return with me that I may worship the
LORD." 26 And Samuel said to Saul, "I will
not return with you. For you have rejected
the word of the LORD, and the LORD has
rejected you from being king over Israel."
27 As Samuel turned to go away, Saul seized
the skirt of his robe, and it tore. 28 And
Samuel said to him, "The LORD has torn
the kingdom of Israel from you this day
and has given it to a neighbor of yours,
who is better than you. 29 And also the
Glory of Israel will not lie or have regret,
for he is not a man, that he should have
regret." 30 Then he said, "I have sinned;
yet honor me now before the elders of my
people and before Israel, and return with
me, that I may bow before the LORD your
God." 31 So Samuel turned back after Saul,
and Saul bowed before the LORD.

32 Then Samuel said, "Bring here to me
Agag the king of the Amalekites." And
Agag came to him cheerfully.[1] Agag said,
"Surely the bitterness of death is past."
33 And Samuel said, "As your sword has
made women childless, so shall your
mother be childless among women." And
Samuel hacked Agag to pieces before the
LORD in Gilgal.

34 Then Samuel went to Ramah, and
Saul went up to his house in Gibeah of
Saul. 35 And Samuel did not see Saul again
until the day of his death, but Samuel
grieved over Saul. And the LORD regretted
that he had made Saul king over Israel.

[1] Or *haltingly* (compare Septuagint); the Hebrew is uncertain

David Anointed King

16 The LORD said to Samuel,
"How long will you grieve
463 over Saul, since I have rejected him
from being king over Israel? Fill
your horn with oil, and go. I will
425 send you to Jesse the Bethlehem-
ite, for I have provided for myself a king
among his sons." 2 And Samuel said, "How
can I go? If Saul hears it, he will kill me."
And the LORD said, "Take a heifer with
you and say, 'I have come to sacrifice to
the LORD.' 3 And invite Jesse to the sacri-
fice, and I will show you what you shall
do. And you shall anoint for me him
whom I declare to you." 4 Samuel did what
the LORD commanded and came to Beth-
lehem. The elders of the city came to meet
him trembling and said, "Do you come
peaceably?" 5 And he said, "Peaceably; I
have come to sacrifice to the LORD.
Consecrate yourselves, and come with me
to the sacrifice." And he consecrated Jesse
and his sons and invited them to the
sacrifice.

6 When they came, he looked on Eliab
and thought, "Surely the LORD's anointed
is before him." 7 But the LORD said to
Samuel, "Do not look on his appearance or
on the height of his stature, because I have
rejected him. For the LORD sees not as man
sees: man looks on the outward
appearance, but the LORD looks on
463 the heart." 8 Then Jesse called
Abinadab and made him pass before
Samuel. And he said, "Neither has the
LORD chosen this one." 9 Then Jesse made
Shammah pass by. And he said, "Neither
has the LORD chosen this one." 10 And Jesse
made seven of his sons pass before Samuel.
And Samuel said to Jesse, "The LORD has
not chosen these." 11 Then Samuel said to
Jesse, "Are all your sons here?" And he said,
"There remains yet the youngest,[1] but
behold, he is keeping the sheep." And
Samuel said to Jesse, "Send and get him, for
we will not sit down till he comes here."

12 And he sent and brought him in.
Now he was ruddy and had beauti-
425 ful eyes and was handsome. And
the LORD said, "Arise, anoint him, for this is
he." 13 Then Samuel took the horn of oil and
anointed him in the midst of his brothers.
And the Spirit of the LORD rushed upon
David from that day forward. And Samuel
rose up and went to Ramah.

David in Saul's Service

14 Now the Spirit of the LORD departed
from Saul, and a harmful spirit from the
LORD tormented him. 15 And Saul's ser-
vants said to him, "Behold now, a harmful
spirit from God is tormenting you. 16 Let
our lord now command your servants

CHARACTER PROFILE

DAVID

David was Israel's second king over Israel. He loved God and served him faithfully. When David was still a boy, he fought and killed the giant Goliath. God gave David victory in battle many times. When David sinned terribly, he confessed his sin and God forgave him. God made a promise to David that one of his descendants would always be king. David wrote many of the psalms.

463, 467, 475, 499, 507

[1] Or *smallest*

who are before you to seek out a man who is skillful in playing the lyre, and when the harmful spirit from God is upon you, he will play it, and you will be well." 17 So Saul said to his servants, "Provide for me a man who can play well and bring him to me." 18 One of the young men answered, "Behold, I have seen a son of Jesse the Bethlehemite, who is skillful in playing, a man of valor, a man of war, prudent in speech, and a man of good presence, and the LORD is with him." 19 Therefore Saul sent messengers to Jesse and said, "Send me David your son, who is with the sheep." 20 And Jesse took a donkey laden with bread and a skin of wine and a young goat and sent them by David his son to Saul. 21 And David came to Saul and entered his service. And Saul loved him greatly, and he became his armor-bearer. 22 And Saul sent to Jesse, saying, "Let David remain in my service, for he has found favor in my sight." 23 And whenever the harmful spirit from God was upon Saul, David took the lyre and played it with his hand. So Saul was refreshed and was well, and the harmful spirit departed from him.

David and Goliath

467

17 Now the Philistines gathered their armies for battle. And they were gathered at Socoh, which belongs to Judah, and encamped between Socoh and Azekah, in Ephes-dammim. 2 And Saul and the men of Israel were gathered, and encamped in the Valley of Elah, and drew up in line of battle against the Philistines. 3 And the Philistines stood on the mountain on the one side, and Israel stood on the mountain on the other side, with a valley between them. 4 And there came out from the camp of the Philistines a champion named Goliath of Gath, whose height was six[1] cubits and a span. 5 He had a helmet of bronze on his head, and he was armed with a coat of mail, and the weight of the coat was five thousand shekels[2] of bronze. 6 And he had bronze armor on his legs, and a javelin of bronze slung between his shoulders. 7 The shaft of his spear was like a weaver's beam, and his spear's head weighed six hundred shekels of iron. And his shield-bearer went before him. 8 He stood and shouted to the ranks of Israel, "Why have you come out to draw up for battle? Am I not a Philistine, and are you not servants of Saul? Choose a man for yourselves, and let him come down to me. 9 If he is able to fight with me and kill me, then we will be your servants. But if I prevail against him and kill him, then you shall be our servants and serve us." 10 And the Philistine said, "I defy the ranks of Israel this day. Give me a man, that we may fight together." 11 When Saul and all Israel heard these words of the Philistine, they were dismayed and greatly afraid.

12 Now David was the son of an Ephrathite of Bethlehem in Judah, named Jesse, who had eight sons. In the days of Saul the man was already old and advanced in years.[3] 13 The three oldest sons of Jesse had followed Saul to the battle. And the names of his three sons who went to the battle were Eliab the firstborn, and next to him Abinadab, and the third Shammah. 14 David was the youngest. The three eldest followed Saul, 15 but David went back and forth from Saul to feed his father's sheep at Bethlehem. 16 For forty days the Philistine came forward and took his stand, morning and evening.

17 And Jesse said to David his son, "Take for your brothers an ephah[4] of this parched grain, and these ten loaves, and carry them quickly to the camp to your brothers. 18 Also take these ten cheeses to the commander of their thousand. See if your brothers are well, and bring some token from them."

19 Now Saul and they and all the men of Israel were in the Valley of Elah, fighting with the Philistines. 20 And David rose early in the morning and left the sheep

[1] Hebrew; Septuagint, Dead Sea Scroll and Josephus *four* [2] A *shekel* was about 2/5 ounce or 11 grams [3] Septuagint, Syriac; Hebrew *years among men* [4] An *ephah* was about 3/5 bushel or 22 liters

David Anointed As King

Over and over King Saul disobeyed God! He would not turn from his wicked ways. God rejected Saul as king over Israel—and He chose someone else to be king.

God told His prophet Samuel to take his jar of anointing oil and go to the home of a man named Jesse, who lived in Bethlehem. From Jesse's house God said, "I have provided for Myself a king among his sons."

Jesse's oldest son was tall and handsome. Samuel was sure God must have chosen him to be the next king. But God told Samuel that this was not the one. God said that Samuel shouldn't look at how tall someone is or how handsome he is. "For the LORD sees not as man sees," God told Samuel. "Man looks on the outward appearance, but the LORD looks on the heart."

One by one, Jesse's sons met Samuel until he had met seven of his sons! "The LORD has not chosen these," Samuel told Jesse. "Are all your sons here?"

Jesse said there was one more son, named David. He was the youngest and was out in the fields with the sheep. Samuel told Jesse to send for David—and they would all wait for him to come.

When David came to Samuel, God told Samuel, "Arise,

anoint him, for this is he." So, Samuel poured the oil on David's head, to anoint David as the next king over Israel. At that moment, God's Holy Spirit filled David. Then David went back to watching the sheep, and Samuel went home. When he was older, David began to lead God's people.

David became a good king. The Bible calls him "a man after [God's] own heart." David showed God's love to the people. He led them in worshiping God and in obeying Him. David was not a perfect king, though. There were several times when he did things that were very wrong, that brought trouble on David and on God's people.

God sent Jesus to be our perfect King. Jesus showed God's love to His people by dying on the cross to pay for all their sins. King Jesus leads His people in obeying and worshiping God. Through faith in Him, He even changes our sinful hearts, so that we will love one another and obey Him. Jesus never did anything that was sinful or wrong. And He only does what is good for His people. What a wonderful King!

SEEK and FIND

WHERE TO FIND THE STORY

1 Samuel 16:1–13

KEY BIBLE VERSE

"Man looks on the outward appearance, but the LORD looks on the heart." (1 Samuel 16:7)

THREE KEY QUESTIONS

- Who did God choose to be king over Israel, after Saul sinned against God?

- What kind of person did God say that He wanted to be king?
- Why is Jesus the perfect King for God's people?

RELATED BIBLE READINGS

1 Samuel 13:13–14; Psalm 78:70–72; 89:19–21; Acts 13:21–23

with a keeper and took the provisions and went, as Jesse had commanded him. And he came to the encampment as the host was going out to the battle line, shouting the war cry. 21 And Israel and the Philistines drew up for battle, army against army. 22 And David left the things in charge of the keeper of the baggage and ran to the ranks and went and greeted his brothers. 23 As he talked with them, behold, the champion, the Philistine of Gath, Goliath by name, came up out of the ranks of the Philistines and spoke the same words as before. And David heard him.

24 All the men of Israel, when they saw the man, fled from him and were much afraid. 25 And the men of Israel said, "Have you seen this man who has come up? Surely he has come up to defy Israel. And the king will enrich the man who kills him with great riches and will give him his daughter and make his father's house free in Israel." 26 And David said to the men who stood by him, "What shall be done for the man who kills this Philistine and takes away the reproach from Israel? For who is this uncircumcised Philistine, that he should defy the armies of the living God?" 27 And the people answered him in the same way, "So shall it be done to the man who kills him."

28 Now Eliab his eldest brother heard when he spoke to the men. And Eliab's anger was kindled against David, and he said, "Why have you come down? And with whom have you left those few sheep in the wilderness? I know your presumption and the evil of your heart, for you have come down to see the battle." 29 And David said, "What have I done now? Was it not but a word?" 30 And he turned away from him toward another, and spoke in the same way, and the people answered him again as before.

31 When the words that David spoke were heard, they repeated them before Saul, and he sent for him. 32 And David said to Saul, "Let no man's heart fail because of him. Your servant will go and fight with this Philistine." 33 And Saul said to David, "You are not able to go against this Philistine to fight with him, for you are but a youth, and he has been a man of war from his youth." 34 But David said to Saul, "Your servant used to keep sheep for his father. And when there came a lion, or a bear, and took a lamb from the flock, 35 I went after him and struck him and delivered it out of his mouth. And if he arose against me, I caught him by his beard and struck him and killed him. 36 Your servant has struck down both lions and bears, and this uncircumcised Philistine shall be like one of them, for he has defied the armies of the living God." 37 And David said, "The LORD who delivered me from the paw of the lion and from the paw of the bear will deliver me from the hand of

David and Goliath

After David had been anointed to become king, Saul still reigned as king of Israel for several years. During this time, King Saul's men were fighting the Philistine army, which often harassed Israel. King Saul and his men were gathered in the valley of Elah, and the Philistine army was gathered on the mountain on the other side of the valley.

The Philistine army had an enormous soldier, named Goliath, who stood over nine feet tall! Goliath had a helmet of bronze and strong armor. He carried a javelin and spear. Every day, Goliath called out to Saul's army, "Choose a man for yourselves, and let him come down to me. If he is able to fight with me and kill me, then we will be your servants. But if I prevail against him and kill him, then you shall be our servants and serve us."

Goliath did this every day for 40 days, and none of the men in Saul's army would fight him. They were all afraid of Goliath and ran away whenever they saw him.

Now there was a man named Jesse, who had three sons fighting in Saul's army. Jesse also had a much younger son named David, who was a shepherd. (This is the same David that Samuel had anointed a few years earlier to become king of Israel.)

One day, David was sent to bring food to his brothers and

the other men in the army. While he was there, David heard the giant making fun of the people of God. David said that the Israelite army should not allow Goliath to make fun of God's army. When someone told King Saul what David had said, Saul sent for David. So David told Saul that he would fight Goliath.

Saul wondered how this young man could fight such an enormous giant. But David told Saul how he had fought lions and bears when he was caring for sheep. This Philistine, David said, "shall be like one of them, for he has defied the armies of the living God. The LORD who delivered me from the paw of the lion and the paw of the bear will deliver me from the hand of this Philistine."

Finally, Saul agreed to let David fight. He gave David armor, but David did not want to wear it. Instead he picked up five smooth stones from a stream, and he put them in his shepherd's pouch. With his slingshot and his shepherd's staff, he walked toward the giant Goliath.

When Goliath saw David, he said, "Am I a dog, that you come to me with sticks?"

David replied, "You come to me with a sword and with a spear and with a javelin, but I come to you in the name of the LORD of hosts, the God of the armies of Israel, whom you have defied. This day the LORD will deliver you into my hand, and I will strike you down." Then, David said, everyone will "know that there is a God in Israel" and that "the LORD saves not with sword and spear. For the battle is the LORD's."

David put his hand in his bag and took out one smooth *round stone*. Then he put the stone in his sling and hurled it at the giant. And the stone struck Goliath on the forehead and killed him!

So David won a great victory over the Philistine with a sling and a stone. When the Philistines saw that their champion was dead, they ran away. And the people of Israel didn't need to be afraid any longer.

Later in his life, David went on to become a great king in Israel. Through David's faith and trust in the one true God, God gave David many victories over Israel's enemies. Many centuries later, the greatest King of all was born, our Savior Jesus Christ. Through Jesus' death on the cross, God gives us the victory over our enemies—sin, death, and the devil—and life with Him forever in heaven.

SEEK and FIND

WHERE TO FIND THE STORY

1 Samuel 17

KEY BIBLE VERSE

"The LORD saves not with sword and spear. For the battle is the LORD's." (1 Samuel 17:47)

THREE KEY QUESTIONS

- Why was David so upset with the things that Goliath said?
- How was David able to defeat the enormous giant Goliath and the Philistine army?
- What powerful enemies did our King and Savior Jesus defeat for us?

RELATED BIBLE READINGS

Psalm 27:1–3; Romans 8:35–37; Hebrews 11:32–34

this Philistine." And Saul said to David,
"Go, and the LORD be with you!"
38 Then Saul clothed David with his
armor. He put a helmet of bronze on his
head and clothed him with a coat of mail,
39 and David strapped his sword over his
armor. And he tried in vain to go, for he
had not tested them. Then David said to
Saul, "I cannot go with these, for I have
not tested them." So David put them
off. 40 Then he took his staff in his hand
and chose five smooth stones from the
brook and put them in his shepherd's
pouch. His sling was in his hand, and he
approached the Philistine.

41 And the Philistine moved forward
and came near to David, with his shield-
bearer in front of him. 42 And when the
Philistine looked and saw David, he dis-
dained him, for he was but a youth, ruddy
and handsome in appearance. 43 And the
Philistine said to David, "Am I a dog, that
you come to me with sticks?" And the
Philistine cursed David by his gods. 44 The
Philistine said to David, "Come to me, and
I will give your flesh to the birds of the air
and to the beasts of the field." 45 Then
David said to the Philistine, "You come to
me with a sword and with a spear and with
a javelin, but I come to you in the name of
the LORD of hosts, the God of the armies of
Israel, whom you have defied. 46 This day
the LORD will deliver you into my hand,
and I will strike you down and cut off your
head. And I will give the dead bodies of the
host of the Philistines this day to the birds
of the air and to the wild beasts of the
earth, that all the earth may know that
there is a God in Israel, 47 and that all this
assembly may know that the LORD
saves not with sword and spear.
467 For the battle is the LORD's, and he
will give you into our hand."

48 When the Philistine arose and came
and drew near to meet David, David ran
quickly toward the battle line to meet the
Philistine. 49 And David put his hand in his
bag and took out a stone and slung it and
struck the Philistine on his forehead. The
stone sank into his forehead, and he fell
on his face to the ground.

50 So David prevailed over the Philistine
with a sling and with a stone, and struck
the Philistine and killed him. There was
no sword in the hand of David. 51 Then
David ran and stood over the Philistine
and took his sword and drew it out of its
sheath and killed him and cut off his head
with it. When the Philistines saw that
their champion was dead, they fled. 52 And
the men of Israel and Judah rose with a
shout and pursued the Philistines as far
as Gath[1] and the gates of Ekron, so that the
wounded Philistines fell on the way from
Shaaraim as far as Gath and Ekron. 53 And
the people of Israel came back from chas-
ing the Philistines, and they plundered
their camp. 54 And David took the head of
the Philistine and brought it to Jerusalem,
but he put his armor in his tent.

55 As soon as Saul saw David go out
against the Philistine, he said to Abner,
the commander of the army, "Abner, whose
son is this youth?" And Abner said, "As
your soul lives, O king, I do not know."
56 And the king said, "Inquire whose
son the boy is." 57 And as soon as David
returned from the striking down of the
Philistine, Abner took him, and brought
him before Saul with the head of the
Philistine in his hand. 58 And Saul said to
him, "Whose son are you, young man?"
And David answered, "I am the son of
your servant Jesse the Bethlehemite."

David and Jonathan's Friendship

18 As soon as he had finished
speaking to Saul, the soul of
475 Jonathan was knit to the soul of
David, and Jonathan loved him as his own
soul. 2 And Saul took him that day and
would not let him return to his father's
house. 3 Then Jonathan made a covenant
with David, because he loved him as his

[1] Septuagint; Hebrew *Gai*

own soul. 4 And Jonathan stripped himself of the robe that was on him and gave it to David, and his armor, and even his sword and his bow and his belt. 5 And David went out and was successful wherever Saul sent him, so that Saul set him over the men of war. And this was good in the sight of all the people and also in the sight of Saul's servants.

Saul's Jealousy of David

6 As they were coming home, when David returned from striking down the Philistine, the women came out of all the cities of Israel, singing and dancing, to meet King Saul, with tambourines, with songs of joy, and with musical instruments.[1] 7 And the women sang to one another as they celebrated,

> "Saul has struck down his thousands,
> and David his ten thousands."

8 And Saul was very angry, and this saying displeased him. He said, "They have ascribed to David ten thousands, and to me they have ascribed thousands, and what more can he have but the kingdom?" 9 And Saul eyed David from that day on.

10 The next day a harmful spirit from God rushed upon Saul, and he raved within his house while David was playing the lyre, as he did day by day. Saul had his spear in his hand. 11 And Saul hurled the spear, for he thought, "I will pin David to the wall." But David evaded him twice.

12 Saul was afraid of David because the LORD was with him but had departed from Saul. 13 So Saul removed him from his presence and made him a commander of a thousand. And he went out and came in before the people. 14 And David had success in all his undertakings, for the LORD was with him. 15 And when Saul saw that he had great success, he stood in fearful awe of him. 16 But all Israel and Judah loved David, for he went out and came in before them.

David Marries Michal

17 Then Saul said to David, "Here is my elder daughter Merab. I will give her to you for a wife. Only be valiant for me and fight the LORD's battles." For Saul thought, "Let not my hand be against him, but let the hand of the Philistines be against him." 18 And David said to Saul, "Who am I, and who are my relatives, my father's clan in Israel, that I should be son-in-law to the king?" 19 But at the time when Merab, Saul's daughter, should have been given to David, she was given to Adriel the Meholathite for a wife.

20 Now Saul's daughter Michal loved David. And they told Saul, and the thing pleased him. 21 Saul thought, "Let me give her to him, that she may be a snare for him and that the hand of the Philistines may be against him." Therefore Saul said to David a second time,[2] "You shall now be my son-in-law." 22 And Saul commanded his servants, "Speak to David in private and say, 'Behold, the king has delight in you, and all his servants love you. Now then become the king's son-in-law.'" 23 And Saul's servants spoke those words in the ears of David. And David said, "Does it seem to you a little thing to become the king's son-in-law, since I am a poor man and have no reputation?" 24 And the servants of Saul told him, "Thus and so did David speak." 25 Then Saul said, "Thus shall you say to David, 'The king desires no bride-price except a hundred foreskins of the Philistines, that he may be avenged of the king's enemies.'" Now Saul thought to make David fall by the hand of the Philistines. 26 And when his servants told David these words, it pleased David well to be the king's son-in-law. Before the time had expired, 27 David arose and went, along with his men, and killed two hundred of the Philistines. And David brought their foreskins, which were given in full number to the king, that he might become the king's son-in-law. And Saul

[1] Or *triangles*, or *three-stringed instruments* [2] Hebrew *by two*

gave him his daughter Michal for a wife. 28 But when Saul saw and knew that the LORD was with David, and that Michal, Saul's daughter, loved him, 29 Saul was even more afraid of David. So Saul was David's enemy continually.

30 Then the princes of the Philistines came out to battle, and as often as they came out David had more success than all the servants of Saul, so that his name was highly esteemed.

Saul Tries to Kill David

19 And Saul spoke to Jonathan his son and to all his servants, that they should kill David. But Jonathan, Saul's son, delighted much in David. 2 And Jonathan told David, "Saul my father seeks to kill you. Therefore be on your guard in the morning. Stay in a secret place and hide yourself. 3 And I will go out and stand beside my father in the field where you are, and I will speak to my father about you. And if I learn anything I will tell you." 4 And Jonathan spoke well of David to Saul his father and said to him, "Let not the king sin against his servant David, because he has not sinned against you, and because his deeds have brought good to you. 5 For he took his life in his hand and he struck down the Philistine, and the LORD worked a great salvation for all Israel. You saw it, and rejoiced. Why then will you sin against innocent blood by killing David without cause?" 6 And Saul listened to the voice of Jonathan. Saul swore, "As the LORD lives, he shall not be put to death." 7 And Jonathan called David, and Jonathan reported to him all these things. And Jonathan brought David to Saul, and he was in his presence as before.

8 And there was war again. And David went out and fought with the Philistines and struck them with a great blow, so that they fled before him. 9 Then a harmful spirit from the LORD came upon Saul, as he sat in his house with his spear in his hand. And David was playing the lyre. 10 And Saul sought to pin David to the wall with the spear, but he eluded Saul, so that he struck the spear into the wall. And David fled and escaped that night.

11 Saul sent messengers to David's house to watch him, that he might kill him in the morning. But Michal, David's wife, told him, "If you do not escape with your life tonight, tomorrow you will be killed." 12 So Michal let David down through the window, and he fled away and escaped. 13 Michal took an image and laid it on the bed and put a pillow of goats' hair at its head and covered it with the clothes. 14 And when Saul sent messengers to take David, she said, "He is sick." 15 Then Saul sent the messengers to see David, saying, "Bring him up to me in the bed, that I may kill him." 16 And when the messengers came in, behold, the image was in the bed, with the pillow of goats' hair at its head. 17 Saul said to Michal, "Why have you deceived me thus and let my enemy go, so that he has escaped?" And Michal answered Saul, "He said to me, 'Let me go. Why should I kill you?'"

18 Now David fled and escaped, and he came to Samuel at Ramah and told him all that Saul had done to him. And he and Samuel went and lived at Naioth. 19 And it was told Saul, "Behold, David is at Naioth in Ramah." 20 Then Saul sent messengers to take David, and when they saw the company of the prophets prophesying, and Samuel standing as head over them, the Spirit of God came upon the messengers of Saul, and they also prophesied. 21 When it was told Saul, he sent other messengers, and they also prophesied. And Saul sent messengers again the third time, and they also prophesied. 22 Then he himself went to Ramah and came to the great well that is in Secu. And he asked, "Where are Samuel and David?" And one said, "Behold, they are at Naioth in Ramah." 23 And he went there to Naioth in

Ramah. And the Spirit of God came upon
him also, and as he went he prophesied
until he came to Naioth in Ramah. 24 And
he too stripped off his clothes, and he too
prophesied before Samuel and lay naked
all that day and all that night. Thus it is
said, "Is Saul also among the prophets?"

Jonathan Warns David

20 Then David fled from Naioth in
Ramah and came and said before
Jonathan, "What have I done? What is my
guilt? And what is my sin before your
father, that he seeks my life?" 2 And he
said to him, "Far from it! You shall not
die. Behold, my father does nothing either
great or small without disclosing it to me.
And why should my father hide this from
me? It is not so." 3 But David vowed again,
saying, "Your father knows well that I have
found favor in your eyes, and he thinks,
'Do not let Jonathan know this, lest he
be grieved.' But truly, as the LORD lives
and as your soul lives, there is but a step
between me and death." 4 Then Jonathan
said to David, "Whatever you say, I will do
for you." 5 David said to Jonathan, "Behold,
tomorrow is the new moon, and I should
not fail to sit at table with the king. But let
me go, that I may hide myself in the field
till the third day at evening. 6 If your father
misses me at all, then say, 'David earnestly
asked leave of me to run to Bethlehem his
city, for there is a yearly sacrifice there for
all the clan.' 7 If he says, 'Good!' it will be
well with your servant, but if he is angry,
then know that harm is determined by
him. 8 Therefore deal kindly with your ser-
vant, for you have brought your servant
into a covenant of the LORD with you. But
if there is guilt in me, kill me yourself, for
why should you bring me to your father?"
9 And Jonathan said, "Far be it from you!
If I knew that it was determined by my
father that harm should come to you,
would I not tell you?" 10 Then David said to
Jonathan, "Who will tell me if your father
answers you roughly?" 11 And Jonathan
said to David, "Come, let us go out into the
field." So they both went out into the field.

12 And Jonathan said to David, "The
LORD, the God of Israel, be witness![1] When
I have sounded out my father, about this
time tomorrow, or the third day, behold,
if he is well disposed toward David, shall I
not then send and disclose it to you? 13 But
should it please my father to do you harm,
the LORD do so to Jonathan and more also
if I do not disclose it to you and send you
away, that you may go in safety. May the
LORD be with you, as he has been with
my father. 14 If I am still alive, show me
the steadfast love of the LORD, that I may
not die; 15 and do not cut off[2] your stead-
fast love from my house forever, when the
LORD cuts off every one of the enemies of
David from the face of the earth." 16 And
Jonathan made a covenant with the house
of David, saying, "May[3] the LORD take
vengeance on David's enemies." 17 And
Jonathan made David swear again by his
love for him, for he loved him as he loved
his own soul.

18 Then Jonathan said to him, "Tomor-
row is the new moon, and you will be
missed, because your seat will be empty.
19 On the third day go down quickly to the
place where you hid yourself when the
matter was in hand, and remain beside
the stone heap.[4] 20 And I will shoot three
arrows to the side of it, as though I shot
at a mark. 21 And behold, I will send the
young man, saying, 'Go, find the arrows.' If
I say to the young man, 'Look, the arrows
are on this side of you, take them,' then
you are to come, for, as the LORD lives, it is
safe for you and there is no danger. 22 But
if I say to the youth, 'Look, the arrows are
beyond you,' then go, for the LORD has
sent you away. 23 And as for the matter of
which you and I have spoken, behold, the
LORD is between you and me forever."

24 So David hid himself in the field. And
when the new moon came, the king sat

[1] Hebrew lacks *be witness* [2] Or *but if I die, do not cut off* [3] Septuagint *earth,* [16]*let not the name of Jonathan be cut off from the house of David. And may* [4] Septuagint; Hebrew *the stone Ezel*

David and Jonathan

After David fought for King Saul and killed the giant Goliath, King Saul asked David to come and live with him and his family. David became one of Saul's soldiers.

Saul's son, Jonathan, was a soldier too. When David met Prince Jonathan, the two became best friends. They were such good friends that Jonathan gave David many amazing gifts—even his armor, his sword, and his bow.

As the leader of Saul's army, David won many battles. Then one day, when King Saul returned from battle, the women of Israel came out, singing and dancing with tambourines. They sang that King Saul was a good soldier, but that David was much, much better. This made King Saul jealous. Instead of loving David, Saul became so angry that he tried to kill David.

David knew that Saul wanted to kill him, but Jonathan did not believe it. So the two friends made a plan to find out if David really was in danger. David went away and hid, while Jonathan talked with King Saul and learned of his plans.

While King Saul and Jonathan were eating together, Saul told Jonathan that he really did want to kill David—and if he didn't kill David, someday David would be king instead of Jonathan. Now Jonathan knew that David was right. His father, King Saul, really did want to kill David.

Jonathan hurried out into the field to the place he and David had planned to meet. There David was hiding behind a pile of stones. Jonathan and David had worked out a special signal so that David would know if it was safe to come home or whether he should go away. Jonathan shot arrows into the field far away. When he sent his servant to get the arrows and told him to go home, he told him that the arrows were "beyond" him—which was Jonathan's signal to David that he must hurry and go far away, because King Saul wanted to kill him.

Right after that, David came out from behind the pile of stones, and Jonathan told David that his father was very angry and wanted to kill David. The two friends were sad and cried. But Jonathan reminded David that the Lord would always keep them both. They would always be friends. They would always love each other. And they would always help each other's families.

In His love, God has given us families and friends to love and care for us. He helps us love and care for our friends and for others too. The very best friend we will ever have is Jesus, our Savior. Jesus loves us so much that He died on the cross for us, even before we ever loved Him. Jesus promises to be with us always. Now and in eternity, we can always count on His love.

SEEK and FIND

WHERE TO FIND THE STORY

1 Samuel 18–20

KEY BIBLE VERSE

"Greater love has no one than this, that someone lay down

his life for his friends." (John 15:13)

THREE KEY QUESTIONS

- What were the amazing gifts that Jonathan gave to David?
- What was more important to Jonathan? To be king or to save David's life?
- What has God given to show His love to us?

RELATED BIBLE READINGS

1 Samuel 23:15–18; 2 Samuel 1:17–27; 9:1–13

down to eat food. 25 The king sat on his
seat, as at other times, on the seat by the
wall. Jonathan sat opposite,[1] and Abner sat
by Saul's side, but David's place was empty.
26 Yet Saul did not say anything that
day, for he thought, "Something has hap-
pened to him. He is not clean; surely he
is not clean." 27 But on the second day,
the day after the new moon, David's place
was empty. And Saul said to Jonathan
his son, "Why has not the son of Jesse
come to the meal, either yesterday or
today?" 28 Jonathan answered Saul, "David
earnestly asked leave of me to go to
Bethlehem. 29 He said, 'Let me go, for our
clan holds a sacrifice in the city, and my
brother has commanded me to be there. So
now, if I have found favor in your eyes, let
me get away and see my brothers.' For this
reason he has not come to the king's table."
30 Then Saul's anger was kindled against
Jonathan, and he said to him, "You son of a
perverse, rebellious woman, do I not know
that you have chosen the son of Jesse to
your own shame, and to the shame of your
mother's nakedness? 31 For as long as the
son of Jesse lives on the earth, neither you
nor your kingdom shall be established.
Therefore send and bring him to me,
for he shall surely die." 32 Then Jonathan
answered Saul his father, "Why should
he be put to death? What has he done?"
33 But Saul hurled his spear at him to strike
him. So Jonathan knew that his father was
determined to put David to death. 34 And
Jonathan rose from the table in fierce
anger and ate no food the second day of
the month, for he was grieved for David,
because his father had disgraced him.
35 In the morning Jonathan went out
into the field to the appointment with
David, and with him a little boy. 36 And
he said to his boy, "Run and find the
arrows that I shoot." As the boy ran, he
shot an arrow beyond him. 37 And when
the boy came to the place of the arrow
that Jonathan had shot, Jonathan called
after the boy and said, "Is not the arrow
beyond you?" 38 And Jonathan called after
the boy, "Hurry! Be quick! Do not stay!"
So Jonathan's boy gathered up the arrows
and came to his master. 39 But the boy
knew nothing. Only Jonathan and David
knew the matter. 40 And Jonathan gave
his weapons to his boy and said to him,
"Go and carry them to the city." 41 And
as soon as the boy had gone, David rose
from beside the stone heap[2] and fell on
his face to the ground and bowed three
times. And they kissed one another and

[1] Compare Septuagint; Hebrew *stood up* [2] Septuagint; Hebrew *from beside the south*

wept with one another, David weeping the
most. 42 Then Jonathan said to David, "Go
in peace, because we have sworn both of
us in the name of the LORD, saying, 'The
LORD shall be between me and you, and
between my offspring and your offspring,
forever.'" And he rose and departed, and
Jonathan went into the city.[1]

David and the Holy Bread

21 [2] Then David came to Nob to Ahim-
elech the priest. And Ahimelech
came to meet David trembling and said to
him, "Why are you alone, and no one with
you?" 2 And David said to Ahimelech the
priest, "The king has charged me with a
matter and said to me, 'Let no one know
anything of the matter about which I send
you, and with which I have charged you.' I
have made an appointment with the young
men for such and such a place. 3 Now then,
what do you have on hand? Give me five
loaves of bread, or whatever is here." 4 And
the priest answered David, "I have no
common bread on hand, but there is holy
bread—if the young men have kept them-
selves from women." 5 And David answered
the priest, "Truly women have been kept
from us as always when I go on an expe-
dition. The vessels of the young men are
holy even when it is an ordinary journey.
How much more today will their vessels
be holy?" 6 So the priest gave him the holy
bread, for there was no bread there but the
bread of the Presence, which is removed
from before the LORD, to be replaced by hot
bread on the day it is taken away.

7 Now a certain man of the servants of
Saul was there that day, detained before the
LORD. His name was Doeg the Edomite,
the chief of Saul's herdsmen.

8 Then David said to Ahimelech, "Then
have you not here a spear or a sword at
hand? For I have brought neither my
sword nor my weapons with me, because
the king's business required haste." 9 And
the priest said, "The sword of Goliath the
Philistine, whom you struck down in the
Valley of Elah, behold, it is here wrapped
in a cloth behind the ephod. If you will
take that, take it, for there is none but that
here." And David said, "There is none like
that; give it to me."

David Flees to Gath

10 And David rose and fled that day from
Saul and went to Achish the king of Gath.
11 And the servants of Achish said to him,
"Is not this David the king of the land?
Did they not sing to one another of him
in dances,

'Saul has struck down his thousands,
and David his ten thousands'?"

12 And David took these words to heart
and was much afraid of Achish the king of
Gath. 13 So he changed his behavior before
them and pretended to be insane in their
hands and made marks on the doors of
the gate and let his spittle run down his
beard. 14 Then Achish said to his servants,
"Behold, you see the man is mad. Why then
have you brought him to me? 15 Do I lack
madmen, that you have brought this fellow
to behave as a madman in my presence?
Shall this fellow come into my house?"

David at the Cave of Adullam

22 David departed from there and
escaped to the cave of Adullam.
And when his brothers and all his
father's house heard it, they went down
there to him. 2 And everyone who was in
distress, and everyone who was in debt,
and everyone who was bitter in soul,[3]
gathered to him. And he became cap-
tain over them. And there were with him
about four hundred men.

3 And David went from there to Mizpeh
of Moab. And he said to the king of Moab,
"Please let my father and my mother
stay[4] with you, till I know what God will
do for me." 4 And he left them with the
king of Moab, and they stayed with him
all the time that David was in the strong-

[1] This sentence is 21:1 in Hebrew [2] Ch 21:2 in Hebrew [3] Or *discontented* [4] Syriac, Vulgate; Hebrew *go out*

hold. 5 Then the prophet Gad said to David, "Do not remain in the stronghold; depart, and go into the land of Judah." So David departed and went into the forest of Hereth.

Saul Kills the Priests at Nob

6 Now Saul heard that David was discovered, and the men who were with him. Saul was sitting at Gibeah under the tamarisk tree on the height with his spear in his hand, and all his servants were standing about him. 7 And Saul said to his servants who stood about him, "Hear now, people of Benjamin; will the son of Jesse give every one of you fields and vineyards, will he make you all commanders of thousands and commanders of hundreds, 8 that all of you have conspired against me? No one discloses to me when my son makes a covenant with the son of Jesse. None of you is sorry for me or discloses to me that my son has stirred up my servant against me, to lie in wait, as at this day." 9 Then answered Doeg the Edomite, who stood by the servants of Saul, "I saw the son of Jesse coming to Nob, to Ahimelech the son of Ahitub, 10 and he inquired of the LORD for him and gave him provisions and gave him the sword of Goliath the Philistine."

11 Then the king sent to summon Ahimelech the priest, the son of Ahitub, and all his father's house, the priests who were at Nob, and all of them came to the king. 12 And Saul said, "Hear now, son of Ahitub." And he answered, "Here I am, my lord." 13 And Saul said to him, "Why have you conspired against me, you and the son of Jesse, in that you have given him bread and a sword and have inquired of God for him, so that he has risen against me, to lie in wait, as at this day?" 14 Then Ahimelech answered the king, "And who among all your servants is so faithful as David, who is the king's son-in-law, and captain over[1] your bodyguard, and honored in your house? 15 Is today the first time that I have inquired of God for him? No! Let not the king impute anything to his servant or to all the house of my father, for your servant has known nothing of all this, much or little." 16 And the king said, "You shall surely die, Ahimelech, you and all your father's house." 17 And the king said to the guard who stood about him, "Turn and kill the priests of the LORD, because their hand also is with David, and they knew that he fled and did not disclose it to me." But the servants of the king would not put out their hand to strike the priests of the LORD. 18 Then the king said to Doeg, "You turn and strike the priests." And Doeg the Edomite turned and struck down the priests, and he killed on that day eighty-five persons who wore the linen ephod. 19 And Nob, the city of the priests, he put to the sword; both man and woman, child and infant, ox, donkey and sheep, he put to the sword.

20 But one of the sons of Ahimelech the son of Ahitub, named Abiathar, escaped and fled after David. 21 And Abiathar told David that Saul had killed the priests of the LORD. 22 And David said to Abiathar, "I knew on that day, when Doeg the Edomite was there, that he would surely tell Saul. I have occasioned the death of all the persons of your father's house. 23 Stay with me; do not be afraid, for he who seeks my life seeks your life. With me you shall be in safekeeping."

David Saves the City of Keilah

23 Now they told David, "Behold, the Philistines are fighting against Keilah and are robbing the threshing floors." 2 Therefore David inquired of the LORD, "Shall I go and attack these Philistines?" And the LORD said to David, "Go and attack the Philistines and save Keilah." 3 But David's men said to him, "Behold, we are afraid here in Judah; how much more then if we go to Keilah against the armies of the Philistines?" 4 Then

[1] Septuagint, Targum; Hebrew *and has turned aside to*

David inquired of the LORD again. And the LORD answered him, "Arise, go down to Keilah, for I will give the Philistines into your hand." 5 And David and his men went to Keilah and fought with the Philistines and brought away their livestock and struck them with a great blow. So David saved the inhabitants of Keilah.

6 When Abiathar the son of Ahimelech had fled to David to Keilah, he had come down with an ephod in his hand. 7 Now it was told Saul that David had come to Keilah. And Saul said, "God has given him into my hand, for he has shut himself in by entering a town that has gates and bars." 8 And Saul summoned all the people to war, to go down to Keilah, to besiege David and his men. 9 David knew that Saul was plotting harm against him. And he said to Abiathar the priest, "Bring the ephod here." 10 Then said David, "O LORD, the God of Israel, your servant has surely heard that Saul seeks to come to Keilah, to destroy the city on my account. 11 Will the men of Keilah surrender me into his hand? Will Saul come down, as your servant has heard? O LORD, the God of Israel, please tell your servant." And the LORD said, "He will come down." 12 Then David said, "Will the men of Keilah surrender me and my men into the hand of Saul?" And the LORD said, "They will surrender you." 13 Then David and his men, who were about six hundred, arose and departed from Keilah, and they went wherever they could go. When Saul was told that David had escaped from Keilah, he gave up the expedition. 14 And David remained in the strongholds in the wilderness, in the hill country of the wilderness of Ziph. And Saul sought him every day, but God did not give him into his hand.

Saul Pursues David

475

15 David saw that Saul had come out to seek his life. David was in the wilderness of Ziph at Horesh. 16 And Jonathan, Saul's son, rose and went to David at Horesh, and strengthened his hand in God. 17 And he said to him, "Do not fear, for the hand of Saul my father shall not find you. You shall be king over Israel, and I shall be next to you. Saul my father also knows this." 18 And the two of them made a covenant before the LORD. David remained at Horesh, and Jonathan went home.

19 Then the Ziphites went up to Saul at Gibeah, saying, "Is not David hiding among us in the strongholds at Horesh, on the hill of Hachilah, which is south of Jeshimon? 20 Now come down, O king, according to all your heart's desire to come down, and our part shall be to surrender him into the king's hand." 21 And Saul said, "May you be blessed by the LORD, for you have had compassion on me. 22 Go, make yet more sure. Know and see the place where his foot is, and who has seen him there, for it is told me that he is very cunning. 23 See therefore and take note of all the lurking places where he hides, and come back to me with sure information. Then I will go with you. And if he is in the land, I will search him out among all the thousands of Judah." 24 And they arose and went to Ziph ahead of Saul.

Now David and his men were in the wilderness of Maon, in the Arabah to the south of Jeshimon. 25 And Saul and his men went to seek him. And David was told, so he went down to the rock and lived in the wilderness of Maon. And when Saul heard that, he pursued after David in the wilderness of Maon. 26 Saul went on one side of the mountain, and David and his men on the other side of the mountain. And David was hurrying to get away from Saul. As Saul and his men were closing in on David and his men to capture them, 27 a messenger came to Saul, saying, "Hurry and come, for the Philistines have made a raid against the land." 28 So Saul returned from pursuing after David and went against the Philistines. Therefore that place was called the Rock of Escape.[1]

[1] Or *Rock of Divisions*

29 [1] And David went up from there and
lived in the strongholds of Engedi.

David Spares Saul's Life

24 [2] When Saul returned from follow-
ing the Philistines, he was told,
"Behold, David is in the wilderness of
Engedi." 2 Then Saul took three thousand
chosen men out of all Israel and went to
seek David and his men in front of the
Wildgoats' Rocks. 3 And he came to the
sheepfolds by the way, where there was a
cave, and Saul went in to relieve himself.[3]
Now David and his men were sitting in
the innermost parts of the cave. 4 And the
men of David said to him, "Here is the day
of which the LORD said to you, 'Behold, I
will give your enemy into your hand, and
you shall do to him as it shall seem good
to you.'" Then David arose and stealthily
cut off a corner of Saul's robe. 5 And after-
ward David's heart struck him, because
he had cut off a corner of Saul's robe. 6 He
said to his men, "The LORD forbid that I
should do this thing to my lord, the LORD's
anointed, to put out my hand against
him, seeing he is the LORD's anointed."
7 So David persuaded his men with these
words and did not permit them to attack
Saul. And Saul rose up and left the cave
and went on his way.

8 Afterward David also arose and went
out of the cave, and called after Saul, "My
lord the king!" And when Saul looked
behind him, David bowed with his face
to the earth and paid homage. 9 And David
said to Saul, "Why do you listen to the
words of men who say, 'Behold, David
seeks your harm'? 10 Behold, this day your
eyes have seen how the LORD gave you
today into my hand in the cave. And some
told me to kill you, but I spared you.[4] I said,
'I will not put out my hand against my lord,
for he is the LORD's anointed.' 11 See, my
father, see the corner of your robe in my
hand. For by the fact that I cut off the cor-
ner of your robe and did not kill you, you
may know and see that there is no wrong
or treason in my hands. I have not sinned
against you, though you hunt my life to
take it. 12 May the LORD judge between me
and you, may the LORD avenge me against
you, but my hand shall not be against you.
13 As the proverb of the ancients says, 'Out
of the wicked comes wickedness.' But my
hand shall not be against you. 14 After
whom has the king of Israel come out?
After whom do you pursue? After a dead
dog! After a flea! 15 May the LORD therefore
be judge and give sentence between me
and you, and see to it and plead my cause
and deliver me from your hand."

16 As soon as David had finished speak-
ing these words to Saul, Saul said, "Is this
your voice, my son David?" And Saul lifted
up his voice and wept. 17 He said to David,
"You are more righteous than I, for you
have repaid me good, whereas I have repaid
you evil. 18 And you have declared this day
how you have dealt well with me, in that
you did not kill me when the LORD put me
into your hands. 19 For if a man finds his
enemy, will he let him go away safe? So
may the LORD reward you with good for
what you have done to me this day. 20 And
now, behold, I know that you shall surely
be king, and that the kingdom of Israel
shall be established in your hand. 21 Swear
to me therefore by the LORD that you will
not cut off my offspring after me, and that
you will not destroy my name out of my
father's house." 22 And David swore this to
Saul. Then Saul went home, but David and
his men went up to the stronghold.

The Death of Samuel

25 Now Samuel died. And all Israel
assembled and mourned for
him, and they buried him in his house at
Ramah.

David and Abigail

Then David rose and went down to the
wilderness of Paran. 2 And there was a man
in Maon whose business was in Carmel.

[1] Ch 24:1 in Hebrew [2] Ch 24:2 in Hebrew [3] Hebrew *cover his feet* [4] Septuagint, Syriac, Targum; Hebrew *it* [my eye] *spared you*

The man was very rich; he had three thou-
sand sheep and a thousand goats. He
was shearing his sheep in Carmel. 3 Now
the name of the man was Nabal, and the
name of his wife Abigail. The woman was
discerning and beautiful, but the man
was harsh and badly behaved; he was a
Calebite. 4 David heard in the wilderness
that Nabal was shearing his sheep. 5 So
David sent ten young men. And David
said to the young men, "Go up to Carmel,
and go to Nabal and greet him in my
name. 6 And thus you shall greet him:
'Peace be to you, and peace be to your
house, and peace be to all that you have.
7 I hear that you have shearers. Now your
shepherds have been with us, and we did
them no harm, and they missed nothing
all the time they were in Carmel. 8 Ask
your young men, and they will tell you.
Therefore let my young men find favor
in your eyes, for we come on a feast day.
Please give whatever you have at hand to
your servants and to your son David.'"

9 When David's young men came,
they said all this to Nabal in the name of
David, and then they waited. 10 And Nabal
answered David's servants, "Who is David?
Who is the son of Jesse? There are many
servants these days who are breaking away
from their masters. 11 Shall I take my bread
and my water and my meat that I have
killed for my shearers and give it to men
who come from I do not know where?"
12 So David's young men turned away and
came back and told him all this. 13 And
David said to his men, "Every man strap
on his sword!" And every man of them
strapped on his sword. David also strapped
on his sword. And about four hundred
men went up after David, while two hun-
dred remained with the baggage.

14 But one of the young men told Abigail,
Nabal's wife, "Behold, David sent mes-
sengers out of the wilderness to greet our
master, and he railed at them. 15 Yet the
men were very good to us, and we suffered
no harm, and we did not miss anything
when we were in the fields, as long as we
went with them. 16 They were a wall to
us both by night and by day, all the while
we were with them keeping the sheep.
17 Now therefore know this and consider
what you should do, for harm is deter-
mined against our master and against all
his house, and he is such a worthless man
that one cannot speak to him."

18 Then Abigail made haste and took two
hundred loaves and two skins of wine
and five sheep already prepared and five
seahs[1] of parched grain and a hundred
clusters of raisins and two hundred cakes
of figs, and laid them on donkeys. 19 And
she said to her young men, "Go on before
me; behold, I come after you." But she did
not tell her husband Nabal. 20 And as she
rode on the donkey and came down under
cover of the mountain, behold, David and
his men came down toward her, and she
met them. 21 Now David had said, "Surely
in vain have I guarded all that this fellow
has in the wilderness, so that nothing was
missed of all that belonged to him, and he
has returned me evil for good. 22 God do so
to the enemies of David[2] and more also, if
by morning I leave so much as one male of
all who belong to him."

23 When Abigail saw David, she hurried
and got down from the donkey and fell
before David on her face and bowed to the
ground. 24 She fell at his feet and said, "On
me alone, my lord, be the guilt. Please let
your servant speak in your ears, and hear
the words of your servant. 25 Let not my
lord regard this worthless fellow, Nabal, for
as his name is, so is he. Nabal[3] is his name,
and folly is with him. But I your servant did
not see the young men of my lord, whom
you sent. 26 Now then, my lord, as the LORD
lives, and as your soul lives, because the
LORD has restrained you from bloodguilt
and from saving with your own hand, now
then let your enemies and those who seek
to do evil to my lord be as Nabal. 27 And

[1] A *seah* was about 7 quarts or 7.3 liters [2] Septuagint *to David* [3] *Nabal* means *fool*

now let this present that your servant has brought to my lord be given to the young men who follow my lord. 28 Please forgive the trespass of your servant. For the LORD will certainly make my lord a sure house, because my lord is fighting the battles of the LORD, and evil shall not be found in you so long as you live. 29 If men rise up to pursue you and to seek your life, the life of my lord shall be bound in the bundle of the living in the care of the LORD your God. And the lives of your enemies he shall sling out as from the hollow of a sling. 30 And when the LORD has done to my lord according to all the good that he has spoken concerning you and has appointed you prince over Israel, 31 my lord shall have no cause of grief or pangs of conscience for having shed blood without cause or for my lord taking vengeance himself. And when the LORD has dealt well with my lord, then remember your servant."

32 And David said to Abigail, "Blessed be the LORD, the God of Israel, who sent you this day to meet me! 33 Blessed be your discretion, and blessed be you, who have kept me this day from bloodguilt and from avenging myself with my own hand! 34 For as surely as the LORD, the God of Israel, lives, who has restrained me from hurting you, unless you had hurried and come to meet me, truly by morning there had not been left to Nabal so much as one male." 35 Then David received from her hand what she had brought him. And he said to her, "Go up in peace to your house. See, I have obeyed your voice, and I have granted your petition."

36 And Abigail came to Nabal, and behold, he was holding a feast in his house, like the feast of a king. And Nabal's heart was merry within him, for he was very drunk. So she told him nothing at all until the morning light. 37 In the morning, when the wine had gone out of Nabal, his wife told him these things, and his heart died within him, and he became as a stone. 38 And about ten days later the LORD struck Nabal, and he died.

39 When David heard that Nabal was dead, he said, "Blessed be the LORD who has avenged the insult I received at the hand of Nabal, and has kept back his servant from wrongdoing. The LORD has returned the evil of Nabal on his own head." Then David sent and spoke to Abigail, to take her as his wife. 40 When the servants of David came to Abigail at Carmel, they said to her, "David has sent us to you to take you to him as his wife." 41 And she rose and bowed with her face to the ground and said, "Behold, your handmaid is a servant to wash the feet of the servants of my lord." 42 And Abigail hurried and rose and mounted a donkey, and her five young women attended her. She followed the messengers of David and became his wife.

43 David also took Ahinoam of Jezreel, and both of them became his wives. 44 Saul had given Michal his daughter, David's wife, to Palti the son of Laish, who was of Gallim.

David Spares Saul Again

26 Then the Ziphites came to Saul at Gibeah, saying, "Is not David hiding himself on the hill of Hachilah, which is on the east of Jeshimon?" 2 So Saul arose and went down to the wilderness of Ziph with three thousand chosen men of Israel to seek David in the wilderness of Ziph. 3 And Saul encamped on the hill of Hachilah, which is beside the road on the east of Jeshimon. But David remained in the wilderness. When he saw that Saul came after him into the wilderness, 4 David sent out spies and learned that Saul had come. 5 Then David rose and came to the place where Saul had encamped. And David saw the place where Saul lay, with Abner the son of Ner, the commander of his army. Saul was lying within the encampment, while the army was encamped around him.

6 Then David said to Ahimelech the

Hittite, and to Joab's brother Abishai the
son of Zeruiah, "Who will go down with
me into the camp to Saul?" And Abishai
said, "I will go down with you." 7 So David
and Abishai went to the army by night.
And there lay Saul sleeping within the
encampment, with his spear stuck in
the ground at his head, and Abner and the
army lay around him. 8 Then said Abishai
to David, "God has given your enemy into
your hand this day. Now please let me pin
him to the earth with one stroke of the
spear, and I will not strike him twice." 9 But
David said to Abishai, "Do not destroy him,
for who can put out his hand against the
LORD's anointed and be guiltless?" 10 And
David said, "As the LORD lives, the LORD
will strike him, or his day will come to die,
or he will go down into battle and perish.
11 The LORD forbid that I should put out
my hand against the LORD's anointed. But
take now the spear that is at his head and
the jar of water, and let us go." 12 So David
took the spear and the jar of water from
Saul's head, and they went away. No man
saw it or knew it, nor did any awake, for
they were all asleep, because a deep sleep
from the LORD had fallen upon them.

13 Then David went over to the other
side and stood far off on the top of the hill,
with a great space between them. 14 And
David called to the army, and to Abner the
son of Ner, saying, "Will you not answer,
Abner?" Then Abner answered, "Who are
you who calls to the king?" 15 And David
said to Abner, "Are you not a man? Who is
like you in Israel? Why then have you not
kept watch over your lord the king? For
one of the people came in to destroy the
king your lord. 16 This thing that you have
done is not good. As the LORD lives, you
deserve to die, because you have not kept
watch over your lord, the LORD's anointed.
And now see where the king's spear is and
the jar of water that was at his head."

17 Saul recognized David's voice and said,
"Is this your voice, my son David?" And
David said, "It is my voice, my lord, O king."
18 And he said, "Why does my lord pursue
after his servant? For what have I done?
What evil is on my hands? 19 Now there-
fore let my lord the king hear the words of
his servant. If it is the LORD who has stirred
you up against me, may he accept an offer-
ing, but if it is men, may they be cursed
before the LORD, for they have driven me
out this day that I should have no share in
the heritage of the LORD, saying, 'Go, serve
other gods.' 20 Now therefore, let not my
blood fall to the earth away from the pres-
ence of the LORD, for the king of Israel has
come out to seek a single flea like one who
hunts a partridge in the mountains."

21 Then Saul said, "I have sinned. Return,
my son David, for I will no more do you
harm, because my life was precious in
your eyes this day. Behold, I have acted
foolishly, and have made a great mistake."
22 And David answered and said, "Here
is the spear, O king! Let one of the young
men come over and take it. 23 The LORD
rewards every man for his righteousness
and his faithfulness, for the LORD gave you
into my hand today, and I would not put
out my hand against the LORD's anointed.
24 Behold, as your life was precious this day
in my sight, so may my life be precious in
the sight of the LORD, and may he deliver
me out of all tribulation." 25 Then Saul said
to David, "Blessed be you, my son David!
You will do many things and will succeed
in them." So David went his way, and Saul
returned to his place.

David Flees to the Philistines

27 Then David said in his heart,
"Now I shall perish one day by the
hand of Saul. There is nothing better for
me than that I should escape to the land
of the Philistines. Then Saul will despair
of seeking me any longer within the bor-
ders of Israel, and I shall escape out of his
hand." 2 So David arose and went over, he
and the six hundred men who were with

him, to Achish the son of Maoch, king of Gath. 3 And David lived with Achish at Gath, he and his men, every man with his household, and David with his two wives, Ahinoam of Jezreel, and Abigail of Carmel, Nabal's widow. 4 And when it was told Saul that David had fled to Gath, he no longer sought him.

5 Then David said to Achish, "If I have found favor in your eyes, let a place be given me in one of the country towns, that I may dwell there. For why should your servant dwell in the royal city with you?" 6 So that day Achish gave him Ziklag. Therefore Ziklag has belonged to the kings of Judah to this day. 7 And the number of the days that David lived in the country of the Philistines was a year and four months.

8 Now David and his men went up and made raids against the Geshurites, the Girzites, and the Amalekites, for these were the inhabitants of the land from of old, as far as Shur, to the land of Egypt. 9 And David would strike the land and would leave neither man nor woman alive, but would take away the sheep, the oxen, the donkeys, the camels, and the garments, and come back to Achish. 10 When Achish asked, "Where have you made a raid today?" David would say, "Against the Negeb of Judah," or, "Against the Negeb of the Jerahmeelites," or, "Against the Negeb of the Kenites." 11 And David would leave neither man nor woman alive to bring news to Gath, thinking, "lest they should tell about us and say, 'So David has done.'" Such was his custom all the while he lived in the country of the Philistines. 12 And Achish trusted David, thinking, "He has made himself an utter stench to his people Israel; therefore he shall always be my servant."

Saul and the Medium of En-dor

28 In those days the Philistines gathered their forces for war, to fight against Israel. And Achish said to David, "Understand that you and your men are to go out with me in the army." 2 David said to Achish, "Very well, you shall know what your servant can do." And Achish said to David, "Very well, I will make you my bodyguard for life."

3 Now Samuel had died, and all Israel had mourned for him and buried him in Ramah, his own city. And Saul had put the mediums and the necromancers out of the land. 4 The Philistines assembled and came and encamped at Shunem. And Saul gathered all Israel, and they encamped at Gilboa. 5 When Saul saw the army of the Philistines, he was afraid, and his heart trembled greatly. 6 And when Saul inquired of the LORD, the LORD did not answer him, either by dreams, or by Urim, or by prophets. 7 Then Saul said to his servants, "Seek out for me a woman who is a medium, that I may go to her and inquire of her." And his servants said to him, "Behold, there is a medium at En-dor."

8 So Saul disguised himself and put on other garments and went, he and two men with him. And they came to the woman by night. And he said, "Divine for me by a spirit and bring up for me whomever I shall name to you." 9 The woman said to him, "Surely you know what Saul has done, how he has cut off the mediums and the necromancers from the land. Why then are you laying a trap for my life to bring about my death?" 10 But Saul swore to her by the LORD, "As the LORD lives, no punishment shall come upon you for this thing." 11 Then the woman said, "Whom shall I bring up for you?" He said, "Bring up Samuel for me." 12 When the woman saw Samuel, she cried out with a loud voice. And the woman said to Saul, "Why have you deceived me? You are Saul." 13 The king said to her, "Do not be afraid. What do you see?" And the woman said to Saul, "I see a god coming up out of the earth." 14 He said to her, "What is his appearance?" And she said, "An old man is coming up, and he is wrapped in a robe." And Saul knew that

it was Samuel, and he bowed with his face to the ground and paid homage.

15 Then Samuel said to Saul, "Why have you disturbed me by bringing me up?" Saul answered, "I am in great distress, for the Philistines are warring against me, and God has turned away from me and answers me no more, either by prophets or by dreams. Therefore I have summoned you to tell me what I shall do." 16 And Samuel said, "Why then do you ask me, since the LORD has turned from you and become your enemy? 17 The LORD has done to you as he spoke by me, for the LORD has torn the kingdom out of your hand and given it to your neighbor, David. 18 Because you did not obey the voice of the LORD and did not carry out his fierce wrath against Amalek, therefore the LORD has done this thing to you this day. 19 Moreover, the LORD will give Israel also with you into the hand of the Philistines, and tomorrow you and your sons shall be with me. The LORD will give the army of Israel also into the hand of the Philistines."

20 Then Saul fell at once full length on the ground, filled with fear because of the words of Samuel. And there was no strength in him, for he had eaten nothing all day and all night. 21 And the woman came to Saul, and when she saw that he was terrified, she said to him, "Behold, your servant has obeyed you. I have taken my life in my hand and have listened to what you have said to me. 22 Now therefore, you also obey your servant. Let me set a morsel of bread before you; and eat, that you may have strength when you go on your way." 23 He refused and said, "I will not eat." But his servants, together with the woman, urged him, and he listened to their words. So he arose from the earth and sat on the bed. 24 Now the woman had a fattened calf in the house, and she quickly killed it, and she took flour and kneaded it and baked unleavened bread of it, 25 and she put it before Saul and his servants, and they ate. Then they rose and went away that night.

The Philistines Reject David

29 Now the Philistines had gathered all their forces at Aphek. And the Israelites were encamped by the spring that is in Jezreel. 2 As the lords of the Philistines were passing on by hundreds and by thousands, and David and his men were passing on in the rear with Achish, 3 the commanders of the Philistines said, "What are these Hebrews doing here?" And Achish said to the commanders of the Philistines, "Is this not David, the servant of Saul, king of Israel, who has been with me now for days and years, and since he deserted to me I have found no fault in him to this day." 4 But the commanders of the Philistines were angry with him. And the commanders of the Philistines said to him, "Send the man back, that he may return to the place to which you have assigned him. He shall not go down with us to battle, lest in the battle he become an adversary to us. For how could this fellow reconcile himself to his lord? Would it not be with the heads of the men here? 5 Is not this David, of whom they sing to one another in dances,

'Saul has struck down his thousands,
and David his ten thousands'?"

6 Then Achish called David and said to him, "As the LORD lives, you have been honest, and to me it seems right that you should march out and in with me in the campaign. For I have found nothing wrong in you from the day of your coming to me to this day. Nevertheless, the lords do not approve of you. 7 So go back now; and go peaceably, that you may not displease the lords of the Philistines." 8 And David said to Achish, "But what have I done? What have you found in your servant from the day I entered your service until now, that I may not go and fight against the ene-

mies of my lord the king?" 9 And Achish answered David and said, "I know that you are as blameless in my sight as an angel of God. Nevertheless, the commanders of the Philistines have said, 'He shall not go up with us to the battle.' 10 Now then rise early in the morning with the servants of your lord who came with you, and start early in the morning, and depart as soon as you have light." 11 So David set out with his men early in the morning to return to the land of the Philistines. But the Philistines went up to Jezreel.

David's Wives Are Captured

30 Now when David and his men came to Ziklag on the third day, the Amalekites had made a raid against the Negeb and against Ziklag. They had overcome Ziklag and burned it with fire 2 and taken captive the women and all[1] who were in it, both small and great. They killed no one, but carried them off and went their way. 3 And when David and his men came to the city, they found it burned with fire, and their wives and sons and daughters taken captive. 4 Then David and the people who were with him raised their voices and wept until they had no more strength to weep. 5 David's two wives also had been taken captive, Ahinoam of Jezreel and Abigail the widow of Nabal of Carmel. 6 And David was greatly distressed, for the people spoke of stoning him, because all the people were bitter in soul,[2] each for his sons and daughters. But David strengthened himself in the LORD his God.

7 And David said to Abiathar the priest, the son of Ahimelech, "Bring me the ephod." So Abiathar brought the ephod to David. 8 And David inquired of the LORD, "Shall I pursue after this band? Shall I overtake them?" He answered him, "Pursue, for you shall surely overtake and shall surely rescue." 9 So David set out, and the six hundred men who were with him, and they came to the brook Besor, where those who were left behind stayed. 10 But David pursued, he and four hundred men. Two hundred stayed behind, who were too exhausted to cross the brook Besor.

11 They found an Egyptian in the open country and brought him to David. And they gave him bread and he ate. They gave him water to drink, 12 and they gave him a piece of a cake of figs and two clusters of raisins. And when he had eaten, his spirit revived, for he had not eaten bread or drunk water for three days and three nights. 13 And David said to him, "To whom do you belong? And where are you from?" He said, "I am a young man of Egypt, servant to an Amalekite, and my master left me behind because I fell sick three days ago. 14 We had made a raid against the Negeb of the Cherethites and against that which belongs to Judah and against the Negeb of Caleb, and we burned Ziklag with fire." 15 And David said to him, "Will you take me down to this band?" And he said, "Swear to me by God that you will not kill me or deliver me into the hands of my master, and I will take you down to this band."

David Defeats the Amalekites

16 And when he had taken him down, behold, they were spread abroad over all the land, eating and drinking and dancing, because of all the great spoil they had taken from the land of the Philistines and from the land of Judah. 17 And David struck them down from twilight until the evening of the next day, and not a man of them escaped, except four hundred young men, who mounted camels and fled. 18 David recovered all that the Amalekites had taken, and David rescued his two wives. 19 Nothing was missing, whether small or great, sons or daughters, spoil or anything that had been taken. David brought back all. 20 David also captured all the flocks and herds, and the people drove the livestock before him,[3] and said, "This is David's spoil."

[1] Septuagint; Hebrew lacks *and all* [2] Compare 22:2 [3] The meaning of the Hebrew clause is uncertain

21 Then David came to the two hundred
men who had been too exhausted to fol-
low David, and who had been left at the
brook Besor. And they went out to meet
David and to meet the people who were
with him. And when David came near
to the people he greeted them. 22 Then all
the wicked and worthless fellows among
the men who had gone with David said,
"Because they did not go with us, we
will not give them any of the spoil that
we have recovered, except that each man
may lead away his wife and children, and
depart." 23 But David said, "You shall not
do so, my brothers, with what the LORD
has given us. He has preserved us and
given into our hand the band that came
against us. 24 Who would listen to you in
this matter? For as his share is who goes
down into the battle, so shall his share
be who stays by the baggage. They shall
share alike." 25 And he made it a statute
and a rule for Israel from that day forward
to this day.

26 When David came to Ziklag, he sent
part of the spoil to his friends, the elders
of Judah, saying, "Here is a present for
you from the spoil of the enemies of the
LORD." 27 It was for those in Bethel, in
Ramoth of the Negeb, in Jattir, 28 in Aroer,
in Siphmoth, in Eshtemoa, 29 in Racal, in
the cities of the Jerahmeelites, in the cities
of the Kenites, 30 in Hormah, in Bor-ashan,
in Athach, 31 in Hebron, for all the places
where David and his men had roamed.

The Death of Saul

31

449

Now the Philistines fought
against Israel, and the men
of Israel fled before the Philistines
and fell slain on Mount Gilboa. 2 And the
Philistines overtook Saul and his sons,
and the Philistines struck down Jonathan
and Abinadab and Malchi-shua, the sons
of Saul. 3 The battle pressed hard against
Saul, and the archers found him, and he
was badly wounded by the archers. 4 Then
Saul said to his armor-bearer, "Draw your
sword, and thrust me through with it, lest
these uncircumcised come and thrust me
through, and mistreat me." But his armor-
bearer would not, for he feared greatly.
Therefore Saul took his own sword and
fell upon it. 5 And when his armor-bearer
saw that Saul was dead, he also fell upon
his sword and died with him. 6 Thus Saul
died, and his three sons, and his armor-
bearer, and all his men, on the same day
together. 7 And when the men of Israel
who were on the other side of the valley
and those beyond the Jordan saw that the
men of Israel had fled and that Saul and
his sons were dead, they abandoned their
cities and fled. And the Philistines came
and lived in them.

8 The next day, when the Philistines
came to strip the slain, they found Saul
and his three sons fallen on Mount Gilboa.
9 So they cut off his head and stripped off
his armor and sent messengers through-
out the land of the Philistines, to carry the
good news to the house of their idols and
to the people. 10 They put his armor in the
temple of Ashtaroth, and they fastened
his body to the wall of Beth-shan. 11 But
when the inhabitants of Jabesh-gilead
heard what the Philistines had done to
Saul, 12 all the valiant men arose and went
all night and took the body of Saul and the
bodies of his sons from the wall of Beth-
shan, and they came to Jabesh and burned
them there. 13 And they took their bones
and buried them under the tamarisk tree
in Jabesh and fasted seven days.

2 Samuel

For the introduction, see the introduction to 1–2 Samuel (p. 431)

David Hears of Saul's Death

1 After the death of Saul, when David
had returned from striking down the
Amalekites, David remained two days in
Ziklag. 2 And on the third day, behold, a
man came from Saul's camp, with his
clothes torn and dirt on his head. And
when he came to David, he fell to the
ground and paid homage. 3 David said to
him, "Where do you come from?" And
he said to him, "I have escaped from the
camp of Israel." 4 And David said to him,
"How did it go? Tell me." And he answered,
"The people fled from the battle, and also
many of the people have fallen and are
dead, and Saul and his son Jonathan are
also dead." 5 Then David said to the young
man who told him, "How do you know
that Saul and his son Jonathan are dead?"
6 And the young man who told him said,
"By chance I happened to be on Mount
Gilboa, and there was Saul leaning on his
spear, and behold, the chariots and the
horsemen were close upon him. 7 And
when he looked behind him, he saw me,
and called to me. And I answered, 'Here I
am.' 8 And he said to me, 'Who are you?' I
answered him, 'I am an Amalekite.' 9 And
he said to me 'Stand beside me and kill
me, for anguish has seized me, and yet my
life still lingers.' 10 So I stood beside him
and killed him, because I was sure that
he could not live after he had fallen. And
I took the crown that was on his head and
the armlet that was on his arm, and I have
brought them here to my lord."

11 Then David took hold of his clothes
and tore them, and so did all the men who
were with him. 12 And they mourned and
wept and fasted until evening for Saul and
for Jonathan his son and for the people
of the LORD and for the house of Israel,
because they had fallen by the sword.
13 And David said to the young man who
told him, "Where do you come from?" And
he answered, "I am the son of a sojourner,
an Amalekite." 14 David said to him, "How is
it you were not afraid to put out your hand
to destroy the LORD's anointed?" 15 Then
David called one of the young men and
said, "Go, execute him." And he struck him
down so that he died. 16 And David said to
him, "Your blood be on your head, for your
own mouth has testified against you, say-
ing, 'I have killed the LORD's anointed.'"

David's Lament for Saul and Jonathan

17 And David lamented with this
lamentation over Saul and Jon-
475 athan his son, 18 and he said it[1]
should be taught to the people of Judah;
behold, it is written in the Book of Jashar.[2]
He said:

19 "Your glory, O Israel, is slain on your
high places!
How the mighty have fallen!
20 Tell it not in Gath,
publish it not in the streets of
Ashkelon,
lest the daughters of the Philistines
rejoice,
lest the daughters of the
uncircumcised exult.
21 "You mountains of Gilboa,
let there be no dew or rain upon
you,
nor fields of offerings![3]
For there the shield of the mighty
was defiled,
the shield of Saul, not anointed
with oil.

[1] Septuagint; Hebrew *the Bow*, which may be the name of the lament's tune [2] Or *of the upright* [3] Septuagint *firstfruits*

22 "From the blood of the slain,
from the fat of the mighty,
the bow of Jonathan turned not back,
and the sword of Saul returned not empty.

23 "Saul and Jonathan, beloved and lovely!
In life and in death they were not divided;
they were swifter than eagles;
they were stronger than lions.

24 "You daughters of Israel, weep over Saul,
who clothed you luxuriously in scarlet,
who put ornaments of gold on your apparel.

25 "How the mighty have fallen
in the midst of the battle!

"Jonathan lies slain on your high places.
26 I am distressed for you, my brother Jonathan;
very pleasant have you been to me;
your love to me was extraordinary,
surpassing the love of women.

27 "How the mighty have fallen,
and the weapons of war perished!"

David Anointed King of Judah

2 After this David inquired of the LORD,
"Shall I go up into any of the cities of
Judah?" And the LORD said to him, "Go
up." David said, "To which shall I go up?"
And he said, "To Hebron." 2 So David went
up there, and his two wives also, Ahinoam
of Jezreel and Abigail the widow of Nabal
of Carmel. 3 And David brought up his
men who were with him, everyone with
his household, and they lived in the towns
of Hebron. 4 And the men of Judah came,
and there they anointed David king over
the house of Judah.

When they told David, "It was the men
of Jabesh-gilead who buried Saul," 5 David
sent messengers to the men of Jabesh-
gilead and said to them, "May you be
blessed by the LORD, because you showed
this loyalty to Saul your lord and buried
him. 6 Now may the LORD show steadfast
love and faithfulness to you. And I will do
good to you because you have done this
thing. 7 Now therefore let your hands be
strong, and be valiant, for Saul your lord is
dead, and the house of Judah has anointed
me king over them."

Ish-bosheth Made King of Israel

8 But Abner the son of Ner, commander
of Saul's army, took Ish-bosheth the son of
Saul and brought him over to Mahanaim,
9 and he made him king over Gilead and
the Ashurites and Jezreel and Ephraim
and Benjamin and all Israel. 10 Ish-bosheth,
Saul's son, was forty years old when he
began to reign over Israel, and he reigned
two years. But the house of Judah followed
David. 11 And the time that David was king
in Hebron over the house of Judah was
seven years and six months.

The Battle of Gibeon

12 Abner the son of Ner, and the servants
of Ish-bosheth the son of Saul, went out
from Mahanaim to Gibeon. 13 And Joab
the son of Zeruiah and the servants of
David went out and met them at the pool
of Gibeon. And they sat down, the one on
the one side of the pool, and the other on
the other side of the pool. 14 And Abner
said to Joab, "Let the young men arise and
compete before us." And Joab said, "Let
them arise." 15 Then they arose and passed
over by number, twelve for Benjamin and
Ish-bosheth the son of Saul, and twelve of
the servants of David. 16 And each caught
his opponent by the head and thrust his
sword in his opponent's side, so they fell
down together. Therefore that place was
called Helkath-hazzurim,[1] which is at
Gibeon. 17 And the battle was very fierce

[1] *Helkath-hazzurim* means *the field of sword-edges*

that day. And Abner and the men of Israel were beaten before the servants of David.

18 And the three sons of Zeruiah were there, Joab, Abishai, and Asahel. Now Asahel was as swift of foot as a wild gazelle. 19 And Asahel pursued Abner, and as he went, he turned neither to the right hand nor to the left from following Abner. 20 Then Abner looked behind him and said, "Is it you, Asahel?" And he answered, "It is I." 21 Abner said to him, "Turn aside to your right hand or to your left, and seize one of the young men and take his spoil." But Asahel would not turn aside from following him. 22 And Abner said again to Asahel, "Turn aside from following me. Why should I strike you to the ground? How then could I lift up my face to your brother Joab?" 23 But he refused to turn aside. Therefore Abner struck him in the stomach with the butt of his spear, so that the spear came out at his back. And he fell there and died where he was. And all who came to the place where Asahel had fallen and died, stood still.

24 But Joab and Abishai pursued Abner. And as the sun was going down they came to the hill of Ammah, which lies before Giah on the way to the wilderness of Gibeon. 25 And the people of Benjamin gathered themselves together behind Abner and became one group and took their stand on the top of a hill. 26 Then Abner called to Joab, "Shall the sword devour forever? Do you not know that the end will be bitter? How long will it be before you tell your people to turn from the pursuit of their brothers?" 27 And Joab said, "As God lives, if you had not spoken, surely the men would not have given up the pursuit of their brothers until the morning." 28 So Joab blew the trumpet, and all the men stopped and pursued Israel no more, nor did they fight anymore.

29 And Abner and his men went all that night through the Arabah. They crossed the Jordan, and marching the whole morning, they came to Mahanaim. 30 Joab returned from the pursuit of Abner. And when he had gathered all the people together, there were missing from David's servants nineteen men besides Asahel. 31 But the servants of David had struck down of Benjamin 360 of Abner's men. 32 And they took up Asahel and buried him in the tomb of his father, which was at Bethlehem. And Joab and his men marched all night, and the day broke upon them at Hebron.

Abner Joins David

3 There was a long war between the house of Saul and the house of David. And David grew stronger and stronger, while the house of Saul became weaker and weaker.

2 And sons were born to David at Hebron: his firstborn was Amnon, of Ahinoam of Jezreel; 3 and his second, Chileab, of Abigail the widow of Nabal of Carmel; and the third, Absalom the son of Maacah the daughter of Talmai king of Geshur; 4 and the fourth, Adonijah the son of Haggith; and the fifth, Shephatiah the son of Abital; 5 and the sixth, Ithream, of Eglah, David's wife. These were born to David in Hebron.

6 While there was war between the house of Saul and the house of David, Abner was making himself strong in the house of Saul. 7 Now Saul had a concubine whose name was Rizpah, the daughter of Aiah. And Ish-bosheth said to Abner, "Why have you gone in to my father's concubine?" 8 Then Abner was very angry over the words of Ish-bosheth and said, "Am I a dog's head of Judah? To this day I keep showing steadfast love to the house of Saul your father, to his brothers, and to his friends, and have not given you into the hand of David. And yet you charge me today with a fault concerning a woman. 9 God do so to Abner and more also, if I do not accomplish for David what the LORD has sworn to him, 10 to transfer the kingdom from the house

of Saul and set up the throne of David
over Israel and over Judah, from Dan to
Beersheba." 11 And Ish-bosheth could not
answer Abner another word, because he
feared him.

12 And Abner sent messengers to David
on his behalf,[1] saying, "To whom does the
land belong? Make your covenant with me,
and behold, my hand shall be with you to
bring over all Israel to you." 13 And he said,
"Good; I will make a covenant with you.
But one thing I require of you; that is, you
shall not see my face unless you first bring
Michal, Saul's daughter, when you come
to see my face." 14 Then David sent mes-
sengers to Ish-bosheth, Saul's son, saying,
"Give me my wife Michal, for whom I paid
the bridal price of a hundred foreskins of
the Philistines." 15 And Ish-bosheth sent
and took her from her husband Paltiel
the son of Laish. 16 But her husband went
with her, weeping after her all the way to
Bahurim. Then Abner said to him, "Go,
return." And he returned.

17 And Abner conferred with the elders
of Israel, saying, "For some time past you
have been seeking David as king over you.
18 Now then bring it about, for the LORD
has promised David, saying, 'By the hand
of my servant David I will save my people
Israel from the hand of the Philistines,
and from the hand of all their enemies.'"
19 Abner also spoke to Benjamin. And then
Abner went to tell David at Hebron all that
Israel and the whole house of Benjamin
thought good to do.

20 When Abner came with twenty men
to David at Hebron, David made a feast for
Abner and the men who were with him.
21 And Abner said to David, "I will arise
and go and will gather all Israel to my lord
the king, that they may make a covenant
with you, and that you may reign over
all that your heart desires." So David sent
Abner away, and he went in peace.

22 Just then the servants of David arrived
with Joab from a raid, bringing much spoil
with them. But Abner was not with David
at Hebron, for he had sent him away, and
he had gone in peace. 23 When Joab and
all the army that was with him came, it
was told Joab, "Abner the son of Ner came
to the king, and he has let him go, and he
has gone in peace." 24 Then Joab went to
the king and said, "What have you done?
Behold, Abner came to you. Why is it
that you have sent him away, so that he
is gone? 25 You know that Abner the son
of Ner came to deceive you and to know
your going out and your coming in, and
to know all that you are doing."

Joab Murders Abner

26 When Joab came out from David's
presence, he sent messengers after Abner,
and they brought him back from the cis-
tern of Sirah. But David did not know about
it. 27 And when Abner returned to Hebron,
Joab took him aside into the midst of the
gate to speak with him privately, and
there he struck him in the stomach, so
that he died, for the blood of Asahel his
brother. 28 Afterward, when David heard of
it, he said, "I and my kingdom are forever
guiltless before the LORD for the blood of
Abner the son of Ner. 29 May it fall upon
the head of Joab and upon all his father's
house, and may the house of Joab never be
without one who has a discharge or who
is leprous or who holds a spindle or who
falls by the sword or who lacks bread!"
30 So Joab and Abishai his brother killed
Abner, because he had put their brother
Asahel to death in the battle at Gibeon.

David Mourns Abner

31 Then David said to Joab and to all the
people who were with him, "Tear your
clothes and put on sackcloth and mourn
before Abner." And King David followed
the bier. 32 They buried Abner at Hebron.
And the king lifted up his voice and wept at
the grave of Abner, and all the people wept.
33 And the king lamented for Abner, saying,

[1] Or *where he was*; Septuagint *at Hebron*

"Should Abner die as a fool dies?
34 Your hands were not bound;
your feet were not fettered;
as one falls before the wicked
you have fallen."

And all the people wept again over him.
35 Then all the people came to persuade
David to eat bread while it was yet day. But
David swore, saying, "God do so to me and
more also, if I taste bread or anything else
till the sun goes down!" 36 And all the peo-
ple took notice of it, and it pleased them,
as everything that the king did pleased all
the people. 37 So all the people and all Israel
understood that day that it had not been
the king's will to put to death Abner the
son of Ner. 38 And the king said to his ser-
vants, "Do you not know that a prince and
a great man has fallen this day in Israel?
39 And I was gentle today, though anointed
king. These men, the sons of Zeruiah, are
more severe than I. The LORD repay the
evildoer according to his wickedness!"

Ish-bosheth Murdered

4 When Ish-bosheth, Saul's son, heard
that Abner had died at Hebron, his
courage failed, and all Israel was dismayed.
2 Now Saul's son had two men who were
captains of raiding bands; the name of
the one was Baanah, and the name of the
other Rechab, sons of Rimmon a man
of Benjamin from Beeroth (for Beeroth
also is counted part of Benjamin; 3 the
Beerothites fled to Gittaim and have been
sojourners there to this day).

4 Jonathan, the son of Saul, had a son
who was crippled in his feet. He was five
years old when the news about Saul and
Jonathan came from Jezreel, and his nurse
took him up and fled, and as she fled in
her haste, he fell and became lame. And
his name was Mephibosheth.

5 Now the sons of Rimmon the Beeroth-
ite, Rechab and Baanah, set out, and about
the heat of the day they came to the house
of Ish-bosheth as he was taking his noon-
day rest. 6 And they came into the midst
of the house as if to get wheat, and they
stabbed him in the stomach. Then Rechab
and Baanah his brother escaped.[1] 7 When
they came into the house, as he lay on
his bed in his bedroom, they struck him
and put him to death and beheaded him.
They took his head and went by the way
of the Arabah all night, 8 and brought the
head of Ish-bosheth to David at Hebron.
And they said to the king, "Here is the
head of Ish-bosheth, the son of Saul, your
enemy, who sought your life. The LORD
has avenged my lord the king this day
on Saul and on his offspring." 9 But David
answered Rechab and Baanah his brother,
the sons of Rimmon the Beerothite, "As
the LORD lives, who has redeemed my life
out of every adversity, 10 when one told
me, 'Behold, Saul is dead,' and thought
he was bringing good news, I seized him
and killed him at Ziklag, which was the
reward I gave him for his news. 11 How
much more, when wicked men have
killed a righteous man in his own house
on his bed, shall I not now require his
blood at your hand and destroy you from
the earth?" 12 And David commanded his
young men, and they killed them and cut
off their hands and feet and hanged them
beside the pool at Hebron. But they took
the head of Ish-bosheth and buried it in
the tomb of Abner at Hebron.

David Anointed King of Israel

5 Then all the tribes of Israel came to
David at Hebron and said, "Behold,
we are your bone and flesh. 2 In times past,
when Saul was king over us, it was you who
led out and brought in Israel. And the LORD
said to you, 'You shall be shepherd of my
people Israel, and you shall be prince over
Israel.'" 3 So all the elders of Israel came to
the king at Hebron, and King David made
a covenant with them at Hebron before the
LORD, and they anointed David king over
Israel. 4 David was thirty years old when he

[1] Septuagint *And behold, the doorkeeper of the house had been cleaning wheat, but she grew drowsy and slept. So Rechab and Baanah his brother slipped in*

Jerusalem in the Time of David (about 1010–970 B.C.)

When Abraham was living in Canaan in tents he met Melchizidek who was the king of Jerusalem at that time. When Melchizidek was its king, the city was called "Salem" (Genesis 14:18).

Later, the Jebusites captured the city, built a wall around it, and named it "Jebus" (1 Chronicles 11:4).

King David captured this city, even though it was strongly fortified. His commander-in-chief, Joab, entered the city secretly through its water system. Joab opened the gates for David and David's men, and they took the city. From then on, David ruled Israel from Jerusalem.

Later in his life, David built an altar on a threshing floor belonging to a man named Araunah. David offered sacrifices on this altar, asking God to stop a plague that was killing Israelites.

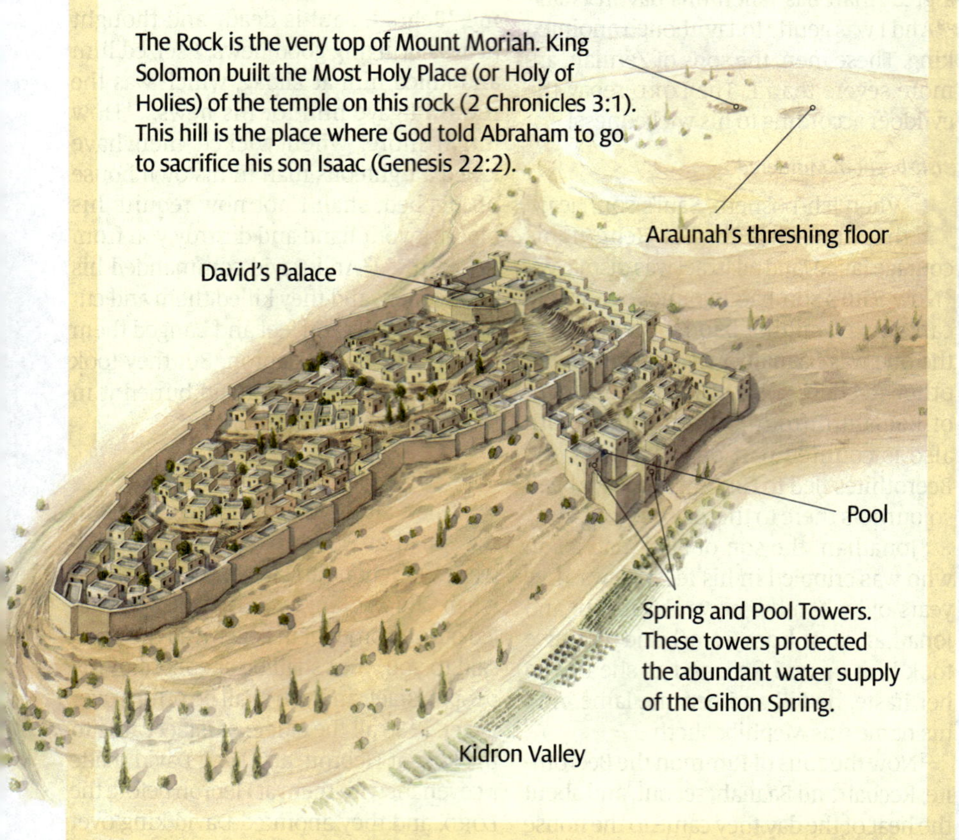

began to reign, and he reigned forty years. 5 At Hebron he reigned over Judah seven years and six months, and at Jerusalem he reigned over all Israel and Judah thirty-three years.[1]

6 And the king and his men went to Jerusalem against the Jebusites, the inhabitants of the land, who said to David, "You will not come in here, but the blind and the lame will ward you off"—thinking, "David cannot come in here." 7 Nevertheless, David took the stronghold of Zion, that is, the city of David. 8 And David said on that day, "Whoever would strike the Jebusites, let him get up the water shaft to attack 'the lame and the blind,' who are hated by David's soul." Therefore it is said, "The blind and the lame shall not come into the house." 9 And David lived in the stronghold and called it the city of David. And David built the city all around from the Millo inward. 10 And David became greater and greater, for the LORD, the God of hosts, was with him.

11 And Hiram king of Tyre sent messengers to David, and cedar trees, also carpenters and masons who built David a house. 12 And David knew that the LORD had established him king over Israel, and that he had exalted his kingdom for the sake of his people Israel.

13 And David took more concubines and wives from Jerusalem, after he came from Hebron, and more sons and daughters were born to David. 14 And these are the names of those who were born to him in Jerusalem: Shammua, Shobab, Nathan, Solomon, 15 Ibhar, Elishua, Nepheg, Japhia, 16 Elishama, Eliada, and Eliphelet.

David Defeats the Philistines

17 When the Philistines heard that David had been anointed king over Israel, all the Philistines went up to search for David. But David heard of it and went down to the stronghold. 18 Now the Philistines had come and spread out in the Valley of Rephaim. 19 And David inquired of the LORD, "Shall I go up against the Philistines? Will you give them into my hand?" And the LORD said to David, "Go up, for I will certainly give the Philistines into your hand." 20 And David came to Baal-perazim, and David defeated them there. And he said, "The LORD has burst through my enemies before me like a bursting flood." Therefore the name of that place is called Baal-perazim.[2] 21 And the Philistines left their idols there, and David and his men carried them away.

22 And the Philistines came up yet again and spread out in the Valley of Rephaim. 23 And when David inquired of the LORD, he said, "You shall not go up; go around to their rear, and come against them opposite the balsam trees. 24 And when you hear the sound of marching in the tops of the balsam trees, then rouse yourself, for then the LORD has gone out before you to strike down the army of the Philistines." 25 And David did as the LORD commanded him, and struck down the Philistines from Geba to Gezer.

The Ark Brought to Jerusalem

6 David again gathered all the chosen men of Israel, thirty thousand. 2 And David arose and went with all the people who were with him from Baale-judah to bring up from there the ark of God, which is called by the name of the LORD of hosts who sits enthroned on the cherubim. 3 And they carried the ark of God on a new cart and brought it out of the house of Abinadab, which was on the hill. And Uzzah and Ahio,[3] the sons of Abinadab, were driving the new cart,[4] 4 with the ark of God, and Ahio went before the ark.

Uzzah and the Ark

5 And David and all the house of Israel were making merry before the LORD, with songs[5] and lyres and harps and tambourines and castanets and cymbals. 6 And

[1] Dead Sea Scroll lacks verses 4-5 [2] *Baal-perazim* means *lord of bursting through* [3] Or *and his brother;* also verse 4 [4] Compare Septuagint; Hebrew *the new cart, and brought it out of the house of Abinadab, which was on the hill* [5] Septuagint, 1 Chronicles 13:8; Hebrew *fir trees*

when they came to the threshing floor of Nacon, Uzzah put out his hand to the ark of God and took hold of it, for the oxen stumbled. 7 And the anger of the LORD was kindled against Uzzah, and God struck him down there because of his error, and he died there beside the ark of God. 8 And David was angry because the LORD had burst forth against Uzzah. And that place is called Perez-uzzah,[1] to this day. 9 And David was afraid of the LORD that day, and he said, "How can the ark of the LORD come to me?" 10 So David was not willing to take the ark of the LORD into the city of David. But David took it aside to the house of Obed-edom the Gittite. 11 And the ark of the LORD remained in the house of Obed-edom the Gittite three months, and the LORD blessed Obed-edom and all his household.

12 And it was told King David, "The LORD has blessed the household of Obed-edom and all that belongs to him, because of the ark of God." So David went and brought up the ark of God from the house of Obed-edom to the city of David with rejoicing. 13 And when those who bore the ark of the LORD had gone six steps, he sacrificed an ox and a fattened animal. 14 And David danced before the LORD with all his might. And David was wearing a linen ephod. 15 So David and all the house of Israel brought up the ark of the LORD with shouting and with the sound of the horn.

David and Michal

16 As the ark of the LORD came into the city of David, Michal the daughter of Saul looked out of the window and saw King David leaping and dancing before the LORD, and she despised him in her heart. 17 And they brought in the ark of the LORD and set it in its place, inside the tent that David had pitched for it. And David offered burnt offerings and peace offerings before the LORD. 18 And when David had finished offering the burnt offerings and the peace offerings, he blessed the people in the name of the LORD of hosts 19 and distributed among all the people, the whole multitude of Israel, both men and women, a cake of bread, a portion of meat,[2] and a cake of raisins to each one. Then all the people departed, each to his house.

20 And David returned to bless his household. But Michal the daughter of Saul came out to meet David and said, "How the king of Israel honored himself today, uncovering himself today before the eyes of his servants' female servants, as one of the vulgar fellows shamelessly uncovers himself!" 21 And David said to Michal, "It was before the LORD, who chose me above your father and above all his house, to appoint me as prince over Israel, the people of the LORD—and I will make merry before the LORD. 22 I will make myself yet more contemptible than this, and I will be abased in your[3] eyes. But by the female servants of whom you have spoken, by them I shall be held in honor." 23 And Michal the daughter of Saul had no child to the day of her death.

God's Covenant with David

499

7 Now when the king lived in his house and the LORD had given him rest from all his surrounding enemies, 2 the king said to Nathan the prophet, "See now, I dwell in a house of cedar, but the ark of God dwells in a tent." 3 And Nathan said to the king, "Go, do all that is in your heart, for the LORD is with you."

4 But that same night the word of the LORD came to Nathan, 5 "Go and tell my servant David, 'Thus says the LORD: Would you build me a house to dwell in? 6 I have not lived in a house since the day I brought up the people of Israel from Egypt to this day, but I have been moving about in a tent for my dwelling. 7 In all places where I have moved with all the people of Israel, did I speak a word with any of the judges[4] of Israel, whom I commanded to shepherd my people Israel, saying, "Why have you

[1] *Perez-uzzah* means *the bursting forth upon Uzzah* [2] Vulgate; the meaning of the Hebrew term is uncertain [3] Septuagint; Hebrew *my* [4] Compare 1 Chronicles 17:6; Hebrew *tribes*

not built me a house of cedar?"' 8 Now, therefore, thus you shall say to my servant David, 'Thus says the LORD of hosts, I took you from the pasture, from following the sheep, that you should be prince over my people Israel. 9 And I have been with you wherever you went and have cut off all your enemies from before you. And I will make for you a great name, like the name of the great ones of the earth. 10 And I will appoint a place for my people Israel and will plant them, so that they may dwell in their own place and be disturbed no more. And violent men shall afflict them no more, as formerly, 11 from the time that I appointed judges over my people Israel. And I will give you rest from all your enemies. Moreover, the LORD declares to you that the LORD will make you a house. 12 When your days are fulfilled and you lie down with your fathers, I 1433 will raise up your offspring after you, who shall come from your body, and I will establish his kingdom. 13 He shall build a house for my name, and I will establish the throne of his kingdom forever. 14 I will be to him a father, and he shall be to me a son. When he commits iniquity, I will discipline him with the rod of men, with the stripes of the sons of men, 15 but my steadfast love will not depart from him, as I took it from Saul, whom I put away from before you. 16 And your house and your kingdom shall be made sure forever before me.[1] Your throne shall be established forever.'" 17 In accordance with all these words, and in accordance with all this vision, Nathan spoke to David.

David's Prayer of Gratitude

18 Then King David went in and sat before the LORD and said, "Who 87 am I, O Lord GOD, and what is my house, that you have brought me thus far? 19 And yet this was a small thing in your eyes, O Lord GOD. You have spoken also of your servant's house for a great while to come, and this is instruction for mankind, O Lord GOD! 20 And what more can David say to you? For you know your servant, O Lord GOD! 21 Because of your promise, and according to your own heart, you have brought about all this greatness, to make your servant know it. 22 Therefore you are great, O LORD God. For there is none like you, and there is no God besides you, according to all that we have heard with our ears. 23 And who is like your people Israel, the one nation on earth whom God went to redeem to be his people, making himself a name and doing for them[2] great and awesome things by driving out[3] before your people, whom you redeemed for yourself from Egypt, a nation and its gods? 24 And you established for yourself your people Israel to be your people forever. And you, O LORD, became their God. 25 And now, O LORD God, confirm forever the word that you have spoken concerning your servant and concerning his house, and do as you have spoken. 26 And your name will be magnified forever, saying, 'The LORD of hosts is God over Israel,' and the house of your servant David will be established before you. 27 For you, O LORD of hosts, the God of Israel, have made this revelation to your servant, saying, 'I will build you a house.' Therefore your servant has found courage to pray this prayer to you. 28 And now, O Lord GOD, you are God, and your words are true, and you have promised this good thing to your servant. 29 Now therefore may it please you to bless the house of your servant, so that it may continue forever before you. For you, O Lord GOD, have spoken, and with your blessing shall the house of your servant be blessed forever."

David's Victories

8 After this David defeated the Philistines and subdued them, and David took Metheg-ammah out of the hand of the Philistines.

[1] Septuagint; Hebrew *you* [2] With a few Targums, Vulgate, Syriac; Hebrew *you* [3] Septuagint (compare 1 Chronicles 17:21); Hebrew *for your land*

God's Promise to King David

God had blessed King David and defeated all his enemies. A time of peace came to the people of Israel, and David was able to build a fine royal house to live in. But while David lived in a beautiful house, the ark of the covenant was still in the tabernacle tent. So David told his friend Nathan that he wanted to build a beautiful temple that could hold God's ark of the covenant. Nathan said, "Go, do all that is in your heart, for the LORD is with you."

But that night, God told Nathan something different. God told Nathan to tell David, "I have not lived in a house. I have been moving about in a tent for My dwelling." God said that David would not be the one to build a temple for God. Even though David would not be the one to build the Temple, God reaffirmed His love for David through the prophet Nathan. God told Nathan: "Say to My servant David, 'I took you from the pasture, from following the sheep, that you should be prince over My people Israel. And I have been with you wherever you went.'"

Then God made some wonderful promises to David. God promised that David's son would be the next king after David, and God would make David's son a great king. He would be the one to build the temple for God. God would always love David's son and would make his kingdom strong. God ended

His promises to David by saying, "And your house and your kingdom shall be made sure forever before Me. Your throne shall be established forever."

Nathan told King David about God's great promise. After King David heard it, he went into the tabernacle and prayed one of the most beautiful prayers in the Bible: "Who am I, O Lord God," David prayed, "that You have brought me thus far? You have spoken also of Your servant's house for a great while to come. And now, O Lord God, You are God, and Your words are true, and You have promised this good thing to Your servant. With Your blessing shall the house of Your servant be blessed forever."

God kept His promise to David. As long as there were kings in Jerusalem, they were from David's family. But God's promises to David were wonderfully fulfilled many years later when Jesus our Lord and eternal King was born. As a human being, Jesus was descended from David's family and is called the "Son of David." But born of the Virgin Mary by the power of the Holy Spirit, Jesus is the Son of God! Jesus is our King! He defeats our greatest enemies, and He takes away our sins. And His kingdom will never end!

SEEK and FIND

WHERE TO FIND THE STORY

2 Samuel 7

KEY BIBLE VERSE

"You shall call his name Jesus. He will be great and will be called the Son of the Most High. And the Lord God will give to him the throne of his father David, and he will reign over the house of Jacob forever, and of his kingdom there will be no end." (Luke 1:31–33)

THREE KEY QUESTIONS

- What did God promise to David?
- How was God's promise wonderfully fulfilled many years later?
- Why do we call Jesus the "son of David" and the "Son of God"?

RELATED BIBLE READINGS

2 Samuel 22:50–23:7; 1 Kings 8:12–26; 11:9–13; Psalm 89:20–37; Isaiah 9:6–7; 55:3; Ezekiel 37:24–28; Acts 2:29–32

[2] And he defeated Moab and he mea-
sured them with a line, making them lie
down on the ground. Two lines he mea-
sured to be put to death, and one full line
to be spared. And the Moabites became
servants to David and brought tribute.
[3] David also defeated Hadadezer
the son of Rehob, king of Zobah, as he
went to restore his power at the river
Euphrates. [4] And David took from him
1,700 horsemen, and 20,000 foot sol-
diers. And David hamstrung all the
chariot horses but left enough for 100
chariots. [5] And when the Syrians of
Damascus came to help Hadadezer king
of Zobah, David struck down 22,000 men
of the Syrians. [6] Then David put garrisons
in Aram of Damascus, and the Syrians
became servants to David and brought
tribute. And the LORD gave victory to
David wherever he went. [7] And David
took the shields of gold that were carried
by the servants of Hadadezer and brought
them to Jerusalem. [8] And from Betah and
from Berothai, cities of Hadadezer, King
David took very much bronze.
[9] When Toi king of Hamath heard that
David had defeated the whole army of
Hadadezer, [10] Toi sent his son Joram to
King David, to ask about his health and to
bless him because he had fought against
Hadadezer and defeated him, for Hadad-
ezer had often been at war with Toi. And
Joram brought with him articles of silver,
of gold, and of bronze. [11] These also King
David dedicated to the LORD, together
with the silver and gold that he dedi-
cated from all the nations he subdued,
[12] from Edom, Moab, the Ammonites, the
Philistines, Amalek, and from the spoil
of Hadadezer the son of Rehob, king of
Zobah.
[13] And David made a name for him-
self when he returned from striking
down 18,000 Edomites in the Valley of
Salt. [14] Then he put garrisons in Edom;
throughout all Edom he put garrisons,
and all the Edomites became David's ser-

vants. And the LORD gave victory to David
wherever he went.

David's Officials

15 So David reigned over all Israel. And
David administered justice and equity to
all his people. 16 Joab the son of Zeruiah
was over the army, and Jehoshaphat the
son of Ahilud was recorder, 17 and Zadok
the son of Ahitub and Ahimelech the
son of Abiathar were priests, and Seraiah
was secretary, 18 and Benaiah the son of
Jehoiada was over[1] the Cherethites and the
Pelethites, and David's sons were priests.

David's Kindness to Mephibosheth

9 And David said, "Is there still
anyone left of the house of Saul,
475 that I may show him kindness for
Jonathan's sake?" 2 Now there was a servant
of the house of Saul whose name was Ziba,
and they called him to David. And the king
said to him, "Are you Ziba?" And he said, "I
am your servant." 3 And the king said, "Is
there not still someone of the house of
Saul, that I may show the kindness of God
to him?" Ziba said to the king, "There is still
a son of Jonathan; he is crippled in his feet."
4 The king said to him, "Where is he?" And
Ziba said to the king, "He is in the house of
Machir the son of Ammiel, at Lo-debar."
5 Then King David sent and brought him
from the house of Machir the son of
Ammiel, at Lo-debar. 6 And Mephibosheth
the son of Jonathan, son of Saul, came to
David and fell on his face and paid homage.
And David said, "Mephibosheth!" And he
answered, "Behold, I am your servant."
7 And David said to him, "Do not fear, for I
will show you kindness for the sake of your
father Jonathan, and I will restore to you all
the land of Saul your father, and you shall
eat at my table always." 8 And he paid hom-
age and said, "What is your servant, that
you should show regard for a dead dog
such as I?"

9 Then the king called Ziba, Saul's ser-
vant, and said to him, "All that belonged
to Saul and to all his house I have given to
your master's grandson. 10 And you and
your sons and your servants shall till the
land for him and shall bring in the pro-
duce, that your master's grandson may
have bread to eat. But Mephibosheth
your master's grandson shall always eat
at my table." Now Ziba had fifteen sons
and twenty servants. 11 Then Ziba said to
the king, "According to all that my lord
the king commands his servant, so will
your servant do." So Mephibosheth ate at
David's[2] table, like one of the king's sons.
12 And Mephibosheth had a young son,
whose name was Mica. And all who lived
in Ziba's house became Mephibosheth's
servants. 13 So Mephibosheth lived in
Jerusalem, for he ate always at the king's
table. Now he was lame in both his feet.

David Defeats Ammon and Syria

10 After this the king of the Ammon-
ites died, and Hanun his son
reigned in his place. 2 And David said, "I
will deal loyally[3] with Hanun the son of
Nahash, as his father dealt loyally with
me." So David sent by his servants to
console him concerning his father. And
David's servants came into the land of
the Ammonites. 3 But the princes of the
Ammonites said to Hanun their lord, "Do
you think, because David has sent com-
forters to you, that he is honoring your
father? Has not David sent his servants to
you to search the city and to spy it out and
to overthrow it?" 4 So Hanun took David's
servants and shaved off half the beard
of each and cut off their garments in the
middle, at their hips, and sent them away.
5 When it was told David, he sent to meet
them, for the men were greatly ashamed.
And the king said, "Remain at Jericho until
your beards have grown and then return."

6 When the Ammonites saw that they
had become a stench to David, the Am-
monites sent and hired the Syrians of
Beth-rehob, and the Syrians of Zobah,

[1] Compare 20:23, 1 Chronicles 18:17, Syriac, Targum, Vulgate; Hebrew lacks *was over* [2] Septuagint; Hebrew *my* [3] Or *kindly*; twice in this verse

20,000 foot soldiers, and the king of Maacah with 1,000 men, and the men of Tob, 12,000 men. 7 And when David heard of it, he sent Joab and all the host of the mighty men. 8 And the Ammonites came out and drew up in battle array at the entrance of the gate, and the Syrians of Zobah and of Rehob and the men of Tob and Maacah were by themselves in the open country.

9 When Joab saw that the battle was set against him both in front and in the rear, he chose some of the best men of Israel and arrayed them against the Syrians. 10 The rest of his men he put in the charge of Abishai his brother, and he arrayed them against the Ammonites. 11 And he said, "If the Syrians are too strong for me, then you shall help me, but if the Ammonites are too strong for you, then I will come and help you. 12 Be of good courage, and let us be courageous for our people, and for the cities of our God, and may the LORD do what seems good to him." 13 So Joab and the people who were with him drew near to battle against the Syrians, and they fled before him. 14 And when the Ammonites saw that the Syrians fled, they likewise fled before Abishai and entered the city. Then Joab returned from fighting against the Ammonites and came to Jerusalem.

15 But when the Syrians saw that they had been defeated by Israel, they gathered themselves together. 16 And Hadadezer sent and brought out the Syrians who were beyond the Euphrates.[1] They came to Helam, with Shobach the commander of the army of Hadadezer at their head. 17 And when it was told David, he gathered all Israel together and crossed the Jordan and came to Helam. The Syrians arrayed themselves against David and fought with him. 18 And the Syrians fled before Israel, and David killed of the Syrians the men of 700 chariots, and 40,000 horsemen, and wounded Shobach the commander of their army, so that he died there. 19 And when all the kings who were servants of Hadadezer saw that they had been defeated by Israel, they made peace with Israel and became subject to them. So the Syrians were afraid to save the Ammonites anymore.

David and Bathsheba

11 In the spring of the year, the time when kings go out to battle, David sent Joab, and his servants with him, and all Israel. And they ravaged the Ammonites and besieged Rabbah. But David remained at Jerusalem.

2 It happened, late one afternoon, when David arose from his couch and was walking on the roof of the king's house, that he saw from the roof a woman bathing; and the woman was very beautiful. 3 And David sent and inquired about the woman. And one said, "Is not this Bathsheba, the daughter of Eliam, the wife of Uriah the Hittite?" 4 So David sent messengers and took her, and she came to him, and he lay with her. (Now she had been purifying herself from her uncleanness.) Then she returned to her house. 5 And the woman conceived, and she sent and told David, "I am pregnant."

6 So David sent word to Joab, "Send me Uriah the Hittite." And Joab sent Uriah to David. 7 When Uriah came to him, David asked how Joab was doing and how the people were doing and how the war was going. 8 Then David said to Uriah, "Go down to your house and wash your feet." And Uriah went out of the king's house, and there followed him a present from the king. 9 But Uriah slept at the door of the king's house with all the servants of his lord, and did not go down to his house. 10 When they told David, "Uriah did not go down to his house," David said to Uriah, "Have you not come from a journey? Why did you not go down to your house?" 11 Uriah said to David, "The ark and Israel and Judah dwell in booths, and

[1] Hebrew *the River*

my lord Joab and the servants of my lord are camping in the open field. Shall I then go to my house, to eat and to drink and to lie with my wife? As you live, and as your soul lives, I will not do this thing." 12 Then David said to Uriah, "Remain here today also, and tomorrow I will send you back." So Uriah remained in Jerusalem that day and the next. 13 And David invited him, and he ate in his presence and drank, so that he made him drunk. And in the evening he went out to lie on his couch with the servants of his lord, but he did not go down to his house.

14 In the morning David wrote a letter to Joab and sent it by the hand of Uriah. 15 In the letter he wrote, "Set Uriah in the forefront of the hardest fighting, and then draw back from him, that he may be struck down, and die." 16 And as Joab was besieging the city, he assigned Uriah to the place where he knew there were valiant men. 17 And the men of the city came out and fought with Joab, and some of the servants of David among the people fell. Uriah the Hittite also died. 18 Then Joab sent and told David all the news about the fighting. 19 And he instructed the messenger, "When you have finished telling all the news about the fighting to the king, 20 then, if the king's anger rises, and if he says to you, 'Why did you go so near the city to fight? Did you not know that they would shoot from the wall? 21 Who killed Abimelech the son of Jerubbesheth? Did not a woman cast an upper millstone on him from the wall, so that he died at Thebez? Why did you go so near the wall?' then you shall say, 'Your servant Uriah the Hittite is dead also.'"

22 So the messenger went and came and told David all that Joab had sent him to tell. 23 The messenger said to David, "The men gained an advantage over us and came out against us in the field, but we drove them back to the entrance of the gate. 24 Then the archers shot at your servants from the wall. Some of the king's servants are dead, and your servant Uriah the Hittite is dead also." 25 David said to the messenger, "Thus shall you say to Joab, 'Do not let this matter trouble you, for the sword devours now one and now another. Strengthen your attack against the city and overthrow it.' And encourage him."

26 When the wife of Uriah heard that Uriah her husband was dead, she lamented over her husband. 27 And when the mourning was over, David sent and brought her to his house, and she became his wife and bore him a son. But the thing that David had done displeased the LORD.

Nathan Rebukes David

12 And the LORD sent Nathan to David. He came to him and said to him, "There were two men in a certain city, the one rich and the other poor. 2 The rich man had very many flocks and herds, 3 but the poor man had nothing but one little ewe lamb, which he had bought. And he brought it up, and it grew up with him and with his children. It used to eat of his morsel and drink from his cup and lie in his arms,[1] and it was like a daughter to him. 4 Now there came a traveler to the rich man, and he was unwilling to take one of his own flock or herd to prepare for the guest who had come to him, but he took the poor man's lamb and prepared it for the man who had come to him." 5 Then David's anger was greatly kindled against the man, and he said to Nathan, "As the LORD lives, the man who has done this deserves to die, 6 and he shall restore the lamb fourfold, because he did this thing, and because he had no pity."

507

7 Nathan said to David, "You are the man! Thus says the LORD, the God of Israel, 'I anointed you king over Israel, and I delivered you out of the hand of Saul. 8 And I gave you your master's house and your master's wives into your arms and gave you the house of Israel and of Judah. And

[1] Hebrew *bosom*; also verse 8

if this were too little, I would add to you as much more. 9 Why have you despised the word of the LORD, to do what is evil in his sight? You have struck down Uriah the Hittite with the sword and have taken his wife to be your wife and have killed him with the sword of the Ammonites. 10 Now therefore the sword shall never depart from your house, because you have despised me and have taken the wife of Uriah the Hittite to be your wife.' 11 Thus says the LORD, 'Behold, I will raise up evil against you out of your own house. And I will take your wives before your eyes and give them to your neighbor, and he shall lie with your wives in the sight of this sun. 12 For you did it secretly, but I will do this thing before all Israel and before the sun.'" 13 David said to Nathan, "I have sinned against the LORD." And Nathan said to David, "The LORD also has put away your sin; you shall not die. 14 Nevertheless, because by this deed you have utterly scorned the LORD,[1] the child who is born to you shall die." 15 Then Nathan went to his house.

David's Child Dies

And the LORD afflicted the child that Uriah's wife bore to David, and he became sick. 16 David therefore sought God on behalf of the child. And David fasted and went in and lay all night on the ground. 17 And the elders of his house stood beside him, to raise him from the ground, but he would not, nor did he eat food with them. 18 On the seventh day the child died. And the servants of David were afraid to tell him that the child was dead, for they said, "Behold, while the child was yet alive, we spoke to him, and he did not listen to us. How then can we say to him the child is dead? He may do himself some harm." 19 But when David saw that his servants were whispering together, David understood that the child was dead. And David said to his servants, "Is the child dead?" They said, "He is dead." 20 Then David arose from the earth and washed and anointed himself and changed his clothes. And he went into the house of the LORD and worshiped. He then went to his own house. And when he asked, they set food before him, and he ate. 21 Then his servants said to him, "What is this thing that you have done? You fasted and wept for the child while he was alive; but when the child died, you arose and ate food." 22 He said, "While the child was still alive, I fasted and wept, for I said, 'Who knows whether the LORD will be gracious to me, that the child may live?' 23 But now he is dead. Why should I fast? Can I bring him back again? I shall go to him, but he will not return to me."

Solomon's Birth

24 Then David comforted his wife, Bathsheba, and went in to her and lay with her, and she bore a son, and he called his name Solomon. And the LORD loved him 25 and sent a message by Nathan the prophet. So he called his name Jedidiah,[2] because of the LORD.

Rabbah Is Captured

26 Now Joab fought against Rabbah of the Ammonites and took the royal city. 27 And Joab sent messengers to David and said, "I have fought against Rabbah; moreover, I have taken the city of waters. 28 Now then gather the rest of the people together and encamp against the city and take it, lest I take the city and it be called by my name." 29 So David gathered all the people together and went to Rabbah and fought against it and took it. 30 And he took the crown of their king from his head. The weight of it was a talent[3] of gold, and in it was a precious stone, and it was placed on David's head. And he brought out the spoil of the city, a very great amount. 31 And he brought out the people who were in it and set them to labor with saws and iron picks and iron

[1] Masoretic Text *the enemies of the LORD*; Dead Sea Scroll *the word of the LORD* [2] *Jedidiah* means *beloved of the LORD* [3] A *talent* was about 75 pounds or 34 kilograms

David Confesses His Terrible Sin

Once while David was king, he did something that was terribly wrong. David took another man's wife and had the man killed in battle. He thought no one knew about it. But God knew, and God wanted David to confess his sin, repent, and be sorry for what he had done. So God sent His prophet, Nathan, to confront King David about his sin.

Nathan told King David a story to help David see how terribly he had sinned. Nathan told him about someone who had done something really bad, but it was not as wrong as what David had done. After David heard the story, he was very angry and said: "The man who has done this deserves to die."

Then Nathan told him, "You are the man!" Nathan reminded King David of all God had done for him—how God had made David king over all the people of Israel; how God had delivered David from all his enemies; how God had given David everything he needed and more.

"Why," Nathan asked, "have you despised the word of the LORD, to do what is evil in His sight?" Nathan told David that God would punish him for the wrong he had done.

Right away, King David knew that what he had done was terribly wrong. "I have sinned against the LORD," David confessed.

Nathan told David, "The LORD also has put away your sin; you shall not die."

Nathan went back to his own house. Later God did punish King David, but David remembered God's forgiveness for him. Even when God punished David, David went to God's house to worship God.

We sin each day. We do and say things that break God's commandments and we deserve God's punishment. But God sent Jesus to die on the cross to take away our sins. He wants us to come to Him in prayer and to say, "I'm sorry. Please forgive me." God will always love and care for us. He promises always to forgive us for Jesus' sake.

SEEK and FIND

WHERE TO FIND THE STORY

2 Samuel 12:1–24

KEY BIBLE VERSE

"If we confess our sins, he is faithful and just to forgive us our sins and to cleanse us from all unrighteousness." (1 John 1:9)

THREE KEY QUESTIONS

- What did David do when the prophet Nathan confronted David about his terrible sin?
- What should we do when we sin?
- What has God promised that He will do when we confess our sins?

RELATED BIBLE READINGS

Psalm 32:1–11; 51:1–19; Romans 4:5–8; 1 John 1:5–10

axes and made them toil at[1] the brick kilns. And thus he did to all the cities of the Ammonites. Then David and all the people returned to Jerusalem.

Amnon and Tamar

13 Now Absalom, David's son, had a
beautiful sister, whose name was
Tamar. And after a time Amnon, David's
son, loved her. 2 And Amnon was so tor-
mented that he made himself ill because
of his sister Tamar, for she was a virgin,
and it seemed impossible to Amnon to
do anything to her. 3 But Amnon had a
friend, whose name was Jonadab, the son
of Shimeah, David's brother. And Jonadab
was a very crafty man. 4 And he said to
him, "O son of the king, why are you so
haggard morning after morning? Will
you not tell me?" Amnon said to him, "I
love Tamar, my brother Absalom's sister."
5 Jonadab said to him, "Lie down on your
bed and pretend to be ill. And when your
father comes to see you, say to him, 'Let
my sister Tamar come and give me bread
to eat, and prepare the food in my sight,
that I may see it and eat it from her hand.'"
6 So Amnon lay down and pretended to be
ill. And when the king came to see him,
Amnon said to the king, "Please let my sis-
ter Tamar come and make a couple of cakes
in my sight, that I may eat from her hand."
7 Then David sent home to Tamar, say-
ing, "Go to your brother Amnon's house
and prepare food for him." 8 So Tamar went
to her brother Amnon's house, where he
was lying down. And she took dough and
kneaded it and made cakes in his sight
and baked the cakes. 9 And she took the
pan and emptied it out before him, but
he refused to eat. And Amnon said, "Send
out everyone from me." So everyone went
out from him. 10 Then Amnon said to
Tamar, "Bring the food into the cham-
ber, that I may eat from your hand." And
Tamar took the cakes she had made and
brought them into the chamber to Amnon
her brother. 11 But when she brought them
near him to eat, he took hold of her and
said to her, "Come, lie with me, my sister."
12 She answered him, "No, my brother, do
not violate[2] me, for such a thing is not
done in Israel; do not do this outrageous
thing. 13 As for me, where could I carry my
shame? And as for you, you would be as
one of the outrageous fools in Israel. Now
therefore, please speak to the king, for he
will not withhold me from you." 14 But he
would not listen to her, and being stronger
than she, he violated her and lay with her.
15 Then Amnon hated her with very great
hatred, so that the hatred with which he
hated her was greater than the love with
which he had loved her. And Amnon said
to her, "Get up! Go!" 16 But she said to him,
"No, my brother, for this wrong in sending
me away is greater than the other that you
did to me."[3] But he would not listen to her.
17 He called the young man who served him
and said, "Put this woman out of my pres-
ence and bolt the door after her." 18 Now
she was wearing a long robe[4] with sleeves,
for thus were the virgin daughters of the
king dressed. So his servant put her out
and bolted the door after her. 19 And Tamar
put ashes on her head and tore the long
robe that she wore. And she laid her hand
on her head and went away, crying aloud
as she went.
20 And her brother Absalom said to her,
"Has Amnon your brother been with you?
Now hold your peace, my sister. He is
your brother; do not take this to heart."
So Tamar lived, a desolate woman, in
her brother Absalom's house. 21 When
King David heard of all these things, he
was very angry.[5] 22 But Absalom spoke to
Amnon neither good nor bad, for Absalom
hated Amnon, because he had violated his
sister Tamar.

Absalom Murders Amnon

23 After two full years Absalom had
sheepshearers at Baal-hazor, which is

[1] Hebrew *pass through* [2] Or *humiliate*; also verses 14, 22, 32 [3] Compare Septuagint, Vulgate; the meaning of the Hebrew is uncertain [4] Or *a robe of many colors* (compare Genesis 37:3); also verse 19 [5] Dead Sea Scroll, Septuagint add *But he would not punish his son Amnon, because he loved him, since he was his firstborn*

near Ephraim, and Absalom invited all the king's sons. 24 And Absalom came to the king and said, "Behold, your servant has sheepshearers. Please let the king and his servants go with your servant." 25 But the king said to Absalom, "No, my son, let us not all go, lest we be burdensome to you." He pressed him, but he would not go but gave him his blessing. 26 Then Absalom said, "If not, please let my brother Amnon go with us." And the king said to him, "Why should he go with you?" 27 But Absalom pressed him until he let Amnon and all the king's sons go with him. 28 Then Absalom commanded his servants, "Mark when Amnon's heart is merry with wine, and when I say to you, 'Strike Amnon,' then kill him. Do not fear; have I not commanded you? Be courageous and be valiant." 29 So the servants of Absalom did to Amnon as Absalom had commanded. Then all the king's sons arose, and each mounted his mule and fled.

30 While they were on the way, news came to David, "Absalom has struck down all the king's sons, and not one of them is left." 31 Then the king arose and tore his garments and lay on the earth. And all his servants who were standing by tore their garments. 32 But Jonadab the son of Shimeah, David's brother, said, "Let not my lord suppose that they have killed all the young men, the king's sons, for Amnon alone is dead. For by the command of Absalom this has been determined from the day he violated his sister Tamar. 33 Now therefore let not my lord the king so take it to heart as to suppose that all the king's sons are dead, for Amnon alone is dead."

Absalom Flees to Geshur

34 But Absalom fled. And the young man who kept the watch lifted up his eyes and looked, and behold, many people were coming from the road behind him[1] by the side of the mountain. 35 And Jonadab said to the king, "Behold, the king's sons have come; as your servant said, so it has come about." 36 And as soon as he had finished speaking, behold, the king's sons came and lifted up their voice and wept. And the king also and all his servants wept very bitterly.

37 But Absalom fled and went to Talmai the son of Ammihud, king of Geshur. And David mourned for his son day after day. 38 So Absalom fled and went to Geshur, and was there three years. 39 And the spirit of the king[2] longed to go out[3] to Absalom, because he was comforted about Amnon, since he was dead.

Absalom Returns to Jerusalem

14 Now Joab the son of Zeruiah knew that the king's heart went out to Absalom. 2 And Joab sent to Tekoa and brought from there a wise woman and said to her, "Pretend to be a mourner and put on mourning garments. Do not anoint yourself with oil, but behave like a woman who has been mourning many days for the dead. 3 Go to the king and speak thus to him." So Joab put the words in her mouth.

4 When the woman of Tekoa came to the king, she fell on her face to the ground and paid homage and said, "Save me, O king." 5 And the king said to her, "What is your trouble?" She answered, "Alas, I am a widow; my husband is dead. 6 And your servant had two sons, and they quarreled with one another in the field. There was no one to separate them, and one struck the other and killed him. 7 And now the whole clan has risen against your servant, and they say, 'Give up the man who struck his brother, that we may put him to death for the life of his brother whom he killed.' And so they would destroy the heir also. Thus they would quench my coal that is left and leave to my husband neither name nor remnant on the face of the earth."

8 Then the king said to the woman, "Go

[1] Septuagint *the Horonaim Road* [2] Dead Sea Scroll, Septuagint; Hebrew *David* [3] Compare Vulgate *ceased to go out*

to your house, and I will give orders con-
cerning you." 9 And the woman of Tekoa
said to the king, "On me be the guilt, my
lord the king, and on my father's house;
let the king and his throne be guiltless."
10 The king said, "If anyone says anything
to you, bring him to me, and he shall never
touch you again." 11 Then she said, "Please
let the king invoke the LORD your God,
that the avenger of blood kill no more, and
my son be not destroyed." He said, "As the
LORD lives, not one hair of your son shall
fall to the ground."

12 Then the woman said, "Please let your
servant speak a word to my lord the king."
He said, "Speak." 13 And the woman said,
"Why then have you planned such a thing
against the people of God? For in giving
this decision the king convicts himself,
inasmuch as the king does not bring his
banished one home again. 14 We must
all die; we are like water spilled on the
ground, which cannot be gathered up
again. But God will not take away life, and
he devises means so that the banished
one will not remain an outcast. 15 Now I
have come to say this to my lord the king
because the people have made me afraid,
and your servant thought, 'I will speak to
the king; it may be that the king will per-
form the request of his servant. 16 For the
king will hear and deliver his servant from
the hand of the man who would destroy
me and my son together from the heritage
of God.' 17 And your servant thought, 'The
word of my lord the king will set me at
rest,' for my lord the king is like the angel
of God to discern good and evil. The LORD
your God be with you!"

18 Then the king answered the woman,
"Do not hide from me anything I ask you."
And the woman said, "Let my lord the
king speak." 19 The king said, "Is the hand
of Joab with you in all this?" The woman
answered and said, "As surely as you live,
my lord the king, one cannot turn to the
right hand or to the left from anything
that my lord the king has said. It was your
servant Joab who commanded me; it was
he who put all these words in the mouth
of your servant. 20 In order to change the
course of things your servant Joab did this.
But my lord has wisdom like the wisdom
of the angel of God to know all things that
are on the earth."

21 Then the king said to Joab, "Behold
now, I grant this; go, bring back the young
man Absalom." 22 And Joab fell on his
face to the ground and paid homage and
blessed the king. And Joab said, "Today
your servant knows that I have found favor
in your sight, my lord the king, in that the
king has granted the request of his ser-
vant." 23 So Joab arose and went to Geshur
and brought Absalom to Jerusalem. 24 And
the king said, "Let him dwell apart in his
own house; he is not to come into my
presence." So Absalom lived apart in his
own house and did not come into the
king's presence.

25 Now in all Israel there was no one
so much to be praised for his handsome
appearance as Absalom. From the sole
of his foot to the crown of his head there
was no blemish in him. 26 And when he
cut the hair of his head (for at the end of
every year he used to cut it; when it was
heavy on him, he cut it), he weighed the
hair of his head, two hundred shekels[1]
by the king's weight. 27 There were born
to Absalom three sons, and one daughter
whose name was Tamar. She was a beau-
tiful woman.

28 So Absalom lived two full years in
Jerusalem, without coming into the king's
presence. 29 Then Absalom sent for Joab,
to send him to the king, but Joab would
not come to him. And he sent a second
time, but Joab would not come. 30 Then
he said to his servants, "See, Joab's field
is next to mine, and he has barley there;
go and set it on fire." So Absalom's ser-
vants set the field on fire.[2] 31 Then Joab
arose and went to Absalom at his house

[1] A *shekel* was about 2/5 ounce or 11 grams [2] Septuagint, Dead Sea Scroll add *So Joab's servants came to him with their clothes torn, and they said to him, "The servants of Absalom have set your field on fire."*

and said to him, "Why have your servants set my field on fire?" 32 Absalom answered Joab, "Behold, I sent word to you, 'Come here, that I may send you to the king, to ask, "Why have I come from Geshur? It would be better for me to be there still." Now therefore let me go into the presence of the king, and if there is guilt in me, let him put me to death.'" 33 Then Joab went to the king and told him, and he summoned Absalom. So he came to the king and bowed himself on his face to the ground before the king, and the king kissed Absalom.

Absalom's Conspiracy

15 After this Absalom got himself a chariot and horses, and fifty men to run before him. 2 And Absalom used to rise early and stand beside the way of the gate. And when any man had a dispute to come before the king for judgment, Absalom would call to him and say, "From what city are you?" And when he said, "Your servant is of such and such a tribe in Israel," 3 Absalom would say to him, "See, your claims are good and right, but there is no man designated by the king to hear you." 4 Then Absalom would say, "Oh that I were judge in the land! Then every man with a dispute or cause might come to me, and I would give him justice." 5 And whenever a man came near to pay homage to him, he would put out his hand and take hold of him and kiss him. 6 Thus Absalom did to all of Israel who came to the king for judgment. So Absalom stole the hearts of the men of Israel.

7 And at the end of four[1] years Absalom said to the king, "Please let me go and pay my vow, which I have vowed to the LORD, in Hebron. 8 For your servant vowed a vow while I lived at Geshur in Aram, saying, 'If the LORD will indeed bring me back to Jerusalem, then I will offer worship to[2] the LORD.'" 9 The king said to him, "Go in peace." So he arose and went to Hebron. 10 But Absalom sent secret messengers throughout all the tribes of Israel, saying, "As soon as you hear the sound of the trumpet, then say, 'Absalom is king at Hebron!'" 11 With Absalom went two hundred men from Jerusalem who were invited guests, and they went in their innocence and knew nothing. 12 And while Absalom was offering the sacrifices, he sent for[3] Ahithophel the Gilonite, David's counselor, from his city Giloh. And the conspiracy grew strong, and the people with Absalom kept increasing.

David Flees Jerusalem

13 And a messenger came to David, saying, "The hearts of the men of Israel have gone after Absalom." 14 Then David said to all his servants who were with him at Jerusalem, "Arise, and let us flee, or else there will be no escape for us from Absalom. Go quickly, lest he overtake us quickly and bring down ruin on us and strike the city with the edge of the sword." 15 And the king's servants said to the king, "Behold, your servants are ready to do whatever my lord the king decides." 16 So the king went out, and all his household after him. And the king left ten concubines to keep the house. 17 And the king went out, and all the people after him. And they halted at the last house.

18 And all his servants passed by him, and all the Cherethites, and all the Pelethites, and all the six hundred Gittites who had followed him from Gath, passed on before the king. 19 Then the king said to Ittai the Gittite, "Why do you also go with us? Go back and stay with the king, for you are a foreigner and also an exile from your home. 20 You came only yesterday, and shall I today make you wander about with us, since I go I know not where? Go back and take your brothers with you, and may the LORD show[4] steadfast love and faithfulness to you." 21 But Ittai answered the king, "As the LORD lives, and as my

[1] Septuagint, Syriac; Hebrew *forty* [2] Or *will serve* [3] Or *sent* [4] Septuagint; Hebrew lacks *may the LORD show*

lord the king lives, wherever my lord the
king shall be, whether for death or for life,
there also will your servant be." 22 And
David said to Ittai, "Go then, pass on." So
Ittai the Gittite passed on with all his men
and all the little ones who were with him.
23 And all the land wept aloud as all the
people passed by, and the king crossed the
brook Kidron, and all the people passed
on toward the wilderness.

24 And Abiathar came up, and behold,
Zadok came also with all the Levites, bear-
ing the ark of the covenant of God. And
they set down the ark of God until the
people had all passed out of the city.
25 Then the king said to Zadok, "Carry the
ark of God back into the city. If I find favor
in the eyes of the LORD, he will bring me
back and let me see both it and his dwell-
ing place. 26 But if he says, 'I have no plea-
sure in you,' behold, here I am, let him do
to me what seems good to him." 27 The
king also said to Zadok the priest, "Are you
not a seer? Go back[1] to the city in peace,
with your two sons, Ahimaaz your son,
and Jonathan the son of Abiathar. 28 See,
I will wait at the fords of the wilderness
until word comes from you to inform
me." 29 So Zadok and Abiathar carried the
ark of God back to Jerusalem, and they
remained there.

30 But David went up the ascent of the
Mount of Olives, weeping as he went, bare-
foot and with his head covered. And all the
people who were with him covered their
heads, and they went up, weeping as they
went. 31 And it was told David, "Ahithophel
is among the conspirators with Absalom."
And David said, "O LORD, please turn the
counsel of Ahithophel into foolishness."

32 While David was coming to the sum-
mit, where God was worshiped, behold,
Hushai the Archite came to meet him with
his coat torn and dirt on his head. 33 David
said to him, "If you go on with me, you
will be a burden to me. 34 But if you return
to the city and say to Absalom, 'I will be
your servant, O king; as I have been your
father's servant in time past, so now I will
be your servant,' then you will defeat for
me the counsel of Ahithophel. 35 Are not
Zadok and Abiathar the priests with you
there? So whatever you hear from the king's
house, tell it to Zadok and Abiathar the
priests. 36 Behold, their two sons are with
them there, Ahimaaz, Zadok's son, and
Jonathan, Abiathar's son, and by them you
shall send to me everything you hear." 37 So
Hushai, David's friend, came into the city,
just as Absalom was entering Jerusalem.

David and Ziba

16 When David had passed a little
beyond the summit, Ziba the
servant of Mephibosheth met him, with
a couple of donkeys saddled, bearing
two hundred loaves of bread, a hundred
bunches of raisins, a hundred of sum-
mer fruits, and a skin of wine. 2 And the
king said to Ziba, "Why have you brought
these?" Ziba answered, "The donkeys are
for the king's household to ride on, the
bread and summer fruit for the young
men to eat, and the wine for those who
faint in the wilderness to drink." 3 And
the king said, "And where is your master's
son?" Ziba said to the king, "Behold, he
remains in Jerusalem, for he said, 'Today
the house of Israel will give me back the
kingdom of my father.'" 4 Then the king
said to Ziba, "Behold, all that belonged to
Mephibosheth is now yours." And Ziba
said, "I pay homage; let me ever find favor
in your sight, my lord the king."

Shimei Curses David

5 When King David came to Bahurim,
there came out a man of the family of the
house of Saul, whose name was Shimei,
the son of Gera, and as he came he cursed
continually. 6 And he threw stones at David
and at all the servants of King David, and
all the people and all the mighty men
were on his right hand and on his left.
7 And Shimei said as he cursed, "Get out,

[1] Septuagint *The king also said to Zadok the priest, "Look, go back*

get out, you man of blood, you worthless man! 8 The LORD has avenged on you all the blood of the house of Saul, in whose place you have reigned, and the LORD has given the kingdom into the hand of your son Absalom. See, your evil is on you, for you are a man of blood."

9 Then Abishai the son of Zeruiah said to the king, "Why should this dead dog curse my lord the king? Let me go over and take off his head." 10 But the king said, "What have I to do with you, you sons of Zeruiah? If he is cursing because the LORD has said to him, 'Curse David,' who then shall say, 'Why have you done so?'" 11 And David said to Abishai and to all his servants, "Behold, my own son seeks my life; how much more now may this Benjaminite! Leave him alone, and let him curse, for the LORD has told him to. 12 It may be that the LORD will look on the wrong done to me,[1] and that the LORD will repay me with good for his cursing today." 13 So David and his men went on the road, while Shimei went along on the hillside opposite him and cursed as he went and threw stones at him and flung dust. 14 And the king, and all the people who were with him, arrived weary at the Jordan.[2] And there he refreshed himself.

Absalom Enters Jerusalem

15 Now Absalom and all the people, the men of Israel, came to Jerusalem, and Ahithophel with him. 16 And when Hushai the Archite, David's friend, came to Absalom, Hushai said to Absalom, "Long live the king! Long live the king!" 17 And Absalom said to Hushai, "Is this your loyalty to your friend? Why did you not go with your friend?" 18 And Hushai said to Absalom, "No, for whom the LORD and this people and all the men of Israel have chosen, his I will be, and with him I will remain. 19 And again, whom should I serve? Should it not be his son? As I have served your father, so I will serve you."

20 Then Absalom said to Ahithophel, "Give your counsel. What shall we do?" 21 Ahithophel said to Absalom, "Go in to your father's concubines, whom he has left to keep the house, and all Israel will hear that you have made yourself a stench to your father, and the hands of all who are with you will be strengthened." 22 So they pitched a tent for Absalom on the roof. And Absalom went in to his father's concubines in the sight of all Israel. 23 Now in those days the counsel that Ahithophel gave was as if one consulted the word of God; so was all the counsel of Ahithophel esteemed, both by David and by Absalom.

Hushai Saves David

17 Moreover, Ahithophel said to Absalom, "Let me choose twelve thousand men, and I will arise and pursue David tonight. 2 I will come upon him while he is weary and discouraged and throw him into a panic, and all the people who are with him will flee. I will strike down only the king, 3 and I will bring all the people back to you as a bride comes home to her husband. You seek the life of only one man,[3] and all the people will be at peace." 4 And the advice seemed right in the eyes of Absalom and all the elders of Israel.

5 Then Absalom said, "Call Hushai the Archite also, and let us hear what he has to say." 6 And when Hushai came to Absalom, Absalom said to him, "Thus has Ahithophel spoken; shall we do as he says? If not, you speak." 7 Then Hushai said to Absalom, "This time the counsel that Ahithophel has given is not good." 8 Hushai said, "You know that your father and his men are mighty men, and that they are enraged,[4] like a bear robbed of her cubs in the field. Besides, your father is expert in war; he will not spend the night with the people. 9 Behold, even now he has hidden himself in one of the pits or in some other place. And as soon as some of the people fall[5] at the first attack, whoever hears

[1] Septuagint, Vulgate *will look upon my affliction* [2] Septuagint; Hebrew lacks *at the Jordan* [3] Septuagint; Hebrew *back to you. Like the return of the whole is the man whom you seek* [4] Hebrew *bitter of soul* [5] Or *And as he falls on them*

it will say, 'There has been a slaughter
among the people who follow Absalom.'
10 Then even the valiant man, whose heart
is like the heart of a lion, will utterly melt
with fear, for all Israel knows that your
father is a mighty man, and that those
who are with him are valiant men. 11 But
my counsel is that all Israel be gathered to
you, from Dan to Beersheba, as the sand
by the sea for multitude, and that you go
to battle in person. 12 So we shall come
upon him in some place where he is to be
found, and we shall light upon him as the
dew falls on the ground, and of him and
all the men with him not one will be left.
13 If he withdraws into a city, then all Israel
will bring ropes to that city, and we shall
drag it into the valley, until not even a peb-
ble is to be found there." 14 And Absalom
and all the men of Israel said, "The coun-
sel of Hushai the Archite is better than the
counsel of Ahithophel." For the LORD had
ordained[1] to defeat the good counsel of
Ahithophel, so that the LORD might bring
harm upon Absalom.

15 Then Hushai said to Zadok and
Abiathar the priests, "Thus and so did
Ahithophel counsel Absalom and the
elders of Israel, and thus and so have I
counseled. 16 Now therefore send quickly
and tell David, 'Do not stay tonight at the
fords of the wilderness, but by all means
pass over, lest the king and all the peo-
ple who are with him be swallowed up.'"
17 Now Jonathan and Ahimaaz were wait-
ing at En-rogel. A female servant was to go
and tell them, and they were to go and tell
King David, for they were not to be seen
entering the city. 18 But a young man saw
them and told Absalom. So both of them
went away quickly and came to the house
of a man at Bahurim, who had a well in
his courtyard. And they went down into
it. 19 And the woman took and spread a
covering over the well's mouth and scat-
tered grain on it, and nothing was known
of it. 20 When Absalom's servants came
to the woman at the house, they said,
"Where are Ahimaaz and Jonathan?" And
the woman said to them, "They have gone
over the brook[2] of water." And when they
had sought and could not find them, they
returned to Jerusalem.

21 After they had gone, the men came
up out of the well, and went and told King
David. They said to David, "Arise, and go
quickly over the water, for thus and so
has Ahithophel counseled against you."
22 Then David arose, and all the people
who were with him, and they crossed the
Jordan. By daybreak not one was left who
had not crossed the Jordan.

23 When Ahithophel saw that his coun-
sel was not followed, he saddled his don-
key and went off home to his own city. He
set his house in order and hanged him-
self, and he died and was buried in the
tomb of his father.

24 Then David came to Mahanaim. And
Absalom crossed the Jordan with all the
men of Israel. 25 Now Absalom had set
Amasa over the army instead of Joab.
Amasa was the son of a man named Ithra
the Ishmaelite,[3] who had married Abigal
the daughter of Nahash, sister of Zeruiah,
Joab's mother. 26 And Israel and Absalom
encamped in the land of Gilead.

27 When David came to Mahanaim,
Shobi the son of Nahash from Rabbah of
the Ammonites, and Machir the son of
Ammiel from Lo-debar, and Barzillai the
Gileadite from Rogelim, 28 brought beds,
basins, and earthen vessels, wheat, barley,
flour, parched grain, beans and lentils,[4]
29 honey and curds and sheep and cheese
from the herd, for David and the people
with him to eat, for they said, "The people
are hungry and weary and thirsty in the
wilderness."

Absalom Killed

18 Then David mustered the men
who were with him and set over
them commanders of thousands and

[1] Hebrew *commanded* [2] The meaning of the Hebrew word is uncertain [3] Compare 1 Chronicles 2:17; Hebrew *Israelite* [4] Hebrew adds *and parched grain*

commanders of hundreds. 2 And David
sent out the army, one third under the
command of Joab, one third under the
command of Abishai the son of Zeruiah,
Joab's brother, and one third under the
command of Ittai the Gittite. And the king
said to the men, "I myself will also go out
with you." 3 But the men said, "You shall
not go out. For if we flee, they will not
care about us. If half of us die, they will
not care about us. But you are worth ten
thousand of us. Therefore it is better that
you send us help from the city." 4 The king
said to them, "Whatever seems best to you
I will do." So the king stood at the side of
the gate, while all the army marched out
by hundreds and by thousands. 5 And the
king ordered Joab and Abishai and Ittai,
"Deal gently for my sake with the young
man Absalom." And all the people heard
when the king gave orders to all the com-
manders about Absalom.

6 So the army went out into the field
against Israel, and the battle was fought
in the forest of Ephraim. 7 And the men of
Israel were defeated there by the servants
of David, and the loss there was great on
that day, twenty thousand men. 8 The bat-
tle spread over the face of all the country,
and the forest devoured more people that
day than the sword.

9 And Absalom happened to meet the
servants of David. Absalom was riding on
his mule, and the mule went under the
thick branches of a great oak,[1] and his
head caught fast in the oak, and he was
suspended between heaven and earth,
while the mule that was under him went
on. 10 And a certain man saw it and told
Joab, "Behold, I saw Absalom hanging in
an oak." 11 Joab said to the man who told
him, "What, you saw him! Why then did
you not strike him there to the ground?
I would have been glad to give you ten
pieces of silver and a belt." 12 But the man
said to Joab, "Even if I felt in my hand the
weight of a thousand pieces of silver, I
would not reach out my hand against the
king's son, for in our hearing the king com-
manded you and Abishai and Ittai, 'For
my sake protect the young man Absalom.'
13 On the other hand, if I had dealt treach-
erously against his life[2] (and there is
nothing hidden from the king), then you
yourself would have stood aloof." 14 Joab
said, "I will not waste time like this with
you." And he took three javelins in his
hand and thrust them into the heart of
Absalom while he was still alive in the
oak. 15 And ten young men, Joab's armor-
bearers, surrounded Absalom and struck
him and killed him.

16 Then Joab blew the trumpet, and the
troops came back from pursuing Israel,
for Joab restrained them. 17 And they took
Absalom and threw him into a great pit in
the forest and raised over him a very great
heap of stones. And all Israel fled every
one to his own home. 18 Now Absalom in
his lifetime had taken and set up for him-
self the pillar that is in the King's Valley, for
he said, "I have no son to keep my name in
remembrance." He called the pillar after
his own name, and it is called Absalom's
monument[3] to this day.

David Hears of Absalom's Death

19 Then Ahimaaz the son of Zadok said,
"Let me run and carry news to the king
that the LORD has delivered him from the
hand of his enemies." 20 And Joab said to
him, "You are not to carry news today.
You may carry news another day, but
today you shall carry no news, because
the king's son is dead." 21 Then Joab said
to the Cushite, "Go, tell the king what you
have seen." The Cushite bowed before
Joab, and ran. 22 Then Ahimaaz the son
of Zadok said again to Joab, "Come what
may, let me also run after the Cushite."
And Joab said, "Why will you run, my son,
seeing that you will have no reward for
the news?" 23 "Come what may," he said, "I
will run." So he said to him, "Run." Then

[1] Or *terebinth*; also verses 10, 14 [2] Or *at the risk of my life* [3] Or *Absalom's hand*

Ahimaaz ran by the way of the plain, and outran the Cushite.

24 Now David was sitting between the two gates, and the watchman went up to the roof of the gate by the wall, and when he lifted up his eyes and looked, he saw a man running alone. 25 The watchman called out and told the king. And the king said, "If he is alone, there is news in his mouth." And he drew nearer and nearer. 26 The watchman saw another man running. And the watchman called to the gate and said, "See, another man running alone!" The king said, "He also brings news." 27 The watchman said, "I think the running of the first is like the running of Ahimaaz the son of Zadok." And the king said, "He is a good man and comes with good news."

28 Then Ahimaaz cried out to the king, "All is well." And he bowed before the king with his face to the earth and said, "Blessed be the LORD your God, who has delivered up the men who raised their hand against my lord the king." 29 And the king said, "Is it well with the young man Absalom?" Ahimaaz answered, "When Joab sent the king's servant, your servant, I saw a great commotion, but I do not know what it was." 30 And the king said, "Turn aside and stand here." So he turned aside and stood still.

David's Grief

31 And behold, the Cushite came, and the Cushite said, "Good news for my lord the king! For the LORD has delivered you this day from the hand of all who rose up against you." 32 The king said to the Cushite, "Is it well with the young man Absalom?" And the Cushite answered, "May the enemies of my lord the king and all who rise up against you for evil be like that young man." 33 [1] And the king was deeply moved and went up to the chamber over the gate and wept. And as he went, he said, "O my son Absalom, my son, my son Absalom! Would I had died instead of you, O Absalom, my son, my son!"

Joab Rebukes David

19 It was told Joab, "Behold, the king is weeping and mourning for Absalom." 2 So the victory that day was turned into mourning for all the people, for the people heard that day, "The king is grieving for his son." 3 And the people stole into the city that day as people steal in who are ashamed when they flee in battle. 4 The king covered his face, and the king cried with a loud voice, "O my son Absalom, O Absalom, my son, my son!" 5 Then Joab came into the house to the king and said, "You have today covered with shame the faces of all your servants, who have this day saved your life and the lives of your sons and your daughters and the lives of your wives and your concubines, 6 because you love those who hate you and hate those who love you. For you have made it clear today that commanders and servants are nothing to you, for today I know that if Absalom were alive and all of us were dead today, then you would be pleased. 7 Now therefore arise, go out and speak kindly to your servants, for I swear by the LORD, if you do not go, not a man will stay with you this night, and this will be worse for you than all the evil that has come upon you from your youth until now." 8 Then the king arose and took his seat in the gate. And the people were all told, "Behold, the king is sitting in the gate." And all the people came before the king.

David Returns to Jerusalem

Now Israel had fled every man to his own home. 9 And all the people were arguing throughout all the tribes of Israel, saying, "The king delivered us from the hand of our enemies and saved us from the hand of the Philistines, and now he has fled out of the land from Absalom. 10 But Absalom, whom we anointed over us, is dead in battle. Now therefore why do

[1] Ch 19:1 in Hebrew

you say nothing about bringing the king back?"

11 And King David sent this message to Zadok and Abiathar the priests: "Say to the elders of Judah, 'Why should you be the last to bring the king back to his house, when the word of all Israel has come to the king?[1] 12 You are my brothers; you are my bone and my flesh. Why then should you be the last to bring back the king?' 13 And say to Amasa, 'Are you not my bone and my flesh? God do so to me and more also, if you are not commander of my army from now on in place of Joab.'" 14 And he swayed the heart of all the men of Judah as one man, so that they sent word to the king, "Return, both you and all your servants." 15 So the king came back to the Jordan, and Judah came to Gilgal to meet the king and to bring the king over the Jordan.

David Pardons His Enemies

16 And Shimei the son of Gera, the Benjaminite, from Bahurim, hurried to come down with the men of Judah to meet King David. 17 And with him were a thousand men from Benjamin. And Ziba the servant of the house of Saul, with his fifteen sons and his twenty servants, rushed down to the Jordan before the king, 18 and they crossed the ford to bring over the king's household and to do his pleasure. And Shimei the son of Gera fell down before the king, as he was about to cross the Jordan, 19 and said to the king, "Let not my lord hold me guilty or remember how your servant did wrong on the day my lord the king left Jerusalem. Do not let the king take it to heart. 20 For your servant knows that I have sinned. Therefore, behold, I have come this day, the first of all the house of Joseph to come down to meet my lord the king." 21 Abishai the son of Zeruiah answered, "Shall not Shimei be put to death for this, because he cursed the LORD's anointed?" 22 But David said, "What have I to do with you, you sons of Zeruiah, that you should this day be as an adversary to me? Shall anyone be put to death in Israel this day? For do I not know that I am this day king over Israel?" 23 And the king said to Shimei, "You shall not die." And the king gave him his oath.

24 And Mephibosheth the son of Saul came down to meet the king. He had neither taken care of his feet nor trimmed his beard nor washed his clothes, from the day the king departed until the day he came back in safety. 25 And when he came to Jerusalem to meet the king, the king said to him, "Why did you not go with me, Mephibosheth?" 26 He answered, "My lord, O king, my servant deceived me, for your servant said to him, 'I will saddle a donkey for myself,[2] that I may ride on it and go with the king.' For your servant is lame. 27 He has slandered your servant to my lord the king. But my lord the king is like the angel of God; do therefore what seems good to you. 28 For all my father's house were but men doomed to death before my lord the king, but you set your servant among those who eat at your table. What further right have I, then, to cry to the king?" 29 And the king said to him, "Why speak any more of your affairs? I have decided: you and Ziba shall divide the land." 30 And Mephibosheth said to the king, "Oh, let him take it all, since my lord the king has come safely home."

31 Now Barzillai the Gileadite had come down from Rogelim, and he went on with the king to the Jordan, to escort him over the Jordan. 32 Barzillai was a very aged man, eighty years old. He had provided the king with food while he stayed at Mahanaim, for he was a very wealthy man. 33 And the king said to Barzillai, "Come over with me, and I will provide for you with me in Jerusalem." 34 But Barzillai said to the king, "How many years have I still to live, that I should go up with the king to

[1] Septuagint; Hebrew *to the king, to his house* [2] Septuagint, Syriac, Vulgate *Saddle a donkey for me*

Jerusalem? 35 I am this day eighty years
old. Can I discern what is pleasant and
what is not? Can your servant taste what
he eats or what he drinks? Can I still listen
to the voice of singing men and singing
women? Why then should your servant
be an added burden to my lord the king?
36 Your servant will go a little way over
the Jordan with the king. Why should
the king repay me with such a reward?
37 Please let your servant return, that I
may die in my own city near the grave
of my father and my mother. But here is
your servant Chimham. Let him go over
with my lord the king, and do for him
whatever seems good to you." 38 And the
king answered, "Chimham shall go over
with me, and I will do for him whatever
seems good to you, and all that you desire
of me I will do for you." 39 Then all the
people went over the Jordan, and the king
went over. And the king kissed Barzillai
and blessed him, and he returned to his
own home. 40 The king went on to Gilgal,
and Chimham went on with him. All the
people of Judah, and also half the people
of Israel, brought the king on his way.

41 Then all the men of Israel came to
the king and said to the king, "Why have
our brothers the men of Judah stolen
you away and brought the king and
his household over the Jordan, and all
David's men with him?" 42 All the men
of Judah answered the men of Israel,
"Because the king is our close relative.
Why then are you angry over this matter?
Have we eaten at all at the king's expense?
Or has he given us any gift?" 43 And the
men of Israel answered the men of Judah,
"We have ten shares in the king, and in
David also we have more than you. Why
then did you despise us? Were we not
the first to speak of bringing back our
king?" But the words of the men of Judah
were fiercer than the words of the men
of Israel.

The Rebellion of Sheba

20 Now there happened to be there a
worthless man, whose name was
Sheba, the son of Bichri, a Benjaminite.
And he blew the trumpet and said,

"We have no portion in David,
and we have no inheritance in the
son of Jesse;
every man to his tents, O Israel!"

2 So all the men of Israel withdrew from
David and followed Sheba the son of Bichri.
But the men of Judah followed their king
steadfastly from the Jordan to Jerusalem.

3 And David came to his house at
Jerusalem. And the king took the ten
concubines whom he had left to care
for the house and put them in a house
under guard and provided for them, but
did not go in to them. So they were shut
up until the day of their death, living as
if in widowhood.

4 Then the king said to Amasa, "Call
the men of Judah together to me within
three days, and be here yourself." 5 So
Amasa went to summon Judah, but he
delayed beyond the set time that had
been appointed him. 6 And David said
to Abishai, "Now Sheba the son of Bichri
will do us more harm than Absalom.
Take your lord's servants and pursue him,
lest he get himself to fortified cities and
escape from us."[1] 7 And there went out
after him Joab's men and the Cherethites
and the Pelethites, and all the mighty men.
They went out from Jerusalem to pursue
Sheba the son of Bichri. 8 When they were
at the great stone that is in Gibeon, Amasa
came to meet them. Now Joab was wear-
ing a soldier's garment, and over it was a
belt with a sword in its sheath fastened
on his thigh, and as he went forward it fell
out. 9 And Joab said to Amasa, "Is it well
with you, my brother?" And Joab took
Amasa by the beard with his right hand
to kiss him. 10 But Amasa did not observe
the sword that was in Joab's hand. So Joab

[1] Hebrew *and snatch away our eyes*

struck him with it in the stomach and spilled his entrails to the ground without striking a second blow, and he died.

Then Joab and Abishai his brother pursued Sheba the son of Bichri. 11 And one of Joab's young men took his stand by Amasa and said, "Whoever favors Joab, and whoever is for David, let him follow Joab." 12 And Amasa lay wallowing in his blood in the highway. And anyone who came by, seeing him, stopped. And when the man saw that all the people stopped, he carried Amasa out of the highway into the field and threw a garment over him. 13 When he was taken out of the highway, all the people went on after Joab to pursue Sheba the son of Bichri.

14 And Sheba passed through all the tribes of Israel to Abel of Beth-maacah,[1] and all the Bichrites[2] assembled and followed him in. 15 And all the men who were with Joab came and besieged him in Abel of Beth-maacah. They cast up a mound against the city, and it stood against the rampart, and they were battering the wall to throw it down. 16 Then a wise woman called from the city, "Listen! Listen! Tell Joab, 'Come here, that I may speak to you.'" 17 And he came near her, and the woman said, "Are you Joab?" He answered, "I am." Then she said to him, "Listen to the words of your servant." And he answered, "I am listening." 18 Then she said, "They used to say in former times, 'Let them but ask counsel at Abel,' and so they settled a matter. 19 I am one of those who are peaceable and faithful in Israel. You seek to destroy a city that is a mother in Israel. Why will you swallow up the heritage of the LORD?" 20 Joab answered, "Far be it from me, far be it, that I should swallow up or destroy! 21 That is not true. But a man of the hill country of Ephraim, called Sheba the son of Bichri, has lifted up his hand against King David. Give up him alone, and I will withdraw from the city." And the woman said to Joab, "Behold, his head shall be thrown to you over the wall." 22 Then the woman went to all the people in her wisdom. And they cut off the head of Sheba the son of Bichri and threw it out to Joab. So he blew the trumpet, and they dispersed from the city, every man to his home. And Joab returned to Jerusalem to the king.

23 Now Joab was in command of all the army of Israel; and Benaiah the son of Jehoiada was in command of the Cherethites and the Pelethites; 24 and Adoram was in charge of the forced labor; and Jehoshaphat the son of Ahilud was the recorder; 25 and Sheva was secretary; and Zadok and Abiathar were priests; 26 and Ira the Jairite was also David's priest.

David Avenges the Gibeonites

21 Now there was a famine in the days of David for three years, year after year. And David sought the face of the LORD. And the LORD said, "There is bloodguilt on Saul and on his house, because he put the Gibeonites to death." 2 So the king called the Gibeonites and spoke to them. Now the Gibeonites were not of the people of Israel but of the remnant of the Amorites. Although the people of Israel had sworn to spare them, Saul had sought to strike them down in his zeal for the people of Israel and Judah. 3 And David said to the Gibeonites, "What shall I do for you? And how shall I make atonement, that you may bless the heritage of the LORD?" 4 The Gibeonites said to him, "It is not a matter of silver or gold between us and Saul or his house; neither is it for us to put any man to death in Israel." And he said, "What do you say that I shall do for you?" 5 They said to the king, "The man who consumed us and planned to destroy us, so that we should have no place in all the territory of Israel, 6 let seven of his sons be given to us, so that we may hang them before the LORD at Gibeah of Saul, the chosen of the LORD." And the king said, "I will give them."

[1] Compare 20:15; Hebrew *and Beth-maacah* [2] Hebrew *Berites*

7 But the king spared Mephibosheth, the son of Saul's son Jonathan, because of the oath of the LORD that was between them, between David and Jonathan the son of Saul. 8 The king took the two sons of Rizpah the daughter of Aiah, whom she bore to Saul, Armoni and Mephibosheth; and the five sons of Merab[1] the daughter of Saul, whom she bore to Adriel the son of Barzillai the Meholathite; 9 and he gave them into the hands of the Gibeonites, and they hanged them on the mountain before the LORD, and the seven of them perished together. They were put to death in the first days of harvest, at the beginning of barley harvest.

10 Then Rizpah the daughter of Aiah took sackcloth and spread it for herself on the rock, from the beginning of harvest until rain fell upon them from the heavens. And she did not allow the birds of the air to come upon them by day, or the beasts of the field by night. 11 When David was told what Rizpah the daughter of Aiah, the concubine of Saul, had done, 12 David went and took the bones of Saul and the bones of his son Jonathan from the men of Jabesh-gilead, who had stolen them from the public square of Beth-shan, where the Philistines had hanged them, on the day the Philistines killed Saul on Gilboa. 13 And he brought up from there the bones of Saul and the bones of his son Jonathan; and they gathered the bones of those who were hanged. 14 And they buried the bones of Saul and his son Jonathan in the land of Benjamin in Zela, in the tomb of Kish his father. And they did all that the king commanded. And after that God responded to the plea for the land.

War with the Philistines

15 There was war again between the Philistines and Israel, and David went down together with his servants, and they fought against the Philistines. And David grew weary. 16 And Ishbi-benob, one of the descendants of the giants, whose spear weighed three hundred shekels[2] of bronze, and who was armed with a new sword, thought to kill David. 17 But Abishai the son of Zeruiah came to his aid and attacked the Philistine and killed him. Then David's men swore to him, "You shall no longer go out with us to battle, lest you quench the lamp of Israel."

18 After this there was again war with the Philistines at Gob. Then Sibbecai the Hushathite struck down Saph, who was one of the descendants of the giants. 19 And there was again war with the Philistines at Gob, and Elhanan the son of Jaare-oregim, the Bethlehemite, struck down Goliath the Gittite, the shaft of whose spear was like a weaver's beam.[3] 20 And there was again war at Gath, where there was a man of great stature, who had six fingers on each hand, and six toes on each foot, twenty-four in number, and he also was descended from the giants. 21 And when he taunted Israel, Jonathan the son of Shimei, David's brother, struck him down. 22 These four were descended from the giants in Gath, and they fell by the hand of David and by the hand of his servants.

David's Song of Deliverance

22 And David spoke to the LORD the words of this song on the day when the LORD delivered him from the hand of all his enemies, and from the hand of Saul. 2 He said,

"The LORD is my rock and my fortress and my deliverer,
3 my[4] God, my rock, in whom I take refuge,
my shield, and the horn of my salvation,
my stronghold and my refuge,
my savior; you save me from violence.

[1] Two Hebrew manuscripts, Septuagint; most Hebrew manuscripts *Michal* [2] A *shekel* was about 2/5 ounce or 11 grams [3] Contrast 1 Chronicles 20:5, which may preserve the original reading [4] Septuagint (compare Psalm 18:2); Hebrew lacks *my*

4 I call upon the LORD, who is worthy
to be praised,
and I am saved from my enemies.

5 "For the waves of death
encompassed me,
the torrents of destruction
assailed me;[1]
6 the cords of Sheol entangled me;
the snares of death confronted me.

7 "In my distress I called upon the
LORD;
to my God I called.
From his temple he heard my voice,
and my cry came to his ears.

8 "Then the earth reeled and rocked;
the foundations of the heavens
trembled
and quaked, because he was angry.
9 Smoke went up from his nostrils,[2]
and devouring fire from his
mouth;
glowing coals flamed forth from
him.
10 He bowed the heavens and came
down;
thick darkness was under his feet.
11 He rode on a cherub and flew;
he was seen on the wings of the
wind.
12 He made darkness around him his
canopy,
thick clouds, a gathering of water.
13 Out of the brightness before him
coals of fire flamed forth.
14 The LORD thundered from heaven,
and the Most High uttered his
voice.
15 And he sent out arrows and
scattered them;
lightning, and routed them.
16 Then the channels of the sea were
seen;
the foundations of the world were
laid bare,
at the rebuke of the LORD,
at the blast of the breath of his
nostrils.

17 "He sent from on high, he took me;
he drew me out of many waters.
18 He rescued me from my strong
enemy,
from those who hated me,
for they were too mighty for me.
19 They confronted me in the day of
my calamity,
but the LORD was my support.
20 He brought me out into a broad
place;
he rescued me, because he
delighted in me.

21 "The LORD dealt with me according
to my righteousness;
according to the cleanness of my
hands he rewarded me.
22 For I have kept the ways of the LORD
and have not wickedly departed
from my God.
23 For all his rules were before me,
and from his statutes I did not
turn aside.
24 I was blameless before him,
and I kept myself from guilt.
25 And the LORD has rewarded
me according to my
righteousness,
according to my cleanness in his
sight.

26 "With the merciful you show
yourself merciful;
with the blameless man you show
yourself blameless;
27 with the purified you deal purely,
and with the crooked you make
yourself seem tortuous.
28 You save a humble people,
but your eyes are on the haughty
to bring them down.
29 For you are my lamp, O LORD,
and my God lightens my
darkness.

[1] Or *terrified me* [2] Or *in his wrath*

30 For by you I can run against a troop,
and by my God I can leap over a wall.
31 This God—his way is perfect;
the word of the LORD proves true;
he is a shield for all those who take refuge in him.

32 "For who is God, but the LORD?
And who is a rock, except our God?
33 This God is my strong refuge
and has made my[1] way blameless.[2]
34 He made my feet like the feet of a deer
and set me secure on the heights.
35 He trains my hands for war,
so that my arms can bend a bow of bronze.
36 You have given me the shield of your salvation,
and your gentleness made me great.
37 You gave a wide place for my steps under me,
and my feet[3] did not slip;
38 I pursued my enemies and destroyed them,
and did not turn back until they were consumed.
39 I consumed them; I thrust them through, so that they did not rise;
they fell under my feet.
40 For you equipped me with strength for the battle;
you made those who rise against me sink under me.
41 You made my enemies turn their backs to me,[4]
those who hated me, and I destroyed them.
42 They looked, but there was none to save;
they cried to the LORD, but he did not answer them.
43 I beat them fine as the dust of the earth;
I crushed them and stamped them down like the mire of the streets.

44 "You delivered me from strife with my people;[5]
you kept me as the head of the nations;
people whom I had not known served me.
45 Foreigners came cringing to me;
as soon as they heard of me, they obeyed me.
46 Foreigners lost heart
and came trembling[6] out of their fortresses.

47 "The LORD lives, and blessed be my rock,
and exalted be my God, the rock of my salvation,
48 the God who gave me vengeance
and brought down peoples under me,
49 who brought me out from my enemies;
you exalted me above those who rose against me;
you delivered me from men of violence.

499
50 "For this I will praise you, O Lord, among the nations,
and sing praises to your name.
51 Great salvation he brings[7] to his king,
and shows steadfast love to his anointed,
to David and his offspring forever."

The Last Words of David

23 Now these are the last words of David:

The oracle of David, the son of Jesse,

[1] Or *his*; also verse 34 [2] Compare Psalm 18:32; Hebrew *he has blamelessly set my way free*, or *he has made my way spring up blamelessly* [3] Hebrew *ankles* [4] Or *You gave me my enemies' necks* [5] Septuagint *with the peoples* [6] Compare Psalm 18:45; Hebrew *equipped themselves* [7] Or *He is a tower of salvation*

the oracle of the man who was
raised on high,
the anointed of the God of Jacob,
the sweet psalmist of Israel:[1]

2 "The Spirit of the LORD speaks by me;
his word is on my tongue.
3 The God of Israel has spoken;
the Rock of Israel has said to me:
When one rules justly over men,
ruling in the fear of God,
4 he dawns on them like the morning
light,
like the sun shining forth on a
cloudless morning,
like rain[2] that makes grass to
sprout from the earth.

5 "For does not my house stand so
with God?
For he has made with me an
everlasting covenant,
ordered in all things and secure.
For will he not cause to prosper
all my help and my desire?
6 But worthless men[3] are all like
thorns that are thrown away,
for they cannot be taken with the
hand;
7 but the man who touches them
arms himself with iron and the
shaft of a spear,
and they are utterly consumed
with fire."[4]

David's Mighty Men

8 These are the names of the mighty men
whom David had: Josheb-basshebeth a
Tahchemonite; he was chief of the three.[5]
He wielded his spear[6] against eight hun-
dred whom he killed at one time.

9 And next to him among the three
mighty men was Eleazar the son of Dodo,
son of Ahohi. He was with David when
they defied the Philistines who were gath-
ered there for battle, and the men of Israel
withdrew. **10** He rose and struck down the
Philistines until his hand was weary, and
his hand clung to the sword. And the LORD
brought about a great victory that day, and
the men returned after him only to strip
the slain.

11 And next to him was Shammah, the
son of Agee the Hararite. The Philistines
gathered together at Lehi, where there was
a plot of ground full of lentils, and the men
fled from the Philistines. **12** But he took his
stand in the midst of the plot and defended
it and struck down the Philistines, and the
LORD worked a great victory.

13 And three of the thirty chief men
went down and came about harvest time
to David at the cave of Adullam, when a
band of Philistines was encamped in the
Valley of Rephaim. **14** David was then in
the stronghold, and the garrison of the
Philistines was then at Bethlehem. **15** And
David said longingly, "Oh, that someone
would give me water to drink from the well
of Bethlehem that is by the gate!" **16** Then
the three mighty men broke through the
camp of the Philistines and drew water out
of the well of Bethlehem that was by the
gate and carried and brought it to David.
But he would not drink of it. He poured it
out to the LORD **17** and said, "Far be it from
me, O LORD, that I should do this. Shall I
drink the blood of the men who went at
the risk of their lives?" Therefore he would
not drink it. These things the three mighty
men did.

18 Now Abishai, the brother of Joab, the
son of Zeruiah, was chief of the thirty.[7]
And he wielded his spear against three
hundred men[8] and killed them and won
a name beside the three. **19** He was the
most renowned of the thirty[9] and became
their commander, but he did not attain
to the three.

20 And Benaiah the son of Jehoiada
was a valiant man[10] of Kabzeel, a doer of
great deeds. He struck down two ariels[11]
of Moab. He also went down and struck

[1] Or *the favorite of the songs of Israel* [2] Hebrew *from rain* [3] Hebrew *worthlessness* [4] Hebrew *consumed with fire in the sitting* [5] Or *of the captains* [6] 1 Chronicles 11:11; the meaning of the Hebrew expression is uncertain [7] Two Hebrew manuscripts, Syriac; most Hebrew manuscripts *three* [8] Or *slain ones* [9] 1 Chronicles 11:25; Hebrew *Was he the most renowned of the three?* [10] Or *the son of Ishhai* [11] The meaning of the word *ariel* is unknown

down a lion in a pit on a day when snow had fallen. 21 And he struck down an Egyptian, a handsome man. The Egyptian had a spear in his hand, but Benaiah went down to him with a staff and snatched the spear out of the Egyptian's hand and killed him with his own spear. 22 These things did Benaiah the son of Jehoiada, and won a name beside the three mighty men. 23 He was renowned among the thirty, but he did not attain to the three. And David set him over his bodyguard.

24 Asahel the brother of Joab was one of the thirty; Elhanan the son of Dodo of Bethlehem, 25 Shammah of Harod, Elika of Harod, 26 Helez the Paltite, Ira the son of Ikkesh of Tekoa, 27 Abiezer of Anathoth, Mebunnai the Hushathite, 28 Zalmon the Ahohite, Maharai of Netophah, 29 Heleb the son of Baanah of Netophah, Ittai the son of Ribai of Gibeah of the people of Benjamin, 30 Benaiah of Pirathon, Hiddai of the brooks of Gaash, 31 Abi-albon the Arbathite, Azmaveth of Bahurim, 32 Eliahba the Shaalbonite, the sons of Jashen, Jonathan, 33 Shammah the Hararite, Ahiam the son of Sharar the Hararite, 34 Eliphelet the son of Ahasbai of Maacah, Eliam the son of Ahithophel of Gilo, 35 Hezro[1] of Carmel, Paarai the Arbite, 36 Igal the son of Nathan of Zobah, Bani the Gadite, 37 Zelek the Ammonite, Naharai of Beeroth, the armor-bearer of Joab the son of Zeruiah, 38 Ira the Ithrite, Gareb the Ithrite, 39 Uriah the Hittite: thirty-seven in all.

David's Census

24 Again the anger of the LORD was kindled against Israel, and he incited David against them, saying, "Go, number Israel and Judah." 2 So the king said to Joab, the commander of the army,[2] who was with him, "Go through all the tribes of Israel, from Dan to Beersheba, and number the people, that I may know the number of the people." 3 But Joab said to the king, "May the LORD your God add to the people a hundred times as many as they are, while the eyes of my lord the king still see it, but why does my lord the king delight in this thing?" 4 But the king's word prevailed against Joab and the commanders of the army. So Joab and the commanders of the army went out from the presence of the king to number the people of Israel. 5 They crossed the Jordan and began from Aroer,[3] and from the city that is in the middle of the valley, toward Gad and on to Jazer. 6 Then they came to Gilead, and to Kadesh in the land of the Hittites;[4] and they came to Dan, and from Dan[5] they went around to Sidon, 7 and came to the fortress of Tyre and to all the cities of the Hivites and Canaanites; and they went out to the Negeb of Judah at Beersheba. 8 So when they had gone through all the land, they came to Jerusalem at the end of nine months and twenty days. 9 And Joab gave the sum of the numbering of the people to the king: in Israel there were 800,000 valiant men who drew the sword, and the men of Judah were 500,000.

The LORD's Judgment of David's Sin

10 But David's heart struck him after he had numbered the people. And David said to the LORD, "I have sinned greatly in what I have done. But now, O LORD, please take away the iniquity of your servant, for I have done very foolishly." 11 And when David arose in the morning, the word of the LORD came to the prophet Gad, David's seer, saying, 12 "Go and say to David, 'Thus says the LORD, Three things I offer[6] you. Choose one of them, that I may do it to you.'" 13 So Gad came to David and told him, and said to him, "Shall three[7] years of famine come to you in your land? Or will you flee three months before your foes while they pursue you? Or shall there be three days' pestilence in your land? Now consider, and decide what answer I shall return to him who sent me." 14 Then

[1] Or *Hezrai* [2] Septuagint *to Joab and the commanders of the army* [3] Septuagint; Hebrew *encamped in Aroer* [4] Septuagint; Hebrew *to the land of Tahtim-hodshi* [5] Septuagint; Hebrew *they came to Dan-jaan and* [6] Or *hold over* [7] Compare 1 Chronicles 21:12, Septuagint; Hebrew *seven*

David said to Gad, "I am in great distress.
Let us fall into the hand of the LORD, for
his mercy is great; but let me not fall into
the hand of man."
15 So the LORD sent a pestilence on Israel
from the morning until the appointed
time. And there died of the people from
Dan to Beersheba 70,000 men. 16 And
when the angel stretched out his hand
toward Jerusalem to destroy it, the LORD
relented from the calamity and said to
the angel who was working destruction
among the people, "It is enough; now stay
your hand." And the angel of the LORD
was by the threshing floor of Araunah the
Jebusite. 17 Then David spoke to the LORD
when he saw the angel who was striking the people, and said, "Behold, I have
sinned, and I have done wickedly. But
these sheep, what have they done? Please
let your hand be against me and against
my father's house."

David Builds an Altar

18 And Gad came that day to David and
said to him, "Go up, raise an altar to the
LORD on the threshing floor of Araunah
the Jebusite." 19 So David went up at Gad's
word, as the LORD commanded. 20 And
when Araunah looked down, he saw the
king and his servants coming on toward
him. And Araunah went out and paid homage to the king with his face to the ground.
21 And Araunah said, "Why has my lord
the king come to his servant?" David said,
"To buy the threshing floor from you, in
order to build an altar to the LORD, that the
plague may be averted from the people."
22 Then Araunah said to David, "Let my
lord the king take and offer up what seems
good to him. Here are the oxen for the
burnt offering and the threshing sledges
and the yokes of the oxen for the wood.
23 All this, O king, Araunah gives to the
king." And Araunah said to the king, "May
the LORD your God accept you." 24 But the
king said to Araunah, "No, but I will buy it
from you for a price. I will not offer burnt
offerings to the LORD my God that cost
me nothing." So David bought the threshing floor and the oxen for fifty shekels[1] of
silver. 25 And David built there an altar to
the LORD and offered burnt offerings and
peace offerings. So the LORD responded to
the plea for the land, and the plague was
averted from Israel.

[1] A *shekel* was about 2/5 ounce or 11 grams

Introduction to

1–2 Kings

Author and Date

Author unknown. Stories cover the last years of David through when the book was written, about 560 B.C.

People

David; Solomon; queen of Sheba; Rehoboam; Jeroboam; Ahab; Jezebel; Elijah; Elisha; Joash; Sennacherib; Hezekiah; Manasseh; Josiah; Nebuchadnezzar

Purpose

These books show that the Lord of history keeps both the promises and the threats of His holy covenant. This explains why the Israelites were defeated by their enemies and driven from the land God had given them.

Central Themes

God keeps His promises for blessing; God establishes and preserves kings from David's line; God provides a place for His worship; God keeps His promises for judgment; Solomon's kingdom is divided because of his idolatry; first Israel, then Judah go into captivity because of their idolatry and failure to keep God's covenant.

Memory Verses

Solomon prays for wisdom (1 Kings 3:6–9); Solomon's benediction (1 Kings 8:56–61)

Introduction

First and Second Kings tell the history of Israel from the end of David's reign until the people are taken into captivity. They tell what happened so readers will understand why it happened. Solomon's reign begins well with his prayer for wisdom (1 Kings 3). The kingdom prospers and the temple is built (1 Kings 4–8). But because Solomon worships his foreign wives' idols along with God, God causes the kingdom to divide into 10 tribes (Israel) and two tribes for David's house (Judah) (1 Kings 11–12). Every king in Israel leads the people in the worship of idols. God sends prophets to warn them, including the two most famous, Elijah and Elisha (1 Kings 17–18; 2 Kings 2; 4–7). Israel never truly repents, and God sends Assyrian soldiers to carry the people of Israel away as captives (2 Kings 17). The kingdom of Judah lasts longer; even though they have some ungodly rulers, they have several godly kings who destroy idols and bring back the worship of the true God. God sends prophets to warn His people in Judah too. Eventually, though, Judah's return again and again to idolatry has to be punished, and God sends the Babylonians to destroy Jerusalem and the temple and to carry the people away into captivity (2 Kings 25).

971, 931 B.C.	**722 B.C.**	**586 B.C.**
Reign of Solomon, Israel divided	Fall of Israel	Fall of Judah

1 Kings

David in His Old Age

1 Now King David was old and advanced in years. And although they covered him with clothes, he could not get warm. **2** Therefore his servants said to him, "Let a young woman be sought for my lord the king, and let her wait on the king and be in his service. Let her lie in your arms,[1] that my lord the king may be warm." **3** So they sought for a beautiful young woman throughout all the territory of Israel, and found Abishag the Shunammite, and brought her to the king. **4** The young woman was very beautiful, and she was of service to the king and attended to him, but the king knew her not.

Adonijah Sets Himself Up as King

5 Now Adonijah the son of Haggith exalted himself, saying, "I will be king." And he prepared for himself chariots and horsemen, and fifty men to run before him. **6** His father had never at any time displeased him by asking, "Why have you done thus and so?" He was also a very handsome man, and he was born next after Absalom. **7** He conferred with Joab the son of Zeruiah and with Abiathar the priest. And they followed Adonijah and helped him. **8** But Zadok the priest and Benaiah the son of Jehoiada and Nathan the prophet and Shimei and Rei and David's mighty men were not with Adonijah.

9 Adonijah sacrificed sheep, oxen, and fattened cattle by the Serpent's Stone, which is beside En-rogel, and he invited all his brothers, the king's sons, and all the royal officials of Judah, **10** but he did not invite Nathan the prophet or Benaiah or the mighty men or Solomon his brother.

Nathan and Bathsheba Before David

11 Then Nathan said to Bathsheba the mother of Solomon, "Have you not heard that Adonijah the son of Haggith has become king and David our lord does not know it? **12** Now therefore come, let me give you advice, that you may save your own life and the life of your son Solomon. **13** Go in at once to King David, and say to him, 'Did you not, my lord the king, swear to your servant, saying, "Solomon your son shall reign after me, and he shall sit on my throne"? Why then is Adonijah king?' **14** Then while you are still speaking with the king, I also will come in after you and confirm[2] your words."

15 So Bathsheba went to the king in his chamber (now the king was very old, and Abishag the Shunammite was attending to the king). **16** Bathsheba bowed and paid homage to the king, and the king said, "What do you desire?" **17** She said to him, "My lord, you swore to your servant by the LORD your God, saying, 'Solomon your son shall reign after me, and he shall sit on my throne.' **18** And now, behold, Adonijah is king, although you, my lord the king, do not know it. **19** He has sacrificed oxen, fattened cattle, and sheep in abundance, and has invited all the sons of the king, Abiathar the priest, and Joab the commander of the army, but Solomon your servant he has not invited. **20** And now, my lord the king, the eyes of all Israel are on you, to tell them who shall sit on the throne of my lord the king after him. **21** Otherwise it will come to pass, when my lord the king sleeps with his fathers, that I and my son Solomon will be counted offenders."

22 While she was still speaking with the

[1] Or *in your bosom* [2] Or *expand on*

king, Nathan the prophet came in. 23 And
they told the king, "Here is Nathan the
prophet." And when he came in before
the king, he bowed before the king, with
his face to the ground. 24 And Nathan said,
"My lord the king, have you said, 'Adonijah
shall reign after me, and he shall sit on
my throne'? 25 For he has gone down this
day and has sacrificed oxen, fattened
cattle, and sheep in abundance, and has
invited all the king's sons, the command-
ers[1] of the army, and Abiathar the priest.
And behold, they are eating and drinking
before him, and saying, 'Long live King
Adonijah!' 26 But me, your servant, and
Zadok the priest, and Benaiah the son of
Jehoiada, and your servant Solomon he
has not invited. 27 Has this thing been
brought about by my lord the king and
you have not told your servants who
should sit on the throne of my lord the
king after him?"

Solomon Anointed King

28 Then King David answered, "Call
Bathsheba to me." So she came into the
king's presence and stood before the king.
29 And the king swore, saying, "As the LORD
lives, who has redeemed my soul out of
every adversity, 30 as I swore to you by the
LORD, the God of Israel, saying, 'Solomon
your son shall reign after me, and he shall
sit on my throne in my place,' even so will
I do this day." 31 Then Bathsheba bowed
with her face to the ground and paid hom-
age to the king and said, "May my lord
King David live forever!"

32 King David said, "Call to me Zadok the
priest, Nathan the prophet, and Benaiah
the son of Jehoiada." So they came before
the king. 33 And the king said to them,
"Take with you the servants of your lord
and have Solomon my son ride on my
own mule, and bring him down to Gihon.
34 And let Zadok the priest and Nathan the
prophet there anoint him king over Israel.
Then blow the trumpet and say, 'Long live
King Solomon!' 35 You shall then come
up after him, and he shall come and sit
on my throne, for he shall be king in my
place. And I have appointed him to be
ruler over Israel and over Judah." 36 And
Benaiah the son of Jehoiada answered the
king, "Amen! May the LORD, the God of my
lord the king, say so. 37 As the LORD has
been with my lord the king, even so may
he be with Solomon, and make his throne
greater than the throne of my lord King
David."

38 So Zadok the priest, Nathan the
prophet, and Benaiah the son of Jehoiada,
and the Cherethites and the Pelethites
went down and had Solomon ride on King
David's mule and brought him to Gihon.
39 There Zadok the priest took the horn of
oil from the tent and anointed Solomon.
Then they blew the trumpet, and all the
people said, "Long live King Solomon!"
40 And all the people went up after him,
playing on pipes, and rejoicing with great
joy, so that the earth was split by their
noise.

41 Adonijah and all the guests who were
with him heard it as they finished feast-
ing. And when Joab heard the sound of
the trumpet, he said, "What does this
uproar in the city mean?" 42 While he was
still speaking, behold, Jonathan the son
of Abiathar the priest came. And Adonijah
said, "Come in, for you are a worthy
man and bring good news." 43 Jonathan
answered Adonijah, "No, for our lord King
David has made Solomon king, 44 and the
king has sent with him Zadok the priest,
Nathan the prophet, and Benaiah the
son of Jehoiada, and the Cherethites and
the Pelethites. And they had him ride on
the king's mule. 45 And Zadok the priest
and Nathan the prophet have anointed
him king at Gihon, and they have gone
up from there rejoicing, so that the city
is in an uproar. This is the noise that you
have heard. 46 Solomon sits on the royal
throne. 47 Moreover, the king's servants

[1] Hebrew; Septuagint *Joab the commander*

came to congratulate our lord King David,
saying, 'May your God make the name of
Solomon more famous than yours, and
make his throne greater than your throne.'
And the king bowed himself on the bed.
48 And the king also said, 'Blessed be the
LORD, the God of Israel, who has granted
someone[1] to sit on my throne this day, my
own eyes seeing it.'"

49 Then all the guests of Adonijah trem-
bled and rose, and each went his own way.
50 And Adonijah feared Solomon. So he
arose and went and took hold of the horns
of the altar. 51 Then it was told Solomon,
"Behold, Adonijah fears King Solomon,
for behold, he has laid hold of the horns
of the altar, saying, 'Let King Solomon
swear to me first that he will not put his
servant to death with the sword.'" 52 And
Solomon said, "If he will show himself a
worthy man, not one of his hairs shall fall
to the earth, but if wickedness is found
in him, he shall die." 53 So King Solomon
sent, and they brought him down from
the altar. And he came and paid homage
to King Solomon, and Solomon said to
him, "Go to your house."

David's Instructions to Solomon

2 When David's time to die drew near,
he commanded Solomon his son,
saying, 2 "I am about to go the way of all
the earth. Be strong, and show yourself
a man, 3 and keep the charge of the LORD
your God, walking in his ways and keep-
ing his statutes, his commandments, his
rules, and his testimonies, as it is written
in the Law of Moses, that you may prosper
in all that you do and wherever you turn,
4 that the LORD may establish his word
that he spoke concerning me, saying,
'If your sons pay close attention to their
way, to walk before me in faithfulness
with all their heart *and with* all their soul,
you shall not lack[2] a man on the throne
of Israel.'

5 "Moreover, you also know what Joab
the son of Zeruiah did to me, how he dealt
with the two commanders of the armies
of Israel, Abner the son of Ner, and Amasa
the son of Jether, whom he killed, aveng-
ing[3] in time of peace for blood that had
been shed in war, and putting the blood
of war[4] on the belt around his[5] waist and
on the sandals on his feet. 6 Act therefore
according to your wisdom, but do not let
his gray head go down to Sheol in peace.
7 But deal loyally with the sons of Barzillai
the Gileadite, and let them be among
those who eat at your table, for with such
loyalty[6] they met me when I fled from
Absalom your brother. 8 And there is
also with you Shimei the son of Gera, the
Benjaminite from Bahurim, who cursed
me with a grievous curse on the day when
I went to Mahanaim. But when he came
down to meet me at the Jordan, I swore
to him by the LORD, saying, 'I will not put
you to death with the sword.' 9 Now there-
fore do not hold him guiltless, for you
are a wise man. You will know what you
ought to do to him, and you shall bring
his gray head down with blood to Sheol."

The Death of David

10 Then David slept with his fathers
and was buried in the city of David.
11 And the time that David reigned over
Israel was forty years. He reigned seven
years in Hebron and thirty-three years
in Jerusalem. 12 So Solomon sat on the
throne of David his father, and his king-
dom was firmly established.

Solomon's Reign Established

13 Then Adonijah the son of Haggith
came to Bathsheba the mother of Sol-
omon. And she said, "Do you come peace-
fully?" He said, "Peacefully." 14 Then he
said, "I have something to say to you." She
said, "Speak." 15 He said, "You know that
the kingdom was mine, and that all Israel
fully expected me to reign. However, the
kingdom has turned about and become

[1] Septuagint *one of my offspring* [2] Hebrew *there shall not be cut off for you* [3] Septuagint; Hebrew *placing* [4] Septuagint *innocent blood* [5] Septuagint *my;* twice in this verse
[6] Or *steadfast love*

my brother's, for it was his from the LORD.
16 And now I have one request to make of
you; do not refuse me." She said to him,
"Speak." 17 And he said, "Please ask King
Solomon—he will not refuse you—to give
me Abishag the Shunammite as my wife."
18 Bathsheba said, "Very well; I will speak
for you to the king."

19 So Bathsheba went to King Solomon
to speak to him on behalf of Adonijah. And
the king rose to meet her and bowed down
to her. Then he sat on his throne and had
a seat brought for the king's mother, and
she sat on his right. 20 Then she said, "I
have one small request to make of you;
do not refuse me." And the king said to
her, "Make your request, my mother, for
I will not refuse you." 21 She said, "Let
Abishag the Shunammite be given to
Adonijah your brother as his wife." 22 King
Solomon answered his mother, "And why
do you ask Abishag the Shunammite for
Adonijah? Ask for him the kingdom also,
for he is my older brother, and on his
side are Abiathar[1] the priest and Joab the
son of Zeruiah." 23 Then King Solomon
swore by the LORD, saying, "God do so to
me and more also if this word does not
cost Adonijah his life! 24 Now therefore as
the LORD lives, who has established me
and placed me on the throne of David my
father, and who has made me a house,
as he promised, Adonijah shall be put
to death today." 25 So King Solomon sent
Benaiah the son of Jehoiada, and he struck
him down, and he died.

26 And to Abiathar the priest the king
said, "Go to Anathoth, to your estate, for
you deserve death. But I will not at this
time put you to death, because you carried
the ark of the Lord GOD before David my
father, and because you shared in all my
father's affliction." 27 So Solomon expelled
Abiathar from being priest to the LORD,
thus fulfilling the word of the LORD that
he had spoken concerning the house of
Eli in Shiloh.

28 When the news came to Joab—for
Joab had supported Adonijah although he
had not supported Absalom—Joab fled to
the tent of the LORD and caught hold of
the horns of the altar. 29 And when it was
told King Solomon, "Joab has fled to the
tent of the LORD, and behold, he is beside
the altar," Solomon sent Benaiah the son
of Jehoiada, saying, "Go, strike him down."
30 So Benaiah came to the tent of the LORD
and said to him, "The king commands,
'Come out.'" But he said, "No, I will die
here." Then Benaiah brought the king word
again, saying, "Thus said Joab, and thus he
answered me." 31 The king replied to him,
"Do as he has said, strike him down and
bury him, and thus take away from me and
from my father's house the guilt for the
blood that Joab shed without cause. 32 The
LORD will bring back his bloody deeds on
his own head, because, without the knowl-
edge of my father David, he attacked and
killed with the sword two men more righ-
teous and better than himself, Abner the
son of Ner, commander of the army of
Israel, and Amasa the son of Jether, com-
mander of the army of Judah. 33 So shall
their blood come back on the head of
Joab and on the head of his descendants
forever. But for David and for his descen-
dants and for his house and for his throne
there shall be peace from the LORD for-
evermore." 34 Then Benaiah the son of
Jehoiada went up and struck him down
and put him to death. And he was buried
in his own house in the wilderness. 35 The
king put Benaiah the son of Jehoiada over
the army in place of Joab, and the king put
Zadok the priest in the place of Abiathar.

36 Then the king sent and summoned
Shimei and said to him, "Build yourself
a house in Jerusalem and dwell there,
and do not go out from there to any place
whatever. 37 For on the day you go out and
cross the brook Kidron, know for certain
that you shall die. Your blood shall be on
your own head." 38 And Shimei said to the

[1] Septuagint, Syriac, Vulgate; Hebrew *and for him and for Abiathar*

king, "What you say is good; as my lord
the king has said, so will your servant do."
So Shimei lived in Jerusalem many days.
39 But it happened at the end of three
years that two of Shimei's servants ran
away to Achish, son of Maacah, king
of Gath. And when it was told Shimei,
"Behold, your servants are in Gath,"
40 Shimei arose and saddled a donkey and
went to Gath to Achish to seek his servants.
Shimei went and brought his servants
from Gath. 41 And when Solomon was told
that Shimei had gone from Jerusalem to
Gath and returned, 42 the king sent and
summoned Shimei and said to him, "Did I
not make you swear by the LORD and sol-
emnly warn you, saying, 'Know for certain
that on the day you go out and go to any
place whatever, you shall die'? And you
said to me, 'What you say is good; I will
obey.' 43 Why then have you not kept your
oath to the LORD and the commandment
with which I commanded you?" 44 The
king also said to Shimei, "You know in
your own heart all the harm that you did
to David my father. So the LORD will bring
back your harm on your own head. 45 But
King Solomon shall be blessed, and the
throne of David shall be established before
the LORD forever." 46 Then the king com-
manded Benaiah the son of Jehoiada, and
he went out and struck him down, and
he died.

So the kingdom was established in the
hand of Solomon.

Solomon's Prayer for Wisdom

535

3 Solomon made a marriage alli-
ance with Pharaoh king of
Egypt. He took Pharaoh's daughter
and brought her into the city of David
until he had finished building his own
house and the house of the LORD and the
wall around Jerusalem. 2 The people were
sacrificing at the high places, however,
because no house had yet been built for
the name of the LORD.

3 Solomon loved the LORD, walking in
the statutes of David his father, only he
sacrificed and made offerings at the high
places. 4 And the king went to Gibeon to
sacrifice there, for that was the great high
place. Solomon used to offer a thousand
burnt offerings on that altar. 5 At Gibeon
the LORD appeared to Solomon in a dream
by night, and God said, "Ask what I shall
give you." 6 And Solomon said, "You
have shown great and steadfast love to
your servant David my father, because
he walked before you in faithfulness,
in righteousness, and in uprightness of
heart toward you. And you have kept for
him this great and steadfast love and have
given him a son to sit on his throne this
day. 7 And now, O LORD my God, you have
made your servant king in place of David
my father, although I am but a little child.
I do not know how to go out or come
in. 8 And your servant is in the midst of
your people whom you have chosen, a
great people, too many to be numbered
or counted for multitude. 9 Give your ser-
vant therefore an understanding mind
to govern your people, that I may discern
between good and evil, for who is able to
govern this your great people?"

Jerusalem in the Time of Solomon (about 970–930 B.C.)

King Solomon built a temple on Mount Moriah (2 Chronicles 3:1), as his father, King David, had told him to do. Before this, the only house of the Lord had been the tabernacle tent, which could move from place to place as the Israelites traveled. It took Solomon seven years to build the temple (1 Kings 6:38). When he had finished, he spent 13 years building the royal complex (1 Kings 7:1). The royal complex included Solomon's palace, a smaller house for his Egyptian queen, the House of the Forest of Lebanon where armor was kept, the Hall of Pillars, and the Hall of the Throne (1 Kings 7:2–8). A special "ascent" led up from the royal complex to the temple. Solomon had the temple and the royal complex built outside and to the north of the part of Jerusalem where David had lived and ruled (the City of David). New city walls were probably built to include Solomon's additions.

Solomon Asks God for Wisdom

When King David died, his son Solomon became the king of God's people. King Solomon loved God and worshiped Him. One night while King Solomon was sleeping, God came to him in a dream. Solomon could ask whatever he wanted, and God would give it to him.

Solomon thanked God for His faithfulness to his father, David. And Solomon thanked God for making him king. But Solomon told God that he did not know how to be king—that he was young and there was so much he did not know! The Israelites were God's people, so they must have a wise and godly king. Then Solomon asked God for the one thing he most wanted—that God would give Solomon a wise and "understanding mind to govern Your people," so that Solomon would be able to "discern between good and evil."

God was pleased that Solomon had asked Him for wisdom to know right from wrong in ruling God's people. God told Solomon that because he had not asked for riches or for long life or for victory over his enemies, God would give him what he asked for—and everything else as well! "I give you a wise and discerning mind," God told Solomon, "so that none like you has been before you and none like you shall arise after you. I give you also what you have not asked, both riches and honor, so that no other king shall compare with you, all your days." Then God reminded Solomon that he must obey God's commandments as his father David had done.

Solomon woke up and realized God had spoken to him. He went to the tabernacle to pray and to burn an offering in thanksgiving to God.

We need God's wisdom and help, too, because we are sinners and often do things that are wrong. But God has given us His wisdom in His Word, and He has given the Lord Jesus Christ. Jesus forgives our sins through faith in Him, and He changes our sinful hearts so that we want to obey God. God also gives His Holy Spirit to live in His people, helping us to understand and follow God's Word. Just as God gave wisdom to Solomon, God gives us wisdom too—through His Word, His Son, and His Holy Spirit.

SEEK and FIND

WHERE TO FIND THE STORY

1 Kings 3:1–15

KEY BIBLE VERSE

"If any of you lacks wisdom, let him ask God, who gives generously to all without reproach, and it will be given him." (James 1:5)

THREE KEY QUESTIONS

- When God asked Solomon what he wanted most, what did Solomon ask for?
- Why was wisdom so important to Solomon?
- How can we find wisdom to understand and follow God today?

RELATED BIBLE READINGS

1 Kings 3:16–28; 4:20–34; 2 Chronicles 1:7–13; 9:1–12; Proverbs 1:1–7; Matthew 12:42; 1 Corinthians 1:27–31; 2:6–13; James 1:5–8

10 It pleased the Lord that Solomon had asked this. 11 And God said to him, "Because you have asked this, and have not asked for yourself long life or riches or the life of your enemies, but have asked for yourself understanding to discern what is right, 12 behold, I now do according to your word. Behold, I give you a wise and discerning mind, so that none like you has been before you and none like you shall arise after you. 13 I give you also what you have not asked, both riches and honor, so that no other king shall compare with you, all your days. 14 And if you will walk in my ways, keeping my statutes and my commandments, as your father David walked, then I will lengthen your days."

15 And Solomon awoke, and behold, it was a dream. Then he came to Jerusalem and stood before the ark of the covenant of the Lord, and offered up burnt offerings and peace offerings, and made a feast for all his servants.

Solomon's Wisdom

535

16 Then two prostitutes came to the king and stood before him. 17 The one woman said, "Oh, my lord, this woman and I live in the same house, and I gave birth to a child while she was in the house. 18 Then on the third day after I gave birth, this woman also gave birth. And we were alone. There was no one else with us in the house; only we two were in the house. 19 And this woman's son died in the night, because she lay on him. 20 And she arose at midnight and took my son from beside me, while your servant slept, and laid him at her breast, and laid her dead son at my breast. 21 When I rose in the morning to nurse my child, behold, he was dead. But when I looked at him closely in the morning, behold, he was not the child that I had borne." 22 But the other woman said, "No, the living child is mine, and the dead child is yours." The first said, "No, the dead child is yours, and the living child is mine." Thus they spoke before the king.

23 Then the king said, "The one says, 'This is my son that is alive, and your son is dead'; and the other says, 'No; but your son is dead, and my son is the living one.'" 24 And the king said, "Bring me a sword." So a sword was brought before the king. 25 And the king said, "Divide the living child in two, and give half to the one and half to the other." 26 Then the woman whose son was alive said to the king, because her heart yearned for her son, "Oh, my lord, give her the living child, and by no means put him to death." But the other said, "He shall be neither mine nor yours; divide him." 27 Then the king answered and said, "Give the living child to the first woman, and by no means put him to death; she is his mother." 28 And all Israel heard of the judgment that the king had rendered, and they stood in awe of the king, because they perceived that the wisdom of God was in him to do justice.

Solomon's Officials

4 King Solomon was king over all Israel, 2 and these were his high officials: Azariah the son of Zadok was the priest; 3 Elihoreph and Ahijah the sons of Shisha were secretaries; Jehoshaphat the son of Ahilud was recorder; 4 Benaiah the son of Jehoiada was in command of the army; Zadok and Abiathar were priests; 5 Azariah the son of Nathan was over the officers; Zabud the son of Nathan was priest and king's friend; 6 Ahishar was in charge of the palace; and Adoniram the son of Abda was in charge of the forced labor.

7 Solomon had twelve officers over all Israel, who provided food for the king and his household. Each man had to make provision for one month in the year. 8 These were their names: Ben-hur, in the hill country of Ephraim; 9 Ben-deker, in Makaz, Shaalbim, Beth-shemesh, and Elonbeth-hanan; 10 Ben-hesed, in Arubboth (to him belonged Socoh and all the land of Hepher); 11 Ben-abinadab, in all Naphath-dor (he had Taphath the daughter of Solomon as his wife); 12 Baana the son of Ahilud, in Taanach, Megiddo, and all Beth-shean that is beside Zarethan below Jezreel, and from Beth-shean to Abel-meholah, as far as the other side of Jokmeam; 13 Ben-geber, in Ramoth-gilead (he had the villages of Jair the son of Manasseh, which are in Gilead, and he had the region of Argob, which is in Bashan, sixty great cities with walls and bronze bars); 14 Ahinadab the son of Iddo, in Mahanaim; 15 Ahimaaz, in Naphtali (he had taken Basemath the daughter of Solomon as his wife); 16 Baana the son of Hushai, in Asher and Bealoth; 17 Jehoshaphat the son of Paruah, in Issachar; 18 Shimei the son of Ela, in Benjamin; 19 Geber the son of Uri, in the land of Gilead, the country of Sihon king of the Amorites and of Og king of Bashan. And there was one governor who was over the land.

Solomon's Wealth and Wisdom

535

20 Judah and Israel were as many as the sand by the sea. They ate and drank and were happy. 21 [1] Solomon ruled over all the kingdoms from the Euphrates to the land of the Philistines and to the border of Egypt. They brought tribute and served Solomon all the days of his life.

22 Solomon's provision for one day was thirty cors[2] of fine flour and sixty cors of meal, 23 ten fat oxen, and twenty pasture-fed cattle, a hundred sheep, besides deer, gazelles, roebucks, and fattened fowl. 24 For he had dominion over all the region west of the Euphrates from Tiphsah to Gaza, over all the kings west of the Euphrates. And he had peace on all sides around him. 25 And Judah and Israel lived in safety, from Dan even to Beersheba, every man under his vine and under his fig tree, all the days of Solomon. 26 Solomon also had 40,000 stalls of horses for his chariots, and 12,000 horsemen. 27 And those officers supplied provisions for King Solomon, and for all who came to King Solomon's table, each one in his month. They let nothing be lacking. 28 Barley also and straw for the horses and swift steeds they brought to the place where it was required, each according to his duty.

29 And God gave Solomon wisdom and understanding beyond measure, and breadth of mind like the sand on the seashore, 30 so that Solomon's wisdom surpassed the wisdom of all the people of the east and all the wisdom of Egypt. 31 For he was wiser than all other men, wiser than Ethan the Ezrahite, and Heman, Calcol, and Darda, the sons of Mahol, and his fame was in all the surrounding nations. 32 He also spoke 3,000 proverbs, and his songs were 1,005. 33 He spoke of trees, from the cedar that is in Lebanon to the hyssop that grows out of the wall. He spoke also of beasts, and of birds, and of reptiles, and of fish. 34 And people of all nations came to hear the wisdom of

[1] Ch 5:1 in Hebrew [2] A *cor* was about 6 bushels or 220 liters

Solomon, and from all the kings of the earth, who had heard of his wisdom.

Preparations for Building the Temple

545

5 [1]Now Hiram king of Tyre sent his servants to Solomon when he heard that they had anointed him king in place of his father, for Hiram always loved David. 2 And Solomon sent word to Hiram, 3 "You know that David my father could not build a house for the name of the LORD his God because of the warfare with which his enemies surrounded him, until the LORD put them under the soles of his feet. 4 But now the LORD my God has given me rest on every side. There is neither adversary nor misfortune. 5 And so I intend to build a house for the name of the LORD my God, as the LORD said to David my father, 'Your son, whom I will set on your throne in your place, shall build the house for my name.' 6 Now therefore command that cedars of Lebanon be cut for me. And my servants will join your servants, and I will pay you for your servants such wages as you set, for you know that there is no one among us who knows how to cut timber like the Sidonians."

7 As soon as Hiram heard the words of Solomon, he rejoiced greatly and said, "Blessed be the LORD this day, who has given to David a wise son to be over this great people." 8 And Hiram sent to Solomon, saying, "I have heard the message that you have sent to me. I am ready to do all you desire in the matter of cedar and cypress timber. 9 My servants shall bring it down to the sea from Lebanon, and I will make it into rafts to go by sea to the place you direct. And I will have them broken up there, and you shall receive it. And you shall meet my wishes by providing food for my household." 10 So Hiram supplied Solomon with all the timber of cedar and cypress that he desired, 11 while Solomon gave Hiram 20,000 cors[2] of wheat as food for his household, and 20,000[3] cors of beaten oil. Solomon gave this to Hiram year by year. 12 And the LORD gave Solomon wisdom, as he promised him. And there was peace between Hiram and Solomon, and the two of them made a treaty.

13 King Solomon drafted forced labor out of all Israel, and the draft numbered 30,000 men. 14 And he sent them to Lebanon, 10,000 a month in shifts. They would be a month in Lebanon and two months at home. Adoniram was in charge of the draft. 15 Solomon also had 70,000 burden-bearers and 80,000 stonecutters in the hill country, 16 besides Solomon's 3,300 chief officers who were over the work, who had charge of the people who carried on the work. 17 At the king's command they quarried out great, costly stones in order to lay the foundation of the house with dressed stones. 18 So Solomon's builders and Hiram's builders and the men of Gebal did the cutting and prepared the timber and the stone to build the house.

Solomon Builds the Temple

6 In the four hundred and eightieth year after the people of Israel came out of the land of Egypt, in the fourth year of Solomon's reign over Israel, in the month of Ziv, which is the second month, he began to build the house of the LORD. 2 The house that King Solomon built for the LORD was sixty cubits[4] long, twenty cubits wide, and thirty cubits high. 3 The vestibule in front of the nave of the house was twenty cubits long, equal to the width of the house, and ten cubits deep in front of the house. 4 And he made for the house windows with recessed frames.[5] 5 He also built a structure[6] against the wall of the house, running around the walls of the house, both the nave and the inner sanctuary. And he made side chambers all around. 6 The lowest story[7]

[1] Ch 5:15 in Hebrew [2] A *cor* was about 6 bushels or 220 liters [3] Septuagint; Hebrew *twenty* [4] A *cubit* was about 18 inches or 45 centimeters [5] Or *blocked lattice windows* [6] Or *platform*; also verse 10 [7] Septuagint; Hebrew *structure*, or *platform*

was five cubits broad, the middle one was six cubits broad, and the third was seven cubits broad. For around the outside of the house he made offsets on the wall in order that the supporting beams should not be inserted into the walls of the house.

7 When the house was built, it was with stone prepared at the quarry, so that neither hammer nor axe nor any tool of iron was heard in the house while it was being built.

8 The entrance for the lowest[1] story was on the south side of the house, and one went up by stairs to the middle story, and from the middle story to the third. **9** So he built the house and finished it, and he made the ceiling of the house of beams and planks of cedar. **10** He built the structure against the whole house, five cubits high, and it was joined to the house with timbers of cedar.

11 Now the word of the LORD came to Solomon, **12** "Concerning this house that you are building, if you will walk in my statutes and obey my rules and keep all my commandments and walk in them, then I will establish my word with you, which I spoke to David your father. **13** And I will dwell among the children of Israel and will not forsake my people Israel."

14 So Solomon built the house and finished it. **15** He lined the walls of the house on the inside with boards of cedar. From the floor of the house to the walls of the ceiling, he covered them on the inside with wood, and he covered the floor of the house with boards of cypress. **16** He built twenty cubits of the rear of the house with boards of cedar from the floor to the walls, and he built this within as an inner sanctuary, as the Most Holy Place. **17** The house, that is, the nave in front of the inner sanctuary, was forty cubits long. **18** The cedar within the house was carved in the form of gourds and open flowers. All was cedar; no stone was seen. **19** The inner sanctuary he prepared in the innermost part of the house, to set there the ark of the covenant of the LORD. **20** The inner sanctuary[2] was twenty cubits long, twenty cubits wide, and twenty cubits high, and he overlaid it with pure gold. He also overlaid[3] an altar of cedar. **21** And Solomon overlaid the inside of the house with pure gold, and he drew chains of gold across, in front of the inner sanctuary, and overlaid it with gold. **22** And he overlaid the whole house with gold, until all the house was finished. Also the whole altar that belonged to the inner sanctuary he overlaid with gold.

23 In the inner sanctuary he made two cherubim of olivewood, each ten cubits high. **24** Five cubits was the length of one wing of the cherub, and five cubits the length of the other wing of the cherub; it was ten cubits from the tip of one wing to the tip of the other. **25** The other cherub also measured ten cubits; both cherubim had the same measure and the same form. **26** The height of one cherub was ten cubits, and so was that of the other cherub. **27** He put the cherubim in the innermost part of the house. And the wings of the cherubim were spread out so that a wing of one touched the one wall, and a wing of the other cherub touched the other wall; their other wings touched each other in the middle of the house. **28** And he overlaid the cherubim with gold.

29 Around all the walls of the house he carved engraved figures of cherubim and palm trees and open flowers, in the inner and outer rooms. **30** The floor of the house he overlaid with gold in the inner and outer rooms.

31 For the entrance to the inner sanctuary he made doors of olivewood; the lintel and the doorposts were five-sided.[4] **32** He covered the two doors of olivewood with carvings of cherubim, palm trees, and open flowers. He overlaid them with gold and spread gold on the cherubim and on the palm trees.

[1] Septuagint, Targum; Hebrew *middle* [2] Vulgate; Hebrew *and before the inner sanctuary* [3] Septuagint *made* [4] The meaning of the Hebrew phrase is uncertain

33 So also he made for the entrance to the nave doorposts of olivewood, in the form of a square, 34 and two doors of cypress wood. The two leaves of the one door were folding, and the two leaves of the other door were folding. 35 On them he carved cherubim and palm trees and open flowers, and he overlaid them with gold evenly applied on the carved work. 36 He built the inner court with three courses of cut stone and one course of cedar beams.

37 In the fourth year the foundation of the house of the LORD was laid, in the month of Ziv. 38 And in the eleventh year, in the month of Bul, which is the eighth month, the house was finished in all its parts, and according to all its specifications. He was seven years in building it.

Solomon Builds His Palace

7 Solomon was building his own house thirteen years, and he finished his entire house.

2 He built the House of the Forest of Lebanon. Its length was a hundred cubits[1] and its breadth fifty cubits and its height thirty cubits, and it was built on four[2] rows of cedar pillars, with cedar beams on the pillars. 3 And it was covered with cedar above the chambers that were on the forty-five pillars, fifteen in each row. 4 There were window frames in three rows, and window opposite window in three tiers. 5 All the doorways and windows[3] had square frames, and window was opposite window in three tiers.

6 And he made the Hall of Pillars; its length was fifty cubits, and its breadth thirty cubits. There was a porch in front with pillars, and a canopy in front of them.

7 And he made the Hall of the Throne where he was to pronounce judgment, even the Hall of Judgment. It was finished with cedar from floor to rafters.[4]

8 His own house where he was to dwell, in the other court back of the hall, was of like workmanship. Solomon also made a house like this hall for Pharaoh's daughter whom he had taken in marriage.

9 All these were made of costly stones, cut according to measure, sawed with saws, back and front, even from the foundation to the coping, and from the outside to the great court. 10 The foundation was of costly stones, huge stones, stones of eight and ten cubits. 11 And above were costly stones, cut according to measurement, and cedar. 12 The great court had three courses of cut stone all around, and a course of cedar beams; so had the inner court of the house of the LORD and the vestibule of the house.

The Temple Furnishings

545

13 And King Solomon sent and brought Hiram from Tyre. 14 He was the son of a widow of the tribe of Naphtali, and his father was a man of Tyre, a worker in bronze. And he was full of wisdom, understanding, and skill for making any work in bronze. He came to King Solomon and did all his work.

15 He cast two pillars of bronze. Eighteen cubits was the height of one pillar, and a line of twelve cubits measured its circumference. It was hollow, and its thickness was four fingers. The second pillar was the same.[5] 16 He also made two capitals of cast bronze to set on the tops of the pillars. The height of the one capital was five cubits, and the height of the other capital was five cubits. 17 There were lattices of checker work with wreaths of chain work for the capitals on the tops of the pillars, a lattice[6] for the one capital and a lattice for the other capital. 18 Likewise he made pomegranates[7] in two rows around the one latticework to cover the capital that was on the top of the pillar, and he did the same with the other capital. 19 Now the capitals that were on the tops of the pillars in the vestibule were of lily-work,

[1] A *cubit* was about 18 inches or 45 centimeters [2] Septuagint *three* [3] Septuagint; Hebrew *posts* [4] Syriac, Vulgate; Hebrew *floor* [5] Targum, Syriac (compare Septuagint and Jeremiah 52:21); Hebrew *fingers. And a line of twelve cubits measured the circumference of the second pillar* [6] Septuagint; Hebrew *seven*; twice in this verse [7] Two manuscripts (compare Septuagint); Hebrew *pillars*

Solomon's Temple

Solomon built "the house of the LORD" in Jerusalem on Mount Moriah. It took seven years to build (1 Kings 6:38). The temple itself (not including the chambers, or rooms, on the sides) was 90 feet (27 m) long, 30 feet (9 m) wide, and 45 (14 m) high. It stood in the middle of a court with walls all around it.

Extra chambers, or rooms, were added to three sides of the temple. These chambers were on three levels. The lower chamber was 7.5 feet (2.3 m) wide, the middle chamber was 9 feet (2.7 m) wide, and the upper chamber was 10.5 feet (3.2 m) wide (1 Kings 6:5–6, 8, 10).

The Most Holy Place was a 30-foot (9.1 m) cube (1 Kings 6:15–29; 2 Chronicles 3:8–14). In temples of those times, rooms like this one were often higher than the rest of the building. Two giant golden cherubim stood on each side of the ark, each 15 feet (4.6 m) tall with 15-foot (4.6 m) wingspans (1 Kings 6:23–28). The ark of the covenant stood between the two cherubim (1 Kings 8:1–11; cf. 2 Chronicles 5:2–14).

The Holy Place of the temple was 60 feet (18 m) long and 30 feet (9.1 m) wide (1 Kings 6:17; 2 Chronicles 3:5–7). Inside the Holy Place were the golden altar of incense, the golden table for the bread of the Presence, and 10 golden lampstands, five on the north and five on the south (1 Kings 7:48–49; cf. 2 Chronicles 4:7)

Ten bronze stands on wheels each held a large basin full of water for rinsing off the animal parts that were used in burnt offerings (1 Kings 7:27–38; cf. 2 Chronicles 4:6).

The Holy Place and the Most Holy Place were separated by doors with carvings on them of cherubim, palm trees, and flowers. These doors were completely covered with gold (1 Kings 6:31–32).

The Holy Place had windows (1 Kings 6:4).

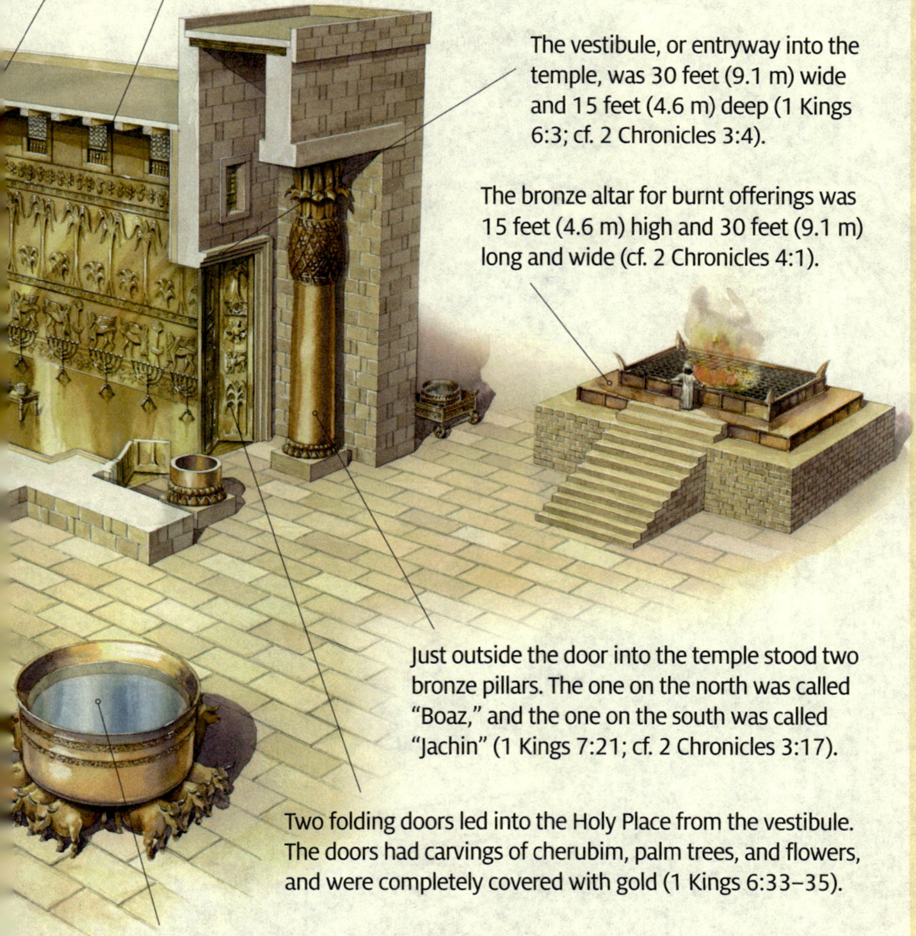

The vestibule, or entryway into the temple, was 30 feet (9.1 m) wide and 15 feet (4.6 m) deep (1 Kings 6:3; cf. 2 Chronicles 3:4).

The bronze altar for burnt offerings was 15 feet (4.6 m) high and 30 feet (9.1 m) long and wide (cf. 2 Chronicles 4:1).

Just outside the door into the temple stood two bronze pillars. The one on the north was called "Boaz," and the one on the south was called "Jachin" (1 Kings 7:21; cf. 2 Chronicles 3:17).

Two folding doors led into the Holy Place from the vestibule. The doors had carvings of cherubim, palm trees, and flowers, and were completely covered with gold (1 Kings 6:33–35).

The "sea" was a large metal basin with water for the priests to wash in. It was 7.5 feet (2.3 m) high and 15 feet (4.6 m) in diameter. It held 12,000 gallons (44,000 liters) of water. The "sea" was held up by twelve bronze oxen in sets of three, facing in each of the four directions (1 Kings 7:23–26; cf. 2 Chronicles 4:2–5).

Solomon Builds the Temple

God gave King Solomon a wise heart just as He had promised, and King Solomon loved God.

Solomon's father, King David, had wanted to build a temple where the people could worship God. But God told David that his son, Solomon, should be the one to build the temple. David collected all the materials so that everything was ready for Solomon to begin building the Temple, according to the Lord's plan.

Solomon enlisted many thousands of workers in his country and in the city of Tyre to do the work. Solomon traded wheat and olive oil from his country for fine logs from Lebanon. In the hill country, thousands of workers cut big, white stone blocks to make the outside walls of the temple. Other workers cut cedar and cypress wood to cover the inside of the walls with fine wood. The temple was 90 feet long, 30 feet wide, and 45 feet high. A large porch went across the front of the temple.

After the large white stones were all in place, Solomon's workers finished the inside rooms of the temple. The Most Holy Place was in the back of the temple, separated by wooden doors covered with gold. The temple's main room was 60 feet long, and was located in front of the Most Holy Place. On all the walls inside the temple, workers carved beautiful pictures of angels, palm trees, and flowers. Then Solomon had the workers cover all the walls and all the floors with pure gold. This would show that the temple was a very special building—the central place for the people of Israel to worship the one true God!

Other workers made curtains, furniture, bowls, and lamps for the temple. All the bowls, lamps, and furniture inside the temple building were also covered with pure gold. The temple was amazingly beautiful—the magnificent house for worshiping the Lord, the great God of Israel.

It took seven years to build the temple. When the temple was completed, King Solomon called the people together, and they brought their best offerings to God. Many sang songs and played musical instruments to praise and thank God.

Then King Solomon stood before the bronze altar in the courtyard—the place where sacrifices would be offered to God—and he began to pray: "O LORD, God of Israel, there is no God like You." Solomon praised God for His great goodness to His people. He asked that God would hear the prayers offered from this temple. Solomon prayed that when the Israelites sinned against God, they would repent and pray toward the temple—and God would hear their prayers and forgive their sin.

The people praised and thanked God for seven days. On the eighth day they went home with joyful hearts for all the goodness that God had shown to King Solomon and to all the people of Israel.

God loves us and is good to us too. He gives us everything we have. God gives us good gifts when we go to church to worship Him. He forgives our sins for Jesus' sake. He talks to us through His Word and answers our prayers. He gives us thankful hearts to praise Him.

SEEK and FIND

WHERE TO FIND THE STORY

1 Kings 5:1–6:38; 7:13–8:66

KEY BIBLE VERSE

"Behold, heaven and the highest heaven cannot contain you; how much less this house that I have built!" (1 Kings 8:27)

THREE KEY QUESTIONS

- What did the inside of the temple look like and what was it made of?
- Why did Solomon use so much gold—even on the floor!—in building the temple?
- What are some of the good gifts that God gives to us?

RELATED BIBLE READINGS

2 Chronicles 2:1–7:22; Acts 7:44–50; Revelation 21:1–4, 22

four cubits. 20 The capitals were on the two
pillars and also above the rounded pro-
jection which was beside the latticework.
There were two hundred pomegranates in
two rows all around, and so with the other
capital. 21 He set up the pillars at the ves-
tibule of the temple. He set up the pillar
on the south and called its name Jachin,
and he set up the pillar on the north and
called its name Boaz. 22 And on the tops of
the pillars was lily-work. Thus the work of
the pillars was finished.

23 Then he made the sea of cast metal.
It was round, ten cubits from brim to
brim, and five cubits high, and a line of
thirty cubits measured its circumfer-
ence. 24 Under its brim were gourds, for
ten cubits, compassing the sea all around.
The gourds were in two rows, cast with
it when it was cast. 25 It stood on twelve
oxen, three facing north, three facing
west, three facing south, and three facing
east. The sea was set on them, and all their
rear parts were inward. 26 Its thickness was
a handbreadth,[1] and its brim was made
like the brim of a cup, like the flower of a
lily. It held two thousand baths.[2]

27 He also made the ten stands of
bronze. Each stand was four cubits long,
four cubits wide, and three cubits high.
28 This was the construction of the stands:
they had panels, and the panels were set
in the frames, 29 and on the panels that
were set in the frames were lions, oxen,
and cherubim. On the frames, both above
and below the lions and oxen, there were
wreaths of beveled work. 30 Moreover,
each stand had four bronze wheels and
axles of bronze, and at the four corners
were supports for a basin. The supports
were cast with wreaths at the side of each.
31 Its opening was within a crown that
projected upward one cubit. Its opening
was round, as a pedestal is made, a cubit
and a half deep. At its opening there were
carvings, and its panels were square, not

[1] A *handbreadth* was about 3 inches or 7.5 centimeters [2] A *bath* was about 6 gallons or 22 liters

round. [32]And the four wheels were under-
neath the panels. The axles of the wheels
were of one piece with the stands, and the
height of a wheel was a cubit and a half.
[33]The wheels were made like a chariot
wheel; their axles, their rims, their spokes,
and their hubs were all cast. [34]There were
four supports at the four corners of each
stand. The supports were of one piece
with the stands. [35]And on the top of the
stand there was a round band half a cubit
high; and on the top of the stand its stays
and its panels were of one piece with it.
[36]And on the surfaces of its stays and on
its panels, he carved cherubim, lions, and
palm trees, according to the space of each,
with wreaths all around. [37]After this man-
ner he made the ten stands. All of them
were cast alike, of the same measure and
the same form.

[38]And he made ten basins of bronze.
Each basin held forty baths, each basin
measured four cubits, and there was a
basin for each of the ten stands. [39]And he
set the stands, five on the south side of the
house, and five on the north side of the
house. And he set the sea at the southeast
corner of the house.

[40]Hiram also made the pots, the shov-
els, and the basins. So Hiram finished all
the work that he did for King Solomon on
the house of the LORD: [41]the two pillars,

Bronze Basins and Stands

In the temple courtyard there were 10 bronze stands on wheels. On each stand was a basin filled with water. There were five of these on the north side and five of them on the south side of the temple. The water in the basins was for rinsing off animal parts that were used in the burnt offerings (1 Kings 7:27–38; 2 Chronicles 4:6). Each stand was 6 feet (1.8 m) long, 6 feet (1.8 m) wide, and 4.5 feet (1.4 m) high. Each basin was 4.5 feet (1.4 m) in diameter and held 240 gallons (909 l) of water.

the two bowls of the capitals that were on the tops of the pillars, and the two latticeworks to cover the two bowls of the capitals that were on the tops of the pillars; 42 and the four hundred pomegranates for the two latticeworks, two rows of pomegranates for each latticework, to cover the two bowls of the capitals that were on the pillars; 43 the ten stands, and the ten basins on the stands; 44 and the one sea, and the twelve oxen underneath the sea.

45 Now the pots, the shovels, and the basins, all these vessels in the house of the LORD, which Hiram made for King Solomon, were of burnished bronze. 46 In the plain of the Jordan the king cast them, in the clay ground between Succoth and Zarethan. 47 And Solomon left all the vessels unweighed, because there were so many of them; the weight of the bronze was not ascertained.

48 So Solomon made all the vessels that were in the house of the LORD: the golden altar, the golden table for the bread of the Presence, 49 the lampstands of pure gold, five on the south side and five on the north, before the inner sanctuary; the flowers, the lamps, and the tongs, of gold; 50 the cups, snuffers, basins, dishes for incense, and fire pans, of pure gold; and the sockets of gold, for the doors of the innermost part of the house, the Most Holy Place, and for the doors of the nave of the temple.

51 Thus all the work that King Solomon did on the house of the LORD was finished. And Solomon brought in the things that David his father had dedicated, the silver, the gold, and the vessels, and stored them in the treasuries of the house of the LORD.

The Ark Brought into the Temple

8 Then Solomon assembled the elders of Israel and all the heads of the tribes, the leaders of the fathers' houses of the people of Israel, before King Solomon in Jerusalem, to bring up the ark of the covenant of the LORD out of the city of David, which is Zion. 2 And all the men of Israel assembled to King Solomon at the feast in the month Ethanim, which is the seventh month. 3 And all the elders of Israel came, and the priests took up the ark. 4 And they brought up the ark of the LORD, the tent of meeting, and all the holy vessels that were in the tent; the priests and the Levites brought them up. 5 And King Solomon and all the congregation of Israel, who had assembled before him, were with him before the ark, sacrificing so many sheep and oxen that they could not be counted or numbered. 6 Then the priests brought the ark of the covenant of the LORD to its place in the inner sanctuary of the house, in the Most Holy Place, underneath the wings of the cherubim. 7 For the cherubim spread out their wings over the place of the ark, so that the cherubim overshadowed the ark and its poles. 8 And the poles were so long that the ends of the poles were seen from the Holy Place before the inner sanctuary; but they could not be seen from outside. And they are there to this day. 9 There was nothing in the ark except the two tablets of stone that Moses put there at Horeb, where the LORD made a covenant with the people of Israel, when they came out of the land of Egypt. 10 And when the priests came out of the Holy Place, a cloud filled the house of the LORD, 11 so that the priests could not stand to minister because of the cloud, for the glory of the LORD filled the house of the LORD.

Solomon Blesses the LORD

499

12 Then Solomon said, "The LORD[1] has said that he would dwell in thick darkness. 13 I have indeed built you an exalted house, a place for you to dwell in forever." 14 Then the king turned around and blessed all the assembly of Israel, while all the assembly of Israel stood. 15 And he said, "Blessed be the LORD, the God of Israel, who with his hand

[1] Septuagint *The LORD has set the sun in the heavens, but*

has fulfilled what he promised with his mouth to David my father, saying, 16 'Since the day that I brought my people Israel out of Egypt, I chose no city out of all the tribes of Israel in which to build a house, that my name might be there. But I chose David to be over my people Israel.' 17 Now it was in the heart of David my father to build a house for the name of the LORD, the God of Israel. 18 But the LORD said to David my father, 'Whereas it was in your heart to build a house for my name, you did well that it was in your heart. 19 Nevertheless, you shall not build the house, but your son who shall be born to you shall build the house for my name.' 20 Now the LORD has fulfilled his promise that he made. For I have risen in the place of David my father, and sit on the throne of Israel, as the LORD promised, and I have built the house for the name of the LORD, the God of Israel. 21 And there I have provided a place for the ark, in which is the covenant of the LORD that he made with our fathers, when he brought them out of the land of Egypt."

Solomon's Prayer of Dedication

22 Then Solomon stood before the altar of the LORD in the presence of all the assembly of Israel and spread out his hands toward heaven, 23 and said, "O LORD, God of Israel, there is no God like you, in heaven above or on earth beneath, keeping covenant and showing steadfast love to your servants who walk before you with all their heart, 24 who have kept with your servant David my father what you declared to him. You spoke with your mouth, and with your hand have fulfilled it this day. 25 Now therefore, O LORD, God of Israel, keep for your servant David my father what you have promised him, saying, 'You shall not lack a man to sit before me on the throne of Israel, if only your sons pay close attention to their way, to walk before me as you have walked before me.' 26 Now therefore, O God of Israel, let your word be confirmed, which you have spoken to your servant David my father.

27 "But will God indeed dwell on the earth? Behold, heaven and the highest heaven cannot contain you; how much less this house that I have built! 28 Yet have regard to the prayer of your servant and to his plea, O LORD my God, listening to the cry and to the prayer that your servant prays before you this day, 29 that your eyes may be open night and day toward this house, the place of which you have said, 'My name shall be there,' that you may listen to the prayer that your servant offers toward this place. 30 And listen to the plea of your servant and of your people Israel, when they pray toward this place. And listen in heaven your dwelling place, and when you hear, forgive.

545

31 "If a man sins against his neighbor and is made to take an oath and comes and swears his oath before your altar in this house, 32 then hear in heaven and act and judge your servants, condemning the guilty by bringing his conduct on his own head, and vindicating the righteous by rewarding him according to his righteousness.

33 "When your people Israel are defeated before the enemy because they have sinned against you, and if they turn again to you and acknowledge your name and pray and plead with you in this house, 34 then hear in heaven and forgive the sin of your people Israel and bring them again to the land that you gave to their fathers.

35 "When heaven is shut up and there is no rain because they have sinned against you, if they pray toward this place and acknowledge your name and turn from their sin, when you afflict them, 36 then hear in heaven and forgive the sin of your servants, your people Israel, when you teach them the good way in which they should walk, and grant rain upon your

land, which you have given to your people
as an inheritance.
37 "If there is famine in the land, if
there is pestilence or blight or mildew
or locust or caterpillar, if their enemy
besieges them in the land at their gates,[1]
whatever plague, whatever sickness there
is, 38 whatever prayer, whatever plea is
made by any man or by all your people
Israel, each knowing the affliction of his
own heart and stretching out his hands
toward this house, 39 then hear in heaven
your dwelling place and forgive and act
and render to each whose heart you know,
according to all his ways (for you, you
only, know the hearts of all the children
of mankind), 40 that they may fear you all
the days that they live in the land that you
gave to our fathers.
41 "Likewise, when a foreigner, who is
not of your people Israel, comes from a far
country for your name's sake 42 (for they
shall hear of your great name and your
mighty hand, and of your outstretched
arm), when he comes and prays toward
this house, 43 hear in heaven your dwelling
place and do according to all for which the
foreigner calls to you, in order that all the
peoples of the earth may know your name
and fear you, as do your people Israel, and
that they may know that this house that I
have built is called by your name.
44 "If your people go out to battle against
their enemy, by whatever way you shall
send them, and they pray to the Lord
toward the city that you have chosen and
the house that I have built for your name,
45 then hear in heaven their prayer and
their plea, and maintain their cause.
46 "If they sin against you—for there
is no one who does not sin—and you
are angry with them and give them to
an enemy, so that they are carried away
captive to the land of the enemy, far off
or near, 47 yet if they turn their heart in
the land to which they have been carried
captive, and repent and plead with you in
the land of their captors, saying, 'We have
sinned and have acted perversely and
wickedly,' 48 if they repent with all their
mind and with all their heart in the land of
their enemies, who carried them captive,
and pray to you toward their land, which
you gave to their fathers, the city that you
have chosen, and the house that I have
built for your name, 49 then hear in heaven
your dwelling place their prayer and their
plea, and maintain their cause 50 and for-
give your people who have sinned against
you, and all their transgressions that they
have committed against you, and grant
them compassion in the sight of those
who carried them captive, that they may
have compassion on them 51 (for they are
your people, and your heritage, which
you brought out of Egypt, from the midst
of the iron furnace). 52 Let your eyes be
open to the plea of your servant and to
the plea of your people Israel, giving ear
to them whenever they call to you. 53 For
you separated them from among all the
peoples of the earth to be your heritage,
as you declared through Moses your ser-
vant, when you brought our fathers out of
Egypt, O Lord God."

Solomon's Benediction

54 Now as Solomon finished offering all
this prayer and plea to the Lord, he arose
from before the altar of the Lord, where
he had knelt with hands outstretched
toward heaven. 55 And he stood and
blessed all the assembly of Israel with a
loud voice, saying, 56 "Blessed be the Lord
who has given rest to his people Israel,
according to all that he promised. Not
one word has failed of all his good prom-
ise, which he spoke by Moses his servant.
57 The Lord our God be with us, as he
was with our fathers. May he not leave us
or forsake us, 58 that he may incline our
hearts to him, to walk in all his ways and
to keep his commandments, his statutes,
and his rules, which he commanded our

[1] Septuagint, Syriac *in any of their cities*

fathers. 59 Let these words of mine, with which I have pleaded before the LORD, be near to the LORD our God day and night, and may he maintain the cause of his servant and the cause of his people Israel, as each day requires, 60 that all the peoples of the earth may know that the LORD is God; there is no other. 61 Let your heart therefore be wholly true to the LORD our God, walking in his statutes and keeping his commandments, as at this day."

Solomon's Sacrifices

62 Then the king, and all Israel with him, offered sacrifice before the LORD. 63 Solomon offered as peace offerings to the LORD 22,000 oxen and 120,000 sheep. So the king and all the people of Israel dedicated the house of the LORD. 64 The same day the king consecrated the middle of the court that was before the house of the LORD, for there he offered the burnt offering and the grain offering and the fat pieces of the peace offerings, because the bronze altar that was before the LORD was too small to receive the burnt offering and the grain offering and the fat pieces of the peace offerings.

65 So Solomon held the feast at that time, and all Israel with him, a great assembly, from Lebo-hamath to the Brook of Egypt, before the LORD our God, seven days.[1] 66 On the eighth day he sent the people away, and they blessed the king and went to their homes joyful and glad of heart for all the goodness that the LORD had shown to David his servant and to Israel his people.

The LORD Appears to Solomon

9 As soon as Solomon had finished building the house of the LORD and the king's house and all that Solomon desired to build, 2 the LORD appeared to Solomon a second time, as he had appeared to him at Gibeon. 3 And the LORD said to him, "I have heard your prayer and your plea, which you have made before me. I have consecrated this house that you have built, by putting my name there forever. My eyes and my heart will be there for all time. 4 And as for you, if you will walk before me, as David your father walked, with integrity of heart and uprightness, doing according to all that I have commanded you, and keeping my statutes and my rules, 5 then I will establish your royal throne over Israel forever, as I promised David your father, saying, 'You shall not lack a man on the throne of Israel.' 6 But if you turn aside from following me, you or your children, and do not keep my commandments and my statutes that I have set before you, but go and serve other gods and worship them, 7 then I will cut off Israel from the land that I have given them, and the house that I have consecrated for my name I will cast out of my sight, and Israel will become a proverb and a byword among all peoples. 8 And this house will become a heap of ruins.[2] Everyone passing by it will be astonished and will hiss, and they will say, 'Why has the LORD done thus to this land and to this house?' 9 Then they will say, 'Because they abandoned the LORD their God who brought their fathers out of the land of Egypt and laid hold on other gods and worshiped them and served them. Therefore the LORD has brought all this disaster on them.'"

Solomon's Other Acts

10 At the end of twenty years, in which Solomon had built the two houses, the house of the LORD and the king's house, 11 and Hiram king of Tyre had supplied Solomon with cedar and cypress timber and gold, as much as he desired, King Solomon gave to Hiram twenty cities in the land of Galilee. 12 But when Hiram came from Tyre to see the cities that Solomon had given him, they did not please him. 13 Therefore he said, "What kind of cities are these that you have given

[1] Septuagint; Hebrew *seven days and seven days, fourteen days* [2] Syriac, Old Latin; Hebrew *will become high*

me, my brother?" So they are called the
land of Cabul to this day. 14 Hiram had sent
to the king 120 talents[1] of gold.
15 And this is the account of the
forced labor that King Solomon drafted
to build the house of the LORD and his
own house and the Millo and the wall
of Jerusalem and Hazor and Megiddo
and Gezer 16 (Pharaoh king of Egypt had
gone up and captured Gezer and burned
it with fire, and had killed the Canaanites
who lived in the city, and had given it as
dowry to his daughter, Solomon's wife;
17 so Solomon rebuilt Gezer) and Lower
Beth-horon 18 and Baalath and Tamar
in the wilderness, in the land of Judah,[2]
19 and all the store cities that Solomon
had, and the cities for his chariots, and
the cities for his horsemen, and whatever
Solomon desired to build in Jerusalem, in
Lebanon, and in all the land of his domin-
ion. 20 All the people who were left of the
Amorites, the Hittites, the Perizzites, the
Hivites, and the Jebusites, who were not
of the people of Israel— 21 their descen-
dants who were left after them in the land,
whom the people of Israel were unable to
devote to destruction[3]—these Solomon
drafted to be slaves, and so they are to this
day. 22 But of the people of Israel Solomon
made no slaves. They were the soldiers,
they were his officials, his commanders,
his captains, his chariot commanders and
his horsemen.
23 These were the chief officers who were
over Solomon's work: 550 who had charge
of the people who carried on the work.
24 But Pharaoh's daughter went up from
the city of David to her own house that
Solomon had built for her. Then he built
the Millo.
25 Three times a year Solomon used to
offer up burnt offerings and peace offer-
ings on the altar that he built to the LORD,
making offerings with it[4] before the LORD.
So he finished the house.
26 King Solomon built a fleet of ships
at Ezion-geber, which is near Eloth on
the shore of the Red Sea, in the land of
Edom. 27 And Hiram sent with the fleet
his servants, seamen who were familiar
with the sea, together with the servants of
Solomon. 28 And they went to Ophir and
brought from there gold, 420 talents, and
they brought it to King Solomon.

The Queen of Sheba

10 Now when the queen of Sheba
heard of the fame of Solomon
concerning the name of the LORD, she
came to test him with hard questions.
2 She came to Jerusalem with a very great
retinue, with camels bearing spices and
very much gold and precious stones. And
when she came to Solomon, she told him
all that was on her mind. 3 And Solomon
answered all her questions; there was
nothing hidden from the king that he
could not explain to her. 4 And when the
queen of Sheba had seen all the wisdom
of Solomon, the house that he had built,
5 the food of his table, the seating of his
officials, and the attendance of his ser-
vants, their clothing, his cupbearers, and
his burnt offerings that he offered at the
house of the LORD, there was no more
breath in her.
6 And she said to the king, "The report
was true that I heard in my own land of
your words and of your wisdom, 7 but I did
not believe the reports until I came and
my own eyes had seen it. And behold, the
half was not told me. Your wisdom and
prosperity surpass the report that I heard.
8 Happy are your men! Happy are your
servants, who continually stand before
you and hear your wisdom! 9 Blessed be
the LORD your God, who has delighted in
you and set you on the throne of Israel!
Because the LORD loved Israel forever, he
has made you king, that you may execute
justice and righteousness." 10 Then she
gave the king 120 talents[5] of gold, and a
very great quantity of spices and precious

[1] A *talent* was about 75 pounds or 34 kilograms [2] Hebrew lacks *of Judah* [3] That is, set apart (devote) as an offering to the Lord (for destruction) [4] Septuagint lacks *with it* [5] A *talent* was about 75 pounds or 34 kilograms

stones. Never again came such an abun-
dance of spices as these that the queen of
Sheba gave to King Solomon.
11 Moreover, the fleet of Hiram, which
brought gold from Ophir, brought from
Ophir a very great amount of almug wood
and precious stones. 12 And the king made
of the almug wood supports for the house
of the LORD and for the king's house, also
lyres and harps for the singers. No such
almug wood has come or been seen to
this day.
13 And King Solomon gave to the queen
of Sheba all that she desired, whatever she
asked besides what was given her by the
bounty of King Solomon. So she turned
and went back to her own land with her
servants.

Solomon's Great Wealth

14 Now the weight of gold that came
to Solomon in one year was 666 talents
of gold, 15 besides that which came from
the explorers and from the business of the
merchants, and from all the kings of the
west and from the governors of the land.
16 King Solomon made 200 large shields
of beaten gold; 600 shekels[1] of gold went
into each shield. 17 And he made 300
shields of beaten gold; three minas[2] of
gold went into each shield. And the king
put them in the House of the Forest of
Lebanon. 18 The king also made a great
ivory throne and overlaid it with the fin-
est gold. 19 The throne had six steps, and
at the back of the throne was a calf's head,
and on each side of the seat were armrests
and two lions standing beside the arm-
rests, 20 while twelve lions stood there,
one on each end of a step on the six steps.
The like of it was never made in any king-
dom. 21 All King Solomon's drinking ves-
sels were of gold, and all the vessels of the
House of the Forest of Lebanon were of
pure gold. None were of silver; silver was
not considered as anything in the days
of Solomon. 22 For the king had a fleet of
ships of Tarshish at sea with the fleet of
Hiram. Once every three years the fleet of
ships of Tarshish used to come bringing
gold, silver, ivory, apes, and peacocks.[3]
23 Thus King Solomon excelled all the
kings of the earth in riches and in wis-
dom. 24 And the whole earth sought the
presence of Solomon to hear his wisdom,
which God had put into his mind. 25 Every
one of them brought his present, arti-
cles of silver and gold, garments, myrrh,
spices, horses, and mules, so much year
by year.
26 And Solomon gathered together char-
iots and horsemen. He had 1,400 chariots
and 12,000 horsemen, whom he stationed
in the chariot cities and with the king in
Jerusalem. 27 And the king made silver as
common in Jerusalem as stone, and he
made cedar as plentiful as the sycamore of
the Shephelah. 28 And Solomon's import
of horses was from Egypt and Kue, and the
king's traders received them from Kue at a
price. 29 A chariot could be imported from
Egypt for 600 shekels of silver and a horse
for 150, and so through the king's traders
they were exported to all the kings of the
Hittites and the kings of Syria.

Solomon Turns from the LORD

11 Now King Solomon loved many
foreign women, along with the
daughter of Pharaoh: Moabite, Ammonite,
Edomite, Sidonian, and Hittite women,
2 from the nations concerning which the
LORD had said to the people of Israel, "You
shall not enter into marriage with them,
neither shall they with you, for surely
they will turn away your heart after their
gods." Solomon clung to these in love.
3 He had 700 wives, princesses, and 300
concubines. And his wives turned away
his heart. 4 For when Solomon was old his
wives turned away his heart after other
gods, and his heart was not wholly true
to the LORD his God, as was the heart of
David his father. 5 For Solomon went after

[1] A *shekel* was about 2/5 ounce or 11 grams [2] A *mina* was about 1 1/4 pounds or 0.6 kilogram [3] Or *baboons*

Ashtoreth the goddess of the Sidonians, and after Milcom the abomination of the Ammonites. 6 So Solomon did what was evil in the sight of the LORD and did not wholly follow the LORD, as David his father had done. 7 Then Solomon built a high place for Chemosh the abomination of Moab, and for Molech the abomination of the Ammonites, on the mountain east of Jerusalem. 8 And so he did for all his foreign wives, who made offerings and sacrificed to their gods.

The LORD Raises Adversaries

9 And the LORD was angry with
Solomon, because his heart had
499 turned away from the LORD, the
God of Israel, who had appeared to him twice 10 and had commanded him concerning this thing, that he should not go after other gods. But he did not keep what the LORD commanded. 11 Therefore the LORD said to Solomon, "Since this has been your practice and you have not kept my covenant and my statutes that I have commanded you, I will surely tear the kingdom from you and will give it to your servant. 12 Yet for the sake of David your father I will not do it in your days, but I will tear it out of the hand of your son. 13 However, I will not tear away all the kingdom, but I will give one tribe to your son, for the sake of David my servant and for the sake of Jerusalem that I have chosen."

14 And the LORD raised up an adversary against Solomon, Hadad the Edomite. He was of the royal house in Edom. 15 For when David was in Edom, and Joab the commander of the army went up to bury the slain, he struck down every male in Edom 16 (for Joab and all Israel remained there six months, until he had cut off every male in Edom). 17 But Hadad fled to Egypt, together with certain Edomites of his father's servants, Hadad still being a little child. 18 They set out from Midian and came to Paran and took men with them from Paran and came to Egypt, to Pharaoh king of Egypt, who gave him a house and assigned him an allowance of food and gave him land. 19 And Hadad found great favor in the sight of Pharaoh, so that he gave him in marriage the sister of his own wife, the sister of Tahpenes the queen. 20 And the sister of Tahpenes bore him Genubath his son, whom Tahpenes weaned in Pharaoh's house. And Genubath was in Pharaoh's house among the sons of Pharaoh. 21 But when Hadad heard in Egypt that David slept with his fathers and that Joab the commander of the army was dead, Hadad said to Pharaoh, "Let me depart, that I may go to my own country." 22 But Pharaoh said to him, "What have you lacked with me that you are now seeking to go to your own country?" And he said to him, "Only let me depart."

23 God also raised up as an adversary to him, Rezon the son of Eliada, who had fled from his master Hadadezer king of Zobah. 24 And he gathered men about him and became leader of a marauding band, after the killing by David. And they went to Damascus and lived there and made him king in Damascus. 25 He was an adversary of Israel all the days of Solomon, doing harm as Hadad did. And he loathed Israel and reigned over Syria.

26 Jeroboam the son of Nebat, an Ephraimite of Zeredah, a servant of Solomon, whose mother's name was Zeruah, a widow, also lifted up his hand against the king. 27 And this was the reason why he lifted up his hand against the king. Solomon built the Millo, and closed up the breach of the city of David his father. 28 The man Jeroboam was very able, and when Solomon saw that the young man was industrious he gave him charge over all the forced labor of the house of Joseph. 29 And at that time, when Jeroboam went out of Jerusalem,

the prophet Ahijah the Shilonite found him on the road. Now Ahijah had dressed himself in a new garment, and the two of them were alone in the open country.
[30]Then Ahijah laid hold of the new garment that was on him, and tore it into twelve pieces.
[31]And he said to Jeroboam, "Take for yourself ten pieces, for thus says the LORD, the God of Israel, 'Behold, I am about to tear the kingdom from the hand of Solomon and will give you ten tribes
[32](but he shall have one tribe, for the sake of my servant David and for the sake of Jerusalem, the city that I have chosen out of all the tribes of Israel),
[33]because they have[1] forsaken me and worshiped Ashtoreth the goddess of the Sidonians, Chemosh the god of Moab, and Milcom the god of the Ammonites, and they have not walked in my ways, doing what is right in my sight and keeping my statutes and my rules, as David his father did.
[34]Nevertheless, I will not take the whole kingdom out of his hand, but I will make him ruler all the days of his life, for the sake of David my servant whom I chose, who kept my commandments and my statutes.
[35]But I will take the kingdom out of his son's hand and will give it to you, ten tribes.
[36]Yet to his son I will give one tribe, that David my servant may always have a lamp before me in Jerusalem, the city where I have chosen to put my name.
[37]And I will take you, and you shall reign over all that your soul desires, and you shall be king over Israel.
[38]And if you will listen to all that I command you, and will walk in my ways, and do what is right in my eyes by keeping my statutes and my commandments, as David my servant did, I will be with you and will build you a sure house, as I built for David, and I will give Israel to you.
[39]And I will afflict the offspring of David because of this, but not forever.'"
[40]Solomon sought therefore to kill Jeroboam. But Jeroboam arose and fled into Egypt, to Shishak king of Egypt, and was in Egypt until the death of Solomon.

[41]Now the rest of the acts of Solomon, and all that he did, and his wisdom, are they not written in the Book of the Acts of Solomon?
[42]And the time that Solomon reigned in Jerusalem over all Israel was forty years.
[43]And Solomon slept with his fathers and was buried in the city of David his father. And Rehoboam his son reigned in his place.

Rehoboam's Folly

12 Rehoboam went to Shechem, for all Israel had come to Shechem to make him king.
[2]And as soon as Jeroboam the son of Nebat heard of it (for he was still in Egypt, where he had fled from King Solomon), then Jeroboam returned from[2] Egypt.
[3]And they sent and called him, and Jeroboam and all the assembly of Israel came and said to Rehoboam,
[4]"Your father made our yoke heavy. Now therefore lighten the hard service of your father and his heavy yoke on us, and we will serve you."
[5]He said to them, "Go away for three days, then come again to me." So the people went away.

[6]Then King Rehoboam took counsel with the old men, who had stood before Solomon his father while he was yet alive, saying, "How do you advise me to answer this people?"
[7]And they said to him, "If you will be a servant to this people today and serve them, and speak good words to them when you answer them, then they will be your servants forever."
[8]But he abandoned the counsel that the old men gave him and took counsel with the young men who had grown up with him and stood before him.
[9]And he said to them, "What do you advise that we answer this people who have said to me, 'Lighten the yoke that your father put on us'?"
[10]And the young men who had grown up with him said to him, "Thus shall you speak to this people who said to

[1] Septuagint, Syriac, Vulgate *he has*; twice in this verse [2] Septuagint, Vulgate (compare 2 Chronicles 10:2); Hebrew *lived in*

you, 'Your father made our yoke heavy, but you lighten it for us,' thus shall you say to them, 'My little finger is thicker than my father's thighs. 11 And now, whereas my father laid on you a heavy yoke, I will add to your yoke. My father disciplined you with whips, but I will discipline you with scorpions.'"

12 So Jeroboam and all the people came to Rehoboam the third day, as the king said, "Come to me again the third day." 13 And the king answered the people harshly, and forsaking the counsel that the old men had given him, 14 he spoke to them according to the counsel of the young men, saying, "My father made your yoke heavy, but I will add to your yoke. My father disciplined you with whips, but I will discipline you with scorpions." 15 So the king did not listen to the people, for it was a turn of affairs brought about by the LORD that he might fulfill his word, which the LORD spoke by Ahijah the Shilonite to Jeroboam the son of Nebat.

The Kingdom Divided

16 And when all Israel saw that the king did not listen to them, the people answered the king, "What portion do we have in David? We have no inheritance in the son of Jesse. To your tents, O Israel! Look now to your own house, David." So Israel went to their tents. 17 But Rehoboam reigned over the people of Israel who lived in the cities of Judah. 18 Then King Rehoboam sent Adoram, who was taskmaster over the forced labor, and all Israel stoned him to death with stones. And King Rehoboam hurried to mount his chariot to flee to Jerusalem. 19 So Israel has been in rebellion against the house of David to this day. 20 And when all Israel heard that Jeroboam had returned, they sent and called him to the assembly and made him king over all Israel. There was none that followed the house of David but the tribe of Judah only.

21 When Rehoboam came to Jerusalem, he assembled all the house of Judah and the tribe of Benjamin, 180,000 chosen warriors, to fight against the house of Israel, to restore the kingdom to Rehoboam the son of Solomon. 22 But the word of God came to Shemaiah the man of God: 23 "Say to Rehoboam the son of Solomon, king of Judah, and to all the house of Judah and Benjamin, and to the rest of the people, 24 'Thus says the LORD, You shall not go up or fight against your relatives the people of Israel. Every man return to his home, for this thing is from me.'" So they listened to the word of the LORD and went home again, according to the word of the LORD.

CHARACTER PROFILE

REHOBOAM

Rehoboam was king of Israel after Solomon. When the people asked him to be less harsh than Solomon had been, he told them he would be even harsher. This caused the kingdom to divide into two separate kingdoms. Ten tribes chose a different king and formed the northern kingdom of "Israel." Rehoboam's smaller kingdom was called "Judah."

Jeroboam's Golden Calves

25 Then Jeroboam built Shechem in the hill country of Ephraim and lived there. And he went out from there and built Penuel. 26 And Jeroboam said in his heart, "Now the kingdom will turn back to the house of David. 27 If this people go up to offer sacrifices in the temple of the LORD at Jerusalem, then the heart of this people will turn again to their lord, to Rehoboam king of Judah, and they will kill me and return to Rehoboam king of Judah." 28 So the king took counsel and made two calves of gold. And he said to the people, "You have gone up to Jerusalem long enough. Behold your gods, O Israel, who brought you up out of the land of Egypt." 29 And he set one in Bethel, and the other he put in Dan. 30 Then this thing became a sin, for the people went as far as Dan to be before one.[1] 31 He also made temples on high places and appointed priests from among all the people, who were not of the Levites. 32 And Jeroboam appointed a feast on the fifteenth day of the eighth month like the feast that was in Judah, and he offered sacrifices on the altar. So he did in Bethel, sacrificing to the calves that he made. And he placed in Bethel the priests of the high places that he had made. 33 He went up to the altar that he had made in Bethel on the fifteenth day in the eighth month, in the month that he had devised from his own heart. And he instituted a feast for the people of Israel and went up to the altar to make offerings.

A Man of God Confronts Jeroboam

13 And behold, a man of God came out of Judah by the word of the LORD to Bethel. Jeroboam was standing by the altar to make offerings. 2 And the man cried against the altar by the word of the LORD and said, "O altar, altar, thus says the LORD: 'Behold, a son shall be born to the house of David, Josiah by name, and he shall sacrifice on you the priests of the high places who make offerings on you, and human bones shall be burned on you.'" 3 And he gave a sign the same day, saying, "This is the sign that the LORD has spoken: 'Behold, the altar shall be torn down, and the ashes that are on it shall be poured out.'" 4 And when the king heard the saying of the man of God, which he cried against the altar at Bethel, Jeroboam stretched out his hand from the altar, saying, "Seize him." And his hand, which he stretched out against him, dried up, so that he could not draw it back to himself. 5 The altar also was torn down, and the ashes poured out from the altar, according to the sign that the man of God had given by the word of the LORD. 6 And the king said to the man of God, "Entreat now the favor of the LORD your God, and pray for me, that my hand may be restored to me." And the man of God entreated the LORD, and the king's hand was restored to him and became as it was before. 7 And the king said to the man of God, "Come home with me, and refresh yourself, and I will give you a reward." 8 And the man of God said to the king, "If you give me half your house, I will not go in with you. And I will not eat bread or drink water in this place, 9 for so was it commanded me by the word of the LORD, saying, 'You shall neither eat bread nor drink water nor return by the way that you came.'" 10 So he went another way and did not return by the way that he came to Bethel.

The Prophet's Disobedience

11 Now an old prophet lived in Bethel. And his sons[2] came and told him all that the man of God had done that day in Bethel. They also told to their father the words that he had spoken to the king. 12 And their father said to them, "Which way did he go?" And his sons showed him the way that the man of God who came from Judah had gone. 13 And he said to his sons, "Saddle the donkey for me." So they saddled the donkey for him and he

[1] Septuagint *went to the one at Bethel and to the other as far as Dan* [2] Septuagint, Syriac, Vulgate; Hebrew *son*

mounted it. 14 And he went after the man of God and found him sitting under an oak. And he said to him, "Are you the man of God who came from Judah?" And he said, "I am." 15 Then he said to him, "Come home with me and eat bread." 16 And he said, "I may not return with you, or go in with you, neither will I eat bread nor drink water with you in this place, 17 for it was said to me by the word of the LORD, 'You shall neither eat bread nor drink water there, nor return by the way that you came.'" 18 And he said to him, "I also am a prophet as you are, and an angel spoke to me by the word of the LORD, saying, 'Bring him back with you into your house that he may eat bread and drink water.'" But he lied to him. 19 So he went back with him and ate bread in his house and drank water.

20 And as they sat at the table, the word of the LORD came to the prophet who had brought him back. 21 And he cried to the man of God who came from Judah, "Thus says the LORD, 'Because you have disobeyed the word of the LORD and have not kept the command that the LORD your God commanded you, 22 but have come back and have eaten bread and drunk water in the place of which he said to you, "Eat no bread and drink no water," your body shall not come to the tomb of your fathers.'" 23 And after he had eaten bread and drunk, he saddled the donkey for the prophet whom he had brought back. 24 And as he went away a lion met him on the road and killed him. And his body was thrown in the road, and the donkey stood beside it; the lion also stood beside the body. 25 And behold, men passed by and saw the body thrown in the road and the lion standing by the body. And they came and told it in the city where the old prophet lived.

26 And when the prophet who had brought him back from the way heard of it, he said, "It is the man of God who disobeyed the word of the LORD; therefore the LORD has given him to the lion, which has torn him and killed him, according to the word that the LORD spoke to him." 27 And he said to his sons, "Saddle the donkey for me." And they saddled it. 28 And he went and found his body thrown in the road, and the donkey and the lion standing beside the body. The lion had not eaten the body or torn the donkey. 29 And the prophet took up the body of the man of God and laid it on the donkey and brought it back to the city[1] to mourn and to bury him. 30 And he laid the body in his own grave. And they mourned over him, saying, "Alas, my brother!" 31 And after he had buried him, he said to his sons, "When I die, bury me in the grave in which the man of God is buried; lay my bones beside his bones. 32 For the saying that he called out by the word of the LORD against the altar in Bethel and against all the houses of the high places that are in the cities of Samaria shall surely come to pass."

33 After this thing Jeroboam did not turn from his evil way, but made priests for the high places again from among all the people. Any who would, he ordained to be priests of the high places. 34 And this thing became sin to the house of Jeroboam, so as to cut it off and to destroy it from the face of the earth.

Prophecy Against Jeroboam

14 At that time Abijah the son of Jeroboam fell sick. 2 And Jeroboam said to his wife, "Arise, and disguise yourself, that it not be known that you are the wife of Jeroboam, and go to Shiloh. Behold, Ahijah the prophet is there, who said of me that I should be king over this people. 3 Take with you ten loaves, some cakes, and a jar of honey, and go to him. He will tell you what shall happen to the child."

4 Jeroboam's wife did so. She arose and went to Shiloh and came to the house of Ahijah. Now Ahijah could not see, for his

[1] Septuagint; Hebrew *he came to the city of the old prophet*

eyes were dim because of his age. 5 And
the LORD said to Ahijah, "Behold, the wife
of Jeroboam is coming to inquire of you
concerning her son, for he is sick. Thus
and thus shall you say to her."

When she came, she pretended to be
another woman. 6 But when Ahijah heard
the sound of her feet, as she came in at the
door, he said, "Come in, wife of Jeroboam.
Why do you pretend to be another? For
I am charged with unbearable news for
you. 7 Go, tell Jeroboam, 'Thus says the
LORD, the God of Israel: "Because I exalted
you from among the people and made you
leader over my people Israel 8 and tore the
kingdom away from the house of David
and gave it to you, and yet you have not
been like my servant David, who kept
my commandments and followed me
with all his heart, doing only that which
was right in my eyes, 9 but you have done
evil above all who were before you and
have gone and made for yourself other
gods and metal images, provoking me
to anger, and have cast me behind your
back, 10 therefore behold, I will bring harm
upon the house of Jeroboam and will cut
off from Jeroboam every male, both bond
and free in Israel, and will burn up the
house of Jeroboam, as a man burns up
dung until it is all gone. 11 Anyone belong-
ing to Jeroboam who dies in the city the
dogs shall eat, and anyone who dies in
the open country the birds of the heav-
ens shall eat, for the LORD has spoken it."'
12 Arise therefore, go to your house. When
your feet enter the city, the child shall
die. 13 And all Israel shall mourn for him
and bury him, for he only of Jeroboam
shall come to the grave, because in him
there is found something pleasing to the
LORD, the God of Israel, in the house of
Jeroboam. 14 Moreover, the LORD will raise
up for himself a king over Israel who shall
cut off the house of Jeroboam today. And
henceforth, 15 the LORD will strike Israel as
a reed is shaken in the water, and root up
Israel out of this good land that he gave to
their fathers and scatter them beyond the
Euphrates, because they have made their
Asherim, provoking the LORD to anger.
16 And he will give Israel up because of the
sins of Jeroboam, which he sinned and
made Israel to sin."

17 Then Jeroboam's wife arose and
departed and came to Tirzah. And as she
came to the threshold of the house, the
child died. 18 And all Israel buried him and
mourned for him, according to the word
of the LORD, which he spoke by his servant
Ahijah the prophet.

The Death of Jeroboam

19 Now the rest of the acts of Jeroboam,
how he warred and how he reigned,

CHARACTER PROFILE

JEROBOAM

Jeroboam set up a rebel kingdom in the north, splitting the kingdom of Israel. Ten tribes followed him and were called "Israel." Two tribes stayed with King Rehoboam and were called "Judah." Jeroboam set up idols throughout all of Israel. The northern kingdom of Israel worshiped idols until it was destroyed.

behold, they are written in the Book of
the Chronicles of the Kings of Israel.
20 And the time that Jeroboam reigned
was twenty-two years. And he slept with
his fathers, and Nadab his son reigned in
his place.

Rehoboam Reigns in Judah

21 Now Rehoboam the son of Solomon
reigned in Judah. Rehoboam was forty-
one years old when he began to reign, and
he reigned seventeen years in Jerusalem,
the city that the LORD had chosen out of
all the tribes of Israel, to put his name
there. His mother's name was Naamah
the Ammonite. 22 And Judah did what was
evil in the sight of the LORD, and they pro-
voked him to jealousy with their sins that
they committed, more than all that their
fathers had done. 23 For they also built for
themselves high places and pillars and
Asherim on every high hill and under
every green tree, 24 and there were also
male cult prostitutes in the land. They did
according to all the abominations of the
nations that the LORD drove out before the
people of Israel.

25 In the fifth year of King Rehoboam,
Shishak king of Egypt came up against
Jerusalem. 26 He took away the treasures
of the house of the LORD and the treasures
of the king's house. He took away every-
thing. He also took away all the shields of
gold that Solomon had made, 27 and King
Rehoboam made in their place shields of
bronze, and committed them to the hands
of the officers of the guard, who kept the
door of the king's house. 28 And as often as
the king went into the house of the LORD,
the guard carried them and brought them
back to the guardroom.

29 Now the rest of the acts of Rehoboam
and all that he did, are they not written in
the Book of the Chronicles of the Kings
of Judah? 30 And there was war between
Rehoboam and Jeroboam continually.
31 And Rehoboam slept with his fathers
and was buried with his fathers in the
city of David. His mother's name was
Naamah the Ammonite. And Abijam his
son reigned in his place.

Abijam Reigns in Judah

15 Now in the eighteenth year of
King Jeroboam the son of Nebat,
Abijam began to reign over Judah. 2 He
reigned for three years in Jerusalem. His
mother's name was Maacah the daughter
of Abishalom. 3 And he walked in all the
sins that his father did before him, and
his heart was not wholly true to the LORD
his God, as the heart of David his father.
4 Nevertheless, for David's sake the LORD
his God gave him a lamp in Jerusalem,
setting up his son after him, and estab-
lishing Jerusalem, 5 because David did
what was right in the eyes of the LORD
and did not turn aside from anything
that he commanded him all the days of
his life, except in the matter of Uriah the
Hittite. 6 Now there was war between
Rehoboam and Jeroboam all the days of
his life. 7 The rest of the acts of Abijam
and all that he did, are they not written
in the Book of the Chronicles of the Kings
of Judah? And there was war between
Abijam and Jeroboam. 8 And Abijam slept
with his fathers, and they buried him in
the city of David. And Asa his son reigned
in his place.

Asa Reigns in Judah

9 In the twentieth year of Jeroboam
king of Israel, Asa began to reign over
Judah, 10 and he reigned forty-one years
in Jerusalem. His mother's name was
Maacah the daughter of Abishalom.
11 And Asa did what was right in the eyes
of the LORD, as David his father had done.
12 He put away the male cult prostitutes
out of the land and removed all the idols
that his fathers had made. 13 He also
removed Maacah his mother from being
queen mother because she had made an
abominable image for Asherah. And Asa

cut down her image and burned it at the
brook Kidron. 14 But the high places were
not taken away. Nevertheless, the heart of
Asa was wholly true to the LORD all his
days. 15 And he brought into the house of
the LORD the sacred gifts of his father and
his own sacred gifts, silver, and gold, and
vessels.

16 And there was war between Asa
and Baasha king of Israel all their days.
17 Baasha king of Israel went up against
Judah and built Ramah, that he might
permit no one to go out or come in to
Asa king of Judah. 18 Then Asa took all the
silver and the gold that were left in the
treasures of the house of the LORD and
the treasures of the king's house and gave
them into the hands of his servants. And
King Asa sent them to Ben-hadad the son
of Tabrimmon, the son of Hezion, king
of Syria, who lived in Damascus, saying,
19 "Let there be a covenant[1] between me
and you, as there was between my father
and your father. Behold, I am sending to
you a present of silver and gold. Go, break
your covenant with Baasha king of Israel,
that he may withdraw from me." 20 And
Ben-hadad listened to King Asa and sent
the commanders of his armies against the
cities of Israel and conquered Ijon, Dan,
Abel-beth-maacah, and all Chinneroth,
with all the land of Naphtali. 21 And when
Baasha heard of it, he stopped building
Ramah, and he lived in Tirzah. 22 Then
King Asa made a proclamation to all
Judah, none was exempt, and they car-
ried away the stones of Ramah and its
timber, with which Baasha had been
building, and with them King Asa built
Geba of Benjamin and Mizpah. 23 Now the
rest of all the acts of Asa, all his might,
and all that he did, and the cities that he
built, are they not written in the Book
of the Chronicles of the Kings of Judah?
But in his old age he was diseased in his
feet. 24 And Asa slept with his fathers and
was buried with his fathers in the city of
David his father, and Jehoshaphat his son
reigned in his place.

Nadab Reigns in Israel

25 Nadab the son of Jeroboam began to
reign over Israel in the second year of Asa
king of Judah, and he reigned over Israel
two years. 26 He did what was evil in the
sight of the LORD and walked in the way
of his father, and in his sin which he made
Israel to sin.

27 Baasha the son of Ahijah, of the house
of Issachar, conspired against him. And
Baasha struck him down at Gibbethon,
which belonged to the Philistines, for
Nadab and all Israel were laying siege to
Gibbethon. 28 So Baasha killed him in the
third year of Asa king of Judah and reigned
in his place. 29 And as soon as he was
king, he killed all the house of Jeroboam.
He left to the house of Jeroboam not one
that breathed, until he had destroyed it,
according to the word of the LORD that he
spoke by his servant Ahijah the Shilonite.
30 It was for the sins of Jeroboam that he
sinned and that he made Israel to sin,
and because of the anger to which he pro-
voked the LORD, the God of Israel.

31 Now the rest of the acts of Nadab and
all that he did, are they not written in the
Book of the Chronicles of the Kings of
Israel? 32 And there was war between Asa
and Baasha king of Israel all their days.

Baasha Reigns in Israel

33 In the third year of Asa king of Judah,
Baasha the son of Ahijah began to reign
over all Israel at Tirzah, and he reigned
twenty-four years. 34 He did what was evil
in the sight of the LORD and walked in the
way of Jeroboam and in his sin which he
made Israel to sin.

16 And the word of the LORD came
to Jehu the son of Hanani against
Baasha, saying, 2 "Since I exalted you out
of the dust and made you leader over
my people Israel, and you have walked
in the way of Jeroboam and have made

[1] Or *treaty*; twice in this verse

my people Israel to sin, provoking me to anger with their sins, 3 behold, I will utterly sweep away Baasha and his house, and I will make your house like the house of Jeroboam the son of Nebat. 4 Anyone belonging to Baasha who dies in the city the dogs shall eat, and anyone of his who dies in the field the birds of the heavens shall eat."

5 Now the rest of the acts of Baasha and what he did, and his might, are they not written in the Book of the Chronicles of the Kings of Israel? 6 And Baasha slept with his fathers and was buried at Tirzah, and Elah his son reigned in his place. 7 Moreover, the word of the LORD came by the prophet Jehu the son of Hanani against Baasha and his house, both because of all the evil that he did in the sight of the LORD, provoking him to anger with the work of his hands, in being like the house of Jeroboam, and also because he destroyed it.

Elah Reigns in Israel

8 In the twenty-sixth year of Asa king of Judah, Elah the son of Baasha began to reign over Israel in Tirzah, and he reigned two years. 9 But his servant Zimri, commander of half his chariots, conspired against him. When he was at Tirzah, drinking himself drunk in the house of Arza, who was over the household in Tirzah, 10 Zimri came in and struck him down and killed him, in the twenty-seventh year of Asa king of Judah, and reigned in his place.

11 When he began to reign, as soon as he had seated himself on his throne, he struck down all the house of Baasha. He did not leave him a single male of his relatives or his friends. 12 Thus Zimri destroyed all the house of Baasha, according to the word of the LORD, which he spoke against Baasha by Jehu the prophet, 13 for all the sins of Baasha and the sins of Elah his son, which they sinned and which they made Israel to sin, provoking the LORD God of Israel to anger with their idols. 14 Now the rest of the acts of Elah and all that he did, are they not written in the Book of the Chronicles of the Kings of Israel?

Zimri Reigns in Israel

15 In the twenty-seventh year of Asa king of Judah, Zimri reigned seven days in Tirzah. Now the troops were encamped against Gibbethon, which belonged to the Philistines, 16 and the troops who were encamped heard it said, "Zimri has conspired, and he has killed the king." Therefore all Israel made Omri, the commander of the army, king over Israel that day in the camp. 17 So Omri went up from Gibbethon, and all Israel with him, and they besieged Tirzah. 18 And when Zimri saw that the city was taken, he went into the citadel of the king's house and burned the king's house over him with fire and died, 19 because of his sins that he committed, doing evil in the sight of the LORD, walking in the way of Jeroboam, and for his sin which he committed, making Israel to sin. 20 Now the rest of the acts of Zimri, and the conspiracy that he made, are they not written in the Book of the Chronicles of the Kings of Israel?

Omri Reigns in Israel

21 Then the people of Israel were divided into two parts. Half of the people followed Tibni the son of Ginath, to make him king, and half followed Omri. 22 But the people who followed Omri overcame the people who followed Tibni the son of Ginath. So Tibni died, and Omri became king. 23 In the thirty-first year of Asa king of Judah, Omri began to reign over Israel, and he reigned for twelve years; six years he reigned in Tirzah. 24 He bought the hill of Samaria from Shemer for two talents[1] of silver, and he fortified the hill and called the name of the city that he built Samaria, after the name of Shemer, the owner of the hill.

[1] A *talent* was about 75 pounds or 34 kilograms

25 Omri did what was evil in the sight of the LORD, and did more evil than all who were before him. 26 For he walked in all the way of Jeroboam the son of Nebat, and in the sins that he made Israel to sin, provoking the LORD, the God of Israel, to anger by their idols. 27 Now the rest of the acts of Omri that he did, and the might that he showed, are they not written in the Book of the Chronicles of the Kings of Israel? 28 And Omri slept with his fathers and was buried in Samaria, and Ahab his son reigned in his place.

Ahab Reigns in Israel

29 In the thirty-eighth year of Asa king of Judah, Ahab the son of Omri began to reign over Israel, and Ahab the son of Omri reigned over Israel in Samaria twenty-two years. 30 And Ahab the son of Omri did evil in the sight of the LORD, more than all who were before him. 31 And as if it had been a light thing for him to walk in the sins of Jeroboam the son of Nebat, he took for his wife Jezebel the daughter of Ethbaal king of the Sidonians, and went and served Baal and worshiped him. 32 He erected an altar for Baal in the house of Baal, which he built in Samaria. 33 And Ahab made an Asherah. Ahab did more to provoke the LORD, the God of Israel, to anger than all the kings of Israel who were before him. 34 In his days Hiel of Bethel built Jericho. He laid its foundation at the cost of Abiram his firstborn, and set up its gates at the cost of his youngest son Segub, according to the word of the LORD, which he spoke by Joshua the son of Nun.

CHARACTER PROFILE

AHAB AND JEZEBEL

Ahab and Jezebel were a wicked king and queen in Israel. They taught the Israelites to worship a false god called Baal. Ahab and Jezebel killed many of God's prophets. Ahab wanted to steal the vineyard of a man named Naboth, so Jezebel had Naboth killed. God promised that Ahab and Jezebel would be severely punished.

567, 573

Elijah Predicts a Drought

567

17 Now Elijah the Tishbite, of Tishbe[1] in Gilead, said to Ahab, "As the LORD, the God of Israel, lives, before whom I stand, there shall be neither dew nor rain these years, except by my word." 2 And the word of the LORD came to him: 3 "Depart from here and turn eastward and hide yourself by the brook Cherith, which is east of the Jordan. 4 You shall drink from the brook, and I have commanded the ravens to feed you there." 5 So he went and did according to the word of the LORD. He went and lived by the brook Cherith that is east of the Jordan. 6 And the ravens brought him bread and meat in the morning, and bread and meat in the evening, and he drank from the brook. 7 And after a while the brook dried up, because there was no rain in the land.

The Widow of Zarephath

1459

8 Then the word of the LORD came to him, 9 "Arise, go to Zarephath, which belongs to Sidon, and dwell there. Behold, I have commanded a widow there to feed you." 10 So he arose and went

[1] Septuagint; Hebrew *of the settlers*

to Zarephath. And when he came to the gate of the city, behold, a widow was there gathering sticks. And he called to her and said, "Bring me a little water in a vessel, that I may drink." 11 And as she was going to bring it, he called to her and said, "Bring me a morsel of bread in your hand." 12 And she said, "As the LORD your God lives, I have nothing baked, only a handful of flour in a jar and a little oil in a jug. And now I am gathering a couple of sticks that I may go in and prepare it for myself and my son, that we may eat it and die." 13 And Elijah said to her, "Do not fear; go and do as you have said. But first make me a little cake of it and bring it to me, and afterward make something for yourself and your son. 14 For thus says the LORD, the God of Israel, 'The jar of flour shall not be spent, and the jug of oil shall not be empty, until the day that the LORD sends rain upon the earth.'" 15 And she went and did as Elijah said. And she and he and her household ate for many days. 16 The jar of flour was not spent, neither did the jug of oil become empty, according to the word of the LORD that he spoke by Elijah.

Elijah Raises the Widow's Son

17 After this the son of the woman, the mistress of the house, became ill. And his illness was so severe that there was no breath left in him. 18 And she said to Elijah, "What have you against me, O man of God? You have come to me to bring my sin to remembrance and to cause the death of my son!" 19 And he said to her, "Give me your son." And he took him from her arms and carried him up into the upper chamber where he lodged, and laid him on his own bed. 20 And he cried to the LORD, "O LORD my God, have you brought calamity even upon the widow with whom I sojourn, by killing her son?" 21 Then he stretched himself upon the child three times and cried to the LORD, "O LORD my God, let this child's life[1] come into him again." 22 And the LORD listened to the voice of Elijah. And the life of the child came into him again, and he revived. 23 And Elijah took the child and brought him down from the upper chamber into the house and delivered him to his mother. And Elijah said, "See, your son lives." 24 And the woman said to Elijah, "Now I know that you are a man of God, and that the word of the LORD in your mouth is truth."

Elijah Confronts Ahab

573

18 After many days the word of the LORD came to Elijah, in the third year, saying, "Go, show yourself to Ahab, and I will send rain upon the earth." 2 So Elijah went to show himself to Ahab. Now the famine was severe in Samaria. 3 And Ahab called Obadiah, who was over the household. (Now Obadiah feared the LORD greatly, 4 and when Jezebel cut off the prophets of the LORD, Obadiah took a hundred prophets and hid them by fifties in a cave and fed them with bread and water.) 5 And Ahab said to Obadiah, "Go through the land to all the springs of water and to all the valleys. Perhaps we may find grass and save the horses and mules alive, and not lose some of the animals." 6 So they divided the land between them to pass through it. Ahab went in one direction by himself, and Obadiah went in another direction by himself.

7 And as Obadiah was on the way, behold, Elijah met him. And Obadiah recognized him and fell on his face and said, "Is it you, my lord Elijah?" 8 And he answered him, "It is I. Go, tell your lord, 'Behold, Elijah is here.'" 9 And he said, "How have I sinned, that you would give your servant into the hand of Ahab, to kill me? 10 As the LORD your God lives, there is no nation or kingdom where my lord has not sent to seek you. And when they would say, 'He is not here,' he would take an oath

[1] Or *soul*; also verse 22

Elijah and the Woman Who Trusted God's Word

Elijah was one of the great prophets of the Old Testament—a man of God who did many miracles by the power of God and who spoke the word of God. Elijah is even mentioned by Jesus in the New Testament.

God was with the prophet Elijah, and God used him to tell the evil King Ahab about God's coming judgment. Because wicked King Ahab was leading the Israelites in idol worship, God said no rain would fall on the land of Israel. That meant no food would grow and there would be a great famine.

But God provided for Elijah during this time. God told Elijah to hide near a brook so that Ahab could not find him. Then God commanded ravens to bring Elijah food. Morning and evening, the birds brought bread and meat to Elijah, and Elijah drank fresh water from the brook.

After some time, though, the brook dried up because there had been no rain. So God told Elijah to go to a city called Zarephath, where God had commanded a widow to prepare food for Elijah.

Elijah walked to the city and found the woman. He asked her for food—but she said she had only enough flour and oil to make one last small loaf of bread for herself and her son. Elijah told her to make food for herself and her son, but to make some for him first. He told her what God had said: "The jar of flour shall not be spent, and the jug of oil shall not be empty, until the day that the LORD sends rain upon the earth."

The woman trusted God's word through Elijah. She used her last flour and oil to make bread for Elijah. But then there was more flour in the flour jar and more oil in the oil jug, so she had enough to make food for herself and her son too! Every day there was more flour and more oil. God took care of them, just as Elijah said God would. The woman's flour jar and jug of oil were never empty, and she baked many loaves of bread for Elijah, herself, and her son.

Some time later, the woman's little boy got very sick. He grew worse and worse and finally stopped breathing and died. The boy's mother was heartbroken and didn't know what to do. Elijah said, "Give me your son." He then carried the little boy upstairs and laid him on his bed. Elijah prayed and asked God to make him alive again.

God answered Elijah's prayer and the boy started breathing—"and the life of the child came into him again." Elijah carried the boy back downstairs and gave him to his mother. "Now I know," his mother said, "that you are a man of God, and that the word of the LORD in your mouth is truth."

We can trust our loving heavenly Father to take care of us too. He knows what we need—food, drink, clothes, home, family, and friends—and He gives us whatever we need in order to follow him faithfully. He gives us His Word through His Son Jesus Christ, which is even better than the word He spoke through His prophet Elijah. He gives us forgiveness of our sins through Jesus, too. And He gives us eternal life. God is so good! He cares for us forever.

SEEK and FIND

WHERE TO FIND THE STORY
1 Kings 17

KEY BIBLE VERSE
"Therefore do not be anxious, saying, 'What shall we eat?' or 'What shall we drink?' or 'What shall we wear?' For . . . your heavenly Father knows that you need them all. But seek first the kingdom of God and his righteousness, and all these things will be added to you." (Matthew 6:31–33)

THREE KEY QUESTIONS
- What happened when the woman used her last bit of flour and oil to make bread for Elijah?
- What happened when the woman's son died?
- What does God give to those who trust in Jesus?

RELATED BIBLE READINGS
Matthew 6:25–33; Luke 4:24–26; Hebrews 11:33–35; James 5:17–18

of the kingdom or nation, that they had
not found you. 11 And now you say, 'Go, tell
your lord, "Behold, Elijah is here."' 12 And as
soon as I have gone from you, the Spirit of
the LORD will carry you I know not where.
And so, when I come and tell Ahab and he
cannot find you, he will kill me, although
I your servant have feared the LORD from
my youth. 13 Has it not been told my lord
what I did when Jezebel killed the proph-
ets of the LORD, how I hid a hundred men
of the LORD's prophets by fifties in a cave
and fed them with bread and water? 14 And
now you say, 'Go, tell your lord, "Behold,
Elijah is here"'; and he will kill me." 15 And
Elijah said, "As the LORD of hosts lives,
before whom I stand, I will surely show
myself to him today." 16 So Obadiah went to
meet Ahab, and told him. And Ahab went
to meet Elijah.

17 When Ahab saw Elijah, Ahab said to
him, "Is it you, you troubler of Israel?"
18 And he answered, "I have not troubled
Israel, but you have, and your father's
house, because you have abandoned the
commandments of the LORD and fol-
lowed the Baals. 19 Now therefore send
and gather all Israel to me at Mount
Carmel, and the 450 prophets of Baal and
the 400 prophets of Asherah, who eat at
Jezebel's table."

The Prophets of Baal Defeated

20 So Ahab sent to all the people of Israel
and gathered the prophets together at
Mount Carmel. 21 And Elijah came near
to all the people and said, "How long
will you go limping between two differ-
ent opinions? If the LORD is God, follow
him; but if Baal, then follow him." And the

people did not answer him a word. 22 Then Elijah said to the people, "I, even I only, am left a prophet of the LORD, but Baal's prophets are 450 men. 23 Let two bulls be given to us, and let them choose one bull for themselves and cut it in pieces and lay it on the wood, but put no fire to it. And I will prepare the other bull and lay it on the wood and put no fire to it. 24 And you call upon the name of your god, and I will call upon the name of the LORD, and the God who answers by fire, he is God." And all the people answered, "It is well spoken." 25 Then Elijah said to the prophets of Baal, "Choose for yourselves one bull and prepare it first, for you are many, and call upon the name of your god, but put no fire to it." 26 And they took the bull that was given them, and they prepared it and called upon the name of Baal from morning until noon, saying, "O Baal, answer us!" But there was no voice, and no one answered. And they limped around the altar that they had made. 27 And at noon Elijah mocked them, saying, "Cry aloud, for he is a god. Either he is musing, or he is relieving himself, or he is on a journey, or perhaps he is asleep and must be awakened." 28 And they cried aloud and cut themselves after their custom with swords and lances, until the blood gushed out upon them. 29 And as midday passed, they raved on until the time of the offering of the oblation, but there was no voice. No one answered; no one paid attention.

30 Then Elijah said to all the people, "Come near to me." And all the people came near to him. And he repaired the altar of the LORD that had been thrown down. 31 Elijah took twelve stones, according to the number of the tribes of the sons of Jacob, to whom the word of the LORD came, saying, "Israel shall be your name," 32 and with the stones he built an altar in the name of the LORD. And he made a trench about the altar, as great as would contain two seahs[1] of seed. 33 And he put the wood in order and cut the bull in pieces and laid it on the wood. And he said, "Fill four jars with water and pour it on the burnt offering and on the wood." 34 And he said, "Do it a second time." And they did it a second time. And he said, "Do it a third time." And they did it a third time. 35 And the water ran around the altar and filled the trench also with water.

36 And at the time of the offering of the oblation, Elijah the prophet came near and said, "O LORD, God of Abraham, Isaac, and Israel, let it be known this day that you are God in Israel, and that I am your servant, and that I have done all these things at your word. 37 Answer me, O LORD, answer me, that this people may know that you, O LORD, are God, and that you have turned their hearts back." 38 Then the fire of the LORD fell and consumed the burnt offering and the wood and the stones and the dust, and licked up the water that was in the trench. 39 And when all the people saw it, they fell on their faces and said, "The LORD, he is God; the LORD, he is God." 40 And Elijah said to them, "Seize the prophets of Baal; let not one of them escape." And they seized them. And Elijah brought them down to the brook Kishon and slaughtered them there.

The LORD Sends Rain

41 And Elijah said to Ahab, "Go up, eat and drink, for there is a sound of the rushing of rain." 42 So Ahab went up to eat and to drink. And Elijah went up to the top of Mount Carmel. And he bowed himself down on the earth and put his face between his knees. 43 And he said to his servant, "Go up now, look toward the sea." And he went up and looked and said, "There is nothing." And he said, "Go again," seven times. 44 And at the seventh time he said, "Behold, a little cloud like a man's hand is rising from the sea." And he said, "Go up, say to Ahab, 'Prepare your chariot and go down, lest the rain stop you.'"

[1] A *seah* was about 7 quarts or 7.3 liters

45 And in a little while the heavens grew black with clouds and wind, and there was a great rain. And Ahab rode and went to Jezreel. 46 And the hand of the LORD was on Elijah, and he gathered up his garment and ran before Ahab to the entrance of Jezreel.

Elijah Flees Jezebel

19 Ahab told Jezebel all that Elijah had done, and how he had killed all the prophets with the sword. 2 Then Jezebel sent a messenger to Elijah, saying, "So may the gods do to me and more also, if I do not make your life as the life of one of them by this time tomorrow." 3 Then he was afraid, and he arose and ran for his life and came to Beersheba, which belongs to Judah, and left his servant there.

4 But he himself went a day's journey into the wilderness and came and sat down under a broom tree. And he asked that he might die, saying, "It is enough; now, O LORD, take away my life, for I am no better than my fathers." 5 And he lay down and slept under a broom tree. And behold, an angel touched him and said to him, "Arise and eat." 6 And he looked, and behold, there was at his head a cake baked on hot stones and a jar of water. And he ate and drank and lay down again. 7 And the angel of the LORD came again a second time and touched him and said, "Arise and eat, for the journey is too great for you." 8 And he arose and ate and drank, and went in the strength of that food forty days and forty nights to Horeb, the mount of God.

The LORD Speaks to Elijah

9 There he came to a cave and lodged in it. And behold, the word of the LORD came to him, and he said to him, "What are you doing here, Elijah?" 10 He said, "I have been very jealous for the LORD, the God of hosts. For the people of Israel have forsaken your covenant, thrown down your altars, and killed your prophets with the sword, and I, even I only, am left, and they seek my life, to take it away." 11 And he said, "Go out and stand on the mount before the LORD." And behold, the LORD passed by, and a great and strong wind tore the mountains and broke in pieces the rocks before the LORD, but the LORD was not in the wind. And after the wind an earthquake, but the LORD was not in the earthquake. 12 And after the earthquake a fire, but the LORD was not in the fire. And after the fire the sound of a low whisper.[1] 13 And when Elijah heard it, he wrapped his face in his cloak and went out and stood at the entrance of the cave. And behold, there came a voice to him and said, "What are you doing here, Elijah?" 14 He said, "I have been very jealous for the LORD, the God of hosts. For the people of Israel have forsaken your covenant, thrown down your altars, and killed your

CHARACTER PROFILE

ELIJAH

Elijah was a prophet who stood boldly for God against King Ahab and Queen Jezebel. While most of Israel worshiped Baal, Elijah insisted that God is the one true God. God did amazing miracles through him. Elijah did not die, because God took him up to heaven in a fiery chariot.

567, 573, 587

[1] Or a sound, a thin silence

Elijah and the False Prophets of Baal

For three years no rain fell in the land of Israel. There was almost nothing to eat. Many people had forgotten about God and prayed to idols instead. God sent His prophet Elijah to meet wicked King Ahab. Elijah told King Ahab that the king and his family had turned their backs on the one true God and broken His commandments. Ahab was leading the Israelites in worshiping the idol Baal.

So Elijah told King Ahab to bring the Israelites to Mount Carmel, along with all the prophets of the false god Baal. When the people gathered on the mountain, Elijah asked them how long they would keep switching back and forth between worshiping God and worshiping the idol Baal. "If the LORD is God, follow Him," Elijah told them, "but if Baal, then follow him." But the people did not answer a word.

So Elijah challenged Israel to a test. He told the people of Israel to bring two bulls and to choose one of the bulls for the false prophets of Baal. Then Elijah told the false prophets to prepare the bull as an offering to the idol Baal, and to place it on an altar of wood. Elijah said that he too would prepare an offering and put it on the altar of the LORD. Then Elijah told the 450 prophets of Baal, "You call upon the name of your god, and I will call upon the name of the LORD—and the God who answers by fire, He is God." The Israelites agreed that this would be a good test.

Baal's prophets prepared an offering for the false god Baal. They prayed all morning, but no fire came. They danced around the altar, but nothing happened. At noon, they prayed louder and louder. They kept it up all afternoon, but still there was no answer from Baal of any kind.

Then Elijah built an altar with 12 large stones to honor God, one for each of the tribes of Israel. Elijah put the offering on the altar and dug a ditch around the altar. Elijah poured water all over the offering three times, so that it was completely soaked. Water ran off the offering, down the altar, into the ditch, until the ditch was full of water. The wood and the offering were soaking wet! How could they ever catch on fire? Then Elijah prayed. "Answer me, O LORD, answer me, that this people may know that You, O LORD, are God, and that You have turned their hearts back."

Immediately, God sent fire from heaven and burned up the sacrifice! The fire burned up all the wood, it dried up all the water in the ditch, and it even burned up the 12 large stones! The people fell down and shouted, "The LORD, He is God; the LORD, He is God." Then, finally, after God sent fire, He sent rain to water the land and to take away the famine.

The true God is the Father, Son, and Holy Spirit. He is the God who made us, loves us, and cares for us. God the Father sent Jesus to die on the cross to take away our sins. God sends the Holy Spirit to give His people faith. Our God wants us to worship only Him. He wants everyone to know that He is the true God and that He sent Jesus to be our Savior.

SEEK and FIND

WHERE TO FIND THE STORY

1 Kings 18

KEY BIBLE VERSE

"But as for me and my house, we will serve the LORD." (Joshua 24:15)

THREE KEY QUESTIONS

- What was the name of the false god—the idol that the wicked King Ahab worshiped?
- What was Elijah's test to show who is the one true God? What happened?
- Who is the true God and what has He done for us?

RELATED BIBLE READINGS

Joshua 24:14–24; Isaiah 43:10–13; 44:6–20; 1 John 5:21

prophets with the sword, and I, even I
only, am left, and they seek my life, to take
it away." 15 And the LORD said to him, "Go,
return on your way to the wilderness of
Damascus. And when you arrive, you shall
anoint Hazael to be king over Syria. 16 And
Jehu the son of Nimshi you shall anoint
to be king over Israel, and Elisha the son
of Shaphat of Abel-meholah you shall
anoint to be prophet in your place. 17 And
the one who escapes from the sword of
Hazael shall Jehu put to death, and the one
who escapes from the sword of Jehu shall
Elisha put to death. 18 Yet I will leave seven
thousand in Israel, all the knees that have
not bowed to Baal, and every mouth that
has not kissed him."

The Call of Elisha

19 So he departed from there and found
Elisha the son of Shaphat, who was plow-
ing with twelve yoke of oxen in front of
him, and he was with the twelfth. Elijah
passed by him and cast his cloak upon him.
20 And he left the oxen and ran after Elijah
and said, "Let me kiss my father and my
mother, and then I will follow you." And he
said to him, "Go back again, for what have
I done to you?" 21 And he returned from
following him and took the yoke of oxen
and sacrificed them and boiled their flesh
with the yokes of the oxen and gave it to
the people, and they ate. Then he arose and
went after Elijah and assisted him.

Ahab's Wars with Syria

20 Ben-hadad the king of Syria gath-
ered all his army together. Thirty-
two kings were with him, and horses and
chariots. And he went up and closed in
on Samaria and fought against it. 2 And
he sent messengers into the city to Ahab
king of Israel and said to him, "Thus says
Ben-hadad: 3 'Your silver and your gold
are mine; your best wives and children
also are mine.'" 4 And the king of Israel

answered, "As you say, my lord, O king, I am yours, and all that I have." **5** The messengers came again and said, "Thus says Ben-hadad: 'I sent to you, saying, "Deliver to me your silver and your gold, your wives and your children." **6** Nevertheless I will send my servants to you tomorrow about this time, and they shall search your house and the houses of your servants and lay hands on whatever pleases you and take it away.'"

7 Then the king of Israel called all the elders of the land and said, "Mark, now, and see how this man is seeking trouble, for he sent to me for my wives and my children, and for my silver and my gold, and I did not refuse him." **8** And all the elders and all the people said to him, "Do not listen or consent." **9** So he said to the messengers of Ben-hadad, "Tell my lord the king, 'All that you first demanded of your servant I will do, but this thing I cannot do.'" And the messengers departed and brought him word again. **10** Ben-hadad sent to him and said, "The gods do so to me and more also, if the dust of Samaria shall suffice for handfuls for all the people who follow me." **11** And the king of Israel answered, "Tell him, 'Let not him who straps on his armor boast himself as he who takes it off.'" **12** When Ben-hadad heard this message as he was drinking with the kings in the booths, he said to his men, "Take your positions." And they took their positions against the city.

Ahab Defeats Ben-hadad

13 And behold, a prophet came near to Ahab king of Israel and said, "Thus says the LORD, Have you seen all this great multitude? Behold, I will give it into your hand this day, and you shall know that I am the LORD." **14** And Ahab said, "By whom?" He said, "Thus says the LORD, By the servants of the governors of the districts." Then he said, "Who shall begin the battle?" He answered, "You." **15** Then he mustered the servants of the governors of the districts, and they were 232. And after them he mustered all the people of Israel, seven thousand.

16 And they went out at noon, while Ben-hadad was drinking himself drunk in the booths, he and the thirty-two kings who helped him. **17** The servants of the governors of the districts went out first. And Ben-hadad sent out scouts, and they reported to him, "Men are coming out from Samaria." **18** He said, "If they have come out for peace, take them alive. Or if they have come out for war, take them alive."

19 So these went out of the city, the servants of the governors of the districts and the army that followed them. **20** And each struck down his man. The Syrians fled, and Israel pursued them, but Ben-hadad king of Syria escaped on a horse with horsemen. **21** And the king of Israel went out and struck the horses and chariots, and struck the Syrians with a great blow.

22 Then the prophet came near to the king of Israel and said to him, "Come, strengthen yourself, and consider well what you have to do, for in the spring the king of Syria will come up against you."

23 And the servants of the king of Syria said to him, "Their gods are gods of the hills, and so they were stronger than we. But let us fight against them in the plain, and surely we shall be stronger than they. **24** And do this: remove the kings, each from his post, and put commanders in their places, **25** and muster an army like the army that you have lost, horse for horse, and chariot for chariot. Then we will fight against them in the plain, and surely we shall be stronger than they." And he listened to their voice and did so.

Ahab Defeats Ben-hadad Again

26 In the spring, Ben-hadad mustered the Syrians and went up to Aphek to fight against Israel. **27** And the people of Israel were mustered and were provisioned and went against them. The people of Israel encamped before them like two little flocks of goats, but the Syrians filled the country. 28 And a man of God came near and said to the king of Israel, "Thus says the LORD, 'Because the Syrians have said, "The LORD is a god of the hills but he is not a god of the valleys," therefore I will give all this great multitude into your hand, and you shall know that I am the LORD.'" 29 And they encamped opposite one another seven days. Then on the seventh day the battle was joined. And the people of Israel struck down of the Syrians 100,000 foot soldiers in one day. 30 And the rest fled into the city of Aphek, and the wall fell upon 27,000 men who were left.

Ben-hadad also fled and entered an inner chamber in the city. 31 And his servants said to him, "Behold now, we have heard that the kings of the house of Israel are merciful kings. Let us put sackcloth around our waists and ropes on our heads and go out to the king of Israel. Perhaps he will spare your life." 32 So they tied sackcloth around their waists and put ropes on their heads and went to the king of Israel and said, "Your servant Ben-hadad says, 'Please, let me live.'" And he said, "Does he still live? He is my brother." 33 Now the men were watching for a sign, and they quickly took it up from him and said, "Yes, your brother Ben-hadad." Then he said, "Go and bring him." Then Ben-hadad came out to him, and he caused him to come up into the chariot. 34 And Ben-hadad said to him, "The cities that my father took from your father I will restore, and you may establish bazaars for yourself in Damascus, as my father did in Samaria." And Ahab said, "I will let you go on these terms." So he made a covenant with him and let him go.

A Prophet Condemns Ben-hadad's Release

35 And a certain man of the sons of the prophets said to his fellow at the command of the LORD, "Strike me, please." But the man refused to strike him. 36 Then he said to him, "Because you have not obeyed the voice of the LORD, behold, as soon as you have gone from me, a lion shall strike you down." And as soon as he had departed from him, a lion met him and struck him down. 37 Then he found another man and said, "Strike me, please." And the man struck him—struck him and wounded him. 38 So the prophet departed and waited for the king by the way, disguising himself with a bandage over his eyes. 39 And as the king passed, he cried to the king and said, "Your servant went out into the midst of the battle, and behold, a soldier turned and brought a man to me and said, 'Guard this man; if by any means he is missing, your life shall be for his life, or else you shall pay a talent[1] of silver.' 40 And as your servant was busy here and there, he was gone." The king of Israel said to him, "So shall your judgment be; you yourself have decided it." 41 Then he hurried to take the bandage away from his eyes, and the king of Israel recognized him as one of the prophets. 42 And he said to him, "Thus says the LORD, 'Because you have let go out of your hand the man whom I had devoted to destruction,[2] therefore your life shall be for his life, and your people for his people.'" 43 And the king of Israel went to his house vexed and sullen and came to Samaria.

Naboth's Vineyard

21 Now Naboth the Jezreelite had a vineyard in Jezreel, beside the palace of Ahab king of Samaria. 2 And after this Ahab said to Naboth, "Give me your vineyard, that I may have it for a vegetable garden, because it is near my house, and I will give you a better vineyard for it; or, if it seems good to you, I will give you its value in money." 3 But Naboth said to Ahab, "The LORD forbid that I should give

[1] A *talent* was about 75 pounds or 34 kilograms [2] That is, set apart (devoted) as an offering to the Lord (for destruction)

you the inheritance of my fathers." 4 And Ahab went into his house vexed and sullen because of what Naboth the Jezreelite had said to him, for he had said, "I will not give you the inheritance of my fathers." And he lay down on his bed and turned away his face and would eat no food.

5 But Jezebel his wife came to him and said to him, "Why is your spirit so vexed that you eat no food?" 6 And he said to her, "Because I spoke to Naboth the Jezreelite and said to him, 'Give me your vineyard for money, or else, if it please you, I will give you another vineyard for it.' And he answered, 'I will not give you my vineyard.'" 7 And Jezebel his wife said to him, "Do you now govern Israel? Arise and eat bread and let your heart be cheerful; I will give you the vineyard of Naboth the Jezreelite."

8 So she wrote letters in Ahab's name and sealed them with his seal, and she sent the letters to the elders and the leaders who lived with Naboth in his city. 9 And she wrote in the letters, "Proclaim a fast, and set Naboth at the head of the people. 10 And set two worthless men opposite him, and let them bring a charge against him, saying, 'You have cursed[1] God and the king.' Then take him out and stone him to death." 11 And the men of his city, the elders and the leaders who lived in his city, did as Jezebel had sent word to them. As it was written in the letters that she had sent to them, 12 they proclaimed a fast and set Naboth at the head of the people. 13 And the two worthless men came in and sat opposite him. And the worthless men brought a charge against Naboth in the presence of the people, saying, "Naboth cursed God and the king." So they took him outside the city and stoned him to death with stones. 14 Then they sent to Jezebel, saying, "Naboth has been stoned; he is dead."

15 As soon as Jezebel heard that Naboth had been stoned and was dead, Jezebel said to Ahab, "Arise, take possession of the vineyard of Naboth the Jezreelite, which he refused to give you for money, for Naboth is not alive, but dead." 16 And as soon as Ahab heard that Naboth was dead, Ahab arose to go down to the vineyard of Naboth the Jezreelite, to take possession of it.

The LORD Condemns Ahab

17 Then the word of the LORD came to Elijah the Tishbite, saying, 18 "Arise, go down to meet Ahab king of Israel, who is in Samaria; behold, he is in the vineyard of Naboth, where he has gone to take possession. 19 And you shall say to him, 'Thus says the LORD, "Have you killed and also taken possession?"' And you shall say to him, 'Thus says the LORD: "In the place where dogs licked up the blood of Naboth shall dogs lick your own blood."'"

20 Ahab said to Elijah, "Have you found me, O my enemy?" He answered, "I have found you, because you have sold yourself to do what is evil in the sight of the LORD. 21 Behold, I will bring disaster upon you. I will utterly burn you up, and will cut off from Ahab every male, bond or free, in Israel. 22 And I will make your house like the house of Jeroboam the son of Nebat, and like the house of Baasha the son of Ahijah, for the anger to which you have provoked me, and because you have made Israel to sin. 23 And of Jezebel the LORD also said, 'The dogs shall eat Jezebel within the walls of Jezreel.' 24 Anyone belonging to Ahab who dies in the city the dogs shall eat, and anyone of his who dies in the open country the birds of the heavens shall eat."

Ahab's Repentance

25 (There was none who sold himself to do what was evil in the sight of the LORD like Ahab, whom Jezebel his wife incited. 26 He acted very abominably in going after idols, as the Amorites had done, whom the LORD cast out before the people of Israel.)

27 And when Ahab heard those words,

[1] Hebrew *blessed*; also verse 13

he tore his clothes and put sackcloth on his flesh and fasted and lay in sackcloth and went about dejectedly. 28 And the word of the LORD came to Elijah the Tishbite, saying, 29 "Have you seen how Ahab has humbled himself before me? Because he has humbled himself before me, I will not bring the disaster in his days; but in his son's days I will bring the disaster upon his house."

Ahab and the False Prophets

22 For three years Syria and Israel continued without war. 2 But in the third year Jehoshaphat the king of Judah came down to the king of Israel. 3 And the king of Israel said to his servants, "Do you know that Ramoth-gilead belongs to us, and we keep quiet and do not take it out of the hand of the king of Syria?" 4 And he said to Jehoshaphat, "Will you go with me to battle at Ramoth-gilead?" And Jehoshaphat said to the king of Israel, "I am as you are, my people as your people, my horses as your horses."

5 And Jehoshaphat said to the king of Israel, "Inquire first for the word of the LORD." 6 Then the king of Israel gathered the prophets together, about four hundred men, and said to them, "Shall I go to battle against Ramoth-gilead, or shall I refrain?" And they said, "Go up, for the Lord will give it into the hand of the king." 7 But Jehoshaphat said, "Is there not here another prophet of the LORD of whom we may inquire?" 8 And the king of Israel said to Jehoshaphat, "There is yet one man by whom we may inquire of the LORD, Micaiah the son of Imlah, but I hate him, for he never prophesies good concerning me, but evil." And Jehoshaphat said, "Let not the king say so." 9 Then the king of Israel summoned an officer and said, "Bring quickly Micaiah the son of Imlah." 10 Now the king of Israel and Jehoshaphat the king of Judah were sitting on their thrones, arrayed in their robes, at the threshing floor at the entrance of the gate of Samaria, and all the prophets were prophesying before them. 11 And Zedekiah the son of Chenaanah made for himself horns of iron and said, "Thus says the LORD, 'With these you shall push the Syrians until they are destroyed.'" 12 And all the prophets prophesied so and said, "Go up to Ramoth-gilead and triumph; the LORD will give it into the hand of the king."

Micaiah Prophesies Against Ahab

13 And the messenger who went to summon Micaiah said to him, "Behold, the words of the prophets with one accord are favorable to the king. Let your word be like the word of one of them, and speak favorably." 14 But Micaiah said, "As the LORD lives, what the LORD says to me, that I will speak." 15 And when he had come to the king, the king said to him, "Micaiah, shall we go to Ramoth-gilead to battle, or shall we refrain?" And he answered him, "Go up and triumph; the LORD will give it into the hand of the king." 16 But the king said to him, "How many times shall I make you swear that you speak to me nothing but the truth in the name of the LORD?" 17 And he said, "I saw all Israel scattered on the mountains, as sheep that have no shepherd. And the LORD said, 'These have no master; let each return to his home in peace.'" 18 And the king of Israel said to Jehoshaphat, "Did I not tell you that he would not prophesy good concerning me, but evil?" 19 And Micaiah said, "Therefore hear the word of the LORD: I saw the LORD sitting on his throne, and all the host of heaven standing beside him on his right hand and on his left; 20 and the LORD said, 'Who will entice Ahab, that he may go up and fall at Ramoth-gilead?' And one said one thing, and another said another. 21 Then a spirit came forward and stood before the LORD, saying, 'I will entice him.' 22 And

the LORD said to him, 'By what means?' And he said, 'I will go out, and will be a lying spirit in the mouth of all his prophets.' And he said, 'You are to entice him, and you shall succeed; go out and do so.' **23** Now therefore behold, the LORD has put a lying spirit in the mouth of all these your prophets; the LORD has declared disaster for you."

24 Then Zedekiah the son of Chenaanah came near and struck Micaiah on the cheek and said, "How did the Spirit of the LORD go from me to speak to you?" **25** And Micaiah said, "Behold, you shall see on that day when you go into an inner chamber to hide yourself." **26** And the king of Israel said, "Seize Micaiah, and take him back to Amon the governor of the city and to Joash the king's son, **27** and say, 'Thus says the king, "Put this fellow in prison and feed him meager rations of bread and water, until I come in peace."'" **28** And Micaiah said, "If you return in peace, the LORD has not spoken by me." And he said, "Hear, all you peoples!"

Ahab Killed in Battle

29 So the king of Israel and Jehoshaphat the king of Judah went up to Ramoth-gilead. **30** And the king of Israel said to Jehoshaphat, "I will disguise myself and go into battle, but you wear your robes." And the king of Israel disguised himself and went into battle. **31** Now the king of Syria had commanded the thirty-two captains of his chariots, "Fight with neither small nor great, but only with the king of Israel." **32** And when the captains of the chariots saw Jehoshaphat, they said, "It is surely the king of Israel." So they turned to fight against him. And Jehoshaphat cried out. **33** And when the captains of the chariots saw that it was not the king of Israel, they turned back from pursuing him. **34** But a certain man drew his bow at random[1] and struck the king of Israel between the scale armor and the breastplate. Therefore he said to the driver of his chariot, "Turn around and carry me out of the battle, for I am wounded." **35** And the battle continued that day, and the king was propped up in his chariot facing the Syrians, until at evening he died. And the blood of the wound flowed into the bottom of the chariot. **36** And about sunset a cry went through the army, "Every man to his city, and every man to his country!"

37 So the king died, and was brought to Samaria. And they buried the king in Samaria. **38** And they washed the chariot by the pool of Samaria, and the dogs licked up his blood, and the prostitutes washed themselves in it, according to the word of the LORD that he had spoken. **39** Now the rest of the acts of Ahab and all that he did, and the ivory house that he built and all the cities that he built, are they not written in the Book of the Chronicles of the Kings of Israel? **40** So Ahab slept with his fathers, and Ahaziah his son reigned in his place.

Jehoshaphat Reigns in Judah

41 Jehoshaphat the son of Asa began to reign over Judah in the fourth year of Ahab king of Israel. **42** Jehoshaphat was thirty-five years old when he began to reign, and he reigned twenty-five years in Jerusalem. His mother's name was Azubah the daughter of Shilhi. **43** He walked in all the way of Asa his father. He did not turn aside from it, doing what was right in the sight of the LORD. Yet the high places were not taken away, and the people still sacrificed and made offerings on the high places. **44** Jehoshaphat also made peace with the king of Israel.

45 Now the rest of the acts of Jehoshaphat, and his might that he showed, and how he warred, are they not written in the Book of the Chronicles of the Kings of Judah? **46** And from the land he exterminated the remnant of the male cult

[1] Hebrew *in his innocence*

prostitutes who remained in the days of
his father Asa.
47 There was no king in Edom; a
deputy was king. 48 Jehoshaphat made
ships of Tarshish to go to Ophir for gold,
but they did not go, for the ships were
wrecked at Ezion-geber. 49 Then Ahaziah
the son of Ahab said to Jehoshaphat, "Let
my servants go with your servants in the
ships," but Jehoshaphat was not willing.
50 And Jehoshaphat slept with his fathers
and was buried with his fathers in the
city of David his father, and Jehoram his
son reigned in his place.

Ahaziah Reigns in Israel

51 Ahaziah the son of Ahab began to
reign over Israel in Samaria in the seven-
teenth year of Jehoshaphat king of Judah,
and he reigned two years over Israel. 52 He
did what was evil in the sight of the LORD
and walked in the way of his father and
in the way of his mother and in the way
of Jeroboam the son of Nebat, who made
Israel to sin. 53 He served Baal and wor-
shiped him and provoked the LORD, the
God of Israel, to anger in every way that his
father had done.

2 Kings

For the introduction, see the introduction to 1–2 Kings (p. 527)

Elijah Denounces Ahaziah

1 After the death of Ahab, Moab rebelled against Israel.

2 Now Ahaziah fell through the lattice in his upper chamber in Samaria, and lay sick; so he sent messengers, telling them, "Go, inquire of Baal-zebub, the god of Ekron, whether I shall recover from this sickness." 3 But the angel of the LORD said to Elijah the Tishbite, "Arise, go up to meet the messengers of the king of Samaria, and say to them, 'Is it because there is no God in Israel that you are going to inquire of Baal-zebub, the god of Ekron? 4 Now therefore thus says the LORD, You shall not come down from the bed to which you have gone up, but you shall surely die.'" So Elijah went.

5 The messengers returned to the king, and he said to them, "Why have you returned?" 6 And they said to him, "There came a man to meet us, and said to us, 'Go back to the king who sent you, and say to him, Thus says the LORD, Is it because there is no God in Israel that you are sending to inquire of Baal-zebub, the god of Ekron? Therefore you shall not come down from the bed to which you have gone up, but you shall surely die.'" 7 He said to them, "What kind of man was he who came to meet you and told you these things?" 8 They answered him, "He wore a garment of hair, with a belt of leather about his waist." And he said, "It is Elijah the Tishbite."

9 Then the king sent to him a captain of fifty men with his fifty. He went up to Elijah, who was sitting on the top of a hill, and said to him, "O man of God, the king says, 'Come down.'" 10 But Elijah answered the captain of fifty, "If I am a man of God, let fire come down from heaven and consume you and your fifty." Then fire came down from heaven and consumed him and his fifty.

11 Again the king sent to him another captain of fifty men with his fifty. And he answered and said to him, "O man of God, this is the king's order, 'Come down quickly!'" 12 But Elijah answered them, "If I am a man of God, let fire come down from heaven and consume you and your fifty." Then the fire of God came down from heaven and consumed him and his fifty.

13 Again the king sent the captain of a third fifty with his fifty. And the third captain of fifty went up and came and fell on his knees before Elijah and entreated him, "O man of God, please let my life, and the life of these fifty servants of yours, be precious in your sight. 14 Behold, fire came down from heaven and consumed the two former captains of fifty men with their fifties, but now let my life be precious in your sight." 15 Then the angel of the LORD said to Elijah, "Go down with him; do not be afraid of him." So he arose and went down with him to the king 16 and said to him, "Thus says the LORD, 'Because you have sent messengers to inquire of Baal-zebub, the god of Ekron—is it because there is no God in Israel to inquire of his word?—therefore you shall not come down from the bed to which you have gone up, but you shall surely die.'"

17 So he died according to the word of the LORD that Elijah had spoken. Jehoram became king in his place in the second year of Jehoram the son of Jehoshaphat, king of Judah, because Ahaziah had no son. 18 Now the rest of the acts of Ahaziah that he did, are they not written in the Book of the Chronicles of the Kings of Israel?

Elijah Taken to Heaven

2 Now when the LORD was about
to take Elijah up to heaven by
587 a whirlwind, Elijah and Elisha were
on their way from Gilgal. 2 And Elijah said
to Elisha, "Please stay here, for the LORD
has sent me as far as Bethel." But Elisha
said, "As the LORD lives, and as you your-
self live, I will not leave you." So they
went down to Bethel. 3 And the sons of the
prophets who were in Bethel came out to
Elisha and said to him, "Do you know that
today the LORD will take away your master
from over you?" And he said, "Yes, I know
it; keep quiet."

4 Elijah said to him, "Elisha, please stay
here, for the LORD has sent me to Jericho."
But he said, "As the LORD lives, and as you
yourself live, I will not leave you." So they
came to Jericho. 5 The sons of the prophets
who were at Jericho drew near to Elisha
and said to him, "Do you know that today
the LORD will take away your master from
over you?" And he answered, "Yes, I know
it; keep quiet."

6 Then Elijah said to him, "Please stay
here, for the LORD has sent me to the
Jordan." But he said, "As the LORD lives, and
as you yourself live, I will not leave you." So
the two of them went on. 7 Fifty men of the
sons of the prophets also went and stood
at some distance from them, as they both
were standing by the Jordan. 8 Then Elijah
took his cloak and rolled it up and struck
the water, and the water was parted to the
one side and to the other, till the two of
them could go over on dry ground.

9 When they had crossed, Elijah said to
Elisha, "Ask what I shall do for you, before
I am taken from you." And Elisha said,
"Please let there be a double portion of your
spirit on me." 10 And he said, "You have
asked a hard thing; yet, if you see me as I
am being taken from you, it shall be so for
you, but if you do not see me, it shall not be
so." 11 And as they still went on and talked,
behold, chariots of fire and horses of fire
separated the two of them. And Elijah went
up by a whirlwind into heaven. 12 And
Elisha saw it and he cried, "My father, my
father! The chariots of Israel and its horse-
men!" And he saw him no more.

Then he took hold of his own clothes
and tore them in two pieces. 13 And he took
up the cloak of Elijah that had fallen from
him and went back and stood on the bank
of the Jordan. 14 Then he took the cloak of
Elijah that had fallen from him and struck
the water, saying, "Where is the LORD, the
God of Elijah?" And when he had struck
the water, the water was parted to the one
side and to the other, and Elisha went over.

Elisha Succeeds Elijah

15 Now when the sons of the prophets
who were at Jericho saw him opposite
them, they said, "The spirit of Elijah rests
on Elisha." And they came to meet him
and bowed to the ground before him.
16 And they said to him, "Behold now, there
are with your servants fifty strong men.
Please let them go and seek your master.
It may be that the Spirit of the LORD has
caught him up and cast him upon some
mountain or into some valley." And he
said, "You shall not send." 17 But when they
urged him till he was ashamed, he said,
"Send." They sent therefore fifty men. And
for three days they sought him but did not
find him. 18 And they came back to him
while he was staying at Jericho, and he said
to them, "Did I not say to you, 'Do not go'?"

19 Now the men of the city said to Elisha,
"Behold, the situation of this city is pleas-
ant, as my lord sees, but the water is bad,
and the land is unfruitful." 20 He said,
"Bring me a new bowl, and put salt in it."
So they brought it to him. 21 Then he went
to the spring of water and threw salt in
it and said, "Thus says the LORD, I have
healed this water; from now on neither
death nor miscarriage shall come from it."
22 So the water has been healed to this day,
according to the word that Elisha spoke.

23 He went up from there to Bethel, and while he was going up on the way, some small boys came out of the city and jeered at him, saying, "Go up, you baldhead! Go up, you baldhead!" 24 And he turned around, and when he saw them, he cursed them in the name of the LORD. And two she-bears came out of the woods and tore forty-two of the boys. 25 From there he went on to Mount Carmel, and from there he returned to Samaria.

Moab Rebels Against Israel

3 In the eighteenth year of Jehoshaphat king of Judah, Jehoram the son of Ahab became king over Israel in Samaria, and he reigned twelve years. 2 He did what was evil in the sight of the LORD, though not like his father and mother, for he put away the pillar of Baal that his father had made. 3 Nevertheless, he clung to the sin of Jeroboam the son of Nebat, which he made Israel to sin; he did not depart from it.

4 Now Mesha king of Moab was a sheep breeder, and he had to deliver to the king of Israel 100,000 lambs and the wool of 100,000 rams. 5 But when Ahab died, the king of Moab rebelled against the king of Israel. 6 So King Jehoram marched out of Samaria at that time and mustered all Israel. 7 And he went and sent word to Jehoshaphat king of Judah, "The king of Moab has rebelled against me. Will you go with me to battle against Moab?" And he said, "I will go. I am as you are, my people as your people, my horses as your horses." 8 Then he said, "By which way shall we march?" Jehoram answered, "By the way of the wilderness of Edom."

9 So the king of Israel went with the king of Judah and the king of Edom. And when they had made a circuitous march of seven days, there was no water for the army or for the animals that followed them. 10 Then the king of Israel said, "Alas! The LORD has called these three kings to give them into the hand of Moab." 11 And Jehoshaphat said, "Is there no prophet of the LORD here, through whom we may inquire of the LORD?" Then one of the king of Israel's servants answered, "Elisha the son of Shaphat is here, who poured water on the hands of Elijah." 12 And Jehoshaphat said, "The word of the LORD is with him." So the king of Israel and Jehoshaphat and the king of Edom went down to him.

13 And Elisha said to the king of Israel, "What have I to do with you? Go to the prophets of your father and to the prophets of your mother." But the king of Israel said to him, "No; it is the LORD who has called these three kings to give them into the hand of Moab." 14 And Elisha said, "As the LORD of hosts lives, before whom I stand, were it not that I have regard for Jehoshaphat the king of Judah, I would neither look at you nor see you. 15 But now bring me a musician." And when the musician played, the hand of the LORD came upon him. 16 And he said, "Thus says the LORD, 'I will make this dry streambed full of pools.' 17 For thus says the LORD, 'You shall not see wind or rain, but that streambed shall be filled with water, so that you shall drink, you, your livestock, and your animals.' 18 This is a light thing in the sight of the LORD. He will also give the Moabites into your hand, 19 and you shall attack every fortified city and every choice city, and shall fell every good tree and stop up all springs of water and ruin every good piece of land with stones." 20 The next morning, about the time of offering the sacrifice, behold, water came from the direction of Edom, till the country was filled with water.

21 When all the Moabites heard that the kings had come up to fight against them, all who were able to put on armor, from the youngest to the oldest, were called out and were drawn up at the border. 22 And when they rose early in the morning and the sun shone on the water, the Moabites saw the water opposite them as red as blood.

Elijah and the Chariots of Fire

After Elijah had faithfully spoken God's word to Israel for many years, God gave Elijah a helper whose name was Elisha. God chose Elisha to replace the prophet Elijah, and now God was about to take Elijah up to heaven by a whirlwind.

While Elijah was on a journey with Elisha, they came to the Jordan River. Elijah took off his cloak, rolled it up, and hit the water with his cloak. Immediately the water separated—some water going to the right and some to the left. And the men walked to the other side on dry ground right through the river.

After they crossed the river, Elijah told Elisha, "Ask what I shall do for you, before I am taken from you." Elisha said, "Please let there be a double portion of your spirit on me." Elisha wanted to be a mighty prophet like Elijah, faithfully speaking God's word to His people.

Elijah told Elisha, "You have asked a hard thing." But, he said, if you see me when the LORD takes me to heaven, "it shall be so for you."

As they were walking, suddenly chariots of fire and horses of fire came down from the sky, and Elisha was separated from Elijah. God took Elijah to heaven in a whirlwind as Elisha watched and cried out to Elijah. Elisha never saw Elijah again.

Elisha took the cloak that had fallen from Elijah and

walked back to the Jordan River. He hit the water with the cloak and called out, "Where is the LORD, the God of Elijah?" When Elijah's cloak hit the water, the river separated again, just as it had done for Elijah. Elisha walked on dry ground right through the river. God had blessed Elisha and had answered his prayer. He too became a mighty prophet like Elijah, faithfully speaking God's word to His people.

God has given us Jesus, the greatest Prophet of all—much greater even than Elijah or Elisha. Jesus shows us exactly what God is like because Jesus is God's only Son. God speaks through His Word today when pastors faithfully preach the Bible. God gives His Spirit to us, so that we can understand His Word and faithfully serve Him.

SEEK and FIND

WHERE TO FIND THE STORY

2 Kings 2:1–14

KEY BIBLE VERSE

"Long ago, at many times and in many ways, God spoke to our fathers by the prophets, but in these last days he has spoken to us by his Son." (Hebrews 1:1–2)

THREE KEY QUESTIONS

- When Elijah asked Elisha what he wanted, what did Elisha say?
- Who is the greatest Prophet that ever lived, and why is He the greatest?
- How does God speak to His people today?

RELATED BIBLE READINGS

Matthew 7:28–29; John 1:1–8; 1 Corinthians 2:1–16; Hebrews 1:1–3

23 And they said, "This is blood; the kings have surely fought together and struck one another down. Now then, Moab, to the spoil!" 24 But when they came to the camp of Israel, the Israelites rose and struck the Moabites, till they fled before them. And they went forward, striking the Moabites as they went.[1] 25 And they overthrew the cities, and on every good piece of land every man threw a stone until it was covered. They stopped every spring of water and felled all the good trees, till only its stones were left in Kir-hareseth, and the slingers surrounded and attacked it. 26 When the king of Moab saw that the battle was going against him, he took with him 700 swordsmen to break through, opposite the king of Edom, but they could not. 27 Then he took his oldest son who was to reign in his place and offered him for a burnt offering on the wall. And there came great wrath against Israel. And they withdrew from him and returned to their own land.

CHARACTER PROFILE

ELISHA

Elisha was chosen by Elijah to be his helper. Elisha saw Elijah go up to heaven in a fiery chariot; then Elisha took over Elijah's ministry as prophet of God to Israel. God did amazing miracles through Elisha, as he had done with Elijah.

587, 593

Elisha and the Widow's Oil

4 Now the wife of one of the sons of the prophets cried to Elisha, "Your servant my husband is dead, and you know that your servant feared the LORD, but the creditor has come to take my two children to be his slaves." 2 And Elisha said to her, "What shall I do for you? Tell me; what have you in the house?" And she said, "Your servant has nothing in the house except a jar of oil." 3 Then he said, "Go outside, borrow vessels from all your neighbors, empty vessels and not too few. 4 Then go in and shut the door behind yourself and your sons and pour into all these vessels. And when one is full, set it aside." 5 So she went from him and shut the door behind herself and her sons. And as she poured they brought the vessels to her. 6 When the vessels were full, she said to her son, "Bring me another vessel." And he said to her, "There is not another." Then the oil stopped flowing. 7 She came and told the man of God, and he said, "Go, sell the oil and pay your debts, and you and your sons can live on the rest."

Elisha and the Shunammite Woman

8 One day Elisha went on to Shunem, where a wealthy woman lived, who urged him to eat some food. So whenever he passed that way, he would turn in there to eat food. 9 And she said to her husband, "Behold now, I know that this is a holy man of God who is continually passing our way. 10 Let us make a small room on the roof with walls and put there for him a bed, a table, a chair, and a lamp, so that whenever he comes to us, he can go in there."

11 One day he came there, and he turned into the chamber and rested there. 12 And he said to Gehazi his servant, "Call this Shunammite." When he had called her, she stood before him. 13 And he said to

[1] Septuagint; the meaning of the Hebrew is uncertain

him, "Say now to her, 'See, you have taken all this trouble for us; what is to be done for you? Would you have a word spoken on your behalf to the king or to the commander of the army?'" She answered, "I dwell among my own people." 14 And he said, "What then is to be done for her?" Gehazi answered, "Well, she has no son, and her husband is old." 15 He said, "Call her." And when he had called her, she stood in the doorway. 16 And he said, "At this season, about this time next year, you shall embrace a son." And she said, "No, my lord, O man of God; do not lie to your servant." 17 But the woman conceived, and she bore a son about that time the following spring, as Elisha had said to her.

Elisha Raises the Shunammite's Son

18 When the child had grown, he went out one day to his father among the reapers. 19 And he said to his father, "Oh, my head, my head!" The father said to his servant, "Carry him to his mother." 20 And when he had lifted him and brought him to his mother, the child sat on her lap till noon, and then he died. 21 And she went up and laid him on the bed of the man of God and shut the door behind him and went out. 22 Then she called to her husband and said, "Send me one of the servants and one of the donkeys, that I may quickly go to the man of God and come back again." 23 And he said, "Why will you go to him today? It is neither new moon nor Sabbath." She said, "All is well." 24 Then she saddled the donkey, and she said to her servant, "Urge the animal on; do not slacken the pace for me unless I tell you." 25 So she set out and came to the man of God at Mount Carmel.

When the man of God saw her coming, he said to Gehazi his servant, "Look, there is the Shunammite. 26 Run at once to meet her and say to her, 'Is all well with you? Is all well with your husband? Is all well with the child?'" And she answered, "All is well." 27 And when she came to the mountain to the man of God, she caught hold of his feet. And Gehazi came to push her away. But the man of God said, "Leave her alone, for she is in bitter distress, and the LORD has hidden it from me and has not told me." 28 Then she said, "Did I ask my lord for a son? Did I not say, 'Do not deceive me?'" 29 He said to Gehazi, "Tie up your garment and take my staff in your hand and go. If you meet anyone, do not greet him, and if anyone greets you, do not reply. And lay my staff on the face of the child." 30 Then the mother of the child said, "As the LORD lives and as you yourself live, I will not leave you." So he arose and followed her. 31 Gehazi went on ahead and laid the staff on the face of the child, but there was no sound or sign of life. Therefore he returned to meet him and told him, "The child has not awakened."

32 When Elisha came into the house, he saw the child lying dead on his bed. 33 So he went in and shut the door behind the two of them and prayed to the LORD. 34 Then he went up and lay on the child, putting his mouth on his mouth, his eyes on his eyes, and his hands on his hands. And as he stretched himself upon him, the flesh of the child became warm. 35 Then he got up again and walked once back and forth in the house, and went up and stretched himself upon him. The child sneezed seven times, and the child opened his eyes. 36 Then he summoned Gehazi and said, "Call this Shunammite." So he called her. And when she came to him, he said, "Pick up your son." 37 She came and fell at his feet, bowing to the ground. Then she picked up her son and went out.

Elisha Purifies the Deadly Stew

38 And Elisha came again to Gilgal when there was a famine in the land. And as the sons of the prophets were sitting before him, he said to his servant, "Set on the large pot, and boil stew for the sons of the

prophets." **39** One of them went out into the field to gather herbs, and found a wild vine and gathered from it his lap full of wild gourds, and came and cut them up into the pot of stew, not knowing what they were. **40** And they poured out some for the men to eat. But while they were eating of the stew, they cried out, "O man of God, there is death in the pot!" And they could not eat it. **41** He said, "Then bring flour." And he threw it into the pot and said, "Pour some out for the men, that they may eat." And there was no harm in the pot.

42 A man came from Baal-shalishah, bringing the man of God bread of the firstfruits, twenty loaves of barley and fresh ears of grain in his sack. And Elisha said, "Give to the men, that they may eat." **43** But his servant said, "How can I set this before a hundred men?" So he repeated, "Give them to the men, that they may eat, for thus says the LORD, 'They shall eat and have some left.'" **44** So he set it before them. And they ate and had some left, according to the word of the LORD.

Naaman Healed of Leprosy

593
1459

5 Naaman, commander of the army of the king of Syria, was a great man with his master and in high favor, because by him the LORD had given victory to Syria. He was a mighty man of valor, but he was a leper.[1] **2** Now the Syrians on one of their raids had carried off a little girl from the land of Israel, and she worked in the service of Naaman's wife. **3** She said to her mistress, "Would that my lord were with the prophet who is in Samaria! He would cure him of his leprosy." **4** So Naaman went in and told his lord, "Thus and so spoke the girl from the land of Israel." **5** And the king of Syria said, "Go now, and I will send a letter to the king of Israel."

So he went, taking with him ten talents of silver, six thousand shekels[2] of gold, and ten changes of clothing. **6** And he brought the letter to the king of Israel, which read, "When this letter reaches you, know that I have sent to you Naaman my servant, that you may cure him of his leprosy." **7** And when the king of Israel read the letter, he tore his clothes and said, "Am I God, to kill and to make alive, that this man sends word to me to cure a man of his leprosy? Only consider, and see how he is seeking a quarrel with me."

8 But when Elisha the man of God heard that the king of Israel had torn his clothes, he sent to the king, saying, "Why have you torn your clothes? Let him come now to me, that he may know that there is a prophet in Israel." **9** So Naaman came with his horses and chariots and stood at the door of Elisha's house. **10** And Elisha sent a messenger to him, saying, "Go and wash in the Jordan seven times, and your flesh shall be restored, and you shall be clean." **11** But Naaman was angry and went away, saying, "Behold, I thought that he would surely come out to me and stand and call upon the name of the LORD his God, and wave his hand over the place and cure the leper. **12** Are not Abana[3] and Pharpar, the rivers of Damascus, better than all the waters of Israel? Could I not wash in them and be clean?" So he turned and went away in a rage. **13** But his servants came near and said to him, "My father, it is a great word the prophet has spoken to you; will you not do it? Has he actually said to you, 'Wash, and be clean'?" **14** So he went down and dipped himself seven times in the Jordan, according to the word of the man of God, and his flesh was restored like the flesh of a little child, and he was clean.

Gehazi's Greed and Punishment

15 Then he returned to the man of God, he and all his company, and he came and stood before him. And he said, "Behold, I know that there is no God in all the earth but in Israel; so accept now a present from your servant." **16** But he said, "As the LORD

[1] *Leprosy* was a term for several skin diseases; see Leviticus 13 [2] A *talent* was about 75 pounds or 34 kilograms; a *shekel* was about 2/5 ounce or 11 grams [3] Or *Amana*

God Heals Naaman of Leprosy

Long ago a little girl lived in her home with the people of God in Israel. But soldiers came and took the little girl far away to live in a land where people worshiped idols and did not know the one true God.

The little girl stayed in the home of a rich man named Naaman, where she worked as a servant helping his wife. Naaman had a terrible skin disease called leprosy. Doctors could not make him better.

The little girl knew that God could help Naaman. She told his wife about Elisha the prophet who lived in Israel, where the little girl used to live. She said Naaman should go see Elisha, and he would cure Naaman of his leprosy.

So Naaman rode to Elisha's house, in his chariot pulled by horses. When Elisha heard that Naaman was coming, he said, "Let him come now to me" so that he will know that there is a prophet of God in the land of Israel. When Naaman arrived at Elisha's house, Elisha sent his servant out to tell Naaman, "Go and wash in the Jordan seven times." If he washed in the Jordan River, he would be healed and his skin would be as good as new.

This made Naaman angry! He didn't want to wash in the Jordan. He wanted Elisha to come outside and wave his hands over him and heal him. But his servants begged Naaman to do what Elisha said.

So Naaman went down to the Jordan River. He walked into the water and dipped down one, two, three, four, five, six, seven times. All at once, Naaman's skin was clear, and he was healed! Overjoyed, Naaman went back to Elisha's house to thank him. Naaman said, "Behold, I know that there is no God in all the earth but in Israel."

God worked through the little girl and Elisha to help Naaman. He made Naaman well again, and Naaman learned about God's love.

God gives us helpers like our parents and teachers and pastors. They take care of us and tell us about the true God and about Jesus, His Son. And God can use us to tell others about His love, just like the little girl helped Naaman to learn about God. God helps us to show His love to the people we meet.

SEEK and FIND

WHERE TO FIND THE STORY

2 Kings 5:1–14

KEY BIBLE VERSE

"Sing to the LORD, bless his name;
tell of his salvation from day to day.
Declare his glory among the nations,
his marvelous works among all the peoples!"
(Psalm 96:2–3)

THREE KEY QUESTIONS

- How do we know that the little girl trusted God even though she lived in a faraway land?
- What happened to Naaman when he washed in the River

Jordan seven times?

- What are some ways that we can show God's love to the people we meet?

RELATED BIBLE READINGS

Psalm 98:1–3; 115:1–8; Isaiah 45:22–24; Matthew 28:19–20; Luke 4:24–27; Romans 15:9–12

lives, before whom I stand, I will receive none." And he urged him to take it, but he refused. 17 Then Naaman said, "If not, please let there be given to your servant two mules' load of earth, for from now on your servant will not offer burnt offering or sacrifice to any god but the LORD. 18 In this matter may the LORD pardon your servant: when my master goes into the house of Rimmon to worship there, leaning on my arm, and I bow myself in the house of Rimmon, when I bow myself in the house of Rimmon, the LORD pardon your servant in this matter." 19 He said to him, "Go in peace."

But when Naaman had gone from him a short distance, 20 Gehazi, the servant of Elisha the man of God, said, "See, my master has spared this Naaman the Syrian, in not accepting from his hand what he brought. As the LORD lives, I will run after him and get something from him." 21 So Gehazi followed Naaman. And when Naaman saw someone running after him, he got down from the chariot to meet him and said, "Is all well?" 22 And he said, "All is well. My master has sent me to say, 'There have just now come to me from the hill country of Ephraim two young men of the sons of the prophets. Please give them a talent of silver and two changes of clothing.'" 23 And Naaman said, "Be pleased to accept two talents." And he urged him and tied up two talents of silver in two bags, with two changes of clothing, and laid them on two of his servants. And they carried them before Gehazi. 24 And when he came to the hill, he took them from their hand and put them in the house, and he sent the men away, and they departed. 25 He went in and stood before his master, and Elisha said to him, "Where have you been, Gehazi?" And he said, "Your servant went nowhere." 26 But he said to him, "Did not my heart go when the man turned from his chariot to meet you? Was it a time to accept money and garments, olive orchards and vineyards, sheep and oxen, male servants and female servants? 27 Therefore the leprosy of Naaman shall cling to you and to your descendants forever." So he went out from his presence a leper, like snow.

The Axe Head Recovered

6 Now the sons of the prophets said to Elisha, "See, the place where we dwell under your charge is too small for us. 2 Let us go to the Jordan and each of us get there a log, and let us make a place for us to dwell there." And he answered, "Go." 3 Then one of them said, "Be pleased to go with your servants." And he answered, "I will go." 4 So he went with them. And when they came to the Jordan, they cut down trees. 5 But as one was felling a log, his axe head fell into the water, and he cried out, "Alas, my master! It was borrowed." 6 Then

the man of God said, "Where did it fall?" When he showed him the place, he cut off a stick and threw it in there and made the iron float. 7 And he said, "Take it up." So he reached out his hand and took it.

Horses and Chariots of Fire

8 Once when the king of Syria was warring against Israel, he took counsel with his servants, saying, "At such and such a place shall be my camp." 9 But the man of God sent word to the king of Israel, "Beware that you do not pass this place, for the Syrians are going down there." 10 And the king of Israel sent to the place about which the man of God told him. Thus he used to warn him, so that he saved himself there more than once or twice.

11 And the mind of the king of Syria was greatly troubled because of this thing, and he called his servants and said to them, "Will you not show me who of us is for the king of Israel?" 12 And one of his servants said, "None, my lord, O king; but Elisha, the prophet who is in Israel, tells the king of Israel the words that you speak in your bedroom." 13 And he said, "Go and see where he is, that I may send and seize him." It was told him, "Behold, he is in Dothan." 14 So he sent there horses and chariots and a great army, and they came by night and surrounded the city.

15 When the servant of the man of God rose early in the morning and went out, behold, an army with horses and chariots was all around the city. And the servant said, "Alas, my master! What shall we do?" 16 He said, "Do not be afraid, for those who are with us are more than those who are with them." 17 Then Elisha prayed and said, "O LORD, please open his eyes that he may see." So the LORD opened the eyes of the young man, and he saw, and behold, the mountain was full of horses and chariots of fire all around Elisha. 18 And when the Syrians came down against him, Elisha prayed to the LORD and said, "Please strike this people with blindness." So he struck them with blindness in accordance with the prayer of Elisha. 19 And Elisha said to them, "This is not the way, and this is not the city. Follow me, and I will bring you to the man whom you seek." And he led them to Samaria.

20 As soon as they entered Samaria, Elisha said, "O LORD, open the eyes of these men, that they may see." So the LORD opened their eyes and they saw, and behold, they were in the midst of Samaria. 21 As soon as the king of Israel saw them, he said to Elisha, "My father, shall I strike them down? Shall I strike them down?" 22 He answered, "You shall not strike them down. Would you strike down those whom you have taken captive with your sword and with your bow? Set bread and water before them, that they may eat and drink and go to their master." 23 So he prepared for them a great feast, and when they had eaten and drunk, he sent them away, and they went to their master. And the Syrians did not come again on raids into the land of Israel.

Ben-hadad's Siege of Samaria

24 Afterward Ben-hadad king of Syria mustered his entire army and went up and besieged Samaria. 25 And there was a great famine in Samaria, as they besieged it, until a donkey's head was sold for eighty shekels of silver, and the fourth part of a kab[1] of dove's dung for five shekels of silver. 26 Now as the king of Israel was passing by on the wall, a woman cried out to him, saying, "Help, my lord, O king!" 27 And he said, "If the LORD will not help you, how shall I help you? From the threshing floor, or from the winepress?" 28 And the king asked her, "What is your trouble?" She answered, "This woman said to me, 'Give your son, that we may eat him today, and we will eat my son tomorrow.' 29 So we boiled my son and ate him. And on the next day I said to her, 'Give your son, that we may eat him.'

[1] A *shekel* was about 2/5 ounce or 11 grams; a *kab* was about 1 quart or 1 liter

But she has hidden her son." 30 When the king heard the words of the woman, he tore his clothes—now he was passing by on the wall—and the people looked, and behold, he had sackcloth beneath on his body— 31 and he said, "May God do so to me and more also, if the head of Elisha the son of Shaphat remains on his shoulders today."

32 Elisha was sitting in his house, and the elders were sitting with him. Now the king had dispatched a man from his presence, but before the messenger arrived Elisha said to the elders, "Do you see how this murderer has sent to take off my head? Look, when the messenger comes, shut the door and hold the door fast against him. Is not the sound of his master's feet behind him?" 33 And while he was still speaking with them, the messenger came down to him and said, "This trouble is from the LORD! Why should I wait for the LORD any longer?"

Elisha Promises Food

7 But Elisha said, "Hear the word of the LORD: thus says the LORD, Tomorrow about this time a seah[1] of fine flour shall be sold for a shekel,[2] and two seahs of barley for a shekel, at the gate of Samaria." 2 Then the captain on whose hand the king leaned said to the man of God, "If the LORD himself should make windows in heaven, could this thing be?" But he said, "You shall see it with your own eyes, but you shall not eat of it."

The Syrians Flee

3 Now there were four men who were lepers[3] at the entrance to the gate. And they said to one another, "Why are we sitting here until we die? 4 If we say, 'Let us enter the city,' the famine is in the city, and we shall die there. And if we sit here, we die also. So now come, let us go over to the camp of the Syrians. If they spare our lives we shall live, and if they kill us we shall but die." 5 So they arose at twilight to go to the camp of the Syrians. But when they came to the edge of the camp of the Syrians, behold, there was no one there. 6 For the Lord had made the army of the Syrians hear the sound of chariots and of horses, the sound of a great army, so that they said to one another, "Behold, the king of Israel has hired against us the kings of the Hittites and the kings of Egypt to come against us." 7 So they fled away in the twilight and abandoned their tents, their horses, and their donkeys, leaving the camp as it was, and fled for their lives. 8 And when these lepers came to the edge of the camp, they went into a tent and ate and drank, and they carried off silver and gold and clothing and went and hid them. Then they came back and entered another tent and carried off things from it and went and hid them.

9 Then they said to one another, "We are not doing right. This day is a day of good news. If we are silent and wait until the morning light, punishment will overtake us. Now therefore come; let us go and tell the king's household." 10 So they came and called to the gatekeepers of the city and told them, "We came to the camp of the Syrians, and behold, there was no one to be seen or heard there, nothing but the horses tied and the donkeys tied and the tents as they were." 11 Then the gatekeepers called out, and it was told within the king's household. 12 And the king rose in the night and said to his servants, "I will tell you what the Syrians have done to us. They know that we are hungry. Therefore they have gone out of the camp to hide themselves in the open country, thinking, 'When they come out of the city, we shall take them alive and get into the city.'" 13 And one of his servants said, "Let some men take five of the remaining horses, seeing that those who are left here will fare like the whole multitude of Israel who have already perished. Let us send and see." 14 So they took two horsemen, and the king sent them after the army of the Syrians, saying, "Go and see." 15 So they

[1] A *seah* was about 7 quarts or 7.3 liters [2] A *shekel* was about 2/5 ounce or 11 grams [3] *Leprosy* was a term for several skin diseases; see Leviticus 13

went after them as far as the Jordan, and behold, all the way was littered with garments and equipment that the Syrians had thrown away in their haste. And the messengers returned and told the king.

16 Then the people went out and plundered the camp of the Syrians. So a seah of fine flour was sold for a shekel, and two seahs of barley for a shekel, according to the word of the LORD. 17 Now the king had appointed the captain on whose hand he leaned to have charge of the gate. And the people trampled him in the gate, so that he died, as the man of God had said when the king came down to him. 18 For when the man of God had said to the king, "Two seahs of barley shall be sold for a shekel, and a seah of fine flour for a shekel, about this time tomorrow in the gate of Samaria," 19 the captain had answered the man of God, "If the LORD himself should make windows in heaven, could such a thing be?" And he had said, "You shall see it with your own eyes, but you shall not eat of it." 20 And so it happened to him, for the people trampled him in the gate and he died.

The Shunammite's Land Restored

8 Now Elisha had said to the woman whose son he had restored to life, "Arise, and depart with your household, and sojourn wherever you can, for the LORD has called for a famine, and it will come upon the land for seven years." 2 So the woman arose and did according to the word of the man of God. She went with her household and sojourned in the land of the Philistines seven years. 3 And at the end of the seven years, when the woman returned from the land of the Philistines, she went to appeal to the king for her house and her land. 4 Now the king was talking with Gehazi the servant of the man of God, saying, "Tell me all the great things that Elisha has done." 5 And while he was telling the king how Elisha had restored the dead to life, behold, the woman whose son he had restored to life appealed to the king for her house and her land. And Gehazi said, "My lord, O king, here is the woman, and here is her son whom Elisha restored to life." 6 And when the king asked the woman, she told him. So the king appointed an official for her, saying, "Restore all that was hers, together with all the produce of the fields from the day that she left the land until now."

Hazael Murders Ben-hadad

7 Now Elisha came to Damascus. Ben-hadad the king of Syria was sick. And when it was told him, "The man of God has come here," 8 the king said to Hazael, "Take a present with you and go to meet the man of God, and inquire of the LORD through him, saying, 'Shall I recover from this sickness?'" 9 So Hazael went to meet him, and took a present with him, all kinds of goods of Damascus, forty camel loads. When he came and stood before him, he said, "Your son Ben-hadad king of Syria has sent me to you, saying, 'Shall I recover from this sickness?'" 10 And Elisha said to him, "Go, say to him, 'You shall certainly recover,' but the LORD has shown me that he shall certainly die." 11 And he fixed his gaze and stared at him, until he was embarrassed. And the man of God wept. 12 And Hazael said, "Why does my lord weep?" He answered, "Because I know the evil that you will do to the people of Israel. You will set on fire their fortresses, and you will kill their young men with the sword and dash in pieces their little ones and rip open their pregnant women." 13 And Hazael said, "What is your servant, who is but a dog, that he should do this great thing?" Elisha answered, "The LORD has shown me that you are to be king over Syria." 14 Then he departed from Elisha and came to his master, who said to him, "What did Elisha say to you?" And he answered, "He told me that you would certainly recover." 15 But the next day he took the bed cloth[1] and dipped

[1] The meaning of the Hebrew is uncertain

it in water and spread it over his face, till he died. And Hazael became king in his place.

Jehoram Reigns in Judah

16 In the fifth year of Joram the son of Ahab, king of Israel, when Jehoshaphat was king of Judah,[1] Jehoram the son of Jehoshaphat, king of Judah, began to reign. 17 He was thirty-two years old when he became king, and he reigned eight years in Jerusalem. 18 And he walked in the way of the kings of Israel, as the house of Ahab had done, for the daughter of Ahab was his wife. And he did what was evil in the sight of the LORD. 19 Yet the LORD was not willing to destroy Judah, for the sake of David his servant, since he promised to give a lamp to him and to his sons forever.

20 In his days Edom revolted from the rule of Judah and set up a king of their own. 21 Then Joram[2] passed over to Zair with all his chariots and rose by night, and he and his chariot commanders struck the Edomites who had surrounded him, but his army fled home. 22 So Edom revolted from the rule of Judah to this day. Then Libnah revolted at the same time. 23 Now the rest of the acts of Joram, and all that he did, are they not written in the Book of the Chronicles of the Kings of Judah? 24 So Joram slept with his fathers and was buried with his fathers in the city of David, and Ahaziah his son reigned in his place.

Ahaziah Reigns in Judah

25 In the twelfth year of Joram the son of Ahab, king of Israel, Ahaziah the son of Jehoram, king of Judah, began to reign. 26 Ahaziah was twenty-two years old when he began to reign, and he reigned one year in Jerusalem. His mother's name was Athaliah; she was a granddaughter of Omri king of Israel. 27 He also walked in the way of the house of Ahab and did what was evil in the sight of the LORD, as the house of Ahab had done, for he was son-in-law to the house of Ahab.

28 He went with Joram the son of Ahab to make war against Hazael king of Syria at Ramoth-gilead, and the Syrians wounded Joram. 29 And King Joram returned to be healed in Jezreel of the wounds that the Syrians had given him at Ramah, when he fought against Hazael king of Syria. And Ahaziah the son of Jehoram king of Judah went down to see Joram the son of Ahab in Jezreel, because he was sick.

Jehu Anointed King of Israel

9 Then Elisha the prophet called one of the sons of the prophets and said to him, "Tie up your garments, and take this flask of oil in your hand, and go to Ramoth-gilead. 2 And when you arrive, look there for Jehu the son of Jehoshaphat, son of Nimshi. And go in and have him rise from among his fellows, and lead him to an inner chamber. 3 Then take the flask of oil and pour it on his head and say, 'Thus says the LORD, I anoint you king over Israel.' Then open the door and flee; do not linger."

4 So the young man, the servant of the prophet, went to Ramoth-gilead. 5 And when he came, behold, the commanders of the army were in council. And he said, "I have a word for you, O commander." And Jehu said, "To which of us all?" And he said, "To you, O commander." 6 So he arose and went into the house. And the young man poured the oil on his head, saying to him, "Thus says the LORD, the God of Israel, I anoint you king over the people of the LORD, over Israel. 7 And you shall strike down the house of Ahab your master, so that I may avenge on Jezebel the blood of my servants the prophets, and the blood of all the servants of the LORD. 8 For the whole house of Ahab shall perish, and I will cut off from Ahab every male, bond or free, in Israel. 9 And I will make the house of Ahab like the house of Jeroboam the son of Nebat, and like the house of Baasha the son of Ahijah. 10 And the dogs shall eat Jezebel in the territory of

[1] Septuagint, Syriac lack *when Jehoshaphat was king of Judah* [2] *Joram* is another spelling of *Jehoram* (the son of Jehoshaphat) as in verse 16; also verses 23, 24

Jezreel, and none shall bury her." Then he opened the door and fled.

11 When Jehu came out to the servants of his master, they said to him, "Is all well? Why did this mad fellow come to you?" And he said to them, "You know the fellow and his talk." 12 And they said, "That is not true; tell us now." And he said, "Thus and so he spoke to me, saying, 'Thus says the LORD, I anoint you king over Israel.'" 13 Then in haste every man of them took his garment and put it under him on the bare[1] steps, and they blew the trumpet and proclaimed, "Jehu is king."

Jehu Assassinates Joram and Ahaziah

14 Thus Jehu the son of Jehoshaphat the son of Nimshi conspired against Joram. (Now Joram with all Israel had been on guard at Ramoth-gilead against Hazael king of Syria, 15 but King Joram had returned to be healed in Jezreel of the wounds that the Syrians had given him, when he fought with Hazael king of Syria.) So Jehu said, "If this is your decision, then let no one slip out of the city to go and tell the news in Jezreel." 16 Then Jehu mounted his chariot and went to Jezreel, for Joram lay there. And Ahaziah king of Judah had come down to visit Joram.

17 Now the watchman was standing on the tower in Jezreel, and he saw the company of Jehu as he came and said, "I see a company." And Joram said, "Take a horseman and send to meet them, and let him say, 'Is it peace?'" 18 So a man on horseback went to meet him and said, "Thus says the king, 'Is it peace?'" And Jehu said, "What do you have to do with peace? Turn around and ride behind me." And the watchman reported, saying, "The messenger reached them, but he is not coming back." 19 Then he sent out a second horseman, who came to them and said, "Thus the king has said, 'Is it peace?'" And Jehu answered, "What do you have to do with peace? Turn around and ride behind me." 20 Again the watchman reported, "He reached them, but he is not coming back. And the driving is like the driving of Jehu the son of Nimshi, for he drives furiously."

21 Joram said, "Make ready." And they made ready his chariot. Then Joram king of Israel and Ahaziah king of Judah set out, each in his chariot, and went to meet Jehu, and met him at the property of Naboth the Jezreelite. 22 And when Joram saw Jehu, he said, "Is it peace, Jehu?" He answered, "What peace can there be, so long as the whorings and the sorceries of your mother Jezebel are so many?" 23 Then Joram reined about and fled, saying to Ahaziah, "Treachery, O Ahaziah!" 24 And Jehu drew his bow with his full strength, and shot Joram between the shoulders, so that the arrow pierced his heart, and he sank in his chariot. 25 Jehu said to Bidkar his aide, "Take him up and throw him on the plot of ground belonging to Naboth the Jezreelite. For remember, when you and I rode side by side behind Ahab his father, how the LORD made this pronouncement against him: 26 'As surely as I saw yesterday the blood of Naboth and the blood of his sons—declares the LORD—I will repay you on this plot of ground.' Now therefore take him up and throw him on the plot of ground, in accordance with the word of the LORD."

27 When Ahaziah the king of Judah saw this, he fled in the direction of Beth-haggan. And Jehu pursued him and said, "Shoot him also." And they shot him[2] in the chariot at the ascent of Gur, which is by Ibleam. And he fled to Megiddo and died there. 28 His servants carried him in a chariot to Jerusalem, and buried him in his tomb with his fathers in the city of David.

29 In the eleventh year of Joram the son of Ahab, Ahaziah began to reign over Judah.

Jehu Executes Jezebel

30 When Jehu came to Jezreel, Jezebel heard of it. And she painted her eyes and adorned her head and looked out of the

[1] The meaning of the Hebrew word is uncertain [2] Syriac, Vulgate (compare Septuagint); Hebrew lacks *and they shot him*

window. 31 And as Jehu entered the gate, she said, "Is it peace, you Zimri, murderer of your master?" 32 And he lifted up his face to the window and said, "Who is on my side? Who?" Two or three eunuchs looked out at him. 33 He said, "Throw her down." So they threw her down. And some of her blood spattered on the wall and on the horses, and they trampled on her. 34 Then he went in and ate and drank. And he said, "See now to this cursed woman and bury her, for she is a king's daughter." 35 But when they went to bury her, they found no more of her than the skull and the feet and the palms of her hands. 36 When they came back and told him, he said, "This is the word of the LORD, which he spoke by his servant Elijah the Tishbite, 'In the territory of Jezreel the dogs shall eat the flesh of Jezebel, 37 and the corpse of Jezebel shall be as dung on the face of the field in the territory of Jezreel, so that no one can say, This is Jezebel.'"

Jehu Slaughters Ahab's Descendants

10 Now Ahab had seventy sons in Samaria. So Jehu wrote letters and sent them to Samaria, to the rulers of the city,[1] to the elders, and to the guardians of the sons[2] of Ahab, saying, 2 "Now then, as soon as this letter comes to you, seeing your master's sons are with you, and there are with you chariots and horses, fortified cities also, and weapons, 3 select the best and fittest of your master's sons and set him on his father's throne and fight for your master's house." 4 But they were exceedingly afraid and said, "Behold, the two kings could not stand before him. How then can we stand?" 5 So he who was over the palace, and he who was over the city, together with the elders and the guardians, sent to Jehu, saying, "We are your servants, and we will do all that you tell us. We will not make anyone king. Do whatever is good in your eyes." 6 Then he wrote to them a second letter, saying, "If you are on my side, and if you are ready to obey me, take the heads of your master's sons and come to me at Jezreel tomorrow at this time." Now the king's sons, seventy persons, were with the great men of the city, who were bringing them up. 7 And as soon as the letter came to them, they took the king's sons and slaughtered them, seventy persons, and put their heads in baskets and sent them to him at Jezreel. 8 When the messenger came and told him, "They have brought the heads of the king's sons," he said, "Lay them in two heaps at the entrance of the gate until the morning." 9 Then in the morning, when he went out, he stood and said to all the people, "You are innocent. It was I who conspired against my master and killed him, but who struck down all these? 10 Know then that there shall fall to the earth nothing of the word of the LORD, which the LORD spoke concerning the house of Ahab, for the LORD has done what he said by his servant Elijah." 11 So Jehu struck down all who remained of the house of Ahab in Jezreel, all his great men and his close friends and his priests, until he left him none remaining.

12 Then he set out and went to Samaria. On the way, when he was at Beth-eked of the Shepherds, 13 Jehu met the relatives of Ahaziah king of Judah, and he said, "Who are you?" And they answered, "We are the relatives of Ahaziah, and we came down to visit the royal princes and the sons of the queen mother." 14 He said, "Take them alive." And they took them alive and slaughtered them at the pit of Beth-eked, forty-two persons, and he spared none of them.

15 And when he departed from there, he met Jehonadab the son of Rechab coming to meet him. And he greeted him and said to him, "Is your heart true to my heart as mine is to yours?" And Jehonadab answered, "It is." Jehu said,[3] "If it is, give me your hand." So he gave him his hand. And Jehu took him up with him into the

[1] Septuagint, Vulgate; Hebrew *rulers of Jezreel* [2] Hebrew lacks *of the sons* [3] Septuagint; Hebrew lacks *Jehu said*

chariot. 16 And he said, "Come with me, and see my zeal for the LORD." So he[1] had him ride in his chariot. 17 And when he came to Samaria, he struck down all who remained to Ahab in Samaria, till he had wiped them out, according to the word of the LORD that he spoke to Elijah.

Jehu Strikes Down the Prophets of Baal

18 Then Jehu assembled all the people and said to them, "Ahab served Baal a little, but Jehu will serve him much. 19 Now therefore call to me all the prophets of Baal, all his worshipers and all his priests. Let none be missing, for I have a great sacrifice to offer to Baal. Whoever is missing shall not live." But Jehu did it with cunning in order to destroy the worshipers of Baal. 20 And Jehu ordered, "Sanctify a solemn assembly for Baal." So they proclaimed it. 21 And Jehu sent throughout all Israel, and all the worshipers of Baal came, so that there was not a man left who did not come. And they entered the house of Baal, and the house of Baal was filled from one end to the other. 22 He said to him who was in charge of the wardrobe, "Bring out the vestments for all the worshipers of Baal." So he brought out the vestments for them. 23 Then Jehu went into the house of Baal with Jehonadab the son of Rechab, and he said to the worshipers of Baal, "Search, and see that there is no servant of the LORD here among you, but only the worshipers of Baal." 24 Then they[2] went in to offer sacrifices and burnt offerings.

Now Jehu had stationed eighty men outside and said, "The man who allows any of those whom I give into your hands to escape shall forfeit his life." 25 So as soon as he had made an end of offering the burnt offering, Jehu said to the guard and to the officers, "Go in and strike them down; let not a man escape." So when they put them to the sword, the guard and the officers cast them out and went into the inner room of the house of Baal, 26 and they brought out the pillar that was in the house of Baal and burned it. 27 And they demolished the pillar of Baal, and demolished the house of Baal, and made it a latrine to this day.

Jehu Reigns in Israel

28 Thus Jehu wiped out Baal from Israel. 29 But Jehu did not turn aside from the sins of Jeroboam the son of Nebat, which he made Israel to sin—that is, the golden calves that were in Bethel and in Dan. 30 And the LORD said to Jehu, "Because you have done well in carrying out what is right in my eyes, and have done to the house of Ahab according to all that was in my heart, your sons of the fourth generation shall sit on the throne of Israel." 31 But Jehu was not careful to walk in the law of the LORD, the God of Israel, with all his heart. He did not turn from the sins of Jeroboam, which he made Israel to sin.

32 In those days the LORD began to cut off parts of Israel. Hazael defeated them throughout the territory of Israel: 33 from the Jordan eastward, all the land of Gilead, the Gadites, and the Reubenites, and the Manassites, from Aroer, which is by the Valley of the Arnon, that is, Gilead and Bashan. 34 Now the rest of the acts of Jehu and all that he did, and all his might, are they not written in the Book of the Chronicles of the Kings of Israel? 35 So Jehu slept with his fathers, and they buried him in Samaria. And Jehoahaz his son reigned in his place. 36 The time that Jehu reigned over Israel in Samaria was twenty-eight years.

Athaliah Reigns in Judah

11 Now when Athaliah the mother of Ahaziah saw that her son was dead, she arose and destroyed all the royal family. 2 But Jehosheba, the daughter of King Joram, sister of Ahaziah, took Joash the son of Ahaziah and stole him away from among the king's sons who were being put to death, and she put[3] him and

[1] Septuagint, Syriac, Targum; Hebrew *they* [2] Septuagint *he* (compare verse 25) [3] Compare 2 Chronicles 22:11; Hebrew lacks *and she put*

his nurse in a bedroom. Thus they[1] hid him from Athaliah, so that he was not put to death. 3 And he remained with her six years, hidden in the house of the LORD, while Athaliah reigned over the land.

Joash Anointed King in Judah

4 But in the seventh year Jehoiada sent and brought the captains of the Carites and of the guards, and had them come to him in the house of the LORD. And he made a covenant with them and put them under oath in the house of the LORD, and he showed them the king's son. 5 And he commanded them, "This is the thing that you shall do: one third of you, those who come off duty on the Sabbath and guard the king's house 6 (another third being at the gate Sur and a third at the gate behind the guards) shall guard the palace.[2] 7 And the two divisions of you, which come on duty in force on the Sabbath and guard the house of the LORD on behalf of the king, 8 shall surround the king, each with his weapons in his hand. And whoever approaches the ranks is to be put to death. Be with the king when he goes out and when he comes in."

9 The captains did according to all that Jehoiada the priest commanded, and they each brought his men who were to go off duty on the Sabbath, with those who were to come on duty on the Sabbath, and came to Jehoiada the priest. 10 And the priest gave to the captains the spears and shields that had been King David's, which were in the house of the LORD. 11 And the guards stood, every man with his weapons in his hand, from the south side of the house to the north side of the house, around the altar and the house on behalf of the king. 12 Then he brought out the king's son and put the crown on him and gave him the testimony. And they proclaimed him king and anointed him, and they clapped their hands and said, "Long live the king!"

13 When Athaliah heard the noise of the guard and of the people, she went into the house of the LORD to the people. 14 And when she looked, there was the king standing by the pillar, according to the custom, and the captains and the trumpeters beside the king, and all the people of the land rejoicing and blowing trumpets. And Athaliah tore her clothes and cried, "Treason! Treason!" 15 Then Jehoiada the priest commanded the captains who were set over the army, "Bring her out between the ranks, and put to death with the sword anyone who follows her." For the priest said, "Let her not be put to death in the house of the LORD." 16 So they laid hands on her; and she went through the horses' entrance to the king's house, and there she was put to death.

17 And Jehoiada made a covenant between the LORD and the king and people, that they should be the LORD's people, and also between the king and the people. 18 Then all the people of the land went to the house of Baal and tore it down; his altars and his images they broke in pieces, and they killed Mattan the priest of Baal before the altars. And the priest posted watchmen over the house of the LORD. 19 And he took the captains, the Carites, the guards, and all the people of the land, and they brought the king down from the house of the LORD, marching through the gate of the guards to the king's house. And he took his seat on the throne of the kings. 20 So all the people of the land rejoiced, and the city was quiet after Athaliah had been put to death with the sword at the king's house.

Jehoash Reigns in Judah

21 [3] Jehoash[4] was seven years old when he began to reign.

12 In the seventh year of Jehu, Jehoash[5] began to reign, and he reigned forty years in Jerusalem. His mother's name was Zibiah of Beersheba. 2 And Jehoash did what was right in the eyes of the LORD all his days, because Jehoiada the priest instructed him. 3 Nevertheless,

[1] Septuagint, Syriac, Vulgate (compare 2 Chronicles 22:11) *she* [2] The meaning of the Hebrew word is uncertain [3] Ch 12:1 in Hebrew [4] *Jehoash* is another spelling of *Joash* (son of Ahaziah) as in verse 2 [5] *Jehoash* is another spelling of *Joash* (son of Ahaziah) as in 11:2; also verses 2, 4, 6, 7, 18

the high places were not taken away; the people continued to sacrifice and make offerings on the high places.

Jehoash Repairs the Temple

4 Jehoash said to the priests, "All the money of the holy things that is brought into the house of the LORD, the money for which each man is assessed—the money from the assessment of persons—and the money that a man's heart prompts him to bring into the house of the LORD, 5 let the priests take, each from his donor, and let them repair the house wherever any need of repairs is discovered." 6 But by the twenty-third year of King Jehoash, the priests had made no repairs on the house. 7 Therefore King Jehoash summoned Jehoiada the priest and the other priests and said to them, "Why are you not repairing the house? Now therefore take no more money from your donors, but hand it over for the repair of the house." 8 So the priests agreed that they should take no more money from the people, and that they should not repair the house.

9 Then Jehoiada the priest took a chest and bored a hole in the lid of it and set it beside the altar on the right side as one entered the house of the LORD. And the priests who guarded the threshold put in it all the money that was brought into the house of the LORD. 10 And whenever they saw that there was much money in the chest, the king's secretary and the high priest came up and they bagged and counted the money that was found in the house of the LORD. 11 Then they would give the money that was weighed out into the hands of the workmen who had the oversight of the house of the LORD. And they paid it out to the carpenters and the builders who worked on the house of the LORD, 12 and to the masons and the stonecutters, as well as to buy timber and quarried stone for making repairs on the house of the LORD, and for any outlay for the repairs of the house. 13 But there were not made for the house of the LORD basins of silver, snuffers, bowls, trumpets, or any vessels of gold, or of silver, from the money that was brought into the house of the LORD, 14 for that was given to the workmen who were repairing the house of the LORD with it. 15 And they did not ask an accounting from the men into whose hand they delivered the money to pay out to the workmen, for they dealt honestly. 16 The money from the guilt offerings and the money from the sin offerings was not brought into the house of the LORD; it belonged to the priests.

17 At that time Hazael king of Syria went up and fought against Gath and took it. But when Hazael set his face to go up against Jerusalem, 18 Jehoash king of Judah took all the sacred gifts that Jehoshaphat and Jehoram and Ahaziah his fathers, the kings of Judah, had dedicated, and his own sacred gifts, and all the gold that was found in the treasuries of the house of the LORD and of the king's house, and sent these to Hazael king of Syria. Then Hazael went away from Jerusalem.

The Death of Joash

19 Now the rest of the acts of Joash and all that he did, are they not written in the Book of the Chronicles of the Kings of Judah? 20 His servants arose and made a conspiracy and struck down Joash in the house of Millo, on the way that goes down to Silla. 21 It was Jozacar the son of Shimeath and Jehozabad the son of Shomer, his servants, who struck him down, so that he died. And they buried him with his fathers in the city of David, and Amaziah his son reigned in his place.

Jehoahaz Reigns in Israel

13 In the twenty-third year of Joash the son of Ahaziah, king of Judah, Jehoahaz the son of Jehu began to reign over Israel in Samaria, and he reigned seventeen years. 2 He did what was evil in the sight of the LORD and followed the sins of

Jeroboam the son of Nebat, which he made
Israel to sin; he did not depart from them.
3 And the anger of the LORD was kindled
against Israel, and he gave them continu-
ally into the hand of Hazael king of Syria
and into the hand of Ben-hadad the son
of Hazael. 4 Then Jehoahaz sought the
favor of the LORD, and the LORD listened
to him, for he saw the oppression of Israel,
how the king of Syria oppressed them.
5 (Therefore the LORD gave Israel a savior,
so that they escaped from the hand of the
Syrians, and the people of Israel lived in
their homes as formerly. 6 Nevertheless,
they did not depart from the sins of the
house of Jeroboam, which he made Israel
to sin, but walked[1] in them; and the
Asherah also remained in Samaria.) 7 For
there was not left to Jehoahaz an army of
more than fifty horsemen and ten chariots
and ten thousand footmen, for the king
of Syria had destroyed them and made
them like the dust at threshing. 8 Now the
rest of the acts of Jehoahaz and all that he
did, and his might, are they not written in
the Book of the Chronicles of the Kings of
Israel? 9 So Jehoahaz slept with his fathers,
and they buried him in Samaria, and Joash
his son reigned in his place.

Jehoash Reigns in Israel

10 In the thirty-seventh year of Joash
king of Judah, Jehoash[2] the son of Jehoahaz
began to reign over Israel in Samaria, and
he reigned sixteen years. 11 He also did
what was evil in the sight of the LORD.
He did not depart from all the sins of
Jeroboam the son of Nebat, which he
made Israel to sin, but he walked in them.
12 Now the rest of the acts of Joash and all
that he did, and the might with which he
fought against Amaziah king of Judah,
are they not written in the Book of the
Chronicles of the Kings of Israel? 13 So
Joash slept with his fathers, and Jeroboam
sat on his throne. And Joash was buried in
Samaria with the kings of Israel.

The Death of Elisha

14 Now when Elisha had fallen sick with
the illness of which he was to die, Joash
king of Israel went down to him and wept
before him, crying, "My father, my father!
The chariots of Israel and its horsemen!"
15 And Elisha said to him, "Take a bow and
arrows." So he took a bow and arrows.
16 Then he said to the king of Israel, "Draw
the bow," and he drew it. And Elisha laid
his hands on the king's hands. 17 And he
said, "Open the window eastward," and he
opened it. Then Elisha said, "Shoot," and
he shot. And he said, "The LORD's arrow of
victory, the arrow of victory over Syria! For
you shall fight the Syrians in Aphek until
you have made an end of them." 18 And he
said, "Take the arrows," and he took them.
And he said to the king of Israel, "Strike
the ground with them." And he struck
three times and stopped. 19 Then the man
of God was angry with him and said, "You
should have struck five or six times; then
you would have struck down Syria until
you had made an end of it, but now you
will strike down Syria only three times."

20 So Elisha died, and they buried him.
Now bands of Moabites used to invade
the land in the spring of the year. 21 And
as a man was being buried, behold, a
marauding band was seen and the man
was thrown into the grave of Elisha, and
as soon as the man touched the bones of
Elisha, he revived and stood on his feet.

22 Now Hazael king of Syria oppressed
Israel all the days of Jehoahaz. 23 But the
LORD was gracious to them and had com-
passion on them, and he turned toward
them, because of his covenant with
Abraham, Isaac, and Jacob, and would not
destroy them, nor has he cast them from
his presence until now.

24 When Hazael king of Syria died, Ben-
hadad his son became king in his place.
25 Then Jehoash the son of Jehoahaz
took again from Ben-hadad the son of
Hazael the cities that he had taken from

[1] Septuagint, Syriac, Targum, Vulgate; Hebrew *he walked* [2] *Jehoash* is another spelling for *Joash* (son of Jehoahaz) as in verses 9, 12-14; also verse 25

Jehoahaz his father in war. Three times
Joash defeated him and recovered the cit-
ies of Israel.

Amaziah Reigns in Judah

14 In the second year of Joash the
son of Joahaz, king of Israel,
Amaziah the son of Joash, king of Judah,
began to reign. 2 He was twenty-five
years old when he began to reign, and he
reigned twenty-nine years in Jerusalem.
His mother's name was Jehoaddin of
Jerusalem. 3 And he did what was right in
the eyes of the LORD, yet not like David
his father. He did in all things as Joash his
father had done. 4 But the high places were
not removed; the people still sacrificed
and made offerings on the high places.
5 And as soon as the royal power was
firmly in his hand, he struck down his
servants who had struck down the king
his father. 6 But he did not put to death
the children of the murderers, according
to what is written in the Book of the Law
of Moses, where the LORD commanded,
"Fathers shall not be put to death because
of their children, nor shall children be put
to death because of their fathers. But each
one shall die for his own sin."

7 He struck down ten thousand Edomites
in the Valley of Salt and took Sela by storm,
and called it Joktheel, which is its name to
this day.

8 Then Amaziah sent messengers to
Jehoash[1] the son of Jehoahaz, son of Jehu,
king of Israel, saying, "Come, let us look
one another in the face." 9 And Jehoash
king of Israel sent word to Amaziah king
of Judah, "A thistle on Lebanon sent to
a cedar on Lebanon, saying, 'Give your
daughter to my son for a wife,' and a wild
beast of Lebanon passed by and trampled
down the thistle. 10 You have indeed struck
down Edom, and your heart has lifted you
up. Be content with your glory, and stay at
home, for why should you provoke trouble
so that you fall, you and Judah with you?"

11 But Amaziah would not listen. So
Jehoash king of Israel went up, and he
and Amaziah king of Judah faced one an-
other in battle at Beth-shemesh, which
belongs to Judah. 12 And Judah was de-
feated by Israel, and every man fled to his
home. 13 And Jehoash king of Israel cap-
tured Amaziah king of Judah, the son of
Jehoash, son of Ahaziah, at Beth-shemesh,
and came to Jerusalem and broke down
the wall of Jerusalem for four hundred
cubits,[2] from the Ephraim Gate to the
Corner Gate. 14 And he seized all the gold
and silver, and all the vessels that were
found in the house of the LORD and in the
treasuries of the king's house, also hos-
tages, and he returned to Samaria.

15 Now the rest of the acts of Jehoash that
he did, and his might, and how he fought
with Amaziah king of Judah, are they not
written in the Book of the Chronicles of
the Kings of Israel? 16 And Jehoash slept
with his fathers and was buried in Samaria
with the kings of Israel, and Jeroboam his
son reigned in his place.

17 Amaziah the son of Joash, king of
Judah, lived fifteen years after the death
of Jehoash son of Jehoahaz, king of Israel.
18 Now the rest of the deeds of Amaziah,
are they not written in the Book of the
Chronicles of the Kings of Judah? 19 And
they made a conspiracy against him in
Jerusalem, and he fled to Lachish. But they
sent after him to Lachish and put him to
death there. 20 And they brought him on
horses; and he was buried in Jerusalem
with his fathers in the city of David. 21 And
all the people of Judah took Azariah, who
was sixteen years old, and made him king
instead of his father Amaziah. 22 He built
Elath and restored it to Judah, after the king
slept with his fathers.

Jeroboam II Reigns in Israel

23 In the fifteenth year of Amaziah the
son of Joash, king of Judah, Jeroboam the
son of Joash, king of Israel, began to reign

[1] *Jehoash* is another spelling for *Joash* (son of Jehoahaz) as in 13:9, 12-14; also verses 9, 11-16 [2] A *cubit* was about 18 inches or 45 centimeters

in Samaria, and he reigned forty-one years.
24 And he did what was evil in the sight of
the LORD. He did not depart from all the
sins of Jeroboam the son of Nebat, which
he made Israel to sin. 25 He restored the
border of Israel from Lebo-hamath as far
as the Sea of the Arabah, according to the
word of the LORD, the God of Israel, which
he spoke by his servant Jonah the son of
Amittai, the prophet, who was from Gath-
hepher. 26 For the LORD saw that the afflic-
tion of Israel was very bitter, for there was
none left, bond or free, and there was none
to help Israel. 27 But the LORD had not said
that he would blot out the name of Israel
from under heaven, so he saved them by
the hand of Jeroboam the son of Joash.
28 Now the rest of the acts of Jeroboam
and all that he did, and his might, how
he fought, and how he restored Damascus
and Hamath to Judah in Israel, are they
not written in the Book of the Chronicles
of the Kings of Israel? 29 And Jeroboam
slept with his fathers, the kings of Israel,
and Zechariah his son reigned in his place.

Azariah Reigns in Judah

15 In the twenty-seventh year of
Jeroboam king of Israel, Azariah
the son of Amaziah, king of Judah, began
to reign. 2 He was sixteen years old when
he began to reign, and he reigned fifty-two
years in Jerusalem. His mother's name was
Jecoliah of Jerusalem. 3 And he did what
was right in the eyes of the LORD, accord-
ing to all that his father Amaziah had done.
4 Nevertheless, the high places were not
taken away. The people still sacrificed and
made offerings on the high places. 5 And
the LORD touched the king, so that he was
a leper[1] to the day of his death, and he lived
in a separate house.[2] And Jotham the king's
son was over the household, governing the
people of the land. 6 Now the rest of the
acts of Azariah, and all that he did, are they
not written in the Book of the Chronicles
of the Kings of Judah? 7 And Azariah slept
with his fathers, and they buried him with
his fathers in the city of David, and Jotham
his son reigned in his place.

Zechariah Reigns in Israel

8 In the thirty-eighth year of Azariah king
of Judah, Zechariah the son of Jeroboam
reigned over Israel in Samaria six months.
9 And he did what was evil in the sight
of the LORD, as his fathers had done. He
did not depart from the sins of Jeroboam
the son of Nebat, which he made Israel
to sin. 10 Shallum the son of Jabesh con-
spired against him and struck him down at
Ibleam and put him to death and reigned
in his place. 11 Now the rest of the deeds
of Zechariah, behold, they are written in
the Book of the Chronicles of the Kings of
Israel. 12 (This was the promise of the LORD
that he gave to Jehu, "Your sons shall sit on
the throne of Israel to the fourth genera-
tion." And so it came to pass.)

Shallum Reigns in Israel

13 Shallum the son of Jabesh began to
reign in the thirty-ninth year of Uzziah[3]
king of Judah, and he reigned one month
in Samaria. 14 Then Menahem the son of
Gadi came up from Tirzah and came to
Samaria, and he struck down Shallum the
son of Jabesh in Samaria and put him to
death and reigned in his place. 15 Now the
rest of the deeds of Shallum, and the con-
spiracy that he made, behold, they are writ-
ten in the Book of the Chronicles of the
Kings of Israel. 16 At that time Menahem
sacked Tiphsah and all who were in it
and its territory from Tirzah on, because
they did not open it to him. Therefore
he sacked it, and he ripped open all the
women in it who were pregnant.

Menahem Reigns in Israel

17 In the thirty-ninth year of Azariah
king of Judah, Menahem the son of Gadi
began to reign over Israel, and he reigned
ten years in Samaria. 18 And he did what
was evil in the sight of the LORD. He did

[1] *Leprosy* was a term for several skin diseases; see Leviticus 13 [2] The meaning of the Hebrew word is uncertain [3] Another name for *Azariah*

not depart all his days from all the sins of
Jeroboam the son of Nebat, which he made
Israel to sin. 19 Pul[1] the king of Assyria
came against the land, and Menahem gave
Pul a thousand talents[2] of silver, that he
might help him to confirm his hold on
the royal power. 20 Menahem exacted the
money from Israel, that is, from all the
wealthy men, fifty shekels[3] of silver from
every man, to give to the king of Assyria.
So the king of Assyria turned back and
did not stay there in the land. 21 Now the
rest of the deeds of Menahem and all that
he did, are they not written in the Book
of the Chronicles of the Kings of Israel?
22 And Menahem slept with his fathers,
and Pekahiah his son reigned in his place.

Pekahiah Reigns in Israel

23 In the fiftieth year of Azariah king
of Judah, Pekahiah the son of Menahem
began to reign over Israel in Samaria, and
he reigned two years. 24 And he did what
was evil in the sight of the LORD. He did not
turn away from the sins of Jeroboam the
son of Nebat, which he made Israel to sin.
25 And Pekah the son of Remaliah, his cap-
tain, conspired against him with fifty men
of the people of Gilead, and struck him
down in Samaria, in the citadel of the king's
house with Argob and Arieh; he put him to
death and reigned in his place. 26 Now the
rest of the deeds of Pekahiah and all that he
did, behold, they are written in the Book of
the Chronicles of the Kings of Israel.

Pekah Reigns in Israel

27 In the fifty-second year of Azariah
king of Judah, Pekah the son of Remaliah
began to reign over Israel in Samaria, and
he reigned twenty years. 28 And he did what
was evil in the sight of the LORD. He did not
depart from the sins of Jeroboam the son of
Nebat, which he made Israel to sin.
29 In the days of Pekah king of Israel,
Tiglath-pileser king of Assyria came and
captured Ijon, Abel-beth-maacah, Janoah,
Kedesh, Hazor, Gilead, and Galilee, all the
land of Naphtali, and he carried the people
captive to Assyria. 30 Then Hoshea the son
of Elah made a conspiracy against Pekah
the son of Remaliah and struck him down
and put him to death and reigned in his
place, in the twentieth year of Jotham the
son of Uzziah. 31 Now the rest of the acts
of Pekah and all that he did, behold, they
are written in the Book of the Chronicles
of the Kings of Israel.

Jotham Reigns in Judah

32 In the second year of Pekah the son of
Remaliah, king of Israel, Jotham the son of
Uzziah, king of Judah, began to reign. 33 He
was twenty-five years old when he began
to reign, and he reigned sixteen years
in Jerusalem. His mother's name was
Jerusha the daughter of Zadok. 34 And he
did what was right in the eyes of the LORD,
according to all that his father Uzziah had
done. 35 Nevertheless, the high places were
not removed. The people still sacrificed
and made offerings on the high places. He
built the upper gate of the house of the
LORD. 36 Now the rest of the acts of Jotham
and all that he did, are they not written in
the Book of the Chronicles of the Kings of
Judah? 37 In those days the LORD began to
send Rezin the king of Syria and Pekah the
son of Remaliah against Judah. 38 Jotham
slept with his fathers and was buried with
his fathers in the city of David his father,
and Ahaz his son reigned in his place.

Ahaz Reigns in Judah

16 In the seventeenth year of Pekah
the son of Remaliah, Ahaz the
son of Jotham, king of Judah, began to
reign. 2 Ahaz was twenty years old when
he began to reign, and he reigned sixteen
years in Jerusalem. And he did not do
what was right in the eyes of the LORD his
God, as his father David had done, 3 but he
walked in the way of the kings of Israel.
He even burned his son as an offering,[4]

[1] Another name for *Tiglath-pileser III* (compare verse 29) [2] A *talent* was about 75 pounds or 34 kilograms [3] A *shekel* was about 2/5 ounce or 11 grams [4] Or *made his son pass through the fire*

according to the despicable practices of the nations whom the LORD drove out before the people of Israel. 4 And he sacrificed and made offerings on the high places and on the hills and under every green tree.

5 Then Rezin king of Syria and Pekah the son of Remaliah, king of Israel, came up to wage war on Jerusalem, and they besieged Ahaz but could not conquer him. 6 At that time Rezin the king of Syria recovered Elath for Syria and drove the men of Judah from Elath, and the Edomites came to Elath, where they dwell to this day. 7 So Ahaz sent messengers to Tiglath-pileser king of Assyria, saying, "I am your servant and your son. Come up and rescue me from the hand of the king of Syria and from the hand of the king of Israel, who are attacking me." 8 Ahaz also took the silver and gold that was found in the house of the LORD and in the treasures of the king's house and sent a present to the king of Assyria. 9 And the king of Assyria listened to him. The king of Assyria marched up against Damascus and took it, carrying its people captive to Kir, and he killed Rezin.

10 When King Ahaz went to Damascus to meet Tiglath-pileser king of Assyria, he saw the altar that was at Damascus. And King Ahaz sent to Uriah the priest a model of the altar, and its pattern, exact in all its details. 11 And Uriah the priest built the altar; in accordance with all that King Ahaz had sent from Damascus, so Uriah the priest made it, before King Ahaz arrived from Damascus. 12 And when the king came from Damascus, the king viewed the altar. Then the king drew near to the altar and went up on it 13 and burned his burnt offering and his grain offering and poured his drink offering and threw the blood of his peace offerings on the altar. 14 And the bronze altar that was before the LORD he removed from the front of the house, from the place between his altar and the house of the LORD, and put it on the north side of his altar. 15 And King Ahaz commanded Uriah the priest, saying, "On the great altar burn the morning burnt offering and the evening grain offering and the king's burnt offering and his grain offering, with the burnt offering of all the people of the land, and their grain offering and their drink offering. And throw on it all the blood of the burnt offering and all the blood of the sacrifice, but the bronze altar shall be for me to inquire by." 16 Uriah the priest did all this, as King Ahaz commanded.

17 And King Ahaz cut off the frames of the stands and removed the basin from them, and he took down the sea[1] from off the bronze oxen that were under it and put it on a stone pedestal. 18 And the covered way for the Sabbath that had been built inside the house and the outer entrance for the king he caused to go around the house of the LORD, because of the king of Assyria. 19 Now the rest of the acts of Ahaz that he did, are they not written in the Book of the Chronicles of the Kings of Judah? 20 And Ahaz slept with his fathers and was buried with his fathers in the city of David, and Hezekiah his son reigned in his place.

17 In the twelfth year of Ahaz king of Judah, Hoshea the son of Elah began to reign in Samaria over Israel, and he reigned nine years. 2 And he did what was evil in the sight of the LORD, yet not as the kings of Israel who were before him. 3 Against him came up Shalmaneser king of Assyria. And Hoshea became his vassal and paid him tribute. 4 But the king of Assyria found treachery in Hoshea, for he had sent messengers to So, king of Egypt, and offered no tribute to the king of Assyria, as he had done year by year. Therefore the king of Assyria shut him up and bound him in prison. 5 Then the king of Assyria invaded all the land and came to Samaria, and for three years he besieged it.

The Fall of Israel

6 In the ninth year of Hoshea, the king of Assyria captured Samaria, and he carried

[1] Compare 1 Kings 7:23

the Israelites away to Assyria and placed them in Halah, and on the Habor, the river of Gozan, and in the cities of the Medes.

Exile Because of Idolatry

7 And this occurred because the people of Israel had sinned against the LORD their God, who had brought them up out of the land of Egypt from under the hand of Pharaoh king of Egypt, and had feared other gods 8 and walked in the customs of the nations whom the LORD drove out before the people of Israel, and in the customs that the kings of Israel had practiced. 9 And the people of Israel did secretly against the LORD their God things that were not right. They built for themselves high places in all their towns, from watchtower to fortified city. 10 They set up for themselves pillars and Asherim on every high hill and under every green tree, 11 and there they made offerings on all the high places, as the nations did whom the LORD carried away before them. And they did wicked things, provoking the LORD to anger, 12 and they served idols, of which the LORD had said to them, "You shall not do this." 13 Yet the LORD warned Israel and Judah by every prophet and every seer, saying, "Turn from your evil ways and keep my commandments and my statutes, in accordance with all the Law that I commanded your fathers, and that I sent to you by my servants the prophets."

14 But they would not listen, but were stubborn, as their fathers had been, who did not believe in the LORD their God. 15 They despised his statutes and his covenant that he made with their fathers and the warnings that he gave them. They went after false idols and became false, and they followed the nations that were around them, concerning whom the LORD had commanded them that they should not do like them. 16 And they abandoned all the commandments of the LORD their God, and made for themselves metal images of two calves; and they made an Asherah and worshiped all the host of heaven and served Baal. 17 And they burned their sons and their daughters as offerings[1] and used divination and omens and sold themselves to do evil in the sight of the LORD, provoking him to anger. 18 Therefore the LORD was very angry with Israel and removed them out of his sight. None was left but the tribe of Judah only.

19 Judah also did not keep the commandments of the LORD their God, but walked in the customs that Israel had introduced. 20 And the LORD rejected all the descendants of Israel and afflicted them and gave them into the hand of plunderers, until he had cast them out of his sight.

21 When he had torn Israel from the house of David, they made Jeroboam the son of Nebat king. And Jeroboam drove Israel from following the LORD and made them commit great sin. 22 The people of Israel walked in all the sins that Jeroboam did. They did not depart from them, 23 until the LORD removed Israel out of his sight, as he had spoken by all his servants the prophets. So Israel was exiled from their own land to Assyria until this day.

Assyria Resettles Samaria

24 And the king of Assyria brought people from Babylon, Cuthah, Avva, Hamath, and Sepharvaim, and placed them in the cities of Samaria instead of the people of Israel. And they took possession of Samaria and lived in its cities. 25 And at the beginning of their dwelling there, they did not fear the LORD. Therefore the LORD sent lions among them, which killed some of them. 26 So the king of Assyria was told, "The nations that you have carried away and placed in the cities of Samaria do not know the law of the god of the land. Therefore he has sent lions among them, and behold, they are killing them, because they do not know the law of the god of the land." 27 Then the king of Assyria commanded,

[1] Or *made their sons and their daughters pass through the fire*

"Send there one of the priests whom you carried away from there, and let him[1] go and dwell there and teach them the law of the god of the land." 28 So one of the priests whom they had carried away from Samaria came and lived in Bethel and taught them how they should fear the LORD.

29 But every nation still made gods of its own and put them in the shrines of the high places that the Samaritans had made, every nation in the cities in which they lived. 30 The men of Babylon made Succoth-benoth, the men of Cuth made Nergal, the men of Hamath made Ashima, 31 and the Avvites made Nibhaz and Tartak; and the Sepharvites burned their children in the fire to Adrammelech and Anammelech, the gods of Sepharvaim. 32 They also feared the LORD and appointed from among themselves all sorts of people as priests of the high places, who sacrificed for them in the shrines of the high places. 33 So they feared the LORD but also served their own gods, after the manner of the nations from among whom they had been carried away.

34 To this day they do according to the former manner. They do not fear the LORD, and they do not follow the statutes or the rules or the law or the commandment that the LORD commanded the children of Jacob, whom he named Israel. 35 The LORD made a covenant with them and commanded them, "You shall not fear other gods or bow yourselves to them or serve them or sacrifice to them, 36 but you shall fear the LORD, who brought you out of the land of Egypt with great power and with an outstretched arm. You shall bow yourselves to him, and to him you shall sacrifice. 37 And the statutes and the rules and the law and the commandment that he wrote for you, you shall always be careful to do. You shall not fear other gods, 38 and you shall not forget the covenant that I have made with you. You shall not fear other gods, 39 but you shall fear the LORD your God, and he will deliver you out of the hand of all your enemies." 40 However, they would not listen, but they did according to their former manner.

41 So these nations feared the LORD and also served their carved images. Their children did likewise, and their children's children—as their fathers did, so they do to this day.

Hezekiah Reigns in Judah

615

18 In the third year of Hoshea son of Elah, king of Israel, Hezekiah the son of Ahaz, king of Judah, began to reign. 2 He was twenty-five years old when he began to reign, and he reigned twenty-nine years in Jerusalem. His mother's name was Abi the daughter of Zechariah. 3 And he did what was right in the eyes of the LORD, according to all that David his father had done. 4 He removed the high places and broke the pillars and cut down the Asherah. And he broke in pieces the bronze serpent that Moses had made, for until those days the people of Israel had made offerings to it (it was called Nehushtan).[2] 5 He trusted in the LORD, the God of Israel, so that there was none like him among all the kings of Judah after him, nor among those who were before him. 6 For he held fast to the LORD. He did not depart from following him, but kept the commandments that the LORD commanded Moses. 7 And the LORD was with him; wherever he went out, he prospered. He rebelled against the king of Assyria and would not serve him. 8 He struck down the Philistines as far as Gaza and its territory, from watchtower to fortified city.

9 In the fourth year of King Hezekiah, which was the seventh year of Hoshea son of Elah, king of Israel, Shalmaneser king of Assyria came up against Samaria and besieged it, 10 and at the end of three years he took it. In the sixth year of Hezekiah, which was the ninth year of Hoshea king of Israel, Samaria was taken. 11 The king

[1] Syriac, Vulgate; Hebrew *them* [2] *Nehushtan* sounds like the Hebrew for both *bronze* and *serpent*

of Assyria carried the Israelites away to Assyria and put them in Halah, and on the Habor, the river of Gozan, and in the cities of the Medes, 12 because they did not obey the voice of the LORD their God but transgressed his covenant, even all that Moses the servant of the LORD commanded. They neither listened nor obeyed.

Sennacherib Attacks Judah

13 In the fourteenth year of King Hezekiah, Sennacherib king of Assyria came up against all the fortified cities of Judah and took them. 14 And Hezekiah king of Judah sent to the king of Assyria at Lachish, saying, "I have done wrong; withdraw from me. Whatever you impose on me I will bear." And the king of Assyria required of Hezekiah king of Judah three hundred talents[1] of silver and thirty talents of gold. 15 And Hezekiah gave him all the silver that was found in the house of the LORD and in the treasuries of the king's house. 16 At that time Hezekiah stripped the gold from the doors of the temple of the LORD and from the doorposts that Hezekiah king of Judah had overlaid and gave it to the king of Assyria. 17 And the king of Assyria sent the Tartan, the Rab-saris, and the Rabshakeh with a great army from Lachish to King Hezekiah at Jerusalem. And they went up and came to Jerusalem. When they arrived, they came and stood by the conduit of the upper pool, which is on the highway to the Washer's Field. 18 And when they called for the king, there came out to them Eliakim the son of Hilkiah, who was over the household, and Shebnah the secretary, and Joah the son of Asaph, the recorder.

19 And the Rabshakeh said to them, "Say to Hezekiah, 'Thus says the great king, the king of Assyria: On what do you rest this trust of yours? 20 Do you think that mere words are strategy and power for war? In whom do you now trust, that you have rebelled against me? 21 Behold, you are trusting now in Egypt, that broken reed of a staff, which will pierce the hand of any man who leans on it. Such is Pharaoh king of Egypt to all who trust in him. 22 But if you say to me, "We trust in the LORD our God," is it not he whose high places and altars Hezekiah has removed, saying to Judah and to Jerusalem, "You shall worship before this altar in Jerusalem"? 23 Come now, make a wager with my master the king of Assyria: I will give you two thousand horses, if you are able on your part to set riders on them. 24 How then can you repulse a single captain among the least of my master's servants, when you trust in Egypt for chariots and for horsemen? 25 Moreover, is it without the LORD that I have come up against this place to destroy it? The LORD said to me, Go up against this land, and destroy it.'"

26 Then Eliakim the son of Hilkiah, and Shebnah, and Joah, said to the Rabshakeh, "Please speak to your servants in Aramaic, for we understand it. Do not speak to us in the language of Judah within the hearing of the people who are on the wall." 27 But the Rabshakeh said to them, "Has my master sent me to speak these words to your master and to you, and not to the men sitting on the wall, who are doomed with you to eat their own dung and to drink their own urine?"

28 Then the Rabshakeh stood and called out in a loud voice in the language of Judah: "Hear the word of the great king, the king of Assyria! 29 Thus says the king: 'Do not let Hezekiah deceive you, for he will not be able to deliver you out of my[2] hand. 30 Do not let Hezekiah make you trust in the LORD by saying, The LORD will surely deliver us, and this city will not be given into the hand of the king of Assyria.' 31 Do not listen to Hezekiah, for thus says the king of Assyria: 'Make your peace with me[3] and come out to me. Then each one of you will eat of his own vine, and each one of his own fig tree, and each one of you will drink the water of

[1] A *talent* was about 75 pounds or 34 kilograms [2] Hebrew *his* [3] Hebrew *Make a blessing with me*

his own cistern, 32 until I come and take you away to a land like your own land, a land of grain and wine, a land of bread and vineyards, a land of olive trees and honey, that you may live, and not die. And do not listen to Hezekiah when he misleads you by saying, The LORD will deliver us. 33 Has any of the gods of the nations ever delivered his land out of the hand of the king of Assyria? 34 Where are the gods of Hamath and Arpad? Where are the gods of Sepharvaim, Hena, and Ivvah? Have they delivered Samaria out of my hand? 35 Who among all the gods of the lands have delivered their lands out of my hand, that the LORD should deliver Jerusalem out of my hand?'"

36 But the people were silent and answered him not a word, for the king's command was, "Do not answer him." 37 Then Eliakim the son of Hilkiah, who was over the household, and Shebna the secretary, and Joah the son of Asaph, the recorder, came to Hezekiah with their clothes torn and told him the words of the Rabshakeh.

Isaiah Reassures Hezekiah

19 As soon as King Hezekiah heard it, he tore his clothes and covered himself with sackcloth and went into the house of the LORD. 2 And he sent Eliakim, who was over the household, and Shebna the secretary, and the senior priests, covered with sackcloth, to the prophet Isaiah the son of Amoz. 3 They said to him, "Thus says Hezekiah, This day is a day of distress, of rebuke, and of disgrace; children have come to the point of birth, and there is no strength to bring them forth. 4 It may be that the LORD your God heard all the words of the Rabshakeh, whom his master the king of Assyria has sent to mock the living God, and will rebuke the words that the LORD your God has heard; therefore lift up your prayer for the remnant that is left." 5 When the servants of King Hezekiah came to Isaiah, 6 Isaiah said to them, "Say to your master, 'Thus says the LORD: Do not be afraid because of the words that you have heard, with which the servants of the king of Assyria have reviled me. 7 Behold, I will put a spirit in him, so that he shall hear a rumor and return to his own land, and I will make him fall by the sword in his own land.'"

Sennacherib Defies the LORD

8 The Rabshakeh returned, and found the king of Assyria fighting against Libnah, for he heard that the king had left Lachish. 9 Now the king heard concerning Tirhakah king of Cush, "Behold, he has set out to fight against you." So he sent messengers again to Hezekiah, saying, 10 "Thus shall you speak to Hezekiah king of Judah: 'Do not let your God in whom you trust deceive you by promising that Jerusalem will not be given into the hand of the king of Assyria. 11 Behold, you have heard what the kings of Assyria have done to all lands, devoting them to destruction. And shall you be delivered? 12 Have the gods of the nations delivered them, the nations that my fathers destroyed, Gozan, Haran, Rezeph, and the people of Eden who were in Telassar? 13 Where is the king of Hamath, the king of Arpad, the king of the city of Sepharvaim, the king of Hena, or the king of Ivvah?'"

Hezekiah's Prayer

14 Hezekiah received the letter from the hand of the messengers and read it; and Hezekiah went up to the house of the LORD and spread it before the LORD. 15 And Hezekiah prayed before the LORD and said: "O LORD, the God of Israel, enthroned above the cherubim, you are the God, you alone, of all the kingdoms of the earth; you have made heaven and earth. 16 Incline your ear, O LORD, and hear; open your eyes, O LORD, and see; and hear the words of Sennacherib, which he has sent to mock the living God. 17 Truly, O LORD, the kings of Assyria have laid waste the nations and their lands

God Answers Hezekiah's Prayer

Hezekiah was a good king for God's people. He trusted God, and God helped him. Hezekiah "did what was right in the eyes of the Lord" as King David had done many years before.

One day, Hezekiah had a huge problem. A great army of enemy soldiers came to fight against his city, Jerusalem. This army had already conquered all the cities in the land around Jerusalem.

The leader of the army sent King Hezekiah a letter. The letter told Hezekiah that if he did not surrender his city, the army would destroy it. Then the leader of the army made fun of Hezekiah's soldiers. And he made fun of God too! He told the Israelite soldiers that none of "the gods of the lands have delivered their lands out of my hand." There's no way, he said, that the Lord could save Jerusalem from the army's attack.

When the messengers brought the letter to Hezekiah, he took it to the temple and prayed: "O Lord, the God of Israel, You are the God, You alone, of all the kingdoms of the earth; You have made heaven and earth." Hezekiah told God that the enemy army had destroyed many other cities, because the gods of those cities were only idols. Hezekiah asked God to hear how enemy soldiers had made fun of God. "So now," King Hezekiah prayed, "O Lord our God, save us, please, from his hand, that all the kingdoms of the earth may know that You, O Lord, are God alone."

After Hezekiah prayed, God sent His prophet Isaiah to Hezekiah. Isaiah told King Hezekiah that God said He had heard Hezekiah's prayer. God told Isaiah that it was wrong of the enemy army to make fun of God. And God promised that He would turn the enemy army away before they could shoot even one arrow at Jerusalem. "For I will defend this city to save it," God said.

That night the angel of the LORD went into the army camp and killed 185,000 enemy soldiers. The few soldiers who were left and the leader of the army turned around and went home, completely defeated by the angel of the LORD.

God had answered Hezekiah's prayer. He had saved His people from their enemies. He had shown that He was the true God, completely different from the false gods and idols of the other nations.

God loves us and cares for us too. He wants us to pray to Him. He sent Jesus to save us from our enemies—sin, death, and the devil. He wants to show other people through us that He is the true God. He promises to answer our prayers for Jesus' sake.

SEEK and FIND

WHERE TO FIND THE STORY

2 Kings 18–19

KEY BIBLE VERSE

"They were not gods, but the work of men's hands, wood and stone. Therefore they were destroyed. So now, O LORD our God, save us, please, from his hand, that all the kingdoms of the earth may know that you, O LORD, are God alone." (2 Kings 19:18–19)

THREE KEY QUESTIONS

- What was King Hezekiah's huge problem and what did he do about his problem?
- How did God answer Hezekiah's prayer?
- What should we do when we have a huge problem, and why does God answer our prayers?

RELATED BIBLE READINGS

2 Chronicles 32:1–23; Isaiah 36:1–37:38

18 and have cast their gods into the fire,
for they were not gods, but the
work of men's hands, wood and
stone. Therefore they were
destroyed. 19 So now, O LORD our God,
save us, please, from his hand, that all the
kingdoms of the earth may know that you,
O LORD, are God alone."

615

Isaiah Prophesies Sennacherib's Fall

20 Then Isaiah the son of Amoz sent to
Hezekiah, saying, "Thus says the LORD,
the God of Israel: Your prayer to me about
Sennacherib king of Assyria I have heard.
21 This is the word that the LORD has spo-
ken concerning him:

"She despises you, she scorns you—
the virgin daughter of Zion;
she wags her head behind you—
the daughter of Jerusalem.

22 "Whom have you mocked and reviled?
Against whom have you raised your voice
and lifted your eyes to the heights?
Against the Holy One of Israel!
23 By your messengers you have mocked the Lord,
and you have said, 'With my many chariots
I have gone up the heights of the mountains,
to the far recesses of Lebanon;
I felled its tallest cedars,
its choicest cypresses;
I entered its farthest lodging place,
its most fruitful forest.
24 I dug wells
and drank foreign waters,
and I dried up with the sole of my foot
all the streams of Egypt.'

25 "Have you not heard
that I determined it long ago?
I planned from days of old
what now I bring to pass,
that you should turn fortified cities
into heaps of ruins,
26 while their inhabitants, shorn of strength,
are dismayed and confounded,
and have become like plants of the field
and like tender grass,
like grass on the housetops,
blighted before it is grown.

27 "But I know your sitting down
and your going out and coming in,
and your raging against me.

28 Because you have raged against me
and your complacency has come
into my ears,
I will put my hook in your nose
and my bit in your mouth,
and I will turn you back on the way
by which you came.

29 “And this shall be the sign for you: this
year eat what grows of itself, and in the sec-
ond year what springs of the same. Then in
the third year sow and reap and plant vine-
yards, and eat their fruit. 30 And the surviv-
ing remnant of the house of Judah shall
again take root downward and bear fruit
upward. 31 For out of Jerusalem shall go a
remnant, and out of Mount Zion a band of
survivors. The zeal of the LORD will do this.
32 “Therefore thus says the LORD con-
cerning the king of Assyria: He shall not
come into this city or shoot an arrow
there, or come before it with a shield or
cast up a siege mound against it. 33 By the
way that he came, by the same he shall
return, and he shall not come into this
city, declares the LORD. 34 For I will defend
this city to save it, for my own sake and for
the sake of my servant David.”
35 And that night the angel of the LORD
went out and struck down 185,000 in the
camp of the Assyrians. And when people
arose early in the morning, behold, these
were all dead bodies. 36 Then Sennacherib
king of Assyria departed and went home
and lived at Nineveh. 37 And as he was
worshiping in the house of Nisroch
his god, Adrammelech and Sharezer, his
sons, struck him down with the sword
and escaped into the land of Ararat. And
Esarhaddon his son reigned in his place.

Hezekiah’s Illness and Recovery

20 In those days Hezekiah became
sick and was at the point of death.
And Isaiah the prophet the son of Amoz
came to him and said to him, “Thus says
the LORD, ‘Set your house in order, for you
shall die; you shall not recover.’” 2 Then
Hezekiah turned his face to the wall and
prayed to the LORD, saying, 3 “Now, O
LORD, please remember how I have walked
before you in faithfulness and with a
whole heart, and have done what is good
in your sight.” And Hezekiah wept bitterly.
4 And before Isaiah had gone out of the
middle court, the word of the LORD came
to him: 5 “Turn back, and say to Hezekiah
the leader of my people, Thus says the
LORD, the God of David your father: I have
heard your prayer; I have seen your tears.
Behold, I will heal you. On the third day
you shall go up to the house of the LORD,
6 and I will add fifteen years to your life.
I will deliver you and this city out of the
hand of the king of Assyria, and I will
defend this city for my own sake and for
my servant David’s sake.” 7 And Isaiah said,
“Bring a cake of figs. And let them take and
lay it on the boil, that he may recover.”
8 And Hezekiah said to Isaiah, “What
shall be the sign that the LORD will heal
me, and that I shall go up to the house of
the LORD on the third day?” 9 And Isaiah
said, “This shall be the sign to you from
the LORD, that the LORD will do the thing
that he has promised: shall the shadow go
forward ten steps, or go back ten steps?”
10 And Hezekiah answered, “It is an easy
thing for the shadow to lengthen ten
steps. Rather let the shadow go back ten
steps.” 11 And Isaiah the prophet called
to the LORD, and he brought the shadow
back ten steps, by which it had gone down
on the steps of Ahaz.

Hezekiah and the Babylonian Envoys

12 At that time Merodach-baladan the
son of Baladan, king of Babylon, sent
envoys with letters and a present to Heze-
kiah, for he heard that Hezekiah had
been sick. 13 And Hezekiah welcomed
them, and he showed them all his trea-
sure house, the silver, the gold, the spices,
the precious oil, his armory, all that was
found in his storehouses. There was noth-
ing in his house or in all his realm that

Hezekiah did not show them. 14 Then Isaiah the prophet came to King Hezekiah, and said to him, "What did these men say? And from where did they come to you?" And Hezekiah said, "They have come from a far country, from Babylon." 15 He said, "What have they seen in your house?" And Hezekiah answered, "They have seen all that is in my house; there is nothing in my storehouses that I did not show them."

16 Then Isaiah said to Hezekiah, "Hear the word of the LORD: 17 Behold, the days are coming, when all that is in your house, and that which your fathers have stored up till this day, shall be carried to Babylon. Nothing shall be left, says the LORD. 18 And some of your own sons, who shall be born to you, shall be taken away, and they shall be eunuchs in the palace of the king of Babylon." 19 Then said Hezekiah to Isaiah, "The word of the LORD that you have spoken is good." For he thought, "Why not, if there will be peace and security in my days?"

20 The rest of the deeds of Hezekiah and all his might and how he made the pool and the conduit and brought water into the city, are they not written in the Book of the Chronicles of the Kings of Judah? 21 And Hezekiah slept with his fathers, and Manasseh his son reigned in his place.

Manasseh Reigns in Judah

21 Manasseh was twelve years old when he began to reign, and he reigned fifty-five years in Jerusalem. His mother's name was Hephzibah. 2 And he did what was evil in the sight of the LORD, according to the despicable practices of the nations whom the LORD drove out before the people of Israel. 3 For he rebuilt the high places that Hezekiah his father had destroyed, and he erected altars for Baal and made an Asherah, as Ahab king of Israel had done, and worshiped all the host of heaven and served them. 4 And he built altars in the house of the LORD, of which the LORD had said, "In Jerusalem will I put my name." 5 And he built altars for all the host of heaven in the two courts of the house of the LORD. 6 And he burned his son as an offering[1] and used fortune-telling and omens and dealt with mediums and with necromancers. He did much evil in the sight of the LORD, provoking him to anger. 7 And the carved image of Asherah that he had made he set in the house of which the LORD said to David and to Solomon his son, "In this house, and in Jerusalem, which I have chosen out of all the tribes of Israel, I will put my name forever. 8 And I will not cause the feet of Israel to wander anymore out of the land that I gave to their fathers, if only they will be careful to do according to all that I have commanded them, and according to all the Law that my servant Moses commanded them." 9 But they did not listen, and Manasseh led them astray to do more evil than the nations had done whom the LORD destroyed before the people of Israel.

Manasseh's Idolatry Denounced

10 And the LORD said by his servants the prophets, 11 "Because Manasseh king of Judah has committed these abominations and has done things more evil than all that the Amorites did, who were before him, and has made Judah also to sin with his idols, 12 therefore thus says the LORD, the God of Israel: Behold, I am bringing upon Jerusalem and Judah such disaster[2] that the ears of everyone who hears of it will tingle. 13 And I will stretch over Jerusalem the measuring line of Samaria, and the plumb line of the house of Ahab, and I will wipe Jerusalem as one wipes a dish, wiping it and turning it upside down. 14 And I will forsake the remnant of my heritage and give them into the hand of their enemies, and they shall become a prey and a spoil to all their enemies, 15 because they have done what is evil in my sight and have provoked me to anger, since the day their fathers came out of Egypt, even to this day."

16 Moreover, Manasseh shed very much

[1] Hebrew *made his son pass through the fire* [2] Or *evil*

innocent blood, till he had filled Jerusalem
from one end to another, besides the sin
that he made Judah to sin so that they did
what was evil in the sight of the LORD.
17 Now the rest of the acts of Manasseh
and all that he did, and the sin that he
committed, are they not written in the
Book of the Chronicles of the Kings of
Judah? 18 And Manasseh slept with his
fathers and was buried in the garden of
his house, in the garden of Uzza, and
Amon his son reigned in his place.

Amon Reigns in Judah

19 Amon was twenty-two years old
when he began to reign, and he reigned
two years in Jerusalem. His mother's
name was Meshullemeth the daughter of
Haruz of Jotbah. 20 And he did what was
evil in the sight of the LORD, as Manasseh
his father had done. 21 He walked in all the
way in which his father walked and served
the idols that his father served and wor-
shiped them. 22 He abandoned the LORD,
the God of his fathers, and did not walk in
the way of the LORD. 23 And the servants
of Amon conspired against him and put
the king to death in his house. 24 But the
people of the land struck down all those
who had conspired against King Amon,
and the people of the land made Josiah
his son king in his place. 25 Now the rest
of the acts of Amon that he did, are they
not written in the Book of the Chronicles
of the Kings of Judah? 26 And he was bur-
ied in his tomb in the garden of Uzza, and
Josiah his son reigned in his place.

Josiah Reigns in Judah

22 Josiah was eight years old
when he began to reign,
697 and he reigned thirty-one years in
Jerusalem. His mother's name was Jedidah
the daughter of Adaiah of Bozkath. 2 And he
did what was right in the eyes of the LORD
and walked in all the way of David his
father, and he did not turn aside to the
right or to the left.

Josiah Repairs the Temple

3 In the eighteenth year of King Josiah,
the king sent Shaphan the son of Azaliah,
son of Meshullam, the secretary, to the
house of the LORD, saying, 4 "Go up to
Hilkiah the high priest, that he may count
the money that has been brought into
the house of the LORD, which the keepers
of the threshold have collected from the
people. 5 And let it be given into the hand
of the workmen who have the oversight of
the house of the LORD, and let them give
it to the workmen who are at the house of
the LORD, repairing the house 6 (that is,
to the carpenters, and to the builders, and
to the masons), and let them use it for buy-
ing timber and quarried stone to repair the
house. 7 But no accounting shall be asked
from them for the money that is delivered
into their hand, for they deal honestly."

Hilkiah Finds the Book of the Law

8 And Hilkiah the high priest said to
Shaphan the secretary, "I have found the
Book of the Law in the house of the LORD."
And Hilkiah gave the book to Shaphan,
and he read it. 9 And Shaphan the secre-
tary came to the king, and reported to the
king, "Your servants have emptied out
the money that was found in the house
and have delivered it into the hand of
the workmen who have the oversight
of the house of the LORD." 10 Then Shaphan
the secretary told the king, "Hilkiah the
priest has given me a book." And Shaphan
read it before the king.
11 When the king heard the words of
the Book of the Law, he tore his clothes.
12 And the king commanded Hilkiah the
priest, and Ahikam the son of Shaphan,
and Achbor the son of Micaiah, and
Shaphan the secretary, and Asaiah the
king's servant, saying, 13 "Go, inquire of
the LORD for me, and for the people, and
for all Judah, concerning the words of this
book that has been found. For great is the
wrath of the LORD that is kindled against

us, because our fathers have not obeyed
the words of this book, to do according to
all that is written concerning us."
14 So Hilkiah the priest, and Ahikam,
and Achbor, and Shaphan, and Asaiah
went to Huldah the prophetess, the wife
of Shallum the son of Tikvah, son of
Harhas, keeper of the wardrobe (now she
lived in Jerusalem in the Second Quarter),
and they talked with her. 15 And she said
to them, "Thus says the LORD, the God of
Israel: 'Tell the man who sent you to me,
16 Thus says the LORD, Behold, I will bring
disaster upon this place and upon its
inhabitants, all the words of the book that
the king of Judah has read. 17 Because they
have forsaken me and have made offerings
to other gods, that they might provoke me
to anger with all the work of their hands,
therefore my wrath will be kindled against
this place, and it will not be quenched.
18 But to the king of Judah, who sent you to
inquire of the LORD, thus shall you say to
him, Thus says the LORD, the God of Israel:
Regarding the words that you have heard,
19 because your heart was penitent, and
you humbled yourself before the LORD,
when you heard how I spoke against this
place and against its inhabitants, that
they should become a desolation and a
curse, and you have torn your clothes and
wept before me, I also have heard you,
declares the LORD. 20 Therefore, behold, I
will gather you to your fathers, and you
shall be gathered to your grave in peace,
and your eyes shall not see all the disaster
that I will bring upon this place.'" And they
brought back word to the king.

CHARACTER PROFILE

JOSIAH

Josiah became king after Judah had worshiped idols for many years. He had workers clean and repair the temple, and they found the Book of God's Law. Josiah read the Book and understood that Judah must repent and turn from idols. Then he read it to the people—and the people turned from idol worship to obey God.

697

Josiah's Reforms

23 Then the king sent, and all the
elders of Judah and Jerusalem
were gathered to him. 2 And the king went
up to the house of the LORD, and with him
all the men of Judah and all the inhabi-
tants of Jerusalem and the priests and
the prophets, all the people, both small
and great. And he read in their hearing
all the words of the Book of the Covenant
that had been found in the house of the
LORD. 3 And the king stood by the pillar
and made a covenant before the LORD, to
walk after the LORD and to keep his com-
mandments and his testimonies and his
statutes with all his heart and all his soul,
to perform the words of this covenant
that were written in this book. And all
the people joined in the covenant.
4 And the king commanded Hilkiah the
high priest and the priests of the second
order and the keepers of the threshold to
bring out of the temple of the LORD all the
vessels made for Baal, for Asherah, and for
all the host of heaven. He burned them out-
side Jerusalem in the fields of the Kidron
and carried their ashes to Bethel. 5 And he
deposed the priests whom the kings of

Judah had ordained to make offerings in the high places at the cities of Judah and around Jerusalem; those also who burned incense to Baal, to the sun and the moon and the constellations and all the host of the heavens. 6 And he brought out the Asherah from the house of the LORD, outside Jerusalem, to the brook Kidron, and burned it at the brook Kidron and beat it to dust and cast the dust of it upon the graves of the common people. 7 And he broke down the houses of the male cult prostitutes who were in the house of the LORD, where the women wove hangings for the Asherah. 8 And he brought all the priests out of the cities of Judah, and defiled the high places where the priests had made offerings, from Geba to Beersheba. And he broke down the high places of the gates that were at the entrance of the gate of Joshua the governor of the city, which were on one's left at the gate of the city. 9 However, the priests of the high places did not come up to the altar of the LORD in Jerusalem, but they ate unleavened bread among their brothers. 10 And he defiled Topheth, which is in the Valley of the Son of Hinnom, that no one might burn his son or his daughter as an offering to Molech.[1] 11 And he removed the horses that the kings of Judah had dedicated to the sun, at the entrance to the house of the LORD, by the chamber of Nathan-melech the chamberlain, which was in the precincts.[2] And he burned the chariots of the sun with fire. 12 And the altars on the roof of the upper chamber of Ahaz, which the kings of Judah had made, and the altars that Manasseh had made in the two courts of the house of the LORD, he pulled down and broke in pieces[3] and cast the dust of them into the brook Kidron. 13 And the king defiled the high places that were east of Jerusalem, to the south of the mount of corruption, which Solomon the king of Israel had built for Ashtoreth the abomination of the Sidonians, and for Chemosh the abomination of Moab, and for Milcom the abomination of the Ammonites. 14 And he broke in pieces the pillars and cut down the Asherim and filled their places with the bones of men.

15 Moreover, the altar at Bethel, the high place erected by Jeroboam the son of Nebat, who made Israel to sin, that altar with the high place he pulled down and burned,[4] reducing it to dust. He also burned the Asherah. 16 And as Josiah turned, he saw the tombs there on the mount. And he sent and took the bones out of the tombs and burned them on the altar and defiled it, according to the word of the LORD that the man of God proclaimed, who had predicted these things. 17 Then he said, "What is that monument that I see?" And the men of the city told him, "It is the tomb of the man of God who came from Judah and predicted[5] these things that you have done against the altar at Bethel." 18 And he said, "Let him be; let no man move his bones." So they let his bones alone, with the bones of the prophet who came out of Samaria. 19 And Josiah removed all the shrines also of the high places that were in the cities of Samaria, which kings of Israel had made, provoking the LORD to anger. He did to them according to all that he had done at Bethel. 20 And he sacrificed all the priests of the high places who were there, on the altars, and burned human bones on them. Then he returned to Jerusalem.

Josiah Restores the Passover

21 And the king commanded all the people, "Keep the Passover to the LORD your God, as it is written in this Book of the Covenant." 22 For no such Passover had been kept since the days of the judges who judged Israel, or during all the days of the kings of Israel or of the kings of Judah. 23 But in the eighteenth year of King Josiah this Passover was kept to the LORD in Jerusalem.

24 Moreover, Josiah put away the mediums and the necromancers and the house-

[1] Hebrew *might cause his son or daughter to pass through the fire for Molech* [2] The meaning of the Hebrew word is uncertain [3] Hebrew *pieces from there* [4] Septuagint *broke in pieces its stones* [5] Hebrew *called*

hold gods and the idols and all the abominations that were seen in the land of Judah and in Jerusalem, that he might establish the words of the law that were written in the book that Hilkiah the priest found in the house of the LORD. 25 Before him there was no king like him, who turned to the LORD with all his heart and with all his soul and with all his might, according to all the Law of Moses, nor did any like him arise after him.

26 Still the LORD did not turn from the burning of his great wrath, by which his anger was kindled against Judah, because of all the provocations with which Manasseh had provoked him. 27 And the LORD said, "I will remove Judah also out of my sight, as I have removed Israel, and I will cast off this city that I have chosen, Jerusalem, and the house of which I said, My name shall be there."

Josiah's Death in Battle

28 Now the rest of the acts of Josiah and all that he did, are they not written in the Book of the Chronicles of the Kings of Judah? 29 In his days Pharaoh Neco king of Egypt went up to the king of Assyria to the river Euphrates. King Josiah went to meet him, and Pharaoh Neco killed him at Megiddo, as soon as he saw him. 30 And his servants carried him dead in a chariot from Megiddo and brought him to Jerusalem and buried him in his own tomb. And the people of the land took Jehoahaz the son of Josiah, and anointed him, and made him king in his father's place.

Jehoahaz's Reign and Captivity

31 Jehoahaz was twenty-three years old when he began to reign, and he reigned three months in Jerusalem. His mother's name was Hamutal the daughter of Jeremiah of Libnah. 32 And he did what was evil in the sight of the LORD, according to all that his fathers had done. 33 And Pharaoh Neco put him in bonds at Riblah in the land of Hamath, that he might not reign in Jerusalem, and laid on the land a tribute of a hundred talents[1] of silver and a talent of gold. 34 And Pharaoh Neco made Eliakim the son of Josiah king in the place of Josiah his father, and changed his name to Jehoiakim. But he took Jehoahaz away, and he came to Egypt and died there. 35 And Jehoiakim gave the silver and the gold to Pharaoh, but he taxed the land to give the money according to the command of Pharaoh. He exacted the silver and the gold of the people of the land, from everyone according to his assessment, to give it to Pharaoh Neco.

Jehoiakim Reigns in Judah

36 Jehoiakim was twenty-five years old when he began to reign, and he reigned eleven years in Jerusalem. His mother's name was Zebidah the daughter of Pedaiah of Rumah. 37 And he did what was evil in the sight of the LORD, according to all that his fathers had done.

24 In his days, Nebuchadnezzar king of Babylon came up, and Jehoiakim became his servant three years. Then he turned and rebelled against him. 2 And the LORD sent against him bands of the Chaldeans and bands of the Syrians and bands of the Moabites and bands of the Ammonites, and sent them against Judah to destroy it, according to the word of the LORD that he spoke by his servants the prophets. 3 Surely this came upon Judah at the command of the LORD, to remove them out of his sight, for the sins of Manasseh, according to all that he had done, 4 and also for the innocent blood that he had shed. For he filled Jerusalem with innocent blood, and the LORD would not pardon. 5 Now the rest of the deeds of Jehoiakim and all that he did, are they not written in the Book of the Chronicles of the Kings of Judah? 6 So Jehoiakim slept with his fathers, and Jehoiachin his son reigned in his place. 7 And the king of

[1] A *talent* was about 75 pounds or 34 kilograms

Egypt did not come again out of his land,
for the king of Babylon had taken all that
belonged to the king of Egypt from the
Brook of Egypt to the river Euphrates.

Jehoiachin Reigns in Judah

8 Jehoiachin was eighteen years old
when he became king, and he reigned
three months in Jerusalem. His mother's
name was Nehushta the daughter of
Elnathan of Jerusalem. 9 And he did what
was evil in the sight of the LORD, accord-
ing to all that his father had done.

Jerusalem Captured

10 At that time the servants of Nebu-
chadnezzar king of Babylon came up to
Jerusalem, and the city was besieged.
11 And Nebuchadnezzar king of Babylon
came to the city while his servants were
besieging it, 12 and Jehoiachin the king
of Judah gave himself up to the king of
Babylon, himself and his mother and his
servants and his officials and his palace
officials. The king of Babylon took him
prisoner in the eighth year of his reign
13 and carried off all the treasures of the
house of the LORD and the treasures of
the king's house, and cut in pieces all
the vessels of gold in the temple of the
LORD, which Solomon king of Israel had
made, as the LORD had foretold. 14 He
carried away all Jerusalem and all the
officials and all the mighty men of valor,
10,000 captives, and all the craftsmen
and the smiths. None remained, except
the poorest people of the land. 15 And
he carried away Jehoiachin to Babylon.
The king's mother, the king's wives, his
officials, and the chief men of the land
he took into captivity from Jerusalem
to Babylon. 16 And the king of Babylon
brought captive to Babylon all the men
of valor, 7,000, and the craftsmen and the
metal workers, 1,000, all of them strong
and fit for war. 17 And the king of Babylon
made Mattaniah, Jehoiachin's uncle,
king in his place, and changed his name
to Zedekiah.

Zedekiah Reigns in Judah

18 Zedekiah was twenty-one years old
when he became king, and he reigned
eleven years in Jerusalem. His moth-
er's name was Hamutal the daughter of
Jeremiah of Libnah. 19 And he did what
was evil in the sight of the LORD, accord-
ing to all that Jehoiakim had done. 20 For
because of the anger of the LORD it came
to the point in Jerusalem and Judah that
he cast them out from his presence.

And Zedekiah rebelled against the king
of Babylon.

Fall and Captivity of Judah

25 And in the ninth year of his
reign, in the tenth month, on the
tenth day of the month, Nebuchadnezzar
king of Babylon came with all his army
against Jerusalem and laid siege to it. And
they built siegeworks all around it. 2 So
the city was besieged till the eleventh
year of King Zedekiah. 3 On the ninth day
of the fourth month the famine was so
severe in the city that there was no food
for the people of the land. 4 Then a breach
was made in the city, and all the men of
war fled by night by the way of the gate
between the two walls, by the king's gar-
den, though the Chaldeans were around
the city. And they went in the direc-
tion of the Arabah. 5 But the army of the
Chaldeans pursued the king and over-
took him in the plains of Jericho, and all
his army was scattered from him. 6 Then
they captured the king and brought him
up to the king of Babylon at Riblah, and
they passed sentence on him. 7 They
slaughtered the sons of Zedekiah before
his eyes, and put out the eyes of Zedekiah
and bound him in chains and took him
to Babylon.

8 In the fifth month, on the seventh
day of the month—that was the nine-
teenth year of King Nebuchadnezzar,

king of Babylon—Nebuzaradan, the captain of the bodyguard, a servant of the king of Babylon, came to Jerusalem. 9 And he burned the house of the LORD and the king's house and all the houses of Jerusalem; every great house he burned down. 10 And all the army of the Chaldeans, who were with the captain of the guard, broke down the walls around Jerusalem. 11 And the rest of the people who were left in the city and the deserters who had deserted to the king of Babylon, together with the rest of the multitude, Nebuzaradan the captain of the guard carried into exile. 12 But the captain of the guard left some of the poorest of the land to be vinedressers and plowmen.

13 And the pillars of bronze that were in the house of the LORD, and the stands and the bronze sea that were in the house of the LORD, the Chaldeans broke in pieces and carried the bronze to Babylon. 14 And they took away the pots and the shovels and the snuffers and the dishes for incense and all the vessels of bronze used in the temple service, 15 the fire pans also and the bowls. What was of gold the captain of the guard took away as gold, and what was of silver, as silver. 16 As for the two pillars, the one sea, and the stands that Solomon had made for the house of the LORD, the bronze of all these vessels was beyond weight. 17 The height of the one pillar was eighteen cubits,[1] and on it was a capital of bronze. The height of the capital was three cubits. A latticework and pomegranates, all of bronze, were all around the capital. And the second pillar had the same, with the latticework.

18 And the captain of the guard took Seraiah the chief priest and Zephaniah the second priest and the three keepers of the threshold, 19 and from the city he took an officer who had been in command of the men of war, and five men of the king's council who were found in the city, and the secretary of the commander of the army who mustered the people of the land, and sixty men of the people of the land who were found in the city. 20 And Nebuzaradan the captain of the guard took them and brought them to the king of Babylon at Riblah. 21 And the king of Babylon struck them down and put them to death at Riblah in the land of Hamath. So Judah was taken into exile out of its land.

Gedaliah Made Governor of Judah

22 And over the people who remained in the land of Judah, whom Nebuchadnezzar king of Babylon had left, he appointed Gedaliah the son of Ahikam, son of Shaphan, governor. 23 Now when all the captains and their men heard that the king of Babylon had appointed Gedaliah governor, they came with their men to Gedaliah at Mizpah, namely, Ishmael the son of Nethaniah, and Johanan the son of Kareah, and Seraiah the son of Tanhumeth the Netophathite, and Jaazaniah the son of the Maacathite. 24 And Gedaliah swore to them and their men, saying, "Do not be afraid because of the Chaldean officials. Live in the land and serve the king of Babylon, and it shall be well with you." 25 But in the seventh month, Ishmael the son of Nethaniah, son of Elishama, of the royal family, came with ten men and struck down Gedaliah and put him to death along with the Jews and the Chaldeans who were with him at Mizpah. 26 Then all the people, both small and great, and the captains of the forces arose and went to Egypt, for they were afraid of the Chaldeans.

Jehoiachin Released from Prison

27 And in the thirty-seventh year of the exile of Jehoiachin king of Judah, in the twelfth month, on the twenty-seventh day of the month, Evil-merodach king of Babylon, in the year that he began to

[1] A *cubit* was about 18 inches or 45 centimeters

reign, graciously freed[1] Jehoiachin king
of Judah from prison. 28 And he spoke
kindly to him and gave him a seat above
the seats of the kings who were with him
in Babylon. 29 So Jehoiachin put off his
prison garments. And every day of his
life he dined regularly at the king's table,
30 and for his allowance, a regular allow-
ance was given him by the king, according
to his daily needs, as long as he lived.

[1] Hebrew *reign, lifted up the head of*

Introduction to

1–2 Chronicles

Author and Date

Author unknown. Written about 430 B.C.

People

David; Solomon; Rehoboam; Asa; Jehoshaphat; Athaliah; Joash; Uzziah; Hezekiah; Manasseh; Josiah; Cyrus

Purpose

These books remind God's people of God's faithfulness in keeping His covenant with David, and to call them to worship and live for God now that He had brought them back to their land after exile.

Central Themes

God provides a godly king in David; God is faithful to His promise to establish kings from David's line; temple worship is central to God's purposes for His people; God's blessing is a result of obedience and His judgment is a result of disobedience; God is faithful in bringing His exiled people back to the land.

Memory Verses

My God is with you (1 Chronicles 28:20); David's doxology and prayer (1 Chronicles 29:11, 16–17); the eyes of the Lord (2 Chronicles 16:9); Jehoshaphat's battle plan (2 Chronicles 20:20–22)

Introduction

After 70 years of captivity in Babylon, God's people have returned to their land. The writer of Chronicles begins his two-part book with lists showing descendants of Adam, Abraham, and Jacob's 12 sons (1 Chronicles 1–7). His list of the exiles who have come back shows them that they are also a part of God's chosen people (1 Chronicles 9). The writer describes God's gift of good kings in David and Solomon (1 Chronicles 11–2 Chronicles 9). The writer wants the returned Israelites to worship God in their rebuilt temple, so he describes how the first temple had been built and how worship in it had been established (1 Chronicles 22–25; 29; 2 Chronicles 2–7). He recounts how God has raised up king after king from David's line, keeping His promise to David. These stories provide examples of godly living to follow and of ungodly living to avoid (2 Chronicles 10–35). The two-part book ends with the story of Jerusalem's destruction as God's judgment for disobedience (2 Chronicles 36:1–21). The last story reminds readers of God's grace. It describes the Persian emperor, Cyrus, allowing the people to return to their land to rebuild Jerusalem and the temple—just as God had said would happen (2 Chronicles 36:22–23).

1010 B.C.	931 B.C.	722 B.C.	586 B.C.
Reign of David begins	Israel divided	Fall of Israel	Fall of Judah

1 Chronicles

From Adam to Abraham

1 [1]Adam, Seth, Enosh; 2 Kenan, Mahalalel, Jared; 3 Enoch, Methuselah, Lamech; 4 Noah, Shem, Ham, and Japheth.

5 The sons of Japheth: Gomer, Magog, Madai, Javan, Tubal, Meshech, and Tiras. 6 The sons of Gomer: Ashkenaz, Riphath,[2] and Togarmah. 7 The sons of Javan: Elishah, Tarshish, Kittim, and Rodanim.

8 The sons of Ham: Cush, Egypt, Put, and Canaan. 9 The sons of Cush: Seba, Havilah, Sabta, Raama, and Sabteca. The sons of Raamah: Sheba and Dedan. 10 Cush fathered Nimrod. He was the first on earth to be a mighty man.[3]

11 Egypt fathered Ludim, Anamim, Lehabim, Naphtuhim, 12 Pathrusim, Casluhim (from whom the Philistines came), and Caphtorim.

13 Canaan fathered Sidon his firstborn and Heth, 14 and the Jebusites, the Amorites, the Girgashites, 15 the Hivites, the Arkites, the Sinites, 16 the Arvadites, the Zemarites, and the Hamathites.

17 The sons of Shem: Elam, Asshur, Arpachshad, Lud, and Aram. And the sons of Aram:[4] Uz, Hul, Gether, and Meshech. 18 Arpachshad fathered Shelah, and Shelah fathered Eber. 19 To Eber were born two sons: the name of the one was Peleg[5] (for in his days the earth was divided), and his brother's name was Joktan. 20 Joktan fathered Almodad, Sheleph, Hazarmaveth, Jerah, 21 Hadoram, Uzal, Diklah, 22 Obal,[6] Abimael, Sheba, 23 Ophir, Havilah, and Jobab; all these were the sons of Joktan.

24 Shem, Arpachshad, Shelah; 25 Eber, Peleg, Reu; 26 Serug, Nahor, Terah; 27 Abram, that is, Abraham.

From Abraham to Jacob

28 The sons of Abraham: Isaac and Ishmael. 29 These are their genealogies: the firstborn of Ishmael, Nebaioth, and Kedar, Adbeel, Mibsam, 30 Mishma, Dumah, Massa, Hadad, Tema, 31 Jetur, Naphish, and Kedemah. These are the sons of Ishmael. 32 The sons of Keturah, Abraham's concubine: she bore Zimran, Jokshan, Medan, Midian, Ishbak, and Shuah. The sons of Jokshan: Sheba and Dedan. 33 The sons of Midian: Ephah, Epher, Hanoch, Abida, and Eldaah. All these were the descendants of Keturah.

34 Abraham fathered Isaac. The sons of Isaac: Esau and Israel. 35 The sons of Esau: Eliphaz, Reuel, Jeush, Jalam, and Korah. 36 The sons of Eliphaz: Teman, Omar, Zepho, Gatam, Kenaz, and of Timna,[7] Amalek. 37 The sons of Reuel: Nahath, Zerah, Shammah, and Mizzah.

38 The sons of Seir: Lotan, Shobal, Zibeon, Anah, Dishon, Ezer, and Dishan. 39 The sons of Lotan: Hori and Hemam;[8] and Lotan's sister was Timna. 40 The sons of Shobal: Alvan,[9] Manahath, Ebal, Shepho,[10] and Onam. The sons of Zibeon: Aiah and Anah. 41 The son[11] of Anah: Dishon. The sons of Dishon: Hemdan,[12] Eshban, Ithran, and Cheran. 42 The sons of Ezer: Bilhan, Zaavan, and Akan.[13] The sons of Dishan: Uz and Aran.

43 These are the kings who reigned in the land of Edom before any king reigned over the people of Israel: Bela the son of Beor, the name of his city being Dinhabah. 44 Bela died, and Jobab the son of Zerah of Bozrah reigned in his place. 45 Jobab died, and Husham of the land of the Temanites reigned in his place. 46 Husham died, and

[1] Many names in these genealogies are spelled differently in other biblical books [2] Septuagint; Hebrew *Diphath* [3] *Or He began to be a mighty man on the earth* [4] Septuagint; Hebrew lacks *And the sons of Aram* [5] *Peleg* means *division* [6] Septuagint, Syriac (compare Genesis 10:28); Hebrew *Ebal* [7] Septuagint (compare Genesis 36:12); Hebrew lacks *and of* [8] Septuagint (compare Genesis 36:22); Hebrew *Homam* [9] Septuagint (compare Genesis 36:23); Hebrew *Alian* [10] Septuagint (compare Genesis 36:23); Hebrew *Shephi* [11] Hebrew *sons* [12] Septuagint (compare Genesis 36:26); Hebrew *Hamran* [13] Septuagint (compare Genesis 36:27); Hebrew *Jaakan*

Hadad the son of Bedad, who defeated Midian in the country of Moab, reigned in his place, the name of his city being Avith. 47 Hadad died, and Samlah of Masrekah reigned in his place. 48 Samlah died, and Shaul of Rehoboth on the Euphrates reigned in his place. 49 Shaul died, and Baal-hanan, the son of Achbor, reigned in his place. 50 Baal-hanan died, and Hadad reigned in his place, the name of his city being Pai; and his wife's name was Mehetabel, the daughter of Matred, the daughter of Mezahab. 51 And Hadad died.

The chiefs of Edom were: chiefs Timna, Alvah, Jetheth, 52 Oholibamah, Elah, Pinon, 53 Kenaz, Teman, Mibzar, 54 Magdiel, and Iram; these are the chiefs of Edom.

A Genealogy of David

2 These are the sons of Israel: Reuben, Simeon, Levi, Judah, Issachar, Zebulun, 2 Dan, Joseph, Benjamin, Naphtali, Gad, and Asher. 3 The sons of Judah: Er, Onan and Shelah; these three Bath-shua the Canaanite bore to him. Now Er, Judah's firstborn, was evil in the sight of the LORD, and he put him to death. 4 His daughter-in-law Tamar also bore him Perez and Zerah. Judah had five sons in all.

5 The sons of Perez: Hezron and Hamul. 6 The sons of Zerah: Zimri, Ethan, Heman, Calcol, and Dara, five in all. 7 The son[1] of Carmi: Achan, the troubler of Israel, who broke faith in the matter of the devoted thing; 8 and Ethan's son was Azariah.

9 The sons of Hezron that were born to him: Jerahmeel, Ram, and Chelubai. 10 Ram fathered Amminadab, and Amminadab fathered Nahshon, prince of the sons of Judah. 11 Nahshon fathered Salmon,[2] Salmon fathered Boaz, 12 Boaz fathered Obed, Obed fathered Jesse. 13 Jesse fathered Eliab his firstborn, Abinadab the second, Shimea the third, 14 Nethanel the fourth, Raddai the fifth, 15 Ozem the sixth, David the seventh. 16 And their sisters were Zeruiah and Abigail. The sons of Zeruiah: Abishai, Joab, and Asahel, three. 17 Abigail bore Amasa, and the father of Amasa was Jether the Ishmaelite.

18 Caleb the son of Hezron fathered children by his wife Azubah, and by Jerioth; and these were her sons: Jesher, Shobab, and Ardon. 19 When Azubah died, Caleb married Ephrath, who bore him Hur. 20 Hur fathered Uri, and Uri fathered Bezalel.

21 Afterward Hezron went in to the daughter of Machir the father of Gilead, whom he married when he was sixty years old, and she bore him Segub. 22 And Segub fathered Jair, who had twenty-three cities in the land of Gilead. 23 But Geshur and Aram took from them Havvoth-jair, Kenath, and its villages, sixty towns. All these were descendants of Machir, the father of Gilead. 24 After the death of Hezron, Caleb went in to Ephrathah,[3] the wife of Hezron his father, and she bore him Ashhur, the father of Tekoa.

25 The sons of Jerahmeel, the firstborn of Hezron: Ram, his firstborn, Bunah, Oren, Ozem, and Ahijah. 26 Jerahmeel also had another wife, whose name was Atarah; she was the mother of Onam. 27 The sons of Ram, the firstborn of Jerahmeel: Maaz, Jamin, and Eker. 28 The sons of Onam: Shammai and Jada. The sons of Shammai: Nadab and Abishur. 29 The name of Abishur's wife was Abihail, and she bore him Ahban and Molid. 30 The sons of Nadab: Seled and Appaim; and Seled died childless. 31 The son[4] of Appaim: Ishi. The son of Ishi: Sheshan. The son of Sheshan: Ahlai. 32 The sons of Jada, Shammai's brother: Jether and Jonathan; and Jether died childless. 33 The sons of Jonathan: Peleth and Zaza. These were the descendants of Jerahmeel. 34 Now Sheshan had no sons, only daughters, but Sheshan had an Egyptian slave whose name was Jarha. 35 So Sheshan gave his daughter in marriage to Jarha his slave, and she bore

[1] Hebrew *sons* [2] Septuagint (compare Ruth 4:21); Hebrew *Salma* [3] Septuagint, Vulgate; Hebrew *in Caleb Ephrathah* [4] Hebrew *sons*; three times in this verse

him Attai. 36 Attai fathered Nathan, and Nathan fathered Zabad. 37 Zabad fathered Ephlal, and Ephlal fathered Obed. 38 Obed fathered Jehu, and Jehu fathered Azariah. 39 Azariah fathered Helez, and Helez fathered Eleasah. 40 Eleasah fathered Sismai, and Sismai fathered Shallum. 41 Shallum fathered Jekamiah, and Jekamiah fathered Elishama.

42 The sons of Caleb the brother of Jerahmeel: Mareshah[1] his firstborn, who fathered Ziph. The son[2] of Mareshah: Hebron.[3] 43 The sons of Hebron: Korah, Tappuah, Rekem and Shema. 44 Shema fathered Raham, the father of Jorkeam; and Rekem fathered Shammai. 45 The son of Shammai: Maon; and Maon fathered Beth-zur. 46 Ephah also, Caleb's concubine, bore Haran, Moza, and Gazez; and Haran fathered Gazez. 47 The sons of Jahdai: Regem, Jotham, Geshan, Pelet, Ephah, and Shaaph. 48 Maacah, Caleb's concubine, bore Sheber and Tirhanah. 49 She also bore Shaaph the father of Madmannah, Sheva the father of Machbenah and the father of Gibea; and the daughter of Caleb was Achsah. 50 These were the descendants of Caleb.

The sons[4] of Hur the firstborn of Ephrathah: Shobal the father of Kiriath-jearim, 51 Salma, the father of Bethlehem, and Hareph the father of Beth-gader. 52 Shobal the father of Kiriath-jearim had other sons: Haroeh, half of the Menuhoth. 53 And the clans of Kiriath-jearim: the Ithrites, the Puthites, the Shumathites, and the Mishraites; from these came the Zorathites and the Eshtaolites. 54 The sons of Salma: Bethlehem, the Netophathites, Atroth-beth-joab and half of the Manahathites, the Zorites. 55 The clans also of the scribes who lived at Jabez: the Tirathites, the Shimeathites and the Sucathites. These are the Kenites who came from Hammath, the father of the house of Rechab.

Descendants of David

3 These are the sons of David who were born to him in Hebron: the firstborn, Amnon, by Ahinoam the Jezreelite; the second, Daniel, by Abigail the Carmelite, 2 the third, Absalom, whose mother was Maacah, the daughter of Talmai, king of Geshur; the fourth, Adonijah, whose mother was Haggith; 3 the fifth, Shephatiah, by Abital; the sixth, Ithream, by his wife Eglah; 4 six were born to him in Hebron, where he reigned for seven years and six months. And he reigned thirty-three years in Jerusalem. 5 These were born to him in Jerusalem: Shimea, Shobab, Nathan and Solomon, four by Bath-shua, the daughter of Ammiel; 6 then Ibhar, Elishama, Eliphelet, 7 Nogah, Nepheg, Japhia, 8 Elishama, Eliada, and Eliphelet, nine. 9 All these were David's sons, besides the sons of the concubines, and Tamar was their sister.

10 The son of Solomon was Rehoboam, Abijah his son, Asa his son, Jehoshaphat his son, 11 Joram his son, Ahaziah his son, Joash his son, 12 Amaziah his son, Azariah his son, Jotham his son, 13 Ahaz his son, Hezekiah his son, Manasseh his son, 14 Amon his son, Josiah his son. 15 The sons of Josiah: Johanan the firstborn, the second Jehoiakim, the third Zedekiah, the fourth Shallum. 16 The descendants of Jehoiakim: Jeconiah his son, Zedekiah his son; 17 and the sons of Jeconiah, the captive: Shealtiel his son, 18 Malchiram, Pedaiah, Shenazzar, Jekamiah, Hoshama and Nedabiah; 19 and the sons of Pedaiah: Zerubbabel and Shimei; and the sons of Zerubbabel: Meshullam and Hananiah, and Shelomith was their sister; 20 and Hashubah, Ohel, Berechiah, Hasadiah, and Jushab-hesed, five. 21 The sons of Hananiah: Pelatiah and Jeshaiah, his son[5] Rephaiah, his son Arnan, his son Obadiah, his son Shecaniah. 22 The son[6] of Shecaniah: Shemaiah. And the sons

[1] Septuagint; Hebrew *Mesha* [2] Hebrew *sons* [3] Hebrew *the father of Hebron* [4] Septuagint, Vulgate; Hebrew *son* [5] Septuagint (compare Syriac, Vulgate); Hebrew *sons of*, four times in this verse [6] Hebrew *sons*

of Shemaiah: Hattush, Igal, Bariah, Neariah, and Shaphat, six. 23 The sons of Neariah: Elioenai, Hizkiah, and Azrikam, three. 24 The sons of Elioenai: Hodaviah, Eliashib, Pelaiah, Akkub, Johanan, Delaiah, and Anani, seven.

Descendants of Judah

4 The sons of Judah: Perez, Hezron, Carmi, Hur, and Shobal. 2 Reaiah the son of Shobal fathered Jahath, and Jahath fathered Ahumai and Lahad. These were the clans of the Zorathites. 3 These were the sons[1] of Etam: Jezreel, Ishma, and Idbash; and the name of their sister was Hazzelelponi, 4 and Penuel fathered Gedor, and Ezer fathered Hushah. These were the sons of Hur, the firstborn of Ephrathah, the father of Bethlehem. 5 Ashhur, the father of Tekoa, had two wives, Helah and Naarah; 6 Naarah bore him Ahuzzam, Hepher, Temeni, and Haahashtari. These were the sons of Naarah. 7 The sons of Helah: Zereth, Izhar, and Ethnan. 8 Koz fathered Anub, Zobebah, and the clans of Aharhel, the son of Harum. 9 Jabez was more honorable than his brothers; and his mother called his name Jabez, saying, "Because I bore him in pain."[2] 10 Jabez called upon the God of Israel, saying, "Oh that you would bless me and enlarge my border, and that your hand might be with me, and that you would keep me from harm[3] so that it might not bring me pain!" And God granted what he asked. 11 Chelub, the brother of Shuhah, fathered Mehir, who fathered Eshton. 12 Eshton fathered Beth-rapha, Paseah, and Tehinnah, the father of Ir-nahash. These are the men of Recah. 13 The sons of Kenaz: Othniel and Seraiah; and the sons of Othniel: Hathath and Meonothai.[4] 14 Meonothai fathered Ophrah; and Seraiah fathered Joab, the father of Ge-harashim,[5] so-called because they were craftsmen. 15 The sons of Caleb the son of Jephunneh: Iru, Elah, and Naam; and the son[6] of Elah: Kenaz. 16 The sons of Jehallelel: Ziph, Ziphah, Tiria, and Asarel. 17 The sons of Ezrah: Jether, Mered, Epher, and Jalon. These are the sons of Bithiah, the daughter of Pharaoh, whom Mered married;[7] and she conceived and bore[8] Miriam, Shammai, and Ishbah, the father of Eshtemoa. 18 And his Judahite wife bore Jered the father of Gedor, Heber the father of Soco, and Jekuthiel the father of Zanoah. 19 The sons of the wife of Hodiah, the sister of Naham, were the fathers of Keilah the Garmite and Eshtemoa the Maacathite. 20 The sons of Shimon: Amnon, Rinnah, Ben-hanan, and Tilon. The sons of Ishi: Zoheth and Ben-zoheth. 21 The sons of Shelah the son of Judah: Er the father of Lecah, Laadah the father of Mareshah, and the clans of the house of linen workers at Beth-ashbea; 22 and Jokim, and the men of Cozeba, and Joash, and Saraph, who ruled in Moab and returned to Lehem[9] (now the records[10] are ancient). 23 These were the potters who were inhabitants of Netaim and Gederah. They lived there in the king's service.

Descendants of Simeon

24 The sons of Simeon: Nemuel, Jamin, Jarib, Zerah, Shaul; 25 Shallum was his son, Mibsam his son, Mishma his son. 26 The sons of Mishma: Hammuel his son, Zaccur his son, Shimei his son. 27 Shimei had sixteen sons and six daughters; but his brothers did not have many children, nor did all their clan multiply like the men of Judah. 28 They lived in Beersheba, Moladah, Hazar-shual, 29 Bilhah, Ezem, Tolad, 30 Bethuel, Hormah, Ziklag, 31 Beth-marcaboth, Hazar-susim, Beth-biri, and Shaaraim. These were their cities until David reigned. 32 And their villages were Etam, Ain, Rimmon, Tochen, and Ashan, five cities, 33 along with all their villages that were around these cities as far as

[1] Septuagint (compare Vulgate); Hebrew *father* [2] *Jabez* sounds like the Hebrew for *pain* [3] Or *evil* [4] Septuagint, Vulgate; Hebrew lacks *Meonothai* [5] *Ge-harashim* means *valley of craftsmen* [6] Hebrew *sons* [7] The clause *These are . . . married* is transposed from verse 18 [8] Hebrew lacks *and bore* [9] Vulgate (compare Septuagint); Hebrew *and Jashubi-lahem* [10] Or *matters*

Baal. These were their settlements, and
they kept a genealogical record.
34 Meshobab, Jamlech, Joshah the
son of Amaziah, 35 Joel, Jehu the son of
Joshibiah, son of Seraiah, son of Asiel,
36 Elioenai, Jaakobah, Jeshohaiah, Asaiah,
Adiel, Jesimiel, Benaiah, 37 Ziza the son of
Shiphi, son of Allon, son of Jedaiah, son
of Shimri, son of Shemaiah— 38 these
mentioned by name were princes in
their clans, and their fathers' houses
increased greatly. 39 They journeyed to
the entrance of Gedor, to the east side of
the valley, to seek pasture for their flocks,
40 where they found rich, good pasture,
and the land was very broad, quiet, and
peaceful, for the former inhabitants there
belonged to Ham. 41 These, registered by
name, came in the days of Hezekiah, king
of Judah, and destroyed their tents and
the Meunites who were found there, and
marked them for destruction to this day,
and settled in their place, because there
was pasture there for their flocks. 42 And
some of them, five hundred men of the
Simeonites, went to Mount Seir, having as
their leaders Pelatiah, Neariah, Rephaiah,
and Uzziel, the sons of Ishi. 43 And they
defeated the remnant of the Amalekites
who had escaped, and they have lived
there to this day.

Descendants of Reuben

5 The sons of Reuben the firstborn of
Israel (for he was the firstborn, but
because he defiled his father's couch, his
birthright was given to the sons of Joseph
the son of Israel, so that he could not be
enrolled as the oldest son; 2 though Judah
became strong among his brothers and
a chief came from him, yet the birth-
right belonged to Joseph), 3 the sons of
Reuben, the firstborn of Israel: Hanoch,
Pallu, Hezron, and Carmi. 4 The sons
of Joel: Shemaiah his son, Gog his son,
Shimei his son, 5 Micah his son, Reaiah
his son, Baal his son, 6 Beerah his son,
whom Tiglath-pileser[1] king of Assyria
carried away into exile; he was a chief
of the Reubenites. 7 And his kinsmen by
their clans, when the genealogy of their
generations was recorded: the chief, Jeiel,
and Zechariah, 8 and Bela the son of Azaz,
son of Shema, son of Joel, who lived in
Aroer, as far as Nebo and Baal-meon. 9 He
also lived to the east as far as the entrance
of the desert this side of the Euphrates,
because their livestock had multiplied in
the land of Gilead. 10 And in the days of
Saul they waged war against the Hagrites,
who fell into their hand. And they lived in
their tents throughout all the region east
of Gilead.

Descendants of Gad

11 The sons of Gad lived over against
them in the land of Bashan as far as
Salecah: 12 Joel the chief, Shapham the sec-
ond, Janai, and Shaphat in Bashan. 13 And
their kinsmen according to their fathers'
houses: Michael, Meshullam, Sheba, Jorai,
Jacan, Zia and Eber, seven. 14 These were
the sons of Abihail the son of Huri, son
of Jaroah, son of Gilead, son of Michael,
son of Jeshishai, son of Jahdo, son of Buz.
15 Ahi the son of Abdiel, son of Guni, was
chief in their fathers' houses, 16 and they
lived in Gilead, in Bashan and in its towns,
and in all the pasturelands of Sharon to
their limits. 17 All of these were recorded
in genealogies in the days of Jotham king
of Judah, and in the days of Jeroboam king
of Israel.
18 The Reubenites, the Gadites, and
the half-tribe of Manasseh had valiant
men who carried shield and sword, and
drew the bow, expert in war, 44,760, able
to go to war. 19 They waged war against
the Hagrites, Jetur, Naphish, and Nodab.
20 And when they prevailed over them, the
Hagrites and all who were with them were
given into their hands, for they cried out
to God in the battle, and he granted their
urgent plea because they trusted in him.

[1] Hebrew *Tilgath-pilneser*; also verse 26

21 They carried off their livestock: 50,000
of their camels, 250,000 sheep, 2,000 don-
keys, and 100,000 men alive. 22 For many
fell, because the war was of God. And they
lived in their place until the exile.

The Half-Tribe of Manasseh

23 The members of the half-tribe of
Manasseh lived in the land. They were
very numerous from Bashan to Baal-
hermon, Senir, and Mount Hermon.
24 These were the heads of their fathers'
houses: Epher,[1] Ishi, Eliel, Azriel,
Jeremiah, Hodaviah, and Jahdiel, mighty
warriors, famous men, heads of their
fathers' houses. 25 But they broke faith
with the God of their fathers, and whored
after the gods of the peoples of the land,
whom God had destroyed before them.
26 So the God of Israel stirred up the spirit
of Pul king of Assyria, the spirit of Tiglath-
pileser king of Assyria, and he took them
into exile, namely, the Reubenites, the
Gadites, and the half-tribe of Manasseh,
and brought them to Halah, Habor, Hara,
and the river Gozan, to this day.

Descendants of Levi

6 [2] The sons of Levi: Gershon, Kohath,
and Merari. 2 The sons of Kohath:
Amram, Izhar, Hebron, and Uzziel. 3 The
children of Amram: Aaron, Moses, and
Miriam. The sons of Aaron: Nadab, Abihu,
Eleazar, and Ithamar. 4 Eleazar fathered
Phinehas, Phinehas fathered Abishua,
5 Abishua fathered Bukki, Bukki fathered
Uzzi, 6 Uzzi fathered Zerahiah, Zerahiah
fathered Meraioth, 7 Meraioth fathered
Amariah, Amariah fathered Ahitub, 8 Ahi-
tub fathered Zadok, Zadok fathered
Ahimaaz, 9 Ahimaaz fathered Azariah,
Azariah fathered Johanan, 10 and Johanan
fathered Azariah (it was he who served as
priest in the house that Solomon built in
Jerusalem). 11 Azariah fathered Amariah,
Amariah fathered Ahitub, 12 Ahitub
fathered Zadok, Zadok fathered Shallum,
13 Shallum fathered Hilkiah, Hilkiah
fathered Azariah, 14 Azariah fathered
Seraiah, Seraiah fathered Jehozadak; 15 and
Jehozadak went into exile when the LORD
sent Judah and Jerusalem into exile by the
hand of Nebuchadnezzar.

16 [3] The sons of Levi: Gershom, Kohath,
and Merari. 17 And these are the names of
the sons of Gershom: Libni and Shimei.
18 The sons of Kohath: Amram, Izhar,
Hebron and Uzziel. 19 The sons of Merari:
Mahli and Mushi. These are the clans of
the Levites according to their fathers. 20 Of
Gershom: Libni his son, Jahath his son,
Zimmah his son, 21 Joah his son, Iddo his
son, Zerah his son, Jeatherai his son. 22 The
sons of Kohath: Amminadab his son,
Korah his son, Assir his son, 23 Elkanah
his son, Ebiasaph his son, Assir his son,
24 Tahath his son, Uriel his son, Uzziah
his son, and Shaul his son. 25 The sons of
Elkanah: Amasai and Ahimoth, 26 Elkanah
his son, Zophai his son, Nahath his son,
27 Eliab his son, Jeroham his son, Elkanah
his son. 28 The sons of Samuel: Joel[4] his
firstborn, the second Abijah.[5] 29 The sons
of Merari: Mahli, Libni his son, Shimei
his son, Uzzah his son, 30 Shimea his son,
Haggiah his son, and Asaiah his son.

31 These are the men whom David put in
charge of the service of song in the house
of the LORD after the ark rested there.
32 They ministered with song before the
tabernacle of the tent of meeting until
Solomon built the house of the LORD in
Jerusalem, and they performed their ser-
vice according to their order. 33 These are
the men who served and their sons. Of the
sons of the Kohathites: Heman the singer
the son of Joel, son of Samuel, 34 son of
Elkanah, son of Jeroham, son of Eliel, son
of Toah, 35 son of Zuph, son of Elkanah,
son of Mahath, son of Amasai, 36 son of
Elkanah, son of Joel, son of Azariah, son of
Zephaniah, 37 son of Tahath, son of Assir,
son of Ebiasaph, son of Korah, 38 son of
Izhar, son of Kohath, son of Levi, son

[1] Septuagint, Vulgate; Hebrew *and Epher* [2] Ch 5:27 in Hebrew [3] Ch 6:1 in Hebrew [4] Septuagint, Syriac (compare verse 33 and 1 Samuel 8:2); Hebrew lacks *Joel*
[5] Hebrew *and Abijah*

of Israel; 39 and his brother Asaph, who stood on his right hand, namely, Asaph the son of Berechiah, son of Shimea, 40 son of Michael, son of Baaseiah, son of Malchijah, 41 son of Ethni, son of Zerah, son of Adaiah, 42 son of Ethan, son of Zimmah, son of Shimei, 43 son of Jahath, son of Gershom, son of Levi. 44 On the left hand were their brothers, the sons of Merari: Ethan the son of Kishi, son of Abdi, son of Malluch, 45 son of Hashabiah, son of Amaziah, son of Hilkiah, 46 son of Amzi, son of Bani, son of Shemer, 47 son of Mahli, son of Mushi, son of Merari, son of Levi. 48 And their brothers the Levites were appointed for all the service of the tabernacle of the house of God.

49 But Aaron and his sons made offerings on the altar of burnt offering and on the altar of incense for all the work of the Most Holy Place, and to make atonement for Israel, according to all that Moses the servant of God had commanded. 50 These are the sons of Aaron: Eleazar his son, Phinehas his son, Abishua his son, 51 Bukki his son, Uzzi his son, Zerahiah his son, 52 Meraioth his son, Amariah his son, Ahitub his son, 53 Zadok his son, Ahimaaz his son.

54 These are their dwelling places according to their settlements within their borders: to the sons of Aaron of the clans of Kohathites, for theirs was the first lot, 55 to them they gave Hebron in the land of Judah and its surrounding pasturelands, 56 but the fields of the city and its villages they gave to Caleb the son of Jephunneh. 57 To the sons of Aaron they gave the cities of refuge: Hebron, Libnah with its pasturelands, Jattir, Eshtemoa with its pasturelands, 58 Hilen with its pasturelands, Debir with its pasturelands, 59 Ashan with its pasturelands, and Beth-shemesh with its pasturelands; 60 and from the tribe of Benjamin, Gibeon,[1] Geba with its pasturelands, Alemeth with its pasturelands, and Anathoth with its pasturelands. All their cities throughout their clans were thirteen.

61 To the rest of the Kohathites were given by lot out of the clan of the tribe, out of the half-tribe, the half of Manasseh, ten cities. 62 To the Gershomites according to their clans were allotted thirteen cities out of the tribes of Issachar, Asher, Naphtali and Manasseh in Bashan. 63 To the Merarites according to their clans were allotted twelve cities out of the tribes of Reuben, Gad, and Zebulun. 64 So the people of Israel gave the Levites the cities with their pasturelands. 65 They gave by lot out of the tribes of Judah, Simeon, and Benjamin these cities that are mentioned by name.

66 And some of the clans of the sons of Kohath had cities of their territory out of the tribe of Ephraim. 67 They were given the cities of refuge: Shechem with its pasturelands in the hill country of Ephraim, Gezer with its pasturelands, 68 Jokmeam with its pasturelands, Beth-horon with its pasturelands, 69 Aijalon with its pasturelands, Gath-rimmon with its pasturelands, 70 and out of the half-tribe of Manasseh, Aner with its pasturelands, and Bileam with its pasturelands, for the rest of the clans of the Kohathites.

71 To the Gershomites were given out of the clan of the half-tribe of Manasseh: Golan in Bashan with its pasturelands and Ashtaroth with its pasturelands; 72 and out of the tribe of Issachar: Kedesh with its pasturelands, Daberath with its pasturelands, 73 Ramoth with its pasturelands, and Anem with its pasturelands; 74 out of the tribe of Asher: Mashal with its pasturelands, Abdon with its pasturelands, 75 Hukok with its pasturelands, and Rehob with its pasturelands; 76 and out of the tribe of Naphtali: Kedesh in Galilee with its pasturelands, Hammon with its pasturelands, and Kiriathaim with its pasturelands. 77 To the rest of the Merarites were allotted out of the tribe of Zebulun:

[1] Septuagint, Syriac (compare Joshua 21:17); Hebrew lacks *Gibeon*

Rimmono with its pasturelands, Tabor with its pasturelands, 78 and beyond the Jordan at Jericho, on the east side of the Jordan, out of the tribe of Reuben: Bezer in the wilderness with its pasturelands, Jahzah with its pasturelands, 79 Kedemoth with its pasturelands, and Mephaath with its pasturelands; 80 and out of the tribe of Gad: Ramoth in Gilead with its pasturelands, Mahanaim with its pasturelands, 81 Heshbon with its pasturelands, and Jazer with its pasturelands.

Descendants of Issachar

7 The sons[1] of Issachar: Tola, Puah, Jashub, and Shimron, four. 2 The sons of Tola: Uzzi, Rephaiah, Jeriel, Jahmai, Ibsam, and Shemuel, heads of their fathers' houses, namely of Tola, mighty warriors of their generations, their number in the days of David being 22,600. 3 The son[2] of Uzzi: Izrahiah. And the sons of Izrahiah: Michael, Obadiah, Joel, and Isshiah, all five of them were chief men. 4 And along with them, by their generations, according to their fathers' houses, were units of the army for war, 36,000, for they had many wives and sons. 5 Their kinsmen belonging to all the clans of Issachar were in all 87,000 mighty warriors, enrolled by genealogy.

Descendants of Benjamin

6 The sons of Benjamin: Bela, Becher, and Jediael, three. 7 The sons of Bela: Ezbon, Uzzi, Uzziel, Jerimoth, and Iri, five, heads of fathers' houses, mighty warriors. And their enrollment by genealogies was 22,034. 8 The sons of Becher: Zemirah, Joash, Eliezer, Elioenai, Omri, Jeremoth, Abijah, Anathoth, and Alemeth. All these were the sons of Becher. 9 And their enrollment by genealogies, according to their generations, as heads of their fathers' houses, mighty warriors, was 20,200. 10 The son of Jediael: Bilhan. And the sons of Bilhan: Jeush, Benjamin, Ehud, Chenaanah, Zethan, Tarshish, and Ahishahar. 11 All these were the sons of Jediael according to the heads of their fathers' houses, mighty warriors, 17,200, able to go to war. 12 And Shuppim and Huppim were the sons of Ir, Hushim the son of Aher.

Descendants of Naphtali

13 The sons of Naphtali: Jahziel, Guni, Jezer and Shallum, the descendants of Bilhah.

Descendants of Manasseh

14 The sons of Manasseh: Asriel, whom his Aramean concubine bore; she bore Machir the father of Gilead. 15 And Machir took a wife for Huppim and for Shuppim. The name of his sister was Maacah. And the name of the second was Zelophehad, and Zelophehad had daughters. 16 And Maacah the wife of Machir bore a son, and she called his name Peresh; and the name of his brother was Sheresh; and his sons were Ulam and Rakem. 17 The son of Ulam: Bedan. These were the sons of Gilead the son of Machir, son of Manasseh. 18 And his sister Hammolecheth bore Ishhod, Abiezer and Mahlah. 19 The sons of Shemida were Ahian, Shechem, Likhi, and Aniam.

Descendants of Ephraim

20 The sons of Ephraim: Shuthelah, and Bered his son, Tahath his son, Eleadah his son, Tahath his son, 21 Zabad his son, Shuthelah his son, and Ezer and Elead, whom the men of Gath who were born in the land killed, because they came down to raid their livestock. 22 And Ephraim their father mourned many days, and his brothers came to comfort him. 23 And Ephraim went in to his wife, and she conceived and bore a son. And he called his name Beriah, because disaster had befallen his house.[3] 24 His daughter was Sheerah, who built both Lower and Upper Beth-horon, and Uzzen-sheerah. 25 Rephah was his son, Resheph his son,

[1] Syriac (compare Vulgate); Hebrew *And to the sons* [2] Hebrew *sons*; also verses 10, 12, 17 [3] *Beriah* sounds like the Hebrew for *disaster*

Telah his son, Tahan his son, 26 Ladan his son, Ammihud his son, Elishama his son, 27 Nun[1] his son, Joshua his son. 28 Their possessions and settlements were Bethel and its towns, and to the east Naaran, and to the west Gezer and its towns, Shechem and its towns, and Ayyah and its towns; 29 also in possession of the Manassites, Beth-shean and its towns, Taanach and its towns, Megiddo and its towns, Dor and its towns. In these lived the sons of Joseph the son of Israel.

Descendants of Asher

30 The sons of Asher: Imnah, Ishvah, Ishvi, Beriah, and their sister Serah. 31 The sons of Beriah: Heber, and Malchiel, who fathered Birzaith. 32 Heber fathered Japhlet, Shomer, Hotham, and their sister Shua. 33 The sons of Japhlet: Pasach, Bimhal, and Ashvath. These are the sons of Japhlet. 34 The sons of Shemer his brother: Rohgah, Jehubbah, and Aram. 35 The sons of Helem his brother: Zophah, Imna, Shelesh, and Amal. 36 The sons of Zophah: Suah, Harnepher, Shual, Beri, Imrah. 37 Bezer, Hod, Shamma, Shilshah, Ithran, and Beera. 38 The sons of Jether: Jephunneh, Pispa, and Ara. 39 The sons of Ulla: Arah, Hanniel, and Rizia. 40 All of these were men of Asher, heads of fathers' houses, approved, mighty warriors, chiefs of the princes. Their number enrolled by genealogies, for service in war, was 26,000 men.

A Genealogy of Saul

8 Benjamin fathered Bela his firstborn, Ashbel the second, Aharah the third, 2 Nohah the fourth, and Rapha the fifth. 3 And Bela had sons: Addar, Gera, Abihud, 4 Abishua, Naaman, Ahoah, 5 Gera, Shephuphan, and Huram. 6 These are the sons of Ehud (they were heads of fathers' houses of the inhabitants of Geba, and they were carried into exile to Manahath): 7 Naaman,[2] Ahijah, and Gera, that is, Heglam,[3] who fathered Uzza and Ahihud. 8 And Shaharaim fathered sons in the country of Moab after he had sent away Hushim and Baara his wives. 9 He fathered sons by Hodesh his wife: Jobab, Zibia, Mesha, Malcam, 10 Jeuz, Sachia, and Mirmah. These were his sons, heads of fathers' houses. 11 He also fathered sons by Hushim: Abitub and Elpaal. 12 The sons of Elpaal: Eber, Misham, and Shemed, who built Ono and Lod with its towns, 13 and Beriah and Shema (they were heads of fathers' houses of the inhabitants of Aijalon, who caused the inhabitants of Gath to flee); 14 and Ahio, Shashak, and Jeremoth. 15 Zebadiah, Arad, Eder, 16 Michael, Ishpah, and Joha were sons of Beriah. 17 Zebadiah, Meshullam, Hizki, Heber, 18 Ishmerai, Izliah, and Jobab were the sons of Elpaal. 19 Jakim, Zichri, Zabdi, 20 Elienai, Zillethai, Eliel, 21 Adaiah, Beraiah, and Shimrath were the sons of Shimei. 22 Ishpan, Eber, Eliel, 23 Abdon, Zichri, Hanan, 24 Hananiah, Elam, Anthothijah, 25 Iphdeiah, and Penuel were the sons of Shashak. 26 Shamsherai, Shehariah, Athaliah, 27 Jaareshiah, Elijah, and Zichri were the sons of Jeroham. 28 These were the heads of fathers' houses, according to their generations, chief men. These lived in Jerusalem.

29 Jeiel[4] the father of Gibeon lived in Gibeon, and the name of his wife was Maacah. 30 His firstborn son: Abdon, then Zur, Kish, Baal, Nadab, 31 Gedor, Ahio, Zecher, 32 and Mikloth (he fathered Shimeah). Now these also lived opposite their kinsmen in Jerusalem, with their kinsmen. 33 Ner was the father of Kish, Kish of Saul, Saul of Jonathan, Malchi-shua, Abinadab and Eshbaal; 34 and the son of Jonathan was Merib-baal; and Merib-baal was the father of Micah. 35 The sons of Micah: Pithon, Melech, Tarea, and Ahaz. 36 Ahaz fathered Jehoaddah, and Jehoaddah fathered Alemeth, Azmaveth, and Zimri. Zimri fathered Moza. 37 Moza fathered Binea; Raphah was his son, Eleasah his son, Azel his son. 38 Azel had six sons, and

[1] Hebrew *Non* [2] Hebrew *and Naaman* [3] Or *he carried them into exile* [4] Compare 9:35; Hebrew lacks *Jeiel*

these are their names: Azrikam, Bocheru,
Ishmael, Sheariah, Obadiah, and Hanan.
All these were the sons of Azel. 39 The sons
of Eshek his brother: Ulam his firstborn,
Jeush the second, and Eliphelet the third.
40 The sons of Ulam were men who were
mighty warriors, bowmen, having many
sons and grandsons, 150. All these were
Benjaminites.

A Genealogy of the Returned Exiles

9 So all Israel was recorded in gene-
alogies, and these are written in the
Book of the Kings of Israel. And Judah
was taken into exile in Babylon because
of their breach of faith. 2 Now the first to
dwell again in their possessions in their
cities were Israel, the priests, the Levites,
and the temple servants. 3 And some of
the people of Judah, Benjamin, Ephraim,
and Manasseh lived in Jerusalem: 4 Uthai
the son of Ammihud, son of Omri, son of
Imri, son of Bani, from the sons of Perez
the son of Judah. 5 And of the Shilonites:
Asaiah the firstborn, and his sons. 6 Of the
sons of Zerah: Jeuel and their kinsmen,
690. 7 Of the Benjaminites: Sallu the son
of Meshullam, son of Hodaviah, son of
Hassenuah, 8 Ibneiah the son of Jeroham,
Elah the son of Uzzi, son of Michri, and
Meshullam the son of Shephatiah, son
of Reuel, son of Ibnijah; 9 and their kins-
men according to their generations, 956.
All these were heads of fathers' houses
according to their fathers' houses.

10 Of the priests: Jedaiah, Jehoiarib,
Jachin, 11 and Azariah the son of Hilkiah,
son of Meshullam, son of Zadok, son of
Meraioth, son of Ahitub, the chief officer
of the house of God; 12 and Adaiah the
son of Jeroham, son of Pashhur, son of
Malchijah, and Maasai the son of Adiel,
son of Jahzerah, son of Meshullam, son
of Meshillemith, son of Immer; 13 besides
their kinsmen, heads of their fathers'
houses, 1,760, mighty men for the work of
the service of the house of God.

14 Of the Levites: Shemaiah the son
of Hasshub, son of Azrikam, son of
Hashabiah, of the sons of Merari; 15 and
Bakbakkar, Heresh, Galal and Mattaniah
the son of Mica, son of Zichri, son of Asaph;
16 and Obadiah the son of Shemaiah, son of
Galal, son of Jeduthun, and Berechiah the
son of Asa, son of Elkanah, who lived in
the villages of the Netophathites.

17 The gatekeepers were Shallum,
Akkub, Talmon, Ahiman, and their kins-
men (Shallum was the chief); 18 until
then they were in the king's gate on
the east side as the gatekeepers of the
camps of the Levites. 19 Shallum the son
of Kore, son of Ebiasaph, son of Korah,
and his kinsmen of his fathers' house,
the Korahites, were in charge of the work
of the service, keepers of the thresholds
of the tent, as their fathers had been in
charge of the camp of the LORD, keepers
of the entrance. 20 And Phinehas the son
of Eleazar was the chief officer over them
in time past; the LORD was with him.
21 Zechariah the son of Meshelemiah was
gatekeeper at the entrance of the tent of
meeting. 22 All these, who were chosen as
gatekeepers at the thresholds, were 212.
They were enrolled by genealogies in
their villages. David and Samuel the seer
established them in their office of trust.
23 So they and their sons were in charge
of the gates of the house of the LORD,
that is, the house of the tent, as guards.
24 The gatekeepers were on the four sides,
east, west, north, and south. 25 And their
kinsmen who were in their villages were
obligated to come in every seven days,
in turn, to be with these, 26 for the four
chief gatekeepers, who were Levites,
were entrusted to be over the chambers
and the treasures of the house of God.
27 And they lodged around the house of
God, for on them lay the duty of watch-
ing, and they had charge of opening it
every morning.

28 Some of them had charge of the

utensils of service, for they were required to count them when they were brought in and taken out. 29 Others of them were appointed over the furniture and over all the holy utensils, also over the fine flour, the wine, the oil, the incense, and the spices. 30 Others, of the sons of the priests, prepared the mixing of the spices, 31 and Mattithiah, one of the Levites, the firstborn of Shallum the Korahite, was entrusted with making the flat cakes. 32 Also some of their kinsmen of the Kohathites had charge of the showbread, to prepare it every Sabbath.

33 Now these, the singers, the heads of fathers' houses of the Levites, were in the chambers of the temple free from other service, for they were on duty day and night. 34 These were heads of fathers' houses of the Levites, according to their generations, leaders. These lived in Jerusalem.

Saul's Genealogy Repeated

35 In Gibeon lived the father of Gibeon, Jeiel, and the name of his wife was Maacah, 36 and his firstborn son Abdon, then Zur, Kish, Baal, Ner, Nadab, 37 Gedor, Ahio, Zechariah, and Mikloth; 38 and Mikloth was the father of Shimeam; and these also lived opposite their kinsmen in Jerusalem, with their kinsmen. 39 Ner fathered Kish, Kish fathered Saul, Saul fathered Jonathan, Malchi-shua, Abinadab, and Eshbaal. 40 And the son of Jonathan was Merib-baal, and Merib-baal fathered Micah. 41 The sons of Micah: Pithon, Melech, Tahrea, and Ahaz.[1] 42 And Ahaz fathered Jarah, and Jarah fathered Alemeth, Azmaveth, and Zimri. And Zimri fathered Moza. 43 Moza fathered Binea, and Rephaiah was his son, Eleasah his son, Azel his son. 44 Azel had six sons and these are their names: Azrikam, Bocheru, Ishmael, Sheariah, Obadiah, and Hanan; these were the sons of Azel.

The Death of Saul and His Sons

10 Now the Philistines fought against Israel, and the men
449 of Israel fled before the Philistines and fell slain on Mount Gilboa. 2 And the Philistines overtook Saul and his sons, and the Philistines struck down Jonathan and Abinadab and Malchi-shua, the sons of Saul. 3 The battle pressed hard against Saul, and the archers found him, and he was wounded by the archers. 4 Then Saul said to his armor-bearer, "Draw your sword and thrust me through with it, lest these uncircumcised come and mistreat me." But his armor-bearer would not, for he feared greatly. Therefore Saul took his own sword and fell upon it. 5 And when his armor-bearer saw that Saul was dead, he also fell upon his sword and died. 6 Thus Saul died; he and his three sons and all his house died together. 7 And when all the men of Israel who were in the valley saw that the army[2] had fled and that Saul and his sons were dead, they abandoned their cities and fled, and the Philistines came and lived in them.

8 The next day, when the Philistines came to strip the slain, they found Saul and his sons fallen on Mount Gilboa. 9 And they stripped him and took his head and his armor, and sent messengers throughout the land of the Philistines to carry the good news to their idols and to the people. 10 And they put his armor in the temple of their gods and fastened his head in the temple of Dagon. 11 But when all Jabesh-gilead heard all that the Philistines had done to Saul, 12 all the valiant men arose and took away the body of Saul and the bodies of his sons, and brought them to Jabesh. And they buried their bones under the oak in Jabesh and fasted seven days.

13 So Saul died for his breach of faith. He broke faith with the LORD in that he did not keep the command of the LORD, and also consulted a medium, seeking guidance. 14 He did not seek guidance from

[1] Compare 8:35; Hebrew lacks *and Ahaz* [2] Hebrew *they*

the LORD. Therefore the LORD put him
to death and turned the kingdom over to
David the son of Jesse.

David Anointed King

11 Then all Israel gathered together to
David at Hebron and said, "Behold,
we are your bone and flesh. 2 In times past,
even when Saul was king, it was you who
led out and brought in Israel. And the
LORD your God said to you, 'You shall be
shepherd of my people Israel, and you
shall be prince over my people Israel.'" 3 So
all the elders of Israel came to the king at
Hebron, and David made a covenant with
them at Hebron before the LORD. And they
anointed David king over Israel, according
to the word of the LORD by Samuel.

David Takes Jerusalem

4 And David and all Israel went to
Jerusalem, that is, Jebus, where the
Jebusites were, the inhabitants of the land.
5 The inhabitants of Jebus said to David,
"You will not come in here." Nevertheless,
David took the stronghold of Zion, that is,
the city of David. 6 David said, "Whoever
strikes the Jebusites first shall be chief and
commander." And Joab the son of Zeruiah
went up first, so he became chief. 7 And
David lived in the stronghold; therefore it
was called the city of David. 8 And he built
the city all around from the Millo in com-
plete circuit, and Joab repaired the rest of
the city. 9 And David became greater and
greater, for the LORD of hosts was with him.

David's Mighty Men

10 Now these are the chiefs of David's
mighty men, who gave him strong sup-
port in his kingdom, together with all
Israel, to make him king, according to
the word of the LORD concerning Israel.
11 This is an account of David's mighty
men: Jashobeam, a Hachmonite, was
chief of the three.[1] He wielded his spear
against 300 whom he killed at one time.

12 And next to him among the three
mighty men was Eleazar the son of Dodo,
the Ahohite. 13 He was with David at Pas-
dammim when the Philistines were
gathered there for battle. There was a
plot of ground full of barley, and the men
fled from the Philistines. 14 But he took
his[2] stand in the midst of the plot and
defended it and killed the Philistines. And
the LORD saved them by a great victory.

15 Three of the thirty chief men went
down to the rock to David at the cave of
Adullam, when the army of Philistines
was encamped in the Valley of Rephaim.
16 David was then in the stronghold, and
the garrison of the Philistines was then at
Bethlehem. 17 And David said longingly,
"Oh that someone would give me water
to drink from the well of Bethlehem that
is by the gate!" 18 Then the three mighty
men broke through the camp of the
Philistines and drew water out of the well
of Bethlehem that was by the gate and
took it and brought it to David. But David
would not drink it. He poured it out to the
LORD 19 and said, "Far be it from me before
my God that I should do this. Shall I drink
the lifeblood of these men? For at the risk
of their lives they brought it." Therefore he
would not drink it. These things did the
three mighty men.

20 Now Abishai, the brother of Joab, was
chief of the thirty.[3] And he wielded his
spear against 300 men and killed them
and won a name beside the three. 21 He
was the most renowned[4] of the thirty[5] and
became their commander, but he did not
attain to the three.

22 And Benaiah the son of Jehoiada
was a valiant man[6] of Kabzeel, a doer of
great deeds. He struck down two heroes
of Moab. He also went down and struck
down a lion in a pit on a day when snow
had fallen. 23 And he struck down an
Egyptian, a man of great stature, five
cubits[7] tall. The Egyptian had in his hand
a spear like a weaver's beam, but Benaiah

[1] Compare 2 Samuel 23:8; Hebrew *thirty*, or *captains* [2] Compare 2 Samuel 23:12; Hebrew *they . . . their* [3] Syriac; Hebrew *three* [4] Compare 2 Samuel 23:19; Hebrew *more renowned among the two* [5] Syriac; Hebrew *three* [6] Syriac; Hebrew *the son of a valiant man* [7] A *cubit* was about 18 inches or 45 centimeters

went down to him with a staff and snatched the spear out of the Egyptian's hand and killed him with his own spear. 24 These things did Benaiah the son of Jehoiada and won a name beside the three mighty men. 25 He was renowned among the thirty, but he did not attain to the three. And David set him over his bodyguard.

26 The mighty men were Asahel the brother of Joab, Elhanan the son of Dodo of Bethlehem, 27 Shammoth of Harod,[1] Helez the Pelonite, 28 Ira the son of Ikkesh of Tekoa, Abiezer of Anathoth, 29 Sibbecai the Hushathite, Ilai the Ahohite, 30 Maharai of Netophah, Heled the son of Baanah of Netophah, 31 Ithai the son of Ribai of Gibeah of the people of Benjamin, Benaiah of Pirathon, 32 Hurai of the brooks of Gaash, Abiel the Arbathite, 33 Azmaveth of Baharum, Eliahba the Shaalbonite, 34 Hashem[2] the Gizonite, Jonathan the son of Shagee the Hararite, 35 Ahiam the son of Sachar the Hararite, Eliphal the son of Ur, 36 Hepher the Mecherathite, Ahijah the Pelonite, 37 Hezro of Carmel, Naarai the son of Ezbai, 38 Joel the brother of Nathan, Mibhar the son of Hagri, 39 Zelek the Ammonite, Naharai of Beeroth, the armor-bearer of Joab the son of Zeruiah, 40 Ira the Ithrite, Gareb the Ithrite, 41 Uriah the Hittite, Zabad the son of Ahlai, 42 Adina the son of Shiza the Reubenite, a leader of the Reubenites, and thirty with him, 43 Hanan the son of Maacah, and Joshaphat the Mithnite, 44 Uzzia the Ashterathite, Shama and Jeiel the sons of Hotham the Aroerite, 45 Jediael the son of Shimri, and Joha his brother, the Tizite, 46 Eliel the Mahavite, and Jeribai, and Joshaviah, the sons of Elnaam, and Ithmah the Moabite, 47 Eliel, and Obed, and Jaasiel the Mezobaite.

The Mighty Men Join David

12 Now these are the men who came to David at Ziklag, while he could not move about freely because of Saul the son of Kish. And they were among the mighty men who helped him in war. 2 They were bowmen and could shoot arrows and sling stones with either the right or the left hand; they were Benjaminites, Saul's kinsmen. 3 The chief was Ahiezer, then Joash, both sons of Shemaah of Gibeah; also Jeziel and Pelet, the sons of Azmaveth; Beracah, Jehu of Anathoth, 4 Ishmaiah of Gibeon, a mighty man among the thirty and a leader over the thirty; Jeremiah,[3] Jahaziel, Johanan, Jozabad of Gederah, 5 Eluzai,[4] Jerimoth, Bealiah, Shemariah, Shephatiah the Haruphite; 6 Elkanah, Isshiah, Azarel, Joezer, and Jashobeam, the Korahites; 7 And Joelah and Zebadiah, the sons of Jeroham of Gedor.

8 From the Gadites there went over to David at the stronghold in the wilderness mighty and experienced warriors, expert with shield and spear, whose faces were like the faces of lions and who were swift as gazelles upon the mountains: 9 Ezer the chief, Obadiah second, Eliab third, 10 Mishmannah fourth, Jeremiah fifth, 11 Attai sixth, Eliel seventh, 12 Johanan eighth, Elzabad ninth, 13 Jeremiah tenth, Machbannai eleventh. 14 These Gadites were officers of the army; the least was a match for a hundred men and the greatest for a thousand. 15 These are the men who crossed the Jordan in the first month, when it was overflowing all its banks, and put to flight all those in the valleys, to the east and to the west.

16 And some of the men of Benjamin and Judah came to the stronghold to David. 17 David went out to meet them and said to them, "If you have come to me in friendship to help me, my heart will be joined to you; but if to betray me to my adversaries, although there is no wrong in my hands, then may the God of our fathers see and rebuke you." 18 Then the Spirit clothed Amasai, chief of the thirty, and he said,

[1] Compare 2 Samuel 23:25; Hebrew *the Harorite* [2] Compare Septuagint and 2 Samuel 23:32; Hebrew *the sons of Hashem* [3] Hebrew verse 5 [4] Hebrew verse 6

"We are yours, O David,
and with you, O son of Jesse!
Peace, peace to you,
and peace to your helpers!
For your God helps you."

Then David received them and made them officers of his troops.

19 Some of the men of Manasseh deserted to David when he came with the Philistines for the battle against Saul. (Yet he did not help them, for the rulers of the Philistines took counsel and sent him away, saying, "At peril to our heads he will desert to his master Saul.") 20 As he went to Ziklag, these men of Manasseh deserted to him: Adnah, Jozabad, Jediael, Michael, Jozabad, Elihu, and Zillethai, chiefs of thousands in Manasseh. 21 They helped David against the band of raiders, for they were all mighty men of valor and were commanders in the army. 22 For from day to day men came to David to help him, until there was a great army, like an army of God.

23 These are the numbers of the divisions of the armed troops who came to David in Hebron to turn the kingdom of Saul over to him, according to the word of the LORD. 24 The men of Judah bearing shield and spear were 6,800 armed troops. 25 Of the Simeonites, mighty men of valor for war, 7,100. 26 Of the Levites 4,600. 27 The prince Jehoiada, of the house of Aaron, and with him 3,700. 28 Zadok, a young man mighty in valor, and twenty-two commanders from his own fathers' house. 29 Of the Benjaminites, the kinsmen of Saul, 3,000, of whom the majority had to that point kept their allegiance to the house of Saul. 30 Of the Ephraimites 20,800, mighty men of valor, famous men in their fathers' houses. 31 Of the half-tribe of Manasseh 18,000, who were expressly named to come and make David king. 32 Of Issachar, men who had understanding of the times, to know what Israel ought to do, 200 chiefs, and all their kinsmen under their command. 33 Of Zebulun 50,000 seasoned troops, equipped for battle with all the weapons of war, to help David[1] with singleness of purpose. 34 Of Naphtali 1,000 commanders with whom were 37,000 men armed with shield and spear. 35 Of the Danites 28,600 men equipped for battle. 36 Of Asher 40,000 seasoned troops ready for battle. 37 Of the Reubenites and Gadites and the half-tribe of Manasseh from beyond the Jordan, 120,000 men armed with all the weapons of war.

38 All these, men of war, arrayed in battle order, came to Hebron with full intent to make David king over all Israel. Likewise, all the rest of Israel were of a single mind to make David king. 39 And they were there with David for three days, eating and drinking, for their brothers had made preparation for them. 40 And also their relatives, from as far as Issachar and Zebulun and Naphtali, came bringing food on donkeys and on camels and on mules and on oxen, abundant provisions of flour, cakes of figs, clusters of raisins, and wine and oil, oxen and sheep, for there was joy in Israel.

The Ark Brought from Kiriath-Jearim

13 David consulted with the commanders of thousands and of hundreds, with every leader. 2 And David said to all the assembly of Israel, "If it seems good to you and from the LORD our God, let us send abroad to our brothers who remain in all the lands of Israel, as well as to the priests and Levites in the cities that have pasturelands, that they may be gathered to us. 3 Then let us bring again the ark of our God to us, for we did not seek it[2] in the days of Saul." 4 All the assembly agreed to do so, for the thing was right in the eyes of all the people.

Uzzah and the Ark

5 So David assembled all Israel from the Nile[3] of Egypt to Lebo-hamath, to bring the ark of God from Kiriath-jearim. 6 And David and all Israel went up to Baalah, that is, to Kiriath-jearim that belongs to Judah,

[1] Septuagint; Hebrew lacks *David* [2] Or *him* [3] Hebrew *Shihor*

to bring up from there the ark of God, which is called by the name of the LORD who sits enthroned above the cherubim. 7 And they carried the ark of God on a new cart, from the house of Abinadab, and Uzzah and Ahio[1] were driving the cart. 8 And David and all Israel were rejoicing before God with all their might, with song and lyres and harps and tambourines and cymbals and trumpets.

9 And when they came to the threshing floor of Chidon, Uzzah put out his hand to take hold of the ark, for the oxen stumbled. 10 And the anger of the LORD was kindled against Uzzah, and he struck him down because he put out his hand to the ark, and he died there before God. 11 And David was angry because the LORD had broken out against Uzzah. And that place is called Perez-uzza[2] to this day. 12 And David was afraid of God that day, and he said, "How can I bring the ark of God home to me?" 13 So David did not take the ark home into the city of David, but took it aside to the house of Obed-edom the Gittite. 14 And the ark of God remained with the household of Obed-edom in his house three months. And the LORD blessed the household of Obed-edom and all that he had.

David's Wives and Children

14 And Hiram king of Tyre sent messengers to David, and cedar trees, also masons and carpenters to build a house for him. 2 And David knew that the LORD had established him as king over Israel, and that his kingdom was highly exalted for the sake of his people Israel.

3 And David took more wives in Jerusalem, and David fathered more sons and daughters. 4 These are the names of the children born to him in Jerusalem: Shammua, Shobab, Nathan, Solomon, 5 Ibhar, Elishua, Elpelet, 6 Nogah, Nepheg, Japhia, 7 Elishama, Beeliada and Eliphelet.

Philistines Defeated

8 When the Philistines heard that David had been anointed king over all Israel, all the Philistines went up to search for David. But David heard of it and went out against them. 9 Now the Philistines had come and made a raid in the Valley of Rephaim. 10 And David inquired of God, "Shall I go up against the Philistines? Will you give them into my hand?" And the LORD said to him, "Go up, and I will give them into your hand." 11 And he went up to Baal-perazim, and David struck them down there. And David said, "God has broken through[3] my enemies by my hand, like a bursting flood." Therefore the name of that place is called Baal-perazim. 12 And they left their gods there, and David gave command, and they were burned.

13 And the Philistines yet again made a raid in the valley. 14 And when David again inquired of God, God said to him, "You shall not go up after them; go around and come against them opposite the balsam trees. 15 And when you hear the sound of marching in the tops of the balsam trees, then go out to battle, for God has gone out before you to strike down the army of the Philistines." 16 And David did as God commanded him, and they struck down the Philistine army from Gibeon to Gezer. 17 And the fame of David went out into all lands, and the LORD brought the fear of him upon all nations.

The Ark Brought to Jerusalem

15 David[4] built houses for himself in the city of David. And he prepared a place for the ark of God and pitched a tent for it. 2 Then David said that no one but the Levites may carry the ark of God, for the LORD had chosen them to carry the ark of the LORD and to minister to him forever. 3 And David assembled all Israel at Jerusalem to bring up the ark of the LORD to its place, which he had prepared for it. 4 And David gathered together the sons

[1] Or *and his brother* [2] *Perez-uzza* means *the breaking out against Uzzah* [3] *Baal-perazim* means *Lord of breaking through* [4] Hebrew *He*

of Aaron and the Levites: 5 of the sons of
Kohath, Uriel the chief, with 120 of his
brothers; 6 of the sons of Merari, Asaiah
the chief, with 220 of his brothers; 7 of the
sons of Gershom, Joel the chief, with 130
of his brothers; 8 of the sons of Elizaphan,
Shemaiah the chief, with 200 of his broth-
ers; 9 of the sons of Hebron, Eliel the chief,
with 80 of his brothers; 10 of the sons of
Uzziel, Amminadab the chief, with 112 of
his brothers. 11 Then David summoned
the priests Zadok and Abiathar, and the
Levites Uriel, Asaiah, Joel, Shemaiah, Eliel,
and Amminadab, 12 and said to them,
"You are the heads of the fathers' houses
of the Levites. Consecrate yourselves,
you and your brothers, so that you may
bring up the ark of the LORD, the God of
Israel, to the place that I have prepared for
it. 13 Because you did not carry it the first
time, the LORD our God broke out against
us, because we did not seek him accord-
ing to the rule." 14 So the priests and the
Levites consecrated themselves to bring
up the ark of the LORD, the God of Israel.
15 And the Levites carried the ark of God
on their shoulders with the poles, as
Moses had commanded according to the
word of the LORD.

16 David also commanded the chiefs
of the Levites to appoint their brothers
as the singers who should play loudly
on musical instruments, on harps and
lyres and cymbals, to raise sounds of joy.
17 So the Levites appointed Heman the
son of Joel; and of his brothers Asaph
the son of Berechiah; and of the sons of
Merari, their brothers, Ethan the son of
Kushaiah; 18 and with them their broth-
ers of the second order, Zechariah,
Jaaziel, Shemiramoth, Jehiel, Unni,
Eliab, Benaiah, Maaseiah, Mattithiah,
Eliphelehu, and Mikneiah, and the gate-
keepers Obed-edom and Jeiel. 19 The
singers, Heman, Asaph, and Ethan, were
to sound bronze cymbals; 20 Zechariah,
Aziel, Shemiramoth, Jehiel, Unni, Eliab,
Maaseiah, and Benaiah were to play harps
according to Alamoth; 21 but Mattithiah,
Eliphelehu, Mikneiah, Obed-edom,
Jeiel, and Azaziah were to lead with lyres
according to the Sheminith. 22 Chenaniah,
leader of the Levites in music, should
direct the music, for he understood it.
23 Berechiah and Elkanah were to be
gatekeepers for the ark. 24 Shebaniah,
Joshaphat, Nethanel, Amasai, Zechariah,
Benaiah, and Eliezer, the priests, should
blow the trumpets before the ark of God.
Obed-edom and Jehiah were to be gate-
keepers for the ark.

25 So David and the elders of Israel and
the commanders of thousands went to
bring up the ark of the covenant of the
LORD from the house of Obed-edom with
rejoicing. 26 And because God helped the
Levites who were carrying the ark of the
covenant of the LORD, they sacrificed
seven bulls and seven rams. 27 David was
clothed with a robe of fine linen, as also
were all the Levites who were carrying the
ark, and the singers and Chenaniah the
leader of the music of the singers. And
David wore a linen ephod. 28 So all Israel
brought up the ark of the covenant of the
LORD with shouting, to the sound of the
horn, trumpets, and cymbals, and made
loud music on harps and lyres.

29 And as the ark of the covenant of the
LORD came to the city of David, Michal the
daughter of Saul looked out of the window
and saw King David dancing and rejoic-
ing, and she despised him in her heart.

The Ark Placed in a Tent

16 And they brought in the ark of God
and set it inside the tent that David
had pitched for it, and they offered burnt
offerings and peace offerings before God.
2 And when David had finished offering the
burnt offerings and the peace offerings, he
blessed the people in the name of the LORD
3 and distributed to all Israel, both men and

women, to each a loaf of bread, a portion of
meat,[1] and a cake of raisins.
4 Then he appointed some of the Levites
as ministers before the ark of the LORD, to
invoke, to thank, and to praise the LORD,
the God of Israel. 5 Asaph was the chief,
and second to him were Zechariah, Jeiel,
Shemiramoth, Jehiel, Mattithiah, Eliab,
Benaiah, Obed-edom, and Jeiel, who
were to play harps and lyres; Asaph was
to sound the cymbals, 6 and Benaiah and
Jahaziel the priests were to blow trumpets
regularly before the ark of the covenant
of God. 7 Then on that day David first
appointed that thanksgiving be sung to
the LORD by Asaph and his brothers.

David's Song of Thanks

8 Oh give thanks to the LORD; call upon his name;
make known his deeds among the peoples!
9 Sing to him; sing praises to him;
tell of all his wondrous works!
10 Glory in his holy name;
let the hearts of those who seek the LORD rejoice!
11 Seek the LORD and his strength;
seek his presence continually!
12 Remember the wondrous works that he has done,
his miracles and the judgments he uttered,
13 O offspring of Israel his servant,
sons of Jacob, his chosen ones!

14 He is the LORD our God;
his judgments are in all the earth.
15 Remember his covenant forever,
the word that he commanded, for a thousand generations,
16 the covenant that he made with Abraham,
his sworn promise to Isaac,
17 which he confirmed as a statute to Jacob,
as an everlasting covenant to Israel,
18 saying, "To you I will give the land of Canaan,
as your portion for an inheritance."
19 When you were few in number,
and of little account, and sojourners in it,
20 wandering from nation to nation,
from one kingdom to another people,
21 he allowed no one to oppress them;
he rebuked kings on their account,
22 saying, "Touch not my anointed ones,
do my prophets no harm!"

23 Sing to the LORD, all the earth!
Tell of his salvation from day to day.
24 Declare his glory among the nations,
his marvelous works among all the peoples!
25 For great is the LORD, and greatly to be praised,
and he is to be held in awe above all gods.
26 For all the gods of the peoples are idols,
but the LORD made the heavens.
27 Splendor and majesty are before him;
strength and joy are in his place.

28 Ascribe to the LORD, O clans of the peoples,
ascribe to the LORD glory and strength!
29 Ascribe to the LORD the glory due his name;
bring an offering and come before him!
Worship the LORD in the splendor of holiness;[2]
30 tremble before him, all the earth;
yes, the world is established; it shall never be moved.
31 Let the heavens be glad, and let the earth rejoice,

[1] Compare Septuagint, Syriac, Vulgate; the meaning of the Hebrew is uncertain [2] Or *in holy attire*

and let them say among the
nations, "The LORD reigns!"
32 Let the sea roar, and all that fills it;
let the field exult, and everything
in it!
33 Then shall the trees of the forest
sing for joy
before the LORD, for he comes to
judge the earth.
34 Oh give thanks to the LORD, for he is
good;
for his steadfast love endures
forever!

35 Say also:

"Save us, O God of our salvation,
and gather and deliver us from
among the nations,
that we may give thanks to your
holy name,
and glory in your praise.
36 Blessed be the LORD, the God of Israel,
from everlasting to everlasting!"

Then all the people said, "Amen!" and
praised the LORD.

Worship Before the Ark

37 So David left Asaph and his brothers
there before the ark of the covenant of the
LORD to minister regularly before the ark
as each day required, 38 and also Obed-
edom and his[1] sixty-eight brothers, while
Obed-edom, the son of Jeduthun, and
Hosah were to be gatekeepers. 39 And he
left Zadok the priest and his brothers the
priests before the tabernacle of the LORD
in the high place that was at Gibeon 40 to
offer burnt offerings to the LORD on the
altar of burnt offering regularly morning
and evening, to do all that is written in
the Law of the LORD that he commanded
Israel. 41 With them were Heman and
Jeduthun and the rest of those chosen
and expressly named to give thanks to
the LORD, for his steadfast love endures
forever. 42 Heman and Jeduthun had
trumpets and cymbals for the music and
instruments for sacred song. The sons of
Jeduthun were appointed to the gate.
43 Then all the people departed each to
his house, and David went home to bless
his household.

The LORD's Covenant with David

17 Now when David lived in his
house, David said to Nathan
205 the prophet, "Behold, I dwell in a
house of cedar, but the ark of the covenant
of the LORD is under a tent." 2 And Nathan
said to David, "Do all that is in your heart,
for God is with you."
3 But that same night the word of the
LORD came to Nathan, 4 "Go and tell my
servant David, 'Thus says the LORD: It
is not you who will build me a house to
dwell in. 5 For I have not lived in a house
since the day I brought up Israel to this
day, but I have gone from tent to tent and
from dwelling to dwelling. 6 In all places
where I have moved with all Israel, did
I speak a word with any of the judges
of Israel, whom I commanded to shep-
herd my people, saying, "Why have you
not built me a house of cedar?"' 7 Now,
therefore, thus shall you say to my ser-
vant David, 'Thus says the LORD of hosts,
I took you from the pasture, from fol-
lowing the sheep, to be prince over my
people Israel, 8 and I have been with you
wherever you have gone and have cut off
all your enemies from before you. And I
will make for you a name, like the name
of the great ones of the earth. 9 And I will
appoint a place for my people Israel and
will plant them, that they may dwell in
their own place and be disturbed no
more. And violent men shall waste them
no more, as formerly, 10 from the time
that I appointed judges over my people
Israel. And I will subdue all your enemies.
Moreover, I declare to you that the LORD
will build you a house. 11 When your days
are fulfilled to walk with your fathers, I
will raise up your offspring after you, one

[1] Hebrew *their*

of your own sons, and I will establish his kingdom. 12 He shall build a house for me, and I will establish his throne forever. 13 I will be to him a father, and he shall be to me a son. I will not take my steadfast love from him, as I took it from him who was before you, 14 but I will confirm him in my house and in my kingdom forever, and his throne shall be established forever.'" 15 In accordance with all these words, and in accordance with all this vision, Nathan spoke to David.

David's Prayer

16 Then King David went in and sat before the LORD and said, "Who am I, O LORD God, and what is my house, that you have brought me thus far? 17 And this was a small thing in your eyes, O God. You have also spoken of your servant's house for a great while to come, and have shown me future generations,[1] O LORD God! 18 And what more can David say to you for honoring your servant? For you know your servant. 19 For your servant's sake, O LORD, and according to your own heart, you have done all this greatness, in making known all these great things. 20 There is none like you, O LORD, and there is no God besides you, according to all that we have heard with our ears. 21 And who is like your people Israel, the one[2] nation on earth whom God went to redeem to be his people, making for yourself a name for great and awesome things, in driving out nations before your people whom you redeemed from Egypt? 22 And you made your people Israel to be your people forever, and you, O LORD, became their God. 23 And now, O LORD, let the word that you have spoken concerning your servant and concerning his house be established forever, and do as you have spoken, 24 and your name will be established and magnified forever, saying, 'The LORD of hosts, the God of Israel, is Israel's God,' and the house of your servant David will be established before you. 25 For you, my God, have revealed to your servant that you will build a house for him. Therefore your servant has found courage to pray before you. 26 And now, O LORD, you are God, and you have promised this good thing to your servant. 27 Now you have been pleased to bless the house of your servant, that it may continue forever before you, for it is you, O LORD, who have blessed, and it is blessed forever."

David Defeats His Enemies

18 After this David defeated the Philistines and subdued them, and he took Gath and its villages out of the hand of the Philistines.

2 And he defeated Moab, and the Moabites became servants to David and brought tribute.

3 David also defeated Hadadezer king of Zobah-Hamath, as he went to set up his monument[3] at the river Euphrates. 4 And David took from him 1,000 chariots, 7,000 horsemen, and 20,000 foot soldiers. And David hamstrung all the chariot horses, but left enough for 100 chariots. 5 And when the Syrians of Damascus came to help Hadadezer king of Zobah, David struck down 22,000 men of the Syrians. 6 Then David put garrisons[4] in Syria of Damascus, and the Syrians became servants to David and brought tribute. And the LORD gave victory to David[5] wherever he went. 7 And David took the shields of gold that were carried by the servants of Hadadezer and brought them to Jerusalem. 8 And from Tibhath and from Cun, cities of Hadadezer, David took a large amount of bronze. With it Solomon made the bronze sea and the pillars and the vessels of bronze.

9 When Tou king of Hamath heard that David had defeated the whole army of Hadadezer, king of Zobah, 10 he sent his son Hadoram to King David, to ask about his health and to bless him because he had

[1] The meaning of the Hebrew is uncertain [2] Septuagint, Vulgate *other* [3] Hebrew *hand* [4] Septuagint, Vulgate, 2 Samuel 8:6 (compare Syriac); Hebrew lacks *garrisons* [5] Hebrew *the LORD saved David*; also verse 13

fought against Hadadezer and defeated him; for Hadadezer had often been at war with Tou. And he sent all sorts of articles of gold, of silver, and of bronze. 11 These also King David dedicated to the LORD, together with the silver and gold that he had carried off from all the nations, from Edom, Moab, the Ammonites, the Philistines, and Amalek.

12 And Abishai, the son of Zeruiah, killed 18,000 Edomites in the Valley of Salt. 13 Then he put garrisons in Edom, and all the Edomites became David's servants. And the LORD gave victory to David wherever he went.

David's Administration

14 So David reigned over all Israel, and he administered justice and equity to all his people. 15 And Joab the son of Zeruiah was over the army; and Jehoshaphat the son of Ahilud was recorder; 16 and Zadok the son of Ahitub and Ahimelech the son of Abiathar were priests; and Shavsha was secretary; 17 and Benaiah the son of Jehoiada was over the Cherethites and the Pelethites; and David's sons were the chief officials in the service of the king.

The Ammonites Disgrace David's Men

19 Now after this Nahash the king of the Ammonites died, and his son reigned in his place. 2 And David said, "I will deal kindly with Hanun the son of Nahash, for his father dealt kindly with me." So David sent messengers to console him concerning his father. And David's servants came to the land of the Ammonites to Hanun to console him. 3 But the princes of the Ammonites said to Hanun, "Do you think, because David has sent comforters to you, that he is honoring your father? Have not his servants come to you to search and to overthrow and to spy out the land?" 4 So Hanun took David's servants and shaved them and cut off their garments in the middle, at their hips, and sent them away; 5 and they departed. When David was told concerning the men, he sent messengers to meet them, for the men were greatly ashamed. And the king said, "Remain at Jericho until your beards have grown and then return."

6 When the Ammonites saw that they had become a stench to David, Hanun and the Ammonites sent 1,000 talents[1] of silver to hire chariots and horsemen from Mesopotamia, from Aram-maacah, and from Zobah. 7 They hired 32,000 chariots and the king of Maacah with his army, who came and encamped before Medeba. And the Ammonites were mustered from their cities and came to battle. 8 When David heard of it, he sent Joab and all the army of the mighty men. 9 And the Ammonites came out and drew up in battle array at the entrance of the city, and the kings who had come were by themselves in the open country.

Ammonites and Syrians Defeated

10 When Joab saw that the battle was set against him both in front and in the rear, he chose some of the best men of Israel and arrayed them against the Syrians. 11 The rest of his men he put in the charge of Abishai his brother, and they were arrayed against the Ammonites. 12 And he said, "If the Syrians are too strong for me, then you shall help me, but if the Ammonites are too strong for you, then I will help you. 13 Be strong, and let us use our strength for our people and for the cities of our God, and may the LORD do what seems good to him." 14 So Joab and the people who were with him drew near before the Syrians for battle, and they fled before him. 15 And when the Ammonites saw that the Syrians fled, they likewise fled before Abishai, Joab's brother, and entered the city. Then Joab came to Jerusalem.

16 But when the Syrians saw that they had been defeated by Israel, they sent messengers and brought out the Syrians who were beyond the Euphrates, with

[1] A *talent* was about 75 pounds or 34 kilograms

Shophach the commander of the army of Hadadezer at their head. 17 And when it was told to David, he gathered all Israel together and crossed the Jordan and came to them and drew up his forces against them. And when David set the battle in array against the Syrians, they fought with him. 18 And the Syrians fled before Israel, and David killed of the Syrians the men of 7,000 chariots and 40,000 foot soldiers, and put to death also Shophach the commander of their army. 19 And when the servants of Hadadezer saw that they had been defeated by Israel, they made peace with David and became subject to him. So the Syrians were not willing to save the Ammonites anymore.

The Capture of Rabbah

20 In the spring of the year, the time when kings go out to battle, Joab led out the army and ravaged the country of the Ammonites and came and besieged Rabbah. But David remained at Jerusalem. And Joab struck down Rabbah and overthrew it. 2 And David took the crown of their king from his head. He found that it weighed a talent[1] of gold, and in it was a precious stone. And it was placed on David's head. And he brought out the spoil of the city, a very great amount. 3 And he brought out the people who were in it and set them to labor[2] with saws and iron picks and axes.[3] And thus David did to all the cities of the Ammonites. Then David and all the people returned to Jerusalem.

Philistine Giants Killed

4 And after this there arose war with the Philistines at Gezer. Then Sibbecai the Hushathite struck down Sippai, who was one of the descendants of the giants, and the Philistines were subdued. 5 And there was again war with the Philistines, and Elhanan the son of Jair struck down Lahmi the brother of Goliath the Gittite, the shaft of whose spear was like a weaver's beam. 6 And there was again war at Gath, where there was a man of great stature, who had six fingers on each hand and six toes on each foot, twenty-four in number, and he also was descended from the giants. 7 And when he taunted Israel, Jonathan the son of Shimea, David's brother, struck him down. 8 These were descended from the giants in Gath, and they fell by the hand of David and by the hand of his servants.

David's Census Brings Pestilence

21 Then Satan stood against Israel and incited David to number Israel. 2 So David said to Joab and the commanders of the army, "Go, number Israel, from Beersheba to Dan, and bring me a report, that I may know their number." 3 But Joab said, "May the LORD add to his people a hundred times as many as they are! Are they not, my lord the king, all of them my lord's servants? Why then should my lord require this? Why should it be a cause of guilt for Israel?" 4 But the king's word prevailed against Joab. So Joab departed and went throughout all Israel and came back to Jerusalem. 5 And Joab gave the sum of the numbering of the people to David. In all Israel there were 1,100,000 men who drew the sword, and in Judah 470,000 who drew the sword. 6 But he did not include Levi and Benjamin in the numbering, for the king's command was abhorrent to Joab.

7 But God was displeased with this thing, and he struck Israel. 8 And David said to God, "I have sinned greatly in that I have done this thing. But now, please take away the iniquity of your servant, for I have acted very foolishly." 9 And the LORD spoke to Gad, David's seer, saying, 10 "Go and say to David, 'Thus says the LORD, Three things I offer you; choose one of them, that I may do it to you.'" 11 So Gad came to David and said to him, "Thus says the LORD, 'Choose what you will: 12 either three years of famine, or three months of devastation by your foes while the sword

[1] A *talent* was about 75 pounds or 34 kilograms [2] Compare 2 Samuel 12:31; Hebrew *he sawed* [3] Compare 2 Samuel 12:31; Hebrew *saws*

of your enemies overtakes you, or else
three days of the sword of the LORD, pes-
tilence on the land, with the angel of the
LORD destroying throughout all the terri-
tory of Israel.' Now decide what answer I
shall return to him who sent me." 13 Then
David said to Gad, "I am in great distress.
Let me fall into the hand of the LORD, for
his mercy is very great, but do not let me
fall into the hand of man."

14 So the LORD sent a pestilence on
Israel, and 70,000 men of Israel fell.
15 And God sent the angel to Jerusalem to
destroy it, but as he was about to destroy
it, the LORD saw, and he relented from the
calamity. And he said to the angel who
was working destruction, "It is enough;
now stay your hand." And the angel of
the LORD was standing by the threshing
floor of Ornan the Jebusite. 16 And David
lifted his eyes and saw the angel of the
LORD standing between earth and heaven,
and in his hand a drawn sword stretched
out over Jerusalem. Then David and the
elders, clothed in sackcloth, fell upon
their faces. 17 And David said to God, "Was
it not I who gave command to number the
people? It is I who have sinned and done
great evil. But these sheep, what have
they done? Please let your hand, O LORD
my God, be against me and against my
father's house. But do not let the plague
be on your people."

David Builds an Altar

18 Now the angel of the LORD had com-
manded Gad to say to David that David
should go up and raise an altar to the
LORD on the threshing floor of Ornan
the Jebusite. 19 So David went up at Gad's
word, which he had spoken in the name
of the LORD. 20 Now Ornan was thresh-
ing wheat. He turned and saw the angel,
and his four sons who were with him hid
themselves. 21 As David came to Ornan,
Ornan looked and saw David and went out
from the threshing floor and paid hom-
age to David with his face to the ground.
22 And David said to Ornan, "Give me the
site of the threshing floor that I may build
on it an altar to the LORD—give it to me
at its full price—that the plague may be
averted from the people." 23 Then Ornan
said to David, "Take it, and let my lord the
king do what seems good to him. See, I
give the oxen for burnt offerings and the
threshing sledges for the wood and the
wheat for a grain offering; I give it all."
24 But King David said to Ornan, "No, but
I will buy them for the full price. I will
not take for the LORD what is yours, nor
offer burnt offerings that cost me noth-
ing." 25 So David paid Ornan 600 shekels[1]
of gold by weight for the site. 26 And David
built there an altar to the LORD and pre-
sented burnt offerings and peace offerings
and called on the LORD, and the LORD[2]
answered him with fire from heaven
upon the altar of burnt offering. 27 Then
the LORD commanded the angel, and he
put his sword back into its sheath.

28 At that time, when David saw that the
LORD had answered him at the threshing
floor of Ornan the Jebusite, he sacrificed
there. 29 For the tabernacle of the LORD,
which Moses had made in the wilderness,
and the altar of burnt offering were at that
time in the high place at Gibeon, 30 but
David could not go before it to inquire of
God, for he was afraid of the sword of the
angel of the LORD.

22 Then David said, "Here shall be
the house of the LORD God and
here the altar of burnt offering for Israel."

David Prepares for Temple Building

2 David commanded to gather together
the resident aliens who were in the land of
Israel, and he set stonecutters to prepare
dressed stones for building the house of
God. 3 David also provided great quantities
of iron for nails for the doors of the gates
and for clamps, as well as bronze in quanti-
ties beyond weighing, 4 and cedar timbers

[1] A *shekel* was about 2/5 ounce or 11 grams [2] Hebrew *he*

without number, for the Sidonians and Tyrians brought great quantities of cedar to David. 5 For David said, "Solomon my son is young and inexperienced, and the house that is to be built for the LORD must be exceedingly magnificent, of fame and glory throughout all lands. I will therefore make preparation for it." So David provided materials in great quantity before his death.

Solomon Charged to Build the Temple

6 Then he called for Solomon his son and charged him to build a house for the LORD, the God of Israel. 7 David said to Solomon, "My son, I had it in my heart to build a house to the name of the LORD my God. 8 But the word of the LORD came to me, saying, 'You have shed much blood and have waged great wars. You shall not build a house to my name, because you have shed so much blood before me on the earth. 9 Behold, a son shall be born to you who shall be a man of rest. I will give him rest from all his surrounding enemies. For his name shall be Solomon, and I will give peace and quiet to Israel in his days. 10 He shall build a house for my name. He shall be my son, and I will be his father, and I will establish his royal throne in Israel forever.'

11 "Now, my son, the LORD be with you, so that you may succeed in building the house of the LORD your God, as he has spoken concerning you. 12 Only, may the LORD grant you discretion and understanding, that when he gives you charge over Israel you may keep the law of the LORD your God. 13 Then you will prosper if you are careful to observe the statutes and the rules that the LORD commanded Moses for Israel. Be strong and courageous. Fear not; do not be dismayed. 14 With great pains I have provided for the house of the LORD 100,000 talents[1] of gold, a million talents of silver, and bronze and iron beyond weighing, for there is so much of it; timber and stone, too, I have provided. To these you must add. 15 You have an abundance of workmen: stonecutters, masons, carpenters, and all kinds of craftsmen without number, skilled in working 16 gold, silver, bronze, and iron. Arise and work! The LORD be with you!"

17 David also commanded all the leaders of Israel to help Solomon his son, saying, 18 "Is not the LORD your God with you? And has he not given you peace on every side? For he has delivered the inhabitants of the land into my hand, and the land is subdued before the LORD and his people. 19 Now set your mind and heart to seek the LORD your God. Arise and build the sanctuary of the LORD God, so that the ark of the covenant of the LORD and the holy vessels of God may be brought into a house built for the name of the LORD."

David Organizes the Levites

23 When David was old and full of days, he made Solomon his son king over Israel.

2 David[2] assembled all the leaders of Israel and the priests and the Levites. 3 The Levites, thirty years old and upward, were numbered, and the total was 38,000 men. 4 "Twenty-four thousand of these," David said,[3] "shall have charge of the work in the house of the LORD, 6,000 shall be officers and judges, 5 4,000 gatekeepers, and 4,000 shall offer praises to the LORD with the instruments that I have made for praise." 6 And David organized them in divisions corresponding to the sons of Levi: Gershon, Kohath, and Merari.

7 The sons of Gershon[4] were Ladan and Shimei. 8 The sons of Ladan: Jehiel the chief, and Zetham, and Joel, three. 9 The sons of Shimei: Shelomoth, Haziel, and Haran, three. These were the heads of the fathers' houses of Ladan. 10 And the sons of Shimei: Jahath, Zina, and Jeush and Beriah. These four were the sons of Shimei. 11 Jahath was the chief, and Zizah

[1] A *talent* was about 75 pounds or 34 kilograms [2] Hebrew *He* [3] Hebrew lacks *David said* [4] Vulgate (compare Septuagint, Syriac); Hebrew *to the Gershonite*

the second; but Jeush and Beriah did not have many sons, therefore they became counted as a single father's house.

12 The sons of Kohath: Amram, Izhar, Hebron, and Uzziel, four. 13 The sons of Amram: Aaron and Moses. Aaron was set apart to dedicate the most holy things, that he and his sons forever should make offerings before the LORD and minister to him and pronounce blessings in his name forever. 14 But the sons of Moses the man of God were named among the tribe of Levi. 15 The sons of Moses: Gershom and Eliezer. 16 The sons of Gershom: Shebuel the chief. 17 The sons of Eliezer: Rehabiah the chief. Eliezer had no other sons, but the sons of Rehabiah were very many. 18 The sons of Izhar: Shelomith the chief. 19 The sons of Hebron: Jeriah the chief, Amariah the second, Jahaziel the third, and Jekameam the fourth. 20 The sons of Uzziel: Micah the chief and Isshiah the second.

21 The sons of Merari: Mahli and Mushi. The sons of Mahli: Eleazar and Kish. 22 Eleazar died having no sons, but only daughters; their kinsmen, the sons of Kish, married them. 23 The sons of Mushi: Mahli, Eder, and Jeremoth, three.

24 These were the sons of Levi by their fathers' houses, the heads of fathers' houses as they were listed according to the number of the names of the individuals from twenty years old and upward who were to do the work for the service of the house of the LORD. 25 For David said, "The LORD, the God of Israel, has given rest to his people, and he dwells in Jerusalem forever. 26 And so the Levites no longer need to carry the tabernacle or any of the things for its service." 27 For by the last words of David the sons of Levi were numbered from twenty years old and upward. 28 For their duty was to assist the sons of Aaron for the service of the house of the LORD, having the care of the courts and the chambers, the cleansing of all that is holy, and any work for the service of the house of God. 29 Their duty was also to assist with the showbread, the flour for the grain offering, the wafers of unleavened bread, the baked offering, the offering mixed with oil, and all measures of quantity or size. 30 And they were to stand every morning, thanking and praising the LORD, and likewise at evening, 31 and whenever burnt offerings were offered to the LORD on Sabbaths, new moons, and feast days, according to the number required of them, regularly before the LORD. 32 Thus they were to keep charge of the tent of meeting and the sanctuary, and to attend the sons of Aaron, their brothers, for the service of the house of the LORD.

David Organizes the Priests

24 The divisions of the sons of Aaron were these. The sons of Aaron: Nadab, Abihu, Eleazar, and Ithamar. 2 But Nadab and Abihu died before their father and had no children, so Eleazar and Ithamar became the priests. 3 With the help of Zadok of the sons of Eleazar, and Ahimelech of the sons of Ithamar, David organized them according to the appointed duties in their service. 4 Since more chief men were found among the sons of Eleazar than among the sons of Ithamar, they organized them under sixteen heads of fathers' houses of the sons of Eleazar, and eight of the sons of Ithamar. 5 They divided them by lot, all alike, for there were sacred officers and officers of God among both the sons of Eleazar and the sons of Ithamar. 6 And the scribe Shemaiah, the son of Nethanel, a Levite, recorded them in the presence of the king and the princes and Zadok the priest and Ahimelech the son of Abiathar and the heads of the fathers' houses of the priests and of the Levites, one father's house being chosen for Eleazar and one chosen for Ithamar.

7 The first lot fell to Jehoiarib, the second to Jedaiah, 8 the third to Harim, the

fourth to Seorim, 9 the fifth to Malchijah,
the sixth to Mijamin, 10 the seventh
to Hakkoz, the eighth to Abijah, 11 the
ninth to Jeshua, the tenth to Shecaniah,
12 the eleventh to Eliashib, the twelfth to
Jakim, 13 the thirteenth to Huppah, the
fourteenth to Jeshebeab, 14 the fifteenth
to Bilgah, the sixteenth to Immer, 15 the
seventeenth to Hezir, the eighteenth to
Happizzez, 16 the nineteenth to Pethahiah,
the twentieth to Jehezkel, 17 the twenty-
first to Jachin, the twenty-second to
Gamul, 18 the twenty-third to Delaiah, the
twenty-fourth to Maaziah. 19 These had
as their appointed duty in their service to
come into the house of the LORD accord-
ing to the procedure established for them
by Aaron their father, as the LORD God of
Israel had commanded him.

20 And of the rest of the sons of Levi: of
the sons of Amram, Shubael; of the sons
of Shubael, Jehdeiah. 21 Of Rehabiah: of
the sons of Rehabiah, Isshiah the chief.
22 Of the Izharites, Shelomoth; of the
sons of Shelomoth, Jahath. 23 The sons of
Hebron:[1] Jeriah the chief,[2] Amariah the
second, Jahaziel the third, Jekameam the
fourth. 24 The sons of Uzziel, Micah; of
the sons of Micah, Shamir. 25 The brother
of Micah, Isshiah; of the sons of Isshiah,
Zechariah. 26 The sons of Merari: Mahli
and Mushi. The sons of Jaaziah: Beno.[3]
27 The sons of Merari: of Jaaziah, Beno,
Shoham, Zaccur, and Ibri. 28 Of Mahli:
Eleazar, who had no sons. 29 Of Kish, the
sons of Kish: Jerahmeel. 30 The sons of
Mushi: Mahli, Eder, and Jerimoth. These
were the sons of the Levites accord-
ing to their fathers' houses. 31 These
also, the head of each father's house
and his younger brother alike, cast lots,
just as their brothers the sons of Aaron,
in the presence of King David, Zadok,
Ahimelech, and the heads of fathers'
houses of the priests and of the Levites.

David Organizes the Musicians

25 David and the chiefs of the ser-
vice also set apart for the service
the sons of Asaph, and of Heman, and
of Jeduthun, who prophesied with lyres,
with harps, and with cymbals. The list
of those who did the work and of their
duties was: 2 Of the sons of Asaph: Zaccur,
Joseph, Nethaniah, and Asharelah, sons
of Asaph, under the direction of Asaph,
who prophesied under the direction of the
king. 3 Of Jeduthun, the sons of Jeduthun:
Gedaliah, Zeri, Jeshaiah, Shimei,[4]
Hashabiah, and Mattithiah, six, under
the direction of their father Jeduthun,
who prophesied with the lyre in thanks-
giving and praise to the LORD. 4 Of Heman,
the sons of Heman: Bukkiah, Mattaniah,
Uzziel, Shebuel and Jerimoth, Hananiah,
Hanani, Eliathah, Giddalti, and Romamti-
ezer, Joshbekashah, Mallothi, Hothir,
Mahazioth. 5 All these were the sons of
Heman the king's seer, according to the
promise of God to exalt him, for God had
given Heman fourteen sons and three
daughters. 6 They were all under the direc-
tion of their father in the music in the
house of the LORD with cymbals, harps,
and lyres for the service of the house of
God. Asaph, Jeduthun, and Heman were
under the order of the king. 7 The num-
ber of them along with their brothers,
who were trained in singing to the LORD,
all who were skillful, was 288. 8 And they
cast lots for their duties, small and great,
teacher and pupil alike.

9 The first lot fell for Asaph to Joseph;
the second to Gedaliah, to him and his
brothers and his sons, twelve; 10 the
third to Zaccur, his sons and his broth-
ers, twelve; 11 the fourth to Izri, his sons
and his brothers, twelve; 12 the fifth to
Nethaniah, his sons and his brothers,
twelve; 13 the sixth to Bukkiah, his sons
and his brothers, twelve; 14 the seventh
to Jesharelah, his sons and his brothers,

[1] Compare 23:19; Hebrew lacks *Hebron* [2] Compare 23:19; Hebrew lacks *the chief* [3] Or *his son*; also verse 27 [4] One Hebrew manuscript, Septuagint; most Hebrew manuscripts lack *Shimei*

twelve; 15 the eighth to Jeshaiah, his sons and his brothers, twelve; 16 the ninth to Mattaniah, his sons and his brothers, twelve; 17 the tenth to Shimei, his sons and his brothers, twelve; 18 the eleventh to Azarel, his sons and his brothers, twelve; 19 the twelfth to Hashabiah, his sons and his brothers, twelve; 20 to the thirteenth, Shubael, his sons and his brothers, twelve; 21 to the fourteenth, Mattithiah, his sons and his brothers, twelve; 22 to the fifteenth, to Jeremoth, his sons and his brothers, twelve; 23 to the sixteenth, to Hananiah, his sons and his brothers, twelve; 24 to the seventeenth, to Joshbekashah, his sons and his brothers, twelve; 25 to the eighteenth, to Hanani, his sons and his brothers, twelve; 26 to the nineteenth, to Mallothi, his sons and his brothers, twelve; 27 to the twentieth, to Eliathah, his sons and his brothers, twelve; 28 to the twenty-first, to Hothir, his sons and his brothers, twelve; 29 to the twenty-second, to Giddalti, his sons and his brothers, twelve; 30 to the twenty-third, to Mahazioth, his sons and his brothers, twelve; 31 to the twenty-fourth, to Romamti-ezer, his sons and his brothers, twelve.

Divisions of the Gatekeepers

26 As for the divisions of the gatekeepers: of the Korahites, Meshelemiah the son of Kore, of the sons of Asaph. 2 And Meshelemiah had sons: Zechariah the firstborn, Jediael the second, Zebadiah the third, Jathniel the fourth, 3 Elam the fifth, Jehohanan the sixth, Eliehoenai the seventh. 4 And Obed-edom had sons: Shemaiah the firstborn, Jehozabad the second, Joah the third, Sachar the fourth, Nethanel the fifth, 5 Ammiel the sixth, Issachar the seventh, Peullethai the eighth, for God blessed him. 6 Also to his son Shemaiah were sons born who were rulers in their fathers' houses, for they were men of great ability. 7 The sons of Shemaiah: Othni, Rephael, Obed and Elzabad, whose brothers were able men, Elihu and Semachiah. 8 All these were of the sons of Obed-edom with their sons and brothers, able men qualified for the service; sixty-two of Obed-edom. 9 And Meshelemiah had sons and brothers, able men, eighteen. 10 And Hosah, of the sons of Merari, had sons: Shimri the chief (for though he was not the firstborn, his father made him chief), 11 Hilkiah the second, Tebaliah the third, Zechariah the fourth: all the sons and brothers of Hosah were thirteen.

12 These divisions of the gatekeepers, corresponding to their chief men, had duties, just as their brothers did, ministering in the house of the LORD. 13 And they cast lots by fathers' houses, small and great alike, for their gates. 14 The lot for the east fell to Shelemiah. They cast lots also for his son Zechariah, a shrewd counselor, and his lot came out for the north. 15 Obed-edom's came out for the south, and to his sons was allotted the gatehouse. 16 For Shuppim and Hosah it came out for the west, at the gate of Shallecheth on the road that goes up. Watch corresponded to watch. 17 On the east there were six each day,[1] on the north four each day, on the south four each day, as well as two and two at the gatehouse. 18 And for the colonnade[2] on the west there were four at the road and two at the colonnade. 19 These were the divisions of the gatekeepers among the Korahites and the sons of Merari.

Treasurers and Other Officials

20 And of the Levites, Ahijah had charge of the treasuries of the house of God and the treasuries of the dedicated gifts. 21 The sons of Ladan, the sons of the Gershonites belonging to Ladan, the heads of the fathers' houses belonging to Ladan the Gershonite: Jehieli.[3]

22 The sons of Jehieli, Zetham, and Joel his brother, were in charge of the treasuries

[1] Septuagint; Hebrew *six Levites* [2] Or *court*; Hebrew *parbar* (meaning unknown); twice in this verse [3] The Hebrew of verse 21 is uncertain

of the house of the LORD. 23 Of the Amramites, the Izharites, the Hebronites, and the Uzzielites— 24 and Shebuel the son of Gershom, son of Moses, was chief officer in charge of the treasuries. 25 His brothers: from Eliezer were his son Rehabiah, and his son Jeshaiah, and his son Joram, and his son Zichri, and his son Shelomoth. 26 This Shelomoth and his brothers were in charge of all the treasuries of the dedicated gifts that David the king and the heads of the fathers' houses and the officers of the thousands and the hundreds and the commanders of the army had dedicated. 27 From spoil won in battles they dedicated gifts for the maintenance of the house of the LORD. 28 Also all that Samuel the seer and Saul the son of Kish and Abner the son of Ner and Joab the son of Zeruiah had dedicated—all dedicated gifts were in the care of Shelomoth[1] and his brothers.

29 Of the Izharites, Chenaniah and his sons were appointed to external duties for Israel, as officers and judges. 30 Of the Hebronites, Hashabiah and his brothers, 1,700 men of ability, had the oversight of Israel westward of the Jordan for all the work of the LORD and for the service of the king. 31 Of the Hebronites, Jerijah was chief of the Hebronites of whatever genealogy or fathers' houses. (In the fortieth year of David's reign search was made and men of great ability among them were found at Jazer in Gilead.) 32 King David appointed him and his brothers, 2,700 men of ability, heads of fathers' houses, to have the oversight of the Reubenites, the Gadites and the half-tribe of the Manassites for everything pertaining to God and for the affairs of the king.

Military Divisions

27 This is the number of the people of Israel, the heads of fathers' houses, the commanders of thousands and hundreds, and their officers who served the king in all matters concerning the divisions that came and went, month after month throughout the year, each division numbering 24,000:

2 Jashobeam the son of Zabdiel was in charge of the first division in the first month; in his division were 24,000. 3 He was a descendant of Perez and was chief of all the commanders. He served for the first month. 4 Dodai the Ahohite[2] was in charge of the division of the second month; in his division were 24,000. 5 The third commander, for the third month, was Benaiah, the son of Jehoiada the chief priest; in his division were 24,000. 6 This is the Benaiah who was a mighty man of the thirty and in command of the thirty; Ammizabad his son was in charge of his division.[3] 7 Asahel the brother of Joab was fourth, for the fourth month, and his son Zebadiah after him; in his division were 24,000. 8 The fifth commander, for the fifth month, was Shamhuth the Izrahite; in his division were 24,000. 9 Sixth, for the sixth month, was Ira, the son of Ikkesh the Tekoite; in his division were 24,000. 10 Seventh, for the seventh month, was Helez the Pelonite, of the sons of Ephraim; in his division were 24,000. 11 Eighth, for the eighth month, was Sibbecai the Hushathite, of the Zerahites; in his division were 24,000. 12 Ninth, for the ninth month, was Abiezer of Anathoth, a Benjaminite; in his division were 24,000. 13 Tenth, for the tenth month, was Maharai of Netophah, of the Zerahites; in his division were 24,000. 14 Eleventh, for the eleventh month, was Benaiah of Pirathon, of the sons of Ephraim; in his division were 24,000. 15 Twelfth, for the twelfth month, was Heldai the Netophathite, of Othniel; in his division were 24,000.

Leaders of Tribes

16 Over the tribes of Israel, for the Reubenites, Eliezer the son of Zichri was chief officer; for the Simeonites, Shephatiah the son of Maacah; 17 for Levi, Hashabiah the son of Kemuel; for

[1] Hebrew *Shelomith* [2] Septuagint; Hebrew *Ahohite and his division and Mikloth the chief officer* [3] Septuagint, Vulgate; Hebrew *was his division*

Aaron, Zadok; 18 for Judah, Elihu, one of
David's brothers; for Issachar, Omri the
son of Michael; 19 for Zebulun, Ishmaiah
the son of Obadiah; for Naphtali, Jeremoth
the son of Azriel; 20 for the Ephraimites,
Hoshea the son of Azaziah; for the half-
tribe of Manasseh, Joel the son of Pedaiah;
21 for the half-tribe of Manasseh in Gilead,
Iddo the son of Zechariah; for Benjamin,
Jaasiel the son of Abner; 22 for Dan, Azarel
the son of Jeroham. These were the lead-
ers of the tribes of Israel. 23 David did not
count those below twenty years of age, for
the LORD had promised to make Israel as
many as the stars of heaven. 24 Joab the
son of Zeruiah began to count, but did not
finish. Yet wrath came upon Israel for this,
and the number was not entered in the
chronicles of King David.

25 Over the king's treasuries was
Azmaveth the son of Adiel; and over the
treasuries in the country, in the cities,
in the villages, and in the towers, was
Jonathan the son of Uzziah; 26 and over
those who did the work of the field for
tilling the soil was Ezri the son of Chelub;
27 and over the vineyards was Shimei the
Ramathite; and over the produce of the
vineyards for the wine cellars was Zabdi
the Shiphmite. 28 Over the olive and syc-
amore trees in the Shephelah was Baal-
hanan the Gederite; and over the stores of
oil was Joash. 29 Over the herds that pas-
tured in Sharon was Shitrai the Sharonite;
over the herds in the valleys was Shaphat
the son of Adlai. 30 Over the camels was
Obil the Ishmaelite; and over the donkeys
was Jehdeiah the Meronothite. Over the
flocks was Jaziz the Hagrite. 31 All these
were stewards of King David's property.

32 Jonathan, David's uncle, was a
counselor, being a man of understand-
ing and a scribe. He and Jehiel the son
of Hachmoni attended the king's sons.
33 Ahithophel was the king's counselor,
and Hushai the Archite was the king's
friend. 34 Ahithophel was succeeded by
Jehoiada the son of Benaiah, and Abiathar.
Joab was commander of the king's army.

David's Charge to Israel

28 David assembled at Jerusalem all
the officials of Israel, the officials
of the tribes, the officers of the divisions
that served the king, the commanders of
thousands, the commanders of hundreds,
the stewards of all the property and live-
stock of the king and his sons, together
with the palace officials, the mighty men
and all the seasoned warriors. 2 Then King
David rose to his feet and said: "Hear me,
my brothers and my people. I had it in my
heart to build a house of rest for the ark of
the covenant of the LORD and for the foot-
stool of our God, and I made preparations
for building. 3 But God said to me, 'You
may not build a house for my name, for
you are a man of war and have shed blood.'
4 Yet the LORD God of Israel chose me from
all my father's house to be king over Israel
forever. For he chose Judah as leader, and
in the house of Judah my father's house,
and among my father's sons he took
pleasure in me to make me king over all
Israel. 5 And of all my sons (for the LORD
has given me many sons) he has chosen
Solomon my son to sit on the throne of
the kingdom of the LORD over Israel. 6 He
said to me, 'It is Solomon your son who
shall build my house and my courts, for I
have chosen him to be my son, and I will
be his father. 7 I will establish his kingdom
forever if he continues strong in keeping
my commandments and my rules, as he
is today.' 8 Now therefore in the sight of all
Israel, the assembly of the LORD, and in
the hearing of our God, observe and seek
out all the commandments of the LORD
your God, that you may possess this good
land and leave it for an inheritance to your
children after you forever.

David's Charge to Solomon

9 "And you, Solomon my son, know the
God of your father and serve him with a

whole heart and with a willing mind, for the LORD searches all hearts and understands every plan and thought. If you seek him, he will be found by you, but if you forsake him, he will cast you off forever. **10** Be careful now, for the LORD has chosen you to build a house for the sanctuary; be strong and do it."

11 Then David gave Solomon his son the plan of the vestibule of the temple,[1] and of its houses, its treasuries, its upper rooms, and its inner chambers, and of the room for the mercy seat; **12** and the plan of all that he had in mind for the courts of the house of the LORD, all the surrounding chambers, the treasuries of the house of God, and the treasuries for dedicated gifts; **13** for the divisions of the priests and of the Levites, and all the work of the service in the house of the LORD; for all the vessels for the service in the house of the LORD, **14** the weight of gold for all golden vessels for each service, the weight of silver vessels for each service, **15** the weight of the golden lampstands and their lamps, the weight of gold for each lampstand and its lamps, the weight of silver for a lampstand and its lamps, according to the use of each lampstand in the service, **16** the weight of gold for each table for the showbread, the silver for the silver tables, **17** and pure gold for the forks, the basins and the cups; for the golden bowls and the weight of each; for the silver bowls and the weight of each; **18** for the altar of incense made of refined gold, and its weight; also his plan for the golden chariot of the cherubim that spread their wings and covered the ark of the covenant of the LORD. **19** "All this he made clear to me in writing from the hand of the LORD, all the work to be done according to the plan."

20 Then David said to Solomon his son, "Be strong and courageous and do it. Do not be afraid and do not be dismayed, for the LORD God, even my God, is with you. He will not leave you or forsake you, until all the work for the service of the house of the LORD is finished. **21** And behold the divisions of the priests and the Levites for all the service of the house of God; and with you in all the work will be every willing man who has skill for any kind of service; also the officers and all the people will be wholly at your command."

Offerings for the Temple

29 And David the king said to all the assembly, "Solomon my son, whom alone God has chosen, is young and inexperienced, and the work is great, for the palace will not be for man but for the LORD God. **2** So I have provided for the house of my God, so far as I was able, the gold for the things of gold, the silver for the things of silver, and the bronze for the things of bronze, the iron for the things of iron, and wood for the things of wood, besides great quantities of onyx and stones for setting, antimony, colored stones, all sorts of precious stones and marble. **3** Moreover, in addition to all that I have provided for the holy house, I have a treasure of my own of gold and silver, and because of my devotion to the house of my God I give it to the house of my God: **4** 3,000 talents[2] of gold, of the gold of Ophir, and 7,000 talents of refined silver, for overlaying the walls of the house,[3] **5** and for all the work to be done by craftsmen, gold for the things of gold and silver for the things of silver. Who then will offer willingly, consecrating himself[4] today to the LORD?"

6 Then the leaders of fathers' houses made their freewill offerings, as did also the leaders of the tribes, the commanders of thousands and of hundreds, and the officers over the king's work. **7** They gave for the service of the house of God 5,000 talents and 10,000 darics[5] of gold, 10,000 talents of silver, 18,000 talents of bronze and 100,000 talents of iron. **8** And whoever had precious stones gave them to the treasury of the house of the LORD, in the

[1] Hebrew lacks *of the temple* [2] A *talent* was about 75 pounds or 34 kilograms [3] Septuagint; Hebrew *houses* [4] Or *ordaining himself*; Hebrew *filling his hand* [5] A *daric* was a coin weighing about 1/4 ounce or 8.5 grams

care of Jehiel the Gershonite. 9 Then the people rejoiced because they had given willingly, for with a whole heart they had offered freely to the LORD. David the king also rejoiced greatly.

David Prays in the Assembly

10 Therefore David blessed the LORD in the presence of all the assembly. And David said: "Blessed are you, O LORD, the God of Israel our father, forever and ever. 11 Yours, O LORD, is the greatness and the power and the glory and the victory and the majesty, for all that is in the heavens and in the earth is yours. Yours is the kingdom, O LORD, and you are exalted as head above all. 12 Both riches and honor come from you, and you rule over all. In your hand are power and might, and in your hand it is to make great and to give strength to all. 13 And now we thank you, our God, and praise your glorious name.

14 "But who am I, and what is my people, that we should be able thus to offer willingly? For all things come from you, and of your own have we given you. 15 For we are strangers before you and sojourners, as all our fathers were. Our days on the earth are like a shadow, and there is no abiding.[1] 16 O LORD our God, all this abundance that we have provided for building you a house for your holy name comes from your hand and is all your own. 17 I know, my God, that you test the heart and have pleasure in uprightness. In the uprightness of my heart I have freely offered all these things, and now I have seen your people, who are present here, offering freely and joyously to you. 18 O LORD, the God of Abraham, Isaac, and Israel, our fathers, keep forever such purposes and thoughts in the hearts of your people, and direct their hearts toward you. 19 Grant to Solomon my son a whole heart that he may keep your commandments, your testimonies, and your statutes, performing all, and that he may build the palace for which I have made provision."

20 Then David said to all the assembly, "Bless the LORD your God." And all the assembly blessed the LORD, the God of their fathers, and bowed their heads and paid homage to the LORD and to the king. 21 And they offered sacrifices to the LORD, and on the next day offered burnt offerings to the LORD, 1,000 bulls, 1,000 rams, and 1,000 lambs, with their drink offerings, and sacrifices in abundance for all Israel. 22 And they ate and drank before the LORD on that day with great gladness.

Solomon Anointed King

And they made Solomon the son of David king the second time, and they anointed him as prince for the LORD, and Zadok as priest.

23 Then Solomon sat on the throne of the LORD as king in place of David his father. And he prospered, and all Israel obeyed him. 24 All the leaders and the mighty men, and also all the sons of King David, pledged their allegiance to King Solomon. 25 And the LORD made Solomon very great in the sight of all Israel and bestowed on him such royal majesty as had not been on any king before him in Israel.

The Death of David

26 Thus David the son of Jesse reigned over all Israel. 27 The time that he reigned over Israel was forty years. He reigned seven years in Hebron and thirty-three years in Jerusalem. 28 Then he died at a good age, full of days, riches, and honor. And Solomon his son reigned in his place. 29 Now the acts of King David, from first to last, are written in the Chronicles of Samuel the seer, and in the Chronicles of Nathan the prophet, and in the Chronicles of Gad the seer, 30 with accounts of all his rule and his might and of the circumstances that came upon him and upon Israel and upon all the kingdoms of the countries.

[1] Septuagint, Vulgate; Hebrew *hope*, or *prospect*

2 Chronicles

For the introduction, see the introduction to 1–2 Chronicles (p. 627)

Solomon Worships at Gibeon

1 Solomon the son of David established
himself in his kingdom, and the LORD
his God was with him and made him
exceedingly great.
2 Solomon spoke to all Israel, to the
commanders of thousands and of hun-
dreds, to the judges, and to all the leaders
in all Israel, the heads of fathers' houses.
3 And Solomon, and all the assembly
with him, went to the high place that
was at Gibeon, for the tent of meeting
of God, which Moses the servant of the
LORD had made in the wilderness, was
there. 4 (But David had brought up the
ark of God from Kiriath-jearim to the
place that David had prepared for it, for
he had pitched a tent for it in Jerusalem.)
5 Moreover, the bronze altar that Bezalel
the son of Uri, son of Hur, had made, was
there before the tabernacle of the LORD.
And Solomon and the assembly sought
it[1] out. 6 And Solomon went up there to
the bronze altar before the LORD, which
was at the tent of meeting, and offered a
thousand burnt offerings on it.

Solomon Prays for Wisdom

7 In that night God appeared to
Solomon, and said to him, "Ask
535 what I shall give you." 8 And
Solomon said to God, "You have shown
great and steadfast love to David my father,
and have made me king in his place. 9 O
LORD God, let your word to David my father
be now fulfilled, for you have made me
king over a people as numerous as the
dust of the earth. 10 Give me now wisdom
and knowledge to go out and come in
before this people, for who can govern this
people of yours, which is so great?" 11 God
answered Solomon, "Because this was in
your heart, and you have not asked pos-
sessions, wealth, honor, or the life of those
who hate you, and have not even asked
long life, but have asked wisdom and
knowledge for yourself that you may gov-
ern my people over whom I have made
you king, 12 wisdom and knowledge are
granted to you. I will also give you riches,
possessions, and honor, such as none of
the kings had who were before you, and
none after you shall have the like." 13 So
Solomon came from[2] the high place at

CHARACTER PROFILE

SOLOMON

Solomon was David's son and the third king of Israel. God gave him great wisdom. Solomon wrote most of Proverbs. While he was king, Israel was wealthy and a great nation. Solomon built a beautiful temple for God in Jerusalem. Solomon married many wives from idol-worshiping nations, leading Solomon into idol worship too.

535, 545

[1] Or *him* [2] Septuagint, Vulgate; Hebrew *to*

Gibeon, from before the tent of meeting, to Jerusalem. And he reigned over Israel.

Solomon Given Wealth

14 Solomon gathered together chariots and horsemen. He had 1,400 chariots and 12,000 horsemen, whom he stationed in the chariot cities and with the king in Jerusalem. 15 And the king made silver and gold as common in Jerusalem as stone, and he made cedar as plentiful as the sycamore of the Shephelah. 16 And Solomon's import of horses was from Egypt and Kue, and the king's traders would buy them from Kue for a price. 17 They imported a chariot from Egypt for 600 shekels[1] of silver, and a horse for 150. Likewise through them these were exported to all the kings of the Hittites and the kings of Syria.

Preparing to Build the Temple

545

2 [2] Now Solomon purposed to build a temple for the name of the LORD, and a royal palace for himself. 2[3] And Solomon assigned 70,000 men to bear burdens and 80,000 to quarry in the hill country, and 3,600 to oversee them. 3 And Solomon sent word to Hiram the king of Tyre: "As you dealt with David my father and sent him cedar to build himself a house to dwell in, so deal with me. 4 Behold, I am about to build a house for the name of the LORD my God and dedicate it to him for the burning of incense of sweet spices before him, and for the regular arrangement of the showbread, and for burnt offerings morning and evening, on the Sabbaths and the new moons and the appointed feasts of the LORD our God, as ordained forever for Israel. 5 The house that I am to build will be great, for our God is greater than all gods. 6 But who is able to build him a house, since heaven, even highest heaven, cannot contain him? Who am I to build a house for him, except as a place to make offerings before him? 7 So now send me a man skilled to work in gold, silver, bronze, and iron, and in purple, crimson, and blue fabrics, trained also in engraving, to be with the skilled workers who are with me in Judah and Jerusalem, whom David my father provided. 8 Send me also cedar, cypress, and algum timber from Lebanon, for I know that your servants know how to cut timber in Lebanon. And my servants will be with your servants, 9 to prepare timber for me in abundance, for the house I am to build will be great and wonderful. 10 I will give for your servants, the woodsmen who cut timber, 20,000 cors[4] of crushed wheat, 20,000 cors of barley, 20,000 baths[5] of wine, and 20,000 baths of oil."

11 Then Hiram the king of Tyre answered in a letter that he sent to Solomon, "Because the LORD loves his people, he has made you king over them." 12 Hiram also said, "Blessed be the LORD God of Israel, who made heaven and earth, who has given King David a wise son, who has discretion and understanding, who will build a temple for the LORD and a royal palace for himself.

13 "Now I have sent a skilled man, who has understanding, Huram-abi, 14 the son of a woman of the daughters of Dan, and his father was a man of Tyre. He is trained to work in gold, silver, bronze, iron, stone, and wood, and in purple, blue, and crimson fabrics and fine linen, and to do all sorts of engraving and execute any design that may be assigned him, with your craftsmen, the craftsmen of my lord, David your father. 15 Now therefore the wheat and barley, oil and wine, of which my lord has spoken, let him send to his servants. 16 And we will cut whatever timber you need from Lebanon and bring it to you in rafts by sea to Joppa, so that you may take it up to Jerusalem."

17 Then Solomon counted all the resident aliens who were in the land of Israel, after the census of them that David his father had taken, and there were found 153,600. 18 Seventy thousand of them he

[1] A *shekel* was about 2/5 ounce or 11 grams [2] Ch 1:18 in Hebrew [3] Ch 2:1 in Hebrew [4] A *cor* was about 6 bushels or 220 liters [5] A *bath* was about 6 gallons or 22 liters

assigned to bear burdens, 80,000 to quarry in the hill country, and 3,600 as overseers to make the people work.

Solomon Builds the Temple

3 Then Solomon began to build the house of the LORD in Jerusalem on Mount Moriah, where the LORD[1] had appeared to David his father, at the place that David had appointed, on the threshing floor of Ornan the Jebusite. 2 He began to build in the second month of the fourth year of his reign. 3 These are Solomon's measurements[2] for building the house of God: the length, in cubits[3] of the old standard, was sixty cubits, and the breadth twenty cubits. 4 The vestibule in front of the nave of the house was twenty cubits long, equal to the width of the house,[4] and its height was 120 cubits. He overlaid it on the inside with pure gold. 5 The nave he lined with cypress and covered it with fine gold and made palms and chains on it. 6 He adorned the house with settings of precious stones. The gold was gold of Parvaim. 7 So he lined the house with gold—its beams, its thresholds, its walls, and its doors—and he carved cherubim on the walls.

8 And he made the Most Holy Place. Its length, corresponding to the breadth of the house, was twenty cubits, and its breadth was twenty cubits. He overlaid it with 600 talents[5] of fine gold. 9 The weight of gold for the nails was fifty shekels.[6] And he overlaid the upper chambers with gold.

10 In the Most Holy Place he made two cherubim of wood[7] and overlaid[8] them with gold. 11 The wings of the cherubim together extended twenty cubits: one wing of the one, of five cubits, touched the wall of the house, and its other wing, of five cubits, touched the wing of the other cherub; 12 and of this cherub, one wing, of five cubits, touched the wall of the house, and the other wing, also of five cubits, was joined to the wing of the first cherub. 13 The wings of these cherubim extended twenty cubits. The cherubim[9] stood on their feet, facing the nave. 14 And he made the veil of blue and purple and crimson fabrics and fine linen, and he worked cherubim on it.

15 In front of the house he made two pillars thirty-five cubits high, with a capital of five cubits on the top of each. 16 He made chains like a necklace[10] and put them on the tops of the pillars, and he made a hundred pomegranates and put them on the chains. 17 He set up the pillars in front of the temple, one on the south, the other on the north; that on the south he called Jachin, and that on the north Boaz.

The Temple's Furnishings

4 He made an altar of bronze, twenty cubits[11] long and twenty cubits wide and ten cubits high. 2 Then he made the sea of cast metal. It was round, ten cubits from brim to brim, and five cubits high, and a line of thirty cubits measured its circumference. 3 Under it were figures of gourds,[12] for ten cubits, compassing the sea all around. The gourds were in two rows, cast with it when it was cast. 4 It stood on twelve oxen, three facing north, three facing west, three facing south, and three facing east. The sea was set on them, and all their rear parts were inward. 5 Its thickness was a handbreadth.[13] And its brim was made like the brim of a cup, like the flower of a lily. It held 3,000 baths.[14] 6 He also made ten basins in which to wash, and set five on the south side, and five on the north side. In these they were to rinse off what was used for the burnt offering, and the sea was for the priests to wash in.

7 And he made ten golden lampstands as prescribed, and set them in the temple, five on the south side and five on the north. 8 He also made ten tables and placed them in the temple, five on the south side and five on the north. And he

[1] Septuagint; Hebrew lacks *the LORD* [2] Syriac; Hebrew *foundations* [3] A *cubit* was about 18 inches or 45 centimeters [4] Compare 1 Kings 6:3; the meaning of the Hebrew is uncertain [5] A *talent* was about 75 pounds or 34 kilograms [6] A *shekel* was about 2/5 ounce or 11 grams [7] Septuagint; the meaning of the Hebrew is uncertain [8] Hebrew *they overlaid* [9] Hebrew *they* [10] Hebrew *chains in the inner sanctuary* [11] A *cubit* was about 18 inches or 45 centimeters [12] Compare 1 Kings 7:24; Hebrew *oxen*; twice in this verse [13] A *handbreadth* was about 3 inches or 7.5 centimeters [14] A *bath* was about 6 gallons or 22 liters

made a hundred basins of gold. 9 He made the court of the priests and the great court and doors for the court and overlaid their doors with bronze. 10 And he set the sea at the southeast corner of the house.

11 Hiram also made the pots, the shovels, and the basins. So Hiram finished the work that he did for King Solomon on the house of God: 12 the two pillars, the bowls, and the two capitals on the top of the pillars; and the two latticeworks to cover the two bowls of the capitals that were on the top of the pillars; 13 and the 400 pomegranates for the two latticeworks, two rows of pomegranates for each latticework, to cover the two bowls of the capitals that were on the pillars. 14 He made the stands also, and the basins on the stands, 15 and the one sea, and the twelve oxen underneath it. 16 The pots, the shovels, the forks, and all the equipment for these Huram-abi made of burnished bronze for King Solomon for the house of the LORD. 17 In the plain of the Jordan the king cast them, in the clay ground between Succoth and Zeredah.[1] 18 Solomon made all these things in great quantities, for the weight of the bronze was not sought.

19 So Solomon made all the vessels that were in the house of God: the golden altar, the tables for the bread of the Presence, 20 the lampstands and their lamps of pure gold to burn before the inner sanctuary, as prescribed; 21 the flowers, the lamps, and the tongs, of purest gold; 22 the snuffers, basins, dishes for incense, and fire pans, of pure gold, and the sockets[2] of the temple, for the inner doors to the Most Holy Place and for the doors of the nave of the temple were of gold.

5 Thus all the work that Solomon did for the house of the LORD was finished. And Solomon brought in the things that David his father had dedicated, and stored the silver, the gold, and all the vessels in the treasuries of the house of God.

The Ark Brought to the Temple

2 Then Solomon assembled the elders of Israel and all the heads of the tribes, the leaders of the fathers' houses of the people of Israel, in Jerusalem, to bring up the ark of the covenant of the LORD out of the city of David, which is Zion. 3 And all the men of Israel assembled before the king at the feast that is in the seventh month. 4 And all the elders of Israel came, and the Levites took up the ark. 5 And they brought up the ark, the tent of meeting, and all the holy vessels that were in the tent; the Levitical priests brought them up. 6 And King Solomon and all the congregation of Israel, who had assembled before him, were before the ark, sacrificing so many sheep and oxen that they could not be counted or numbered. 7 Then the priests brought the ark of the covenant of the LORD to its place, in the inner sanctuary of the house, in the Most Holy Place, underneath the wings of the cherubim. 8 The cherubim spread out their wings over the place of the ark, so that the cherubim made a covering above the ark and its poles. 9 And the poles were so long that the ends of the poles were seen from the Holy Place before the inner sanctuary, but they could not be seen from outside. And they are[3] there to this day. 10 There was nothing in the ark except the two tablets that Moses put there at Horeb, where the LORD made a covenant with the people of Israel, when they came out of Egypt. 11 And when the priests came out of the Holy Place (for all the priests who were present had consecrated themselves, without regard to their divisions, 12 and all the Levitical singers, Asaph, Heman, and Jeduthun, their sons and kinsmen, arrayed in fine linen, with cymbals, harps, and lyres, stood east of the altar with 120 priests who were trumpeters; 13 and it was the duty of the trumpeters and singers to make themselves heard in unison in praise and thanksgiving to the LORD), and when the song was raised, with

[1] Spelled *Zarethan* in 1 Kings 7:46 [2] Compare 1 Kings 7:50; Hebrew *the entrance of the house* [3] Hebrew *it is*

trumpets and cymbals and other musical instruments, in praise to the LORD,

"For he is good,
for his steadfast love endures
forever,"

the house, the house of the LORD, was filled with a cloud, 14 so that the priests could not stand to minister because of the cloud, for the glory of the LORD filled the house of God.

Solomon Blesses the People

6 Then Solomon said, "The LORD has said that he would dwell in thick darkness. 2 But I have built you an exalted house, a place for you to dwell in forever." 3 Then the king turned around and blessed all the assembly of Israel, while all the assembly of Israel stood. 4 And he said, "Blessed be the LORD, the God of Israel, who with his hand has fulfilled what he promised with his mouth to David my father, saying, 5 'Since the day that I brought my people out of the land of Egypt, I chose no city out of all the tribes of Israel in which to build a house, that my name might be there, and I chose no man as prince over my people Israel; 6 but I have chosen Jerusalem that my name may be there, and I have chosen David to be over my people Israel.' 7 Now it was in the heart of David my father to build a house for the name of the LORD, the God of Israel. 8 But the LORD said to David my father, 'Whereas it was in your heart to build a house for my name, you did well that it was in your heart. 9 Nevertheless, it is not you who shall build the house, but your son who shall be born to you shall build the house for my name.' 10 Now the LORD has fulfilled his promise that he made. For I have risen in the place of David my father and sit on the throne of Israel, as the LORD promised, and I have built the house for the name of the LORD, the God of Israel. 11 And there I have set the ark, in which is the covenant of the LORD that he made with the people of Israel."

Solomon's Prayer of Dedication

12 Then Solomon stood before the altar of the LORD in the presence of all the assembly of Israel and spread out his hands. 13 Solomon had made a bronze platform five cubits[1] long, five cubits wide, and three cubits high, and had set it in the court, and he stood on it. Then he knelt on his knees in the presence of all the assembly of Israel, and spread out his hands toward heaven, 14 and said, "O LORD, God of Israel, there is no God like you, in heaven or on earth, keeping covenant and showing steadfast love to your servants who walk before you with all their heart, 15 who have kept with your servant David my father what you declared to him. You spoke with your mouth, and with your hand have fulfilled it this day. 16 Now therefore, O LORD, God of Israel, keep for your servant David my father what you have promised him, saying, 'You shall not lack a man to sit before me on the throne of Israel, if only your sons pay close attention to their way, to walk in my law as you have walked before me.' 17 Now therefore, O LORD, God of Israel, let your word be confirmed, which you have spoken to your servant David.

18 "But will God indeed dwell with man on the earth? Behold, heaven and the highest heaven cannot contain you, how much less this house that I have built! 19 Yet have regard to the prayer of your servant and to his plea, O LORD my God, listening to the cry and to the prayer that your servant prays before you, 20 that your eyes may be open day and night toward this house, the place where you have promised to set your name, that you may listen to the prayer that your servant offers toward this place. 21 And listen to the pleas of your servant and of your people Israel, when they pray toward this place. And listen from heaven your dwelling place, and when you hear, forgive.

[1] A *cubit* was about 18 inches or 45 centimeters

22 “If a man sins against his neighbor
and is made to take an oath and comes
and swears his oath before your altar
in this house, 23 then hear from heaven
and act and judge your servants, repay-
ing the guilty by bringing his conduct on
his own head, and vindicating the righ-
teous by rewarding him according to his
righteousness.

24 “If your people Israel are defeated
before the enemy because they have
sinned against you, and they turn again
and acknowledge your name and pray and
plead with you in this house, 25 then hear
from heaven and forgive the sin of your
people Israel and bring them again to the
land that you gave to them and to their
fathers.

26 “When heaven is shut up and there is
no rain because they have sinned against
you, if they pray toward this place and
acknowledge your name and turn from
their sin, when you afflict[1] them, 27 then
hear in heaven and forgive the sin of your
servants, your people Israel, when you
teach them the good way[2] in which they
should walk, and grant rain upon your
land, which you have given to your people
as an inheritance.

28 “If there is famine in the land, if there
is pestilence or blight or mildew or locust
or caterpillar, if their enemies besiege
them in the land at their gates, what-
ever plague, whatever sickness there is,
29 whatever prayer, whatever plea is made
by any man or by all your people Israel,
each knowing his own affliction and his
own sorrow and stretching out his hands
toward this house, 30 then hear from
heaven your dwelling place and forgive
and render to each whose heart you know,
according to all his ways, for you, you only,
know the hearts of the children of man-
kind, 31 that they may fear you and walk in
your ways all the days that they live in the
land that you gave to our fathers.

32 “Likewise, when a foreigner, who is
not of your people Israel, comes from a far
country for the sake of your great name and
your mighty hand and your outstretched
arm, when he comes and prays toward this
house, 33 hear from heaven your dwelling
place and do according to all for which the
foreigner calls to you, in order that all the
peoples of the earth may know your name
and fear you, as do your people Israel, and
that they may know that this house that I
have built is called by your name.

34 “If your people go out to battle against
their enemies, by whatever way you shall
send them, and they pray to you toward
this city that you have chosen and the
house that I have built for your name,
35 then hear from heaven their prayer and
their plea, and maintain their cause.

36 “If they sin against you—for there
is no one who does not sin—and you
are angry with them and give them to an
enemy, so that they are carried away cap-
tive to a land far or near, 37 yet if they turn
their heart in the land to which they have
been carried captive, and repent and plead
with you in the land of their captivity, say-
ing, ‘We have sinned and have acted per-
versely and wickedly,’ 38 if they repent with
all their mind and with all their heart in
the land of their captivity to which they
were carried captive, and pray toward their
land, which you gave to their fathers, the
city that you have chosen and the house
that I have built for your name, 39 then
hear from heaven your dwelling place their
prayer and their pleas, and maintain their
cause and forgive your people who have
sinned against you. 40 Now, O my God, let
your eyes be open and your ears attentive
to the prayer of this place.

41 “And now arise, O LORD God, and go
to your resting place,
you and the ark of your might.
Let your priests, O LORD God, be
clothed with salvation,
and let your saints rejoice in your
goodness.

[1] Septuagint, Vulgate; Hebrew *answer* [2] Septuagint, Syriac, Vulgate (compare 1 Kings 8:36); Hebrew *toward the good way*

42 O LORD God, do not turn away the
face of your anointed one!
Remember your steadfast love for
David your servant."

Fire from Heaven

7 As soon as Solomon finished his
prayer, fire came down from heaven
and consumed the burnt offering and the
sacrifices, and the glory of the LORD filled
the temple. 2 And the priests could not
enter the house of the LORD, because the
glory of the LORD filled the LORD's house.
3 When all the people of Israel saw the fire
come down and the glory of the LORD on
the temple, they bowed down with their
faces to the ground on the pavement and
worshiped and gave thanks to the LORD,
saying, "For he is good, for his steadfast
love endures forever."

The Dedication of the Temple

4 Then the king and all the people
offered sacrifice before the LORD. 5 King
Solomon offered as a sacrifice 22,000
oxen and 120,000 sheep. So the king
and all the people dedicated the house
of God. 6 The priests stood at their posts;
the Levites also, with the instruments for
music to the LORD that King David had
made for giving thanks to the LORD—for
his steadfast love endures forever—when-
ever David offered praises by their minis-
try;[1] opposite them the priests sounded
trumpets, and all Israel stood.
7 And Solomon consecrated the middle
of the court that was before the house of
the LORD, for there he offered the burnt
offering and the fat of the peace offerings,
because the bronze altar Solomon had
made could not hold the burnt offering
and the grain offering and the fat.
8 At that time Solomon held the feast
for seven days, and all Israel with him, a
very great assembly, from Lebo-hamath
to the Brook of Egypt. 9 And on the eighth
day they held a solemn assembly, for they
had kept the dedication of the altar seven
days and the feast seven days. 10 On the
twenty-third day of the seventh month
he sent the people away to their homes,
joyful and glad of heart for the prosperity
that the LORD had granted to David and to
Solomon and to Israel his people.

If My People Pray

11 Thus Solomon finished the house of
the LORD and the king's house. All that
Solomon had planned to do in the house
of the LORD and in his own house he suc-
cessfully accomplished. 12 Then the LORD
appeared to Solomon in the night and said
to him: "I have heard your prayer and have
chosen this place for myself as a house of
sacrifice. 13 When I shut up the heavens
so that there is no rain, or command the
locust to devour the land, or send pesti-
lence among my people, 14 if my people
who are called by my name humble them-
selves, and pray and seek my face and turn
from their wicked ways, then I will hear
from heaven and will forgive their sin and
heal their land. 15 Now my eyes will be
open and my ears attentive to the prayer
that is made in this place. 16 For now I have
chosen and consecrated this house that
my name may be there forever. My eyes
and my heart will be there for all time.
17 And as for you, if you will walk before
me as David your father walked, doing
according to all that I have commanded
you and keeping my statutes and my rules,
18 then I will establish your royal throne, as
I covenanted with David your father, say-
ing, 'You shall not lack a man to rule Israel.'
19 "But if you[2] turn aside and forsake
my statutes and my commandments that
I have set before you, and go and serve
other gods and worship them, 20 then
I will pluck you[3] up from my land that I
have given you, and this house that I have
consecrated for my name, I will cast out
of my sight, and I will make it a proverb
and a byword among all peoples. 21 And at
this house, which was exalted, everyone

[1] Hebrew *by their hand* [2] The Hebrew for *you* is plural here [3] Hebrew *them*; twice in this verse

passing by will be astonished and say, 'Why
has the LORD done thus to this land and to
this house?' 22 Then they will say, 'Because
they abandoned the LORD, the God of
their fathers who brought them out of the
land of Egypt and laid hold on other gods
and worshiped them and served them.
Therefore he has brought all this disaster
on them.'"

Solomon's Accomplishments

8 At the end of twenty years, in which
Solomon had built the house of the
LORD and his own house, 2 Solomon rebuilt
the cities that Hiram had given to him, and
settled the people of Israel in them.

3 And Solomon went to Hamath-zobah
and took it. 4 He built Tadmor in the wilder-
ness and all the store cities that he built in
Hamath. 5 He also built Upper Beth-horon
and Lower Beth-horon, fortified cities with
walls, gates, and bars, 6 and Baalath, and
all the store cities that Solomon had and
all the cities for his chariots and the cities
for his horsemen, and whatever Solomon
desired to build in Jerusalem, in Lebanon,
and in all the land of his dominion. 7 All
the people who were left of the Hittites, the
Amorites, the Perizzites, the Hivites, and
the Jebusites, who were not of Israel, 8 from
their descendants who were left after them
in the land, whom the people of Israel had
not destroyed—these Solomon drafted as
forced labor, and so they are to this day.
9 But of the people of Israel Solomon made
no slaves for his work; they were soldiers,
and his officers, the commanders of his
chariots, and his horsemen. 10 And these
were the chief officers of King Solomon,
250, who exercised authority over the
people.

11 Solomon brought Pharaoh's daughter
up from the city of David to the house that
he had built for her, for he said, "My wife
shall not live in the house of David king
of Israel, for the places to which the ark of
the LORD has come are holy."

12 Then Solomon offered up burnt offer-
ings to the LORD on the altar of the LORD
that he had built before the vestibule,
13 as the duty of each day required, offer-
ing according to the commandment of
Moses for the Sabbaths, the new moons,
and the three annual feasts—the Feast of
Unleavened Bread, the Feast of Weeks, and
the Feast of Booths. 14 According to the rul-
ing of David his father, he appointed the
divisions of the priests for their service,
and the Levites for their offices of praise
and ministry before the priests as the duty
of each day required, and the gatekeepers
in their divisions at each gate, for so David
the man of God had commanded. 15 And
they did not turn aside from what the king
had commanded the priests and Levites
concerning any matter and concerning
the treasuries.

16 Thus was accomplished all the work
of Solomon from[1] the day the foundation
of the house of the LORD was laid until
it was finished. So the house of the LORD
was completed.

17 Then Solomon went to Ezion-geber
and Eloth on the shore of the sea, in the
land of Edom. 18 And Hiram sent to him
by the hand of his servants ships and
servants familiar with the sea, and they
went to Ophir together with the servants
of Solomon and brought from there 450
talents[2] of gold and brought it to King
Solomon.

The Queen of Sheba

9 Now when the queen of Sheba
heard of the fame of Solomon,
535 she came to Jerusalem to test him
with hard questions, having a very great
retinue and camels bearing spices and
very much gold and precious stones. And
when she came to Solomon, she told him
all that was on her mind. 2 And Solomon
answered all her questions. There was
nothing hidden from Solomon that he
could not explain to her. 3 And when the
queen of Sheba had seen the wisdom of
Solomon, the house that he had built,

[1] Septuagint, Syriac, Vulgate; Hebrew *to* [2] A *talent* was about 75 pounds or 34 kilograms

4 the food of his table, the seating of his officials, and the attendance of his servants, and their clothing, his cupbearers, and their clothing, and his burnt offerings that he offered at the house of the LORD, there was no more breath in her.

5 And she said to the king, "The report was true that I heard in my own land of your words and of your wisdom, **6** but I did not believe the[1] reports until I came and my own eyes had seen it. And behold, half the greatness of your wisdom was not told me; you surpass the report that I heard. **7** Happy are your wives![2] Happy are these your servants, who continually stand before you and hear your wisdom! **8** Blessed be the LORD your God, who has delighted in you and set you on his throne as king for the LORD your God! Because your God loved Israel and would establish them forever, he has made you king over them, that you may execute justice and righteousness." **9** Then she gave the king 120 talents[3] of gold, and a very great quantity of spices, and precious stones. There were no spices such as those that the queen of Sheba gave to King Solomon.

10 Moreover, the servants of Hiram and the servants of Solomon, who brought gold from Ophir, brought algum wood and precious stones. **11** And the king made from the algum wood supports for the house of the LORD and for the king's house, lyres also and harps for the singers. There never was seen the like of them before in the land of Judah.

12 And King Solomon gave to the queen of Sheba all that she desired, whatever she asked besides what she had brought to the king. So she turned and went back to her own land with her servants.

Solomon's Wealth

13 Now the weight of gold that came to Solomon in one year was 666 talents of gold, **14** besides that which the explorers and merchants brought. And all the kings of Arabia and the governors of the land brought gold and silver to Solomon. **15** King Solomon made 200 large shields of beaten gold; 600 shekels[4] of beaten gold went into each shield. **16** And he made 300 shields of beaten gold; 300 shekels of gold went into each shield; and the king put them in the House of the Forest of Lebanon. **17** The king also made a great ivory throne and overlaid it with pure gold. **18** The throne had six steps and a footstool of gold, which were attached to the throne, and on each side of the seat were armrests and two lions standing beside the armrests, **19** while twelve lions stood there, one on each end of a step on the six steps. Nothing like it was ever made for any kingdom. **20** All King Solomon's drinking vessels were of gold, and all the vessels of the House of the Forest of Lebanon were of pure gold. Silver was not considered as anything in the days of Solomon. **21** For the king's ships went to Tarshish with the servants of Hiram. Once every three years the ships of Tarshish used to come bringing gold, silver, ivory, apes, and peacocks.[5]

22 Thus King Solomon excelled all the kings of the earth in riches and in wisdom. **23** And all the kings of the earth sought the presence of Solomon to hear his wisdom, which God had put into his mind. **24** Every one of them brought his present, articles of silver and of gold, garments, myrrh, spices, horses, and mules, so much year by year. **25** And Solomon had 4,000 stalls for horses and chariots, and 12,000 horsemen, whom he stationed in the chariot cities and with the king in Jerusalem. **26** And he ruled over all the kings from the Euphrates to the land of the Philistines and to the border of Egypt. **27** And the king made silver as common in Jerusalem as stone, and he made cedar as plentiful as the sycamore of the Shephelah. **28** And horses were imported for Solomon from Egypt and from all lands.

[1] Hebrew *their* [2] Septuagint (compare 1 Kings 10:8); Hebrew *men* [3] A *talent* was about 75 pounds or 34 kilograms [4] A *shekel* was about 2/5 ounce or 11 grams
[5] Or *baboons*

Solomon's Death

29 Now the rest of the acts of Solomon,
from first to last, are they not written in
the history of Nathan the prophet, and in
the prophecy of Ahijah the Shilonite, and
in the visions of Iddo the seer concerning
Jeroboam the son of Nebat? 30 Solomon
reigned in Jerusalem over all Israel forty
years. 31 And Solomon slept with his
fathers and was buried in the city of David
his father, and Rehoboam his son reigned
in his place.

The Revolt Against Rehoboam

10 Rehoboam went to Shechem, for
all Israel had come to Shechem to
make him king. 2 And as soon as Jeroboam
the son of Nebat heard of it (for he was
in Egypt, where he had fled from King
Solomon), then Jeroboam returned from
Egypt. 3 And they sent and called him. And
Jeroboam and all Israel came and said to
Rehoboam, 4 "Your father made our yoke
heavy. Now therefore lighten the hard
service of your father and his heavy yoke
on us, and we will serve you." 5 He said to
them, "Come to me again in three days."
So the people went away.
6 Then King Rehoboam took counsel
with the old men,[1] who had stood before
Solomon his father while he was yet alive,
saying, "How do you advise me to answer
this people?" 7 And they said to him, "If
you will be good to this people and please
them and speak good words to them, then
they will be your servants forever." 8 But he
abandoned the counsel that the old men
gave him, and took counsel with the young
men who had grown up with him and
stood before him. 9 And he said to them,
"What do you advise that we answer this
people who have said to me, 'Lighten the
yoke that your father put on us'?" 10 And
the young men who had grown up with
him said to him, "Thus shall you speak to
the people who said to you, 'Your father
made our yoke heavy, but you lighten it for
us'; thus shall you say to them, 'My little
finger is thicker than my father's thighs.
11 And now, whereas my father laid on you
a heavy yoke, I will add to your yoke. My
father disciplined you with whips, but I
will discipline you with scorpions.'"
12 So Jeroboam and all the people came
to Rehoboam the third day, as the king said,
"Come to me again the third day." 13 And
the king answered them harshly; and for-
saking the counsel of the old men, 14 King
Rehoboam spoke to them according to the
counsel of the young men, saying, "My
father made your yoke heavy, but I will add
to it. My father disciplined you with whips,
but I will discipline you with scorpions."
15 So the king did not listen to the people,
for it was a turn of affairs brought about by
God that the LORD might fulfill his word,
which he spoke by Ahijah the Shilonite to
Jeroboam the son of Nebat.
16 And when all Israel saw that the
king did not listen to them, the people
answered the king, "What portion have
we in David? We have no inheritance in
the son of Jesse. Each of you to your tents,
O Israel! Look now to your own house,
David." So all Israel went to their tents.
17 But Rehoboam reigned over the people
of Israel who lived in the cities of Judah.
18 Then King Rehoboam sent Hadoram,[2]
who was taskmaster over the forced labor,
and the people of Israel stoned him to
death with stones. And King Rehoboam
quickly mounted his chariot to flee to
Jerusalem. 19 So Israel has been in rebel-
lion against the house of David to this day.

Rehoboam Secures His Kingdom

11 When Rehoboam came to Jeru-
salem, he assembled the house
of Judah and Benjamin, 180,000 chosen
warriors, to fight against Israel, to restore
the kingdom to Rehoboam. 2 But the word
of the LORD came to Shemaiah the man
of God: 3 "Say to Rehoboam the son of
Solomon, king of Judah, and to all Israel

[1] Or *the elders*; also verses 8, 13 [2] Spelled *Adoram* in 1 Kings 12:18

in Judah and Benjamin, 4 'Thus says the
LORD, You shall not go up or fight against
your relatives. Return every man to his
home, for this thing is from me.'" So they
listened to the word of the LORD and
returned and did not go against Jeroboam.
5 Rehoboam lived in Jerusalem, and
he built cities for defense in Judah. 6 He
built Bethlehem, Etam, Tekoa, 7 Beth-zur,
Soco, Adullam, 8 Gath, Mareshah, Ziph,
9 Adoraim, Lachish, Azekah, 10 Zorah,
Aijalon, and Hebron, fortified cities that
are in Judah and in Benjamin. 11 He made
the fortresses strong, and put command-
ers in them, and stores of food, oil, and
wine. 12 And he put shields and spears in
all the cities and made them very strong.
So he held Judah and Benjamin.

Priests and Levites Come to Jerusalem

13 And the priests and the Levites who
were in all Israel presented themselves
to him from all places where they lived.
14 For the Levites left their common lands
and their holdings and came to Judah
and Jerusalem, because Jeroboam and
his sons cast them out from serving as
priests of the LORD, 15 and he appointed
his own priests for the high places and for
the goat idols and for the calves that he
had made. 16 And those who had set their
hearts to seek the LORD God of Israel came
after them from all the tribes of Israel to
Jerusalem to sacrifice to the LORD, the
God of their fathers. 17 They strengthened
the kingdom of Judah, and for three years
they made Rehoboam the son of Solomon
secure, for they walked for three years in
the way of David and Solomon.

Rehoboam's Family

18 Rehoboam took as wife Mahalath the
daughter of Jerimoth the son of David, and
of Abihail the daughter of Eliab the son
of Jesse, 19 and she bore him sons, Jeush,
Shemariah, and Zaham. 20 After her he
took Maacah the daughter of Absalom,
who bore him Abijah, Attai, Ziza, and
Shelomith. 21 Rehoboam loved Maacah
the daughter of Absalom above all his
wives and concubines (he took eighteen
wives and sixty concubines, and fathered
twenty-eight sons and sixty daughters).
22 And Rehoboam appointed Abijah the
son of Maacah as chief prince among his
brothers, for he intended to make him
king. 23 And he dealt wisely and distributed
some of his sons through all the districts
of Judah and Benjamin, in all the fortified
cities, and he gave them abundant provi-
sions and procured wives for them.[1]

Egypt Plunders Jerusalem

12 When the rule of Rehoboam was
established and he was strong,
he abandoned the law of the LORD, and
all Israel with him. 2 In the fifth year of
King Rehoboam, because they had been
unfaithful to the LORD, Shishak king of
Egypt came up against Jerusalem 3 with
1,200 chariots and 60,000 horsemen. And
the people were without number who
came with him from Egypt—Libyans,
Sukkiim, and Ethiopians. 4 And he took
the fortified cities of Judah and came as far
as Jerusalem. 5 Then Shemaiah the prophet
came to Rehoboam and to the princes
of Judah, who had gathered at Jerusalem
because of Shishak, and said to them,
"Thus says the LORD, 'You abandoned
me, so I have abandoned you to the hand
of Shishak.'" 6 Then the princes of Israel
and the king humbled themselves and
said, "The LORD is righteous." 7 When the
LORD saw that they humbled themselves,
the word of the LORD came to Shemaiah:
"They have humbled themselves. I will
not destroy them, but I will grant them
some deliverance, and my wrath shall not
be poured out on Jerusalem by the hand
of Shishak. 8 Nevertheless, they shall be
servants to him, that they may know my
service and the service of the kingdoms
of the countries."
9 So Shishak king of Egypt came up

[1] Hebrew *and sought a multitude of wives*

against Jerusalem. He took away the trea-
sures of the house of the LORD and the
treasures of the king's house. He took
away everything. He also took away the
shields of gold that Solomon had made,
10 and King Rehoboam made in their place
shields of bronze and committed them to
the hands of the officers of the guard, who
kept the door of the king's house. 11 And
as often as the king went into the house
of the LORD, the guard came and carried
them and brought them back to the guard-
room. 12 And when he humbled himself
the wrath of the LORD turned from him,
so as not to make a complete destruction.
Moreover, conditions were good[1] in Judah.

13 So King Rehoboam grew strong in
Jerusalem and reigned. Rehoboam was
forty-one years old when he began to
reign, and he reigned seventeen years in
Jerusalem, the city that the LORD had cho-
sen out of all the tribes of Israel to put
his name there. His mother's name was
Naamah the Ammonite. 14 And he did evil,
for he did not set his heart to seek the LORD.

15 Now the acts of Rehoboam, from
first to last, are they not written in the
chronicles of Shemaiah the prophet and
of Iddo the seer?[2] There were continual
wars between Rehoboam and Jeroboam.
16 And Rehoboam slept with his fathers
and was buried in the city of David, and
Abijah[3] his son reigned in his place.

Abijah Reigns in Judah

13 In the eighteenth year of King
Jeroboam, Abijah began to reign
over Judah. 2 He reigned for three years
in Jerusalem. His mother's name was
Micaiah[4] the daughter of Uriel of Gibeah.

Now there was war between Abijah and
Jeroboam. 3 Abijah went out to battle,
having an army of valiant men of war,
400,000 chosen men. And Jeroboam drew
up his line of battle against him with
800,000 chosen mighty warriors. 4 Then
Abijah stood up on Mount Zemaraim
that is in the hill country of Ephraim and
said, "Hear me, O Jeroboam and all Israel!
5 Ought you not to know that the LORD God
of Israel gave the kingship over Israel for-
ever to David and his sons by a covenant of
salt? 6 Yet Jeroboam the son of Nebat, a ser-
vant of Solomon the son of David, rose up
and rebelled against his lord, 7 and certain
worthless scoundrels gathered about him
and defied Rehoboam the son of Solomon,
when Rehoboam was young and irreso-
lute[5] and could not withstand them.

8 "And now you think to withstand the
kingdom of the LORD in the hand of the
sons of David, because you are a great
multitude and have with you the golden
calves that Jeroboam made you for gods.
9 Have you not driven out the priests of the
LORD, the sons of Aaron, and the Levites,
and made priests for yourselves like the
peoples of other lands? Whoever comes
for ordination[6] with a young bull or seven
rams becomes a priest of what are no
gods. 10 But as for us, the LORD is our God,
and we have not forsaken him. We have
priests ministering to the LORD who are
sons of Aaron, and Levites for their ser-
vice. 11 They offer to the LORD every morn-
ing and every evening burnt offerings and
incense of sweet spices, set out the show-
bread on the table of pure gold, and care
for the golden lampstand that its lamps
may burn every evening. For we keep the
charge of the LORD our God, but you have
forsaken him. 12 Behold, God is with us
at our head, and his priests with their
battle trumpets to sound the call to battle
against you. O sons of Israel, do not fight
against the LORD, the God of your fathers,
for you cannot succeed."

13 Jeroboam had sent an ambush around
to come upon them from behind. Thus
his troops[7] were in front of Judah, and the
ambush was behind them. 14 And when
Judah looked, behold, the battle was in
front of and behind them. And they cried
to the LORD, and the priests blew the trum-

[1] Hebrew *good things were found* [2] After *seer*, Hebrew adds *according to genealogy* [3] Spelled *Abijam* in 1 Kings 14:31 [4] Spelled *Maacah* in 1 Kings 15:2 [5] Hebrew *soft of heart* [6] Hebrew *to fill his hand* [7] Hebrew *they*

pets. 15 Then the men of Judah raised the battle shout. And when the men of Judah shouted, God defeated Jeroboam and all Israel before Abijah and Judah. 16 The men of Israel fled before Judah, and God gave them into their hand. 17 Abijah and his people struck them with great force, so there fell slain of Israel 500,000 chosen men. 18 Thus the men of Israel were subdued at that time, and the men of Judah prevailed, because they relied on the LORD, the God of their fathers. 19 And Abijah pursued Jeroboam and took cities from him, Bethel with its villages and Jeshanah with its villages and Ephron[1] with its villages. 20 Jeroboam did not recover his power in the days of Abijah. And the LORD struck him down, and he died. 21 But Abijah grew mighty. And he took fourteen wives and had twenty-two sons and sixteen daughters. 22 The rest of the acts of Abijah, his ways and his sayings, are written in the story of the prophet Iddo.

Asa Reigns in Judah

14 [2] Abijah slept with his fathers, and they buried him in the city of David. And Asa his son reigned in his place. In his days the land had rest for ten years. 2[3] And Asa did what was good and right in the eyes of the LORD his God. 3 He took away the foreign altars and the high places and broke down the pillars and cut down the Asherim 4 and commanded Judah to seek the LORD, the God of their fathers, and to keep the law and the commandment. 5 He also took out of all the cities of Judah the high places and the incense altars. And the kingdom had rest under him. 6 He built fortified cities in Judah, for the land had rest. He had no war in those years, for the LORD gave him peace. 7 And he said to Judah, "Let us build these cities and surround them with walls and towers, gates and bars. The land is still ours, because we have sought the LORD our God. We have sought him, and he has given us peace on every side." So they built and prospered. 8 And Asa had an army of 300,000 from Judah, armed with large shields and spears, and 280,000 men from Benjamin that carried shields and drew bows. All these were mighty men of valor.

9 Zerah the Ethiopian came out against them with an army of a million men and 300 chariots, and came as far as Mareshah. 10 And Asa went out to meet him, and they drew up their lines of battle in the Valley of Zephathah at Mareshah. 11 And Asa cried to the LORD his God, "O LORD, there is none like you to help, between the mighty and the weak. Help us, O LORD our God, for we rely on you, and in your name we have come against this multitude. O LORD, you are our God; let not man prevail against you." 12 So the LORD defeated the Ethiopians before Asa and before Judah, and the Ethiopians fled. 13 Asa and the people who were with him pursued them as far as Gerar, and the Ethiopians fell until none remained alive, for they were broken before the LORD and his army. The men of Judah[4] carried away very much spoil. 14 And they attacked all the cities around Gerar, for the fear of the LORD was upon them. They plundered all the cities, for there was much plunder in them. 15 And they struck down the tents of those who had livestock and carried away sheep in abundance and camels. Then they returned to Jerusalem.

Asa's Religious Reforms

15 The Spirit of God came upon Azariah the son of Oded, 2 and he went out to meet Asa and said to him, "Hear me, Asa, and all Judah and Benjamin: The LORD is with you while you are with him. If you seek him, he will be found by you, but if you forsake him, he will forsake you. 3 For a long time Israel was without the true God, and without a teaching priest and without law, 4 but when in their distress they turned to the LORD, the God of Israel, and sought him, he was found by them. 5 In

[1] Or *Ephrain* [2] Ch 13:23 in Hebrew [3] Ch 14:1 in Hebrew [4] Hebrew *they*

those times there was no peace to him who went out or to him who came in, for great disturbances afflicted all the inhabitants of the lands. 6 They were broken in pieces. Nation was crushed by nation and city by city, for God troubled them with every sort of distress. 7 But you, take courage! Do not let your hands be weak, for your work shall be rewarded."

8 As soon as Asa heard these words, the prophecy of Azariah the son of Oded, he took courage and put away the detestable idols from all the land of Judah and Benjamin and from the cities that he had taken in the hill country of Ephraim, and he repaired the altar of the LORD that was in front of the vestibule of the house of the LORD.[1] 9 And he gathered all Judah and Benjamin, and those from Ephraim, Manasseh, and Simeon who were residing with them, for great numbers had deserted to him from Israel when they saw that the LORD his God was with him. 10 They were gathered at Jerusalem in the third month of the fifteenth year of the reign of Asa. 11 They sacrificed to the LORD on that day from the spoil that they had brought 700 oxen and 7,000 sheep. 12 And they entered into a covenant to seek the LORD, the God of their fathers, with all their heart and with all their soul, 13 but that whoever would not seek the LORD, the God of Israel, should be put to death, whether young or old, man or woman. 14 They swore an oath to the LORD with a loud voice and with shouting and with trumpets and with horns. 15 And all Judah rejoiced over the oath, for they had sworn with all their heart and had sought him with their whole desire, and he was found by them, and the LORD gave them rest all around.

16 Even Maacah, his mother, King Asa removed from being queen mother because she had made a detestable image for Asherah. Asa cut down her image, crushed it, and burned it at the brook Kidron. 17 But the high places were not taken out of Israel. Nevertheless, the heart of Asa was wholly true all his days. 18 And he brought into the house of God the sacred gifts of his father and his own sacred gifts, silver, and gold, and vessels. 19 And there was no more war until the thirty-fifth year of the reign of Asa.

Asa's Last Years

16 In the thirty-sixth year of the reign of Asa, Baasha king of Israel went up against Judah and built Ramah, that he might permit no one to go out or come in to Asa king of Judah. 2 Then Asa took silver and gold from the treasures of the house of the LORD and the king's house and sent them to Ben-hadad king of Syria, who lived in Damascus, saying, 3 "There is a covenant[2] between me and you, as there was between my father and your father. Behold, I am sending to you silver and gold. Go, break your covenant with Baasha king of Israel, that he may withdraw from me." 4 And Ben-hadad listened to King Asa and sent the commanders of his armies against the cities of Israel, and they conquered Ijon, Dan, Abel-maim, and all the store cities of Naphtali. 5 And when Baasha heard of it, he stopped building Ramah and let his work cease. 6 Then King Asa took all Judah, and they carried away the stones of Ramah and its timber, with which Baasha had been building, and with them he built Geba and Mizpah.

7 At that time Hanani the seer came to Asa king of Judah and said to him, "Because you relied on the king of Syria, and did not rely on the LORD your God, the army of the king of Syria has escaped you. 8 Were not the Ethiopians and the Libyans a huge army with very many chariots and horsemen? Yet because you relied on the LORD, he gave them into your hand. 9 For the eyes of the LORD run to and fro throughout the whole earth, to give strong support to those whose heart is blameless toward him. You have done foolishly in this, for from now on you will have wars."

[1] Hebrew *the vestibule of the LORD* [2] Or *treaty;* twice in this verse

10 Then Asa was angry with the seer and
put him in the stocks in prison, for he was
in a rage with him because of this. And
Asa inflicted cruelties upon some of the
people at the same time.
11 The acts of Asa, from first to last, are
written in the Book of the Kings of Judah
and Israel. 12 In the thirty-ninth year of his
reign Asa was diseased in his feet, and his
disease became severe. Yet even in his dis-
ease he did not seek the LORD, but sought
help from physicians. 13 And Asa slept with
his fathers, dying in the forty-first year of
his reign. 14 They buried him in the tomb
that he had cut for himself in the city of
David. They laid him on a bier that had
been filled with various kinds of spices
prepared by the perfumer's art, and they
made a very great fire in his honor.

CHARACTER PROFILE

JEHOSHAPHAT

Jehoshaphat was one of Judah's good kings. He taught the people of Judah what God's Word said, and he led them in worshiping God. When an enemy army came against Judah, Jehoshaphat prayed. God promised him victory, and Jehoshaphat sent a choir praising God to lead the army into battle.

Jehoshaphat Reigns in Judah

17 Jehoshaphat his son reigned in his
place and strengthened himself
against Israel. 2 He placed forces in all the
fortified cities of Judah and set garrisons
in the land of Judah, and in the cities of
Ephraim that Asa his father had captured.
3 The LORD was with Jehoshaphat, because
he walked in the earlier ways of his father
David. He did not seek the Baals, 4 but
sought the God of his father and walked in
his commandments, and not according to
the practices of Israel. 5 Therefore the LORD
established the kingdom in his hand. And
all Judah brought tribute to Jehoshaphat,
and he had great riches and honor. 6 His
heart was courageous in the ways of the
LORD. And furthermore, he took the high
places and the Asherim out of Judah.
7 In the third year of his reign he sent
his officials, Ben-hail, Obadiah, Zechariah,
Nethanel, and Micaiah, to teach in the cit-
ies of Judah; 8 and with them the Levites,
Shemaiah, Nethaniah, Zebadiah, Asahel,
Shemiramoth, Jehonathan, Adonijah,
Tobijah, and Tobadonijah; and with these
Levites, the priests Elishama and Jehoram.
9 And they taught in Judah, having the
Book of the Law of the LORD with them.
They went about through all the cities of
Judah and taught among the people.
10 And the fear of the LORD fell upon
all the kingdoms of the lands that were
around Judah, and they made no war
against Jehoshaphat. 11 Some of the Phil-
istines brought Jehoshaphat presents and
silver for tribute, and the Arabians also
brought him 7,700 rams and 7,700 goats.
12 And Jehoshaphat grew steadily greater.
He built in Judah fortresses and store cit-
ies, 13 and he had large supplies in the
cities of Judah. He had soldiers, mighty
men of valor, in Jerusalem. 14 This was
the muster of them by fathers' houses:
Of Judah, the commanders of thousands:
Adnah the commander, with 300,000
mighty men of valor; 15 and next to him

Jehohanan the commander, with 280,000;
16 and next to him Amasiah the son of
Zichri, a volunteer for the service of the
LORD, with 200,000 mighty men of valor.
17 Of Benjamin: Eliada, a mighty man of
valor, with 200,000 men armed with bow
and shield; 18 and next to him Jehozabad
with 180,000 armed for war. 19 These were
in the service of the king, besides those
whom the king had placed in the fortified
cities throughout all Judah.

Jehoshaphat Allies with Ahab

18 Now Jehoshaphat had great riches
and honor, and he made a marriage
alliance with Ahab. 2 After some years he
went down to Ahab in Samaria. And Ahab
killed an abundance of sheep and oxen
for him and for the people who were with
him, and induced him to go up against
Ramoth-gilead. 3 Ahab king of Israel said
to Jehoshaphat king of Judah, "Will you go
with me to Ramoth-gilead?" He answered
him, "I am as you are, my people as your
people. We will be with you in the war."

4 And Jehoshaphat said to the king of
Israel, "Inquire first for the word of the
LORD." 5 Then the king of Israel gathered the
prophets together, four hundred men, and
said to them, "Shall we go to battle against
Ramoth-gilead, or shall I refrain?" And they
said, "Go up, for God will give it into the
hand of the king." 6 But Jehoshaphat said,
"Is there not here another prophet of the
LORD of whom we may inquire?" 7 And the
king of Israel said to Jehoshaphat, "There
is yet one man by whom we may inquire
of the LORD, Micaiah the son of Imlah;
but I hate him, for he never prophesies
good concerning me, but always evil." And
Jehoshaphat said, "Let not the king say so."
8 Then the king of Israel summoned an
officer and said, "Bring quickly Micaiah the
son of Imlah." 9 Now the king of Israel and
Jehoshaphat the king of Judah were sitting
on their thrones, arrayed in their robes.
And they were sitting at the threshing
floor at the entrance of the gate of Samaria,
and all the prophets were prophesying
before them. 10 And Zedekiah the son of
Chenaanah made for himself horns of iron
and said, "Thus says the LORD, 'With these
you shall push the Syrians until they are
destroyed.'" 11 And all the prophets proph-
esied so and said, "Go up to Ramoth-gilead
and triumph. The LORD will give it into the
hand of the king."

12 And the messenger who went to sum-
mon Micaiah said to him, "Behold, the
words of the prophets with one accord
are favorable to the king. Let your word be
like the word of one of them, and speak
favorably." 13 But Micaiah said, "As the LORD
lives, what my God says, that I will speak."
14 And when he had come to the king, the
king said to him, "Micaiah, shall we go to
Ramoth-gilead to battle, or shall I refrain?"
And he answered, "Go up and triumph;
they will be given into your hand." 15 But
the king said to him, "How many times
shall I make you swear that you speak to
me nothing but the truth in the name of
the LORD?" 16 And he said, "I saw all Israel
scattered on the mountains, as sheep that
have no shepherd. And the LORD said,
'These have no master; let each return
to his home in peace.'" 17 And the king of
Israel said to Jehoshaphat, "Did I not tell
you that he would not prophesy good con-
cerning me, but evil?" 18 And Micaiah said,
"Therefore hear the word of the LORD: I saw
the LORD sitting on his throne, and all the
host of heaven standing on his right hand
and on his left. 19 And the LORD said, 'Who
will entice Ahab the king of Israel, that
he may go up and fall at Ramoth-gilead?'
And one said one thing, and another said
another. 20 Then a spirit came forward and
stood before the LORD, saying, 'I will entice
him.' And the LORD said to him, 'By what
means?' 21 And he said, 'I will go out, and
will be a lying spirit in the mouth of all his
prophets.' And he said, 'You are to entice
him, and you shall succeed; go out and

do so.' 22 Now therefore behold, the LORD has put a lying spirit in the mouth of these your prophets. The LORD has declared disaster concerning you."

23 Then Zedekiah the son of Chenaanah came near and struck Micaiah on the cheek and said, "Which way did the Spirit of the LORD go from me to speak to you?" 24 And Micaiah said, "Behold, you shall see on that day when you go into an inner chamber to hide yourself." 25 And the king of Israel said, "Seize Micaiah and take him back to Amon the governor of the city and to Joash the king's son, 26 and say, 'Thus says the king, Put this fellow in prison and feed him with meager rations of bread and water until I return in peace.'" 27 And Micaiah said, "If you return in peace, the LORD has not spoken by me." And he said, "Hear, all you peoples!"

The Defeat and Death of Ahab

28 So the king of Israel and Jehoshaphat the king of Judah went up to Ramoth-gilead. 29 And the king of Israel said to Jehoshaphat, "I will disguise myself and go into battle, but you wear your robes." And the king of Israel disguised himself, and they went into battle. 30 Now the king of Syria had commanded the captains of his chariots, "Fight with neither small nor great, but only with the king of Israel." 31 As soon as the captains of the chariots saw Jehoshaphat, they said, "It is the king of Israel." So they turned to fight against him. And Jehoshaphat cried out, and the LORD helped him; God drew them away from him. 32 For as soon as the captains of the chariots saw that it was not the king of Israel, they turned back from pursuing him. 33 But a certain man drew his bow at random[1] and struck the king of Israel between the scale armor and the breastplate. Therefore he said to the driver of his chariot, "Turn around and carry me out of the battle, for I am wounded." 34 And the battle continued that day, and the king of Israel was propped up in his chariot facing the Syrians until evening. Then at sunset he died.

Jehoshaphat's Reforms

19 Jehoshaphat the king of Judah returned in safety to his house in Jerusalem. 2 But Jehu the son of Hanani the seer went out to meet him and said to King Jehoshaphat, "Should you help the wicked and love those who hate the LORD? Because of this, wrath has gone out against you from the LORD. 3 Nevertheless, some good is found in you, for you destroyed the Asherahs out of the land, and have set your heart to seek God."

4 Jehoshaphat lived at Jerusalem. And he went out again among the people, from Beersheba to the hill country of Ephraim, and brought them back to the LORD, the God of their fathers. 5 He appointed judges in the land in all the fortified cities of Judah, city by city, 6 and said to the judges, "Consider what you do, for you judge not for man but for the LORD. He is with you in giving judgment. 7 Now then, let the fear of the LORD be upon you. Be careful what you do, for there is no injustice with the LORD our God, or partiality or taking bribes."

8 Moreover, in Jerusalem Jehoshaphat appointed certain Levites and priests and heads of families of Israel, to give judgment for the LORD and to decide disputed cases. They had their seat at Jerusalem. 9 And he charged them: "Thus you shall do in the fear of the LORD, in faithfulness, and with your whole heart: 10 whenever a case comes to you from your brothers who live in their cities, concerning bloodshed, law or commandment, statutes or rules, then you shall warn them, that they may not incur guilt before the LORD and wrath may not come upon you and your brothers. Thus you shall do, and you will not incur guilt. 11 And behold, Amariah the chief priest is over you in all matters of the LORD; and Zebadiah the son of Ishmael,

[1] Hebrew *in his innocence*

the governor of the house of Judah, in all
the king's matters, and the Levites will
serve you as officers. Deal courageously,
and may the LORD be with the upright!"[1]

Jehoshaphat's Prayer

20 After this the Moabites and Am-
monites, and with them some of
the Meunites,[2] came against Jehoshaphat
for battle. 2 Some men came and told Je-
hoshaphat, "A great multitude is coming
against you from Edom,[3] from beyond
the sea; and, behold, they are in Hazazon-
tamar" (that is, Engedi). 3 Then Jehoshaphat
was afraid and set his face to seek the
LORD, and proclaimed a fast throughout all
Judah. 4 And Judah assembled to seek help
from the LORD; from all the cities of Judah
they came to seek the LORD.

5 And Jehoshaphat stood in the assembly
of Judah and Jerusalem, in the house of the
LORD, before the new court, 6 and said, "O
LORD, God of our fathers, are you not God
in heaven? You rule over all the kingdoms
of the nations. In your hand are power and
might, so that none is able to withstand
you. 7 Did you not, our God, drive out the
inhabitants of this land before your people
Israel, and give it forever to the descen-
dants of Abraham your friend? 8 And they
have lived in it and have built for you in it a
sanctuary for your name, saying, 9 'If disas-
ter comes upon us, the sword, judgment,[4]
or pestilence, or famine, we will stand
before this house and before you—for
your name is in this house—and cry out
to you in our affliction, and you will hear
and save.' 10 And now behold, the men of
Ammon and Moab and Mount Seir, whom
you would not let Israel invade when
they came from the land of Egypt, and
whom they avoided and did not destroy—
11 behold, they reward us by coming to
drive us out of your possession, which you
have given us to inherit. 12 O our God, will
you not execute judgment on them? For
we are powerless against this great horde
that is coming against us. We do not know
what to do, but our eyes are on you."

13 Meanwhile all Judah stood before the
LORD, with their little ones, their wives,
and their children. 14 And the Spirit of
the LORD came upon Jahaziel the son of
Zechariah, son of Benaiah, son of Jeiel, son
of Mattaniah, a Levite of the sons of Asaph,
in the midst of the assembly. 15 And he
said, "Listen, all Judah and inhabitants of
Jerusalem and King Jehoshaphat: Thus says
the LORD to you, 'Do not be afraid and do
not be dismayed at this great horde, for the
battle is not yours but God's. 16 Tomorrow
go down against them. Behold, they will
come up by the ascent of Ziz. You will find
them at the end of the valley, east of the
wilderness of Jeruel. 17 You will not need
to fight in this battle. Stand firm, hold your
position, and see the salvation of the LORD
on your behalf, O Judah and Jerusalem.'
Do not be afraid and do not be dismayed.
Tomorrow go out against them, and the
LORD will be with you."

18 Then Jehoshaphat bowed his head
with his face to the ground, and all Judah
and the inhabitants of Jerusalem fell down
before the LORD, worshiping the LORD.
19 And the Levites, of the Kohathites and
the Korahites, stood up to praise the LORD,
the God of Israel, with a very loud voice.

20 And they rose early in the morning
and went out into the wilderness of Tekoa.
And when they went out, Jehoshaphat
stood and said, "Hear me, Judah and inhab-
itants of Jerusalem! Believe in the LORD
your God, and you will be established;
believe his prophets, and you will suc-
ceed." 21 And when he had taken counsel
with the people, he appointed those who
were to sing to the LORD and praise him in
holy attire, as they went before the army,
and say,

"Give thanks to the LORD,
for his steadfast love endures
forever."

[1] Hebrew *the good* [2] Compare 26:7; Hebrew *Ammonites* [3] One Hebrew manuscript; most Hebrew manuscripts *Aram* (Syria) [4] Or *the sword of judgment*

22 And when they began to sing and praise, the LORD set an ambush against the men of Ammon, Moab, and Mount Seir, who had come against Judah, so that they were routed. 23 For the men of Ammon and Moab rose against the inhabitants of Mount Seir, devoting them to destruction, and when they had made an end of the inhabitants of Seir, they all helped to destroy one another.

The LORD Delivers Judah

24 When Judah came to the watchtower of the wilderness, they looked toward the horde, and behold, there[1] were dead bodies lying on the ground; none had escaped. 25 When Jehoshaphat and his people came to take their spoil, they found among them, in great numbers, goods, clothing, and precious things, which they took for themselves until they could carry no more. They were three days in taking the spoil, it was so much. 26 On the fourth day they assembled in the Valley of Beracah,[2] for there they blessed the LORD. Therefore the name of that place has been called the Valley of Beracah to this day. 27 Then they returned, every man of Judah and Jerusalem, and Jehoshaphat at their head, returning to Jerusalem with joy, for the LORD had made them rejoice over their enemies. 28 They came to Jerusalem with harps and lyres and trumpets, to the house of the LORD. 29 And the fear of God came on all the kingdoms of the countries when they heard that the LORD had fought against the enemies of Israel. 30 So the realm of Jehoshaphat was quiet, for his God gave him rest all around.

31 Thus Jehoshaphat reigned over Judah. He was thirty-five years old when he began to reign, and he reigned twenty-five years in Jerusalem. His mother's name was Azubah the daughter of Shilhi. 32 He walked in the way of Asa his father and did not turn aside from it, doing what was right in the sight of the LORD. 33 The high places, however, were not taken away; the people had not yet set their hearts upon the God of their fathers.

34 Now the rest of the acts of Jehoshaphat, from first to last, are written in the chronicles of Jehu the son of Hanani, which are recorded in the Book of the Kings of Israel.

The End of Jehoshaphat's Reign

35 After this Jehoshaphat king of Judah joined with Ahaziah king of Israel, who acted wickedly. 36 He joined him in building ships to go to Tarshish, and they built the ships in Ezion-geber. 37 Then Eliezer the son of Dodavahu of Mareshah prophesied against Jehoshaphat, saying, "Because you have joined with Ahaziah, the LORD will destroy what you have made." And the ships were wrecked and were not able to go to Tarshish.

Jehoram Reigns in Judah

21 Jehoshaphat slept with his fathers and was buried with his fathers in the city of David, and Jehoram his son reigned in his place. 2 He had brothers, the sons of Jehoshaphat: Azariah, Jehiel, Zechariah, Azariah, Michael, and Shephatiah; all these were the sons of Jehoshaphat king of Israel.[3] 3 Their father gave them great gifts of silver, gold, and valuable possessions, together with fortified cities in Judah, but he gave the kingdom to Jehoram, because he was the firstborn. 4 When Jehoram had ascended the throne of his father and was established, he killed all his brothers with the sword, and also some of the princes of Israel. 5 Jehoram was thirty-two years old when he became king, and he reigned eight years in Jerusalem. 6 And he walked in the way of the kings of Israel, as the house of Ahab had done, for the daughter of Ahab was his wife. And he did what was evil in the sight of the LORD. 7 Yet the LORD was not willing to destroy the house of David, because of the covenant that he had made with David, and since he had promised to give a lamp to him and to his sons forever.

[1] Hebrew *they* [2] *Beracah* means *blessing* [3] That is, Judah

8 In his days Edom revolted from the
rule of Judah and set up a king of their
own. 9 Then Jehoram passed over with his
commanders and all his chariots, and he
rose by night and struck the Edomites who
had surrounded him and his chariot com-
manders. 10 So Edom revolted from the rule
of Judah to this day. At that time Libnah
also revolted from his rule, because he had
forsaken the LORD, the God of his fathers.

11 Moreover, he made high places in
the hill country of Judah and led the in-
habitants of Jerusalem into whoredom
and made Judah go astray. 12 And a let-
ter came to him from Elijah the prophet,
saying, "Thus says the LORD, the God
of David your father, 'Because you have
not walked in the ways of Jehoshaphat
your father, or in the ways of Asa king of
Judah, 13 but have walked in the way of
the kings of Israel and have enticed Judah
and the inhabitants of Jerusalem into
whoredom, as the house of Ahab led Israel
into whoredom, and also you have killed
your brothers, of your father's house, who
were better than yourself, 14 behold, the
LORD will bring a great plague on your
people, your children, your wives, and all
your possessions, 15 and you yourself will
have a severe sickness with a disease of
your bowels, until your bowels come out
because of the disease, day by day.'"

16 And the LORD stirred up against
Jehoram the anger[1] of the Philistines
and of the Arabians who are near the
Ethiopians. 17 And they came up against
Judah and invaded it and carried away all
the possessions they found that belonged
to the king's house, and also his sons and
his wives, so that no son was left to him
except Jehoahaz, his youngest son.

18 And after all this the LORD struck him
in his bowels with an incurable disease.
19 In the course of time, at the end of two
years, his bowels came out because of the
disease, and he died in great agony. His
people made no fire in his honor, like the
fires made for his fathers. 20 He was thirty-
two years old when he began to reign, and
he reigned eight years in Jerusalem. And
he departed with no one's regret. They
buried him in the city of David, but not in
the tombs of the kings.

Ahaziah Reigns in Judah

22 And the inhabitants of Jerusalem
made Ahaziah, his youngest son,
king in his place, for the band of men that
came with the Arabians to the camp had
killed all the older sons. So Ahaziah the
son of Jehoram king of Judah reigned.
2 Ahaziah was twenty-two years old when
he began to reign, and he reigned one
year in Jerusalem. His mother's name was
Athaliah, the granddaughter of Omri. 3 He
also walked in the ways of the house of
Ahab, for his mother was his counselor
in doing wickedly. 4 He did what was evil
in the sight of the LORD, as the house of
Ahab had done. For after the death of his
father they were his counselors, to his
undoing. 5 He even followed their counsel
and went with Jehoram the son of Ahab
king of Israel to make war against Hazael
king of Syria at Ramoth-gilead. And the
Syrians wounded Joram, 6 and he returned
to be healed in Jezreel of the wounds that
he had received at Ramah, when he fought
against Hazael king of Syria. And Ahaziah
the son of Jehoram king of Judah went
down to see Joram the son of Ahab in
Jezreel, because he was wounded.

7 But it was ordained by God that the
downfall of Ahaziah should come about
through his going to visit Joram. For when
he came there, he went out with Jehoram
to meet Jehu the son of Nimshi, whom the
LORD had anointed to destroy the house
of Ahab. 8 And when Jehu was executing
judgment on the house of Ahab, he met
the princes of Judah and the sons of Aha-
ziah's brothers, who attended Ahaziah,
and he killed them. 9 He searched for Aha-
ziah, and he was captured while hiding in

[1] Hebrew *spirit*

Samaria, and he was brought to Jehu and put to death. They buried him, for they said, "He is the grandson of Jehoshaphat, who sought the LORD with all his heart." And the house of Ahaziah had no one able to rule the kingdom.

Athaliah Reigns in Judah

10 Now when Athaliah the mother of Ahaziah saw that her son was dead, she arose and destroyed all the royal family of the house of Judah. 11 But Jehoshabeath,[1] the daughter of the king, took Joash the son of Ahaziah and stole him away from among the king's sons who were about to be put to death, and she put him and his nurse in a bedroom. Thus Jehoshabeath, the daughter of King Jehoram and wife of Jehoiada the priest, because she was a sister of Ahaziah, hid him[2] from Athaliah, so that she did not put him to death. 12 And he remained with them six years, hidden in the house of God, while Athaliah reigned over the land.

Joash Made King

23 But in the seventh year Jehoiada took courage and entered into a covenant with the commanders of hundreds, Azariah the son of Jeroham, Ishmael the son of Jehohanan, Azariah the son of Obed, Maaseiah the son of Adaiah, and Elishaphat the son of Zichri. 2 And they went about through Judah and gathered the Levites from all the cities of Judah, and the heads of fathers' houses of Israel, and they came to Jerusalem. 3 And all the assembly made a covenant with the king in the house of God. And Jehoiada[3] said to them, "Behold, the king's son! Let him reign, as the LORD spoke concerning the sons of David. 4 This is the thing that you shall do: of you priests and Levites who come off duty on the Sabbath, one third shall be gatekeepers, 5 and one third shall be at the king's house and one third at the Gate of the Foundation. And all the people shall be in the courts of the house of the LORD. 6 Let no one enter the house of the LORD except the priests and ministering Levites. They may enter, for they are holy, but all the people shall keep the charge of the LORD. 7 The Levites shall surround the king, each with his weapons in his hand. And whoever enters the house shall be put to death. Be with the king when he comes in and when he goes out."

8 The Levites and all Judah did according to all that Jehoiada the priest commanded, and they each brought his men, who were to go off duty on the Sabbath, with those who were to come on duty on the Sabbath, for Jehoiada the priest did not dismiss the divisions. 9 And Jehoiada the priest gave to the captains the spears and the large and small shields that had been King David's, which were in the house of God. 10 And he set all the people as a guard for the king, every man with his weapon in his hand, from the south side of the house to the north side of the house, around the altar and the house. 11 Then they brought out the king's son and put the crown on him and gave him the testimony. And they proclaimed him king, and Jehoiada and his sons anointed him, and they said, "Long live the king."

Athaliah Executed

12 When Athaliah heard the noise of the people running and praising the king, she went into the house of the LORD to the people. 13 And when she looked, there was the king standing by his pillar at the entrance, and the captains and the trumpeters beside the king, and all the people of the land rejoicing and blowing trumpets, and the singers with their musical instruments leading in the celebration. And Athaliah tore her clothes and cried, "Treason! Treason!" 14 Then Jehoiada the priest brought out the captains who were set over the army, saying to them, "Bring her out between the ranks, and anyone who follows her is to be put to death with

[1] Spelled *Jehosheba* in 2 Kings 11:2 [2] That is, Joash [3] Hebrew *he*

the sword." For the priest said, "Do not put her to death in the house of the LORD." 15 So they laid hands on her,[1] and she went into the entrance of the horse gate of the king's house, and they put her to death there.

Jehoiada's Reforms

16 And Jehoiada made a covenant between himself and all the people and the king that they should be the LORD's people. 17 Then all the people went to the house of Baal and tore it down; his altars and his images they broke in pieces, and they killed Mattan the priest of Baal before the altars. 18 And Jehoiada posted watchmen for the house of the LORD under the direction of the Levitical priests and the Levites whom David had organized to be in charge of the house of the LORD, to offer burnt offerings to the LORD, as it is written in the Law of Moses, with rejoicing and with singing, according to the order of David. 19 He stationed the gatekeepers at the gates of the house of the LORD so that no one should enter who was in any way unclean. 20 And he took the captains, the nobles, the governors of the people, and all the people of the land, and they brought the king down from the house of the LORD, marching through the upper gate to the king's house. And they set the king on the royal throne. 21 So all the people of the land rejoiced, and the city was quiet after Athaliah had been put to death with the sword.

Joash Repairs the Temple

24 Joash[2] was seven years old when he began to reign, and he reigned forty years in Jerusalem. His mother's name was Zibiah of Beersheba. 2 And Joash did what was right in the eyes of the LORD all the days of Jehoiada the priest. 3 Jehoiada got for him two wives, and he had sons and daughters.

4 After this Joash decided to restore the house of the LORD. 5 And he gathered the priests and the Levites and said to them, "Go out to the cities of Judah and gather from all Israel money to repair the house of your God from year to year, and see that you act quickly." But the Levites did not act quickly. 6 So the king summoned Jehoiada the chief and said to him, "Why have you not required the Levites to bring in from Judah and Jerusalem the tax levied by Moses, the servant of the LORD, and the congregation of Israel for the tent of testimony?" 7 For the sons of Athaliah, that wicked woman, had broken into the house of God, and had also used all the dedicated things of the house of the LORD for the Baals.

8 So the king commanded, and they made a chest and set it outside the gate of the house of the LORD. 9 And proclamation was made throughout Judah and Jerusalem to bring in for the LORD the tax that Moses the servant of God laid on Israel in the wilderness. 10 And all the princes and all the people rejoiced and brought their tax and dropped it into the chest until they had finished.[3] 11 And whenever the chest was brought to the king's officers by the Levites, when they saw that there was much money in it, the king's secretary and the officer of the chief priest would come and empty the chest and take it and return it to its place. Thus they did day after day, and collected money in abundance. 12 And the king and Jehoiada gave it to those who had charge of the work of the house of the LORD, and they hired masons and carpenters to restore the house of the LORD, and also workers in iron and bronze to repair the house of the LORD. 13 So those who were engaged in the work labored, and the repairing went forward in their hands, and they restored the house of God to its proper condition and strengthened it. 14 And when they had finished, they brought the rest of the money before the king and Jehoiada, and with it were made utensils for the house of the LORD, both for the service and for the burnt offerings, and dishes for incense and vessels of gold

[1] Or *they made a passage for her* [2] Spelled *Jehoash* in 2 Kings 12:1 [3] Or *until it was full*

and silver. And they offered burnt offerings in the house of the LORD regularly all the days of Jehoiada.

15 But Jehoiada grew old and full of days, and died. He was 130 years old at his death. 16 And they buried him in the city of David among the kings, because he had done good in Israel, and toward God and his house.

17 Now after the death of Jehoiada the princes of Judah came and paid homage to the king. Then the king listened to them. 18 And they abandoned the house of the LORD, the God of their fathers, and served the Asherim and the idols. And wrath came upon Judah and Jerusalem for this guilt of theirs. 19 Yet he sent prophets among them to bring them back to the LORD. These testified against them, but they would not pay attention.

Joash's Treachery

20 Then the Spirit of God clothed Zechariah the son of Jehoiada the priest, and he stood above the people, and said to them, "Thus says God, 'Why do you break the commandments of the LORD, so that you cannot prosper? Because you have forsaken the LORD, he has forsaken you.'" 21 But they conspired against him, and by command of the king they stoned him with stones in the court of the house of the LORD. 22 Thus Joash the king did not remember the kindness that Jehoiada, Zechariah's father, had shown him, but killed his son. And when he was dying, he said, "May the LORD see and avenge!"[1]

Joash Assassinated

23 At the end of the year the army of the Syrians came up against Joash. They came to Judah and Jerusalem and destroyed all the princes of the people from among the people and sent all their spoil to the king of Damascus. 24 Though the army of the Syrians had come with few men, the LORD delivered into their hand a very great army, because Judah[2] had forsaken the LORD, the God of their fathers. Thus they executed judgment on Joash.

25 When they had departed from him, leaving him severely wounded, his servants conspired against him because of the blood of the son[3] of Jehoiada the priest, and killed him on his bed. So he died, and they buried him in the city of David, but they did not bury him in the tombs of the kings. 26 Those who conspired against him were Zabad the son of Shimeath the Ammonite, and Jehozabad the son of Shimrith the Moabite. 27 Accounts of his sons and of the many oracles against him and of the rebuilding[4] of the house of God are written in the Story of the Book of the Kings. And Amaziah his son reigned in his place.

Amaziah Reigns in Judah

25 Amaziah was twenty-five years old when he began to reign, and he reigned twenty-nine years in Jerusalem. His mother's name was Jehoaddan of Jerusalem. 2 And he did what was right in the eyes of the LORD, yet not with a whole heart. 3 And as soon as the royal power was firmly his, he killed his servants who had struck down the king his father. 4 But he did not put their children to death, according to what is written in the Law, in the Book of Moses, where the LORD commanded, "Fathers shall not die because of their children, nor children die because of their fathers, but each one shall die for his own sin."

Amaziah's Victories

5 Then Amaziah assembled the men of Judah and set them by fathers' houses under commanders of thousands and of hundreds for all Judah and Benjamin. He mustered those twenty years old and upward, and found that they were 300,000 choice men, fit for war, able to handle spear and shield. 6 He hired also 100,000 mighty men of valor from Israel for 100 talents[5] of silver. 7 But a man of God came

[1] Hebrew *and seek* [2] Hebrew *they* [3] Septuagint, Vulgate; Hebrew *sons* [4] Hebrew *founding* [5] A *talent* was about 75 pounds or 34 kilograms

to him and said, "O king, do not let the
army of Israel go with you, for the LORD is
not with Israel, with all these Ephraimites.
8 But go, act, be strong for the battle. Why
should you suppose that God will cast
you down before the enemy? For God
has power to help or to cast down." 9 And
Amaziah said to the man of God, "But what
shall we do about the hundred talents that
I have given to the army of Israel?" The
man of God answered, "The LORD is able
to give you much more than this." 10 Then
Amaziah discharged the army that had
come to him from Ephraim to go home
again. And they became very angry with
Judah and returned home in fierce anger.
11 But Amaziah took courage and led out
his people and went to the Valley of Salt
and struck down 10,000 men of Seir. 12 The
men of Judah captured another 10,000
alive and took them to the top of a rock
and threw them down from the top of the
rock, and they were all dashed to pieces.
13 But the men of the army whom Amaziah
sent back, not letting them go with him
to battle, raided the cities of Judah, from
Samaria to Beth-horon, and struck down
3,000 people in them and took much spoil.

Amaziah's Idolatry

14 After Amaziah came from striking
down the Edomites, he brought the gods
of the men of Seir and set them up as
his gods and worshiped them, making
offerings to them. 15 Therefore the LORD
was angry with Amaziah and sent to him
a prophet, who said to him, "Why have
you sought the gods of a people who did
not deliver their own people from your
hand?" 16 But as he was speaking, the
king said to him, "Have we made you a
royal counselor? Stop! Why should you be
struck down?" So the prophet stopped, but
said, "I know that God has determined to
destroy you, because you have done this
and have not listened to my counsel."

Israel Defeats Amaziah

17 Then Amaziah king of Judah took
counsel and sent to Joash the son of
Jehoahaz, son of Jehu, king of Israel, say-
ing, "Come, let us look one another in the
face." 18 And Joash the king of Israel sent
word to Amaziah king of Judah, "A thistle
on Lebanon sent to a cedar on Lebanon,
saying, 'Give your daughter to my son for
a wife,' and a wild beast of Lebanon passed
by and trampled down the thistle. 19 You
say, 'See, I[1] have struck down Edom,' and
your heart has lifted you up in boastful-
ness. But now stay at home. Why should
you provoke trouble so that you fall, you
and Judah with you?"
20 But Amaziah would not listen, for it
was of God, in order that he might give
them into the hand of their enemies,
because they had sought the gods of
Edom. 21 So Joash king of Israel went up,
and he and Amaziah king of Judah faced
one another in battle at Beth-shemesh,
which belongs to Judah. 22 And Judah was
defeated by Israel, and every man fled to
his home. 23 And Joash king of Israel cap-
tured Amaziah king of Judah, the son of
Joash, son of Ahaziah, at Beth-shemesh,
and brought him to Jerusalem and broke
down the wall of Jerusalem for 400 cubits,[2]
from the Ephraim Gate to the Corner Gate.
24 And he seized all the gold and silver,
and all the vessels that were found in the
house of God, in the care of Obed-edom.
He seized also the treasuries of the king's
house, also hostages, and he returned to
Samaria.
25 Amaziah the son of Joash, king of
Judah, lived fifteen years after the death
of Joash the son of Jehoahaz, king of Israel.
26 Now the rest of the deeds of Amaziah,
from first to last, are they not written in
the Book of the Kings of Judah and Israel?
27 From the time when he turned away
from the LORD they made a conspiracy
against him in Jerusalem, and he fled to
Lachish. But they sent after him to Lachish

[1] Hebrew *you* [2] A *cubit* was about 18 inches or 45 centimeters

and put him to death there. 28 And they brought him upon horses, and he was buried with his fathers in the city of David.[1]

Uzziah Reigns in Judah

26 And all the people of Judah took Uzziah, who was sixteen years old, and made him king instead of his father Amaziah. 2 He built Eloth and restored it to Judah, after the king slept with his fathers. 3 Uzziah was sixteen years old when he began to reign, and he reigned fifty-two years in Jerusalem. His mother's name was Jecoliah of Jerusalem. 4 And he did what was right in the eyes of the LORD, according to all that his father Amaziah had done. 5 He set himself to seek God in the days of Zechariah, who instructed him in the fear of God, and as long as he sought the LORD, God made him prosper.

6 He went out and made war against the Philistines and broke through the wall of Gath and the wall of Jabneh and the wall of Ashdod, and he built cities in the territory of Ashdod and elsewhere among the Philistines. 7 God helped him against the Philistines and against the Arabians who lived in Gurbaal and against the Meunites. 8 The Ammonites paid tribute to Uzziah, and his fame spread even to the border of Egypt, for he became very strong. 9 Moreover, Uzziah built towers in Jerusalem at the Corner Gate and at the Valley Gate and at the Angle, and fortified them. 10 And he built towers in the wilderness and cut out many cisterns, for he had large herds, both in the Shephelah and in the plain, and he had farmers and vinedressers in the hills and in the fertile lands, for he loved the soil. 11 Moreover, Uzziah had an army of soldiers, fit for war, in divisions according to the numbers in the muster made by Jeiel the secretary and Maaseiah the officer, under the direction of Hananiah, one of the king's commanders. 12 The whole number of the heads of fathers' houses of mighty men of valor was 2,600. 13 Under their command was an army of 307,500, who could make war with mighty power, to help the king against the enemy. 14 And Uzziah prepared for all the army shields, spears, helmets, coats of mail, bows, and stones for slinging. 15 In Jerusalem he made engines, invented by skillful men, to be on the towers and the corners, to shoot arrows and great stones. And his fame spread far, for he was marvelously helped, till he was strong.

Uzziah's Pride and Punishment

16 But when he was strong, he grew proud, to his destruction. For he was unfaithful to the LORD his God and entered the temple of the LORD to burn incense on the altar of incense. 17 But Azariah the priest went in after him, with eighty priests of the LORD who were men of valor, 18 and they withstood King Uzziah and said to him, "It is not for you, Uzziah, to burn incense to the LORD, but for the priests, the sons of Aaron, who are consecrated to burn incense. Go out of the sanctuary, for you have done wrong, and it will bring you no honor from the LORD God." 19 Then Uzziah was angry. Now he had a censer in his hand to burn incense, and when he became angry with the priests, leprosy[2] broke out on his forehead in the presence of the priests in the house of the LORD, by the altar of incense. 20 And Azariah the chief priest and all the priests looked at him, and behold, he was leprous in his forehead! And they rushed him out quickly, and he himself hurried to go out, because the LORD had struck him. 21 And King Uzziah was a leper to the day of his death, and being a leper lived in a separate house, for he was excluded from the house of the LORD. And Jotham his son was over the king's household, governing the people of the land.

22 Now the rest of the acts of Uzziah, from first to last, Isaiah the prophet the son of Amoz wrote. 23 And Uzziah slept

[1] Hebrew *of Judah* [2] *Leprosy* was a term for several skin diseases; see Leviticus 13

with his fathers, and they buried him with his fathers in the burial field that belonged to the kings, for they said, "He is a leper." And Jotham his son reigned in his place.

Jotham Reigns in Judah

27 Jotham was twenty-five years old when he began to reign, and he reigned sixteen years in Jerusalem. His mother's name was Jerushah the daughter of Zadok. **2** And he did what was right in the eyes of the LORD according to all that his father Uzziah had done, except he did not enter the temple of the LORD. But the people still followed corrupt practices. **3** He built the upper gate of the house of the LORD and did much building on the wall of Ophel. **4** Moreover, he built cities in the hill country of Judah, and forts and towers on the wooded hills. **5** He fought with the king of the Ammonites and prevailed against them. And the Ammonites gave him that year 100 talents[1] of silver, and 10,000 cors[2] of wheat and 10,000 of barley. The Ammonites paid him the same amount in the second and the third years. **6** So Jotham became mighty, because he ordered his ways before the LORD his God. **7** Now the rest of the acts of Jotham, and all his wars and his ways, behold, they are written in the Book of the Kings of Israel and Judah. **8** He was twenty-five years old when he began to reign, and he reigned sixteen years in Jerusalem. **9** And Jotham slept with his fathers, and they buried him in the city of David, and Ahaz his son reigned in his place.

Ahaz Reigns in Judah

28 Ahaz was twenty years old when he began to reign, and he reigned sixteen years in Jerusalem. And he did not do what was right in the eyes of the LORD, as his father David had done, **2** but he walked in the ways of the kings of Israel. He even made metal images for the Baals, **3** and he made offerings in the Valley of the Son of Hinnom and burned his sons as an offering,[3] according to the abominations of the nations whom the LORD drove out before the people of Israel. **4** And he sacrificed and made offerings on the high places and on the hills and under every green tree.

Judah Defeated

5 Therefore the LORD his God gave him into the hand of the king of Syria, who defeated him and took captive a great number of his people and brought them to Damascus. He was also given into the hand of the king of Israel, who struck him with great force. **6** For Pekah the son of Remaliah killed 120,000 from Judah in one day, all of them men of valor, because they had forsaken the LORD, the God of their fathers. **7** And Zichri, a mighty man of Ephraim, killed Maaseiah the king's son and Azrikam the commander of the palace and Elkanah the next in authority to the king.

8 The men of Israel took captive 200,000 of their relatives, women, sons, and daughters. They also took much spoil from them and brought the spoil to Samaria. **9** But a prophet of the LORD was there, whose name was Oded, and he went out to meet the army that came to Samaria and said to them, "Behold, because the LORD, the God of your fathers, was angry with Judah, he gave them into your hand, but you have killed them in a rage that has reached up to heaven. **10** And now you intend to subjugate the people of Judah and Jerusalem, male and female, as your slaves. Have you not sins of your own against the LORD your God? **11** Now hear me, and send back the captives from your relatives whom you have taken, for the fierce wrath of the LORD is upon you."

12 Certain chiefs also of the men of Ephraim, Azariah the son of Johanan, Berechiah the son of Meshillemoth, Jehizkiah the son of Shallum, and Amasa the son of Hadlai, stood up against those who were coming from the war **13** and

[1] A *talent* was about 75 pounds or 34 kilograms [2] A *cor* was about 6 bushels or 220 liters [3] Hebrew *made his sons pass through the fire*

said to them, "You shall not bring the captives in here, for you propose to bring upon us guilt against the LORD in addition to our present sins and guilt. For our guilt is already great, and there is fierce wrath against Israel." 14 So the armed men left the captives and the spoil before the princes and all the assembly. 15 And the men who have been mentioned by name rose and took the captives, and with the spoil they clothed all who were naked among them. They clothed them, gave them sandals, provided them with food and drink, and anointed them, and carrying all the feeble among them on donkeys, they brought them to their kinsfolk at Jericho, the city of palm trees. Then they returned to Samaria.

16 At that time King Ahaz sent to the king[1] of Assyria for help. 17 For the Edomites had again invaded and defeated Judah and carried away captives. 18 And the Philistines had made raids on the cities in the Shephelah and the Negeb of Judah, and had taken Beth-shemesh, Aijalon, Gederoth, Soco with its villages, Timnah with its villages, and Gimzo with its villages. And they settled there. 19 For the LORD humbled Judah because of Ahaz king of Israel, for he had made Judah act sinfully[2] and had been very unfaithful to the LORD. 20 So Tiglath-pileser[3] king of Assyria came against him and afflicted him instead of strengthening him. 21 For Ahaz took a portion from the house of the LORD and the house of the king and of the princes, and gave tribute to the king of Assyria, but it did not help him.

Ahaz's Idolatry

22 In the time of his distress he became yet more faithless to the LORD—this same King Ahaz. 23 For he sacrificed to the gods of Damascus that had defeated him and said, "Because the gods of the kings of Syria helped them, I will sacrifice to them that they may help me." But they were the ruin of him and of all Israel. 24 And Ahaz gathered together the vessels of the house of God and cut in pieces the vessels of the house of God, and he shut up the doors of the house of the LORD, and he made himself altars in every corner of Jerusalem. 25 In every city of Judah he made high places to make offerings to other gods, provoking to anger the LORD, the God of his fathers. 26 Now the rest of his acts and all his ways, from first to last, behold, they are written in the Book of the Kings of Judah and Israel. 27 And Ahaz slept with his fathers, and they buried him in the city, in Jerusalem, for they did not bring him into the tombs of the kings of Israel. And Hezekiah his son reigned in his place.

Hezekiah Reigns in Judah

29 Hezekiah began to reign when he was twenty-five years old, and he reigned twenty-nine years in Jerusalem. His mother's name was Abijah[4] the daughter of Zechariah. 2 And he did what was right in the eyes of the LORD, according to all that David his father had done.

Hezekiah Cleanses the Temple

3 In the first year of his reign, in the first month, he opened the doors of the house of the LORD and repaired them. 4 He brought in the priests and the Levites and assembled them in the square on the east 5 and said to them, "Hear me, Levites! Now consecrate yourselves, and consecrate the house of the LORD, the God of your fathers, and carry out the filth from the Holy Place. 6 For our fathers have been unfaithful and have done what was evil in the sight of the LORD our God. They have forsaken him and have turned away their faces from the habitation of the LORD and turned their backs. 7 They also shut the doors of the vestibule and put out the lamps and have not burned incense or offered burnt offerings in the Holy Place to the God of Israel. 8 Therefore the wrath of the LORD came on Judah and Jerusalem,

[1] Septuagint, Syriac, Vulgate (compare 2 Kings 16:7); Hebrew *kings* [2] Or *wildly* [3] Hebrew *Tilgath-pilneser* [4] Spelled *Abi* in 2 Kings 18:2

and he has made them an object of hor-
ror, of astonishment, and of hissing, as
you see with your own eyes. 9 For behold,
our fathers have fallen by the sword, and
our sons and our daughters and our wives
are in captivity for this. 10 Now it is in my
heart to make a covenant with the LORD,
the God of Israel, in order that his fierce
anger may turn away from us. 11 My sons,
do not now be negligent, for the LORD has
chosen you to stand in his presence, to
minister to him and to be his ministers
and make offerings to him."

12 Then the Levites arose, Mahath the
son of Amasai, and Joel the son of Azariah,
of the sons of the Kohathites; and of the
sons of Merari, Kish the son of Abdi, and
Azariah the son of Jehallelel; and of the
Gershonites, Joah the son of Zimmah, and
Eden the son of Joah; 13 and of the sons
of Elizaphan, Shimri and Jeuel; and of the
sons of Asaph, Zechariah and Mattaniah;
14 and of the sons of Heman, Jehuel and
Shimei; and of the sons of Jeduthun,
Shemaiah and Uzziel. 15 They gathered
their brothers and consecrated themselves
and went in as the king had commanded,
by the words of the LORD, to cleanse the
house of the LORD. 16 The priests went
into the inner part of the house of the
LORD to cleanse it, and they brought out
all the uncleanness that they found in the
temple of the LORD into the court of the
house of the LORD. And the Levites took
it and carried it out to the brook Kidron.
17 They began to consecrate on the first
day of the first month, and on the eighth
day of the month they came to the vesti-
bule of the LORD. Then for eight days they
consecrated the house of the LORD, and on
the sixteenth day of the first month they
finished. 18 Then they went in to Hezekiah
the king and said, "We have cleansed all
the house of the LORD, the altar of burnt
offering and all its utensils, and the table
for the showbread and all its utensils. 19 All
the utensils that King Ahaz discarded in
his reign when he was faithless, we have
made ready and consecrated, and behold,
they are before the altar of the LORD."

Hezekiah Restores Temple Worship

20 Then Hezekiah the king rose early
and gathered the officials of the city and
went up to the house of the LORD. 21 And
they brought seven bulls, seven rams,
seven lambs, and seven male goats for a
sin offering for the kingdom and for the
sanctuary and for Judah. And he com-
manded the priests, the sons of Aaron, to
offer them on the altar of the LORD. 22 So
they slaughtered the bulls, and the priests
received the blood and threw it against the
altar. And they slaughtered the rams, and
their blood was thrown against the altar.

CHARACTER PROFILE

HEZEKIAH

Hezekiah was a godly king in Judah. When the Assyrian army came to attack Jerusalem, Hezekiah prayed, and the angel of the LORD killed 185,000 enemy soldiers in the night. When Hezekiah was sick, he prayed, and God healed him. The sundial's shadow went backward as a sign that Hezekiah would get well.

615

And they slaughtered the lambs, and their blood was thrown against the altar. 23 Then the goats for the sin offering were brought to the king and the assembly, and they laid their hands on them, 24 and the priests slaughtered them and made a sin offering with their blood on the altar, to make atonement for all Israel. For the king commanded that the burnt offering and the sin offering should be made for all Israel.

25 And he stationed the Levites in the house of the LORD with cymbals, harps, and lyres, according to the commandment of David and of Gad the king's seer and of Nathan the prophet, for the commandment was from the LORD through his prophets. 26 The Levites stood with the instruments of David, and the priests with the trumpets. 27 Then Hezekiah commanded that the burnt offering be offered on the altar. And when the burnt offering began, the song to the LORD began also, and the trumpets, accompanied by the instruments of David king of Israel. 28 The whole assembly worshiped, and the singers sang, and the trumpeters sounded. All this continued until the burnt offering was finished. 29 When the offering was finished, the king and all who were present with him bowed themselves and worshiped. 30 And Hezekiah the king and the officials commanded the Levites to sing praises to the LORD with the words of David and of Asaph the seer. And they sang praises with gladness, and they bowed down and worshiped.

31 Then Hezekiah said, "You have now consecrated yourselves to[1] the LORD. Come near; bring sacrifices and thank offerings to the house of the LORD." And the assembly brought sacrifices and thank offerings, and all who were of a willing heart brought burnt offerings. 32 The number of the burnt offerings that the assembly brought was 70 bulls, 100 rams, and 200 lambs; all these were for a burnt offering to the LORD. 33 And the consecrated offerings were 600 bulls and 3,000 sheep. 34 But the priests were too few and could not flay all the burnt offerings, so until other priests had consecrated themselves, their brothers the Levites helped them, until the work was finished—for the Levites were more upright in heart than the priests in consecrating themselves. 35 Besides the great number of burnt offerings, there was the fat of the peace offerings, and there were the drink offerings for the burnt offerings. Thus the service of the house of the LORD was restored. 36 And Hezekiah and all the people rejoiced because God had prepared for the people, for the thing came about suddenly.

Passover Celebrated

30 Hezekiah sent to all Israel and Judah, and wrote letters also to Ephraim and Manasseh, that they should come to the house of the LORD at Jerusalem to keep the Passover to the LORD, the God of Israel. 2 For the king and his princes and all the assembly in Jerusalem had taken counsel to keep the Passover in the second month— 3 for they could not keep it at that time because the priests had not consecrated themselves in sufficient number, nor had the people assembled in Jerusalem— 4 and the plan seemed right to the king and all the assembly. 5 So they decreed to make a proclamation throughout all Israel, from Beersheba to Dan, that the people should come and keep the Passover to the LORD, the God of Israel, at Jerusalem, for they had not kept it as often as prescribed. 6 So couriers went throughout all Israel and Judah with letters from the king and his princes, as the king had commanded, saying, "O people of Israel, return to the LORD, the God of Abraham, Isaac, and Israel, that he may turn again to the remnant of you who have escaped from the hand of the kings of Assyria. 7 Do not be like your fathers and your brothers, who were faithless to the

[1] Hebrew *filled your hand for*

LORD God of their fathers, so that he made them a desolation, as you see. 8 Do not now be stiff-necked as your fathers were, but yield yourselves to the LORD and come to his sanctuary, which he has consecrated forever, and serve the LORD your God, that his fierce anger may turn away from you. 9 For if you return to the LORD, your brothers and your children will find compassion with their captors and return to this land. For the LORD your God is gracious and merciful and will not turn away his face from you, if you return to him."

10 So the couriers went from city to city through the country of Ephraim and Manasseh, and as far as Zebulun, but they laughed them to scorn and mocked them. 11 However, some men of Asher, of Manasseh, and of Zebulun humbled themselves and came to Jerusalem. 12 The hand of God was also on Judah to give them one heart to do what the king and the princes commanded by the word of the LORD.

13 And many people came together in Jerusalem to keep the Feast of Unleavened Bread in the second month, a very great assembly. 14 They set to work and removed the altars that were in Jerusalem, and all the altars for burning incense they took away and threw into the Kidron Valley. 15 And they slaughtered the Passover lamb on the fourteenth day of the second month. And the priests and the Levites were ashamed, so that they consecrated themselves and brought burnt offerings into the house of the LORD. 16 They took their accustomed posts according to the Law of Moses the man of God. The priests threw the blood that they received from the hand of the Levites. 17 For there were many in the assembly who had not consecrated themselves. Therefore the Levites had to slaughter the Passover lamb for everyone who was not clean, to consecrate it to the LORD. 18 For a majority of the people, many of them from Ephraim, Manasseh, Issachar, and Zebulun, had not cleansed themselves, yet they ate the Passover otherwise than as prescribed. For Hezekiah had prayed for them, saying, "May the good LORD pardon everyone 19 who sets his heart to seek God, the LORD, the God of his fathers, even though not according to the sanctuary's rules of cleanness."[1] 20 And the LORD heard Hezekiah and healed the people. 21 And the people of Israel who were present at Jerusalem kept the Feast of Unleavened Bread seven days with great gladness, and the Levites and the priests praised the LORD day by day, singing with all their might[2] to the LORD. 22 And Hezekiah spoke encouragingly to all the Levites who showed good skill in the service of the LORD. So they ate the food of the festival for seven days, sacrificing peace offerings and giving thanks to the LORD, the God of their fathers.

23 Then the whole assembly agreed together to keep the feast for another seven days. So they kept it for another seven days with gladness. 24 For Hezekiah king of Judah gave the assembly 1,000 bulls and 7,000 sheep for offerings, and the princes gave the assembly 1,000 bulls and 10,000 sheep. And the priests consecrated themselves in great numbers. 25 The whole assembly of Judah, and the priests and the Levites, and the whole assembly that came out of Israel, and the sojourners who came out of the land of Israel, and the sojourners who lived in Judah, rejoiced. 26 So there was great joy in Jerusalem, for since the time of Solomon the son of David king of Israel there had been nothing like this in Jerusalem. 27 Then the priests and the Levites arose and blessed the people, and their voice was heard, and their prayer came to his holy habitation in heaven.

Hezekiah Organizes the Priests

31 Now when all this was finished, all Israel who were present went out to the cities of Judah and broke in pieces the pillars and cut down the

[1] Hebrew *not according to the cleanness of holiness* [2] Compare 1 Chronicles 13:8; Hebrew *with instruments of might*

Asherim and broke down the high places
and the altars throughout all Judah and
Benjamin, and in Ephraim and Manasseh,
until they had destroyed them all. Then
all the people of Israel returned to their
cities, every man to his possession.
2 And Hezekiah appointed the divisions
of the priests and of the Levites, division
by division, each according to his service,
the priests and the Levites, for burnt offer-
ings and peace offerings, to minister in the
gates of the camp of the LORD and to give
thanks and praise. 3 The contribution of
the king from his own possessions was for
the burnt offerings: the burnt offerings of
morning and evening, and the burnt offer-
ings for the Sabbaths, the new moons, and
the appointed feasts, as it is written in the
Law of the LORD. 4 And he commanded
the people who lived in Jerusalem to give
the portion due to the priests and the
Levites, that they might give themselves
to the Law of the LORD. 5 As soon as the
command was spread abroad, the people
of Israel gave in abundance the firstfruits
of grain, wine, oil, honey, and of all the
produce of the field. And they brought in
abundantly the tithe of everything. 6 And
the people of Israel and Judah who lived
in the cities of Judah also brought in the
tithe of cattle and sheep, and the tithe of
the dedicated things that had been dedi-
cated to the LORD their God, and laid them
in heaps. 7 In the third month they began
to pile up the heaps, and finished them
in the seventh month. 8 When Hezekiah
and the princes came and saw the heaps,
they blessed the LORD and his people
Israel. 9 And Hezekiah questioned the
priests and the Levites about the heaps.
10 Azariah the chief priest, who was of the
house of Zadok, answered him, "Since
they began to bring the contributions into
the house of the LORD, we have eaten and
had enough and have plenty left, for the
LORD has blessed his people, so that we
have this large amount left."
11 Then Hezekiah commanded them
to prepare chambers in the house of the
LORD, and they prepared them. 12 And they
faithfully brought in the contributions, the
tithes, and the dedicated things. The chief
officer in charge of them was Conaniah the
Levite, with Shimei his brother as second,
13 while Jehiel, Azaziah, Nahath, Asahel,
Jerimoth, Jozabad, Eliel, Ismachiah,
Mahath, and Benaiah were overseers
assisting Conaniah and Shimei his brother,
by the appointment of Hezekiah the king
and Azariah the chief officer of the house
of God. 14 And Kore the son of Imnah the
Levite, keeper of the east gate, was over
the freewill offerings to God, to appor-
tion the contribution reserved for the
LORD and the most holy offerings. 15 Eden,
Miniamin, Jeshua, Shemaiah, Amariah,
and Shecaniah were faithfully assisting
him in the cities of the priests, to distrib-
ute the portions to their brothers, old and
young alike, by divisions, 16 except those
enrolled by genealogy, males from three
years old and upward—all who entered
the house of the LORD as the duty of each
day required—for their service according
to their offices, by their divisions. 17 The
enrollment of the priests was according
to their fathers' houses; that of the Levites
from twenty years old and upward was
according to their offices, by their divi-
sions. 18 They were enrolled with all their
little children, their wives, their sons, and
their daughters, the whole assembly, for
they were faithful in keeping themselves
holy. 19 And for the sons of Aaron, the
priests, who were in the fields of common
land belonging to their cities, there were
men in the several cities who were des-
ignated by name to distribute portions to
every male among the priests and to every-
one among the Levites who was enrolled.
20 Thus Hezekiah did throughout all
Judah, and he did what was good and
right and faithful before the LORD his God.
21 And every work that he undertook in the

Jerusalem in the Time of Hezekiah (about 725–686 B.C.)

During the time of King Hezekiah, the city of Jerusalem grew to be larger than it had ever been before. Assyrians had invaded Judah and captured many cities. The Jews who had lived in the captured cities fled to Jerusalem. There was not enough room in the older city on the Eastern Hill, so they settled on the Western Hill.

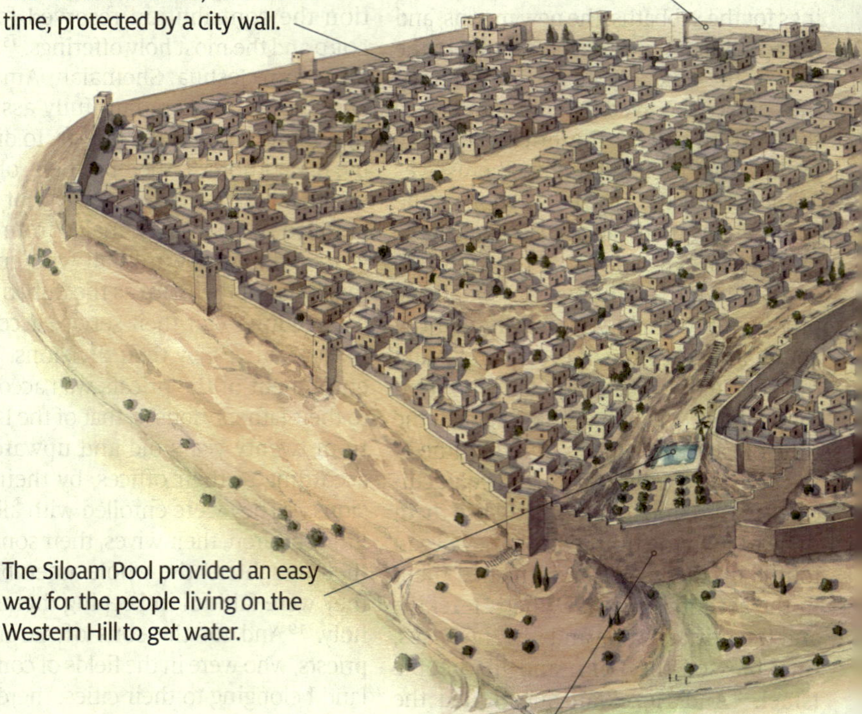

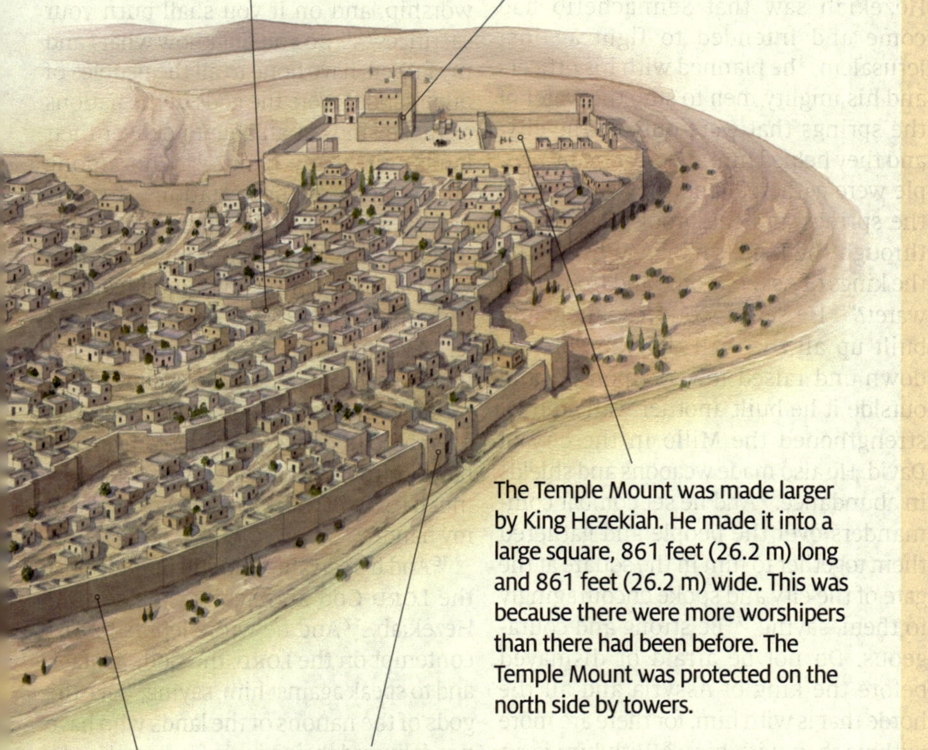
Long ago, a king named Melchizedek had ruled Jerusalem (Genesis 14:18). This Eastern Hill was where the city was located then.
The temple itself was completely rebuilt by Hezekiah. It was probably higher than it had been under King Solomon.
The Temple Mount was made larger by King Hezekiah. He made it into a large square, 861 feet (26.2 m) long and 861 feet (26.2 m) wide. This was because there were more worshipers than there had been before. The Temple Mount was protected on the north side by towers.
The Spring Tower was built over the Gihon Spring. King Hezekiah built an underground tunnel that would take the waters from this spring to the newly built Siloam Pool. This was so the people who lived on the Western Hill could have water.
An outer wall was built to protect the new part of the city, east of the old City of David.

service of the house of God and in accor-
dance with the law and the command-
ments, seeking his God, he did with all
his heart, and prospered.

Sennacherib Invades Judah

32 After these things and
these acts of faithfulness,
615 Sennacherib king of Assyria came
and invaded Judah and encamped
against the fortified cities, thinking to
win them for himself. 2 And when
Hezekiah saw that Sennacherib had
come and intended to fight against
Jerusalem, 3 he planned with his officers
and his mighty men to stop the water of
the springs that were outside the city;
and they helped him. 4 A great many peo-
ple were gathered, and they stopped all
the springs and the brook that flowed
through the land, saying, "Why should
the kings of Assyria come and find much
water?" 5 He set to work resolutely and
built up all the wall that was broken
down and raised towers upon it,[1] and
outside it he built another wall, and he
strengthened the Millo in the city of
David. He also made weapons and shields
in abundance. 6 And he set combat com-
manders over the people and gathered
them together to him in the square at the
gate of the city and spoke encouragingly
to them, saying, 7 "Be strong and coura-
geous. Do not be afraid or dismayed
before the king of Assyria and all the
horde that is with him, for there are more
with us than with him. 8 With him is an
arm of flesh, but with us is the LORD our
God, to help us and to fight our battles."
And the people took confidence from the
words of Hezekiah king of Judah.

Sennacherib Blasphemes

9 After this, Sennacherib king of Assyria,
who was besieging Lachish with all his
forces, sent his servants to Jerusalem
to Hezekiah king of Judah and to all the
people of Judah who were in Jerusalem,
saying, 10 "Thus says Sennacherib king of
Assyria, 'On what are you trusting, that
you endure the siege in Jerusalem? 11 Is
not Hezekiah misleading you, that he
may give you over to die by famine and
by thirst, when he tells you, "The LORD
our God will deliver us from the hand of
the king of Assyria"? 12 Has not this same
Hezekiah taken away his high places and
his altars and commanded Judah and
Jerusalem, "Before one altar you shall
worship, and on it you shall burn your
sacrifices"? 13 Do you not know what I and
my fathers have done to all the peoples of
other lands? Were the gods of the nations
of those lands at all able to deliver their
lands out of my hand? 14 Who among
all the gods of those nations that my
fathers devoted to destruction was able
to deliver his people from my hand, that
your God should be able to deliver you
from my hand? 15 Now, therefore, do not
let Hezekiah deceive you or mislead you
in this fashion, and do not believe him,
for no god of any nation or kingdom has
been able to deliver his people from my
hand or from the hand of my fathers. How
much less will your God deliver you out of
my hand!'"

16 And his servants said still more against
the LORD God and against his servant
Hezekiah. 17 And he wrote letters to cast
contempt on the LORD, the God of Israel,
and to speak against him, saying, "Like the
gods of the nations of the lands who have
not delivered their people from my hands,
so the God of Hezekiah will not deliver
his people from my hand." 18 And they
shouted it with a loud voice in the lan-
guage of Judah to the people of Jerusalem
who were on the wall, to frighten and ter-
rify them, in order that they might take
the city. 19 And they spoke of the God of
Jerusalem as they spoke of the gods of the
peoples of the earth, which are the work
of men's hands.

[1] Vulgate; Hebrew *and raised upon the towers*

The LORD Delivers Jerusalem

20 Then Hezekiah the king and Isaiah
the prophet, the son of Amoz, prayed
because of this and cried to heaven. 21 And
the LORD sent an angel, who cut off all the
mighty warriors and commanders and
officers in the camp of the king of Assyria.
So he returned with shame of face to his
own land. And when he came into the
house of his god, some of his own sons
struck him down there with the sword.
22 So the LORD saved Hezekiah and the
inhabitants of Jerusalem from the hand
of Sennacherib king of Assyria and from
the hand of all his enemies, and he pro-
vided for them on every side. 23 And many
brought gifts to the LORD to Jerusalem and
precious things to Hezekiah king of Judah,
so that he was exalted in the sight of all
nations from that time onward.

Hezekiah's Pride and Achievements

24 In those days Hezekiah became sick
and was at the point of death, and he
prayed to the LORD, and he answered him
and gave him a sign. 25 But Hezekiah did
not make return according to the bene-
fit done to him, for his heart was proud.
Therefore wrath came upon him and Judah
and Jerusalem. 26 But Hezekiah humbled
himself for the pride of his heart, both he
and the inhabitants of Jerusalem, so that
the wrath of the LORD did not come upon
them in the days of Hezekiah.

27 And Hezekiah had very great riches
and honor, and he made for himself trea-
suries for silver, for gold, for precious
stones, for spices, for shields, and for all
kinds of costly vessels; 28 storehouses also
for the yield of grain, wine, and oil; and
stalls for all kinds of cattle, and sheepfolds.
29 He likewise provided cities for himself,
and flocks and herds in abundance, for
God had given him very great possessions.
30 This same Hezekiah closed the upper
outlet of the waters of Gihon and directed
them down to the west side of the city
of David. And Hezekiah prospered in all
his works. 31 And so in the matter of the
envoys of the princes of Babylon, who had
been sent to him to inquire about the sign
that had been done in the land, God left
him to himself, in order to test him and to
know all that was in his heart.

32 Now the rest of the acts of Hezekiah
and his good deeds, behold, they are writ-
ten in the vision of Isaiah the prophet the
son of Amoz, in the Book of the Kings of
Judah and Israel. 33 And Hezekiah slept
with his fathers, and they buried him in
the upper part of the tombs of the sons of
David, and all Judah and the inhabitants of
Jerusalem did him honor at his death. And
Manasseh his son reigned in his place.

Manasseh Reigns in Judah

33 Manasseh was twelve years old
when he began to reign, and he
reigned fifty-five years in Jerusalem.
2 And he did what was evil in the sight of
the LORD, according to the abominations
of the nations whom the LORD drove out
before the people of Israel. 3 For he rebuilt
the high places that his father Hezekiah
had broken down, and he erected altars to
the Baals, and made Asherahs, and wor-
shiped all the host of heaven and served
them. 4 And he built altars in the house of
the LORD, of which the LORD had said, "In
Jerusalem shall my name be forever." 5 And
he built altars for all the host of heaven in
the two courts of the house of the LORD.
6 And he burned his sons as an offering
in the Valley of the Son of Hinnom, and
used fortune-telling and omens and sor-
cery, and dealt with mediums and with
necromancers. He did much evil in the
sight of the LORD, provoking him to anger.
7 And the carved image of the idol that he
had made he set in the house of God, of
which God said to David and to Solomon
his son, "In this house, and in Jerusalem,
which I have chosen out of all the tribes
of Israel, I will put my name forever, 8 and

I will no more remove the foot of Israel from the land that I appointed for your fathers, if only they will be careful to do all that I have commanded them, all the law, the statutes, and the rules given through Moses." 9 Manasseh led Judah and the inhabitants of Jerusalem astray, to do more evil than the nations whom the LORD destroyed before the people of Israel.

Manasseh's Repentance

10 The LORD spoke to Manasseh and to his people, but they paid no attention. 11 Therefore the LORD brought upon them the commanders of the army of the king of Assyria, who captured Manasseh with hooks and bound him with chains of bronze and brought him to Babylon. 12 And when he was in distress, he entreated the favor of the LORD his God and humbled himself greatly before the God of his fathers. 13 He prayed to him, and God was moved by his entreaty and heard his plea and brought him again to Jerusalem into his kingdom. Then Manasseh knew that the LORD was God.

14 Afterward he built an outer wall for the city of David west of Gihon, in the valley, and for the entrance into the Fish Gate, and carried it around Ophel, and raised it to a very great height. He also put commanders of the army in all the fortified cities in Judah. 15 And he took away the foreign gods and the idol from the house of the LORD, and all the altars that he had built on the mountain of the house of the LORD and in Jerusalem, and he threw them outside of the city. 16 He also restored the altar of the LORD and offered on it sacrifices of peace offerings and of thanksgiving, and he commanded Judah to serve the LORD, the God of Israel. 17 Nevertheless, the people still sacrificed at the high places, but only to the LORD their God.

18 Now the rest of the acts of Manasseh, and his prayer to his God, and the words of the seers who spoke to him in the name of the LORD, the God of Israel, behold, they are in the Chronicles of the Kings of Israel. 19 And his prayer, and how God was moved by his entreaty, and all his sin and his faithlessness, and the sites on which he built high places and set up the Asherim and the images, before he humbled himself, behold, they are written in the Chronicles of the Seers.[1] 20 So Manasseh slept with his fathers, and they buried him in his house, and Amon his son reigned in his place.

Amon's Reign and Death

21 Amon was twenty-two years old when he began to reign, and he reigned two years in Jerusalem. 22 And he did what was evil in the sight of the LORD, as Manasseh his father had done. Amon sacrificed to all the images that Manasseh his father had made, and served them. 23 And he did not humble himself before the LORD, as Manasseh his father had humbled himself, but this Amon incurred guilt more and more. 24 And his servants conspired against him and put him to death in his house. 25 But the people of the land struck down all those who had conspired against King Amon. And the people of the land made Josiah his son king in his place.

Josiah Reigns in Judah

697

34 Josiah was eight years old when he began to reign, and he reigned thirty-one years in Jerusalem. 2 And he did what was right in the eyes of the LORD, and walked in the ways of David his father; and he did not turn aside to the right hand or to the left. 3 For in the eighth year of his reign, while he was yet a boy, he began to seek the God of David his father, and in the twelfth year he began to purge Judah and Jerusalem of the high places, the Asherim, and the carved and the metal images. 4 And they chopped down the altars of the Baals in his presence, and he cut down the incense altars that stood above them. And he broke in pieces the Asherim and the carved and

[1] One Hebrew manuscript, Septuagint; most Hebrew manuscripts *of Hozai*

the metal images, and he made dust of them and scattered it over the graves of those who had sacrificed to them. 5 He also burned the bones of the priests on their altars and cleansed Judah and Jerusalem.
6 And in the cities of Manasseh, Ephraim, and Simeon, and as far as Naphtali, in their ruins[1] all around, 7 he broke down the altars and beat the Asherim and the images into powder and cut down all the incense altars throughout all the land of Israel. Then he returned to Jerusalem.

The Book of the Law Found

8 Now in the eighteenth year of his reign, when he had cleansed the land and the house, he sent Shaphan the son of Azaliah, and Maaseiah the governor of the city, and Joah the son of Joahaz, the recorder, to repair the house of the LORD his God.
9 They came to Hilkiah the high priest and gave him the money that had been brought into the house of God, which the Levites, the keepers of the threshold, had collected from Manasseh and Ephraim and from all the remnant of Israel and from all Judah and Benjamin and from the inhabitants of
Jerusalem. 10 And they gave it to the workmen who were working in the house of the LORD. And the workmen who were working in the house of the LORD gave it for
repairing and restoring the house. 11 They gave it to the carpenters and the builders to buy quarried stone, and timber for binders and beams for the buildings that the kings
of Judah had let go to ruin. 12 And the men did the work faithfully. Over them were set Jahath and Obadiah the Levites, of the sons of Merari, and Zechariah and Meshullam, of the sons of the Kohathites, to have oversight. The Levites, all who were skillful
with instruments of music, 13 were over the burden-bearers and directed all who did work in every kind of service, and some of the Levites were scribes and officials and gatekeepers.
14 While they were bringing out the money that had been brought into the house of the LORD, Hilkiah the priest found the Book of the Law of the LORD given
through Moses. 15 Then Hilkiah answered and said to Shaphan the secretary, "I have found the Book of the Law in the house of the LORD." And Hilkiah gave the book to
Shaphan. 16 Shaphan brought the book to the king, and further reported to the king, "All that was committed to your servants
they are doing. 17 They have emptied out the money that was found in the house of the LORD and have given it into the hand
of the overseers and the workmen." 18 Then Shaphan the secretary told the king, "Hilkiah the priest has given me a book." And Shaphan read from it before the king.
19 And when the king heard the words
of the Law, he tore his clothes. 20 And the king commanded Hilkiah, Ahikam the son of Shaphan, Abdon the son of Micah, Shaphan the secretary, and Asaiah the
king's servant, saying, 21 "Go, inquire of the LORD for me and for those who are left in Israel and in Judah, concerning the words of the book that has been found. For great is the wrath of the LORD that is poured out on us, because our fathers have not kept the word of the LORD, to do according to all that is written in this book."

Huldah Prophesies Disaster

22 So Hilkiah and those whom the king had sent[2] went to Huldah the prophetess, the wife of Shallum the son of Tokhath, son of Hasrah, keeper of the wardrobe (now she lived in Jerusalem in the Second Quarter) and spoke to her to that effect.
23 And she said to them, "Thus says the LORD, the God of Israel: 'Tell the man who
sent you to me, 24 Thus says the LORD, Behold, I will bring disaster upon this place and upon its inhabitants, all the curses that are written in the book that was read
before the king of Judah. 25 Because they have forsaken me and have made offerings to other gods, that they might provoke me

[1] The meaning of the Hebrew is uncertain [2] Syriac, Vulgate; Hebrew lacks *had sent*

Josiah and the Priest Who Found God's Word

Once a long time ago, a young boy named Josiah became king of Judah. Josiah tried to follow the ways of the Lord. He destroyed all the altars to other gods that other kings before him had built in Jerusalem. The Bible tells us that Josiah "did what was right in the eyes of the LORD," and he walked in the right ways of King David who reigned many years before Josiah.

When he was a young man, Josiah ordered some men to repair the house of the Lord, which was known as the Temple. Carpenters and builders bought stone and wood to fix beams and timbers, in order to rebuild the Temple and make it beautiful again.

While the workers were fixing and cleaning some rooms, the high priest named Hilkiah found a book. He said, "I have found the Book of the Law in the house of the LORD." The Book of the Law was God's Word that Moses had written down many years before.

Hilkiah gave the book to a secretary named Shaphan, who read the book to King Josiah.

When the king heard the words of the Law, he was very sad. He even tore his clothes to show he was terribly upset. The king listened to what God's Law said about what God's people must do. He knew that for years God's people had disobeyed God. He knew that the people deserved God's judgment for all the sin and evil they had done.

Josiah did not want his people to forget God's Word and to live under God's judgment. So he sent messengers throughout the land to call the people to come to Jerusalem. When they arrived, the king went to the Temple, stood before the people, and read the Book of the Law to them. Then the king made a covenant with God. He pledged that he would keep the Law and serve the Lord. He commanded the people to make the same promise. And they did.

The two kings before Josiah had led God's people in worshiping idols. As long as Josiah was king in Jerusalem, the people did not turn away from following the Lord. After he died, the next kings went back to idol worship and led the people, once again, in sinning against the Lord.

Josiah was a good king, but he was king only for a while. God has given us a much better King in Jesus, who will be King forever. Jesus leads His people in loving and obeying God. But He lives forever and His heavenly kingdom will have no end. Jesus also changes our hearts, to help us always love and serve God faithfully.

SEEK and FIND

WHERE TO FIND THE STORY

2 Chronicles 34

KEY BIBLE VERSE

"And the king stood in his place and made a covenant before the LORD, to walk after the LORD and to keep his commandments and his testimonies and his statutes, with all his heart and all his soul, to perform the words of the covenant that were written in this book." (2 Chronicles 34:31)

THREE KEY QUESTIONS

- What did the priest Hilkiah do when the workers were repairing the temple?
- What did King Josiah do when he heard the words of God's Law?
- Who is our King today and what does He do for us?

RELATED BIBLE READINGS

Deuteronomy 17:14–15, 18–20; 2 Kings 22:1–23:30; 2 Chronicles 35:1–27; Psalm 119:121–136; Zephaniah 1:1

to anger with all the works of their hands,
therefore my wrath will be poured out
on this place and will not be quenched.
26 But to the king of Judah, who sent you to
inquire of the LORD, thus shall you say to
him, Thus says the LORD, the God of Israel:
Regarding the words that you have heard,
27 because your heart was tender and you
humbled yourself before God when you
heard his words against this place and its
inhabitants, and you have humbled your-
self before me and have torn your clothes
and wept before me, I also have heard you,
declares the LORD. 28 Behold, I will gather
you to your fathers, and you shall be gath-
ered to your grave in peace, and your eyes
shall not see all the disaster that I will bring
upon this place and its inhabitants.'" And
they brought back word to the king.
29 Then the king sent and gathered
together all the elders of Judah and
Jerusalem. 30 And the king went up to the
house of the LORD, with all the men of
Judah and the inhabitants of Jerusalem
and the priests and the Levites, all the peo-
ple both great and small. And he read in
their hearing all the words of the Book of
the Covenant that had been found in the
house of the LORD. 31 And the king stood
in his place and made a covenant
before the LORD, to walk after the
697 LORD and to keep his command-
ments and his testimonies and his stat-
utes, with all his heart and all his soul, to
perform the words of the covenant that
were written in this book. 32 Then he made
all who were present in Jerusalem and in
Benjamin join in it. And the inhabitants of
Jerusalem did according to the covenant of
God, the God of their fathers. 33 And Josiah
took away all the abominations from all
the territory that belonged to the people of
Israel and made all who were present in
Israel serve the LORD their God. All his
days they did not turn away from follow-
ing the LORD, the God of their fathers.

Josiah Keeps the Passover

35 Josiah kept a Passover to
the LORD in Jerusalem. And
697 they slaughtered the Passover lamb
on the fourteenth day of the first month.

2 He appointed the priests to their offices and encouraged them in the service of the house of the LORD. 3 And he said to the Levites who taught all Israel and who were holy to the LORD, "Put the holy ark in the house that Solomon the son of David, king of Israel, built. You need not carry it on your shoulders. Now serve the LORD your God and his people Israel. 4 Prepare yourselves according to your fathers' houses by your divisions, as prescribed in the writing of David king of Israel and the document of Solomon his son. 5 And stand in the Holy Place according to the groupings of the fathers' houses of your brothers the lay people, and according to the division of the Levites by fathers' household. 6 And slaughter the Passover lamb, and consecrate yourselves, and prepare for your brothers, to do according to the word of the LORD by Moses."

7 Then Josiah contributed to the lay people, as Passover offerings for all who were present, lambs and young goats from the flock to the number of 30,000, and 3,000 bulls; these were from the king's possessions. 8 And his officials contributed willingly to the people, to the priests, and to the Levites. Hilkiah, Zechariah, and Jehiel, the chief officers of the house of God, gave to the priests for the Passover offerings 2,600 Passover lambs and 300 bulls. 9 Conaniah also, and Shemaiah and Nethanel his brothers, and Hashabiah and Jeiel and Jozabad, the chiefs of the Levites, gave to the Levites for the Passover offerings 5,000 lambs and young goats and 500 bulls.

10 When the service had been prepared for, the priests stood in their place, and the Levites in their divisions according to the king's command. 11 And they slaughtered the Passover lamb, and the priests threw the blood that they received from them while the Levites flayed the sacrifices. 12 And they set aside the burnt offerings that they might distribute them according to the groupings of the fathers' houses of the lay people, to offer to the LORD, as it is written in the Book of Moses. And so they did with the bulls. 13 And they roasted the Passover lamb with fire according to the rule; and they boiled the holy offerings in pots, in cauldrons, and in pans, and carried them quickly to all the lay people. 14 And afterward they prepared for themselves and for the priests, because the priests, the sons of Aaron, were offering the burnt offerings and the fat parts until night; so the Levites prepared for themselves and for the priests, the sons of Aaron. 15 The singers, the sons of Asaph, were in their place according to the command of David, and Asaph, and Heman, and Jeduthun the king's seer; and the gatekeepers were at each gate. They did not need to depart from their service, for their brothers the Levites prepared for them.

16 So all the service of the LORD was prepared that day, to keep the Passover and to offer burnt offerings on the altar of the LORD, according to the command of King Josiah. 17 And the people of Israel who were present kept the Passover at that time, and the Feast of Unleavened Bread seven days. 18 No Passover like it had been kept in Israel since the days of Samuel the prophet. None of the kings of Israel had kept such a Passover as was kept by Josiah, and the priests and the Levites, and all Judah and Israel who were present, and the inhabitants of Jerusalem. 19 In the eighteenth year of the reign of Josiah this Passover was kept.

Josiah Killed in Battle

20 After all this, when Josiah had prepared the temple, Neco king of Egypt went up to fight at Carchemish on the Euphrates, and Josiah went out to meet him. 21 But he sent envoys to him, saying, "What have we to do with each other, king of Judah? I am not coming against you this day, but against the house with which I

am at war. And God has commanded me to hurry. Cease opposing God, who is with me, lest he destroy you." 22 Nevertheless, Josiah did not turn away from him, but disguised himself in order to fight with him. He did not listen to the words of Neco from the mouth of God, but came to fight in the plain of Megiddo. 23 And the archers shot King Josiah. And the king said to his servants, "Take me away, for I am badly wounded." 24 So his servants took him out of the chariot and carried him in his second chariot and brought him to Jerusalem. And he died and was buried in the tombs of his fathers. All Judah and Jerusalem mourned for Josiah. 25 Jeremiah also uttered a lament for Josiah; and all the singing men and singing women have spoken of Josiah in their laments to this day. They made these a rule in Israel; behold, they are written in the Laments. 26 Now the rest of the acts of Josiah, and his good deeds according to what is written in the Law of the LORD, 27 and his acts, first and last, behold, they are written in the Book of the Kings of Israel and Judah.

Judah's Decline

36 The people of the land took Jehoahaz the son of Josiah and made him king in his father's place in Jerusalem. 2 Jehoahaz was twenty-three years old when he began to reign, and he reigned three months in Jerusalem. 3 Then the king of Egypt deposed him in Jerusalem and laid on the land a tribute of a hundred talents of silver and a talent[1] of gold. 4 And the king of Egypt made Eliakim his brother king over Judah and Jerusalem, and changed his name to Jehoiakim. But Neco took Jehoahaz his brother and carried him to Egypt.

5 Jehoiakim was twenty-five years old when he began to reign, and he reigned eleven years in Jerusalem. He did what was evil in the sight of the LORD his God. 6 Against him came up Nebuchadnezzar king of Babylon and bound him in chains to take him to Babylon. 7 Nebuchadnezzar also carried part of the vessels of the house of the LORD to Babylon and put them in his palace in Babylon. 8 Now the rest of the acts of Jehoiakim, and the abominations that he did, and what was found against him, behold, they are written in the Book of the Kings of Israel and Judah. And Jehoiachin his son reigned in his place.

9 Jehoiachin was eighteen[2] years old when he became king, and he reigned three months and ten days in Jerusalem. He did what was evil in the sight of the LORD. 10 In the spring of the year King Nebuchadnezzar sent and brought him to Babylon, with the precious vessels of the house of the LORD, and made his brother Zedekiah king over Judah and Jerusalem.

11 Zedekiah was twenty-one years old when he began to reign, and he reigned eleven years in Jerusalem. 12 He did what was evil in the sight of the LORD his God. He did not humble himself before Jeremiah the prophet, who spoke from the mouth of the LORD. 13 He also rebelled against King Nebuchadnezzar, who had made him swear by God. He stiffened his neck and hardened his heart against turning to the LORD, the God of Israel. 14 All the officers of the priests and the people likewise were exceedingly unfaithful, following all the abominations of the nations. And they polluted the house of the LORD that he had made holy in Jerusalem.

15 The LORD, the God of their fathers, sent persistently to them by his messengers, because he had compassion on his people and on his dwelling place. 16 But they kept mocking the messengers of God, despising his words and scoffing at his prophets, until the wrath of the LORD rose against his people, until there was no remedy.

Jerusalem Captured and Burned

17 Therefore he brought up against them the king of the Chaldeans, who killed their

[1] A *talent* was about 75 pounds or 34 kilograms [2] Septuagint (compare 2 Kings 24:8); most Hebrew manuscripts *eight*

young men with the sword in the house of
their sanctuary and had no compassion
on young man or virgin, old man or aged.
He gave them all into his hand. 18 And all
the vessels of the house of God, great and
small, and the treasures of the house of
the LORD, and the treasures of the king
and of his princes, all these he brought to
Babylon. 19 And they burned the house of
God and broke down the wall of Jerusalem
and burned all its palaces with fire and
destroyed all its precious vessels. 20 He
took into exile in Babylon those who had
escaped from the sword, and they became
servants to him and to his sons until the
establishment of the kingdom of Persia,
21 to fulfill the word of the LORD by the
mouth of Jeremiah, until the land had
enjoyed its Sabbaths. All the days that it
lay desolate it kept Sabbath, to fulfill sev-
enty years.

The Proclamation of Cyrus

22 Now in the first year of Cyrus king of
Persia, that the word of the LORD by the
mouth of Jeremiah might be fulfilled, the
LORD stirred up the spirit of Cyrus king of
Persia, so that he made a proclamation
throughout all his kingdom and also put
it in writing: 23 "Thus says Cyrus king of
Persia, 'The LORD, the God of heaven, has
given me all the kingdoms of the earth, and
he has charged me to build him a house at
Jerusalem, which is in Judah. Whoever is
among you of all his people, may the LORD
his God be with him. Let him go up.'"

Introduction to

Ezra

Author

Ezra the scribe

Date

About 440 B.C.

People

Cyrus; Zerubbabel; Jeshua; Haggai; Zechariah; Darius; Ezra

Purpose

The purpose of Ezra is to show how God kept His powerful Word by bringing the Israelites back to their land to rebuild the temple, and to call the returned Israelites to live in obedience to God.

Central Themes

God keeps His promises of a return to the land and a rebuilt temple; God rules over rulers and all circumstances; enemies of God's people seek to hinder their worship; God's people must worship Him and obey His commands; God calls His people to repent when they fail to obey.

Memory Verses

Temple dedication (Ezra 3:10–13); Ezra's heart (Ezra 7:10); Ezra's prayer (Ezra 9:6–9)

Introduction

Ezra opens with a fulfilled prophecy of the Lord: King Cyrus of Persia decrees that the Jews living in exile can return to Israel and rebuild the temple (Ezra 1:1–4). Many Israelites return (Ezra 2). The first thing they do is rebuild the altar of the Lord so they can again offer sacrifices to God (Ezra 3:1–6). The Israelites then begin rebuilding the temple (Ezra 3), but stop when neighboring nations stir up trouble. The Jews' enemies threaten them, pay local leaders to prevent them from building, and, later, send letters with false accusations about the Israelites to the king (Ezra 4). Years later, the prophets Haggai and Zechariah urge the Jews to begin rebuilding the temple again and the people obey, led by Zerubbabel the governor and Jeshua the priest (Ezra 5:1–2). Enemy nations again try to stop them, by a letter to King Darius, but he decrees that the work should continue—and the enemies have to pay for it (Ezra 5:3–6:12)! So the temple is finished, and Ezra the scribe comes to Jerusalem to teach the people God's Law (Ezra 7–8). He finds the people already living in disobedience to God and leads them in confession and repentance (Ezra 9–10).

586 B.C.	538 B.C.	516 B.C.	458 B.C.
Fall of Judah/ temple destroyed	Decree of Cyrus/ end of exile	Temple rebuilt	Ezra arrives in Jerusalem

Ezra

The Proclamation of Cyrus

1 In the first year of Cyrus king of Persia, that the word of the LORD by the mouth of Jeremiah might be fulfilled, the LORD stirred up the spirit of Cyrus king of Persia, so that he made a proclamation throughout all his kingdom and also put it in writing:

2 "Thus says Cyrus king of Persia: The LORD, the God of heaven, has given me all the kingdoms of the earth, and he has charged me to build him a house at Jerusalem, which is in Judah. 3 Whoever is among you of all his people, may his God be with him, and let him go up to Jerusalem, which is in Judah, and rebuild the house of the LORD, the God of Israel—he is the God who is in Jerusalem. 4 And let each survivor, in whatever place he sojourns, be assisted by the men of his place with silver and gold, with goods and with beasts, besides freewill offerings for the house of God that is in Jerusalem."

5 Then rose up the heads of the fathers' houses of Judah and Benjamin, and the priests and the Levites, everyone whose spirit God had stirred to go up to rebuild the house of the LORD that is in Jerusalem. 6 And all who were about them aided them with vessels of silver, with gold, with goods, with beasts, and with costly wares, besides all that was freely offered. 7 Cyrus the king also brought out the vessels of the house of the LORD that Nebuchadnezzar had carried away from Jerusalem and placed in the house of his gods. 8 Cyrus king of Persia brought these out in the charge of Mithredath the treasurer, who counted them out to Sheshbazzar the prince of Judah. 9 And this was the number of them: 30 basins of gold, 1,000 basins of silver, 29 censers, 10 30 bowls of gold, 410 bowls of silver, and 1,000 other vessels; 11 all the vessels of gold and of silver were 5,400. All these did Sheshbazzar bring up, when the exiles were brought up from Babylonia to Jerusalem.

The Exiles Return

2 Now these were the people of the province who came up out of the captivity of those exiles whom Nebuchadnezzar the king of Babylon had carried captive to Babylonia. They returned to Jerusalem and Judah, each to his own town. 2 They came with Zerubbabel, Jeshua, Nehemiah, Seraiah, Reelaiah, Mordecai, Bilshan, Mispar, Bigvai, Rehum, and Baanah.

The number of the men of the people of Israel: 3 the sons of Parosh, 2,172. 4 The sons of Shephatiah, 372. 5 The sons of Arah, 775. 6 The sons of Pahath-moab, namely the sons of Jeshua and Joab, 2,812. 7 The sons of Elam, 1,254. 8 The sons of Zattu, 945. 9 The sons of Zaccai, 760. 10 The sons of Bani, 642. 11 The sons of Bebai, 623. 12 The sons of Azgad, 1,222. 13 The sons of Adonikam, 666. 14 The sons of Bigvai, 2,056. 15 The sons of Adin, 454. 16 The sons of Ater, namely of Hezekiah, 98. 17 The sons of Bezai, 323. 18 The sons of Jorah, 112. 19 The sons of Hashum, 223. 20 The sons of Gibbar, 95. 21 The sons of Bethlehem, 123. 22 The men of Netophah, 56. 23 The men of Anathoth, 128. 24 The sons of Azmaveth, 42. 25 The sons of Kiriath-arim, Chephirah, and Beeroth, 743. 26 The sons of Ramah and Geba, 621. 27 The men of Michmas, 122. 28 The men of Bethel and Ai, 223. 29 The sons of Nebo, 52. 30 The sons of Magbish, 156. 31 The sons of the other Elam, 1,254. 32 The sons of Harim, 320. 33 The sons of

Lod, Hadid, and Ono, 725. 34 The sons of Jericho, 345. 35 The sons of Senaah, 3,630.

36 The priests: the sons of Jedaiah, of the house of Jeshua, 973. 37 The sons of Immer, 1,052. 38 The sons of Pashhur, 1,247. 39 The sons of Harim, 1,017.

40 The Levites: the sons of Jeshua and Kadmiel, of the sons of Hodaviah, 74. 41 The singers: the sons of Asaph, 128. 42 The sons of the gatekeepers: the sons of Shallum, the sons of Ater, the sons of Talmon, the sons of Akkub, the sons of Hatita, and the sons of Shobai, in all 139.

43 The temple servants: the sons of Ziha, the sons of Hasupha, the sons of Tabbaoth, 44 the sons of Keros, the sons of Siaha, the sons of Padon, 45 the sons of Lebanah, the sons of Hagabah, the sons of Akkub, 46 the sons of Hagab, the sons of Shamlai, the sons of Hanan, 47 the sons of Giddel, the sons of Gahar, the sons of Reaiah, 48 the sons of Rezin, the sons of Nekoda, the sons of Gazzam, 49 the sons of Uzza, the sons of Paseah, the sons of Besai, 50 the sons of Asnah, the sons of Meunim, the sons of Nephisim, 51 the sons of Bakbuk, the sons of Hakupha, the sons of Harhur, 52 the sons of Bazluth, the sons of Mehida, the sons of Harsha, 53 the sons of Barkos, the sons of Sisera, the sons of Temah, 54 the sons of Neziah, and the sons of Hatipha.

55 The sons of Solomon's servants: the sons of Sotai, the sons of Hassophereth, the sons of Peruda, 56 the sons of Jaalah, the sons of Darkon, the sons of Giddel, 57 the sons of Shephatiah, the sons of Hattil, the sons of Pochereth-hazzebaim, and the sons of Ami.

58 All the temple servants and the sons of Solomon's servants were 392.

59 The following were those who came up from Tel-melah, Tel-harsha, Cherub, Addan, and Immer, though they could not prove their fathers' houses or their descent, whether they belonged to Israel: 60 the sons of Delaiah, the sons of Tobiah, and the sons of Nekoda, 652. 61 Also, of the sons of the priests: the sons of Habaiah, the sons of Hakkoz, and the sons of Barzillai (who had taken a wife from the daughters of Barzillai the Gileadite, and was called by their name). 62 These sought their registration among those enrolled in the genealogies, but they were not found there, and so they were excluded from the priesthood as unclean. 63 The governor told them that they were not to partake of the most holy food, until there should be a priest to consult Urim and Thummim.

64 The whole assembly together was 42,360, 65 besides their male and female servants, of whom there were 7,337, and they had 200 male and female singers. 66 Their horses were 736, their mules were 245, 67 their camels were 435, and their donkeys were 6,720.

68 Some of the heads of families, when they came to the house of the LORD that is in Jerusalem, made freewill offerings for the house of God, to erect it on its site. 69 According to their ability they gave to the treasury of the work 61,000 darics[1] of gold, 5,000 minas[2] of silver, and 100 priests' garments.

70 Now the priests, the Levites, some of the people, the singers, the gatekeepers, and the temple servants lived in their towns, and all the rest of Israel[3] in their towns.

Rebuilding the Altar

3 When the seventh month came, and the children of Israel were in the towns, the people gathered as one man to Jerusalem. 2 Then arose Jeshua the son of Jozadak, with his fellow priests, and Zerubbabel the son of Shealtiel with his kinsmen, and they built the altar of the God of Israel, to offer burnt offerings on it, as it is written in the Law of Moses the man of God. 3 They set the altar in its place, for fear was on them because of the peoples of the lands, and they offered burnt offerings on it to the LORD, burnt

[1] A *daric* was a coin weighing about 1/4 ounce or 8.5 grams [2] A *mina* was about 1 1/4 pounds or 0.6 kilogram [3] Hebrew *all Israel*

offerings morning and evening. 4 And they
kept the Feast of Booths, as it is written,
and offered the daily burnt offerings by
number according to the rule, as each day
required, 5 and after that the regular burnt
offerings, the offerings at the new moon
and at all the appointed feasts of the LORD,
and the offerings of everyone who made
a freewill offering to the LORD. 6 From the
first day of the seventh month they began
to offer burnt offerings to the LORD. But
the foundation of the temple of the LORD
was not yet laid. 7 So they gave money to
the masons and the carpenters, and food,
drink, and oil to the Sidonians and the
Tyrians to bring cedar trees from Lebanon
to the sea, to Joppa, according to the grant
that they had from Cyrus king of Persia.

Rebuilding the Temple

8 Now in the second year after their
coming to the house of God at Jerusalem,
in the second month, Zerubbabel the
son of Shealtiel and Jeshua the son of
Jozadak made a beginning, together with
the rest of their kinsmen, the priests
and the Levites and all who had come
to Jerusalem from the captivity. They
appointed the Levites, from twenty years
old and upward, to supervise the work of
the house of the LORD. 9 And Jeshua with
his sons and his brothers, and Kadmiel
and his sons, the sons of Judah, together
supervised the workmen in the house of
God, along with the sons of Henadad and
the Levites, their sons and brothers.

10 And when the builders laid the foun-
dation of the temple of the LORD, the
priests in their vestments came forward
with trumpets, and the Levites, the sons of
Asaph, with cymbals, to praise the LORD,
according to the directions of David king
of Israel. 11 And they sang responsively,
praising and giving thanks to the LORD,

"For he is good,
for his steadfast love endures
forever toward Israel."

And all the people shouted with a great
shout when they praised the LORD,
because the foundation of the house of
the LORD was laid. 12 But many of the
priests and Levites and heads of fathers'
houses, old men who had seen the first
house, wept with a loud voice when they
saw the foundation of this house being
laid, though many shouted aloud for joy,
13 so that the people could not distinguish
the sound of the joyful shout from the
sound of the people's weeping, for the
people shouted with a great shout, and
the sound was heard far away.

Adversaries Oppose the Rebuilding

4 Now when the adversaries of Judah
and Benjamin heard that the returned
exiles were building a temple to the
LORD, the God of Israel, 2 they approached
Zerubbabel and the heads of fathers'
houses and said to them, "Let us build
with you, for we worship your God as you
do, and we have been sacrificing to him
ever since the days of Esarhaddon king
of Assyria who brought us here." 3 But
Zerubbabel, Jeshua, and the rest of the
heads of fathers' houses in Israel said to
them, "You have nothing to do with us in
building a house to our God; but we alone
will build to the LORD, the God of Israel,
as King Cyrus the king of Persia has com-
manded us."

4 Then the people of the land discour-
aged the people of Judah and made them
afraid to build 5 and bribed counselors
against them to frustrate their purpose, all
the days of Cyrus king of Persia, even until
the reign of Darius king of Persia.

6 And in the reign of Ahasuerus, in
the beginning of his reign, they wrote
an accusation against the inhabitants of
Judah and Jerusalem.

The Letter to King Artaxerxes

7 In the days of Artaxerxes, Bishlam
and Mithredath and Tabeel and the rest
of their associates wrote to Artaxerxes

king of Persia. The letter was written in Aramaic and translated.[1] 8 Rehum the commander and Shimshai the scribe wrote a letter against Jerusalem to Artaxerxes the king as follows: 9 Rehum the commander, Shimshai the scribe, and the rest of their associates, the judges, the governors, the officials, the Persians, the men of Erech, the Babylonians, the men of Susa, that is, the Elamites, 10 and the rest of the nations whom the great and noble Osnappar deported and settled in the cities of Samaria and in the rest of the province Beyond the River. 11 (This is a copy of the letter that they sent.) "To Artaxerxes the king: Your servants, the men of the province Beyond the River, send greeting. And now 12 be it known to the king that the Jews who came up from you to us have gone to Jerusalem. They are rebuilding that rebellious and wicked city. They are finishing the walls and repairing the foundations. 13 Now be it known to the king that if this city is rebuilt and the walls finished, they will not pay tribute, custom, or toll, and the royal revenue will be impaired. 14 Now because we eat the salt of the palace and it is not fitting for us to witness the king's dishonor, therefore we send and inform the king, 15 in order that search may be made in the book of the records of your fathers. You will find in the book of the records and learn that this city is a rebellious city, hurtful to kings and provinces, and that sedition was stirred up in it from of old. That was why this city was laid waste. 16 We make known to the king that if this city is rebuilt and its walls finished, you will then have no possession in the province Beyond the River."

The King Orders the Work to Cease

17 The king sent an answer: "To Rehum the commander and Shimshai the scribe and the rest of their associates who live in Samaria and in the rest of the province Beyond the River, greeting. And now 18 the letter that you sent to us has been plainly read before me. 19 And I made a decree, and search has been made, and it has been found that this city from of old has risen against kings, and that rebellion and sedition have been made in it. 20 And mighty kings have been over Jerusalem, who ruled over the whole province Beyond the River, to whom tribute, custom, and toll were paid. 21 Therefore make a decree that these men be made to cease, and that this city be not rebuilt, until a decree is made by me. 22 And take care not to be slack in this matter. Why should damage grow to the hurt of the king?"

23 Then, when the copy of King Artaxerxes' letter was read before Rehum and Shimshai the scribe and their associates, they went in haste to the Jews at Jerusalem and by force and power made them cease. 24 Then the work on the house of God that is in Jerusalem stopped, and it ceased until the second year of the reign of Darius king of Persia.

Rebuilding Begins Anew

5 Now the prophets, Haggai and Zechariah the son of Iddo, prophesied to the Jews who were in Judah and Jerusalem, in the name of the God of Israel who was over them. 2 Then Zerubbabel the son of Shealtiel and Jeshua the son of Jozadak arose and began to rebuild the house of God that is in Jerusalem, and the prophets of God were with them, supporting them.

3 At the same time Tattenai the governor of the province Beyond the River and Shethar-bozenai and their associates came to them and spoke to them thus: "Who gave you a decree to build this house and to finish this structure?" 4 They[2] also asked them this: "What are the names of the men who are building this building?" 5 But the eye of their God was on the elders of the Jews, and they did not stop them until the report should reach Darius

[1] Hebrew *written in Aramaic and translated in Aramaic*, indicating that 4:8–6:18 is in Aramaic; another interpretation is *The letter was written in the Aramaic script and set forth in the Aramaic language* [2] Septuagint, Syriac; Aramaic *We*

and then an answer be returned by letter concerning it.

Tattenai's Letter to King Darius

6 This is a copy of the letter that Tattenai the governor of the province Beyond the River and Shethar-bozenai and his associates, the governors who were in the province Beyond the River, sent to Darius the king. 7 They sent him a report, in which was written as follows: "To Darius the king, all peace. 8 Be it known to the king that we went to the province of Judah, to the house of the great God. It is being built with huge stones, and timber is laid in the walls. This work goes on diligently and prospers in their hands. 9 Then we asked those elders and spoke to them thus: 'Who gave you a decree to build this house and to finish this structure?' 10 We also asked them their names, for your information, that we might write down the names of their leaders.[1] 11 And this was their reply to us: 'We are the servants of the God of heaven and earth, and we are rebuilding the house that was built many years ago, which a great king of Israel built and finished. 12 But because our fathers had angered the God of heaven, he gave them into the hand of Nebuchadnezzar king of Babylon, the Chaldean, who destroyed this house and carried away the people to Babylonia. 13 However, in the first year of Cyrus king of Babylon, Cyrus the king made a decree that this house of God should be rebuilt. 14 And the gold and silver vessels of the house of God, which Nebuchadnezzar had taken out of the temple that was in Jerusalem and brought into the temple of Babylon, these Cyrus the king took out of the temple of Babylon, and they were delivered to one whose name was Sheshbazzar, whom he had made governor; 15 and he said to him, "Take these vessels, go and put them in the temple that is in Jerusalem, and let the house of God be rebuilt on its site." 16 Then this Sheshbazzar came and laid the foundations of the house of God that is in Jerusalem, and from that time until now it has been in building, and it is not yet finished.' 17 Therefore, if it seems good to the king, let search be made in the royal archives there in Babylon, to see whether a decree was issued by Cyrus the king for the rebuilding of this house of God in Jerusalem. And let the king send us his pleasure in this matter."

The Decree of Darius

6 Then Darius the king made a decree, and search was made in Babylonia, in the house of the archives where the documents were stored. 2 And in Ecbatana, the capital that is in the province of Media, a scroll was found on which this was written: "A record. 3 In the first year of Cyrus the king, Cyrus the king issued a decree: Concerning the house of God at Jerusalem, let the house be rebuilt, the place where sacrifices were offered, and let its foundations be retained. Its height shall be sixty cubits[2] and its breadth sixty cubits, 4 with three layers of great stones and one layer of timber. Let the cost be paid from the royal treasury. 5 And also let the gold and silver vessels of the house of God, which Nebuchadnezzar took out of the temple that is in Jerusalem and brought to Babylon, be restored and brought back to the temple that is in Jerusalem, each to its place. You shall put them in the house of God."

6 "Now therefore, Tattenai, governor of the province Beyond the River, Shethar-bozenai, and your associates the governors who are in the province Beyond the River, keep away. 7 Let the work on this house of God alone. Let the governor of the Jews and the elders of the Jews rebuild this house of God on its site. 8 Moreover, I make a decree regarding what you shall do for these elders of the Jews for the rebuilding of this house of God. The

[1] Aramaic *of the men at their heads* [2] A *cubit* was about 18 inches or 45 centimeters

cost is to be paid to these men in full and without delay from the royal revenue, the tribute of the province from Beyond the River. 9 And whatever is needed—bulls, rams, or sheep for burnt offerings to the God of heaven, wheat, salt, wine, or oil, as the priests at Jerusalem require—let that be given to them day by day without fail, 10 that they may offer pleasing sacrifices to the God of heaven and pray for the life of the king and his sons. 11 Also I make a decree that if anyone alters this edict, a beam shall be pulled out of his house, and he shall be impaled on it, and his house shall be made a dunghill. 12 May the God who has caused his name to dwell there overthrow any king or people who shall put out a hand to alter this, or to destroy this house of God that is in Jerusalem. I Darius make a decree; let it be done with all diligence."

The Temple Finished and Dedicated

13 Then, according to the word sent by Darius the king, Tattenai, the governor of the province Beyond the River, Shethar-bozenai, and their associates did with all diligence what Darius the king had ordered. 14 And the elders of the Jews built and prospered through the prophesying of Haggai the prophet and Zechariah the son of Iddo. They finished their building by decree of the God of Israel and by decree of Cyrus and Darius and Artaxerxes king of Persia; 15 and this house was finished on the third day of the month of Adar, in the sixth year of the reign of Darius the king.

16 And the people of Israel, the priests and the Levites, and the rest of the returned exiles, celebrated the dedication of this house of God with joy. 17 They offered at the dedication of this house of God 100 bulls, 200 rams, 400 lambs, and as a sin offering for all Israel 12 male goats, according to the number of the tribes of Israel. 18 And they set the priests in their divisions and the Levites in their divisions, for the service of God at Jerusalem, as it is written in the Book of Moses.

Passover Celebrated

19 On the fourteenth day of the first month, the returned exiles kept the Passover. 20 For the priests and the Levites had purified themselves together; all of them were clean. So they slaughtered the Passover lamb for all the returned exiles, for their fellow priests, and for themselves. 21 It was eaten by the people of Israel who had returned from exile, and also by every one who had joined them and separated himself from the uncleanness of the peoples of the land to worship the LORD, the God of Israel. 22 And they kept the Feast of Unleavened Bread seven days with joy, for the LORD had made them joyful and had turned the heart of the king of Assyria to them, so that he aided them in the work of the house of God, the God of Israel.

Ezra Sent to Teach the People

7 Now after this, in the reign of Artaxerxes king of Persia, Ezra the son of Seraiah, son of Azariah, son of Hilkiah, 2 son of Shallum, son of Zadok, son of Ahitub, 3 son of Amariah, son of Azariah, son of Meraioth, 4 son of Zerahiah, son of Uzzi, son of Bukki, 5 son of Abishua, son of Phinehas, son of Eleazar, son of Aaron the chief priest— 6 this Ezra went up from Babylonia. He was a scribe skilled in the Law of Moses that the LORD, the God of Israel, had given, and the king granted him all that he asked, for the hand of the LORD his God was on him.

7 And there went up also to Jerusalem, in the seventh year of Artaxerxes the king, some of the people of Israel, and some of the priests and Levites, the singers and gatekeepers, and the temple servants. 8 And Ezra[1] came to Jerusalem in the fifth month, which was in the seventh year of the king. 9 For on the first day of the first month he began to go up from Babylonia,

[1] Aramaic *he*

and on the first day of the fifth month he
came to Jerusalem, for the good hand of
his God was on him. 10 For Ezra had set his
heart to study the Law of the LORD, and to
do it and to teach his statutes and rules
in Israel.

11 This is a copy of the letter that King
Artaxerxes gave to Ezra the priest, the
scribe, a man learned in matters of the
commandments of the LORD
and his statutes for Israel: 12 "Artaxerxes,
king of kings, to Ezra the priest, the scribe
of the Law of the God of heaven. Peace.[1]
And now 13 I make a decree that anyone
of the people of Israel or their priests
or Levites in my kingdom, who freely
offers to go to Jerusalem, may go with
you. 14 For you are sent by the king and

[1] Aramaic *Perfect* (probably a greeting)

Zerubbabel's Temple

When the Jews came back to Jerusalem, they rebuilt the temple in three stages (about 536–516 B.C.). First, the altar was built, so the Jews could offer sacrifices once more (Ezra 3:2–3). Next, the Jews laid the foundation for the temple. Some people rejoiced because the temple was being rebuilt. Older people, who had seen the old temple, which the Babylonians had destroyed, were sad because this one would not be nearly so beautiful. Neighboring enemy nations tried to discourage the building of the temple. The Jews themselves got busy building their own houses instead. Twenty years went by before the temple was finally completed.

The only information we have in the Bible about this temple is that it was 90 feet (27 m) high and 90 feet (27 m) wide (Ezra 6:3). This must have been for the front of the temple, or the Porch. Nothing tells how long the temple was.

his seven counselors to make inquiries about Judah and Jerusalem according to the Law of your God, which is in your hand, 15 and also to carry the silver and gold that the king and his counselors have freely offered to the God of Israel, whose dwelling is in Jerusalem, 16 with all the silver and gold that you shall find in the whole province of Babylonia, and with the freewill offerings of the people and the priests, vowed willingly for the house of their God that is in Jerusalem. 17 With this money, then, you shall with all diligence buy bulls, rams, and lambs, with their grain offerings and their drink offerings, and you shall offer them on the altar of the house of your God that is in Jerusalem. 18 Whatever seems good to you and your brothers to do with the rest of the silver and gold, you may do, according to the will of your God. 19 The vessels that have been given you for the service of the house of your God, you shall deliver before the God of Jerusalem. 20 And whatever else is required for the house of your God, which it falls to you to provide, you may provide it out of the king's treasury.

21 "And I, Artaxerxes the king, make a decree to all the treasurers in the province Beyond the River: Whatever Ezra the priest, the scribe of the Law of the God of heaven, requires of you, let it be done with all diligence, 22 up to 100 talents[1] of silver, 100 cors[2] of wheat, 100 baths[3] of wine, 100 baths of oil, and salt without prescribing how much. 23 Whatever is decreed by the God of heaven, let it be done in full for the house of the God of heaven, lest his wrath be against the realm of the king and his sons. 24 We also notify you that it shall not be lawful to impose tribute, custom, or toll on anyone of the priests, the Levites, the singers, the doorkeepers, the temple servants, or other servants of this house of God.

25 "And you, Ezra, according to the wisdom of your God that is in your hand, appoint magistrates and judges who may judge all the people in the province Beyond the River, all such as know the laws of your God. And those who do not know them, you shall teach. 26 Whoever will not obey the law of your God and the law of the king, let judgment be strictly executed on him, whether for death or for banishment or for confiscation of his goods or for imprisonment."

27 Blessed be the LORD, the God of our fathers, who put such a thing as this into the heart of the king, to beautify the house of the LORD that is in Jerusalem, 28 and who extended to me his steadfast love before the king and his counselors, and before all the king's mighty officers. I took courage, for the hand of the LORD my God was on me, and I gathered leading men from Israel to go up with me.

CHARACTER PROFILE

EZRA

Ezra was a priest and a scribe, a teacher of God's Law. The Jews who had been living in exile in Babylonia had been allowed to return to Jerusalem. Ezra went to Jerusalem to teach them the commandments and laws of God.

[1] A *talent* was about 75 pounds or 34 kilograms [2] A *cor* was about 6 bushels or 220 liters [3] A *bath* was about 6 gallons or 22 liters

Genealogy of Those Who Returned with Ezra

8 These are the heads of their fathers'
houses, and this is the genealogy
of those who went up with me from
Babylonia, in the reign of Artaxerxes the
king: 2 Of the sons of Phinehas, Gershom.
Of the sons of Ithamar, Daniel. Of the
sons of David, Hattush. 3 Of the sons
of Shecaniah, who was of the sons of
Parosh, Zechariah, with whom were reg-
istered 150 men. 4 Of the sons of Pahath-
moab, Eliehoenai the son of Zerahiah,
and with him 200 men. 5 Of the sons of
Zattu,[1] Shecaniah the son of Jahaziel, and
with him 300 men. 6 Of the sons of Adin,
Ebed the son of Jonathan, and with him
50 men. 7 Of the sons of Elam, Jeshaiah
the son of Athaliah, and with him 70 men.
8 Of the sons of Shephatiah, Zebadiah the
son of Michael, and with him 80 men. 9 Of
the sons of Joab, Obadiah the son of Jehiel,
and with him 218 men. 10 Of the sons of
Bani,[2] Shelomith the son of Josiphiah,
and with him 160 men. 11 Of the sons of
Bebai, Zechariah, the son of Bebai, and
with him 28 men. 12 Of the sons of Azgad,
Johanan the son of Hakkatan, and with
him 110 men. 13 Of the sons of Adonikam,
those who came later, their names being
Eliphelet, Jeuel, and Shemaiah, and with
them 60 men. 14 Of the sons of Bigvai,
Uthai and Zaccur, and with them 70 men.

Ezra Sends for Levites

15 I gathered them to the river that runs
to Ahava, and there we camped three days.
As I reviewed the people and the priests,
I found there none of the sons of Levi.
16 Then I sent for Eliezer, Ariel, Shemaiah,
Elnathan, Jarib, Elnathan, Nathan,
Zechariah, and Meshullam, leading men,
and for Joiarib and Elnathan, who were
men of insight, 17 and sent them to Iddo,
the leading man at the place Casiphia,
telling them what to say to Iddo and his
brothers and[3] the temple servants at the
place Casiphia, namely, to send us minis-
ters for the house of our God. 18 And by the
good hand of our God on us, they brought
us a man of discretion, of the sons of
Mahli the son of Levi, son of Israel, namely
Sherebiah with his sons and kinsmen, 18;
19 also Hashabiah, and with him Jeshaiah
of the sons of Merari, with his kinsmen
and their sons, 20; 20 besides 220 of the
temple servants, whom David and his offi-
cials had set apart to attend the Levites.
These were all mentioned by name.

Fasting and Prayer for Protection

21 Then I proclaimed a fast there, at the
river Ahava, that we might humble our-
selves before our God, to seek from him
a safe journey for ourselves, our children,
and all our goods. 22 For I was ashamed
to ask the king for a band of soldiers and
horsemen to protect us against the enemy
on our way, since we had told the king,
"The hand of our God is for good on all
who seek him, and the power of his wrath
is against all who forsake him." 23 So we
fasted and implored our God for this, and
he listened to our entreaty.

Priests to Guard Offerings

24 Then I set apart twelve of the leading
priests: Sherebiah, Hashabiah, and ten of
their kinsmen with them. 25 And I weighed
out to them the silver and the gold and
the vessels, the offering for the house of
our God that the king and his counselors
and his lords and all Israel there present
had offered. 26 I weighed out into their
hand 650 talents[4] of silver, and silver ves-
sels worth 200 talents,[5] and 100 talents of
gold, 27 20 bowls of gold worth 1,000 dar-
ics,[6] and two vessels of fine bright bronze
as precious as gold. 28 And I said to them,
"You are holy to the LORD, and the vessels
are holy, and the silver and the gold are
a freewill offering to the LORD, the God
of your fathers. 29 Guard them and keep
them until you weigh them before the
chief priests and the Levites and the heads

[1] Septuagint; Hebrew lacks *of Zattu* [2] Septuagint; Hebrew lacks *Bani* [3] Hebrew lacks *and* [4] A *talent* was about 75 pounds or 34 kilograms [5] Revocalization; the number is missing in the Masoretic Text [6] A *daric* was a coin weighing about 1/4 ounce or 8.5 grams

of fathers' houses in Israel at Jerusalem,
within the chambers of the house of the
LORD." 30 So the priests and the Levites
took over the weight of the silver and the
gold and the vessels, to bring them to
Jerusalem, to the house of our God.

31 Then we departed from the river
Ahava on the twelfth day of the first
month, to go to Jerusalem. The hand
of our God was on us, and he delivered
us from the hand of the enemy and
from ambushes by the way. 32 We came
to Jerusalem, and there we remained
three days. 33 On the fourth day, within
the house of our God, the silver and the
gold and the vessels were weighed into
the hands of Meremoth the priest, son
of Uriah, and with him was Eleazar the
son of Phinehas, and with them were the
Levites, Jozabad the son of Jeshua and
Noadiah the son of Binnui. 34 The whole
was counted and weighed, and the weight
of everything was recorded.

35 At that time those who had come
from captivity, the returned exiles, offered
burnt offerings to the God of Israel, twelve
bulls for all Israel, ninety-six rams, sev-
enty-seven lambs, and as a sin offering
twelve male goats. All this was a burnt
offering to the LORD. 36 They also deliv-
ered the king's commissions to the king's
satraps[1] and to the governors of the prov-
ince Beyond the River, and they aided the
people and the house of God.

Ezra Prays About Intermarriage

9 After these things had been done, the
officials approached me and said,
"The people of Israel and the priests and
the Levites have not separated themselves
from the peoples of the lands with their
abominations, from the Canaanites, the
Hittites, the Perizzites, the Jebusites, the
Ammonites, the Moabites, the Egyptians,
and the Amorites. 2 For they have taken
some of their daughters to be wives for
themselves and for their sons, so that the
holy race[2] has mixed itself with the peo-
ples of the lands. And in this faithlessness
the hand of the officials and chief men
has been foremost." 3 As soon as I heard
this, I tore my garment and my cloak and
pulled hair from my head and beard and
sat appalled. 4 Then all who trembled at
the words of the God of Israel, because of
the faithlessness of the returned exiles,
gathered around me while I sat appalled
until the evening sacrifice. 5 And at the
evening sacrifice I rose from my fasting,
with my garment and my cloak torn, and
fell upon my knees and spread out my
hands to the LORD my God, 6 saying:

"O my God, I am ashamed and blush to
lift my face to you, my God, for our iniqui-
ties have risen higher than our heads, and
our guilt has mounted up to the heavens.
7 From the days of our fathers to this day
we have been in great guilt. And for our
iniquities we, our kings, and our priests
have been given into the hand of the kings
of the lands, to the sword, to captivity, to
plundering, and to utter shame, as it is
today. 8 But now for a brief moment favor
has been shown by the LORD our God, to
leave us a remnant and to give us a secure
hold[3] within his holy place, that our God
may brighten our eyes and grant us a
little reviving in our slavery. 9 For we are
slaves. Yet our God has not forsaken us
in our slavery, but has extended to us his
steadfast love before the kings of Persia, to
grant us some reviving to set up the house
of our God, to repair its ruins, and to give
us protection[4] in Judea and Jerusalem.

10 "And now, O our God, what shall we
say after this? For we have forsaken your
commandments, 11 which you com-
manded by your servants the prophets,
saying, 'The land that you are entering, to
take possession of it, is a land impure with
the impurity of the peoples of the lands,
with their abominations that have filled
it from end to end with their uncleanness.
12 Therefore do not give your daughters to

[1] A *satrap* was a Persian official [2] Hebrew *offspring* [3] Hebrew *nail*, or *tent-pin* [4] Hebrew *a wall*

their sons, neither take their daughters for your sons, and never seek their peace or prosperity, that you may be strong and eat the good of the land and leave it for an inheritance to your children forever.' 13 And after all that has come upon us for our evil deeds and for our great guilt, seeing that you, our God, have punished us less than our iniquities deserved and have given us such a remnant as this, 14 shall we break your commandments again and intermarry with the peoples who practice these abominations? Would you not be angry with us until you consumed us, so that there should be no remnant, nor any to escape? 15 O LORD, the God of Israel, you are just, for we are left a remnant that has escaped, as it is today. Behold, we are before you in our guilt, for none can stand before you because of this."

The People Confess Their Sin

10 While Ezra prayed and made confession, weeping and casting himself down before the house of God, a very great assembly of men, women, and children, gathered to him out of Israel, for the people wept bitterly. 2 And Shecaniah the son of Jehiel, of the sons of Elam, addressed Ezra: "We have broken faith with our God and have married foreign women from the peoples of the land, but even now there is hope for Israel in spite of this. 3 Therefore let us make a covenant with our God to put away all these wives and their children, according to the counsel of my lord[1] and of those who tremble at the commandment of our God, and let it be done according to the Law. 4 Arise, for it is your task, and we are with you; be strong and do it." 5 Then Ezra arose and made the leading priests and Levites and all Israel take oath that they would do as had been said. So they took the oath.

6 Then Ezra withdrew from before the house of God and went to the chamber of Jehohanan the son of Eliashib, where he spent the night,[2] neither eating bread nor drinking water, for he was mourning over the faithlessness of the exiles. 7 And a proclamation was made throughout Judah and Jerusalem to all the returned exiles that they should assemble at Jerusalem, 8 and that if anyone did not come within three days, by order of the officials and the elders all his property should be forfeited, and he himself banned from the congregation of the exiles.

9 Then all the men of Judah and Benjamin assembled at Jerusalem within the three days. It was the ninth month, on the twentieth day of the month. And all the people sat in the open square before the house of God, trembling because of this matter and because of the heavy rain. 10 And Ezra the priest stood up and said to them, "You have broken faith and married foreign women, and so increased the guilt of Israel. 11 Now then make confession to the LORD, the God of your fathers and do his will. Separate yourselves from the peoples of the land and from the foreign wives." 12 Then all the assembly answered with a loud voice, "It is so; we must do as you have said. 13 But the people are many, and it is a time of heavy rain; we cannot stand in the open. Nor is this a task for one day or for two, for we have greatly transgressed in this matter. 14 Let our officials stand for the whole assembly. Let all in our cities who have taken foreign wives come at appointed times, and with them the elders and judges of every city, until the fierce wrath of our God over this matter is turned away from us." 15 Only Jonathan the son of Asahel and Jahzeiah the son of Tikvah opposed this, and Meshullam and Shabbethai the Levite supported them.

16 Then the returned exiles did so. Ezra the priest selected men,[3] heads of fathers' houses, according to their fathers' houses, each of them designated by name. On the first day of the tenth month they sat down

[1] Or *of the Lord* [2] Probable reading; Hebrew *where he went* [3] Syriac; Hebrew *And there were selected Ezra . . .*

to examine the matter; **17** and by the first
day of the first month they had come to
the end of all the men who had married
foreign women.

Those Guilty of Intermarriage

18 Now there were found some of the
sons of the priests who had married for-
eign women: Maaseiah, Eliezer, Jarib, and
Gedaliah, some of the sons of Jeshua the
son of Jozadak and his brothers. **19** They
pledged themselves to put away their
wives, and their guilt offering was a ram
of the flock for their guilt.[1] **20** Of the sons
of Immer: Hanani and Zebadiah. **21** Of
the sons of Harim: Maaseiah, Elijah,
Shemaiah, Jehiel, and Uzziah. **22** Of the
sons of Pashhur: Elioenai, Maaseiah,
Ishmael, Nethanel, Jozabad, and Elasah.

23 Of the Levites: Jozabad, Shimei,
Kelaiah (that is, Kelita), Pethahiah, Judah,
and Eliezer. **24** Of the singers: Eliashib. Of
the gatekeepers: Shallum, Telem, and Uri.

25 And of Israel: of the sons of Parosh:
Ramiah, Izziah, Malchijah, Mijamin,
Eleazar, Hashabiah,[2] and Benaiah. **26** Of the
sons of Elam: Mattaniah, Zechariah, Jehiel,
Abdi, Jeremoth, and Elijah. **27** Of the sons
of Zattu: Elioenai, Eliashib, Mattaniah,
Jeremoth, Zabad, and Aziza. **28** Of the
sons of Bebai were Jehohanan, Hananiah,
Zabbai, and Athlai. **29** Of the sons of Bani
were Meshullam, Malluch, Adaiah,
Jashub, Sheal, and Jeremoth. **30** Of the sons
of Pahath-moab: Adna, Chelal, Benaiah,
Maaseiah, Mattaniah, Bezalel, Binnui,
and Manasseh. **31** Of the sons of Harim:
Eliezer, Isshijah, Malchijah, Shemaiah,
Shimeon, **32** Benjamin, Malluch, and
Shemariah. **33** Of the sons of Hashum:
Mattenai, Mattattah, Zabad, Eliphelet,
Jeremai, Manasseh, and Shimei. **34** Of
the sons of Bani: Maadai, Amram, Uel,
35 Benaiah, Bedeiah, Cheluhi, **36** Vaniah,
Meremoth, Eliashib, **37** Mattaniah,
Mattenai, Jaasu. **38** Of the sons of Binnui:[3]
Shimei, **39** Shelemiah, Nathan, Adaiah,
40 Machnadebai, Shashai, Sharai, **41** Azarel,
Shelemiah, Shemariah, **42** Shallum,
Amariah, and Joseph. **43** Of the sons of
Nebo: Jeiel, Mattithiah, Zabad, Zebina,
Jaddai, Joel, and Benaiah. **44** All these had
married foreign women, and some of the
women had even borne children.[4]

[1] Or *as their reparation* [2] Septuagint; Hebrew *Malchijah* [3] Septuagint; Hebrew *Bani, Binnui* [4] Or *and they put them away with their children*

Introduction to

Nehemiah

Author
Nehemiah, governor of Judah

Date
About 445–432 B.C.

People
Nehemiah; Artaxerxes; Ezra; Sanballat; Tobiah

Purpose
The purpose of Nehemiah is to show God's strength and protection as His people rebuild the walls of Jerusalem, and to call God's people to worship and obey Him.

Central Themes
God answers prayer; God works through rulers and circumstances to carry out His purposes; God protects His people; God provides strength to do His work; God's people worship, hear His Word, and obey Him; when God's people sin, they must repent.

Memory Verses
Nehemiah's prayer (Nehemiah 1:4–11); building the wall (Nehemiah 4:18–23); attending to the Word (Nehemiah 8:7b–8)

Introduction

Nehemiah was cupbearer to the king of Persia. This book opens when Nehemiah hears a report of the ruined walls of Jerusalem, where God's people have returned after exile. Nehemiah prays, then asks the king for permission to go to Jerusalem to rebuild. The king agrees, and Nehemiah goes (Nehemiah 1–2). In Jerusalem, with Nehemiah leading them, many different people work on the different sections of the wall (Nehemiah 3). Enemy neighbors try to stop the building, first by mocking, then by threatening the builders. Nehemiah prays, arms the builders, trusts God, and continues working (Nehemiah 4). In just 52 days, the wall is finished (Nehemiah 6). Then Nehemiah gathers the people and has Ezra the scribe read God's Law to them. The people rejoice before God and then confess their sins. Afterward, they commit themselves anew to the covenant God had made with them (Nehemiah 8–10). Later, they dedicate the wall with praise to God, and organize the service of priests and Levites in temple worship (Nehemiah 12). Years later, Nehemiah returns to visit Jerusalem. He finds many ways in which the people have already turned back to sin, and he calls them once more to repentance (Nehemiah 13).

516 B.C.	458 B.C.	445 B.C.	About 433–423 B.C.
Temple rebuilt	Ezra arrives in Jerusalem	Nehemiah rebuilds walls	Nehemiah's absence and return

Nehemiah

Report from Jerusalem

1 The words of Nehemiah the son of Hacaliah.

Now it happened in the month of Chislev, in the twentieth year, as I was in Susa the capital,[1] 2 that Hanani, one of my brothers, came with certain men from Judah. And I asked them concerning the Jews who escaped, who had survived the exile, and concerning Jerusalem. 3 And they said to me, "The remnant there in the province who had survived the exile is in great trouble and shame. The wall of Jerusalem is broken down, and its gates are destroyed by fire."

Nehemiah's Prayer

4 As soon as I heard these words I sat down and wept and mourned for days, and I continued fasting and praying before the God of heaven. 5 And I said, "O LORD God of heaven, the great and awesome God who keeps covenant and steadfast love with those who love him and keep his commandments, 6 let your ear be attentive and your eyes open, to hear the prayer of your servant that I now pray before you day and night for the people of Israel your servants, confessing the sins of the people of Israel, which we have sinned against you. Even I and my father's house have sinned. 7 We have acted very corruptly against you and have not kept the commandments, the statutes, and the rules that you commanded your servant Moses. 8 Remember the word that you commanded your servant Moses, saying, 'If you are unfaithful, I will scatter you among the peoples, 9 but if you return to me and keep my commandments and do them, though your outcasts are in the uttermost parts of heaven, from there I will gather them and bring them to the place that I have chosen, to make my name dwell there.' 10 They are your servants and your people, whom you have redeemed by your great power and by your strong hand. 11 O Lord, let your ear be attentive to the prayer of your servant, and to the prayer of your servants who delight to fear your name, and give success to your servant today, and grant him mercy in the sight of this man."

Now I was cupbearer to the king.

Nehemiah Sent to Judah

2 In the month of Nisan, in the twentieth year of King Artaxerxes, when wine was before him, I took up the wine and gave it to the king. Now I had not been sad in his presence. 2 And the king said to me, "Why is your face sad, seeing you are not sick? This is nothing but sadness of the heart." Then I was very much afraid. 3 I said to the king, "Let the king live forever! Why should not my face be sad, when the city, the place of my fathers' graves, lies in ruins, and its gates have been destroyed by fire?" 4 Then the king said to me, "What are you requesting?" So I prayed to the God of heaven. 5 And I said to the king, "If it pleases the king, and if your servant has found favor in your sight, that you send me to Judah, to the city of my fathers' graves, that I may rebuild it." 6 And the king said to me (the queen sitting beside him), "How long will you be gone, and when will you return?" So it pleased the king to send me when I had given him a time. 7 And I said to the king, "If it pleases the king, let letters be given me to the governors of the province Beyond the River, that they may let me pass through until I come to Judah, 8 and a letter to Asaph,

[1] Or *the fortified city*

the keeper of the king's forest, that he
may give me timber to make beams for
the gates of the fortress of the temple, and
for the wall of the city, and for the house
that I shall occupy." And the king granted
me what I asked, for the good hand of my
God was upon me.

Nehemiah Inspects Jerusalem's Walls

9 Then I came to the governors of the
province Beyond the River and gave them
the king's letters. Now the king had sent
with me officers of the army and horse-
men. 10 But when Sanballat the Horonite
and Tobiah the Ammonite servant heard
this, it displeased them greatly that some-
one had come to seek the welfare of the
people of Israel.

11 So I went to Jerusalem and was there
three days. 12 Then I arose in the night,
I and a few men with me. And I told no
one what my God had put into my heart
to do for Jerusalem. There was no animal
with me but the one on which I rode. 13 I
went out by night by the Valley Gate to the
Dragon Spring and to the Dung Gate, and I
inspected the walls of Jerusalem that were
broken down and its gates that had been
destroyed by fire. 14 Then I went on to the
Fountain Gate and to the King's Pool, but
there was no room for the animal that
was under me to pass. 15 Then I went up
in the night by the valley and inspected
the wall, and I turned back and entered
by the Valley Gate, and so returned. 16 And
the officials did not know where I had
gone or what I was doing, and I had not
yet told the Jews, the priests, the nobles,
the officials, and the rest who were to do
the work.

17 Then I said to them, "You see the
trouble we are in, how Jerusalem lies in
ruins with its gates burned. Come, let us
build the wall of Jerusalem, that we may
no longer suffer derision." 18 And I told
them of the hand of my God that had been
upon me for good, and also of the words
that the king had spoken to me. And they
said, "Let us rise up and build." So they
strengthened their hands for the good
work. 19 But when Sanballat the Horonite
and Tobiah the Ammonite servant and
Geshem the Arab heard of it, they jeered at
us and despised us and said, "What is this
thing that you are doing? Are you rebel-
ling against the king?" 20 Then I replied to
them, "The God of heaven will make us
prosper, and we his servants will arise and
build, but you have no portion or right or
claim[1] in Jerusalem."

Rebuilding the Wall

3 Then Eliashib the high priest rose up
with his brothers the priests, and they
built the Sheep Gate. They consecrated it
and set its doors. They consecrated it as
far as the Tower of the Hundred, as far

CHARACTER PROFILE

NEHEMIAH

Nehemiah served the king of Persia while the Jews were living in exile. With the king's permission, Nehemiah went back to Jerusalem to rebuild its city walls. Although enemy neighbors kept trying to stop him, Nehemiah trusted God and led the Jews in rebuilding the walls of Jerusalem.

[1] Or *memorial*

as the Tower of Hananel. 2 And next to
him the men of Jericho built. And next to
them[1] Zaccur the son of Imri built.

3 The sons of Hassenaah built the Fish
Gate. They laid its beams and set its doors,
its bolts, and its bars. 4 And next to them
Meremoth the son of Uriah, son of Hakkoz
repaired. And next to them Meshullam
the son of Berechiah, son of Meshezabel
repaired. And next to them Zadok the son
of Baana repaired. 5 And next to them the
Tekoites repaired, but their nobles would
not stoop to serve their Lord.[2]

6 Joiada the son of Paseah and Meshul-
lam the son of Besodeiah repaired the
Gate of Yeshanah.[3] They laid its beams
and set its doors, its bolts, and its bars.
7 And next to them repaired Melatiah the
Gibeonite and Jadon the Meronothite, the
men of Gibeon and of Mizpah, the seat
of the governor of the province Beyond
the River. 8 Next to them Uzziel the son
of Harhaiah, goldsmiths, repaired. Next
to him Hananiah, one of the perfumers,
repaired, and they restored Jerusalem
as far as the Broad Wall. 9 Next to them
Rephaiah the son of Hur, ruler of half the
district of[4] Jerusalem, repaired. 10 Next
to them Jedaiah the son of Harumaph
repaired opposite his house. And next
to him Hattush the son of Hashabneiah
repaired. 11 Malchijah the son of Harim
and Hasshub the son of Pahath-moab
repaired another section and the Tower of
the Ovens. 12 Next to him Shallum the son
of Hallohesh, ruler of half the district of
Jerusalem, repaired, he and his daughters.

13 Hanun and the inhabitants of Zanoah
repaired the Valley Gate. They rebuilt it
and set its doors, its bolts, and its bars,
and repaired a thousand cubits[5] of the
wall, as far as the Dung Gate.

14 Malchijah the son of Rechab, ruler of
the district of Beth-haccherem, repaired
the Dung Gate. He rebuilt it and set its
doors, its bolts, and its bars.

15 And Shallum the son of Col-hozeh,
ruler of the district of Mizpah, repaired the
Fountain Gate. He rebuilt it and covered
it and set its doors, its bolts, and its bars.
And he built the wall of the Pool of Shelah
of the king's garden, as far as the stairs that
go down from the city of David. 16 After
him Nehemiah the son of Azbuk, ruler of
half the district of Beth-zur, repaired to
a point opposite the tombs of David, as
far as the artificial pool, and as far as the
house of the mighty men. 17 After him the
Levites repaired: Rehum the son of Bani.
Next to him Hashabiah, ruler of half the
district of Keilah, repaired for his district.
18 After him their brothers repaired: Bavvai
the son of Henadad, ruler of half the dis-
trict of Keilah. 19 Next to him Ezer the
son of Jeshua, ruler of Mizpah, repaired
another section opposite the ascent to
the armory at the buttress.[6] 20 After him
Baruch the son of Zabbai repaired another
section from the buttress to the door of
the house of Eliashib the high priest.
21 After him Meremoth the son of Uriah,
son of Hakkoz repaired another section
from the door of the house of Eliashib to
the end of the house of Eliashib. 22 After
him the priests, the men of the surround-
ing area, repaired. 23 After them Benjamin
and Hasshub repaired opposite their
house. After them Azariah the son of
Maaseiah, son of Ananiah repaired beside
his own house. 24 After him Binnui the
son of Henadad repaired another section,
from the house of Azariah to the buttress
25 and to the corner. Palal the son of Uzai
repaired opposite the buttress and the
tower projecting from the upper house of
the king at the court of the guard. After
him Pedaiah the son of Parosh 26 and the
temple servants living on Ophel repaired
to a point opposite the Water Gate on the
east and the projecting tower. 27 After him
the Tekoites repaired another section
opposite the great projecting tower as far
as the wall of Ophel.

28 Above the Horse Gate the priests

[1] Hebrew *him* [2] Or *lords* [3] Or *of the old city* [4] Or *foreman of half the portion assigned to*; also verses 12, 14, 15, 16, 17, 18 [5] A *cubit* was about 18 inches or 45 centimeters [6] Or *corner*; also verses 20, 24, 25

repaired, each one opposite his own house. 29 After them Zadok the son of Immer repaired opposite his own house. After him Shemaiah the son of Shecaniah, the keeper of the East Gate, repaired. 30 After him Hananiah the son of Shelemiah and Hanun the sixth son of Zalaph repaired another section. After him Meshullam the son of Berechiah repaired opposite his chamber. 31 After him Malchijah, one of the goldsmiths, repaired as far as the house of the temple servants and of the merchants, opposite the Muster Gate,[1] and to the upper chamber of the corner. 32 And between the upper chamber of the corner and the Sheep Gate the goldsmiths and the merchants repaired.

Opposition to the Work

4 [2]Now when Sanballat heard that we were building the wall, he was angry and greatly enraged, and he jeered at the Jews. 2 And he said in the presence of his brothers and of the army of Samaria, "What are these feeble Jews doing? Will they restore it for themselves?[3] Will they sacrifice? Will they finish up in a day? Will they revive the stones out of the heaps of rubbish, and burned ones at that?" 3 Tobiah the Ammonite was beside him, and he said, "Yes, what they are building—if a fox goes up on it he will break down their stone wall!" 4 Hear, O our God, for we are despised. Turn back their taunt on their own heads and give them up to be plundered in a land where they are captives. 5 Do not cover their guilt, and let not their sin be blotted out from your sight, for they have provoked you to anger in the presence of the builders.

6 So we built the wall. And all the wall was joined together to half its height, for the people had a mind to work.

7 [4] But when Sanballat and Tobiah and the Arabs and the Ammonites and the Ashdodites heard that the repairing of the walls of Jerusalem was going forward and that the breaches were beginning to be closed, they were very angry. 8 And they all plotted together to come and fight against Jerusalem and to cause confusion in it. 9 And we prayed to our God and set a guard as a protection against them day and night.

10 In Judah it was said,[5] "The strength of those who bear the burdens is failing. There is too much rubble. By ourselves we will not be able to rebuild the wall." 11 And our enemies said, "They will not know or see till we come among them and kill them and stop the work." 12 At that time the Jews who lived near them came from all directions and said to us ten times, "You must return to us."[6] 13 So in the lowest parts of the space behind the wall, in open places, I stationed the people by their clans, with their swords, their spears, and their bows. 14 And I looked and arose and said to the nobles and to the officials and to the rest of the people, "Do not be afraid of them. Remember the Lord, who is great and awesome, and fight for your brothers, your sons, your daughters, your wives, and your homes."

The Work Resumes

15 When our enemies heard that it was known to us and that God had frustrated their plan, we all returned to the wall, each to his work. 16 From that day on, half of my servants worked on construction, and half held the spears, shields, bows, and coats of mail. And the leaders stood behind the whole house of Judah, 17 who were building on the wall. Those who carried burdens were loaded in such a way that each labored on the work with one hand and held his weapon with the other. 18 And each of the builders had his sword strapped at his side while he built. The man who sounded the trumpet was beside me. 19 And I said to the nobles and to the officials and to the rest of the people, "The

[1] Or *Hammiphkad Gate* [2] Ch 3:33 in Hebrew [3] Or *Will they commit themselves to God?* [4] Ch 4:1 in Hebrew [5] Hebrew *Judah said* [6] The meaning of the Hebrew is uncertain

Jerusalem in the Time of Nehemiah (about 444–420? B.C.)

Jerusalem was destroyed by the Babylonians in 586 B.C. When the Jews returned to Jerusalem in 536 B.C., they first rebuilt the altar, then laid the foundations for the temple. Zerubbabel and Jeshua were their leaders. Later, Nehemiah rebuilt the city wall (Nehemiah 3).

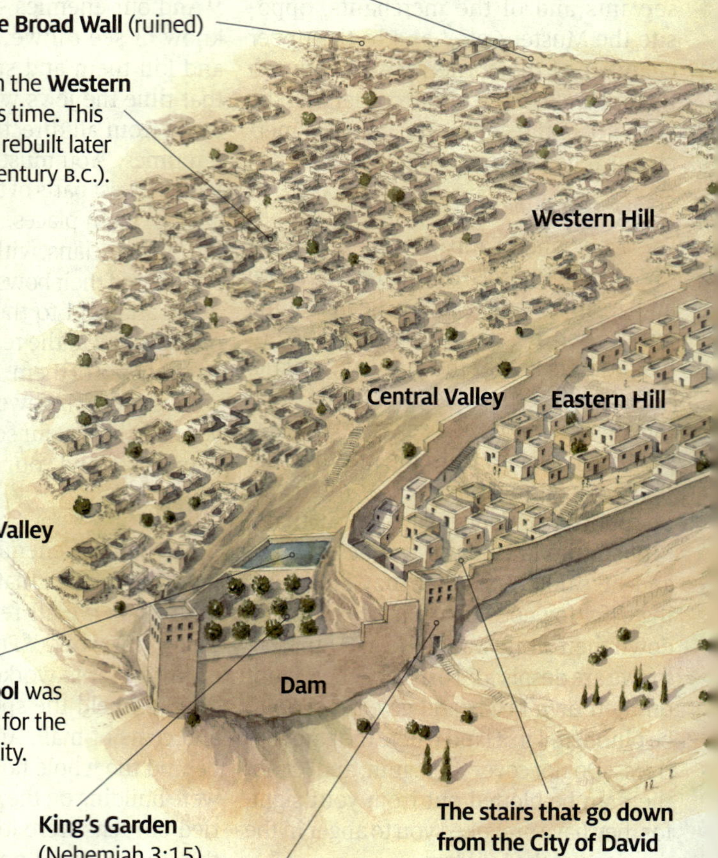

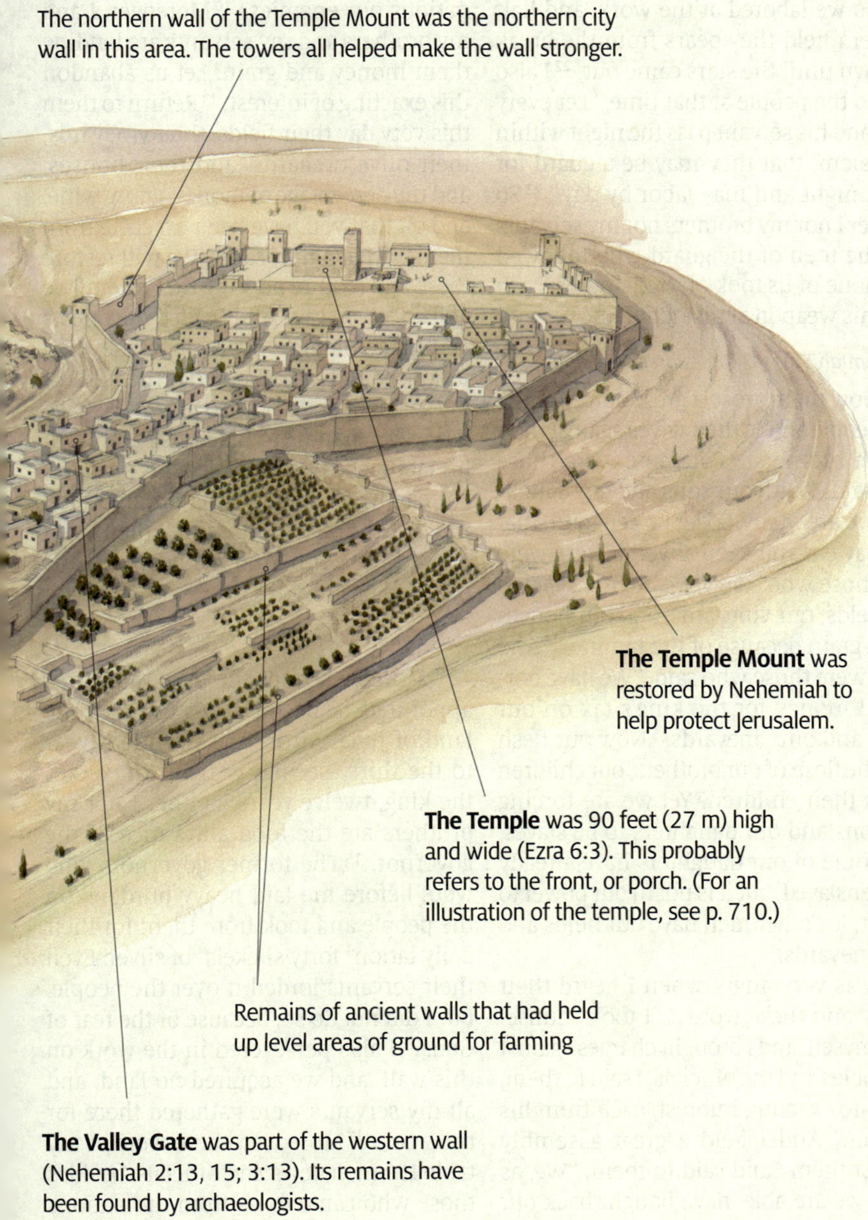

The northern wall of the Temple Mount was the northern city wall in this area. The towers all helped make the wall stronger.
The Temple Mount was restored by Nehemiah to help protect Jerusalem.
The Temple was 90 feet (27 m) high and wide (Ezra 6:3). This probably refers to the front, or porch. (For an illustration of the temple, see p. 710.)
Remains of ancient walls that had held up level areas of ground for farming
The Valley Gate was part of the western wall (Nehemiah 2:13, 15; 3:13). Its remains have been found by archaeologists.

work is great and widely spread, and we
are separated on the wall, far from one
another. 20 In the place where you hear
the sound of the trumpet, rally to us there.
Our God will fight for us."

21 So we labored at the work, and half
of them held the spears from the break
of dawn until the stars came out. 22 I also
said to the people at that time, "Let every
man and his servant pass the night within
Jerusalem, that they may be a guard for
us by night and may labor by day." 23 So
neither I nor my brothers nor my servants
nor the men of the guard who followed
me, none of us took off our clothes; each
kept his weapon at his right hand.[1]

Nehemiah Stops Oppression of the Poor

5 Now there arose a great outcry of the
people and of their wives against their
Jewish brothers. 2 For there were those
who said, "With our sons and our daugh-
ters, we are many. So let us get grain, that
we may eat and keep alive." 3 There were
also those who said, "We are mortgaging
our fields, our vineyards, and our houses
to get grain because of the famine." 4 And
there were those who said, "We have bor-
rowed money for the king's tax on our
fields and our vineyards. 5 Now our flesh
is as the flesh of our brothers, our children
are as their children. Yet we are forcing
our sons and our daughters to be slaves,
and some of our daughters have already
been enslaved, but it is not in our power to
help it, for other men have our fields and
our vineyards."

6 I was very angry when I heard their
outcry and these words. 7 I took counsel
with myself, and I brought charges against
the nobles and the officials. I said to them,
"You are exacting interest, each from his
brother." And I held a great assembly
against them 8 and said to them, "We, as
far as we are able, have bought back our
Jewish brothers who have been sold to the
nations, but you even sell your brothers
that they may be sold to us!" They were
silent and could not find a word to say.
9 So I said, "The thing that you are doing
is not good. Ought you not to walk in the
fear of our God to prevent the taunts of the
nations our enemies? 10 Moreover, I and
my brothers and my servants are lending
them money and grain. Let us abandon
this exacting of interest. 11 Return to them
this very day their fields, their vineyards,
their olive orchards, and their houses,
and the percentage of money, grain, wine,
and oil that you have been exacting from
them." 12 Then they said, "We will restore
these and require nothing from them. We
will do as you say." And I called the priests
and made them swear to do as they had
promised. 13 I also shook out the fold[2] of
my garment and said, "So may God shake
out every man from his house and from
his labor who does not keep this promise.
So may he be shaken out and emptied."
And all the assembly said "Amen" and
praised the LORD. And the people did as
they had promised.

Nehemiah's Generosity

14 Moreover, from the time that I was
appointed to be their governor in the
land of Judah, from the twentieth year
to the thirty-second year of Artaxerxes
the king, twelve years, neither I nor my
brothers ate the food allowance of the
governor. 15 The former governors who
were before me laid heavy burdens on
the people and took from them for their
daily ration[3] forty shekels[4] of silver. Even
their servants lorded it over the people.
But I did not do so, because of the fear of
God. 16 I also persevered in the work on
this wall, and we acquired no land, and
all my servants were gathered there for
the work. 17 Moreover, there were at my
table 150 men, Jews and officials, besides
those who came to us from the nations
that were around us. 18 Now what was pre-
pared at my expense[5] for each day was one

[1] Probable reading; Hebrew *each his weapon the water* [2] Hebrew *bosom* [3] Compare Vulgate; Hebrew *took from them with food and wine afterward* [4] A *shekel* was about 2/5 ounce or 11 grams [5] Or *prepared for me*

ox and six choice sheep and birds, and
every ten days all kinds of wine in abun-
dance. Yet for all this I did not demand the
food allowance of the governor, because
the service was too heavy on this people.
19 Remember for my good, O my God, all
that I have done for this people.

Conspiracy Against Nehemiah

6 Now when Sanballat and Tobiah
and Geshem the Arab and the rest
of our enemies heard that I had built the
wall and that there was no breach left in
it (although up to that time I had not set
up the doors in the gates), 2 Sanballat and
Geshem sent to me, saying, "Come and
let us meet together at Hakkephirim in
the plain of Ono." But they intended to
do me harm. 3 And I sent messengers to
them, saying, "I am doing a great work
and I cannot come down. Why should the
work stop while I leave it and come down
to you?" 4 And they sent to me four times
in this way, and I answered them in the
same manner. 5 In the same way Sanballat
for the fifth time sent his servant to me
with an open letter in his hand. 6 In it was
written, "It is reported among the nations,
and Geshem[1] also says it, that you and the
Jews intend to rebel; that is why you are
building the wall. And according to these
reports you wish to become their king.
7 And you have also set up prophets to pro-
claim concerning you in Jerusalem, 'There
is a king in Judah.' And now the king will
hear of these reports. So now come and
let us take counsel together." 8 Then I sent
to him, saying, "No such things as you
say have been done, for you are inventing
them out of your own mind." 9 For they
all wanted to frighten us, thinking, "Their
hands will drop from the work, and it will
not be done." But now, O God,[2] strengthen
my hands.

10 Now when I went into the house
of Shemaiah the son of Delaiah, son of
Mehetabel, who was confined to his
home, he said, "Let us meet together in
the house of God, within the temple. Let
us close the doors of the temple, for they
are coming to kill you. They are coming
to kill you by night." 11 But I said, "Should
such a man as I run away? And what man
such as I could go into the temple and
live?[3] I will not go in." 12 And I understood
and saw that God had not sent him, but he
had pronounced the prophecy against me
because Tobiah and Sanballat had hired
him. 13 For this purpose he was hired,
that I should be afraid and act in this way
and sin, and so they could give me a bad
name in order to taunt me. 14 Remember
Tobiah and Sanballat, O my God, accord-
ing to these things that they did, and also
the prophetess Noadiah and the rest of the
prophets who wanted to make me afraid.

The Wall Is Finished

15 So the wall was finished on the
twenty-fifth day of the month Elul, in
fifty-two days. 16 And when all our ene-
mies heard of it, all the nations around
us were afraid and fell greatly in their
own esteem, for they perceived that this
work had been accomplished with the
help of our God. 17 Moreover, in those
days the nobles of Judah sent many let-
ters to Tobiah, and Tobiah's letters came
to them. 18 For many in Judah were bound
by oath to him, because he was the son-
in-law of Shecaniah the son of Arah: and
his son Jehohanan had taken the daughter
of Meshullam the son of Berechiah as his
wife. 19 Also they spoke of his good deeds
in my presence and reported my words
to him. And Tobiah sent letters to make
me afraid.

7 Now when the wall had been built
and I had set up the doors, and the
gatekeepers, the singers, and the Levites
had been appointed, 2 I gave my brother
Hanani and Hananiah the governor of the
castle charge over Jerusalem, for he was a
more faithful and God-fearing man than

[1] Hebrew *Gashmu* [2] Hebrew lacks *O God* [3] Or *would go into the temple to save his life*

many. 3 And I said to them, "Let not the
gates of Jerusalem be opened until the sun
is hot. And while they are still standing
guard, let them shut and bar the doors.
Appoint guards from among the inhab-
itants of Jerusalem, some at their guard
posts and some in front of their own
homes." 4 The city was wide and large,
but the people within it were few, and no
houses had been rebuilt.

Lists of Returned Exiles

5 Then my God put it into my heart to
assemble the nobles and the officials and
the people to be enrolled by genealogy.
And I found the book of the genealogy
of those who came up at the first, and I
found written in it:

6 These were the people of the province
who came up out of the captivity of those
exiles whom Nebuchadnezzar the king
of Babylon had carried into exile. They
returned to Jerusalem and Judah, each to
his town. 7 They came with Zerubbabel,
Jeshua, Nehemiah, Azariah, Raamiah,
Nahamani, Mordecai, Bilshan, Mispereth,
Bigvai, Nehum, Baanah.

The number of the men of the people
of Israel: 8 the sons of Parosh, 2,172. 9 The
sons of Shephatiah, 372. 10 The sons of
Arah, 652. 11 The sons of Pahath-moab,
namely the sons of Jeshua and Joab, 2,818.
12 The sons of Elam, 1,254. 13 The sons
of Zattu, 845. 14 The sons of Zaccai, 760.
15 The sons of Binnui, 648. 16 The sons of
Bebai, 628. 17 The sons of Azgad, 2,322.
18 The sons of Adonikam, 667. 19 The sons
of Bigvai, 2,067. 20 The sons of Adin, 655.
21 The sons of Ater, namely of Hezekiah,
98. 22 The sons of Hashum, 328. 23 The
sons of Bezai, 324. 24 The sons of Hariph,
112. 25 The sons of Gibeon, 95. 26 The men
of Bethlehem and Netophah, 188. 27 The
men of Anathoth, 128. 28 The men of
Beth-azmaveth, 42. 29 The men of Kiriath-
jearim, Chephirah, and Beeroth, 743. 30 The
men of Ramah and Geba, 621. 31 The men
of Michmas, 122. 32 The men of Bethel and
Ai, 123. 33 The men of the other Nebo, 52.
34 The sons of the other Elam, 1,254. 35 The
sons of Harim, 320. 36 The sons of Jericho,
345. 37 The sons of Lod, Hadid, and Ono,
721. 38 The sons of Senaah, 3,930.

39 The priests: the sons of Jedaiah,
namely the house of Jeshua, 973. 40 The
sons of Immer, 1,052. 41 The sons of
Pashhur, 1,247. 42 The sons of Harim, 1,017.

43 The Levites: the sons of Jeshua, namely
of Kadmiel of the sons of Hodevah, 74.
44 The singers: the sons of Asaph, 148.
45 The gatekeepers: the sons of Shallum,
the sons of Ater, the sons of Talmon, the
sons of Akkub, the sons of Hatita, the sons
of Shobai, 138.

46 The temple servants: the sons of Ziha,
the sons of Hasupha, the sons of Tabbaoth,
47 the sons of Keros, the sons of Sia, the
sons of Padon, 48 the sons of Lebana, the
sons of Hagaba, the sons of Shalmai,
49 the sons of Hanan, the sons of Giddel,
the sons of Gahar, 50 the sons of Reaiah, the
sons of Rezin, the sons of Nekoda, 51 the
sons of Gazzam, the sons of Uzza, the sons
of Paseah, 52 the sons of Besai, the sons of
Meunim, the sons of Nephushesim, 53 the
sons of Bakbuk, the sons of Hakupha, the
sons of Harhur, 54 the sons of Bazlith,
the sons of Mehida, the sons of Harsha,
55 the sons of Barkos, the sons of Sisera,
the sons of Temah, 56 the sons of Neziah,
the sons of Hatipha.

57 The sons of Solomon's servants: the
sons of Sotai, the sons of Sophereth, the
sons of Perida, 58 the sons of Jaala, the sons
of Darkon, the sons of Giddel, 59 the sons of
Shephatiah, the sons of Hattil, the sons of
Pochereth-hazzebaim, the sons of Amon.

60 All the temple servants and the sons
of Solomon's servants were 392.

61 The following were those who came
up from Tel-melah, Tel-harsha, Cherub,
Addon, and Immer, but they could not
prove their fathers' houses nor their
descent, whether they belonged to Israel:

62 the sons of Delaiah, the sons of Tobiah, the sons of Nekoda, 642. 63 Also, of the priests: the sons of Hobaiah, the sons of Hakkoz, the sons of Barzillai (who had taken a wife of the daughters of Barzillai the Gileadite and was called by their name). 64 These sought their registration among those enrolled in the genealogies, but it was not found there, so they were excluded from the priesthood as unclean. 65 The governor told them that they were not to partake of the most holy food until a priest with Urim and Thummim should arise.

Totals of People and Gifts

66 The whole assembly together was 42,360, 67 besides their male and female servants, of whom there were 7,337. And they had 245 singers, male and female. 68 Their horses were 736, their mules 245,[1] 69 their camels 435, and their donkeys 6,720.

70 Now some of the heads of fathers' houses gave to the work. The governor gave to the treasury 1,000 darics[2] of gold, 50 basins, 30 priests' garments and 500 minas[3] of silver.[4] 71 And some of the heads of fathers' houses gave into the treasury of the work 20,000 darics of gold and 2,200 minas of silver. 72 And what the rest of the people gave was 20,000 darics of gold, 2,000 minas of silver, and 67 priests' garments.

73 So the priests, the Levites, the gatekeepers, the singers, some of the people, the temple servants, and all Israel, lived in their towns.

And when the seventh month had come, the people of Israel were in their towns.

Ezra Reads the Law

8 And all the people gathered as one man into the square before the Water Gate. And they told Ezra the scribe to bring the Book of the Law of Moses that the LORD had commanded Israel. 2 So Ezra the priest brought the Law before the assembly, both men and women and all who could understand what they heard, on the first day of the seventh month. 3 And he read from it facing the square before the Water Gate from early morning until midday, in the presence of the men and the women and those who could understand. And the ears of all the people were attentive to the Book of the Law. 4 And Ezra the scribe stood on a wooden platform that they had made for the purpose. And beside him stood Mattithiah, Shema, Anaiah, Uriah, Hilkiah, and Maaseiah on his right hand, and Pedaiah, Mishael, Malchijah, Hashum, Hashbaddanah, Zechariah, and Meshullam on his left hand. 5 And Ezra opened the book in the sight of all the people, for he was above all the people, and as he opened it all the people stood. 6 And Ezra blessed the LORD, the great God, and all the people answered, "Amen, Amen," lifting up their hands. And they bowed their heads and worshiped the LORD with their faces to the ground. 7 Also Jeshua, Bani, Sherebiah, Jamin, Akkub, Shabbethai, Hodiah, Maaseiah, Kelita, Azariah, Jozabad, Hanan, Pelaiah, the Levites,[5] helped the people to understand the Law, while the people remained in their places. 8 They read from the book, from the Law of God, clearly,[6] and they gave the sense, so that the people understood the reading.

This Day Is Holy

9 And Nehemiah, who was the governor, and Ezra the priest and scribe, and the Levites who taught the people said to all the people, "This day is holy to the LORD your God; do not mourn or weep." For all the people wept as they heard the words of the Law. 10 Then he said to them, "Go your way. Eat the fat and drink sweet wine and send portions to anyone who has nothing ready, for this day is holy to our Lord. And do not be grieved, for the joy of the LORD

[1] Ezra 2:66 and the margins of some Hebrew manuscripts; Hebrew lacks *Their horses . . . 245* [2] A *daric* was a coin weighing about 1/4 ounce or 8.5 grams [3] A *mina* was about 1 1/4 pounds or 0.6 kilogram [4] Probable reading; Hebrew lacks *minas of silver* [5] Vulgate; Hebrew *and the Levites* [6] Or *with interpretation*, or *paragraph by paragraph*

is your strength." 11 So the Levites calmed all the people, saying, "Be quiet, for this day is holy; do not be grieved." 12 And all the people went their way to eat and drink and to send portions and to make great rejoicing, because they had understood the words that were declared to them.

Feast of Booths Celebrated

13 On the second day the heads of fathers' houses of all the people, with the priests and the Levites, came together to Ezra the scribe in order to study the words of the Law. 14 And they found it written in the Law that the LORD had commanded by Moses that the people of Israel should dwell in booths[1] during the feast of the seventh month, 15 and that they should proclaim it and publish it in all their towns and in Jerusalem, "Go out to the hills and bring branches of olive, wild olive, myrtle, palm, and other leafy trees to make booths, as it is written." 16 So the people went out and brought them and made booths for themselves, each on his roof, and in their courts and in the courts of the house of God, and in the square at the Water Gate and in the square at the Gate of Ephraim. 17 And all the assembly of those who had returned from the captivity made booths and lived in the booths, for from the days of Jeshua the son of Nun to that day the people of Israel had not done so. And there was very great rejoicing. 18 And day by day, from the first day to the last day, he read from the Book of the Law of God. They kept the feast seven days, and on the eighth day there was a solemn assembly, according to the rule.

The People of Israel Confess Their Sin

9 Now on the twenty-fourth day of this month the people of Israel were assembled with fasting and in sackcloth, and with earth on their heads. 2 And the Israelites separated themselves from all foreigners and stood and confessed their sins and the iniquities of their fathers. 3 And they stood up in their place and read from the Book of the Law of the LORD their God for a quarter of the day; for another quarter of it they made confession and worshiped the LORD their God. 4 On the stairs of the Levites stood Jeshua, Bani, Kadmiel, Shebaniah, Bunni, Sherebiah, Bani, and Chenani; and they cried with a loud voice to the LORD their God. 5 Then the Levites, Jeshua, Kadmiel, Bani, Hashabneiah, Sherebiah, Hodiah, Shebaniah, and Pethahiah, said, "Stand up and bless the LORD your God from everlasting to everlasting. Blessed be your glorious name, which is exalted above all blessing and praise.

6 [2] "You are the LORD, you alone. You have made heaven, the heaven of heavens, with all their host, the earth and all that is on it, the seas and all that is in them; and you preserve all of them; and the host of heaven worships you. 7 You are the LORD, the God who chose Abram and brought him out of Ur of the Chaldeans and gave him the name Abraham. 8 You found his heart faithful before you, and made with him the covenant to give to his offspring the land of the Canaanite, the Hittite, the Amorite, the Perizzite, the Jebusite, and the Girgashite. And you have kept your promise, for you are righteous.

161

9 "And you saw the affliction of our fathers in Egypt and heard their cry at the Red Sea, 10 and performed signs and wonders against Pharaoh and all his servants and all the people of his land, for you knew that they acted arrogantly against our fathers. And you made a name for yourself, as it is to this day. 11 And you divided the sea before them, so that they went through the midst of the sea on dry land, and you cast their pursuers into the depths, as a stone into mighty waters. 12 By a pillar of cloud you led them in the day, and by a pillar of fire in the night to light for them the way in which they should go. 13 You came down on

[1] Or *temporary shelters* [2] Septuagint adds *And Ezra said*

Mount Sinai and spoke with them from
heaven and gave them right rules and true
laws, good statutes and commandments,
14 and you made known to them your holy
Sabbath and commanded them com-
mandments and statutes and a law by
Moses your servant. 15 You gave them
bread from heaven for their hunger and
brought water for them out of the rock for
their thirst, and you told them to go in to
possess the land that you had sworn to
give them.

16 "But they and our fathers acted pre-
sumptuously and stiffened their neck
and did not obey your commandments.
17 They refused to obey and were not
mindful of the wonders that you per-
formed among them, but they stiffened
their neck and appointed a leader to
return to their slavery in Egypt. But you
are a God ready to forgive, gracious and
merciful, slow to anger and abounding in
steadfast love, and did not forsake them.
18 Even when they had made for them-
selves a golden[1] calf and said, 'This is your
God who brought you up out of Egypt,' and
had committed great blasphemies, 19 you
in your great mercies did not forsake them
in the wilderness. The pillar of cloud to
lead them in the way did not depart from
them by day, nor the pillar of fire by night
to light for them the way by which they
should go. 20 You gave your good Spirit to
instruct them and did not withhold your
manna from their mouth and gave them
water for their thirst. 21 Forty years you
sustained them in the wilderness, and
they lacked nothing. Their clothes did not
wear out and their feet did not swell.

22 "And you gave them kingdoms and
peoples and allotted to them every cor-
ner. So they took possession of the land
of Sihon king of Heshbon and the land
of Og king of Bashan. 23 You multiplied
their children as the stars of heaven, and
you brought them into the land that you
had told their fathers to enter and pos-
sess. 24 So the descendants went in and
possessed the land, and you subdued
before them the inhabitants of the land,
the Canaanites, and gave them into their
hand, with their kings and the peoples of
the land, that they might do with them
as they would. 25 And they captured forti-
fied cities and a rich land, and took pos-
session of houses full of all good things,
cisterns already hewn, vineyards, olive
orchards and fruit trees in abundance. So
they ate and were filled and became fat
and delighted themselves in your great
goodness.

26 "Nevertheless, they were disobedient
and rebelled against you and cast your
law behind their back and killed your
prophets, who had warned them in order
to turn them back to you, and they com-
mitted great blasphemies. 27 Therefore
you gave them into the hand of their
enemies, who made them suffer. And in
the time of their suffering they cried out
to you and you heard them from heaven,
and according to your great mercies you
gave them saviors who saved them from
the hand of their enemies. 28 But after they
had rest they did evil again before you,
and you abandoned them to the hand of
their enemies, so that they had domin-
ion over them. Yet when they turned and
cried to you, you heard from heaven, and
many times you delivered them accord-
ing to your mercies. 29 And you warned
them in order to turn them back to your
law. Yet they acted presumptuously and
did not obey your commandments, but
sinned against your rules, which if a
person does them, he shall live by them,
and they turned a stubborn shoulder and
stiffened their neck and would not obey.
30 Many years you bore with them and
warned them by your Spirit through your
prophets. Yet they would not give ear.
Therefore you gave them into the hand of
the peoples of the lands. 31 Nevertheless,
in your great mercies you did not make an

[1] Hebrew *metal*

end of them or forsake them, for you are a
gracious and merciful God.
32 "Now, therefore, our God, the great,
the mighty, and the awesome God, who
keeps covenant and steadfast love, let
not all the hardship seem little to you
that has come upon us, upon our kings,
our princes, our priests, our prophets,
our fathers, and all your people, since
the time of the kings of Assyria until this
day. 33 Yet you have been righteous in
all that has come upon us, for you have
dealt faithfully and we have acted wick-
edly. 34 Our kings, our princes, our priests,
and our fathers have not kept your law or
paid attention to your commandments
and your warnings that you gave them.
35 Even in their own kingdom, and amid
your great goodness that you gave them,
and in the large and rich land that you
set before them, they did not serve you or
turn from their wicked works. 36 Behold,
we are slaves this day; in the land that you
gave to our fathers to enjoy its fruit and its
good gifts, behold, we are slaves. 37 And
its rich yield goes to the kings whom you
have set over us because of our sins. They
rule over our bodies and over our livestock
as they please, and we are in great distress.
38 [1] "Because of all this we make a firm
covenant in writing; on the sealed docu-
ment are the names of[2] our princes, our
Levites, and our priests.

The People Who Sealed the Covenant

10 [3] "On the seals are the names of[4]
Nehemiah the governor, the son
of Hacaliah, Zedekiah, 2 Seraiah, Azariah,
Jeremiah, 3 Pashhur, Amariah, Malchijah,
4 Hattush, Shebaniah, Malluch, 5 Harim,
Meremoth, Obadiah, 6 Daniel, Ginnethon,
Baruch, 7 Meshullam, Abijah, Mijamin,
8 Maaziah, Bilgai, Shemaiah; these are the
priests. 9 And the Levites: Jeshua the son of
Azaniah, Binnui of the sons of Henadad,
Kadmiel; 10 and their brothers, Shebaniah,
Hodiah, Kelita, Pelaiah, Hanan, 11 Mica,
Rehob, Hashabiah, 12 Zaccur, Sherebiah,
Shebaniah, 13 Hodiah, Bani, Beninu.
14 The chiefs of the people: Parosh,
Pahath-moab, Elam, Zattu, Bani, 15 Bunni,
Azgad, Bebai, 16 Adonijah, Bigvai, Adin,
17 Ater, Hezekiah, Azzur, 18 Hodiah,
Hashum, Bezai, 19 Hariph, Anathoth,
Nebai, 20 Magpiash, Meshullam, Hezir,
21 Meshezabel, Zadok, Jaddua, 22 Pelatiah,
Hanan, Anaiah, 23 Hoshea, Hananiah,
Hasshub, 24 Hallohesh, Pilha, Shobek,
25 Rehum, Hashabnah, Maaseiah, 26 Ahiah,
Hanan, Anan, 27 Malluch, Harim, Baanah.

The Obligations of the Covenant

28 "The rest of the people, the priests,
the Levites, the gatekeepers, the singers,
the temple servants, and all who have sep-
arated themselves from the peoples of the
lands to the Law of God, their wives, their
sons, their daughters, all who have knowl-
edge and understanding, 29 join with their
brothers, their nobles, and enter into a
curse and an oath to walk in God's Law
that was given by Moses the servant of
God, and to observe and do all the com-
mandments of the LORD our Lord and his
rules and his statutes. 30 We will not give
our daughters to the peoples of the land or
take their daughters for our sons. 31 And if
the peoples of the land bring in goods or
any grain on the Sabbath day to sell, we
will not buy from them on the Sabbath
or on a holy day. And we will forego the
crops of the seventh year and the exaction
of every debt.
32 "We also take on ourselves the obliga-
tion to give yearly a third part of a shekel[5]
for the service of the house of our God:
33 for the showbread, the regular grain
offering, the regular burnt offering, the
Sabbaths, the new moons, the appointed
feasts, the holy things, and the sin offer-
ings to make atonement for Israel, and
for all the work of the house of our God.
34 We, the priests, the Levites, and the peo-
ple, have likewise cast lots for the wood

[1] Ch 10:1 in Hebrew [2] Hebrew lacks *the names of* [3] Ch 10:2 in Hebrew [4] Hebrew lacks *the names of* [5] A *shekel* was about 2/5 ounce or 11 grams

offering, to bring it into the house of our God, according to our fathers' houses, at times appointed, year by year, to burn on the altar of the LORD our God, as it is written in the Law. 35 We obligate ourselves to bring the firstfruits of our ground and the firstfruits of all fruit of every tree, year by year, to the house of the LORD; 36 also to bring to the house of our God, to the priests who minister in the house of our God, the firstborn of our sons and of our cattle, as it is written in the Law, and the firstborn of our herds and of our flocks; 37 and to bring the first of our dough, and our contributions, the fruit of every tree, the wine and the oil, to the priests, to the chambers of the house of our God; and to bring to the Levites the tithes from our ground, for it is the Levites who collect the tithes in all our towns where we labor. 38 And the priest, the son of Aaron, shall be with the Levites when the Levites receive the tithes. And the Levites shall bring up the tithe of the tithes to the house of our God, to the chambers of the storehouse. 39 For the people of Israel and the sons of Levi shall bring the contribution of grain, wine, and oil to the chambers, where the vessels of the sanctuary are, as well as the priests who minister, and the gatekeepers and the singers. We will not neglect the house of our God."

The Leaders in Jerusalem

11 Now the leaders of the people lived in Jerusalem. And the rest of the people cast lots to bring one out of ten to live in Jerusalem the holy city, while nine out of ten[1] remained in the other towns. 2 And the people blessed all the men who willingly offered to live in Jerusalem.

3 These are the chiefs of the province who lived in Jerusalem; but in the towns of Judah everyone lived on his property in their towns: Israel, the priests, the Levites, the temple servants, and the descendants of Solomon's servants. 4 And in Jerusalem lived certain of the sons of Judah and of the sons of Benjamin. Of the sons of Judah: Athaiah the son of Uzziah, son of Zechariah, son of Amariah, son of Shephatiah, son of Mahalalel, of the sons of Perez; 5 and Maaseiah the son of Baruch, son of Col-hozeh, son of Hazaiah, son of Adaiah, son of Joiarib, son of Zechariah, son of the Shilonite. 6 All the sons of Perez who lived in Jerusalem were 468 valiant men.

7 And these are the sons of Benjamin: Sallu the son of Meshullam, son of Joed, son of Pedaiah, son of Kolaiah, son of Maaseiah, son of Ithiel, son of Jeshaiah, 8 and his brothers, men of valor, 928.[2] 9 Joel the son of Zichri was their overseer; and Judah the son of Hassenuah was second over the city.

10 Of the priests: Jedaiah the son of Joiarib, Jachin, 11 Seraiah the son of Hilkiah, son of Meshullam, son of Zadok, son of Meraioth, son of Ahitub, ruler of the house of God, 12 and their brothers who did the work of the house, 822; and Adaiah the son of Jeroham, son of Pelaliah, son of Amzi, son of Zechariah, son of Pashhur, son of Malchijah, 13 and his brothers, heads of fathers' houses, 242; and Amashsai, the son of Azarel, son of Ahzai, son of Meshillemoth, son of Immer, 14 and their brothers, mighty men of valor, 128; their overseer was Zabdiel the son of Haggedolim.

15 And of the Levites: Shemaiah the son of Hasshub, son of Azrikam, son of Hashabiah, son of Bunni; 16 and Shabbethai and Jozabad, of the chiefs of the Levites, who were over the outside work of the house of God; 17 and Mattaniah the son of Mica, son of Zabdi, son of Asaph, who was the leader of the praise,[3] who gave thanks, and Bakbukiah, the second among his brothers; and Abda the son of Shammua, son of Galal, son of Jeduthun. 18 All the Levites in the holy city were 284.

[1] Hebrew *nine hands* [2] Compare Septuagint; Hebrew *Jeshaiah, and after him Gabbai, Sallai, 928* [3] Compare Septuagint, Vulgate; Hebrew *beginning*

19 The gatekeepers, Akkub, Talmon and their brothers, who kept watch at the gates, were 172. 20 And the rest of Israel, and of the priests and the Levites, were in all the towns of Judah, every one in his inheritance. 21 But the temple servants lived on Ophel; and Ziha and Gishpa were over the temple servants.

22 The overseer of the Levites in Jerusalem was Uzzi the son of Bani, son of Hashabiah, son of Mattaniah, son of Mica, of the sons of Asaph, the singers, over the work of the house of God. 23 For there was a command from the king concerning them, and a fixed provision for the singers, as every day required. 24 And Pethahiah the son of Meshezabel, of the sons of Zerah the son of Judah, was at the king's side[1] in all matters concerning the people.

Villages Outside Jerusalem

25 And as for the villages, with their fields, some of the people of Judah lived in Kiriath-arba and its villages, and in Dibon and its villages, and in Jekabzeel and its villages, 26 and in Jeshua and in Moladah and Beth-pelet, 27 in Hazar-shual, in Beersheba and its villages, 28 in Ziklag, in Meconah and its villages, 29 in En-rimmon, in Zorah, in Jarmuth, 30 Zanoah, Adullam, and their villages, Lachish and its fields, and Azekah and its villages. So they encamped from Beersheba to the Valley of Hinnom. 31 The people of Benjamin also lived from Geba onward, at Michmash, Aija, Bethel and its villages, 32 Anathoth, Nob, Ananiah, 33 Hazor, Ramah, Gittaim, 34 Hadid, Zeboim, Neballat, 35 Lod, and Ono, the valley of craftsmen. 36 And certain divisions of the Levites in Judah were assigned to Benjamin.

Priests and Levites

12 These are the priests and the Levites who came up with Zerubbabel the son of Shealtiel, and Jeshua: Seraiah, Jeremiah, Ezra, 2 Amariah, Malluch, Hattush, 3 Shecaniah, Rehum, Meremoth, 4 Iddo, Ginnethoi, Abijah, 5 Mijamin, Maadiah, Bilgah, 6 Shemaiah, Joiarib, Jedaiah, 7 Sallu, Amok, Hilkiah, Jedaiah. These were the chiefs of the priests and of their brothers in the days of Jeshua.

8 And the Levites: Jeshua, Binnui, Kadmiel, Sherebiah, Judah, and Mattaniah, who with his brothers was in charge of the songs of thanksgiving. 9 And Bakbukiah and Unni and their brothers stood opposite them in the service. 10 And Jeshua was the father of Joiakim, Joiakim the father of Eliashib, Eliashib the father of Joiada, 11 Joiada the father of Jonathan, and Jonathan the father of Jaddua.

12 And in the days of Joiakim were priests, heads of fathers' houses: of Seraiah, Meraiah; of Jeremiah, Hananiah; 13 of Ezra, Meshullam; of Amariah, Jehohanan; 14 of Malluchi, Jonathan; of Shebaniah, Joseph; 15 of Harim, Adna; of Meraioth, Helkai; 16 of Iddo, Zechariah; of Ginnethon, Meshullam; 17 of Abijah, Zichri; of Miniamin, of Moadiah, Piltai; 18 of Bilgah, Shammua; of Shemaiah, Jehonathan; 19 of Joiarib, Mattenai; of Jedaiah, Uzzi; 20 of Sallai, Kallai; of Amok, Eber; 21 of Hilkiah, Hashabiah; of Jedaiah, Nethanel.

22 In the days of Eliashib, Joiada, Johanan, and Jaddua, the Levites were recorded as heads of fathers' houses; so too were the priests in the reign of Darius the Persian. 23 As for the sons of Levi, their heads of fathers' houses were written in the Book of the Chronicles until the days of Johanan the son of Eliashib. 24 And the chiefs of the Levites: Hashabiah, Sherebiah, and Jeshua the son of Kadmiel, with their brothers who stood opposite them, to praise and to give thanks, according to the commandment of David the man of God, watch by watch. 25 Mattaniah, Bakbukiah, Obadiah, Meshullam, Talmon, and Akkub were gatekeepers standing

[1] Hebrew *hand*

guard at the storehouses of the gates. 26 These were in the days of Joiakim the son of Jeshua son of Jozadak, and in the days of Nehemiah the governor and of Ezra, the priest and scribe.

Dedication of the Wall

27 And at the dedication of the wall of Jerusalem they sought the Levites in all their places, to bring them to Jerusalem to celebrate the dedication with gladness, with thanksgivings and with singing, with cymbals, harps, and lyres. 28 And the sons of the singers gathered together from the district surrounding Jerusalem and from the villages of the Netophathites; 29 also from Beth-gilgal and from the region of Geba and Azmaveth, for the singers had built for themselves villages around Jerusalem. 30 And the priests and the Levites purified themselves, and they purified the people and the gates and the wall.

31 Then I brought the leaders of Judah up onto the wall and appointed two great choirs that gave thanks. One went to the south on the wall to the Dung Gate. 32 And after them went Hoshaiah and half of the leaders of Judah, 33 and Azariah, Ezra, Meshullam, 34 Judah, Benjamin, Shemaiah, and Jeremiah, 35 and certain of the priests' sons with trumpets: Zechariah the son of Jonathan, son of Shemaiah, son of Mattaniah, son of Micaiah, son of Zaccur, son of Asaph; 36 and his relatives, Shemaiah, Azarel, Milalai, Gilalai, Maai, Nethanel, Judah, and Hanani, with the musical instruments of David the man of God. And Ezra the scribe went before them. 37 At the Fountain Gate they went up straight before them by the stairs of the city of David, at the ascent of the wall, above the house of David, to the Water Gate on the east.

38 The other choir of those who gave thanks went to the north, and I followed them with half of the people, on the wall, above the Tower of the Ovens, to the Broad Wall, 39 and above the Gate of Ephraim, and by the Gate of Yeshanah,[1] and by the Fish Gate and the Tower of Hananel and the Tower of the Hundred, to the Sheep Gate; and they came to a halt at the Gate of the Guard. 40 So both choirs of those who gave thanks stood in the house of God, and I and half of the officials with me; 41 and the priests Eliakim, Maaseiah, Miniamin, Micaiah, Elioenai, Zechariah, and Hananiah, with trumpets; 42 and Maaseiah, Shemaiah, Eleazar, Uzzi, Jehohanan, Malchijah, Elam, and Ezer. And the singers sang with Jezrahiah as their leader. 43 And they offered great sacrifices that day and rejoiced, for God had made them rejoice with great joy; the women and children also rejoiced. And the joy of Jerusalem was heard far away.

Service at the Temple

44 On that day men were appointed over the storerooms, the contributions, the firstfruits, and the tithes, to gather into them the portions required by the Law for the priests and for the Levites according to the fields of the towns, for Judah rejoiced over the priests and the Levites who ministered. 45 And they performed the service of their God and the service of purification, as did the singers and the gatekeepers, according to the command of David and his son Solomon. 46 For long ago in the days of David and Asaph there were directors of the singers, and there were songs[2] of praise and thanksgiving to God. 47 And all Israel in the days of Zerubbabel and in the days of Nehemiah gave the daily portions for the singers and the gatekeepers; and they set apart that which was for the Levites; and the Levites set apart that which was for the sons of Aaron.

Nehemiah's Final Reforms

13 On that day they read from the Book of Moses in the hearing of the people. And in it was found written that no Ammonite or Moabite should ever

[1] Or *of the old city* [2] Or *leaders*

enter the assembly of God, 2 for they did not meet the people of Israel with bread and water, but hired Balaam against them to curse them—yet our God turned the curse into a blessing. 3 As soon as the people heard the law, they separated from Israel all those of foreign descent.

4 Now before this, Eliashib the priest, who was appointed over the chambers of the house of our God, and who was related to Tobiah, 5 prepared for Tobiah a large chamber where they had previously put the grain offering, the frankincense, the vessels, and the tithes of grain, wine, and oil, which were given by commandment to the Levites, singers, and gatekeepers, and the contributions for the priests. 6 While this was taking place, I was not in Jerusalem, for in the thirty-second year of Artaxerxes king of Babylon I went to the king. And after some time I asked leave of the king 7 and came to Jerusalem, and I then discovered the evil that Eliashib had done for Tobiah, preparing for him a chamber in the courts of the house of God. 8 And I was very angry, and I threw all the household furniture of Tobiah out of the chamber. 9 Then I gave orders, and they cleansed the chambers, and I brought back there the vessels of the house of God, with the grain offering and the frankincense.

10 I also found out that the portions of the Levites had not been given to them, so that the Levites and the singers, who did the work, had fled each to his field. 11 So I confronted the officials and said, “Why is the house of God forsaken?” And I gathered them together and set them in their stations. 12 Then all Judah brought the tithe of the grain, wine, and oil into the storehouses. 13 And I appointed as treasurers over the storehouses Shelemiah the priest, Zadok the scribe, and Pedaiah of the Levites, and as their assistant Hanan the son of Zaccur, son of Mattaniah, for they were considered reliable, and their duty was to distribute to their brothers. 14 Remember me, O my God, concerning this, and do not wipe out my good deeds that I have done for the house of my God and for his service.

15 In those days I saw in Judah people treading winepresses on the Sabbath, and bringing in heaps of grain and loading them on donkeys, and also wine, grapes, figs, and all kinds of loads, which they brought into Jerusalem on the Sabbath day. And I warned them on the day when they sold food. 16 Tyrians also, who lived in the city, brought in fish and all kinds of goods and sold them on the Sabbath to the people of Judah, in Jerusalem itself! 17 Then I confronted the nobles of Judah and said to them, “What is this evil thing that you are doing, profaning the Sabbath day? 18 Did not your fathers act in this way, and did not our God bring all this disaster[1] on us and on this city? Now you are bringing more wrath on Israel by profaning the Sabbath.”

19 As soon as it began to grow dark at the gates of Jerusalem before the Sabbath, I commanded that the doors should be shut and gave orders that they should not be opened until after the Sabbath. And I stationed some of my servants at the gates, that no load might be brought in on the Sabbath day. 20 Then the merchants and sellers of all kinds of wares lodged outside Jerusalem once or twice. 21 But I warned them and said to them, “Why do you lodge outside the wall? If you do so again, I will lay hands on you.” From that time on they did not come on the Sabbath. 22 Then I commanded the Levites that they should purify themselves and come and guard the gates, to keep the Sabbath day holy. Remember this also in my favor, O my God, and spare me according to the greatness of your steadfast love.

23 In those days also I saw the Jews who had married women of Ashdod, Ammon, and Moab. 24 And half of their children

[1] The Hebrew word can mean *evil*, *harm*, or *disaster*, depending on the context

spoke the language of Ashdod, and they
could not speak the language of Judah,
but only the language of each people.
25 And I confronted them and cursed
them and beat some of them and pulled
out their hair. And I made them take oath
in the name of God, saying, "You shall not
give your daughters to their sons, or take
their daughters for your sons or for your-
selves. 26 Did not Solomon king of Israel
sin on account of such women? Among
the many nations there was no king like
him, and he was beloved by his God,
and God made him king over all Israel.
Nevertheless, foreign women made even
him to sin. 27 Shall we then listen to you
and do all this great evil and act treacher-
ously against our God by marrying for-
eign women?"

28 And one of the sons of Jehoiada, the
son of Eliashib the high priest, was the son-
in-law of Sanballat the Horonite. Therefore
I chased him from me. 29 Remember them,
O my God, because they have desecrated
the priesthood and the covenant of the
priesthood and the Levites.

30 Thus I cleansed them from everything
foreign, and I established the duties of
the priests and Levites, each in his work;
31 and I provided for the wood offering at
appointed times, and for the firstfruits.

Remember me, O my God, for good.

Introduction to

Esther

Author
Unknown

Date
About 400 B.C.

People
King Ahasuerus (Xerxes); Esther; Mordecai; Haman

Purpose
The purpose of Esther is to show God's work through circumstances to protect His people from destruction by their enemies.

Central Themes
God's is sovereign; God's power can protect and preserve; love for God and His people requires action; it is foolish to exalt self rather than to exalt God.

Memory Verses
Mordecai's counsel about courage (Esther 4:13–17)

Introduction

Many Jews had returned to their land, but some, like Mordecai and his cousin Esther, lived in Susa, where Mordecai worked for the Persian king. The book of Esther begins when King Ahasuerus holds a beauty contest to choose a new queen. He likes Esther better than all the other young women and chooses her (Esther 1:1–2:18). Haman, who also works for the king, hates Mordecai and plans to kill him, as well as all Mordecai's people, the Jews, throughout the Persian Empire. Not knowing that Esther is Jewish, the king agrees to Haman's plan (Esther 3). Mordecai tells Esther that God may have made her queen so she can help. Although death is the punishment for going to the king without an invitation, Esther goes to him anyway and is welcomed (Esther 4:1–5:8). At a banquet Esther gives for the king and Haman, she tells the king of Haman's wicked plot and the king is so furious that he has Haman hanged (Esther 7). The Jews are saved, and Haman's high position goes to Mordecai. God is never mentioned in the book of Esther, but we see Him in all the seeming "coincidences" He brings to accomplish His purposes.

516 B.C.	478–473 B.C.	445 B.C.
Temple rebuilt (in Jerusalem)	Events of Esther (in Persia)	Walls rebuilt (in Jerusalem)

Esther

The King's Banquets

1 Now in the days of Ahasuerus,
the Ahasuerus who reigned
747 from India to Ethiopia over 127
provinces, 2 in those days when King
Ahasuerus sat on his royal throne in Susa,
the capital,[1] 3 in the third year of his reign
he gave a feast for all his officials and ser-
vants. The army of Persia and Media and
the nobles and governors of the provinces
were before him, 4 while he showed the
riches of his royal glory and the splendor
and pomp of his greatness for many days,
180 days. 5 And when these days were
completed, the king gave for all the people
present in Susa, the citadel, both great and
small, a feast lasting for seven days in the
court of the garden of the king's palace.
6 There were white cotton curtains and
violet hangings fastened with cords of
fine linen and purple to silver rods[2] and
marble pillars, and also couches of gold
and silver on a mosaic pavement of por-
phyry, marble, mother-of-pearl and pre-
cious stones. 7 Drinks were served in
golden vessels, vessels of different kinds,
and the royal wine was lavished according
to the bounty of the king. 8 And drinking
was according to this edict: "There is no
compulsion." For the king had given
orders to all the staff of his palace to do as
each man desired. 9 Queen Vashti also
gave a feast for the women in the palace
that belonged to King Ahasuerus.

Queen Vashti's Refusal

10 On the seventh day, when the heart
of the king was merry with wine, he com-
manded Mehuman, Biztha, Harbona,
Bigtha and Abagtha, Zethar and Carkas,
the seven eunuchs who served in the pres-
ence of King Ahasuerus, 11 to bring Queen
Vashti before the king with her royal
crown,[3] in order to show the peoples and
the princes her beauty, for she was lovely
to look at. 12 But Queen Vashti refused to
come at the king's command delivered
by the eunuchs. At this the king became
enraged, and his anger burned within him.

13 Then the king said to the wise men
who knew the times (for this was the
king's procedure toward all who were
versed in law and judgment, 14 the men
next to him being Carshena, Shethar,
Admatha, Tarshish, Meres, Marsena, and
Memucan, the seven princes of Persia
and Media, who saw the king's face, and
sat first in the kingdom): 15 "According
to the law, what is to be done to Queen
Vashti, because she has not performed
the command of King Ahasuerus deliv-
ered by the eunuchs?" 16 Then Memucan
said in the presence of the king and
the officials, "Not only against the king
has Queen Vashti done wrong, but also
against all the officials and all the peo-
ples who are in all the provinces of King
Ahasuerus. 17 For the queen's behav-
ior will be made known to all women,
causing them to look at their husbands
with contempt, since they will say, 'King
Ahasuerus commanded Queen Vashti to
be brought before him, and she did not
come.' 18 This very day the noble women
of Persia and Media who have heard of
the queen's behavior will say the same
to all the king's officials, and there will
be contempt and wrath in plenty. 19 If it
please the king, let a royal order go out
from him, and let it be written among
the laws of the Persians and the Medes
so that it may not be repealed, that
Vashti is never again to come before
King Ahasuerus. And let the king give

[1] Or *the fortified city* [2] Or *rings* [3] Or *headdress*

her royal position to another who is better than she. 20 So when the decree made by the king is proclaimed throughout all his kingdom, for it is vast, all women will give honor to their husbands, high and low alike." 21 This advice pleased the king and the princes, and the king did as Memucan proposed. 22 He sent letters to all the royal provinces, to every province in its own script and to every people in its own language, that every man be master in his own household and speak according to the language of his people.

Esther Chosen Queen

2 After these things, when the anger of King Ahasuerus had abated, he remembered Vashti and what she had done and what had been decreed against her. 2 Then the king's young men who attended him said, "Let beautiful young virgins be sought out for the king. 3 And let the king appoint officers in all the provinces of his kingdom to gather all the beautiful young virgins to the harem in Susa the capital, under custody of Hegai, the king's eunuch, who is in charge of the women. Let their cosmetics be given them. 4 And let the young woman who pleases the king be queen instead of Vashti." This pleased the king, and he did so.

5 Now there was a Jew in Susa the citadel whose name was Mordecai, the son of Jair, son of Shimei, son of Kish, a Benjaminite, 6 who had been carried away from Jerusalem among the captives carried away with Jeconiah king of Judah, whom Nebuchadnezzar king of Babylon had carried away. 7 He was bringing up Hadassah, that is Esther, the daughter of his uncle, for she had neither father nor mother. The young woman had a beautiful figure and was lovely to look at, and when her father and her mother died, Mordecai took her as his own daughter. 8 So when the king's order and his edict were proclaimed, and when many young women were gathered in Susa the citadel in custody of Hegai, Esther also was taken into the king's palace and put in custody of Hegai, who had charge of the women. 9 And the young woman pleased him and won his favor. And he quickly provided her with her cosmetics and her portion of food, and with seven chosen young women from the king's palace, and advanced her and her young women to the best place in the harem. 10 Esther had not made known her people or kindred, for Mordecai had commanded her not to make it known. 11 And every day Mordecai walked in front of the court of the harem to learn how Esther was and what was happening to her.

12 Now when the turn came for each young woman to go in to King Ahasuerus,

CHARACTER PROFILE

ESTHER

Esther was a Jew living in Persia. She became queen to the Persian king. When one of the king's men planned to kill all the Jews, Esther went to the king, even though she could have been killed for doing it. The king listened to her request and the Jewish people were saved.

747

after being twelve months under the regu-
lations for the women, since this was the
regular period of their beautifying, six
months with oil of myrrh and six months
with spices and ointments for women—
13 when the young woman went in to the
king in this way, she was given whatever
she desired to take with her from the
harem to the king's palace. 14 In the eve-
ning she would go in, and in the morning
she would return to the second harem in
custody of Shaashgaz, the king's eunuch,
who was in charge of the concubines. She
would not go in to the king again, unless
the king delighted in her and she was sum-
moned by name.

15 When the turn came for Esther the
daughter of Abihail the uncle of Mordecai,
who had taken her as his own daughter,
to go in to the king, she asked for nothing
except what Hegai the king's eunuch, who
had charge of the women, advised. Now
Esther was winning favor in the eyes of
all who saw her. 16 And when Esther was
taken to King Ahasuerus, into his royal
palace, in the tenth month, which is the
month of Tebeth, in the seventh year of
his reign, 17 the king loved Esther more
than all the women, and she won grace
and favor in his sight more than all the
virgins, so that he set the royal crown[1] on
her head and made her queen instead of
Vashti. 18 Then the king gave a great feast
for all his officials and servants; it was
Esther's feast. He also granted a remis-
sion of taxes to the provinces and gave
gifts with royal generosity.

Mordecai Discovers a Plot

19 Now when the virgins were gathered
together the second time, Mordecai was
sitting at the king's gate. 20 Esther had not
made known her kindred or her people,
as Mordecai had commanded her, for
Esther obeyed Mordecai just as when she
was brought up by him. 21 In those days,
as Mordecai was sitting at the king's gate,
Bigthan and Teresh, two of the king's
eunuchs, who guarded the threshold,
became angry and sought to lay hands on
King Ahasuerus. 22 And this came to the
knowledge of Mordecai, and he told it to
Queen Esther, and Esther told the king in
the name of Mordecai. 23 When the affair
was investigated and found to be so, the
men were both hanged on the gallows.[2]
And it was recorded in the book of the
chronicles in the presence of the king.

Haman Plots Against the Jews

3 After these things King Ahasuerus
promoted Haman the Agagite, the
son of Hammedatha, and advanced him
and set his throne above all the officials
who were with him. 2 And all the king's
servants who were at the king's gate
bowed down and paid homage to Haman,
for the king had so commanded con-
cerning him. But Mordecai did not bow
down or pay homage. 3 Then the king's
servants who were at the king's gate said
to Mordecai, "Why do you transgress
the king's command?" 4 And when they
spoke to him day after day and he would
not listen to them, they told Haman, in
order to see whether Mordecai's words
would stand, for he had told them that
he was a Jew. 5 And when Haman saw
that Mordecai did not bow down or pay
homage to him, Haman was filled with
fury. 6 But he disdained to lay hands on
Mordecai alone. So, as they had made
known to him the people of Mordecai,
Haman sought to destroy all the Jews,
the people of Mordecai, throughout the
whole kingdom of Ahasuerus.

7 In the first month, which is the month
of Nisan, in the twelfth year of King
Ahasuerus, they cast Pur (that is, they
cast lots) before Haman day after day;
and they cast it month after month till
the twelfth month, which is the month
of Adar. 8 Then Haman said to King
Ahasuerus, "There is a certain people

[1] Or *headdress* [2] Or *suspended on a stake*

scattered abroad and dispersed among
the peoples in all the provinces of your
kingdom. Their laws are different from
those of every other people, and they do
not keep the king's laws, so that it is not
to the king's profit to tolerate them. 9 If it
please the king, let it be decreed that they
be destroyed, and I will pay 10,000 tal-
ents[1] of silver into the hands of those who
have charge of the king's business, that
they may put it into the king's treasuries."
10 So the king took his signet ring from his
hand and gave it to Haman the Agagite,
the son of Hammedatha, the enemy of the
Jews. 11 And the king said to Haman, "The
money is given to you, the people also,
to do with them as it seems good to you."
12 Then the king's scribes were sum-
moned on the thirteenth day of the first
month, and an edict, according to all that
Haman commanded, was written to the
king's satraps and to the governors over
all the provinces and to the officials of all
the peoples, to every province in its own
script and every people in its own lan-
guage. It was written in the name of King
Ahasuerus and sealed with the king's sig-
net ring. 13 Letters were sent by couriers to
all the king's provinces with instruction to
destroy, to kill, and to annihilate all Jews,
young and old, women and children, in
one day, the thirteenth day of the twelfth
month, which is the month of Adar, and
to plunder their goods. 14 A copy of the
document was to be issued as a decree
in every province by proclamation to all
the peoples to be ready for that day. 15 The
couriers went out hurriedly by order of
the king, and the decree was issued in
Susa the citadel. And the king and Haman
sat down to drink, but the city of Susa was
thrown into confusion.

Esther Agrees to Help the Jews

4 When Mordecai learned all that had
been done, Mordecai tore his clothes
and put on sackcloth and ashes, and went
out into the midst of the city, and he cried
out with a loud and bitter cry. 2 He went
up to the entrance of the king's gate, for
no one was allowed to enter the king's
gate clothed in sackcloth. 3 And in every
province, wherever the king's command
and his decree reached, there was great
mourning among the Jews, with fasting
and weeping and lamenting, and many of
them lay in sackcloth and ashes.
4 When Esther's young women and her
eunuchs came and told her, the queen
was deeply distressed. She sent garments
to clothe Mordecai, so that he might take
off his sackcloth, but he would not accept
them. 5 Then Esther called for Hathach,
one of the king's eunuchs, who had been
appointed to attend her, and ordered him
to go to Mordecai to learn what this was

CHARACTER PROFILE

HAMAN

Haman worked for the king of Persia. A Jew named Mordecai would not bow to Haman, so Haman planned to kill all the Jews and hang Mordecai. But Queen Esther told the king about the plan. The Jews were saved, and Haman was hung on the gallows he had built for Mordecai.

747

[1] A *talent* was about 75 pounds or 34 kilograms

and why it was. 6 Hathach went out to
Mordecai in the open square of the city
in front of the king's gate, 7 and Mordecai
told him all that had happened to him,
and the exact sum of money that Haman
had promised to pay into the king's trea-
suries for the destruction of the Jews.
8 Mordecai also gave him a copy of the
written decree issued in Susa for their
destruction, that he might show it to
Esther and explain it to her and command
her to go to the king to beg his favor and
plead with him on behalf of her people.
9 And Hathach went and told Esther what
Mordecai had said. 10 Then Esther spoke
to Hathach and commanded him to go
to Mordecai and say, 11 "All the king's ser-
vants and the people of the king's prov-
inces know that if any man or woman
goes to the king inside the inner court
without being called, there is but one
law—to be put to death, except the one
to whom the king holds out the golden
scepter so that he may live. But as for me,
I have not been called to come in to the
king these thirty days."

12 And they told Mordecai what Esther
had said. 13 Then Mordecai told them to
reply to Esther, "Do not think to yourself
that in the king's palace you will escape
any more than all the other Jews. 14 For
if you keep silent at this time, relief and
deliverance will rise for the Jews from
another place, but you and your father's
house will perish. And who knows
whether you have not come to the king-
dom for such a time as this?" 15 Then
Esther told them to reply to Mordecai,
16 "Go, gather all the Jews to be found in
Susa, and hold a fast on my behalf, and
do not eat or drink for three days, night
or day. I and my young women will
also fast as you do. Then I will go to the
king, though it is against the law, and if
I perish, I perish." 17 Mordecai then went
away and did everything as Esther had
ordered him.

Esther Prepares a Banquet

5 On the third day Esther put on her
royal robes and stood in the inner
court of the king's palace, in front of the
king's quarters, while the king was sit-
ting on his royal throne inside the throne
room opposite the entrance to the palace.
2 And when the king saw Queen Esther
standing in the court, she won favor in his
sight, and he held out to Esther the golden
scepter that was in his hand. Then Esther
approached and touched the tip of the
scepter. 3 And the king said to her, "What
is it, Queen Esther? What is your request?
It shall be given you, even to the half of my
kingdom." 4 And Esther said, "If it please
the king, let the king and Haman come
today to a feast that I have prepared for the
king." 5 Then the king said, "Bring Haman
quickly, so that we may do as Esther has
asked." So the king and Haman came to
the feast that Esther had prepared. 6 And
as they were drinking wine after the feast,
the king said to Esther, "What is your
wish? It shall be granted you. And what is
your request? Even to the half of my king-
dom, it shall be fulfilled." 7 Then Esther
answered, "My wish and my request is:
8 If I have found favor in the sight of the
king, and if it please the king to grant my
wish and fulfill my request, let the king
and Haman come to the feast that I will
prepare for them, and tomorrow I will do
as the king has said."

Haman Plans to Hang Mordecai

9 And Haman went out that day joy-
ful and glad of heart. But when Haman
saw Mordecai in the king's gate, that he
neither rose nor trembled before him, he
was filled with wrath against Mordecai.
10 Nevertheless, Haman restrained him-
self and went home, and he sent and
brought his friends and his wife Zeresh.
11 And Haman recounted to them the
splendor of his riches, the number of his
sons, all the promotions with which the

king had honored him, and how he had advanced him above the officials and the servants of the king. **12** Then Haman said, "Even Queen Esther let no one but me come with the king to the feast she prepared. And tomorrow also I am invited by her together with the king. **13** Yet all this is worth nothing to me, so long as I see Mordecai the Jew sitting at the king's gate." **14** Then his wife Zeresh and all his friends said to him, "Let a gallows[1] fifty cubits[2] high be made, and in the morning tell the king to have Mordecai hanged upon it. Then go joyfully with the king to the feast." This idea pleased Haman, and he had the gallows made.

The King Honors Mordecai

6 On that night the king could not sleep. And he gave orders to bring the book of memorable deeds, the chronicles, and they were read before the king. **2** And it was found written how Mordecai had told about Bigthana and Teresh, two of the king's eunuchs, who guarded the threshold, and who had sought to lay hands on King Ahasuerus. **3** And the king said, "What honor or distinction has been bestowed on Mordecai for this?" The king's young men who attended him said, "Nothing has been done for him." **4** And the king said, "Who is in the court?" Now Haman had just entered the outer court of the king's palace to speak to the king about having Mordecai hanged on the gallows[3] that he had prepared for him. **5** And the king's young men told him, "Haman is there, standing in the court." And the king said, "Let him come in." **6** So Haman came in, and the king said to him, "What should be done to the man whom the king delights to honor?" And Haman said to himself, "Whom would the king delight to honor more than me?" **7** And Haman said to the king, "For the man whom the king delights to honor, **8** let royal robes be brought, which the king has worn, and the horse that the king has ridden, and on whose head a royal crown[4] is set. **9** And let the robes and the horse be handed over to one of the king's most noble officials. Let them dress the man whom the king delights to honor, and let them lead him on the horse through the square of the city, proclaiming before him: 'Thus shall it be done to the man whom the king delights to honor.'" **10** Then the king said to Haman, "Hurry; take the robes and the horse, as you have said, and do so to Mordecai the Jew, who sits at the king's gate. Leave out nothing that you have mentioned." **11** So Haman took the robes and the horse, and he dressed Mordecai and led him through the square of the city, proclaiming before him, "Thus shall it be done to the man whom the king delights to honor."

12 Then Mordecai returned to the king's gate. But Haman hurried to his house, mourning and with his head covered. **13** And Haman told his wife Zeresh and all his friends everything that had happened to him. Then his wise men and his wife Zeresh said to him, "If Mordecai, before whom you have begun to fall, is of the Jewish people, you will not overcome him but will surely fall before him."

Esther Reveals Haman's Plot

14 While they were yet talking with him, the king's eunuchs arrived and hurried to bring Haman to the feast that Esther had prepared.

7 So the king and Haman went in to feast with Queen Esther. **2** And on the second day, as they were drinking wine after the feast, the king again said to Esther, "What is your wish, Queen Esther? It shall be granted you. And what is your request? Even to the half of my kingdom, it shall be fulfilled." **3** Then Queen Esther answered, "If I have found favor in your sight, O king, and if it please the king, let my life be granted me for my wish, and my people for my request. **4** For we have been

[1] Or *stake*; twice in this verse [2] A *cubit* was about 18 inches or 45 centimeters [3] Or *suspended on a stake* [4] Or *headdress*

sold, I and my people, to be destroyed,
to be killed, and to be annihilated. If we
had been sold merely as slaves, men and
women, I would have been silent, for our
affliction is not to be compared with the
loss to the king." 5 Then King Ahasuerus
said to Queen Esther, "Who is he, and
where is he, who has dared[1] to do this?"
6 And Esther said, "A foe and enemy! This
wicked Haman!" Then Haman was terri-
fied before the king and the queen.

Haman Is Hanged

7 And the king arose in his wrath from
the wine-drinking and went into the pal-
ace garden, but Haman stayed to beg for
his life from Queen Esther, for he saw that
harm was determined against him by the
king. 8 And the king returned from the pal-
ace garden to the place where they were
drinking wine, as Haman was falling on
the couch where Esther was. And the king
said, "Will he even assault the queen in
my presence, in my own house?" As the
word left the mouth of the king, they cov-
ered Haman's face. 9 Then Harbona, one
of the eunuchs in attendance on the king,
said, "Moreover, the gallows[2] that Haman
has prepared for Mordecai, whose word
saved the king, is standing at Haman's
house, fifty cubits[3] high." 10 And the king
said, "Hang him on that." So they hanged
Haman on the gallows that he had pre-
pared for Mordecai. Then the wrath of the
king abated.

Esther Saves the Jews

8 On that day King Ahasuerus gave to
Queen Esther the house of Haman,
the enemy of the Jews. And Mordecai
came before the king, for Esther had told
what he was to her. 2 And the king took
off his signet ring, which he had taken
from Haman, and gave it to Mordecai.
And Esther set Mordecai over the house
of Haman.
3 Then Esther spoke again to the
king. She fell at his feet and wept and
pleaded with him to avert the evil plan
of Haman the Agagite and the plot that
he had devised against the Jews. 4 When
the king held out the golden scepter to
Esther, 5 Esther rose and stood before the
king. And she said, "If it please the king,
and if I have found favor in his sight,
and if the thing seems right before the
king, and I am pleasing in his eyes, let
an order be written to revoke the letters
devised by Haman the Agagite, the son of
Hammedatha, which he wrote to destroy
the Jews who are in all the provinces of
the king. 6 For how can I bear to see the
calamity that is coming to my people?
Or how can I bear to see the destruction
of my kindred?" 7 Then King Ahasuerus
said to Queen Esther and to Mordecai
the Jew, "Behold, I have given Esther the
house of Haman, and they have hanged
him on the gallows,[4] because he intended
to lay hands on the Jews. 8 But you may
write as you please with regard to the
Jews, in the name of the king, and seal it
with the king's ring, for an edict written in
the name of the king and sealed with the
king's ring cannot be revoked."
9 The king's scribes were summoned at
that time, in the third month, which is the
month of Sivan, on the twenty-third day.
And an edict was written, according to all
that Mordecai commanded concerning the
Jews, to the satraps and the governors and
the officials of the provinces from India to
Ethiopia, 127 provinces, to each province
in its own script and to each people in its
own language, and also to the Jews in their
script and their language. 10 And he wrote
in the name of King Ahasuerus and sealed
it with the king's signet ring. Then he sent
the letters by mounted couriers riding on
swift horses that were used in the king's
service, bred from the royal stud, 11 saying
that the king allowed the Jews who were in
every city to gather and defend their lives,
to destroy, to kill, and to annihilate any
armed force of any people or province that

[1] Hebrew *whose heart has filled him* [2] Or *stake*; also verse 10 [3] A *cubit* was about 18 inches or 45 centimeters [4] Or *stake*

might attack them, children and women included, and to plunder their goods, 12 on one day throughout all the provinces of King Ahasuerus, on the thirteenth day of the twelfth month, which is the month of Adar. 13 A copy of what was written was to be issued as a decree in every province, being publicly displayed to all peoples, and the Jews were to be ready on that day to take vengeance on their enemies. 14 So the couriers, mounted on their swift horses that were used in the king's service, rode out hurriedly, urged by the king's command. And the decree was issued in Susa the citadel.

15 Then Mordecai went out from the presence of the king in royal robes of blue and white, with a great golden crown[1] and a robe of fine linen and purple, and the city of Susa shouted and rejoiced. 16 The Jews had light and gladness and joy and honor. 17 And in every province and in every city, wherever the king's command and his edict reached, there was gladness and joy among the Jews, a feast and a holiday. And many from the peoples of the country declared themselves Jews, for fear of the Jews had fallen on them.

The Jews Destroy Their Enemies

9 Now in the twelfth month, which is the month of Adar, on the thirteenth day of the same, when the king's command and edict were about to be carried out, on the very day when the enemies of the Jews hoped to gain the mastery over them, the reverse occurred: the Jews gained mastery over those who hated them. 2 The Jews gathered in their cities throughout all the provinces of King Ahasuerus to lay hands on those who sought their harm. And no one could stand against them, for the fear of them had fallen on all peoples. 3 All the officials of the provinces and the satraps and the governors and the royal agents also helped the Jews, for the fear of Mordecai had fallen on them. 4 For Mordecai was great in the king's house, and his fame spread throughout all the provinces, for the man Mordecai grew more and more powerful. 5 The Jews struck all their enemies with the sword, killing and destroying them, and did as they pleased to those who hated them. 6 In Susa the citadel itself the Jews killed and destroyed 500 men, 7 and also killed Parshandatha and Dalphon and Aspatha 8 and Poratha and Adalia and Aridatha 9 and Parmashta and Arisai and Aridai and Vaizatha, 10 the ten sons of Haman the son of Hammedatha, the enemy of the Jews, but they laid no hand on the plunder.

11 That very day the number of those killed in Susa the citadel was reported to the king. 12 And the king said to Queen Esther, "In Susa the citadel the Jews have killed and destroyed 500 men and also the ten sons of Haman. What then have they done in the rest of the king's provinces! Now what is your wish? It shall be granted you. And what further is your request? It shall be fulfilled." 13 And Esther said, "If it please the king, let the Jews who are in Susa be allowed tomorrow also to do according to this day's edict. And let the ten sons of Haman be hanged on the gallows."[2] 14 So the king commanded this to be done. A decree was issued in Susa, and the ten sons of Haman were hanged. 15 The Jews who were in Susa gathered also on the fourteenth day of the month of Adar and they killed 300 men in Susa, but they laid no hands on the plunder.

16 Now the rest of the Jews who were in the king's provinces also gathered to defend their lives, and got relief from their enemies and killed 75,000 of those who hated them, but they laid no hands on the plunder. 17 This was on the thirteenth day of the month of Adar, and on the fourteenth day they rested and made that a day of feasting and gladness. 18 But the Jews who were in Susa gathered on the

[1] Or *headdress* [2] Or *stake*

Esther and God's People

King Ahasuerus, the king of Persia, reigned over a vast empire, stretching all the way from Ethiopia to India. After Queen Vashti offended him, King Ahasuerus decided that he wanted a wife who would not offend him again. So the king held an enormous beauty contest for every girl in his kingdom. The contest lasted more than a year, with young women coming from all over the kingdom.

One of the young women—a beautiful woman named Esther—was an Israelite, one of God's own people. Esther was so beautiful that King Ahasuerus chose her over all the other young women to be his queen.

Esther had a cousin named Mordecai. He had raised Esther and had been like a father to her, because Esther didn't have a father. One day, Esther saw her cousin Mordecai crying loudly near the palace gate. So Esther sent a messenger to him to find out what was wrong.

Mordecai sent a message back, telling Esther that a man named Haman—a man who hated God's people—had tricked the king into making a new law. This law said that on a certain day all God's people would be killed. Mordecai told Queen Esther she must go to the king and beg him to save her people.

Esther sent another message to Mordecai. She explained to him that no one was allowed to go to the king without an invitation. If someone went to the king and had not been invited, that person would be put to death. And the king had not invited Esther to come see him for 30 days!

Mordecai sent his answer back to Esther, urging her to go see the king. Who knows, Mordecai said, maybe this was the whole reason Esther had become queen—to save God's people from death! Esther sent back one last message. She told Mordecai to ask God's people everywhere to fast for three days for her, and then she would go to the king. "And if I perish, I perish," she said.

Three days later, when Esther went to the king, he was glad to see her, even though he had not invited her. He told her he would do anything she wanted and asked what she wanted him to do. Esther simply invited the king to a feast she had prepared, and she asked him to bring Haman too.

The king and Haman came to Esther's feast. After they had eaten, the king asked Esther again what she wanted him to do for her. Once more Esther asked the king to come to a feast, on the very next day, and to bring Haman too. At the feast the next day the king asked Esther one last time what she wanted him to do. Finally, Esther told him—she wanted the king to save her life from Haman, who wanted to kill her and all God's people too!

When King Ahasuerus saw that Haman was going to kill Esther and all of God's people, he was furious. Haman was put to death for his evil plan. And the king made a new law that saved the Israelites from all their enemies who wanted to kill them.

God used Esther to save His people. Mordecai and Queen

Esther praised and thanked God, and all God's people shouted and rejoiced! Even today, the people of Israel still sing and dance and celebrate every year, in remembrance of how God chose Esther to help them and how God saved them from their enemies.

God saved His people from being destroyed, more than 400 years before Jesus our Savior was born. How thankful we are to God for sending Jesus to save us and take our sins away!

SEEK and FIND

WHERE TO FIND THE STORY

Esther 1–10

KEY BIBLE VERSE

"Many are the plans in the mind of a man,
but it is the purpose of the LORD that will stand."
(Proverbs 19:21)

THREE KEY QUESTIONS

- What was Haman's evil plan for God's people?
- How did Esther trust God and stop Haman's evil plan?
- What is God's plan to save us?

RELATED BIBLE READINGS

Isaiah 46:8–10; 55:10–11; Ephesians 1:11

thirteenth day and on the fourteenth, and rested on the fifteenth day, making that a day of feasting and gladness. 19 Therefore the Jews of the villages, who live in the rural towns, hold the fourteenth day of the month of Adar as a day for gladness and feasting, as a holiday, and as a day on which they send gifts of food to one another.

The Feast of Purim Inaugurated

20 And Mordecai recorded these things and sent letters to all the Jews who were in all the provinces of King Ahasuerus, both near and far, 21 obliging them to keep the fourteenth day of the month Adar and also the fifteenth day of the same, year by year, 22 as the days on which the Jews got relief from their enemies, and as the month that

had been turned for them from sorrow
into gladness and from mourning into a
holiday; that they should make them days
of feasting and gladness, days for sending
gifts of food to one another and gifts to
the poor.
23 So the Jews accepted what they
had started to do, and what Mordecai
had written to them. 24 For Haman the
Agagite, the son of Hammedatha, the
enemy of all the Jews, had plotted against
the Jews to destroy them, and had cast
Pur (that is, cast lots), to crush and to
destroy them. 25 But when it came before
the king, he gave orders in writing that
his evil plan that he had devised against
the Jews should return on his own
head, and that he and his sons should
be hanged on the gallows.[1] 26 Therefore
they called these days Purim, after the
term Pur. Therefore, because of all that
was written in this letter, and of what
they had faced in this matter, and of
what had happened to them, 27 the Jews
firmly obligated themselves and their
offspring and all who joined them, that
without fail they would keep these two
days according to what was written and
at the time appointed every year, 28 that
these days should be remembered and
kept throughout every generation, in
every clan, province, and city, and that
these days of Purim should never fall
into disuse among the Jews, nor should
the commemoration of these days cease
among their descendants.
29 Then Queen Esther, the daughter of
Abihail, and Mordecai the Jew gave full
written authority, confirming this second
letter about Purim. 30 Letters were sent to
all the Jews, to the 127 provinces of the
kingdom of Ahasuerus, in words of peace
and truth, 31 that these days of Purim
should be observed at their appointed
seasons, as Mordecai the Jew and Queen
Esther obligated them, and as they had
obligated themselves and their offspring,
with regard to their fasts and their lament-
ing. 32 The command of Queen Esther
confirmed these practices of Purim, and
it was recorded in writing.

The Greatness of Mordecai

10 King Ahasuerus imposed tax on
the land and on the coastlands of
the sea. 2 And all the acts of his power and
might, and the full account of the high
honor of Mordecai, to which the king
advanced him, are they not written in
the Book of the Chronicles of the kings of
Media and Persia? 3 For Mordecai the Jew
was second in rank to King Ahasuerus,
and he was great among the Jews and pop-
ular with the multitude of his brothers, for
he sought the welfare of his people and
spoke peace to all his people.

[1] Or *suspended on a stake*

Introduction to

Job

Author

Job, or someone who lived when he did

Date

Late third or early second millennium B.C.

People

Job; Eliphaz; Bildad; Zophar; Elihu

Purpose

The purpose of Job is to show that suffering in a fallen world is not always because the sufferer has done something very sinful; suffering can be a way of bringing great glory to God.

Central Themes

Satan accuses people before God and tempts God's people, but he can do nothing apart from God's permission; God's people who suffer may not know the reason for their suffering, but they honor Him when they continue to trust Him; it is harmful and wrong to believe that the righteous always prosper and only the sinful suffer; God can be trusted because He is all-powerful, wise, and good.

Memory Verses

Job's resolve (Job 1:21; 2:9–10); Job's comfort (Job 19:25–27); the Lord's answer (Job 38:1–2)

Introduction

Job is famous for trusting God during great suffering. When the book begins, Job is a God-fearing, righteous man. He has a large family and great riches. When Satan tells God that Job only obeys God for what he gets out of it, God gives Satan permission, first, to take away all of Job's possessions and his 10 children, and then to cover Job himself with ugly, painful sores. Job does not curse God as Satan said he would (Job 1:1–2:10). Job's friends come to comfort him, but they only tell him, over and over, that if he had not sinned greatly, God would not have allowed him to suffer so. Job insists that he has not sinned. He never curses God, but he does complain (Job 2:11–37:24). God answers Job by describing things He has done in creation that Job could never do, things that show God's great power and wisdom. Job admits that God is greater than he is and that God knows better than Job what should be done (Job 38:1–42:6). God rebukes Job's friends, but forgives them when Job prays for them. Then God gives Job double of what he had before, including 10 more children (Job 42:7–17).

2166 B.C.	?	1446 B.C.
Abraham born	Events of Job	Exodus from Egypt

Job

Job's Character and Wealth

1 There was a man in the land of Uz whose name was Job, and that man was blameless and upright, one who feared God and turned away from evil. 2 There were born to him seven sons and three daughters. 3 He possessed 7,000 sheep, 3,000 camels, 500 yoke of oxen, and 500 female donkeys, and very many servants, so that this man was the greatest of all the people of the east. 4 His sons used to go and hold a feast in the house of each one on his day, and they would send and invite their three sisters to eat and drink with them. 5 And when the days of the feast had run their course, Job would send and consecrate them, and he would rise early in the morning and offer burnt offerings according to the number of them all. For Job said, "It may be that my children have sinned, and cursed[1] God in their hearts." Thus Job did continually.

Satan Allowed to Test Job

6 Now there was a day when the sons of God came to present themselves before the LORD, and Satan[2] also came among them. 7 The LORD said to Satan, "From where have you come?" Satan answered the LORD and said, "From going to and fro on the earth, and from walking up and down on it." 8 And the LORD said to Satan, "Have you considered my servant Job, that there is none like him on the earth, a blameless and upright man, who fears God and turns away from evil?" 9 Then Satan answered the LORD and said, "Does Job fear God for no reason? 10 Have you not put a hedge around him and his house and all that he has, on every side? You have blessed the work of his hands, and his possessions have increased in the land. 11 But stretch out your hand and touch all that he has, and he will curse you to your face." 12 And the LORD said to Satan, "Behold, all that he has is in your hand. Only against him do not stretch out your hand." So Satan went out from the presence of the LORD.

Satan Takes Job's Property and Children

13 Now there was a day when his sons and daughters were eating and drinking wine in their oldest brother's house, 14 and there came a messenger to Job and said, "The oxen were plowing and the donkeys feeding beside them, 15 and the Sabeans

CHARACTER PROFILE

JOB

Job suddenly lost all his children and all his riches, and became sick with painful boils. But, Job continued to love and trust God. His three friends said Job must have sinned greatly. God rebuked the three friends, restored Job's wealth and health, and gave him more children.

[1] The Hebrew word *bless* is used euphemistically for *curse* in 1:5, 11; 2:5, 9 [2] Hebrew *the Adversary*; so throughout chapters 1–2

fell upon them and took them and struck
down the servants[1] with the edge of the
sword, and I alone have escaped to tell
you." 16 While he was yet speaking, there
came another and said, "The fire of God
fell from heaven and burned up the sheep
and the servants and consumed them,
and I alone have escaped to tell you."
17 While he was yet speaking, there came
another and said, "The Chaldeans formed
three groups and made a raid on the cam-
els and took them and struck down the
servants with the edge of the sword, and
I alone have escaped to tell you." 18 While
he was yet speaking, there came another
and said, "Your sons and daughters were
eating and drinking wine in their oldest
brother's house, 19 and behold, a great
wind came across the wilderness and
struck the four corners of the house, and
it fell upon the young people, and they are
dead, and I alone have escaped to tell you."
20 Then Job arose and tore his robe and
shaved his head and fell on the ground
and worshiped. 21 And he said, "Naked
I came from my mother's womb, and
naked shall I return. The LORD gave, and
the LORD has taken away; blessed be the
name of the LORD."
22 In all this Job did not sin or charge
God with wrong.

Satan Attacks Job's Health

2 Again there was a day when the sons
of God came to present themselves
before the LORD, and Satan also came
among them to present himself before the
LORD. 2 And the LORD said to Satan, "From
where have you come?" Satan answered
the LORD and said, "From going to and fro
on the earth, and from walking up and
down on it." 3 And the LORD said to Satan,
"Have you considered my servant Job,
that there is none like him on the earth, a
blameless and upright man, who fears God
and turns away from evil? He still holds
fast his integrity, although you incited me
against him to destroy him without rea-
son." 4 Then Satan answered the LORD and
said, "Skin for skin! All that a man has he
will give for his life. 5 But stretch out your
hand and touch his bone and his flesh,
and he will curse you to your face." 6 And
the LORD said to Satan, "Behold, he is in
your hand; only spare his life."
7 So Satan went out from the presence
of the LORD and struck Job with loath-
some sores from the sole of his foot to the
crown of his head. 8 And he took a piece of
broken pottery with which to scrape him-
self while he sat in the ashes.
9 Then his wife said to him, "Do you still
hold fast your integrity? Curse God and
die." 10 But he said to her, "You speak as
one of the foolish women would speak.
Shall we receive good from God, and shall
we not receive evil?"[2] In all this Job did not
sin with his lips.

Job's Three Friends

11 Now when Job's three friends heard of
all this evil that had come upon him, they
came each from his own place, Eliphaz the
Temanite, Bildad the Shuhite, and Zophar
the Naamathite. They made an appoint-
ment together to come to show him
sympathy and comfort him. 12 And when
they saw him from a distance, they did
not recognize him. And they raised their
voices and wept, and they tore their robes
and sprinkled dust on their heads toward
heaven. 13 And they sat with him on the
ground seven days and seven nights, and
no one spoke a word to him, for they saw
that his suffering was very great.

Job Laments His Birth

3 After this Job opened his mouth and
cursed the day of his birth. 2 And Job
said:

3 "Let the day perish on which I was
born,
and the night that said,
'A man is conceived.'

[1] Hebrew *the young men*; also verses 16, 17 [2] Or *disaster*; also verse 11

4 Let that day be darkness!
May God above not seek it,
nor light shine upon it.
5 Let gloom and deep darkness claim it.
Let clouds dwell upon it;
let the blackness of the day terrify it.
6 That night—let thick darkness seize it!
Let it not rejoice among the days of the year;
let it not come into the number of the months.
7 Behold, let that night be barren;
let no joyful cry enter it.
8 Let those curse it who curse the day,
who are ready to rouse up Leviathan.
9 Let the stars of its dawn be dark;
let it hope for light, but have none,
nor see the eyelids of the morning,
10 because it did not shut the doors of my mother's womb,
nor hide trouble from my eyes.

11 "Why did I not die at birth,
come out from the womb and expire?
12 Why did the knees receive me?
Or why the breasts, that I should nurse?
13 For then I would have lain down and been quiet;
I would have slept; then I would have been at rest,
14 with kings and counselors of the earth
who rebuilt ruins for themselves,
15 or with princes who had gold,
who filled their houses with silver.
16 Or why was I not as a hidden stillborn child,
as infants who never see the light?
17 There the wicked cease from troubling,
and there the weary are at rest.
18 There the prisoners are at ease together;
they hear not the voice of the taskmaster.
19 The small and the great are there,
and the slave is free from his master.

20 "Why is light given to him who is in misery,
and life to the bitter in soul,
21 who long for death, but it comes not,
and dig for it more than for hidden treasures,
22 who rejoice exceedingly
and are glad when they find the grave?
23 Why is light given to a man whose way is hidden,
whom God has hedged in?
24 For my sighing comes instead of[1] my bread,
and my groanings are poured out like water.
25 For the thing that I fear comes upon me,
and what I dread befalls me.
26 I am not at ease, nor am I quiet;
I have no rest, but trouble comes."

Eliphaz Speaks: The Innocent Prosper

4 Then Eliphaz the Temanite answered and said:

2 "If one ventures a word with you, will you be impatient?
Yet who can keep from speaking?
3 Behold, you have instructed many,
and you have strengthened the weak hands.
4 Your words have upheld him who was stumbling,
and you have made firm the feeble knees.

[1] Or *like*; Hebrew *before*

5 But now it has come to you, and you
are impatient;
it touches you, and you are
dismayed.
6 Is not your fear of God[1] your
confidence,
and the integrity of your ways
your hope?

7 "Remember: who that was innocent
ever perished?
Or where were the upright cut off?
8 As I have seen, those who plow
iniquity
and sow trouble reap the same.
9 By the breath of God they perish,
and by the blast of his anger they
are consumed.
10 The roar of the lion, the voice of the
fierce lion,
the teeth of the young lions are
broken.
11 The strong lion perishes for lack of
prey,
and the cubs of the lioness are
scattered.

12 "Now a word was brought to me
stealthily;
my ear received the whisper of it.
13 Amid thoughts from visions of the
night,
when deep sleep falls on men,
14 dread came upon me, and trembling,
which made all my bones shake.
15 A spirit glided past my face;
the hair of my flesh stood up.
16 It stood still,
but I could not discern its
appearance.
A form was before my eyes;
there was silence, then I heard a
voice:
17 'Can mortal man be in the right
before[2] God?
Can a man be pure before his
Maker?
18 Even in his servants he puts no
trust,
and his angels he charges with
error;
19 how much more those who dwell in
houses of clay,
whose foundation is in the dust,
who are crushed like the moth.
20 Between morning and evening they
are beaten to pieces;
they perish forever without
anyone regarding it.
21 Is not their tent-cord plucked up
within them,
do they not die, and that without
wisdom?'

5 "Call now; is there anyone who will
answer you?
To which of the holy ones will you
turn?
2 Surely vexation kills the fool,
and jealousy slays the simple.
3 I have seen the fool taking root,
but suddenly I cursed his
dwelling.
4 His children are far from safety;
they are crushed in the gate,
and there is no one to deliver
them.
5 The hungry eat his harvest,
and he takes it even out of
thorns,[3]
and the thirsty pant[4] after his[5]
wealth.
6 For affliction does not come from
the dust,
nor does trouble sprout from the
ground,
7 but man is born to trouble
as the sparks fly upward.

8 "As for me, I would seek God,
and to God would I commit my
cause,

[1] Hebrew lacks *of God* [2] Or *more than*; twice in this verse [3] The meaning of the Hebrew is uncertain [4] Aquila, Symmachus, Syriac, Vulgate; Hebrew could be read as *and the snare pants* [5] Hebrew *their*

9 who does great things and
unsearchable,
marvelous things without
number:
10 he gives rain on the earth
and sends waters on the fields;
11 he sets on high those who are lowly,
and those who mourn are lifted to
safety.
12 He frustrates the devices of the
crafty,
so that their hands achieve no
success.
13 He catches the wise in their own
craftiness,
and the schemes of the wily are
brought to a quick end.
14 They meet with darkness in the
daytime
and grope at noonday as in the
night.
15 But he saves the needy from the
sword of their mouth
and from the hand of the mighty.
16 So the poor have hope,
and injustice shuts her mouth.

17 "Behold, blessed is the one whom
God reproves;
therefore despise not the
discipline of the Almighty.
18 For he wounds, but he binds up;
he shatters, but his hands heal.
19 He will deliver you from six
troubles;
in seven no evil[1] shall touch you.
20 In famine he will redeem you from
death,
and in war from the power of the
sword.
21 You shall be hidden from the lash of
the tongue,
and shall not fear destruction
when it comes.
22 At destruction and famine you shall
laugh,
and shall not fear the beasts of the
earth.
23 For you shall be in league with the
stones of the field,
and the beasts of the field shall be
at peace with you.
24 You shall know that your tent is at
peace,
and you shall inspect your fold
and miss nothing.
25 You shall know also that your
offspring shall be many,
and your descendants as the grass
of the earth.
26 You shall come to your grave in ripe
old age,
like a sheaf gathered up in its
season.
27 Behold, this we have searched out;
it is true.
Hear, and know it for your good."[2]

Job Replies: My Complaint Is Just

6 Then Job answered and said:

2 "Oh that my vexation were weighed,
and all my calamity laid in the
balances!
3 For then it would be heavier than
the sand of the sea;
therefore my words have been
rash.
4 For the arrows of the Almighty are
in me;
my spirit drinks their poison;
the terrors of God are arrayed
against me.
5 Does the wild donkey bray when he
has grass,
or the ox low over his fodder?
6 Can that which is tasteless be eaten
without salt,
or is there any taste in the juice of
the mallow?[3]
7 My appetite refuses to touch them;
they are as food that is loathsome
to me.[4]

8 "Oh that I might have my request,
and that God would fulfill my hope,

[1] Or *disaster* [2] Hebrew *for yourself* [3] The meaning of the Hebrew word is uncertain [4] The meaning of the Hebrew is uncertain

9 that it would please God to crush me,
that he would let loose his hand
and cut me off!
10 This would be my comfort;
I would even exult[1] in pain
unsparing,
for I have not denied the words of
the Holy One.
11 What is my strength, that I should
wait?
And what is my end, that I should
be patient?
12 Is my strength the strength of
stones, or is my flesh bronze?
13 Have I any help in me,
when resource is driven from me?

14 "He who withholds[2] kindness from a
friend
forsakes the fear of the Almighty.
15 My brothers are treacherous as a
torrent-bed,
as torrential streams that pass
away,
16 which are dark with ice,
and where the snow hides itself.
17 When they melt, they disappear;
when it is hot, they vanish from
their place.
18 The caravans turn aside from their
course;
they go up into the waste and
perish.
19 The caravans of Tema look,
the travelers of Sheba hope.
20 They are ashamed because they
were confident;
they come there and are
disappointed.
21 For you have now become nothing;
you see my calamity and are afraid.
22 Have I said, 'Make me a gift'?
Or, 'From your wealth offer a
bribe for me'?
23 Or, 'Deliver me from the adversary's
hand'?
Or, 'Redeem me from the hand of
the ruthless'?

24 "Teach me, and I will be silent;
make me understand how I have
gone astray.
25 How forceful are upright words!
But what does reproof from you
reprove?
26 Do you think that you can reprove
words,
when the speech of a despairing
man is wind?
27 You would even cast lots over the
fatherless,
and bargain over your friend.

28 "But now, be pleased to look at me,
for I will not lie to your face.
29 Please turn; let no injustice be done.
Turn now; my vindication is at
stake.
30 Is there any injustice on my tongue?
Cannot my palate discern the
cause of calamity?

Job Continues: My Life Has No Hope

7 "Has not man a hard service on earth,
and are not his days like the days of
a hired hand?
2 Like a slave who longs for the
shadow,
and like a hired hand who looks
for his wages,
3 so I am allotted months of
emptiness,
and nights of misery are
apportioned to me.
4 When I lie down I say, 'When shall I
arise?'
But the night is long,
and I am full of tossing till the
dawn.
5 My flesh is clothed with worms and
dirt;
my skin hardens, then breaks out
afresh.
6 My days are swifter than a weaver's
shuttle
and come to their end without
hope.

[1] The meaning of the Hebrew word is uncertain [2] Syriac, Vulgate (compare Targum); the meaning of the Hebrew word is uncertain

7 "Remember that my life is a breath;
my eye will never again see good.
8 The eye of him who sees me will
behold me no more;
while your eyes are on me, I shall
be gone.
9 As the cloud fades and vanishes,
so he who goes down to Sheol
does not come up;
10 he returns no more to his house,
nor does his place know him
anymore.

11 "Therefore I will not restrain my
mouth;
I will speak in the anguish of my
spirit;
I will complain in the bitterness
of my soul.
12 Am I the sea, or a sea monster,
that you set a guard over me?
13 When I say, 'My bed will comfort me,
my couch will ease my
complaint,'
14 then you scare me with dreams
and terrify me with visions,
15 so that I would choose strangling
and death rather than my bones.
16 I loathe my life; I would not live
forever.
Leave me alone, for my days are a
breath.
17 What is man, that you make so
much of him,
and that you set your heart on
him,
18 visit him every morning
and test him every moment?
19 How long will you not look away
from me,
nor leave me alone till I swallow
my spit?
20 If I sin, what do I do to you, you
watcher of mankind?
Why have you made me your
mark?
Why have I become a burden to
you?
21 Why do you not pardon my
transgression
and take away my iniquity?
For now I shall lie in the earth;
you will seek me, but I shall not be."

Bildad Speaks: Job Should Repent

8 Then Bildad the Shuhite answered and said:

2 "How long will you say these things,
and the words of your mouth be a
great wind?
3 Does God pervert justice?
Or does the Almighty pervert the
right?
4 If your children have sinned against
him,
he has delivered them into the
hand of their transgression.
5 If you will seek God
and plead with the Almighty for
mercy,
6 if you are pure and upright,
surely then he will rouse himself
for you
and restore your rightful
habitation.
7 And though your beginning was
small,
your latter days will be very great.

8 "For inquire, please, of bygone ages,
and consider what the fathers
have searched out.
9 For we are but of yesterday and
know nothing,
for our days on earth are a shadow.
10 Will they not teach you and tell you
and utter words out of their
understanding?

11 "Can papyrus grow where there is no
marsh?
Can reeds flourish where there is
no water?
12 While yet in flower and not cut
down,
they wither before any other plant.

13 Such are the paths of all who forget
God;
the hope of the godless shall
perish.
14 His confidence is severed,
and his trust is a spider's web.[1]
15 He leans against his house, but it
does not stand;
he lays hold of it, but it does not
endure.
16 He is a lush plant before the sun,
and his shoots spread over his
garden.
17 His roots entwine the stone heap;
he looks upon a house of stones.
18 If he is destroyed from his place,
then it will deny him, saying, 'I
have never seen you.'
19 Behold, this is the joy of his way,
and out of the soil others will
spring.

20 "Behold, God will not reject a
blameless man,
nor take the hand of evildoers.
21 He will yet fill your mouth with
laughter,
and your lips with shouting.
22 Those who hate you will be clothed
with shame,
and the tent of the wicked will be
no more."

Job Replies: There Is No Arbiter

9 Then Job answered and said:

2 "Truly I know that it is so:
But how can a man be in the right
before God?
3 If one wished to contend with him,
one could not answer him once
in a thousand times.
4 He is wise in heart and mighty in
strength
—who has hardened himself
against him, and succeeded?—
5 he who removes mountains, and
they know it not,
when he overturns them in his
anger,
6 who shakes the earth out of its
place,
and its pillars tremble;
7 who commands the sun, and it
does not rise;
who seals up the stars;
8 who alone stretched out the
heavens
and trampled the waves of the sea;
9 who made the Bear and Orion,
the Pleiades and the chambers of
the south;
10 who does great things beyond
searching out,
and marvelous things beyond
number.
11 Behold, he passes by me, and I see
him not;
he moves on, but I do not
perceive him.
12 Behold, he snatches away; who can
turn him back?
Who will say to him, 'What are
you doing?'

13 "God will not turn back his anger;
beneath him bowed the helpers
of Rahab.
14 How then can I answer him,
choosing my words with him?
15 Though I am in the right, I cannot
answer him;
I must appeal for mercy to my
accuser.[2]
16 If I summoned him and he
answered me,
I would not believe that he was
listening to my voice.
17 For he crushes me with a tempest
and multiplies my wounds
without cause;
18 he will not let me get my breath,
but fills me with bitterness.

[1] Hebrew *house* [2] Or *to my judge*

19 If it is a contest of strength, behold,
he is mighty!
If it is a matter of justice, who can
summon him?[1]
20 Though I am in the right, my own
mouth would condemn me;
though I am blameless, he would
prove me perverse.
21 I am blameless; I regard not myself;
I loathe my life.
22 It is all one; therefore I say,
He destroys both the blameless
and the wicked.
23 When disaster brings sudden death,
he mocks at the calamity[2] of the
innocent.
24 The earth is given into the hand of
the wicked;
he covers the faces of its judges—
if it is not he, who then is it?

25 "My days are swifter than a runner;
they flee away; they see no good.
26 They go by like skiffs of reed,
like an eagle swooping on the
prey.
27 If I say, 'I will forget my complaint,
I will put off my sad face, and be
of good cheer,'
28 I become afraid of all my suffering,
for I know you will not hold me
innocent.
29 I shall be condemned;
why then do I labor in vain?
30 If I wash myself with snow
and cleanse my hands with lye,
31 yet you will plunge me into a pit,
and my own clothes will abhor
me.
32 For he is not a man, as I am, that I
might answer him,
that we should come to trial
together.
33 There is no[3] arbiter between us,
who might lay his hand on us
both.
34 Let him take his rod away from me,
and let not dread of him terrify
me.
35 Then I would speak without fear of
him,
for I am not so in myself.

Job Continues: A Plea to God

10 "I loathe my life;
I will give free utterance to my
complaint;
I will speak in the bitterness of
my soul.
2 I will say to God, Do not condemn
me;
let me know why you contend
against me.
3 Does it seem good to you to oppress,
to despise the work of your hands
and favor the designs of the
wicked?
4 Have you eyes of flesh?
Do you see as man sees?
5 Are your days as the days of man,
or your years as a man's years,
6 that you seek out my iniquity
and search for my sin,
7 although you know that I am not
guilty,
and there is none to deliver out of
your hand?
8 Your hands fashioned and made me,
and now you have destroyed me
altogether.
9 Remember that you have made me
like clay;
and will you return me to the
dust?
10 Did you not pour me out like milk
and curdle me like cheese?
11 You clothed me with skin and flesh,
and knit me together with bones
and sinews.
12 You have granted me life and
steadfast love,
and your care has preserved my
spirit.

[1] Compare Septuagint; Hebrew *me* [2] The meaning of the Hebrew word is uncertain [3] Or *Would that there were an*

13 Yet these things you hid in your
heart;
I know that this was your purpose.
14 If I sin, you watch me
and do not acquit me of my
iniquity.
15 If I am guilty, woe to me!
If I am in the right, I cannot lift up
my head,
for I am filled with disgrace
and look on my affliction.
16 And were my head lifted up,[1] you
would hunt me like a lion
and again work wonders against
me.
17 You renew your witnesses against
me
and increase your vexation
toward me;
you bring fresh troops against me.

18 "Why did you bring me out from the
womb?
Would that I had died before any
eye had seen me
19 and were as though I had not been,
carried from the womb to the
grave.
20 Are not my days few?
Then cease, and leave me alone,
that I may find a little cheer
21 before I go—and I shall not return—
to the land of darkness and deep
shadow,
22 the land of gloom like thick darkness,
like deep shadow without any
order,
where light is as thick darkness."

Zophar Speaks: You Deserve Worse

11 Then Zophar the Naamathite answered and said:

2 "Should a multitude of words go
unanswered,
and a man full of talk be judged
right?
3 Should your babble silence men,
and when you mock, shall no one
shame you?
4 For you say, 'My doctrine is pure,
and I am clean in God's[2] eyes.'
5 But oh, that God would speak
and open his lips to you,
6 and that he would tell you the
secrets of wisdom!
For he is manifold in
understanding.[3]
Know then that God exacts of you
less than your guilt deserves.

7 "Can you find out the deep things of
God?
Can you find out the limit of the
Almighty?
8 It is higher than heaven[4]—what can
you do?
Deeper than Sheol—what can you
know?
9 Its measure is longer than the earth
and broader than the sea.
10 If he passes through and imprisons
and summons the court, who can
turn him back?
11 For he knows worthless men;
when he sees iniquity, will he not
consider it?
12 But a stupid man will get
understanding
when a wild donkey's colt is born
a man!

13 "If you prepare your heart,
you will stretch out your hands
toward him.
14 If iniquity is in your hand, put it far
away,
and let not injustice dwell in your
tents.
15 Surely then you will lift up your face
without blemish;
you will be secure and will not
fear.

[1] Hebrew lacks *my head* [2] Hebrew *your* [3] The meaning of the Hebrew is uncertain [4] Hebrew *The heights of heaven*

16 You will forget your misery;
you will remember it as waters
that have passed away.
17 And your life will be brighter than
the noonday;
its darkness will be like the
morning.
18 And you will feel secure, because
there is hope;
you will look around and take
your rest in security.
19 You will lie down, and none will
make you afraid;
many will court your favor.
20 But the eyes of the wicked will fail;
all way of escape will be lost to
them,
and their hope is to breathe their
last."

Job Replies: The LORD Has Done This

12 Then Job answered and said:

2 "No doubt you are the people,
and wisdom will die with you.
3 But I have understanding as well as
you;
I am not inferior to you.
Who does not know such things
as these?
4 I am a laughingstock to my friends;
I, who called to God and he
answered me,
a just and blameless man, am a
laughingstock.
5 In the thought of one who is at
ease there is contempt for
misfortune;
it is ready for those whose feet slip.
6 The tents of robbers are at peace,
and those who provoke God are
secure,
who bring their god in their hand.[1]

7 "But ask the beasts, and they will
teach you;
the birds of the heavens, and they
will tell you;
8 or the bushes of the earth,[2] and they
will teach you;
and the fish of the sea will declare
to you.
9 Who among all these does not know
that the hand of the LORD has
done this?
10 In his hand is the life of every living
thing
and the breath of all mankind.
11 Does not the ear test words
as the palate tastes food?
12 Wisdom is with the aged,
and understanding in length of
days.

13 "With God[3] are wisdom and might;
he has counsel and
understanding.
14 If he tears down, none can rebuild;
if he shuts a man in, none can
open.
15 If he withholds the waters, they dry
up;
if he sends them out, they
overwhelm the land.
16 With him are strength and sound
wisdom;
the deceived and the deceiver are
his.
17 He leads counselors away stripped,
and judges he makes fools.
18 He looses the bonds of kings
and binds a waistcloth on their
hips.
19 He leads priests away stripped
and overthrows the mighty.
20 He deprives of speech those who
are trusted
and takes away the discernment
of the elders.
21 He pours contempt on princes
and loosens the belt of the strong.
22 He uncovers the deeps out of
darkness
and brings deep darkness to light.

[1] The meaning of the Hebrew is uncertain [2] Or *speak to the earth* [3] Hebrew *him*

23 He makes nations great, and he
destroys them;
he enlarges nations, and leads
them away.
24 He takes away understanding from
the chiefs of the people of the
earth
and makes them wander in a
pathless waste.
25 They grope in the dark without
light,
and he makes them stagger like a
drunken man.

Job Continues: Still I Will Hope in God

13 "Behold, my eye has seen all this,
my ear has heard and
understood it.
2 What you know, I also know;
I am not inferior to you.
3 But I would speak to the Almighty,
and I desire to argue my case with
God.
4 As for you, you whitewash with lies;
worthless physicians are you all.
5 Oh that you would keep silent,
and it would be your wisdom!
6 Hear now my argument
and listen to the pleadings of my
lips.
7 Will you speak falsely for God
and speak deceitfully for him?
8 Will you show partiality toward him?
Will you plead the case for God?
9 Will it be well with you when he
searches you out?
Or can you deceive him, as one
deceives a man?
10 He will surely rebuke you
if in secret you show partiality.
11 Will not his majesty terrify you,
and the dread of him fall upon
you?
12 Your maxims are proverbs of ashes;
your defenses are defenses of clay.
13 "Let me have silence, and I will speak,
and let come on me what may.
14 Why should I take my flesh in my
teeth
and put my life in my hand?
15 Though he slay me, I will hope in
him;[1]
yet I will argue my ways to his
face.
16 This will be my salvation,
that the godless shall not come
before him.
17 Keep listening to my words,
and let my declaration be in your
ears.
18 Behold, I have prepared my case;
I know that I shall be in the right.
19 Who is there who will contend with
me?
For then I would be silent and die.
20 Only grant me two things,
then I will not hide myself from
your face:
21 withdraw your hand far from me,
and let not dread of you terrify
me.
22 Then call, and I will answer;
or let me speak, and you reply to
me.
23 How many are my iniquities and
my sins?
Make me know my transgression
and my sin.
24 Why do you hide your face
and count me as your enemy?
25 Will you frighten a driven leaf
and pursue dry chaff?
26 For you write bitter things against
me
and make me inherit the
iniquities of my youth.
27 You put my feet in the stocks
and watch all my paths;
you set a limit for[2] the soles of my
feet.
28 Man[3] wastes away like a rotten
thing,
like a garment that is moth-eaten.

[1] *Or Behold, he will slay me; I have no hope* [2] *Or you marked* [3] Hebrew *He*

Job Continues: Death Comes Soon to All

14 "Man who is born of a woman
is few of days and full of trouble.
2 He comes out like a flower and withers;
he flees like a shadow and continues not.
3 And do you open your eyes on such a one
and bring me into judgment with you?
4 Who can bring a clean thing out of an unclean?
There is not one.
5 Since his days are determined,
and the number of his months is with you,
and you have appointed his limits that he cannot pass,
6 look away from him and leave him alone,[1]
that he may enjoy, like a hired hand, his day.

7 "For there is hope for a tree,
if it be cut down, that it will sprout again,
and that its shoots will not cease.
8 Though its root grow old in the earth,
and its stump die in the soil,
9 yet at the scent of water it will bud
and put out branches like a young plant.
10 But a man dies and is laid low;
man breathes his last, and where is he?
11 As waters fail from a lake
and a river wastes away and dries up,
12 so a man lies down and rises not again;
till the heavens are no more he will not awake
or be roused out of his sleep.
13 Oh that you would hide me in Sheol,
that you would conceal me until your wrath be past,
that you would appoint me a set time, and remember me!
14 If a man dies, shall he live again?
All the days of my service I would wait,
till my renewal[2] should come.
15 You would call, and I would answer you;
you would long for the work of your hands.
16 For then you would number my steps;
you would not keep watch over my sin;
17 my transgression would be sealed up in a bag,
and you would cover over my iniquity.

18 "But the mountain falls and crumbles away,
and the rock is removed from its place;
19 the waters wear away the stones;
the torrents wash away the soil of the earth;
so you destroy the hope of man.
20 You prevail forever against him, and he passes;
you change his countenance, and send him away.
21 His sons come to honor, and he does not know it;
they are brought low, and he perceives it not.
22 He feels only the pain of his own body,
and he mourns only for himself."

Eliphaz Accuses: Job Does Not Fear God

15 Then Eliphaz the Temanite answered and said:
2 "Should a wise man answer with windy knowledge,
and fill his belly with the east wind?

[1] Probable reading; Hebrew *look away from him, that he may cease* [2] Or *relief*

3 Should he argue in unprofitable talk,
or in words with which he can do no good?
4 But you are doing away with the fear of God[1]
and hindering meditation before God.
5 For your iniquity teaches your mouth,
and you choose the tongue of the crafty.
6 Your own mouth condemns you, and not I;
your own lips testify against you.

7 "Are you the first man who was born?
Or were you brought forth before the hills?
8 Have you listened in the council of God?
And do you limit wisdom to yourself?
9 What do you know that we do not know?
What do you understand that is not clear to us?
10 Both the gray-haired and the aged are among us,
older than your father.
11 Are the comforts of God too small for you,
or the word that deals gently with you?
12 Why does your heart carry you away,
and why do your eyes flash,
13 that you turn your spirit against God
and bring such words out of your mouth?
14 What is man, that he can be pure?
Or he who is born of a woman, that he can be righteous?
15 Behold, God[2] puts no trust in his holy ones,
and the heavens are not pure in his sight;
16 how much less one who is abominable and corrupt,
a man who drinks injustice like water!

17 "I will show you; hear me,
and what I have seen I will declare
18 (what wise men have told,
without hiding it from their fathers,
19 to whom alone the land was given,
and no stranger passed among them).
20 The wicked man writhes in pain all his days,
through all the years that are laid up for the ruthless.
21 Dreadful sounds are in his ears;
in prosperity the destroyer will come upon him.
22 He does not believe that he will return out of darkness,
and he is marked for the sword.
23 He wanders abroad for bread, saying, 'Where is it?'
He knows that a day of darkness is ready at his hand;
24 distress and anguish terrify him;
they prevail against him, like a king ready for battle.
25 Because he has stretched out his hand against God
and defies the Almighty,
26 running stubbornly against him
with a thickly bossed shield;
27 because he has covered his face with his fat
and gathered fat upon his waist
28 and has lived in desolate cities,
in houses that none should inhabit,
which were ready to become heaps of ruins;
29 he will not be rich, and his wealth will not endure,
nor will his possessions spread over the earth;[3]

[1] Hebrew lacks *of God* [2] Hebrew *he* [3] Or *nor will his produce bend down to the earth*

30 he will not depart from darkness;
the flame will dry up his shoots,
and by the breath of his mouth he will depart.
31 Let him not trust in emptiness, deceiving himself,
for emptiness will be his payment.
32 It will be paid in full before his time,
and his branch will not be green.
33 He will shake off his unripe grape like the vine,
and cast off his blossom like the olive tree.
34 For the company of the godless is barren,
and fire consumes the tents of bribery.
35 They conceive trouble and give birth to evil,
and their womb prepares deceit."

Job Replies: Miserable Comforters Are You

16 Then Job answered and said:
2 "I have heard many such things;
miserable comforters are you all.
3 Shall windy words have an end?
Or what provokes you that you answer?
4 I also could speak as you do,
if you were in my place;
I could join words together against you
and shake my head at you.
5 I could strengthen you with my mouth,
and the solace of my lips would assuage your pain.

6 "If I speak, my pain is not assuaged,
and if I forbear, how much of it leaves me?
7 Surely now God has worn me out;
he has[1] made desolate all my company.
8 And he has shriveled me up,
which is a witness against me,
and my leanness has risen up against me;
it testifies to my face.
9 He has torn me in his wrath and hated me;
he has gnashed his teeth at me;
my adversary sharpens his eyes against me.
10 Men have gaped at me with their mouth;
they have struck me insolently on the cheek;
they mass themselves together against me.
11 God gives me up to the ungodly
and casts me into the hands of the wicked.
12 I was at ease, and he broke me apart;
he seized me by the neck and dashed me to pieces;
he set me up as his target;
13 his archers surround me.
He slashes open my kidneys and does not spare;
he pours out my gall on the ground.
14 He breaks me with breach upon breach;
he runs upon me like a warrior.
15 I have sewed sackcloth upon my skin
and have laid my strength in the dust.
16 My face is red with weeping,
and on my eyelids is deep darkness,
17 although there is no violence in my hands,
and my prayer is pure.

18 "O earth, cover not my blood,
and let my cry find no resting place.
19 Even now, behold, my witness is in heaven,
and he who testifies for me is on high.

[1] Hebrew *you have*; also verse 8

20 My friends scorn me;
my eye pours out tears to God,
21 that he would argue the case of a man with God,
as[1] a son of man does with his neighbor.
22 For when a few years have come
I shall go the way from which I shall not return.

Job Continues: Where Then Is My Hope?

17 "My spirit is broken; my days are extinct;
the graveyard is ready for me.
2 Surely there are mockers about me,
and my eye dwells on their provocation.

3 "Lay down a pledge for me with yourself;
who is there who will put up security for me?
4 Since you have closed their hearts to understanding,
therefore you will not let them triumph.
5 He who informs against his friends to get a share of their property—
the eyes of his children will fail.

6 "He has made me a byword of the peoples,
and I am one before whom men spit.
7 My eye has grown dim from vexation,
and all my members are like a shadow.
8 The upright are appalled at this,
and the innocent stirs himself up against the godless.
9 Yet the righteous holds to his way,
and he who has clean hands grows stronger and stronger.
10 But you, come on again, all of you,
and I shall not find a wise man among you.
11 My days are past; my plans are broken off,
the desires of my heart.
12 They make night into day:
'The light,' they say, 'is near to the darkness.'[2]
13 If I hope for Sheol as my house,
if I make my bed in darkness,
14 if I say to the pit, 'You are my father,'
and to the worm, 'My mother,' or 'My sister,'
15 where then is my hope?
Who will see my hope?
16 Will it go down to the bars of Sheol?
Shall we descend together into the dust?"

Bildad Speaks: God Punishes the Wicked

18 Then Bildad the Shuhite answered and said:

2 "How long will you hunt for words?
Consider, and then we will speak.
3 Why are we counted as cattle?
Why are we stupid in your sight?
4 You who tear yourself in your anger,
shall the earth be forsaken for you,
or the rock be removed out of its place?

5 "Indeed, the light of the wicked is put out,
and the flame of his fire does not shine.
6 The light is dark in his tent,
and his lamp above him is put out.
7 His strong steps are shortened,
and his own schemes throw him down.
8 For he is cast into a net by his own feet,
and he walks on its mesh.
9 A trap seizes him by the heel;
a snare lays hold of him.
10 A rope is hidden for him in the ground,
a trap for him in the path.

[1] Hebrew *and* [2] The meaning of the Hebrew is uncertain

11 Terrors frighten him on every side,
and chase him at his heels.
12 His strength is famished,
and calamity is ready for his stumbling.
13 It consumes the parts of his skin;
the firstborn of death consumes his limbs.
14 He is torn from the tent in which he trusted
and is brought to the king of terrors.
15 In his tent dwells that which is none of his;
sulfur is scattered over his habitation.
16 His roots dry up beneath,
and his branches wither above.
17 His memory perishes from the earth,
and he has no name in the street.
18 He is thrust from light into darkness,
and driven out of the world.
19 He has no posterity or progeny among his people,
and no survivor where he used to live.
20 They of the west are appalled at his day,
and horror seizes them of the east.
21 Surely such are the dwellings of the unrighteous,
such is the place of him who knows not God."

Job Replies: My Redeemer Lives

19 Then Job answered and said:
2 "How long will you torment me
and break me in pieces with words?
3 These ten times you have cast reproach upon me;
are you not ashamed to wrong me?
4 And even if it be true that I have erred,
my error remains with myself.
5 If indeed you magnify yourselves against me
and make my disgrace an argument against me,
6 know then that God has put me in the wrong
and closed his net about me.
7 Behold, I cry out, 'Violence!' but I am not answered;
I call for help, but there is no justice.
8 He has walled up my way, so that I cannot pass,
and he has set darkness upon my paths.
9 He has stripped from me my glory
and taken the crown from my head.
10 He breaks me down on every side, and I am gone,
and my hope has he pulled up like a tree.
11 He has kindled his wrath against me
and counts me as his adversary.
12 His troops come on together;
they have cast up their siege ramp[1] against me
and encamp around my tent.
13 "He has put my brothers far from me,
and those who knew me are wholly estranged from me.
14 My relatives have failed me,
my close friends have forgotten me.
15 The guests in my house and my maidservants count me as a stranger;
I have become a foreigner in their eyes.
16 I call to my servant, but he gives me no answer;
I must plead with him with my mouth for mercy.

[1] Hebrew *their way*

17 My breath is strange to my wife,
and I am a stench to the children
of my own mother.
18 Even young children despise me;
when I rise they talk against me.
19 All my intimate friends abhor me,
and those whom I loved have
turned against me.
20 My bones stick to my skin and to
my flesh,
and I have escaped by the skin of
my teeth.
21 Have mercy on me, have mercy on
me, O you my friends,
for the hand of God has touched
me!
22 Why do you, like God, pursue me?
Why are you not satisfied with
my flesh?

23 "Oh that my words were written!
Oh that they were inscribed in a
book!
24 Oh that with an iron pen and lead
they were engraved in the rock
forever!
25 For I know that my Redeemer lives,
and at the last he will stand upon
the earth.[1]
26 And after my skin has been thus
destroyed,
yet in[2] my flesh I shall see God,
27 whom I shall see for myself,
and my eyes shall behold, and not
another.
My heart faints within me!
28 If you say, 'How we will pursue him!'
and, 'The root of the matter is
found in him,'
29 be afraid of the sword,
for wrath brings the punishment
of the sword,
that you may know there is a
judgment."

Zophar Speaks: The Wicked Will Suffer

20 Then Zophar the Naamathite answered and said:

2 "Therefore my thoughts answer me,
because of my haste within me.
3 I hear censure that insults me,
and out of my understanding a
spirit answers me.
4 Do you not know this from of old,
since man was placed on earth,
5 that the exulting of the wicked is
short,
and the joy of the godless but for a
moment?
6 Though his height mount up to the
heavens,
and his head reach to the clouds,
7 he will perish forever like his own
dung;
those who have seen him will say,
'Where is he?'
8 He will fly away like a dream and
not be found;
he will be chased away like a
vision of the night.
9 The eye that saw him will see him
no more,
nor will his place any more
behold him.
10 His children will seek the favor of
the poor,
and his hands will give back his
wealth.
11 His bones are full of his youthful
vigor,
but it will lie down with him in
the dust.

12 "Though evil is sweet in his mouth,
though he hides it under his
tongue,
13 though he is loath to let it go
and holds it in his mouth,
14 yet his food is turned in his
stomach;
it is the venom of cobras within
him.
15 He swallows down riches and
vomits them up again;
God casts them out of his belly.

[1] Hebrew *dust* [2] Or *without*

16 He will suck the poison of cobras;
the tongue of a viper will kill him.
17 He will not look upon the rivers,
the streams flowing with honey and curds.
18 He will give back the fruit of his toil
and will not swallow it down;
from the profit of his trading
he will get no enjoyment.
19 For he has crushed and abandoned the poor;
he has seized a house that he did not build.

20 "Because he knew no contentment in his belly,
he will not let anything in which he delights escape him.
21 There was nothing left after he had eaten;
therefore his prosperity will not endure.
22 In the fullness of his sufficiency he will be in distress;
the hand of everyone in misery will come against him.
23 To fill his belly to the full,
God[1] will send his burning anger against him
and rain it upon him into his body.
24 He will flee from an iron weapon;
a bronze arrow will strike him through.
25 It is drawn forth and comes out of his body;
the glittering point comes out of his gallbladder;
terrors come upon him.
26 Utter darkness is laid up for his treasures;
a fire not fanned will devour him;
what is left in his tent will be consumed.
27 The heavens will reveal his iniquity,
and the earth will rise up against him.
28 The possessions of his house will be carried away,
dragged off in the day of God's[2] wrath.
29 This is the wicked man's portion from God,
the heritage decreed for him by God."

Job Replies: The Wicked Do Prosper

21 Then Job answered and said:

2 "Keep listening to my words,
and let this be your comfort.
3 Bear with me, and I will speak,
and after I have spoken, mock on.
4 As for me, is my complaint against man?
Why should I not be impatient?
5 Look at me and be appalled,
and lay your hand over your mouth.
6 When I remember, I am dismayed,
and shuddering seizes my flesh.
7 Why do the wicked live,
reach old age, and grow mighty in power?
8 Their offspring are established in their presence,
and their descendants before their eyes.
9 Their houses are safe from fear,
and no rod of God is upon them.
10 Their bull breeds without fail;
their cow calves and does not miscarry.
11 They send out their little boys like a flock,
and their children dance.
12 They sing to the tambourine and the lyre
and rejoice to the sound of the pipe.
13 They spend their days in prosperity,
and in peace they go down to Sheol.

[1] Hebrew *he* [2] Hebrew *his*

14 They say to God, 'Depart from us!
We do not desire the knowledge
of your ways.
15 What is the Almighty, that we
should serve him?
And what profit do we get if we
pray to him?'
16 Behold, is not their prosperity in
their hand?
The counsel of the wicked is far
from me.

17 "How often is it that the lamp of the
wicked is put out?
That their calamity comes upon
them?
That God[1] distributes pains in his
anger?
18 That they are like straw before the
wind,
and like chaff that the storm
carries away?
19 You say, 'God stores up their
iniquity for their children.'
Let him pay it out to them, that
they may know it.
20 Let their own eyes see their
destruction,
and let them drink of the wrath of
the Almighty.
21 For what do they care for their
houses after them,
when the number of their
months is cut off?
22 Will any teach God knowledge,
seeing that he judges those who
are on high?
23 One dies in his full vigor,
being wholly at ease and secure,
24 his pails[2] full of milk
and the marrow of his bones moist.
25 Another dies in bitterness of soul,
never having tasted of prosperity.
26 They lie down alike in the dust,
and the worms cover them.

27 "Behold, I know your thoughts
and your schemes to wrong me.
28 For you say, 'Where is the house of
the prince?
Where is the tent in which the
wicked lived?'
29 Have you not asked those who
travel the roads,
and do you not accept their
testimony
30 that the evil man is spared in the
day of calamity,
that he is rescued in the day of
wrath?
31 Who declares his way to his face,
and who repays him for what he
has done?
32 When he is carried to the grave,
watch is kept over his tomb.
33 The clods of the valley are sweet to
him;
all mankind follows after him,
and those who go before him are
innumerable.
34 How then will you comfort me with
empty nothings?
There is nothing left of your
answers but falsehood."

Eliphaz Speaks: Job's Wickedness Is Great

22 Then Eliphaz the Temanite answered and said:

2 "Can a man be profitable to God?
Surely he who is wise is profitable
to himself.
3 Is it any pleasure to the Almighty if
you are in the right,
or is it gain to him if you make
your ways blameless?
4 Is it for your fear of him that he
reproves you
and enters into judgment with
you?
5 Is not your evil abundant?
There is no end to your iniquities.
6 For you have exacted pledges of
your brothers for nothing
and stripped the naked of their
clothing.

[1] Hebrew *he* [2] The meaning of the Hebrew word is uncertain

7 You have given no water to the
weary to drink,
and you have withheld bread
from the hungry.
8 The man with power possessed the
land,
and the favored man lived in it.
9 You have sent widows away empty,
and the arms of the fatherless
were crushed.
10 Therefore snares are all around you,
and sudden terror overwhelms
you,
11 or darkness, so that you cannot see,
and a flood of water covers you.

12 "Is not God high in the heavens?
See the highest stars, how lofty
they are!
13 But you say, 'What does God know?
Can he judge through the deep
darkness?
14 Thick clouds veil him, so that he
does not see,
and he walks on the vault of
heaven.'
15 Will you keep to the old way
that wicked men have trod?
16 They were snatched away before
their time;
their foundation was washed away.
17 They said to God, 'Depart from us,'
and 'What can the Almighty do to
us?'[1]
18 Yet he filled their houses with good
things—
but the counsel of the wicked is
far from me.
19 The righteous see it and are glad;
the innocent one mocks at them,
20 saying, 'Surely our adversaries are
cut off,
and what they left the fire has
consumed.'

21 "Agree with God, and be at peace;
thereby good will come to you.
22 Receive instruction from his
mouth,
and lay up his words in your
heart.
23 If you return to the Almighty you
will be built up;
if you remove injustice far from
your tents,
24 if you lay gold in the dust,
and gold of Ophir among the
stones of the torrent-bed,
25 then the Almighty will be your gold
and your precious silver.
26 For then you will delight yourself in
the Almighty
and lift up your face to God.
27 You will make your prayer to him,
and he will hear you,
and you will pay your vows.
28 You will decide on a matter, and it
will be established for you,
and light will shine on your ways.
29 For when they are humbled you say,
'It is because of pride';[2]
but he saves the lowly.
30 He delivers even the one who is not
innocent,[3]
who will be delivered through the
cleanness of your hands."

Job Replies: Where Is God?

23 Then Job answered and said:

2 "Today also my complaint is bitter;[4]
my hand is heavy on account of
my groaning.
3 Oh, that I knew where I might find
him,
that I might come even to his seat!
4 I would lay my case before him
and fill my mouth with
arguments.
5 I would know what he would
answer me
and understand what he would
say to me.

[1] Hebrew *them* [2] Or *you say, 'It is exaltation'* [3] Septuagint, Syriac, Vulgate; Hebrew *him that is not innocent* [4] Or *defiant*

6 Would he contend with me in the
greatness of his power?
No; he would pay attention to
me.
7 There an upright man could argue
with him,
and I would be acquitted forever
by my judge.
8 "Behold, I go forward, but he is not
there,
and backward, but I do not
perceive him;
9 on the left hand when he is
working, I do not behold
him;
he turns to the right hand, but I
do not see him.
10 But he knows the way that I take;
when he has tried me, I shall
come out as gold.
11 My foot has held fast to his steps;
I have kept his way and have not
turned aside.
12 I have not departed from the
commandment of his lips;
I have treasured the words of his
mouth more than my portion
of food.
13 But he is unchangeable,[1] and who
can turn him back?
What he desires, that he does.
14 For he will complete what he
appoints for me,
and many such things are in his
mind.
15 Therefore I am terrified at his
presence;
when I consider, I am in dread of
him.
16 God has made my heart faint;
the Almighty has terrified me;
17 yet I am not silenced because of the
darkness,
nor because thick darkness covers
my face.

24 "Why are not times of judgment
kept by the Almighty,
and why do those who know him
never see his days?
2 Some move landmarks;
they seize flocks and pasture them.
3 They drive away the donkey of the
fatherless;
they take the widow's ox for a
pledge.
4 They thrust the poor off the road;
the poor of the earth all hide
themselves.
5 Behold, like wild donkeys in the
desert
the poor[2] go out to their toil,
seeking game;
the wasteland yields food for their
children.
6 They gather their[3] fodder in the
field,
and they glean the vineyard of the
wicked man.
7 They lie all night naked, without
clothing,
and have no covering in the cold.
8 They are wet with the rain of the
mountains
and cling to the rock for lack of
shelter.
9 (There are those who snatch the
fatherless child from the
breast,
and they take a pledge against the
poor.)
10 They go about naked, without
clothing;
hungry, they carry the sheaves;
11 among the olive rows of the wicked[4]
they make oil;
they tread the winepresses, but
suffer thirst.
12 From out of the city the dying groan,
and the soul of the wounded cries
for help;
yet God charges no one with
wrong.

[1] Or *one* [2] Hebrew *they* [3] Hebrew *his* [4] Hebrew *their olive rows*

13 "There are those who rebel against
the light,
who are not acquainted with its
ways,
and do not stay in its paths.
14 The murderer rises before it is light,
that he may kill the poor and
needy,
and in the night he is like a thief.
15 The eye of the adulterer also waits
for the twilight,
saying, 'No eye will see me';
and he veils his face.
16 In the dark they dig through houses;
by day they shut themselves up;
they do not know the light.
17 For deep darkness is morning to all
of them;
for they are friends with the
terrors of deep darkness.

18 "You say, 'Swift are they on the face
of the waters;
their portion is cursed in the land;
no treader turns toward their
vineyards.
19 Drought and heat snatch away the
snow waters;
so does Sheol those who have
sinned.
20 The womb forgets them;
the worm finds them sweet;
they are no longer remembered,
so wickedness is broken like a
tree.'

21 "They wrong the barren, childless
woman,
and do no good to the widow.
22 Yet God[1] prolongs the life of the
mighty by his power;
they rise up when they despair of
life.
23 He gives them security, and they are
supported,
and his eyes are upon their ways.
24 They are exalted a little while, and
then are gone;
they are brought low and
gathered up like all others;
they are cut off like the heads of
grain.
25 If it is not so, who will prove me a
liar
and show that there is nothing in
what I say?"

Bildad Speaks: Man Cannot Be Righteous

25 Then Bildad the Shuhite answered
and said:

2 "Dominion and fear are with God;[2]
he makes peace in his high
heaven.
3 Is there any number to his armies?
Upon whom does his light not
arise?
4 How then can man be in the right
before God?
How can he who is born of
woman be pure?
5 Behold, even the moon is not bright,
and the stars are not pure in his
eyes;
6 how much less man, who is a
maggot,
and the son of man, who is a
worm!"

Job Replies: God's Majesty Is Unsearchable

26 Then Job answered and said:

2 "How you have helped him who has
no power!
How you have saved the arm that
has no strength!
3 How you have counseled him who
has no wisdom,
and plentifully declared sound
knowledge!
4 With whose help have you uttered
words,
and whose breath has come out
from you?

[1] Hebrew *he* [2] Hebrew *him*

5 The dead tremble
under the waters and their inhabitants.
6 Sheol is naked before God,[1]
and Abaddon has no covering.
7 He stretches out the north over the void
and hangs the earth on nothing.
8 He binds up the waters in his thick clouds,
and the cloud is not split open under them.
9 He covers the face of the full moon[2]
and spreads over it his cloud.
10 He has inscribed a circle on the face of the waters
at the boundary between light and darkness.
11 The pillars of heaven tremble
and are astounded at his rebuke.
12 By his power he stilled the sea;
by his understanding he shattered Rahab.
13 By his wind the heavens were made fair;
his hand pierced the fleeing serpent.
14 Behold, these are but the outskirts of his ways,
and how small a whisper do we hear of him!
But the thunder of his power who can understand?"

Job Continues: I Will Maintain My Integrity

27 And Job again took up his discourse, and said:

2 "As God lives, who has taken away my right,
and the Almighty, who has made my soul bitter,
3 as long as my breath is in me,
and the spirit of God is in my nostrils,
4 my lips will not speak falsehood,
and my tongue will not utter deceit.
5 Far be it from me to say that you are right;
till I die I will not put away my integrity from me.
6 I hold fast my righteousness and will not let it go;
my heart does not reproach me for any of my days.

7 "Let my enemy be as the wicked,
and let him who rises up against me be as the unrighteous.
8 For what is the hope of the godless when God cuts him off,
when God takes away his life?
9 Will God hear his cry
when distress comes upon him?
10 Will he take delight in the Almighty?
Will he call upon God at all times?
11 I will teach you concerning the hand of God;
what is with the Almighty I will not conceal.
12 Behold, all of you have seen it yourselves;
why then have you become altogether vain?

13 "This is the portion of a wicked man with God,
and the heritage that oppressors receive from the Almighty:
14 If his children are multiplied, it is for the sword,
and his descendants have not enough bread.
15 Those who survive him the pestilence buries,
and his widows do not weep.
16 Though he heap up silver like dust,
and pile up clothing like clay,
17 he may pile it up, but the righteous will wear it,
and the innocent will divide the silver.

[1] Hebrew *him* [2] Or *his throne*

18 He builds his house like a moth's,
like a booth that a watchman makes.
19 He goes to bed rich, but will do so no more;
he opens his eyes, and his wealth is gone.
20 Terrors overtake him like a flood;
in the night a whirlwind carries him off.
21 The east wind lifts him up and he is gone;
it sweeps him out of his place.
22 It[1] hurls at him without pity;
he flees from its[2] power in headlong flight.
23 It claps its hands at him
and hisses at him from its place.

Job Continues: Where Is Wisdom?

28 "Surely there is a mine for silver,
and a place for gold that they refine.
2 Iron is taken out of the earth,
and copper is smelted from the ore.
3 Man puts an end to darkness
and searches out to the farthest limit
the ore in gloom and deep darkness.
4 He opens shafts in a valley away from where anyone lives;
they are forgotten by travelers;
they hang in the air, far away from mankind; they swing to and fro.
5 As for the earth, out of it comes bread,
but underneath it is turned up as by fire.
6 Its stones are the place of sapphires,[3]
and it has dust of gold.

7 "That path no bird of prey knows,
and the falcon's eye has not seen it.
8 The proud beasts have not trodden it;
the lion has not passed over it.
9 "Man puts his hand to the flinty rock
and overturns mountains by the roots.
10 He cuts out channels in the rocks,
and his eye sees every precious thing.
11 He dams up the streams so that they do not trickle,
and the thing that is hidden he brings out to light.

12 "But where shall wisdom be found?
And where is the place of understanding?
13 Man does not know its worth,
and it is not found in the land of the living.
14 The deep says, 'It is not in me,'
and the sea says, 'It is not with me.'
15 It cannot be bought for gold,
and silver cannot be weighed as its price.
16 It cannot be valued in the gold of Ophir,
in precious onyx or sapphire.
17 Gold and glass cannot equal it,
nor can it be exchanged for jewels of fine gold.
18 No mention shall be made of coral or of crystal;
the price of wisdom is above pearls.
19 The topaz of Ethiopia cannot equal it,
nor can it be valued in pure gold.

20 "From where, then, does wisdom come?
And where is the place of understanding?
21 It is hidden from the eyes of all living
and concealed from the birds of the air.
22 Abaddon and Death say,
'We have heard a rumor of it with our ears.'

[1] Or *He* (that is, God); also verse 23 [2] Or *his*; also verse 23 [3] Or *lapis lazuli*; also verse 16

23 "God understands the way to it,
and he knows its place.
24 For he looks to the ends of the earth
and sees everything under the heavens.
25 When he gave to the wind its weight
and apportioned the waters by measure,
26 when he made a decree for the rain
and a way for the lightning of the thunder,
27 then he saw it and declared it;
he established it, and searched it out.
28 And he said to man,
'Behold, the fear of the Lord, that is wisdom,
and to turn away from evil is understanding.'"

Job's Summary Defense

29 And Job again took up his discourse, and said:

2 "Oh, that I were as in the months of old,
as in the days when God watched over me,
3 when his lamp shone upon my head,
and by his light I walked through darkness,
4 as I was in my prime,[1]
when the friendship of God was upon my tent,
5 when the Almighty was yet with me,
when my children were all around me,
6 when my steps were washed with butter,
and the rock poured out for me streams of oil!
7 When I went out to the gate of the city,
when I prepared my seat in the square,
8 the young men saw me and withdrew,
and the aged rose and stood;
9 the princes refrained from talking
and laid their hand on their mouth;
10 the voice of the nobles was hushed,
and their tongue stuck to the roof of their mouth.
11 When the ear heard, it called me blessed,
and when the eye saw, it approved,
12 because I delivered the poor who cried for help,
and the fatherless who had none to help him.
13 The blessing of him who was about to perish came upon me,
and I caused the widow's heart to sing for joy.
14 I put on righteousness, and it clothed me;
my justice was like a robe and a turban.
15 I was eyes to the blind
and feet to the lame.
16 I was a father to the needy,
and I searched out the cause of him whom I did not know.
17 I broke the fangs of the unrighteous
and made him drop his prey from his teeth.
18 Then I thought, 'I shall die in my nest,
and I shall multiply my days as the sand,
19 my roots spread out to the waters,
with the dew all night on my branches,
20 my glory fresh with me,
and my bow ever new in my hand.'

21 "Men listened to me and waited
and kept silence for my counsel.
22 After I spoke they did not speak again,
and my word dropped upon them.

[1] Hebrew *my autumn days*

23 They waited for me as for the rain,
and they opened their mouths as for the spring rain.
24 I smiled on them when they had no confidence,
and the light of my face they did not cast down.
25 I chose their way and sat as chief,
and I lived like a king among his troops,
like one who comforts mourners.

30 "But now they laugh at me,
men who are younger than I,
whose fathers I would have disdained
to set with the dogs of my flock.
2 What could I gain from the strength of their hands,
men whose vigor is gone?
3 Through want and hard hunger
they gnaw the dry ground by night in waste and desolation;
4 they pick saltwort and the leaves of bushes,
and the roots of the broom tree for their food.[1]
5 They are driven out from human company;
they shout after them as after a thief.
6 In the gullies of the torrents they must dwell,
in holes of the earth and of the rocks.
7 Among the bushes they bray;
under the nettles they huddle together.
8 A senseless, a nameless brood,
they have been whipped out of the land.

9 "And now I have become their song;
I am a byword to them.
10 They abhor me; they keep aloof from me;
they do not hesitate to spit at the sight of me.
11 Because God has loosed my cord and humbled me,
they have cast off restraint[2] in my presence.
12 On my right hand the rabble rise;
they push away my feet;
they cast up against me their ways of destruction.
13 They break up my path;
they promote my calamity;
they need no one to help them.
14 As through a wide breach they come;
amid the crash they roll on.
15 Terrors are turned upon me;
my honor is pursued as by the wind,
and my prosperity has passed away like a cloud.

16 "And now my soul is poured out within me;
days of affliction have taken hold of me.
17 The night racks my bones,
and the pain that gnaws me takes no rest.
18 With great force my garment is disfigured;
it binds me about like the collar of my tunic.
19 God[3] has cast me into the mire,
and I have become like dust and ashes.
20 I cry to you for help and you do not answer me;
I stand, and you only look at me.
21 You have turned cruel to me;
with the might of your hand you persecute me.
22 You lift me up on the wind; you make me ride on it,
and you toss me about in the roar of the storm.
23 For I know that you will bring me to death
and to the house appointed for all living.

[1] Or *warmth* [2] Hebrew *the bridle* [3] Hebrew *He*

24 "Yet does not one in a heap of ruins
stretch out his hand,
and in his disaster cry for help?[1]
25 Did not I weep for him whose day
was hard?
Was not my soul grieved for the
needy?
26 But when I hoped for good, evil
came,
and when I waited for light,
darkness came.
27 My inward parts are in turmoil and
never still;
days of affliction come to meet
me.
28 I go about darkened, but not by the
sun;
I stand up in the assembly and cry
for help.
29 I am a brother of jackals
and a companion of ostriches.
30 My skin turns black and falls from
me,
and my bones burn with heat.
31 My lyre is turned to mourning,
and my pipe to the voice of those
who weep.

Job's Final Appeal

31 "I have made a covenant with my
eyes;
how then could I gaze at a virgin?
2 What would be my portion from
God above
and my heritage from the
Almighty on high?
3 Is not calamity for the unrighteous,
and disaster for the workers of
iniquity?
4 Does not he see my ways
and number all my steps?
5 "If I have walked with falsehood
and my foot has hastened to
deceit;
6 (Let me be weighed in a just
balance,
and let God know my integrity!)
7 if my step has turned aside from the
way
and my heart has gone after my
eyes,
and if any spot has stuck to my
hands,
8 then let me sow, and another eat,
and let what grows for me[2] be
rooted out.

9 "If my heart has been enticed toward
a woman,
and I have lain in wait at my
neighbor's door,
10 then let my wife grind for another,
and let others bow down on her.
11 For that would be a heinous crime;
that would be an iniquity to be
punished by the judges;
12 for that would be a fire that
consumes as far as Abaddon,
and it would burn to the root all
my increase.

13 "If I have rejected the cause of my
manservant or my maidservant,
when they brought a complaint
against me,
14 what then shall I do when God rises
up?
When he makes inquiry, what
shall I answer him?
15 Did not he who made me in the
womb make him?
And did not one fashion us in the
womb?

16 "If I have withheld anything that the
poor desired,
or have caused the eyes of the
widow to fail,
17 or have eaten my morsel alone,
and the fatherless has not eaten
of it
18 (for from my youth the fatherless[3]
grew up with me as with a
father,
and from my mother's womb I
guided the widow[4]),

[1] The meaning of the Hebrew is uncertain [2] Or *let my descendants* [3] Hebrew *he* [4] Hebrew *her*

19 if I have seen anyone perish for lack
of clothing,
or the needy without covering,
20 if his body has not blessed me,[1]
and if he was not warmed with
the fleece of my sheep,
21 if I have raised my hand against the
fatherless,
because I saw my help in the gate,
22 then let my shoulder blade fall from
my shoulder,
and let my arm be broken from its
socket.
23 For I was in terror of calamity from
God,
and I could not have faced his
majesty.

24 "If I have made gold my trust
or called fine gold my confidence,
25 if I have rejoiced because my wealth
was abundant
or because my hand had found
much,
26 if I have looked at the sun[2] when it
shone,
or the moon moving in splendor,
27 and my heart has been secretly
enticed,
and my mouth has kissed my
hand,
28 this also would be an iniquity to be
punished by the judges,
for I would have been false to God
above.

29 "If I have rejoiced at the ruin of him
who hated me,
or exulted when evil overtook him
30 (I have not let my mouth sin
by asking for his life with a curse),
31 if the men of my tent have not said,
'Who is there that has not been
filled with his meat?'
32 (the sojourner has not lodged in the
street;
I have opened my doors to the
traveler),
33 if I have concealed my
transgressions as others do[3]
by hiding my iniquity in my
bosom,
34 because I stood in great fear of the
multitude,
and the contempt of families
terrified me,
so that I kept silence, and did not
go out of doors—
35 Oh, that I had one to hear me!
(Here is my signature! Let the
Almighty answer me!)
Oh, that I had the indictment
written by my adversary!
36 Surely I would carry it on my
shoulder;
I would bind it on me as a crown;
37 I would give him an account of all
my steps;
like a prince I would approach
him.

38 "If my land has cried out against me
and its furrows have wept
together,
39 if I have eaten its yield without
payment
and made its owners breathe their
last,
40 let thorns grow instead of wheat,
and foul weeds instead of barley."
The words of Job are ended.

Elihu Rebukes Job's Three Friends

32 So these three men ceased to
answer Job, because he was righ-
teous in his own eyes. 2 Then Elihu the
son of Barachel the Buzite, of the family of
Ram, burned with anger. He burned with
anger at Job because he justified himself
rather than God. 3 He burned with anger
also at Job's three friends because they
had found no answer, although they had
declared Job to be in the wrong. 4 Now
Elihu had waited to speak to Job because
they were older than he. 5 And when

[1] Hebrew *if his loins have not blessed me* [2] Hebrew *the light* [3] Or *as Adam did*

Elihu saw that there was no answer in the mouth of these three men, he burned with anger.

6 And Elihu the son of Barachel the Buzite answered and said:

"I am young in years,
and you are aged;
therefore I was timid and afraid
to declare my opinion to you.
7 I said, 'Let days speak,
and many years teach wisdom.'
8 But it is the spirit in man,
the breath of the Almighty, that makes him understand.
9 It is not the old[1] who are wise,
nor the aged who understand what is right.
10 Therefore I say, 'Listen to me;
let me also declare my opinion.'

11 "Behold, I waited for your words,
I listened for your wise sayings,
while you searched out what to say.
12 I gave you my attention,
and, behold, there was none among you who refuted Job
or who answered his words.
13 Beware lest you say, 'We have found wisdom;
God may vanquish him, not a man.'
14 He has not directed his words against me,
and I will not answer him with your speeches.

15 "They are dismayed; they answer no more;
they have not a word to say.
16 And shall I wait, because they do not speak,
because they stand there, and answer no more?
17 I also will answer with my share;
I also will declare my opinion.
18 For I am full of words;
the spirit within me constrains me.
19 Behold, my belly is like wine that has no vent;
like new wineskins ready to burst.
20 I must speak, that I may find relief;
I must open my lips and answer.
21 I will not show partiality to any man
or use flattery toward any person.
22 For I do not know how to flatter,
else my Maker would soon take me away.

Elihu Rebukes Job

33 "But now, hear my speech, O Job,
and listen to all my words.
2 Behold, I open my mouth;
the tongue in my mouth speaks.
3 My words declare the uprightness of my heart,
and what my lips know they speak sincerely.
4 The Spirit of God has made me,
and the breath of the Almighty gives me life.
5 Answer me, if you can;
set your words in order before me; take your stand.
6 Behold, I am toward God as you are;
I too was pinched off from a piece of clay.
7 Behold, no fear of me need terrify you;
my pressure will not be heavy upon you.

8 "Surely you have spoken in my ears,
and I have heard the sound of your words.
9 You say, 'I am pure, without transgression;
I am clean, and there is no iniquity in me.
10 Behold, he finds occasions against me,
he counts me as his enemy,
11 he puts my feet in the stocks
and watches all my paths.'

[1] Hebrew *many* [in years]

12 "Behold, in this you are not right. I
will answer you,
for God is greater than man.
13 Why do you contend against him,
saying, 'He will answer none of
man's[1] words'?[2]
14 For God speaks in one way,
and in two, though man does not
perceive it.
15 In a dream, in a vision of the night,
when deep sleep falls on men,
while they slumber on their
beds,
16 then he opens the ears of men
and terrifies them with warnings,
17 that he may turn man aside from
his deed
and conceal pride from a man;
18 he keeps back his soul from the pit,
his life from perishing by the
sword.

19 "Man is also rebuked with pain on
his bed
and with continual strife in his
bones,
20 so that his life loathes bread,
and his appetite the choicest
food.
21 His flesh is so wasted away that it
cannot be seen,
and his bones that were not seen
stick out.
22 His soul draws near the pit,
and his life to those who bring
death.
23 If there be for him an angel,
a mediator, one of the thousand,
to declare to man what is right for
him,
24 and he is merciful to him, and says,
'Deliver him from going down
into the pit;
I have found a ransom;
25 let his flesh become fresh with
youth;
let him return to the days of his
youthful vigor';
26 then man[3] prays to God, and he
accepts him;
he sees his face with a shout of
joy,
and he restores to man his
righteousness.
27 He sings before men and says:
'I sinned and perverted what was
right,
and it was not repaid to me.
28 He has redeemed my soul from
going down into the pit,
and my life shall look upon the
light.'

29 "Behold, God does all these things,
twice, three times, with a man,
30 to bring back his soul from the pit,
that he may be lighted with the
light of life.
31 Pay attention, O Job, listen to me;
be silent, and I will speak.
32 If you have any words, answer me;
speak, for I desire to justify you.
33 If not, listen to me;
be silent, and I will teach you
wisdom."

Elihu Asserts God's Justice

34 Then Elihu answered and said:

2 "Hear my words, you wise men,
and give ear to me, you who know;
3 for the ear tests words
as the palate tastes food.
4 Let us choose what is right;
let us know among ourselves
what is good.
5 For Job has said, 'I am in the right,
and God has taken away my right;
6 in spite of my right I am counted a
liar;
my wound is incurable, though I
am without transgression.'
7 What man is like Job,
who drinks up scoffing like water,

[1] Hebrew *his* [2] Or *He will not answer for any of his own words* [3] Hebrew *he*

8 who travels in company with
evildoers
and walks with wicked men?
9 For he has said, 'It profits a man
nothing
that he should take delight in God.'

10 "Therefore, hear me, you men of
understanding:
far be it from God that he should
do wickedness,
and from the Almighty that he
should do wrong.
11 For according to the work of a man
he will repay him,
and according to his ways he will
make it befall him.
12 Of a truth, God will not do wickedly,
and the Almighty will not pervert
justice.
13 Who gave him charge over the
earth,
and who laid on him[1] the whole
world?
14 If he should set his heart to it
and gather to himself his spirit
and his breath,
15 all flesh would perish together,
and man would return to dust.

16 "If you have understanding, hear
this;
listen to what I say.
17 Shall one who hates justice govern?
Will you condemn him who is
righteous and mighty,
18 who says to a king, 'Worthless one,'
and to nobles, 'Wicked man,'
19 who shows no partiality to princes,
nor regards the rich more than
the poor,
for they are all the work of his
hands?
20 In a moment they die;
at midnight the people are shaken
and pass away,
and the mighty are taken away by
no human hand.

21 "For his eyes are on the ways of a
man,
and he sees all his steps.
22 There is no gloom or deep darkness
where evildoers may hide
themselves.
23 For God[2] has no need to consider a
man further,
that he should go before God in
judgment.
24 He shatters the mighty without
investigation
and sets others in their place.
25 Thus, knowing their works,
he overturns them in the night,
and they are crushed.
26 He strikes them for their
wickedness
in a place for all to see,
27 because they turned aside from
following him
and had no regard for any of his
ways,
28 so that they caused the cry of the
poor to come to him,
and he heard the cry of the
afflicted—
29 When he is quiet, who can
condemn?
When he hides his face, who can
behold him,
whether it be a nation or a man?—
30 that a godless man should not
reign,
that he should not ensnare the
people.

31 "For has anyone said to God,
'I have borne punishment; I will
not offend any more;
32 teach me what I do not see;
if I have done iniquity, I will do it
no more'?
33 Will he then make repayment to
suit you,
because you reject it?
For you must choose, and not I;
therefore declare what you know.[3]

[1] Hebrew lacks *on him* [2] Hebrew *he* [3] The meaning of the Hebrew in verses 29-33 is uncertain

34 Men of understanding will say to me,
and the wise man who hears me will say:
35 'Job speaks without knowledge;
his words are without insight.'
36 Would that Job were tried to the end,
because he answers like wicked men.
37 For he adds rebellion to his sin;
he claps his hands among us
and multiplies his words against God."

Elihu Condemns Job

35 And Elihu answered and said:
2 "Do you think this to be just?
Do you say, 'It is my right before God,'
3 that you ask, 'What advantage have I?
How am I better off than if I had sinned?'
4 I will answer you
and your friends with you.
5 Look at the heavens, and see;
and behold the clouds, which are higher than you.
6 If you have sinned, what do you accomplish against him?
And if your transgressions are multiplied, what do you do to him?
7 If you are righteous, what do you give to him?
Or what does he receive from your hand?
8 Your wickedness concerns a man like yourself,
and your righteousness a son of man.
9 "Because of the multitude of oppressions people cry out;
they call for help because of the arm of the mighty.[1]
10 But none says, 'Where is God my Maker,
who gives songs in the night,
11 who teaches us more than the beasts of the earth
and makes us wiser than the birds of the heavens?'
12 There they cry out, but he does not answer,
because of the pride of evil men.
13 Surely God does not hear an empty cry,
nor does the Almighty regard it.
14 How much less when you say that you do not see him,
that the case is before him, and you are waiting for him!
15 And now, because his anger does not punish,
and he does not take much note of transgression,[2]
16 Job opens his mouth in empty talk;
he multiplies words without knowledge."

Elihu Extols God's Greatness

36 And Elihu continued, and said:
2 "Bear with me a little, and I will show you,
for I have yet something to say on God's behalf.
3 I will get my knowledge from afar
and ascribe righteousness to my Maker.
4 For truly my words are not false;
one who is perfect in knowledge is with you.
5 "Behold, God is mighty, and does not despise any;
he is mighty in strength of understanding.
6 He does not keep the wicked alive,
but gives the afflicted their right.

[1] Or *the many* [2] Theodotion, Symmachus (compare Vulgate); the meaning of the Hebrew word is uncertain

7 He does not withdraw his eyes from the righteous,
but with kings on the throne
he sets them forever, and they are exalted.
8 And if they are bound in chains
and caught in the cords of affliction,
9 then he declares to them their work
and their transgressions, that they are behaving arrogantly.
10 He opens their ears to instruction
and commands that they return from iniquity.
11 If they listen and serve him,
they complete their days in prosperity,
and their years in pleasantness.
12 But if they do not listen, they perish by the sword
and die without knowledge.

13 "The godless in heart cherish anger;
they do not cry for help when he binds them.
14 They die in youth,
and their life ends among the cult prostitutes.
15 He delivers the afflicted by their affliction
and opens their ear by adversity.
16 He also allured you out of distress
into a broad place where there was no cramping,
and what was set on your table was full of fatness.

17 "But you are full of the judgment on the wicked;
judgment and justice seize you.
18 Beware lest wrath entice you into scoffing,
and let not the greatness of the ransom turn you aside.
19 Will your cry for help avail to keep you from distress,
or all the force of your strength?
20 Do not long for the night,
when peoples vanish in their place.
21 Take care; do not turn to iniquity,
for this you have chosen rather than affliction.
22 Behold, God is exalted in his power;
who is a teacher like him?
23 Who has prescribed for him his way,
or who can say, 'You have done wrong'?

24 "Remember to extol his work,
of which men have sung.
25 All mankind has looked on it;
man beholds it from afar.
26 Behold, God is great, and we know him not;
the number of his years is unsearchable.
27 For he draws up the drops of water;
they distill his mist in rain,
28 which the skies pour down
and drop on mankind abundantly.
29 Can anyone understand the spreading of the clouds,
the thunderings of his pavilion?
30 Behold, he scatters his lightning about him
and covers the roots of the sea.
31 For by these he judges peoples;
he gives food in abundance.
32 He covers his hands with the lightning
and commands it to strike the mark.
33 Its crashing declares his presence;[1]
the cattle also declare that he rises.

Elihu Proclaims God's Majesty

37 "At this also my heart trembles
and leaps out of its place.
2 Keep listening to the thunder of his voice
and the rumbling that comes from his mouth.

[1] Hebrew *declares concerning him*

3 Under the whole heaven he lets it go,
and his lightning to the corners of the earth.
4 After it his voice roars;
he thunders with his majestic voice,
and he does not restrain the lightnings[1] when his voice is heard.
5 God thunders wondrously with his voice;
he does great things that we cannot comprehend.
6 For to the snow he says, 'Fall on the earth,'
likewise to the downpour, his mighty downpour.
7 He seals up the hand of every man,
that all men whom he made may know it.
8 Then the beasts go into their lairs,
and remain in their dens.
9 From its chamber comes the whirlwind,
and cold from the scattering winds.
10 By the breath of God ice is given,
and the broad waters are frozen fast.
11 He loads the thick cloud with moisture;
the clouds scatter his lightning.
12 They turn around and around by his guidance,
to accomplish all that he commands them
on the face of the habitable world.
13 Whether for correction or for his land
or for love, he causes it to happen.

14 "Hear this, O Job;
stop and consider the wondrous works of God.
15 Do you know how God lays his command upon them
and causes the lightning of his cloud to shine?
16 Do you know the balancings[2] of the clouds,
the wondrous works of him who is perfect in knowledge,
17 you whose garments are hot
when the earth is still because of the south wind?
18 Can you, like him, spread out the skies,
hard as a cast metal mirror?
19 Teach us what we shall say to him;
we cannot draw up our case because of darkness.
20 Shall it be told him that I would speak?
Did a man ever wish that he would be swallowed up?

21 "And now no one looks on the light
when it is bright in the skies,
when the wind has passed and cleared them.
22 Out of the north comes golden splendor;
God is clothed with awesome majesty.
23 The Almighty—we cannot find him;
he is great in power;
justice and abundant righteousness he will not violate.
24 Therefore men fear him;
he does not regard any who are wise in their own conceit."[3]

The LORD Answers Job

38 Then the LORD answered Job out of the whirlwind and said:

2 "Who is this that darkens counsel by words without knowledge?
3 Dress for action[4] like a man;
I will question you, and you make it known to me.

4 "Where were you when I laid the foundation of the earth?
Tell me, if you have understanding.

[1] Hebrew *them* [2] Or *hoverings* [3] Hebrew *in heart* [4] Hebrew *Gird up your loins*

5 Who determined its measurements—
surely you know!
Or who stretched the line upon it?
6 On what were its bases sunk,
or who laid its cornerstone,
7 when the morning stars sang
together
and all the sons of God shouted
for joy?

8 "Or who shut in the sea with doors
when it burst out from the womb,
9 when I made clouds its garment
and thick darkness its swaddling
band,
10 and prescribed limits for it
and set bars and doors,
11 and said, 'Thus far shall you come,
and no farther,
and here shall your proud waves
be stayed'?

12 "Have you commanded the morning
since your days began,
and caused the dawn to know its
place,
13 that it might take hold of the skirts
of the earth,
and the wicked be shaken out of
it?
14 It is changed like clay under the seal,
and its features stand out like a
garment.
15 From the wicked their light is
withheld,
and their uplifted arm is broken.

16 "Have you entered into the springs
of the sea,
or walked in the recesses of the
deep?
17 Have the gates of death been
revealed to you,
or have you seen the gates of deep
darkness?
18 Have you comprehended the
expanse of the earth?
Declare, if you know all this.

19 "Where is the way to the dwelling of
light,
and where is the place of
darkness,
20 that you may take it to its territory
and that you may discern the
paths to its home?
21 You know, for you were born then,
and the number of your days is
great!

22 "Have you entered the storehouses
of the snow,
or have you seen the storehouses
of the hail,
23 which I have reserved for the time
of trouble,
for the day of battle and war?
24 What is the way to the place where
the light is distributed,
or where the east wind is
scattered upon the earth?

25 "Who has cleft a channel for the
torrents of rain
and a way for the thunderbolt,
26 to bring rain on a land where no
man is,
on the desert in which there is no
man,
27 to satisfy the waste and desolate
land,
and to make the ground sprout
with grass?

28 "Has the rain a father,
or who has begotten the drops of
dew?
29 From whose womb did the ice come
forth,
and who has given birth to the
frost of heaven?
30 The waters become hard like stone,
and the face of the deep is frozen.

31 "Can you bind the chains of the
Pleiades
or loose the cords of Orion?

32 Can you lead forth the Mazzaroth[1]
in their season,
or can you guide the Bear with its
children?
33 Do you know the ordinances of the
heavens?
Can you establish their rule on
the earth?

34 "Can you lift up your voice to the
clouds,
that a flood of waters may cover
you?
35 Can you send forth lightnings, that
they may go
and say to you, 'Here we are'?
36 Who has put wisdom in the inward
parts[2]
or given understanding to the
mind?[3]
37 Who can number the clouds by
wisdom?
Or who can tilt the waterskins of
the heavens,
38 when the dust runs into a mass
and the clods stick fast together?

39 "Can you hunt the prey for the lion,
or satisfy the appetite of the
young lions,
40 when they crouch in their dens
or lie in wait in their thicket?
41 Who provides for the raven its prey,
when its young ones cry to God
for help,
and wander about for lack of food?

39 "Do you know when the
mountain goats give birth?
Do you observe the calving of the
does?
2 Can you number the months that
they fulfill,
and do you know the time when
they give birth,
3 when they crouch, bring forth their
offspring,
and are delivered of their young?
4 Their young ones become strong;
they grow up in the open;
they go out and do not return to
them.

5 "Who has let the wild donkey go
free?
Who has loosed the bonds of the
swift donkey,
6 to whom I have given the arid plain
for his home
and the salt land for his dwelling
place?
7 He scorns the tumult of the city;
he hears not the shouts of the
driver.
8 He ranges the mountains as his
pasture,
and he searches after every green
thing.

9 "Is the wild ox willing to serve you?
Will he spend the night at your
manger?
10 Can you bind him in the furrow
with ropes,
or will he harrow the valleys after
you?
11 Will you depend on him because
his strength is great,
and will you leave to him your
labor?
12 Do you have faith in him that he
will return your grain
and gather it to your threshing
floor?

13 "The wings of the ostrich wave
proudly,
but are they the pinions and
plumage of love?[4]
14 For she leaves her eggs to the earth
and lets them be warmed on the
ground,
15 forgetting that a foot may crush
them
and that the wild beast may
trample them.

[1] Probably the name of a constellation [2] Or *in the ibis* [3] Or *rooster* [4] The meaning of the Hebrew is uncertain

16 She deals cruelly with her young, as if they were not hers;
though her labor be in vain, yet she has no fear,
17 because God has made her forget wisdom
and given her no share in understanding.
18 When she rouses herself to flee,[1]
she laughs at the horse and his rider.

19 "Do you give the horse his might?
Do you clothe his neck with a mane?
20 Do you make him leap like the locust?
His majestic snorting is terrifying.
21 He paws[2] in the valley and exults in his strength;
he goes out to meet the weapons.
22 He laughs at fear and is not dismayed;
he does not turn back from the sword.
23 Upon him rattle the quiver,
the flashing spear, and the javelin.
24 With fierceness and rage he swallows the ground;
he cannot stand still at the sound of the trumpet.
25 When the trumpet sounds, he says 'Aha!'
He smells the battle from afar,
the thunder of the captains, and the shouting.

26 "Is it by your understanding that the hawk soars
and spreads his wings toward the south?
27 Is it at your command that the eagle mounts up
and makes his nest on high?
28 On the rock he dwells and makes his home,
on the rocky crag and stronghold.
29 From there he spies out the prey;
his eyes behold it from far away.
30 His young ones suck up blood,
and where the slain are, there is he."

40 And the LORD said to Job:
2 "Shall a faultfinder contend with the Almighty?
He who argues with God, let him answer it."

Job Promises Silence

3 Then Job answered the LORD and said:
4 "Behold, I am of small account; what shall I answer you?
I lay my hand on my mouth.
5 I have spoken once, and I will not answer;
twice, but I will proceed no further."

The LORD Challenges Job

6 Then the LORD answered Job out of the whirlwind and said:

7 "Dress for action[3] like a man;
I will question you, and you make it known to me.
8 Will you even put me in the wrong?
Will you condemn me that you may be in the right?
9 Have you an arm like God,
and can you thunder with a voice like his?

10 "Adorn yourself with majesty and dignity;
clothe yourself with glory and splendor.
11 Pour out the overflowings of your anger,
and look on everyone who is proud and abase him.
12 Look on everyone who is proud and bring him low
and tread down the wicked where they stand.

[1] The meaning of the Hebrew is uncertain [2] Hebrew *They paw* [3] Hebrew *Gird up your loins*

13 Hide them all in the dust together;
bind their faces in the world below.[1]
14 Then will I also acknowledge to you
that your own right hand can save you.

15 "Behold, Behemoth,[2]
which I made as I made you;
he eats grass like an ox.
16 Behold, his strength in his loins,
and his power in the muscles of his belly.
17 He makes his tail stiff like a cedar;
the sinews of his thighs are knit together.
18 His bones are tubes of bronze,
his limbs like bars of iron.

19 "He is the first of the works[3] of God;
let him who made him bring near his sword!
20 For the mountains yield food for him
where all the wild beasts play.
21 Under the lotus plants he lies,
in the shelter of the reeds and in the marsh.
22 For his shade the lotus trees cover him;
the willows of the brook surround him.
23 Behold, if the river is turbulent he is not frightened;
he is confident though Jordan rushes against his mouth.
24 Can one take him by his eyes,[4]
or pierce his nose with a snare?

41 [5]"Can you draw out Leviathan[6] with a fishhook
or press down his tongue with a cord?
2 Can you put a rope in his nose
or pierce his jaw with a hook?
3 Will he make many pleas to you?
Will he speak to you soft words?
4 Will he make a covenant with you
to take him for your servant forever?
5 Will you play with him as with a bird,
or will you put him on a leash for your girls?
6 Will traders bargain over him?
Will they divide him up among the merchants?
7 Can you fill his skin with harpoons
or his head with fishing spears?
8 Lay your hands on him;
remember the battle—you will not do it again!
9[7] Behold, the hope of a man is false;
he is laid low even at the sight of him.
10 No one is so fierce that he dares to stir him up.
Who then is he who can stand before me?
11 Who has first given to me, that I should repay him?
Whatever is under the whole heaven is mine.

12 "I will not keep silence concerning his limbs,
or his mighty strength, or his goodly frame.
13 Who can strip off his outer garment?
Who would come near him with a bridle?
14 Who can open the doors of his face?
Around his teeth is terror.
15 His back is made of[8] rows of shields,
shut up closely as with a seal.
16 One is so near to another
that no air can come between them.
17 They are joined one to another;
they clasp each other and cannot be separated.

[1] Hebrew *in the hidden place* [2] A large animal, exact identity unknown [3] Hebrew *ways* [4] Or *in his sight* [5] Ch 40:25 in Hebrew [6] A large sea animal, exact identity unknown [7] Ch 41:1 in Hebrew [8] Or *His pride is in his*

18 His sneezings flash forth light,
and his eyes are like the eyelids of the dawn.
19 Out of his mouth go flaming torches;
sparks of fire leap forth.
20 Out of his nostrils comes forth smoke,
as from a boiling pot and burning rushes.
21 His breath kindles coals,
and a flame comes forth from his mouth.
22 In his neck abides strength,
and terror dances before him.
23 The folds of his flesh stick together,
firmly cast on him and immovable.
24 His heart is hard as a stone,
hard as the lower millstone.
25 When he raises himself up the mighty[1] are afraid;
at the crashing they are beside themselves.
26 Though the sword reaches him, it does not avail,
nor the spear, the dart, or the javelin.
27 He counts iron as straw,
and bronze as rotten wood.
28 The arrow cannot make him flee;
for him sling stones are turned to stubble.
29 Clubs are counted as stubble;
he laughs at the rattle of javelins.
30 His underparts are like sharp potsherds;
he spreads himself like a threshing sledge on the mire.
31 He makes the deep boil like a pot;
he makes the sea like a pot of ointment.
32 Behind him he leaves a shining wake;
one would think the deep to be white-haired.
33 On earth there is not his like,
a creature without fear.
34 He sees everything that is high;
he is king over all the sons of pride."

Job's Confession and Repentance

42 Then Job answered the LORD and said:

2 "I know that you can do all things,
and that no purpose of yours can be thwarted.
3 'Who is this that hides counsel without knowledge?'
Therefore I have uttered what I did not understand,
things too wonderful for me,
which I did not know.
4 'Hear, and I will speak;
I will question you, and you make it known to me.'
5 I had heard of you by the hearing of the ear,
but now my eye sees you;
6 therefore I despise myself,
and repent[2] in dust and ashes."

The LORD Rebukes Job's Friends

7 After the LORD had spoken these
words to Job, the LORD said to Eliphaz the
Temanite: "My anger burns against you
and against your two friends, for you have
not spoken of me what is right, as my ser-
vant Job has. 8 Now therefore take seven
bulls and seven rams and go to my servant
Job and offer up a burnt offering for your-
selves. And my servant Job shall pray for
you, for I will accept his prayer not to deal
with you according to your folly. For you
have not spoken of me what is right, as my
servant Job has." 9 So Eliphaz the Temanite
and Bildad the Shuhite and Zophar the
Naamathite went and did what the LORD
had told them, and the LORD accepted
Job's prayer.

The LORD Restores Job's Fortunes

10 And the LORD restored the fortunes
of Job, when he had prayed for his friends.

[1] Or *gods* [2] Or *and am comforted*

And the LORD gave Job twice as much as
he had before. 11 Then came to him all
his brothers and sisters and all who had
known him before, and ate bread with
him in his house. And they showed him
sympathy and comforted him for all the
evil[1] that the LORD had brought upon
him. And each of them gave him a piece
of money[2] and a ring of gold.
12 And the LORD blessed the latter days of
Job more than his beginning. And he had
14,000 sheep, 6,000 camels, 1,000 yoke of
oxen, and 1,000 female donkeys. 13 He had
also seven sons and three daughters. 14 And
he called the name of the first daughter
Jemimah, and the name of the second
Keziah, and the name of the third Keren-
happuch. 15 And in all the land there were
no women so beautiful as Job's daughters.
And their father gave them an inheritance
among their brothers. 16 And after this Job
lived 140 years, and saw his sons, and his
sons' sons, four generations. 17 And Job
died, an old man, and full of days.

[1] Or *disaster* [2] Hebrew *a qesitah;* a unit of money of unknown value

Introduction to

The Psalms

Author(s)
King David; Asaph; the sons of Korah; others

Date
Eleventh century to sixth century B.C.

People
David; Asaph; the sons of Korah

Purpose
The purpose of the book of Psalms is to provide a collection of hymns for all kinds of occasions, happy or sad, that can be used to praise God in all circumstances of life.

Central Themes
One true God rules as King over all; God made and sustains all created things; God has made a covenant with His people and is always faithful to it; God's people must repent when they sin and must walk in His ways; the righteous often face persecution; God's salvation is for all the nations.

Memory Verses
The Shepherd Psalm (Psalm 23); sincere repentance (Psalm 51:7–12); the Lord reigns (Psalm 110); the Psalm of the Word (Psalm 119:105–107); the Mission Psalm (Psalm 145:4–13)

Introduction

The Psalms were written by different authors over a period of centuries. For example, David wrote many of them, Solomon wrote at least one, men who served in the temple wrote others; there is even one by Moses! They were gathered together by an unknown person or persons into a book to be used as Israel's hymnbook when the people came together in worship. Some psalms praise God with great joy for victory (Psalm 18); others for His acts of creation (Psalm 104) or for His provision and care (Psalm 105). Others are laments, songs of mourning that praise God by bringing to Him deep feelings of sadness (Psalm 88). Many psalms are cries for protection against persecuting enemies (Psalm 7). Other psalms confess sin and pray for forgiveness (Psalm 51). Still others express deep longings to know God better and follow Him more closely (Psalm 27). The longest psalm praises the Word of God from many different perspectives (Psalm 119). Several psalms look ahead to the Messiah in His sufferings (Psalm 22) and in His glory (Psalm 110). The book of Psalms is one of the best loved books of the entire Bible, having something for every believer, no matter what their specific circumstances or feelings.

1526 B.C.	1050/1030–1010 B.C.	1010–971 B.C.	971–931 B.C.
Moses born	Reign of Saul	Reign of David	Reign of Solomon

The Psalms

BOOK ONE

The Way of the Righteous and the Wicked

101

1 Blessed is the man[1]
who walks not in the counsel of the wicked,
nor stands in the way of sinners,
nor sits in the seat of scoffers;
2 but his delight is in the law[2] of the LORD,
and on his law he meditates day and night.

3 He is like a tree
planted by streams of water
that yields its fruit in its season,
and its leaf does not wither.
In all that he does, he prospers.
4 The wicked are not so,
but are like chaff that the wind drives away.

5 Therefore the wicked will not stand in the judgment,
nor sinners in the congregation of the righteous;
6 for the LORD knows the way of the righteous,
but the way of the wicked will perish.

The Reign of the LORD's Anointed

2 Why do the nations rage[3]
and the peoples plot in vain?
2 The kings of the earth set themselves,
and the rulers take counsel together,
against the LORD and against his Anointed, saying,
3 "Let us burst their bonds apart
and cast away their cords from us."

4 He who sits in the heavens laughs;
the Lord holds them in derision.
5 Then he will speak to them in his wrath,
and terrify them in his fury, saying,
6 "As for me, I have set my King
on Zion, my holy hill."

7 I will tell of the decree:
The LORD said to me, "You are my Son;
today I have begotten you.
8 Ask of me, and I will make the nations your heritage,
and the ends of the earth your possession.
9 You shall break[4] them with a rod of iron
and dash them in pieces like a potter's vessel."

10 Now therefore, O kings, be wise;
be warned, O rulers of the earth.
11 Serve the LORD with fear,
and rejoice with trembling.
12 Kiss the Son,
lest he be angry, and you perish in the way,
for his wrath is quickly kindled.
Blessed are all who take refuge in him.

Save Me, O My God

3 A PSALM OF DAVID, WHEN HE FLED FROM ABSALOM HIS SON.

1 O LORD, how many are my foes!
Many are rising against me;
2 many are saying of my soul,
there is no salvation for him in God. *Selah*[5]

[1] The singular Hebrew word for *man* (*ish*) is used here to portray a representative example of a godly person [2] Or *instruction* [3] Or *nations noisily assemble*
[4] Revocalization yields (compare Septuagint) *You shall rule* [5] The meaning of the Hebrew word *Selah*, used frequently in the Psalms, is uncertain. It may be a musical or liturgical direction

3 But you, O LORD, are a shield about me,
my glory, and the lifter of my head.
4 I cried aloud to the LORD,
and he answered me from his holy hill. *Selah*

5 I lay down and slept;
I woke again, for the LORD sustained me.
6 I will not be afraid of many thousands of people
who have set themselves against me all around.

7 Arise, O LORD!
Save me, O my God!
For you strike all my enemies on the cheek;
you break the teeth of the wicked.

8 Salvation belongs to the LORD;
your blessing be on your people! *Selah*

Answer Me When I Call

4 TO THE CHOIRMASTER: WITH STRINGED INSTRUMENTS. A PSALM OF DAVID.

1 Answer me when I call, O God of my righteousness!
You have given me relief when I was in distress.
Be gracious to me and hear my prayer!

2 O men,[1] how long shall my honor be turned into shame?
How long will you love vain words and seek after lies? *Selah*

3 But know that the LORD has set apart the godly for himself;
the LORD hears when I call to him.

4 Be angry,[2] and do not sin;
ponder in your own hearts on your beds, and be silent. *Selah*
5 Offer right sacrifices,
and put your trust in the LORD.

6 There are many who say, "Who will show us some good?
Lift up the light of your face upon us, O LORD!"
7 You have put more joy in my heart
than they have when their grain and wine abound.

8 In peace I will both lie down and sleep;
for you alone, O LORD, make me dwell in safety.

Lead Me in Your Righteousness

5 TO THE CHOIRMASTER: FOR THE FLUTES. A PSALM OF DAVID.

1 Give ear to my words, O LORD;
consider my groaning.
2 Give attention to the sound of my cry,
my King and my God,
for to you do I pray.
3 O LORD, in the morning you hear my voice;
in the morning I prepare a sacrifice for you[3] and watch.

4 For you are not a God who delights in wickedness;
evil may not dwell with you.
5 The boastful shall not stand before your eyes;
you hate all evildoers.
6 You destroy those who speak lies;
the LORD abhors the bloodthirsty and deceitful man.

7 But I, through the abundance of your steadfast love,
will enter your house.
I will bow down toward your holy temple
in the fear of you.
8 Lead me, O LORD, in your righteousness
because of my enemies;
make your way straight before me.

[1] Or *O men of rank* [2] Or *Be agitated* [3] Or *I direct my prayer to you*

9 For there is no truth in their mouth;
their inmost self is destruction;
their throat is an open grave;
they flatter with their tongue.
10 Make them bear their guilt, O God;
let them fall by their own
counsels;
because of the abundance of their
transgressions cast them out,
for they have rebelled against you.

11 But let all who take refuge in you
rejoice;
let them ever sing for joy,
and spread your protection over
them,
that those who love your name
may exult in you.
12 For you bless the righteous, O LORD;
you cover him with favor as with
a shield.

O LORD, Deliver My Life

6 TO THE CHOIRMASTER: WITH STRINGED INSTRUMENTS; ACCORDING TO THE SHEMINITH.[1] A PSALM OF DAVID.

1 O LORD, rebuke me not in your
anger,
nor discipline me in your wrath.
2 Be gracious to me, O LORD, for I am
languishing;
heal me, O LORD, for my bones are
troubled.
3 My soul also is greatly troubled.
But you, O LORD—how long?

4 Turn, O LORD, deliver my life;
save me for the sake of your
steadfast love.
5 For in death there is no
remembrance of you;
in Sheol who will give you praise?

6 I am weary with my moaning;
every night I flood my bed with
tears;
I drench my couch with my
weeping.
7 My eye wastes away because of
grief;
it grows weak because of all my
foes.

8 Depart from me, all you workers of
evil,
for the LORD has heard the sound
of my weeping.
9 The LORD has heard my plea;
the LORD accepts my prayer.
10 All my enemies shall be ashamed
and greatly troubled;
they shall turn back and be put to
shame in a moment.

In You Do I Take Refuge

7 A SHIGGAION[2] OF DAVID, WHICH HE SANG TO THE LORD CONCERNING THE WORDS OF CUSH, A BENJAMINITE.

1 O LORD my God, in you do I take
refuge;
save me from all my pursuers and
deliver me,
2 lest like a lion they tear my soul
apart,
rending it in pieces, with none to
deliver.

3 O LORD my God, if I have done this,
if there is wrong in my hands,
4 if I have repaid my friend[3] with
evil
or plundered my enemy without
cause,
5 let the enemy pursue my soul and
overtake it,
and let him trample my life to the
ground
and lay my glory in the dust. *Selah*

6 Arise, O LORD, in your anger;
lift yourself up against the fury of
my enemies;
awake for me; you have appointed
a judgment.

[1] Probably a musical or liturgical term [2] Probably a musical or liturgical term [3] Hebrew *the one at peace with me*

7 Let the assembly of the peoples be
gathered about you;
over it return on high.
8 The LORD judges the peoples;
judge me, O LORD, according to
my righteousness
and according to the integrity that
is in me.
9 Oh, let the evil of the wicked come
to an end,
and may you establish the
righteous—
you who test the minds and
hearts,[1]
O righteous God!
10 My shield is with God,
who saves the upright in heart.
11 God is a righteous judge,
and a God who feels indignation
every day.
12 If a man[2] does not repent, God[3] will
whet his sword;
he has bent and readied his bow;
13 he has prepared for him his deadly
weapons,
making his arrows fiery shafts.
14 Behold, the wicked man conceives
evil
and is pregnant with mischief
and gives birth to lies.
15 He makes a pit, digging it out,
and falls into the hole that he has
made.
16 His mischief returns upon his own
head,
and on his own skull his violence
descends.

17 I will give to the LORD the thanks
due to his righteousness,
and I will sing praise to the name
of the LORD, the Most High.

How Majestic Is Your Name

8 TO THE CHOIRMASTER: ACCORDING TO THE GITTITH.[4] A PSALM OF DAVID.

1 O LORD, our Lord,
how majestic is your name in all
the earth!
You have set your glory above the
heavens.
2 Out of the mouth of babies and
infants,
you have established strength
because of your foes,
to still the enemy and the
avenger.

3 When I look at your heavens, the
work of your fingers,
the moon and the stars, which
you have set in place,
4 what is man that you are mindful of
him,
and the son of man that you care
for him?

5 Yet you have made him a little
lower than the heavenly
beings[5]
and crowned him with glory and
honor.
6 You have given him dominion over
the works of your hands;
you have put all things under his
feet,
7 all sheep and oxen,
and also the beasts of the field,
8 the birds of the heavens, and the
fish of the sea,
whatever passes along the paths
of the seas.

9 O LORD, our Lord,
how majestic is your name in all
the earth!

[1] Hebrew *the hearts and kidneys* [2] Hebrew *he* [3] Hebrew *he* [4] Probably a musical or liturgical term [5] Or *than God*; Septuagint *than the angels*

I Will Recount Your Wonderful Deeds

9

[1] To the choirmaster: according to Muth-labben.[2] A Psalm of David.

1 I will give thanks to the LORD with
my whole heart;
I will recount all of your
wonderful deeds.
2 I will be glad and exult in you;
I will sing praise to your name, O
Most High.

3 When my enemies turn back,
they stumble and perish before[3]
your presence.
4 For you have maintained my just
cause;
you have sat on the throne, giving
righteous judgment.

5 You have rebuked the nations; you
have made the wicked perish;
you have blotted out their name
forever and ever.
6 The enemy came to an end in
everlasting ruins;
their cities you rooted out;
the very memory of them has
perished.

7 But the LORD sits enthroned
forever;
he has established his throne for
justice,
8 and he judges the world with
righteousness;
he judges the peoples with
uprightness.

9 The LORD is a stronghold for the
oppressed,
a stronghold in times of trouble.
10 And those who know your name
put their trust in you,
for you, O LORD, have not
forsaken those who seek you.

11 Sing praises to the LORD, who sits
enthroned in Zion!
Tell among the peoples his deeds!
12 For he who avenges blood is
mindful of them;
he does not forget the cry of the
afflicted.

13 Be gracious to me, O LORD!
See my affliction from those who
hate me,
O you who lift me up from the
gates of death,
14 that I may recount all your praises,
that in the gates of the daughter
of Zion
I may rejoice in your salvation.

15 The nations have sunk in the pit
that they made;
in the net that they hid, their own
foot has been caught.
16 The LORD has made himself known;
he has executed judgment;
the wicked are snared in the
work of their own hands.
Higgaion.[4] *Selah*

17 The wicked shall return to Sheol,
all the nations that forget God.

18 For the needy shall not always be
forgotten,
and the hope of the poor shall not
perish forever.

19 Arise, O LORD! Let not man prevail;
let the nations be judged before
you!
20 Put them in fear, O LORD!
Let the nations know that they are
but men! *Selah*

Why Do You Hide Yourself?

10

Why, O LORD, do you stand far
away?
Why do you hide yourself in
times of trouble?

[1] Psalms 9 and 10 together follow an acrostic pattern, each stanza beginning with the successive letters of the Hebrew alphabet. In the Septuagint they form one psalm
[2] Probably a musical or liturgical term [3] Or *because of* [4] Probably a musical or liturgical term

2 In arrogance the wicked hotly
pursue the poor;
let them be caught in the schemes
that they have devised.
3 For the wicked boasts of the desires
of his soul,
and the one greedy for gain
curses[1] and renounces the
LORD.
4 In the pride of his face[2] the wicked
does not seek him;[3]
all his thoughts are, "There is no
God."
5 His ways prosper at all times;
your judgments are on high, out
of his sight;
as for all his foes, he puffs at
them.
6 He says in his heart, "I shall not be
moved;
throughout all generations I shall
not meet adversity."
7 His mouth is filled with cursing and
deceit and oppression;
under his tongue are mischief
and iniquity.
8 He sits in ambush in the villages;
in hiding places he murders the
innocent.
His eyes stealthily watch for the
helpless;
9 he lurks in ambush like a lion in
his thicket;
he lurks that he may seize the poor;
he seizes the poor when he draws
him into his net.
10 The helpless are crushed, sink
down,
and fall by his might.
11 He says in his heart, "God has
forgotten,
he has hidden his face, he will
never see it."
12 Arise, O LORD; O God, lift up your
hand;
forget not the afflicted.
13 Why does the wicked renounce God
and say in his heart, "You will not
call to account"?
14 But you do see, for you note
mischief and vexation,
that you may take it into your
hands;
to you the helpless commits
himself;
you have been the helper of the
fatherless.
15 Break the arm of the wicked and
evildoer;
call his wickedness to account till
you find none.

16 The LORD is king forever and ever;
the nations perish from his land.
17 O LORD, you hear the desire of the
afflicted;
you will strengthen their heart;
you will incline your ear
18 to do justice to the fatherless and
the oppressed,
so that man who is of the earth
may strike terror no more.

The LORD Is in His Holy Temple

11 TO THE CHOIRMASTER. OF DAVID.
In the LORD I take refuge;
how can you say to my soul,
"Flee like a bird to your mountain,
2 for behold, the wicked bend the
bow;
they have fitted their arrow to the
string
to shoot in the dark at the upright
in heart;
3 if the foundations are destroyed,
what can the righteous do?"[4]

4 The LORD is in his holy temple;
the LORD's throne is in heaven;
his eyes see, his eyelids test the
children of man.
5 The LORD tests the righteous,
but his soul hates the wicked and
the one who loves violence.

[1] *Or and he blesses the one greedy for gain* [2] *Or of his anger* [3] *Or the wicked says, "He will not call to account"* [4] *Or for the foundations will be destroyed; what has the righteous done?*

6 Let him rain coals on the wicked;
fire and sulfur and a scorching wind shall be the portion of their cup.
7 For the LORD is righteous;
he loves righteous deeds;
the upright shall behold his face.

The Faithful Have Vanished

12 TO THE CHOIRMASTER: ACCORDING TO THE SHEMINITH.[1] A PSALM OF DAVID.

1 Save, O LORD, for the godly one is gone;
for the faithful have vanished from among the children of man.
2 Everyone utters lies to his neighbor;
with flattering lips and a double heart they speak.

3 May the LORD cut off all flattering lips,
the tongue that makes great boasts,
4 those who say, "With our tongue we will prevail,
our lips are with us; who is master over us?"

5 "Because the poor are plundered, because the needy groan,
I will now arise," says the LORD;
"I will place him in the safety for which he longs."
6 The words of the LORD are pure words,
like silver refined in a furnace on the ground,
purified seven times.

7 You, O LORD, will keep them;
you will guard us[2] from this generation forever.
8 On every side the wicked prowl,
as vileness is exalted among the children of man.

How Long, O LORD?

13 TO THE CHOIRMASTER. A PSALM OF DAVID.

1 How long, O LORD? Will you forget me forever?
How long will you hide your face from me?
2 How long must I take counsel in my soul
and have sorrow in my heart all the day?
How long shall my enemy be exalted over me?

3 Consider and answer me, O LORD my God;
light up my eyes, lest I sleep the sleep of death,
4 lest my enemy say, "I have prevailed over him,"
lest my foes rejoice because I am shaken.

5 But I have trusted in your steadfast love;
my heart shall rejoice in your salvation.
6 I will sing to the LORD,
because he has dealt bountifully with me.

The Fool Says, There Is No God

14 TO THE CHOIRMASTER. OF DAVID.
The fool says in his heart,
"There is no God."
They are corrupt, they do abominable deeds,
there is none who does good.

2 The LORD looks down from heaven on the children of man,
to see if there are any who understand,[3]
who seek after God.

3 They have all turned aside; together they have become corrupt;
there is none who does good,
not even one.

[1] Probably a musical or liturgical term [2] Or *guard him* [3] Or *that act wisely*

4 Have they no knowledge, all the evildoers
who eat up my people as they eat bread
and do not call upon the LORD?

5 There they are in great terror,
for God is with the generation of the righteous.
6 You would shame the plans of the poor,
but[1] the LORD is his refuge.

7 Oh, that salvation for Israel would come out of Zion!
When the LORD restores the fortunes of his people,
let Jacob rejoice, let Israel be glad.

Who Shall Dwell on Your Holy Hill?

15

A PSALM OF DAVID.

O LORD, who shall sojourn in your tent?
Who shall dwell on your holy hill?

2 He who walks blamelessly and does what is right
and speaks truth in his heart;
3 who does not slander with his tongue
and does no evil to his neighbor,
nor takes up a reproach against his friend;
4 in whose eyes a vile person is despised,
but who honors those who fear the LORD;
who swears to his own hurt and does not change;
5 who does not put out his money at interest
and does not take a bribe against the innocent.
He who does these things shall never be moved.

You Will Not Abandon My Soul

16

A MIKTAM[2] OF DAVID.

Preserve me, O God, for in you I take refuge.
2 I say to the LORD, "You are my Lord;
I have no good apart from you."

3 As for the saints in the land, they are the excellent ones,
in whom is all my delight.[3]
4 The sorrows of those who run after[4] another god shall multiply;
their drink offerings of blood I will not pour out
or take their names on my lips.

5 The LORD is my chosen portion and my cup;
you hold my lot.
6 The lines have fallen for me in pleasant places;
indeed, I have a beautiful inheritance.

7 I bless the LORD who gives me counsel;
in the night also my heart instructs me.[5]
8 I have set the LORD always before me;
because he is at my right hand, I shall not be shaken.

9 Therefore my heart is glad, and my whole being[6] rejoices;
my flesh also dwells secure.
10 For you will not abandon my soul to Sheol,
or let your holy one see corruption.[7]

11 You make known to me the path of life;
in your presence there is fullness of joy;
at your right hand are pleasures forevermore.

[1] Or *for* [2] Probably a musical or liturgical term [3] Or *To the saints in the land, the excellent in whom is all my delight, I say:* [4] Or *who acquire* [5] Hebrew *my kidneys instruct me*
[6] Hebrew *my glory* [7] Or *see the pit*

In the Shadow of Your Wings

17 A Prayer of David.
Hear a just cause, O Lord;
attend to my cry!
Give ear to my prayer from lips
free of deceit!
2 From your presence let my
vindication come!
Let your eyes behold the right!

3 You have tried my heart, you have
visited me by night,
you have tested me, and you will
find nothing;
I have purposed that my mouth
will not transgress.
4 With regard to the works of man, by
the word of your lips
I have avoided the ways of the
violent.
5 My steps have held fast to your
paths;
my feet have not slipped.

6 I call upon you, for you will answer
me, O God;
incline your ear to me; hear my
words.
7 Wondrously show[1] your steadfast
love,
O Savior of those who seek refuge
from their adversaries at your
right hand.

8 Keep me as the apple of your eye;
hide me in the shadow of your
wings,
9 from the wicked who do me
violence,
my deadly enemies who
surround me.

10 They close their hearts to pity;
with their mouths they speak
arrogantly.
11 They have now surrounded our
steps;
they set their eyes to cast us to the
ground.
12 He is like a lion eager to tear,
as a young lion lurking in
ambush.

13 Arise, O Lord! Confront him,
subdue him!
Deliver my soul from the wicked
by your sword,
14 from men by your hand, O Lord,
from men of the world whose
portion is in this life.[2]
You fill their womb with treasure;[3]
they are satisfied with children,
and they leave their abundance to
their infants.

15 As for me, I shall behold your face
in righteousness;
when I awake, I shall be satisfied
with your likeness.

The Lord Is My Rock and My Fortress

18 To the choirmaster. A Psalm of
David, the servant of the Lord, who
addressed the words of this song to
the Lord on the day when the Lord
rescued him from the hand of all
his enemies, and from the hand of
Saul. He said:

1 I love you, O Lord, my strength.
2 The Lord is my rock and my
fortress and my deliverer,
my God, my rock, in whom I take
refuge,
my shield, and the horn of my
salvation, my stronghold.
3 I call upon the Lord, who is worthy
to be praised,
and I am saved from my enemies.

4 The cords of death encompassed
me;
the torrents of destruction
assailed me;[4]
5 the cords of Sheol entangled me;
the snares of death confronted
me.

[1] Or *Distinguish me by* [2] Or *from men whose portion in life is of the world* [3] Or *As for your treasured ones, you fill their womb* [4] Or *terrified me*

6 In my distress I called upon the
LORD;
to my God I cried for help.
From his temple he heard my voice,
and my cry to him reached his
ears.

7 Then the earth reeled and rocked;
the foundations also of the
mountains trembled
and quaked, because he was angry.
8 Smoke went up from his nostrils,[1]
and devouring fire from his
mouth;
glowing coals flamed forth from
him.
9 He bowed the heavens and came
down;
thick darkness was under his feet.
10 He rode on a cherub and flew;
he came swiftly on the wings of
the wind.
11 He made darkness his covering, his
canopy around him,
thick clouds dark with water.
12 Out of the brightness before him
hailstones and coals of fire broke
through his clouds.

13 The LORD also thundered in the
heavens,
and the Most High uttered his
voice,
hailstones and coals of fire.
14 And he sent out his arrows and
scattered them;
he flashed forth lightnings and
routed them.
15 Then the channels of the sea were
seen,
and the foundations of the world
were laid bare
at your rebuke, O LORD,
at the blast of the breath of your
nostrils.

16 He sent from on high, he took me;
he drew me out of many waters.
17 He rescued me from my strong
enemy
and from those who hated me,
for they were too mighty for me.
18 They confronted me in the day of
my calamity,
but the LORD was my support.
19 He brought me out into a broad
place;
he rescued me, because he
delighted in me.

20 The LORD dealt with me according
to my righteousness;
according to the cleanness of my
hands he rewarded me.
21 For I have kept the ways of the
LORD,
and have not wickedly departed
from my God.
22 For all his rules[2] were before me,
and his statutes I did not put away
from me.
23 I was blameless before him,
and I kept myself from my guilt.
24 So the LORD has rewarded
me according to my
righteousness,
according to the cleanness of my
hands in his sight.

25 With the merciful you show
yourself merciful;
with the blameless man you show
yourself blameless;
26 with the purified you show yourself
pure;
and with the crooked you make
yourself seem tortuous.
27 For you save a humble people,
but the haughty eyes you bring
down.
28 For it is you who light my lamp;
the LORD my God lightens my
darkness.
29 For by you I can run against a troop,
and by my God I can leap over a
wall.

[1] Or *in his wrath* [2] Or *just decrees*

30 This God—his way is perfect;[1]
the word of the LORD proves true;
he is a shield for all those who take refuge in him.

31 For who is God, but the LORD?
And who is a rock, except our God?—
32 the God who equipped me with strength
and made my way blameless.
33 He made my feet like the feet of a deer
and set me secure on the heights.
34 He trains my hands for war,
so that my arms can bend a bow of bronze.
35 You have given me the shield of your salvation,
and your right hand supported me,
and your gentleness made me great.
36 You gave a wide place for my steps under me,
and my feet did not slip.
37 I pursued my enemies and overtook them,
and did not turn back till they were consumed.
38 I thrust them through, so that they were not able to rise;
they fell under my feet.
39 For you equipped me with strength for the battle;
you made those who rise against me sink under me.
40 You made my enemies turn their backs to me,[2]
and those who hated me I destroyed.
41 They cried for help, but there was none to save;
they cried to the LORD, but he did not answer them.
42 I beat them fine as dust before the wind;
I cast them out like the mire of the streets.

43 You delivered me from strife with the people;
you made me the head of the nations;
people whom I had not known served me.
44 As soon as they heard of me they obeyed me;
foreigners came cringing to me.
45 Foreigners lost heart
and came trembling out of their fortresses.

46 The LORD lives, and blessed be my rock,
and exalted be the God of my salvation—
47 the God who gave me vengeance
and subdued peoples under me,
48 who delivered me from my enemies;
yes, you exalted me above those who rose against me;
you rescued me from the man of violence.

49 For this I will praise you, O LORD, among the nations,
and sing to your name.
50 Great salvation he brings to his king,
and shows steadfast love to his anointed,
to David and his offspring forever.

The Law of the LORD Is Perfect

19

TO THE CHOIRMASTER. A PSALM OF DAVID.

5

1 The heavens declare the glory of God,
and the sky above[3] proclaims his handiwork.
2 Day to day pours out speech,
and night to night reveals knowledge.
3 There is no speech, nor are there words,
whose voice is not heard.

[1] Or *blameless* [2] Or *You gave me my enemies' necks* [3] Hebrew *the expanse*; compare Genesis 1:6-8

4 Their voice[1] goes out through all the earth,
and their words to the end of the world.
In them he has set a tent for the sun,
5 which comes out like a bridegroom leaving his chamber,
and, like a strong man, runs its course with joy.
6 Its rising is from the end of the heavens,
and its circuit to the end of them,
and there is nothing hidden from its heat.

7 The law of the LORD is perfect,[2]
reviving the soul;
the testimony of the LORD is sure,
making wise the simple;
8 the precepts of the LORD are right,
rejoicing the heart;
the commandment of the LORD is pure,
enlightening the eyes;
9 the fear of the LORD is clean,
enduring forever;
the rules[3] of the LORD are true,
and righteous altogether.
10 More to be desired are they than gold,
even much fine gold;
sweeter also than honey
and drippings of the honeycomb.
11 Moreover, by them is your servant warned;
in keeping them there is great reward.

12 Who can discern his errors?
Declare me innocent from hidden faults.
13 Keep back your servant also from presumptuous sins;
let them not have dominion over me!
Then I shall be blameless,
and innocent of great transgression.

[1] Or *Their measuring line* [2] Or *blameless* [3] Or *just decrees*

14 Let the words of my mouth and the meditation of my heart
be acceptable in your sight,
O LORD, my rock and my redeemer.

Trust in the Name of the LORD Our God

20 TO THE CHOIRMASTER. A PSALM OF DAVID.
May the LORD answer you in the day of trouble!
May the name of the God of Jacob protect you!
2 May he send you help from the sanctuary
and give you support from Zion!
3 May he remember all your offerings
and regard with favor your burnt sacrifices! *Selah*

4 May he grant you your heart's desire
and fulfill all your plans!
5 May we shout for joy over your salvation,
and in the name of our God set up our banners!
May the LORD fulfill all your petitions!

6 Now I know that the LORD saves his anointed;
he will answer him from his holy heaven
with the saving might of his right hand.
7 Some trust in chariots and some in horses,
but we trust in the name of the LORD our God.
8 They collapse and fall,
but we rise and stand upright.

9 O LORD, save the king!
May he answer us when we call.

The King Rejoices in the LORD's Strength

21 TO THE CHOIRMASTER. A PSALM OF DAVID.
O LORD, in your strength the king rejoices,
and in your salvation how greatly he exults!

2 You have given him his heart's desire
and have not withheld the request
of his lips. *Selah*
3 For you meet him with rich
blessings;
you set a crown of fine gold upon
his head.
4 He asked life of you; you gave it to
him,
length of days forever and ever.
5 His glory is great through your
salvation;
splendor and majesty you bestow
on him.
6 For you make him most blessed
forever;[1]
you make him glad with the joy of
your presence.
7 For the king trusts in the LORD,
and through the steadfast love of
the Most High he shall not be
moved.

8 Your hand will find out all your
enemies;
your right hand will find out
those who hate you.
9 You will make them as a blazing
oven
when you appear.
The LORD will swallow them up in
his wrath,
and fire will consume them.
10 You will destroy their descendants
from the earth,
and their offspring from among
the children of man.
11 Though they plan evil against you,
though they devise mischief, they
will not succeed.
12 For you will put them to flight;
you will aim at their faces with
your bows.

13 Be exalted, O LORD, in your
strength!
We will sing and praise your
power.

Why Have You Forsaken Me?

22

TO THE CHOIRMASTER: ACCORDING TO THE DOE OF THE DAWN. A PSALM OF DAVID.

1 My God, my God, why have you
forsaken me?
Why are you so far from saving
me, from the words of my
groaning?
2 O my God, I cry by day, but you do
not answer,
and by night, but I find no rest.

3 Yet you are holy,
enthroned on the praises[2] of
Israel.
4 In you our fathers trusted;
they trusted, and you delivered
them.
5 To you they cried and were rescued;
in you they trusted and were not
put to shame.

6 But I am a worm and not a man,
scorned by mankind and
despised by the people.
7 All who see me mock me;
they make mouths at me; they
wag their heads;
8 "He trusts in the LORD; let him
deliver him;
let him rescue him, for he
delights in him!"

9 Yet you are he who took me from
the womb;
you made me trust you at my
mother's breasts.
10 On you was I cast from my birth,
and from my mother's womb you
have been my God.
11 Be not far from me,
for trouble is near,
and there is none to help.

12 Many bulls encompass me;
strong bulls of Bashan surround
me;

[1] Or *make him a source of blessing forever* [2] Or *dwelling in the praises*

13 they open wide their mouths at me,
like a ravening and roaring lion.

14 I am poured out like water,
and all my bones are out of joint;
my heart is like wax;
it is melted within my breast;
15 my strength is dried up like a potsherd,
and my tongue sticks to my jaws;
you lay me in the dust of death.

16 For dogs encompass me;
a company of evildoers encircles me;
they have pierced my hands and feet[1]—
17 I can count all my bones—
they stare and gloat over me;
18 they divide my garments among them,
and for my clothing they cast lots.

19 But you, O LORD, do not be far off!
O you my help, come quickly to my aid!
20 Deliver my soul from the sword,
my precious life from the power of the dog!
21 Save me from the mouth of the lion!
You have rescued[2] me from the horns of the wild oxen!

22 I will tell of your name to my brothers;
in the midst of the congregation I will praise you:
23 You who fear the LORD, praise him!
All you offspring of Jacob, glorify him,
and stand in awe of him, all you offspring of Israel!
24 For he has not despised or abhorred
the affliction of the afflicted,
and he has not hidden his face from him,
but has heard, when he cried to him.

25 From you comes my praise in the great congregation;
my vows I will perform before those who fear him.
26 The afflicted[3] shall eat and be satisfied;
those who seek him shall praise the LORD!
May your hearts live forever!

27 All the ends of the earth shall remember
and turn to the LORD,
and all the families of the nations
shall worship before you.
28 For kingship belongs to the LORD,
and he rules over the nations.

29 All the prosperous of the earth eat and worship;
before him shall bow all who go down to the dust,
even the one who could not keep himself alive.
30 Posterity shall serve him;
it shall be told of the Lord to the coming generation;
31 they shall come and proclaim his righteousness to a people yet unborn,
that he has done it.

The LORD Is My Shepherd

23

A PSALM OF DAVID.

1571

The LORD is my shepherd;
I shall not want.
2 He makes me lie down in green pastures.
He leads me beside still waters.[4]
3 He restores my soul.
He leads me in paths of righteousness[5]
for his name's sake.

[1] Some Hebrew manuscripts, Septuagint, Vulgate, Syriac; most Hebrew manuscripts *like a lion* [they are at] *my hands and feet* [2] Hebrew *answered* [3] Or *The meek*
[4] Hebrew *beside waters of rest* [5] Or *in right paths*

4 Even though I walk through the
valley of the shadow of death,[1]
I will fear no evil,
for you are with me;
your rod and your staff,
they comfort me.

5 You prepare a table before me
in the presence of my enemies;
you anoint my head with oil;
my cup overflows.
6 Surely[2] goodness and mercy[3] shall
follow me
all the days of my life,
and I shall dwell[4] in the house of
the LORD
forever.[5]

The King of Glory

24

A PSALM OF DAVID.
The earth is the LORD's and the
fullness thereof,[6]
the world and those who dwell
therein,
2 for he has founded it upon the seas
and established it upon the rivers.

3 Who shall ascend the hill of the
LORD?
And who shall stand in his holy
place?
4 He who has clean hands and a pure
heart,
who does not lift up his soul to
what is false
and does not swear deceitfully.
5 He will receive blessing from the
LORD
and righteousness from the God
of his salvation.
6 Such is the generation of those who
seek him,
who seek the face of the God of
Jacob.[7] *Selah*

7 Lift up your heads, O gates!
And be lifted up, O ancient doors,
that the King of glory may come in.
8 Who is this King of glory?
The LORD, strong and mighty,
the LORD, mighty in battle!
9 Lift up your heads, O gates!
And lift them up, O ancient
doors,
that the King of glory may come
in.
10 Who is this King of glory?
The LORD of hosts,
he is the King of glory! *Selah*

Teach Me Your Paths

25

95

[8] OF DAVID.
To you, O LORD, I lift up
my soul.
2 O my God, in you I trust;
let me not be put to shame;
let not my enemies exult over me.
3 Indeed, none who wait for you shall
be put to shame;
they shall be ashamed who are
wantonly treacherous.

4 Make me to know your ways, O
LORD;
teach me your paths.
5 Lead me in your truth and teach me,
for you are the God of my
salvation;
for you I wait all the day long.

6 Remember your mercy, O LORD, and
your steadfast love,
for they have been from of old.
7 Remember not the sins of my youth
or my transgressions;
according to your steadfast love
remember me,
for the sake of your goodness, O
LORD!

8 Good and upright is the LORD;
therefore he instructs sinners in
the way.
9 He leads the humble in what is
right,
and teaches the humble his way.

[1] Or *the valley of deep darkness* [2] Or *Only* [3] Or *steadfast love* [4] Or *shall return to dwell* [5] Hebrew *for length of days* [6] Or *and all that fills it* [7] Septuagint, Syriac, and two Hebrew manuscripts; Masoretic Text *Jacob, who seek your face* [8] This psalm is an acrostic poem, each verse beginning with the successive letters of the Hebrew alphabet

43

10 All the paths of the LORD are
steadfast love and faithfulness,
for those who keep his covenant
and his testimonies.

11 For your name's sake, O LORD,
pardon my guilt, for it is great.
12 Who is the man who fears the LORD?
Him will he instruct in the way
that he should choose.
13 His soul shall abide in well-being,
and his offspring shall inherit the
land.
14 The friendship[1] of the LORD is for
those who fear him,
and he makes known to them his
covenant.
15 My eyes are ever toward the LORD,
for he will pluck my feet out of
the net.

16 Turn to me and be gracious to me,
for I am lonely and afflicted.
17 The troubles of my heart are
enlarged;
bring me out of my distresses.
18 Consider my affliction and my
trouble,
and forgive all my sins.

19 Consider how many are my foes,
and with what violent hatred they
hate me.
20 Oh, guard my soul, and deliver me!
Let me not be put to shame, for I
take refuge in you.
21 May integrity and uprightness
preserve me,
for I wait for you.

22 Redeem Israel, O God,
out of all his troubles.

I Will Bless the LORD

26

OF DAVID.
Vindicate me, O LORD,
for I have walked in my integrity,
and I have trusted in the LORD
without wavering.
2 Prove me, O LORD, and try me;
test my heart and my mind.[2]
3 For your steadfast love is before my
eyes,
and I walk in your faithfulness.

4 I do not sit with men of falsehood,
nor do I consort with hypocrites.
5 I hate the assembly of evildoers,
and I will not sit with the wicked.

6 I wash my hands in innocence
and go around your altar, O LORD,
7 proclaiming thanksgiving aloud,
and telling all your wondrous
deeds.

8 O LORD, I love the habitation of your
house
and the place where your glory
dwells.
9 Do not sweep my soul away with
sinners,
nor my life with bloodthirsty
men,
10 in whose hands are evil devices,
and whose right hands are full of
bribes.

11 But as for me, I shall walk in my
integrity;
redeem me, and be gracious to
me.
12 My foot stands on level ground;
in the great assembly I will bless
the LORD.

The LORD Is My Light and My Salvation

467, 1191

27

OF DAVID.
The LORD is my light and
my salvation;
whom shall I fear?
The LORD is the stronghold[3] of my
life;
of whom shall I be afraid?

2 When evildoers assail me
to eat up my flesh,
my adversaries and foes,
it is they who stumble and fall.

[1] Or *The secret counsel* [2] Hebrew *test my kidneys and my heart* [3] Or *refuge*

3 Though an army encamp against me,
my heart shall not fear;
though war arise against me,
yet[1] I will be confident.

4 One thing have I asked of the LORD,
that will I seek after:
that I may dwell in the house of the LORD
all the days of my life,
to gaze upon the beauty of the LORD
and to inquire[2] in his temple.

5 For he will hide me in his shelter
in the day of trouble;
he will conceal me under the cover of his tent;
he will lift me high upon a rock.

6 And now my head shall be lifted up
above my enemies all around me,
and I will offer in his tent
sacrifices with shouts of joy;
I will sing and make melody to the LORD.

7 Hear, O LORD, when I cry aloud;
be gracious to me and answer me!
8 You have said, "Seek[3] my face."
My heart says to you,
"Your face, LORD, do I seek."[4]
9 Hide not your face from me.
Turn not your servant away in anger,
O you who have been my help.
Cast me not off; forsake me not,
O God of my salvation!
10 For my father and my mother have forsaken me,
but the LORD will take me in.

11 Teach me your way, O LORD,
and lead me on a level path
because of my enemies.
12 Give me not up to the will of my adversaries;
for false witnesses have risen against me,
and they breathe out violence.

13 I believe[5] that I shall look upon the goodness of the LORD
in the land of the living!
14 Wait for the LORD;
be strong, and let your heart take courage;
wait for the LORD!

The LORD Is My Strength and My Shield

28 OF DAVID.
To you, O LORD, I call;
my rock, be not deaf to me,
lest, if you be silent to me,
I become like those who go down to the pit.
2 Hear the voice of my pleas for mercy,
when I cry to you for help,
when I lift up my hands
toward your most holy sanctuary.[6]

3 Do not drag me off with the wicked,
with the workers of evil,
who speak peace with their neighbors
while evil is in their hearts.
4 Give to them according to their work
and according to the evil of their deeds;
give to them according to the work of their hands;
render them their due reward.
5 Because they do not regard the works of the LORD
or the work of his hands,
he will tear them down and build them up no more.

6 Blessed be the LORD!
For he has heard the voice of my pleas for mercy.
7 The LORD is my strength and my shield;
in him my heart trusts, and I am helped;
my heart exults,
and with my song I give thanks to him.

[1] Or *in this* [2] Or *meditate* [3] The command (*seek*) is addressed to more than one person [4] The meaning of the Hebrew verse is uncertain [5] Other Hebrew manuscripts *Oh! Had I not believed* [6] Hebrew *your innermost sanctuary*

8 The LORD is the strength of his people;[1]
he is the saving refuge of his anointed.
9 Oh, save your people and bless your heritage!
Be their shepherd and carry them forever.

Ascribe to the LORD Glory

29

A PSALM OF DAVID.

Ascribe to the LORD, O heavenly beings,[2]
ascribe to the LORD glory and strength.
2 Ascribe to the LORD the glory due his name;
worship the LORD in the splendor of holiness.[3]

3 The voice of the LORD is over the waters;
the God of glory thunders,
the LORD, over many waters.
4 The voice of the LORD is powerful;
the voice of the LORD is full of majesty.

5 The voice of the LORD breaks the cedars;
the LORD breaks the cedars of Lebanon.
6 He makes Lebanon to skip like a calf,
and Sirion like a young wild ox.

7 The voice of the LORD flashes forth flames of fire.
8 The voice of the LORD shakes the wilderness;
the LORD shakes the wilderness of Kadesh.

9 The voice of the LORD makes the deer give birth[4]
and strips the forests bare,
and in his temple all cry, "Glory!"

10 The LORD sits enthroned over the flood;
the LORD sits enthroned as king forever.
11 May the LORD give strength to his people!
May the LORD bless[5] his people with peace!

Joy Comes with the Morning

30

A PSALM OF DAVID. A SONG AT THE DEDICATION OF THE TEMPLE.

1 I will extol you, O LORD, for you have drawn me up
and have not let my foes rejoice over me.
2 O LORD my God, I cried to you for help,
and you have healed me.
3 O LORD, you have brought up my soul from Sheol;
you restored me to life from among those who go down to the pit.[6]

4 Sing praises to the LORD, O you his saints,
and give thanks to his holy name.[7]
5 For his anger is but for a moment,
and his favor is for a lifetime.[8]
Weeping may tarry for the night,
but joy comes with the morning.

6 As for me, I said in my prosperity,
"I shall never be moved."
7 By your favor, O LORD,
you made my mountain stand strong;
you hid your face;
I was dismayed.

8 To you, O LORD, I cry,
and to the Lord I plead for mercy:
9 "What profit is there in my death,[9]
if I go down to the pit?[10]
Will the dust praise you?
Will it tell of your faithfulness?

[1] Some Hebrew manuscripts, Septuagint, Syriac; most Hebrew manuscripts *is their strength* [2] Hebrew *sons of God, or sons of might* [3] Or *in holy attire* [4] Revocalization yields *makes the oaks to shake* [5] Or *The LORD will give . . . The LORD will bless* [6] Or *to life, that I should not go down to the pit* [7] Hebrew *to the memorial of his holiness* (see Exodus 3:15) [8] Or *and in his favor is life* [9] Hebrew *in my blood* [10] Or *to corruption*

10 Hear, O LORD, and be merciful to
me!
O LORD, be my helper!"
11 You have turned for me my
mourning into dancing;
you have loosed my sackcloth
and clothed me with gladness,
12 that my glory may sing your praise
and not be silent.
O LORD my God, I will give thanks
to you forever!

Into Your Hand I Commit My Spirit

31 TO THE CHOIRMASTER. A PSALM OF DAVID.

1 In you, O LORD, do I take refuge;
let me never be put to shame;
in your righteousness deliver me!
2 Incline your ear to me;
rescue me speedily!
Be a rock of refuge for me,
a strong fortress to save me!
3 For you are my rock and my
fortress;
and for your name's sake you lead
me and guide me;
4 you take me out of the net they have
hidden for me,
for you are my refuge.
5 Into your hand I commit my spirit;
you have redeemed me, O LORD,
faithful God.
6 I hate[1] those who pay regard to
worthless idols,
but I trust in the LORD.
7 I will rejoice and be glad in your
steadfast love,
because you have seen my
affliction;
you have known the distress of
my soul,
8 and you have not delivered me into
the hand of the enemy;
you have set my feet in a broad
place.
9 Be gracious to me, O LORD, for I am
in distress;
my eye is wasted from grief;
my soul and my body also.
10 For my life is spent with sorrow,
and my years with sighing;
my strength fails because of my
iniquity,
and my bones waste away.
11 Because of all my adversaries I have
become a reproach,
especially to my neighbors,
and an object of dread to my
acquaintances;
those who see me in the street
flee from me.
12 I have been forgotten like one who
is dead;
I have become like a broken vessel.
13 For I hear the whispering of many—
terror on every side!—
as they scheme together against me,
as they plot to take my life.
14 But I trust in you, O LORD;
I say, "You are my God."
15 My times are in your hand;
rescue me from the hand of
my enemies and from my
persecutors!
16 Make your face shine on your servant;
save me in your steadfast love!
17 O LORD, let me not be put to shame,
for I call upon you;
let the wicked be put to shame;
let them go silently to Sheol.
18 Let the lying lips be mute,
which speak insolently against
the righteous
in pride and contempt.
19 Oh, how abundant is your goodness,
which you have stored up for
those who fear you
and worked for those who take
refuge in you,
in the sight of the children of
mankind!

[1] Masoretic Text; one Hebrew manuscript, Septuagint, Syriac, Jerome *You hate*

20 In the cover of your presence you
hide them
from the plots of men;
you store them in your shelter
from the strife of tongues.

21 Blessed be the LORD,
for he has wondrously shown his
steadfast love to me
when I was in a besieged city.
22 I had said in my alarm,[1]
"I am cut off from your sight."
But you heard the voice of my pleas
for mercy
when I cried to you for help.

23 Love the LORD, all you his saints!
The LORD preserves the faithful
but abundantly repays the one
who acts in pride.
24 Be strong, and let your heart take
courage,
all you who wait for the LORD!

Blessed Are the Forgiven

507

32

A MASKIL[2] OF DAVID.

Blessed is the one whose
transgression is forgiven,
whose sin is covered.
2 Blessed is the man against whom
the LORD counts no iniquity,
and in whose spirit there is no
deceit.

3 For when I kept silent, my bones
wasted away
through my groaning all day long.
4 For day and night your hand was
heavy upon me;
my strength was dried up[3] as by
the heat of summer. *Selah*

5 I acknowledged my sin to you,
and I did not cover my iniquity;
I said, "I will confess my
transgressions to the LORD,"
and you forgave the iniquity of
my sin. *Selah*

6 Therefore let everyone who is
godly
offer prayer to you at a time when
you may be found;
surely in the rush of great waters,
they shall not reach him.
7 You are a hiding place for me;
you preserve me from trouble;
you surround me with shouts of
deliverance. *Selah*

8 I will instruct you and teach you in
the way you should go;
I will counsel you with my eye
upon you.
9 Be not like a horse or a mule,
without understanding,
which must be curbed with bit
and bridle,
or it will not stay near you.

10 Many are the sorrows of the
wicked,
but steadfast love surrounds the
one who trusts in the LORD.
11 Be glad in the LORD, and rejoice, O
righteous,
and shout for joy, all you upright
in heart!

The Steadfast Love of the LORD

33

Shout for joy in the LORD, O you
righteous!
Praise befits the upright.
2 Give thanks to the LORD with the
lyre;
make melody to him with the
harp of ten strings!
3 Sing to him a new song;
play skillfully on the strings, with
loud shouts.

4 For the word of the LORD is upright,
and all his work is done in
faithfulness.
5 He loves righteousness and justice;
the earth is full of the steadfast
love of the LORD.

[1] Or *in my haste* [2] Probably a musical or liturgical term [3] Hebrew *my vitality was changed*

6 By the word of the LORD the
heavens were made,
and by the breath of his mouth all
their host.
7 He gathers the waters of the sea as a
heap;
he puts the deeps in storehouses.

8 Let all the earth fear the LORD;
let all the inhabitants of the world
stand in awe of him!
9 For he spoke, and it came to be;
he commanded, and it stood
firm.

10 The LORD brings the counsel of the
nations to nothing;
he frustrates the plans of the
peoples.
11 The counsel of the LORD stands
forever,
the plans of his heart to all
generations.
12 Blessed is the nation whose God is
the LORD,
the people whom he has chosen
as his heritage!

13 The LORD looks down from heaven;
he sees all the children of man;
14 from where he sits enthroned he
looks out
on all the inhabitants of the earth,
15 he who fashions the hearts of them
all
and observes all their deeds.
16 The king is not saved by his great
army;
a warrior is not delivered by his
great strength.
17 The war horse is a false hope for
salvation,
and by its great might it cannot
rescue.

18 Behold, the eye of the LORD is on
those who fear him,
on those who hope in his
steadfast love,
19 that he may deliver their soul from
death
and keep them alive in famine.

20 Our soul waits for the LORD;
he is our help and our shield.
21 For our heart is glad in him,
because we trust in his holy
name.
22 Let your steadfast love, O LORD, be
upon us,
even as we hope in you.

Taste and See That the LORD Is Good

34

[1] OF DAVID, WHEN HE CHANGED HIS BEHAVIOR BEFORE ABIMELECH, SO THAT HE DROVE HIM OUT, AND HE WENT AWAY.

1 I will bless the LORD at all times;
his praise shall continually be in
my mouth.
2 My soul makes its boast in the LORD;
let the humble hear and be glad.
3 Oh, magnify the LORD with me,
and let us exalt his name
together!

4 I sought the LORD, and he answered
me
and delivered me from all my
fears.
5 Those who look to him are radiant,
and their faces shall never be
ashamed.
6 This poor man cried, and the LORD
heard him
and saved him out of all his
troubles.
7 The angel of the LORD encamps
around those who fear him, and
delivers them.

8 Oh, taste and see that the LORD is
good!
Blessed is the man who takes
refuge in him!
9 Oh, fear the LORD, you his saints,
for those who fear him have no
lack!

[1] This psalm is an acrostic poem, each verse beginning with the successive letters of the Hebrew alphabet

10 The young lions suffer want and hunger;
but those who seek the LORD lack no good thing.

11 Come, O children, listen to me;
I will teach you the fear of the LORD.
12 What man is there who desires life
and loves many days, that he may see good?
13 Keep your tongue from evil
and your lips from speaking deceit.
14 Turn away from evil and do good;
seek peace and pursue it.

15 The eyes of the LORD are toward the righteous
1191 and his ears toward their cry.
16 The face of the LORD is against those who do evil,
to cut off the memory of them from the earth.
17 When the righteous cry for help, the LORD hears
and delivers them out of all their troubles.
18 The LORD is near to the brokenhearted
and saves the crushed in spirit.

19 Many are the afflictions of the righteous,
but the LORD delivers him out of them all.
20 He keeps all his bones;
not one of them is broken.
21 Affliction will slay the wicked,
and those who hate the righteous will be condemned.
22 The LORD redeems the life of his servants;
none of those who take refuge in him will be condemned.

Great Is the LORD

35

OF DAVID.

Contend, O LORD, with those who contend with me;
fight against those who fight against me!
2 Take hold of shield and buckler
and rise for my help!
3 Draw the spear and javelin[1]
against my pursuers!
Say to my soul,
"I am your salvation!"

4 Let them be put to shame and dishonor
who seek after my life!
Let them be turned back and disappointed
who devise evil against me!
5 Let them be like chaff before the wind,
with the angel of the LORD driving them away!
6 Let their way be dark and slippery,
with the angel of the LORD pursuing them!

7 For without cause they hid their net for me;
without cause they dug a pit for my life.[2]
8 Let destruction come upon him when he does not know it!
And let the net that he hid ensnare him;
let him fall into it—to his destruction!

9 Then my soul will rejoice in the LORD,
exulting in his salvation.
10 All my bones shall say,
"O LORD, who is like you,
delivering the poor
from him who is too strong for him,
the poor and needy from him who robs him?"

11 Malicious[3] witnesses rise up;
they ask me of things that I do not know.

[1] Or *and close the way* [2] The word *pit* is transposed from the preceding line; Hebrew *For without cause they hid the pit of their net for me; without cause they dug for my life*
[3] Or *Violent*

12 They repay me evil for good;
my soul is bereft.[1]
13 But I, when they were sick—
I wore sackcloth;
I afflicted myself with fasting;
I prayed with head bowed[2] on my chest.
14 I went about as though I grieved for my friend or my brother;
as one who laments his mother,
I bowed down in mourning.

15 But at my stumbling they rejoiced and gathered;
they gathered together against me;
wretches whom I did not know
tore at me without ceasing;
16 like profane mockers at a feast,[3]
they gnash at me with their teeth.

17 How long, O Lord, will you look on?
Rescue me from their destruction,
my precious life from the lions!
18 I will thank you in the great congregation;
in the mighty throng I will praise you.

19 Let not those rejoice over me
who are wrongfully my foes,
and let not those wink the eye
who hate me without cause.
20 For they do not speak peace,
but against those who are quiet in the land
they devise words of deceit.
21 They open wide their mouths against me;
they say, "Aha, Aha!
Our eyes have seen it!"

22 You have seen, O LORD; be not silent!
O Lord, be not far from me!
23 Awake and rouse yourself for my vindication,
for my cause, my God and my Lord!
24 Vindicate me, O LORD, my God,
according to your righteousness,
and let them not rejoice over me!
25 Let them not say in their hearts,
"Aha, our heart's desire!"
Let them not say, "We have swallowed him up."

26 Let them be put to shame and disappointed altogether
who rejoice at my calamity!
Let them be clothed with shame and dishonor
who magnify themselves against me!

27 Let those who delight in my righteousness
shout for joy and be glad
and say evermore,
"Great is the LORD,
who delights in the welfare of his servant!"
28 Then my tongue shall tell of your righteousness
and of your praise all the day long.

How Precious Is Your Steadfast Love

36

TO THE CHOIRMASTER. OF DAVID, THE SERVANT OF THE LORD.

1 Transgression speaks to the wicked deep in his heart;[4]
there is no fear of God
before his eyes.
2 For he flatters himself in his own eyes
that his iniquity cannot be found out and hated.
3 The words of his mouth are trouble and deceit;
he has ceased to act wisely and do good.
4 He plots trouble while on his bed;
he sets himself in a way that is not good;
he does not reject evil.

[1] Hebrew *it is bereavement to my soul* [2] Or *my prayer shall turn back* [3] The meaning of the Hebrew phrase is uncertain [4] Some Hebrew manuscripts, Syriac, Jerome (compare Septuagint); most Hebrew manuscripts *in my heart*

5 Your steadfast love, O LORD, extends
to the heavens,
your faithfulness to the clouds.
6 Your righteousness is like the
mountains of God;
your judgments are like the great
deep;
man and beast you save, O LORD.

7 How precious is your steadfast love,
O God!
The children of mankind take
refuge in the shadow of your
wings.
8 They feast on the abundance of
your house,
and you give them drink from the
river of your delights.
9 For with you is the fountain of life;
in your light do we see light.

10 Oh, continue your steadfast love to
those who know you,
and your righteousness to the
upright of heart!
11 Let not the foot of arrogance come
upon me,
nor the hand of the wicked drive
me away.
12 There the evildoers lie fallen;
they are thrust down, unable to
rise.

He Will Not Forsake His Saints

37 [1] Of David.
Fret not yourself because of
evildoers;
be not envious of wrongdoers!
2 For they will soon fade like the
grass
and wither like the green herb.

3 Trust in the LORD, and do good;
dwell in the land and befriend
faithfulness.[2]
4 Delight yourself in the LORD,
and he will give you the desires of
your heart.

5 Commit your way to the LORD;
trust in him, and he will act.
101 6 He will bring forth your
righteousness as the light,
and your justice as the noonday.

7 Be still before the LORD and wait
patiently for him;
fret not yourself over the one who
prospers in his way,
over the man who carries out evil
devices!

8 Refrain from anger, and forsake
wrath!
Fret not yourself; it tends only to
evil.
9 For the evildoers shall be cut off,
but those who wait for the LORD
shall inherit the land.

10 In just a little while, the wicked will
be no more;
though you look carefully at his
place, he will not be there.
11 But the meek shall inherit the land
and delight themselves in
abundant peace.

12 The wicked plots against the
righteous
and gnashes his teeth at him,
13 but the Lord laughs at the wicked,
for he sees that his day is coming.

14 The wicked draw the sword and
bend their bows
to bring down the poor and
needy,
to slay those whose way is
upright;
15 their sword shall enter their own
heart,
and their bows shall be broken.

16 Better is the little that the righteous
has
than the abundance of many
wicked.

[1] This psalm is an acrostic poem, each stanza beginning with the successive letters of the Hebrew alphabet [2] Or *and feed on faithfulness*, or *and find safe pasture*

17 For the arms of the wicked shall be broken,
but the LORD upholds the righteous.

18 The LORD knows the days of the blameless,
and their heritage will remain forever;
19 they are not put to shame in evil times;
in the days of famine they have abundance.

20 But the wicked will perish;
the enemies of the LORD are like the glory of the pastures;
they vanish—like smoke they vanish away.

21 The wicked borrows but does not pay back,
but the righteous is generous and gives;
22 for those blessed by the LORD[1] shall inherit the land,
but those cursed by him shall be cut off.

23 The steps of a man are established by the LORD,
when he delights in his way;
24 though he fall, he shall not be cast headlong,
for the LORD upholds his hand.

25 I have been young, and now am old,
yet I have not seen the righteous forsaken
or his children begging for bread.
26 He is ever lending generously,
and his children become a blessing.

27 Turn away from evil and do good;
so shall you dwell forever.
28 For the LORD loves justice;
he will not forsake his saints.
They are preserved forever,
but the children of the wicked shall be cut off.
29 The righteous shall inherit the land
and dwell upon it forever.

30 The mouth of the righteous utters wisdom,
and his tongue speaks justice.
31 The law of his God is in his heart;
his steps do not slip.

32 The wicked watches for the righteous
and seeks to put him to death.
33 The LORD will not abandon him to his power
or let him be condemned when he is brought to trial.

34 Wait for the LORD and keep his way,
and he will exalt you to inherit the land;
you will look on when the wicked are cut off.

35 I have seen a wicked, ruthless man,
spreading himself like a green laurel tree.[2]
36 But he passed away,[3] and behold, he was no more;
though I sought him, he could not be found.

37 Mark the blameless and behold the upright,
for there is a future for the man of peace.
38 But transgressors shall be altogether destroyed;
the future of the wicked shall be cut off.

101
39 The salvation of the righteous is from the LORD;
he is their stronghold in the time of trouble.
40 The LORD helps them and delivers them;
he delivers them from the wicked and saves them,
because they take refuge in him.

[1] Hebrew *by him* [2] The identity of this tree is uncertain [3] Or *But one passed by*

Do Not Forsake Me, O Lord

38

A PSALM OF DAVID, FOR THE MEMORIAL OFFERING.

1 O LORD, rebuke me not in your anger,
nor discipline me in your wrath!
2 For your arrows have sunk into me,
and your hand has come down on me.

3 There is no soundness in my flesh
because of your indignation;
there is no health in my bones
because of my sin.
4 For my iniquities have gone over my head;
like a heavy burden, they are too heavy for me.

5 My wounds stink and fester
because of my foolishness,
6 I am utterly bowed down and prostrate;
all the day I go about mourning.
7 For my sides are filled with burning,
and there is no soundness in my flesh.
8 I am feeble and crushed;
I groan because of the tumult of my heart.

9 O Lord, all my longing is before you;
my sighing is not hidden from you.
10 My heart throbs; my strength fails me,
and the light of my eyes—it also has gone from me.
11 My friends and companions stand aloof from my plague,
and my nearest kin stand far off.

12 Those who seek my life lay their snares;
those who seek my hurt speak of ruin
and meditate treachery all day long.

13 But I am like a deaf man; I do not hear,
like a mute man who does not open his mouth.
14 I have become like a man who does not hear,
and in whose mouth are no rebukes.

15 But for you, O LORD, do I wait;
it is you, O Lord my God, who will answer.
16 For I said, "Only let them not rejoice over me,
who boast against me when my foot slips!"

17 For I am ready to fall,
and my pain is ever before me.
18 I confess my iniquity;
I am sorry for my sin.
19 But my foes are vigorous, they are mighty,
and many are those who hate me wrongfully.
20 Those who render me evil for good
accuse me because I follow after good.

21 Do not forsake me, O LORD!
O my God, be not far from me!
22 Make haste to help me,
O Lord, my salvation!

What Is the Measure of My Days?

39

TO THE CHOIRMASTER: TO JEDUTHUN. A PSALM OF DAVID.

1 I said, "I will guard my ways,
that I may not sin with my tongue;
I will guard my mouth with a muzzle,
so long as the wicked are in my presence."
2 I was mute and silent;
I held my peace to no avail,
and my distress grew worse.
3 My heart became hot within me.
As I mused, the fire burned;
then I spoke with my tongue:

4 "O LORD, make me know my end
and what is the measure of my days;
let me know how fleeting I am!
5 Behold, you have made my days a few handbreadths,
and my lifetime is as nothing before you.
Surely all mankind stands as a mere breath! *Selah*
6 Surely a man goes about as a shadow!
Surely for nothing[1] they are in turmoil;
man heaps up wealth and does not know who will gather!

7 "And now, O Lord, for what do I wait?
My hope is in you.
8 Deliver me from all my transgressions.
Do not make me the scorn of the fool!
9 I am mute; I do not open my mouth,
for it is you who have done it.
10 Remove your stroke from me;
I am spent by the hostility of your hand.
11 When you discipline a man
with rebukes for sin,
you consume like a moth what is dear to him;
surely all mankind is a mere breath! *Selah*

12 "Hear my prayer, O LORD,
and give ear to my cry;
hold not your peace at my tears!
For I am a sojourner with you,
a guest, like all my fathers.
13 Look away from me, that I may smile again,
before I depart and am no more!"

My Help and My Deliverer

40 TO THE CHOIRMASTER. A PSALM OF DAVID.
I waited patiently for the LORD;
he inclined to me and heard my cry.
2 He drew me up from the pit of destruction,
out of the miry bog,
and set my feet upon a rock,
making my steps secure.
3 He put a new song in my mouth,
a song of praise to our God.
Many will see and fear,
and put their trust in the LORD.

4 Blessed is the man who makes the LORD his trust,
who does not turn to the proud,
to those who go astray after a lie!
5 You have multiplied, O LORD my God,
your wondrous deeds and your thoughts toward us;
none can compare with you!
I will proclaim and tell of them,
yet they are more than can be told.

6 In sacrifice and offering you have not delighted,
but you have given me an open ear.[2]
Burnt offering and sin offering
you have not required.
7 Then I said, "Behold, I have come;
in the scroll of the book it is written of me:
8 I delight to do your will, O my God;
your law is within my heart."

9 I have told the glad news of deliverance[3]
in the great congregation;
behold, I have not restrained my lips,
as you know, O LORD.
10 I have not hidden your deliverance within my heart;
I have spoken of your faithfulness and your salvation;
I have not concealed your steadfast love and your faithfulness
from the great congregation.

[1] Hebrew *Surely as a breath* [2] Hebrew *ears you have dug for me* [3] Hebrew *righteousness*; also verse 10

11 As for you, O LORD, you will not
restrain
your mercy from me;
your steadfast love and your
faithfulness will
ever preserve me!
12 For evils have encompassed me
beyond number;
my iniquities have overtaken me,
and I cannot see;
they are more than the hairs of my
head;
my heart fails me.

13 Be pleased, O LORD, to deliver me!
O LORD, make haste to help me!
14 Let those be put to shame and
disappointed altogether
who seek to snatch away my life;
let those be turned back and
brought to dishonor
who delight in my hurt!
15 Let those be appalled because of
their shame
who say to me, "Aha, Aha!"

16 But may all who seek you
rejoice and be glad in you;
may those who love your salvation
say continually, "Great is the
LORD!"
17 As for me, I am poor and needy,
but the Lord takes thought for me.
You are my help and my deliverer;
do not delay, O my God!

O LORD, Be Gracious to Me

41

TO THE CHOIRMASTER. A PSALM OF DAVID.

1 Blessed is the one who considers
the poor![1]
In the day of trouble the LORD
delivers him;
2 the LORD protects him and keeps
him alive;
he is called blessed in the land;
you do not give him up to the will
of his enemies.
3 The LORD sustains him on his
sickbed;
in his illness you restore him to
full health.[2]

4 As for me, I said, "O LORD, be
gracious to me;
heal me,[3] for I have sinned
against you!"
5 My enemies say of me in malice,
"When will he die, and his name
perish?"
6 And when one comes to see me, he
utters empty words,
while his heart gathers iniquity;
when he goes out, he tells it
abroad.
7 All who hate me whisper together
about me;
they imagine the worst for me.[4]

8 They say, "A deadly thing is poured
out[5] on him;
he will not rise again from where
he lies."
9 Even my close friend in whom I
trusted,
who ate my bread, has lifted his
heel against me.
10 But you, O LORD, be gracious to
me,
and raise me up, that I may repay
them!

11 By this I know that you delight in
me:
my enemy will not shout in
triumph over me.
12 But you have upheld me because of
my integrity,
and set me in your presence
forever.

13 Blessed be the LORD, the God of
Israel,
from everlasting to everlasting!
Amen and Amen.

[1] Or *weak* [2] Hebrew *you turn all his bed* [3] Hebrew *my soul* [4] Or *they devise evil against me* [5] Or *has fastened*

BOOK TWO

Why Are You Cast Down, O My Soul?

42

TO THE CHOIRMASTER. A MASKIL[1] OF THE SONS OF KORAH.

1 As a deer pants for flowing
streams,
so pants my soul for you, O God.
2 My soul thirsts for God,
for the living God.
When shall I come and appear
before God?[2]
3 My tears have been my food
day and night,
while they say to me all the day
long,
"Where is your God?"
4 These things I remember,
as I pour out my soul:
how I would go with the throng
and lead them in procession to
the house of God
with glad shouts and songs of
praise,
a multitude keeping festival.

5 Why are you cast down, O my soul,
and why are you in turmoil
within me?
Hope in God; for I shall again praise
him,
my salvation[3] 6 and my God.

My soul is cast down within me;
therefore I remember you
from the land of Jordan and of
Hermon,
from Mount Mizar.
7 Deep calls to deep
at the roar of your waterfalls;
all your breakers and your waves
have gone over me.
8 By day the LORD commands his
steadfast love,
and at night his song is with me,
a prayer to the God of my life.

9 I say to God, my rock:
"Why have you forgotten me?
Why do I go mourning
because of the oppression of the
enemy?"
10 As with a deadly wound in my
bones,
my adversaries taunt me,
while they say to me all the day
long,
"Where is your God?"

11 Why are you cast down, O my soul,
and why are you in turmoil
within me?
Hope in God; for I shall again praise
him,
my salvation and my God.

Send Out Your Light and Your Truth

43

Vindicate me, O God, and defend
my cause
against an ungodly people,
from the deceitful and unjust man
deliver me!
2 For you are the God in whom I take
refuge;
why have you rejected me?
Why do I go about mourning
because of the oppression of the
enemy?

3 Send out your light and your truth;
let them lead me;
let them bring me to your holy hill
and to your dwelling!
4 Then I will go to the altar of God,
to God my exceeding joy,
and I will praise you with the lyre,
O God, my God.

5 Why are you cast down, O my soul,
and why are you in turmoil
within me?
Hope in God; for I shall again praise
him,
my salvation and my God.

[1] Probably a musical or liturgical term [2] Revocalization yields *and see the face of God* [3] Hebrew *the salvation of my face*; also verse 11 and 43:5

Come to Our Help

44

To the choirmaster. A Maskil[1] of the Sons of Korah.

1 O God, we have heard with our ears,
our fathers have told us,
what deeds you performed in their days,
in the days of old:
2 you with your own hand drove out the nations,
but them you planted;
you afflicted the peoples,
but them you set free;
3 for not by their own sword did they win the land,
nor did their own arm save them,
but your right hand and your arm,
and the light of your face,
for you delighted in them.

4 You are my King, O God;
ordain salvation for Jacob!
5 Through you we push down our foes;
through your name we tread down those who rise up against us.
6 For not in my bow do I trust,
nor can my sword save me.
7 But you have saved us from our foes
and have put to shame those who hate us.
8 In God we have boasted continually,
and we will give thanks to your name forever. *Selah*

9 But you have rejected us and disgraced us
and have not gone out with our armies.
10 You have made us turn back from the foe,
and those who hate us have gotten spoil.
11 You have made us like sheep for slaughter
and have scattered us among the nations.
12 You have sold your people for a trifle,
demanding no high price for them.
13 You have made us the taunt of our neighbors,
the derision and scorn of those around us.
14 You have made us a byword among the nations,
a laughingstock[2] among the peoples.
15 All day long my disgrace is before me,
and shame has covered my face
16 at the sound of the taunter and reviler,
at the sight of the enemy and the avenger.

17 All this has come upon us,
though we have not forgotten you,
and we have not been false to your covenant.
18 Our heart has not turned back,
nor have our steps departed from your way;
19 yet you have broken us in the place of jackals
and covered us with the shadow of death.
20 If we had forgotten the name of our God
or spread out our hands to a foreign god,
21 would not God discover this?
For he knows the secrets of the heart.
22 Yet for your sake we are killed all the day long;
we are regarded as sheep to be slaughtered.

23 Awake! Why are you sleeping, O Lord?
Rouse yourself! Do not reject us forever!
24 Why do you hide your face?
Why do you forget our affliction and oppression?

[1] Probably a musical or liturgical term [2] Hebrew *a shaking of the head*

25 For our soul is bowed down to the dust;
our belly clings to the ground.
26 Rise up; come to our help!
Redeem us for the sake of your steadfast love!

Your Throne, O God, Is Forever

45

TO THE CHOIRMASTER: ACCORDING TO LILIES. A MASKIL[1] OF THE SONS OF KORAH; A LOVE SONG.

1 My heart overflows with a pleasing theme;
I address my verses to the king;
my tongue is like the pen of a ready scribe.

2 You are the most handsome of the sons of men;
grace is poured upon your lips;
therefore God has blessed you forever.
3 Gird your sword on your thigh, O mighty one,
in your splendor and majesty!

4 In your majesty ride out victoriously
for the cause of truth and meekness and righteousness;
let your right hand teach you awesome deeds!
5 Your arrows are sharp
in the heart of the king's enemies;
the peoples fall under you.

6 Your throne, O God, is forever and ever.
The scepter of your kingdom is a scepter of uprightness;
7 you have loved righteousness and hated wickedness.
Therefore God, your God, has anointed you
with the oil of gladness beyond your companions;
8 your robes are all fragrant with myrrh and aloes and cassia.
From ivory palaces stringed instruments make you glad;
9 daughters of kings are among your ladies of honor;
at your right hand stands the queen in gold of Ophir.

10 Hear, O daughter, and consider, and incline your ear:
forget your people and your father's house,
11 and the king will desire your beauty.
Since he is your lord, bow to him.
12 The people[2] of Tyre will seek your favor with gifts,
the richest of the people.[3]

13 All glorious is the princess in her chamber, with robes interwoven with gold.
14 In many-colored robes she is led to the king,
with her virgin companions following behind her.
15 With joy and gladness they are led along
as they enter the palace of the king.

16 In place of your fathers shall be your sons;
you will make them princes in all the earth.
17 I will cause your name to be remembered in all generations;
therefore nations will praise you forever and ever.

God Is Our Fortress

46

TO THE CHOIRMASTER. OF THE SONS OF KORAH. ACCORDING TO ALAMOTH.[4] A SONG.

1 God is our refuge and strength,
a very present[5] help in trouble.

[1] Probably a musical or liturgical term [2] Hebrew *daughter* [3] Or *The daughter of Tyre is here with gifts, the richest of people seek your favor* [4] Probably a musical or liturgical term [5] Or *well proved*

2 Therefore we will not fear though
the earth gives way,
though the mountains be moved
into the heart of the sea,
3 though its waters roar and foam,
though the mountains tremble at
its swelling. *Selah*
4 There is a river whose streams make
glad the city of God,
the holy habitation of the Most
High.
5 God is in the midst of her; she shall
not be moved;
God will help her when morning
dawns.
6 The nations rage, the kingdoms
totter;
he utters his voice, the earth melts.
7 The LORD of hosts is with us;
the God of Jacob is our fortress.
Selah

8 Come, behold the works of the LORD,
how he has brought desolations
on the earth.
9 He makes wars cease to the end of
the earth;
he breaks the bow and shatters
the spear;
he burns the chariots with fire.
10 "Be still, and know that I am God.
I will be exalted among the
nations,
I will be exalted in the earth!"
11 The LORD of hosts is with us;
the God of Jacob is our fortress.
Selah

God Is King over All the Earth

47

TO THE CHOIRMASTER. A PSALM OF THE SONS OF KORAH.

1 Clap your hands, all peoples!
Shout to God with loud songs of
joy!
2 For the LORD, the Most High, is to be
feared,
a great king over all the earth.
3 He subdued peoples under us,
and nations under our feet.
4 He chose our heritage for us,
the pride of Jacob whom he loves.
Selah

5 God has gone up with a shout,
the LORD with the sound of a
trumpet.
6 Sing praises to God, sing praises!
Sing praises to our King, sing
praises!
7 For God is the King of all the earth;
sing praises with a psalm![1]
8 God reigns over the nations;
God sits on his holy throne.
9 The princes of the peoples gather
as the people of the God of
Abraham.
For the shields of the earth belong
to God;
he is highly exalted!

Zion, the City of Our God

48

A SONG. A PSALM OF THE SONS OF KORAH.

Great is the LORD and greatly to
be praised
in the city of our God!
His holy mountain, 2 beautiful in
elevation,
is the joy of all the earth,
Mount Zion, in the far north,
the city of the great King.
3 Within her citadels God
has made himself known as a
fortress.

4 For behold, the kings assembled;
they came on together.
5 As soon as they saw it, they were
astounded;
they were in panic; they took to
flight.
6 Trembling took hold of them there,
anguish as of a woman in labor.
7 By the east wind you shattered
the ships of Tarshish.

[1] Hebrew *maskil*

8 As we have heard, so have we seen
in the city of the LORD of hosts,
in the city of our God,
which God will establish forever.
Selah

9 We have thought on your steadfast
love, O God,
in the midst of your temple.
10 As your name, O God,
so your praise reaches to the ends
of the earth.
Your right hand is filled with
righteousness.
11 Let Mount Zion be glad!
Let the daughters of Judah rejoice
because of your judgments!

12 Walk about Zion, go around her,
number her towers,
13 consider well her ramparts,
go through her citadels,
that you may tell the next generation
14 that this is God,
our God forever and ever.
He will guide us forever.[1]

Why Should I Fear in Times of Trouble?

49

TO THE CHOIRMASTER. A PSALM OF THE SONS OF KORAH.

1 Hear this, all peoples!
Give ear, all inhabitants of the
world,
2 both low and high,
rich and poor together!
3 My mouth shall speak wisdom;
the meditation of my heart shall
be understanding.
4 I will incline my ear to a proverb;
I will solve my riddle to the music
of the lyre.

5 Why should I fear in times of trouble,
when the iniquity of those who
cheat me surrounds me,
6 those who trust in their wealth
and boast of the abundance of
their riches?
7 Truly no man can ransom another,
or give to God the price of his life,
8 for the ransom of their life is costly
and can never suffice,
9 that he should live on forever
and never see the pit.

10 For he sees that even the wise die;
the fool and the stupid alike must
perish
and leave their wealth to others.
11 Their graves are their homes
forever,[2]
their dwelling places to all
generations,
though they called lands by their
own names.
12 Man in his pomp will not remain;
he is like the beasts that perish.

13 This is the path of those who have
foolish confidence;
yet after them people approve of
their boasts.[3] *Selah*
14 Like sheep they are appointed for
Sheol;
death shall be their shepherd,
and the upright shall rule over them
in the morning.
Their form shall be consumed in
Sheol, with no place to dwell.
15 But God will ransom my soul from
the power of Sheol,
for he will receive me. *Selah*

16 Be not afraid when a man becomes
rich,
when the glory of his house
increases.
17 For when he dies he will carry
nothing away;
his glory will not go down after
him.
18 For though, while he lives, he
counts himself blessed
—and though you get praise when
you do well for yourself—

[1] Septuagint; another reading is (compare Jerome, Syriac) *He will guide us beyond death* [2] Septuagint, Syriac, Targum; Hebrew *Their inward thought was that their homes were forever* [3] Or *and of those after them who approve of their boasts*

19 his soul will go to the generation of his fathers,
who will never again see light.
20 Man in his pomp yet without understanding is like the beasts that perish.

God Himself Is Judge

50

A Psalm of Asaph.

The Mighty One, God the Lord,
speaks and summons the earth
from the rising of the sun to its setting.
2 Out of Zion, the perfection of beauty,
God shines forth.

3 Our God comes; he does not keep silence;[1]
before him is a devouring fire,
around him a mighty tempest.
4 He calls to the heavens above
and to the earth, that he may judge his people:
5 "Gather to me my faithful ones,
who made a covenant with me by sacrifice!"
6 The heavens declare his righteousness,
for God himself is judge! *Selah*

7 "Hear, O my people, and I will speak;
O Israel, I will testify against you.
I am God, your God.
8 Not for your sacrifices do I rebuke you;
your burnt offerings are continually before me.
9 I will not accept a bull from your house
or goats from your folds.
10 For every beast of the forest is mine,
the cattle on a thousand hills.
11 I know all the birds of the hills,
and all that moves in the field is mine.

12 "If I were hungry, I would not tell you,
for the world and its fullness are mine.
13 Do I eat the flesh of bulls
or drink the blood of goats?
14 Offer to God a sacrifice of thanksgiving,[2]
and perform your vows to the Most High,
15 and call upon me in the day of trouble;
I will deliver you, and you shall glorify me."

16 But to the wicked God says:
"What right have you to recite my statutes
or take my covenant on your lips?
17 For you hate discipline,
and you cast my words behind you.
18 If you see a thief, you are pleased with him,
and you keep company with adulterers.

19 "You give your mouth free rein for evil,
and your tongue frames deceit.
20 You sit and speak against your brother;
you slander your own mother's son.
21 These things you have done, and I have been silent;
you thought that I[3] was one like yourself.
But now I rebuke you and lay the charge before you.

22 "Mark this, then, you who forget God,
lest I tear you apart, and there be none to deliver!
23 The one who offers thanksgiving as his sacrifice glorifies me;
to one who orders his way rightly
I will show the salvation of God!"

[1] Or *May our God come, and not keep silence* [2] Or *Make thanksgiving your sacrifice to God* [3] Or *that the I AM*

Create in Me a Clean Heart, O God

51

507

TO THE CHOIRMASTER. A PSALM OF DAVID, WHEN NATHAN THE PROPHET WENT TO HIM, AFTER HE HAD GONE IN TO BATHSHEBA.

1 Have mercy on me,[1] O God,
according to your steadfast love;
according to your abundant mercy
blot out my transgressions.
2 Wash me thoroughly from my iniquity,
and cleanse me from my sin!
3 For I know my transgressions,
and my sin is ever before me.
4 Against you, you only, have I sinned
and done what is evil in your sight,
so that you may be justified in your words
and blameless in your judgment.
5 Behold, I was brought forth in iniquity,
and in sin did my mother conceive me.
6 Behold, you delight in truth in the inward being,
and you teach me wisdom in the secret heart.
7 Purge me with hyssop, and I shall be clean;
wash me, and I shall be whiter than snow.
8 Let me hear joy and gladness;
let the bones that you have broken rejoice.
9 Hide your face from my sins,
and blot out all my iniquities.
10 Create in me a clean heart, O God,
and renew a right[2] spirit within me.
11 Cast me not away from your presence,
and take not your Holy Spirit from me.
12 Restore to me the joy of your salvation,
and uphold me with a willing spirit.
13 Then I will teach transgressors your ways,
and sinners will return to you.
14 Deliver me from bloodguiltiness, O God,
O God of my salvation,
and my tongue will sing aloud of your righteousness.
15 O Lord, open my lips,
and my mouth will declare your praise.
16 For you will not delight in sacrifice, or I would give it;
you will not be pleased with a burnt offering.
17 The sacrifices of God are a broken spirit;
a broken and contrite heart, O God, you will not despise.
18 Do good to Zion in your good pleasure;
build up the walls of Jerusalem;
19 then will you delight in right sacrifices,
in burnt offerings and whole burnt offerings;
then bulls will be offered on your altar.

The Steadfast Love of God Endures

52

TO THE CHOIRMASTER. A MASKIL[3] OF DAVID, WHEN DOEG, THE EDOMITE, CAME AND TOLD SAUL, "DAVID HAS COME TO THE HOUSE OF AHIMELECH."

1 Why do you boast of evil, O mighty man?
The steadfast love of God endures all the day.
2 Your tongue plots destruction,
like a sharp razor, you worker of deceit.

[1] Or *Be gracious to me* [2] Or *steadfast* [3] Probably a musical or liturgical term

3 You love evil more than good,
and lying more than speaking
what is right. *Selah*
4 You love all words that devour,
O deceitful tongue.
5 But God will break you down
forever;
he will snatch and tear you from
your tent;
he will uproot you from the land
of the living. *Selah*
6 The righteous shall see and fear,
and shall laugh at him, saying,
7 "See the man who would not make
God his refuge,
but trusted in the abundance of his
riches
and sought refuge in his own
destruction!"[1]
8 But I am like a green olive tree
in the house of God.
I trust in the steadfast love of God
forever and ever.
9 I will thank you forever,
because you have done it.
I will wait for your name, for it is
good,
in the presence of the godly.

There Is None Who Does Good

53 To the choirmaster: according to Mahalath. A Maskil[2] of David.

1 The fool says in his heart, "There is
no God."
They are corrupt, doing
abominable iniquity;
there is none who does good.
2 God looks down from heaven
on the children of man
to see if there are any who
understand,[3]
who seek after God.
3 They have all fallen away;
together they have become
corrupt;
there is none who does good,
not even one.
4 Have those who work evil no
knowledge,
who eat up my people as they eat
bread,
and do not call upon God?
5 There they are, in great terror,
where there is no terror!
For God scatters the bones of him
who encamps against you;
you put them to shame, for God
has rejected them.
6 Oh, that salvation for Israel would
come out of Zion!
When God restores the fortunes
of his people,
let Jacob rejoice, let Israel be glad.

The Lord Upholds My Life

54 To the choirmaster: with stringed instruments. A Maskil[4] of David, when the Ziphites went and told Saul, "Is not David hiding among us?"

1 O God, save me by your name,
and vindicate me by your might.
2 O God, hear my prayer;
give ear to the words of my
mouth.
3 For strangers[5] have risen against
me;
ruthless men seek my life;
they do not set God before
themselves. *Selah*
4 Behold, God is my helper;
the Lord is the upholder of my
life.
5 He will return the evil to my
enemies;
in your faithfulness put an end to
them.

[1] Or *in his work of destruction* [2] Probably musical or liturgical terms [3] Or *who act wisely* [4] Probably a musical or liturgical term [5] Some Hebrew manuscripts and Targum *insolent men* (compare Psalm 86:14)

6 With a freewill offering I will
sacrifice to you;
I will give thanks to your name,
O LORD, for it is good.
7 For he has delivered me from every
trouble,
and my eye has looked in triumph
on my enemies.

Cast Your Burden on the LORD

55

TO THE CHOIRMASTER: WITH STRINGED INSTRUMENTS. A MASKIL[1] OF DAVID.

1 Give ear to my prayer, O God,
and hide not yourself from my
plea for mercy!
2 Attend to me, and answer me;
I am restless in my complaint and
I moan,
3 because of the noise of the enemy,
because of the oppression of the
wicked.
For they drop trouble upon me,
and in anger they bear a grudge
against me.

4 My heart is in anguish within me;
the terrors of death have fallen
upon me.
5 Fear and trembling come upon me,
and horror overwhelms me.
6 And I say, "Oh, that I had wings like
a dove!
I would fly away and be at rest;
7 yes, I would wander far away;
I would lodge in the wilderness;
Selah
8 I would hurry to find a shelter
from the raging wind and tempest."

9 Destroy, O Lord, divide their tongues;
for I see violence and strife in the
city.
10 Day and night they go around it
on its walls,
and iniquity and trouble are within it;
11 ruin is in its midst;
oppression and fraud
do not depart from its marketplace.

12 For it is not an enemy who taunts
me—
then I could bear it;
it is not an adversary who deals
insolently with me—
then I could hide from him.
13 But it is you, a man, my equal,
my companion, my familiar friend.
14 We used to take sweet counsel
together;
within God's house we walked in
the throng.
15 Let death steal over them;
let them go down to Sheol alive;
for evil is in their dwelling place
and in their heart.

16 But I call to God,
and the LORD will save me.
17 Evening and morning and at noon
I utter my complaint and moan,
and he hears my voice.
18 He redeems my soul in safety
from the battle that I wage,
for many are arrayed against me.
19 God will give ear and humble them,
he who is enthroned from of old,
Selah
because they do not change
and do not fear God.

20 My companion[2] stretched out his
hand against his friends;
he violated his covenant.
21 His speech was smooth as butter,
yet war was in his heart;
his words were softer than oil,
yet they were drawn swords.

22 Cast your burden on the LORD,
and he will sustain you;
he will never permit
the righteous to be moved.

23 But you, O God, will cast them down
into the pit of destruction;
men of blood and treachery
shall not live out half their days.
But I will trust in you.

[1] Probably a musical or liturgical term [2] Hebrew *He*

In God I Trust

56

To the choirmaster: according to The Dove on Far-off Terebinths. A Miktam[1] of David, when the Philistines seized him in Gath.

1 Be gracious to me, O God, for man
tramples on me;
all day long an attacker
oppresses me;
2 my enemies trample on me all day
long,
for many attack me proudly.
3 When I am afraid,
I put my trust in you.
4 In God, whose word I praise,
in God I trust; I shall not be afraid.
What can flesh do to me?

5 All day long they injure my cause;[2]
all their thoughts are against me
for evil.
6 They stir up strife, they lurk;
they watch my steps,
as they have waited for my life.
7 For their crime will they escape?
In wrath cast down the peoples,
O God!

8 You have kept count of my tossings;[3]
put my tears in your bottle.
Are they not in your book?
9 Then my enemies will turn back
in the day when I call.
This I know, that[4] God is for me.
10 In God, whose word I praise,
in the LORD, whose word I praise,
11 in God I trust; I shall not be afraid.
What can man do to me?

12 I must perform my vows to you,
O God;
I will render thank offerings to you.
13 For you have delivered my soul
from death,
yes, my feet from falling,
that I may walk before God
in the light of life.

Let Your Glory Be over All the Earth

57

To the choirmaster: according to Do Not Destroy. A Miktam[5] of David, when he fled from Saul, in the cave.

1 Be merciful to me, O God, be
merciful to me,
for in you my soul takes refuge;
in the shadow of your wings I will
take refuge,
till the storms of destruction
pass by.
2 I cry out to God Most High,
to God who fulfills his purpose
for me.
3 He will send from heaven and save
me;
he will put to shame him who
tramples on me. *Selah*
God will send out his steadfast love
and his faithfulness!

4 My soul is in the midst of lions;
I lie down amid fiery beasts—
the children of man, whose teeth
are spears and arrows,
whose tongues are sharp swords.

5 Be exalted, O God, above the
heavens!
Let your glory be over all the
earth!

6 They set a net for my steps;
my soul was bowed down.
They dug a pit in my way,
but they have fallen into it
themselves. *Selah*
7 My heart is steadfast, O God,
my heart is steadfast!
I will sing and make melody!
8 Awake, my glory![6]
Awake, O harp and lyre!
I will awake the dawn!
9 I will give thanks to you, O Lord,
among the peoples;
I will sing praises to you among
the nations.

[1] Probably a musical or liturgical term [2] Or *they twist my words* [3] Or *wanderings* [4] Or *because* [5] Probably a musical or liturgical term [6] Or *my whole being*

10 For your steadfast love is great to
the heavens,
your faithfulness to the clouds.

11 Be exalted, O God, above the heavens!
Let your glory be over all the
earth!

God Who Judges the Earth

58

TO THE CHOIRMASTER: ACCORDING TO DO NOT DESTROY. A MIKTAM[1] OF DAVID.

1 Do you indeed decree what is right,
you gods?[2]
Do you judge the children of man
uprightly?
2 No, in your hearts you devise
wrongs;
your hands deal out violence on
earth.
3 The wicked are estranged from the
womb;
they go astray from birth,
speaking lies.
4 They have venom like the venom of
a serpent,
like the deaf adder that stops its
ear,
5 so that it does not hear the voice of
charmers
or of the cunning enchanter.

6 O God, break the teeth in their
mouths;
tear out the fangs of the young
lions, O LORD!
7 Let them vanish like water that runs
away;
when he aims his arrows, let
them be blunted.
8 Let them be like the snail that
dissolves into slime,
like the stillborn child who never
sees the sun.
9 Sooner than your pots can feel the
heat of thorns,
whether green or ablaze, may he
sweep them away![3]

10 The righteous will rejoice when he
sees the vengeance;
he will bathe his feet in the blood
of the wicked.
11 Mankind will say, "Surely there is a
reward for the righteous;
surely there is a God who judges
on earth."

Deliver Me from My Enemies

59

TO THE CHOIRMASTER: ACCORDING TO DO NOT DESTROY. A MIKTAM[4] OF DAVID, WHEN SAUL SENT MEN TO WATCH HIS HOUSE IN ORDER TO KILL HIM.

1 Deliver me from my enemies, O my
God;
protect me from those who rise
up against me;
2 deliver me from those who work
evil,
and save me from bloodthirsty
men.

3 For behold, they lie in wait for my
life;
fierce men stir up strife against
me.
For no transgression or sin of mine,
O LORD,
4 for no fault of mine, they run and
make ready.
Awake, come to meet me, and see!
5 You, LORD God of hosts, are God
of Israel.
Rouse yourself to punish all the
nations;
spare none of those who
treacherously plot evil. *Selah*

6 Each evening they come back,
howling like dogs
and prowling about the city.
7 There they are, bellowing with their
mouths
with swords in their lips—
for "Who," they think,[5] "will hear
us?"

[1] Probably a musical or liturgical term [2] Or *mighty lords* (by revocalization; Hebrew *in silence*) [3] The meaning of the Hebrew verse is uncertain [4] Probably a musical or liturgical term [5] Hebrew lacks *they think*

8 But you, O LORD, laugh at them;
you hold all the nations in derision.
9 O my Strength, I will watch for you,
for you, O God, are my fortress.
10 My God in his steadfast love[1] will meet me;
God will let me look in triumph on my enemies.

11 Kill them not, lest my people forget;
make them totter[2] by your power and bring them down,
O Lord, our shield!
12 For the sin of their mouths, the words of their lips,
let them be trapped in their pride.
For the cursing and lies that they utter,
13 consume them in wrath;
consume them till they are no more,
that they may know that God rules over Jacob
to the ends of the earth. *Selah*
14 Each evening they come back,
howling like dogs
and prowling about the city.
15 They wander about for food
and growl if they do not get their fill.

16 But I will sing of your strength;
I will sing aloud of your steadfast love in the morning.
For you have been to me a fortress
and a refuge in the day of my distress.
17 O my Strength, I will sing praises to you,
for you, O God, are my fortress,
the God who shows me steadfast love.

He Will Tread Down Our Foes

60

TO THE CHOIRMASTER: ACCORDING TO SHUSHAN EDUTH. A MIKTAM[3] OF DAVID; FOR INSTRUCTION; WHEN HE STROVE WITH ARAM-NAHARAIM AND WITH ARAM-ZOBAH, AND WHEN JOAB ON HIS RETURN STRUCK DOWN TWELVE THOUSAND OF EDOM IN THE VALLEY OF SALT.

1 O God, you have rejected us, broken our defenses;
you have been angry; oh, restore us.
2 You have made the land to quake;
you have torn it open;
repair its breaches, for it totters.
3 You have made your people see hard things;
you have given us wine to drink that made us stagger.

4 You have set up a banner for those who fear you,
that they may flee to it from the bow.[4] *Selah*
5 That your beloved ones may be delivered,
give salvation by your right hand and answer us!

6 God has spoken in his holiness:[5]
"With exultation I will divide up Shechem
and portion out the Vale of Succoth.
7 Gilead is mine; Manasseh is mine;
Ephraim is my helmet;
Judah is my scepter.
8 Moab is my washbasin;
upon Edom I cast my shoe;
over Philistia I shout in triumph."[6]

9 Who will bring me to the fortified city?
Who will lead me to Edom?
10 Have you not rejected us, O God?
You do not go forth, O God, with our armies.

[1] Or *The God who shows me steadfast love* [2] Or *wander* [3] Probably musical or liturgical terms [4] Or *that it may be displayed because of truth* [5] Or *sanctuary* [6] Revocalization (compare Psalm 108:10); Masoretic Text *over me, O Philistia, shout in triumph*

11 Oh, grant us help against the foe,
for vain is the salvation of man!
12 With God we shall do valiantly;
it is he who will tread down our foes.

Lead Me to the Rock

61

To the choirmaster: with stringed instruments. Of David.

1 Hear my cry, O God,
listen to my prayer;
2 from the end of the earth I call to you
when my heart is faint.
Lead me to the rock
that is higher than I,
3 for you have been my refuge,
a strong tower against the enemy.

4 Let me dwell in your tent forever!
Let me take refuge under the shelter of your wings! *Selah*
5 For you, O God, have heard my vows;
you have given me the heritage of those who fear your name.

6 Prolong the life of the king;
may his years endure to all generations!
7 May he be enthroned forever before God;
appoint steadfast love and faithfulness to watch over him!

8 So will I ever sing praises to your name,
as I perform my vows day after day.

My Soul Waits for God Alone

62

To the choirmaster: according to Jeduthun. A Psalm of David.

1 For God alone my soul waits in silence;
from him comes my salvation.
2 He only is my rock and my salvation,
my fortress; I shall not be greatly shaken.

3 How long will all of you attack a man
to batter him,
like a leaning wall, a tottering fence?
4 They only plan to thrust him down from his high position.
They take pleasure in falsehood.
They bless with their mouths,
but inwardly they curse. *Selah*

5 For God alone, O my soul, wait in silence,
for my hope is from him.
6 He only is my rock and my salvation,
my fortress; I shall not be shaken.
7 On God rests my salvation and my glory;
my mighty rock, my refuge is God.

8 Trust in him at all times, O people;
pour out your heart before him;
God is a refuge for us. *Selah*

9 Those of low estate are but a breath;
those of high estate are a delusion;
in the balances they go up;
they are together lighter than a breath.
10 Put no trust in extortion;
set no vain hopes on robbery;
if riches increase, set not your heart on them.

11 Once God has spoken;
twice have I heard this:
that power belongs to God,
12 and that to you, O Lord, belongs steadfast love.
For you will render to a man
according to his work.

My Soul Thirsts for You

63

A Psalm of David, when he was in the wilderness of Judah.

1 O God, you are my God; earnestly I seek you;
my soul thirsts for you;
my flesh faints for you,
as in a dry and weary land where there is no water.
2 So I have looked upon you in the sanctuary,
beholding your power and glory.
3 Because your steadfast love is better than life,
my lips will praise you.
4 So I will bless you as long as I live;
in your name I will lift up my hands.

5 My soul will be satisfied as with fat and rich food,
and my mouth will praise you with joyful lips,
6 when I remember you upon my bed,
and meditate on you in the watches of the night;
7 for you have been my help,
and in the shadow of your wings I will sing for joy.
8 My soul clings to you;
your right hand upholds me.

9 But those who seek to destroy my life
shall go down into the depths of the earth;
10 they shall be given over to the power of the sword;
they shall be a portion for jackals.
11 But the king shall rejoice in God;
all who swear by him shall exult,
for the mouths of liars will be stopped.

Hide Me from the Wicked

64

To the choirmaster. A Psalm of David.

Hear my voice, O God, in my complaint;
preserve my life from dread of the enemy.
2 Hide me from the secret plots of the wicked,
from the throng of evildoers,
3 who whet their tongues like swords,
who aim bitter words like arrows,
4 shooting from ambush at the blameless,
shooting at him suddenly and without fear.
5 They hold fast to their evil purpose;
they talk of laying snares secretly,
thinking, "Who can see them?"
6 They search out injustice,
saying, "We have accomplished a diligent search."
For the inward mind and heart of a man are deep!

7 But God shoots his arrow at them;
they are wounded suddenly.
8 They are brought to ruin, with their own tongues turned against them;
all who see them will wag their heads.
9 Then all mankind fears;
they tell what God has brought about
and ponder what he has done.

10 Let the righteous one rejoice in the Lord
and take refuge in him!
Let all the upright in heart exult!

O God of Our Salvation

65

To the choirmaster. A Psalm of David. A Song.

1 Praise is due to you,[1] O God, in Zion,
and to you shall vows be performed.

[1] Or *Praise waits for you in silence*

2 O you who hear prayer,
to you shall all flesh come.
3 When iniquities prevail against
me,
you atone for our transgressions.
4 Blessed is the one you choose and
bring near,
to dwell in your courts!
We shall be satisfied with the
goodness of your house,
the holiness of your temple!

5 By awesome deeds you answer us
with righteousness,
O God of our salvation,
the hope of all the ends of the earth
and of the farthest seas;
6 the one who by his strength
established the mountains,
being girded with might;
7 who stills the roaring of the seas,
the roaring of their waves,
the tumult of the peoples,
8 so that those who dwell at the ends
of the earth are in awe at your
signs.
You make the going out of the
morning and the evening to
shout for joy.

9 You visit the earth and water it;[1]
you greatly enrich it;
the river of God is full of water;
you provide their grain,
for so you have prepared it.
10 You water its furrows abundantly,
settling its ridges,
softening it with showers,
and blessing its growth.
11 You crown the year with your bounty;
your wagon tracks overflow with
abundance.
12 The pastures of the wilderness
overflow,
the hills gird themselves with joy,
13 the meadows clothe themselves
with flocks,
the valleys deck themselves with
grain,
they shout and sing together for
joy.

[1] Or *and make it overflow*

How Awesome Are Your Deeds

66 To the choirmaster. A Song. A Psalm.
Shout for joy to God, all the earth;
2 sing the glory of his name;
give to him glorious praise!
3 Say to God, "How awesome are your
deeds!
So great is your power that your
enemies come cringing to you.
4 All the earth worships you
and sings praises to you;
they sing praises to your name."
Selah

5 Come and see what God has
done:
161 he is awesome in his deeds
toward the children of man.
6 He turned the sea into dry land;
they passed through the river on
foot.
There did we rejoice in him,
7 who rules by his might forever,
whose eyes keep watch on the
nations—
let not the rebellious exalt
themselves. *Selah*

8 Bless our God, O peoples;
let the sound of his praise be heard,
9 who has kept our soul among the
living
and has not let our feet slip.
10 For you, O God, have tested us;
you have tried us as silver is tried.
11 You brought us into the net;
you laid a crushing burden on our
backs;
12 you let men ride over our heads;
we went through fire and through
water;
yet you have brought us out to a
place of abundance.

13 I will come into your house with
burnt offerings;
I will perform my vows to you,
14 that which my lips uttered
and my mouth promised when I
was in trouble.
15 I will offer to you burnt offerings of
fattened animals,
with the smoke of the sacrifice of
rams;
I will make an offering of bulls and
goats. *Selah*

16 Come and hear, all you who fear
God,
and I will tell what he has done
for my soul.
17 I cried to him with my mouth,
and high praise was on[1] my
tongue.[2]
18 If I had cherished iniquity in my
heart,
the Lord would not have
listened.
19 But truly God has listened;
he has attended to the voice of my
prayer.

20 Blessed be God,
because he has not rejected my
prayer
or removed his steadfast love
from me!

Make Your Face Shine upon Us

67

TO THE CHOIRMASTER: WITH STRINGED INSTRUMENTS. A PSALM. A SONG.

1 May God be gracious to us and
bless us
and make his face to shine upon
us, *Selah*
2 that your way may be known on
earth,
your saving power among all
nations.
3 Let the peoples praise you, O God;
let all the peoples praise you!

4 Let the nations be glad and sing for
joy,
for you judge the peoples with
equity
and guide the nations upon earth.
Selah
5 Let the peoples praise you, O God;
let all the peoples praise you!

6 The earth has yielded its increase;
God, our God, shall bless us.
7 God shall bless us;
let all the ends of the earth fear him!

God Shall Scatter His Enemies

68

TO THE CHOIRMASTER. A PSALM OF DAVID. A SONG.

1 God shall arise, his enemies shall be
scattered;
and those who hate him shall flee
before him!
2 As smoke is driven away, so you
shall drive them away;
as wax melts before fire,
so the wicked shall perish before
God!
3 But the righteous shall be glad;
they shall exult before God;
they shall be jubilant with joy!

4 Sing to God, sing praises to his name;
lift up a song to him who rides
through the deserts;
his name is the LORD;
exult before him!
5 Father of the fatherless and
protector of widows
is God in his holy habitation.
6 God settles the solitary in a home;
he leads out the prisoners to
prosperity,
but the rebellious dwell in a
parched land.

7 O God, when you went out before
your people,
when you marched through the
wilderness, *Selah*

[1] Hebrew *under* [2] Or *and he was exalted with my tongue*

8 the earth quaked, the heavens
poured down rain,
before God, the One of Sinai,
before God, the God of Israel.
9 Rain in abundance, O God, you shed
abroad;
you restored your inheritance as
it languished;
10 your flock[1] found a dwelling in it;
in your goodness, O God, you
provided for the needy.

11 The Lord gives the word;
the women who announce the
news are a great host:
12 "The kings of the armies—they
flee, they flee!"
The women at home divide the
spoil—
13 though you men lie among the
sheepfolds—
the wings of a dove covered with
silver,
its pinions with shimmering
gold.
14 When the Almighty scatters kings
there,
let snow fall on Zalmon.

15 O mountain of God, mountain of
Bashan;
O many-peaked[2] mountain,
mountain of Bashan!
16 Why do you look with hatred, O
many-peaked mountain,
at the mount that God desired for
his abode,
yes, where the LORD will dwell
forever?
17 The chariots of God are twice ten
thousand,
thousands upon thousands;
the Lord is among them; Sinai is
now in the sanctuary.
18 You ascended on high,
leading a host of captives in your
train
and receiving gifts among men,
even among the rebellious, that the
LORD God may dwell there.

19 Blessed be the Lord,
who daily bears us up;
God is our salvation. *Selah*
20 Our God is a God of salvation,
and to GOD, the Lord, belong
deliverances from death.
21 But God will strike the heads of his
enemies,
the hairy crown of him who walks
in his guilty ways.
22 The Lord said,
"I will bring them back from
Bashan,
I will bring them back from the
depths of the sea,
23 that you may strike your feet in
their blood,
that the tongues of your dogs may
have their portion from the
foe."

24 Your procession is[3] seen, O God,
the procession of my God, my
King, into the sanctuary—
25 the singers in front, the musicians
last,
between them virgins playing
tambourines:
26 "Bless God in the great
congregation,
the LORD, O you[4] who are of
Israel's fountain!"
27 There is Benjamin, the least of
them, in the lead,
the princes of Judah in their
throng,
the princes of Zebulun, the
princes of Naphtali.

28 Summon your power, O God,[5]
the power, O God, by which you
have worked for us.

[1] Or *your congregation* [2] Or *hunch-backed*; also verse 16 [3] Or *has been* [4] The Hebrew for *you* is plural here [5] Probable reading; Hebrew *Your God has summoned your power*

29 Because of your temple at Jerusalem
kings shall bear gifts to you.
30 Rebuke the beasts that dwell among
the reeds,
the herd of bulls with the calves
of the peoples.
Trample underfoot those who lust
after tribute;
scatter the peoples who delight in
war.[1]
31 Nobles shall come from Egypt;
Cush shall hasten to stretch out
her hands to God.

32 O kingdoms of the earth, sing to
God;
sing praises to the Lord, *Selah*
33 to him who rides in the heavens,
the ancient heavens;
behold, he sends out his voice, his
mighty voice.
34 Ascribe power to God,
whose majesty is over Israel,
and whose power is in the skies.
35 Awesome is God from his[2]
sanctuary;
the God of Israel—he is the one
who gives power and strength
to his people.
Blessed be God!

Save Me, O God

69

TO THE CHOIRMASTER: ACCORDING TO LILIES. OF DAVID.

1 Save me, O God!
For the waters have come up to
my neck.[3]
2 I sink in deep mire,
where there is no foothold;
I have come into deep waters,
and the flood sweeps over me.
3 I am weary with my crying out;
my throat is parched.
My eyes grow dim
with waiting for my God.

4 More in number than the hairs of
my head
are those who hate me without
cause;
mighty are those who would
destroy me,
those who attack me with lies.
What I did not steal
must I now restore?
5 O God, you know my folly;
the wrongs I have done are not
hidden from you.

6 Let not those who hope in you be
put to shame through me,
O Lord GOD of hosts;
let not those who seek you be brought
to dishonor through me,
O God of Israel.
7 For it is for your sake that I have
borne reproach,
that dishonor has covered my face.
8 I have become a stranger to my
brothers,
an alien to my mother's sons.

1545

9 For zeal for your house has
consumed me,
and the reproaches of those
who reproach you have fallen
on me.
10 When I wept and humbled[4] my soul
with fasting,
it became my reproach.
11 When I made sackcloth my
clothing,
I became a byword to them.
12 I am the talk of those who sit in the
gate,
and the drunkards make songs
about me.

13 But as for me, my prayer is to you,
O LORD.
At an acceptable time, O God,
in the abundance of your
steadfast love answer me in
your saving faithfulness.

[1] The meaning of the Hebrew verse is uncertain [2] Septuagint; Hebrew *your* [3] Or *waters threaten my life* [4] Hebrew lacks *and humbled*

14 Deliver me
from sinking in the mire;
let me be delivered from my enemies
and from the deep waters.
15 Let not the flood sweep over me,
or the deep swallow me up,
or the pit close its mouth over me.
16 Answer me, O LORD, for your
steadfast love is good;
according to your abundant
mercy, turn to me.
17 Hide not your face from your
servant;
for I am in distress; make haste to
answer me.
18 Draw near to my soul, redeem me;
ransom me because of my
enemies!
19 You know my reproach,
and my shame and my dishonor;
my foes are all known to you.
20 Reproaches have broken my heart,
so that I am in despair.
I looked for pity, but there was none,
and for comforters, but I found
none.
21 They gave me poison for food,
and for my thirst they gave me
sour wine to drink.
22 Let their own table before them
become a snare;
and when they are at peace, let it
become a trap.[1]
23 Let their eyes be darkened, so that
they cannot see,
and make their loins tremble
continually.
24 Pour out your indignation upon
them,
and let your burning anger
overtake them.
25 May their camp be a desolation;
let no one dwell in their tents.
26 For they persecute him whom you
have struck down,
and they recount the pain of
those you have wounded.
27 Add to them punishment upon
punishment;
may they have no acquittal from
you.[2]
28 Let them be blotted out of the book
of the living;
let them not be enrolled among
the righteous.
29 But I am afflicted and in pain;
let your salvation, O God, set me
on high!
30 I will praise the name of God with a
song;
I will magnify him with
thanksgiving.
31 This will please the LORD more than
an ox
or a bull with horns and hoofs.
32 When the humble see it they will be
glad;
you who seek God, let your hearts
revive.
33 For the LORD hears the needy
and does not despise his own
people who are prisoners.
34 Let heaven and earth praise him,
the seas and everything that
moves in them.
35 For God will save Zion
and build up the cities of Judah,
and people shall dwell there and
possess it;
36 the offspring of his servants shall
inherit it,
and those who love his name
shall dwell in it.

O LORD, Do Not Delay

70

TO THE CHOIRMASTER. OF DAVID, FOR THE MEMORIAL OFFERING.

1 Make haste, O God, to deliver me!
O LORD, make haste to help me!

[1] Hebrew; a slight revocalization yields (compare Septuagint, Syriac, Jerome) *a snare, and retribution and a trap* [2] Hebrew *may they not come into your righteousness*

2 Let them be put to shame and
confusion
who seek my life!
Let them be turned back and
brought to dishonor
who delight in my hurt!
3 Let them turn back because of their
shame
who say, "Aha, Aha!"

4 May all who seek you
rejoice and be glad in you!
May those who love your salvation
say evermore, "God is great!"
5 But I am poor and needy;
hasten to me, O God!
You are my help and my deliverer;
O LORD, do not delay!

Forsake Me Not When My Strength Is Spent

71 In you, O LORD, do I take refuge;
let me never be put to shame!
2 In your righteousness deliver me
and rescue me;
incline your ear to me, and save
me!
3 Be to me a rock of refuge,
to which I may continually come;
you have given the command to
save me,
for you are my rock and my
fortress.

4 Rescue me, O my God, from the
hand of the wicked,
from the grasp of the unjust and
cruel man.
5 For you, O Lord, are my hope,
my trust, O LORD, from my youth.
6 Upon you I have leaned from before
my birth;
you are he who took me from my
mother's womb.
My praise is continually of you.

7 I have been as a portent to many,
but you are my strong refuge.
8 My mouth is filled with your praise,
and with your glory all the day.
9 Do not cast me off in the time of old
age;
forsake me not when my strength
is spent.
10 For my enemies speak concerning
me;
those who watch for my life
consult together
11 and say, "God has forsaken him;
pursue and seize him,
for there is none to deliver him."

12 O God, be not far from me;
O my God, make haste to help
me!
13 May my accusers be put to shame
and consumed;
with scorn and disgrace may they
be covered
who seek my hurt.
14 But I will hope continually
and will praise you yet more and
more.
15 My mouth will tell of your righteous
acts,
of your deeds of salvation all the
day,
for their number is past my
knowledge.
16 With the mighty deeds of the Lord
GOD I will come;
I will remind them of your
righteousness, yours alone.

17 O God, from my youth you have
taught me,
and I still proclaim your
wondrous deeds.
18 So even to old age and gray hairs,
O God, do not forsake me,
until I proclaim your might to
another generation,
your power to all those to come.
19 Your righteousness, O God,
reaches the high heavens.
You who have done great things,
O God, who is like you?

20 You who have made me see many troubles and calamities
will revive me again;
from the depths of the earth
you will bring me up again.
21 You will increase my greatness
and comfort me again.

22 I will also praise you with the harp
for your faithfulness, O my God;
I will sing praises to you with the lyre,
O Holy One of Israel.
23 My lips will shout for joy,
when I sing praises to you;
my soul also, which you have redeemed.
24 And my tongue will talk of your righteous help all the day long,
for they have been put to shame and disappointed
who sought to do me hurt.

Give the King Your Justice

72

OF SOLOMON.

Give the king your justice, O God,
and your righteousness to the royal son!
2 May he judge your people with righteousness,
and your poor with justice!
3 Let the mountains bear prosperity for the people,
and the hills, in righteousness!
4 May he defend the cause of the poor of the people,
give deliverance to the children of the needy,
and crush the oppressor!

5 May they fear you[1] while the sun endures,
and as long as the moon,
throughout all generations!
6 May he be like rain that falls on the mown grass,
like showers that water the earth!
7 In his days may the righteous flourish,
and peace abound, till the moon be no more!

8 May he have dominion from sea to sea,
and from the River[2] to the ends of the earth!
9 May desert tribes bow down before him,
and his enemies lick the dust!
10 May the kings of Tarshish and of the coastlands
render him tribute;
may the kings of Sheba and Seba
bring gifts!
11 May all kings fall down before him,
all nations serve him!
12 For he delivers the needy when he calls,
the poor and him who has no helper.
13 He has pity on the weak and the needy,
and saves the lives of the needy.
14 From oppression and violence he redeems their life,
and precious is their blood in his sight.

15 Long may he live;
may gold of Sheba be given to him!
May prayer be made for him continually,
and blessings invoked for him all the day!
16 May there be abundance of grain in the land;
on the tops of the mountains may it wave;
may its fruit be like Lebanon;
and may people blossom in the cities
like the grass of the field!

[1] Septuagint *He shall endure* [2] That is, the Euphrates

17 May his name endure forever,
his fame continue as long as the sun!
May people be blessed in him,
all nations call him blessed!

18 Blessed be the LORD, the God of Israel,
who alone does wondrous things.
19 Blessed be his glorious name forever;
may the whole earth be filled with his glory!
Amen and Amen!

20 The prayers of David, the son of Jesse, are ended.

BOOK THREE

God Is My Strength and Portion Forever

73 A PSALM OF ASAPH.
Truly God is good to Israel,
to those who are pure in heart.
2 But as for me, my feet had almost stumbled,
my steps had nearly slipped.
3 For I was envious of the arrogant
when I saw the prosperity of the wicked.

4 For they have no pangs until death;
their bodies are fat and sleek.
5 They are not in trouble as others are;
they are not stricken like the rest of mankind.
6 Therefore pride is their necklace;
violence covers them as a garment.
7 Their eyes swell out through fatness;
their hearts overflow with follies.
8 They scoff and speak with malice;
loftily they threaten oppression.
9 They set their mouths against the heavens,
and their tongue struts through the earth.
10 Therefore his people turn back to them,
and find no fault in them.[1]
11 And they say, "How can God know?
Is there knowledge in the Most High?"
12 Behold, these are the wicked;
always at ease, they increase in riches.
13 All in vain have I kept my heart clean
and washed my hands in innocence.
14 For all the day long I have been stricken
and rebuked every morning.
15 If I had said, "I will speak thus,"
I would have betrayed the generation of your children.

16 But when I thought how to understand this,
it seemed to me a wearisome task,
17 until I went into the sanctuary of God;
then I discerned their end.

18 Truly you set them in slippery places;
you make them fall to ruin.
19 How they are destroyed in a moment,
swept away utterly by terrors!
20 Like a dream when one awakes,
O Lord, when you rouse yourself,
you despise them as phantoms.
21 When my soul was embittered,
when I was pricked in heart,
22 I was brutish and ignorant;
I was like a beast toward you.

23 Nevertheless, I am continually with you;
you hold my right hand.
24 You guide me with your counsel,
and afterward you will receive me to glory.

[1] Probable reading; Hebrew *the waters of a full cup are drained by them*

37
25 Whom have I in heaven but you?
And there is nothing on earth
that I desire besides you.
26 My flesh and my heart may fail,
but God is the strength[1] of my
heart and my portion forever.

27 For behold, those who are far from
you shall perish;
you put an end to everyone who
is unfaithful to you.
28 But for me it is good to be near God;
I have made the Lord GOD my
refuge,
that I may tell of all your works.

Arise, O God, Defend Your Cause

74

A MASKIL[2] OF ASAPH.

O God, why do you cast us off
forever?
Why does your anger smoke
against the sheep of your
pasture?
2 Remember your congregation, which
you have purchased of old,
which you have redeemed to be
the tribe of your heritage!
Remember Mount Zion, where
you have dwelt.
3 Direct your steps to the perpetual
ruins;
the enemy has destroyed
everything in the sanctuary!

4 Your foes have roared in the midst
of your meeting place;
they set up their own signs for
signs.
5 They were like those who swing
axes
in a forest of trees.[3]
6 And all its carved wood
they broke down with hatchets
and hammers.
7 They set your sanctuary on fire;
they profaned the dwelling place
of your name,
bringing it down to the ground.
8 They said to themselves, "We will
utterly subdue them";
they burned all the meeting
places of God in the land.

9 We do not see our signs;
there is no longer any prophet,
and there is none among us who
knows how long.
10 How long, O God, is the foe to scoff?
Is the enemy to revile your name
forever?
11 Why do you hold back your hand,
your right hand?
Take it from the fold of your
garment[4] and destroy them!

12 Yet God my King is from of old,
working salvation in the midst of
the earth.
13 You divided the sea by your might;
you broke the heads of the sea
monsters[5] on the waters.
14 You crushed the heads of Leviathan;
you gave him as food for the
creatures of the wilderness.
15 You split open springs and brooks;
you dried up ever-flowing streams.
16 Yours is the day, yours also the night;
you have established the heavenly
lights and the sun.
17 You have fixed all the boundaries of
the earth;
you have made summer and
winter.

18 Remember this, O LORD, how the
enemy scoffs,
and a foolish people reviles your
name.
19 Do not deliver the soul of your dove
to the wild beasts;
do not forget the life of your poor
forever.

20 Have regard for the covenant,
for the dark places of the land
are full of the habitations of
violence.

[1] Hebrew *rock* [2] Probably a musical or liturgical term [3] The meaning of the Hebrew is uncertain [4] Hebrew *from your bosom* [5] Or *the great sea creatures*

21 Let not the downtrodden turn back
in shame;
let the poor and needy praise your
name.
22 Arise, O God, defend your cause;
remember how the foolish scoff
at you all the day!
23 Do not forget the clamor of your
foes,
the uproar of those who rise
against you, which goes up
continually!

God Will Judge with Equity

75

To the choirmaster: according to Do Not Destroy. A Psalm of Asaph. A Song.

1 We give thanks to you, O God;
we give thanks, for your name is
near.
We[1] recount your wondrous deeds.

2 "At the set time that I appoint
I will judge with equity.
3 When the earth totters, and all its
inhabitants,
it is I who keep steady its pillars.
Selah
4 I say to the boastful, 'Do not boast,'
and to the wicked, 'Do not lift up
your horn;
5 do not lift up your horn on high,
or speak with haughty neck.'"

6 For not from the east or from the
west
and not from the wilderness
comes lifting up,
7 but it is God who executes
judgment,
putting down one and lifting up
another.
8 For in the hand of the LORD there is
a cup
with foaming wine, well mixed,
and he pours out from it,
and all the wicked of the earth
shall drain it down to the dregs.

9 But I will declare it forever;
I will sing praises to the God of
Jacob.
10 All the horns of the wicked I will cut
off,
but the horns of the righteous
shall be lifted up.

Who Can Stand Before You?

76

To the choirmaster: with stringed instruments. A Psalm of Asaph. A Song.

1 In Judah God is known;
his name is great in Israel.
2 His abode has been established in
Salem,
his dwelling place in Zion.
3 There he broke the flashing
arrows,
the shield, the sword, and the
weapons of war. *Selah*

4 Glorious are you, more majestic
than the mountains of prey.
5 The stouthearted were stripped of
their spoil;
they sank into sleep;
all the men of war
were unable to use their hands.
6 At your rebuke, O God of Jacob,
both rider and horse lay stunned.

7 But you, you are to be feared!
Who can stand before you
when once your anger is roused?
8 From the heavens you uttered
judgment;
the earth feared and was still,
9 when God arose to establish
judgment,
to save all the humble of the
earth. *Selah*

10 Surely the wrath of man shall praise
you;
the remnant[2] of wrath you will
put on like a belt.

[1] Hebrew *They* [2] Or *extremity*

11 Make your vows to the LORD your
God and perform them;
let all around him bring gifts
to him who is to be feared,
12 who cuts off the spirit of princes,
who is to be feared by the kings of
the earth.

In the Day of Trouble I Seek the Lord

77

TO THE CHOIRMASTER: ACCORDING TO JEDUTHUN. A PSALM OF ASAPH.

1 I cry aloud to God,
aloud to God, and he will hear
me.
2 In the day of my trouble I seek the
Lord;
in the night my hand is stretched
out without wearying;
my soul refuses to be comforted.
3 When I remember God, I moan;
when I meditate, my spirit faints.
Selah

4 You hold my eyelids open;
I am so troubled that I cannot
speak.
5 I consider the days of old,
the years long ago.
6 I said,[1] "Let me remember my song
in the night;
let me meditate in my heart."
Then my spirit made a diligent
search:
7 "Will the Lord spurn forever,
and never again be favorable?
8 Has his steadfast love forever
ceased?
Are his promises at an end for all
time?
9 Has God forgotten to be gracious?
Has he in anger shut up his
compassion?" Selah
10 Then I said, "I will appeal to this,
to the years of the right hand of
the Most High."[2]
11 I will remember the deeds of the
LORD;
yes, I will remember your
wonders of old.
12 I will ponder all your work,
and meditate on your mighty
deeds.
13 Your way, O God, is holy.
What god is great like our God?
14 You are the God who works wonders;
you have made known your
might among the peoples.
15 You with your arm redeemed your
people,
the children of Jacob and Joseph.
Selah

161, 351

16 When the waters saw you,
O God,
when the waters saw you, they
were afraid;
indeed, the deep trembled.
17 The clouds poured out water;
the skies gave forth thunder;
your arrows flashed on every
side.
18 The crash of your thunder was in
the whirlwind;
your lightnings lighted up the
world;
the earth trembled and shook.
19 Your way was through the sea,
your path through the great
waters;
yet your footprints were unseen.[3]
20 You led your people like a flock
by the hand of Moses and Aaron.

Tell the Coming Generation

78

A MASKIL[4] OF ASAPH.

Give ear, O my people, to my
teaching;
incline your ears to the words of
my mouth!
2 I will open my mouth in a parable;
I will utter dark sayings from of
old,

[1] Hebrew lacks *I said* [2] Or *This is my grief: that the right hand of the Most High has changed* [3] Hebrew *unknown* [4] Probably a musical or liturgical term

3 things that we have heard and known,
that our fathers have told us.
4 We will not hide them from their children,
but tell to the coming generation
the glorious deeds of the LORD, and his might,
and the wonders that he has done.

5 He established a testimony in Jacob
and appointed a law in Israel,
which he commanded our fathers
to teach to their children,
6 that the next generation might know them,
the children yet unborn,
and arise and tell them to their children,
7 so that they should set their hope in God
and not forget the works of God,
but keep his commandments;
8 and that they should not be like their fathers,
a stubborn and rebellious generation,
a generation whose heart was not steadfast,
whose spirit was not faithful to God.

9 The Ephraimites, armed with[1] the bow,
turned back on the day of battle.
10 They did not keep God's covenant,
but refused to walk according to his law.
11 They forgot his works
and the wonders that he had shown them.
12 In the sight of their fathers he performed wonders
in the land of Egypt, in the fields of Zoan.
13 He divided the sea and let them pass through it,
and made the waters stand like a heap.
14 In the daytime he led them with a cloud,
and all the night with a fiery light.
15 He split rocks in the wilderness
and gave them drink abundantly as from the deep.
16 He made streams come out of the rock
and caused waters to flow down like rivers.

17 Yet they sinned still more against him,
rebelling against the Most High in the desert.
18 They tested God in their heart
by demanding the food they craved.
19 They spoke against God, saying,
"Can God spread a table in the wilderness?
20 He struck the rock so that water gushed out
and streams overflowed.
Can he also give bread
or provide meat for his people?"

21 Therefore, when the LORD heard, he was full of wrath;
a fire was kindled against Jacob;
his anger rose against Israel,
22 because they did not believe in God
and did not trust his saving power.
23 Yet he commanded the skies above
and opened the doors of heaven,
24 and he rained down on them manna to eat
and gave them the grain of heaven.
25 Man ate of the bread of the angels;
he sent them food in abundance.
26 He caused the east wind to blow in the heavens,
and by his power he led out the south wind;

[1] Hebrew *armed and shooting*

27 he rained meat on them like dust,
winged birds like the sand of the seas;
28 he let them fall in the midst of their camp,
all around their dwellings.
29 And they ate and were well filled,
for he gave them what they craved.
30 But before they had satisfied their craving,
while the food was still in their mouths,
31 the anger of God rose against them,
and he killed the strongest of them
and laid low the young men of Israel.
32 In spite of all this, they still sinned;
despite his wonders, they did not believe.
33 So he made their days vanish like[1] a breath,[2]
and their years in terror.
34 When he killed them, they sought him;
they repented and sought God earnestly.
35 They remembered that God was their rock,
the Most High God their redeemer.
36 But they flattered him with their mouths;
they lied to him with their tongues.
37 Their heart was not steadfast toward him;
265
they were not faithful to his covenant.
38 Yet he, being compassionate,
atoned for their iniquity
and did not destroy them;
he restrained his anger often
and did not stir up all his wrath.
39 He remembered that they were but flesh,
a wind that passes and comes not again.
40 How often they rebelled against him in the wilderness
and grieved him in the desert!
41 They tested God again and again
and provoked the Holy One of Israel.
42 They did not remember his power[3]
or the day when he redeemed them from the foe,
43 when he performed his signs in Egypt
145
and his marvels in the fields of Zoan.
44 He turned their rivers to blood,
so that they could not drink of their streams.
45 He sent among them swarms of flies, which devoured them,
and frogs, which destroyed them.
46 He gave their crops to the destroying locust
and the fruit of their labor to the locust.
47 He destroyed their vines with hail
and their sycamores with frost.
48 He gave over their cattle to the hail
and their flocks to thunderbolts.
49 He let loose on them his burning anger,
wrath, indignation, and distress,
a company of destroying angels.
50 He made a path for his anger;
he did not spare them from death,
but gave their lives over to the plague.
51 He struck down every firstborn in Egypt,
the firstfruits of their strength in the tents of Ham.
52 Then he led out his people like sheep
and guided them in the wilderness like a flock.

[1] Hebrew *in* [2] Or *vapor* [3] Hebrew *hand*

53 He led them in safety, so that they
were not afraid,
but the sea overwhelmed their
enemies.
54 And he brought them to his holy
land,
357 to the mountain which his right
hand had won.
55 He drove out nations before them;
he apportioned them for a
possession
and settled the tribes of Israel in
their tents.

56 Yet they tested and rebelled against
the Most High God
and did not keep his testimonies,
57 but turned away and acted
treacherously like their
fathers;
they twisted like a deceitful bow.
58 For they provoked him to anger
with their high places;
they moved him to jealousy with
their idols.
59 When God heard, he was full of
wrath,
and he utterly rejected Israel.
60 He forsook his dwelling at Shiloh,
the tent where he dwelt among
mankind,
61 and delivered his power to captivity,
his glory to the hand of the foe.
62 He gave his people over to the
sword
and vented his wrath on his
heritage.
63 Fire devoured their young men,
and their young women had no
marriage song.
64 Their priests fell by the sword,
and their widows made no
lamentation.
65 Then the Lord awoke as from sleep,
like a strong man shouting
because of wine.
66 And he put his adversaries to rout;
he put them to everlasting shame.
67 He rejected the tent of Joseph;
he did not choose the tribe of
Ephraim,
68 but he chose the tribe of Judah,
Mount Zion, which he loves.
69 He built his sanctuary like the high
heavens,
like the earth, which he has
founded forever.
70 He chose David his servant
and took him from the
463, sheepfolds;
1571 71 from following the nursing
ewes he brought him
to shepherd Jacob his people,
Israel his inheritance.
72 With upright heart he shepherded
them
and guided them with his skillful
hand.

How Long, O Lord?

79 A Psalm of Asaph.
O God, the nations have come
into your inheritance;
they have defiled your holy
temple;
they have laid Jerusalem in ruins.
2 They have given the bodies of your
servants
to the birds of the heavens for
food,
the flesh of your faithful to the
beasts of the earth.
3 They have poured out their blood
like water
all around Jerusalem,
and there was no one to bury
them.
4 We have become a taunt to our
neighbors,
mocked and derided by those
around us.
5 How long, O Lord? Will you be
angry forever?
Will your jealousy burn like fire?

6 Pour out your anger on the nations
that do not know you,
and on the kingdoms
that do not call upon your name!
7 For they have devoured Jacob
and laid waste his habitation.

8 Do not remember against us our
former iniquities;[1]
let your compassion come
speedily to meet us,
for we are brought very low.
9 Help us, O God of our salvation,
for the glory of your name;
deliver us, and atone for our sins,
for your name's sake!
10 Why should the nations say,
"Where is their God?"
Let the avenging of the outpoured
blood of your servants
be known among the nations
before our eyes!

11 Let the groans of the prisoners
come before you;
according to your great power,
preserve those doomed to die!
12 Return sevenfold into the lap of our
neighbors
the taunts with which they have
taunted you, O Lord!
13 But we your people, the sheep of
your pasture,
will give thanks to you forever;
from generation to generation we
will recount your praise.

Restore Us, O God

80

TO THE CHOIRMASTER: ACCORDING TO LILIES. A TESTIMONY. OF ASAPH, A PSALM.

1 Give ear, O Shepherd of Israel,
you who lead Joseph like a flock!
You who are enthroned upon the
cherubim, shine forth.
2 Before Ephraim and Benjamin
and Manasseh,
stir up your might
and come to save us!

3 Restore us,[2] O God;
let your face shine, that we may
be saved!

4 O LORD God of hosts,
how long will you be angry with
your people's prayers?
5 You have fed them with the bread of
tears
and given them tears to drink in
full measure.
6 You make us an object of
contention for our neighbors,
and our enemies laugh among
themselves.

7 Restore us, O God of hosts;
let your face shine, that we may
be saved!

8 You brought a vine out of Egypt;
you drove out the nations and
planted it.
9 You cleared the ground for it;
it took deep root and filled the
land.
10 The mountains were covered with
its shade,
the mighty cedars with its
branches.
11 It sent out its branches to the sea
and its shoots to the River.[3]
12 Why then have you broken down its
walls,
so that all who pass along the way
pluck its fruit?
13 The boar from the forest ravages it,
and all that move in the field feed
on it.

14 Turn again, O God of hosts!
Look down from heaven, and
see;
have regard for this vine,
15 the stock that your right hand
planted,
and for the son whom you made
strong for yourself.

[1] Or *the iniquities of former generations* [2] Or *Turn us again*; also verses 7, 19 [3] That is, the Euphrates

16 They have burned it with fire; they have cut it down;
may they perish at the rebuke of your face!
17 But let your hand be on the man of your right hand,
the son of man whom you have made strong for yourself!
18 Then we shall not turn back from you;
give us life, and we will call upon your name!

19 Restore us, O LORD God of hosts!
Let your face shine, that we may be saved!

Oh, That My People Would Listen to Me

81

TO THE CHOIRMASTER: ACCORDING TO THE GITTITH.[1] OF ASAPH.

1 Sing aloud to God our strength;
shout for joy to the God of Jacob!
2 Raise a song; sound the tambourine,
the sweet lyre with the harp.
3 Blow the trumpet at the new moon,
at the full moon, on our feast day.

4 For it is a statute for Israel,
a rule[2] of the God of Jacob.
5 He made it a decree in Joseph
when he went out over[3] the land of Egypt.
I hear a language I had not known:
6 "I relieved your[4] shoulder of the burden;
your hands were freed from the basket.
7 In distress you called, and I delivered you;
I answered you in the secret place of thunder;
I tested you at the waters of Meribah. *Selah*
8 Hear, O my people, while I admonish you!
O Israel, if you would but listen to me!
9 There shall be no strange god among you;
you shall not bow down to a foreign god.
10 I am the LORD your God,
who brought you up out of the land of Egypt.
Open your mouth wide, and I will fill it.

11 "But my people did not listen to my voice;
Israel would not submit to me.
12 So I gave them over to their stubborn hearts,
to follow their own counsels.
13 Oh, that my people would listen to me,
that Israel would walk in my ways!
14 I would soon subdue their enemies
and turn my hand against their foes.
15 Those who hate the LORD would cringe toward him,
and their fate would last forever.
16 But he would feed you[5] with the finest of the wheat,
and with honey from the rock I would satisfy you."

Rescue the Weak and Needy

82

A PSALM OF ASAPH.

God has taken his place in the divine council;
in the midst of the gods he holds judgment:
2 "How long will you judge unjustly
and show partiality to the wicked? *Selah*
3 Give justice to the weak and the fatherless;
maintain the right of the afflicted and the destitute.
4 Rescue the weak and the needy;
deliver them from the hand of the wicked."

[1] Probably a musical or liturgical term [2] Or *just decree* [3] Or *against* [4] Hebrew *his*; also next line [5] That is, Israel; Hebrew *him*

5 They have neither knowledge nor
understanding,
they walk about in darkness;
all the foundations of the earth
are shaken.

6 I said, "You are gods,
sons of the Most High, all of you;
7 nevertheless, like men you shall die,
and fall like any prince."[1]

8 Arise, O God, judge the earth;
for you shall inherit all the nations!

O God, Do Not Keep Silence

83

A SONG. A PSALM OF ASAPH.

O God, do not keep silence;
do not hold your peace or be still,
O God!
2 For behold, your enemies make an
uproar;
those who hate you have raised
their heads.
3 They lay crafty plans against your
people;
they consult together against
your treasured ones.
4 They say, "Come, let us wipe them
out as a nation;
let the name of Israel be
remembered no more!"
5 For they conspire with one accord;
against you they make a
covenant—
6 the tents of Edom and the
Ishmaelites,
Moab and the Hagrites,
7 Gebal and Ammon and Amalek,
Philistia with the inhabitants of
Tyre;
8 Asshur also has joined them;
they are the strong arm of the
children of Lot. *Selah*

9 *Do to them as you did to Midian,*
as to Sisera and Jabin at the river
Kishon,
10 who were destroyed at En-dor,
who became dung for the ground.

389,
397

11 Make their nobles like Oreb and
Zeeb,
all their princes like Zebah and
Zalmunna,
12 who said, "Let us take possession
for ourselves
of the pastures of God."

13 O my God, make them like whirling
dust,[2]
like chaff before the wind.
14 As fire consumes the forest,
as the flame sets the mountains
ablaze,
15 so may you pursue them with your
tempest
and terrify them with your
hurricane!
16 Fill their faces with shame,
that they may seek your name,
O LORD.
17 Let them be put to shame and
dismayed forever;
let them perish in disgrace,
18 that they may know that you alone,
whose name is the LORD,
are the Most High over all the
earth.

My Soul Longs for the Courts of the LORD

84

TO THE CHOIRMASTER: ACCORDING TO
THE GITTITH.[3] A PSALM OF THE SONS OF
KORAH.

1 How lovely is your dwelling place,
O LORD of hosts!
2 My soul longs, yes, faints
for the courts of the LORD;
my heart and flesh sing for joy
to the living God.

3 Even the sparrow finds a home,
and the swallow a nest for herself,
where she may lay her young,
at your altars, O LORD of hosts,
my King and my God.
4 Blessed are those who dwell in your
house,
ever singing your praise! *Selah*

[1] Or *fall as one man, O princes* [2] Or *like a tumbleweed* [3] Probably a musical or liturgical term

5 Blessed are those whose strength is in you,
in whose heart are the highways to Zion.[1]
6 As they go through the Valley of Baca
they make it a place of springs;
the early rain also covers it with pools.
7 They go from strength to strength;
each one appears before God in Zion.

8 O LORD God of hosts, hear my prayer;
give ear, O God of Jacob! *Selah*
9 Behold our shield, O God;
look on the face of your anointed!

10 For a day in your courts is better than a thousand elsewhere.
I would rather be a doorkeeper in the house of my God
than dwell in the tents of wickedness.
11 For the LORD God is a sun and shield;
the LORD bestows favor and honor.
No good thing does he withhold from those who walk uprightly.
12 O LORD of hosts,
blessed is the one who trusts in you!

Revive Us Again

85

To the choirmaster. A Psalm of the Sons of Korah.

1 LORD, you were favorable to your land;
you restored the fortunes of Jacob.
2 You forgave the iniquity of your people;
you covered all their sin. *Selah*
3 You withdrew all your wrath;
you turned from your hot anger.

4 Restore us again, O God of our salvation,
and put away your indignation toward us!
5 Will you be angry with us forever?
Will you prolong your anger to all generations?
6 Will you not revive us again,
that your people may rejoice in you?
7 Show us your steadfast love, O LORD,
and grant us your salvation.

8 Let me hear what God the LORD will speak,
for he will speak peace to his people, to his saints;
but let them not turn back to folly.
9 Surely his salvation is near to those who fear him,
that glory may dwell in our land.

10 Steadfast love and faithfulness meet;
righteousness and peace kiss each other.
11 Faithfulness springs up from the ground,
and righteousness looks down from the sky.
12 Yes, the LORD will give what is good,
and our land will yield its increase.
13 Righteousness will go before him
and make his footsteps a way.

Great Is Your Steadfast Love

86

A Prayer of David.

Incline your ear, O LORD, and answer me,
for I am poor and needy.
2 Preserve my life, for I am godly;
save your servant, who trusts in you—you are my God.
3 Be gracious to me, O Lord,
for to you do I cry all the day.
4 Gladden the soul of your servant,
for to you, O Lord, do I lift up my soul.

[1] Hebrew lacks *to Zion*

5 For you, O Lord, are good and forgiving,
abounding in steadfast love to all who call upon you.
6 Give ear, O LORD, to my prayer;
listen to my plea for grace.
7 In the day of my trouble I call upon you,
for you answer me.

8 There is none like you among the gods, O Lord,
nor are there any works like yours.
9 All the nations you have made shall come
and worship before you, O Lord,
and shall glorify your name.
10 For you are great and do wondrous things;
you alone are God.
11 Teach me your way, O LORD,
that I may walk in your truth;
unite my heart to fear your name.
12 I give thanks to you, O Lord my God, with my whole heart,
and I will glorify your name forever.
13 For great is your steadfast love toward me;
you have delivered my soul from the depths of Sheol.

14 O God, insolent men have risen up against me;
a band of ruthless men seeks my life,
and they do not set you before them.
15 But you, O Lord, are a God merciful and gracious,
slow to anger and abounding in steadfast love and faithfulness.
16 *Turn to me and be gracious to me;*
give your strength to your servant,
and save the son of your maidservant.
17 Show me a sign of your favor,
that those who hate me may see and be put to shame
because you, LORD, have helped me and comforted me.

Glorious Things of You Are Spoken

87 A PSALM OF THE SONS OF KORAH. A SONG.

On the holy mount stands the city he founded;
2 the LORD loves the gates of Zion
more than all the dwelling places of Jacob.
3 Glorious things of you are spoken,
O city of God. *Selah*

4 Among those who know me I mention Rahab and Babylon;
behold, Philistia and Tyre, with Cush[1]—
"This one was born there," they say.
5 And of Zion it shall be said,
"This one and that one were born in her";
for the Most High himself will establish her.
6 The LORD records as he registers the peoples,
"This one was born there." *Selah*

7 Singers and dancers alike say,
"All my springs are in you."

I Cry Out Day and Night Before You

88 A SONG. A PSALM OF THE SONS OF KORAH. TO THE CHOIRMASTER: ACCORDING TO MAHALATH LEANNOTH. A MASKIL[2] OF HEMAN THE EZRAHITE.

1 O LORD, God of my salvation;
I cry out day and night before you.
2 Let my prayer come before you;
incline your ear to my cry!

3 For my soul is full of troubles,
and my life draws near to Sheol.
4 I am counted among those who go down to the pit;
I am a man who has no strength,

[1] Probably *Nubia* [2] Probably musical or liturgical terms

5 like one set loose among the dead,
like the slain that lie in the grave,
like those whom you remember no more,
for they are cut off from your hand.
6 You have put me in the depths of the pit,
in the regions dark and deep.
7 Your wrath lies heavy upon me,
and you overwhelm me with all your waves. *Selah*
8 You have caused my companions to shun me;
you have made me a horror[1] to them.
I am shut in so that I cannot escape;
9 my eye grows dim through sorrow.
Every day I call upon you, O LORD;
I spread out my hands to you.
10 Do you work wonders for the dead?
Do the departed rise up to praise you? *Selah*
11 Is your steadfast love declared in the grave,
or your faithfulness in Abaddon?
12 Are your wonders known in the darkness,
or your righteousness in the land of forgetfulness?
13 But I, O LORD, cry to you;
in the morning my prayer comes before you.
14 O LORD, why do you cast my soul away?
Why do you hide your face from me?
15 Afflicted and close to death from my youth up,
I suffer your terrors; I am helpless.[2]
16 Your wrath has swept over me;
your dreadful assaults destroy me.
17 They surround me like a flood all day long;
they close in on me together.
18 You have caused my beloved and my friend to shun me;
my companions have become darkness.[3]

I Will Sing of the Steadfast Love of the LORD

89

A MASKIL[4] OF ETHAN THE EZRAHITE.

I will sing of the steadfast love of the LORD, forever;
with my mouth I will make known your faithfulness to all generations.
2 For I said, "Steadfast love will be built up forever;
in the heavens you will establish your faithfulness."
3 You have said, "I have made a covenant with my chosen one;
I have sworn to David my servant:
4 'I will establish your offspring forever,
and build your throne for all generations.'" *Selah*

5 Let the heavens praise your wonders, O LORD,
your faithfulness in the assembly of the holy ones!
6 For who in the skies can be compared to the LORD?
Who among the heavenly beings[5] is like the LORD,
7 a God greatly to be feared in the council of the holy ones,
and awesome above all who are around him?
8 O LORD God of hosts,
who is mighty as you are, O LORD,
with your faithfulness all around you?
9 You rule the raging of the sea;
when its waves rise, you still them.
10 You crushed Rahab like a carcass;
you scattered your enemies with your mighty arm.

[1] Or *an abomination* [2] The meaning of the Hebrew word is uncertain [3] Or *darkness has become my only companion* [4] Probably a musical or liturgical term [5] Hebrew *the sons of God, or the sons of might*

11 The heavens are yours; the earth
also is yours;
the world and all that is in it, you
have founded them.
12 The north and the south, you have
created them;
Tabor and Hermon joyously
praise your name.
13 You have a mighty arm;
strong is your hand, high your
right hand.
14 Righteousness and justice are the
foundation of your throne;
steadfast love and faithfulness go
before you.
15 Blessed are the people who know
the festal shout,
who walk, O LORD, in the light of
your face,
16 who exult in your name all the day
and in your righteousness are
exalted.
17 For you are the glory of their strength;
by your favor our horn is exalted.
18 For our shield belongs to the LORD,
our king to the Holy One of Israel.

19 Of old you spoke in a vision to
your godly one,[1] and said:
463
"I have granted help to one who
is mighty;
I have exalted one chosen from
the people.
20 I have found David, my servant;
with my holy oil I have anointed
499
him,
21 so that my hand shall be established
with him;
my arm also shall strengthen him.
22 The enemy shall not outwit him;
the wicked shall not humble him.
23 I will crush his foes before him
and strike down those who hate
him.
24 My faithfulness and my steadfast
love shall be with him,
and in my name shall his horn be
exalted.
25 I will set his hand on the sea
and his right hand on the rivers.
26 He shall cry to me, 'You are my Father,
my God, and the Rock of my
salvation.'
27 And I will make him the firstborn,
the highest of the kings of the earth.
28 My steadfast love I will keep for him
forever,
and my covenant will stand firm[2]
for him.
29 I will establish his offspring forever
and his throne as the days of the
heavens.
30 If his children forsake my law
and do not walk according to my
rules,[3]
31 if they violate my statutes
and do not keep my
commandments,
32 then I will punish their
transgression with the rod
and their iniquity with stripes,
33 but I will not remove from him my
steadfast love
or be false to my faithfulness.
34 I will not violate my covenant
or alter the word that went forth
from my lips.
35 Once for all I have sworn by my
holiness;
I will not lie to David.
36 His offspring shall endure forever,
his throne as long as the sun
before me.
37 Like the moon it shall be
established forever,
a faithful witness in the skies."
Selah

38 But now you have cast off and
rejected;
you are full of wrath against your
anointed.
39 You have renounced the covenant
with your servant;
you have defiled his crown in the
dust.

[1] Some Hebrew manuscripts *godly ones* [2] Or *will remain faithful* [3] Or *my just decrees*

40 You have breached all his walls;
you have laid his strongholds in ruins.
41 All who pass by plunder him;
he has become the scorn of his neighbors.
42 You have exalted the right hand of his foes;
you have made all his enemies rejoice.
43 You have also turned back the edge of his sword,
and you have not made him stand in battle.
44 You have made his splendor to cease
and cast his throne to the ground.
45 You have cut short the days of his youth;
you have covered him with shame. *Selah*

46 How long, O LORD? Will you hide yourself forever?
How long will your wrath burn like fire?
47 Remember how short my time is!
For what vanity you have created all the children of man!
48 What man can live and never see death?
Who can deliver his soul from the power of Sheol? *Selah*

49 Lord, where is your steadfast love of old,
which by your faithfulness you swore to David?
50 Remember, O Lord, how your servants are mocked,
and how I bear in my heart the insults[1] of all the many nations,
51 with which your enemies mock, O LORD,
with which they mock the footsteps of your anointed.

52 Blessed be the LORD forever!
Amen and Amen.

BOOK FOUR

From Everlasting to Everlasting

90

A PRAYER OF MOSES, THE MAN OF GOD.

Lord, you have been our dwelling place[2]
in all generations.
2 Before the mountains were brought forth,
or ever you had formed the earth and the world,
from everlasting to everlasting you are God.

3 You return man to dust
and say, "Return, O children of man!"[3]
4 For a thousand years in your sight
are but as yesterday when it is past,
or as a watch in the night.

5 You sweep them away as with a flood; they are like a dream,
like grass that is renewed in the morning:
6 in the morning it flourishes and is renewed;
in the evening it fades and withers.

7 For we are brought to an end by your anger;
by your wrath we are dismayed.
8 You have set our iniquities before you,
our secret sins in the light of your presence.

9 For all our days pass away under your wrath;
we bring our years to an end like a sigh.
10 The years of our life are seventy,
or even by reason of strength eighty;
yet their span[4] is but toil and trouble;
they are soon gone, and we fly away.

[1] Hebrew lacks *the insults* [2] Some Hebrew manuscripts (compare Septuagint) *our refuge* [3] Or *of Adam* [4] Or *pride*

11 Who considers the power of your anger,
and your wrath according to the fear of you?
12 So teach us to number our days
that we may get a heart of wisdom.
13 Return, O LORD! How long?
Have pity on your servants!
14 Satisfy us in the morning with your steadfast love,
that we may rejoice and be glad all our days.
15 Make us glad for as many days as you have afflicted us,
and for as many years as we have seen evil.
16 Let your work be shown to your servants,
and your glorious power to their children.
17 Let the favor[1] of the Lord our God be upon us,
and establish the work of our hands upon us;
yes, establish the work of our hands!

My Refuge and My Fortress

91 He who dwells in the shelter of the Most High
will abide in the shadow of the Almighty.
2 I will say[2] to the LORD, "My refuge and my fortress,
my God, in whom I trust."

3 For he will deliver you from the snare of the fowler
and from the deadly pestilence.
4 He will cover you with his pinions,
and under his wings you will find refuge;
his faithfulness is a shield and buckler.
5 You will not fear the terror of the night,
nor the arrow that flies by day,
6 nor the pestilence that stalks in darkness,
nor the destruction that wastes at noonday.

7 A thousand may fall at your side,
ten thousand at your right hand,
but it will not come near you.
8 You will only look with your eyes
and see the recompense of the wicked.

9 Because you have made the LORD your dwelling place—
the Most High, who is my refuge[3]—
10 no evil shall be allowed to befall you,
no plague come near your tent.

11 For he will command his angels concerning you
to guard you in all your ways.
12 On their hands they will bear you up,
lest you strike your foot against a stone.
13 You will tread on the lion and the adder;
the young lion and the serpent you will trample underfoot.

14 "Because he holds fast to me in love,
I will deliver him;
I will protect him, because he knows my name.
15 When he calls to me, I will answer him;
I will be with him in trouble;
I will rescue him and honor him.
16 With long life I will satisfy him
and show him my salvation."

How Great Are Your Works

92 A PSALM. A SONG FOR THE SABBATH.
It is good to give thanks to the LORD,
to sing praises to your name, O Most High;

[1] Or *beauty* [2] Septuagint *He will say* [3] Or *For you, O LORD, are my refuge! You have made the Most High your dwelling place*

2 to declare your steadfast love in the morning,
and your faithfulness by night,
3 to the music of the lute and the harp,
to the melody of the lyre.
4 For you, O LORD, have made me glad by your work;
at the works of your hands I sing for joy.

5 How great are your works, O LORD!
Your thoughts are very deep!
6 The stupid man cannot know;
the fool cannot understand this:
7 that though the wicked sprout like grass
and all evildoers flourish,
they are doomed to destruction forever;
8 but you, O LORD, are on high forever.
9 For behold, your enemies, O LORD,
for behold, your enemies shall perish;
all evildoers shall be scattered.

10 But you have exalted my horn like that of the wild ox;
you have poured over me[1] fresh oil.
11 My eyes have seen the downfall of my enemies;
my ears have heard the doom of my evil assailants.

12 The righteous flourish like the palm tree
and grow like a cedar in Lebanon.
13 They are planted in the house of the LORD;
they flourish in the courts of our God.
14 They still bear fruit in old age;
they are ever full of sap and green,
15 to declare that the LORD is upright;
he is my rock, and there is no unrighteousness in him.

[1] Compare Syriac; the meaning of the Hebrew is uncertain

The LORD Reigns

93 The LORD reigns; he is robed in majesty;
the LORD is robed; he has put on strength as his belt.
Yes, the world is established; it shall never be moved.
2 Your throne is established from of old;
you are from everlasting.

3 The floods have lifted up, O LORD,
the floods have lifted up their voice;
the floods lift up their roaring.
4 Mightier than the thunders of many waters,
mightier than the waves of the sea,
the LORD on high is mighty!

5 Your decrees are very trustworthy;
holiness befits your house,
O LORD, forevermore.

The LORD Will Not Forsake His People

94 O LORD, God of vengeance,
O God of vengeance, shine forth!
2 Rise up, O judge of the earth;
repay to the proud what they deserve!
3 O LORD, how long shall the wicked,
how long shall the wicked exult?
4 They pour out their arrogant words;
all the evildoers boast.
5 They crush your people, O LORD,
and afflict your heritage.
6 They kill the widow and the sojourner,
and murder the fatherless;
7 and they say, "The LORD does not see;
the God of Jacob does not perceive."

8 Understand, O dullest of the people!
Fools, when will you be wise?
9 He who planted the ear, does he not hear?
He who formed the eye, does he not see?

10 He who disciplines the nations,
does he not rebuke?
He who teaches man knowledge—
11 the LORD—knows the thoughts of man,
that they are but a breath.[1]

12 Blessed is the man whom you discipline, O LORD,
and whom you teach out of your law,
13 to give him rest from days of trouble,
until a pit is dug for the wicked.
14 For the LORD will not forsake his people;
he will not abandon his heritage;
15 for justice will return to the righteous,
and all the upright in heart will follow it.

16 Who rises up for me against the wicked?
Who stands up for me against evildoers?
17 If the LORD had not been my help,
my soul would soon have lived in the land of silence.
18 When I thought, "My foot slips,"
your steadfast love, O LORD, held me up.
19 When the cares of my heart are many,
your consolations cheer my soul.
20 Can wicked rulers be allied with you,
those who frame injustice by statute?
21 They band together against the life of the righteous
and condemn the innocent to death.[2]
22 But the LORD has become my stronghold,
and my God the rock of my refuge.
23 He will bring back on them their iniquity
and wipe them out for their wickedness;
the LORD our God will wipe them out.

Let Us Sing Songs of Praise

95 Oh come, let us sing to the LORD;
let us make a joyful noise to the rock of our salvation!
2 Let us come into his presence with thanksgiving;
let us make a joyful noise to him with songs of praise!
3 For the LORD is a great God,
and a great King above all gods.
4 In his hand are the depths of the earth;
the heights of the mountains are his also.
5 The sea is his, for he made it,
and his hands formed the dry land.

6 Oh come, let us worship and bow down;
let us kneel before the LORD, our Maker!
7 For he is our God,
and we are the people of his pasture,
and the sheep of his hand.
Today, if you hear his voice,
8 do not harden your hearts, as at Meribah,
as on the day at Massah in the wilderness,
9 when your fathers put me to the test
and put me to the proof, though they had seen my work.
10 For forty years I loathed that generation
and said, "They are a people who go astray in their heart,
and they have not known my ways."
11 Therefore I swore in my wrath,
"They shall not enter my rest."

[1] Septuagint *they are futile* [2] Hebrew *condemn innocent blood*

Worship in the Splendor of Holiness

96 Oh sing to the LORD a new song;
sing to the LORD, all the earth!
2 Sing to the LORD, bless his name;
tell of his salvation from day to day.

593

3 Declare his glory among the nations,
his marvelous works among all the peoples!
4 For great is the LORD, and greatly to be praised;
he is to be feared above all gods.
5 For all the gods of the peoples are worthless idols,
but the LORD made the heavens.
6 Splendor and majesty are before him;
strength and beauty are in his sanctuary.

7 Ascribe to the LORD, O families of the peoples,
ascribe to the LORD glory and strength!
8 Ascribe to the LORD the glory due his name;
bring an offering, and come into his courts!
9 Worship the LORD in the splendor of holiness;[1]
tremble before him, all the earth!

10 Say among the nations, "The LORD reigns!
Yes, the world is established; it shall never be moved;
he will judge the peoples with equity."

11 Let the heavens be glad, and let the earth rejoice;
let the sea roar, and all that fills it;
12 let the field exult, and everything in it!
Then shall all the trees of the forest sing for joy
13 before the LORD, for he comes,
for he comes to judge the earth.
He will judge the world in righteousness,
and the peoples in his faithfulness.

The LORD Reigns

97 The LORD reigns, let the earth rejoice;
let the many coastlands be glad!
2 Clouds and thick darkness are all around him;
righteousness and justice are the foundation of his throne.
3 Fire goes before him
and burns up his adversaries all around.
4 His lightnings light up the world;
the earth sees and trembles.
5 The mountains melt like wax before the LORD,
before the Lord of all the earth.

6 The heavens proclaim his righteousness,
and all the peoples see his glory.
7 All worshipers of images are put to shame,
who make their boast in worthless idols;
worship him, all you gods!

8 Zion hears and is glad,
and the daughters of Judah rejoice,
because of your judgments, O LORD.
9 For you, O LORD, are most high over all the earth;
you are exalted far above all gods.

10 O you who love the LORD, hate evil!
He preserves the lives of his saints;
he delivers them from the hand of the wicked.
11 Light is sown[2] for the righteous,
and joy for the upright in heart.
12 Rejoice in the LORD, O you righteous,
and give thanks to his holy name!

[1] Or *in holy attire* [2] Most Hebrew manuscripts; one Hebrew manuscript, Septuagint, Syriac, Jerome *Light dawns*

Make a Joyful Noise to the LORD

593

98 A PSALM.
Oh sing to the LORD a new song,
for he has done marvelous things!
His right hand and his holy arm
have worked salvation for him.

1449

2 The LORD has made known his salvation;
he has revealed his righteousness in the sight of the nations.
3 He has remembered his steadfast love and faithfulness
to the house of Israel.
All the ends of the earth have seen
the salvation of our God.

4 Make a joyful noise to the LORD, all the earth;
break forth into joyous song and sing praises!
5 Sing praises to the LORD with the lyre,
with the lyre and the sound of melody!
6 With trumpets and the sound of the horn
make a joyful noise before the King, the LORD!

7 Let the sea roar, and all that fills it;
the world and those who dwell in it!
8 Let the rivers clap their hands;
let the hills sing for joy together
9 before the LORD, for he comes
to judge the earth.
He will judge the world with righteousness,
and the peoples with equity.

The LORD Our God Is Holy

99 The LORD reigns; let the peoples tremble!
He sits enthroned upon the cherubim; let the earth quake!
2 The LORD is great in Zion;
he is exalted over all the peoples.
3 Let them praise your great and awesome name!
Holy is he!
4 The King in his might loves justice.[1]
You have established equity;
you have executed justice
and righteousness in Jacob.
5 Exalt the LORD our God;
worship at his footstool!
Holy is he!

6 Moses and Aaron were among his priests,
Samuel also was among those who called upon his name.
They called to the LORD, and he answered them.
7 In the pillar of the cloud he spoke to them;
they kept his testimonies
and the statute that he gave them.

8 O LORD our God, you answered them;
you were a forgiving God to them,
but an avenger of their wrongdoings.
9 Exalt the LORD our God,
and worship at his holy mountain;
for the LORD our God is holy!

His Steadfast Love Endures Forever

100 A PSALM FOR GIVING THANKS.
Make a joyful noise to the LORD, all the earth!
2 Serve the LORD with gladness!
Come into his presence with singing!

3 Know that the LORD, he is God!
It is he who made us, and we are his;[2]
we are his people, and the sheep of his pasture.

4 Enter his gates with thanksgiving,
and his courts with praise!
Give thanks to him; bless his name!

[1] Or *The might of the King loves justice* [2] Or *and not we ourselves*

5 For the LORD is good;
his steadfast love endures
forever,
and his faithfulness to all
generations.

I Will Walk with Integrity

101 A PSALM OF DAVID.
I will sing of steadfast love
and justice;
to you, O LORD, I will make
music.
2 I will ponder the way that is
blameless.
Oh when will you come to me?
I will walk with integrity of heart
within my house;
3 I will not set before my eyes
anything that is worthless.
I hate the work of those who fall
away;
it shall not cling to me.
4 A perverse heart shall be far from
me;
I will know nothing of evil.
5 Whoever slanders his neighbor
secretly
I will destroy.
Whoever has a haughty look and an
arrogant heart
I will not endure.

6 I will look with favor on the faithful
in the land,
that they may dwell with me;
he who walks in the way that is
blameless
shall minister to me.

7 No one who practices deceit
shall dwell in my house;
no one who utters lies
shall continue before my eyes.

8 Morning by morning I will destroy
all the wicked in the land,
cutting off all the evildoers
from the city of the LORD.

Do Not Hide Your Face from Me

102 A PRAYER OF ONE AFFLICTED, WHEN HE IS FAINT AND POURS OUT HIS COMPLAINT BEFORE THE LORD.

1 Hear my prayer, O LORD;
let my cry come to you!
2 Do not hide your face from me
in the day of my distress!
Incline your ear to me;
answer me speedily in the day
when I call!

3 For my days pass away like smoke,
and my bones burn like a furnace.
4 My heart is struck down like grass
and has withered;
I forget to eat my bread.
5 Because of my loud groaning
my bones cling to my flesh.
6 I am like a desert owl of the
wilderness,
like an owl[1] of the waste places;
7 I lie awake;
I am like a lonely sparrow on the
housetop.
8 All the day my enemies taunt me;
those who deride me use my
name for a curse.
9 For I eat ashes like bread
and mingle tears with my drink,
10 because of your indignation and
anger;
for you have taken me up and
thrown me down.
11 My days are like an evening shadow;
I wither away like grass.

12 But you, O LORD, are enthroned
forever;
you are remembered throughout
all generations.
13 You will arise and have pity on Zion;
it is the time to favor her;
the appointed time has come.
14 For your servants hold her stones
dear
and have pity on her dust.

[1] The precise identity of these birds is uncertain

15 Nations will fear the name of the LORD,
and all the kings of the earth will fear your glory.
16 For the LORD builds up Zion;
he appears in his glory;
17 he regards the prayer of the destitute
and does not despise their prayer.

18 Let this be recorded for a generation to come,
so that a people yet to be created may praise the LORD:
19 that he looked down from his holy height;
from heaven the LORD looked at the earth,
20 to hear the groans of the prisoners,
to set free those who were doomed to die,
21 that they may declare in Zion the name of the LORD,
and in Jerusalem his praise,
22 when peoples gather together,
and kingdoms, to worship the LORD.

23 He has broken my strength in midcourse;
he has shortened my days.
24 "O my God," I say, "take me not away
in the midst of my days—
you whose years endure
throughout all generations!"

25 Of old you laid the foundation of the earth,
and the heavens are the work of your hands.
26 They will perish, but you will remain;
they will all wear out like a garment.
You will change them like a robe,
and they will pass away,
27 but you are the same, and your years have no end.
28 The children of your servants shall dwell secure;
their offspring shall be established before you.

Bless the LORD, O My Soul

103

OF DAVID.

Bless the LORD, O my soul,
and all that is within me,
bless his holy name!
2 Bless the LORD, O my soul,
and forget not all his benefits,
3 who forgives all your iniquity,
who heals all your diseases,
4 who redeems your life from the pit,
who crowns you with steadfast love and mercy,
5 who satisfies you with good
so that your youth is renewed like the eagle's.

6 The LORD works righteousness
and justice for all who are oppressed.
7 He made known his ways to Moses,
his acts to the people of Israel.
1239
8 The LORD is merciful and gracious,
slow to anger and abounding in steadfast love.
9 He will not always chide,
nor will he keep his anger forever.
1239
10 He does not deal with us according to our sins,
nor repay us according to our iniquities.
11 For as high as the heavens are above the earth,
so great is his steadfast love toward those who fear him;
12 as far as the east is from the west,
so far does he remove our transgressions from us.
13 As a father shows compassion to his children,
so the LORD shows compassion to those who fear him.

14 For he knows our frame;[1]
he remembers that we are dust.

15 As for man, his days are like grass;
he flourishes like a flower of the
field;
16 for the wind passes over it, and it is
gone,
and its place knows it no more.
17 But the steadfast love of the
LORD is from everlasting to
61 everlasting on those who fear
him,
and his righteousness to
children's children,
18 to those who keep his covenant
and remember to do his
commandments.
19 The LORD has established his
throne in the heavens,
and his kingdom rules over all.

20 Bless the LORD, O you his angels,
you mighty ones who do his
word,
obeying the voice of his word!
21 Bless the LORD, all his hosts,
his ministers, who do his will!
22 Bless the LORD, all his works,
in all places of his dominion.
Bless the LORD, O my soul!

O LORD My God, You Are Very Great

104

Bless the LORD, O my
soul!
5 O LORD my God, you are very great!
You are clothed with splendor and
majesty,
2 covering yourself with light as
with a garment,
stretching out the heavens like a
tent.
3 He lays the beams of his chambers
on the waters;
he makes the clouds his chariot;
he rides on the wings of the wind;
4 he makes his messengers winds,
his ministers a flaming fire.

5 He set the earth on its foundations,
so that it should never be moved.
6 You covered it with the deep as with
a garment;
the waters stood above the
mountains.
7 At your rebuke they fled;
at the sound of your thunder they
took to flight.
8 The mountains rose, the valleys
sank down
to the place that you appointed
for them.
9 You set a boundary that they may
not pass,
so that they might not again cover
the earth.

10 You make springs gush forth in the
valleys;
they flow between the hills;
11 they give drink to every beast of the
field;
the wild donkeys quench their
thirst.
12 Beside them the birds of the
heavens dwell;
they sing among the branches.
13 From your lofty abode you water
the mountains;
the earth is satisfied with the fruit
of your work.

14 You cause the grass to grow for the
livestock
and plants for man to cultivate,
that he may bring forth food from
the earth
15 and wine to gladden the heart of
man,
oil to make his face shine
and bread to strengthen man's
heart.
16 The trees of the LORD are watered
abundantly,
the cedars of Lebanon that he
planted.

[1] *Or knows how we are formed*

17 In them the birds build their nests;
the stork has her home in the fir trees.
18 The high mountains are for the wild goats;
the rocks are a refuge for the rock badgers.

19 He made the moon to mark the seasons;[1]
the sun knows its time for setting.
20 You make darkness, and it is night,
when all the beasts of the forest creep about.
21 The young lions roar for their prey,
seeking their food from God.
22 When the sun rises, they steal away
and lie down in their dens.
23 Man goes out to his work
and to his labor until the evening.

24 O LORD, how manifold are your works!
In wisdom have you made them all;
the earth is full of your creatures.
25 Here is the sea, great and wide,
which teems with creatures innumerable,
living things both small and great.
26 There go the ships,
and Leviathan, which you formed to play in it.[2]

27 These all look to you,
to give them their food in due season.
28 When you give it to them, they gather it up;
when you open your hand, they are filled with good things.
29 When you hide your face, they are dismayed;
when you take away their breath, they die
and return to their dust.
30 When you send forth your Spirit,[3] they are created,
and you renew the face of the ground.

31 May the glory of the LORD endure forever;
may the LORD rejoice in his works,
32 who looks on the earth and it trembles,
who touches the mountains and they smoke!
33 I will sing to the LORD as long as I live;
I will sing praise to my God while I have being.
34 May my meditation be pleasing to him,
for I rejoice in the LORD.
35 Let sinners be consumed from the earth,
and let the wicked be no more!
Bless the LORD, O my soul!
Praise the LORD!

Tell of All His Wonderful Works

105 Oh give thanks to the LORD; call upon his name;
make known his deeds among the peoples!
2 Sing to him, sing praises to him;
tell of all his wondrous works!
3 Glory in his holy name;
let the hearts of those who seek the LORD rejoice!
4 Seek the LORD and his strength;
seek his presence continually!
5 Remember the wondrous works that he has done,
his miracles, and the judgments he uttered,
6 O offspring of Abraham, his servant,
children of Jacob, his chosen ones!

7 He is the LORD our God;
his judgments are in all the earth.
8 He remembers his covenant forever,
the word that he commanded, for a thousand generations,
9 the covenant that he made with Abraham,
his sworn promise to Isaac,

[1] Or *the appointed times* (compare Genesis 1:14) [2] Or *you formed to play with* [3] Or *breath*

10 which he confirmed to Jacob as a
statute,
to Israel as an everlasting covenant,
11 saying, "To you I will give the land
of Canaan
as your portion for an inheritance."

12 When they were few in number,
of little account, and sojourners
in it,
13 wandering from nation to nation,
from one kingdom to another
people,
14 he allowed no one to oppress them;
he rebuked kings on their
account,
15 saying, "Touch not my anointed ones,
do my prophets no harm!"

16 When he summoned a famine on
the land
and broke all supply[1] of bread,
17 he had sent a man ahead of them,
Joseph, who was sold as a slave.
18 His feet were hurt with fetters;
his neck was put in a collar of iron;
19 until what he had said came to pass,
the word of the LORD tested him.
20 The king sent and released him;
the ruler of the peoples set him
free;
21 he made him lord of his house
and ruler of all his possessions,
22 to bind[2] his princes at his pleasure
and to teach his elders wisdom.

23 Then Israel came to Egypt;
Jacob sojourned in the land of
Ham.
24 And the LORD made his people very
fruitful
and made them stronger than
their foes.
25 He turned their hearts to hate his
people,
to deal craftily with his servants.

26 He sent Moses, his servant,
and Aaron, whom he had chosen.
27 They performed his signs among
them
and miracles in the land of Ham.
28 He sent darkness, and made the
land dark;
they did not rebel[3] against his
words.

[1] Hebrew *staff* [2] Septuagint, Syriac, Jerome *instruct* [3] Septuagint, Syriac omit *not*

Psalm 105—Remembering God's Works

Psalm 105 is a song that describes how God has always been faithful and good to His people. The Israelites would sing this song to help them remember all the ways in which God had cared for them in the past. This helped them to grow in trusting God with their futures. To read the stories in detail, go to the following pages.

105:8–11 .... Jacob's Dream 75
105:16–22......... Joseph Saves People from Famine 107
105:23–27......... Moses and the Burning Bush............ 137
105:28–36......... Moses and the Plagues 145
105:36–38......... The Passover 153
105:40–42......... God Provides Manna, Water, and Quail.... 167
105:43–45......... The Walls Come Crashing Down 357

29 He turned their waters into blood
and caused their fish to die.
30 Their land swarmed with frogs,
even in the chambers of their kings.
31 He spoke, and there came swarms of flies,
and gnats throughout their country.
32 He gave them hail for rain,
and fiery lightning bolts through their land.
33 He struck down their vines and fig trees,
and shattered the trees of their country.
34 He spoke, and the locusts came,
young locusts without number,
35 which devoured all the vegetation in their land
and ate up the fruit of their ground.
36 He struck down all the firstborn in their land,
the firstfruits of all their strength.

37 Then he brought out Israel with silver and gold,
and there was none among his tribes who stumbled.
38 Egypt was glad when they departed,
for dread of them had fallen upon it.

39 He spread a cloud for a covering,
and fire to give light by night.
40 They asked, and he brought quail,
and gave them bread from heaven in abundance.
41 He opened the rock, and water gushed out;
it flowed through the desert like a river.
42 For he remembered his holy promise,
and Abraham, his servant.

43 So he brought his people out with joy,
his chosen ones with singing.
44 And he gave them the lands of the nations,
and they took possession of the fruit of the peoples' toil,
45 that they might keep his statutes
and observe his laws.
Praise the LORD!

Give Thanks to the LORD, for He Is Good

106 Praise the LORD!
Oh give thanks to the LORD, for he is good,
for his steadfast love endures forever!
2 Who can utter the mighty deeds of the LORD,
or declare all his praise?
3 Blessed are they who observe justice,
who do righteousness at all times!

4 Remember me, O LORD, when you show favor to your people;
help me when you save them,[1]
5 that I may look upon the prosperity of your chosen ones,
that I may rejoice in the gladness of your nation,
that I may glory with your inheritance.

6 Both we and our fathers have sinned;
we have committed iniquity; we have done wickedness.
161
7 Our fathers, when they were in Egypt,
did not consider your wondrous works;
they did not remember the abundance of your steadfast love,
but rebelled by the sea, at the Red Sea.
8 Yet he saved them for his name's sake,
that he might make known his mighty power.

[1] Or *Remember me, O LORD, with the favor you show to your people; help me with your salvation*

9 He rebuked the Red Sea, and it became dry,
and he led them through the deep as through a desert.
10 So he saved them from the hand of the foe
and redeemed them from the power of the enemy.
11 And the waters covered their adversaries;
not one of them was left.
12 Then they believed his words;
they sang his praise.

13 But they soon forgot his works;
they did not wait for his counsel.
14 But they had a wanton craving in the wilderness,
and put God to the test in the desert;
15 he gave them what they asked,
but sent a wasting disease among them.

16 When men in the camp were jealous of Moses
and Aaron, the holy one of the LORD,
17 the earth opened and swallowed up Dathan,
and covered the company of Abiram.
18 Fire also broke out in their company;
the flame burned up the wicked.

19 They made a calf in Horeb
and worshiped a metal image.
20 They exchanged the glory of God
for the image of an ox that eats grass.
21 They forgot God, their Savior,
who had done great things in Egypt,
22 wondrous works in the land of Ham,
and awesome deeds by the Red Sea.
23 Therefore he said he would destroy them—
had not Moses, his chosen one,
stood in the breach before him,
to turn away his wrath from destroying them.

265
24 Then they despised the pleasant land,
having no faith in his promise.
25 They murmured in their tents,
and did not obey the voice of the LORD.
26 Therefore he raised his hand and swore to them
that he would make them fall in the wilderness,
27 and would make their offspring fall among the nations,
scattering them among the lands.

28 Then they yoked themselves to the Baal of Peor,
and ate sacrifices offered to the dead;
29 they provoked the LORD to anger with their deeds,
and a plague broke out among them.
30 Then Phinehas stood up and intervened,
and the plague was stayed.
31 And that was counted to him as righteousness
from generation to generation forever.

32 They angered him at the waters of Meribah,
and it went ill with Moses on their account,
33 for they made his spirit bitter,[1]
and he spoke rashly with his lips.

34 They did not destroy the peoples,
as the LORD commanded them,
35 but they mixed with the nations
and learned to do as they did.
36 They served their idols,

[1] *Or they rebelled against God's Spirit*

which became a snare to them.
37 They sacrificed their sons
and their daughters to the demons;
38 they poured out innocent blood,
the blood of their sons and daughters,
whom they sacrificed to the idols of Canaan,
and the land was polluted with blood.
39 Thus they became unclean by their acts,
and played the whore in their deeds.

40 Then the anger of the LORD was kindled against his people,
and he abhorred his heritage;
41 he gave them into the hand of the nations,
so that those who hated them ruled over them.
42 Their enemies oppressed them,
and they were brought into subjection under their power.
43 Many times he delivered them,
but they were rebellious in their purposes
and were brought low through their iniquity.

44 Nevertheless, he looked upon their distress,
when he heard their cry.
45 For their sake he remembered his covenant,
and relented according to the abundance of his steadfast love.
46 He caused them to be pitied
by all those who held them captive.

47 Save us, O LORD our God,
and gather us from among the nations,
that we may give thanks to your holy name
and glory in your praise.

48 Blessed be the LORD, the God of Israel,
from everlasting to everlasting!
And let all the people say, "Amen!"
Praise the LORD!

BOOK FIVE

Let the Redeemed of the LORD Say So

107 Oh give thanks to the LORD, for he is good,
for his steadfast love endures forever!
2 Let the redeemed of the LORD say so,
whom he has redeemed from trouble[1]
3 and gathered in from the lands,
from the east and from the west,
from the north and from the south.

4 Some wandered in desert wastes,
finding no way to a city to dwell in;
5 hungry and thirsty,
their soul fainted within them.
6 Then they cried to the LORD in their trouble,
and he delivered them from their distress.
7 He led them by a straight way
till they reached a city to dwell in.
8 Let them thank the LORD for his steadfast love,
for his wondrous works to the children of man!
9 For he satisfies the longing soul,
and the hungry soul he fills with good things.

10 Some sat in darkness and in the shadow of death,
prisoners in affliction and in irons,
11 for they had rebelled against the words of God,
and spurned the counsel of the Most High.

[1] Or *from the hand of the foe*

12 So he bowed their hearts down with hard labor;
they fell down, with none to help.
13 Then they cried to the LORD in their trouble,
and he delivered them from their distress.
14 He brought them out of darkness and the shadow of death,
and burst their bonds apart.
15 Let them thank the LORD for his steadfast love,
for his wondrous works to the children of man!
16 For he shatters the doors of bronze
and cuts in two the bars of iron.

17 Some were fools through their sinful ways,
and because of their iniquities suffered affliction;
18 they loathed any kind of food,
and they drew near to the gates of death.
19 Then they cried to the LORD in their trouble,
and he delivered them from their distress.
20 He sent out his word and healed them,
and delivered them from their destruction.
21 Let them thank the LORD for his steadfast love,
for his wondrous works to the children of man!
22 And let them offer sacrifices of thanksgiving,
and tell of his deeds in songs of joy!

1689
23 Some went down to the sea in ships,
doing business on the great waters;
24 they saw the deeds of the LORD,
his wondrous works in the deep.
25 For he commanded and raised the stormy wind,
which lifted up the waves of the sea.
26 They mounted up to heaven; they went down to the depths;
their courage melted away in their evil plight;
27 they reeled and staggered like drunken men
and were at their wits' end.[1]
28 Then they cried to the LORD in their trouble,
and he delivered them from their distress.
1689
29 He made the storm be still,
and the waves of the sea were hushed.
30 Then they were glad that the waters[2] were quiet,
and he brought them to their desired haven.
31 Let them thank the LORD for his steadfast love,
for his wondrous works to the children of man!
32 Let them extol him in the congregation of the people,
and praise him in the assembly of the elders.

33 He turns rivers into a desert,
springs of water into thirsty ground,
34 a fruitful land into a salty waste,
because of the evil of its inhabitants.
35 He turns a desert into pools of water,
a parched land into springs of water.
36 And there he lets the hungry dwell,
and they establish a city to live in;
37 they sow fields and plant vineyards
and get a fruitful yield.
38 By his blessing they multiply greatly,
and he does not let their livestock diminish.

[1] Hebrew *and all their wisdom was swallowed up* [2] Hebrew *they*

39 When they are diminished and
brought low
through oppression, evil, and
sorrow,
40 he pours contempt on princes
and makes them wander in
trackless wastes;
41 but he raises up the needy out of
affliction
and makes their families like
flocks.
42 The upright see it and are glad,
and all wickedness shuts its
mouth.

43 Whoever is wise, let him attend to
these things;
let them consider the steadfast
love of the LORD.

With God We Shall Do Valiantly

108

A SONG. A PSALM OF DAVID.

My heart is steadfast, O God!
I will sing and make melody with
all my being![1]
2 Awake, O harp and lyre!
I will awake the dawn!
3 I will give thanks to you, O LORD,
among the peoples;
I will sing praises to you among
the nations.
4 For your steadfast love is great
above the heavens;
your faithfulness reaches to the
clouds.

5 Be exalted, O God, above the
heavens!
Let your glory be over all the earth!
6 That your beloved ones may be
delivered,
give salvation by your right hand
and answer me!
7 God has promised in his holiness:[2]
"With exultation I will divide up
Shechem
and portion out the Valley of
Succoth.
8 Gilead is mine; Manasseh is mine;
Ephraim is my helmet,
Judah my scepter.
9 Moab is my washbasin;
upon Edom I cast my shoe;
over Philistia I shout in triumph."

10 Who will bring me to the fortified
city?
Who will lead me to Edom?
11 Have you not rejected us, O God?
You do not go out, O God, with
our armies.
12 Oh grant us help against the foe,
for vain is the salvation of man!
13 With God we shall do valiantly;
it is he who will tread down our
foes.

Help Me, O LORD My God

109

TO THE CHOIRMASTER. A PSALM OF
DAVID.

1 Be not silent, O God of my praise!
2 For wicked and deceitful mouths
are opened against me,
speaking against me with lying
tongues.
3 They encircle me with words of hate,
and attack me without cause.
4 In return for my love they accuse me,
but I give myself to prayer.[3]
5 So they reward me evil for good,
and hatred for my love.

6 Appoint a wicked man against him;
let an accuser stand at his right
hand.
7 When he is tried, let him come
forth guilty;
let his prayer be counted as sin!
8 May his days be few;
may another take his office!
9 May his children be fatherless
and his wife a widow!
10 May his children wander about and
beg,
seeking food far from the ruins
they inhabit!

[1] Hebrew *with my glory* [2] Or *sanctuary* [3] Hebrew *but I am prayer*

11 May the creditor seize all that he has;
may strangers plunder the fruits of his toil!
12 Let there be none to extend kindness to him,
nor any to pity his fatherless children!
13 May his posterity be cut off;
may his name be blotted out in the second generation!
14 May the iniquity of his fathers be remembered before the LORD,
and let not the sin of his mother be blotted out!
15 Let them be before the LORD continually,
that he may cut off the memory of them from the earth!

16 For he did not remember to show kindness,
but pursued the poor and needy and the brokenhearted, to put them to death.
17 He loved to curse; let curses come[1] upon him!
He did not delight in blessing; may it be far[2] from him!
18 He clothed himself with cursing as his coat;
may it soak[3] into his body like water,
like oil into his bones!
19 May it be like a garment that he wraps around him,
like a belt that he puts on every day!
20 May this be the reward of my accusers from the LORD,
of those who speak evil against my life!
21 But you, O GOD my Lord,
deal on my behalf for your name's sake;
because your steadfast love is good, deliver me!
22 For I am poor and needy,
and my heart is stricken within me.
23 I am gone like a shadow at evening;
I am shaken off like a locust.
24 My knees are weak through fasting;
my body has become gaunt, with no fat.
25 I am an object of scorn to my accusers;
when they see me, they wag their heads.

26 Help me, O LORD my God!
Save me according to your steadfast love!
27 Let them know that this is your hand;
you, O LORD, have done it!
28 Let them curse, but you will bless!
They arise and are put to shame, but your servant will be glad!
29 May my accusers be clothed with dishonor;
may they be wrapped in their own shame as in a cloak!

30 With my mouth I will give great thanks to the LORD;
I will praise him in the midst of the throng.
31 For he stands at the right hand of the needy one,
to save him from those who condemn his soul to death.

Sit at My Right Hand

110

A PSALM OF DAVID.
The LORD says to my Lord:
"Sit at my right hand,
until I make your enemies your footstool."

2 The LORD sends forth from Zion your mighty scepter.
Rule in the midst of your enemies!
3 Your people will offer themselves freely
on the day of your power,[4]
in holy garments;[5]
from the womb of the morning,

[1] Revocalization; Masoretic Text *curses have come* [2] Revocalization; Masoretic Text *it is far* [3] Revocalization; Masoretic Text *it has soaked* [4] Or *on the day you lead your forces* [5] Masoretic Text; some Hebrew manuscripts and Jerome *on the holy mountains*

the dew of your youth will be
yours.[1]

4 The LORD has sworn
and will not change his mind,
"You are a priest forever
after the order of Melchizedek."

5 The Lord is at your right hand;
he will shatter kings on the day of
his wrath.
6 He will execute judgment among
the nations,
filling them with corpses;
he will shatter chiefs[2]
over the wide earth.
7 He will drink from the brook by the
way;
therefore he will lift up his head.

Great Are the LORD's Works

111 [3] Praise the LORD!
I will give thanks to the
LORD with my whole heart,
in the company of the upright, in
the congregation.
2 Great are the works of the LORD,
studied by all who delight in them.
3 Full of splendor and majesty is his
work,
and his righteousness endures
forever.
4 He has caused his wondrous works
to be remembered;
the LORD is gracious and merciful.
5 He provides food for those who fear
him;
he remembers his covenant forever.
6 He has shown his people the power
of his works,
in giving them the inheritance of
the nations.
7 The works of his hands are faithful
and just;
all his precepts are trustworthy;
8 they are established forever and ever,
to be performed with faithfulness
and uprightness.
9 He sent redemption to his people;
he has commanded his covenant
forever.
Holy and awesome is his name!
10 The fear of the LORD is the
beginning of wisdom;
all those who practice it have a
good understanding.
His praise endures forever!

The Righteous Will Never Be Moved

112 [4] Praise the LORD!
Blessed is the man who fears
the LORD,
who greatly delights in his
commandments!
2 His offspring will be mighty in the
land;
the generation of the upright will
be blessed.
3 Wealth and riches are in his house,
and his righteousness endures
forever.
4 Light dawns in the darkness for the
upright;
he is gracious, merciful, and
righteous.
5 It is well with the man who deals
generously and lends;
who conducts his affairs with
justice.
6 For the righteous will never be
moved;
he will be remembered forever.
7 He is not afraid of bad news;
his heart is firm, trusting in the
LORD.
8 His heart is steady; he will not be
afraid,
until he looks in triumph on his
adversaries.
9 He has distributed freely; he has
given to the poor;
his righteousness endures
forever;
his horn is exalted in honor.

[1] The meaning of the Hebrew is uncertain [2] Or *the head* [3] This psalm is an acrostic poem, each line beginning with the successive letters of the Hebrew alphabet [4] This psalm is an acrostic poem, each line beginning with the successive letters of the Hebrew alphabet

10 The wicked man sees it and is angry;
he gnashes his teeth and melts away;
the desire of the wicked will perish!

Who Is like the LORD Our God?

113 Praise the LORD!
Praise, O servants of the LORD,
praise the name of the LORD!

2 Blessed be the name of the LORD
from this time forth and forevermore!

3 From the rising of the sun to its setting,
the name of the LORD is to be praised!

4 The LORD is high above all nations,
and his glory above the heavens!

5 Who is like the LORD our God,
who is seated on high,

6 who looks far down
on the heavens and the earth?

7 He raises the poor from the dust
and lifts the needy from the ash heap,

8 to make them sit with princes,
with the princes of his people.

9 He gives the barren woman a home,
making her the joyous mother of children.
Praise the LORD!

Tremble at the Presence of the Lord

351

114 When Israel went out from Egypt,
the house of Jacob from a people of strange language,

2 Judah became his sanctuary,
Israel his dominion.

3 The sea looked and fled;
Jordan turned back.

4 The mountains skipped like rams,
the hills like lambs.

5 What ails you, O sea, that you flee?
O Jordan, that you turn back?

6 O mountains, that you skip like rams?
O hills, like lambs?

7 Tremble, O earth, at the presence of the Lord,
at the presence of the God of Jacob,

8 who turns the rock into a pool of water,
the flint into a spring of water.

To Your Name Give Glory

593

115 Not to us, O LORD, not to us, but to your name give glory,
for the sake of your steadfast love and your faithfulness!

2 Why should the nations say,
"Where is their God?"

3 Our God is in the heavens;
he does all that he pleases.

4 Their idols are silver and gold,
the work of human hands.

5 They have mouths, but do not speak;
eyes, but do not see.

6 They have ears, but do not hear;
noses, but do not smell.

7 They have hands, but do not feel;
feet, but do not walk;
and they do not make a sound in their throat.

8 Those who make them become like them;
so do all who trust in them.

9 O Israel,[1] trust in the LORD!
He is their help and their shield.

10 O house of Aaron, trust in the LORD!
He is their help and their shield.

11 You who fear the LORD, trust in the LORD!
He is their help and their shield.

12 The LORD has remembered us; he will bless us;
he will bless the house of Israel;
he will bless the house of Aaron;

[1] Masoretic Text; many Hebrew manuscripts, Septuagint, Syriac *O house of Israel*

13 he will bless those who fear the LORD,
both the small and the great.

14 May the LORD give you increase,
you and your children!
15 May you be blessed by the LORD,
who made heaven and earth!

16 The heavens are the LORD's heavens,
but the earth he has given to the
children of man.
17 The dead do not praise the LORD,
nor do any who go down into
silence.
18 But we will bless the LORD
from this time forth and
forevermore.
Praise the LORD!

I Love the LORD

116 I love the LORD, because he
has heard
my voice and my pleas for mercy.
2 Because he inclined his ear to me,
therefore I will call on him as long
as I live.
3 The snares of death encompassed
me;
the pangs of Sheol laid hold on me;
I suffered distress and anguish.
4 Then I called on the name of the
LORD:
"O LORD, I pray, deliver my soul!"

5 Gracious is the LORD, and righteous;
our God is merciful.
6 The LORD preserves the simple;
when I was brought low, he
saved me.
7 Return, O my soul, to your rest;
for the LORD has dealt bountifully
with you.

8 For you have delivered my soul
from death,
my eyes from tears,
my feet from stumbling;
9 I will walk before the LORD
in the land of the living.

10 I believed, even when[1] I spoke,
"I am greatly afflicted";
11 I said in my alarm,
"All mankind are liars."

12 What shall I render to the LORD
for all his benefits to me?
13 I will lift up the cup of salvation
and call on the name of the LORD,
14 I will pay my vows to the LORD
in the presence of all his people.

15 Precious in the sight of the LORD
is the death of his saints.
16 O LORD, I am your servant;
I am your servant, the son of your
maidservant.
You have loosed my bonds.
17 I will offer to you the sacrifice of
thanksgiving
and call on the name of the LORD.
18 I will pay my vows to the LORD
in the presence of all his people,
19 in the courts of the house of the LORD,
in your midst, O Jerusalem.
Praise the LORD!

The LORD's Faithfulness Endures Forever

117 Praise the LORD, all nations!
Extol him, all peoples!
2 For great is his steadfast love
toward us,
and the faithfulness of the LORD
endures forever.
Praise the LORD!

His Steadfast Love Endures Forever

118 Oh give thanks to the LORD,
for he is good;
for his steadfast love endures
forever!

2 Let Israel say,
"His steadfast love endures forever."
3 Let the house of Aaron say,
"His steadfast love endures forever."
4 Let those who fear the LORD say,
"His steadfast love endures forever."

[1] Or *believed, indeed*; Septuagint *believed, therefore*

35 Lead me in the path of your
commandments,
for I delight in it.
36 Incline my heart to your testimonies,
and not to selfish gain!
37 Turn my eyes from looking at
worthless things;
and give me life in your ways.
38 Confirm to your servant your
promise,
that you may be feared.
39 Turn away the reproach that I dread,
for your rules are good.
40 Behold, I long for your precepts;
in your righteousness give me life!

Waw

41 Let your steadfast love come to me,
O Lord,
your salvation according to your
promise;
42 then shall I have an answer for him
who taunts me,
for I trust in your word.
43 And take not the word of truth
utterly out of my mouth,
for my hope is in your rules.
44 I will keep your law continually,
forever and ever,
45 and I shall walk in a wide place,
for I have sought your precepts.
46 I will also speak of your testimonies
before kings
and shall not be put to shame,
47 for I find my delight in your
commandments,
which I love.
48 I will lift up my hands toward your
commandments, which I love,
and I will meditate on your
statutes.

Zayin

49 Remember your word to your
servant,
in which you have made me hope.
50 This is my comfort in my affliction,
that your promise gives me life.
51 The insolent utterly deride me,
but I do not turn away from your
law.
52 When I think of your rules from of
old,
I take comfort, O Lord.
53 Hot indignation seizes me because
of the wicked,
who forsake your law.
54 Your statutes have been my songs
in the house of my sojourning.
55 I remember your name in the night,
O Lord,
and keep your law.
56 This blessing has fallen to me,
that I have kept your precepts.

Heth

57 The Lord is my portion;
I promise to keep your words.
58 I entreat your favor with all my heart;
be gracious to me according to
your promise.
59 When I think on my ways,
I turn my feet to your testimonies;
60 I hasten and do not delay
to keep your commandments.
61 Though the cords of the wicked
ensnare me,
I do not forget your law.
62 At midnight I rise to praise you,
because of your righteous rules.
63 I am a companion of all who fear you,
of those who keep your precepts.
64 The earth, O Lord, is full of your
steadfast love;
teach me your statutes!

Teth

65 You have dealt well with your
servant,
O Lord, according to your word.
66 Teach me good judgment and
knowledge,
for I believe in your
commandments.
67 Before I was afflicted I went astray,
but now I keep your word.

68 You are good and do good;
teach me your statutes.
69 The insolent smear me with lies,
but with my whole heart I keep
your precepts;
70 their heart is unfeeling like fat,
but I delight in your law.
71 It is good for me that I was afflicted,
that I might learn your statutes.
72 The law of your mouth is better to me
than thousands of gold and silver
pieces.

Yodh

73 Your hands have made and
fashioned me;
give me understanding that I may
learn your commandments.
74 Those who fear you shall see me
and rejoice,
because I have hoped in your word.
75 I know, O Lord, that your rules are
righteous,
and that in faithfulness you have
afflicted me.
76 Let your steadfast love comfort me
according to your promise to your
servant.
77 Let your mercy come to me, that I
may live;
for your law is my delight.
78 Let the insolent be put to shame,
because they have wronged me
with falsehood;
as for me, I will meditate on your
precepts.
79 Let those who fear you turn to me,
that they may know your
testimonies.
80 May my heart be blameless in your
statutes,
that I may not be put to shame!

Kaph

81 My soul longs for your salvation;
I hope in your word.
82 My eyes long for your promise;
I ask, "When will you comfort me?"
83 For I have become like a wineskin
in the smoke,
yet I have not forgotten your
statutes.
84 How long must your servant
endure?[1]
When will you judge those who
persecute me?
85 The insolent have dug pitfalls for me;
they do not live according to your
law.
86 All your commandments are sure;
they persecute me with
falsehood; help me!
87 They have almost made an end of
me on earth,
but I have not forsaken your
precepts.
88 In your steadfast love give me life,
that I may keep the testimonies of
your mouth.

Lamedh

89 Forever, O Lord, your word
is firmly fixed in the heavens.
90 Your faithfulness endures to all
generations;
you have established the earth,
and it stands fast.
91 By your appointment they stand
this day,
for all things are your servants.
92 If your law had not been my delight,
I would have perished in my
affliction.
93 I will never forget your precepts,
for by them you have given me life.
94 I am yours; save me,
for I have sought your precepts.
95 The wicked lie in wait to destroy me,
but I consider your testimonies.
96 I have seen a limit to all perfection,
but your commandment is
exceedingly broad.

Mem

97 Oh how I love your law!
It is my meditation all the day.

[1] Hebrew *How many are the days of your servant?*

98 Your commandment makes me
wiser than my enemies,
for it is ever with me.
99 I have more understanding than all
my teachers,
for your testimonies are my
meditation.
100 I understand more than the aged,[1]
for I keep your precepts.
101 I hold back my feet from every evil
way,
in order to keep your word.
102 I do not turn aside from your rules,
for you have taught me.
103 How sweet are your words to my
taste,
sweeter than honey to my mouth!
104 Through your precepts I get
understanding;
therefore I hate every false way.

Nun

105 Your word is a lamp to my feet
and a light to my path.
106 I have sworn an oath and
confirmed it,
to keep your righteous rules.
107 I am severely afflicted;
give me life, O LORD, according to
your word!
108 Accept my freewill offerings of
praise, O LORD,
and teach me your rules.
109 I hold my life in my hand continually,
but I do not forget your law.
110 The wicked have laid a snare for me,
but I do not stray from your
precepts.
111 Your testimonies are my heritage
forever,
for they are the joy of my heart.
112 I incline my heart to perform your
statutes
forever, to the end.[2]

Samekh

113 I hate the double-minded,
but I love your law.
114 You are my hiding place and my
shield;
I hope in your word.
115 Depart from me, you evildoers,
that I may keep the
commandments of my God.
116 Uphold me according to your
promise, that I may live,
and let me not be put to shame in
my hope!
117 Hold me up, that I may be safe
and have regard for your statutes
continually!
118 You spurn all who go astray from
your statutes,
for their cunning is in vain.
119 All the wicked of the earth you
discard like dross,
therefore I love your testimonies.
120 My flesh trembles for fear of you,
and I am afraid of your
judgments.

Ayin

697
121 I have done what is just and right;
do not leave me to my oppressors.
122 Give your servant a pledge of
good;
let not the insolent oppress me.
123 My eyes long for your salvation
and for the fulfillment of your
righteous promise.
124 Deal with your servant according to
your steadfast love,
and teach me your statutes.
125 I am your servant; give me
understanding,
that I may know your
testimonies!
126 It is time for the LORD to act,
for your law has been broken.
127 Therefore I love your
commandments
above gold, above fine gold.
128 Therefore I consider all your
precepts to be right;
I hate every false way.

[1] *Or the elders* [2] *Or statutes; the reward is eternal*

PE

129 Your testimonies are wonderful;
therefore my soul keeps them.
130 The unfolding of your words gives light;
it imparts understanding to the simple.
131 I open my mouth and pant,
because I long for your commandments.
132 Turn to me and be gracious to me,
as is your way with those who love your name.
133 Keep steady my steps according to your promise,
and let no iniquity get dominion over me.
134 Redeem me from man's oppression,
that I may keep your precepts.
135 Make your face shine upon your servant,
and teach me your statutes.
136 My eyes shed streams of tears,
because people do not keep your law.

TSADHE

137 Righteous are you, O LORD,
and right are your rules.
138 You have appointed your testimonies in righteousness
and in all faithfulness.
139 My zeal consumes me,
because my foes forget your words.
140 Your promise is well tried,
and your servant loves it.
141 I am small and despised,
yet I do not forget your precepts.
142 Your righteousness is righteous forever,
and your law is true.
143 Trouble and anguish have found me out,
but your commandments are my delight.
144 Your testimonies are righteous forever;
give me understanding that I may live.

QOPH

145 With my whole heart I cry; answer me, O LORD!
I will keep your statutes.
146 I call to you; save me,
that I may observe your testimonies.
147 I rise before dawn and cry for help;
I hope in your words.
148 My eyes are awake before the watches of the night,
that I may meditate on your promise.
149 Hear my voice according to your steadfast love;
O LORD, according to your justice give me life.
150 They draw near who persecute me with evil purpose;
they are far from your law.
151 But you are near, O LORD,
and all your commandments are true.
152 Long have I known from your testimonies
that you have founded them forever.

RESH

153 Look on my affliction and deliver me,
for I do not forget your law.
154 Plead my cause and redeem me;
give me life according to your promise!
155 Salvation is far from the wicked,
for they do not seek your statutes.
156 Great is your mercy, O LORD;
give me life according to your rules.
157 Many are my persecutors and my adversaries,
but I do not swerve from your testimonies.

158 I look at the faithless with disgust,
because they do not keep your commands.
159 Consider how I love your precepts!
Give me life according to your steadfast love.
160 The sum of your word is truth,
and every one of your righteous rules endures forever.

SIN AND SHIN

161 Princes persecute me without cause,
but my heart stands in awe of your words.
162 I rejoice at your word
like one who finds great spoil.
163 I hate and abhor falsehood,
but I love your law.
164 Seven times a day I praise you
for your righteous rules.
165 Great peace have those who love your law;
nothing can make them stumble.
166 I hope for your salvation, O LORD,
and I do your commandments.
167 My soul keeps your testimonies;
I love them exceedingly.
168 I keep your precepts and testimonies,
for all my ways are before you.

TAW

169 Let my cry come before you, O LORD;
give me understanding according to your word!
170 Let my plea come before you;
deliver me according to your word.
171 My lips will pour forth praise,
for you teach me your statutes.
172 My tongue will sing of your word,
for all your commandments are right.
173 Let your hand be ready to help me,
for I have chosen your precepts.
174 I long for your salvation, O LORD,
and your law is my delight.
175 Let my soul live and praise you,
and let your rules help me.

1501

176 I have gone astray like a lost sheep; seek your servant,
for I do not forget your commandments.

Deliver Me, O LORD

120 A SONG OF ASCENTS.
In my distress I called to the LORD,
and he answered me.
2 Deliver me, O LORD,
from lying lips,
from a deceitful tongue.

3 What shall be given to you,
and what more shall be done to you,
you deceitful tongue?
4 A warrior's sharp arrows,
with glowing coals of the broom tree!

5 Woe to me, that I sojourn in Meshech,
that I dwell among the tents of Kedar!
6 Too long have I had my dwelling
among those who hate peace.
7 I am for peace,
but when I speak, they are for war!

My Help Comes from the LORD

121 A SONG OF ASCENTS.
I lift up my eyes to the hills.
From where does my help come?
2 My help comes from the LORD,
who made heaven and earth.

3 He will not let your foot be moved;
he who keeps you will not slumber.
4 Behold, he who keeps Israel
will neither slumber nor sleep.

5 The LORD is your keeper;
the LORD is your shade on your right hand.
6 The sun shall not strike you by day,
nor the moon by night.

7 The LORD will keep you from all evil;
he will keep your life.
8 The LORD will keep
your going out and your coming in
from this time forth and
forevermore.

Let Us Go to the House of the LORD

122 A SONG OF ASCENTS. OF DAVID.
I was glad when they said to
me,
"Let us go to the house of the
LORD!"
2 Our feet have been standing
within your gates, O Jerusalem!

3 Jerusalem—built as a city
that is bound firmly together,
4 to which the tribes go up,
the tribes of the LORD,
as was decreed for[1] Israel,
to give thanks to the name of the
LORD.
5 There thrones for judgment were set,
the thrones of the house of David.

6 Pray for the peace of Jerusalem!
"May they be secure who love you!
7 Peace be within your walls
and security within your towers!"
8 For my brothers and companions'
sake
I will say, "Peace be within you!"
9 For the sake of the house of the
LORD our God,
I will seek your good.

Our Eyes Look to the LORD Our God

123 A SONG OF ASCENTS.
To you I lift up my eyes,
O you who are enthroned in the
heavens!
2 Behold, as the eyes of servants
look to the hand of their master,
as the eyes of a maidservant
to the hand of her mistress,
so our eyes look to the LORD our God,
till he has mercy upon us.

3 Have mercy upon us, O LORD, have
mercy upon us,
for we have had more than
enough of contempt.
4 Our soul has had more than enough
of the scorn of those who are at ease,
of the contempt of the proud.

Our Help Is in the Name of the LORD

124 A SONG OF ASCENTS. OF DAVID.
If it had not been the LORD
who was on our side—
let Israel now say—
2 if it had not been the LORD who was
on our side
when people rose up against us,
3 then they would have swallowed us
up alive,
when their anger was kindled
against us;
4 then the flood would have swept us
away,
the torrent would have gone over
us;
5 then over us would have gone
the raging waters.

6 Blessed be the LORD,
who has not given us
as prey to their teeth!
7 We have escaped like a bird
from the snare of the fowlers;
the snare is broken,
and we have escaped!

8 Our help is in the name of the LORD,
who made heaven and earth.

The LORD Surrounds His People

125 A SONG OF ASCENTS.
Those who trust in the LORD
are like Mount Zion,
which cannot be moved, but
abides forever.
2 As the mountains surround
Jerusalem,
so the LORD surrounds his people,
from this time forth and
forevermore.

[1] *Or as a testimony for*

3 For the scepter of wickedness shall not rest
on the land allotted to the righteous,
lest the righteous stretch out
their hands to do wrong.
4 Do good, O LORD, to those who are good,
and to those who are upright in their hearts!
5 But those who turn aside to their crooked ways
the LORD will lead away with evildoers!
Peace be upon Israel!

Restore Our Fortunes, O LORD

126 A SONG OF ASCENTS.
When the LORD restored the fortunes of Zion,
we were like those who dream.
2 Then our mouth was filled with laughter,
and our tongue with shouts of joy;
then they said among the nations,
"The LORD has done great things for them."
3 The LORD has done great things for us;
we are glad.
4 Restore our fortunes, O LORD,
like streams in the Negeb!
5 Those who sow in tears
shall reap with shouts of joy!
6 He who goes out weeping,
bearing the seed for sowing,
shall come home with shouts of joy,
bringing his sheaves with him.

Unless the LORD Builds the House

127 A SONG OF ASCENTS. OF SOLOMON.
Unless the LORD builds the house,
those who build it labor in vain.
Unless the LORD watches over the city,
the watchman stays awake in vain.
2 It is in vain that you rise up early
and go late to rest,
eating the bread of anxious toil;
for he gives to his beloved sleep.

3 Behold, children are a heritage from the LORD,
the fruit of the womb a reward.
4 Like arrows in the hand of a warrior
are the children[1] of one's youth.
5 Blessed is the man
who fills his quiver with them!
He shall not be put to shame
when he speaks with his enemies in the gate.[2]

Blessed Is Everyone Who Fears the LORD

128 A SONG OF ASCENTS.
Blessed is everyone who fears the LORD,
who walks in his ways!
2 You shall eat the fruit of the labor of your hands;
you shall be blessed, and it shall be well with you.

3 Your wife will be like a fruitful vine
within your house;
your children will be like olive shoots
around your table.
4 Behold, thus shall the man be blessed
who fears the LORD.

5 The LORD bless you from Zion!
May you see the prosperity of Jerusalem
all the days of your life!
6 May you see your children's children!
Peace be upon Israel!

They Have Afflicted Me from My Youth

129 A SONG OF ASCENTS.
"Greatly[3] have they afflicted me from my youth"—
let Israel now say—
2 "Greatly have they afflicted me from my youth,
yet they have not prevailed against me.

[1] Or *sons* [2] Or *They shall not be put to shame when they speak with their enemies in the gate* [3] Or *Often*; also verse 2

3 The plowers plowed upon my back;
they made long their furrows."
4 The LORD is righteous;
he has cut the cords of the wicked.
5 May all who hate Zion
be put to shame and turned backward!
6 Let them be like the grass on the housetops,
which withers before it grows up,
7 with which the reaper does not fill his hand
nor the binder of sheaves his arms,
8 nor do those who pass by say,
"The blessing of the LORD be upon you!
We bless you in the name of the LORD!"

My Soul Waits for the Lord

130

A SONG OF ASCENTS.

Out of the depths I cry to you, O LORD!
2 O Lord, hear my voice!
Let your ears be attentive
to the voice of my pleas for mercy!

3 If you, O LORD, should mark iniquities,
O Lord, who could stand?
4 But with you there is forgiveness,
that you may be feared.

5 I wait for the LORD, my soul waits,
and in his word I hope;
6 my soul waits for the Lord
more than watchmen for the morning,
more than watchmen for the morning.

7 O Israel, hope in the LORD!
For with the LORD there is steadfast love,
and with him is plentiful redemption.
8 And he will redeem Israel
from all his iniquities.

I Have Calmed and Quieted My Soul

131

A SONG OF ASCENTS. OF DAVID.

O LORD, my heart is not lifted up;
my eyes are not raised too high;
I do not occupy myself with things
too great and too marvelous for me.
2 But I have calmed and quieted my soul,
like a weaned child with its mother;
like a weaned child is my soul within me.

3 O Israel, hope in the LORD
from this time forth and forevermore.

The LORD Has Chosen Zion

132

A SONG OF ASCENTS.

Remember, O LORD, in David's favor,
all the hardships he endured,
2 how he swore to the LORD
and vowed to the Mighty One of Jacob,
3 "I will not enter my house
or get into my bed,
4 I will not give sleep to my eyes
or slumber to my eyelids,
5 until I find a place for the LORD,
a dwelling place for the Mighty One of Jacob."

6 Behold, we heard of it in Ephrathah;
we found it in the fields of Jaar.
7 "Let us go to his dwelling place;
let us worship at his footstool!"

8 Arise, O LORD, and go to your resting place,
you and the ark of your might.
9 Let your priests be clothed with righteousness,
and let your saints shout for joy.
10 For the sake of your servant David,
do not turn away the face of your anointed one.

11 The LORD swore to David a sure oath
from which he will not turn back:
"One of the sons of your body[1]
I will set on your throne.
12 If your sons keep my covenant
and my testimonies that I shall teach them,
their sons also forever
shall sit on your throne."

13 For the LORD has chosen Zion;
he has desired it for his dwelling place:
14 "This is my resting place forever;
here I will dwell, for I have desired it.
15 I will abundantly bless her provisions;
I will satisfy her poor with bread.
16 Her priests I will clothe with salvation,
and her saints will shout for joy.
17 There I will make a horn to sprout for David;
I have prepared a lamp for my anointed.
18 His enemies I will clothe with shame,
but on him his crown will shine."

When Brothers Dwell in Unity

133

A SONG OF ASCENTS. OF DAVID.

Behold, how good and pleasant it is
when brothers dwell in unity![2]
2 It is like the precious oil on the head,
running down on the beard,
on the beard of Aaron,
running down on the collar of his robes!
3 It is like the dew of Hermon,
which falls on the mountains of Zion!
For there the LORD has commanded the blessing,
life forevermore.

Come, Bless the LORD

134

A SONG OF ASCENTS.

Come, bless the LORD, all you servants of the LORD,
who stand by night in the house of the LORD!
2 Lift up your hands to the holy place
and bless the LORD!

3 May the LORD bless you from Zion,
he who made heaven and earth!

Your Name, O LORD, Endures Forever

135

Praise the LORD!
Praise the name of the LORD,
give praise, O servants of the LORD,
2 who stand in the house of the LORD,
in the courts of the house of our God!
3 Praise the LORD, for the LORD is good;
sing to his name, for it is pleasant![3]
4 For the LORD has chosen Jacob for himself,
Israel as his own possession.

5 For I know that the LORD is great,
and that our Lord is above all gods.
6 Whatever the LORD pleases, he does,
in heaven and on earth,
in the seas and all deeps.
7 He it is who makes the clouds rise at the end of the earth,
who makes lightnings for the rain
and brings forth the wind from his storehouses.

153
8 He it was who struck down the firstborn of Egypt,
both of man and of beast;
9 who in your midst, O Egypt,
sent signs and wonders
against Pharaoh and all his servants;
10 who struck down many nations
and killed mighty kings,
11 Sihon, king of the Amorites,
and Og, king of Bashan,
and all the kingdoms of Canaan,

[1] Hebrew *of your fruit of the womb* [2] Or *dwell together* [3] Or *for he is beautiful*

12 and gave their land as a heritage,
a heritage to his people Israel.

13 Your name, O LORD, endures forever,
your renown,[1] O LORD,
throughout all ages.
14 For the LORD will vindicate his
people
and have compassion on his
servants.

15 The idols of the nations are silver
and gold,
the work of human hands.
16 They have mouths, but do not speak;
they have eyes, but do not see;
17 they have ears, but do not hear,
nor is there any breath in their
mouths.
18 Those who make them become like
them,
so do all who trust in them!

19 O house of Israel, bless the LORD!
O house of Aaron, bless the LORD!
20 O house of Levi, bless the LORD!
You who fear the LORD, bless the
LORD!
21 Blessed be the LORD from Zion,
he who dwells in Jerusalem!
Praise the LORD!

His Steadfast Love Endures Forever

136 Give thanks to the LORD, for
he is good,
for his steadfast love endures
forever.
2 Give thanks to the God of gods,
for his steadfast love endures
forever.
3 Give thanks to the Lord of lords,
for his steadfast love endures
forever;

4 to him who alone does great
wonders,
for his steadfast love endures
forever;
5 to him who by understanding made
the heavens,
for his steadfast love endures
forever;
6 to him who spread out the earth
above the waters,
for his steadfast love endures
forever;
7 to him who made the great lights,
for his steadfast love endures
forever;
8 the sun to rule over the day,
for his steadfast love endures
forever;
9 the moon and stars to rule over the
night,
for his steadfast love endures
forever;

10 to him who struck down the
firstborn of Egypt,
for his steadfast love endures
forever;
11 and brought Israel out from among
them,
for his steadfast love endures
forever;
12 with a strong hand and an
outstretched arm,
for his steadfast love endures
forever;
13 to him who divided the Red Sea in
two,
for his steadfast love endures
forever;
14 and made Israel pass through the
midst of it,
for his steadfast love endures
forever;
15 but overthrew[2] Pharaoh and his
host in the Red Sea,
for his steadfast love endures
forever;
16 to him who led his people through
the wilderness,
for his steadfast love endures
forever;

[1] Or *remembrance* [2] Hebrew *shook off*

17 to him who struck down great kings,
for his steadfast love endures forever;
18 and killed mighty kings,
for his steadfast love endures forever;
19 Sihon, king of the Amorites,
for his steadfast love endures forever;
20 and Og, king of Bashan,
for his steadfast love endures forever;
21 and gave their land as a heritage,
for his steadfast love endures forever;
22 a heritage to Israel his servant,
for his steadfast love endures forever.

23 It is he who remembered us in our low estate,
for his steadfast love endures forever;
24 and rescued us from our foes,
for his steadfast love endures forever;
25 he who gives food to all flesh,
for his steadfast love endures forever.

26 Give thanks to the God of heaven,
for his steadfast love endures forever.

How Shall We Sing the LORD's Song?

137 By the waters of Babylon,
there we sat down and wept,
when we remembered Zion.
2 On the willows[1] there
we hung up our lyres.
3 For there our captors
required of us songs,
and our tormentors, mirth, saying,
"Sing us one of the songs of Zion!"

4 How shall we sing the LORD's song
in a foreign land?
5 If I forget you, O Jerusalem,
let my right hand forget its skill!
6 Let my tongue stick to the roof of my mouth,
if I do not remember you,
if I do not set Jerusalem
above my highest joy!

7 Remember, O LORD, against the Edomites
the day of Jerusalem,
how they said, "Lay it bare, lay it bare,
down to its foundations!"
8 O daughter of Babylon, doomed to be destroyed,
blessed shall he be who repays you
with what you have done to us!
9 Blessed shall he be who takes your little ones
and dashes them against the rock!

Give Thanks to the LORD

138 OF DAVID.
I give you thanks, O LORD,
with my whole heart;
before the gods I sing your praise;
2 I bow down toward your holy temple
and give thanks to your name for your steadfast love and your faithfulness,
for you have exalted above all things
your name and your word.[2]
3 On the day I called, you answered me;
my strength of soul you increased.[3]

4 All the kings of the earth shall give you thanks, O LORD,
for they have heard the words of your mouth,
5 and they shall sing of the ways of the LORD,
for great is the glory of the LORD.
6 For though the LORD is high, he regards the lowly,
but the haughty he knows from afar.

[1] Or *poplars* [2] Or *you have exalted your word above all your name* [3] Hebrew *you made me bold in my soul with strength*

7 Though I walk in the midst of
trouble,
you preserve my life;
you stretch out your hand against
the wrath of my enemies,
and your right hand delivers me.
8 The LORD will fulfill his purpose
for me;
your steadfast love, O LORD,
endures forever.
Do not forsake the work of your
hands.

Search Me, O God, and Know My Heart

139

TO THE CHOIRMASTER. A PSALM OF DAVID.

1 O LORD, you have searched me and
known me!
2 You know when I sit down and
when I rise up;
you discern my thoughts from
afar.
3 You search out my path and my
lying down
and are acquainted with all my
ways.
4 Even before a word is on my tongue,
behold, O LORD, you know it
altogether.
5 You hem me in, behind and before,
and lay your hand upon me.
6 Such knowledge is too wonderful
for me;
it is high; I cannot attain it.

7 Where shall I go from your
Spirit?
75 Or where shall I flee from your
presence?
8 If I ascend to heaven, you are there!
If I make my bed in Sheol, you are
there!
9 If I take the wings of the morning
and dwell in the uttermost parts
of the sea,
10 even there your hand shall lead me,
and your right hand shall hold me.
11 If I say, "Surely the darkness shall
cover me,
and the light about me be night,"
12 even the darkness is not dark to
you;
the night is bright as the day,
for darkness is as light with you.

13 For you formed my inward parts;
you knitted me together in my
mother's womb.
14 I praise you, for I am fearfully and
wonderfully made.[1]
Wonderful are your works;
my soul knows it very well.
15 My frame was not hidden from you,
when I was being made in secret,
intricately woven in the depths of
the earth.
16 Your eyes saw my unformed
substance;
in your book were written, every
one of them,
the days that were formed for me,
when as yet there was none of
them.

17 How precious to me are your
thoughts, O God!
How vast is the sum of them!
18 If I would count them, they are
more than the sand.
I awake, and I am still with you.

19 Oh that you would slay the wicked,
O God!
O men of blood, depart from me!
20 They speak against you with
malicious intent;
your enemies take your name in
vain![2]
21 Do I not hate those who hate you,
O LORD?
And do I not loathe those who rise
up against you?
22 I hate them with complete hatred;
I count them my enemies.

[1] Or *for I am fearfully set apart* [2] Hebrew lacks *your name*

23 Search me, O God, and know my
heart!
Try me and know my thoughts![1]
24 And see if there be any grievous way
in me,
and lead me in the way
everlasting![2]

Deliver Me, O LORD, from Evil Men

140 TO THE CHOIRMASTER. A PSALM OF DAVID.

1 Deliver me, O LORD, from evil men;
preserve me from violent men,
2 who plan evil things in their heart
and stir up wars continually.
3 They make their tongue sharp as a
serpent's,
and under their lips is the venom
of asps. *Selah*
4 Guard me, O LORD, from the hands
of the wicked;
preserve me from violent men,
who have planned to trip up my
feet.
5 The arrogant have hidden a trap for
me,
and with cords they have spread a
net;[3]
beside the way they have set
snares for me. *Selah*
6 I say to the LORD, You are my God;
give ear to the voice of my pleas
for mercy, O LORD!
7 O LORD, my Lord, the strength of my
salvation,
you have covered my head in the
day of battle.
8 Grant not, O LORD, the desires of the
wicked;
do not further their[4] evil plot, or
they will be exalted! *Selah*
9 As for the head of those who
surround me,
let the mischief of their lips
overwhelm them!
10 Let burning coals fall upon them!
Let them be cast into fire,
into miry pits, no more to rise!
11 Let not the slanderer be established
in the land;
let evil hunt down the violent
man speedily!
12 I know that the LORD will maintain
the cause of the afflicted,
and will execute justice for the
needy.
13 Surely the righteous shall give
thanks to your name;
the upright shall dwell in your
presence.

Give Ear to My Voice

141 A PSALM OF DAVID.

O LORD, I call upon you;
hasten to me!
Give ear to my voice when I call to
you!
2 Let my prayer be counted as incense
before you,
and the lifting up of my hands as
the evening sacrifice!
3 Set a guard, O LORD, over my mouth;
keep watch over the door of my
lips!
4 Do not let my heart incline to any evil,
to busy myself with wicked deeds
in company with men who work
iniquity,
and let me not eat of their
delicacies!
5 Let a righteous man strike me—it is
a kindness;
let him rebuke me—it is oil for
my head;
let my head not refuse it.
Yet my prayer is continually against
their evil deeds.
6 When their judges are thrown over
the cliff,[5]
then they shall hear my words, for
they are pleasant.

[1] Or *cares* [2] Or *in the ancient way* (compare Jeremiah 6:16) [3] Or *they have spread cords as a net* [4] Hebrew *his* [5] Or *When their judges fall into the hands of the Rock*

7 As when one plows and breaks up
the earth,
so shall our bones be scattered at
the mouth of Sheol.[1]

8 But my eyes are toward you, O GOD,
my Lord;
in you I seek refuge; leave me not
defenseless![2]
9 Keep me from the trap that they
have laid for me
and from the snares of evildoers!
10 Let the wicked fall into their own nets,
while I pass by safely.

You Are My Refuge

142

A MASKIL[3] OF DAVID, WHEN HE WAS IN THE CAVE. A PRAYER.

1 With my voice I cry out to the LORD;
with my voice I plead for mercy to
the LORD.
2 I pour out my complaint before him;
I tell my trouble before him.
3 When my spirit faints within me,
you know my way!
In the path where I walk
they have hidden a trap for me.
4 Look to the right and see:
there is none who takes notice of
me;
no refuge remains to me;
no one cares for my soul.

5 I cry to you, O LORD;
I say, "You are my refuge,
my portion in the land of the
living."
6 Attend to my cry,
for I am brought very low!
Deliver me from my persecutors,
for they are too strong for me!
7 Bring me out of prison,
that I may give thanks to your
name!
The righteous will surround me,
for you will deal bountifully with
me.

My Soul Thirsts for You

143

A PSALM OF DAVID.

Hear my prayer, O LORD;
give ear to my pleas for mercy!
In your faithfulness answer me,
in your righteousness!
2 Enter not into judgment with your
servant,
for no one living is righteous
before you.

3 For the enemy has pursued my soul;
he has crushed my life to the
ground;
he has made me sit in darkness
like those long dead.
4 Therefore my spirit faints within me;
my heart within me is appalled.

5 I remember the days of old;
I meditate on all that you have
done;
I ponder the work of your hands.
6 I stretch out my hands to you;
my soul thirsts for you like a
parched land. *Selah*

7 Answer me quickly, O LORD!
My spirit fails!
Hide not your face from me,
lest I be like those who go down
to the pit.
8 Let me hear in the morning of your
steadfast love,
for in you I trust.
Make me know the way I should go,
for to you I lift up my soul.

9 Deliver me from my enemies, O LORD!
I have fled to you for refuge![4]
10 Teach me to do your will,
for you are my God!
Let your good Spirit lead me
on level ground!

11 For your name's sake, O LORD,
preserve my life!
In your righteousness bring my
soul out of trouble!

[1] The meaning of the Hebrew in verses 6, 7 is uncertain [2] Hebrew *refuge; do not pour out my life!* [3] Probably a musical or liturgical term [4] One Hebrew manuscript, Septuagint; most Hebrew manuscripts *To you I have covered*

12 And in your steadfast love you will
cut off my enemies,
and you will destroy all the
adversaries of my soul,
for I am your servant.

My Rock and My Fortress

144 OF DAVID.
Blessed be the LORD, my rock,
who trains my hands for war,
and my fingers for battle;
2 he is my steadfast love and my
fortress,
my stronghold and my deliverer,
my shield and he in whom I take
refuge,
who subdues peoples[1] under me.

3 O LORD, what is man that you
regard him,
or the son of man that you think
of him?
4 Man is like a breath;
his days are like a passing
shadow.

5 Bow your heavens, O LORD, and
come down!
Touch the mountains so that they
smoke!
6 Flash forth the lightning and scatter
them;
send out your arrows and rout
them!
7 Stretch out your hand from on high;
rescue me and deliver me from
the many waters,
from the hand of foreigners,
8 whose mouths speak lies
and whose right hand is a right
hand of falsehood.

9 I will sing a new song to you, O God;
upon a ten-stringed harp I will
play to you,
10 who gives victory to kings,
who rescues David his servant
from the cruel sword.

11 Rescue me and deliver me
from the hand of foreigners,
whose mouths speak lies
and whose right hand is a right
hand of falsehood.

12 May our sons in their youth
be like plants full grown,
our daughters like corner pillars
cut for the structure of a palace;
13 may our granaries be full,
providing all kinds of produce;
may our sheep bring forth
thousands
and ten thousands in our fields;
14 may our cattle be heavy with young,
suffering no mishap or failure in
bearing;[2]
may there be no cry of distress in
our streets!
15 Blessed are the people to whom
such blessings fall!
Blessed are the people whose God
is the LORD!

Great Is the LORD

145 [3] A SONG OF PRAISE. OF DAVID.
I will extol you, my God and
King,
and bless your name forever and
ever.
2 Every day I will bless you
and praise your name forever and
ever.
3 Great is the LORD, and greatly to be
praised,
and his greatness is unsearchable.

4 One generation shall commend
your works to another,
and shall declare your mighty acts.
5 On the glorious splendor of your
majesty,
and on your wondrous works, I
will meditate.
6 They shall speak of the might of
your awesome deeds,
and I will declare your greatness.

[1] Many Hebrew manuscripts, Dead Sea Scroll, Jerome, Syriac, Aquila; most Hebrew manuscripts *subdues my people* [2] Hebrew *with no breaking in or going out* [3] This psalm is an acrostic poem, each verse beginning with the successive letters of the Hebrew alphabet

7 They shall pour forth the fame of
your abundant goodness
and shall sing aloud of your
righteousness.

8 The LORD is gracious and merciful,
slow to anger and abounding in
steadfast love.
9 The LORD is good to all,
and his mercy is over all that he
has made.

10 All your works shall give thanks to
you, O LORD,
and all your saints shall bless you!
11 They shall speak of the glory of your
kingdom
and tell of your power,
12 to make known to the children of
man your[1] mighty deeds,
and the glorious splendor of your
kingdom.
13 Your kingdom is an everlasting
kingdom,
and your dominion endures
throughout all generations.

[The LORD is faithful in all his words
and kind in all his works.][2]
14 The LORD upholds all who are
falling
and raises up all who are bowed
down.
15 The eyes of all look to you,
and you give them their food in
due season.
16 You open your hand;
you satisfy the desire of every
living thing.
17 The LORD is righteous in all his
ways
and kind in all his works.
18 The LORD is near to all who call on
him,
to all who call on him in truth.
19 He fulfills the desire of those who
fear him;
he also hears their cry and saves
them.
20 The LORD preserves all who love him,
but all the wicked he will destroy.

21 My mouth will speak the praise of
the LORD,
and let all flesh bless his holy
name forever and ever.

Put Not Your Trust in Princes

146 Praise the LORD!
Praise the LORD, O my soul!
2 I will praise the LORD as long as I
live;
I will sing praises to my God while
I have my being.

3 Put not your trust in princes,
in a son of man, in whom there is
no salvation.
4 When his breath departs, he returns
to the earth;
on that very day his plans perish.

5 Blessed is he whose help is the God
of Jacob,
whose hope is in the LORD his
God,
6 who made heaven and earth,
the sea, and all that is in them,
who keeps faith forever;
7 who executes justice for the
oppressed,
who gives food to the hungry.

The LORD sets the prisoners free;
8 the LORD opens the eyes of the
blind.
The LORD lifts up those who are
bowed down;
the LORD loves the righteous.
9 The LORD watches over the
sojourners;
he upholds the widow and the
fatherless,
but the way of the wicked he
brings to ruin.

10 The LORD will reign forever,
your God, O Zion, to all generations.
Praise the LORD!

[1] Hebrew *his*; also next line [2] These two lines are supplied by one Hebrew manuscript, Septuagint, Syriac (compare Dead Sea Scroll)

He Heals the Brokenhearted

147 Praise the LORD!
For it is good to sing praises to our God;
for it is pleasant,[1] and a song of praise is fitting.
2 The LORD builds up Jerusalem;
he gathers the outcasts of Israel.
3 He heals the brokenhearted
and binds up their wounds.
4 He determines the number of the stars;
he gives to all of them their names.
5 Great is our Lord, and abundant in power;
his understanding is beyond measure.
6 The LORD lifts up the humble;[2]
he casts the wicked to the ground.

7 Sing to the LORD with thanksgiving;
make melody to our God on the lyre!
8 He covers the heavens with clouds;
he prepares rain for the earth;
he makes grass grow on the hills.
9 He gives to the beasts their food,
and to the young ravens that cry.
10 His delight is not in the strength of the horse,
nor his pleasure in the legs of a man,
11 but the LORD takes pleasure in those who fear him,
in those who hope in his steadfast love.

12 Praise the LORD, O Jerusalem!
Praise your God, O Zion!
13 For he strengthens the bars of your gates;
he blesses your children within you.
14 He makes peace in your borders;
he fills you with the finest of the wheat.
15 He sends out his command to the earth;
his word runs swiftly.
16 He gives snow like wool;
he scatters hoarfrost like ashes.
17 He hurls down his crystals of ice like crumbs;
who can stand before his cold?
18 He sends out his word, and melts them;
he makes his wind blow and the waters flow.
19 He declares his word to Jacob,
his statutes and rules[3] to Israel.
20 He has not dealt thus with any other nation;
they do not know his rules.[4]
Praise the LORD!

Praise the Name of the LORD

148 Praise the LORD!
Praise the LORD from the heavens;
praise him in the heights!
2 Praise him, all his angels;
praise him, all his hosts!

3 Praise him, sun and moon,
praise him, all you shining stars!
4 Praise him, you highest heavens,
and you waters above the heavens!

5 Let them praise the name of the LORD!
For he commanded and they were created.
6 And he established them forever and ever;
he gave a decree, and it shall not pass away.[5]

7 Praise the LORD from the earth,
you great sea creatures and all deeps,
8 fire and hail, snow and mist,
stormy wind fulfilling his word!
9 Mountains and all hills,
fruit trees and all cedars!

[1] Or *for he is beautiful* [2] Or *afflicted* [3] Or *and just decrees* [4] Or *his just decrees* [5] Or *it shall not be transgressed*

10 Beasts and all livestock,
creeping things and flying birds!
11 Kings of the earth and all peoples,
princes and all rulers of the earth!
12 Young men and maidens together,
old men and children!

13 Let them praise the name of the LORD,
for his name alone is exalted;
his majesty is above earth and
heaven.
14 He has raised up a horn for his
people,
praise for all his saints,
for the people of Israel who are
near to him.
Praise the LORD!

Sing to the LORD a New Song

149 Praise the LORD!
Sing to the LORD a new song,
his praise in the assembly of the
godly!

449
2 Let Israel be glad in his Maker;
let the children of Zion rejoice
in their King!
3 Let them praise his name with
dancing,
making melody to him with
tambourine and lyre!
4 For the LORD takes pleasure in his
people;
he adorns the humble with
salvation.

5 Let the godly exult in glory;
let them sing for joy on their beds.
6 Let the high praises of God be in
their throats
and two-edged swords in their
hands,
7 to execute vengeance on the nations
and punishments on the peoples,
8 to bind their kings with chains
and their nobles with fetters of
iron,
9 to execute on them the judgment
written!
This is honor for all his godly ones.
Praise the LORD!

Let Everything Praise the LORD

150 Praise the LORD!
Praise God in his sanctuary;
praise him in his mighty heavens![1]
2 Praise him for his mighty deeds;
praise him according to his
excellent greatness!

3 Praise him with trumpet sound;
praise him with lute and harp!
4 Praise him with tambourine and
dance;
praise him with strings and pipe!
5 Praise him with sounding cymbals;
praise him with loud clashing
cymbals!
6 Let everything that has breath
praise the LORD!
Praise the LORD!

[1] Hebrew *expanse* (compare Genesis 1:6-8)

Introduction to

Proverbs

Author(s)

Solomon; Agur; Lemuel; Lemuel's mother; unnamed wise men

Date

Tenth century B.C. for most of the book; late eighth or early seventh century for some parts

People

King Solomon; Solomon's son (Rehoboam) or a student

Purpose

The purpose of the book of Proverbs is to pass on God's wisdom, especially to young people.

Central Themes

Fear of the Lord is the beginning of wisdom; wisdom is right and folly is destructive; God's wisdom can and should be applied to practical details of life; wisdom doesn't just happen—it must be studied, loved, and diligently pursued.

Memory Verses

Fear of the Lord (Proverbs 1:2–7); wisdom and creation (Proverbs 8:22–31); the woman who fears the Lord (Proverbs 31:10–31)

Introduction

Many of the proverbs were written by Solomon. In the opening chapters, he calls his own son to live wisely by fearing God. He urges him to remember, honor, and obey what his parents have taught him (Proverbs 4:1–4, 20–27). Solomon tells his son to value wisdom, study hard for it, and seek it diligently. Living wisely protects a person from many troubles and provides a person with many benefits (Proverbs 4:5–9). Solomon warns his son against several dangers, including bad companions (Proverbs 1:8–19), laziness and a foolish use of money (Proverbs 6:1–11), and wrong relationships with women who are not his wife (Proverbs 7:1–27). The middle section of the book has collections of proverbs—wise sayings that describe the good things that usually happen when people live wisely in the fear of God and the bad things that usually happen when people disobey God and live as fools. These cover many everyday things, such as money, speech, family, emotions, and friendships, showing how God's wisdom should impact them all. A final chapter is a poem praising the godly woman (Proverbs 31:10–31). Proverbs often reminds readers that "the fear of the LORD is the beginning of wisdom" (Proverbs 9:10).

1010–971 B.C. Reign of David

971–931 B.C. Reign of Solomon

715–686 B.C. Reign of Hezekiah

Proverbs

The Beginning of Knowledge

535

1 The proverbs of Solomon, son of David, king of Israel:

2 To know wisdom and instruction,
to understand words of insight,
3 to receive instruction in wise dealing,
in righteousness, justice, and equity;
4 to give prudence to the simple,
knowledge and discretion to the youth—
5 Let the wise hear and increase in learning,
and the one who understands obtain guidance,
6 to understand a proverb and a saying,
the words of the wise and their riddles.
7 The fear of the LORD is the beginning of knowledge;
fools despise wisdom and instruction.

The Enticement of Sinners

8 Hear, my son, your father's instruction,
and forsake not your mother's teaching,
9 for they are a graceful garland for your head
and pendants for your neck.
10 My son, if sinners entice you,
do not consent.
11 If they say, "Come with us, let us lie in wait for blood;
let us ambush the innocent without reason;
12 like Sheol let us swallow them alive,
and whole, like those who go down to the pit;
13 we shall find all precious goods,
we shall fill our houses with plunder;
14 throw in your lot among us;
we will all have one purse"—
15 my son, do not walk in the way with them;
hold back your foot from their paths,
16 for their feet run to evil,
and they make haste to shed blood.
17 For in vain is a net spread
in the sight of any bird,
18 but these men lie in wait for their own blood;
they set an ambush for their own lives.
19 Such are the ways of everyone who is greedy for unjust gain;
it takes away the life of its possessors.

The Call of Wisdom

20 Wisdom cries aloud in the street,
in the markets she raises her voice;
21 at the head of the noisy streets she cries out;
at the entrance of the city gates she speaks:
22 "How long, O simple ones, will you love being simple?
How long will scoffers delight in their scoffing
and fools hate knowledge?
23 If you turn at my reproof,[1]
behold, I will pour out my spirit to you;
I will make my words known to you.

[1] Or *Will you turn away at my reproof?*

24 Because I have called and you
refused to listen,
have stretched out my hand and
no one has heeded,
25 because you have ignored all my
counsel
and would have none of my
reproof,
26 I also will laugh at your calamity;
I will mock when terror strikes
you,
27 when terror strikes you like a storm
and your calamity comes like a
whirlwind,
when distress and anguish come
upon you.
28 Then they will call upon me, but I
will not answer;
they will seek me diligently but
will not find me.
29 Because they hated knowledge
and did not choose the fear of the
LORD,
30 would have none of my counsel
and despised all my reproof,
31 therefore they shall eat the fruit of
their way,
and have their fill of their own
devices.
32 For the simple are killed by their
turning away,
and the complacency of fools
destroys them;
33 but whoever listens to me will dwell
secure
and will be at ease, without dread
of disaster."

The Value of Wisdom

2 My son, if you receive my words
and treasure up my
commandments with you,
2 making your ear attentive to
wisdom
and inclining your heart to
understanding;
3 yes, if you call out for insight
and raise your voice for
understanding,
4 if you seek it like silver
and search for it as for hidden
treasures,
5 then you will understand the fear of
the LORD
and find the knowledge of God.
6 For the LORD gives wisdom;
from his mouth come knowledge
and understanding;
7 he stores up sound wisdom for the
upright;
he is a shield to those who walk in
integrity,
8 guarding the paths of justice
and watching over the way of his
saints.
9 Then you will understand
righteousness and justice
and equity, every good path;
10 for wisdom will come into your
heart,
and knowledge will be pleasant to
your soul;
11 discretion will watch over you,
understanding will guard you,
12 delivering you from the way of evil,
from men of perverted speech,
13 who forsake the paths of
uprightness
to walk in the ways of darkness,
14 who rejoice in doing evil
and delight in the perverseness of
evil,
15 men whose paths are crooked,
and who are devious in their ways.
16 So you will be delivered from the
forbidden[1] woman,
from the adulteress[2] with her
smooth words,
17 who forsakes the companion of her
youth
and forgets the covenant of her
God;

[1] Hebrew *strange* [2] Hebrew *foreign woman*

18 for her house sinks down to death,
and her paths to the departed;[1]
19 none who go to her come back,
nor do they regain the paths of life.

20 So you will walk in the way of the good
and keep to the paths of the righteous.
21 For the upright will inhabit the land,
and those with integrity will remain in it,
22 but the wicked will be cut off from the land,
and the treacherous will be rooted out of it.

Trust in the LORD with All Your Heart

3 My son, do not forget my teaching,
but let your heart keep my commandments,
2 for length of days and years of life
and peace they will add to you.

3 Let not steadfast love and faithfulness forsake you;
bind them around your neck;
write them on the tablet of your heart.
4 So you will find favor and good success[2]
in the sight of God and man.

5 Trust in the LORD with all your heart,
61 and do not lean on your own understanding.
6 In all your ways acknowledge him,
and he will make straight your paths.
7 Be not wise in your own eyes;
fear the LORD, and turn away from evil.
8 It will be healing to your flesh[3]
and refreshment[4] to your bones.

9 Honor the LORD with your wealth
and with the firstfruits of all your produce;
10 then your barns will be filled with plenty,
and your vats will be bursting with wine.

11 My son, do not despise the LORD's discipline
or be weary of his reproof,
12 for the LORD reproves him whom he loves,
as a father the son in whom he delights.

Blessed Is the One Who Finds Wisdom

13 Blessed is the one who finds wisdom,
and the one who gets understanding,
14 for the gain from her is better than gain from silver
and her profit better than gold.
15 She is more precious than jewels,
and nothing you desire can compare with her.
16 Long life is in her right hand;
in her left hand are riches and honor.
17 Her ways are ways of pleasantness,
and all her paths are peace.
18 She is a tree of life to those who lay hold of her;
those who hold her fast are called blessed.

19 The LORD by wisdom founded the earth;
by understanding he established the heavens;
20 by his knowledge the deeps broke open,
and the clouds drop down the dew.

21 My son, do not lose sight of these—
keep sound wisdom and discretion,
22 and they will be life for your soul
and adornment for your neck.

[1] Hebrew *to the Rephaim* [2] Or *repute* [3] Hebrew *navel* [4] Or *medicine*

23 Then you will walk on your way
securely,
and your foot will not stumble.
24 If you lie down, you will not be
afraid;
when you lie down, your sleep
will be sweet.
25 Do not be afraid of sudden terror
or of the ruin[1] of the wicked,
when it comes,
26 for the LORD will be your confidence
and will keep your foot from
being caught.
27 Do not withhold good from those to
whom it is due,[2]
when it is in your power to do it.
28 Do not say to your neighbor, "Go,
and come again,
tomorrow I will give it"—when
you have it with you.
29 Do not plan evil against your
neighbor,
who dwells trustingly beside you.
30 Do not contend with a man for no
reason,
when he has done you no harm.
31 Do not envy a man of violence
and do not choose any of his ways,
32 for the devious person is an
abomination to the LORD,
but the upright are in his
confidence.
33 The LORD's curse is on the house of
the wicked,
but he blesses the dwelling of the
righteous.
34 Toward the scorners he is scornful,
but to the humble he gives favor.[3]
35 The wise will inherit honor,
but fools get[4] disgrace.

A Father's Wise Instruction

4 Hear, O sons, a father's instruction,
and be attentive, that you may gain[5]
insight,
2 for I give you good precepts;
do not forsake my teaching.
3 When I was a son with my father,
tender, the only one in the sight
of my mother,
4 he taught me and said to me,
"Let your heart hold fast my words;
keep my commandments, and
live.
5 Get wisdom; get insight;
do not forget, and do not turn away
from the words of my mouth.
6 Do not forsake her, and she will
keep you;
love her, and she will guard you.
7 The beginning of wisdom is this:
Get wisdom,
and whatever you get, get insight.
8 Prize her highly, and she will exalt
you;
she will honor you if you embrace
her.
9 She will place on your head a
graceful garland;
she will bestow on you a beautiful
crown."
10 Hear, my son, and accept my words,
that the years of your life may be
many.
11 I have taught you the way of wisdom;
I have led you in the paths of
uprightness.
12 When you walk, your step will not
be hampered,
and if you run, you will not
stumble.
13 Keep hold of instruction; do not let
go;
guard her, for she is your life.
14 Do not enter the path of the wicked,
and do not walk in the way of the
evil.
15 Avoid it; do not go on it;
turn away from it and pass on.
16 For they cannot sleep unless they
have done wrong;
they are robbed of sleep unless
they have made someone
stumble.

[1] Hebrew *storm* [2] Hebrew *Do not withhold good from its owners* [3] Or *grace* [4] The meaning of the Hebrew word is uncertain [5] Hebrew *know*

17 For they eat the bread of wickedness
and drink the wine of violence.
18 But the path of the righteous is like the light of dawn,
which shines brighter and brighter until full day.
19 The way of the wicked is like deep darkness;
they do not know over what they stumble.

20 My son, be attentive to my words;
incline your ear to my sayings.
21 Let them not escape from your sight;
keep them within your heart.
22 For they are life to those who find them,
and healing to all their[1] flesh.
23 Keep your heart with all vigilance,
for from it flow the springs of life.
24 Put away from you crooked speech,
and put devious talk far from you.
25 Let your eyes look directly forward,
and your gaze be straight before you.
26 Ponder[2] the path of your feet;
then all your ways will be sure.
27 Do not swerve to the right or to the left;
turn your foot away from evil.

Warning Against Adultery

5 My son, be attentive to my wisdom;
incline your ear to my understanding,
2 that you may keep discretion,
and your lips may guard knowledge.
3 For the lips of a forbidden[3] woman drip honey,
and her speech[4] is smoother than oil,
4 but in the end she is bitter as wormwood,
sharp as a two-edged sword.
5 Her feet go down to death;
her steps follow the path to[5] Sheol;
6 she does not ponder the path of life;
her ways wander, and she does not know it.

7 And now, O sons, listen to me,
and do not depart from the words of my mouth.
8 Keep your way far from her,
and do not go near the door of her house,
9 lest you give your honor to others
and your years to the merciless,
10 lest strangers take their fill of your strength,
and your labors go to the house of a foreigner,
11 and at the end of your life you groan,
when your flesh and body are consumed,
12 and you say, "How I hated discipline,
and my heart despised reproof!
13 I did not listen to the voice of my teachers
or incline my ear to my instructors.
14 I am at the brink of utter ruin
in the assembled congregation."

15 Drink water from your own cistern,
flowing water from your own well.
16 Should your springs be scattered abroad,
streams of water in the streets?
17 Let them be for yourself alone,
and not for strangers with you.
18 Let your fountain be blessed,
and rejoice in the wife of your youth,
19 a lovely deer, a graceful doe.
Let her breasts fill you at all times with delight;
be intoxicated[6] always in her love.

[1] Hebrew *his* [2] Or *Make level* [3] Hebrew *strange*; also verse 20 [4] Hebrew *palate* [5] Hebrew *lay hold of* [6] Hebrew *be led astray*; also verse 20

20 Why should you be intoxicated, my son, with a forbidden woman
and embrace the bosom of an adulteress?[1]
21 For a man's ways are before the eyes of the LORD,
and he ponders[2] all his paths.
22 The iniquities of the wicked ensnare him,
and he is held fast in the cords of his sin.
23 He dies for lack of discipline,
and because of his great folly he is led astray.

Practical Warnings

6 My son, if you have put up security for your neighbor,
have given your pledge for a stranger,
2 if you are snared in the words of your mouth,
caught in the words of your mouth,
3 then do this, my son, and save yourself,
for you have come into the hand of your neighbor:
go, hasten,[3] and plead urgently with your neighbor.
4 Give your eyes no sleep
and your eyelids no slumber;
5 save yourself like a gazelle from the hand of the hunter,[4]
like a bird from the hand of the fowler.

6 Go to the ant, O sluggard;
consider her ways, and be wise.
7 Without having any chief,
officer, or ruler,
8 she prepares her bread in summer
and gathers her food in harvest.
9 How long will you lie there, O sluggard?
When will you arise from your sleep?
10 A little sleep, a little slumber,
a little folding of the hands to rest,
11 and poverty will come upon you like a robber,
and want like an armed man.

12 A worthless person, a wicked man,
goes about with crooked speech,
13 winks with his eyes, signals[5] with his feet,
points with his finger,
14 with perverted heart devises evil,
continually sowing discord;
15 therefore calamity will come upon him suddenly;
in a moment he will be broken beyond healing.

16 There are six things that the LORD hates,
seven that are an abomination to him:
17 haughty eyes, a lying tongue,
and hands that shed innocent blood,
18 a heart that devises wicked plans,
feet that make haste to run to evil,
19 a false witness who breathes out lies,
and one who sows discord among brothers.

Warnings Against Adultery

20 My son, keep your father's commandment,
and forsake not your mother's teaching.
21 Bind them on your heart always;
tie them around your neck.
22 When you walk, they[6] will lead you;
when you lie down, they will watch over you;
and when you awake, they will talk with you.
23 For the commandment is a lamp
and the teaching a light,
and the reproofs of discipline are the way of life,

[1] Hebrew *a foreign woman* [2] Or *makes level* [3] Or *humble yourself* [4] Hebrew lacks *of the hunter* [5] Hebrew *scrapes* [6] Hebrew *it*; three times in this verse

24 to preserve you from the evil woman,[1]
from the smooth tongue of the adulteress.[2]
25 Do not desire her beauty in your heart,
and do not let her capture you with her eyelashes;
26 for the price of a prostitute is only a loaf of bread,[3]
but a married woman[4] hunts down a precious life.
27 Can a man carry fire next to his chest
and his clothes not be burned?
28 Or can one walk on hot coals
and his feet not be scorched?
29 So is he who goes in to his neighbor's wife;
none who touches her will go unpunished.
30 People do not despise a thief if he steals
to satisfy his appetite when he is hungry,
31 but if he is caught, he will pay sevenfold;
he will give all the goods of his house.
32 He who commits adultery lacks sense;
he who does it destroys himself.
33 He will get wounds and dishonor,
and his disgrace will not be wiped away.
34 For jealousy makes a man furious,
and he will not spare when he takes revenge.
35 He will accept no compensation;
he will refuse though you multiply gifts.

Warning Against the Adulteress

7 My son, keep my words
and treasure up my commandments with you;
2 keep my commandments and live;
keep my teaching as the apple of your eye;
3 bind them on your fingers;
write them on the tablet of your heart.
4 Say to wisdom, "You are my sister,"
and call insight your intimate friend,
5 to keep you from the forbidden[5] woman,
from the adulteress[6] with her smooth words.

6 For at the window of my house
I have looked out through my lattice,
7 and I have seen among the simple,
I have perceived among the youths,
a young man lacking sense,
8 passing along the street near her corner,
taking the road to her house
9 in the twilight, in the evening,
at the time of night and darkness.

10 And behold, the woman meets him,
dressed as a prostitute, wily of heart.[7]
11 She is loud and wayward;
her feet do not stay at home;
12 now in the street, now in the market,
and at every corner she lies in wait.
13 She seizes him and kisses him,
and with bold face she says to him,
14 "I had to offer sacrifices,[8]
and today I have paid my vows;
15 so now I have come out to meet you,
to seek you eagerly, and I have found you.
16 I have spread my couch with coverings,
colored linens from Egyptian linen;
17 I have perfumed my bed with myrrh,
aloes, and cinnamon.

[1] Revocalization (compare Septuagint) yields *from the wife of a neighbor* [2] Hebrew *the foreign woman* [3] Or (compare Septuagint, Syriac, Vulgate) *for a prostitute leaves a man with nothing but a loaf of bread* [4] Hebrew *a man's wife* [5] Hebrew *strange* [6] Hebrew *the foreign woman* [7] Hebrew *guarded in heart* [8] Hebrew *peace offerings*

18 Come, let us take our fill of love till morning;
let us delight ourselves with love.
19 For my husband is not at home;
he has gone on a long journey;
20 he took a bag of money with him;
at full moon he will come home."
21 With much seductive speech she persuades him;
with her smooth talk she compels him.
22 All at once he follows her,
as an ox goes to the slaughter,
or as a stag is caught fast[1]
23 till an arrow pierces its liver;
as a bird rushes into a snare;
he does not know that it will cost him his life.

24 And now, O sons, listen to me,
and be attentive to the words of my mouth.
25 Let not your heart turn aside to her ways;
do not stray into her paths,
26 for many a victim has she laid low,
and all her slain are a mighty throng.
27 Her house is the way to Sheol,
going down to the chambers of death.

The Blessings of Wisdom

8 Does not wisdom call?
Does not understanding raise her voice?
2 On the heights beside the way,
at the crossroads she takes her stand;
3 beside the gates in front of the town,
at the entrance of the portals she cries aloud:
4 "To you, O men, I call,
and my cry is to the children of man.
5 O simple ones, learn prudence;
O fools, learn sense.
6 Hear, for I will speak noble things,
and from my lips will come what is right,
7 for my mouth will utter truth;
wickedness is an abomination to my lips.
8 All the words of my mouth are righteous;
there is nothing twisted or crooked in them.
9 They are all straight to him who understands,
and right to those who find knowledge.
10 Take my instruction instead of silver,
and knowledge rather than choice gold,
11 for wisdom is better than jewels,
and all that you may desire cannot compare with her.

12 "I, wisdom, dwell with prudence,
and I find knowledge and discretion.
13 The fear of the LORD is hatred of evil.
Pride and arrogance and the way of evil
and perverted speech I hate.
14 I have counsel and sound wisdom;
I have insight; I have strength.
15 By me kings reign,
and rulers decree what is just;
16 by me princes rule,
and nobles, all who govern justly.[2]
17 I love those who love me,
and those who seek me diligently find me.
18 Riches and honor are with me,
enduring wealth and righteousness.
19 My fruit is better than gold, even fine gold,
and my yield than choice silver.

[1] Probable reading (compare Septuagint, Vulgate, Syriac); Hebrew *as an anklet for the discipline of a fool* [2] Most Hebrew manuscripts; many Hebrew manuscripts, Septuagint *govern the earth*

20 I walk in the way of righteousness,
in the paths of justice,
21 granting an inheritance to those who love me,
and filling their treasuries.

22 "The LORD possessed[1] me at the beginning of his work,[2]
the first of his acts of old.
23 Ages ago I was set up,
at the first, before the beginning of the earth.
24 When there were no depths I was brought forth,
when there were no springs abounding with water.
25 Before the mountains had been shaped,
before the hills, I was brought forth,
26 before he had made the earth with its fields,
or the first of the dust of the world.
27 When he established the heavens, I was there;
when he drew a circle on the face of the deep,
28 when he made firm the skies above,
when he established[3] the fountains of the deep,
29 when he assigned to the sea its limit,
so that the waters might not transgress his command,
when he marked out the foundations of the earth,
30 then I was beside him, like a master workman,
and I was daily his[4] delight,
rejoicing before him always,
31 rejoicing in his inhabited world
and delighting in the children of man.

32 "And now, O sons, listen to me:
blessed are those who keep my ways.
33 Hear instruction and be wise,
and do not neglect it.
34 Blessed is the one who listens to me,
watching daily at my gates,
waiting beside my doors.
35 For whoever finds me finds life
and obtains favor from the LORD,
36 but he who fails to find me injures himself;
all who hate me love death."

The Way of Wisdom

9 Wisdom has built her house;
she has hewn her seven pillars.
2 She has slaughtered her beasts; she has mixed her wine;
she has also set her table.
3 She has sent out her young women to call
from the highest places in the town,
4 "Whoever is simple, let him turn in here!"
To him who lacks sense she says,
5 "Come, eat of my bread
and drink of the wine I have mixed.
6 Leave your simple ways,[5] and live,
and walk in the way of insight."

7 Whoever corrects a scoffer gets himself abuse,
and he who reproves a wicked man incurs injury.
8 Do not reprove a scoffer, or he will hate you;
reprove a wise man, and he will love you.
9 Give instruction[6] to a wise man,
and he will be still wiser;
teach a righteous man, and he will increase in learning.
10 The fear of the LORD is the beginning of wisdom,
and the knowledge of the Holy One is insight.

[1] Or *fathered;* Septuagint *created* [2] Hebrew *way* [3] The meaning of the Hebrew is uncertain [4] Or *daily filled with* [5] Or *Leave the company of the simple* [6] Hebrew lacks *instruction*

11 For by me your days will be
multiplied,
and years will be added to your
life.
12 If you are wise, you are wise for
yourself;
if you scoff, you alone will bear it.

The Way of Folly

13 The woman Folly is loud;
she is seductive[1] and knows
nothing.
14 She sits at the door of her house;
she takes a seat on the highest
places of the town,
15 calling to those who pass by,
who are going straight on their
way,
16 "Whoever is simple, let him turn in
here!"
And to him who lacks sense she
says,
17 "Stolen water is sweet,
and bread eaten in secret is
pleasant."
18 But he does not know that the dead[2]
are there,
that her guests are in the depths
of Sheol.

The Proverbs of Solomon

10 The proverbs of Solomon.

A wise son makes a glad father,
but a foolish son is a sorrow to his
mother.
2 Treasures gained by wickedness do
not profit,
but righteousness delivers from
death.
3 The LORD does not let the righteous
go hungry,
but he thwarts the craving of the
wicked.
4 A slack hand causes poverty,
but the hand of the diligent
makes rich.
5 He who gathers in summer is a
prudent son,
but he who sleeps in harvest is a
son who brings shame.
6 Blessings are on the head of the
righteous,
but the mouth of the wicked
conceals violence.
7 The memory of the righteous is a
blessing,
but the name of the wicked will
rot.
8 The wise of heart will receive
commandments,
but a babbling fool will come to
ruin.
9 Whoever walks in integrity walks
securely,
but he who makes his ways
crooked will be found out.
10 Whoever winks the eye causes
trouble,
but a babbling fool will come to
ruin.
11 The mouth of the righteous is a
fountain of life,
but the mouth of the wicked
conceals violence.
12 Hatred stirs up strife,
but love covers all offenses.
13 On the lips of him who has
understanding, wisdom is
found,
but a rod is for the back of him
who lacks sense.
14 The wise lay up knowledge,
but the mouth of a fool brings
ruin near.
15 A rich man's wealth is his strong city;
the poverty of the poor is their ruin.
16 The wage of the righteous leads to
life,
the gain of the wicked to sin.
17 Whoever heeds instruction is on
the path to life,
but he who rejects reproof leads
others astray.

[1] Or *full of simpleness* [2] Hebrew *Rephaim*

18 The one who conceals hatred has lying lips,
and whoever utters slander is a fool.
19 When words are many, transgression is not lacking,
but whoever restrains his lips is prudent.
20 The tongue of the righteous is choice silver;
the heart of the wicked is of little worth.
21 The lips of the righteous feed many,
but fools die for lack of sense.
22 The blessing of the LORD makes rich,
and he adds no sorrow with it.[1]
23 Doing wrong is like a joke to a fool,
but wisdom is pleasure to a man of understanding.
24 What the wicked dreads will come upon him,
but the desire of the righteous will be granted.
25 When the tempest passes, the wicked is no more,
but the righteous is established forever.
26 Like vinegar to the teeth and smoke to the eyes,
so is the sluggard to those who send him.
27 The fear of the LORD prolongs life,
but the years of the wicked will be short.
28 The hope of the righteous brings joy,
but the expectation of the wicked will perish.
29 The way of the LORD is a stronghold to the blameless,
but destruction to evildoers.
30 The righteous will never be removed,
but the wicked will not dwell in the land.
31 The mouth of the righteous brings forth wisdom,
but the perverse tongue will be cut off.
32 The lips of the righteous know what is acceptable,
but the mouth of the wicked, what is perverse.

11 A false balance is an abomination to the LORD,
but a just weight is his delight.
2 When pride comes, then comes disgrace,
but with the humble is wisdom.
3 The integrity of the upright guides them,
but the crookedness of the treacherous destroys them.
4 Riches do not profit in the day of wrath,
but righteousness delivers from death.
5 The righteousness of the blameless keeps his way straight,
but the wicked falls by his own wickedness.
6 The righteousness of the upright delivers them,
but the treacherous are taken captive by their lust.
7 When the wicked dies, his hope will perish,
and the expectation of wealth[2] perishes too.
8 The righteous is delivered from trouble,
and the wicked walks into it instead.
9 With his mouth the godless man would destroy his neighbor,
but by knowledge the righteous are delivered.
10 When it goes well with the righteous, the city rejoices,
and when the wicked perish there are shouts of gladness.

[1] Or *and toil adds nothing to it* [2] Or *of his strength*, or *of iniquity*

11 By the blessing of the upright a city
is exalted,
but by the mouth of the wicked it
is overthrown.
12 Whoever belittles his neighbor
lacks sense,
but a man of understanding
remains silent.
13 Whoever goes about slandering
reveals secrets,
but he who is trustworthy in
spirit keeps a thing covered.
14 Where there is no guidance, a
people falls,
but in an abundance of
counselors there is safety.
15 Whoever puts up security for a
stranger will surely suffer
harm,
but he who hates striking hands
in pledge is secure.
16 A gracious woman gets honor,
and violent men get riches.
17 A man who is kind benefits himself,
but a cruel man hurts himself.
18 The wicked earns deceptive wages,
but one who sows righteousness
gets a sure reward.
19 Whoever is steadfast in
righteousness will live,
but he who pursues evil will die.
20 Those of crooked heart are an
abomination to the LORD,
but those of blameless ways are
his delight.
21 Be assured, an evil person will not
go unpunished,
but the offspring of the righteous
will be delivered.
22 Like a gold ring in a pig's snout
is a beautiful woman without
discretion.
23 The desire of the righteous ends
only in good;
the expectation of the wicked in
wrath.
24 One gives freely, yet grows all the
richer;
another withholds what he should
give, and only suffers want.
25 Whoever brings blessing will be
enriched,
and one who waters will himself
be watered.
26 The people curse him who holds
back grain,
but a blessing is on the head of
him who sells it.
27 Whoever diligently seeks good
seeks favor,[1]
but evil comes to him who
searches for it.
28 Whoever trusts in his riches will fall,
but the righteous will flourish like
a green leaf.
29 Whoever troubles his own
household will inherit the
wind,
and the fool will be servant to the
wise of heart.
30 The fruit of the righteous is a tree of
life,
and whoever captures souls is
wise.
31 If the righteous is repaid on earth,
how much more the wicked and
the sinner!

12 Whoever loves discipline loves
knowledge,
but he who hates reproof is
stupid.
2 A good man obtains favor from the
LORD,
but a man of evil devices he
condemns.
3 No one is established by
wickedness,
but the root of the righteous will
never be moved.
4 An excellent wife is the crown of
her husband,
but she who brings shame is like
rottenness in his bones.

[1] Or *acceptance*

5 The thoughts of the righteous are just;
the counsels of the wicked are deceitful.
6 The words of the wicked lie in wait for blood,
but the mouth of the upright delivers them.
7 The wicked are overthrown and are no more,
but the house of the righteous will stand.
8 A man is commended according to his good sense,
but one of twisted mind is despised.
9 Better to be lowly and have a servant
than to play the great man and lack bread.
10 Whoever is righteous has regard for the life of his beast,
but the mercy of the wicked is cruel.
11 Whoever works his land will have plenty of bread,
but he who follows worthless pursuits lacks sense.
12 Whoever is wicked covets the spoil of evildoers,
but the root of the righteous bears fruit.
13 An evil man is ensnared by the transgression of his lips,
but the righteous escapes from trouble.
14 From the fruit of his mouth a man is satisfied with good,
and the work of a man's hand comes back to him.
15 The way of a fool is right in his own eyes,
but a wise man listens to advice.
16 The vexation of a fool is known at once,
but the prudent ignores an insult.
17 Whoever speaks[1] the truth gives honest evidence,
but a false witness utters deceit.
18 There is one whose rash words are like sword thrusts,
but the tongue of the wise brings healing.
19 Truthful lips endure forever,
but a lying tongue is but for a moment.
20 Deceit is in the heart of those who devise evil,
but those who plan peace have joy.
21 No ill befalls the righteous,
but the wicked are filled with trouble.
22 Lying lips are an abomination to the LORD,
but those who act faithfully are his delight.
23 A prudent man conceals knowledge,
but the heart of fools proclaims folly.
24 The hand of the diligent will rule,
while the slothful will be put to forced labor.
25 Anxiety in a man's heart weighs him down,
but a good word makes him glad.
26 One who is righteous is a guide to his neighbor,[2]
but the way of the wicked leads them astray.
27 Whoever is slothful will not roast his game,
but the diligent man will get precious wealth.[3]
28 In the path of righteousness is life,
and in its pathway there is no death.

13 A wise son hears his father's instruction,
but a scoffer does not listen to rebuke.
2 From the fruit of his mouth a man eats what is good,
but the desire of the treacherous is for violence.

[1] Hebrew *breathes out* [2] Or *The righteous chooses his friends carefully* [3] Or *but diligence is precious wealth*

3 Whoever guards his mouth
preserves his life;
he who opens wide his lips comes
to ruin.
4 The soul of the sluggard craves and
gets nothing,
while the soul of the diligent is
richly supplied.
5 The righteous hates falsehood,
but the wicked brings shame[1] and
disgrace.
6 Righteousness guards him whose
way is blameless,
but sin overthrows the wicked.
7 One pretends to be rich, yet has
nothing;
another pretends to be poor, yet
has great wealth.
8 The ransom of a man's life is his
wealth,
but a poor man hears no threat.
9 The light of the righteous rejoices,
but the lamp of the wicked will be
put out.
10 By insolence comes nothing but
strife,
but with those who take advice is
wisdom.
11 Wealth gained hastily[2] will dwindle,
but whoever gathers little by little
will increase it.
12 Hope deferred makes the heart sick,
but a desire fulfilled is a tree of
life.
13 Whoever despises the word brings
destruction on himself,
but he who reveres the
commandment will be
rewarded.
14 The teaching of the wise is a
fountain of life,
that one may turn away from the
snares of death.
15 Good sense wins favor,
but the way of the treacherous is
their ruin.[3]
16 In everything the prudent acts with
knowledge,
but a fool flaunts his folly.
17 A wicked messenger falls into
trouble,
but a faithful envoy brings
healing.
18 Poverty and disgrace come to him
who ignores instruction,
but whoever heeds reproof is
honored.
19 A desire fulfilled is sweet to the
soul,
but to turn away from evil is an
abomination to fools.
20 Whoever walks with the wise
becomes wise,
but the companion of fools will
suffer harm.
21 Disaster[4] pursues sinners,
but the righteous are rewarded
with good.
22 A good man leaves an inheritance to
his children's children,
but the sinner's wealth is laid up
for the righteous.
23 The fallow ground of the poor
would yield much food,
but it is swept away through
injustice.
24 Whoever spares the rod hates his
son,
but he who loves him is diligent
to discipline him.[5]
25 The righteous has enough to satisfy
his appetite,
but the belly of the wicked suffers
want.

14 The wisest of women builds her
house,
but folly with her own hands
tears it down.
2 Whoever walks in uprightness fears
the LORD,
but he who is devious in his ways
despises him.

[1] Or *stench* [2] Or *by fraud* [3] Probable reading (compare Septuagint, Syriac, Vulgate); Hebrew *is rugged*, or *is an enduring rut* [4] Or *Evil* [5] Or *who loves him disciplines him early*

3 By the mouth of a fool comes a rod
for his back,[1]
but the lips of the wise will
preserve them.
4 Where there are no oxen, the
manger is clean,
but abundant crops come by the
strength of the ox.
5 A faithful witness does not lie,
but a false witness breathes out
lies.
6 A scoffer seeks wisdom in vain,
but knowledge is easy for a man
of understanding.
7 Leave the presence of a fool,
for there you do not meet words
of knowledge.
8 The wisdom of the prudent is to
discern his way,
but the folly of fools is deceiving.
9 Fools mock at the guilt offering,
but the upright enjoy acceptance.[2]
10 The heart knows its own bitterness,
and no stranger shares its joy.
11 The house of the wicked will be
destroyed,
but the tent of the upright will
flourish.
12 There is a way that seems right to a
man,
but its end is the way to death.[3]
13 Even in laughter the heart may
ache,
and the end of joy may be grief.
14 The backslider in heart will be filled
with the fruit of his ways,
and a good man will be filled with
the fruit of his ways.
15 The simple believes everything,
but the prudent gives thought to
his steps.
16 One who is wise is cautious[4] and
turns away from evil,
but a fool is reckless and careless.
17 A man of quick temper acts
foolishly,
and a man of evil devices is hated.
18 The simple inherit folly,
but the prudent are crowned with
knowledge.
19 The evil bow down before the good,
the wicked at the gates of the
righteous.
20 The poor is disliked even by his
neighbor,
but the rich has many friends.
21 Whoever despises his neighbor is a
sinner,
but blessed is he who is generous
to the poor.
22 Do they not go astray who devise
evil?
Those who devise good
meet[5] steadfast love and
faithfulness.
23 In all toil there is profit,
but mere talk tends only to
poverty.
24 The crown of the wise is their
wealth,
but the folly of fools brings folly.
25 A truthful witness saves lives,
but one who breathes out lies is
deceitful.
26 In the fear of the LORD one has
strong confidence,
and his children will have a
refuge.
27 The fear of the LORD is a fountain of
life,
that one may turn away from the
snares of death.
28 In a multitude of people is the glory
of a king,
but without people a prince is
ruined.
29 Whoever is slow to anger has great
understanding,
but he who has a hasty temper
exalts folly.
30 A tranquil[6] heart gives life to the
flesh,
but envy[7] makes the bones rot.

[1] Or *In the mouth of a fool is a rod of pride* [2] Hebrew *but among the upright is acceptance* [3] Hebrew *ways of death* [4] Or *fears* [the LORD] [5] Or *show* [6] Or *healing*
[7] Or *jealousy*

31 Whoever oppresses a poor man
insults his Maker,
but he who is generous to the
needy honors him.
32 The wicked is overthrown through
his evildoing,
but the righteous finds refuge in
his death.
33 Wisdom rests in the heart of a man
of understanding,
but it makes itself known even in
the midst of fools.[1]
34 Righteousness exalts a nation,
but sin is a reproach to any
people.
35 A servant who deals wisely has the
king's favor,
but his wrath falls on one who
acts shamefully.

15 A soft answer turns away wrath,
but a harsh word stirs up anger.
2 The tongue of the wise commends
knowledge,
but the mouths of fools pour out
folly.
3 The eyes of the LORD are in every
place,
keeping watch on the evil and the
good.
4 A gentle[2] tongue is a tree of life,
but perverseness in it breaks the
spirit.
5 A fool despises his father's
instruction,
but whoever heeds reproof is
prudent.
6 In the house of the righteous there
is much treasure,
but trouble befalls the income of
the wicked.
7 The lips of the wise spread
knowledge;
not so the hearts of fools.[3]
8 The sacrifice of the wicked is an
abomination to the LORD,
but the prayer of the upright is
acceptable to him.
9 The way of the wicked is an
abomination to the LORD,
but he loves him who pursues
righteousness.
10 There is severe discipline for him
who forsakes the way;
whoever hates reproof will die.
11 Sheol and Abaddon lie open before
the LORD;
how much more the hearts of the
children of man!
12 A scoffer does not like to be
reproved;
he will not go to the wise.
13 A glad heart makes a cheerful face,
but by sorrow of heart the spirit is
crushed.
14 The heart of him who has
understanding seeks
knowledge,
but the mouths of fools feed on
folly.
15 All the days of the afflicted are evil,
but the cheerful of heart has a
continual feast.
16 Better is a little with the fear of the
LORD
than great treasure and trouble
with it.
17 Better is a dinner of herbs where
love is
than a fattened ox and hatred
with it.
18 A hot-tempered man stirs up strife,
but he who is slow to anger quiets
contention.
19 The way of a sluggard is like a hedge
of thorns,
but the path of the upright is a
level highway.
20 A wise son makes a glad father,
but a foolish man despises his
mother.
21 Folly is a joy to him who lacks
sense,
but a man of understanding
walks straight ahead.

[1] Or *Wisdom rests quietly in the heart of a man of understanding, but makes itself known in the midst of fools* [2] Or *healing* [3] Or *the hearts of fools are not steadfast*

22 Without counsel plans fail,
but with many advisers they succeed.
23 To make an apt answer is a joy to a man,
and a word in season, how good it is!
24 The path of life leads upward for the prudent,
that he may turn away from Sheol beneath.
25 The LORD tears down the house of the proud
but maintains the widow's boundaries.
26 The thoughts of the wicked are an abomination to the LORD,
but gracious words are pure.
27 Whoever is greedy for unjust gain troubles his own household,
but he who hates bribes will live.
28 The heart of the righteous ponders how to answer,
but the mouth of the wicked pours out evil things.
29 The LORD is far from the wicked,
but he hears the prayer of the righteous.
30 The light of the eyes rejoices the heart,
and good news refreshes[1] the bones.
31 The ear that listens to life-giving reproof
will dwell among the wise.
32 Whoever ignores instruction despises himself,
but he who listens to reproof gains intelligence.
33 The fear of the LORD is instruction in wisdom,
and humility comes before honor.

16 The plans of the heart belong to man,
but the answer of the tongue is from the LORD.
2 All the ways of a man are pure in his own eyes,
but the LORD weighs the spirit.
3 Commit your work to the LORD,
and your plans will be established.
4 The LORD has made everything for its purpose,
even the wicked for the day of trouble.
5 Everyone who is arrogant in heart is an abomination to the LORD;
be assured, he will not go unpunished.
6 By steadfast love and faithfulness iniquity is atoned for,
and by the fear of the LORD one turns away from evil.
7 When a man's ways please the LORD,
he makes even his enemies to be at peace with him.
8 Better is a little with righteousness
than great revenues with injustice.
9 The heart of man plans his way,
but the LORD establishes his steps.
10 An oracle is on the lips of a king;
his mouth does not sin in judgment.
11 A just balance and scales are the LORD's;
all the weights in the bag are his work.
12 It is an abomination to kings to do evil,
for the throne is established by righteousness.
13 Righteous lips are the delight of a king,
and he loves him who speaks what is right.
14 A king's wrath is a messenger of death,
and a wise man will appease it.

[1] Hebrew *makes fat*

15 In the light of a king's face there is life,
and his favor is like the clouds that bring the spring rain.
16 How much better to get wisdom than gold!
To get understanding is to be chosen rather than silver.
17 The highway of the upright turns aside from evil;
whoever guards his way preserves his life.
18 Pride goes before destruction,
and a haughty spirit before a fall.
19 It is better to be of a lowly spirit with the poor
than to divide the spoil with the proud.
20 Whoever gives thought to the word[1] will discover good,
and blessed is he who trusts in the LORD.
21 The wise of heart is called discerning,
and sweetness of speech increases persuasiveness.
22 Good sense is a fountain of life to him who has it,
but the instruction of fools is folly.
23 The heart of the wise makes his speech judicious
and adds persuasiveness to his lips.
24 Gracious words are like a honeycomb,
sweetness to the soul and health to the body.
25 There is a way that seems right to a man,
but its end is the way to death.[2]
26 A worker's appetite works for him;
his mouth urges him on.
27 A worthless man plots evil,
and his speech[3] is like a scorching fire.
28 A dishonest man spreads strife,
and a whisperer separates close friends.
29 A man of violence entices his neighbor
and leads him in a way that is not good.
30 Whoever winks his eyes plans[4] dishonest things;
he who purses his lips brings evil to pass.
31 Gray hair is a crown of glory;
it is gained in a righteous life.
32 Whoever is slow to anger is better than the mighty,
and he who rules his spirit than he who takes a city.
33 The lot is cast into the lap,
but its every decision is from the LORD.

17 Better is a dry morsel with quiet
than a house full of feasting[5] with strife.
2 A servant who deals wisely will rule over a son who acts shamefully
and will share the inheritance as one of the brothers.
3 The crucible is for silver, and the furnace is for gold,
and the LORD tests hearts.
4 An evildoer listens to wicked lips,
and a liar gives ear to a mischievous tongue.
5 Whoever mocks the poor insults his Maker;
he who is glad at calamity will not go unpunished.
6 Grandchildren are the crown of the aged,
and the glory of children is their fathers.
7 Fine speech is not becoming to a fool;
still less is false speech to a prince.
8 A bribe is like a magic stone in the eyes of the one who gives it;
wherever he turns he prospers.

[1] Or *to a matter* [2] Hebrew *ways of death* [3] Hebrew *what is on his lips* [4] Hebrew *to plan* [5] Hebrew *sacrifices*

9 Whoever covers an offense seeks love,
but he who repeats a matter separates close friends.
10 A rebuke goes deeper into a man of understanding
than a hundred blows into a fool.
11 An evil man seeks only rebellion,
and a cruel messenger will be sent against him.
12 Let a man meet a she-bear robbed of her cubs
rather than a fool in his folly.
13 If anyone returns evil for good,
evil will not depart from his house.
14 The beginning of strife is like letting out water,
so quit before the quarrel breaks out.
15 He who justifies the wicked and he who condemns the righteous
are both alike an abomination to the LORD.
16 Why should a fool have money in his hand to buy wisdom
when he has no sense?
17 A friend loves at all times,
and a brother is born for adversity.
18 One who lacks sense gives a pledge
and puts up security in the presence of his neighbor.
19 Whoever loves transgression loves strife;
he who makes his door high seeks destruction.
20 A man of crooked heart does not discover good,
and one with a dishonest tongue falls into calamity.
21 He who sires a fool gets himself sorrow,
and the father of a fool has no joy.
22 A joyful heart is good medicine,
but a crushed spirit dries up the bones.
23 The wicked accepts a bribe in secret[1]
to pervert the ways of justice.
24 The discerning sets his face toward wisdom,
but the eyes of a fool are on the ends of the earth.
25 A foolish son is a grief to his father
and bitterness to her who bore him.
26 To impose a fine on a righteous man is not good,
nor to strike the noble for their uprightness.
27 Whoever restrains his words has knowledge,
and he who has a cool spirit is a man of understanding.
28 Even a fool who keeps silent is considered wise;
when he closes his lips, he is deemed intelligent.

18 Whoever isolates himself seeks his own desire;
he breaks out against all sound judgment.
2 A fool takes no pleasure in understanding,
but only in expressing his opinion.
3 When wickedness comes, contempt comes also,
and with dishonor comes disgrace.
4 The words of a man's mouth are deep waters;
the fountain of wisdom is a bubbling brook.
5 It is not good to be partial to[2] the wicked
or to deprive the righteous of justice.
6 A fool's lips walk into a fight,
and his mouth invites a beating.
7 A fool's mouth is his ruin,
and his lips are a snare to his soul.

[1] Hebrew *a bribe from the bosom* [2] Hebrew *to lift the face of*

8 The words of a whisperer are like delicious morsels;
they go down into the inner parts of the body.
9 Whoever is slack in his work
is a brother to him who destroys.
10 The name of the LORD is a strong tower;
the righteous man runs into it and is safe.
11 A rich man's wealth is his strong city,
and like a high wall in his imagination.
12 Before destruction a man's heart is haughty,
but humility comes before honor.
13 If one gives an answer before he hears,
it is his folly and shame.
14 A man's spirit will endure sickness,
but a crushed spirit who can bear?
15 An intelligent heart acquires knowledge,
and the ear of the wise seeks knowledge.
16 A man's gift makes room for him
and brings him before the great.
17 The one who states his case first seems right,
until the other comes and examines him.
18 The lot puts an end to quarrels
and decides between powerful contenders.
19 A brother offended is more unyielding than a strong city,
and quarreling is like the bars of a castle.
20 From the fruit of a man's mouth his stomach is satisfied;
he is satisfied by the yield of his lips.
21 Death and life are in the power of the tongue,
and those who love it will eat its fruits.
22 He who finds a wife finds a good thing
and obtains favor from the LORD.
23 The poor use entreaties,
but the rich answer roughly.
24 A man of many companions may come to ruin,
but there is a friend who sticks closer than a brother.

19 Better is a poor person who walks in his integrity
than one who is crooked in speech and is a fool.
2 Desire[1] without knowledge is not good,
and whoever makes haste with his feet misses his way.
3 When a man's folly brings his way to ruin,
his heart rages against the LORD.
4 Wealth brings many new friends,
but a poor man is deserted by his friend.
5 A false witness will not go unpunished,
and he who breathes out lies will not escape.
6 Many seek the favor of a generous man,[2]
and everyone is a friend to a man who gives gifts.
7 All a poor man's brothers hate him;
how much more do his friends go far from him!
He pursues them with words, but does not have them.[3]
8 Whoever gets sense loves his own soul;
he who keeps understanding will discover good.
9 A false witness will not go unpunished,
and he who breathes out lies will perish.
10 It is not fitting for a fool to live in luxury,

[1] Or *A soul* [2] Or *of a noble* [3] The meaning of the Hebrew sentence is uncertain

much less for a slave to rule over
princes.

11 Good sense makes one slow to
anger,
and it is his glory to overlook an
offense.

12 A king's wrath is like the growling of
a lion,
but his favor is like dew on the
grass.

13 A foolish son is ruin to his father,
and a wife's quarreling is a
continual dripping of rain.

14 House and wealth are inherited
from fathers,
61
but a prudent wife is from the
LORD.

15 Slothfulness casts into a deep sleep,
and an idle person will suffer
hunger.

16 Whoever keeps the commandment
keeps his life;
he who despises his ways will die.

17 Whoever is generous to the poor
lends to the LORD,
and he will repay him for his
deed.

18 Discipline your son, for there is
hope;
do not set your heart on putting
him to death.

19 A man of great wrath will pay the
penalty,
for if you deliver him, you will
only have to do it again.

20 Listen to advice and accept
instruction,
that you may gain wisdom in the
future.

21 Many are the plans in the mind
of a man,
747
but it is the purpose of the LORD
that will stand.

22 What is desired in a man is
steadfast love,
and a poor man is better than a
liar.

23 The fear of the LORD leads to life,
and whoever has it rests satisfied;
he will not be visited by harm.

24 The sluggard buries his hand in the
dish
and will not even bring it back to
his mouth.

25 Strike a scoffer, and the simple will
learn prudence;
reprove a man of understanding,
and he will gain knowledge.

26 He who does violence to his father
and chases away his mother
is a son who brings shame and
reproach.

27 Cease to hear instruction, my son,
and you will stray from the words
of knowledge.

28 A worthless witness mocks at
justice,
and the mouth of the wicked
devours iniquity.

29 Condemnation is ready for scoffers,
and beating for the backs of fools.

20 Wine is a mocker, strong drink a
brawler,
and whoever is led astray by it is
not wise.[1]

2 The terror of a king is like the
growling of a lion;
whoever provokes him to anger
forfeits his life.

3 It is an honor for a man to keep
aloof from strife,
but every fool will be quarreling.

4 The sluggard does not plow in the
autumn;
he will seek at harvest and have
nothing.

5 The purpose in a man's heart is like
deep water,
but a man of understanding will
draw it out.

6 Many a man proclaims his own
steadfast love,
but a faithful man who can find?

[1] Or *will not become wise*

7 The righteous who walks in his
integrity—
blessed are his children after him!
8 A king who sits on the throne of
judgment
winnows all evil with his eyes.
9 Who can say, "I have made my heart
pure;
I am clean from my sin"?
10 Unequal[1] weights and unequal
measures
are both alike an abomination to
the LORD.
11 Even a child makes himself known
by his acts,
by whether his conduct is pure
and upright.[2]
12 The hearing ear and the seeing eye,
the LORD has made them both.
13 Love not sleep, lest you come to
poverty;
open your eyes, and you will have
plenty of bread.
14 "Bad, bad," says the buyer,
but when he goes away, then he
boasts.
15 There is gold and abundance of
costly stones,
but the lips of knowledge are a
precious jewel.
16 Take a man's garment when he has
put up security for a stranger,
and hold it in pledge when
he puts up security for
foreigners.[3]
17 Bread gained by deceit is sweet to a
man,
but afterward his mouth will be
full of gravel.
18 Plans are established by counsel;
by wise guidance wage war.
19 Whoever goes about slandering
reveals secrets;
therefore do not associate with a
simple babbler.[4]
20 If one curses his father or his
mother,
his lamp will be put out in utter
darkness.
21 An inheritance gained hastily in the
beginning
will not be blessed in the end.
22 Do not say, "I will repay evil";
wait for the LORD, and he will
deliver you.
23 Unequal weights are an
abomination to the LORD,
and false scales are not good.
24 A man's steps are from the LORD;
how then can man understand
his way?
25 It is a snare to say rashly, "It is holy,"
and to reflect only after making
vows.
26 A wise king winnows the wicked
and drives the wheel over them.
27 The spirit[5] of man is the lamp of the
LORD,
searching all his innermost parts.
28 Steadfast love and faithfulness
preserve the king,
and by steadfast love his throne is
upheld.
29 The glory of young men is their
strength,
but the splendor of old men is
their gray hair.
30 Blows that wound cleanse away evil;
strokes make clean the innermost
parts.

21 The king's heart is a stream of
water in the hand of the LORD;
he turns it wherever he will.
2 Every way of a man is right in his
own eyes,
but the LORD weighs the heart.
3 To do righteousness and justice
is more acceptable to the LORD
than sacrifice.
4 Haughty eyes and a proud heart,
the lamp[6] of the wicked, are sin.

[1] Or *Two kinds of*; also verse 23 [2] Or *Even a child can dissemble in his actions, though his conduct seems pure and upright* [3] Or *for an adulteress* (compare 27:13) [4] Hebrew *with one who is simple in his lips* [5] Hebrew *breath* [6] Or *the plowing*

5 The plans of the diligent lead surely
to abundance,
but everyone who is hasty comes
only to poverty.
6 The getting of treasures by a lying
tongue
is a fleeting vapor and a snare of
death.[1]
7 The violence of the wicked will
sweep them away,
because they refuse to do what is
just.
8 The way of the guilty is crooked,
but the conduct of the pure is
upright.
9 It is better to live in a corner of the
housetop
than in a house shared with a
quarrelsome wife.
10 The soul of the wicked desires evil;
his neighbor finds no mercy in
his eyes.
11 When a scoffer is punished, the
simple becomes wise;
when a wise man is instructed, he
gains knowledge.
12 The Righteous One observes the
house of the wicked;
he throws the wicked down to ruin.
13 Whoever closes his ear to the cry of
the poor
will himself call out and not be
answered.
14 A gift in secret averts anger,
and a concealed bribe,[2] strong
wrath.
15 When justice is done, it is a joy to
the righteous
but terror to evildoers.
16 One who wanders from the way of
good sense
will rest in the assembly of the
dead.
17 Whoever loves pleasure will be a
poor man;
he who loves wine and oil will not
be rich.
18 The wicked is a ransom for the
righteous,
and the traitor for the upright.
19 It is better to live in a desert land
than with a quarrelsome and
fretful woman.
20 Precious treasure and oil are in a
wise man's dwelling,
but a foolish man devours it.
21 Whoever pursues righteousness
and kindness
will find life, righteousness, and
honor.
22 A wise man scales the city of the
mighty
and brings down the stronghold
in which they trust.
23 Whoever keeps his mouth and his
tongue
keeps himself out of trouble.
24 "Scoffer" is the name of the arrogant,
haughty man
who acts with arrogant pride.
25 The desire of the sluggard kills
him,
for his hands refuse to labor.
26 All day long he craves and craves,
but the righteous gives and does
not hold back.
27 The sacrifice of the wicked is an
abomination;
how much more when he brings
it with evil intent.
28 A false witness will perish,
but the word of a man who hears
will endure.
29 A wicked man puts on a bold face,
but the upright gives thought to[3]
his ways.
30 No wisdom, no understanding, no
counsel
can avail against the LORD.
31 The horse is made ready for the day
of battle,
but the victory belongs to the
LORD.

[1] Some Hebrew manuscripts, Septuagint, Latin; most Hebrew manuscripts *vapor for those who seek death* [2] Hebrew *a bribe in the bosom* [3] Or *establishes*

22 A good name is to be chosen
rather than great riches,
and favor is better than silver or
gold.
2 The rich and the poor meet
together;
the LORD is the maker of them all.
3 The prudent sees danger and hides
himself,
but the simple go on and suffer
for it.
4 The reward for humility and fear of
the LORD
is riches and honor and life.[1]
5 Thorns and snares are in the way of
the crooked;
whoever guards his soul will keep
far from them.
6 Train up a child in the way he
should go;
even when he is old he will not
depart from it.
7 The rich rules over the poor,
and the borrower is the slave of
the lender.
8 Whoever sows injustice will reap
calamity,
and the rod of his fury will fail.
9 Whoever has a bountiful[2] eye will
be blessed,
for he shares his bread with the
poor.
10 Drive out a scoffer, and strife will go
out,
and quarreling and abuse will
cease.
11 He who loves purity of heart,
and whose speech is gracious,
will have the king as his
friend.
12 The eyes of the LORD keep watch
over knowledge,
but he overthrows the words of
the traitor.
13 The sluggard says, "There is a lion
outside!
I shall be killed in the streets!"
14 The mouth of forbidden[3] women is
a deep pit;
he with whom the LORD is angry
will fall into it.
15 Folly is bound up in the heart of a
child,
but the rod of discipline drives it
far from him.
16 Whoever oppresses the poor to
increase his own wealth,
or gives to the rich, will only
come to poverty.

Words of the Wise

17 Incline your ear, and hear the words
of the wise,
and apply your heart to my
knowledge,
18 for it will be pleasant if you keep
them within you,
if all of them are ready on your
lips.
19 That your trust may be in the LORD,
I have made them known to you
today, even to you.
20 Have I not written for you thirty
sayings
of counsel and knowledge,
21 to make you know what is right and
true,
that you may give a true answer to
those who sent you?

22 Do not rob the poor, because he is
poor,
or crush the afflicted at the gate,
23 for the LORD will plead their cause
and rob of life those who rob
them.
24 Make no friendship with a man
given to anger,
nor go with a wrathful man,
25 lest you learn his ways
and entangle yourself in a snare.
26 Be not one of those who give
pledges,
who put up security for debts.

[1] Or *The reward for humility is the fear of the LORD, riches and honor and life* [2] Hebrew *good* [3] Hebrew *strange*

27 If you have nothing with which to pay,
why should your bed be taken from under you?
28 Do not move the ancient landmark
that your fathers have set.
29 Do you see a man skillful in his work?
He will stand before kings;
he will not stand before obscure men.

23 When you sit down to eat with a ruler,
observe carefully what[1] is before you,
2 and put a knife to your throat
if you are given to appetite.
3 Do not desire his delicacies,
for they are deceptive food.
4 Do not toil to acquire wealth;
be discerning enough to desist.
5 When your eyes light on it, it is gone,
for suddenly it sprouts wings,
flying like an eagle toward heaven.
6 Do not eat the bread of a man who is stingy;[2]
do not desire his delicacies,
7 for he is like one who is inwardly calculating.[3]
"Eat and drink!" he says to you,
but his heart is not with you.
8 You will vomit up the morsels that you have eaten,
and waste your pleasant words.
9 Do not speak in the hearing of a fool,
for he will despise the good sense of your words.
10 Do not move an ancient landmark
or enter the fields of the fatherless,
11 for their Redeemer is strong;
he will plead their cause against you.
12 Apply your heart to instruction
and your ear to words of knowledge.
13 Do not withhold discipline from a child;
if you strike him with a rod, he will not die.
14 If you strike him with the rod,
you will save his soul from Sheol.
15 My son, if your heart is wise,
my heart too will be glad.
16 My inmost being[4] will exult
when your lips speak what is right.
17 Let not your heart envy sinners,
but continue in the fear of the LORD all the day.
18 Surely there is a future,
and your hope will not be cut off.

19 Hear, my son, and be wise,
and direct your heart in the way.
20 Be not among drunkards[5]
or among gluttonous eaters of meat,
21 for the drunkard and the glutton will come to poverty,
and slumber will clothe them with rags.

22 Listen to your father who gave you life,
and do not despise your mother when she is old.
23 Buy truth, and do not sell it;
buy wisdom, instruction, and understanding.
24 The father of the righteous will greatly rejoice;
he who fathers a wise son will be glad in him.
25 Let your father and mother be glad;
let her who bore you rejoice.

26 My son, give me your heart,
and let your eyes observe[6] my ways.
27 For a prostitute is a deep pit;
an adulteress[7] is a narrow well.

[1] Or *who* [2] Hebrew *whose eye is evil* [3] Or *for as he calculates in his soul, so is he* [4] Hebrew *My kidneys* [5] Hebrew *those who drink too much wine* [6] Or *delight in* [7] Hebrew *a foreign woman*

28 She lies in wait like a robber
and increases the traitors among mankind.

29 Who has woe? Who has sorrow?
Who has strife? Who has complaining?
Who has wounds without cause?
Who has redness of eyes?
30 Those who tarry long over wine;
those who go to try mixed wine.
31 Do not look at wine when it is red,
when it sparkles in the cup
and goes down smoothly.
32 In the end it bites like a serpent
and stings like an adder.
33 Your eyes will see strange things,
and your heart utter perverse things.
34 You will be like one who lies down in the midst of the sea,
like one who lies on the top of a mast.[1]
35 "They struck me," you will say,[2] "but I was not hurt;
they beat me, but I did not feel it.
When shall I awake?
I must have another drink."

24 Be not envious of evil men,
nor desire to be with them,
2 for their hearts devise violence,
and their lips talk of trouble.

3 By wisdom a house is built,
and by understanding it is established;
4 by knowledge the rooms are filled
with all precious and pleasant riches.
5 A wise man is full of strength,
and a man of knowledge enhances his might,
6 for by wise guidance you can wage your war,
and in abundance of counselors there is victory.
7 Wisdom is too high for a fool;
in the gate he does not open his mouth.

8 Whoever plans to do evil
will be called a schemer.
9 The devising[3] of folly is sin,
and the scoffer is an abomination to mankind.

10 If you faint in the day of adversity,
your strength is small.
11 Rescue those who are being taken away to death;
hold back those who are stumbling to the slaughter.
12 If you say, "Behold, we did not know this,"
does not he who weighs the heart perceive it?
Does not he who keeps watch over your soul know it,
and will he not repay man according to his work?

13 My son, eat honey, for it is good,
and the drippings of the honeycomb are sweet to your taste.
14 Know that wisdom is such to your soul;
if you find it, there will be a future,
and your hope will not be cut off.

15 Lie not in wait as a wicked man against the dwelling of the righteous;
do no violence to his home;
16 for the righteous falls seven times and rises again,
but the wicked stumble in times of calamity.

17 Do not rejoice when your enemy falls,
and let not your heart be glad when he stumbles,

[1] Or *of the rigging* [2] Hebrew lacks *you will say* [3] Or *scheming*

18 lest the LORD see it and be
displeased,
and turn away his anger from him.

19 Fret not yourself because of
evildoers,
and be not envious of the wicked,
20 for the evil man has no future;
the lamp of the wicked will be put
out.

21 My son, fear the LORD and the king,
and do not join with those who
do otherwise,
22 for disaster will arise suddenly from
them,
and who knows the ruin that will
come from them both?

More Sayings of the Wise

23 These also are sayings of the wise.

Partiality in judging is not good.
24 Whoever says to the wicked, "You
are in the right,"
will be cursed by peoples,
abhorred by nations,
25 but those who rebuke the wicked
will have delight,
and a good blessing will come
upon them.
26 Whoever gives an honest answer
kisses the lips.
27 Prepare your work outside;
get everything ready for yourself
in the field,
and after that build your house.

28 Be not a witness against your
neighbor without cause,
and do not deceive with your lips.
29 Do not say, "I will do to him as he
has done to me;
I will pay the man back for what
he has done."

30 I passed by the field of a sluggard,
by the vineyard of a man lacking
sense,
31 and behold, it was all overgrown
with thorns;
the ground was covered with
nettles,
and its stone wall was broken
down.
32 Then I saw and considered it;
I looked and received instruction.
33 A little sleep, a little slumber,
a little folding of the hands to
rest,
34 and poverty will come upon you
like a robber,
and want like an armed man.

More Proverbs of Solomon

25 These also are proverbs of Solomon which the men of Hezekiah king of Judah copied.

2 It is the glory of God to conceal
things,
but the glory of kings is to search
things out.
3 As the heavens for height, and the
earth for depth,
so the heart of kings is
unsearchable.
4 Take away the dross from the silver,
and the smith has material for a
vessel;
5 take away the wicked from the
presence of the king,
and his throne will be established
in righteousness.
6 Do not put yourself forward in the
king's presence
or stand in the place of the great,
7 for it is better to be told, "Come up
here,"
than to be put lower in the
presence of a noble.

What your eyes have seen
8 do not hastily bring into court,
for[1] what will you do in the end,
when your neighbor puts you to
shame?

[1] Hebrew *or else*

9 Argue your case with your neighbor
himself,
and do not reveal another's secret,
10 lest he who hears you bring shame
upon you,
and your ill repute have no end.

11 A word fitly spoken
is like apples of gold in a setting
of silver.
12 Like a gold ring or an ornament of
gold
is a wise reprover to a listening
ear.
13 Like the cold of snow in the time of
harvest
is a faithful messenger to those
who send him;
he refreshes the soul of his
masters.
14 Like clouds and wind without rain
is a man who boasts of a gift he
does not give.

15 With patience a ruler may be
persuaded,
and a soft tongue will break a bone.
16 If you have found honey, eat only
enough for you,
lest you have your fill of it and
vomit it.
17 Let your foot be seldom in your
neighbor's house,
lest he have his fill of you and
hate you.
18 A man who bears false witness
against his neighbor
is like a war club, or a sword, or a
sharp arrow.
19 Trusting in a treacherous man in
time of trouble
is like a bad tooth or a foot that
slips.
20 Whoever sings songs to a heavy
heart
is like one who takes off a
garment on a cold day,
and like vinegar on soda.

21 If your enemy is hungry, give him
bread to eat,
and if he is thirsty, give him water
to drink,
22 for you will heap burning coals on
his head,
and the LORD will reward you.
23 The north wind brings forth rain,
and a backbiting tongue, angry
looks.
24 It is better to live in a corner of the
housetop
than in a house shared with a
quarrelsome wife.
25 Like cold water to a thirsty soul,
so is good news from a far
country.
26 Like a muddied spring or a polluted
fountain
is a righteous man who gives way
before the wicked.

27 It is not good to eat much honey,
nor is it glorious to seek one's
own glory.[1]
28 A man without self-control
is like a city broken into and left
without walls.

26 Like snow in summer or rain in
harvest,
so honor is not fitting for a fool.
2 Like a sparrow in its flitting, like a
swallow in its flying,
a curse that is causeless does not
alight.
3 A whip for the horse, a bridle for the
donkey,
and a rod for the back of fools.
4 Answer not a fool according to his
folly,
lest you be like him yourself.
5 Answer a fool according to his folly,
lest he be wise in his own eyes.
6 Whoever sends a message by the
hand of a fool
cuts off his own feet and drinks
violence.

[1] The meaning of the Hebrew line is uncertain

7 Like a lame man's legs, which hang
useless,
is a proverb in the mouth of fools.
8 Like one who binds the stone in the
sling
is one who gives honor to a fool.
9 Like a thorn that goes up into the
hand of a drunkard
is a proverb in the mouth of fools.
10 Like an archer who wounds
everyone
is one who hires a passing fool or
drunkard.[1]
11 Like a dog that returns to his vomit
is a fool who repeats his folly.
12 Do you see a man who is wise in his
own eyes?
There is more hope for a fool than
for him.
13 The sluggard says, "There is a lion
in the road!
There is a lion in the streets!"
14 As a door turns on its hinges,
so does a sluggard on his bed.
15 The sluggard buries his hand in the
dish;
it wears him out to bring it back
to his mouth.
16 The sluggard is wiser in his own
eyes
than seven men who can answer
sensibly.
17 Whoever meddles in a quarrel not
his own
is like one who takes a passing
dog by the ears.
18 Like a madman who throws
firebrands, arrows, and death
19 is the man who deceives his
neighbor
and says, "I am only joking!"
20 For lack of wood the fire goes out,
and where there is no whisperer,
quarreling ceases.
21 As charcoal to hot embers and wood
to fire,
so is a quarrelsome man for
kindling strife.
22 The words of a whisperer are like
delicious morsels;
they go down into the inner parts
of the body.
23 Like the glaze[2] covering an earthen
vessel
are fervent lips with an evil heart.
24 Whoever hates disguises himself
with his lips
and harbors deceit in his heart;
25 when he speaks graciously, believe
him not,
for there are seven abominations
in his heart;
26 though his hatred be covered with
deception,
his wickedness will be exposed in
the assembly.
27 Whoever digs a pit will fall into it,
and a stone will come back on
him who starts it rolling.
28 A lying tongue hates its victims,
and a flattering mouth works
ruin.

27 Do not boast about tomorrow,
for you do not know what a day
may bring.
2 Let another praise you, and not your
own mouth;
a stranger, and not your own lips.
3 A stone is heavy, and sand is
weighty,
but a fool's provocation is heavier
than both.
4 Wrath is cruel, anger is
overwhelming,
but who can stand before jealousy?
5 Better is open rebuke
than hidden love.
6 Faithful are the wounds of a friend;
profuse are the kisses of an
enemy.
7 One who is full loathes honey,
but to one who is hungry
everything bitter is sweet.

[1] Or *hires a fool or passersby* [2] By revocalization; Hebrew *silver of dross*

8 Like a bird that strays from its nest
is a man who strays from his home.
9 Oil and perfume make the heart glad,
and the sweetness of a friend comes from his earnest counsel.[1]
10 Do not forsake your friend and your father's friend,
and do not go to your brother's house in the day of your calamity.
Better is a neighbor who is near
than a brother who is far away.
11 Be wise, my son, and make my heart glad,
that I may answer him who reproaches me.
12 The prudent sees danger and hides himself,
but the simple go on and suffer for it.
13 Take a man's garment when he has put up security for a stranger,
and hold it in pledge when he puts up security for an adulteress.[2]
14 Whoever blesses his neighbor with a loud voice,
rising early in the morning,
will be counted as cursing.
15 A continual dripping on a rainy day
and a quarrelsome wife are alike;
16 to restrain her is to restrain the wind
or to grasp[3] oil in one's right hand.
17 Iron sharpens iron,
and one man sharpens another.[4]
18 Whoever tends a fig tree will eat its fruit,
and he who guards his master will be honored.
19 As in water face reflects face,
so the heart of man reflects the man.
20 Sheol and Abaddon are never satisfied,
and never satisfied are the eyes of man.
21 The crucible is for silver, and the furnace is for gold,
and a man is tested by his praise.
22 Crush a fool in a mortar with a pestle
along with crushed grain,
yet his folly will not depart from him.

23 Know well the condition of your flocks,
and give attention to your herds,
24 for riches do not last forever;
and does a crown endure to all generations?
25 When the grass is gone and the new growth appears
and the vegetation of the mountains is gathered,
26 the lambs will provide your clothing,
and the goats the price of a field.
27 There will be enough goats' milk for your food,
for the food of your household
and maintenance for your girls.

28 The wicked flee when no one pursues,
but the righteous are bold as a lion.
2 When a land transgresses, it has many rulers,
but with a man of understanding and knowledge,
its stability will long continue.
3 A poor man who oppresses the poor
is a beating rain that leaves no food.
4 Those who forsake the law praise the wicked,
but those who keep the law strive against them.

[1] Or *and so does the sweetness of a friend that comes from his earnest counsel* [2] Hebrew *a foreign woman*; a slight emendation yields (compare Vulgate; see also 20:16) *foreigners* [3] Hebrew *to meet with* [4] Hebrew *sharpens the face of another*

5 Evil men do not understand justice,
but those who seek the LORD
understand it completely.
6 Better is a poor man who walks in
his integrity
than a rich man who is crooked in
his ways.
7 The one who keeps the law is a son
with understanding,
but a companion of gluttons
shames his father.
8 Whoever multiplies his wealth by
interest and profit[1]
gathers it for him who is generous
to the poor.
9 If one turns away his ear from
hearing the law,
even his prayer is an
abomination.
10 Whoever misleads the upright into
an evil way
will fall into his own pit,
but the blameless will have a
goodly inheritance.
11 A rich man is wise in his own eyes,
but a poor man who has
understanding will find him
out.
12 When the righteous triumph, there
is great glory,
but when the wicked rise, people
hide themselves.
13 Whoever conceals his
transgressions will not
prosper,
but he who confesses and
forsakes them will obtain
mercy.
14 Blessed is the one who fears the
LORD always,
but whoever hardens his heart
will fall into calamity.
15 Like a roaring lion or a charging
bear
is a wicked ruler over a poor
people.
16 A ruler who lacks understanding is
a cruel oppressor,
but he who hates unjust gain will
prolong his days.
17 If one is burdened with the blood of
another,
he will be a fugitive until death;[2]
let no one help him.
18 Whoever walks in integrity will be
delivered,
but he who is crooked in his ways
will suddenly fall.
19 Whoever works his land will have
plenty of bread,
but he who follows worthless
pursuits will have plenty of
poverty.
20 A faithful man will abound with
blessings,
but whoever hastens to be rich
will not go unpunished.
21 To show partiality is not good,
but for a piece of bread a man will
do wrong.
22 A stingy man[3] hastens after wealth
and does not know that poverty
will come upon him.
23 Whoever rebukes a man will
afterward find more favor
than he who flatters with his
tongue.
24 Whoever robs his father or his
mother
and says, "That is no transgression,"
is a companion to a man who
destroys.
25 A greedy man stirs up strife,
but the one who trusts in the
LORD will be enriched.
26 Whoever trusts in his own mind is a
fool,
but he who walks in wisdom will
be delivered.
27 Whoever gives to the poor will not
want,
but he who hides his eyes will get
many a curse.

[1] That is, profit that comes from charging interest to the poor [2] Hebrew *until the pit* [3] Hebrew *A man whose eye is evil*

28 When the wicked rise, people hide
themselves,
but when they perish, the
righteous increase.

29

He who is often reproved, yet
stiffens his neck,
will suddenly be broken beyond
healing.
2 When the righteous increase, the
people rejoice,
but when the wicked rule, the
people groan.
3 He who loves wisdom makes his
father glad,
but a companion of prostitutes
squanders his wealth.
4 By justice a king builds up the land,
but he who exacts gifts[1] tears it
down.
5 A man who flatters his neighbor
spreads a net for his feet.
6 An evil man is ensnared in his
transgression,
but a righteous man sings and
rejoices.
7 A righteous man knows the rights
of the poor;
a wicked man does not
understand such knowledge.
8 Scoffers set a city aflame,
but the wise turn away wrath.
9 If a wise man has an argument with
a fool,
the fool only rages and laughs,
and there is no quiet.
10 Bloodthirsty men hate one who is
blameless
and seek the life of the upright.[2]
11 A fool gives full vent to his spirit,
but a wise man quietly holds it
back.
12 If a ruler listens to falsehood,
all his officials will be wicked.
13 The poor man and the oppressor
meet together;
the LORD gives light to the eyes of
both.
14 If a king faithfully judges the poor,
his throne will be established
forever.
15 The rod and reproof give wisdom,
but a child left to himself brings
shame to his mother.
16 When the wicked increase,
transgression increases,
but the righteous will look upon
their downfall.
17 Discipline your son, and he will
give you rest;
he will give delight to your heart.
18 Where there is no prophetic vision
the people cast off restraint,[3]
but blessed is he who keeps the
law.
19 By mere words a servant is not
disciplined,
for though he understands, he
will not respond.
20 Do you see a man who is hasty in
his words?
There is more hope for a fool than
for him.
21 Whoever pampers his servant from
childhood
will in the end find him his heir.[4]
22 A man of wrath stirs up strife,
and one given to anger causes
much transgression.
23 One's pride will bring him low,
but he who is lowly in spirit will
obtain honor.
24 The partner of a thief hates his own
life;
he hears the curse, but discloses
nothing.
25 The fear of man lays a snare,
but whoever trusts in the LORD is
safe.
26 Many seek the face of a ruler,
but it is from the LORD that a man
gets justice.

[1] Or *who taxes heavily* [2] Or *but the upright seek his soul* [3] Or *the people are discouraged* [4] The meaning of the Hebrew word rendered *his heir* is uncertain

27 An unjust man is an abomination
to the righteous,
but one whose way is straight is
an abomination to the wicked.

The Words of Agur

30 The words of Agur son of Jakeh. The oracle.[1]

The man declares, I am weary, O God;
I am weary, O God, and worn out.[2]
2 Surely I am too stupid to be a man.
I have not the understanding of a
man.
3 I have not learned wisdom,
nor have I knowledge of the Holy
One.
4 Who has ascended to heaven and
come down?
Who has gathered the wind in his
fists?
Who has wrapped up the waters in a
garment?
Who has established all the ends
of the earth?
What is his name, and what is his
son's name?
Surely you know!

5 Every word of God proves true;
he is a shield to those who take
refuge in him.
6 Do not add to his words,
lest he rebuke you and you be
found a liar.

7 Two things I ask of you;
deny them not to me before I die:
8 Remove far from me falsehood and
lying;
give me neither poverty nor
riches;
feed me with the food that is
needful for me,
9 lest I be full and deny you
and say, "Who is the LORD?"
or lest I be poor and steal
and profane the name of my God.

10 Do not slander a servant to his
master,
lest he curse you, and you be held
guilty.

11 There are those[3] who curse their
fathers
and do not bless their mothers.
12 There are those who are clean in
their own eyes
but are not washed of their filth.
13 There are those—how lofty are their
eyes,
how high their eyelids lift!
14 There are those whose teeth are
swords,
whose fangs are knives,
to devour the poor from off the
earth,
the needy from among mankind.

15 The leech has two daughters:
Give and Give.[4]
Three things are never satisfied;
four never say, "Enough":
16 Sheol, the barren womb,
the land never satisfied with
water,
and the fire that never says,
"Enough."

17 The eye that mocks a father
and scorns to obey a mother
will be picked out by the ravens of
the valley
and eaten by the vultures.

18 Three things are too wonderful for
me;
four I do not understand:
19 the way of an eagle in the sky,
the way of a serpent on a rock,
the way of a ship on the high seas,
and the way of a man with a
virgin.

20 This is the way of an adulteress:
she eats and wipes her mouth
and says, "I have done no wrong."

[1] Or *Jakeh, the man of Massa* [2] Revocalization; Hebrew *The man declares to Ithiel, to Ithiel and Ucal* [3] Hebrew *There is a generation*; also verses 12, 13, 14 [4] Or *"Give, give," they cry*

21 Under three things the earth
trembles;
under four it cannot bear up:
22 a slave when he becomes king,
and a fool when he is filled with
food;
23 an unloved woman when she gets a
husband,
and a maidservant when she
displaces her mistress.

24 Four things on earth are small,
but they are exceedingly wise:
25 the ants are a people not strong,
yet they provide their food in the
summer;
26 the rock badgers are a people not
mighty,
yet they make their homes in the
cliffs;
27 the locusts have no king,
yet all of them march in rank;
28 the lizard you can take in your
hands,
yet it is in kings' palaces.

29 Three things are stately in their
tread;
four are stately in their stride:
30 the lion, which is mightiest among
beasts
and does not turn back before
any;
31 the strutting rooster,[1] the he-goat,
and a king whose army is with
him.[2]

32 If you have been foolish, exalting
yourself,
or if you have been devising evil,
put your hand on your mouth.
33 For pressing milk produces curds,
pressing the nose produces blood,
and pressing anger produces
strife.

The Words of King Lemuel

31 The words of King Lemuel. An
oracle that his mother taught him:

2 What are you doing, my son?[3] What
are you doing, son of my
womb?
What are you doing, son of my
vows?
3 Do not give your strength to
women,
your ways to those who destroy
kings.
4 It is not for kings, O Lemuel,
it is not for kings to drink wine,
or for rulers to take strong drink,
5 lest they drink and forget what has
been decreed
and pervert the rights of all the
afflicted.
6 Give strong drink to the one who is
perishing,
and wine to those in bitter
distress;[4]
7 let them drink and forget their
poverty
and remember their misery no
more.
8 Open your mouth for the mute,
for the rights of all who are
destitute.[5]
9 Open your mouth, judge
righteously,
defend the rights of the poor and
needy.

The Woman Who Fears the LORD

10[6] An excellent wife who can find?
She is far more precious than
jewels.
11 The heart of her husband trusts in
her,
and he will have no lack of gain.
12 She does him good, and not harm,
all the days of her life.
13 She seeks wool and flax,
and works with willing hands.

[1] Or *the magpie*, or *the greyhound*; Hebrew *girt-of-loins* [2] Or *against whom there is no rising up* [3] Hebrew *What, my son?* [4] Hebrew *those bitter in soul* [5] Hebrew *are sons of passing away* [6] Verses 10-31 are an acrostic poem, each verse beginning with the successive letters of the Hebrew alphabet

14 She is like the ships of the merchant;
she brings her food from afar.
15 She rises while it is yet night
and provides food for her household
and portions for her maidens.
16 She considers a field and buys it;
with the fruit of her hands she plants a vineyard.
17 She dresses herself[1] with strength
and makes her arms strong.
18 She perceives that her merchandise is profitable.
Her lamp does not go out at night.
19 She puts her hands to the distaff,
and her hands hold the spindle.
20 She opens her hand to the poor
and reaches out her hands to the needy.
21 She is not afraid of snow for her household,
for all her household are clothed in scarlet.[2]
22 She makes bed coverings for herself;
her clothing is fine linen and purple.
23 Her husband is known in the gates
when he sits among the elders of the land.
24 She makes linen garments and sells them;
she delivers sashes to the merchant.
25 Strength and dignity are her clothing,
and she laughs at the time to come.
26 She opens her mouth with wisdom,
and the teaching of kindness is on her tongue.
27 She looks well to the ways of her household
and does not eat the bread of idleness.
28 Her children rise up and call her blessed;
her husband also, and he praises her:
29 "Many women have done excellently,
but you surpass them all."
30 Charm is deceitful, and beauty is vain,
but a woman who fears the LORD is to be praised.
31 Give her of the fruit of her hands,
and let her works praise her in the gates.

[1] Hebrew *She girds her loins* [2] Or *in double thickness*

Introduction to

Ecclesiastes

Author
King Solomon

Date
About 931 B.C. (end of Solomon's reign)

Purpose
The purpose of Ecclesiastes is to give wisdom and knowledge to the people of God, especially concerning the troubles and frustrations of life.

Central Themes
The fall brought sad results; life is "vain" (frustrating, not the way it should be); sin and death are painful; work is both joyful and frustrating; God's gifts can be gratefully enjoyed; God must be feared.

Memory Verses
Vanity (Ecclesiastes 1:2–3; 2:9–11); seasons and times under heaven (Ecclesiastes 3:1–8); the end of the matter (Ecclesiastes 12:13–14)

Introduction

The "Preacher," probably Solomon, begins the book of Ecclesiastes with a poem about the vanity of life (Ecclesiastes 1:2–11). Everything continues the same, he says, and nothing we do makes any difference. Most of the rest of the book says the same thing in different ways, usually describing life "under the sun," that is, in a fallen world. Because sin is in the world with all its sad consequences, life is full of trouble and frustration. The Preacher describes the many things he has tried in the hope of finding something truly worthwhile: wisdom (Ecclesiastes 1:12–18, 2:12–17), pleasure and possessions (Ecclesiastes 2:1–11), hard work (Ecclesiastes 2:18–26). None of it will last, he concludes, and all "under the sun"—in a fallen world—is vanity. The Preacher considers how everyone will die (Ecclesiastes 3:16–4:3), whether they are good or evil. He describes the difficulties of growing old (Ecclesiastes 11:7–12:7). The writer paints a gloomy picture of life in a fallen world, but this is what God has ordained for now. Solomon's conclusion: we must fear God (Ecclesiastes 12:13–14) and trust Him. He alone gives life meaning. Even in this fallen world, God gives good gifts to those who live for Him (Ecclesiastes 2:24–26, 9:7–10).

1010–971 B.C.	**971–931 B.C.**	**586 B.C.**
Reign of David	Reign of Solomon	Fall of Judah

Ecclesiastes

All Is Vanity

1 The words of the Preacher,[1] the son of
David, king in Jerusalem.

2 Vanity[2] of vanities, says the Preacher,
vanity of vanities! All is vanity.
3 What does man gain by all the toil
at which he toils under the sun?
4 A generation goes, and a generation
comes,
but the earth remains forever.
5 The sun rises, and the sun goes
down,
and hastens[3] to the place where it
rises.
6 The wind blows to the south
and goes around to the north;
around and around goes the wind,
and on its circuits the wind returns.
7 All streams run to the sea,
but the sea is not full;
to the place where the streams flow,
there they flow again.
8 All things are full of weariness;
a man cannot utter it;
the eye is not satisfied with seeing,
nor the ear filled with hearing.
9 What has been is what will be,
and what has been done is what
will be done,
and there is nothing new under
the sun.
10 Is there a thing of which it is said,
"See, this is new"?
It has been already
in the ages before us.
11 There is no remembrance of former
things,[4]
nor will there be any remembrance
of later things[5] yet to be
among those who come after.

The Vanity of Wisdom

12 I the Preacher have been king over
Israel in Jerusalem. **13** And I applied my
heart[6] to seek and to search out by wis-
dom all that is done under heaven. It is an
unhappy business that God has given to
the children of man to be busy with. **14** I
have seen everything that is done under
the sun, and behold, all is vanity and a
striving after wind.[7]

15 What is crooked cannot be made
straight,
and what is lacking cannot be
counted.

16 I said in my heart, "I have acquired
great wisdom, surpassing all who were
over Jerusalem before me, and my heart
has had great experience of wisdom and
knowledge." **17** And I applied my heart
to know wisdom and to know madness
and folly. I perceived that this also is but a
striving after wind.

18 For in much wisdom is much
vexation,
and he who increases knowledge
increases sorrow.

The Vanity of Self-Indulgence

2 I said in my heart, "Come now, I will
test you with pleasure; enjoy your-
self." But behold, this also was vanity. **2** I
said of laughter, "It is mad," and of plea-
sure, "What use is it?" **3** I searched with my
heart how to cheer my body with wine—
my heart still guiding me with wisdom—
and how to lay hold on folly, till I might
see what was good for the children of man
to do under heaven during the few days
of their life. **4** I made great works. I built

[1] Or *Convener*, or *Collector*; Hebrew *Qoheleth* (so throughout Ecclesiastes) [2] Hebrew *vapor* (so throughout Ecclesiastes) [3] Or *and returns panting* [4] Or *former people* [5] Or *later people* [6] The Hebrew term denotes the center of one's inner life, including mind, will, and emotions [7] Or *a feeding on wind*; compare Hosea 12:1 (so throughout Ecclesiastes)

houses and planted vineyards for myself. 5 I made myself gardens and parks, and planted in them all kinds of fruit trees. 6 I made myself pools from which to water the forest of growing trees. 7 I bought male and female slaves, and had slaves who were born in my house. I had also great possessions of herds and flocks, more than any who had been before me in Jerusalem. 8 I also gathered for myself silver and gold and the treasure of kings and provinces. I got singers, both men and women, and many concubines,[1] the delight of the children of man.

9 So I became great and surpassed all who were before me in Jerusalem. Also my wisdom remained with me. 10 And whatever my eyes desired I did not keep from them. I kept my heart from no pleasure, for my heart found pleasure in all my toil, and this was my reward for all my toil. 11 Then I considered all that my hands had done and the toil I had expended in doing it, and behold, all was vanity and a striving after wind, and there was nothing to be gained under the sun.

The Vanity of Living Wisely

12 So I turned to consider wisdom and madness and folly. For what can the man do who comes after the king? Only what has already been done. 13 Then I saw that there is more gain in wisdom than in folly, as there is more gain in light than in darkness. 14 The wise person has his eyes in his head, but the fool walks in darkness. And yet I perceived that the same event happens to all of them. 15 Then I said in my heart, "What happens to the fool will happen to me also. Why then have I been so very wise?" And I said in my heart that this also is vanity. 16 For of the wise as of the fool there is no enduring remembrance, seeing that in the days to come all will have been long forgotten. How the wise dies just like the fool! 17 So I hated life, because what is done under the sun was grievous to me, for all is vanity and a striving after wind.

The Vanity of Toil

18 I hated all my toil in which I toil under the sun, seeing that I must leave it to the man who will come after me, 19 and who knows whether he will be wise or a fool? Yet he will be master of all for which I toiled and used my wisdom under the sun. This also is vanity. 20 So I turned about and gave my heart up to despair over all the toil of my labors under the sun, 21 because sometimes a person who has toiled with wisdom and knowledge and skill must leave everything to be enjoyed by someone who did not toil for it. This also is vanity and a great evil. 22 What has a man from all the toil and striving of heart with which he toils beneath the sun? 23 For all his days are full of sorrow, and his work is a vexation. Even in the night his heart does not rest. This also is vanity.

24 There is nothing better for a person than that he should eat and drink and find enjoyment[2] in his toil. This also, I saw, is from the hand of God, 25 for apart from him[3] who can eat or who can have enjoyment? 26 For to the one who pleases him God has given wisdom and knowledge and joy, but to the sinner he has given the business of gathering and collecting, only to give to one who pleases God. This also is vanity and a striving after wind.

A Time for Everything

3 For everything there is a season, and a time for every matter under heaven:

2 a time to be born, and a time to die;
a time to plant, and a time to pluck
up what is planted;
3 a time to kill, and a time to heal;
a time to break down, and a time to
build up;
4 a time to weep, and a time to laugh;

[1] The meaning of the Hebrew word is uncertain [2] Or *and make his soul see good* [3] Some Hebrew manuscripts, Septuagint, Syriac; most Hebrew manuscripts *apart from me*

a time to mourn, and a time to
dance;
5 a time to cast away stones, and a
time to gather stones together;
a time to embrace, and a time to
refrain from embracing;
6 a time to seek, and a time to lose;
a time to keep, and a time to cast
away;
7 a time to tear, and a time to sew;
a time to keep silence, and a time to
speak;
8 a time to love, and a time to hate;
a time for war, and a time for peace.

The God-Given Task

9 What gain has the worker from his toil? 10 I have seen the business that God has given to the children of man to be busy with. 11 He has made everything beautiful in its time. Also, he has put eternity into man's heart, yet so that he cannot find out what God has done from the beginning to the end. 12 I perceived that there is nothing better for them than to be joyful and to do good as long as they live; 13 also that everyone should eat and drink and take pleasure in all his toil—this is God's gift to man.

14 I perceived that whatever God does endures forever; nothing can be added to it, nor anything taken from it. God has done it, so that people fear before him. 15 That which is, already has been; that which is to be, already has been; and God seeks what has been driven away.[1]

From Dust to Dust

16 Moreover, I saw under the sun that in the place of justice, even there was wickedness, and in the place of righteousness, even there was wickedness. 17 I said in my heart, God will judge the righteous and the wicked, *for there is a time for* every matter and for every work. 18 I said in my heart with regard to the children of man that God is testing them that they may see that they themselves are but beasts. 19 For what happens to the children of man and what happens to the beasts is the same; as one dies, so dies the other. They all have the same breath, and man has no advantage over the beasts, for all is vanity. 20 All go to one place. All are from the dust, and to dust all return. 21 Who knows whether the spirit of man goes upward and the spirit of the beast goes down into the earth? 22 So I saw that there is nothing better than that a man should rejoice in his work, for that is his lot. Who can bring him to see what will be after him?

Evil Under the Sun

4 Again I saw all the oppressions that are done under the sun. And behold, the tears of the oppressed, and they had no one to comfort them! On the side of their oppressors there was power, and there was no one to comfort them. 2 And I thought the dead who are already dead more fortunate than the living who are still alive. 3 But better than both is he who has not yet been and has not seen the evil deeds that are done under the sun.

4 Then I saw that all toil and all skill in work come from a man's envy of his neighbor. This also is vanity and a striving after wind.

5 The fool folds his hands and eats his own flesh.

6 Better is a handful of quietness than two hands full of toil and a striving after wind.

7 Again, I saw vanity under the sun: 8 one person who has no other, either son or brother, yet there is no end to all his toil, and his eyes are never satisfied with riches, so that he never asks, "For whom am I toiling and depriving myself of pleasure?" This also is vanity and an unhappy business.

9 Two are better than one, because they have a good reward for their toil. 10 For if they fall, one will lift up his fellow. But woe to him who is alone when he falls and

[1] Hebrew *what has been pursued*

has not another to lift him up! 11 Again, if
two lie together, they keep warm, but how
can one keep warm alone? 12 And though
a man might prevail against one who is
alone, two will withstand him—a three-
fold cord is not quickly broken.
13 Better was a poor and wise youth than
an old and foolish king who no longer
knew how to take advice. 14 For he went
from prison to the throne, though in his
own kingdom he had been born poor. 15 I
saw all the living who move about under
the sun, along with that[1] youth who was
to stand in the king's[2] place. 16 There was
no end of all the people, all of whom he
led. Yet those who come later will not
rejoice in him. Surely this also is vanity
and a striving after wind.

Fear God

5 [3]Guard your steps when you go to the
house of God. To draw near to listen
is better than to offer the sacrifice of fools,
for they do not know that they are doing
evil. 2 [4] Be not rash with your mouth, nor
let your heart be hasty to utter a word
before God, for God is in heaven and you
are on earth. Therefore let your words be
few. 3 For a dream comes with much busi-
ness, and a fool's voice with many words.
4 When you vow a vow to God, do not
delay paying it, for he has no pleasure in
fools. Pay what you vow. 5 It is better that
you should not vow than that you should
vow and not pay. 6 Let not your mouth
lead you[5] into sin, and do not say before
the messenger[6] that it was a mistake.
Why should God be angry at your voice
and destroy the work of your hands? 7 For
when dreams increase and words grow
many, there is vanity;[7] but God is the one
you must fear.

The Vanity of Wealth and Honor

8 If you see in a province the oppression
of the poor and the violation of justice
and righteousness, do not be amazed at
the matter, for the high official is watched
by a higher, and there are yet higher ones
over them. 9 But this is gain for a land in
every way: a king committed to cultivated
fields.[8]
10 He who loves money will not be
satisfied with money, nor he who loves
wealth with his income; this also is van-
ity. 11 When goods increase, they increase
who eat them, and what advantage has
their owner but to see them with his eyes?
12 Sweet is the sleep of a laborer, whether
he eats little or much, but the full stomach
of the rich will not let him sleep.
13 There is a grievous evil that I have
seen under the sun: riches were kept by
their owner to his hurt, 14 and those riches
were lost in a bad venture. And he is father
of a son, but he has nothing in his hand.
15 As he came from his mother's womb he
shall go again, naked as he came, and shall
take nothing for his toil that he may carry
away in his hand. 16 This also is a grievous
evil: just as he came, so shall he go, and
what gain is there to him who toils for the
wind? 17 Moreover, all his days he eats in
darkness in much vexation and sickness
and anger.
18 Behold, what I have seen to be good
and fitting is to eat and drink and find
enjoyment[9] in all the toil with which
one toils under the sun the few days of
his life that God has given him, for this
is his lot. 19 Everyone also to whom God
has given wealth and possessions and
power to enjoy them, and to accept his lot
and rejoice in his toil—this is the gift of
God. 20 For he will not much remember
the days of his life because God keeps him
occupied with joy in his heart.

6 There is an evil that I have seen under
the sun, and it lies heavy on man-
kind: 2 a man to whom God gives wealth,
possessions, and honor, so that he lacks
nothing of all that he desires, yet God does
not give him power to enjoy them, but a
stranger enjoys them. This is vanity; it is a

[1] Hebrew *the second* [2] Hebrew *his* [3] Ch 4:17 in Hebrew [4] Ch 5:1 in Hebrew [5] Hebrew *your flesh* [6] Or *angel* [7] Or *For when dreams and vanities increase, words also grow many* [8] The meaning of the Hebrew verse is uncertain [9] Or *and see good*

grievous evil. 3 If a man fathers a hundred
children and lives many years, so that the
days of his years are many, but his soul is
not satisfied with life's good things, and
he also has no burial, I say that a stillborn
child is better off than he. 4 For it comes in
vanity and goes in darkness, and in dark-
ness its name is covered. 5 Moreover, it has
not seen the sun or known anything, yet it
finds rest rather than he. 6 Even though he
should live a thousand years twice over,
yet enjoy[1] no good—do not all go to the
one place?

7 All the toil of man is for his mouth,
yet his appetite is not satisfied.[2] 8 For what
advantage has the wise man over the fool?
And what does the poor man have who
knows how to conduct himself before the
living? 9 Better is the sight of the eyes than
the wandering of the appetite: this also is
vanity and a striving after wind.

10 Whatever has come to be has already
been named, and it is known what man is,
and that he is not able to dispute with one
stronger than he. 11 The more words, the
more vanity, and what is the advantage to
man? 12 For who knows what is good for
man while he lives the few days of his vain
life, which he passes like a shadow? For
who can tell man what will be after him
under the sun?

The Contrast of Wisdom and Folly

7 A good name is better than precious ointment,
and the day of death than the day of birth.
2 It is better to go to the house of mourning
than to go to the house of feasting,
for this is the end of all mankind,
and the living will lay it to heart.
3 Sorrow is better than laughter,
for by sadness of face the heart is made glad.
4 The heart of the wise is in the house of mourning,
but the heart of fools is in the house of mirth.
5 It is better for a man to hear the rebuke of the wise
than to hear the song of fools.
6 For as the crackling of thorns under a pot,
so is the laughter of the fools;
this also is vanity.
7 Surely oppression drives the wise into madness,
and a bribe corrupts the heart.
8 Better is the end of a thing than its beginning,
and the patient in spirit is better than the proud in spirit.
9 Be not quick in your spirit to become angry,
for anger lodges in the bosom of fools.
10 Say not, "Why were the former days better than these?"
For it is not from wisdom that you ask this.
11 Wisdom is good with an inheritance,
an advantage to those who see the sun.
12 For the protection of wisdom is like the protection of money,
and the advantage of knowledge is that wisdom preserves the life of him who has it.
13 Consider the work of God:
who can make straight what he has made crooked?

14 In the day of prosperity be joyful, and
in the day of adversity consider: God has
made the one as well as the other, so that
man may not find out anything that will
be after him.

15 In my vain life I have seen everything.
There is a righteous man who perishes in
his righteousness, and there is a wicked
man who prolongs his life in his evildoing.
16 Be not overly righteous, and do not make
yourself too wise. Why should you destroy
yourself? 17 Be not overly wicked, neither

[1] Or *see* [2] Hebrew *filled*

be a fool. Why should you die before your time? 18 It is good that you should take hold of this, and from that withhold not your hand, for the one who fears God shall come out from both of them.

19 Wisdom gives strength to the wise man more than ten rulers who are in a city.

20 Surely there is not a righteous man on earth who does good and never sins.

21 Do not take to heart all the things that people say, lest you hear your servant cursing you. 22 Your heart knows that many times you yourself have cursed others.

23 All this I have tested by wisdom. I said, "I will be wise," but it was far from me. 24 That which has been is far off, and deep, very deep; who can find it out?

25 I turned my heart to know and to search out and to seek wisdom and the scheme of things, and to know the wickedness of folly and the foolishness that is madness. 26 And I find something more bitter than death: the woman whose heart is snares and nets, and whose hands are fetters. He who pleases God escapes her, but the sinner is taken by her. 27 Behold, this is what I found, says the Preacher, while adding one thing to another to find the scheme of things— 28 which my soul has sought repeatedly, but I have not found. One man among a thousand I found, but a woman among all these I have not found. 29 See, this alone I found, that God made man upright, but they have sought out many schemes.

Keep the King's Command

8 Who is like the wise?
And who knows the interpretation of a thing?
A man's wisdom makes his face shine,
and the hardness of his face is changed.

2 I say:[1] Keep the king's command, because of God's oath to him.[2] 3 Be not hasty to go from his presence. Do not take your stand in an evil cause, for he does whatever he pleases. 4 For the word of the king is supreme, and who may say to him, "What are you doing?" 5 Whoever keeps a command will know no evil thing, and the wise heart will know the proper time and the just way. 6 For there is a time and a way for everything, although man's trouble[3] lies heavy on him. 7 For he does not know what is to be, for who can tell him how it will be? 8 No man has power to retain the spirit, or power over the day of death. There is no discharge from war, nor will wickedness deliver those who are given to it. 9 All this I observed while applying my heart to all that is done under the sun, when man had power over man to his hurt.

Those Who Fear God Will Do Well

10 Then I saw the wicked buried. They used to go in and out of the holy place and were praised[4] in the city where they had done such things. This also is vanity. 11 Because the sentence against an evil deed is not executed speedily, the heart of the children of man is fully set to do evil. 12 Though a sinner does evil a hundred times and prolongs his life, yet I know that it will be well with those who fear God, because they fear before him. 13 But it will not be well with the wicked, neither will he prolong his days like a shadow, because he does not fear before God.

Man Cannot Know God's Ways

14 There is a vanity that takes place on earth, that there are righteous people to whom it happens according to the deeds of the wicked, and there are wicked people to whom it happens according to the deeds of the righteous. I said that this also is vanity. 15 And I commend joy, for man has no good thing under the sun but to eat and drink and be joyful, for this will go with him in his toil through the days of his life that God has given him under the sun.

16 When I applied my heart to know wisdom, and to see the business that is

[1] Hebrew lacks *say* [2] Or *because of your oath to God* [3] Or *evil* [4] Some Hebrew manuscripts, Septuagint, Vulgate; most Hebrew manuscripts *forgotten*

done on earth, how neither day nor night
do one's eyes see sleep, **17** then I saw all
the work of God, that man cannot find
out the work that is done under the sun.
However much man may toil in seeking,
he will not find it out. Even though a wise
man claims to know, he cannot find it out.

Death Comes to All

9 But all this I laid to heart, examin-
ing it all, how the righteous and the
wise and their deeds are in the hand of
God. Whether it is love or hate, man does
not know; both are before him. **2** It is the
same for all, since the same event hap-
pens to the righteous and the wicked, to
the good and the evil,[1] to the clean and the
unclean, to him who sacrifices and him
who does not sacrifice. As the good one
is, so is the sinner, and he who swears is
as he who shuns an oath. **3** This is an evil
in all that is done under the sun, that the
same event happens to all. Also, the hearts
of the children of man are full of evil, and
madness is in their hearts while they live,
and after that they go to the dead. **4** But he
who is joined with all the living has hope,
for a living dog is better than a dead lion.
5 For the living know that they will die, but
the dead know nothing, and they have no
more reward, for the memory of them is
forgotten. **6** Their love and their hate and
their envy have already perished, and for-
ever they have no more share in all that is
done under the sun.

Enjoy Life with the One You Love

7 Go, eat your bread with joy, and drink
your wine with a merry heart, for God has
already approved what you do.

8 Let your garments be always white. Let
not oil be lacking on your head.

9 Enjoy life with the wife whom you
love, all the days of your vain life that he
has given you under the sun, because that
is your portion in life and in your toil at
which you toil under the sun. **10** Whatever
your hand finds to do, do it with your
might,[2] for there is no work or thought or
knowledge or wisdom in Sheol, to which
you are going.

Wisdom Better than Folly

11 Again I saw that under the sun the
race is not to the swift, nor the battle to the
strong, nor bread to the wise, nor riches
to the intelligent, nor favor to those with
knowledge, but time and chance happen
to them all. **12** For man does not know his
time. Like fish that are taken in an evil net,
and like birds that are caught in a snare, so
the children of man are snared at an evil
time, when it suddenly falls upon them.

13 I have also seen this example of wis-
dom under the sun, and it seemed great
to me. **14** There was a little city with few
men in it, and a great king came against it
and besieged it, building great siegeworks
against it. **15** But there was found in it a
poor, wise man, and he by his wisdom
delivered the city. Yet no one remem-
bered that poor man. **16** But I say that
wisdom is better than might, though the
poor man's wisdom is despised and his
words are not heard.

17 The words of the wise heard in quiet
are better than the shouting of a ruler
among fools. **18** Wisdom is better than
weapons of war, but one sinner destroys
much good.

10 Dead flies make the perfumer's
ointment give off a stench;
so a little folly outweighs wisdom
and honor.

2 A wise man's heart inclines him to
the right,
but a fool's heart to the left.

3 Even when the fool walks on the
road, he lacks sense,
and he says to everyone that he is
a fool.

4 If the anger of the ruler rises against
you, do not leave your place,
for calmness[3] will lay great
offenses to rest.

[1] Septuagint, Syriac, Vulgate; Hebrew lacks *and the evil* [2] Or *finds to do with your might, do it* [3] Hebrew *healing*

[5]There is an evil that I have seen under
the sun, as it were an error proceeding
from the ruler: [6]folly is set in many high
places, and the rich sit in a low place. [7]I
have seen slaves on horses, and princes
walking on the ground like slaves.

8 He who digs a pit will fall into it,
and a serpent will bite him who breaks through a wall.
9 He who quarries stones is hurt by them,
and he who splits logs is endangered by them.
10 If the iron is blunt, and one does not sharpen the edge,
he must use more strength,
but wisdom helps one to succeed.[1]
11 If the serpent bites before it is charmed,
there is no advantage to the charmer.
12 The words of a wise man's mouth win him favor,[2]
but the lips of a fool consume him.
13 The beginning of the words of his mouth is foolishness,
and the end of his talk is evil madness.
14 A fool multiplies words,
though no man knows what is to be,
and who can tell him what will be after him?
15 The toil of a fool wearies him,
for he does not know the way to the city.

16 Woe to you, O land, when your king is a child,
and your princes feast in the morning!
17 Happy are you, O land, when your king is the son of the nobility,
and your princes feast at the proper time,
for strength, and not for drunkenness!
18 Through sloth the roof sinks in,
and through indolence the house leaks.
19 Bread is made for laughter,
and wine gladdens life,
and money answers everything.
20 Even in your thoughts, do not curse the king,
nor in your bedroom curse the rich,
for a bird of the air will carry your voice,
or some winged creature tell the matter.

Cast Your Bread upon the Waters

11 Cast your bread upon the waters,
for you will find it after many days.
2 Give a portion to seven, or even to eight,
for you know not what disaster may happen on earth.
3 If the clouds are full of rain,
they empty themselves on the earth,
and if a tree falls to the south or to the north,
in the place where the tree falls, there it will lie.
4 He who observes the wind will not sow,
and he who regards the clouds will not reap.

[5]As you do not know the way the spirit
comes to the bones in the womb[3] of a
woman with child, so you do not know
the work of God who makes everything.
[6]In the morning sow your seed, and at
evening withhold not your hand, for you
do not know which will prosper, this or
that, or whether both alike will be good.
[7]Light is sweet, and it is pleasant for the
eyes to see the sun.

[1] Or *wisdom is an advantage for success* [2] Or *are gracious* [3] Some Hebrew manuscripts, Targum; most Hebrew manuscripts *As you do not know the way of the wind, or how the bones grow in the womb*

8 So if a person lives many years, let him rejoice in them all; but let him remember that the days of darkness will be many. All that comes is vanity.

9 Rejoice, O young man, in your youth, and let your heart cheer you in the days of your youth. Walk in the ways of your heart and the sight of your eyes. But know that for all these things God will bring you into judgment.

10 Remove vexation from your heart, and put away pain[1] from your body, for youth and the dawn of life are vanity.

Remember Your Creator in Your Youth

12 Remember also your Creator in the days of your youth, before the evil days come and the years draw near of which you will say, "I have no pleasure in them"; 2 before the sun and the light and the moon and the stars are darkened and the clouds return after the rain, 3 in the day when the keepers of the house tremble, and the strong men are bent, and the grinders cease because they are few, and those who look through the windows are dimmed, 4 and the doors on the street are shut—when the sound of the grinding is low, and one rises up at the sound of a bird, and all the daughters of song are brought low— 5 they are afraid also of what is high, and terrors are in the way; the almond tree blossoms, the grasshopper drags itself along,[2] and desire fails, because man is going to his eternal home, and the mourners go about the streets— 6 before the silver cord is snapped, or the golden bowl is broken, or the pitcher is shattered at the fountain, or the wheel broken at the cistern, 7 and the dust returns to the earth as it was, and the spirit returns to God who gave it. 8 Vanity of vanities, says the Preacher; all is vanity.

Fear God and Keep His Commandments

9 Besides being wise, the Preacher also taught the people knowledge, weighing and studying and arranging many proverbs with great care. 10 The Preacher sought to find words of delight, and uprightly he wrote words of truth.

11 The words of the wise are like goads, and like nails firmly fixed are the collected sayings; they are given by one Shepherd. 12 My son, beware of anything beyond these. Of making many books there is no end, and much study is a weariness of the flesh.

13 The end of the matter; all has been heard. Fear God and keep his commandments, for this is the whole duty of man.[3] 14 For God will bring every deed into judgment, with[4] every secret thing, whether good or evil.

[1] *Or evil* [2] *Or is a burden* [3] *Or the duty of all mankind* [4] *Or into the judgment on*

Introduction to

The Song of Solomon

Author
King Solomon

Date
971 B.C., the beginning of Solomon's reign

People
A young man ("HE"); a young woman ("SHE"); and a chorus ("OTHERS")

Purpose
The purpose of the Song of Solomon is to show the beauty of God's good gifts of love and marriage.

Central Themes
The book celebrates the delight that a man and a woman have for each other when they are in love; the longing of a man and woman for each other when they are soon to be married; and the joy and fulfillment of married love.

Memory Verses
Love that pleases (Song of Solomon 2:3–7); captivated by the bride (Song of Solomon 4:9–10); the gift and power of love (Song of Solomon 8:6–7)

Introduction

The Song of Solomon is a collection of love poems. The poems have two main characters: a young man and a young woman who are in love with each other. The poetry is not like what we're used to in English poetry. The expressions the lovers use to praise and compliment each other are not like what we're used to, although they were the kinds of things lovers would say about each other in the culture of that day. Where a modern man might tell his fiancée that he loves her long, black, silky hair that always smells so nice, this young man says, "Your hair is like a flock of goats leaping down the slopes of Gilead" (Song of Solomon 4:1). In most of the poems, the couple is not married, but in love. They long to be together and to be married. At the end of the book, the couple come together to enjoy married love. God's covenant requires a man and a woman to be committed to each other in marriage, treating no one else in the same special way a husband or wife should be treated. When people are faithful to honor God's covenant in this way, married love can be a rich joy and a gift from God. The poems of the Song of Solomon give us a picture of this romantic and married love at its best.

1010 B.C.	971 B.C.	931 B.C.
Reign of David begins	Reign of Solomon begins	Israel divided

The Song of Solomon

1 The Song of Songs, which is Solomon's.

The Bride Confesses Her Love

SHE[1]

2 Let him kiss me with the kisses of his mouth!
For your love is better than wine;
3 your anointing oils are fragrant;
your name is oil poured out;
therefore virgins love you.
4 Draw me after you; let us run.
The king has brought me into his chambers.

OTHERS

We will exult and rejoice in you;
we will extol your love more than wine;
rightly do they love you.

SHE

5 I am very dark, but lovely,
O daughters of Jerusalem,
like the tents of Kedar,
like the curtains of Solomon.
6 Do not gaze at me because I am dark,
because the sun has looked upon me.
My mother's sons were angry with me;
they made me keeper of the vineyards,
but my own vineyard I have not kept!
7 Tell me, you whom my soul loves,
where you pasture your flock,
where you make it lie down at noon;
for why should I be like one who veils herself
beside the flocks of your companions?

Solomon and His Bride Delight in Each Other

HE

8 If you do not know,
O most beautiful among women,
follow in the tracks of the flock,
and pasture your young goats
beside the shepherds' tents.
9 I compare you, my love,
to a mare among Pharaoh's chariots.
10 Your cheeks are lovely with ornaments,
your neck with strings of jewels.

OTHERS

11 We will make for you[2] ornaments of gold,
studded with silver.

SHE

12 While the king was on his couch,
my nard gave forth its fragrance.
13 My beloved is to me a sachet of myrrh
that lies between my breasts.
14 My beloved is to me a cluster of henna blossoms
in the vineyards of Engedi.

HE

15 Behold, you are beautiful, my love;
behold, you are beautiful;
your eyes are doves.

SHE

16 Behold, you are beautiful, my beloved, truly delightful.
Our couch is green;
17 the beams of our house are cedar;
our rafters are pine.

[1] The translators have added speaker identifications based on the gender and number of the Hebrew words [2] The Hebrew for *you* is feminine singular

2 I am a rose[1] of Sharon,
a lily of the valleys.

HE

2 As a lily among brambles,
so is my love among the young women.

SHE

3 As an apple tree among the trees of the forest,
so is my beloved among the young men.
With great delight I sat in his shadow,
and his fruit was sweet to my taste.
4 He brought me to the banqueting house,[2]
and his banner over me was love.
5 Sustain me with raisins;
refresh me with apples,
for I am sick with love.
6 His left hand is under my head,
and his right hand embraces me!
7 I adjure you,[3] O daughters of Jerusalem,
by the gazelles or the does of the field,
that you not stir up or awaken love
until it pleases.

The Bride Adores Her Beloved

8 The voice of my beloved!
Behold, he comes,
leaping over the mountains,
bounding over the hills.
9 My beloved is like a gazelle
or a young stag.
Behold, there he stands
behind our wall,
gazing through the windows,
looking through the lattice.
10 My beloved speaks and says to me:
"Arise, my love, my beautiful one,
and come away,
11 for behold, the winter is past;
the rain is over and gone.
12 The flowers appear on the earth,
the time of singing[4] has come,
and the voice of the turtledove
is heard in our land.
13 The fig tree ripens its figs,
and the vines are in blossom;
they give forth fragrance.
Arise, my love, my beautiful one,
and come away.
14 O my dove, in the clefts of the rock,
in the crannies of the cliff,
let me see your face,
let me hear your voice,
for your voice is sweet,
and your face is lovely.
15 Catch the foxes[5] for us,
the little foxes
that spoil the vineyards,
for our vineyards are in blossom."
16 My beloved is mine, and I am his;
he grazes[6] among the lilies.
17 Until the day breathes
and the shadows flee,
turn, my beloved, be like a gazelle
or a young stag on cleft mountains.[7]

The Bride's Dream

3 On my bed by night
I sought him whom my soul loves;
I sought him, but found him not.
2 I will rise now and go about the city,
in the streets and in the squares;
I will seek him whom my soul loves.
I sought him, but found him not.
3 The watchmen found me
as they went about in the city.
"Have you seen him whom my soul loves?"
4 Scarcely had I passed them
when I found him whom my soul loves.
I held him, and would not let him go
until I had brought him into my mother's house,
and into the chamber of her who conceived me.

[1] Probably a bulb, such as a crocus, asphodel, or narcissus [2] Hebrew *the house of wine* [3] That is, I put you on oath; so throughout the Song [4] Or *pruning* [5] Or *jackals*
[6] Or *he pastures his flock* [7] Or *mountains of Bether*

5 I adjure you, O daughters of Jerusalem,
by the gazelles or the does of the field,
that you not stir up or awaken love
until it pleases.

Solomon Arrives for the Wedding

6 What is that coming up from the wilderness
like columns of smoke,
perfumed with myrrh and frankincense,
with all the fragrant powders of a merchant?
7 Behold, it is the litter[1] of Solomon!
Around it are sixty mighty men,
some of the mighty men of Israel,
8 all of them wearing swords
and expert in war,
each with his sword at his thigh,
against terror by night.
9 King Solomon made himself a carriage[2]
from the wood of Lebanon.
10 He made its posts of silver,
its back of gold, its seat of purple;
its interior was inlaid with love
by the daughters of Jerusalem.
11 Go out, O daughters of Zion,
and look upon King Solomon,
with the crown with which his mother crowned him
on the day of his wedding,
on the day of the gladness of his heart.

Solomon Admires His Bride's Beauty

HE

4 Behold, you are beautiful, my love,
behold, you are beautiful!
Your eyes are doves
behind your veil.
Your hair is like a flock of goats
leaping down the slopes of Gilead.
2 Your teeth are like a flock of shorn ewes
that have come up from the washing,
all of which bear twins,
and not one among them has lost its young.
3 Your lips are like a scarlet thread,
and your mouth is lovely.
Your cheeks are like halves of a pomegranate
behind your veil.
4 Your neck is like the tower of David,
built in rows of stone;[3]
on it hang a thousand shields,
all of them shields of warriors.
5 Your two breasts are like two fawns,
twins of a gazelle,
that graze among the lilies.
6 Until the day breathes
and the shadows flee,
I will go away to the mountain of myrrh
and the hill of frankincense.
7 You are altogether beautiful, my love;
there is no flaw in you.
8 Come with me from Lebanon, my bride;
come with me from Lebanon.
Depart[4] from the peak of Amana,
from the peak of Senir and Hermon,
from the dens of lions,
from the mountains of leopards.

9 You have captivated my heart, my sister, my bride;
you have captivated my heart
with one glance of your eyes,
with one jewel of your necklace.
10 How beautiful is your love, my sister, my bride!
How much better is your love than wine,
and the fragrance of your oils than any spice!

[1] That is, the couch on which servants carry a king [2] Or *sedan chair* [3] The meaning of the Hebrew word is uncertain [4] Or *Look*

11 Your lips drip nectar, my bride;
honey and milk are under your tongue;
the fragrance of your garments is like the fragrance of Lebanon.
12 A garden locked is my sister, my bride,
a spring locked, a fountain sealed.
13 Your shoots are an orchard of pomegranates
with all choicest fruits,
henna with nard,
14 nard and saffron, calamus and cinnamon,
with all trees of frankincense,
myrrh and aloes,
with all choice spices—
15 a garden fountain, a well of living water,
and flowing streams from Lebanon.

16 Awake, O north wind,
and come, O south wind!
Blow upon my garden,
let its spices flow.

Together in the Garden of Love

SHE

Let my beloved come to his garden,
and eat its choicest fruits.

HE

5 I came to my garden, my sister, my bride,
I gathered my myrrh with my spice,
I ate my honeycomb with my honey,
I drank my wine with my milk.

OTHERS

Eat, friends, drink,
and be drunk with love!

The Bride Searches for Her Beloved

SHE

2 I slept, but my heart was awake.
A sound! My beloved is knocking.
"Open to me, my sister, my love,
my dove, my perfect one,
for my head is wet with dew,
my locks with the drops of the night."
3 I had put off my garment;
how could I put it on?
I had bathed my feet;
how could I soil them?
4 My beloved put his hand to the latch,
and my heart was thrilled within me.
5 I arose to open to my beloved,
and my hands dripped with myrrh,
my fingers with liquid myrrh,
on the handles of the bolt.
6 I opened to my beloved,
but my beloved had turned and gone.
My soul failed me when he spoke.
I sought him, but found him not;
I called him, but he gave no answer.
7 The watchmen found me
as they went about in the city;
they beat me, they bruised me,
they took away my veil,
those watchmen of the walls.
8 I adjure you, O daughters of Jerusalem,
if you find my beloved,
that you tell him
I am sick with love.

OTHERS

9 What is your beloved more than another beloved,
O most beautiful among women?
What is your beloved more than another beloved,
that you thus adjure us?

The Bride Praises Her Beloved

SHE

10 My beloved is radiant and ruddy,
distinguished among ten thousand.
11 His head is the finest gold;
his locks are wavy,
black as a raven.

12 His eyes are like doves
beside streams of water,
bathed in milk,
sitting beside a full pool.[1]
13 His cheeks are like beds of spices,
mounds of sweet-smelling herbs.
His lips are lilies,
dripping liquid myrrh.
14 His arms are rods of gold,
set with jewels.
His body is polished ivory,[2]
bedecked with sapphires.[3]
15 His legs are alabaster columns,
set on bases of gold.
His appearance is like Lebanon,
choice as the cedars.
16 His mouth[4] is most sweet,
and he is altogether desirable.
This is my beloved and this is my friend,
O daughters of Jerusalem.

OTHERS

6 Where has your beloved gone,
O most beautiful among women?
Where has your beloved turned,
that we may seek him with you?

Together in the Garden of Love

SHE

2 My beloved has gone down to his garden
to the beds of spices,
to graze[5] in the gardens
and to gather lilies.
3 I am my beloved's and my beloved is mine;
he grazes among the lilies.

Solomon and His Bride Delight in Each Other

HE

4 You are beautiful as Tirzah, my love,
lovely as Jerusalem,
awesome as an army with banners.
5 Turn away your eyes from me,
for they overwhelm me—
Your hair is like a flock of goats
leaping down the slopes of Gilead.
6 Your teeth are like a flock of ewes
that have come up from the washing;
all of them bear twins;
not one among them has lost its young.
7 Your cheeks are like halves of a pomegranate
behind your veil.
8 There are sixty queens and eighty concubines,
and virgins without number.
9 My dove, my perfect one, is the only one,
the only one of her mother,
pure to her who bore her.
The young women saw her and called her blessed;
the queens and concubines also,
and they praised her.

10 "Who is this who looks down like the dawn,
beautiful as the moon, bright as the sun,
awesome as an army with banners?"

SHE

11 I went down to the nut orchard
to look at the blossoms of the valley,
to see whether the vines had budded,
whether the pomegranates were in bloom.
12 Before I was aware, my desire set me
among the chariots of my kinsman, a prince.[6]

OTHERS

13[7] Return, return, O Shulammite,
return, return, that we may look upon you.

[1] The meaning of the Hebrew is uncertain [2] The meaning of the Hebrew word is uncertain [3] Hebrew *lapis lazuli* [4] Hebrew *palate* [5] Or *to pasture his flock*; also verse 3 [6] Or *chariots of Ammi-Nadib* [7] Ch 7:1 in Hebrew

HE

Why should you look upon the
Shulammite,
as upon a dance before two
armies?[1]

7 How beautiful are your feet in
sandals,
O noble daughter!
Your rounded thighs are like jewels,
the work of a master hand.
2 Your navel is a rounded bowl
that never lacks mixed wine.
Your belly is a heap of wheat,
encircled with lilies.
3 Your two breasts are like two fawns,
twins of a gazelle.
4 Your neck is like an ivory tower.
Your eyes are pools in Heshbon,
by the gate of Bath-rabbim.
Your nose is like a tower of
Lebanon,
which looks toward Damascus.
5 Your head crowns you like Carmel,
and your flowing locks are like
purple;
a king is held captive in the tresses.

6 How beautiful and pleasant you are,
O loved one, with all your
delights![2]
7 Your stature is like a palm tree,
and your breasts are like its
clusters.
8 I say I will climb the palm tree
and lay hold of its fruit.
Oh may your breasts be like clusters
of the vine,
and the scent of your breath like
apples,
9 and your mouth[3] like the best wine.

SHE

It goes down smoothly for my
beloved,
gliding over lips and teeth.[4]

10 I am my beloved's,
and his desire is for me.

The Bride Gives Her Love

11 Come, my beloved,
let us go out into the fields
and lodge in the villages;[5]
12 let us go out early to the vineyards
and see whether the vines have
budded,
whether the grape blossoms have
opened
and the pomegranates are in
bloom.
There I will give you my love.
13 The mandrakes give forth fragrance,
and beside our doors are all
choice fruits,
new as well as old,
which I have laid up for you, O my
beloved.

Longing for Her Beloved

8 Oh that you were like a brother to me
who nursed at my mother's breasts!
If I found you outside, I would kiss
you,
and none would despise me.
2 I would lead you and bring you
into the house of my mother—
she who used to teach me.
I would give you spiced wine to
drink,
the juice of my pomegranate.
3 His left hand is under my head,
and his right hand embraces me!
4 I adjure you, O daughters of
Jerusalem,
that you not stir up or awaken
love
until it pleases.

5 Who is that coming up from the
wilderness,
leaning on her beloved?

Under the apple tree I awakened you.
There your mother was in labor
with you;
there she who bore you was in
labor.

[1] Or *dance of Mahanaim* [2] Or *among delights* [3] Hebrew *palate* [4] Septuagint, Syriac, Vulgate; Hebrew *causing the lips of sleepers to speak* [5] Or *among the henna plants*

6 Set me as a seal upon your heart,
as a seal upon your arm,
for love is strong as death,
jealousy[1] is fierce as the grave.[2]
Its flashes are flashes of fire,
the very flame of the LORD.
7 Many waters cannot quench love,
neither can floods drown it.
If a man offered for love
all the wealth of his house,
he[3] would be utterly despised.

Final Advice

OTHERS

8 We have a little sister,
and she has no breasts.
What shall we do for our sister
on the day when she is spoken for?
9 If she is a wall,
we will build on her a battlement of silver,
but if she is a door,
we will enclose her with boards of cedar.

SHE

10 I was a wall,
and my breasts were like towers;
then I was in his eyes
as one who finds[4] peace.

11 Solomon had a vineyard at Baal-hamon;
he let out the vineyard to keepers;
each one was to bring for its fruit
a thousand pieces of silver.
12 My vineyard, my very own, is before me;
you, O Solomon, may have the thousand,
and the keepers of the fruit two hundred.

HE

13 O you who dwell in the gardens,
with companions listening for your voice;
let me hear it.

SHE

14 Make haste, my beloved,
and be like a gazelle
or a young stag
on the mountains of spices.

[1] Or *ardor* [2] Hebrew *as Sheol* [3] Or *it* [4] Or *brings out*

Introduction to

Isaiah

Author

Isaiah the prophet

Date

About 740–681 B.C.

People

Isaiah; Hezekiah; Sennacherib; the coming servant of the Lord

Purpose

The purpose of Isaiah is to call God's rebellious people to repentance and to encourage God's discouraged people by showing them God's greatness, God's glory, and God's plan for the future.

Central Themes

God is holy; what God says always happens; there are no gods but God; God will judge all mankind for their sin; God will return His people to their land; God will send a Savior to be "God with us" and to suffer for His people; God's people will have a glorious future.

Memory Verses

Let us reason together (Isaiah 1:18–19); song of the vineyard (Isaiah 5:1–7); temple vision (Isaiah 6:1–13); Immanuel and His reign (Isaiah 7:14; 9:2–7); the Branch and the Spirit (Isaiah 11:1–9); the feast (Isaiah 25); comfort (Isaiah 40:1–5); the Suffering Servant (Isaiah 52:13–53:12); the Lord's ways (Isaiah 55:6–11); new heavens and a new earth (Isaiah 65:17–25)

Introduction

Isaiah tells of his call to be a prophet. He describes seeing God on a throne, glorious and holy. Isaiah is afraid because of his sin, but an angel tells him his sin has been atoned for and he is forgiven (Isaiah 6). The things Isaiah saw in his vision come up in everything else Isaiah says in his book: God rules the nations (Isaiah 44:24–45:14); God is great and there is no one like Him (Isaiah 43:8–15; 44:6–8); God is holy and judges sin (Isaiah 5; 24); God provides atonement for sin so His people can be forgiven (Isaiah 53). Isaiah warns of coming judgment on Judah and on the neighboring nations if they do not repent of their sin (Isaiah 1:1–23; Isaiah 14–21). He describes God's wrath at sin, but he also describes a glorious future for God's people (Isaiah 65–66). Isaiah writes more than any other prophet about the Savior God will provide (Isaiah 9:1–7, 49:1–7), and gives some of the most wonderful descriptions of the greatness and character of God in all Scripture (Isaiah 40).

767 B.C.	740 B.C.	722 B.C.	715 B.C.
Reign of Uzziah begins	Prophetic ministry of Isaiah begins	Fall of Israel	Reign of Hezekiah begins

Isaiah

1 The vision of Isaiah the son of Amoz, which he saw concerning Judah and Jerusalem in the days of Uzziah, Jotham, Ahaz, and Hezekiah, kings of Judah.

The Wickedness of Judah

2 Hear, O heavens, and give ear, O earth;
for the LORD has spoken:
"Children[1] have I reared and brought up,
but they have rebelled against me.
3 The ox knows its owner,
and the donkey its master's crib,
but Israel does not know,
my people do not understand."

4 Ah, sinful nation,
a people laden with iniquity,
offspring of evildoers,
children who deal corruptly!
They have forsaken the LORD,
they have despised the Holy One of Israel,
they are utterly estranged.

5 Why will you still be struck down?
Why will you continue to rebel?
The whole head is sick,
and the whole heart faint.
6 From the sole of the foot even to the head,
there is no soundness in it,
but bruises and sores
and raw wounds;
they are not pressed out or bound up
or softened with oil.

7 Your country lies desolate;
your cities are burned with fire;
in your very presence
foreigners devour your land;
it is desolate, as overthrown by foreigners.
8 And the daughter of Zion is left
like a booth in a vineyard,
like a lodge in a cucumber field,
like a besieged city.

9 If the LORD of hosts
had not left us a few survivors,
we should have been like Sodom,
and become like Gomorrah.

10 Hear the word of the LORD,
you rulers of Sodom!
Give ear to the teaching[2] of our God,
you people of Gomorrah!
11 "What to me is the multitude of your sacrifices?
says the LORD;
I have had enough of burnt offerings of rams
and the fat of well-fed beasts;
I do not delight in the blood of bulls,
or of lambs, or of goats.

12 "When you come to appear before me,
who has required of you
this trampling of my courts?
13 Bring no more vain offerings;
incense is an abomination to me.
New moon and Sabbath and the calling of convocations—
I cannot endure iniquity and solemn assembly.
14 Your new moons and your appointed feasts
my soul hates;
they have become a burden to me;
I am weary of bearing them.
15 When you spread out your hands,
I will hide my eyes from you;
even though you make many prayers,
I will not listen;
your hands are full of blood.

[1] Or *Sons*; also verse 4 [2] Or *law*

16 Wash yourselves; make yourselves
clean;
remove the evil of your deeds
from before my eyes;
cease to do evil,
17 learn to do good;
seek justice,
correct oppression;
bring justice to the fatherless,
plead the widow's cause.

18 "Come now, let us reason[1] together,
says the LORD:
though your sins are like scarlet,
they shall be as white as snow;
though they are red like crimson,
they shall become like wool.
19 If you are willing and obedient,
you shall eat the good of the land;
20 but if you refuse and rebel,
you shall be eaten by the sword;
for the mouth of the LORD has
spoken."

The Unfaithful City

21 How the faithful city
has become a whore,[2]
she who was full of justice!
Righteousness lodged in her,
but now murderers.
22 Your silver has become dross,
your best wine mixed with water.
23 Your princes are rebels
and companions of thieves.
Everyone loves a bribe
and runs after gifts.
They do not bring justice to the
fatherless,
and the widow's cause does not
come to them.

24 Therefore the Lord declares,
the LORD of hosts,
the Mighty One of Israel:
"Ah, I will get relief from my
enemies
and avenge myself on my foes.
25 I will turn my hand against you
and will smelt away your dross as
with lye
and remove all your alloy.
26 And I will restore your judges as at
the first,
and your counselors as at the
beginning.
Afterward you shall be called the
city of righteousness,
the faithful city."

27 Zion shall be redeemed by justice,
and those in her who repent, by
righteousness.
28 But rebels and sinners shall be
broken together,
and those who forsake the LORD
shall be consumed.
29 For they[3] shall be ashamed of the
oaks
that you desired;
and you shall blush for the gardens
that you have chosen.
30 For you shall be like an oak
whose leaf withers,
and like a garden without water.
31 And the strong shall become tinder,
and his work a spark,
and both of them shall burn
together,
with none to quench them.

The Mountain of the LORD

2 The word that Isaiah the son of Amoz saw concerning Judah and Jerusalem.

2 It shall come to pass in the latter
days
that the mountain of the house of
the LORD
shall be established as the highest
of the mountains,
and shall be lifted up above the
hills;
and all the nations shall flow to it,
3 and many peoples shall come,
and say:

[1] Or *dispute* [2] Or *become unchaste* [3] Some Hebrew manuscripts *you*

"Come, let us go up to the mountain
of the LORD,
to the house of the God of Jacob,
that he may teach us his ways
and that we may walk in his paths."
For out of Zion shall go the law,[1]
and the word of the LORD from
Jerusalem.

4 He shall judge between the nations,
and shall decide disputes for
many peoples;
and they shall beat their swords
into plowshares,
and their spears into pruning
hooks;
nation shall not lift up sword
against nation,
neither shall they learn war
anymore.

5 O house of Jacob,
come, let us walk
in the light of the LORD.

The Day of the LORD

6 For you have rejected your people,
the house of Jacob,
because they are full of things from
the east
and of fortune-tellers like the
Philistines,
and they strike hands with the
children of foreigners.

7 Their land is filled with silver and
gold,
and there is no end to their
treasures;
their land is filled with horses,
and there is no end to their
chariots.

8 Their land is filled with idols;
they bow down to the work of
their hands,
to what their own fingers have
made.

9 So man is humbled,
and each one is brought low—
do not forgive them!

10 Enter into the rock
and hide in the dust
from before the terror of the LORD,
and from the splendor of his
majesty.

11 The haughty looks of man shall be
brought low,
and the lofty pride of men shall be
humbled,
and the LORD alone will be exalted
in that day.

12 For the LORD of hosts has a day
against all that is proud and lofty,
against all that is lifted up—and it
shall be brought low;

13 against all the cedars of Lebanon,
lofty and lifted up;
and against all the oaks of
Bashan;

14 against all the lofty mountains,
and against all the uplifted hills;

15 against every high tower,
and against every fortified wall;

16 against all the ships of Tarshish,
and against all the beautiful craft.

17 And the haughtiness of man shall
be humbled,
and the lofty pride of men shall be
brought low,
and the LORD alone will be
exalted in that day.

18 And the idols shall utterly pass
away.

19 And people shall enter the caves of
the rocks
and the holes of the ground,[2]
from before the terror of the LORD,
and from the splendor of his
majesty,
when he rises to terrify the earth.

20 In that day mankind will cast away
their idols of silver and their idols
of gold,
which they made for themselves to
worship,
to the moles and to the bats,

[1] Or *teaching* [2] Hebrew *dust*

21 to enter the caverns of the rocks
and the clefts of the cliffs,
from before the terror of the LORD,
and from the splendor of his majesty,
when he rises to terrify the earth.
22 Stop regarding man
in whose nostrils is breath,
for of what account is he?

Judgment on Judah and Jerusalem

3 For behold, the Lord GOD of hosts
is taking away from Jerusalem and from Judah
support and supply,[1]
all support of bread,
and all support of water;
2 the mighty man and the soldier,
the judge and the prophet,
the diviner and the elder,
3 the captain of fifty
and the man of rank,
the counselor and the skillful magician
and the expert in charms.
4 And I will make boys their princes,
and infants[2] shall rule over them.
5 And the people will oppress one another,
every one his fellow
and every one his neighbor;
the youth will be insolent to the elder,
and the despised to the honorable.

6 For a man will take hold of his brother
in the house of his father, saying:
"You have a cloak;
you shall be our leader,
and this heap of ruins
shall be under your rule";
7 in that day he will speak out, saying:
"I will not be a healer;[3]
in my house there is neither bread nor cloak;
you shall not make me
leader of the people."
8 For Jerusalem has stumbled,
and Judah has fallen,
because their speech and their deeds are against the LORD,
defying his glorious presence.[4]
9 For the look on their faces bears witness against them;
they proclaim their sin like Sodom;
they do not hide it.
Woe to them!
For they have brought evil on themselves.
10 Tell the righteous that it shall be well with them,
for they shall eat the fruit of their deeds.
11 Woe to the wicked! It shall be ill with him,
for what his hands have dealt out
shall be done to him.
12 My people—infants are their oppressors,
and women rule over them.
O my people, your guides mislead you
and they have swallowed up[5] the course of your paths.

13 The LORD has taken his place to contend;
he stands to judge peoples.
14 The LORD will enter into judgment
with the elders and princes of his people:
"It is you who have devoured[6] the vineyard,
the spoil of the poor is in your houses.
15 What do you mean by crushing my people,
by grinding the face of the poor?"
declares the Lord GOD of hosts.

16 The LORD said:
Because the daughters of Zion are haughty
and walk with outstretched necks,
glancing wantonly with their eyes,

[1] Hebrew *staff* [2] Or *caprice* [3] Hebrew *binder of wounds* [4] Hebrew *the eyes of his glory* [5] Or *they have confused* [6] Or *grazed over;* compare Exodus 22:5

mincing along as they go,
tinkling with their feet,
17 therefore the Lord will strike with a scab
the heads of the daughters of Zion,
and the LORD will lay bare their secret parts.

18 In that day the Lord will take away
the finery of the anklets, the headbands,
and the crescents; 19 the pendants, the
bracelets, and the scarves; 20 the head-
dresses, the armlets, the sashes, the per-
fume boxes, and the amulets; 21 the signet
rings and nose rings; 22 the festal robes,
the mantles, the cloaks, and the handbags;
23 the mirrors, the linen garments, the tur-
bans, and the veils.

24 Instead of perfume there will be rottenness;
and instead of a belt, a rope;
and instead of well-set hair, baldness;
and instead of a rich robe, a skirt of sackcloth;
and branding instead of beauty.
25 Your men shall fall by the sword
and your mighty men in battle.
26 And her gates shall lament and mourn;
empty, she shall sit on the ground.

4 And seven women shall take hold
of one man in that day, saying, "We
will eat our own bread and wear our own
clothes, only let us be called by your name;
take away our reproach."

The Branch of the LORD Glorified

2 In that day the branch of the LORD shall
be beautiful and glorious, and the fruit of
the land shall be the pride and honor of
the survivors of Israel. 3 And he who is
left in Zion and remains in Jerusalem will
be called holy, everyone who has been
recorded for life in Jerusalem, 4 when the
Lord shall have washed away the filth of
the daughters of Zion and cleansed the
bloodstains of Jerusalem from its midst
by a spirit of judgment and by a spirit of
burning.[1] 5 Then the LORD will create over
the whole site of Mount Zion and over her
assemblies a cloud by day, and smoke and
the shining of a flaming fire by night; for
over all the glory there will be a canopy.
6 There will be a booth for shade by day
from the heat, and for a refuge and a shel-
ter from the storm and rain.

The Vineyard of the LORD Destroyed

5 Let me sing for my beloved
my love song concerning his vineyard:
My beloved had a vineyard
on a very fertile hill.
2 He dug it and cleared it of stones,
and planted it with choice vines;
he built a watchtower in the midst of it,
and hewed out a wine vat in it;
and he looked for it to yield grapes,
but it yielded wild grapes.

3 And now, O inhabitants of Jerusalem
and men of Judah,
judge between me and my vineyard.
4 What more was there to do for my vineyard,
that I have not done in it?
When I looked for it to yield grapes,
why did it yield wild grapes?

5 And now I will tell you
what I will do to my vineyard.
I will remove its hedge,
and it shall be devoured;[2]
I will break down its wall,
and it shall be trampled down.
6 I will make it a waste;
it shall not be pruned or hoed,
and briers and thorns shall grow up;
I will also command the clouds
that they rain no rain upon it.

7 For the vineyard of the LORD of hosts
is the house of Israel,

[1] Or *purging* [2] Or *grazed over;* compare Exodus 22:5

and the men of Judah
are his pleasant planting;
and he looked for justice,
but behold, bloodshed;[1]
for righteousness,
but behold, an outcry![2]

Woe to the Wicked

8 Woe to those who join house to
house,
who add field to field,
until there is no more room,
and you are made to dwell alone
in the midst of the land.
9 The LORD of hosts has sworn in my
hearing:
"Surely many houses shall be
desolate,
large and beautiful houses,
without inhabitant.
10 For ten acres[3] of vineyard shall yield
but one bath,
and a homer of seed shall yield
but an ephah."[4]

11 Woe to those who rise early in the
morning,
that they may run after strong
drink,
who tarry late into the evening
as wine inflames them!
12 They have lyre and harp,
tambourine and flute and wine at
their feasts,
but they do not regard the deeds of
the LORD,
or see the work of his hands.

13 Therefore my people go into exile
for lack of knowledge;[5]
their honored men go hungry,[6]
and their multitude is parched
with thirst.
14 Therefore Sheol has enlarged its
appetite
and opened its mouth beyond
measure,
and the nobility of Jerusalem[7] and
her multitude will go down,
her revelers and he who exults in
her.
15 Man is humbled, and each one is
brought low,
and the eyes of the haughty[8] are
brought low.
16 But the LORD of hosts is exalted[9] in
justice,
and the Holy God shows himself
holy in righteousness.
17 Then shall the lambs graze as in
their pasture,
and nomads shall eat among the
ruins of the rich.

18 Woe to those who draw iniquity
with cords of falsehood,
who draw sin as with cart ropes,
19 who say: "Let him be quick,
let him speed his work
that we may see it;
let the counsel of the Holy One of
Israel draw near,
and let it come, that we may know
it!"
20 Woe to those who call evil good
and good evil,
who put darkness for light
and light for darkness,
who put bitter for sweet
and sweet for bitter!
21 Woe to those who are wise in their
own eyes,
and shrewd in their own sight!
22 Woe to those who are heroes at
drinking wine,
and valiant men in mixing strong
drink,
23 who acquit the guilty for a bribe,
and deprive the innocent of his
right!

[1] The Hebrew words for *justice* and *bloodshed* sound alike [2] The Hebrew words for *righteous* and *outcry* sound alike [3] Hebrew *ten yoke*, the area ten yoke of oxen can plow in a day [4] A *bath* was about 6 gallons or 22 liters; a *homer* was about 6 bushels or 220 liters; an *ephah* was about 3/5 bushel or 22 liters [5] Or *without their knowledge* [6] Or *die of hunger* [7] Hebrew *her nobility* [8] Hebrew *high* [9] Hebrew *high*

24 Therefore, as the tongue of fire
devours the stubble,
and as dry grass sinks down in the
flame,
so their root will be as rottenness,
and their blossom go up like dust;
for they have rejected the law of the
LORD of hosts,
and have despised the word of the
Holy One of Israel.
25 Therefore the anger of the LORD was
kindled against his people,
and he stretched out his hand
against them and struck them,
and the mountains quaked;
and their corpses were as refuse
in the midst of the streets.

CHARACTER PROFILE

ISAIAH

Isaiah saw a vision of God's glory and of angels praising God's holiness. When Isaiah was told his sin was forgiven, he volunteered to go to God's people with God's messages. Through Isaiah, God rebuked His people for praying to idols, and He promised that a Savior would come who would take away sin.

For all this his anger has not turned
away,
and his hand is stretched out still.
26 He will raise a signal for nations far
away,
and whistle for them from the
ends of the earth;
and behold, quickly, speedily they
come!
27 None is weary, none stumbles,
none slumbers or sleeps,
not a waistband is loose,
not a sandal strap broken;
28 their arrows are sharp,
all their bows bent,
their horses' hoofs seem like flint,
and their wheels like the whirlwind.
29 Their roaring is like a lion,
like young lions they roar;
they growl and seize their prey;
they carry it off, and none can
rescue.
30 They will growl over it on that day,
like the growling of the sea.
And if one looks to the land,
behold, darkness and distress;
and the light is darkened by its clouds.

Isaiah's Vision of the Lord

6 In the year that King Uzziah died I saw
the Lord sitting upon a throne, high
and lifted up; and the train[1] of his robe
filled the temple. 2 Above him stood the
seraphim. Each had six wings: with two
he covered his face, and with two he cov-
ered his feet, and with two he flew. 3 And
one called to another and said:

"Holy, holy, holy is the LORD of hosts;
the whole earth is full of his glory!"[2]

4 And the foundations of the thresholds
shook at the voice of him who called, and
the house was filled with smoke. 5 And
I said: "Woe is me! For I am lost; for I am
a man of unclean lips, and I dwell in the
midst of a people of unclean lips; for my
eyes have seen the King, the LORD of hosts!"

[1] *Or hem* [2] *Or may his glory fill the whole earth*

6 Then one of the seraphim flew to me,
having in his hand a burning coal that he
had taken with tongs from the altar. **7** And
he touched my mouth and said: "Behold,
this has touched your lips; your guilt is
taken away, and your sin atoned for."

Isaiah's Commission from the LORD

8 And I heard the voice of the Lord say-
ing, "Whom shall I send, and who will go
for us?" Then I said, "Here am I! Send me."
9 And he said, "Go, and say to this people:

"'Keep on hearing,[1] but do not
  understand;
keep on seeing,[2] but do not perceive.'
10 Make the heart of this people dull,[3]
  and their ears heavy,
  and blind their eyes;
lest they see with their eyes,
  and hear with their ears,
and understand with their hearts,
  and turn and be healed."
11 Then I said, "How long, O Lord?"
And he said:
"Until cities lie waste
  without inhabitant,
and houses without people,
  and the land is a desolate waste,
12 and the LORD removes people far
    away,
  and the forsaken places are many
    in the midst of the land.
13 And though a tenth remain in it,
  it will be burned[4] again,
like a terebinth or an oak,
  whose stump remains
  when it is felled."
The holy seed[5] is its stump.

Isaiah Sent to King Ahaz

7 In the days of Ahaz the son of Jotham,
son of Uzziah, king of Judah, Rezin
the king of Syria and Pekah the son of
Remaliah the king of Israel came up to
Jerusalem to wage war against it, but could
not yet mount an attack against it. **2** When
the house of David was told, "Syria is in
league with[6] Ephraim," the heart of Ahaz[7]
and the heart of his people shook as the
trees of the forest shake before the wind.
3 And the LORD said to Isaiah, "Go out to
meet Ahaz, you and Shear-jashub[8] your
son, at the end of the conduit of the upper
pool on the highway to the Washer's Field.
4 And say to him, 'Be careful, be quiet,
do not fear, and do not let your heart be
faint because of these two smoldering
stumps of firebrands, at the fierce anger of
Rezin and Syria and the son of Remaliah.
5 Because Syria, with Ephraim and the son
of Remaliah, has devised evil against you,
saying, **6** "Let us go up against Judah and
terrify it, and let us conquer it[9] for our-
selves, and set up the son of Tabeel as king
in the midst of it," **7** thus says the Lord GOD:

"'It shall not stand,
  and it shall not come to pass.
8 For the head of Syria is Damascus,
  and the head of Damascus is Rezin.
And within sixty-five years
  Ephraim will be shattered from
    being a people.
9 And the head of Ephraim is Samaria,
  and the head of Samaria is the son
    of Remaliah.
If you[10] are not firm in faith,
  you will not be firm at all.'"

The Sign of Immanuel

10 Again the LORD spoke to Ahaz, **11** "Ask
a sign of the LORD your[11] God; let it be deep
as Sheol or high as heaven." **12** But Ahaz
said, "I will not ask, and I will not put the
LORD to the test." **13** And he[12] said, "Hear
then, O house of David! Is it too little for
you to weary men, that you weary my God
also? **14** Therefore the Lord himself
will give you a sign. Behold, the vir-
gin shall conceive and bear a son,
and shall call his name Imman-
uel.[13] **15** He shall eat curds and honey when
he knows how to refuse the evil and

1293, 1433

[1] Or *Hear indeed* [2] Or *see indeed* [3] Hebrew *fat* [4] Or *purged* [5] Or *offspring* [6] Hebrew *Syria has rested upon* [7] Hebrew *his heart* [8] *Shear-jashub* means *A remnant shall return* [9] Hebrew *let us split it open* [10] The Hebrew for *you* is plural in verses 9, 13, 14 [11] The Hebrew for *you* and *your* is singular in verses 11, 16, 17 [12] That is, Isaiah [13] *Immanuel* means *God is with us*

choose the good. 16 For before the boy knows how to refuse the evil and choose the good, the land whose two kings you dread will be deserted. 17 The LORD will bring upon you and upon your people and upon your father's house such days as have not come since the day that Ephraim departed from Judah—the king of Assyria."

18 In that day the LORD will whistle for the fly that is at the end of the streams of Egypt, and for the bee that is in the land of Assyria. 19 And they will all come and settle in the steep ravines, and in the clefts of the rocks, and on all the thornbushes, and on all the pastures.[1]

20 In that day the Lord will shave with a razor that is hired beyond the River—with the king of Assyria—the head and the hair of the feet, and it will sweep away the beard also.

21 In that day a man will keep alive a young cow and two sheep, 22 and because of the abundance of milk that they give, he will eat curds, for everyone who is left in the land will eat curds and honey.

23 In that day every place where there used to be a thousand vines, worth a thousand shekels[2] of silver, will become briers and thorns. 24 With bow and arrows a man will come there, for all the land will be briers and thorns. 25 And as for all the hills that used to be hoed with a hoe, you will not come there for fear of briers and thorns, but they will become a place where cattle are let loose and where sheep tread.

The Coming Assyrian Invasion

8 Then the LORD said to me, "Take a large tablet and write on it in common characters,[3] 'Belonging to Maher-shalal-hash-baz.'[4] 2 And I will get reliable witnesses, Uriah the priest and Zechariah the son of Jeberechiah, to attest for me."

3 And I went to the prophetess, and she conceived and bore a son. Then the LORD said to me, "Call his name Maher-shalal-hash-baz; 4 for before the boy knows how to cry 'My father' or 'My mother,' the wealth of Damascus and the spoil of Samaria will be carried away before the king of Assyria."

5 The LORD spoke to me again: 6 "Because this people has refused the waters of Shiloah that flow gently, and rejoice over Rezin and the son of Remaliah, 7 therefore, behold, the Lord is bringing up against them the waters of the River, mighty and many, the king of Assyria and all his glory. And it will rise over all its channels and go over all its banks, 8 and it will sweep on into Judah, it will overflow and pass on, reaching even to the neck, and its outspread wings will fill the breadth of your land, O Immanuel."

9 Be broken,[5] you peoples, and be
shattered;[6]
give ear, all you far countries;
strap on your armor and be shattered;
strap on your armor and be
shattered.
10 Take counsel together, but it will
come to nothing;
speak a word, but it will not stand,
for God is with us.[7]

Fear God, Wait for the LORD

11 For the LORD spoke thus to me with his strong hand upon me, and warned me not to walk in the way of this people, saying: 12 "Do not call conspiracy all that this people calls conspiracy, and do not fear what they fear, nor be in dread. 13 But the LORD of hosts, him you shall honor as holy. Let him be your fear, and let him be your dread. 14 And he will become a sanctuary and a stone of offense and a rock of stumbling to both houses of Israel, a trap and a snare to the inhabitants of Jerusalem. 15 And many shall stumble on it. They shall fall and be broken; they shall be snared and taken."

16 Bind up the testimony; seal the teaching[8] among my disciples. 17 I will wait for the LORD, who is hiding his face from the

[1] Or *watering holes, or brambles* [2] A *shekel* was about 2/5 ounce or 11 grams [3] Hebrew *with a man's stylus* [4] *Maher-shalal-hash-baz* means *The spoil speeds, the prey hastens* [5] Or *Be evil* [6] Or *dismayed* [7] The Hebrew for *God is with us* is *Immanuel* [8] Or *law*; also verse 20

house of Jacob, and I will hope in him.
18 Behold, I and the children whom the
LORD has given me are signs and por-
tents in Israel from the LORD of hosts, who
dwells on Mount Zion. 19 And when they
say to you, "Inquire of the mediums and
the necromancers who chirp and mutter,"
should not a people inquire of their God?
Should they inquire of the dead on behalf
of the living? 20 To the teaching and to the
testimony! If they will not speak accord-
ing to this word, it is because they have no
dawn. 21 They will pass through the land,[1]
greatly distressed and hungry. And when
they are hungry, they will be enraged and
will speak contemptuously against[2] their
king and their God, and turn their faces
upward. 22 And they will look to the earth,
but behold, distress and darkness, the
gloom of anguish. And they will be thrust
into thick darkness.

For to Us a Child Is Born

9 [3] But there will be no gloom for her
who was in anguish. In the former
time he brought into contempt the land
of Zebulun and the land of Naphtali, but
in the latter time he has made glorious
the way of the sea, the land beyond the
Jordan, Galilee of the nations.[4]

2 [5] The people who walked in darkness
have seen a great light;
those who dwelt in a land of deep
darkness,
on them has light shined.
3 You have multiplied the nation;
you have increased its joy;
they rejoice before you
as with joy at the harvest,
as they are glad when they divide
the spoil.
4 For the yoke of his burden,
and the staff for his shoulder,
the rod of his oppressor,
you have broken as on the day of
Midian.
5 For every boot of the tramping
warrior in battle tumult
and every garment rolled in blood
will be burned as fuel for the fire.
6 For to us a child is born,
to us a son is given;
449, and the government shall be
499, upon[6] his shoulder,
1433, 1445 and his name shall be called[7]
Wonderful Counselor, Mighty God,
Everlasting Father, Prince of Peace.
7 Of the increase of his government
and of peace
there will be no end,
on the throne of David and over his
kingdom,
to establish it and to uphold it
with justice and with righteousness
from this time forth and
forevermore.
The zeal of the LORD of hosts will do
this.

Judgment on Arrogance and Oppression

8 The Lord has sent a word against
Jacob,
and it will fall on Israel;
9 and all the people will know,
Ephraim and the inhabitants of
Samaria,
who say in pride and in arrogance
of heart:
10 "The bricks have fallen,
but we will build with dressed
stones;
the sycamores have been cut down,
but we will put cedars in their
place."
11 But the LORD raises the adversaries
of Rezin against him,
and stirs up his enemies.
12 The Syrians on the east and the
Philistines on the west
devour Israel with open mouth.
For all this his anger has not turned
away,
and his hand is stretched out still.

[1] Hebrew *it* [2] Or *speak contemptuously by* [3] Ch 8:23 in Hebrew [4] Or *of the Gentiles* [5] Ch 9:1 in Hebrew [6] Or *is upon* [7] Or *is called*

13 The people did not turn to him who struck them,
nor inquire of the LORD of hosts.
14 So the LORD cut off from Israel head and tail,
palm branch and reed in one day—
15 the elder and honored man is the head,
and the prophet who teaches lies is the tail;
16 for those who guide this people have been leading them astray,
and those who are guided by them are swallowed up.
17 Therefore the Lord does not rejoice over their young men,
and has no compassion on their fatherless and widows;
for everyone is godless and an evildoer,
and every mouth speaks folly.[1]
For all this his anger has not turned away,
and his hand is stretched out still.

18 For wickedness burns like a fire;
it consumes briers and thorns;
it kindles the thickets of the forest,
and they roll upward in a column of smoke.
19 Through the wrath of the LORD of hosts
the land is scorched,
and the people are like fuel for the fire;
no one spares another.
20 They slice meat on the right, but are still hungry,
and they devour on the left, but are not satisfied;
each devours the flesh of his own arm,
21 Manasseh devours Ephraim, and Ephraim devours Manasseh;
together they are against Judah.
For all this his anger has not turned away,
and his hand is stretched out still.

10 Woe to those who decree iniquitous decrees,
and the writers who keep writing oppression,
2 to turn aside the needy from justice
and to rob the poor of my people of their right,
that widows may be their spoil,
and that they may make the fatherless their prey!
3 What will you do on the day of punishment,
in the ruin that will come from afar?
To whom will you flee for help,
and where will you leave your wealth?
4 Nothing remains but to crouch among the prisoners
or fall among the slain.
For all this his anger has not turned away,
and his hand is stretched out still.

Judgment on Arrogant Assyria

5 Ah, Assyria, the rod of my anger;
the staff in their hands is my fury!
6 Against a godless nation I send him,
and against the people of my wrath I command him,
to take spoil and seize plunder,
and to tread them down like the mire of the streets.
7 But he does not so intend,
and his heart does not so think;
but it is in his heart to destroy,
and to cut off nations not a few;
8 for he says:
"Are not my commanders all kings?
9 Is not Calno like Carchemish?
Is not Hamath like Arpad?
Is not Samaria like Damascus?
10 As my hand has reached to the kingdoms of the idols,
whose carved images were greater than those of Jerusalem and Samaria,

[1] Or *speaks disgraceful things*

11 shall I not do to Jerusalem and her
idols
as I have done to Samaria and her
images?"

[12]When the Lord has finished all his
work on Mount Zion and on Jerusalem,
he[1] will punish the speech of the arrogant
heart of the king of Assyria and the boast-
ful look in his eyes. [13]For he says:

"By the strength of my hand I have
done it,
and by my wisdom, for I have
understanding;
I remove the boundaries of peoples,
and plunder their treasures;
like a bull I bring down those who
sit on thrones.
14 My hand has found like a nest
the wealth of the peoples;
and as one gathers eggs that have
been forsaken,
so I have gathered all the earth;
and there was none that moved a
wing
or opened the mouth or chirped."
15 Shall the axe boast over him who
hews with it,
or the saw magnify itself against
him who wields it?
As if a rod should wield him who
lifts it,
or as if a staff should lift him who
is not wood!
16 Therefore the Lord GOD of hosts
will send wasting sickness among
his stout warriors,
and under his glory a burning will
be kindled,
like the burning of fire.
17 The light of Israel will become a fire,
and his Holy One a flame,
and it will burn and devour
his thorns and briers in one day.
18 The glory of his forest and of his
fruitful land
the LORD will destroy, both soul
and body,
and it will be as when a sick man
wastes away.
19 The remnant of the trees of his
forest will be so few
that a child can write them down.

The Remnant of Israel Will Return

[20]In that day the remnant of Israel and
the survivors of the house of Jacob will
no more lean on him who struck them,
but will lean on the LORD, the Holy One of
Israel, in truth. [21]A remnant will return,
the remnant of Jacob, to the mighty God.
[22]For though your people Israel be as the
sand of the sea, only a remnant of them
will return. Destruction is decreed, over-
flowing with righteousness. [23]For the
Lord GOD of hosts will make a full end, as
decreed, in the midst of all the earth.

[24]Therefore thus says the Lord GOD of
hosts: "O my people, who dwell in Zion,
be not afraid of the Assyrians when they
strike with the rod and lift up their staff
against you as the Egyptians did. [25]For in
a very little while my fury will come to an
end, and my anger will be directed to their
destruction. [26]And the LORD of hosts will
wield against them a whip, as when he
struck Midian at the rock of Oreb. And his
staff will be over the sea, and he will lift it
as he did in Egypt. [27]And in that day his
burden will depart from your shoulder,
and his yoke from your neck; and the yoke
will be broken because of the fat."[2]

28 He has come to Aiath;
he has passed through Migron;
at Michmash he stores his baggage;
29 they have crossed over the pass;
at Geba they lodge for the night;
Ramah trembles;
Gibeah of Saul has fled.
30 Cry aloud, O daughter of Gallim!
Give attention, O Laishah!
O poor Anathoth!
31 Madmenah is in flight;

[1] Hebrew *I* / [2] The meaning of the Hebrew is uncertain

the inhabitants of Gebim flee for
safety.
32 This very day he will halt at Nob;
he will shake his fist
at the mount of the daughter of
Zion,
the hill of Jerusalem.

33 Behold, the Lord GOD of hosts
will lop the boughs with terrifying
power;
the great in height will be hewn
down,
and the lofty will be brought low.
34 He will cut down the thickets of the
forest with an axe,
and Lebanon will fall by the
Majestic One.

The Righteous Reign of the Branch

11 There shall come forth a shoot
from the stump of Jesse,
and a branch from his roots shall
bear fruit.
2 And the Spirit of the LORD shall rest
upon him,
the Spirit of wisdom and
understanding,
the Spirit of counsel and might,
the Spirit of knowledge and the
fear of the LORD.
3 And his delight shall be in the fear
of the LORD.
He shall not judge by what his eyes
see,
or decide disputes by what his
ears hear,
4 but with righteousness he shall
judge the poor,
and decide with equity for the
meek of the earth;
and he shall strike the earth with
the rod of his mouth,
and with the breath of his lips he
shall kill the wicked.
5 Righteousness shall be the belt of
his waist,
and faithfulness the belt of his
loins.

6 The wolf shall dwell with the lamb,
and the leopard shall lie down
with the young goat,
and the calf and the lion and the
fattened calf together;
and a little child shall lead them.
7 The cow and the bear shall graze;
their young shall lie down
together;
and the lion shall eat straw like
the ox.
8 The nursing child shall play over
the hole of the cobra,
and the weaned child shall put
his hand on the adder's den.
9 They shall not hurt or destroy
in all my holy mountain;
for the earth shall be full of the
knowledge of the LORD
as the waters cover the sea.

10 In that day the root of Jesse, who shall
stand as a signal for the peoples—of him
shall the nations inquire, and his resting
place shall be glorious.
11 In that day the Lord will extend his
hand yet a second time to recover the
remnant that remains of his people,
from Assyria, from Egypt, from Pathros,
from Cush,[1] from Elam, from Shinar, from
Hamath, and from the coastlands of the
sea.

12 He will raise a signal for the nations
and will assemble the banished of
Israel,
and gather the dispersed of Judah
from the four corners of the earth.
13 The jealousy of Ephraim shall
depart,
and those who harass Judah shall
be cut off;
Ephraim shall not be jealous of
Judah,

[1] Probably *Nubia*

and Judah shall not harass
Ephraim.
14 But they shall swoop down on the
shoulder of the Philistines in
the west,
and together they shall plunder
the people of the east.
They shall put out their hand
against Edom and Moab,
and the Ammonites shall obey
them.
15 And the LORD will utterly destroy[1]
the tongue of the Sea of Egypt,
and will wave his hand over the
River
with his scorching breath,[2]
and strike it into seven channels,
and he will lead people across in
sandals.
16 And there will be a highway from
Assyria
for the remnant that remains of
his people,
as there was for Israel
when they came up from the land
of Egypt.

The LORD Is My Strength and My Song

12 You[3] will say in that day:
"I will give thanks to you, O LORD,
for though you were angry with
me,
your anger turned away,
that you might comfort me.
2 "Behold, God is my salvation;
I will trust, and will not be afraid;
for the LORD GOD[4] is my strength
and my song,
and he has become my salvation."
3 With joy you[5] will draw water from the
wells of salvation. 4 And you will say in
that day:
"Give thanks to the LORD,
call upon his name,
make known his deeds among the
peoples,
proclaim that his name is exalted.
5 "Sing praises to the LORD, for he has
done gloriously;
let this be made known[6] in all the
earth.
6 Shout, and sing for joy, O inhabitant
of Zion,
for great in your[7] midst is the
Holy One of Israel."

The Judgment of Babylon

13 The oracle concerning Babylon
which Isaiah the son of Amoz saw.
2 On a bare hill raise a signal;
cry aloud to them;
wave the hand for them to enter
the gates of the nobles.
3 I myself have commanded my
consecrated ones,
and have summoned my mighty
men to execute my anger,
my proudly exulting ones.[8]

4 The sound of a tumult is on the
mountains
as of a great multitude!
The sound of an uproar of
kingdoms,
of nations gathering together!
The LORD of hosts is mustering
a host for battle.
5 They come from a distant land,
from the end of the heavens,
the LORD and the weapons of his
indignation,
to destroy the whole land.[9]
6 Wail, for the day of the LORD is near;
as destruction from the
Almighty[10] it will come!
7 Therefore all hands will be feeble,
and every human heart will melt.
8 They will be dismayed:
pangs and agony will seize them;

[1] Hebrew *devote to destruction* [2] Or *wind* [3] The Hebrew for *you* is singular in verse 1 [4] Hebrew *for Yah, the LORD* [5] The Hebrew for *you* is plural in verses 3, 4 [6] Or *this is made known* [7] The Hebrew for *your* in verse 6 is singular, referring to the *inhabitant of Zion* [8] Or *those who exult in my majesty* [9] Or *earth*; also verse 9 [10] The Hebrew words for *destruction* and *almighty* sound alike

they will be in anguish like a
woman in labor.
They will look aghast at one
another;
their faces will be aflame.

9 Behold, the day of the LORD comes,
cruel, with wrath and fierce anger,
to make the land a desolation
and to destroy its sinners from it.
10 For the stars of the heavens and
their constellations
will not give their light;
the sun will be dark at its rising,
and the moon will not shed its
light.
11 I will punish the world for its evil,
and the wicked for their iniquity;
I will put an end to the pomp of the
arrogant,
and lay low the pompous pride of
the ruthless.
12 I will make people more rare than
fine gold,
and mankind than the gold of
Ophir.
13 Therefore I will make the heavens
tremble,
and the earth will be shaken out
of its place,
at the wrath of the LORD of hosts
in the day of his fierce anger.
14 And like a hunted gazelle,
or like sheep with none to gather
them,
each will turn to his own people,
and each will flee to his own land.
15 Whoever is found will be thrust
through,
and whoever is caught will fall by
the sword.
16 Their infants will be dashed in pieces
before their eyes;
their houses will be plundered
and their wives ravished.
17 Behold, I am stirring up the Medes
against them,
who have no regard for silver
and do not delight in gold.
18 Their bows will slaughter[1] the
young men;
they will have no mercy on the
fruit of the womb;
their eyes will not pity children.
19 And Babylon, the glory of kingdoms,
the splendor and pomp of the
Chaldeans,
will be like Sodom and Gomorrah
when God overthrew them.
20 It will never be inhabited
or lived in for all generations;
no Arab will pitch his tent there;
no shepherds will make their
flocks lie down there.
21 But wild animals will lie down there,
and their houses will be full of
howling creatures;
there ostriches[2] will dwell,
and there wild goats will dance.
22 Hyenas[3] will cry in its towers,
and jackals in the pleasant palaces;
its time is close at hand
and its days will not be prolonged.

The Restoration of Jacob

14 For the LORD will have compassion
on Jacob and will again choose
Israel, and will set them in their own land,
and sojourners will join them and will
attach themselves to the house of Jacob.
2 And the peoples will take them and bring
them to their place, and the house of Israel
will possess them in the LORD's land as
male and female slaves. They will take
captive those who were their captors, and
rule over those who oppressed them.

Israel's Remnant Taunts Babylon

3 When the LORD has given you rest from
your pain and turmoil and the hard ser-
vice with which you were made to serve,
4 you will take up this taunt against the
king of Babylon:

[1] Hebrew *dash in pieces* [2] Or *owls* [3] Or *foxes*

"How the oppressor has ceased,
the insolent fury[1] ceased!
5 The LORD has broken the staff of the wicked,
the scepter of rulers,
6 that struck the peoples in wrath
with unceasing blows,
that ruled the nations in anger
with unrelenting persecution.
7 The whole earth is at rest and quiet;
they break forth into singing.
8 The cypresses rejoice at you,
the cedars of Lebanon, saying,
'Since you were laid low,
no woodcutter comes up against us.'
9 Sheol beneath is stirred up
to meet you when you come;
it rouses the shades to greet you,
all who were leaders of the earth;
it raises from their thrones
all who were kings of the nations.
10 All of them will answer
and say to you:
'You too have become as weak as we!
You have become like us!'
11 Your pomp is brought down to Sheol,
the sound of your harps;
maggots are laid as a bed beneath you,
and worms are your covers.

12 "How you are fallen from heaven,
O Day Star, son of Dawn!
How you are cut down to the ground,
you who laid the nations low!
13 You said in your heart,
'I will ascend to heaven;
above the stars of God
I will set my throne on high;
I will sit on the mount of assembly
in the far reaches of the north;[2]
14 I will ascend above the heights of the clouds;
I will make myself like the Most High.'
15 But you are brought down to Sheol,
to the far reaches of the pit.
16 Those who see you will stare at you
and ponder over you:
'Is this the man who made the earth tremble,
who shook kingdoms,
17 who made the world like a desert
and overthrew its cities,
who did not let his prisoners go home?'
18 All the kings of the nations lie in glory,
each in his own tomb;[3]
19 but you are cast out, away from your grave,
like a loathed branch,
clothed with the slain, those pierced by the sword,
who go down to the stones of the pit,
like a dead body trampled underfoot.
20 You will not be joined with them in burial,
because you have destroyed your land,
you have slain your people.

"May the offspring of evildoers
nevermore be named!
21 Prepare slaughter for his sons
because of the guilt of their fathers,
lest they rise and possess the earth,
and fill the face of the world with cities."

22 "I will rise up against them," declares
the LORD of hosts, "and will cut off from
Babylon name and remnant, descendants
and posterity," declares the LORD. 23 "And
I will make it a possession of the hedge-
hog,[4] and pools of water, and I will sweep
it with the broom of destruction," declares
the LORD of hosts.

[1] Dead Sea Scroll (compare Septuagint, Syriac, Vulgate); the meaning of the word in the Masoretic Text is uncertain [2] Or *in the remote parts of Zaphon* [3] Hebrew *house*
[4] Possibly *porcupine*, or *owl*

An Oracle Concerning Assyria

24 The LORD of hosts has sworn:
"As I have planned,
so shall it be,
and as I have purposed,
so shall it stand,
25 that I will break the Assyrian in my land,
and on my mountains trample him underfoot;
and his yoke shall depart from them,
and his burden from their shoulder."

26 This is the purpose that is purposed concerning the whole earth,
and this is the hand that is stretched out
over all the nations.
27 For the LORD of hosts has purposed,
and who will annul it?
His hand is stretched out,
and who will turn it back?

An Oracle Concerning Philistia

28 In the year that King Ahaz died came
this oracle:

29 Rejoice not, O Philistia, all of you,
that the rod that struck you is broken,
for from the serpent's root will come forth an adder,
and its fruit will be a flying fiery serpent.
30 And the firstborn of the poor will graze,
and the needy lie down in safety;
but I will kill your root with famine,
and your remnant it will slay.
31 Wail, O gate; cry out, O city;
melt in fear, O Philistia, all of you!
For smoke comes out of the north,
and there is no straggler in his ranks.
32 What will one answer the messengers of the nation?
"The LORD has founded Zion,
and in her the afflicted of his people find refuge."

An Oracle Concerning Moab

15 An oracle concerning Moab.

Because Ar of Moab is laid waste in a night,
Moab is undone;
because Kir of Moab is laid waste in a night,
Moab is undone.
2 He has gone up to the temple,[1] and to Dibon,
to the high places[2] to weep;
over Nebo and over Medeba
Moab wails.
On every head is baldness;
every beard is shorn;
3 in the streets they wear sackcloth;
on the housetops and in the squares
everyone wails and melts in tears.
4 Heshbon and Elealeh cry out;
their voice is heard as far as Jahaz;
therefore the armed men of Moab cry aloud;
his soul trembles.
5 My heart cries out for Moab;
her fugitives flee to Zoar,
to Eglath-shelishiyah.
For at the ascent of Luhith
they go up weeping;
on the road to Horonaim
they raise a cry of destruction;
6 the waters of Nimrim
are a desolation;
the grass is withered, the vegetation fails,
the greenery is no more.
7 Therefore the abundance they have gained
and what they have laid up
they carry away
over the Brook of the Willows.

[1] Hebrew *the house* [2] Or *temple, even Dibon to the high places*

8 For a cry has gone
around the land of Moab;
her wailing reaches to Eglaim;
her wailing reaches to Beer-elim.
9 For the waters of Dibon[1] are full of
blood;
for I will bring upon Dibon even
more,
a lion for those of Moab who escape,
for the remnant of the land.

16 Send the lamb to the ruler of
the land,
from Sela, by way of the desert,
to the mount of the daughter of
Zion.
2 Like fleeing birds,
like a scattered nest,
so are the daughters of Moab
at the fords of the Arnon.

3 "Give counsel;
grant justice;
make your shade like night
at the height of noon;
shelter the outcasts;
do not reveal the fugitive;
4 let the outcasts of Moab
sojourn among you;
be a shelter to them[2]
from the destroyer.
When the oppressor is no more,
and destruction has ceased,
and he who tramples underfoot has
vanished from the land,
5 then a throne will be established in
steadfast love,
and on it will sit in faithfulness
in the tent of David
one who judges and seeks justice
and is swift to do righteousness."

6 We have heard of the pride of
Moab—
how proud he is!—
of his arrogance, his pride, and his
insolence;
in his idle boasting he is not right.
7 Therefore let Moab wail for Moab,
let everyone wail.
Mourn, utterly stricken,
for the raisin cakes of
Kir-hareseth.
8 For the fields of Heshbon languish,
and the vine of Sibmah;
the lords of the nations
have struck down its branches,
which reached to Jazer
and strayed to the desert;
its shoots spread abroad
and passed over the sea.
9 Therefore I weep with the weeping
of Jazer
for the vine of Sibmah;
I drench you with my tears,
O Heshbon and Elealeh;
for over your summer fruit and
your harvest
the shout has ceased.
10 And joy and gladness are taken
away from the fruitful field,
and in the vineyards no songs are
sung,
no cheers are raised;
no treader treads out wine in the
presses;
I have put an end to the shouting.
11 Therefore my inner parts moan like
a lyre for Moab,
and my inmost self for
Kir-hareseth.

12 And when Moab presents himself,
when he wearies himself on the high place,
when he comes to his sanctuary to pray,
he will not prevail.
13 This is the word that the LORD spoke
concerning Moab in the past. 14 But now
the LORD has spoken, saying, "In three
years, like the years of a hired worker, the
glory of Moab will be brought into con-
tempt, in spite of all his great multitude,
and those who remain will be very few
and feeble."

[1] Dead Sea Scroll, Vulgate (compare Syriac); Masoretic Text *Dimon* (twice in this verse) [2] Some Hebrew manuscripts, Septuagint, Syriac; Masoretic Text *let my outcasts sojourn among you; as for Moab, be a shelter to them*

An Oracle Concerning Damascus

17 An oracle concerning Damascus.

Behold, Damascus will cease to be a city
and will become a heap of ruins.
2 The cities of Aroer are deserted;
they will be for flocks,
which will lie down, and none will make them afraid.
3 The fortress will disappear from Ephraim,
and the kingdom from Damascus;
and the remnant of Syria will be
like the glory of the children of Israel,
declares the LORD of hosts.

4 And in that day the glory of Jacob will be brought low,
and the fat of his flesh will grow lean.
5 And it shall be as when the reaper gathers standing grain
and his arm harvests the ears,
and as when one gleans the ears of grain
in the Valley of Rephaim.
6 Gleanings will be left in it,
as when an olive tree is beaten—
two or three berries
in the top of the highest bough,
four or five
on the branches of a fruit tree,
declares the LORD God of Israel.

7 In that day man will look to his Maker,
and his eyes will look on the Holy One of
Israel. 8 He will not look to the altars, the
work of his hands, and he will not look on
what his own fingers have made, either
the Asherim or the altars of incense.
9 In that day their strong cities will be
like the deserted places of the wooded
heights and the hilltops, which they
deserted because of the children of Israel,
and there will be desolation.

10 For you have forgotten the God of your salvation
and have not remembered the Rock of your refuge;
therefore, though you plant pleasant plants
and sow the vine-branch of a stranger,
11 though you make them grow[1] on the day that you plant them,
and make them blossom in the morning that you sow,
yet the harvest will flee away[2]
in a day of grief and incurable pain.

12 Ah, the thunder of many peoples;
they thunder like the thundering of the sea!
Ah, the roar of nations;
they roar like the roaring of mighty waters!
13 The nations roar like the roaring of many waters,
but he will rebuke them, and they will flee far away,
chased like chaff on the mountains before the wind
and whirling dust before the storm.
14 At evening time, behold, terror!
Before morning, they are no more!
This is the portion of those who loot us,
and the lot of those who plunder us.

An Oracle Concerning Cush

18 Ah, land of whirring wings
that is beyond the rivers of Cush,[3]
2 which sends ambassadors by the sea,
in vessels of papyrus on the waters!
Go, you swift messengers,
to a nation, tall and smooth,
to a people feared near and far,
a nation mighty and conquering,
whose land the rivers divide.

[1] Or *though you carefully fence them* [2] Or *will be a heap* [3] Probably *Nubia*

3 All you inhabitants of the world,
you who dwell on the earth,
when a signal is raised on the
mountains, look!
When a trumpet is blown, hear!
4 For thus the LORD said to me:
"I will quietly look from my dwelling
like clear heat in sunshine,
like a cloud of dew in the heat of
harvest."
5 For before the harvest, when the
blossom is over,
and the flower becomes a
ripening grape,
he cuts off the shoots with pruning
hooks,
and the spreading branches he
lops off and clears away.
6 They shall all of them be left
to the birds of prey of the
mountains
and to the beasts of the earth.
And the birds of prey will summer
on them,
and all the beasts of the earth will
winter on them.

7 At that time tribute will be brought to
the LORD of hosts

from a people tall and smooth,
from a people feared near and far,
a nation mighty and conquering,
whose land the rivers divide,

to Mount Zion, the place of the name of
the LORD of hosts.

An Oracle Concerning Egypt

19 An oracle concerning Egypt.

Behold, the LORD is riding on a swift
cloud
and comes to Egypt;
and the idols of Egypt will tremble
at his presence,
and the heart of the Egyptians will
melt within them.
2 And I will stir up Egyptians against
Egyptians,
and they will fight, each against
another
and each against his neighbor,
city against city, kingdom against
kingdom;
3 and the spirit of the Egyptians within
them will be emptied out,
and I will confound[1] their counsel;
and they will inquire of the idols
and the sorcerers,
and the mediums and the
necromancers;
4 and I will give over the Egyptians
into the hand of a hard master,
and a fierce king will rule over them,
declares the Lord GOD of hosts.

5 And the waters of the sea will be
dried up,
and the river will be dry and
parched,
6 and its canals will become foul,
and the branches of Egypt's Nile
will diminish and dry up,
reeds and rushes will rot away.
7 There will be bare places by the Nile,
on the brink of the Nile,
and all that is sown by the Nile will
be parched,
will be driven away, and will be
no more.
8 The fishermen will mourn and
lament,
all who cast a hook in the Nile;
and they will languish
who spread nets on the water.
9 The workers in combed flax will be
in despair,
and the weavers of white cotton.
10 Those who are the pillars of the
land will be crushed,
and all who work for pay will be
grieved.

[1] Or *I will swallow up*

11 The princes of Zoan are utterly
foolish;
the wisest counselors of Pharaoh
give stupid counsel.
How can you say to Pharaoh,
"I am a son of the wise,
a son of ancient kings"?
12 Where then are your wise men?
Let them tell you
that they might know what the
LORD of hosts has purposed
against Egypt.
13 The princes of Zoan have become
fools,
and the princes of Memphis are
deluded;
those who are the cornerstones of
her tribes
have made Egypt stagger.
14 The LORD has mingled within her a
spirit of confusion,
and they will make Egypt stagger in
all its deeds,
as a drunken man staggers in his
vomit.
15 And there will be nothing for Egypt
that head or tail, palm branch or
reed, may do.

Egypt, Assyria, Israel Blessed

16 In that day the Egyptians will be like
women, and tremble with fear before
the hand that the LORD of hosts shakes
over them. 17 And the land of Judah will
become a terror to the Egyptians. Everyone
to whom it is mentioned will fear because
of the purpose that the LORD of hosts has
purposed against them.

18 In that day there will be five cities in
the land of Egypt that speak the language
of Canaan and swear allegiance to the
LORD of hosts. One of these will be called
the City of Destruction.[1]

19 In that day there will be an altar to the
LORD in the midst of the land of Egypt,
and a pillar to the LORD at its border. 20 It
will be a sign and a witness to the LORD
of hosts in the land of Egypt. When they
cry to the LORD because of oppressors, he
will send them a savior and defender, and
deliver them. 21 And the LORD will make
himself known to the Egyptians, and the
Egyptians will know the LORD in that day
and worship with sacrifice and offering,
and they will make vows to the LORD and
perform them. 22 And the LORD will strike
Egypt, striking and healing, and they will
return to the LORD, and he will listen to
their pleas for mercy and heal them.

23 In that day there will be a highway
from Egypt to Assyria, and Assyria will
come into Egypt, and Egypt into Assyria,
and the Egyptians will worship with the
Assyrians.

24 In that day Israel will be the third with
Egypt and Assyria, a blessing in the midst
of the earth, 25 whom the LORD of hosts
has blessed, saying, "Blessed be Egypt my
people, and Assyria the work of my hands,
and Israel my inheritance."

A Sign Against Egypt and Cush

20 In the year that the commander
in chief, who was sent by Sargon
the king of Assyria, came to Ashdod and
fought against it and captured it— 2 at that
time the LORD spoke by Isaiah the son of
Amoz, saying, "Go, and loose the sack-
cloth from your waist and take off your
sandals from your feet," and he did so,
walking naked and barefoot.

3 Then the LORD said, "As my servant
Isaiah has walked naked and barefoot for
three years as a sign and a portent against
Egypt and Cush,[2] 4 so shall the king of
Assyria lead away the Egyptian captives
and the Cushite exiles, both the young
and the old, naked and barefoot, with
buttocks uncovered, the nakedness of
Egypt. 5 Then they shall be dismayed and
ashamed because of Cush their hope and
of Egypt their boast. 6 And the inhabi-
tants of this coastland will say in that day,
'Behold, this is what has happened to those

[1] Dead Sea Scroll and some other manuscripts *City of the Sun* [2] Probably *Nubia*

in whom we hoped and to whom we fled
for help to be delivered from the king of
Assyria! And we, how shall we escape?'"

Fallen, Fallen Is Babylon

21 The oracle concerning the wilderness of the sea.

As whirlwinds in the Negeb sweep
on,
it comes from the wilderness,
from a terrible land.
2 A stern vision is told to me;
the traitor betrays,
and the destroyer destroys.
Go up, O Elam;
lay siege, O Media;
all the sighing she has caused
I bring to an end.
3 Therefore my loins are filled with
anguish;
pangs have seized me,
like the pangs of a woman in
labor;
I am bowed down so that I cannot
hear;
I am dismayed so that I cannot
see.
4 My heart staggers; horror has
appalled me;
the twilight I longed for
has been turned for me into
trembling.
5 They prepare the table,
they spread the rugs,[1]
they eat, they drink.
Arise, O princes;
oil the shield!
6 For thus the Lord said to me:
"Go, set a watchman;
let him announce what he sees.
7 When he sees riders, horsemen in
pairs,
riders on donkeys, riders on
camels,
let him listen diligently,
very diligently."
8 Then he who saw cried out:[2]
"Upon a watchtower I stand, O Lord,
continually by day,
and at my post I am stationed
whole nights.
9 And behold, here come riders,
horsemen in pairs!"
And he answered,
"Fallen, fallen is Babylon;
and all the carved images of her
gods
he has shattered to the ground."
10 O my threshed and winnowed one,
what I have heard from the LORD
of hosts,
the God of Israel, I announce to
you.

11 The oracle concerning Dumah.

One is calling to me from Seir,
"Watchman, what time of the
night?
Watchman, what time of the
night?"
12 The watchman says:
"Morning comes, and also the night.
If you will inquire, inquire;
come back again."

13 The oracle concerning Arabia.

In the thickets in Arabia you will
lodge,
O caravans of Dedanites.
14 To the thirsty bring water;
meet the fugitive with bread,
O inhabitants of the land of Tema.
15 For they have fled from the swords,
from the drawn sword,
from the bent bow,
and from the press of battle.

16 For thus the Lord said to me, "Within
a year, according to the years of a hired
worker, all the glory of Kedar will come
to an end. 17 And the remainder of the
archers of the mighty men of the sons of
Kedar will be few, for the LORD, the God of
Israel, has spoken."

[1] Or *they set the watchman* [2] Dead Sea Scroll, Syriac; Masoretic Text *Then a lion cried out*, or *Then he cried out like a lion*

An Oracle Concerning Jerusalem

22 The oracle concerning the valley of vision.

What do you mean that you have
gone up,
all of you, to the housetops,
2 you who are full of shoutings,
tumultuous city, exultant town?
Your slain are not slain with the
sword
or dead in battle.
3 All your leaders have fled together;
without the bow they were
captured.
All of you who were found were
captured,
though they had fled far away.
4 Therefore I said:
"Look away from me;
let me weep bitter tears;
do not labor to comfort me
concerning the destruction of the
daughter of my people."

5 For the Lord GOD of hosts has a day
of tumult and trampling and
confusion
in the valley of vision,
a battering down of walls
and a shouting to the mountains.
6 And Elam bore the quiver
with chariots and horsemen,
and Kir uncovered the shield.
7 Your choicest valleys were full of
chariots,
and the horsemen took their
stand at the gates.
8 He has taken away the covering of
Judah.

In that day you looked to the weap-
ons of the House of the Forest, 9 and you
saw that the breaches of the city of David
were many. You collected the waters of
the lower pool, 10 and you counted the
houses of Jerusalem, and you broke down
the houses to fortify the wall. 11 You made
a reservoir between the two walls for the
water of the old pool. But you did not look
to him who did it, or see him who planned
it long ago.

12 In that day the Lord GOD of hosts
called for weeping and mourning,
for baldness and wearing
sackcloth;
13 and behold, joy and gladness,
killing oxen and slaughtering
sheep,
eating flesh and drinking wine.
"Let us eat and drink,
for tomorrow we die."
14 The LORD of hosts has revealed
himself in my ears:
"Surely this iniquity will not be
atoned for you until you die,"
says the Lord GOD of hosts.

15 Thus says the Lord GOD of hosts,
"Come, go to this steward, to Shebna, who
is over the household, and say to him:
16 What have you to do here, and whom
have you here, that you have cut out here a
tomb for yourself, you who cut out a tomb
on the height and carve a dwelling for
yourself in the rock? 17 Behold, the LORD
will hurl you away violently, O you strong
man. He will seize firm hold on you 18 and
whirl you around and around, and throw
you like a ball into a wide land. There you
shall die, and there shall be your glori-
ous chariots, you shame of your master's
house. 19 I will thrust you from your office,
and you will be pulled down from your
station. 20 In that day I will call my servant
Eliakim the son of Hilkiah, 21 and I will
clothe him with your robe, and will bind
your sash on him, and will commit your
authority to his hand. And he shall be a
father to the inhabitants of Jerusalem and
to the house of Judah. 22 And I will place on
his shoulder the key of the house of David.
He shall open, and none shall shut; and he
shall shut, and none shall open. 23 And I
will fasten him like a peg in a secure place,

and he will become a throne of honor to
his father's house. 24 And they will hang on
him the whole honor of his father's house,
the offspring and issue, every small vessel,
from the cups to all the flagons. 25 In that
day, declares the LORD of hosts, the peg
that was fastened in a secure place will
give way, and it will be cut down and fall,
and the load that was on it will be cut off,
for the LORD has spoken."

An Oracle Concerning Tyre and Sidon

23 The oracle concerning Tyre.

Wail, O ships of Tarshish,
for Tyre is laid waste, without
house or harbor!
From the land of Cyprus[1]
it is revealed to them.
2 Be still, O inhabitants of the coast;
the merchants of Sidon, who
cross the sea, have filled you.
3 And on many waters
your revenue was the grain of Shihor,
the harvest of the Nile;
you were the merchant of the
nations.
4 Be ashamed, O Sidon, for the sea
has spoken,
the stronghold of the sea, saying:
"I have neither labored nor given birth,
I have neither reared young men
nor brought up young women."
5 When the report comes to Egypt,
they will be in anguish[2] over the
report about Tyre.
6 Cross over to Tarshish;
wail, O inhabitants of the coast!
7 Is this your exultant city
whose origin is from days of old,
whose feet carried her
to settle far away?
8 Who has purposed this
against Tyre, the bestower of
crowns,
whose merchants were princes,
whose traders were the honored
of the earth?
9 The LORD of hosts has purposed it,
to defile the pompous pride of all
glory,[3]
to dishonor all the honored of the
earth.
10 Cross over your land like the Nile,
O daughter of Tarshish;
there is no restraint anymore.
11 He has stretched out his hand over
the sea;
he has shaken the kingdoms;
the LORD has given command
concerning Canaan
to destroy its strongholds.
12 And he said:
"You will no more exult,
O oppressed virgin daughter of
Sidon;
arise, cross over to Cyprus,
even there you will have no rest."

13 Behold the land of the Chaldeans!
This is the people that was not;[4] Assyria
destined it for wild beasts. They erected
their siege towers, they stripped her pal-
aces bare, they made her a ruin.

14 Wail, O ships of Tarshish,
for your stronghold is laid waste.

15 In that day Tyre will be forgotten for sev-
enty years, like the days[5] of one king. At
the end of seventy years, it will happen to
Tyre as in the song of the prostitute:

16 "Take a harp;
go about the city,
O forgotten prostitute!
Make sweet melody;
sing many songs,
that you may be remembered."

17 At the end of seventy years, the LORD will
visit Tyre, and she will return to her wages
and will prostitute herself with all the
kingdoms of the world on the face of the
earth. 18 Her merchandise and her wages
will be holy to the LORD. It will not be

[1] Hebrew *Kittim*; also verse 12 [2] Hebrew *they will have labor pains* [3] The Hebrew words for *glory* and *hosts* sound alike [4] Or *that has become nothing* [5] Or *lifetime*

stored or hoarded, but her merchandise will supply abundant food and fine clothing for those who dwell before the LORD.

Judgment on the Whole Earth

24 Behold, the LORD will empty the
earth[1] and make it desolate,
and he will twist its surface and
scatter its inhabitants.
2 And it shall be, as with the people,
so with the priest;
as with the slave, so with his
master;
as with the maid, so with her
mistress;
as with the buyer, so with the seller;
as with the lender, so with the
borrower;
as with the creditor, so with the
debtor.
3 The earth shall be utterly empty and
utterly plundered;
for the LORD has spoken this word.
4 The earth mourns and withers;
the world languishes and withers;
the highest people of the earth
languish.
5 The earth lies defiled
under its inhabitants;
for they have transgressed the laws,
violated the statutes,
broken the everlasting covenant.
6 Therefore a curse devours the earth,
and its inhabitants suffer for their
guilt;
therefore the inhabitants of the
earth are scorched,
and few men are left.
7 The wine mourns,
the vine languishes,
all the merry-hearted sigh.
8 The mirth of the tambourines is
stilled,
the noise of the jubilant has ceased,
the mirth of the lyre is stilled.
9 No more do they drink wine with
singing;
strong drink is bitter to those who
drink it.
10 The wasted city is broken down;
every house is shut up so that
none can enter.
11 There is an outcry in the streets for
lack of wine;
all joy has grown dark;
the gladness of the earth is
banished.
12 Desolation is left in the city;
the gates are battered into ruins.
13 For thus it shall be in the midst of
the earth
among the nations,
as when an olive tree is beaten,
as at the gleaning when the grape
harvest is done.
14 They lift up their voices, they sing
for joy;
over the majesty of the LORD they
shout from the west.[2]
15 Therefore in the east[3] give glory to
the LORD;
in the coastlands of the sea, give
glory to the name of the LORD,
the God of Israel.
16 From the ends of the earth we hear
songs of praise,
of glory to the Righteous One.
But I say, "I waste away,
I waste away. Woe is me!
For the traitors have betrayed,
with betrayal the traitors have
betrayed."
17 Terror and the pit and the snare[4]
are upon you, O inhabitant of the
earth!
18 He who flees at the sound of the
terror
shall fall into the pit,
and he who climbs out of the pit
shall be caught in the snare.
For the windows of heaven are
opened,

[1] Or *land*; also throughout this chapter [2] Hebrew *from the sea* [3] Hebrew *in the realm of light* [4] The Hebrew words for *terror*, *pit*, and *snare* sound alike

and the foundations of the earth
tremble.
19 The earth is utterly broken,
the earth is split apart,
the earth is violently shaken.
20 The earth staggers like a drunken
man;
it sways like a hut;
its transgression lies heavy upon it,
and it falls, and will not rise again.

21 On that day the LORD will punish
the host of heaven, in heaven,
and the kings of the earth, on the
earth.
22 They will be gathered together
as prisoners in a pit;
they will be shut up in a prison,
and after many days they will be
punished.
23 Then the moon will be confounded
and the sun ashamed,
for the LORD of hosts reigns
on Mount Zion and in Jerusalem,
and his glory will be before his elders.

God Will Swallow Up Death Forever

25 O LORD, you are my God;
I will exalt you; I will praise your
name,
for you have done wonderful things,
plans formed of old, faithful and
sure.
2 For you have made the city a heap,
the fortified city a ruin;
the foreigners' palace is a city no
more;
it will never be rebuilt.
3 Therefore strong peoples will
glorify you;
cities of ruthless nations will fear
you.
4 For you have been a stronghold to
the poor,
a stronghold to the needy in his
distress,
a shelter from the storm and a
shade from the heat;
for the breath of the ruthless is like
a storm against a wall,
5 like heat in a dry place.
You subdue the noise of the
foreigners;
as heat by the shade of a cloud,
so the song of the ruthless is put
down.

1847
6 On this mountain the LORD of
hosts will make for all peoples
a feast of rich food, a feast of
well-aged wine,
of rich food full of marrow, of
aged wine well refined.
7 And he will swallow up on this
mountain
the covering that is cast over all
peoples,
the veil that is spread over all
nations.
8 He will swallow up death forever;
and the Lord GOD will wipe away
tears from all faces,
and the reproach of his people
he will take away from all the
earth,
for the LORD has spoken.
9 It will be said on that day,
"Behold, this is our God; we have
waited for him, that he might
save us.
This is the LORD; we have waited
for him;
let us be glad and rejoice in his
salvation."
10 For the hand of the LORD will rest
on this mountain,
and Moab shall be trampled down
in his place,
as straw is trampled down in a
dunghill.[1]
11 And he will spread out his hands in
the midst of it
as a swimmer spreads his hands
out to swim,

[1] The Hebrew words for *dunghill* and for the Moabite town *Madmen* (Jeremiah 48:2) sound alike

but the LORD will lay low his
pompous pride together with
the skill[1] of his hands.
12 And the high fortifications of his
walls he will bring down,
lay low, and cast to the ground, to
the dust.

You Keep Him in Perfect Peace

26 In that day this song will be sung in the land of Judah:

"We have a strong city;
he sets up salvation
as walls and bulwarks.
2 Open the gates,
that the righteous nation that
keeps faith may enter in.
3 You keep him in perfect peace
whose mind is stayed on you,
because he trusts in you.
4 Trust in the LORD forever,
for the LORD GOD is an everlasting
rock.
5 For he has humbled
the inhabitants of the height,
the lofty city.
He lays it low, lays it low to the
ground,
casts it to the dust.
6 The foot tramples it,
the feet of the poor,
the steps of the needy."

7 The path of the righteous is level;
you make level the way of the
righteous.
8 In the path of your judgments,
O LORD, we wait for you;
your name and remembrance
are the desire of our soul.
9 My soul yearns for you in the night;
my spirit within me earnestly
seeks you.
For when your judgments are in the
earth,
the inhabitants of the world learn
righteousness.
10 If favor is shown to the wicked,
he does not learn righteousness;
in the land of uprightness he deals
corruptly
and does not see the majesty of
the LORD.
11 O LORD, your hand is lifted up,
but they do not see it.
Let them see your zeal for your
people, and be ashamed.
Let the fire for your adversaries
consume them.
12 O LORD, you will ordain peace for us,
for you have indeed done for us
all our works.
13 O LORD our God,
other lords besides you have ruled
over us,
but your name alone we bring to
remembrance.
14 They are dead, they will not live;
they are shades, they will not arise;
to that end you have visited them
with destruction
and wiped out all remembrance
of them.
15 But you have increased the nation,
O LORD,
you have increased the nation;
you are glorified;
you have enlarged all the borders
of the land.

16 O LORD, in distress they sought you;
they poured out a whispered prayer
when your discipline was upon
them.
17 Like a pregnant woman
who writhes and cries out in her
pangs
when she is near to giving birth,
so were we because of you, O LORD;
18 we were pregnant, we writhed,
but we have given birth to wind.
We have accomplished no
deliverance in the earth,
and the inhabitants of the world
have not fallen.

[1] Or *in spite of the skill*

19 Your dead shall live; their bodies
shall rise.
You who dwell in the dust, awake
and sing for joy!
For your dew is a dew of light,
and the earth will give birth to the
dead.

20 Come, my people, enter your
chambers,
and shut your doors behind you;
hide yourselves for a little while
until the fury has passed by.
21 For behold, the LORD is coming out
from his place
to punish the inhabitants of the
earth for their iniquity,
and the earth will disclose the blood
shed on it,
and will no more cover its slain.

The Redemption of Israel

27 In that day the LORD with his hard
and great and strong sword will
punish Leviathan the fleeing serpent,
Leviathan the twisting serpent, and he
will slay the dragon that is in the sea.

2 In that day,
"A pleasant vineyard,[1] sing of it!
3 I, the LORD, am its keeper;
every moment I water it.
Lest anyone punish it,
I keep it night and day;
4 I have no wrath.
Would that I had thorns and briers
to battle!
I would march against them,
I would burn them up together.
5 Or let them lay hold of my protection,
let them make peace with me,
let them make peace with me."

6 In days to come[2] Jacob shall take root,
Israel shall blossom and put forth
shoots
and fill the whole world with fruit.
7 Has he struck them as he struck
those who struck them?
Or have they been slain as their
slayers were slain?
8 Measure by measure,[3] by exile you
contended with them;
he removed them with his fierce
breath[4] in the day of the east
wind.
9 Therefore by this the guilt of Jacob
will be atoned for,
and this will be the full fruit of the
removal of his sin:[5]
when he makes all the stones of the
altars
like chalkstones crushed to
pieces,
no Asherim or incense altars will
remain standing.
10 For the fortified city is solitary,
a habitation deserted and
forsaken, like the wilderness;
there the calf grazes;
there it lies down and strips its
branches.
11 When its boughs are dry, they are
broken;
women come and make a fire of
them.
For this is a people without
discernment;
therefore he who made them
will not have compassion on
them;
he who formed them will show
them no favor.

12 In that day from the river Euphrates
to the Brook of Egypt the LORD will thresh
out the grain, and you will be gleaned one
by one, O people of Israel. 13 And in that
day a great trumpet will be blown, and
those who were lost in the land of Assyria
and those who were driven out to the land
of Egypt will come and worship the LORD
on the holy mountain at Jerusalem.

[1] Many Hebrew manuscripts *A vineyard of wine* [2] Hebrew *In those to come* [3] Or *By driving her away*; the meaning of the Hebrew word is uncertain [4] Or *wind*
[5] Septuagint *and this is the blessing when I take away his sin*

Judgment on Ephraim and Jerusalem

28 Ah, the proud crown of the drunkards of Ephraim,
and the fading flower of its glorious beauty,
which is on the head of the rich valley of those overcome with wine!
2 Behold, the Lord has one who is mighty and strong;
like a storm of hail, a destroying tempest,
like a storm of mighty, overflowing waters,
he casts down to the earth with his hand.
3 The proud crown of the drunkards of Ephraim
will be trodden underfoot;
4 and the fading flower of its glorious beauty,
which is on the head of the rich valley,
will be like a first-ripe fig before the summer:
when someone sees it, he swallows it
as soon as it is in his hand.
5 In that day the LORD of hosts will be a crown of glory,[1]
and a diadem of beauty, to the remnant of his people,
6 and a spirit of justice to him who sits in judgment,
and strength to those who turn back the battle at the gate.

7 These also reel with wine
and stagger with strong drink;
the priest and the prophet reel with strong drink,
they are swallowed by[2] wine,
they stagger with strong drink,
they reel in vision,
they stumble in giving judgment.
8 For all tables are full of filthy vomit,
with no space left.
9 "To whom will he teach knowledge,
and to whom will he explain the message?
Those who are weaned from the milk,
those taken from the breast?
10 For it is precept upon precept,
precept upon precept,
line upon line, line upon line,
here a little, there a little."

11 For by people of strange lips
and with a foreign tongue
the LORD will speak to this people,
12 to whom he has said,
"This is rest;
give rest to the weary;
and this is repose";
yet they would not hear.
13 And the word of the LORD will be to them
precept upon precept, precept upon precept,
line upon line, line upon line,
here a little, there a little,
that they may go, and fall backward,
and be broken, and snared, and taken.

A Cornerstone in Zion

14 Therefore hear the word of the LORD, you scoffers,
who rule this people in Jerusalem!
15 Because you have said, "We have made a covenant with death,
and with Sheol we have an agreement,
when the overwhelming whip passes through
it will not come to us,
for we have made lies our refuge,
and in falsehood we have taken shelter";
16 therefore thus says the Lord GOD,
"Behold, I am the one who has laid[3] as a foundation in Zion,
a stone, a tested stone,
a precious cornerstone, of a sure foundation:

[1] The Hebrew words for *glory* and *hosts* sound alike [2] Or *confused by* [3] Dead Sea Scroll *I am laying*

'Whoever believes will not be in
haste.'
17 And I will make justice the line,
and righteousness the plumb line;
and hail will sweep away the refuge
of lies,
and waters will overwhelm the
shelter."
18 Then your covenant with death will
be annulled,
and your agreement with Sheol
will not stand;
when the overwhelming scourge
passes through,
you will be beaten down by it.
19 As often as it passes through it will
take you;
for morning by morning it will
pass through,
by day and by night;
and it will be sheer terror to
understand the message.
20 For the bed is too short to stretch
oneself on,
and the covering too narrow to
wrap oneself in.
21 For the LORD will rise up as on
Mount Perazim;
as in the Valley of Gibeon he will
be roused;
to do his deed—strange is his deed!
and to work his work—alien is his
work!
22 Now therefore do not scoff,
lest your bonds be made strong;
for I have heard a decree of
destruction
from the Lord GOD of hosts
against the whole land.
23 Give ear, and hear my voice;
give attention, and hear my speech.
24 Does he who plows for sowing plow
continually?
Does he continually open and
harrow his ground?
25 When he has leveled its surface,
does he not scatter dill, sow cumin,
and put in wheat in rows
and barley in its proper place,
and emmer[1] as the border?
26 For he is rightly instructed;
his God teaches him.
27 Dill is not threshed with a threshing
sledge,
nor is a cart wheel rolled over
cumin,
but dill is beaten out with a stick,
and cumin with a rod.
28 Does one crush grain for bread?
No, he does not thresh it forever;[2]
when he drives his cart wheel over it
with his horses, he does not
crush it.
29 This also comes from the LORD of
hosts;
he is wonderful in counsel
and excellent in wisdom.

The Siege of Jerusalem

29 Ah, Ariel, Ariel,
the city where David encamped!
Add year to year;
let the feasts run their round.
2 Yet I will distress Ariel,
and there shall be moaning and
lamentation,
and she shall be to me like an Ariel.[3]
3 And I will encamp against you all
around,
and will besiege you with towers
and I will raise siegeworks against
you.
4 And you will be brought low; from
the earth you shall speak,
and from the dust your speech
will be bowed down;
your voice shall come from the
ground like the voice of a ghost,
and from the dust your speech
shall whisper.

[1] A type of wheat [2] Or *Grain is crushed for bread; he will surely thresh it, but not forever* [3] *Ariel* could mean *lion of God*, or *hero* (2 Samuel 23:20), or *altar hearth* (Ezekiel 43:15-16)

5 But the multitude of your foreign
foes shall be like small dust,
and the multitude of the ruthless
like passing chaff.
And in an instant, suddenly,
6 you will be visited by the LORD of
hosts
with thunder and with earthquake
and great noise,
with whirlwind and tempest, and
the flame of a devouring fire.
7 And the multitude of all the nations
that fight against Ariel,
all that fight against her and her
stronghold and distress her,
shall be like a dream, a vision of
the night.
8 As when a hungry man dreams he
is eating
and awakes with his hunger not
satisfied,
or as when a thirsty man dreams he
is drinking
and awakes faint, with his thirst
not quenched,
so shall the multitude of all the
nations be
that fight against Mount Zion.

9 Astonish yourselves[1] and be
astonished;
blind yourselves and be blind!
Be drunk, but not with wine;
stagger, but not with strong drink!
10 For the LORD has poured out upon
you
a spirit of deep sleep,
and has closed your eyes (the
prophets),
and covered your heads (the seers).

11 And the vision of all this has become
to you like the words of a book that is
sealed. When men give it to one who can
read, saying, "Read this," he says, "I can-
not, for it is sealed." 12 And when they give
the book to one who cannot read, saying,
"Read this," he says, "I cannot read."

13 And the Lord said:
"Because this people draw near with
their mouth
and honor me with their lips,
while their hearts are far from me,
and their fear of me is a
commandment taught by men,
14 therefore, behold, I will again
do wonderful things with this
people,
with wonder upon wonder;
and the wisdom of their wise men
shall perish,
and the discernment of their
discerning men shall be
hidden."

15 Ah, you who hide deep from the
LORD your counsel,
whose deeds are in the dark,
and who say, "Who sees us? Who
knows us?"
16 You turn things upside down!
Shall the potter be regarded as the
clay,
that the thing made should say of
its maker,
"He did not make me";
or the thing formed say of him who
formed it,
"He has no understanding"?
17 Is it not yet a very little while
until Lebanon shall be turned
into a fruitful field,
and the fruitful field shall be
regarded as a forest?
18 In that day the deaf shall hear
the words of a book,
and out of their gloom and darkness
the eyes of the blind shall see.
19 The meek shall obtain fresh joy in
the LORD,
and the poor among mankind shall
exult in the Holy One of Israel.
20 For the ruthless shall come to nothing
and the scoffer cease,

[1] Or *Linger awhile*

and all who watch to do evil shall
be cut off,
21 who by a word make a man out to
be an offender,
and lay a snare for him who
reproves in the gate,
and with an empty plea turn aside
him who is in the right.

22 Therefore thus says the LORD, who
redeemed Abraham, concerning the house
of Jacob:

"Jacob shall no more be ashamed,
no more shall his face grow pale.
23 For when he sees his children,
the work of my hands, in his midst,
they will sanctify my name;
they will sanctify the Holy One of
Jacob
and will stand in awe of the God
of Israel.
24 And those who go astray in spirit
will come to understanding,
and those who murmur will
accept instruction."

Do Not Go Down to Egypt

30 "Ah, stubborn children," declares
the LORD,
"who carry out a plan, but not mine,
and who make an alliance,[1] but not
of my Spirit,
that they may add sin to sin;
2 who set out to go down to Egypt,
without asking for my direction,
to take refuge in the protection of
Pharaoh
and to seek shelter in the shadow
of Egypt!
3 Therefore shall the protection of
Pharaoh turn to your shame,
and the shelter in the shadow of
Egypt to your humiliation.
4 For though his officials are at Zoan
and his envoys reach Hanes,
5 everyone comes to shame
through a people that cannot
profit them,
that brings neither help nor profit,
but shame and disgrace."

6 An oracle on the beasts of the Negeb.

Through a land of trouble and
anguish,
from where come the lioness and
the lion,
the adder and the flying fiery
serpent,
they carry their riches on the backs
of donkeys,
and their treasures on the humps
of camels,
to a people that cannot profit them.
7 Egypt's help is worthless and empty;
therefore I have called her
"Rahab who sits still."

A Rebellious People

8 And now, go, write it before them
on a tablet
and inscribe it in a book,
that it may be for the time to come
as a witness forever.[2]
9 For they are a rebellious people,
lying children,
children unwilling to hear
the instruction of the LORD;
10 who say to the seers, "Do not see,"
and to the prophets, "Do not
prophesy to us what is right;
speak to us smooth things,
prophesy illusions,
11 leave the way, turn aside from the
path,
let us hear no more about the
Holy One of Israel."
12 Therefore thus says the Holy One of
Israel,
"Because you despise this word
and trust in oppression and
perverseness
and rely on them,
13 therefore this iniquity shall be to you

[1] Hebrew *who weave a web* [2] Some Hebrew manuscripts, Syriac, Targum, Vulgate, and Greek versions; Masoretic Text *forever and ever*

like a breach in a high wall, bulging
out, and about to collapse,
whose breaking comes suddenly,
in an instant;
14 and its breaking is like that of a
potter's vessel
that is smashed so ruthlessly
that among its fragments not a
shard is found
with which to take fire from the
hearth,
or to dip up water out of the
cistern."

15 For thus said the Lord GOD, the Holy
One of Israel,
"In returning[1] and rest you shall be
saved;
in quietness and in trust shall be
your strength."
But you were unwilling, 16 and you
said,
"No! We will flee upon horses";
therefore you shall flee away;
and, "We will ride upon swift steeds";
therefore your pursuers shall be
swift.
17 A thousand shall flee at the threat of
one;
at the threat of five you shall flee,
till you are left
like a flagstaff on the top of a
mountain,
like a signal on a hill.

The LORD Will Be Gracious

18 Therefore the LORD waits to be
gracious to you,
and therefore he exalts himself to
show mercy to you.
For the LORD is a God of justice;
blessed are all those who wait for
him.

19 For a people shall dwell in Zion, in
Jerusalem; you shall weep no more. He
will surely be gracious to you at the sound
of your cry. As soon as he hears it, he
answers you. 20 And though the Lord give
you the bread of adversity and the water of
affliction, yet your Teacher will not hide
himself anymore, but your eyes shall see
your Teacher. 21 And your ears shall hear a
word behind you, saying, "This is the way,
walk in it," when you turn to the right or
when you turn to the left. 22 Then you will
defile your carved idols overlaid with sil-
ver and your gold-plated metal images.
You will scatter them as unclean things.
You will say to them, "Be gone!"

23 And he will give rain for the seed with
which you sow the ground, and bread,
the produce of the ground, which will be
rich and plenteous. In that day your live-
stock will graze in large pastures, 24 and
the oxen and the donkeys that work the
ground will eat seasoned fodder, which
has been winnowed with shovel and fork.
25 And on every lofty mountain and every
high hill there will be brooks running
with water, in the day of the great slaugh-
ter, when the towers fall. 26 Moreover, the
light of the moon will be as the light of
the sun, and the light of the sun will be
sevenfold, as the light of seven days, in the
day when the LORD binds up the broken-
ness of his people, and heals the wounds
inflicted by his blow.

27 Behold, the name of the LORD
comes from afar,
burning with his anger, and in
thick rising smoke;[2]
his lips are full of fury,
and his tongue is like a devouring
fire;
28 his breath is like an overflowing
stream
that reaches up to the neck;
to sift the nations with the sieve of
destruction,
and to place on the jaws of the
peoples a bridle that leads
astray.

29 You shall have a song as in the night

[1] Or *repentance* [2] Hebrew *in weight of uplifted clouds*

when a holy feast is kept, and gladness of
heart, as when one sets out to the sound
of the flute to go to the mountain of the
LORD, to the Rock of Israel. 30 And the
LORD will cause his majestic voice to be
heard and the descending blow of his arm
to be seen, in furious anger and a flame
of devouring fire, with a cloudburst and
storm and hailstones. 31 The Assyrians
will be terror-stricken at the voice of the
LORD, when he strikes with his rod. 32 And
every stroke of the appointed staff that the
LORD lays on them will be to the sound of
tambourines and lyres. Battling with bran-
dished arm, he will fight with them. 33 For
a burning place[1] has long been prepared;
indeed, for the king it is made ready, its
pyre made deep and wide, with fire and
wood in abundance; the breath of the
LORD, like a stream of sulfur, kindles it.

Woe to Those Who Go Down to Egypt

31 Woe to those who go down to Egypt for help
and rely on horses,
who trust in chariots because they are many
and in horsemen because they are very strong,
but do not look to the Holy One of Israel
or consult the LORD!

2 And yet he is wise and brings disaster;
he does not call back his words,
but will arise against the house of the evildoers
and against the helpers of those who work iniquity.

3 The Egyptians are man, and not God,
and their horses are flesh, and not spirit.
When the LORD stretches out his hand,
the helper will stumble, and he who is helped will fall,
and they will all perish together.

4 For thus the LORD said to me,
"As a lion or a young lion growls over his prey,
and when a band of shepherds is called out against him
he is not terrified by their shouting or daunted at their noise,
so the LORD of hosts will come down to fight[2] on Mount Zion and on its hill.

5 Like birds hovering, so the LORD of hosts
will protect Jerusalem;
he will protect and deliver it;
he will spare and rescue it."

6 Turn to him from whom people[3] have
deeply revolted, O children of Israel. 7 For
in that day everyone shall cast away his
idols of silver and his idols of gold, which
your hands have sinfully made for you.

8 "And the Assyrian shall fall by a sword, not of man;
and a sword, not of man, shall devour him;
and he shall flee from the sword,
and his young men shall be put to forced labor.

9 His rock shall pass away in terror,
and his officers desert the standard in panic,"
declares the LORD, whose fire is in Zion,
and whose furnace is in Jerusalem.

A King Will Reign in Righteousness

32 Behold, a king will reign in righteousness,
and princes will rule in justice.

2 Each will be like a hiding place from the wind,
a shelter from the storm,
like streams of water in a dry place,
like the shade of a great rock in a weary land.

3 Then the eyes of those who see will not be closed,

[1] Or *For Topheth* [2] The Hebrew words for *hosts* and *to fight* sound alike [3] Hebrew *they*

and the ears of those who hear
will give attention.
4 The heart of the hasty will
understand and know,
and the tongue of the stammerers
will hasten to speak distinctly.
5 The fool will no more be called noble,
nor the scoundrel said to be
honorable.
6 For the fool speaks folly,
and his heart is busy with iniquity,
to practice ungodliness,
to utter error concerning the LORD,
to leave the craving of the hungry
unsatisfied,
and to deprive the thirsty of drink.
7 As for the scoundrel—his devices
are evil;
he plans wicked schemes
to ruin the poor with lying words,
even when the plea of the needy
is right.
8 But he who is noble plans noble
things,
and on noble things he stands.

Complacent Women Warned of Disaster

9 Rise up, you women who are at
ease, hear my voice;
you complacent daughters, give
ear to my speech.
10 In little more than a year
you will shudder, you complacent
women;
for the grape harvest fails,
the fruit harvest will not come.
11 Tremble, you women who are at ease,
shudder, you complacent ones;
strip, and make yourselves bare,
and tie sackcloth around your
waist.
12 Beat your breasts for the pleasant
fields,
for the fruitful vine,
13 for the soil of my people
growing up in thorns and briers,
yes, for all the joyous houses
in the exultant city.
14 For the palace is forsaken,
the populous city deserted;
the hill and the watchtower
will become dens forever,
a joy of wild donkeys,
a pasture of flocks;
15 until the Spirit is poured upon us
from on high,
and the wilderness becomes a
fruitful field,
and the fruitful field is deemed a
forest.
16 Then justice will dwell in the
wilderness,
and righteousness abide in the
fruitful field.
17 And the effect of righteousness will
be peace,
and the result of righteousness,
quietness and trust[1] forever.
18 My people will abide in a peaceful
habitation,
in secure dwellings, and in quiet
resting places.
19 And it will hail when the forest falls
down,
and the city will be utterly laid low.
20 Happy are you who sow beside all
waters,
who let the feet of the ox and the
donkey range free.

O LORD, Be Gracious to Us

33 Ah, you destroyer,
who yourself have not been
destroyed,
you traitor,
whom none has betrayed!
When you have ceased to destroy,
you will be destroyed;
and when you have finished
betraying,
they will betray you.

2 O LORD, be gracious to us; we wait
for you.
Be our arm every morning,

[1] Or *security*

our salvation in the time of trouble.
3 At the tumultuous noise peoples flee;
when you lift yourself up, nations are scattered,
4 and your spoil is gathered as the caterpillar gathers;
as locusts leap, it is leapt upon.

5 The LORD is exalted, for he dwells on high;
he will fill Zion with justice and righteousness,
6 and he will be the stability of your times,
abundance of salvation, wisdom, and knowledge;
the fear of the LORD is Zion's[1] treasure.

7 Behold, their heroes cry in the streets;
the envoys of peace weep bitterly.
8 The highways lie waste;
the traveler ceases.
Covenants are broken;
cities[2] are despised;
there is no regard for man.
9 The land mourns and languishes;
Lebanon is confounded and withers away;
Sharon is like a desert,
and Bashan and Carmel shake off their leaves.

10 "Now I will arise," says the LORD,
"now I will lift myself up;
now I will be exalted.
11 You conceive chaff; you give birth to stubble;
your breath is a fire that will consume you.
12 And the peoples will be as if burned to lime,
like thorns cut down, that are burned in the fire."

13 Hear, you who are far off, what I have done;
and you who are near, acknowledge my might.
14 The sinners in Zion are afraid;
trembling has seized the godless:
"Who among us can dwell with the consuming fire?
Who among us can dwell with everlasting burnings?"
15 He who walks righteously and speaks uprightly,
who despises the gain of oppressions,
who shakes his hands, lest they hold a bribe,
who stops his ears from hearing of bloodshed
and shuts his eyes from looking on evil,
16 he will dwell on the heights;
his place of defense will be the fortresses of rocks;
his bread will be given him; his water will be sure.

17 Your eyes will behold the king in his beauty;
they will see a land that stretches afar.
18 Your heart will muse on the terror:
"Where is he who counted, where is he who weighed the tribute?
Where is he who counted the towers?"
19 You will see no more the insolent people,
the people of an obscure speech that you cannot comprehend,
stammering in a tongue that you cannot understand.
20 Behold Zion, the city of our appointed feasts!
Your eyes will see Jerusalem,
an untroubled habitation, an immovable tent,
whose stakes will never be plucked up,
nor will any of its cords be broken.
21 But there the LORD in majesty will be for us
a place of broad rivers and streams,

[1] Hebrew *his* [2] Masoretic Text; Dead Sea Scroll *witnesses*

where no galley with oars can go,
nor majestic ship can pass.
22 For the LORD is our judge; the LORD is our lawgiver;
the LORD is our king; he will save us.
23 Your cords hang loose;
they cannot hold the mast firm in its place
or keep the sail spread out.
Then prey and spoil in abundance will be divided;
even the lame will take the prey.
24 And no inhabitant will say, "I am sick";
the people who dwell there will be forgiven their iniquity.

Judgment on the Nations

34 Draw near, O nations, to hear,
and give attention, O peoples!
Let the earth hear, and all that fills it;
the world, and all that comes from it.
2 For the LORD is enraged against all the nations,
and furious against all their host;
he has devoted them to destruction,[1] has given them over for slaughter.
3 Their slain shall be cast out,
and the stench of their corpses shall rise;
the mountains shall flow with their blood.
4 All the host of heaven shall rot away,
and the skies roll up like a scroll.
All their host shall fall,
as leaves fall from the vine,
like leaves falling from the fig tree.
5 For my sword has drunk its fill in the heavens;
behold, it descends for judgment upon Edom,
upon the people I have devoted to destruction.
6 The LORD has a sword; it is sated with blood;
it is gorged with fat,
with the blood of lambs and goats,
with the fat of the kidneys of rams.
For the LORD has a sacrifice in Bozrah,
a great slaughter in the land of Edom.
7 Wild oxen shall fall with them,
and young steers with the mighty bulls.
Their land shall drink its fill of blood,
and their soil shall be gorged with fat.
8 For the LORD has a day of vengeance,
a year of recompense for the cause of Zion.
9 And the streams of Edom[2] shall be turned into pitch,
and her soil into sulfur;
her land shall become burning pitch.
10 Night and day it shall not be quenched;
its smoke shall go up forever.
From generation to generation it shall lie waste;
none shall pass through it forever and ever.
11 But the hawk and the porcupine[3] shall possess it,
the owl and the raven shall dwell in it.
He shall stretch the line of confusion[4] over it,
and the plumb line of emptiness.
12 Its nobles—there is no one there to call it a kingdom,
and all its princes shall be nothing.
13 Thorns shall grow over its strongholds,
nettles and thistles in its fortresses.
It shall be the haunt of jackals,
an abode for ostriches.[5]

[1] That is, set apart (devoted) as an offering to the Lord (for destruction); also verse 5 [2] Hebrew *her streams* [3] The identity of the animals rendered *hawk* and *porcupine* is uncertain [4] Hebrew *formlessness* [5] Or *owls*

14 And wild animals shall meet with hyenas;
the wild goat shall cry to his fellow;
indeed, there the night bird[1] settles
and finds for herself a resting place.
15 There the owl nests and lays
and hatches and gathers her young in her shadow;
indeed, there the hawks are gathered,
each one with her mate.
16 Seek and read from the book of the LORD:
Not one of these shall be missing;
none shall be without her mate.
For the mouth of the LORD has commanded,
and his Spirit has gathered them.
17 He has cast the lot for them;
his hand has portioned it out to them with the line;
they shall possess it forever;
from generation to generation they shall dwell in it.

The Ransomed Shall Return

35 The wilderness and the dry land shall be glad;
the desert shall rejoice and blossom like the crocus;
2 it shall blossom abundantly
and rejoice with joy and singing.
The glory of Lebanon shall be given to it,
the majesty of Carmel and Sharon.
They shall see the glory of the LORD,
the majesty of our God.
3 Strengthen the weak hands,
and make firm the feeble knees.
4 Say to those who have an anxious heart,
"Be strong; fear not!
Behold, your God
will come with vengeance,
with the recompense of God.
He will come and save you."
5 Then the eyes of the blind shall be opened,
and the ears of the deaf unstopped;
6 then shall the lame man leap like a deer,
and the tongue of the mute sing for joy.
For waters break forth in the wilderness,
and streams in the desert;
7 the burning sand shall become a pool,
and the thirsty ground springs of water;
in the haunt of jackals, where they lie down,
the grass shall become reeds and rushes.

8 And a highway shall be there,
and it shall be called the Way of Holiness;
the unclean shall not pass over it.
It shall belong to those who walk on the way;
even if they are fools, they shall not go astray.[2]
9 No lion shall be there,
nor shall any ravenous beast come up on it;
they shall not be found there,
but the redeemed shall walk there.
10 And the ransomed of the LORD shall return
and come to Zion with singing;
everlasting joy shall be upon their heads;
they shall obtain gladness and joy,
and sorrow and sighing shall flee away.

Sennacherib Invades Judah

615
36 In the fourteenth year of
King Hezekiah, Sennach-
erib king of Assyria came up
against all the fortified cities of Judah and
took them. 2 And the king of Assyria sent
the Rabshakeh[3] from Lachish to King

[1] Identity uncertain [2] Or *if they are fools, they shall not wander in it* [3] *Rabshakeh* is the title of a high-ranking Assyrian military officer

Hezekiah at Jerusalem, with a great army. And he stood by the conduit of the upper pool on the highway to the Washer's Field. 3 And there came out to him Eliakim the son of Hilkiah, who was over the household, and Shebna the secretary, and Joah the son of Asaph, the recorder.

4 And the Rabshakeh said to them, "Say to Hezekiah, 'Thus says the great king, the king of Assyria: On what do you rest this trust of yours? 5 Do you think that mere words are strategy and power for war? In whom do you now trust, that you have rebelled against me? 6 Behold, you are trusting in Egypt, that broken reed of a staff, which will pierce the hand of any man who leans on it. Such is Pharaoh king of Egypt to all who trust in him. 7 But if you say to me, "We trust in the LORD our God," is it not he whose high places and altars Hezekiah has removed, saying to Judah and to Jerusalem, "You shall worship before this altar"? 8 Come now, make a wager with my master the king of Assyria: I will give you two thousand horses, if you are able on your part to set riders on them. 9 How then can you repulse a single captain among the least of my master's servants, when you trust in Egypt for chariots and for horsemen? 10 Moreover, is it without the LORD that I have come up against this land to destroy it? The LORD said to me, Go up against this land and destroy it.'"

11 Then Eliakim, Shebna, and Joah said to the Rabshakeh, "Please speak to your servants in Aramaic, for we understand it. Do not speak to us in the language of Judah within the hearing of the people who are on the wall." 12 But the Rabshakeh said, "Has my master sent me to speak these words to your master and to you, and not to the men sitting on the wall, who are doomed with you to eat their own dung and drink their own urine?"

13 Then the Rabshakeh stood and called out in a loud voice in the language of Judah: "Hear the words of the great king, the king of Assyria! 14 Thus says the king: 'Do not let Hezekiah deceive you, for he will not be able to deliver you. 15 Do not let Hezekiah make you trust in the LORD by saying, "The LORD will surely deliver us. This city will not be given into the hand of the king of Assyria." 16 Do not listen to Hezekiah. For thus says the king of Assyria: Make your peace with me[1] and come out to me. Then each one of you will eat of his own vine, and each one of his own fig tree, and each one of you will drink the water of his own cistern, 17 until I come and take you away to a land like your own land, a land of grain and wine, a land of bread and vineyards. 18 Beware lest Hezekiah mislead you by saying, "The LORD will deliver us." Has any of the gods of the nations delivered his land out of the hand of the king of Assyria? 19 Where are the gods of Hamath and Arpad? Where are the gods of Sepharvaim? Have they delivered Samaria out of my hand? 20 Who among all the gods of these lands have delivered their lands out of my hand, that the LORD should deliver Jerusalem out of my hand?'"

21 But they were silent and answered him not a word, for the king's command was, "Do not answer him." 22 Then Eliakim the son of Hilkiah, who was over the household, and Shebna the secretary, and Joah the son of Asaph, the recorder, came to Hezekiah with their clothes torn, and told him the words of the Rabshakeh.

Hezekiah Seeks Isaiah's Help

37 As soon as King Hezekiah heard it, he tore his clothes and covered himself with sackcloth and went into the house of the LORD. 2 And he sent Eliakim, who was over the household, and Shebna the secretary, and the senior priests, covered with sackcloth, to the prophet Isaiah the son of Amoz. 3 They said to him, "Thus says Hezekiah, 'This day is a day of distress, of rebuke, and of disgrace; children have come to the point of birth, and there

[1] Hebrew *Make a blessing with me*

is no strength to bring them forth. 4 It may be that the LORD your God will hear the words of the Rabshakeh, whom his master the king of Assyria has sent to mock the living God, and will rebuke the words that the LORD your God has heard; therefore lift up your prayer for the remnant that is left.'"

5 When the servants of King Hezekiah came to Isaiah, 6 Isaiah said to them, "Say to your master, 'Thus says the LORD: Do not be afraid because of the words that you have heard, with which the young men of the king of Assyria have reviled me. 7 Behold, I will put a spirit in him, so that he shall hear a rumor and return to his own land, and I will make him fall by the sword in his own land.'"

8 The Rabshakeh returned, and found the king of Assyria fighting against Libnah, for he had heard that the king had left Lachish. 9 Now the king heard concerning Tirhakah king of Cush,[1] "He has set out to fight against you." And when he heard it, he sent messengers to Hezekiah, saying, 10 "Thus shall you speak to Hezekiah king of Judah: 'Do not let your God in whom you trust deceive you by promising that Jerusalem will not be given into the hand of the king of Assyria. 11 Behold, you have heard what the kings of Assyria have done to all lands, devoting them to destruction. And shall you be delivered? 12 Have the gods of the nations delivered them, the nations that my fathers destroyed, Gozan, Haran, Rezeph, and the people of Eden who were in Telassar? 13 Where is the king of Hamath, the king of Arpad, the king of the city of Sepharvaim, the king of Hena, or the king of Ivvah?'"

Hezekiah's Prayer for Deliverance

14 Hezekiah received the letter from the hand of the messengers, and read it; and Hezekiah went up to the house of the LORD, and spread it before the LORD. 15 And Hezekiah prayed to the LORD: 16 "O LORD of hosts, God of Israel, enthroned above the cherubim, you are the God, you alone, of all the kingdoms of the earth; you have made heaven and earth. 17 Incline your ear, O LORD, and hear; open your eyes, O LORD, and see; and hear all the words of Sennacherib, which he has sent to mock the living God. 18 Truly, O LORD, the kings of Assyria have laid waste all the nations and their lands, 19 and have cast their gods into the fire. For they were no gods, but the work of men's hands, wood and stone. Therefore they were destroyed. 20 So now, O LORD our God, save us from his hand, that all the kingdoms of the earth may know that you alone are the LORD."

Sennacherib's Fall

21 Then Isaiah the son of Amoz sent to Hezekiah, saying, "Thus says the LORD, the God of Israel: Because you have prayed to me concerning Sennacherib king of Assyria, 22 this is the word that the LORD has spoken concerning him:

"'She despises you, she scorns you—
the virgin daughter of Zion;
she wags her head behind you—
the daughter of Jerusalem.

23 "'Whom have you mocked and reviled?
Against whom have you raised your voice
and lifted your eyes to the heights?
Against the Holy One of Israel!
24 By your servants you have mocked the Lord,
and you have said, With my many chariots
I have gone up the heights of the mountains,
to the far recesses of Lebanon,
to cut down its tallest cedars,
its choicest cypresses,
to come to its remotest height,
its most fruitful forest.

[1] Probably *Nubia*

25 I dug wells
and drank waters,
to dry up with the sole of my foot
all the streams of Egypt.

26 "'Have you not heard
that I determined it long ago?
I planned from days of old
what now I bring to pass,
that you should make fortified
cities
crash into heaps of ruins,
27 while their inhabitants, shorn of
strength,
are dismayed and confounded,
and have become like plants of the
field
and like tender grass,
like grass on the housetops,
blighted[1] before it is grown.

28 "'I know your sitting down
and your going out and coming in,
and your raging against me.
29 Because you have raged against me
and your complacency has come
to my ears,
I will put my hook in your nose
and my bit in your mouth,
and I will turn you back on the way
by which you came.'

30 "And this shall be the sign for you: this
year you shall eat what grows of itself, and
in the second year what springs from that.
Then in the third year sow and reap, and
plant vineyards, and eat their fruit. 31 And
the surviving remnant of the house of
Judah shall again take root downward and
bear fruit upward. 32 For out of Jerusalem
shall go a remnant, and out of Mount Zion
a band of survivors. The zeal of the LORD
of hosts will do this.

33 "Therefore thus says the LORD con-
cerning the king of Assyria: He shall not
come into this city or shoot an arrow there
or come before it with a shield or cast up a
siege mound against it. 34 By the way that
he came, by the same he shall return, and
he shall not come into this city, declares
the LORD. 35 For I will defend this city to
save it, for my own sake and for the sake
of my servant David."

36 And the angel of the LORD went
out and struck down a hundred and
eighty-five thousand in the camp of the
Assyrians. And when people arose early
in the morning, behold, these were all
dead bodies. 37 Then Sennacherib king of
Assyria departed and returned home and
lived at Nineveh. 38 And as he was wor-
shiping in the house of Nisroch his god,
Adrammelech and Sharezer, his sons,
struck him down with the sword. And
after they escaped into the land of Ararat,
Esarhaddon his son reigned in his place.

Hezekiah's Sickness and Recovery

38 In those days Hezekiah became
sick and was at the point of death.
And Isaiah the prophet the son of Amoz
came to him, and said to him, "Thus says
the LORD: Set your house in order, for you
shall die, you shall not recover."[2] 2 Then
Hezekiah turned his face to the wall and
prayed to the LORD, 3 and said, "Please, O
LORD, remember how I have walked before
you in faithfulness and with a whole heart,
and have done what is good in your sight."
And Hezekiah wept bitterly.

4 Then the word of the LORD came to
Isaiah: 5 "Go and say to Hezekiah, Thus
says the LORD, the God of David your
father: I have heard your prayer; I have
seen your tears. Behold, I will add fifteen
years to your life.[3] 6 I will deliver you and
this city out of the hand of the king of
Assyria, and will defend this city.

7 "This shall be the sign to you from
the LORD, that the LORD will do this
thing that he has promised: 8 Behold, I
will make the shadow cast by the declin-
ing sun on the dial of Ahaz turn back ten
steps." So the sun turned back on the dial
the ten steps by which it had declined.[4]

[1] Some Hebrew manuscripts and 2 Kings 19:26; most Hebrew manuscripts *like a field* [2] Or *live*; also verses 9, 21 [3] Hebrew *to your days* [4] The meaning of the Hebrew verse is uncertain

9 A writing of Hezekiah king of Judah, after he had been sick and had recovered from his sickness:

10 I said, In the middle[1] of my days
I must depart;
I am consigned to the gates of Sheol
for the rest of my years.
11 I said, I shall not see the LORD,
the LORD in the land of the living;
I shall look on man no more
among the inhabitants of the world.
12 My dwelling is plucked up and removed from me
like a shepherd's tent;
like a weaver I have rolled up my life;
he cuts me off from the loom;
from day to night you bring me to an end;
13 I calmed myself[2] until morning;
like a lion he breaks all my bones;
from day to night you bring me to an end.

14 Like a swallow or a crane I chirp;
I moan like a dove.
My eyes are weary with looking upward.
O Lord, I am oppressed; be my pledge of safety!
15 What shall I say? For he has spoken to me,
and he himself has done it.
I walk slowly all my years
because of the bitterness of my soul.

16 O Lord, by these things men live,
and in all these is the life of my spirit.
Oh restore me to health and make me live!
17 Behold, it was for my welfare
that I had great bitterness;
but in love you have delivered my life
from the pit of destruction,
for you have cast all my sins
behind your back.
18 For Sheol does not thank you;
death does not praise you;
those who go down to the pit do not hope
for your faithfulness.
19 The living, the living, he thanks you,
as I do this day;
the father makes known to the children
your faithfulness.

20 The LORD will save me,
and we will play my music on stringed instruments
all the days of our lives,
at the house of the LORD.

21 Now Isaiah had said, "Let them take
a cake of figs and apply it to the boil, that
he may recover." 22 Hezekiah also had said,
"What is the sign that I shall go up to the
house of the LORD?"

Envoys from Babylon

39 At that time Merodach-baladan
the son of Baladan, king of Bab-
ylon, sent envoys with letters and a pres-
ent to Hezekiah, for he heard that he
had been sick and had recovered. 2 And
Hezekiah welcomed them gladly. And he
showed them his treasure house, the sil-
ver, the gold, the spices, the precious oil,
his whole armory, all that was found in
his storehouses. There was nothing in his
house or in all his realm that Hezekiah did
not show them. 3 Then Isaiah the prophet
came to King Hezekiah, and said to him,
"What did these men say? And from where
did they come to you?" Hezekiah said,
"They have come to me from a far country,
from Babylon." 4 He said, "What have they
seen in your house?" Hezekiah answered,
"They have seen all that is in my house.
There is nothing in my storehouses that I
did not show them."
5 Then Isaiah said to Hezekiah, "Hear
the word of the LORD of hosts: 6 Behold,
the days are coming, when all that is in

[1] Or *In the quiet* [2] Or (with Targum) *I cried for help*

your house, and that which your fathers
have stored up till this day, shall be car-
ried to Babylon. Nothing shall be left, says
the LORD. 7 And some of your own sons,
who will come from you, whom you will
father, shall be taken away, and they shall
be eunuchs in the palace of the king of
Babylon." 8 Then said Hezekiah to Isaiah,
"The word of the LORD that you have spo-
ken is good." For he thought, "There will
be peace and security in my days."

Comfort for God's People

40 Comfort, comfort my people,
says your God.
2 Speak tenderly to Jerusalem,
and cry to her
that her warfare[1] is ended,
that her iniquity is pardoned,
that she has received from the
LORD's hand
double for all her sins.

1297, 1441

3 A voice cries:[2]
"In the wilderness prepare the
way of the LORD;
make straight in the desert a
highway for our God.
4 Every valley shall be lifted up,
and every mountain and hill be
made low;
the uneven ground shall become
level,
and the rough places a plain.
5 And the glory of the LORD shall be
revealed,
and all flesh shall see it together,
for the mouth of the LORD has
spoken."

The Word of God Stands Forever

6 A voice says, "Cry!"
And I said,[3] "What shall I cry?"
All flesh is grass,
and all its beauty[4] is like the
flower of the field.
7 The grass withers, the flower fades
when the breath of the LORD
blows on it;
surely the people are grass.
8 The grass withers, the flower fades,
but the word of our God will stand
forever.

The Greatness of God

9 Get you up to a high mountain,
O Zion, herald of good news;[5]
lift up your voice with strength,
O Jerusalem, herald of good news;[6]
lift it up, fear not;
say to the cities of Judah,
"Behold your God!"
10 Behold, the Lord GOD comes with
might,
and his arm rules for him;
behold, his reward is with him,
and his recompense before him.
11 He will tend his flock like a shepherd;
he will gather the lambs in his
arms;
he will carry them in his bosom,
and gently lead those that are
with young.
12 Who has measured the waters in
the hollow of his hand
and marked off the heavens with
a span,
enclosed the dust of the earth in a
measure
and weighed the mountains in
scales
and the hills in a balance?
13 Who has measured[7] the Spirit of the
LORD,
or what man shows him his
counsel?
14 Whom did he consult,
and who made him understand?
Who taught him the path of justice,
and taught him knowledge,
and showed him the way of
understanding?

[1] Or *time of service* [2] Or *A voice of one crying* [3] Revocalization based on Dead Sea Scroll, Septuagint, Vulgate; Masoretic Text *And someone says* [4] Or *all its constancy* [5] Or *O herald of good news to Zion* [6] Or *O herald of good news to Jerusalem* [7] Or *has directed*

15 Behold, the nations are like a drop
from a bucket,
and are accounted as the dust on
the scales;
behold, he takes up the
coastlands like fine dust.
16 Lebanon would not suffice for fuel,
nor are its beasts enough for a
burnt offering.
17 All the nations are as nothing
before him,
they are accounted by him as less
than nothing and emptiness.

18 To whom then will you liken God,
or what likeness compare with
him?
19 An idol! A craftsman casts it,
and a goldsmith overlays it with
gold
and casts for it silver chains.
20 He who is too impoverished for an
offering
chooses wood[1] that will not rot;
he seeks out a skillful craftsman
to set up an idol that will not move.

21 Do you not know? Do you not hear?
Has it not been told you from the
beginning?
Have you not understood from
the foundations of the earth?
22 It is he who sits above the circle of
the earth,
and its inhabitants are like
grasshoppers;
who stretches out the heavens like a
curtain,
and spreads them like a tent to
dwell in;
23 who brings princes to nothing,
and makes the rulers of the earth
as emptiness.

24 Scarcely are they planted, scarcely
sown,
scarcely has their stem taken root
in the earth,
when he blows on them, and they
wither,
and the tempest carries them off
like stubble.

25 To whom then will you compare me,
that I should be like him? says the
Holy One.
26 Lift up your eyes on high and see:
who created these?
He who brings out their host by
number,
calling them all by name,
by the greatness of his might,
and because he is strong in power
not one is missing.

27 Why do you say, O Jacob,
and speak, O Israel,
"My way is hidden from the LORD,
and my right is disregarded by my
God"?
28 Have you not known? Have you not
heard?
The LORD is the everlasting God,
the Creator of the ends of the earth.
He does not faint or grow weary;
his understanding is
unsearchable.
29 He gives power to the faint,
and to him who has no might he
increases strength.
30 Even youths shall faint and be weary,
and young men shall fall
exhausted;
31 but they who wait for the LORD shall
renew their strength;
they shall mount up with wings
like eagles;
they shall run and not be weary;
they shall walk and not faint.

Fear Not, For I Am with You

41 Listen to me in silence,
O coastlands;
let the peoples renew their
strength;

[1] Or *He chooses valuable wood*

let them approach, then let them
speak;
let us together draw near for
judgment.

2 Who stirred up one from the east
whom victory meets at every step?[1]
He gives up nations before him,
so that he tramples kings
underfoot;
he makes them like dust with his
sword,
like driven stubble with his bow.
3 He pursues them and passes on
safely,
by paths his feet have not trod.
4 Who has performed and done this,
calling the generations from the
beginning?
I, the LORD, the first,
and with the last; I am he.

5 The coastlands have seen and are
afraid;
the ends of the earth tremble;
they have drawn near and come.
6 Everyone helps his neighbor
and says to his brother, "Be strong!"
7 The craftsman strengthens the
goldsmith,
and he who smooths with the
hammer him who strikes the
anvil,
saying of the soldering, "It is good";
and they strengthen it with nails
so that it cannot be moved.

8 But you, Israel, my servant,
Jacob, whom I have chosen,
the offspring of Abraham, my
friend;
9 you whom I took from the ends of
the earth,
and called from its farthest corners,
saying to you, "You are my servant,
I have chosen you and not cast
you off";
10 fear not, for I am with you;
be not dismayed, for I am your God;
I will strengthen you, I will help you,
I will uphold you with my
righteous right hand.

11 Behold, all who are incensed
against you
shall be put to shame and
confounded;
those who strive against you
shall be as nothing and shall perish.
12 You shall seek those who contend
with you,
but you shall not find them;
those who war against you
shall be as nothing at all.
13 For I, the LORD your God,
hold your right hand;
it is I who say to you, "Fear not,
I am the one who helps you."

14 Fear not, you worm Jacob,
you men of Israel!
I am the one who helps you,
declares the LORD;
your Redeemer is the Holy One of
Israel.
15 Behold, I make of you a threshing
sledge,
new, sharp, and having teeth;
you shall thresh the mountains and
crush them,
and you shall make the hills like
chaff;
16 you shall winnow them, and the
wind shall carry them away,
and the tempest shall scatter them.
And you shall rejoice in the LORD;
in the Holy One of Israel you shall
glory.

17 When the poor and needy seek water,
and there is none,
and their tongue is parched with
thirst,
I the LORD will answer them;
I the God of Israel will not forsake
them.
18 I will open rivers on the bare heights,

[1] Or *whom righteousness calls to follow?*

and fountains in the midst of the
valleys.
I will make the wilderness a pool of
water,
and the dry land springs of water.
19 I will put in the wilderness the cedar,
the acacia, the myrtle, and the olive.
I will set in the desert the cypress,
the plane and the pine together,
20 that they may see and know,
may consider and understand
together,
that the hand of the LORD has done
this,
the Holy One of Israel has created it.

The Futility of Idols

21 Set forth your case, says the LORD;
bring your proofs, says the King of
Jacob.
22 Let them bring them, and tell us
what is to happen.
Tell us the former things, what they
are,
that we may consider them,
that we may know their outcome;
or declare to us the things to come.
23 Tell us what is to come hereafter,
that we may know that you are
gods;
do good, or do harm,
that we may be dismayed and
terrified.[1]
24 Behold, you are nothing,
and your work is less than nothing;
an abomination is he who
chooses you.
25 I stirred up one from the north, and
he has come,
from the rising of the sun, and he
shall call upon my name;
he shall trample on rulers as on
mortar,
as the potter treads clay.
26 Who declared it from the beginning,
that we might know,
and beforehand, that we might
say, "He is right"?
There was none who declared it,
none who proclaimed,
none who heard your words.
27 I was the first to say[2] to Zion,
"Behold, here they are!"
and I give to Jerusalem a herald of
good news.
28 But when I look, there is no one;
among these there is no counselor
who, when I ask, gives an answer.
29 Behold, they are all a delusion;
their works are nothing;
their metal images are empty wind.

The LORD's Chosen Servant

42 Behold my servant, whom I
uphold,
my chosen, in whom my soul
delights;
I have put my Spirit upon him;
he will bring forth justice to the
nations.
2 He will not cry aloud or lift up his
voice,
or make it heard in the street;
3 a bruised reed he will not break,
and a faintly burning wick he will
not quench;
he will faithfully bring forth justice.
4 He will not grow faint or be
discouraged[3]
till he has established justice in
the earth;
and the coastlands wait for his law.

5 Thus says God, the LORD,
who created the heavens and
stretched them out,
who spread out the earth and
what comes from it,
who gives breath to the people on it
and spirit to those who walk in it:
6 "I am the LORD; I have called you
in righteousness;
1449
I will take you by the hand and
keep you;

[1] Or *that we may both be dismayed and see* [2] Or *Formerly I said* [3] Or *bruised*

I will give you as a covenant for the people,
a light for the nations,
7 to open the eyes that are blind,
to bring out the prisoners from the dungeon,
from the prison those who sit in darkness.
8 I am the LORD; that is my name;
my glory I give to no other,
nor my praise to carved idols.
9 Behold, the former things have come to pass,
and new things I now declare;
before they spring forth
I tell you of them."

Sing to the LORD a New Song

10 Sing to the LORD a new song,
his praise from the end of the earth,
you who go down to the sea, and all that fills it,
the coastlands and their inhabitants.
11 Let the desert and its cities lift up their voice,
the villages that Kedar inhabits;
let the habitants of Sela sing for joy,
let them shout from the top of the mountains.
12 Let them give glory to the LORD,
and declare his praise in the coastlands.
13 The LORD goes out like a mighty man,
like a man of war he stirs up his zeal;
he cries out, he shouts aloud,
he shows himself mighty against his foes.
14 For a long time I have held my peace;
I have kept still and restrained myself;
now I will cry out like a woman in labor;
I will gasp and pant.
15 I will lay waste mountains and hills,
and dry up all their vegetation;
I will turn the rivers into islands,[1]
and dry up the pools.
16 And I will lead the blind
in a way that they do not know,
in paths that they have not known
I will guide them.
I will turn the darkness before them into light,
the rough places into level ground.
These are the things I do,
and I do not forsake them.
17 They are turned back and utterly put to shame,
who trust in carved idols,
who say to metal images,
"You are our gods."

Israel's Failure to Hear and See

18 Hear, you deaf,
and look, you blind, that you may see!
19 Who is blind but my servant,
or deaf as my messenger whom I send?
Who is blind as my dedicated one,[2]
or blind as the servant of the LORD?
20 He sees many things, but does not observe them;
his ears are open, but he does not hear.
21 The LORD was pleased, for his righteousness' sake,
to magnify his law and make it glorious.
22 But this is a people plundered and looted;
they are all of them trapped in holes
and hidden in prisons;
they have become plunder with none to rescue,
spoil with none to say, "Restore!"
23 Who among you will give ear to this,
will attend and listen for the time to come?
24 Who gave up Jacob to the looter,
and Israel to the plunderers?

[1] Or *into coastlands* [2] Or *as the one at peace with me*

Was it not the LORD, against whom
we have sinned,
in whose ways they would not
walk,
and whose law they would not
obey?
25 So he poured on him the heat of his
anger
and the might of battle;
it set him on fire all around, but he
did not understand;
it burned him up, but he did not
take it to heart.

Israel's Only Savior

43 But now thus says the LORD,
he who created you, O Jacob,
he who formed you, O Israel:
"Fear not, for I have redeemed you;
I have called you by name, you are
mine.
2 When you pass through the waters,
I will be with you;
and through the rivers, they shall
not overwhelm you;
when you walk through fire you
shall not be burned,
and the flame shall not consume
you.
3 For I am the LORD your God,
the Holy One of Israel, your Savior.
I give Egypt as your ransom,
Cush and Seba in exchange for you.
4 Because you are precious in my eyes,
and honored, and I love you,
I give men in return for you,
peoples in exchange for your life.
5 Fear not, for I am with you;
I will bring your offspring from
the east,
and from the west I will gather you.
6 I will say to the north, Give up,
and to the south, Do not withhold;
bring my sons from afar
and my daughters from the end of
the earth,
7 everyone who is called by my name,
whom I created for my glory,
whom I formed and made."
8 Bring out the people who are blind,
yet have eyes,
who are deaf, yet have ears!
9 All the nations gather together,
and the peoples assemble.
Who among them can declare this,
and show us the former things?
Let them bring their witnesses to
prove them right,
and let them hear and say, It is true.
10 "You are my witnesses," declares
the LORD,
573
"and my servant whom I have
chosen,
that you may know and believe me
and understand that I am he.
Before me no god was formed,
nor shall there be any after me.
11 I, I am the LORD,
and besides me there is no savior.
12 I declared and saved and proclaimed,
when there was no strange god
among you;
and you are my witnesses," declares
the LORD, "and I am God.
13 Also henceforth I am he;
there is none who can deliver
from my hand;
I work, and who can turn it back?"

14 Thus says the LORD,
your Redeemer, the Holy One of
Israel:
"For your sake I send to Babylon
and bring them all down as
fugitives,
even the Chaldeans, in the ships
in which they rejoice.
15 I am the LORD, your Holy One,
the Creator of Israel, your King."

16 Thus says the LORD,
who makes a way in the sea,
a path in the mighty waters,
17 who brings forth chariot and horse,
army and warrior;

they lie down, they cannot rise,
they are extinguished, quenched like a wick:
18 "Remember not the former things,
nor consider the things of old.
19 Behold, I am doing a new thing;
now it springs forth, do you not perceive it?
I will make a way in the wilderness
and rivers in the desert.
20 The wild beasts will honor me,
the jackals and the ostriches,
for I give water in the wilderness,
rivers in the desert,
to give drink to my chosen people,
21 the people whom I formed for myself
that they might declare my praise.

22 "Yet you did not call upon me, O Jacob;
but you have been weary of me, O Israel!
23 You have not brought me your sheep for burnt offerings,
or honored me with your sacrifices.
I have not burdened you with offerings,
or wearied you with frankincense.
24 You have not bought me sweet cane with money,
or satisfied me with the fat of your sacrifices.
But you have burdened me with your sins;
you have wearied me with your iniquities.

25 "I, I am he
who blots out your transgressions for my own sake,
and I will not remember your sins.
26 Put me in remembrance; let us argue together;
set forth your case, that you may be proved right.
27 Your first father sinned,
and your mediators transgressed against me.
28 Therefore I will profane the princes of the sanctuary,
and deliver Jacob to utter destruction
and Israel to reviling.

Israel the LORD's Chosen

44 "But now hear, O Jacob my servant,
Israel whom I have chosen!
2 Thus says the LORD who made you,
who formed you from the womb and will help you:
Fear not, O Jacob my servant,
Jeshurun whom I have chosen.
3 For I will pour water on the thirsty land,
and streams on the dry ground;
I will pour my Spirit upon your offspring,
and my blessing on your descendants.
4 They shall spring up among the grass
like willows by flowing streams.
5 This one will say, 'I am the LORD's,'
another will call on the name of Jacob,
and another will write on his hand, 'The LORD's,'
and name himself by the name of Israel."

Besides Me There Is No God

573

6 Thus says the LORD, the King of Israel
and his Redeemer, the LORD of hosts:
"I am the first and I am the last;
besides me there is no god.
7 Who is like me? Let him proclaim it.[1]
Let him declare and set it before me,
since I appointed an ancient people.
Let them declare what is to come,
and what will happen.
8 Fear not, nor be afraid;
have I not told you from of old and declared it?
And you are my witnesses!

[1] Or *Who like me can proclaim it?*

Is there a God besides me?
There is no Rock; I know not any."

The Folly of Idolatry

9 All who fashion idols are nothing, and
the things they delight in do not profit.
Their witnesses neither see nor know, that
they may be put to shame. 10 Who fash-
ions a god or casts an idol that is profitable
for nothing? 11 Behold, all his companions
shall be put to shame, and the craftsmen
are only human. Let them all assemble, let
them stand forth. They shall be terrified;
they shall be put to shame together.

12 The ironsmith takes a cutting tool
and works it over the coals. He fashions
it with hammers and works it with his
strong arm. He becomes hungry, and his
strength fails; he drinks no water and is
faint. 13 The carpenter stretches a line; he
marks it out with a pencil. He shapes it
with planes and marks it with a compass.
He shapes it into the figure of a man, with
the beauty of a man, to dwell in a house.
14 He cuts down cedars, or he chooses a
cypress tree or an oak and lets it grow
strong among the trees of the forest. He
plants a cedar and the rain nourishes it.
15 Then it becomes fuel for a man. He takes
a part of it and warms himself; he kindles
a fire and bakes bread. Also he makes a
god and worships it; he makes it an idol
and falls down before it. 16 Half of it he
burns in the fire. Over the half he eats
meat; he roasts it and is satisfied. Also he
warms himself and says, "Aha, I am warm,
I have seen the fire!" 17 And the rest of it he
makes into a god, his idol, and falls down
to it and worships it. He prays to it and
says, "Deliver me, for you are my god!"

18 They know not, nor do they discern,
for he has shut their eyes, so that they can-
not see, and their hearts, so that they can-
not understand. 19 No one considers, nor
is there knowledge or discernment to say,
"Half of it I burned in the fire; I also baked
bread on its coals; I roasted meat and have
eaten. And shall I make the rest of it an
abomination? Shall I fall down before a
block of wood?" 20 He feeds on ashes; a
deluded heart has led him astray, and he
cannot deliver himself or say, "Is there not
a lie in my right hand?"

The LORD Redeems Israel

21 Remember these things, O Jacob,
and Israel, for you are my servant;
I formed you; you are my servant;
O Israel, you will not be forgotten
by me.
22 I have blotted out your
transgressions like a cloud
and your sins like mist;
return to me, for I have redeemed
you.

23 Sing, O heavens, for the LORD has
done it;
shout, O depths of the earth;
break forth into singing, O
mountains,
O forest, and every tree in it!
For the LORD has redeemed Jacob,
and will be glorified[1] in Israel.

24 Thus says the LORD, your Redeemer,
who formed you from the womb:
"I am the LORD, who made all things,
who alone stretched out the
heavens,
who spread out the earth by myself,
25 who frustrates the signs of liars
and makes fools of diviners,
who turns wise men back
and makes their knowledge foolish,
26 who confirms the word of his servant
and fulfills the counsel of his
messengers,
who says of Jerusalem, 'She shall be
inhabited,'
and of the cities of Judah, 'They
shall be built,
and I will raise up their ruins';
27 who says to the deep, 'Be dry;
I will dry up your rivers';

[1] Or *will display his beauty*

28 who says of Cyrus, 'He is my
shepherd,
and he shall fulfill all my
purpose';
saying of Jerusalem, 'She shall be
built,'
and of the temple, 'Your
foundation shall be laid.'"

Cyrus, God's Instrument

45 Thus says the LORD to his
anointed, to Cyrus,
whose right hand I have grasped,
to subdue nations before him
and to loose the belts of kings,
to open doors before him
that gates may not be closed:
2 "I will go before you
and level the exalted places,[1]
I will break in pieces the doors of
bronze
and cut through the bars of iron,
3 I will give you the treasures of
darkness
and the hoards in secret places,
that you may know that it is I, the
LORD,
the God of Israel, who call you by
your name.
4 For the sake of my servant Jacob,
and Israel my chosen,
I call you by your name,
I name you, though you do not
know me.
5 I am the LORD, and there is no other,
besides me there is no God;
I equip you, though you do not
know me,
6 that people may know, from the
rising of the sun
and from the west, that there is
none besides me;
I am the LORD, and there is no
other.
7 I form light and create darkness,
I make well-being and create
calamity,
I am the LORD, who does all these
things.
8 "Shower, O heavens, from above,
and let the clouds rain down
righteousness;
let the earth open, that salvation and
righteousness may bear fruit;
let the earth cause them both to
sprout;
I the LORD have created it.
9 "Woe to him who strives with him
who formed him,
a pot among earthen pots!
Does the clay say to him who forms
it, 'What are you making?'
or 'Your work has no handles'?
10 Woe to him who says to a father,
'What are you begetting?'
or to a woman, 'With what are
you in labor?'"
11 Thus says the LORD,
the Holy One of Israel, and the
one who formed him:
"Ask me of things to come;
will you command me
concerning my children and
the work of my hands?[2]
12 I made the earth
and created man on it;
it was my hands that stretched out
the heavens,
and I commanded all their host.
13 I have stirred him up in
righteousness,
and I will make all his ways level;
he shall build my city
and set my exiles free,
not for price or reward,"
says the LORD of hosts.

[1] Masoretic Text; Dead Sea Scroll, Septuagint *level the mountains* [2] A slight emendation yields *will you question me about my children, or command me concerning the work of my hands?*

The LORD, the Only Savior

14 Thus says the LORD:
"The wealth of Egypt and the
merchandise of Cush,
and the Sabeans, men of stature,
shall come over to you and be yours;
they shall follow you;
they shall come over in chains
and bow down to you.
They will plead with you, saying:
'Surely God is in you, and there is
no other,
no god besides him.'"

15 Truly, you are a God who hides
himself,
O God of Israel, the Savior.
16 All of them are put to shame and
confounded;
the makers of idols go in
confusion together.
17 But Israel is saved by the LORD
with everlasting salvation;
you shall not be put to shame or
confounded
to all eternity.

18 For thus says the LORD,
who created the heavens
(he is God!),
who formed the earth and made it
(he established it;
he did not create it empty,
he formed it to be inhabited!):
"I am the LORD, and there is no other.
19 I did not speak in secret,
in a land of darkness;
I did not say to the offspring of Jacob,
'Seek me in vain.'[1]
I the LORD speak the truth;
I declare what is right.

20 "Assemble yourselves and come;
draw near together,
you survivors of the nations!
They have no knowledge
who carry about their wooden
idols,
and keep on praying to a god
that cannot save.
21 Declare and present your case;
let them take counsel together!
Who told this long ago?
Who declared it of old?
Was it not I, the LORD?
And there is no other god besides
me,
a righteous God and a Savior;
there is none besides me.

593
22 "Turn to me and be saved,
all the ends of the earth!
For I am God, and there is no
other.
23 By myself I have sworn;
from my mouth has gone out in
righteousness
a word that shall not return:
'To me every knee shall bow,
every tongue shall swear
allegiance.'[2]

24 "Only in the LORD, it shall be said of
me,
are righteousness and strength;
to him shall come and be ashamed
all who were incensed against
him.
25 In the LORD all the offspring of Israel
shall be justified and shall glory."

The Idols of Babylon and the One True God

46 Bel bows down; Nebo stoops;
their idols are on beasts and
livestock;
these things you carry are borne
as burdens on weary beasts.
2 They stoop; they bow down together;
they cannot save the burden,
but themselves go into captivity.

3 "Listen to me, O house of Jacob,
all the remnant of the house of
Israel,
who have been borne by me from
before your birth,
carried from the womb;

[1] Hebrew *in emptiness* [2] Septuagint *every tongue shall confess to God*

4 even to your old age I am he,
and to gray hairs I will carry you.
I have made, and I will bear;
I will carry and will save.

5 "To whom will you liken me and
make me equal,
and compare me, that we may be
alike?
6 Those who lavish gold from the purse,
and weigh out silver in the scales,
hire a goldsmith, and he makes it
into a god;
then they fall down and worship!
7 They lift it to their shoulders, they
carry it,
they set it in its place, and it
stands there;
it cannot move from its place.
If one cries to it, it does not answer
or save him from his trouble.

747
8 "Remember this and stand firm,
recall it to mind, you
transgressors,
9 remember the former things of old;
for I am God, and there is no other;
I am God, and there is none like me,
10 declaring the end from the beginning
and from ancient times things
not yet done,
saying, 'My counsel shall stand,
and I will accomplish all my
purpose,'
11 calling a bird of prey from the east,
the man of my counsel from a far
country.
I have spoken, and I will bring it to
pass;
I have purposed, and I will do it.

12 "Listen to me, you stubborn of heart,
you who are far from
righteousness:
13 I bring near my righteousness; it is
not far off,
and my salvation will not delay;
I will put salvation in Zion,
for Israel my glory."

The Humiliation of Babylon

47 Come down and sit in the dust,
O virgin daughter of Babylon;
sit on the ground without a throne,
O daughter of the Chaldeans!
For you shall no more be called
tender and delicate.
2 Take the millstones and grind flour,
put off your veil,
strip off your robe, uncover your legs,
pass through the rivers.
3 Your nakedness shall be uncovered,
and your disgrace shall be seen.
I will take vengeance,
and I will spare no one.
4 Our Redeemer—the LORD of hosts
is his name—
is the Holy One of Israel.

5 Sit in silence, and go into darkness,
O daughter of the Chaldeans;
for you shall no more be called
the mistress of kingdoms.
6 I was angry with my people;
I profaned my heritage;
I gave them into your hand;
you showed them no mercy;
on the aged you made your yoke
exceedingly heavy.
7 You said, "I shall be mistress forever,"
so that you did not lay these
things to heart
or remember their end.

8 Now therefore hear this, you lover
of pleasures,
who sit securely,
who say in your heart,
"I am, and there is no one besides
me;
I shall not sit as a widow
or know the loss of children":
9 These two things shall come to you
in a moment, in one day;
the loss of children and widowhood
shall come upon you in full
measure,

in spite of your many sorceries
and the great power of your enchantments.
10 You felt secure in your wickedness,
you said, "No one sees me";
your wisdom and your knowledge led you astray,
and you said in your heart,
"I am, and there is no one besides me."
11 But evil shall come upon you,
which you will not know how to charm away;
disaster shall fall upon you,
for which you will not be able to atone;
and ruin shall come upon you suddenly,
of which you know nothing.
12 Stand fast in your enchantments
and your many sorceries,
with which you have labored from your youth;
perhaps you may be able to succeed;
perhaps you may inspire terror.
13 You are wearied with your many counsels;
let them stand forth and save you,
those who divide the heavens,
who gaze at the stars,
who at the new moons make known
what shall come upon you.
14 Behold, they are like stubble;
the fire consumes them;
they cannot deliver themselves
from the power of the flame.
No coal for warming oneself is this,
no fire to sit before!
15 Such to you are those with whom you have labored,
who have done business with you from your youth;
they wander about, each in his own direction;
there is no one to save you.

Israel Refined for God's Glory

48 Hear this, O house of Jacob,
who are called by the name of Israel,
and who came from the waters of Judah,
who swear by the name of the LORD
and confess the God of Israel,
but not in truth or right.
2 For they call themselves after the holy city,
and stay themselves on the God of Israel;
the LORD of hosts is his name.
3 "The former things I declared of old;
they went out from my mouth, and I announced them;
then suddenly I did them, and they came to pass.
4 Because I know that you are obstinate,
and your neck is an iron sinew
and your forehead brass,
5 I declared them to you from of old,
before they came to pass I announced them to you,
lest you should say, 'My idol did them,
my carved image and my metal image commanded them.'
6 "You have heard; now see all this;
and will you not declare it?
From this time forth I announce to you new things,
hidden things that you have not known.
7 They are created now, not long ago;
before today you have never heard of them,
lest you should say, 'Behold, I knew them.'
8 You have never heard, you have never known,
from of old your ear has not been opened.

For I knew that you would surely deal treacherously,
and that from before birth you were called a rebel.

9 "For my name's sake I defer my anger,
for the sake of my praise I restrain it for you,
that I may not cut you off.
10 Behold, I have refined you, but not as silver;
I have tried[1] you in the furnace of affliction.
11 For my own sake, for my own sake, I do it,
for how should my name[2] be profaned?
My glory I will not give to another.

The LORD's Call to Israel

12 "Listen to me, O Jacob,
and Israel, whom I called!
I am he; I am the first,
and I am the last.
13 My hand laid the foundation of the earth,
and my right hand spread out the heavens;
when I call to them,
they stand forth together.

14 "Assemble, all of you, and listen!
Who among them has declared these things?
The LORD loves him;
he shall perform his purpose on Babylon,
and his arm shall be against the Chaldeans.
15 I, even I, have spoken and called him;
I have brought him, and he will prosper in his way.
16 Draw near to me, hear this:
from the beginning I have not spoken in secret,
from the time it came to be I have been there."
And now the Lord GOD has sent me,
and his Spirit.

17 Thus says the LORD,
your Redeemer, the Holy One of Israel:
"I am the LORD your God,
who teaches you to profit,
who leads you in the way you should go.
18 Oh that you had paid attention to my commandments!
Then your peace would have been like a river,
and your righteousness like the waves of the sea;
19 your offspring would have been like the sand,
and your descendants like its grains;
their name would never be cut off
or destroyed from before me."

20 Go out from Babylon, flee from Chaldea,
declare this with a shout of joy, proclaim it,
send it out to the end of the earth;
say, "The LORD has redeemed his servant Jacob!"
21 They did not thirst when he led them through the deserts;
he made water flow for them from the rock;
he split the rock and the water gushed out.

22 "There is no peace," says the LORD,
"for the wicked."

The Servant of the LORD

49 Listen to me, O coastlands,
and give attention, you peoples from afar.
The LORD called me from the womb,
from the body of my mother he named my name.

[1] Or *I have chosen* [2] Hebrew lacks *my name*

2 He made my mouth like a sharp
sword;
in the shadow of his hand he hid
me;
he made me a polished arrow;
in his quiver he hid me away.
3 And he said to me, "You are my
servant,
Israel, in whom I will be glorified."[1]
4 But I said, "I have labored in vain;
I have spent my strength for
nothing and vanity;
yet surely my right is with the LORD,
and my recompense with my God."

1297
5 And now the LORD says,
he who formed me from the
womb to be his servant,
to bring Jacob back to him;
and that Israel might be gathered
to him—
for I am honored in the eyes of the
LORD,
and my God has become my
strength—
1449
6 he says:
"It is too light a thing that you
should be my servant
to raise up the tribes of Jacob
and to bring back the preserved of
Israel;
I will make you as a light for the
nations,
that my salvation may reach to
the end of the earth."

7 Thus says the LORD,
the Redeemer of Israel and his
Holy One,
to one deeply despised, abhorred by
the nation,
the servant of rulers:
"Kings shall see and arise;
princes, and they shall prostrate
themselves;
because of the LORD, who is faithful,
the Holy One of Israel, who has
chosen you."

The Restoration of Israel

8 Thus says the LORD:
"In a time of favor I have answered
you;
in a day of salvation I have helped
you;
I will keep you and give you
as a covenant to the people,
to establish the land,
to apportion the desolate heritages,
9 saying to the prisoners, 'Come out,'
to those who are in darkness,
'Appear.'
They shall feed along the ways;
on all bare heights shall be their
pasture;
10 they shall not hunger or thirst,
neither scorching wind nor sun
shall strike them,
for he who has pity on them will
lead them,
and by springs of water will guide
them.
11 And I will make all my mountains a
road,
and my highways shall be raised
up.
12 Behold, these shall come from afar,
and behold, these from the north
and from the west,[2]
and these from the land of Syene."[3]

13 Sing for joy, O heavens, and exult, O
earth;
break forth, O mountains, into
singing!
For the LORD has comforted his
people
and will have compassion on his
afflicted.

14 But Zion said, "The LORD has
forsaken me;
my Lord has forgotten me."

[1] Or *I will display my beauty* [2] Hebrew *from the sea* [3] Dead Sea Scroll; Masoretic Text *Sinim*

15 "Can a woman forget her nursing child,
that she should have no compassion on the son of her womb?
Even these may forget,
yet I will not forget you.
16 Behold, I have engraved you on the palms of my hands;
your walls are continually before me.
17 Your builders make haste;[1]
your destroyers and those who laid you waste go out from you.
18 Lift up your eyes around and see;
they all gather, they come to you.
As I live, declares the LORD,
you shall put them all on as an ornament;
you shall bind them on as a bride does.
19 "Surely your waste and your desolate places
and your devastated land—
surely now you will be too narrow for your inhabitants,
and those who swallowed you up will be far away.
20 The children of your bereavement will yet say in your ears:
'The place is too narrow for me;
make room for me to dwell in.'
21 Then you will say in your heart:
'Who has borne me these?
I was bereaved and barren,
exiled and put away,
but who has brought up these?
Behold, I was left alone;
from where have these come?'"
22 Thus says the Lord GOD:
"Behold, I will lift up my hand to the nations,
and raise my signal to the peoples;
and they shall bring your sons in their bosom,
and your daughters shall be carried on their shoulders.
23 Kings shall be your foster fathers,
and their queens your nursing mothers.
With their faces to the ground they shall bow down to you,
and lick the dust of your feet.
Then you will know that I am the LORD;
those who wait for me shall not be put to shame."
24 Can the prey be taken from the mighty,
or the captives of a tyrant[2] be rescued?
25 For thus says the LORD:
"Even the captives of the mighty shall be taken,
and the prey of the tyrant be rescued,
for I will contend with those who contend with you,
and I will save your children.
26 I will make your oppressors eat their own flesh,
and they shall be drunk with their own blood as with wine.
Then all flesh shall know
that I am the LORD your Savior,
and your Redeemer, the Mighty One of Jacob."

Israel's Sin and the Servant's Obedience

50 Thus says the LORD:
"Where is your mother's certificate of divorce,
with which I sent her away?
Or which of my creditors is it
to whom I have sold you?
Behold, for your iniquities you were sold,
and for your transgressions your mother was sent away.
2 Why, when I came, was there no man;
why, when I called, was there no one to answer?

[1] Dead Sea Scroll; Masoretic Text *Your children make haste* [2] Dead Sea Scroll, Syriac, Vulgate (see also verse 25); Masoretic Text *of a righteous man*

Is my hand shortened, that it
cannot redeem?
Or have I no power to deliver?
Behold, by my rebuke I dry up the sea,
I make the rivers a desert;
their fish stink for lack of water
and die of thirst.
3 I clothe the heavens with blackness
and make sackcloth their covering."

4 The Lord GOD has given me
the tongue of those who are taught,
that I may know how to sustain
with a word
him who is weary.
Morning by morning he awakens;
he awakens my ear
to hear as those who are taught.
5 The Lord GOD has opened my ear,
and I was not rebellious;
I turned not backward.
6 I gave my back to those who strike,
and my cheeks to those who pull
out the beard;
I hid not my face
from disgrace and spitting.

7 But the Lord GOD helps me;
therefore I have not been disgraced;
therefore I have set my face like a
flint,
and I know that I shall not be put
to shame.
8 He who vindicates me is near.
Who will contend with me?
Let us stand up together.
Who is my adversary?
Let him come near to me.
9 Behold, the Lord GOD helps me;
who will declare me guilty?
Behold, all of them will wear out
like a garment;
the moth will eat them up.

10 Who among you fears the LORD
and obeys the voice of his servant?
Let him who walks in darkness
and has no light
trust in the name of the LORD
and rely on his God.
11 Behold, all you who kindle a fire,
who equip yourselves with
burning torches!
Walk by the light of your fire,
and by the torches that you have
kindled!
This you have from my hand:
you shall lie down in torment.

The LORD's Comfort for Zion

51 "Listen to me, you who pursue
righteousness,
you who seek the LORD:
look to the rock from which you
were hewn,
and to the quarry from which you
were dug.
2 Look to Abraham your father
and to Sarah who bore you;
for he was but one when I called him,
that I might bless him and
multiply him.
3 For the LORD comforts Zion;
he comforts all her waste places
and makes her wilderness like Eden,
her desert like the garden of the
LORD;
joy and gladness will be found in her,
thanksgiving and the voice of song.

4 "Give attention to me, my people,
and give ear to me, my nation;
for a law[1] will go out from me,
and I will set my justice for a light
to the peoples.
5 My righteousness draws near,
my salvation has gone out,
and my arms will judge the
peoples;
the coastlands hope for me,
and for my arm they wait.
6 Lift up your eyes to the heavens,
and look at the earth beneath;
for the heavens vanish like smoke,
the earth will wear out like a
garment,

[1] Or *for teaching*; also verse 7

and they who dwell in it will die
in like manner;[1]
but my salvation will be forever,
and my righteousness will never
be dismayed.

7 "Listen to me, you who know
righteousness,
the people in whose heart is my
law;
fear not the reproach of man,
nor be dismayed at their revilings.
8 For the moth will eat them up like a
garment,
and the worm will eat them like
wool;
but my righteousness will be forever,
and my salvation to all
generations."

9 Awake, awake, put on strength,
O arm of the LORD;
awake, as in days of old,
the generations of long ago.
Was it not you who cut Rahab in
pieces,
who pierced the dragon?
10 Was it not you who dried up the
sea,
161 the waters of the great deep,
who made the depths of the sea a way
for the redeemed to pass over?
11 And the ransomed of the LORD shall
return
and come to Zion with singing;
everlasting joy shall be upon their
heads;
they shall obtain gladness and joy,
and sorrow and sighing shall flee
away.

12 "I, I am he who comforts you;
who are you that you are afraid of
man who dies,
of the son of man who is made
like grass,
13 and have forgotten the LORD, your
Maker,
who stretched out the heavens
and laid the foundations of the
earth,
and you fear continually all the day
because of the wrath of the
oppressor,
when he sets himself to destroy?
And where is the wrath of the
oppressor?
14 He who is bowed down shall
speedily be released;
he shall not die and go down to
the pit,
neither shall his bread be lacking.
15 I am the LORD your God,
who stirs up the sea so that its
waves roar—
the LORD of hosts is his name.
16 And I have put my words in your
mouth
and covered you in the shadow of
my hand,
establishing[2] the heavens
and laying the foundations of the
earth,
and saying to Zion, 'You are my
people.'"

17 Wake yourself, wake yourself,
stand up, O Jerusalem,
you who have drunk from the hand
of the LORD
the cup of his wrath,
who have drunk to the dregs
the bowl, the cup of staggering.
18 There is none to guide her
among all the sons she has borne;
there is none to take her by the hand
among all the sons she has
brought up.
19 These two things have happened to
you—
who will console you?—
devastation and destruction,
famine and sword;
who will comfort you?[3]
20 Your sons have fainted;
they lie at the head of every street
like an antelope in a net;

[1] Or *will die like gnats* [2] Or *planting* [3] Dead Sea Scroll, Septuagint, Syriac, Vulgate; Masoretic Text *how shall I comfort you*

they are full of the wrath of the LORD,
the rebuke of your God.

21 Therefore hear this, you who are afflicted,
who are drunk, but not with wine:
22 Thus says your Lord, the LORD,
your God who pleads the cause of his people:
"Behold, I have taken from your hand the cup of staggering;
the bowl of my wrath you shall drink no more;
23 and I will put it into the hand of your tormentors,
who have said to you,
'Bow down, that we may pass over';
and you have made your back like the ground
and like the street for them to pass over."

The LORD's Coming Salvation

52 Awake, awake,
put on your strength, O Zion;
put on your beautiful garments,
O Jerusalem, the holy city;
for there shall no more come into you
the uncircumcised and the unclean.
2 Shake yourself from the dust and arise;
be seated, O Jerusalem;
loose the bonds from your neck,
O captive daughter of Zion.

3 For thus says the LORD: "You were sold
for nothing, and you shall be redeemed
without money." 4 For thus says the Lord
GOD: "My people went down at the first
into Egypt to sojourn there, and the
Assyrian oppressed them for nothing.
5 Now therefore what have I here," declares
the LORD, "seeing that my people are
taken away for nothing? Their rulers wail,"
declares the LORD, "and continually all the
day my name is despised. 6 Therefore my
people shall know my name. Therefore in
that day they shall know that it is I who
speak; here am I."

7 How beautiful upon the mountains
are the feet of him who brings good news,
who publishes peace, who brings good news of happiness,
who publishes salvation,
who says to Zion, "Your God reigns."
8 The voice of your watchmen—they lift up their voice;
together they sing for joy;
for eye to eye they see
the return of the LORD to Zion.
9 Break forth together into singing,
you waste places of Jerusalem,
for the LORD has comforted his people;
he has redeemed Jerusalem.
1449
10 The LORD has bared his holy arm
before the eyes of all the nations,
and all the ends of the earth shall see
the salvation of our God.

11 Depart, depart, go out from there;
touch no unclean thing;
go out from the midst of her; purify yourselves,
you who bear the vessels of the LORD.
12 For you shall not go out in haste,
and you shall not go in flight,
for the LORD will go before you,
and the God of Israel will be your rear guard.

He Was Wounded for Our Transgressions

13 Behold, my servant shall act wisely;[1]
he shall be high and lifted up,
and shall be exalted.
14 As many were astonished at you—
his appearance was so marred,
beyond human semblance,
and his form beyond that of the children of mankind—

[1] Or *shall prosper*

15 so shall he sprinkle[1] many nations;
kings shall shut their mouths
because of him;
for that which has not been told
them they see,
and that which they have not
heard they understand.

53

1361,
1633

Who has believed what
he has heard from us?[2]
And to whom has the arm of
the LORD been revealed?
2 For he grew up before him like a
young plant,
and like a root out of dry ground;
he had no form or majesty that we
should look at him,
and no beauty that we should
desire him.
3 He was despised and rejected[3] by
men;
a man of sorrows,[4] and
acquainted with[5] grief;[6]
and as one from whom men hide
their faces[7]
he was despised, and we
esteemed him not.

4 Surely he has borne our griefs
and carried our sorrows;
yet we esteemed him stricken,
smitten by God, and afflicted.
5 But he was wounded for our
transgressions;
he was crushed for our iniquities;
upon him was the chastisement
that brought us peace,
and with his stripes we are
healed.
6 All we like sheep have gone astray;
we have turned—every one—to
his own way;
and the LORD has laid on him
the iniquity of us all.

7 He was oppressed, and he was
afflicted,
yet he opened not his mouth;
like a lamb that is led to the
slaughter,
and like a sheep that before its
shearers is silent,
so he opened not his mouth.
8 By oppression and judgment he was
taken away;
and as for his generation, who
considered
that he was cut off out of the land of
the living,
stricken for the transgression of
my people?
9 And they made his grave with the
wicked
and with a rich man in his death,
although he had done no violence,
and there was no deceit in his
mouth.

10 Yet it was the will of the LORD to
crush him;
he has put him to grief;[8]
when his soul makes[9] an offering
for guilt,
he shall see his offspring; he shall
prolong his days;
the will of the LORD shall prosper in
his hand.
11 Out of the anguish of his soul he
shall see[10] and be satisfied;
by his knowledge shall the
righteous one, my servant,
make many to be accounted
righteous,
and he shall bear their iniquities.
12 Therefore I will divide him a
portion with the many,[11]
and he shall divide the spoil with
the strong,[12]
because he poured out his soul to
death
and was numbered with the
transgressors;
yet he bore the sin of many,
and makes intercession for the
transgressors.

[1] *Or startle* [2] *Or Who has believed what we have heard?* [3] *Or forsaken* [4] *Or pains;* also verse 4 [5] *Or and knowing* [6] *Or sickness;* also verse 4 [7] *Or as one who hides his face from us* [8] *Or he has made him sick* [9] *Or when you make his soul* [10] Masoretic Text; Dead Sea Scroll *he shall see light* [11] *Or with the great* [12] *Or with the numerous*

The Eternal Covenant of Peace

54 "Sing, O barren one, who did not bear;
break forth into singing and cry aloud,
you who have not been in labor!
For the children of the desolate one will be more
than the children of her who is married," says the LORD.
2 "Enlarge the place of your tent,
and let the curtains of your habitations be stretched out;
do not hold back; lengthen your cords
and strengthen your stakes.
3 For you will spread abroad to the right and to the left,
and your offspring will possess the nations
and will people the desolate cities.

4 "Fear not, for you will not be ashamed;
be not confounded, for you will not be disgraced;
for you will forget the shame of your youth,
and the reproach of your widowhood you will remember no more.
5 For your Maker is your husband,
the LORD of hosts is his name;
and the Holy One of Israel is your Redeemer,
the God of the whole earth he is called.
6 For the LORD has called you
like a wife deserted and grieved in spirit,
like a wife of youth when she is cast off,
says your God.
7 For a brief moment I deserted you,
but with great compassion I will gather you.
8 In overflowing anger for a moment
I hid my face from you,
but with everlasting love I will have compassion on you,"
says the LORD, your Redeemer.

9 "This is like the days of Noah[1] to me:
as I swore that the waters of Noah should no more go over the earth,
so I have sworn that I will not be angry with you,
and will not rebuke you.
10 For the mountains may depart
and the hills be removed,
but my steadfast love shall not depart from you,
and my covenant of peace shall not be removed,"
says the LORD, who has compassion on you.

11 "O afflicted one, storm-tossed and not comforted,
behold, I will set your stones in antimony,
and lay your foundations with sapphires.[2]
12 I will make your pinnacles of agate,[3]
your gates of carbuncles,[4]
and all your wall of precious stones.
13 All your children shall be taught by the LORD,
and great shall be the peace of your children.
14 In righteousness you shall be established;
you shall be far from oppression,
for you shall not fear;
and from terror, for it shall not come near you.
15 If anyone stirs up strife,
it is not from me;
whoever stirs up strife with you
shall fall because of you.
16 Behold, I have created the smith
who blows the fire of coals
and produces a weapon for its purpose.
I have also created the ravager to destroy;

[1] Some manuscripts *For this is as the waters of Noah* [2] Or *lapis lazuli* [3] Or *jasper, or ruby* [4] Or *crystal*

17 no weapon that is fashioned
against you shall succeed,
and you shall confute every
tongue that rises against you
in judgment.
This is the heritage of the servants
of the LORD
and their vindication[1] from me,
declares the LORD."

The Compassion of the LORD

55 "Come, everyone who
thirsts,
1553 come to the waters;
and he who has no money,
come, buy and eat!
Come, buy wine and milk
without money and without price.
2 Why do you spend your money for
that which is not bread,
and your labor for that which
does not satisfy?
Listen diligently to me, and eat what
is good,
and delight yourselves in rich food.
3 Incline your ear, and come to
me;
499 hear, that your soul may live;
and I will make with you an
everlasting covenant,
my steadfast, sure love for David.
4 Behold, I made him a witness to the
peoples,
a leader and commander for the
peoples.
5 Behold, you shall call a nation that
you do not know,
and a nation that did not know
you shall run to you,
because of the LORD your God, and
of the Holy One of Israel,
for he has glorified you.

6 "Seek the LORD while he may be
found;
call upon him while he is near;
7 let the wicked forsake his way,
and the unrighteous man his
thoughts;
let him return to the LORD, that he
may have compassion on him,
and to our God, for he will
abundantly pardon.
8 For my thoughts are not your
thoughts,
neither are your ways my ways,
declares the LORD.
9 For as the heavens are higher than
the earth,
so are my ways higher than your
ways
and my thoughts than your
thoughts.

10 "For as the rain and the snow
come down from heaven
747 and do not return there but
water the earth,
making it bring forth and sprout,
giving seed to the sower and
bread to the eater,
11 so shall my word be that goes out
from my mouth;
it shall not return to me empty,
but it shall accomplish that which I
purpose,
and shall succeed in the thing for
which I sent it.

12 "For you shall go out in joy
and be led forth in peace;
the mountains and the hills before
you
shall break forth into singing,
and all the trees of the field shall
clap their hands.
13 Instead of the thorn shall come up
the cypress;
instead of the brier shall come up
the myrtle;
and it shall make a name for the
LORD,
an everlasting sign that shall not
be cut off."

[1] Or *righteousness*

Salvation for Foreigners

56 Thus says the LORD:
"Keep justice, and do righteousness,
for soon my salvation will come,
and my deliverance be revealed.
2 Blessed is the man who does this,
and the son of man who holds it fast,
who keeps the Sabbath, not profaning it,
and keeps his hand from doing any evil."

3 Let not the foreigner who has joined himself to the LORD say,
"The LORD will surely separate me from his people";
and let not the eunuch say,
"Behold, I am a dry tree."
4 For thus says the LORD:
"To the eunuchs who keep my Sabbaths,
who choose the things that please me
and hold fast my covenant,
5 I will give in my house and within my walls
a monument and a name
better than sons and daughters;
I will give them an everlasting name
that shall not be cut off.

6 "And the foreigners who join themselves to the LORD,
to minister to him, to love the name of the LORD,
and to be his servants,
everyone who keeps the Sabbath and does not profane it,
and holds fast my covenant—
7 these I will bring to my holy mountain,
and make them joyful in my house of prayer;
their burnt offerings and their sacrifices
will be accepted on my altar;
for my house shall be called a house of prayer
for all peoples."
8 The Lord GOD,
who gathers the outcasts of Israel, declares,
"I will gather yet others to him
besides those already gathered."

Israel's Irresponsible Leaders

9 All you beasts of the field, come to devour—
all you beasts in the forest.
10 His watchmen are blind;
they are all without knowledge;
they are all silent dogs;
they cannot bark,
dreaming, lying down,
loving to slumber.
11 The dogs have a mighty appetite;
they never have enough.
But they are shepherds who have no understanding;
they have all turned to their own way,
each to his own gain, one and all.
12 "Come," they say, "let me get wine;
let us fill ourselves with strong drink;
and tomorrow will be like this day,
great beyond measure."

Israel's Futile Idolatry

57 The righteous man perishes,
and no one lays it to heart;
devout men are taken away,
while no one understands.
For the righteous man is taken away from calamity;
2 he enters into peace;
they rest in their beds
who walk in their uprightness.
3 But you, draw near,
sons of the sorceress,
offspring of the adulterer and the loose woman.
4 Whom are you mocking?

Against whom do you open your
mouth wide
and stick out your tongue?
Are you not children of transgression,
the offspring of deceit,
5 you who burn with lust among the
oaks,[1]
under every green tree,
who slaughter your children in the
valleys,
under the clefts of the rocks?
6 Among the smooth stones of the
valley is your portion;
they, they, are your lot;
to them you have poured out a
drink offering,
you have brought a grain offering.
Shall I relent for these things?
7 On a high and lofty mountain
you have set your bed,
and there you went up to offer
sacrifice.
8 Behind the door and the doorpost
you have set up your memorial;
for, deserting me, you have
uncovered your bed,
you have gone up to it,
you have made it wide;
and you have made a covenant for
yourself with them,
you have loved their bed,
you have looked on nakedness.[2]
9 You journeyed to the king with oil
and multiplied your perfumes;
you sent your envoys far off,
and sent down even to Sheol.
10 You were wearied with the length of
your way,
but you did not say, "It is hopeless";
you found new life for your strength,
and so you were not faint.[3]
11 Whom did you dread and fear,
so that you lied,
and did not remember me,
did not lay it to heart?
Have I not held my peace, even for a
long time,
and you do not fear me?
12 I will declare your righteousness
and your deeds,
but they will not profit you.
13 When you cry out, let your
collection of idols deliver you!
The wind will carry them off,
a breath will take them away.
But he who takes refuge in me shall
possess the land
and shall inherit my holy
mountain.

Comfort for the Contrite

14 And it shall be said,
"Build up, build up, prepare the way,
remove every obstruction from
my people's way."
15 For thus says the One who is high
and lifted up,
who inhabits eternity, whose
name is Holy:
"I dwell in the high and holy place,
and also with him who is of a
contrite and lowly spirit,
to revive the spirit of the lowly,
and to revive the heart of the
contrite.
16 For I will not contend forever,
nor will I always be angry;
for the spirit would grow faint
before me,
and the breath of life that I made.
17 Because of the iniquity of his unjust
gain I was angry,
I struck him; I hid my face and
was angry,
but he went on backsliding in the
way of his own heart.
18 I have seen his ways, but I will heal
him;
I will lead him and restore comfort
to him and his mourners,
19 creating the fruit of the lips.
Peace, peace, to the far and to the
near," says the LORD,
"and I will heal him.

[1] *Or among the terebinths* [2] *Or on a monument* (see 56:5); *Hebrew on a hand* [3] *Hebrew and so you were not sick*

20 But the wicked are like the tossing
sea;
for it cannot be quiet,
and its waters toss up mire and dirt.
21 There is no peace," says my God,
"for the wicked."

True and False Fasting

58 "Cry aloud; do not hold back;
lift up your voice like a trumpet;
declare to my people their
transgression,
to the house of Jacob their sins.
2 Yet they seek me daily
and delight to know my ways,
as if they were a nation that did
righteousness
and did not forsake the judgment
of their God;
they ask of me righteous judgments;
they delight to draw near to God.
3 'Why have we fasted, and you see it
not?
Why have we humbled
ourselves, and you take no
knowledge of it?'
Behold, in the day of your fast you
seek your own pleasure,[1]
and oppress all your workers.
4 Behold, you fast only to quarrel and
to fight
and to hit with a wicked fist.
Fasting like yours this day
will not make your voice to be
heard on high.
5 Is such the fast that I choose,
a day for a person to humble
himself?
Is it to bow down his head like a reed,
and to spread sackcloth and ashes
under him?
Will you call this a fast,
and a day acceptable to the LORD?
6 "Is not this the fast that I choose:
to loose the bonds of wickedness,
to undo the straps of the yoke,
to let the oppressed[2] go free,
and to break every yoke?
7 Is it not to share your bread with the
hungry
and bring the homeless poor into
your house;
when you see the naked, to cover
him,
and not to hide yourself from
your own flesh?
8 Then shall your light break forth
like the dawn,
and your healing shall spring up
speedily;
your righteousness shall go before
you;
the glory of the LORD shall be your
rear guard.
9 Then you shall call, and the LORD
will answer;
you shall cry, and he will say,
'Here I am.'
If you take away the yoke from your
midst,
the pointing of the finger, and
speaking wickedness,
10 if you pour yourself out for the
hungry
and satisfy the desire of the
afflicted,
then shall your light rise in the
darkness
and your gloom be as the noonday.
11 And the LORD will guide you
continually
and satisfy your desire in
scorched places
and make your bones strong;
and you shall be like a watered
garden,
like a spring of water,
whose waters do not fail.
12 And your ancient ruins shall be
rebuilt;
you shall raise up the foundations
of many generations;

[1] *Or pursue your own business* [2] *Or bruised*

you shall be called the repairer of
the breach,
the restorer of streets to dwell in.

13 "If you turn back your foot from the
Sabbath,
from doing your pleasure[1] on my
holy day,
and call the Sabbath a delight
and the holy day of the LORD
honorable;
if you honor it, not going your own
ways,
or seeking your own pleasure,[2] or
talking idly;[3]
14 then you shall take delight in the
LORD,
and I will make you ride on the
heights of the earth;[4]
I will feed you with the heritage of
Jacob your father,
for the mouth of the LORD has
spoken."

Evil and Oppression

59 Behold, the LORD's hand is not
shortened, that it cannot save,
or his ear dull, that it cannot hear;
2 but your iniquities have made a
separation
between you and your God,
and your sins have hidden his face
from you
so that he does not hear.
3 For your hands are defiled with blood
and your fingers with iniquity;
your lips have spoken lies;
your tongue mutters wickedness.
4 No one enters suit justly;
no one goes to law honestly;
they rely on empty pleas, they speak
lies,
they conceive mischief and give
birth to iniquity.
5 They hatch adders' eggs;
they weave the spider's web;
he who eats their eggs dies,
and from one that is crushed a
viper is hatched.
6 Their webs will not serve as clothing;
men will not cover themselves
with what they make.
Their works are works of iniquity,
and deeds of violence are in their
hands.
7 Their feet run to evil,
and they are swift to shed
innocent blood;
their thoughts are thoughts of
iniquity;
desolation and destruction are in
their highways.
8 The way of peace they do not know,
and there is no justice in their
paths;
they have made their roads crooked;
no one who treads on them
knows peace.
9 Therefore justice is far from us,
and righteousness does not
overtake us;
we hope for light, and behold,
darkness,
and for brightness, but we walk in
gloom.
10 We grope for the wall like the blind;
we grope like those who have no
eyes;
we stumble at noon as in the twilight,
among those in full vigor we are
like dead men.
11 We all growl like bears;
we moan and moan like doves;
we hope for justice, but there is none;
for salvation, but it is far from us.
12 For our transgressions are
multiplied before you,
and our sins testify against us;
for our transgressions are with us,
and we know our iniquities:
13 transgressing, and denying the LORD,
and turning back from following
our God,

[1] *Or business* [2] *Or pursuing your own business* [3] *Hebrew or speaking a word* [4] *Or of the land*

speaking oppression and revolt,
conceiving and uttering from the heart lying words.
14 Justice is turned back,
and righteousness stands far away;
for truth has stumbled in the public squares,
and uprightness cannot enter.
15 Truth is lacking,
and he who departs from evil makes himself a prey.

Judgment and Redemption

The LORD saw it, and it displeased him[1]
that there was no justice.
16 He saw that there was no man,
and wondered that there was no one to intercede;
then his own arm brought him salvation,
and his righteousness upheld him.
17 He put on righteousness as a breastplate,
and a helmet of salvation on his head;
he put on garments of vengeance for clothing,
and wrapped himself in zeal as a cloak.
18 According to their deeds, so will he repay,
wrath to his adversaries, repayment to his enemies;
to the coastlands he will render repayment.
19 So they shall fear the name of the LORD from the west,
and his glory from the rising of the sun;
for he will come like a rushing stream,[2]
which the wind of the LORD drives.
20 "And a Redeemer will come to Zion,
to those in Jacob who turn from transgression," declares the LORD.

21 "And as for me, this is my covenant with
them," says the LORD: "My Spirit that is
upon you, and my words that I have put in
your mouth, shall not depart out of your
mouth, or out of the mouth of your off-
spring, or out of the mouth of your chil-
dren's offspring," says the LORD, "from
this time forth and forevermore."

The Future Glory of Israel

60 Arise, shine, for your light has come,
and the glory of the LORD has risen upon you.
2 For behold, darkness shall cover the earth,
and thick darkness the peoples;
but the LORD will arise upon you,
and his glory will be seen upon you.
3 And nations shall come to your light,
and kings to the brightness of your rising.

4 Lift up your eyes all around, and see;
they all gather together, they come to you;
your sons shall come from afar,
and your daughters shall be carried on the hip.
5 Then you shall see and be radiant;
your heart shall thrill and exult,[3]
because the abundance of the sea shall be turned to you,
the wealth of the nations shall come to you.
6 A multitude of camels shall cover you,
the young camels of Midian and Ephah;
all those from Sheba shall come.
They shall bring gold and frankincense,
and shall bring good news, the praises of the LORD.
7 All the flocks of Kedar shall be gathered to you;
the rams of Nebaioth shall minister to you;

[1] Hebrew *and it was evil in his eyes* [2] Hebrew *a narrow river* [3] Hebrew *your heart shall tremble and grow wide*

they shall come up with acceptance
on my altar,
and I will beautify my beautiful
house.

8 Who are these that fly like a cloud,
and like doves to their windows?
9 For the coastlands shall hope for me,
the ships of Tarshish first,
to bring your children from afar,
their silver and gold with them,
for the name of the LORD your God,
and for the Holy One of Israel,
because he has made you beautiful.

10 Foreigners shall build up your walls,
and their kings shall minister to
you;
for in my wrath I struck you,
but in my favor I have had mercy
on you.
11 Your gates shall be open continually;
day and night they shall not be
shut,
that people may bring to you the
wealth of the nations,
with their kings led in procession.
12 For the nation and kingdom
that will not serve you shall perish;
those nations shall be utterly laid
waste.
13 The glory of Lebanon shall come to
you,
the cypress, the plane, and the pine,
to beautify the place of my sanctuary,
and I will make the place of my
feet glorious.
14 The sons of those who afflicted you
shall come bending low to you,
and all who despised you
shall bow down at your feet;
they shall call you the City of the
LORD,
the Zion of the Holy One of Israel.

15 Whereas you have been forsaken
and hated,
with no one passing through,
I will make you majestic forever,
a joy from age to age.
16 You shall suck the milk of nations;
you shall nurse at the breast of
kings;
and you shall know that I, the LORD,
am your Savior
and your Redeemer, the Mighty
One of Jacob.

1847
17 Instead of bronze I will bring gold,
and instead of iron I will bring
silver;
instead of wood, bronze,
instead of stones, iron.
I will make your overseers peace
and your taskmasters
righteousness.
18 Violence shall no more be heard in
your land,
devastation or destruction within
your borders;
you shall call your walls Salvation,
and your gates Praise.

19 The sun shall be no more
your light by day,
nor for brightness shall the moon
give you light;[1]
but the LORD will be your
everlasting light,
and your God will be your glory.[2]
20 Your sun shall no more go down,
nor your moon withdraw itself;
for the LORD will be your everlasting
light,
and your days of mourning shall
be ended.
21 Your people shall all be righteous;
they shall possess the land
forever,
the branch of my planting, the work
of my hands,
that I might be glorified.[3]
22 The least one shall become a clan,
and the smallest one a mighty
nation;
I am the LORD;
in its time I will hasten it.

[1] Masoretic Text; Dead Sea Scroll, Septuagint, Targum add *by night* [2] Or *your beauty* [3] Or *that I might display my beauty*

The Year of the LORD's Favor

61 The Spirit of the Lord GOD is upon me,
because the LORD has anointed me
to bring good news to the poor;[1]
he has sent me to bind up the brokenhearted,
to proclaim liberty to the captives,
and the opening of the prison to those who are bound;[2]
2 to proclaim the year of the LORD's favor,
and the day of vengeance of our God;
to comfort all who mourn;
3 to grant to those who mourn in Zion—
to give them a beautiful headdress instead of ashes,
the oil of gladness instead of mourning,
the garment of praise instead of a faint spirit;
that they may be called oaks of righteousness,
the planting of the LORD, that he may be glorified.[3]
4 They shall build up the ancient ruins;
they shall raise up the former devastations;
they shall repair the ruined cities,
the devastations of many generations.

5 Strangers shall stand and tend your flocks;
foreigners shall be your plowmen and vinedressers;
6 but you shall be called the priests of the LORD;
they shall speak of you as the ministers of our God;
you shall eat the wealth of the nations,
and in their glory you shall boast.
7 Instead of your shame there shall be a double portion;
instead of dishonor they shall rejoice in their lot;
therefore in their land they shall possess a double portion;
they shall have everlasting joy.

8 For I the LORD love justice;
I hate robbery and wrong;[4]
I will faithfully give them their recompense,
and I will make an everlasting covenant with them.
9 Their offspring shall be known among the nations,
and their descendants in the midst of the peoples;
all who see them shall acknowledge them,
that they are an offspring the LORD has blessed.

10 I will greatly rejoice in the LORD;
my soul shall exult in my God,
for he has clothed me with the garments of salvation;
he has covered me with the robe of righteousness,
as a bridegroom decks himself like a priest with a beautiful headdress,
and as a bride adorns herself with her jewels.
11 For as the earth brings forth its sprouts,
and as a garden causes what is sown in it to sprout up,
so the Lord GOD will cause righteousness and praise
to sprout up before all the nations.

Zion's Coming Salvation

62 For Zion's sake I will not keep silent,
and for Jerusalem's sake I will not be quiet,
until her righteousness goes forth as brightness,

[1] *Or afflicted* [2] *Or the opening* [of the eyes] *to those who are blind; Septuagint and recovery of sight to the blind* [3] *Or that he may display his beauty* [4] *Or robbery with a burnt offering*

and her salvation as a burning
torch.
2 The nations shall see your
righteousness,
and all the kings your glory,
and you shall be called by a new
name
that the mouth of the LORD will
give.
3 You shall be a crown of beauty in
the hand of the LORD,
and a royal diadem in the hand of
your God.
4 You shall no more be termed
Forsaken,[1]
and your land shall no more be
termed Desolate,[2]
but you shall be called My Delight Is
in Her,[3]
and your land Married;[4]
for the LORD delights in you,
and your land shall be married.
5 For as a young man marries a young
woman,
so shall your sons marry you,
and as the bridegroom rejoices over
the bride,
so shall your God rejoice over you.

6 On your walls, O Jerusalem,
I have set watchmen;
all the day and all the night
they shall never be silent.
You who put the LORD in
remembrance,
take no rest,
7 and give him no rest
until he establishes Jerusalem
and makes it a praise in the earth.
8 The LORD has sworn by his right hand
and by his mighty arm:
"I will not again give your grain
to be food for your enemies,
and foreigners shall not drink your
wine
for which you have labored;
9 but those who garner it shall eat it
and praise the LORD,
and those who gather it shall drink it
in the courts of my sanctuary."[5]

10 Go through, go through the gates;
prepare the way for the people;
build up, build up the highway;
clear it of stones;
lift up a signal over the peoples.
11 Behold, the LORD has proclaimed
to the end of the earth:
Say to the daughter of Zion,
"Behold, your salvation comes;
behold, his reward is with him,
and his recompense before him."
12 And they shall be called The Holy
People,
The Redeemed of the LORD;
and you shall be called Sought Out,
A City Not Forsaken.

The LORD's Day of Vengeance

63 Who is this who comes from
Edom,
in crimsoned garments from
Bozrah,
he who is splendid in his apparel,
marching in the greatness of his
strength?
"It is I, speaking in righteousness,
mighty to save."

2 Why is your apparel red,
and your garments like his who
treads in the winepress?

3 "I have trodden the winepress alone,
and from the peoples no one was
with me;
I trod them in my anger
and trampled them in my wrath;
their lifeblood[6] spattered on my
garments,
and stained all my apparel.
4 For the day of vengeance was in my
heart,
and my year of redemption[7] had
come.
5 I looked, but there was no one to help;

[1] Hebrew *Azubah* [2] Hebrew *Shemamah* [3] Hebrew *Hephzibah* [4] Hebrew *Beulah* [5] Or *in my holy courts* [6] Or *their juice*; also verse 6 [7] Or *the year of my redeemed*

I was appalled, but there was no
one to uphold;
so my own arm brought me
salvation,
and my wrath upheld me.
6 I trampled down the peoples in my
anger;
I made them drunk in my wrath,
and I poured out their lifeblood
on the earth."

The LORD's Mercy Remembered

7 I will recount the steadfast love of
the LORD,
the praises of the LORD,
according to all that the LORD has
granted us,
and the great goodness to the
house of Israel
that he has granted them according
to his compassion,
according to the abundance of his
steadfast love.
8 For he said, "Surely they are my
people,
children who will not deal falsely."
And he became their Savior.
9 In all their affliction he was afflicted,[1]
and the angel of his presence
saved them;
in his love and in his pity he
redeemed them;
he lifted them up and carried
them all the days of old.
10 But they rebelled
and grieved his Holy Spirit;
therefore he turned to be their enemy,
and himself fought against them.
11 Then he remembered the days of old,
of Moses and his people.[2]
Where is he who brought them up
out of the sea
with the shepherds of his flock?
Where is he who put in the midst of
them
his Holy Spirit,
12 who caused his glorious arm
to go at the right hand of Moses,
who divided the waters before them
to make for himself an everlasting
name,
13 who led them through the depths?
Like a horse in the desert,
they did not stumble.
14 Like livestock that go down into the
valley,
the Spirit of the LORD gave them
rest.
So you led your people,
to make for yourself a glorious
name.

Prayer for Mercy

15 Look down from heaven and see,
from your holy and beautiful[3]
habitation.
Where are your zeal and your might?
The stirring of your inner parts
and your compassion
are held back from me.
16 For you are our Father,
though Abraham does not know us,
and Israel does not acknowledge
us;
you, O LORD, are our Father,
our Redeemer from of old is your
name.
17 O LORD, why do you make us
wander from your ways
and harden our heart, so that we
fear you not?
Return for the sake of your servants,
the tribes of your heritage.
18 Your holy people held possession
for a little while;[4]
our adversaries have trampled
down your sanctuary.
19 We have become like those over
whom you have never ruled,
like those who are not called by
your name.

[1] *Or he did not afflict* [2] *Or Then his people remembered the days of old, of Moses* [3] *Or holy and glorious* [4] *Or They have dispossessed your holy people for a little while*

64 Oh that you would rend the
heavens and come down,
that the mountains might quake
at your presence—
2[1] as when fire kindles brushwood
and the fire causes water to boil—
to make your name known to your
adversaries,
and that the nations might
tremble at your presence!
3 When you did awesome things that
we did not look for,
you came down, the mountains
quaked at your presence.
4 From of old no one has heard
or perceived by the ear,
no eye has seen a God besides you,
who acts for those who wait for
him.
5 You meet him who joyfully works
righteousness,
those who remember you in your
ways.
Behold, you were angry, and we
sinned;
in our sins we have been a long
time, and shall we be saved?[2]
6 We have all become like one who is
unclean,
and all our righteous deeds are
like a polluted garment.
We all fade like a leaf,
and our iniquities, like the wind,
take us away.
7 There is no one who calls upon your
name,
who rouses himself to take hold
of you;
for you have hidden your face from
us,
and have made us melt in[3] the
hand of our iniquities.
8 But now, O LORD, you are our Father;
we are the clay, and you are our
potter;
we are all the work of your hand.
9 Be not so terribly angry, O LORD,
and remember not iniquity forever.
Behold, please look, we are all
your people.
10 Your holy cities have become a
wilderness;
Zion has become a wilderness,
Jerusalem a desolation.
11 Our holy and beautiful[4] house,
where our fathers praised you,
has been burned by fire,
and all our pleasant places have
become ruins.
12 Will you restrain yourself at these
things, O LORD?
Will you keep silent, and afflict us
so terribly?

Judgment and Salvation

65 I was ready to be sought by
those who did not ask for me;
I was ready to be found by those
who did not seek me.
I said, "Here am I, here am I,"
to a nation that was not called by[5]
my name.
2 I spread out my hands all the day
to a rebellious people,
who walk in a way that is not good,
following their own devices;
3 a people who provoke me
to my face continually,
sacrificing in gardens
and making offerings on bricks;
4 who sit in tombs,
and spend the night in secret
places;
who eat pig's flesh,
and broth of tainted meat is in
their vessels;
5 who say, "Keep to yourself,
do not come near me, for I am too
holy for you."
These are a smoke in my nostrils,
a fire that burns all the day.
6 Behold, it is written before me:

[1] Ch 64:1 in Hebrew [2] Or *in your ways is continuance, that we might be saved* [3] Masoretic Text; Septuagint, Syriac, Targum *have delivered us into* [4] Or *holy and glorious*
[5] Or *that did not call upon*

"I will not keep silent, but I will
repay;
I will indeed repay into their bosom
7 both your iniquities and your
fathers' iniquities together,
says the LORD;
because they made offerings on the
mountains
and insulted me on the hills,
I will measure into their bosom
payment for their former deeds."[1]

8 Thus says the LORD:
"As the new wine is found in the
cluster,
and they say, 'Do not destroy it,
for there is a blessing in it,'
so I will do for my servants' sake,
and not destroy them all.
9 I will bring forth offspring from Jacob,
and from Judah possessors of my
mountains;
my chosen shall possess it,
and my servants shall dwell there.
10 Sharon shall become a pasture for
flocks,
and the Valley of Achor a place for
herds to lie down,
for my people who have sought me.
11 But you who forsake the LORD,
who forget my holy mountain,
who set a table for Fortune
and fill cups of mixed wine for
Destiny,
12 I will destine you to the sword,
and all of you shall bow down to
the slaughter,
because, when I called, you did not
answer;
when I spoke, you did not listen,
but you did what was evil in my eyes
and chose what I did not delight in."

13 Therefore thus says the Lord GOD:
"Behold, my servants shall eat,
but you shall be hungry;
behold, my servants shall drink,
but you shall be thirsty;
behold, my servants shall rejoice,
but you shall be put to shame;
14 behold, my servants shall sing for
gladness of heart,
but you shall cry out for pain of
heart
and shall wail for breaking of spirit.
15 You shall leave your name to my
chosen for a curse,
and the Lord GOD will put you to
death,
but his servants he will call by
another name.
16 So that he who blesses himself in
the land
shall bless himself by the God of
truth,
and he who takes an oath in the land
shall swear by the God of truth;
because the former troubles are
forgotten
and are hidden from my eyes.

New Heavens and a New Earth

1847

17 "For behold, I create new heavens
and a new earth,
and the former things shall not
be remembered
or come into mind.
18 But be glad and rejoice forever
in that which I create;
for behold, I create Jerusalem to be a
joy,
and her people to be a gladness.
19 I will rejoice in Jerusalem
and be glad in my people;
no more shall be heard in it the
sound of weeping
and the cry of distress.
20 No more shall there be in it
an infant who lives but a few days,
or an old man who does not fill
out his days,
for the young man shall die a
hundred years old,
and the sinner a hundred years
old shall be accursed.

[1] Or *I will first measure their payment into their bosom*

21 They shall build houses and inhabit them;
they shall plant vineyards and eat their fruit.
22 They shall not build and another inhabit;
they shall not plant and another eat;
for like the days of a tree shall the days of my people be,
and my chosen shall long enjoy[1] the work of their hands.
23 They shall not labor in vain
or bear children for calamity,[2]
for they shall be the offspring of the blessed of the LORD,
and their descendants with them.
24 Before they call I will answer;
while they are yet speaking I will hear.
25 The wolf and the lamb shall graze together;
the lion shall eat straw like the ox,
and dust shall be the serpent's food.
They shall not hurt or destroy
in all my holy mountain,"
says the LORD.

The Humble and Contrite in Spirit

66 Thus says the LORD:
"Heaven is my throne,
and the earth is my footstool;
what is the house that you would build for me,
and what is the place of my rest?
2 All these things my hand has made,
and so all these things came to be,
declares the LORD.
But this is the one to whom I will look:
he who is humble and contrite in spirit
and trembles at my word.

3 "He who slaughters an ox is like one who kills a man;
he who sacrifices a lamb, like one who breaks a dog's neck;
he who presents a grain offering, like one who offers pig's blood;
he who makes a memorial offering of frankincense, like one who blesses an idol.
These have chosen their own ways,
and their soul delights in their abominations;
4 I also will choose harsh treatment for them
and bring their fears upon them,
because when I called, no one answered,
when I spoke, they did not listen;
but they did what was evil in my eyes
and chose that in which I did not delight."

5 Hear the word of the LORD,
you who tremble at his word:
"Your brothers who hate you
and cast you out for my name's sake
have said, 'Let the LORD be glorified,
that we may see your joy';
but it is they who shall be put to shame.

6 "The sound of an uproar from the city!
A sound from the temple!
The sound of the LORD,
rendering recompense to his enemies!

Rejoice with Jerusalem

7 "Before she was in labor
she gave birth;
before her pain came upon her
she delivered a son.
8 Who has heard such a thing?
Who has seen such things?
Shall a land be born in one day?
Shall a nation be brought forth in one moment?
For as soon as Zion was in labor
she brought forth her children.

[1] Hebrew *shall wear out* [2] Or *for sudden terror*

9 Shall I bring to the point of birth
and not cause to bring forth?"
says the LORD;
"shall I, who cause to bring forth,
shut the womb?"
says your God.

10 "Rejoice with Jerusalem, and be glad
for her,
all you who love her;
rejoice with her in joy,
all you who mourn over her;
11 that you may nurse and be satisfied
from her consoling breast;
that you may drink deeply with
delight
from her glorious abundance."[1]

12 For thus says the LORD:
"Behold, I will extend peace to her
like a river,
and the glory of the nations like
an overflowing stream;
and you shall nurse, you shall be
carried upon her hip,
and bounced upon her knees.
13 As one whom his mother comforts,
so I will comfort you;
you shall be comforted in
Jerusalem.
14 You shall see, and your heart shall
rejoice;
your bones shall flourish like the
grass;
and the hand of the LORD shall be
known to his servants,
and he shall show his indignation
against his enemies.

Final Judgment and Glory of the LORD

15 "For behold, the LORD will come in
fire,
and his chariots like the whirlwind,
to render his anger in fury,
and his rebuke with flames of fire.
16 For by fire will the LORD enter into
judgment,
and by his sword, with all flesh;
and those slain by the LORD shall
be many.

17 "Those who sanctify and purify themselves to go into the gardens, following one in the midst, eating pig's flesh and the abomination and mice, shall come to an end together, declares the LORD.

18 "For I know[2] their works and their
thoughts, and the time is coming[3] to
gather all nations and tongues. And they
shall come and shall see my glory,
19 and
I will set a sign among them. And from
them I will send survivors to the nations,
to Tarshish, Pul, and Lud, who draw the
bow, to Tubal and Javan, to the coastlands
far away, that have not heard my fame
or seen my glory. And they shall declare
my glory among the nations.
20 And they
shall bring all your brothers from all the
nations as an offering to the LORD, on
horses and in chariots and in litters and
on mules and on dromedaries, to my holy
mountain Jerusalem, says the LORD, just
as the Israelites bring their grain offering
in a clean vessel to the house of the LORD.
21 And some of them also I will take for
priests and for Levites, says the LORD.

22 "For as the new heavens and the new
earth
that I make
shall remain before me, says the
LORD,
so shall your offspring and your
name remain.
23 From new moon to new moon,
and from Sabbath to Sabbath,
all flesh shall come to worship
before me,
declares the LORD.

24 "And they shall go out and look on the dead bodies of the men who have rebelled against me. For their worm shall not die, their fire shall not be quenched, and they shall be an abhorrence to all flesh."

[1] Or *breast* [2] Septuagint, Syriac; Hebrew lacks *know* [3] Hebrew *and it is coming*

Introduction to

Jeremiah

Author
Jeremiah the prophet, with his scribe, Baruch

Date
About 627–580 B.C.

People
Jeremiah; Baruch; Pashur; Hananiah and other false prophets; Jehoiakim; Ebed-melech; Zedekiah

Purpose
Jeremiah's purpose was to call Judah to repentance, to announce the Babylonian exile, and to prophesy the new covenant.

Central Themes
God will judge Judah's sin with 70 years of exile in Babylon; the people must submit to this judgment; God will bring the people back to the land; God will make a new covenant, changing His people's hearts; God will judge the nations; God will provide a King on David's throne.

Memory Verses
Broken cisterns (Jeremiah 2:11–13); amend your ways (Jeremiah 7:3); a proper boast (Jeremiah 9:23–24); delight in the Word (Jeremiah 15:15–21); the Lord tests the heart (Jeremiah 17:5–10); the potter and the clay (Jeremiah 18:6–11); the new covenant (Jeremiah 31:31–34)

Introduction

Jeremiah is sometimes called "the weeping prophet." From his first call to prophesy, he understood that his message could cause great sadness because it told of God's judgment on His people (Jeremiah 1). Jeremiah called Judah to repent by accepting their punishment of the Babylonian soldiers destroying Jerusalem and the temple and taking the Jews away to Babylon (Jeremiah 27). Jeremiah was grieved by his message, but he was also grieved by how people responded to it. False prophets argued with it (Jeremiah 28); the king cut it in pieces and burned it in the fire (Jeremiah 36); the priest beat Jeremiah for speaking it (Jeremiah 20); Jeremiah was imprisoned in a pit because of it (Jeremiah 38:1–6). Just as God had said, Jerusalem was destroyed and its people taken into captivity. Jeremiah saw this take place and wrote about it (Jeremiah 39:1–10). In Jeremiah's sorrowful message, though, there is also a message of great hope. God will bring His exiled people back to the land (Jeremiah 32). He will raise up Someone from David's family to be King forever (Jeremiah 33:14–22), and God will make a new covenant for His people (Jeremiah 31:31–34). He will forgive their sins and put His laws in their hearts.

701 B.C.	627 B.C.	586 B.C.
Assyria attacks Judah	Prophetic ministry of Jeremiah begins	Fall of Judah

Jeremiah

1033

1 The words of Jeremiah, the son
of Hilkiah, one of the priests
who were in Anathoth in the land
of Benjamin, 2 to whom the word of the
LORD came in the days of Josiah the son of
Amon, king of Judah, in the thirteenth
year of his reign. 3 It came also in the days
of Jehoiakim the son of Josiah, king of
Judah, and until the end of the eleventh
year of Zedekiah, the son of Josiah, king of
Judah, until the captivity of Jerusalem in
the fifth month.

The Call of Jeremiah

4 Now the word of the LORD came to me,
saying,

5 "Before I formed you in the womb I
knew you,
and before you were born I
consecrated you;
I appointed you a prophet to the
nations."

6 Then I said, "Ah, Lord GOD! Behold, I do
not know how to speak, for I am only a
youth." 7 But the LORD said to me,

"Do not say, 'I am only a youth';
for to all to whom I send you, you
shall go,
and whatever I command you, you
shall speak.
8 Do not be afraid of them,
for I am with you to deliver you,
declares the LORD."

9 Then the LORD put out his hand and
touched my mouth. And the LORD said
to me,

"Behold, I have put my words in your
mouth.
10 See, I have set you this day over
nations and over kingdoms,
to pluck up and to break down,
to destroy and to overthrow,
to build and to plant."

11 And the word of the LORD came to me,
saying, "Jeremiah, what do you see?" And I
said, "I see an almond[1] branch." 12 Then the
LORD said to me, "You have seen well, for I
am watching over my word to perform it."
13 The word of the LORD came to me a
second time, saying, "What do you see?"
And I said, "I see a boiling pot, facing away
from the north." 14 Then the LORD said to

CHARACTER PROFILE

JEREMIAH

Jeremiah was God's prophet when the Babylonians came and destroyed Jerusalem. God's people did not like Jeremiah's messages. They put him in jail, put him in a muddy pit, beat him, and made fun of him. This made Jeremiah sad, but he kept telling God's messages to God's people.

1033

[1] *Almond* sounds like the Hebrew for *watching* (compare verse 12) [2] The Hebrew word can mean *evil*, *harm*, or *disaster*, depending on the context; so throughout Jeremiah

me, "Out of the north disaster[2] shall be let
loose upon all the inhabitants of the land.
15 For behold, I am calling all the tribes of
the kingdoms of the north, declares the
LORD, and they shall come, and every
one shall set his throne at the entrance
of the gates of Jerusalem, against all its
walls all around and against all the cities
of Judah. 16 And I will declare my judg-
ments against them, for all their evil in
forsaking me. They have made offerings
to other gods and worshiped the works of
their own hands. 17 But you, dress yourself
for work;[1] arise, and say to them every-
thing that I command you. Do not be dis-
mayed by them, lest I dismay you before
them. 18 And I, behold, I make you this day
a fortified city, an iron pillar, and bronze
walls, against the whole land, against the
kings of Judah, its officials, its priests, and
the people of the land. 19 They will fight
against you, but they shall not prevail
against you, for I am with you, declares
the LORD, to deliver you."

Israel Forsakes the LORD

2 The word of the LORD came to me,
saying, 2 "Go and proclaim in the
hearing of Jerusalem, Thus says the LORD,

"I remember the devotion of your youth,
your love as a bride,
how you followed me in the wilderness,
in a land not sown.
3 Israel was holy to the LORD,
the firstfruits of his harvest.
All who ate of it incurred guilt;
disaster came upon them,
declares the LORD."

4 Hear the word of the LORD, O house
of Jacob, and all the clans of the house of
Israel. 5 Thus says the LORD:

"What wrong did your fathers find in me
that they went far from me,
and went after worthlessness, and became worthless?
6 They did not say, 'Where is the LORD
who brought us up from the land of Egypt,
who led us in the wilderness,
in a land of deserts and pits,
in a land of drought and deep darkness,
in a land that none passes through,
where no man dwells?'
7 And I brought you into a plentiful land
to enjoy its fruits and its good things.
But when you came in, you defiled my land
and made my heritage an abomination.
8 The priests did not say, 'Where is the LORD?'
Those who handle the law did not know me;
the shepherds[2] transgressed against me;
the prophets prophesied by Baal
and went after things that do not profit.

9 "Therefore I still contend with you,
declares the LORD,
and with your children's children I will contend.
10 For cross to the coasts of Cyprus and see,
or send to Kedar and examine with care;
see if there has been such a thing.
11 Has a nation changed its gods,
even though they are no gods?
But my people have changed their glory
for that which does not profit.
12 Be appalled, O heavens, at this;
be shocked, be utterly desolate,
declares the LORD,
13 for my people have committed two evils:

[1] Hebrew *gird up your loins* [2] Or *rulers*

Jeremiah and the Great Promise

At the time Josiah was king of Judah, Jeremiah was growing up as the son of a priest named Hilkiah. While Jeremiah was still a young man, the Lord spoke to him. God told Jeremiah that even before he was born, God had planned for Jeremiah to be a prophet. God wanted Jeremiah to bring the word of the Lord to His people and also to the people of other nations.

When the word of the Lord first came to Jeremiah he was surprised. Jeremiah did not think he would be a good prophet because he was too young. He said to the Lord, "I do not know how to speak."

But the Lord told Jeremiah not to think about how young he was, but to remember that it was God who was sending him. God did not want Jeremiah to be afraid, for He would be with Jeremiah. Then God put out His hand and touched Jeremiah's mouth. God said, "I have put My words in your mouth. See, I have set you this day over nations and over kingdoms."

God gave Jeremiah a sad message of judgment for the people of God. God was sending the nation of Babylon to conquer His people Israel because of all the sin God's people had done. Jerusalem would be destroyed and God's people would be taken away as prisoners to live in Babylon. But God also gave Jeremiah a message of hope for His people. After 70 years, God would bring His people back to Jerusalem to rebuild the city and to rebuild God's temple.

Even better, the Lord gave Jeremiah the great promise that He would send someone who would be a perfect King for His people. He would rule wisely and with righteousness. "In His days," God promised through Jeremiah, "Judah will be saved, and Israel will dwell securely. And this is the name by which He will be called: 'The LORD is our righteousness.'"

The Lord also told Jeremiah that He would make a new covenant with His people. It would not be like the covenant Israel had broken so many times. Instead, God said, "I will put My law within them, and I will write it on their hearts. And I will be their God, and they shall be My people. They shall all know Me, from the least of them to the greatest. I will forgive their iniquity, and I will remember their sin no more."

Just as God promised through Jeremiah, the Babylonian army destroyed Jerusalem and took the people to Babylon. Just as God promised, the Israelites were allowed to return to Jerusalem after 70 years. And just as God promised, He made a new covenant with His people—by sending His Son Jesus to die for our sins on the cross, so that all who trust in Him will know "The LORD is our righteousness."

SEEK and FIND

WHERE TO FIND THE STORY

Jeremiah 1:1–19; 23:5–6; 31:31–37

KEY BIBLE VERSE

"But this is the covenant that I will make with the house of

Israel after those days, declares the LORD: I will put my law within them, and I will write it on their hearts. And I will be their God, and they shall be my people." (Jeremiah 31:33)

THREE KEY QUESTIONS

- When Jeremiah thought he was too young and couldn't speak well, what did God do?
- Why did God allow the Babylonian army to conquer Jerusalem, and what did God promise would happen seventy years later?
- What is the great promise that God made to His people, and how does Jesus fulfill God's promise?

RELATED BIBLE READINGS

Jeremiah 29:1–32; 36:1–38:28; Ezekiel 37:24–28; Matthew 26:26–29; Hebrews 8:6–13

they have forsaken me,
the fountain of living waters,
and hewed out cisterns for themselves,
broken cisterns that can hold no water.

14 "Is Israel a slave? Is he a homeborn servant?
Why then has he become a prey?
15 The lions have roared against him;
they have roared loudly.
They have made his land a waste;
his cities are in ruins, without inhabitant.
16 Moreover, the men of Memphis and Tahpanhes
have shaved[1] the crown of your head.
17 Have you not brought this upon yourself
by forsaking the LORD your God,
when he led you in the way?
18 And now what do you gain by going to Egypt
to drink the waters of the Nile?
Or what do you gain by going to Assyria
to drink the waters of the Euphrates?
19 Your evil will chastise you,
and your apostasy will reprove you.
Know and see that it is evil and bitter
for you to forsake the LORD your God;
the fear of me is not in you,
declares the Lord GOD of hosts.

20 "For long ago I broke your yoke
and burst your bonds;
but you said, 'I will not serve.'
Yes, on every high hill
and under every green tree
you bowed down like a whore.
21 Yet I planted you a choice vine,
wholly of pure seed.
How then have you turned degenerate

[1] Hebrew *grazed*

and become a wild vine?
22 Though you wash yourself with lye
and use much soap,
the stain of your guilt is still
before me,
declares the Lord GOD.
23 How can you say, 'I am not unclean,
I have not gone after the Baals'?
Look at your way in the valley;
know what you have done—
a restless young camel running
here and there,
24 a wild donkey used to the
wilderness,
in her heat sniffing the wind!
Who can restrain her lust?
None who seek her need weary
themselves;
in her month they will find her.
25 Keep your feet from going unshod
and your throat from thirst.
But you said, 'It is hopeless,
for I have loved foreigners,
and after them I will go.'

26 "As a thief is shamed when caught,
so the house of Israel shall be
shamed:
they, their kings, their officials,
their priests, and their prophets,
27 who say to a tree, 'You are my father,'
and to a stone, 'You gave me birth.'
For they have turned their back to me,
and not their face.
But in the time of their trouble they
say,
'Arise and save us!'
28 But where are your gods
that you made for yourself?
Let them arise, if they can save you,
in your time of trouble;
for as many as your cities
are your gods, O Judah.

29 "Why do you contend with me?
You have all transgressed against
me,
declares the LORD.
30 In vain have I struck your children;
they took no correction;
your own sword devoured your
prophets
like a ravening lion.
31 And you, O generation, behold the
word of the LORD.
Have I been a wilderness to Israel,
or a land of thick darkness?
Why then do my people say, 'We are
free,
we will come no more to you'?
32 Can a virgin forget her ornaments,
or a bride her attire?
Yet my people have forgotten me
days without number.

33 "How well you direct your course
to seek love!
So that even to wicked women
you have taught your ways.
34 Also on your skirts is found
the lifeblood of the guiltless poor;
you did not find them breaking in.
Yet in spite of all these things
35 you say, 'I am innocent;
surely his anger has turned from
me.'
Behold, I will bring you to judgment
for saying, 'I have not sinned.'
36 How much you go about,
changing your way!
You shall be put to shame by Egypt
as you were put to shame by
Assyria.
37 From it too you will come away
with your hands on your head,
for the LORD has rejected those in
whom you trust,
and you will not prosper by them.

3 "If[1] a man divorces his wife
and she goes from him
and becomes another man's wife,
will he return to her?
Would not that land be greatly
polluted?

[1] Septuagint, Syriac; Hebrew *Saying, "If*

You have played the whore with
many lovers;
and would you return to me?
declares the LORD.
2 Lift up your eyes to the bare heights,
and see!
Where have you not been ravished?
By the waysides you have sat
awaiting lovers
like an Arab in the wilderness.
You have polluted the land
with your vile whoredom.
3 Therefore the showers have been
withheld,
and the spring rain has not come;
yet you have the forehead of a whore;
you refuse to be ashamed.
4 Have you not just now called to me,
'My father, you are the friend of
my youth—
5 will he be angry forever,
will he be indignant to the end?'
Behold, you have spoken,
but you have done all the evil that
you could."

Faithless Israel Called to Repentance

6 The LORD said to me in the days of King
Josiah: "Have you seen what she did, that
faithless one, Israel, how she went up
on every high hill and under every green
tree, and there played the whore? 7 And I
thought, 'After she has done all this she will
return to me,' but she did not return, and
her treacherous sister Judah saw it. 8 She
saw that for all the adulteries of that faith-
less one, Israel, I had sent her away with
a decree of divorce. Yet her treacherous
sister Judah did not fear, but she too went
and played the whore. 9 Because she took
her whoredom lightly, she polluted the
land, committing adultery with stone and
tree. 10 Yet for all this her treacherous sister
Judah did not return to me with her whole
heart, but in pretense, declares the LORD."
11 And the LORD said to me, "Faithless
Israel has shown herself more righteous
than treacherous Judah. 12 Go, and proclaim
these words toward the north, and say,

"'Return, faithless Israel,
declares the LORD.
I will not look on you in anger,
for I am merciful,
declares the LORD;
I will not be angry forever.
13 Only acknowledge your guilt,
that you rebelled against the LORD
your God
and scattered your favors among
foreigners under every green
tree,
and that you have not obeyed my
voice,
declares the LORD.
14 Return, O faithless children,
declares the LORD;
for I am your master;
I will take you, one from a city and
two from a family,
and I will bring you to Zion.

15 "'And I will give you shepherds after
my own heart, who will feed you with
knowledge and understanding. 16 And
when you have multiplied and increased
in the land, in those days, declares the
LORD, they shall no more say, "The ark
of the covenant of the LORD." It shall
not come to mind or be remembered or
missed; it shall not be made again. 17 At
that time Jerusalem shall be called the
throne of the LORD, and all nations shall
gather to it, to the presence of the LORD in
Jerusalem, and they shall no more stub-
bornly follow their own evil heart. 18 In
those days the house of Judah shall join
the house of Israel, and together they shall
come from the land of the north to the
land that I gave your fathers for a heritage.

19 "'I said,
How I would set you among my
sons,

and give you a pleasant land,
a heritage most beautiful of all nations.
And I thought you would call me, My Father,
and would not turn from following me.
20 Surely, as a treacherous wife leaves her husband,
so have you been treacherous to me, O house of Israel,
declares the LORD.'"

21 A voice on the bare heights is heard,
the weeping and pleading of Israel's sons
because they have perverted their way;
they have forgotten the LORD their God.
22 "Return, O faithless sons;
I will heal your faithlessness."
"Behold, we come to you,
for you are the LORD our God.
23 Truly the hills are a delusion,
the orgies[1] on the mountains.
Truly in the LORD our God
is the salvation of Israel.

24 "But from our youth the shameful
thing has devoured all for which our
fathers labored, their flocks and their
herds, their sons and their daughters.
25 Let us lie down in our shame, and let
our dishonor cover us. For we have sinned
against the LORD our God, we and our
fathers, from our youth even to this day,
and we have not obeyed the voice of the
LORD our God."

4 "If you return, O Israel,
declares the LORD,
to me you should return.
If you remove your detestable things from my presence,
and do not waver,
2 and if you swear, 'As the LORD lives,'
in truth, in justice, and in righteousness,
then nations shall bless themselves in him,
and in him shall they glory."

3 For thus says the LORD to the men of
Judah and Jerusalem:

"Break up your fallow ground,
and sow not among thorns.
4 Circumcise yourselves to the LORD;
remove the foreskin of your hearts,
O men of Judah and inhabitants of Jerusalem;
lest my wrath go forth like fire,
and burn with none to quench it,
because of the evil of your deeds."

Disaster from the North

5 Declare in Judah, and proclaim in Jeru-
salem, and say,

"Blow the trumpet through the land;
cry aloud and say,
'Assemble, and let us go
into the fortified cities!'
6 Raise a standard toward Zion,
flee for safety, stay not,
for I bring disaster from the north,
and great destruction.
7 A lion has gone up from his thicket,
a destroyer of nations has set out;
he has gone out from his place
to make your land a waste;
your cities will be ruins
without inhabitant.
8 For this put on sackcloth,
lament and wail,
for the fierce anger of the LORD
has not turned back from us."

9 "In that day, declares the LORD, cour-
age shall fail both king and officials. The
priests shall be appalled and the prophets
astounded." 10 Then I said, "Ah, Lord GOD,
surely you have utterly deceived this peo-
ple and Jerusalem, saying, 'It shall be well
with you,' whereas the sword has reached
their very life."

[1] Hebrew *commotion*

11 At that time it will be said to this peo-
ple and to Jerusalem, "A hot wind from
the bare heights in the desert toward the
daughter of my people, not to winnow or
cleanse, 12 a wind too full for this comes
for me. Now it is I who speak in judgment
upon them."

13 Behold, he comes up like clouds;
his chariots like the whirlwind;
his horses are swifter than eagles—
woe to us, for we are ruined!
14 O Jerusalem, wash your heart from evil,
that you may be saved.
How long shall your wicked thoughts
lodge within you?
15 For a voice declares from Dan
and proclaims trouble from
Mount Ephraim.
16 Warn the nations that he is coming;
announce to Jerusalem,
"Besiegers come from a distant land;
they shout against the cities of
Judah.
17 Like keepers of a field are they
against her all around,
because she has rebelled against
me,
declares the LORD.
18 Your ways and your deeds
have brought this upon you.
This is your doom, and it is bitter;
it has reached your very heart."

Anguish over Judah's Desolation

19 My anguish, my anguish! I writhe in
pain!
Oh the walls of my heart!
My heart is beating wildly;
I cannot keep silent,
for I hear the sound of the trumpet,
the alarm of war.
20 Crash follows hard on crash;
the whole land is laid waste.
Suddenly my tents are laid waste,
my curtains in a moment.
21 How long must I see the standard
and hear the sound of the trumpet?

22 "For my people are foolish;
they know me not;
they are stupid children;
they have no understanding.
They are 'wise'—in doing evil!
But how to do good they know not."

23 I looked on the earth, and behold, it
was without form and void;
and to the heavens, and they had
no light.
24 I looked on the mountains, and
behold, they were quaking,
and all the hills moved to and fro.
25 I looked, and behold, there was no
man,
and all the birds of the air had fled.
26 I looked, and behold, the fruitful
land was a desert,
and all its cities were laid in ruins
before the LORD, before his fierce
anger.

27 For thus says the LORD, "The whole
land shall be a desolation; yet I will not
make a full end.

28 "For this the earth shall mourn,
and the heavens above be dark;
for I have spoken; I have purposed;
I have not relented, nor will I turn
back."

29 At the noise of horseman and archer
every city takes to flight;
they enter thickets; they climb
among rocks;
all the cities are forsaken,
and no man dwells in them.
30 And you, O desolate one,
what do you mean that you dress in
scarlet,
that you adorn yourself with
ornaments of gold,
that you enlarge your eyes with
paint?

In vain you beautify yourself.
Your lovers despise you;
they seek your life.
31 For I heard a cry as of a woman in labor,
anguish as of one giving birth to her first child,
the cry of the daughter of Zion gasping for breath,
stretching out her hands,
"Woe is me! I am fainting before murderers."

Jerusalem Refused to Repent

5 Run to and fro through the streets of Jerusalem,
look and take note!
Search her squares to see
if you can find a man,
one who does justice
and seeks truth,
that I may pardon her.
2 Though they say, "As the LORD lives,"
yet they swear falsely.
3 O LORD, do not your eyes look for truth?
You have struck them down,
but they felt no anguish;
you have consumed them,
but they refused to take correction.
They have made their faces harder than rock;
they have refused to repent.
4 Then I said, "These are only the poor;
they have no sense;
for they do not know the way of the LORD,
the justice of their God.
5 I will go to the great
and will speak to them,
for they know the way of the LORD,
the justice of their God."
But they all alike had broken the yoke;
they had burst the bonds.
6 Therefore a lion from the forest shall strike them down;
a wolf from the desert shall devastate them.
A leopard is watching their cities;
everyone who goes out of them shall be torn in pieces,
because their transgressions are many,
their apostasies are great.
7 "How can I pardon you?
Your children have forsaken me
and have sworn by those who are no gods.
When I fed them to the full,
they committed adultery
and trooped to the houses of whores.
8 They were well-fed, lusty stallions,
each neighing for his neighbor's wife.
9 Shall I not punish them for these things?
declares the LORD;
and shall I not avenge myself
on a nation such as this?
10 "Go up through her vine rows and destroy,
but make not a full end;
strip away her branches,
for they are not the LORD's.
11 For the house of Israel and the house of Judah
have been utterly treacherous to me,
declares the LORD.
12 They have spoken falsely of the LORD
and have said, 'He will do nothing;
no disaster will come upon us,
nor shall we see sword or famine.
13 The prophets will become wind;
the word is not in them.
Thus shall it be done to them!'"

The Lord Proclaims Judgment

14 Therefore thus says the LORD, the God of hosts:
"Because you have spoken this word,
behold, I am making my words in your mouth a fire,
and this people wood, and the fire shall consume them.
15 Behold, I am bringing against you
a nation from afar, O house of Israel,
declares the LORD.
It is an enduring nation;
it is an ancient nation,
a nation whose language you do not know,
nor can you understand what they say.
16 Their quiver is like an open tomb;
they are all mighty warriors.
17 They shall eat up your harvest and your food;
they shall eat up your sons and your daughters;
they shall eat up your flocks and your herds;
they shall eat up your vines and your fig trees;
your fortified cities in which you trust
they shall beat down with the sword."

18 "But even in those days, declares the
LORD, I will not make a full end of you.
19 And when your people say, 'Why has
the LORD our God done all these things
to us?' you shall say to them, 'As you have
forsaken me and served foreign gods in
your land, so you shall serve foreigners in
a land that is not yours.'"

20 Declare this in the house of Jacob;
proclaim it in Judah:
21 "Hear this, O foolish and senseless people,
who have eyes, but see not,
who have ears, but hear not.
22 Do you not fear me? declares the LORD.
Do you not tremble before me?
I placed the sand as the boundary for the sea,
a perpetual barrier that it cannot pass;
though the waves toss, they cannot prevail;
though they roar, they cannot pass over it.
23 But this people has a stubborn and rebellious heart;
they have turned aside and gone away.
24 They do not say in their hearts,
'Let us fear the LORD our God,
who gives the rain in its season,
the autumn rain and the spring rain,
and keeps for us
the weeks appointed for the harvest.'
25 Your iniquities have turned these away,
and your sins have kept good from you.
26 For wicked men are found among my people;
they lurk like fowlers lying in wait.[1]
They set a trap;
they catch men.
27 Like a cage full of birds,
their houses are full of deceit;
therefore they have become great and rich;
28 they have grown fat and sleek.
They know no bounds in deeds of evil;
they judge not with justice
the cause of the fatherless, to make it prosper,
and they do not defend the rights of the needy.

[1] The meaning of the Hebrew is uncertain

29 Shall I not punish them for these
things?
declares the LORD,
and shall I not avenge myself
on a nation such as this?"

30 An appalling and horrible thing
has happened in the land:
31 the prophets prophesy falsely,
and the priests rule at their
direction;
my people love to have it so,
but what will you do when the
end comes?

Impending Disaster for Jerusalem

6 Flee for safety, O people of Benjamin,
from the midst of Jerusalem!
Blow the trumpet in Tekoa,
and raise a signal on
Beth-haccherem,
for disaster looms out of the north,
and great destruction.
2 The lovely and delicately bred I will
destroy,
the daughter of Zion.[1]
3 Shepherds with their flocks shall
come against her;
they shall pitch their tents around
her;
they shall pasture, each in his place.
4 "Prepare war against her;
arise, and let us attack at noon!
Woe to us, for the day declines,
for the shadows of evening
lengthen!
5 Arise, and let us attack by night
and destroy her palaces!"

6 For thus says the LORD of hosts:
"Cut down her trees;
cast up a siege mound against
Jerusalem.
This is the city that must be punished;
there is nothing but oppression
within her.
7 As a well keeps its water fresh,
so she keeps fresh her evil;
violence and destruction are heard
within her;
sickness and wounds are ever
before me.
8 Be warned, O Jerusalem,
lest I turn from you in disgust,
lest I make you a desolation,
an uninhabited land."

9 Thus says the LORD of hosts:
"They shall glean thoroughly as a vine
the remnant of Israel;
like a grape-gatherer pass your hand
again
over its branches."
10 To whom shall I speak and give
warning,
that they may hear?
Behold, their ears are
uncircumcised,
they cannot listen;
behold, the word of the LORD is to
them an object of scorn;
they take no pleasure in it.
11 Therefore I am full of the wrath of
the LORD;
I am weary of holding it in.
"Pour it out upon the children in the
street,
and upon the gatherings of young
men, also;
both husband and wife shall be taken,
the elderly and the very aged.
12 Their houses shall be turned over to
others,
their fields and wives together,
for I will stretch out my hand
against the inhabitants of the land,"
declares the LORD.
13 "For from the least to the greatest of
them,
everyone is greedy for unjust gain;
and from prophet to priest,
everyone deals falsely.
14 They have healed the wound of my
people lightly,
saying, 'Peace, peace,'
when there is no peace.

[1] Or *I have likened the daughter of Zion to the loveliest pasture*

15 Were they ashamed when they
committed abomination?
No, they were not at all ashamed;
they did not know how to blush.
Therefore they shall fall among
those who fall;
at the time that I punish them,
they shall be overthrown,"
says the LORD.

16 Thus says the LORD:
"Stand by the roads, and look,
and ask for the ancient paths,
where the good way is; and walk in
it,
and find rest for your souls.
But they said, 'We will not walk in
it.'
17 I set watchmen over you, saying,
'Pay attention to the sound of the
trumpet!'
But they said, 'We will not pay
attention.'
18 Therefore hear, O nations,
and know, O congregation, what
will happen to them.
19 Hear, O earth; behold, I am bringing
disaster upon this people,
the fruit of their devices,
because they have not paid
attention to my words;
and as for my law, they have
rejected it.
20 What use to me is frankincense that
comes from Sheba,
or sweet cane from a distant land?
Your burnt offerings are not
acceptable,
nor your sacrifices pleasing to me.
21 Therefore thus says the LORD:
'Behold, I will lay before this people
stumbling blocks against which
they shall stumble;
fathers and sons together,
neighbor and friend shall perish.'"

22 Thus says the LORD:
"Behold, a people is coming from the
north country,
a great nation is stirring from the
farthest parts of the earth.
23 They lay hold on bow and javelin;
they are cruel and have no mercy;
the sound of them is like the
roaring sea;
they ride on horses,
set in array as a man for battle,
against you, O daughter of Zion!"
24 We have heard the report of it;
our hands fall helpless;
anguish has taken hold of us,
pain as of a woman in labor.
25 Go not out into the field,
nor walk on the road,
for the enemy has a sword;
terror is on every side.
26 O daughter of my people, put on
sackcloth,
and roll in ashes;
make mourning as for an only son,
most bitter lamentation,
for suddenly the destroyer
will come upon us.

27 "I have made you a tester of metals
among my people,
that you may know and test their
ways.
28 They are all stubbornly rebellious,
going about with slanders;
they are bronze and iron;
all of them act corruptly.
29 The bellows blow fiercely;
the lead is consumed by the fire;
in vain the refining goes on,
for the wicked are not removed.
30 Rejected silver they are called,
for the LORD has rejected them."

Evil in the Land

7 The word that came to Jeremiah from
the LORD: 2 "Stand in the gate of the
LORD's house, and proclaim there this
word, and say, Hear the word of the LORD,

all you men of Judah who enter these gates to worship the LORD. 3 Thus says the LORD of hosts, the God of Israel: Amend your ways and your deeds, and I will let you dwell in this place. 4 Do not trust in these deceptive words: 'This is the temple of the LORD, the temple of the LORD, the temple of the LORD.'

5 "For if you truly amend your ways and your deeds, if you truly execute justice one with another, 6 if you do not oppress the sojourner, the fatherless, or the widow, or shed innocent blood in this place, and if you do not go after other gods to your own harm, 7 then I will let you dwell in this place, in the land that I gave of old to your fathers forever.

8 "Behold, you trust in deceptive words to no avail. 9 Will you steal, murder, commit adultery, swear falsely, make offerings to Baal, and go after other gods that you have not known, 10 and then come and stand before me in this house, which is called by my name, and say, 'We are delivered!'—only to go on doing all these abominations? 11 Has this house, which is called by my name, become a den of robbers in your eyes? Behold, I myself have seen it, declares the LORD. 12 Go now to my place that was in Shiloh, where I made my name dwell at first, and see what I did to it because of the evil of my people Israel. 13 And now, because you have done all these things, declares the LORD, and when I spoke to you persistently you did not listen, and when I called you, you did not answer, 14 therefore I will do to the house that is called by my name, and in which you trust, and to the place that I gave to you and to your fathers, as I did to Shiloh. 15 And I will cast you out of my sight, as I cast out all your kinsmen, all the offspring of Ephraim.

16 "As for you, do not pray for this people, or lift up a cry or prayer for them, and do not intercede with me, for I will not hear you. 17 Do you not see what they are doing in the cities of Judah and in the streets of Jerusalem? 18 The children gather wood, the fathers kindle fire, and the women knead dough, to make cakes for the queen of heaven. And they pour out drink offerings to other gods, to provoke me to anger. 19 Is it I whom they provoke? declares the LORD. Is it not themselves, to their own shame? 20 Therefore thus says the Lord GOD: behold, my anger and my wrath will be poured out on this place, upon man and beast, upon the trees of the field and the fruit of the ground; it will burn and not be quenched."

21 Thus says the LORD of hosts, the God of Israel: "Add your burnt offerings to your sacrifices, and eat the flesh. 22 For in the day that I brought them out of the land of Egypt, I did not speak to your fathers or command them concerning burnt offerings and sacrifices. 23 But this command I gave them: 'Obey my voice, and I will be your God, and you shall be my people. And walk in all the way that I command you, that it may be well with you.' 24 But they did not obey or incline their ear, but walked in their own counsels and the stubbornness of their evil hearts, and went backward and not forward. 25 From the day that your fathers came out of the land of Egypt to this day, I have persistently sent all my servants the prophets to them, day after day. 26 Yet they did not listen to me or incline their ear, but stiffened their neck. They did worse than their fathers.

27 "So you shall speak all these words to them, but they will not listen to you. You shall call to them, but they will not answer you. 28 And you shall say to them, 'This is the nation that did not obey the voice of the LORD their God, and did not accept discipline; truth has perished; it is cut off from their lips.

29 "'Cut off your hair and cast it away;
raise a lamentation on the bare heights,

for the LORD has rejected and
forsaken
the generation of his wrath.'

The Valley of Slaughter

30 "For the sons of Judah have done
evil in my sight, declares the LORD. They
have set their detestable things in the
house that is called by my name, to defile
it. 31 And they have built the high places
of Topheth, which is in the Valley of the
Son of Hinnom, to burn their sons and
their daughters in the fire, which I did not
command, nor did it come into my mind.
32 Therefore, behold, the days are coming,
declares the LORD, when it will no more be
called Topheth, or the Valley of the Son of
Hinnom, but the Valley of Slaughter; for
they will bury in Topheth, because there is
no room elsewhere. 33 And the dead bod-
ies of this people will be food for the birds
of the air, and for the beasts of the earth,
and none will frighten them away. 34 And
I will silence in the cities of Judah and in
the streets of Jerusalem the voice of mirth
and the voice of gladness, the voice of the
bridegroom and the voice of the bride, for
the land shall become a waste.

8 "At that time, declares the LORD, the
bones of the kings of Judah, the bones
of its officials, the bones of the priests, the
bones of the prophets, and the bones of the
inhabitants of Jerusalem shall be brought
out of their tombs. 2 And they shall be
spread before the sun and the moon and all
the host of heaven, which they have loved
and served, which they have gone after, and
which they have sought and worshiped.
And they shall not be gathered or buried.
They shall be as dung on the surface of the
ground. 3 Death shall be preferred to life by
all the remnant that remains of this evil
family in all the places where I have driven
them, declares the LORD of hosts.

Sin and Treachery

4 "You shall say to them, Thus says the
LORD:
When men fall, do they not rise
again?
If one turns away, does he not
return?
5 Why then has this people turned
away
in perpetual backsliding?
They hold fast to deceit;
they refuse to return.
6 I have paid attention and listened,
but they have not spoken rightly;
no man relents of his evil,
saying, 'What have I done?'
Everyone turns to his own course,
like a horse plunging headlong
into battle.
7 Even the stork in the heavens
knows her times,
and the turtledove, swallow, and
crane[1]
keep the time of their coming,
but my people know not
the rules[2] of the LORD.

8 "How can you say, 'We are wise,
and the law of the LORD is with us'?
But behold, the lying pen of the
scribes
has made it into a lie.
9 The wise men shall be put to shame;
they shall be dismayed and taken;
behold, they have rejected the word
of the LORD,
so what wisdom is in them?
10 Therefore I will give their wives to
others
and their fields to conquerors,
because from the least to the
greatest
everyone is greedy for unjust
gain;
from prophet to priest,
everyone deals falsely.
11 They have healed the wound of my
people lightly,
saying, 'Peace, peace,'
when there is no peace.

[1] The meaning of the Hebrew word is uncertain [2] Or *just decrees*

12 Were they ashamed when they
committed abomination?
No, they were not at all ashamed;
they did not know how to blush.
Therefore they shall fall among the
fallen;
when I punish them, they shall be
overthrown,
says the LORD.
13 When I would gather them, declares
the LORD,
there are no grapes on the vine,
nor figs on the fig tree;
even the leaves are withered,
and what I gave them has passed
away from them."[1]

14 Why do we sit still?
Gather together; let us go into the
fortified cities
and perish there,
for the LORD our God has doomed
us to perish
and has given us poisoned water
to drink,
because we have sinned against
the LORD.
15 We looked for peace, but no good
came;
for a time of healing, but behold,
terror.

16 "The snorting of their horses is heard
from Dan;
at the sound of the neighing of
their stallions
the whole land quakes.
They come and devour the land and
all that fills it,
the city and those who dwell in it.
17 For behold, I am sending among
you serpents,
adders that cannot be charmed,
and they shall bite you,"
declares the LORD.

Jeremiah Grieves for His People

18 My joy is gone; grief is upon me;[2]
my heart is sick within me.
19 Behold, the cry of the daughter of
my people
from the length and breadth of
the land:
"Is the LORD not in Zion?
Is her King not in her?"
"Why have they provoked me to
anger with their carved images
and with their foreign idols?"
20 "The harvest is past, the summer is
ended,
and we are not saved."
21 For the wound of the daughter of my
people is my heart wounded;
I mourn, and dismay has taken
hold on me.

22 Is there no balm in Gilead?
Is there no physician there?
Why then has the health of the
daughter of my people
not been restored?

9 [3] Oh that my head were waters,
and my eyes a fountain of tears,
that I might weep day and night
for the slain of the daughter of my
people!
2[4] Oh that I had in the desert
a travelers' lodging place,
that I might leave my people
and go away from them!
For they are all adulterers,
a company of treacherous men.
3 They bend their tongue like a bow;
falsehood and not truth has
grown strong[5] in the land;
for they proceed from evil to evil,
and they do not know me,
declares the LORD.

4 Let everyone beware of his neighbor,
and put no trust in any brother,

[1] The meaning of the Hebrew is uncertain [2] Compare Septuagint; the meaning of the Hebrew is uncertain [3] Ch 8:23 in Hebrew [4] Ch 9:1 in Hebrew [5] Septuagint; Hebrew *and not for truth they have grown strong*

for every brother is a deceiver,
and every neighbor goes about as a slanderer.
5 Everyone deceives his neighbor,
and no one speaks the truth;
they have taught their tongue to speak lies;
they weary themselves committing iniquity.
6 Heaping oppression upon oppression, and deceit upon deceit,
they refuse to know me, declares the LORD.

7 Therefore thus says the LORD of hosts:
"Behold, I will refine them and test them,
for what else can I do, because of my people?
8 Their tongue is a deadly arrow;
it speaks deceitfully;
with his mouth each speaks peace to his neighbor,
but in his heart he plans an ambush for him.
9 Shall I not punish them for these things? declares the LORD,
and shall I not avenge myself on a nation such as this?

10 "I will take up weeping and wailing for the mountains,
and a lamentation for the pastures of the wilderness,
because they are laid waste so that no one passes through,
and the lowing of cattle is not heard;
both the birds of the air and the beasts
have fled and are gone.
11 I will make Jerusalem a heap of ruins,
a lair of jackals,
and I will make the cities of Judah a desolation,
without inhabitant."

12 Who is the man so wise that he can
understand this? To whom has the mouth
of the LORD spoken, that he may declare
it? Why is the land ruined and laid waste
like a wilderness, so that no one passes
through? 13 And the LORD says: "Because
they have forsaken my law that I set before
them, and have not obeyed my voice or
walked in accord with it, 14 but have stub-
bornly followed their own hearts and have
gone after the Baals, as their fathers taught
them. 15 Therefore thus says the LORD of
hosts, the God of Israel: Behold, I will feed
this people with bitter food, and give them
poisonous water to drink. 16 I will scatter
them among the nations whom neither
they nor their fathers have known, and
I will send the sword after them, until I
have consumed them."

17 Thus says the LORD of hosts:
"Consider, and call for the mourning women to come;
send for the skillful women to come;
18 let them make haste and raise a wailing over us,
that our eyes may run down with tears
and our eyelids flow with water.
19 For a sound of wailing is heard from Zion:
'How we are ruined!
We are utterly shamed,
because we have left the land,
because they have cast down our dwellings.'"

20 Hear, O women, the word of the LORD,
and let your ear receive the word of his mouth;
teach to your daughters a lament,
and each to her neighbor a dirge.
21 For death has come up into our windows;
it has entered our palaces,

cutting off the children from the
streets
and the young men from the
squares.
22 Speak, "Thus declares the LORD:
'The dead bodies of men shall fall
like dung upon the open field,
like sheaves after the reaper,
and none shall gather them.'"

23 Thus says the LORD: "Let not the wise
man boast in his wisdom, let not the
mighty man boast in his might, let not the
rich man boast in his riches, 24 but let him
who boasts boast in this, that he under-
stands and knows me, that I am the LORD
who practices steadfast love, justice, and
righteousness in the earth. For in these
things I delight, declares the LORD."
25 "Behold, the days are coming, declares
the LORD, when I will punish all those
who are circumcised merely in the
flesh— 26 Egypt, Judah, Edom, the sons of
Ammon, Moab, and all who dwell in the
desert who cut the corners of their hair,
for all these nations are uncircumcised,
and all the house of Israel are uncircum-
cised in heart."

Idols and the Living God

10 Hear the word that the LORD speaks
to you, O house of Israel. 2 Thus
says the LORD:

"Learn not the way of the nations,
nor be dismayed at the signs of
the heavens
because the nations are dismayed
at them,
3 for the customs of the peoples are
vanity.[1]
A tree from the forest is cut down
and worked with an axe by the
hands of a craftsman.
4 They decorate it with silver and gold;
they fasten it with hammer and
nails
so that it cannot move.
5 Their idols[2] are like scarecrows in a
cucumber field,
and they cannot speak;
they have to be carried,
for they cannot walk.
Do not be afraid of them,
for they cannot do evil,
neither is it in them to do good."

6 There is none like you, O LORD;
you are great, and your name is
great in might.
7 Who would not fear you, O King of
the nations?
For this is your due;
for among all the wise ones of the
nations
and in all their kingdoms
there is none like you.
8 They are both stupid and foolish;
the instruction of idols is but wood!
9 Beaten silver is brought from
Tarshish,
and gold from Uphaz.
They are the work of the craftsman
and of the hands of the
goldsmith;
their clothing is violet and purple;
they are all the work of skilled men.
10 But the LORD is the true God;
he is the living God and the
everlasting King.
At his wrath the earth quakes,
and the nations cannot endure
his indignation.

11 Thus shall you say to them: "The gods
who did not make the heavens and the
earth shall perish from the earth and from
under the heavens."[3]

12 It is he who made the earth by his
power,
who established the world by his
wisdom,
and by his understanding
stretched out the heavens.

[1] Or *vapor*, or *mist* [2] Hebrew *They* [3] This verse is in Aramaic

13 When he utters his voice, there
is a tumult of waters in the
heavens,
and he makes the mist rise from
the ends of the earth.
He makes lightning for the rain,
and he brings forth the wind from
his storehouses.
14 Every man is stupid and without
knowledge;
every goldsmith is put to shame
by his idols,
for his images are false,
and there is no breath in them.
15 They are worthless, a work of
delusion;
at the time of their punishment
they shall perish.
16 Not like these is he who is the
portion of Jacob,
for he is the one who formed all
things,
and Israel is the tribe of his
inheritance;
the LORD of hosts is his name.
17 Gather up your bundle from the
ground,
O you who dwell under siege!
18 For thus says the LORD:
"Behold, I am slinging out the
inhabitants of the land
at this time,
and I will bring distress on them,
that they may feel it."
19 Woe is me because of my hurt!
My wound is grievous.
But I said, "Truly this is an affliction,
and I must bear it."
20 My tent is destroyed,
and all my cords are broken;
my children have gone from me,
and they are not;
there is no one to spread my tent
again
and to set up my curtains.
21 For the shepherds are stupid
and do not inquire of the LORD;
therefore they have not prospered,
and all their flock is scattered.
22 A voice, a rumor! Behold, it comes!—
a great commotion out of the
north country
to make the cities of Judah a
desolation,
a lair of jackals.
23 I know, O LORD, that the way of man
is not in himself,
that it is not in man who walks to
direct his steps.
24 Correct me, O LORD, but in justice;
not in your anger, lest you bring
me to nothing.
25 Pour out your wrath on the nations
that know you not,
and on the peoples that call not
on your name,
for they have devoured Jacob;
they have devoured him and
consumed him,
and have laid waste his habitation.

The Broken Covenant

11 The word that came to Jeremiah
from the LORD: 2 "Hear the words
of this covenant, and speak to the men of
Judah and the inhabitants of Jerusalem.
3 You shall say to them, Thus says the LORD,
the God of Israel: Cursed be the man who
does not hear the words of this covenant
4 that I commanded your fathers when
I brought them out of the land of Egypt,
from the iron furnace, saying, Listen to my
voice, and do all that I command you. So
shall you be my people, and I will be your
God, 5 that I may confirm the oath that I
swore to your fathers, to give them a land
flowing with milk and honey, as at this
day." Then I answered, "So be it, LORD."
6 And the LORD said to me, "Proclaim
all these words in the cities of Judah
and in the streets of Jerusalem: Hear the
words of this covenant and do them. 7 For

I solemnly warned your fathers when I
brought them up out of the land of Egypt,
warning them persistently, even to this
day, saying, Obey my voice. 8 Yet they did
not obey or incline their ear, but every-
one walked in the stubbornness of his evil
heart. Therefore I brought upon them all
the words of this covenant, which I com-
manded them to do, but they did not."

9 Again the LORD said to me, "A conspir-
acy exists among the men of Judah and
the inhabitants of Jerusalem. 10 They have
turned back to the iniquities of their fore-
fathers, who refused to hear my words.
They have gone after other gods to serve
them. The house of Israel and the house
of Judah have broken my covenant that
I made with their fathers. 11 Therefore,
thus says the LORD, Behold, I am bring-
ing disaster upon them that they cannot
escape. Though they cry to me, I will not
listen to them. 12 Then the cities of Judah
and the inhabitants of Jerusalem will go
and cry to the gods to whom they make
offerings, but they cannot save them in the
time of their trouble. 13 For your gods have
become as many as your cities, O Judah,
and as many as the streets of Jerusalem
are the altars you have set up to shame,
altars to make offerings to Baal.

14 "Therefore do not pray for this people,
or lift up a cry or prayer on their behalf, for
I will not listen when they call to me in the
time of their trouble. 15 What right has my
beloved in my house, when she has done
many vile deeds? Can even sacrificial flesh
avert your doom? Can you then exult?
16 The LORD once called you 'a green olive
tree, beautiful with good fruit.' But with
the roar of a great tempest he will set fire
to it, and its branches will be consumed.
17 The LORD of hosts, who planted you, has
decreed disaster against you, because of
the evil that the house of Israel and the
house of Judah have done, provoking me
to anger by making offerings to Baal."

18 The LORD made it known to me and
I knew;
then you showed me their deeds.
19 But I was like a gentle lamb
led to the slaughter.
I did not know it was against me
they devised schemes, saying,
"Let us destroy the tree with its fruit,
let us cut him off from the land of
the living,
that his name be remembered no
more."
20 But, O LORD of hosts, who judges
righteously,
who tests the heart and the mind,
let me see your vengeance upon
them,
for to you have I committed my
cause.

21 Therefore thus says the LORD con-
cerning the men of Anathoth, who seek
your life, and say, "Do not prophesy in the
name of the LORD, or you will die by our
hand"— 22 therefore thus says the LORD
of hosts: "Behold, I will punish them. The
young men shall die by the sword, their
sons and their daughters shall die by fam-
ine, 23 and none of them shall be left. For
I will bring disaster upon the men of
Anathoth, the year of their punishment."

Jeremiah's Complaint

12 Righteous are you, O LORD,
when I complain to you;
yet I would plead my case before
you.
Why does the way of the wicked
prosper?
Why do all who are treacherous
thrive?
2 You plant them, and they take root;
they grow and produce fruit;
you are near in their mouth
and far from their heart.
3 But you, O LORD, know me;
you see me, and test my heart
toward you.

Pull them out like sheep for the
slaughter,
and set them apart for the day of
slaughter.
4 How long will the land mourn
and the grass of every field wither?
For the evil of those who dwell in it
the beasts and the birds are swept
away,
because they said, "He will not
see our latter end."

The Lord Answers Jeremiah

5 "If you have raced with men on foot,
and they have wearied you,
how will you compete with horses?
And if in a safe land you are so
trusting,
what will you do in the thicket of
the Jordan?
6 For even your brothers and the
house of your father,
even they have dealt
treacherously with you;
they are in full cry after you;
do not believe them,
though they speak friendly words
to you."

7 "I have forsaken my house;
I have abandoned my heritage;
I have given the beloved of my soul
into the hands of her enemies.
8 My heritage has become to me
like a lion in the forest;
she has lifted up her voice against me;
therefore I hate her.
9 Is my heritage to me like a hyena's
lair?
Are the birds of prey against her
all around?
Go, assemble all the wild beasts;
bring them to devour.
10 Many shepherds have destroyed my
vineyard;
they have trampled down my
portion;
they have made my pleasant portion
a desolate wilderness.
11 They have made it a desolation;
desolate, it mourns to me.
The whole land is made desolate,
but no man lays it to heart.
12 Upon all the bare heights in the
desert
destroyers have come,
for the sword of the Lord devours
from one end of the land to the
other;
no flesh has peace.
13 They have sown wheat and have
reaped thorns;
they have tired themselves out
but profit nothing.
They shall be ashamed of their[1]
harvests
because of the fierce anger of the
Lord."

14 Thus says the Lord concerning all
my evil neighbors who touch the heri-
tage that I have given my people Israel to
inherit: "Behold, I will pluck them up from
their land, and I will pluck up the house
of Judah from among them. 15 And after
I have plucked them up, I will again have
compassion on them, and I will bring
them again each to his heritage and each
to his land. 16 And it shall come to pass, if
they will diligently learn the ways of my
people, to swear by my name, 'As the Lord
lives,' even as they taught my people to
swear by Baal, then they shall be built up in
the midst of my people. 17 But if any nation
will not listen, then I will utterly pluck it
up and destroy it, declares the Lord."

The Ruined Loincloth

13 Thus says the Lord to me, "Go
and buy a linen loincloth and put
it around your waist, and do not dip it in
water." 2 So I bought a loincloth accord-
ing to the word of the Lord, and put it
around my waist. 3 And the word of the
Lord came to me a second time, 4 "Take

[1] Hebrew *your*

the loincloth that you have bought, which
is around your waist, and arise, go to the
Euphrates and hide it there in a cleft of
the rock." 5 So I went and hid it by the
Euphrates, as the LORD commanded me.
6 And after many days the LORD said to
me, "Arise, go to the Euphrates, and take
from there the loincloth that I commanded
you to hide there." 7 Then I went to the
Euphrates, and dug, and I took the loin-
cloth from the place where I had hidden
it. And behold, the loincloth was spoiled;
it was good for nothing.
8 Then the word of the LORD came to me:
9 "Thus says the LORD: Even so will I spoil
the pride of Judah and the great pride of
Jerusalem. 10 This evil people, who refuse
to hear my words, who stubbornly follow
their own heart and have gone after other
gods to serve them and worship them, shall
be like this loincloth, which is good for
nothing. 11 For as the loincloth clings to the
waist of a man, so I made the whole house
of Israel and the whole house of Judah cling
to me, declares the LORD, that they might
be for me a people, a name, a praise, and a
glory, but they would not listen.

The Jars Filled with Wine

12 "You shall speak to them this word:
'Thus says the LORD, the God of Israel,
"Every jar shall be filled with wine."' And
they will say to you, 'Do we not indeed
know that every jar will be filled with
wine?' 13 Then you shall say to them,
'Thus says the LORD: Behold, I will fill
with drunkenness all the inhabitants of
this land: the kings who sit on David's
throne, the priests, the prophets, and all
the inhabitants of Jerusalem. 14 And I will
dash them one against another, fathers
and sons together, declares the LORD. I
will not pity or spare or have compassion,
that I should not destroy them.'"

Exile Threatened

15 Hear and give ear; be not proud,
for the LORD has spoken.
16 Give glory to the LORD your God
before he brings darkness,
before your feet stumble
on the twilight mountains,
and while you look for light
he turns it into gloom
and makes it deep darkness.
17 But if you will not listen,
my soul will weep in secret for
your pride;
my eyes will weep bitterly and run
down with tears,
because the LORD's flock has been
taken captive.

18 Say to the king and the queen mother:
"Take a lowly seat,
for your beautiful crown
has come down from your head."
19 The cities of the Negeb are shut up,
with none to open them;
all Judah is taken into exile,
wholly taken into exile.

20 "Lift up your eyes and see
those who come from the north.
Where is the flock that was given you,
your beautiful flock?
21 What will you say when they set as
head over you
those whom you yourself have
taught to be friends to you?
Will not pangs take hold of you
like those of a woman in labor?
22 And if you say in your heart,
'Why have these things come
upon me?'
it is for the greatness of your iniquity
that your skirts are lifted up
and you suffer violence.
23 Can the Ethiopian change his skin
or the leopard his spots?
Then also you can do good
who are accustomed to do evil.
24 I will scatter you[1] like chaff
driven by the wind from the desert.

[1] Hebrew *them*

25 This is your lot,
the portion I have measured out
to you, declares the LORD,
because you have forgotten me
and trusted in lies.
26 I myself will lift up your skirts over
your face,
and your shame will be seen.
27 I have seen your abominations,
your adulteries and neighings,
your lewd whorings,
on the hills in the field.
Woe to you, O Jerusalem!
How long will it be before you are
made clean?"

Famine, Sword, and Pestilence

14 The word of the LORD that came to Jeremiah concerning the drought:

2 "Judah mourns,
and her gates languish;
her people lament on the ground,
and the cry of Jerusalem goes up.
3 Her nobles send their servants for
water;
they come to the cisterns;
they find no water;
they return with their vessels
empty;
they are ashamed and confounded
and cover their heads.
4 Because of the ground that is
dismayed,
since there is no rain on the land,
the farmers are ashamed;
they cover their heads.
5 Even the doe in the field forsakes
her newborn fawn
because there is no grass.
6 The wild donkeys stand on the bare
heights;
they pant for air like jackals;
their eyes fail
because there is no vegetation.
7 "Though our iniquities testify
against us,
act, O LORD, for your name's sake;
for our backslidings are many;
we have sinned against you.
8 O you hope of Israel,
its savior in time of trouble,
why should you be like a stranger in
the land,
like a traveler who turns aside to
tarry for a night?
9 Why should you be like a man
confused,
like a mighty warrior who cannot
save?
Yet you, O LORD, are in the midst of
us,
and we are called by your name;
do not leave us."

10 Thus says the LORD concerning this
people:
"They have loved to wander thus;
they have not restrained their feet;
therefore the LORD does not accept
them;
now he will remember their
iniquity
and punish their sins."

11 The LORD said to me: "Do not pray for
the welfare of this people. 12 Though they
fast, I will not hear their cry, and though
they offer burnt offering and grain offer-
ing, I will not accept them. But I will con-
sume them by the sword, by famine, and
by pestilence."

Lying Prophets

13 Then I said: "Ah, Lord GOD, behold,
the prophets say to them, 'You shall not
see the sword, nor shall you have fam-
ine, but I will give you assured peace in
this place.'" 14 And the LORD said to me:
"The prophets are prophesying lies in
my name. I did not send them, nor did I
command them or speak to them. They
are prophesying to you a lying vision,

worthless divination, and the deceit of
their own minds. 15 Therefore thus says the
LORD concerning the prophets who proph-
esy in my name although I did not send
them, and who say, 'Sword and famine
shall not come upon this land': By sword
and famine those prophets shall be con-
sumed. 16 And the people to whom they
prophesy shall be cast out in the streets of
Jerusalem, victims of famine and sword,
with none to bury them—them, their
wives, their sons, and their daughters. For
I will pour out their evil upon them.

17 "You shall say to them this word:
'Let my eyes run down with tears
night and day,
and let them not cease,
for the virgin daughter of my people
is shattered with a great
wound,
with a very grievous blow.
18 If I go out into the field,
behold, those pierced by the sword!
And if I enter the city,
behold, the diseases of famine!
For both prophet and priest ply
their trade through the land
and have no knowledge.'"

19 Have you utterly rejected Judah?
Does your soul loathe Zion?
Why have you struck us down
so that there is no healing for us?
We looked for peace, but no good
came;
for a time of healing, but behold,
terror.
20 We acknowledge our wickedness,
O LORD,
and the iniquity of our fathers,
for we have sinned against you.
21 Do not spurn us, for your name's
sake;
do not dishonor your glorious
throne;
remember and do not break your
covenant with us.
22 Are there any among the false gods of
the nations that can bring rain?
Or can the heavens give showers?
Are you not he, O LORD our God?
We set our hope on you,
for you do all these things.

The LORD Will Not Relent

15 Then the LORD said to me, "Though
Moses and Samuel stood before
me, yet my heart would not turn toward
this people. Send them out of my sight,
and let them go! 2 And when they ask you,
'Where shall we go?' you shall say to them,
'Thus says the LORD:

"'Those who are for pestilence, to
pestilence,
and those who are for the sword,
to the sword;
those who are for famine, to famine,
and those who are for captivity, to
captivity.'

3 I will appoint over them four kinds of
destroyers, declares the LORD: the sword
to kill, the dogs to tear, and the birds of the
air and the beasts of the earth to devour
and destroy. 4 And I will make them a
horror to all the kingdoms of the earth
because of what Manasseh the son of
Hezekiah, king of Judah, did in Jerusalem.

5 "Who will have pity on you,
O Jerusalem,
or who will grieve for you?
Who will turn aside
to ask about your welfare?
6 You have rejected me, declares the
LORD;
you keep going backward,
so I have stretched out my hand
against you and destroyed
you—
I am weary of relenting.
7 I have winnowed them with a
winnowing fork
in the gates of the land;

I have bereaved them; I have
destroyed my people;
they did not turn from their ways.
8 I have made their widows more in
number
than the sand of the seas;
I have brought against the mothers
of young men
a destroyer at noonday;
I have made anguish and terror
fall upon them suddenly.
9 She who bore seven has grown feeble;
she has fainted away;
her sun went down while it was yet
day;
she has been shamed and
disgraced.
And the rest of them I will give to
the sword
before their enemies,
declares the LORD."

Jeremiah's Complaint

10 Woe is me, my mother, that you bore
me, a man of strife and contention to the
whole land! I have not lent, nor have I bor-
rowed, yet all of them curse me. 11 The
LORD said, "Have I not[1] set you free for their
good? Have I not pleaded for you before the
enemy in the time of trouble and in the
time of distress? 12 Can one break iron, iron
from the north, and bronze?
13 "Your wealth and your treasures I will
give as spoil, without price, for all your
sins, throughout all your territory. 14 I will
make you serve your enemies in a land
that you do not know, for in my anger a
fire is kindled that shall burn forever."

15 O LORD, you know;
remember me and visit me,
and take vengeance for me on my
persecutors.
In your forbearance take me not
away;
know that for your sake I bear
reproach.

16 Your words were found, and I ate
them,
and your words became to me a joy
and the delight of my heart,
for I am called by your name,
O LORD, God of hosts.
17 I did not sit in the company of
revelers,
nor did I rejoice;
I sat alone, because your hand was
upon me,
for you had filled me with
indignation.
18 Why is my pain unceasing,
my wound incurable,
refusing to be healed?
Will you be to me like a deceitful
brook,
like waters that fail?

19 Therefore thus says the LORD:
"If you return, I will restore you,
and you shall stand before me.
If you utter what is precious, and
not what is worthless,
you shall be as my mouth.
They shall turn to you,
but you shall not turn to them.
20 And I will make you to this people
a fortified wall of bronze;
they will fight against you,
but they shall not prevail over you,
for I am with you
to save you and deliver you,
declares the LORD.
21 I will deliver you out of the hand of
the wicked,
and redeem you from the grasp of
the ruthless."

Famine, Sword, and Death

16 The word of the LORD came to me:
2 "You shall not take a wife, nor
shall you have sons or daughters in this
place. 3 For thus says the LORD concern-
ing the sons and daughters who are born
in this place, and concerning the moth-
ers who bore them and the fathers who

[1] The meaning of the Hebrew is uncertain

fathered them in this land: 4 They shall
die of deadly diseases. They shall not be
lamented, nor shall they be buried. They
shall be as dung on the surface of the
ground. They shall perish by the sword
and by famine, and their dead bodies shall
be food for the birds of the air and for the
beasts of the earth.

5 "For thus says the LORD: Do not enter
the house of mourning, or go to lament or
grieve for them, for I have taken away my
peace from this people, my steadfast love
and mercy, declares the LORD. 6 Both great
and small shall die in this land. They shall
not be buried, and no one shall lament
for them or cut himself or make himself
bald for them. 7 No one shall break bread
for the mourner, to comfort him for the
dead, nor shall anyone give him the cup
of consolation to drink for his father or his
mother. 8 You shall not go into the house
of feasting to sit with them, to eat and
drink. 9 For thus says the LORD of hosts,
the God of Israel: Behold, I will silence in
this place, before your eyes and in your
days, the voice of mirth and the voice of
gladness, the voice of the bridegroom and
the voice of the bride.

10 "And when you tell this people all
these words, and they say to you, 'Why
has the LORD pronounced all this great
evil against us? What is our iniquity? What
is the sin that we have committed against
the LORD our God?' 11 then you shall say
to them: 'Because your fathers have for-
saken me, declares the LORD, and have
gone after other gods and have served and
worshiped them, and have forsaken me
and have not kept my law, 12 and because
you have done worse than your fathers,
for behold, every one of you follows his
stubborn, evil will, refusing to listen to
me. 13 Therefore I will hurl you out of this
land into a land that neither you nor your
fathers have known, and there you shall
serve other gods day and night, for I will
show you no favor.'

The LORD Will Restore Israel

14 "Therefore, behold, the days are com-
ing, declares the LORD, when it shall no
longer be said, 'As the LORD lives who
brought up the people of Israel out of the
land of Egypt,' 15 but 'As the LORD lives who
brought up the people of Israel out of the
north country and out of all the countries
where he had driven them.' For I will bring
them back to their own land that I gave to
their fathers.

16 "Behold, I am sending for many fish-
ers, declares the LORD, and they shall catch
them. And afterward I will send for many
hunters, and they shall hunt them from
every mountain and every hill, and out of
the clefts of the rocks. 17 For my eyes are on
all their ways. They are not hidden from
me, nor is their iniquity concealed from
my eyes. 18 But first I will doubly repay
their iniquity and their sin, because they
have polluted my land with the carcasses
of their detestable idols, and have filled
my inheritance with their abominations."

19 O LORD, my strength and my
stronghold,
my refuge in the day of trouble,
to you shall the nations come
from the ends of the earth and say:
"Our fathers have inherited nothing
but lies,
worthless things in which there is
no profit.
20 Can man make for himself gods?
Such are not gods!"

21 "Therefore, behold, I will make them
know, this once I will make them know
my power and my might, and they shall
know that my name is the LORD."

The Sin of Judah

17 "The sin of Judah is written with
a pen of iron; with a point of dia-
mond it is engraved on the tablet of their
heart, and on the horns of their altars,
2 while their children remember their

altars and their Asherim, beside every
green tree and on the high hills, 3 on the
mountains in the open country. Your
wealth and all your treasures I will give
for spoil as the price of your high places
for sin throughout all your territory. 4 You
shall loosen your hand from your heritage
that I gave to you, and I will make you
serve your enemies in a land that you do
not know, for in my anger a fire is kindled
that shall burn forever."

5 Thus says the LORD:
"Cursed is the man who trusts in man
and makes flesh his strength,[1]
whose heart turns away from the LORD.
6 He is like a shrub in the desert,
and shall not see any good come.
He shall dwell in the parched places of the wilderness,
in an uninhabited salt land.

7 "Blessed is the man who trusts in the LORD,
whose trust is the LORD.
8 He is like a tree planted by water,
that sends out its roots by the stream,
and does not fear when heat comes,
for its leaves remain green,
and is not anxious in the year of drought,
for it does not cease to bear fruit."

9 The heart is deceitful above all things,
and desperately sick;
who can understand it?
10 "I the LORD search the heart
and test the mind,[2]
to give every man according to his ways,
according to the fruit of his deeds."
11 Like the partridge that gathers a brood that she did not hatch,
so is he who gets riches but not by justice;
in the midst of his days they will leave him,
and at his end he will be a fool.

12 A glorious throne set on high from the beginning
is the place of our sanctuary.
13 O LORD, the hope of Israel,
all who forsake you shall be put to shame;
those who turn away from you[3]
shall be written in the earth,
for they have forsaken the LORD,
the fountain of living water.

Jeremiah Prays for Deliverance

14 Heal me, O LORD, and I shall be healed;
save me, and I shall be saved,
for you are my praise.
15 Behold, they say to me,
"Where is the word of the LORD?
Let it come!"
16 I have not run away from being your shepherd,
nor have I desired the day of sickness.
You know what came out of my lips;
it was before your face.
17 Be not a terror to me;
you are my refuge in the day of disaster.
18 Let those be put to shame who persecute me,
but let me not be put to shame;
let them be dismayed,
but let me not be dismayed;
bring upon them the day of disaster;
destroy them with double destruction!

Keep the Sabbath Holy

19 Thus said the LORD to me: "Go and
stand in the People's Gate, by which the
kings of Judah enter and by which they
go out, and in all the gates of Jerusalem,
20 and say: 'Hear the word of the LORD, you
kings of Judah, and all Judah, and all the

[1] Hebrew *arm* [2] Hebrew *kidneys* [3] Hebrew *me*

inhabitants of Jerusalem, who enter by
these gates. 21 Thus says the LORD: Take
care for the sake of your lives, and do not
bear a burden on the Sabbath day or bring
it in by the gates of Jerusalem. 22 And do
not carry a burden out of your houses on
the Sabbath or do any work, but keep the
Sabbath day holy, as I commanded your
fathers. 23 Yet they did not listen or incline
their ear, but stiffened their neck, that they
might not hear and receive instruction.

24 "'But if you listen to me, declares the
LORD, and bring in no burden by the gates
of this city on the Sabbath day, but keep
the Sabbath day holy and do no work on
it, 25 then there shall enter by the gates of
this city kings and princes who sit on the
throne of David, riding in chariots and on
horses, they and their officials, the men of
Judah and the inhabitants of Jerusalem.
And this city shall be inhabited forever.
26 And people shall come from the cities
of Judah and the places around Jerusalem,
from the land of Benjamin, from the
Shephelah, from the hill country, and
from the Negeb, bringing burnt offerings
and sacrifices, grain offerings and frank-
incense, and bringing thank offerings to
the house of the LORD. 27 But if you do not
listen to me, to keep the Sabbath day holy,
and not to bear a burden and enter by the
gates of Jerusalem on the Sabbath day,
then I will kindle a fire in its gates, and it
shall devour the palaces of Jerusalem and
shall not be quenched.'"

The Potter and the Clay

18 The word that came to Jeremiah
from the LORD: 2 "Arise, and go
down to the potter's house, and there I will
let you hear my words." 3 So I went down to
the potter's house, and there he was work-
ing at his wheel. 4 And the vessel he was
making of clay was spoiled in the potter's
hand, and he reworked it into another ves-
sel, as it seemed good to the potter to do.

5 Then the word of the LORD came to
me: 6 "O house of Israel, can I not do with
you as this potter has done? declares the
LORD. Behold, like the clay in the potter's
hand, so are you in my hand, O house of
Israel. 7 If at any time I declare concerning
a nation or a kingdom, that I will pluck
up and break down and destroy it, 8 and
if that nation, concerning which I have
spoken, turns from its evil, I will relent
of the disaster that I intended to do to it.
9 And if at any time I declare concerning a
nation or a kingdom that I will build and
plant it, 10 and if it does evil in my sight,
not listening to my voice, then I will relent
of the good that I had intended to do to it.
11 Now, therefore, say to the men of Judah
and the inhabitants of Jerusalem: 'Thus
says the LORD, Behold, I am shaping disas-
ter against you and devising a plan against
you. Return, every one from his evil way,
and amend your ways and your deeds.'

12 "But they say, 'That is in vain! We will
follow our own plans, and will every one
act according to the stubbornness of his
evil heart.'

13 "Therefore thus says the LORD:
Ask among the nations,
  Who has heard the like of this?
The virgin Israel
  has done a very horrible thing.
14 Does the snow of Lebanon leave
  the crags of Sirion?[1]
Do the mountain waters run dry,[2]
  the cold flowing streams?
15 But my people have forgotten me;
  they make offerings to false gods;
they made them stumble in their
    ways,
  in the ancient roads,
and to walk into side roads,
  not the highway,
16 making their land a horror,
  a thing to be hissed at forever.
Everyone who passes by it is horrified
  and shakes his head.
17 Like the east wind I will scatter them
  before the enemy.

[1] Hebrew *of the field* [2] Hebrew *Are foreign waters plucked up*

I will show them my back, not my
face,
in the day of their calamity."

[18] Then they said, "Come, let us make plots against Jeremiah, for the law shall not perish from the priest, nor counsel from the wise, nor the word from the prophet. Come, let us strike him with the tongue, and let us not pay attention to any of his words."

19 Hear me, O LORD,
and listen to the voice of my
adversaries.
20 Should good be repaid with evil?
Yet they have dug a pit for my life.
Remember how I stood before you
to speak good for them,
to turn away your wrath from them.
21 Therefore deliver up their children
to famine;
give them over to the power of the
sword;
let their wives become childless and
widowed.
May their men meet death by
pestilence,
their youths be struck down by
the sword in battle.
22 May a cry be heard from their houses,
when you bring the plunderer
suddenly upon them!
For they have dug a pit to take me
and laid snares for my feet.
23 Yet you, O LORD, know
all their plotting to kill me.
Forgive not their iniquity,
nor blot out their sin from your
sight.
Let them be overthrown before you;
deal with them in the time of
your anger.

The Broken Flask

19 Thus says the LORD, "Go, buy a pot-
ter's earthenware flask, and take
some of the elders of the people and some
of the elders of the priests, [2] and go out
to the Valley of the Son of Hinnom at the
entry of the Potsherd Gate, and proclaim
there the words that I tell you. [3] You shall
say, 'Hear the word of the LORD, O kings of
Judah and inhabitants of Jerusalem. Thus
says the LORD of hosts, the God of Israel:
Behold, I am bringing such disaster upon
this place that the ears of everyone who
hears of it will tingle. [4] Because the people
have forsaken me and have profaned this
place by making offerings in it to other
gods whom neither they nor their fathers
nor the kings of Judah have known; and
because they have filled this place with
the blood of innocents, [5] and have built the
high places of Baal to burn their sons in
the fire as burnt offerings to Baal, which
I did not command or decree, nor did it
come into my mind— [6] therefore, behold,
days are coming, declares the LORD, when
this place shall no more be called Topheth,
or the Valley of the Son of Hinnom, but
the Valley of Slaughter. [7] And in this place
I will make void the plans of Judah and
Jerusalem, and will cause their people to
fall by the sword before their enemies,
and by the hand of those who seek their
life. I will give their dead bodies for food
to the birds of the air and to the beasts
of the earth. [8] And I will make this city a
horror, a thing to be hissed at. Everyone
who passes by it will be horrified and will
hiss because of all its wounds. [9] And I will
make them eat the flesh of their sons and
their daughters, and everyone shall eat
the flesh of his neighbor in the siege and
in the distress, with which their enemies
and those who seek their life afflict them.'

[10] "Then you shall break the flask in the
sight of the men who go with you, [11] and
shall say to them, 'Thus says the LORD
of hosts: So will I break this people and
this city, as one breaks a potter's vessel,
so that it can never be mended. Men shall
bury in Topheth because there will be no
place else to bury. [12] Thus will I do to this

place, declares the LORD, and to its inhabitants, making this city like Topheth. 13 The houses of Jerusalem and the houses of the kings of Judah—all the houses on whose roofs offerings have been offered to all the host of heaven, and drink offerings have been poured out to other gods—shall be defiled like the place of Topheth.'"

14 Then Jeremiah came from Topheth, where the LORD had sent him to prophesy, and he stood in the court of the LORD's house and said to all the people: 15 "Thus says the LORD of hosts, the God of Israel, behold, I am bringing upon this city and upon all its towns all the disaster that I have pronounced against it, because they have stiffened their neck, refusing to hear my words."

Jeremiah Persecuted by Pashhur

20 Now Pashhur the priest, the son of Immer, who was chief officer in the house of the LORD, heard Jeremiah prophesying these things. 2 Then Pashhur beat Jeremiah the prophet, and put him in the stocks that were in the upper Benjamin Gate of the house of the LORD. 3 The next day, when Pashhur released Jeremiah from the stocks, Jeremiah said to him, "The LORD does not call your name Pashhur, but Terror On Every Side. 4 For thus says the LORD: Behold, I will make you a terror to yourself and to all your friends. They shall fall by the sword of their enemies while you look on. And I will give all Judah into the hand of the king of Babylon. He shall carry them captive to Babylon, and shall strike them down with the sword. 5 Moreover, I will give all the wealth of the city, all its gains, all its prized belongings, and all the treasures of the kings of Judah into the hand of their enemies, who shall plunder them and seize them and carry them to Babylon. 6 And you, Pashhur, and all who dwell in your house, shall go into captivity. To Babylon you shall go, and there you shall die, and there you shall be buried, you and all your friends, to whom you have prophesied falsely."

7 O LORD, you have deceived me,
and I was deceived;
you are stronger than I,
and you have prevailed.
I have become a laughingstock all the day;
everyone mocks me.
8 For whenever I speak, I cry out,
I shout, "Violence and destruction!"
For the word of the LORD has become for me
a reproach and derision all day long.
9 If I say, "I will not mention him,
or speak any more in his name,"
there is in my heart as it were a burning fire
shut up in my bones,
and I am weary with holding it in,
and I cannot.
10 For I hear many whispering.
Terror is on every side!
"Denounce him! Let us denounce him!"
say all my close friends,
watching for my fall.
"Perhaps he will be deceived;
then we can overcome him
and take our revenge on him."
11 But the LORD is with me as a dread warrior;
therefore my persecutors will stumble;
they will not overcome me.
They will be greatly shamed,
for they will not succeed.
Their eternal dishonor
will never be forgotten.
12 O LORD of hosts, who tests the righteous,
who sees the heart and the mind,[1]
let me see your vengeance upon them,
for to you have I committed my cause.

[1] Hebrew *kidneys*

13 Sing to the LORD;
praise the LORD!
For he has delivered the life of the
needy
from the hand of evildoers.

14 Cursed be the day
on which I was born!
The day when my mother bore me,
let it not be blessed!
15 Cursed be the man who brought the
news to my father,
"A son is born to you,"
making him very glad.
16 Let that man be like the cities
that the LORD overthrew without
pity;
let him hear a cry in the morning
and an alarm at noon,
17 because he did not kill me in the
womb;
so my mother would have been
my grave,
and her womb forever great.
18 Why did I come out from the womb
to see toil and sorrow,
and spend my days in shame?

Jerusalem Will Fall to Nebuchadnezzar

21 This is the word that came to
Jeremiah from the LORD, when
King Zedekiah sent to him Pashhur the
son of Malchiah and Zephaniah the priest,
the son of Maaseiah, saying, 2 "Inquire
of the LORD for us, for Nebuchadnezzar[1]
king of Babylon is making war against us.
Perhaps the LORD will deal with us according to all his wonderful deeds and will
make him withdraw from us."
3 Then Jeremiah said to them: 4 "Thus
you shall say to Zedekiah, 'Thus says the
LORD, the God of Israel: Behold, I will turn
back the weapons of war that are in your
hands and with which you are fighting
against the king of Babylon and against the
Chaldeans who are besieging you outside
the walls. And I will bring them together
into the midst of this city. 5 I myself will
fight against you with outstretched hand
and strong arm, in anger and in fury and
in great wrath. 6 And I will strike down
the inhabitants of this city, both man and
beast. They shall die of a great pestilence.
7 Afterward, declares the LORD, I will give
Zedekiah king of Judah and his servants
and the people in this city who survive
the pestilence, sword, and famine into the
hand of Nebuchadnezzar king of Babylon
and into the hand of their enemies, into
the hand of those who seek their lives. He
shall strike them down with the edge of
the sword. He shall not pity them or spare
them or have compassion.'
8 "And to this people you shall say: 'Thus
says the LORD: Behold, I set before you the
way of life and the way of death. 9 He who
stays in this city shall die by the sword,
by famine, and by pestilence, but he who
goes out and surrenders to the Chaldeans
who are besieging you shall live and shall
have his life as a prize of war. 10 For I have
set my face against this city for harm and
not for good, declares the LORD: it shall be
given into the hand of the king of Babylon,
and he shall burn it with fire.'

Message to the House of David

11 "And to the house of the king of Judah
say, 'Hear the word of the LORD, 12 O house
of David! Thus says the LORD:

"'Execute justice in the morning,
and deliver from the hand of the
oppressor
him who has been robbed,
lest my wrath go forth like fire,
and burn with none to quench it,
because of your evil deeds.'"

13 "Behold, I am against you, O
inhabitant of the valley,
O rock of the plain,
declares the LORD;

[1] Hebrew *Nebuchadrezzar*, another spelling for *Nebuchadnezzar* (king of Babylon) occurring frequently from Jeremiah 21–52; this latter spelling is used throughout Jeremiah for consistency

you who say, 'Who shall come down
against us,
or who shall enter our habitations?'
14 I will punish you according to the
fruit of your deeds,
declares the LORD;
I will kindle a fire in her forest,
and it shall devour all that is
around her."

22 Thus says the LORD: "Go down to
the house of the king of Judah and
speak there this word, 2 and say, 'Hear the
word of the LORD, O king of Judah, who
sits on the throne of David, you, and your
servants, and your people who enter these
gates. 3 Thus says the LORD: Do justice
and righteousness, and deliver from the
hand of the oppressor him who has been
robbed. And do no wrong or violence to
the resident alien, the fatherless, and the
widow, nor shed innocent blood in this
place. 4 For if you will indeed obey this
word, then there shall enter the gates of
this house kings who sit on the throne of
David, riding in chariots and on horses,
they and their servants and their people.
5 But if you will not obey these words, I
swear by myself, declares the LORD, that
this house shall become a desolation. 6 For
thus says the LORD concerning the house
of the king of Judah:

"'You are like Gilead to me,
like the summit of Lebanon,
yet surely I will make you a desert,
an uninhabited city.[1]
7 I will prepare destroyers against you,
each with his weapons,
and they shall cut down your
choicest cedars
and cast them into the fire.

8 "'And many nations will pass by this
city, and every man will say to his neigh-
bor, "Why has the LORD dealt thus with
this great city?" 9 And they will answer,
"Because they have forsaken the cov-
enant of the LORD their God and wor-
shiped other gods and served them."'"

10 Weep not for him who is dead,
nor grieve for him,
but weep bitterly for him who goes
away,
for he shall return no more
to see his native land.

Message to the Sons of Josiah

11 For thus says the LORD concerning
Shallum the son of Josiah, king of Judah,
who reigned instead of Josiah his father,
and who went away from this place: "He
shall return here no more, 12 but in the
place where they have carried him cap-
tive, there shall he die, and he shall never
see this land again."

13 "Woe to him who builds his house
by unrighteousness,
and his upper rooms by injustice,
who makes his neighbor serve him
for nothing
and does not give him his wages,
14 who says, 'I will build myself a great
house
with spacious upper rooms,'
who cuts out windows for it,
paneling it with cedar
and painting it with vermilion.
15 Do you think you are a king
because you compete in cedar?
Did not your father eat and drink
and do justice and righteousness?
Then it was well with him.
16 He judged the cause of the poor and
needy;
then it was well.
Is not this to know me?
declares the LORD.
17 But you have eyes and heart
only for your dishonest gain,
for shedding innocent blood,
and for practicing oppression and
violence."

18 Therefore thus says the LORD con-

[1] Hebrew *cities*

cerning Jehoiakim the son of Josiah, king
of Judah:

"They shall not lament for him, saying,
'Ah, my brother!' or 'Ah, sister!'
They shall not lament for him, saying,
'Ah, lord!' or 'Ah, his majesty!'
19 With the burial of a donkey he shall
be buried,
dragged and dumped beyond the
gates of Jerusalem."

20 "Go up to Lebanon, and cry out,
and lift up your voice in Bashan;
cry out from Abarim,
for all your lovers are destroyed.
21 I spoke to you in your prosperity,
but you said, 'I will not listen.'
This has been your way from your
youth,
that you have not obeyed my voice.
22 The wind shall shepherd all your
shepherds,
and your lovers shall go into
captivity;
then you will be ashamed and
confounded
because of all your evil.
23 O inhabitant of Lebanon,
nested among the cedars,
how you will be pitied when pangs
come upon you,
pain as of a woman in labor!"

24 "As I live, declares the LORD, though
Coniah the son of Jehoiakim, king of Judah,
were the signet ring on my right hand, yet
I would tear you off 25 and give you into
the hand of those who seek your life, into
the hand of those of whom you are afraid,
even into the hand of Nebuchadnezzar
king of Babylon and into the hand of the
Chaldeans. 26 I will hurl you and the mother
who bore you into another country, where
you were not born, and there you shall die.
27 But to the land to which they will long to
return, there they shall not return."

28 Is this man Coniah a despised,
broken pot,
a vessel no one cares for?
Why are he and his children hurled
and cast
into a land that they do not know?
29 O land, land, land,
hear the word of the LORD!
30 Thus says the LORD:
"Write this man down as childless,
a man who shall not succeed in
his days,
for none of his offspring shall
succeed
in sitting on the throne of David
and ruling again in Judah."

The Righteous Branch

23 "Woe to the shepherds who destroy
and scatter the sheep of my pas-
ture!" declares the LORD. 2 Therefore thus
says the LORD, the God of Israel, concern-
ing the shepherds who care for my peo-
ple: "You have scattered my flock and
have driven them away, and you have not
attended to them. Behold, I will attend to
you for your evil deeds, declares the LORD.
3 Then I will gather the remnant of my
flock out of all the countries where I have
driven them, and I will bring them back
to their fold, and they shall be fruitful and
multiply. 4 I will set shepherds over them
who will care for them, and they shall fear
no more, nor be dismayed, neither shall
any be missing, declares the LORD.

5 "Behold, the days are coming,
declares the LORD, when I will raise
1033
up for David a righteous Branch,
and he shall reign as king and deal
wisely, and shall execute justice
1345
and righteousness in the land. 6 In
his days Judah will be saved, and Israel
will dwell securely. And this is the name
by which he will be called: 'The LORD is
our righteousness.'

7 "Therefore, behold, the days are com-
ing, declares the LORD, when they shall no

longer say, 'As the LORD lives who brought
up the people of Israel out of the land of
Egypt,' 8 but 'As the LORD lives who brought
up and led the offspring of the house of
Israel out of the north country and out of all
the countries where he[1] had driven them.'
Then they shall dwell in their own land."

Lying Prophets

9 Concerning the prophets:

My heart is broken within me;
all my bones shake;
I am like a drunken man,
like a man overcome by wine,
because of the LORD
and because of his holy words.
10 For the land is full of adulterers;
because of the curse the land
mourns,
and the pastures of the
wilderness are dried up.
Their course is evil,
and their might is not right.
11 "Both prophet and priest are ungodly;
even in my house I have found
their evil,
declares the LORD.
12 Therefore their way shall be to them
like slippery paths in the darkness,
into which they shall be driven
and fall,
for I will bring disaster upon them
in the year of their punishment,
declares the LORD.
13 In the prophets of Samaria
I saw an unsavory thing:
they prophesied by Baal
and led my people Israel astray.
14 But in the prophets of Jerusalem
I have seen a horrible thing:
they commit adultery and walk in
lies;
they strengthen the hands of
evildoers,
so that no one turns from his evil;
all of them have become like Sodom
to me,
and its inhabitants like Gomorrah."
15 Therefore thus says the LORD of
hosts concerning the prophets:
"Behold, I will feed them with bitter
food
and give them poisoned water to
drink,
for from the prophets of Jerusalem
ungodliness has gone out into all
the land."

16 Thus says the LORD of hosts: "Do not
listen to the words of the prophets who
prophesy to you, filling you with vain
hopes. They speak visions of their own
minds, not from the mouth of the LORD.
17 They say continually to those who
despise the word of the LORD, 'It shall be
well with you'; and to everyone who stub-
bornly follows his own heart, they say, 'No
disaster shall come upon you.'"

18 For who among them has stood in
the council of the LORD
to see and to hear his word,
or who has paid attention to his
word and listened?
19 Behold, the storm of the LORD!
Wrath has gone forth,
a whirling tempest;
it will burst upon the head of the
wicked.
20 The anger of the LORD will not turn
back
until he has executed and
accomplished
the intents of his heart.
In the latter days you will
understand it clearly.
21 "I did not send the prophets,
yet they ran;
I did not speak to them,
yet they prophesied.
22 But if they had stood in my council,
then they would have proclaimed
my words to my people,

[1] Septuagint; Hebrew *I*

and they would have turned them
from their evil way,
and from the evil of their deeds.

23 "Am I a God at hand, declares the LORD,
and not a God far away? 24 Can a man hide
himself in secret places so that I cannot
see him? declares the LORD. Do I not fill
heaven and earth? declares the LORD. 25 I
have heard what the prophets have said
who prophesy lies in my name, saying,
'I have dreamed, I have dreamed!' 26 How
long shall there be lies in the heart of the
prophets who prophesy lies, and who
prophesy the deceit of their own heart,
27 who think to make my people forget my
name by their dreams that they tell one
another, even as their fathers forgot my
name for Baal? 28 Let the prophet who has
a dream tell the dream, but let him who
has my word speak my word faithfully.
What has straw in common with wheat?
declares the LORD. 29 Is not my word like
fire, declares the LORD, and like a hammer
that breaks the rock in pieces? 30 Therefore,
behold, I am against the prophets, declares
the LORD, who steal my words from one
another. 31 Behold, I am against the proph-
ets, declares the LORD, who use their
tongues and declare, 'declares the LORD.'
32 Behold, I am against those who prophesy
lying dreams, declares the LORD, and who
tell them and lead my people astray by their
lies and their recklessness, when I did not
send them or charge them. So they do not
profit this people at all, declares the LORD.

33 "When one of this people, or a prophet
or a priest asks you, 'What is the burden
of the LORD?' you shall say to them, 'You are
the burden,[1] and I will cast you off, declares
the LORD.' 34 And as for the prophet, priest,
or one of the people who says, 'The burden
of the LORD,' I will punish that man and
his household. 35 Thus shall you say, every
one to his neighbor and every one to his
brother, 'What has the LORD answered?'
or 'What has the LORD spoken?' 36 But 'the
burden of the LORD' you shall mention no
more, for the burden is every man's own
word, and you pervert the words of the
living God, the LORD of hosts, our God.
37 Thus you shall say to the prophet, 'What
has the LORD answered you?' or 'What has
the LORD spoken?' 38 But if you say, 'The
burden of the LORD,' thus says the LORD,
'Because you have said these words, "The
burden of the LORD," when I sent to you,
saying, "You shall not say, 'The burden
of the LORD,'" 39 therefore, behold, I will
surely lift you up and cast you away from
my presence, you and the city that I gave
to you and your fathers. 40 And I will bring
upon you everlasting reproach and perpet-
ual shame, which shall not be forgotten.'"

The Good Figs and the Bad Figs

24 After Nebuchadnezzar king of
Babylon had taken into exile from
Jerusalem Jeconiah the son of Jehoiakim,
king of Judah, together with the officials of
Judah, the craftsmen, and the metal work-
ers, and had brought them to Babylon, the
LORD showed me this vision: behold, two
baskets of figs placed before the temple of
the LORD. 2 One basket had very good figs,
like first-ripe figs, but the other basket had
very bad figs, so bad that they could not be
eaten. 3 And the LORD said to me, "What do
you see, Jeremiah?" I said, "Figs, the good
figs very good, and the bad figs very bad,
so bad that they cannot be eaten."

4 Then the word of the LORD came to me:
5 "Thus says the LORD, the God of Israel:
Like these good figs, so I will regard as
good the exiles from Judah, whom I have
sent away from this place to the land of
the Chaldeans. 6 I will set my eyes on them
for good, and I will bring them back to this
land. I will build them up, and not tear
them down; I will plant them, and not
uproot them. 7 I will give them a heart to
know that I am the LORD, and they shall be
my people and I will be their God, for they
shall return to me with their whole heart.

8 "But thus says the LORD: Like the bad

[1] Septuagint, Vulgate; Hebrew *What burden?*

figs that are so bad they cannot be eaten, so will I treat Zedekiah the king of Judah, his officials, the remnant of Jerusalem who remain in this land, and those who dwell in the land of Egypt. 9 I will make them a horror[1] to all the kingdoms of the earth, to be a reproach, a byword, a taunt, and a curse in all the places where I shall drive them. 10 And I will send sword, famine, and pestilence upon them, until they shall be utterly destroyed from the land that I gave to them and their fathers."

Seventy Years of Captivity

25 The word that came to Jeremiah concerning all the people of Judah, in the fourth year of Jehoiakim the son of Josiah, king of Judah (that was the first year of Nebuchadnezzar king of Babylon), 2 which Jeremiah the prophet spoke to all the people of Judah and all the inhabitants of Jerusalem: 3 "For twenty-three years, from the thirteenth year of Josiah the son of Amon, king of Judah, to this day, the word of the LORD has come to me, and I have spoken persistently to you, but you have not listened. 4 You have neither listened nor inclined your ears to hear, although the LORD persistently sent to you all his servants the prophets, 5 saying, 'Turn now, every one of you, from his evil way and evil deeds, and dwell upon the land that the LORD has given to you and your fathers from of old and forever. 6 Do not go after other gods to serve and worship them, or provoke me to anger with the work of your hands. Then I will do you no harm.' 7 Yet you have not listened to me, declares the LORD, that you might provoke me to anger with the work of your hands to your own harm.

8 "Therefore thus says the LORD of hosts: Because you have not obeyed my words, 9 behold, I will send for all the tribes of the north, declares the LORD, and for Nebuchadnezzar the king of Babylon, my servant, and I will bring them against this land and its inhabitants, and against all these surrounding nations. I will devote them to destruction, and make them a horror, a hissing, and an everlasting desolation. 10 Moreover, I will banish from them the voice of mirth and the voice of gladness, the voice of the bridegroom and the voice of the bride, the grinding of the millstones and the light of the lamp. 11 This whole land shall become a ruin and a waste, and these nations shall serve the king of Babylon seventy years. 12 Then after seventy years are completed, I will punish the king of Babylon and that nation, the land of the Chaldeans, for their iniquity, declares the LORD, making the land an everlasting waste. 13 I will bring upon that land all the words that I have uttered against it, everything written in this book, which Jeremiah prophesied against all the nations. 14 For many nations and great kings shall make slaves even of them, and I will recompense them according to their deeds and the work of their hands."

The Cup of the LORD's Wrath

15 Thus the LORD, the God of Israel, said to me: "Take from my hand this cup of the wine of wrath, and make all the nations to whom I send you drink it. 16 They shall drink and stagger and be crazed because of the sword that I am sending among them."

17 So I took the cup from the LORD's hand, and made all the nations to whom the LORD sent me drink it: 18 Jerusalem and the cities of Judah, its kings and officials, to make them a desolation and a waste, a hissing and a curse, as at this day; 19 Pharaoh king of Egypt, his servants, his officials, all his people, 20 and all the mixed tribes among them; all the kings of the land of Uz and all the kings of the land of the Philistines (Ashkelon, Gaza, Ekron, and the remnant of Ashdod); 21 Edom, Moab, and the sons of Ammon; 22 all the kings of Tyre, all the kings of Sidon, and the kings of the coastland across the sea; 23 Dedan, Tema,

[1] Compare Septuagint; Hebrew *horror for evil*

Buz, and all who cut the corners of their
hair; 24 all the kings of Arabia and all the
kings of the mixed tribes who dwell in the
desert; 25 all the kings of Zimri, all the kings
of Elam, and all the kings of Media; 26 all
the kings of the north, far and near, one
after another, and all the kingdoms of the
world that are on the face of the earth. And
after them the king of Babylon[1] shall drink.
27 "Then you shall say to them, 'Thus
says the LORD of hosts, the God of Israel:
Drink, be drunk and vomit, fall and rise
no more, because of the sword that I am
sending among you.'
28 "And if they refuse to accept the cup
from your hand to drink, then you shall
say to them, 'Thus says the LORD of hosts:
You must drink! 29 For behold, I begin to
work disaster at the city that is called by my
name, and shall you go unpunished? You
shall not go unpunished, for I am summoning a sword against all the inhabitants
of the earth, declares the LORD of hosts.'
30 "You, therefore, shall prophesy against
them all these words, and say to them:

"'The LORD will roar from on high,
and from his holy habitation utter his voice;
he will roar mightily against his fold,
and shout, like those who tread grapes,
against all the inhabitants of the earth.
31 The clamor will resound to the ends of the earth,
for the LORD has an indictment against the nations;
he is entering into judgment with all flesh,
and the wicked he will put to the sword,
declares the LORD.'
32 "Thus says the LORD of hosts:
Behold, disaster is going forth
from nation to nation,
and a great tempest is stirring
from the farthest parts of the earth!

33 "And those pierced by the LORD on
that day shall extend from one end of
the earth to the other. They shall not be
lamented, or gathered, or buried; they shall
be dung on the surface of the ground.

34 "Wail, you shepherds, and cry out,
and roll in ashes, you lords of the flock,
for the days of your slaughter and dispersion have come,
and you shall fall like a choice vessel.
35 No refuge will remain for the shepherds,
nor escape for the lords of the flock.
36 A voice—the cry of the shepherds,
and the wail of the lords of the flock!
For the LORD is laying waste their pasture,
37 and the peaceful folds are devastated
because of the fierce anger of the LORD.
38 Like a lion he has left his lair,
for their land has become a waste
because of the sword of the oppressor,
and because of his fierce anger."

Jeremiah Threatened with Death

26 In the beginning of the reign of
Jehoiakim the son of Josiah, king
of Judah, this word came from the LORD:
2 "Thus says the LORD: Stand in the court of
the LORD's house, and speak to all the cities
of Judah that come to worship in the house
of the LORD all the words that I command
you to speak to them; do not hold back a
word. 3 It may be they will listen, and every
one turn from his evil way, that I may
relent of the disaster that I intend to do
to them because of their evil deeds. 4 You
shall say to them, 'Thus says the LORD: If

[1] Hebrew *Sheshach*, a code name for Babylon

you will not listen to me, to walk in my law
that I have set before you, 5 and to listen
to the words of my servants the prophets
whom I send to you urgently, though you
have not listened, 6 then I will make this
house like Shiloh, and I will make this city
a curse for all the nations of the earth.'"

7 The priests and the prophets and all
the people heard Jeremiah speaking these
words in the house of the LORD. 8 And
when Jeremiah had finished speaking all
that the LORD had commanded him to
speak to all the people, then the priests and
the prophets and all the people laid hold of
him, saying, "You shall die! 9 Why have you
prophesied in the name of the LORD, say-
ing, 'This house shall be like Shiloh, and
this city shall be desolate, without inhabi-
tant'?" And all the people gathered around
Jeremiah in the house of the LORD.

10 When the officials of Judah heard
these things, they came up from the king's
house to the house of the LORD and took
their seat in the entry of the New Gate of
the house of the LORD. 11 Then the priests
and the prophets said to the officials and
to all the people, "This man deserves the
sentence of death, because he has proph-
esied against this city, as you have heard
with your own ears."

12 Then Jeremiah spoke to all the offi-
cials and all the people, saying, "The
LORD sent me to prophesy against this
house and this city all the words you have
heard. 13 Now therefore mend your ways
and your deeds, and obey the voice of the
LORD your God, and the LORD will relent
of the disaster that he has pronounced
against you. 14 But as for me, behold, I am
in your hands. Do with me as seems good
and right to you. 15 Only know for certain
that if you put me to death, you will bring
innocent blood upon yourselves and
upon this city and its inhabitants, for in
truth the LORD sent me to you to speak all
these words in your ears."

Jeremiah Spared from Death

16 Then the officials and all the people
said to the priests and the prophets, "This
man does not deserve the sentence of
death, for he has spoken to us in the name
of the LORD our God." 17 And certain of the
elders of the land arose and spoke to all
the assembled people, saying, 18 "Micah
of Moresheth prophesied in the days of
Hezekiah king of Judah, and said to all the
people of Judah: 'Thus says the LORD of
hosts,

"'Zion shall be plowed as a field;
Jerusalem shall become a heap of ruins,
and the mountain of the house a wooded height.'

19 Did Hezekiah king of Judah and all Judah
put him to death? Did he not fear the LORD
and entreat the favor of the LORD, and did
not the LORD relent of the disaster that
he had pronounced against them? But
we are about to bring great disaster upon
ourselves."

20 There was another man who proph-
esied in the name of the LORD, Uriah the
son of Shemaiah from Kiriath-jearim. He
prophesied against this city and against
this land in words like those of Jeremiah.
21 And when King Jehoiakim, with all
his warriors and all the officials, heard
his words, the king sought to put him
to death. But when Uriah heard of it, he
was afraid and fled and escaped to Egypt.
22 Then King Jehoiakim sent to Egypt cer-
tain men, Elnathan the son of Achbor and
others with him, 23 and they took Uriah
from Egypt and brought him to King
Jehoiakim, who struck him down with the
sword and dumped his dead body into the
burial place of the common people.

24 But the hand of Ahikam the son of
Shaphan was with Jeremiah so that he
was not given over to the people to be put
to death.

The Yoke of Nebuchadnezzar

27 In the beginning of the reign of Zedekiah[1] the son of Josiah, king of Judah, this word came to Jeremiah from the LORD. 2 Thus the LORD said to me: "Make yourself straps and yoke-bars, and put them on your neck. 3 Send word[2] to the king of Edom, the king of Moab, the king of the sons of Ammon, the king of Tyre, and the king of Sidon by the hand of the envoys who have come to Jerusalem to Zedekiah king of Judah. 4 Give them this charge for their masters: 'Thus says the LORD of hosts, the God of Israel: This is what you shall say to your masters: 5 "It is I who by my great power and my outstretched arm have made the earth, with the men and animals that are on the earth, and I give it to whomever it seems right to me. 6 Now I have given all these lands into the hand of Nebuchadnezzar, the king of Babylon, my servant, and I have given him also the beasts of the field to serve him. 7 All the nations shall serve him and his son and his grandson, until the time of his own land comes. Then many nations and great kings shall make him their slave.

8 "'"But if any nation or kingdom will not serve this Nebuchadnezzar king of Babylon, and put its neck under the yoke of the king of Babylon, I will punish that nation with the sword, with famine, and with pestilence, declares the LORD, until I have consumed it by his hand. 9 So do not listen to your prophets, your diviners, your dreamers, your fortune-tellers, or your sorcerers, who are saying to you, 'You shall not serve the king of Babylon.' 10 For it is a lie that they are prophesying to you, with the result that you will be removed far from your land, and I will drive you out, and you will perish. 11 But any nation that will bring its neck under the yoke of the king of Babylon and serve him, I will leave on its own land, to work it and dwell there, declares the LORD."'"

12 To Zedekiah king of Judah I spoke in like manner: "Bring your necks under the yoke of the king of Babylon, and serve him and his people and live. 13 Why will you and your people die by the sword, by famine, and by pestilence, as the LORD has spoken concerning any nation that will not serve the king of Babylon? 14 Do not listen to the words of the prophets who are saying to you, 'You shall not serve the king of Babylon,' for it is a lie that they are prophesying to you. 15 I have not sent them, declares the LORD, but they are prophesying falsely in my name, with the result that I will drive you out and you will perish, you and the prophets who are prophesying to you."

16 Then I spoke to the priests and to all this people, saying, "Thus says the LORD: Do not listen to the words of your prophets who are prophesying to you, saying, 'Behold, the vessels of the LORD's house will now shortly be brought back from Babylon,' for it is a lie that they are prophesying to you. 17 Do not listen to them; serve the king of Babylon and live. Why should this city become a desolation? 18 If they are prophets, and if the word of the LORD is with them, then let them intercede with the LORD of hosts, that the vessels that are left in the house of the LORD, in the house of the king of Judah, and in Jerusalem may not go to Babylon. 19 For thus says the LORD of hosts concerning the pillars, the sea, the stands, and the rest of the vessels that are left in this city, 20 which Nebuchadnezzar king of Babylon did not take away, when he took into exile from Jerusalem to Babylon Jeconiah the son of Jehoiakim, king of Judah, and all the nobles of Judah and Jerusalem— 21 thus says the LORD of hosts, the God of Israel, concerning the vessels that are left in the house of the LORD, in the house of the king of Judah, and in Jerusalem: 22 They shall be carried to Babylon and remain there until the day when I visit them,

[1] Or *Jehoiakim* [2] Hebrew *Send them*

declares the LORD. Then I will bring them back and restore them to this place."

Hananiah the False Prophet

28 In that same year, at the beginning of the reign of Zedekiah king of Judah, in the fifth month of the fourth year, Hananiah the son of Azzur, the prophet from Gibeon, spoke to me in the house of the LORD, in the presence of the priests and all the people, saying, 2 "Thus says the LORD of hosts, the God of Israel: I have broken the yoke of the king of Babylon. 3 Within two years I will bring back to this place all the vessels of the LORD's house, which Nebuchadnezzar king of Babylon took away from this place and carried to Babylon. 4 I will also bring back to this place Jeconiah the son of Jehoiakim, king of Judah, and all the exiles from Judah who went to Babylon, declares the LORD, for I will break the yoke of the king of Babylon."

5 Then the prophet Jeremiah spoke to Hananiah the prophet in the presence of the priests and all the people who were standing in the house of the LORD, 6 and the prophet Jeremiah said, "Amen! May the LORD do so; may the LORD make the words that you have prophesied come true, and bring back to this place from Babylon the vessels of the house of the LORD, and all the exiles. 7 Yet hear now this word that I speak in your hearing and in the hearing of all the people. 8 The prophets who preceded you and me from ancient times prophesied war, famine, and pestilence against many countries and great kingdoms. 9 As for the prophet who prophesies peace, when the word of that prophet comes to pass, then it will be known that the LORD has truly sent the prophet."

10 Then the prophet Hananiah took the yoke-bars from the neck of Jeremiah the prophet and broke them. 11 And Hananiah spoke in the presence of all the people, saying, "Thus says the LORD: Even so will I break the yoke of Nebuchadnezzar king of Babylon from the neck of all the nations within two years." But Jeremiah the prophet went his way.

12 Sometime after the prophet Hananiah had broken the yoke-bars from off the neck of Jeremiah the prophet, the word of the LORD came to Jeremiah: 13 "Go, tell Hananiah, 'Thus says the LORD: You have broken wooden bars, but you have made in their place bars of iron. 14 For thus says the LORD of hosts, the God of Israel: I have put upon the neck of all these nations an iron yoke to serve Nebuchadnezzar king of Babylon, and they shall serve him, for I have given to him even the beasts of the field.'" 15 And Jeremiah the prophet said to the prophet Hananiah, "Listen, Hananiah, the LORD has not sent you, and you have made this people trust in a lie. 16 Therefore thus says the LORD: 'Behold, I will remove you from the face of the earth. This year you shall die, because you have uttered rebellion against the LORD.'"

17 In that same year, in the seventh month, the prophet Hananiah died.

Jeremiah's Letter to the Exiles

1033

29 These are the words of the letter that Jeremiah the prophet sent from Jerusalem to the surviving elders of the exiles, and to the priests, the prophets, and all the people, whom Nebuchadnezzar had taken into exile from Jerusalem to Babylon. 2 This was after King Jeconiah and the queen mother, the eunuchs, the officials of Judah and Jerusalem, the craftsmen, and the metal workers had departed from Jerusalem. 3 The letter was sent by the hand of Elasah the son of Shaphan and Gemariah the son of Hilkiah, whom Zedekiah king of Judah sent to Babylon to Nebuchadnezzar king of Babylon. It said: 4 "Thus says the LORD of hosts, the God of Israel, to all the exiles whom I have sent into exile from Jerusalem to Babylon: 5 Build houses and live in them; plant gardens and eat their produce. 6 Take wives and have sons and daughters; take wives for your sons, and give your daughters in marriage, that they may bear sons and daughters; multiply there, and do not decrease. 7 But seek the welfare of the city where I have sent you into exile, and pray to the LORD on its behalf, for in its welfare you will find your welfare. 8 For thus says the LORD of hosts, the God of Israel: Do not let your prophets and your diviners who are among you deceive you, and do not listen to the dreams that they dream,[1] 9 for it is a lie that they are prophesying to you in my name; I did not send them, declares the LORD.

10 "For thus says the LORD: When seventy years are completed for Babylon, I will visit you, and I will fulfill to you my promise and bring you back to this place. 11 For I know the plans I have for you, declares the LORD, plans for welfare[2] and not for evil, to give you a future and a hope. 12 Then you will call upon me and come and pray to me, and I will hear you. 13 You will seek me and find me, when you seek me with all your heart. 14 I will be found by you, declares the LORD, and I will restore your fortunes and gather you from all the nations and all the places where I have driven you, declares the LORD, and I will bring you back to the place from which I sent you into exile.

15 "Because you have said, 'The LORD has raised up prophets for us in Babylon,' 16 thus says the LORD concerning the king who sits on the throne of David, and concerning all the people who dwell in this city, your kinsmen who did not go out with you into exile: 17 'Thus says the LORD of hosts, behold, I am sending on them sword, famine, and pestilence, and I will make them like vile figs that are so rotten they cannot be eaten. 18 I will pursue them with sword, famine, and pestilence, and will make them a horror to all the kingdoms of the earth, to be a curse, a terror, a hissing, and a reproach among all the nations where I have driven them, 19 because they did not pay attention to my words, declares the LORD, that I persistently sent to you by my servants the prophets, but you would not listen, declares the LORD.' 20 Hear the word of the LORD, all you exiles whom I sent away from Jerusalem to Babylon: 21 'Thus says the LORD of hosts, the God of Israel, concerning Ahab the son of Kolaiah and Zedekiah the son of Maaseiah, who are prophesying a lie to you in my name: Behold, I will deliver them into the hand of Nebuchadnezzar king of Babylon, and he shall strike them down before your eyes. 22 Because of them this curse shall be used by all the exiles from Judah in Babylon: "The LORD make you like Zedekiah and Ahab, whom the king of Babylon roasted in the fire," 23 because they have done an outrageous thing in Israel, they have committed adultery with their neighbors' wives, and they have spoken in my name lying words that I did not command them. I am the one who knows, and I am witness, declares the LORD.'"

Shemaiah's False Prophecy

24 To Shemaiah of Nehelam you shall say: 25 "Thus says the LORD of hosts, the God of Israel: You have sent letters in your name to all the people who are in Jerusalem, and to Zephaniah the son of Maaseiah the priest, and to all the priests, saying, 26 'The LORD has made you priest instead of Jehoiada the priest, to have charge in the house of the LORD over every madman who prophesies, to put him in the stocks and neck irons. 27 Now why have you not rebuked Jeremiah of Anathoth who is prophesying to you? 28 For he has sent to us in Babylon, saying, "Your exile will be long; build houses and live in them, and plant gardens and eat their produce."'"

29 Zephaniah the priest read this letter in the hearing of Jeremiah the prophet. 30 Then the word of the LORD came to Jeremiah: 31 "Send to all the exiles, saying, 'Thus says the LORD concerning Shemaiah

[1] Hebrew *your dreams, which you cause to dream* [2] Or *peace*

of Nehelam: Because Shemaiah had proph-
esied to you when I did not send him, and
has made you trust in a lie, 32 therefore
thus says the LORD: Behold, I will punish
Shemaiah of Nehelam and his descen-
dants. He shall not have anyone living
among this people, and he shall not see the
good that I will do to my people, declares
the LORD, for he has spoken rebellion
against the LORD.'"

Restoration for Israel and Judah

30 The word that came to Jeremiah
from the LORD: 2 "Thus says the
LORD, the God of Israel: Write in a book
all the words that I have spoken to you.
3 For behold, days are coming, declares
the LORD, when I will restore the fortunes
of my people, Israel and Judah, says the
LORD, and I will bring them back to the
land that I gave to their fathers, and they
shall take possession of it."

4 These are the words that the LORD
spoke concerning Israel and Judah:

5 "Thus says the LORD:
We have heard a cry of panic,
of terror, and no peace.
6 Ask now, and see,
can a man bear a child?
Why then do I see every man
with his hands on his stomach
like a woman in labor?
Why has every face turned pale?
7 Alas! That day is so great
there is none like it;
it is a time of distress for Jacob;
yet he shall be saved out of it.

8 "And it shall come to pass in that day,
declares the LORD of hosts, that I will break
his yoke from off your neck, and I will
burst your bonds, and foreigners shall no
more make a servant of him.[1] 9 But they
shall serve the LORD their God and David
their king, whom I will raise up for them.

10 "Then fear not, O Jacob my servant,
declares the LORD,
nor be dismayed, O Israel;
for behold, I will save you from far
away,
and your offspring from the land
of their captivity.
Jacob shall return and have quiet
and ease,
and none shall make him afraid.
11 For I am with you to save you,
declares the LORD;
I will make a full end of all the nations
among whom I scattered you,
but of you I will not make a full end.
I will discipline you in just measure,
and I will by no means leave you
unpunished.

12 "For thus says the LORD:
Your hurt is incurable,
and your wound is grievous.
13 There is none to uphold your cause,
no medicine for your wound,
no healing for you.
14 All your lovers have forgotten you;
they care nothing for you;
for I have dealt you the blow of an
enemy,
the punishment of a merciless foe,
because your guilt is great,
because your sins are flagrant.
15 Why do you cry out over your hurt?
Your pain is incurable.
Because your guilt is great,
because your sins are flagrant,
I have done these things to you.
16 Therefore all who devour you shall
be devoured,
and all your foes, every one of
them, shall go into captivity;
those who plunder you shall be
plundered,
and all who prey on you I will
make a prey.
17 For I will restore health to you,
and your wounds I will heal,
declares the LORD,

[1] Or *serve him*

because they have called you an outcast:
'It is Zion, for whom no one cares!'

18 "Thus says the LORD:
Behold, I will restore the fortunes of the tents of Jacob
and have compassion on his dwellings;
the city shall be rebuilt on its mound,
and the palace shall stand where it used to be.
19 Out of them shall come songs of thanksgiving,
and the voices of those who celebrate.
I will multiply them, and they shall not be few;
I will make them honored, and they shall not be small.
20 Their children shall be as they were of old,
and their congregation shall be established before me,
and I will punish all who oppress them.
21 Their prince shall be one of themselves;
their ruler shall come out from their midst;
I will make him draw near, and he shall approach me,
for who would dare of himself to approach me?
declares the LORD.
22 And you shall be my people,
and I will be your God."
23 Behold the storm of the LORD!
Wrath has gone forth,
a whirling tempest;
it will burst upon the head of the wicked.
24 The fierce anger of the LORD will not turn back
until he has executed and accomplished
the intentions of his mind.
In the latter days you will understand this.

The LORD Will Turn Mourning to Joy

31 "At that time, declares the LORD, I will be the God of all the clans of Israel, and they shall be my people."

2 Thus says the LORD:
"The people who survived the sword found grace in the wilderness;
when Israel sought for rest,
3 the LORD appeared to him[1] from far away.
I have loved you with an everlasting love;
therefore I have continued my faithfulness to you.
4 Again I will build you, and you shall be built,
O virgin Israel!
Again you shall adorn yourself with tambourines
and shall go forth in the dance of the merrymakers.
5 Again you shall plant vineyards on the mountains of Samaria;
the planters shall plant
and shall enjoy the fruit.
6 For there shall be a day when watchmen will call
in the hill country of Ephraim:
'Arise, and let us go up to Zion,
to the LORD our God.'"

7 For thus says the LORD:
"Sing aloud with gladness for Jacob,
and raise shouts for the chief of the nations;
proclaim, give praise, and say,
'O LORD, save your people,
the remnant of Israel.'
8 Behold, I will bring them from the north country

[1] Septuagint; Hebrew *me*

and gather them from the farthest
parts of the earth,
among them the blind and the lame,
the pregnant woman and she
who is in labor, together;
a great company, they shall return
here.
9 With weeping they shall come,
and with pleas for mercy I will
lead them back,
I will make them walk by brooks of
water,
in a straight path in which they
shall not stumble,
for I am a father to Israel,
and Ephraim is my firstborn.

10 "Hear the word of the LORD, O nations,
and declare it in the coastlands
far away;
say, 'He who scattered Israel will
gather him,
and will keep him as a shepherd
keeps his flock.'
11 For the LORD has ransomed Jacob
and has redeemed him from
hands too strong for him.
12 They shall come and sing aloud on
the height of Zion,
and they shall be radiant over the
goodness of the LORD,
over the grain, the wine, and the oil,
and over the young of the flock
and the herd;
their life shall be like a watered
garden,
and they shall languish no more.
13 Then shall the young women
rejoice in the dance,
and the young men and the old
shall be merry.
I will turn their mourning into joy;
I will comfort them, and give
them gladness for sorrow.
14 I will feast the soul of the priests
with abundance,
and my people shall be satisfied
with my goodness,
declares the LORD."

15 Thus says the LORD:
"A voice is heard in Ramah,
lamentation and bitter weeping.
Rachel is weeping for her children;
she refuses to be comforted for
her children,
because they are no more."

16 Thus says the LORD:
"Keep your voice from weeping,
and your eyes from tears,
for there is a reward for your work,
declares the LORD,
and they shall come back from
the land of the enemy.
17 There is hope for your future,
declares the LORD,
and your children shall come
back to their own country.
18 I have heard Ephraim grieving,
'You have disciplined me, and I was
disciplined,
like an untrained calf;
bring me back that I may be restored,
for you are the LORD my God.
19 For after I had turned away, I relented,
and after I was instructed, I struck
my thigh;
I was ashamed, and I was
confounded,
because I bore the disgrace of my
youth.'
20 Is Ephraim my dear son?
Is he my darling child?
For as often as I speak against him,
I do remember him still.
Therefore my heart[1] yearns for him;
I will surely have mercy on him,
declares the LORD.

21 "Set up road markers for yourself;
make yourself guideposts;
consider well the highway,
the road by which you went.

[1] Hebrew *bowels*

Return, O virgin Israel,
return to these your cities.
22 How long will you waver,
O faithless daughter?
For the LORD has created a new
thing on the earth:
a woman encircles a man."

23 Thus says the LORD of hosts, the God
of Israel: "Once more they shall use these
words in the land of Judah and in its cities,
when I restore their fortunes:

"'The LORD bless you, O habitation of
righteousness,
O holy hill!'

24 And Judah and all its cities shall dwell
there together, and the farmers and those
who wander with their flocks. 25 For I will
satisfy the weary soul, and every languish-
ing soul I will replenish."
26 At this I awoke and looked, and my
sleep was pleasant to me.
27 "Behold, the days are coming, declares
the LORD, when I will sow the house of
Israel and the house of Judah with the
seed of man and the seed of beast. 28 And it
shall come to pass that as I have watched
over them to pluck up and break down, to
overthrow, destroy, and bring harm, so I
will watch over them to build and to plant,
declares the LORD. 29 In those days they
shall no longer say:

"'The fathers have eaten sour grapes,
and the children's teeth are set on
edge.'

30 But everyone shall die for his own sin.
Each man who eats sour grapes, his teeth
shall be set on edge.

The New Covenant

1033
31 "Behold, the days are coming,
declares the LORD, when I will make
a new covenant with the house of
Israel and the house of Judah, 32 not like
the covenant that I made with their fathers
on the day when I took them by the hand
to bring them out of the land of Egypt,
my covenant that they broke, though I
was their husband, declares the LORD.
1033
33 But this is the covenant that I will
make with the house of Israel after
those days, declares the LORD: I will
put my law within them, and I will write it
on their hearts. And I will be their God, and
they shall be my people. 34 And no longer
shall each one teach his neighbor and each
his brother, saying, 'Know the LORD,' for
they shall all know me, from the least of
them to the greatest, declares the LORD. For
I will forgive their iniquity, and I will
remember their sin no more."

35 Thus says the LORD,
who gives the sun for light by day
and the fixed order of the moon
and the stars for light by night,
who stirs up the sea so that its
waves roar—
the LORD of hosts is his name:
36 "If this fixed order departs
from before me, declares the LORD,
then shall the offspring of Israel cease
from being a nation before me
forever."
37 Thus says the LORD:
"If the heavens above can be
measured,
and the foundations of the earth
below can be explored,
then I will cast off all the offspring
of Israel
for all that they have done,
declares the LORD."

38 "Behold, the days are coming, declares
the LORD, when the city shall be rebuilt
for the LORD from the Tower of Hananel
to the Corner Gate. 39 And the measuring
line shall go out farther, straight to the
hill Gareb, and shall then turn to Goah.
40 The whole valley of the dead bodies and
the ashes, and all the fields as far as the
brook Kidron, to the corner of the Horse
Gate toward the east, shall be sacred to

the LORD. It shall not be uprooted or overthrown anymore forever."

Jeremiah Buys a Field During the Siege

32 The word that came to Jeremiah from the LORD in the tenth year of Zedekiah king of Judah, which was the eighteenth year of Nebuchadnezzar. 2 At that time the army of the king of Babylon was besieging Jerusalem, and Jeremiah the prophet was shut up in the court of the guard that was in the palace of the king of Judah. 3 For Zedekiah king of Judah had imprisoned him, saying, "Why do you prophesy and say, 'Thus says the LORD: Behold, I am giving this city into the hand of the king of Babylon, and he shall capture it; 4 Zedekiah king of Judah shall not escape out of the hand of the Chaldeans, but shall surely be given into the hand of the king of Babylon, and shall speak with him face to face and see him eye to eye. 5 And he shall take Zedekiah to Babylon, and there he shall remain until I visit him, declares the LORD. Though you fight against the Chaldeans, you shall not succeed'?"

6 Jeremiah said, "The word of the LORD came to me: 7 Behold, Hanamel the son of Shallum your uncle will come to you and say, 'Buy my field that is at Anathoth, for the right of redemption by purchase is yours.' 8 Then Hanamel my cousin came to me in the court of the guard, in accordance with the word of the LORD, and said to me, 'Buy my field that is at Anathoth in the land of Benjamin, for the right of possession and redemption is yours; buy it for yourself.' Then I knew that this was the word of the LORD.

9 "And I bought the field at Anathoth from Hanamel my cousin, and weighed out the money to him, seventeen shekels of silver. 10 I signed the deed, sealed it, got witnesses, and weighed the money on scales. 11 Then I took the sealed deed of purchase, containing the terms and conditions and the open copy. 12 And I gave the deed of purchase to Baruch the son of Neriah son of Mahseiah, in the presence of Hanamel my cousin, in the presence of the witnesses who signed the deed of purchase, and in the presence of all the Judeans who were sitting in the court of the guard. 13 I charged Baruch in their presence, saying, 14 'Thus says the LORD of hosts, the God of Israel: Take these deeds, both this sealed deed of purchase and this open deed, and put them in an earthenware vessel, that they may last for a long time. 15 For thus says the LORD of hosts, the God of Israel: Houses and fields and vineyards shall again be bought in this land.'

Jeremiah Prays for Understanding

16 "After I had given the deed of purchase to Baruch the son of Neriah, I prayed to the LORD, saying: 17 'Ah, Lord GOD! It is you who have made the heavens and the earth by your great power and by
47 your outstretched arm! Nothing is too hard for you. 18 You show steadfast love to thousands, but you repay the guilt of fathers to their children after them, O great and mighty God, whose name is the LORD of hosts, 19 great in counsel and mighty in deed, whose eyes are open to all the ways of the children of man, rewarding each one according to his ways and according to the fruit of his deeds. 20 You have shown signs and wonders in the land of Egypt, and to this day in Israel and among all mankind, and have made a name for yourself, as at this day. 21 You brought your people Israel out of the land of Egypt with signs and wonders, with a strong hand and outstretched arm, and with great terror. 22 And you gave them this land, which you swore to their fathers to give them, a land flowing with milk and honey. 23 And they entered and took possession of it. But they did not obey your voice or walk in your law. They did nothing of all you commanded them to do. Therefore you have made all this disaster come upon them. 24 Behold, the siege

mounds have come up to the city to take it, and because of sword and famine and pestilence the city is given into the hands of the Chaldeans who are fighting against it. What you spoke has come to pass, and behold, you see it. 25 Yet you, O Lord GOD, have said to me, "Buy the field for money and get witnesses"—though the city is given into the hands of the Chaldeans.'"

26 The word of the LORD came to Jeremiah: 27 "Behold, I am the LORD, the God of all flesh. Is anything too hard for me? 28 Therefore, thus says the LORD: Behold, I am giving this city into the hands of the Chaldeans and into the hand of Nebuchadnezzar king of Babylon, and he shall capture it. 29 The Chaldeans who are fighting against this city shall come and set this city on fire and burn it, with the houses on whose roofs offerings have been made to Baal and drink offerings have been poured out to other gods, to provoke me to anger. 30 For the children of Israel and the children of Judah have done nothing but evil in my sight from their youth. The children of Israel have done nothing but provoke me to anger by the work of their hands, declares the LORD. 31 This city has aroused my anger and wrath, from the day it was built to this day, so that I will remove it from my sight 32 because of all the evil of the children of Israel and the children of Judah that they did to provoke me to anger—their kings and their officials, their priests and their prophets, the men of Judah and the inhabitants of Jerusalem. 33 They have turned to me their back and not their face. And though I have taught them persistently, they have not listened to receive instruction. 34 They set up their abominations in the house that is called by my name, to defile it. 35 They built the high places of Baal in the Valley of the Son of Hinnom, to offer up their sons and daughters to Molech, though I did not command them, nor did it enter into my mind, that they should do this abomination, to cause Judah to sin.

They Shall Be My People; I Will Be Their God

36 "Now therefore thus says the LORD, the God of Israel, concerning this city of which you say, 'It is given into the hand of the king of Babylon by sword, by famine, and by pestilence': 37 Behold, I will gather them from all the countries to which I drove them in my anger and my wrath and in great indignation. I will bring them back to this place, and I will make them dwell in safety. 38 And they shall be my people, and I will be their God. 39 I will give them one heart and one way, that they may fear me forever, for their own good and the good of their children after them. 40 I will make with them an everlasting covenant, that I will not turn away from doing good to them. And I will put the fear of me in their hearts, that they may not turn from me. 41 I will rejoice in doing them good, and I will plant them in this land in faithfulness, with all my heart and all my soul.

42 "For thus says the LORD: Just as I have brought all this great disaster upon this people, so I will bring upon them all the good that I promise them. 43 Fields shall be bought in this land of which you are saying, 'It is a desolation, without man or beast; it is given into the hand of the Chaldeans.' 44 Fields shall be bought for money, and deeds shall be signed and sealed and witnessed, in the land of Benjamin, in the places about Jerusalem, and in the cities of Judah, in the cities of the hill country, in the cities of the Shephelah, and in the cities of the Negeb; for I will restore their fortunes, declares the LORD."

The LORD Promises Peace

33 The word of the LORD came to Jeremiah a second time, while he was still shut up in the court of the guard: 2 "Thus says the LORD who made the earth,[1] the LORD who formed it to establish it—the LORD is his name: 3 Call to me and I will

[1] Septuagint; Hebrew *it*

answer you, and will tell you great and
hidden things that you have not known.
4 For thus says the LORD, the God of Israel,
concerning the houses of this city and the
houses of the kings of Judah that were torn
down to make a defense against the siege
mounds and against the sword: 5 They are
coming in to fight against the Chaldeans
and to fill them[1] with the dead bodies
of men whom I shall strike down in my
anger and my wrath, for I have hidden my
face from this city because of all their evil.
6 Behold, I will bring to it health and heal-
ing, and I will heal them and reveal to them
abundance of prosperity and security. 7 I
will restore the fortunes of Judah and the
fortunes of Israel, and rebuild them as they
were at first. 8 I will cleanse them from all
the guilt of their sin against me, and I will
forgive all the guilt of their sin and rebel-
lion against me. 9 And this city[2] shall be
to me a name of joy, a praise and a glory
before all the nations of the earth who shall
hear of all the good that I do for them. They
shall fear and tremble because of all the
good and all the prosperity I provide for it.

10 "Thus says the LORD: In this place
of which you say, 'It is a waste without
man or beast,' in the cities of Judah and
the streets of Jerusalem that are desolate,
without man or inhabitant or beast, there
shall be heard again 11 the voice of mirth
and the voice of gladness, the voice of the
bridegroom and the voice of the bride, the
voices of those who sing, as they bring
thank offerings to the house of the LORD:

"'Give thanks to the LORD of hosts,
for the LORD is good,
for his steadfast love endures
forever!'

For I will restore the fortunes of the land
as at first, says the LORD.

12 "Thus says the LORD of hosts: In this
place that is waste, without man or beast,
and in all of its cities, there shall again
be habitations of shepherds resting their
flocks. 13 In the cities of the hill country, in
the cities of the Shephelah, and in the cit-
ies of the Negeb, in the land of Benjamin,
the places about Jerusalem, and in the cit-
ies of Judah, flocks shall again pass under
the hands of the one who counts them,
says the LORD.

The LORD's Eternal Covenant with David

14 "Behold, the days are coming, declares
the LORD, when I will fulfill the promise I
made to the house of Israel and the house
of Judah. 15 In those days and at that time
I will cause a righteous Branch to spring
up for David, and he shall execute justice
and righteousness in the land. 16 In those
days Judah will be saved, and Jerusalem
will dwell securely. And this is the name
by which it will be called: 'The LORD is our
righteousness.'

17 "For thus says the LORD: David shall
never lack a man to sit on the throne of
the house of Israel, 18 and the Levitical
priests shall never lack a man in my pres-
ence to offer burnt offerings, to burn grain
offerings, and to make sacrifices forever."

19 The word of the LORD came to Jere-
miah: 20 "Thus says the LORD: If you can
break my covenant with the day and my
covenant with the night, so that day and
night will not come at their appointed
time, 21 then also my covenant with David
my servant may be broken, so that he shall
not have a son to reign on his throne, and
my covenant with the Levitical priests my
ministers. 22 As the host of heaven can-
not be numbered and the sands of the sea
cannot be measured, so I will multiply
the offspring of David my servant, and
the Levitical priests who minister to me."

23 The word of the LORD came to Jere-
miah: 24 "Have you not observed that these
people are saying, 'The LORD has rejected
the two clans that he chose'? Thus they
have despised my people so that they are
no longer a nation in their sight. 25 Thus
says the LORD: If I have not established

[1] That is, the torn-down houses [2] Hebrew *And it*

my covenant with day and night and the fixed order of heaven and earth, 26 then I will reject the offspring of Jacob and David my servant and will not choose one of his offspring to rule over the offspring of Abraham, Isaac, and Jacob. For I will restore their fortunes and will have mercy on them."

Zedekiah to Die in Babylon

34 The word that came to Jeremiah from the LORD, when Nebuchadnezzar king of Babylon and all his army and all the kingdoms of the earth under his dominion and all the peoples were fighting against Jerusalem and all of its cities: 2 "Thus says the LORD, the God of Israel: Go and speak to Zedekiah king of Judah and say to him, 'Thus says the LORD: Behold, I am giving this city into the hand of the king of Babylon, and he shall burn it with fire. 3 You shall not escape from his hand but shall surely be captured and delivered into his hand. You shall see the king of Babylon eye to eye and speak with him face to face. And you shall go to Babylon.' 4 Yet hear the word of the LORD, O Zedekiah king of Judah! Thus says the LORD concerning you: 'You shall not die by the sword. 5 You shall die in peace. And as spices were burned for your fathers, the former kings who were before you, so people shall burn spices for you and lament for you, saying, "Alas, lord!"' For I have spoken the word, declares the LORD."

6 Then Jeremiah the prophet spoke all these words to Zedekiah king of Judah, in Jerusalem, 7 when the army of the king of Babylon was fighting against Jerusalem and against all the cities of Judah that were left, Lachish and Azekah, for these were the only fortified cities of Judah that remained.

8 The word that came to Jeremiah from the LORD, after King Zedekiah had made a covenant with all the people in Jerusalem to make a proclamation of liberty to them, 9 that everyone should set free his Hebrew slaves, male and female, so that no one should enslave a Jew, his brother. 10 And they obeyed, all the officials and all the people who had entered into the covenant that everyone would set free his slave, male or female, so that they would not be enslaved again. They obeyed and set them free. 11 But afterward they turned around and took back the male and female slaves they had set free, and brought them into subjection as slaves. 12 The word of the LORD came to Jeremiah from the LORD: 13 "Thus says the LORD, the God of Israel: I myself made a covenant with your fathers when I brought them out of the land of Egypt, out of the house of bondage, saying, 14 'At the end of seven years each of you must set free the fellow Hebrew who has been sold to you and has served you six years; you must set him free from your service.' But your fathers did not listen to me or incline their ears to me. 15 You recently repented and did what was right in my eyes by proclaiming liberty, each to his neighbor, and you made a covenant before me in the house that is called by my name, 16 but then you turned around and profaned my name when each of you took back his male and female slaves, whom you had set free according to their desire, and you brought them into subjection to be your slaves.

17 "Therefore, thus says the LORD: You have not obeyed me by proclaiming liberty, every one to his brother and to his neighbor; behold, I proclaim to you liberty to the sword, to pestilence, and to famine, declares the LORD. I will make you a horror to all the kingdoms of the earth. 18 And the men who transgressed my covenant and did not keep the terms of the covenant that they made before me, I will make them like[1] the calf that they cut in two and passed between its parts— 19 the officials of Judah, the officials of Jerusalem, the eunuchs, the priests, and all the people of the land who passed between the parts of the calf. 20 And I will give them into the

[1] Hebrew lacks *them like*

hand of their enemies and into the hand of those who seek their lives. Their dead bodies shall be food for the birds of the air and the beasts of the earth. 21 And Zedekiah king of Judah and his officials I will give into the hand of their enemies and into the hand of those who seek their lives, into the hand of the army of the king of Babylon which has withdrawn from you. 22 Behold, I will command, declares the LORD, and will bring them back to this city. And they will fight against it and take it and burn it with fire. I will make the cities of Judah a desolation without inhabitant."

The Obedience of the Rechabites

35 The word that came to Jeremiah from the LORD in the days of Jehoiakim the son of Josiah, king of Judah: 2 "Go to the house of the Rechabites and speak with them and bring them to the house of the LORD, into one of the chambers; then offer them wine to drink." 3 So I took Jaazaniah the son of Jeremiah, son of Habazziniah and his brothers and all his sons and the whole house of the Rechabites. 4 I brought them to the house of the LORD into the chamber of the sons of Hanan the son of Igdaliah, the man of God, which was near the chamber of the officials, above the chamber of Maaseiah the son of Shallum, keeper of the threshold. 5 Then I set before the Rechabites pitchers full of wine, and cups, and I said to them, "Drink wine." 6 But they answered, "We will drink no wine, for Jonadab the son of Rechab, our father, commanded us, 'You shall not drink wine, neither you nor your sons forever. 7 You shall not build a house; you shall not sow seed; you shall not plant or have a vineyard; but you shall live in tents all your days, that you may live many days in the land where you sojourn.' 8 We have obeyed the voice of Jonadab the son of Rechab, our father, in all that he commanded us, to drink no wine all our days, ourselves, our wives, our sons, or our daughters, 9 and not to build houses to dwell in. We have no vineyard or field or seed, 10 but we have lived in tents and have obeyed and done all that Jonadab our father commanded us. 11 But when Nebuchadnezzar king of Babylon came up against the land, we said, 'Come, and let us go to Jerusalem for fear of the army of the Chaldeans and the army of the Syrians.' So we are living in Jerusalem."

12 Then the word of the LORD came to Jeremiah: 13 "Thus says the LORD of hosts, the God of Israel: Go and say to the people of Judah and the inhabitants of Jerusalem, Will you not receive instruction and listen to my words? declares the LORD. 14 The command that Jonadab the son of Rechab gave to his sons, to drink no wine, has been kept, and they drink none to this day, for they have obeyed their father's command. I have spoken to you persistently, but you have not listened to me. 15 I have sent to you all my servants the prophets, sending them persistently, saying, 'Turn now every one of you from his evil way, and amend your deeds, and do not go after other gods to serve them, and then you shall dwell in the land that I gave to you and your fathers.' But you did not incline your ear or listen to me. 16 The sons of Jonadab the son of Rechab have kept the command that their father gave them, but this people has not obeyed me. 17 Therefore, thus says the LORD, the God of hosts, the God of Israel: Behold, I am bringing upon Judah and all the inhabitants of Jerusalem all the disaster that I have pronounced against them, because I have spoken to them and they have not listened, I have called to them and they have not answered."

18 But to the house of the Rechabites Jeremiah said, "Thus says the LORD of hosts, the God of Israel: Because you have obeyed the command of Jonadab your father and kept all his precepts and done all that he commanded you, 19 therefore thus says the LORD of hosts, the God of

Israel: Jonadab the son of Rechab shall never lack a man to stand before me."

Jehoiakim Burns Jeremiah's Scroll

36 In the fourth year of Jehoiakim the son of Josiah,
1033 king of Judah, this word came to Jeremiah from the LORD: 2 "Take a scroll and write on it all the words that I have spoken to you against Israel and Judah and all the nations, from the day I spoke to you, from the days of Josiah until today. 3 It may be that the house of Judah will hear all the disaster that I intend to do to them, so that every one may turn from his evil way, and that I may forgive their iniquity and their sin."

4 Then Jeremiah called Baruch the son of Neriah, and Baruch wrote on a scroll at the dictation of Jeremiah all the words of the LORD that he had spoken to him. 5 And Jeremiah ordered Baruch, saying, "I am banned from going to the house of the LORD, 6 so you are to go, and on a day of fasting in the hearing of all the people in the LORD's house you shall read the words of the LORD from the scroll that you have written at my dictation. You shall read them also in the hearing of all the men of Judah who come out of their cities. 7 It may be that their plea for mercy will come before the LORD, and that every one will turn from his evil way, for great is the anger and wrath that the LORD has pronounced against this people." 8 And Baruch the son of Neriah did all that Jeremiah the prophet ordered him about reading from the scroll the words of the LORD in the LORD's house.

9 In the fifth year of Jehoiakim the son of Josiah, king of Judah, in the ninth month, all the people in Jerusalem and all the people who came from the cities of Judah to Jerusalem proclaimed a fast before the LORD. 10 Then, in the hearing of all the people, Baruch read the words of Jeremiah from the scroll, in the house of the LORD, in the chamber of Gemariah the son of Shaphan the secretary, which was in the upper court, at the entry of the New Gate of the LORD's house.

11 When Micaiah the son of Gemariah, son of Shaphan, heard all the words of the LORD from the scroll, 12 he went down to the king's house, into the secretary's chamber, and all the officials were sitting there: Elishama the secretary, Delaiah the son of Shemaiah, Elnathan the son of Achbor, Gemariah the son of Shaphan, Zedekiah the son of Hananiah, and all the officials. 13 And Micaiah told them all the words that he had heard, when Baruch read the scroll in the hearing of the people. 14 Then all the officials sent Jehudi the son of Nethaniah, son of Shelemiah, son of Cushi, to say to Baruch, "Take in your hand the scroll that you read in the hearing of the people, and come." So Baruch the son of Neriah took the scroll in his hand and came to them. 15 And they said to him, "Sit down and read it." So Baruch read it to them. 16 When they heard all the words, they turned one to another in fear. And they said to Baruch, "We must report all these words to the king." 17 Then they asked Baruch, "Tell us, please, how did you write all these words? Was it at his dictation?" 18 Baruch answered them, "He dictated all these words to me, while I wrote them with ink on the scroll." 19 Then the officials said to Baruch, "Go and hide, you and Jeremiah, and let no one know where you are."

20 So they went into the court to the king, having put the scroll in the chamber of Elishama the secretary, and they reported all the words to the king. 21 Then the king sent Jehudi to get the scroll, and he took it from the chamber of Elishama the secretary. And Jehudi read it to the king and all the officials who stood beside the king. 22 It was the ninth month, and the king was sitting in the winter house, and there was a fire burning in the fire pot before him. 23 As Jehudi read three or four columns, the king would cut them off

with a knife and throw them into the fire in the fire pot, until the entire scroll was consumed in the fire that was in the fire pot. 24 Yet neither the king nor any of his servants who heard all these words was afraid, nor did they tear their garments. 25 Even when Elnathan and Delaiah and Gemariah urged the king not to burn the scroll, he would not listen to them. 26 And the king commanded Jerahmeel the king's son and Seraiah the son of Azriel and Shelemiah the son of Abdeel to seize Baruch the secretary and Jeremiah the prophet, but the LORD hid them.

27 Now after the king had burned the scroll with the words that Baruch wrote at Jeremiah's dictation, the word of the LORD came to Jeremiah: 28 "Take another scroll and write on it all the former words that were in the first scroll, which Jehoiakim the king of Judah has burned. 29 And concerning Jehoiakim king of Judah you shall say, 'Thus says the LORD, You have burned this scroll, saying, "Why have you written in it that the king of Babylon will certainly come and destroy this land, and will cut off from it man and beast?" 30 Therefore thus says the LORD concerning Jehoiakim king of Judah: He shall have none to sit on the throne of David, and his dead body shall be cast out to the heat by day and the frost by night. 31 And I will punish him and his offspring and his servants for their iniquity. I will bring upon them and upon the inhabitants of Jerusalem and upon the people of Judah all the disaster that I have pronounced against them, but they would not hear.'"

32 Then Jeremiah took another scroll and gave it to Baruch the scribe, the son of Neriah, who wrote on it at the dictation of Jeremiah all the words of the scroll that Jehoiakim king of Judah had burned in the fire. And many similar words were added to them.

Jeremiah Warns Zedekiah

37 Zedekiah the son of Josiah, whom Nebuchadnezzar king of Babylon made king in the land of Judah, reigned instead of Coniah the son of Jehoiakim. 2 But neither he nor his servants nor the people of the land listened to the words of the LORD that he spoke through Jeremiah the prophet.

3 King Zedekiah sent Jehucal the son of Shelemiah, and Zephaniah the priest, the son of Maaseiah, to Jeremiah the prophet, saying, "Please pray for us to the LORD our God." 4 Now Jeremiah was still going in and out among the people, for he had not yet been put in prison. 5 The army of Pharaoh had come out of Egypt. And when the Chaldeans who were besieging Jerusalem heard news about them, they withdrew from Jerusalem.

6 Then the word of the LORD came to Jeremiah the prophet: 7 "Thus says the LORD, God of Israel: Thus shall you say to the king of Judah who sent you to me to inquire of me, 'Behold, Pharaoh's army that came to help you is about to return to Egypt, to its own land. 8 And the Chaldeans shall come back and fight against this city. They shall capture it and burn it with fire. 9 Thus says the LORD, Do not deceive yourselves, saying, "The Chaldeans will surely go away from us," for they will not go away. 10 For even if you should defeat the whole army of Chaldeans who are fighting against you, and there remained of them only wounded men, every man in his tent, they would rise up and burn this city with fire.'"

Jeremiah Imprisoned

11 Now when the Chaldean army had withdrawn from Jerusalem at the approach of Pharaoh's army, 12 Jeremiah set out from Jerusalem to go to the land of Benjamin to receive his portion there among the people. 13 When he was at the Benjamin Gate, a sentry there named Irijah the son of Shelemiah, son of Hananiah,

seized Jeremiah the prophet, saying, "You
are deserting to the Chaldeans." 14 And
Jeremiah said, "It is a lie; I am not desert-
ing to the Chaldeans." But Irijah would
not listen to him, and seized Jeremiah
and brought him to the officials. 15 And
the officials were enraged at Jeremiah, and
they beat him and imprisoned him in the
house of Jonathan the secretary, for it had
been made a prison.

16 When Jeremiah had come to the dun-
geon cells and remained there many days,
17 King Zedekiah sent for him and received
him. The king questioned him secretly in
his house and said, "Is there any word
from the LORD?" Jeremiah said, "There
is." Then he said, "You shall be delivered
into the hand of the king of Babylon."
18 Jeremiah also said to King Zedekiah,
"What wrong have I done to you or your
servants or this people, that you have put
me in prison? 19 Where are your prophets
who prophesied to you, saying, 'The king
of Babylon will not come against you and
against this land'? 20 Now hear, please, O
my lord the king: let my humble plea come
before you and do not send me back to the
house of Jonathan the secretary, lest I die
there." 21 So King Zedekiah gave orders,
and they committed Jeremiah to the court
of the guard. And a loaf of bread was given
him daily from the bakers' street, until all
the bread of the city was gone. So Jeremiah
remained in the court of the guard.

Jeremiah Cast into the Cistern

38 Now Shephatiah the son of Mattan,
Gedaliah the son of Pashhur, Jucal
the son of Shelemiah, and Pashhur the son
of Malchiah heard the words that Jeremiah
was saying to all the people, 2 "Thus says
the LORD: He who stays in this city shall die
by the sword, by famine, and by pestilence,
but he who goes out to the Chaldeans shall
live. He shall have his life as a prize of war,
and live. 3 Thus says the LORD: This city
shall surely be given into the hand of the
army of the king of Babylon and be taken."
4 Then the officials said to the king, "Let
this man be put to death, for he is weaken-
ing the hands of the soldiers who are left
in this city, and the hands of all the people,
by speaking such words to them. For this
man is not seeking the welfare of this peo-
ple, but their harm." 5 King Zedekiah said,
"Behold, he is in your hands, for the king
can do nothing against you." 6 So they took
Jeremiah and cast him into the cistern of
Malchiah, the king's son, which was in the
court of the guard, letting Jeremiah down
by ropes. And there was no water in the
cistern, but only mud, and Jeremiah sank
in the mud.

Jeremiah Rescued from the Cistern

7 When Ebed-melech the Ethiopian, a
eunuch who was in the king's house, heard
that they had put Jeremiah into the cis-
tern—the king was sitting in the Benjamin
Gate— 8 Ebed-melech went from the king's
house and said to the king, 9 "My lord the
king, these men have done evil in all that
they did to Jeremiah the prophet by cast-
ing him into the cistern, and he will die
there of hunger, for there is no bread left
in the city." 10 Then the king commanded
Ebed-melech the Ethiopian, "Take thirty
men with you from here, and lift Jeremiah
the prophet out of the cistern before he
dies." 11 So Ebed-melech took the men with
him and went to the house of the king,
to a wardrobe in the storehouse, and took
from there old rags and worn-out clothes,
which he let down to Jeremiah in the cis-
tern by ropes. 12 Then Ebed-melech the
Ethiopian said to Jeremiah, "Put the rags
and clothes between your armpits and the
ropes." Jeremiah did so. 13 Then they drew
Jeremiah up with ropes and lifted him out
of the cistern. And Jeremiah remained in
the court of the guard.

Jeremiah Warns Zedekiah Again

14 King Zedekiah sent for Jeremiah the
prophet and received him at the third

entrance of the temple of the LORD. The king said to Jeremiah, "I will ask you a question; hide nothing from me." 15 Jeremiah said to Zedekiah, "If I tell you, will you not surely put me to death? And if I give you counsel, you will not listen to me." 16 Then King Zedekiah swore secretly to Jeremiah, "As the LORD lives, who made our souls, I will not put you to death or deliver you into the hand of these men who seek your life."

17 Then Jeremiah said to Zedekiah, "Thus says the LORD, the God of hosts, the God of Israel: If you will surrender to the officials of the king of Babylon, then your life shall be spared, and this city shall not be burned with fire, and you and your house shall live. 18 But if you do not surrender to the officials of the king of Babylon, then this city shall be given into the hand of the Chaldeans, and they shall burn it with fire, and you shall not escape from their hand." 19 King Zedekiah said to Jeremiah, "I am afraid of the Judeans who have deserted to the Chaldeans, lest I be handed over to them and they deal cruelly with me." 20 Jeremiah said, "You shall not be given to them. Obey now the voice of the LORD in what I say to you, and it shall be well with you, and your life shall be spared. 21 But if you refuse to surrender, this is the vision which the LORD has shown to me: 22 Behold, all the women left in the house of the king of Judah were being led out to the officials of the king of Babylon and were saying,

"'Your trusted friends have deceived you
and prevailed against you;
now that your feet are sunk in the mud,
they turn away from you.'

23 All your wives and your sons shall be led out to the Chaldeans, and you yourself shall not escape from their hand, but shall be seized by the king of Babylon, and this city shall be burned with fire."

24 Then Zedekiah said to Jeremiah, "Let no one know of these words, and you shall not die. 25 If the officials hear that I have spoken with you and come to you and say to you, 'Tell us what you said to the king and what the king said to you; hide nothing from us and we will not put you to death,' 26 then you shall say to them, 'I made a humble plea to the king that he would not send me back to the house of Jonathan to die there.'" 27 Then all the officials came to Jeremiah and asked him, and he answered them as the king had instructed him. So they stopped speaking with him, for the conversation had not been overheard. 28 And Jeremiah remained in the court of the guard until the day that Jerusalem was taken.

The Fall of Jerusalem

39 In the ninth year of Zedekiah king of Judah, in the tenth month, Nebuchadnezzar king of Babylon and all his army came against Jerusalem and besieged it. 2 In the eleventh year of Zedekiah, in the fourth month, on the ninth day of the month, a breach was made in the city. 3 Then all the officials of the king of Babylon came and sat in the middle gate: Nergal-sar-ezer, Samgar-nebu, Sar-sekim the Rab-saris, Nergal-sar-ezer the Rab-mag, with all the rest of the officers of the king of Babylon. 4 When Zedekiah king of Judah and all the soldiers saw them, they fled, going out of the city at night by way of the king's garden through the gate between the two walls; and they went toward the Arabah. 5 But the army of the Chaldeans pursued them and overtook Zedekiah in the plains of Jericho. And when they had taken him, they brought him up to Nebuchadnezzar king of Babylon, at Riblah, in the land of Hamath; and he passed sentence on him. 6 The king of Babylon slaughtered the sons of

Zedekiah at Riblah before his eyes, and the
king of Babylon slaughtered all the nobles
of Judah. 7 He put out the eyes of Zedekiah
and bound him in chains to take him to
Babylon. 8 The Chaldeans burned the king's
house and the house of the people, and
broke down the walls of Jerusalem. 9 Then
Nebuzaradan, the captain of the guard,
carried into exile to Babylon the rest of the
people who were left in the city, those who
had deserted to him, and the people who
remained. 10 Nebuzaradan, the captain of
the guard, left in the land of Judah some
of the poor people who owned nothing,
and gave them vineyards and fields at the
same time.

The LORD Delivers Jeremiah

11 Nebuchadnezzar king of Babylon gave
command concerning Jeremiah through
Nebuzaradan, the captain of the guard,
saying, 12 "Take him, look after him well,
and do him no harm, but deal with him
as he tells you." 13 So Nebuzaradan the
captain of the guard, Nebushazban the
Rab-saris, Nergal-sar-ezer the Rab-mag,
and all the chief officers of the king of
Babylon 14 sent and took Jeremiah from
the court of the guard. They entrusted
him to Gedaliah the son of Ahikam, son of
Shaphan, that he should take him home.
So he lived among the people.

15 The word of the LORD came to Jere-
miah while he was shut up in the court
of the guard: 16 "Go, and say to Ebed-
melech the Ethiopian, 'Thus says the LORD
of hosts, the God of Israel: Behold, I will
fulfill my words against this city for harm
and not for good, and they shall be accom-
plished before you on that day. 17 But I will
deliver you on that day, declares the LORD,
and you shall not be given into the hand
of the men of whom you are afraid. 18 For
I will surely save you, and you shall not
fall by the sword, but you shall have your
life as a prize of war, because you have put
your trust in me, declares the LORD.'"

Jeremiah Remains in Judah

40 The word that came to Jeremiah
from the LORD after Nebuzaradan
the captain of the guard had let him go
from Ramah, when he took him bound
in chains along with all the captives of
Jerusalem and Judah who were being
exiled to Babylon. 2 The captain of the
guard took Jeremiah and said to him,
"The LORD your God pronounced this
disaster against this place. 3 The LORD has
brought it about, and has done as he said.
Because you sinned against the LORD and
did not obey his voice, this thing has
come upon you. 4 Now, behold, I release
you today from the chains on your hands.
If it seems good to you to come with me
to Babylon, come, and I will look after you
well, but if it seems wrong to you to come
with me to Babylon, do not come. See,
the whole land is before you; go wher-
ever you think it good and right to go. 5 If
you remain,[1] then return to Gedaliah the
son of Ahikam, son of Shaphan, whom
the king of Babylon appointed governor
of the cities of Judah, and dwell with him
among the people. Or go wherever you
think it right to go." So the captain of the
guard gave him an allowance of food and
a present, and let him go. 6 Then Jeremiah
went to Gedaliah the son of Ahikam, at
Mizpah, and lived with him among the
people who were left in the land.

7 When all the captains of the forces in
the open country and their men heard
that the king of Babylon had appointed
Gedaliah the son of Ahikam governor in
the land and had committed to him men,
women, and children, those of the poorest
of the land who had not been taken into
exile to Babylon, 8 they went to Gedaliah
at Mizpah—Ishmael the son of Nethaniah,
Johanan the son of Kareah, Seraiah the son
of Tanhumeth, the sons of Ephai the
Netophathite, Jezaniah the son of the
Maacathite, they and their men. 9 Gedaliah
the son of Ahikam, son of Shaphan, swore

[1] Syriac; the meaning of the Hebrew phrase is uncertain

to them and their men, saying, "Do not be
afraid to serve the Chaldeans. Dwell in the
land and serve the king of Babylon, and it
shall be well with you. 10 As for me, I will
dwell at Mizpah, to represent you before
the Chaldeans who will come to us. But as
for you, gather wine and summer fruits
and oil, and store them in your vessels, and
dwell in your cities that you have taken."
11 Likewise, when all the Judeans who were
in Moab and among the Ammonites and
in Edom and in other lands heard that
the king of Babylon had left a remnant
in Judah and had appointed Gedaliah the
son of Ahikam, son of Shaphan, as gov-
ernor over them, 12 then all the Judeans
returned from all the places to which they
had been driven and came to the land of
Judah, to Gedaliah at Mizpah. And they
gathered wine and summer fruits in great
abundance.

13 Now Johanan the son of Kareah and
all the leaders of the forces in the open
country came to Gedaliah at Mizpah 14 and
said to him, "Do you know that Baalis the
king of the Ammonites has sent Ishmael
the son of Nethaniah to take your life?"
But Gedaliah the son of Ahikam would
not believe them. 15 Then Johanan the
son of Kareah spoke secretly to Gedaliah
at Mizpah, "Please let me go and strike
down Ishmael the son of Nethaniah, and
no one will know it. Why should he take
your life, so that all the Judeans who are
gathered about you would be scattered,
and the remnant of Judah would perish?"
16 But Gedaliah the son of Ahikam said to
Johanan the son of Kareah, "You shall not
do this thing, for you are speaking falsely
of Ishmael."

Gedaliah Murdered

41 In the seventh month, Ishmael the
son of Nethaniah, son of Elishama,
of the royal family, one of the chief offi-
cers of the king, came with ten men to
Gedaliah the son of Ahikam, at Mizpah.
As they ate bread together there at Mizpah,
2 Ishmael the son of Nethaniah and the
ten men with him rose up and struck
down Gedaliah the son of Ahikam, son of
Shaphan, with the sword, and killed him,
whom the king of Babylon had appointed
governor in the land. 3 Ishmael also struck
down all the Judeans who were with
Gedaliah at Mizpah, and the Chaldean
soldiers who happened to be there.

4 On the day after the murder of
Gedaliah, before anyone knew of it, 5 eighty
men arrived from Shechem and Shiloh
and Samaria, with their beards shaved and
their clothes torn, and their bodies gashed,
bringing grain offerings and incense to
present at the temple of the LORD. 6 And
Ishmael the son of Nethaniah came out
from Mizpah to meet them, weeping as
he came. As he met them, he said to them,
"Come in to Gedaliah the son of Ahikam."
7 When they came into the city, Ishmael
the son of Nethaniah and the men with
him slaughtered them and cast them into
a cistern. 8 But there were ten men among
them who said to Ishmael, "Do not put us
to death, for we have stores of wheat, bar-
ley, oil, and honey hidden in the fields."
So he refrained and did not put them to
death with their companions.

9 Now the cistern into which Ishmael
had thrown all the bodies of the men
whom he had struck down along with[1]
Gedaliah was the large cistern that
King Asa had made for defense against
Baasha king of Israel; Ishmael the son of
Nethaniah filled it with the slain. 10 Then
Ishmael took captive all the rest of the
people who were in Mizpah, the king's
daughters and all the people who were
left at Mizpah, whom Nebuzaradan, the
captain of the guard, had committed to
Gedaliah the son of Ahikam. Ishmael the
son of Nethaniah took them captive and
set out to cross over to the Ammonites.

11 But when Johanan the son of Kareah
and all the leaders of the forces with him

[1] Hebrew *by the hand of*

heard of all the evil that Ishmael the son of
Nethaniah had done, 12 they took all their
men and went to fight against Ishmael
the son of Nethaniah. They came upon
him at the great pool that is in Gibeon.
13 And when all the people who were with
Ishmael saw Johanan the son of Kareah
and all the leaders of the forces with him,
they rejoiced. 14 So all the people whom
Ishmael had carried away captive from
Mizpah turned around and came back,
and went to Johanan the son of Kareah.
15 But Ishmael the son of Nethaniah
escaped from Johanan with eight men,
and went to the Ammonites. 16 Then
Johanan the son of Kareah and all the
leaders of the forces with him took from
Mizpah all the rest of the people whom
he had recovered from Ishmael the son
of Nethaniah, after he had struck down
Gedaliah the son of Ahikam—soldiers,
women, children, and eunuchs, whom
Johanan brought back from Gibeon. 17 And
they went and stayed at Geruth Chimham
near Bethlehem, intending to go to Egypt
18 because of the Chaldeans. For they were
afraid of them, because Ishmael the son of
Nethaniah had struck down Gedaliah the
son of Ahikam, whom the king of Babylon
had made governor over the land.

Warning Against Going to Egypt

42 Then all the commanders of the
forces, and Johanan the son of
Kareah and Jezaniah the son of Hoshaiah,
and all the people from the least to the
greatest, came near 2 and said to Jeremiah
the prophet, "Let our plea for mercy come
before you, and pray to the LORD your God
for us, for all this remnant—because we
are left with but a few, as your eyes see
us— 3 that the LORD your God may show
us the way we should go, and the thing
that we should do." 4 Jeremiah the prophet
said to them, "I have heard you. Behold, I
will pray to the LORD your God according
to your request, and whatever the LORD
answers you I will tell you. I will keep
nothing back from you." 5 Then they said
to Jeremiah, "May the LORD be a true and
faithful witness against us if we do not act
according to all the word with which the
LORD your God sends you to us. 6 Whether
it is good or bad, we will obey the voice of
the LORD our God to whom we are send-
ing you, that it may be well with us when
we obey the voice of the LORD our God."

7 At the end of ten days the word of the
LORD came to Jeremiah. 8 Then he sum-
moned Johanan the son of Kareah and all
the commanders of the forces who were
with him, and all the people from the
least to the greatest, 9 and said to them,
"Thus says the LORD, the God of Israel, to
whom you sent me to present your plea
for mercy before him: 10 If you will remain
in this land, then I will build you up and
not pull you down; I will plant you, and
not pluck you up; for I relent of the disas-
ter that I did to you. 11 Do not fear the king
of Babylon, of whom you are afraid. Do
not fear him, declares the LORD, for I am
with you, to save you and to deliver you
from his hand. 12 I will grant you mercy,
that he may have mercy on you and let
you remain in your own land. 13 But if you
say, 'We will not remain in this land,' dis-
obeying the voice of the LORD your God
14 and saying, 'No, we will go to the land of
Egypt, where we shall not see war or hear
the sound of the trumpet or be hungry
for bread, and we will dwell there,' 15 then
hear the word of the LORD, O remnant
of Judah. Thus says the LORD of hosts,
the God of Israel: If you set your faces to
enter Egypt and go to live there, 16 then
the sword that you fear shall overtake you
there in the land of Egypt, and the famine
of which you are afraid shall follow close
after you to Egypt, and there you shall die.
17 All the men who set their faces to go to
Egypt to live there shall die by the sword,
by famine, and by pestilence. They shall

have no remnant or survivor from the
disaster that I will bring upon them.
18 "For thus says the LORD of hosts, the
God of Israel: As my anger and my wrath
were poured out on the inhabitants of
Jerusalem, so my wrath will be poured out
on you when you go to Egypt. You shall
become an execration, a horror, a curse,
and a taunt. You shall see this place no
more. 19 The LORD has said to you, O rem-
nant of Judah, 'Do not go to Egypt.' Know
for a certainty that I have warned you this
day 20 that you have gone astray at the cost
of your lives. For you sent me to the LORD
your God, saying, 'Pray for us to the LORD
our God, and whatever the LORD our God
says declare to us and we will do it.' 21 And
I have this day declared it to you, but you
have not obeyed the voice of the LORD
your God in anything that he sent me
to tell you. 22 Now therefore know for a
certainty that you shall die by the sword,
by famine, and by pestilence in the place
where you desire to go to live."

Jeremiah Taken to Egypt

43 When Jeremiah finished speaking
to all the people all these words of
the LORD their God, with which the LORD
their God had sent him to them, 2 Azariah
the son of Hoshaiah and Johanan the son
of Kareah and all the insolent men said to
Jeremiah, "You are telling a lie. The LORD
our God did not send you to say, 'Do not go
to Egypt to live there,' 3 but Baruch the son
of Neriah has set you against us, to deliver
us into the hand of the Chaldeans, that
they may kill us or take us into exile in
Babylon." 4 So Johanan the son of Kareah
and all the commanders of the forces and
all the people did not obey the voice of
the LORD, to remain in the land of Judah.
5 But Johanan the son of Kareah and all
the commanders of the forces took all the
remnant of Judah who had returned to live
in the land of Judah from all the nations to
which they had been driven— 6 the men,
the women, the children, the princesses,
and every person whom Nebuzaradan the
captain of the guard had left with Gedaliah
the son of Ahikam, son of Shaphan; also
Jeremiah the prophet and Baruch the son
of Neriah. 7 And they came into the land
of Egypt, for they did not obey the voice of
the LORD. And they arrived at Tahpanhes.
8 Then the word of the LORD came to
Jeremiah in Tahpanhes: 9 "Take in your
hands large stones and hide them in the
mortar in the pavement that is at the
entrance to Pharaoh's palace in Tahpanhes,
in the sight of the men of Judah, 10 and say
to them, 'Thus says the LORD of hosts, the
God of Israel: Behold, I will send and take
Nebuchadnezzar the king of Babylon, my
servant, and I will set his throne above
these stones that I have hidden, and he
will spread his royal canopy over them.
11 He shall come and strike the land of
Egypt, giving over to the pestilence those
who are doomed to the pestilence, to cap-
tivity those who are doomed to captivity,
and to the sword those who are doomed to
the sword. 12 I shall kindle a fire in the tem-
ples of the gods of Egypt, and he shall burn
them and carry them away captive. And he
shall clean the land of Egypt as a shepherd
cleans his cloak of vermin, and he shall go
away from there in peace. 13 He shall break
the obelisks of Heliopolis, which is in the
land of Egypt, and the temples of the gods
of Egypt he shall burn with fire.'"

Judgment for Idolatry

44 The word that came to Jeremiah
concerning all the Judeans who
lived in the land of Egypt, at Migdol, at
Tahpanhes, at Memphis, and in the land of
Pathros, 2 "Thus says the LORD of hosts, the
God of Israel: You have seen all the disaster
that I brought upon Jerusalem and upon all
the cities of Judah. Behold, this day they are
a desolation, and no one dwells in them,
3 because of the evil that they committed,
provoking me to anger, in that they went to

make offerings and serve other gods that they knew not, neither they, nor you, nor your fathers. 4 Yet I persistently sent to you all my servants the prophets, saying, 'Oh, do not do this abomination that I hate!' 5 But they did not listen or incline their ear, to turn from their evil and make no offerings to other gods. 6 Therefore my wrath and my anger were poured out and kindled in the cities of Judah and in the streets of Jerusalem, and they became a waste and a desolation, as at this day. 7 And now thus says the LORD God of hosts, the God of Israel: Why do you commit this great evil against yourselves, to cut off from you man and woman, infant and child, from the midst of Judah, leaving you no remnant? 8 Why do you provoke me to anger with the works of your hands, making offerings to other gods in the land of Egypt where you have come to live, so that you may be cut off and become a curse and a taunt among all the nations of the earth? 9 Have you forgotten the evil of your fathers, the evil of the kings of Judah, the evil of their[1] wives, your own evil, and the evil of your wives, which they committed in the land of Judah and in the streets of Jerusalem? 10 They have not humbled themselves even to this day, nor have they feared, nor walked in my law and my statutes that I set before you and before your fathers.

11 "Therefore thus says the LORD of hosts, the God of Israel: Behold, I will set my face against you for harm, to cut off all Judah. 12 I will take the remnant of Judah who have set their faces to come to the land of Egypt to live, and they shall all be consumed. In the land of Egypt they shall fall; by the sword and by famine they shall be consumed. From the least to the greatest, they shall die by the sword and by famine, and they shall become an oath, a horror, a curse, and a taunt. 13 I will punish those who dwell in the land of Egypt, as I have punished Jerusalem, with the sword, with famine, and with pestilence, 14 so that none of the remnant of Judah who have come to live in the land of Egypt shall escape or survive or return to the land of Judah, to which they desire to return to dwell there. For they shall not return, except some fugitives."

15 Then all the men who knew that their wives had made offerings to other gods, and all the women who stood by, a great assembly, all the people who lived in Pathros in the land of Egypt, answered Jeremiah: 16 "As for the word that you have spoken to us in the name of the LORD, we will not listen to you. 17 But we will do everything that we have vowed, make offerings to the queen of heaven and pour out drink offerings to her, as we did, both we and our fathers, our kings and our officials, in the cities of Judah and in the streets of Jerusalem. For then we had plenty of food, and prospered, and saw no disaster. 18 But since we left off making offerings to the queen of heaven and pouring out drink offerings to her, we have lacked everything and have been consumed by the sword and by famine." 19 And the women said,[2] "When we made offerings to the queen of heaven and poured out drink offerings to her, was it without our husbands' approval that we made cakes for her bearing her image and poured out drink offerings to her?"

20 Then Jeremiah said to all the people, men and women, all the people who had given him this answer: 21 "As for the offerings that you offered in the cities of Judah and in the streets of Jerusalem, you and your fathers, your kings and your officials, and the people of the land, did not the LORD remember them? Did it not come into his mind? 22 The LORD could no longer bear your evil deeds and the abominations that you committed. Therefore your land has become a desolation and a waste and a curse, without inhabitant, as it is this day. 23 It is because you made offerings and because you sinned against the LORD and did not obey the voice of the LORD or walk in his law and in his statutes

[1] Hebrew *his* [2] Compare Syriac; Hebrew lacks *And the women said*

and in his testimonies that this disaster
has happened to you, as at this day."
24 Jeremiah said to all the people and all
the women, "Hear the word of the LORD,
all you of Judah who are in the land of
Egypt. 25 Thus says the LORD of hosts, the
God of Israel: You and your wives have
declared with your mouths, and have ful-
filled it with your hands, saying, 'We will
surely perform our vows that we have
made, to make offerings to the queen of
heaven and to pour out drink offerings to
her.' Then confirm your vows and perform
your vows! 26 Therefore hear the word of
the LORD, all you of Judah who dwell in the
land of Egypt: Behold, I have sworn by my
great name, says the LORD, that my name
shall no more be invoked by the mouth of
any man of Judah in all the land of Egypt,
saying, 'As the Lord GOD lives.' 27 Behold, I
am watching over them for disaster and
not for good. All the men of Judah who are
in the land of Egypt shall be consumed by
the sword and by famine, until there is an
end of them. 28 And those who escape the
sword shall return from the land of Egypt
to the land of Judah, few in number; and
all the remnant of Judah, who came to the
land of Egypt to live, shall know whose
word will stand, mine or theirs. 29 This
shall be the sign to you, declares the LORD,
that I will punish you in this place, in order
that you may know that my words will
surely stand against you for harm: 30 Thus
says the LORD, Behold, I will give Pharaoh
Hophra king of Egypt into the hand of his
enemies and into the hand of those who
seek his life, as I gave Zedekiah king of
Judah into the hand of Nebuchadnezzar
king of Babylon, who was his enemy and
sought his life."

Message to Baruch

45 The word that Jeremiah the
prophet spoke to Baruch the son
of Neriah, when he wrote these words
in a book at the dictation of Jeremiah,
in the fourth year of Jehoiakim the son
of Josiah, king of Judah: 2 "Thus says the
LORD, the God of Israel, to you, O Baruch:
3 You said, 'Woe is me! For the LORD has
added sorrow to my pain. I am weary with
my groaning, and I find no rest.' 4 Thus
shall you say to him, Thus says the LORD:
Behold, what I have built I am breaking
down, and what I have planted I am pluck-
ing up—that is, the whole land. 5 And do
you seek great things for yourself? Seek
them not, for behold, I am bringing disas-
ter upon all flesh, declares the LORD. But I
will give you your life as a prize of war in
all places to which you may go."

Judgment on Egypt

46 The word of the LORD that came to
Jeremiah the prophet concerning
the nations.
2 About Egypt. Concerning the army of
Pharaoh Neco, king of Egypt, which was
by the river Euphrates at Carchemish and
which Nebuchadnezzar king of Babylon
defeated in the fourth year of Jehoiakim
the son of Josiah, king of Judah:

3 "Prepare buckler and shield,
  and advance for battle!
4 Harness the horses;
  mount, O horsemen!
Take your stations with your helmets,
  polish your spears,
  put on your armor!
5 Why have I seen it?
They are dismayed
  and have turned backward.
Their warriors are beaten down
  and have fled in haste;
they look not back—
  terror on every side!
    declares the LORD.

6 "The swift cannot flee away,
  nor the warrior escape;
in the north by the river Euphrates
  they have stumbled and fallen.

7 "Who is this, rising like the Nile,
like rivers whose waters surge?
8 Egypt rises like the Nile,
like rivers whose waters surge.
He said, 'I will rise, I will cover the earth,
I will destroy cities and their inhabitants.'
9 Advance, O horses,
and rage, O chariots!
Let the warriors go out:
men of Cush and Put who handle the shield,
men of Lud, skilled in handling the bow.
10 That day is the day of the Lord GOD of hosts,
a day of vengeance,
to avenge himself on his foes.
The sword shall devour and be sated
and drink its fill of their blood.
For the Lord GOD of hosts holds a sacrifice
in the north country by the river Euphrates.
11 Go up to Gilead, and take balm,
O virgin daughter of Egypt!
In vain you have used many medicines;
there is no healing for you.
12 The nations have heard of your shame,
and the earth is full of your cry;
for warrior has stumbled against warrior;
they have both fallen together."

13 The word that the LORD spoke to Jer-
emiah the prophet about the coming of
Nebuchadnezzar king of Babylon to strike
the land of Egypt:

14 "Declare in Egypt, and proclaim in Migdol;
proclaim in Memphis and Tahpanhes;
say, 'Stand ready and be prepared,
for the sword shall devour around you.'
15 Why are your mighty ones face down?
They do not stand[1]
because the LORD thrust them down.
16 He made many stumble, and they fell,
and they said one to another,
'Arise, and let us go back to our own people
and to the land of our birth,
because of the sword of the oppressor.'
17 Call the name of Pharaoh, king of Egypt,
'Noisy one who lets the hour go by.'

18 "As I live, declares the King,
whose name is the LORD of hosts,
like Tabor among the mountains
and like Carmel by the sea, shall one come.
19 Prepare yourselves baggage for exile,
O inhabitants of Egypt!
For Memphis shall become a waste,
a ruin, without inhabitant.

20 "A beautiful heifer is Egypt,
but a biting fly from the north has come upon her.
21 Even her hired soldiers in her midst
are like fattened calves;
yes, they have turned and fled together;
they did not stand,
for the day of their calamity has come upon them,
the time of their punishment.

22 "She makes a sound like a serpent gliding away;
for her enemies march in force
and come against her with axes
like those who fell trees.
23 They shall cut down her forest,
declares the LORD,
though it is impenetrable,

[1] Hebrew *He does not stand*

because they are more numerous
than locusts;
they are without number.
24 The daughter of Egypt shall be put
to shame;
she shall be delivered into the hand
of a people from the north."

25 The LORD of hosts, the God of Israel,
said: "Behold, I am bringing punishment
upon Amon of Thebes, and Pharaoh and
Egypt and her gods and her kings, upon
Pharaoh and those who trust in him. 26 I
will deliver them into the hand of those
who seek their life, into the hand of
Nebuchadnezzar king of Babylon and his
officers. Afterward Egypt shall be inhabited
as in the days of old, declares the LORD.

27 "But fear not, O Jacob my servant,
nor be dismayed, O Israel,
for behold, I will save you from far
away,
and your offspring from the land
of their captivity.
Jacob shall return and have quiet
and ease,
and none shall make him afraid.
28 Fear not, O Jacob my servant,
declares the LORD,
for I am with you.
I will make a full end of all the nations
to which I have driven you,
but of you I will not make a full end.
I will discipline you in just measure,
and I will by no means leave you
unpunished."

Judgment on the Philistines

47 The word of the LORD that came
to Jeremiah the prophet concern-
ing the Philistines, before Pharaoh struck
down Gaza.

2 "Thus says the LORD:
Behold, waters are rising out of the
north,
and shall become an overflowing
torrent;
they shall overflow the land and all
that fills it,
the city and those who dwell in it.
Men shall cry out,
and every inhabitant of the land
shall wail.
3 At the noise of the stamping of the
hoofs of his stallions,
at the rushing of his chariots, at
the rumbling of their wheels,
the fathers look not back to their
children,
so feeble are their hands,
4 because of the day that is coming to
destroy
all the Philistines,
to cut off from Tyre and Sidon
every helper that remains.
For the LORD is destroying the
Philistines,
the remnant of the coastland of
Caphtor.
5 Baldness has come upon Gaza;
Ashkelon has perished.
O remnant of their valley,
how long will you gash yourselves?
6 Ah, sword of the LORD!
How long till you are quiet?
Put yourself into your scabbard;
rest and be still!
7 How can it[1] be quiet
when the LORD has given it a
charge?
Against Ashkelon and against the
seashore
he has appointed it."

Judgment on Moab

48 Concerning Moab.
Thus says the LORD of hosts, the
God of Israel:

"Woe to Nebo, for it is laid waste!
Kiriathaim is put to shame, it is
taken;
the fortress is put to shame and
broken down;
2 the renown of Moab is no more.

[1] Septuagint, Vulgate; Hebrew *you*

In Heshbon they planned disaster
against her:
'Come, let us cut her off from
being a nation!'
You also, O Madmen, shall be
brought to silence;
the sword shall pursue you.

3 "A voice! A cry from Horonaim,
'Desolation and great destruction!'
4 Moab is destroyed;
her little ones have made a cry.
5 For at the ascent of Luhith
they go up weeping;[1]
for at the descent of Horonaim
they have heard the distressed
cry[2] of destruction.
6 Flee! Save yourselves!
You will be like a juniper in the
desert!
7 For, because you trusted in your
works and your treasures,
you also shall be taken;
and Chemosh shall go into exile
with his priests and his officials.
8 The destroyer shall come upon
every city,
and no city shall escape;
the valley shall perish,
and the plain shall be destroyed,
as the LORD has spoken.

9 "Give wings to Moab,
for she would fly away;
her cities shall become a desolation,
with no inhabitant in them.

10 "Cursed is he who does the work of the
LORD with slackness, and cursed is he who
keeps back his sword from bloodshed.

11 "Moab has been at ease from his youth
and has settled on his dregs;
he has not been emptied from
vessel to vessel,
nor has he gone into exile;
so his taste remains in him,
and his scent is not changed.

12 "Therefore, behold, the days are com-
ing, declares the LORD, when I shall send
to him pourers who will pour him, and
empty his vessels and break his[3] jars in
pieces. 13 Then Moab shall be ashamed
of Chemosh, as the house of Israel was
ashamed of Bethel, their confidence.

14 "How do you say, 'We are heroes
and mighty men of war'?
15 The destroyer of Moab and his cities
has come up,
and the choicest of his young men
have gone down to slaughter,
declares the King, whose name is
the LORD of hosts.
16 The calamity of Moab is near at hand,
and his affliction hastens swiftly.
17 Grieve for him, all you who are
around him,
and all who know his name;
say, 'How the mighty scepter is
broken,
the glorious staff.'

18 "Come down from your glory,
and sit on the parched ground,
O inhabitant of Dibon!
For the destroyer of Moab has come
up against you;
he has destroyed your strongholds.
19 Stand by the way and watch,
O inhabitant of Aroer!
Ask him who flees and her who
escapes;
say, 'What has happened?'
20 Moab is put to shame, for it is broken;
wail and cry!
Tell it beside the Arnon,
that Moab is laid waste.

21 "Judgment has come upon the table-
land, upon Holon, and Jahzah, and
Mephaath, 22 and Dibon, and Nebo,
and Beth-diblathaim, 23 and Kiriathaim,
and Beth-gamul, and Beth-meon, 24 and
Kerioth, and Bozrah, and all the cities of
the land of Moab, far and near. 25 The horn

[1] Hebrew *weeping goes up with weeping* [2] Septuagint (compare Isaiah 15:5) *heard the cry* [3] Septuagint, Aquila; Hebrew *their*

of Moab is cut off, and his arm is broken,
declares the LORD.
26 "Make him drunk, because he mag-
nified himself against the LORD, so that
Moab shall wallow in his vomit, and he
too shall be held in derision. 27 Was not
Israel a derision to you? Was he found
among thieves, that whenever you spoke
of him you wagged your head?

28 "Leave the cities, and dwell in the rock,
O inhabitants of Moab!
Be like the dove that nests
in the sides of the mouth of a gorge.
29 We have heard of the pride of Moab—
he is very proud—
of his loftiness, his pride, and his arrogance,
and the haughtiness of his heart.
30 I know his insolence, declares the LORD;
his boasts are false,
his deeds are false.
31 Therefore I wail for Moab;
I cry out for all Moab;
for the men of Kir-hareseth I mourn.
32 More than for Jazer I weep for you,
O vine of Sibmah!
Your branches passed over the sea,
reached to the Sea of Jazer;
on your summer fruits and your grapes
the destroyer has fallen.
33 Gladness and joy have been taken away
from the fruitful land of Moab;
I have made the wine cease from the winepresses;
no one treads them with shouts of joy;
the shouting is not the shout of joy.

34 "From the outcry at Heshbon even
to Elealeh, as far as Jahaz they utter their
voice, from Zoar to Horonaim and Eglath-
shelishiyah. For the waters of Nimrim also
have become desolate. 35 And I will bring
to an end in Moab, declares the LORD, him
who offers sacrifice in the high place and
makes offerings to his god. 36 Therefore
my heart moans for Moab like a flute, and
my heart moans like a flute for the men
of Kir-hareseth. Therefore the riches they
gained have perished.
37 "For every head is shaved and every
beard cut off. On all the hands are gashes,
and around the waist is sackcloth. 38 On all
the housetops of Moab and in the squares
there is nothing but lamentation, for I
have broken Moab like a vessel for which
no one cares, declares the LORD. 39 How it
is broken! How they wail! How Moab has
turned his back in shame! So Moab has
become a derision and a horror to all that
are around him."

40 For thus says the LORD:
"Behold, one shall fly swiftly like an eagle
and spread his wings against Moab;
41 the cities shall be taken
and the strongholds seized.
The heart of the warriors of Moab
shall be in that day
like the heart of a woman in her birth pains;
42 Moab shall be destroyed and be no longer a people,
because he magnified himself against the LORD.
43 Terror, pit, and snare
are before you, O inhabitant of Moab!
declares the LORD.
44 He who flees from the terror
shall fall into the pit,
and he who climbs out of the pit
shall be caught in the snare.
For I will bring these things upon Moab,
the year of their punishment,
declares the LORD.

45 "In the shadow of Heshbon
fugitives stop without strength,

for fire came out from Heshbon,
flame from the house of Sihon;
it has destroyed the forehead of Moab,
the crown of the sons of tumult.
46 Woe to you, O Moab!
The people of Chemosh are undone,
for your sons have been taken captive,
and your daughters into captivity.
47 Yet I will restore the fortunes of Moab
in the latter days, declares the LORD."
Thus far is the judgment on Moab.

Judgment on Ammon

49 Concerning the Ammonites.
Thus says the LORD:
"Has Israel no sons?
Has he no heir?
Why then has Milcom dispossessed Gad,
and his people settled in its cities?
2 Therefore, behold, the days are coming,
declares the LORD,
when I will cause the battle cry to be heard
against Rabbah of the Ammonites;
it shall become a desolate mound,
and its villages shall be burned with fire;
then Israel shall dispossess those who dispossessed him,
says the LORD.
3 "Wail, O Heshbon, for Ai is laid waste!
Cry out, O daughters of Rabbah!
Put on sackcloth,
lament, and run to and fro among the hedges!
For Milcom shall go into exile,
with his priests and his officials.
4 Why do you boast of your valleys,[1]
O faithless daughter,
who trusted in her treasures, saying,
'Who will come against me?'
5 Behold, I will bring terror upon you,
declares the Lord GOD of hosts,
from all who are around you,
and you shall be driven out, every man straight before him,
with none to gather the fugitives.
6 "But afterward I will restore the fortunes
of the Ammonites, declares the LORD."

Judgment on Edom

7 Concerning Edom.
Thus says the LORD of hosts:
"Is wisdom no more in Teman?
Has counsel perished from the prudent?
Has their wisdom vanished?
8 Flee, turn back, dwell in the depths,
O inhabitants of Dedan!
For I will bring the calamity of Esau upon him,
the time when I punish him.
9 If grape-gatherers came to you,
would they not leave gleanings?
If thieves came by night,
would they not destroy only enough for themselves?
10 But I have stripped Esau bare;
I have uncovered his hiding places,
and he is not able to conceal himself.
His children are destroyed, and his brothers,
and his neighbors; and he is no more.
11 Leave your fatherless children; I will keep them alive;
and let your widows trust in me."
12 For thus says the LORD: "If those who
did not deserve to drink the cup must
drink it, will you go unpunished? You shall
not go unpunished, but you must drink.
13 For I have sworn by myself, declares the
LORD, that Bozrah shall become a horror,
a taunt, a waste, and a curse, and all her
cities shall be perpetual wastes."

[1] Hebrew *boast of your valleys, your valley flows*

14 I have heard a message from the LORD,
and an envoy has been sent among the nations:
"Gather yourselves together and come against her,
and rise up for battle!
15 For behold, I will make you small among the nations,
despised among mankind.
16 The horror you inspire has deceived you,
and the pride of your heart,
you who live in the clefts of the rock,[1]
who hold the height of the hill.
Though you make your nest as high as the eagle's,
I will bring you down from there,
declares the LORD.

17 "Edom shall become a horror. Every-
one who passes by it will be horrified and
will hiss because of all its disasters. 18 As
when Sodom and Gomorrah and their
neighboring cities were overthrown, says
the LORD, no man shall dwell there, no
man shall sojourn in her. 19 Behold, like
a lion coming up from the jungle of the
Jordan against a perennial pasture, I will
suddenly make him[2] run away from her.
And I will appoint over her whomever
I choose. For who is like me? Who will
summon me? What shepherd can stand
before me? 20 Therefore hear the plan that
the LORD has made against Edom and the
purposes that he has formed against the
inhabitants of Teman: Even the little ones
of the flock shall be dragged away. Surely
their fold shall be appalled at their fate. 21 At
the sound of their fall the earth shall trem-
ble; the sound of their cry shall be heard at
the Red Sea. 22 Behold, one shall mount up
and fly swiftly like an eagle and spread his
wings against Bozrah, and the heart of the
warriors of Edom shall be in that day like
the heart of a woman in her birth pains."

[1] Or *of Sela* [2] Septuagint, Syriac *them*

Judgment on Damascus

23 Concerning Damascus:
"Hamath and Arpad are confounded,
for they have heard bad news;
they melt in fear,
they are troubled like the sea that cannot be quiet.
24 Damascus has become feeble, she turned to flee,
and panic seized her;
anguish and sorrows have taken hold of her,
as of a woman in labor.
25 How is the famous city not forsaken,
the city of my joy?
26 Therefore her young men shall fall in her squares,
and all her soldiers shall be destroyed in that day,
declares the LORD of hosts.
27 And I will kindle a fire in the wall of Damascus,
and it shall devour the strongholds of Ben-hadad."

Judgment on Kedar and Hazor

28 Concerning Kedar and the kingdoms
of Hazor that Nebuchadnezzar king of
Babylon struck down.

Thus says the LORD:
"Rise up, advance against Kedar!
Destroy the people of the east!
29 Their tents and their flocks shall be taken,
their curtains and all their goods;
their camels shall be led away from them,
and men shall cry to them: 'Terror on every side!'
30 Flee, wander far away, dwell in the depths,
O inhabitants of Hazor!
declares the LORD.
For Nebuchadnezzar king of Babylon
has made a plan against you
and formed a purpose against you.

31 "Rise up, advance against a nation at
ease,
that dwells securely,
declares the LORD,
that has no gates or bars,
that dwells alone.
32 Their camels shall become plunder,
their herds of livestock a spoil.
I will scatter to every wind
those who cut the corners of their
hair,
and I will bring their calamity
from every side of them,
declares the LORD.
33 Hazor shall become a haunt of
jackals,
an everlasting waste;
no man shall dwell there;
no man shall sojourn in her."

Judgment on Elam

34 The word of the LORD that came to
Jeremiah the prophet concerning Elam,
in the beginning of the reign of Zedekiah
king of Judah.
35 Thus says the LORD of hosts: "Behold,
I will break the bow of Elam, the main-
stay of their might. 36 And I will bring
upon Elam the four winds from the four
quarters of heaven. And I will scatter them
to all those winds, and there shall be no
nation to which those driven out of Elam
shall not come. 37 I will terrify Elam before
their enemies and before those who seek
their life. I will bring disaster upon them,
my fierce anger, declares the LORD. I will
send the sword after them, until I have
consumed them, 38 and I will set my throne
in Elam and destroy their king and offi-
cials, declares the LORD.
39 "But in the latter days I will restore
the fortunes of Elam, declares the LORD."

Judgment on Babylon

50 The word that the LORD spoke
concerning Babylon, concerning
the land of the Chaldeans, by Jeremiah the
prophet:

2 "Declare among the nations and
proclaim,
set up a banner and proclaim,
conceal it not, and say:
'Babylon is taken,
Bel is put to shame,
Merodach is dismayed.
Her images are put to shame,
her idols are dismayed.'

3 "For out of the north a nation has come
up against her, which shall make her land
a desolation, and none shall dwell in it;
both man and beast shall flee away.

4 "In those days and in that time, declares
the LORD, the people of Israel and the peo-
ple of Judah shall come together, weep-
ing as they come, and they shall seek the
LORD their God. 5 They shall ask the way to
Zion, with faces turned toward it, saying,
'Come, let us join ourselves to the LORD in
an everlasting covenant that will never be
forgotten.'

6 "My people have been lost sheep. Their
shepherds have led them astray, turning
them away on the mountains. From moun-
tain to hill they have gone. They have for-
gotten their fold. 7 All who found them
have devoured them, and their enemies
have said, 'We are not guilty, for they have
sinned against the LORD, their habitation
of righteousness, the LORD, the hope of
their fathers.'

8 "Flee from the midst of Babylon, and go
out of the land of the Chaldeans, and be as
male goats before the flock. 9 For behold,
I am stirring up and bringing against
Babylon a gathering of great nations,
from the north country. And they shall
array themselves against her. From there
she shall be taken. Their arrows are like
a skilled warrior who does not return
empty-handed. 10 Chaldea shall be plun-
dered; all who plunder her shall be sated,
declares the LORD.

11 "Though you rejoice, though you exult,
O plunderers of my heritage,
though you frolic like a heifer in the pasture,
and neigh like stallions,
12 your mother shall be utterly shamed,
and she who bore you shall be disgraced.
Behold, she shall be the last of the nations,
a wilderness, a dry land, and a desert.
13 Because of the wrath of the LORD
she shall not be inhabited
but shall be an utter desolation;
everyone who passes by Babylon shall be appalled,
and hiss because of all her wounds.
14 Set yourselves in array against Babylon all around,
all you who bend the bow;
shoot at her, spare no arrows,
for she has sinned against the LORD.
15 Raise a shout against her all around;
she has surrendered;
her bulwarks have fallen;
her walls are thrown down.
For this is the vengeance of the LORD:
take vengeance on her;
do to her as she has done.
16 Cut off from Babylon the sower,
and the one who handles the sickle in time of harvest;
because of the sword of the oppressor,
every one shall turn to his own people,
and every one shall flee to his own land.

17 "Israel is a hunted sheep driven away
by lions. First the king of Assyria devoured
him, and now at last Nebuchadnezzar
king of Babylon has gnawed his bones.
18 Therefore, thus says the LORD of hosts,
the God of Israel: Behold, I am bringing
punishment on the king of Babylon and
his land, as I punished the king of Assyria.
19 I will restore Israel to his pasture, and he
shall feed on Carmel and in Bashan, and
his desire shall be satisfied on the hills of
Ephraim and in Gilead. 20 In those days
and in that time, declares the LORD, iniq-
uity shall be sought in Israel, and there
shall be none, and sin in Judah, and none
shall be found, for I will pardon those
whom I leave as a remnant.

21 "Go up against the land of Merathaim,[1]
and against the inhabitants of Pekod.[2]
Kill, and devote them to destruction,[3]
declares the LORD,
and do all that I have commanded you.
22 The noise of battle is in the land,
and great destruction!
23 How the hammer of the whole earth
is cut down and broken!
How Babylon has become
a horror among the nations!
24 I set a snare for you and you were taken, O Babylon,
and you did not know it;
you were found and caught,
because you opposed the LORD.
25 The LORD has opened his armory
and brought out the weapons of his wrath,
for the Lord GOD of hosts has a work to do
in the land of the Chaldeans.
26 Come against her from every quarter;
open her granaries;
pile her up like heaps of grain, and devote her to destruction;
let nothing be left of her.
27 Kill all her bulls;
let them go down to the slaughter.
Woe to them, for their day has come,
the time of their punishment.

28 "A voice! They flee and escape from
the land of Babylon, to declare in Zion

[1] *Merathaim* means *double rebellion* [2] *Pekod* means *punishment* [3] That is, set apart (devote) as an offering to the Lord (for destruction)

the vengeance of the LORD our God, ven-
geance for his temple.

29 "Summon archers against Babylon, all
those who bend the bow. Encamp around
her; let no one escape. Repay her accord-
ing to her deeds; do to her according to
all that she has done. For she has proudly
defied the LORD, the Holy One of Israel.
30 Therefore her young men shall fall in
her squares, and all her soldiers shall be
destroyed on that day, declares the LORD.

31 "Behold, I am against you, O proud
one,
declares the Lord GOD of hosts,
for your day has come,
the time when I will punish you.
32 The proud one shall stumble and fall,
with none to raise him up,
and I will kindle a fire in his cities,
and it will devour all that is
around him.

33 "Thus says the LORD of hosts: The
people of Israel are oppressed, and the
people of Judah with them. All who took
them captive have held them fast; they
refuse to let them go. 34 Their Redeemer
is strong; the LORD of hosts is his name.
He will surely plead their cause, that he
may give rest to the earth, but unrest to
the inhabitants of Babylon.

35 "A sword against the Chaldeans,
declares the LORD,
and against the inhabitants of
Babylon,
and against her officials and her
wise men!
36 A sword against the diviners,
that they may become fools!
A sword against her warriors,
that they may be destroyed!
37 A sword against her horses and
against her chariots,
and against all the foreign troops
in her midst,
that they may become women!
A sword against all her treasures,
that they may be plundered!
38 A drought against her waters,
that they may be dried up!
For it is a land of images,
and they are mad over idols.

39 "Therefore wild beasts shall dwell
with hyenas in Babylon, and ostriches
shall dwell in her. She shall never again
have people, nor be inhabited for all gener-
ations. 40 As when God overthrew Sodom
and Gomorrah and their neighboring cit-
ies, declares the LORD, so no man shall
dwell there, and no son of man shall
sojourn in her.

41 "Behold, a people comes from the
north;
a mighty nation and many kings
are stirring from the farthest parts
of the earth.
42 They lay hold of bow and spear;
they are cruel and have no mercy.
The sound of them is like the
roaring of the sea;
they ride on horses,
arrayed as a man for battle
against you, O daughter of Babylon!

43 "The king of Babylon heard the
report of them,
and his hands fell helpless;
anguish seized him,
pain as of a woman in labor.

44 "Behold, like a lion coming up from
the thicket of the Jordan against a peren-
nial pasture, I will suddenly make them
run away from her, and I will appoint over
her whomever I choose. For who is like me?
Who will summon me? What shepherd can
stand before me? 45 Therefore hear the plan
that the LORD has made against Babylon,
and the purposes that he has formed
against the land of the Chaldeans: Surely
the little ones of their flock shall be dragged
away; surely their fold shall be appalled at
their fate. 46 At the sound of the capture of

Babylon the earth shall tremble, and her cry shall be heard among the nations."

The Utter Destruction of Babylon

51 Thus says the LORD:
"Behold, I will stir up the spirit of
a destroyer
against Babylon,
against the inhabitants of
Leb-kamai,[1]
2 and I will send to Babylon
winnowers,
and they shall winnow her,
and they shall empty her land,
when they come against her from
every side
on the day of trouble.
3 Let not the archer bend his bow,
and let him not stand up in his
armor.
Spare not her young men;
devote to destruction[2] all her army.
4 They shall fall down slain in the
land of the Chaldeans,
and wounded in her streets.
5 For Israel and Judah have not been
forsaken
by their God, the LORD of hosts,
but the land of the Chaldeans[3] is
full of guilt
against the Holy One of Israel.

6 "Flee from the midst of Babylon;
let every one save his life!
Be not cut off in her punishment,
for this is the time of the LORD's
vengeance,
the repayment he is rendering her.
7 Babylon was a golden cup in the
LORD's hand,
making all the earth drunken;
the nations drank of her wine;
therefore the nations went mad.
8 Suddenly Babylon has fallen and
been broken;
wail for her!
Take balm for her pain;
perhaps she may be healed.
9 We would have healed Babylon,
but she was not healed.
Forsake her, and let us go
each to his own country,
for her judgment has reached up to
heaven
and has been lifted up even to the
skies.
10 The LORD has brought about our
vindication;
come, let us declare in Zion
the work of the LORD our God.

11 "Sharpen the arrows!
Take up the shields!

The LORD has stirred up the spirit of the
kings of the Medes, because his purpose
concerning Babylon is to destroy it, for
that is the vengeance of the LORD, the ven-
geance for his temple.

12 "Set up a standard against the walls
of Babylon;
make the watch strong;
set up watchmen;
prepare the ambushes;
for the LORD has both planned and
done
what he spoke concerning the
inhabitants of Babylon.
13 O you who dwell by many waters,
rich in treasures,
your end has come;
the thread of your life is cut.
14 The LORD of hosts has sworn by
himself:
Surely I will fill you with men, as
many as locusts,
and they shall raise the shout of
victory over you.

15 "It is he who made the earth by his
power,
who established the world by his
wisdom,
and by his understanding stretched
out the heavens.

[1] A code name for Chaldea [2] That is, set apart (devote) as an offering to the Lord (for destruction) [3] Hebrew *their land*

16 When he utters his voice there
is a tumult of waters in the
heavens,
and he makes the mist rise from
the ends of the earth.
He makes lightning for the rain,
and he brings forth the wind from
his storehouses.
17 Every man is stupid and without
knowledge;
every goldsmith is put to shame
by his idols,
for his images are false,
and there is no breath in them.
18 They are worthless, a work of
delusion;
at the time of their punishment
they shall perish.
19 Not like these is he who is the
portion of Jacob,
for he is the one who formed all
things,
and Israel is the tribe of his
inheritance;
the LORD of hosts is his name.

20 "You are my hammer and weapon of
war:
with you I break nations in pieces;
with you I destroy kingdoms;
21 with you I break in pieces the horse
and his rider;
with you I break in pieces the
chariot and the charioteer;
22 with you I break in pieces man and
woman;
with you I break in pieces the old
man and the youth;
with you I break in pieces the young
man and the young woman;
23 with you I break in pieces the
shepherd and his flock;
with you I break in pieces the
farmer and his team;
with you I break in pieces
governors and commanders.

24 "I will repay Babylon and all the inhab-
itants of Chaldea before your very eyes for
all the evil that they have done in Zion,
declares the LORD.

25 "Behold, I am against you,
O destroying mountain,
declares the LORD,
which destroys the whole earth;
I will stretch out my hand against
you,
and roll you down from the crags,
and make you a burnt mountain.
26 No stone shall be taken from you
for a corner
and no stone for a foundation,
but you shall be a perpetual waste,
declares the LORD.

27 "Set up a standard on the earth;
blow the trumpet among the
nations;
prepare the nations for war against
her;
summon against her the
kingdoms,
Ararat, Minni, and Ashkenaz;
appoint a marshal against her;
bring up horses like bristling
locusts.
28 Prepare the nations for war against
her,
the kings of the Medes, with their
governors and deputies,
and every land under their
dominion.
29 The land trembles and writhes in
pain,
for the LORD's purposes against
Babylon stand,
to make the land of Babylon a
desolation,
without inhabitant.
30 The warriors of Babylon have ceased
fighting;
they remain in their strongholds;
their strength has failed;
they have become women;

her dwellings are on fire;
her bars are broken.
31 One runner runs to meet another,
and one messenger to meet another,
to tell the king of Babylon
that his city is taken on every side;
32 the fords have been seized,
the marshes are burned with fire,
and the soldiers are in panic.
33 For thus says the LORD of hosts, the God of Israel:
The daughter of Babylon is like a threshing floor
at the time when it is trodden;
yet a little while
and the time of her harvest will come."

34 "Nebuchadnezzar the king of Babylon has devoured me;
he has crushed me;
he has made me an empty vessel;
he has swallowed me like a monster;
he has filled his stomach with my delicacies;
he has rinsed me out.[1]
35 The violence done to me and to my kinsmen be upon Babylon,"
let the inhabitant of Zion say.
"My blood be upon the inhabitants of Chaldea,"
let Jerusalem say.
36 Therefore thus says the LORD:
"Behold, I will plead your cause
and take vengeance for you.
I will dry up her sea
and make her fountain dry,
37 and Babylon shall become a heap of ruins,
the haunt of jackals,
a horror and a hissing,
without inhabitant.

38 "They shall roar together like lions;
they shall growl like lions' cubs.
39 While they are inflamed I will prepare them a feast
and make them drunk, that they may become merry,
then sleep a perpetual sleep
and not wake, declares the LORD.
40 I will bring them down like lambs to the slaughter,
like rams and male goats.

41 "How Babylon[2] is taken,
the praise of the whole earth seized!
How Babylon has become
a horror among the nations!
42 The sea has come up on Babylon;
she is covered with its tumultuous waves.
43 Her cities have become a horror,
a land of drought and a desert,
a land in which no one dwells,
and through which no son of man passes.
44 And I will punish Bel in Babylon,
and take out of his mouth what he has swallowed.
The nations shall no longer flow to him;
the wall of Babylon has fallen.

45 "Go out of the midst of her, my people!
Let every one save his life
from the fierce anger of the LORD!
46 Let not your heart faint, and be not fearful
at the report heard in the land,
when a report comes in one year
and afterward a report in another year,
and violence is in the land,
and ruler is against ruler.

47 "Therefore, behold, the days are coming
when I will punish the images of Babylon;
her whole land shall be put to shame,
and all her slain shall fall in the midst of her.

[1] Or *he has expelled me* [2] Hebrew *Sheshach*, a code name for Babylon

48 Then the heavens and the earth,
and all that is in them,
shall sing for joy over Babylon,
for the destroyers shall come
against them out of the north,
declares the LORD.
49 Babylon must fall for the slain of
Israel,
just as for Babylon have fallen the
slain of all the earth.

50 "You who have escaped from the
sword,
go, do not stand still!
Remember the LORD from far away,
and let Jerusalem come into your
mind:
51 'We are put to shame, for we have
heard reproach;
dishonor has covered our face,
for foreigners have come
into the holy places of the LORD's
house.'

52 "Therefore, behold, the days are
coming, declares the LORD,
when I will execute judgment
upon her images,
and through all her land
the wounded shall groan.
53 Though Babylon should mount up
to heaven,
and though she should fortify her
strong height,
yet destroyers would come from me
against her,
declares the LORD.

54 "A voice! A cry from Babylon!
The noise of great destruction from
the land of the Chaldeans!
55 For the LORD is laying Babylon waste
and stilling her mighty voice.
Their waves roar like many waters;
the noise of their voice is raised,
56 for a destroyer has come upon her,
upon Babylon;
her warriors are taken;
their bows are broken in pieces,
for the LORD is a God of recompense;
he will surely repay.
57 I will make drunk her officials and
her wise men,
her governors, her commanders,
and her warriors;
they shall sleep a perpetual sleep
and not wake,
declares the King, whose name is
the LORD of hosts.

58 "Thus says the LORD of hosts:
The broad wall of Babylon
shall be leveled to the ground,
and her high gates
shall be burned with fire.
The peoples labor for nothing,
and the nations weary themselves
only for fire."

59 The word that Jeremiah the prophet
commanded Seraiah the son of Neriah, son
of Mahseiah, when he went with Zedekiah
king of Judah to Babylon, in the fourth year
of his reign. Seraiah was the quartermaster.
60 Jeremiah wrote in a book all the disaster
that should come upon Babylon, all these
words that are written concerning Babylon.
61 And Jeremiah said to Seraiah: "When you
come to Babylon, see that you read all these
words, 62 and say, 'O LORD, you have said
concerning this place that you will cut it
off, so that nothing shall dwell in it, neither
man nor beast, and it shall be desolate for-
ever.' 63 When you finish reading this book,
tie a stone to it and cast it into the midst
of the Euphrates, 64 and say, 'Thus shall
Babylon sink, to rise no more, because of
the disaster that I am bringing upon her,
and they shall become exhausted.'"
Thus far are the words of Jeremiah.

The Fall of Jerusalem Recounted

52 Zedekiah was twenty-one years
old when he became king; and
he reigned eleven years in Jerusalem. His
mother's name was Hamutal the daughter

of Jeremiah of Libnah. 2 And he did what was evil in the sight of the LORD, according to all that Jehoiakim had done. 3 For because of the anger of the LORD things came to the point in Jerusalem and Judah that he cast them out from his presence.

And Zedekiah rebelled against the king of Babylon. 4 And in the ninth year of his reign, in the tenth month, on the tenth day of the month, Nebuchadnezzar king of Babylon came with all his army against Jerusalem, and laid siege to it. And they built siegeworks all around it. 5 So the city was besieged till the eleventh year of King Zedekiah. 6 On the ninth day of the fourth month the famine was so severe in the city that there was no food for the people of the land. 7 Then a breach was made in the city, and all the men of war fled and went out from the city by night by the way of a gate between the two walls, by the king's garden, while the Chaldeans were around the city. And they went in the direction of the Arabah. 8 But the army of the Chaldeans pursued the king and overtook Zedekiah in the plains of Jericho. And all his army was scattered from him. 9 Then they captured the king and brought him up to the king of Babylon at Riblah in the land of Hamath, and he passed sentence on him. 10 The king of Babylon slaughtered the sons of Zedekiah before his eyes, and also slaughtered all the officials of Judah at Riblah. 11 He put out the eyes of Zedekiah, and bound him in chains, and the king of Babylon took him to Babylon, and put him in prison till the day of his death.

The Temple Burned

12 In the fifth month, on the tenth day of the month—that was the nineteenth year of King Nebuchadnezzar, king of Babylon—Nebuzaradan the captain of the bodyguard, who served the king of Babylon, entered Jerusalem. 13 And he burned the house of the LORD, and the king's house and all the houses of Jerusalem; every great house he burned down. 14 And all the army of the Chaldeans, who were with the captain of the guard, broke down all the walls around Jerusalem. 15 And Nebuzaradan the captain of the guard carried away captive some of the poorest of the people and the rest of the people who were left in the city and the deserters who had deserted to the king of Babylon, together with the rest of the artisans. 16 But Nebuzaradan the captain of the guard left some of the poorest of the land to be vinedressers and plowmen.

17 And the pillars of bronze that were in the house of the LORD, and the stands and the bronze sea that were in the house of the LORD, the Chaldeans broke in pieces, and carried all the bronze to Babylon. 18 And they took away the pots and the shovels and the snuffers and the basins and the dishes for incense and all the vessels of bronze used in the temple service; 19 also the small bowls and the fire pans and the basins and the pots and the lampstands and the dishes for incense and the bowls for drink offerings. What was of gold the captain of the guard took away as gold, and what was of silver, as silver. 20 As for the two pillars, the one sea, the twelve bronze bulls that were under the sea,[1] and the stands, which Solomon the king had made for the house of the LORD, the bronze of all these things was beyond weight. 21 As for the pillars, the height of the one pillar was eighteen cubits,[2] its circumference was twelve cubits, and its thickness was four fingers, and it was hollow. 22 On it was a capital of bronze. The height of the one capital was five cubits. A network and pomegranates, all of bronze, were around the capital. And the second pillar had the same, with pomegranates. 23 There were ninety-six pomegranates on the sides; all the pomegranates were a hundred upon the network all around.

[1] Hebrew lacks *the sea* [2] A *cubit* was about 18 inches or 45 centimeters

The People Exiled to Babylon

24 And the captain of the guard took
Seraiah the chief priest, and Zephaniah
the second priest, and the three keepers
of the threshold; 25 and from the city he
took an officer who had been in command
of the men of war, and seven men of the
king's council, who were found in the city;
and the secretary of the commander of the
army who mustered the people of the land;
and sixty men of the people of the land,
who were found in the midst of the city.
26 And Nebuzaradan the captain of the
guard took them and brought them to the
king of Babylon at Riblah. 27 And the king of
Babylon struck them down, and put them
to death at Riblah in the land of Hamath. So
Judah was taken into exile out of its land.

28 This is the number of the people
whom Nebuchadnezzar carried away cap-
tive: in the seventh year, 3,023 Judeans; 29 in
the eighteenth year of Nebuchadnezzar
he carried away captive from Jerusalem
832 persons; 30 in the twenty-third year of
Nebuchadnezzar, Nebuzaradan the cap-
tain of the guard carried away captive of
the Judeans 745 persons; all the persons
were 4,600.

Jehoiachin Released from Prison

31 And in the thirty-seventh year of the
exile of Jehoiachin king of Judah, in the
twelfth month, on the twenty-fifth day
of the month, Evil-merodach king of
Babylon, in the year that he became king,
graciously freed[1] Jehoiachin king of Judah
and brought him out of prison. 32 And he
spoke kindly to him, and gave him a seat
above the seats of the kings who were
with him in Babylon. 33 So Jehoiachin put
off his prison garments. And every day
of his life he dined regularly at the king's
table, 34 and for his allowance, a regular
allowance was given him by the king
according to his daily need, until the day
of his death, as long as he lived.

[1] Hebrew *king, lifted up the head of*

Introduction to

Lamentations

Author
Jeremiah the prophet

Date
586 B.C.

Purpose
The purpose of Lamentations is to express sorrow over Jerusalem's destruction and the sin that caused it, and to remind the people of God's steadfast love even in suffering.

Central Themes
Sin separates from God and results in suffering; sinners must humbly repent; God shows mercy; God's steadfast love never ends; God can restore His sinful people.

Memory Verses
God's mercies never cease (Lamentations 3:21–24); compassion and steadfast love (Lamentations 3:31–33); examine your ways (Lamentations 3:40–42)

Introduction

Lamentations is a book of five poems. Each poem expresses great sadness over the destruction of Jerusalem. The poems express even greater sadness over the separation between God and His people and the disobedience that caused Jerusalem's destruction. It was hard for the people of Judah to see their homes destroyed and to be carried away to another country by their enemies. But what made it even worse was that they knew they had brought this on themselves through their disobedience to God. Now, when they needed God to comfort them, they had only the realization that they had made Him angry.

The five poems are long, and each piles up one expression of sorrow after another. The middle poem (Lamentations 3) is the one bright spot in the book, and it is a very bright spot! After admitting that sinners have no right to complain when they suffer for their sin, the poem goes on to describe God's steadfast love and His mercies as being never ending—no matter what! This middle poem calls on sinners to suffer patiently and to call on God, trusting Him to refrain His anger and to turn again to His people in compassion.

701 B.C. Assyria attacks Judah

627 B.C. Prophetic ministry of Jeremiah begins

586 B.C. Fall of Judah

Lamentations

How Lonely Sits the City

1 How lonely sits the city
that was full of people!
How like a widow has she become,
she who was great among the nations!
She who was a princess among the provinces
has become a slave.

2 She weeps bitterly in the night,
with tears on her cheeks;
among all her lovers
she has none to comfort her;
all her friends have dealt treacherously with her;
they have become her enemies.

3 Judah has gone into exile because of affliction
and hard servitude;
she dwells now among the nations,
but finds no resting place;
her pursuers have all overtaken her
in the midst of her distress.[1]

4 The roads to Zion mourn,
for none come to the festival;
all her gates are desolate;
her priests groan;
her virgins have been afflicted,[2]
and she herself suffers bitterly.

5 Her foes have become the head;
her enemies prosper,
because the LORD has afflicted her
for the multitude of her transgressions;
her children have gone away,
captives before the foe.

6 From the daughter of Zion
all her majesty has departed.
Her princes have become like deer
that find no pasture;
they fled without strength
before the pursuer.

7 Jerusalem remembers
in the days of her affliction and wandering
all the precious things
that were hers from days of old.
When her people fell into the hand of the foe,
and there was none to help her,
her foes gloated over her;
they mocked at her downfall.

8 Jerusalem sinned grievously;
therefore she became filthy;
all who honored her despise her,
for they have seen her nakedness;
she herself groans
and turns her face away.

9 Her uncleanness was in her skirts;
she took no thought of her future;[3]
therefore her fall is terrible;
she has no comforter.
"O LORD, behold my affliction,
for the enemy has triumphed!"

10 The enemy has stretched out his hands
over all her precious things;
for she has seen the nations
enter her sanctuary,
those whom you forbade
to enter your congregation.

11 All her people groan
as they search for bread;
they trade their treasures for food
to revive their strength.
"Look, O LORD, and see,
for I am despised."

[1] Or *in the narrow passes* [2] Septuagint, Old Latin *dragged away* [3] Or *end*

12 "Is it nothing to you, all you who
pass by?
Look and see
if there is any sorrow like my sorrow,
which was brought upon me,
which the LORD inflicted
on the day of his fierce anger.

13 "From on high he sent fire;
into my bones[1] he made it descend;
he spread a net for my feet;
he turned me back;
he has left me stunned,
faint all the day long.

14 "My transgressions were bound[2] into
a yoke;
by his hand they were fastened
together;
they were set upon my neck;
he caused my strength to fail;
the Lord gave me into the hands
of those whom I cannot withstand.

15 "The Lord rejected
all my mighty men in my midst;
he summoned an assembly against
me
to crush my young men;
the Lord has trodden as in a
winepress
the virgin daughter of Judah.

16 "For these things I weep;
my eyes flow with tears;
for a comforter is far from me,
one to revive my spirit;
my children are desolate,
for the enemy has prevailed."

17 Zion stretches out her hands,
but there is none to comfort her;
the LORD has commanded against
Jacob
that his neighbors should be his
foes;
Jerusalem has become
a filthy thing among them.

18 "The LORD is in the right,
for I have rebelled against his word;
but hear, all you peoples,
and see my suffering;
my young women and my young
men
have gone into captivity.

19 "I called to my lovers,
but they deceived me;
my priests and elders
perished in the city,
while they sought food
to revive their strength.

20 "Look, O LORD, for I am in distress;
my stomach churns;
my heart is wrung within me,
because I have been very rebellious.
In the street the sword bereaves;
in the house it is like death.

21 "They heard[3] my groaning,
yet there is no one to comfort me.
All my enemies have heard of my
trouble;
they are glad that you have done it.
You have brought[4] the day you
announced;
now let them be as I am.

22 "Let all their evildoing come before
you,
and deal with them
as you have dealt with me
because of all my transgressions;
for my groans are many,
and my heart is faint."

The Lord Has Destroyed Without Pity

2 How the Lord in his anger
has set the daughter of Zion under a
cloud!
He has cast down from heaven to
earth
the splendor of Israel;
he has not remembered his footstool
in the day of his anger.

[1] Septuagint; Hebrew *bones and* [2] The meaning of the Hebrew is uncertain [3] Septuagint, Syriac *Hear* [4] Syriac *Bring*

2 The Lord has swallowed up without mercy
all the habitations of Jacob;
in his wrath he has broken down
the strongholds of the daughter of Judah;
he has brought down to the ground in dishonor
the kingdom and its rulers.

3 He has cut down in fierce anger
all the might of Israel;
he has withdrawn from them his right hand
in the face of the enemy;
he has burned like a flaming fire in Jacob,
consuming all around.

4 He has bent his bow like an enemy,
with his right hand set like a foe;
and he has killed all who were delightful in our eyes
in the tent of the daughter of Zion;
he has poured out his fury like fire.

5 The Lord has become like an enemy;
he has swallowed up Israel;
he has swallowed up all its palaces;
he has laid in ruins its strongholds,
and he has multiplied in the daughter of Judah
mourning and lamentation.

6 He has laid waste his booth like a garden,
laid in ruins his meeting place;
the LORD has made Zion forget
festival and Sabbath,
and in his fierce indignation has spurned king and priest.

7 The Lord has scorned his altar,
disowned his sanctuary;
he has delivered into the hand of the enemy
the *walls of her* palaces;
they raised a clamor in the house of the LORD
as on the day of festival.

8 The LORD determined to lay in ruins
the wall of the daughter of Zion;
he stretched out the measuring line;
he did not restrain his hand from destroying;
he caused rampart and wall to lament;
they languished together.

9 Her gates have sunk into the ground;
he has ruined and broken her bars;
her king and princes are among the nations;
the law is no more,
and her prophets find
no vision from the LORD.

10 The elders of the daughter of Zion
sit on the ground in silence;
they have thrown dust on their heads
and put on sackcloth;
the young women of Jerusalem
have bowed their heads to the ground.

11 My eyes are spent with weeping;
my stomach churns;
my bile is poured out to the ground
because of the destruction of the daughter of my people,
because infants and babies faint
in the streets of the city.

12 They cry to their mothers,
"Where is bread and wine?"
as they faint like a wounded man
in the streets of the city,
as their life is poured out
on their mothers' bosom.

13 What can I say for you, to what compare you,
O daughter of Jerusalem?
What can I liken to you, that I may comfort you,
O virgin daughter of Zion?
For your ruin is vast as the sea;
who can heal you?

14 Your prophets have seen for you
false and deceptive visions;
they have not exposed your iniquity
to restore your fortunes,
but have seen for you oracles
that are false and misleading.

15 All who pass along the way
clap their hands at you;
they hiss and wag their heads
at the daughter of Jerusalem:
"Is this the city that was called
the perfection of beauty,
the joy of all the earth?"

16 All your enemies
rail against you;
they hiss, they gnash their teeth,
they cry: "We have swallowed her!
Ah, this is the day we longed for;
now we have it; we see it!"

17 The LORD has done what he
purposed;
he has carried out his word,
which he commanded long ago;
he has thrown down without pity;
he has made the enemy rejoice over
you
and exalted the might of your
foes.

18 Their heart cried to the Lord.
O wall of the daughter of Zion,
let tears stream down like a torrent
day and night!
Give yourself no rest,
your eyes no respite!

19 "Arise, cry out in the night,
at the beginning of the night
watches!
Pour out your heart like water
before the presence of the Lord!
Lift your hands to him
for the lives of your children,
who faint for hunger
at the head of every street."

20 Look, O LORD, and see!
With whom have you dealt thus?
Should women eat the fruit of their
womb,
the children of their tender care?
Should priest and prophet be killed
in the sanctuary of the Lord?

21 In the dust of the streets
lie the young and the old;
my young women and my young
men
have fallen by the sword;
you have killed them in the day of
your anger,
slaughtering without pity.

22 You summoned as if to a festival
day
my terrors on every side,
and on the day of the anger of the
LORD
no one escaped or survived;
those whom I held and raised
my enemy destroyed.

Great Is Your Faithfulness

3 I am the man who has seen
affliction
under the rod of his wrath;
2 he has driven and brought me
into darkness without any light;
3 surely against me he turns his hand
again and again the whole day
long.

4 He has made my flesh and my skin
waste away;
he has broken my bones;
5 he has besieged and enveloped me
with bitterness and tribulation;
6 he has made me dwell in darkness
like the dead of long ago.

7 He has walled me about so that I
cannot escape;
he has made my chains heavy;
8 though I call and cry for help,
he shuts out my prayer;

9 he has blocked my ways with blocks
of stones;
he has made my paths crooked.

10 He is a bear lying in wait for me,
a lion in hiding;
11 he turned aside my steps and tore
me to pieces;
he has made me desolate;
12 he bent his bow and set me
as a target for his arrow.

13 He drove into my kidneys
the arrows of his quiver;
14 I have become the laughingstock of
all peoples,
the object of their taunts all day
long.
15 He has filled me with bitterness;
he has sated me with wormwood.

16 He has made my teeth grind on
gravel,
and made me cower in ashes;
17 my soul is bereft of peace;
I have forgotten what happiness[1] is;
18 so I say, "My endurance has perished;
so has my hope from the LORD."

19 Remember my affliction and my
wanderings,
the wormwood and the gall!
20 My soul continually remembers it
and is bowed down within me.
21 But this I call to mind,
and therefore I have hope:

22 The steadfast love of the LORD never
ceases;[2]
his mercies never come to an end;
23 they are new every morning;
great is your faithfulness.
24 "The LORD is my portion," says my
soul,
"therefore I will hope in him."

25 The LORD is good to those who wait
for him,
to the soul who seeks him.
26 It is good that one should wait quietly
for the salvation of the LORD.
27 It is good for a man that he bear
the yoke in his youth.

28 Let him sit alone in silence
when it is laid on him;
29 let him put his mouth in the dust—
there may yet be hope;
30 let him give his cheek to the one
who strikes,
and let him be filled with insults.

31 For the Lord will not
cast off forever,
32 but, though he cause grief, he will
have compassion
according to the abundance of his
steadfast love;
33 for he does not willingly afflict
or grieve the children of men.

34 To crush underfoot
all the prisoners of the earth,
35 to deny a man justice
in the presence of the Most High,
36 to subvert a man in his lawsuit,
the Lord does not approve.

37 Who has spoken and it came to pass,
unless the Lord has commanded it?
38 Is it not from the mouth of the Most
High
that good and bad come?
39 Why should a living man complain,
a man, about the punishment of
his sins?

40 Let us test and examine our ways,
and return to the LORD!
41 Let us lift up our hearts and hands
to God in heaven:
42 "We have transgressed and rebelled,
and you have not forgiven.

43 "You have wrapped yourself with
anger and pursued us,
killing without pity;
44 you have wrapped yourself with a
cloud
so that no prayer can pass through.

[1] Hebrew *good* [2] Syriac, Targum; Hebrew *Because of the steadfast love of the LORD, we are not cut off*

45 You have made us scum and garbage
among the peoples.

46 "All our enemies
open their mouths against us;
47 panic and pitfall have come upon us,
devastation and destruction;
48 my eyes flow with rivers of tears
because of the destruction of the
daughter of my people.

49 "My eyes will flow without ceasing,
without respite,
50 until the LORD from heaven
looks down and sees;
51 my eyes cause me grief
at the fate of all the daughters of
my city.

52 "I have been hunted like a bird
by those who were my enemies
without cause;
53 they flung me alive into the pit
and cast stones on me;
54 water closed over my head;
I said, 'I am lost.'

55 "I called on your name, O LORD,
from the depths of the pit;
56 you heard my plea, 'Do not close
your ear to my cry for help!'
57 You came near when I called on you;
you said, 'Do not fear!'

58 "You have taken up my cause, O Lord;
you have redeemed my life.
59 You have seen the wrong done to
me, O LORD;
judge my cause.
60 You have seen all their vengeance,
all their plots against me.

61 "You have heard their taunts, O LORD,
all their plots against me.
62 The lips and thoughts of my
assailants
are against me all the day long.
63 Behold their sitting and their rising;
I am the object of their taunts.

64 "You will repay them,[1] O LORD,
according to the work of their
hands.
65 You will give them[2] dullness of heart;
your curse will be[3] on them.
66 You will pursue them[4] in anger and
destroy them
from under your heavens,
O LORD."[5]

The Holy Stones Lie Scattered

4 How the gold has grown dim,
how the pure gold is changed!
The holy stones lie scattered
at the head of every street.

2 The precious sons of Zion,
worth their weight in fine gold,
how they are regarded as earthen
pots,
the work of a potter's hands!

3 Even jackals offer the breast;
they nurse their young,
but the daughter of my people has
become cruel,
like the ostriches in the wilderness.
4 The tongue of the nursing infant
sticks
to the roof of its mouth for thirst;
the children beg for food,
but no one gives to them.

5 Those who once feasted on delicacies
perish in the streets;
those who were brought up in purple
embrace ash heaps.

6 For the chastisement[6] of the daughter
of my people has been greater
than the punishment[7] of Sodom,
which was overthrown in a moment,
and no hands were wrung for her.[8]

7 Her princes were purer than snow,
whiter than milk;

[1] Or *Repay them* [2] Or *Give them* [3] Or *place your curse* [4] Or *Pursue them* [5] Syriac (compare Septuagint, Vulgate); Hebrew *the heavens of the LORD* [6] Or *iniquity* [7] Or *sin*
[8] The meaning of the Hebrew is uncertain

their bodies were more ruddy than
coral,
the beauty of their form[1] was like
sapphire.[2]

8 Now their face is blacker than soot;
they are not recognized in the
streets;
their skin has shriveled on their
bones;
it has become as dry as wood.

9 Happier were the victims of the
sword
than the victims of hunger,
who wasted away, pierced
by lack of the fruits of the field.

10 The hands of compassionate women
have boiled their own children;
they became their food
during the destruction of the
daughter of my people.

11 The LORD gave full vent to his wrath;
he poured out his hot anger,
and he kindled a fire in Zion
that consumed its foundations.

12 The kings of the earth did not believe,
nor any of the inhabitants of the
world,
that foe or enemy could enter
the gates of Jerusalem.

13 This was for the sins of her prophets
and the iniquities of her priests,
who shed in the midst of her
the blood of the righteous.

14 They wandered, blind, through the
streets;
they were so defiled with blood
that no one was able to touch
their garments.

15 "Away! Unclean!" people cried at them.
"Away! Away! Do not touch!"
So they became fugitives and
wanderers;
people said among the nations,
"They shall stay with us no longer."

16 The LORD himself[3] has scattered
them;
he will regard them no more;
no honor was shown to the priests,
no favor to the elders.

17 Our eyes failed, ever watching
vainly for help;
in our watching we watched
for a nation which could not save.

18 They dogged our steps
so that we could not walk in our
streets;
our end drew near; our days were
numbered,
for our end had come.

19 Our pursuers were swifter
than the eagles in the heavens;
they chased us on the mountains;
they lay in wait for us in the
wilderness.

20 The breath of our nostrils, the
LORD's anointed,
was captured in their pits,
of whom we said, "Under his shadow
we shall live among the nations."

21 Rejoice and be glad, O daughter of
Edom,
you who dwell in the land of Uz;
but to you also the cup shall pass;
you shall become drunk and strip
yourself bare.

22 The punishment of your iniquity,
O daughter of Zion, is
accomplished;
he will keep you in exile no longer;[4]
but your iniquity, O daughter of
Edom, he will punish;
he will uncover your sins.

[1] The meaning of the Hebrew is uncertain [2] Hebrew *lapis lazuli* [3] Hebrew *The face of the LORD* [4] Or *he will not exile you again*

Restore Us to Yourself, O Lord

5 Remember, O Lord, what has befallen us;
look, and see our disgrace!
2 Our inheritance has been turned over to strangers,
our homes to foreigners.
3 We have become orphans, fatherless;
our mothers are like widows.
4 We must pay for the water we drink;
the wood we get must be bought.
5 Our pursuers are at our necks;[1]
we are weary; we are given no rest.
6 We have given the hand to Egypt, and to Assyria,
to get bread enough.
7 Our fathers sinned, and are no more;
and we bear their iniquities.
8 Slaves rule over us;
there is none to deliver us from their hand.
9 We get our bread at the peril of our lives,
because of the sword in the wilderness.
10 Our skin is hot as an oven
with the burning heat of famine.
11 Women are raped in Zion,
young women in the towns of Judah.
12 Princes are hung up by their hands;
no respect is shown to the elders.
13 Young men are compelled to grind at the mill,
and boys stagger under loads of wood.
14 The old men have left the city gate,
the young men their music.
15 The joy of our hearts has ceased;
our dancing has been turned to mourning.
16 The crown has fallen from our head;
woe to us, for we have sinned!
17 For this our heart has become sick,
for these things our eyes have grown dim,
18 for Mount Zion which lies desolate;
jackals prowl over it.
19 But you, O Lord, reign forever;
your throne endures to all generations.
20 Why do you forget us forever,
why do you forsake us for so many days?
21 Restore us to yourself, O Lord, that we may be restored!
Renew our days as of old—
22 unless you have utterly rejected us,
and you remain exceedingly angry with us.

[1] Symmachus *With a yoke on our necks*

Introduction to

Ezekiel

Author
Ezekiel the prophet

Date
593–573 B.C.

Purpose
The purpose of Ezekiel is to explain why God's glory left Israel and how His glory would return.

Central Themes
God is glorious and holy; God's people can be very sinful; God's presence and God's blessings were taken from Israel because of their sin; God is faithful to His covenant; God gives His people great gifts: His Spirit, forgiveness, a Good Shepherd, and new hearts.

Memory Verses
The watchman's calling (Ezekiel 3:17–19); a new heart (Ezekiel 11:19–20); the Lord desires to save us (Ezekiel 18:21–23, 32); the Good Shepherd (Ezekiel 34:20–24); the new covenant (Ezekiel 36:25–27); the Lord's glory returns (Ezekiel 43:2–5)

Introduction

Ezekiel was carried away to Babylon as a prisoner. He writes to explain that the coming Babylonian destruction of Jerusalem and the temple is not because God doesn't keep His promises, but because His people have sinned. Ezekiel's first vision is of God in His glory; it overwhelms him for seven days (Ezekiel 1:1–3:15)! Ezekiel speaks against the sins of God's people. In one vision, he sees God's glory leave the temple and the city; God is leaving His people because of their sin (Ezekiel 8–11). Ezekiel describes God's judgment on the nations, too, for their pride and idolatry (Ezekiel 25–32). But Ezekiel also promises a glorious future. In one vision, when he preaches to thousands of dry bones, God puts them together and breathes life into them, a picture of God's Spirit giving new life to people dead in sin (Ezekiel 37:1–14). Ezekiel writes that God will seek His lost sheep and set a Shepherd over them (Ezekiel 34:11–24). God will forgive His people and give them new hearts to obey Him (Ezekiel 36:22–32). In one of the last of Ezekiel's visions, he sees a new temple and the glory of the Lord returning to remain with His people forever (Ezekiel 40:1–43:5).

593 B.C.	586 B.C.	573 B.C.
Ezekiel's first vision	Fall of Judah/ temple destroyed	Ezekiel's vision of second temple

Ezekiel

Ezekiel in Babylon

1 In the thirtieth year, in the fourth
month, on the fifth day of the month,
as I was among the exiles by the Chebar
canal, the heavens were opened, and I saw
visions of God.[1] 2 On the fifth day of the
month (it was the fifth year of the exile of
King Jehoiachin), 3 the word of the LORD
came to Ezekiel the priest, the son of Buzi,
in the land of the Chaldeans by the Chebar
canal, and the hand of the LORD was upon
him there.

The Glory of the LORD

4 As I looked, behold, a stormy wind
came out of the north, and a great cloud,
with brightness around it, and fire flash-
ing forth continually, and in the midst of
the fire, as it were gleaming metal.[2] 5 And
from the midst of it came the likeness of
four living creatures. And this was their
appearance: they had a human likeness,
6 but each had four faces, and each of them
had four wings. 7 Their legs were straight,
and the soles of their feet were like the sole
of a calf's foot. And they sparkled like bur-
nished bronze. 8 Under their wings on their
four sides they had human hands. And
the four had their faces and their wings
thus: 9 their wings touched one another.
Each one of them went straight forward,
without turning as they went. 10 As for the
likeness of their faces, each had a human
face. The four had the face of a lion on the
right side, the four had the face of an ox on
the left side, and the four had the face of an
eagle. 11 Such were their faces. And their
wings were spread out above. Each crea-
ture had two wings, each of which touched
the wing of another, while two covered
their bodies. 12 And each went straight for-
ward. Wherever the spirit would go, they
went, without turning as they went. 13 As
for the likeness of the living creatures,
their appearance was like burning coals of
fire, like the appearance of torches moving
to and fro among the living creatures. And
the fire was bright, and out of the fire went
forth lightning. 14 And the living creatures
darted to and fro, like the appearance of a
flash of lightning.

15 Now as I looked at the living crea-
tures, I saw a wheel on the earth beside
the living creatures, one for each of the
four of them.[3] 16 As for the appearance of

CHARACTER PROFILE

EZEKIEL

Ezekiel was a prophet who lived in Babylon with other Jews. They had been taken there when Babylonian soldiers had destroyed Jerusalem. Ezekiel said this happened because God's people had sinned. He promised God would make a new and better covenant with His people and would live with them forever.

[1] Or *from God* [2] Or *amber*; also verse 27 [3] Hebrew *of their faces*

the wheels and their construction: their appearance was like the gleaming of beryl. And the four had the same likeness, their appearance and construction being as it were a wheel within a wheel. **17** When they went, they went in any of their four directions[1] without turning as they went. **18** And their rims were tall and awesome, and the rims of all four were full of eyes all around. **19** And when the living creatures went, the wheels went beside them; and when the living creatures rose from the earth, the wheels rose. **20** Wherever the spirit wanted to go, they went, and the wheels rose along with them, for the spirit of the living creatures[2] was in the wheels. **21** When those went, these went; and when those stood, these stood; and when those rose from the earth, the wheels rose along with them, for the spirit of the living creatures was in the wheels.

22 Over the heads of the living creatures there was the likeness of an expanse, shining like awe-inspiring crystal, spread out above their heads. **23** And under the expanse their wings were stretched out straight, one toward another. And each creature had two wings covering its body. **24** And when they went, I heard the sound of their wings like the sound of many waters, like the sound of the Almighty, a sound of tumult like the sound of an army. When they stood still, they let down their wings. **25** And there came a voice from above the expanse over their heads. When they stood still, they let down their wings.

26 And above the expanse over their heads there was the likeness of a throne, in appearance like sapphire;[3] and seated above the likeness of a throne was a likeness with a human appearance. **27** And upward from what had the appearance of his waist I saw as it were gleaming metal, like the appearance of fire enclosed all around. And downward from what had the appearance of his waist I saw as it were the appearance of fire, and there was brightness around him.[4] **28** Like the appearance of the bow that is in the cloud on the day of rain, so was the appearance of the brightness all around.

Such was the appearance of the likeness of the glory of the LORD. And when I saw it, I fell on my face, and I heard the voice of one speaking.

Ezekiel's Call

2 And he said to me, "Son of man,[5] stand on your feet, and I will speak with you." **2** And as he spoke to me, the Spirit entered into me and set me on my feet, and I heard him speaking to me. **3** And he said to me, "Son of man, I send you to the people of Israel, to nations of rebels, who have rebelled against me. They and their fathers have transgressed against me to this very day. **4** The descendants also are impudent and stubborn: I send you to them, and you shall say to them, 'Thus says the Lord GOD.' **5** And whether they hear or refuse to hear (for they are a rebellious house) they will know that a prophet has been among them. **6** And you, son of man, be not afraid of them, nor be afraid of their words, though briers and thorns are with you and you sit on scorpions.[6] Be not afraid of their words, nor be dismayed at their looks, for they are a rebellious house. **7** And you shall speak my words to them, whether they hear or refuse to hear, for they are a rebellious house.

8 "But you, son of man, hear what I say to you. Be not rebellious like that rebellious house; open your mouth and eat what I give you." **9** And when I looked, behold, a hand was stretched out to me, and behold, a scroll of a book was in it. **10** And he spread it before me. And it had writing on the front and on the back, and there were written on it words of lamentation and mourning and woe.

3 And he said to me, "Son of man, eat whatever you find here. Eat this scroll, and go, speak to the house of Israel." **2** So I

[1] Hebrew *on their four sides* [2] Or *the spirit of life*; also verse 21 [3] Or *lapis lazuli* [4] Or *it* [5] Or *Son of Adam*; so throughout Ezekiel [6] Or *on scorpion plants*

opened my mouth, and he gave me this scroll to eat. 3 And he said to me, "Son of man, feed your belly with this scroll that I give you and fill your stomach with it." Then I ate it, and it was in my mouth as sweet as honey.

4 And he said to me, "Son of man, go to the house of Israel and speak with my words to them. 5 For you are not sent to a people of foreign speech and a hard language, but to the house of Israel— 6 not to many peoples of foreign speech and a hard language, whose words you cannot understand. Surely, if I sent you to such, they would listen to you. 7 But the house of Israel will not be willing to listen to you, for they are not willing to listen to me: because all the house of Israel have a hard forehead and a stubborn heart. 8 Behold, I have made your face as hard as their faces, and your forehead as hard as their foreheads. 9 Like emery harder than flint have I made your forehead. Fear them not, nor be dismayed at their looks, for they are a rebellious house." 10 Moreover, he said to me, "Son of man, all my words that I shall speak to you receive in your heart, and hear with your ears. 11 And go to the exiles, to your people, and speak to them and say to them, 'Thus says the Lord GOD,' whether they hear or refuse to hear."

12 Then the Spirit[1] lifted me up, and I heard behind me the voice[2] of a great earthquake: "Blessed be the glory of the LORD from its place!" 13 It was the sound of the wings of the living creatures as they touched one another, and the sound of the wheels beside them, and the sound of a great earthquake. 14 The Spirit lifted me up and took me away, and I went in bitterness in the heat of my spirit, the hand of the LORD being strong upon me. 15 And I came to the exiles at Tel-abib, who were dwelling by the Chebar canal, and I sat where they were dwelling.[3] And I sat there overwhelmed among them seven days.

A Watchman for Israel

16 And at the end of seven days, the word of the LORD came to me: 17 "Son of man, I have made you a watchman for the house of Israel. Whenever you hear a word from my mouth, you shall give them warning from me. 18 If I say to the wicked, 'You shall surely die,' and you give him no warning, nor speak to warn the wicked from his wicked way, in order to save his life, that wicked person shall die for[4] his iniquity, but his blood I will require at your hand. 19 But if you warn the wicked, and he does not turn from his wickedness, or from his wicked way, he shall die for his iniquity, but you will have delivered your soul. 20 Again, if a righteous person turns from his righteousness and commits injustice, and I lay a stumbling block before him, he shall die. Because you have not warned him, he shall die for his sin, and his righteous deeds that he has done shall not be remembered, but his blood I will require at your hand. 21 But if you warn the righteous person not to sin, and he does not sin, he shall surely live, because he took warning, and you will have delivered your soul."

22 And the hand of the LORD was upon me there. And he said to me, "Arise, go out into the valley,[5] and there I will speak with you." 23 So I arose and went out into the valley, and behold, the glory of the LORD stood there, like the glory that I had seen by the Chebar canal, and I fell on my face. 24 But the Spirit entered into me and set me on my feet, and he spoke with me and said to me, "Go, shut yourself within your house. 25 And you, O son of man, behold, cords will be placed upon you, and you shall be bound with them, so that you cannot go out among the people. 26 And I will make your tongue cling to the roof of your mouth, so that you shall be mute and unable to reprove them, for they are a rebellious house. 27 But when I speak with you, I will open your mouth, and you shall say to them, 'Thus says the Lord GOD.' He

[1] Or *the wind*; also verse 14 [2] Or *sound* [3] Or *Chebar, and to where they dwelt* [4] Or *in*; also verses 19, 20 [5] Or *plain*; also verse 23

who will hear, let him hear; and he who will refuse to hear, let him refuse, for they are a rebellious house.

The Siege of Jerusalem Symbolized

4 "And you, son of man, take a brick and lay it before you, and engrave on it a city, even Jerusalem. **2** And put siegeworks against it, and build a siege wall against it, and cast up a mound against it. Set camps also against it, and plant battering rams against it all around. **3** And you, take an iron griddle, and place it as an iron wall between you and the city; and set your face toward it, and let it be in a state of siege, and press the siege against it. This is a sign for the house of Israel.

4 "Then lie on your left side, and place the punishment[1] of the house of Israel upon it. For the number of the days that you lie on it, you shall bear their punishment. **5** For I assign to you a number of days, 390 days, equal to the number of the years of their punishment. So long shall you bear the punishment of the house of Israel. **6** And when you have completed these, you shall lie down a second time, but on your right side, and bear the punishment of the house of Judah. Forty days I assign you, a day for each year. **7** And you shall set your face toward the siege of Jerusalem, with your arm bared, and you shall prophesy against the city. **8** And behold, I will place cords upon you, so that you cannot turn from one side to the other, till you have completed the days of your siege.

9 "And you, take wheat and barley, beans and lentils, millet and emmer,[2] and put them into a single vessel and make your bread from them. During the number of days that you lie on your side, 390 days, you shall eat it. **10** And your food that you eat shall be by weight, twenty shekels[3] a day; from day to day[4] you shall eat it. **11** And water you shall drink by measure, the sixth part of a hin;[5] from day to day you shall drink. **12** And you shall eat it as a barley cake, baking it in their sight on human dung." **13** And the LORD said, "Thus shall the people of Israel eat their bread unclean, among the nations where I will drive them." **14** Then I said, "Ah, Lord GOD! Behold, I have never defiled myself.[6] From my youth up till now I have never eaten what died of itself or was torn by beasts, nor has tainted meat come into my mouth." **15** Then he said to me, "See, I assign to you cow's dung instead of human dung, on which you may prepare your bread." **16** Moreover, he said to me, "Son of man, behold, I will break the supply[7] of bread in Jerusalem. They shall eat bread by weight and with anxiety, and they shall drink water by measure and in dismay. **17** I will do this that they may lack bread and water, and look at one another in dismay, and rot away because of their punishment.

Jerusalem Will Be Destroyed

5 "And you, O son of man, take a sharp sword. Use it as a barber's razor and pass it over your head and your beard. Then take balances for weighing and divide the hair. **2** A third part you shall burn in the fire in the midst of the city, when the days of the siege are completed. And a third part you shall take and strike with the sword all around the city. And a third part you shall scatter to the wind, and I will unsheathe the sword after them. **3** And you shall take from these a small number and bind them in the skirts of your robe. **4** And of these again you shall take some and cast them into the midst of the fire and burn them in the fire. From there a fire will come out into all the house of Israel.

5 "Thus says the Lord GOD: This is Jerusalem. I have set her in the center of the nations, with countries all around her. **6** And she has rebelled against my rules by doing wickedness more than the nations, and against my statutes more than the countries all around her; for they have rejected my rules and have not walked

[1] Or *iniquity;* also verses 5, 6, 17 [2] A type of wheat [3] A *shekel* was about 2/5 ounce or 11 grams [4] Or *at a set time daily;* also verse 11 [5] A *hin* was about 4 quarts or 3.5 liters [6] Hebrew *my soul* (or *throat*) *has never been made unclean* [7] Hebrew *staff*

in my statutes. 7 Therefore thus says the Lord GOD: Because you are more turbulent than the nations that are all around you, and have not walked in my statutes or obeyed my rules, and have not[1] even acted according to the rules of the nations that are all around you, 8 therefore thus says the Lord GOD: Behold, I, even I, am against you. And I will execute judgments[2] in your midst in the sight of the nations. 9 And because of all your abominations I will do with you what I have never yet done, and the like of which I will never do again. 10 Therefore fathers shall eat their sons in your midst, and sons shall eat their fathers. And I will execute judgments on you, and any of you who survive I will scatter to all the winds. 11 Therefore, as I live, declares the Lord GOD, surely, because you have defiled my sanctuary with all your detestable things and with all your abominations, therefore I will withdraw.[3] My eye will not spare, and I will have no pity. 12 A third part of you shall die of pestilence and be consumed with famine in your midst; a third part shall fall by the sword all around you; and a third part I will scatter to all the winds and will unsheathe the sword after them.

13 "Thus shall my anger spend itself, and I will vent my fury upon them and satisfy myself. And they shall know that I am the LORD—that I have spoken in my jealousy—when I spend my fury upon them. 14 Moreover, I will make you a desolation and an object of reproach among the nations all around you and in the sight of all who pass by. 15 You shall be[4] a reproach and a taunt, a warning and a horror, to the nations all around you, when I execute judgments on you in anger and fury, and with furious rebukes—I am the LORD; I have spoken— 16 when I send against you[5] the deadly arrows of famine, arrows for destruction, which I will send to destroy you, and when I bring more and more famine upon you and break your supply[6] of bread. 17 I will send famine and wild beasts against you, and they will rob you of your children. Pestilence and blood shall pass through you, and I will bring the sword upon you. I am the LORD; I have spoken."

Judgment Against Idolatry

6 The word of the LORD came to me: 2 "Son of man, set your face toward the mountains of Israel, and prophesy against them, 3 and say, You mountains of Israel, hear the word of the Lord GOD! Thus says the Lord GOD to the mountains and the hills, to the ravines and the valleys: Behold, I, even I, will bring a sword upon you, and I will destroy your high places. 4 Your altars shall become desolate, and your incense altars shall be broken, and I will cast down your slain before your idols. 5 And I will lay the dead bodies of the people of Israel before their idols, and I will scatter your bones around your altars. 6 Wherever you dwell, the cities shall be waste and the high places ruined, so that your altars will be waste and ruined,[7] your idols broken and destroyed, your incense altars cut down, and your works wiped out. 7 And the slain shall fall in your midst, and you shall know that I am the LORD.

8 "Yet I will leave some of you alive. When you have among the nations some who escape the sword, and when you are scattered through the countries, 9 then those of you who escape will remember me among the nations where they are carried captive, how I have been broken over their whoring heart that has departed from me and over their eyes that go whoring after their idols. And they will be loathsome in their own sight for the evils that they have committed, for all their abominations. 10 And they shall know that I am the LORD. I have not said in vain that I would do this evil to them."

11 Thus says the Lord GOD: "Clap your hands and stamp your foot and say, Alas, because of all the evil abominations of

[1] Some Hebrew manuscripts and Syriac lack *not* [2] The same Hebrew expression can mean *obey rules*, or *execute judgments*, depending on the context [3] Some Hebrew manuscripts *I will cut you down* [4] Dead Sea Scroll, Septuagint, Syriac, Vulgate, Targum; Masoretic Text *And it shall be* [5] Hebrew *them* [6] Hebrew *staff* [7] Or *and punished*

the house of Israel, for they shall fall by
the sword, by famine, and by pestilence.
12 He who is far off shall die of pestilence,
and he who is near shall fall by the sword,
and he who is left and is preserved shall
die of famine. Thus I will spend my fury
upon them. 13 And you shall know that I
am the LORD, when their slain lie among
their idols around their altars, on every
high hill, on all the mountaintops, under
every green tree, and under every leafy oak,
wherever they offered pleasing aroma to
all their idols. 14 And I will stretch out my
hand against them and make the land
desolate and waste, in all their dwelling
places, from the wilderness to Riblah.[1]
Then they will know that I am the LORD."

The Day of the Wrath of the LORD

7 The word of the LORD came to me:
2 "And you, O son of man, thus says the
Lord GOD to the land of Israel: An end! The
end has come upon the four corners of the
land.[2] 3 Now the end is upon you, and I will
send my anger upon you; I will judge you
according to your ways, and I will punish
you for all your abominations. 4 And my
eye will not spare you, nor will I have pity,
but I will punish you for your ways, while
your abominations are in your midst. Then
you will know that I am the LORD.

5 "Thus says the Lord GOD: Disaster after
disaster![3] Behold, it comes. 6 An end has
come; the end has come; it has awakened
against you. Behold, it comes. 7 Your doom[4]
has come to you, O inhabitant of the land.
The time has come; the day is near, a day
of tumult, and not of joyful shouting on
the mountains. 8 Now I will soon pour out
my wrath upon you, and spend my anger
against you, and judge you according to
your ways, and I will punish you for all
your abominations. 9 And my eye will not
spare, nor will I have pity. I will punish you
according to your ways, while your abomi-
nations are in your midst. Then you will
know that I am the LORD, who strikes.

10 "Behold, the day! Behold, it comes! Your
doom has come; the rod has blossomed;
pride has budded. 11 Violence has grown
up into a rod of wickedness. None of them
shall remain, nor their abundance, nor their
wealth; neither shall there be preeminence
among them.[5] 12 The time has come; the
day has arrived. Let not the buyer rejoice,
nor the seller mourn, for wrath is upon all
their multitude.[6] 13 For the seller shall not
return to what he has sold, while they live.
For the vision concerns all their multitude;
it shall not turn back; and because of his
iniquity, none can maintain his life.[7]

14 "They have blown the trumpet and
made everything ready, but none goes to
battle, for my wrath is upon all their mul-
titude. 15 The sword is without; pestilence
and famine are within. He who is in the
field dies by the sword, and him who is
in the city famine and pestilence devour.
16 And if any survivors escape, they will be
on the mountains, like doves of the val-
leys, all of them moaning, each one over
his iniquity. 17 All hands are feeble, and all
knees turn to water. 18 They put on sack-
cloth, and horror covers them. Shame is on
all faces, and baldness on all their heads.
19 They cast their silver into the streets, and
their gold is like an unclean thing. Their sil-
ver and gold are not able to deliver them in
the day of the wrath of the LORD. They can-
not satisfy their hunger or fill their stom-
achs with it. For it was the stumbling block
of their iniquity. 20 His beautiful ornament
they used for pride, and they made their
abominable images and their detestable
things of it. Therefore I make it an unclean
thing to them. 21 And I will give it into the
hands of foreigners for prey, and to the
wicked of the earth for spoil, and they shall
profane it. 22 I will turn my face from them,
and they shall profane my treasured[8] place.
Robbers shall enter and profane it.

[1] Some Hebrew manuscripts; most Hebrew manuscripts *Diblah* [2] Or *earth* [3] Some Hebrew manuscripts (compare Syriac, Targum); most Hebrew manuscripts *Disaster! A unique disaster!* [4] The meaning of the Hebrew word is uncertain; also verse 10 [5] The meaning of this last Hebrew sentence is uncertain [6] Or *abundance*; also verses 13, 14 [7] The meaning of this last Hebrew sentence is uncertain [8] Or *secret*

23 "Forge a chain![1] For the land is full of bloody crimes and the city is full of violence. 24 I will bring the worst of the nations to take possession of their houses. I will put an end to the pride of the strong, and their holy places[2] shall be profaned. 25 When anguish comes, they will seek peace, but there shall be none. 26 Disaster comes upon disaster; rumor follows rumor. They seek a vision from the prophet, while the law[3] perishes from the priest and counsel from the elders. 27 The king mourns, the prince is wrapped in despair, and the hands of the people of the land are paralyzed by terror. According to their way I will do to them, and according to their judgments I will judge them, and they shall know that I am the LORD."

Abominations in the Temple

8 In the sixth year, in the sixth month, on the fifth day of the month, as I sat in my house, with the elders of Judah sitting before me, the hand of the Lord GOD fell upon me there. 2 Then I looked, and behold, a form that had the appearance of a man.[4] Below what appeared to be his waist was fire, and above his waist was something like the appearance of brightness, like gleaming metal.[5] 3 He put out the form of a hand and took me by a lock of my head, and the Spirit lifted me up between earth and heaven and brought me in visions of God to Jerusalem, to the entrance of the gateway of the inner court that faces north, where was the seat of the image of jealousy, which provokes to jealousy. 4 And behold, the glory of the God of Israel was there, like the vision that I saw in the valley.

5 Then he said to me, "Son of man, lift up your eyes now toward the north." So I lifted up my eyes toward the north, and behold, north of the altar gate, in the entrance, was *this* image of jealousy. 6 And he said to me, "Son of man, do you see what they are doing, the great abominations that the house of Israel are committing here, to drive me far from my sanctuary? But you will see still greater abominations."

7 And he brought me to the entrance of the court, and when I looked, behold, there was a hole in the wall. 8 Then he said to me, "Son of man, dig in the wall." So I dug in the wall, and behold, there was an entrance. 9 And he said to me, "Go in, and see the vile abominations that they are committing here." 10 So I went in and saw. And there, engraved on the wall all around, was every form of creeping things and loathsome beasts, and all the idols of the house of Israel. 11 And before them stood seventy men of the elders of the house of Israel, with Jaazaniah the son of Shaphan standing among them. Each had his censer in his hand, and the smoke of the cloud of incense went up. 12 Then he said to me, "Son of man, have you seen what the elders of the house of Israel are doing in the dark, each in his room of pictures? For they say, 'The LORD does not see us, the LORD has forsaken the land.'" 13 He said also to me, "You will see still greater abominations that they commit."

14 Then he brought me to the entrance of the north gate of the house of the LORD, and behold, there sat women weeping for Tammuz. 15 Then he said to me, "Have you seen this, O son of man? You will see still greater abominations than these."

16 And he brought me into the inner court of the house of the LORD. And behold, at the entrance of the temple of the LORD, between the porch and the altar, were about twenty-five men, with their backs to the temple of the LORD, and their faces toward the east, worshiping the sun toward the east. 17 Then he said to me, "Have you seen this, O son of man? Is it too light a thing for the house of Judah to commit the abominations that they commit here, that they should fill the land with violence and provoke me still further to anger? Behold, they put the branch to their[6] nose. 18 Therefore I will act in wrath.

[1] Probably refers to an instrument of captivity [2] By revocalization (compare Septuagint); Hebrew *and those who sanctify them* [3] Or *instruction* [4] By revocalization (compare Septuagint); Hebrew *of fire* [5] Or *amber* [6] Or *my*

My eye will not spare, nor will I have pity. And though they cry in my ears with a loud voice, I will not hear them."

Idolaters Killed

9 Then he cried in my ears with a loud voice, saying, "Bring near the executioners of the city, each with his destroying weapon in his hand." 2 And behold, six men came from the direction of the upper gate, which faces north, each with his weapon for slaughter in his hand, and with them was a man clothed in linen, with a writing case at his waist. And they went in and stood beside the bronze altar.

3 Now the glory of the God of Israel had gone up from the cherub on which it rested to the threshold of the house. And he called to the man clothed in linen, who had the writing case at his waist. 4 And the LORD said to him, "Pass through the city, through Jerusalem, and put a mark on the foreheads of the men who sigh and groan over all the abominations that are committed in it." 5 And to the others he said in my hearing, "Pass through the city after him, and strike. Your eye shall not spare, and you shall show no pity. 6 Kill old men outright, young men and maidens, little children and women, but touch no one on whom is the mark. And begin at my sanctuary." So they began with the elders who were before the house. 7 Then he said to them, "Defile the house, and fill the courts with the slain. Go out." So they went out and struck in the city. 8 And while they were striking, and I was left alone, I fell upon my face, and cried, "Ah, Lord GOD! Will you destroy all the remnant of Israel in the outpouring of your wrath on Jerusalem?"

9 Then he said to me, "The guilt of the house of Israel and Judah is exceedingly great. The land is full of blood, and the city full of injustice. For they say, 'The LORD has forsaken the land, and the LORD does not see.' 10 As for me, my eye will not spare, nor will I have pity; I will bring their deeds upon their heads."

11 And behold, the man clothed in linen, with the writing case at his waist, brought back word, saying, "I have done as you commanded me."

The Glory of the LORD Leaves the Temple

10 Then I looked, and behold, on the expanse that was over the heads of the cherubim there appeared above them something like a sapphire,[1] in appearance like a throne. 2 And he said to the man clothed in linen, "Go in among the whirling wheels underneath the cherubim. Fill your hands with burning coals from between the cherubim, and scatter them over the city."

And he went in before my eyes. 3 Now the cherubim were standing on the south side of the house, when the man went in, and a cloud filled the inner court. 4 And the glory of the LORD went up from the cherub to the threshold of the house, and the house was filled with the cloud, and the court was filled with the brightness of the glory of the LORD. 5 And the sound of the wings of the cherubim was heard as far as the outer court, like the voice of God Almighty when he speaks.

6 And when he commanded the man clothed in linen, "Take fire from between the whirling wheels, from between the cherubim," he went in and stood beside a wheel. 7 And a cherub stretched out his hand from between the cherubim to the fire that was between the cherubim, and took some of it and put it into the hands of the man clothed in linen, who took it and went out. 8 The cherubim appeared to have the form of a human hand under their wings.

9 And I looked, and behold, there were four wheels beside the cherubim, one beside each cherub, and the appearance of the wheels was like sparkling beryl. 10 And as for their appearance, the four had the

[1] Or *lapis lazuli*

same likeness, as if a wheel were within a wheel. 11 When they went, they went in any of their four directions[1] without turning as they went, but in whatever direction the front wheel[2] faced, the others followed without turning as they went. 12 And their whole body, their rims, and their spokes, their wings,[3] and the wheels were full of eyes all around—the wheels that the four of them had. 13 As for the wheels, they were called in my hearing "the whirling wheels." 14 And every one had four faces: the first face was the face of the cherub, and the second face was a human face, and the third the face of a lion, and the fourth the face of an eagle.

15 And the cherubim mounted up. These were the living creatures that I saw by the Chebar canal. 16 And when the cherubim went, the wheels went beside them. And when the cherubim lifted up their wings to mount up from the earth, the wheels did not turn from beside them. 17 When they stood still, these stood still, and when they mounted up, these mounted up with them, for the spirit of the living creatures[4] was in them.

18 Then the glory of the LORD went out from the threshold of the house, and stood over the cherubim. 19 And the cherubim lifted up their wings and mounted up from the earth before my eyes as they went out, with the wheels beside them. And they stood at the entrance of the east gate of the house of the LORD, and the glory of the God of Israel was over them.

20 These were the living creatures that I saw underneath the God of Israel by the Chebar canal; and I knew that they were cherubim. 21 Each had four faces, and each four wings, and underneath their wings the likeness of human hands. 22 And as for the likeness of their faces, they were the same faces whose appearance I had seen by the Chebar canal. Each one of them went straight forward.

Judgment on Wicked Counselors

11 The Spirit lifted me up and brought me to the east gate of the house of the LORD, which faces east. And behold, at the entrance of the gateway there were twenty-five men. And I saw among them Jaazaniah the son of Azzur, and Pelatiah the son of Benaiah, princes of the people. 2 And he said to me, "Son of man, these are the men who devise iniquity and who give wicked counsel in this city; 3 who say, 'The time is not near[5] to build houses. This city is the cauldron, and we are the meat.' 4 Therefore prophesy against them, prophesy, O son of man."

5 And the Spirit of the LORD fell upon me, and he said to me, "Say, Thus says the LORD: So you think, O house of Israel. For I know the things that come into your mind. 6 You have multiplied your slain in this city and have filled its streets with the slain. 7 Therefore thus says the Lord GOD: Your slain whom you have laid in the midst of it, they are the meat, and this city is the cauldron, but you shall be brought out of the midst of it. 8 You have feared the sword, and I will bring the sword upon you, declares the Lord GOD. 9 And I will bring you out of the midst of it, and give you into the hands of foreigners, and execute judgments upon you. 10 You shall fall by the sword. I will judge you at the border of Israel, and you shall know that I am the LORD. 11 This city shall not be your cauldron, nor shall you be the meat in the midst of it. I will judge you at the border of Israel, 12 and you shall know that I am the LORD. For you have not walked in my statutes, nor obeyed my rules, but have acted according to the rules of the nations that are around you."

13 And it came to pass, while I was prophesying, that Pelatiah the son of Benaiah died. Then I fell down on my face and cried out with a loud voice and said, "Ah, Lord GOD! Will you make a full end of the remnant of Israel?"

[1] Hebrew *to their four sides* [2] Hebrew *the head* [3] Or *their whole body, their backs, their hands, and their wings* [4] Or *spirit of life* [5] Or *Is not the time near . . . ?*

Israel's New Heart and Spirit

14 And the word of the LORD came to me:
15 "Son of man, your brothers, even your
brothers, your kinsmen,[1] the whole house
of Israel, all of them, are those of whom the
inhabitants of Jerusalem have said, 'Go far
from the LORD; to us this land is given for a
possession.' 16 Therefore say, 'Thus says the
Lord GOD: Though I removed them far off
among the nations, and though I scattered
them among the countries, yet I have been a
sanctuary to them for a while[2] in the coun-
tries where they have gone.' 17 Therefore say,
'Thus says the Lord GOD: I will gather you
from the peoples and assemble you out of
the countries where you have been scat-
tered, and I will give you the land of Israel.'
18 And when they come there, they will
remove from it all its detestable things and
all its abominations. 19 And I will give them
one heart, and a new spirit I will put within
them. I will remove the heart of stone from
their flesh and give them a heart of flesh,
20 that they may walk in my statutes and
keep my rules and obey them. And they
shall be my people, and I will be their God.
21 But as for those whose heart goes after
their detestable things and their abomina-
tions, I will[3] bring their deeds upon their
own heads, declares the Lord GOD."

22 Then the cherubim lifted up their
wings, with the wheels beside them, and
the glory of the God of Israel was over
them. 23 And the glory of the LORD went
up from the midst of the city and stood
on the mountain that is on the east side
of the city. 24 And the Spirit lifted me
up and brought me in the vision by the
Spirit of God into Chaldea, to the exiles.
Then the vision that I had seen went up
from me. 25 And I told the exiles all the
things that the LORD had shown me.

Judah's Captivity Symbolized

12 The word of the LORD came to me:
2 "Son of man, you dwell in the
midst of a rebellious house, who have
eyes to see, but see not, who have ears to
hear, but hear not, for they are a rebellious
house. 3 As for you, son of man, prepare
for yourself an exile's baggage, and go
into exile by day in their sight. You shall
go like an exile from your place to another
place in their sight. Perhaps they will
understand, though[4] they are a rebellious
house. 4 You shall bring out your baggage
by day in their sight, as baggage for exile,
and you shall go out yourself at evening in
their sight, as those do who must go into
exile. 5 In their sight dig through the wall,
and bring your baggage out through it. 6 In
their sight you shall lift the baggage upon
your shoulder and carry it out at dusk. You
shall cover your face that you may not see
the land, for I have made you a sign for the
house of Israel."

7 And I did as I was commanded. I
brought out my baggage by day, as bag-
gage for exile, and in the evening I dug
through the wall with my own hands. I
brought out my baggage at dusk, carrying
it on my shoulder in their sight.

8 In the morning the word of the LORD
came to me: 9 "Son of man, has not the
house of Israel, the rebellious house, said
to you, 'What are you doing?' 10 Say to them,
'Thus says the Lord GOD: This oracle con-
cerns[5] the prince in Jerusalem and all the
house of Israel who are in it.'[6] 11 Say, 'I am
a sign for you: as I have done, so shall it
be done to them. They shall go into exile,
into captivity.' 12 And the prince who is
among them shall lift his baggage upon his
shoulder at dusk, and shall go out. They
shall dig through the wall to bring him out
through it. He shall cover his face, that he
may not see the land with his eyes. 13 And
I will spread my net over him, and he shall
be taken in my snare. And I will bring him
to Babylon, the land of the Chaldeans, yet
he shall not see it, and he shall die there.
14 And I will scatter toward every wind all
who are around him, his helpers and all
his troops, and I will unsheathe the sword

[1] Hebrew *the men of your redemption* [2] Or *in small measure* [3] Hebrew *To the heart of their detestable things and their abominations their heart goes; I will* [4] Or *will see that* [5] Or *This burden is* [6] Hebrew *in the midst of them*

after them. 15 And they shall know that I am the LORD, when I disperse them among the nations and scatter them among the countries. 16 But I will let a few of them escape from the sword, from famine and pestilence, that they may declare all their abominations among the nations where they go, and may know that I am the LORD."

17 And the word of the LORD came to me: 18 "Son of man, eat your bread with quaking, and drink water with trembling and with anxiety. 19 And say to the people of the land, Thus says the Lord GOD concerning the inhabitants of Jerusalem in the land of Israel: They shall eat their bread with anxiety, and drink water in dismay. In this way her land will be stripped of all it contains, on account of the violence of all those who dwell in it. 20 And the inhabited cities shall be laid waste, and the land shall become a desolation; and you shall know that I am the LORD."

21 And the word of the LORD came to me: 22 "Son of man, what is this proverb that you[1] have about the land of Israel, saying, 'The days grow long, and every vision comes to nothing'? 23 Tell them therefore, 'Thus says the Lord GOD: I will put an end to this proverb, and they shall no more use it as a proverb in Israel.' But say to them, The days are near, and the fulfillment[2] of every vision. 24 For there shall be no more any false vision or flattering divination within the house of Israel. 25 For I am the LORD; I will speak the word that I will speak, and it will be performed. It will no longer be delayed, but in your days, O rebellious house, I will speak the word and perform it, declares the Lord GOD."

26 And the word of the LORD came to me: 27 "Son of man, behold, they of the house of Israel say, 'The vision that he sees is for many days from now, and he prophesies of times far off.' 28 Therefore say to them, Thus says the Lord GOD: None of my words will be delayed any longer, but the word that I speak will be performed, declares the Lord GOD."

False Prophets Condemned

13 The word of the LORD came to me: 2 "Son of man, prophesy against the prophets of Israel, who are prophesying, and say to those who prophesy from their own hearts: 'Hear the word of the LORD!' 3 Thus says the Lord GOD, Woe to the foolish prophets who follow their own spirit, and have seen nothing! 4 Your prophets have been like jackals among ruins, O Israel. 5 You have not gone up into the breaches, or built up a wall for the house of Israel, that it might stand in battle in the day of the LORD. 6 They have seen false visions and lying divinations. They say, 'Declares the LORD,' when the LORD has not sent them, and yet they expect him to fulfill their word. 7 Have you not seen a false vision and uttered a lying divination, whenever you have said, 'Declares the LORD,' although I have not spoken?"

8 Therefore thus says the Lord GOD: "Because you have uttered falsehood and seen lying visions, therefore behold, I am against you, declares the Lord GOD. 9 My hand will be against the prophets who see false visions and who give lying divinations. They shall not be in the council of my people, nor be enrolled in the register of the house of Israel, nor shall they enter the land of Israel. And you shall know that I am the Lord GOD. 10 Precisely because they have misled my people, saying, 'Peace,' when there is no peace, and because, when the people build a wall, these prophets smear it with whitewash,[3] 11 say to those who smear it with whitewash that it shall fall! There will be a deluge of rain, and you, O great hailstones, will fall, and a stormy wind break out. 12 And when the wall falls, will it not be said to you, 'Where is the coating with which you smeared it?' 13 Therefore thus says the Lord GOD: I will make a stormy wind break out in my

[1] The Hebrew for *you* is plural [2] Hebrew *word* [3] Or *plaster*; also verses 11, 14, 15

wrath, and there shall be a deluge of rain in my anger, and great hailstones in wrath to make a full end. 14 And I will break down the wall that you have smeared with whitewash, and bring it down to the ground, so that its foundation will be laid bare. When it falls, you shall perish in the midst of it, and you shall know that I am the LORD. 15 Thus will I spend my wrath upon the wall and upon those who have smeared it with whitewash, and I will say to you, The wall is no more, nor those who smeared it, 16 the prophets of Israel who prophesied concerning Jerusalem and saw visions of peace for her, when there was no peace, declares the Lord GOD.

17 "And you, son of man, set your face against the daughters of your people, who prophesy out of their own minds. Prophesy against them 18 and say, Thus says the Lord GOD: Woe to the women who sew magic bands upon all wrists, and make veils for the heads of persons of every stature, in the hunt for souls! Will you hunt down souls belonging to my people and keep your own souls alive? 19 You have profaned me among my people for handfuls of barley and for pieces of bread, putting to death souls who should not die and keeping alive souls who should not live, by your lying to my people, who listen to lies.

20 "Therefore thus says the Lord GOD: Behold, I am against your magic bands with which you hunt the souls like birds, and I will tear them from your arms, and I will let the souls whom you hunt go free, the souls like birds. 21 Your veils also I will tear off and deliver my people out of your hand, and they shall be no more in your hand as prey, and you shall know that I am the LORD. 22 Because you have disheartened the righteous falsely, although I have not grieved him, and you have encouraged the wicked, that he should not turn from his evil way to save his life, 23 therefore you shall no more see false visions nor practice divination. I will deliver my people out of your hand. And you shall know that I am the LORD."

Idolatrous Elders Condemned

14 Then certain of the elders of Israel came to me and sat before me. 2 And the word of the LORD came to me: 3 "Son of man, these men have taken their idols into their hearts, and set the stumbling block of their iniquity before their faces. Should I indeed let myself be consulted by them? 4 Therefore speak to them and say to them, Thus says the Lord GOD: Any one of the house of Israel who takes his idols into his heart and sets the stumbling block of his iniquity before his face, and yet comes to the prophet, I the LORD will answer him as he comes with the multitude of his idols, 5 that I may lay hold of the hearts of the house of Israel, who are all estranged from me through their idols.

6 "Therefore say to the house of Israel, Thus says the Lord GOD: Repent and turn away from your idols, and turn away your faces from all your abominations. 7 For any one of the house of Israel, or of the strangers who sojourn in Israel, who separates himself from me, taking his idols into his heart and putting the stumbling block of his iniquity before his face, and yet comes to a prophet to consult me through him, I the LORD will answer him myself. 8 And I will set my face against that man; I will make him a sign and a byword and cut him off from the midst of my people, and you shall know that I am the LORD. 9 And if the prophet is deceived and speaks a word, I, the LORD, have deceived that prophet, and I will stretch out my hand against him and will destroy him from the midst of my people Israel. 10 And they shall bear their punishment[1]—the punishment of the prophet and the punishment of the inquirer shall be alike— 11 that the house of Israel may no more go astray from me, nor defile themselves anymore with all their transgressions, but that they may be

[1] Or *iniquity*; three times in this verse

my people and I may be their God, declares the Lord GOD."

Jerusalem Will Not Be Spared

12 And the word of the LORD came to me: 13 "Son of man, when a land sins against me by acting faithlessly, and I stretch out my hand against it and break its supply[1] of bread and send famine upon it, and cut off from it man and beast, 14 even if these three men, Noah, Daniel, and Job, were in it, they would deliver but their own lives by their righteousness, declares the Lord GOD.

15 "If I cause wild beasts to pass through the land, and they ravage it, and it be made desolate, so that no one may pass through because of the beasts, 16 even if these three men were in it, as I live, declares the Lord GOD, they would deliver neither sons nor daughters. They alone would be delivered, but the land would be desolate.

17 "Or if I bring a sword upon that land and say, Let a sword pass through the land, and I cut off from it man and beast, 18 though these three men were in it, as I live, declares the Lord GOD, they would deliver neither sons nor daughters, but they alone would be delivered.

19 "Or if I send a pestilence into that land and pour out my wrath upon it with blood, to cut off from it man and beast, 20 even if Noah, Daniel, and Job were in it, as I live, declares the Lord GOD, they would deliver neither son nor daughter. They would deliver but their own lives by their righteousness.

21 "For thus says the Lord GOD: How much more when I send upon Jerusalem my four disastrous acts of judgment, sword, famine, wild beasts, and pestilence, to cut off from it man and beast! 22 But behold, some survivors will be left in it, sons and daughters who will be brought out; behold, when they come out to you, and you see their ways and their deeds, you will be consoled for the disaster that I have brought upon Jerusalem, for all that I have brought upon it. 23 They will console you, when you see their ways and their deeds, and you shall know that I have not done without cause all that I have done in it, declares the Lord GOD."

Jerusalem, a Useless Vine

15 And the word of the LORD came to me: 2 "Son of man, how does the wood of the vine surpass any wood, the vine branch that is among the trees of the forest? 3 Is wood taken from it to make anything? Do people take a peg from it to hang any vessel on it? 4 Behold, it is given to the fire for fuel. When the fire has consumed both ends of it, and the middle of it is charred, is it useful for anything? 5 Behold, when it was whole, it was used for nothing. How much less, when the fire has consumed it and it is charred, can it ever be used for anything! 6 Therefore thus says the Lord GOD: Like the wood of the vine among the trees of the forest, which I have given to the fire for fuel, so have I given up the inhabitants of Jerusalem. 7 And I will set my face against them. Though they escape from the fire, the fire shall yet consume them, and you will know that I am the LORD, when I set my face against them. 8 And I will make the land desolate, because they have acted faithlessly, declares the Lord GOD."

The LORD's Faithless Bride

16 Again the word of the LORD came to me: 2 "Son of man, make known to Jerusalem her abominations, 3 and say, Thus says the Lord GOD to Jerusalem: Your origin and your birth are of the land of the Canaanites; your father was an Amorite and your mother a Hittite. 4 And as for your birth, on the day you were born your cord was not cut, nor were you washed with water to cleanse you, nor rubbed with salt, nor wrapped in swaddling cloths. 5 No eye pitied you, to do any of these things to you out of compassion for you, but you were

[1] Hebrew *staff*

cast out on the open field, for you were
abhorred, on the day that you were born.
6 "And when I passed by you and saw
you wallowing in your blood, I said to you
in your blood, 'Live!' I said to you in your
blood, 'Live!' 7 I made you flourish like a
plant of the field. And you grew up and
became tall and arrived at full adornment.
Your breasts were formed, and your hair
had grown; yet you were naked and bare.
8 "When I passed by you again and saw
you, behold, you were at the age for love,
and I spread the corner of my garment
over you and covered your nakedness; I
made my vow to you and entered into a
covenant with you, declares the Lord GOD,
and you became mine. 9 Then I bathed you
with water and washed off your blood
from you and anointed you with oil. 10 I
clothed you also with embroidered cloth
and shod you with fine leather. I wrapped
you in fine linen and covered you with
silk.[1] 11 And I adorned you with ornaments
and put bracelets on your wrists and a
chain on your neck. 12 And I put a ring on
your nose and earrings in your ears and
a beautiful crown on your head. 13 Thus
you were adorned with gold and silver,
and your clothing was of fine linen and
silk and embroidered cloth. You ate fine
flour and honey and oil. You grew exceed-
ingly beautiful and advanced to royalty.
14 And your renown went forth among the
nations because of your beauty, for it was
perfect through the splendor that I had
bestowed on you, declares the Lord GOD.
15 "But you trusted in your beauty and
played the whore[2] because of your renown
and lavished your whorings[3] on any pass-
erby; your beauty[4] became his. 16 You took
some of your garments and made for
yourself colorful shrines, and on them
played the whore. The like has never been,
nor ever shall be.[5] 17 You also took your
beautiful jewels of my gold and of my sil-
ver, which I had given you, and made for
yourself images of men, and with them
played the whore. 18 And you took your
embroidered garments to cover them, and
set my oil and my incense before them.
19 Also my bread that I gave you—I fed you
with fine flour and oil and honey—you set
before them for a pleasing aroma; and so
it was, declares the Lord GOD. 20 And you
took your sons and your daughters, whom
you had borne to me, and these you sacri-
ficed to them to be devoured. Were your
whorings so small a matter 21 that you
slaughtered my children and delivered
them up as an offering by fire to them?
22 And in all your abominations and your
whorings you did not remember the days
of your youth, when you were naked and
bare, wallowing in your blood.
23 "And after all your wickedness (woe,
woe to you! declares the Lord GOD), 24 you
built yourself a vaulted chamber and made
yourself a lofty place in every square. 25 At
the head of every street you built your lofty
place and made your beauty an abomina-
tion, offering yourself[6] to any passerby
and multiplying your whoring. 26 You also
played the whore with the Egyptians, your
lustful neighbors, multiplying your whor-
ing, to provoke me to anger. 27 Behold,
therefore, I stretched out my hand against
you and diminished your allotted portion
and delivered you to the greed of your
enemies, the daughters of the Philistines,
who were ashamed of your lewd behav-
ior. 28 You played the whore also with the
Assyrians, because you were not satisfied;
yes, you played the whore with them, and
still you were not satisfied. 29 You multi-
plied your whoring also with the trading
land of Chaldea, and even with this you
were not satisfied.
30 "How sick is your heart,[7] declares
the Lord GOD, because you did all these
things, the deeds of a brazen prostitute,
31 building your vaulted chamber at the
head of every street, and making your
lofty place in every square. Yet you were
not like a prostitute, because you scorned

[1] Or *with rich fabric* [2] Or *were unfaithful*; also verses 16, 17, 26, 28 [3] Or *unfaithfulness*; also verses 20, 22, 25, 26, 29, 33, 34, 36 [4] Hebrew *it* [5] The meaning of this Hebrew sentence is uncertain [6] Hebrew *spreading your legs* [7] Revocalization yields *How I am filled with anger against you*

payment. 32 Adulterous wife, who receives strangers instead of her husband! 33 Men give gifts to all prostitutes, but you gave your gifts to all your lovers, bribing them to come to you from every side with your whorings. 34 So you were different from other women in your whorings. No one solicited you to play the whore, and you gave payment, while no payment was given to you; therefore you were different.

35 "Therefore, O prostitute, hear the word of the LORD: 36 Thus says the Lord GOD, Because your lust was poured out and your nakedness uncovered in your whorings with your lovers, and with all your abominable idols, and because of the blood of your children that you gave to them, 37 therefore, behold, I will gather all your lovers with whom you took pleasure, all those you loved and all those you hated. I will gather them against you from every side and will uncover your nakedness to them, that they may see all your nakedness. 38 And I will judge you as women who commit adultery and shed blood are judged, and bring upon you the blood of wrath and jealousy. 39 And I will give you into their hands, and they shall throw down your vaulted chamber and break down your lofty places. They shall strip you of your clothes and take your beautiful jewels and leave you naked and bare. 40 They shall bring up a crowd against you, and they shall stone you and cut you to pieces with their swords. 41 And they shall burn your houses and execute judgments upon you in the sight of many women. I will make you stop playing the whore, and you shall also give payment no more. 42 So will I satisfy my wrath on you, and my jealousy shall depart from you. I will be calm and will no more be angry. 43 Because you have not remembered the days of your youth, but have enraged me with all these things, therefore, behold, I have returned your deeds upon your head, declares the Lord GOD. Have you not committed lewdness in addition to all your abominations?

44 "Behold, everyone who uses proverbs will use this proverb about you: 'Like mother, like daughter.' 45 You are the daughter of your mother, who loathed her husband and her children; and you are the sister of your sisters, who loathed their husbands and their children. Your mother was a Hittite and your father an Amorite. 46 And your elder sister is Samaria, who lived with her daughters to the north of you; and your younger sister, who lived to the south of you, is Sodom with her daughters. 47 Not only did you walk in their ways and do according to their abominations; within a very little time you were more corrupt than they in all your ways. 48 As I live, declares the Lord GOD, your sister Sodom and her daughters have not done as you and your daughters have done. 49 Behold, this was the guilt of your sister Sodom: she and her daughters had pride, excess of food, and prosperous ease, but did not aid the poor and needy. 50 They were haughty and did an abomination before me. So I removed them, when I saw it. 51 Samaria has not committed half your sins. You have committed more abominations than they, and have made your sisters appear righteous by all the abominations that you have committed. 52 Bear your disgrace, you also, for you have intervened on behalf of your sisters. Because of your sins in which you acted more abominably than they, they are more in the right than you. So be ashamed, you also, and bear your disgrace, for you have made your sisters appear righteous.

53 "I will restore their fortunes, both the fortunes of Sodom and her daughters, and the fortunes of Samaria and her daughters, and I will restore your own fortunes in their midst, 54 that you may bear your disgrace and be ashamed of all that you have done, becoming a consolation to them. 55 As for your sisters, Sodom

and her daughters shall return to their
former state, and Samaria and her daugh-
ters shall return to their former state, and
you and your daughters shall return to
your former state. 56 Was not your sister
Sodom a byword in your mouth in the day
of your pride, 57 before your wickedness
was uncovered? Now you have become
an object of reproach for the daughters of
Syria[1] and all those around her, and for
the daughters of the Philistines, those all
around who despise you. 58 You bear the
penalty of your lewdness and your abomi-
nations, declares the LORD.

The LORD's Everlasting Covenant

59 "For thus says the Lord GOD: I will
deal with you as you have done, you who
have despised the oath in breaking the
covenant, 60 yet I will remember my cov-
enant with you in the days of your youth,
and I will establish for you an everlasting
covenant. 61 Then you will remember your
ways and be ashamed when you take your
sisters, both your elder and your younger,
and I give them to you as daughters, but not
on account of[2] the covenant with you. 62 I
will establish my covenant with you, and
you shall know that I am the LORD, 63 that
you may remember and be confounded,
and never open your mouth again because
of your shame, when I atone for you for all
that you have done, declares the Lord GOD."

Parable of Two Eagles and a Vine

17 The word of the LORD came to me:
2 "Son of man, propound a riddle,
and speak a parable to the house of Israel;
3 say, Thus says the Lord GOD: A great eagle
with great wings and long pinions, rich in
plumage of many colors, came to Lebanon
and took the top of the cedar. 4 He broke
off the topmost of its young twigs and car-
ried it to a land of trade and set it in a city
of merchants. 5 Then he took of the seed
of the land and planted it in fertile soil.[3]
He placed it beside abundant waters. He
set it like a willow twig, 6 and it sprouted
and became a low spreading vine, and its
branches turned toward him, and its roots
remained where it stood. So it became a
vine and produced branches and put out
boughs.

7 "And there was another great eagle
with great wings and much plumage, and
behold, this vine bent its roots toward him
and shot forth its branches toward him
from the bed where it was planted, that
he might water it. 8 It had been planted
on good soil by abundant waters, that it
might produce branches and bear fruit
and become a noble vine.

9 "Say, Thus says the Lord GOD: Will it
thrive? Will he not pull up its roots and cut
off its fruit, so that it withers, so that all its
fresh sprouting leaves wither? It will not
take a strong arm or many people to pull it
from its roots. 10 Behold, it is planted; will
it thrive? Will it not utterly wither when
the east wind strikes it—wither away on
the bed where it sprouted?"

11 Then the word of the LORD came to
me: 12 "Say now to the rebellious house,
Do you not know what these things mean?
Tell them, behold, the king of Babylon
came to Jerusalem, and took her king and
her princes and brought them to him to
Babylon. 13 And he took one of the royal
offspring[4] and made a covenant with
him, putting him under oath (the chief
men of the land he had taken away), 14 that
the kingdom might be humble and not
lift itself up, and keep his covenant that
it might stand. 15 But he rebelled against
him by sending his ambassadors to Egypt,
that they might give him horses and a
large army. Will he thrive? Can one escape
who does such things? Can he break the
covenant and yet escape?

16 "As I live, declares the Lord GOD, surely
in the place where the king dwells who
made him king, whose oath he despised,
and whose covenant with him he broke,
in Babylon he shall die. 17 Pharaoh with his
mighty army and great company will not

[1] Some manuscripts (compare Syriac) *of Edom* [2] Or *not apart from* [3] Hebrew *in a field of seed* [4] Hebrew *seed*

help him in war, when mounds are cast up and siege walls built to cut off many lives. 18 He despised the oath in breaking the covenant, and behold, he gave his hand and did all these things; he shall not escape. 19 Therefore thus says the Lord GOD: As I live, surely it is my oath that he despised, and my covenant that he broke. I will return it upon his head. 20 I will spread my net over him, and he shall be taken in my snare, and I will bring him to Babylon and enter into judgment with him there for the treachery he has committed against me. 21 And all the pick[1] of his troops shall fall by the sword, and the survivors shall be scattered to every wind, and you shall know that I am the LORD; I have spoken."

22 Thus says the Lord GOD: "I myself will take a sprig from the lofty top of the cedar and will set it out. I will break off from the topmost of its young twigs a tender one, and I myself will plant it on a high and lofty mountain. 23 On the mountain height of Israel will I plant it, that it may bear branches and produce fruit and become a noble cedar. And under it will dwell every kind of bird; in the shade of its branches birds of every sort will nest. 24 And all the trees of the field shall know that I am the LORD; I bring low the high tree, and make high the low tree, dry up the green tree, and make the dry tree flourish. I am the LORD; I have spoken, and I will do it."

The Soul Who Sins Shall Die

18 The word of the LORD came to me: 2 "What do you[2] mean by repeating this proverb concerning the land of Israel, 'The fathers have eaten sour grapes, and the children's teeth are set on edge'? 3 As I live, declares the Lord GOD, this proverb shall no more be used by you in Israel. 4 Behold, all souls are mine; the soul of the father as well as the soul of the son is mine: the soul who sins shall die.

5 "If a man is righteous and does what is just and right— 6 if he does not eat upon the mountains or lift up his eyes to the idols of the house of Israel, does not defile his neighbor's wife or approach a woman in her time of menstrual impurity, 7 does not oppress anyone, but restores to the debtor his pledge, commits no robbery, gives his bread to the hungry and covers the naked with a garment, 8 does not lend at interest or take any profit,[3] withholds his hand from injustice, executes true justice between man and man, 9 walks in my statutes, and keeps my rules by acting faithfully—he is righteous; he shall surely live, declares the Lord GOD.

10 "If he fathers a son who is violent, a shedder of blood, who does any of these things 11 (though he himself did none of these things), who even eats upon the mountains, defiles his neighbor's wife, 12 oppresses the poor and needy, commits robbery, does not restore the pledge, lifts up his eyes to the idols, commits abomination, 13 lends at interest, and takes profit; shall he then live? He shall not live. He has done all these abominations; he shall surely die; his blood shall be upon himself.

14 "Now suppose this man fathers a son who sees all the sins that his father has done; he sees, and does not do likewise: 15 he does not eat upon the mountains or lift up his eyes to the idols of the house of Israel, does not defile his neighbor's wife, 16 does not oppress anyone, exacts no pledge, commits no robbery, but gives his bread to the hungry and covers the naked with a garment, 17 withholds his hand from iniquity,[4] takes no interest or profit, obeys my rules, and walks in my statutes; he shall not die for his father's iniquity; he shall surely live. 18 As for his father, because he practiced extortion, robbed his brother, and did what is not good among his people, behold, he shall die for his iniquity.

19 "Yet you say, 'Why should not the son suffer for the iniquity of the father?' When the son has done what is just and right, and has been careful to observe all my

[1] Some Hebrew manuscripts, Syriac, Targum; most Hebrew manuscripts *all the fugitives* [2] The Hebrew for *you* is plural [3] That is, profit that comes from charging interest to the poor; also verses 13, 17 (compare Leviticus 25:36) [4] Septuagint; Hebrew *from the poor*

statutes, he shall surely live. 20 The soul
who sins shall die. The son shall not suf-
fer for the iniquity of the father, nor the
father suffer for the iniquity of the son.
The righteousness of the righteous shall
be upon himself, and the wickedness of
the wicked shall be upon himself.
21 "But if a wicked person turns away
from all his sins that he has committed
and keeps all my statutes and does what
is just and right, he shall surely live; he
shall not die. 22 None of the transgressions
that he has committed shall be remem-
bered against him; for the righteousness
that he has done he shall live. 23 Have I
any pleasure in the death of the wicked,
declares the Lord GOD, and not rather that
he should turn from his way and live?
24 But when a righteous person turns away
from his righteousness and does injustice
and does the same abominations that the
wicked person does, shall he live? None
of the righteous deeds that he has done
shall be remembered; for the treachery of
which he is guilty and the sin he has com-
mitted, for them he shall die.
25 "Yet you say, 'The way of the Lord is
not just.' Hear now, O house of Israel: Is
my way not just? Is it not your ways that
are not just? 26 When a righteous person
turns away from his righteousness and
does injustice, he shall die for it; for the
injustice that he has done he shall die.
27 Again, when a wicked person turns away
from the wickedness he has committed
and does what is just and right, he shall
save his life. 28 Because he considered and
turned away from all the transgressions
that he had committed, he shall surely
live; he shall not die. 29 Yet the house of
Israel says, 'The way of the Lord is not just.'
O house of Israel, are my ways not just? Is
it not your ways that are not just?
30 "Therefore I will judge you, O house
of Israel, every one according to his ways,
declares the Lord GOD. Repent and turn
from all your transgressions, lest iniquity
be your ruin.[1] 31 Cast away from you all
the transgressions that you have commit-
ted, and make yourselves a new heart and
a new spirit! Why will you die, O house
of Israel? 32 For I have no pleasure in the
death of anyone, declares the Lord GOD;
so turn, and live."

A Lament for the Princes of Israel

19 And you, take up a lamentation for
the princes of Israel, 2 and say:

What was your mother? A lioness!
  Among lions she crouched;
in the midst of young lions
  she reared her cubs.
3 And she brought up one of her cubs;
  he became a young lion,
and he learned to catch prey;
  he devoured men.
4 The nations heard about him;
  he was caught in their pit,
and they brought him with hooks
  to the land of Egypt.
5 When she saw that she waited in vain,
  that her hope was lost,
she took another of her cubs
  and made him a young lion.
6 He prowled among the lions;
  he became a young lion,
and he learned to catch prey;
  he devoured men,
7 and seized[2] their widows.
  He laid waste their cities,
and the land was appalled and all
    who were in it
  at the sound of his roaring.
8 Then the nations set against him
  from provinces on every side;
they spread their net over him;
  he was taken in their pit.
9 With hooks they put him in a cage[3]
  and brought him to the king of
    Babylon;
  they brought him into custody,
that his voice should no more be
    heard
  on the mountains of Israel.

[1] Or *lest iniquity be your stumbling block* [2] Hebrew *knew* [3] Or *in a wooden collar*

10 Your mother was like a vine in a
vineyard[1]
planted by the water,
fruitful and full of branches
by reason of abundant water.
11 Its strong stems became
rulers' scepters;
it towered aloft
among the thick boughs;[2]
it was seen in its height
with the mass of its branches.
12 But the vine was plucked up in fury,
cast down to the ground;
the east wind dried up its fruit;
they were stripped off and
withered.
As for its strong stem,
fire consumed it.
13 Now it is planted in the wilderness,
in a dry and thirsty land.
14 And fire has gone out from the stem
of its shoots,
has consumed its fruit,
so that there remains in it no strong
stem,
no scepter for ruling.

This is a lamentation and has become
a lamentation.

Israel's Continuing Rebellion

20 In the seventh year, in the fifth
month, on the tenth day of the
month, certain of the elders of Israel came
to inquire of the LORD, and sat before me.
2 And the word of the LORD came to me:
3 "Son of man, speak to the elders of Israel,
and say to them, Thus says the Lord GOD,
Is it to inquire of me that you come? As I
live, declares the Lord GOD, I will not be
inquired of by you. 4 Will you judge them,
son of man, will you judge them? Let them
know the abominations of their fathers,
5 and say to them, Thus says the Lord GOD:
On the day when I chose Israel, I swore[3] to
the offspring of the house of Jacob, making
myself known to them in the land of Egypt;
I swore to them, saying, I am the LORD your
God. 6 On that day I swore to them that I
would bring them out of the land of Egypt
into a land that I had searched out for
them, a land flowing with milk and honey,
the most glorious of all lands. 7 And I said
to them, Cast away the detestable things
your eyes feast on, every one of you, and
do not defile yourselves with the idols of
Egypt; I am the LORD your God. 8 But they
rebelled against me and were not willing
to listen to me. None of them cast away the
detestable things their eyes feasted on, nor
did they forsake the idols of Egypt.

"Then I said I would pour out my wrath
upon them and spend my anger against
them in the midst of the land of Egypt.
9 But I acted for the sake of my name, that
it should not be profaned in the sight of
the nations among whom they lived, in
whose sight I made myself known to them
in bringing them out of the land of Egypt.
10 So I led them out of the land of Egypt
and brought them into the wilderness. 11 I
gave them my statutes and made known
to them my rules, by which, if a person
does them, he shall live. 12 Moreover, I
gave them my Sabbaths, as a sign between
me and them, that they might know that
I am the LORD who sanctifies them. 13 But
the house of Israel rebelled against me in
the wilderness. They did not walk in my
statutes but rejected my rules, by which, if
a person does them, he shall live; and my
Sabbaths they greatly profaned.

"Then I said I would pour out my wrath
upon them in the wilderness, to make a
full end of them. 14 But I acted for the sake
of my name, that it should not be pro-
faned in the sight of the nations, in whose
sight I had brought them out. 15 Moreover,
I swore to them in the wilderness that I
would not bring them into the land that I
had given them, a land flowing with milk
and honey, the most glorious of all lands,
16 because they rejected my rules and did
not walk in my statutes, and profaned
my Sabbaths; for their heart went after

[1] Some Hebrew manuscripts; most Hebrew manuscripts *in your blood* [2] Or *the clouds* [3] Hebrew *I lifted my hand*; twice in this verse; also verses 6, 15, 23, 28, 42

their idols. 17 Nevertheless, my eye spared them, and I did not destroy them or make a full end of them in the wilderness.

18 "And I said to their children in the wilderness, Do not walk in the statutes of your fathers, nor keep their rules, nor defile yourselves with their idols. 19 I am the LORD your God; walk in my statutes, and be careful to obey my rules, 20 and keep my Sabbaths holy that they may be a sign between me and you, that you may know that I am the LORD your God. 21 But the children rebelled against me. They did not walk in my statutes and were not careful to obey my rules, by which, if a person does them, he shall live; they profaned my Sabbaths.

"Then I said I would pour out my wrath upon them and spend my anger against them in the wilderness. 22 But I withheld my hand and acted for the sake of my name, that it should not be profaned in the sight of the nations, in whose sight I had brought them out. 23 Moreover, I swore to them in the wilderness that I would scatter them among the nations and disperse them through the countries, 24 because they had not obeyed my rules, but had rejected my statutes and profaned my Sabbaths, and their eyes were set on their fathers' idols. 25 Moreover, I gave them statutes that were not good and rules by which they could not have life, 26 and I defiled them through their very gifts in their offering up all their firstborn, that I might devastate them. I did it that they might know that I am the LORD.

27 "Therefore, son of man, speak to the house of Israel and say to them, Thus says the Lord GOD: In this also your fathers blasphemed me, by dealing treacherously with me. 28 For when I had brought them into the land that I swore to give them, then wherever they saw any high hill or any leafy tree, there they offered their sacrifices and there they presented the provocation of their offering; there they sent up their pleasing aromas, and there they poured out their drink offerings. 29 (I said to them, What is the high place to which you go? So its name is called Bamah[1] to this day.)

30 "Therefore say to the house of Israel, Thus says the Lord GOD: Will you defile yourselves after the manner of your fathers and go whoring after their detestable things? 31 When you present your gifts and offer up your children in fire,[2] you defile yourselves with all your idols to this day. And shall I be inquired of by you, O house of Israel? As I live, declares the Lord GOD, I will not be inquired of by you.

32 "What is in your mind shall never happen—the thought, 'Let us be like the nations, like the tribes of the countries, and worship wood and stone.'

The LORD Will Restore Israel

33 "As I live, declares the Lord GOD, surely with a mighty hand and an outstretched arm and with wrath poured out I will be king over you. 34 I will bring you out from the peoples and gather you out of the countries where you are scattered, with a mighty hand and an outstretched arm, and with wrath poured out. 35 And I will bring you into the wilderness of the peoples, and there I will enter into judgment with you face to face. 36 As I entered into judgment with your fathers in the wilderness of the land of Egypt, so I will enter into judgment with you, declares the Lord GOD. 37 I will make you pass under the rod, and I will bring you into the bond of the covenant. 38 I will purge out the rebels from among you, and those who transgress against me. I will bring them out of the land where they sojourn, but they shall not enter the land of Israel. Then you will know that I am the LORD.

39 "As for you, O house of Israel, thus says the Lord GOD: Go serve every one of you his idols, now and hereafter, if you will not listen to me; but my holy name you shall no more profane with your gifts and your idols.

[1] *Bamah* means *high place* [2] Hebrew *and make your children pass through the fire*

40 "For on my holy mountain, the mountain height of Israel, declares the Lord GOD, there all the house of Israel, all of them, shall serve me in the land. There I will accept them, and there I will require your contributions and the choicest of your gifts, with all your sacred offerings. **41** As a pleasing aroma I will accept you, when I bring you out from the peoples and gather you out of the countries where you have been scattered. And I will manifest my holiness among you in the sight of the nations. **42** And you shall know that I am the LORD, when I bring you into the land of Israel, the country that I swore to give to your fathers. **43** And there you shall remember your ways and all your deeds with which you have defiled yourselves, and you shall loathe yourselves for all the evils that you have committed. **44** And you shall know that I am the LORD, when I deal with you for my name's sake, not according to your evil ways, nor according to your corrupt deeds, O house of Israel, declares the Lord GOD."

45[1] And the word of the LORD came to me: **46** "Son of man, set your face toward the southland;[2] preach against the south, and prophesy against the forest land in the Negeb. **47** Say to the forest of the Negeb, Hear the word of the LORD: Thus says the Lord GOD, Behold, I will kindle a fire in you, and it shall devour every green tree in you and every dry tree. The blazing flame shall not be quenched, and all faces from south to north shall be scorched by it. **48** All flesh shall see that I the LORD have kindled it; it shall not be quenched." **49** Then I said, "Ah, Lord GOD! They are saying of me, 'Is he not a maker of parables?' "

The LORD Has Drawn His Sword

21 [3] The word of the LORD came to me: **2** "Son of man, set your face toward Jerusalem and preach against the sanctuaries.[4] Prophesy against the land of Israel **3** and say to the land of Israel, Thus says the LORD: Behold, I am against you and will draw my sword from its sheath and will cut off from you both righteous and wicked. **4** Because I will cut off from you both righteous and wicked, therefore my sword shall be drawn from its sheath against all flesh from south to north. **5** And all flesh shall know that I am the LORD. I have drawn my sword from its sheath; it shall not be sheathed again.

6 "As for you, son of man, groan; with breaking heart and bitter grief, groan before their eyes. **7** And when they say to you, 'Why do you groan?' you shall say, 'Because of the news that it is coming. Every heart will melt, and all hands will be feeble; every spirit will faint, and all knees will be weak as water. Behold, it is coming, and it will be fulfilled,'" declares the Lord GOD.

8 And the word of the LORD came to me: **9** "Son of man, prophesy and say, Thus says the Lord, say:

"A sword, a sword is sharpened
    and also polished,
10 sharpened for slaughter,
    polished to flash like lightning!

(Or shall we rejoice? You have despised the rod, my son, with everything of wood.)[5] **11** So the sword is given to be polished, that it may be grasped in the hand. It is sharpened and polished to be given into the hand of the slayer. **12** Cry out and wail, son of man, for it is against my people. It is against all the princes of Israel. They are delivered over to the sword with my people. Strike therefore upon your thigh. **13** For it will not be a testing—what could it do if you despise the rod?"[6] declares the Lord GOD.

14 "As for you, son of man, prophesy. Clap your hands and let the sword come down twice, yes, three times,[7] the sword for those to be slain. It is the sword for the great slaughter, which surrounds them, **15** that their hearts may melt, and many

[1] Ch 21:1 in Hebrew [2] Or *toward Teman* [3] Ch 21:6 in Hebrew [4] Some Hebrew manuscripts, compare Septuagint, Syriac *against their sanctuary* [5] Probable reading; Hebrew *The rod of my son despises everything of wood* [6] Or *For it is a testing; and what if even the rod despises? It shall not be!* [7] Hebrew *its third*

stumble.[1] At all their gates I have given the glittering sword. Ah, it is made like lightning; it is taken up[2] for slaughter. 16 Cut sharply to the right; set yourself to the left, wherever your face is directed. 17 I also will clap my hands, and I will satisfy my fury; I the LORD have spoken."

18 The word of the LORD came to me again: 19 "As for you, son of man, mark two ways for the sword of the king of Babylon to come. Both of them shall come from the same land. And make a signpost; make it at the head of the way to a city. 20 Mark a way for the sword to come to Rabbah of the Ammonites and to Judah, into Jerusalem the fortified. 21 For the king of Babylon stands at the parting of the way, at the head of the two ways, to use divination. He shakes the arrows; he consults the teraphim;[3] he looks at the liver. 22 Into his right hand comes the divination for Jerusalem, to set battering rams, to open the mouth with murder, to lift up the voice with shouting, to set battering rams against the gates, to cast up mounds, to build siege towers. 23 But to them it will seem like a false divination. They have sworn solemn oaths, but he brings their guilt to remembrance, that they may be taken.

24 "Therefore thus says the Lord GOD: Because you have made your guilt to be remembered, in that your transgressions are uncovered, so that in all your deeds your sins appear—because you have come to remembrance, you shall be taken in hand. 25 And you, O profane[4] wicked one, prince of Israel, whose day has come, the time of your final punishment, 26 thus says the Lord GOD: Remove the turban and take off the crown. Things shall not remain as they are. Exalt that which is low, and bring low that which is exalted. 27 A ruin, ruin, ruin I will make it. This also shall not be, until he comes, the one to whom judgment belongs, and I will give it to him.

28 "And you, son of man, prophesy, and say, Thus says the Lord GOD concerning the Ammonites and concerning their reproach; say, A sword, a sword is drawn for the slaughter. It is polished to consume and to flash like lightning— 29 while they see for you false visions, while they divine lies for you—to place you on the necks of the profane wicked, whose day has come, the time of their final punishment. 30 Return it to its sheath. In the place where you were created, in the land of your origin, I will judge you. 31 And I will pour out my indignation upon you; I will blow upon you with the fire of my wrath, and I will deliver you into the hands of brutish men, skillful to destroy. 32 You shall be fuel for the fire. Your blood shall be in the midst of the land. You shall be no more remembered, for I the LORD have spoken."

Israel's Shedding of Blood

22 And the word of the LORD came to me, saying, 2 "And you, son of man, will you judge, will you judge the bloody city? Then declare to her all her abominations. 3 You shall say, Thus says the Lord GOD: A city that sheds blood in her midst, so that her time may come, and that makes idols to defile herself! 4 You have become guilty by the blood that you have shed, and defiled by the idols that you have made, and you have brought your days near, the appointed time of[5] your years has come. Therefore I have made you a reproach to the nations, and a mockery to all the countries. 5 Those who are near and those who are far from you will mock you; your name is defiled; you are full of tumult.

6 "Behold, the princes of Israel in you, every one according to his power, have been bent on shedding blood. 7 Father and mother are treated with contempt in you; the sojourner suffers extortion in your midst; the fatherless and the widow are wronged in you. 8 You have despised my holy things and profaned my Sabbaths. 9 There are men in you who slander to shed blood, and people in you who eat on the

[1] Hebrew *many stumbling blocks* [2] The meaning of the Hebrew word rendered *taken up* is uncertain [3] Or *household idols* [4] Or *slain*; also verse 29 [5] Some Hebrew manuscripts, Septuagint, Syriac, Vulgate, Targum; most Hebrew manuscripts *until*

mountains; they commit lewdness in your midst. 10 In you men uncover their fathers' nakedness; in you they violate women who are unclean in their menstrual impurity. 11 One commits abomination with his neighbor's wife; another lewdly defiles his daughter-in-law; another in you violates his sister, his father's daughter. 12 In you they take bribes to shed blood; you take interest and profit[1] and make gain of your neighbors by extortion; but me you have forgotten, declares the Lord GOD.

13 "Behold, I strike my hand at the dishonest gain that you have made, and at the blood that has been in your midst. 14 Can your courage endure, or can your hands be strong, in the days that I shall deal with you? I the LORD have spoken, and I will do it. 15 I will scatter you among the nations and disperse you through the countries, and I will consume your uncleanness out of you. 16 And you shall be profaned by your own doing in the sight of the nations, and you shall know that I am the LORD."

17 And the word of the LORD came to me: 18 "Son of man, the house of Israel has become dross to me; all of them are bronze and tin and iron and lead in the furnace; they are dross of silver. 19 Therefore thus says the Lord GOD: Because you have all become dross, therefore, behold, I will gather you into the midst of Jerusalem. 20 As one gathers silver and bronze and iron and lead and tin into a furnace, to blow the fire on it in order to melt it, so I will gather you in my anger and in my wrath, and I will put you in and melt you. 21 I will gather you and blow on you with the fire of my wrath, and you shall be melted in the midst of it. 22 As silver is melted in a furnace, so you shall be melted in the midst of it, and you shall know that I am the LORD; I have poured out my wrath upon you."

23 And the word of the LORD came to me: 24 "Son of man, say to her, You are a land that is not cleansed or rained upon in the day of indignation. 25 The conspiracy of her prophets in her midst is like a roaring lion tearing the prey; they have devoured human lives; they have taken treasure and precious things; they have made many widows in her midst. 26 Her priests have done violence to my law and have profaned my holy things. They have made no distinction between the holy and the common, neither have they taught the difference between the unclean and the clean, and they have disregarded my Sabbaths, so that I am profaned among them. 27 Her princes in her midst are like wolves tearing the prey, shedding blood, destroying lives to get dishonest gain. 28 And her prophets have smeared whitewash for them, seeing false visions and divining lies for them, saying, 'Thus says the Lord GOD,' when the LORD has not spoken. 29 The people of the land have practiced extortion and committed robbery. They have oppressed the poor and needy, and have extorted from the sojourner without justice. 30 And I sought for a man among them who should build up the wall and stand in the breach before me for the land, that I should not destroy it, but I found none. 31 Therefore I have poured out my indignation upon them. I have consumed them with the fire of my wrath. I have returned their way upon their heads, declares the Lord GOD."

Oholah and Oholibah

23 The word of the LORD came to me: 2 "Son of man, there were two women, the daughters of one mother. 3 They played the whore in Egypt; they played the whore in their youth; there their breasts were pressed and their virgin bosoms[2] handled. 4 Oholah was the name of the elder and Oholibah the name of her sister. They became mine, and they bore sons and daughters. As for their names, Oholah is Samaria, and Oholibah is Jerusalem.

5 "Oholah played the whore while she was mine, and she lusted after her lovers

[1] That is, profit that comes from charging interest to the poor (compare Leviticus 25:36) [2] Hebrew *nipples*; also verses 8, 21

the Assyrians, warriors 6 clothed in purple,
governors and commanders, all of them
desirable young men, horsemen riding on
horses. 7 She bestowed her whoring upon
them, the choicest men of Assyria all of
them, and she defiled herself with all the
idols of everyone after whom she lusted.
8 She did not give up her whoring that she
had begun in Egypt; for in her youth men
had lain with her and handled her virgin
bosom and poured out their whoring lust
upon her. 9 Therefore I delivered her into
the hands of her lovers, into the hands
of the Assyrians, after whom she lusted.
10 These uncovered her nakedness; they
seized her sons and her daughters; and
as for her, they killed her with the sword;
and she became a byword among women,
when judgment had been executed on her.

11 "Her sister Oholibah saw this, and she
became more corrupt than her sister[1] in
her lust and in her whoring, which was
worse than that of her sister. 12 She lusted
after the Assyrians, governors and com-
manders, warriors clothed in full armor,
horsemen riding on horses, all of them
desirable young men. 13 And I saw that
she was defiled; they both took the same
way. 14 But she carried her whoring fur-
ther. She saw men portrayed on the wall,
the images of the Chaldeans portrayed in
vermilion, 15 wearing belts on their waists,
with flowing turbans on their heads, all of
them having the appearance of officers, a
likeness of Babylonians whose native land
was Chaldea. 16 When she saw them, she
lusted after them and sent messengers to
them in Chaldea. 17 And the Babylonians
came to her into the bed of love, and they
defiled her with their whoring lust. And
after she was defiled by them, she turned
from them in disgust. 18 When she carried
on her whoring so openly and flaunted her
nakedness, I turned in disgust from her,
as I had turned in disgust from her sister.
19 Yet she increased her whoring, remem-
bering the days of her youth, when she
played the whore in the land of Egypt 20 and
lusted after her paramours there, whose
members were like those of donkeys, and
whose issue was like that of horses. 21 Thus
you longed for the lewdness of your youth,
when the Egyptians handled your bosom
and pressed[2] your young breasts."

22 Therefore, O Oholibah, thus says the
Lord GOD: "Behold, I will stir up against
you your lovers from whom you turned
in disgust, and I will bring them against
you from every side: 23 the Babylonians
and all the Chaldeans, Pekod and Shoa
and Koa, and all the Assyrians with them,
desirable young men, governors and com-
manders all of them, officers and men
of renown, all of them riding on horses.
24 And they shall come against you from
the north[3] with chariots and wagons and a
host of peoples. They shall set themselves
against you on every side with buckler,
shield, and helmet; and I will commit the
judgment to them, and they shall judge
you according to their judgments. 25 And
I will direct my jealousy against you, that
they may deal with you in fury. They shall
cut off your nose and your ears, and your
survivors shall fall by the sword. They
shall seize your sons and your daughters,
and your survivors shall be devoured by
fire. 26 They shall also strip you of your
clothes and take away your beautiful jew-
els. 27 Thus I will put an end to your lewd-
ness and your whoring begun in the land
of Egypt, so that you shall not lift up your
eyes to them or remember Egypt anymore.

28 "For thus says the Lord GOD: Behold,
I will deliver you into the hands of those
whom you hate, into the hands of those
from whom you turned in disgust,
29 and they shall deal with you in hatred
and take away all the fruit of your labor and
leave you naked and bare, and the naked-
ness of your whoring shall be uncovered.
Your lewdness and your whoring 30 have
brought this upon you, because you played
the whore with the nations and defiled

[1] Hebrew *than she* [2] Vulgate, Syriac; Hebrew *bosom for the sake of* [3] Septuagint; the meaning of the Hebrew word is unknown

yourself with their idols. 31 You have gone
the way of your sister; therefore I will give
her cup into your hand. 32 Thus says the
Lord GOD:

"You shall drink your sister's cup
that is deep and large;
you shall be laughed at and held in
derision,
for it contains much;
33 you will be filled with drunkenness
and sorrow.
A cup of horror and desolation,
the cup of your sister Samaria;
34 you shall drink it and drain it out,
and gnaw its shards,
and tear your breasts;

for I have spoken, declares the Lord GOD.
35 Therefore thus says the Lord GOD:
Because you have forgotten me and cast
me behind your back, you yourself must
bear the consequences of your lewdness
and whoring."

36 The LORD said to me: "Son of man, will
you judge Oholah and Oholibah? Declare
to them their abominations. 37 For they
have committed adultery, and blood is
on their hands. With their idols they have
committed adultery, and they have even
offered up[1] to them for food the children
whom they had borne to me. 38 Moreover,
this they have done to me: they have
defiled my sanctuary on the same day
and profaned my Sabbaths. 39 For when
they had slaughtered their children in sac-
rifice to their idols, on the same day they
came into my sanctuary to profane it. And
behold, this is what they did in my house.
40 They even sent for men to come from
afar, to whom a messenger was sent; and
behold, they came. For them you bathed
yourself, painted your eyes, and adorned
yourself with ornaments. 41 You sat on a
stately couch, with a table spread before
it on which you had placed my incense
and my oil. 42 The sound of a carefree mul-
titude was with her; and with men of the
common sort, drunkards[2] were brought
from the wilderness; and they put brace-
lets on the hands of the women, and beau-
tiful crowns on their heads.

43 "Then I said of her who was worn out
by adultery, Now they will continue to use
her for a whore, even her![3] 44 For they have
gone in to her, as men go in to a prosti-
tute. Thus they went in to Oholah and to
Oholibah, lewd women! 45 But righteous
men shall pass judgment on them with
the sentence of adulteresses, and with
the sentence of women who shed blood,
because they are adulteresses, and blood
is on their hands."

46 For thus says the Lord GOD: "Bring up a
vast host against them, and make them an
object of terror and a plunder. 47 And the
host shall stone them and cut them down
with their swords. They shall kill their sons
and their daughters, and burn up their
houses. 48 Thus will I put an end to lewd-
ness in the land, that all women may take
warning and not commit lewdness as you
have done. 49 And they shall return your
lewdness upon you, and you shall bear the
penalty for your sinful idolatry, and you
shall know that I am the Lord GOD."

The Siege of Jerusalem

24 In the ninth year, in the tenth
month, on the tenth day of the
month, the word of the LORD came to me:
2 "Son of man, write down the name of this
day, this very day. The king of Babylon has
laid siege to Jerusalem this very day. 3 And
utter a parable to the rebellious house and
say to them, Thus says the Lord GOD:

"Set on the pot, set it on;
pour in water also;
4 put in it the pieces of meat,
all the good pieces, the thigh and
the shoulder;
fill it with choice bones.
5 Take the choicest one of the flock;
pile the logs[4] under it;

[1] Or *have even made pass through the fire* [2] Or *Sabeans* [3] The meaning of the Hebrew verse is uncertain [4] Compare verse 10; Hebrew *the bones*

boil it well;
seethe also its bones in it.

6 "Therefore thus says the Lord GOD: Woe to the bloody city, to the pot whose corrosion is in it, and whose corrosion has not gone out of it! Take out of it piece after piece, without making any choice.[1] 7 For the blood she has shed is in her midst; she put it on the bare rock; she did not pour it out on the ground to cover it with dust. 8 To rouse my wrath, to take vengeance, I have set on the bare rock the blood she has shed, that it may not be covered. 9 Therefore thus says the Lord GOD: Woe to the bloody city! I also will make the pile great. 10 Heap on the logs, kindle the fire, boil the meat well, mix in the spices,[2] and let the bones be burned up. 11 Then set it empty upon the coals, that it may become hot, and its copper may burn, that its uncleanness may be melted in it, its corrosion consumed. 12 She has wearied herself with toil;[3] its abundant corrosion does not go out of it. Into the fire with its corrosion! 13 On account of your unclean lewdness, because I would have cleansed you and you were not cleansed from your uncleanness, you shall not be cleansed anymore till I have satisfied my fury upon you. 14 I am the LORD. I have spoken; it shall come to pass; I will do it. I will not go back; I will not spare; I will not relent; according to your ways and your deeds you will be judged, declares the Lord GOD."

Ezekiel's Wife Dies

15 The word of the LORD came to me: 16 "Son of man, behold, I am about to take the delight of your eyes away from you at a stroke; yet you shall not mourn or weep, nor shall your tears run down. 17 Sigh, but not aloud; make no mourning for the dead. Bind on your turban, and put your shoes on your feet; do not cover your lips, nor eat the bread of men." 18 So I spoke to the people in the morning, and at evening my wife died. And on the next morning I did as I was commanded.

19 And the people said to me, "Will you not tell us what these things mean for us, that you are acting thus?" 20 Then I said to them, "The word of the LORD came to me: 21 'Say to the house of Israel, Thus says the Lord GOD: Behold, I will profane my sanctuary, the pride of your power, the delight of your eyes, and the yearning of your soul, and your sons and your daughters whom you left behind shall fall by the sword. 22 And you shall do as I have done; you shall not cover your lips, nor eat the bread of men. 23 Your turbans shall be on your heads and your shoes on your feet; you shall not mourn or weep, but you shall rot away in your iniquities and groan to one another. 24 Thus shall Ezekiel be to you a sign; according to all that he has done you shall do. When this comes, then you will know that I am the Lord GOD.'

25 "As for you, son of man, surely on the day when I take from them their stronghold, their joy and glory, the delight of their eyes and their soul's desire, and also their sons and daughters, 26 on that day a fugitive will come to you to report to you the news. 27 On that day your mouth will be opened to the fugitive, and you shall speak and be no longer mute. So you will be a sign to them, and they will know that I am the LORD."

Prophecy Against Ammon

25 The word of the LORD came to me: 2 "Son of man, set your face toward the Ammonites and prophesy against them. 3 Say to the Ammonites, Hear the word of the Lord GOD: Thus says the Lord GOD, Because you said, 'Aha!' over my sanctuary when it was profaned, and over the land of Israel when it was made desolate, and over the house of Judah when they went into exile, 4 therefore behold, I am handing you over to the people of the East for a possession, and they shall set their encampments among you and make

[1] Hebrew *no lot has fallen upon it* [2] Or *empty out the broth* [3] The meaning of the Hebrew is uncertain

their dwellings in your midst. They shall eat your fruit, and they shall drink your milk. 5 I will make Rabbah a pasture for camels and Ammon[1] a fold for flocks. Then you will know that I am the LORD. 6 For thus says the Lord GOD: Because you have clapped your hands and stamped your feet and rejoiced with all the malice within your soul against the land of Israel, 7 therefore, behold, I have stretched out my hand against you, and will hand you over as plunder to the nations. And I will cut you off from the peoples and will make you perish out of the countries; I will destroy you. Then you will know that I am the LORD.

Prophecy Against Moab and Seir

8 "Thus says the Lord GOD: Because Moab and Seir[2] said, 'Behold, the house of Judah is like all the other nations,' 9 therefore I will lay open the flank of Moab from the cities, from its cities on its frontier, the glory of the country, Beth-jeshimoth, Baal-meon, and Kiriathaim. 10 I will give it along with the Ammonites to the people of the East as a possession, that the Ammonites may be remembered no more among the nations, 11 and I will execute judgments upon Moab. Then they will know that I am the LORD.

Prophecy Against Edom

12 "Thus says the Lord GOD: Because Edom acted revengefully against the house of Judah and has grievously offended in taking vengeance on them, 13 therefore thus says the Lord GOD, I will stretch out my hand against Edom and cut off from it man and beast. And I will make it desolate; from Teman even to Dedan they shall fall by the sword. 14 And I will lay my vengeance upon Edom by the hand of my people Israel, and they shall do in Edom according to my anger and according to my wrath, and they shall know my vengeance, declares the Lord GOD.

Prophecy Against Philistia

15 "Thus says the Lord GOD: Because the Philistines acted revengefully and took vengeance with malice of soul to destroy in never-ending enmity, 16 therefore thus says the Lord GOD, Behold, I will stretch out my hand against the Philistines, and I will cut off the Cherethites and destroy the rest of the seacoast. 17 I will execute great vengeance on them with wrathful rebukes. Then they will know that I am the LORD, when I lay my vengeance upon them."

Prophecy Against Tyre

26 In the eleventh year, on the first day of the month, the word of the LORD came to me: 2 "Son of man, because Tyre said concerning Jerusalem, 'Aha, the gate of the peoples is broken; it has swung open to me. I shall be replenished, now that she is laid waste,' 3 therefore thus says the Lord GOD: Behold, I am against you, O Tyre, and will bring up many nations against you, as the sea brings up its waves. 4 They shall destroy the walls of Tyre and break down her towers, and I will scrape her soil from her and make her a bare rock. 5 She shall be in the midst of the sea a place for the spreading of nets, for I have spoken, declares the Lord GOD. And she shall become plunder for the nations, 6 and her daughters on the mainland shall be killed by the sword. Then they will know that I am the LORD.

7 "For thus says the Lord GOD: Behold, I will bring against Tyre from the north Nebuchadnezzar[3] king of Babylon, king of kings, with horses and chariots, and with horsemen and a host of many soldiers. 8 He will kill with the sword your daughters on the mainland. He will set up a siege wall against you and throw up a mound against you, and raise a roof of shields against you. 9 He will direct the shock of his battering rams against your walls, and with his axes he will break down your towers. 10 His horses will be so many that their

[1] Hebrew *and the Ammonites* [2] Septuagint lacks *and Seir* [3] Hebrew *Nebuchadrezzar*, so throughout Ezekiel

dust will cover you. Your walls will shake
at the noise of the horsemen and wagons
and chariots, when he enters your gates as
men enter a city that has been breached.
11 With the hoofs of his horses he will
trample all your streets. He will kill your
people with the sword, and your mighty
pillars will fall to the ground. 12 They will
plunder your riches and loot your mer-
chandise. They will break down your
walls and destroy your pleasant houses.
Your stones and timber and soil they will
cast into the midst of the waters. 13 And I
will stop the music of your songs, and the
sound of your lyres shall be heard no more.
14 I will make you a bare rock. You shall be
a place for the spreading of nets. You shall
never be rebuilt, for I am the LORD; I have
spoken, declares the Lord GOD.

15 "Thus says the Lord GOD to Tyre: Will
not the coastlands shake at the sound of
your fall, when the wounded groan, when
slaughter is made in your midst? 16 Then
all the princes of the sea will step down
from their thrones and remove their robes
and strip off their embroidered garments.
They will clothe themselves with trem-
bling; they will sit on the ground and
tremble every moment and be appalled at
you. 17 And they will raise a lamentation
over you and say to you,

"'How you have perished,
you who were inhabited from the seas,
O city renowned,
who was mighty on the sea;
she and her inhabitants imposed their terror
on all her inhabitants!
18 Now the coastlands tremble
on the day of your fall,
and the coastlands that are on the sea
are dismayed at your passing.'

19 "For thus says the Lord GOD: When I
make you a city laid waste, like the cities
that are not inhabited, when I bring up the
deep over you, and the great waters cover
you, 20 then I will make you go down with
those who go down to the pit, to the people
of old, and I will make you to dwell in the
world below, among ruins from of old, with
those who go down to the pit, so that you
will not be inhabited; but I will set beauty
in the land of the living. 21 I will bring you
to a dreadful end, and you shall be no more.
Though you be sought for, you will never
be found again, declares the Lord GOD."

A Lament for Tyre

27 The word of the LORD came to
me: 2 "Now you, son of man, raise
a lamentation over Tyre, 3 and say to Tyre,
who dwells at the entrances to the sea,
merchant of the peoples to many coast-
lands, thus says the Lord GOD:

"O Tyre, you have said,
'I am perfect in beauty.'
4 Your borders are in the heart of the seas;
your builders made perfect your beauty.
5 They made all your planks
of fir trees from Senir;
they took a cedar from Lebanon
to make a mast for you.
6 Of oaks of Bashan
they made your oars;
they made your deck of pines
from the coasts of Cyprus,
inlaid with ivory.
7 Of fine embroidered linen from Egypt
was your sail,
serving as your banner;
blue and purple from the coasts of Elishah
was your awning.
8 The inhabitants of Sidon and Arvad
were your rowers;
your skilled men, O Tyre, were in you;
they were your pilots.
9 The elders of Gebal and her skilled
men were in you,
caulking your seams;

all the ships of the sea with their
mariners were in you
to barter for your wares.

10 "Persia and Lud and Put were in your
army as your men of war. They hung the
shield and helmet in you; they gave you
splendor. 11 Men of Arvad and Helech
were on your walls all around, and men
of Gamad were in your towers. They hung
their shields on your walls all around;
they made perfect your beauty.
12 "Tarshish did business with you be-
cause of your great wealth of every kind;
silver, iron, tin, and lead they exchanged
for your wares. 13 Javan, Tubal, and
Meshech traded with you; they exchanged
human beings and vessels of bronze for
your merchandise. 14 From Beth-togarmah
they exchanged horses, war horses, and
mules for your wares. 15 The men of Dedan[1]
traded with you. Many coastlands were
your own special markets; they brought
you in payment ivory tusks and ebony.
16 Syria did business with you because of
your abundant goods; they exchanged
for your wares emeralds, purple, embroi-
dered work, fine linen, coral, and ruby.
17 Judah and the land of Israel traded with
you; they exchanged for your merchandise
wheat of Minnith, meal,[2] honey, oil, and
balm. 18 Damascus did business with you
for your abundant goods, because of your
great wealth of every kind; wine of Helbon
and wool of Sahar 19 and casks of wine[3]
from Uzal they exchanged for your wares;
wrought iron, cassia, and calamus were
bartered for your merchandise. 20 Dedan
traded with you in saddlecloths for riding.
21 Arabia and all the princes of Kedar were
your favored dealers in lambs, rams, and
goats; in these they did business with you.
22 The traders of Sheba and Raamah traded
with you; they exchanged for your wares
the best of all kinds of spices and all pre-
cious stones and gold. 23 Haran, Canneh,
Eden, traders of Sheba, Asshur, and
Chilmad traded with you. 24 In your market
these traded with you in choice garments,
in clothes of blue and embroidered work,
and in carpets of colored material, bound
with cords and made secure. 25 The ships
of Tarshish traveled for you with your mer-
chandise. So you were filled and heavily
laden in the heart of the seas.

26 "Your rowers have brought you out
into the high seas.
The east wind has wrecked you
in the heart of the seas.
27 Your riches, your wares, your
merchandise,
your mariners and your pilots,
your caulkers, your dealers in
merchandise,
and all your men of war who are
in you,
with all your crew
that is in your midst,
sink into the heart of the seas
on the day of your fall.
28 At the sound of the cry of your pilots
the countryside shakes,
29 and down from their ships
come all who handle the oar.
The mariners and all the pilots of
the sea
stand on the land
30 and shout aloud over you
and cry out bitterly.
They cast dust on their heads
and wallow in ashes;
31 they make themselves bald for you
and put sackcloth on their waist,
and they weep over you in
bitterness of soul,
with bitter mourning.
32 In their wailing they raise a
lamentation for you
and lament over you:
'Who is like Tyre,
like one destroyed in the midst of
the sea?
33 When your wares came from the
seas,
you satisfied many peoples;

[1] Hebrew; Septuagint *Rhodes* [2] The meaning of the Hebrew word is unknown [3] Probable reading; Hebrew *wool of Sahar, Vedan, and Javan*

with your abundant wealth and
merchandise
you enriched the kings of the earth.
34 Now you are wrecked by the seas,
in the depths of the waters;
your merchandise and all your crew
in your midst
have sunk with you.
35 All the inhabitants of the coastlands
are appalled at you,
and the hair of their kings bristles
with horror;
their faces are convulsed.
36 The merchants among the peoples
hiss at you;
you have come to a dreadful end
and shall be no more forever.'"

Prophecy Against the Prince of Tyre

28 The word of the LORD came to me:
2 "Son of man, say to the prince of
Tyre, Thus says the Lord GOD:

"Because your heart is proud,
and you have said, 'I am a god,
I sit in the seat of the gods,
in the heart of the seas,'
yet you are but a man, and no god,
though you make your heart like
the heart of a god—
3 you are indeed wiser than Daniel;
no secret is hidden from you;
4 by your wisdom and your
understanding
you have made wealth for yourself,
and have gathered gold and silver
into your treasuries;
5 by your great wisdom in your trade
you have increased your wealth,
and your heart has become proud
in your wealth—
6 therefore thus says the Lord GOD:
Because you make your heart
like the heart of a god,
7 therefore, behold, I will bring
foreigners upon you,
the most ruthless of the nations;
and they shall draw their swords
against the beauty of your
wisdom
and defile your splendor.
8 They shall thrust you down into the
pit,
and you shall die the death of the
slain
in the heart of the seas.
9 Will you still say, 'I am a god,'
in the presence of those who kill
you,
though you are but a man, and no
god,
in the hands of those who slay you?
10 You shall die the death of the
uncircumcised
by the hand of foreigners;
for I have spoken, declares the
Lord GOD."

A Lament over the King of Tyre

11 Moreover, the word of the LORD came
to me: 12 "Son of man, raise a lamentation
over the king of Tyre, and say to him, Thus
says the Lord GOD:

"You were the signet of perfection,[1]
full of wisdom and perfect in
beauty.
13 You were in Eden, the garden of God;
every precious stone was your
covering,
sardius, topaz, and diamond,
beryl, onyx, and jasper,
sapphire,[2] emerald, and carbuncle;
and crafted in gold were your
settings
and your engravings.[3]
On the day that you were created
they were prepared.
14 You were an anointed guardian
cherub.
I placed you;[4] you were on the
holy mountain of God;
in the midst of the stones of fire
you walked.
15 You were blameless in your ways

[1] The meaning of the Hebrew phrase is uncertain [2] Or *lapis lazuli* [3] The meaning of the Hebrew phrase is uncertain [4] The meaning of the Hebrew phrase is uncertain

from the day you were created,
till unrighteousness was found in you.
16 In the abundance of your trade
you were filled with violence in your midst, and you sinned;
so I cast you as a profane thing from the mountain of God,
and I destroyed you,[1] O guardian cherub,
from the midst of the stones of fire.
17 Your heart was proud because of your beauty;
you corrupted your wisdom for the sake of your splendor.
I cast you to the ground;
I exposed you before kings,
to feast their eyes on you.
18 By the multitude of your iniquities,
in the unrighteousness of your trade
you profaned your sanctuaries;
so I brought fire out from your midst;
it consumed you,
and I turned you to ashes on the earth
in the sight of all who saw you.
19 All who know you among the peoples
are appalled at you;
you have come to a dreadful end
and shall be no more forever."

Prophecy Against Sidon

20 The word of the LORD came to me:
21 "Son of man, set your face toward Sidon,
and prophesy against her 22 and say, Thus
says the Lord GOD:

"Behold, I am against you, O Sidon,
and I will manifest my glory in your midst.
And they shall know that I am the LORD
when I execute judgments in her
and manifest my holiness in her;
23 for I will send pestilence into her,
and blood into her streets;
and the slain shall fall in her midst,
by the sword that is against her on every side.
Then they will know that I am the LORD.

24 "And for the house of Israel there shall
be no more a brier to prick or a thorn to
hurt them among all their neighbors who
have treated them with contempt. Then
they will know that I am the Lord GOD.

Israel Gathered in Security

25 "Thus says the Lord GOD: When I
gather the house of Israel from the peo-
ples among whom they are scattered, and
manifest my holiness in them in the sight
of the nations, then they shall dwell in
their own land that I gave to my servant
Jacob. 26 And they shall dwell securely in
it, and they shall build houses and plant
vineyards. They shall dwell securely, when
I execute judgments upon all their neigh-
bors who have treated them with con-
tempt. Then they will know that I am the
LORD their God."

Prophecy Against Egypt

29 In the tenth year, in the tenth
month, on the twelfth day of the
month, the word of the LORD came to
me: 2 "Son of man, set your face against
Pharaoh king of Egypt, and prophesy
against him and against all Egypt; 3 speak,
and say, Thus says the Lord GOD:

"Behold, I am against you,
Pharaoh king of Egypt,
the great dragon that lies
in the midst of his streams,
that says, 'My Nile is my own;
I made it for myself.'
4 I will put hooks in your jaws,
and make the fish of your streams stick to your scales;
and I will draw you up out of the midst of your streams,
with all the fish of your streams that stick to your scales.

[1] Or *banished you*

5 And I will cast you out into the
wilderness,
you and all the fish of your streams;
you shall fall on the open field,
and not be brought together or
gathered.
To the beasts of the earth and to the
birds of the heavens
I give you as food.

6 Then all the inhabitants of Egypt shall
know that I am the LORD.

"Because you[1] have been a staff of reed
to the house of Israel, 7 when they grasped
you with the hand, you broke and tore all
their shoulders; and when they leaned on
you, you broke and made all their loins
to shake.[2] 8 Therefore thus says the Lord
GOD: Behold, I will bring a sword upon
you, and will cut off from you man and
beast, 9 and the land of Egypt shall be a
desolation and a waste. Then they will
know that I am the LORD.

"Because you[3] said, 'The Nile is mine,
and I made it,' 10 therefore, behold, I am
against you and against your streams, and I
will make the land of Egypt an utter waste
and desolation, from Migdol to Syene, as
far as the border of Cush. 11 No foot of man
shall pass through it, and no foot of beast
shall pass through it; it shall be uninhab-
ited forty years. 12 And I will make the land
of Egypt a desolation in the midst of deso-
lated countries, and her cities shall be a
desolation forty years among cities that
are laid waste. I will scatter the Egyptians
among the nations, and disperse them
through the countries.

13 "For thus says the Lord GOD: At the end
of forty years I will gather the Egyptians
from the peoples among whom they were
scattered, 14 and I will restore the fortunes
of Egypt and bring them back to the land of
Pathros, the land of their origin, and there
they shall be a lowly kingdom. 15 It shall be
the most lowly of the kingdoms, and never
again exalt itself above the nations. And
I will make them so small that they will
never again rule over the nations. 16 And
it shall never again be the reliance of the
house of Israel, recalling their iniquity,
when they turn to them for aid. Then they
will know that I am the Lord GOD."

17 In the twenty-seventh year, in the first
month, on the first day of the month, the
word of the LORD came to me: 18 "Son of
man, Nebuchadnezzar king of Babylon
made his army labor hard against Tyre.
Every head was made bald, and every
shoulder was rubbed bare, yet neither he
nor his army got anything from Tyre to
pay for the labor that he had performed
against her. 19 Therefore thus says the Lord
GOD: Behold, I will give the land of Egypt
to Nebuchadnezzar king of Babylon; and
he shall carry off its wealth[4] and despoil
it and plunder it; and it shall be the wages
for his army. 20 I have given him the land of
Egypt as his payment for which he labored,
because they worked for me, declares the
Lord GOD.

21 "On that day I will cause a horn to
spring up for the house of Israel, and I will
open your lips among them. Then they
will know that I am the LORD."

A Lament for Egypt

30 The word of the LORD came to me:
2 "Son of man, prophesy, and say,
Thus says the Lord GOD:

"Wail, 'Alas for the day!'
3 For the day is near,
the day of the LORD is near;
it will be a day of clouds,
a time of doom for[5] the nations.
4 A sword shall come upon Egypt,
and anguish shall be in Cush,
when the slain fall in Egypt,
and her wealth[6] is carried away,
and her foundations are torn down.

5 Cush, and Put, and Lud, and all Arabia, and
Libya,[7] and the people of the land that is in
league,[8] shall fall with them by the sword.

[1] Hebrew *they* [2] Syriac (compare Psalm 69:23); Hebrew *to stand* [3] Hebrew *he* [4] Or *multitude* [5] Hebrew lacks *doom for* [6] Or *multitude*; also verse 10 [7] With Septuagint; Hebrew *Cub* [8] Hebrew *and the sons of the land of the covenant*

6 "Thus says the LORD:
Those who support Egypt shall fall,
and her proud might shall come down;
from Migdol to Syene
they shall fall within her by the sword,
declares the Lord GOD.
7 And they shall be desolated in the midst of desolated countries,
and their cities shall be in the midst of cities that are laid waste.
8 Then they will know that I am the LORD,
when I have set fire to Egypt,
and all her helpers are broken.

9 "On that day messengers shall go out
from me in ships to terrify the unsus-
pecting people of Cush, and anguish shall
come upon them on the day of Egypt's
doom;[1] for, behold, it comes!
10 "Thus says the Lord GOD:

"I will put an end to the wealth of Egypt,
by the hand of Nebuchadnezzar king of Babylon.
11 He and his people with him, the most ruthless of nations,
shall be brought in to destroy the land,
and they shall draw their swords against Egypt
and fill the land with the slain.
12 And I will dry up the Nile
and will sell the land into the hand of evildoers;
I will bring desolation upon the land and everything in it,
by the hand of foreigners;
I am the LORD; I have spoken.

13 "Thus says the Lord GOD:

"I will destroy the idols
and put an end to the images in Memphis;
there shall no longer be a prince from the land of Egypt;
so I will put fear in the land of Egypt.
14 I will make Pathros a desolation
and will set fire to Zoan
and will execute judgments on Thebes.
15 And I will pour out my wrath on Pelusium,
the stronghold of Egypt,
and cut off the multitude[2] of Thebes.
16 And I will set fire to Egypt;
Pelusium shall be in great agony;
Thebes shall be breached,
and Memphis shall face enemies[3] by day.
17 The young men of On and of Pi-beseth shall fall by the sword,
and the women[4] shall go into captivity.
18 At Tehaphnehes the day shall be dark,
when I break there the yoke bars of Egypt,
and her proud might shall come to an end in her;
she shall be covered by a cloud,
and her daughters shall go into captivity.
19 Thus I will execute judgments on Egypt.
Then they will know that I am the LORD."

Egypt Shall Fall to Babylon

20 In the eleventh year, in the first month,
on the seventh day of the month, the word
of the LORD came to me: 21 "Son of man,
I have broken the arm of Pharaoh king of
Egypt, and behold, it has not been bound
up, to heal it by binding it with a bandage,
so that it may become strong to wield the
sword. 22 Therefore thus says the Lord GOD:
Behold, I am against Pharaoh king of Egypt
and will break his arms, both the strong

[1] Hebrew *the day of Egypt* [2] Or *wealth* [3] Or *distress* [4] Or *the cities*; Hebrew *they*

arm and the one that was broken, and I will
make the sword fall from his hand. 23 I will
scatter the Egyptians among the nations
and disperse them through the countries.
24 And I will strengthen the arms of the
king of Babylon and put my sword in his
hand, but I will break the arms of Pharaoh,
and he will groan before him like a man
mortally wounded. 25 I will strengthen the
arms of the king of Babylon, but the arms
of Pharaoh shall fall. Then they shall know
that I am the LORD, when I put my sword
into the hand of the king of Babylon and he
stretches it out against the land of Egypt.
26 And I will scatter the Egyptians among
the nations and disperse them throughout
the countries. Then they will know that I
am the LORD."

Pharaoh to Be Slain

31 In the eleventh year, in the third
month, on the first day of the
month, the word of the LORD came to me:
2 "Son of man, say to Pharaoh king of Egypt
and to his multitude:

"Whom are you like in your greatness?
3 Behold, Assyria was a cedar in
Lebanon,
with beautiful branches and forest
shade,
and of towering height,
its top among the clouds.[1]
4 The waters nourished it;
the deep made it grow tall,
making its rivers flow
around the place of its planting,
sending forth its streams
to all the trees of the field.
5 So it towered high
above all the trees of the field;
its boughs grew large
and its branches long
from abundant water in its shoots.
6 All the birds of the heavens
made their nests in its boughs;
under its branches all the beasts of
the field
gave birth to their young,
and under its shadow
lived all great nations.
7 It was beautiful in its greatness,
in the length of its branches;
for its roots went down
to abundant waters.
8 The cedars in the garden of God
could not rival it,
nor the fir trees equal its boughs;
neither were the plane trees
like its branches;
no tree in the garden of God
was its equal in beauty.
9 I made it beautiful
in the mass of its branches,
and all the trees of Eden envied it,
that were in the garden of God.

10 "Therefore thus says the Lord GOD:
Because it[2] towered high and set its top
among the clouds, and its heart was proud
of its height, 11 I will give it into the hand of
a mighty one of the nations. He shall surely
deal with it as its wickedness deserves. I
have cast it out. 12 Foreigners, the most
ruthless of nations, have cut it down and
left it. On the mountains and in all the
valleys its branches have fallen, and its
boughs have been broken in all the ravines
of the land, and all the peoples of the earth
have gone away from its shadow and left it.
13 On its fallen trunk dwell all the birds of
the heavens, and on its branches are all the
beasts of the field. 14 All this is in order that
no trees by the waters may grow to tow-
ering height or set their tops among the
clouds, and that no trees that drink water
may reach up to them in height. For they
are all given over to death, to the world
below, among the children of man,[3] with
those who go down to the pit.

15 "Thus says the Lord GOD: On the day
the cedar[4] went down to Sheol I caused
mourning; I closed the deep over it, and
restrained its rivers, and many waters were
stopped. I clothed Lebanon in gloom for
it, and all the trees of the field fainted

[1] Or *its top went through the thick boughs*; also verses 10, 14 [2] Syriac, Vulgate; Hebrew *you* [3] Or *of Adam* [4] Hebrew *it*

because of it. 16 I made the nations quake
at the sound of its fall, when I cast it down
to Sheol with those who go down to the
pit. And all the trees of Eden, the choice
and best of Lebanon, all that drink water,
were comforted in the world below. 17 They
also went down to Sheol with it, to those
who are slain by the sword; yes, those who
were its arm, who lived under its shadow
among the nations.

18 "Whom are you thus like in glory and
in greatness among the trees of Eden?
You shall be brought down with the trees
of Eden to the world below. You shall lie
among the uncircumcised, with those who
are slain by the sword.

"This is Pharaoh and all his multitude,
declares the Lord GOD."

A Lament over Pharaoh and Egypt

32 In the twelfth year, in the twelfth
month, on the first day of the
month, the word of the LORD came to me:
2 "Son of man, raise a lamentation over
Pharaoh king of Egypt and say to him:

"You consider yourself a lion of the nations,
but you are like a dragon in the seas;
you burst forth in your rivers,
trouble the waters with your feet,
and foul their rivers.
3 Thus says the Lord GOD:
I will throw my net over you
with a host of many peoples,
and they will haul you up in my dragnet.
4 And I will cast you on the ground;
on the open field I will fling you,
and will cause all the birds of the heavens to settle on you,
and I will gorge the beasts of the whole earth with you.
5 I will strew your flesh upon the mountains
and fill the valleys with your carcass.[1]
6 I will drench the land even to the mountains
with your flowing blood,
and the ravines will be full of you.
7 When I blot you out, I will cover the heavens
and make their stars dark;
I will cover the sun with a cloud,
and the moon shall not give its light.
8 All the bright lights of heaven
will I make dark over you,
and put darkness on your land,
declares the Lord GOD.

9 "I will trouble the hearts of many peo-
ples, when I bring your destruction among
the nations, into the countries that you
have not known. 10 I will make many peo-
ples appalled at you, and the hair of their
kings shall bristle with horror because of
you, when I brandish my sword before
them. They shall tremble every moment,
every one for his own life, on the day of
your downfall.

11 "For thus says the Lord GOD: The sword
of the king of Babylon shall come upon
you. 12 I will cause your multitude to fall
by the swords of mighty ones, all of them
most ruthless of nations.

"They shall bring to ruin the pride of Egypt,
and all its multitude[2] shall perish.
13 I will destroy all its beasts
from beside many waters;
and no foot of man shall trouble them anymore,
nor shall the hoofs of beasts trouble them.
14 Then I will make their waters clear,
and cause their rivers to run like oil,
declares the Lord GOD.
15 When I make the land of Egypt desolate,
and when the land is desolate of all that fills it,

[1] Hebrew *your height* [2] Or *wealth*

when I strike down all who dwell in it,
then they will know that I am the
LORD.

16 This is a lamentation that shall be chant-
ed; the daughters of the nations shall
chant it; over Egypt, and over all her mul-
titude, shall they chant it, declares the
Lord GOD."
17 In the twelfth year, in the twelfth
month,[1] on the fifteenth day of the month,
the word of the LORD came to me: 18 "Son of
man, wail over the multitude of Egypt, and
send them down, her and the daughters
of majestic nations, to the world below, to
those who have gone down to the pit:

19 'Whom do you surpass in beauty?
Go down and be laid to rest with
the uncircumcised.'

20 They shall fall amid those who are slain
by the sword. Egypt[2] is delivered to the
sword; drag her away, and all her multi-
tudes. 21 The mighty chiefs shall speak of
them, with their helpers, out of the midst of
Sheol: 'They have come down, they lie still,
the uncircumcised, slain by the sword.'
22 "Assyria is there, and all her company,
its graves all around it, all of them slain,
fallen by the sword, 23 whose graves are
set in the uttermost parts of the pit; and
her company is all around her grave, all
of them slain, fallen by the sword, who
spread terror in the land of the living.
24 "Elam is there, and all her multitude
around her grave; all of them slain, fallen
by the sword, who went down uncircum-
cised into the world below, who spread
their terror in the land of the living; and
they bear their shame with those who go
down to the pit. 25 They have made her a
bed among the slain with all her multi-
tude, her graves all around it, all of them
uncircumcised, slain by the sword; for
terror of them was spread in the land of
the living, and they bear their shame with
those who go down to the pit; they are
placed among the slain.
26 "Meshech-Tubal is there, and all her
multitude, her graves all around it, all of
them uncircumcised, slain by the sword;
for they spread their terror in the land of
the living. 27 And they do not lie with the
mighty, the fallen from among the uncir-
cumcised, who went down to Sheol with
their weapons of war, whose swords were
laid under their heads, and whose iniqui-
ties are upon their bones; for the terror of
the mighty men was in the land of the liv-
ing. 28 But as for you, you shall be broken
and lie among the uncircumcised, with
those who are slain by the sword.
29 "Edom is there, her kings and all her
princes, who for all their might are laid
with those who are killed by the sword;
they lie with the uncircumcised, with
those who go down to the pit.
30 "The princes of the north are there,
all of them, and all the Sidonians, who
have gone down in shame with the slain,
for all the terror that they caused by their
might; they lie uncircumcised with those
who are slain by the sword, and bear their
shame with those who go down to the pit.
31 "When Pharaoh sees them, he will be
comforted for all his multitude, Pharaoh
and all his army, slain by the sword,
declares the Lord GOD. 32 For I spread ter-
ror in the land of the living; and he shall
be laid to rest among the uncircumcised,
with those who are slain by the sword,
Pharaoh and all his multitude, declares
the Lord GOD."

Ezekiel Is Israel's Watchman

33 The word of the LORD came to me:
2 "Son of man, speak to your peo-
ple and say to them, If I bring the sword
upon a land, and the people of the land
take a man from among them, and make
him their watchman, 3 and if he sees the
sword coming upon the land and blows
the trumpet and warns the people, 4 then if
anyone who hears the sound of the trum-
pet does not take warning, and the sword

[1] Hebrew lacks *in the twelfth month* [2] Hebrew *She*

comes and takes him away, his blood shall be upon his own head. 5 He heard the sound of the trumpet and did not take warning; his blood shall be upon himself. But if he had taken warning, he would have saved his life. 6 But if the watchman sees the sword coming and does not blow the trumpet, so that the people are not warned, and the sword comes and takes any one of them, that person is taken away in his iniquity, but his blood I will require at the watchman's hand.

7 "So you, son of man, I have made a watchman for the house of Israel. Whenever you hear a word from my mouth, you shall give them warning from me. 8 If I say to the wicked, O wicked one, you shall surely die, and you do not speak to warn the wicked to turn from his way, that wicked person shall die in his iniquity, but his blood I will require at your hand. 9 But if you warn the wicked to turn from his way, and he does not turn from his way, that person shall die in his iniquity, but you will have delivered your soul.

Why Will You Die, Israel?

10 "And you, son of man, say to the house of Israel, Thus have you said: 'Surely our transgressions and our sins are upon us, and we rot away because of them. How then can we live?' 11 Say to them, As I live, declares the Lord GOD, I have no pleasure in the death of the wicked, but that the wicked turn from his way and live; turn back, turn back from your evil ways, for why will you die, O house of Israel?

12 "And you, son of man, say to your people, The righteousness of the righteous shall not deliver him when he transgresses, and as for the wickedness of the wicked, he shall not fall by it when he turns from his wickedness, and the righteous shall not be able to live by his righteousness[1] when he sins. 13 Though I say to the righteous that he shall surely live, yet if he trusts in his righteousness and does injustice, none of his righteous deeds shall be remembered, but in his injustice that he has done he shall die. 14 Again, though I say to the wicked, 'You shall surely die,' yet if he turns from his sin and does what is just and right, 15 if the wicked restores the pledge, gives back what he has taken by robbery, and walks in the statutes of life, not doing injustice, he shall surely live; he shall not die. 16 None of the sins that he has committed shall be remembered against him. He has done what is just and right; he shall surely live.

17 "Yet your people say, 'The way of the Lord is not just,' when it is their own way that is not just. 18 When the righteous turns from his righteousness and does injustice, he shall die for it. 19 And when the wicked turns from his wickedness and does what is just and right, he shall live by this. 20 Yet you say, 'The way of the Lord is not just.' O house of Israel, I will judge each of you according to his ways."

Jerusalem Struck Down

21 In the twelfth year of our exile, in the tenth month, on the fifth day of the month, a fugitive from Jerusalem came to me and said, "The city has been struck down." 22 Now the hand of the LORD had been upon me the evening before the fugitive came; and he had opened my mouth by the time the man came to me in the morning, so my mouth was opened, and I was no longer mute.

23 The word of the LORD came to me: 24 "Son of man, the inhabitants of these waste places in the land of Israel keep saying, 'Abraham was only one man, yet he got possession of the land; but we are many; the land is surely given us to possess.' 25 Therefore say to them, Thus says the Lord GOD: You eat flesh with the blood and lift up your eyes to your idols and shed blood; shall you then possess the land? 26 You rely on the sword, you commit abominations, and each of you defiles his neighbor's wife;

[1] Hebrew *by it*

shall you then possess the land? 27 Say this to them, Thus says the Lord GOD: As I live, surely those who are in the waste places shall fall by the sword, and whoever is in the open field I will give to the beasts to be devoured, and those who are in strongholds and in caves shall die by pestilence. 28 And I will make the land a desolation and a waste, and her proud might shall come to an end, and the mountains of Israel shall be so desolate that none will pass through. 29 Then they will know that I am the LORD, when I have made the land a desolation and a waste because of all their abominations that they have committed.

30 "As for you, son of man, your people who talk together about you by the walls and at the doors of the houses, say to one another, each to his brother, 'Come, and hear what the word is that comes from the LORD.' 31 And they come to you as people come, and they sit before you as my people, and they hear what you say but they will not do it; for with lustful talk in their mouths they act; their heart is set on their gain. 32 And behold, you are to them like one who sings lustful songs with a beautiful voice and plays[1] well on an instrument, for they hear what you say, but they will not do it. 33 When this comes—and come it will!—then they will know that a prophet has been among them."

Prophecy Against the Shepherds of Israel

34 The word of the LORD came to me: 2 "Son of man, prophesy against the shepherds of Israel; prophesy, and say to them, even to the shepherds, Thus says the Lord GOD: Ah, shepherds of Israel who have been feeding yourselves! Should not shepherds feed the sheep? 3 You eat the fat, you clothe yourselves with the wool, you slaughter the fat ones, but you do not feed the sheep. 4 The weak you have not strengthened, the sick you have not healed, the injured you have not bound up, the strayed you have not brought back, the lost you have not sought, and with force and harshness you have ruled them. 5 So they were scattered, because there was no shepherd, and they became food for all the wild beasts. 6 My sheep were scattered; they wandered over all the mountains and on every high hill. My sheep were scattered over all the face of the earth, with none to search or seek for them.

7 "Therefore, you shepherds, hear the word of the LORD: 8 As I live, declares the Lord GOD, surely because my sheep have become a prey, and my sheep have become food for all the wild beasts, since there was no shepherd, and because my shepherds have not searched for my sheep, but the shepherds have fed themselves, and have not fed my sheep, 9 therefore, you shepherds, hear the word of the LORD: 10 Thus says the Lord GOD, Behold, I am against the shepherds, and I will require my sheep at their hand and put a stop to their feeding the sheep. No longer shall the shepherds feed themselves. I will rescue my sheep from their mouths, that they may not be food for them.

The Lord GOD Will Seek Them Out

11 "For thus says the Lord GOD: Behold, I, I myself will search for my sheep and will seek them out. 12 As a shepherd seeks out his flock when he is among his sheep that have been scattered, so will I seek out my sheep, and I will rescue them from all places where they have been scattered on a day of clouds and thick darkness. 13 And I will bring them out from the peoples and gather them from the countries, and will bring them into their own land. And I will feed them on the mountains of Israel, by the ravines, and in all the inhabited places of the country. 14 I will feed them with good pasture, and on the mountain heights of Israel shall be their grazing land. There they shall lie down in good grazing land, and on rich pasture they shall feed on the mountains of Israel. 15 I myself

[1] Hebrew *like the singing of lustful songs with a beautiful voice and one who plays*

will be the shepherd of my sheep, and I myself will make them lie down, declares the Lord GOD. 16 I will seek the lost, and I will bring back the strayed, and I will bind up the injured, and I will strengthen the weak, and the fat and the strong I will destroy.[1] I will feed them in justice.

17 "As for you, my flock, thus says the Lord GOD: Behold, I judge between sheep and sheep, between rams and male goats. 18 Is it not enough for you to feed on the good pasture, that you must tread down with your feet the rest of your pasture; and to drink of clear water, that you must muddy the rest of the water with your feet? 19 And must my sheep eat what you have trodden with your feet, and drink what you have muddied with your feet?

20 "Therefore, thus says the Lord GOD to them: Behold, I, I myself will judge between the fat sheep and the lean sheep. 21 Because you push with side and shoulder, and thrust at all the weak with your horns, till you have scattered them abroad, 22 I will rescue[2] my flock; they shall no longer be a prey. And I will judge between sheep and sheep. 23 And I will set up over them one shepherd, my servant David, and he shall feed them: he shall feed them and be their shepherd. 24 And I, the LORD, will be their God, and my servant David shall be prince among them. I am the LORD; I have spoken.

The LORD's Covenant of Peace

25 "I will make with them a covenant of peace and banish wild beasts from the land, so that they may dwell securely in the wilderness and sleep in the woods. 26 And I will make them and the places all around my hill a blessing, and I will send down the showers in their season; they shall be showers of blessing. 27 And the trees of the field *shall yield* their fruit, and the earth shall yield its increase, and they shall be secure in their land. And they shall know that I am the LORD, when I break the bars of their yoke, and deliver them from the hand of those who enslaved them. 28 They shall no more be a prey to the nations, nor shall the beasts of the land devour them. They shall dwell securely, and none shall make them afraid. 29 And I will provide for them renowned plantations so that they shall no more be consumed with hunger in the land, and no longer suffer the reproach of the nations. 30 And they shall know that I am the LORD their God with them, and that they, the house of Israel, are my people, declares the Lord GOD. 31 And you are my sheep, human sheep of my pasture, and I am your God, declares the Lord GOD."

Prophecy Against Mount Seir

35 The word of the LORD came to me: 2 "Son of man, set your face against Mount Seir, and prophesy against it, 3 and say to it, Thus says the Lord GOD: Behold, I am against you, Mount Seir, and I will stretch out my hand against you, and I will make you a desolation and a waste. 4 I will lay your cities waste, and you shall become a desolation, and you shall know that I am the LORD. 5 Because you cherished perpetual enmity and gave over the people of Israel to the power of the sword at the time of their calamity, at the time of their final punishment, 6 therefore, as I live, declares the Lord GOD, I will prepare you for blood, and blood shall pursue you; because you did not hate bloodshed, therefore blood shall pursue you. 7 I will make Mount Seir a waste and a desolation, and I will cut off from it all who come and go. 8 And I will fill its mountains with the slain. On your hills and in your valleys and in all your ravines those slain with the sword shall fall. 9 I will make you a perpetual desolation, and your cities shall not be inhabited. Then you will know that I am the LORD.

10 "Because you said, 'These two nations and these two countries shall be mine, and we will take possession of them'—although

[1] Septuagint, Syriac, Vulgate *I will watch over* [2] Or *save*

the LORD was there— 11 therefore, as I live,
declares the Lord GOD, I will deal with you
according to the anger and envy that you
showed because of your hatred against
them. And I will make myself known
among them, when I judge you. 12 And you
shall know that I am the LORD.

"I have heard all the revilings that you
uttered against the mountains of Israel,
saying, 'They are laid desolate; they are
given us to devour.' 13 And you magnified
yourselves against me with your mouth,
and multiplied your words against me; I
heard it. 14 Thus says the Lord GOD: While
the whole earth rejoices, I will make you
desolate. 15 As you rejoiced over the inheri-
tance of the house of Israel, because it was
desolate, so I will deal with you; you shall
be desolate, Mount Seir, and all Edom, all of
it. Then they will know that I am the LORD.

Prophecy to the Mountains of Israel

36 "And you, son of man, prophesy to
the mountains of Israel, and say, O
mountains of Israel, hear the word of the
LORD. 2 Thus says the Lord GOD: Because
the enemy said of you, 'Aha!' and, 'The
ancient heights have become our posses-
sion,' 3 therefore prophesy, and say, Thus
says the Lord GOD: Precisely because they
made you desolate and crushed you from
all sides, so that you became the posses-
sion of the rest of the nations, and you
became the talk and evil gossip of the peo-
ple, 4 therefore, O mountains of Israel, hear
the word of the Lord GOD: Thus says the
Lord GOD to the mountains and the hills,
the ravines and the valleys, the desolate
wastes and the deserted cities, which have
become a prey and derision to the rest of
the nations all around, 5 therefore thus
says the Lord GOD: Surely I have spoken
in my hot jealousy against the rest of the
nations and against all Edom, who gave
my land to themselves as a possession
with wholehearted joy and utter contempt,
that they might make its pasturelands a
prey. 6 Therefore prophesy concerning
the land of Israel, and say to the moun-
tains and hills, to the ravines and valleys,
Thus says the Lord GOD: Behold, I have
spoken in my jealous wrath, because you
have suffered the reproach of the nations.
7 Therefore thus says the Lord GOD: I swear
that the nations that are all around you
shall themselves suffer reproach.

8 "But you, O mountains of Israel, shall
shoot forth your branches and yield your
fruit to my people Israel, for they will soon
come home. 9 For behold, I am for you, and
I will turn to you, and you shall be tilled
and sown. 10 And I will multiply people
on you, the whole house of Israel, all of it.
The cities shall be inhabited and the waste
places rebuilt. 11 And I will multiply on
you man and beast, and they shall multi-
ply and be fruitful. And I will cause you to
be inhabited as in your former times, and
will do more good to you than ever before.
Then you will know that I am the LORD. 12 I
will let people walk on you, even my people
Israel. And they shall possess you, and you
shall be their inheritance, and you shall no
longer bereave them of children. 13 Thus
says the Lord GOD: Because they say to you,
'You devour people, and you bereave your
nation of children,' 14 therefore you shall
no longer devour people and no longer
bereave your nation of children, declares
the Lord GOD. 15 And I will not let you hear
anymore the reproach of the nations, and
you shall no longer bear the disgrace of the
peoples and no longer cause your nation to
stumble, declares the Lord GOD."

The LORD's Concern for His Holy Name

16 The word of the LORD came to me:
17 "Son of man, when the house of Israel
lived in their own land, they defiled it by
their ways and their deeds. Their ways
before me were like the uncleanness of a
woman in her menstrual impurity. 18 So I
poured out my wrath upon them for the
blood that they had shed in the land, for

the idols with which they had defiled it. 19 I scattered them among the nations, and they were dispersed through the countries. In accordance with their ways and their deeds I judged them. 20 But when they came to the nations, wherever they came, they profaned my holy name, in that people said of them, 'These are the people of the LORD, and yet they had to go out of his land.' 21 But I had concern for my holy name, which the house of Israel had profaned among the nations to which they came.

I Will Put My Spirit Within You

22 "Therefore say to the house of Israel, Thus says the Lord GOD: It is not for your sake, O house of Israel, that I am about to act, but for the sake of my holy name, which you have profaned among the nations to which you came. 23 And I will vindicate the holiness of my great name, which has been profaned among the nations, and which you have profaned among them. And the nations will know that I am the LORD, declares the Lord GOD, when through you I vindicate my holiness before their eyes. 24 I will take you from the nations and gather you from all the countries and bring you into your own land. 25 I will sprinkle clean water on you, and you shall be clean from all your uncleannesses, and from all your idols I will cleanse you. 26 And I will give you a new heart, and a new spirit I will put within you. And I will remove the heart of stone from your flesh and give you a heart of flesh. 27 And I will put my Spirit within you, and cause you to walk in my statutes and be careful to obey my rules.[1] 28 You shall dwell in the land that I gave to your fathers, and you shall be my people, and I will be your God. 29 And I will deliver you from all your uncleannesses. And I will summon the grain and make *it* abundant and lay no famine upon you. 30 I will make the fruit of the tree and the increase of the field abundant, that you may never again suffer the disgrace of famine among the nations. 31 Then you will remember your evil ways, and your deeds that were not good, and you will loathe yourselves for your iniquities and your abominations. 32 It is not for your sake that I will act, declares the Lord GOD; let that be known to you. Be ashamed and confounded for your ways, O house of Israel.

33 "Thus says the Lord GOD: On the day that I cleanse you from all your iniquities, I will cause the cities to be inhabited, and the waste places shall be rebuilt. 34 And the land that was desolate shall be tilled, instead of being the desolation that it was in the sight of all who passed by. 35 And they will say, 'This land that was desolate has become like the garden of Eden, and the waste and desolate and ruined cities are now fortified and inhabited.' 36 Then the nations that are left all around you shall know that I am the LORD; I have rebuilt the ruined places and replanted that which was desolate. I am the LORD; I have spoken, and I will do it.

37 "Thus says the Lord GOD: This also I will let the house of Israel ask me to do for them: to increase their people like a flock. 38 Like the flock for sacrifices,[2] like the flock at Jerusalem during her appointed feasts, so shall the waste cities be filled with flocks of people. Then they will know that I am the LORD."

The Valley of Dry Bones

37 The hand of the LORD was upon me, and he brought me out in the Spirit of the LORD and set me down in the middle of the valley;[3] it was full of bones. 2 And he led me around among them, and behold, there were very many on the surface of the valley, and behold, they were very dry. 3 And he said to me, "Son of man, can these bones live?" And I answered, "O Lord GOD, you know." 4 Then he said to me, "Prophesy over these bones, and say to them, O dry bones, hear the word of the LORD. 5 Thus says the Lord GOD to these

[1] Or *my just decrees* [2] Hebrew *flock of holy things* [3] Or *plain*; also verse 2

bones: Behold, I will cause breath[1] to enter you, and you shall live. 6 And I will lay sinews upon you, and will cause flesh to come upon you, and cover you with skin, and put breath in you, and you shall live, and you shall know that I am the LORD."

7 So I prophesied as I was commanded. And as I prophesied, there was a sound, and behold, a rattling,[2] and the bones came together, bone to its bone. 8 And I looked, and behold, there were sinews on them, and flesh had come upon them, and skin had covered them. But there was no breath in them. 9 Then he said to me, "Prophesy to the breath; prophesy, son of man, and say to the breath, Thus says the Lord GOD: Come from the four winds, O breath, and breathe on these slain, that they may live." 10 So I prophesied as he commanded me, and the breath came into them, and they lived and stood on their feet, an exceedingly great army.

11 Then he said to me, "Son of man, these bones are the whole house of Israel. Behold, they say, 'Our bones are dried up, and our hope is lost; we are indeed cut off.' 12 Therefore prophesy, and say to them, Thus says the Lord GOD: Behold, I will open your graves and raise you from your graves, O my people. And I will bring you into the land of Israel. 13 And you shall know that I am the LORD, when I open your graves, and raise you from your graves, O my people. 14 And I will put my Spirit within you, and you shall live, and I will place you in your own land. Then you shall know that I am the LORD; I have spoken, and I will do it, declares the LORD."

I Will Be Their God, They Shall Be My People

15 The word of the LORD came to me: 16 "Son of man, take a stick[3] and write on it, 'For Judah, and the people of Israel associated with him'; then take another stick and write on it, 'For Joseph (the stick of Ephraim) and all the house of Israel associated with him.' 17 And join them one to another into one stick, that they may become one in your hand. 18 And when your people say to you, 'Will you not tell us what you mean by these?' 19 say to them, Thus says the Lord GOD: Behold, I am about to take the stick of Joseph (that is in the hand of Ephraim) and the tribes of Israel associated with him. And I will join with it the stick of Judah,[4] and make them one stick, that they may be one in my hand. 20 When the sticks on which you write are in your hand before their eyes, 21 then say to them, Thus says the Lord GOD: Behold, I will take the people of Israel from the nations among which they have gone, and will gather them from all around, and bring them to their own land. 22 And I will make them one nation in the land, on the mountains of Israel. And one king shall be king over them all, and they shall be no longer two nations, and no longer divided into two kingdoms. 23 They shall not defile themselves anymore with their idols and their detestable things, or with any of their transgressions. But I will save them from all the backslidings[5] in which they have sinned, and will cleanse them; and they shall be my people, and I will be their God.

24 "My servant David shall be king
over them, and they shall all have
499, one shepherd. They shall walk
1033, in my rules and be careful to obey
1433 my statutes. 25 They shall dwell in the land that I gave to my servant Jacob, where your fathers lived. They and their children and their children's children shall dwell there forever, and David my servant shall be their prince forever. 26 I will make a covenant of peace with them. It shall be an everlasting covenant with them. And I will set them in their land[6] and multiply them, and will set my sanctuary in their midst forevermore. 27 My dwelling place shall be with them, and I will be their God, and they shall be my people. 28 Then the nations will know that I am the LORD who

[1] Or *spirit*; also verses 6, 9, 10 [2] Or *an earthquake* (compare 3:12, 13) [3] Or *one piece of wood*; also verses 17, 19, 20 [4] Hebrew *And I will place them on it, the stick of Judah* [5] Many Hebrew manuscripts; other Hebrew manuscripts *dwellings* [6] Hebrew lacks *in their land*

sanctifies Israel, when my sanctuary is in their midst forevermore."

Prophecy Against Gog

38 The word of the LORD came to me: 2 "Son of man, set your face toward Gog, of the land of Magog, the chief prince of Meshech[1] and Tubal, and prophesy against him 3 and say, Thus says the Lord GOD: Behold, I am against you, O Gog, chief prince of Meshech[2] and Tubal. 4 And I will turn you about and put hooks into your jaws, and I will bring you out, and all your army, horses and horsemen, all of them clothed in full armor, a great host, all of them with buckler and shield, wielding swords. 5 Persia, Cush, and Put are with them, all of them with shield and helmet; 6 Gomer and all his hordes; Beth-togarmah from the uttermost parts of the north with all his hordes—many peoples are with you.

7 "Be ready and keep ready, you and all your hosts that are assembled about you, and be a guard for them. 8 After many days you will be mustered. In the latter years you will go against the land that is restored from war, the land whose people were gathered from many peoples upon the mountains of Israel, which had been a continual waste. Its people were brought out from the peoples and now dwell securely, all of them. 9 You will advance, coming on like a storm. You will be like a cloud covering the land, you and all your hordes, and many peoples with you.

10 "Thus says the Lord GOD: On that day, thoughts will come into your mind, and you will devise an evil scheme 11 and say, 'I will go up against the land of unwalled villages. I will fall upon the quiet people who dwell securely, all of them dwelling without walls, and having no bars or gates,' 12 to seize spoil and carry off plunder, to turn your hand against the waste places that are now inhabited, and the people who were gathered from the nations, who have acquired livestock and goods, who dwell at the center of the earth. 13 Sheba and Dedan and the merchants of Tarshish and all its leaders[3] will say to you, 'Have you come to seize spoil? Have you assembled your hosts to carry off plunder, to carry away silver and gold, to take away livestock and goods, to seize great spoil?'

14 "Therefore, son of man, prophesy, and say to Gog, Thus says the Lord GOD: On that day when my people Israel are dwelling securely, will you not know it? 15 You will come from your place out of the uttermost parts of the north, you and many peoples with you, all of them riding on horses, a great host, a mighty army. 16 You will come up against my people Israel, like a cloud covering the land. In the latter days I will bring you against my land, that the nations may know me, when through you, O Gog, I vindicate my holiness before their eyes.

17 "Thus says the Lord GOD: Are you he of whom I spoke in former days by my servants the prophets of Israel, who in those days prophesied for years that I would bring you against them? 18 But on that day, the day that Gog shall come against the land of Israel, declares the Lord GOD, my wrath will be roused in my anger. 19 For in my jealousy and in my blazing wrath I declare, On that day there shall be a great earthquake in the land of Israel. 20 The fish of the sea and the birds of the heavens and the beasts of the field and all creeping things that creep on the ground, and all the people who are on the face of the earth, shall quake at my presence. And the mountains shall be thrown down, and the cliffs shall fall, and every wall shall tumble to the ground. 21 I will summon a sword against Gog[4] on all my mountains, declares the Lord GOD. Every man's sword will be against his brother. 22 With pestilence and bloodshed I will enter into judgment with him, and I will rain upon him and his hordes and the many peoples who are with him torrential rains and hailstones, fire and sulfur. 23 So I will show

[1] Or *Magog, the prince of Rosh, Meshech* [2] Or *Gog, prince of Rosh, Meshech* [3] Hebrew *young lions* [4] Hebrew *against him*

my greatness and my holiness and make
myself known in the eyes of many nations.
Then they will know that I am the LORD.

39 "And you, son of man, prophesy
against Gog and say, Thus says the
Lord GOD: Behold, I am against you, O Gog,
chief prince of Meshech[1] and Tubal. 2 And I
will turn you about and drive you forward,
and bring you up from the uttermost parts
of the north, and lead you against the
mountains of Israel. 3 Then I will strike
your bow from your left hand, and will
make your arrows drop out of your right
hand. 4 You shall fall on the mountains
of Israel, you and all your hordes and the
peoples who are with you. I will give you
to birds of prey of every sort and to the
beasts of the field to be devoured. 5 You
shall fall in the open field, for I have spo-
ken, declares the Lord GOD. 6 I will send
fire on Magog and on those who dwell
securely in the coastlands, and they shall
know that I am the LORD.

7 "And my holy name I will make known
in the midst of my people Israel, and I will
not let my holy name be profaned any-
more. And the nations shall know that I am
the LORD, the Holy One in Israel. 8 Behold,
it is coming and it will be brought about,
declares the Lord GOD. That is the day of
which I have spoken.

9 "Then those who dwell in the cit-
ies of Israel will go out and make fires
of the weapons and burn them, shields
and bucklers, bow and arrows, clubs[2] and
spears; and they will make fires of them
for seven years, 10 so that they will not
need to take wood out of the field or cut
down any out of the forests, for they will
make their fires of the weapons. They will
seize the spoil of those who despoiled
them, and plunder those who plundered
them, declares the Lord GOD.

11 "On that day I will give to Gog a
place for burial in Israel, the Valley of the
Travelers, east of the sea. It will block the
travelers, for there Gog and all his mul-
titude will be buried. It will be called the
Valley of Hamon-gog.[3] 12 For seven months
the house of Israel will be burying them,
in order to cleanse the land. 13 All the peo-
ple of the land will bury them, and it will
bring them renown on the day that I show
my glory, declares the Lord GOD. 14 They
will set apart men to travel through the
land regularly and bury those travelers
remaining on the face of the land, so as
to cleanse it. At[4] the end of seven months
they will make their search. 15 And when
these travel through the land and anyone
sees a human bone, then he shall set up a
sign by it, till the buriers have buried it in
the Valley of Hamon-gog. 16 (Hamonah[5] is
also the name of the city.) Thus shall they
cleanse the land.

17 "As for you, son of man, thus says the
Lord GOD: Speak to the birds of every sort
and to all beasts of the field, 'Assemble
and come, gather from all around to the
sacrificial feast that I am preparing for
you, a great sacrificial feast on the moun-
tains of Israel, and you shall eat flesh and
drink blood. 18 You shall eat the flesh of
the mighty, and drink the blood of the
princes of the earth—of rams, of lambs,
and of he-goats, of bulls, all of them fat
beasts of Bashan. 19 And you shall eat fat
till you are filled, and drink blood till you
are drunk, at the sacrificial feast that I
am preparing for you. 20 And you shall be
filled at my table with horses and chari-
oteers, with mighty men and all kinds of
warriors,' declares the Lord GOD.

21 "And I will set my glory among the
nations, and all the nations shall see
my judgment that I have executed, and
my hand that I have laid on them. 22 The
house of Israel shall know that I am the
LORD their God, from that day forward.
23 And the nations shall know that the
house of Israel went into captivity for
their iniquity, because they dealt so
treacherously with me that I hid my face
from them and gave them into the hand

[1] Or *Gog, prince of Rosh, Meshech* [2] Or *javelins* [3] *Hamon-gog* means *the multitude of Gog* [4] Or *Until* [5] *Hamonah* means *multitude*

of their adversaries, and they all fell by the sword. **24** I dealt with them according to their uncleanness and their transgressions, and hid my face from them.

The LORD Will Restore Israel

25 "Therefore thus says the Lord GOD: Now I will restore the fortunes of Jacob and have mercy on the whole house of Israel, and I will be jealous for my holy name. **26** They shall forget their shame and all the treachery they have practiced against me, when they dwell securely in their land with none to make them afraid, **27** when I have brought them back from the peoples and gathered them from their enemies' lands, and through them have vindicated my holiness in the sight of many nations. **28** Then they shall know that I am the LORD their God, because I sent them into exile among the nations and then assembled them into their own land. I will leave none of them remaining among the nations anymore. **29** And I will not hide my face anymore from them, when I pour out my Spirit upon the house of Israel, declares the Lord GOD."

Vision of the New Temple

40 In the twenty-fifth year of our exile, at the beginning of the year, on the tenth day of the month, in the fourteenth year after the city was struck down, on that very day, the hand of the LORD was upon me, and he brought me to the city.[1] **2** In visions of God he brought me to the land of Israel, and set me down on a very high mountain, on which was a structure like a city to the south. **3** When he brought me there, behold, there was a man whose appearance was like bronze, with a linen cord and a measuring reed in his hand. And he was standing in the gateway. **4** And the man said to me, "Son of man, look with your eyes, and hear with your ears, and set your heart upon all that I shall show you, for you were brought here in order that I might show it to you. Declare all that you see to the house of Israel."

The East Gate to the Outer Court

5 And behold, there was a wall all around the outside of the temple area, and the length of the measuring reed in the man's hand was six long cubits, each being a cubit and a handbreadth[2] in length. So he measured the thickness of the wall, one reed; and the height, one reed. **6** Then he went into the gateway facing east, going up its steps, and measured the threshold of the gate, one reed deep.[3] **7** And the side rooms, one reed long and one reed broad; and the space between the side rooms, five cubits; and the threshold of the gate by the vestibule of the gate at the inner end, one reed. **8** Then he measured the vestibule of the gateway, on the inside, one reed. **9** Then he measured the vestibule of the gateway, eight cubits; and its jambs, two cubits; and the vestibule of the gate was at the inner end. **10** And there were three side rooms on either side of the east gate. The three were of the same size, and the jambs on either side were of the same size. **11** Then he measured the width of the opening of the gateway, ten cubits; and the length of the gateway, thirteen cubits. **12** There was a barrier before the side rooms, one cubit on either side. And the side rooms were six cubits on either side. **13** Then he measured the gate from the ceiling of the one side room to the ceiling of the other, a breadth of twenty-five cubits; the openings faced each other. **14** He measured also the vestibule, twenty cubits. And around the vestibule of the gateway was the court.[4] **15** From the front of the gate at the entrance to the front of the inner vestibule of the gate was fifty cubits. **16** And the gateway had windows all around, narrowing inwards toward the side rooms and toward their jambs, and likewise the vestibule had windows all around inside, and on the jambs were palm trees.

[1] Hebrew *brought me there* [2] A *cubit* was about 18 inches or 45 centimeters; a *handbreadth* was about 3 inches or 7.5 centimeters [3] Hebrew *deep, and one threshold, one reed deep* [4] Text uncertain; Hebrew *And he made the jambs sixty cubits, and to the jamb of the court was the gateway all around*

The Outer Court

17 Then he brought me into the outer court. And behold, there were chambers and a pavement, all around the court. Thirty chambers faced the pavement. 18 And the pavement ran along the side of the gates, corresponding to the length of the gates. This was the lower pavement. 19 Then he measured the distance from the inner front of the lower gate to the outer front of the inner court,[1] a hundred cubits on the east side and on the north side.[2]

The North Gate

20 As for the gate that faced toward the north, belonging to the outer court, he measured its length and its breadth. 21 Its side rooms, three on either side, and its jambs and its vestibule were of the same size as those of the first gate. Its length was fifty cubits, and its breadth twenty-five cubits. 22 And its windows, its vestibule, and its palm trees were of the same size as those of the gate that faced toward the east. And by seven steps people would go up to it, and find its vestibule before them. 23 And opposite the gate on the north, as on the east, was a gate to the inner court. And he measured from gate to gate, a hundred cubits.

The South Gate

24 And he led me toward the south, and behold, there was a gate on the south. And he measured its jambs and its vestibule; they had the same size as the others. 25 Both it and its vestibule had windows all around, like the windows of the others. Its length was fifty cubits, and its breadth twenty-five cubits. 26 And there were seven steps leading up to it, and its vestibule was before them, and it had palm trees on its jambs, one on either side. 27 And there was a gate on the south of the inner court. And he measured from gate to gate toward the south, a hundred cubits.

The Inner Court

28 Then he brought me to the inner court through the south gate, and he measured the south gate. It was of the same size as the others. 29 Its side rooms, its jambs, and its vestibule were of the same size as the others, and both it and its vestibule had windows all around. Its length was fifty cubits, and its breadth twenty-five cubits. 30 And there were vestibules all around, twenty-five cubits long and five cubits broad. 31 Its vestibule faced the outer court, and palm trees were on its jambs, and its stairway had eight steps.

32 Then he brought me to the inner court on the east side, and he measured the gate. It was of the same size as the others. 33 Its side rooms, its jambs, and its vestibule were of the same size as the others, and both it and its vestibule had windows all around. Its length was fifty cubits, and its breadth twenty-five cubits. 34 Its vestibule faced the outer court, and it had palm trees on its jambs, on either side, and its stairway had eight steps.

35 Then he brought me to the north gate, and he measured it. It had the same size as the others. 36 Its side rooms, its jambs, and its vestibule were of the same size as the others,[3] and it had windows all around. Its length was fifty cubits, and its breadth twenty-five cubits. 37 Its vestibule[4] faced the outer court, and it had palm trees on its jambs, on either side, and its stairway had eight steps.

38 There was a chamber with its door in the vestibule of the gate,[5] where the burnt offering was to be washed. 39 And in the vestibule of the gate were two tables on either side, on which the burnt offering and the sin offering and the guilt offering were to be slaughtered. 40 And off to the side, on the outside as one goes up to the entrance of the north gate, were two tables; and off to the other side of the vestibule of the gate were two tables. 41 Four

[1] Hebrew *distance from before the low gate before the inner court to the outside* [2] Or *cubits. So far the eastern gate; now to the northern gate.* [3] One manuscript (compare verses 29 and 33); most manuscripts lack *were of the same size as the others* [4] Septuagint, Vulgate (compare verses 26, 31, 34); Hebrew *jambs* [5] Hebrew *at the jambs, the gates*

tables were on either side of the gate, eight tables, on which to slaughter. 42 And there were four tables of hewn stone for the burnt offering, a cubit and a half long, and a cubit and a half broad, and one cubit high, on which the instruments were to be laid with which the burnt offerings and the sacrifices were slaughtered. 43 And hooks,[1] a handbreadth long, were fastened all around within. And on the tables the flesh of the offering was to be laid.

Chambers for the Priests

44 On the outside of the inner gateway there were two chambers[2] in the inner court, one[3] at the side of the north gate facing south, the other at the side of the south[4] gate facing north. 45 And he said to me, This chamber that faces south is for the priests who have charge of the temple, 46 and the chamber that faces north is for the priests who have charge of the altar. These are the sons of Zadok, who alone[5] among the sons of Levi may come near to the LORD to minister to him. 47 And he measured the court, a hundred cubits long and a hundred cubits broad, a square. And the altar was in front of the temple.

The Vestibule of the Temple

48 Then he brought me to the vestibule of the temple and measured the jambs of the vestibule, five cubits on either side. And the breadth of the gate was fourteen cubits, and the sidewalls of the gate[6] were three cubits on either side. 49 The length of the vestibule was twenty cubits, and the breadth twelve[7] cubits, and people would go up to it by ten steps.[8] And there were pillars beside the jambs, one on either side.

The Inner Temple

41 Then he brought me to the nave and measured the jambs. On each side six cubits[9] was the breadth of the jambs.[10] 2 And the breadth of the entrance was ten cubits, and the sidewalls of the entrance were five cubits on either side. And he measured the length of the nave,[11] forty cubits, and its breadth, twenty cubits. 3 Then he went into the inner room and measured the jambs of the entrance, two cubits; and the entrance, six cubits; and the sidewalls on either side[12] of the entrance, seven cubits. 4 And he measured the length of the room, twenty cubits, and its breadth, twenty cubits, across the nave. And he said to me, "This is the Most Holy Place."

5 Then he measured the wall of the temple, six cubits thick, and the breadth of the side chambers, four cubits, all around the temple. 6 And the side chambers were in three stories, one over another, thirty in each story. There were offsets[13] all around the wall of the temple to serve as supports for the side chambers, so that they should not be supported by the wall of the temple. 7 And it became broader as it wound upward to the side chambers, because the temple was enclosed upward all around the temple. Thus the temple had a broad area upward, and so one went up from the lowest story to the top story through the middle story. 8 I saw also that the temple had a raised platform all around; the foundations of the side chambers measured a full reed of six long cubits. 9 The thickness of the outer wall of the side chambers was five cubits. The free space between the side chambers of the temple and the 10 other chambers was a breadth of twenty cubits all around the temple on every side. 11 And the doors of the side chambers opened on the free space, one door toward the north, and another door toward the south. And the breadth of the free space was five cubits all around.

12 The building that was facing the separate yard on the west side was seventy cubits broad, and the wall of the building

[1] Or *shelves* [2] Septuagint; Hebrew *were chambers for singers* [3] Hebrew lacks *one* [4] Septuagint; Hebrew *east* [5] Hebrew lacks *alone* [6] Septuagint; Hebrew lacks *was fourteen cubits, and the sidewalls of the gate* [7] Septuagint; Hebrew *eleven* [8] Septuagint; Hebrew *and by steps that would go up to it* [9] *A cubit* was about 18 inches or 45 centimeters [10] Compare Septuagint; Hebrew *tent* [11] Hebrew *its length* [12] Septuagint; Hebrew *and the breadth* [13] Septuagint, compare 1 Kings 6:6; the meaning of the Hebrew word is uncertain

was five cubits thick all around, and its length ninety cubits.

13 Then he measured the temple, a hundred cubits long; and the yard and the building with its walls, a hundred cubits long; 14 also the breadth of the east front of the temple and the yard, a hundred cubits.

15 Then he measured the length of the building facing the yard that was at the back and its galleries[1] on either side, a hundred cubits.

The inside of the nave and the vestibules of the court, 16 the thresholds and the narrow windows and the galleries all around the three of them, opposite the threshold, were paneled with wood all around, from the floor up to the windows (now the windows were covered), 17 to the space above the door, even to the inner room, and on the outside. And on all the walls all around, inside and outside, was a measured pattern.[2] 18 It was carved of cherubim and palm trees, a palm tree between cherub and cherub. Every cherub had two faces: 19 a human face toward the palm tree on the one side, and the face of a young lion toward the palm tree on the other side. They were carved on the whole temple all around. 20 From the floor to above the door, cherubim and palm trees were carved; similarly the wall of the nave.

21 The doorposts of the nave were squared, and in front of the Holy Place was something resembling 22 an altar of wood, three cubits high, two cubits long, and two cubits broad.[3] Its corners, its base,[4] and its walls were of wood. He said to me, "This is the table that is before the LORD." 23 The nave and the Holy Place had each a double door. 24 The double doors had two leaves apiece, two swinging leaves for each door. 25 And on the doors of the nave were carved cherubim and palm trees, such as were carved on the walls. And there was a canopy[5] of wood in front of the vestibule outside. 26 And there were narrow windows and palm trees on either side, on the sidewalls of the vestibule, the side chambers of the temple, and the canopies.

The Temple's Chambers

42 Then he led me out into the outer court, toward the north, and he brought me to the chambers that were opposite the separate yard and opposite the building on the north. 2 The length of the building whose door faced north was a hundred cubits,[6] and the breadth fifty cubits. 3 Facing the twenty cubits that belonged to the inner court, and facing the pavement that belonged to the outer court, was gallery[7] against gallery in three stories. 4 And before the chambers was a passage inward, ten cubits wide and a hundred cubits long,[8] and their doors were on the north. 5 Now the upper chambers were narrower, for the galleries took more away from them than from the lower and middle chambers of the building. 6 For they were in three stories, and they had no pillars like the pillars of the courts. Thus the upper chambers were set back from the ground more than the lower and the middle ones. 7 And there was a wall outside parallel to the chambers, toward the outer court, opposite the chambers, fifty cubits long. 8 For the chambers on the outer court were fifty cubits long, while those opposite the nave[9] were a hundred cubits long. 9 Below these chambers was an entrance on the east side, as one enters them from the outer court.

10 In the thickness of the wall of the court, on the south[10] also, opposite the yard and opposite the building, there were chambers 11 with a passage in front of them. They were similar to the chambers on the north, of the same length and breadth, with the same exits[11] and arrangements and doors, 12 as were the entrances of the chambers on the south. There was an entrance at the beginning of the passage,

[1] The meaning of the Hebrew term is unknown; also verse 16 [2] Hebrew *were measurements* [3] Septuagint; Hebrew lacks *two cubits broad* [4] Septuagint; Hebrew *length* [5] The meaning of the Hebrew word is unknown; also verse 26 [6] A *cubit* was about 18 inches or 45 centimeters [7] The meaning of the Hebrew word is unknown; also verse 5 [8] Septuagint, Syriac; Hebrew *and a way of one cubit* [9] Or *temple* [10] Septuagint; Hebrew *east* [11] Hebrew *and all their exits*

the passage before the corresponding wall on the east as one enters them.[1]

13 Then he said to me, "The north chambers and the south chambers opposite the yard are the holy chambers, where the priests who approach the LORD shall eat the most holy offerings. There they shall put the most holy offerings—the grain offering, the sin offering, and the guilt offering—for the place is holy. 14 When the priests enter the Holy Place, they shall not go out of it into the outer court without laying there the garments in which they minister, for these are holy. They shall put on other garments before they go near to that which is for the people."

15 Now when he had finished measuring the interior of the temple area, he led me out by the gate that faced east, and measured the temple area all around. 16 He measured the east side with the measuring reed, 500 cubits by the measuring reed all around. 17 He measured the north side, 500 cubits by the measuring reed all around. 18 He measured the south side, 500 cubits by the measuring reed. 19 Then he turned to the west side and measured, 500 cubits by the measuring reed. 20 He measured it on the four sides. It had a wall around it, 500 cubits long and 500 cubits broad, to make a separation between the holy and the common.

The Glory of the LORD Fills the Temple

43 Then he led me to the gate, the gate facing east. 2 And behold, the glory of the God of Israel was coming from the east. And the sound of his coming was like the sound of many waters, and the earth shone with his glory. 3 And the vision I saw was just like the vision that I had seen when he[2] came to destroy the city, and just like the vision that I had seen by the Chebar canal. And I fell on my face. 4 As the glory of the LORD entered the temple by the gate facing east, 5 the Spirit lifted me up and brought me into the inner court; and behold, the glory of the LORD filled the temple.

6 While the man was standing beside me, I heard one speaking to me out of the temple, 7 and he said to me, "Son of man, this is the place of my throne and the place of the soles of my feet, where I will dwell in the midst of the people of Israel forever. And the house of Israel shall no more defile my holy name, neither they, nor their kings, by their whoring and by the dead bodies[3] of their kings at their high places,[4] 8 by setting their threshold by my threshold and their doorposts beside my doorposts, with only a wall between me and them. They have defiled my holy name by their abominations that they have committed, so I have consumed them in my anger. 9 Now let them put away their whoring and the dead bodies of their kings far from me, and I will dwell in their midst forever.

10 "As for you, son of man, describe to the house of Israel the temple, that they may be ashamed of their iniquities; and they shall measure the plan. 11 And if they are ashamed of all that they have done, make known to them the design of the temple, its arrangement, its exits and its entrances, that is, its whole design; and make known to them as well all its statutes and its whole design and all its laws, and write it down in their sight, so that they may observe all its laws and all its statutes and carry them out. 12 This is the law of the temple: the whole territory on the top of the mountain all around shall be most holy. Behold, this is the law of the temple.

The Altar

13 "These are the measurements of the altar by cubits (the cubit being a cubit and a handbreadth):[5] its base shall be one cubit high[6] and one cubit broad, with a rim of one span[7] around its edge. And this shall be the height of the altar: 14 from the

[1] The meaning of the Hebrew verse is uncertain [2] Some Hebrew manuscripts and Vulgate; most Hebrew manuscripts *when I* [3] Or *the monuments*; also verse 9 [4] Or *at their deaths* [5] A *cubit* was about 18 inches or 45 centimeters; a *handbreadth* was about 3 inches or 7.5 centimeters [6] Or *its gutter shall be one cubit deep* [7] A *span* was about 9 inches or 22 centimeters

base on the ground to the lower ledge, two cubits, with a breadth of one cubit; and from the smaller ledge to the larger ledge, four cubits, with a breadth of one cubit; 15 and the altar hearth, four cubits; and from the altar hearth projecting upward, four horns. 16 The altar hearth shall be square, twelve cubits long by twelve broad. 17 The ledge also shall be square, fourteen cubits long by fourteen broad, with a rim around it half a cubit broad, and its base one cubit all around. The steps of the altar shall face east."

18 And he said to me, "Son of man, thus says the Lord GOD: These are the ordinances for the altar: On the day when it is erected for offering burnt offerings upon it and for throwing blood against it, 19 you shall give to the Levitical priests of the family of Zadok, who draw near to me to minister to me, declares the Lord GOD, a bull from the herd for a sin offering. 20 And you shall take some of its blood and put it on the four horns of the altar and on the four corners of the ledge and upon the rim all around. Thus you shall purify the altar and make atonement for it. 21 You shall also take the bull of the sin offering, and it shall be burned in the appointed place belonging to the temple, outside the sacred area. 22 And on the second day you shall offer a male goat without blemish for a sin offering; and the altar shall be purified, as it was purified with the bull. 23 When you have finished purifying it, you shall offer a bull from the herd without blemish and a ram from the flock without blemish. 24 You shall present them before the LORD, and the priests shall sprinkle salt on them and offer them up as a burnt offering to the LORD. 25 For seven days you shall provide daily a male goat for a sin offering; also, a bull from the herd and a ram from the flock, without blemish, shall be provided. 26 Seven days shall they make atonement for the altar and cleanse it, and so consecrate it.[1] 27 And when they have completed these days, then from the eighth day onward the priests shall offer on the altar your burnt offerings and your peace offerings, and I will accept you, declares the Lord GOD."

The Gate for the Prince

44 Then he brought me back to the outer gate of the sanctuary, which faces east. And it was shut. 2 And the LORD said to me, "This gate shall remain shut; it shall not be opened, and no one shall enter by it, for the LORD, the God of Israel, has entered by it. Therefore it shall remain shut. 3 Only the prince may sit in it to eat bread before the LORD. He shall enter by way of the vestibule of the gate, and shall go out by the same way."

4 Then he brought me by way of the north gate to the front of the temple, and I looked, and behold, the glory of the LORD filled the temple of the LORD. And I fell on my face. 5 And the LORD said to me, "Son of man, mark well, see with your eyes, and hear with your ears all that I shall tell you concerning all the statutes of the temple of the LORD and all its laws. And mark well the entrance to the temple and all the exits from the sanctuary. 6 And say to the rebellious house,[2] to the house of Israel, Thus says the Lord GOD: O house of Israel, enough of all your abominations, 7 in admitting foreigners, uncircumcised in heart and flesh, to be in my sanctuary, profaning my temple, when you offer to me my food, the fat and the blood. You[3] have broken my covenant, in addition to all your abominations. 8 And you have not kept charge of my holy things, but you have set others to keep my charge for you in my sanctuary.

9 "Thus says the Lord GOD: No foreigner, uncircumcised in heart and flesh, of all the foreigners who are among the people of Israel, shall enter my sanctuary. 10 But the Levites who went far from me, going astray from me after their idols when Israel went astray, shall bear their punishment.[4]

[1] Hebrew *fill its hand* [2] Septuagint; Hebrew lacks *house* [3] Septuagint, Syriac, Vulgate; Hebrew *They* [4] Or *iniquity*; also verse 12

11 They shall be ministers in my sanctuary, having oversight at the gates of the temple and ministering in the temple. They shall slaughter the burnt offering and the sacrifice for the people, and they shall stand before the people, to minister to them. 12 Because they ministered to them before their idols and became a stumbling block of iniquity to the house of Israel, therefore I have sworn concerning them, declares the Lord GOD, and they shall bear their punishment. 13 They shall not come near to me, to serve me as priest, nor come near any of my holy things and the things that are most holy, but they shall bear their shame and the abominations that they have committed. 14 Yet I will appoint them to keep charge of the temple, to do all its service and all that is to be done in it.

Rules for Levitical Priests

15 "But the Levitical priests, the sons of Zadok, who kept the charge of my sanctuary when the people of Israel went astray from me, shall come near to me to minister to me. And they shall stand before me to offer me the fat and the blood, declares the Lord GOD. 16 They shall enter my sanctuary, and they shall approach my table, to minister to me, and they shall keep my charge. 17 When they enter the gates of the inner court, they shall wear linen garments. They shall have nothing of wool on them, while they minister at the gates of the inner court, and within. 18 They shall have linen turbans on their heads, and linen undergarments around their waists. They shall not bind themselves with anything that causes sweat. 19 And when they go out into the outer court to the people, they shall put off the garments in which they have been ministering and lay them in the holy chambers. And they shall put on other garments, lest they transmit holiness to the people with their garments. 20 They shall not shave their heads or let their locks grow long; they shall surely trim the hair of their heads. 21 No priest shall drink wine when he enters the inner court. 22 They shall not marry a widow or a divorced woman, but only virgins of the offspring of the house of Israel, or a widow who is the widow of a priest. 23 They shall teach my people the difference between the holy and the common, and show them how to distinguish between the unclean and the clean. 24 In a dispute, they shall act as judges, and they shall judge it according to my judgments. They shall keep my laws and my statutes in all my appointed feasts, and they shall keep my Sabbaths holy. 25 They shall not defile themselves by going near to a dead person. However, for father or mother, for son or daughter, for brother or unmarried sister they may defile themselves. 26 After he has become clean, they shall count seven days for him. 27 And on the day that he goes into the Holy Place, into the inner court, to minister in the Holy Place, he shall offer his sin offering, declares the Lord GOD.

28 "This shall be their inheritance: I am their inheritance: and you shall give them no possession in Israel; I am their possession. 29 They shall eat the grain offering, the sin offering, and the guilt offering, and every devoted thing in Israel shall be theirs. 30 And the first of all the firstfruits of all kinds, and every offering of all kinds from all your offerings, shall belong to the priests. You shall also give to the priests the first of your dough, that a blessing may rest on your house. 31 The priests shall not eat of anything, whether bird or beast, that has died of itself or is torn by wild animals.

The Holy District

45 "When you allot the land as an inheritance, you shall set apart for the LORD a portion of the land as a holy district, 25,000 cubits[1] long and 20,000[2] cubits broad. It shall be holy throughout its whole extent. 2 Of this a square plot of 500 by 500 cubits shall be for the sanctu-

[1] A *cubit* was about 18 inches or 45 centimeters [2] Septuagint; Hebrew *ten*

ary, with fifty cubits for an open space
around it. 3 And from this measured dis-
trict you shall measure off a section 25,000
cubits long and 10,000 broad, in which
shall be the sanctuary, the Most Holy Place.
4 It shall be the holy portion of the land.
It shall be for the priests, who minister
in the sanctuary and approach the LORD
to minister to him, and it shall be a place
for their houses and a holy place for the
sanctuary. 5 Another section, 25,000 cubits
long and 10,000 cubits broad, shall be for
the Levites who minister at the temple, as
their possession for cities to live in.[1]
6 "Alongside the portion set apart as the
holy district you shall assign for the prop-
erty of the city an area 5,000 cubits broad
and 25,000 cubits long. It shall belong to
the whole house of Israel.

The Portion for the Prince

7 "And to the prince shall belong the
land on both sides of the holy district and
the property of the city, alongside the holy
district and the property of the city, on the
west and on the east, corresponding in
length to one of the tribal portions, and
extending from the western to the eastern
boundary 8 of the land. It is to be his prop-
erty in Israel. And my princes shall no
more oppress my people, but they shall let
the house of Israel have the land accord-
ing to their tribes.
9 "Thus says the Lord GOD: Enough, O
princes of Israel! Put away violence and
oppression, and execute justice and righ-
teousness. Cease your evictions of my peo-
ple, declares the Lord GOD.
10 "You shall have just balances, a just
ephah, and a just bath.[2] 11 The ephah and
the bath shall be of the same measure, the
bath containing one tenth of a homer,[3]
and the ephah one tenth of a homer; the
homer shall be the standard measure.
12 The shekel shall be twenty gerahs;[4]
twenty shekels plus twenty-five shekels
plus fifteen shekels shall be your mina.[5]
13 "This is the offering that you shall
make: one sixth of an ephah from each
homer of wheat, and one sixth of an ephah
from each homer of barley, 14 and as the
fixed portion of oil, measured in baths,
one tenth of a bath from each cor[6] (the
cor, like the homer, contains ten baths).[7]
15 And one sheep from every flock of two
hundred, from the watering places of
Israel for grain offering, burnt offering,
and peace offerings, to make atonement
for them, declares the Lord GOD. 16 All the
people of the land shall be obliged to give
this offering to the prince in Israel. 17 It
shall be the prince's duty to furnish the
burnt offerings, grain offerings, and drink
offerings, at the feasts, the new moons,
and the Sabbaths, all the appointed feasts
of the house of Israel: he shall provide the
sin offerings, grain offerings, burnt offer-
ings, and peace offerings, to make atone-
ment on behalf of the house of Israel.
18 "Thus says the Lord GOD: In the first
month, on the first day of the month, you
shall take a bull from the herd without
blemish, and purify the sanctuary. 19 The
priest shall take some of the blood of the
sin offering and put it on the doorposts of
the temple, the four corners of the ledge
of the altar, and the posts of the gate of the
inner court. 20 You shall do the same on the
seventh day of the month for anyone who
has sinned through error or ignorance; so
you shall make atonement for the temple.
21 "In the first month, on the fourteenth
day of the month, you shall celebrate the
Feast of the Passover, and for seven days
unleavened bread shall be eaten. 22 On that
day the prince shall provide for himself and
all the people of the land a young bull for a
sin offering. 23 And on the seven days of the
festival he shall provide as a burnt offering
to the LORD seven young bulls and seven
rams without blemish, on each of the

1 Septuagint; Hebrew *as their possession, twenty chambers* 2 An *ephah* was about 3/5 of a bushel or 22 liters; a *bath* was about 6 gallons or 22 liters 3 A *homer* was about 6 bushels or 220 liters 4 A *shekel* was about 2/5 ounce or 11 grams; a *gerah* was about 1/50 ounce or 0.6 gram 5 A *mina* was about 1 1/4 pounds or 0.6 kilogram 6 A cor was about 6 bushels or 220 liters 7 See Vulgate; Hebrew *(ten baths are a homer, for ten baths are a homer)*

seven days; and a male goat daily for a sin offering. 24 And he shall provide as a grain offering an ephah for each bull, an ephah for each ram, and a hin[1] of oil to each ephah. 25 In the seventh month, on the fifteenth day of the month and for the seven days of the feast, he shall make the same provision for sin offerings, burnt offerings, and grain offerings, and for the oil.

The Prince and the Feasts

46 "Thus says the Lord GOD: The gate of the inner court that faces east shall be shut on the six working days, but on the Sabbath day it shall be opened, and on the day of the new moon it shall be opened. 2 The prince shall enter by the vestibule of the gate from outside, and shall take his stand by the post of the gate. The priests shall offer his burnt offering and his peace offerings, and he shall worship at the threshold of the gate. Then he shall go out, but the gate shall not be shut until evening. 3 The people of the land shall bow down at the entrance of that gate before the LORD on the Sabbaths and on the new moons. 4 The burnt offering that the prince offers to the LORD on the Sabbath day shall be six lambs without blemish and a ram without blemish. 5 And the grain offering with the ram shall be an ephah,[2] and the grain offering with the lambs shall be as much as he is able, together with a hin[3] of oil to each ephah. 6 On the day of the new moon he shall offer a bull from the herd without blemish, and six lambs and a ram, which shall be without blemish. 7 As a grain offering he shall provide an ephah with the bull and an ephah with the ram, and with the lambs as much as he is able, together with a hin of oil to each ephah. 8 When the prince enters, he shall enter by the vestibule of the gate, and he shall go out by the same way.

9 "When the people of the land come before the LORD at the appointed feasts, he who enters by the north gate to worship shall go out by the south gate, and he who enters by the south gate shall go out by the north gate: no one shall return by way of the gate by which he entered, but each shall go out straight ahead. 10 When they enter, the prince shall enter with them, and when they go out, he shall go out.

11 "At the feasts and the appointed festivals, the grain offering with a young bull shall be an ephah, and with a ram an ephah, and with the lambs as much as one is able to give, together with a hin of oil to an ephah. 12 When the prince provides a freewill offering, either a burnt offering or peace offerings as a freewill offering to the LORD, the gate facing east shall be opened for him. And he shall offer his burnt offering or his peace offerings as he does on the Sabbath day. Then he shall go out, and after he has gone out the gate shall be shut.

13 "You shall provide a lamb a year old without blemish for a burnt offering to the LORD daily; morning by morning you shall provide it. 14 And you shall provide a grain offering with it morning by morning, one sixth of an ephah, and one third of a hin of oil to moisten the flour, as a grain offering to the LORD. This is a perpetual statute. 15 Thus the lamb and the meal offering and the oil shall be provided, morning by morning, for a regular burnt offering.

16 "Thus says the Lord GOD: If the prince makes a gift to any of his sons as his inheritance, it shall belong to his sons. It is their property by inheritance. 17 But if he makes a gift out of his inheritance to one of his servants, it shall be his to the year of liberty. Then it shall revert to the prince; surely it is his inheritance—it shall belong to his sons. 18 The prince shall not take any of the inheritance of the people, thrusting them out of their property. He shall give his sons their inheritance out of his own property, so that none of my people shall be scattered from his property."

[1] A *hin* was about 4 quarts or 3.5 liters [2] An *ephah* was about 3/5 bushel or 22 liters [3] A *hin* was about 4 quarts or 3.5 liters

Boiling Places for Offerings

19 Then he brought me through the entrance, which was at the side of the gate, to the north row of the holy chambers for the priests, and behold, a place was there at the extreme western end of them. **20** And he said to me, "This is the place where the priests shall boil the guilt offering and the sin offering, and where they shall bake the grain offering, in order not to bring them out into the outer court and so transmit holiness to the people."

21 Then he brought me out to the outer court and led me around to the four corners of the court. And behold, in each corner of the court there was another court— **22** in the four corners of the court were small[1] courts, forty cubits[2] long and thirty broad; the four were of the same size. **23** On the inside, around each of the four courts was a row of masonry, with hearths made at the bottom of the rows all around. **24** Then he said to me, "These are the kitchens where those who minister at the temple shall boil the sacrifices of the people."

Water Flowing from the Temple

47 Then he brought me back to the door of the temple, and behold, water was issuing from below the threshold of the temple toward the east (for the temple faced east). The water was flowing down from below the south end of the threshold of the temple, south of the altar. **2** Then he brought me out by way of the north gate and led me around on the outside to the outer gate that faces toward the east; and behold, the water was trickling out on the south side.

3 Going on eastward with a measuring line in his hand, the man measured a thousand cubits,[3] and then led me through the water, and it was ankle-deep. **4** Again he measured a thousand, and led me through the water, and it was knee-deep. Again he measured a thousand, and led me through the water, and it was waist-deep. **5** Again he measured a thousand, and it was a river that I could not pass through, for the water had risen. It was deep enough to swim in, a river that could not be passed through. **6** And he said to me, "Son of man, have you seen this?"

Then he led me back to the bank of the river. **7** As I went back, I saw on the bank of the river very many trees on the one side and on the other. **8** And he said to me, "This water flows toward the eastern region and goes down into the Arabah, and enters the sea;[4] when the water flows into the sea, the water will become fresh.[5] **9** And wherever the river goes,[6] every living creature that swarms will live, and there will be very many fish. For this water goes there, that the waters of the sea[7] may become fresh; so everything will live where the river goes. **10** Fishermen will stand beside the sea. From Engedi to Eneglaim it will be a place for the spreading of nets. Its fish will be of very many kinds, like the fish of the Great Sea.[8] **11** But its swamps and marshes will not become fresh; they are to be left for salt. **12** And on the banks, on both sides of the river, there will grow all kinds of trees for food. Their leaves will not wither, nor their fruit fail, but they will bear fresh fruit every month, because the water for them flows from the sanctuary. Their fruit will be for food, and their leaves for healing."

Division of the Land

13 Thus says the Lord GOD: "This is the boundary[9] by which you shall divide the land for inheritance among the twelve tribes of Israel. Joseph shall have two portions. **14** And you shall divide equally what I swore to give to your fathers. This land shall fall to you as your inheritance.

15 "This shall be the boundary of the land: On the north side, from the Great Sea by way of Hethlon to Lebo-hamath, and on to Zedad,[10] **16** Berothah, Sibraim (which

[1] Septuagint, Syriac, Vulgate; the meaning of the Hebrew word is uncertain [2] A *cubit* was about 18 inches or 45 centimeters [3] A *cubit* was about 18 inches or 45 centimeters [4] That is, the Dead Sea [5] Hebrew *will be healed*; also verses 9, 11 [6] Septuagint, Syriac, Vulgate, Targum; Hebrew *the two rivers go* [7] Hebrew lacks *the waters of the sea* [8] That is, the Mediterranean Sea; also verses 15, 19, 20 [9] Probable reading; Hebrew *The valley of the boundary* [10] Septuagint; Hebrew *the entrance of Zedad, Hamath*

lies on the border between Damascus
and Hamath), as far as Hazer-hatticon,
which is on the border of Hauran. 17 So the
boundary shall run from the sea to Hazar-
enan, which is on the northern border of
Damascus, with the border of Hamath to
the north.[1] This shall be the north side.[2]
18 "On the east side, the boundary shall
run between Hauran and Damascus; along
the Jordan between Gilead and the land
of Israel; to the eastern sea and as far as
Tamar.[3] This shall be the east side.
19 "On the south side, it shall run from
Tamar as far as the waters of Meribah-
kadesh, from there along the Brook of
Egypt[4] to the Great Sea. This shall be the
south side.
20 "On the west side, the Great Sea shall
be the boundary to a point opposite Lebo-
hamath. This shall be the west side.
21 "So you shall divide this land among
you according to the tribes of Israel. 22 You
shall allot it as an inheritance for your-
selves and for the sojourners who reside
among you and have had children among
you. They shall be to you as native-born
children of Israel. With you they shall be
allotted an inheritance among the tribes
of Israel. 23 In whatever tribe the sojourner
resides, there you shall assign him his
inheritance, declares the Lord GOD.

48 "These are the names of the
tribes: Beginning at the northern
extreme, beside the way of Hethlon to
Lebo-hamath, as far as Hazar-enan (which
is on the northern border of Damascus over
against Hamath), and[5] extending from the
east side to the west,[6] Dan, one portion.
2 Adjoining the territory of Dan, from the
east side to the west, Asher, one portion.
3 Adjoining the territory of Asher, from the
east side to the west, Naphtali, one por-
tion. 4 Adjoining the territory of Naphtali,
from the east side to the west, Manasseh,
one portion. 5 Adjoining the territory of
Manasseh, from the east side to the west,
Ephraim, one portion. 6 Adjoining the ter-
ritory of Ephraim, from the east side to the
west, Reuben, one portion. 7 Adjoining the
territory of Reuben, from the east side to
the west, Judah, one portion.
8 "Adjoining the territory of Judah, from
the east side to the west, shall be the por-
tion which you shall set apart, 25,000
cubits[7] in breadth, and in length equal to
one of the tribal portions, from the east
side to the west, with the sanctuary in the
midst of it. 9 The portion that you shall set
apart for the LORD shall be 25,000 cubits
in length, and 20,000[8] in breadth. 10 These
shall be the allotments of the holy por-
tion: the priests shall have an allotment
measuring 25,000 cubits on the northern
side, 10,000 cubits in breadth on the west-
ern side, 10,000 in breadth on the eastern
side, and 25,000 in length on the southern
side, with the sanctuary of the LORD in the
midst of it. 11 This shall be for the conse-
crated priests, the sons of Zadok, who kept
my charge, who did not go astray when the
people of Israel went astray, as the Levites
did. 12 And it shall belong to them as a spe-
cial portion from the holy portion of the
land, a most holy place, adjoining the terri-
tory of the Levites. 13 And alongside the ter-
ritory of the priests, the Levites shall have
an allotment 25,000 cubits in length and
10,000 in breadth. The whole length shall
be 25,000 cubits and the breadth 20,000.[9]
14 They shall not sell or exchange any of it.
They shall not alienate this choice portion
of the land, for it is holy to the LORD.
15 "The remainder, 5,000 cubits in
breadth and 25,000 in length, shall be for
common use for the city, for dwellings and
for open country. In the midst of it shall
be the city, 16 and these shall be its mea-
surements: the north side 4,500 cubits,
the south side 4,500, the east side 4,500,
and the west side 4,500. 17 And the city
shall have open land: on the north 250
cubits, on the south 250, on the east 250,

[1] The meaning of the Hebrew is uncertain [2] Probable reading; Hebrew *and as for the north side* [3] Compare Syriac; Hebrew *to the eastern sea you shall measure* [4] Hebrew lacks *of Egypt* [5] Probable reading; Hebrew *and they shall be his* [6] Septuagint (compare verses 2-8); Hebrew *the east side the west* [7] A *cubit* was about 18 inches or 45 centimeters [8] Compare 45:1; Hebrew *ten* [9] Septuagint; Hebrew *10,000*

and on the west 250. 18 The remainder of the length alongside the holy portion shall be 10,000 cubits to the east, and 10,000 to the west, and it shall be alongside the holy portion. Its produce shall be food for the workers of the city. 19 And the workers of the city, from all the tribes of Israel, shall till it. 20 The whole portion that you shall set apart shall be 25,000 cubits square, that is, the holy portion together with the property of the city.

21 "What remains on both sides of the holy portion and of the property of the city shall belong to the prince. Extending from the 25,000 cubits of the holy portion to the east border, and westward from the 25,000 cubits to the west border, parallel to the tribal portions, it shall belong to the prince. The holy portion with the sanctuary of the temple shall be in its midst. 22 It shall be separate from the property of the Levites and the property of the city, which are in the midst of that which belongs to the prince. The portion of the prince shall lie between the territory of Judah and the territory of Benjamin.

23 "As for the rest of the tribes: from the east side to the west, Benjamin, one portion. 24 Adjoining the territory of Benjamin, from the east side to the west, Simeon, one portion. 25 Adjoining the territory of Simeon, from the east side to the west, Issachar, one portion. 26 Adjoining the territory of Issachar, from the east side to the west, Zebulun, one portion. 27 Adjoining the territory of Zebulun, from the east side to the west, Gad, one portion. 28 And adjoining the territory of Gad to the south, the boundary shall run from Tamar to the waters of Meribah-kadesh, from there along the Brook of Egypt[1] to the Great Sea.[2] 29 This is the land that you shall allot as an inheritance among the tribes of Israel, and these are their portions, declares the Lord GOD.

The Gates of the City

30 "These shall be the exits of the city: On the north side, which is to be 4,500 cubits by measure, 31 three gates, the gate of Reuben, the gate of Judah, and the gate of Levi, the gates of the city being named after the tribes of Israel. 32 On the east side, which is to be 4,500 cubits, three gates, the gate of Joseph, the gate of Benjamin, and the gate of Dan. 33 On the south side, which is to be 4,500 cubits by measure, three gates, the gate of Simeon, the gate of Issachar, and the gate of Zebulun. 34 On the west side, which is to be 4,500 cubits, three gates,[3] the gate of Gad, the gate of Asher, and the gate of Naphtali. 35 The circumference of the city shall be 18,000 cubits. And the name of the city from that time on shall be, The LORD Is There."

[1] Hebrew lacks *of Egypt* [2] That is, the Mediterranean Sea [3] One Hebrew manuscript, Syriac (compare Septuagint); most Hebrew manuscripts *their gates three*

Daniel

Daniel Taken to Babylon

1 In the third year of the reign of Jehoiakim king of Judah, Nebuchadnezzar king of Babylon came to Jerusalem and besieged it. 2 And the Lord gave Jehoiakim king of Judah into his hand, with some of the vessels of the house of God. And he brought them to the land of Shinar, to the house of his god, and placed the vessels in the treasury of his god. 3 Then the king commanded Ashpenaz, his chief eunuch, to bring some of the people of Israel, both of the royal family[1] and of the nobility, 4 youths without blemish, of good appearance and skillful in all wisdom, endowed with knowledge, understanding learning, and competent to stand in the king's palace, and to teach them the literature and language of the Chaldeans. 5 The king assigned them a daily portion of the food that the king ate, and of the wine that he drank. They were to be educated for three years, and at the end of that time they were to stand before the king. 6 Among these were Daniel, Hananiah, Mishael, and Azariah of the tribe of Judah. 7 And the chief of the eunuchs gave them names: Daniel he called Belteshazzar, Hananiah he called Shadrach, Mishael he called Meshach, and Azariah he called Abednego.

Daniel's Faithfulness

8 But Daniel resolved that he would not defile himself with the king's food, or with the wine that he drank. Therefore he asked the chief of the eunuchs to allow him not to defile himself. 9 And God gave Daniel favor and compassion in the sight of the chief of the eunuchs, 10 and the chief of the eunuchs said to Daniel, "I fear my lord the king, who assigned your food and your drink; for why should he see that you were in worse condition than the youths who are of your own age? So you would endanger my head with the king." 11 Then Daniel said to the steward whom the chief of the eunuchs had assigned over Daniel, Hananiah, Mishael, and Azariah, 12 "Test your servants for ten days; let us be given vegetables to eat and water to drink. 13 Then let our appearance and the appearance of the youths who eat the king's food be observed by you, and deal with your servants according to what you see." 14 So he listened to them in this matter, and tested

CHARACTER PROFILE

DANIEL

Daniel was taken to Babylon to serve the king who had destroyed Jerusalem. Daniel always obeyed God, even when it wasn't easy. When Daniel was put in a lions' den for praying to God, God closed the lions' mouths and kept Daniel safe. Daniel's message was that God is the greatest King of all and the only true God.

1191

[1] Hebrew *of the seed of the kingdom*

Introduction to

Daniel

Author
Daniel

Date
About 605–536 B.C.

People
Daniel; Shadrach, Meshach, and Abednego; Nebuchadnezzar; Belshazzar; Darius

Purpose
The purpose of Daniel is to encourage God's people who suffer under the rule of unbelieving leaders by showing God as the King over all kings.

Central Themes
God rules all of history; God raises up and takes down all rulers; God's people must trust and serve Him faithfully under ungodly rulers; though believers may suffer, they will finally triumph in God's kingdom which alone will last forever.

Memory Verses
The everlasting Kingdom (Daniel 2:44–45); the King of heaven (Daniel 4:37); the Son of Man receives dominion (Daniel 7:13–14); the saints receive dominion (Daniel 7:27); God's great mercy (Daniel 9:18); the resurrection (Daniel 12:2–3)

Introduction

Daniel was taken as a prisoner from Jerusalem to serve Babylon's King Nebuchadnezzar. Daniel faithfully serves several kings who rise to power, then pass away. Daniel always serves God first. The stories in this book tell of God's care for His people when unbelievers rule them. Daniel's obedience makes him healthier than the other young men (Daniel 1); Daniel's prayers result in wisdom (Daniel 2); Daniel's friends refuse to bow to an image, and God saves them from the fiery furnace (Daniel 3); Daniel interprets visions (Daniel 4–5); and God saves Daniel from lions when he breaks the king's law by praying (Daniel 6). In these stories, we also see God as the highest Ruler of all. Nebuchadnezzar sees great kingdoms in his dream, all falling before God's kingdom (Daniel 2); Nebuchadnezzar's punishment doesn't work against God's servants (Daniel 3); Nebuchadnezzar himself loses his mind for failing to acknowledge God (Daniel 4). Belshazzar doesn't honor God and loses his throne (Daniel 5); Darius's order is disobeyed by Daniel, whom God protects (Daniel 6). These same messages are given through Daniel's visions: God's rule is over all others and lasts forever; God's people must remain faithful; they will suffer but triumph at last (Daniel 7–12).

About 605 B.C.	586 B.C.	538 B.C.	522 B.C.
Prophetic ministry of Daniel begins	Fall of Judah	Decree of Cyrus/ end of exile	Reign of Darius begins

them for ten days. 15 At the end of ten days it was seen that they were better in appearance and fatter in flesh than all the youths who ate the king's food. 16 So the steward took away their food and the wine they were to drink, and gave them vegetables.

17 As for these four youths, God gave them learning and skill in all literature and wisdom, and Daniel had understanding in all visions and dreams. 18 At the end of the time, when the king had commanded that they should be brought in, the chief of the eunuchs brought them in before Nebuchadnezzar. 19 And the king spoke with them, and among all of them none was found like Daniel, Hananiah, Mishael, and Azariah. Therefore they stood before the king. 20 And in every matter of wisdom and understanding about which the king inquired of them, he found them ten times better than all the magicians and enchanters that were in all his kingdom. 21 And Daniel was there until the first year of King Cyrus.

Nebuchadnezzar's Dream

2 In the second year of the reign of Nebuchadnezzar, Nebuchadnezzar had dreams; his spirit was troubled, and his sleep left him. 2 Then the king commanded that the magicians, the enchanters, the sorcerers, and the Chaldeans be summoned to tell the king his dreams. So they came in and stood before the king. 3 And the king said to them, "I had a dream, and my spirit is troubled to know the dream." 4 Then the Chaldeans said to the king in Aramaic,[1] "O king, live forever! Tell your servants the dream, and we will show the interpretation." 5 The king answered and said to the Chaldeans, "The word from me is firm: if you do not make known to me the dream and its interpretation, you shall be torn limb from limb, and your houses shall be laid in ruins. 6 But if you show the dream and its interpretation, you shall receive from me gifts and rewards and great honor. Therefore show me the dream and its interpretation." 7 They answered a second time and said, "Let the king tell his servants the dream, and we will show its interpretation." 8 The king answered and said, "I know with certainty that you are trying to gain time, because you see that the word from me is firm— 9 if you do not make the dream known to me, there is but one sentence for you. You have agreed to speak lying and corrupt words before me till the times change. Therefore tell me the dream, and I shall know that you can show me its interpretation." 10 The Chaldeans answered the king and said, "There is not a man on earth who can meet the king's demand, for no great and powerful king has asked such a thing of any magician or enchanter or Chaldean. 11 The thing that the king asks is difficult, and no one can show it to the king except the gods, whose dwelling is not with flesh."

12 Because of this the king was angry and very furious, and commanded that all the wise men of Babylon be destroyed. 13 So the decree went out, and the wise men were about to be killed; and they sought Daniel and his companions, to kill them. 14 Then Daniel replied with prudence and discretion to Arioch, the captain of the king's guard, who had gone out to kill the wise men of Babylon. 15 He declared[2] to Arioch, the king's captain, "Why is the decree of the king so urgent?" Then Arioch made the matter known to Daniel. 16 And Daniel went in and requested the king to appoint him a time, that he might show the interpretation to the king.

God Reveals Nebuchadnezzar's Dream

17 Then Daniel went to his house and made the matter known to Hananiah, Mishael, and Azariah, his companions, 18 and told them to seek mercy from the God of heaven concerning this mystery, so that Daniel and his companions might not be destroyed with the rest of the wise

[1] The text from this point to the end of chapter 7 is in Aramaic [2] Aramaic *answered and said*; also verse 26

men of Babylon. 19 Then the mystery was
revealed to Daniel in a vision of the night.
Then Daniel blessed the God of heaven.
20 Daniel answered and said:

"Blessed be the name of God forever
and ever,
to whom belong wisdom and
might.
21 He changes times and seasons;
he removes kings and sets up kings;
he gives wisdom to the wise
and knowledge to those who have
understanding;
22 he reveals deep and hidden things;
he knows what is in the darkness,
and the light dwells with him.
23 To you, O God of my fathers,
I give thanks and praise,
for you have given me wisdom and
might,
and have now made known to me
what we asked of you,
for you have made known to us
the king's matter."

24 Therefore Daniel went in to Arioch,
whom the king had appointed to destroy
the wise men of Babylon. He went and said
thus to him: "Do not destroy the wise men
of Babylon; bring me in before the king,
and I will show the king the interpretation."
25 Then Arioch brought in Daniel before
the king in haste and said thus to him: "I
have found among the exiles from Judah
a man who will make known to the king
the interpretation." 26 The king declared
to Daniel, whose name was Belteshazzar,
"Are you able to make known to me the
dream that I have seen and its interpre-
tation?" 27 Daniel answered the king and
said, "No wise men, enchanters, magi-
cians, or astrologers can show to the king
the mystery that the king has asked, 28 but
there is a God in heaven who reveals mys-
teries, and he has made known to King
Nebuchadnezzar what will be in the latter
days. Your dream and the visions of your
head as you lay in bed are these: 29 To you,
O king, as you lay in bed came thoughts
of what would be after this, and he who
reveals mysteries made known to you
what is to be. 30 But as for me, this mystery
has been revealed to me, not because of
any wisdom that I have more than all the
living, but in order that the interpretation
may be made known to the king, and that
you may know the thoughts of your mind.

Daniel Interprets the Dream

31 "You saw, O king, and behold, a great
image. This image, mighty and of exceed-
ing brightness, stood before you, and its
appearance was frightening. 32 The head of
this image was of fine gold, its chest and
arms of silver, its middle and thighs of
bronze, 33 its legs of iron, its feet partly of
iron and partly of clay. 34 As you looked, a
stone was cut out by no human hand, and
it struck the image on its feet of iron and
clay, and broke them in pieces. 35 Then
the iron, the clay, the bronze, the silver,
and the gold, all together were broken in
pieces, and became like the chaff of the
summer threshing floors; and the wind
carried them away, so that not a trace of
them could be found. But the stone that
struck the image became a great moun-
tain and filled the whole earth.
36 "This was the dream. Now we will tell
the king its interpretation. 37 You, O king,
the king of kings, to whom the God of
heaven has given the kingdom, the power,
and the might, and the glory, 38 and into
whose hand he has given, wherever they
dwell, the children of man, the beasts of
the field, and the birds of the heavens,
making you rule over them all—you are
the head of gold. 39 Another kingdom
inferior to you shall arise after you, and
yet a third kingdom of bronze, which
shall rule over all the earth. 40 And there
shall be a fourth kingdom, strong as iron,
because iron breaks to pieces and shatters
all things. And like iron that crushes, it

shall break and crush all these. 41 And as you saw the feet and toes, partly of potter's clay and partly of iron, it shall be a divided kingdom, but some of the firmness of iron shall be in it, just as you saw iron mixed with the soft clay. 42 And as the toes of the feet were partly iron and partly clay, so the kingdom shall be partly strong and partly brittle. 43 As you saw the iron mixed with soft clay, so they will mix with one another in marriage,[1] but they will not hold together, just as iron does not mix with clay. 44 And in the days of those kings the God of heaven will set up a kingdom that shall never be destroyed, nor shall the kingdom be left to another people. It shall break in pieces all these kingdoms and bring them to an end, and it shall stand forever, 45 just as you saw that a stone was cut from a mountain by no human hand, and that it broke in pieces the iron, the bronze, the clay, the silver, and the gold. A great God has made known to the king what shall be after this. The dream is certain, and its interpretation sure."

Daniel Is Promoted

46 Then King Nebuchadnezzar fell upon his face and paid homage to Daniel, and commanded that an offering and incense be offered up to him. 47 The king answered and said to Daniel, "Truly, your God is God of gods and Lord of kings, and a revealer of mysteries, for you have been able to reveal this mystery." 48 Then the king gave Daniel high honors and many great gifts, and made him ruler over the whole province of Babylon and chief prefect over all the wise men of Babylon. 49 Daniel made a request of the king, and he appointed Shadrach, Meshach, and Abednego over the affairs of the province of Babylon. But Daniel remained at the king's court.

Nebuchadnezzar's Golden Image

1181

3 King Nebuchadnezzar made an image of gold, whose height was sixty cubits[2] and its breadth six cubits. He set it up on the plain of Dura, in the province of Babylon. 2 Then King Nebuchadnezzar sent to gather the satraps, the prefects, and the governors, the counselors, the treasurers, the justices, the magistrates, and all the officials of the provinces to come to the dedication of the image that King Nebuchadnezzar had set up. 3 Then the satraps, the prefects, and the governors, the counselors, the treasurers, the justices, the magistrates, and all the officials of the provinces gathered for the dedication of the image that King Nebuchadnezzar had set up. And they stood before the image that Nebuchadnezzar had set up. 4 And the herald proclaimed aloud, "You are commanded, O peoples, nations, and languages, 5 that when you hear the sound of the horn, pipe, lyre, trigon, harp, bagpipe, and every kind of music, you are to fall down and worship the golden image that King Nebuchadnezzar has set up. 6 And whoever does not fall down and worship shall immediately be cast into a burning fiery furnace." 7 Therefore, as soon as all the peoples heard the sound of the horn, pipe, lyre, trigon, harp, bagpipe, and every kind of music, all the peoples, nations, and languages fell down and worshiped the golden image that King Nebuchadnezzar had set up.

The Fiery Furnace

8 Therefore at that time certain Chaldeans came forward and maliciously accused the Jews. 9 They declared[3] to King Nebuchadnezzar, "O king, live forever! 10 You, O king, have made a decree, that every man who hears the sound of the horn, pipe, lyre, trigon, harp, bagpipe, and every kind of music, shall fall down and worship the golden image. 11 And whoever does not fall down and worship shall be cast into a burning fiery furnace. 12 There are certain Jews whom you have appointed over the affairs of the province of Babylon: Shadrach, Meshach, and Abednego. These

[1] Aramaic *by the seed of men* [2] A *cubit* was about 18 inches or 45 centimeters [3] Aramaic *answered and said*; also verses 24, 26

Three Young Men and the Fiery Furnace

Shadrach, Meshach, and Abednego were three young men who believed in God and worshiped Him. Enemy soldiers took them to a faraway country where the king and the people did not love God.

One day, King Nebuchadnezzar made a huge golden idol that was 90 feet tall. The king had his servant command everyone, "When you hear the sound of music, you are to fall down and worship the golden image that King Nebuchadnezzar has set up. And whoever does not fall down and worship shall immediately be cast into a burning fiery furnace."

When the music started to play, most of the people bowed down—but not Shadrach, Meshach, and Abednego. They loved the one true God, and they refused to bow to the idol.

This made King Nebuchadnezzar furious. He warned the three young men that they must bow down to the idol, or he would throw them into the fiery furnace. "And who is the god who will deliver you out of my hands?" he asked.

The three young men were very respectful to the king. But they told him, "Our God whom we serve is able to deliver us from the burning fiery furnace, and He will deliver us out of your hand, O king. But if not, O king, we will not serve your gods or worship the golden image that you have set up." Now King Nebuchadnezzar was even more furious!

He ordered that the fire should be heated seven times hotter than it had been before. Then he told his soldiers to tie up Shadrach, Meshach, and Abednego and throw them into the burning fiery furnace.

But when King Nebuchadnezzar looked into the furnace to see what had happened, he was amazed. He saw Shadrach, Meshach, and Abednego walking around in the fire—not hurt at all!

Then the king said, "Did we not cast three men into the fire?" Yes, his servants answered. "But I see four men walking in the midst of the fire," Nebuchadnezzar said, "and they are not hurt!" And the fourth man looks like "a son of the gods."

The king had Shadrach, Meshach, and Abednego taken out of the furnace. Not even their hair or the clothes had been burned. And they didn't even smell like smoke!

Then the king said to all the people, "Blessed be the God of Shadrach, Meshach, and Abednego, who has sent His angel and delivered His servants, who trusted in Him." Shadrach, Meshach, and Abednego were willing to give up their lives to worship and trust only the one true God. God protected them and saved them from the fiery furnace!

God calls us to worship and trust Him alone, for only He can save us. God sent His Son Jesus to die on the cross for us—to take the punishment we deserve and to save us from our sins. Jesus is our Savior and our God.

SEEK and FIND

WHERE TO FIND THE STORY

Daniel 3

KEY BIBLE VERSE

"Blessed be the God of Shadrach, Meshach, and Abednego, who has sent his angel and delivered his servants, who trusted in him." (Daniel 3:28)

THREE KEY QUESTIONS

- Why wouldn't Shadrach, Meshach, and Abednego bow to King Nebuchadnezzar's idol?
- What happened when King Nebuchadnezzar threw Shadrach, Meshach, and Abednego in the fiery furnace?
- Why should we trust only in Jesus to save us from our sins?

RELATED BIBLE READINGS

Exodus 20:3–6; Acts 4:18–31; 5:27–29; Romans 12:1–2; 1 Peter 2:21–23; 5:6–10

men, O king, pay no attention to you; they
do not serve your gods or worship the
golden image that you have set up."
13 Then Nebuchadnezzar in furious rage
commanded that Shadrach, Meshach, and
Abednego be brought. So they brought
these men before the king. 14 Nebuchad-
nezzar answered and said to them, "Is it
true, O Shadrach, Meshach, and Abednego,
that you do not serve my gods or worship
the golden image that I have set up? 15 Now
if you are ready when you hear the sound
of the horn, pipe, lyre, trigon, harp, bag-
pipe, and every kind of music, to fall down
and worship the image that I have made,
well and good.[1] But if you do not worship,
you shall immediately be cast into a burn-
ing fiery furnace. And who is the god who
will deliver you out of my hands?"
16 Shadrach, Meshach, and Abednego
answered and said to the king, "O Nebu-
chadnezzar, we have no need to answer
you in this matter. 17 If this be so, our God
whom we serve is able to deliver us from
the burning fiery furnace, and he will
deliver us out of your hand, O king.[2] 18 But
if not, be it known to you, O king, that we
will not serve your gods or worship the
golden image that you have set up."
19 Then Nebuchadnezzar was filled with
fury, and the expression of his face was
changed against Shadrach, Meshach, and
Abednego. He ordered the furnace heated
seven times more than it was usually
heated. 20 And he ordered some of the
mighty men of his army to bind Shadrach,
Meshach, and Abednego, and to cast them
into the burning fiery furnace. 21 Then
these men were bound in their cloaks,
their tunics,[3] their hats, and their other

[1] Aramaic lacks *well and good* [2] Or *If our God whom we serve is able to deliver us, he will deliver us from the burning fiery furnace and out of your hand, O king.* [3] The meaning of the Aramaic words rendered *cloaks* and *tunics* is uncertain; also verse 27

garments, and they were thrown into the burning fiery furnace. **22** Because the king's order was urgent and the furnace overheated, the flame of the fire killed those men who took up Shadrach, Meshach, and Abednego. **23** And these three men, Shadrach, Meshach, and Abednego, fell bound into the burning fiery furnace.

24 Then King Nebuchadnezzar was astonished and rose up in haste. He declared to his counselors, "Did we not cast three men bound into the fire?" They answered and said to the king, "True, O king." **25** He answered and said, "But I see four men unbound, walking in the midst of the fire, and they are not hurt; and the appearance of the fourth is like a son of the gods."

26 Then Nebuchadnezzar came near to the door of the burning fiery furnace; he declared, "Shadrach, Meshach, and Abednego, servants of the Most High God, come out, and come here!" Then Shadrach, Meshach, and Abednego came out from the fire. **27** And the satraps, the prefects, the governors, and the king's counselors gathered together and saw that the fire had not had any power over the bodies of those men. The hair of their heads was not singed, their cloaks were not harmed, and no smell of fire had come upon them. **28** Nebuchadnezzar answered and said, "Blessed be the God of Shadrach, Meshach, and Abednego, who has sent his angel and delivered his servants, who trusted in him, and set aside[1] the king's command, and yielded up their bodies rather than serve and worship any god except their own God. **29** Therefore I make a decree: Any people, nation, or language that speaks anything against the God of Shadrach, Meshach, and Abednego shall be torn limb from limb, and their houses laid in ruins, for there is no other god who is able to rescue in this way." **30** Then the king promoted Shadrach, Meshach, and Abednego in the province of Babylon.

1181

Nebuchadnezzar Praises God

4 [2] King Nebuchadnezzar to all peoples, nations, and languages, that dwell in all the earth: Peace be multiplied to you! **2** It has seemed good to me to show the signs and wonders that the Most High God has done for me.

3 How great are his signs,
how mighty his wonders!
His kingdom is an everlasting
kingdom,
and his dominion endures from
generation to generation.

Nebuchadnezzar's Second Dream

4 [3] I, Nebuchadnezzar, was at ease in my house and prospering in my palace. **5** I saw a dream that made me afraid. As I lay in bed the fancies and the visions of my head alarmed me. **6** So I made a decree that all the wise men of Babylon should be brought before me, that they might make known to me the interpretation of the dream. **7** Then the magicians, the enchanters, the Chaldeans, and the astrologers came in, and I told them the dream, but they could not make known to me its interpretation. **8** At last Daniel came in before me—he who was named Belteshazzar after the name of my god, and in whom is the spirit of the holy gods[4]—and I told him the dream, saying, **9** "O Belteshazzar, chief of the magicians, because I know that the spirit of the holy gods is in you and that no mystery is too difficult for you, tell me the visions of my dream that I saw and their interpretation. **10** The visions of my head as I lay in bed were these: I saw, and behold, a tree in the midst of the earth, and its height was great. **11** The tree grew and became strong, and its top reached to heaven, and it was visible to the end of the whole earth. **12** Its leaves were beautiful and its fruit abundant, and in it was food for all. The beasts of the field found shade under it, and the birds of the heavens lived in its branches, and all flesh was fed from it.

[1] Aramaic *and changed* [2] Ch 3:31 in Aramaic [3] Ch 4:1 in Aramaic [4] Or *Spirit of the holy God*; also verses 9, 18

[13]"I saw in the visions of my head as I
lay in bed, and behold, a watcher, a holy
one, came down from heaven. [14]He pro-
claimed aloud and said thus: 'Chop down
the tree and lop off its branches, strip off
its leaves and scatter its fruit. Let the beasts
flee from under it and the birds from its
branches. [15]But leave the stump of its roots
in the earth, bound with a band of iron and
bronze, amid the tender grass of the field.
Let him be wet with the dew of heaven. Let
his portion be with the beasts in the grass
of the earth. [16]Let his mind be changed
from a man's, and let a beast's mind be
given to him; and let seven periods of time
pass over him. [17]The sentence is by the
decree of the watchers, the decision by the
word of the holy ones, to the end that the
living may know that the Most High rules
the kingdom of men and gives it to whom
he will and sets over it the lowliest of men.'
[18]This dream I, King Nebuchadnezzar, saw.
And you, O Belteshazzar, tell me the inter-
pretation, because all the wise men of my
kingdom are not able to make known to
me the interpretation, but you are able, for
the spirit of the holy gods is in you."

Daniel Interprets the Second Dream

[19]Then Daniel, whose name was Bel-
teshazzar, was dismayed for a while,
and his thoughts alarmed him. The king
answered and said, "Belteshazzar, let not
the dream or the interpretation alarm
you." Belteshazzar answered and said, "My
lord, may the dream be for those who hate
you and its interpretation for your ene-
mies! [20]The tree you saw, which grew and
became strong, so that its top reached to
heaven, and it was visible to the end of the
whole earth, [21]whose leaves were beautiful
and its fruit abundant, and in which was
food for all, under which beasts of the field
found shade, and in whose branches the
birds of the heavens lived— [22]it is you, O
king, who have grown and become strong.
Your greatness has grown and reaches to
heaven, and your dominion to the ends
of the earth. [23]And because the king saw
a watcher, a holy one, coming down from
heaven and saying, 'Chop down the tree
and destroy it, but leave the stump of its
roots in the earth, bound with a band of
iron and bronze, in the tender grass of the
field, and let him be wet with the dew of
heaven, and let his portion be with the
beasts of the field, till seven periods of
time pass over him,' [24]this is the interpreta-
tion, O king: It is a decree of the Most High,
which has come upon my lord the king,
[25]that you shall be driven from among
men, and your dwelling shall be with the
beasts of the field. You shall be made to
eat grass like an ox, and you shall be wet

CHARACTER PROFILE

NEBUCHADNEZZAR

Nebuchadnezzar destroyed Jerusalem. He was the proud king of Babylon, and did not give God glory for his kingdom. God caused Nebuchadnezzar to lose his mind. He lived outside like an animal and ate grass for seven years. When God restored his mind, Nebuchadnezzar gave God glory as the highest King and the only true God.

1181

with the dew of heaven, and seven periods
of time shall pass over you, till you know
that the Most High rules the kingdom of
men and gives it to whom he will. 26 And
as it was commanded to leave the stump
of the roots of the tree, your kingdom shall
be confirmed for you from the time that
you know that Heaven rules. 27 Therefore,
O king, let my counsel be acceptable to
you: break off your sins by practicing righ-
teousness, and your iniquities by showing
mercy to the oppressed, that there may per-
haps be a lengthening of your prosperity."

Nebuchadnezzar's Humiliation

28 All this came upon King Nebuchad-
nezzar. 29 At the end of twelve months he
was walking on the roof of the royal pal-
ace of Babylon, 30 and the king answered
and said, "Is not this great Babylon, which
I have built by my mighty power as a royal
residence and for the glory of my majesty?"
31 While the words were still in the king's
mouth, there fell a voice from heaven, "O
King Nebuchadnezzar, to you it is spoken:
The kingdom has departed from you, 32 and
you shall be driven from among men, and
your dwelling shall be with the beasts of
the field. And you shall be made to eat grass
like an ox, and seven periods of time shall
pass over you, until you know that the Most
High rules the kingdom of men and gives it
to whom he will." 33 Immediately the word
was fulfilled against Nebuchadnezzar. He
was driven from among men and ate grass
like an ox, and his body was wet with the
dew of heaven till his hair grew as long
as eagles' feathers, and his nails were like
birds' claws.

Nebuchadnezzar Restored

34 At the end of the days I, Nebuchadnez-
zar, lifted my eyes to heaven, and my rea-
son returned to me, and I blessed the Most
High, and praised and honored him who
lives forever,

for his dominion is an everlasting
    dominion,
  and his kingdom endures from
    generation to generation;
35 all the inhabitants of the earth are
    accounted as nothing,
  and he does according to his will
    among the host of heaven
  and among the inhabitants of the
    earth;
and none can stay his hand
  or say to him, "What have you
    done?"

36 At the same time my reason returned to
me, and for the glory of my kingdom, my
majesty and splendor returned to me. My
counselors and my lords sought me, and I
was established in my kingdom, and still
more greatness was added to me. 37 Now
I, Nebuchadnezzar, praise and extol and
honor the King of heaven, for all his works
are right and his ways are just; and those
who walk in pride he is able to humble.

The Handwriting on the Wall

5 King Belshazzar made a great feast
for a thousand of his lords and drank
wine in front of the thousand.

2 Belshazzar, when he tasted the wine,
commanded that the vessels of gold and
of silver that Nebuchadnezzar his father[1]
had taken out of the temple in Jerusalem
be brought, that the king and his lords,
his wives, and his concubines might drink
from them. 3 Then they brought in the
golden vessels that had been taken out of
the temple, the house of God in Jerusalem,
and the king and his lords, his wives, and
his concubines drank from them. 4 They
drank wine and praised the gods of gold
and silver, bronze, iron, wood, and stone.

5 Immediately the fingers of a human
hand appeared and wrote on the plas-
ter of the wall of the king's palace, oppo-
site the lampstand. And the king saw the
hand as it wrote. 6 Then the king's color
changed, and his thoughts alarmed him;

[1] Or *predecessor;* also verses 11, 13, 18

his limbs gave way, and his knees knocked
together. **7** The king called loudly to bring
in the enchanters, the Chaldeans, and the
astrologers. The king declared[1] to the wise
men of Babylon, "Whoever reads this writ-
ing, and shows me its interpretation, shall
be clothed with purple and have a chain of
gold around his neck and shall be the third
ruler in the kingdom." **8** Then all the king's
wise men came in, but they could not read
the writing or make known to the king the
interpretation. **9** Then King Belshazzar was
greatly alarmed, and his color changed,
and his lords were perplexed.

10 The queen,[2] because of the words of
the king and his lords, came into the ban-
queting hall, and the queen declared, "O
king, live forever! Let not your thoughts
alarm you or your color change. **11** There
is a man in your kingdom in whom is
the spirit of the holy gods.[3] In the days of
your father, light and understanding and
wisdom like the wisdom of the gods were
found in him, and King Nebuchadnezzar,
your father—your father the king—made
him chief of the magicians, enchanters,
Chaldeans, and astrologers, **12** because an
excellent spirit, knowledge, and under-
standing to interpret dreams, explain
riddles, and solve problems were found
in this Daniel, whom the king named
Belteshazzar. Now let Daniel be called,
and he will show the interpretation."

Daniel Interprets the Handwriting

13 Then Daniel was brought in before
the king. The king answered and said to
Daniel, "You are that Daniel, one of the
exiles of Judah, whom the king my father
brought from Judah. **14** I have heard of you
that the spirit of the gods[4] is in you, and
that light and understanding and excellent
wisdom are found in you. **15** Now the wise
men, the enchanters, have been brought in
before me to read this writing and make
known to me its interpretation, but they
could not show the interpretation of the
matter. **16** But I have heard that you can
give interpretations and solve problems.
Now if you can read the writing and make
known to me its interpretation, you shall
be clothed with purple and have a chain
of gold around your neck and shall be the
third ruler in the kingdom."

17 Then Daniel answered and said before
the king, "Let your gifts be for yourself, and
give your rewards to another. Nevertheless,
I will read the writing to the king and make
known to him the interpretation. **18** O king,
the Most High God gave Nebuchadnezzar
your father kingship and greatness and
glory and majesty. **19** And because of the
greatness that he gave him, all peoples,
nations, and languages trembled and
feared before him. Whom he would,
he killed, and whom he would, he kept
alive; whom he would, he raised up, and
whom he would, he humbled. **20** But when
his heart was lifted up and his spirit was
hardened so that he dealt proudly, he was
brought down from his kingly throne,
and his glory was taken from him. **21** He
was driven from among the children of
mankind, and his mind was made like
that of a beast, and his dwelling was with
the wild donkeys. He was fed grass like an
ox, and his body was wet with the dew of
heaven, until he knew that the Most High
God rules the kingdom of mankind and
sets over it whom he will. **22** And you his
son,[5] Belshazzar, have not humbled your
heart, though you knew all this, **23** but you
have lifted up yourself against the Lord of
heaven. And the vessels of his house have
been brought in before you, and you and
your lords, your wives, and your concu-
bines have drunk wine from them. And you
have praised the gods of silver and gold, of
bronze, iron, wood, and stone, which do
not see or hear or know, but the God in
whose hand is your breath, and whose are
all your ways, you have not honored.

24 "Then from his presence the hand was
sent, and this writing was inscribed. **25** And

[1] Aramaic *answered and said;* also verse 10 [2] Or *queen mother;* twice in this verse [3] Or *Spirit of the holy God* [4] Or *Spirit of God* [5] Or *successor*

this is the writing that was inscribed: MENE, MENE, TEKEL, and PARSIN. 26 This is the interpretation of the matter: MENE, God has numbered[1] the days of your kingdom and brought it to an end; 27 TEKEL, you have been weighed[2] in the balances and found wanting; 28 PERES, your kingdom is divided and given to the Medes and Persians."[3]

29 Then Belshazzar gave the command, and Daniel was clothed with purple, a chain of gold was put around his neck, and a proclamation was made about him, that he should be the third ruler in the kingdom.

30 That very night Belshazzar the Chaldean king was killed. 31 [4] And Darius the Mede received the kingdom, being about sixty-two years old.

Daniel and the Lions' Den

1191

6 It pleased Darius to set over the kingdom 120 satraps, to be throughout the whole kingdom; 2 and over them three presidents, of whom Daniel was one, to whom these satraps should give account, so that the king might suffer no loss. 3 Then this Daniel became distinguished above all the other presidents and satraps, because an excellent spirit was in him. And the king planned to set him over the whole kingdom. 4 Then the presidents and the satraps sought to find a ground for complaint against Daniel with regard to the kingdom, but they could find no ground for complaint or any fault, because he was faithful, and no error or fault was found in him. 5 Then these men said, "We shall not find any ground for complaint against this Daniel unless we find it in connection with the law of his God."

6 Then these presidents and satraps came by agreement[5] to the king and said to him, "O King Darius, live forever! 7 All the presidents of the kingdom, the prefects and the satraps, the counselors and the governors are agreed that the king should establish an ordinance and enforce an injunction, that whoever makes petition to any god or man for thirty days, except to you, O king, shall be cast into the den of lions. 8 Now, O king, establish the injunction and sign the document, so that it cannot be changed, according to the law of the Medes and the Persians, which cannot be revoked." 9 Therefore King Darius signed the document and injunction.

10 When Daniel knew that the document had been signed, he went to his house where he had windows in his upper chamber open toward Jerusalem. He got down on his knees three times a day and prayed and gave thanks before his God, as he had done previously. 11 Then these men came by agreement and found Daniel making petition and plea before his God. 12 Then they came near and said before the king, concerning the injunction, "O king! Did you not sign an injunction, that anyone who makes petition to any god or man within thirty days except to you, O king, shall be cast into the den of lions?" The king answered and said, "The thing stands fast, according to the law of the Medes and Persians, which cannot be revoked." 13 Then they answered and said before the king, "Daniel, who is one of the exiles from Judah, pays no attention to you, O king, or the injunction you have signed, but makes his petition three times a day."

14 Then the king, when he heard these words, was much distressed and set his mind to deliver Daniel. And he labored till the sun went down to rescue him. 15 Then these men came by agreement to the king and said to the king, "Know, O king, that it is a law of the Medes and Persians that no injunction or ordinance that the king establishes can be changed."

16 Then the king commanded, and Daniel was brought and cast into the den of lions. The king declared[6] to Daniel, "May your God, whom you serve con-

[1] *MENE* sounds like the Aramaic for *numbered* [2] *TEKEL* sounds like the Aramaic for *weighed* [3] *PERES* (the singular of *Parsin*) sounds like the Aramaic for *divided* and for *Persia* [4] Ch 6:1 in Aramaic [5] Or *came thronging*; also verses 11, 15 [6] Aramaic *answered and said*; also verse 20

tinually, deliver you!" 17 And a stone was
brought and laid on the mouth of the
den, and the king sealed it with his own
signet and with the signet of his lords,
that nothing might be changed concern-
ing Daniel. 18 Then the king went to his
palace and spent the night fasting; no
diversions were brought to him, and sleep
fled from him.

19 Then, at break of day, the king arose
and went in haste to the den of lions. 20 As
he came near to the den where Daniel
was, he cried out in a tone of anguish.
The king declared to Daniel, "O Daniel,
servant of the living God, has your God,
whom you serve continually, been able
to deliver you from the lions?" 21 Then
Daniel said to the king, "O king, live for-
ever! 22 My God sent his angel and shut
the lions' mouths, and they have not
harmed me, because I was found blame-
less before him; and also before you, O
king, I have done no harm." 23 Then the
king was exceedingly glad, and com-
manded that Daniel be taken up out of
the den. So Daniel was taken up out of
the den, and no kind of harm was found
on him, because he had trusted in his
God. 24 And the king commanded, and
those men who had maliciously accused
Daniel were brought and cast into the den
of lions—they, their children, and their
wives. And before they reached the bot-
tom of the den, the lions overpowered
them and broke all their bones in pieces.

25 Then King Darius wrote to all the peo-
ples, nations, and languages that dwell in
all the earth: "Peace be multiplied to you.
26 I make a decree, that in all my royal
dominion people are to tremble and fear
before the God of Daniel,

for he is the living God,
  enduring forever;
his kingdom shall never be destroyed,
  and his dominion shall be to the
    end.
27 He delivers and rescues;
  he works signs and wonders
  in heaven and on earth,
he who has saved Daniel
  from the power of the lions."

28 So this Daniel prospered during the
reign of Darius and the reign of Cyrus the
Persian.

Daniel's Vision of the Four Beasts

7 In the first year of Belshazzar king
of Babylon, Daniel saw a dream and
visions of his head as he lay in his bed.
Then he wrote down the dream and told
the sum of the matter. 2 Daniel declared,[1]
"I saw in my vision by night, and behold,
the four winds of heaven were stirring
up the great sea. 3 And four great beasts
came up out of the sea, different from one
another. 4 The first was like a lion and had
eagles' wings. Then as I looked its wings
were plucked off, and it was lifted up from
the ground and made to stand on two feet
like a man, and the mind of a man was
given to it. 5 And behold, another beast,
a second one, like a bear. It was raised up
on one side. It had three ribs in its mouth
between its teeth; and it was told, 'Arise,
devour much flesh.' 6 After this I looked,
and behold, another, like a leopard, with
four wings of a bird on its back. And the
beast had four heads, and dominion was
given to it. 7 After this I saw in the night
visions, and behold, a fourth beast, terrify-
ing and dreadful and exceedingly strong.
It had great iron teeth; it devoured and
broke in pieces and stamped what was
left with its feet. It was different from
all the beasts that were before it, and it
had ten horns. 8 I considered the horns,
and behold, there came up among them
another horn, a little one, before which
three of the first horns were plucked up
by the roots. And behold, in this horn were
eyes like the eyes of a man, and a mouth
speaking great things.

[1] Aramaic *answered and said*

Daniel in the Lions' Den

King Darius chose three leaders to help rule his kingdom. Daniel was one of the three, but Daniel was the best leader of them all.

Daniel believed in God and prayed to Him every day. The king's other workers did not like Daniel. So together they went to the king with a plan to get Daniel in trouble. They told the king that all the king's helpers wanted him to make a new law. The law would say that, for 30 days, people could only ask the king for things they wanted. If someone asked another person for something, or if anyone asked a god for something, that person would be thrown into a den filled with hungry lions.

The king agreed and made the new law. When Daniel heard about the law, he went home to his upstairs room, got down on his knees by the window, and prayed to God, just as he always did.

Daniel's enemies saw him praying to God. They hurried to the king and told him that Daniel was not obeying the new law—Daniel was asking God for something, instead of the king!

The king liked Daniel, and he was upset that the new law got Daniel in trouble. He tried to think of a way to save Daniel, but once a law had been made, it could not be changed.

King Darius had no choice. He had to throw Daniel into the lions' den. The king told Daniel, "May your God, Whom you serve continually, deliver you!" Then the king's helpers threw Daniel into the den of hungry lions. That night the king did not sleep or eat, because he was so afraid that Daniel would be devoured by the lions.

At the first light of dawn, the king ran to the lions' den and shouted, "O Daniel, servant of the living God, has your God, whom you serve continually, been able to deliver you from the lions?"

Daniel answered, "My God sent His angel and shut the lions' mouths, and they have not harmed me."

The king was so happy! Daniel was alive! The king gave orders to lift Daniel out of the lions' den. Then King Darius threw Daniel's accusers into the lions' den. The king wrote to everyone in his kingdom saying, "I make a decree, that in all my royal dominion people are to tremble and fear before the God of Daniel, for He is the living God, enduring forever; His kingdom shall never be destroyed, and His dominion shall be to the end. He delivers and rescues; He works signs and wonders in heaven and on earth, He who has saved Daniel from the power of the lions."

God watches over you and me each day too. He sent Jesus to be our Savior and rescue us from all our sins. We can trust God to care for us.

SEEK and FIND

WHERE TO FIND THE STORY

Daniel 6

KEY BIBLE VERSE

"The eyes of the LORD are toward the righteous
and his ears toward their cry."
(Psalm 34:15)

THREE KEY QUESTIONS

- When the new law said that no one could pray to God, what did Daniel do?
- What happened to Daniel when he was thrown into the lions' den?
- What did the king write to everyone in his kingdom because God delivered Daniel from the lions?

RELATED BIBLE READINGS

Psalm 27:1–14; 118:5–9; Romans 8:35–39; Hebrews 11:32–34

The Ancient of Days Reigns

9 "As I looked,
thrones were placed,
and the Ancient of Days took his seat;
his clothing was white as snow,
and the hair of his head like pure wool;
his throne was fiery flames;
its wheels were burning fire.
10 A stream of fire issued
and came out from before him;
a thousand thousands served him,
and ten thousand times ten thousand stood before him;
the court sat in judgment,
and the books were opened.

11 "I looked then because of the sound of
the great words that the horn was speak-
ing. And as I looked, the beast was killed,
and its body destroyed and given over to
be burned with fire. 12 As for the rest of the
beasts, their dominion was taken away,
but their lives were prolonged for a season
and a time.

The Son of Man Is Given Dominion

13 "I saw in the night visions,
and behold, with the clouds of heaven
there came one like a son of man,
and he came to the Ancient of Days
and was presented before him.
14 And to him was given dominion
and glory and a kingdom,
that all peoples, nations, and languages
should serve him;
his dominion is an everlasting dominion,

which shall not pass away,
and his kingdom one
that shall not be destroyed.

Daniel's Vision Interpreted

15 "As for me, Daniel, my spirit within
me[1] was anxious, and the visions of my
head alarmed me. 16 I approached one of
those who stood there and asked him the
truth concerning all this. So he told me
and made known to me the interpretation
of the things. 17 'These four great beasts
are four kings who shall arise out of the
earth. 18 But the saints of the Most High
shall receive the kingdom and possess the
kingdom forever, forever and ever.'

19 "Then I desired to know the truth
about the fourth beast, which was dif-
ferent from all the rest, exceedingly ter-
rifying, with its teeth of iron and claws of
bronze, and which devoured and broke in
pieces and stamped what was left with its
feet, 20 and about the ten horns that were
on its head, and the other horn that came
up and before which three of them fell, the
horn that had eyes and a mouth that spoke
great things, and that seemed greater than
its companions. 21 As I looked, this horn
made war with the saints and prevailed
over them, 22 until the Ancient of Days
came, and judgment was given for the
saints of the Most High, and the time came
when the saints possessed the kingdom.

23 "Thus he said: 'As for the fourth beast,

there shall be a fourth kingdom on
earth,
which shall be different from all
the kingdoms,
and it shall devour the whole earth,
and trample it down, and break it
to pieces.
24 As for the ten horns,
out of this kingdom ten kings shall
arise,
and another shall arise after them;
he shall be different from the
former ones,
and shall put down three kings.
25 He shall speak words against the
Most High,
and shall wear out the saints of
the Most High,
and shall think to change the
times and the law;
and they shall be given into his hand
for a time, times, and half a time.
26 But the court shall sit in judgment,
and his dominion shall be taken
away,
to be consumed and destroyed to
the end.
27 And the kingdom and the dominion
and the greatness of the kingdoms
under the whole heaven
shall be given to the people of the
saints of the Most High;
their kingdom shall be an
everlasting kingdom,
and all dominions shall serve and
obey them.'[2]

28 "Here is the end of the matter. As for
me, Daniel, my thoughts greatly alarmed
me, and my color changed, but I kept the
matter in my heart."

Daniel's Vision of the Ram and the Goat

8 In the third year of the reign of King
Belshazzar a vision appeared to me,
Daniel, after that which appeared to me
at the first. 2 And I saw in the vision; and
when I saw, I was in Susa the capital,[3]
which is in the province of Elam. And I
saw in the vision, and I was at the Ulai
canal. 3 I raised my eyes and saw, and
behold, a ram standing on the bank of the
canal. It had two horns, and both horns
were high, but one was higher than the
other, and the higher one came up last.
4 I saw the ram charging westward and
northward and southward. No beast could
stand before him, and there was no one
who could rescue from his power. He did
as he pleased and became great.
5 As I was considering, behold, a male

[1] Aramaic *within its sheath* [2] Or *his kingdom shall be an everlasting kingdom, and all dominions shall serve and obey him* [3] Or *the fortified city*

goat came from the west across the face of the whole earth, without touching the ground. And the goat had a conspicuous horn between his eyes. 6 He came to the ram with the two horns, which I had seen standing on the bank of the canal, and he ran at him in his powerful wrath. 7 I saw him come close to the ram, and he was enraged against him and struck the ram and broke his two horns. And the ram had no power to stand before him, but he cast him down to the ground and trampled on him. And there was no one who could rescue the ram from his power. 8 Then the goat became exceedingly great, but when he was strong, the great horn was broken, and instead of it there came up four conspicuous horns toward the four winds of heaven.

9 Out of one of them came a little horn, which grew exceedingly great toward the south, toward the east, and toward the glorious land. 10 It grew great, even to the host of heaven. And some of the host and some[1] of the stars it threw down to the ground and trampled on them. 11 It became great, even as great as the Prince of the host. And the regular burnt offering was taken away from him, and the place of his sanctuary was overthrown. 12 And a host will be given over to it together with the regular burnt offering because of transgression,[2] and it will throw truth to the ground, and it will act and prosper. 13 Then I heard a holy one speaking, and another holy one said to the one who spoke, "For how long is the vision concerning the regular burnt offering, the transgression that makes desolate, and the giving over of the sanctuary and host to be trampled underfoot?" 14 And he said to me,[3] "For 2,300 evenings and mornings. Then the sanctuary shall be restored to its rightful state."

The Interpretation of the Vision

15 When I, Daniel, had seen the vision, I sought to understand it. And behold, there stood before me one having the appearance of a man. 16 And I heard a man's voice between the banks of the Ulai, and it called, "Gabriel, make this man understand the vision." 17 So he came near where I stood. And when he came, I was frightened and fell on my face. But he said to me, "Understand, O son of man, that the vision is for the time of the end."

18 And when he had spoken to me, I fell into a deep sleep with my face to the ground. But he touched me and made me stand up. 19 He said, "Behold, I will make known to you what shall be at the latter end of the indignation, for it refers to the appointed time of the end. 20 As for the ram that you saw with the two horns, these are the kings of Media and Persia. 21 And the goat[4] is the king of Greece. And the great horn between his eyes is the first king. 22 As for the horn that was broken, in place of which four others arose, four kingdoms shall arise from his[5] nation, but not with his power. 23 And at the latter end of their kingdom, when the transgressors have reached their limit, a king of bold face, one who understands riddles, shall arise. 24 His power shall be great—but not by his own power; and he shall cause fearful destruction and shall succeed in what he does, and destroy mighty men and the people who are the saints. 25 By his cunning he shall make deceit prosper under his hand, and in his own mind he shall become great. Without warning he shall destroy many. And he shall even rise up against the Prince of princes, and he shall be broken—but by no human hand. 26 The vision of the evenings and the mornings that has been told is true, but seal up the vision, for it refers to many days from now."

27 And I, Daniel, was overcome and lay sick for some days. Then I rose and went about the king's business, but I was appalled by the vision and did not understand it.

[1] Or *host, that is, some* [2] Or *in an act of rebellion* [3] Hebrew; Septuagint, Theodotion, Vulgate *to him* [4] Or *the shaggy goat* [5] Theodotion, Septuagint, Vulgate; Hebrew *the*

Daniel's Prayer for His People

9 In the first year of Darius the son of Ahasuerus, by descent a Mede, who was made king over the realm of the Chaldeans— 2 in the first year of his reign, I, Daniel, perceived in the books the number of years that, according to the word of the LORD to Jeremiah the prophet, must pass before the end of the desolations of Jerusalem, namely, seventy years.

3 Then I turned my face to the Lord God, seeking him by prayer and pleas for mercy with fasting and sackcloth and ashes. 4 I prayed to the LORD my God and made confession, saying, "O Lord, the great and awesome God, who keeps covenant and steadfast love with those who love him and keep his commandments, 5 we have sinned and done wrong and acted wickedly and rebelled, turning aside from your commandments and rules. 6 We have not listened to your servants the prophets, who spoke in your name to our kings, our princes, and our fathers, and to all the people of the land. 7 To you, O Lord, belongs righteousness, but to us open shame, as at this day, to the men of Judah, to the inhabitants of Jerusalem, and to all Israel, those who are near and those who are far away, in all the lands to which you have driven them, because of the treachery that they have committed against you. 8 To us, O LORD, belongs open shame, to our kings, to our princes, and to our fathers, because we have sinned against you. 9 To the Lord our God belong mercy and forgiveness, for we have rebelled against him 10 and have not obeyed the voice of the LORD our God by walking in his laws, which he set before us by his servants the prophets. 11 All Israel has transgressed your law and turned aside, refusing to obey your voice. And the curse and oath that are written in the Law of Moses the servant of God have been poured out upon us, because we have sinned against him. 12 He has confirmed his words, which he spoke against us and against our rulers who ruled us,[1] by bringing upon us a great calamity. For under the whole heaven there has not been done anything like what has been done against Jerusalem. 13 As it is written in the Law of Moses, all this calamity has come upon us; yet we have not entreated the favor of the LORD our God, turning from our iniquities and gaining insight by your truth. 14 Therefore the LORD has kept ready the calamity and has brought it upon us, for the LORD our God is righteous in all the works that he has done, and we have not obeyed his voice. 15 And now, O Lord our God, who brought your people out of the land of Egypt with a mighty hand, and have made a name for yourself, as at this day, we have sinned, we have done wickedly.

16 "O Lord, according to all your righteous acts, let your anger and your wrath turn away from your city Jerusalem, your holy hill, because for our sins, and for the iniquities of our fathers, Jerusalem and your people have become a byword among all who are around us. 17 Now therefore, O our God, listen to the prayer of your servant and to his pleas for mercy, and for your own sake, O Lord,[2] make your face to shine upon your sanctuary, which is desolate. 18 O my God, incline your ear and hear. Open your eyes and see our desolations, and the city that is called by your name. For we do not present our pleas before you because of our righteousness, but because of your great mercy. 19 O Lord, hear; O Lord, forgive. O Lord, pay attention and act. Delay not, for your own sake, O my God, because your city and your people are called by your name."

Gabriel Brings an Answer

20 While I was speaking and praying, confessing my sin and the sin of my people Israel, and presenting my plea before the LORD my God for the holy hill of my God, 21 while I was speaking in prayer, the man Gabriel, whom I had seen in the vision at

[1] *Or our judges who judged us* [2] *Hebrew for the Lord's sake*

the first, came to me in swift flight at the
time of the evening sacrifice. 22 He made
me understand, speaking with me and say-
ing, "O Daniel, I have now come out to give
you insight and understanding. 23 At the
beginning of your pleas for mercy a word
went out, and I have come to tell it to you,
for you are greatly loved. Therefore con-
sider the word and understand the vision.

The Seventy Weeks

24 "Seventy weeks[1] are decreed about
your people and your holy city, to finish
the transgression, to put an end to sin, and
to atone for iniquity, to bring in everlast-
ing righteousness, to seal both vision and
prophet, and to anoint a most holy place.[2]
25 Know therefore and understand that
from the going out of the word to restore
and build Jerusalem to the coming of an
anointed one, a prince, there shall be seven
weeks. Then for sixty-two weeks it shall be
built again with squares and moat, but in
a troubled time. 26 And after the sixty-two
weeks, an anointed one shall be cut off and
shall have nothing. And the people of the
prince who is to come shall destroy the city
and the sanctuary. Its[3] end shall come with
a flood, and to the end there shall be war.
Desolations are decreed. 27 And he shall
make a strong covenant with many for one
week,[4] and for half of the week he shall put
an end to sacrifice and offering. And on the
wing of abominations shall come one who
makes desolate, until the decreed end is
poured out on the desolator."

Daniel's Terrifying Vision of a Man

10 In the third year of Cyrus king
of Persia a word was revealed to
Daniel, who was named Belteshazzar. And
the word was true, and it was a great con-
flict.[5] And he understood the word and
had understanding of the vision.

2 In those days I, Daniel, was mourn-
ing for three weeks. 3 I ate no delicacies,
no meat or wine entered my mouth, nor
did I anoint myself at all, for the full three
weeks. 4 On the twenty-fourth day of the
first month, as I was standing on the bank
of the great river (that is, the Tigris) 5 I lifted
up my eyes and looked, and behold, a man
clothed in linen, with a belt of fine gold
from Uphaz around his waist. 6 His body
was like beryl, his face like the appear-
ance of lightning, his eyes like flaming
torches, his arms and legs like the gleam
of burnished bronze, and the sound of his
words like the sound of a multitude. 7 And
I, Daniel, alone saw the vision, for the men
who were with me did not see the vision,
but a great trembling fell upon them, and
they fled to hide themselves. 8 So I was left
alone and saw this great vision, and no
strength was left in me. My radiant appear-
ance was fearfully changed,[6] and I retained
no strength. 9 Then I heard the sound of
his words, and as I heard the sound of his
words, I fell on my face in deep sleep with
my face to the ground.

10 And behold, a hand touched me and
set me trembling on my hands and knees.
11 And he said to me, "O Daniel, man greatly
loved, understand the words that I speak
to you, and stand upright, for now I have
been sent to you." And when he had spo-
ken this word to me, I stood up trembling.
12 Then he said to me, "Fear not, Daniel, for
from the first day that you set your heart to
understand and humbled yourself before
your God, your words have been heard, and
I have come because of your words. 13 The
prince of the kingdom of Persia withstood
me twenty-one days, but Michael, one of
the chief princes, came to help me, for I
was left there with the kings of Persia,
14 and came to make you understand what
is to happen to your people in the latter
days. For the vision is for days yet to come."

15 When he had spoken to me according
to these words, I turned my face toward
the ground and was mute. 16 And behold,
one in the likeness of the children of man
touched my lips. Then I opened my mouth

[1] *Or sevens; also twice in verse 25 and once in verse 26* [2] *Or thing, or one* [3] *Or His* [4] *Or seven; twice in this verse* [5] *Or and it was about a great conflict* [6] Hebrew *My splendor was changed to ruin*

and spoke. I said to him who stood before
me, "O my lord, by reason of the vision
pains have come upon me, and I retain
no strength. 17 How can my lord's servant
talk with my lord? For now no strength
remains in me, and no breath is left in me."

18 Again one having the appearance of
a man touched me and strengthened me.
19 And he said, "O man greatly loved, fear
not, peace be with you; be strong and of
good courage." And as he spoke to me, I was
strengthened and said, "Let my lord speak,
for you have strengthened me." 20 Then he
said, "Do you know why I have come to
you? But now I will return to fight against
the prince of Persia; and when I go out,
behold, the prince of Greece will come.
21 But I will tell you what is inscribed in the
book of truth: there is none who contends
by my side against these except Michael,
your prince.

The Kings of the South and the North

11 "And as for me, in the first year
of Darius the Mede, I stood up to
confirm and strengthen him.

2 "And now I will show you the truth.
Behold, three more kings shall arise in
Persia, and a fourth shall be far richer
than all of them. And when he has become
strong through his riches, he shall stir up
all against the kingdom of Greece. 3 Then a
mighty king shall arise, who shall rule with
great dominion and do as he wills. 4 And as
soon as he has arisen, his kingdom shall
be broken and divided toward the four
winds of heaven, but not to his posterity,
nor according to the authority with which
he ruled, for his kingdom shall be plucked
up and go to others besides these.

5 "Then the king of the south shall be
strong, but one of his princes shall be
stronger than he and shall rule, and his
authority shall be a great authority. 6 After
some years they shall make an alliance,
and the daughter of the king of the south
shall come to the king of the north to make
an agreement. But she shall not retain the
strength of her arm, and he and his arm
shall not endure, but she shall be given up,
and her attendants, he who fathered her,
and he who supported[1] her in those times.

7 "And from a branch from her roots
one shall arise in his place. He shall come
against the army and enter the fortress of
the king of the north, and he shall deal
with them and shall prevail. 8 He shall
also carry off to Egypt their gods with their
metal images and their precious vessels
of silver and gold, and for some years he
shall refrain from attacking the king of the
north. 9 Then the latter shall come into the
realm of the king of the south but shall
return to his own land.

10 "His sons shall wage war and assem-
ble a multitude of great forces, which
shall keep coming and overflow and pass
through, and again shall carry the war as
far as his fortress. 11 Then the king of the
south, moved with rage, shall come out
and fight against the king of the north.
And he shall raise a great multitude, but it
shall be given into his hand. 12 And when
the multitude is taken away, his heart shall
be exalted, and he shall cast down tens of
thousands, but he shall not prevail. 13 For
the king of the north shall again raise a
multitude, greater than the first. And after
some years[2] he shall come on with a great
army and abundant supplies.

14 "In those times many shall rise against
the king of the south, and the violent
among your own people shall lift them-
selves up in order to fulfill the vision,
but they shall fail. 15 Then the king of the
north shall come and throw up siege-
works and take a well-fortified city. And
the forces of the south shall not stand, or
even his best troops, for there shall be no
strength to stand. 16 But he who comes
against him shall do as he wills, and none
shall stand before him. And he shall stand
in the glorious land, with destruction in
his hand. 17 He shall set his face to come

[1] Or *obtained* [2] Hebrew *at the end of the times*

with the strength of his whole kingdom, and he shall bring terms of an agreement and perform them. He shall give him the daughter of women to destroy the kingdom,[1] but it shall not stand or be to his advantage. 18 Afterward he shall turn his face to the coastlands and shall capture many of them, but a commander shall put an end to his insolence. Indeed,[2] he shall turn his insolence back upon him. 19 Then he shall turn his face back toward the fortresses of his own land, but he shall stumble and fall, and shall not be found.

20 "Then shall arise in his place one who shall send an exactor of tribute for the glory of the kingdom. But within a few days he shall be broken, neither in anger nor in battle. 21 In his place shall arise a contemptible person to whom royal majesty has not been given. He shall come in without warning and obtain the kingdom by flatteries. 22 Armies shall be utterly swept away before him and broken, even the prince of the covenant. 23 And from the time that an alliance is made with him he shall act deceitfully, and he shall become strong with a small people. 24 Without warning he shall come into the richest parts[3] of the province, and he shall do what neither his fathers nor his fathers' fathers have done, scattering among them plunder, spoil, and goods. He shall devise plans against strongholds, but only for a time. 25 And he shall stir up his power and his heart against the king of the south with a great army. And the king of the south shall wage war with an exceedingly great and mighty army, but he shall not stand, for plots shall be devised against him. 26 Even those who eat his food shall break him. His army shall be swept away, and many shall fall down slain. 27 And as for the two kings, their hearts shall be bent on doing evil. They shall speak lies at the same table, but to no avail, for the end is yet to be at the time appointed. 28 And he shall return to his land with great wealth, but his heart shall be set against the holy covenant. And he shall work his will and return to his own land.

29 "At the time appointed he shall return and come into the south, but it shall not be this time as it was before. 30 For ships of Kittim shall come against him, and he shall be afraid and withdraw, and shall turn back and be enraged and take action against the holy covenant. He shall turn back and pay attention to those who forsake the holy covenant. 31 Forces from him shall appear and profane the temple and fortress, and shall take away the regular burnt offering. And they shall set up the abomination that makes desolate. 32 He shall seduce with flattery those who violate the covenant, but the people who know their God shall stand firm and take action. 33 And the wise among the people shall make many understand, though for some days they shall stumble by sword and flame, by captivity and plunder. 34 When they stumble, they shall receive a little help. And many shall join themselves to them with flattery, 35 and some of the wise shall stumble, so that they may be refined, purified, and made white, until the time of the end, for it still awaits the appointed time.

36 "And the king shall do as he wills. He shall exalt himself and magnify himself above every god, and shall speak astonishing things against the God of gods. He shall prosper till the indignation is accomplished; for what is decreed shall be done. 37 He shall pay no attention to the gods of his fathers, or to the one beloved by women. He shall not pay attention to any other god, for he shall magnify himself above all. 38 He shall honor the god of fortresses instead of these. A god whom his fathers did not know he shall honor with gold and silver, with precious stones and costly gifts. 39 He shall deal with the strongest fortresses with the help of a foreign god. Those who acknowledge him he shall load with honor. He shall make them

[1] Hebrew *her*, or *it* [2] The meaning of the Hebrew is uncertain [3] Or *among the richest men*

rulers over many and shall divide the land for a price.[1]

40 "At the time of the end, the king of the south shall attack[2] him, but the king of the north shall rush upon him like a whirlwind, with chariots and horsemen, and with many ships. And he shall come into countries and shall overflow and pass through. 41 He shall come into the glorious land. And tens of thousands shall fall, but these shall be delivered out of his hand: Edom and Moab and the main part of the Ammonites. 42 He shall stretch out his hand against the countries, and the land of Egypt shall not escape. 43 He shall become ruler of the treasures of gold and of silver, and all the precious things of Egypt, and the Libyans and the Cushites shall follow in his train. 44 But news from the east and the north shall alarm him, and he shall go out with great fury to destroy and devote many to destruction. 45 And he shall pitch his palatial tents between the sea and the glorious holy mountain. Yet he shall come to his end, with none to help him.

The Time of the End

12 "At that time shall arise Michael, the great prince who has charge of your people. And there shall be a time of trouble, such as never has been since there was a nation till that time. But at that time your people shall be delivered, everyone whose name shall be found written in the book. 2 And many of those who sleep in the dust of the earth shall awake, some to everlasting life, and some to shame and everlasting contempt. 3 And those who are wise shall shine like the brightness of the sky above;[3] and those who turn many to righteousness, like the stars forever and ever. 4 But you, Daniel, shut up the words and seal the book, until the time of the end. Many shall run to and fro, and knowledge shall increase."

5 Then I, Daniel, looked, and behold, two others stood, one on this bank of the stream and one on that bank of the stream. 6 And someone said to the man clothed in linen, who was above the waters of the stream,[4] "How long shall it be till the end of these wonders?" 7 And I heard the man clothed in linen, who was above the waters of the stream; he raised his right hand and his left hand toward heaven and swore by him who lives forever that it would be for a time, times, and half a time, and that when the shattering of the power of the holy people comes to an end all these things would be finished. 8 I heard, but I did not understand. Then I said, "O my lord, what shall be the outcome of these things?" 9 He said, "Go your way, Daniel, for the words are shut up and sealed until the time of the end. 10 Many shall purify themselves and make themselves white and be refined, but the wicked shall act wickedly. And none of the wicked shall understand, but those who are wise shall understand. 11 And from the time that the regular burnt offering is taken away and the abomination that makes desolate is set up, there shall be 1,290 days. 12 Blessed is he who waits and arrives at the 1,335 days. 13 But go your way till the end. And you shall rest and shall stand in your allotted place at the end of the days."

[1] Or *land as payment* [2] Hebrew *thrust at* [3] Hebrew *the expanse*; compare Genesis 1:6-8 [4] Or *who was upstream*; also verse 7

Introduction to

Hosea

Author

Hosea the prophet

Date

About 740–715 B.C.

People

Hosea; Gomer

Purpose

The purpose of Hosea is to show the people of the northern kingdom of Israel the evil of their sin and idol worship, while showing God's faithfulness and compassion in spite of their sin.

Central Themes

God uses an unfaithful wife and a forgiving husband as a picture of unfaithful Israel and her forgiving God; idol worship is evil; Israel is sinful and will face the coming judgment; God is faithful and merciful; God calls His people to repentance; God promises forgiveness.

Memory Verses

My husband (Hosea 2:16–17); lack of knowledge (Hosea 4:4–6); God will revive us (Hosea 6:1–3); break the fallow ground (Hosea 10:11–12); bands of love (Hosea 11:1–4); dew to Israel (Hosea 14:4–9)

Introduction

God gave Hosea to His people as a prophet and as a picture. Hosea lived in the northern kingdom of Israel, whose kings had always led the people in worshiping idols along with God. God would soon send the Assyrians to destroy Israel and carry its people away as captives. Hosea calls Israel to repent and promises God's forgiveness if they do. Hosea has a wife, Gomer, who treats other men in the special way she should treat only her husband. God tells Hosea to love Gomer anyway and to take her back as his wife. God says the Israelites are like Gomer. They have a covenant with God, but they worship idols. God is like Hosea; He still loves His unfaithful people and takes them back (Hosea 1–3). In another picture from family life, Hosea says Israel is like a child, and God is like the loving Father who has always cared for him. Now Israel has rebelled, grieving God's Father heart. Although God must punish His people, He will not give them up; He will come to them in compassion (Hosea 11).

793/781 B.C.	About 755 B.C.	722 B.C.
Reign of Jeroboam II begins	Prophetic ministry of Hosea begins	Fall of Israel

Hosea

1 The word of the LORD that came to Hosea, the son of Beeri, in the days of Uzziah, Jotham, Ahaz, and Hezekiah, kings of Judah, and in the days of Jeroboam the son of Joash, king of Israel.

Hosea's Wife and Children

2 When the LORD first spoke through Hosea, the LORD said to Hosea, "Go, take to yourself a wife of whoredom and have children of whoredom, for the land commits great whoredom by forsaking the LORD." 3 So he went and took Gomer, the daughter of Diblaim, and she conceived and bore him a son.

4 And the LORD said to him, "Call his name Jezreel, for in just a little while I will punish the house of Jehu for the blood of Jezreel, and I will put an end to the kingdom of the house of Israel. 5 And on that day I will break the bow of Israel in the Valley of Jezreel."

6 She conceived again and bore a daughter. And the LORD said to him, "Call her name No Mercy,[1] for I will no more have mercy on the house of Israel, to forgive them at all. 7 But I will have mercy on the house of Judah, and I will save them by the LORD their God. I will not save them by bow or by sword or by war or by horses or by horsemen."

8 When she had weaned No Mercy, she conceived and bore a son. 9 And the LORD said, "Call his name Not My People,[2] for you are not my people, and I am not your God."[3]

10 [4] Yet the number of the children of Israel shall be like the sand of the sea, which cannot be measured or numbered. And in the place where it was said to them, "You are not my people," it shall be said to them, "Children[5] of the living God." 11 And the children of Judah and the children of Israel shall be gathered together, and they shall appoint for themselves one head. And they shall go up from the land, for great shall be the day of Jezreel.

Israel's Unfaithfulness Punished

2 [6] Say to your brothers, "You are my people,"[7] and to your sisters, "You have received mercy."[8]

2 "Plead with your mother, plead—
for she is not my wife,
and I am not her husband—
that she put away her whoring from her face,
and her adultery from between her breasts;
3 lest I strip her naked
and make her as in the day she was born,
and make her like a wilderness,
and make her like a parched land,
and kill her with thirst.
4 Upon her children also I will have no mercy,
because they are children of whoredom.
5 For their mother has played the whore;
she who conceived them has acted shamefully.
For she said, 'I will go after my lovers,
who give me my bread and my water,
my wool and my flax, my oil and my drink.'
6 Therefore I will hedge up her[9] way with thorns,
and I will build a wall against her,
so that she cannot find her paths.

[1] Hebrew *Lo-ruhama*, which means *she has not received mercy* [2] Hebrew *Lo-ammi*, which means *not my people* [3] Hebrew *I am not yours* [4] Ch 2:1 in Hebrew [5] Or *Sons* [6] Ch 2:3 in Hebrew [7] Hebrew *ammi*, which means *my people* [8] Hebrew *ruhama*, which means *she has received mercy* [9] Hebrew *your*

7 She shall pursue her lovers
but not overtake them,
and she shall seek them
but shall not find them.
Then she shall say,
'I will go and return to my first
husband,
for it was better for me then than
now.'
8 And she did not know
that it was I who gave her
the grain, the wine, and the oil,
and who lavished on her silver and
gold,
which they used for Baal.
9 Therefore I will take back
my grain in its time,
and my wine in its season,
and I will take away my wool and
my flax,
which were to cover her
nakedness.
10 Now I will uncover her lewdness
in the sight of her lovers,
and no one shall rescue her out of
my hand.
11 And I will put an end to all her
mirth,
her feasts, her new moons, her
Sabbaths,
and all her appointed feasts.
12 And I will lay waste her vines and
her fig trees,
of which she said,
'These are my wages,
which my lovers have given me.'
I will make them a forest,
and the beasts of the field shall
devour them.
13 And I will punish her for the feast
days of the Baals
when she burned offerings to
them
and adorned herself with her ring
and jewelry,
and went after her lovers
and forgot me, declares the LORD.

The LORD's Mercy on Israel

14 "Therefore, behold, I will allure her,
and bring her into the wilderness,
and speak tenderly to her.
15 And there I will give her her vineyards
and make the Valley of Achor[1] a
door of hope.
And there she shall answer as in the
days of her youth,
as at the time when she came out
of the land of Egypt.

16 "And in that day, declares the LORD,
you will call me 'My Husband,' and no long-
er will you call me 'My Baal.' 17 For I will
remove the names of the Baals from her
mouth, and they shall be remembered by
name no more. 18 And I will make for them
a covenant on that day with the beasts of
the field, the birds of the heavens, and the
creeping things of the ground. And I will
abolish[2] the bow, the sword, and war from
the land, and I will make you lie down in
safety. 19 And I will betroth you to me for-
ever. I will betroth you to me in righteous-
ness and in justice, in steadfast love and in
mercy. 20 I will betroth you to me in faith-
fulness. And you shall know the LORD.

21 "And in that day I will answer,
declares the LORD,
I will answer the heavens,
and they shall answer the earth,
22 and the earth shall answer the
grain, the wine, and the oil,
and they shall answer Jezreel,[3]
23 and I will sow her for myself in
the land.
And I will have mercy on No Mercy,[4]
and I will say to Not My People,[5]
'You are my people';
and he shall say, 'You are my God.'"

Hosea Redeems His Wife

3 And the LORD said to me, "Go again,
love a woman who is loved by another
man and is an adulteress, even as the
LORD loves the children of Israel, though

[1] *Achor* means *trouble*; compare Joshua 7:26 [2] Hebrew *break* [3] *Jezreel* means *God will sow* [4] Hebrew *Lo-ruhama* [5] Hebrew *Lo-ammi*

they turn to other gods and love cakes of
raisins." 2 So I bought her for fifteen shek-
els of silver and a homer and a lethech[1] of
barley. 3 And I said to her, "You must dwell
as mine for many days. You shall not play
the whore, or belong to another man; so
will I also be to you." 4 For the children of
Israel shall dwell many days without king
or prince, without sacrifice or pillar, with-
out ephod or household gods. 5 Afterward
the children of Israel shall return and seek
the LORD their God, and David their king,
and they shall come in fear to the LORD
and to his goodness in the latter days.

The LORD Accuses Israel

4 Hear the word of the LORD, O children of Israel,
for the LORD has a controversy with the inhabitants of the land.
There is no faithfulness or steadfast love,
and no knowledge of God in the land;
2 there is swearing, lying, murder, stealing, and committing adultery;
they break all bounds, and bloodshed follows bloodshed.
3 Therefore the land mourns,
and all who dwell in it languish,
and also the beasts of the field
and the birds of the heavens,
and even the fish of the sea are taken away.

4 Yet let no one contend,
and let none accuse,
for with you is my contention, O priest.[2]
5 You shall stumble by day;
the prophet also shall stumble with you by night;
and I will destroy your mother.
6 My people are destroyed for lack of knowledge;
because you have rejected knowledge,
I reject you from being a priest to me.
And since you have forgotten the law of your God,
I also will forget your children.

7 The more they increased,
the more they sinned against me;
I will change their glory into shame.
8 They feed on the sin[3] of my people;
they are greedy for their iniquity.
9 And it shall be like people, like priest;
I will punish them for their ways
and repay them for their deeds.
10 They shall eat, but not be satisfied;
they shall play the whore, but not multiply,
because they have forsaken the LORD
to cherish 11 whoredom, wine, and new wine,
which take away the understanding.
12 My people inquire of a piece of wood,
and their walking staff gives them oracles.
For a spirit of whoredom has led them astray,
and they have left their God to play the whore.
13 They sacrifice on the tops of the mountains
and burn offerings on the hills,
under oak, poplar, and terebinth,
because their shade is good.
Therefore your daughters play the whore,
and your brides commit adultery.
14 I will not punish your daughters when they play the whore,
nor your brides when they commit adultery;

[1] A *shekel* was about 2/5 ounce or 11 grams; a *homer* was about 6 bushels or 220 liters; a *lethech* was about 3 bushels or 110 liters [2] Or *for your people are like those who contend with the priest* [3] Or *sin offering*

for the men themselves go aside
with prostitutes
and sacrifice with cult prostitutes,
and a people without understanding
shall come to ruin.
15 Though you play the whore, O
Israel,
let not Judah become guilty.
Enter not into Gilgal,
nor go up to Beth-aven,
and swear not, "As the LORD lives."
16 Like a stubborn heifer,
Israel is stubborn;
can the LORD now feed them
like a lamb in a broad pasture?
17 Ephraim is joined to idols;
leave him alone.
18 When their drink is gone, they give
themselves to whoring;
their rulers[1] dearly love shame.
19 A wind has wrapped them[2] in its
wings,
and they shall be ashamed
because of their sacrifices.

Punishment Coming for Israel and Judah

5 Hear this, O priests!
Pay attention, O house of Israel!
Give ear, O house of the king!
For the judgment is for you;
for you have been a snare at Mizpah
and a net spread upon Tabor.
2 And the revolters have gone deep
into slaughter,
but I will discipline all of them.
3 I know Ephraim,
and Israel is not hidden from me;
for now, O Ephraim, you have
played the whore;
Israel is defiled.
4 Their deeds do not permit them
to return to their God.
For the spirit of whoredom is
within them,
and they know not the LORD.
5 The pride of Israel testifies to his face;[3]
Israel and Ephraim shall stumble
in his guilt;
Judah also shall stumble with them.
6 With their flocks and herds they
shall go
to seek the LORD,
but they will not find him;
he has withdrawn from them.
7 They have dealt faithlessly with the
LORD;
for they have borne alien children.
Now the new moon shall devour
them with their fields.
8 Blow the horn in Gibeah,
the trumpet in Ramah.
Sound the alarm at Beth-aven;
we follow you,[4] O Benjamin!
9 Ephraim shall become a desolation
in the day of punishment;
among the tribes of Israel
I make known what is sure.
10 The princes of Judah have become
like those who move the
landmark;
upon them I will pour out
my wrath like water.
11 Ephraim is oppressed, crushed in
judgment,
because he was determined to go
after filth.[5]
12 But I am like a moth to Ephraim,
and like dry rot to the house of
Judah.
13 When Ephraim saw his sickness,
and Judah his wound,
then Ephraim went to Assyria,
and sent to the great king.[6]
But he is not able to cure you
or heal your wound.
14 For I will be like a lion to Ephraim,
and like a young lion to the house
of Judah.
I, even I, will tear and go away;
I will carry off, and no one shall
rescue.

[1] Hebrew *shields* [2] Hebrew *her* [3] Or *in his presence* [4] Or *after you* [5] Or *to follow human precepts* [6] Or *to King Jareb*

15 I will return again to my place,
until they acknowledge their guilt
and seek my face,
and in their distress earnestly
seek me.

Israel and Judah Are Unrepentant

6 "Come, let us return to the LORD;
for he has torn us, that he may heal
us;
he has struck us down, and he
will bind us up.
2 After two days he will revive us;
on the third day he will raise us up,
that we may live before him.
3 Let us know; let us press on to know
the LORD;
his going out is sure as the dawn;
he will come to us as the showers,
as the spring rains that water the
earth."
4 What shall I do with you, O Ephraim?
What shall I do with you, O Judah?
Your love is like a morning cloud,
like the dew that goes early away.
5 Therefore I have hewn them by the
prophets;
I have slain them by the words of
my mouth,
and my judgment goes forth as
the light.
6 For I desire steadfast love[1] and not
sacrifice,
the knowledge of God rather than
burnt offerings.
7 But like Adam they transgressed the
covenant;
there they dealt faithlessly with me.
8 Gilead is a city of evildoers,
tracked with blood.
9 As robbers lie in wait for a man,
so the priests band together;
they murder on the way to
Shechem;
they commit villainy.
10 In the house of Israel I have seen a
horrible thing;
Ephraim's whoredom is there;
Israel is defiled.
11 For you also, O Judah, a harvest is
appointed,
when I restore the fortunes of my
people.

7 When I would heal Israel,
the iniquity of Ephraim is revealed,
and the evil deeds of Samaria;
for they deal falsely;
the thief breaks in,
and the bandits raid outside.
2 But they do not consider
that I remember all their evil.
Now their deeds surround them;
they are before my face.
3 By their evil they make the king
glad,
and the princes by their treachery.
4 They are all adulterers;
they are like a heated oven
whose baker ceases to stir the fire,
from the kneading of the dough
until it is leavened.
5 On the day of our king, the princes
became sick with the heat of wine;
he stretched out his hand with
mockers.
6 For with hearts like an oven they
approach their intrigue;
all night their anger smolders;
in the morning it blazes like a
flaming fire.
7 All of them are hot as an oven,
and they devour their rulers.
All their kings have fallen,
and none of them calls upon me.
8 Ephraim mixes himself with the
peoples;
Ephraim is a cake not turned.
9 Strangers devour his strength,
and he knows it not;
gray hairs are sprinkled upon him,
and he knows it not.

[1] Septuagint *mercy*

10 The pride of Israel testifies to his
face;[1]
yet they do not return to the LORD
their God,
nor seek him, for all this.

11 Ephraim is like a dove,
silly and without sense,
calling to Egypt, going to Assyria.
12 As they go, I will spread over them
my net;
I will bring them down like birds
of the heavens;
I will discipline them according
to the report made to their
congregation.
13 Woe to them, for they have strayed
from me!
Destruction to them, for they
have rebelled against me!
I would redeem them,
but they speak lies against me.

14 They do not cry to me from the heart,
but they wail upon their beds;
for grain and wine they gash
themselves;
they rebel against me.
15 Although I trained and
strengthened their arms,
yet they devise evil against me.
16 They return, but not upward;[2]
they are like a treacherous bow;
their princes shall fall by the sword
because of the insolence of their
tongue.
This shall be their derision in the
land of Egypt.

Israel Will Reap the Whirlwind

8 Set the trumpet to your lips!
One like a vulture is over the house
of the LORD,
because they have transgressed my
covenant
and rebelled against my law.
2 To me they cry,
"My God, we—Israel—know you."
3 Israel has spurned the good;
the enemy shall pursue him.

4 They made kings, but not through me.
They set up princes, but I knew it
not.
With their silver and gold they
made idols
for their own destruction.
5 I have[3] spurned your calf, O Samaria.
My anger burns against them.
How long will they be incapable of
innocence?
6 For it is from Israel;
a craftsman made it;
it is not God.
The calf of Samaria
shall be broken to pieces.[4]

7 For they sow the wind,
and they shall reap the whirlwind.
The standing grain has no heads;
it shall yield no flour;
if it were to yield,
strangers would devour it.
8 Israel is swallowed up;
already they are among the nations
as a useless vessel.
9 For they have gone up to Assyria,
a wild donkey wandering alone;
Ephraim has hired lovers.
10 Though they hire allies among the
nations,
I will soon gather them up.
And the king and princes shall soon
writhe
because of the tribute.

11 Because Ephraim has multiplied
altars for sinning,
they have become to him altars
for sinning.
12 Were I to write for him my laws by
the ten thousands,
they would be regarded as a
strange thing.
13 As for my sacrificial offerings,
they sacrifice meat and eat it,
but the LORD does not accept them.

[1] Or *in his presence* [2] Or *to the Most High* [3] Hebrew *He has* [4] Or *shall go up in flames*

Now he will remember their iniquity
and punish their sins;
they shall return to Egypt.
14 For Israel has forgotten his Maker
and built palaces,
and Judah has multiplied fortified cities;
so I will send a fire upon his cities,
and it shall devour her strongholds.

The LORD Will Punish Israel

9 Rejoice not, O Israel!
Exult not like the peoples;
for you have played the whore,
forsaking your God.
You have loved a prostitute's wages
on all threshing floors.
2 Threshing floor and wine vat shall not feed them,
and the new wine shall fail them.
3 They shall not remain in the land of the LORD,
but Ephraim shall return to Egypt,
and they shall eat unclean food in Assyria.

4 They shall not pour drink offerings of wine to the LORD,
and their sacrifices shall not please him.
It shall be like mourners' bread to them;
all who eat of it shall be defiled;
for their bread shall be for their hunger only;
it shall not come to the house of the LORD.

5 What will you do on the day of the appointed festival,
and on the day of the feast of the LORD?
6 For behold, they are going away from destruction;
but Egypt shall gather them;
Memphis shall bury them.
Nettles shall possess their precious things of silver;
thorns shall be in their tents.
7 The days of punishment have come;
the days of recompense have come;
Israel shall know it.
The prophet is a fool;
the man of the spirit is mad,
because of your great iniquity
and great hatred.
8 The prophet is the watchman of Ephraim with my God;
yet a fowler's snare is on all his ways,
and hatred in the house of his God.
9 They have deeply corrupted themselves
as in the days of Gibeah:
he will remember their iniquity;
he will punish their sins.

10 Like grapes in the wilderness,
I found Israel.
Like the first fruit on the fig tree
in its first season,
I saw your fathers.
But they came to Baal-peor
and consecrated themselves to the thing of shame,
and became detestable like the thing they loved.
11 Ephraim's glory shall fly away like a bird—
no birth, no pregnancy, no conception!
12 Even if they bring up children,
I will bereave them till none is left.
Woe to them
when I depart from them!
13 Ephraim, as I have seen, was like a young palm[1] planted in a meadow;
but Ephraim must lead his children out to slaughter.[2]
14 Give them, O LORD—
what will you give?
Give them a miscarrying womb
and dry breasts.

15 Every evil of theirs is in Gilgal;
there I began to hate them.

[1] Or *like Tyre* [2] Hebrew *to him who slaughters*

Because of the wickedness of their deeds
I will drive them out of my house.
I will love them no more;
all their princes are rebels.

16 Ephraim is stricken;
their root is dried up;
they shall bear no fruit.
Even though they give birth,
I will put their beloved children to death.

17 My God will reject them
because they have not listened to him;
they shall be wanderers among the nations.

10 Israel is a luxuriant vine
that yields its fruit.
The more his fruit increased,
the more altars he built;
as his country improved,
he improved his pillars.

2 Their heart is false;
now they must bear their guilt.
The LORD[1] will break down their altars
and destroy their pillars.

3 For now they will say:
"We have no king,
for we do not fear the LORD;
and a king—what could he do for us?"

4 They utter mere words;
with empty oaths they make covenants;
so judgment springs up like poisonous weeds
in the furrows of the field.

5 The inhabitants of Samaria tremble
for the calf[2] of Beth-aven.
Its people mourn for it, and so do its idolatrous priests—
those who rejoiced over it and over its glory—
for it has departed[3] from them.

6 The thing itself shall be carried to Assyria
as tribute to the great king.[4]
Ephraim shall be put to shame,
and Israel shall be ashamed of his idol.[5]

7 Samaria's king shall perish
like a twig on the face of the waters.

8 The high places of Aven, the sin of Israel,
shall be destroyed.
Thorn and thistle shall grow up
on their altars,
and they shall say to the mountains,
"Cover us,"
and to the hills, "Fall on us."

9 From the days of Gibeah, you have sinned, O Israel;
there they have continued.
Shall not the war against the unjust[6]
overtake them in Gibeah?

10 When I please, I will discipline them,
and nations shall be gathered against them
when they are bound up for their double iniquity.

11 Ephraim was a trained calf
that loved to thresh,
and I spared her fair neck;
but I will put Ephraim to the yoke;
Judah must plow;
Jacob must harrow for himself.

12 Sow for yourselves righteousness;
reap steadfast love;
break up your fallow ground,
for it is the time to seek the LORD,
that he may come and rain
righteousness upon you.

13 You have plowed iniquity;
you have reaped injustice;
you have eaten the fruit of lies.
Because you have trusted in your own way
and in the multitude of your warriors,

[1] Hebrew *He* [2] Or *calves* [3] Or *has gone into exile* [4] Or *to King Jareb* [5] Or *counsel* [6] Hebrew *the children of injustice*

14 therefore the tumult of war shall arise among your people,
and all your fortresses shall be destroyed,
as Shalman destroyed Beth-arbel on the day of battle;
mothers were dashed in pieces with their children.
15 Thus it shall be done to you, O Bethel,
because of your great evil.
At dawn the king of Israel
shall be utterly cut off.

The LORD's Love for Israel

11 When Israel was a child, I loved him,
and out of Egypt I called my son.
2 The more they were called,
the more they went away;
they kept sacrificing to the Baals
and burning offerings to idols.

3 Yet it was I who taught Ephraim to walk;
I took them up by their arms,
but they did not know that I healed them.
4 I led them with cords of kindness,[1]
with the bands of love,
and I became to them as one who eases the yoke on their jaws,
and I bent down to them and fed them.

5 They shall not[2] return to the land of Egypt,
but Assyria shall be their king,
because they have refused to return to me.
6 The sword shall rage against their cities,
consume the bars of their gates,
and devour them because of their own counsels.
7 My people are bent on turning away from me,
and though they call out to the Most High,
he shall not raise them up at all.
8 How can I give you up, O Ephraim?
How can I hand you over, O Israel?
How can I make you like Admah?
How can I treat you like Zeboiim?
My heart recoils within me;
my compassion grows warm and tender.
9 I will not execute my burning anger;
I will not again destroy Ephraim;
for I am God and not a man,
the Holy One in your midst,
and I will not come in wrath.[3]

10 They shall go after the LORD;
he will roar like a lion;
when he roars,
his children shall come trembling from the west;
11 they shall come trembling like birds from Egypt,
and like doves from the land of Assyria,
and I will return them to their homes, declares the LORD.
12[4] Ephraim has surrounded me with lies,
and the house of Israel with deceit,
but Judah still walks with God
and is faithful to the Holy One.

12 Ephraim feeds on the wind
and pursues the east wind all day long;
they multiply falsehood and violence;
they make a covenant with Assyria,
and oil is carried to Egypt.

The LORD's Indictment of Israel and Judah

87

2 The LORD has an indictment against Judah
and will punish Jacob according to his ways;
he will repay him according to his deeds.
3 In the womb he took his brother by the heel,

[1] Or *humaneness*; Hebrew *man* [2] Or *surely* [3] Or *into the city* [4] Ch 12:1 in Hebrew

and in his manhood he strove
with God.
4 He strove with the angel and
prevailed;
he wept and sought his favor.
He met God[1] at Bethel,
and there God spoke with us—
5 the LORD, the God of hosts,
the LORD is his memorial name:
6 "So you, by the help of your God,
return,
hold fast to love and justice,
and wait continually for your God."

7 A merchant, in whose hands are
false balances,
he loves to oppress.
8 Ephraim has said, "Ah, but I am rich;
I have found wealth for myself;
in all my labors they cannot find in
me iniquity or sin."
9 I am the LORD your God
from the land of Egypt;
I will again make you dwell in tents,
as in the days of the appointed
feast.

10 I spoke to the prophets;
it was I who multiplied visions,
and through the prophets gave
parables.
11 If there is iniquity in Gilead,
they shall surely come to nothing:
in Gilgal they sacrifice bulls;
their altars also are like stone heaps
on the furrows of the field.
12 Jacob fled to the land of Aram;
there Israel served for a wife,
and for a wife he guarded sheep.
13 By a prophet the LORD brought
Israel up from Egypt,
and by a prophet he was guarded.
14 Ephraim has given bitter
provocation;
so his Lord will leave his
bloodguilt on him
and will repay him for his
disgraceful deeds.

The LORD's Relentless Judgment on Israel

13 When Ephraim spoke, there was
trembling;
he was exalted in Israel,
but he incurred guilt through Baal
and died.
2 And now they sin more and more,
and make for themselves metal
images,
idols skillfully made of their silver,
all of them the work of craftsmen.
It is said of them,
"Those who offer human sacrifice
kiss calves!"
3 Therefore they shall be like the
morning mist
or like the dew that goes early
away,
like the chaff that swirls from the
threshing floor
or like smoke from a window.

4 But I am the LORD your God
from the land of Egypt;
you know no God but me,
and besides me there is no savior.
5 It was I who knew you in the
wilderness,
in the land of drought;
6 but when they had grazed,[2] they
became full,
they were filled, and their heart
was lifted up;
therefore they forgot me.
7 So I am to them like a lion;
like a leopard I will lurk beside
the way.
8 I will fall upon them like a bear
robbed of her cubs;
I will tear open their breast,
and there I will devour them like a
lion,
as a wild beast would rip them
open.
9 He destroys[3] you, O Israel,
for you are against me, against
your helper.

[1] Hebrew *him* [2] Hebrew *according to their pasture* [3] Or *I will destroy*

10 Where now is your king, to save you
in all your cities?
Where are all your rulers—
those of whom you said,
"Give me a king and princes"?
11 I gave you a king in my anger,
and I took him away in my wrath.

12 The iniquity of Ephraim is bound up;
his sin is kept in store.
13 The pangs of childbirth come for him,
but he is an unwise son,
for at the right time he does not
present himself
at the opening of the womb.
14 Shall I ransom them from the power
of Sheol?
Shall I redeem them from Death?
O Death, where are your plagues?
O Sheol, where is your sting?
Compassion is hidden from my
eyes.

15 Though he may flourish among his
brothers,
the east wind, the wind of the
LORD, shall come,
rising from the wilderness,
and his fountain shall dry up;
his spring shall be parched;
it shall strip his treasury
of every precious thing.
16 [1] Samaria shall bear her guilt,
because she has rebelled against
her God;
they shall fall by the sword;
their little ones shall be dashed in
pieces,
and their pregnant women ripped
open.

A Plea to Return to the LORD

14 Return, O Israel, to the LORD
your God,
for you have stumbled because of
your iniquity.
2 Take with you words
and return to the LORD;
say to him,
"Take away all iniquity;
accept what is good,
and we will pay with bulls
the vows[2] of our lips.
3 Assyria shall not save us;
we will not ride on horses;
and we will say no more, 'Our God,'
to the work of our hands.
In you the orphan finds mercy."

4 I will heal their apostasy;
I will love them freely,
for my anger has turned from
them.
5 I will be like the dew to Israel;
he shall blossom like the lily;
he shall take root like the trees of
Lebanon;
6 his shoots shall spread out;
his beauty shall be like the olive,
and his fragrance like Lebanon.
7 They shall return and dwell beneath
my[3] shadow;
they shall flourish like the grain;
they shall blossom like the vine;
their fame shall be like the wine
of Lebanon.

8 O Ephraim, what have I to do with
idols?
It is I who answer and look after
you.[4]
I am like an evergreen cypress;
from me comes your fruit.

9 Whoever is wise, let him
understand these things;
whoever is discerning, let him
know them;
for the ways of the LORD are right,
and the upright walk in them,
but transgressors stumble in
them.

[1] Ch 14:1 in Hebrew [2] Septuagint, Syriac *pay the fruit* [3] Hebrew *his* [4] Hebrew *him*

Introduction to

Joel

Author
Joel the prophet

Date
About 500 B.C. ?

Purpose
The purpose of Joel is to warn God's people of disaster because of God's judgment on their sin and to call them to repent.

Central Themes
The day of the Lord is a time of judgment for sinners and blessing for God's people; a locust plague is a picture of the coming disaster; salvation is for those who call on the Lord; God's Spirit is poured out.

Memory Verses
The day of the Lord (Joel 2:1–2); return to the Lord (Joel 2:12–13); the outpouring of the Spirit (Joel 2:28–29)

Introduction

Joel tells of a locust plague in Judah so terrible that no grain and wine are left (Joel 1). In a kingdom like Judah, where almost everyone was a farmer, a locust plague destroying all the crops was a disaster! Joel says the judgment against sin on the day of the Lord will be much worse and calls God's people to repent (Joel 2:1–17). Joel promises God's grace and mercy on those who do repent. He says that God will pour out His Spirit on all His people (Joel 2:28–32), a promise which was fulfilled when the Lord Jesus Christ sent the Holy Spirit to live in His people on the day of Pentecost (Acts 2). Joel writes of God's future judgment against all nations and the future glory of God's people (Joel 3). He promises that "everyone who calls on the name of the LORD shall be saved" (Joel 2:32), a promise Peter quoted in his gospel sermon telling about Jesus (Acts 2:21).

586 B.C.
Fall of Judah/ temple destroyed

538 B.C.
Decree of Cyrus/ end of exile

About 500 B.C. ?
Prophetic ministry of Joel begins

Joel

1 The word of the LORD that came to
Joel, the son of Pethuel:

An Invasion of Locusts

2 Hear this, you elders;
give ear, all inhabitants of the land!
Has such a thing happened in your days,
or in the days of your fathers?
3 Tell your children of it,
and let your children tell their children,
and their children to another generation.

4 What the cutting locust left,
the swarming locust has eaten.
What the swarming locust left,
the hopping locust has eaten,
and what the hopping locust left,
the destroying locust has eaten.

5 Awake, you drunkards, and weep,
and wail, all you drinkers of wine,
because of the sweet wine,
for it is cut off from your mouth.
6 For a nation has come up against my land,
powerful and beyond number;
its teeth are lions' teeth,
and it has the fangs of a lioness.
7 It has laid waste my vine
and splintered my fig tree;
it has stripped off their bark and thrown it down;
their branches are made white.

8 Lament like a virgin[1] wearing sackcloth
for the bridegroom of her youth.
9 The grain offering and the drink offering are cut off
from the house of the LORD.
The priests mourn,
the ministers of the LORD.
10 The fields are destroyed,
the ground mourns,
because the grain is destroyed,
the wine dries up,
the oil languishes.

11 Be ashamed,[2] O tillers of the soil;
wail, O vinedressers,
for the wheat and the barley,
because the harvest of the field has perished.
12 The vine dries up;
the fig tree languishes.
Pomegranate, palm, and apple,
all the trees of the field are dried up,
and gladness dries up
from the children of man.

A Call to Repentance

13 Put on sackcloth and lament, O priests;
wail, O ministers of the altar.
Go in, pass the night in sackcloth,
O ministers of my God!
Because grain offering and drink offering
are withheld from the house of your God.

14 Consecrate a fast;
call a solemn assembly.
Gather the elders
and all the inhabitants of the land
to the house of the LORD your God,
and cry out to the LORD.

15 Alas for the day!
For the day of the LORD is near,
and as destruction from the Almighty[3] it comes.

[1] Or *young woman* [2] The Hebrew words for *dry up* and *be ashamed* in verses 10-12, 17 sound alike [3] *Destruction* sounds like the Hebrew for *Almighty*

16 Is not the food cut off
before our eyes,
joy and gladness
from the house of our God?
17 The seed shrivels under the clods;[1]
the storehouses are desolate;
the granaries are torn down
because the grain has dried up.
18 How the beasts groan!
The herds of cattle are perplexed
because there is no pasture for
them;
even the flocks of sheep suffer.[2]
19 To you, O LORD, I call.
For fire has devoured
the pastures of the wilderness,
and flame has burned
all the trees of the field.
20 Even the beasts of the field pant for
you
because the water brooks are
dried up,
and fire has devoured
the pastures of the wilderness.

The Day of the LORD

2 Blow a trumpet in Zion;
sound an alarm on my holy
mountain!
Let all the inhabitants of the land
tremble,
for the day of the LORD is coming;
it is near,
2 a day of darkness and gloom,
a day of clouds and thick
darkness!
Like blackness there is spread upon
the mountains
a great and powerful people;
their like has never been before,
nor will be again after them
through the years of all
generations.
3 Fire devours before them,
and behind them a flame burns.
The land is like the garden of Eden
before them,
but behind them a desolate
wilderness,
and nothing escapes them.
4 Their appearance is like the
appearance of horses,
and like war horses they run.
5 As with the rumbling of chariots,
they leap on the tops of the
mountains,
like the crackling of a flame of fire
devouring the stubble,
like a powerful army
drawn up for battle.
6 Before them peoples are in anguish;
all faces grow pale.
7 Like warriors they charge;
like soldiers they scale the wall.
They march each on his way;
they do not swerve from their
paths.
8 They do not jostle one another;
each marches in his path;
they burst through the weapons
and are not halted.
9 They leap upon the city,
they run upon the walls,
they climb up into the houses,
they enter through the windows
like a thief.
10 The earth quakes before them;
the heavens tremble.
The sun and the moon are
darkened,
and the stars withdraw their
shining.
11 The LORD utters his voice
before his army,
for his camp is exceedingly great;
he who executes his word is
powerful.
For the day of the LORD is great and
very awesome;
who can endure it?

[1] The meaning of the Hebrew line is uncertain [2] Or *are made desolate*

Return to the LORD

12 "Yet even now," declares the LORD,
"return to me with all your heart,
with fasting, with weeping, and
with mourning;
13 and rend your hearts and not your
garments."
Return to the LORD your God,
for he is gracious and merciful,
slow to anger, and abounding in
steadfast love;
and he relents over disaster.
14 Who knows whether he will not
turn and relent,
and leave a blessing behind him,
a grain offering and a drink offering
for the LORD your God?

15 Blow the trumpet in Zion;
consecrate a fast;
call a solemn assembly;
16 gather the people.
Consecrate the congregation;
assemble the elders;
gather the children,
even nursing infants.
Let the bridegroom leave his room,
and the bride her chamber.

17 Between the vestibule and the altar
let the priests, the ministers of
the LORD, weep
and say, "Spare your people, O LORD,
and make not your heritage a
reproach,
a byword among the nations.[1]
Why should they say among the
peoples,
'Where is their God?'"

The LORD Had Pity

18 Then the LORD became jealous for
his land
and had pity on his people.
19 The LORD answered and said to his
people,
"Behold, I am sending to you
grain, wine, and oil,
and you will be satisfied;
and I will no more make you
a reproach among the nations.

20 "I will remove the northerner far
from you,
and drive him into a parched and
desolate land,
his vanguard[2] into the eastern sea,
and his rear guard[3] into the
western sea;
the stench and foul smell of him
will rise,
for he has done great things.

21 "Fear not, O land;
be glad and rejoice,
for the LORD has done great things!
22 Fear not, you beasts of the field,
for the pastures of the wilderness
are green;
the tree bears its fruit;
the fig tree and vine give their full
yield.

23 "Be glad, O children of Zion,
and rejoice in the LORD your God,
for he has given the early rain for
your vindication;
he has poured down for you
abundant rain,
the early and the latter rain, as
before.

24 "The threshing floors shall be full of
grain;
the vats shall overflow with wine
and oil.
25 I will restore to you the years
that the swarming locust has eaten,
the hopper, the destroyer, and the
cutter,
my great army, which I sent
among you.

[1] Or *reproach, that the nations should rule over them* [2] Hebrew *face* [3] Hebrew *his end*

26 "You shall eat in plenty and be
satisfied,
and praise the name of the LORD
your God,
who has dealt wondrously with
you.
And my people shall never again be
put to shame.
27 You shall know that I am in the
midst of Israel,
and that I am the LORD your God
and there is none else.
And my people shall never again be
put to shame.

The LORD Will Pour Out His Spirit

28 [1] "And it shall come to pass
afterward,
1615
that I will pour out my Spirit on
all flesh;
your sons and your daughters shall
prophesy,
your old men shall dream dreams,
and your young men shall see
visions.
29 Even on the male and female servants
in those days I will pour out my
Spirit.

30 "And I will show wonders in the
heavens and on the earth, blood and fire
and columns of smoke. 31 The sun shall
be turned to darkness, and the moon to
blood, before the great and awesome day
of the LORD comes. 32 And it shall come
to pass that everyone who calls on the
name of the LORD shall be saved. For in
Mount Zion and in Jerusalem there shall
be those who escape, as the LORD has said,
and among the survivors shall be those
whom the LORD calls.

The LORD Judges the Nations

3 [2] "For behold, in those days and at that
time, when I restore the fortunes of
Judah and Jerusalem, 2 I will gather all the
nations and bring them down to the Valley
of Jehoshaphat. And I will enter into judg-
ment with them there, on behalf of my
people and my heritage Israel, because they
have scattered them among the nations
and have divided up my land, 3 and have
cast lots for my people, and have traded a
boy for a prostitute, and have sold a girl for
wine and have drunk it.
4 "What are you to me, O Tyre and Sidon,
and all the regions of Philistia? Are you
paying me back for something? If you
are paying me back, I will return your
payment on your own head swiftly and
speedily. 5 For you have taken my silver
and my gold, and have carried my rich
treasures into your temples.[3] 6 You have
sold the people of Judah and Jerusalem
to the Greeks in order to remove them far
from their own border. 7 Behold, I will stir
them up from the place to which you have
sold them, and I will return your payment
on your own head. 8 I will sell your sons
and your daughters into the hand of the
people of Judah, and they will sell them
to the Sabeans, to a nation far away, for the
LORD has spoken."

9 Proclaim this among the nations:
Consecrate for war;[4]
stir up the mighty men.
Let all the men of war draw near;
let them come up.
10 Beat your plowshares into swords,
and your pruning hooks into
spears;
let the weak say, "I am a warrior."

11 Hasten and come,
all you surrounding nations,
and gather yourselves there.
Bring down your warriors, O LORD.
12 Let the nations stir themselves up
and come up to the Valley of
Jehoshaphat;
for there I will sit to judge
all the surrounding nations.

13 Put in the sickle,
for the harvest is ripe.

[1] Ch 3:1 in Hebrew [2] Ch 4:1 in Hebrew [3] Or *palaces* [4] Or *Consecrate a war*

Go in, tread,
for the winepress is full.
The vats overflow,
for their evil is great.

14 Multitudes, multitudes,
in the valley of decision!
For the day of the LORD is near
in the valley of decision.
15 The sun and the moon are darkened,
and the stars withdraw their
shining.
16 The LORD roars from Zion,
and utters his voice from
Jerusalem,
and the heavens and the earth
quake.
But the LORD is a refuge to his people,
a stronghold to the people of Israel.

The Glorious Future of Judah

17 "So you shall know that I am the
LORD your God,
who dwells in Zion, my holy
mountain.
And Jerusalem shall be holy,
and strangers shall never again
pass through it.

18 "And in that day
the mountains shall drip sweet wine,
and the hills shall flow with milk,
and all the streambeds of Judah
shall flow with water;
and a fountain shall come forth
from the house of the LORD
and water the Valley of Shittim.

19 "Egypt shall become a desolation
and Edom a desolate wilderness,
for the violence done to the people
of Judah,
because they have shed innocent
blood in their land.
20 But Judah shall be inhabited forever,
and Jerusalem to all generations.
21 I will avenge their blood,
blood I have not avenged,[1]
for the LORD dwells in Zion."

[1] Or *I will acquit their bloodguilt that I have not acquitted*

Introduction to

Amos

Author
Amos the prophet

Date
About 760 B.C.

Purpose
The purpose of Amos is to call God's people in the kingdoms of Judah and Israel to repent before God's judgment fell on them for their sin.

Central Themes
The day of the Lord is coming; God will judge the nations for their sin; God will judge His unrepentant people; God does not accept worship unless it is sincere and unless the worshipers live to please Him; God requires His people to show justice to others and to care for the poor.

Memory Verses
Let justice roll down (Amos 5:21–24); the fortunes of Israel restored (Amos 9:13–15)

Introduction

Amos was a shepherd from the southern kingdom of Judah whom God sent to the northern kingdom of Israel with a message of judgment. The people in the northern kingdom did not like his message and did not want him there (Amos 7:10–15). The people probably did not mind so much when Amos spoke judgment against the sins of the neighboring nations (Amos 1:2–2:3), but they didn't like hearing that God would judge *them* (Amos 2:4–16); *they* were God's people! Amos told them that the day of the Lord that they hoped for, a day of blessing for God's people, would not be good for them. On that day, God would judge them for their sin (Amos 5:18–20). He told them that God hated their worship because they showed no justice or compassion to the poor (Amos 5:21–24). At the end of Amos's prophecy, though, Amos wrote of God's promise to raise up His people again and bring other nations to worship Him as well (Amos 9:11–15).

793/781 B.C.	About 760 B.C.	722 B.C.
Reign of Jeroboam II begins	Prophetic ministry of Amos begins	Fall of Israel

Amos

1 The words of Amos, who was among the shepherds[1] of Tekoa, which he saw concerning Israel in the days of Uzziah king of Judah and in the days of Jeroboam the son of Joash, king of Israel, two years[2] before the earthquake.

Judgment on Israel's Neighbors

2 And he said:

"The LORD roars from Zion
and utters his voice from Jerusalem;
the pastures of the shepherds mourn,
and the top of Carmel withers."

3 Thus says the LORD:

"For three transgressions of Damascus,
and for four, I will not revoke the punishment,[3]
because they have threshed Gilead
with threshing sledges of iron.
4 So I will send a fire upon the house of Hazael,
and it shall devour the strongholds of Ben-hadad.
5 I will break the gate-bar of Damascus,
and cut off the inhabitants from the Valley of Aven,[4]
and him who holds the scepter from Beth-eden;
and the people of Syria shall go into exile to Kir,"
says the LORD.

6 Thus says the LORD:

"For three transgressions of Gaza,
and for four, I will not revoke the punishment,
because they carried into exile a whole people
to deliver them up to Edom.
7 So I will send a fire upon the wall of Gaza,
and it shall devour her strongholds.
8 I will cut off the inhabitants from Ashdod,
and him who holds the scepter from Ashkelon;
I will turn my hand against Ekron,
and the remnant of the Philistines shall perish,"
says the Lord GOD.

9 Thus says the LORD:

"For three transgressions of Tyre,
and for four, I will not revoke the punishment,
because they delivered up a whole people to Edom,
and did not remember the covenant of brotherhood.
10 So I will send a fire upon the wall of Tyre,
and it shall devour her strongholds."

11 Thus says the LORD:

"For three transgressions of Edom,
and for four, I will not revoke the punishment,
because he pursued his brother with the sword
and cast off all pity,
and his anger tore perpetually,
and he kept his wrath forever.
12 So I will send a fire upon Teman,
and it shall devour the strongholds of Bozrah."

13 Thus says the LORD:

[1] Or *sheep breeders* [2] Or *during two years* [3] Hebrew *I will not turn it back*; also verses 6, 9, 11, 13 [4] Or *On*

"For three transgressions of the
Ammonites,
and for four, I will not revoke the
punishment,
because they have ripped open
pregnant women in Gilead,
that they might enlarge their border.
14 So I will kindle a fire in the wall of
Rabbah,
and it shall devour her strongholds,
with shouting on the day of battle,
with a tempest in the day of the
whirlwind;
15 and their king shall go into exile,
he and his princes[1] together,"
says the LORD.

2 Thus says the LORD:

"For three transgressions of Moab,
and for four, I will not revoke the
punishment,[2]
because he burned to lime
the bones of the king of Edom.
2 So I will send a fire upon Moab,
and it shall devour the
strongholds of Kerioth,
and Moab shall die amid uproar,
amid shouting and the sound of
the trumpet;
3 I will cut off the ruler from its midst,
and will kill all its princes[3] with
him,"
says the LORD.

Judgment on Judah

4 Thus says the LORD:

"For three transgressions of Judah,
and for four, I will not revoke the
punishment,
because they have rejected the law
of the LORD,
and have not kept his statutes,
but their lies have led them astray,
those after which their fathers
walked.
5 So I will send a fire upon Judah,
and it shall devour the
strongholds of Jerusalem."

Judgment on Israel

6 Thus says the LORD:

"For three transgressions of Israel,
and for four, I will not revoke the
punishment,
because they sell the righteous for
silver,
and the needy for a pair of
sandals—
7 those who trample the head of the
poor into the dust of the earth
and turn aside the way of the
afflicted;
a man and his father go in to the
same girl,
so that my holy name is profaned;
8 they lay themselves down beside
every altar
on garments taken in pledge,
and in the house of their God they
drink
the wine of those who have been
fined.

9 "Yet it was I who destroyed the
Amorite before them,
whose height was like the height
of the cedars
and who was as strong as the oaks;
I destroyed his fruit above
and his roots beneath.
10 Also it was I who brought you up
out of the land of Egypt
and led you forty years in the
wilderness,
to possess the land of the Amorite.
11 And I raised up some of your sons
for prophets,
and some of your young men for
Nazirites.
Is it not indeed so, O people of
Israel?"
declares the LORD.

[1] Or *officials* [2] Hebrew *I will not turn it back*; also verses 4, 6 [3] Or *officials*

12 "But you made the Nazirites drink
wine,
and commanded the prophets,
saying, 'You shall not prophesy.'
13 "Behold, I will press you down in
your place,
as a cart full of sheaves presses
down.
14 Flight shall perish from the swift,
and the strong shall not retain his
strength,
nor shall the mighty save his life;
15 he who handles the bow shall not
stand,
and he who is swift of foot shall
not save himself,
nor shall he who rides the horse
save his life;
16 and he who is stout of heart among
the mighty
shall flee away naked in that day,"
declares the LORD.

Israel's Guilt and Punishment

3 Hear this word that the LORD has spoken against you, O people of Israel, against the whole family that I brought up out of the land of Egypt:

2 "You only have I known
of all the families of the earth;
therefore I will punish you
for all your iniquities.
3 "Do two walk together,
unless they have agreed to meet?
4 Does a lion roar in the forest,
when he has no prey?
Does a young lion cry out from his
den,
if he has taken nothing?
5 Does a bird fall in a snare on the earth,
when there is no trap for it?
Does a snare spring up from the
ground,
when it has taken nothing?
6 Is a trumpet blown in a city,
and the people are not afraid?
Does disaster come to a city,
unless the LORD has done it?
7 "For the Lord GOD does nothing
without revealing his secret
to his servants the prophets.
8 The lion has roared;
who will not fear?
The Lord GOD has spoken;
who can but prophesy?"
9 Proclaim to the strongholds in
Ashdod
and to the strongholds in the land
of Egypt,
and say, "Assemble yourselves on
the mountains of Samaria,
and see the great tumults within
her,
and the oppressed in her midst."
10 "They do not know how to do right,"
declares the LORD,
"those who store up violence and
robbery in their strongholds."

11 Therefore thus says the Lord GOD:

"An adversary shall surround the land
and bring down[1] your defenses
from you,
and your strongholds shall be
plundered."

12 Thus says the LORD: "As the shep-
herd rescues from the mouth of the lion
two legs, or a piece of an ear, so shall the
people of Israel who dwell in Samaria be
rescued, with the corner of a couch and
part[2] of a bed.

13 "Hear, and testify against the house
of Jacob,"
declares the Lord GOD, the God of
hosts,
14 "that on the day I punish Israel for
his transgressions,
I will punish the altars of Bethel,
and the horns of the altar shall be
cut off
and fall to the ground.

[1] Hebrew *An adversary, one who surrounds the land—he shall bring down* [2] The meaning of the Hebrew word is uncertain

15 I will strike the winter house along
with the summer house,
and the houses of ivory shall perish,
and the great houses[1] shall come to
an end,"
declares the LORD.

4 "Hear this word, you cows of Bashan,
who are on the mountain of Samaria,
who oppress the poor, who crush
the needy,
who say to your husbands, 'Bring,
that we may drink!'
2 The Lord GOD has sworn by his
holiness
that, behold, the days are coming
upon you,
when they shall take you away with
hooks,
even the last of you with fishhooks.
3 And you shall go out through the
breaches,
each one straight ahead;
and you shall be cast out into
Harmon,"
declares the LORD.

4 "Come to Bethel, and transgress;
to Gilgal, and multiply
transgression;
bring your sacrifices every morning,
your tithes every three days;
5 offer a sacrifice of thanksgiving of
that which is leavened,
and proclaim freewill offerings,
publish them;
for so you love to do, O people of
Israel!"
declares the Lord GOD.

Israel Has Not Returned to the LORD

6 "I gave you cleanness of teeth in all
your cities,
and lack of bread in all your
places,
yet you did not return to me,"
declares the LORD.

7 "I also withheld the rain from you
when there were yet three
months to the harvest;
I would send rain on one city,
and send no rain on another city;
one field would have rain,
and the field on which it did not
rain would wither;
8 so two or three cities would wander
to another city
to drink water, and would not be
satisfied;
yet you did not return to me,"
declares the LORD.

9 "I struck you with blight and
mildew;
your many gardens and your
vineyards,
your fig trees and your olive trees
the locust devoured;
yet you did not return to me,"
declares the LORD.

10 "I sent among you a pestilence after
the manner of Egypt;
I killed your young men with the
sword,
and carried away your horses,[2]
and I made the stench of your
camp go up into your nostrils;
yet you did not return to me,"
declares the LORD.

11 "I overthrew some of you,
as when God overthrew Sodom
and Gomorrah,
and you were as a brand[3] plucked
out of the burning;
yet you did not return to me,"
declares the LORD.

12 "Therefore thus I will do to you, O
Israel;
because I will do this to you,
prepare to meet your God, O
Israel!"

[1] Or *and many houses* [2] Hebrew *along with the captivity of your horses* [3] That is, a burning stick

13 For behold, he who forms the
mountains and creates the
wind,
and declares to man what is his
thought,
who makes the morning darkness,
and treads on the heights of the
earth—
the LORD, the God of hosts, is his
name!

Seek the LORD and Live

5 Hear this word that I take up over you
in lamentation, O house of Israel:

2 "Fallen, no more to rise,
is the virgin Israel;
forsaken on her land,
with none to raise her up."

3 For thus says the Lord GOD:

"The city that went out a thousand
shall have a hundred left,
and that which went out a hundred
shall have ten left
to the house of Israel."

4 For thus says the LORD to the house of
Israel:

"Seek me and live;
5 but do not seek Bethel,
and do not enter into Gilgal
or cross over to Beersheba;
for Gilgal shall surely go into exile,
and Bethel shall come to nothing."

6 Seek the LORD and live,
lest he break out like fire in the
house of Joseph,
and it devour, with none to
quench it for Bethel,
7 O you who turn justice to wormwood[1]
and cast down righteousness to
the earth!

8 He who made the Pleiades and Orion,
and turns deep darkness into the
morning
and darkens the day into night,
who calls for the waters of the sea
and pours them out on the
surface of the earth,
the LORD is his name;
9 who makes destruction flash forth
against the strong,
so that destruction comes upon
the fortress.
10 They hate him who reproves in the
gate,
and they abhor him who speaks
the truth.
11 Therefore because you trample on[2]
the poor
and you exact taxes of grain from
him,
you have built houses of hewn
stone,
but you shall not dwell in them;
you have planted pleasant
vineyards,
but you shall not drink their wine.
12 For I know how many are your
transgressions
and how great are your sins—
you who afflict the righteous, who
take a bribe,
and turn aside the needy in the
gate.
13 Therefore he who is prudent will
keep silent in such a time,
for it is an evil time.

14 Seek good, and not evil,
that you may live;
and so the LORD, the God of hosts,
will be with you,
as you have said.
15 Hate evil, and love good,
and establish justice in the gate;
it may be that the LORD, the God of
hosts,
will be gracious to the remnant of
Joseph.

16 Therefore thus says the LORD, the God of
hosts, the Lord:

[1] Or *to bitter fruit* [2] Or *you tax*

"In all the squares there shall be
wailing,
and in all the streets they shall
say, 'Alas! Alas!'
They shall call the farmers to
mourning
and to wailing those who are
skilled in lamentation,
17 and in all vineyards there shall be
wailing,
for I will pass through your midst,"
says the LORD.

Let Justice Roll Down

18 Woe to you who desire the day of
the LORD!
Why would you have the day of
the LORD?
It is darkness, and not light,
19 as if a man fled from a lion,
and a bear met him,
or went into the house and leaned
his hand against the wall,
and a serpent bit him.
20 Is not the day of the LORD darkness,
and not light,
and gloom with no brightness in it?

21 "I hate, I despise your feasts,
and I take no delight in your
solemn assemblies.
22 Even though you offer me your
burnt offerings and grain
offerings,
I will not accept them;
and the peace offerings of your
fattened animals,
I will not look upon them.
23 Take away from me the noise of
your songs;
to the melody of your harps I will
not listen.
24 But let justice roll down like waters,
and righteousness like an ever-
flowing stream.

25 "Did you bring to me sacrifices and
offerings during the forty years in the wil-
derness, O house of Israel? 26 You shall take
up Sikkuth your king, and Kiyyun your
star-god—your images that you made for
yourselves, 27 and I will send you into exile
beyond Damascus," says the LORD, whose
name is the God of hosts.

Woe to Those at Ease in Zion

6 "Woe to those who are at ease in
Zion,
and to those who feel secure on
the mountain of Samaria,
the notable men of the first of the
nations,
to whom the house of Israel
comes!
2 Pass over to Calneh, and see,
and from there go to Hamath the
great;
then go down to Gath of the
Philistines.
Are you better than these
kingdoms?
Or is their territory greater than
your territory,
3 O you who put far away the day of
disaster
and bring near the seat of
violence?

4 "Woe to those who lie on beds of
ivory
and stretch themselves out on
their couches,
and eat lambs from the flock
and calves from the midst of the
stall,
5 who sing idle songs to the sound of
the harp
and like David invent for
themselves instruments of
music,
6 who drink wine in bowls
and anoint themselves with the
finest oils,
but are not grieved over the ruin
of Joseph!

7 Therefore they shall now be the first
of those who go into exile,
and the revelry of those who
stretch themselves out shall
pass away."

8 The Lord GOD has sworn by himself,
declares the LORD, the God of hosts:

"I abhor the pride of Jacob
and hate his strongholds,
and I will deliver up the city and
all that is in it."

9 And if ten men remain in one house,
they shall die. 10 And when one's relative,
the one who anoints him for burial, shall
take him up to bring the bones out of the
house, and shall say to him who is in the
innermost parts of the house, "Is there
still anyone with you?" he shall say, "No";
and he shall say, "Silence! We must not
mention the name of the LORD."

11 For behold, the LORD commands,
and the great house shall be
struck down into fragments,
and the little house into bits.
12 Do horses run on rocks?
Does one plow there[1] with oxen?
But you have turned justice into
poison
and the fruit of righteousness
into wormwood[2]—
13 you who rejoice in Lo-debar,[3]
who say, "Have we not by our own
strength
captured Karnaim[4] for
ourselves?"
14 "For behold, I will raise up against
you a nation,
O house of Israel," declares the
LORD, the God of hosts;
"and they shall oppress you from
Lebo-hamath
to the Brook of the Arabah."

Warning Visions

7 This is what the Lord GOD showed me:
behold, he was forming locusts when
the latter growth was just beginning to
sprout, and behold, it was the latter growth
after the king's mowings. 2 When they had
finished eating the grass of the land, I said,

"O Lord GOD, please forgive!
How can Jacob stand?
He is so small!"
3 The LORD relented concerning this:
"It shall not be," said the LORD.

4 This is what the Lord GOD showed
me: behold, the Lord GOD was calling for
a judgment by fire, and it devoured the
great deep and was eating up the land.
5 Then I said,

"O Lord GOD, please cease!
How can Jacob stand?
He is so small!"
6 The LORD relented concerning this:
"This also shall not be," said the
Lord GOD.

7 This is what he showed me: behold,
the Lord was standing beside a wall built
with a plumb line, with a plumb line in his
hand. 8 And the LORD said to me, "Amos,
what do you see?" And I said, "A plumb
line." Then the Lord said,

"Behold, I am setting a plumb line
in the midst of my people Israel;
I will never again pass by them;
9 the high places of Isaac shall be
made desolate,
and the sanctuaries of Israel shall
be laid waste,
and I will rise against the house of
Jeroboam with the sword."

Amos Accused

10 Then Amaziah the priest of Bethel
sent to Jeroboam king of Israel, saying,
"Amos has conspired against you in the
midst of the house of Israel. The land is

[1] Or *the sea* [2] Or *into bitter fruit* [3] *Lo-debar* means *nothing* [4] *Karnaim* means *horns* (a symbol of strength)

not able to bear all his words. 11 For thus
Amos has said,

"'Jeroboam shall die by the sword,
and Israel must go into exile
away from his land.'"

12 And Amaziah said to Amos, "O seer, go,
flee away to the land of Judah, and eat
bread there, and prophesy there, 13 but
never again prophesy at Bethel, for it is
the king's sanctuary, and it is a temple of
the kingdom."

14 Then Amos answered and said to
Amaziah, "I was[1] no prophet, nor a proph-
et's son, but I was a herdsman and a dresser
of sycamore figs. 15 But the LORD took me
from following the flock, and the LORD
said to me, 'Go, prophesy to my people
Israel.' 16 Now therefore hear the word of
the LORD.

"You say, 'Do not prophesy against
Israel,
and do not preach against the
house of Isaac.'

17 Therefore thus says the LORD:

"'Your wife shall be a prostitute in the
city,
and your sons and your daughters
shall fall by the sword,
and your land shall be divided up
with a measuring line;
you yourself shall die in an unclean
land,
and Israel shall surely go into
exile away from its land.'"

The Coming Day of Bitter Mourning

8 This is what the Lord GOD showed
me: behold, a basket of summer fruit.
2 And he said, "Amos, what do you see?"
And I said, "A basket of summer fruit."
Then the LORD said to me,

"The end[2] has come upon my people
Israel;
I will never again pass by them.

3 The songs of the temple[3] shall
become wailings[4] in that day,"
declares the Lord GOD.
"So many dead bodies!"
"They are thrown everywhere!"
"Silence!"

4 Hear this, you who trample on the
needy
and bring the poor of the land to
an end,
5 saying, "When will the new moon
be over,
that we may sell grain?
And the Sabbath,
that we may offer wheat for sale,
that we may make the ephah small
and the shekel[5] great
and deal deceitfully with false
balances,
6 that we may buy the poor for silver
and the needy for a pair of sandals
and sell the chaff of the wheat?"

7 The LORD has sworn by the pride of
Jacob:
"Surely I will never forget any of
their deeds.
8 Shall not the land tremble on this
account,
and everyone mourn who dwells
in it,
and all of it rise like the Nile,
and be tossed about and sink
again, like the Nile of Egypt?"

9 "And on that day," declares the Lord
GOD,
"I will make the sun go down at
noon
and darken the earth in broad
daylight.
10 I will turn your feasts into mourning
and all your songs into
lamentation;
I will bring sackcloth on every waist
and baldness on every head;

[1] Or *am*; twice in this verse [2] The Hebrew words for *end* and *summer fruit* sound alike [3] Or *palace* [4] Or *The singing women of the palace shall wail* [5] An *ephah* was about 3/5 bushel or 22 liters; a *shekel* was about 2/5 ounce or 11 grams

I will make it like the mourning for
an only son
and the end of it like a bitter day.

11 "Behold, the days are coming,"
declares the Lord GOD,
"when I will send a famine on the
land—
not a famine of bread, nor a thirst
for water,
but of hearing the words of the
LORD.
12 They shall wander from sea to sea,
and from north to east;
they shall run to and fro, to seek the
word of the LORD,
but they shall not find it.

13 "In that day the lovely virgins and
the young men
shall faint for thirst.
14 Those who swear by the Guilt of
Samaria,
and say, 'As your god lives, O Dan,'
and, 'As the Way of Beersheba lives,'
they shall fall, and never rise again."

The Destruction of Israel

9 I saw the Lord standing beside[1] the
altar, and he said:

"Strike the capitals until the
thresholds shake,
and shatter them on the heads of
all the people;[2]
and those who are left of them I will
kill with the sword;
not one of them shall flee away;
not one of them shall escape.

2 "If they dig into Sheol,
from there shall my hand take
them;
if they climb up to heaven,
from there I will bring them down.
3 If they hide themselves on the top
of Carmel,
from there I will search them out
and take them;
and if they hide from my sight at
the bottom of the sea,
there I will command the serpent,
and it shall bite them.
4 And if they go into captivity before
their enemies,
there I will command the sword,
and it shall kill them;
and I will fix my eyes upon them
for evil and not for good."
5 The Lord GOD of hosts,
he who touches the earth and it
melts,
and all who dwell in it mourn,
and all of it rises like the Nile,
and sinks again, like the Nile of
Egypt;
6 who builds his upper chambers in
the heavens
and founds his vault upon the
earth;
who calls for the waters of the sea
and pours them out upon the
surface of the earth—
the LORD is his name.

7 "Are you not like the Cushites to me,
O people of Israel?" declares the
LORD.
"Did I not bring up Israel from the
land of Egypt,
and the Philistines from Caphtor
and the Syrians from Kir?
8 Behold, the eyes of the Lord GOD are
upon the sinful kingdom,
and I will destroy it from the
surface of the ground,
except that I will not utterly
destroy the house of Jacob,"
declares the LORD.

9 "For behold, I will command,
and shake the house of Israel
among all the nations
as one shakes with a sieve,
but no pebble shall fall to the
earth.

[1] *Or on* [2] *Hebrew all of them*

10 All the sinners of my people shall
die by the sword,
who say, 'Disaster shall not
overtake or meet us.'

The Restoration of Israel

11 "In that day I will raise up
the booth of David that is fallen
and repair its breaches,
and raise up its ruins
and rebuild it as in the days of old,
12 that they may possess the remnant
of Edom
and all the nations who are called
by my name,"[1]
declares the LORD who does this.

13 "Behold, the days are coming,"
declares the LORD,
"when the plowman shall overtake
the reaper
and the treader of grapes him
who sows the seed;
the mountains shall drip sweet
wine,
and all the hills shall flow with it.
14 I will restore the fortunes of my
people Israel,
and they shall rebuild the ruined
cities and inhabit them;
they shall plant vineyards and drink
their wine,
and they shall make gardens and
eat their fruit.
15 I will plant them on their land,
and they shall never again be
uprooted
out of the land that I have given
them,"
says the LORD your God.

[1] Hebrew; Septuagint (compare Acts 15:17) *that the remnant of mankind and all the nations who are called by my name may seek the Lord*

Introduction to

Obadiah

Author
Obadiah the prophet

Date
About 570 B.C.

Purpose
The purpose of Obadiah is to promise salvation to God's people and judgment to the enemies who caused them to suffer.

Central Themes
God will judge His enemies for their actions against His people; God will shame the proud and boastful; God will restore His suffering people; God will rule the nations.

Memory Verses
Retribution (Obadiah 15); the Lord's kingdom (Obadiah 21)

Introduction

Jacob and Esau were twin brothers who had quarreled with each other (Genesis 27). The nation of Israel had come from Jacob. The nation of Edom had come from Esau. Obadiah was written to the nation of Edom. Some calamity had happened to the Israelites, probably the destruction of Jerusalem by Babylon (Obadiah 11). Instead of helping their brothers, the people of Edom had mocked them and helped their enemies. The people of Edom had helped themselves to the defeated Israelites' things (Obadiah 10–14). God promised to judge Edom for this, and for their pride that made them think they had built their cities so well that no one could destroy them (Obadiah 3–4). God promised that His people would be restored to their land, and that the kingdom would be the Lord's (Obadiah 17–21).

586 B.C.	About 570 B.C.	553 B.C.
Fall of Judah	Prophetic ministry of Obadiah	Babylon's campaign against Edom

Obadiah

1 The vision of Obadiah.

Edom Will Be Humbled

Thus says the Lord GOD concerning
Edom:
We have heard a report from the
LORD,
and a messenger has been sent
among the nations:
"Rise up! Let us rise against her for
battle!"
2 Behold, I will make you small
among the nations;
you shall be utterly despised.[1]
3 The pride of your heart has deceived
you,
you who live in the clefts of the
rock,[2]
in your lofty dwelling,
who say in your heart,
"Who will bring me down to the
ground?"
4 Though you soar aloft like the eagle,
though your nest is set among the
stars,
from there I will bring you down,
declares the LORD.

5 If thieves came to you,
if plunderers came by night—
how you have been destroyed!—
would they not steal only enough
for themselves?
If grape gatherers came to you,
would they not leave gleanings?
6 How Esau has been pillaged,
his treasures sought out!
7 All your allies have driven you to
your border;
those at peace with you have
deceived you;
they have prevailed against you;
those who eat your bread[3] have
set a trap beneath you—
you have[4] no understanding.

8 Will I not on that day, declares the
LORD,
destroy the wise men out of
Edom,
and understanding out of Mount
Esau?
9 And your mighty men shall be
dismayed, O Teman,
so that every man from Mount
Esau will be cut off by
slaughter.

Edom's Violence Against Jacob

10 Because of the violence done to
your brother Jacob,
shame shall cover you,
and you shall be cut off forever.
11 On the day that you stood aloof,
on the day that strangers carried
off his wealth
and foreigners entered his gates
and cast lots for Jerusalem,
you were like one of them.
12 But do not gloat over the day of your
brother
in the day of his misfortune;
do not rejoice over the people of
Judah
in the day of their ruin;
do not boast[5]
in the day of distress.
13 Do not enter the gate of my people
in the day of their calamity;
do not gloat over his disaster
in the day of his calamity;
do not loot his wealth
in the day of his calamity.

[1] Or *Behold, I have made you small among the nations; you are utterly despised* [2] Or *Sela* [3] Hebrew lacks *those who eat* [4] Hebrew *he has* [5] Hebrew *do not enlarge your mouth*

14 Do not stand at the crossroads
to cut off his fugitives;
do not hand over his survivors
in the day of distress.

The Day of the LORD Is Near

15 For the day of the LORD is near upon
all the nations.
As you have done, it shall be done to
you;
your deeds shall return on your
own head.
16 For as you have drunk on my holy
mountain,
so all the nations shall drink
continually;
they shall drink and swallow,
and shall be as though they had
never been.
17 But in Mount Zion there shall be
those who escape,
69 and it shall be holy,
and the house of Jacob shall possess
their own possessions.
18 The house of Jacob shall be a fire,
and the house of Joseph a flame,
and the house of Esau stubble;
they shall burn them and consume
them,
and there shall be no survivor for
the house of Esau,
for the LORD has spoken.

The Kingdom of the LORD

19 Those of the Negeb shall possess
Mount Esau,
and those of the Shephelah
shall possess the land of the
Philistines;
they shall possess the land of
Ephraim and the land of
Samaria,
and Benjamin shall possess Gilead.
20 The exiles of this host of the people
of Israel
shall possess the land of the
Canaanites as far as Zarephath,
and the exiles of Jerusalem who are
in Sepharad
shall possess the cities of the
Negeb.
21 Saviors shall go up to Mount Zion
to rule Mount Esau,
and the kingdom shall be the
LORD's.

Introduction to

Jonah

Author
Jonah the prophet

Date
About 760 B.C.

People
Jonah; sailors; king of Nineveh; people of Nineveh

Purpose
The purpose of Jonah is to show God's mercy and grace to sinners of all nations.

Central Themes
God rules over all His creatures; God is in all places; God's mercy is for all nations; God corrects His people when they sin; people must repent of sin; God's people must show concern for others as God does.

Memory Verses
God's powerful Word (Jonah 3:6–10); God's character (Jonah 4:2)

Introduction

This book tells the story of Jonah, God's disobedient prophet, in a way that teaches us about God and shows how we are to imitate God's compassion. When God calls Jonah to go tell the people of Nineveh that God will destroy them for their great wickedness, Jonah doesn't want to go. He gets on a boat and heads the other way (Jonah 1:1–3). One thing we learn from this story, though, is that God is everywhere. God sends a storm after Jonah's ship and the fearful sailors, realizing the storm is Jonah's fault, throw him overboard. The storm stops (Jonah 1:4–16). At God's command, a large fish swallows Jonah. From inside it, Jonah asks for God's help. God answers by having the fish vomit Jonah out onto the land (Jonah 1:17–2:10). Now Jonah obeys God, going to Nineveh and preaching. The people repent and God says He won't destroy them after all (Jonah 3). Now we learn why Jonah didn't want to preach to these people in the first place; he wanted God to punish them! When God forgives them, Jonah is very angry. God shows him that God's people must show mercy to others, the way God shows mercy (Jonah 4).

793/781 B.C.	**About 760 B.C.**	**722 B.C.**
Reign of Jeroboam II begins	Prophetic ministry of Jonah	Fall of Israel

Jonah

Jonah Flees the Presence of the LORD

1 Now the word of the LORD came
to Jonah the son of Amittai, say-
1239 ing, 2 "Arise, go to Nineveh, that
great city, and call out against it, for their
evil[1] has come up before me." 3 But Jonah
rose to flee to Tarshish from the presence
of the LORD. He went down to Joppa and
found a ship going to Tarshish. So he paid
the fare and went on board, to go with
them to Tarshish, away from the presence
of the LORD.

CHARACTER PROFILE

JONAH

Jonah ran away when God told him to go to Nineveh to preach. God sent a storm after Jonah's ship, and the sailors threw Jonah overboard. Jonah prayed from inside the large fish that swallowed him, and God made the great fish spit Jonah out onto dry land. Finally Jonah obeyed God and went to Nineveh. The people of Nineveh repented and believed God.

1239

4 But the LORD hurled a great wind
upon the sea, and there was a
1689 mighty tempest on the sea, so that
the ship threatened to break up. 5 Then the
mariners were afraid, and each cried out
to his god. And they hurled the cargo that
was in the ship into the sea to lighten it for
them. But Jonah had gone down into the
inner part of the ship and had lain down
and was fast asleep. 6 So the captain came
and said to him, "What do you mean, you
sleeper? Arise, call out to your god! Perhaps
the god will give a thought to us, that we
may not perish."

Jonah Is Thrown into the Sea

7 And they said to one another, "Come,
let us cast lots, that we may know on whose
account this evil has come upon us." So
they cast lots, and the lot fell on Jonah.
8 Then they said to him, "Tell us on whose
account this evil has come upon us. What
is your occupation? And where do you
come from? What is your country? And
of what people are you?" 9 And he said to
them, "I am a Hebrew, and I fear the LORD,
the God of heaven, who made the sea and
the dry land." 10 Then the men were exceed-
ingly afraid and said to him, "What is this
that you have done!" For the men knew
that he was fleeing from the presence of
the LORD, because he had told them.

11 Then they said to him, "What shall
we do to you, that the sea may quiet down
for us?" For the sea grew more and more
tempestuous. 12 He said to them, "Pick
me up and hurl me into the sea; then the
sea will quiet down for you, for I know it
is because of me that this great tempest
has come upon you." 13 Nevertheless, the
men rowed hard[2] to get back to dry land,
but they could not, for the sea grew more

[1] The same Hebrew word can mean *evil* or *disaster*, depending on the context; so throughout Jonah [2] Hebrew *the men dug in* [their oars]

and more tempestuous against them.
14 Therefore they called out to the LORD,
"O LORD, let us not perish for this man's
life, and lay not on us innocent blood, for
you, O LORD, have done as it pleased you."
15 So they picked up Jonah and hurled him
into the sea, and the sea ceased from its
raging. **16** Then the men feared the LORD
exceedingly, and they offered a sacrifice
to the LORD and made vows.

A Great Fish Swallows Jonah

17[1] And the LORD appointed[2] a great fish
to swallow up Jonah. And Jonah was in the
belly of the fish three days and three nights.

Jonah's Prayer

2 Then Jonah prayed to the LORD his
God from the belly of the fish, **2** saying,

"I called out to the LORD, out of my distress,
and he answered me;
out of the belly of Sheol I cried,
and you heard my voice.
3 For you cast me into the deep,
into the heart of the seas,
and the flood surrounded me;
all your waves and your billows
passed over me.
4 Then I said, 'I am driven away
from your sight;
yet I shall again look
upon your holy temple.'
5 The waters closed in over me to take my life;
the deep surrounded me;
weeds were wrapped about my head
6 at the roots of the mountains.
I went down to the land
whose bars closed upon me forever;
yet you brought up my life from the pit,
O LORD my God.
7 When my life was fainting away,
I remembered the LORD,
and my prayer came to you,
into your holy temple.
8 Those who pay regard to vain idols
forsake their hope of steadfast love.
9 But I with the voice of thanksgiving
will sacrifice to you;
what I have vowed I will pay.
Salvation belongs to the LORD!"

10 And the LORD spoke to the fish, and it
vomited Jonah out upon the dry land.

Jonah Goes to Nineveh

3 Then the word of the LORD came
to Jonah the second time, saying,
2 "Arise, go to Nineveh, that great city,
and call out against it the message that
I tell you." **3** So Jonah arose and went to
Nineveh, according to the word of the
LORD. Now Nineveh was an exceedingly
great city,[3] three days' journey in breadth.[4]
4 Jonah began to go into the city, going a
day's journey. And he called out, "Yet forty
days, and Nineveh shall be overthrown!"
5 And the people of Nineveh believed God.
They called for a fast and put on sack-
cloth, from the greatest of them to the
least of them.

The People of Nineveh Repent

6 The word reached[5] the king of Nineveh,
and he arose from his throne, removed
his robe, covered himself with sackcloth,
and sat in ashes. **7** And he issued a procla-
mation and published through Nineveh,
"By the decree of the king and his nobles:
Let neither man nor beast, herd nor flock,
taste anything. Let them not feed or drink
water, **8** but let man and beast be covered
with sackcloth, and let them call out
mightily to God. Let everyone turn from
his evil way and from the violence that is
in his hands. **9** Who knows? God may turn
and relent and turn from his fierce anger,
so that we may not perish."

10 When God saw what they did, how
they turned from their evil way, God
relented of the disaster that he had said
he would do to them, and he did not do it.

[1] Ch 2:1 in Hebrew [2] Or *had appointed* [3] Hebrew *a great city to God* [4] Or *a visit was a three days' journey* [5] Or *had reached*

Jonah and the Great Fish

Jonah was a prophet. He was one of the people called by God to tell people the word of the Lord.

One day God told Jonah to go to the city of Nineveh. Jonah was supposed to tell the people of Nineveh that God was very angry with them because of their great sin, and that God was going to overthrow their city.

But Jonah did not want to go to Nineveh. He was afraid that the people would listen to God and repent. Then God would forgive them. Jonah did not want that to happen. Instead, he wanted Nineveh to be destroyed. So Jonah bought a ticket to sail far away on a ship.

Jonah tried to run away from God. But God knew where Jonah was, and God knew that Jonah had disobeyed Him. Jonah had sinned against God.

At first, Jonah thought he was safe on the ship, sailing away from the presence of the Lord. But God knew where Jonah was, and God sent a strong wind over the sea. Huge waves crashed over the ship's deck, and the ship was about to sink. The sailors were terrified. They threw things overboard to make the ship lighter. They prayed to their gods. But nothing helped.

Finally, the ship's captain found Jonah asleep below the deck. The captain woke Jonah up and asked Jonah to pray to God. But still the winds kept blowing and the waves kept crashing over the ship.

At last the sailors discovered that God had caused the great storm because of Jonah! Jonah told the sailors they must throw him into the sea. Then God would stop the storm.

The sailors did not want to hurt Jonah, so they tried instead to row to shore. When that did not work, they prayed to the Lord and asked Him not to hold them guilty for Jonah's life. Then they picked up Jonah and threw him overboard as far as they could. And immediately the storm stopped raging.

Jonah did not die, though. God sent a great fish to swallow Jonah and keep him safe from drowning. Jonah was inside the fish three days and three nights. He prayed and asked God to help him. He promised to obey God.

God heard Jonah's prayer. God still loved Jonah, and He forgave Jonah for disobeying Him. God told the big fish to throw up Jonah onto the dry land, and the fish obeyed.

Once more God told Jonah to go to Nineveh and give the word of the Lord to the people of Nineveh. This time Jonah obeyed. He went to Nineveh and announced God's message. Jonah told them that God was going to destroy the city because of all the evil they had done.

The people of Nineveh believed God. They put on sackcloth instead of clothes, and they stopped eating to show how sorry they were for their sins. Their king told all the people to call out to God for forgiveness. When God saw the people repent, He told Jonah He would not destroy the city after all, because the people had turned from their evil ways.

This made Jonah angry. He did not want God to forgive

the people of Nineveh. He wanted them to be destroyed. But God is loving and patient—and He helped Jonah see that he too must be loving and patient like God is. Jonah should care about other people, even evil people, praying that they would repent and love God too. Jonah should forgive, just as God forgives all who ask for His forgiveness.

Our God is gracious and merciful. He is slow to anger. He abounds in steadfast love. Our God is a God who loves to save. He sent a fish to save Jonah. He sent Jonah with a message to save the people of Nineveh. Best of all, He sent Jesus to save us. Jesus died on the cross to pay for our sins. After three days in the grave, Jesus came back to life so that everyone would hear the message about His forgiveness and His love, and trust Him as their Savior.

SEEK and FIND

WHERE TO FIND THE STORY

Jonah 1–4

KEY BIBLE VERSE

"The LORD is merciful and gracious,
slow to anger and abounding in steadfast love.
. . . He does not deal with us according to our sins,
nor repay us according to our iniquities."
(Psalm 103:8, 10)

THREE KEY QUESTIONS

- How did God show His love and mercy to the people of Nineveh?
- How did God show His love and mercy to Jonah?
- How has God shown His love and mercy to you?

RELATED BIBLE READINGS

Matthew 9:10–13; 12:38–41; Luke 15:1–7

Jonah's Anger and the LORD's Compassion

4 But it displeased Jonah exceedingly,[1] and he was angry. **2** And he prayed to the LORD and said, "O LORD, is not this what I said when I was yet in my country? That is why I made haste to flee to Tarshish; for I knew that you are a gracious God and merciful, slow to anger and abounding in steadfast love, and relenting from disaster. **3** Therefore now, O LORD, please take my life from me, for it is better for me to die than to live." **4** And the LORD said, "Do you do well to be angry?"

5 Jonah went out of the city and sat to the east of the city and made a booth for himself there. He sat under it in the shade, till he should see what would become of the city. **6** Now the LORD God appointed a plant[2] and made it come up over Jonah, that it might be a shade over his head, to save him from his discomfort.[3] So Jonah was exceedingly glad because of the plant. **7** But when dawn came up the next day, God appointed a worm that attacked the plant, so that it withered. **8** When the sun rose, God appointed a scorching east wind, and the sun beat down on the head of Jonah so that he was faint. And he asked that he might die and said, "It is better for me to die than to live." **9** But God said to Jonah, "Do you do well to be angry for the plant?" And he said, "Yes, I do well to be angry, angry enough to die." **10** And the LORD said, "You pity the plant, for which you did not labor, nor did you make it grow, which came into being in a night and perished in a night. **11** And should not I pity Nineveh, that great city, in which there are more than 120,000 persons who do not know their right hand from their left, and also much cattle?"

[1] Hebrew *it was exceedingly evil to Jonah* [2] Hebrew *qiqayon*, probably the castor oil plant; also verses 7, 9, 10 [3] Or *his evil*

Introduction to

Micah

Author
Micah the prophet

Date
About 742 B.C.

Purpose
The purpose of Micah is to announce the guilt of God's people and their leaders, while promising God's Shepherd-King who would forgive, gather, and care for God's people.

Central Themes
God, the just Judge, brings a "lawsuit" against His people and pronounces judgment; true worship requires a life of justice, mercy, and faithfulness; God's Shepherd-King will gather and care for His people; the nations will come and join God's people in the worship of the true God.

Memory Verses
Remnant gathered (Micah 2:12–13); the Ruler from Bethlehem (Micah 5:2–5a); what is good (Micah 6:8); God's compassion (Micah 7:18–20)

Introduction

Micah announces God's court case against Israel and Judah. God is the Judge and finds His people guilty of idol worship, of cheating and oppressing the poor, and of violence. Those who should lead the people in faithfulness to God are poor examples themselves. God pronounces their punishment, promising to bring enemy nations against both Israel and Judah (Micah 1–3; 6:1–2). Because of God's great mercy and grace, He also promises to raise up a Ruler from Bethlehem who will shepherd His flock in the strength of the Lord, causing God's people to dwell in peace and safety (Micah 5:2–5a). God promises that one day the nations will repent and turn humbly to the true God (Micah 7:14–17). The book closes with a song that praises God because no one is like Him: delighting in steadfast love, forgiving the sins of His people, and keeping the promises He made long ago in His covenant (Micah 7:18–20).

750 B.C.	About 742 B.C.	722 B.C.	715 B.C.
Reign of Jotham begins	Prophetic ministry of Micah	Fall of Israel	Reign of Hezekiah begins

Micah

1 The word of the LORD that came to Micah of Moresheth in the days of Jotham, Ahaz, and Hezekiah, kings of Judah, which he saw concerning Samaria and Jerusalem.

The Coming Destruction

2 Hear, you peoples, all of you;[1]
pay attention, O earth, and all that is in it,
and let the Lord GOD be a witness against you,
the Lord from his holy temple.
3 For behold, the LORD is coming out of his place,
and will come down and tread upon the high places of the earth.
4 And the mountains will melt under him,
and the valleys will split open,
like wax before the fire,
like waters poured down a steep place.
5 All this is for the transgression of Jacob
and for the sins of the house of Israel.
What is the transgression of Jacob?
Is it not Samaria?
And what is the high place of Judah?
Is it not Jerusalem?
6 Therefore I will make Samaria a heap in the open country,
a place for planting vineyards,
and I will pour down her stones into the valley
and uncover her foundations.
7 All her carved images shall be beaten to pieces,
all her wages shall be burned with fire,
and all her idols I will lay waste,
for from the fee of a prostitute she gathered them,
and to the fee of a prostitute they shall return.

8 For this I will lament and wail;
I will go stripped and naked;
I will make lamentation like the jackals,
and mourning like the ostriches.
9 For her wound is incurable,
and it has come to Judah;
it has reached to the gate of my people,
to Jerusalem.

10 Tell it not in Gath;
weep not at all;
in Beth-le-aphrah
roll yourselves in the dust.
11 Pass on your way,
inhabitants of Shaphir,
in nakedness and shame;
the inhabitants of Zaanan
do not come out;
the lamentation of Beth-ezel
shall take away from you its standing place.
12 For the inhabitants of Maroth
wait anxiously for good,
because disaster has come down from the LORD
to the gate of Jerusalem.
13 Harness the steeds to the chariots,
inhabitants of Lachish;
it was the beginning of sin
to the daughter of Zion,
for in you were found
the transgressions of Israel.
14 Therefore you shall give parting gifts[2]
to Moresheth-gath;

[1] Hebrew *all of them* [2] Or *give dowry*

the houses of Achzib shall be a
deceitful thing
to the kings of Israel.
15 I will again bring a conqueror to you,
inhabitants of Mareshah;
the glory of Israel
shall come to Adullam.
16 Make yourselves bald and cut off
your hair,
for the children of your delight;
make yourselves as bald as the eagle,
for they shall go from you into
exile.

Woe to the Oppressors

2 Woe to those who devise wickedness
and work evil on their beds!
When the morning dawns, they
perform it,
because it is in the power of their
hand.
2 They covet fields and seize them,
and houses, and take them away;
they oppress a man and his house,
a man and his inheritance.
3 Therefore thus says the LORD:
behold, against this family I am
devising disaster,[1]
from which you cannot remove
your necks,
and you shall not walk haughtily,
for it will be a time of disaster.
4 In that day they shall take up a taunt
song against you
and moan bitterly,
and say, "We are utterly ruined;
he changes the portion of my
people;
how he removes it from me!
To an apostate he allots our fields."
5 Therefore you will have none to cast
the line by lot
in the assembly of the LORD.
6 "Do not preach"—thus they preach—
"one should not preach of such
things;
disgrace will not overtake us."
7 Should this be said, O house of Jacob?
Has the LORD grown impatient?[2]
Are these his deeds?
Do not my words do good
to him who walks uprightly?
8 But lately my people have risen up
as an enemy;
you strip the rich robe from those
who pass by trustingly
with no thought of war.[3]
9 The women of my people you drive
out
from their delightful houses;
from their young children you take
away
my splendor forever.
10 Arise and go,
for this is no place to rest,
because of uncleanness that
destroys
with a grievous destruction.
11 If a man should go about and utter
wind and lies,
saying, "I will preach to you of
wine and strong drink,"
he would be the preacher for this
people!
12 I will surely assemble all of you, O
Jacob;
I will gather the remnant of Israel;
I will set them together
like sheep in a fold,
like a flock in its pasture,
a noisy multitude of men.
13 He who opens the breach goes up
before them;
they break through and pass the
gate,
going out by it.
Their king passes on before them,
the LORD at their head.

Rulers and Prophets Denounced

3 And I said:
Hear, you heads of Jacob
and rulers of the house of Israel!
Is it not for you to know justice?—

[1] The same Hebrew word can mean *evil* or *disaster*, depending on the context [2] Hebrew *Has the spirit of the LORD grown short?* [3] Or *returning from war*

2 you who hate the good and love
the evil,
who tear the skin from off my
people[1]
and their flesh from off their
bones,
3 who eat the flesh of my people,
and flay their skin from off them,
and break their bones in pieces
and chop them up like meat in a
pot,
like flesh in a cauldron.

4 Then they will cry to the LORD,
but he will not answer them;
he will hide his face from them at
that time,
because they have made their
deeds evil.

5 Thus says the LORD concerning the
prophets
who lead my people astray,
who cry "Peace"
when they have something to eat,
but declare war against him
who puts nothing into their
mouths.
6 Therefore it shall be night to you,
without vision,
and darkness to you, without
divination.
The sun shall go down on the
prophets,
and the day shall be black over
them;
7 the seers shall be disgraced,
and the diviners put to shame;
they shall all cover their lips,
for there is no answer from God.
8 But as for me, I am filled with power,
with the Spirit of the LORD,
and with justice and might,
to declare to Jacob his transgression
and to Israel his sin.

9 Hear this, you heads of the house of
Jacob
and rulers of the house of Israel,
who detest justice
and make crooked all that is
straight,
10 who build Zion with blood
and Jerusalem with iniquity.
11 Its heads give judgment for a bribe;
its priests teach for a price;
its prophets practice divination
for money;
yet they lean on the LORD and say,
"Is not the LORD in the midst of us?
No disaster shall come upon us."
12 Therefore because of you
Zion shall be plowed as a field;
Jerusalem shall become a heap of
ruins,
and the mountain of the house a
wooded height.

The Mountain of the LORD

4 It shall come to pass in the latter days
that the mountain of the house of
the LORD
shall be established as the highest
of the mountains,
and it shall be lifted up above the
hills;
and peoples shall flow to it,
2 and many nations shall come,
and say:
"Come, let us go up to the mountain
of the LORD,
to the house of the God of Jacob,
that he may teach us his ways
and that we may walk in his paths."
For out of Zion shall go forth the
law,[2]
and the word of the LORD from
Jerusalem.
3 He shall judge between many
peoples,
and shall decide for strong
nations far away;
and they shall beat their swords
into plowshares,
and their spears into pruning
hooks;

[1] Hebrew *from off them* [2] Or *teaching*

nation shall not lift up sword
against nation,
neither shall they learn war
anymore;
4 but they shall sit every man under
his vine and under his fig tree,
and no one shall make them afraid,
for the mouth of the LORD of
hosts has spoken.
5 For all the peoples walk
each in the name of its god,
but we will walk in the name of the
LORD our God
forever and ever.

The LORD Shall Rescue Zion

6 In that day, declares the LORD,
I will assemble the lame
and gather those who have been
driven away
and those whom I have afflicted;
7 and the lame I will make the
remnant,
and those who were cast off, a
strong nation;
and the LORD will reign over them
in Mount Zion
from this time forth and
forevermore.

8 And you, O tower of the flock,
hill of the daughter of Zion,
to you shall it come,
the former dominion shall come,
kingship for the daughter of
Jerusalem.

9 Now why do you cry aloud?
Is there no king in you?
Has your counselor perished,
that pain seized you like a woman
in labor?
10 Writhe and groan,[1] O daughter of
Zion,
like a woman in labor,
for now you shall go out from the city
and dwell in the open country;
you shall go to Babylon.
There you shall be rescued;
there the LORD will redeem you
from the hand of your enemies.

11 Now many nations
are assembled against you,
saying, "Let her be defiled,
and let our eyes gaze upon Zion."
12 But they do not know
the thoughts of the LORD;
they do not understand his plan,
that he has gathered them as
sheaves to the threshing floor.
13 Arise and thresh,
O daughter of Zion,
for I will make your horn iron,
and I will make your hoofs
bronze;
you shall beat in pieces many
peoples;
and shall devote[2] their gain to the
LORD,
their wealth to the Lord of the
whole earth.

The Ruler to Be Born in Bethlehem

5 [3] Now muster your troops, O
daughter[4] of troops;
siege is laid against us;
with a rod they strike the judge of
Israel
on the cheek.

2[5] But you, O Bethlehem
Ephrathah,
1297, 1445
who are too little to be among
the clans of Judah,
from you shall come forth for me
one who is to be ruler in Israel,
whose coming forth is from of old,
from ancient days.
3 Therefore he shall give them up
until the time
when she who is in labor has
given birth;
then the rest of his brothers shall
return
to the people of Israel.

[1] Or *push* [2] Hebrew *devote to destruction* [3] Ch 4:14 in Hebrew [4] That is, city [5] Ch 5:1 in Hebrew

4 And he shall stand and shepherd
his flock in the strength of the
LORD,
in the majesty of the name of the
LORD his God.
And they shall dwell secure, for now
he shall be great
to the ends of the earth.
5 And he shall be their peace.

When the Assyrian comes into our
land
and treads in our palaces,
then we will raise against him seven
shepherds
and eight princes of men;
6 they shall shepherd the land of
Assyria with the sword,
and the land of Nimrod at its
entrances;
and he shall deliver us from the
Assyrian
when he comes into our land
and treads within our border.

A Remnant Shall Be Delivered

7 Then the remnant of Jacob shall be
in the midst of many peoples
like dew from the LORD,
like showers on the grass,
which delay not for a man
nor wait for the children of man.
8 And the remnant of Jacob shall be
among the nations,
in the midst of many peoples,
like a lion among the beasts of the
forest,
like a young lion among the
flocks of sheep,
which, when it goes through, treads
down
and tears in pieces, and there is
none to deliver.
9 *Your hand* shall be lifted up over
your adversaries,
and all your enemies shall be cut
off.

10 And in that day, declares the LORD,
I will cut off your horses from
among you
and will destroy your chariots;
11 and I will cut off the cities of your land
and throw down all your
strongholds;
12 and I will cut off sorceries from
your hand,
and you shall have no more
tellers of fortunes;
13 and I will cut off your carved images
and your pillars from among you,
and you shall bow down no more
to the work of your hands;
14 and I will root out your Asherah
images from among you
and destroy your cities.
15 And in anger and wrath I will
execute vengeance
on the nations that did not obey.

The Indictment of the LORD

6 Hear what the LORD says:
Arise, plead your case before the
mountains,
and let the hills hear your voice.
2 Hear, you mountains, the
indictment of the LORD,
and you enduring foundations of
the earth,
for the LORD has an indictment
against his people,
and he will contend with Israel.

3 "O my people, what have I done
to you?
131 How have I wearied you?
Answer me!
4 For I brought you up from the land
of Egypt
and redeemed you from the
house of slavery,
and I sent before you Moses,
Aaron, and Miriam.
5 O my people, remember what Balak
king of Moab devised,

and what Balaam the son of Beor
answered him,
and what happened from Shittim to
Gilgal,
that you may know the saving
acts of the LORD."

What Does the LORD Require?

6 "With what shall I come before the
LORD,
and bow myself before God on
high?
Shall I come before him with burnt
offerings,
with calves a year old?
7 Will the LORD be pleased with[1]
thousands of rams,
with ten thousands of rivers of oil?
Shall I give my firstborn for my
transgression,
the fruit of my body for the sin of
my soul?"
8 He has told you, O man, what is good;
and what does the LORD require
of you
but to do justice, and to love
kindness,[2]
and to walk humbly with your God?

Destruction of the Wicked

9 The voice of the LORD cries to the
city—
and it is sound wisdom to fear
your name:
"Hear of the rod and of him who
appointed it![3]
10 Can I forget any longer the
treasures[4] of wickedness in
the house of the wicked,
and the scant measure that is
accursed?
11 Shall I acquit the man with wicked
scales
and with a bag of deceitful weights?
12 Your[5] rich men are full of violence;
your inhabitants speak lies,
and their tongue is deceitful in
their mouth.
13 Therefore I strike you with a
grievous blow,
making you desolate because of
your sins.
14 You shall eat, but not be satisfied,
and there shall be hunger within
you;
you shall put away, but not preserve,
and what you preserve I will give
to the sword.
15 You shall sow, but not reap;
you shall tread olives, but not
anoint yourselves with oil;
you shall tread grapes, but not
drink wine.
16 For you have kept the statutes of
Omri,[6]
and all the works of the house of
Ahab;
and you have walked in their
counsels,
that I may make you a desolation, and
your[7] inhabitants a hissing;
so you shall bear the scorn of my
people."

Wait for the God of Salvation

7 Woe is me! For I have become
as when the summer fruit has been
gathered,
as when the grapes have been
gleaned:
there is no cluster to eat,
no first-ripe fig that my soul desires.
2 The godly has perished from the
earth,
and there is no one upright
among mankind;
they all lie in wait for blood,
and each hunts the other with a net.
3 Their hands are on what is evil, to
do it well;
the prince and the judge ask for a
bribe,

[1] Or *Will the LORD accept* [2] Or *steadfast love* [3] The meaning of the Hebrew is uncertain [4] Or *Are there still treasures* [5] Hebrew *whose* [6] Hebrew *For the statutes of Omri are kept* [7] Hebrew *its*

and the great man utters the evil
desire of his soul;
thus they weave it together.
4 The best of them is like a brier,
the most upright of them a thorn
hedge.
The day of your watchmen, of your
punishment, has come;
now their confusion is at hand.
5 Put no trust in a neighbor;
have no confidence in a friend;
guard the doors of your mouth
from her who lies in your arms;[1]
6 for the son treats the father with
contempt,
the daughter rises up against her
mother,
the daughter-in-law against her
mother-in-law;
a man's enemies are the men of
his own house.
7 But as for me, I will look to the LORD;
I will wait for the God of my
salvation;
my God will hear me.

8 Rejoice not over me, O my enemy;
when I fall, I shall rise;
when I sit in darkness,
the LORD will be a light to me.
9 I will bear the indignation of the LORD
because I have sinned against him,
until he pleads my cause
and executes judgment for me.
He will bring me out to the light;
I shall look upon his vindication.
10 Then my enemy will see,
and shame will cover her who
said to me,
"Where is the LORD your God?"
My eyes will look upon her;
now she will be trampled down
like the mire of the streets.
11 A day for the building of your walls!
In that day the boundary shall be
far extended.
12 In that day they[2] will come to you,
from Assyria and the cities of Egypt,
and from Egypt to the River,
from sea to sea and from
mountain to mountain.
13 But the earth will be desolate
because of its inhabitants,
for the fruit of their deeds.

14 Shepherd your people with your staff,
the flock of your inheritance,
who dwell alone in a forest
in the midst of a garden land;[3]
let them graze in Bashan and Gilead
as in the days of old.
15 As in the days when you came out
of the land of Egypt,
I will show them[4] marvelous things.
16 The nations shall see and be
ashamed of all their might;
they shall lay their hands on their
mouths;
their ears shall be deaf;
17 they shall lick the dust like a serpent,
like the crawling things of the earth;
they shall come trembling out of
their strongholds;
they shall turn in dread to the
LORD our God,
and they shall be in fear of you.

God's Steadfast Love and Compassion

18 Who is a God like you, pardoning
iniquity
and passing over transgression
for the remnant of his
inheritance?
He does not retain his anger forever,
because he delights in steadfast
love.
19 He will again have compassion on us;
he will tread our iniquities
underfoot.
You will cast all our[5] sins
into the depths of the sea.
20 You will show faithfulness to Jacob
and steadfast love to Abraham,
as you have sworn to our fathers
from the days of old.

[1] Hebrew *bosom* [2] Hebrew *he* [3] Hebrew *of Carmel* [4] Hebrew *him* [5] Hebrew *their*

Introduction to

Nahum

Author
Nahum the prophet

Date
About 660 B.C.

Purpose
The purpose of Nahum is to announce the destruction of Nineveh, the capital city of Assyria, as God's judgment on the Assyrians.

Central Themes
God's judgment is dreadful and terrifying; God will judge Nineveh for its idolatry, cruelty, and pride; God will save His people and restore their greatness; God is good and protects those who take refuge in Him.

Memory Verses
The Lord's promise (Nahum 1:7–8); good news for Judah (Nahum 1:15); the Lord opposes Assyria (Nahum 2:13)

Introduction

When Jonah preached in Nineveh, the people repented and God forgave their sin. But when Nahum writes, many years have passed. Now the people of Nineveh, the capital city of Assyria, are even more evil than they were before. They have risen to power and have destroyed other nations, treating their captives with great cruelty. Nahum announces the sure fall of Nineveh as judgment from God. The book begins praising God for His character: slow to anger, but punishing His enemies and great in power. His wrath is terrible and no one can bear it, but He is good and protects those who take refuge in Him (Nahum 1:1–7). God had used the Assyrians to discipline His sinful people of Israel and Judah, but now He promises to free His people from Assyria's power (Nahum 1:12–13, 15). He will restore His people's majesty (Nahum 2:2). God promises to destroy Nineveh, and Nahum uses his words to paint a picture of a confused, noisy, frightening battle scene, all taking place in Nineveh, with death and destruction all around (Nahum 2:2–3:19). This time, there will be no help for Nineveh, for they have treated too many people with "unceasing evil" (Nahum 3:18–19).

686 B.C.	About 660 B.C.	640 B.C.	612 B.C.
Reign of Manasseh begins	Prophetic ministry of Nahum begins	Reign of Josiah begins	Ninevah destroyed

Nahum

1 An oracle concerning Nineveh. The book of the vision of Nahum of Elkosh.

God's Wrath Against Nineveh

2 The LORD is a jealous and avenging God;
the LORD is avenging and wrathful;
the LORD takes vengeance on his adversaries
and keeps wrath for his enemies.
3 The LORD is slow to anger and great in power,
and the LORD will by no means clear the guilty.
His way is in whirlwind and storm,
and the clouds are the dust of his feet.
4 He rebukes the sea and makes it dry;
he dries up all the rivers;
Bashan and Carmel wither;
the bloom of Lebanon withers.
5 The mountains quake before him;
the hills melt;
the earth heaves before him,
the world and all who dwell in it.

6 Who can stand before his indignation?
Who can endure the heat of his anger?
His wrath is poured out like fire,
and the rocks are broken into pieces by him.
7 The LORD is good,
a stronghold in the day of trouble;
he knows those who take refuge in him.
8 But with an overflowing flood
he *will* make a complete end of the adversaries,[1]
and will pursue his enemies into darkness.
9 What do you plot against the LORD?
He will make a complete end;
trouble will not rise up a second time.
10 For they are like entangled thorns,
like drunkards as they drink;
they are consumed like stubble fully dried.
11 From you came one
who plotted evil against the LORD,
a worthless counselor.

12 Thus says the LORD,
"Though they are at full strength and many,
they will be cut down and pass away.
Though I have afflicted you,
I will afflict you no more.
13 And now I will break his yoke from off you
and will burst your bonds apart."

14 The LORD has given commandment about you:
"No more shall your name be perpetuated;
from the house of your gods I will cut off
the carved image and the metal image.
I will make your grave, for you are vile."

15[2] Behold, upon the mountains, the feet of him
who brings good news,
who publishes peace!
Keep your feasts, O Judah;
fulfill your vows,
for never again shall the worthless pass through you;
he is utterly cut off.

[1] Hebrew *of her place* [2] Ch 2:1 in Hebrew

The Destruction of Nineveh

2 The scatterer has come up against you.
Man the ramparts;
watch the road;
dress for battle;[1]
collect all your strength.

2 For the LORD is restoring the majesty of Jacob
as the majesty of Israel,
for plunderers have plundered them
and ruined their branches.

3 The shield of his mighty men is red;
his soldiers are clothed in scarlet.
The chariots come with flashing metal
on the day he musters them;
the cypress spears are brandished.
4 The chariots race madly through the streets;
they rush to and fro through the squares;
they gleam like torches;
they dart like lightning.
5 He remembers his officers;
they stumble as they go,
they hasten to the wall;
the siege tower[2] is set up.
6 The river gates are opened;
the palace melts away;
7 its mistress[3] is stripped;[4] she is carried off,
her slave girls lamenting,
moaning like doves
and beating their breasts.
8 Nineveh is like a pool
whose waters run away.[5]
"Halt! Halt!" they cry,
but none turns back.
9 Plunder the silver,
plunder the gold!
There is no end of the treasure
or of the wealth of all precious things.
10 Desolate! Desolation and ruin!
Hearts melt and knees tremble;
anguish is in all loins;
all faces grow pale!
11 Where is the lions' den,
the feeding place of the young lions,
where the lion and lioness went,
where his cubs were, with none to disturb?
12 The lion tore enough for his cubs
and strangled prey for his lionesses;
he filled his caves with prey
and his dens with torn flesh.

13 Behold, I am against you, declares the
LORD of hosts, and I will burn your[6] chari-
ots in smoke, and the sword shall devour
your young lions. I will cut off your prey
from the earth, and the voice of your mes-
sengers shall no longer be heard.

Woe to Nineveh

3 Woe to the bloody city,
all full of lies and plunder—
no end to the prey!
2 The crack of the whip, and rumble of the wheel,
galloping horse and bounding chariot!
3 Horsemen charging,
flashing sword and glittering spear,
hosts of slain,
heaps of corpses,
dead bodies without end—
they stumble over the bodies!
4 And all for the countless whorings of the prostitute,
graceful and of deadly charms,
who betrays nations with her whorings,
and peoples with her charms.

5 Behold, I am against you,
declares the LORD of hosts,
and will lift up your skirts over your face;

[1] Hebrew *gird your loins* [2] Or *the mantelet* [3] The meaning of the Hebrew word rendered *its mistress* is uncertain [4] Or *exiled* [5] Compare Septuagint; the meaning of the Hebrew is uncertain [6] Hebrew *her*

and I will make nations look at your nakedness
and kingdoms at your shame.
6 I will throw filth at you
and treat you with contempt
and make you a spectacle.
7 And all who look at you will shrink from you and say,
Wasted is Nineveh; who will grieve for her?
Where shall I seek comforters for you?

8 Are you better than Thebes[1]
that sat by the Nile,
with water around her,
her rampart a sea,
and water her wall?
9 Cush was her strength;
Egypt too, and that without limit;
Put and the Libyans were her[2] helpers.

10 Yet she became an exile;
she went into captivity;
her infants were dashed in pieces
at the head of every street;
for her honored men lots were cast,
and all her great men were bound in chains.
11 You also will be drunken;
you will go into hiding;
you will seek a refuge from the enemy.
12 All your fortresses are like fig trees
with first-ripe figs—
if shaken they fall
into the mouth of the eater.
13 Behold, your troops
are women in your midst.
The gates of your land
are wide open to your enemies;
fire has devoured your bars.

14 Draw water for the siege;
strengthen your forts;
go into the clay;
tread the mortar;
take hold of the brick mold!
15 There will the fire devour you;
the sword will cut you off.
It will devour you like the locust.
Multiply yourselves like the locust;
multiply like the grasshopper!
16 You increased your merchants
more than the stars of the heavens.
The locust spreads its wings and flies away.

17 Your princes are like grasshoppers,
your scribes[3] like clouds of locusts
settling on the fences
in a day of cold—
when the sun rises, they fly away;
no one knows where they are.

18 Your shepherds are asleep,
O king of Assyria;
your nobles slumber.
Your people are scattered on the mountains
with none to gather them.
19 There is no easing your hurt;
your wound is grievous.
All who hear the news about you
clap their hands over you.
For upon whom has not come
your unceasing evil?

[1] Hebrew *No-amon* [2] Hebrew *your* [3] Or *marshals*

Introduction to

Habakkuk

Author

Habakkuk the prophet

Date

About 640 B.C.

Purpose

The purpose of Habakkuk is to show that even through evil God works to accomplish His good purpose of bringing glory to Himself.

Central Themes

God disciplines His sinful people; God uses even evil people and nations to accomplish His purposes; God will judge all evil; God's goal is to bring glory to Himself; God's people must trust Him and live by faith while they wait for Him to accomplish His purposes.

Memory Verses

Habakkuk's complaint (Habakkuk 1:2–4); a message for the arrogant and the righteous (Habakkuk 2:2–4); prayer for mercy (Habakkuk 3:2); rejoice always in the Lord (Habakkuk 3:17–19)

Introduction

This book is a conversation between Habakkuk and God. Habakkuk begins by complaining that God's people are wicked and God does nothing about it (Habakkuk 1:2–4). God answers Habakkuk; He will bring the Babylonians against Judah, to defeat it and take its people captive (Habakkuk 1:5–11). This upsets Habakkuk greatly, because the Babylonians are more wicked than the Jews. Habakkuk complains that if God is really holy and just, evil people should not be allowed to harm those who are more righteous than they are (Habakkuk 1:12–2:1). God answers by promising that He will also punish the Babylonians for their great evil (Habakkuk 2:2–20). God assures Habakkuk that He will accomplish His one great purpose, that "the earth will be filled with the knowledge of the glory of the LORD as the waters cover the sea" (Habakkuk 2:14). While God's people wait for God to carry out His plans, they must live by faith (Habakkuk 2:4). Habakkuk ends with the prophet's prayer for God's mercy, praise for God's acts for His people in the past, and prayer of confidence that, even though he will suffer with God's people under the Babylonians, he can trust in God and rejoice in Him (Habakkuk 3).

722 B.C.	**About 640 B.C.**	**586 B.C.**
Fall of Israel	Prophetic ministry of Habakkuk	Fall of Judah

Habakkuk

1 The oracle that Habakkuk the prophet
saw.

Habakkuk's Complaint

2 O LORD, how long shall I cry for help,
and you will not hear?
Or cry to you "Violence!"
and you will not save?
3 Why do you make me see iniquity,
and why do you idly look at wrong?
Destruction and violence are
before me;
strife and contention arise.
4 So the law is paralyzed,
and justice never goes forth.
For the wicked surround the
righteous;
so justice goes forth perverted.

The LORD's Answer

5 "Look among the nations, and see;
wonder and be astounded.
For I am doing a work in your days
that you would not believe if told.
6 For behold, I am raising up the
Chaldeans,
that bitter and hasty nation,
who march through the breadth of
the earth,
to seize dwellings not their own.
7 They are dreaded and fearsome;
their justice and dignity go forth
from themselves.
8 Their horses are swifter than leopards,
more fierce than the evening
wolves;
their horsemen press proudly on.
Their horsemen come from afar;
they fly like an eagle swift to devour.
9 They all come for violence,
all their faces forward.
They gather captives like sand.
10 At kings they scoff,
and at rulers they laugh.
They laugh at every fortress,
for they pile up earth and take it.
11 Then they sweep by like the wind
and go on,
guilty men, whose own might is
their god!"

Habakkuk's Second Complaint

12 Are you not from everlasting,
O LORD my God, my Holy One?
We shall not die.
O LORD, you have ordained them as
a judgment,
and you, O Rock, have established
them for reproof.
13 You who are of purer eyes than to
see evil
and cannot look at wrong,
why do you idly look at traitors
and remain silent when the
wicked swallows up
the man more righteous than he?
14 You make mankind like the fish of
the sea,
like crawling things that have no
ruler.
15 He brings all of them up with a
hook;
he drags them out with his net;
he gathers them in his dragnet;
so he rejoices and is glad.
16 Therefore he sacrifices to his net
and makes offerings to his
dragnet;
for by them he lives in luxury,[1]
and his food is rich.
17 Is he then to keep on emptying his
net
and mercilessly killing nations
forever?

[1] Hebrew *his portion is fat*

2 I will take my stand at my watchpost
and station myself on the tower,
and look out to see what he will say
to me,
and what I will answer
concerning my complaint.

The Righteous Shall Live by His Faith

2 And the LORD answered me:

"Write the vision;
make it plain on tablets,
so he may run who reads it.
3 For still the vision awaits its
appointed time;
it hastens to the end—it will not lie.
If it seems slow, wait for it;
it will surely come; it will not delay.
4 "Behold, his soul is puffed up; it is
not upright within him,
but the righteous shall live by his
faith.[1]

5 "Moreover, wine[2] is a traitor,
an arrogant man who is never at
rest.[3]
His greed is as wide as Sheol;
like death he has never enough.
He gathers for himself all nations
and collects as his own all peoples."

Woe to the Chaldeans

6 Shall not all these take up their taunt
against him, with scoffing and riddles for
him, and say,

"Woe to him who heaps up what is
not his own—
for how long?—
and loads himself with pledges!"
7 Will not your debtors suddenly arise,
and those awake who will make
you tremble?
Then you will be spoil for them.
8 Because you have plundered many
nations,
all the remnant of the peoples
shall plunder you,
for the blood of man and violence to
the earth,
to cities and all who dwell in them.

9 "Woe to him who gets evil gain for
his house,
to set his nest on high,
to be safe from the reach of harm!
10 You have devised shame for your
house
by cutting off many peoples;
you have forfeited your life.
11 For the stone will cry out from the
wall,
and the beam from the woodwork
respond.

12 "Woe to him who builds a town with
blood
and founds a city on iniquity!
13 Behold, is it not from the LORD of
hosts
that peoples labor merely for fire,
and nations weary themselves for
nothing?
14 For the earth will be filled
with the knowledge of the glory
of the LORD
as the waters cover the sea.

15 "Woe to him who makes his
neighbors drink—
you pour out your wrath and
make them drunk,
in order to gaze at their nakedness!
16 You will have your fill of shame
instead of glory.
Drink, yourself, and show your
uncircumcision!
The cup in the LORD's right hand
will come around to you,
and utter shame will come upon
your glory!
17 The violence done to Lebanon will
overwhelm you,
as will the destruction of the
beasts that terrified them,

[1] Or *faithfulness* [2] Masoretic Text; Dead Sea Scroll *wealth* [3] The meaning of the Hebrew of these two lines is uncertain

for the blood of man and violence to
the earth,
to cities and all who dwell in them.

18 "What profit is an idol
when its maker has shaped it,
a metal image, a teacher of lies?
For its maker trusts in his own
creation
when he makes speechless idols!
19 Woe to him who says to a wooden
thing, Awake;
to a silent stone, Arise!
Can this teach?
Behold, it is overlaid with gold and
silver,
and there is no breath at all in it.
20 But the LORD is in his holy temple;
let all the earth keep silence
before him."

Habakkuk's Prayer

3 A prayer of Habakkuk the prophet, according to Shigionoth.

2 O LORD, I have heard the report of you,
and your work, O LORD, do I fear.
In the midst of the years revive it;
in the midst of the years make it
known;
in wrath remember mercy.
3 God came from Teman,
and the Holy One from Mount
Paran.
His splendor covered the heavens,
and the earth was full of his
praise. *Selah*
4 His brightness was like the light;
rays flashed from his hand;
and there he veiled his power.
5 Before him went pestilence,
and plague followed at his heels.[1]
6 He stood and measured the earth;
he looked and shook the nations;
then the eternal mountains were
scattered;
the everlasting hills sank low.
His were the everlasting ways.
7 I saw the tents of Cushan in affliction;
the curtains of the land of Midian
did tremble.
8 Was your wrath against the rivers,
O LORD?
Was your anger against the rivers,
or your indignation against the sea,
when you rode on your horses,
on your chariot of salvation?
9 You stripped the sheath from your
bow,
calling for many arrows.[2] *Selah*
You split the earth with rivers.
10 The mountains saw you and writhed;
the raging waters swept on;
the deep gave forth its voice;
it lifted its hands on high.
11 The sun and moon stood still in
their place
at the light of your arrows as they
sped,
at the flash of your glittering
spear.
12 You marched through the earth in
fury;
you threshed the nations in anger.
13 You went out for the salvation of
your people,
for the salvation of your anointed.
You crushed the head of the house
of the wicked,
laying him bare from thigh to
neck.[3] *Selah*
14 You pierced with his own arrows
the heads of his warriors,
who came like a whirlwind to
scatter me,
rejoicing as if to devour the poor
in secret.
15 You trampled the sea with your
horses,
the surging of mighty waters.
16 I hear, and my body trembles;
my lips quiver at the sound;
rottenness enters into my bones;
my legs tremble beneath me.

[1] Hebrew *feet* [2] The meaning of the Hebrew line is uncertain [3] The meaning of the Hebrew line is uncertain

Yet I will quietly wait for the day of trouble
to come upon people who invade us.

Habakkuk Rejoices in the LORD

17 Though the fig tree should not blossom,
nor fruit be on the vines,
the produce of the olive fail
and the fields yield no food,
the flock be cut off from the fold
and there be no herd in the stalls,
18 yet I will rejoice in the LORD;
I will take joy in the God of my salvation.
19 GOD, the Lord, is my strength;
he makes my feet like the deer's;
he makes me tread on my high places.

To the choirmaster: with stringed[1] instruments.

[1] Hebrew *my stringed*

Introduction to
Zephaniah

Author
Zephaniah the prophet

Date
About 620 B.C.

Purpose
The purpose of Zephaniah is to announce the day of the Lord as a time of blessing for God's people and of judgment for His enemies, both soon and especially in the future.

Central Themes
The Day of the Lord will give blessing for God's people and judgment for God's enemies; Judah must repent to avoid God's judgment and receive His blessing; God will judge all nations and will cause people from all nations to turn to Him; God will save His people and be among them forever.

Introduction

When Zephaniah wrote his book, the northern kingdom of Israel had already been carried away into captivity because of the sin of the people. The same thing would probably happen to Judah, because the sin of its people had also become great. The good King Josiah ruled, but was the repentance of the people under him real? If they did not truly repent, Zephaniah promised that when the day of the Lord came, the people would be counted as God's enemies to receive His judgment, not as His people to receive His blessing (Zephaniah 1). God threatened judgment against all Judah's neighbors, then against Jerusalem itself (Zephaniah 2:4–3:8). God also promised that, one day, He would bring people from all nations to call upon Him and to serve Him (Zephaniah 3:9–13). He would forgive the sins of His people and would live among them, loving and rejoicing in them forever (Zephaniah 3:14–20).

722 B.C.
Fall of Israel

About 620 B.C.
Prophetic ministry of Zephaniah

586 B.C.
Fall of Judah

Zephaniah

697

1 The word of the LORD that came to Zephaniah the son of Cushi, son of Gedaliah, son of Amariah, son of Hezekiah, in the days of Josiah the son of Amon, king of Judah.

The Coming Judgment on Judah

2 "I will utterly sweep away everything
from the face of the earth,"
declares the LORD.
3 "I will sweep away man and beast;
I will sweep away the birds of the heavens
and the fish of the sea,
and the rubble[1] with the wicked.
I will cut off mankind
from the face of the earth,"
declares the LORD.
4 "I will stretch out my hand against Judah
and against all the inhabitants of Jerusalem;
and I will cut off from this place the remnant of Baal
and the name of the idolatrous priests along with the priests,
5 those who bow down on the roofs
to the host of the heavens,
those who bow down and swear to the LORD
and yet swear by Milcom,
6 those who have turned back from following the LORD,
who do not seek the LORD or inquire of him."

The Day of the LORD Is Near

7 Be silent before the Lord GOD!
For the day of the LORD is near;
the LORD has prepared a sacrifice
and consecrated his guests.
8 And on the day of the LORD's sacrifice—
"I will punish the officials and the king's sons
and all who array themselves in foreign attire.
9 On that day I will punish
everyone who leaps over the threshold,
and those who fill their master's[2] house
with violence and fraud.

10 "On that day," declares the LORD,
"a cry will be heard from the Fish Gate,
a wail from the Second Quarter,
a loud crash from the hills.
11 Wail, O inhabitants of the Mortar!
For all the traders[3] are no more;
all who weigh out silver are cut off.
12 At that time I will search Jerusalem with lamps,
and I will punish the men
who are complacent,[4]
those who say in their hearts,
'The LORD will not do good,
nor will he do ill.'
13 Their goods shall be plundered,
and their houses laid waste.
Though they build houses,
they shall not inhabit them;
though they plant vineyards,
they shall not drink wine from them."

14 The great day of the LORD is near,
near and hastening fast;
the sound of the day of the LORD is bitter;
the mighty man cries aloud there.
15 A day of wrath is that day,
a day of distress and anguish,

[1] Or *stumbling blocks* (that is, idols) [2] Or *their Lord's* [3] Or *all the people of Canaan* [4] Hebrew *are thickening on the dregs* [of their wine]

a day of ruin and devastation,
a day of darkness and gloom,
a day of clouds and thick darkness,
16 a day of trumpet blast and battle cry
against the fortified cities
and against the lofty battlements.

17 I will bring distress on mankind,
so that they shall walk like the blind,
because they have sinned against the LORD;
their blood shall be poured out like dust,
and their flesh like dung.
18 Neither their silver nor their gold
shall be able to deliver them
on the day of the wrath of the LORD.
In the fire of his jealousy,
all the earth shall be consumed;
for a full and sudden end
he will make of all the inhabitants of the earth.

Judgment on Judah's Enemies

2 Gather together, yes, gather,
O shameless nation,
2 before the decree takes effect[1]
—before the day passes away like chaff—
before there comes upon you
the burning anger of the LORD,
before there comes upon you
the day of the anger of the LORD.
3 Seek the LORD, all you humble of the land,
who do his just commands;[2]
seek righteousness; seek humility;
perhaps you may be hidden
on the day of the anger of the LORD.
4 For Gaza shall be deserted,
and Ashkelon shall become a desolation;
Ashdod's people shall be driven out at noon,
and Ekron shall be uprooted.

5 Woe to you inhabitants of the seacoast,
you nation of the Cherethites!
The word of the LORD is against you,
O Canaan, land of the Philistines;
and I will destroy you until no inhabitant is left.
6 And you, O seacoast, shall be pastures,
with meadows[3] for shepherds
and folds for flocks.
7 The seacoast shall become the possession
of the remnant of the house of Judah,
on which they shall graze,
and in the houses of Ashkelon
they shall lie down at evening.
For the LORD their God will be mindful of them
and restore their fortunes.

8 "I have heard the taunts of Moab
and the revilings of the Ammonites,
how they have taunted my people
and made boasts against their territory.
9 Therefore, as I live," declares the LORD of hosts,
the God of Israel,
"Moab shall become like Sodom,
and the Ammonites like Gomorrah,
a land possessed by nettles and salt pits,
and a waste forever.
The remnant of my people shall plunder them,
and the survivors of my nation
shall possess them."
10 This shall be their lot in return for their pride,
because they taunted and boasted
against the people of the LORD of hosts.
11 The LORD will be awesome against them;
for he will famish all the gods of the earth,

[1] Hebrew *gives birth* [2] Or *who carry out his judgment* [3] Or *caves*

and to him shall bow down,
each in its place,
all the lands of the nations.

12 You also, O Cushites,
shall be slain by my sword.

13 And he will stretch out his hand
against the north
and destroy Assyria,
and he will make Nineveh a
desolation,
a dry waste like the desert.

14 Herds shall lie down in her midst,
all kinds of beasts;[1]
even the owl and the hedgehog[2]
shall lodge in her capitals;
a voice shall hoot in the window;
devastation will be on the
threshold;
for her cedar work will be laid bare.

15 This is the exultant city
that lived securely,
that said in her heart,
"I am, and there is no one else."
What a desolation she has become,
a lair for wild beasts!
Everyone who passes by her
hisses and shakes his fist.

Judgment on Jerusalem and the Nations

3 Woe to her who is rebellious and
defiled,
the oppressing city!

2 She listens to no voice;
she accepts no correction.
She does not trust in the LORD;
she does not draw near to her God.

3 Her officials within her
are roaring lions;
her judges are evening wolves
that leave nothing till the morning.

4 Her prophets are fickle, treacherous
men;
her priests profane what is holy;
they do violence to the law.

5 The LORD within her is righteous;
he does no injustice;
every morning he shows forth his
justice;
each dawn he does not fail;
but the unjust knows no shame.

6 "I have cut off nations;
their battlements are in ruins;
I have laid waste their streets
so that no one walks in them;
their cities have been made desolate,
without a man, without an
inhabitant.

7 I said, 'Surely you will fear me;
you will accept correction.
Then your[3] dwelling would not be
cut off
according to all that I have
appointed against you.'[4]
But all the more they were eager
to make all their deeds corrupt.

8 "Therefore wait for me," declares the
LORD,
"for the day when I rise up to seize
the prey.
For my decision is to gather nations,
to assemble kingdoms,
to pour out upon them my
indignation,
all my burning anger;
for in the fire of my jealousy
all the earth shall be consumed.

The Conversion of the Nations

9 "For at that time I will change the
speech of the peoples
to a pure speech,
that all of them may call upon the
name of the LORD
and serve him with one accord.

10 From beyond the rivers of Cush
my worshipers, the daughter of
my dispersed ones,
shall bring my offering.

11 "On that day you shall not be put to
shame
because of the deeds by which
you have rebelled against me;

[1] Hebrew *beasts of every nation* [2] The identity of the animals rendered *owl* and *hedgehog* is uncertain [3] Hebrew *her* [4] Hebrew *her*

for then I will remove from your midst
your proudly exultant ones,
and you shall no longer be haughty
in my holy mountain.
12 But I will leave in your midst
a people humble and lowly.
They shall seek refuge in the name of the LORD,
13 those who are left in Israel;
they shall do no injustice
and speak no lies,
nor shall there be found in their mouth
a deceitful tongue.
For they shall graze and lie down,
and none shall make them afraid."

Israel's Joy and Restoration

14 Sing aloud, O daughter of Zion;
shout, O Israel!
Rejoice and exult with all your heart,
O daughter of Jerusalem!
15 The LORD has taken away the judgments against you;
he has cleared away your enemies.
The King of Israel, the LORD, is in your midst;
you shall never again fear evil.
16 On that day it shall be said to Jerusalem:
"Fear not, O Zion;
let not your hands grow weak.
17 The LORD your God is in your midst,
a mighty one who will save;
he will rejoice over you with gladness;
he will quiet you by his love;
he will exult over you with loud singing.
18 I will gather those of you who mourn for the festival,
so that you will no longer suffer reproach.[1]
19 Behold, at that time I will deal
with all your oppressors.
And I will save the lame
and gather the outcast,
and I will change their shame into praise
and renown in all the earth.
20 At that time I will bring you in,
at the time when I gather you together;
for I will make you renowned and praised
among all the peoples of the earth,
when I restore your fortunes
before your eyes," says the LORD.

[1] The meaning of the Hebrew is uncertain

Introduction to

Haggai

Author
Haggai the prophet

Date
520 B.C.

People
Haggai; Zerubbabel the governor of Judah; Joshua the high priest

Purpose
The purpose of Haggai is to call the Jews who had returned from exile to finish building the temple so God would be among them and bless them again.

Central Themes
God's people are to give to His work, not selfishly keeping everything for themselves; God will withhold blessing from His people when they will not give to His work; God will fill His temple with great glory and bring the nations to it.

Memory Verses
Shaking the nations (Haggai 2:7–9)

Introduction

The Jews had returned to Jerusalem from their exile in Babylon. They had begun to rebuild the temple, but because the enemy neighbors were causing problems they had stopped their work. The Jews didn't mind this too much, because that gave them time to build their own houses and make them more and more luxurious. Now years had gone by, and still there was no temple in Jerusalem. Haggai scolded the Jews, saying they would never have enough food and money if they kept holding back from giving to finish the temple (Haggai 1:1–11). God caused the people to listen to Haggai and they went back to work (Haggai 1:12–15). Some of the people were sad because this rebuilt temple was not nearly as glorious as Solomon's temple had been. God promised that the day would come when He would fill the temple with glory greater than it had known under Solomon. The nations would come, bringing their treasures to the temple (Haggai 2:1–9). God also promised to overthrow the rule of other nations, making the descendant of David God's chosen ruler over all (Haggai 2:20–23).

586 B.C.	**538 B.C.**	**520–516 B.C.**
Fall of Judah/ temple destroyed	Decree of Cyrus/ end of exile	Haggai prophesies/ temple rebuilt

Haggai

The Command to Rebuild the Temple

1 In the second year of Darius the king, in the sixth month, on the first day of the month, the word of the LORD came by the hand of Haggai the prophet to Zerubbabel the son of Shealtiel, governor of Judah, and to Joshua the son of Jehozadak, the high priest: 2 "Thus says the LORD of hosts: These people say the time has not yet come to rebuild the house of the LORD." 3 Then the word of the LORD came by the hand of Haggai the prophet, 4 "Is it a time for you yourselves to dwell in your paneled houses, while this house lies in ruins? 5 Now, therefore, thus says the LORD of hosts: Consider your ways. 6 You have sown much, and harvested little. You eat, but you never have enough; you drink, but you never have your fill. You clothe yourselves, but no one is warm. And he who earns wages does so to put them into a bag with holes.

7 "Thus says the LORD of hosts: Consider your ways. 8 Go up to the hills and bring wood and build the house, that I may take pleasure in it and that I may be glorified, says the LORD. 9 You looked for much, and behold, it came to little. And when you brought it home, I blew it away. Why? declares the LORD of hosts. Because of my house that lies in ruins, while each of you busies himself with his own house. 10 Therefore the heavens above you have withheld the dew, and the earth has withheld its produce. 11 And I have called for a drought on the land and the hills, on the grain, the new wine, the oil, on what the ground brings forth, on man and beast, and on all their labors."

The People Obey the LORD

12 Then Zerubbabel the son of Shealtiel, and Joshua the son of Jehozadak, the high priest, with all the remnant of the people, obeyed the voice of the LORD their God, and the words of Haggai the prophet, as the LORD their God had sent him. And the people feared the LORD. 13 Then Haggai, the messenger of the LORD, spoke to the people with the LORD's message, "I am with you, declares the LORD." 14 And the LORD stirred up the spirit of Zerubbabel the son of Shealtiel, governor of Judah, and the spirit of Joshua the son of Jehozadak, the high priest, and the spirit of all the remnant of the people. And they came and worked on the house of the LORD of hosts, their God, 15 on the twenty-fourth day of the month, in the sixth month, in the second year of Darius the king.

The Coming Glory of the Temple

2 In the seventh month, on the twenty-first day of the month, the word of the LORD came by the hand of Haggai the prophet, 2 "Speak now to Zerubbabel the son of Shealtiel, governor of Judah, and to Joshua the son of Jehozadak, the high priest, and to all the remnant of the people, and say, 3 'Who is left among you who saw this house in its former glory? How do you see it now? Is it not as nothing in your eyes? 4 Yet now be strong, O Zerubbabel, declares the LORD. Be strong, O Joshua, son of Jehozadak, the high priest. Be strong, all you people of the land, declares the LORD. Work, for I am with you, declares the LORD of hosts, 5 according to the covenant that I made with you when you came out of Egypt. My Spirit remains in your midst. Fear not. 6 For thus says the LORD of hosts:

Yet once more, in a little while, I will shake
the heavens and the earth and the sea and
the dry land. 7 And I will shake all nations,
so that the treasures of all nations shall
come in, and I will fill this house with
glory, says the LORD of hosts. 8 The silver
is mine, and the gold is mine, declares
the LORD of hosts. 9 The latter glory of
this house shall be greater than the for-
mer, says the LORD of hosts. And in this
place I will give peace, declares the LORD
of hosts.'"

Blessings for a Defiled People

10 On the twenty-fourth day of the
ninth month, in the second year of
Darius, the word of the LORD came by
Haggai the prophet, 11 "Thus says the
LORD of hosts: Ask the priests about the
law: 12 'If someone carries holy meat in
the fold of his garment and touches with
his fold bread or stew or wine or oil or
any kind of food, does it become holy?'"
The priests answered and said, "No."
13 Then Haggai said, "If someone who
is unclean by contact with a dead body
touches any of these, does it become
unclean?" The priests answered and
said, "It does become unclean." 14 Then
Haggai answered and said, "So is it with
this people, and with this nation before
me, declares the LORD, and so with every
work of their hands. And what they offer
there is unclean. 15 Now then, consider
from this day onward.[1] Before stone was
placed upon stone in the temple of the
LORD, 16 how did you fare? When[2] one
came to a heap of twenty measures, there
were but ten. When one came to the wine
vat to draw fifty measures, there were but
twenty. 17 I struck you and all the prod-
ucts of your toil with blight and with mil-
dew and with hail, yet you did not turn to
me, declares the LORD. 18 Consider from
this day onward, from the twenty-fourth
day of the ninth month. Since the day
that the foundation of the LORD's temple
was laid, consider: 19 Is the seed yet in
the barn? Indeed, the vine, the fig tree,
the pomegranate, and the olive tree have
yielded nothing. But from this day on I
will bless you."

Zerubbabel Chosen as a Signet

20 The word of the LORD came a second
time to Haggai on the twenty-fourth day
of the month, 21 "Speak to Zerubbabel,
governor of Judah, saying, I am about to
shake the heavens and the earth, 22 and to
overthrow the throne of kingdoms. I am
about to destroy the strength of the king-
doms of the nations, and overthrow the
chariots and their riders. And the horses
and their riders shall go down, every one
by the sword of his brother. 23 On that
day, declares the LORD of hosts, I will take
you, O Zerubbabel my servant, the son of
Shealtiel, declares the LORD, and make
you like a[3] signet ring, for I have chosen
you, declares the LORD of hosts."

[1] Or *backward*; also verse 18 [2] Probable reading (compare Septuagint); Hebrew *LORD, since they were. When* [3] Hebrew *the*

Introduction to

Zechariah

Author
Zechariah the prophet

Date
520–518 B.C.

People
Zechariah; Joshua the high priest; Zerubbabel the governor

Purpose
The purpose of Zechariah is to encourage the Jews who had returned to Jerusalem from exile in Babylon as they rebuilt the temple.

Central Themes
God welcomes the return of His people in repentance; God will punish the nations that are enemies of Judah; God will bring glory to His people and live among them forever; God will forgive and remove the sins of His people; God's work is done in the power of His Spirit, not in human strength.

Memory Verses
The vision of Joshua (Zechariah 3); by the Lord's Spirit (Zechariah 4:6); the humble King (Zechariah 9:9); the doomed flock (Zechariah 11:4–6); they are My people (Zechariah 13:7–9)

Introduction

The Jews had been back from exile for nearly 20 years. They had begun to rebuild the temple but had stopped, discouraged because of the opposition of enemy neighbors. They had recently begun rebuilding again, but this new temple was nothing like the glorious one Solomon had built. Jerusalem's walls were still in ruins, and God's promises to David seemed unfulfilled. Zechariah wrote to encourage these Jews and to call them to a fresh commitment to their covenant with God. Zechariah promised good things for God's people. The nations that were their enemies would be judged, while Jerusalem would be rebuilt and filled with glory (Zechariah 1:7–2:12). God would provide forgiveness of sins for His people (Zechariah 3; 13:1), would remove their evil and sin (Zechariah 5), and would cover them in righteousness (Zechariah 3). He would give them power by His Spirit to do His will (Zechariah 4:1–10a). Zechariah included promises of the Messiah as well: He would be both King and Priest (Zechariah 6:9–13); He would come as a King bringing peace and salvation (Zechariah 9:9–17); He would suffer for His people (Zechariah 13:7). A day of judgment and salvation would come, "And the LORD will be King over all the earth" (Zechariah 14:9a).

586 B.C.	538 B.C.	520–516 B.C.
Fall of Judah/ temple destroyed	Decree of Cyrus/ end of exile	Zechariah prophesies/ temple rebuilt

Zechariah

A Call to Return to the LORD

1 In the eighth month, in the second year of Darius, the word of the LORD came to the prophet Zechariah, the son of Berechiah, son of Iddo, saying, 2 "The LORD was very angry with your fathers. 3 Therefore say to them, Thus declares the LORD of hosts: Return to me, says the LORD of hosts, and I will return to you, says the LORD of hosts. 4 Do not be like your fathers, to whom the former prophets cried out, 'Thus says the LORD of hosts, Return from your evil ways and from your evil deeds.' But they did not hear or pay attention to me, declares the LORD. 5 Your fathers, where are they? And the prophets, do they live forever? 6 But my words and my statutes, which I commanded my servants the prophets, did they not overtake your fathers? So they repented and said, As the LORD of hosts purposed to deal with us for our ways and deeds, so has he dealt with us."

A Vision of a Horseman

7 On the twenty-fourth day of the eleventh month, which is the month of Shebat, in the second year of Darius, the word of the LORD came to the prophet Zechariah, the son of Berechiah, son of Iddo, saying, 8 "I saw in the night, and behold, a man riding on a red horse! He was standing among the myrtle trees in the glen, and behind him were red, sorrel, and white horses. 9 Then I said, 'What are these, my lord?' The angel who talked with me said to me, 'I will show you what they are.' 10 So the man who was standing among the myrtle trees answered, 'These are they whom the LORD has sent to patrol the earth.' 11 And they answered the angel of the LORD who was standing among the myrtle trees, and said, 'We have patrolled the earth, and behold, all the earth remains at rest.' 12 Then the angel of the LORD said, 'O LORD of hosts, how long will you have no mercy on Jerusalem and the cities of Judah, against which you have been angry these seventy years?' 13 And the LORD answered gracious and comforting words to the angel who talked with me. 14 So the angel who talked with me said to me, 'Cry out, Thus says the LORD of hosts: I am exceedingly jealous for Jerusalem and for Zion. 15 And I am exceedingly angry with the nations that are at ease; for while I was angry but a little, they furthered the disaster. 16 Therefore, thus says the LORD, I have returned to Jerusalem with mercy; my house shall be built in it, declares the LORD of hosts, and the measuring line shall be stretched out over Jerusalem. 17 Cry out again, Thus says the LORD of hosts: My cities shall again overflow with prosperity, and the LORD will again comfort Zion and again choose Jerusalem.'"

A Vision of Horns and Craftsmen

18 [1] And I lifted my eyes and saw, and behold, four horns! 19 And I said to the angel who talked with me, "What are these?" And he said to me, "These are the horns that have scattered Judah, Israel, and Jerusalem." 20 Then the LORD showed me four craftsmen. 21 And I said, "What are these coming to do?" He said, "These are the horns that scattered Judah, so that no one raised his head. And these have come to terrify them, to cast down the horns of the nations who lifted up their horns against the land of Judah to scatter it."

[1] Ch 2:1 in Hebrew

A Vision of a Man with a Measuring Line

2 [1]And I lifted my eyes and saw, and
behold, a man with a measuring line
in his hand! 2 Then I said, "Where are you
going?" And he said to me, "To measure
Jerusalem, to see what is its width and
what is its length." 3 And behold, the angel
who talked with me came forward, and
another angel came forward to meet him
4 and said to him, "Run, say to that young
man, 'Jerusalem shall be inhabited as vil-
lages without walls, because of the mul-
titude of people and livestock in it. 5 And
I will be to her a wall of fire all around,
declares the LORD, and I will be the glory
in her midst.'"

6 Up! Up! Flee from the land of the north,
declares the LORD. For I have spread you
abroad as the four winds of the heav-
ens, declares the LORD. 7 Up! Escape to
Zion, you who dwell with the daughter of
Babylon. 8 For thus said the LORD of hosts,
after his glory sent me[2] to the nations who
plundered you, for he who touches you
touches the apple of his eye: 9 "Behold, I
will shake my hand over them, and they
shall become plunder for those who served
them. Then you will know that the LORD
of hosts has sent me. 10 Sing and rejoice,
O daughter of Zion, for behold, I come
and I will dwell in your midst, declares
the LORD. 11 And many nations shall join
themselves to the LORD in that day, and
shall be my people. And I will dwell in your
midst, and you shall know that the LORD of
hosts has sent me to you. 12 And the LORD
will inherit Judah as his portion in the holy
land, and will again choose Jerusalem."

13 Be silent, all flesh, before the LORD,
for he has roused himself from his holy
dwelling.

A Vision of Joshua the High Priest

3 Then he showed me Joshua the high
priest standing before the angel of
the LORD, and Satan[3] standing at his right
hand to accuse him. 2 And the LORD said to
Satan, "The LORD rebuke you, O Satan! The
LORD who has chosen Jerusalem rebuke
you! Is not this a brand[4] plucked from the
fire?" 3 Now Joshua was standing before the
angel, clothed with filthy garments. 4 And
the angel said to those who were standing
before him, "Remove the filthy garments
from him." And to him he said, "Behold,
I have taken your iniquity away from you,
and I will clothe you with pure vestments."
5 And I said, "Let them put a clean turban
on his head." So they put a clean turban on
his head and clothed him with garments.
And the angel of the LORD was standing by.

6 And the angel of the LORD solemnly
assured Joshua, 7 "Thus says the LORD of
hosts: If you will walk in my ways and
keep my charge, then you shall rule my
house and have charge of my courts, and
I will give you the right of access among
those who are standing here. 8 Hear now,
O Joshua the high priest, you and your
friends who sit before you, for they are
men who are a sign: behold, I will bring
my servant the Branch. 9 For behold, on
the stone that I have set before Joshua,
on a single stone with seven eyes,[5] I will
engrave its inscription, declares the LORD
of hosts, and I will remove the iniquity
of this land in a single day. 10 In that day,
declares the LORD of hosts, every one of
you will invite his neighbor to come under
his vine and under his fig tree."

A Vision of a Golden Lampstand

4 And the angel who talked with me
came again and woke me, like a man
who is awakened out of his sleep. 2 And
he said to me, "What do you see?" I said, "I
see, and behold, a lampstand all of gold,
with a bowl on the top of it, and seven
lamps on it, with seven lips on each of
the lamps that are on the top of it. 3 And
there are two olive trees by it, one on the
right of the bowl and the other on its left."
4 And I said to the angel who talked with
me, "What are these, my lord?" 5 Then the

[1] Ch 2:5 in Hebrew [2] Or *he sent me after glory* [3] *Satan* means *the accuser* [4] That is, a burning stick [5] Or *facets*

angel who talked with me answered and
said to me, "Do you not know what these
are?" I said, "No, my lord." 6 Then he said
to me, "This is the word of the LORD to
Zerubbabel: Not by might, nor by power,
but by my Spirit, says the LORD of hosts.
7 Who are you, O great mountain? Before
Zerubbabel you shall become a plain. And
he shall bring forward the top stone amid
shouts of 'Grace, grace to it!'"

8 Then the word of the LORD came to
me, saying, 9 "The hands of Zerubbabel
have laid the foundation of this house; his
hands shall also complete it. Then you will
know that the LORD of hosts has sent me
to you. 10 For whoever has despised the day
of small things shall rejoice, and shall see
the plumb line in the hand of Zerubbabel.

"These seven are the eyes of the LORD,
which range through the whole earth."
11 Then I said to him, "What are these two
olive trees on the right and the left of
the lampstand?" 12 And a second time I
answered and said to him, "What are these
two branches of the olive trees, which are
beside the two golden pipes from which
the golden oil[1] is poured out?" 13 He said to
me, "Do you not know what these are?" I
said, "No, my lord." 14 Then he said, "These
are the two anointed ones[2] who stand by
the Lord of the whole earth."

A Vision of a Flying Scroll

5 Again I lifted my eyes and saw, and
behold, a flying scroll! 2 And he said to
me, "What do you see?" I answered, "I see
a flying scroll. Its length is twenty cubits,
and its width ten cubits."[3] 3 Then he said
to me, "This is the curse that goes out over
the face of the whole land. For everyone
who steals shall be cleaned out according
to what is on one side, and everyone who
swears falsely[4] shall be cleaned out accord-
ing to what is on the other side. 4 I will send
it out, *declares* the LORD of hosts, and it
shall enter the house of the thief, and the
house of him who swears falsely by my
name. And it shall remain in his house
and consume it, both timber and stones."

A Vision of a Woman in a Basket

5 Then the angel who talked with me
came forward and said to me, "Lift your
eyes and see what this is that is going out."
6 And I said, "What is it?" He said, "This is
the basket[5] that is going out." And he said,
"This is their iniquity[6] in all the land." 7 And
behold, the leaden cover was lifted, and
there was a woman sitting in the basket!
8 And he said, "This is Wickedness." And he
thrust her back into the basket, and thrust
down the leaden weight on its opening.

9 Then I lifted my eyes and saw, and
behold, two women coming forward! The
wind was in their wings. They had wings
like the wings of a stork, and they lifted
up the basket between earth and heaven.
10 Then I said to the angel who talked with
me, "Where are they taking the basket?"
11 He said to me, "To the land of Shinar,
to build a house for it. And when this is
prepared, they will set the basket down
there on its base."

A Vision of Four Chariots

6 Again I lifted my eyes and saw, and
behold, four chariots came out from
between two mountains. And the moun-
tains were mountains of bronze. 2 The first
chariot had red horses, the second black
horses, 3 the third white horses, and the
fourth chariot dappled horses—all of them
strong.[7] 4 Then I answered and said to the
angel who talked with me, "What are these,
my lord?" 5 And the angel answered and
said to me, "These are going out to the four
winds of heaven, after presenting them-
selves before the LORD of all the earth. 6 The
chariot with the black horses goes toward
the north country, the white ones go after
them, and the dappled ones go toward the
south country." 7 When the strong horses
came out, they were impatient to go and
patrol the earth. And he said, "Go, patrol

[1] Hebrew lacks *oil* [2] Hebrew *two sons of new oil* [3] A *cubit* was about 18 inches or 45 centimeters [4] Hebrew lacks *falsely* (supplied from verse 4) [5] Hebrew *ephah*; also verses 7-11. An *ephah* was about 3/5 bushel or 22 liters [6] One Hebrew manuscript, Septuagint, Syriac; most Hebrew manuscripts *eye* [7] Or *and the fourth chariot strong dappled horses*

the earth." So they patrolled the earth. 8 Then he cried to me, "Behold, those who go toward the north country have set my Spirit at rest in the north country."

The Crown and the Temple

9 And the word of the LORD came to me: 10 "Take from the exiles Heldai, Tobijah, and Jedaiah, who have arrived from Babylon, and go the same day to the house of Josiah, the son of Zephaniah. 11 Take from them silver and gold, and make a crown, and set it on the head of Joshua, the son of Jehozadak, the high priest. 12 And say to him, 'Thus says the LORD of hosts, "Behold, the man whose name is the Branch: for he shall branch out from his place, and he shall build the temple of the LORD. 13 It is he who shall build the temple of the LORD and shall bear royal honor, and shall sit and rule on his throne. And there shall be a priest on his throne, and the counsel of peace shall be between them both."' 14 And the crown shall be in the temple of the LORD as a reminder to Helem,[1] Tobijah, Jedaiah, and Hen the son of Zephaniah.

15 "And those who are far off shall come and help to build the temple of the LORD. And you shall know that the LORD of hosts has sent me to you. And this shall come to pass, if you will diligently obey the voice of the LORD your God."

A Call for Justice and Mercy

7 In the fourth year of King Darius, the word of the LORD came to Zechariah on the fourth day of the ninth month, which is Chislev. 2 Now the people of Bethel had sent Sharezer and Regem-melech and their men to entreat the favor of the LORD, 3 saying to the priests of the house of the LORD of hosts and the prophets, "Should I weep and abstain in the fifth month, as I have done for so many years?"

4 Then the word of the LORD of hosts came to me: 5 "Say to all the people of the land and the priests, When you fasted and mourned in the fifth month and in the seventh, for these seventy years, was it for me that you fasted? 6 And when you eat and when you drink, do you not eat for yourselves and drink for yourselves? 7 Were not these the words that the LORD proclaimed by the former prophets, when Jerusalem was inhabited and prosperous, with her cities around her, and the South and the lowland were inhabited?"

8 And the word of the LORD came to Zechariah, saying, 9 "Thus says the LORD of hosts, Render true judgments, show kindness and mercy to one another, 10 do not oppress the widow, the fatherless, the sojourner, or the poor, and let none of you devise evil against another in your heart." 11 But they refused to pay attention and turned a stubborn shoulder and stopped their ears that they might not hear.[2] 12 They made their hearts diamond-hard lest they should hear the law and the words that the LORD of hosts had sent by his Spirit through the former prophets. Therefore great anger came from the LORD of hosts. 13 "As I[3] called, and they would not hear, so they called, and I would not hear," says the LORD of hosts, 14 "and I scattered them with a whirlwind among all the nations that they had not known. Thus the land they left was desolate, so that no one went to and fro, and the pleasant land was made desolate."

The Coming Peace and Prosperity of Zion

8 And the word of the LORD of hosts came, saying, 2 "Thus says the LORD of hosts: I am jealous for Zion with great jealousy, and I am jealous for her with great wrath. 3 Thus says the LORD: I have returned to Zion and will dwell in the midst of Jerusalem, and Jerusalem shall be called the faithful city, and the mountain of the LORD of hosts, the holy mountain. 4 Thus says the LORD of hosts: Old men and old women shall again sit in the streets of Jerusalem, each with staff in

[1] An alternate spelling of *Heldai* (verse 10) [2] Hebrew *and made their ears too heavy to hear* [3] Hebrew *he*

hand because of great age. 5 And the streets of the city shall be full of boys and girls playing in its streets. 6 Thus says the LORD of hosts: If it is marvelous in the sight of the remnant of this people in those days, should it also be marvelous in my sight, declares the LORD of hosts? 7 Thus says the LORD of hosts: behold, I will save my people from the east country and from the west country, 8 and I will bring them to dwell in the midst of Jerusalem. And they shall be my people, and I will be their God, in faithfulness and in righteousness."

9 Thus says the LORD of hosts: "Let your hands be strong, you who in these days have been hearing these words from the mouth of the prophets who were present on the day that the foundation of the house of the LORD of hosts was laid, that the temple might be built. 10 For before those days there was no wage for man or any wage for beast, neither was there any safety from the foe for him who went out or came in, for I set every man against his neighbor. 11 But now I will not deal with the remnant of this people as in the former days, declares the LORD of hosts. 12 For there shall be a sowing of peace. The vine shall give its fruit, and the ground shall give its produce, and the heavens shall give their dew. And I will cause the remnant of this people to possess all these things. 13 And as you have been a byword of cursing among the nations, O house of Judah and house of Israel, so will I save you, and you shall be a blessing. Fear not, but let your hands be strong."

14 For thus says the LORD of hosts: "As I purposed to bring disaster to you when your fathers provoked me to wrath, and I did not relent, says the LORD of hosts, 15 so again have I purposed in these days to bring good to Jerusalem and to the house of Judah; fear not. 16 These are the things that you shall do: Speak the truth to one another; render in your gates judgments that are true and make for peace; 17 do not devise evil in your hearts against one another, and love no false oath, for all these things I hate, declares the LORD."

18 And the word of the LORD of hosts came to me, saying, 19 "Thus says the LORD of hosts: The fast of the fourth month and the fast of the fifth and the fast of the seventh and the fast of the tenth shall be to the house of Judah seasons of joy and gladness and cheerful feasts. Therefore love truth and peace.

20 "Thus says the LORD of hosts: Peoples shall yet come, even the inhabitants of many cities. 21 The inhabitants of one city shall go to another, saying, 'Let us go at once to entreat the favor of the LORD and to seek the LORD of hosts; I myself am going.' 22 Many peoples and strong nations shall come to seek the LORD of hosts in Jerusalem and to entreat the favor of the LORD. 23 Thus says the LORD of hosts: In those days ten men from the nations of every tongue shall take hold of the robe of a Jew, saying, 'Let us go with you, for we have heard that God is with you.'"

Judgment on Israel's Enemies

9 The burden of the word of the LORD is against the land of Hadrach
and Damascus is its resting place.
For the LORD has an eye on mankind
and on all the tribes of Israel,[1]
2 and on Hamath also, which borders on it,
Tyre and Sidon, though they are very wise.
3 Tyre has built herself a rampart
and heaped up silver like dust,
and fine gold like the mud of the streets.
4 But behold, the Lord will strip her of her possessions
and strike down her power on the sea,
and she shall be devoured by fire.

[1] A slight emendation yields *For to the* LORD *belongs the capital of Syria and all the tribes of Israel*

5 Ashkelon shall see it, and be afraid;
Gaza too, and shall writhe in anguish;
Ekron also, because its hopes are confounded.
The king shall perish from Gaza;
Ashkelon shall be uninhabited;
6 a mixed people[1] shall dwell in Ashdod,
and I will cut off the pride of Philistia.
7 I will take away its blood from its mouth,
and its abominations from between its teeth;
it too shall be a remnant for our God;
it shall be like a clan in Judah,
and Ekron shall be like the Jebusites.
8 Then I will encamp at my house as a guard,
so that none shall march to and fro;
no oppressor shall again march over them,
for now I see with my own eyes.

The Coming King of Zion

9 Rejoice greatly, O daughter of Zion!
1345
Shout aloud, O daughter of Jerusalem!
Behold, your king is coming to you;
righteous and having salvation is he,
humble and mounted on a donkey,
on a colt, the foal of a donkey.
10 I will cut off the chariot from Ephraim
and the war horse from Jerusalem;
and the battle bow shall be cut off,
and he shall speak peace to the nations;
his rule shall be from sea to sea,
and from the River to the ends of the earth.
11 As for you also, because of the blood of my covenant with you,
I will set your prisoners free from the waterless pit.
12 Return to your stronghold, O prisoners of hope;
today I declare that I will restore to you double.
13 For I have bent Judah as my bow;
I have made Ephraim its arrow.
I will stir up your sons, O Zion,
against your sons, O Greece,
and wield you like a warrior's sword.

The Lord Will Save His People

14 Then the Lord will appear over them,
and his arrow will go forth like lightning;
the Lord God will sound the trumpet
and will march forth in the whirlwinds of the south.
15 The Lord of hosts will protect them,
and they shall devour, and tread down the sling stones,
and they shall drink and roar as if drunk with wine,
and be full like a bowl,
drenched like the corners of the altar.
16 On that day the Lord their God will save them,
as the flock of his people;
for like the jewels of a crown
they shall shine on his land.
17 For how great is his goodness, and how great his beauty!
Grain shall make the young men flourish,
and new wine the young women.

The Restoration for Judah and Israel

10 Ask rain from the Lord
in the season of the spring rain,
from the Lord who makes the storm clouds,
and he will give them showers of rain,
to everyone the vegetation in the field.

[1] Or *a foreign people*; Hebrew *a bastard*

2 For the household gods utter nonsense,
and the diviners see lies;
they tell false dreams
and give empty consolation.
Therefore the people wander like sheep;
they are afflicted for lack of a shepherd.

3 "My anger is hot against the shepherds,
and I will punish the leaders;[1]
for the LORD of hosts cares for his flock, the house of Judah,
and will make them like his majestic steed in battle.
4 From him shall come the cornerstone,
from him the tent peg,
from him the battle bow,
from him every ruler—all of them together.
5 They shall be like mighty men in battle,
trampling the foe in the mud of the streets;
they shall fight because the LORD is with them,
and they shall put to shame the riders on horses.

6 "I will strengthen the house of Judah,
and I will save the house of Joseph.
I will bring them back because I have compassion on them,
and they shall be as though I had not rejected them,
for I am the LORD their God and I will answer them.
7 Then Ephraim shall become like a mighty warrior,
and their hearts shall be glad as with wine.
Their children shall see it and be glad;
their hearts shall rejoice in the LORD.

8 "I will whistle for them and gather them in,
for I have redeemed them,
and they shall be as many as they were before.
9 Though I scattered them among the nations,
yet in far countries they shall remember me,
and with their children they shall live and return.
10 I will bring them home from the land of Egypt,
and gather them from Assyria,
and I will bring them to the land of Gilead and to Lebanon,
till there is no room for them.
11 He shall pass through the sea of troubles
and strike down the waves of the sea,
and all the depths of the Nile shall be dried up.
The pride of Assyria shall be laid low,
and the scepter of Egypt shall depart.
12 I will make them strong in the LORD,
and they shall walk in his name,"
declares the LORD.

The Flock Doomed to Slaughter

11 Open your doors, O Lebanon,
that the fire may devour your cedars!
2 Wail, O cypress, for the cedar has fallen,
for the glorious trees are ruined!
Wail, oaks of Bashan,
for the thick forest has been felled!
3 The sound of the wail of the shepherds,
for their glory is ruined!
The sound of the roar of the lions,
for the thicket of the Jordan is ruined!

4 Thus said the LORD my God: "Become
shepherd of the flock doomed to slaugh-

[1] Hebrew *the male goats*

ter. 5Those who buy them slaughter them
and go unpunished, and those who sell
them say, 'Blessed be the LORD, I have
become rich,' and their own shepherds
have no pity on them. 6For I will no longer
have pity on the inhabitants of this land,
declares the LORD. Behold, I will cause
each of them to fall into the hand of his
neighbor, and each into the hand of his
king, and they shall crush the land, and I
will deliver none from their hand."

7So I became the shepherd of the
flock doomed to be slaughtered by the
sheep traders. And I took two staffs, one
I named Favor, the other I named Union.
And I tended the sheep. 8In one month
I destroyed the three shepherds. But I
became impatient with them, and they also
detested me. 9So I said, "I will not be your
shepherd. What is to die, let it die. What
is to be destroyed, let it be destroyed. And
let those who are left devour the flesh of
one another." 10And I took my staff Favor,
and I broke it, annulling the covenant that
I had made with all the peoples. 11So it was
annulled on that day, and the sheep trad-
ers, who were watching me, knew that it
was the word of the LORD. 12Then I said
to them, "If it seems good to you, give me
my wages; but if not, keep them." And they
weighed out as my wages thirty pieces of
silver. 13Then the LORD said to me, "Throw
it to the potter"—the lordly price at which
I was priced by them. So I took the thirty
pieces of silver and threw them into the
house of the LORD, to the potter. 14Then
I broke my second staff Union, annulling
the brotherhood between Judah and Israel.

15Then the LORD said to me, "Take once
more the equipment of a foolish shep-
herd. 16For behold, I am raising up in the
land a shepherd who does not care for
those being destroyed, or seek the young or
heal the maimed or nourish the healthy,
but devours the flesh of the fat ones, tear-
ing off even their hoofs.

17 "Woe to my worthless shepherd,
who deserts the flock!
May the sword strike his arm
and his right eye!
Let his arm be wholly withered,
his right eye utterly blinded!"

The LORD Will Give Salvation

12 The burden of the word of the LORD
concerning Israel: Thus declares
the LORD, who stretched out the heavens
and founded the earth and formed the
spirit of man within him: 2"Behold, I am
about to make Jerusalem a cup of stagger-
ing to all the surrounding peoples. The
siege of Jerusalem will also be against
Judah. 3On that day I will make Jerusalem
a heavy stone for all the peoples. All who
lift it will surely hurt themselves. And all
the nations of the earth will gather against
it. 4On that day, declares the LORD, I will
strike every horse with panic, and its rider
with madness. But for the sake of the
house of Judah I will keep my eyes open,
when I strike every horse of the peoples
with blindness. 5Then the clans of Judah
shall say to themselves, 'The inhabitants
of Jerusalem have strength through the
LORD of hosts, their God.'

6"On that day I will make the clans of
Judah like a blazing pot in the midst of
wood, like a flaming torch among sheaves.
And they shall devour to the right and to
the left all the surrounding peoples, while
Jerusalem shall again be inhabited in its
place, in Jerusalem.

7"And the LORD will give salvation to
the tents of Judah first, that the glory of
the house of David and the glory of the
inhabitants of Jerusalem may not sur-
pass that of Judah. 8On that day the LORD
will protect the inhabitants of Jerusalem,
so that the feeblest among them on that
day shall be like David, and the house of
David shall be like God, like the angel of
the LORD, going before them. 9And on that

day I will seek to destroy all the nations
that come against Jerusalem.

Him Whom They Have Pierced

10 "And I will pour out on the house of
David and the inhabitants of Jerusalem a
spirit of grace and pleas for mercy, so that,
when they look on me, on him whom they
have pierced, they shall mourn for him, as
one mourns for an only child, and weep
bitterly over him, as one weeps over a
firstborn. 11 On that day the mourning in
Jerusalem will be as great as the mourn-
ing for Hadad-rimmon in the plain of
Megiddo. 12 The land shall mourn, each
family[1] by itself: the family of the house
of David by itself, and their wives by them-
selves; the family of the house of Nathan
by itself, and their wives by themselves;
13 the family of the house of Levi by itself,
and their wives by themselves; the family
of the Shimeites by itself, and their wives
by themselves; 14 and all the families that
are left, each by itself, and their wives by
themselves.

13 "On that day there shall be a
fountain opened for the house of
David and the inhabitants of Jerusalem, to
cleanse them from sin and uncleanness.

Idolatry Cut Off

2 "And on that day, declares the LORD of
hosts, I will cut off the names of the idols
from the land, so that they shall be remem-
bered no more. And also I will remove
from the land the prophets and the spirit of
uncleanness. 3 And if anyone again proph-
esies, his father and mother who bore him
will say to him, 'You shall not live, for you
speak lies in the name of the LORD.' And
his father and mother who bore him shall
pierce him through when he prophesies.

4 "On that day every prophet will be
ashamed of his vision when he proph-
esies. He *will* not put on a hairy cloak in
order to deceive, 5 but he will say, 'I am no
prophet, I am a worker of the soil, for a
man sold me in my youth.'[2] 6 And if one
asks him, 'What are these wounds on your
back?'[3] he will say, 'The wounds I received
in the house of my friends.'

The Shepherd Struck

7 "Awake, O sword, against my
 shepherd,
against the man who stands next
 to me,"
 declares the LORD of hosts.

"Strike the shepherd, and the sheep
 will be scattered;
I will turn my hand against the
 little ones.
8 In the whole land, declares the LORD,
two thirds shall be cut off and
 perish,
and one third shall be left alive.
9 And I will put this third into the fire,
and refine them as one refines
 silver,
and test them as gold is tested.
They will call upon my name,
and I will answer them.
I will say, 'They are my people';
and they will say, 'The LORD is my
 God.'"

The Coming Day of the LORD

14 Behold, a day is coming for the
LORD, when the spoil taken from
you will be divided in your midst. 2 For I
will gather all the nations against Jeru-
salem to battle, and the city shall be taken
and the houses plundered and the women
raped. Half of the city shall go out into
exile, but the rest of the people shall not
be cut off from the city. 3 Then the LORD
will go out and fight against those nations
as when he fights on a day of battle. 4 On
that day his feet shall stand on the Mount
of Olives that lies before Jerusalem on
the east, and the Mount of Olives shall
be split in two from east to west by a very
wide valley, so that one half of the Mount
shall move northward, and the other half
southward. 5 And you shall flee to the val-

[1] Or *clan*; also verses 13, 14 [2] Or *for the land has been my possession since my youth* [3] Or *on your chest*; Hebrew *wounds between your hands*

ley of my mountains, for the valley of the
mountains shall reach to Azal. And you
shall flee as you fled from the earthquake
in the days of Uzziah king of Judah. Then
the LORD my God will come, and all the
holy ones with him.
6 On that day there shall be no light, cold,
or frost.[1] 7 And there shall be a unique[2] day,
which is known to the LORD, neither day
nor night, but at evening time there shall
be light.
8 On that day living waters shall flow out
from Jerusalem, half of them to the eastern
sea[3] and half of them to the western sea.[4]
It shall continue in summer as in winter.
9 And the LORD will be king over all the
earth. On that day the LORD will be one
and his name one.
10 The whole land shall be turned into
a plain from Geba to Rimmon south of
Jerusalem. But Jerusalem shall remain aloft
on its site from the Gate of Benjamin to
the place of the former gate, to the Corner
Gate, and from the Tower of Hananel to
the king's winepresses. 11 And it shall be
inhabited, for there shall never again be
a decree of utter destruction.[5] Jerusalem
shall dwell in security.
12 And this shall be the plague with
which the LORD will strike all the peoples
that wage war against Jerusalem: their
flesh will rot while they are still standing
on their feet, their eyes will rot in their
sockets, and their tongues will rot in their
mouths.
13 And on that day a great panic from
the LORD shall fall on them, so that each
will seize the hand of another, and the
hand of the one will be raised against the
hand of the other. 14 Even Judah will fight
at Jerusalem. And the wealth of all the sur-
rounding nations shall be collected, gold,
silver, and garments in great abundance.
15 And a plague like this plague shall fall
on the horses, the mules, the camels, the
donkeys, and whatever beasts may be in
those camps.
16 Then everyone who survives of all the
nations that have come against Jerusalem
shall go up year after year to worship the
King, the LORD of hosts, and to keep the
Feast of Booths. 17 And if any of the fami-
lies of the earth do not go up to Jerusalem
to worship the King, the LORD of hosts,
there will be no rain on them. 18 And if the
family of Egypt does not go up and pre-
sent themselves, then on them there shall
be no rain;[6] there shall be the plague with
which the LORD afflicts the nations that
do not go up to keep the Feast of Booths.
19 This shall be the punishment to Egypt
and the punishment to all the nations that
do not go up to keep the Feast of Booths.
20 And on that day there shall be in-
scribed on the bells of the horses, "Holy
to the LORD." And the pots in the house
of the LORD shall be as the bowls before
the altar. 21 And every pot in Jerusalem and
Judah shall be holy to the LORD of hosts,
so that all who sacrifice may come and
take of them and boil the meat of the sac-
rifice in them. And there shall no longer
be a trader[7] in the house of the LORD of
hosts on that day.

[1] Compare Septuagint, Syriac, Vulgate, Targum; the meaning of the Hebrew is uncertain [2] Hebrew *one* [3] That is, the Dead Sea [4] That is, the Mediterranean Sea [5] The Hebrew term rendered *decree of utter destruction* refers to things devoted (or set apart) to the Lord (or by the Lord) for destruction [6] Hebrew lacks *rain* [7] Or *Canaanite*

Introduction to

Malachi

Author

Malachi the prophet

Date

About 460 B.C.

Purpose

The purpose of Malachi is to call God's people to repentance from sin and to continued perseverance in faith when they weren't seeing how God was working.

Central Themes

God loves His people; tithes and offerings are to be offered to God; God is offended by divorce, adultery, and other sins; God deserves honor; God will send the Messiah after sending someone to prepare the people for His coming.

Memory Verses

God our Father (Malachi 1:6–7); a priest's chief duty (Malachi 2:4–7); the messenger of the covenant (Malachi 3:1–3); the day of the Lord (Malachi 4:1–6)

Introduction

Malachi wrote around 100 years after the Jews had returned to Jerusalem from exile in Babylon. No great miracles were being done, and Jerusalem was nothing special in the world's eyes. It was easy for the Jews to wonder what had happened to their special relationship with God and His promises to them. Malachi wrote six short arguments between God and His people. In each one, God accused His people of wrongdoing; the people asked in what way they were committing that wrong; God explained. God assured His people that they were His people, knowing His love in a special way (Malachi 1:2–3; 3:16–18). He reminded them that they owed Him honor and they should show such honor in their offerings (Malachi 1:6–2:2; 3:6–12). God rebuked His people for marrying idol worshipers and for divorcing their spouses (Malachi 2:10–16). God also assured His people that He would send the promised Messiah, who would purify God's people and bring righteousness and healing (Malachi 3:1–4; 4:1–3), but first God would send someone to prepare the people for the Messiah's coming (Malachi 4:5–6).

516 B.C.
Temple rebuilt

About 460 B.C.
Prophetic ministry of Malachi

334–323 B.C.
Reign of Alexander the Great

Malachi

1 The oracle of the word of the LORD to Israel by Malachi.[1]

The LORD's Love for Israel

69

²"I have loved you," says the LORD. But you say, "How have you loved us?" "Is not Esau Jacob's brother?" declares the LORD. "Yet I have loved Jacob ³but Esau I have hated. I have laid waste his hill country and left his heritage to jackals of the desert." ⁴If Edom says, "We are shattered but we will rebuild the ruins," the LORD of hosts says, "They may build, but I will tear down, and they will be called 'the wicked country,' and 'the people with whom the LORD is angry forever.'" ⁵Your own eyes shall see this, and you shall say, "Great is the LORD beyond the border of Israel!"

The Priests' Polluted Offerings

⁶"A son honors his father, and a servant his master. If then I am a father, where is my honor? And if I am a master, where is my fear? says the LORD of hosts to you, O priests, who despise my name. But you say, 'How have we despised your name?' ⁷By offering polluted food upon my altar. But you say, 'How have we polluted you?' By saying that the LORD's table may be despised. ⁸When you offer blind animals in sacrifice, is that not evil? And when you offer those that are lame or sick, is that not evil? Present that to your governor; will he accept you or show you favor? says the LORD of hosts. ⁹And now entreat the favor of God, that he may be gracious to us. With such a gift from your hand, will he show favor to any of you? says the LORD of hosts. ¹⁰Oh that there were one among you who would shut the doors, that you might not kindle fire on my altar in vain! I have no pleasure in you, says the LORD of hosts, and I will not accept an offering from your hand. ¹¹For from the rising of the sun to its setting my name will be[2] great among the nations, and in every place incense will be offered to my name, and a pure offering. For my name will be great among the nations, says the LORD of hosts. ¹²But you profane it when you say that the Lord's table is polluted, and its fruit, that is, its food may be despised. ¹³But you say, 'What a weariness this is,' and you snort at it, says the LORD of hosts. You bring what has been taken by violence or is lame or sick, and this you bring as your offering! Shall I accept that from your hand? says the LORD. ¹⁴Cursed be the cheat who has a male in his flock, and vows it, and yet sacrifices to the Lord what is blemished. For I am a great King, says the LORD of hosts, and my name will be feared among the nations.

The LORD Rebukes the Priests

2 "And now, O priests, this command is for you. ²If you will not listen, if you will not take it to heart to give honor to my name, says the LORD of hosts, then I will send the curse upon you and I will curse your blessings. Indeed, I have already cursed them, because you do not lay it to heart. ³Behold, I will rebuke your offspring,[3] and spread dung on your faces, the dung of your offerings, and you shall be taken away with it.[4] ⁴So shall you know that I have sent this command to you, that my covenant with Levi may stand, says the LORD of hosts. ⁵My covenant with him was one of life and peace, and I gave them to him. It was a covenant of fear, and he feared me. He stood in awe of my name. ⁶True instruction[5] was in his mouth, and no wrong was found on his lips. He

[1] *Malachi* means *my messenger* [2] Or *is* (three times in verse 11; also verse 14) [3] Hebrew *seed* [4] Or *to it* [5] Or *law*; also verses 7, 8, 9

walked with me in peace and uprightness, and he turned many from iniquity. **7** For the lips of a priest should guard knowledge, and people[1] should seek instruction from his mouth, for he is the messenger of the LORD of hosts. **8** But you have turned aside from the way. You have caused many to stumble by your instruction. You have corrupted the covenant of Levi, says the LORD of hosts, **9** and so I make you despised and abased before all the people, inasmuch as you do not keep my ways but show partiality in your instruction."

Judah Profaned the Covenant

10 Have we not all one Father? Has not one God created us? Why then are we faithless to one another, profaning the covenant of our fathers? **11** Judah has been faithless, and abomination has been committed in Israel and in Jerusalem. For Judah has profaned the sanctuary of the LORD, which he loves, and has married the daughter of a foreign god. **12** May the LORD cut off from the tents of Jacob any descendant[2] of the man who does this, who brings an offering to the LORD of hosts!

13 And this second thing you do. You cover the LORD's altar with tears, with weeping and groaning because he no longer regards the offering or accepts it with favor from your hand. **14** But you say, "Why does he not?" Because the LORD was witness between you and the wife of your youth, to whom you have been faithless, though she is your companion and your wife by covenant. **15** Did he not make them one, with a portion of the Spirit in their union?[3] And what was the one God[4] seeking?[5] Godly offspring. So guard yourselves[6] in your spirit, and let none of you be faithless to the wife of your youth. **16** "For the man who does not love his wife but divorces her,[7] says the LORD, the God of Israel, covers[8] his garment with violence, says the LORD of hosts. So guard yourselves in your spirit, and do not be faithless."

The Messenger of the LORD

17 You have wearied the LORD with your words. But you say, "How have we wearied him?" By saying, "Everyone who does evil is good in the sight of the LORD, and he delights in them." Or by asking, "Where is the God of justice?"

3 "Behold, I send my messenger, and he will prepare the way
1441 before me. And the Lord whom you seek will suddenly come to his temple; and the messenger of the covenant in whom you delight, behold, he is coming, says the LORD of hosts. **2** But who can endure the day of his coming, and who can stand when he appears? For he is like a refiner's fire and like fullers' soap. **3** He will sit as a refiner and purifier of silver, and he will purify the sons of Levi and refine them like gold and silver, and they will bring offerings in righteousness to the LORD.[9] **4** Then the offering of Judah and Jerusalem will be pleasing to the LORD as in the days of old and as in former years.

5 "Then I will draw near to you for judgment. I will be a swift witness against the sorcerers, against the adulterers, against those who swear falsely, against those who oppress the hired worker in his wages, the widow and the fatherless, against those who thrust aside the sojourner, and do not fear me, says the LORD of hosts.

Robbing God

6 "For I the LORD do not change; therefore you, O children of Jacob, are not consumed. **7** From the days of your fathers you have turned aside from my statutes and have not kept them. Return to me, and I will return to you, says the LORD of hosts. But you say, 'How shall we return?' **8** Will man rob God? Yet you are robbing me. But you say, 'How have we robbed you?'

[1] Hebrew *they* [2] Hebrew *any who wakes and answers* [3] Hebrew *in it* [4] Hebrew *the one* [5] Or *And not one has done this who has a portion of the Spirit. And what was that one seeking?* [6] Or *So take care*; also verse 16 [7] Hebrew *who hates and divorces* [8] Probable meaning (compare Septuagint and Deuteronomy 24:1-4); or *"The LORD, the God of Israel, says that he hates divorce, and him who covers* [9] Or *and they will belong to the LORD, bringers of an offering in righteousness*

In your tithes and contributions. **9** You are cursed with a curse, for you are robbing me, the whole nation of you. **10** Bring the full tithe into the storehouse, that there may be food in my house. And thereby put me to the test, says the LORD of hosts, if I will not open the windows of heaven for you and pour down for you a blessing until there is no more need. **11** I will rebuke the devourer[1] for you, so that it will not destroy the fruits of your soil, and your vine in the field shall not fail to bear, says the LORD of hosts. **12** Then all nations will call you blessed, for you will be a land of delight, says the LORD of hosts.

13 "Your words have been hard against me, says the LORD. But you say, 'How have we spoken against you?' **14** You have said, 'It is vain to serve God. What is the profit of our keeping his charge or of walking as in mourning before the LORD of hosts? **15** And now we call the arrogant blessed. Evildoers not only prosper but they put God to the test and they escape.'"

The Book of Remembrance

16 Then those who feared the LORD spoke with one another. The LORD paid attention and heard them, and a book of remembrance was written before him of those who feared the LORD and esteemed his name. **17** "They shall be mine, says the LORD of hosts, in the day when I make up my treasured possession, and I will spare them as a man spares his son who serves him. **18** Then once more you shall see the distinction between the righteous and the wicked, between one who serves God and one who does not serve him.

The Great Day of the LORD

4 [2] "For behold, the day is coming, burning like an oven, when all the arrogant and all evildoers will be stubble. The day that is coming shall set them ablaze, says the LORD of hosts, so that it will leave them neither root nor branch. **2** But for you who fear my name, the sun of righteousness shall rise with healing in its wings. You shall go out leaping like calves from the stall. **3** And you shall tread down the wicked, for they will be ashes under the soles of your feet, on the day when I act, says the LORD of hosts.

4 "Remember the law of my servant Moses, the statutes and rules[3] that I commanded him at Horeb for all Israel.

5 "Behold, I will send you Elijah the prophet before the great and awesome day of the LORD comes. **6** And 1429, 1441 he will turn the hearts of fathers to their children and the hearts of children to their fathers, lest I come and strike the land with a decree of utter destruction."[4]

[1] Probably a name for some crop-destroying pest or pests [2] Ch 4:1-6 is ch 3:19-24 in the Hebrew [3] Or *and just decrees* [4] The Hebrew term rendered *decree of utter destruction* refers to things devoted (or set apart) to the Lord (or by the Lord) for destruction

The
New Testament

Introduction to

Matthew

Author

Matthew the apostle

Date

About A.D. 55–65

Key People

Jesus; Joseph and Mary; the Wise Men; Herod the Great; John the Baptist; Peter; James; John; Pharisees; Sadducees; Judas Iscariot; Pontius Pilate

Purpose

The purpose of Matthew is to announce that God's promises of a Messiah have been kept in the person and ministry of Jesus Christ, who has brought the kingdom of heaven to earth.

Central Themes

Jesus is the promised Messiah (or King); the kingdom of heaven has arrived but is not yet fully completed; Old Testament prophecy is fulfilled in Christ; disciples of Jesus should follow Him and obey His teaching; the good news of the kingdom is for all nations.

Memory Verses

Jesus' birth (Matthew 1:18–25); the Beatitudes (Matthew 5:1–12); prayer and the Golden Rule (Matthew 7:7–14); rest in Jesus (Matthew 11:28–30); parable of the net interpreted (Matthew 13:47–50); forgiveness and the Church (Matthew 18:15–20); the call to make disciples (Matthew 28:18–20)

Introduction

Matthew was a Jewish tax collector whom Jesus called to be one of His disciples. He had been an eyewitness of Jesus' ministry. Matthew wanted Jews to see that Jesus was the promised Messiah, the King who would set free and victoriously rule His people, so Matthew's Gospel often shows how Jesus fulfills Old Testament prophecy. Matthew tells of Jesus' supernatural birth, of the visit of the Wise Men, and of John the Baptist preparing people for Jesus' coming (Matthew 1–3). He describes Jesus resisting Satan's temptation in the wilderness and beginning His ministry (Matthew 4). Matthew moves back and forth from chapters telling what Jesus taught to chapters describing what Jesus did. One of the sermons Matthew records is the famous Sermon on the Mount (Matthew 5–7). Matthew describes many miracles Jesus did, especially healing sick people. He also records many of the parables Jesus told (Matthew 13:1–51; 18:10–14, 21–35; 20:1–16; 21:28–22:14; 25:1–30). Matthew tells of Jesus' suffering in His unfair trial and in His death on the cross (Matthew 26:47–27:66). The story ends on the triumphant note of Jesus' resurrection from the dead and ascension into heaven (Matthew 28).

About 5 B.C.	About A.D. 28–33	About A.D. 55–65
Birth of Jesus	Jesus' ministry, death, resurrection	Matthew's Gospel written

The Gospel According to

Matthew

The Genealogy of Jesus Christ

1 The book of the genealogy of
Jesus Christ, the son of David,
425 the son of Abraham.
2 Abraham was the father of Isaac, and
Isaac the father of Jacob, and Jacob the
father of Judah and his brothers, 3 and
Judah the father of Perez and Zerah by
Tamar, and Perez the father of Hezron,
and Hezron the father of Ram,[1] 4 and Ram
the father of Amminadab, and Ammin-
adab the father of Nahshon, and Nahshon
the father of Salmon, 5 and Salmon the
father of Boaz by Rahab, and Boaz
the father of Obed by Ruth, and
345, Obed the father of Jesse, 6 and Jesse
425 the father of David the king.
And David was the father of Solomon
by the wife of Uriah, 7 and Solomon the
father of Rehoboam, and Rehoboam the
father of Abijah, and Abijah the father of
Asaph,[2] 8 and Asaph the father of Jehosh-
aphat, and Jehoshaphat the father of Jo-
ram, and Joram the father of Uzziah, 9 and
Uzziah the father of Jotham, and Jotham
the father of Ahaz, and Ahaz the father
of Hezekiah, 10 and Hezekiah the father of
Manasseh, and Manasseh the father of
Amos,[3] and Amos the father of Josiah,
11 and Josiah the father of Jechoniah and
his brothers, at the time of the deporta-
tion to Babylon.
12 And after the deportation to Babylon:
Jechoniah was the father of Shealtiel,[4]
and Shealtiel the father of Zerubbabel,
13 and Zerubbabel the father of Abiud,
and Abiud the father of Eliakim, and
Eliakim the father of Azor, 14 and Azor
the father of Zadok, and Zadok the
father of Achim, and Achim the father of
Eliud, 15 and Eliud the father of Eleazar,
and Eleazar the father of Matthan, and
Matthan the father of Jacob, 16 and Jacob
the father of Joseph the husband of Mary,
of whom Jesus was born, who is called
Christ.
17 So all the generations from Abraham
to David were fourteen generations, and
from David to the deportation to Babylon
fourteen generations, and from the depor-
tation to Babylon to the Christ fourteen
generations.

The Birth of Jesus Christ

18 Now the birth of Jesus Christ[5]
took place in this way. When his
1293 mother Mary had been betrothed[6]
to Joseph, before they came to-
gether she was found to be with
1433 child from the Holy Spirit. 19 And
her husband Joseph, being a just man
and unwilling to put her to shame, re-
solved to divorce her quietly. 20 But as he
considered these things, behold,
an angel of the Lord appeared to
13 him in a dream, saying, "Joseph,
son of David, do not fear to take Mary as
your wife, for that which is conceived in
her is from the Holy Spirit. 21 She will bear
a son, and you shall call his name Jesus,
for he will save his people from their sins."
22 All this took place to fulfill what the Lord
had spoken by the prophet:

23 "Behold, the virgin shall conceive
and bear a son,
1293 and they shall call his name
Immanuel"

(which means, God with us). 24 When
Joseph woke from sleep, he did as the
angel of the Lord commanded him: he
took his wife, 25 but knew her not until she

[1] Greek *Aram*; also verse 4 [2] *Asaph* is probably an alternate spelling for *Asa*; some manuscripts read *Asa*; also verse 8 [3] *Amos* is probably an alternate spelling for *Amon*; some manuscripts read *Amon*; twice in this verse [4] Greek *Salathiel*; twice in this verse [5] Some manuscripts *of the Christ* [6] That is, legally pledged to be married

had given birth to a son. And he called his name Jesus.

The Visit of the Wise Men

2 Now after Jesus was born in
Bethlehem of Judea in the
1297 days of Herod the king, behold,
wise men[1] from the east came to Jeru-
salem, 2 saying, "Where is he who
has been born king of the Jews? For
1297 we saw his star when it rose[2] and
have come to worship him." 3 When Herod the king heard this, he was troubled, and all Jerusalem with him; 4 and assembling all the chief priests and scribes of the people, he inquired of them where the Christ was to be born. 5 They told him, "In Bethlehem of Judea, for so it is written by the prophet:

> 6 "'And you, O Bethlehem, in the land
> of Judah,
> are by no means least among the
> rulers of Judah;
> for from you shall come a ruler
> who will shepherd my people
> Israel.'"

7 Then Herod summoned the wise men secretly and ascertained from them what time the star had appeared. 8 And he sent them to Bethlehem, saying, "Go and search diligently for the child, and when you have found him, bring me word, that I too may come and worship him." 9 After listening to the king, they went on their way. And behold, the star that they had seen when it rose went before them until it came to rest over the place where the child was. 10 When they saw the star, they rejoiced exceedingly with great joy. 11 And going into the house they saw the child with Mary his mother, and they fell down and worshiped him. Then, opening their treasures, they offered him gifts, gold and frankincense and myrrh. 12 And being warned in a dream not to return to Herod, they departed to their own country by another way.

The Flight to Egypt

13 Now when they had departed,
behold, an angel of the Lord
1293 appeared to Joseph in a dream and
said, "Rise, take the child and his mother, and flee to Egypt, and remain there until I tell you, for Herod is about to search for the child, to destroy him." 14 And he rose and took the child and his mother by night and departed to Egypt 15 and remained there until the death of Herod. This was to fulfill what the Lord had spoken by the prophet, "Out of Egypt I called my son."

Herod Kills the Children

16 Then Herod, when he saw that he had been tricked by the wise men, became furious, and he sent and killed all the male children in Bethlehem and in all that region who were two years old or under, according to the time that he had ascertained from the wise men. 17 Then was fulfilled what was spoken by the prophet Jeremiah:

> 18 "A voice was heard in Ramah,
> weeping and loud lamentation,
> Rachel weeping for her children;
> she refused to be comforted,
> because they are no more."

The Return to Nazareth

19 But when Herod died, behold, an
angel of the Lord appeared in a
1293 dream to Joseph in Egypt, 20 saying,
"Rise, take the child and his mother and go to the land of Israel, for those who sought the child's life are dead." 21 And he rose and took the child and his mother and went to the land of Israel. 22 But when he heard that Archelaus was reigning over Judea in place of his father Herod, he was afraid to go there, and being warned in a dream he withdrew to the district of Galilee. 23 And
he went and lived in a city called
Nazareth, that what was spoken by
1459 the prophets might be fulfilled: "He
shall be called a Nazarene."

[1] Greek *magi*; also verses 7, 16 [2] Or *in the east*; also verse 9

An Angel Visits Joseph

Joseph and Mary had promised to marry each other. But one day Joseph found out that Mary was going to have a baby. This made Joseph sad because he knew that he was not the baby's father. He thought that another man was the father, and he did not want to marry Mary if she was going to have another man's baby. So Joseph decided it would be best if he and Mary did not get married after all.

While Joseph was thinking about these things, an angel appeared to him in a dream. The angel said, "Joseph, son of David, do not fear to take Mary as your wife." The angel told Joseph that the baby growing inside Mary was from the Holy Spirit. "She will bear a son," the angel said, "and you shall call His name Jesus, for He will save His people from their sins."

Long ago, the prophet Isaiah had written that a virgin—a woman who was not yet married—would have a son and people would call Him Immanuel. Immanuel means "God with us."

When Joseph woke up, he did what the angel had told him. He married Mary, and she later gave birth to a son. Joseph called His name Jesus. God loved Joseph and gave him the faith he needed to take Mary as his wife.

For a long, long time, God had been promising to send someone who would save God's people from their sins. The time had finally come!

SEEK and FIND

WHERE TO FIND THE STORY

Matthew 1:18–25

KEY BIBLE VERSE

"'Behold, the virgin shall conceive and bear a son, and they shall call his name Immanuel' (which means, God with us)." (Matthew 1:23)

THREE KEY QUESTIONS

- How did Joseph find out about the baby that Mary was going to have?
- What did the angel tell Joseph?
- What does "Immanuel" mean?

RELATED BIBLE READINGS

Isaiah 7:14; Matthew 2:13–15, 19–23; Luke 2:4–5; John 1:14

John the Baptist Prepares the Way

3 In those days John the Baptist
came preaching in the wilder-
1301 ness of Judea, 2 "Repent, for the
kingdom of heaven is at hand."
3 For this is he who was spoken of
1373, by the prophet Isaiah when he said,
1429

> "The voice of one crying in the wilderness:
> 'Prepare[1] the way of the Lord;
> make his paths straight.'"

4 Now John wore a garment of camel's hair and a leather belt around his waist, and his food was locusts and wild honey. 5 Then Jerusalem and all Judea and all the region about the Jordan were going out to him, 6 and they were baptized by him in the river Jordan, confessing their sins.

7 But when he saw many of the Pharisees and Sadducees coming to his baptism, he said to them, "You brood of vipers! Who warned you to flee from the wrath to come? 8 Bear fruit in keeping with repentance. 9 And do not presume to say to yourselves, 'We have Abraham as our father,' for I tell you, God is able from these stones to raise up children for Abraham. 10 Even now the axe is laid to the root of the trees. Every tree therefore that does not bear good fruit is cut down and thrown into the fire.

11 "I baptize you with water for
repentance, but he who is coming
1301 after me is mightier than I, whose
sandals I am not worthy to carry. He will baptize you with the Holy Spirit and fire. 12 His winnowing fork is in his hand, and he will clear his threshing floor and gather his wheat into the barn, but the chaff he will burn with unquenchable fire."

The Baptism of Jesus

13 Then Jesus came from Galilee to
the Jordan to John, to be baptized
1305 by him. 14 John would have pre-

[1] Or *crying: Prepare in the wilderness*

vented him, saying, "I need to be baptized
by you, and do you come to me?" 15 But
Jesus answered him, "Let it be so now, for
thus it is fitting for us to fulfill all righ-
teousness." Then he consented. 16 And
when Jesus was baptized, immediately he
went up from the water, and behold, the
heavens were opened to him,[1] and he saw
the Spirit of God descending like a dove
and coming to rest on him; 17 and behold,
a voice from heaven said, "This is
my beloved Son,[2] with whom I am
1305 well pleased."

The Temptation of Jesus

4 Then Jesus was led up by the
Spirit into the wilderness to be
1309 tempted by the devil. 2 And after
fasting forty days and forty nights,
he was hungry. 3 And the tempter
13 came and said to him, "If you are
the Son of God, command these stones to
become loaves of bread." 4 But he answered,
"It is written,

> "'Man shall not live by bread alone,
> but by every word that comes
> from the mouth of God.'"

5 Then the devil took him to the holy city
and set him on the pinnacle of the temple
6 and said to him, "If you are the Son of
God, throw yourself down, for it is written,

> "'He will command his angels
> concerning you,'

and

> "'On their hands they will bear you up,
> lest you strike your foot against a
> stone.'"

7 Jesus said to him, "Again it is written,
'You shall not put the Lord your God to
the test.'" 8 Again, the devil took him to
a very high mountain and showed him
all the kingdoms of the world and their
glory. 9 And he said to him, "All these I will
give you, if you will fall down and worship
me." 10 Then Jesus said to him, "Be gone,
Satan! For it is written,

> "'You shall worship the Lord your God
> and him only shall you serve.'"

11 Then the devil left him, and behold,
angels came and were ministering to him.

Jesus Begins His Ministry

12 Now when he heard that John
had been arrested, he withdrew
1313 into Galilee. 13 And leaving Naza-
reth he went and lived in Capernaum by
the sea, in the territory of Zebulun and
Naphtali, 14 so that what was spoken by
the prophet Isaiah might be fulfilled:

> 15 "The land of Zebulun and the land of
> Naphtali,
> the way of the sea, beyond
> the Jordan, Galilee of the
> Gentiles—
> 16 the people dwelling in darkness
> have seen a great light,
> and for those dwelling in the region
> and shadow of death,
> on them a light has dawned."

17 From that time Jesus began to preach,
saying, "Repent, for the kingdom of
heaven is at hand."

Jesus Calls the First Disciples

18 While walking by the Sea of
Galilee, he saw two brothers,
1467 Simon (who is called Peter) and
Andrew his brother, casting a net into the
sea, for they were fishermen. 19 And he
said to them, "Follow me, and I
will make you fishers of men."
1313 20 Immediately they left their nets
and followed him. 21 And going on from
there he saw two other brothers, James the
son of Zebedee and John his brother, in the
boat with Zebedee their father, mending
their nets, and he called them.
22 Immediately they left the boat and their
father and followed him.

[1] Some manuscripts omit *to him* [2] Or *my Son, my* (or *the*) *Beloved*

The Visit of the Wise Men

When Jesus was born in Bethlehem, God displayed a special star in the sky. Far away from Bethlehem, some wise men saw this special star. They knew it meant a king had been born for God's people. They set out on a long journey to follow the star and find the baby Jesus.

The wise men traveled until they came to Jerusalem. There, they asked King Herod, "Where is He who has been born king of the Jews? For we saw His star when it rose and have come to worship Him."

Herod was very angry when he heard this. He did not want anyone else to be king. He asked the teachers and priests to tell him where the new King would be born. They told him what the prophet Micah had written long before—that God's Ruler would come from the town of Bethlehem.

Then Herod told the wise men to go to Bethlehem to look for the new King. If they found Him, Herod said, they should come back to Jerusalem and tell him where to find this new King. Herod said that he would go worship Him too. But Herod was lying. He did not want to worship Jesus. He wanted to kill Him!

The wise men went on to Bethlehem. There, the special star stopped—right over the house where Jesus was. The wise men were so happy to find the baby with His mother Mary. They bowed down and worshiped Jesus. And they gave Him gifts of gold, frankincense, and myrrh.

God used the star to lead the wise men to Jesus, even though they were not from among the Jewish people. God wanted to show that Jesus came to pay for the sins of people from every nation. Jesus is our Savior, too. Because of Jesus, God forgives our sins. Someday we will live with Jesus forever.

SEEK and FIND

WHERE TO FIND THE STORY

Matthew 2:1–12

KEY BIBLE VERSE

"Where is he who has been born king of the Jews? For we saw his star when it rose and have come to worship him." (Matthew 2:2)

THREE KEY QUESTIONS

- Where did the prophet Micah say that Jesus would be born?
- How did the wise men know exactly where Jesus was?
- What did the wise men do when they found Jesus? What should we do about Jesus?

RELATED BIBLE READINGS

Genesis 12:1–3; Isaiah 40:3–5; 49:5–7; Micah 5:2

Jesus Ministers to Great Crowds

23 And he went throughout all Galilee, teaching in their synagogues and proclaiming the gospel of the kingdom and healing every disease and every affliction among the people. 24 So his fame spread throughout all Syria, and they brought him all the sick, those afflicted with various diseases and pains, those oppressed by demons, epileptics, and paralytics, and he healed them. 25 And great crowds followed him from Galilee and the Decapolis, and from Jerusalem and Judea, and from beyond the Jordan.

The Sermon on the Mount

5 Seeing the crowds, he went up
on the mountain, and when he
1317 sat down, his disciples came to him.

The Beatitudes

2 And he opened his mouth and taught them, saying:

3 "Blessed are the poor in spirit, for theirs is the kingdom of heaven.

4 "Blessed are those who mourn, for they shall be comforted.

5 "Blessed are the meek, for they shall inherit the earth.

6 "Blessed are those who hunger and thirst for righteousness, for they shall be satisfied.

7 "Blessed are the merciful, for they shall receive mercy.

8 "Blessed are the pure in heart, for they shall see God.

9 "Blessed are the peacemakers, for they shall be called sons of God.

10 "Blessed are those who are persecuted for righteousness' sake, for theirs is the kingdom of heaven.

11 "Blessed are you when others revile you and persecute you and utter all kinds of evil against you falsely on my account. 12 Rejoice and be glad, for your reward is great in heaven, for so they persecuted the prophets who were before you.

Salt and Light

13 "You are the salt of the earth, but
if salt has lost its taste, how shall its
1317 saltiness be restored? It is no longer
good for anything except to be thrown out
and trampled under people's feet.
14 "You are the light of the world. A
city set on a hill cannot be hidden.
1317 15 Nor do people light a lamp and
put it under a basket, but on a stand, and it
gives light to all in the house. 16 In the same
way, let your light shine before others, so that they may see your good
1317 works and give glory to your Father
who is in heaven.

Christ Came to Fulfill the Law

17 "Do not think that I have come to abolish the Law or the Prophets; I have not come to abolish them but to fulfill them. 18 For truly, I say to you, until heaven and earth pass away, not an iota, not a dot, will pass from the Law until all is accomplished. 19 Therefore whoever relaxes one of the least of these commandments and teaches others to do the same will be called least in the kingdom of heaven, but whoever does them and teaches them will be called great in the kingdom of heaven. 20 For I tell you, unless your righteousness exceeds that of the scribes and Pharisees, you will never enter the kingdom of heaven.

Anger

21 "You have heard that it was said to those of old, 'You shall not murder; and whoever murders will be liable to judgment.' 22 But I say to you that everyone who is angry with his brother[1] will be liable to judgment; whoever insults[2] his brother will be liable to the council; and whoever says, 'You fool!' will be liable to the hell[3] of fire. 23 So if you are offering your gift at the altar and there remember that your brother has something against you, 24 leave your gift there before the altar

[1] Some manuscripts insert *without cause* [2] Greek *says Raca to* (a term of abuse) [3] Greek *Gehenna*; also verses 29, 30

John the Baptist Prepares the Way

God chose a man named John to do a very important work. God wanted John to prepare the way for Jesus! God chose John to tell people that Jesus, our Savior, had come to earth. John prepared the way by telling people they must repent—they must turn away from their sins and turn to God. When people repented, John baptized them in the Jordan River as a sign or picture of God's washing away their sins. This is why John was called "John the Baptist."

John the Baptist wore clothing made from camel's hair and a leather belt. He ate locusts and wild honey. He spent his time doing the work God called him to do. John told the people, "Repent, for the kingdom of heaven is at hand." And he told them that those who truly turned to God and away from their sins would have lives that looked different than before.

Some people did not want to repent. They were proud of themselves and thought they were already good enough. They did not think they had any sins about which they needed to repent. But many people did listen and repent. They confessed their sins and were baptized by John to show their repentance and prepare the way for Jesus' coming.

Today God uses His people to tell others about God's Word and that Jesus came to save them. All of us are sinners who need to repent and trust in Jesus. Jesus loves us so much that He came to save us from our sins.

SEEK and FIND

WHERE TO FIND THE STORY

Matthew 3:1–12

KEY BIBLE VERSE

"I baptize you with water for repentance, but he who is coming after me is mightier than I. . . . He will baptize you with the Holy Spirit and fire." (Matthew 3:11)

THREE KEY QUESTIONS

- What was the important work that God chose John to do?
- What does it mean to repent from our sins?
- What does Jesus do when we repent from sin and trust in Him?

RELATED BIBLE READINGS

Matthew 11:10–15; 17:10–13; John 1:6–8, 19–36

and go. First be reconciled to your brother,
and then come and offer your gift. 25 Come
to terms quickly with your accuser while
you are going with him to court, lest your
accuser hand you over to the judge, and
the judge to the guard, and you be put in
prison. 26 Truly, I say to you, you will never
get out until you have paid the last penny.[1]

Lust

27 "You have heard that it was said, 'You
shall not commit adultery.' 28 But I say to
you that everyone who looks at a woman
with lustful intent has already committed
adultery with her in his heart. 29 If your
right eye causes you to sin, tear it out
and throw it away. For it is better that you
lose one of your members than that your
whole body be thrown into hell. 30 And if
your right hand causes you to sin, cut it
off and throw it away. For it is better that
you lose one of your members than that
your whole body go into hell.

Divorce

31 "It was also said, 'Whoever divorces
his wife, let him give her a certificate of
divorce.' 32 But I say to you that everyone
who divorces his wife, except on the
ground of sexual immorality, makes her
commit adultery, and whoever marries a
divorced woman commits adultery.

Oaths

33 "Again you have heard that it was
said to those of old, 'You shall not
swear falsely, but shall perform to the
Lord what you have sworn.' 34 But I say
to you, Do not take an oath at all, either
by heaven, for it is the throne of God,
35 or by the earth, for it is his footstool,
or by Jerusalem, for it is the city of the
great King. 36 And do not take an oath by
your head, for you cannot make one hair
white or black. 37 Let what you say be sim-
ply 'Yes' or 'No'; anything more than this
comes from evil.[2]

[1] Greek *kodrantes*, Roman copper coin (Latin *quadrans*) worth about 1/64 of a *denarius* (which was a day's wage for a laborer) [2] Or *the evil one*

Retaliation

38 “You have heard that it was said, ‘An eye for an eye and a tooth for a tooth.’ 39 But I say to you, Do not resist the one who is evil. But if anyone slaps you on the right cheek, turn to him the other also. 40 And if anyone would sue you and take your tunic,[1] let him have your cloak as well. 41 And if anyone forces you to go one mile, go with him two miles. 42 Give to the one who begs from you, and do not refuse the one who would borrow from you.

Love Your Enemies

43 “You have heard that it was said, ‘You shall love your neighbor and hate your enemy.’ 44 But I say to you, Love your enemies and pray for those who persecute you, 45 so that you may be sons of your Father who is in heaven. For he makes his sun rise on the evil and on the good, and sends rain on the just and on the unjust. 46 For if you love those who love you, what reward do you have? Do not even the tax collectors do the same? 47 And if you greet only your brothers,[2] what more are you doing than others? Do not even the Gentiles do the same? 48 You therefore must be perfect, as your heavenly Father is perfect.

Giving to the Needy

6 “Beware of practicing your righteousness before other people in order to be seen by them, for then you will have no reward from your Father who is in heaven.

2 “Thus, when you give to the needy, sound no trumpet before you, as the hypocrites do in the synagogues and in the streets, that they may be praised by others. Truly, I say to you, they have received their reward. 3 But when you give to the needy, do not let your left hand know what your right hand is doing, 4 so that your giving may be in secret. And your Father who sees in secret will reward you.

The Lord’s Prayer

1493

5 “And when you pray, you must not be like the hypocrites. For they love to stand and pray in the synagogues and at the street corners, that they may be seen by others. Truly, I say to you, they have received their reward. 6 But when you pray, go into your room and shut the door and pray to your Father who is in secret. And your Father who sees in secret will reward you.

7 “And when you pray, do not heap up empty phrases as the Gentiles do, for they think that they will be heard for their many words. 8 Do not be like them, for your Father knows what you need before you ask him. 9 Pray then like this:

1783

“Our Father in heaven,
hallowed be your name.[3]
10 Your kingdom come,
your will be done,[4]
on earth as it is in heaven.
11 Give us this day our daily bread,[5]
12 and forgive us our debts,
as we also have forgiven our debtors.
13 And lead us not into temptation,
but deliver us from evil.[6]

14 For if you forgive others their trespasses, your heavenly Father will also forgive you, 15 but if you do not forgive others their trespasses, neither will your Father forgive your trespasses.

Fasting

16 “And when you fast, do not look gloomy like the hypocrites, for they disfigure their faces that their fasting may be seen by others. Truly, I say to you, they have received their reward. 17 But when you fast, anoint your head and wash your face, 18 that your fasting may not be seen by others but by your Father who is in

[1] Greek *chiton*, a long garment worn under the cloak next to the skin [2] Or *brothers and sisters*. The plural Greek word *adelphoi* (translated “brothers”) refers to siblings in a family. In New Testament usage, depending on the context, *adelphoi* may refer either to *brothers* or to *brothers and sisters* [3] Or *Let your name be kept holy*, or *Let your name be treated with reverence* [4] Or *Let your kingdom come, let your will be done* [5] Or *our bread for tomorrow* [6] Or *the evil one*; some manuscripts add *For yours is the kingdom and the power and the glory, forever. Amen*

The Baptism of Jesus

One day Jesus came from Galilee to see John the Baptist at the Jordan River. Jesus asked John to baptize Him. John was surprised because the people who were baptized had repented from their sins and turned to God. John knew that Jesus had never done anything wrong. Jesus didn't have any sins to be sorry for or to turn from!

John tried to prevent Jesus from being baptized. "I need to be baptized by You," John said. John couldn't understand why Jesus wanted to be baptized by him.

Jesus answered John that His baptism would "fulfill all righteousness." It was something God wanted Him to do. Then John agreed to baptize Jesus. He took Jesus into the Jordan River and baptized Him.

When Jesus came up out of the water, suddenly the heavens opened! The Spirit of God came down like a dove and came to rest on Jesus! At the same time, a voice from heaven said, "This is My beloved Son, with whom I am well pleased." The voice was the voice of God the Father.

After His baptism, Jesus taught and preached about who He was and why He had come to earth. He did many miracles to show that He was truly God. After three years of ministry,

Jesus died on the cross to pay for the sins of the world. Then after three days, He rose from the dead—in glorious triumph over sin and death.

SEEK and FIND

WHERE TO FIND THE STORY

Matthew 3:13–17

KEY BIBLE VERSE

"This is my beloved Son, with whom I am well pleased." (Matthew 3:17)

THREE KEY QUESTIONS

- What happened when Jesus came up out of the water when He was baptized?
- Whose voice came from heaven and what did He say?
- Why did Jesus die on the cross and what happened after three days?

RELATED BIBLE READINGS

Mark 1:9–11; Luke 3:21–22; John 1:29–34

secret. And your Father who sees in secret
will reward you.

Lay Up Treasures in Heaven

19“Do not lay up for yourselves trea-
sures on earth, where moth and
1321 rust[1] destroy and where thieves
break in and steal, 20but lay up for your-
selves treasures in heaven, where neither
moth nor rust destroys and where thieves
do not break in and steal. 21For where your
treasure is, there your heart will be also.
22“The eye is the lamp of the body. So, if
your eye is healthy, your whole body will
be full of light, 23but if your eye is bad,
your whole body will be full of darkness.
If then the light in you is darkness, how
great is the darkness!
24“No one can serve two masters, for
either he will hate the one and love the
other, or he will be devoted to the one and
despise the other. You cannot serve God
and money.[2]

Do Not Be Anxious

25“Therefore I tell you, do not be
anxious about your life, what you
567 will eat or what you will drink, nor

[1] Or *worm*; also verse 20 [2] Greek *mammon*, a Semitic word for money or possessions

about your body, what you will put on. Is not life more than food, and the body more than clothing? 26 Look at the birds of the air: they neither sow nor reap nor gather into barns, and yet your heavenly Father feeds them. Are you not of more value than they? 27 And which of you by being anxious can add a single hour to his span of life?[1] 28 And why are you anxious about clothing? Consider the lilies of the field, how they grow: they neither toil nor spin, 29 yet I tell you, even Solomon in all his glory was not arrayed like one of these. 30 But if God so clothes the grass of the field, which today is alive and tomorrow is thrown into the oven, will he not much more clothe you, O
you of little faith? 31 Therefore do not be
anxious, saying, 'What shall we eat?'
or 'What shall we drink?' or 'What
567 shall we wear?' 32 For the Gentiles
seek after all these things, and your heavenly Father knows that you need them all.
33 But seek first the kingdom of God
and his righteousness, and all these
1321 things will be added to you.

34 "Therefore do not be anxious about tomorrow, for tomorrow will be anxious for itself. Sufficient for the day is its own trouble.

Judging Others

7 "Judge not, that you be not judged. 2 For with the judgment you pronounce you will be judged, and with the measure you use it will be measured to you. 3 Why do you see the speck that is in your brother's eye, but do not notice the log that is in your own eye? 4 Or how can you say to your brother, 'Let me take the speck out of your eye,' when there is the log in your own eye? 5 You hypocrite, first take the log out of your own eye, and then you will see clearly to take the speck out of your brother's eye.

6 "Do not give dogs what is holy, and do not throw your pearls before pigs, lest they trample them underfoot and turn to attack you.

Ask, and It Will Be Given

7 "Ask, and it will be given to you;
seek, and you will find; knock, and
1493 it will be opened to you. 8 For every-
one who asks receives, and the one who seeks finds, and to the one who knocks it will be opened. 9 Or which one of you, if his son asks him for bread, will give him a stone? 10 Or if he asks for a fish, will give
him a serpent? 11 If you then, who are evil,
know how to give good gifts to
your children, how much more
1493 will your Father who is in heaven
give good things to those who ask him!

The Golden Rule

12 "So whatever you wish that others would do to you, do also to them, for this is the Law and the Prophets.

13 "Enter by the narrow gate. For the gate is wide and the way is easy[2] that leads to destruction, and those who enter by it are many. 14 For the gate is narrow and the way is hard that leads to life, and those who find it are few.

A Tree and Its Fruit

15 "Beware of false prophets, who come to you in sheep's clothing but inwardly are ravenous wolves. 16 You will recognize them by their fruits. Are grapes gathered from thornbushes, or figs from thistles? 17 So, every healthy tree bears good fruit, but the diseased tree bears bad fruit. 18 A healthy tree cannot bear bad fruit, nor can a diseased tree bear good fruit. 19 Every tree that does not bear good fruit is cut down and thrown into the fire. 20 Thus you will recognize them by their fruits.

I Never Knew You

21 "Not everyone who says to me, 'Lord, Lord,' will enter the kingdom of heaven, but the one who does the will of my Father who is in heaven. 22 On that day many will say to me, 'Lord, Lord, did we not prophesy in your name, and cast out demons in your name, and do many mighty works in

[1] Or *a single cubit to his stature;* a *cubit* was about 18 inches or 45 centimeters [2] Some manuscripts *For the way is wide and easy*

The Temptation of Jesus

After Jesus was baptized, He was led by the Holy Spirit into the wilderness, where He was tempted by the devil.

Jesus did not eat for 40 days and 40 nights. At the end of this time, He was very hungry. God's enemy, the devil, knew Jesus was hungry. He came to Jesus and tried to get Him to sin. The devil said to Jesus, "If You are the Son of God, command these stones to become loaves of bread."

"It is written," Jesus answered him, "'Man shall not live by bread alone, but by every word that comes from the mouth of God.'"

Then the devil took Jesus to Jerusalem and had Him stand on the very highest point on top of the temple. Again the devil quoted words from the Bible, trying to trick Jesus and make Him sin. The devil told Jesus to jump off the top of the temple. If you really are the Son of God, the devil said, God "will command His angels, and 'On their hands they will bear You up,'" so that You won't even "strike Your foot against a stone."

Again Jesus answered him, "It is written, 'You shall not put the Lord your God to the test.'"

Then the devil took Jesus to the top of a high mountain and showed Him all the glorious kingdoms of the world. "All these I will give You," the devil said, "if You will worship me."

Then Jesus said to the devil, "Be gone, Satan! For it is written, 'You shall worship the Lord your God, and Him only shall you serve.'"

Then the devil left Him, and angels came to help Jesus.

Jesus was tempted by the devil to sin, but Jesus overcame the devil with God's Word. Through faith in Jesus, we too can overcome temptation by turning to God's Word and by looking to Jesus. Jesus never sinned, but always obeyed God. Through faith in Jesus as our Savior, God sees Jesus' perfect righteousness when He looks at us. Therefore, we can trust in Jesus as we fight against the devil's temptations.

SEEK and FIND

WHERE TO FIND THE STORY

Matthew 4:1–11

KEY BIBLE VERSE

"For we do not have a high priest who is unable to sympathize with our weaknesses, but one who in every respect has been tempted as we are, yet without sin." (Hebrews 4:15)

THREE KEY QUESTIONS

- What did Jesus use all three times to overcome the devil's temptations?
- Did Jesus ever give in to temptation and sin?
- What should we do when we are tempted?

RELATED BIBLE READINGS

Mark 1:12–13; Luke 4:1–13; Hebrews 2:14–18; 4:14–16; 7:26

your name?' 23 And then will I declare to
them, 'I never knew you; depart from me,
you workers of lawlessness.'

Build Your House on the Rock

24 "Everyone then who hears these
words of mine and does them will be like
a wise man who built his house on the
rock. 25 And the rain fell, and the floods
came, and the winds blew and beat on
that house, but it did not fall, because
it had been founded on the rock. 26 And
everyone who hears these words of mine
and does not do them will be like a fool-
ish man who built his house on the sand.
27 And the rain fell, and the floods came,
and the winds blew and beat against that
house, and it fell, and great was the fall
of it."

The Authority of Jesus

28 And when Jesus finished these
sayings, the crowds were aston-
587 ished at his teaching, 29 for he was
teaching them as one who had authority,
and not as their scribes.

Jesus Cleanses a Leper

8 When he came down from the moun-
tain, great crowds followed him.
2 And behold, a leper[1] came to him and
knelt before him, saying, "Lord, if you
will, you can make me clean." 3 And Jesus[2]
stretched out his hand and touched him,
saying, "I will; be clean." And immediately
his leprosy was cleansed. 4 And Jesus said
to him, "See that you say nothing to any-
one, but go, show yourself to the priest
and offer the gift that Moses commanded,
for a proof to them."

The Faith of a Centurion

5 When he entered Capernaum, a cen-
turion came forward to him, appealing
to him, 6 "Lord, my servant is lying para-
lyzed at home, suffering terribly." 7 And he
said to him, "I will come and heal him."
8 But the centurion replied, "Lord, I am
not worthy to have you come under my
roof, but only say the word, and my ser-
vant will be healed. 9 For I too am a man
under authority, with soldiers under me.
And I say to one, 'Go,' and he goes, and to
another, 'Come,' and he comes, and to my
servant,[3] 'Do this,' and he does it." 10 When
Jesus heard this, he marveled and said to
those who followed him, "Truly, I tell you,
with no one in Israel[4] have I found such
faith. 11 I tell you, many will come from
east and west and recline at table with
Abraham, Isaac, and Jacob in the kingdom
of heaven, 12 while the sons of the kingdom
will be thrown into the outer darkness. In
that place there will be weeping and gnash-
ing of teeth." 13 And to the centurion Jesus
said, "Go; let it be done for you as you have
believed." And the servant was healed at
that very moment.

Jesus Heals Many

14 And when Jesus entered Peter's house,
he saw his mother-in-law lying sick with
a fever. 15 He touched her hand, and the
fever left her, and she rose and began to
serve him. 16 That evening they brought
to him many who were oppressed by
demons, and he cast out the spirits with
a word and healed all who were sick.
17 This was to fulfill what was spoken by
the prophet Isaiah: "He took our illnesses
and bore our diseases."

The Cost of Following Jesus

18 Now when Jesus saw a crowd around
him, he gave orders to go over to the
other side. 19 And a scribe came up and
said to him, "Teacher, I will follow you
wherever you go." 20 And Jesus said to
him, "Foxes have holes, and birds of the
air have nests, but the Son of Man has
nowhere to lay his head." 21 Another of
the disciples said to him, "Lord, let me
first go and bury my father." 22 And Jesus
said to him, "Follow me, and leave the
dead to bury their own dead."

[1] *Leprosy* was a term for several skin diseases; see Leviticus 13 [2] Greek *he* [3] Greek *bondservant* [4] Some manuscripts *not even in Israel*

Jesus Calls the First Disciples

When Jesus was about 30 years old, He went to live in Capernaum, by the Sea of Galilee. There He began his ministry, preaching: "Repent, for the kingdom of heaven is at hand."

One day, while Jesus was walking by the Sea of Galilee, He saw two brothers named Andrew and Peter. They were fishermen and were throwing their fishing net into the water just as Jesus walked nearby them.

Jesus called to Andrew and Peter, saying, "Follow Me, and I will make you fishers of men." Right away, Peter and Andrew left their fishing nets and followed Jesus.

Jesus walked a little farther and saw two more brothers named James and John. They were sitting in a boat with their father, Zebedee, repairing their fishing nets. Jesus called them to follow Him too. Right away, James and John left what they were doing and followed Jesus.

Peter and Andrew, and James and John, were Jesus' first disciples. Jesus chose these men to be His friends and helpers, and to go with Him wherever He went. They would learn from Him and they would help Him with His work while He lived here on earth. Later, when Jesus went to heaven, His disciples continued His work and told everyone about Him.

God wants all people to know that He sent Jesus to earth

to take away our sins. He gives us pastors and teachers and parents who teach us about Jesus. And He gives us the Bible to read and learn about everything God had done for us. Through faith in Jesus, God makes us His children so we, too, can follow Jesus and share His love with others.

SEEK and FIND

WHERE TO FIND THE STORY

Matthew 4:12–22

KEY BIBLE VERSE

"And he said to them, 'Follow me, and I will make you fishers of men.' Immediately they left their nets and followed him." (Matthew 4:19–20)

THREE KEY QUESTIONS

- What did Peter and Andrew do when Jesus called out to them, saying, "Follow Me"?
- What does it mean to be "fishers of men"?
- How can we learn to follow Jesus today?

RELATED BIBLE READINGS

Matthew 10:1–7; Mark 1:16–20; Luke 5:1–11; John 1:35–42

Jesus Calms a Storm

23 And when he got into the boat,
his disciples followed him. 24 And
1331, 1385 behold, there arose a great storm
on the sea, so that the boat was
being swamped by the waves; but he was
asleep. 25 And they went and woke him,
saying, "Save us, Lord; we are perishing."
26 And he said to them, "Why are you
afraid, O you of little faith?" Then he rose
and rebuked the winds and the sea, and
there was a great calm. 27 And the men
marveled, saying, "What sort of man is
this, that even winds and sea obey him?"

Jesus Heals Two Men with Demons

28 And when he came to the other side,
to the country of the Gadarenes,[1] two
demon-possessed[2] men met him, coming out of the tombs, so fierce that no one
could pass that way. 29 And behold, they
cried out, "What have you to do with us,
O Son of God? Have you come here to

[1] Some manuscripts *Gergesenes*; some *Gerasenes* [2] Greek *daimonizomai*; also verse 33; elsewhere rendered *oppressed by demons*

torment us before the time?" 30 Now a
herd of many pigs was feeding at some
distance from them. 31 And the demons
begged him, saying, "If you cast us out,
send us away into the herd of pigs." 32 And
he said to them, "Go." So they came out
and went into the pigs, and behold, the
whole herd rushed down the steep bank
into the sea and drowned in the waters.
33 The herdsmen fled, and going into the
city they told everything, especially what
had happened to the demon-possessed
men. 34 And behold, all the city came out
to meet Jesus, and when they saw him,
they begged him to leave their region.

Jesus Heals a Paralytic

9 And getting into a boat he
crossed over and came to his
1377 own city. 2 And behold, some peo-
ple brought to him a paralytic, lying on a
bed. And when Jesus saw their faith, he
said to the paralytic, "Take heart, my son;
your sins are forgiven." 3 And behold, some
of the scribes said to themselves, "This
man is blaspheming." 4 But Jesus, knowing[1]
their thoughts, said, "Why do you think
evil in your hearts? 5 For which is easier, to
say, 'Your sins are forgiven,' or to say, 'Rise
and walk'? 6 But that you may know that the
Son of Man has authority on earth to for-
give sins"—he then said to the paralytic—
"Rise, pick up your bed and go home." 7 And
he rose and went home. 8 When the crowds
saw it, they were afraid, and they glorified
God, who had given such authority to men.

Jesus Calls Matthew

9 As Jesus passed on from there, he
saw a man called Matthew sitting
1381, at the tax booth, and he said to
1511 him, "Follow me." And he rose and
followed him.

10 And as Jesus[2] reclined at table in
the house, behold, many tax collec-
1239, tors and sinners came and were
1473, reclining with Jesus and his disci-
1501 ples. 11 And when the Pharisees saw
this, they said to his disciples, "Why does
your teacher eat with tax collectors and
sinners?" 12 But when he heard it, he said,
"Those who are well have no need of a
physician, but those who are sick. 13 Go
and learn what this means, 'I desire mercy,
and not sacrifice.' For I came not to call the
righteous, but sinners."

A Question About Fasting

14 Then the disciples of John came
to him, saying, "Why do we and the
Pharisees fast,[3] but your disciples do not
fast?" 15 And Jesus said to them, "Can the
wedding guests mourn as long as the
bridegroom is with them? The days will

CHARACTER PROFILE

MATTHEW

Matthew, who was also called Levi, was one of Jesus' 12 disciples. Matthew worked as a tax collector for the Roman government. Tax collectors were disliked by the Jewish people because of the power that Rome had over the Jewish nation and because tax collectors were often unfair. When Jesus called Matthew, he left his work and followed Jesus. Matthew wrote the Gospel of Matthew.

1381

[1] Some manuscripts *perceiving* [2] Greek *he* [3] Some manuscripts add *much,* or *often*

Jesus Teaches How to Be Blessed

After Jesus had chosen His 12 disciples, He began to teach them how He wanted them to live and what He wanted them to be like. One day Jesus took His disciples up a mountain, where He taught them with these words:

"Blessed are the poor in spirit, for theirs is the kingdom of heaven.

"Blessed are those who mourn, for they shall be comforted.

"Blessed are the meek, for they shall inherit the earth.

"Blessed are those who hunger and thirst for righteousness, for they will be satisfied.

"Blessed are the merciful, for they shall receive mercy.

"Blessed are the pure in heart, for they shall see God.

"Blessed are the peacemakers, for they shall be called sons of God.

"Blessed are those who are persecuted for righteousness' sake, for theirs is the kingdom of heaven.

"Blessed are you when others revile you and persecute you and utter all kinds of evil against you falsely on My account. Rejoice and be glad, for your reward is great in heaven, for so they persecuted the prophets who were before you."

People don't usually think it's a good thing to mourn or to be meek or to be persecuted. But Jesus said people were "blessed" for these things. To be "blessed" means to be happy, but it also means much more than this. To be "blessed" means that we have great joy in knowing that we love God, that He loves us, that we are His children, and that we are living the way Jesus wants us to live. Jesus calls us to be His followers—to think differently and to live differently than the rest of the world—and so to know that we are truly "blessed."

SEEK and FIND

WHERE TO FIND THE STORY

Matthew 5:1–12

KEY BIBLE VERSE

"You are the light of the world. . . . Let your light shine before others, so that they may see your good works and give glory to your Father who is in heaven." (Matthew 5:14a, 16)

THREE KEY QUESTIONS

- How many times did Jesus say "Blessed"? Can you remember some of the ways that Jesus said we would be "blessed"?
- What does it mean to be "blessed"?
- What are some of the ways that Christians think and live differently from the way the world thinks and lives?

RELATED BIBLE READINGS

Matthew 5:13–7:29; Luke 6:20–26

come when the bridegroom is taken away from them, and then they will fast. 16 No one puts a piece of unshrunk cloth on an old garment, for the patch tears away from the garment, and a worse tear is made. 17 Neither is new wine put into old wineskins. If it is, the skins burst and the wine is spilled and the skins are destroyed. But new wine is put into fresh wineskins, and so both are preserved."

A Girl Restored to Life and a Woman Healed

18 While he was saying these things
to them, behold, a ruler came in
1389 and knelt before him, saying, "My
daughter has just died, but come and lay your hand on her, and she will live." 19 And Jesus rose and followed him, with his disciples. 20 And behold, a woman who had suffered from a discharge of blood for twelve years came up behind him and touched the fringe of his garment, 21 for she said to herself, "If I only touch his garment, I will be made well." 22 Jesus turned, and seeing her he said, "Take heart, daughter; your faith has made you well." And instantly[1] the woman was made well. 23 And when Jesus came to the ruler's house and saw the flute players and the crowd making a commotion, 24 he said, "Go away, for the girl is not dead but sleeping." And they laughed at him. 25 But when the crowd had been put outside, he went in and took her by the hand, and the girl arose. 26 And the report of this went through all that district.

Jesus Heals Two Blind Men

27 And as Jesus passed on from there, two blind men followed him, crying aloud, "Have mercy on us, Son of David." 28 When he entered the house, the blind men came to him, and Jesus said to them, "Do you believe that I am able to do this?" They said to him, "Yes, Lord." 29 Then he touched their eyes, saying, "According to your faith be it done to you." 30 And their eyes were opened. And Jesus sternly warned them, "See that no one knows about it." 31 But they went away and spread his fame through all that district.

Jesus Heals a Man Unable to Speak

32 As they were going away, behold, a demon-oppressed man who was mute was brought to him. 33 And when the demon had been cast out, the mute man spoke. And the crowds marveled, saying, "Never was anything like this seen in Israel." 34 But the Pharisees said, "He casts out demons by the prince of demons."

The Harvest Is Plentiful, the Laborers Few

35 And Jesus went throughout all
the cities and villages, teaching in
1483 their synagogues and proclaiming
the gospel of the kingdom and healing every disease and every affliction. 36 When he saw the crowds, he had compassion for them, because they were harassed and helpless, like sheep without a shepherd. 37 Then he said to his disciples, "The harvest is plentiful, but the laborers are few; 38 therefore pray earnestly to the Lord of the harvest to send out laborers into his harvest."

The Twelve Apostles

10 And he called to him his
twelve disciples and gave
1313 them authority over unclean spir-
its, to cast them out, and to heal every disease and every affliction. 2 The names of the twelve apostles are these: first, Simon, who is called Peter, and Andrew his brother; James the son of Zebedee, and John his brother; 3 Philip and Bartholomew; Thomas and Matthew the tax collector; James the son of Alphaeus, and Thaddaeus;[2] 4 Simon the Cananaean, and Judas Iscariot, who betrayed him.

Jesus Sends Out the Twelve Apostles

5 These twelve Jesus sent out, instructing them, "Go nowhere among the Gentiles and enter no town of the Samaritans, 6 but

[1] Greek *from that hour* [2] Some manuscripts *Lebbaeus*, or *Lebbaeus called Thaddaeus*

Why We Never Need to Worry

After Jesus taught His disciples about what it means to be blessed, He taught them many other important things—things that are very important for us too.

Jesus taught the disciples that they should make sure their treasures are in heaven and not on earth. He told them they should not give all their time and energy to earning money and getting things, but they should serve God and trust Him to provide what they needed.

Jesus said to them, "Do not be anxious about what you will eat or what you will drink, nor about your body, what you will put on. Look at the birds." They don't grow food and store it up in barns. "Yet your heavenly Father feeds them." Jesus wanted His people to know that they were more special than birds. He wanted them to trust that God would give them food.

Jesus also said they should look at the flowers growing out in the fields. Flowers don't work, and they don't make clothes. But not even King Solomon, in his best royal robes, was dressed as beautifully as the flowers.

Jesus wanted His people to have faith that God loves each one of them very much, and that He will always take care of them. Then they would be free to spend their time and energy seeking God, and enjoying God, and doing His work. Jesus tells us not to worry about food and clothing. "Your heavenly Father knows that you need them all," Jesus said. "But seek first the kingdom of God and His righteousness, and all these things will be added to you."

God cared for us so much that He sent Jesus to be our Savior from sin, death, and the devil. Because He loves us so much, He will surely give us all the smaller things we need, like food and clothing. Jesus calls us into His kingdom through faith in Him. Jesus takes away all our worries, and tells us always to trust in Him.

SEEK and FIND

WHERE TO FIND THE STORY

Matthew 6:19–34

KEY BIBLE VERSE

"But seek first the kingdom of God and his righteousness, and all these things will be added to you." (Matthew 6:33)

THREE KEY QUESTIONS

- Who feeds the birds and makes the flowers look so beautiful?
- What is the most important thing that we can do?
- If we seek God's kingdom first, what does He promise that He will do?

RELATED BIBLE READINGS

Matthew 19:16–30; Luke 12:13–34; 16:1–13, 19–31; 2 Corinthians 9:6–11

go rather to the lost sheep of the house of Israel. **7** And proclaim as you go, saying, 'The kingdom of heaven is at hand.' **8** Heal the sick, raise the dead, cleanse lepers,[1] cast out demons. You received without paying; give without pay. **9** Acquire no gold nor silver nor copper for your belts, **10** no bag for your journey, nor two tunics[2] nor sandals nor a staff, for the laborer deserves his food. **11** And whatever town or village you enter, find out who is worthy in it and stay there until you depart. **12** As you enter the house, greet it. **13** And if the house is worthy, let your peace come upon it, but if it is not worthy, let your peace return to you. **14** And if anyone will not receive you or listen to your words, shake off the dust from your feet when you leave that house or town. **15** Truly, I say to you, it will be more bearable on the day of judgment for the land of Sodom and Gomorrah than for that town.

Persecution Will Come

16 "Behold, I am sending you out as sheep in the midst of wolves, so be wise as serpents and innocent as doves. **17** Beware of men, for they will deliver you over to courts and flog you in their synagogues, **18** and you will be dragged before governors and kings for my sake, to bear witness before them and the Gentiles. **19** When they deliver you over, do not be anxious how you are to speak or what you are to say, for what you are to say will be given to you in that hour. **20** For it is not you who speak, but the Spirit of your Father speaking through you. **21** Brother will deliver brother over to death, and the father his child, and children will rise against parents and have them put to death, **22** and you will be hated by all for my name's sake. But the one who endures to the end will be saved. **23** When they persecute you in one town, flee to the next, for truly, I say to you, you will not have gone through all the towns of Israel before the Son of Man comes.

24 "A disciple is not above his teacher, nor a servant[3] above his master. **25** It is enough for the disciple to be like his teacher, and the servant like his master. If they have called the master of the house Beelzebul, how much more will they malign[4] those of his household.

Have No Fear

26 "So have no fear of them, for nothing is covered that will not be revealed, or hidden that will not be known. **27** What I tell you in the dark, say in the light, and what you hear whispered, proclaim on the housetops. **28** And do not fear those who kill the body but cannot kill the soul. Rather fear him who can destroy both soul and body in hell.[5] **29** Are not two sparrows sold for a penny?[6] And not one of them will fall to the ground apart from your Father. **30** But even the hairs of your head are all numbered. **31** Fear not, therefore; you are of more value than many sparrows. **32** So everyone who acknowledges me before men, I also will acknowledge before my Father who is in heaven, **33** but whoever denies me before men, I also will deny before my Father who is in heaven.

Not Peace, but a Sword

34 "Do not think that I have come to bring peace to the earth. I have not come to bring peace, but a sword. **35** For I have come to set a man against his father, and a daughter against her mother, and a daughter-in-law against her mother-in-law. **36** And a person's enemies will be those of his own household. **37** Whoever loves father or mother more than me is not worthy of me, and whoever loves son or daughter more than me is not worthy of me. **38** And whoever does not take his cross and follow me is not worthy of me. **39** Whoever finds his life will lose it, and whoever loses his life for my sake will find it.

[1] *Leprosy* was a term for several skin diseases; see Leviticus 13 [2] Greek *chiton*, a long garment worn under the cloak next to the skin [3] Greek *bondservant*; also verse 25
[4] Greek lacks *will they malign* [5] Greek *Gehenna* [6] Greek *assarion*, Roman copper coin (Latin *quadrans*) worth about 1/16 of a *denarius* (which was a day's wage for a laborer)

Rewards

40 "Whoever receives you receives me, and whoever receives me receives him who sent me. 41 The one who receives a prophet because he is a prophet will receive a prophet's reward, and the one who receives a righteous person because he is a righteous person will receive a righteous person's reward. 42 And whoever gives one of these little ones even a cup of cold water because he is a disciple, truly, I say to you, he will by no means lose his reward."

Messengers from John the Baptist

11 When Jesus had finished instructing his twelve disciples, he went on from there to teach and preach in their cities.

2 Now when John heard in prison about the deeds of the Christ, he sent word by his disciples 3 and said to him, "Are you the one who is to come, or shall we look for another?" 4 And Jesus answered them, "Go and tell John what you hear and see: 5 the blind receive their sight and the lame walk, lepers[1] are cleansed and the deaf hear, and the dead are raised up, and the poor have good news preached to them. 6 And blessed is the one who is not offended by me."

7 As they went away, Jesus began to speak to the crowds concerning John: "What did you go out into the wilderness to see? A reed shaken by the wind? 8 What then did you go out to see? A man[2] dressed in soft clothing? Behold, those who wear soft clothing are in kings' houses. 9 What then did you go out to see? A prophet?[3] Yes, I tell you, and more than a prophet. 10 This is he of whom it is written,

"'Behold, I send my messenger
before your face,
who will prepare your way
before you.'

1301, 1429

11 Truly, I say to you, among those born of women there has arisen no one greater than John the Baptist. Yet the one who is least in the kingdom of heaven is greater than he. 12 From the days of John the Baptist until now the kingdom of heaven has suffered violence,[4] and the violent take it by force. 13 For all the Prophets and the Law prophesied until John, 14 and if you are willing to accept it, he is Elijah who is to come. 15 He who has ears to hear,[5] let him hear.

16 "But to what shall I compare this generation? It is like children sitting in the marketplaces and calling to their playmates,

17 "'We played the flute for you, and you
did not dance;
we sang a dirge, and you did not
mourn.'

18 For John came neither eating nor drinking, and they say, 'He has a demon.' 19 The Son of Man came eating and drinking, and they say, 'Look at him! A glutton and a drunkard, a friend of tax collectors and sinners!' Yet wisdom is justified by her deeds."[6]

Woe to Unrepentant Cities

20 Then he began to denounce the cities where most of his mighty works had been done, because they did not repent. 21 "Woe to you, Chorazin! Woe to you, Bethsaida! For if the mighty works done in you had been done in Tyre and Sidon, they would have repented long ago in sackcloth and ashes. 22 But I tell you, it will be more bearable on the day of judgment for Tyre and Sidon than for you. 23 And you, Capernaum, will you be exalted to heaven? You will be brought down to Hades. For if the mighty works done in you had been done in Sodom, it would have remained until this day. 24 But I tell you that it will be more tolerable on the day of judgment for the land of Sodom than for you."

[1] *Leprosy* was a term for several skin diseases; see Leviticus 13 [2] Or *Why then did you go out? To see a man . . .* [3] Some manuscripts *Why then did you go out? To see a prophet?* [4] Or *has been coming violently* [5] Some manuscripts omit *to hear* [6] Some manuscripts *children* (compare Luke 7:35)

Come to Me, and I Will Give You Rest

25 At that time Jesus declared, "I thank you, Father, Lord of heaven and earth, that you have hidden these things from the wise and understanding and revealed them to little children; 26 yes, Father, for such was your gracious will.[1] 27 All things have been handed over to me by my Father, and no one knows the Son except the Father, and no one knows the Father except the Son and anyone to whom the Son chooses to reveal him. 28 Come to me, all who labor and are heavy laden, and I will give you rest. 29 Take my yoke upon you, and learn from me, for I am gentle and lowly in heart, and you will find rest for your souls. 30 For my yoke is easy, and my burden is light."

Jesus Is Lord of the Sabbath

12 At that time Jesus went through the grainfields on the Sabbath. His disciples were hungry, and they began to pluck heads of grain and to eat. 2 But when the Pharisees saw it, they said to him, "Look, your disciples are doing what is not lawful to do on the Sabbath." 3 He said to them, "Have you not read what David did when he was hungry, and those who were with him: 4 how he entered the house of God and ate the bread of the Presence, which it was not lawful for him to eat nor for those who were with him, but only for the priests? 5 Or have you not read in the Law how on the Sabbath the priests in the temple profane the Sabbath and are guiltless? 6 I tell you, something greater than the temple is here. 7 And if you had known what this means, 'I desire mercy, and not sacrifice,' you would not have condemned the guiltless. 8 For the Son of Man is lord of the Sabbath."

A Man with a Withered Hand

9 He went on from there and entered their synagogue. 10 And a man was there with a withered hand. And they asked him, "Is it lawful to heal on the Sabbath?"—so that they might accuse him. 11 He said to them, "Which one of you who has a sheep, if it falls into a pit on the Sabbath, will not take hold of it and lift it out? 12 Of how much more value is a man than a sheep! So it is lawful to do good on the Sabbath." 13 Then he said to the man, "Stretch out your hand." And the man stretched it out, and it was restored, healthy like the other. 14 But the Pharisees went out and conspired against him, how to destroy him.

God's Chosen Servant

15 Jesus, aware of this, withdrew from there. And many followed him, and he healed them all 16 and ordered them not to make him known. 17 This was to fulfill what was spoken by the prophet Isaiah:

18 "Behold, my servant whom I have chosen,
my beloved with whom my soul is well pleased.
I will put my Spirit upon him,
and he will proclaim justice to the Gentiles.
19 He will not quarrel or cry aloud,
nor will anyone hear his voice in the streets;
20 a bruised reed he will not break,
and a smoldering wick he will not quench,
until he brings justice to victory;
21 and in his name the Gentiles will hope."

Blasphemy Against the Holy Spirit

22 Then a demon-oppressed man who was blind and mute was brought to him, and he healed him, so that the man spoke and saw. 23 And all the people were amazed, and said, "Can this be the Son of David?" 24 But when the Pharisees heard it, they said, "It is only by Beelzebul, the prince of demons, that this man casts out demons." 25 Knowing their thoughts, he said to them, "Every kingdom divided

[1] *Or for so it pleased you well*

against itself is laid waste, and no city or
house divided against itself will stand.
26 And if Satan casts out Satan, he is
divided against himself. How then will
his kingdom stand? 27 And if I cast out
demons by Beelzebul, by whom do your
sons cast them out? Therefore they will
be your judges. 28 But if it is by the Spirit of
God that I cast out demons, then the king-
dom of God has come upon you. 29 Or how
can someone enter a strong man's house
and plunder his goods, unless he first
binds the strong man? Then indeed he
may plunder his house. 30 Whoever is not
with me is against me, and whoever does
not gather with me scatters. 31 Therefore
I tell you, every sin and blasphemy will
be forgiven people, but the blasphemy
against the Spirit will not be forgiven.
32 And whoever speaks a word against the
Son of Man will be forgiven, but whoever
speaks against the Holy Spirit will not be
forgiven, either in this age or in the age
to come.

A Tree Is Known by Its Fruit

33 "Either make the tree good and its
fruit good, or make the tree bad and its
fruit bad, for the tree is known by its fruit.
34 You brood of vipers! How can you speak
good, when you are evil? For out of the
abundance of the heart the mouth speaks.
35 The good person out of his good trea-
sure brings forth good, and the evil person
out of his evil treasure brings forth evil. 36 I
tell you, on the day of judgment people
will give account for every careless word
they speak, 37 for by your words you will
be justified, and by your words you will be
condemned."

The Sign of Jonah

38 Then some of the scribes and
Pharisees answered him, saying,
1239 "Teacher, we wish to see a sign
from you." 39 But he answered them, "An
evil and adulterous generation seeks for a
sign, but no sign will be given to it except
the sign of the prophet Jonah. 40 For just as
Jonah was three days and three nights in
the belly of the great fish, so will the Son
of Man be three days and three nights in
the heart of the earth. 41 The men of
Nineveh will rise up at the judgment with
this generation and condemn it, for they
repented at the preaching of Jonah, and
behold, something greater than Jonah is
here. 42 The queen of the South will
rise up at the judgment with this
535 generation and condemn it, for she
came from the ends of the earth to hear
the wisdom of Solomon, and behold,
something greater than Solomon is here.

Return of an Unclean Spirit

43 "When the unclean spirit has gone
out of a person, it passes through water-
less places seeking rest, but finds none.
44 Then it says, 'I will return to my house
from which I came.' And when it comes,
it finds the house empty, swept, and put
in order. 45 Then it goes and brings with it
seven other spirits more evil than itself,
and they enter and dwell there, and the
last state of that person is worse than
the first. So also will it be with this evil
generation."

Jesus' Mother and Brothers

46 While he was still speaking to the
people, behold, his mother and his broth-
ers stood outside, asking to speak to him.[1]
48 But he replied to the man who told him,
"Who is my mother, and who are my
brothers?" 49 And stretching out his hand
toward his disciples, he said, "Here are my
mother and my brothers! 50 For whoever
does the will of my Father in heaven is my
brother and sister and mother."

The Parable of the Sower

13 That same day Jesus went out of
the house and sat beside the sea.
2 And great crowds gathered about him, so
that he got into a boat and sat down. And
the whole crowd stood on the beach. 3 And

[1] Some manuscripts insert verse 47: *Someone told him, "Your mother and your brothers are standing outside, asking to speak to you"*

he told them many things in parables,
saying: "A sower went out to sow. 4 And
as he sowed, some seeds fell along the
path, and the birds came and devoured
them. 5 Other seeds fell on rocky ground,
where they did not have much soil, and
immediately they sprang up, since they
had no depth of soil, 6 but when the sun
rose they were scorched. And since they
had no root, they withered away. 7 Other
seeds fell among thorns, and the thorns
grew up and choked them. 8 Other seeds
fell on good soil and produced grain, some
a hundredfold, some sixty, some thirty.
9 He who has ears,[1] let him hear."

The Purpose of the Parables

10 Then the disciples came and said
to him, "Why do you speak to them in
parables?" 11 And he answered them, "To
you it has been given to know the secrets
of the kingdom of heaven, but to them it
has not been given. 12 For to the one who
has, more will be given, and he will have
an abundance, but from the one who has
not, even what he has will be taken away.
13 This is why I speak to them in parables,
because seeing they do not see, and hear-
ing they do not hear, nor do they under-
stand. 14 Indeed, in their case the proph-
ecy of Isaiah is fulfilled that says:

"'You will indeed hear but never
understand,
and you will indeed see but never
perceive.
15 For this people's heart has grown
dull,
and with their ears they can
barely hear,
and their eyes they have closed,
lest they should see with their eyes
and hear with their ears
and understand with their heart
and turn, and I would heal them.'

16 But blessed are your eyes, for they see,
and your ears, for they hear. 17 For truly, I
say to you, many prophets and righteous
people longed to see what you see, and did
not see it, and to hear what you hear, and
did not hear it.

The Parable of the Sower Explained

18 "Hear then the parable of the sower:
19 When anyone hears the word of the
kingdom and does not understand it, the
evil one comes and snatches away what
has been sown in his heart. This is what
was sown along the path. 20 As for what was
sown on rocky ground, this is the one who
hears the word and immediately receives
it with joy, 21 yet he has no root in himself,
but endures for a while, and when tribula-
tion or persecution arises on account of the
word, immediately he falls away.[2] 22 As for
what was sown among thorns, this is the
one who hears the word, but the cares of
the world and the deceitfulness of riches
choke the word, and it proves unfruitful.
23 As for what was sown on good soil, this
is the one who hears the word and under-
stands it. He indeed bears fruit and yields,
in one case a hundredfold, in another sixty,
and in another thirty."

The Parable of the Weeds

24 He put another parable before them,
saying, "The kingdom of heaven may be
compared to a man who sowed good seed
in his field, 25 but while his men were
sleeping, his enemy came and sowed
weeds[3] among the wheat and went away.
26 So when the plants came up and bore
grain, then the weeds appeared also.
27 And the servants[4] of the master of the
house came and said to him, 'Master,
did you not sow good seed in your field?
How then does it have weeds?' 28 He said
to them, 'An enemy has done this.' So the
servants said to him, 'Then do you want
us to go and gather them?' 29 But he said,
'No, lest in gathering the weeds you root
up the wheat along with them. 30 Let both
grow together until the harvest, and at
harvest time I will tell the reapers, Gather

[1] Some manuscripts add here and in verse 43 *to hear* [2] Or *stumbles* [3] Probably *darnel*, a wheat-like weed [4] Greek *bondservants*; also verse 28

the weeds first and bind them in bundles to be burned, but gather the wheat into my barn.'"

The Mustard Seed and the Leaven

31 He put another parable before them, saying, "The kingdom of heaven is like a grain of mustard seed that a man took and sowed in his field. **32** It is the smallest of all seeds, but when it has grown it is larger than all the garden plants and becomes a tree, so that the birds of the air come and make nests in its branches."

33 He told them another parable. "The kingdom of heaven is like leaven that a woman took and hid in three measures of flour, till it was all leavened."

Prophecy and Parables

34 All these things Jesus said to the crowds in parables; indeed, he said nothing to them without a parable. **35** This was to fulfill what was spoken by the prophet:[1]

"I will open my mouth in parables;
 I will utter what has been hidden
  since the foundation of the
  world."

The Parable of the Weeds Explained

36 Then he left the crowds and went into the house. And his disciples came to him, saying, "Explain to us the parable of the weeds of the field." **37** He answered, "The one who sows the good seed is the Son of Man. **38** The field is the world, and the good seed is the sons of the kingdom. The weeds are the sons of the evil one, **39** and the enemy who sowed them is the devil. The harvest is the close of the age, and the reapers are angels. **40** Just as the weeds are gathered and burned with fire, so will it be at the close of the age. **41** The Son of Man will send his angels, and they will gather out of his kingdom all causes of sin and all law-breakers, **42** and throw them into the fiery furnace. In that place there will be weeping and gnashing of teeth. **43** Then the righteous will shine like the sun in the kingdom of their Father. He who has ears, let him hear.

The Parable of the Hidden Treasure

44 "The kingdom of heaven is like treasure hidden in a field, which a man found and covered up. Then in his joy he goes and sells all that he has and buys that field.

The Parable of the Pearl of Great Value

45 "Again, the kingdom of heaven is like a merchant in search of fine pearls, **46** who, on finding one pearl of great value, went and sold all that he had and bought it.

The Parable of the Net

47 "Again, the kingdom of heaven is like a net that was thrown into the sea and gathered fish of every kind. **48** When it was full, men drew it ashore and sat down and sorted the good into containers but threw away the bad. **49** So it will be at the close of the age. The angels will come out and separate the evil from the righteous **50** and throw them into the fiery furnace. In that place there will be weeping and gnashing of teeth.

New and Old Treasures

51 "Have you understood all these things?" They said to him, "Yes." **52** And he said to them, "Therefore every scribe who has been trained for the kingdom of heaven is like a master of a house, who brings out of his treasure what is new and what is old."

Jesus Rejected at Nazareth

53 And when Jesus had finished these parables, he went away from there, **54** and coming to his hometown he taught them in their synagogue, so that 1459 they were astonished, and said, "Where did this man get this wisdom and these mighty works? **55** Is not this the carpenter's son? Is not his mother called Mary? And are not his brothers James and

[1] Some manuscripts *Isaiah the prophet*

Joseph and Simon and Judas? 56And are not all his sisters with us? Where then did this man get all these things?" 57And they took offense at him. But Jesus said to them, "A prophet is not without honor except in his hometown and in his own household." 58And he did not do many mighty works there, because of their unbelief.

The Death of John the Baptist

14 At that time Herod the tetrarch heard about the fame of Jesus, 2and he said to his servants, "This is John the Baptist. He has been raised from the dead; that is why these miraculous powers are at work in him." 3For Herod had seized John and bound him and put him in prison for the sake of Herodias, his brother Philip's wife,[1] 4because John had been saying to him, "It is not lawful for you to have her." 5And though he wanted to put him to death, he feared the people, because they held him to be a prophet. 6But when Herod's birthday came, the daughter of Herodias danced before the company and pleased Herod, 7so that he promised with an oath to give her whatever she might ask. 8Prompted by her mother, she said, "Give me the head of John the Baptist here on a platter." 9And the king was sorry, but because of his oaths and his guests he commanded it to be given. 10He sent and had John beheaded in the prison, 11and his head was brought on a platter and given to the girl, and she brought it to her mother. 12And his disciples came and took the body and buried it, and they went and told Jesus.

[1] Some manuscripts *his brother's wife*

Galilean Fishing Boat

Jesus and His disciples probably used a boat like this one that fishermen typically used. It could have held 15 men and was 26.5 feet long, 7.5 feet wide, and 4.5 feet high (8.1 x 2.3 x 1.4 m).

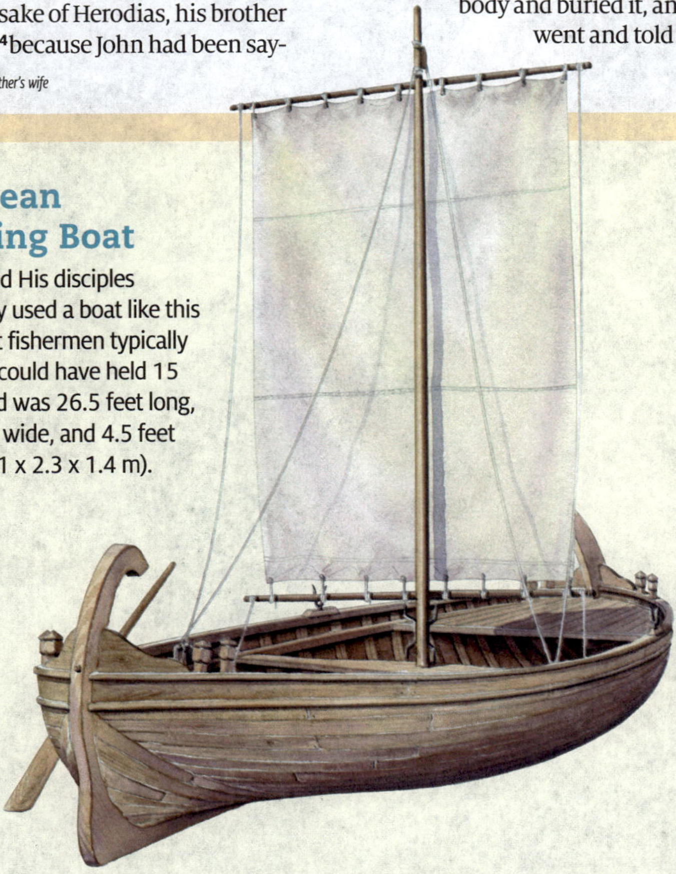

Jesus Walks on Water

Many people had come out from the towns into the countryside to hear Jesus teach. Jesus had compassion on the crowds, and He healed the sick and taught them all day long.

When evening came, Jesus saw that the people were hungry and had nothing to eat. Jesus took five pieces of bread and two small fish, and he made enough food to feed the huge crowd of 5,000 men plus women and children—probably more than 10,000 people altogether!

When everyone had eaten, Jesus told His disciples to get into a boat and go to the other side of the big lake, called the Sea of Galilee. The disciples started out in the boat, but Jesus was not yet ready to go. He stayed behind to send the crowds away. Then He went up on a mountain where He could be alone and pray.

By then it was dark, and the disciples were in the boat, a long way from shore. The wind was blowing hard and big waves were crashing against the boat. Just before morning, Jesus started walking—on the water!—toward the disciples in the boat. When the disciples saw Jesus walking on the water, they were terrified. They thought Jesus was a ghost, and they cried out in fear.

Immediately, Jesus spoke to them, saying, "Take heart; it is I. Do not be afraid."

Peter answered, "Lord, if it is You, command me to come to You on the water."

Jesus replied, "Come."

So Peter got out of the boat and walked on the water toward Jesus. But when Peter saw how the strong wind was blowing the waves, he was afraid and started to sink. He called out, "Lord, save me."

Immediately, Jesus reached out and took hold of Peter's hand, lifting Peter up so he wouldn't drown. "O you of little faith," Jesus asked, "why did you doubt?"

As soon as Jesus and Peter got into the boat, the wind stopped. The disciples in the boat worshiped Jesus, saying, "Truly You are the Son of God."

Jesus was gracious to Peter and the disciples. Jesus is gracious to us. Just as Jesus reached out to Peter and the disciples in their fear and disbelief, so He reaches out to us. Jesus calls us to Himself through His Word and His Church. He gives us faith to believe in Him. And He wants us to keep our eyes fixed on Him. Jesus saved Peter from drowning in the lake, and He saves us from sin and death.

SEEK and FIND

WHERE TO FIND THE STORY

Matthew 14:22–33

KEY BIBLE VERSE

"And those in the boat worshiped him, saying, 'Truly you are the Son of God.'" (Matthew 14:33)

THREE KEY QUESTIONS

- Why were the disciples afraid when they saw Jesus walking on the water?
- When Peter was walking to Jesus on the water, why did he suddenly start to sink?
- What did Jesus do when Peter started to sink? How does Jesus reach out to us to save us?

RELATED BIBLE READINGS

Matthew 8:23–27; Mark 6:45–51; Luke 8:22–25; John 6:16–21

Jesus Feeds the Five Thousand

13 Now when Jesus heard this, he
withdrew from there in a boat to a
1559 desolate place by himself. But
when the crowds heard it, they followed
him on foot from the towns. 14 When he
went ashore he saw a great crowd, and he
had compassion on them and healed their
sick. 15 Now when it was evening, the dis-
ciples came to him and said, "This is a
desolate place, and the day is now over;
send the crowds away to go into the vil-
lages and buy food for themselves." 16 But
Jesus said, "They need not go away; you
give them something to eat." 17 They said
to him, "We have only five loaves here and
two fish." 18 And he said, "Bring them here
to me." 19 Then he ordered the crowds to
sit down on the grass, and taking the five
loaves and the two fish, he looked up to
heaven and said a blessing. Then he broke
the loaves and gave them to the disciples,
and the disciples gave them to the crowds.
20 And they all ate and were satisfied. And
they took up twelve baskets full of the bro-
ken pieces left over. 21 And those who ate
were about five thousand men, besides
women and children.

Jesus Walks on the Water

22 Immediately he made the disci-
ples get into the boat and go before
1331 him to the other side, while he dis-
missed the crowds. 23 And after he
had dismissed the crowds, he went
1385 up on the mountain by himself to
pray. When evening came, he was there
alone, 24 but the boat by this time was a
long way[1] from the land,[2] beaten
by the waves, for the wind was
1601 against them. 25 And in the fourth
watch of the night he came to them, walk-
ing on the sea. 26 But when the disciples
saw him walking on the sea, they were
terrified, and said, "It is a ghost!" and they
cried out in fear. 27 But immediately Jesus
spoke to them, saying, "Take heart; it is I.
Do not be afraid."

28 And Peter answered him, "Lord, if it is
you, command me to come to you on the
water." 29 He said, "Come." So Peter got out
of the boat and walked on the water and
came to Jesus. 30 But when he saw the
wind,[3] he was afraid, and beginning to
sink he cried out, "Lord, save me." 31 Jesus
immediately reached out his hand and
took hold of him, saying to him, "O you of

[1] Greek *many stadia*, a *stadion* was about 607 feet or 185 meters [2] Some manuscripts *was out on the sea* [3] Some manuscripts *strong wind*

little faith, why did you doubt?" 32 And when they got into the boat, the wind ceased. 33 And those in the boat worshiped him, saying, "Truly you are the Son of God."

1331

Jesus Heals the Sick in Gennesaret

34 And when they had crossed over, they came to land at Gennesaret. 35 And when the men of that place recognized him, they sent around to all that region and brought to him all who were sick 36 and implored him that they might only touch the fringe of his garment. And as many as touched it were made well.

Traditions and Commandments

15 Then Pharisees and scribes came to Jesus from Jerusalem and said, 2 "Why do your disciples break the tradition of the elders? For they do not wash their hands when they eat." 3 He answered them, "And why do you break the commandment of God for the sake of your tradition? 4 For God commanded, 'Honor your father and your mother,' and, 'Whoever reviles father or mother must surely die.' 5 But you say, 'If anyone tells his father or his mother, "What you would have gained from me is given to God,"[1] 6 he need not honor his father.' So for the sake of your tradition you have made void the word[2] of God. 7 You hypocrites! Well did Isaiah prophesy of you, when he said:

8 "'This people honors me with their
lips,
but their heart is far from me;
9 in vain do they worship me,
teaching as doctrines the
commandments of men.'"

What Defiles a Person

10 And he called the people to him and said to them, "Hear and understand: 11 it is not what goes into the mouth that defiles a person, but what comes out of the mouth; this defiles a person." 12 Then the disciples came and said to him, "Do you know that the Pharisees were offended when they heard this saying?" 13 He answered, "Every plant that my heavenly Father has not planted will be rooted up. 14 Let them alone; they are blind guides.[3] And if the blind lead the blind, both will fall into a pit." 15 But Peter said to him, "Explain the parable to us." 16 And he said, "Are you also still without understanding? 17 Do you not see that whatever goes into the mouth passes into the stomach and is expelled?[4] 18 But what comes out of the mouth proceeds from the heart, and this defiles a person. 19 For out of the heart come evil thoughts, murder, adultery, sexual immorality, theft, false witness, slander. 20 These are what defile a person. But to eat with unwashed hands does not defile anyone."

The Faith of a Canaanite Woman

21 And Jesus went away from there and withdrew to the district of Tyre and Sidon. 22 And behold, a Canaanite woman from that region came out and was crying, "Have mercy on me, O Lord, Son of David; my daughter is severely oppressed by a demon." 23 But he did not answer her a word. And his disciples came and begged him, saying, "Send her away, for she is crying out after us." 24 He answered, "I was sent only to the lost sheep of the house of Israel." 25 But she came and knelt before him, saying, "Lord, help me." 26 And he answered, "It is not right to take the children's bread and throw it to the dogs." 27 She said, "Yes, Lord, yet even the dogs eat the crumbs that fall from their masters' table." 28 Then Jesus answered her, "O woman, great is your faith! Be it done for you as you desire." And her daughter was healed instantly.[5]

Jesus Heals Many

29 Jesus went on from there and walked beside the Sea of Galilee. And he went up on the mountain and sat down there.

[1] Or *is an offering* [2] Some manuscripts *law* [3] Some manuscripts add *of the blind* [4] Greek *is expelled into the latrine* [5] Greek *from that hour*

30 And great crowds came to him, bring-
ing with them the lame, the blind, the
crippled, the mute, and many others, and
they put them at his feet, and he healed
them, 31 so that the crowd wondered,
when they saw the mute speaking, the
crippled healthy, the lame walking, and
the blind seeing. And they glorified the
God of Israel.

Jesus Feeds the Four Thousand

32 Then Jesus called his disciples to
him and said, "I have compassion on the
crowd because they have been with me
now three days and have nothing to eat.
And I am unwilling to send them away
hungry, lest they faint on the way." 33 And
the disciples said to him, "Where are we to
get enough bread in such a desolate place
to feed so great a crowd?" 34 And Jesus said
to them, "How many loaves do you have?"
They said, "Seven, and a few small fish."
35 And directing the crowd to sit down on
the ground, 36 he took the seven loaves
and the fish, and having given thanks he
broke them and gave them to the disci-
ples, and the disciples gave them to the
crowds. 37 And they all ate and were satis-
fied. And they took up seven baskets full
of the broken pieces left over. 38 Those
who ate were four thousand men, besides
women and children. 39 And after sending
away the crowds, he got into the boat and
went to the region of Magadan.

The Pharisees and Sadducees Demand Signs

16 And the Pharisees and Sadducees
came, and to test him they asked
him to show them a sign from heaven. 2 He
answered them,[1] "When it is evening, you
say, 'It will be fair weather, for the sky is
red.' 3 And in the morning, 'It will be stormy
today, for the sky is red and threatening.'
You know how to interpret the appearance
of the sky, but you cannot interpret the
signs of the times. 4 An evil and adulterous
generation seeks for a sign, but no sign will
be given to it except the sign of Jonah." So
he left them and departed.

The Leaven of the Pharisees and Sadducees

5 When the disciples reached the other
side, they had forgotten to bring any
bread. 6 Jesus said to them, "Watch and
beware of the leaven of the Pharisees and
Sadducees." 7 And they began discussing it
among themselves, saying, "We brought
no bread." 8 But Jesus, aware of this, said,
"O you of little faith, why are you discuss-
ing among yourselves the fact that you
have no bread? 9 Do you not yet perceive?
Do you not remember the five loaves for
the five thousand, and how many baskets
you gathered? 10 Or the seven loaves for
the four thousand, and how many bas-
kets you gathered? 11 How is it that you
fail to understand that I did not speak
about bread? Beware of the leaven of the
Pharisees and Sadducees." 12 Then they
understood that he did not tell them to
beware of the leaven of bread, but of the
teaching of the Pharisees and Sadducees.

Peter Confesses Jesus as the Christ

13 Now when Jesus came into the dis-
trict of Caesarea Philippi, he asked his
disciples, "Who do people say that the
Son of Man is?" 14 And they said, "Some
say John the Baptist, others say Elijah, and
others Jeremiah or one of the prophets."
15 He said to them, "But who do you say
that I am?" 16 Simon Peter replied, "You
are the Christ, the Son of the living God."
17 And Jesus answered him, "Blessed are
you, Simon Bar-Jonah! For flesh and blood
has not revealed this to you, but my Father
who is in heaven. 18 And I tell you, you are
Peter, and on this rock[2] I will build my
church, and the gates of hell[3] shall not
prevail against it. 19 I will give you the
keys of the kingdom of heaven, and what-
ever you bind on earth shall be bound in
heaven, and whatever you loose on earth
shall be loosed[4] in heaven." 20 Then he

[1] Some manuscripts omit the following words to the end of verse 3 [2] The Greek words for *Peter* and *rock* sound similar [3] Greek *the gates of Hades* [4] Or *shall have been bound . . . shall have been loosed*

strictly charged the disciples to tell no one that he was the Christ.

Jesus Foretells His Death and Resurrection

21 From that time Jesus began to
show his disciples that he must
1365 go to Jerusalem and suffer many
things from the elders and chief priests and scribes, and be killed, and on the third day be raised. 22 And Peter took him aside and began to rebuke him, saying, "Far be it from you, Lord![1] This shall never happen to you." 23 But he turned and said to Peter, "Get behind me, Satan! You are a hindrance[2] to me. For you are not setting your mind on the things of God, but on the things of man."

Take Up Your Cross and Follow Jesus

24 Then Jesus told his disciples, "If anyone would come after me, let him deny himself and take up his cross and follow me. 25 For whoever would save his life[3] will lose it, but whoever loses his life for my sake will find it. 26 For what will it profit a man if he gains the whole world and forfeits his soul? Or what shall a man give in return for his soul? 27 For the Son of Man is going to come with his angels in the glory of his Father, and then he will repay each person according to what he has done. 28 Truly, I say to you, there are some standing here who will not taste death until they see the Son of Man coming in his kingdom."

The Transfiguration

17 And after six days Jesus took
with him Peter and James,
1339 and John his brother, and led them
up a high mountain by themselves.
2 And he was transfigured before
1397 them, and his face shone like the
sun, and his clothes became white as light. 3 And behold, there appeared to them Moses and Elijah, talking with him. 4 And Peter said to Jesus, "Lord, it is good that we are here. If you wish, I will make three tents here, one for you and one for Moses and one for Elijah." 5 He was still speaking when, behold, a bright cloud overshadowed them, and a voice from the cloud said, "This is my beloved Son,[4] with whom I am well pleased; listen to him." 6 When the disciples heard this, they fell on their faces and were terrified. 7 But Jesus came and touched them, saying, "Rise, and have no fear." 8 And when they lifted up their eyes, they saw no one but Jesus only.

9 And as they were coming down the mountain, Jesus commanded them, "Tell no one the vision, until the Son of Man is
raised from the dead." 10 And the
disciples asked him, "Then why
1301 do the scribes say that first Elijah
must come?" 11 He answered, "Elijah does come, and he will restore all things. 12 But I tell you that Elijah has already come, and they did not recognize him, but did to him whatever they pleased. So also the Son of Man will certainly suffer at their hands." 13 Then the disciples understood that he was speaking to them of John the Baptist.

Jesus Heals a Boy with a Demon

14 And when they came to the crowd, a man came up to him and, kneeling before him, 15 said, "Lord, have mercy on my son, for he is an epileptic and he suffers terribly. For often he falls into the fire, and often into the water. 16 And I brought him to your disciples, and they could not heal him." 17 And Jesus answered, "O faithless and twisted generation, how long am I to be with you? How long am I to bear with you? Bring him here to me." 18 And Jesus rebuked the demon,[5] and it[6] came out of him, and the boy was healed instantly.[7] 19 Then the disciples came to Jesus privately and said, "Why could we not cast it out?" 20 He said to them, "Because of your little faith. For truly, I say to you, if you have faith like a grain of mustard seed,

[1] Or "[May God be] *merciful to you, Lord!*" [2] Greek *stumbling block* [3] The same Greek word can mean either *soul* or *life*, depending on the context; twice in this verse and twice in verse 26 [4] Or *my Son, my* (or *the*) *Beloved* [5] Greek *it* [6] Greek *the demon* [7] Greek *from that hour*

you will say to this mountain, 'Move from
here to there,' and it will move, and noth-
ing will be impossible for you."[1]

Jesus Again Foretells Death, Resurrection

22 As they were gathering[2] in Galilee,
Jesus said to them, "The Son of Man is
about to be delivered into the hands of
men, 23 and they will kill him, and he will
be raised on the third day." And they were
greatly distressed.

The Temple Tax

24 When they came to Capernaum, the
collectors of the two-drachma tax went up
to Peter and said, "Does your teacher not
pay the tax?" 25 He said, "Yes." And when
he came into the house, Jesus spoke to
him first, saying, "What do you think,
Simon? From whom do kings of the earth
take toll or tax? From their sons or from
others?" 26 And when he said, "From oth-
ers," Jesus said to him, "Then the sons
are free. 27 However, not to give offense
to them, go to the sea and cast a hook
and take the first fish that comes up, and
when you open its mouth you will find a
shekel.[3] Take that and give it to them for
me and for yourself."

Who Is the Greatest?

18 At that time the disciples
came to Jesus, saying, "Who
1403 is the greatest in the kingdom of
heaven?" 2 And calling to him a child, he
put him in the midst of them 3 and said,
"Truly, I say to you, unless you turn and
become like children, you will never enter
the kingdom of heaven. 4 Whoever hum-
bles himself like this child is the greatest
in the kingdom of heaven.

5 "Whoever receives one such child in
my name receives me, 6 but whoever causes
one of these little ones who believe in me
to sin,[4] it would be better for him to have a
great millstone fastened around his neck
and to be drowned in the depth of the sea.

Temptations to Sin

7 "Woe to the world for temptations to
sin![5] For it is necessary that temptations
come, but woe to the one by whom the
temptation comes! 8 And if your hand or
your foot causes you to sin, cut it off and
throw it away. It is better for you to enter
life crippled or lame than with two hands
or two feet to be thrown into the eternal
fire. 9 And if your eye causes you to sin,
tear it out and throw it away. It is better for
you to enter life with one eye than with
two eyes to be thrown into the hell[6] of fire.

The Parable of the Lost Sheep

10 "See that you do not despise one of
these little ones. For I tell you that in
heaven their angels always see the face of
my Father who is in heaven.[7] 12 What do
you think? If a man has a hundred
sheep, and one of them has gone
1501 astray, does he not leave the ninety-
nine on the mountains and go in search of
the one that went astray? 13 And if he finds
it, truly, I say to you, he rejoices over it
more than over the ninety-nine that never
went astray. 14 So it is not the will of my[8]
Father who is in heaven that one of these
little ones should perish.

If Your Brother Sins Against You

15 "If your brother sins against you, go
and tell him his fault, between you and
him alone. If he listens to you, you have
gained your brother. 16 But if he does not
listen, take one or two others along with
you, that every charge may be established
by the evidence of two or three witnesses.
17 If he refuses to listen to them, tell it to
the church. And if he refuses to listen
even to the church, let him be to you as a
Gentile and a tax collector. 18 Truly, I say
to you, whatever you bind on earth shall
be bound in heaven, and whatever you
loose on earth shall be loosed[9] in heaven.
19 Again I say to you, if two of you agree

[1] Some manuscripts insert verse 21: *But this kind never comes out except by prayer and fasting* [2] Some manuscripts *remained* [3] Greek *stater*, a silver coin worth four drachmas or approximately one shekel [4] Greek *causes . . . to stumble*; also verses 8, 9 [5] Greek *stumbling blocks* [6] Greek *Gehenna* [7] Some manuscripts add verse 11: *For the Son of Man came to save the lost* [8] Some manuscripts *your* [9] Or *shall have been bound . . . shall have been loosed*

The Transfiguration

One day Jesus took three of His disciples—Peter, James, and John—up on a high mountain. When they got to the top of the mountain, something happened that amazed the disciples.

All of a sudden, Jesus was transfigured right in front of His disciples. He suddenly changed greatly in the way He looked. His face became as bright as the sun, and His clothes became as white as light.

Then something else happened that also amazed the disciples. Moses and Elijah suddenly appeared and stood by Jesus. Moses and Elijah were great prophets who had lived centuries before, but now they didn't live on earth any more. God had sent them from heaven at this very moment to talk with Jesus on the mountain.

The disciples knew who Moses and Elijah were, and they were excited to see them. Peter said, "Lord, it is good that we are here. If You wish, I will make three tents here, one for You and one for Moses and one for Elijah."

While Peter was still talking, a bright cloud came and overshadowed everyone. The disciples heard a voice from the cloud say, "This is My beloved Son, with whom I am well pleased; listen to Him."

When the disciples heard God's voice, they were so afraid

that they fell with their faces to the ground. Jesus came and touched them and told them not to be afraid. When the disciples looked up, they saw only Jesus—and Jesus looked once again like He usually did.

As they came down the mountain, Jesus told Peter, James, and John not to tell anyone what they had seen until He had risen from the dead. The disciples obeyed the Lord—they didn't tell anyone what they had seen. But later, after Jesus rose from the grave, they told many people that they had seen Jesus' glory there on the mountain. They knew He was the Son of God and the Savior.

SEEK and FIND

WHERE TO FIND THE STORY

Matthew 17:1–9

KEY BIBLE VERSE

"And the Word became flesh and dwelt among us, and we have seen his glory, glory as of the only Son from the Father, full of grace and truth." (John 1:14)

THREE KEY QUESTIONS

- What are some of the amazing things that happened on the mountain when Jesus was transfigured?
- Whose voice came from heaven, and what did He say?
- What did the disciples do when they heard the voice from heaven? And what did Jesus do so they wouldn't be afraid?

RELATED BIBLE READINGS

Mark 9:2–10; Luke 9:28–36; 2 Peter 1:16–18

on earth about anything they ask, it will be done for them by my Father in heaven. 20 For where two or three are gathered in my name, there am I among them."

The Parable of the Unforgiving Servant

21 Then Peter came up and said to
him, "Lord, how often will my
1783 brother sin against me, and I for-
give him? As many as seven times?"
22 Jesus said to him, "I do not say to you seven times, but seventy times seven.[1]

23 "Therefore the kingdom of heaven may be compared to a king who wished to settle accounts with his servants.[2] 24 When he began to settle, one was brought to him who owed him ten thousand talents.[3] 25 And since he could not pay, his master ordered him to be sold, with his wife and children and all that he had, and payment to be made. 26 So the servant[4] fell on his knees, imploring him, 'Have patience with me, and I will pay you everything.' 27 And out of pity for him, the master of that servant released him and forgave him the debt. 28 But when that same servant went out, he found one of his fellow servants who owed him a hundred denarii,[5] and seizing him, he began to choke him, saying, 'Pay what you owe.' 29 So his fellow servant fell down and pleaded with him, 'Have patience with me, and I will pay you.' 30 He refused and went and put him in prison until he should pay the debt. 31 When his fellow servants saw what had taken place, they were greatly distressed, and they went and reported to their master all that had taken place. 32 Then his master summoned him and said to him, 'You wicked servant! I forgave you all that debt because you pleaded with me. 33 And should not you have had mercy on your fellow servant, as I had mercy on you?' 34 And in anger his master delivered him to the jailers,[6] until he should pay all his debt. 35 So also my heavenly Father will do to every one of you, if you do not forgive your brother from your heart."

Teaching About Divorce

19 Now when Jesus had finished these sayings, he went away from Galilee and entered the region of Judea beyond the Jordan. 2 And large crowds followed him, and he healed them there.

3 And Pharisees came up to him and
tested him by asking, "Is it lawful to divorce
one's wife for any cause?" 4 He answered,
"Have you not read that he who cre-
ated them from the beginning
9 made them male and female, 5 and
said, 'Therefore a man shall leave his father and his mother and hold fast to his wife, and the two shall become one flesh'? 6 So they are no longer two but one flesh. What therefore God has joined together, let not man separate." 7 They said to him, "Why then did Moses command one to give a certificate of divorce and to send her away?" 8 He said to them, "Because of your hardness of heart Moses allowed you to divorce your wives, but from the beginning it was not so. 9 And I say to you: whoever divorces his wife, except for sexual immorality, and marries another, commits adultery."[7]

10 The disciples said to him, "If such is the case of a man with his wife, it is better not to marry." 11 But he said to them, "Not everyone can receive this saying, but only those to whom it is given. 12 For there are eunuchs who have been so from birth, and there are eunuchs who have been made eunuchs by men, and there are eunuchs who have made themselves eunuchs for the sake of the kingdom of heaven. Let the one who is able to receive this receive it."

Let the Children Come to Me

13 Then children were brought to
him that he might lay his hands
1403 on them and pray. The disciples
rebuked the people, 14 but Jesus said, "Let

[1] Or *seventy-seven times* [2] Greek *bondservants;* also verses 28, 31 [3] A *talent* was a monetary unit worth about twenty years' wages for a laborer [4] Greek *bondservant;* also verses 27, 28, 29, 32, 33 [5] A *denarius* was a day's wage for a laborer [6] Greek *torturers* [7] Some manuscripts add *and whoever marries a divorced woman commits adultery;* other manuscripts *except for sexual immorality, makes her commit adultery, and whoever marries a divorced woman commits adultery*

the little children come to me and do not hinder them, for to such belongs the kingdom of heaven." 15 And he laid his hands on them and went away.

The Rich Young Man

175, 1321

16 And behold, a man came up to him, saying, "Teacher, what good deed must I do to have eternal life?" 17 And he said to him, "Why do you ask me about what is good? There is only one who is good. If you would enter life, keep the commandments." 18 He said to him, "Which ones?" And Jesus said, "You shall not murder, You shall not commit adultery, You shall not steal, You shall not bear false witness, 19 Honor your father and mother, and, You shall love your neighbor as yourself." 20 The young man said to him, "All these I have kept. What do I still lack?" 21 Jesus said to him, "If you would be perfect, go, sell what you possess and give to the poor, and you will have treasure in heaven; and come, follow me." 22 When the young man heard this he went away sorrowful, for he had great possessions.

23 And Jesus said to his disciples, "Truly, I say to you, only with difficulty will a rich person enter the kingdom of heaven. 24 Again I tell you, it is easier for a camel to go through the eye of a needle than for a rich person to enter the kingdom of God." 25 When the disciples heard this, they were greatly astonished, saying, "Who then can be saved?" 26 But Jesus looked at them and said, "With man this is impossible, but with God all things are possible." 27 Then Peter said in reply, "See, we have left everything and followed you. What then will we have?" 28 Jesus said to them, "Truly, I say to you, in the new world,[1] when the Son of Man will sit on his glorious throne, you who have followed me will also sit on twelve thrones, judging the twelve tribes of Israel. 29 And everyone who has left houses or brothers or sisters or father or mother or children or lands, for my name's sake, will receive a hundredfold[2] and will inherit eternal life. 30 But many who are first will be last, and the last first.

Laborers in the Vineyard

20 "For the kingdom of heaven is like a master of a house who went out early in the morning to hire laborers for his vineyard. 2 After agreeing with the laborers for a denarius[3] a day, he sent them into his vineyard. 3 And going out about the third hour he saw others standing idle in the marketplace, 4 and to them he said, 'You go into the vineyard too, and whatever is right I will give you.' 5 So they went. Going out again about the sixth hour and the ninth hour, he did the same. 6 And about the eleventh hour he went out and found others standing. And he said to them, 'Why do you stand here idle all day?' 7 They said to him, 'Because no one has hired us.' He said to them, 'You go into the vineyard too.' 8 And when evening came, the owner of the vineyard said to his foreman, 'Call the laborers and pay them their wages, beginning with the last, up to the first.' 9 And when those hired about the eleventh hour came, each of them received a denarius. 10 Now when those hired first came, they thought they would receive more, but each of them also received a denarius. 11 And on receiving it they grumbled at the master of the house, 12 saying, 'These last worked only one hour, and you have made them equal to us who have borne the burden of the day and the scorching heat.' 13 But he replied to one of them, 'Friend, I am doing you no wrong. Did you not agree with me for a denarius? 14 Take what belongs to you and go. I choose to give to this last worker as I give to you. 15 Am I not allowed to do what I choose with what belongs to me? Or do you begrudge my generosity?'[4] 16 So the last will be first, and the first last."

Jesus Foretells His Death a Third Time

17 And as Jesus was going up to Jerusalem, he took the twelve disciples aside,

[1] Greek *in the regeneration* [2] Some manuscripts *manifold* [3] A *denarius* was a day's wage for a laborer [4] Or *is your eye bad because I am good?*

and on the way he said to them, 18“See, we are going up to Jerusalem. And the Son of Man will be delivered over to the chief priests and scribes, and they will condemn him to death 19and deliver him over to the Gentiles to be mocked and flogged and crucified, and he will be raised on the third day.”

A Mother's Request

20Then the mother of the sons of Zebedee came up to him with her sons, and kneeling before him she asked him for something. 21And he said to her, “What do you want?” She said to him, “Say that these two sons of mine are to sit, one at your right hand and one at your left, in your kingdom.” 22Jesus answered, “You do not know what you are asking. Are you able to drink the cup that I am to drink?” They said to him, “We are able.” 23He said to them, “You will drink my cup, but to sit at my right hand and at my left is not mine to grant, but it is for those for whom it has been prepared by my Father.” 24And when the ten heard it, they were indignant at the two brothers. 25But Jesus called them to him and said, “You know that the rulers of the Gentiles lord it over them, and their great ones exercise authority over them. 26It shall not be so among you. But whoever would be great among you must be your servant,[1] 27and whoever would be first among you must be your slave,[2] 28even as the Son of Man came not to be served but to serve, and to give his life as a ransom for many.”

Jesus Heals Two Blind Men

29And as they went out of Jericho, a great crowd followed him. 30And behold, there were two blind men sitting by the roadside, and when they heard that Jesus was passing by, they cried out, “Lord,[3] have mercy on us, Son of David!” 31The crowd rebuked them, telling them to be silent, but they cried out all the more, “Lord, have mercy on us, Son of David!” 32And stopping, Jesus called them and said, “What do you want me to do for you?” 33They said to him, “Lord, let our eyes be opened.” 34And Jesus in pity touched their eyes, and immediately they recovered their sight and followed him.

The Triumphal Entry

21 Now when they drew near
to Jerusalem and came to
1345 Bethphage, to the Mount of Olives,
then Jesus sent two disciples, 2saying to them, “Go into the village in
449 front of you, and immediately you
will find a donkey tied, and a colt with her. Untie them and bring them to me. 3If anyone says anything to you, you shall say, ‘The Lord needs them,’ and he will send them at once.” 4This took place to fulfill what was spoken by the prophet, saying,

> 5“Say to the daughter of Zion,
> ‘Behold, your king is coming to
1345
> you,
> humble, and mounted on a donkey,
> and[4] on a colt, the foal of a beast of burden.’”

6The disciples went and did as Jesus had directed them. 7They brought the donkey and the colt and put on them their cloaks, and he sat on them. 8Most of the crowd spread their cloaks on the road, and others cut branches from the trees and spread them on the road. 9And the crowds that went before him and that followed him were shouting, “Hosanna to the Son of David! Blessed is he who comes in the name of the Lord! Hosanna in the highest!” 10And when he entered Jerusalem, the whole city was stirred up, saying, “Who is this?” 11And the crowds said, “This is the prophet Jesus, from Nazareth of Galilee.”

Jesus Cleanses the Temple

12And Jesus entered the temple[5]
and drove out all who sold and
1545 bought in the temple, and he

[1] Greek *diakonos* [2] Greek *bondservant (doulos)* [3] Some manuscripts omit *Lord* [4] Or *even* [5] Some manuscripts add *of God*

KUEKER

The Triumphal Entry

When Jesus and His disciples were coming to Jerusalem, He sent two disciples ahead of Him with a special job. They were to go to the village and find a donkey and her colt. Then they were to bring the donkey and colt to Jesus.

Jesus told the disciples if anyone asked them what they were doing, they should say, "The Lord needs them." Then the people would know that the donkey and its colt were needed for a very special purpose. In fact, this happened to fulfill a prophecy, found in the book of Zechariah. Long before, the prophet Zechariah had written that a king would ride into Jerusalem, mounted on a donkey. Jesus was that King.

The disciples found the donkey and colt and brought them back to Jesus. Then they put their cloaks on the animals. Jesus sat on their cloaks and began to ride toward Jerusalem. All along the way, people spread their cloaks on the road. Others cut branches from trees and put them on the road. The people shouted, "Hosanna to the Son of David!" and "Hosanna in the highest!"

As Jesus entered Jerusalem, the people of the city were amazed by the excited crowd. "Who is this?" the people asked. The crowds who were following Jesus answered, "This is the Prophet Jesus, from Nazareth of Galilee."

Jesus is the great Teacher, Savior, and King that God had promised for His people. The people were right to worship and praise Jesus. And as our King and Savior, Jesus deserves our trust, our praise, and our worship too.

SEEK and FIND

WHERE TO FIND THE STORY

Matthew 21:1–11

KEY BIBLE VERSE

"Behold, your king is coming to you,
humble, and mounted on a donkey."
(Matthew 21:5)

THREE KEY QUESTIONS

- What did Zechariah prophesy was going to happen in Jerusalem many years later?
- What did the crowds of people do when they saw Jesus riding on the donkey toward Jerusalem?
- As our King and our Savior, how should we respond to Jesus?

RELATED BIBLE READINGS

Jeremiah 23:5–6; Zechariah 9:9; Mark 11:1–11; Luke 19:28–40

overturned the tables of the money-changers and the seats of those who sold pigeons. 13 He said to them, "It is written, 'My house shall be called a house of prayer,' but you make it a den of robbers."

14 And the blind and the lame came to him in the temple, and he healed them.

1403

15 But when the chief priests and the scribes saw the wonderful things that he did, and the children crying out in the temple, "Hosanna to the Son of David!" they were indignant, 16 and they said to him, "Do you hear what these are saying?" And Jesus said to them, "Yes; have you never read,

"'Out of the mouth of infants and
nursing babies
you have prepared praise'?"

17 And leaving them, he went out of the city to Bethany and lodged there.

Jesus Curses the Fig Tree

18 In the morning, as he was returning to the city, he became hungry. 19 And seeing a fig tree by the wayside, he went to it

and found nothing on it but only leaves. And he said to it, "May no fruit ever come from you again!" And the fig tree withered at once.

20 When the disciples saw it, they marveled, saying, "How did the fig tree wither at once?" 21 And Jesus answered them, "Truly, I say to you, if you have faith and do not doubt, you will not only do what has been done to the fig tree, but even if you say to this mountain, 'Be taken up and thrown into the sea,' it will happen. 22 And whatever you ask in prayer, you will receive, if you have faith."

The Authority of Jesus Challenged

23 And when he entered the temple, the chief priests and the elders of the people came up to him as he was teaching, and said, "By what authority are you doing these things, and who gave you this authority?" 24 Jesus answered them, "I also will ask you one question, and if you tell me the answer, then I also will tell you by what authority I do these things. 25 The baptism of John, from where did it come? From heaven or from man?" And they discussed it among themselves, saying, "If we say, 'From heaven,' he will say to us, 'Why then did you not believe him?' 26 But if we say, 'From man,' we are afraid of the crowd, for they all hold that John was a prophet." 27 So they answered Jesus, "We do not know." And he said to them, "Neither will I tell you by what authority I do these things.

The Parable of the Two Sons

28 "What do you think? A man had two sons. And he went to the first and said, 'Son, go and work in the vineyard today.' 29 And he answered, 'I will not,' but afterward he changed his mind and went. 30 And he went to the other son and said the same. And he answered, 'I go, sir,' but did not go. 31 Which of the two did the will of his father?" They said, "The first." Jesus said to them, "Truly, I say to you, the tax collectors and the prostitutes go into the kingdom of God before you. 32 For John came to you in the way of righteousness, and you did not believe him, but the tax collectors and the prostitutes believed him. And even when you saw it, you did not afterward change your minds and believe him.

The Parable of the Tenants

33 "Hear another parable. There was a master of a house who planted a vineyard and put a fence around it and dug a winepress in it and built a tower and leased it to tenants, and went into another country. 34 When the season for fruit drew near, he sent his servants[1] to the tenants to get his fruit. 35 And the tenants took his servants and beat one, killed another, and stoned another. 36 Again he sent other servants, more than the first. And they did the same to them. 37 Finally he sent his son to them, saying, 'They will respect my son.' 38 But when the tenants saw the son, they said to themselves, 'This is the heir. Come, let us kill him and have his inheritance.' 39 And they took him and threw him out of the vineyard and killed him. 40 When therefore the owner of the vineyard comes, what will he do to those tenants?" 41 They said to him, "He will put those wretches to a miserable death and let out the vineyard to other tenants who will give him the fruits in their seasons."

42 Jesus said to them, "Have you never read in the Scriptures:

"'The stone that the builders rejected
 has become the cornerstone;[2]
this was the Lord's doing,
 and it is marvelous in our eyes'?

43 Therefore I tell you, the kingdom of God will be taken away from you and given to a people producing its fruits. 44 And the one who falls on this stone will be broken to pieces; and when it falls on anyone, it will crush him."[3]

[1] Greek *bondservants*; also verses 35, 36 [2] Greek *the head of the corner* [3] Some manuscripts omit verse 44

45 When the chief priests and the
Pharisees heard his parables, they per-
ceived that he was speaking about them.
46 And although they were seeking to
arrest him, they feared the crowds,
because they held him to be a prophet.

The Parable of the Wedding Feast

22 And again Jesus spoke to them in
parables, saying, 2 "The kingdom
of heaven may be compared to a king who
gave a wedding feast for his son, 3 and
sent his servants[1] to call those who were
invited to the wedding feast, but they
would not come. 4 Again he sent other ser-
vants, saying, 'Tell those who are invited,
See, I have prepared my dinner, my oxen
and my fat calves have been slaughtered,
and everything is ready. Come to the wed-
ding feast.' 5 But they paid no attention
and went off, one to his farm, another to
his business, 6 while the rest seized his
servants, treated them shamefully, and
killed them. 7 The king was angry, and he
sent his troops and destroyed those mur-
derers and burned their city. 8 Then he
said to his servants, 'The wedding feast is
ready, but those invited were not worthy.
9 Go therefore to the main roads and invite
to the wedding feast as many as you find.'
10 And those servants went out into the
roads and gathered all whom they found,
both bad and good. So the wedding hall
was filled with guests.

11 "But when the king came in to look at
the guests, he saw there a man who had no
wedding garment. 12 And he said to him,
'Friend, how did you get in here without a
wedding garment?' And he was speechless.
13 Then the king said to the attendants,
'Bind him hand and foot and cast him into
the outer darkness. In that place there will
be weeping and gnashing of teeth.' 14 For
many are called, but few are chosen."

Paying Taxes to Caesar

15 Then the Pharisees went and plotted
how to entangle him in his words. 16 And
they sent their disciples to him, along with
the Herodians, saying, "Teacher, we know
that you are true and teach the way of God
truthfully, and you do not care about any-
one's opinion, for you are not swayed by
appearances.[2] 17 Tell us, then, what you
think. Is it lawful to pay taxes to Caesar,
or not?" 18 But Jesus, aware of their malice,
said, "Why put me to the test, you hypo-
crites? 19 Show me the coin for the tax."
And they brought him a denarius.[3] 20 And
Jesus said to them, "Whose likeness and
inscription is this?" 21 They said, "Caesar's."
Then he said to them, "Therefore render
to Caesar the things that are Caesar's, and
to God the things that are God's." 22 When
they heard it, they marveled. And they left
him and went away.

Sadducees Ask About the Resurrection

23 The same day Sadducees came to
him, who say that there is no resurrection,
and they asked him a question, 24 saying,
"Teacher, Moses said, 'If a man dies hav-
ing no children, his brother must marry
the widow and raise up children for his
brother.' 25 Now there were seven broth-
ers among us. The first married and died,
and having no children left his wife to his
brother. 26 So too the second and third,
down to the seventh. 27 After them all, the
woman died. 28 In the resurrection, there-
fore, of the seven, whose wife will she be?
For they all had her."

29 But Jesus answered them, "You are
wrong, because you know neither the
Scriptures nor the power of God. 30 For
in the resurrection they neither marry
nor are given in marriage, but are like
angels in heaven. 31 And as for the res-
urrection of the dead, have you not read
what was said to you by God: 32 'I am the
God of Abraham, and the God of Isaac,
and the God of Jacob'? He is not God of
the dead, but of the living." 33 And when
the crowd heard it, they were astonished
at his teaching.

[1] Greek *bondservants;* also verses 4, 6, 8, 10 [2] Greek *for you do not look at people's faces* [3] A *denarius* was a day's wage for a laborer

The Great Commandment

34 But when the Pharisees heard that he had silenced the Sadducees, they
1487 gathered together. 35 And one of them, a lawyer, asked him a question to test him. 36 "Teacher, which is the great commandment in the Law?" 37 And he said to him, "You shall love the Lord your God with all your heart and with all your soul and with all your mind. 38 This is the great and first commandment. 39 And a second is like it: You shall love your neighbor as yourself. 40 On these two commandments depend all the Law and the Prophets."

Whose Son Is the Christ?

41 Now while the Pharisees were gathered together, Jesus asked them a question, 42 saying, "What do you think about the Christ? Whose son is he?" They said to him, "The son of David." 43 He said to them, "How is it then that David, in the Spirit, calls him Lord, saying,

44 "'The Lord said to my Lord,
Sit at my right hand,
until I put your enemies under
your feet'?

45 If then David calls him Lord, how is he his son?" 46 And no one was able to answer him a word, nor from that day did anyone dare to ask him any more questions.

Seven Woes to the Scribes and Pharisees

23 Then Jesus said to the crowds and to his disciples, 2 "The scribes and the Pharisees sit on Moses' seat, 3 so practice and observe whatever they tell you—but not what they do. For they preach, but do not practice. 4 They tie up heavy burdens, hard to bear,[1] and lay them on people's shoulders, but they themselves are not willing to move them with their finger. 5 They do all their deeds to be seen by others. For they make their phylacteries broad and their fringes long, 6 and they love the place of honor at feasts and the best seats in the synagogues 7 and greetings in the marketplaces and being called rabbi[2] by others. 8 But you are not to be called rabbi, for you have one teacher, and you are all brothers.[3] 9 And call no man your father on earth, for you have one Father, who is in heaven. 10 Neither be called instructors, for you have one instructor, the Christ. 11 The greatest among you shall be your servant. 12 Whoever exalts himself will be humbled, and whoever humbles himself will be exalted.

13 "But woe to you, scribes and Pharisees, hypocrites! For you shut the kingdom of heaven in people's faces. For you neither enter yourselves nor allow those who would enter to go in.[4] 15 Woe to you, scribes and Pharisees, hypocrites! For you travel across sea and land to make a single proselyte, and when he becomes a proselyte, you make him twice as much a child of hell[5] as yourselves.

16 "Woe to you, blind guides, who say, 'If anyone swears by the temple, it is nothing, but if anyone swears by the gold of the temple, he is bound by his oath.' 17 You blind fools! For which is greater, the gold or the temple that has made the gold sacred? 18 And you say, 'If anyone swears by the altar, it is nothing, but if anyone swears by the gift that is on the altar, he is bound by his oath.' 19 You blind men! For which is greater, the gift or the altar that makes the gift sacred? 20 So whoever swears by the altar swears by it and by everything on it. 21 And whoever swears by the temple swears by it and by him who dwells in it. 22 And whoever swears by heaven swears by the throne of God and by him who sits upon it.

23 "Woe to you, scribes and Pharisees, hypocrites! For you tithe mint and dill and cumin, and have neglected the weightier matters of the law: justice and mercy and faithfulness. These you ought to have done,

[1] Some manuscripts omit *hard to bear* [2] *Rabbi* means *my teacher*, or *my master*; also verse 8 [3] Or *brothers and sisters* [4] Some manuscripts add here (or after verse 12) verse 14: *Woe to you, scribes and Pharisees, hypocrites! For you devour widows' houses and for a pretense you make long prayers; therefore you will receive the greater condemnation* [5] Greek *Gehenna*; also verse 33

without neglecting the others. 24 You blind guides, straining out a gnat and swallowing a camel!

25 "Woe to you, scribes and Pharisees, hypocrites! For you clean the outside of the cup and the plate, but inside they are full of greed and self-indulgence. 26 You blind Pharisee! First clean the inside of the cup and the plate, that the outside also may be clean.

27 "Woe to you, scribes and Pharisees, hypocrites! For you are like whitewashed tombs, which outwardly appear beautiful, but within are full of dead people's bones and all uncleanness. 28 So you also outwardly appear righteous to others, but within you are full of hypocrisy and lawlessness.

29 "Woe to you, scribes and Pharisees, hypocrites! For you build the tombs of the prophets and decorate the monuments of the righteous, 30 saying, 'If we had lived in the days of our fathers, we would not have taken part with them in shedding the blood of the prophets.' 31 Thus you witness against yourselves that you are sons of those who murdered the prophets. 32 Fill up, then, the measure of your fathers. 33 You serpents, you brood of vipers, how are you to escape being sentenced to hell? 34 Therefore I send you prophets and wise men and scribes, some of whom you will kill and crucify, and some you will flog in your synagogues and persecute from town to town, 35 so that on you may come all the righteous blood shed on earth, from the blood of innocent Abel to the blood of Zechariah the son of Barachiah,[1] whom you murdered between the sanctuary and the altar. 36 Truly, I say to you, all these things will come upon this generation.

Lament over Jerusalem

37 "O Jerusalem, Jerusalem, the city that kills the prophets and stones those who are sent to it! How often would I have gathered your children together as a hen gathers her brood under her wings, and you would not! 38 See, your house is left to you desolate. 39 For I tell you, you will not see me again, until you say, 'Blessed is he who comes in the name of the Lord.'"

Jesus Foretells Destruction of the Temple

24 Jesus left the temple and was going away, when his disciples came to point out to him the buildings of the temple. 2 But he answered them, "You see all these, do you not? Truly, I say to you, there will not be left here one stone upon another that will not be thrown down."

Signs of the Close of the Age

3 As he sat on the Mount of Olives, the disciples came to him privately, saying, "Tell us, when will these things be, and what will be the sign of your coming and of the close of the age?" 4 And Jesus answered them, "See that no one leads you astray. 5 For many will come in my name, saying, 'I am the Christ,' and they will lead many astray. 6 And you will hear of wars and rumors of wars. See that you are not alarmed, for this must take place, but the end is not yet. 7 For nation will rise against nation, and kingdom against kingdom, and there will be famines and earthquakes in various places. 8 All these are but the beginning of the birth pains.

9 "Then they will deliver you up to tribulation and put you to death, and you will be hated by all nations for my name's sake. 10 And then many will fall away[2] and betray one another and hate one another. 11 And many false prophets will arise and lead many astray. 12 And because lawlessness will be increased, the love of many will grow cold. 13 But the one who endures to the end will be saved. 14 And this gospel of the kingdom will be proclaimed throughout the whole world as a testimony to all nations, and then the end will come.

[1] Some manuscripts omit *the son of Barachiah* [2] Or *stumble*

The Abomination of Desolation

15 "So when you see the abomination of desolation spoken of by the prophet Daniel, standing in the holy place (let the reader understand), **16** then let those who are in Judea flee to the mountains. **17** Let the one who is on the housetop not go down to take what is in his house, **18** and let the one who is in the field not turn back to take his cloak. **19** And alas for women who are pregnant and for those who are nursing infants in those days! **20** Pray that your flight may not be in winter or on a Sabbath. **21** For then there will be great tribulation, such as has not been from the beginning of the world until now, no, and never will be. **22** And if those days had not been cut short, no human being would be saved. But for the sake of the elect those days will be cut short. **23** Then if anyone says to you, 'Look, here is the Christ!' or 'There he is!' do not believe it. **24** For false christs and false prophets will arise and perform great signs and wonders, so as to lead astray, if possible, even the elect. **25** See, I have told you beforehand. **26** So, if they say to you, 'Look, he is in the wilderness,' do not go out. If they say, 'Look, he is in the inner rooms,' do not believe it. **27** For as the lightning comes from the east and shines as far as the west, so will be the coming of the Son of Man. **28** Wherever the corpse is, there the vultures will gather.

The Coming of the Son of Man

29 "Immediately after the tribulation of those days the sun will be darkened, and the moon will not give its light, and the stars will fall from heaven, and the powers of the heavens will be shaken. **30** Then will appear in heaven the sign of the Son of Man, and then all the tribes of the earth will mourn, and they will see the Son of Man coming on the clouds of heaven with power and great glory. **31** And he will send out his angels with a loud trumpet call, and they will gather his elect from the four winds, from one end of heaven to the other.

The Lesson of the Fig Tree

32 "From the fig tree learn its lesson: as soon as its branch becomes tender and puts out its leaves, you know that summer is near. **33** So also, when you see all these things, you know that he is near, at the very gates. **34** Truly, I say to you, this generation will not pass away until all these things take place. **35** Heaven and earth will pass away, but my words will not pass away.

No One Knows That Day and Hour

36 "But concerning that day and
hour no one knows, not even the
25 angels of heaven, nor the Son,[1] but
the Father only. **37** For as were the days of Noah, so will be the coming of the Son of Man. **38** For as in those days before the flood they were eating and drinking, marrying and giving in marriage, until the day when Noah entered the ark, **39** and they were unaware until the flood came and swept them all away, so will be the coming of the Son of Man. **40** Then two men will be in the field; one will be taken and one left. **41** Two women will be grinding at the mill; one will be taken and one left. **42** Therefore, stay awake, for you do not know on what day your Lord is coming. **43** But know this, that if the master of the house had known in what part of the night the thief was coming, he would have stayed awake and would not have let his house be broken into. **44** Therefore you also must be ready, for the Son of Man is coming at an hour you do not expect.

45 "Who then is the faithful and wise servant,[2] whom his master has set over his household, to give them their food at the proper time? **46** Blessed is that servant whom his master will find so doing when he comes. **47** Truly, I say to you, he will set him over all his possessions. **48** But if that wicked servant says to himself, 'My master

[1] Some manuscripts omit *nor the Son* [2] Greek *bondservant*; also verses 46, 48, 50

is delayed,' 49 and begins to beat his fellow servants[1] and eats and drinks with drunkards, 50 the master of that servant will come on a day when he does not expect him and at an hour he does not know 51 and will cut him in pieces and put him with the hypocrites. In that place there will be weeping and gnashing of teeth.

The Parable of the Ten Virgins

25 "Then the kingdom of heaven will be like ten virgins who took their lamps[2] and went to meet the bridegroom.[3] 2 Five of them were foolish, and five were wise. 3 For when the foolish took their lamps, they took no oil with them, 4 but the wise took flasks of oil with their lamps. 5 As the bridegroom was delayed, they all became drowsy and slept. 6 But at midnight there was a cry, 'Here is the bridegroom! Come out to meet him.' 7 Then all those virgins rose and trimmed their lamps. 8 And the foolish said to the wise, 'Give us some of your oil, for our lamps are going out.' 9 But the wise answered, saying, 'Since there will not be enough for us and for you, go rather to the dealers and buy for yourselves.' 10 And while they were going to buy, the bridegroom came, and those who were ready went in with him to the marriage feast, and the door was shut. 11 Afterward the other virgins came also, saying, 'Lord, lord, open to us.' 12 But he answered, 'Truly, I say to you, I do not know you.' 13 Watch therefore, for you know neither the day nor the hour.

The Parable of the Talents

14 "For it will be like a man going on a journey, who called his servants[4] and entrusted to them his property. 15 To one he gave five talents,[5] to another two, to another one, to each according to his ability. Then he went away. 16 He who had received the five talents went at once and traded with them, and he made five talents more. 17 So also he who had the two talents made two talents more. 18 But he who had received the one talent went and dug in the ground and hid his master's money. 19 Now after a long time the master of those servants came and settled accounts with them. 20 And he who had received the five talents came forward, bringing five talents more, saying, 'Master, you delivered to me five talents; here I have made five talents more.' 21 His master said to him, 'Well done, good and faithful servant.[6] You have been faithful over a little; I will set you over much. Enter into the joy of your master.' 22 And he also who had the two talents came forward, saying, 'Master, you delivered to me two talents; here I have made two talents more.' 23 His master said to him, 'Well done, good and faithful servant. You have been faithful over a little; I will set you over much. Enter into the joy of your master.' 24 He also who had received the one talent came forward, saying, 'Master, I knew you to be a hard man, reaping where you did not sow, and gathering where you scattered no seed, 25 so I was afraid, and I went and hid your talent in the ground. Here you have what is yours.' 26 But his master answered him, 'You wicked and slothful servant! You knew that I reap where I have not sown and gather where I scattered no seed? 27 Then you ought to have invested my money with the bankers, and at my coming I should have received what was my own with interest. 28 So take the talent from him and give it to him who has the ten talents. 29 For to everyone who has will more be given, and he will have an abundance. But from the one who has not, even what he has will be taken away. 30 And cast the worthless servant into the outer darkness. In that place there will be weeping and gnashing of teeth.'

The Final Judgment

31 "When the Son of Man comes in his glory, and all the angels with him, then he will sit on his glorious throne. 32 Before

[1] Greek *bondservants* [2] Or *torches* [3] Some manuscripts add *and the bride* [4] Greek *bondservants*; also verse 19 [5] A *talent* was a monetary unit worth about twenty years' wages for a laborer [6] Greek *bondservant*; also verses 23, 26, 30

him will be gathered all the nations, and
he will separate people one from another
as a shepherd separates the sheep from
the goats. 33 And he will place the sheep
on his right, but the goats on the left.
34 Then the King will say to those on his
right, 'Come, you who are blessed by my
Father, inherit the kingdom prepared for
you from the foundation of the world.
35 For I was hungry and you gave me food,
I was thirsty and you gave me drink, I was
a stranger and you welcomed me, 36 I was
naked and you clothed me, I was sick and
you visited me, I was in prison and you
came to me.' 37 Then the righteous will
answer him, saying, 'Lord, when did we
see you hungry and feed you, or thirsty
and give you drink? 38 And when did we
see you a stranger and welcome you, or
naked and clothe you? 39 And when did
we see you sick or in prison and visit you?'
40 And the King will answer them, 'Truly, I
say to you, as you did it to one of the least
of these my brothers,[1] you did it to me.'

41 "Then he will say to those on his left,
'Depart from me, you cursed, into the
eternal fire prepared for the devil and his
angels. 42 For I was hungry and you gave
me no food, I was thirsty and you gave me
no drink, 43 I was a stranger and you did
not welcome me, naked and you did not
clothe me, sick and in prison and you did
not visit me.' 44 Then they also will answer,
saying, 'Lord, when did we see you hun-
gry or thirsty or a stranger or naked or
sick or in prison, and did not minister to
you?' 45 Then he will answer them, saying,
'Truly, I say to you, as you did not do it to
one of the least of these, you did not do it
to me.' 46 And these will go away into eter-
nal punishment, but the righteous into
eternal life."

The Plot to Kill Jesus

26 When Jesus had finished all
these sayings, he said to his dis-
ciples, 2 "You know that after two days the
Passover is coming, and the Son of Man
will be delivered up to be crucified."

3 Then the chief priests and the elders
of the people gathered in the palace of the
high priest, whose name was Caiaphas,
4 and plotted together in order to arrest
Jesus by stealth and kill him. 5 But they
said, "Not during the feast, lest there be
an uproar among the people."

Jesus Anointed at Bethany

6 Now when Jesus was at Bethany in
the house of Simon the leper,[2] 7 a
1473 woman came up to him with an
alabaster flask of very expensive ointment,
and she poured it on his head as he reclined
at table. 8 And when the disciples saw it,
they were indignant, saying, "Why this
waste? 9 For this could have been sold for a
large sum and given to the poor." 10 But
Jesus, aware of this, said to them, "Why do
you trouble the woman? For she has done
a beautiful thing to me. 11 For you always
have the poor with you, but you will not
always have me. 12 In pouring this oint-
ment on my body, she has done it to pre-
pare me for burial. 13 Truly, I say to you,
wherever this gospel is proclaimed in the
whole world, what she has done will also
be told in memory of her."

Judas to Betray Jesus

14 Then one of the twelve, whose name
was Judas Iscariot, went to the chief
priests 15 and said, "What will you give me
if I deliver him over to you?" And they paid
him thirty pieces of silver. 16 And from
that moment he sought an opportunity
to betray him.

The Passover with the Disciples

17 Now on the first day of Unleav-
ened Bread the disciples came to
153 Jesus, saying, "Where will you have
us prepare for you to eat the Passover?"
18 He said, "Go into the city to a certain
man and say to him, 'The Teacher says, My
time is at hand. I will keep the Passover at

[1] Or *brothers and sisters* [2] *Leprosy* was a term for several skin diseases; see Leviticus 13

1. The **Gate of the Essenes** was used by certain Jews who had very strict rules about personal cleanliness.
2. **Herod's Palace** was where Herod the Great lived from 23 to 4 B.C. When the governor, Pilate, visited Jerusalem, he would stay in this palace.
3. The **Praetorium** was in Herod's Palace. This was both a fortress and Pilate's official headquarters. A raised stone platform stood outside the palace. From this stone pavement, Pilate sent Jesus to be crucified (John 19:13).

4–6. Herod the Great fortified these three towers to protect his palace.

7. The **Palatial Mansion** (6,500 sq. feet/604 sq. m) may have been the Palace of Annas. Annas was high priest from A.D. 6 to 15.
8. This is probably where **Golgotha** was, the place where Jesus died on the cross. It was on a hill outside the Second Wall of the city.
9. Herod the Great lived in the luxurious **Hasmonean Palace** while he was waiting for his own new palace to be built (mid-30's to 23 B.C.). Herod Antipas (or "Herod the Tetrarch") lived in this palace while Jesus was on earth.

10. The **Archives** was where official records and legal documents were kept.
11. The **Xystus** was a place where large meetings with many people were held.
12. The **Council House** was a public building, maybe used as a city office.
13. The **Temple** had been rebuilt by Herod the Great, beginning in 20/19 B.C.
14. The **Bethesda Pools** were twin pools. Jesus healed a man who lay every day by these pools (John 5:2).
15. Jesus was praying in the **Garden of Gethsemane** when He was arrested (Matthew 26:36–47).
16. The ravine of the **Kidron Valley** has always been Jerusalem's eastern boundary.
17. The **Pool of Siloam** received water from the Gihon Spring. When Jesus put mud on a blind man's eyes to heal him, He told him to go wash in this pool (John 9:6–7).
18. The **Hinnom Valley** was south of the hill that held the original city of David.
19. The **Upper City** had large luxurious houses of wealthy people.

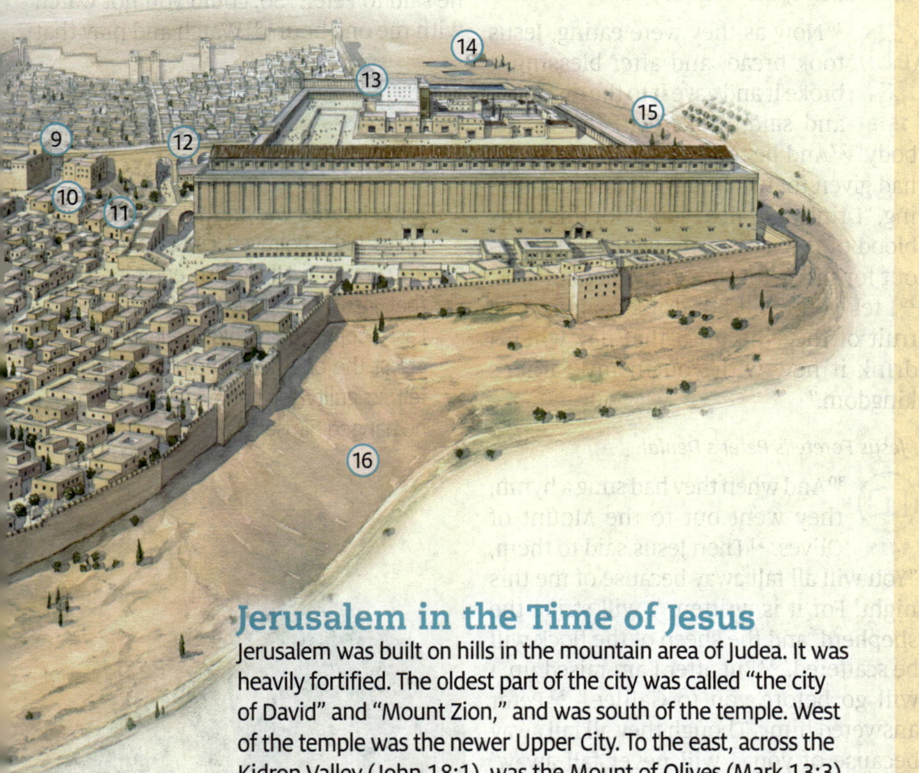

Jerusalem in the Time of Jesus

Jerusalem was built on hills in the mountain area of Judea. It was heavily fortified. The oldest part of the city was called "the city of David" and "Mount Zion," and was south of the temple. West of the temple was the newer Upper City. To the east, across the Kidron Valley (John 18:1), was the Mount of Olives (Mark 13:3). This is how Jerusalem would have looked around A.D. 30.

your house with my disciples.'" 19 And the
disciples did as Jesus had directed them,
and they prepared the Passover.
20 When it was evening, he reclined at
table with the twelve.[1] 21 And as they were
eating, he said, "Truly, I say to you, one
of you will betray me." 22 And they were
very sorrowful and began to say to him
one after another, "Is it I, Lord?" 23 He
answered, "He who has dipped his hand
in the dish with me will betray me. 24 The
Son of Man goes as it is written of him, but
woe to that man by whom the Son of Man
is betrayed! It would have been better for
that man if he had not been born." 25 Judas,
who would betray him, answered, "Is it I,
Rabbi?" He said to him, "You have said so."

Institution of the Lord's Supper

26 Now as they were eating, Jesus
took bread, and after blessing it
1033, broke it and gave it to the disciples,
1519 and said, "Take, eat; this is my
body." 27 And he took a cup, and when he
had given thanks he gave it to them, say-
ing, "Drink of it, all of you, 28 for this is my
blood of the[2] covenant, which is poured
out for many for the forgiveness of sins.
29 I tell you I will not drink again of this
fruit of the vine until that day when I
drink it new with you in my Father's
kingdom."

Jesus Foretells Peter's Denial

30 And when they had sung a hymn,
they went out to the Mount of
1415 Olives. 31 Then Jesus said to them,
"You will all fall away because of me this
night. For it is written, 'I will strike the
shepherd, and the sheep of the flock will
be scattered.' 32 But after I am raised up, I
will go before you to Galilee." 33 Peter
answered him, "Though they all fall away
because of you, I will never fall away."
34 Jesus said to him, "Truly, I tell you, this
very night, before the rooster crows, you
will deny me three times." 35 Peter said to
him, "Even if I must die with you, I will
not deny you!" And all the disciples said
the same.

Jesus Prays in Gethsemane

36 Then Jesus went with them to a
place called Gethsemane, and he
1361 said to his disciples, "Sit here, while
I go over there and pray." 37 And taking
with him Peter and the two sons of
Zebedee, he began to be sorrowful and
troubled. 38 Then he said to them, "My soul
is very sorrowful, even to death; remain
here, and watch[3] with me." 39 And going a
little farther he fell on his face and prayed,
saying, "My Father, if it be possible, let this
cup pass from me; nevertheless, not as I
will, but as you will." 40 And he came to the
disciples and found them sleeping. And
he said to Peter, "So, could you not watch
with me one hour? 41 Watch and pray that

CHARACTER PROFILE

JUDAS ISCARIOT

Judas Iscariot was one of Jesus' 12 disciples. Judas betrayed Jesus. He turned Jesus over to His Jewish enemies, so that Jesus would be killed. After the Last Supper Judas told the leaders to arrest the one he kissed. Later, Judas felt so guilty for betraying Jesus that he hanged himself.

1361

[1] Some manuscripts add *disciples* [2] Some manuscripts insert *new* [3] Or *keep awake*; also verses 40, 41

you may not enter into temptation. The
spirit indeed is willing, but the flesh is
weak." **42** Again, for the second time, he
went away and prayed, "My Father, if this
cannot pass unless I drink it, your will be
done." **43** And again he came and found
them sleeping, for their eyes were heavy.
44 So, leaving them again, he went away
and prayed for the third time, saying the
same words again. **45** Then he came to the
disciples and said to them, "Sleep and take
your rest later on.[1] See, the hour is at
hand, and the Son of Man is betrayed into
the hands of sinners. **46** Rise, let us be
going; see, my betrayer is at hand."

Betrayal and Arrest of Jesus

47 While he was still speaking, Judas
came, one of the twelve, and with him a
great crowd with swords and clubs, from
the chief priests and the elders of the peo-
ple. **48** Now the betrayer had given them
a sign, saying, "The one I will kiss is the
man; seize him." **49** And he came up to
Jesus at once and said, "Greetings, Rabbi!"
And he kissed him. **50** Jesus said to him,
"Friend, do what you came to do."[2] Then
they came up and laid hands on Jesus and
seized him. **51** And behold, one of those
who were with Jesus stretched out his
hand and drew his sword and struck the
servant[3] of the high priest and cut off his
ear. **52** Then Jesus said to him, "Put your
sword back into its place. For all who
take the sword will perish by the sword.
53 Do you think that I cannot appeal to my
Father, and he will at once send me more
than twelve legions of angels? **54** But how
then should the Scriptures be fulfilled, that
it must be so?" **55** At that hour Jesus said to
the crowds, "Have you come out as against
a robber, with swords and clubs to capture
me? Day after day I sat in the temple teach-
ing, and you did not seize me. **56** But all this
has taken place that the Scriptures of the
prophets might be fulfilled." Then all the
disciples left him and fled.

Jesus Before Caiaphas and the Council

57 Then those who had seized Jesus led
him to Caiaphas the high priest, where the
scribes and the elders had gathered. **58** And
Peter was following him at a distance, as
far as the courtyard of the high priest, and
going inside he sat with the guards to see
the end. **59** Now the chief priests and the
whole Council[4] were seeking false testi-
mony against Jesus that they might put
him to death, **60** but they found none,
though many false witnesses came for-
ward. At last two came forward **61** and said,
"This man said, 'I am able to destroy the
temple of God, and to rebuild it in three
days.'" **62** And the high priest stood up and
said, "Have you no answer to make? What
is it that these men testify against you?"[5]
63 But Jesus remained silent. And the high
priest said to him, "I adjure you by the liv-
ing God, tell us if you are the Christ, the
Son of God." **64** Jesus said to him, "You
have said so. But I tell you, from now on
you will see the Son of Man seated at the
right hand of Power and coming on the
clouds of heaven." **65** Then the high priest
tore his robes and said, "He has uttered
blasphemy. What further witnesses do
we need? You have now heard his blas-
phemy. **66** What is your judgment?" They
answered, "He deserves death." **67** Then
they spit in his face and struck him. And
some slapped him, **68** saying, "Prophesy to
us, you Christ! Who is it that struck you?"

Peter Denies Jesus

69 Now Peter was sitting outside in the
courtyard. And a servant girl came up to
him and said, "You also were with Jesus
the Galilean." **70** But he denied it before
them all, saying, "I do not know what
you mean." **71** And when he went out to
the entrance, another servant girl saw
him, and she said to the bystanders, "This
man was with Jesus of Nazareth." **72** And
again he denied it with an oath: "I do not
know the man." **73** After a little while the

[1] Or *Are you still sleeping and taking your rest?* [2] Or *Friend, why are you here?* [3] Greek *bondservant* [4] Greek *Sanhedrin* [5] Or *Have you no answer to what these men testify against you?*

bystanders came up and said to Peter,
"Certainly you too are one of them, for
your accent betrays you." 74 Then he began
to invoke a curse on himself and to swear,
"I do not know the man." And immedi-
ately the rooster crowed. 75 And Peter
remembered the saying of Jesus, "Before
the rooster crows, you will deny me three
times." And he went out and wept bitterly.

Jesus Delivered to Pilate

27 When morning came, all the chief
priests and the elders of the peo-
ple took counsel against Jesus to put him
to death. 2 And they bound him and led
him away and delivered him over to Pilate
the governor.

Judas Hangs Himself

3 Then when Judas, his betrayer, saw that
Jesus[1] was condemned, he changed his
mind and brought back the thirty pieces
of silver to the chief priests and the elders,
4 saying, "I have sinned by betraying inno-
cent blood." They said, "What is that to us?
See to it yourself." 5 And throwing down
the pieces of silver into the temple, he
departed, and he went and hanged him-
self. 6 But the chief priests, taking the pieces
of silver, said, "It is not lawful to put them
into the treasury, since it is blood money."
7 So they took counsel and bought with
them the potter's field as a burial place for
strangers. 8 Therefore that field has been
called the Field of Blood to this day. 9 Then
was fulfilled what had been spoken by the
prophet Jeremiah, saying, "And they took
the thirty pieces of silver, the price of him
on whom a price had been set by some of
the sons of Israel, 10 and they gave them for
the potter's field, as the Lord directed me."

Jesus Before Pilate

11 Now Jesus stood before the gov-
ernor, and the governor asked him,
1421, "Are you the King of the Jews?"
1523 Jesus said, "You have said so." 12 But
when he was accused by the chief priests
and elders, he gave no answer. 13 Then
Pilate said to him, "Do you not hear how
many things they testify against you?"
14 But he gave him no answer, not even to
a single charge, so that the governor was
greatly amazed.

The Crowd Chooses Barabbas

15 Now at the feast the governor was
accustomed to release for the crowd any
one prisoner whom they wanted. 16 And
they had then a notorious prisoner called
Barabbas. 17 So when they had gathered,
Pilate said to them, "Whom do you want
me to release for you: Barabbas, or Jesus
who is called Christ?" 18 For he knew that
it was out of envy that they had deliv-
ered him up. 19 Besides, while he was sit-
ting on the judgment seat, his wife sent
word to him, "Have nothing to do with
that righteous man, for I have suffered
much because of him today in a dream."
20 Now the chief priests and the elders per-
suaded the crowd to ask for Barabbas and
destroy Jesus. 21 The governor again said
to them, "Which of the two do you want
me to release for you?" And they said,
"Barabbas." 22 Pilate said to them, "Then
what shall I do with Jesus who is called
Christ?" They all said, "Let him be cruci-
fied!" 23 And he said, "Why, what evil has
he done?" But they shouted all the more,
"Let him be crucified!"

Pilate Delivers Jesus to Be Crucified

24 So when Pilate saw that he was gain-
ing nothing, but rather that a riot was
beginning, he took water and washed
his hands before the crowd, saying, "I
am innocent of this man's blood;[2] see
to it yourselves." 25 And all the people
answered, "His blood be on us and on our
children!" 26 Then he released for them
Barabbas, and having scourged[3] Jesus,
delivered him to be crucified.

[1] Greek *he* [2] Some manuscripts *this righteous blood,* or *this righteous man's blood* [3] A Roman judicial penalty, consisting of a severe beating with a multi-lashed whip containing imbedded pieces of bone and metal

Jesus Is Mocked

27 Then the soldiers of the governor took Jesus into the governor's headquarters,[1] and they gathered the whole battalion[2] before him. 28 And they stripped him and put a scarlet robe on him, 29 and twisting together a crown of thorns, they put it on his head and put a reed in his right hand. And kneeling before him, they mocked him, saying, "Hail, King of the Jews!" 30 And they spit on him and took the reed and struck him on the head. 31 And when they had mocked him, they stripped him of the robe and put his own clothes on him and led him away to crucify him.

The Crucifixion

32 As they went out, they found a man of Cyrene, Simon by name. They compelled this man to carry his cross. 33 And when they came to a place called Golgotha (which means Place of a Skull), 34 they offered him wine to drink, mixed with gall, but when he tasted it, he would not drink it. 35 And when they had crucified him, they divided his garments among them by casting lots. 36 Then they sat down and kept watch over him there. 37 And over his head they put the charge against him, which read, "This is Jesus, the King of the Jews." 38 Then two robbers were crucified with him, one on the right and one on the left. 39 And those who passed by derided him, wagging their heads 40 and saying, "You who would destroy the temple and rebuild it in three days, save yourself! If you are the Son of God, come down from the cross." 41 So also the chief priests, with the scribes and elders, mocked him, saying, 42 "He saved others; he cannot save himself. He is the King of Israel; let him come down now from the cross, and we will believe in him. 43 He trusts in God; let God deliver him now, if he desires him. For he said, 'I am the Son of God.'" 44 And the robbers who were crucified with him also reviled him in the same way.

The Death of Jesus

45 Now from the sixth hour[3] there was darkness over all the land[4] until the ninth hour.[5] 46 And about the ninth hour Jesus cried out with a loud voice, saying, "Eli, Eli, lema sabachthani?" that is, "My God, my God, why have you forsaken me?" 47 And some of the bystanders, hearing it, said, "This man is calling Elijah." 48 And one of them at once ran and took a sponge, filled it with sour wine, and put it on a reed and gave it to him to drink. 49 But the others said, "Wait, let us see whether Elijah will come to save him." 50 And Jesus cried out again with a loud voice and yielded up his spirit.

51 And behold, the curtain of the temple was torn in two, from top to bottom. And the earth shook, and the rocks were split. 52 The tombs also were opened. And many bodies of the saints who had fallen asleep were raised, 53 and coming out of the tombs after his resurrection they went into the holy city and appeared to many. 54 When the centurion and those who were with him, keeping watch over Jesus, saw the earthquake and what took place, they were filled with awe and said, "Truly this was the Son[6] of God!"

55 There were also many women there, looking on from a distance, who had followed Jesus from Galilee, ministering to him, 56 among whom were Mary Magdalene and Mary the mother of James and Joseph and the mother of the sons of Zebedee.

Jesus Is Buried

57 When it was evening, there came a rich man from Arimathea, named Joseph, who also was a disciple of Jesus. 58 He went to Pilate and asked for the body of Jesus. Then Pilate ordered it to be given to him. 59 And Joseph took the body and wrapped it in a clean linen shroud 60 and laid it in his own new tomb, which he had cut in the rock. And he rolled a great stone to

[1] Greek *the praetorium* [2] Greek *cohort;* a tenth of a Roman legion, usually about 600 men [3] That is, noon [4] Or *earth* [5] That is, 3 P.M. [6] Or *a son*

The Passion of Jesus

Jesus knew He would soon die on the cross to pay for our sins. So, He went to the Garden of Gethsemane just outside Jerusalem to pray to His Father in heaven for strength. Jesus prayed all night long. He was in great agony, in anticipation of His death on the cross. He even asked His Father in Heaven, "If possible, let this cup pass from Me." Nevertheless, Jesus said, I will do Your will.

When early morning came, a great crowd arrived with swords and clubs. Judas the betrayer was among the crowd. He told the leaders that he would go up to Jesus and kiss his cheek, so that they would know which one was Jesus to arrest Him. So Judas betrayed Jesus with a kiss, and the crowd took Jesus away. And the disciples left Jesus and fled.

The angry crowd with clubs and swords took Jesus to the high priest's house. The high priest and other Jewish leaders did not believe that Jesus was the Savior that God had promised to send. Instead, they thought Jesus was a false teacher, and they wanted to put Jesus to death.

The Jewish leaders, however, had no authority to put Jesus to death by themselves. So they took Jesus to a man named Pilate. Pilate was the Roman governor, the ruler of the region. They told Pilate that Jesus was a troublemaker, who had lied and broken the Jewish law. They said that He called Himself a king, and that He should die.

Pilate did not think Jesus had done anything wrong, but he was afraid of the people. Then Pilate had an idea. It was a Jewish feast day, and the governor usually let a Jewish prisoner go free then. Pilate brought out Jesus and another prisoner named Barabbas, who was a murderer and a thief. Pilate asked the people, "Which of the two do you want me to release for you?"

The Jewish leaders had told the people in the crowd that they should tell Pilate to set Barabbas free and to kill Jesus. So the people shouted to Pilate that they wanted Barabbas!

"Then what shall I do with Jesus who is called Christ?" Pilate asked.

"Let Him be crucified!" the crowd shouted.

"Why, what evil has He done?" Pilate asked.

But the crowd shouted all the more, "Let Him be crucified!"

Pilate let his soldiers put a robe on Jesus and hurt Him cruelly. They twisted thorny branches into a crown and placed it on His head and beat Him with whips. They mocked Jesus, saying, "Hail, King of the Jews!" They spit in His face. Then Pilate let the soldiers take Jesus away and nail Him to a cross. There He hung between two criminals. All of this hurt Jesus terribly, but this is what Jesus had come to do—to die on the cross to take the punishment for our sins.

Jesus hung there on the cross from early morning in great agony. Finally, in the middle of the afternoon, the sky grew dark and the ground shook. Jesus cried out with a loud voice, then it was finished. He died. The soldiers and the others watching Jesus saw the earthquake and the rocks split. The soldiers were amazed at how Jesus had died and at the dark sky and the shaking earth. They were filled with awe and said, "Truly this was the Son of God!"

Then Jesus' friends came and took His body down off the cross, and laid His body in a tomb.

Jesus' disciples and friends and family were very sad. They did not understand yet that Jesus died on the cross for a purpose, to save His people from their sins. They did not understand that this was not the end of the story. Jesus would not stay dead. After three days, on Easter morning, He would come back to life!

Jesus died on the cross in our place because He loves us so very much. Because Jesus suffered and died and rose again, God forgives our sins through faith in Jesus, and we will live with Him in heaven someday.

SEEK and FIND

WHERE TO FIND THE STORY

Matthew 26:36–27:66

KEY BIBLE VERSE

"But God shows his love for us in that while we were still sinners, Christ died for us." (Romans 5:8)

THREE KEY QUESTIONS

- What did Jesus come here on earth to do?
- When Jesus died on the cross, was it the end of the story? What happened three days later?
- What is the true meaning of Jesus' death and resurrection?

RELATED BIBLE READINGS

Isaiah 53:1–12; Mark 14:32–15:47; Luke 22:39–23:56; John 18:1–19:42; Acts 4:27–28; Romans 5:6–11

The Resurrection of Jesus

Very early on Sunday morning, three days after Jesus had died on the cross, something wonderful happened. While it was still dark, a great earthquake came. The ground rumbled and shook, and an angel came down from heaven. The angel rolled away the big stone in front of Jesus' tomb and sat on it! This frightened the guards so much that they fell to the ground trembling with fear.

That same morning, some women who loved Jesus very much walked to the tomb where Jesus was buried. They were bringing spices to put on His body, as a way to show how much they had loved Him. They were very sad that Jesus had died. But when they got to Jesus' tomb, they saw that the huge stone had been rolled away—and the angel was sitting on it!

The angel told the women, "Do not be afraid, for I know that you seek Jesus who was crucified. He is not here, for He has risen, as He said. Come, see the place where He lay. Then go quickly and tell His disciples that He has risen from the dead." The women looked in the tomb and saw that the tomb was empty. Jesus had risen just as He had said He would!

The women were afraid because of the amazing things they saw, but they were also filled with joy. They started back to tell their friends what had happened. All of a sudden, they heard someone say, "Greetings!" It was Jesus! The women ran to Jesus and knelt down to worship Him. Then Jesus told them not to be afraid, but to tell His disciples that He was alive and would meet them in Galilee.

So the women hurried to tell the disciples the amazing news of great joy: Jesus is alive! Never again did they need to be afraid.

This is amazing news of great joy for us too! Because Jesus rose from the dead, we know that He is God and that His death on the cross paid for our sins. We never need to be afraid because we know that He will raise us from the dead, and we will live with Him forever!

SEEK and FIND

WHERE TO FIND THE STORY

Matthew 28

KEY BIBLE VERSE

"He is not here, for he has risen, as he said." (Matthew 28:6a)

THREE KEY QUESTIONS

- What happened early Sunday morning, three days after Jesus died on the cross?
- What did the women do when they saw Jesus was alive?
- Why do we never need to be afraid forever?

RELATED BIBLE READINGS

Matthew 16:21; Mark 16:1–8; Luke 24:1–12; John 20:1–18; Acts 2:22–36

the entrance of the tomb and went away.
61 Mary Magdalene and the other Mary
were there, sitting opposite the tomb.

The Guard at the Tomb

62 The next day, that is, after the day
of Preparation, the chief priests and the
Pharisees gathered before Pilate 63 and
said, "Sir, we remember how that impos-
tor said, while he was still alive, 'After
three days I will rise.' 64 Therefore order
the tomb to be made secure until the
third day, lest his disciples go and steal
him away and tell the people, 'He has risen
from the dead,' and the last fraud will be
worse than the first." 65 Pilate said to them,
"You have a guard[1] of soldiers. Go, make
it as secure as you can." 66 So they went
and made the tomb secure by sealing the
stone and setting a guard.

The Resurrection

28 Now after the Sabbath,
toward the dawn of the first
1365 day of the week, Mary Magdalene
and the other Mary went to see the
tomb. 2 And behold, there was a
1593 great earthquake, for an angel of the
Lord descended from heaven and came and
rolled back the stone and sat on it. 3 His
appearance was like lightning, and his
clothing white as snow. 4 And for fear of
him the guards trembled and became like
dead men. 5 But the angel said to the
women, "Do not be afraid, for I know that
you seek Jesus who was crucified. 6 He is
not here, for he has risen, as he said.
Come, see the place where he[2] lay.
1365 7 Then go quickly and tell his disci-
ples that he has risen from the dead, and
behold, he is going before you to Galilee;
there you will see him. See, I have told you."
8 So they departed quickly from the tomb
with fear and great joy, and ran to tell his
disciples. 9 And behold, Jesus met them and
said, "Greetings!" And they came up and
took hold of his feet and worshiped him.
10 Then Jesus said to them, "Do not be
afraid; go and tell my brothers to go to
Galilee, and there they will see me."

The Report of the Guard

11 While they were going, behold, some
of the guard went into the city and told
the chief priests all that had taken place.
12 And when they had assembled with
the elders and taken counsel, they gave
a sufficient sum of money to the soldiers
13 and said, "Tell people, 'His disciples
came by night and stole him away while
we were asleep.' 14 And if this comes to
the governor's ears, we will satisfy him
and keep you out of trouble." 15 So they
took the money and did as they were
directed. And this story has been spread
among the Jews to this day.

The Great Commission

16 Now the eleven disciples went
to Galilee, to the mountain to
1611 which Jesus had directed them.
17 And when they saw him they wor-
shiped him, but some doubted. 18 And
Jesus came and said to them, "All author-
ity in heaven and on earth has been given
to me. 19 Go therefore and make disciples
of all nations, baptizing them in[3]
the name of the Father and of the
593 Son and of the Holy Spirit,
20 teaching them to observe all that I have
commanded you. And behold, I am with
you always, to the end of the age."

[1] Or *Take a guard* [2] Some manuscripts *the Lord* [3] Or *into*

Introduction to

Mark

Author
John Mark

Date
About A.D. 53–55

Key People
Jesus; John the Baptist; Peter; James; John; the Pharisees; Judas Iscariot; Pontius Pilate

Purpose
The purpose of Mark is to tell the story of Jesus' ministry, death, and resurrection so that it shows who Jesus is—God's Son and promised Messiah who is to be believed and obeyed.

Central Themes
Jesus is man; Jesus is the Son of God; Jesus is the Son of Man with all power and authority; Jesus is Lord; Jesus came to serve and give His life for His people; Jesus' disciples must follow Him in denying themselves and serving God and others.

Memory Verses
Jesus' message (Mark 1:14–15); prayer for faith (Mark 9:23–24); Jesus' mission (Mark 10:42–45); a centurion's confession (Mark 15:39)

Introduction

Even though Mark was not one of Jesus' 12 apostles, he received eyewitness information from the apostle Peter. Mark doesn't tell of Jesus' birth; he begins with Jesus' baptism, when the Holy Spirit descends on Jesus (Mark 1:1–11). Things happen quickly in Mark, and the same chapter goes on to show us Jesus being tempted by Satan, announcing that the kingdom of heaven has come, calling His first disciples, casting out demons, healing, and preaching (Mark 1:12–45). Mark tells of Jesus doing things only God can do—forgiving sins (Mark 2:1–12) and calming storms (Mark 4:35–41). Once Jesus has revealed to His disciples that He is the Messiah (8:27–29), He begins to teach that He will save His people not by force but by suffering for them (Mark 8:31–32; 9:12, 30–32; 10:32–34). The Jewish leaders, refusing to accept Jesus as God's Son and promised Messiah, have Him nailed to a cross. As Jesus dies, the curtain in the temple separating people from God tears apart, and the Roman soldier standing by the cross says, "Truly this man was the Son of God" (Mark 15). Mark tells of Jesus rising from the dead on the third day, just as He had promised (Mark 16).

About 5 B.C.	About A.D. 28–33	About A.D. 53–55
Birth of Jesus	Jesus' ministry, death, resurrection	Mark's Gospel written

The Gospel According to

Mark

John the Baptist Prepares the Way

1 The beginning of the gospel of
Jesus Christ, the Son of God.[1]
1373 2 As it is written in Isaiah the
prophet,[2]

> "Behold, I send my messenger before
> your face,
> who will prepare your way,
> 3 the voice of one crying in the
> wilderness:
> 'Prepare[3] the way of the Lord,
> make his paths straight,'"

4 John appeared, baptizing in the wil-
derness and proclaiming a baptism of
repentance for the forgiveness of sins.
5 And all the country of Judea and all
Jerusalem were going out to him and
were being baptized by him in the river
Jordan, confessing their sins. 6 Now
John was clothed with camel's hair and
wore a leather belt around his waist
and ate locusts and wild honey. 7 And
he preached, saying, "After me comes
he who is mightier than I, the strap of
whose sandals I am not worthy to stoop
down and untie. 8 I have baptized you
with water, but he will baptize you with
the Holy Spirit."

The Baptism of Jesus

9 In those days Jesus came from
Nazareth of Galilee and was
1305 baptized by John in the Jordan.
10 And when he came up out of the water,
immediately he saw the heavens being
torn open and the Spirit descending on
him like a dove. 11 And a voice came from
heaven, "You are my beloved Son;[4] with
you I am well pleased."

The Temptation of Jesus

12 The Spirit immediately drove
him out into the wilderness. 13 And
1309 he was in the wilderness forty
days, being tempted by Satan. And he was
with the wild animals, and the angels
were ministering to him.

Jesus Begins His Ministry

14 Now after John was arrested, Jesus
came into Galilee, proclaiming the gos-
pel of God, 15 and saying, "The time is ful-
filled, and the kingdom of God is at hand;
repent and believe in the gospel."

Jesus Calls the First Disciples

16 Passing alongside the Sea of
Galilee, he saw Simon and Andrew
1313, the brother of Simon casting a net
1467 into the sea, for they were fisher-
men. 17 And Jesus said to them, "Follow
me, and I will make you become fishers of
men." 18 And immediately they left their
nets and followed him. 19 And going on a
little farther, he saw James the son of
Zebedee and John his brother, who were
in their boat mending the nets. 20 And
immediately he called them, and they left
their father Zebedee in the boat with the
hired servants and followed him.

Jesus Heals a Man with an Unclean Spirit

21 And they went into Capernaum,
and immediately on the Sabbath
1463 he entered the synagogue and was
teaching. 22 And they were astonished at
his teaching, for he taught them as one
who had authority, and not as the scribes.
23 And immediately there was in their syn-
agogue a man with an unclean spirit. And
he cried out, 24 "What have you to do with

[1] Some manuscripts omit *the Son of God* [2] Some manuscripts *in the prophets* [3] Or *crying: Prepare in the wilderness* [4] Or *my Son, my (or the) Beloved*

us, Jesus of Nazareth? Have you come to
destroy us? I know who you are—the Holy
One of God." 25 But Jesus rebuked him, say-
ing, "Be silent, and come out of him!"
26 And the unclean spirit, convulsing him
and crying out with a loud voice, came out
of him. 27 And they were all amazed, so
that they questioned among themselves,
saying, "What is this? A new teaching with
authority! He commands even the unclean
spirits, and they obey him." 28 And at once
his fame spread everywhere throughout
all the surrounding region of Galilee.

Jesus Heals Many

29 And immediately he[1] left the syna-
gogue and entered the house of Simon
and Andrew, with James and John. 30 Now
Simon's mother-in-law lay ill with a fever,
and immediately they told him about her.
31 And he came and took her by the hand
and lifted her up, and the fever left her, and
she began to serve them.

32 That evening at sundown they
brought to him all who were sick or
oppressed by demons. 33 And the whole
city was gathered together at the door.
34 And he healed many who were sick
with various diseases, and cast out many
demons. And he would not permit the
demons to speak, because they knew him.

Jesus Preaches in Galilee

35 And rising very early in the morning,
while it was still dark, he departed and
went out to a desolate place, and there he
prayed. 36 And Simon and those who were
with him searched for him, 37 and they
found him and said to him, "Everyone is
looking for you." 38 And he said to them,
"Let us go on to the next towns, that I
may preach there also, for that is why I
came out." 39 And he went throughout all
Galilee, preaching in their synagogues and
casting out demons.

Jesus Cleanses a Leper

40 And a leper[2] came to him,
imploring him, and kneeling said
1507
to him, "If you will, you can make
me clean." 41 Moved with pity, he stretched
out his hand and touched him and said to
him, "I will; be clean." 42 And immediately
the leprosy left him, and he was made
clean. 43 And Jesus[3] sternly charged him
and sent him away at once, 44 and said to
him, "See that you say nothing to anyone,
but go, show yourself to the priest and
offer for your cleansing what Moses com-
manded, for a proof to them." 45 But he
went out and began to talk freely about it,
and to spread the news, so that Jesus
could no longer openly enter a town, but
was out in desolate places, and people
were coming to him from every quarter.

CHARACTER PROFILE

JAMES AND JOHN

James and John were brothers and two of Jesus' closest disciples. After Jesus' resurrection, Herod beheaded James for preaching the gospel. John wrote the Gospel of John as well as 1 John, 2 John, and 3 John. He was exiled to the island of Patmos for preaching the gospel. There, he saw and wrote down the vision that became the book of Revelation.

1313, 1339, 1415, 1847

[1] Some manuscripts *they* [2] *Leprosy* was a term for several skin diseases; see Leviticus 13 [3] Greek *he*; also verse 45

The Baptism and Temptation of Jesus

John was the messenger that God had promised would prepare the way for the Savior. John lived in the desert and wore clothing made of camel's hair. He ate locusts and wild honey. He told the crowds who came to hear him that someone was coming who was more powerful than he was. "I have baptized you with water," John said, "but He will baptize you with the Holy Spirit." John told people to repent of their sins. He told them to stop disobeying God and instead to fear, love, and trust God above all things. When people were baptized by John, they were showing that they were sorry for their sins and wanted to change.

One day, Jesus came from Nazareth to see John in the desert. Although Jesus had never sinned, John still baptized Him in the Jordan River. After Jesus had been baptized, the Holy Spirit came down on Him like a dove. A voice from heaven said, "You are My beloved Son; with You I am well pleased." It was the voice of God the Father talking to His Son.

At once, the Holy Spirit sent Jesus into the desert, where He stayed for 40 days. The devil tried many times to tempt Jesus to disobey God while He was in the desert, but Jesus did not sin. Wild animals lived in the desert. It was also a place where Jesus was hungry and weak. Even with all these troubles, Jesus obeyed God's commands, and God's angels took care of Him.

Long before this, when Satan tempted Adam and Eve, they listened to him and disobeyed God. Because Adam sinned, everyone is born sinful. Jesus is the only person who never sinned. He resisted all of Satan's temptations for us. If He had sinned, even once, He would not have been able to save us from sin. What a wonderful, perfect Savior!

SEEK and FIND

WHERE TO FIND THE STORY

Mark 1:1–13

KEY BIBLE VERSE

"For it was indeed fitting that we should have such a high priest, holy, innocent, unstained, separated from sinners, and exalted above the heavens." (Hebrews 7:26)

THREE KEY QUESTIONS

- Why were people going to John to be baptized?
- What happened when John baptized Jesus?
- Why is it important for us that Jesus never sinned?

RELATED BIBLE READINGS

Matthew 3:1–17; Luke 3:1–22; 4:1–13; Hebrews 2:14–18; 4:14–16

Jesus Heals a Paralytic

1377

2 And when he returned to
Capernaum after some days, it
was reported that he was at home.
2 And many were gathered together, so that
there was no more room, not even at the
door. And he was preaching the word to
them. 3 And they came, bringing to him a
paralytic carried by four men. 4 And when
they could not get near him because of the
crowd, they removed the roof above him,
and when they had made an opening, they
let down the bed on which the paralytic lay.
5 And when Jesus saw their faith, he said to
the paralytic, "Son, your sins are forgiven."
6 Now some of the scribes were sitting
there, questioning in their hearts, 7 "Why
does this man speak like that? He is blas-
pheming! Who can forgive sins but God
alone?" 8 And immediately Jesus, perceiv-
ing in his spirit that they thus questioned
within themselves, said to them, "Why do

you question these things in your hearts?
9 Which is easier, to say to the paralytic,
'Your sins are forgiven,' or to say, 'Rise, take
up your bed and walk'? 10 But that you may
know that the Son of Man has authority on
earth to forgive sins"—he said to the
paralytic— 11 "I say to you, rise, pick
1377 up your bed, and go home." 12 And
he rose and immediately picked up his bed
and went out before them all, so that they
were all amazed and glorified God, saying,
"We never saw anything like this!"

Jesus Calls Levi

13 He went out again beside the sea,
and all the crowd was coming to
1381 him, and he was teaching them.
14 And as he passed by, he saw Levi the son
of Alphaeus sitting at the tax booth, and
he said to him, "Follow me." And he rose
and followed him.

15 And as he reclined at table in his
house, many tax collectors and sinners
were reclining with Jesus and his disciples,
for there were many who followed him.
16 And the scribes of[1] the Pharisees, when
they saw that he was eating with sinners
and tax collectors, said to his disciples,
"Why does he eat[2] with tax collectors and
sinners?" 17 And when Jesus heard it, he
said to them, "Those who are well
have no need of a physician, but
1381 those who are sick. I came not to
call the righteous, but sinners."

A Question About Fasting

18 Now John's disciples and the
Pharisees were fasting. And people came
and said to him, "Why do John's disciples
and the disciples of the Pharisees fast, but
your disciples do not fast?" 19 And Jesus
said to them, "Can the wedding guests
fast while the bridegroom is with them?
As long as they have the bridegroom with
them, they cannot fast. 20 The days will
come when the bridegroom is taken away
from them, and then they will fast in that
day. 21 No one sews a piece of unshrunk
cloth on an old garment. If he does, the
patch tears away from it, the new from the
old, and a worse tear is made. 22 And no
one puts new wine into old wineskins. If
he does, the wine will burst the skins—and
the wine is destroyed, and so are the skins.
But new wine is for fresh wineskins."[3]

Jesus Is Lord of the Sabbath

23 One Sabbath he was going through
the grainfields, and as they made their
way, his disciples began to pluck heads of
grain. 24 And the Pharisees were saying to
him, "Look, why are they doing what is
not lawful on the Sabbath?" 25 And he said
to them, "Have you never read what David
did, when he was in need and was hungry,
he and those who were with him: 26 how
he entered the house of God, in the time of
Abiathar the high priest, and ate the bread
of the Presence, which it is not lawful for
any but the priests to eat, and also gave it
to those who were with him?" 27 And he
said to them, "The Sabbath was made for
man, not man for the Sabbath. 28 So the
Son of Man is lord even of the Sabbath."

A Man with a Withered Hand

3 Again he entered the synagogue, and a
man was there with a withered hand.
2 And they watched Jesus,[4] to see whether
he would heal him on the Sabbath, so that
they might accuse him. 3 And he said to the
man with the withered hand, "Come here."
4 And he said to them, "Is it lawful on the
Sabbath to do good or to do harm, to save
life or to kill?" But they were silent. 5 And
he looked around at them with anger,
grieved at their hardness of heart, and said
to the man, "Stretch out your hand." He
stretched it out, and his hand was restored.
6 The Pharisees went out and immediately
held counsel with the Herodians against
him, how to destroy him.

A Great Crowd Follows Jesus

7 Jesus withdrew with his disciples to
the sea, and a great crowd followed, from

[1] Some manuscripts *and* [2] Some manuscripts add *and drink* [3] Some manuscripts omit *But new wine is for fresh wineskins* [4] Greek *him*

Jesus Heals a Paralyzed Man

The people in Capernaum had heard about the miracles Jesus had done in other places. When He came to their town, they were eager to see Him. Crowds gathered inside and outside of the house where Jesus was preaching.

While Jesus was there, along came four people carrying a paralyzed man on a mat. They wanted Jesus to heal their friend, so he could walk again. But the crowd was so large that there was no way the men could get him through the door to Jesus. So the four friends carried the paralyzed man up to the flat roof of the house. They made an opening in the roof large enough for the mat to pass through. Then taking ropes, they gently lowered their friend into the house until he was right in front of Jesus.

When Jesus saw their faith, He said to the paralyzed man, "Son, your sins are forgiven."

Some teachers of the law heard Jesus' words. They wondered, "Why does this man speak like that. Who can forgive sins but God alone?" They did not believe that Jesus could forgive sins, because they did not believe that Jesus was God.

Right away Jesus knew what they were thinking. So He asked them, "Which is easier, to say to the paralytic, 'Your sins are forgiven,' or to say, 'Rise, take up your bed and walk'?"

Then, to show them that He really is God and really can forgive sins, Jesus said to the paralyzed man, "I say to you, rise, pick up your bed, and go home." And right away, the man got up. He picked up his mat and left.

Everyone was amazed. They praised God, saying, "We never saw anything like this!"

Jesus healed many people while He was on earth. But people need to have their sins forgiven even more than they need to have their bodies healed. Jesus doesn't always heal us when we're sick or when we've been hurt. But He will always forgive our sins when we ask Him in faith, believing that He is our Savior.

SEEK and FIND

WHERE TO FIND THE STORY

Mark 2:1–12

KEY BIBLE VERSE

"The Son of Man has authority on earth to forgive sins" (Mark 2:10)

THREE KEY QUESTIONS

- What did the paralyzed man need even more than healing?
- How could Jesus know what the teachers of the law were thinking?
- How would healing the paralyzed man show that Jesus could also forgive sins?

RELATED BIBLE READINGS

Matthew 9:1–7; Luke 5:17–26; 7:48–49

Galilee and Judea 8 and Jerusalem and
Idumea and from beyond the Jordan and
from around Tyre and Sidon. When the
great crowd heard all that he was doing,
they came to him. 9 And he told his disci-
ples to have a boat ready for him because of
the crowd, lest they crush him, 10 for he had
healed many, so that all who had diseases
pressed around him to touch him. 11 And
whenever the unclean spirits saw him,
they fell down before him and cried out,
"You are the Son of God." 12 And he strictly
ordered them not to make him known.

The Twelve Apostles

13 And he went up on the mountain and
called to him those whom he desired, and
they came to him. 14 And he appointed
twelve (whom he also named apostles)
so that they might be with him and he
might send them out to preach 15 and
have authority to cast out demons. 16 He
appointed the twelve: Simon (to whom
he gave the name Peter); 17 James the son
of Zebedee and John the brother of James
(to whom he gave the name Boanerges,
that is, Sons of Thunder); 18 Andrew, and
Philip, and Bartholomew, and Matthew,
and Thomas, and James the son of
Alphaeus, and Thaddaeus, and Simon
the Cananaean, 19 and Judas Iscariot, who
betrayed him.

20 Then he went home, and the crowd
gathered again, so that they could not
even eat. 21 And when his family heard it,
they went out to seize him, for they were
saying, "He is out of his mind."

Blasphemy Against the Holy Spirit

22 And the scribes who came down
from Jerusalem were saying, "He is pos-
sessed by Beelzebul," and "by the prince
of demons he casts out the demons."
23 And he called them to him and said to
them in parables, "How can Satan cast out
Satan? 24 If a kingdom is divided against
itself, that kingdom cannot stand. 25 And
if a house is divided against itself, that
house will not be able to stand. 26 And if
Satan has risen up against himself and is
divided, he cannot stand, but is coming
to an end. 27 But no one can enter a strong
man's house and plunder his goods,
unless he first binds the strong man. Then
indeed he may plunder his house.

28 "Truly, I say to you, all sins will be for-
given the children of man, and whatever
blasphemies they utter, 29 but whoever
blasphemes against the Holy Spirit never
has forgiveness, but is guilty of an eternal
sin"— 30 for they were saying, "He has an
unclean spirit."

Jesus' Mother and Brothers

31 And his mother and his brothers
came, and standing outside they sent to
him and called him. 32 And a crowd was
sitting around him, and they said to him,
"Your mother and your brothers[1] are out-
side, seeking you." 33 And he answered
them, "Who are my mother and my broth-
ers?" 34 And looking about at those who sat
around him, he said, "Here are my mother
and my brothers! 35 For whoever does the
will of God, he is my brother and sister
and mother."

The Parable of the Sower

4 Again he began to teach beside the
sea. And a very large crowd gathered
about him, so that he got into a boat and
sat in it on the sea, and the whole crowd
was beside the sea on the land. 2 And he
was teaching them many things in para-
bles, and in his teaching he said to them:
3 "Listen! A sower went out to sow. 4 And
as he sowed, some seed fell along the
path, and the birds came and devoured it.
5 Other seed fell on rocky ground, where
it did not have much soil, and immedi-
ately it sprang up, since it had no depth
of soil. 6 And when the sun rose, it was
scorched, and since it had no root, it with-
ered away. 7 Other seed fell among thorns,
and the thorns grew up and choked it, and
it yielded no grain. 8 And other seeds fell

[1] Other early manuscripts add *and your sisters*

Jesus Eats at Matthew's House

One day Jesus went out by the Sea of Galilee. The whole crowd was coming to Him, and He was teaching them. As He passed by, Jesus saw Matthew (whose other name was Levi) sitting at the tax booth, doing his work. Matthew's job was to collect money from his fellow Jews for the Roman government, which ruled over them. People did not like tax collectors because of all the corruption. But Jesus loved Matthew. He said to the tax collector, "Follow Me."

Matthew got up and followed Him. Later, Jesus and His disciples ate a meal at Matthew's house. Jesus sat down with many tax collectors and other people who were known to be sinners. By eating with these people, Jesus was showing that He loved them.

Some Pharisees who were proud of knowing God's rules saw Jesus eating with sinners and tax collectors. They did not like Jesus being so friendly with such sinful people. So they asked Jesus' disciples, "Why does He eat with tax collectors and sinners?"

Jesus heard the question and answered it Himself. He told the Pharisees that it is sick people who need a doctor, not healthy people. He told them, "I came not to call the righteous, but sinners."

Sometimes, people think they must become good before they can come to Jesus. Jesus knows we are sinners who do wrong things every day. He came to save sinners. He calls sinners like us to believe in Him and follow Him. Then He heals us from our sin.

SEEK and FIND

WHERE TO FIND THE STORY

Mark 2:13–17

KEY BIBLE VERSE

"And when Jesus heard it, he said to them, 'Those who are well have no need of a physician, but those who are sick. I came not to call the righteous, but sinners.'" (Mark 2:17)

THREE KEY QUESTIONS

- What did Jesus do that the Pharisees did not like?
- What did Jesus tell the Pharisees?
- Do we need to make ourselves good before we can come to Jesus?

RELATED BIBLE READINGS

Matthew 9:9–13; Luke 5:27–32; 15:1–32

into good soil and produced grain, grow-
ing up and increasing and yielding thir-
tyfold and sixtyfold and a hundredfold."
9 And he said, "He who has ears to hear,
let him hear."

The Purpose of the Parables

10 And when he was alone, those around
him with the twelve asked him about the
parables. 11 And he said to them, "To you
has been given the secret of the kingdom
of God, but for those outside everything is
in parables, 12 so that

"they may indeed see but not perceive,
and may indeed hear but not understand,
lest they should turn and be forgiven."

13 And he said to them, "Do you not under-
stand this parable? How then will you
understand all the parables? 14 The sower
sows the word. 15 And these are the ones
along the path, where the word is sown:
when they hear, Satan immediately comes
and takes away the word that is sown in

them. 16 And these are the ones sown on rocky ground: the ones who, when they hear the word, immediately receive it with joy. 17 And they have no root in themselves, but endure for a while; then, when tribulation or persecution arises on account of the word, immediately they fall away.[1] 18 And others are the ones sown among thorns. They are those who hear the word, 19 but the cares of the world and the deceitfulness of riches and the desires for other things enter in and choke the word, and it proves unfruitful. 20 But those that were sown on the good soil are the ones who hear the word and accept it and bear fruit, thirtyfold and sixtyfold and a hundredfold."

A Lamp Under a Basket

21 And he said to them, "Is a lamp brought in to be put under a basket, or under a bed, and not on a stand? 22 For nothing is hidden except to be made manifest; nor is anything secret except to come to light. 23 If anyone has ears to hear, let him hear." 24 And he said to them, "Pay attention to what you hear: with the measure you use, it will be measured to you, and still more will be added to you. 25 For to the one who has, more will be given, and from the one who has not, even what he has will be taken away."

The Parable of the Seed Growing

26 And he said, "The kingdom of God is as if a man should scatter seed on the ground. 27 He sleeps and rises night and day, and the seed sprouts and grows; he knows not how. 28 The earth produces by itself, first the blade, then the ear, then the full grain in the ear. 29 But when the grain is ripe, at once he puts in the sickle, because the harvest has come."

The Parable of the Mustard Seed

30 And he said, "With what can we compare the kingdom of God, or what parable shall we use for it? 31 It is like a grain of mustard seed, which, when sown on the ground, is the smallest of all the seeds on earth, 32 yet when it is sown it grows up and becomes larger than all the garden plants and puts out large branches, so that the birds of the air can make nests in its shade."

33 With many such parables he spoke the word to them, as they were able to hear it. 34 He did not speak to them without a parable, but privately to his own disciples he explained everything.

Jesus Calms a Storm

1385

35 On that day, when evening had come, he said to them, "Let us go across to the other side." 36 And leaving the crowd, they took him with them in the boat, just as he was. And other boats were with him. 37 And a great windstorm arose, and the waves were breaking into the boat, so that the boat was already filling. 38 But he was in the stern, asleep on the cushion. And they woke him and said to him, "Teacher, do you not care that we are perishing?" 39 And he awoke and rebuked the wind and said to the sea, "Peace! Be still!" And the wind ceased, and there was a great calm. 40 He said to them, "Why are you so afraid? Have you still no faith?" 41 And they were filled with great fear and said to one another, "Who then is this, that even the wind and the sea obey him?"

1385

Jesus Heals a Man with a Demon

5 They came to the other side of the sea, to the country of the Gerasenes.[2] 2 And when Jesus[3] had stepped out of the boat, immediately there met him out of the tombs a man with an unclean spirit. 3 He lived among the tombs. And no one could bind him anymore, not even with a chain, 4 for he had often been bound with shackles and chains, but he wrenched the chains apart, and he broke the shackles in pieces. No one had the strength to subdue him. 5 Night and day among the tombs and on the mountains he was always crying

[1] Or *stumble* [2] Some manuscripts *Gergesenes*; some *Gadarenes* [3] Greek *he*; also verse 9

Jesus Calms the Storm

One evening, after a day of teaching by the Sea of Galilee, Jesus was very tired. He said to His disciples, "Let us go across to the other side." So they left the crowd and got in a boat. As they started across the water, some other boats followed.

While they were in the boat, the weather changed. A strong wind began to blow. The wind tossed the waves higher and higher until water splashed over the side of the boat and began to fill it. The disciples began to worry that the boat might sink—with them in it!

While the storm was raging, Jesus was asleep on a pillow in the back of the boat. He did not seem worried at all. But the disciples were afraid that they were about to drown. They woke Jesus and said, "Teacher, do You not care that we are perishing?"

Jesus got up. He ordered the wind and water to be quiet. He said to them, "Peace! Be still!" And just then, the wind stopped blowing and the water was calm.

Then Jesus turned to His disciples and said, "Why are you so afraid? Have you still no faith?"

After seeing this miracle, the disciples were filled with great fear at Jesus' power and authority. They said to one another, "Who then is this, that even the wind and the sea obey Him?"

Jesus became a human like us, but He is also God. Jesus is able to control the wind and the sea because He is the One who created them! Jesus did amazing things like calming storms so that we would know He really is the Son of God. We don't need to worry when trouble comes our way. We can trust Jesus at all times because He is in control.

SEEK and FIND

WHERE TO FIND THE STORY

Mark 4:35–41

KEY BIBLE VERSE

"And they were filled with great fear and said to one another, 'Who then is this, that even the wind and the sea obey Him?'" (Mark 4:41)

THREE KEY QUESTIONS

- Why were the disciples afraid when the storm was raging?
- What did Jesus say and what happened when He said it?
- Why was Jesus able to tell the wind and the waves what to do?

RELATED BIBLE READINGS

Matthew 8:23–27; 14:22–33; Mark 6:45–51; Luke 8:22–25; John 6:16–21

out and cutting himself with stones. 6 And
when he saw Jesus from afar, he ran and
fell down before him. 7 And crying out
with a loud voice, he said, "What have you
to do with me, Jesus, Son of the Most High
God? I adjure you by God, do not torment
me." 8 For he was saying to him, "Come
out of the man, you unclean spirit!" 9 And
Jesus asked him, "What is your name?"
He replied, "My name is Legion, for we are
many." 10 And he begged him earnestly not
to send them out of the country. 11 Now a
great herd of pigs was feeding there on the
hillside, 12 and they begged him, saying,
"Send us to the pigs; let us enter them."
13 So he gave them permission. And the
unclean spirits came out, and entered the
pigs, and the herd, numbering about two
thousand, rushed down the steep bank
into the sea and were drowned in the sea.

14 The herdsmen fled and told it in the city and in the country. And people came to see what it was that had happened. 15 And they came to Jesus and saw the demon-possessed[1] man, the one who had had the legion, sitting there, clothed and in his right mind, and they were afraid. 16 And those who had seen it described to them what had happened to the demon-possessed man and to the pigs. 17 And they began to beg Jesus[2] to depart from their region. 18 As he was getting into the boat, the man who had been possessed with demons begged him that he might be with him. 19 And he did not permit him but said to him, "Go home to your friends and tell them how much the Lord has done for you, and how he has had mercy on you." 20 And he went away and began to proclaim in the Decapolis how much Jesus had done for him, and everyone marveled.

Jesus Heals a Woman and Jairus's Daughter

1389

21 And when Jesus had crossed again in the boat to the other side, a great crowd gathered about him, and he was beside the sea. 22 Then came one of the rulers of the synagogue, Jairus by name, and seeing him, he fell at his feet 23 and implored him earnestly, saying, "My little daughter is at the point of death. Come and lay your hands on her, so that she may be made well and live." 24 And he went with him.

And a great crowd followed him and thronged about him. 25 And there was a woman who had had a discharge of blood for twelve years, 26 and who had suffered much under many physicians, and had spent all that she had, and was no better but rather grew worse. 27 She had heard the reports about Jesus and came up behind him in the crowd and touched his garment. 28 For she said, "If I touch even his garments, I will be made well." 29 And immediately the flow of blood dried up, and she felt in her body that she was healed of her disease. 30 And Jesus, perceiving in himself that power had gone out from him, immediately turned about in the crowd and said, "Who touched my garments?" 31 And his disciples said to him, "You see the crowd pressing around you, and yet you say, 'Who touched me?'" 32 And he looked around to see who had done it. 33 But the woman, knowing what had happened to her, came in fear and trembling and fell down before him and told him the whole truth. 34 And he said to her, "Daughter, your faith has made you well; go in peace, and be healed of your disease."

1389

1577, 1641

35 While he was still speaking, there came from the ruler's house some who said, "Your daughter is dead. Why trouble the Teacher any further?" 36 But overhearing[3] what they said, Jesus said to the ruler of the synagogue, "Do not fear, only believe." 37 And he allowed no one to follow him except Peter and James and John the brother of James. 38 They came to the house of the ruler of the synagogue, and Jesus[4] saw a commotion, people weeping and wailing loudly. 39 And when he had entered, he said to them, "Why are you making a commotion and weeping? The child is not dead but sleeping." 40 And they laughed at him. But he put them all outside and took the child's father and mother and those who were with him and went in where the child was. 41 Taking her by the hand he said to her, "Talitha cumi," which means, "Little girl, I say to you, arise." 42 And immediately the girl got up and began walking (for she was twelve years of age), and they were immediately overcome with amazement. 43 And he strictly charged them that no one should know this, and told them to give her something to eat.

Jesus Rejected at Nazareth

1459

6 He went away from there and came to his hometown, and his disciples followed him. 2 And on

[1] Greek *daimonizomai*; also verses 16, 18; elsewhere rendered *oppressed by demons* [2] Greek *him* [3] Or *ignoring*; some manuscripts *hearing* [4] Greek *he*

Jesus Makes a Little Girl Alive

One day, after Jesus had crossed back to the other side of the lake, a large crowd gathered around Him. Jairus, a person in charge of a Jewish meeting place, saw Jesus and went over to Him. Jairus knelt down at Jesus' feet. He asked Jesus for help, because his 12-year-old daughter was so sick she was about to die. "Come and lay Your hands on her," Jairus begged Jesus, "so that she may be made well and live." Jesus had healed many people by touching them. He was willing to heal this girl, too.

Jesus and His disciples went with Jairus, but it took a long time for them to get to Jairus's house. Many people were eager to see Jesus and talk with Him, and the crowd slowed them down. While Jesus was still on the way, some men came from Jairus's home with bad news. They said to Jairus, "Your daughter is dead. Why trouble the Teacher any further?"

Jesus heard them and said to Jairus, "Do not fear, only believe." Jesus sent everyone away except three of His disciples—Peter, James, and John—and they continued on the way to Jairus's house.

Finally, they arrived at the house. Jesus could hear people crying loudly, mourning for the girl who had died. Jesus went inside and said to them, "Why are you making a commotion and weeping?" He told them the girl would live.

The mourners did not believe Jesus. They knew the child had died, so they laughed at Jesus. Jesus told the people who were crying to leave the house. Then Jesus took the child's parents along with Peter and James and John into the room where she lay. Jesus took the girl's hand and said, "Little girl, I say to you, arise."

Immediately, the girl got up and began walking. Jesus told someone to give her food. What an amazing miracle!

Only God can make a dead person come back to life. Jesus is God. After Jesus died, He Himself came back to life. Even if we die, Jesus promises that He will raise us from the dead—if we trust Him. And if we truly know Jesus, we will live with Him forever.

SEEK and FIND

WHERE TO FIND THE STORY

Mark 5:21–24, 35–43

KEY BIBLE VERSE

"For as the Father raises the dead and gives them life, so also the Son gives life to whom he will." (John 5:21)

THREE KEY QUESTIONS

- Why did the people at Jairus's house think Jesus had come too late?
- How did Jesus raise the little girl from the dead?
- What will Jesus do some day for all who have trusted Jesus?

RELATED BIBLE READINGS

Matthew 9:18–26; Luke 7:11–17; 8:40–42, 49–56; John 5:19–29; 11:1–44

the Sabbath he began to teach in the synagogue, and many who heard him were astonished, saying, "Where did this man get these things? What is the wisdom given to him? How are such mighty works done by his hands? 3 Is not this the carpenter, the son of Mary and brother of James and Joses and Judas and Simon? And are not his sisters here with us?" And they took offense at him. 4 And Jesus said to them, "A prophet is not without honor, except in his hometown and among his relatives and in his own household." 5 And he could do no mighty work there, except that he laid his hands on a few sick people and healed them. 6 And he marveled because of their unbelief.

And he went about among the villages teaching.

Jesus Sends Out the Twelve Apostles

7 And he called the twelve and began to send them out two by two, and gave them authority over the unclean spirits. 8 He charged them to take nothing for their journey except a staff—no bread, no bag, no money in their belts— 9 but to wear sandals and not put on two tunics.[1] 10 And he said to them, "Whenever you enter a house, stay there until you depart from there. 11 And if any place will not receive you and they will not listen to you, when you leave, shake off the dust that is on your feet as a testimony against them." 12 So they went out and proclaimed that people should repent. 13 And they cast out many demons and anointed with oil many who were sick and healed them.

The Death of John the Baptist

14 King Herod heard of it, for Jesus'[2] name had become known. Some[3] said, "John the Baptist[4] has been raised from the dead. That is why these miraculous powers are at work in him." 15 But others said, "He is Elijah." And others said, "He is a prophet, like one of the prophets of old." 16 But when Herod heard of it, he said, "John, whom I beheaded, has been raised." 17 For it was Herod who had sent and seized John and bound him in prison for the sake of Herodias, his brother Philip's wife, because he had married her. 18 For John had been saying to Herod, "It is not lawful for you to have your brother's wife." 19 And Herodias had a grudge against him and wanted to put him to death. But she could not, 20 for Herod feared John, knowing that he was a righteous and holy man, and he kept him safe. When he heard him, he was greatly perplexed, and yet he heard him gladly.

21 But an opportunity came when Herod on his birthday gave a banquet for his nobles and military commanders and the leading men of Galilee. 22 For when Herodias's daughter came in and danced, she pleased Herod and his guests. And the king said to the girl, "Ask me for whatever you wish, and I will give it to you." 23 And he vowed to her, "Whatever you ask me, I will give you, up to half of my kingdom." 24 And she went out and said to her mother, "For what should I ask?" And she said, "The head of John the Baptist." 25 And she came in immediately with haste to the king and asked, saying, "I want you to give me at once the head of John the Baptist on a platter." 26 And the king was exceedingly sorry, but because of his oaths and his guests he did not want to break his word to her. 27 And immediately the king sent an executioner with orders to bring John's[5] head. He went and beheaded him in the prison 28 and brought his head on a platter and gave it to the girl, and the girl gave it to her mother. 29 When his disciples heard of it, they came and took his body and laid it in a tomb.

Jesus Feeds the Five Thousand

30 The apostles returned to Jesus and told him all that they had done and taught. 31 And he said to them, "Come away by yourselves to a desolate place and rest a while." For many were coming and going, and they had no leisure even to eat.

[1] Greek *chiton*, a long garment worn under the cloak next to the skin [2] Greek *his* [3] Some manuscripts *He* [4] Greek *baptizer*; also verse 24 [5] Greek *his*

32 And they went away in the boat to
a desolate place by themselves.
1559 33 Now many saw them going and
recognized them, and they ran there on
foot from all the towns and got there ahead
of them. 34 When he went ashore he
saw a great crowd, and he had com-
1571 passion on them, because they
were like sheep without a shepherd. And
he began to teach them many things.
35 And when it grew late, his disciples came
to him and said, "This is a desolate place,
and the hour is now late. 36 Send them
away to go into the surrounding country-
side and villages and buy themselves
something to eat." 37 But he answered
them, "You give them something to eat."
And they said to him, "Shall we go and buy
two hundred denarii[1] worth of bread and
give it to them to eat?" 38 And he said to
them, "How many loaves do you have? Go
and see." And when they had found out,
they said, "Five, and two fish." 39 Then he
commanded them all to sit down in groups
on the green grass. 40 So they sat down in
groups, by hundreds and by fifties. 41 And
taking the five loaves and the two fish he
looked up to heaven and said a blessing
and broke the loaves and gave them to the
disciples to set before the people. And he
divided the two fish among them all. 42 And
they all ate and were satisfied. 43 And they
took up twelve baskets full of broken
pieces and of the fish. 44 And those who ate
the loaves were five thousand men.

Jesus Walks on the Water

45 Immediately he made his disci-
ples get into the boat and go before
1331, him to the other side, to Bethsaida,
1385 while he dismissed the crowd.
46 And after he had taken leave of them, he
went up on the mountain to pray. 47 And
when evening came, the *boat* was out on
the sea, and he was alone on the land.
48 And he saw that they were making head-
way painfully, for the wind was against
them. And about the fourth watch of the
night[2] he came to them, walking on the sea.
He meant to pass by them, 49 but when they
saw him walking on the sea they thought it
was a ghost, and cried out, 50 for they all saw
him and were terrified. But immediately he
spoke to them and said, "Take heart; it is I.
Do not be afraid." 51 And he got into the boat
with them, and the wind ceased. And they
were utterly astounded, 52 for they did not
understand about the loaves, but their
hearts were hardened.

Jesus Heals the Sick in Gennesaret

53 When they had crossed over, they
came to land at Gennesaret and moored to
the shore. 54 And when they got out of the
boat, the people immediately recognized
him 55 and ran about the whole region
and began to bring the sick people on
their beds to wherever they heard he was.
56 And wherever he came, in villages, cit-
ies, or countryside, they laid the sick in the
marketplaces and implored him that they
might touch even the fringe of his garment.
And as many as touched it were made well.

Traditions and Commandments

7 Now when the Pharisees gathered to
him, with some of the scribes who
had come from Jerusalem, 2 they saw that
some of his disciples ate with hands that
were defiled, that is, unwashed. 3 (For
the Pharisees and all the Jews do not eat
unless they wash[3] their hands, holding
to the tradition of the elders, 4 and when
they come from the marketplace, they do
not eat unless they wash.[4] And there are
many other traditions that they observe,
such as the washing of cups and pots and
copper vessels and dining couches.[5]) 5 And
the Pharisees and the scribes asked him,
"Why do your disciples not walk accord-
ing to the tradition of the elders, but eat
with defiled hands?" 6 And he said to
them, "Well did Isaiah prophesy of you
hypocrites, as it is written,

[1] A *denarius* was a day's wage for a laborer [2] That is, between 3 A.M. and 6 A.M. [3] Greek *unless they wash with a fist*, probably indicating a kind of ceremonial washing [4] Greek *unless they baptize*; some manuscripts *unless they purify themselves* [5] Some manuscripts omit *and dining couches*

"'This people honors me with their
lips,
but their heart is far from me;
7 in vain do they worship me,
teaching as doctrines the
commandments of men.'

8 You leave the commandment of God and
hold to the tradition of men."
9 And he said to them, "You have a fine
way of rejecting the commandment of
God in order to establish your tradition!
10 For Moses said, 'Honor your father and
your mother'; and, 'Whoever reviles father
or mother must surely die.' 11 But you say,
'If a man tells his father or his mother,
"Whatever you would have gained from
me is Corban"' (that is, given to God)[1]—
12 then you no longer permit him to do
anything for his father or mother, 13 thus
making void the word of God by your tra-
dition that you have handed down. And
many such things you do."

What Defiles a Person

14 And he called the people to him again
and said to them, "Hear me, all of you, and
understand: 15 There is nothing outside a
person that by going into him can defile
him, but the things that come out of a
person are what defile him."[2] 17 And when
he had entered the house and left the
people, his disciples asked him about the
parable. 18 And he said to them, "Then are
you also without understanding? Do you
not see that whatever goes into a person
from outside cannot defile him, 19 since it
enters not his heart but his stomach, and
is expelled?"[3] (Thus he declared all foods
clean.) 20 And he said, "What comes out of
a person is what defiles him. 21 For from
within, out of the heart of man, come evil
thoughts, sexual immorality, theft, mur-
der, adultery, 22 coveting, wickedness,
deceit, sensuality, envy, slander, pride,
foolishness. 23 All these evil things come
from within, and they defile a person."

The Syrophoenician Woman's Faith

24 And from there he arose and went
away to the region of Tyre and Sidon.[4]
And he entered a house and did not want
anyone to know, yet he could not be hid-
den. 25 But immediately a woman whose
little daughter had an unclean spirit heard
of him and came and fell down at his
feet. 26 Now the woman was a Gentile, a
Syrophoenician by birth. And she begged
him to cast the demon out of her daugh-
ter. 27 And he said to her, "Let the children
be fed first, for it is not right to take the
children's bread and throw it to the dogs."
28 But she answered him, "Yes, Lord; yet
even the dogs under the table eat the chil-
dren's crumbs." 29 And he said to her, "For
this statement you may go your way; the
demon has left your daughter." 30 And she
went home and found the child lying in
bed and the demon gone.

Jesus Heals a Deaf Man

31 Then he returned from the region of
Tyre and went through Sidon to the Sea
of Galilee, in the region of the Decapolis.
32 And they brought to him a man who was
deaf and had a speech impediment, and
they begged him to lay his hand on him.
33 And taking him aside from the crowd
privately, he put his fingers into his ears,
and after spitting touched his tongue.
34 And looking up to heaven, he sighed
and said to him, "Ephphatha," that is, "Be
opened." 35 And his ears were opened, his
tongue was released, and he spoke plainly.
36 And Jesus[5] charged them to tell no one.
But the more he charged them, the more
zealously they proclaimed it. 37 And they
were astonished beyond measure, say-
ing, "He has done all things well. He even
makes the deaf hear and the mute speak."

Jesus Feeds the Four Thousand

8 In those days, when again a great
crowd had gathered, and they had
nothing to eat, he called his disciples to

[1] Or *an offering* [2] Some manuscripts add verse 16: *If anyone has ears to hear, let him hear* [3] Greek *goes out into the latrine* [4] Some manuscripts omit *and Sidon* [5] Greek *he*

him and said to them, 2 "I have compassion on the crowd, because they have been with me now three days and have nothing to eat. 3 And if I send them away hungry to their homes, they will faint on the way. And some of them have come from far away." 4 And his disciples answered him, "How can one feed these people with bread here in this desolate place?" 5 And he asked them, "How many loaves do you have?" They said, "Seven." 6 And he directed the crowd to sit down on the ground. And he took the seven loaves, and having given thanks, he broke them and gave them to his disciples to set before the people; and they set them before the crowd. 7 And they had a few small fish. And having blessed them, he said that these also should be set before them. 8 And they ate and were satisfied. And they took up the broken pieces left over, seven baskets full. 9 And there were about four thousand people. And he sent them away. 10 And immediately he got into the boat with his disciples and went to the district of Dalmanutha.[1]

The Pharisees Demand a Sign

11 The Pharisees came and began to argue with him, seeking from him a sign from heaven to test him. 12 And he sighed deeply in his spirit and said, "Why does this generation seek a sign? Truly, I say to you, no sign will be given to this generation." 13 And he left them, got into the boat again, and went to the other side.

The Leaven of the Pharisees and Herod

14 Now they had forgotten to bring bread, and they had only one loaf with them in the boat. 15 And he cautioned them, saying, "Watch out; beware of the leaven of the Pharisees and the leaven of Herod."[2] 16 And they began discussing with one another the fact that they had no bread. 17 And Jesus, aware of this, said to them, "Why are you discussing the fact that you have no bread? Do you not yet perceive or understand? Are your hearts hardened? 18 Having eyes do you not see, and having ears do you not hear? And do you not remember? 19 When I broke the five loaves for the five thousand, how many baskets full of broken pieces did you take up?" They said to him, "Twelve." 20 "And the seven for the four thousand, how many baskets full of broken pieces did you take up?" And they said to him, "Seven." 21 And he said to them, "Do you not yet understand?"

Jesus Heals a Blind Man at Bethsaida

1567
22 And they came to Bethsaida. And some people brought to him a blind man and begged him to touch him. 23 And he took the blind man by the hand and led him out of the village, and when he had spit on his eyes and laid his hands on him, he asked him, "Do you see anything?" 24 And he looked up and said, "I see men, but they look like trees, walking." 25 Then Jesus[3] laid his hands on his eyes again; and he opened his eyes, his sight was restored, and he saw everything clearly. 26 And he sent him to his home, saying, "Do not even enter the village."

Peter Confesses Jesus as the Christ

27 And Jesus went on with his disciples to the villages of Caesarea Philippi. And on the way he asked his disciples, "Who do people say that I am?" 28 And they told him, "John the Baptist; and others say, Elijah; and others, one of the prophets." 29 And he asked them, "But who do you say that I am?" Peter answered him, "You are the Christ." 30 And he strictly charged them to tell no one about him.

Jesus Foretells His Death and Resurrection

31 And he began to teach them that the Son of Man must suffer many things and be rejected by the elders and the chief priests and the scribes and be killed, and after three days rise again. 32 And he said this plainly. And Peter took him aside and began to rebuke him. 33 But turning and seeing his disciples, he rebuked Peter

[1] Some manuscripts *Magadan*, or *Magdala* [2] Some manuscripts *the Herodians* [3] Greek *he*

and said, "Get behind me, Satan! For you are not setting your mind on the things of God, but on the things of man."

34 And calling the crowd to him with his disciples, he said to them, "If anyone would come after me, let him deny himself and take up his cross and follow me. 35 For whoever would save his life[1] will lose it, but whoever loses his life for my sake and the gospel's will save it. 36 For what does it profit a man to gain the whole world and forfeit his soul? 37 For what can a man give in return for his soul? 38 For whoever is ashamed of me and of my words in this adulterous and sinful generation, of him will the Son of Man also be ashamed when he comes in the glory of his Father with the holy angels."

9 And he said to them, "Truly, I say to you, there are some standing here who will not taste death until they see the kingdom of God after it has come with power."

The Transfiguration

1397

1339

2 And after six days Jesus took with him Peter and James and John, and led them up a high mountain by themselves. And he was transfigured before them, 3 and his clothes became radiant, intensely white, as no one[2] on earth could bleach them. 4 And there appeared to them Elijah with Moses, and they were talking with Jesus. 5 And Peter said to Jesus, "Rabbi,[3] it is good that we are here. Let us make three tents, one for you and one for Moses and one for Elijah." 6 For he did not know what to say, for they were terrified. 7 And a cloud overshadowed them, and a voice came out of the cloud, "This is my beloved Son;[4] listen to him." 8 And suddenly, looking around, they no longer saw anyone with them but Jesus only.

9 And as they were coming down the mountain, he charged them to tell no one what they had seen, until the Son of Man had risen from the dead. 10 So they kept the matter to themselves, questioning what this rising from the dead might mean. 11 And they asked him, "Why do the scribes say that first Elijah must come?" 12 And he said to them, "Elijah does come first to restore all things. And how is it written of the Son of Man that he should suffer many things and be treated with contempt? 13 But I tell you that Elijah has come, and they did to him whatever they pleased, as it is written of him."

Jesus Heals a Boy with an Unclean Spirit

14 And when they came to the disciples, they saw a great crowd around them, and scribes arguing with them. 15 And immediately all the crowd, when they saw him, were greatly amazed and ran up to him and greeted him. 16 And he asked them, "What are you arguing about with them?" 17 And someone from the crowd answered him, "Teacher, I brought my son to you, for he has a spirit that makes him mute. 18 And whenever it seizes him, it throws him down, and he foams and grinds his teeth and becomes rigid. So I asked your disciples to cast it out, and they were not able." 19 And he answered them, "O faithless generation, how long am I to be with you? How long am I to bear with you? Bring him to me." 20 And they brought the boy to him. And when the spirit saw him, immediately it convulsed the boy, and he fell on the ground and rolled about, foaming at the mouth. 21 And Jesus asked his father, "How long has this been happening to him?" And he said, "From childhood. 22 And it has often cast him into fire and into water, to destroy him. But if you can do anything, have compassion on us and help us." 23 And Jesus said to him, "'If you can'! All things are possible for one who believes." 24 Immediately the father of the child cried out[5] and said, "I believe; help my unbelief!" 25 And when Jesus saw that a crowd came running together, he rebuked the unclean spirit, saying to it,

[1] The same Greek word can mean either *soul* or *life*, depending on the context; twice in this verse and once in verse 36 and once in verse 37 [2] Greek *no cloth refiner*
[3] *Rabbi* means *my teacher*, or *my master* [4] Or *my Son, my* (or *the*) *Beloved* [5] Some manuscripts add *with tears*

The Transfiguration

One day Jesus took Peter, James, and John with Him on a journey. He led them up a high mountain. When they reached a certain spot, something amazing happened: Jesus was transfigured. His appearance completely changed. The glory of God began shining from Jesus' face. His clothes became radiant, whiter than anyone could ever make them with soap or bleach.

While they were on the mountain, Moses and Elijah appeared and talked with Jesus. Both of these men had lived long ago. Moses lived at the time when God first gave the Ten Commandments. And Elijah was one of God's prophets. Both of them had gone to be with the Lord a long, long time ago, but now here they were on earth, talking with Jesus!

The disciples were surprised and terrified. Not knowing what else to say, Peter said to Jesus, "It is good that we are here. Let us make three tents—one for You and one for Moses and one for Elijah."

Then a cloud came over them. God's voice came out of the cloud with a message about Jesus. God said, "This is My beloved Son; listen to Him."

Suddenly, looking around, Peter, James, and John saw only Jesus. Moses and Elijah were gone. The cloud was gone. And Jesus looked like a normal man again.

As they were coming down the mountain, Jesus told the three disciples not to tell anyone what they had seen or heard until He had risen from the dead. And even though they had some questions about what Jesus meant, the disciples did as He asked.

The three disciples saw Jesus glorified as God's Son. They heard God's voice telling them to listen to Jesus. Later, after Jesus had risen from the dead, they would remember what they had seen and they would tell everyone. People would know that Jesus was truly human, but He was also God and shared in the glory of God. He left that glory to come save His people from their sin. What a great Savior!

SEEK and FIND

WHERE TO FIND THE STORY

Mark 9:2–10

KEY BIBLE VERSE

"We were eyewitnesses of his majesty. For when he received honor and glory from God the Father, and the voice was borne to him by the Majestic Glory, 'This is my beloved Son, with whom I am well pleased,' we ourselves heard this very voice borne from heaven, for we were with him on the holy mountain." (2 Peter 1:16–18)

THREE KEY QUESTIONS

- What did Jesus look like on the mountain?
- Who were Moses and Elijah?
- When God's voice came out of the cloud, who did God say Jesus is?

RELATED BIBLE READINGS

Matthew 17:1–9; Luke 9:28–36; John 1:18; 17:4–5

"You mute and deaf spirit, I command you, come out of him and never enter him again." **26** And after crying out and convulsing him terribly, it came out, and the boy was like a corpse, so that most of them said, "He is dead." **27** But Jesus took him by the hand and lifted him up, and he arose. **28** And when he had entered the house, his disciples asked him privately, "Why could we not cast it out?" **29** And he said to them, "This kind cannot be driven out by anything but prayer."[1]

Jesus Again Foretells Death, Resurrection

30 They went on from there and passed through Galilee. And he did not want anyone to know, **31** for he was teaching his disciples, saying to them, "The Son of Man is going to be delivered into the hands of men, and they will kill him. And when he is killed, after three days he will rise." **32** But they did not understand the saying, and were afraid to ask him.

Who Is the Greatest?

33 And they came to Capernaum. And when he was in the house he asked them, "What were you discussing on the way?" **34** But they kept silent, for on the way they had argued with one another about who was the greatest. **35** And he sat down and called the twelve. And he said to them, "If anyone would be first, he must be last of all and servant of all." **36** And he took a child and put him in the midst of them, and taking him in his arms, he said to them, **37** "Whoever receives one such child in my name receives me, and whoever receives me, receives not me but him who sent me."

Anyone Not Against Us Is for Us

38 John said to him, "Teacher, we saw someone casting out demons in your name,[2] and we tried to stop him, because he was not following us." **39** But Jesus said, "Do not stop him, for no one who does a mighty work in my name will be able soon afterward to speak evil of me. **40** For the one who is not against us is for us. **41** For truly, I say to you, whoever gives you a cup of water to drink because you belong to Christ will by no means lose his reward.

Temptations to Sin

42 "Whoever causes one of these little ones who believe in me to sin,[3] it would be better for him if a great millstone were hung around his neck and he were thrown into the sea. **43** And if your hand causes you to sin, cut it off. It is better for you to enter life crippled than with two hands to go to hell,[4] to the unquenchable fire.[5] **45** And if your foot causes you to sin, cut it off. It is better for you to enter life lame than with two feet to be thrown into hell. **47** And if your eye causes you to sin, tear it out. It is better for you to enter the kingdom of God with one eye than with two eyes to be thrown into hell, **48** 'where their worm does not die and the fire is not quenched.' **49** For everyone will be salted with fire.[6] **50** Salt is good, but if the salt has lost its saltiness, how will you make it salty again? Have salt in yourselves, and be at peace with one another."

Teaching About Divorce

10 And he left there and went to the region of Judea and beyond the Jordan, and crowds gathered to him again. And again, as was his custom, he taught them.

2 And Pharisees came up and in order to test him asked, "Is it lawful for a man to divorce his wife?" **3** He answered them, "What did Moses command you?" **4** They said, "Moses allowed a man to write a certificate of divorce and to send her away." **5** And Jesus said to them, "Because of your hardness of heart he wrote you this commandment. **6** But from the beginning of creation, 'God made them male and female.' **7** 'Therefore a man shall leave

[1] Some manuscripts add *and fasting* [2] Some manuscripts add *who does not follow us* [3] Greek *to stumble*; also verses 43, 45, 47 [4] Greek *Gehenna*; also verse 47 [5] Some manuscripts add verses 44 and 46 (which are identical with verse 48) [6] Some manuscripts add *and every sacrifice will be salted with salt*

his father and mother and hold fast to his wife,[1] 8 and the two shall become one flesh.' So they are no longer two but one flesh. 9 What therefore God has joined together, let not man separate."

10 And in the house the disciples asked him again about this matter. 11 And he said to them, "Whoever divorces his wife and marries another commits adultery against her, 12 and if she divorces her husband and marries another, she commits adultery."

Let the Children Come to Me

1403

13 And they were bringing children to him that he might touch them, and the disciples rebuked them. 14 But when Jesus saw it, he was indignant and said to them, "Let the children come to me; do not hinder them, for to such belongs the kingdom of God. 15 Truly, I say to you, whoever does not receive the kingdom of God like a child shall not enter it." 16 And he took them in his arms and blessed them, laying his hands on them.

1403

The Rich Young Man

17 And as he was setting out on his journey, a man ran up and knelt before him and asked him, "Good Teacher, what must I do to inherit eternal life?" 18 And Jesus said to him, "Why do you call me good? No one is good except God alone. 19 You know the commandments: 'Do not murder, Do not commit adultery, Do not steal, Do not bear false witness, Do not defraud, Honor your father and mother.'" 20 And he said to him, "Teacher, all these I have kept from my youth." 21 And Jesus, looking at him, loved him, and said to him, "You lack one thing: go, sell all that you have and give to the poor, and you will have treasure in heaven; and come, follow me." 22 Disheartened by the saying, he went away sorrowful, for he had great possessions.

23 And Jesus looked around and said to his disciples, "How difficult it will be for those who have wealth to enter the kingdom of God!" 24 And the disciples were amazed at his words. But Jesus said to them again, "Children, how difficult it is[2] to enter the kingdom of God! 25 It is easier for a camel to go through the eye of a needle than for a rich person to enter the kingdom of God." 26 And they were exceedingly astonished, and said to him,[3] "Then who can be saved?" 27 Jesus looked at them and said, "With man it is impossible, but not with God. For all things are possible with God." 28 Peter began to say to him, "See, we have left everything and followed you." 29 Jesus said, "Truly, I say to you, there is no one who has left house or brothers or sisters or mother or father or children or lands, for my sake and for the gospel, 30 who will not receive a hundredfold now in this time, houses and brothers and sisters and mothers and children and lands, with persecutions, and in the age to come eternal life. 31 But many who are first will be last, and the last first."

Jesus Foretells His Death a Third Time

32 And they were on the road, going up to Jerusalem, and Jesus was walking ahead of them. And they were amazed, and those who followed were afraid. And taking the twelve again, he began to tell them what was to happen to him, 33 saying, "See, we are going up to Jerusalem, and the Son of Man will be delivered over to the chief priests and the scribes, and they will condemn him to death and deliver him over to the Gentiles. 34 And they will mock him and spit on him, and flog him and kill him. And after three days he will rise."

The Request of James and John

35 And James and John, the sons of Zebedee, came up to him and said to him, "Teacher, we want you to do for us whatever we ask of you." 36 And he said to them, "What do you want me to do for you?" 37 And they said to him, "Grant us to sit, one at your right hand and one at your

[1] Some manuscripts omit *and hold fast to his wife* [2] Some manuscripts add *for those who trust in riches* [3] Some manuscripts *to one another*

left, in your glory." 38 Jesus said to them, "You do not know what you are asking. Are you able to drink the cup that I drink, or to be baptized with the baptism with which I am baptized?" 39 And they said to him, "We are able." And Jesus said to them, "The cup that I drink you will drink, and with the baptism with which I am baptized, you will be baptized, 40 but to sit at my right hand or at my left is not mine to grant, but it is for those for whom it has been prepared." 41 And when the ten heard it, they began to be indignant at James and John. 42 And Jesus called them to him and said to them, "You know that those who are considered rulers of the Gentiles lord it over them, and their great ones exercise authority over them. 43 But it shall not be so among you. But whoever would be great among you must be your servant,[1] 44 and whoever would be first among you must be slave[2] of all. 45 For even the Son of Man came not to be served but to serve, and to give his life as a ransom for many."

Jesus Heals Blind Bartimaeus

46 And they came to Jericho. And as he was leaving Jericho with his disciples and a great crowd, Bartimaeus, a blind beggar, the son of Timaeus, was sitting by the roadside. 47 And when he heard that it was Jesus of Nazareth, he began to cry out and say, "Jesus, Son of David, have mercy on me!" 48 And many rebuked him, telling him to be silent. But he cried out all the more, "Son of David, have mercy on me!" 49 And Jesus stopped and said, "Call him." And they called the blind man, saying to him, "Take heart. Get up; he is calling you." 50 And throwing off his cloak, he sprang up and came to Jesus. 51 And Jesus said to him, "What do you want me to do for you?" And the blind man said to him, "Rabbi, let me recover my sight." 52 And Jesus said to him, "Go your way; your faith has made you well." And immediately he recovered his sight and followed him on the way.

The Triumphal Entry

11 Now when they drew near to Jerusalem, to Bethphage and
1345 Bethany, at the Mount of Olives,
Jesus[3] sent two of his disciples 2 and said to them, "Go into the village in front of you, and immediately as you enter it you will find a colt tied, on which no one has ever sat. Untie it and bring it. 3 If anyone says to you, 'Why are you doing this?' say, 'The Lord has need of it and will send it back here immediately.'" 4 And they went away and found a colt tied at a door outside in the street, and they untied it. 5 And some of those standing there said to them, "What are you doing, untying the colt?" 6 And they told them what Jesus had said, and they let them go. 7 And they brought the colt to Jesus and threw their cloaks on it, and he sat on it. 8 And many spread their cloaks on the road, and others spread leafy branches that they had cut from the fields. 9 And those who went before and those who followed were shouting, "Hosanna! Blessed is he who comes in the name of the Lord! 10 Blessed is the coming kingdom of our father David! Hosanna in the highest!"

11 And he entered Jerusalem and went into the temple. And when he had looked around at everything, as it was already late, he went out to Bethany with the twelve.

Jesus Curses the Fig Tree

12 On the following day, when they came from Bethany, he was hungry. 13 And seeing in the distance a fig tree in leaf, he went to see if he could find anything on it. When he came to it, he found nothing but leaves, for it was not the season for figs. 14 And he said to it, "May no one ever eat fruit from you again." And his disciples heard it.

Jesus Cleanses the Temple

15 And they came to Jerusalem. And he entered the temple and began
1545 to drive out those who sold and
those who bought in the temple, and he

[1] Greek *diakonos* [2] Greek *bondservant (doulos)* [3] Greek *he*

Jesus Blesses the Little Children

One day, while Jesus was with His disciples, some people brought their little children to Jesus. They wanted Jesus to put His hands on their children and to bless them. But the disciples thought Jesus had more important things to do. They told the people to stop bothering Jesus.

When Jesus saw what was happening, He became angry and said to His disciples, "Let the children come to Me; do not hinder them, for to such belongs the kingdom of God. Truly, I say to you, whoever does not receive the kingdom of God like a child shall not enter it." Jesus wanted all people to humbly trust Him, like children.

Then Jesus took the children in His arms and blessed them, laying His hands on them.

Jesus loves and receives all kinds of people. We don't have to be grown up or wise or rich or good to come to Jesus. We simply need to believe that He will receive us and that He is everything we need.

SEEK and FIND

WHERE TO FIND THE STORY

Mark 10:13–16

KEY BIBLE VERSE

"Let the children come to me; do not hinder them, for to such belongs the kingdom of God." (Mark 10:14b)

THREE KEY QUESTIONS

- Why were people bringing their children to Jesus?
- Why did Jesus become angry with His disciples?
- In what ways does Jesus want everyone to be like a little child?

RELATED BIBLE READINGS

Matthew 18:1–6; 19:13–15; 21:15–16; Luke 18:15–17

overturned the tables of the money-changers and the seats of those who sold pigeons. 16 And he would not allow anyone to carry anything through the temple. 17 And he was teaching them and saying to them, "Is it not written, 'My house shall be called a house of prayer for all the nations'? But you have made it a den of robbers." 18 And the chief priests and the scribes heard it and were seeking a way to destroy him, for they feared him, because all the crowd was astonished at his teaching. 19 And when evening came they[1] went out of the city.

The Lesson from the Withered Fig Tree

20 As they passed by in the morning, they saw the fig tree withered away to its roots. 21 And Peter remembered and said to him, "Rabbi, look! The fig tree that you cursed has withered." 22 And Jesus answered them, "Have faith in God. 23 Truly, I say to you, whoever says to this mountain, 'Be taken up and thrown into the sea,' and does not doubt in his heart, but believes that what he says will come to pass, it will be done for him. 24 Therefore I tell you, whatever you ask in prayer, believe that you have received[2] it, and it will be yours. 25 And whenever you stand praying, forgive, if you have anything against anyone, so that your Father also who is in heaven may forgive you your trespasses."[3]

The Authority of Jesus Challenged

27 And they came again to Jerusalem. And as he was walking in the temple, the chief priests and the scribes and the elders came to him, 28 and they said to him, "By what authority are you doing these things, or who gave you this authority to do them?" 29 Jesus said to them, "I will ask you one question; answer me, and I will tell you by what authority I do these things. 30 Was the baptism of John from heaven or from man? Answer me." 31 And they discussed it with one another, saying, "If we say, 'From heaven,' he will say, 'Why then did you not believe him?' 32 But shall we say, 'From

[1] Some manuscripts *he* [2] Some manuscripts *are receiving* [3] Some manuscripts add verse 26: *But if you do not forgive, neither will your Father who is in heaven forgive your trespasses*

man'?"—they were afraid of the people, for
they all held that John really was a prophet.
33 So they answered Jesus, "We do not know."
And Jesus said to them, "Neither will I tell
you by what authority I do these things."

The Parable of the Tenants

12 And he began to speak to them in
parables. "A man planted a vine-
yard and put a fence around it and dug a
pit for the winepress and built a tower, and
leased it to tenants and went into another
country. 2 When the season came, he sent
a servant[1] to the tenants to get from them
some of the fruit of the vineyard. 3 And
they took him and beat him and sent
him away empty-handed. 4 Again he sent
to them another servant, and they struck
him on the head and treated him shame-
fully. 5 And he sent another, and him they
killed. And so with many others: some they
beat, and some they killed. 6 He had still
one other, a beloved son. Finally he sent
him to them, saying, 'They will respect my
son.' 7 But those tenants said to one another,
'This is the heir. Come, let us kill him, and
the inheritance will be ours.' 8 And they
took him and killed him and threw him out
of the vineyard. 9 What will the owner of
the vineyard do? He will come and destroy
the tenants and give the vineyard to others.
10 Have you not read this Scripture:

"'The stone that the builders rejected
has become the cornerstone;[2]
11 this was the Lord's doing,
and it is marvelous in our eyes'?"

12 And they were seeking to arrest him
but feared the people, for they perceived
that he had told the parable against them.
So they left him and went away.

Paying Taxes to Caesar

13 And they sent to him some of the
Pharisees and some of the Herodians,
to trap him in his talk. 14 And they came
and said to him, "Teacher, we know that
you are true and do not care about any-
one's opinion. For you are not swayed by
appearances,[3] but truly teach the way of
God. Is it lawful to pay taxes to Caesar, or
not? Should we pay them, or should we
not?" 15 But, knowing their hypocrisy, he
said to them, "Why put me to the test?
Bring me a denarius[4] and let me look at
it." 16 And they brought one. And he said to
them, "Whose likeness and inscription is
this?" They said to him, "Caesar's." 17 Jesus
said to them, "Render to Caesar the things
that are Caesar's, and to God the things
that are God's." And they marveled at him.

The Sadducees Ask About the Resurrection

18 And Sadducees came to him, who say
that there is no resurrection. And they
asked him a question, saying, 19 "Teacher,
Moses wrote for us that if a man's brother
dies and leaves a wife, but leaves no child,
the man[5] must take the widow and raise
up offspring for his brother. 20 There were
seven brothers; the first took a wife, and
when he died left no offspring. 21 And
the second took her, and died, leaving no
offspring. And the third likewise. 22 And
the seven left no offspring. Last of all the
woman also died. 23 In the resurrection,
when they rise again, whose wife will she
be? For the seven had her as wife."

24 Jesus said to them, "Is this not the
reason you are wrong, because you know
neither the Scriptures nor the power of
God? 25 For when they rise from the dead,
they neither marry nor are given in mar-
riage, but are like angels in heaven. 26 And
as for the dead being raised, have you not
read in the book of Moses, in the passage
about the bush, how God spoke to him,
saying, 'I am the God of Abraham, and the
God of Isaac, and the God of Jacob'? 27 He is
not God of the dead, but of the living. You
are quite wrong."

The Great Commandment

28 And one of the scribes came up
and heard them disputing with
175 one another, and seeing that he

[1] Greek *bondservant*; also verse 4 [2] Greek *the head of the corner* [3] Greek *you do not look at people's faces* [4] A *denarius* was a day's wage for a laborer [5] Greek *his brother*

answered them well, asked him, "Which commandment is the most important of all?" 29 Jesus answered, "The most important is, 'Hear, O Israel: The Lord our God, the Lord is one. 30 And you shall love the Lord your God with all your heart and with all your soul and with all your mind and with all your strength.' 31 The second is this: 'You shall love your neighbor as yourself.' There is no other commandment greater than these." 32 And the scribe said to him, "You are right, Teacher. You have truly said that he is one, and there is no other besides him. 33 And to love him with all the heart and with all the understanding and with all the strength, and to love one's neighbor as oneself, is much more than all whole burnt offerings and sacrifices." 34 And when Jesus saw that he answered wisely, he said to him, "You are not far from the kingdom of God." And after that no one dared to ask him any more questions.

Whose Son Is the Christ?

35 And as Jesus taught in the temple, he said, "How can the scribes say that the Christ is the son of David? 36 David himself, in the Holy Spirit, declared,

"'The Lord said to my Lord,
Sit at my right hand,
until I put your enemies under
your feet.'

37 David himself calls him Lord. So how is he his son?" And the great throng heard him gladly.

Beware of the Scribes

38 And in his teaching he said, "Beware of the scribes, who like to walk around in long robes and like greetings in the marketplaces 39 and have the best seats in the synagogues and the places of honor at feasts, 40 who devour widows' houses and for a pretense make long prayers. They will receive the greater condemnation."

The Widow's Offering

1411

41 And he sat down opposite the treasury and watched the people putting money into the offering box. Many rich people put in large sums. 42 And a poor widow came and put in two small copper coins, which make a penny.[1] 43 And he called his disciples to him and said to them, "Truly, I say to you, this poor widow has put in more than all those who are contributing to the offering box. 44 For they all contributed out of their abundance, but she out of her poverty has put in everything she had, all she had to live on."

Jesus Foretells Destruction of the Temple

13 And as he came out of the temple, one of his disciples said to him, "Look, Teacher, what wonderful stones and what wonderful buildings!" 2 And Jesus said to him, "Do you see these great buildings? There will not be left here one stone upon another that will not be thrown down."

Signs of the Close of the Age

3 And as he sat on the Mount of Olives opposite the temple, Peter and James and John and Andrew asked him privately, 4 "Tell us, when will these things be, and what will be the sign when all these things are about to be accomplished?" 5 And Jesus began to say to them, "See that no one leads you astray. 6 Many will come in my name, saying, 'I am he!' and they will lead many astray. 7 And when you hear of wars and rumors of wars, do not be alarmed. This must take place, but the end is not yet. 8 For nation will rise against nation, and kingdom against kingdom. There will be earthquakes in various places; there will be famines. These are but the beginning of the birth pains.

9 "But be on your guard. For they will deliver you over to councils, and you will be beaten in synagogues, and you will stand before governors and kings for my

[1] Greek *two lepta*, which make a *kodrantes*; a *kodrantes* (Latin *quadrans*) was a Roman copper coin worth about 1/64 of a *denarius* (which was a day's wage for a laborer)

sake, to bear witness before them. 10 And the gospel must first be proclaimed to all nations. 11 And when they bring you to trial and deliver you over, do not be anxious beforehand what you are to say, but say whatever is given you in that hour, for it is not you who speak, but the Holy Spirit. 12 And brother will deliver brother over to death, and the father his child, and children will rise against parents and have them put to death. 13 And you will be hated by all for my name's sake. But the one who endures to the end will be saved.

The Abomination of Desolation

14 "But when you see the abomination of desolation standing where he ought not to be (let the reader understand), then let those who are in Judea flee to the mountains. 15 Let the one who is on the housetop not go down, nor enter his house, to take anything out, 16 and let the one who is in the field not turn back to take his cloak. 17 And alas for women who are pregnant and for those who are nursing infants in those days! 18 Pray that it may not happen in winter. 19 For in those days there will be such tribulation as has not been from the beginning of the creation that God created until now, and never will be. 20 And if the Lord had not cut short the days, no human being would be saved. But for the sake of the elect, whom he chose, he shortened the days. 21 And then if anyone says to you, 'Look, here is the Christ!' or 'Look, there he is!' do not believe it. 22 For false christs and false prophets will arise and perform signs and wonders, to lead astray, if possible, the elect. 23 But be on guard; I have told you all things beforehand.

The Coming of the Son of Man

24 "But in those days, after that tribulation, the sun will be darkened, and the moon will not give its light, 25 and the stars will be falling from heaven, and the powers in the heavens will be shaken. 26 And then they will see the Son of Man coming in clouds with great power and glory. 27 And then he will send out the angels and gather his elect from the four winds, from the ends of the earth to the ends of heaven.

The Lesson of the Fig Tree

28 "From the fig tree learn its lesson: as soon as its branch becomes tender and puts out its leaves, you know that summer is near. 29 So also, when you see these things taking place, you know that he is near, at the very gates. 30 Truly, I say to you, this generation will not pass away until all these things take place. 31 Heaven and earth will pass away, but my words will not pass away.

No One Knows That Day or Hour

32 "But concerning that day or that hour, no one knows, not even the angels in heaven, nor the Son, but only the Father. 33 Be on guard, keep awake.[1] For you do not know when the time will come. 34 It is like a man going on a journey, when he leaves home and puts his servants[2] in charge, each with his work, and commands the doorkeeper to stay awake. 35 Therefore stay awake—for you do not know when the master of the house will come, in the evening, or at midnight, or when the rooster crows,[3] or in the morning— 36 lest he come suddenly and find you asleep. 37 And what I say to you I say to all: Stay awake."

The Plot to Kill Jesus

14 It was now two days before the Passover and the Feast of Unleavened Bread. And the chief priests and the scribes were seeking how to arrest him by stealth and kill him, 2 for they said, "Not during the feast, lest there be an uproar from the people."

Jesus Anointed at Bethany

1473

3 And while he was at Bethany in the house of Simon the leper,[4] as he was reclining at table, a woman

[1] Some manuscripts add *and pray* [2] Greek *bondservants* [3] That is, the third watch of the night, between midnight and 3 A.M. [4] *Leprosy* was a term for several skin diseases; see Leviticus 13

The Temple Mount in the Time of Jesus

The most important part of Jerusalem during the time of Jesus was the Temple Mount. It was up on a ridge and it filled one-sixth of the city's space. Herod the Great had made the foundation of the temple larger, so that it filled 1.5 million square feet (140,000 square meters). Gigantic stones were used to build the walls, some as large as 45 feet long, 11.5 feet high, and 12 feet thick (13.7 m x 3.5 m x 3.7 m).

A bridge leading to the Temple Mount crossed the Tyropoeon Valley. There is a section of the western wall near this bridge that is sometimes called the Wailing Wall. It has been a place of prayer for Jews for hundreds of years.

A massive stairway and a great arch led up from the street to the Royal Stoa.

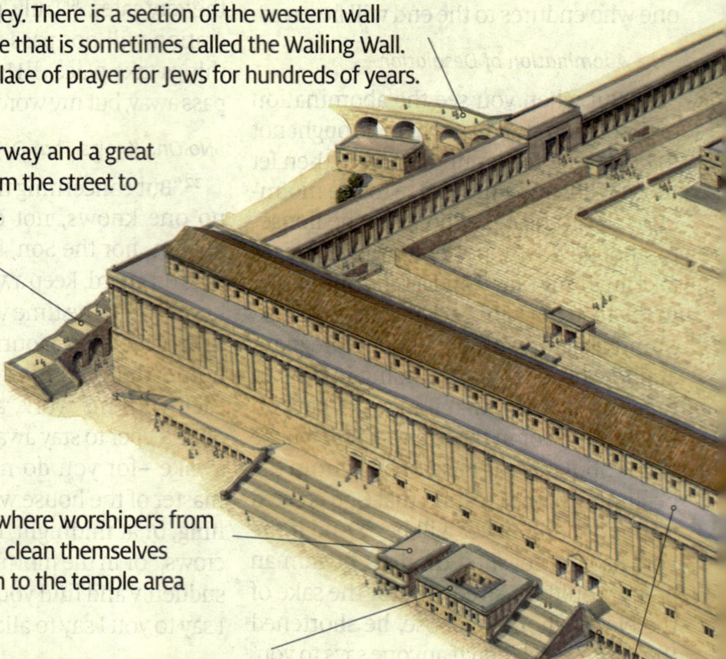

A bath-house where worshipers from far away could clean themselves before going in to the temple area

A Council House for meetings about laws

Small shops were built along the southern wall of the Temple Mount. A narrow street was built above them.

The Royal Stoa was a long, covered walkway. This may have been the area where Jesus found merchants and money-changers, and drove them out (Matthew 21:12–13). It was a long way down to the street below (140 feet/ 43 m), and even farther to the bottom of the valley (300 feet/ 91 m). This may be the place Satan told Jesus to jump from, in order to prove that He was the Son of God (Matthew 4:5).

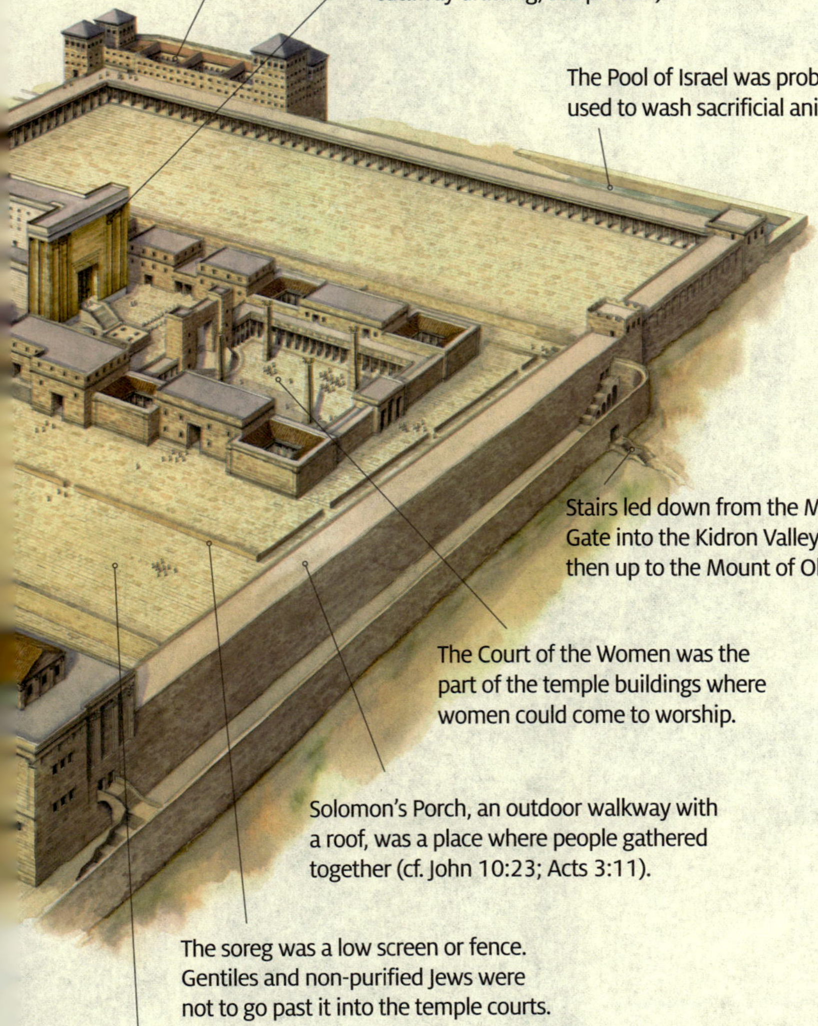

The Antonia Fortress was where Roman soldiers stayed.
Herod's temple (for a detailed cutaway drawing, see p.1427).
The Pool of Israel was probably used to wash sacrificial animals.
Stairs led down from the Muster Gate into the Kidron Valley, then up to the Mount of Olives.
The Court of the Women was the part of the temple buildings where women could come to worship.
Solomon's Porch, an outdoor walkway with a roof, was a place where people gathered together (cf. John 10:23; Acts 3:11).
The soreg was a low screen or fence. Gentiles and non-purified Jews were not to go past it into the temple courts.
The Court of the Gentiles was the only part of the Temple Mount where worshipers who were not Jews could come.

The Widow's Great Gift

Inside the temple courts in Jerusalem, people gave offerings to God. Jesus sat down one day and watched people put their money in the offering box. The disciples were there too.

Jesus watched many rich people put large amounts of money in the box. They were wealthy and had a lot of money to give. Then Jesus saw a poor widow. Her husband had died, and she had only a very small amount of money left. Still, she was thankful to God, and she trusted Him to provide all that she needed.

The widow dropped two copper coins into the offering box. It wasn't much money. In fact, it was all she had. But it was a great gift, because she gave it all to God.

Then Jesus gathered His disciples around Him. He said that the poor widow had given more than all the rich people who were giving their great big gifts. That was because the rich people had plenty left for themselves after they gave their gifts, but the poor woman had nothing left.

The widow gave all she had to God, and kept nothing back for herself. Jesus gave all He had—even His life—and held nothing back, so that He could do the will of the Father and show us His deep and lasting love by saving us from our sins.

SEEK and FIND

WHERE TO FIND THE STORY
Mark 12:41–44

KEY BIBLE VERSE
“God loves a cheerful giver.” (2 Corinthians 9:7)

THREE KEY QUESTIONS
- When the rich people gave large amounts of money, how much did they have left?
- Why did Jesus say the poor widow gave more than the rich people had given?
- How much did Jesus give for us?

RELATED BIBLE READINGS
Luke 21:1–4; 2 Corinthians 8:9; 9:6–15

came with an alabaster flask of ointment
of pure nard, very costly, and she broke
the flask and poured it over his head.
4 There were some who said to themselves
indignantly, “Why was the ointment
wasted like that? 5 For this ointment could
have been sold for more than three hun-
dred denarii[1] and given to the poor.” And
they scolded her. 6 But Jesus said, “Leave
her alone. Why do you trouble her? She
has done a beautiful thing to me. 7 For you
always have the poor with you, and when-
ever you want, you can do good for them.
But you will not always have me. 8 She has
done what she could; she has anointed my
body beforehand for burial. 9 And truly, I
say to you, wherever the gospel is pro-
claimed in the whole world, what she has
done will be told in memory of her.”

Judas to Betray Jesus

10 Then Judas Iscariot, who was one of
the twelve, went to the chief priests in
order to betray him to them. 11 And when
they heard it, they were glad and prom-
ised to give him money. And he sought an
opportunity to betray him.

The Passover with the Disciples

12 And on the first day of Unleavened
Bread, when they sacrificed the Passover
lamb, his disciples said to him, “Where will
you have us go and prepare for you to eat
the Passover?” 13 And he sent two of his dis-
ciples and said to them, “Go into the city,
and a man carrying a jar of water will meet
you. Follow him, 14 and wherever he enters,
say to the master of the house, ‘The Teacher
says, Where is my guest room, where I may
eat the Passover with my disciples?’ 15 And
he will show you a large upper room fur-
nished and ready; there prepare for us.”
16 And the disciples set out and went to the
city and found it just as he had told them,
and they prepared the Passover.

17 And when it was evening, he came
with the twelve. 18 And as they were reclin-
ing at table and eating, Jesus said, “Truly, I

[1] A *denarius* was a day’s wage for a laborer

say to you, one of you will betray me, one
who is eating with me." 19 They began to
be sorrowful and to say to him one after
another, "Is it I?" 20 He said to them, "It
is one of the twelve, one who is dipping
bread into the dish with me. 21 For the Son
of Man goes as it is written of him, but
woe to that man by whom the Son of Man
is betrayed! It would have been better for
that man if he had not been born."

Institution of the Lord's Supper

22 And as they were eating, he took
bread, and after blessing it broke it
1519 and gave it to them, and said, "Take;
this is my body." 23 And he took a cup, and
when he had given thanks he gave it to
them, and they all drank of it. 24 And he
said to them, "This is my blood of the[1] cov-
enant, which is poured out for many.
25 Truly, I say to you, I will not drink again
of the fruit of the vine until that day when
I drink it new in the kingdom of God."

Jesus Foretells Peter's Denial

26 And when they had sung a hymn,
they went out to the Mount of
1415 Olives. 27 And Jesus said to them,
"You will all fall away, for it is written, 'I
will strike the shepherd, and the sheep
will be scattered.' 28 But after I am raised
up, I will go before you to Galilee." 29 Peter
said to him, "Even though they all fall
away, I will not." 30 And Jesus said to him,
"Truly, I tell you, this very night, before the
rooster crows twice, you will deny me
three times." 31 But he said emphatically,
"If I must die with you, I will not deny
you." And they all said the same.

Jesus Prays in Gethsemane

32 And they went to a place called
Gethsemane. And he said to his dis-
1361 ciples, "Sit here while I pray." 33 And
he took with him Peter and James and
John, and began to be greatly distressed
and troubled. 34 And he said to them, "My
soul is very sorrowful, even to death.
Remain here and watch."[2] 35 And going a
little farther, he fell on the ground and
prayed that, if it were possible, the hour
might pass from him. 36 And he said, "Abba,
Father, all things are possible for you.
Remove this cup from me. Yet not what I
will, but what you will." 37 And he came and
found them sleeping, and he said to Peter,
"Simon, are you asleep? Could you not
watch one hour? 38 Watch and pray that you
may not enter into temptation. The spirit
indeed is willing, but the flesh is weak."
39 And again he went away and prayed, say-
ing the same words. 40 And again he came
and found them sleeping, for their eyes
were very heavy, and they did not know
what to answer him. 41 And he came the
third time and said to them, "Are you still
sleeping and taking your rest? It is enough;
the hour has come. The Son of Man is
betrayed into the hands of sinners. 42 Rise,
let us be going; see, my betrayer is at hand."

Betrayal and Arrest of Jesus

43 And immediately, while he was still
speaking, Judas came, one of the twelve,
and with him a crowd with swords and
clubs, from the chief priests and the
scribes and the elders. 44 Now the betrayer
had given them a sign, saying, "The one
I will kiss is the man. Seize him and lead
him away under guard." 45 And when he
came, he went up to him at once and
said, "Rabbi!" And he kissed him. 46 And
they laid hands on him and seized him.
47 But one of those who stood by drew his
sword and struck the servant[3] of the high
priest and cut off his ear. 48 And Jesus said
to them, "Have you come out as against a
robber, with swords and clubs to capture
me? 49 Day after day I was with you in the
temple teaching, and you did not seize
me. But let the Scriptures be fulfilled."
50 And they all left him and fled.

A Young Man Flees

51 And a young man followed him, with
nothing but a linen cloth about his body.

[1] Some manuscripts insert *new* [2] Or *keep awake*; also verses 37, 38 [3] Greek *bondservant*

Peter Denies Jesus

After eating the Passover meal, Jesus led His disciples out of Jerusalem to the Mount of Olives—a large hill with a garden nearby. Jesus knew He was about to be arrested. And He knew His disciples would be afraid and would run away and leave Him alone. Jesus told them, "You will all fall away."

When Peter heard this, he said, "Even though they all fall away, I will not."

Jesus knew this was not true. He told Peter that that very night, before a rooster crowed twice, Peter would say that he did not know Jesus. Jesus even told Peter that he would deny him not just once, but three times. Peter protested. He was sure he would never deny that he knew Jesus. Peter said, "If I must die with You, I will not deny You." The other disciples all said the same thing.

When Jesus and the disciples reached the Garden of Gethsemane on the Mount of Olives, Jesus told most of His disciples to sit and wait for Him. Jesus was troubled and sad. He knew He would soon suffer death for the sins of His people. He asked Peter, James, and John to come with Him a little farther into the garden.

Then Jesus went off by Himself. Jesus asked His heavenly Father if it might be possible to take away the suffering that

Jesus would have to go through. But Jesus also said that, if that was not possible, He would do His Father's will.

When Jesus came back to the three disciples, He found Peter and the others sleeping. Jesus asked Peter, "Could you not watch one hour? Watch and pray that you may not enter into temptation."

Three times, Jesus came back from praying. And three times, Peter, James, and John were sleeping. The third time Jesus woke Peter and the others. He knew it was time for Him to be handed over to His enemies. Soon Judas, another one of Jesus' disciples, came with a mob of men who carried swords and clubs to arrest Jesus. Judas had agreed to betray Jesus for money. So Judas walked up to Jesus and greeted Him with a kiss on the cheek. It was a signal to show the guards which man to arrest.

Peter and the other disciples were so afraid that they all ran away and left Jesus with the guards and the angry men. Secretly, Peter followed the crowd to the house of Caiaphas, the high priest. Inside, Caiaphas and other leaders put Jesus on trial. They wanted people to say bad things about Jesus—things that weren't true. But the leaders were having trouble. People kept saying different things about Jesus, and no one could agree about what Jesus really said.

Outside, Peter watched and waited in the courtyard. As he was warming himself by the fire, a servant girl came up to Peter. She said he had been with Jesus. Peter said that was not true. Peter walked to a gateway. Then a rooster crowed.

The servant girl saw him again and began to tell other people that Peter was one of Jesus' followers. Again, Peter denied it. Soon more people questioned Peter. They said, "Certainly you are one of them."

Peter insisted, "I do not know this man of whom you speak." Just then, the rooster crowed again. Then Peter remembered how Jesus had told him that, before the rooster crowed twice, he would deny Jesus three times. Peter began to cry. He was very sorry that he had denied Jesus.

Inside the high priest's house, Jesus did not deny who He was. He told the high priest and others that He was God's Son. And because of this, Jesus was condemned to die on the cross.

Jesus forgave Peter for denying Him. We, like Peter, are sometimes afraid to let others know that we are followers of Jesus. Jesus tells us that we should never be ashamed of Him. But even when we fail, He will never stop loving all who trust in Him, and He will forgive us for our many sins.

SEEK and FIND

WHERE TO FIND THE STORY

Mark 14:26–72

KEY BIBLE VERSE

"But if anyone does sin, we have an advocate with the Father, Jesus Christ the righteous." (1 John 2:1b)

THREE KEY QUESTIONS

- What did Peter say he would never do?
- What did Jesus do for Peter after Jesus rose from the dead?
- What are some ways that we deny Jesus?

RELATED BIBLE READINGS

Matthew 26:30–75; Luke 22:31–62; John 13:36–38; 18:15–27

And they seized him, 52 but he left the
linen cloth and ran away naked.

Jesus Before the Council

53 And they led Jesus to the high priest.
And all the chief priests and the elders
and the scribes came together. 54 And
Peter had followed him at a distance,
right into the courtyard of the high priest.
And he was sitting with the guards and
warming himself at the fire. 55 Now the
chief priests and the whole Council[1]
were seeking testimony against Jesus to
put him to death, but they found none.
56 For many bore false witness against
him, but their testimony did not agree.
57 And some stood up and bore false wit-
ness against him, saying, 58 "We heard
him say, 'I will destroy this temple that
is made with hands, and in three days I
will build another, not made with hands.'"
59 Yet even about this their testimony did
not agree. 60 And the high priest stood
up in the midst and asked Jesus, "Have
you no answer to make? What is it that
these men testify against you?"[2] 61 But he
remained silent and made no answer.
Again the high priest asked him, "Are you
the Christ, the Son of the Blessed?" 62 And
Jesus said, "I am, and you will see the Son
of Man seated at the right hand of Power,
and coming with the clouds of heaven."
63 And the high priest tore his garments
and said, "What further witnesses do we
need? 64 You have heard his blasphemy.
What is your decision?" And they all con-
demned him as deserving death. 65 And
some began to spit on him and to cover
his face and to strike him, saying to him,
"Prophesy!" And the guards received him
with blows.

Peter Denies Jesus

66 And as Peter was below in the court-
yard, one of the servant girls of the high
priest came, 67 and seeing Peter warm-
ing himself, she looked at him and said,
"You also were with the Nazarene, Jesus."
68 But he denied it, saying, "I neither
know nor understand what you mean."
And he went out into the gateway[3] and
the rooster crowed.[4] 69 And the servant
girl saw him and began again to say to the
bystanders, "This man is one of them."
70 But again he denied it. And after a little
while the bystanders again said to Peter,
"Certainly you are one of them, for you
are a Galilean." 71 But he began to invoke
a curse on himself and to swear, "I do
not know this man of whom you speak."
72 And immediately the rooster crowed a
second time. And Peter remembered how
Jesus had said to him, "Before the rooster
crows twice, you will deny me three
times." And he broke down and wept.[5]

Jesus Delivered to Pilate

15 And as soon as it was
morning, the chief priests
1421 held a consultation with the elders
and scribes and the whole Council.
And they bound Jesus and led him
1523 away and delivered him over to
Pilate. 2 And Pilate asked him, "Are you the
King of the Jews?" And he answered him,
"You have said so." 3 And the chief priests
accused him of many things. 4 And Pilate
again asked him, "Have you no answer to
make? See how many charges they bring
against you." 5 But Jesus made no further
answer, so that Pilate was amazed.

Pilate Delivers Jesus to Be Crucified

6 Now at the feast he used to release for
them one prisoner for whom they asked.
7 And among the rebels in prison, who
had committed murder in the insurrec-
tion, there was a man called Barabbas.
8 And the crowd came up and began to
ask Pilate to do as he usually did for them.
9 And he answered them, saying, "Do you
want me to release for you the King of the
Jews?" 10 For he perceived that it was out of
envy that the chief priests had delivered

[1] Greek *Sanhedrin* [2] Or *Have you no answer to what these men testify against you?* [3] Or *forecourt* [4] Some manuscripts omit *and the rooster crowed* [5] Or *And when he had thought about it, he wept*

him up. 11 But the chief priests stirred up the crowd to have him release for them Barabbas instead. 12 And Pilate again said to them, "Then what shall I do with the man you call the King of the Jews?" 13 And they cried out again, "Crucify him." 14 And Pilate said to them, "Why, what evil has he done?" But they shouted all the more, "Crucify him." 15 So Pilate, wishing to satisfy the crowd, released for them Barabbas, and having scourged[1] Jesus, he delivered him to be crucified.

Jesus Is Mocked

16 And the soldiers led him away inside the palace (that is, the governor's headquarters),[2] and they called together the whole battalion.[3] 17 And they clothed him in a purple cloak, and twisting together a crown of thorns, they put it on him. 18 And they began to salute him, "Hail, King of the Jews!" 19 And they were striking his head with a reed and spitting on him and kneeling down in homage to him. 20 And when they had mocked him, they stripped him of the purple cloak and put his own clothes on him. And they led him out to crucify him.

The Crucifixion

21 And they compelled a passerby, Simon of Cyrene, who was coming in from the country, the father of Alexander and Rufus, to carry his cross. 22 And they brought him to the place called Golgotha (which means Place of a Skull). 23 And they offered him wine mixed with myrrh, but he did not take it. 24 And they crucified him and divided his garments among them, casting lots for them, to decide what each should take. 25 And it was the third hour[4] when they crucified him. 26 And the inscription of the charge against him read, "The King of the Jews." 27 And with him they crucified two robbers, one on his right and one on his left.[5] 29 And those who passed by derided him, wagging their heads and saying, "Aha! You who would destroy the temple and rebuild it in three days, 30 save yourself, and come down from the cross!" 31 So also the chief priests with the scribes mocked him to one another, saying, "He saved others; he cannot save himself. 32 Let the Christ, the King of Israel, come down now from the cross that we may see and believe." Those who were crucified with him also reviled him.

The Death of Jesus

33 And when the sixth hour[6] had come, there was darkness over the whole land until the ninth hour.[7] 34 And at the ninth hour Jesus cried with a loud voice, "Eloi, Eloi, lema sabachthani?" which means, "My God, my God, why have you forsaken me?" 35 And some of the bystanders hearing it said, "Behold, he is calling Elijah." 36 And someone ran and filled a sponge with sour wine, put it on a reed and gave it to him to drink, saying, "Wait, let us see whether Elijah will come to take him down." 37 And Jesus uttered a loud cry and breathed his last. 38 And the curtain of the temple was torn in two, from top to bottom. 39 And when the centurion, who stood facing him, saw that in this way he[8] breathed his last, he said, "Truly this man was the Son[9] of God!"

40 There were also women looking on from a distance, among whom were Mary Magdalene, and Mary the mother of James the younger and of Joses, and Salome. 41 When he was in Galilee, they followed him and ministered to him, and there were also many other women who came up with him to Jerusalem.

Jesus Is Buried

42 And when evening had come, since it was the day of Preparation, that is, the day before the Sabbath, 43 Joseph of

[1] A Roman judicial penalty, consisting of a severe beating with a multi-lashed whip containing imbedded pieces of bone and metal [2] Greek *the praetorium* [3] Greek *cohort*; a tenth of a Roman legion, usually about 600 men [4] That is, 9 A.M. [5] Some manuscripts insert verse 28: *And the Scripture was fulfilled that says, "He was numbered with the transgressors"* [6] That is, noon [7] That is, 3 P.M. [8] Some manuscripts insert *cried out and* [9] Or *a son*

Jesus Dies and Lives Again

Early Friday morning, the chief priests took Jesus to the governor, Pilate. They accused Jesus of many bad things, but Pilate could find nothing wrong with Him. So Pilate had an idea of how to free Jesus. At Passover time, he always let one prisoner go free. Pilate asked the crowd if they wanted Jesus, the King of the Jews, set free. But the Jewish leaders stirred up the crowd to ask for another prisoner instead—a murderer named Barabbas. Pilate asked them what he should do with the King of the Jews, and they cried out, "Crucify Him."

"Why, what evil has He done?" Pilate asked, but the crowd yelled even louder, "Crucify Him."

Wanting to please the crowd, Pilate set the murderer Barabbas free. Then Pilate had the soldiers whip Jesus, and sent Him away to be crucified.

Before they crucified Jesus, though, the soldiers taunted Jesus and made fun of Him. They put a purple robe on Him so that He looked like a foolish king. They twisted together a crown of thorns and pushed it onto His head. They laughed at Jesus, and they spat on Him, and they pretended to bow down to Him. They said, "Hail, King of the Jews!" But they didn't really mean it.

Finally, they led Jesus out to be crucified. By now, Jesus was too weak to carry His cross. The soldiers saw a man walking by, Simon of Cyrene, and made him carry Jesus' cross. When they reached a place called Golgotha, which means "Place of a Skull," the soldiers nailed Jesus' hands and feet to the cross. They put a sign on the cross that said, "The King of the Jews." They crucified two robbers at the same time, one on each side of Jesus. Then they took Jesus' clothing and divided it among themselves.

While Jesus hung there, people made fun of Him. They said, "Let the Christ, the King of Israel, come down now from the cross."

For three hours in the afternoon, the sky grew very dark. Finally, Jesus called out, "My God, My God, why have You forsaken Me?" Then He made a loud cry, breathed His last breath, and died on the cross. At that moment, the big curtain in the temple was torn from the top to the bottom—God Himself had opened the way to the Most Holy Place. A soldier standing by the cross saw all that happened and believed, saying: "Truly this man was the Son of God!"

A man named Joseph took Jesus' body down, wrapped it in a cloth, and placed it in a tomb cut out of rock. Mary Magdalene and Mary, Jesus' mother, saw the tomb where Joseph had buried Jesus' body. A large stone was rolled against the entrance to the tomb.

Early on Sunday morning, the third day since Jesus had died, Mary Magdalene, Mary the mother of James, and Salome went to the tomb to anoint Jesus' body with spices. They asked each other, "Who will roll away the stone for us from the entrance of the tomb?"

When they got there, they were surprised to find that the stone had already been rolled away! They walked inside the tomb and were frightened by an angel in a white robe! The angel told them not to be afraid. He told them, "You seek Jesus of Nazareth, who was crucified. He has risen; He is not here. Go, tell His disciples and Peter that He is going before you to Galilee. There you will see Him, just as He told you." Quickly, the women left the tomb trembling and astonished.

When Jesus suffered and died on the cross, He paid the price for the sins of the world. Those who trust in Jesus are no longer separated from God by their sin. When Jesus rose from the dead, He proved that He is God's Son and He opened the gate to heaven for all who believe in Him. He is the King of kings and He now sits at the right hand of God the Father in heaven.

SEEK and FIND

WHERE TO FIND THE STORY

Mark 15:1–16:8

KEY BIBLE VERSE

"Jesus our Lord . . . was delivered up for our trespasses and raised for our justification." (Romans 4:24–25)

THREE KEY QUESTIONS

- What did the crowd tell Pilate to do with Jesus?
- What did the soldier say when Jesus died?
- What did Jesus do to open the gate to heaven for us?

RELATED BIBLE READINGS

Matthew 27:11–28:10; Luke 22:66–24:12; John 18:1–20:29; Romans 1:4; Ephesians 2:13–18

Arimathea, a respected member of the Council, who was also himself looking for the kingdom of God, took courage and went to Pilate and asked for the body of Jesus. 44 Pilate was surprised to hear that he should have already died.[1] And summoning the centurion, he asked him whether he was already dead. 45 And when he learned from the centurion that he was dead, he granted the corpse to Joseph. 46 And Joseph[2] bought a linen shroud, and taking him down, wrapped him in the linen shroud and laid him in a tomb that had been cut out of the rock. And he rolled a stone against the entrance of the tomb. 47 Mary Magdalene and Mary the mother of Joses saw where he was laid.

The Resurrection

16 When the Sabbath was
past, Mary Magdalene and
1365, Mary the mother of James and
1593 Salome bought spices, so that they
might go and anoint him. 2 And very early
on the first day of the week, when the
sun had risen, they went to the tomb.
3 And they were saying to one another,
"Who will roll away the stone for us from
the entrance of the tomb?" 4 And looking
up, they saw that the stone had been
rolled back—it was very large. 5 And
entering the tomb, they saw a young man
sitting on the right side, dressed in a
white robe, and they were alarmed. 6 And
he said to them, "Do not be alarmed. You
seek Jesus of Nazareth, who was crucified. He has risen; he is not here. See the
place where they laid him. 7 But go, tell
his disciples and Peter that he is going
before you to Galilee. There you will see
him, just as he told you." 8 And they went
out and fled from the tomb, for trembling
and astonishment had seized them, and
they said nothing to anyone, for they
were afraid.

[SOME OF THE EARLIEST MANUSCRIPTS DO NOT INCLUDE 16:9-20.][3]

Jesus Appears to Mary Magdalene

9 [[Now when he rose early on the first day of the week, he appeared first to Mary Magdalene, from whom he had cast out seven demons. 10 She went and told those who had been with him, as they mourned and wept. 11 But when they heard that he was alive and had been seen by her, they would not believe it.

Jesus Appears to Two Disciples

12 After these things he appeared in another form to two of them, as they were walking into the country. 13 And they went back and told the rest, but they did not believe them.

The Great Commission

14 Afterward he appeared to the eleven themselves as they were reclining at table, and he rebuked them for their unbelief and hardness of heart, because they had not believed those who saw him after he had risen. 15 And he said to them, "Go into all the world and proclaim the gospel to the whole creation. 16 Whoever believes and is baptized will be saved, but whoever does not believe will be condemned. 17 And these signs will accompany those who believe: in my name they will cast out demons; they will speak in new tongues; 18 they will pick up serpents with their hands; and if they drink any deadly poison, it will not hurt them; they will lay their hands on the sick, and they will recover."

19 So then the Lord Jesus, after he had spoken to them, was taken up into heaven and sat down at the right hand of God. 20 And they went out and preached everywhere, while the Lord worked with them and confirmed the message by accompanying signs.]]

[1] Or *Pilate wondered whether he had already died* [2] Greek *he* [3] Some manuscripts end the book with 16:8; others include verses 9-20 immediately after verse 8. A few manuscripts insert additional material after verse 14; one Latin manuscript adds after verse 8 the following: *But they reported briefly to Peter and those with him all that they had been told. And after this, Jesus himself sent out by means of them, from east to west, the sacred and imperishable proclamation of eternal salvation.* Other manuscripts include this same wording after verse 8, then continue with verses 9-20

Introduction to

Luke

Author

Luke

Date

About A.D. 62

Key People

Jesus; Peter; James; John; Mary, the mother of Jesus; Zechariah; Elizabeth; John the Baptist; Simeon; Anna; Mary Magdalene; Zacchaeus; Mary; Martha

Purpose

The purpose of Luke is to show the truthfulness of the stories early Christians had heard about Jesus, and to assure them that Jesus' gospel is for everyone.

Central Themes

God's kingdom has come in Jesus, as Scripture promised; the gospel is for Gentiles as well as Jews; Jesus welcomes the lowly, outcasts, and sinners; following Jesus is costly; Jesus depended on prayer and the Holy Spirit, and so must His followers; God's people must not live for riches.

Memory Verses

The annunciation (Luke 1:30–33); the *Magnificat* (Luke 1:46–55); the *Gloria in Excelsis* (Luke 2:10–14); the *Nunc Dimittis* (Luke 2:29–32); parable of the lost sons (Luke 15:11–32); Jesus fulfills the Scriptures (Luke 24:44–49)

Introduction

Luke was a Gentile doctor who sometimes traveled with the apostle Paul. Luke got the material for his Gospel from eyewitnesses of Jesus' birth, ministry, death, and resurrection. Luke shows Jesus carrying out His mission "to seek and to save the lost" (Luke 19:10). He tells of Jesus' determination to go to Jerusalem, even knowing that He would suffer and die there (Luke 9:43–45, 51). Luke records Jesus calling His disciples to be willing to suffer and to lay down their lives for Him (Luke 14:25–33). Luke emphasizes Jesus' welcome for Gentiles, sinners, and outcasts. Only Luke tells the story of shepherds, social outcasts of the day, worshiping Jesus at His birth (Luke 2:8–20). Only Luke tells us that Jesus visited Zacchaeus, a wicked tax collector who had cheated many (Luke 19:1–10). Only Luke records the parable of the prodigal son, showing how heaven rejoices over sinners who repent (Luke 15:11–32). He alone gives us the parables of the good Samaritan, where the hero is a despised Samaritan (Luke 10:29–37), and of the Pharisee and the tax collector, where the hero is a hated tax collector (Luke 18:9–14).

About 5 B.C.	About A.D. 28–33	About A.D. 62
Birth of Jesus	Jesus' ministry, death, resurrection	Luke's Gospel written

The Gospel According to

Luke

Dedication to Theophilus

1 Inasmuch as many have undertaken
to compile a narrative of the things
that have been accomplished among
us, 2 just as those who from the begin-
ning were eyewitnesses and ministers of
the word have delivered them to us, 3 it
seemed good to me also, having followed
all things closely for some time past, to
write an orderly account for you, most
excellent Theophilus, 4 that you may have
certainty concerning the things you have
been taught.

Birth of John the Baptist Foretold

5 In the days of Herod, king of
Judea, there was a priest named
1429 Zechariah,[1] of the division of
Abijah. And he had a wife from the
daughters of Aaron, and her name
1437, was Elizabeth. 6 And they were
1441 both righteous before God, walk-
ing blamelessly in all the commandments
and statutes of the Lord. 7 But they had no
child, because Elizabeth was barren, and
both were advanced in years.

8 Now while he was serving as priest
before God when his division was on duty,
9 according to the custom of the priest-
hood, he was chosen by lot to enter the
temple of the Lord and burn incense.
10 And the whole multitude of the people
were praying outside at the hour of
incense. 11 And there appeared to him an
angel of the Lord standing on the right side
of the altar of incense. 12 And Zechariah
was troubled when he saw him, and fear
fell upon him. 13 But the angel said to him,
"Do not be afraid, Zechariah, for your
prayer has been heard, and your wife
Elizabeth will bear you a son, and you shall
call his name John. 14 And you will have joy
and gladness, and many will rejoice at his
birth, 15 for he will be great before the Lord.
And he must not drink wine or strong
drink, and he will be filled with the Holy
Spirit, even from his mother's womb.
16 And he will turn many of the children of
Israel to the Lord their God, 17 and he will go
before him in the spirit and power
of Elijah, to turn the hearts of the
1429 fathers to the children, and the dis-
obedient to the wisdom of the just, to make
ready for the Lord a people prepared."

[1] Greek *Zacharias*

CHARACTER PROFILE

ZECHARIAH AND ELIZABETH

Zechariah and Elizabeth had grown old without having any children. One year, when Zechariah was able to offer incense in the temple as a priest, an angel told him that Elizabeth would have a baby and they should name him "John." This baby grew up to be John the Baptist, who prepared the way for Jesus.

1429, 1437, 1441

Herod's Temple in the Time of Jesus

King Herod built this magnificent temple in 20/19 B.C. Most of the building was completed in about 10 years. Years after Jesus' death and resurrection, in A.D. 70, the Roman army captured Jerusalem and destroyed this temple. The temple was 172 feet (52 m) long, 172 feet wide, and 172 feet high (the height of a 16–20-story building).

There was an upper chamber, or room, above the sanctuary. There were holes in the floor of this chamber through which someone could clean the gold-covered walls of the sanctuary below.

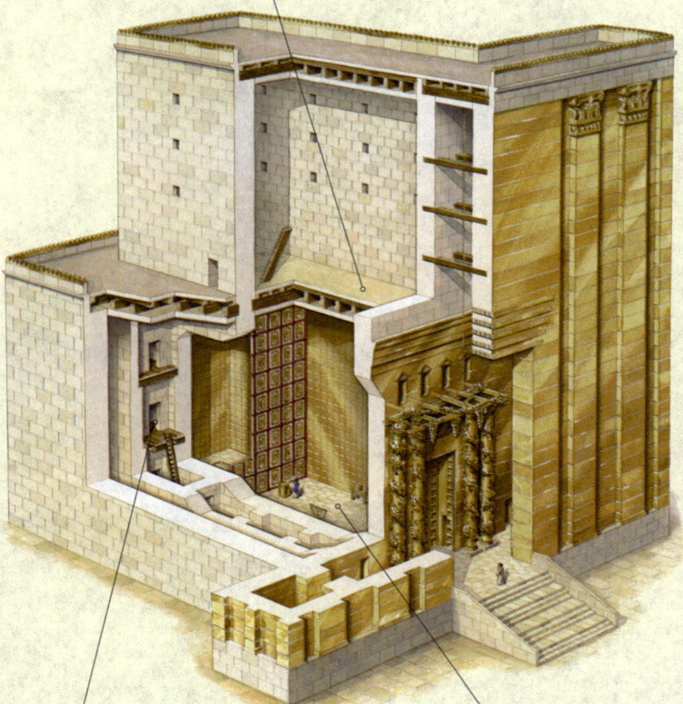

On three sides of the temple, between the outside walls and the Holy Place and Most Holy Place on the inside, were small chambers or rooms used for storing supplies used in temple ceremonies.

This is where the angel Gabriel appeared to Zechariah as he was offering incense (Luke 1:11).

The Birth of John Foretold

During the time when Herod was king of Judea, Zechariah served as a priest in the temple in Jerusalem. Zechariah and his wife, Elizabeth, were quite old. They loved God, but they were sad because they had no children.

One day, Zechariah went to the temple to burn incense and pray. Suddenly, an angel of the Lord appeared, standing on the right side of the incense altar.

God sent the angel to Zechariah in order to give him a message. The angel told Zechariah that he and Elizabeth were going to have a baby boy, and that they were to name him John. He would bring joy to his parents and to many other people—and he would be great before the Lord. He would be filled with the Holy Spirit even before he was born. And when John was grown up, God would use John in a powerful way—to call people to repent of their sins and to prepare the way for the Lord Jesus.

But to Zechariah this seemed too good to be true. "How shall I know this?" Zechariah asked the angel, "for I am an old man, and my wife is advanced in years." People their age were too old to have babies!

Then the angel told Zechariah an amazing thing: "I am Gabriel. I stand in the presence of God." Gabriel had been sent directly from God to tell Zechariah the good news about John!

But because Zechariah didn't believe, Gabriel said to him: "You will be silent and unable to speak until the day that these things take place." Immediately Zechariah couldn't speak. He could only use his hands to show people what the angel said.

After the angel went away, Zechariah met with the people who were waiting for him to come out of the temple. When Zechariah was unable to speak, the people realized that he had seen a vision in the temple.

Many days later, after Zechariah's time of serving in the temple was finished, Zechariah went home. Soon after that, Elizabeth found out she was going to have a baby. She and Zechariah were so happy!

God sent His angel to give Zechariah good news. God gives us Good News too. He tells us in the Bible that He sent His Son, Jesus, to be our Savior. He gives us parents and pastors and to tell us this Good News and teach us about God's love for us in Jesus.

SEEK and FIND

WHERE TO FIND THE STORY

Luke 1:5–25

KEY BIBLE VERSE

"He will go before him in the spirit and power of Elijah,
to turn the hearts of the fathers to the children, and the disobedient to the wisdom of the just, to make ready for the Lord a people prepared." (Luke 1:17)

THREE KEY QUESTIONS

- What was the message of good news that the angel Gabriel brought to Zechariah?

- What happened to Zechariah when he didn't believe Gabriel?
- What is the message of Good News that God has given to us?

RELATED BIBLE READINGS

Malachi 4:5–6; Matthew 3:1–12; 11:10–15; John 1:6–8, 19–36

18 And Zechariah said to the angel, "How shall I know this? For I am an old man, and my wife is advanced in years." 19 And the angel answered him, "I am Gabriel. I stand in the presence of God, and I was sent to speak to you and to bring you this good news. 20 And behold, you will be silent and unable to speak until the day that these things take place, because you did not believe my words, which will be fulfilled in their time." 21 And the people were waiting for Zechariah, and they were wondering at his delay in the temple. 22 And when he came out, he was unable to speak to them, and they realized that he had seen a vision in the temple. And he kept making signs to them and remained mute. 23 And when his time of service was ended, he went to his home.

24 After these days his wife Elizabeth conceived, and for five months she kept herself hidden, saying, 25 "Thus the Lord has done for me in the days when he looked on me, to take away my reproach among people."

Birth of Jesus Foretold

26 In the sixth month the angel
Gabriel was sent from God to a city
1433 of Galilee named Nazareth, 27 to a
virgin betrothed[1] to a man whose name was Joseph, of the house of David. And the virgin's name was Mary. 28 And he came to her and said, "Greetings, O favored one, the Lord is with you!"[2] 29 But she was greatly troubled at the saying, and tried to discern what sort of greeting this might be.

30 And the angel said to her, "Do not
be afraid, Mary, for you have found
47 favor with God. 31 And behold, you
will conceive in your womb and bear a
son, and you shall call his name
Jesus. 32 He will be great and will be
499, called the Son of the Most High.
1433 And the Lord God will give to him
the throne of his father David, 33 and he will reign over the house of Jacob forever, and of his kingdom there will be no end."

34 And Mary said to the angel, "How will this be, since I am a virgin?"[3]

35 And the angel answered her, "The Holy Spirit will come upon you, and the power of the Most High will overshadow you; therefore the child to be born[4] will be called holy—the Son of God. 36 And behold, your relative Elizabeth in her old age has also conceived a son, and this is the sixth month with her who was called barren. 37 For nothing will be impossible with God." 38 And Mary said, "Behold, I am the servant[5] of the Lord; let it be to me according to your word." And the angel departed from her.

Mary Visits Elizabeth

39 In those days Mary arose and
went with haste into the hill coun-
1437 try, to a town in Judah, 40 and she
entered the house of Zechariah
and greeted Elizabeth. 41 And when
435 Elizabeth heard the greeting of

[1] That is, legally pledged to be married [2] Some manuscripts add *Blessed are you among women!* [3] Greek *since I do not know a man* [4] Some manuscripts add *of you*
[5] Greek *bondservant*; also verse 48

The Birth of Jesus Foretold

God sent the angel Gabriel again, this time with a message for a virgin named Mary, who was engaged to Joseph.

The angel greeted Mary and told her that God had favored her. "The Lord is with you!" Gabriel said.

When Mary saw the angel, she was afraid and wondered what the angel meant. "Do not be afraid," the angel said, "for you have found favor with God."

Then Gabriel told Mary that she was going to have a baby. "You will bear a Son," Gabriel said, "and you shall call His name Jesus. He will be great and will be called the Son of the Most High. And the Lord God will give to Him the throne of His father David, and He will reign over the house of Jacob forever, and of His kingdom there will be no end."

"How will this be?" Mary asked the angel. She had no husband. She had not been with a man. Who would be the baby's father?

The angel told her this would happen by the power of the Holy Spirit. God would be this baby's Father! "The child to be born will be called holy—the Son of God," the angel said.

Then the angel told Mary that her cousin Elizabeth was six months pregnant—even though she was too old to have a baby! "For nothing will be impossible with God," Gabriel said.

"I am the servant of the Lord," Mary answered. "Let it be to me according to your word." Then, just as suddenly as he had come, the angel Gabriel left Mary.

God kept His promise to Mary. She conceived and gave birth to Jesus. God's Son—our Lord Jesus—lived perfectly, died for our sins, and rose victorious on Easter morning.

SEEK and FIND

WHERE TO FIND THE STORY

Luke 1:26–38

KEY BIBLE VERSE

"He will be great and will be called the Son of the Most High. And the Lord God will give to him the throne of his father David, and he will reign over the house of Jacob forever, and of his kingdom there will be no end." (Luke 1:32–33)

THREE KEY QUESTIONS

- What did the angel Gabriel tell Mary?
- Who would be the Father of the baby that Mary was going to have?
- Is anything impossible for God? How do we know that this is true?

RELATED BIBLE READINGS

2 Samuel 7:12–17; Isaiah 7:14; 9:6–7; Ezekiel 37:24–25; Matthew 1:18–25

Mary, the baby leaped in her womb. And
Elizabeth was filled with the Holy Spirit,
42 and she exclaimed with a loud cry,
"Blessed are you among women, and
blessed is the fruit of your womb! 43 And
why is this granted to me that the mother
of my Lord should come to me? 44 For
behold, when the sound of your greeting
came to my ears, the baby in my womb
leaped for joy. 45 And blessed is she who
believed that there would be[1] a fulfillment
of what was spoken to her from the Lord."

[1] Or *believed, for there will be*

Mary's Song of Praise: The Magnificat

1437
[46] And Mary said,

"My soul magnifies the Lord,
[47] and my spirit rejoices in God my
Savior,

43
[48] for he has looked on the humble
estate of his servant.
For behold, from now on all
generations will call me
blessed;
49 for he who is mighty has done great
things for me,
and holy is his name.
50 And his mercy is for those who fear
him
from generation to generation.
51 He has shown strength with his arm;
he has scattered the proud in the
thoughts of their hearts;
52 he has brought down the mighty
from their thrones
and exalted those of humble
estate;
53 he has filled the hungry with good
things,
and the rich he has sent away
empty.
54 He has helped his servant Israel,
in remembrance of his mercy,
55 as he spoke to our fathers,
to Abraham and to his offspring
forever."

[56] And Mary remained with her about
three months and returned to her home.

The Birth of John the Baptist

[57] Now the time came for Elizabeth
to give birth, and she bore a son.
1441
[58] And her neighbors and relatives
heard that the Lord had shown great
mercy to her, and they rejoiced with her.
[59] And on the eighth day they came to cir-
cumcise the child. And they would have
called him Zechariah after his father,
[60] but his mother answered, "No; he shall
be called John." [61] And they said to her,
"None of your relatives is called by this
name." [62] And they made signs to his
father, inquiring what he wanted him to
be called. [63] And he asked for a writing
tablet and wrote, "His name is John." And
they all wondered. [64] And immediately
his mouth was opened and his tongue
loosed, and he spoke, blessing God. [65] And
fear came on all their neighbors. And all
these things were talked about through
all the hill country of Judea, [66] and all who
heard them laid them up in their hearts,
saying, "What then will this child be?" For
the hand of the Lord was with him.

Zechariah's Prophecy

[67] And his father Zechariah was
filled with the Holy Spirit and
43
prophesied, saying,

CHARACTER PROFILE

MARY

Mary was Jesus' mother. An angel came to her and told her she would have a baby boy in a special way, even though she and Joseph were not yet married. The baby would be the Son of God and God's promised King. Mary was present at Jesus' very first miracle.

1293, 1433, 1445, 1449, 1453, 1541

Mary Visits Elizabeth

Some time after the angel Gabriel came to Mary and told her that she was going to have the baby Jesus, Mary went to visit her cousin Elizabeth. Elizabeth lived with her husband Zechariah in a town located in the hill country of Judea. The angel Gabriel had come to Zechariah, too, telling him that Elizabeth was going to have a baby who would be called John the Baptist.

When Mary entered Elizabeth's house and greeted her, Elizabeth was filled with the Holy Spirit and her baby John jumped for joy, even while he was still inside Elizabeth!

Elizabeth told Mary how amazed and thankful she was: "Blessed are you among women," Elizabeth said—because Mary was the mother of the Lord and because Mary had believed "what was spoken to her from the Lord."

Mary responded to Elizabeth with some of the most beautiful words in the Bible. We call this song of Mary "The Magnificat." Here is part of what Mary said: "My soul magnifies the Lord, and my spirit rejoices in God my Savior. For He who is mighty has done great things for me, and holy is His name. And His mercy is for those who fear Him, from generation to generation."

Mary stayed with Elizabeth for about three months. During

this time, Mary and Elizabeth rejoiced that God was sending Jesus to be their Savior. We rejoice too that God sent Jesus to be our Savior!

SEEK and FIND

WHERE TO FIND THE STORY

Luke 1:39–56

KEY BIBLE VERSE

"And Mary said, 'My soul magnifies the Lord, and my spirit rejoices in God my Savior.'" (Luke 1:46–47)

THREE KEY QUESTIONS

- Who did Mary go to visit in the hill country of Judea?
- What was the name of Elizabeth's baby? What did he do when Mary greeted Elizabeth?
- Why did Mary and Elizabeth rejoice? Why do we rejoice, too?

RELATED BIBLE READINGS

1 Samuel 2:1–10; Luke 1:5–25

389
425

68 "Blessed be the Lord God of Israel,
for he has visited and redeemed his people
69 and has raised up a horn of salvation for us
in the house of his servant David,
70 as he spoke by the mouth of his holy prophets from of old,
389
71 that we should be saved from our enemies
and from the hand of all who hate us;
72 to show the mercy promised to our fathers
and to remember his holy covenant,
73 the oath that he swore to our father Abraham, to grant us
74 that we, being delivered from the hand of our enemies,
might serve him without fear,
75 in holiness and righteousness before him all our days.
1441
76 And you, child, will be called the prophet of the Most High;
for you will go before the Lord to prepare his ways,
77 to give knowledge of salvation to his people
in the forgiveness of their sins,

78 because of the tender mercy of our
God,
whereby the sunrise shall visit us[1]
from on high
79 to give light to those who sit in
darkness and in the shadow
of death,
to guide our feet into the way of
peace."

80 And the child grew and became strong
in spirit, and he was in the wilderness
until the day of his public appearance to
Israel.

The Birth of Jesus Christ

2 In those days a decree went out
from Caesar Augustus that all
1445 the world should be registered.
2 This was the first registration when[2]
Quirinius was governor of Syria. 3 And all
went to be registered, each to his own
town. 4 And Joseph also went up
from Galilee, from the town of
1293 Nazareth, to Judea, to the city of
David, which is called Bethlehem, because
he was of the house and lineage of David,
5 to be registered with Mary, his betrothed,[3]
who was with child. 6 And while they were
there, the time came for her to give birth.
7 And she gave birth to her firstborn son
and wrapped him in swaddling cloths and
laid him in a manger, because there was
no place for them in the inn.

The Shepherds and the Angels

8 And in the same region there were
shepherds out in the field, keeping watch
over their flock by night. 9 And an angel
of the Lord appeared to them, and the
glory of the Lord shone around them, and
they were filled with fear. 10 And the
angel said to them, "Fear not, for behold,
I bring you good news of great joy that
will be for all the people. 11 For unto you
is born this day in the city of
David a Savior, who is Christ the
1445 Lord. 12 And this will be a sign for
you: you will find a baby wrapped in
swaddling cloths and lying in a manger."
13 And suddenly there was with the angel
a multitude of the heavenly host praising
God and saying,

14 "Glory to God in the highest,
and on earth peace among those
with whom he is pleased!"[4]

15 When the angels went away from
them into heaven, the shepherds said to
one another, "Let us go over to Bethlehem
and see this thing that has happened,
which the Lord has made known to us."
16 And they went with haste and found
Mary and Joseph, and the baby lying in
a manger. 17 And when they saw it, they
made known the saying that had been told
them concerning this child. 18 And all who
heard it wondered at what the shepherds
told them. 19 But Mary treasured up all
these things, pondering them in her heart.
20 And the shepherds returned, glorifying
and praising God for all they had heard
and seen, as it had been told them.

21 And at the end of eight days, when he
was circumcised, he was called Jesus, the
name given by the angel before he was
conceived in the womb.

Jesus Presented at the Temple

22 And when the time came for
their purification according to the
1449 Law of Moses, they brought him up
to Jerusalem to present him to the Lord
23 (as it is written in the Law of the Lord,
"Every male who first opens the womb
shall be called holy to the Lord") 24 and to
offer a sacrifice according to what is said
in the Law of the Lord, "a pair of turtle-
doves, or two young pigeons." 25 Now
there was a man in Jerusalem, whose
name was Simeon, and this man was righ-
teous and devout, waiting for the consola-
tion of Israel, and the Holy Spirit was
upon him. 26 And it had been revealed to
him by the Holy Spirit that he would not

[1] Or *when the sunrise shall dawn upon us*; some manuscripts *since the sunrise has visited us* [2] Or *This was the registration before* [3] That is, one legally pledged to be married
[4] Some manuscripts *peace, good will among men*

The Birth of John

Zechariah and Elizabeth were very old when their baby John was born. They were very happy! God had kept His promise to give them a baby even in their old age!

On the eighth day after John was born, their family and neighbors came to see the new baby. They thought the baby would be named Zechariah after his father, but his mother, Elizabeth, said, "No; he shall be called John."

The friends were surprised. No one in the family was named John! They looked at Zechariah to see what he wanted to name the baby. Zechariah was not able to speak, so he wrote on a tablet, "His name is John"—the name that the angel Gabriel had told Zechariah to give to the baby.

Right away, Zechariah could speak again. Then Zechariah sang a song to praise God. He said that God sent John to do something very important. When John grew up, he would be the promised prophet who would prepare the way for the coming of Jesus. John would tell people to repent from their sins, so that God through His grace and mercy would forgive their sins.

Today God gives us pastors and parents to tell us about Jesus. He gives us His Word, the Bible, so we will know that Jesus came to be our Savior. God wants us to be sorry for our sins and believe in Jesus so that we can go to heaven and live with Him forever.

SEEK and FIND

WHERE TO FIND THE STORY

Luke 1:57–80

KEY BIBLE VERSE

"And you, child, will be called the prophet of the Most High;
for you will go before the Lord to prepare his ways,
to give knowledge of salvation to his people
in the forgiveness of their sins."
(Luke 1:76–77)

THREE KEY QUESTIONS

- Why did Elizabeth and Zechariah want to name their baby John?
- Why did Zechariah have to write, "His name is John," instead of just saying his name?
- What would John do when he was grown up?

RELATED BIBLE READINGS

Isaiah 40:3–5; Malachi 3:1; 4:5–6; Luke 1:5–25; 3:1–6

see death before he had seen the Lord's
Christ. 27 And he came in the Spirit into
the temple, and when the parents brought
in the child Jesus, to do for him according
to the custom of the Law, 28 he took him
up in his arms and blessed God and said,

29 "Lord, now you are letting your
servant[1] depart in peace,
according to your word;
30 for my eyes have seen your
salvation
31 that you have prepared in the
presence of all peoples,
32 a light for revelation to the Gentiles,
and for glory to your people
Israel."

1449

33 And his father and his mother mar-
veled at what was said about him. 34 And
Simeon blessed them and said to Mary his
mother, "Behold, this child is appointed
for the fall and rising of many in Israel,
and for a sign that is opposed 35 (and a
sword will pierce through your own soul
also), so that thoughts from many hearts
may be revealed."
36 And there was a prophetess, Anna, the

[1] Greek *bondservant*

daughter of Phanuel, of the tribe of Asher. She was advanced in years, having lived with her husband seven years from when she was a virgin, 37 and then as a widow until she was eighty-four.[1] She did not depart from the temple, worshiping with fasting and prayer night and day. 38 And coming up at that very hour she began to give thanks to God and to speak of him to all who were waiting for the redemption of Jerusalem.

The Return to Nazareth

39 And when they had performed everything according to the Law of the Lord, they returned into Galilee, to their own town of Nazareth. 40 And the child grew and became strong, filled with wisdom. And the favor of God was upon him.

The Boy Jesus in the Temple

41 Now his parents went to
Jerusalem every year at the Feast of
1453 the Passover. 42 And when he was
twelve years old, they went up according to custom. 43 And when the feast was ended, as they were returning, the boy Jesus stayed behind in Jerusalem. His parents did not know it, 44 but supposing him to be in the group they went a day's journey, but then they began to search for him among their relatives and acquaintances, 45 and when they did not find him, they returned to Jerusalem, searching for him. 46 After three days they found him in the temple, sitting among the teachers, listening to them and asking them questions. 47 And all who heard him were amazed at his understanding and his answers. 48 And when his parents[2] saw him, they were astonished. And his mother said to him, "Son, why have you treated us so? Behold, your father and I have been searching for you in great distress." 49 And he said to them, "Why were you looking for me? Did you not know that I must be in my Father's house?"[3] 50 And they did not understand the saying that he spoke to them. 51 And he went down with them and came to Nazareth and was submissive to them. And his mother treasured up all these things in her heart.

52 And Jesus increased in wisdom and in stature[4] and in favor with God and man.

John the Baptist Prepares the Way

3 In the fifteenth year of the reign
of Tiberius Caesar, Pontius
1373, Pilate being governor of Judea, and
1441 Herod being tetrarch of Galilee, and
his brother Philip tetrarch of the region of Ituraea and Trachonitis, and Lysanias tetrarch of Abilene, 2 during the high priesthood of Annas and Caiaphas, the word of God came to John the son of Zechariah in the wilderness. 3 And he went into all the region around the Jordan, proclaiming a baptism of repentance for the forgiveness of sins. 4 As it is written in the book of the words of Isaiah the prophet,

> "The voice of one crying in the
> wilderness:
> 'Prepare the way of the Lord,[5]
> make his paths straight.
> 5 Every valley shall be filled,
> and every mountain and hill shall
> be made low,
> and the crooked shall become
> straight,
> and the rough places shall
> become level ways,
> 6 and all flesh shall see the salvation
> of God.'"

7 He said therefore to the crowds that came out to be baptized by him, "You
brood of vipers! Who warned you to flee
from the wrath to come? 8 Bear fruits in
keeping with repentance. And do
not begin to say to yourselves, 'We
1511 have Abraham as our father.' For I
tell you, God is able from these stones to raise up children for Abraham. 9 Even now the axe is laid to the root of the trees. Every tree therefore that does not bear good fruit is cut down and thrown into the fire."

[1] *Or as a widow for eighty-four years* [2] *Greek they* [3] *Or about my Father's business* [4] *Or years* [5] *Or crying, Prepare in the wilderness the way of the Lord*

The Birth of Jesus

In those days long ago, a ruler named Caesar Augustus wanted to take a census. Caesar wanted to count all the people that he ruled by making them register their name in official records. Everyone would have to travel back to their family's hometown. Joseph had to travel to Bethlehem, the little town where his family was from. And he had to take Mary, his wife, with him on the long journey to Bethlehem, even though Mary was about to have a baby.

When Mary and Joseph got to Bethlehem, they found it was crowded with all the people who had come to register. There was no room for them to stay in an inn. So Joseph and Mary had to stay in a stable where the animals were kept.

While they were there, the time came for Jesus to be born. Mary wrapped Him in strips of cloth and laid Him in a manger, a place to put food for donkeys and cows.

That night there were shepherds watching their flocks near Bethlehem. Suddenly, an angel of the Lord appeared to them and the glory of the Lord shone brightly around them. The shepherds were very afraid.

But the angel said to them, "Fear not. I bring you good news of great joy that will be for all the people. For unto you is born this day in the city of David a Savior, who is Christ the Lord."

The angel told the shepherds they would know that they had found the right baby when they found baby Jesus wrapped in strips of cloth and lying in a manger.

Suddenly, thousands of angels appeared in the heavens, praising God and saying, "Glory to God in the highest, and on earth peace among those with whom He is pleased!"

When the angels left, the shepherds hurried to Bethlehem to find Jesus. Just as the angel had said, they found Joseph, Mary, and baby Jesus lying in the manger. The shepherds spread the amazing news—the Savior had been born! All who heard the news wondered what this could mean. But Mary treasured all these things in her heart. Then the shepherds returned to their sheep, glorifying and praising God for all they had seen and heard.

Jesus grew up to be a man, and He taught about the kingdom of God. When the time was right, according to God's will, Jesus suffered and died on the cross for the sins of the world. Three days later, He rose in victory over sin and death and the devil. Jesus is the Savior God promised, for all who believe in Him and trust Him for the forgiveness of their sins.

SEEK and FIND

WHERE TO FIND THE STORY

Luke 2:1–20

KEY BIBLE VERSE

"For unto you is born this day in the city of David a Savior, who is Christ the Lord." (Luke 2:11)

THREE KEY QUESTIONS

- Why did Joseph and Mary have to go to Bethlehem?
- Why did Mary have to lay her baby in a manger, where animals ate?
- What was the good news the angel told the shepherds?

RELATED BIBLE READINGS

Isaiah 9:6–7; Micah 5:2; John 1:9–14

10 And the crowds asked him, "What then shall we do?" 11 And he answered them, "Whoever has two tunics[1] is to share with him who has none, and whoever has food is to do likewise." 12 Tax collectors also came to be baptized and said to him, "Teacher, what shall we do?" 13 And he said to them, "Collect no more than you are authorized to do." 14 Soldiers also asked him, "And we, what shall we do?" And he said to them, "Do not extort money from anyone by threats or by false accusation, and be content with your wages."

15 As the people were in expectation, and all were questioning in their hearts concerning John, whether he might be the Christ, 16 John answered them all, saying, "I baptize you with water, but he who is mightier than I is coming, the strap of whose sandals I am not worthy to untie. He will baptize you with the Holy Spirit and with fire. 17 His winnowing fork is in his hand, to clear his threshing floor and to gather the wheat into his barn, but the chaff he will burn with unquenchable fire."

18 So with many other exhortations he preached good news to the people. 19 But Herod the tetrarch, who had been reproved by him for Herodias, his brother's wife, and for all the evil things that Herod had done, 20 added this to them all, that he locked up John in prison.

21 Now when all the people were
baptized, and when Jesus also had
1305 been baptized and was praying, the
heavens were opened, 22 and the Holy Spirit descended on him in bodily form, like a dove; and a voice came from heaven, "You are my beloved Son;[2] with you I am well pleased."[3]

The Genealogy of Jesus Christ

23 Jesus, when he began his minis-
try, was about thirty years of age,
425 being the son (as was supposed) of
Joseph, the son of Heli, 24 the son of Matthat, the son of Levi, the son of Melchi, the son of Jannai, the son of Joseph, 25 the son of Mattathias, the son of Amos, the son of Nahum, the son of Esli, the son of Naggai, 26 the son of Maath, the son of Mattathias, the son of Semein, the son of Josech, the son of Joda, 27 the son of Joanan, the son of Rhesa, the son of Zerubbabel, the son of Shealtiel,[4] the son of Neri, 28 the son of Melchi, the son of Addi, the son of Cosam, the son of Elmadam, the son of Er, 29 the son of Joshua, the son of Eliezer, the son of Jorim, the son of Matthat, the son of Levi, 30 the son of Simeon, the son of Judah, the son of Joseph, the son of Jonam, the

[1] Greek *chiton*, a long garment worn under the cloak next to the skin [2] Or *my Son, my* (or *the*) *Beloved* [3] Some manuscripts *beloved Son; today I have begotten you* [4] Greek *Salathiel*

The Presentation of Jesus

Mary and Joseph called their baby Jesus, just as the angel of the Lord had told them. The name Jesus means "God Saves," because Jesus came to save His people from their sins.

When Jesus was six weeks old, Mary and Joseph took Him to the temple in Jerusalem, to present Him to the Lord. They also brought an offering to give to God. They did these things in obedience to God's Law.

There was a man named Simeon at the temple that day, who was a very godly man. The Holy Spirit had revealed to Simeon that, before he died, he would see the One God had been promising to send. When Simeon saw the baby Jesus, he knew right away that He was the Savior God had promised.

Simeon took the baby Jesus in his arms and praised God. He said, "Lord, now You are letting Your servant depart in peace, according to Your word; for my eyes have seen Your salvation." Mary and Joseph were amazed at the things Simeon said. Then Simeon blessed Mary and Joseph and Jesus.

There was also an old woman in the temple that day. Her name was Anna, and she often came to the temple to worship and pray. At that very same time Anna came over to see Jesus. She thanked God for the gift of the baby Jesus, and she told everyone there in the temple that Jesus was the Savior God had promised.

Simeon and Anna had waited a long time for God to fulfill His promise and send the Savior. They rejoiced when they saw Him. We are thankful that God sent Jesus to earth to be our Savior too. Because Jesus died on the cross to save us from our sins, someday, through faith in Him, we too will see Jesus!

SEEK and FIND

WHERE TO FIND THE STORY

Luke 2:22–38

KEY BIBLE VERSES

"Lord, now you are letting your servant depart in peace,
according to your word;
for my eyes have seen your salvation."
(Luke 2:29–30)

THREE KEY QUESTIONS

- Where did Mary and Joseph bring Jesus when he was six weeks old? Why did they bring Him there?
- What had Simeon and Anna been waiting for?
- What does the name "Jesus" mean?

RELATED BIBLE READINGS

Psalm 98:2; Isaiah 42:6; 49:6; 52:10

son of Eliakim, 31 the son of Melea, the son
of Menna, the son of Mattatha, the
son of Nathan, the son of David,
425 32 the son of Jesse, the son of Obed,
the son of Boaz, the son of Sala, the son of
Nahshon, 33 the son of Amminadab, the
son of Admin, the son of Arni, the son of
Hezron, the son of Perez, the son of Judah,
34 the son of Jacob, the son of Isaac, the
son of Abraham, the son of Terah, the son
of Nahor, 35 the son of Serug, the son of
Reu, the son of Peleg, the son of Eber, the
son of Shelah, 36 the son of Cainan, the son
of Arphaxad, the son of Shem, the son of
Noah, the son of Lamech, 37 the son of Me-
thuselah, the son of Enoch, the son of

Jared, the son of Mahalaleel, the son of Cainan, 38 the son of Enos, the son of Seth, the son of Adam, the son of God.

The Temptation of Jesus

4 And Jesus, full of the Holy
Spirit, returned from the
1309, Jordan and was led by the Spirit in
1373 the wilderness 2 for forty days,
being tempted by the devil. And he ate nothing during those days. And when they were ended, he was hungry. 3 The devil said to him, "If you are the Son of God, command this stone to become bread." 4 And Jesus answered him, "It is written, 'Man shall not live by bread alone.'" 5 And the devil took him up and showed him all the kingdoms of the world in a moment of time, 6 and said to him, "To you I will give all this authority and their glory, for it has been delivered to me, and I give it to whom I will. 7 If you, then, will worship me, it will all be yours." 8 And Jesus answered him, "It is written,

> "'You shall worship the Lord your God,
> and him only shall you serve.'"

9 And he took him to Jerusalem and set him on the pinnacle of the temple and said to him, "If you are the Son of God, throw yourself down from here, 10 for it is written,

> "'He will command his angels
> concerning you,
> to guard you,'

11 and

> "'On their hands they will bear you up,
> lest you strike your foot against a
> stone.'"

12 And Jesus answered him, "It is said, 'You shall not put the Lord your God to the test.'" 13 And when the devil had ended every temptation, he departed from him until an opportune time.

Jesus Begins His Ministry

14 And Jesus returned in the power of the Spirit to Galilee, and a report about him went out through all the surrounding country. 15 And he taught in their synagogues, being glorified by all.

Jesus Rejected at Nazareth

16 And he came to Nazareth, where
he had been brought up. And as
1459 was his custom, he went to the
synagogue on the Sabbath day, and he stood up to read. 17 And the scroll of the prophet Isaiah was given to him. He unrolled the scroll and found the place where it was written,

> 18 "The Spirit of the Lord is upon me,
> because he has anointed me
> 1459 to proclaim good news to the
> poor.

CHARACTER PROFILE

JOHN THE BAPTIST

John the Baptist's birth was predicted by an angel to parents too old to have a child. The prophets had promised that someone would prepare the way for the Savior; John was that person. He preached that people should repent, then he baptized those who did. At Jesus' request, John baptized Jesus, too.

1301, 1305, 1441

The Boy Jesus in the Temple

Every year Mary and Joseph took Jesus to Jerusalem to celebrate the Feast of the Passover. When He was 12 years old, Jesus went as usual with His parents to Jerusalem.

That year, when the Passover festival was over, Joseph and Mary started on the journey back to their home in Nazareth. They traveled for a whole day thinking that Jesus was with them—they didn't know that Jesus had stayed back in Jerusalem. When they realized He was missing, they looked everywhere for Him among all their friends and relatives traveling together. Worried and troubled, Mary and Joseph went back to Jerusalem to find Jesus.

They searched everywhere for Him for three days in Jerusalem. At last they found Him in the temple, sitting among the Jewish teachers, listening and asking questions.

Everyone who heard Jesus was astonished at His understanding and answers. When His parents saw Him, they were amazed. Jesus' mother asked Him why He had treated them this way. She told Him they had been looking everywhere for Him, greatly worried.

"Why were you looking for Me?" Jesus asked them. "Did you not know that I must be in My Father's house?"

Mary and Joseph did not understand what Jesus meant.

"But Mary treasured up all these things in her heart."

Jesus went back with His parents to Nazareth and was submissive to them. And Jesus grew in wisdom and stature, and in favor with God and other people.

The years went by, and Jesus grew up to be a man. He continued to do His heavenly Father's will, by His preaching and all the miracles He did. Finally, Jesus suffered and died for the sins of the world. Jesus, our Savior, rose victorious over sin and death, fulfilling all of Scripture for you and for me.

SEEK and FIND

WHERE TO FIND THE STORY

Luke 2:41–52

KEY BIBLE VERSE

"For I have come down from heaven, not to do my own will but the will of him who sent me." (John 6:38)

THREE KEY QUESTIONS

- Where did Joseph and Mary find Jesus when they went back to Jerusalem?
- What was Jesus doing when they found Him?
- What did Jesus do when He grew up to be a man?

RELATED BIBLE READINGS

Exodus 20:12; John 4:31–34; 17:4, 6–8; Ephesians 6:1

He has sent me to proclaim liberty
to the captives
and recovering of sight to the
blind,
to set at liberty those who are
oppressed,
19 to proclaim the year of the Lord's
favor."

20 And he rolled up the scroll and gave it
back to the attendant and sat down. And
the eyes of all in the synagogue were fixed
on him. 21 And he began to say to
them, "Today this Scripture has
been fulfilled in your hearing."
22 And all spoke well of him and marveled
at the gracious words that were coming

1459

from his mouth. And they said, "Is not
this Joseph's son?" 23 And he said to them,
"Doubtless you will quote to me this prov-
erb, 'Physician, heal yourself.' What we
have heard you did at Capernaum, do here
in your hometown as well." 24 And he said,
"Truly, I say to you, no prophet is
acceptable in his hometown. 25 But
567, in truth, I tell you, there were
593 many widows in Israel in the days
of Elijah, when the heavens were shut up
three years and six months, and a great
famine came over all the land, 26 and
Elijah was sent to none of them but only
to Zarephath, in the land of Sidon, to a
woman who was a widow. 27 And there
were many lepers[1] in Israel in the time of
the prophet Elisha, and none of them was
cleansed, but only Naaman the Syrian."
28 When they heard these things, all in the
synagogue were filled with wrath. 29 And
they rose up and drove him out of the
town and brought him to the brow of the
hill on which their town was built, so that
they could throw him down the cliff.
30 But passing through their midst, he
went away.

Jesus Heals a Man with an Unclean Demon

31 And he went down to Caper-
naum, a city of Galilee. And he was
1463 teaching them on the Sabbath,
32 and they were astonished at his teach-
ing, for his word possessed authority.
33 And in the synagogue there was a man
who had the spirit of an unclean demon,
and he cried out with a loud voice, 34 "Ha![2]
What have you to do with us, Jesus of
Nazareth? Have you come to destroy us? I
know who you are—the Holy One of God."
35 But Jesus rebuked him, saying, "Be
silent and come out of him!" And when
the demon had thrown him down in their
midst, he came out of him, having done
him no harm. 36 And they were all amazed
and said to one another, "What is this
word? For with authority and power he
commands the unclean spirits, and they
come out!" 37 And reports about him went
out into every place in the surrounding
region.

Jesus Heals Many

38 And he arose and left the synagogue
and entered Simon's house. Now Simon's
mother-in-law was ill with a high fever,
and they appealed to him on her behalf.
39 And he stood over her and rebuked the
fever, and it left her, and immediately she
rose and began to serve them.
40 Now when the sun was setting,
all those who had any who were
1463 sick with various diseases brought
them to him, and he laid his hands on
every one of them and healed them. 41 And
demons also came out of many, crying,
"You are the Son of God!" But he rebuked
them and would not allow them to speak,
because they knew that he was the Christ.

Jesus Preaches in Synagogues

42 And when it was day, he departed
and went into a desolate place. And the
people sought him and came to him, and
would have kept him from leaving them,
43 but he said to them, "I must preach the
good news of the kingdom of God to the
other towns as well; for I was sent for this
purpose." 44 And he was preaching in the
synagogues of Judea.[3]

Jesus Calls the First Disciples

5 On one occasion, while the
crowd was pressing in on him
1467 to hear the word of God, he was
standing by the lake of Gennesaret,
2 and he saw two boats by the lake,
1313, but the fishermen had gone out of
1601 them and were washing their nets.
3 Getting into one of the boats, which was
Simon's, he asked him to put out a little
from the land. And he sat down and
taught the people from the boat. 4 And
when he had finished speaking, he said to
Simon, "Put out into the deep and let

[1] *Leprosy* was a term for several skin diseases; see Leviticus 13 [2] Or *Leave us alone* [3] Some manuscripts *Galilee*

Herod's Temple Complex in the Time of Jesus

In the Gospels and in Acts, when "the temple" is mentioned, it often refers to this whole group of buildings and courtyards. It was the buildings of this temple complex that the disciples pointed out to Jesus when they said, ". . . what wonderful stones and what wonderful buildings" (Mark 13:1–2).

In the Temple Court near the door to the temple stood the altar where sacrifices were offered to God, the brass basin where the priests washed themselves according to the rules for offering sacrifice, and the place where the sacrificial animals were slaughtered.

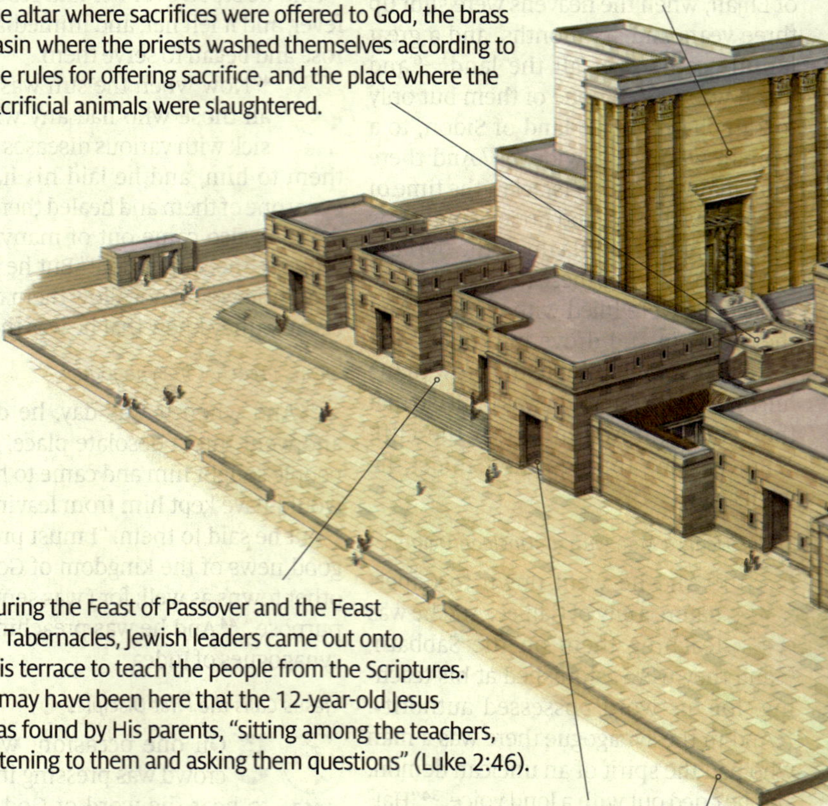

During the Feast of Passover and the Feast of Tabernacles, Jewish leaders came out onto this terrace to teach the people from the Scriptures. It may have been here that the 12-year-old Jesus was found by His parents, "sitting among the teachers, listening to them and asking them questions" (Luke 2:46).

The Chamber of Hewn Stone was where the Sanhedrin Council, a group of Jewish leaders, met until around A.D. 30.

The soreg (a low screen or railing) separated the temple courts from the Court of the Gentiles, keeping Gentiles or non-purified Jews from entering any farther. Paul may have been thinking of this railing when he wrote of how Jesus had done away with "the dividing wall of hostility" between Jews and Gentiles (Ephesians 2:14).

The Chamber of the Hearth was the building where the priests who were on duty lived during their time of service (cf. Zechariah in Luke 1:8).

The Nicanor Gate divided the Court of the Israelites and the Court of the Women

Lepers who had been healed were examined by priests in the Chamber of Lepers to be sure the healing was genuine. (cf. Matthew 8:4; Mark 1:44; Luke 5:14).

Four large lampstands 86 feet (26 m) high stood in the Court of the Women to provide lighting at night.

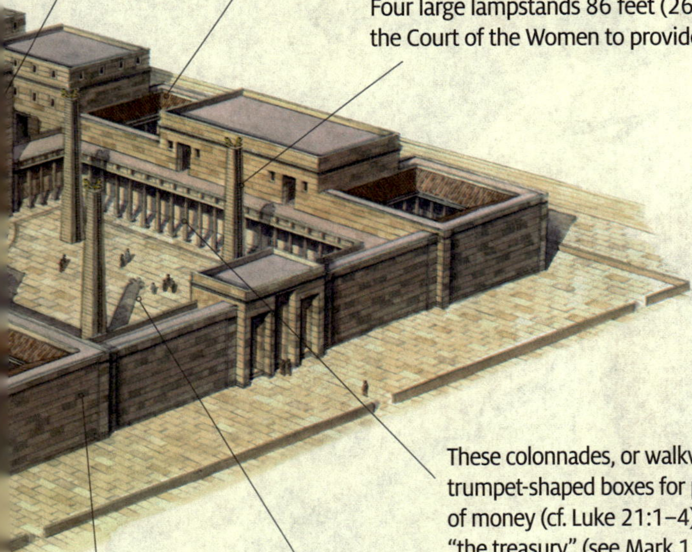

These colonnades, or walkways, contained 13 trumpet-shaped boxes for people's offerings of money (cf. Luke 21:1–4); this was called "the treasury" (see Mark 12:41; John 8:20).

The Court of the Women was a 233 feet/71 m square courtyard where 6,000 worshipers could gather at a time. Both men and women could gather here, but women could go no farther than this into the temple courts. It was in this court that the infant Jesus and His parents were met by Simeon and Anna (Luke 2:25–38).

The Chamber of the Nazirites was where a Nazirite, someone who had taken a vow to live a certain way, would bring his sacrifices when his vows had been completed.

Jesus Rejected at Nazareth

After Jesus was baptized by John, and after He had been tempted by the devil, Jesus began His ministry of teaching and miracles. The news about Jesus spread quickly throughout the countryside.

When Jesus returned to His hometown of Nazareth, the people had heard about Jesus' new ministry. Now they wanted to see and hear this man who had grown up in their town.

On the Sabbath, Jesus stood up in the synagogue to read from the Scripture. And a great crowd of people from His hometown came out to see Him. The leader of the synagogue brought Him the Book of Isaiah. Jesus unrolled the scroll and found words about the promised Savior, and He read aloud to everyone.

"The Spirit of the Lord is upon Me," He read, "because He has anointed Me to proclaim Good News to the poor. He has sent Me to proclaim liberty to the captives and recovering of sight to the blind, to set at liberty those who are oppressed, to proclaim the year of the Lord's favor."

After He read these words, Jesus sat down to explain their meaning. Everyone waited for Jesus to speak. "Today," Jesus said, "this Scripture has been fulfilled in your hearing."

Everyone liked what Jesus said and how well He said it.

But they did not believe that Jesus was the Savior God had promised. "Is not this Joseph's son?" they asked.

Jesus knew they did not believe He was more than Joseph's son—that He was also the Son of God the Father in heaven. He knew that no prophet ever received honor in his own town. Jesus told them that even Elijah and Elisha were not respected in their towns as God's prophets.

The people became angry at these words. They grabbed Jesus and pulled Him outside the synagogue. The people turned into an angry mob and drove Jesus to the top of a hill outside Nazareth—hoping to throw Him over the cliff. But miraculously, Jesus walked quietly through the crowd and went away without being hurt.

Jesus wanted to spread the news that He was the promised Savior, so He went on to His hometown of Capernaum and throughout all the surrounding countryside. When He taught on the Sabbath, the people were glad to hear Him at first. But soon many people did not believe that He was Son of God and the only Savior. Today Jesus wants us always to believe in Him and who He really is—Jesus Christ, the Son of God the Father, and our only Savior.

SEEK and FIND

WHERE TO FIND THE STORY

Luke 4:16–30

KEY BIBLE VERSE

"'The Spirit of the Lord is upon me, because he has anointed me to proclaim good news to the poor . . .' And he began to say to them, 'Today this Scripture has been fulfilled in your hearing.'" (Luke 4:18, 21)

THREE KEY QUESTIONS

- After Jesus read Isaiah's prophecy, what did Jesus say had happened that very day?
- Why did the people of Nazareth become angry with the things that Jesus said?
- How did Jesus escape from the angry mob?

RELATED BIBLE READINGS

1 Kings 17:8–16; 2 Kings 5:1–14; Matthew 2:23; 13:54–58; Mark 6:1–6

down your nets for a catch." **5** And Simon answered, "Master, we toiled all night and took nothing! But at your word I will let down the nets." **6** And when they had done this, they enclosed a large number of fish, and their nets were breaking. **7** They signaled to their partners in the other boat to come and help them. And they came and filled both the boats, so that they began to sink. **8** But when Simon Peter saw it, he fell down at Jesus' knees, saying, "Depart from me, for I am a sinful man, O Lord." **9** For he and all who were with him were astonished at the catch of fish that they had taken, **10** and so also were James and John, sons of Zebedee, who were partners with Simon. And Jesus said to Simon, "Do not be afraid; from now on you
1467 will be catching men." **11** And when they had brought their boats to land, they left everything and followed him.

Jesus Cleanses a Leper

12 While he was in one of the cities, there came a man full of leprosy.[1] And when he saw Jesus, he fell on his face and begged him, "Lord, if you will, you can make me clean." **13** And Jesus[2] stretched out his hand and touched him, saying, "I will; be clean." And immediately the leprosy left him. **14** And he charged him to tell no one, but "go and show yourself to the priest, and make an offering for your cleansing, as Moses commanded, for a proof to them." **15** But now even more the report about him went abroad, and great crowds gathered to hear him and to be healed of their infirmities. **16** But he would withdraw to desolate places and pray.

Jesus Heals a Paralytic

17 On one of those days, as he was teaching, Pharisees and teachers of
1377 the law were sitting there, who had come from every village of Galilee and Judea and from Jerusalem. And the power of the Lord was with him to heal.[3] **18** And behold, some men were bringing on a bed a man who was paralyzed, and they were seeking to bring him in and lay him before Jesus, **19** but finding no way to bring him in, because of the crowd, they went up on the roof and let him down with his bed through the tiles into the midst before

[1] *Leprosy* was a term for several skin diseases; see Leviticus 13 [2] Greek *he* [3] Some manuscripts *was present to heal them*

Jesus Heals Many

After Jesus left His hometown of Nazareth, He traveled to Capernaum. He taught again in the synagogue on the Sabbath day. All the people who heard Him were astonished at His teaching, because He spoke with great authority.

In the synagogue there was a man with an evil spirit who cried out with a loud voice. The evil spirit recognized that Jesus had great authority. "I know who You are," the evil spirit said, "the Holy One of God."

Jesus rebuked the evil spirit. He told the evil spirit to "be silent and come out of him!" The evil spirit obeyed and came out of the man! The people in the synagogue were amazed.

"What is this word?" they asked. "For with authority and power He commands the unclean spirits, and they come out!"

After Jesus left the synagogue, He went to Peter's home. Peter's mother-in-law was sick with a high fever. Jesus stood over her and rebuked the fever. Immediately, the fever left her, and she began to serve Jesus and His followers.

Later, as the sun was going down, many people came to Jesus with family members or friends who were sick. Jesus laid His hands on every one of them and healed them. Jesus also cast out more evil spirits.

When the morning came, Jesus went away to be alone.

Once people found Him, they begged Him to stay, but Jesus told them He had come to preach the Good News of the kingdom of God in other places too.

During His life on earth, Jesus preached and healed many people. When He died on the cross, Jesus provided the complete healing from sin, for all who by faith believe in Him.

SEEK and FIND

WHERE TO FIND THE STORY

Luke 4:31–44

KEY BIBLE VERSE

"Now when the sun was setting, all those who had any who were sick with various diseases brought them to him, and he laid his hands on every one of them and healed them." (Luke 4:40)

THREE KEY QUESTIONS

- What happened when Jesus rebuked the evil spirit?
- What happened when Jesus rebuked the fever in Peter's mother-in-law?
- How did Jesus have the power and authority to cast out evil spirits and to heal the sick?

RELATED BIBLE READINGS

Mark 1:21–28; Luke 8:25; Acts 2:22

Jesus. 20 And when he saw their faith, he
said, "Man, your sins are forgiven you."
21 And the scribes and the Pharisees began
to question, saying, "Who is this who
speaks blasphemies? Who can forgive sins
but God alone?" 22 When Jesus perceived
their thoughts, he answered them, "Why
do you question in your hearts? 23 Which
is easier, to say, 'Your sins are forgiven
you,' or to say, 'Rise and walk'? 24 But that
you may know that the Son of Man has
authority on earth to forgive sins"—he
said to the man who was paralyzed—"I say
to you, rise, pick up your bed and go
home." 25 And immediately he rose up
before them and picked up what he had
been lying on and went home, glorifying
God. 26 And amazement seized them all,

and they glorified God and were filled with awe, saying, "We have seen extraordinary things today."

Jesus Calls Levi

27 After this he went out and saw a
tax collector named Levi, sitting at
1381 the tax booth. And he said to him,
"Follow me." 28 And leaving everything, he
rose and followed him.

29 And Levi made him a great feast in his
house, and there was a large company of
tax collectors and others reclining at table
with them. 30 And the Pharisees and their
scribes grumbled at his disciples, saying,
"Why do you eat and drink with tax collec-
tors and sinners?" 31 And Jesus answered
them, "Those who are well have no need
of a physician, but those who are sick. 32 I
have not come to call the righteous but
sinners to repentance."

A Question About Fasting

33 And they said to him, "The disciples
of John fast often and offer prayers, and so
do the disciples of the Pharisees, but yours
eat and drink." 34 And Jesus said to them,
"Can you make wedding guests fast while
the bridegroom is with them? 35 The days
will come when the bridegroom is taken
away from them, and then they will fast in
those days." 36 He also told them a parable:
"No one tears a piece from a new garment
and puts it on an old garment. If he does,
he will tear the new, and the piece from
the new will not match the old. 37 And no
one puts new wine into old wineskins. If
he does, the new wine will burst the skins
and it will be spilled, and the skins will be
destroyed. 38 But new wine must be put
into fresh wineskins. 39 And no one after
drinking old wine desires new, for he says,
'The old is good.'"[1]

Jesus Is Lord of the Sabbath

6 On a Sabbath,[2] while he was going
through the grainfields, his disciples
plucked and ate some heads of grain, rub-
bing them in their hands. 2 But some of
the Pharisees said, "Why are you doing
what is not lawful to do on the Sabbath?"
3 And Jesus answered them, "Have you not
read what David did when he was hungry,
he and those who were with him: 4 how
he entered the house of God and took and
ate the bread of the Presence, which is not
lawful for any but the priests to eat, and
also gave it to those with him?" 5 And he
said to them, "The Son of Man is lord of
the Sabbath."

A Man with a Withered Hand

6 On another Sabbath, he entered the
synagogue and was teaching, and a man
was there whose right hand was with-
ered. 7 And the scribes and the Pharisees

CHARACTER PROFILE

SIMON PETER

Simon Peter was a fisherman who became one of Jesus' closest disciples, often the spokesman for the other disciples. After Jesus' resurrection, Peter preached bold sermons to the Jewish leaders. He also was the first Apostle to preach to a gathering of Gentiles. Peter wrote the letters we call First and Second Peter.

1313, 1415, 1593, 1601, 1645, 1651

[1] Some manuscripts *better* [2] Some manuscripts *On the second first Sabbath* (that is, on the second Sabbath after the first)

Jesus Calls the First Disciples

One day, Jesus was teaching a crowd of people by the Lake of Gennesaret (another name for the Sea of Galilee). The people were so eager to hear Jesus' teaching that they pressed in on Him at the waters' edge. In fact, they almost pushed Him into the water! Then Jesus saw two boats that had been left there by the fishermen who were washing their nets. He got into the one belonging to Simon Peter and asked Peter to move the boat a little distance from shore. Then Jesus sat down in the boat and taught the people who were gathered at the edge of the water.

When Jesus finished teaching, He asked Simon Peter to move out into deeper water and to put down his nets for a catch. Peter, who had just returned from fishing, replied, "Master, we toiled all night and took nothing!" Then he added, "But at Your word I will let down the nets."

Peter and his partner rowed out from land and let down their nets. To their surprise, the nets filled up with fish. In fact, the nets were so full that they began to break. Quickly, Simon Peter and his partner motioned to James and John, who were in a nearby boat, to come and help. Soon, both boats were so full of fish that they began to sink.

When Peter saw all of the fish, he fell down at Jesus' knees and begged Jesus to go away. "I am a sinful man!" he cried. Peter was sorry that he had not believed Jesus at first. He felt unworthy to be in Jesus' presence.

Then Jesus said to Peter, "Do not be afraid; from now on you will be catching men." Jesus was referring to the people who would later believe in Him through Peter's preaching.

So the fishermen pulled to shore their boats filled with fish. They left everything and followed Jesus. From that day on they were His disciples.

Soon Jesus had 12 disciples. These men went all over the land with Jesus. They listened to Jesus and helped Him as He taught the people. Later, after Jesus ascended into heaven, the Holy Spirit gave these men power to tell others that Jesus was the Savior God had promised. They also wrote down what Jesus had done and taught.

SEEK and FIND

WHERE TO FIND THE STORY

Luke 5:1–11

KEY BIBLE VERSE

"And Jesus said to Simon, 'Do not be afraid; from now on you will be catching men.'" (Luke 5:10)

THREE KEY QUESTIONS

- Why did Peter think there was no use going out into deep water to let down his nets?
- After the fish had been caught, why did Peter want Jesus to go away?
- What did Jesus do with Peter instead?

RELATED BIBLE READINGS

Matthew 4:18–22; Mark 1:16–20; John 1:40–42; 21:1–14

watched him, to see whether he would heal on the Sabbath, so that they might find a reason to accuse him. 8 But he knew their thoughts, and he said to the man with the withered hand, "Come and stand here." And he rose and stood there. 9 And Jesus said to them, "I ask you, is it lawful on the Sabbath to do good or to do harm, to save life or to destroy it?" 10 And after looking around at them all he said to him, "Stretch out your hand." And he did so, and his hand was restored. 11 But they were filled with fury and discussed with one another what they might do to Jesus.

The Twelve Apostles

12 In these days he went out to the mountain to pray, and all night he continued in prayer to God. 13 And when day came, he called his disciples and chose from them twelve, whom he named apostles: 14 Simon, whom he named Peter, and Andrew his brother, and James and John, and Philip, and Bartholomew, 15 and Matthew, and Thomas, and James the son of Alphaeus, and Simon who was called the Zealot, 16 and Judas the son of James, and Judas Iscariot, who became a traitor.

Jesus Ministers to a Great Multitude

17 And he came down with them and stood on a level place, with a great crowd of his disciples and a great multitude of people from all Judea and Jerusalem and the seacoast of Tyre and Sidon, 18 who came to hear him and to be healed of their diseases. And those who were troubled with unclean spirits were cured. 19 And all the crowd sought to touch him, for power came out from him and healed them all.

The Beatitudes

20 And he lifted up his eyes on his disciples, and said:

1317 "Blessed are you who are poor, for yours is the kingdom of God.

21 "Blessed are you who are hungry now, for you shall be satisfied.

"Blessed are you who weep now, for you shall laugh.

22 "Blessed are you when people hate you and when they exclude you and revile you and spurn your name as evil, on account of the Son of Man! 23 Rejoice in that day, and leap for joy, for behold, your reward is great in heaven; for so their fathers did to the prophets.

Jesus Pronounces Woes

24 "But woe to you who are rich, for you have received your consolation.

25 "Woe to you who are full now, for you shall be hungry.

"Woe to you who laugh now, for you shall mourn and weep.

26 "Woe to you, when all people speak well of you, for so their fathers did to the false prophets.

Love Your Enemies

27 "But I say to you who hear, Love your enemies, do good to those who hate you, 28 bless those who curse you, pray for those who abuse you. 29 To one who strikes you on the cheek, offer the other also, and from one who takes away your cloak do not withhold your tunic[1] either. 30 Give to everyone who begs from you, and from one who takes away your goods do not demand them back. 31 And as you wish that others would do to you, do so to them.

32 "If you love those who love you, what benefit is that to you? For even sinners love those who love them. 33 And if you do good to those who do good to you, what benefit is that to you? For even sinners do the same. 34 And if you lend to those from whom you expect to receive, what credit is that to you? Even sinners lend to sinners, to get back the same amount. 35 But love your enemies, and do good, and lend, expecting nothing in return, and your reward will be great, and you will be sons of the Most High, for he is kind to the ungrateful and the evil. 36 Be merciful, even as your Father is merciful.

[1] Greek *chiton*, a long garment worn under the cloak next to the skin

The Synagogue and Jewish Worship

Jerusalem had the temple. Other cities had synagogues as centers of Jewish worship during the time Jesus was on earth. Most of Israel's leading towns had synagogues. This illustration is based on ruins that were found in Gamla, about 6 miles (9.7 km) northeast of the Sea of Galilee. The synagogues Jesus worshiped and taught in would probably have been very similar to this one.

Inside was an unpaved area in the shape of a rectangle. This was where the people gathered. Pillars holding the roof were all around the edges of this area. Four rows of stone benches lined the walls and could probably hold a few hundred people.

The building itself was made of basalt stone blocks. The building was 84 x 56 feet (26 x 17 m).

The entrance to the synagogue faced Jerusalem.

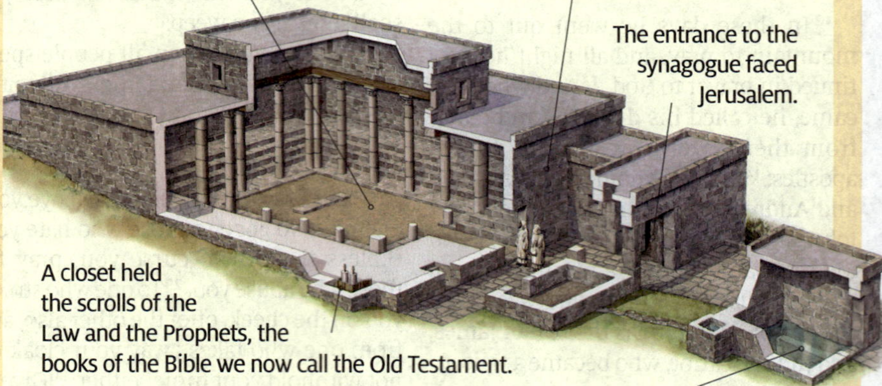

A closet held the scrolls of the Law and the Prophets, the books of the Bible we now call the Old Testament.

A covered water channel ran to the mikveh, a stone bath with seven steps down into it. The mikveh held just enough water for a person to be completely immersed. People needing purification, as well as jars and utensils or other items used for worship, would be cleansed here.

Judging Others

37 "Judge not, and you will not be
judged; condemn not, and you will not be
condemned; forgive, and you will be for-
given; 38 give, and it will be given to you.
Good measure, pressed down, shaken
together, running over, will be put into
your *lap*. For with the measure you use it
will be measured back to you."
39 He also told them a parable: "Can a
blind man lead a blind man? Will they
not both fall into a pit? 40 A disciple is not
above his teacher, but everyone when he
is fully trained will be like his teacher.
41 Why do you see the speck that is in your
brother's eye, but do not notice the log
that is in your own eye? 42 How can you
say to your brother, 'Brother, let me take
out the speck that is in your eye,' when
you yourself do not see the log that is in
your own eye? You hypocrite, first take the
log out of your own eye, and then you will

see clearly to take out the speck that is in
your brother's eye.

A Tree and Its Fruit

43 "For no good tree bears bad fruit, nor
again does a bad tree bear good fruit, 44 for
each tree is known by its own fruit. For
figs are not gathered from thornbushes,
nor are grapes picked from a bramble
bush. 45 The good person out of the good
treasure of his heart produces good, and
the evil person out of his evil treasure pro-
duces evil, for out of the abundance of the
heart his mouth speaks.

Build Your House on the Rock

46 "Why do you call me 'Lord, Lord,' and
not do what I tell you? 47 Everyone who
comes to me and hears my words and
does them, I will show you what he is like:
48 he is like a man building a house, who
dug deep and laid the foundation on the
rock. And when a flood arose, the stream
broke against that house and could not
shake it, because it had been well built.[1]
49 But the one who hears and does not do
them is like a man who built a house on
the ground without a foundation. When
the stream broke against it, immediately it
fell, and the ruin of that house was great."

Jesus Heals a Centurion's Servant

7 After he had finished all his say-
ings in the hearing of the people, he
entered Capernaum. 2 Now a centurion
had a servant[2] who was sick and at the
point of death, who was highly valued
by him. 3 When the centurion[3] heard
about Jesus, he sent to him elders of the
Jews, asking him to come and heal his
servant. 4 And when they came to Jesus,
they pleaded with him earnestly, saying,
"He is worthy to have you do this for him,
5 for he loves our nation, and he is the
one who built us our synagogue." 6 And
Jesus went with them. When he was not
far from the house, the centurion sent
friends, saying to him, "Lord, do not trou-
ble yourself, for I am not worthy to have
you come under my roof. 7 Therefore I did
not presume to come to you. But say the
word, and let my servant be healed. 8 For
I too am a man set under authority, with
soldiers under me: and I say to one, 'Go,'
and he goes; and to another, 'Come,' and
he comes; and to my servant, 'Do this,'
and he does it." 9 When Jesus heard these
things, he marveled at him, and turning
to the crowd that followed him, said, "I
tell you, not even in Israel have I found
such faith." 10 And when those who had
been sent returned to the house, they
found the servant well.

Jesus Raises a Widow's Son

11 Soon afterward[4] he went to a
town called Nain, and his disciples
1389, and a great crowd went with him.
1577 12 As he drew near to the gate of the
town, behold, a man who had died was
being carried out, the only son of his
mother, and she was a widow, and a con-
siderable crowd from the town was with
her. 13 And when the Lord saw her, he had
compassion on her and said to her, "Do
not weep." 14 Then he came up and
touched the bier, and the bearers stood
still. And he said, "Young man, I say to
you, arise." 15 And the dead man sat up and
began to speak, and Jesus[5] gave him to his
mother. 16 Fear seized them all, and they
glorified God, saying, "A great prophet has
arisen among us!" and "God has visited
his people!" 17 And this report about him
spread through the whole of Judea and all
the surrounding country.

Messengers from John the Baptist

18 The disciples of John reported all
these things to him. And John, 19 calling
two of his disciples to him, sent them to
the Lord, saying, "Are you the one who is
to come, or shall we look for another?"
20 And when the men had come to him,
they said, "John the Baptist has sent us
to you, saying, 'Are you the one who is to

[1] Some manuscripts *founded upon the rock* [2] Greek *bondservant*; also verses 3, 8, 10 [3] Greek *he* [4] Some manuscripts *The next day* [5] Greek *he*

Jesus is Anointed

Simon the Pharisee heard Jesus teach and decided to invite Him to dinner along with other guests. Now the Pharisees were very careful about whom they invited to dinner, because they did not want to be around people who disobeyed God's laws.

While Jesus was reclining at the table in Simon's house, a woman entered and stood near Jesus. The woman was known to be a sinner. But she loved Jesus, because He had forgiven her sins.

The woman saw that Simon was treating Jesus poorly. No one had washed Jesus' feet, which were still dusty from the road. She knew that He deserved better than that. The woman began to cry. She wet Jesus' feet with her tears. She took her long hair and dried the tears. Then, she kissed Jesus' feet and anointed His feet with expensive perfume she had brought in a beautiful little bottle.

Simon and the other people who were eating with Jesus were shocked. They looked at each other and said, "If this man were a prophet, He would have known who and what sort of woman this is who is touching Him, for she is a sinner."

Jesus was not only a Prophet but the Son of God. He told Simon a story to teach him about God's love.

Jesus said that two people owed money to a moneylender. One owed 500 pieces of money. The other person owed 50 pieces. Neither person had enough money to pay back what they owed. Since the moneylender knew that neither person could pay, he said that the two people did not have to pay back any of the money at all. He forgave both of their debts.

After telling this story, Jesus asked Simon which one of the two people would love the moneylender more.

Simon said that the man who had owed the most money would love the moneylender the most.

Jesus told Simon that he was right. Then He turned toward the woman and said to Simon, "Do you see this woman? I entered your house; you gave Me no water for My feet, but she has wet My feet with her tears and wiped them with her hair. You gave Me no kiss, but from the time I came in she has not ceased to kiss My feet. You did not anoint My head with oil, but she has anointed My feet with ointment. Therefore I tell you, her sins, which are many, are forgiven—for she loved much. But he who is forgiven little, loves little."

Then Jesus said to the woman, "Your sins are forgiven."

The other people at the table began to whisper to each other, "Who is this, who even forgives sins?"

Jesus said to the woman, "Your faith has saved you; go in peace."

In faith, a sinful woman anointed Jesus' feet. He had forgiven her sins, and she wanted to show her love and thankfulness to Him. In faith, we receive the forgiveness for our sins and show love and praise for Jesus.

SEEK and FIND

WHERE TO FIND THE STORY

Luke 7:36–50

KEY BIBLE VERSE

"Therefore I tell you, her sins, which are many, are forgiven—for she loved much. But he who is forgiven little, loves little." (Luke 7:47)

THREE KEY QUESTIONS

- Why did the woman wash Jesus' feet with her tears, dry them with her hair, and then put expensive perfume on them? Why did she love Jesus so much?
- Why did Simon think Jesus should not let her touch Him?
- Why was Jesus able to forgive her sins?

RELATED BIBLE READINGS

Matthew 9:10–13; 26:6–13; Mark 14:3–9; John 12:1–8

come, or shall we look for another?'" 21 In that hour he healed many people of diseases and plagues and evil spirits, and on many who were blind he bestowed sight. 22 And he answered them, "Go and tell John what you have seen and heard: the blind receive their sight, the lame walk, lepers[1] are cleansed, and the deaf hear, the dead are raised up, the poor have good news preached to them. 23 And blessed is the one who is not offended by me."

24 When John's messengers had gone, Jesus[2] began to speak to the crowds concerning John: "What did you go out into the wilderness to see? A reed shaken by the wind? 25 What then did you go out to see? A man dressed in soft clothing? Behold, those who are dressed in splendid clothing and live in luxury are in kings' courts. 26 What then did you go out to see? A prophet? Yes, I tell you, and more than a prophet. 27 This is he of whom it is written,

> "'Behold, I send my messenger before
> your face,
> who will prepare your way before
> you.'

28 I tell you, among those born of women none is greater than John. Yet the one who is least in the kingdom of God is greater than he." 29 (When all the people heard this, and the tax collectors too, they declared God just,[3] having been baptized with the baptism of John, 30 but the Pharisees and the lawyers rejected the purpose of God for themselves, not having been baptized by him.)

31 "To what then shall I compare the people of this generation, and what are they like? 32 They are like children sitting in the marketplace and calling to one another,

[1] *Leprosy* was a term for several skin diseases; see Leviticus 13 [2] Greek *he* [3] Greek *they justified God*

"'We played the flute for you, and you
did not dance;
we sang a dirge, and you did not
weep.'

33 For John the Baptist has come eating no bread and drinking no wine, and you say, 'He has a demon.' 34 The Son of Man has come eating and drinking, and you say, 'Look at him! A glutton and a drunkard, a friend of tax collectors and sinners!' 35 Yet wisdom is justified by all her children."

A Sinful Woman Forgiven

36 One of the Pharisees asked him
to eat with him, and he went into
1473 the Pharisee's house and took his
place at the table. 37 And behold, a
woman of the city, who was a sin-
1501 ner, when she learned that he was
reclining at table in the Pharisee's house, brought an alabaster flask of ointment, 38 and standing behind him at his feet, weeping, she began to wet his feet with her tears and wiped them with the hair of her head and kissed his feet and anointed them with the ointment. 39 Now when the Pharisee who had invited him saw this, he said to himself, "If this man were a prophet, he would have known who and what sort of woman this is who is touching him, for she is a sinner." 40 And Jesus answering said to him, "Simon, I have something to say to you." And he answered, "Say it, Teacher."

41 "A certain moneylender had two debtors. One owed five hundred denarii, and the other fifty. 42 When they could not pay, he cancelled the debt of both. Now which of them will love him more?" 43 Simon answered, "The one, I suppose, for whom he cancelled the larger debt." And he said to him, "You have judged rightly." 44 Then turning toward the woman he said to Simon, "Do you see this woman? I entered your house; you gave me no water for my feet, but she has wet my feet with her tears and wiped them with her hair. 45 You gave me no kiss, but from the time I came in she has not ceased to kiss my feet. 46 You did not anoint my head with oil, but she has anointed my feet with ointment.
47 Therefore I tell you, her sins,
which are many, are forgiven—for
1473 she loved much. But he who is for-
given little, loves little." 48 And he said to
her, "Your sins are forgiven." 49 Then
those who were at table with him
1377 began to say among[1] themselves,
"Who is this, who even forgives sins?" 50 And he said to the woman, "Your faith has saved you; go in peace."

Women Accompanying Jesus

8 Soon afterward he went on through cities and villages, proclaiming and bringing the good news of the kingdom of God. And the twelve were with him, 2 and also some women who had been healed of evil spirits and infirmities: Mary, called Magdalene, from whom seven demons had gone out, 3 and Joanna, the wife of Chuza, Herod's household manager, and Susanna, and many others, who provided for them[2] out of their means.

The Parable of the Sower

4 And when a great crowd was gathering and people from town after town came to him, he said in a parable: 5 "A sower went out to sow his seed. And as he sowed, some fell along the path and was trampled underfoot, and the birds of the air devoured it. 6 And some fell on the rock, and as it grew up, it withered away, because it had no moisture. 7 And some fell among thorns, and the thorns grew up with it and choked it. 8 And some fell into good soil and grew and yielded a hundredfold." As he said these things, he called out, "He who has ears to hear, let him hear."

The Purpose of the Parables

9 And when his disciples asked him what this parable meant, 10 he said, "To you it has been given to know the secrets

[1] Or *to* [2] Some manuscripts *him*

of the kingdom of God, but for others they are in parables, so that 'seeing they may not see, and hearing they may not understand.' [11]Now the parable is this: The seed is the word of God. [12]The ones along the path are those who have heard; then the devil comes and takes away the word from their hearts, so that they may not believe and be saved. [13]And the ones on the rock are those who, when they hear the word, receive it with joy. But these have no root; they believe for a while, and in time of testing fall away. [14]And as for what fell among the thorns, they are those who hear, but as they go on their way they are choked by the cares and riches and pleasures of life, and their fruit does not mature. [15]As for that in the good soil, they are those who, hearing the word, hold it fast in an honest and good heart, and bear fruit with patience.

A Lamp Under a Jar

[16]"No one after lighting a lamp covers it with a jar or puts it under a bed, but puts it on a stand, so that those who enter may see the light. [17]For nothing is hidden that will not be made manifest, nor is anything secret that will not be known and come to light. [18]Take care then how you hear, for to the one who has, more will be given, and from the one who has not, even what he thinks that he has will be taken away."

Jesus' Mother and Brothers

[19]Then his mother and his brothers came to him, but they could not reach him because of the crowd. [20]And he was told, "Your mother and your brothers are standing outside, desiring to see you." [21]But he answered them, "My mother and my brothers are those who hear the word of God and do it."

Jesus Calms a Storm

[22]One day he got into a boat with his disciples, and he said to them,
1331, "Let us go across to the other side
1385 of the lake." So they set out, [23]and as they sailed he fell asleep. And a windstorm came down on the lake, and they were filling with water and were in danger. [24]And they went and woke him, saying, "Master, Master, we are perishing!" And he awoke and rebuked the wind and the raging waves, and they ceased, and there was a calm. [25]He said to them, "Where is your faith?" And they were afraid, and they marveled,
1463 saying to one another, "Who then is this, that he commands even winds and water, and they obey him?"

Jesus Heals a Man with a Demon

[26]Then they sailed to the country of the Gerasenes,[1] which is opposite Galilee.

CHARACTER PROFILE

MARY MAGDALENE

Mary Magdalene was a follower of Jesus, who had cast seven demons out of her. Mary was at the cross when Jesus died and at the tomb when He was buried. She went with other women to the tomb and stayed behind after they saw that Jesus' body was not there. After the resurrection, Jesus appeared first to Mary Magdalene.

1421, 1593

[1] Some manuscripts *Gadarenes*; others *Gergesenes*; also verse 37

27 When Jesus[1] had stepped out on land, there met him a man from the city who had demons. For a long time he had worn no clothes, and he had not lived in a house but among the tombs. 28 When he saw Jesus, he cried out and fell down before him and said with a loud voice, "What have you to do with me, Jesus, Son of the Most High God? I beg you, do not torment me." 29 For he had commanded the unclean spirit to come out of the man. (For many a time it had seized him. He was kept under guard and bound with chains and shackles, but he would break the bonds and be driven by the demon into the desert.) 30 Jesus then asked him, "What is your name?" And he said, "Legion," for many demons had entered him. 31 And they begged him not to command them to depart into the abyss. 32 Now a large herd of pigs was feeding there on the hillside, and they begged him to let them enter these. So he gave them permission. 33 Then the demons came out of the man and entered the pigs, and the herd rushed down the steep bank into the lake and were drowned.

34 When the herdsmen saw what had happened, they fled and told it in the city and in the country. 35 Then people went out to see what had happened, and they came to Jesus and found the man from whom the demons had gone, sitting at the feet of Jesus, clothed and in his right mind, and they were afraid. 36 And those who had seen it told them how the demon-possessed[2] man had been healed. 37 Then all the people of the surrounding country of the Gerasenes asked him to depart from them, for they were seized with great fear. So he got into the boat and returned. 38 The man from whom the demons had gone begged that he might be with him, but Jesus sent him away, saying, 39 "Return to your home, and declare how much God has done for you." And he went away, proclaiming throughout the whole city how much Jesus had done for him.

Jesus Heals a Woman and Jairus's Daughter

40 Now when Jesus returned, the
crowd welcomed him, for they
1389 were all waiting for him. 41 And
there came a man named Jairus, who was a ruler of the synagogue. And falling at Jesus' feet, he implored him to come to his house, 42 for he had an only daughter, about twelve years of age, and she was dying.

As Jesus went, the people pressed around him. 43 And there was a woman who had had a discharge of blood for twelve years, and though she had spent all her living on physicians,[3] she could not be healed by anyone. 44 She came up behind him and touched the fringe of his garment, and immediately her discharge of blood ceased. 45 And Jesus said, "Who was it that touched me?" When all denied it, Peter[4] said, "Master, the crowds surround you and are pressing in on you!" 46 But Jesus said, "Someone touched me, for I perceive that power has gone out from me." 47 And when the woman saw that she was not hidden, she came trembling, and falling down before him declared in the presence of all the people why she had touched him, and how she had been immediately healed. 48 And he said to her, "Daughter, your faith has made you well; go in peace."

49 While he was still speaking,
someone from the ruler's house
1389 came and said, "Your daughter is
dead; do not trouble the Teacher any more." 50 But Jesus on hearing this answered him, "Do not fear; only believe, and she will be well." 51 And when he came to the house, he allowed no one to enter with him, except Peter and John and James, and the father and mother of the child. 52 And all were weeping and mourning for her, but he said, "Do not weep, for she is not dead but sleeping." 53 And they

[1] Greek *he*; also verses 38, 42 [2] Greek *daimonizomai*; elsewhere rendered *oppressed by demons* [3] Some manuscripts omit *and though she had spent all her living on physicians,* [4] Some manuscripts add *and those who were with him*

laughed at him, knowing that she was dead. 54 But taking her by the hand he called, saying, "Child, arise." 55 And her spirit returned, and she got up at once. And he directed that something should be given her to eat. 56 And her parents were amazed, but he charged them to tell no one what had happened.

Jesus Sends Out the Twelve Apostles

9 And he called the twelve
together and gave them power
1483 and authority over all demons and
to cure diseases, 2 and he sent them out to proclaim the kingdom of God and to heal. 3 And he said to them, "Take nothing for your journey, no staff, nor bag, nor bread, nor money; and do not have two tunics.[1] 4 And whatever house you enter, stay there, and from there depart. 5 And wherever they do not receive you, when you leave that town shake off the dust from your feet as a testimony against them." 6 And they departed and went through the villages, preaching the gospel and healing everywhere.

Herod Is Perplexed by Jesus

7 Now Herod the tetrarch heard about all that was happening, and he was perplexed, because it was said by some that John had been raised from the dead, 8 by some that Elijah had appeared, and by others that one of the prophets of old had risen. 9 Herod said, "John I beheaded, but who is this about whom I hear such things?" And he sought to see him.

Jesus Feeds the Five Thousand

10 On their return the apostles told
him all that they had done. And he
1559 took them and withdrew apart to
a town called Bethsaida. 11 When the crowds learned it, they followed him, and he welcomed them and spoke to them of the kingdom of God and cured those who had need of healing. 12 Now the day began to wear away, and the twelve came and said to him, "Send the crowd away to go into the surrounding villages and countryside to find lodging and get provisions, for we are here in a desolate place." 13 But he said to them, "You give them something to eat." They said, "We have no more than five loaves and two fish—unless we are to go and buy food for all these people." 14 For there were about five thousand men. And he said to his disciples, "Have them sit down in groups of about fifty each." 15 And they did so, and had them all sit down. 16 And taking the five loaves and the two fish, he looked up to heaven and said a blessing over them. Then he broke the loaves and gave them to the disciples to set before the crowd. 17 And they all ate and were satisfied. And what was left over was picked up, twelve baskets of broken pieces.

Peter Confesses Jesus as the Christ

18 Now it happened that as he was praying alone, the disciples were with him. And he asked them, "Who do the crowds say that I am?" 19 And they answered, "John the Baptist. But others say, Elijah, and others, that one of the prophets of old has risen." 20 Then he said to them, "But who do you say that I am?" And Peter answered, "The Christ of God."

Jesus Foretells His Death

21 And he strictly charged and commanded them to tell this to no one, 22 saying, "The Son of Man must suffer many things and be rejected by the elders and chief priests and scribes, and be killed, and on the third day be raised."

Take Up Your Cross and Follow Jesus

23 And he said to all, "If anyone would come after me, let him deny himself and take up his cross daily and follow me. 24 For whoever would save his life will lose it, but whoever loses his life for my sake will save it. 25 For what does it profit a man if he gains the whole world and

[1] Greek *chiton*, a long garment worn under the cloak next to the skin

loses or forfeits himself? 26 For whoever is
ashamed of me and of my words, of him
will the Son of Man be ashamed when he
comes in his glory and the glory of the
Father and of the holy angels. 27 But I tell
you truly, there are some standing here
who will not taste death until they see the
kingdom of God."

The Transfiguration

28 Now about eight days after these
sayings he took with him Peter and
1339, John and James and went up on
1397 the mountain to pray. 29 And as he
was praying, the appearance of his face
was altered, and his clothing became daz-
zling white. 30 And behold, two men were
talking with him, Moses and Elijah,
31 who appeared in glory and spoke of his
departure,[1] which he was about to accom-
plish at Jerusalem. 32 Now Peter and those
who were with him were heavy with
sleep, but when they became fully awake
they saw his glory and the two men who
stood with him. 33 And as the men were
parting from him, Peter said to Jesus,
"Master, it is good that we are here. Let us
make three tents, one for you and one for
Moses and one for Elijah"—not knowing
what he said. 34 As he was saying these
things, a cloud came and overshadowed
them, and they were afraid as they
entered the cloud. 35 And a voice came out
of the cloud, saying, "This is my Son, my
Chosen One;[2] listen to him!" 36 And when
the voice had spoken, Jesus was found
alone. And they kept silent and told no
one in those days anything of what they
had seen.

Jesus Heals a Boy with an Unclean Spirit

37 On the next day, when they had come
down from the mountain, a great crowd
met him. 38 And behold, a man from the
crowd cried out, "Teacher, I beg you to
look at my son, for he is my only child.
39 And behold, a spirit seizes him, and he
suddenly cries out. It convulses him so
that he foams at the mouth, and shatters
him, and will hardly leave him. 40 And I
begged your disciples to cast it out, but
they could not." 41 Jesus answered, "O
faithless and twisted generation, how
long am I to be with you and bear with
you? Bring your son here." 42 While he
was coming, the demon threw him to
the ground and convulsed him. But Jesus
rebuked the unclean spirit and healed
the boy, and gave him back to his father.
43 And all were astonished at the majesty
of God.

Jesus Again Foretells His Death

But while they were all marveling at
everything he was doing, Jesus[3] said to
his disciples, 44 "Let these words sink into
your ears: The Son of Man is about to be
delivered into the hands of men." 45 But
they did not understand this saying, and
it was concealed from them, so that they
might not perceive it. And they were
afraid to ask him about this saying.

Who Is the Greatest?

46 An argument arose among them
as to which of them was the greatest.
47 But Jesus, knowing the reasoning of
their hearts, took a child and put him by
his side 48 and said to them, "Whoever
receives this child in my name receives
me, and whoever receives me receives
him who sent me. For he who is least
among you all is the one who is great."

Anyone Not Against Us Is For Us

49 John answered, "Master, we saw
someone casting out demons in your
name, and we tried to stop him, because
he does not follow with us." 50 But Jesus
said to him, "Do not stop him, for the one
who is not against you is for you."

A Samaritan Village Rejects Jesus

51 When the days drew near for him
to be taken up, he set his face to go
1487 to Jerusalem. 52 And he sent mes-

[1] Greek *exodus* [2] Some manuscripts *my Beloved* [3] Greek *he*

sengers ahead of him, who went and
entered a village of the Samaritans, to
make preparations for him. 53 But the peo-
ple did not receive him, because his face
was set toward Jerusalem. 54 And when his
disciples James and John saw it, they said,
"Lord, do you want us to tell fire to come
down from heaven and consume them?"[1]
55 But he turned and rebuked them.[2]
56 And they went on to another village.

The Cost of Following Jesus

57 As they were going along the road,
someone said to him, "I will follow you
wherever you go." 58 And Jesus said to
him, "Foxes have holes, and birds of the
air have nests, but the Son of Man has
nowhere to lay his head." 59 To another
he said, "Follow me." But he said, "Lord,
let me first go and bury my father." 60 And
Jesus[3] said to him, "Leave the dead to bury
their own dead. But as for you, go and pro-
claim the kingdom of God." 61 Yet another
said, "I will follow you, Lord, but let me
first say farewell to those at my home."
62 Jesus said to him, "No one who puts his
hand to the plow and looks back is fit for
the kingdom of God."

Jesus Sends Out the Seventy-Two

10 After this the Lord ap-
pointed seventy-two[4] oth-
1483 ers and sent them on ahead of
him, two by two, into every town and
place where he himself was about to go.
2 And he said to them, "The harvest
is plentiful, but the laborers are
1483 few. Therefore pray earnestly to
the Lord of the harvest to send out labor-
ers into his harvest. 3 Go your way; be-
hold, I am sending you out as lambs in the
midst of wolves. 4 Carry no moneybag, no
knapsack, no sandals, and greet no one
on the road. 5 Whatever house you enter,
first say, 'Peace be to this house!' 6 And if a
son of peace is there, your peace will rest
upon him. But if not, it will return to you.
7 And remain in the same house, eating
and drinking what they provide, for the
laborer deserves his wages. Do not go
from house to house. 8 Whenever you
enter a town and they receive you, eat
what is set before you. 9 Heal the sick in it
and say to them, 'The kingdom of God has
come near to you.' 10 But whenever you
enter a town and they do not receive you,
go into its streets and say, 11 'Even the dust
of your town that clings to our feet we
wipe off against you. Nevertheless know
this, that the kingdom of God has come
near.' 12 I tell you, it will be more bearable
on that day for Sodom than for that town.

Woe to Unrepentant Cities

13 "Woe to you, Chorazin! Woe to you,
Bethsaida! For if the mighty works done
in you had been done in Tyre and Sidon,

CHARACTER PROFILE

MARY AND MARTHA

Mary and Martha were the sisters of Lazarus, whom Jesus raised from the dead. All three were close friends of Jesus and He often stayed with them when in Bethany. The sisters sent word to Jesus when Lazarus became very sick.

1577

[1] Some manuscripts add *as Elijah did* [2] Some manuscripts add *and he said, "You do not know what manner of spirit you are of; for the Son of Man came not to destroy people's lives but to save them"* [3] Greek *he* [4] Some manuscripts *seventy;* also verse 17

Jesus Sends the Seventy-Two

Jesus was planning to visit people in the cities and villages of Israel, to tell them about God and His kingdom. Before He went, He chose 72 men to go ahead of Him in groups of two.

Before the men left, Jesus talked to them about their work. He said, "The harvest is plentiful, but the laborers (or workers) are few. Pray to the Lord of the harvest to send out laborers into His harvest." Jesus wasn't talking about workers to pick wheat or olives. He was talking about people who would tell others about the coming of the kingdom of God. Jesus told the men that He would take care of their needs. They didn't even need money.

Jesus also gave the men special directions about their work. He said, "Whenever you enter a town and they receive you, eat what is set before you. Heal the sick in it and say to them, 'The kingdom of God has come near to you.'"

Jesus knew that some people would reject the news about Him and His kingdom. When that happened, Jesus said His messengers should leave those people with a warning. They should wipe the dust of that town from their feet, because God's judgment will fall on those who reject Jesus.

Finally, after Jesus had finished teaching them, the 72

went on their way. They did just as Jesus had told them. Through God's power, they healed the sick and cast out evil spirits hiding inside of people. When they had done all that Jesus had asked, they returned with great joy.

The 72 men told Jesus about the great and powerful things that they had done in His name. Although this was good news, Jesus reminded them that they should rejoice about something even more important: their names were written in heaven! Jesus had given them the right to be with Him in heaven when their work on earth was finished.

God chose the 72 for a special task. God places each of us just where He wants us, giving us opportunities to serve Him and share our faith with others. Yet more important than the work we do for Jesus is our faith in Him as our Savior.

SEEK and FIND

WHERE TO FIND THE STORY

Luke 10:1–20

KEY BIBLE VERSE

"And he said to them, 'The harvest is plentiful, but the laborers are few. Therefore pray earnestly to the Lord of the harvest to send out laborers into his harvest.'" (Luke 10:2)

THREE KEY QUESTIONS

- What did Jesus tell His disciples they should pray for?
- When the disciples returned, why were they rejoicing?
- What did Jesus say they should rejoice over even more?

RELATED BIBLE READINGS

Matthew 9:35–38; Luke 9:1–6; John 4:35–38

they would have repented long ago, sitting in sackcloth and ashes. 14 But it will be more bearable in the judgment for Tyre and Sidon than for you. 15 And you, Capernaum, will you be exalted to heaven? You shall be brought down to Hades.

16 "The one who hears you hears me, and the one who rejects you rejects me, and the one who rejects me rejects him who sent me."

The Return of the Seventy-Two

17 The seventy-two returned with joy, saying, "Lord, even the demons are subject to us in your name!" 18 And he said to them, "I saw Satan fall like lightning from heaven. 19 Behold, I have given you authority to tread on serpents and scorpions, and over all the power of the enemy, and nothing shall hurt you. 20 Nevertheless, do not rejoice in this, that the spirits are subject to you, but rejoice that your names are written in heaven."

Jesus Rejoices in the Father's Will

21 In that same hour he rejoiced in the Holy Spirit and said, "I thank you, Father, Lord of heaven and earth, that you have hidden these things from the wise and understanding and revealed them to little children; yes, Father, for such was your gracious will.[1] 22 All things have been handed over to me by my Father, and no one knows who the Son is except the Father, or who the Father is except the Son and anyone to whom the Son chooses to reveal him."

23 Then turning to the disciples he said privately, "Blessed are the eyes that see what you see! 24 For I tell you that many prophets and kings desired to see what you see, and did not see it, and to hear what you hear, and did not hear it."

The Parable of the Good Samaritan

1487

25 And behold, a lawyer stood up to put him to the test, saying, "Teacher, what shall I do to inherit eternal life?" 26 He said to him, "What is written in the Law? How do you read it?" 27 And he answered, "You shall love the Lord your God with all your heart and with all your soul and with all your strength and with all your mind, and your neighbor as yourself." 28 And he said to him, "You have answered correctly; do this, and you will live."

29 But he, desiring to justify himself, said to Jesus, "And who is my neighbor?" 30 Jesus replied, "A man was going down from Jerusalem to Jericho, and he fell among robbers, who stripped him and beat him and departed, leaving him half dead. 31 Now by chance a priest was going down that road, and when he saw him he passed by on the other side. 32 So likewise a Levite, when he came to the place and saw him, passed by on the other side. 33 But a Samaritan, as he journeyed, came to where he was, and when he saw him, he had compassion. 34 He went to him and bound up his wounds, pouring on oil and wine. Then he set him on his own animal and brought him to an inn and took care of him. 35 And the next day he took out two denarii[2] and gave them to the innkeeper, saying, 'Take care of him, and whatever more you spend, I will repay you when I come back.' 36 Which of these three, do you think, proved to be a neighbor to the man who fell among the robbers?" 37 He said, "The one who showed him mercy." And Jesus said to him, "You go, and do likewise."

Martha and Mary

38 Now as they went on their way, Jesus[3] entered a village. And a woman named Martha welcomed him into her house. 39 And she had a sister called Mary, who sat at the Lord's feet and listened to his teaching. 40 But Martha was distracted with much serving. And she went up to him and said, "Lord, do you not care that my sister has left me to serve alone? Tell her then to help me." 41 But the Lord answered her, "Martha, Martha, you are anxious and troubled about many things,

[1] Or *for so it pleased you well* [2] A *denarius* was a day's wage for a laborer [3] Greek *he*

KUEKER

The Good Samaritan

A scholar, an expert in the Law of Moses, stood up and questioned Jesus. He said, "Teacher, what shall I do to inherit eternal life?"

Jesus said, "What is written in the Law?"

The scholar quoted the Scriptures: "You shall love the Lord your God with all your heart and with all your soul and with all your strength and with all your mind, and your neighbor as yourself."

Jesus said, "You have answered correctly; do this, and you will live."

Then the scholar asked, "And who is my neighbor?" He did not think that he needed to love everyone—only those who were like him.

Jesus answered the scholar's question with a story. Jesus described a Jewish man who was going down the road from Jerusalem to Jericho. Now everyone knew this road was dangerous. It passed through a narrow canyon that twisted and turned, full of caves where thieves could hide. Sure enough, the man came upon robbers who beat him and stripped him and left him half dead. After some time, a Jewish priest came down the road. When he saw the man was hurt, he passed by on the other side. He did not help. Next, a Levite, a man who worked with the priests in the temple, came along and saw the man. He did not help either. Both the priest and Levite were probably afraid that the man would die. Touching a dead body would make them unclean and unable to do their work in the temple. Finally, a Samaritan came by. In Jesus' day, Samaritans and Jews did not get along. But this Samaritan saw the hurt Jewish man and had compassion on him. He put bandages and medicine on his wounds and placed the man on his own donkey. The Samaritan took him to an inn where he told the owner to take care of him. The next day when he got ready to leave, he paid the innkeeper for what the injured man would need. He said that he would come back later to check on the man. He even offered to pay for anything else the man might need.

When Jesus had finished the story, He asked the scholar, "Which of these three, do you think, proved to be a neighbor to the man who fell among the robbers?"

The scholar said, "The one who showed him mercy."

Then Jesus told the man to go and do the same.

Jesus tells us how we should live to please God—by loving God and others. These two commands sum up everything in the Law and the Prophets. Thankfully, Jesus died to pay for the many times we fail to do what we should. If we have received mercy from God we will want to show mercy to others. God gives us His Holy Spirit to live inside us, to help us to love Him and love our neighbor as ourselves.

SEEK and FIND

WHERE TO FIND THE STORY

Luke 10:25–37

KEY BIBLE VERSE

"But if anyone has the world's goods and sees his brother in need, yet closes his heart against him, how does God's love abide in him? Little children, let us not love in word or talk but in deed and in truth." (I John 3:17–18)

THREE KEY QUESTIONS

- Why is it surprising that the priest and Levite did not stop to help the hurt man, while the Samaritan did?
- According to Jesus, who is our "neighbor"?
- What are some good ways that we can show love for others?

RELATED BIBLE READINGS

Matthew 22:34–40; Luke 9:51–53; 18:18–23; John 4:7–9

42 but one thing is necessary.[1] Mary has
chosen the good portion, which will not
be taken away from her."

The Lord's Prayer

1493

11 Now Jesus[2] was praying in a
certain place, and when he
finished, one of his disciples said
to him, "Lord, teach us to pray, as John
taught his disciples." **2** And he said to
them, "When you pray, say:

"Father, hallowed be your name.
Your kingdom come.
3 Give us each day our daily bread,[3]
4 and forgive us our sins,
for we ourselves forgive everyone
who is indebted to us.
And lead us not into temptation."

5 And he said to them, "Which of you
who has a friend will go to him at mid-
night and say to him, 'Friend, lend me
three loaves, **6** for a friend of mine has
arrived on a journey, and I have nothing
to set before him'; **7** and he will answer
from within, 'Do not bother me; the door
is now shut, and my children are with
me in bed. I cannot get up and give you
anything'? **8** I tell you, though he will not
get up and give him anything because
he is his friend, yet because of his impu-
dence[4] he will rise and give him what-
ever he needs. **9** And I tell you, ask, and
it will be given to you; seek, and you will
find; knock, and it will be opened to you.
10 For everyone who asks receives, and the
one who seeks finds, and to the one who
knocks it will be opened. **11** What father
among you, if his son asks for[5] a fish,
will instead of a fish give him a serpent;
12 or if he asks for an egg, will give him

[1] Some manuscripts *few things are necessary, or only one* [2] Greek *he* [3] Or *our bread for tomorrow* [4] Or *persistence* [5] Some manuscripts insert *bread, will give him a stone; or if he asks for*

a scorpion? 13 If you then, who are evil,
know how to give good gifts to your chil-
dren, how much more will the heavenly
Father give the Holy Spirit to those who
ask him!"

Jesus and Beelzebul

14 Now he was casting out a demon
that was mute. When the demon had
gone out, the mute man spoke, and the
people marveled. 15 But some of them
said, "He casts out demons by Beelzebul,
the prince of demons," 16 while others, to
test him, kept seeking from him a sign
from heaven. 17 But he, knowing their
thoughts, said to them, "Every kingdom
divided against itself is laid waste, and a
divided household falls. 18 And if Satan
also is divided against himself, how will
his kingdom stand? For you say that I
cast out demons by Beelzebul. 19 And if I
cast out demons by Beelzebul, by whom
do your sons cast them out? Therefore
they will be your judges. 20 But if it is by
the finger of God that I cast out demons,
then the kingdom of God has come upon
you. 21 When a strong man, fully armed,
guards his own palace, his goods are safe;
22 but when one stronger than he attacks
him and overcomes him, he takes away
his armor in which he trusted and divides
his spoil. 23 Whoever is not with me is
against me, and whoever does not gather
with me scatters.

Return of an Unclean Spirit

24 "When the unclean spirit has gone
out of a person, it passes through water-
less places seeking rest, and finding none
it says, 'I will return to my house from
which I came.' 25 And when it comes, it
finds the house swept and put in order.
26 Then it goes and brings seven other
spirits more evil than itself, and they enter
and dwell there. And the last state of that
person is worse than the first."

True Blessedness

27 As he said these things, a woman in
the crowd raised her voice and said to
him, "Blessed is the womb that bore you,
and the breasts at which you nursed!"
28 But he said, "Blessed rather are those
who hear the word of God and keep it!"

The Sign of Jonah

29 When the crowds were increasing,
he began to say, "This generation is an
evil generation. It seeks for a sign, but no
sign will be given to it except the sign of
Jonah. 30 For as Jonah became a sign to
the people of Nineveh, so will the Son of
Man be to this generation. 31 The queen
of the South will rise up at the judg-
ment with the men of this generation
and condemn them, for she came from
the ends of the earth to hear the wisdom
of Solomon, and behold, something
greater than Solomon is here. 32 The men
of Nineveh will rise up at the judgment
with this generation and condemn it, for
they repented at the preaching of Jonah,
and behold, something greater than
Jonah is here.

The Light in You

33 "No one after lighting a lamp puts it in
a cellar or under a basket, but on a stand,
so that those who enter may see the light.
34 Your eye is the lamp of your body. When
your eye is healthy, your whole body is full
of light, but when it is bad, your body is
full of darkness. 35 Therefore be careful
lest the light in you be darkness. 36 If then
your whole body is full of light, having no
part dark, it will be wholly bright, as when
a lamp with its rays gives you light."

Woes to the Pharisees and Lawyers

37 While Jesus[1] was speaking, a Pharisee
asked him to dine with him, so he went
in and reclined at table. 38 The Pharisee
was astonished to see that he did not first
wash before dinner. 39 And the Lord said
to him, "Now you Pharisees cleanse the

[1] Greek *he*

outside of the cup and of the dish, but inside you are full of greed and wickedness. 40 You fools! Did not he who made the outside make the inside also? 41 But give as alms those things that are within, and behold, everything is clean for you.

42 "But woe to you Pharisees! For you tithe the mint and rue and every herb, and neglect justice and the love of God. These you ought to have done, without neglecting the others. 43 Woe to you Pharisees! For you love the best seat in the synagogues and greetings in the marketplaces. 44 Woe to you! For you are like unmarked graves, and people walk over them without knowing it."

45 One of the lawyers answered him, "Teacher, in saying these things you insult us also." 46 And he said, "Woe to you lawyers also! For you load people with burdens hard to bear, and you yourselves do not touch the burdens with one of your fingers. 47 Woe to you! For you build the tombs of the prophets whom your fathers killed. 48 So you are witnesses and you consent to the deeds of your fathers, for they killed them, and you build their tombs. 49 Therefore also the Wisdom of God said, 'I will send them prophets and apostles, some of whom they will kill and persecute,' 50 so that the blood of all the prophets, shed from the foundation of the world, may be charged against this generation, 51 from the blood of Abel to the blood of Zechariah, who perished between the altar and the sanctuary. Yes, I tell you, it will be required of this generation. 52 Woe to you lawyers! For you have taken away the key of knowledge. You did not enter yourselves, and you hindered those who were entering."

53 As he went away from there, the scribes and the Pharisees began to press him hard and to provoke him to speak about many things, 54 lying in wait for him, to catch him in something he might say.

Beware of the Leaven of the Pharisees

12 In the meantime, when so many thousands of the people had gathered together that they were trampling one another, he began to say to his disciples first, "Beware of the leaven of the Pharisees, which is hypocrisy. 2 Nothing is covered up that will not be revealed, or hidden that will not be known. 3 Therefore whatever you have said in the dark shall be heard in the light, and what you have whispered in private rooms shall be proclaimed on the housetops.

Have No Fear

4 "I tell you, my friends, do not fear those who kill the body, and after that have nothing more that they can do. 5 But I will warn you whom to fear: fear him who, after he has killed, has authority to cast into hell.[1] Yes, I tell you, fear him! 6 Are not five sparrows sold for two pennies?[2] And not one of them is forgotten before God. 7 Why, even the hairs of your head are all numbered. Fear not; you are of more value than many sparrows.

Acknowledge Christ Before Men

8 "And I tell you, everyone who acknowledges me before men, the Son of Man also will acknowledge before the angels of God, 9 but the one who denies me before men will be denied before the angels of God. 10 And everyone who speaks a word against the Son of Man will be forgiven, but the one who blasphemes against the Holy Spirit will not be forgiven. 11 And when they bring you before the synagogues and the rulers and the authorities, do not be anxious about how you should defend yourself or what you should say, 12 for the Holy Spirit will teach you in that very hour what you ought to say."

The Parable of the Rich Fool

1321

13 Someone in the crowd said to him, "Teacher, tell my brother to divide the inheritance with me."

[1] Greek *Gehenna* [2] Greek *two assaria*; an *assarion* was a Roman copper coin worth about 1/16 of a *denarius* (which was a day's wage for a laborer)

Jesus Teaches Us to Pray

One day, when Jesus was finished praying, one of His disciples said to Him, "Lord, teach us to pray, as John taught his disciples." And Jesus did.

He said to them, "When you pray, say: Father, hallowed be Your name." This means treating God as holy and very special. Jesus wants us to pray that God will be thought of highly by others, not ignored or hated. We should want all people to worship Him.

Then Jesus said, "Your kingdom come." With these words we ask God to cause His kingdom to grow and spread through the Good News of Jesus' death and resurrection. We also look forward to the Second Coming of Jesus, when He will rule on earth as He does in heaven.

Jesus continued, "Give us each day our daily bread." God provides us with much more than bread. With these words we ask Him to give us what our bodies need: food, drink, clothing, and a home. We do not need to worry; we can trust God to provide for our life on earth.

Jesus continued, "And forgive us our sins, for we ourselves forgive everyone who is indebted to us." With these words, we confess to God that we sin every day. We know that we deserve God's punishment. We ask that our loving heavenly Father would forgive our sins. Knowing that God has forgiven us, we ask Him to give us the power to forgive those who sin against us.

Jesus also said, "And lead us not into temptation." We have three big enemies—the devil, the world, and our own sinful nature. But we have a bigger God who can defeat them all. Our God will protect us and give us His power to win over evil's temptations. And when we sin, He forgives us.

Once Jesus had finished teaching this special prayer, He explained more about prayer to His disciples. He said that just like a father gives what is good to children who ask him for it, so God will give what is good to His children when they ask Him.

Our heavenly Father invites us to pray. Because Jesus has paid for our sins, God listens to our prayers for Jesus' sake. That is why we often end our prayers saying, "in Jesus' name I pray."

How wonderful it is to know that we can pray to God and that He hears our prayers. We can praise God and ask Him to provide for all our needs. Let us give thanks to Him for all things.

SEEK and FIND

WHERE TO FIND THE STORY

Luke 11:1–12

KEY BIBLE VERSE

"If you then, who are evil, know how to give good gifts to your children, how much more will your Father who is in heaven give good things to those who ask him!" (Matthew 7:11)

THREE KEY QUESTIONS

- What is God's attitude toward His children, when we ask Him for what is good?
- Why did Jesus teach us to pray about God first, and then about ourselves?
- When we ask God to forgive our sins, why is it important for us to forgive others for their sins against us?

RELATED BIBLE READINGS

Matthew 6:5–15; 7:7–11; Luke 18:1–6

14 But he said to him, "Man, who made me
a judge or arbitrator over you?" 15 And he
said to them, "Take care, and be on your
guard against all covetousness, for one's
life does not consist in the abundance of
his possessions." 16 And he told them a
parable, saying, "The land of a rich man
produced plentifully, 17 and he thought to
himself, 'What shall I do, for I have
nowhere to store my crops?' 18 And he said,
'I will do this: I will tear down my barns
and build larger ones, and there I will store
all my grain and my goods. 19 And I will say
to my soul, Soul, you have ample goods
laid up for many years; relax, eat, drink, be
merry.' 20 But God said to him, 'Fool! This
night your soul is required of you, and the
things you have prepared, whose will they
be?' 21 So is the one who lays up treasure
for himself and is not rich toward God."

Do Not Be Anxious

22 And he said to his disciples,
"Therefore I tell you, do not be anxious
about your life, what you will eat, nor
about your body, what you will put on.
23 For life is more than food, and the
body more than clothing. 24 Consider the
ravens: they neither sow nor reap, they
have neither storehouse nor barn, and
yet God feeds them. Of how much more
value are you than the birds! 25 And which
of you by being anxious can add a single
hour to his span of life?[1] 26 If then you are
not able to do as small a thing as that, why
are you anxious about the rest? 27 Consider
the lilies, how they grow: they neither toil
nor spin,[2] yet I tell you, even Solomon in
all his glory was not arrayed like one of
these. 28 But if God so clothes the grass,
which is alive in the field today, and
tomorrow is thrown into the oven, how
much more will he clothe you, O you of
little faith! 29 And do not seek what you are
to eat and what you are to drink, nor be
worried. 30 For all the nations of the world
seek after these things, and your Father
knows that you need them. 31 Instead,
seek his[3] kingdom, and these things will
be added to you.

32 "Fear not, little flock, for it is your
Father's good pleasure to give you the
kingdom. 33 Sell your possessions, and
give to the needy. Provide yourselves with
moneybags that do not grow old, with a
treasure in the heavens that does not fail,
where no thief approaches and no moth
destroys. 34 For where your treasure is,
there will your heart be also.

[1] Or *a single cubit to his stature*; a *cubit* was about 18 inches or 45 centimeters [2] Some manuscripts *Consider the lilies; they neither spin nor weave* [3] Some manuscripts *God's*

You Must Be Ready

35 "Stay dressed for action[1] and keep your lamps burning, 36 and be like men who are waiting for their master to come home from the wedding feast, so that they may open the door to him at once when he comes and knocks. 37 Blessed are those servants[2] whom the master finds awake when he comes. Truly, I say to you, he will dress himself for service and have them recline at table, and he will come and serve them. 38 If he comes in the second watch, or in the third, and finds them awake, blessed are those servants! 39 But know this, that if the master of the house had known at what hour the thief was coming, he[3] would not have left his house to be broken into. 40 You also must be ready, for the Son of Man is coming at an hour you do not expect."

41 Peter said, "Lord, are you telling this parable for us or for all?" 42 And the Lord said, "Who then is the faithful and wise manager, whom his master will set over his household, to give them their portion of food at the proper time? 43 Blessed is that servant[4] whom his master will find so doing when he comes. 44 Truly, I say to you, he will set him over all his possessions. 45 But if that servant says to himself, 'My master is delayed in coming,' and begins to beat the male and female servants, and to eat and drink and get drunk, 46 the master of that servant will come on a day when he does not expect him and at an hour he does not know, and will cut him in pieces and put him with the unfaithful. 47 And that servant who knew his master's will but did not get ready or act according to his will, will receive a severe beating. 48 But the one who did not know, and did what deserved a beating, will receive a light beating. Everyone to whom much was given, of him much will be required, and from him to whom they entrusted much, they will demand the more.

Not Peace, but Division

49 "I came to cast fire on the earth, and would that it were already kindled! 50 I have a baptism to be baptized with, and how great is my distress until it is accomplished! 51 Do you think that I have come to give peace on earth? No, I tell you, but rather division. 52 For from now on in one house there will be five divided, three against two and two against three. 53 They will be divided, father against son and son against father, mother against daughter and daughter against mother, mother-in-law against her daughter-in-law and daughter-in-law against mother-in-law."

Interpreting the Time

54 He also said to the crowds, "When you see a cloud rising in the west, you say at once, 'A shower is coming.' And so it happens. 55 And when you see the south wind blowing, you say, 'There will be scorching heat,' and it happens. 56 You hypocrites! You know how to interpret the appearance of earth and sky, but why do you not know how to interpret the present time?

Settle with Your Accuser

57 "And why do you not judge for yourselves what is right? 58 As you go with your accuser before the magistrate, make an effort to settle with him on the way, lest he drag you to the judge, and the judge hand you over to the officer, and the officer put you in prison. 59 I tell you, you will never get out until you have paid the very last penny."[5]

Repent or Perish

13 There were some present at that very time who told him about the Galileans whose blood Pilate had mingled with their sacrifices. 2 And he answered them, "Do you think that these Galileans were worse sinners than all the other Galileans, because they suffered in this way? 3 No, I tell you; but unless you repent,

[1] Greek *Let your loins stay girded*; compare Exodus 12:11 [2] Greek *bondservants* [3] Some manuscripts add *would have stayed awake and* [4] Greek *bondservant*; also verses 45, 46, 47 [5] Greek *lepton*, a Jewish bronze or copper coin worth about 1/128 of a *denarius* (which was a day's wage for a laborer)

you will all likewise perish. 4 Or those eighteen on whom the tower in Siloam fell and killed them: do you think that they were worse offenders than all the others who lived in Jerusalem? 5 No, I tell you; but unless you repent, you will all likewise perish."

The Parable of the Barren Fig Tree

6 And he told this parable: "A man had a fig tree planted in his vineyard, and he came seeking fruit on it and found none. 7 And he said to the vinedresser, 'Look, for three years now I have come seeking fruit on this fig tree, and I find none. Cut it down. Why should it use up the ground?' 8 And he answered him, 'Sir, let it alone this year also, until I dig around it and put on manure. 9 Then if it should bear fruit next year, well and good; but if not, you can cut it down.'"

A Woman with a Disabling Spirit

10 Now he was teaching in one of the synagogues on the Sabbath. 11 And there was a woman who had had a disabling spirit for eighteen years. She was bent over and could not fully straighten herself. 12 When Jesus saw her, he called her over and said to her, "Woman, you are freed from your disability." 13 And he laid his hands on her, and immediately she was made straight, and she glorified God. 14 But the ruler of the synagogue, indignant because Jesus had healed on the Sabbath, said to the people, "There are six days in which work ought to be done. Come on those days and be healed, and not on the Sabbath day." 15 Then the Lord answered him, "You hypocrites! Does not each of you on the Sabbath untie his ox or his donkey from the manger and lead it away to water it? 16 And ought not this woman, a daughter of Abraham whom Satan bound for eighteen years, be loosed from this bond on the Sabbath day?" 17 As he said these things, all his adversaries were put to shame, and all the people rejoiced at all the glorious things that were done by him.

The Mustard Seed and the Leaven

18 He said therefore, "What is the kingdom of God like? And to what shall I compare it? 19 It is like a grain of mustard seed that a man took and sowed in his garden, and it grew and became a tree, and the birds of the air made nests in its branches."

20 And again he said, "To what shall I compare the kingdom of God? 21 It is like leaven that a woman took and hid in three measures of flour, until it was all leavened."

The Narrow Door

22 He went on his way through towns and villages, teaching and journeying toward Jerusalem. 23 And someone said to him, "Lord, will those who are saved be few?" And he said to them, 24 "Strive to enter through the narrow door. For many, I tell you, will seek to enter and will not be able. 25 When once the master of the house has risen and shut the door, and you begin to stand outside and to knock at the door, saying, 'Lord, open to us,' then he will answer you, 'I do not know where you come from.' 26 Then you will begin to say, 'We ate and drank in your presence, and you taught in our streets.' 27 But he will say, 'I tell you, I do not know where you come from. Depart from me, all you workers of evil!' 28 In that place there will be weeping and gnashing of teeth, when you see Abraham and Isaac and Jacob and all the prophets in the kingdom of God but you yourselves cast out. 29 And people will come from east and west, and from north and south, and recline at table in the kingdom of God. 30 And behold, some are last who will be first, and some are first who will be last."

Lament over Jerusalem

31 At that very hour some Pharisees came and said to him, "Get away from

here, for Herod wants to kill you." 32 And he said to them, "Go and tell that fox, 'Behold, I cast out demons and perform cures today and tomorrow, and the third day I finish my course. 33 Nevertheless, I must go on my way today and tomorrow and the day following, for it cannot be that a prophet should perish away from Jerusalem.' 34 O Jerusalem, Jerusalem, the city that kills the prophets and stones those who are sent to it! How often would I have gathered your children together as a hen gathers her brood under her wings, and you would not! 35 Behold, your house is forsaken. And I tell you, you will not see me until you say, 'Blessed is he who comes in the name of the Lord!'"

Healing of a Man on the Sabbath

14 One Sabbath, when he went to dine at the house of a ruler of the Pharisees, they were watching him carefully. 2 And behold, there was a man before him who had dropsy. 3 And Jesus responded to the lawyers and Pharisees, saying, "Is it lawful to heal on the Sabbath, or not?" 4 But they remained silent. Then he took him and healed him and sent him away. 5 And he said to them, "Which of you, having a son[1] or an ox that has fallen into a well on a Sabbath day, will not immediately pull him out?" 6 And they could not reply to these things.

The Parable of the Wedding Feast

7 Now he told a parable to those who were invited, when he noticed how they chose the places of honor, saying to them, 8 "When you are invited by someone to a wedding feast, do not sit down in a place of honor, lest someone more distinguished than you be invited by him, 9 and he who invited you both will come and say to you, 'Give your place to this person,' and then you will begin with shame to take the lowest place. 10 But when you are invited, go and sit in the lowest place, so that when your host comes he may say to you, 'Friend, move up higher.' Then you will be honored in the presence of all who sit at table with you. 11 For everyone who exalts himself will be humbled, and he who humbles himself will be exalted."

The Parable of the Great Banquet

12 He said also to the man who had invited him, "When you give a dinner or a banquet, do not invite your friends or your brothers[2] or your relatives or rich neighbors, lest they also invite you in return and you be repaid. 13 But when you give a feast, invite the poor, the crippled, the lame, the blind, 14 and you will be blessed, because they cannot repay you. For you will be repaid at the resurrection of the just."

15 When one of those who reclined at table with him heard these things, he said to him, "Blessed is everyone who will eat bread in the kingdom of God!" 16 But he said to him, "A man once gave a great banquet and invited many. 17 And at the time for the banquet he sent his servant[3] to say to those who had been invited, 'Come, for everything is now ready.' 18 But they all alike began to make excuses. The first said to him, 'I have bought a field, and I must go out and see it. Please have me excused.' 19 And another said, 'I have bought five yoke of oxen, and I go to examine them. Please have me excused.' 20 And another said, 'I have married a wife, and therefore I cannot come.' 21 So the servant came and reported these things to his master. Then the master of the house became angry and said to his servant, 'Go out quickly to the streets and lanes of the city, and bring in the poor and crippled and blind and lame.' 22 And the servant said, 'Sir, what you commanded has been done, and still there is room.' 23 And the master said to the servant, 'Go out to the highways and hedges and compel people to come in, that my house may be filled. 24 For I tell

[1] Some manuscripts *a donkey* [2] Or *your brothers and sisters.* The plural Greek word *adelphoi* (translated "brothers") refers to siblings in a family. In New Testament usage, depending on the context, *adelphoi* may refer either to *brothers* or to *brothers and sisters* [3] Greek *bondservant;* also verses 21, 22, 23

you,[1] none of those men who were invited
shall taste my banquet.'"

The Cost of Discipleship

25 Now great crowds accompanied him,
and he turned and said to them, 26 "If
anyone comes to me and does not hate
his own father and mother and wife and
children and brothers and sisters, yes, and
even his own life, he cannot be my dis-
ciple. 27 Whoever does not bear his own
cross and come after me cannot be my
disciple. 28 For which of you, desiring to
build a tower, does not first sit down and
count the cost, whether he has enough to
complete it? 29 Otherwise, when he has
laid a foundation and is not able to finish,
all who see it begin to mock him, 30 say-
ing, 'This man began to build and was not
able to finish.' 31 Or what king, going out
to encounter another king in war, will not
sit down first and deliberate whether he is
able with ten thousand to meet him who
comes against him with twenty thou-
sand? 32 And if not, while the other is yet
a great way off, he sends a delegation and
asks for terms of peace. 33 So therefore, any
one of you who does not renounce all that
he has cannot be my disciple.

Salt Without Taste Is Worthless

34 "Salt is good, but if salt has lost its
taste, how shall its saltiness be restored?
35 It is of no use either for the soil or for the
manure pile. It is thrown away. He who
has ears to hear, let him hear."

The Parable of the Lost Sheep

15 Now the tax collectors and
sinners were all drawing
1501 near to hear him. 2 And the
Pharisees and the scribes grum-
bled, saying, "This man receives
1239, sinners and eats with them."
1381, 3 So he told them this parable:
1511, 4 "What man of you, having a hun-
1571 dred sheep, if he has lost one of
them, does not leave the ninety-nine in
the open country, and go after the one that
is lost, until he finds it? 5 And when he has
found it, he lays it on his shoulders, rejoic-
ing. 6 And when he comes home, he calls
together his friends and his neighbors,
saying to them, 'Rejoice with me, for I have
found my sheep that was lost.' 7 Just so, I
tell you, there will be more joy in heaven
over one sinner who repents than over
ninety-nine righteous persons who need
no repentance.

The Parable of the Lost Coin

8 "Or what woman, having ten silver
coins,[2] if she loses one coin, does not light
a lamp and sweep the house and seek dili-
gently until she finds it? 9 And when she
has found it, she calls together her friends
and neighbors, saying, 'Rejoice with me,
for I have found the coin that I had lost.'
10 Just so, I tell you, there is joy
before the angels of God over one
1501 sinner who repents."

The Parable of the Prodigal Son

11 And he said, "There was a man who
had two sons. 12 And the younger of them
said to his father, 'Father, give me the share
of property that is coming to me.' And he
divided his property between them. 13 Not
many days later, the younger son gath-
ered all he had and took a journey into a
far country, and there he squandered his
property in reckless living. 14 And when
he had spent everything, a severe famine
arose in that country, and he began to be in
need. 15 So he went and hired himself out
to[3] one of the citizens of that country, who
sent him into his fields to feed pigs. 16 And
he was longing to be fed with the pods that
the pigs ate, and no one gave him anything.
17 "But when he came to himself, he
said, 'How many of my father's hired ser-
vants have more than enough bread, but
I perish here with hunger! 18 I will arise
and go to my father, and I will say to him,

[1] The Greek word for *you* here is plural [2] Greek *ten drachmas*; a *drachma* was a Greek coin approximately equal in value to a Roman *denarius*, worth about a day's wage for a laborer [3] Greek *joined himself to*

Jesus Seeks the Lost

One day Jesus heard the Pharisees and the teachers of the law complaining about how He was friendly toward sinners and even ate with them. The Pharisees kept such people at a distance and they thought Jesus should do the same. So Jesus told three stories, called parables, to help explain His love for all people.

In the first parable, a man with 100 sheep lost one. He left the 99 other sheep to go look for the lost one. And he didn't quit until he found it. Finally, when he found it, he called his friends and neighbors in to rejoice. Likewise, Jesus said that there would be more rejoicing in heaven over one sinner who repents than over 99 righteous persons who think they do not need to repent.

In the second parable, a woman lost one of her 10 silver coins. She swept the house until she found it. When she found the coin, she called her friends and neighbors to rejoice with her. In the same way, Jesus said there is rejoicing in the presence of the angels of God over one sinner who repents.

The third parable was about a man who had two sons. The younger one asked his father for his share of his father's money. This was an outrageous request! Sons did not receive their inheritance until after the father had died. By asking for the money now, it was as if the younger son wanted his father dead. Even though the father was sad about the request, he gave his son the money.

Soon, the son left home for a faraway country. There, he foolishly spent his money until it was all gone. Then a bad famine came, and food became scarce. The son had no money left to buy food, so he got a job feeding pigs. When the hungry son found himself dreaming about eating the pig's food, he came to his senses. He knew his father's servants had plenty to eat, so he decided to go home and tell his father that he had sinned. He was even willing to become one of his father's servants, just to get some food.

While the son was still a long way off, the father saw him and ran to kiss him. The son began to tell his father about the bad things he had done, but the father was forgiving and filled with joy. He asked the servants to bring his son gifts—the best robe, a special ring, and new shoes. Rather than treating him like a servant, the father treated him like a son again. The father also asked the servants to prepare the fattened calf for a celebration.

The father's older son was angry about this. He had stayed home and worked for his father all this time, and his father hadn't given a party for him. "Son," the father said to this older son, "you are always with me, and all that is mine is yours. It was fitting to celebrate and be glad, for this your brother was dead, and is alive; he was lost, and is found."

We too are lost in our sin apart from Jesus, but thankfully Jesus came to seek us and to find us. Through faith in Him, He brings us back to Himself and forgives us. Then He keeps us *with Him* forever.

SEEK and FIND

WHERE TO FIND THE STORY

Luke 15

KEY BIBLE VERSE

"There is joy before the angels of God over one sinner who repents." (Luke 15:10)

THREE KEY QUESTIONS

- Why were the Pharisees and the teachers of the law upset with Jesus?
- In the story of the father and his two sons, who was the younger son like? Who was the older son like?
- In all three stories, how did the shepherd, the woman, and the father respond when the thing they had lost was found? What does that tell us about God?

RELATED BIBLE READINGS

Psalm 119:176; Matthew 9:10–13; 18:12–14; Luke 7:36–50; John 10:10–16; 1 Peter 2:25

"Father, I have sinned against heaven and before you. 19 I am no longer worthy to be called your son. Treat me as one of your hired servants."' 20 And he arose and came to his father. But while he was still a long way off, his father saw him and felt compassion, and ran and embraced him and kissed him. 21 And the son said to him, 'Father, I have sinned against heaven and before you. I am no longer worthy to be called your son.'[1] 22 But the father said to his servants,[2] 'Bring quickly the best robe, and put it on him, and put a ring on his hand, and shoes on his feet. 23 And bring the fattened calf and kill it, and let us eat and celebrate. 24 For this my son was dead, and is alive again; he was lost, and is found.' And they began to celebrate.

25 "Now his older son was in the field, and as he came and drew near to the house, he heard music and dancing. 26 And he called one of the servants and asked what these things meant. 27 And he said to him, 'Your brother has come, and your father has killed the fattened calf, because he has received him back safe and sound.' 28 But he was angry and refused to go in. His father came out and entreated him, 29 but he answered his father, 'Look, these many years I have served you, and I never disobeyed your command, yet you never gave me a young goat, that I might celebrate with my friends. 30 But when this son of yours came, who has devoured your property with prostitutes, you killed the fattened calf for him!' 31 And he said to him, 'Son, you are always with me, and all that is mine is yours. 32 It was fitting to celebrate and be glad, for this your brother was dead, and is alive; he was lost, and is found.'"

[1] Some manuscripts add *treat me as one of your hired servants* [2] Greek *bondservants*

The Parable of the Dishonest Manager

16 He also said to the disci-
ples, "There was a rich man
1321 who had a manager, and charges
were brought to him that this man was
wasting his possessions. 2 And he called
him and said to him, 'What is this that I
hear about you? Turn in the account of
your management, for you can no longer
be manager.' 3 And the manager said to
himself, 'What shall I do, since my master
is taking the management away from me?
I am not strong enough to dig, and I am
ashamed to beg. 4 I have decided what to
do, so that when I am removed from
management, people may receive me into
their houses.' 5 So, summoning his mas-
ter's debtors one by one, he said to the
first, 'How much do you owe my master?'
6 He said, 'A hundred measures[1] of oil.' He
said to him, 'Take your bill, and sit down
quickly and write fifty.' 7 Then he said to
another, 'And how much do you owe?' He
said, 'A hundred measures[2] of wheat.' He
said to him, 'Take your bill, and write
eighty.' 8 The master commended the dis-
honest manager for his shrewdness. For
the sons of this world[3] are more shrewd
in dealing with their own generation
than the sons of light. 9 And I tell you,
make friends for yourselves by means of
unrighteous wealth,[4] so that when it fails
they may receive you into the eternal
dwellings.

10 "One who is faithful in a very little is
also faithful in much, and one who is
dishonest in a very little is also dishonest
in much. 11 If then you have not been
faithful in the unrighteous wealth, who
will entrust to you the true riches? 12 And
if you have not been faithful in that
which is another's, who will give you that
which is your own? 13 No servant can
serve two masters, for either he
will hate the one and love the
37 other, or he will be devoted to the
one and despise the other. You cannot
serve God and money."

The Law and the Kingdom of God

14 The Pharisees, who were lovers of
money, heard all these things, and they
ridiculed him. 15 And he said to them,
"You are those who justify yourselves
before men, but God knows your hearts.
For what is exalted among men is an
abomination in the sight of God.

16 "The Law and the Prophets were until
John; since then the good news of the
kingdom of God is preached, and every-
one forces his way into it.[5] 17 But it is eas-
ier for heaven and earth to pass away than
for one dot of the Law to become void.

Divorce and Remarriage

18 "Everyone who divorces his wife and
marries another commits adultery, and he
who marries a woman divorced from her
husband commits adultery.

The Rich Man and Lazarus

19 "There was a rich man who was
clothed in purple and fine linen
1321 and who feasted sumptuously
every day. 20 And at his gate was laid a poor
man named Lazarus, covered with sores,
21 who desired to be fed with what fell
from the rich man's table. Moreover, even
the dogs came and licked his sores. 22 The
poor man died and was carried by the
angels to Abraham's side.[6] The rich man
also died and was buried, 23 and in Hades,
being in torment, he lifted up his eyes and
saw Abraham far off and Lazarus at his
side. 24 And he called out, 'Father
Abraham, have mercy on me, and send
Lazarus to dip the end of his finger in
water and cool my tongue, for I am in
anguish in this flame.' 25 But Abraham
said, 'Child, remember that you in your
lifetime received your good things, and
Lazarus in like manner bad things; but
now he is comforted here, and you are in

[1] About 875 gallons [2] Between 1,000 and 1,200 bushels [3] Greek *age* [4] Greek *mammon*, a Semitic word for money or possessions; also verse 11; rendered *money* in verse 13 [5] Or *everyone is forcefully urged into it* [6] Greek *bosom*; also verse 23

anguish. 26 And besides all this, between
us and you a great chasm has been fixed,
in order that those who would pass from
here to you may not be able, and none
may cross from there to us.' 27 And he said,
'Then I beg you, father, to send him to my
father's house— 28 for I have five broth-
ers[1]—so that he may warn them, lest they
also come into this place of torment.'
29 But Abraham said, 'They have Moses
and the Prophets; let them hear them.'
30 And he said, 'No, father Abraham, but if
someone goes to them from the dead,
they will repent.' 31 He said to him, 'If they
do not hear Moses and the Prophets, nei-
ther will they be convinced if someone
should rise from the dead.'"

Temptations to Sin

17 And he said to his disciples,
"Temptations to sin[2] are sure to
come, but woe to the one through whom
they come! 2 It would be better for him if
a millstone were hung around his neck
and he were cast into the sea than that
he should cause one of these little ones
to sin.[3] 3 Pay attention to yourselves! If
your brother sins, rebuke him, and if
he repents, forgive him, 4 and if he sins
against you seven times in the day, and
turns to you seven times, saying, 'I repent,'
you must forgive him."

Increase Our Faith

5 The apostles said to the Lord, "Increase
our faith!" 6 And the Lord said, "If you
had faith like a grain of mustard seed,
you could say to this mulberry tree, 'Be
uprooted and planted in the sea,' and it
would obey you.

Unworthy Servants

7 "Will any one of you who has a ser-
vant[4] plowing or keeping sheep say to
him when he has come in from the field,
'Come at once and recline at table'? 8 Will
he not rather say to him, 'Prepare supper
for me, and dress properly,[5] and serve me
while I eat and drink, and afterward you
will eat and drink'? 9 Does he thank the
servant because he did what was com-
manded? 10 So you also, when you have
done all that you were commanded, say,
'We are unworthy servants;[6] we have only
done what was our duty.'"

Jesus Cleanses Ten Lepers

1507

11 On the way to Jerusalem he was
passing along between Samaria
and Galilee. 12 And as he entered a
village, he was met by ten lepers,[7] who
stood at a distance 13 and lifted up their
voices, saying, "Jesus, Master, have mercy
on us." 14 When he saw them he said to
them, "Go and show yourselves to the
priests." And as they went they were
cleansed. 15 Then one of them, when he
saw that he was healed, turned back, prais-
ing God with a loud voice; 16 and he fell on
his face at Jesus' feet, giving him thanks.
Now he was a Samaritan. 17 Then Jesus
answered, "Were not ten cleansed? Where
are the nine? 18 Was no one found to return
and give praise to God except this for-
eigner?" 19 And he said to him, "Rise and go
your way; your faith has made you well."[8]

The Coming of the Kingdom

20 Being asked by the Pharisees when
the kingdom of God would come, he
answered them, "The kingdom of God
is not coming with signs to be observed,
21 nor will they say, 'Look, here it is!' or
'There!' for behold, the kingdom of God is
in the midst of you."[9]

22 And he said to the disciples, "The
days are coming when you will desire to
see one of the days of the Son of Man, and
you will not see it. 23 And they will say to
you, 'Look, there!' or 'Look, here!' Do not go
out or follow them. 24 For as the lightning
flashes and lights up the sky from one side
to the other, so will the Son of Man be in
his day.[10] 25 But first he must suffer many

[1] Or *brothers and sisters* [2] Greek *Stumbling blocks* [3] Greek *stumble* [4] Greek *bondservant*; also verse 9 [5] Greek *gird yourself* [6] Greek *bondservants* [7] *Leprosy* was a term for several skin diseases; see Leviticus 13 [8] Or *has saved you* [9] Or *within you*, or *within your grasp* [10] Some manuscripts omit *in his day*

Jesus Heals Ten Lepers

On His way to Jerusalem, Jesus traveled along the border between Samaria and Galilee. As He was going into a village, 10 men with leprosy met Him. Sores covered their bodies, and no doctor could help them. Lepers were required by the Law to stay away from other people. Others were afraid of catching leprosy from them. If lepers thought they were getting better, they were to go to a priest, who would look closely at their sores to see if the leprosy was really gone. Only then could lepers go back to live with their families. These 10 men stood at a distance and called out in a loud voice, "Jesus, Master, have mercy on us." They believed that Jesus could help them.

When He saw them, Jesus said, "Go and show yourselves to the priests." The men turned to go, and, as they went, they were completely healed. Their sores were gone! When one of them—a man from Samaria—saw that he was healed, he came back to Jesus, praising God in a loud voice. He fell down on his face at Jesus' feet and thanked Him.

Jesus asked, "Were not ten cleansed? Where are the nine? Was no one found to return and give praise to God except this foreigner?" It bothered Jesus that not one of the Jewish lepers returned to praise God for the healing. They should have known better!

Then Jesus said to him, "Rise and go your way; your faith has made you well."

Jesus healed the men from the deadly sickness of leprosy. Jesus heals us from the deadly sickness of sin and death. In faith, we respond with thankful hearts, praising Him for His love.

SEEK and FIND

WHERE TO FIND THE STORY

Luke 17:11–19

KEY BIBLE VERSE

"Giving thanks to the Father, who has qualified you to share in the inheritance of the saints in light. He has delivered us from the domain of darkness and transferred us to the kingdom of his beloved Son, in whom we have redemption, the forgiveness of sins." (Colossians 1:12–14)

THREE KEY QUESTIONS

- Why is leprosy such a terrible sickness?
- How did Jesus heal the lepers?
- Why did only one man come back?

RELATED BIBLE READINGS

Leviticus 13:15–17, 45–46; Mark 1:40–46; 1 Thessalonians 5:18

things and be rejected by this generation.
[26]Just as it was in the days of Noah, so will
it be in the days of the Son of Man. [27]They
were eating and drinking and marrying
and being given in marriage, until the day
when Noah entered the ark, and the flood
came and destroyed them all. [28]Likewise,
just as it was in the days of Lot—they were
eating and drinking, buying and selling,
planting and building, [29]but on the day
when Lot went out from Sodom, fire and
sulfur rained from heaven and destroyed
them all— [30]so will it be on the day when
the Son of Man is revealed. [31]On that day,
let the one who is on the housetop, with
his goods in the house, not come down
to take them away, and likewise let the
one who is in the field not turn back.

32 Remember Lot's wife. 33 Whoever seeks to preserve his life will lose it, but whoever loses his life will keep it. 34 I tell you, in that night there will be two in one bed. One will be taken and the other left. 35 There will be two women grinding together. One will be taken and the other left."[1] 37 And they said to him, "Where, Lord?" He said to them, "Where the corpse[2] is, there the vultures[3] will gather."

The Parable of the Persistent Widow

18 And he told them a parable
to the effect that they ought
87, always to pray and not lose heart.
1493 2 He said, "In a certain city there
was a judge who neither feared God nor respected man. 3 And there was a widow in that city who kept coming to him and saying, 'Give me justice against my adversary.' 4 For a while he refused, but afterward he said to himself, 'Though I neither fear God nor respect man, 5 yet because this widow keeps bothering me, I will give her justice, so that she will not beat me down by her continual coming.'" 6 And the Lord said, "Hear what the unrighteous judge says. 7 And will not God give justice to his elect, who cry to him day and night? Will he delay long over them? 8 I tell you, he will give justice to them speedily. Nevertheless, when the Son of Man comes, will he find faith on earth?"

The Pharisee and the Tax Collector

9 He also told this parable to some who trusted in themselves that they were righteous, and treated others with contempt: 10 "Two men went up into the temple to pray, one a Pharisee and the other a tax collector. 11 The Pharisee, standing by himself, prayed[4] thus: 'God, I thank you that I am not like other men, extortioners, unjust, adulterers, or even like this tax collector. 12 I fast twice a week; I give tithes of all that I get.' 13 But the tax collector, standing far off, would not even lift up his eyes to heaven, but beat his breast, saying, 'God, be merciful to me, a sinner!' 14 I tell you, this man went down to his house justified, rather than the other. For everyone who exalts himself will be humbled, but the one who humbles himself will be exalted."

Let the Children Come to Me

15 Now they were bringing even
infants to him that he might touch
1403 them. And when the disciples saw
it, they rebuked them. 16 But Jesus called them to him, saying, "Let the children come to me, and do not hinder them, for to such belongs the kingdom of God. 17 Truly, I say to you, whoever does not receive the kingdom of God like a child shall not enter it."

The Rich Ruler

18 And a ruler asked him, "Good
Teacher, what must I do to inherit
1487 eternal life?" 19 And Jesus said to
him, "Why do you call me good? No one is good except God alone. 20 You know the commandments: 'Do not commit adultery, Do not murder, Do not steal, Do not bear false witness, Honor your father and mother.'" 21 And he said, "All these I have kept from my youth." 22 When Jesus heard this, he said to him, "One thing you still lack. Sell all that you have and distribute to the poor, and you will have treasure in heaven; and come, follow me." 23 But when he heard these things, he became very sad, for he was extremely rich. 24 Jesus, seeing that he had become sad, said, "How difficult it is for those who have wealth to enter the kingdom of God! 25 For it is easier for a camel to go through the eye of a needle than for a rich person to enter the kingdom of God." 26 Those who heard it said, "Then who can be saved?" 27 But he said, "What is impossible with men is possible with God." 28 And Peter said, "See, we have left our homes and followed you." 29 And he said to them, "Truly, I say to you, there is no one who has left house or wife

[1] Some manuscripts add verse 36: *Two men will be in the field; one will be taken and the other left* [2] Greek *body* [3] Or *eagles* [4] Or *standing, prayed to himself*

Jesus and Zacchaeus

Jesus walked to Jericho. A big crowd began to follow Him along the road.

Zacchaeus was a chief tax collector in Jericho, and he was very rich. He wanted to see Jesus, too, but he was short and couldn't see over the crowds. So he ran ahead of everyone and climbed up a sycamore tree. From there, he would be able to see Jesus when Jesus passed by.

When Jesus came to the tree, He looked up at Zacchaeus and said, "Zacchaeus, hurry and come down, for I must stay at your house today."

Zacchaeus hurried down. He rejoiced because Jesus was coming to his house. But some people who heard what Jesus said grumbled instead. They said, "He has gone in to be the guest of a man who is a sinner!" They did not think Jesus should be friends with such people.

When they got to the house, Zacchaeus stood up and told Jesus that he would give half of what he had to the poor. To anyone whom he had cheated out of tax money, he would pay back four times what he had taken. By making these promises from his heart, Zacchaeus was showing that he had repented of his sin. Rather than living for himself, he now wanted to live for God.

Jesus said, "Today salvation has come to this house. For the Son of Man came to seek and to save the lost."

We, like Zacchaeus, are among the lost whom the Son of Man seeks. We, too, are called to repent and have faith in Jesus, as Zacchaeus did. Jesus gladly forgives our sins and saves us, too.

SEEK and FIND

WHERE TO FIND THE STORY

Luke 19:1–10

KEY BIBLE VERSE

"For the Son of Man came to seek and to save the lost." (Luke 19:10)

THREE KEY QUESTIONS

- Why did people complain about Jesus going to Zacchaeus' house?
- What kind of people did Jesus come to save?
- How can you tell that Zacchaeus repented and believed in Jesus?

RELATED BIBLE READINGS

Matthew 9:9–13; Luke 3:8; 15:1–7

or brothers[1] or parents or children, for the
sake of the kingdom of God, 30 who will
not receive many times more in this time,
and in the age to come eternal life."

Jesus Foretells His Death a Third Time

31 And taking the twelve, he said to
them, "See, we are going up to Jerusalem,
and everything that is written about
the Son of Man by the prophets will be
accomplished. 32 For he will be delivered
over to the Gentiles and will be mocked
and shamefully treated and spit upon.
33 And after flogging him, they will kill
him, and on the third day he will rise."
34 But they understood none of these
things. This saying was hidden from them,
and they did not grasp what was said.

Jesus Heals a Blind Beggar

35 As he drew near to Jericho, a blind man
was sitting by the roadside begging. 36 And

[1] Or *wife or brothers and sisters*

hearing a crowd going by, he inquired what
this meant. 37 They told him, "Jesus of
Nazareth is passing by." 38 And he cried out,
"Jesus, Son of David, have mercy on me!"
39 And those who were in front rebuked
him, telling him to be silent. But he cried
out all the more, "Son of David, have mercy
on me!" 40 And Jesus stopped and com-
manded him to be brought to him. And
when he came near, he asked him, 41 "What
do you want me to do for you?" He said,
"Lord, let me recover my sight." 42 And Jesus
said to him, "Recover your sight; your faith
has made you well." 43 And immediately he
recovered his sight and followed him, glo-
rifying God. And all the people, when they
saw it, gave praise to God.

Jesus and Zacchaeus

19 He entered Jericho and was
passing through. 2 And
1511 there was a man named Zacchaeus.
He was a chief tax collector and was rich.
3 And he was seeking to see who Jesus was,
but on account of the crowd he could not,
because he was small of stature. 4 So he
ran on ahead and climbed up into a syca-
more tree to see him, for he was about to
pass that way. 5 And when Jesus came to
the place, he looked up and said to him,
"Zacchaeus, hurry and come down, for I
must stay at your house today." 6 So he
hurried and came down and received him
joyfully. 7 And when they saw it, they all
grumbled, "He has gone in to be the guest
of a man who is a sinner." 8 And Zacchaeus
stood and said to the Lord, "Behold, Lord,
the half of my goods I give to the poor. And
if I have defrauded anyone of anything, I
restore it fourfold." 9 And Jesus said to him,
"Today salvation has come to this house,
since he also is a son of Abraham.
10 For the Son of Man came to seek
1511 and to save the lost."

The Parable of the Ten Minas

11 As they heard these things, he pro-
ceeded to tell a parable, because he was
near to Jerusalem, and because they sup-
posed that the kingdom of God was to
appear immediately. 12 He said therefore,
"A nobleman went into a far country to
receive for himself a kingdom and then
return. 13 Calling ten of his servants,[1] he
gave them ten minas,[2] and said to them,
'Engage in business until I come.' 14 But
his citizens hated him and sent a delega-
tion after him, saying, 'We do not want
this man to reign over us.' 15 When he
returned, having received the kingdom,
he ordered these servants to whom he had
given the money to be called to him, that
he might know what they had gained by
doing business. 16 The first came before
him, saying, 'Lord, your mina has made
ten minas more.' 17 And he said to him,
'Well done, good servant![3] Because you
have been faithful in a very little, you shall
have authority over ten cities.' 18 And the
second came, saying, 'Lord, your mina
has made five minas.' 19 And he said to
him, 'And you are to be over five cities.'
20 Then another came, saying, 'Lord, here
is your mina, which I kept laid away in
a handkerchief; 21 for I was afraid of you,
because you are a severe man. You take
what you did not deposit, and reap what
you did not sow.' 22 He said to him, 'I will
condemn you with your own words, you
wicked servant! You knew that I was a
severe man, taking what I did not deposit
and reaping what I did not sow? 23 Why
then did you not put my money in the
bank, and at my coming I might have col-
lected it with interest?' 24 And he said to
those who stood by, 'Take the mina from
him, and give it to the one who has the ten
minas.' 25 And they said to him, 'Lord, he
has ten minas!' 26 'I tell you that to every-
one who has, more will be given, but
from the one who has not, even what he
has will be taken away. 27 But as for these
enemies of mine, who did not want me
to reign over them, bring them here and
slaughter them before me.'"

[1] Greek *bondservants;* also verse 15 [2] A *mina* was about three months' wages for a laborer [3] Greek *bondservant;* also verse 22

The Triumphal Entry

28 And when he had said these
things, he went on ahead, going up
1519 to Jerusalem. 29 When he drew
near to Bethphage and Bethany, at
the mount that is called Olivet, he
1345 sent two of the disciples, 30 saying,
"Go into the village in front of you, where
on entering you will find a colt tied, on
which no one has ever yet sat. Untie it and
bring it here. 31 If anyone asks you, 'Why
are you untying it?' you shall say this: 'The
Lord has need of it.'" 32 So those who were
sent went away and found it just as he had
told them. 33 And as they were untying the
colt, its owners said to them, "Why are
you untying the colt?" 34 And they said,
"The Lord has need of it." 35 And they
brought it to Jesus, and throwing their
cloaks on the colt, they set Jesus on it.
36 And as he rode along, they spread their
cloaks on the road. 37 As he was drawing
near—already on the way down the Mount
of Olives—the whole multitude of his dis-
ciples began to rejoice and praise God
with a loud voice for all the mighty works
that they had seen, 38 saying, "Blessed is
the King who comes in the name of the
Lord! Peace in heaven and glory in the
highest!" 39 And some of the Pharisees in
the crowd said to him, "Teacher, rebuke
your disciples." 40 He answered, "I tell you,
if these were silent, the very stones would
cry out."

Jesus Weeps over Jerusalem

41 And when he drew near and saw the
city, he wept over it, 42 saying, "Would that
you, even you, had known on this day the
things that make for peace! But now they
are hidden from your eyes. 43 For the days
will come upon you, when your enemies
will set up a barricade around you and
surround you and hem you in on every
side 44 and tear you down to the ground,
you and your children within you. And
they will not leave one stone upon
another in you, because you did not know
the time of your visitation."

Jesus Cleanses the Temple

45 And he entered the temple and
began to drive out those who sold,
1545 46 saying to them, "It is written, 'My
house shall be a house of prayer,' but you
have made it a den of robbers."
47 And he was teaching daily in the
temple. The chief priests and the scribes
and the principal men of the people were
seeking to destroy him, 48 but they did not
find anything they could do, for all the
people were hanging on his words.

The Authority of Jesus Challenged

20 One day, as Jesus[1] was teaching
the people in the temple and
preaching the gospel, the chief priests
and the scribes with the elders came up
2 and said to him, "Tell us by what author-
ity you do these things, or who it is that
gave you this authority." 3 He answered
them, "I also will ask you a question. Now
tell me, 4 was the baptism of John from
heaven or from man?" 5 And they dis-
cussed it with one another, saying, "If we
say, 'From heaven,' he will say, 'Why did
you not believe him?' 6 But if we say, 'From
man,' all the people will stone us to death,
for they are convinced that John was a
prophet." 7 So they answered that they did
not know where it came from. 8 And Jesus
said to them, "Neither will I tell you by
what authority I do these things."

The Parable of the Wicked Tenants

9 And he began to tell the people this
parable: "A man planted a vineyard
and let it out to tenants and went into
another country for a long while. 10 When
the time came, he sent a servant[2] to the
tenants, so that they would give him
some of the fruit of the vineyard. But
the tenants beat him and sent him away
empty-handed. 11 And he sent another
servant. But they also beat and treated

[1] Greek *he* [2] Greek *bondservant*; also verse 11

him shamefully, and sent him away empty-handed. 12 And he sent yet a third. This one also they wounded and cast out. 13 Then the owner of the vineyard said, 'What shall I do? I will send my beloved son; perhaps they will respect him.' 14 But when the tenants saw him, they said to themselves, 'This is the heir. Let us kill him, so that the inheritance may be ours.' 15 And they threw him out of the vineyard and killed him. What then will the owner of the vineyard do to them? 16 He will come and destroy those tenants and give the vineyard to others." When they heard this, they said, "Surely not!" 17 But he looked directly at them and said, "What then is this that is written:

> "'The stone that the builders rejected
> has become the cornerstone'?[1]

18 Everyone who falls on that stone will be broken to pieces, and when it falls on anyone, it will crush him."

Paying Taxes to Caesar

19 The scribes and the chief priests sought to lay hands on him at that very hour, for they perceived that he had told this parable against them, but they feared the people. 20 So they watched him and sent spies, who pretended to be sincere, that they might catch him in something he said, so as to deliver him up to the authority and jurisdiction of the governor. 21 So they asked him, "Teacher, we know that you speak and teach rightly, and show no partiality,[2] but truly teach the way of God. 22 Is it lawful for us to give tribute to Caesar, or not?" 23 But he perceived their craftiness, and said to them, 24 "Show me a denarius.[3] Whose likeness and inscription does it have?" They said, "Caesar's." 25 He said to them, "Then render to Caesar the things that are Caesar's, and to God the things that are God's." 26 And they were not able in the presence of the people to catch him in what he said, but marveling at his answer they became silent.

Sadducees Ask About the Resurrection

27 There came to him some Sadducees, those who deny that there is a resurrection, 28 and they asked him a question, saying, "Teacher, Moses wrote for us that if a man's brother dies, having a wife but no children, the man[4] must take the widow and raise up offspring for his brother. 29 Now there were seven brothers. The first took a wife, and died without children. 30 And the second 31 and the third took her, and likewise all seven left no children and died. 32 Afterward the woman also died. 33 In the resurrection, therefore, whose wife will the woman be? For the seven had her as wife."

34 And Jesus said to them, "The sons of this age marry and are given in marriage, 35 but those who are considered worthy to attain to that age and to the resurrection from the dead neither marry nor are given in marriage, 36 for they cannot die anymore, because they are equal to angels and are sons of God, being sons of the resurrection. 37 But that the dead are raised, even Moses showed, in the passage about the bush, where he calls the Lord the God of Abraham and the God of Isaac and the God of Jacob. 38 Now he is not God of the dead, but of the living, for all live to him." 39 Then some of the scribes answered, "Teacher, you have spoken well." 40 For they no longer dared to ask him any question.

Whose Son Is the Christ?

41 But he said to them, "How can they say that the Christ is David's son? 42 For David himself says in the Book of Psalms,

> "'The Lord said to my Lord,
> Sit at my right hand,
> 43 until I make your enemies your
> footstool.'

44 David thus calls him Lord, so how is he his son?"

[1] Greek *the head of the corner* [2] Greek *and do not receive a face* [3] A *denarius* was a day's wage for a laborer [4] Greek *his brother*

Beware of the Scribes

45 And in the hearing of all the people
he said to his disciples, 46 "Beware of the
scribes, who like to walk around in long
robes, and love greetings in the market-
places and the best seats in the syna-
gogues and the places of honor at feasts,
47 who devour widows' houses and for
a pretense make long prayers. They will
receive the greater condemnation."

The Widow's Offering

21 Jesus[1] looked up and saw
the rich putting their gifts
1411 into the offering box, 2 and he saw
a poor widow put in two small copper
coins.[2] 3 And he said, "Truly, I tell you, this
poor widow has put in more than all of
them. 4 For they all contributed out of their
abundance, but she out of her poverty put
in all she had to live on."

Jesus Foretells Destruction of the Temple

5 And while some were speaking of the
temple, how it was adorned with noble
stones and offerings, he said, 6 "As for
these things that you see, the days will
come when there will not be left here
one stone upon another that will not be
thrown down." 7 And they asked him,
"Teacher, when will these things be, and
what will be the sign when these things
are about to take place?" 8 And he said,
"See that you are not led astray. For many
will come in my name, saying, 'I am he!'
and, 'The time is at hand!' Do not go after
them. 9 And when you hear of wars and
tumults, do not be terrified, for these
things must first take place, but the end
will not be at once."

Jesus Foretells Wars and Persecution

10 Then he said to them, "Nation will
rise against nation, and kingdom against
kingdom. 11 There will be great earth-
quakes, and in various places famines
and pestilences. And there will be terrors
and great signs from heaven. 12 But before
all this they will lay their hands on you
and persecute you, delivering you up to
the synagogues and prisons, and you will
be brought before kings and governors
for my name's sake. 13 This will be your
opportunity to bear witness. 14 Settle it
therefore in your minds not to meditate
beforehand how to answer, 15 for I will
give you a mouth and wisdom, which
none of your adversaries will be able to
withstand or contradict. 16 You will be
delivered up even by parents and broth-
ers[3] and relatives and friends, and some
of you they will put to death. 17 You will be
hated by all for my name's sake. 18 But not
a hair of your head will perish. 19 By your
endurance you will gain your lives.

Jesus Foretells Destruction of Jerusalem

20 "But when you see Jerusalem sur-
rounded by armies, then know that its
desolation has come near. 21 Then let
those who are in Judea flee to the moun-
tains, and let those who are inside the city
depart, and let not those who are out in
the country enter it, 22 for these are days
of vengeance, to fulfill all that is written.
23 Alas for women who are pregnant and
for those who are nursing infants in those
days! For there will be great distress upon
the earth and wrath against this people.
24 They will fall by the edge of the sword
and be led captive among all nations,
and Jerusalem will be trampled under-
foot by the Gentiles, until the times of the
Gentiles are fulfilled.

The Coming of the Son of Man

25 "And there will be signs in sun and
moon and stars, and on the earth distress
of nations in perplexity because of the
roaring of the sea and the waves, 26 people
fainting with fear and with foreboding of
what is coming on the world. For the pow-
ers of the heavens will be shaken. 27 And
then they will see the Son of Man com-

[1] Greek *He* [2] Greek *two lepta*; a *lepton* was a Jewish bronze or copper coin worth about 1/128 of a *denarius* (which was a day's wage for a laborer) [3] Or *parents and brothers and sisters*

ing in a cloud with power and great glory. 28 Now when these things begin to take place, straighten up and raise your heads, because your redemption is drawing near."

The Lesson of the Fig Tree

29 And he told them a parable: "Look at the fig tree, and all the trees. 30 As soon as they come out in leaf, you see for yourselves and know that the summer is already near. 31 So also, when you see these things taking place, you know that the kingdom of God is near. 32 Truly, I say to you, this generation will not pass away until all has taken place. 33 Heaven and earth will pass away, but my words will not pass away.

Watch Yourselves

34 "But watch yourselves lest your hearts be weighed down with dissipation and drunkenness and cares of this life, and that day come upon you suddenly like a trap. 35 For it will come upon all who dwell on the face of the whole earth. 36 But stay awake at all times, praying that you may have strength to escape all these things that are going to take place, and to stand before the Son of Man."

37 And every day he was teaching in the temple, but at night he went out and lodged on the mount called Olivet. 38 And early in the morning all the people came to him in the temple to hear him.

The Plot to Kill Jesus

22 Now the Feast of Unleavened Bread drew near, which is called the Passover. 2 And the chief priests and the scribes were seeking how to put him to death, for they feared the people.

Judas to Betray Jesus

3 Then Satan entered into Judas called Iscariot, who was of the number of the twelve. 4 He went away and conferred with the chief priests and officers how he might betray him to them. 5 And they were glad, and agreed to give him money. 6 So he consented and sought an opportunity to betray him to them in the absence of a crowd.

The Passover with the Disciples

1519

7 Then came the day of Unleavened Bread, on which the Passover lamb had to be sacrificed. 8 So Jesus[1] sent Peter and John, saying, "Go and prepare the Passover for us, that we may eat it." 9 They said to him, "Where will you have us prepare it?" 10 He said to them, "Behold, when you have entered the city, a man carrying a jar of water will meet you. Follow him into the house that he enters 11 and tell the master of the house, 'The Teacher says to you, Where is the guest room, where I may eat the Passover with my disciples?' 12 And he will show you a large upper room furnished; prepare it there." 13 And they went and found it just as he had told them, and they prepared the Passover.

Institution of the Lord's Supper

14 And when the hour came, he reclined at table, and the apostles with him. 15 And he said to them, "I have earnestly desired to eat this Passover with you before I suffer. 16 For I tell you I will not eat it[2] until it is fulfilled in the kingdom of God." 17 And he took a cup, and when he had given thanks he said, "Take this, and divide it among yourselves. 18 For I tell you that from now on I will not drink of the fruit of the vine until the kingdom of God comes." 19 And he took bread, and when he had given thanks, he broke it and gave it to them, saying, "This is my body, which is given for you. Do this in remembrance of me." 20 And likewise the cup after they had eaten, saying, "This cup that is poured out for you is the new covenant in my blood.[3] 21 But behold, the hand of him who betrays me is with me on the table. 22 For the Son of Man goes as it has been determined, but woe to that man by whom he is betrayed!" 23 And they began

[1] Greek *he* [2] Some manuscripts *never eat it again* [3] Some manuscripts omit, in whole or in part, verses 19b-20 (*which is given . . . in my blood*)

The Lord's Supper

On the first day of the week Jesus had ridden into Jerusalem on a donkey. Many people in Jerusalem were happy to see Jesus and they wanted Him to be their king. They waved palm branches and put their coats on the ground so that Jesus could ride the donkey over them. As Jesus went by, they rejoiced and praised God, saying, "Blessed is the King who comes in the name of the Lord!"

Later that week, on Thursday, it was time to celebrate the Passover meal. This was a feast where the Jews celebrated how God had saved them from Egypt many years before. It was their most important holiday. So Jesus asked Peter and John to prepare a room so that He could eat the Passover meal with His disciples. To do this, Jesus told them to enter the city gate and follow a man carrying a water jar. He would lead them to the right home with a large upstairs room. They would prepare the meal in that room.

That night, as Jesus and His disciples ate the meal together, Jesus told His disciples that He wanted to eat this Passover meal with them before He suffered and died. Then Jesus took bread and gave thanks to God. He broke the bread and gave it to His disciples saying, "This is My body, which is given for you. Do this in remembrance of Me." And they ate the bread together.

Then Jesus took a cup of wine and said, "This cup that is

poured out for you is the new covenant in My blood." Now a covenant is a very serious promise. God had made a covenant with His people early in the Old Testament, but the people were always breaking it. The prophets had promised a new covenant. Now Jesus was saying that He was making that new covenant. His body would be wounded and His blood would flow so the sins of His people could be forgiven. They would live forever with God under the new covenant. So the disciples drank the wine of the new covenant for the first time.

In the Lord's Supper, we receive Jesus' body and blood and remember what Jesus did for us. He gives us grace to live for Him and glorify Him, as we look ahead to His return.

SEEK and FIND

WHERE TO FIND THE STORY

Luke 19:28–38; 22:7–20

KEY BIBLE VERSE

"In the same way also he took the cup, after supper, saying, 'This cup is the new covenant in my blood. Do this, as often as you drink it, in remembrance of me.' For as often as you eat this bread and drink the cup, you proclaim the Lord's death until he comes." (1 Corinthians 11:25–26)

THREE KEY QUESTIONS

- Why was the Passover meal important to the Jewish people?
- How did Jesus change the meaning of the bread and the cup?
- Why do we celebrate the Lord's Supper today?

RELATED BIBLE READINGS

Matthew 26:26–29; Mark 14:22–25; 1 Corinthians 11:17–34

to question one another, which of them it could be who was going to do this.

Who Is the Greatest?

24 A dispute also arose among them, as to which of them was to be regarded as the greatest. 25 And he said to them, "The kings of the Gentiles exercise lordship over them, and those in authority over them are called benefactors. 26 But not so with you. Rather, let the greatest among you become as the youngest, and the leader as one who serves. 27 For who is the greater, one who reclines at table or one who serves? Is it not the one who reclines at table? But I am among you as the one who serves.

28 "You are those who have stayed with me in my trials, 29 and I assign to you, as my Father assigned to me, a kingdom, 30 that you may eat and drink at my table in my kingdom and sit on thrones judging the twelve tribes of Israel.

Jesus Foretells Peter's Denial

1415
31 "Simon, Simon, behold, Satan demanded to have you,[1] that he might sift you like wheat, 32 but I have prayed for you that your faith may not fail. And when you have turned again, strengthen your brothers." 33 Peter[2] said to him, "Lord, I am ready to go with you both to prison and to death." 34 Jesus[3] said, "I tell you, Peter, the rooster will not crow this day, until you deny three times that you know me."

Scripture Must Be Fulfilled in Jesus

35 And he said to them, "When I sent you out with no moneybag or knapsack or sandals, did you lack anything?" They said, "Nothing." 36 He said to them, "But now let the one who has a moneybag take it, and likewise a knapsack. And let the one who has no sword sell his cloak and buy one. 37 For I tell you that this Scripture must be fulfilled in me: 'And he was numbered with the transgressors.' For what is written about me has its fulfillment." 38 And they said, "Look, Lord, here are two swords." And he said to them, "It is enough."

Jesus Prays on the Mount of Olives

1361
39 And he came out and went, as was his custom, to the Mount of Olives, and the disciples followed him. 40 And when he came to the place, he said to them, "Pray that you may not enter into temptation." 41 And he withdrew from them about a stone's throw, and knelt down and prayed, 42 saying, "Father, if you are willing, remove this cup from me. Nevertheless, not my will, but yours, be done." 43 And there appeared to him an angel from heaven, strengthening him. 44 And being in an agony he prayed more earnestly; and his sweat became like great drops of blood falling down to the ground.[4] 45 And when he rose from prayer, he came to the disciples and found them sleeping for sorrow, 46 and he said to them, "Why are you sleeping? Rise and pray that you may not enter into temptation."

Betrayal and Arrest of Jesus

47 While he was still speaking, there came a crowd, and the man called Judas, one of the twelve, was leading them. He drew near to Jesus to kiss him, 48 but Jesus said to him, "Judas, would you betray the Son of Man with a kiss?" 49 And when those who were around him saw what would follow, they said, "Lord, shall we strike with the sword?" 50 And one of them struck the servant[5] of the high priest and cut off his right ear. 51 But Jesus said, "No more of this!" And he touched his ear and healed him. 52 Then Jesus said to the chief priests and officers of the temple and elders, who had come out against him, "Have you come out as against a robber, with swords and clubs? 53 When I was with you day after day in the temple, you did not lay hands on me. But this is your hour, and the power of darkness."

[1] The Greek word for *you* (twice in this verse) is plural; in verse 32, all four instances are singular [2] Greek *He* [3] Greek *He* [4] Some manuscripts omit verses 43 and 44
[5] Greek *bondservant*

Jesus Dies and Lives Again

Soldiers arrested Jesus. Important religious leaders and government rulers questioned Jesus. Soldiers beat Him and put a crown of thorns on His head. Finally, the Roman governor Pontius Pilate asked the crowd if Jesus should be set free. They yelled, "Crucify Him!" That is just what happened.

On Good Friday, soldiers nailed Jesus to a cross. While He hung on the cross, Jesus prayed for others. He said, "Father, forgive them, for they know not what they do."

Meanwhile, soldiers divided Jesus' clothing while the religious leaders made fun of Him. They said, "He saved others; let Him save Himself, if He is the Christ of God, His Chosen One!" But Jesus said nothing in return.

The soldiers made fun of Jesus too, and offered Him sour wine to drink. They said, "If You are the King of the Jews, save Yourself!" Again, Jesus said nothing.

Two criminals were crucified along with Jesus. One of the criminals said to Jesus, "Are You not the Christ? Save Yourself and us!" Still Jesus said nothing.

The other criminal said the first one was wrong to speak like that. He said that the two of them deserved to die, but that Jesus had done nothing wrong. Then he said to Jesus, "Jesus, remember me when You come into Your kingdom."

Jesus said to that man, "Truly I say to you, today you will

be with Me in Paradise."

At about noon, darkness covered the land until three in the afternoon. At that time, Jesus called out with a loud voice and said, "Father, into Your hands I commit My spirit!" And then Jesus died.

A Roman solider, who was watching all these things nearby, praised God and said, "Certainly, this man was innocent." He knew that Jesus had done nothing to deserve death.

Joseph of Arimathea, a religious leader who had befriended Jesus, wrapped Jesus' body in a linen cloth and laid Him in a new stone tomb. Since the next day was the Sabbath—the day everyone rested according to the Jewish laws—they had to just leave Him there in the tomb, without doing much to His body to show their love for Him.

Early on the first day of the week, when the Sabbath was over, Mary Magdalene, Joanna, Mary the mother of James, and other women went to the tomb. They took spices to put on Jesus' body. But when they got to the tomb, they were surprised. The big stone in front of the grave was rolled away. The women found the tomb empty.

Two angels in dazzling clothes stood by them and said, "Why do you seek the living among the dead? He is not here, but has risen."

With joy, the women left the tomb and returned to tell the disciples.

Jesus' resurrection was a victory over sin, over death, and over the devil. That victory is God's gift to you! Thanks be to God for His gifts through Jesus!

SEEK and FIND

WHERE TO FIND THE STORY

Luke 23:18–24:12

KEY BIBLE VERSE

"Thus it is written, that the Christ should suffer and on the third day rise from the dead, and that repentance and forgiveness of sins should be proclaimed in his name to all nations." (Luke 24:46–47)

THREE KEY QUESTIONS

- For whom did Jesus pray while He was on the cross?
- What did Jesus promise the criminal who asked Jesus to remember him in His kingdom?
- What did the angels at the tomb tell the women who had come to put spices on Jesus' dead body?

RELATED BIBLE READINGS

Matthew 27:11–28:10; Mark 15:1–16:8; John 18:1–20:29

Peter Denies Jesus

1605

54 Then they seized him and led him away, bringing him into the high priest's house, and Peter was following at a distance. 55 And when they had kindled a fire in the middle of the courtyard and sat down together, Peter sat down among them. 56 Then a servant girl, seeing him as he sat in the light and looking closely at him, said, "This man also was with him." 57 But he denied it, saying, "Woman, I do not know him." 58 And a little later someone else saw him and said, "You also are one of them." But Peter said, "Man, I am not." 59 And after an interval of about an hour still another insisted, saying, "Certainly this man also was with him, for he too is a Galilean." 60 But Peter said, "Man, I do not know what you are talking about." And immediately, while he was still speaking, the rooster crowed. 61 And the Lord turned and looked at Peter. And Peter remembered the saying of the Lord, how he had said to him, "Before the rooster crows today, you will deny me three times." 62 And he went out and wept bitterly.

Jesus Is Mocked

63 Now the men who were holding Jesus in custody were mocking him as they beat him. 64 They also blindfolded him and kept asking him, "Prophesy! Who is it that struck you?" 65 And they said many other things against him, blaspheming him.

Jesus Before the Council

1421

66 When day came, the assembly of the elders of the people gathered together, both chief priests and scribes. And they led him away to their council, and they said, 67 "If you are the

Christ, tell us." But he said to them, "If I
tell you, you will not believe, 68 and if I ask
you, you will not answer. 69 But from now
on the Son of Man shall be seated at the
right hand of the power of God." 70 So they
all said, "Are you the Son of God, then?"
And he said to them, "You say that I am."
71 Then they said, "What further testimony
do we need? We have heard it ourselves
from his own lips."

Jesus Before Pilate

23 Then the whole company of them
arose and brought him before
Pilate. 2 And they began to accuse him,
saying, "We found this man misleading
our nation and forbidding us to give trib-
ute to Caesar, and saying that he himself
is Christ, a king." 3 And Pilate asked him,
"Are you the King of the Jews?" And he
answered him, "You have said so." 4 Then
Pilate said to the chief priests and the
crowds, "I find no guilt in this man." 5 But
they were urgent, saying, "He stirs up the
people, teaching throughout all Judea,
from Galilee even to this place."

Jesus Before Herod

6 When Pilate heard this, he asked
whether the man was a Galilean. 7 And
when he learned that he belonged to
Herod's jurisdiction, he sent him over to
Herod, who was himself in Jerusalem at
that time. 8 When Herod saw Jesus, he was
very glad, for he had long desired to see
him, because he had heard about him,
and he was hoping to see some sign done
by him. 9 So he questioned him at some
length, but he made no answer. 10 The
chief priests and the scribes stood by,
vehemently accusing him. 11 And Herod
with his soldiers treated him with con-
tempt and mocked him. Then, arraying
him in splendid clothing, he sent him
back to Pilate. 12 And Herod and Pilate
became friends with each other that
very day, for before this they had been at
enmity with each other.

13 Pilate then called together the chief
priests and the rulers and the people,
14 and said to them, "You brought me
this man as one who was misleading the
people. And after examining him before
you, behold, I did not find this man
guilty of any of your charges against him.
15 Neither did Herod, for he sent him back
to us. Look, nothing deserving death has
been done by him. 16 I will therefore pun-
ish and release him."[1]

Pilate Delivers Jesus to Be Crucified

18 But they all cried out together,
"Away with this man, and release
1523 to us Barabbas"— 19 a man who
had been thrown into prison for an insur-
rection started in the city and for murder.
20 Pilate addressed them once more,
desiring to release Jesus, 21 but they kept
shouting, "Crucify, crucify him!" 22 A
third time he said to them, "Why, what
evil has he done? I have found in him no
guilt deserving death. I will therefore
punish and release him." 23 But they were
urgent, demanding with loud cries that
he should be crucified. And their voices
prevailed. 24 So Pilate decided that their
demand should be granted. 25 He released
the man who had been thrown into
prison for insurrection and murder, for
whom they asked, but he delivered Jesus
over to their will.

The Crucifixion

26 And as they led him away, they seized
one Simon of Cyrene, who was coming
in from the country, and laid on him
the cross, to carry it behind Jesus. 27 And
there followed him a great multitude
of the people and of women who were
mourning and lamenting for him. 28 But
turning to them Jesus said, "Daughters of
Jerusalem, do not weep for me, but weep
for yourselves and for your children. 29 For
behold, the days are coming when they
will say, 'Blessed are the barren and the
wombs that never bore and the breasts

[1] Here, or after verse 19, some manuscripts add verse 17: *Now he was obliged to release one man to them at the festival*

that never nursed!' 30 Then they will begin to say to the mountains, 'Fall on us,' and to the hills, 'Cover us.' 31 For if they do these things when the wood is green, what will happen when it is dry?"

32 Two others, who were criminals, were led away to be put to death with him. 33 And when they came to the place that is called The Skull, there they crucified him, and the criminals, one on his right and one on his left. 34 And Jesus said, "Father, forgive them, for they know not what they do."[1] And they cast lots to divide his garments. 35 And the people stood by, watching, but the rulers scoffed at him, saying, "He saved others; let him save himself, if he is the Christ of God, his Chosen One!" 36 The soldiers also mocked him, coming up and offering him sour wine 37 and saying, "If you are the King of the Jews, save yourself!" 38 There was also an inscription over him,[2] "This is the King of the Jews."

39 One of the criminals who were hanged railed at him,[3] saying, "Are you not the Christ? Save yourself and us!" 40 But the other rebuked him, saying, "Do you not fear God, since you are under the same sentence of condemnation? 41 And we indeed justly, for we are receiving the due reward of our deeds; but this man has done nothing wrong." 42 And he said, "Jesus, remember me when you come into your kingdom." 43 And he said to him, "Truly, I say to you, today you will be with me in Paradise."

The Death of Jesus

44 It was now about the sixth hour,[4] and there was darkness over the whole land until the ninth hour,[5] 45 while the sun's light failed. And the curtain of the temple was torn in two. 46 Then Jesus, calling out with a loud voice, said, "Father, into your hands I commit my spirit!" And having said this he breathed his last. 47 Now when the centurion saw what had taken place, he praised God, saying, "Certainly this man was innocent!" 48 And all the crowds that had assembled for this spectacle, when they saw what had taken place, returned home beating their breasts. 49 And all his acquaintances and the women who had followed him from Galilee stood at a distance watching these things.

Jesus Is Buried

50 Now there was a man named Joseph, from the Jewish town of Arimathea. He was a member of the council, a good and righteous man, 51 who had not consented to their decision and action; and he was looking for the kingdom of God. 52 This man went to Pilate and asked for the body of Jesus. 53 Then he took it down and wrapped it in a linen shroud and laid him in a tomb cut in stone, where no one had ever yet been laid. 54 It was the day of Preparation, and the Sabbath was beginning.[6] 55 The women who had come with him from Galilee followed and saw the tomb and how his body was laid. 56 Then they returned and prepared spices and ointments.

On the Sabbath they rested according to the commandment.

The Resurrection

24 But on the first day of the week, at early dawn, they
1365, went to the tomb, taking the spices
1593 they had prepared. 2 And they found the stone rolled away from the tomb, 3 but when they went in they did not find the body of the Lord Jesus. 4 While they were perplexed about this, behold, two men stood by them in dazzling apparel. 5 And as they were frightened and bowed their faces to the ground, the men said to them, "Why do you seek the living among the dead? 6 He is not here, but has risen. Remember how he told you, while he was still in Galilee, 7 that the Son of Man must be delivered into the hands of sinful men and be crucified and on the

[1] Some manuscripts omit the sentence *And Jesus . . . what they do* [2] Some manuscripts add *in letters of Greek and Latin and Hebrew* [3] Or *blasphemed him* [4] That is, noon [5] That is, 3 P.M. [6] Greek *was dawning*

Jesus Appears on the Emmaus Road

On the third day after Jesus had been crucified, two of His disciples were walking to a town called Emmaus. They were talking about Jesus. They were sad that He had died.

All of a sudden, Jesus came and walked beside them. He asked what they were talking about. The men looked at Jesus but did not know who He was. God kept them from recognizing Jesus.

The men told about Jesus and His death on the cross. They said He "was a Prophet, mighty in deed and word. Our chief priests and rulers delivered Him up to be condemned to death, and crucified Him. But we had hoped that He was the one to redeem Israel." Then the men told how some women had gone to Jesus' tomb that very morning and had come back saying that His body was not there and that they had seen angels who said Jesus was alive again.

Jesus told them they were foolish and slow to believe, because the Old Testament prophets had spoken of this many years before. Then Jesus explained to the men what God's Word said about the Savior. He told them that it was part of God's plan for the Savior to suffer, die, and come alive again. Then Jesus began with the earliest Scriptures written and showed how all of God's Word spoke about Jesus and the salvation He would bring.

When they came to the village where they were staying, the men asked Jesus to stay with them. They sat down to eat their evening meal. Then Jesus let the men see who He was. He took some bread, blessed it, and broke it into pieces. Right away the men knew it was Jesus! They recognized Him. Jesus really was alive! What a happy surprise. Then Jesus disappeared. The men said to each other, "Did not our hearts burn within us while He talked to us on the road, while He opened to us the Scriptures?" They were so happy that they hurried back to Jerusalem to tell their friends that Jesus was alive!

The New Testament is not the only Scripture about Jesus; we also read about Jesus in the Old Testament. Moses and the Prophets predicted that the Christ would come and be the Savior of the world. Jesus fulfilled all of those prophecies.

SEEK and FIND

WHERE TO FIND THE STORY

Luke 24:13–35

KEY BIBLE VERSE

"And beginning with Moses and all the Prophets, he interpreted to them in all the Scriptures the things concerning himself." (Luke 24:27)

THREE KEY QUESTIONS

- Whose plan was it for Jesus to die on the cross?
- What did Jesus show the two men from all of Scripture?
- How did the two men feel while Jesus was explaining the Scriptures to them?

RELATED BIBLE READINGS

Luke 24:36–49; John 20:11–18; 1 Peter 1:10–12

third day rise." 8 And they remembered his
words, 9 and returning from the tomb they
told all these things to the eleven and to
all the rest. 10 Now it was Mary Magdalene
and Joanna and Mary the mother of James
and the other women with them who told
these things to the apostles, 11 but these
words seemed to them an idle tale, and
they did not believe them. 12 But Peter rose
and ran to the tomb; stooping and looking
in, he saw the linen cloths by themselves;
and he went home marveling at what had
happened.

On the Road to Emmaus

13 That very day two of them were
going to a village named Emmaus,
1529 about seven miles[1] from Jeru-
salem, 14 and they were talking with each
other about all these things that had hap-
pened. 15 While they were talking and dis-
cussing together, Jesus himself drew near
and went with them. 16 But their eyes
were kept from recognizing him. 17 And
he said to them, "What is this conversa-
tion that you are holding with each other
as you walk?" And they stood still, looking
sad. 18 Then one of them, named Cleopas,
answered him, "Are you the only visitor to
Jerusalem who does not know the things
that have happened there in these days?"
19 And he said to them, "What things?"
And they said to him, "Concerning Jesus
of Nazareth, a man who was a prophet
mighty in deed and word before God and
all the people, 20 and how our chief priests
and rulers delivered him up to be con-
demned to death, and crucified him.
21 But we had hoped that he was the one to
redeem Israel. Yes, and besides all this, it
is now the third day since these things
happened. 22 Moreover, some women of
our company amazed us. They were at the
tomb early in the morning, 23 and when
they did not find his body, they came back
saying that they had even seen a vision of
angels, who said that he was alive. 24 Some
of those who were with us went to the
tomb and found it just as the women had
said, but him they did not see." 25 And he
said to them, "O foolish ones, and slow of
heart to believe all that the prophets have
spoken! 26 Was it not necessary that the
Christ should suffer these things
and enter into his glory?" 27 And
1529 beginning with Moses and all the
Prophets, he interpreted to them in
all the Scriptures the things con-
1633 cerning himself.

28 So they drew near to the village to
which they were going. He acted as if
he were going farther, 29 but they urged
him strongly, saying, "Stay with us, for it
is toward evening and the day is now far
spent." So he went in to stay with them.
30 When he was at table with them, he
took the bread and blessed and broke
it and gave it to them. 31 And their eyes
were opened, and they recognized him.
And he vanished from their sight. 32 They
said to each other, "Did not our hearts
burn within us while he talked to us
on the road, while he opened to us the
Scriptures?" 33 And they rose that same
hour and returned to Jerusalem. And
they found the eleven and those who
were with them gathered together, 34 say-
ing, "The Lord has risen indeed, and has
appeared to Simon!" 35 Then they told
what had happened on the road, and how
he was known to them in the breaking of
the bread.

Jesus Appears to His Disciples

36 As they were talking about these
things, Jesus himself stood among
1529, them, and said to them, "Peace to
1597 you!" 37 But they were startled and
frightened and thought they saw a spirit.
38 And he said to them, "Why are you trou-
bled, and why do doubts arise in your
hearts? 39 See my hands and my feet, that
it is I myself. Touch me, and see. For a
spirit does not have flesh and bones as

[1] Greek *sixty stadia*; a *stadion* was about 607 feet or 185 meters

you see that I have." [40] And when he had
said this, he showed them his hands and
his feet. [41] And while they still disbelieved
for joy and were marveling, he said to
them, "Have you anything here to eat?"
[42] They gave him a piece of broiled fish,[1]
[43] and he took it and ate before them.

[44] Then he said to them, "These are my
words that I spoke to you while I was still
with you, that everything written about
me in the Law of Moses and the Prophets
and the Psalms must be fulfilled." [45] Then
he opened their minds to understand the
Scriptures, [46] and said to them, "Thus it is
written, that the Christ should suf-
fer and on the third day rise from
1523 the dead, [47] and that repentance
and forgiveness of sins should be pro-
claimed in his name to all nations, begin-
ning from Jerusalem. [48] You are witnesses
of these things. [49] And behold, I am send-
ing the promise of my Father upon you.
But stay in the city until you are clothed
with power from on high."

The Ascension

[50] Then he led them out as far as
Bethany, and lifting up his hands
1611 he blessed them. [51] While he
blessed them, he parted from them and
was carried up into heaven. [52] And they
worshiped him and returned to Jerusalem
with great joy, [53] and were continually in
the temple blessing God.

[1] Some manuscripts add *and some honeycomb*

Introduction to

John

Author
John the apostle

Date
About A.D. 85–95

Key People
Jesus; John the Baptist; John the apostle, the "disciple whom Jesus loved"; Simon Peter; Judas Iscariot; Nicodemus; Lazarus; Mary; Martha; Pontius Pilate; Mary Magdalene

Purpose
The purpose of John is to show that Jesus is the Christ and the Son of God, so that his readers will believe in Him and have eternal life.

Central Themes
Jesus is God; seven signs show Jesus is the Messiah; Jesus gives seven "I am" statements; Jesus gives eternal life; we walk in either light or darkness; the Holy Spirit gives life; Jesus' death is the basis of salvation; Jesus was sent from God with a mission and sends His followers to continue that mission.

Memory Verses
Jesus the Word (John 1:1–5); born of God (John 1:12–14); the new birth (John 3:5–8); God so loved the world (John 3:16–17); resurrection and life (John 11:25–26); the way to the Father (John 14:1–6)

Introduction

John was one of Jesus' 12 disciples. He is probably the person this Gospel calls "the disciple whom Jesus loved." John says he wrote his book so that people would believe that Jesus is the Christ, the Son of God, and that by believing they may have life in His name (John 20:30–31). John writes about seven of Jesus' many miracles, calling them "signs" that point to who Jesus is. The signs are: turning water into wine (John 2:1–11), healing an official's son (John 4:46–54), healing a paralyzed man (John 5:1–9), feeding 5,000 (John 6:1–15), walking on water (John 6:16–21), healing a blind man (John 9), and raising Lazarus from the dead (John 11). John also writes of seven times Jesus said "I am" about Himself, including: "I am the Bread of Life" (John 6:35), "I am the Light of the World" (John 8:12), and "I am the good Shepherd" (John 10:11). John records some long conversations Jesus had with individual people including Nicodemus (John 3:1–21) and the woman at the well (John 4:1–42). Before telling of Jesus' death on the cross and resurrection, John records Jesus' long, private teaching of His disciples after their last meal and His prayer for them and for future believers (John 14–17).

About 5 B.C.	**About A.D. 28–33**	**About A.D. 85–95**
Birth of Jesus	Jesus' ministry, death, resurrection	John's Gospel written

The Gospel According to

John

The Word Became Flesh

1 In the beginning was the Word,
and the Word was with God,
5, and the Word was God. 2 He was in
587 the beginning with God. 3 All
things were made through him, and without him was not any thing made that was
made. 4 In him was life,[1] and the
life was the light of men. 5 The light
1567 shines in the darkness, and the
darkness has not overcome it.

6 There was a man sent from God,
whose name was John. 7 He came
1301, as a witness, to bear witness about
1429 the light, that all might believe
through him. 8 He was not the light, but
came to bear witness about the light.

9 The true light, which enlightens
everyone, was coming into the
1445 world. 10 He was in the world, and
the world was made through him, yet the world did not know him. 11 He came to his own,[2] and his own people[3] did not receive him. 12 But to all who did receive him, who believed in his name, he gave the right to become children of God, 13 who were born, not of blood nor of the will of the flesh nor of the will of man, but of God.

14 And the Word became flesh and
dwelt among us, and we have seen
1339 his glory, glory as of the only Son
from the Father, full of grace and
truth. 15 (John bore witness about
him, and cried out, "This was he of
205, whom I said, 'He who comes after
1293,
1541 me ranks before me, because he
was before me.'") 16 And from his fullness we have all received, grace upon grace. 17 For the law was given through Moses; grace and truth came through Jesus Christ.

18 No one has ever seen God; the
only God,[4] who is at the Father's
1397 side,[5] he has made him known.

The Testimony of John the Baptist

19 And this is the testimony of John,
when the Jews sent priests and
1301, Levites from Jerusalem to ask him,
1429 "Who are you?" 20 He confessed,
and did not deny, but confessed, "I am not the Christ." 21 And they asked him, "What then? Are you Elijah?" He said, "I am not." "Are you the Prophet?" And he answered, "No." 22 So they said to him, "Who are you? We need to give an answer to those who sent us. What do you say about yourself?" 23 He said, "I am the voice of one crying out in the wilderness, 'Make straight[6] the way of the Lord,' as the prophet Isaiah said."

24 (Now they had been sent from the Pharisees.) 25 They asked him, "Then why are you baptizing, if you are neither the Christ, nor Elijah, nor the Prophet?" 26 John answered them, "I baptize with water, but among you stands one you do not know, 27 even he who comes after me, the strap of whose sandal I am not worthy to untie." 28 These things took place in Bethany across the Jordan, where John was baptizing.

Behold, the Lamb of God

29 The next day he saw Jesus coming toward him, and said, "Behold,
57, the Lamb of God, who takes away
1305 the sin of the world! 30 This is he of
whom I said, 'After me comes a man who ranks before me, because he was before me.' 31 I myself did not know him, but for this purpose I came baptizing with water, that he might be revealed to Israel." 32 And John bore witness: "I saw the Spirit

[1] Or *was not any thing made. That which has been made was life in him* [2] Greek *to his own things*; that is, to his own domain, or to his own people [3] *People* is implied in Greek [4] Or *the only One, who is God*; some manuscripts *the only Son* [5] Greek *in the bosom of the Father* [6] Or *crying out, 'In the wilderness make straight*

descend from heaven like a dove, and it
remained on him. 33 I myself did not know
him, but he who sent me to baptize with
water said to me, 'He on whom you see the
Spirit descend and remain, this is he who
baptizes with the Holy Spirit.' 34 And I have
seen and have borne witness that this is
the Son of God."

Jesus Calls the First Disciples

35 The next day again John was
standing with two of his disciples,
1313 36 and he looked at Jesus as he
walked by and said, "Behold, the Lamb of
God!" 37 The two disciples heard him say
this, and they followed Jesus. 38 Jesus
turned and saw them following and said
to them, "What are you seeking?" And
they said to him, "Rabbi" (which means
Teacher), "where are you staying?" 39 He
said to them, "Come and you will see." So
they came and saw where he was staying,
and they stayed with him that day, for it
was about the tenth hour.[1] 40 One of the
two who heard John speak and fol-
lowed Jesus[2] was Andrew, Simon
1467 Peter's brother. 41 He first found his
own brother Simon and said to him, "We
have found the Messiah" (which means
Christ). 42 He brought him to Jesus. Jesus
looked at him and said, "So you are Simon
the son of John? You shall be called
Cephas" (which means Peter[3]).

Jesus Calls Philip and Nathanael

43 The next day Jesus decided to go
to Galilee. He found Philip and said
1537 to him, "Follow me." 44 Now Philip
was from Bethsaida, the city of Andrew
and Peter. 45 Philip found Nathanael and
said to him, "We have found him of
whom Moses in the Law and also the
prophets wrote, Jesus of Nazareth, the son
of Joseph." 46 Nathanael said to him, "Can
anything good come out of Nazareth?"
Philip said to him, "Come and see." 47 Jesus
saw Nathanael coming toward him and
said of him, "Behold, an Israelite indeed, in
whom there is no deceit!" 48 Nathanael said
to him, "How do you know me?" Jesus an-
swered him, "Before Philip called you,
when you were under the fig tree, I saw
you." 49 Nathanael answered him,
"Rabbi, you are the Son of God! You
75 are the King of Israel!" 50 Jesus an-
swered him, "Because I said to you, 'I saw
you under the fig tree,' do you believe? You
will see greater things than these." 51 And
he said to him, "Truly, truly, I say to
you,[4] you will see heaven opened,
1537 and the angels of God ascending
and descending on the Son of Man."

CHARACTER PROFILE

ANDREW

Andrew was a fisherman who listened eagerly to the teaching of John the Baptist. John told people that they must repent and get ready for the promised Messiah. When John called Jesus the Lamb of God, Andrew knew that he must now follow Jesus the Messiah. Andrew found his brother, Simon Peter, and brought him to Jesus, too. So Andrew and his brother Simon Peter became two of the 12 disciples, who were Jesus' closest friends and helpers.

1313

[1] That is, about 4 P.M. [2] Greek *him* [3] *Cephas* and *Peter* are from the word for *rock* in Aramaic and Greek, respectively [4] The Greek for *you* is plural; twice in this verse

Jesus Calls Philip and Nathanael

While Jesus was traveling to Galilee, He found Philip who came from the town of Bethsaida. Jesus said to him, "Follow Me."

Philip was so excited about meeting Jesus that he hurried to look for his friend Nathanael. He wanted to tell Nathanael that he had found the One about whom Moses and the prophets had written. Philip discovered his friend Nathanael sitting under a fig tree.

When Philip told Nathanael that the Messiah was Jesus of Nazareth, the son of Joseph, Nathanael asked, "Can anything good come out of Nazareth?" Nathanael did not expect that anyone important could come from such a little town.

Philip invited Nathanael to "come and see."

When Jesus saw Nathanael, He called him "an Israelite, in whom there is no deceit."

Nathanael was surprised! How did Jesus know that he was an Israelite and a truthful man before they had ever met? Nathanael asked, "How do You know me?"

Jesus told him, "Before Philip called to you, when you were under the fig tree, I saw you."

Now Nathanael was even more amazed! How could Jesus have seen him sitting under that fig tree? Nathanael said to

Jesus, "You are the Son of God! You are the King of Israel!" Nathanael was right!

Jesus replied, "Because I said to you, 'I saw you under the fig tree,' do you believe? You will see greater things than these. You will see heaven opened, and the angels of God ascending and descending on the Son of Man."

Nathanael and Philip followed Jesus when He called them. They became His disciples, and they saw Jesus do many miraculous things. Jesus calls us to follow Him, too—and one day we will see all the amazing wonders of heaven.

SEEK and FIND

WHERE TO FIND THE STORY

John 1:43–51

KEY BIBLE VERSE

"[Jesus] said to him, 'Truly, truly, I say to you, you will see heaven opened, and the angels of God ascending and descending on the Son of Man.' " (John 1:51)

THREE KEY QUESTIONS

- What did Philip and Nathanael do when Jesus called them?
- Who did Nathanael say that Jesus was?
- What does Jesus call us to do and what does this mean?

RELATED BIBLE READINGS

Genesis 28:12; John 12:20–22; 21:1–2

The Wedding at Cana

2 On the third day there was a
wedding at Cana in Galilee, and
1541 the mother of Jesus was there.
2 Jesus also was invited to the wedding with
his disciples. 3 When the wine ran out, the
mother of Jesus said to him, "They have no
wine." 4 And Jesus said to her, "Woman,
what does this have to do with me? My
hour has not yet come." 5 His mother said to
the servants, "Do whatever he tells you."

6 Now there were six stone water jars
there for the Jewish rites of purification,
each holding twenty or thirty gallons.[1]
7 Jesus said to the servants, "Fill the jars
with water." And they filled them up to the
brim. 8 And he said to them, "Now draw
some out and take it to the master of the
feast." So they took it. 9 When the master
of the feast tasted the water now become
wine, and did not know where it came
from (though the servants who had drawn
the water knew), the master of the feast
called the bridegroom 10 and said to him,
"Everyone serves the good wine first, and
when people have drunk freely, then the
poor wine. But you have kept the good
wine until now." 11 This, the first of
his signs, Jesus did at Cana in
1541 Galilee, and manifested his glory.
And his disciples believed in him.

12 After this he went down to Capernaum, with his mother and his brothers[2]
and his disciples, and they stayed there
for a few days.

Jesus Cleanses the Temple

13 The Passover of the Jews was at
hand, and Jesus went up to
1545 Jerusalem. 14 In the temple he
found those who were selling oxen and
sheep and pigeons, and the money-changers sitting there. 15 And making a
whip of cords, he drove them all out of the
temple, with the sheep and oxen. And he
poured out the coins of the money-changers and overturned their tables. 16 And he
told those who sold the pigeons, "Take
these things away; do not make my
Father's house a house of trade." 17 His disciples remembered that it was written,
"Zeal for your house will consume me."

18 So the Jews said to him, "What sign
do you show us for doing these things?"
19 Jesus answered them, "Destroy this
temple, and in three days I will raise it up."
20 The Jews then said, "It has taken forty-six years to build this temple, and will you
raise it up in three days?" 21 But he was
speaking about the temple of his body.
22 When therefore he was raised from the
dead, his disciples remembered that he had
said this, and they believed the Scripture
and the word that Jesus had spoken.

Jesus Knows What Is in Man

23 Now when he was in Jerusalem at
the Passover Feast, many believed in his
name when they saw the signs that he
was doing. 24 But Jesus on his part did not
entrust himself to them, because he knew
all people 25 and needed no one to bear
witness about man, for he himself knew
what was in man.

You Must Be Born Again

3 Now there was a man of the
Pharisees named Nicodemus,
1549 a ruler of the Jews. 2 This man came
to Jesus[3] by night and said to him,
"Rabbi, we know that you are a
1541 teacher come from God, for no one
can do these signs that you do unless God
is with him." 3 Jesus answered him, "Truly,
truly, I say to you, unless one is born
again[4] he cannot see the kingdom of God."
4 Nicodemus said to him, "How can a man
be born when he is old? Can he enter a
second time into his mother's womb and
be born?" 5 Jesus answered, "Truly, truly, I
say to you, unless one is born of water and
the Spirit, he cannot enter the kingdom of

[1] Greek *two or three measures* (*metrētas*); a *metrētēs* was about 10 gallons or 35 liters [2] Or *brothers and sisters*. The plural Greek word *adelphoi* (translated "brothers") refers to siblings in a family. In New Testament usage, depending on the context, *adelphoi* may refer either to *brothers* or to *brothers and sisters* [3] Greek *him* [4] Or *from above*; the Greek is purposely ambiguous and can mean both *again* and *from above*; also verse 7

Jesus Changes Water Into Wine

Not too long after Jesus' cousin John had baptized him, Jesus attended a wedding celebration in a town in Galilee called Cana. Jesus went there with His disciples and His mother, Mary. A marriage celebration was a joyful occasion that lasted a long time, while the guests enjoyed wonderful foods and drank wine. This feast lasted so long that the host ran into a problem: There was no more wine left to serve his guests!

Mary told Jesus about the trouble: "They have no wine."

Jesus asked her, "What does this have to do with Me? My hour has not yet come." Jesus knew that His public ministry of miracles and healing had not yet begun.

But Mary trusted Jesus. She told the servants, "Do whatever He tells you."

Nearby there were six large stone water pots that could each hold between 20 to 30 gallons. The Jews used this water for their religious ceremonies.

Jesus said to the servants, "Fill the jars with water." The obedient servants filled them up to the brim.

Then Jesus said to them, "Now draw some out and take it to the master of the feast." The surprised servants obeyed again.

When the master of the feast tasted what was in the cup, he did not taste water. He tasted wine! The master of the feast did not know where the good wine had come from, but the humble servants who had filled the big jars with water knew!

After tasting the wine, the master of the feast talked to the man who was getting married. He said, "Everyone serves the good wine first, and when people have drunk freely, then the poor wine. But you have kept the good wine until now."

This was Jesus' first miracle. It showed Jesus' glory to His disciples, and they believed in Him.

Jesus did many other miracles, so that people would know that He was not just an ordinary man—He was God's Son, who had come to be their Savior. Jesus' miracles are "signs" that point to who He is, the Son of God. The Gospel writers wrote about these signs so we can see Jesus' glory too, and believe in Him as His disciples did.

SEEK and FIND

WHERE TO FIND THE STORY

John 2:1–11

KEY BIBLE VERSE

"This, the first of his signs, Jesus did at Cana in Galilee, and manifested his glory. And his disciples believed in him." (John 2:11)

THREE KEY QUESTIONS

- What problem happened at the wedding party and what did Jesus do?
- What did the disciples do when they saw the miracle and Jesus' glory?
- What should we do when we read about Jesus' miracles and His glory in the gospels?

RELATED BIBLE READINGS
John 1:14; 3:2; 20:30–31; Acts 2:22

God. 6 That which is born of the flesh is flesh, and that which is born of the Spirit is spirit.[1] 7 Do not marvel that I said to you, 'You[2] must be born again.' 8 The wind[3] blows where it wishes, and you hear its sound, but you do not know where it comes from or where it goes. So it is with everyone who is born of the Spirit."

9 Nicodemus said to him, "How can these things be?" 10 Jesus answered him, "Are you the teacher of Israel and yet you do not understand these things? 11 Truly, truly, I say to you, we speak of what we know, and bear witness to what we have seen, but you[4] do not receive our testimony. 12 If I have told you earthly things and you do not believe, how can you believe if I tell you heavenly things? 13 No one has ascended into heaven except he
who descended from heaven, the
Son of Man.[5] 14 And as Moses lifted
279 up the serpent in the wilderness,
so must the Son of Man be lifted
up, 15 that whoever believes in him
279 may have eternal life.[6]

For God So Loved the World

16 "For God so loved the world,[7] that
he gave his only Son, that whoever
1549 believes in him should not perish
but have eternal life. 17 For God did not send his Son into the world to condemn the world, but in order that the world might be saved through him. 18 Whoever believes in him is not condemned, but whoever does not believe is condemned already, because he has not believed in the name of the only Son of God. 19 And this is the judgment: the light has come into the world, and people loved the darkness rather than the light because their works were evil. 20 For everyone who does wicked things hates the light and does not come to the light, lest his works should be exposed. 21 But whoever does what is true comes to the light, so that it may be clearly seen that his works have been carried out in God."

John the Baptist Exalts Christ

22 After this Jesus and his disciples went into the Judean countryside, and he remained there with them and was baptizing. 23 John also was baptizing at Aenon near Salim, because water was plentiful there, and people were coming and being baptized 24 (for John had not yet been put in prison).

25 Now a discussion arose between some of John's disciples and a Jew over purification. 26 And they came to John and said to him, "Rabbi, he who was with you across the Jordan, to whom you bore witness—look, he is baptizing, and all are going to him." 27 John answered, "A person cannot receive even one thing unless it is given him from heaven. 28 You yourselves bear me witness, that I said, 'I am not the Christ, but I have been sent before him.' 29 The one who has the bride is the bridegroom. The friend of the bridegroom, who stands and hears him, rejoices greatly at the bridegroom's voice. Therefore this joy of mine is now complete. 30 He must increase, but I must decrease."[8]

[1] The same Greek word means both *wind* and *spirit* [2] The Greek for *you* is plural here [3] The same Greek word means both *wind* and *spirit* [4] The Greek for *you* is plural here; also four times in verse 12 [5] Some manuscripts add *who is in heaven* [6] Some interpreters hold that the quotation ends at verse 15 [7] Or *For this is how God loved the world* [8] Some interpreters hold that the quotation continues through verse 36

Jesus Clears the Temple

Jesus walked to Jerusalem for the festival of Passover. During the Passover celebration, the Jewish people ate special foods and worshiped God by offering sacrifices at the temple. They remembered a time long ago when God led Moses and His people out of slavery in Egypt.

When Jesus got to Jerusalem, He went into the temple courts. In the courtyard, He saw men selling animals. But the men were charging people too much for the animals. And there were money-changers, who cheated the people when they exchanged their money.

Jesus was angry and very upset at the people who were cheating those who came to the temple! The temple was supposed to be a place where people could worship and honor God the Father. The cheating merchants dishonored God with their dishonest sales and unfair money exchange.

Jesus told the people who were buying and selling to stop. He commanded, "Take these things away; do not make My Father's house a house of trade!" When they didn't do what Jesus said, He knocked their tables over, poured out their coins, and drove out the animals.

But when they saw what Jesus did, some of the people questioned Jesus. "What sign do You show us for doing these things?" They didn't believe Jesus had the authority to do these things, and they wanted Jesus to do a miracle to prove who He was.

So Jesus told the people about the great miracle that was going to happen very soon. Jesus said, "Destroy this temple, and in three days I will raise it up." The people did not understand. They thought Jesus was talking about the temple building, which had taken many years to build. But Jesus was talking about Himself as God's temple. Jesus knew that His life was going to be destroyed—that soon He would die on the cross to save us from sin, and rise again on the third day.

Later, when Jesus rose from the dead, His disciples remembered these words Jesus had said about raising up the temple in three days. They knew Jesus' resurrection was a great sign, showing that He truly is the Son of God and that all authority belongs to Him.

SEEK and FIND

WHERE TO FIND THE STORY

John 2:13–22

KEY BIBLE VERSE

"Let us offer to God acceptable worship, with reverence and awe." (Hebrews 12:28)

THREE KEY QUESTIONS

- Why was Jesus upset by what was happening in the temple?
- What kind of place was the temple supposed to be?
- How did Jesus show that He truly was the Son of God and that all authority belongs to him?

RELATED BIBLE READINGS
Psalm 69:9; Matthew 21:12–13; Mark 11:15–18; Luke 19:45–46; Acts 17:31; Romans 1:3–4

31 He who comes from above is above all. He who is of the earth belongs to the earth and speaks in an earthly way. He who comes from heaven is above all. 32 He bears witness to what he has seen and heard, yet no one receives his testimony. 33 Whoever receives his testimony sets his seal to this, that God is true. 34 For he whom God has sent utters the words of God, for he gives the Spirit without measure. 35 The Father loves the Son and has given all things into his hand. 36 Whoever believes in the Son has eternal life; whoever does not obey the Son shall not see life, but the wrath of God remains on him.

Jesus and the Woman of Samaria

4 Now when Jesus learned that
the Pharisees had heard that
1553 Jesus was making and baptizing
more disciples than John 2 (although Jesus himself did not baptize, but only his disciples), 3 he left Judea and departed again for Galilee. 4 And he had to pass through Samaria. 5 So he came to a town of Samaria called Sychar, near the field that Jacob had given to his son Joseph. 6 Jacob's well was there; so Jesus, wearied as he was from his journey, was sitting beside the well. It was about the sixth hour.[1]

7 A woman from Samaria came to
draw water. Jesus said to her, "Give
167, me a drink." 8 (For his disciples had
1487 gone away into the city to buy
food.) 9 The Samaritan woman said to him, "How is it that you, a Jew, ask for a drink from me, a woman of Samaria?" (For Jews have no dealings with Samaritans.) 10 Jesus answered her, "If you knew the gift of God, and who it is that is saying to you, 'Give me a drink,' you would have asked him, and he would have given you living water." 11 The woman said to him, "Sir, you have nothing to draw water with, and the well is deep. Where do you get that living water? 12 Are you greater than our father Jacob? He gave us the well and drank from it himself, as did his sons and his livestock." 13 Jesus said to her, "Everyone who drinks of this water will be thirsty again,
14 but whoever drinks of the water
that I will give him will never be
1553 thirsty again.[2] The water that I will
give him will become in him a spring of water welling up to eternal life." 15 The woman said to him, "Sir, give me this water, so that I will not be thirsty or have to come here to draw water."

16 Jesus said to her, "Go, call your husband, and come here." 17 The woman answered him, "I have no husband." Jesus said to her, "You are right in saying, 'I have no husband'; 18 for you have had five husbands, and the one you now have is not your husband. What you have said is true." 19 The woman said to him, "Sir, I perceive that you are a prophet. 20 Our fathers worshiped on this mountain, but you say that in Jerusalem is the place where people ought to worship." 21 Jesus said to her, "Woman, believe me, the hour is coming when neither on this mountain nor in Jerusalem will you worship the Father. 22 You worship what you do not know; we

[1] That is, about noon [2] Greek *forever*

Jesus Teaches Nicodemus

There was a man named Nicodemus, who was one of the leaders of the Jewish people. Late one night, Nicodemus went to visit Jesus. "We know that You are a teacher come from God," said Nicodemus to Jesus. "No one can do these signs that You do unless God is with Him." Nicodemus had seen Jesus' signs and miracles, and he wanted to know more about who Jesus really was.

Jesus told Nicodemus, "Truly, truly, I say to you, unless one is born again he cannot see the kingdom of God."

Nicodemus didn't understand. He thought Jesus meant he had to become a little baby inside his mother and be born a second time! But Jesus explained that He meant a person must be born of water and the Holy Spirit. "That which is born of the flesh is flesh," Jesus said, "and that which is born of the Spirit is spirit. Do not marvel that I said to you, 'You must be born again.'"

Nicodemus had already been born once. But Jesus was telling Nicodemus that he must be "born again," this time into God's family. Jesus told Nicodemus that people who were born of the Spirit would believe in Jesus.

To help Nicodemus understand, Jesus reminded him of a true story in the Old Testament. There was a time once, long before, when the people of Israel had rebelled against God. Because of this, God brought a terrible plague of poisonous snakes, who killed many people with their terrible bites.

But then God told Moses to make a sculpture of a snake and put it on the top of a pole. God healed every person who would fix his eyes on the snake on the pole. Jesus explained: "As Moses lifted up the serpent in the wilderness, so must the Son of Man be lifted up." And whoever believes in him will have eternal life.

Jesus is "the Son of Man" who was "lifted up" on the cross, and everyone who trusts in Him will be "born again" by God's Spirit and have "eternal life."

Then Jesus explained the reason to Nicodemus, "For God so loved the world, that He gave His only Son, that whoever believes in Him should not perish but have eternal life." Because of God's great love, He made a way for people to be born into His family forever. Through faith in Jesus, God forgives our sins for Jesus' sake and promises to take us to live with Him forever in heaven.

SEEK and FIND

WHERE TO FIND THE STORY

John 3:1–16

KEY BIBLE VERSE

"For God so loved the world, that he gave his only Son, that whoever believes in him should not perish but have eternal life." (John 3:16)

THREE KEY QUESTIONS

- What did Jesus mean when He told Nicodemus "You must be born again"?
- What did Jesus mean when He said that He must be "lifted up"?
- Why did God send His only Son into the world and what does God promise to all who believe in Jesus?

RELATED BIBLE READINGS

Numbers 21:6–9; Titus 3:4–7; 1 Peter 1:3; 1 John 5:1, 4, 18

worship what we know, for salvation is from the Jews. 23 But the hour is coming, and is now here, when the true worshipers will worship the Father in spirit and truth, for the Father is seeking such people to worship him. 24 God is spirit, and those who worship him must worship in spirit and truth." 25 The woman said to him, "I know that Messiah is coming (he who is called Christ). When he comes, he will tell us all things." 26 Jesus said to her, "I who speak to you am he."

27 Just then his disciples came back. They marveled that he was talking with a woman, but no one said, "What do you seek?" or, "Why are you talking with her?" 28 So the woman left her water jar and went away into town and said to the people, 29 "Come, see a man who told me all that I ever did. Can this be the Christ?" 30 They went out of the town and were coming to him.

31 Meanwhile the disciples were urging him, saying, "Rabbi, eat."
1453
32 But he said to them, "I have food to eat that you do not know about." 33 So the disciples said to one another, "Has anyone brought him something to eat?" 34 Jesus said to them, "My food is to do the will of him who sent me and to accomplish his work. 35 Do you not say, 'There are yet four months, then comes the harvest'? Look, I tell you, lift up
1483
your eyes, and see that the fields are white for harvest. 36 Already the one who reaps is receiving wages and gathering fruit for eternal life, so that sower and reaper may rejoice together. 37 For here the saying holds true, 'One sows and another reaps.' 38 I sent you to reap that for which you did not labor. Others have labored, and you have entered into their labor."

39 Many Samaritans from that town believed in him because of the woman's testimony, "He told me all that I ever did." 40 So when the Samaritans came to him, they asked him to stay with them, and he stayed there two days. 41 And many more believed because of his word. 42 They said to the woman, "It is no longer because of what you said that we believe, for we have heard for ourselves, and we know that this is indeed the Savior of the world."

43 After the two days he departed for Galilee. 44 (For Jesus himself had testified that a prophet has no honor in his own hometown.) 45 So when he came to Galilee, the Galileans welcomed him, having seen

Jesus and the Samaritan Woman

Jesus and His disciples walked back to Galilee on the dusty roads. Jesus was tired from the hot sun and the long walk, so He stopped to rest by a well, outside the town of Samaria. Jesus sat down by the well while His disciples went into the town to get some food.

Soon a woman came to the well with a large jar to get water for her daily washing and cooking. As she pulled her full water jar up out of the well, Jesus asked her for a drink.

The woman was surprised, and asked, "How is it that You, a Jew, ask for a drink from me, a woman of Samaria?" In those days long ago, the Jewish people and the Samaritans would have nothing to do with each other.

"If you knew the gift of God," Jesus answered, "and who it is that is saying to you, 'Give Me a drink,' you would have asked Him, and He would have given you living water."

The woman didn't understand what Jesus meant. She could see that Jesus did not have a jar or bucket to let down into the deep well. "Where" she asked, "do You get that living water?"

Jesus replied, "Everyone who drinks of this water will be thirsty again, but whoever drinks of the water that I will give him will never be thirsty again. The water that I will give him will become in him a spring of water welling up to eternal life."

Now the woman was really interested! "Sir," she said, "give me this water, so that I will not be thirsty or have to come here to draw water."

Then Jesus told the woman that He knew about the many sins she had committed. She was sure Jesus must be a prophet, a person who spoke truths from God. She said, "I know the Messiah is coming (He who is called Christ). When He comes, He will tell us all things." The woman was amazed when Jesus said, "I who speak to you am He."

Then the woman knew she had met the Messiah! In her excitement, she left her water jar and ran all the way to town to spread the great news. She told the people, "Come, see a man who told me all that I ever did. Can this be the Christ?"

The people were curious and came to see Jesus. Jesus stayed to teach them for two more days, and many of the Samaritans believed in Jesus. "We have heard for ourselves," the people said, "and we know that this is indeed the Savior of the world."

This true story from John's gospel teaches something wonderful and amazing: No matter where we are from or what we have done, the grace of Jesus Christ saves us through faith in Christ. He saves us from our sins and gives us the refreshing water of eternal life.

SEEK and FIND

WHERE TO FIND THE STORY
John 4:1–44

KEY BIBLE VERSE

"Whoever drinks of the water that I will give him will never be thirsty again. The water that I will give him will become in him a spring of water welling up to eternal life." (John 4:14)

THREE KEY QUESTIONS

- What did Jesus ask the Samaritan woman to give Him, and what did Jesus offer to give to her?
- Why did the Samaritan woman need the "living water"?
- What is the wonderful and amazing thing that this true story teaches us?

RELATED BIBLE READINGS

Isaiah 55:1; John 6:35; 7:37–39; Revelation 7:16

all that he had done in Jerusalem at the feast. For they too had gone to the feast.

Jesus Heals an Official's Son

46 So he came again to Cana in Galilee, where he had made the water wine. And at Capernaum there was an official whose son was ill. 47 When this man heard that Jesus had come from Judea to Galilee, he went to him and asked him to come down and heal his son, for he was at the point of death. 48 So Jesus said to him, "Unless you see signs and wonders you will not believe." 49 The official said to him, "Sir, come down before my child dies." 50 Jesus said to him, "Go; your son will live." The man believed the word that Jesus spoke to him and went on his way. 51 As he was going down, his servants[1] met him and told him that his son was recovering. 52 So he asked them the hour when he began to get better, and they said to him, "Yesterday at the seventh hour[2] the fever left him." 53 The father knew that was the hour when Jesus had said to him, "Your son will live." And he himself believed, and all his household. 54 This was now the second sign that Jesus did when he had come from Judea to Galilee.

The Healing at the Pool on the Sabbath

1619

5 After this there was a feast of the Jews, and Jesus went up to Jerusalem.

2 Now there is in Jerusalem by the Sheep Gate a pool, in Aramaic[3] called Bethesda,[4] which has five roofed colonnades. 3 In these lay a multitude of invalids—blind, lame, and paralyzed.[5] 5 One man was there who had been an invalid for thirty-eight years. 6 When Jesus saw him lying there and knew that he had already been there a long time, he said to him, "Do you want to be healed?" 7 The sick man answered him, "Sir, I have no one to put me into the pool when the water is stirred up, and while I am going another steps down before me." 8 Jesus said to him, "Get up, take up your bed, and walk." 9 And at once the man was healed, and he took up his bed and walked.

[1] Greek *bondservants* [2] That is, at 1 P.M. [3] Or *Hebrew* [4] Some manuscripts *Bethsaida* [5] Some manuscripts insert, wholly or in part, *waiting for the moving of the water; 4for an angel of the Lord went down at certain seasons into the pool, and stirred the water: whoever stepped in first after the stirring of the water was healed of whatever disease he had*

Now that day was the Sabbath. 10 So the Jews said to the man who had been healed, "It is the Sabbath, and it is not lawful for you to take up your bed." 11 But he answered them, "The man who healed me, that man said to me, 'Take up your bed, and walk.'" 12 They asked him, "Who is the man who said to you, 'Take up your bed and walk'?" 13 Now the man who had been healed did not know who it was, for Jesus had withdrawn, as there was a crowd in the place. 14 Afterward Jesus found him in the temple and said to him, "See, you are well! Sin no more, that nothing worse may happen to you." 15 The man went away and told the Jews that it was Jesus who had healed him. 16 And this was why the Jews were persecuting Jesus, because he was doing these things on the Sabbath. 17 But Jesus answered them, "My Father is working until now, and I am working."

Jesus Is Equal with God

18 This was why the Jews were seeking all the more to kill him, because not only was he breaking the Sabbath, but he was even calling God his own Father, making himself equal with God.

The Authority of the Son

19 So Jesus said to them, "Truly,
truly, I say to you, the Son can do
1389 nothing of his own accord, but
only what he sees the Father doing. For
whatever the Father[1] does, that the Son
does likewise. 20 For the Father loves the
Son and shows him all that he himself is
doing. And greater works than these will
he show him, so that you may marvel.
21 For as the Father raises the dead
and gives them life, so also the Son
1389 gives life to whom he will. 22 The
Father judges no one, but has given
all judgment to the Son, 23 that all
1577 may honor the Son, just as they
honor the Father. Whoever does not
honor the Son does not honor the Father
who sent him. 24 Truly, truly, I say to you, whoever hears my word and believes him who sent me has eternal life. He does not come into judgment, but has passed from death to life.

25 "Truly, truly, I say to you, an hour is coming, and is now here, when the dead will hear the voice of the Son of God, and those who hear will live. 26 For as the Father has life in himself, so he has granted the Son also to have life in himself. 27 And he has given him authority to execute judgment, because he is the Son of Man. 28 Do not marvel at this, for an hour is coming when all who are in the tombs will hear his voice 29 and come out, those who have done good to the resurrection of life, and those who have done evil to the resurrection of judgment.

Witnesses to Jesus

30 "I can do nothing on my own. As I hear, I judge, and my judgment is just, because I seek not my own will but the will of him who sent me. 31 If I alone bear witness about myself, my testimony is not deemed true. 32 There is another who bears witness about me, and I know that the testimony that he bears about me is true. 33 You sent to John, and he has borne witness to the truth. 34 Not that the testimony that I receive is from man, but I say these things so that you may be saved. 35 He was a burning and shining lamp, and you were willing to rejoice for a while in his light. 36 But the testimony that I have is greater than that of John. For the works that the Father has given me to accomplish, the very works that I am doing, bear witness about me that the Father has sent me. 37 And the Father who sent me has himself borne witness about me. His voice you have never heard, his form you have never seen, 38 and you do not have his word abiding in you, for you do not believe the one whom he has sent. 39 You search the Scriptures because you think that in them you have eternal life; and it is

[1] Greek *he*

they that bear witness about me, 40 yet you
refuse to come to me that you may have
life. 41 I do not receive glory from people.
42 But I know that you do not have the love
of God within you. 43 I have come in my
Father's name, and you do not receive me.
If another comes in his own name, you
will receive him. 44 How can you believe,
when you receive glory from one another
and do not seek the glory that comes from
the only God? 45 Do not think that I will
accuse you to the Father. There is one who
accuses you: Moses, on whom you have
set your hope. 46 For if you believed Moses,
you would believe me; for he wrote of me.
47 But if you do not believe his writings,
how will you believe my words?"

Jesus Feeds the Five Thousand

6 After this Jesus went away to
the other side of the Sea of
1559 Galilee, which is the Sea of Tiberias.
2 And a large crowd was following him,
because they saw the signs that he was
doing on the sick. 3 Jesus went up on the
mountain, and there he sat down with his
disciples. 4 Now the Passover, the feast of
the Jews, was at hand. 5 Lifting up his eyes,
then, and seeing that a large crowd was
coming toward him, Jesus said to Philip,
"Where are we to buy bread, so that these
people may eat?" 6 He said this to test him,
for he himself knew what he would do.
7 Philip answered him, "Two hundred
denarii[1] would not buy enough bread for
each of them to get a little." 8 One of his
disciples, Andrew, Simon Peter's brother,
said to him, 9 "There is a boy here who has
five barley loaves and two fish, but what
are they for so many?" 10 Jesus said, "Have
the people sit down." Now there was
much grass in the place. So the men sat
down, about five thousand in number.
11 Jesus then took the loaves, and when he
had given thanks, he distributed them to
those who were seated. So also the fish, as
much as they wanted. 12 And when they
had eaten their fill, he told his disciples,
"Gather up the leftover fragments, that
nothing may be lost." 13 So they gathered
them up and filled twelve baskets with
fragments from the five barley loaves left
by those who had eaten. 14 When the peo-
ple saw the sign that he had done, they
said, "This is indeed the Prophet who is to
come into the world!"

15 Perceiving then that they were about
to come and take him by force to make
him king, Jesus withdrew again to the
mountain by himself.

Jesus Walks on Water

16 When evening came, his disci-
ples went down to the sea, 17 got
1331, into a boat, and started across the
1385 sea to Capernaum. It was now
dark, and Jesus had not yet come to them.
18 The sea became rough because a strong
wind was blowing. 19 When they had
rowed about three or four miles,[2] they saw
Jesus walking on the sea and coming near
the boat, and they were frightened. 20 But
he said to them, "It is I; do not be afraid."
21 Then they were glad to take him into the
boat, and immediately the boat was at the
land to which they were going.

I Am the Bread of Life

22 On the next day the crowd that
remained on the other side of the
1559 sea saw that there had been only
one boat there, and that Jesus had not
entered the boat with his disciples, but
that his disciples had gone away alone.
23 Other boats from Tiberias came near the
place where they had eaten the bread after
the Lord had given thanks. 24 So when the
crowd saw that Jesus was not there, nor
his disciples, they themselves got into the
boats and went to Capernaum, seeking
Jesus.

25 When they found him on the
other side of the sea, they said to
167 him, "Rabbi, when did you come
here?" 26 Jesus answered them, "Truly,

[1] A *denarius* was a day's wage for a laborer [2] Greek *twenty-five or thirty stadia*; a *stadion* was about 607 feet or 185 meters

Jesus Feeds Five Thousand People

The news was spreading about Jesus' miraculous ministry of healing the sick. Many who were ill or disabled followed Jesus because they wanted Jesus to heal them. Many others followed Jesus because they wanted to hear more about His wise and authoritative teaching. So a great crowd of people followed Jesus from one side of the Sea of Galilee to the other.

When Jesus reached the other side of the Sea of Galilee, He went up a mountainside and sat down with His disciples. Jesus looked out at the huge crowd that had followed Him. He asked Philip, one of His disciples, where they could buy bread for these people to eat.

Philip knew that Jesus and the disciples didn't have enough money to buy even a tiny bit of bread for each person. The crowd was enormous—thousands of people!

Then Andrew, another one of Jesus' disciples, spoke up. "There is a boy here who has five barley loaves and two fish," Andrew said, but what good are these with so many people?

Of course, Jesus knew all along what He was going to do. He told the disciples to have all the people sit down on the grass. About 5,000 men sat down, plus all the women and children. Jesus took the boy's bread, gave thanks, and began giving it out to everyone. Then He did the same with the fish.

Miraculously, the food did not run out, and the people had as much to eat as they wanted.

When the 5,000 men, plus women and children, had finished eating, there was still lots of food left over! The disciples picked up 12 baskets of leftover bread and fish.

After the people saw this miraculous sign of Jesus' power and authority, they said, "This is indeed the Prophet who is to come into the world!" Only God's power could turn five barley loaves and two fish into such a feast!

God has power over all things in heaven and on earth. He is the One who provides us with food and everything else we need every day of our life. But the greatest treasure God gives to us is the gift of His Son, Jesus our Savior.

SEEK and FIND

WHERE TO FIND THE STORY

John 6:1–14

KEY BIBLE VERSE

"For the bread of God is he who comes down from heaven and gives life to the world." (John 6:33)

THREE KEY QUESTIONS

- Why were so many people following Jesus?
- How did Jesus feed all the thousands of people?
- Who provides our food and everything we need every day?

RELATED BIBLE READINGS

Matthew 14:13–21; Mark 6:32–44; Luke 9:10–17; John 6:22–59

truly, I say to you, you are seeking me,
not because you saw signs, but because
you ate your fill of the loaves. 27 Do not
labor for the food that perishes, but for
the food that endures to eternal life,
which the Son of Man will give to you.
For on him God the Father has set his
seal." 28 Then they said to him, "What
must we do, to be doing the works of
God?" 29 Jesus answered them, "This is the
work of God, that you believe in him
whom he has sent." 30 So they said to him,
"Then what sign do you do, that we may
see and believe you? What work do you
perform? 31 Our fathers ate the manna in
the wilderness; as it is written, 'He gave
them bread from heaven to eat.'" 32 Jesus
then said to them, "Truly, truly, I say to
you, it was not Moses who gave you the
bread from heaven, but my Father gives
you the true bread from heaven. 33 For the
bread of God is he who comes
down from heaven and gives life
1559 to the world." 34 They said to him,
"Sir, give us this bread always."

35 Jesus said to them, "I am the
bread of life; whoever comes to me
167 shall not hunger, and whoever
believes in me shall never thirst.
36 But I said to you that you have
1553 seen me and yet do not believe.
37 All that the Father gives me will come to
me, and whoever comes to me I will never
cast out. 38 For I have come down from
heaven, not to do my own will but
the will of him who sent me. 39 And
1453 this is the will of him who sent me,
that I should lose nothing of all that he has
given me, but raise it up on the last day.
40 For this is the will of my Father, that
everyone who looks on the Son and
believes in him should have eternal life,
and I will raise him up on the last day."

41 So the Jews grumbled about him,
because he said, "I am the bread that came
down from heaven." 42 They said, "Is not
this Jesus, the son of Joseph, whose father
and mother we know? How does he now
say, 'I have come down from heaven'?"
43 Jesus answered them, "Do not grumble
among yourselves. 44 No one can come to
me unless the Father who sent me draws
him. And I will raise him up on the last day.
45 It is written in the Prophets, 'And they
will all be taught by God.' Everyone who
has heard and learned from the Father
comes to me— 46 not that anyone has seen
the Father except he who is from God; he
has seen the Father. 47 Truly, truly, I say to
you, whoever believes has eternal life. 48 I
am the bread of life. 49 Your fathers ate the
manna in the wilderness, and they died.
50 This is the bread that comes down from
heaven, so that one may eat of it and not
die. 51 I am the living bread that came down
from heaven. If anyone eats of this bread,
he will live forever. And the bread that I will
give for the life of the world is my flesh."

52 The Jews then disputed among them-
selves, saying, "How can this man give us
his flesh to eat?" 53 So Jesus said to them,
"Truly, truly, I say to you, unless you eat
the flesh of the Son of Man and drink his
blood, you have no life in you. 54 Whoever
feeds on my flesh and drinks my blood
has eternal life, and I will raise him up on
the last day. 55 For my flesh is true food,
and my blood is true drink. 56 Whoever
feeds on my flesh and drinks my blood
abides in me, and I in him. 57 As the liv-
ing Father sent me, and I live because of
the Father, so whoever feeds on me, he
also will live because of me. 58 This is the
bread that came down from heaven, not
like the bread[1] the fathers ate and died.
Whoever feeds on this bread will live
forever." 59 Jesus[2] said these things in the
synagogue, as he taught at Capernaum.

The Words of Eternal Life

60 When many of his disciples heard
it, they said, "This is a hard saying; who
can listen to it?" 61 But Jesus, knowing in
himself that his disciples were grumbling

[1] Greek lacks *the bread* [2] Greek *He*

about this, said to them, "Do you take offense at this? 62 Then what if you were to see the Son of Man ascending to where he was before? 63 It is the Spirit who gives life; the flesh is no help at all. The words that I have spoken to you are spirit and life. 64 But there are some of you who do not believe." (For Jesus knew from the beginning who those were who did not believe, and who it was who would betray him.) 65 And he said, "This is why I told you that no one can come to me unless it is granted him by the Father."

66 After this many of his disciples turned back and no longer walked with him. 67 So Jesus said to the Twelve, "Do you want to go away as well?" 68 Simon Peter answered him, "Lord, to whom shall we go? You have the words of eternal life, 69 and we have believed, and have come to know, that you are the Holy One of God." 70 Jesus answered them, "Did I not choose you, the Twelve? And yet one of you is a devil." 71 He spoke of Judas the son of Simon Iscariot, for he, one of the Twelve, was going to betray him.

Jesus at the Feast of Booths

7 After this Jesus went about in Galilee. He would not go about in Judea, because the Jews[1] were seeking to kill him. 2 Now the Jews' Feast of Booths was at hand. 3 So his brothers[2] said to him, "Leave here and go to Judea, that your disciples also may see the works you are doing. 4 For no one works in secret if he seeks to be known openly. If you do these things, show yourself to the world." 5 For not even his brothers believed in him. 6 Jesus said to them, "My time has not yet come, but your time is always here. 7 The world cannot hate you, but it hates me because I testify about it that its works are evil. 8 You go up to the feast. I am not[3] going up to this feast, for my time has not yet fully come." 9 After saying this, he remained in Galilee.

10 But after his brothers had gone up to the feast, then he also went up, not publicly but in private. 11 The Jews were looking for him at the feast, and saying, "Where is he?" 12 And there was much muttering about him among the people. While some said, "He is a good man," others said, "No, he is leading the people astray." 13 Yet for fear of the Jews no one spoke openly of him.

14 About the middle of the feast Jesus went up into the temple and began teaching. 15 The Jews therefore marveled, saying, "How is it that this man has learning,[4] when he has never studied?" 16 So Jesus answered them, "My teaching is not mine, but his who sent me. 17 If anyone's will is to do God's[5] will, he will know whether the teaching is from God or whether I am speaking on my own authority. 18 The one who speaks on his own authority seeks his own glory; but the one who seeks the glory of him who sent him is true, and in him there is no falsehood. 19 Has not Moses given you the law? Yet none of you keeps the law. Why do you seek to kill me?" 20 The crowd answered, "You have a demon! Who is seeking to kill you?" 21 Jesus answered them, "I did one work, and you all marvel at it. 22 Moses gave you circumcision (not that it is from Moses, but from the fathers), and you circumcise a man on the Sabbath. 23 If on the Sabbath a man receives circumcision, so that the law of Moses may not be broken, are you angry with me because on the Sabbath I made a man's whole body well? 24 Do not judge by appearances, but judge with right judgment."

Can This Be the Christ?

25 Some of the people of Jerusalem therefore said, "Is not this the man whom they seek to kill? 26 And here he is, speaking openly, and they say nothing to him! Can it be that the authorities really know that this is the Christ? 27 But we know where this man comes from, and when the Christ appears, no one will

[1] Or *Judeans* [2] Or *brothers and sisters*; also verses 5, 10 [3] Some manuscripts add *yet* [4] Or *this man knows his letters* [5] Greek *his*

know where he comes from." 28 So Jesus proclaimed, as he taught in the temple, "You know me, and you know where I come from? But I have not come of my own accord. He who sent me is true, and him you do not know. 29 I know him, for I come from him, and he sent me." 30 So they were seeking to arrest him, but no one laid a hand on him, because his hour had not yet come. 31 Yet many of the people believed in him. They said, "When the Christ appears, will he do more signs than this man has done?"

Officers Sent to Arrest Jesus

32 The Pharisees heard the crowd muttering these things about him, and the chief priests and Pharisees sent officers to arrest him. 33 Jesus then said, "I will be with you a little longer, and then I am going to him who sent me. 34 You will seek me and you will not find me. Where I am you cannot come." 35 The Jews said to one another, "Where does this man intend to go that we will not find him? Does he intend to go to the Dispersion among the Greeks and teach the Greeks? 36 What does he mean by saying, 'You will seek me and you will not find me,' and, 'Where I am you cannot come'?"

Rivers of Living Water

1553

37 On the last day of the feast, the great day, Jesus stood up and cried out, "If anyone thirsts, let him come to me and drink. 38 Whoever believes in me, as[1] the Scripture has said, 'Out of his heart will flow rivers of living water.'" 39 Now this he said about the Spirit, whom those who believed in him were to receive, for as yet the Spirit had not been given, because Jesus was not yet glorified.

Division Among the People

40 When they heard these words, some of the people said, "This really is the Prophet." 41 Others said, "This is the Christ." But some said, "Is the Christ to come from Galilee? 42 Has not the Scripture said that the Christ comes from the offspring of David, and comes from Bethlehem, the village where David was?" 43 So there was a division among the people over him. 44 Some of them wanted to arrest him, but no one laid hands on him.

45 The officers then came to the chief priests and Pharisees, who said to them, "Why did you not bring him?" 46 The officers answered, "No one ever spoke like this man!" 47 The Pharisees answered them, "Have you also been deceived? 48 Have any of the authorities or the Pharisees believed in him? 49 But this crowd that does not know the law is accursed." 50 Nicodemus, who had gone to him before, and who was one of them, said to them, 51 "Does our law judge a man without first giving him a hearing and learning what he does?" 52 They replied, "Are you from Galilee too? Search and see that no prophet arises from Galilee."

[THE EARLIEST MANUSCRIPTS DO NOT INCLUDE 7:53–8:11.][2]

The Woman Caught in Adultery

8 53 [[They went each to his own house, 1 but Jesus went to the Mount of Olives. 2 Early in the morning he came again to the temple. All the people came to him, and he sat down and taught them. 3 The scribes and the Pharisees brought a woman who had been caught in adultery, and placing her in the midst 4 they said to him, "Teacher, this woman has been caught in the act of adultery. 5 Now in the Law Moses commanded us to stone such women. So what do you say?" 6 This they said to test him, that they might have some charge to bring against him. Jesus bent down and wrote with his finger on the ground. 7 And as they continued to ask him, he stood up and said to them, "Let him who is without sin among you

[1] Or *let him come to me, and let him who believes in me drink. As* [2] Some manuscripts do not include 7:53–8:11; others add the passage here or after 7:36 or after 21:25 or after Luke 21:38, with variations in the text

be the first to throw a stone at her." 8 And once more he bent down and wrote on the ground. 9 But when they heard it, they went away one by one, beginning with the older ones, and Jesus was left alone with the woman standing before him. 10 Jesus stood up and said to her, "Woman, where are they? Has no one condemned you?" 11 She said, "No one, Lord." And Jesus said, "Neither do I condemn you; go, and from now on sin no more."]]

I Am the Light of the World

1567

12 Again Jesus spoke to them, saying, "I am the light of the world. Whoever follows me will not walk in darkness, but will have the light of life." 13 So the Pharisees said to him, "You are bearing witness about yourself; your testimony is not true." 14 Jesus answered, "Even if I do bear witness about myself, my testimony is true, for I know where I came from and where I am going, but you do not know where I come from or where I am going. 15 You judge according to the flesh; I judge no one. 16 Yet even if I do judge, my judgment is true, for it is not I alone who judge, but I and the Father[1] who sent me. 17 In your Law it is written that the testimony of two people is true. 18 I am the one who bears witness about myself, and the Father who sent me bears witness about me." 19 They said to him therefore, "Where is your Father?" Jesus answered, "You know neither me nor my Father. If you knew me, you would know my Father also." 20 These words he spoke in the treasury, as he taught in the temple; but no one arrested him, because his hour had not yet come.

21 So he said to them again, "I am going away, and you will seek me, and you will die in your sin. Where I am going, you cannot come." 22 So the Jews said, "Will he kill himself, since he says, 'Where I am going, you cannot come'?" 23 He said to them, "You are from below; I am from above. You are of this world; I am not of this world. 24 I told you that you would die in your sins, for unless you believe that I am he you will die in your sins." 25 So they said to him, "Who are you?" Jesus said to them, "Just what I have been telling you from the beginning. 26 I have much to say about you and much to judge, but he who sent me is true, and I declare to the world what I have heard from him." 27 They did not understand that he had been speaking to them about the Father. 28 So Jesus said to them, "When you have lifted up the Son of Man, then you will know that I am he, and that I do nothing on my own authority, but speak just as the Father taught me. 29 And he who sent me is with me. He has not left me alone, for I always do the things that are pleasing to him." 30 As he was saying these things, many believed in him.

The Truth Will Set You Free

31 So Jesus said to the Jews who had believed in him, "If you abide in my word, you are truly my disciples, 32 and you will know the truth, and the truth will set you free." 33 They answered him, "We are offspring of Abraham and have never been enslaved to anyone. How is it that you say, 'You will become free'?"

34 Jesus answered them, "Truly, truly, I say to you, everyone who commits sin is a slave[2] to sin. 35 The slave does not remain in the house forever; the son remains forever. 36 So if the Son sets you free, you will be free indeed. 37 I know that you are offspring of Abraham; yet you seek to kill me because my word finds no place in you. 38 I speak of what I have seen with my Father, and you do what you have heard from your father."

You Are of Your Father the Devil

39 They answered him, "Abraham is our father." Jesus said to them, "If you were Abraham's children, you would be doing the works Abraham did, 40 but now you

[1] Some manuscripts *he* [2] Greek *bondservant*; also verse 35

seek to kill me, a man who has told you the truth that I heard from God. This is not what Abraham did. **41** You are doing the works your father did." They said to him, "We were not born of sexual immorality. We have one Father—even God." **42** Jesus said to them, "If God were your Father, you would love me, for I came from God and I am here. I came not of my own accord, but he sent me. **43** Why do you not understand what I say? It is because you cannot bear to hear my word. **44** You are of your father the devil, and your will is to do your father's desires. He was a murderer from the beginning, and has nothing to do with the truth, because there is no truth in him. When he lies, he speaks out of his own character, for he is a liar and the father of lies. **45** But because I tell the truth, you do not believe me. **46** Which one of you convicts me of sin? If I tell the truth, why do you not believe me? **47** Whoever is of God hears the words of God. The reason why you do not hear them is that you are not of God."

Before Abraham Was, I Am

48 The Jews answered him, "Are we not right in saying that you are a Samaritan and have a demon?" **49** Jesus answered, "I do not have a demon, but I honor my Father, and you dishonor me. **50** Yet I do not seek my own glory; there is One who seeks it, and he is the judge. **51** Truly, truly, I say to you, if anyone keeps my word, he will never see death." **52** The Jews said to him, "Now we know that you have a demon! Abraham died, as did the prophets, yet you say, 'If anyone keeps my word, he will never taste death.' **53** Are you greater than our father Abraham, who died? And the prophets died! Who do you make yourself out to be?" **54** Jesus answered, "If I glorify myself, my glory is nothing. It is my Father who glorifies me, of whom you say, 'He is our God.'[1] **55** But you have not known him. I know him. If I were to say that I do not know him, I would be a liar like you, but I do know him and I keep his word. **56** Your father Abraham rejoiced that he would see my day. He saw it and was glad." **57** So the Jews said to him, "You are not yet fifty years old, and have you seen Abraham?"[2] **58** Jesus said to them, "Truly, truly, I say to you, before Abraham was, I am." **59** So they picked up stones to throw at him, but Jesus hid himself and went out of the temple.

Jesus Heals a Man Born Blind

1567

9 As he passed by, he saw a man blind from birth. **2** And his disciples asked him, "Rabbi, who sinned, this man or his parents, that he was born blind?" **3** Jesus answered, "It was not that this man sinned, or his parents, but that the works of God might be displayed in him. **4** We must work the works of him who sent me while it is day; night is coming, when no one can work. **5** As long as I am in the world, I am the light of the world." **6** Having said these things, he spat on the ground and made mud with the saliva. Then he anointed the man's eyes with the mud **7** and said to him, "Go, wash in the pool of Siloam" (which means Sent). So he went and washed and came back seeing.

8 The neighbors and those who had seen him before as a beggar were saying, "Is this not the man who used to sit and beg?" **9** Some said, "It is he." Others said, "No, but he is like him." He kept saying, "I am the man." **10** So they said to him, "Then how were your eyes opened?" **11** He answered, "The man called Jesus made mud and anointed my eyes and said to me, 'Go to Siloam and wash.' So I went and washed and received my sight." **12** They said to him, "Where is he?" He said, "I do not know."

13 They brought to the Pharisees the man who had formerly been blind. **14** Now it was a Sabbath day when Jesus made the mud and opened his eyes. **15** So the Pharisees again asked him how he had received his sight. And he said to them, "He put mud on my eyes, and I washed, and I see."

[1] Some manuscripts *your God* [2] Some manuscripts *has Abraham seen you?*

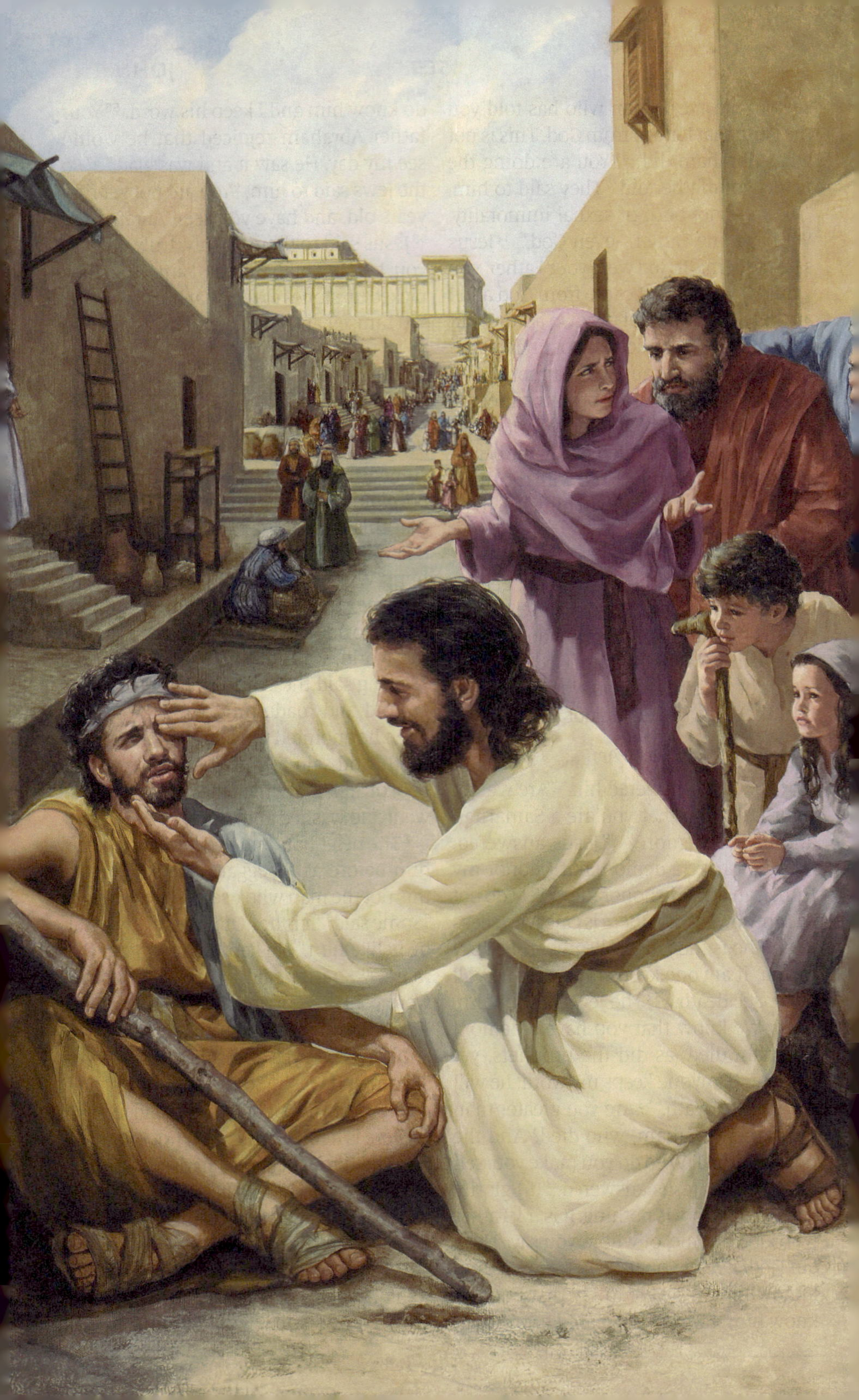

Jesus Heals a Blind Man

While Jesus and His disciples were walking along one day, they saw a man begging for money. The man couldn't work at a regular job because he had been blind since the day he was born. Jesus' disciples asked, "Who sinned, this man or his parents, that he was born blind?" In Jesus' time, many people thought that all their troubles were punishment for sin.

Jesus answered, "It was not that this man sinned, or his parents, but that the works of God might be displayed in him." Jesus knew that the man's blindness would help many people see God's glorious power at work. Jesus explained that He had come to do these works of God. Then He said an amazing thing: "I am the light of the world."

Jesus spit on the ground and made mud to put on the blind man's eyes. After that, Jesus told the blind man, "Go, wash in the pool of Siloam." The man did exactly what Jesus told him to do. When he came back, he was able to see for the first time in his life. Jesus had healed the blind man!

The people in the city were amazed to see the man who used to be a blind beggar. He was rejoicing—he could see! Some of the Jewish religious leaders were angry, however, because so many people were accepting the authority of Jesus. And they didn't like it that Jesus healed people even on the

Sabbath day, the Jewish day of worship and rest. But Jesus knew that His authority and His power to heal came straight from God the Father.

Later Jesus saw the man who had been blind and asked him if he believed in the One God had promised to send. The man answered, "Who is He, Sir, that I may believe in Him?"

Jesus told the man that He—Jesus!—was the Messiah, the promised One. The man responded, "Lord, I believe," and he worshiped Jesus.

The blind man had received the gift of sight for his eyes, but he also received the gift of faith—to believe that Jesus was the promised Savior.

Jesus helped the man born blind so that he could see with his eyes, but also so that he could believe in his heart! Sin makes people blind to God's truth, but Jesus is the "light of the world," who takes away the darkness of our hearts.

SEEK and FIND

WHERE TO FIND THE STORY

John 9

KEY BIBLE VERSE

"Again, Jesus spoke to them, saying, 'I am the light of the world. Whoever follows me will not walk in darkness, but will have the light of life.'" (John 8:12)

THREE KEY QUESTIONS

- How did Jesus heal the blind man?
- Who did Jesus tell the blind man that He was?
- What does it mean that Jesus is "the light of the world"?

RELATED BIBLE READINGS
Mark 8:22–26; John 1:4–9; 2 Corinthians 4:4–6

16 Some of the Pharisees said, "This man is not from God, for he does not keep the Sabbath." But others said, "How can a man who is a sinner do such signs?" And there was a division among them. 17 So they said again to the blind man, "What do you say about him, since he has opened your eyes?" He said, "He is a prophet."

18 The Jews did not believe that he had been blind and had received his sight, until they called the parents of the man who had received his sight 19 and asked them, "Is this your son, who you say was born blind? How then does he now see?" 20 His parents answered, "We know that this is our son and that he was born blind. 21 But how he now sees we do not know, nor do we know who opened his eyes. Ask him; he is of age. He will speak for himself." 22 (His parents said these things because they feared the Jews, for the Jews had already agreed that if anyone should confess Jesus[1] to be Christ, he was to be put out of the synagogue.) 23 Therefore his parents said, "He is of age; ask him."

24 So for the second time they called the man who had been blind and said to him, "Give glory to God. We know that this man is a sinner." 25 He answered, "Whether he is a sinner I do not know. One thing I do know, that though I was blind, now I see." 26 They said to him, "What did he do to you? How did he open your eyes?" 27 He answered them, "I have told you already, and you would not listen. Why do you want to hear it again? Do you also want to become his disciples?" 28 And they reviled him, saying, "You are his disciple, but we are disciples of Moses. 29 We know that God has spoken to Moses, but as for this man, we do not know where he comes from." 30 The man answered, "Why, this is an amazing thing! You do not know where he comes from, and yet he opened my eyes. 31 We know that God does not listen to sinners, but if anyone is a worshiper of God and does his will, God listens to him. 32 Never since the world began has it been heard that anyone opened the eyes of a man born blind. 33 If this man were not from God, he could do nothing." 34 They answered him, "You were born in utter sin, and would you teach us?" And they cast him out.

35 Jesus heard that they had cast him out, and having found him he said, "Do you believe in the Son of Man?"[2] 36 He answered, "And who is he, sir, that I may believe in him?" 37 Jesus said to him, "You have seen him, and it is he who is speaking to you." 38 He said, "Lord, I believe," and he worshiped him. 39 Jesus said, "For judgment I came into this world, that those who do not see may see, and those who see may become blind." 40 Some of the Pharisees near him heard these things, and said to him, "Are we also blind?" 41 Jesus said to them, "If you were blind, you would have no guilt;[3] but now that you say, 'We see,' your guilt remains.

I Am the Good Shepherd

1571

10 "Truly, truly, I say to you, he who does not enter the sheepfold by the door but climbs in by another way, that man is a thief and a

[1] Greek *him* [2] Some manuscripts *the Son of God* [3] Greek *you would not have sin*

Jesus, the Good Shepherd

In Jesus' time and in the country where He lived, many families kept sheep, and the person in charge of the sheep was called a shepherd. Because people understood about sheep and shepherds, Jesus used these familiar things to explain that He was "the Good Shepherd."

A good shepherd provides, protects, and cares for his sheep. Jesus explained how sheep recognize their true shepherd and will not follow a stranger. When a shepherd goes to the sheep pen to get his flock, he stands at the gate and calls to them. He calls each sheep by name. The sheep recognize the shepherd's voice, and they run to follow him. The sheep will not run out to meet a stranger or a thief.

Then Jesus said, "The thief comes only to steal and kill and destroy. I came that they may have life and have it abundantly. I am the Good Shepherd. The Good Shepherd lays down His life for the sheep. I know My own, and My own know Me, just as the Father knows Me and I know the Father."

Later, as Jesus was walking in the temple, some of the unbelieving Jews started to question Him about who He really was. Jesus reminded them that He had already told them, but they did not believe Him. "You do not believe," He said, "because you are not part of My flock. My sheep hear My voice, and I know them, and they follow Me. I give them eternal life, and they will never perish, and no one will snatch them out of My hand. My Father, who has given them to Me, is greater than all, and no one is able to snatch them out of the Father's hand. I and the Father are one."

Jesus tells us that the most important thing in life is that we would believe in who Jesus is—that He is the "Good Shepherd" who laid down His life for us. Jesus died on the cross to pay the penalty for our sins, and He rose again to defeat sin and death and the devil. Through faith in Him, we know that we are His own and that He will always be with us, both now and forever with Him in heaven.

SEEK and FIND

WHERE TO FIND THE STORY

John 10:1–30

KEY BIBLE VERSE

"I am the good shepherd. The good shepherd lays down his life for the sheep." (John 10:11)

THREE KEY QUESTIONS

- What does the Good Shepherd do for the sheep?
- Who is the Good Shepherd and who are the sheep?
- How do we know that Jesus is our Good Shepherd and that He will always be with us?

RELATED BIBLE READINGS

Psalm 23:1–3; 78:70–72; Mark 6:34; Luke 15:3–7; 1 Peter 2:24–25; 5:4

robber. 2 But he who enters by the door is
the shepherd of the sheep. 3 To him the
gatekeeper opens. The sheep hear his
voice, and he calls his own sheep by name
and leads them out. 4 When he has
brought out all his own, he goes before
them, and the sheep follow him, for they
know his voice. 5 A stranger they will not
follow, but they will flee from him, for
they do not know the voice of strangers."
6 This figure of speech Jesus used with
them, but they did not understand what
he was saying to them.

7 So Jesus again said to them, "Truly,
truly, I say to you, I am the door of the
sheep. 8 All who came before me are
thieves and robbers, but the sheep did not
listen to them. 9 I am the door. If anyone
enters by me, he will be saved and will go
in and out and find pasture. 10 The thief
comes only to steal and kill and
destroy. I came that they may have
1501 life and have it abundantly. 11 I am
the good shepherd. The good shep-
herd lays down his life for the
1571 sheep. 12 He who is a hired hand
and not a shepherd, who does not own the
sheep, sees the wolf coming and leaves
the sheep and flees, and the wolf snatches
them and scatters them. 13 He flees
because he is a hired hand and cares noth-
ing for the sheep. 14 I am the good shep-
herd. I know my own and my own know
me, 15 just as the Father knows me and I
know the Father; and I lay down my life
for the sheep. 16 And I have other sheep
that are not of this fold. I must bring them
also, and they will listen to my voice. So
there will be one flock, one shepherd.
17 For this reason the Father loves me,
because I lay down my life that I may take
it up again. 18 No one takes it from me, but
I lay it down of my own accord. I have
authority to lay it down, and I have
authority to take it up again. This charge I
have received from my Father."

19 There was again a division among
the Jews because of these words. 20 Many
of them said, "He has a demon, and is
insane; why listen to him?" 21 Others said,
"These are not the words of one who is
oppressed by a demon. Can a demon open
the eyes of the blind?"

I and the Father Are One

22 At that time the Feast of Dedication
took place at Jerusalem. It was winter,
23 and Jesus was walking in the temple, in
the colonnade of Solomon. 24 So the Jews
gathered around him and said to him,
"How long will you keep us in suspense? If
you are the Christ, tell us plainly." 25 Jesus
answered them, "I told you, and you do
not believe. The works that I do in my
Father's name bear witness about me,
26 but you do not believe because you are
not part of my flock. 27 My sheep hear my
voice, and I know them, and they follow
me. 28 I give them eternal life, and they will
never perish, and no one will snatch them
out of my hand. 29 My Father, who has
given them to me,[1] is greater than all, and
no one is able to snatch them out of the
Father's hand. 30 I and the Father are one."

31 The Jews picked up stones again to
stone him. 32 Jesus answered them, "I have
shown you many good works from the
Father; for which of them are you going to
stone me?" 33 The Jews answered him, "It
is not for a good work that we are going to
stone you but for blasphemy, because you,
being a man, make yourself God." 34 Jesus
answered them, "Is it not written in your
Law, 'I said, you are gods'? 35 If he called
them gods to whom the word of God
came—and Scripture cannot be broken—
36 do you say of him whom the Father
consecrated and sent into the world, 'You
are blaspheming,' because I said, 'I am
the Son of God'? 37 If I am not doing the
works of my Father, then do not believe
me; 38 but if I do them, even though you
do not believe me, believe the works, that

[1] Some manuscripts *What my Father has given to me*

you may know and understand that the Father is in me and I am in the Father." 39 Again they sought to arrest him, but he escaped from their hands.

40 He went away again across the Jordan to the place where John had been baptizing at first, and there he remained. 41 And many came to him. And they said, "John did no sign, but everything that John said about this man was true." 42 And many believed in him there.

The Death of Lazarus

1577

1389

11 Now a certain man was ill, Lazarus of Bethany, the village of Mary and her sister Martha. 2 It was Mary who anointed the Lord with ointment and wiped his feet with her hair, whose brother Lazarus was ill. 3 So the sisters sent to him, saying, "Lord, he whom you love is ill." 4 But when Jesus heard it he said, "This illness does not lead to death. It is for the glory of God, so that the Son of God may be glorified through it."

5 Now Jesus loved Martha and her sister and Lazarus. 6 So, when he heard that Lazarus[1] was ill, he stayed two days longer in the place where he was. 7 Then after this he said to the disciples, "Let us go to Judea again." 8 The disciples said to him, "Rabbi, the Jews were just now seeking to stone you, and are you going there again?" 9 Jesus answered, "Are there not twelve hours in the day? If anyone walks in the day, he does not stumble, because he sees the light of this world. 10 But if anyone walks in the night, he stumbles, because the light is not in him." 11 After saying these things, he said to them, "Our friend Lazarus has fallen asleep, but I go to awaken him." 12 The disciples said to him, "Lord, if he has fallen asleep, he will recover." 13 Now Jesus had spoken of his death, but they thought that he meant taking rest in sleep. 14 Then Jesus told them plainly, "Lazarus has died, 15 and for your sake I am glad that I was not there, so that you may believe. But let us go to him." 16 So Thomas, called the Twin,[2] said to his fellow disciples, "Let us also go, that we may die with him."

I Am the Resurrection and the Life

17 Now when Jesus came, he found that Lazarus had already been in the tomb four days. 18 Bethany was near Jerusalem, about two miles[3] off, 19 and many of the Jews had come to Martha and Mary to console them concerning their brother. 20 So when Martha heard that Jesus was coming, she went and met him, but Mary remained seated in the house. 21 Martha said to Jesus, "Lord, if you had been here, my brother would not have died. 22 But even now I know that whatever you ask from God, God will give you." 23 Jesus said to her, "Your brother will rise again." 24 Martha said to him, "I know that he will rise again in the resurrection on the last day." 25 Jesus said to her, "I am the resurrection and the life.[4] Whoever believes in me, though he die, yet shall he live, 26 and everyone who lives and believes in me shall never die. Do you believe this?" 27 She said to him, "Yes, Lord; I believe that you are the Christ, the Son of God, who is coming into the world."

1577

Jesus Weeps

28 When she had said this, she went and called her sister Mary, saying in private, "The Teacher is here and is calling for you." 29 And when she heard it, she rose quickly and went to him. 30 Now Jesus had not yet come into the village, but was still in the place where Martha had met him. 31 When the Jews who were with her in the house, consoling her, saw Mary rise quickly and go out, they followed her, supposing that she was going to the tomb to weep there. 32 Now when Mary came to where Jesus was and saw him, she fell at his feet, saying to him, "Lord, if you had been here, my brother would not have died." 33 When Jesus saw her weep-

[1] Greek *he*; also verse 17 [2] Greek *Didymus* [3] Greek *fifteen stadia*; a *stadion* was about 607 feet or 185 meters [4] Some manuscripts omit *and the life*

ing, and the Jews who had come with her also weeping, he was deeply moved in his spirit and greatly troubled. 34 And he said, "Where have you laid him?" They said to him, "Lord, come and see." 35 Jesus wept. 36 So the Jews said, "See how he loved him!" 37 But some of them said, "Could not he who opened the eyes of the blind man also have kept this man from dying?"

Jesus Raises Lazarus

38 Then Jesus, deeply moved again, came to the tomb. It was a cave, and a stone lay against it. 39 Jesus said, "Take away the stone." Martha, the sister of the dead man, said to him, "Lord, by this time there will be an odor, for he has been dead four days." 40 Jesus said to her, "Did I not tell you that if you believed you would see the glory of God?" 41 So they took away the stone. And Jesus lifted up his eyes and said, "Father, I thank you that you have heard me. 42 I knew that you always hear me, but I said this on account of the people standing around, that they may believe that you sent me." 43 When he had said these things, he cried out with a loud voice, "Lazarus, come out." 44 The man who had died came out, his hands and feet bound with linen strips, and his face wrapped with a cloth. Jesus said to them, "Unbind him, and let him go."

The Plot to Kill Jesus

45 Many of the Jews therefore, who had come with Mary and had seen what he did, believed in him, 46 but some of them went to the Pharisees and told them what Jesus had done. 47 So the chief priests and the Pharisees gathered the Council and said, "What are we to do? For this man performs many signs. 48 If we let him go on like this, everyone will believe in him, and the Romans will come and take away both our place and our nation." 49 But one of them, Caiaphas, who was high priest that year, said to them, "You know nothing at all. 50 Nor do you understand that it is better for you that one man should die for the people, not that the whole nation should perish." 51 He did not say this of his own accord, but being high priest that year he prophesied that Jesus would die for the nation, 52 and not for the nation only, but also to gather into one the children of God who are scattered abroad. 53 So from that day on they made plans to put him to death.

54 Jesus therefore no longer walked openly among the Jews, but went from there to the region near the wilderness,

CHARACTER PROFILE

LAZARUS

Lazarus lived in Bethany with his sisters, Mary and Martha. Lazarus and his sisters were close friends of Jesus. When messengers told Jesus that Lazarus was very sick, Jesus knew His friends were in trouble. But Jesus did not go to them right away. By the time Jesus arrived, Lazarus had been dead four days, and Mary and Martha were heartbroken. But Jesus knew God had a plan to demonstrate His power over death. Jesus called Lazarus to come out of his tomb, and Lazarus came back to life!

1577

Jesus Raises Lazarus

Mary and Martha were sisters who lived in Bethany. They were sad and worried because their brother Lazarus was very sick, so they sent a message asking their close friend Jesus to come. They knew that if Jesus were there, He could help Lazarus. But when Jesus got the sisters' message, He did not come right away! He waited two days before He began to walk to their home. By the time Jesus arrived at Bethany, Lazarus had been dead for four days and was already buried in a tomb.

When Jesus finally came, Martha ran to meet Him. She said, "Lord, if You had been here, my brother would not have died."

Jesus said, "Your brother will rise again."

Martha thought Jesus meant that Lazarus would be resurrected, or made alive again, in heaven, because he had loved and trusted in God.

Then Jesus told her an amazing thing , "I am the Resurrection and the Life," He said. "Whoever believes in Me, though he die, yet shall he live, and everyone who lives and believes in Me shall never die. Do you believe this?"

Martha said, "Yes, Lord; I believe that You are the Christ, the Son of God!"

Then Mary and some others came to Jesus. Mary fell down at Jesus' feet crying. When Jesus saw her and the others who were weeping and crying, He was terribly sad too—so sad that "Jesus wept."

The sisters took Jesus to the tomb where Lazarus was buried. The tomb was like a cave, with a stone blocking the entrance. Jesus asked for the stone to be rolled away. Jesus knew that the death of Lazarus had been part of God's plan to show the world His glory and power.

In a loud voice, He shouted, "Lazarus, come out." Then Lazarus stood up and walked out of the tomb, still wrapped up in grave cloths. Lazarus was alive! "Unbind him, and let him go," Jesus said. Everyone who saw Lazarus alive again was amazed, and many of them believed in Jesus.

When Jesus brought Lazarus back to life, He showed His power over sin and death. He showed that He is the Savior God promised to send. Jesus cares for us too. He came to die on the cross to pay for our sins. He promises that everyone who believes in Him will live forever in heaven with Him.

SEEK and FIND

WHERE TO FIND THE STORY

John 11:1–44

KEY BIBLE VERSE

"Jesus said to her, 'I am the resurrection and the life. Whoever believes in me, though he die, yet shall he live, and everyone who lives and believes in me shall never die.'" (John 11:25–26)

THREE KEY QUESTIONS

- *What was the amazing thing that Jesus told to Martha?*

- What did many of the people do when Lazarus was raised from the dead?
- When Jesus brought Lazarus back to life, what did it show?

RELATED BIBLE READINGS

Mark 5:35–43; Luke 7:11–17; John 5:21–29

to a town called Ephraim, and there he
stayed with the disciples.
55 Now the Passover of the Jews was at
hand, and many went up from the coun-
try to Jerusalem before the Passover to
purify themselves. 56 They were looking
for[1] Jesus and saying to one another as
they stood in the temple, "What do you
think? That he will not come to the feast
at all?" 57 Now the chief priests and the
Pharisees had given orders that if anyone
knew where he was, he should let them
know, so that they might arrest him.

Mary Anoints Jesus at Bethany

12 Six days before the Passover,
Jesus therefore came to
1473 Bethany, where Lazarus was, whom
Jesus had raised from the dead. 2 So they
gave a dinner for him there. Martha served,
and Lazarus was one of those reclining
with him at table. 3 Mary therefore took a
pound[2] of expensive ointment made from
pure nard, and anointed the feet of Jesus
and wiped his feet with her hair. The house
was filled with the fragrance of the per-
fume. 4 But Judas Iscariot, one of his disci-
ples (he who was about to betray him),
said, 5 "Why was this ointment not sold for
three hundred denarii[3] and given to the
poor?" 6 He said this, not because he cared
about the poor, but because he was a thief,
and having charge of the moneybag he
used to help himself to what was put into
it. 7 Jesus said, "Leave her alone, so that she
may keep it[4] for the day of my burial. 8 For
the poor you always have with you, but you
do not always have me."

The Plot to Kill Lazarus

9 When the large crowd of the Jews
learned that Jesus[5] was there, they came,
not only on account of him but also to see
Lazarus, whom he had raised from the
dead. 10 So the chief priests made plans
to put Lazarus to death as well, 11 because
on account of him many of the Jews were
going away and believing in Jesus.

The Triumphal Entry

12 The next day the large crowd that
had come to the feast heard that Jesus
was coming to Jerusalem. 13 So they took
branches of palm trees and went out to
meet him, crying out, "Hosanna! Blessed
is he who comes in the name of the Lord,
even the King of Israel!" 14 And Jesus
found a young donkey and sat on it, just
as it is written,

15 "Fear not, daughter of Zion;
behold, your king is coming,
sitting on a donkey's colt!"

16 His disciples did not understand these
things at first, but when Jesus was glori-
fied, then they remembered that these
things had been written about him and
had been done to him. 17 The crowd that

[1] Greek *were seeking for* [2] Greek *litra;* a *litra* (or Roman pound) was equal to about 11 1/2 ounces or 327 grams [3] A *denarius* was a day's wage for a laborer [4] Or *Leave her alone; she intended to keep it* [5] Greek *he*

had been with him when he called Lazarus out of the tomb and raised him from the dead continued to bear witness. 18 The reason why the crowd went to meet him was that they heard he had done this sign. 19 So the Pharisees said to one another, "You see that you are gaining nothing. Look, the world has gone after him."

Some Greeks Seek Jesus

20 Now among those who went up to worship at the feast were some

1537

Greeks. 21 So these came to Philip, who was from Bethsaida in Galilee, and asked him, "Sir, we wish to see Jesus." 22 Philip went and told Andrew; Andrew and Philip went and told Jesus. 23 And Jesus answered them, "The hour has come for the Son of Man to be glorified. 24 Truly, truly, I say to you, unless a grain of wheat falls into the earth and dies, it remains alone; but if it dies, it bears much fruit. 25 Whoever loves his life loses it, and whoever hates his life in this world will keep it for eternal life. 26 If anyone serves me, he must follow me; and where I am, there will my servant be also. If anyone serves me, the Father will honor him.

The Son of Man Must Be Lifted Up

27 "Now is my soul troubled. And what shall I say? 'Father, save me from this hour'? But for this purpose I have come to this hour. 28 Father, glorify your name." Then a voice came from heaven: "I have glorified it, and I will glorify it again." 29 The crowd that stood there and heard it said that it had thundered. Others said, "An angel has spoken to him." 30 Jesus answered, "This voice has come for your sake, not mine. 31 Now is the judgment of this world; now will the ruler of this world be cast out. 32 And I, when I am lifted up from the earth, will draw all people to myself." 33 He said this to show by what kind of death he was going to die. 34 So the crowd answered him, "We have heard from the Law that the Christ remains forever. How can you say that the Son of Man must be lifted up? Who is this Son of Man?" 35 So Jesus said to them, "The light is among you for a little while longer. Walk while you have the light, lest darkness overtake you. The one who walks in the darkness does not know where he is going. 36 While you have the light, believe in the light, that you may become sons of light."

The Unbelief of the People

When Jesus had said these things, he departed and hid himself from them. 37 Though he had done so many signs before them, they still did not believe in him, 38 so that the word spoken by the prophet Isaiah might be fulfilled:

"Lord, who has believed what he
heard from us,
and to whom has the arm of the
Lord been revealed?"

39 Therefore they could not believe. For again Isaiah said,

40 "He has blinded their eyes
and hardened their heart,
lest they see with their eyes,
and understand with their heart,
and turn,
and I would heal them."

41 Isaiah said these things because he saw his glory and spoke of him. 42 Nevertheless, many even of the authorities believed in him, but for fear of the Pharisees they did not confess it, so that they would not be put out of the synagogue; 43 for they loved the glory that comes from man more than the glory that comes from God.

Jesus Came to Save the World

44 And Jesus cried out and said, "Whoever believes in me, believes not in me but in him who sent me. 45 And whoever sees me sees him who sent me. 46 I have come into the world as light, so that

whoever believes in me may not remain in darkness. 47 If anyone hears my words and does not keep them, I do not judge him; for I did not come to judge the world but to save the world. 48 The one who rejects me and does not receive my words has a judge; the word that I have spoken will judge him on the last day. 49 For I have not spoken on my own authority, but the Father who sent me has himself given me a commandment—what to say and what to speak. 50 And I know that his commandment is eternal life. What I say, therefore, I say as the Father has told me."

Jesus Washes the Disciples' Feet

13 Now before the Feast of the Passover, when Jesus knew that his hour had come to depart out of this world to the Father, having loved his own who were in the world, he loved them to the end. 2 During supper, when the devil had already put it into the heart of Judas Iscariot, Simon's son, to betray him, 3 Jesus, knowing that the Father had given all things into his hands, and that he had come from God and was going back to God, 4 rose from supper. He laid aside his outer garments, and taking a towel, tied it around his waist. 5 Then he poured water into a basin and began to wash the disciples' feet and to wipe them with the towel that was wrapped around him. 6 He came to Simon Peter, who said to him, "Lord, do you wash my feet?" 7 Jesus answered him, "What I am doing you do not understand now, but afterward you will understand." 8 Peter said to him, "You shall never wash my feet." Jesus answered him, "If I do not wash you, you have no share with me." 9 Simon Peter said to him, "Lord, not my feet only but also my hands and my head!" 10 Jesus said to him, "The one who has bathed does not need to wash, except for his feet,[1] but is completely clean. And you[2] are clean, but not every one of you." 11 For he knew who was to betray him; that was why he said, "Not all of you are clean."

12 When he had washed their feet and put on his outer garments and resumed his place, he said to them, "Do you understand what I have done to you? 13 You call me Teacher and Lord, and you are right, for so I am. 14 If I then, your Lord and Teacher, have washed your feet, you also ought to wash one another's feet. 15 For I have given you an example, that you also should do just as I have done to you. 16 Truly, truly, I say to you, a servant[3] is not greater than his master, nor is a messenger greater than the one who sent him. 17 If you know these things, blessed are you if you do them. 18 I am not speaking of all of you; I know whom I have chosen. But the Scripture will be fulfilled,[4] 'He who ate my bread has lifted his heel against me.' 19 I am telling you this now, before it takes place, that when it does take place you may believe that I am he. 20 Truly, truly, I say to you, whoever receives the one I send receives me, and whoever receives me receives the one who sent me."

One of You Will Betray Me

21 After saying these things, Jesus was troubled in his spirit, and testified, "Truly, truly, I say to you, one of you will betray me." 22 The disciples looked at one another, uncertain of whom he spoke. 23 One of his disciples, whom Jesus loved, was reclining at table close to Jesus,[5] 24 so Simon Peter motioned to him to ask Jesus[6] of whom he was speaking. 25 So that disciple, leaning back against Jesus, said to him, "Lord, who is it?" 26 Jesus answered, "It is he to whom I will give this morsel of bread when I have dipped it." So when he had dipped the morsel, he gave it to Judas, the son of Simon Iscariot. 27 Then after he had taken the morsel, Satan entered into him. Jesus said to him, "What you are going to do, do quickly." 28 Now no one at the table knew why he said this to him.

[1] Some manuscripts omit *except for his feet* [2] The Greek words for *you* in this verse are plural [3] Greek *bondservant* [4] Greek *But in order that the Scripture may be fulfilled* [5] Greek *in the bosom of Jesus* [6] Greek lacks *Jesus*

29 Some thought that, because Judas had the moneybag, Jesus was telling him, "Buy what we need for the feast," or that he should give something to the poor. 30 So, after receiving the morsel of bread, he immediately went out. And it was night.

A New Commandment

31 When he had gone out, Jesus said, "Now is the Son of Man glorified, and God is glorified in him. 32 If God is glorified in him, God will also glorify him in himself, and glorify him at once. 33 Little children, yet a little while I am with you. You will seek me, and just as I said to the Jews, so now I also say to you, 'Where I am going you cannot come.' 34 A new commandment I give to you, that you love one another: just as I have loved you, you also are to love one another. 35 By this all people will know that you are my disciples, if you have love for one another."

Jesus Foretells Peter's Denial

36 Simon Peter said to him, "Lord, where are you going?" Jesus
1415 answered him, "Where I am going you cannot follow me now, but you will follow afterward." 37 Peter said to him, "Lord, why can I not follow you now? I will lay down my life for you." 38 Jesus answered, "Will you lay down your life for me? Truly, truly, I say to you, the rooster will not crow till you have denied me three times.

I Am the Way, and the Truth, and the Life

14 "Let not your hearts be troubled. Believe in God;[1] believe also in me. 2 In my Father's house are many rooms. If it were not so, would I have told you that I go to prepare a place for you?[2] 3 And if I go and prepare a place for you, I will come again and will take you to myself, that where I am you may be also. 4 And you know the way to where I am going."[3] 5 Thomas said to him, "Lord, we do not know where you are going. How can we know the way?" 6 Jesus said to him, "I am the way, and the truth, and the life. No one comes to the Father except through me. 7 If you had known me, you would have known my Father also.[4] From now on you do know him and have seen him."

8 Philip said to him, "Lord, show us the Father, and it is enough for us." 9 Jesus said to him, "Have I been with you so long, and you still do not know me, Philip? Whoever has seen me has seen the Father. How can you say, 'Show us the Father'? 10 Do you not believe that I am in the Father and the Father is in me? The words that I say to you I do not speak on my own authority, but the Father who dwells in me does his works. 11 Believe me that I am in the Father and the Father is in me, or else believe on account of the works themselves.

12 "Truly, truly, I say to you, whoever believes in me will also do the works that I do; and greater works than these will he do, because I am going to the Father. 13 Whatever you ask in my name, this I will do, that the Father may be glorified in the Son. 14 If you ask me[5] anything in my name, I will do it.

Jesus Promises the Holy Spirit

15 "If you love me, you will keep my commandments. 16 And I will ask
1611 the Father, and he will give you another Helper,[6] to be with you forever, 17 even the Spirit of truth, whom the world cannot receive, because it neither sees him nor knows him. You know him, for he dwells with you and will be in you.

18 "I will not leave you as orphans; I will come to you. 19 Yet a little while and the world will see me no more, but you will see me. Because I live, you also will live. 20 In that day you will know that I am in my Father, and you in me, and I in you. 21 Whoever has my commandments and keeps them, he it is who loves me. And he

[1] Or *You believe in God* [2] Or *In my Father's house are many rooms; if it were not so, I would have told you; for I go to prepare a place for you* [3] Some manuscripts *Where I am going you know, and the way you know* [4] Or *If you know me, you will know my Father also*, or *If you have known me, you will know my Father also* [5] Some manuscripts omit *me* [6] Or *Advocate*, or *Counselor*; also 14:26; 15:26; 16:7

who loves me will be loved by my Father,
and I will love him and manifest myself
to him." 22 Judas (not Iscariot) said to
him, "Lord, how is it that you will mani-
fest yourself to us, and not to the world?"
23 Jesus answered him, "If anyone loves
me, he will keep my word, and my Father
will love him, and we will come to him
and make our home with him. 24 Whoever
does not love me does not keep my words.
And the word that you hear is not mine
but the Father's who sent me.

25 "These things I have spoken to you
while I am still with you. 26 But the Helper,
the Holy Spirit, whom the Father will send
in my name, he will teach you all things
and bring to your remembrance all that I
have said to you. 27 Peace I leave with you;
my peace I give to you. Not as the world
gives do I give to you. Let not your hearts
be troubled, neither let them be afraid.
28 You heard me say to you, 'I am going
away, and I will come to you.' If you loved
me, you would have rejoiced, because I am
going to the Father, for the Father is greater
than I. 29 And now I have told you before
it takes place, so that when it does take
place you may believe. 30 I will no longer
talk much with you, for the ruler of this
world is coming. He has no claim on me,
31 but I do as the Father has commanded
me, so that the world may know that I love
the Father. Rise, let us go from here.

I Am the True Vine

15 "I am the true vine, and my Father
is the vinedresser. 2 Every branch
in me that does not bear fruit he takes
away, and every branch that does bear
fruit he prunes, that it may bear more
fruit. 3 Already you are clean because of
the word that I have spoken to you. 4 Abide
in me, and I in you. As the branch cannot
bear fruit by itself, unless it abides in the
vine, neither can you, unless you abide in
me. 5 I am the vine; you are the branches.
Whoever abides in me and I in him, he
it is that bears much fruit, for apart from
me you can do nothing. 6 If anyone does
not abide in me he is thrown away like
a branch and withers; and the branches
are gathered, thrown into the fire, and
burned. 7 If you abide in me, and my words
abide in you, ask whatever you wish, and
it will be done for you. 8 By this my Father
is glorified, that you bear much fruit and
so prove to be my disciples. 9 As the Father
has loved me, so have I loved you. Abide
in my love. 10 If you keep my command-
ments, you will abide in my love, just as
I have kept my Father's commandments
and abide in his love. 11 These things I
have spoken to you, that my joy may be in
you, and that your joy may be full.

12 "This is my commandment, that you
love one another as I have loved you.
13 Greater love has no one than
this, that someone lay down his
475 life for his friends. 14 You are my
friends if you do what I command you.
15 No longer do I call you servants,[1] for the
servant[2] does not know what his master is
doing; but I have called you friends, for all
that I have heard from my Father I have
made known to you. 16 You did not choose
me, but I chose you and appointed you
that you should go and bear fruit and that
your fruit should abide, so that whatever
you ask the Father in my name, he may
give it to you. 17 These things I command
you, so that you will love one another.

The Hatred of the World

18 "If the world hates you, know that
it has hated me before it hated you. 19 If
you were of the world, the world would
love you as its own; but because you are
not of the world, but I chose you out of
the world, therefore the world hates you.
20 Remember the word that I said to you:
'A servant is not greater than his master.'
If they persecuted me, they will also per-
secute you. If they kept my word, they will
also keep yours. 21 But all these things they

[1] Greek *bondservants* [2] Greek *bondservant*; also verse 20

will do to you on account of my name, because they do not know him who sent me. 22 If I had not come and spoken to them, they would not have been guilty of sin,[1] but now they have no excuse for their sin. 23 Whoever hates me hates my Father also. 24 If I had not done among them the works that no one else did, they would not be guilty of sin, but now they have seen and hated both me and my Father. 25 But the word that is written in their Law must be fulfilled: 'They hated me without a cause.'

26 "But when the Helper comes, whom I will send to you from the Father, the Spirit of truth, who proceeds from the Father, he will bear witness about me. 27 And you also will bear witness, because you have been with me from the beginning.

16 "I have said all these things to you to keep you from falling away. 2 They will put you out of the synagogues. Indeed, the hour is coming when whoever kills you will think he is offering service to God. 3 And they will do these things because they have not known the Father, nor me. 4 But I have said these things to you, that when their hour comes you may remember that I told them to you.

The Work of the Holy Spirit

"I did not say these things to you from the beginning, because I was with you. 5 But now I am going to him who sent me, and none of you asks me, 'Where are you going?' 6 But because I have said these things to you, sorrow has filled your heart. 7 Nevertheless, I tell you the truth: it is to your advantage that I go away,
1611 for if I do not go away, the Helper will not come to you. But if I go, I will send him to you. 8 And when he comes, he will convict the world concerning sin and righteousness and judgment: 9 concerning sin, because they do not believe in me; 10 concerning righteousness, because I go to the Father, and you will see me no longer; 11 concerning judgment, because the ruler of this world is judged.

12 "I still have many things to say to you, but you cannot bear them now. 13 When the Spirit of truth comes, he will guide you into all the truth, for he will not speak on his own authority, but whatever he hears he will speak, and he will declare to you the things that are to come. 14 He will glorify me, for he will take what is mine and declare it to you. 15 All that the Father has is mine; therefore I said that he will take what is mine and declare it to you.

Your Sorrow Will Turn into Joy

16 "A little while, and you will see me no longer; and again a little while, and you will see me." 17 So some of his disciples said to one another, "What is this that he says to us, 'A little while, and you will not see me, and again a little while, and you will see me'; and, 'because I am going to the Father'?" 18 So they were saying, "What does he mean by 'a little while'? We do not know what he is talking about." 19 Jesus knew that they wanted to ask him, so he said to them, "Is this what you are asking yourselves, what I meant by saying, 'A little while and you will not see me, and again a little while and you will see me'? 20 Truly, truly, I say to you, you will weep and lament, but the world will rejoice. You will be sorrowful, but your sorrow will turn into joy. 21 When a woman is giving birth, she has sorrow because her hour has come, but when she has delivered the baby, she no longer remembers the anguish, for joy that a human being has been born into the world. 22 So also you have sorrow now, but I will see you again, and your hearts will rejoice, and no one will take your joy from you. 23 In that day you will ask nothing of me. Truly, truly, I say to you, whatever you ask of the Father in my name, he will give it to you. 24 Until now you have asked nothing in my name. Ask, and you will receive, that your joy may be full.

[1] Greek *they would not have sin*; also verse 24

I Have Overcome the World

25 “I have said these things to you in figures of speech. The hour is coming when I will no longer speak to you in figures of speech but will tell you plainly about the Father. 26 In that day you will ask in my name, and I do not say to you that I will ask the Father on your behalf; 27 for the Father himself loves you, because you have loved me and have believed that I came from God.[1] 28 I came from the Father and have come into the world, and now I am leaving the world and going to the Father.”

29 His disciples said, “Ah, now you are speaking plainly and not using figurative speech! 30 Now we know that you know all things and do not need anyone to question you; this is why we believe that you came from God.” 31 Jesus answered them, “Do you now believe? 32 Behold, the hour is coming, indeed it has come, when you will be scattered, each to his own home, and will leave me alone. Yet I am not alone, for the Father is with me. 33 I have said these things to you, that in me you may have peace. In the world you will have tribulation. But take heart; I have overcome the world.”

The High Priestly Prayer

17 When Jesus had spoken these words, he lifted up his eyes to heaven, and said, “Father, the hour has come; glorify your Son that the Son may glorify you, 2 since you have given him authority over all flesh, to give eternal life to all whom you have given him. 3 And this is eternal life, that they know you the only true God, and Jesus Christ whom you have sent. 4 I glorified you on earth, having accomplished the work that you gave me to do. 5 And now, Father,
1397, glorify me in your own presence
1453 with the glory that I had with you
before the world existed.

6 “I have manifested your name to the people whom you gave me out of the world. Yours they were, and you gave them to me, and they have kept your word. 7 Now they know that everything that you have given me is from you. 8 For I have given them the words that you gave me, and they have received them and have come to know in truth that I came from you; and they have believed that you sent me. 9 I am praying for them. I am not praying for the world but for those whom you have given me, for they are yours. 10 All mine are yours, and yours are mine, and I am glorified in them. 11 And I am no longer in the world, but they are in the world, and I am coming to you. Holy Father, keep them in your name, which you have given me, that they may be one, even as we are one. 12 While I was with them, I kept them in your name, which you have given me. I have guarded them, and not one of them has been lost except the son of destruction, that the Scripture might be fulfilled. 13 But now I am coming to you, and these things I speak in the world, that they may have my joy fulfilled in themselves. 14 I have given them your word, and the world has hated them because they are not of the world, just as I am not of the world. 15 I do not ask that you take them out of the world, but that you keep them from the evil one.[2] 16 They are not of the world, just as I am not of the world. 17 Sanctify them[3] in the truth; your word is truth. 18 As you sent me into the world, so I have sent them into the world. 19 And for their sake I consecrate myself,[4] that they also may be sanctified[5] in truth.

20 “I do not ask for these only, but also for those who will believe in me through their word, 21 that they may all be one, just as you, Father, are in me, and I in you, that they also may be in us, so that the world may believe that you have sent me. 22 The glory that you have given me I have given to them, that they may be one even as we are one, 23 I in them and you in me, that they may become perfectly one, so

[1] Some manuscripts *from the Father* [2] Or *from evil* [3] Greek *Set them apart* (for holy service to God) [4] Or *I sanctify myself*; or *I set myself apart* (for holy service to God)
[5] Greek *may be set apart* (for holy service to God)

that the world may know that you sent
me and loved them even as you loved me.
24 Father, I desire that they also, whom you
have given me, may be with me where I
am, to see my glory that you have given
me because you loved me before the foun-
dation of the world. **25** O righteous Father,
even though the world does not know
you, I know you, and these know that you
have sent me. **26** I made known to them
your name, and I will continue to make it
known, that the love with which you have
loved me may be in them, and I in them."

Betrayal and Arrest of Jesus

18 When Jesus had spoken
these words, he went out
with his disciples across the Kidron
1361, 1421, Valley, where there was a garden,
1523 which he and his disciples entered.
2 Now Judas, who betrayed him, also knew
the place, for Jesus often met there with
his disciples. **3** So Judas, having procured a
band of soldiers and some officers from
the chief priests and the Pharisees, went
there with lanterns and torches and weap-
ons. **4** Then Jesus, knowing all that would
happen to him, came forward and said to
them, "Whom do you seek?" **5** They an-
swered him, "Jesus of Nazareth." Jesus
said to them, "I am he."[1] Judas, who be-
trayed him, was standing with them.
6 When Jesus[2] said to them, "I am he," they
drew back and fell to the ground. **7** So he
asked them again, "Whom do you seek?"
And they said, "Jesus of Nazareth." **8** Jesus
answered, "I told you that I am he. So, if
you seek me, let these men go." **9** This was
to fulfill the word that he had spoken: "Of
those whom you gave me I have lost not
one." **10** Then Simon Peter, having a sword,
drew it and struck the high priest's ser-
vant[3] and cut off his right ear. (The ser-
vant's name was Malchus.) **11** So Jesus said
to Peter, "Put your sword into its sheath;
shall I not drink the cup that the Father
has given me?"

Jesus Faces Annas and Caiaphas

12 So the band of soldiers and their cap-
tain and the officers of the Jews arrested
Jesus and bound him. **13** First they led him
to Annas, for he was the father-in-law of
Caiaphas, who was high priest that year.
14 It was Caiaphas who had advised the
Jews that it would be expedient that one
man should die for the people.

Peter Denies Jesus

15 Simon Peter followed Jesus, and
so did another disciple. Since that
1415 disciple was known to the high
priest, he entered with Jesus into the court
of the high priest, **16** but Peter stood out-
side at the door. So the other disciple, who
was known to the high priest, went out
and spoke to the servant girl who kept
watch at the door, and brought Peter in.
17 The servant girl at the door said to Peter,
"You also are not one of this man's disci-
ples, are you?" He said, "I am not." **18** Now
the servants[4] and officers had made a
charcoal fire, because it was cold, and they
were standing and warming themselves.
Peter also was with them, standing and
warming himself.

The High Priest Questions Jesus

19 The high priest then questioned
Jesus about his disciples and his teach-
ing. **20** Jesus answered him, "I have spoken
openly to the world. I have always taught
in synagogues and in the temple, where
all Jews come together. I have said noth-
ing in secret. **21** Why do you ask me? Ask
those who have heard me what I said to
them; they know what I said." **22** When he
had said these things, one of the officers
standing by struck Jesus with his hand,
saying, "Is that how you answer the high
priest?" **23** Jesus answered him, "If what
I said is wrong, bear witness about the
wrong; but if what I said is right, why do
you strike me?" **24** Annas then sent him
bound to Caiaphas the high priest.

[1] Greek *I am*; also verses 6, 8 [2] Greek *he* [3] Greek *bondservant*; twice in this verse [4] Greek *bondservants*; also verse 26

Peter Denies Jesus Again

25 Now Simon Peter was standing and warming himself. So they said to him, "You also are not one of his disciples, are you?" He denied it and said, "I am not." 26 One of the servants of the high priest, a relative of the man whose ear Peter had cut off, asked, "Did I not see you in the garden with him?" 27 Peter again denied it, and at once a rooster crowed.

Jesus Before Pilate

28 Then they led Jesus from the house of Caiaphas to the governor's headquarters.[1] It was early morning. They themselves did not enter the governor's headquarters, so that they would not be defiled, but could eat the Passover. 29 So Pilate went outside to them and said, "What accusation do you bring against this man?" 30 They answered him, "If this man were not doing evil, we would not have delivered him over to you." 31 Pilate said to them, "Take him yourselves and judge him by your own law." The Jews said to him, "It is not lawful for us to put anyone to death." 32 This was to fulfill the word that Jesus had spoken to show by what kind of death he was going to die.

My Kingdom Is Not of This World

33 So Pilate entered his headquarters again and called Jesus and said to him, "Are you the King of the Jews?" 34 Jesus answered, "Do you say this of your own accord, or did others say it to you about me?" 35 Pilate answered, "Am I a Jew? Your own nation and the chief priests have delivered you over to me. What have you done?" 36 Jesus answered, "My kingdom is not of this world. If my kingdom were of this world, my servants would have been fighting, that I might not be delivered over to the Jews. But my kingdom is not from the world." 37 Then Pilate said to him, "So you are a king?" Jesus answered, "You say that I am a king. For this purpose I was born and for this purpose I have come into the world—to bear witness to the truth. Everyone who is of the truth listens to my voice." 38 Pilate said to him, "What is truth?"

After he had said this, he went back outside to the Jews and told them, "I find no guilt in him. 39 But you have a custom that I should release one man for you at the Passover. So do you want me to release to you the King of the Jews?" 40 They cried out again, "Not this man, but Barabbas!" Now Barabbas was a robber.[2]

Jesus Delivered to Be Crucified

19 Then Pilate took Jesus and flogged him. 2 And the soldiers twisted together a crown of thorns and put it on his head and arrayed him in a purple robe. 3 They came up to him, saying, "Hail, King of the Jews!" and struck him with their hands. 4 Pilate went out again and said to them, "See, I am bringing him out to you that you may know that I find no guilt in him." 5 So Jesus came out, wearing the crown of thorns and the purple robe. Pilate said to them, "Behold the man!" 6 When the chief priests and the officers saw him, they cried out, "Crucify him, crucify him!" Pilate said to them, "Take him yourselves and crucify him, for I find no guilt in him." 7 The Jews answered him, "We have a law, and according to that law he ought to die because he has made himself the Son of God." 8 When Pilate heard this statement, he was even more afraid. 9 He entered his headquarters again and said to Jesus, "Where are you from?" But Jesus gave him no answer. 10 So Pilate said to him, "You will not speak to me? Do you not know that I have authority to release you and authority to crucify you?" 11 Jesus answered him, "You would have no authority over me at all unless it had been given you from above. Therefore he who delivered me over to you has the greater sin."

12 From then on Pilate sought to release him, but the Jews cried out, "If you

[1] Greek *the praetorium* [2] Or *an insurrectionist*

Golgotha and the Temple Mount

No one is completely certain where Jesus was crucified, buried, and rose from the dead. A church called the Church of the Holy Sepulcher marks the spot where people think Jesus died and rose again. There are several good reasons for believing that this is the correct location.

The Bible says Jesus was put to death outside of the walls of Jerusalem (Hebrews 13:12). The Church of the Holy Sepulcher was built on a mass of rock. Archaeologists have discovered tombs in this rock from the time when Jesus was alive. We know this spot was outside of the city walls, because people buried the dead outside of the city.

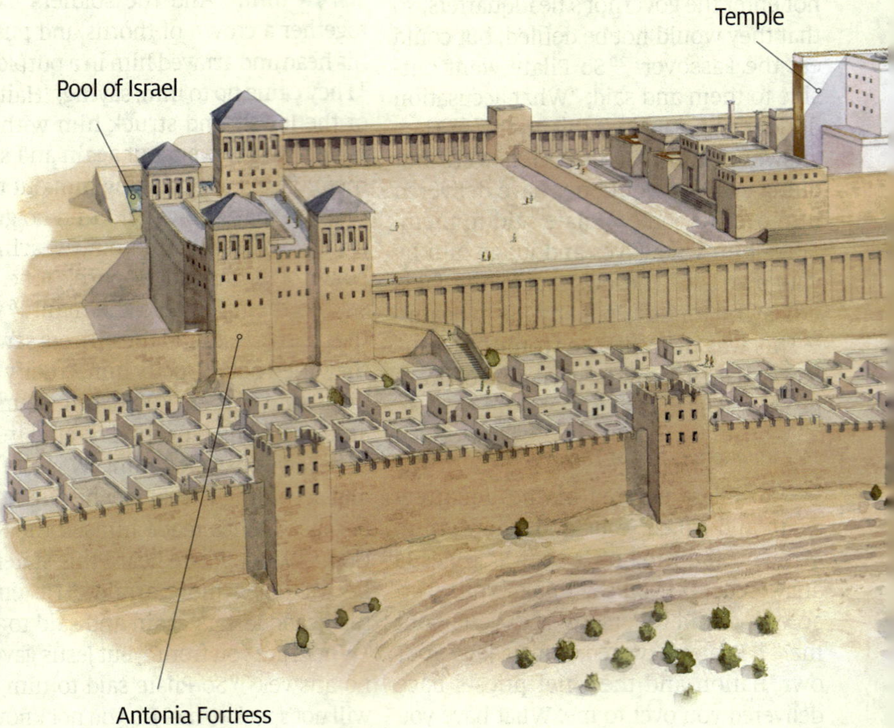

The Bible says there was a garden where Jesus was crucified (John 19:41). Ruins near the Church of the Holy Sepulcher are believed to be the gate to a garden, and soil good for growing plants is near the spot.

The drawing shows the place where it's believed Jesus died and where He may have been buried. Three crosses are shown on the Hill of Golgotha, where Jesus was crucified. The Temple Mount is shown behind Golgotha. To the left is the Roman Fortress, Antonia Fortress, and to the right is the Royal Stoa, a long, covered walkway that was part of the temple complex. A possible location for the tomb of Joseph of Arimathea, where Jesus was buried, is shown near Golgotha.

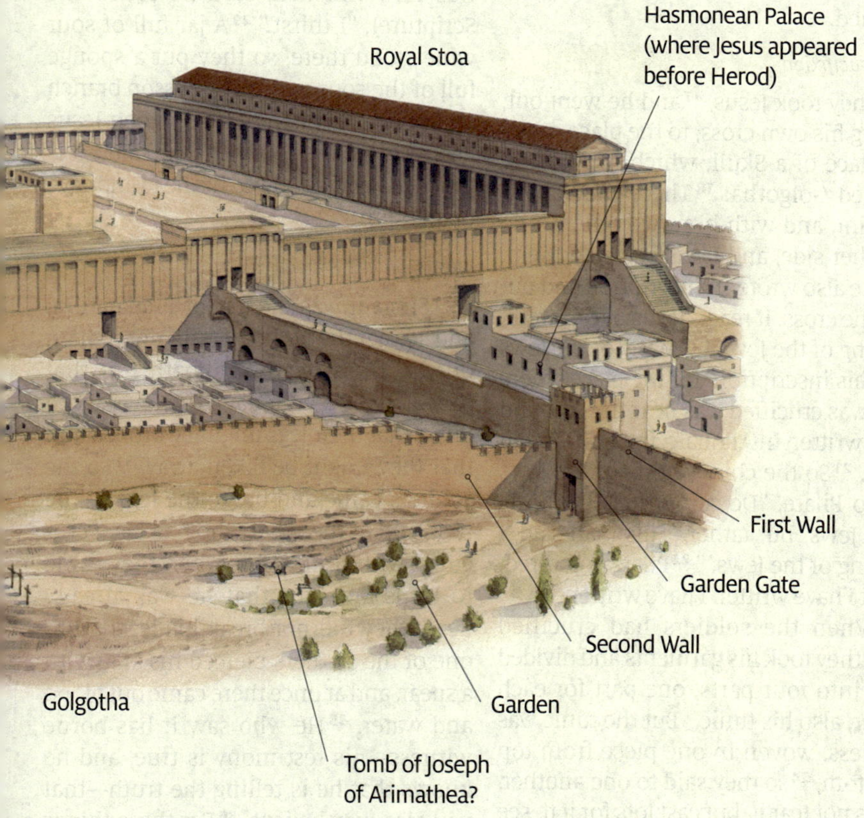

release this man, you are not Caesar's friend. Everyone who makes himself a king opposes Caesar." 13 So when Pilate heard these words, he brought Jesus out and sat down on the judgment seat at a place called The Stone Pavement, and in Aramaic[1] Gabbatha. 14 Now it was the day of Preparation of the Passover. It was about the sixth hour.[2] He said to the Jews, "Behold your King!" 15 They cried out, "Away with him, away with him, crucify him!" Pilate said to them, "Shall I crucify your King?" The chief priests answered, "We have no king but Caesar." 16 So he delivered him over to them to be crucified.

The Crucifixion

So they took Jesus, 17 and he went out, bearing his own cross, to the place called The Place of a Skull, which in Aramaic is called Golgotha. 18 There they crucified him, and with him two others, one on either side, and Jesus between them. 19 Pilate also wrote an inscription and put it on the cross. It read, "Jesus of Nazareth, the King of the Jews." 20 Many of the Jews read this inscription, for the place where Jesus was crucified was near the city, and it was written in Aramaic, in Latin, and in Greek. 21 So the chief priests of the Jews said to Pilate, "Do not write, 'The King of the Jews,' but rather, 'This man said, I am King of the Jews.'" 22 Pilate answered, "What I have written I have written."

23 When the soldiers had crucified Jesus, they took his garments and divided them into four parts, one part for each soldier; also his tunic.[3] But the tunic was seamless, woven in one piece from top to bottom, 24 so they said to one another, "Let us not tear it, but cast lots for it to see whose it shall be." This was to fulfill the Scripture which says,

> "They divided my garments among
> them,
> and for my clothing they cast lots."

So the soldiers did these things, 25 but standing by the cross of Jesus were his mother and his mother's sister, Mary the wife of Clopas, and Mary Magdalene. 26 When Jesus saw his mother and the disciple whom he loved standing nearby, he said to his mother, "Woman, behold, your son!" 27 Then he said to the disciple, "Behold, your mother!" And from that hour the disciple took her to his own home.

The Death of Jesus

28 After this, Jesus, knowing that all was now finished, said (to fulfill the Scripture), "I thirst." 29 A jar full of sour wine stood there, so they put a sponge full of the sour wine on a hyssop branch and held it to his mouth. 30 When Jesus had received the sour wine, he said, "It is finished," and he bowed his head and gave up his spirit.

Jesus' Side Is Pierced

31 Since it was the day of Preparation, and so that the bodies would not remain on the cross on the Sabbath (for that Sabbath was a high day), the Jews asked Pilate that their legs might be broken and that they might be taken away. 32 So the soldiers came and broke the legs of the first, and of the other who had been crucified with him. 33 But when they came to Jesus and saw that he was already dead, they did not break his legs. 34 But one of the soldiers pierced his side with a spear, and at once there came out blood and water. 35 He who saw it has borne witness—his testimony is true, and he knows that he is telling the truth—that you also may believe. 36 For these things took place that the Scripture might be fulfilled: "Not one of his bones will be broken." 37 And again another Scripture says, "They will look on him whom they have pierced."

[1] Or *Hebrew*; also verses 17, 20 [2] That is, about noon [3] Greek *chiton*, a long garment worn under the cloak next to the skin

The Tomb of Jesus

The Gospel writers tell us that after Jesus died, a rich man, Joseph of Arimathea, took His body and placed it in a new tomb he had built for himself and his family. Tombs were built by carving out rooms in rock. They were like man-made caves. In the center of the tomb would be a pit, with benches for dead bodies on three sides of the pit. Jesus was buried in a new tomb; older tombs would have more rooms built into them.

Some women saw where Jesus' body was placed (Mark 15:47). After the resurrection, some disciples saw the grave clothes lying in the tomb and the face cloth folded (John 20:5–6). Jesus' body must have been placed on a bench across from the opening to the tomb.

The entrance to the tomb would have been low, causing the disciples to stoop down to look inside and enter (Luke 24:12; John 20:5). Archaeologists have uncovered almost 1,000 tombs from Jesus' time in and around Jerusalem. Only a few of them had rolling stones to close off the entrance to the tomb. Only very rich people (like Joseph of Arimathea) had this kind of door. Usually, a tomb had a square doorway, and the stone fit in the doorway like a cork in a bottle. The Bible says the stone of Jesus' tomb had been rolled away (Matthew 27:60; Mark 15:46; Luke 24:2). In this cutaway drawing of what Jesus' tomb would have been like, a very large rolling stone is shown for a door, as the tomb of a rich man would have had.

The Empty Tomb

Jesus had been dead since Friday afternoon. His followers and friends were sad and quiet on Saturday, the Sabbath day—the day Jewish people set aside each week for rest and worship.

But early in the morning on Sunday, the first day of the week, Mary Magdalene went to the place where Jesus was buried. How surprised she was when she got there! Someone had rolled away the large stone from the tomb! When she saw this, Mary hurried back to tell Jesus' close friends Peter and John that someone had taken the Lord's body from the tomb, and she did not know where Jesus' body was.

Peter and John ran to Jesus' tomb to see for themselves. John got there first and peeked inside, but he didn't go in. He saw the cloths that had been used to wrap up Jesus' body. Then Peter ran up and went inside. Near the pile of cloths he saw the cloth that had covered Jesus' face, neatly folded. Then John went inside too and "he believed." But they did not see Jesus!

The disciples hurried back home, but Mary stayed in the garden, crying. She did not know Jesus was alive. She looked into the tomb and saw two angels, dressed in white. They asked her why she was crying, and she said, "They have taken away my Lord, and I do not know where they have laid Him."

Then Mary turned around and saw Jesus standing there right in front of her, but she did not recognize Him right away.

She thought maybe the man was the gardener. “Sir,” she said, “if you have carried Him away, tell me where you have laid Him, and I will take Him away.”

Then Jesus said her name: “Mary.” Immediately, Mary knew it was Jesus! Mary stopped crying. She was so happy Jesus was alive!

Jesus told Mary to go and tell His disciples the good news. Mary joyfully hurried to tell them: “I have seen the Lord!”

Jesus’ friends were happy that Jesus was alive. We also share in the joy and excitement that Jesus is alive and our sins are forgiven. We celebrate Jesus’ resurrection every Sunday, but especially on Easter, when we remember Mary’s early morning visit to the empty tomb.

SEEK and FIND

WHERE TO FIND THE STORY

John 20:1–18

KEY BIBLE VERSE

“If Christ has not been raised, your faith is futile and you are still in your sins. . . . But in fact Christ has been raised from the dead.” (1 Corinthians 15:17, 20)

THREE KEY QUESTIONS

- What did Peter and John see when they looked into the tomb?
- How did Mary know that the man she saw in the garden was not the gardener?
- When do we celebrate Jesus’ resurrection?

RELATED BIBLE READINGS

Matthew 28:1–10; Mark 16:1–8; Luke 24:1–12; 1 Corinthians 15:1–22

Jesus Is Buried

38 After these things Joseph of Arimathea, who was a disciple of Jesus, but secretly for fear of the Jews, asked Pilate that he might take away the body of Jesus, and Pilate gave him permission. So he came and took away his body. 39 Nicodemus also, who earlier had come to Jesus[1] by night, came bringing a mixture of myrrh and aloes, about seventy-five pounds[2] in weight. 40 So they took the body of Jesus and bound it in linen cloths with the spices, as is the burial custom of the Jews. 41 Now in the place where he was crucified there was a garden, and in the garden a new tomb in which no one had yet been laid. 42 So because of the Jewish day of Preparation, since the tomb was close at hand, they laid Jesus there.

The Resurrection

1593
1365

20 Now on the first day of the week Mary Magdalene came to the tomb early, while it was still dark, and saw that the stone had been taken away from the tomb. 2 So she ran and went to Simon Peter and the other disciple, the one whom Jesus loved, and said to them, "They have taken the Lord out of the tomb, and we do not know where they have laid him." 3 So Peter went out with the other disciple, and they were going toward the tomb. 4 Both of them were running together, but the other disciple outran Peter and reached the tomb first. 5 And stooping to look in, he saw the linen cloths lying there, but he did not go in. 6 Then Simon Peter came, following him, and went into the tomb. He saw the linen cloths lying there, 7 and the face cloth, which had been on Jesus'[3] head, not lying with the linen cloths but folded up in a place by itself. 8 Then the other disciple, who had reached the tomb first, also went in, and he saw and believed; 9 for as yet they did not understand the Scripture, that he must rise from the dead. 10 Then the disciples went back to their homes.

Jesus Appears to Mary Magdalene

1529

11 But Mary stood weeping outside the tomb, and as she wept she stooped to look into the tomb. 12 And she saw two angels in white, sitting where the body of Jesus had lain, one at the head and one at the feet. 13 They said to her, "Woman, why are you weeping?" She said to them, "They have taken away my Lord, and I do not know where they have laid him." 14 Having said this, she turned around and saw Jesus standing, but she did not know that it was Jesus. 15 Jesus said to her, "Woman, why are you weeping? Whom are you seeking?" Supposing him to be the gardener, she said to him, "Sir, if you have carried him away, tell me where you have laid him, and I will take him away." 16 Jesus said to her, "Mary." She turned and said to him in Aramaic,[4] "Rabboni!" (which means Teacher). 17 Jesus said to her, "Do not cling to me, for I have not yet ascended to the Father; but go to my brothers and say to them, 'I am ascending to my Father and your Father, to my God and your God.'" 18 Mary Magdalene went and announced to the disciples, "I have seen the Lord"—and that he had said these things to her.

Jesus Appears to the Disciples

1597

19 On the evening of that day, the first day of the week, the doors being locked where the disciples were for fear of the Jews, Jesus came and stood among them and said to them, "Peace be with you." 20 When he had said this, he showed them his hands and his side. Then the disciples were glad when they saw the Lord. 21 Jesus said to them again, "Peace be with you. As the Father has sent me, even so I am sending you." 22 And when he had said this, he breathed on them and said to them, "Receive the Holy Spirit. 23 If you forgive the sins of any, they

[1] Greek *him* [2] Greek *one hundred litras*; a *litra* (or Roman pound) was equal to about 11 1/2 ounces or 327 grams [3] Greek *his* [4] Or *Hebrew*

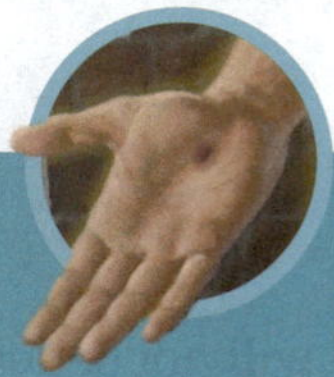

Jesus Appears to the Disciples

Immediately after Mary Magdalene saw Jesus alive in the garden near the tomb, she went back and told Jesus' closest friends and followers. They were excited to hear the good news—that Jesus was alive!

That evening most of the disciples were gathered together in a room indoors. Everyone was there except Thomas. They kept the doors locked because they were afraid of what the Jewish leaders might do. Jesus had been taken away and killed—and they were worried that they might be in danger because they were Jesus' friends. Suddenly Jesus stood there among them! "Peace be with you," He said.

Jesus showed the disciples the marks of the nails in His hands and feet, so they would not be afraid and would know it was really Jesus. The disciples were overjoyed to see that Jesus really was alive! Jesus told the disciples that, just as the Father had sent Him, now He was sending them out into the world. He breathed on them and said, "Receive the Holy Spirit."

Later—after Jesus had left them and Thomas joined the others in the room—the disciples excitedly told Thomas, "We have seen the Lord!" But Thomas could not believe the amazing news. He said, "Unless I see in His hands the mark of the nails, and place my finger into the mark of the nails, and place my hand into His side, I will not believe."

Eight days later, the disciples were together again. This time, Thomas was with them. Even though the doors were locked, suddenly Jesus was in the room again. "Peace be with you," He said again. Then Jesus came near to Thomas and said, "Put your finger here, and see My hands; and put out your hand and place it in My side. Do not disbelieve, but believe." Now Thomas believed that Jesus was alive. "My Lord and my God!" he cried.

Jesus said, "Have you believed because you have seen Me? Blessed are those who have not seen and yet have believed." It is a hard thing to believe that a person could die and come alive again. Thomas believed it when he saw with his own eyes that Jesus was truly living. But Jesus knew that many people all over the world and for many hundreds of years would believe in the truth of His resurrection, even when they couldn't see Him with their eyes.

We believe the truth of Jesus' resurrection through God's Word, the Bible. The Holy Spirit gives us eyes of faith so that we can believe and know that Jesus truly lives!

SEEK and FIND

WHERE TO FIND THE STORY

John 20:19–29

KEY BIBLE VERSE

"Though you have not seen him, you love him. Though you do not now see him, you believe in him and rejoice with joy that is inexpressible and filled with glory." (1 Peter 1:8)

THREE KEY QUESTIONS

- Why did Jesus show His disciples the marks of the nails in His hands and feet?
- Why did Thomas have such a hard time believing the disciples had really seen Jesus alive?
- What did Jesus say about people who have not seen Jesus, but who still believe in Him?

RELATED BIBLE READINGS

Luke 24:36–43; 1 Corinthians 15:3–7

are forgiven them; if you withhold forgiveness from any, it is withheld."

Jesus and Thomas

24 Now Thomas, one of the Twelve, called the Twin,[1] was not with them when Jesus came. 25 So the other disciples told him, "We have seen the Lord." But he said to them, "Unless I see in his hands the mark of the nails, and place my finger into the mark of the nails, and place my hand into his side, I will never believe."

26 Eight days later, his disciples were inside again, and Thomas was with them. Although the doors were locked, Jesus came and stood among them and said, "Peace be with you." 27 Then he said to Thomas, "Put your finger here, and see my hands; and put out your hand, and place it in my side. Do not disbelieve, but believe." 28 Thomas answered him, "My Lord and my God!" 29 Jesus said to him, "Have you believed because you have seen me? Blessed are those who have not seen and yet have believed."

The Purpose of This Book

30 Now Jesus did many other signs
in the presence of the disciples,
1541 which are not written in this book;
31 but these are written so that you may believe that Jesus is the Christ, the Son of God, and that by believing you may have life in his name.

Jesus Appears to Seven Disciples

21 After this Jesus revealed
himself again to the disci-
1601, ples by the Sea of Tiberias, and he
1605 revealed himself in this way.
2 Simon Peter, Thomas (called the
Twin), Nathanael of Cana in Galilee,
1467, the sons of Zebedee, and two others
1537 of his disciples were together.
3 Simon Peter said to them, "I am going fishing." They said to him, "We will go with you." They went out and got into the boat, but that night they caught nothing.

4 Just as day was breaking, Jesus stood on the shore; yet the disciples did not know that it was Jesus. 5 Jesus said to them, "Children, do you have any fish?" They answered him, "No." 6 He said to them, "Cast the net on the right side of the boat, and you will find some." So they cast it, and now they were not able to haul it in, because of the quantity of fish. 7 That disciple whom Jesus loved therefore said to Peter, "It is the Lord!" When Simon Peter heard that it was the Lord,

[1] Greek *Didymus*

The Miraculous Catch of Fish

Many of Jesus' disciples had been fishermen before Jesus called them to walk with Him and become "fishers of men." After Jesus death and resurrection, they still went fishing sometimes. They would especially go at night when the fish they caught at night could be sold fresh in the morning.

One night, not long after the disciples had seen Jesus alive again, Peter went fishing with six other disciples. The men fished all night, but they didn't catch a single fish.

Early in the morning, just as the sun was coming up, someone called out to them from shore: "Do you have any fish?" Tired and discouraged, the disciples yelled back, "No."

Then the man on the shore told them to throw out their net on the right side of the boat. The disciples tossed the net into the water. Suddenly there were so many fish in their net they couldn't even pull it up into the boat! Such an amazing catch was a miracle! Right away the disciple named John knew the man on shore must be Jesus. With joy he said to Peter, "It is the Lord!"

Peter was so excited to see Jesus he jumped in the water and swam to shore, leaving the other disciples and the fish behind. When they all reached the shore, tugging their big net along with them, they saw a charcoal fire, with fish laid out on it, and bread. Jesus told the disciples to bring some of their fish. Peter hauled in the net—filled with 153 large fish.

There on the seashore, Jesus prepared the food and served His disciples. He said, "Come and have breakfast." He took the bread and gave it to them with the fish. Even though He was God's own Son, who had created the whole world, He was glad to show His love by serving His friends.

What a blessing for Jesus' disciples to see Jesus again and to know that He had risen from the dead. Jesus reveals Himself to us, too, through His Word. He gives us joy and confidence that He has risen and is still caring for us.

SEEK and FIND

WHERE TO FIND THE STORY

John 21:1–14

KEY BIBLE VERSE

"The God of peace . . . brought again from the dead our Lord Jesus, the great shepherd of the sheep." (Hebrews 13:20)

THREE KEY QUESTIONS

- How many fish did the disciples catch when they fished all night?
- How did John know the man on the shore must be Jesus?
- How does Jesus care for us today?

RELATED BIBLE READINGS

Matthew 14:24–33; Luke 5:1–11; 1 Corinthians 15:3–7

he put on his outer garment, for he was
stripped for work, and threw himself into
the sea. **8** The other disciples came in the
boat, dragging the net full of fish, for they
were not far from the land, but about a
hundred yards[1] off.

9 When they got out on land, they saw
a charcoal fire in place, with fish laid out
on it, and bread. **10** Jesus said to them,
"Bring some of the fish that you have just
caught." **11** So Simon Peter went aboard
and hauled the net ashore, full of large
fish, 153 of them. And although there were
so many, the net was not torn. **12** Jesus
said to them, "Come and have breakfast."
Now none of the disciples dared ask him,
"Who are you?" They knew it was the Lord.
13 Jesus came and took the bread and gave
it to them, and so with the fish. **14** This was
now the third time that Jesus was revealed
to the disciples after he was raised from
the dead.

Jesus and Peter

15 When they had finished breakfast,
Jesus said to Simon Peter, "Simon, son of
John, do you love me more than these?"
He said to him, "Yes, Lord; you know
that I love you." He said to him, "Feed my
lambs." **16** He said to him a second time,
"Simon, son of John, do you love me?"
He said to him, "Yes, Lord; you know
that I love you." He said to him, "Tend my
sheep." **17** He said to him the third time,
"Simon, son of John, do you love me?"
Peter was grieved because he said to him
the third time, "Do you love me?" and he
said to him, "Lord, you know everything;
you know that I love you." Jesus said to
him, "Feed my sheep. **18** Truly, truly, I say
to you, when you were young, you used
to dress yourself and walk wherever you
wanted, but when you are old, you will
stretch out your hands, and another will
dress you and carry you where you do
not want to go." **19** (This he said to show
by what kind of death he was to glorify
God.) And after saying this he said to him,
"Follow me."

Jesus and the Beloved Apostle

20 Peter turned and saw the disciple
whom Jesus loved following them, the
one who had been reclining at table close
to him and had said, "Lord, who is it that
is going to betray you?" **21** When Peter saw
him, he said to Jesus, "Lord, what about
this man?" **22** Jesus said to him, "If it is my
will that he remain until I come, what is
that to you? You follow me!" **23** So the say-
ing spread abroad among the brothers[2]
that this disciple was not to die; yet Jesus
did not say to him that he was not to die,
but, "If it is my will that he remain until I
come, what is that to you?"

24 This is the disciple who is bearing
witness about these things, and who has
written these things, and we know that
his testimony is true.

25 Now there are also many other things
that Jesus did. Were every one of them to
be written, I suppose that the world itself
could not contain the books that would
be written.

[1] Greek *two hundred cubits*; a *cubit* was about 18 inches or 45 centimeters [2] Or *brothers and sisters*

Jesus Forgives Peter

The Lord Jesus had special plans for His friend, the disciple called Peter. On the night that Jesus was betrayed and taken as a prisoner, Peter had lied three times. Peter pretended that he was not a friend and follower of Jesus. Peter had said that he'd never deny Jesus. But Jesus knew that he would. Because he was afraid of what people might do to him, Peter's fear led him to sin. But Jesus still forgave him.

On the morning when Jesus helped the disciples catch a huge net full of fish, Jesus served them a breakfast of fish and bread. After breakfast, Jesus took Peter aside to talk with him alone.

Jesus asked Peter, "Do you love Me?"

"Yes, Lord," said Peter. "You know that I love You."

Jesus answered. "Feed My lambs." A second time He asked, "Do you love Me?"

"Yes, Lord," said Peter. "You know that I love You."

"Tend My sheep," said Jesus. A third time Jesus asked Peter, "Do you love Me?"

Peter felt sad that Jesus had asked him three times. "Lord," said Peter, "You know everything; You know that I love You."

"Feed My sheep," Jesus said once again. Then He said, "Follow Me."

Who were the sheep that Jesus mentioned three times? Jesus was talking about His own friends and followers. But He was also talking about all the people who would come to believe that Jesus is the Savior. Jesus forgave Peter for denying Him three times on the night when Jesus was betrayed and taken prisoner. He gave Peter important work to do, teaching people about Jesus and caring for God's people.

Sometimes we are like Peter. Sometimes our words and actions seem to say that we are not Jesus' followers or friends. But Jesus is faithful! When we are sorry for our sin and turn to Jesus, He always forgives us and keeps on loving us.

SEEK and FIND

WHERE TO FIND THE STORY

John 21:15–19

KEY BIBLE VERSE

"For you were straying like sheep, but have now returned to the Shepherd and Overseer of your souls." (1 Peter 2:25)

THREE KEY QUESTIONS

- Why did Peter deny Jesus?
- What did Jesus ask Peter and how many times did He ask him?
- What was the important work that Jesus gave Peter to do?

RELATED BIBLE READINGS

Luke 22:54–62; 1 Peter 5:1–4; 1 John 1:9–2:1

Introduction to

Acts

Author
Luke

Date
About A.D. 60–62

Key People
Jesus; Peter; John; Stephen; Barnabas; Philip; Cornelius; Saul/Paul; James, the brother of John; James, the brother of Jesus; John Mark; Timothy; Luke

Purpose
The purpose of Acts is to show how Jesus' ministry continued through the Spirit-filled apostles and church as they witnessed about Jesus from Jerusalem to the ends of the earth.

Central Themes
Jesus sends the Holy Spirit who empowers His followers to carry on His ministry; the gospel spreads to the ends of the earth, to Gentiles as well as Jews; Jesus conquers hearts everywhere the gospel goes; the gospel message calls all to repent and believe in Jesus Christ; Jesus establishes, strengthens, and protects His young Church.

Memory Verses
The mission (Acts 1:7–9); the name of Jesus (Acts 4:11–12); Stephen's prayer (Acts 7:59–60); saved by grace (Acts 15:10–11); counsel for church elders (Acts 20:28–32)

Introduction

Acts begins with Jesus' promise to His followers that He will send the Holy Spirit, who will give them power to be His witnesses in Jerusalem, in all Judea and Samaria, and to the ends of the earth (Acts 1). When the Holy Spirit comes, this empowering begins (Acts 2). People believe their witness, and even though the church in Jerusalem grows by thousands, persecution grows, too (Acts 3–5). When Stephen is stoned to death for his preaching, great persecution arises and many believers leave Jerusalem (Acts 6:1–8:3). Everywhere they go, they tell of Jesus, so that the gospel spreads into Judea and Samaria (8:4–25). Saul, a leading persecutor, sees Jesus in a vision and becomes, not only one of His followers, but a bold, outspoken teacher and missionary for Christ (Acts 9). The rest of Acts follows Saul—later called Paul—as he takes the gospel to places where it hasn't been heard. When Acts ends, Paul is in prison awaiting a trial—but he is in Rome, the capital of the world, still teaching about the Lord Jesus Christ (Acts 28:30–31). So Acts begins in Jerusalem, the center of the Jewish world, highlighting Peter, the apostle to the Jews (Acts 1–12); it ends in Rome, the center of the Gentile world, highlighting Paul, the apostle to the Gentiles (Acts 13–28).

About A.D. 33/34	About A.D. 46–57	About A.D. 64–67
Pentecost, conversion of Paul	Paul's missionary journeys	Peter and Paul martyred in Rome

The Acts of the Apostles

The Promise of the Holy Spirit

1611

1 In the first book, O Theophilus, I have dealt with all that Jesus began to do and teach, 2 until the day when he was taken up, after he had given commands through the Holy Spirit to the apostles whom he had chosen. 3 He presented himself alive to them after his suffering by many proofs, appearing to them during forty days and speaking about the kingdom of God.

1615

4 And while staying[1] with them he ordered them not to depart from Jerusalem, but to wait for the promise of the Father, which, he said, "you heard from me; 5 for John baptized with water, but you will be baptized with[2] the Holy Spirit not many days from now."

The Ascension

6 So when they had come together, they asked him, "Lord, will you at this time restore the kingdom to Israel?" 7 He said to them, "It is not for you to know times or seasons that the Father has fixed by his own authority. 8 But you will receive power when the Holy Spirit has come upon you, and you will be my witnesses in Jerusalem and in all Judea and Samaria, and to the end of the earth." 9 And when he had said these things, as they were looking on, he was lifted up, and a cloud took him out of their sight. 10 And while they were gazing into heaven as he went, behold, two men stood by them in white robes, 11 and said, "Men of Galilee, why do you stand looking into heaven? This Jesus, who was taken up from you into heaven, will come in the same way as you saw him go into heaven."

1657

Matthias Chosen to Replace Judas

12 Then they returned to Jerusalem from the mount called Olivet, which is near Jerusalem, a Sabbath day's journey away. 13 And when they had entered, they went up to the upper room, where they were staying, Peter and John and James and Andrew, Philip and Thomas,

CHARACTER PROFILE

LUKE

Luke was a doctor who became a missionary after he believed in Jesus as Savior. He wrote the Gospel of Luke, which tells the true story of Jesus' time on earth, and the book of Acts, which tells the true story of what happened after Jesus went back to heaven. Luke was a Gentile, a person who was not a Jew, so he gladly wrote about how the Good News of salvation is for people of all nations.

1669

[1] Or *eating* [2] Or *in*

Bartholomew and Matthew, James the son of Alphaeus and Simon the Zealot and Judas the son of James. 14 All these with one accord were devoting themselves to prayer, together with the women and Mary the mother of Jesus, and his brothers.[1]

15 In those days Peter stood up among the brothers (the company of persons was in all about 120) and said, 16 "Brothers, the Scripture had to be fulfilled, which the Holy Spirit spoke beforehand by the mouth of David concerning Judas, who became a guide to those who arrested Jesus. 17 For he was numbered among us and was allotted his share in this ministry." 18 (Now this man acquired a field with the reward of his wickedness, and falling headlong[2] he burst open in the middle and all his bowels gushed out. 19 And it became known to all the inhabitants of Jerusalem, so that the field was called in their own language Akeldama, that is, Field of Blood.) 20 "For it is written in the Book of Psalms,

"'May his camp become desolate,
and let there be no one to dwell in it';

and

"'Let another take his office.'

21 So one of the men who have accompanied us during all the time that the Lord Jesus went in and out among us, 22 beginning from the baptism of John until the day when he was taken up from us—one of these men must become with us a witness to his resurrection." 23 And they put forward two, Joseph called Barsabbas, who was also called Justus, and Matthias. 24 And they prayed and said, "You, Lord, who know the hearts of all, show which one of these two you have chosen 25 to take the place in this ministry and apostleship from which Judas turned aside to go to his own place." 26 And they cast lots for them, and the lot fell on Matthias, and he was numbered with the eleven apostles.

The Coming of the Holy Spirit

1615

2 When the day of Pentecost arrived, they were all together in one place. 2 And suddenly there came from heaven a sound like a mighty rushing wind, and it filled the entire house where they were sitting. 3 And divided tongues as of fire appeared to them and rested[3] on each one of them. 4 And they were all filled with the Holy Spirit and began to speak in other tongues as the Spirit gave them utterance.

5 Now there were dwelling in Jerusalem Jews, devout men from every nation under heaven. 6 And at this sound the multitude came together, and they were bewildered, because each one was hearing them speak in his own language. 7 And they were amazed and astonished, saying, "Are not all these who are speaking Galileans? 8 And how is it that we hear, each of us in his own native language? 9 Parthians and Medes and Elamites and residents of Mesopotamia, Judea and Cappadocia, Pontus and Asia, 10 Phrygia and Pamphylia, Egypt and the parts of Libya belonging to Cyrene, and visitors from Rome, 11 both Jews and proselytes, Cretans and Arabians—we hear them telling in our own tongues the mighty works of God." 12 And all were amazed and perplexed, saying to one another, "What does this mean?" 13 But others mocking said, "They are filled with new wine."

Peter's Sermon at Pentecost

14 But Peter, standing with the eleven, lifted up his voice and addressed them: "Men of Judea and all who dwell in Jerusalem, let this be known to you, and give ear to my words. 15 For these people are not drunk, as you suppose, since it

[1] Or *brothers and sisters*. The plural Greek word *adelphoi* (translated "brothers") refers to siblings in a family. In New Testament usage, depending on the context, *adelphoi* may refer either to men or to both men and women who are siblings (brothers and sisters) in God's family, the church; also verse 15 [2] Or *swelling up* [3] Or *And tongues as of fire appeared to them, distributed among them, and rested*

Jesus Ascends Into Heaven

After His death and resurrection, Jesus visited with His disciples over a period of 40 days. During their time together, Jesus spoke often about the kingdom of God. The disciples listened carefully to everything Jesus commanded, and they were eager to know His plans. After witnessing His resurrection from the dead, the disciples knew that Jesus really was God's Son. They wondered if He might use His power to restore the kingdom of Israel and free the Jewish people from being ruled by the Romans. Jesus helped them understand that God had plans for a different kind of kingdom.

Jesus did give His disciples an exciting promise. He told them to wait in Jerusalem for a gift that His Father would send. They would receive the Holy Spirit. Jesus took His friends and helpers up to a hill outside Jerusalem. Jesus promised them, "You will receive power when the Holy Spirit has come upon you, and you will be My witnesses in Jerusalem and in all Judea and Samaria, and to the end of the earth."

After Jesus had spoken these things, Jesus was lifted up, higher and higher, until He disappeared into a cloud right in front of the disciples' eyes! While the disciples were still gazing up where they had seen Jesus disappear—and before they had a chance to feel too sad or discouraged about Jesus leaving them—two men dressed in white stood beside them. They were angels! The angels had a message for the disciples: "This Jesus, who was taken up from you into heaven, will come in the same way as you saw Him go into heaven." This was great news for Jesus' friends; Jesus would one day come back again!

The disciples did exactly what Jesus had commanded; they returned to Jerusalem to wait for the gift of the Holy Spirit that Jesus had promised. While they waited, Jesus' followers devoted themselves to prayer. Together they worshiped Jesus. Jesus had finished His work on earth and had gone victoriously back to His home in heaven. The disciples had seen Jesus exercise authority over heaven and earth, and they knew He would keep His promises to hear their prayers and care for them, and that He would return one day, in power and great glory, to take them to be with Him forever.

SEEK and FIND

WHERE TO FIND THE STORY

Acts 1:1–14

KEY BIBLE VERSE

"[God] raised him from the dead and seated him at his right hand in the heavenly places, far above all rule and authority and power and dominion, and above every name that is named, not only in this age but also in the one to come." (Ephesians 1:20–21)

THREE KEY QUESTIONS

- How did Jesus' friends know for sure that Jesus really was God's Son?
- What gift did Jesus promise that His followers would receive?

- Once they had received power from God's Holy Spirit, what did Jesus say they would do all over the world?

RELATED BIBLE READINGS

Matthew 28:16–20; Luke 24:50–53; John 14:15–17; 16:7–15; Ephesians 1:19–23; Hebrews 1:4

is only the third hour of the day.[1]
16 But this is what was uttered
1615 through the prophet Joel:

17 "'And in the last days it shall be, God
declares,
that I will pour out my Spirit on all
flesh,
and your sons and your daughters
shall prophesy,
and your young men shall see
visions,
and your old men shall dream
dreams;
18 even on my male servants[2] and
female servants
in those days I will pour out my
Spirit, and they shall prophesy.
19 And I will show wonders in the
heavens above
and signs on the earth below,
blood, and fire, and vapor of smoke;
20 the sun shall be turned to darkness
and the moon to blood,
before the day of the Lord comes,
the great and magnificent day.
21 And it shall come to pass that
everyone who calls upon the
1615 name of the Lord shall be
saved.'

22 "Men of Israel, hear these words:
Jesus of Nazareth, a man attested to
1365, you by God with mighty works and
1463, wonders and signs that God did
1541,
1619 through him in your midst, as you
yourselves know— 23 this Jesus, delivered
up according to the definite plan and fore-
knowledge of God, you crucified and killed
by the hands of lawless men. 24 God raised
him up, loosing the pangs of death, be-
cause it was not possible for him to be held
by it. 25 For David says concerning him,

"'I saw the Lord always before me,
for he is at my right hand that I
may not be shaken;
26 therefore my heart was glad, and
my tongue rejoiced;
my flesh also will dwell in hope.
27 For you will not abandon my soul to
Hades,
or let your Holy One see
corruption.
28 You have made known to me the
paths of life;
you will make me full of gladness
with your presence.'

29 "Brothers, I may say to you with
confidence about the patriarch
499 David that he both died and was
buried, and his tomb is with us to this day.
30 Being therefore a prophet, and knowing
that God had sworn with an oath to him
that he would set one of his descendants
on his throne, 31 he foresaw and spoke
about the resurrection of the Christ, that
he was not abandoned to Hades, nor did
his flesh see corruption. 32 This Jesus God
raised up, and of that we all are witnesses.
33 Being therefore exalted at the right hand

[1] That is, 9 A.M. [2] Greek *bondservants*; twice in this verse

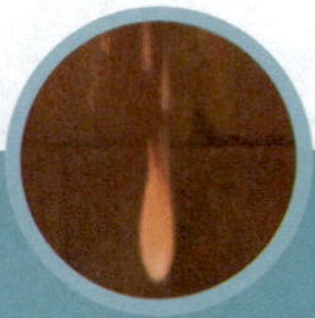

God Sends the Holy Spirit

When the annual harvest celebration day of Pentecost came, God-fearing Jews from all over the world were staying in Jerusalem to observe the festival. Jesus' disciples were meeting together when suddenly a sound like a mighty wind came from heaven. It filled the whole house. Those who were gathered saw what looked like tongues of fire that separated and came to rest on each one of Jesus' followers. They were all filled with the Holy Spirit and began to speak about what Jesus had done in languages other than their own.

The noise of the mighty wind and the bright tongues of fire drew the attention of others, and many people crowded around the disciples. They were amazed at what they saw and heard. Each person was hearing about Jesus in his own language—languages Jesus' followers had never learned to speak!

The people asked how it was that they could hear these people from Galilee declaring the wonders of God in their own native languages. Some people made fun of the disciples, saying they must have been drinking too much wine. It was Peter who silenced the excited crowd. He stood up and spoke to them, explaining how the prophet Joel had said the Holy Spirit would be poured out in just this way. Then Peter preached a powerful sermon about who Jesus was and how He had come to pay for the sins of all who would believe in Him.

Three thousand people repented of their sins and put their faith in Jesus at the end of Peter's sermon.

Just as Jesus had promised, the Holy Spirit came to the disciples on Pentecost. God's Word promises the Holy Spirit to everyone who believes in Jesus as Savior. So the brand-new believers who listened to Peter's sermon received the gift of the Holy Spirit. God gives the Holy Spirit to all of us who believe in Jesus today. The Holy Spirit lives in us and gives us power and wisdom to live for God and to tell about what Jesus has done.

SEEK and FIND

WHERE TO FIND THE STORY

Acts 2:1–41

KEY BIBLE VERSE

"But this is what was uttered through the prophet Joel: 'And in the last days it shall be, God declares, that I will pour out my Spirit on all flesh . . . And it shall come to pass that everyone who calls upon the name of the Lord shall be saved.' " (Acts 2:16–17, 21)

THREE KEY QUESTIONS

- Where did the people come from who heard Peter's sermon on the day of Pentecost?
- Why was Peter able to preach such a powerful sermon?
- How many people believed in Jesus that day when Peter preached to them?

RELATED BIBLE READINGS

Joel 2:28–32; Acts 1:4–8; 10:44–48

of God, and having received from the Father the promise of the Holy Spirit, he has poured out this that you yourselves are seeing and hearing. 34 For David did not ascend into the heavens, but he himself says,

"'The Lord said to my Lord,
Sit at my right hand,
35 until I make your enemies your footstool.'

36 Let all the house of Israel therefore know for certain that God has made him both Lord and Christ, this Jesus whom you crucified."

1673

37 Now when they heard this they were cut to the heart, and said to Peter and the rest of the apostles, "Brothers, what shall we do?" 38 And Peter said to them, "Repent and be baptized every one of you in the name of Jesus Christ for the forgiveness of your sins, and you will receive the gift of the Holy Spirit. 39 For the promise is for you and for your children and for all who are far off, everyone whom the Lord our God calls to himself." 40 And with many other words he bore witness and continued to exhort them, saying, "Save yourselves from this crooked generation." 41 So those who received his word were baptized, and there were added that day about three thousand souls.

The Fellowship of the Believers

42 And they devoted themselves to the apostles' teaching and the fellowship, to the breaking of bread and the prayers.

1619

43 And awe[1] came upon every soul, and many wonders and signs were being done through the apostles. 44 And all who believed were together and had all things in common. 45 And they were selling their possessions and belongings and distributing the proceeds to all, as any had need. 46 And day by day, attending the temple together and breaking bread in their homes, they received their food with glad and generous hearts, 47 praising God and having favor with all the people. And the Lord added to their number day by day those who were being saved.

1669

The Lame Beggar Healed

1619

3 Now Peter and John were going up to the temple at the hour of prayer, the ninth hour.[2] 2 And a man lame from birth was being carried, whom they laid daily at the gate of the temple that is called the Beautiful Gate to ask alms of those entering the temple. 3 Seeing Peter and John about to go into the temple, he asked to receive alms. 4 And Peter directed his gaze at him, as did John, and said, "Look at us." 5 And he fixed his attention on them, expecting to receive something from them. 6 But Peter said, "I have no silver and gold, but what I do have I give to you. In the name of Jesus Christ of Nazareth, rise up and walk!" 7 And he took him by the right hand and raised him up, and immediately his feet and ankles were made strong. 8 And leaping up he stood and began to walk, and entered the temple with them, walking and leaping and praising God. 9 And all the people saw him walking and praising God, 10 and recognized him as the one who sat at the Beautiful Gate of the temple, asking for alms. And they were filled with wonder and amazement at what had happened to him.

Peter Speaks in Solomon's Portico

11 While he clung to Peter and John, all the people, utterly astounded, ran together to them in the portico called Solomon's. 12 And when Peter saw it he addressed the people: "Men of Israel, why do you wonder at this, or why do you stare at us, as though by our own power or piety we have made him walk? 13 The God of Abraham, the God of Isaac, and the God of Jacob, the God of our fathers, glorified his servant[3] Jesus, whom you delivered over and denied in the presence of Pilate, when he had

[1] Or *fear* [2] That is, 3 P.M. [3] Or *child*; also verse 26

The Lame Man Is Healed!

Peter and John, two of Jesus' disciples, were walking to the temple one day to pray. As they approached the temple, a man who couldn't walk was sitting by the temple gates. Since he could not work, the man came to the same place every day, where many people would pass by close to him. When Peter and John came near, he asked them if they would give him some money.

Peter told the man, "I have no silver and gold, but what I do have I give to you. In the name of Jesus Christ of Nazareth, rise up and walk!" Then Peter took the man's hand and helped him stand up. The man began to leap and run and praise God! He was so happy that God had made him well. Right away, he went to the temple to praise God and to give thanks to Him.

The people in the temple recognized the crippled man as the one who used to sit by the temple gates each day. The people were so astonished to see the lame man able to jump and walk around that they came running to Peter and John.

With the people gathered all around, Peter preached a powerful, important sermon about Jesus. Peter explained to the crowd that he and John did not have any power on their own to make the lame man walk. Peter made it clear that it was only the power of God and faith in the Name of Jesus that made this man strong. "The faith that is through Jesus," Peter said, "has given the man this perfect health in the presence of you all."

Then Peter reminded the people that the One who had healed the lame man was the same Jesus whom they had killed!—but whom God had raised from the dead. Peter told the people to repent and turn to God so that He would blot out their sins. Many who heard Peter's message that day believed in Jesus and were baptized.

The man who could now walk praised God for healing him. We too praise God, especially for His gift of repentance and forgiveness of sins, through Jesus our Savior.

SEEK and FIND

WHERE TO FIND THE STORY

Acts 3:1–4:4

KEY BIBLE VERSE

"God, having raised up his servant, sent him to you first, to bless you by turning every one of you from your wickedness." (Acts 3:26)

THREE KEY QUESTIONS

- What did the lame man ask Peter and John to give him? What *did* they give to him?
- Who really healed the lame man?
- Why do we praise God like the lame man did?

RELATED BIBLE READINGS

John 5:1–8; Acts 2:22–41, 43; 5:12–16

decided to release him. 14 But you denied the Holy and Righteous One, and asked for a murderer to be granted to you, 15 and you killed the Author of life, whom God raised from the dead. To this we are witnesses. 16 And his name—by faith in his name—has made this man strong whom you see and know, and the faith that is through Jesus[1] has given the man this perfect health in the presence of you all.

17 "And now, brothers, I know that you acted in ignorance, as did also your rulers. 18 But what God foretold by the mouth of all the prophets, that his Christ would suffer, he thus fulfilled. 19 Repent therefore, and turn again, that your sins may be blotted out, 20 that times of refreshing may come from the presence of the Lord, and that he may send the Christ appointed for you, Jesus, 21 whom heaven must receive until the time for restoring all the things about which God spoke by the mouth of his holy prophets long ago. 22 Moses said, 'The Lord God will raise up for you a prophet like me from your brothers. You shall listen to him in whatever he tells you. 23 And it shall be that every soul who does not listen to that prophet shall be destroyed from the people.' 24 And all the prophets who have spoken, from Samuel and those who came after him, also proclaimed these days. 25 You are the sons of the prophets and of the covenant that God made with your fathers, saying to Abraham, 'And in your offspring shall all the families of the earth be blessed.' 26 God, having raised up his servant, sent him to you first, to bless you by turning every one of you
1619 from your wickedness."

Peter and John Before the Council

4 And as they were speaking to the people, the priests and the captain of the temple and the Sadducees came upon them, 2 greatly annoyed because they were teaching the people and proclaiming in Jesus the resurrection from the dead. 3 And they arrested them and put them in custody until the next day, for it was already evening. 4 But many of those who had heard the word believed, and the number of the men came to about five thousand.

5 On the next day their rulers and elders and scribes gathered together in Jerusalem, 6 with Annas the high priest and Caiaphas and John and Alexander, and all who were of the high-priestly family. 7 And when they had set them in the midst, they inquired, "By what power or by what name did you do this?" 8 Then Peter, filled with the Holy Spirit, said to them, "Rulers of the people and elders, 9 if we are being examined today concerning a good deed done to a crippled man, by what means this man has been healed, 10 let it be known to all of you and to all the people of Israel that by the name of Jesus Christ of Nazareth, whom you crucified, whom God raised from the dead—by him this man is standing before you well. 11 This Jesus[2] is the stone that was rejected by you, the builders, which has become the cornerstone.[3] 12 And there is salvation in no one else, for there is no other name under heaven given among men by which we must be saved."

13 Now when they saw the boldness of Peter and John, and perceived that they were uneducated, common men, they were astonished. And they recognized that they had been with Jesus. 14 But seeing the man who was healed standing beside them, they had nothing to say in opposition. 15 But when they had commanded them to leave the council, they conferred with one another, 16 saying, "What shall we do with these men? For that a notable sign has been performed through them is evident to all the inhabitants of Jerusalem, and we cannot deny it. 17 But in order that it may spread no further among the people, let us warn them to speak no more to anyone in this name."

18 So they called them and charged them not to speak or teach at all in
1181 the name of Jesus. 19 But Peter and

[1] Greek *him* [2] Greek *This one* [3] Greek *the head of the corner*

John answered them, "Whether it is right
in the sight of God to listen to you rather
than to God, you must judge, 20 for we can-
not but speak of what we have seen and
heard." 21 And when they had further
threatened them, they let them go, finding
no way to punish them, because of the
people, for all were praising God for what
had happened. 22 For the man on whom
this sign of healing was performed was
more than forty years old.

The Believers Pray for Boldness

23 When they were released, they
went to their friends and reported
1651 what the chief priests and the
elders had said to them. 24 And when they
heard it, they lifted their voices together to
God and said, "Sovereign Lord, who made
the heaven and the earth and the sea and
everything in them, 25 who through the
mouth of our father David, your servant,[1]
said by the Holy Spirit,

"'Why did the Gentiles rage,
and the peoples plot in vain?
26 The kings of the earth set themselves,
and the rulers were gathered
together,
against the Lord and against his
Anointed'[2]—

27 for truly in this city there were
gathered together against your
1361 holy servant Jesus, whom you
anointed, both Herod and Pontius Pilate,
along with the Gentiles and the peoples of
Israel, 28 to do whatever your hand and
your plan had predestined to take place.
29 And now, Lord, look upon their threats
and grant to your servants[3] to continue to
speak your word with all boldness,
30 while you stretch out your hand to heal,
and signs and wonders are performed
through the name of your holy servant
Jesus." 31 And when they had prayed, the
place in which they were gathered
together was shaken, and they were all
filled with the Holy Spirit and continued
to speak the word of God with boldness.

They Had Everything in Common

32 Now the full number of those who
believed were of one heart and soul, and
no one said that any of the things that
belonged to him was his own, but they
had everything in common. 33 And with
great power the apostles were giving their
testimony to the resurrection of the Lord
Jesus, and great grace was upon them all.
34 There was not a needy person among
them, for as many as were owners of lands
or houses sold them and brought the pro-
ceeds of what was sold 35 and laid it at the
apostles' feet, and it was distributed to
each as any had need. 36 Thus Joseph, who

CHARACTER PROFILE

BARNABAS

Barnabas's name means "Son of Encouragement," and Barnabas lived up to his name. He sold land so he could help poorer people in the church. Then he became the apostle Paul's best support and helper on a missionary journey to spread the gospel. Later Barnabas took another young believer on more missionary travels. Because of Barnabas's faithfulness, the new church grew.

1657

[1] Or *child*; also verses 27, 30 [2] Or *Christ* [3] Greek *bondservants*

was also called by the apostles Barnabas (which means son of encouragement), a Levite, a native of Cyprus, 37 sold a field that belonged to him and brought the money and laid it at the apostles' feet.

Anananias and Sapphira

5 But a man named Ananias, with his wife Sapphira, sold a piece of property, 2 and with his wife's knowledge he kept back for himself some of the proceeds and brought only a part of it and laid it at the apostles' feet. 3 But Peter said, "Ananias, why has Satan filled your heart to lie to the Holy Spirit and to keep back for yourself part of the proceeds of the land? 4 While it remained unsold, did it not remain your own? And after it was sold, was it not at your disposal? Why is it that you have contrived this deed in your heart? You have not lied to men but to God." 5 When Ananias heard these words, he fell down and breathed his last. And great fear came upon all who heard of it. 6 The young men rose and wrapped him up and carried him out and buried him.

7 After an interval of about three hours his wife came in, not knowing what had happened. 8 And Peter said to her, "Tell me whether you[1] sold the land for so much." And she said, "Yes, for so much." 9 But Peter said to her, "How is it that you have agreed together to test the Spirit of the Lord? Behold, the feet of those who have buried your husband are at the door, and they will carry you out." 10 Immediately she fell down at his feet and breathed her last. When the young men came in they found her dead, and they carried her out and buried her beside her husband. 11 And great fear came upon the whole church and upon all who heard of these things.

Many Signs and Wonders Done

12 Now many signs and wonders
were regularly done among the
1619 people by the hands of the apostles. And they were all together in Solomon's Portico. 13 None of the rest dared join them, but the people held them in high esteem. 14 And more than ever believers were added to the Lord, multitudes of both men and women, 15 so that they even carried out the sick into the streets and laid them on cots and mats, that as Peter came by at least his shadow might fall on some of them. 16 The people also gathered from the towns around Jerusalem, bringing the sick and those afflicted with unclean spirits, and they were all healed.

The Apostles Arrested and Freed

17 But the high priest rose up, and
all who were with him (that is, the
1651, party of the Sadducees), and filled
1673 with jealousy 18 they arrested the apostles and put them in the public prison. 19 But during the night an angel of the Lord opened the prison doors and brought them out, and said, 20 "Go and stand in the temple and speak to the people all the words of this Life." 21 And when they heard this, they entered the temple at daybreak and began to teach.

Now when the high priest came, and those who were with him, they called together the council and all the senate of the people of Israel and sent to the prison to have them brought. 22 But when the officers came, they did not find them in the prison, so they returned and reported, 23 "We found the prison securely locked and the guards standing at the doors, but when we opened them we found no one inside." 24 Now when the captain of the temple and the chief priests heard these words, they were greatly perplexed about them, wondering what this would come to. 25 And someone came and told them, "Look! The men whom you put in prison are standing in the temple and teaching the people." 26 Then the captain with the officers went and brought them, but not by force, for they were afraid of being stoned by the people.

[1] The Greek for *you* is plural here

1181
27 And when they had brought
them, they set them before the
council. And the high priest ques-
tioned them, 28 saying, "We strictly
charged you not to teach in this name, yet
here you have filled Jerusalem with your
teaching, and you intend to bring this
man's blood upon us." 29 But Peter and the
apostles answered, "We must obey God
rather than men. 30 The God of our fathers
raised Jesus, whom you killed by hanging
him on a tree. 31 God exalted him at his
right hand as Leader and Savior, to give
repentance to Israel and forgiveness of
sins. 32 And we are witnesses to these
things, and so is the Holy Spirit, whom
God has given to those who obey him."

CHARACTER PROFILE

STEPHEN

Stephen and six other men were chosen to take care of widows in the church. Stephen told everyone the Good News about Jesus. Enemies of the church lied about Stephen and threw stones at him, to kill him. Even while he was dying, Stephen focused on Jesus waiting for him in heaven, and he prayed for God to forgive the men who killed him.

1629

33 When they heard this, they were
enraged and wanted to kill them. 34 But a
Pharisee in the council named Gamaliel, a
teacher of the law held in honor by all the
people, stood up and gave orders to put
the men outside for a little while. 35 And
he said to them, "Men of Israel, take care
what you are about to do with these men.
36 For before these days Theudas rose up,
claiming to be somebody, and a number
of men, about four hundred, joined him.
He was killed, and all who followed him
were dispersed and came to nothing.
37 After him Judas the Galilean rose up
in the days of the census and drew away
some of the people after him. He too per-
ished, and all who followed him were
scattered. 38 So in the present case I tell
you, keep away from these men and let
them alone, for if this plan or this under-
taking is of man, it will fail; 39 but if it is
of God, you will not be able to overthrow
them. You might even be found oppos-
ing God!" So they took his advice, 40 and
when they had called in the apostles,
they beat them and charged them not to
speak in the name of Jesus, and let them
go. 41 Then they left the presence of the
council, rejoicing that they were counted
worthy to suffer dishonor for the name.
42 And every day, in the temple and from
house to house, they did not cease teach-
ing and preaching Jesus as the Christ.

Seven Chosen to Serve

6 Now in these days when the
disciples were increasing in
1629 number, a complaint by the
Hellenists[1] arose against the
Hebrews because their widows
1641 were being neglected in the daily
distribution. 2 And the twelve summoned
the full number of the disciples and said,
"It is not right that we should give up
preaching the word of God to serve tables.
3 Therefore, brothers,[2] pick out from
among you seven men of good repute, full
of the Spirit and of wisdom, whom we will

[1] That is, Greek-speaking Jews [2] Or *brothers and sisters*

appoint to this duty. 4 But we will devote
ourselves to prayer and to the ministry of
the word." 5 And what they said pleased
the whole gathering, and they chose
Stephen, a man full of faith and of the
Holy Spirit, and Philip, and Prochorus,
and Nicanor, and Timon, and Parmenas,
and Nicolaus, a proselyte of Antioch.
6 These they set before the apostles, and
they prayed and laid their hands on them.

7 And the word of God continued to
increase, and the number of the disciples
multiplied greatly in Jerusalem, and a
great many of the priests became obedi-
ent to the faith.

Stephen Is Seized

8 And Stephen, full of grace and power,
was doing great wonders and signs
among the people. 9 Then some of those
who belonged to the synagogue of the
Freedmen (as it was called), and of the
Cyrenians, and of the Alexandrians, and
of those from Cilicia and Asia, rose up
and disputed with Stephen. 10 But they
could not withstand the wisdom and the
Spirit with which he was speaking. 11 Then
they secretly instigated men who said,
"We have heard him speak blasphemous
words against Moses and God." 12 And
they stirred up the people and the elders
and the scribes, and they came upon him
and seized him and brought him before
the council, 13 and they set up false wit-
nesses who said, "This man never ceases
to speak words against this holy place and
the law, 14 for we have heard him say that
this Jesus of Nazareth will destroy this
place and will change the customs that
Moses delivered to us." 15 And gazing at
him, all who sat in the council saw that
his face was like the face of an angel.

Stephen's Speech

7 And the high priest said, "Are these
things so?" 2 And Stephen said:
"Brothers and fathers, hear me. The God
of glory appeared to our father Abraham
when he was in Mesopotamia, before he
lived in Haran, 3 and said to him, 'Go out
from your land and from your kindred
and go into the land that I will show you.'
4 Then he went out from the land of the
Chaldeans and lived in Haran. And after
his father died, God removed him from
there into this land in which you are now
living. 5 Yet he gave him no inheritance in
it, not even a foot's length, but promised
to give it to him as a possession and to
his offspring after him, though he had no
child. 6 And God spoke to this effect—that
his offspring would be sojourners in a land
belonging to others, who would enslave
them and afflict them four hundred years.
7 'But I will judge the nation that they
serve,' said God, 'and after that they shall
come out and worship me in this place.'
8 And he gave him the covenant of cir-
cumcision. And so Abraham became the
father of Isaac, and circumcised him on
the eighth day, and Isaac became the father
of Jacob, and Jacob of the twelve patriarchs.

9 "And the patriarchs, jealous of Joseph,
sold him into Egypt; but God was with
him 10 and rescued him out of all his
afflictions and gave him favor and wis-
dom before Pharaoh, king of Egypt, who
made him ruler over Egypt and over all
his household. 11 Now there came a fam-
ine throughout all Egypt and Canaan, and
great affliction, and our fathers could find
no food. 12 But when Jacob heard that there
was grain in Egypt, he sent out our fathers
on their first visit. 13 And on the second
visit Joseph made himself known to his
brothers, and Joseph's family became
known to Pharaoh. 14 And Joseph sent and
summoned Jacob his father and all his
kindred, seventy-five persons in all. 15 And
Jacob went down into Egypt, and he died,
he and our fathers, 16 and they were car-
ried back to Shechem and laid in the tomb
that Abraham had bought for a sum of sil-
ver from the sons of Hamor in Shechem.

17 "But as the time of the promise

drew near, which God had granted to
Abraham, the people increased and mul-
tiplied in Egypt 18 until there arose over
Egypt another king who did not know
Joseph. 19 He dealt shrewdly with our
race and forced our fathers to expose
their infants, so that they would not be
kept alive. 20 At this time Moses was born;
and he was beautiful in God's sight. And
he was brought up for three months in
his father's house, 21 and when he was
exposed, Pharaoh's daughter adopted
him and brought him up as her own son.
22 And Moses was instructed in all the wis-
dom of the Egyptians, and he was mighty
in his words and deeds.

23 "When he was forty years old, it
came into his heart to visit his brothers,
the children of Israel. 24 And seeing one
of them being wronged, he defended the
oppressed man and avenged him by strik-
ing down the Egyptian. 25 He supposed
that his brothers would understand that
God was giving them salvation by his
hand, but they did not understand. 26 And
on the following day he appeared to them
as they were quarreling and tried to rec-
oncile them, saying, 'Men, you are broth-
ers. Why do you wrong each other?' 27 But
the man who was wronging his neighbor
thrust him aside, saying, 'Who made you
a ruler and a judge over us? 28 Do you want
to kill me as you killed the Egyptian yes-
terday?' 29 At this retort Moses fled and
became an exile in the land of Midian,
where he became the father of two sons.

30 "Now when forty years had passed,
an angel appeared to him in the wilder-
ness of Mount Sinai, in a flame of fire
in a bush. 31 When Moses saw it, he was
amazed at the sight, and as he drew near
to look, there came the voice of the Lord:
32 'I am the God of your fathers, the God of
Abraham and of Isaac and of Jacob.' And
Moses trembled and did not dare to look.
33 Then the Lord said to him, 'Take off the
sandals from your feet, for the place where
you are standing is holy ground. 34 I have
surely seen the affliction of my people who
are in Egypt, and have heard their groan-
ing, and I have come down to deliver them.
And now come, I will send you to Egypt.'

Stephen's Speech—Israel's History

Stephen was falsely accused of saying bad things about Moses and God. Instead of being afraid, Stephen showed love to his enemies by telling them about Jesus. He explained how all of the Old Testament pointed to a coming Savior and how that Savior was Jesus. To read the stories in detail, go to the following pages.

Reference	Story	Page
7:2–5	God Calls Abram	33
7:9–10	Joseph and His Brothers	95
7:9–10	Joseph's Troubles	101
7:9–12	Joseph Saves People from Famine	107
7:17–22	The Birth of Moses	131
7:23–34	Moses and the Burning Bush	137
7:44-45	The Walls Come Crashing Down	357
7:44-50	Solomon Builds the Temple	545

35 "This Moses, whom they rejected,
saying, 'Who made you a ruler and a
judge?'—this man God sent as both ruler
and redeemer by the hand of the angel
who appeared to him in the bush. 36 This
man led them out, performing wonders
and signs in Egypt and at the Red Sea and
in the wilderness for forty years. 37 This is
the Moses who said to the Israelites, 'God
will raise up for you a prophet like me
from your brothers.' 38 This is the one who
was in the congregation in the wilderness
with the angel who spoke to him at Mount
Sinai, and with our fathers. He received
living oracles to give to us. 39 Our fathers
refused to obey him, but thrust him aside,
and in their hearts they turned to Egypt,
40 saying to Aaron, 'Make for us gods who
will go before us. As for this Moses who
led us out from the land of Egypt, we do
not know what has become of him.' 41 And
they made a calf in those days, and offered
a sacrifice to the idol and were rejoicing
in the works of their hands. 42 But God
turned away and gave them over to wor-
ship the host of heaven, as it is written in
the book of the prophets:

"'Did you bring to me slain beasts
and sacrifices,
during the forty years in the
wilderness, O house of Israel?
43 You took up the tent of Moloch
and the star of your god Rephan,
the images that you made to
worship;
and I will send you into exile
beyond Babylon.'

44 "Our fathers had the tent of witness
in the wilderness, just as he who spoke
to Moses directed him to make it, accord-
ing to the pattern that he had seen. 45 Our
fathers in turn brought it in with Joshua
when they dispossessed the nations that
God drove out before our fathers. So it
was until the days of David, 46 who found
favor in the sight of God and asked to find
a dwelling place for the God of Jacob.[1] 47 But
it was Solomon who built a house for him.
48 Yet the Most High does not dwell in
houses made by hands, as the prophet says,

49 "'Heaven is my throne,
and the earth is my footstool.
What kind of house will you build
for me, says the Lord,
or what is the place of my rest?
50 Did not my hand make all these
things?'

51 "You stiff-necked people, uncircum-
cised in heart and ears, you always resist
the Holy Spirit. As your fathers did, so do
you. 52 Which of the prophets did your
fathers not persecute? And they killed
those who announced beforehand the
coming of the Righteous One, whom you
have now betrayed and murdered, 53 you
who received the law as delivered by
angels and did not keep it."

The Stoning of Stephen

54 Now when they heard these things
they were enraged, and they ground their
teeth at him. 55 But he, full of the Holy
Spirit, gazed into heaven and saw the
glory of God, and Jesus standing at the
right hand of God. 56 And he said, "Behold,
I see the heavens opened, and the Son of
Man standing at the right hand of God."
57 But they cried out with a loud voice and
stopped their ears and rushed together[2]
at him. 58 Then they cast him out of the
city and stoned him. And the witnesses
laid down their garments at the feet of a
young man named Saul. 59 And as they
were stoning Stephen, he called out, "Lord
Jesus, receive my spirit." 60 And falling to
his knees he cried out with a loud voice,
"Lord, do not hold this sin against them."
And when he had said this, he fell asleep.

Saul Ravages the Church

8 And Saul approved of his execution.
And there arose on that day a great
persecution against the church in

[1] Some manuscripts *for the house of Jacob* [2] Or *rushed with one mind*

Stephen, God's Servant

After Jesus went up into heaven, He left important work for His followers to do. All those who believed in Jesus helped care for others and spread the Good News about Jesus.

The people in the church in Jerusalem chose Stephen to take special care of widows. These were women whose husbands had died, and who had no way to take care of their needs. Stephen made sure the widows had enough food to eat. He also told the widows, and everyone he met, about Jesus and how He had come to die on the cross for our sins.

Many Jewish leaders did not want people to believe that Jesus is the promised Savior and Messiah. These leaders didn't like Stephen talking about Jesus.

One day, some of the leaders came and took Stephen to meet with the leaders' council. The people who brought Stephen to the council told many lies about him.

But Stephen was not afraid of their lies. Instead he spoke boldly to the council and all who had gathered around. Stephen told them that they weren't listening to God. He said it was terribly wrong that they had killed Jesus, and that God had sent Jesus to save them.

The Holy Spirit gave Stephen great power to preach that day—about the whole history of the Jewish people, and about

God's provision of Jesus to save them from their sins. But the more Stephen preached the truth, the more angry the crowd became.

But Stephen didn't do anything to defend himself. Filled with the Holy Spirit, Stephen looked up into heaven—and saw Jesus and the glory of God! "Behold," Stephen said, "I see the heavens opened, and the Son of Man standing at the right hand of God."

When Stephen said this, the crowd became furious. They rushed at him and threw him out of the city. As soon as they were outside the city, they started throwing big stones at him to kill him.

Stephen knew that God loved him and was with him. He could see Jesus waiting for him in heaven. He cried out, "Lord Jesus, receive my spirit." Then he asked God to forgive the men who were killing him. As soon as Stephen said this, Stephen died and God took him to heaven, to be with Him forever.

Even though the angry people killed Stephen, he knew that no matter what happened, God loved him and had forgiven his sins, for Jesus' sake. He knew that he would be happy with God in heaven, where there is no sadness! We have the same hope of heaven and the same confidence in God's love and forgiveness, no matter what happens.

SEEK and FIND

WHERE TO FIND THE STORY

Acts 6–7

KEY BIBLE VERSE

"As it is written, . . . in all these things we are more than conquerors through him who loved us." (Romans 8:36–37)

THREE KEY QUESTIONS

- What were the special people called that Stephen took care of? Why do these people especially need our help?
- Why did the crowd become furious and what did they do?
- What did Stephen see when he was dying and looked up to heaven?

RELATED BIBLE READINGS

Acts 14:19–20; 2 Timothy 3:12–14

Jerusalem, and they were all scattered throughout the regions of Judea and Samaria, except the apostles. 2 Devout men buried Stephen and made great lamentation over him. 3 But Saul was ravaging the church, and entering house after house, he dragged off men and women and committed them to prison.

Philip Proclaims Christ in Samaria

4 Now those who were scattered went about preaching the word. 5 Philip went down to the city[1] of Samaria and proclaimed to them the Christ.

1633

6 And the crowds with one accord paid attention to what was being said by Philip when they heard him and saw the signs that he did. 7 For unclean spirits, crying out with a loud voice, came out of many who had them, and many who were paralyzed or lame were healed. 8 So there was much joy in that city.

Simon the Magician Believes

9 But there was a man named Simon, who had previously practiced magic in the city and amazed the people of Samaria, saying that he himself was somebody great. 10 They all paid attention to him, from the least to the greatest, saying, "This man is the power of God that is called Great." 11 And they paid attention to him because for a long time he had amazed them with his magic. 12 But when they believed Philip as he preached good news about the kingdom of God and the name of Jesus Christ, they were baptized, both men and women. 13 Even Simon himself believed, and after being baptized he continued with Philip. And seeing signs and great miracles[2] performed, he was amazed.

14 Now when the apostles at Jerusalem heard that Samaria had received the word of God, they sent to them Peter and John, 15 who came down and prayed for them that they might receive the Holy Spirit, 16 for he had not yet fallen on any of them, but they had only been baptized in the name of the Lord Jesus. 17 Then they laid their hands on them and they received the Holy Spirit. 18 Now when Simon saw that the Spirit was given through the laying on of the apostles' hands, he offered them money, 19 saying, "Give me this

[1] Some manuscripts *a city* [2] Greek *works of power*

Philip and the Ethiopian

Philip was one of Jesus 12 disciples, and was quick to obey whatever God wanted him to do. One day, some time after Jesus had ascended to heaven, God sent an angel to Philip, to give him a special message. "Go to the road that goes down from Jerusalem to Gaza," the angel said.

Philip immediately started on his way. Along the road, Philip saw a man from Ethiopia. This man was an important official from the queen of Ethiopia, whose name was Candace. While sitting in his chariot, the Ethiopian man was reading from God's Word in Isaiah. The book of Isaiah is a prophecy, which predicts how the Savior would one day suffer and die for His people.

The Holy Spirit told Philip exactly what to do. So Philip ran up to the chariot and asked the man, "Do you understand what you are reading?" The man replied that he did not understand, but he hoped that Philip could explain what he was reading.

So the Ethiopian man invited Philip to come sit in the chariot with him. Philip began with the Scripture the Ethiopian was reading, explaining that Jesus was the Suffering Servant that Isaiah had written about. Philip told the Ethiopian man the Good News that this prophecy had already come true!—that God's Son, Jesus, had come from heaven to suffer and die on the cross, to save His people from their sins, and that Jesus had risen from the dead! Philip explained that Jesus wants people to repent of their sins and put their faith in Jesus.

As the chariot was passing some water, the Ethiopian said, "See, here is water." The Ethiopian asked Philip to baptize him right away. As soon as Philip had baptized the new believer, the Spirit of the Lord suddenly carried Philip away to preach to other people. Although the Ethiopian didn't see Philip anymore, he got back in his chariot and went on his way rejoicing! He was filled with joy because Philip had explained to him the Good News about Jesus.

The Holy Spirit helps us to find truth in God's Word too, and He gives us faith to believe in Jesus as our Savior. Like the Ethiopian man, we go on our way, rejoicing!

SEEK and FIND

WHERE TO FIND THE STORY

Acts 8:26–40

KEY BIBLE VERSE

"Then Philip opened his mouth, and beginning with this Scripture he told him the good news about Jesus." (Acts 8:35)

THREE KEY QUESTIONS

- What was the Scripture that the Ethiopian man reading?
- What was the prophecy from Isaiah that Philip explained had come true?
- How does the Holy Spirit help us?

RELATED BIBLE READINGS

Isaiah 53:1–12; Luke 24:27; Acts 8:5–8; 16:29–34

power also, so that anyone on whom I lay
my hands may receive the Holy Spirit."
20 But Peter said to him, "May your silver
perish with you, because you thought you
could obtain the gift of God with money!
21 You have neither part nor lot in this
matter, for your heart is not right before
God. 22 Repent, therefore, of this wicked-
ness of yours, and pray to the Lord that, if
possible, the intent of your heart may be
forgiven you. 23 For I see that you are in
the gall[1] of bitterness and in the bond of
iniquity." 24 And Simon answered, "Pray
for me to the Lord, that nothing of what
you have said may come upon me."

25 Now when they had testified and spo-
ken the word of the Lord, they returned to
Jerusalem, preaching the gospel to many
villages of the Samaritans.

Philip and the Ethiopian Eunuch

1633
26 Now an angel of the Lord said to
Philip, "Rise and go toward the
south[2] to the road that goes down
from Jerusalem to Gaza." This is a desert
place. 27 And he rose and went. And there
was an Ethiopian, a eunuch, a court offi-
cial of Candace, queen of the Ethiopians,
who was in charge of all her treasure. He
had come to Jerusalem to worship 28 and
was returning, seated in his chariot, and he
was reading the prophet Isaiah. 29 And the
Spirit said to Philip, "Go over and join this
chariot." 30 So Philip ran to him and heard
him reading Isaiah the prophet and asked,
"Do you understand what you are read-
ing?" 31 And he said, "How can I, unless
someone guides me?" And he invited
Philip to come up and sit with him. 32 Now
the passage of the Scripture that he was
reading was this:

> "Like a sheep he was led to the
> slaughter
> and like a lamb before its shearer
> is silent,
> so he opens not his mouth.
>
> 33 In his humiliation justice was
> denied him.
> Who can describe his generation?
> For his life is taken away from the
> earth."

34 And the eunuch said to Philip, "About
whom, I ask you, does the prophet say
this, about himself or about someone
else?" 35 Then Philip opened his
mouth, and beginning with this
1633
Scripture he told him the good
news about Jesus. 36 And as they were
going along the road they came to some
water, and the eunuch said, "See, here is
water! What prevents me from being bap-
tized?"[3] 38 And he commanded the chariot
to stop, and they both went down into the
water, Philip and the eunuch, and he bap-
tized him. 39 And when they came up out
of the water, the Spirit of the Lord carried
Philip away, and the eunuch saw him no
more, and went on his way rejoicing.
40 But Philip found himself at Azotus, and
as he passed through he preached the gos-
pel to all the towns until he came to
Caesarea.

The Conversion of Saul

9 But Saul, still breathing threats
and murder against the disci-
1637
ples of the Lord, went to the high
priest 2 and asked him for letters to the
synagogues at Damascus, so that if he
found any belonging to the Way, men or
women, he might bring them bound to
Jerusalem. 3 Now as he went on his way,
he approached Damascus, and suddenly a
light from heaven flashed around him.
4 And falling to the ground he heard a
voice saying to him, "Saul, Saul, why are
you persecuting me?" 5 And he said, "Who
are you, Lord?" And he said, "I am Jesus,
whom you are persecuting. 6 But rise and
enter the city, and you will be told what
you are to do." 7 The men who were travel-
ing with him stood speechless, hearing

[1] That is, a bitter fluid secreted by the liver; bile [2] Or *go at about noon* [3] Some manuscripts add all or most of verse 37: *And Philip said, "If you believe with all your heart, you may." And he replied, "I believe that Jesus Christ is the Son of God."*

The Conversion of Saul

Saul was an educated man who did everything as hard as he could. But Saul did not believe that Jesus was the Savior or that He had risen from the dead. Because of this, Saul hated Jesus and he persecuted anyone who believed in Him. He even put believers in jail to try to make them stop believing in Jesus—or at least stop preaching about Him!

Saul decided that Damascus was the next place where he would go to find Christians and put them in jail. While Saul was traveling along the road, suddenly a bright light from heaven shone all around him. Saul was afraid and fell to the ground. Then he heard a voice asking, "Saul, Saul, why are you persecuting Me?"

Saul replied, "Who are You, Lord?"

The voice said, "I am Jesus, whom you are persecuting."

Even though Saul was an enemy of Jesus, Jesus loved Saul and wanted Saul to believe in Him. Jesus had an important work for Saul to do. Jesus told Saul to get up "and enter the city, and you will be told what you are to do." But when Saul opened his eyes, he couldn't see. His friends helped him to the city, where he prayed and waited for God to tell him what to do.

After waiting in the city for three days, Jesus sent a man named Ananias to Saul. Ananias was worried, because everyone knew that Saul was putting believers in jail everywhere he went. Still Ananias obeyed God and went and found Saul. Ananias told Saul that Jesus had sent him, so that Saul could see again and be filled with the Holy Spirit.

As soon as Ananias said this, suddenly Saul could see! He got up, and Ananias baptized him, because now Saul wanted to be a follower of Jesus.

God changed Saul from being God's enemy into His own child. Some time later, God changed Saul's name to Paul. Paul served the Lord with all his heart wherever God sent him to go. God used Paul to become a great missionary and a preacher, to tell thousands of people about Jesus. God's Word tells how He loved us even while we were still enemies of God. How wonderful it is to have our sins forgiven and to be part of His family!

SEEK and FIND

WHERE TO FIND THE STORY

Acts 9:1–20

KEY BIBLE VERSE

"The saying is trustworthy and deserving of full acceptance, that Christ Jesus came into the world to save sinners, of whom I am the foremost." (1 Timothy 1:15)

THREE KEY QUESTIONS

- What was Saul doing before he believed in Jesus?
- What happened to Saul while he was traveling on the road to Damascus?
- What was the new name that God gave to Saul, and what was the great work that he did?

RELATED BIBLE READINGS

Acts 22:1–21; 26:9–23; Philippians 3:4–11;
1 Timothy 1:12–16

the voice but seeing no one. 8 Saul rose from the ground, and although his eyes were opened, he saw nothing. So they led him by the hand and brought him into Damascus. 9 And for three days he was without sight, and neither ate nor drank.

10 Now there was a disciple at Damascus named Ananias. The Lord said to him in a vision, "Ananias." And he said, "Here I am, Lord." 11 And the Lord said to him, "Rise and go to the street called Straight, and at the house of Judas look for a man of Tarsus named Saul, for behold, he is praying, 12 and he has seen in a vision a man named Ananias come in and lay his hands on him so that he might regain his sight." 13 But Ananias answered, "Lord, I have heard from many about this man, how much evil he has done to your saints at Jerusalem. 14 And here he has authority from the chief priests to bind all who call on your name." 15 But the Lord said to him, "Go, for he is a chosen instrument of mine to carry my name before the Gentiles and kings and the children of Israel. 16 For I will show him how much he must suffer for the sake of my name." 17 So Ananias departed and entered the house. And laying his hands on him he said, "Brother Saul, the Lord Jesus who appeared to you on the road by which you came has sent me so that you may regain your sight and be filled with the Holy Spirit." 18 And immediately something like scales fell from his eyes, and he regained his sight. Then he rose and was baptized; 19 and taking food, he was strengthened.

Saul Proclaims Jesus in Synagogues

For some days he was with the disciples at Damascus. 20 And immediately he proclaimed Jesus in the synagogues, saying, "He is the Son of God." 21 And all who heard him were amazed and said, "Is not this the man who made havoc in Jerusalem of those who called upon this name? And has he not come here for this purpose, to bring them bound before the chief priests?" 22 But Saul increased all the more in strength, and confounded the Jews who lived in Damascus by proving that Jesus was the Christ.

Saul Escapes from Damascus

23 When many days had passed, the Jews plotted to kill him, 24 but their plot became known to Saul. They were watching the gates day and night in order to kill him, 25 but his disciples took him by night and let him down through an opening in the wall,[1] lowering him in a basket.

Saul in Jerusalem

26 And when he had come to Jerusalem, he attempted to join the disciples. And they were all afraid of him, for they did not believe that he was a disciple. 27 But Barnabas took him and brought him to the apostles and declared to them how on the road he had seen the Lord, who spoke to him, and how at Damascus he had preached boldly in the name of Jesus. 28 So he went in and out among them at Jerusalem, preaching boldly in the name of the Lord. 29 And he spoke and disputed

[1] Greek *through the wall*

Dorcas Is Alive!

In the city of Joppa there lived a lady named Dorcas, who was also called Tabitha. Everyone who knew Dorcas loved her because she was very kind and often did good things for others. She was known especially because of the clothes she made for the widows in the church, who were too poor to buy their own clothes.

Dorcas was kind and loving to others because she loved Jesus and wanted to please Him. Dorcas was a living example of God's plan for His church—that His followers would love and serve one another, in the same way that Jesus had done. So, when Dorcas became sick and died, all of her friends in Joppa were very sad and heartbroken.

Very soon after Dorcas died, her friends heard that a man named Peter was in a nearby city. Peter was one of the first followers of Jesus, who were called His disciples. So they went to look for Peter thinking that maybe he could help. When they found Peter, they asked if he would please come with them back to Joppa. And Peter agreed to go with them.

When he reached the house in Joppa where Dorcas had lived, the women took Peter upstairs to the room where Dorcas's body was lying dead on the bed. Many poor widow were there, terribly sad and crying because they loved Dorcas so much. They showed Peter the clothing Dorcas had made for them.

Then Peter asked the widows to leave the room. He got down on his knees beside Dorcas and prayed to God that He would make Dorcas alive again. Peter then turned to Dorcas's body and said, "Tabitha, arise."

Dorcas opened her eyes. When she saw Peter, she sat up. Peter gave her his hand and helped her get up. Then Peter called out to the widows and the others who were there. He presented Dorcas to them and showed them that she was alive! How glad they were to see Dorcas alive again—raised up by the power of God! The news about Dorcas spread throughout all of Joppa and many people believed in the Lord.

God raised brought Dorcas back to life, which was a great miracle. But an even greater miracle is that through faith in Jesus, God will raise us up to eternal life!

SEEK and FIND

WHERE TO FIND THE STORY

Acts 9:36–43

KEY BIBLE VERSE

"Love one another with brotherly affection . . . Rejoice with those who rejoice, weep with those who weep." (Romans 12:10a, 15)

THREE KEY QUESTIONS

- How did Dorcas show her love for the Lord?
- What made Dorcas come back to life?
- What is the greater miracle that Jesus does for all who believe in Him?

RELATED BIBLE READINGS

Mark 5:35–43; Acts 6:1–3; 1 Timothy 5:3–5, 9–10, 16

against the Hellenists.[1] But they were
seeking to kill him. 30 And when the broth-
ers learned this, they brought him down
to Caesarea and sent him off to Tarsus.
31 So the church throughout all Judea
and Galilee and Samaria had peace and
was being built up. And walking in the
fear of the Lord and in the comfort of the
Holy Spirit, it multiplied.

The Healing of Aeneas

32 Now as Peter went here and there
among them all, he came down also to
the saints who lived at Lydda. 33 There he
found a man named Aeneas, bedridden
for eight years, who was paralyzed. 34 And
Peter said to him, "Aeneas, Jesus Christ
heals you; rise and make your bed." And
immediately he rose. 35 And all the resi-
dents of Lydda and Sharon saw him, and
they turned to the Lord.

Dorcas Restored to Life

1641
36 Now there was in Joppa a disci-
ple named Tabitha, which, trans-
lated, means Dorcas.[2] She was full
of good works and acts of charity. 37 In
those days she became ill and died, and
when they had washed her, they laid her
in an upper room. 38 Since Lydda was
near Joppa, the disciples, hearing that
Peter was there, sent two men to him,
urging him, "Please come to us without
delay." 39 So Peter rose and went with
them. And when he arrived, they took
him to the upper room. All the widows
stood beside him weeping and showing
tunics[3] and other garments that Dorcas
made while she was with them. 40 But
Peter put them all outside, and knelt
down and prayed; and turning to the
body he said, "Tabitha, arise." And she
opened her eyes, and when she saw Peter
she sat up. 41 And he gave her his hand
and raised her up. Then calling the saints
and widows, he presented her alive.
42 And it became known throughout all
Joppa, and many believed in the Lord.
43 And he stayed in Joppa for many days
with one Simon, a tanner.

Peter and Cornelius

1645
10 At Caesarea there was a man
named Cornelius, a centu-
rion of what was known as the
Italian Cohort, 2 a devout man who feared
God with all his household, gave alms gen-
erously to the people, and prayed continu-
ally to God. 3 About the ninth hour of the
day[4] he saw clearly in a vision an angel of
God come in and say to him, "Cornelius."
4 And he stared at him in terror and said,

CHARACTER PROFILE

PAUL

Paul used to be a Jewish leader named Saul, who hated Jesus and hunted for Christ's followers so he could put them in prison. But Jesus appeared to Saul, and He changed Saul's heart completely. So Saul became Paul, who traveled far and wide to preach the gospel to both Jews and Gentiles. Paul wrote many letters to teach and encourage the new Christians, which are included in the New Testament.

1637, 1657, 1663, 1669, 1673, 1689

[1] That is, Greek-speaking Jews [2] The Aramaic name *Tabitha* and the Greek name *Dorcas* both mean *gazelle* [3] Greek *chiton*, a long garment worn under the cloak next to the skin [4] That is, 3 P.M.

Peter and Cornelius

Cornelius was an important Roman soldier who believed in the one true God of the Jews, but he did not know about Jesus. One day, an angel came to Cornelius. The angel told him, "Send men to Joppa and bring Simon who is called Peter." Cornelius obeyed the angel and sent messengers to Joppa to find Peter.

Before the messengers found Peter in Joppa where he was staying, God gave Peter a strange dream while he was praying. In his dream, Peter saw a large sheet with many animals in it. A voice from heaven told Peter he could eat the animals, even though the Jewish people were forbidden to eat some of these animals. While Peter was still wondering about what his strange dream might mean, the Holy Spirit told him messengers were at the door and that he should go with them to Cornelius's house.

Peter went downstairs and found the messengers waiting for him. And Peter went back to Cornelius's house with them, even though they were Gentiles and Jews were forbidden to go into Gentile homes. Peter understood from his dream that God did not just love the Jews—even though they had been specially chosen by God—but that He loves people from every nation.

When they arrived at Cornelius's home, he was happy to see Peter. Peter went into his home and met many of

Cornelius's family and friends who were there too, ready to hear whatever the Lord had commanded Peter to say.

Peter now understood that God cares for people of every nation. He gladly told Cornelius and his family that God had sent Jesus. "Everyone," Peter said, "who believes in Him receives forgiveness of sins through His name."

While Peter was still speaking, the Holy Spirit fell on all who heard. Cornelius and all his friends believed in Jesus and were baptized. Now they were part of God's family too.

God showed Peter that He does not prefer any one group of people over another. He accepts people from every nation—no matter what language they speak or what color they are. God sent Jesus to die on the cross and rise again for the sins of all people. All who believe in Jesus will be saved and someday will live with Him in heaven.

SEEK and FIND

WHERE TO FIND THE STORY

Acts 10

KEY BIBLE VERSE

"Truly I understand that God shows no partiality, but in every nation anyone who fears him and does what is right is acceptable to him." (Acts 10:34b–35)

THREE KEY QUESTIONS

- What was Peter's dream and how did it show that God loves people from every nation?
- What happens to everyone who believes in Jesus?
- What are the most important things that we can learn from *this* true story in the Bible?

RELATED BIBLE READINGS
Genesis 12:3; Acts 11:1–18; 15:7–17; Ephesians 2:11–22;
Revelation 7:9–10

"What is it, Lord?" And he said to him,
"Your prayers and your alms have ascended
as a memorial before God. 5 And now send
men to Joppa and bring one Simon who is
called Peter. 6 He is lodging with one
Simon, a tanner, whose house is by the
sea." 7 When the angel who spoke to him
had departed, he called two of his servants
and a devout soldier from among those
who attended him, 8 and having related
everything to them, he sent them to Joppa.

Peter's Vision

9 The next day, as they were on their
journey and approaching the city, Peter
went up on the housetop about the sixth
hour[1] to pray. 10 And he became hungry
and wanted something to eat, but while
they were preparing it, he fell into a
trance 11 and saw the heavens opened and
something like a great sheet descending,
being let down by its four corners upon
the earth. 12 In it were all kinds of animals
and reptiles and birds of the air. 13 And
there came a voice to him: "Rise, Peter; kill
and eat." 14 But Peter said, "By no means,
Lord; for I have never eaten anything that
is common or unclean." 15 And the voice
came to him again a second time, "What
God has made clean, do not call com-
mon." 16 This happened three times, and
the thing was taken up at once to heaven.

17 Now while Peter was inwardly per-
plexed as to what the vision that he had
seen might mean, behold, the men who
were sent by Cornelius, having made
inquiry for Simon's house, stood at the
gate 18 and called out to ask whether
Simon who was called Peter was lodging
there. 19 And while Peter was pondering
the vision, the Spirit said to him, "Behold,
three men are looking for you. 20 Rise and
go down and accompany them without
hesitation, for I have sent them." 21 And
Peter went down to the men and said, "I
am the one you are looking for. What is the
reason for your coming?" 22 And they said,
"Cornelius, a centurion, an upright and
God-fearing man, who is well spoken of by
the whole Jewish nation, was directed by
a holy angel to send for you to come to his
house and to hear what you have to say."
23 So he invited them in to be his guests.

The next day he rose and went away
with them, and some of the brothers
from Joppa accompanied him. 24 And on
the following day they entered Caesarea.
Cornelius was expecting them and had
called together his relatives and close
friends. 25 When Peter entered, Cornelius
met him and fell down at his feet and wor-
shiped him. 26 But Peter lifted him up, say-
ing, "Stand up; I too am a man." 27 And as
he talked with him, he went in and found
many persons gathered. 28 And he said to
them, "You yourselves know how unlaw-
ful it is for a Jew to associate with or to
visit anyone of another nation, but God
has shown me that I should not call any
person common or unclean. 29 So when
I was sent for, I came without objection. I
ask then why you sent for me."

30 And Cornelius said, "Four days ago,
about this hour, I was praying in my
house at the ninth hour,[2] and behold, a

[1] That is, noon [2] That is, 3 P.M.

man stood before me in bright clothing 31 and said, 'Cornelius, your prayer has been heard and your alms have been remembered before God. 32 Send therefore to Joppa and ask for Simon who is called Peter. He is lodging in the house of Simon, a tanner, by the sea.' 33 So I sent for you at once, and you have been kind enough to come. Now therefore we are all here in the presence of God to hear all that you have been commanded by the Lord."

Gentiles Hear the Good News

34 So Peter opened his mouth and said: "Truly I understand that God shows no partiality, 35 but in every nation 1645 anyone who fears him and does what is right is acceptable to him. 36 As for the word that he sent to Israel, preaching good news of peace through Jesus Christ (he is Lord of all), 37 you yourselves know what happened throughout all Judea, beginning from Galilee after the baptism that John proclaimed: 38 how God anointed Jesus of Nazareth with the Holy Spirit and with power. He went about doing good and healing all who were oppressed by the devil, for God was with him. 39 And we are witnesses of all that he did both in the country of the Jews and in Jerusalem. They put him to death by hanging him on a tree, 40 but God raised him on the third day and made him to appear, 41 not to all the people but to us who had been chosen by God as witnesses, who ate and drank with him after he rose from the dead. 42 And he commanded us to preach to the people and to testify that he is the one appointed by God to be judge of the living and the dead. 43 To him all the prophets bear witness that everyone who believes in him receives forgiveness of sins through his name."

The Holy Spirit Falls on the Gentiles

44 While Peter was still saying these things, the Holy Spirit fell on all 1615 who heard the word. 45 And the believers from among the circumcised who had come with Peter were amazed, because the gift of the Holy Spirit was poured out even on the Gentiles. 46 For they were hearing them speaking in tongues and extolling God. Then Peter declared, 47 "Can anyone withhold water for baptizing these people, who have received the Holy Spirit just as we have?" 48 And he commanded them to be baptized in the name of Jesus Christ. Then they asked him to remain for some days.

Peter Reports to the Church

11 Now the apostles and the brothers[1] who were through1645 out Judea heard that the Gentiles also had received the word of God. 2 So when Peter went up to Jerusalem, the circumcision party criticized him, saying, 3 "You went to uncircumcised men and ate with them." 4 But Peter began and explained it to them in order: 5 "I was in the city of Joppa praying, and in a trance I saw a vision, something like a great sheet descending, being let down from heaven by its four corners, and it came down to me. 6 Looking at it closely, I observed animals and beasts of prey and reptiles and birds of the air. 7 And I heard a voice saying to me, 'Rise, Peter; kill and eat.' 8 But I said, 'By no means, Lord; for nothing common or unclean has ever entered my mouth.' 9 But the voice answered a second time from heaven, 'What God has made clean, do not call common.' 10 This happened three times, and all was drawn up again into heaven. 11 And behold, at that very moment three men arrived at the house in which we were, sent to me from Caesarea. 12 And the Spirit told me to go with them, making no distinction. These six brothers also accompanied me, and we entered the man's house. 13 And he told us how he had seen the angel stand in his house and say, 'Send to Joppa and bring Simon who is called Peter; 14 he will declare to you a message by which you will be saved, you and

[1] Or *brothers and sisters*

all your household.' 15 As I began to speak, the Holy Spirit fell on them just as on us at the beginning. 16 And I remembered the word of the Lord, how he said, 'John baptized with water, but you will be baptized with the Holy Spirit.' 17 If then God gave the same gift to them as he gave to us when we believed in the Lord Jesus Christ, who was I that I could stand in God's way?" 18 When they heard these things they fell silent. And they glorified God, saying, "Then to the Gentiles also God has granted repentance that leads to life."

The Church in Antioch

19 Now those who were scattered because of the persecution that arose over Stephen traveled as far as Phoenicia and Cyprus and Antioch, speaking the word to no one except Jews. 20 But there were some of them, men of Cyprus and Cyrene, who on coming to Antioch spoke to the Hellenists[1] also, preaching the Lord Jesus. 21 And the hand of the Lord was with them, and a great number who believed turned to the Lord. 22 The report of this came to the ears of the church in Jerusalem, and they sent Barnabas to Antioch. 23 When he came and saw the grace of God, he was glad, and he exhorted them all to remain faithful to the Lord with steadfast purpose, 24 for he was a good man, full of the Holy Spirit and of faith. And a great many people were added to the Lord. 25 So Barnabas went to Tarsus to look for Saul, 26 and when he had found him, he brought him to Antioch. For a whole year they met with the church and taught a great many people. And in Antioch the disciples were first called Christians.

27 Now in these days prophets came down from Jerusalem to Antioch. 28 And one of them named Agabus stood up and foretold by the Spirit that there would be a great famine over all the world (this took place in the days of Claudius). 29 So the disciples determined, everyone according to his ability, to send relief to the brothers[2] living in Judea. 30 And they did so, sending it to the elders by the hand of Barnabas and Saul.

James Killed and Peter Imprisoned

1651
1673

12 About that time Herod the king laid violent hands on some who belonged to the church. 2 He killed James the brother of John with the sword, 3 and when he saw that it pleased the Jews, he proceeded to arrest Peter also. This was during the days of Unleavened Bread. 4 And when he had seized him, he put him in prison, delivering him over to four squads of soldiers to guard him, intending after the Passover to bring him out to the people. 5 So Peter was kept in prison, but earnest prayer for him was made to God by the church.

Peter Is Rescued

6 Now when Herod was about to bring him out, on that very night, Peter was sleeping between two soldiers, bound with two chains, and sentries before the door were guarding the prison. 7 And behold, an angel of the Lord stood next to him, and a light shone in the cell. He struck Peter on the side and woke him, saying, "Get up quickly." And the chains fell off his hands. 8 And the angel said to him, "Dress yourself and put on your sandals." And he did so. And he said to him, "Wrap your cloak around you and follow me." 9 And he went out and followed him. He did not know that what was being done by the angel was real, but thought he was seeing a vision. 10 When they had passed the first and the second guard, they came to the iron gate leading into the city. It opened for them of its own accord, and they went out and went along one street, and immediately the angel left him. 11 When Peter came to himself, he said, "Now I am sure that the Lord has sent his angel and rescued me from the hand of Herod and from all that the Jewish people were expecting."

[1] Or *Greeks* (that is, Greek-speaking non-Jews) [2] Or *brothers and sisters*

Peter Escapes From Prison

Peter loved to tell people how Jesus came from heaven to save us from our sins. The Holy Spirit helped Peter to be a powerful preacher. Many people who listened to Peter believed in Jesus and became part of God's family. Peter was a leader in God's Church, just as Jesus had told him that he would be.

But there were many people who did not believe in Jesus. The Jewish leaders especially wanted Peter to stop telling others about Jesus. One day, King Herod had his Roman soldiers take Peter to jail. They put chains on Peter and stood guard over him night and day.

Peter's friends in the church were sad and worried about him. They did not know what would happen to their friend. They were especially afraid that some violent men might kill Peter, just as they had killed another disciple, James. The believers prayed earnestly that God would keep Peter safe and set him free.

God heard the prayers of His people and sent an angel to help Peter. The angel woke Peter up in the middle of the night, saying, "Get up quickly." Miraculously, the chains fell off of Peter's hands and his feet. The angel told Peter, "Dress yourself and put on your sandals. Wrap your cloak around you and follow me."

Quickly, Peter did what the angel said. But it all happened

so quickly that he thought he must be dreaming. The angel led Peter past the soldiers to the iron gate that led into the city. When they got to the gate, it opened by itself—and the angel and Peter walked right through the open gate.

When Peter was safely outside the prison, the angel disappeared. Now Peter knew he wasn't dreaming—it was real! He hurried to the house where his friends were praying for him. Peter knocked at the door, and a servant girl named Rhoda came to answer. When she heard Peter's voice, Rhoda was so happy that she ran back to tell everyone, but she forgot to open the door and let him in!

At first, Peter's friends did not believe Rhoda. But when Peter kept on knocking, his friends finally opened the door and were astonished! God had miraculously answered their prayers and kept Peter safe.

Our God can do anything! He is all-powerful, and all His plans are always good. We can trust God's sovereign power and plans. God has rescued us, too, from the "prison" of sin, by sending His Son, Jesus, to be our Savior. God always hears our prayers, and He sends His angels to watch over us.

SEEK and FIND

WHERE TO FIND THE STORY

Acts 12:1–19

KEY BIBLE VERSE

"First of all, then, I urge that supplications, prayers, intercessions, and thanksgivings be made for all people, for kings and all who are in high positions, that we may lead a

peaceful and quiet life, godly and dignified in every way."
(1 Timothy 2:1–2)

THREE KEY QUESTIONS

- What did the Roman soldiers do to keep Peter in prison?
- What are all the miracles that happened so that Peter could get out of prison?
- What did God do to set us free from the "prison" of sin?

RELATED BIBLE READINGS

Acts 4:23–31; Acts 5:17–42; Ephesians 6:18–20

12 When he realized this, he went to the
house of Mary, the mother of John whose
other name was Mark, where many were
gathered together and were praying.
13 And when he knocked at the door of
the gateway, a servant girl named Rhoda
came to answer. 14 Recognizing Peter's
voice, in her joy she did not open the gate
but ran in and reported that Peter was
standing at the gate. 15 They said to her,
"You are out of your mind." But she kept
insisting that it was so, and they kept say-
ing, "It is his angel!" 16 But Peter contin-
ued knocking, and when they opened,
they saw him and were amazed. 17 But
motioning to them with his hand to be
silent, he described to them how the Lord
had brought him out of the prison. And
he said, "Tell these things to James and to
the brothers."[1] Then he departed and went
to another place.
18 Now when day came, there was no
little disturbance among the soldiers
over what had become of Peter. 19 And
after Herod searched for him and did
not find him, he examined the sentries
and ordered that they should be put to
death. Then he went down from Judea to
Caesarea and spent time there.

The Death of Herod

20 Now Herod was angry with the people
of Tyre and Sidon, and they came to him
with one accord, and having persuaded
Blastus, the king's chamberlain, they asked
for peace, because their country depended
on the king's country for food. 21 On an
appointed day Herod put on his royal
robes, took his seat upon the throne, and
delivered an oration to them. 22 And the
people were shouting, "The voice of a god,
and not of a man!" 23 Immediately an angel
of the Lord struck him down, because he
did not give God the glory, and he was
eaten by worms and breathed his last.
24 But the word of God increased and
multiplied.
25 And Barnabas and Saul returned
from[2] Jerusalem when they had com-
pleted their service, bringing with them
John, whose other name was Mark.

Barnabas and Saul Sent Off

13 Now there were in the
church at Antioch prophets
1657 and teachers, Barnabas, Simeon
who was called Niger,[3] Lucius of Cyrene,
Manaen a member of the court of Herod
the tetrarch, and Saul. 2 While they were

[1] Or *brothers and sisters* [2] Some manuscripts *to* [3] *Niger* is a Latin word meaning *black*, or *dark*

worshiping the Lord and fasting, the Holy Spirit said, "Set apart for me Barnabas and Saul for the work to which I have called them." 3 Then after fasting and praying they laid their hands on them and sent them off.

Barnabas and Saul on Cyprus

4 So, being sent out by the Holy Spirit, they went down to Seleucia, and from there they sailed to Cyprus. 5 When they arrived at Salamis, they proclaimed the word of God in the synagogues of the Jews. And they had John to assist them. 6 When they had gone through the whole island as far as Paphos, they came upon a certain magician, a Jewish false prophet named Bar-Jesus. 7 He was with the proconsul, Sergius Paulus, a man of intelligence, who summoned Barnabas and Saul and sought to hear the word of God. 8 But Elymas the magician (for that is the meaning of his name) opposed them, seeking to turn the proconsul away from the faith. 9 But Saul, who was also called Paul, filled with the Holy Spirit, looked intently at him 10 and said, "You son of the devil, you enemy of all righteousness, full of all deceit and villainy, will you not stop making crooked the straight paths of the Lord? 11 And now, behold, the hand of the Lord is upon you, and you will be blind and unable to see the sun for a time." Immediately mist and darkness fell upon him, and he went about seeking people to lead him by the hand. 12 Then the proconsul believed, when he saw what had occurred, for he was astonished at the teaching of the Lord.

Paul and Barnabas at Antioch in Pisidia

13 Now Paul and his companions set sail from Paphos and came to Perga in Pamphylia. And John left them and returned to Jerusalem, 14 but they went on from Perga and came to Antioch in Pisidia. And on the Sabbath day they went into the synagogue and sat down. 15 After the reading from the Law and the Prophets, the rulers of the synagogue sent a message to them, saying, "Brothers, if you have any word of encouragement for the people, say it." 16 So Paul stood up, and motioning with his hand said:

"Men of Israel and you who fear God, listen. 17 The God of this people Israel chose our fathers and made the people great during their stay in the land of Egypt, and with uplifted arm he led them out of it. 18 And for about forty years he put up with[1] them in the wilderness. 19 And after destroying seven nations in the land of Canaan, he gave them their land as an inheritance. 20 All this took about 450 years. And after that he gave them judges until Samuel the prophet. 21 Then they asked for a king, and God gave them Saul the son of Kish, a man of the tribe of Benjamin, for forty years. 22 And when he had removed him, he raised up David to be their king, of whom he testified and said, 'I have found in David the son of Jesse a man after my heart, who will do all my will.' 23 Of this man's offspring God has brought to Israel a Savior, Jesus, as he promised. 24 Before his coming, John had proclaimed a baptism of repentance to all the people of Israel. 25 And as John was finishing his course, he said, 'What do you suppose that I am? I am not he. No, but behold, after me one is coming, the sandals of whose feet I am not worthy to untie.'

463

26 "Brothers, sons of the family of Abraham, and those among you who fear God, to us has been sent the message of this salvation. 27 For those who live in Jerusalem and their rulers, because they did not recognize him nor understand the utterances of the prophets, which are read every Sabbath, fulfilled them by condemning him. 28 And though they found in him no guilt worthy of death, they asked Pilate to have him executed. 29 And when they had carried out all that was written of him, they took him down from the tree and laid him in a tomb. 30 But God raised him from the dead, 31 and for many days he appeared

[1] Some manuscripts *he carried* (compare Deuteronomy 1:31)

to those who had come up with him from Galilee to Jerusalem, who are now his witnesses to the people. 32 And we bring you the good news that what God promised to the fathers, 33 this he has fulfilled to us their children by raising Jesus, as also it is written in the second Psalm,

> "'You are my Son,
> today I have begotten you.'

34 And as for the fact that he raised him from the dead, no more to return to corruption, he has spoken in this way,

> "'I will give you the holy and sure
> blessings of David.'

35 Therefore he says also in another psalm,

> "'You will not let your Holy One see
> corruption.'

36 For David, after he had served the purpose of God in his own generation, fell asleep and was laid with his fathers and saw corruption, 37 but he whom God raised up did not see corruption. 38 Let it be known to you therefore, brothers, that through this man forgiveness of sins is proclaimed to you, 39 and by him everyone who believes is freed[1] from everything from which you could not be freed by the law of Moses. 40 Beware, therefore, lest what is said in the Prophets should come about:

> 41 "'Look, you scoffers,
> be astounded and perish;
> for I am doing a work in your days,
> a work that you will not believe,
> even if one tells it to you.'"

42 As they went out, the people begged that these things might be told them the next Sabbath. 43 And after the meeting of the synagogue broke up, many Jews and devout converts to Judaism followed Paul and Barnabas, who, as they spoke with them, urged them to continue in the grace of God.

44 The next Sabbath almost the whole city gathered to hear the word of the Lord. 45 But when the Jews saw the crowds, they were filled with jealousy and began to contradict what was spoken by Paul, reviling him. 46 And Paul and Barnabas spoke out boldly, saying, "It was necessary that the word of God be spoken first to you. Since you thrust it aside and judge yourselves unworthy of eternal life, behold, we are turning to the Gentiles. 47 For so the Lord has commanded us, saying,

> "'I have made you a light for the
> Gentiles,
> that you may bring salvation to
> the ends of the earth.'"

1669

48 And when the Gentiles heard this, they began rejoicing and glorifying the word of the Lord, and as many as were appointed to eternal life believed. 49 And the word of the Lord was spreading throughout the whole region. 50 But the Jews incited the devout women of high standing and the leading men of the city, stirred up persecution against Paul and Barnabas, and drove them out of their district. 51 But they shook off the dust from their feet against them and went to Iconium. 52 And the disciples were filled with joy and with the Holy Spirit.

Paul and Barnabas at Iconium

14 Now at Iconium they entered together into the Jewish synagogue and spoke in such a way that a great number of both Jews and Greeks believed. 2 But the unbelieving Jews stirred up the Gentiles and poisoned their minds against the brothers.[2] 3 So they remained for a long time, speaking boldly for the Lord, who bore witness to the word of his grace, granting signs and wonders to be done by their hands. 4 But the people of the city were divided; some sided with the Jews and some with the apostles. 5 When an attempt was made by both Gentiles and

[1] Greek *justified*; twice in this verse [2] Or *brothers and sisters*

Paul's First Missionary Journey

The Holy Spirit sent Paul and Barnabas on a journey to spread the Good News about Jesus. They began in Antioch and traveled to many towns all around the Mediterranean Sea. Whenever they reached a new place, they would go first to the Jewish meeting house. There Paul and Barnabas told the Jews that God had sent Jesus Christ as their Lord and Savior. Then Paul and Barnabas moved on to tell other people who were not Jews about the gospel. Paul and Barnabas were called missionaries, because they brought the Good News to many people in faraway places.

In each city they went to, there were people who did not believe Paul and Barnabas's message. Sometimes they became very angry and treated Paul and Barnabas badly. But in each city, the Holy Spirit worked in the hearts of other people who then believed. With help and encouragement from Paul and Barnabas, these new believers formed new little churches. When they finished their work in each city, the Holy Spirit would send Paul and Barnabas on to new places.

Once in a town called Lystra, Paul and Barnabas met a crippled man who had never walked before. Paul saw that this man had faith. In a loud voice, Paul said to the man, "Stand upright on your feet."

Immediately, the man jumped up and began to walk! When

the crowds saw the miracle, they thought Paul and Barnabas must be pagan gods of some sort. They said, "The gods have come down to us in the likeness of men!" The pagan priest, who looked after the city's idols, brought garlands of flowers and a bull to sacrifice to Paul and Barnabas. The people even began to call Paul and Barnabas by the names of false gods.

Paul and Barnabas were horrified! Only the Lord should be worshiped. Paul and Barnabas tried to stop the people from worshiping them. Paul said, "Why are you doing these things? We also are men, of like nature with you."

Then Paul explained how he and Barnabas had come for this very reason: to turn people away from these false gods, so that they could know the one true living God, who made heaven and earth. Some people in Lystra believed Paul's message, but others tried to stop him.

Paul and Barnabas journeyed a long time. Then, on their way home, they stopped at all the places they had visited before. They encouraged those who believed in Jesus. All along the way, God continued to protect Paul and Barnabas, leading them and blessing their work.

When they arrived back in Antioch, they reported to the believers all that God had done and how both Jews and Gentiles had believed in Jesus. The Holy Spirit had worked in people's hearts so they would repent of their sins and put their faith in Jesus.

Today the Holy Spirit still sends missionaries to spread the Good News about Jesus, and He still changes people's hearts so they will believe in Him.

SEEK and FIND

WHERE TO FIND THE STORY

Acts 13–14

KEY BIBLE VERSE

"And when they arrived and gathered the church together, they declared all that God had done with them, and how he had opened a door of faith to the Gentiles." (Acts 14:27)

THREE KEY QUESTIONS

- What happened to Paul and Barnabas in the town of Lystra after the crippled man was healed? Who did the people think that Paul and Barnabas were?
- Many of the people who believed were Jews, but what were the other people called?
- How do people in faraway places find out the Good News about Jesus today?

RELATED BIBLE READINGS

Acts 1:8; 15:36–18:22; 18:23–28:31

Jews, with their rulers, to mistreat them
and to stone them, 6 they learned of it and
fled to Lystra and Derbe, cities of Lycaonia,
and to the surrounding country, 7 and
there they continued to preach the gospel.

Paul and Barnabas at Lystra

8 Now at Lystra there was a man sit-
ting who could not use his feet. He was
crippled from birth and had never walked.
9 He listened to Paul speaking. And Paul,
looking intently at him and seeing that
he had faith to be made well,[1] 10 said in a
loud voice, "Stand upright on your feet."
And he sprang up and began walking.
11 And when the crowds saw what Paul
had done, they lifted up their voices, say-
ing in Lycaonian, "The gods have come
down to us in the likeness of men!"
12 Barnabas they called Zeus, and Paul,
Hermes, because he was the chief speaker.
13 And the priest of Zeus, whose temple
was at the entrance to the city, brought
oxen and garlands to the gates and
wanted to offer sacrifice with the crowds.
14 But when the apostles Barnabas and
Paul heard of it, they tore their garments
and rushed out into the crowd, crying out,
15 "Men, why are you doing these things?
We also are men, of like nature with you,
and we bring you good news, that you
should turn from these vain things to a
living God, who made the heaven and the
earth and the sea and all that is in them.
16 In past generations he allowed all the
nations to walk in their own ways. 17 Yet
he did not leave himself without witness,
for he did good by giving you rains from

[1] *Or be saved*

heaven and fruitful seasons, satisfying
your hearts with food and gladness."
18 Even with these words they scarcely
restrained the people from offering sac-
rifice to them.

Paul Stoned at Lystra

19 But Jews came from Antioch and
Iconium, and having persuaded
1629 the crowds, they stoned Paul and
dragged him out of the city, supposing
that he was dead. 20 But when the disciples
gathered about him, he rose up
and entered the city, and on the
1663 next day he went on with Barnabas
to Derbe. 21 When they had preached the
gospel to that city and had made many
disciples, they returned to Lystra and to
Iconium and to Antioch, 22 strengthening
the souls of the disciples, encouraging
them to continue in the faith, and saying
that through many tribulations we must
enter the kingdom of God. 23 And when
they had appointed elders for them in
every church, with prayer and fasting they
committed them to the Lord in whom
they had believed.

Paul and Barnabas Return to Antioch in Syria

24 Then they passed through Pisidia and
came to Pamphylia. 25 And when they had
spoken the word in Perga, they went down
to Attalia, 26 and from there they sailed to
Antioch, where they had been com-
mended to the grace of God for the work
that they had fulfilled. 27 And when they
arrived and gathered the church
together, they declared all that God
1657 had done with them, and how he
had opened a door of faith to the Gentiles.
28 And they remained no little time with
the disciples.

The Jerusalem Council

15 But some men came down
from Judea and were teach-
1663 ing the brothers, "Unless you are
circumcised according to the custom of
Moses, you cannot be saved." 2 And after
Paul and Barnabas had no small dissen-
sion and debate with them, Paul and
Barnabas and some of the others were
appointed to go up to Jerusalem to the
apostles and the elders about this ques-
tion. 3 So, being sent on their way by the
church, they passed through both
Phoenicia and Samaria, describing in
detail the conversion of the Gentiles, and
brought great joy to all the brothers.[1]
4 When they came to Jerusalem, they were
welcomed by the church and the apostles
and the elders, and they declared all that
God had done with them. 5 But some
believers who belonged to the party of the
Pharisees rose up and said, "It is necessary
to circumcise them and to order them to
keep the law of Moses."
6 The apostles and the elders were gath-

CHARACTER PROFILE

JAMES

James (the brother of Jesus) did not believe in Jesus before Jesus died. But after Jesus rose from the dead, James met Jesus again and believed in Him. James became a leader of the church in Jerusalem, and he wrote the New Testament book we call "James."

[1] Or *brothers and sisters;* also verse 22

ered together to consider this matter.
7 And after there had been much
debate, Peter stood up and said to
1645 them, "Brothers, you know that in
the early days God made a choice among
you, that by my mouth the Gentiles should
hear the word of the gospel and believe.
8 And God, who knows the heart, bore wit-
ness to them, by giving them the Holy
Spirit just as he did to us, 9 and he made no
distinction between us and them, having
cleansed their hearts by faith. 10 Now,
therefore, why are you putting God to the
test by placing a yoke on the neck of the
disciples that neither our fathers nor we
have been able to bear? 11 But we believe
that we will be saved through the grace of
the Lord Jesus, just as they will."

12 And all the assembly fell silent, and
they listened to Barnabas and Paul as they
related what signs and wonders God had
done through them among the Gentiles.
13 After they finished speaking, James
replied, "Brothers, listen to me. 14 Simeon
has related how God first visited the
Gentiles, to take from them a people for
his name. 15 And with this the words of the
prophets agree, just as it is written,

16 "'After this I will return,
and I will rebuild the tent of David
that has fallen;
I will rebuild its ruins,
and I will restore it,
17 that the remnant[1] of mankind may
seek the Lord,
and all the Gentiles who are called
by my name,
says the Lord, who makes these
things 18 known from of old.'

19 Therefore my judgment is that we
should not trouble those of the Gentiles
who turn to God, 20 but should write to
them to abstain from the things polluted
by idols, and from sexual immorality, and
from what has been strangled, and from
blood. 21 For from ancient generations
Moses has had in every city those who
proclaim him, for he is read every Sabbath
in the synagogues."

The Council's Letter to Gentile Believers

22 Then it seemed good to the apostles
and the elders, with the whole church, to
choose men from among them and send
them to Antioch with Paul and Barnabas.
They sent Judas called Barsabbas, and
Silas, leading men among the brothers,
23 with the following letter: "The broth-
ers, both the apostles and the elders, to
the brothers[2] who are of the Gentiles in
Antioch and Syria and Cilicia, greetings.
24 Since we have heard that some per-
sons have gone out from us and troubled
you[3] with words, unsettling your minds,
although we gave them no instructions,
25 it has seemed good to us, having come
to one accord, to choose men and send
them to you with our beloved Barnabas
and Paul, 26 men who have risked their
lives for the sake of our Lord Jesus Christ.
27 We have therefore sent Judas and Silas,
who themselves will tell you the same
things by word of mouth. 28 For it has
seemed good to the Holy Spirit and to
us to lay on you no greater burden than
these requirements: 29 that you abstain
from what has been sacrificed to idols,
and from blood, and from what has been
strangled, and from sexual immorality. If
you keep yourselves from these, you will
do well. Farewell."

30 So when they were sent off, they went
down to Antioch, and having gathered the
congregation together, they delivered the
letter. 31 And when they had read it, they
rejoiced because of its encouragement.
32 And Judas and Silas, who were them-
selves prophets, encouraged and strength-
ened the brothers with many words.
33 And after they had spent some time,
they were sent off in peace by the broth-
ers to those who had sent them.[4] 35 But
Paul and Barnabas remained in Antioch,

[1] Or *rest* [2] Or *brothers and sisters*; also verses 32, 33, 36 [3] Some manuscripts *some persons from us have troubled you* [4] Some manuscripts insert verse 34: *But it seemed good to Silas to remain there*

God's One Family

Timothy's father was a Greek, not a Jew who worshiped the one true God. But when Timothy was a boy, his Jewish mother and grandmother taught him about God from the Scriptures. They told him about God's promise to send the Savior. So when their family learned about Jesus—that He was the promised Savior—they were quick to believe in Him. They joined the Christian believers who had planted churches in the cities of Lystra and Iconium.

When Paul came back to visit the followers of Jesus at Lystra, Paul heard good things about Timothy from the people in the church where Timothy worshiped the Lord. So Paul asked Timothy to travel with him on his missionary journey.

There were two main purposes for Paul's missionary journey. The first was to spread the Good News about Jesus. Paul's second purpose was to encourage and teach all the small groups of new believers who had planted churches. He wanted to share with them some important news from an important church meeting that had been held recently in Jerusalem.

This meeting of church leaders in Jerusalem settled a difficult issue. There were people who had been arguing about things they thought everyone had to do as a believer in Jesus. Some thought everyone had to eat special food or do special things to keep the Jewish Law in order to become a true follower of Jesus and to be a member of His Church. But God had shown Paul that there isn't anything we can do to make ourselves good enough to deserve God's love and grace. Paul had tried to keep all the rules and Jewish laws—but he failed! He knew that he was still an unworthy sinner, just like all of us are! That is why God sent Jesus to save us from our sins.

Paul wanted everyone to know that God forgives all our sins because of our faith in Jesus. We don't have to do anything. Jesus did it all for us. Jesus kept God's rules perfectly, and then He died on the cross for our sins, to pay for the punishment that we deserved.

The important church meeting in Jerusalem listened to Paul, and they decided the issue once and for all. They agreed with Paul: no one needs to do anything extra to earn God's love and grace. Jesus has done it all for us. We only need to have faith in Him. Then the church leaders wrote a letter for Paul and Timothy to take with them on their missionary journey to the churches.

Timothy went many places with Paul. Everywhere they went, they told people that Jesus came to save them from their sins and they did not need to do special things, but just believe in Jesus as their Savior. The Holy Spirit helped the people in the churches grow stronger in faith. Many more people, both Jews and Gentiles, believed in Jesus as their Savior. They all became part of God's one family, the church.

SEEK and FIND

WHERE TO FIND THE STORY

Acts 15:1–16:5

KEY BIBLE VERSE

"For we hold that one is justified by faith apart from works of the law." (Romans 3:28)

THREE KEY QUESTIONS

- Who taught Timothy about the one true God?
- What was the important decision that was made by the meeting of church leaders in Jerusalem?
- Who can become part of God's family, the Church?

RELATED BIBLE READINGS

Acts 14:20–21; Romans 3:19–28; Galatians 2:15–21; 2 Timothy 1:5; 3:15

teaching and preaching the word of the Lord, with many others also.

Paul and Barnabas Separate

1657

36 And after some days Paul said to Barnabas, "Let us return and visit the brothers in every city where we proclaimed the word of the Lord, and see how they are." 37 Now Barnabas wanted to take with them John called Mark. 38 But Paul thought best not to take with them one who had withdrawn from them in Pamphylia and had not gone with them to the work. 39 And there arose a sharp disagreement, so that they separated from each other. Barnabas took Mark with him and sailed away to Cyprus, 40 but Paul chose Silas and departed, having been commended by the brothers to the grace of the Lord. 41 And he went through Syria and Cilicia, strengthening the churches.

Timothy Joins Paul and Silas

16 Paul[1] came also to Derbe and to Lystra. A disciple was there, named Timothy, the son of a Jewish woman who was a believer, but his father was a Greek. 2 He was well spoken of by the brothers[2] at Lystra and Iconium. 3 Paul wanted Timothy to accompany him, and he took him and circumcised him because of the Jews who were in those places, for they all knew that his father was a Greek. 4 As they went on their way through the cities, they delivered to them for observance the decisions that had been reached by the apostles and elders who were in Jerusalem. 5 So the churches were strengthened in the faith, and they increased in numbers daily.

The Macedonian Call

6 And they went through the region of Phrygia and Galatia, having been forbidden by the Holy Spirit to speak the word in Asia. 7 And when they had come up to Mysia, they attempted to go into Bithynia, but the Spirit of Jesus did not allow them. 8 So, passing by Mysia, they went down to Troas. 9 And a vision appeared to Paul in the night: a man of Macedonia was standing there, urging him and saying, "Come over to Macedonia and help us." 10 And when Paul[3] had seen the vision, immediately we

[1] Greek *He* [2] Or *brothers and sisters*; also verse 40 [3] Greek *he*

sought to go on into Macedonia, concluding that God had called us to preach the gospel to them.

The Conversion of Lydia

11 So, setting sail from Troas, we
made a direct voyage to Samo-
1669 thrace, and the following day to
Neapolis, 12 and from there to Philippi,
which is a leading city of the[1] district of
Macedonia and a Roman colony. We re-
mained in this city some days. 13 And on
the Sabbath day we went outside the gate
to the riverside, where we supposed there
was a place of prayer, and we sat down and
spoke to the women who had come to-
gether. 14 One who heard us was a woman
named Lydia, from the city of Thyatira, a
seller of purple goods, who was a wor-
shiper of God. The Lord opened her
heart to pay attention to what was
1669 said by Paul. 15 And after she was
baptized, and her household as well, she
urged us, saying, "If you have judged me to
be faithful to the Lord, come to my house
and stay." And she prevailed upon us.

Paul and Silas in Prison

16 As we were going to the place of
prayer, we were met by a slave girl
1673 who had a spirit of divination and
brought her owners much gain by
fortune-telling. 17 She followed
1669 Paul and us, crying out, "These
men are servants[2] of the Most High God,
who proclaim to you the way of salvation."
18 And this she kept doing for many days.
Paul, having become greatly annoyed,
turned and said to the spirit, "I command
you in the name of Jesus Christ to come
out of her." And it came out that very hour.

19 But when her owners saw that their hope of gain was gone, they seized Paul and Silas and dragged them into the marketplace before the rulers. 20 And when they had brought them to the magistrates, they said, "These men are Jews, and they are disturbing our city. 21 They advocate customs that are not lawful for us as Romans to accept or practice." 22 The crowd joined in attacking them, and the magistrates tore the garments off them and gave orders to beat them with rods. 23 And when they had inflicted many blows upon them, they threw them into prison, ordering the jailer to keep them safely. 24 Having received this order, he put them into the inner prison and fastened their feet in the stocks.

The Philippian Jailer Converted

25 About midnight Paul and Silas were
praying and singing hymns to God, and
the prisoners were listening to them,
26 and suddenly there was a great earth-
quake, so that the foundations of the
prison were shaken. And immediately all
the doors were opened, and everyone's
bonds were unfastened. 27 When the jailer
woke and saw that the prison doors were
open, he drew his sword and was about to
kill himself, supposing that the prisoners
had escaped. 28 But Paul cried with a loud
voice, "Do not harm yourself, for we are all
here." 29 And the jailer[3] called for
lights and rushed in, and trem-
1633 bling with fear he fell down before
Paul and Silas. 30 Then he brought them
out and said, "Sirs, what must I do to be
saved?" 31 And they said, "Believe in
the Lord Jesus, and you will be
1673 saved, you and your household."
32 And they spoke the word of the Lord to
him and to all who were in his house.
33 And he took them the same hour of the
night and washed their wounds; and he
was baptized at once, he and all his family.
34 Then he brought them up into his house
and set food before them. And he rejoiced
along with his entire household that he
had believed in God.

35 But when it was day, the magistrates sent the police, saying, "Let those men go." 36 And the jailer reported these words to Paul, saying, "The magistrates have sent to let you go. Therefore come out now and go

[1] Or *that* [2] Greek *bondservants* [3] Greek *he*

in peace." 37 But Paul said to them, "They have beaten us publicly, uncondemned, men who are Roman citizens, and have thrown us into prison; and do they now throw us out secretly? No! Let them come themselves and take us out." 38 The police reported these words to the magistrates, and they were afraid when they heard that they were Roman citizens. 39 So they came and apologized to them. And they took them out and asked them to leave the city. 40 So they went out of the prison and visited Lydia. And when they had seen the brothers, they encouraged them and departed.

Paul and Silas in Thessalonica

17 Now when they had passed through Amphipolis and Apollonia, they came to Thessalonica, where there was a synagogue of the Jews. 2 And Paul went in, as was his custom, and on three Sabbath days he reasoned with them from the Scriptures, 3 explaining and proving that it was necessary for the Christ to suffer and to rise from the dead, and saying, "This Jesus, whom I proclaim to you, is the Christ." 4 And some of them were persuaded and joined Paul and Silas, as did a great many of the devout Greeks and not a few of the leading women. 5 But the Jews were jealous, and taking some wicked men of the rabble, they formed a mob, set the city in an uproar, and attacked the house of Jason, seeking to bring them out to the crowd. 6 And when they could not find them, they dragged Jason and some of the brothers before the city authorities, shouting, "These men who have turned the world upside down have come here also, 7 and Jason has received them, and they are all acting against the decrees of Caesar, saying that there is another king, Jesus." 8 And the people and the city authorities were disturbed when they heard these things. 9 And when they had taken money as security from Jason and the rest, they let them go.

Paul and Silas in Berea

10 The brothers[1] immediately sent Paul and Silas away by night to Berea, and when they arrived they went into the Jewish synagogue. 11 Now these Jews were more noble than those in Thessalonica; they received the word with all eagerness, examining the Scriptures daily to see if these things were so. 12 Many of them therefore believed, with not a few Greek women of high standing as well as men. 13 But when the Jews from Thessalonica learned that the word of God was proclaimed by Paul at Berea also, they came there too, agitating and stirring up the crowds. 14 Then the brothers immediately sent Paul off on his way to the sea, but Silas and Timothy remained there. 15 Those who conducted Paul brought him as far as Athens, and after receiving a command for Silas and Timothy to come to him as soon as possible, they departed.

Paul in Athens

16 Now while Paul was waiting for them at Athens, his spirit was provoked within him as he saw that the city was full of idols. 17 So he reasoned in the synagogue with the Jews and the devout persons, and in the marketplace every day with those who happened to be there. 18 Some of the Epicurean and Stoic philosophers also conversed with him. And some said, "What does this babbler wish to say?" Others said, "He seems to be a preacher of foreign divinities"—because he was preaching Jesus and the resurrection. 19 And they took him and brought him to the Areopagus, saying, "May we know what this new teaching is that you are presenting? 20 For you bring some strange things to our ears. We wish to know therefore what these things mean." 21 Now all the Athenians and the foreigners who lived there would spend their time in nothing except telling or hearing something new.

[1] Or *brothers and sisters*; also verse 14

Lydia Trusts in Jesus

Paul continued on his missionary journeys with three other missionaries: Silas, Luke, and Timothy. They were close friends and co-workers with Paul. They told people that Jesus was the Savior for all who put their trust in Him.

The men made a long journey, and sometimes very hard things happened. Many times they couldn't find a good place to stay, and people often opposed them. But in spite of great persecution, they always obeyed the Holy Spirit and kept on preaching and encouraging new believers.

One of the cities they visited was called Philippi. It was a prosperous city, but there was no place in Philippi to worship the one true God. But Paul discovered that there was a place for prayer outside the city wall along the river. So on the day of worship, the Sabbath day, Paul walked with his friends to the place of prayer along the river.

When they got to the place of prayer, a group of women had gathered there to pray. So Paul told the women about the Good News of Jesus. One of the women was named Lydia, who worshiped the one true God. She also had her own business selling expensive purple cloth.

The Holy Spirit had prepared Lydia's heart and mind to understand and believe the Good News about Jesus the

Savior. Right away she wanted to be baptized to show her commitment to the Lord. Because she was an important businesswoman, she had many servants who made up her household. Lydia brought all of them to hear about the Savior and be baptized, too!

Lydia was so excited about living for Jesus that she urged Paul, Silas, Luke, and Timothy to come and stay in her large home as her guests. There in Lydia's home the new believers in Philippi learned all about the gospel and God's Word from these wise leaders. And because no church buildings had been built yet, they worshiped together in Lydia's home.

Today the Holy Spirit is still at work—giving us a trusting heart to believe in Jesus as our Savior.

SEEK and FIND

WHERE TO FIND THE STORY

Acts 16:11–15

KEY BIBLE VERSE

"The Lord opened her heart to pay attention to what was said by Paul. . . . She was baptized, and her household as well." (Acts 16:14–15)

THREE KEY QUESTIONS

- What was Lydia's important business in the city of Philippi?
- What did Lydia do when she heard the Good News about Jesus?
- Where did the new believers meet before church buildings were built?

RELATED BIBLE READINGS

Acts 2:47; 13:48; 16:16–40; Galatians 1:15–16

Paul Addresses the Areopagus

22 So Paul, standing in the midst of
the Areopagus, said: "Men of Athens, I
perceive that in every way you are very
religious. 23 For as I passed along and
observed the objects of your worship, I
found also an altar with this inscription,
'To the unknown god.' What therefore you
worship as unknown, this I proclaim to
you. 24 The God who made the world and
everything in it, being Lord of heaven and
earth, does not live in temples made by
man,[1] 25 nor is he served by human hands,
as though he needed anything, since he
himself gives to all mankind life and
breath and everything. 26 And he made
from one man every nation of mankind
to live on all the face of the earth, hav-
ing determined allotted periods and the
boundaries of their dwelling place, 27 that
they should seek God, in the hope that
they might feel their way toward him and
find him. Yet he is actually not far from
each one of us, 28 for

> "'In him we live and move and have
> our being';[2]

as even some of your own poets have said,

> "'For we are indeed his offspring.'[3]

29 Being then God's offspring, we ought
not to think that the divine being is like
gold or silver or stone, an image formed
by the art and imagination of man. 30 The
times of ignorance God overlooked, but
now he commands all people everywhere
to repent, 31 because he has fixed a day on
which he will judge the world in
righteousness by a man whom he
1545 has appointed; and of this he has
given assurance to all by raising him from
the dead."

32 Now when they heard of the resurrec-
tion of the dead, some mocked. But oth-
ers said, "We will hear you again about
this." 33 So Paul went out from their midst.
34 But some men joined him and believed,
among whom also were Dionysius the
Areopagite and a woman named Damaris
and others with them.

Paul in Corinth

18 After this Paul[4] left Athens and
went to Corinth. 2 And he found
a Jew named Aquila, a native of Pontus,
recently come from Italy with his wife
Priscilla, because Claudius had com-
manded all the Jews to leave Rome. And
he went to see them, 3 and because he was
of the same trade he stayed with them
and worked, for they were tentmakers by
trade. 4 And he reasoned in the synagogue
every Sabbath, and tried to persuade Jews
and Greeks.

5 When Silas and Timothy arrived from
Macedonia, Paul was occupied with the
word, testifying to the Jews that the Christ
was Jesus. 6 And when they opposed and
reviled him, he shook out his garments
and said to them, "Your blood be on
your own heads! I am innocent. From
now on I will go to the Gentiles." 7 And
he left there and went to the house of a
man named Titius Justus, a worshiper
of God. His house was next door to the
synagogue. 8 Crispus, the ruler of the
synagogue, believed in the Lord, together
with his entire household. And many of
the Corinthians hearing Paul believed and
were baptized. 9 And the Lord said to Paul
one night in a vision, "Do not be afraid,
but go on speaking and do not be silent,
10 for I am with you, and no one will attack
you to harm you, for I have many in this
city who are my people." 11 And he stayed
a year and six months, teaching the word
of God among them.

12 But when Gallio was proconsul of
Achaia, the Jews made a united attack on
Paul and brought him before the tribunal,
13 saying, "This man is persuading people
to worship God contrary to the law." 14 But
when Paul was about to open his mouth,
Gallio said to the Jews, "If it were a matter

[1] Greek *made by hands* [2] Probably from Epimenides of Crete [3] From Aratus's poem "Phainomena" [4] Greek *he*

Paul and Silas in Prison

Not everybody wanted to believe—or even listen to—the Good News that Jesus is the Savior. While Paul and Silas were preaching in Philippi, a wicked man got so angry with them that he started a riot. Then he lied to the officials about Paul and Silas. The officials had them beaten and taken away to prison!

In the prison, a jailer put Paul and Silas in a deep, inner part of the jail and locked their feet in pieces of wood (called "stocks"). The prison was a terrible place, and Paul and Silas did not know what would happen to them when morning came. So they passed the long hours of the night by praying together and singing hymns to God.

Suddenly, around midnight, there was a great earthquake! The foundations of the prison shook, all the prison doors opened, and the chains fell off all the prisoners!

When the jailer woke up, he saw that the prison doors were open. He was sure the prisoners had escaped. He knew he was in trouble and would be held responsible for any prisoners who escaped. He thought it might be better just to fall on his sword and die.

But Paul cried with a loud voice, "Do not harm yourself, for we are all here."

The jailer called for lighted torches to be brought, and rushed in to see for himself. When he found Paul and Silas, he trembled with fear and fell down before them. He recognized it was the power of God that had opened the prison. Immediately, he brought Paul and Silas out of prison and asked them, "Sirs, what must I do to be saved?"

Paul and Silas were glad they could tell the jailer that there was nothing that he needed to do, because Jesus had already done it all! They said, "Believe in the Lord Jesus, and you will be saved, you and your household."

The jailer took Paul and Silas into his home to wash their wounds, where they spoke God's Word to the jailer and to all who were in his house. That very night the jailer and his whole family believed in the Savior and were baptized! Then the new believers shared a meal with Paul and Silas, and the jailer and his family were filled with joy.

The very next day, Paul and Silas were released from prison.

SEEK and FIND

WHERE TO FIND THE STORY

Acts 16:16–40

KEY BIBLE VERSE

"And they said, 'Believe in the Lord Jesus, and you will be saved, you and your household.'" (Acts 16:31)

THREE KEY QUESTIONS

- What did Paul and Silas do at night in prison and why were they able to do this?
- What caused the earthquake in the middle of the night, and

what happened to the prisoners?

- What did Paul and Silas say the jailer should do?

RELATED BIBLE READINGS

Acts 2:37–39; 5:17–25; 12:1–19

of wrongdoing or vicious crime, O Jews,
I would have reason to accept your com-
plaint. 15 But since it is a matter of ques-
tions about words and names and your
own law, see to it yourselves. I refuse to be a
judge of these things." 16 And he drove them
from the tribunal. 17 And they all seized
Sosthenes, the ruler of the synagogue, and
beat him in front of the tribunal. But Gallio
paid no attention to any of this.

Paul Returns to Antioch

18 After this, Paul stayed many days
longer and then took leave of the broth-
ers[1] and set sail for Syria, and with him
Priscilla and Aquila. At Cenchreae he
had cut his hair, for he was under a vow.
19 And they came to Ephesus, and he left
them there, but he himself went into the
synagogue and reasoned with the Jews.
20 When they asked him to stay for a longer
period, he declined. 21 But on taking leave
of them he said, "I will return to you if God
wills," and he set sail from Ephesus.
22 When he had landed at Caesarea, he
went up and greeted the church, and then
went down to Antioch. 23 After spending
some time there, he departed and
went from one place to the next
1657 through the region of Galatia and
Phrygia, strengthening all the disciples.

Apollos Speaks Boldly in Ephesus

24 Now a Jew named Apollos, a native
of Alexandria, came to Ephesus. He was
an eloquent man, competent in the
Scriptures. 25 He had been instructed in
the way of the Lord. And being fervent in
spirit,[2] he spoke and taught accurately the
things concerning Jesus, though he knew
only the baptism of John. 26 He began to
speak boldly in the synagogue, but when
Priscilla and Aquila heard him, they took
him and explained to him the way of God
more accurately. 27 And when he wished to
cross to Achaia, the brothers encouraged
him and wrote to the disciples to welcome
him. When he arrived, he greatly helped
those who through grace had believed,
28 for he powerfully refuted the Jews in
public, showing by the Scriptures that the
Christ was Jesus.

Paul in Ephesus

19 And it happened that while
Apollos was at Corinth, Paul
passed through the inland[3] country and
came to Ephesus. There he found some
disciples. 2 And he said to them, "Did you
receive the Holy Spirit when you believed?"
And they said, "No, we have not even
heard that there is a Holy Spirit." 3 And he
said, "Into what then were you baptized?"
They said, "Into John's baptism." 4 And Paul
said, "John baptized with the baptism of
repentance, telling the people to believe
in the one who was to come after him, that
is, Jesus." 5 On hearing this, they were bap-
tized in[4] the name of the Lord Jesus. 6 And
when Paul had laid his hands on them, the
Holy Spirit came on them, and they began

[1] Or *brothers and sisters*; also verse 27 [2] Or *in the Spirit* [3] Greek *upper* (that is, highland) [4] Or *into*

speaking in tongues and prophesying.
7 There were about twelve men in all.
8 And he entered the synagogue and for
three months spoke boldly, reasoning and
persuading them about the kingdom of
God. 9 But when some became stubborn
and continued in unbelief, speaking evil
of the Way before the congregation, he
withdrew from them and took the dis-
ciples with him, reasoning daily in the
hall of Tyrannus.[1] 10 This continued for
two years, so that all the residents of Asia
heard the word of the Lord, both Jews
and Greeks.

The Sons of Sceva

11 And God was doing extraordinary
miracles by the hands of Paul, 12 so that
even handkerchiefs or aprons that had
touched his skin were carried away to
the sick, and their diseases left them
and the evil spirits came out of them.
13 Then some of the itinerant Jewish exor-
cists undertook to invoke the name of
the Lord Jesus over those who had evil
spirits, saying, "I adjure you by the Jesus
whom Paul proclaims." 14 Seven sons of
a Jewish high priest named Sceva were
doing this. 15 But the evil spirit answered
them, "Jesus I know, and Paul I recog-
nize, but who are you?" 16 And the man in
whom was the evil spirit leaped on them,
mastered all[2] of them and overpowered
them, so that they fled out of that house
naked and wounded. 17 And this became
known to all the residents of Ephesus,
both Jews and Greeks. And fear fell upon
them all, and the name of the Lord Jesus
was extolled. 18 Also many of those who
were now believers came, confessing and
divulging their practices. 19 And a num-
ber of those who had practiced magic arts
brought their books together and burned
them in the sight of all. And they counted
the value of them and found it came to
fifty thousand pieces of silver. 20 So the
word of the Lord continued to increase
and prevail mightily.

A Riot at Ephesus

21 Now after these events Paul resolved
in the Spirit to pass through Macedonia
and Achaia and go to Jerusalem, saying,
"After I have been there, I must also see
Rome." 22 And having sent into Macedonia
two of his helpers, Timothy and Erastus,
he himself stayed in Asia for a while.
23 About that time there arose no little
disturbance concerning the Way. 24 For
a man named Demetrius, a silversmith,
who made silver shrines of Artemis,
brought no little business to the crafts-
men. 25 These he gathered together, with
the workmen in similar trades, and said,
"Men, you know that from this busi-
ness we have our wealth. 26 And you see

CHARACTER PROFILE

JOHN MARK

John Mark wrote the Gospel of Mark, about the life and teaching of Jesus. John Mark went with Paul and Barnabas on their first missionary journey, but left them and went home. After John Mark and Barnabas traveled together for a while, Paul recognized that faithful John Mark was "very useful" and sent for him to come work with him again.

[1] Some manuscripts add *from the fifth hour to the tenth* (that is, from 11 A.M. to 4 P.M.) [2] Or *both*

and hear that not only in Ephesus but in
almost all of Asia this Paul has persuaded
and turned away a great many people,
saying that gods made with hands are not
gods. 27 And there is danger not only that
this trade of ours may come into disrepute
but also that the temple of the great god-
dess Artemis may be counted as nothing,
and that she may even be deposed from
her magnificence, she whom all Asia and
the world worship."
28 When they heard this they were
enraged and were crying out, "Great is
Artemis of the Ephesians!" 29 So the city
was filled with the confusion, and they
rushed together into the theater, drag-
ging with them Gaius and Aristarchus,
Macedonians who were Paul's compan-
ions in travel. 30 But when Paul wished
to go in among the crowd, the disciples
would not let him. 31 And even some of the
Asiarchs,[1] who were friends of his, sent to
him and were urging him not to venture
into the theater. 32 Now some cried out one
thing, some another, for the assembly was
in confusion, and most of them did not
know why they had come together. 33 Some
of the crowd prompted Alexander, whom
the Jews had put forward. And Alexander,
motioning with his hand, wanted to make
a defense to the crowd. 34 But when they
recognized that he was a Jew, for about
two hours they all cried out with one voice,
"Great is Artemis of the Ephesians!"
35 And when the town clerk had quieted
the crowd, he said, "Men of Ephesus, who
is there who does not know that the city
of the Ephesians is temple keeper of the
great Artemis, and of the sacred stone
that fell from the sky?[2] 36 Seeing then that
these things cannot be denied, you ought
to be quiet and do nothing rash. 37 For
you have brought these men here who
are neither sacrilegious nor blasphemers
of our goddess. 38 If therefore Demetrius
and the craftsmen with him have a com-
plaint against anyone, the courts are open,
and there are proconsuls. Let them bring
charges against one another. 39 But if you
seek anything further,[3] it shall be settled
in the regular assembly. 40 For we really
are in danger of being charged with riot-
ing today, since there is no cause that
we can give to justify this commotion."
41 And when he had said these things, he
dismissed the assembly.

Paul in Macedonia and Greece

20 After the uproar ceased, Paul
sent for the disciples, and after
encouraging them, he said farewell and
departed for Macedonia. 2 When he had

CHARACTER PROFILE

AQUILA AND PRISCILLA

Aquila and Priscilla were husband and wife, tentmakers and special friends of the apostle Paul. Paul sometimes stayed with them in Corinth, where a group of Jesus' followers met in their home to worship and learn about God's Kingdom. They sometimes traveled with Paul and helped him in his work of spreading the gospel. Aquila and Priscilla loved the truth about Jesus and helped others teach accurately about the Lord.

[1] That is, high-ranking officers of the province of Asia [2] The meaning of the Greek is uncertain [3] Some manuscripts *seek about other matters*

gone through those regions and had given
them much encouragement, he came to
Greece. 3 There he spent three months,
and when a plot was made against him
by the Jews as he was about to set sail
for Syria, he decided to return through
Macedonia. 4 Sopater the Berean, son of
Pyrrhus, accompanied him; and of the
Thessalonians, Aristarchus and Secundus;
and Gaius of Derbe, and Timothy; and the
Asians, Tychicus and Trophimus. 5 These
went on ahead and were waiting for us at
Troas, 6 but we sailed away from Philippi
after the days of Unleavened Bread, and in
five days we came to them at Troas, where
we stayed for seven days.

Eutychus Raised from the Dead

7 On the first day of the week, when we
were gathered together to break bread,
Paul talked with them, intending to
depart on the next day, and he prolonged
his speech until midnight. 8 There were
many lamps in the upper room where we
were gathered. 9 And a young man named
Eutychus, sitting at the window, sank into
a deep sleep as Paul talked still longer.
And being overcome by sleep, he fell
down from the third story and was taken
up dead. 10 But Paul went down and bent
over him, and taking him in his arms, said,
"Do not be alarmed, for his life is in him."
11 And when Paul had gone up and had
broken bread and eaten, he conversed with
them a long while, until daybreak, and so
departed. 12 And they took the youth away
alive, and were not a little comforted.

13 But going ahead to the ship, we set sail
for Assos, intending to take Paul aboard
there, for so he had arranged, intending
himself to go by land. 14 And when he met
us at Assos, we took him on board and
went to Mitylene. 15 And sailing from there
we came the following day opposite Chios;
the next day we touched at Samos; and[1] the
day after that we went to Miletus. 16 For Paul
had decided to sail past Ephesus, so that he
might not have to spend time in Asia, for
he was hastening to be at Jerusalem, if pos-
sible, on the day of Pentecost.

Paul Speaks to the Ephesian Elders

17 Now from Miletus he sent to Ephesus
and called the elders of the church to
come to him. 18 And when they came to
him, he said to them:

"You yourselves know how I lived
among you the whole time from the first
day that I set foot in Asia, 19 serving the
Lord with all humility and with tears and
with trials that happened to me through
the plots of the Jews; 20 how I did not
shrink from declaring to you anything
that was profitable, and teaching you in
public and from house to house, 21 testify-
ing both to Jews and to Greeks of repen-
tance toward God and of faith in our Lord
Jesus Christ. 22 And now, behold, I am
going to Jerusalem, constrained by[2] the
Spirit, not knowing what will happen to
me there, 23 except that the Holy Spirit
testifies to me in every city that impris-
onment and afflictions await me. 24 But I
do not account my life of any value nor
as precious to myself, if only I may finish
my course and the ministry that I received
from the Lord Jesus, to testify to the gospel
of the grace of God. 25 And now, behold,
I know that none of you among whom I
have gone about proclaiming the king-
dom will see my face again. 26 Therefore
I testify to you this day that I am innocent
of the blood of all of you, 27 for I did not
shrink from declaring to you the whole
counsel of God. 28 Pay careful attention to
yourselves and to all the flock, in which
the Holy Spirit has made you overseers,
to care for the church of God,[3] which he
obtained with his own blood.[4] 29 I know
that after my departure fierce wolves
will come in among you, not sparing the
flock; 30 and from among your own selves
will arise men speaking twisted things,
to draw away the disciples after them.

[1] Some manuscripts add *after remaining at Trogyllium* [2] Or *bound in* [3] Some manuscripts *of the Lord* [4] Or *with the blood of his Own*

31 Therefore be alert, remembering that for three years I did not cease night or day to admonish everyone with tears. 32 And now I commend you to God and to the word of his grace, which is able to build you up and to give you the inheritance among all those who are sanctified. 33 I coveted no one's silver or gold or apparel. 34 You yourselves know that these hands ministered to my necessities and to those who were with me. 35 In all things I have shown you that by working hard in this way we must help the weak and remember the words of the Lord Jesus, how he himself said, 'It is more blessed to give than to receive.'"

36 And when he had said these things, he knelt down and prayed with them all. 37 And there was much weeping on the part of all; they embraced Paul and kissed him, 38 being sorrowful most of all because of the word he had spoken, that they would not see his face again. And they accompanied him to the ship.

Paul Goes to Jerusalem

21 And when we had parted from them and set sail, we came by a straight course to Cos, and the next day to Rhodes, and from there to Patara.[1] 2 And having found a ship crossing to Phoenicia, we went aboard and set sail. 3 When we had come in sight of Cyprus, leaving it on the left we sailed to Syria and landed at Tyre, for there the ship was to unload its cargo. 4 And having sought out the disciples, we stayed there for seven days. And through the Spirit they were telling Paul not to go on to Jerusalem. 5 When our days there were ended, we departed and went on our journey, and they all, with wives and children, accompanied us until we were outside the city. And kneeling down on the beach, we prayed 6 and said farewell to one another. Then we went on board the ship, and they returned home.

7 When we had finished the voyage from Tyre, we arrived at Ptolemais, and we greeted the brothers[2] and stayed with them for one day. 8 On the next day we departed and came to Caesarea, and we entered the house of Philip the evangelist, who was one of the seven, and stayed with him. 9 He had four unmarried daughters, who prophesied. 10 While we were staying for many days, a prophet named Agabus came down from Judea. 11 And coming to us, he took Paul's belt and bound his own feet and hands and said, "Thus says the Holy Spirit, 'This is how the Jews at Jerusalem will bind the man who owns this belt and deliver him into the hands of the Gentiles.'" 12 When we heard this, we and the people there urged him not to go up to Jerusalem. 13 Then Paul answered, "What are you doing, weeping and breaking my heart? For I am ready not only to be imprisoned but even to die in Jerusalem for the name of the Lord Jesus." 14 And since he would not be persuaded, we ceased and said, "Let the will of the Lord be done."

15 After these days we got ready and went up to Jerusalem. 16 And some of the disciples from Caesarea went with us, bringing us to the house of Mnason of Cyprus, an early disciple, with whom we should lodge.

Paul Visits James

17 When we had come to Jerusalem, the brothers received us gladly. 18 On the following day Paul went in with us to James, and all the elders were present. 19 After greeting them, he related one by one the things that God had done among the Gentiles through his ministry. 20 And when they heard it, they glorified God. And they said to him, "You see, brother, how many thousands there are among the Jews of those who have believed. They are all zealous for the law, 21 and they have been told about you that you teach all the Jews who are among the Gentiles to forsake Moses, telling them not to circumcise their children or walk according to our customs. 22 What then is to be done? They

[1] Some manuscripts add *and Myra* [2] Or *brothers and sisters*; also verse 17

will certainly hear that you have come. 23 Do therefore what we tell you. We have four men who are under a vow; 24 take these men and purify yourself along with them and pay their expenses, so that they may shave their heads. Thus all will know that there is nothing in what they have been told about you, but that you yourself also live in observance of the law. 25 But as for the Gentiles who have believed, we have sent a letter with our judgment that they should abstain from what has been sacrificed to idols, and from blood, and from what has been strangled,[1] and from sexual immorality." 26 Then Paul took the men, and the next day he purified himself along with them and went into the temple, giving notice when the days of purification would be fulfilled and the offering presented for each one of them.

Paul Arrested in the Temple

27 When the seven days were almost completed, the Jews from Asia, seeing him in the temple, stirred up the whole crowd and laid hands on him, 28 crying out, "Men of Israel, help! This is the man who is teaching everyone everywhere against the people and the law and this place. Moreover, he even brought Greeks into the temple and has defiled this holy place." 29 For they had previously seen Trophimus the Ephesian with him in the city, and they supposed that Paul had brought him into the temple. 30 Then all the city was stirred up, and the people ran together. They seized Paul and dragged him out of the temple, and at once the gates were shut. 31 And as they were seeking to kill him, word came to the tribune of the cohort that all Jerusalem was in confusion. 32 He at once took soldiers and centurions and ran down to them. And when they saw the tribune and the soldiers, they stopped beating Paul. 33 Then the tribune came up and arrested him and ordered him to be bound with two chains. He inquired who he was and what he had done. 34 Some in the crowd were shouting one thing, some another. And as he could not learn the facts because of the uproar, he ordered him to be brought into the barracks. 35 And when he came to the steps, he was actually carried by the soldiers because of the violence of the crowd, 36 for the mob of the people followed, crying out, "Away with him!"

Paul Speaks to the People

37 As Paul was about to be brought into the barracks, he said to the tribune, "May I say something to you?" And he said, "Do you know Greek? 38 Are you not the Egyptian, then, who recently stirred up a revolt and led the four thousand men of the Assassins out into the wilderness?" 39 Paul replied, "I am a Jew, from Tarsus in Cilicia, a citizen of no obscure city. I beg you, permit me to speak to the people." 40 And when he had given him permission, Paul, standing on the steps, motioned with his hand to the people. And when there was a great hush, he addressed them in the Hebrew language,[2] saying:

22 "Brothers and fathers, hear the defense that I now make before you."

1637

2 And when they heard that he was addressing them in the Hebrew language, they became even more quiet. And he said:

3 "I am a Jew, born in Tarsus in Cilicia, but brought up in this city, educated at the feet of Gamaliel[3] according to the strict manner of the law of our fathers, being zealous for God as all of you are this day. 4 I persecuted this Way to the death, binding and delivering to prison both men and women, 5 as the high priest and the whole council of elders can bear me witness. From them I received letters to the brothers, and I journeyed toward Damascus to take those also who were there and bring them in bonds to Jerusalem to be punished.

6 "As I was on my way and drew near to Damascus, about noon a great light from heaven suddenly shone around me. 7 And I

[1] Some manuscripts omit *and from what has been strangled* [2] Or *the Hebrew dialect* (that is, Aramaic); also 22:2 [3] Or *city at the feet of Gamaliel, educated*

fell to the ground and heard a voice saying
to me, 'Saul, Saul, why are you persecuting
me?' 8 And I answered, 'Who are you, Lord?'
And he said to me, 'I am Jesus of Nazareth,
whom you are persecuting.' 9 Now those
who were with me saw the light but did
not understand[1] the voice of the one who
was speaking to me. 10 And I said, 'What
shall I do, Lord?' And the Lord said to me,
'Rise, and go into Damascus, and there you
will be told all that is appointed for you to
do.' 11 And since I could not see because of
the brightness of that light, I was led by
the hand by those who were with me, and
came into Damascus.

12 "And one Ananias, a devout man
according to the law, well spoken of by all
the Jews who lived there, 13 came to me,
and standing by me said to me, 'Brother
Saul, receive your sight.' And at that very
hour I received my sight and saw him.
14 And he said, 'The God of our fathers
appointed you to know his will, to see the
Righteous One and to hear a voice from
his mouth; 15 for you will be a witness for
him to everyone of what you have seen
and heard. 16 And now why do you wait?
Rise and be baptized and wash away your
sins, calling on his name.'

17 "When I had returned to Jerusalem
and was praying in the temple, I fell into a
trance 18 and saw him saying to me, 'Make
haste and get out of Jerusalem quickly,
because they will not accept your testi-
mony about me.' 19 And I said, 'Lord, they
themselves know that in one synagogue
after another I imprisoned and beat those
who believed in you. 20 And when the blood
of Stephen your witness was being shed, I
myself was standing by and approving and
watching over the garments of those who
killed him.' 21 And he said to me, 'Go, for
I will send you far away to the Gentiles.'"

Paul and the Roman Tribune

22 Up to this word they listened to him.
Then they raised their voices and said,
"Away with such a fellow from the earth!
For he should not be allowed to live."
23 And as they were shouting and throw-
ing off their cloaks and flinging dust into
the air, 24 the tribune ordered him to be
brought into the barracks, saying that he
should be examined by flogging, to find
out why they were shouting against him
like this. 25 But when they had stretched
him out for the whips,[2] Paul said to the
centurion who was standing by, "Is it law-
ful for you to flog a man who is a Roman
citizen and uncondemned?" 26 When
the centurion heard this, he went to the
tribune and said to him, "What are you
about to do? For this man is a Roman
citizen." 27 So the tribune came and said
to him, "Tell me, are you a Roman citi-
zen?" And he said, "Yes." 28 The tribune
answered, "I bought this citizenship for
a large sum." Paul said, "But I am a citizen
by birth." 29 So those who were about to
examine him withdrew from him imme-
diately, and the tribune also was afraid, for
he realized that Paul was a Roman citizen
and that he had bound him.

Paul Before the Council

30 But on the next day, desiring to know
the real reason why he was being accused
by the Jews, he unbound him and com-
manded the chief priests and all the coun-
cil to meet, and he brought Paul down and
set him before them.

23 And looking intently at the coun-
cil, Paul said, "Brothers, I have
lived my life before God in all good con-
science up to this day." 2 And the high priest
Ananias commanded those who stood by
him to strike him on the mouth. 3 Then
Paul said to him, "God is going to strike
you, you whitewashed wall! Are you sit-
ting to judge me according to the law, and
yet contrary to the law you order me to be
struck?" 4 Those who stood by said, "Would
you revile God's high priest?" 5 And Paul
said, "I did not know, brothers, that he was
the high priest, for it is written, 'You shall
not speak evil of a ruler of your people.'"

[1] Or *hear with understanding* [2] Or *when they had tied him up with leather strips*

6 Now when Paul perceived that one part
were Sadducees and the other Pharisees,
he cried out in the council, "Brothers, I am
a Pharisee, a son of Pharisees. It is with
respect to the hope and the resurrection of
the dead that I am on trial." 7 And when he
had said this, a dissension arose between
the Pharisees and the Sadducees, and the
assembly was divided. 8 For the Sadducees
say that there is no resurrection, nor angel,
nor spirit, but the Pharisees acknowledge
them all. 9 Then a great clamor arose, and
some of the scribes of the Pharisees' party
stood up and contended sharply, "We find
nothing wrong in this man. What if a spirit
or an angel spoke to him?" 10 And when the
dissension became violent, the tribune,
afraid that Paul would be torn to pieces by
them, commanded the soldiers to go down
and take him away from among them by
force and bring him into the barracks.

11 The following night the Lord stood
by him and said, "Take courage, for as
you have testified to the facts about me
in Jerusalem, so you must testify also in
Rome."

A Plot to Kill Paul

12 When it was day, the Jews made a plot
and bound themselves by an oath neither
to eat nor drink till they had killed Paul.
13 There were more than forty who made
this conspiracy. 14 They went to the chief
priests and elders and said, "We have
strictly bound ourselves by an oath to taste
no food till we have killed Paul. 15 Now
therefore you, along with the council, give
notice to the tribune to bring him down
to you, as though you were going to deter-
mine his case more exactly. And we are
ready to kill him before he comes near."

16 Now the son of Paul's sister heard of
their ambush, so he went and entered the
barracks and told Paul. 17 Paul called one of
the centurions and said, "Take this young
man to the tribune, for he has something
to tell him." 18 So he took him and brought
him to the tribune and said, "Paul the pris-
oner called me and asked me to bring this
young man to you, as he has something
to say to you." 19 The tribune took him
by the hand, and going aside asked him
privately, "What is it that you have to tell
me?" 20 And he said, "The Jews have agreed
to ask you to bring Paul down to the coun-
cil tomorrow, as though they were going
to inquire somewhat more closely about
him. 21 But do not be persuaded by them,
for more than forty of their men are lying
in ambush for him, who have bound
themselves by an oath neither to eat nor
drink till they have killed him. And now
they are ready, waiting for your consent."
22 So the tribune dismissed the young
man, charging him, "Tell no one that you
have informed me of these things."

Paul Sent to Felix the Governor

23 Then he called two of the centurions
and said, "Get ready two hundred soldiers,
with seventy horsemen and two hundred
spearmen to go as far as Caesarea at the
third hour of the night.[1] 24 Also provide
mounts for Paul to ride and bring him
safely to Felix the governor." 25 And he
wrote a letter to this effect:

26 "Claudius Lysias, to his Excellency
the governor Felix, greetings. 27 This man
was seized by the Jews and was about to
be killed by them when I came upon them
with the soldiers and rescued him, hav-
ing learned that he was a Roman citizen.
28 And desiring to know the charge for
which they were accusing him, I brought
him down to their council. 29 I found that
he was being accused about questions of
their law, but charged with nothing deserv-
ing death or imprisonment. 30 And when it
was disclosed to me that there would be a
plot against the man, I sent him to you at
once, ordering his accusers also to state
before you what they have against him."

31 So the soldiers, according to their
instructions, took Paul and brought him by

[1] That is, 9 P.M.

night to Antipatris. 32 And on the next day
they returned to the barracks, letting the
horsemen go on with him. 33 When they
had come to Caesarea and delivered the
letter to the governor, they presented Paul
also before him. 34 On reading the letter,
he asked what province he was from. And
when he learned that he was from Cilicia,
35 he said, "I will give you a hearing when
your accusers arrive." And he commanded
him to be guarded in Herod's praetorium.

Paul Before Felix at Caesarea

24 And after five days the high priest
Ananias came down with some
elders and a spokesman, one Tertullus.
They laid before the governor their case
against Paul. 2 And when he had been
summoned, Tertullus began to accuse
him, saying:

"Since through you we enjoy much
peace, and since by your foresight, most
excellent Felix, reforms are being made
for this nation, 3 in every way and every-
where we accept this with all gratitude.
4 But, to detain[1] you no further, I beg you
in your kindness to hear us briefly. 5 For
we have found this man a plague, one who
stirs up riots among all the Jews through-
out the world and is a ringleader of the
sect of the Nazarenes. 6 He even tried to
profane the temple, but we seized him.[2]
8 By examining him yourself you will be
able to find out from him about every-
thing of which we accuse him."

9 The Jews also joined in the charge,
affirming that all these things were so.

10 And when the governor had nodded
to him to speak, Paul replied:

"Knowing that for many years you have
been a judge over this nation, I cheerfully
make my defense. 11 You can verify that it
is not more than twelve days since I went
up to worship in Jerusalem, 12 and they
did not find me disputing with anyone or
stirring up a crowd, either in the temple or
in the synagogues or in the city. 13 Neither
can they prove to you what they now bring
up against me. 14 But this I confess to you,
that according to the Way, which they call
a sect, I worship the God of our fathers,
believing everything laid down by the Law
and written in the Prophets, 15 having a
hope in God, which these men themselves
accept, that there will be a resurrection of
both the just and the unjust. 16 So I always
take pains to have a clear conscience
toward both God and man. 17 Now after
several years I came to bring alms to my
nation and to present offerings. 18 While
I was doing this, they found me puri-
fied in the temple, without any crowd or
tumult. But some Jews from Asia— 19 they
ought to be here before you and to make
an accusation, should they have anything
against me. 20 Or else let these men them-
selves say what wrongdoing they found
when I stood before the council, 21 other
than this one thing that I cried out while
standing among them: 'It is with respect
to the resurrection of the dead that I am
on trial before you this day.'"

Paul Kept in Custody

22 But Felix, having a rather accurate
knowledge of the Way, put them off, say-
ing, "When Lysias the tribune comes
down, I will decide your case." 23 Then
he gave orders to the centurion that he
should be kept in custody but have some
liberty, and that none of his friends should
be prevented from attending to his needs.

24 After some days Felix came with his
wife Drusilla, who was Jewish, and he sent
for Paul and heard him speak about faith
in Christ Jesus. 25 And as he reasoned about
righteousness and self-control and the
coming judgment, Felix was alarmed and
said, "Go away for the present. When I get
an opportunity I will summon you." 26 At
the same time he hoped that money would
be given him by Paul. So he sent for him
often and conversed with him. 27 When
two years had elapsed, Felix was succeeded

[1] Or *weary* [2] Some manuscripts add *and we would have judged him according to our law. 7But the chief captain Lysias came and with great violence took him out of our hands, 8commanding his accusers to come before you.*

by Porcius Festus. And desiring to do the Jews a favor, Felix left Paul in prison.

Paul Appeals to Caesar

25 Now three days after Festus had arrived in the province, he went up to Jerusalem from Caesarea. 2 And the chief priests and the principal men of the Jews laid out their case against Paul, and they urged him, 3 asking as a favor against Paul[1] that he summon him to Jerusalem—because they were planning an ambush to kill him on the way. 4 Festus replied that Paul was being kept at Caesarea and that he himself intended to go there shortly. 5 "So," said he, "let the men of authority among you go down with me, and if there is anything wrong about the man, let them bring charges against him."

6 After he stayed among them not more than eight or ten days, he went down to Caesarea. And the next day he took his seat on the tribunal and ordered Paul to be brought. 7 When he had arrived, the Jews who had come down from Jerusalem stood around him, bringing many and serious charges against him that they could not prove. 8 Paul argued in his defense, "Neither against the law of the Jews, nor against the temple, nor against Caesar have I committed any offense." 9 But Festus, wishing to do the Jews a favor, said to Paul, "Do you wish to go up to Jerusalem and there be tried on these charges before me?" 10 But Paul said, "I am standing before Caesar's tribunal, where I ought to be tried. To the Jews I have done no wrong, as you yourself know very well. 11 If then I am a wrongdoer and have committed anything for which I deserve to die, I do not seek to escape death. But if there is nothing to their charges against me, no one can give me up to them. I appeal to Caesar." 12 Then Festus, when he had conferred with his council, answered, "To Caesar you have appealed; to Caesar you shall go."

[1] Greek *him*

Paul Before Agrippa and Bernice

13 Now when some days had passed, Agrippa the king and Bernice arrived at Caesarea and greeted Festus. 14 And as they stayed there many days, Festus laid Paul's case before the king, saying, "There is a man left prisoner by Felix, 15 and when I was at Jerusalem, the chief priests and the elders of the Jews laid out their case against him, asking for a sentence of condemnation against him. 16 I answered them that it was not the custom of the Romans to give up anyone before the accused met the accusers face to face and had opportunity to make his defense concerning the charge laid against him. 17 So when they came together here, I made no delay, but on the next day took my seat on the tribunal and ordered the man to be brought. 18 When the accusers stood up, they brought no charge in his case of such evils as I supposed. 19 Rather they had certain points of dispute with him about their own religion and about a certain Jesus, who was dead, but whom Paul asserted to be alive. 20 Being at a loss how to investigate these questions, I asked whether he wanted to go to Jerusalem and be tried there regarding them. 21 But when Paul had appealed to be kept in custody for the decision of the emperor, I ordered him to be held until I could send him to Caesar." 22 Then Agrippa said to Festus, "I would like to hear the man myself." "Tomorrow," said he, "you will hear him."

23 So on the next day Agrippa and Bernice came with great pomp, and they entered the audience hall with the military tribunes and the prominent men of the city. Then, at the command of Festus, Paul was brought in. 24 And Festus said, "King Agrippa and all who are present with us, you see this man about whom the whole Jewish people petitioned me, both in Jerusalem and here, shouting that he ought not to live any longer. 25 But I found that he had done nothing deserv-

ing death. And as he himself appealed to
the emperor, I decided to go ahead and
send him. 26 But I have nothing definite
to write to my lord about him. Therefore
I have brought him before you all, and
especially before you, King Agrippa, so
that, after we have examined him, I may
have something to write. 27 For it seems to
me unreasonable, in sending a prisoner,
not to indicate the charges against him."

Paul's Defense Before Agrippa

26 So Agrippa said to Paul, "You have
permission to speak for yourself."
Then Paul stretched out his hand and
made his defense:

2 "I consider myself fortunate that it
is before you, King Agrippa, I am going
to make my defense today against all
the accusations of the Jews, 3 espe-
cially because you are familiar with all
the customs and controversies of the
Jews. Therefore I beg you to listen to me
patiently.

4 "My manner of life from my youth,
spent from the beginning among my
own nation and in Jerusalem, is known
by all the Jews. 5 They have known for a
long time, if they are willing to testify, that
according to the strictest party of our reli-
gion I have lived as a Pharisee. 6 And now I
stand here on trial because of my hope in
the promise made by God to our fathers,
7 to which our twelve tribes hope to attain,
as they earnestly worship night and day.
And for this hope I am accused by Jews, O
king! 8 Why is it thought incredible by any
of you that God raises the dead?

9 "I myself was convinced that I
ought to do many things in oppos-
1637 ing the name of Jesus of Nazareth.
10 And I did so in Jerusalem. I not only
locked up many of the saints in prison after
receiving authority from the chief priests,
but when they were put to death I cast my
vote against them. 11 And I punished them
often in all the synagogues and tried to
make them blaspheme, and in raging fury
against them I persecuted them even to
foreign cities.

Paul Tells of His Conversion

12 "In this connection I journeyed to
Damascus with the authority and com-
mission of the chief priests. 13 At mid-
day, O king, I saw on the way a light from
heaven, brighter than the sun, that shone
around me and those who journeyed with
me. 14 And when we had all fallen to the
ground, I heard a voice saying to me in the
Hebrew language,[1] 'Saul, Saul, why are you
persecuting me? It is hard for you to kick
against the goads.' 15 And I said, 'Who are
you, Lord?' And the Lord said, 'I am Jesus
whom you are persecuting. 16 But rise and
stand upon your feet, for I have appeared
to you for this purpose, to appoint you as a
servant and witness to the things in which
you have seen me and to those in which I
will appear to you, 17 delivering you from
your people and from the Gentiles—to
whom I am sending you 18 to open their
eyes, so that they may turn from dark-
ness to light and from the power of Satan
to God, that they may receive forgiveness
of sins and a place among those who are
sanctified by faith in me.'

19 "Therefore, O King Agrippa, I was not
disobedient to the heavenly vision, 20 but
declared first to those in Damascus, then
in Jerusalem and throughout all the region
of Judea, and also to the Gentiles, that they
should repent and turn to God, perform-
ing deeds in keeping with their repen-
tance. 21 For this reason the Jews seized me
in the temple and tried to kill me. 22 To this
day I have had the help that comes from
God, and so I stand here testifying both to
small and great, saying nothing but what
the prophets and Moses said would come
to pass: 23 that the Christ must suffer and
that, by being the first to rise from the
dead, he would proclaim light both to our
people and to the Gentiles."

24 And as he was saying these things in
his defense, Festus said with a loud voice,

[1] Or *the Hebrew dialect* (that is, Aramaic)

"Paul, you are out of your mind; your great
learning is driving you out of your mind."
25 But Paul said, "I am not out of my mind,
most excellent Festus, but I am speaking
true and rational words. 26 For the king
knows about these things, and to him I
speak boldly. For I am persuaded that none
of these things has escaped his notice, for
this has not been done in a corner. 27 King
Agrippa, do you believe the prophets? I
know that you believe." 28 And Agrippa
said to Paul, "In a short time would you
persuade me to be a Christian?"[1] 29 And
Paul said, "Whether short or long, I would
to God that not only you but also all who
hear me this day might become such as I
am—except for these chains."

30 Then the king rose, and the governor
and Bernice and those who were sitting
with them. 31 And when they had with-
drawn, they said to one another, "This
man is doing nothing to deserve death
or imprisonment." 32 And Agrippa said to
Festus, "This man could have been set free
if he had not appealed to Caesar."

Paul Sails for Rome

27 And when it was decided
that we should sail for Italy,
1689 they delivered Paul and some other
prisoners to a centurion of the Augustan
Cohort named Julius. 2 And embarking in
a ship of Adramyttium, which was about
to sail to the ports along the coast of Asia,
we put to sea, accompanied by Aristarchus,
a Macedonian from Thessalonica. 3 The
next day we put in at Sidon. And Julius
treated Paul kindly and gave him leave to
go to his friends and be cared for. 4 And
putting out to sea from there we sailed
under the lee of Cyprus, because the winds
were against us. 5 And when we had sailed
across the open sea along the coast of
Cilicia and Pamphylia, we came to Myra in
Lycia. 6 There the centurion found a ship of
Alexandria sailing for Italy and put us on
board. 7 We sailed slowly for a number of
days and arrived with difficulty off
Cnidus, and as the wind did not allow us
to go farther, we sailed under the lee of
Crete off Salmone. 8 Coasting along it with
difficulty, we came to a place called Fair
Havens, near which was the city of Lasea.

9 Since much time had passed, and the
voyage was now dangerous because even
the Fast[2] was already over, Paul advised
them, 10 saying, "Sirs, I perceive that the
voyage will be with injury and much loss,
not only of the cargo and the ship, but also
of our lives." 11 But the centurion paid more
attention to the pilot and to the owner
of the ship than to what Paul said. 12 And
because the harbor was not suitable to
spend the winter in, the majority decided
to put out to sea from there, on the chance
that somehow they could reach Phoenix, a
harbor of Crete, facing both southwest and
northwest, and spend the winter there.

The Storm at Sea

13 Now when the south wind blew gen-
tly, supposing that they had obtained their
purpose, they weighed anchor and sailed
along Crete, close to the shore. 14 But soon
a tempestuous wind, called the north-
easter, struck down from the land. 15 And
when the ship was caught and could not
face the wind, we gave way to it and were
driven along. 16 Running under the lee of
a small island called Cauda,[3] we managed
with difficulty to secure the ship's boat.
17 After hoisting it up, they used supports
to undergird the ship. Then, fearing that
they would run aground on the Syrtis,
they lowered the gear,[4] and thus they were
driven along. 18 Since we were violently
storm-tossed, they began the next day to
jettison the cargo. 19 And on the third day
they threw the ship's tackle overboard
with their own hands. 20 When neither
sun nor stars appeared for many days, and
no small tempest lay on us, all hope of our
being saved was at last abandoned.

21 Since they had been without food for

[1] Or *In a short time you would persuade me to act like a Christian!* [2] That is, the Day of Atonement [3] Some manuscripts *Clauda* [4] That is, the sea-anchor (or possibly the mainsail)

a long time, Paul stood up among them and said, "Men, you should have listened to me and not have set sail from Crete and incurred this injury and loss. 22 Yet now I urge you to take heart, for there will be no loss of life among you, but only of the ship. 23 For this very night there stood before me an angel of the God to whom I belong and whom I worship, 24 and he said, 'Do not be afraid, Paul; you must stand before Caesar. And behold, God has granted you all those who sail with you.' 25 So take heart, men, for I have faith in God that it will be exactly as I have been told. 26 But we must run aground on some island."

27 When the fourteenth night had come, as we were being driven across the Adriatic Sea, about midnight the sailors suspected that they were nearing land. 28 So they took a sounding and found twenty fathoms.[1] A little farther on they took a sounding again and found fifteen fathoms.[2] 29 And fearing that we might run on the rocks, they let down four anchors from the stern and prayed for day to come. 30 And as the sailors were seeking to escape from the ship, and had lowered the ship's boat into the sea under pretense of laying out anchors from the bow, 31 Paul said to the centurion and the soldiers, "Unless these men stay in the ship, you cannot be saved." 32 Then the soldiers cut away the ropes of the ship's boat and let it go.

33 As day was about to dawn, Paul urged them all to take some food, saying, "Today is the fourteenth day that you have continued in suspense and without food, having taken nothing. 34 Therefore I urge you to take some food. For it will give you strength, for not a hair is to perish from the head of any of you." 35 And when he had said these things, he took bread, and giving thanks to God in the presence of all he broke it and began to eat. 36 Then they all were encouraged and ate some food themselves. 37 (We were in all 276[3] persons in the ship.) 38 And when they had eaten enough, they lightened the ship, throwing out the wheat into the sea.

The Shipwreck

39 Now when it was day, they did not recognize the land, but they noticed a bay with a beach, on which they planned if possible to run the ship ashore. 40 So they cast off the anchors and left them in the sea, at the same time loosening the ropes that tied the rudders. Then hoisting the foresail to the wind they made for the beach. 41 But striking a reef,[4] they ran the vessel aground. The bow stuck and remained immovable, and the stern was being broken up by the surf. 42 The soldiers' plan was to kill the prisoners, lest any should swim away and escape. 43 But the centurion, wishing to save Paul, kept them from carrying out their plan. He ordered those who could swim to jump overboard first and make for the land, 44 and the rest on planks or on pieces of the ship. And so it was that all were brought safely to land.

Paul on Malta

1689

28 After we were brought safely through, we then learned that the island was called Malta. 2 The native people[5] showed us unusual kindness, for they kindled a fire and welcomed us all, because it had begun to rain and was cold. 3 When Paul had gathered a bundle of sticks and put them on the fire, a viper came out because of the heat and fastened on his hand. 4 When the native people saw the creature hanging from his hand, they said to one another, "No doubt this man is a murderer. Though he has escaped from the sea, Justice[6] has not allowed him to live." 5 He, however, shook off the creature into the fire and suffered no harm. 6 They were waiting for him to swell up or suddenly fall down dead. But when they had waited a long time and saw no misfortune come to him, they changed their minds and said that he was a god.

[1] About 120 feet; a fathom (Greek *orguia*) was about 6 feet or 2 meters [2] About 90 feet (see previous note) [3] Some manuscripts *seventy-six*, or *about seventy-six*
[4] Or *sandbank*, or *crosscurrent*; Greek *place between two seas* [5] Greek *barbaroi* (that is, non-Greek speakers); also verse 4 [6] Or *justice*

Paul and the Shipwreck

As soon as Paul saw Jesus on the road to Damascus, he gave his life completely to serving the Lord. He became a traveling missionary, who preached and taught about Jesus and encouraged new believers. The Holy Spirit led Paul on all his travels where ever he went—even when Paul was arrested by those who did not want him to preach about Jesus.

Now that Paul was under arrest, he had to make the long trip by boat, from Jerusalem to Rome. But he was still able preach the gospel wherever he stopped along the way. When Paul would finally arrive in Rome, the ruler of the Roman Empire, Nero Caesar, would decide if Paul should be freed or not.

But it was a bad time of the year for any ship to sail when they started to sail to Rome; the voyage would be filled with danger. Because of this, Paul encouraged the soldiers and sailors to wait. But the ship's owner wanted to sail anyway, hoping to spend the winter in some safe harbor on the way.

As they sailed along close to the shore, a wild wind began to blow. The violent wind and waves crashed against the ship, splashing over the ship and driving it off course. The next day, the sailors were so worried the ship would sink that they began to throw cargo overboard to lighten the ship. The storm went on for many days. Almost all the people on board gave up all hope of being saved. They were afraid that they would either drown or starve to death.

Even though Paul was a prisoner on the ship, he encouraged all the sailors and soldiers not to give up hope. An angel of the Lord had spoken to Paul, saying, "Do not be afraid, Paul; you must stand before Caesar." The angel told Paul that no one on the ship would be harmed, even though the boat would be shipwrecked. Paul believed God, and he wanted the other men to have courage too.

After two weeks of stormy weather, the sailors finally saw land. They decided to sail the ship onto a small beach. But before they got there, the ship crashed into a coral reef and got stuck. The waves pounded against the ship, until it started to break up. The soldiers were afraid their prisoners would escape, so they wanted to kill all of them, including Paul. But the soldier in charge, a man called Julius, wanted Paul to live. He wouldn't let the other soldiers carry out their plan.

Julius ordered those who could swim to jump overboard and get to land.

The rest of the passengers hung on to pieces of the ship to keep from drowning, and were washed safely to the shore. Every single person on the ship safely reached the shore, just as God had promised.

Even though he was a prisoner—and shipwrecked, too!—Paul knew that nothing could stop God's plans for him, and that God was with him wherever he went. Paul trusted in God's power and God's good plans, to bring the Good News of Jesus throughout the Roman Empire. When we trust Jesus, God is with us, too, wherever we go.

SEEK and FIND

WHERE TO FIND THE STORY

Acts 27

KEY BIBLE VERSE

"He made the storm be still,
 and the waves of the sea were hushed.
Then they were glad that the waters were quiet,
 and he brought them to their desired haven.
Let them thank the LORD for his steadfast love,
 for his wondrous works to the children of man!"
(Psalm 107:29-31)

THREE KEY QUESTIONS

- Why was Paul arrested and held a prisoner?
- What did the angel say to Paul?
- Who saved Paul's life and the lives of the people on the ship?

RELATED BIBLE READINGS

Psalm 107:23–32; Jonah 1:4–15; Acts 28:1–31;
2 Corinthians 11:25

7 Now in the neighborhood of that place
were lands belonging to the chief man of
the island, named Publius, who received
us and entertained us hospitably for
three days. 8 It happened that the father of
Publius lay sick with fever and dysentery.
And Paul visited him and prayed, and put-
ting his hands on him healed him. 9 And
when this had taken place, the rest of the
people on the island who had diseases also
came and were cured. 10 They also honored
us greatly,[1] and when we were about to sail,
they put on board whatever we needed.

Paul Arrives at Rome

11 After three months we set sail in a
ship that had wintered in the island, a
ship of Alexandria, with the twin gods[2] as
a figurehead. 12 Putting in at Syracuse, we
stayed there for three days. 13 And from
there we made a circuit and arrived at
Rhegium. And after one day a south wind
sprang up, and on the second day we
came to Puteoli. 14 There we found broth-
ers[3] and were invited to stay with them
for seven days. And so we came to Rome.
15 And the brothers there, when they heard
about us, came as far as the Forum of
Appius and Three Taverns to meet us. On
seeing them, Paul thanked God and took
courage. 16 And when we came into Rome,
Paul was allowed to stay by himself, with
the soldier that guarded him.

Paul in Rome

17 After three days he called together the
local leaders of the Jews, and when they
had gathered, he said to them, "Brothers,

[1] Greek *honored us with many honors* [2] That is, the Greek gods Castor and Pollux [3] Or *brothers and sisters*; also verses 15, 21

though I had done nothing against our
people or the customs of our fathers,
yet I was delivered as a prisoner from
Jerusalem into the hands of the Romans.
18 When they had examined me, they
wished to set me at liberty, because there
was no reason for the death penalty in my
case. **19** But because the Jews objected, I
was compelled to appeal to Caesar—
though I had no charge to bring against
my nation. **20** For this reason, therefore, I
have asked to see you and speak with you,
since it is because of the hope of Israel
that I am wearing this chain." **21** And they
said to him, "We have received no let-
ters from Judea about you, and none of
the brothers coming here has reported
or spoken any evil about you. **22** But we
desire to hear from you what your views
are, for with regard to this sect we know
that everywhere it is spoken against."

23 When they had appointed a day for
him, they came to him at his lodging in
greater numbers. From morning till eve-
ning he expounded to them, testifying
to the kingdom of God and trying to con-
vince them about Jesus both from the Law
of Moses and from the Prophets. **24** And
some were convinced by what he said,
but others disbelieved. **25** And disagreeing
among themselves, they departed after
Paul had made one statement: "The Holy
Spirit was right in saying to your fathers
through Isaiah the prophet:

26 "'Go to this people, and say,
You will indeed hear but never
understand,
and you will indeed see but never
perceive.
27 For this people's heart has grown
dull,
and with their ears they can
barely hear,
and their eyes they have closed;
lest they should see with their eyes
and hear with their ears
and understand with their heart
and turn, and I would heal them.'

28 Therefore let it be known to you that
this salvation of God has been sent to the
Gentiles; they will listen."[1]

30 He lived there two whole years at his
own expense,[2] and welcomed all who
came to him, **31** proclaiming the king-
dom of God and teaching about the Lord
Jesus Christ with all boldness and without
hindrance.

[1] Some manuscripts add verse 29: *And when he had said these words, the Jews departed, having much dispute among themselves* [2] Or *in his own hired dwelling*

Introduction to

Romans

Introduction

The church in Rome had both Jews and Gentiles in it. Paul, who had not yet been to Rome, wanted the Christians in Rome to clearly understand the gospel and to see how it should make a difference in the way they lived before God and before one another. He begins his letter by showing how good people as well as bad people are guilty before God and must believe in the Lord Jesus Christ to be justified (counted as righteous) by Him. God loves to freely justify believers because Jesus took God's judgment for their sin on the cross (Romans 1–3). Paul shows that this is what the Old Testament taught (Romans 4) and that faith in Christ comes with many blessings (Romans 5), including new power to live a new kind of life through the Holy Spirit (Romans 6–8). Paul writes that God's welcoming of Gentiles into His people does not conflict with His Old Testament promises to Israel (Romans 9–11). Paul teaches that believers in Jesus will treat others with the same love they have received from God (Romans 12–13). When Christians disagree, they are eager to put others ahead of themselves, just as Jesus put others ahead of Himself (Romans 14:1–15:13).

Author

Paul the apostle

Date

About A.D. 57

Purpose

The purpose of Romans is to explain the gospel to the Christians in Rome, showing how the gospel freely saves both Jews and Gentiles in a way that fulfills God's Old Testament promises.

Central Themes

All are guilty of breaking God's law; justification—being declared righteous by God—comes by faith in Christ alone; justification is based on Jesus' crucifixion and resurrection; Christians are united to Christ; God chooses whom He will save; faith in Christ results in a holy life and in loving relationships with others; Christians must be careful to do what is best for each other and maintain peace in the church.

Memory Verses

The gospel's power (Romans 1:16–17); justified through Jesus (Romans 3:21–26); peace through Christ (Romans 5:1–2); buried by baptism (Romans 6:3–4); the life-giving Spirit (Romans 8:1–2, 9–11); more than conquerors (Romans 8:31–39); living sacrifices (Romans 12:1–2); pursue peace (Romans 14:17–19)

About A.D. 33/34
Conversion of Paul

About A.D. 57
Paul in Ephesus, writes Romans

About A.D. 64–67
Paul martyred in Rome

The Letter of Paul to the

Romans

Greeting

1 Paul, a servant[1] of Christ Jesus, called to be an apostle, set apart for the gospel of God, 2 which he promised beforehand through his prophets in the holy Scriptures, 3 concerning his Son, who was
descended from David[2] according
to the flesh 4 and was declared to be
1421, the Son of God in power according
1545 to the Spirit of holiness by his resurrection from the dead, Jesus Christ our Lord, 5 through whom we have received grace and apostleship to bring about the obedience of faith for the sake of his name among all the nations, 6 including you who are called to belong to Jesus Christ,

7 To all those in Rome who are loved by God and called to be saints:

Grace to you and peace from God our Father and the Lord Jesus Christ.

Longing to Go to Rome

8 First, I thank my God through Jesus Christ for all of you, because your faith is proclaimed in all the world. 9 For God is my witness, whom I serve with my spirit in the gospel of his Son, that without ceasing I mention you 10 always in my prayers, asking that somehow by God's will I may now at last succeed in coming to you. 11 For I long to see you, that I may impart to you some spiritual gift to strengthen you— 12 that is, that we may be mutually encouraged by each other's faith, both yours and mine. 13 I want you to know, brothers,[3] that I have often intended to come to you (but thus far have been prevented), in order that I may reap some harvest among you as well as among *the rest of* the Gentiles. 14 I am under obligation both to Greeks and to barbarians,[4] both to the wise and to the foolish. 15 So I am eager to preach the gospel to you also who are in Rome.

The Righteous Shall Live by Faith

16 For I am not ashamed of the gospel, for it is the power of God for salvation to everyone who believes, to the Jew first and also to the Greek. 17 For in it the righteousness of God is revealed from faith for faith,[5] as it is written, "The righteous shall live by faith."[6]

God's Wrath on Unrighteousness

18 For the wrath of God is revealed from heaven against all ungodliness and unrighteousness of men, who by their unrighteousness suppress the truth. 19 For what
can be known about God is plain
to them, because God has shown it
5 to them. 20 For his invisible attributes, namely, his eternal power and divine nature, have been clearly perceived, ever since the creation of the world, in the things that have been made. So they are without excuse. 21 For although they knew God, they did not honor him as God or give thanks to him, but they became futile in their thinking, and their foolish hearts were darkened. 22 Claiming to be wise, they became fools, 23 and exchanged the glory of the immortal God for images resembling mortal man and birds and animals and creeping things.

24 Therefore God gave them up in the lusts of their hearts to impurity, to the dishonoring of their bodies among themselves, 25 because they exchanged the truth about God for a lie and worshiped and served the creature rather than the Creator, who is blessed forever! Amen.

26 For this reason God gave them up to dishonorable passions. For their women

[1] Or *slave*; Greek *bondservant* [2] Or *who came from the offspring of David* [3] Or *brothers and sisters*. The plural Greek word *adelphoi* (translated "brothers") refers to siblings in a family. In New Testament usage, depending on the context, *adelphoi* may refer either to men or to both men and women who are siblings (brothers and sisters) in God's family, the church [4] That is, non-Greeks [5] Or *beginning and ending in faith* [6] Or *The one who by faith is righteous shall live*

exchanged natural relations for those that are contrary to nature; 27 and the men likewise gave up natural relations with women and were consumed with passion for one another, men committing shameless acts with men and receiving in themselves the due penalty for their error.

28 And since they did not see fit to acknowledge God, God gave them up to a debased mind to do what ought not to be done. 29 They were filled with all manner of unrighteousness, evil, covetousness, malice. They are full of envy, murder, strife, deceit, maliciousness. They are gossips, 30 slanderers, haters of God, insolent, haughty, boastful, inventors of evil, disobedient to parents, 31 foolish, faithless, heartless, ruthless. 32 Though they know God's decree that those who practice such things deserve to die, they not only do them but give approval to those who practice them.

God's Righteous Judgment

2 Therefore you have no excuse, O man, every one of you who judges. For in passing judgment on another you condemn yourself, because you, the judge, practice the very same things. 2 We know that the judgment of God rightly falls on those who practice such things. 3 Do you suppose, O man—you who judge those who practice such things and yet do them yourself—that you will escape the judgment of God? 4 Or do you presume on the riches of his kindness and forbearance and patience, not knowing that God's kindness is meant to lead you to repentance? 5 But because of your hard and impenitent heart you are storing up wrath for yourself on the day of wrath when God's righteous judgment will be revealed.

6 He will render to each one according to his works: 7 to those who by patience in well-doing seek for glory and honor and immortality, he will give eternal life; 8 but for those who are self-seeking[1] and do not obey the truth, but obey unrighteousness, there will be wrath and fury. 9 There will be tribulation and distress for every human being who does evil, the Jew first and also the Greek, 10 but glory and honor and peace for everyone who does good, the Jew first and also the Greek. 11 For God shows no partiality.

God's Judgment and the Law

12 For all who have sinned without the law will also perish without the law, and all who have sinned under the law will be judged by the law. 13 For it is not the hearers of the law who are righteous before God, but the doers of the law who will be justified. 14 For when Gentiles, who do not have the law, by nature do what the law requires, they are a law to themselves, even though they do not have the law. 15 They show that the work of the law is written on their hearts, while their conscience also bears witness, and their conflicting thoughts accuse or even excuse them 16 on that day when, according to my gospel, God judges the secrets of men by Christ Jesus.

17 But if you call yourself a Jew and rely on the law and boast in God 18 and know his will and approve what is excellent, because you are instructed from the law; 19 and if you are sure that you yourself are a guide to the blind, a light to those who are in darkness, 20 an instructor of the foolish, a teacher of children, having in the law the embodiment of knowledge and truth— 21 you then who teach others, do you not teach yourself? While you preach against stealing, do you steal? 22 You who say that one must not commit adultery, do you commit adultery? You who abhor idols, do you rob temples? 23 You who boast in the law dishonor God by breaking the law. 24 For, as it is written, "The name of God is blasphemed among the Gentiles because of you."

25 For circumcision indeed is of value if you obey the law, but if you break the law, your circumcision becomes uncircumcision. 26 So, if a man who is uncircumcised keeps the precepts of the law,

[1] Or *contentious*

will not his uncircumcision be regarded[1] as circumcision? **27** Then he who is physically uncircumcised but keeps the law will condemn you who have the written code[2] and circumcision but break the law. **28** For no one is a Jew who is merely one outwardly, nor is circumcision outward and physical. **29** But a Jew is one inwardly, and circumcision is a matter of the heart, by the Spirit, not by the letter. His praise is not from man but from God.

God's Righteousness Upheld

3 Then what advantage has the Jew? Or what is the value of circumcision? **2** Much in every way. To begin with, the Jews were entrusted with the oracles of God. **3** What if some were unfaithful? Does their faithlessness nullify the faithfulness of God? **4** By no means! Let God be true though every one were a liar, as it is written,

> "That you may be justified in your words,
> and prevail when you are judged."

5 But if our unrighteousness serves to show the righteousness of God, what shall we say? That God is unrighteous to inflict wrath on us? (I speak in a human way.) **6** By no means! For then how could God judge the world? **7** But if through my lie God's truth abounds to his glory, why am I still being condemned as a sinner? **8** And why not do evil that good may come?—as some people slanderously charge us with saying. Their condemnation is just.

No One Is Righteous

9 What then? Are we Jews[3] any better off?[4] No, not at all. For we have already charged that all, both Jews and Greeks, are under sin, **10** as it is written:

> "None is righteous, no, not one;
> 11 *no one* understands;
> no one seeks for God.
> 12 All have turned aside; together they have become worthless;
> no one does good,
> not even one."
> 13 "Their throat is an open grave;
> they use their tongues to deceive."
> "The venom of asps is under their lips."
> 14 "Their mouth is full of curses and bitterness."
> 15 "Their feet are swift to shed blood;
> 16 in their paths are ruin and misery,
> 17 and the way of peace they have not known."
> 18 "There is no fear of God before their eyes."

1663

19 Now we know that whatever the law says it speaks to those who are under the law, so that every mouth may be stopped, and the whole world may be held accountable to God. **20** For by works of the law no human being[5] will be justified in his sight, since through the law comes knowledge of sin.

The Righteousness of God Through Faith

21 But now the righteousness of God has been manifested apart from the law, although the Law and the Prophets bear witness to it— **22** the righteousness of God through faith in Jesus Christ for all who believe. For there is no distinction: **23** for all have sinned and fall short of the glory of God, **24** and are justified by his grace as a gift, through the redemption that is in Christ Jesus, **25** whom God put forward as a propitiation by his blood, to be received by faith. This was to show God's righteousness, because in his divine forbearance he had passed over former sins. **26** It was to show his righteousness at the present time, so that he might be just and the justifier of the one who has faith in Jesus.

27 Then what becomes of our boasting? It is excluded. By what kind of law? By a law of works? No, but by the law of faith.

1663

28 For we hold that one is justified by faith apart from works of the law. **29** Or is God the God of Jews only? Is he not the God of Gentiles also? Yes,

[1] Or *counted* [2] Or *the letter* [3] Greek *Are we* [4] Or *at any disadvantage?* [5] Greek *flesh*

of Gentiles also, 30 since God is one—who will justify the circumcised by faith and the uncircumcised through faith. 31 Do we then overthrow the law by this faith? By no means! On the contrary, we uphold the law.

Abraham Justified by Faith

43 **4** What then shall we say was gained by[1] Abraham, our forefather according to the flesh? 2 For if Abraham was justified by works, he has something to boast about, but not before God. 3 For what does the Scripture say? "Abraham believed God, and it was counted to him as righteousness." 4 Now to the one who works, his wages are not counted as a gift but as his due. 5 And to
507 the one who does not work but believes in[2] him who justifies the ungodly, his faith is counted as righteousness, 6 just as David also speaks of the blessing of the one to whom God counts righteousness apart from works:

7 "Blessed are those whose lawless
deeds are forgiven,
and whose sins are covered;
8 blessed is the man against whom the
Lord will not count his sin."

9 Is this blessing then only for the circumcised, or also for the uncircumcised? We say that faith was counted to Abraham as righteousness. 10 How then was it counted to him? Was it before or after he had been circumcised? It was not after, but before he was circumcised. 11 He received the sign of circumcision as a seal of the righteousness that he had by faith while he was still uncircumcised. The purpose was to make him the father of all who believe without being circumcised, so that righteousness would be counted to them as well, 12 and to make him the father of the circumcised who are not merely circumcised but who also walk in the footsteps of the faith that our father Abraham had before he was circumcised.

The Promise Realized Through Faith

13 For the promise to Abraham and his offspring that he would be heir of the world did not come through the law but through the righteousness of faith. 14 For if it is the adherents of the law who are to be the heirs, faith is null and the promise is void. 15 For the law brings wrath, but where there is no law there is no transgression.

16 That is why it depends on faith, in order that the promise may rest on grace and be guaranteed to all his offspring—not only to the adherent of the law but also to the one who shares the faith of Abraham, who is the father of us all, 17 as it is written, "I have made you the father of many nations"—in the presence of the God in whom he believed, who gives life to the dead and calls into existence the things that do not exist. 18 In hope he believed against hope, that he should become the father of many nations, as he had been told, "So shall your offspring be." 19 He did not weaken in faith when he considered his own body, which was as good as dead (since he was about a hundred years old), or when he considered the barrenness of Sarah's womb. 20 No distrust made him waver concerning the promise of God, but he grew strong in his faith as he gave glory to God, 21 fully convinced that God was able to do what he had promised. 22 That is why his faith was "counted to him as righteousness." 23 But the words "it was counted to him" were not written for his sake alone, 24 but for ours also. It will be counted to us who believe in him who raised from the dead Jesus our Lord, 25 who was delivered up for our trespasses and
1421 raised for our justification.

Peace with God Through Faith

5 Therefore, since we have been justified by faith, we[3] have peace with God through our Lord Jesus Christ. 2 Through him we have also obtained access by faith[4] into this grace in which we stand, and we[5]

[1] Some manuscripts *say about* [2] Or *but trusts*; compare verse 24 [3] Some manuscripts *let us* [4] Some manuscripts omit *by faith* [5] Or *let us*; also verse 3

rejoice[1] in hope of the glory of God. 3More than that, we rejoice in our sufferings, knowing that suffering produces endurance, 4and endurance produces character, and character produces hope, 5and hope does not put us to shame, because God's love has been poured into our hearts through the Holy Spirit who has been given to us.

6For while we were still weak, at
the right time Christ died for the
1361 ungodly. 7For one will scarcely die
for a righteous person—though perhaps
for a good person one would dare even to
die— 8but God shows his love for
us in that while we were still sin-
397, ners, Christ died for us. 9Since,
1361 therefore, we have now been justi-
fied by his blood, much more shall we be saved by him from the wrath of God. 10For if while we were enemies we were reconciled to God by the death of his Son, much more, now that we are reconciled, shall we be saved by his life. 11More than that, we also rejoice in God through our Lord Jesus Christ, through whom we have now received reconciliation.

Death in Adam, Life in Christ

12Therefore, just as sin came into
the world through one man, and
13 death through sin, and so death
spread to all men because all sinned— 13for sin indeed was in the world before the law was given, but sin is not counted where there is no law. 14Yet death reigned from Adam to Moses, even over those whose sinning was not like the transgression of Adam, who was a type of the one who was to come.

15But the free gift is not like the trespass. For if many died through one man's trespass, much more have the grace of God and the free gift by the grace of that one man Jesus Christ abounded for many. 16And the free gift is not like the result of that one man's sin. For the judgment following one trespass brought condemnation, but the free gift following many trespasses brought justification. 17For if, because of one man's trespass, death reigned through that one man, much more will those who receive the abundance of grace and the free gift of righteousness reign in life through the one man Jesus Christ.

18Therefore, as one trespass[2] led to condemnation for all men, so one act of righteousness[3] leads to justification and life for all men. 19For as by the one man's disobedience the many were made sinners, so by the one man's obedience the many will be made righteous. 20Now the law came in to increase the trespass, but where sin increased, grace abounded all the more, 21so that, as sin reigned in death, grace also might reign through righteousness leading to eternal life through Jesus Christ our Lord.

Dead to Sin, Alive to God

6 What shall we say then? Are we to continue in sin that grace may abound? 2By no means! How can we who died to sin still live in it? 3Do you not know that all of us who have been baptized into Christ Jesus were baptized into his death? 4We were buried therefore with him by baptism into death, in order that, just as Christ was raised from the dead by the glory of the Father, we too might walk in newness of life.

5For if we have been united with him in a death like his, we shall certainly be united with him in a resurrection like his. 6We know that our old self[4] was crucified with him in order that the body of sin might be brought to nothing, so that we would no longer be enslaved to sin. 7For one who has died has been set free[5] from sin. 8Now if we have died with Christ, we believe that we will also live with him. 9We know that Christ, being raised from the dead, will never die again; death no longer has dominion over him. 10For the death he died he died

[1] Or *boast*; also verses 3, 11 [2] Or *the trespass of one* [3] Or *the act of righteousness of one* [4] Greek *man* [5] Greek *has been justified*

to sin, once for all, but the life he lives he lives to God. 11 So you also must consider yourselves dead to sin and alive to God in Christ Jesus.

12 Let not sin therefore reign in your mortal body, to make you obey its passions. 13 Do not present your members to sin as instruments for unrighteousness, but present yourselves to God as those who have been brought from death to life, and your members to God as instruments for righteousness. 14 For sin will have no dominion over you, since you are not under law but under grace.

Slaves to Righteousness

15 What then? Are we to sin because we are not under law but under grace? By no means! 16 Do you not know that if you present yourselves to anyone as obedient slaves,[1] you are slaves of the one whom you obey, either of sin, which leads to death, or of obedience, which leads to righteousness? 17 But thanks be to God, that you who were once slaves of sin have become obedient from the heart to the standard of teaching to which you were committed, 18 and, having been set free from sin, have become slaves of righteousness. 19 I am speaking in human terms, because of your natural limitations. For just as you once presented your members as slaves to impurity and to lawlessness leading to more lawlessness, so now present your members as slaves to righteousness leading to sanctification.

20 For when you were slaves of sin, you were free in regard to righteousness. 21 But what fruit were you getting at that time from the things of which you are now ashamed? For the end of those things is death. 22 But now that you have been set free from sin and have become slaves of God, the fruit you get leads to sanctification and its end, eternal life. 23 For the wages of sin is death, but the free gift of God is eternal life in Christ Jesus our Lord.

Released from the Law

7 Or do you not know, brothers[2]—for I am speaking to those who know the law—that the law is binding on a person only as long as he lives? 2 For a married woman is bound by law to her husband while he lives, but if her husband dies she is released from the law of marriage.[3] 3 Accordingly, she will be called an adulteress if she lives with another man while her husband is alive. But if her husband dies, she is free from that law, and if she marries another man she is not an adulteress.

4 Likewise, my brothers, you also have died to the law through the body of Christ, so that you may belong to another, to him who has been raised from the dead, in order that we may bear fruit for God. 5 For while we were living in the flesh, our sinful passions, aroused by the law, were at work in our members to bear fruit for death. 6 But now we are released from the law, having died to that which held us captive, so that we serve in the new way of the Spirit and not in the old way of the written code.[4]

The Law and Sin

7 What then shall we say? That the law is sin? By no means! Yet if it
175 had not been for the law, I would not have known sin. For I would not have known what it is to covet if the law had not said, "You shall not covet." 8 But sin, seizing an opportunity through the commandment, produced in me all kinds of covetousness. For apart from the law, sin lies dead. 9 I was once alive apart from the law, but when the commandment came, sin came alive and I died. 10 The very commandment that promised life proved to be death to me. 11 For sin, seizing an opportunity through the commandment, deceived me and through it killed me. 12 So the law is holy, and the commandment is holy and righteous and good.

13 Did that which is good, then, bring death to me? By no means! It was sin,

[1] Greek *bondservants.* Twice in this verse and verse 19; also once in verses 17, 20 [2] Or *brothers and sisters;* also verse 4 [3] Greek *law concerning the husband* [4] Greek *of the letter*

producing death in me through what is
good, in order that sin might be shown to
be sin, and through the commandment
might become sinful beyond measure.
14 For we know that the law is spiritual, but
I am of the flesh, sold under sin. 15 For I do
not understand my own actions. For I do
not do what I want, but I do the very thing
I hate. 16 Now if I do what I do not want,
I agree with the law, that it is good. 17 So
now it is no longer I who do it, but sin that
dwells within me. 18 For I know that noth-
ing good dwells in me, that is, in my flesh.
For I have the desire to do what is right,
but not the ability to carry it out. 19 For I
do not do the good I want, but the evil I do
not want is what I keep on doing. 20 Now
if I do what I do not want, it is no longer I
who do it, but sin that dwells within me.

21 So I find it to be a law that when I want
to do right, evil lies close at hand. 22 For I
delight in the law of God, in my inner
being, 23 but I see in my members another
law waging war against the law of my mind
and making me captive to the law of sin
that dwells in my members. 24 Wretched
man that I am! Who will deliver me from
this body of death? 25 Thanks be to God
through Jesus Christ our Lord! So then, I
myself serve the law of God with my mind,
but with my flesh I serve the law of sin.

Life in the Spirit

8 There is therefore now no condem-
nation for those who are in Christ
Jesus.[1] 2 For the law of the Spirit of life has
set you[2] free in Christ Jesus from the law
of sin and death. 3 For God has done what
the law, weakened by the flesh, could not
do. By sending his own Son in the like-
ness of sinful flesh and for sin,[3] he con-
demned sin in the flesh, 4 in order that the
righteous requirement of the law might
be fulfilled in us, *who walk* not accord-
ing to the flesh but according to the Spirit.
5 For those who live according to the flesh
set their minds on the things of the flesh,
but those who live according to the Spirit
set their minds on the things of the Spirit.
6 For to set the mind on the flesh is death,
but to set the mind on the Spirit is life and
peace. 7 For the mind that is set on the
flesh is hostile to God, for it does not sub-
mit to God's law; indeed, it cannot. 8 Those
who are in the flesh cannot please God.

9 You, however, are not in the flesh but
in the Spirit, if in fact the Spirit of God
dwells in you. Anyone who does not have
the Spirit of Christ does not belong to him.
10 But if Christ is in you, although the body
is dead because of sin, the Spirit is life
because of righteousness. 11 If the Spirit of
him who raised Jesus from the dead dwells
in you, he who raised Christ Jesus from the
dead will also give life to your mortal bod-
ies through his Spirit who dwells in you.

Heirs with Christ

12 So then, brothers,[4] we are debtors, not
to the flesh, to live according to the flesh.
13 For if you live according to the flesh
you will die, but if by the Spirit you put to
death the deeds of the body, you will live.
14 For all who are led by the Spirit of God
are sons of God. 15 For you did not receive
the spirit of slavery to fall back into fear,
but you have received the Spirit of adop-
tion as sons, by whom we cry, "Abba!
Father!" 16 The Spirit himself bears witness
with our spirit that we are children of God,
17 and if children, then heirs—heirs of God
and fellow heirs with Christ, provided we
suffer with him in order that we may also
be glorified with him.

Future Glory

18 For I consider that the sufferings of
this present time are not worth comparing
with the glory that is to be revealed to us.
19 For the creation waits with eager longing
for the revealing of the sons of God. 20 For
the creation was subjected to futility, not
willingly, but because of him who sub-
jected it, in hope 21 that the creation itself

[1] Some manuscripts add *who walk not according to the flesh (but according to the Spirit)* [2] Some manuscripts *me* [3] Or *and as a sin offering* [4] Or *brothers and sisters*; also verse 29

will be set free from its bondage to corruption and obtain the freedom of the glory of the children of God. **22** For we know that the whole creation has been groaning together in the pains of childbirth until now. **23** And not only the creation, but we ourselves, who have the firstfruits of the Spirit, groan inwardly as we wait eagerly for adoption as sons, the redemption of our bodies. **24** For in this hope we were saved. Now hope that is seen is not hope. For who hopes for what he sees? **25** But if we hope for what we do not see, we wait for it with patience.

26 Likewise the Spirit helps us in our weakness. For we do not know what to pray for as we ought, but the Spirit himself intercedes for us with groanings too deep for words. **27** And he who searches hearts knows what is the mind of the Spirit, because[1] the Spirit intercedes for the saints according to the will of God. **28** And
we know that for those who love
God all things work together for
107 good,[2] for those who are called
according to his purpose. **29** For those whom he foreknew he also predestined to be conformed to the image of his Son, in order that he might be the firstborn among many brothers. **30** And those whom he predestined he also called, and those whom he called he also justified, and those whom he justified he also glorified.

God's Everlasting Love

31 What then shall we say to these things? If God is for us, who can be[3] against us? **32** He who did not spare his own Son but gave him up for us all, how will he not also with him graciously give us all things? **33** Who shall bring any charge against God's elect? It is God who justifies. **34** Who is to condemn? Christ Jesus is the one who died—more than that, who was raised—
who is at the right hand of God, who
indeed is interceding for us.[4] **35** Who
467, shall separate us from the love of
1191 Christ? Shall tribulation, or distress,
or persecution, or famine, or nakedness, or danger, or sword? **36** As it is written,

> "For your sake we are being killed
> all the day long;
> 1629 we are regarded as sheep to be
> slaughtered."

37 No, in all these things we are more than conquerors through him who loved us. **38** For I am sure that neither death nor life, nor angels nor rulers, nor things present nor things to come, nor powers, **39** nor height nor depth, nor anything else in all creation, will be able to separate us from the love of God in Christ Jesus our Lord.

God's Sovereign Choice

9 I am speaking the truth in Christ—I am not lying; my conscience bears me witness in the Holy Spirit— **2** that I have great sorrow and unceasing anguish in my heart. **3** For I could wish that I myself were accursed and cut off from Christ for the sake of my brothers,[5] my kinsmen according to the flesh. **4** They are Israelites, and to them belong the adoption, the glory, the covenants, the giving of the law, the worship, and the promises. **5** To them belong the patriarchs, and from their race, according to the flesh, is the Christ who is God over all, blessed forever. Amen.

6 But it is not as though the word of
God has failed. For not all who are
53 descended from Israel belong to
Israel, **7** and not all are children of Abraham because they are his offspring, but "Through Isaac shall your offspring be named." **8** This means that it is not the children of the flesh who are the children of God, but the children of the promise are counted as offspring. **9** For this is what the promise said: "About this time next year I will return, and Sarah shall have a son."

10 And not only so, but also when
Rebekah had conceived children
69 by one man, our forefather Isaac,

[1] Or *that* [2] Some manuscripts *God works all things together for good*, or *God works in all things for the good* [3] Or *who is* [4] Or *Is it Christ Jesus who died . . . for us?* [5] Or *brothers and sisters*

11 though they were not yet born
and had done nothing either good
69 or bad—in order that God's pur-
pose of election might continue, not
because of works but because of him who
calls— 12 she was told, "The older will
serve the younger." 13 As it is written,
"Jacob I loved, but Esau I hated."

14 What shall we say then? Is there injustice on God's part? By no means! 15 For he says to Moses, "I will have mercy on whom I have mercy, and I will have compassion on whom I have compassion." 16 So then it depends not on human will or exertion,[1] but on God, who has mercy.

17 For the Scripture says to
Pharaoh, "For this very purpose I
145 have raised you up, that I might
show my power in you, and that my
name might be proclaimed in all the
earth." 18 So then he has mercy on whom-
ever he wills, and he hardens whomever
he wills.

19 You will say to me then, "Why does he still find fault? For who can resist his will?" 20 But who are you, O man, to answer back to God? Will what is molded say to its molder, "Why have you made me like this?" 21 Has the potter no right over the clay, to make out of the same lump one vessel for honorable use and another for dishonorable use? 22 What if God, desiring to show his wrath and to make known his power, has endured with much patience vessels of wrath prepared for destruction, 23 in order to make known the riches of his glory for vessels of mercy, which he has prepared beforehand for glory— 24 even us whom he has called, not from the Jews only but also from the Gentiles? 25 As indeed he says in Hosea,

"Those who were not my people I
will call 'my people,'
and her who was not beloved I
will call 'beloved.'"

26 "And in the very place where it was
said to them, 'You are not my
people,'
there they will be called 'sons of
the living God.'"

27 And Isaiah cries out concerning Israel: "Though the number of the sons of Israel[2] be as the sand of the sea, only a remnant of them will be saved, 28 for the Lord will carry out his sentence upon the earth fully and without delay." 29 And as Isaiah predicted,

"If the Lord of hosts had not left us
offspring,
we would have been like Sodom
and become like Gomorrah."

Israel's Unbelief

30 What shall we say, then? That Gentiles who did not pursue righteousness have attained it, that is, a righteousness that is by faith; 31 but that Israel who pursued a law that would lead to righteousness[3] did not succeed in reaching that law. 32 Why? Because they did not pursue it by faith, but as if it were based on works. They have stumbled over the stumbling stone, 33 as it is written,

"Behold, I am laying in Zion a stone
of stumbling, and a rock of
offense;
and whoever believes in him will
not be put to shame."

10 Brothers,[4] my heart's desire and prayer to God for them is that they may be saved. 2 For I bear them witness that they have a zeal for God, but not according to knowledge. 3 For, being ignorant of the righteousness of God, and seeking to establish their own, they did not submit to God's righteousness. 4 For Christ is the end of the law for righteousness to everyone who believes.[5]

The Message of Salvation to All

5 For Moses writes about the righteousness that is based on the law, that the per-

[1] Greek *not of him who wills or runs* [2] Or *children of Israel* [3] Greek *a law of righteousness* [4] Or *Brothers and sisters* [5] Or *end of the law, that everyone who believes may be justified*

son who does the commandments shall
live by them. 6 But the righteousness based
on faith says, "Do not say in your heart,
'Who will ascend into heaven?'" (that is, to
bring Christ down) 7 or "'Who will descend
into the abyss?'" (that is, to bring Christ up
from the dead). 8 But what does it say? "The
word is near you, in your mouth and in
your heart" (that is, the word of faith that
we proclaim); 9 because, if you confess
with your mouth that Jesus is Lord and
believe in your heart that God raised him
from the dead, you will be saved. 10 For
with the heart one believes and is justi-
fied, and with the mouth one confesses
and is saved. 11 For the Scripture says,
"Everyone who believes in him will not be
put to shame." 12 For there is no distinction
between Jew and Greek; for the same Lord
is Lord of all, bestowing his riches on all
who call on him. 13 For "everyone who calls
on the name of the Lord will be saved."

14 How then will they call on him in
whom they have not believed? And how
are they to believe in him of whom they
have never heard?[1] And how are they to
hear without someone preaching? 15 And
how are they to preach unless they are
sent? As it is written, "How beautiful are
the feet of those who preach the good
news!" 16 But they have not all obeyed the
gospel. For Isaiah says, "Lord, who has
believed what he has heard from us?" 17 So
faith comes from hearing, and hearing
through the word of Christ.

18 But I ask, have they not heard? Indeed
they have, for

"Their voice has gone out to all the
earth,
and their words to the ends of the
world."

19 But I ask, did Israel not understand?
First Moses says,

"I will make you jealous of those
who are not a nation;
with a foolish nation I will make
you angry."

20 Then Isaiah is so bold as to say,

"I have been found by those who did
not seek me;
I have shown myself to those who
did not ask for me."

21 But of Israel he says, "All day long I have
held out my hands to a disobedient and
contrary people."

The Remnant of Israel

11 I ask, then, has God rejected his
people? By no means! For I myself
am an Israelite, a descendant of Abraham,[2]
a member of the tribe of Benjamin. 2 God
has not rejected his people whom he fore-
knew. Do you not know what the Scrip-
ture says of Elijah, how he appeals to God
against Israel? 3 "Lord, they have killed
your prophets, they have demolished your
altars, and I alone am left, and they seek
my life." 4 But what is God's reply to him? "I
have kept for myself seven thousand men
who have not bowed the knee to Baal." 5 So
too at the present time there is a remnant,
chosen by grace. 6 But if it is by grace, it is
no longer on the basis of works; otherwise
grace would no longer be grace.

7 What then? Israel failed to obtain what
it was seeking. The elect obtained it, but
the rest were hardened, 8 as it is written,

"God gave them a spirit of stupor,
eyes that would not see
and ears that would not hear,
down to this very day."

9 And David says,

"Let their table become a snare and a
trap,
a stumbling block and a
retribution for them;
10 let their eyes be darkened so that
they cannot see,
and bend their backs forever."

[1] Or *him whom they have never heard* [2] Or *one of the offspring of Abraham*

Gentiles Grafted In

11 So I ask, did they stumble in order
that they might fall? By no means! Rather
through their trespass salvation has come
to the Gentiles, so as to make Israel jeal-
ous. 12 Now if their trespass means riches
for the world, and if their failure means
riches for the Gentiles, how much more
will their full inclusion[1] mean!

13 Now I am speaking to you Gentiles.
Inasmuch then as I am an apostle to the
Gentiles, I magnify my ministry 14 in order
somehow to make my fellow Jews jealous,
and thus save some of them. 15 For if their
rejection means the reconciliation of the
world, what will their acceptance mean but
life from the dead? 16 If the dough offered
as firstfruits is holy, so is the whole lump,
and if the root is holy, so are the branches.

17 But if some of the branches were bro-
ken off, and you, although a wild olive
shoot, were grafted in among the others
and now share in the nourishing root[2] of
the olive tree, 18 do not be arrogant toward
the branches. If you are, remember it
is not you who support the root, but the
root that supports you. 19 Then you will
say, "Branches were broken off so that I
might be grafted in." 20 That is true. They
were broken off because of their unbelief,
but you stand fast through faith. So do not
become proud, but fear. 21 For if God did
not spare the natural branches, neither will
he spare you. 22 Note then the kindness and
the severity of God: severity toward those
who have fallen, but God's kindness to you,
provided you continue in his kindness.
Otherwise you too will be cut off. 23 And
even they, if they do not continue in their
unbelief, will be grafted in, for God has
the power to graft them in again. 24 For if
you were cut from what is by nature a wild
olive tree, and grafted, *contrary* to nature,
into a cultivated olive tree, how much
more will these, the natural branches, be
grafted back into their own olive tree.

The Mystery of Israel's Salvation

25 Lest you be wise in your own sight,
I want you to understand this mystery,
brothers:[3] a partial hardening has come
upon Israel, until the fullness of the
Gentiles has come in. 26 And in this way
all Israel will be saved, as it is written,

"The Deliverer will come from Zion,
he will banish ungodliness from
Jacob";
27 "and this will be my covenant with
them
when I take away their sins."

28 As regards the gospel, they are enemies
of God for your sake. But as regards elec-
tion, they are beloved for the sake of their
forefathers. 29 For the gifts and the calling
of God are irrevocable. 30 For just as you
were at one time disobedient to God but
now have received mercy because of their
disobedience, 31 so they too have now been
disobedient in order that by the mercy
shown to you they also may now[4] receive
mercy. 32 For God has consigned all to dis-
obedience, that he may have mercy on all.

33 Oh, the depth of the riches and
wisdom and knowledge of God! How
unsearchable are his judgments and how
inscrutable his ways!

34 "For who has known the mind of the
Lord,
or who has been his counselor?"
35 "Or who has given a gift to him
that he might be repaid?"

36 For from him and through him and to
him are all things. To him be glory forever.
Amen.

A Living Sacrifice

12 I appeal to you therefore,
brothers,[5] by the mercies of
1181 God, to present your bodies as a
living sacrifice, holy and acceptable to
God, which is your spiritual worship.[6] 2 Do
not be conformed to this world,[7] but be

[1] Greek *their fullness* [2] Greek *root of richness; some manuscripts richness* [3] Or *brothers and sisters* [4] Some manuscripts omit *now* [5] Or *brothers and sisters* [6] Or *your rational service* [7] Greek *age*

transformed by the renewal of your mind, that by testing you may discern what is the will of God, what is good and acceptable and perfect.[1]

Gifts of Grace

3 For by the grace given to me I say to everyone among you not to think of himself more highly than he ought to think, but to think with sober judgment, each according to the measure of faith that God has assigned. 4 For as in one body we have many members,[2] and the members do not all have the same function, 5 so we, though many, are one body in Christ, and individually members one of another. 6 Having gifts that differ according to the grace given to us, let us use them: if prophecy, in proportion to our faith; 7 if service, in our serving; the one who teaches, in his teaching; 8 the one who exhorts, in his exhortation; the one who contributes, in generosity; the one who leads,[3] with zeal; the one who does acts of mercy, with cheerfulness.

Marks of the True Christian

9 Let love be genuine. Abhor what is evil;
hold fast to what is good. 10 Love
one another with brotherly affec-
1641 tion. Outdo one another in showing
honor. 11 Do not be slothful in zeal, be fervent in spirit,[4] serve the Lord. 12 Rejoice in hope, be patient in tribulation, be constant in prayer. 13 Contribute to the needs of the saints and seek to show hospitality.

14 Bless those who persecute you; bless
and do not curse them. 15 Rejoice
with those who rejoice, weep with
1641 those who weep. 16 Live in harmony
with one another. Do not be haughty, but associate with the lowly.[5] Never be wise in your own sight. 17 Repay no one evil for evil, but give thought to do what is honorable in the sight of all. 18 If possible, so far as it depends on you, live peaceably with all. 19 Beloved, never avenge yourselves, but leave it[6] to the wrath of God, for it is written, "Vengeance is mine, I will repay, says the Lord." 20 To the contrary, "if your enemy is hungry, feed him; if he is thirsty, give him something to drink; for by so doing you will heap burning coals on his head." 21 Do not be overcome by evil, but overcome evil with good.

Submission to the Authorities

13 Let every person be subject to the governing authorities. For there is no authority except from God, and those that exist have been instituted by God. 2 Therefore whoever resists the authorities resists what God has appointed, and those who resist will incur judgment. 3 For rulers are not a terror to good conduct, but to bad. Would you have no fear of the one who is in authority? Then do what is good, and you will receive his approval, 4 for he is God's servant for your good. But if you do wrong, be afraid, for he does not bear the sword in vain. For he is the servant of God, an avenger who carries out God's wrath on the wrongdoer. 5 Therefore one must be in subjection, not only to avoid God's wrath but also for the sake of conscience. 6 For because of this you also pay taxes, for the authorities are ministers of God, attending to this very thing. 7 Pay to all what is owed to them: taxes to whom taxes are owed, revenue to whom revenue is owed, respect to whom respect is owed, honor to whom honor is owed.

Fulfilling the Law Through Love

8 Owe no one anything, except to
love each other, for the one who
175 loves another has fulfilled the law.
9 For the commandments, "You shall not commit adultery, You shall not murder, You shall not steal, You shall not covet," and any other commandment, are summed up in this word: "You shall love your neighbor as yourself." 10 Love does no wrong to a neighbor; therefore love is the fulfilling of the law.

[1] *Or what is the good and acceptable and perfect will of God* [2] Greek *parts*; also verse 5 [3] *Or gives aid* [4] *Or fervent in the Spirit* [5] *Or give yourselves to humble tasks* [6] Greek *give place*

11 Besides this you know the time, that
the hour has come for you to wake from
sleep. For salvation is nearer to us now
than when we first believed. 12 The night
is far gone; the day is at hand. So then let
us cast off the works of darkness and put
on the armor of light. 13 Let us walk prop-
erly as in the daytime, not in orgies and
drunkenness, not in sexual immorality
and sensuality, not in quarreling and jeal-
ousy. 14 But put on the Lord Jesus Christ,
and make no provision for the flesh, to
gratify its desires.

Do Not Pass Judgment on One Another

14 As for the one who is weak in faith,
welcome him, but not to quarrel
over opinions. 2 One person believes he
may eat anything, while the weak per-
son eats only vegetables. 3 Let not the one
who eats despise the one who abstains,
and let not the one who abstains pass
judgment on the one who eats, for God
has welcomed him. 4 Who are you to pass
judgment on the servant of another? It is
before his own master[1] that he stands or
falls. And he will be upheld, for the Lord is
able to make him stand.

5 One person esteems one day as better
than another, while another esteems all
days alike. Each one should be fully con-
vinced in his own mind. 6 The one who
observes the day, observes it in honor of
the Lord. The one who eats, eats in honor
of the Lord, since he gives thanks to God,
while the one who abstains, abstains in
honor of the Lord and gives thanks to God.
7 For none of us lives to himself, and none
of us dies to himself. 8 For if we live, we
live to the Lord, and if we die, we die to the
Lord. So then, whether we live or whether
we die, we are the Lord's. 9 For to this end
Christ died and lived again, that he might
be Lord both of the dead and of the living.

10 Why do you pass judgment on your
brother? Or you, why do you despise your
brother? For we will all stand before the
judgment seat of God; 11 for it is written,

"As I live, says the Lord, every knee
shall bow to me,
and every tongue shall confess[2] to
God."

12 So then each of us will give an account
of himself to God.

Do Not Cause Another to Stumble

13 Therefore let us not pass judgment
on one another any longer, but rather
decide never to put a stumbling block
or hindrance in the way of a brother. 14 I
know and am persuaded in the Lord Jesus
that nothing is unclean in itself, but it is
unclean for anyone who thinks it unclean.
15 For if your brother is grieved by what
you eat, you are no longer walking in love.
By what you eat, do not destroy the one for
whom Christ died. 16 So do not let what
you regard as good be spoken of as evil.
17 For the kingdom of God is not a matter
of eating and drinking but of righteous-
ness and peace and joy in the Holy Spirit.
18 Whoever thus serves Christ is accept-
able to God and approved by men. 19 So
then let us pursue what makes for peace
and for mutual upbuilding.

20 Do not, for the sake of food, destroy the
work of God. Everything is indeed clean,
but it is wrong for anyone to make another
stumble by what he eats. 21 It is good not
to eat meat or drink wine or do anything
that causes your brother to stumble.[3] 22 The
faith that you have, keep between your-
self and God. Blessed is the one who has
no reason to pass judgment on himself
for what he approves. 23 But whoever has
doubts is condemned if he eats, because
the eating is not from faith. For whatever
does not proceed from faith is sin.[4]

The Example of Christ

15 We who are strong have an obli-
gation to bear with the failings
of the weak, and not to please ourselves.
2 Let each of us please his neighbor for his
good, to build him up. 3 For Christ did not

[1] Or *lord* [2] Or *shall give praise* [3] Some manuscripts add *or be hindered or be weakened* [4] Some manuscripts insert here 16:25-27

please himself, but as it is written, "The reproaches of those who reproached you fell on me." 4 For whatever was written in former days was written for our instruction, that through endurance and through the encouragement of the Scriptures we might have hope. 5 May the God of endurance and encouragement grant you to live in such harmony with one another, in accord with Christ Jesus, 6 that together you may with one voice glorify the God and Father of our Lord Jesus Christ. 7 Therefore welcome one another as Christ has welcomed you, for the glory of God.

Christ the Hope of Jews and Gentiles

8 For I tell you that Christ became a servant to the circumcised to show God's truthfulness, in order to confirm the promises given to the patriarchs, 9 and in order that the Gentiles might glorify God for his mercy. As it is written,

593

> "Therefore I will praise you
> among the Gentiles,
> and sing to your name."

10 And again it is said,

> "Rejoice, O Gentiles, with his people."

11 And again,

> "Praise the Lord, all you Gentiles,
> and let all the peoples extol him."

12 And again Isaiah says,

> "The root of Jesse will come,
> even he who arises to rule the
> Gentiles;
> in him will the Gentiles hope."

13 May the God of hope fill you with all joy and peace in believing, so that by the power of the Holy Spirit you may abound in hope.

Paul the Minister to the Gentiles

14 I myself am satisfied about you, my brothers,[1] that you yourselves are full of goodness, filled with all knowledge and able to instruct one another. 15 But on some points I have written to you very boldly by way of reminder, because of the grace given me by God 16 to be a minister of Christ Jesus to the Gentiles in the priestly service of the gospel of God, so that the offering of the Gentiles may be acceptable, sanctified by the Holy Spirit. 17 In Christ Jesus, then, I have reason to be proud of my work for God. 18 For I will not venture to speak of anything except what Christ has accomplished through me to bring the Gentiles to obedience—by word and deed, 19 by the power of signs and wonders, by the power of the Spirit of God—so that from Jerusalem and all the way around to Illyricum I have fulfilled the ministry of the gospel of Christ; 20 and thus I make it my ambition to preach the gospel, not where Christ has already been named, lest I build on someone else's foundation, 21 but as it is written,

> "Those who have never been told of
> him will see,
> and those who have never heard
> will understand."

Paul's Plan to Visit Rome

22 This is the reason why I have so often been hindered from coming to you. 23 But now, since I no longer have any room for work in these regions, and since I have longed for many years to come to you, 24 I hope to see you in passing as I go to Spain, and to be helped on my journey there by you, once I have enjoyed your company for a while. 25 At present, however, I am going to Jerusalem bringing aid to the saints. 26 For Macedonia and Achaia have been pleased to make some contribution for the poor among the saints at Jerusalem. 27 For they were pleased to do it, and indeed they owe it to them. For if the Gentiles have come to share in their spiritual blessings, they ought also to be of service to them in material blessings. 28 When therefore I have completed this and have delivered

[1] Or *brothers and sisters*; also verse 30

to them what has been collected,[1] I will
leave for Spain by way of you. 29 I know
that when I come to you I will come in the
fullness of the blessing[2] of Christ.

30 I appeal to you, brothers, by our Lord
Jesus Christ and by the love of the Spirit,
to strive together with me in your prayers
to God on my behalf, 31 that I may be
delivered from the unbelievers in Judea,
and that my service for Jerusalem may be
acceptable to the saints, 32 so that by God's
will I may come to you with joy and be
refreshed in your company. 33 May the God
of peace be with you all. Amen.

Personal Greetings

16 I commend to you our sister
Phoebe, a servant[3] of the church
at Cenchreae, 2 that you may welcome her
in the Lord in a way worthy of the saints,
and help her in whatever she may need
from you, for she has been a patron of
many and of myself as well.

3 Greet Prisca and Aquila, my fellow
workers in Christ Jesus, 4 who risked
their necks for my life, to whom not
only I give thanks but all the churches of
the Gentiles give thanks as well. 5 Greet
also the church in their house. Greet my
beloved Epaenetus, who was the first
convert[4] to Christ in Asia. 6 Greet Mary,
who has worked hard for you. 7 Greet
Andronicus and Junia,[5] my kinsmen and
my fellow prisoners. They are well known
to the apostles,[6] and they were in Christ
before me. 8 Greet Ampliatus, my beloved
in the Lord. 9 Greet Urbanus, our fellow
worker in Christ, and my beloved Stachys.
10 Greet Apelles, who is approved in Christ.
Greet those who belong to the family
of Aristobulus. 11 Greet my kinsman
Herodion. Greet those in the Lord who
belong to the family of Narcissus. 12 Greet
those workers in the Lord, Tryphaena
and Tryphosa. Greet the beloved Persis,
who has worked hard in the Lord. 13 Greet
Rufus, chosen in the Lord; also his mother,
who has been a mother to me as well.
14 Greet Asyncritus, Phlegon, Hermes,
Patrobas, Hermas, and the brothers[7] who
are with them. 15 Greet Philologus, Julia,
Nereus and his sister, and Olympas, and
all the saints who are with them. 16 Greet
one another with a holy kiss. All the
churches of Christ greet you.

Final Instructions and Greetings

17 I appeal to you, brothers, to watch out
for those who cause divisions and create
obstacles contrary to the doctrine that you
have been taught; avoid them. 18 For such
persons do not serve our Lord Christ, but
their own appetites,[8] and by smooth talk
and flattery they deceive the hearts of the
naive. 19 For your obedience is known to
all, so that I rejoice over you, but I want
you to be wise as to what is good and inno-
cent as to what is evil. 20 The God of peace
will soon crush Satan under your feet. The
grace of our Lord Jesus Christ be with you.

21 Timothy, my fellow worker, greets
you; so do Lucius and Jason and Sosipater,
my kinsmen.

22 I Tertius, who wrote this letter, greet
you in the Lord.

23 Gaius, who is host to me and to the
whole church, greets you. Erastus, the city
treasurer, and our brother Quartus, greet
you.[9]

Doxology

25 Now to him who is able to strengthen
you according to my gospel and the
preaching of Jesus Christ, according to
the revelation of the mystery that was kept
secret for long ages 26 but has now been
disclosed and through the prophetic writ-
ings has been made known to all nations,
according to the command of the eter-
nal God, to bring about the obedience of
faith— 27 to the only wise God be glory
forevermore through Jesus Christ! Amen.

[1] Greek *sealed to them this fruit* [2] Some manuscripts insert *of the gospel* [3] Or *deaconess* [4] Greek *firstfruit* [5] Or *Junias* [6] Or *messengers* [7] Or *brothers and sisters*; also verse 17 [8] Greek *their own belly* [9] Some manuscripts insert verse 24: *The grace of our Lord Jesus Christ be with you all. Amen.*

Introduction to

1 Corinthians

Author
Paul the apostle

Date
About A.D. 53–55

Purpose
The purpose of 1 Corinthians is to remind the Corinthians how different Christianity is from the way the world is, to exhort them to live lives faithful to the gospel and in unity with one another, and to answer questions that the Corinthians had asked.

Central Themes
Man's foolishness is contrasted with God's wisdom; ungodly divisions and lawsuits in the church should stop; the church should pursue purity, not immorality; Christians should follow biblical teaching on marriage and divorce; there should be good order in worship; food offered to idols; spiritual gifts and right attitudes about them; the Lord's table; Christ's resurrection and the future resurrection of believers.

Memory Verses
God's wisdom (1 Corinthians 1:26–2:2); the Lord's Supper (1 Corinthians 11:23–32); love's greatness (1 Corinthians 13:1–13); the resurrection (1 Corinthians 15:50–58)

Introduction

Paul had heard reports about the church in Corinth. Christians there were acting in a way that was not pleasing to Jesus their Lord. Paul writes this letter to correct them. Pride and disunity were the biggest problems. The Corinthians were divided over which Christian leader was the best (1 Corinthians 1:10–4:21); they went to court against each other (1 Corinthians 6:1–11); they were rude to each other at the Lord's Table (1 Corinthians 11:17–34); and they treated some spiritual gifts as better than others (1 Corinthians 12–14). Paul tries to correct these things by telling the Corinthians to think according to God's wisdom, not man's (1 Corinthians 1:17–2:16) and to love each other (1 Corinthians 13). Paul also motivated the Corinthians to leave behind immorality, calling them to purity (1 Corinthians 5:1–13; 6:12–20). In other parts of his letter, Paul answers questions the Corinthians had written to him concerning marriage and divorce (1 Corinthians 7), food offered to idols (1 Corinthians 8:1–11:1), the church's worship service (1 Corinthians 14), and the future resurrection of believers' bodies (1 Corinthians 15).

About A.D. 33/34	About A.D. 48/49–51	About A.D. 53–55
Conversion of Paul	Paul plants church at Corinth	Paul writes 1 Corinthians

The First Letter of Paul to the Corinthians

1 Corinthians

Greeting

1 Paul, called by the will of God to be
an apostle of Christ Jesus, and our
brother Sosthenes,
2 To the church of God that is in Corinth,
to those sanctified in Christ Jesus, called
to be saints together with all those who in
every place call upon the name of our Lord
Jesus Christ, both their Lord and ours:
3 Grace to you and peace from God our
Father and the Lord Jesus Christ.

Thanksgiving

4 I give thanks to my God always for you
because of the grace of God that was given
you in Christ Jesus, 5 that in every way you
were enriched in him in all speech and
all knowledge— 6 even as the testimony
about Christ was confirmed among you—
7 so that you are not lacking in any spiri-
tual gift, as you wait for the revealing of
our Lord Jesus Christ, 8 who will sustain
you to the end, guiltless in the day of our
Lord Jesus Christ. 9 God is faithful, by
whom you were called into the fellowship
of his Son, Jesus Christ our Lord.

Divisions in the Church

10 I appeal to you, brothers,[1] by the
name of our Lord Jesus Christ, that all of
you agree, and that there be no divisions
among you, but that you be united in the
same mind and the same judgment. 11 For
it has been reported to me by Chloe's peo-
ple that there is quarreling among you,
my brothers. 12 What I mean is that each
one of you says, "I follow Paul," or "I fol-
low Apollos," or "I follow Cephas," or "I fol-
low Christ." 13 Is Christ divided? Was Paul
crucified for you? Or were you baptized
in the name of Paul? 14 I thank God that I
baptized none of you except Crispus and
Gaius, 15 so that no one may say that you
were baptized in my name. 16 (I did baptize
also the household of Stephanas. Beyond
that, I do not know whether I baptized
anyone else.) 17 For Christ did not send me
to baptize but to preach the gospel, and
not with words of eloquent wisdom, lest
the cross of Christ be emptied of its power.

Christ the Wisdom and Power of God

18 For the word of the cross is folly to
those who are perishing, but to us who are
being saved it is the power of God. 19 For it
is written,

> "I will destroy the wisdom of the wise,
> and the discernment of the
> discerning I will thwart."

20 Where is the one who is wise? Where is
the scribe? Where is the debater of this age?
Has not God made foolish the wisdom of
the world? 21 For since, in the wisdom of
God, the world did not know God through
wisdom, it pleased God through the folly of
what we preach to save those who believe.
22 For Jews demand signs and Greeks seek
wisdom, 23 but we preach Christ cruci-
fied, a stumbling block to Jews and folly
to Gentiles, 24 but to those who are called,
both Jews and Greeks, Christ the power
of God and the wisdom of God. 25 For the
foolishness of God is wiser than men, and
the weakness of God is stronger than men.
26 For consider your calling, brothers:
not many of you were wise according to
worldly standards,[2] not many were pow-
erful, not many were of noble birth. 27 But
God chose what is foolish in the
world to shame the wise; God
chose what is weak in the world to

[1] Or *brothers and sisters*. The plural Greek word *adelphoi* (translated "brothers") refers to siblings in a family. In New Testament usage, depending on the context, *adelphoi* may refer either to men or to both men and women who are siblings (brothers and sisters) in God's family, the church; also verses 11, 26 [2] Greek *according to the flesh*

shame the strong; 28 God chose what is low and despised in the world, even things that are not, to bring to nothing things that are, 29 so that no human being[1] might boast in the presence of God. 30 And because of him[2] you are in Christ Jesus, who became to us wisdom from God, righteousness and sanctification and redemption, 31 so that, as it is written, "Let the one who boasts, boast in the Lord."

Proclaiming Christ Crucified

2 And I, when I came to you, brothers,[3] did not come pro-
587 claiming to you the testimony[4] of God with lofty speech or wisdom. 2 For I decided to know nothing among you except Jesus Christ and him crucified. 3 And I was with you in weakness and in fear and much trembling, 4 and my speech and my message were not in plausible words of wisdom, but in demonstration of the Spirit and of power, 5 that your faith might not rest in the wisdom of men but in the power of God.

Wisdom from the Spirit

6 Yet among the mature we do impart wisdom, although it is not
535 a wisdom of this age or of the rulers of this age, who are doomed to pass away. 7 But we impart a secret and hidden wisdom of God, which God decreed before the ages for our glory. 8 None of the rulers of this age understood this, for if they had, they would not have crucified the Lord of glory. 9 But, as it is written,

> "What no eye has seen, nor ear heard,
> nor the heart of man imagined,
> what God has prepared for those
> who love him"—

10 these things God has revealed to us through the Spirit. For the Spirit searches everything, even the depths of God. 11 For who knows a person's thoughts except the spirit of that person, which is in him? So also no one comprehends the thoughts of God except the Spirit of God. 12 Now we have received not the spirit of the world, but the Spirit who is from God, that we might understand the things freely given us by God. 13 And we impart this in words not taught by human wisdom but taught by the Spirit, interpreting spiritual truths to those who are spiritual.[5]

14 The natural person does not accept the things of the Spirit of God, for they are folly to him, and he is not able to understand them because they are spiritually discerned. 15 The spiritual person judges all things, but is himself to be judged by no one. 16 "For who has understood the mind of the Lord so as to instruct him?" But we have the mind of Christ.

Divisions in the Church

3 But I, brothers,[6] could not address you as spiritual people, but as people of the flesh, as infants in Christ. 2 I fed you with milk, not solid food, for you were not ready for it. And even now you are not yet ready, 3 for you are still of the flesh. For while there is jealousy and strife among you, are you not of the flesh and behaving only in a human way? 4 For when one says, "I follow Paul," and another, "I follow Apollos," are you not being merely human?

5 What then is Apollos? What is Paul? Servants through whom you believed, as the Lord assigned to each. 6 I planted, Apollos watered, but God gave the growth. 7 So neither he who plants nor he who waters is anything, but only God who gives the growth. 8 He who plants and he who waters are one, and each will receive his wages according to his labor. 9 For we are God's fellow workers. You are God's field, God's building.

10 According to the grace of God given to me, like a skilled master builder I laid a foundation, and someone else is building upon it. Let each one take care how he builds upon it. 11 For no one can lay a

[1] Greek *no flesh* [2] Greek *And from him* [3] Or *brothers and sisters* [4] Some manuscripts *mystery* (or *secret*) [5] Or *interpreting spiritual truths in spiritual language*, or *comparing spiritual things with spiritual* [6] Or *brothers and sisters*

foundation other than that which is laid,
which is Jesus Christ. 12 Now if anyone
builds on the foundation with gold, sil-
ver, precious stones, wood, hay, straw—
13 each one's work will become manifest,
for the Day will disclose it, because it will
be revealed by fire, and the fire will test
what sort of work each one has done. 14 If
the work that anyone has built on the
foundation survives, he will receive a
reward. 15 If anyone's work is burned up,
he will suffer loss, though he himself will
be saved, but only as through fire.

16 Do you not know that you[1] are God's
temple and that God's Spirit dwells in you?
17 If anyone destroys God's temple, God
will destroy him. For God's temple is holy,
and you are that temple.

18 Let no one deceive himself. If any-
one among you thinks that he is wise in
this age, let him become a fool that he
may become wise. 19 For the wisdom of
this world is folly with God. For it is writ-
ten, "He catches the wise in their crafti-
ness," 20 and again, "The Lord knows the
thoughts of the wise, that they are futile."
21 So let no one boast in men. For all things
are yours, 22 whether Paul or Apollos or
Cephas or the world or life or death or the
present or the future—all are yours, 23 and
you are Christ's, and Christ is God's.

The Ministry of Apostles

4 This is how one should regard us, as
servants of Christ and stewards of the
mysteries of God. 2 Moreover, it is required
of stewards that they be found trustwor-
thy. 3 But with me it is a very small thing
that I should be judged by you or by any
human court. In fact, I do not even judge
myself. 4 For I am not aware of anything
against myself, but I am not thereby
acquitted. It is the Lord who judges me.
5 Therefore do not pronounce judgment
before the time, before the Lord comes,
who will bring to light the things now
hidden in darkness and will disclose the
purposes of the heart. Then each one will
receive his commendation from God.

6 I have applied all these things to
myself and Apollos for your benefit,
brothers,[2] that you may learn by us not
to go beyond what is written, that none
of you may be puffed up in favor of one
against another. 7 For who sees anything
different in you? What do you have that
you did not receive? If then you received
it, why do you boast as if you did not
receive it?

8 Already you have all you want! Already
you have become rich! Without us you
have become kings! And would that you
did reign, so that we might share the rule
with you! 9 For I think that God has exhib-
ited us apostles as last of all, like men sen-
tenced to death, because we have become
a spectacle to the world, to angels, and to
men. 10 We are fools for Christ's sake, but
you are wise in Christ. We are weak,
but you are strong. You are held in honor,
but we in disrepute. 11 To the present
hour we hunger and thirst, we are poorly
dressed and buffeted and homeless, 12 and
we labor, working with our own hands.
When reviled, we bless; when persecuted,
we endure; 13 when slandered, we entreat.
We have become, and are still, like the
scum of the world, the refuse of all things.

14 I do not write these things to make
you ashamed, but to admonish you as
my beloved children. 15 For though you
have countless guides in Christ, you do
not have many fathers. For I became your
father in Christ Jesus through the gospel.
16 I urge you, then, be imitators of me.
17 That is why I sent[3] you Timothy, my
beloved and faithful child in the Lord, to
remind you of my ways in Christ,[4] as I
teach them everywhere in every church.
18 Some are arrogant, as though I were not
coming to you. 19 But I will come to you
soon, if the Lord wills, and I will find out
not the talk of these arrogant people but
their power. 20 For the kingdom of God

[1] The Greek for *you* is plural in verses 16 and 17 [2] Or *brothers and sisters* [3] Or *am sending* [4] Some manuscripts add *Jesus*

does not consist in talk but in power. 21 What do you wish? Shall I come to you with a rod, or with love in a spirit of gentleness?

Sexual Immorality Defiles the Church

5 It is actually reported that there is sexual immorality among you, and of a kind that is not tolerated even among pagans, for a man has his father's wife. 2 And you are arrogant! Ought you not rather to mourn? Let him who has done this be removed from among you.

3 For though absent in body, I am present in spirit; and as if present, I have already pronounced judgment on the one who did such a thing. 4 When you are assembled in the name of the Lord Jesus and my spirit is present, with the power of our Lord Jesus, 5 you are to deliver this man to Satan for the destruction of the flesh, so that his spirit may be saved in the day of the Lord.[1]

6 Your boasting is not good. Do you not know that a little leaven leavens the whole lump? 7 Cleanse out the old leaven
153 that you may be a new lump, as you really are unleavened. For Christ, our Passover lamb, has been sacrificed. 8 Let us therefore celebrate
153 the festival, not with the old leaven, the leaven of malice and evil, but with the unleavened bread of sincerity and truth.

9 I wrote to you in my letter not to associate with sexually immoral people— 10 not at all meaning the sexually immoral of this world, or the greedy and swindlers, or idolaters, since then you would need to go out of the world. 11 But now I am writing to you not to associate with anyone who bears the name of brother if he is guilty of sexual immorality or greed, or is an idolater, reviler, drunkard, or swindler—not even to eat with such a one. 12 For what have I to do with judging outsiders? Is it not those inside the church whom you are to judge? 13 God judges[2] those outside. "Purge the evil person from among you."

Lawsuits Against Believers

6 When one of you has a grievance against another, does he dare go to law before the unrighteous instead of the saints? 2 Or do you not know that the saints will judge the world? And if the world is to be judged by you, are you incompetent to try trivial cases? 3 Do you not know that we are to judge angels? How much more, then, matters pertaining to this life! 4 So if you have such cases, why do you lay them before those who have no standing in the church? 5 I say this to your shame. Can it be that there is no one among you wise enough to settle a dispute between the brothers, 6 but brother goes to law against brother, and that before unbelievers? 7 To have lawsuits at all with one another is already a defeat for you. Why not rather suffer wrong? Why not rather be defrauded? 8 But you yourselves wrong and defraud—even your own brothers![3]

9 Or do you not know that the unrighteous[4] will not inherit the kingdom of God? Do not be deceived: neither the sexually immoral, nor idolaters, nor adulterers, nor men who practice homosexuality,[5] 10 nor thieves, nor the greedy, nor drunkards, nor revilers, nor swindlers will inherit the kingdom of God. 11 And such were some of you. But you were washed, you were sanctified, you were justified in the name of the Lord Jesus Christ and by the Spirit of our God.

Flee Sexual Immorality

12 "All things are lawful for me," but not all things are helpful. "All things are lawful for me," but I will not be enslaved by anything. 13 "Food is meant for the stomach and the stomach for food"—and God will destroy both one and the other. The body is not meant for sexual immorality, but for

[1] Some manuscripts add *Jesus* [2] Or *will judge* [3] Or *brothers and sisters* [4] Or *wrongdoers* [5] The two Greek terms translated by this phrase refer to the passive and active partners in consensual homosexual acts

the Lord, and the Lord for the body. 14 And God raised the Lord and will also raise us up by his power. 15 Do you not know that your bodies are members of Christ? Shall I then take the members of Christ and make them members of a prostitute? Never! 16 Or do you not know that he who is joined[1] to a prostitute becomes one body with her? For, as it is written, "The two will become one flesh." 17 But he who is joined to the Lord becomes one spirit with him. 18 Flee from sexual immorality. Every other sin[2] a person commits is outside the body, but the sexually immoral person sins against his own body. 19 Or do you not know that your body is a temple of the Holy Spirit within you, whom you have from God? You are not your own, 20 for you were bought with a price. So glorify God in your body.

Principles for Marriage

7 Now concerning the matters about which you wrote: "It is good for a man not to have sexual relations with a woman." 2 But because of the temptation to sexual immorality, each man should have his own wife and each woman her own husband. 3 The husband should give to his wife her conjugal rights, and likewise the wife to her husband. 4 For the wife does not have authority over her own body, but the husband does. Likewise the husband does not have authority over his own body, but the wife does. 5 Do not deprive one another, except perhaps by agreement for a limited time, that you may devote yourselves to prayer; but then come together again, so that Satan may not tempt you because of your lack of self-control.

6 Now as a concession, not a command, I say this.[3] 7 I wish that all were as I myself am. But each has his own gift from God, one of one kind and one of another.

8 To the unmarried and the widows I say that it is good for them to remain single as I am. 9 But if they cannot exercise self-control, they should marry. For it is better to marry than to burn with passion.

10 To the married I give this charge (not I, but the Lord): the wife should not separate from her husband 11 (but if she does, she should remain unmarried or else be reconciled to her husband), and the husband should not divorce his wife.

12 To the rest I say (I, not the Lord) that if any brother has a wife who is an unbeliever, and she consents to live with him, he should not divorce her. 13 If any woman has a husband who is an unbeliever, and he consents to live with her, she should not divorce him. 14 For the unbelieving husband is made holy because of his wife, and the unbelieving wife is made holy because of her husband. Otherwise your children would be unclean, but as it is, they are holy. 15 But if the unbelieving partner separates, let it be so. In such cases the brother or sister is not enslaved. God has called you[4] to peace. 16 For how do you know, wife, whether you will save your husband? Or how do you know, husband, whether you will save your wife?

Live as You Are Called

17 Only let each person lead the life that the Lord has assigned to him, and to which God has called him. This is my rule in all the churches. 18 Was anyone at the time of his call already circumcised? Let him not seek to remove the marks of circumcision. Was anyone at the time of his call uncircumcised? Let him not seek circumcision. 19 For neither circumcision counts for anything nor uncircumcision, but keeping the commandments of God. 20 Each one should remain in the condition in which he was called. 21 Were you a slave[5] when called? Do not be concerned about it. (But if you can gain your freedom, avail yourself of the opportunity.) 22 For he who was called in the Lord as a slave is a freedman of the Lord. Likewise

[1] Or *who holds fast* (compare Genesis 2:24 and Deuteronomy 10:20); also verse 17 [2] Or *Every sin* [3] Or *I say this:* [4] Some manuscripts *us* [5] Greek *bondservant;* also twice in verse 22 and once in verse 23 (plural)

he who was free when called is a slave of Christ. **23** You were bought with a price; do not become slaves of men. **24** So, brothers,[1] in whatever condition each was called, there let him remain with God.

The Unmarried and the Widowed

25 Now concerning[2] the betrothed,[3] I have no command from the Lord, but I give my judgment as one who by the Lord's mercy is trustworthy. **26** I think that in view of the present[4] distress it is good for a person to remain as he is. **27** Are you bound to a wife? Do not seek to be free. Are you free from a wife? Do not seek a wife. **28** But if you do marry, you have not sinned, and if a betrothed woman[5] marries, she has not sinned. Yet those who marry will have worldly troubles, and I would spare you that. **29** This is what I mean, brothers: the appointed time has grown very short. From now on, let those who have wives live as though they had none, **30** and those who mourn as though they were not mourning, and those who rejoice as though they were not rejoicing, and those who buy as though they had no goods, **31** and those who deal with the world as though they had no dealings with it. For the present form of this world is passing away.

32 I want you to be free from anxieties. The unmarried man is anxious about the things of the Lord, how to please the Lord. **33** But the married man is anxious about worldly things, how to please his wife, **34** and his interests are divided. And the unmarried or betrothed woman is anxious about the things of the Lord, how to be holy in body and spirit. But the married woman is anxious about worldly things, how to please her husband. **35** I say this for your own benefit, not to lay any restraint upon you, but to promote good order and to secure your undivided devotion to the Lord.

36 If anyone thinks that he is not behaving properly toward his betrothed,[6] if his[7] passions are strong, and it has to be, let him do as he wishes: let them marry—it is no sin. **37** But whoever is firmly established in his heart, being under no necessity but having his desire under control, and has determined this in his heart, to keep her as his betrothed, he will do well. **38** So then he who marries his betrothed does well, and he who refrains from marriage will do even better.

39 A wife is bound to her husband as long as he lives. But if her husband dies, she is free to be married to whom she wishes, only in the Lord. **40** Yet in my judgment she is happier if she remains as she is. And I think that I too have the Spirit of God.

Food Offered to Idols

8 Now concerning[8] food offered to idols: we know that "all of us possess knowledge." This "knowledge" puffs up, but love builds up. **2** If anyone imagines that he knows something, he does not yet know as he ought to know. **3** But if anyone loves God, he is known by God.[9]

4 Therefore, as to the eating of food offered to idols, we know that "an idol has no real existence," and that "there is no God but one." **5** For although there may be so-called gods in heaven or on earth—as indeed there are many "gods" and many "lords"— **6** yet for us there is one God, the Father, from whom are all things and for whom we exist, and one Lord, Jesus Christ, through whom are all things and through whom we exist.

7 However, not all possess this knowledge. But some, through former association with idols, eat food as really offered to an idol, and their conscience, being weak, is defiled. **8** Food will not commend us to God. We are no worse off if we do not eat, and no better off if we do. **9** But take care

[1] Or *brothers and sisters*; also verse 29 [2] The expression *Now concerning* introduces a reply to a question in the Corinthians' letter; see 7:1 [3] Greek *virgins* [4] Or *impending* [5] Greek *virgin*; also verse 34 [6] Greek *virgin*; also verses 37, 38 [7] Or *her* [8] The expression *Now concerning* introduces a reply to a question in the Corinthians' letter; see 7:1 [9] Greek *him*

that this right of yours does not somehow become a stumbling block to the weak. 10 For if anyone sees you who have knowledge eating[1] in an idol's temple, will he not be encouraged,[2] if his conscience is weak, to eat food offered to idols? 11 And so by your knowledge this weak person is destroyed, the brother for whom Christ died. 12 Thus, sinning against your brothers[3] and wounding their conscience when it is weak, you sin against Christ. 13 Therefore, if food makes my brother stumble, I will never eat meat, lest I make my brother stumble.

Paul Surrenders His Rights

9 Am I not free? Am I not an apostle? Have I not seen Jesus our Lord? Are not you my workmanship in the Lord? 2 If to others I am not an apostle, at least I am to you, for you are the seal of my apostleship in the Lord.

3 This is my defense to those who would examine me. 4 Do we not have the right to eat and drink? 5 Do we not have the right to take along a believing wife,[4] as do the other apostles and the brothers of the Lord and Cephas? 6 Or is it only Barnabas and I who have no right to refrain from working for a living? 7 Who serves as a soldier at his own expense? Who plants a vineyard without eating any of its fruit? Or who tends a flock without getting some of the milk?

8 Do I say these things on human authority? Does not the Law say the same? 9 For it is written in the Law of Moses, "You shall not muzzle an ox when it treads out the grain." Is it for oxen that God is concerned? 10 Does he not speak entirely for our sake? It was written for our sake, because the plowman should plow in hope and the thresher thresh in hope of sharing in the crop. 11 If we have sown spiritual things among you, is it too much if we reap material things from you? 12 If others share this rightful claim on you, do not we even more?

Nevertheless, we have not made use of this right, but we endure anything rather than put an obstacle in the way of the gospel of Christ. 13 Do you not know that those who are employed in the temple service get their food from the temple, and those who serve at the altar share in the sacrificial offerings? 14 In the same way, the Lord commanded that those who proclaim the gospel should get their living by the gospel.

15 But I have made no use of any of these rights, nor am I writing these things to secure any such provision. For I would rather die than have anyone deprive me of my ground for boasting. 16 For if I preach the gospel, that gives me no ground for boasting. For necessity is laid upon me. Woe to me if I do not preach the gospel! 17 For if I do this of my own will, I have a reward, but if not of my own will, I am still entrusted with a stewardship. 18 What then is my reward? That in my preaching I may present the gospel free of charge, so as not to make full use of my right in the gospel.

19 For though I am free from all, I have made myself a servant to all, that I might win more of them. 20 To the Jews I became as a Jew, in order to win Jews. To those under the law I became as one under the law (though not being myself under the law) that I might win those under the law. 21 To those outside the law I became as one outside the law (not being outside the law of God but under the law of Christ) that I might win those outside the law. 22 To the weak I became weak, that I might win the weak. I have become all things to all people, that by all means I might save some. 23 I do it all for the sake of the gospel, that I may share with them in its blessings.

24 Do you not know that in a race all the runners run, but only one receives the prize? So run that you may obtain it. 25 Every athlete exercises self-control in

[1] Greek *reclining at table* [2] Or *fortified*; Greek *built up* [3] Or *brothers and sisters* [4] Greek *a sister as wife*

all things. They do it to receive a perish-
able wreath, but we an imperishable.
26So I do not run aimlessly; I do not box
as one beating the air. **27**But I discipline
my body and keep it under control,[1] lest
after preaching to others I myself should
be disqualified.

Warning Against Idolatry

10 For I want you to know,
brothers,[2] that our fathers
167, were all under the cloud, and all
265 passed through the sea, **2**and all
were baptized into Moses in the cloud
and in the sea, **3**and all ate the same spiri-
tual food, **4**and all drank the same spiritual
drink. For they drank from the spiritual
Rock that followed them, and the Rock
was Christ. **5**Nevertheless, with most of
them God was not pleased, for they were
overthrown in the wilderness.

6Now these things took place as exam-
ples for us, that we might not desire
evil as they did. **7**Do not be idolaters as
some of them were; as it is written, "The
people sat down to eat and drink and
rose up to play." **8**We must not indulge
in sexual immorality as some of them
did, and twenty-three thousand fell in a
single day. **9**We must not put Christ[3] to
the test, as some of them did and were
destroyed by serpents, **10**nor grumble, as
some of them did and were destroyed by
the Destroyer. **11**Now these things hap-
pened to them as an example, but they
were written down for our instruction,
on whom the end of the ages has come.
12Therefore let anyone who thinks that
he stands take heed lest he fall. **13**No
temptation has overtaken you that is not
common to man. God is faithful, and he
will not let you be tempted beyond your
ability, but with the temptation he will
also provide the way of escape, that you
may be able to endure it.

14Therefore, my beloved, flee from
idolatry. **15**I speak as to sensible people;
judge for yourselves what I say. **16**The
cup of blessing that we bless, is it not a
participation in the blood of Christ? The
bread that we break, is it not a participa-
tion in the body of Christ? **17**Because there
is one bread, we who are many are one
body, for we all partake of the one bread.
18Consider the people of Israel:[4] are not
those who eat the sacrifices participants
in the altar? **19**What do I imply then?
That food offered to idols is anything,
or that an idol is anything? **20**No, I imply
that what pagans sacrifice they offer to
demons and not to God. I do not want you
to be participants with demons. **21**You
cannot drink the cup of the Lord and the
cup of demons. You cannot partake of the
table of the Lord and the table of demons.
22Shall we provoke the Lord to jealousy?
Are we stronger than he?

Do All to the Glory of God

23"All things are lawful," but not all
things are helpful. "All things are law-
ful," but not all things build up. **24**Let no
one seek his own good, but the good of
his neighbor. **25**Eat whatever is sold in the
meat market without raising any ques-
tion on the ground of conscience. **26**For
"the earth is the Lord's, and the fullness
thereof." **27**If one of the unbelievers invites
you to dinner and you are disposed to
go, eat whatever is set before you with-
out raising any question on the ground
of conscience. **28**But if someone says to
you, "This has been offered in sacrifice,"
then do not eat it, for the sake of the one
who informed you, and for the sake of
conscience— **29**I do not mean your con-
science, but his. For why should my lib-
erty be determined by someone else's con-
science? **30**If I partake with thankfulness,
why am I denounced because of that for
which I give thanks?

31So, whether you eat or drink, or what-
ever you do, do all to the glory of God.
32Give no offense to Jews or to Greeks

[1] Greek *I pummel my body and make it a slave* [2] Or *brothers and sisters* [3] Some manuscripts *the Lord* [4] Greek *Consider Israel according to the flesh*

or to the church of God, 33 just as I try to please everyone in everything I do, not seeking my own advantage, but that of many, that they may be saved.

11 Be imitators of me, as I am of Christ.

Head Coverings

2 Now I commend you because you remember me in everything and maintain the traditions even as I delivered them to you. 3 But I want you to understand that the head of every man is Christ, the head of a wife[1] is her husband, and the head of Christ is God. 4 Every man who prays or prophesies with his head covered dishonors his head, 5 but every wife[2] who prays or prophesies with her head uncovered dishonors her head, since it is the same as if her head were shaven. 6 For if a wife will not cover her head, then she should cut her hair short. But since it is disgraceful for a wife to cut off her hair or shave her head, let her cover her head. 7 For a man ought not to cover his head, since he is the image and glory of God, but woman is the glory of man. 8 For man was not made from woman, but woman from man. 9 Neither was man created for woman, but woman for man. 10 That is why a wife ought to have a symbol of authority on her head, because of the angels.[3] 11 Nevertheless, in the Lord woman is not independent of man nor man of woman; 12 for as woman was made from man, so man is now born of woman. And all things are from God. 13 Judge for yourselves: is it proper for a wife to pray to God with her head uncovered? 14 Does not nature itself teach you that if a man wears long hair it is a disgrace for him, 15 but if a woman has long hair, it is her glory? For her hair is given to her for a covering. 16 If anyone is inclined to be contentious, we have no such practice, nor do the churches of God.

The Lord's Supper

17 But in the following instructions
I do not commend you, because
1519 when you come together it is not
for the better but for the worse. 18 For, in the first place, when you come together as a church, I hear that there are divisions among you. And I believe it in part,[4] 19 for there must be factions among you in order that those who are genuine among you may be recognized. 20 When you come together, it is not the Lord's supper that you eat. 21 For in eating, each one goes ahead with his own meal. One goes hungry, another gets drunk. 22 What! Do you not have houses to eat and drink in? Or do you despise the church of God and humiliate those who have nothing? What shall I say to you? Shall I commend you in this? No, I will not.

23 For I received from the Lord what I also delivered to you, that the Lord Jesus on the night when he was betrayed took bread, 24 and when he had given thanks, he broke it, and said, "This is my body which is for[5] you. Do this in remembrance
of me."[6] 25 In the same way also he
took the cup, after supper, saying,
1519 "This cup is the new covenant in
my blood. Do this, as often as you drink it, in remembrance of me." 26 For as often as you eat this bread and drink the cup, you proclaim the Lord's death until he comes.

27 Whoever, therefore, eats the bread or drinks the cup of the Lord in an unworthy manner will be guilty concerning the body and blood of the Lord. 28 Let a person examine himself, then, and so eat of the bread and drink of the cup. 29 For anyone who eats and drinks without discerning the body eats and drinks judgment on himself. 30 That is why many of you are weak and ill, and some have died.[7] 31 But if we judged[8] ourselves truly, we would not be judged. 32 But when we are judged by the Lord, we are disciplined[9] so that

[1] Greek *gunē*. This term may refer to a *woman* or a *wife*, depending on the context [2] In verses 5-13, the Greek word *gunē* is translated *wife* in verses that deal with wearing a veil, a sign of being married in first-century culture [3] Or *messengers*, that is, people sent to observe and report [4] Or *I believe a certain report* [5] Some manuscripts *broken for* [6] Or *as my memorial*; also verse 25 [7] Greek *have fallen asleep* (as in 15:6, 20) [8] Or *discerned* [9] Or *when we are judged we are being disciplined by the Lord*

we may not be condemned along with the world.

33 So then, my brothers,[1] when you come together to eat, wait for[2] one another— **34** if anyone is hungry, let him eat at home—so that when you come together it will not be for judgment. About the other things I will give directions when I come.

Spiritual Gifts

12 Now concerning[3] spiritual gifts,[4] brothers,[5] I do not want you to be uninformed. **2** You know that when you were pagans you were led astray to mute idols, however you were led. **3** Therefore I want you to understand that no one speaking in the Spirit of God ever says "Jesus is accursed!" and no one can say "Jesus is Lord" except in the Holy Spirit.

4 Now there are varieties of gifts, but the same Spirit; **5** and there are varieties of service, but the same Lord; **6** and there are varieties of activities, but it is the same God who empowers them all in everyone. **7** To each is given the manifestation of the Spirit for the common good. **8** For to one is given through the Spirit the utterance of wisdom, and to another the utterance of knowledge according to the same Spirit, **9** to another faith by the same Spirit, to another gifts of healing by the one Spirit, **10** to another the working of miracles, to another prophecy, to another the ability to distinguish between spirits, to another various kinds of tongues, to another the interpretation of tongues. **11** All these are empowered by one and the same Spirit, who apportions to each one individually as he wills.

One Body with Many Members

12 For just as the body is one and has many members, and all the members of the body, though many, are one body, so it is with Christ. **13** For in one Spirit we were all baptized into one body—Jews or Greeks, slaves[6] or free—and all were made to drink of one Spirit.

14 For the body does not consist of one member but of many. **15** If the foot should say, "Because I am not a hand, I do not belong to the body," that would not make it any less a part of the body. **16** And if the ear should say, "Because I am not an eye, I do not belong to the body," that would not make it any less a part of the body. **17** If the whole body were an eye, where would be the sense of hearing? If the whole body were an ear, where would be the sense of smell? **18** But as it is, God arranged the members in the body, each one of them, as he chose. **19** If all were a single member, where would the body be? **20** As it is, there are many parts,[7] yet one body.

21 The eye cannot say to the hand, "I have no need of you," nor again the head to the feet, "I have no need of you." **22** On the contrary, the parts of the body that seem to be weaker are indispensable, **23** and on those parts of the body that we think less honorable we bestow the greater honor, and our unpresentable parts are treated with greater modesty, **24** which our more presentable parts do not require. But God has so composed the body, giving greater honor to the part that lacked it, **25** that there may be no division in the body, but that the members may have the same care for one another. **26** If one member suffers, all suffer together; if one member is honored, all rejoice together.

27 Now you are the body of Christ and individually members of it. **28** And God has appointed in the church first apostles, second prophets, third teachers, then miracles, then gifts of healing, helping, administrating, and various kinds of tongues. **29** Are all apostles? Are all prophets? Are all teachers? Do all work miracles? **30** Do all possess gifts of healing? Do all speak with tongues? Do all interpret? **31** But earnestly desire the higher gifts.

[1] Or *brothers and sisters* [2] Or *share with* [3] The expression *Now concerning* introduces a reply to a question in the Corinthians' letter; see 7:1 [4] Or *spiritual persons* [5] Or *brothers and sisters* [6] Or *servants*; Greek *bondservants* [7] Or *members*; also verse 22

And I will show you a still more excellent way.

The Way of Love

13 If I speak in the tongues of men and of angels, but have not love, I am a noisy gong or a clanging cymbal. 2 And if I have prophetic powers, and understand all mysteries and all knowledge, and if I have all faith, so as to remove mountains, but have not love, I am nothing. 3 If I give away all I have, and if I deliver up my body to be burned,[1] but have not love, I gain nothing.

4 Love is patient and kind; love does not envy or boast; it is not arrogant 5 or rude. It does not insist on its own way; it is not irritable or resentful;[2] 6 it does not rejoice at wrongdoing, but rejoices with the truth. 7 Love bears all things, believes all things, hopes all things, endures all things.

8 Love never ends. As for prophecies, they will pass away; as for tongues, they will cease; as for knowledge, it will pass away. 9 For we know in part and we prophesy in part, 10 but when the perfect comes, the partial will pass away. 11 When I was a child, I spoke like a child, I thought like a child, I reasoned like a child. When I became a man, I gave up childish ways. 12 For now we see in a mirror dimly, but then face to face. Now I know in part; then I shall know fully, even as I have been fully known.

13 So now faith, hope, and love abide, these three; but the greatest of these is love.

Prophecy and Tongues

14 Pursue love, and earnestly desire the spiritual gifts, especially that you may prophesy. 2 For one who speaks in a tongue speaks not to men but to God; for no one understands him, but he utters mysteries in the Spirit. 3 On the other hand, the one who prophesies speaks to people for their upbuilding and encouragement and consolation. 4 The one who speaks in a tongue builds up himself, but the one who prophesies builds up the church. 5 Now I want you all to speak in tongues, but even more to prophesy. The one who prophesies is greater than the one who speaks in tongues, unless someone interprets, so that the church may be built up.

6 Now, brothers,[3] if I come to you speaking in tongues, how will I benefit you unless I bring you some revelation or knowledge or prophecy or teaching? 7 If even lifeless instruments, such as the flute or the harp, do not give distinct notes, how will anyone know what is played? 8 And if the bugle gives an indistinct sound, who will get ready for battle? 9 So with yourselves, if with your tongue you utter speech that is not intelligible, how will anyone know what is said? For you will be speaking into the air. 10 There are doubtless many different languages in the world, and none is without meaning, 11 but if I do not know the meaning of the language, I will be a foreigner to the speaker and the speaker a foreigner to me. 12 So with yourselves, since you are eager for manifestations of the Spirit, strive to excel in building up the church.

13 Therefore, one who speaks in a tongue should pray for the power to interpret. 14 For if I pray in a tongue, my spirit prays but my mind is unfruitful. 15 What am I to do? I will pray with my spirit, but I will pray with my mind also; I will sing praise with my spirit, but I will sing with my mind also. 16 Otherwise, if you give thanks with your spirit, how can anyone in the position of an outsider[4] say "Amen" to your thanksgiving when he does not know what you are saying? 17 For you may be giving thanks well enough, but the other person is not being built up. 18 I thank God that I speak in tongues more than all of you. 19 Nevertheless, in church I would rather speak five words with my

[1] Some manuscripts *deliver up my body* [to death] *that I may boast* [2] Greek *irritable and does not count up wrongdoing* [3] Or *brothers and sisters*; also verses 20, 26, 39
[4] Or *of him that is without gifts*

mind in order to instruct others, than ten thousand words in a tongue.

20 Brothers, do not be children in your thinking. Be infants in evil, but in your thinking be mature. 21 In the Law it is written, "By people of strange tongues and by the lips of foreigners will I speak to this people, and even then they will not listen to me, says the Lord." 22 Thus tongues are a sign not for believers but for unbelievers, while prophecy is a sign[1] not for unbelievers but for believers. 23 If, therefore, the whole church comes together and all speak in tongues, and outsiders or unbelievers enter, will they not say that you are out of your minds? 24 But if all prophesy, and an unbeliever or outsider enters, he is convicted by all, he is called to account by all, 25 the secrets of his heart are disclosed, and so, falling on his face, he will worship God and declare that God is really among you.

Orderly Worship

26 What then, brothers? When you come together, each one has a hymn, a lesson, a revelation, a tongue, or an interpretation. Let all things be done for building up. 27 If any speak in a tongue, let there be only two or at most three, and each in turn, and let someone interpret. 28 But if there is no one to interpret, let each of them keep silent in church and speak to himself and to God. 29 Let two or three prophets speak, and let the others weigh what is said. 30 If a revelation is made to another sitting there, let the first be silent. 31 For you can all prophesy one by one, so that all may learn and all be encouraged, 32 and the spirits of prophets are subject to prophets. 33 For God is not a God of confusion but of peace.

As in all the churches of the saints, 34 the women should keep silent in the churches. For they are not permitted to speak, but should be in submission, as the Law also says. 35 If there is anything they desire to learn, let them ask their husbands at home. For it is shameful for a woman to speak in church.

36 Or was it from you that the word of God came? Or are you the only ones it has reached? 37 If anyone thinks that he is a prophet, or spiritual, he should acknowledge that the things I am writing to you are a command of the Lord. 38 If anyone does not recognize this, he is not recognized. 39 So, my brothers, earnestly desire to prophesy, and do not forbid speaking in tongues. 40 But all things should be done decently and in order.

The Resurrection of Christ

15 Now I would remind you,
brothers,[2] of the gospel I
1593 preached to you, which you
received, in which you stand, 2 and by
which you are being saved, if you hold fast
to the word I preached to you—unless you
believed in vain.

3 For I delivered to you as of first
importance what I also received:
1597, that Christ died for our sins in
1601 accordance with the Scriptures,
4 that he was buried, that he was raised on
the third day in accordance with the
Scriptures, 5 and that he appeared to
Cephas, then to the twelve. 6 Then he
appeared to more than five hundred
brothers at one time, most of whom are
still alive, though some have fallen
asleep. 7 Then he appeared to James, then
to all the apostles. 8 Last of all, as to one
untimely born, he appeared also to me.
9 For I am the least of the apostles, unworthy to be called an apostle, because I persecuted the church of God. 10 But by the grace of God I am what I am, and his grace toward me was not in vain. On the contrary, I worked harder than any of them, though it was not I, but the grace of God that is with me. 11 Whether then it was I or they, so we preach and so you believed.

[1] Greek lacks *a sign* [2] Or *brothers and sisters*; also verses 6, 31, 50, 58

The Resurrection of the Dead

12 Now if Christ is proclaimed as raised from the dead, how can some of you say that there is no resurrection of the dead? 13 But if there is no resurrection of the dead, then not even Christ has been raised. 14 And if Christ has not been raised, then our preaching is in vain and your faith is in vain. 15 We are even found to be misrepresenting God, because we testified about God that he raised Christ, whom he did not raise if it is true that the dead are not raised. 16 For if the dead are not raised, not even Christ has been
raised. 17 And if Christ has not been
raised, your faith is futile and you
1593 are still in your sins. 18 Then those
also who have fallen asleep in Christ have perished. 19 If in Christ we have hope[1] in this life only, we are of all people most to be pitied.

20 But in fact Christ has been raised
from the dead, the firstfruits of
1593 those who have fallen asleep. 21 For
as by a man came death, by a man has come also the resurrection of the dead. 22 For as in Adam all die, so also in Christ shall all be made alive. 23 But each in his own order: Christ the firstfruits, then at his coming those who belong to Christ.

24 Then comes the end, when he
delivers the kingdom to God the
411, Father after destroying every rule
1847 and every authority and power.
25 For he must reign until he has put all his enemies under his feet. 26 The last enemy to be destroyed is death. 27 For "God[2] has put all things in subjection under his feet." But when it says, "all things are put in subjection," it is plain that he is excepted who put all things in subjection under him. 28 When all things are subjected to him, then the Son himself will also be subjected to him who put all things in subjection under him, that God may be all in all.

29 Otherwise, what do people mean by being baptized on behalf of the dead? If the dead are not raised at all, why are people baptized on their behalf? 30 Why are we in danger every hour? 31 I protest, brothers, by my pride in you, which I have in Christ Jesus our Lord, I die every day! 32 What do I gain if, humanly speaking, I fought with beasts at Ephesus? If the dead are not raised, "Let us eat and drink, for tomorrow we die." 33 Do not be deceived: "Bad company ruins good morals."[3] 34 Wake up from your drunken stupor, as is right, and do not go on sinning. For some have no knowledge of God. I say this to your shame.

The Resurrection Body

35 But someone will ask, "How are the dead raised? With what kind of body do they come?" 36 You foolish person! What you sow does not come to life unless it dies. 37 And what you sow is not the body that is to be, but a bare kernel, perhaps of wheat or of some other grain. 38 But God gives it a body as he has chosen, and to each kind of seed its own body. 39 For not all flesh is the same, but there is one kind for humans, another for animals, another for birds, and another for fish. 40 There are heavenly bodies and earthly bodies, but the glory of the heavenly is of one kind, and the glory of the earthly is of another. 41 There is one glory of the sun, and another glory of the moon, and another glory of the stars; for star differs from star in glory.

42 So is it with the resurrection of the dead. What is sown is perishable; what is raised is imperishable. 43 It is sown in dishonor; it is raised in glory. It is sown in weakness; it is raised in power. 44 It is sown a natural body; it is raised a spiritual body. If there is a natural body, there is also a spiritual body. 45 Thus it is written, "The first man Adam became a living being";[4] the last Adam became a life-giving spirit. 46 But it is not the spiritual that is first but the natural, and then the spiritual. 47 The first man was from the earth, a man of

[1] Or *we have hoped* [2] Greek *he* [3] Probably from Menander's comedy *Thais* [4] Greek *a living soul*

dust; the second man is from heaven. 48 As was the man of dust, so also are those who are of the dust, and as is the man of heaven, so also are those who are of heaven. 49 Just as we have borne the image of the man of dust, we shall[1] also bear the image of the man of heaven.

Mystery and Victory

50 I tell you this, brothers: flesh and blood cannot inherit the kingdom of God, nor does the perishable inherit the imperishable. 51 Behold! I tell you a mystery. We shall not all sleep, but we shall all be changed, 52 in a moment, in the twinkling of an eye, at the last trumpet. For the trumpet will sound, and the dead will be raised imperishable, and we shall be changed. 53 For this perishable body must put on the imperishable, and this mortal body must put on immortality. 54 When the perishable puts on the imperishable, and the mortal puts on immortality, then shall come to pass the saying that is written:

> "Death is swallowed up in victory."
> 55 "O death, where is your victory?
> O death, where is your sting?"

56 The sting of death is sin, and the power of sin is the law. 57 But thanks be to God, who gives us the victory
411 through our Lord Jesus Christ.

58 Therefore, my beloved brothers, be steadfast, immovable, always abounding in the work of the Lord, knowing that in the Lord your labor is not in vain.

The Collection for the Saints

16 Now concerning[2] the collection for the saints: as I directed the churches of Galatia, so you also are to do. 2 On the first day of every week, each of you is to put something aside and store it up, as he may prosper, so that there will be no collecting when I come. 3 And when I arrive, I will send those whom you accredit by letter to carry your gift to Jerusalem. 4 If it seems advisable that I should go also, they will accompany me.

Plans for Travel

5 I will visit you after passing through Macedonia, for I intend to pass through Macedonia, 6 and perhaps I will stay with you or even spend the winter, so that you may help me on my journey, wherever I go. 7 For I do not want to see you now just in passing. I hope to spend some time with you, if the Lord permits. 8 But I will stay in Ephesus until Pentecost, 9 for a wide door for effective work has opened to me, and there are many adversaries.

10 When Timothy comes, see that you put him at ease among you, for he is doing the work of the Lord, as I am. 11 So let no one despise him. Help him on his way in peace, that he may return to me, for I am expecting him with the brothers.

Final Instructions

12 Now concerning our brother Apollos, I strongly urged him to visit you with the other brothers, but it was not at all his will[3] to come now. He will come when he has opportunity.

13 Be watchful, stand firm in the faith, act like men, be strong. 14 Let all that you do be done in love.

15 Now I urge you, brothers[4]—you know that the household[5] of Stephanas were the first converts in Achaia, and that they have devoted themselves to the service of the saints— 16 be subject to such as these, and to every fellow worker and laborer. 17 I rejoice at the coming of Stephanas and Fortunatus and Achaicus, because they have made up for your absence, 18 for they refreshed my spirit as well as yours. Give recognition to such men.

Greetings

19 The churches of Asia send you greetings. Aquila and Prisca, together with the

[1] Some manuscripts *let us* [2] The expression *Now concerning* introduces a reply to a question in the Corinthians' letter; see 7:1; also verse 12 [3] Or *God's will for him* [4] Or *brothers and sisters*; also verse 20 [5] Greek *house*

church in their house, send you hearty
greetings in the Lord. 20 All the brothers
send you greetings. Greet one another
with a holy kiss.
21 I, Paul, write this greeting with my
own hand. 22 If anyone has no love for
the Lord, let him be accursed. Our Lord,
come![1] 23 The grace of the Lord Jesus be
with you. 24 My love be with you all in
Christ Jesus. Amen.

[1] Greek *Maranatha* (a transliteration of Aramaic)

Introduction to

2 Corinthians

Author

Paul the apostle

Date

About A.D. 55–56

Purpose

The purpose of 2 Corinthians is to demonstrate that Paul was a true apostle, since false apostles were telling the Corinthians he was not, and to show that Christianity is opposite of the way we normally think about religion.

Central Themes

True apostleship is contrasted with false teachers; God often gives true joy to Christians through the most difficult things in life; suffering with joy for Christ is a response to the gospel; repentance; forgiveness and love should be given to the repentant; God is the Provider and therefore Christians can give generously.

Memory Verses

Amen in Christ (2 Corinthians 1:18–22); the Spirit gives life (2 Corinthians 3:4–6); eternal glory (2 Corinthians 4:16–18); the ministry of reconciliation (2 Corinthians 5:17–21); rich in Christ (2 Corinthians 8:9); a cheerful giver (2 Corinthians 9:6–8); God's wonderful grace (2 Corinthians 12:7–10)

Introduction

Paul had enemies in Corinth who falsely claimed to be apostles and who told the Corinthians that Paul was not a true apostle. Paul writes to the Corinthians to warn them of these false teachers. To show that he is truly an apostle, Paul describes his many sufferings for the gospel (2 Corinthians 11:23–30). He boasts of his weaknesses because God's power is made perfect in weakness (2 Corinthians 12:7–10). Paul describes himself as a minister of the new covenant, resulting in people with changed hearts who were growing ever more like Jesus (2 Corinthians 3). He writes that he is an ambassador for Christ, calling people to be reconciled to God through Christ (2 Corinthians 5:11–6:10). Paul encourages the Corinthian believers to pursue holiness in light of God's promises (2 Corinthians 6:14–7:1). He urges them to give generously to meet the needs of other Christians, because God loves a cheerful giver and He would provide abundantly for their needs (2 Corinthians 8–9). After defending his authority as a leader of God's people (2 Corinthians 10–12), Paul ends his letter by calling on those who rebelled against his authority to repent before he came to Corinth (2 Corinthians 13).

About A.D. 33/34	About A.D. 48/49–51	About A.D. 55–56
Conversion of Paul	Paul plants church at Corinth	Paul writes 2 Corinthians

The Second Letter of Paul to the Corinthians

2 Corinthians

Greeting

1 Paul, an apostle of Christ Jesus by the
will of God, and Timothy our brother,
To the church of God that is at Corinth,
with all the saints who are in the whole
of Achaia:
2 Grace to you and peace from God our
Father and the Lord Jesus Christ.

God of All Comfort

3 Blessed be the God and Father of our
Lord Jesus Christ, the Father of mercies
and God of all comfort, 4 who comforts us
in all our affliction, so that we may be able
to comfort those who are in any affliction,
with the comfort with which we our-
selves are comforted by God. 5 For as we
share abundantly in Christ's sufferings,
so through Christ we share abundantly in
comfort too.[1] 6 If we are afflicted, it is for
your comfort and salvation; and if we are
comforted, it is for your comfort, which
you experience when you patiently en-
dure the same sufferings that we suffer.
7 Our hope for you is unshaken, for we
know that as you share in our sufferings,
you will also share in our comfort.
8 For we do not want you to be ignorant,
brothers,[2] of the affliction we experienced
in Asia. For we were so utterly burdened
beyond our strength that we despaired of
life itself. 9 Indeed, we felt that we had re-
ceived the sentence of death. But that was
to make us rely not on ourselves but on God
who raises the dead. 10 He delivered us from
such a deadly peril, and he will deliver us.
On him we have set our hope that he will
deliver us again. 11 You also must help us by
prayer, so that many will give thanks on our
behalf for the blessing granted us through
the prayers of many.

Paul's Change of Plans

12 For our boast is this, the testimony
of our conscience, that we behaved in the
world with simplicity[3] and godly sincerity,
not by earthly wisdom but by the grace of
God, and supremely so toward you. 13 For
we are not writing to you anything other
than what you read and acknowledge[4] and
I hope you will fully acknowledge— 14 just
as you did partially acknowledge us—that
on the day of our Lord Jesus you will boast
of us as we will boast of you.
15 Because I was sure of this, I wanted to
come to you first, so that you might have
a second experience of grace. 16 I wanted
to visit you on my way to Macedonia, and
to come back to you from Macedonia and
have you send me on my way to Judea.
17 Was I vacillating when I wanted to do
this? Do I make my plans according to
the flesh, ready to say "Yes, yes" and "No,
no" at the same time? 18 As surely as God
is faithful, our word to you has not been
Yes and No. 19 For the Son of God, Jesus
Christ, whom we proclaimed among you,
Silvanus and Timothy and I, was not Yes
and No, but in him it is always Yes. 20 For
all the promises of God find their Yes in
him. That is why it is through him that we
utter our Amen to God for his glory. 21 And
it is God who establishes us with you in
Christ, and has anointed us, 22 and who
has also put his seal on us and given us his
Spirit in our hearts as a guarantee.[5]
23 But I call God to witness against me—
it was to spare you that I refrained from
coming again to Corinth. 24 Not that we
lord it over your faith, but we work with
you for your joy, for you stand firm in
your faith.

[1] Or *For as the sufferings of Christ abound for us, so also our comfort abounds through Christ* [2] Or *brothers and sisters.* The plural Greek word *adelphoi* (translated "brothers") refers to siblings in a family. In New Testament usage, depending on the context, *adelphoi* may refer either to men or to both men and women who are siblings (brothers and sisters) in God's family, the church [3] Some manuscripts *holiness* [4] Or *understand*; twice in this verse; also verse 14 [5] Or *down payment*

2 For I made up my mind not to make another painful visit to you. 2 For if I cause you pain, who is there to make me glad but the one whom I have pained? 3 And I wrote as I did, so that when I came I might not suffer pain from those who should have made me rejoice, for I felt sure of all of you, that my joy would be the joy of you all. 4 For I wrote to you out of much affliction and anguish of heart and with many tears, not to cause you pain but to let you know the abundant love that I have for you.

Forgive the Sinner

5 Now if anyone has caused pain, he has caused it not to me, but in some measure—not to put it too severely—to all of you. 6 For such a one, this punishment by the majority is enough, 7 so you should rather turn to forgive and comfort him, or he may be overwhelmed by excessive sorrow. 8 So I beg you to reaffirm your love for him. 9 For this is why I wrote, that I might test you and know whether you are obedient in everything. 10 Anyone whom you forgive, I also forgive. Indeed, what I have forgiven, if I have forgiven anything, has been for your sake in the presence of Christ, 11 so that we would not be outwitted by Satan; for we are not ignorant of his designs.

Triumph in Christ

12 When I came to Troas to preach the gospel of Christ, even though a door was opened for me in the Lord, 13 my spirit was not at rest because I did not find my brother Titus there. So I took leave of them and went on to Macedonia.

14 But thanks be to God, who in Christ always leads us in triumphal procession, and through us spreads the fragrance of the knowledge of him everywhere. 15 For we are the aroma of Christ to God among those who are being saved and among those who are perishing, 16 to one a fragrance from death to death, to the other a fragrance from life to life. Who is sufficient[1] for these things? 17 For we are not, like so many, peddlers of God's word, but as men of sincerity, as commissioned by God, in the sight of God we speak in Christ.

Ministers of the New Covenant

3 Are we beginning to commend ourselves again? Or do we need, as some do, letters of recommendation to you, or from you? 2 You yourselves are our letter of recommendation, written on our[2] hearts, to be known and read by all. 3 And you show that you are a letter from Christ delivered by us, written not with ink but with the Spirit of the living God, not on tablets of stone but on tablets of human hearts.[3]

4 Such is the confidence that we have through Christ toward God. 5 Not that we are sufficient in ourselves to claim anything as coming from us, but our sufficiency is from God, 6 who has made us competent[4] to be ministers of a new covenant, not of the letter but of the Spirit. For the letter kills, but the Spirit gives life.

7 Now if the ministry of death, carved in letters on stone, came with such glory that the Israelites could not gaze at Moses' face because of its glory, which was being brought to an end, 8 will not the ministry of the Spirit have even more glory? 9 For if there was glory in the ministry of condemnation, the ministry of righteousness must far exceed it in glory. 10 Indeed, in this case, what once had glory has come to have no glory at all, because of the glory that surpasses it. 11 For if what was being brought to an end came with glory, much more will what is permanent have glory.

12 Since we have such a hope, we are very bold, 13 not like Moses, who would put a veil over his face so that the Israelites might not gaze at the outcome of what was being brought to an end. 14 But their minds were hardened. For to this day, when they read the old covenant, that same veil remains unlifted, because only through Christ is it taken away. 15 Yes, to this day whenever Moses is read a veil lies over their hearts. 16 But when one[5] turns to the Lord, the veil

[1] Or *competent* [2] Some manuscripts *your* [3] Greek *fleshly hearts* [4] Or *sufficient* [5] Greek *he*

is removed. 17 Now the Lord[1] is the Spirit,
and where the Spirit of the Lord is, there is
freedom. 18 And we all, with unveiled face,
beholding the glory of the Lord,[2] are being
transformed into the same image from one
degree of glory to another. For this comes
from the Lord who is the Spirit.

The Light of the Gospel

4 Therefore, having this ministry by the
mercy of God,[3] we do not lose heart.
2 But we have renounced disgraceful, un-
derhanded ways. We refuse to practice
cunning or to tamper with God's word, but
by the open statement of the truth we
would commend ourselves to everyone's
conscience in the sight of God. 3 And even
if our gospel is veiled, it is veiled only to
those who are perishing. 4 In their
case the god of this world has
1567 blinded the minds of the unbeliev-
ers, to keep them from seeing the light of
the gospel of the glory of Christ, who is the
image of God. 5 For what we proclaim is
not ourselves, but Jesus Christ as Lord,
with ourselves as your servants[4] for Jesus'
sake. 6 For God, who said, "Let light shine
out of darkness," has shone in our hearts
to give the light of the knowledge of the
glory of God in the face of Jesus Christ.

Treasure in Jars of Clay

7 But we have this treasure in jars of clay,
to show that the surpassing power belongs
to God and not to us. 8 We are afflicted in
every way, but not crushed; perplexed, but
not driven to despair; 9 persecuted, but not
forsaken; struck down, but not destroyed;
10 always carrying in the body the death of
Jesus, so that the life of Jesus may also be
manifested in our bodies. 11 For we who
live are always being given over to death
for Jesus' sake, so that the life of Jesus also
may be manifested in our mortal flesh.
12 So death is at work in us, but life in you.

13 Since we have the same spirit of faith
according to what has been written, "I
believed, and so I spoke," we also believe,
and so we also speak, 14 knowing that he
who raised the Lord Jesus will raise us also
with Jesus and bring us with you into his
presence. 15 For it is all for your sake, so
that as grace extends to more and more
people it may increase thanksgiving, to
the glory of God.

16 So we do not lose heart. Though our
outer self[5] is wasting away, our inner self is
being renewed day by day. 17 For this light
momentary affliction is preparing for us
an eternal weight of glory beyond all com-
parison, 18 as we look not to the things that
are seen but to the things that are unseen.
For the things that are seen are transient,
but the things that are unseen are eternal.

Our Heavenly Dwelling

5 For we know that if the tent that is our
earthly home is destroyed, we have a
building from God, a house not made with
hands, eternal in the heavens. 2 For in this
tent we groan, longing to put on our heav-
enly dwelling, 3 if indeed by putting it on[6]
we may not be found naked. 4 For while we
are still in this tent, we groan, being bur-
dened—not that we would be unclothed,
but that we would be further clothed, so
that what is mortal may be swallowed up
by life. 5 He who has prepared us for this
very thing is God, who has given us the
Spirit as a guarantee.

6 So we are always of good courage. We
know that while we are at home in the
body we are away from the Lord, 7 for we
walk by faith, not by sight. 8 Yes, we are
of good courage, and we would rather be
away from the body and at home with the
Lord. 9 So whether we are at home or away,
we make it our aim to please him. 10 For
we must all appear before the judgment
seat of Christ, so that each one may receive
what is due for what he has done in the
body, whether good or evil.

The Ministry of Reconciliation

11 Therefore, knowing the fear of the
Lord, we persuade others. But what we are

[1] Or *this Lord* [2] Or *reflecting the glory of the Lord* [3] Greek *as we have received mercy* [4] Greek *bondservants* [5] Greek *man* [6] Some manuscripts *putting it off*

is known to God, and I hope it is known also
to your conscience. 12 We are not commend-
ing ourselves to you again but giving you
cause to boast about us, so that you may be
able to answer those who boast about out-
ward appearance and not about what is in
the heart. 13 For if we are beside ourselves,
it is for God; if we are in our right mind, it
is for you. 14 For the love of Christ controls
us, because we have concluded this: that
one has died for all, therefore all have died;
15 and he died for all, that those who live
might no longer live for themselves but for
him who for their sake died and was raised.

16 From now on, therefore, we regard no
one according to the flesh. Even though we
once regarded Christ according to the flesh,
we regard him thus no longer. 17 Therefore,
if anyone is in Christ, he is a new creation.[1]
The old has passed away; behold, the new
has come. 18 All this is from God, who
through Christ reconciled us to himself
and gave us the ministry of reconciliation;
19 that is, in Christ God was reconciling[2] the
world to himself, not counting their tres-
passes against them, and entrusting to us
the message of reconciliation. 20 Therefore,
we are ambassadors for Christ, God making
his appeal through us. We implore you on
behalf of Christ, be reconciled to God. 21 For
our sake he made him to be sin who knew
no sin, so that in him we might become the
righteousness of God.

6 Working together with him, then, we
appeal to you not to receive the grace
of God in vain. 2 For he says,

"In a favorable time I listened to you,
and in a day of salvation I have
helped you."

Behold, now is the favorable time; behold,
now is the day of salvation. 3 We put no
obstacle in anyone's way, so that no fault
may be found with our ministry, 4 but as
servants of God we commend ourselves
in every way: by great endurance, in afflic-
tions, hardships, calamities, 5 beatings, im-
prisonments, riots, labors, sleepless nights,
hunger; 6 by purity, knowledge, patience,
kindness, the Holy Spirit, genuine love;
7 by truthful speech, and the power of God;
with the weapons of righteousness for the
right hand and for the left; 8 through honor
and dishonor, through slander and praise.
We are treated as impostors, and yet are
true; 9 as unknown, and yet well known;
as dying, and behold, we live; as punished,
and yet not killed; 10 as sorrowful, yet al-
ways rejoicing; as poor, yet making many
rich; as having nothing, yet possessing
everything.

11 We have spoken freely to you,[3] Corin-
thians; our heart is wide open. 12 You are
not restricted by us, but you are restricted
in your own affections. 13 In return (I speak
as to children) widen your hearts also.

The Temple of the Living God

14 Do not be unequally yoked with
unbelievers. For what partnership has
righteousness with lawlessness? Or
what fellowship has light with darkness?
15 What accord has Christ with Belial?[4] Or
what portion does a believer share with
an unbeliever? 16 What agreement has the
temple of God with idols? For we are the
temple of the living God; as God said,

"I will make my dwelling among
them and walk among them,
and I will be their God,
and they shall be my people.
17 Therefore go out from their midst,
and be separate from them, says
the Lord,
and touch no unclean thing;
then I will welcome you,
18 and I will be a father to you,
and you shall be sons and
daughters to me,
says the Lord Almighty."

7 Since we have these promises, beloved,
let us cleanse ourselves from every de-
filement of body[5] and spirit, bringing holi-
ness to completion in the fear of God.

[1] Or *creature* [2] Or *God was in Christ, reconciling* [3] Greek *Our mouth is open to you* [4] Greek *Beliar* [5] Greek *flesh*

Paul's Joy

2 Make room in your hearts[1] for us. We have wronged no one, we have corrupted no one, we have taken advantage of no one. 3 I do not say this to condemn you, for I said before that you are in our hearts, to die together and to live together. 4 I am acting with great boldness toward you; I have great pride in you; I am filled with comfort. In all our affliction, I am overflowing with joy.

5 For even when we came into Macedonia, our bodies had no rest, but we were afflicted at every turn—fighting without and fear within. 6 But God, who comforts the downcast, comforted us by the coming of Titus, 7 and not only by his coming but also by the comfort with which he was comforted by you, as he told us of your longing, your mourning, your zeal for me, so that I rejoiced still more. 8 For even if I made you grieve with my letter, I do not regret it—though I did regret it, for I see that that letter grieved you, though only for a while. 9 As it is, I rejoice, not because you were grieved, but because you were grieved into repenting. For you felt a godly grief, so that you suffered no loss through us.

10 For godly grief produces a repentance that leads to salvation without regret, whereas worldly grief produces death. 11 For see what earnestness this godly grief has produced in you, but also what eagerness to clear yourselves, what indignation, what fear, what longing, what zeal, what punishment! At every point you have proved yourselves innocent in the matter. 12 So although I wrote to you, it was not for the sake of the one who did the wrong, nor for the sake of the one who suffered the wrong, but in order that your earnestness for us might be revealed to you in the sight of God. 13 Therefore we are comforted.

And besides our own comfort, we rejoiced still more at the joy of Titus, because his spirit has been refreshed by you all. 14 For whatever boasts I made to him about you, I was not put to shame. But just as everything we said to you was true, so also our boasting before Titus has proved true. 15 And his affection for you is even greater, as he remembers the obedience of you all, how you received him with fear and trembling. 16 I rejoice, because I have perfect confidence in you.

Encouragement to Give Generously

8 We want you to know, brothers,[2] about the grace of God that has been given among the churches of Macedonia, 2 for in a severe test of affliction, their abundance of joy and their extreme poverty have overflowed in a wealth of generosity on their part. 3 For they gave according to their means, as I can testify, and beyond their means, of their own accord, 4 begging us earnestly for the favor[3] of taking part in the relief of the saints— 5 and this, not as we expected, but they gave themselves first to the Lord and then by the will of God to us. 6 Accordingly, we urged Titus that as he had started, so he should complete among you this act of grace. 7 But as you excel in everything—in faith, in speech, in knowledge, in all earnestness, and in our love for you[4]—see that you excel in this act of grace also.

8 I say this not as a command, but to prove by the earnestness of others that your love also is genuine. 9 For you know the grace of our Lord Jesus Christ, that though he was rich, yet for your sake he became poor, so that you by his poverty might become rich. 10 And in this matter I give my judgment: this benefits you, who a year ago started not only to do this work but also to desire to do it. 11 So now finish doing it as well, so that your readiness in desiring it may be matched by your completing it out of what you have. 12 For if the readiness is there, it is acceptable according to what a person has, not according to what he does not

1411

[1] Greek lacks *in your hearts* [2] Or *brothers and sisters* [3] The Greek word *charis* can mean *favor* or *grace* or *thanks*, depending on the context [4] Some manuscripts *in your love for us*

have. **13** For I do not mean that others should be eased and you burdened, but that as a matter of fairness **14** your abundance at the present time should supply their need, so that their abundance may supply your need, that there may be fairness. **15** As it is written, "Whoever gathered much had nothing left over, and whoever gathered little had no lack."

Commendation of Titus

16 But thanks be to God, who put into the heart of Titus the same earnest care I have for you. **17** For he not only accepted our appeal, but being himself very earnest he is going[1] to you of his own accord. **18** With him we are sending[2] the brother who is famous among all the churches for his preaching of the gospel. **19** And not only that, but he has been appointed by the churches to travel with us as we carry out this act of grace that is being ministered by us, for the glory of the Lord himself and to show our good will. **20** We take this course so that no one should blame us about this generous gift that is being administered by us, **21** for we aim at what is honorable not only in the Lord's sight but also in the sight of man. **22** And with them we are sending our brother whom we have often tested and found earnest in many matters, but who is now more earnest than ever because of his great confidence in you. **23** As for Titus, he is my partner and fellow worker for your benefit. And as for our brothers, they are messengers[3] of the churches, the glory of Christ. **24** So give proof before the churches of your love and of our boasting about you to these men.

The Collection for Christians in Jerusalem

9 Now it is superfluous for me to write to you about the ministry for the saints, **2** for I know your readiness, of which I boast about you to the people of Macedonia, saying that Achaia has been ready since last year. And your zeal has stirred up most of them. **3** But I am sending[4] the brothers so that our boasting about you may not prove empty in this matter, so that you may be ready, as I said you would be. **4** Otherwise, if some Macedonians come with me and find that you are not ready, we would be humiliated—to say nothing of you—for being so confident. **5** So I thought it necessary to urge the brothers to go on ahead to you and arrange in advance for the gift[5] you have promised, so that it may be ready as a willing gift, not as an exaction.[6]

The Cheerful Giver

6 The point is this: whoever sows
sparingly will also reap sparingly,
and whoever sows bountifully[7] will
1321, 1411 also reap bountifully. **7** Each one
must give as he has decided in his heart,
not reluctantly or under compulsion, for
God loves a cheerful giver. **8** And
God is able to make all grace
1411 abound to you, so that having all
sufficiency[8] in all things at all times, you
may abound in every good work. **9** As it is
written,

> "He has distributed freely, he has
> given to the poor;
> his righteousness endures forever."

10 He who supplies seed to the sower and bread for food will supply and multiply your seed for sowing and increase the harvest of your righteousness. **11** You will be enriched in every way to be generous in every way, which through us will produce thanksgiving to God. **12** For the ministry of this service is not only supplying the needs of the saints but is also overflowing in many thanksgivings to God. **13** By their approval of this service, they[9] will glorify God because of your submission flowing from your confession of the gospel of Christ, and the generosity of your contribution for them and for all others, **14** while they long for you and pray for

[1] Or *he went* [2] Or *we sent*; also verse 22 [3] Greek *apostles* [4] Or *I have sent* [5] Greek *blessing*; twice in this verse [6] Or *a gift expecting something in return*; Greek *greed* [7] Greek *with blessings*; twice in this verse [8] Or *all contentment* [9] Or *you*

you, because of the surpassing grace of God upon you. 15 Thanks be to God for his inexpressible gift!

Paul Defends His Ministry

10 I, Paul, myself entreat you, by the meekness and gentleness of Christ—I who am humble when face to face with you, but bold toward you when I am away!— 2 I beg of you that when I am present I may not have to show boldness with such confidence as I count on showing against some who suspect us of walking according to the flesh. 3 For though we walk in the flesh, we are not waging war according to the flesh. 4 For the weapons of our warfare are not of the flesh but have divine power to destroy strongholds. 5 We destroy arguments and every lofty opinion raised against the knowledge of God, and take every thought captive to obey Christ, 6 being ready to punish every disobedience, when your obedience is complete.

7 Look at what is before your eyes. If anyone is confident that he is Christ's, let him remind himself that just as he is Christ's, so also are we. 8 For even if I boast a little too much of our authority, which the Lord gave for building you up and not for destroying you, I will not be ashamed. 9 I do not want to appear to be frightening you with my letters. 10 For they say, "His letters are weighty and strong, but his bodily presence is weak, and his speech of no account." 11 Let such a person understand that what we say by letter when absent, we do when present. 12 Not that we dare to classify or compare ourselves with some of those who are commending themselves. But when they measure themselves by one another and compare themselves with one another, they are without understanding.

13 But we will not boast beyond limits, but will boast only with regard to the area of influence God assigned to us, to reach even to you. 14 For we are not overextending ourselves, as though we did not reach you. For we were the first to come all the way to you with the gospel of Christ. 15 We do not boast beyond limit in the labors of others. But our hope is that as your faith increases, our area of influence among you may be greatly enlarged, 16 so that we may preach the gospel in lands beyond you, without boasting of work already done in another's area of influence. 17 "Let the one who boasts, boast in the Lord." 18 For it is not the one who commends himself who is approved, but the one whom the Lord commends.

Paul and the False Apostles

11 I wish you would bear with me in a little foolishness. Do bear with me! 2 For I feel a divine jealousy for you, since I betrothed you to one husband, to present you as a pure virgin to Christ. 3 But I am afraid that as the serpent deceived Eve by his cunning, your thoughts will be led astray from a sincere and pure devotion to Christ. 4 For if someone comes and proclaims another Jesus than the one we proclaimed, or if you receive a different spirit from the one you received, or if you accept a different gospel from the one you accepted, you put up with it readily enough. 5 Indeed, I consider that I am not in the least inferior to these super-apostles. 6 Even if I am unskilled in speaking, I am not so in knowledge; indeed, in every way we have made this plain to you in all things.

7 Or did I commit a sin in humbling myself so that you might be exalted, because I preached God's gospel to you free of charge? 8 I robbed other churches by accepting support from them in order to serve you. 9 And when I was with you and was in need, I did not burden anyone, for the brothers who came from Macedonia supplied my need. So I refrained and will refrain from burdening you in any way. 10 As the truth of Christ is in me, this boasting of mine will not be silenced in the regions of Achaia. 11 And why? Because I do not love you? God knows I do!

12 And what I do I will continue to do,

in order to undermine the claim of those who would like to claim that in their boasted mission they work on the same terms as we do. 13 For such men are false apostles, deceitful workmen, disguising themselves as apostles of Christ. 14 And no wonder, for even Satan disguises himself as an angel of light. 15 So it is no surprise if his servants, also, disguise themselves as servants of righteousness. Their end will correspond to their deeds.

Paul's Sufferings as an Apostle

16 I repeat, let no one think me foolish. But even if you do, accept me as a fool, so that I too may boast a little. 17 What I am saying with this boastful confidence, I say not with the Lord's authority but as a fool. 18 Since many boast according to the flesh, I too will boast. 19 For you gladly bear with fools, being wise yourselves! 20 For you bear it if someone makes slaves of you, or devours you, or takes advantage of you, or puts on airs, or strikes you in the face. 21 To my shame, I must say, we were too weak for that!

But whatever anyone else dares to boast of—I am speaking as a fool—I also dare to boast of that. 22 Are they Hebrews? So am I. Are they Israelites? So am I. Are they offspring of Abraham? So am I. 23 Are they servants of Christ? I am a better one—I am talking like a madman—with far greater labors, far more imprisonments, with countless beatings, and often near death. 24 Five times I received at the hands of the Jews the forty lashes less one. 25 Three times I was beaten with rods. Once I was stoned. Three times I was shipwrecked; a night and a day I was adrift at sea; 26 on frequent journeys, in danger from rivers, danger from robbers, danger from my own people, danger from Gentiles, danger in the city, danger in the wilderness, danger at sea, danger from false brothers; 27 in toil and hardship, through many a sleepless night, in hunger and thirst, often without food,[1] in cold and exposure. 28 And, apart from other things, there is the daily pressure on me of my anxiety for all the churches. 29 Who is weak, and I am not weak? Who is made to fall, and I am not indignant?

1689

30 If I must boast, I will boast of the things that show my weakness. 31 The God and Father of the Lord Jesus, he who is blessed forever, knows that I am not lying. 32 At Damascus, the governor under King Aretas was guarding the city of Damascus in order to seize me, 33 but I was let down in a basket through a window in the wall and escaped his hands.

Paul's Visions and His Thorn

12 I must go on boasting. Though there is nothing to be gained by it, I will go on to visions and revelations of the Lord. 2 I know a man in Christ who fourteen years ago was caught up to the third heaven—whether in the body or out of the body I do not know, God knows. 3 And I know that this man was caught up into paradise—whether in the body or out of the body I do not know, God knows— 4 and he heard things that cannot be told, which man may not utter. 5 On behalf of this man I will boast, but on my own behalf I will not boast, except of my weaknesses. 6 Though if I should wish to boast, I would not be a fool, for I would be speaking the truth. But I refrain from it, so that no one may think more of me than he sees in me or hears from me. 7 So to keep me from becoming conceited because of the surpassing greatness of the revelations,[2] a thorn was given me in the flesh, a messenger of Satan to harass me, to keep me from becoming conceited. 8 Three times I pleaded with the Lord about this, that it should leave me. 9 But he said to me, "My grace is sufficient for you, for my power is made perfect in weakness." Therefore I will boast all the more gladly of my weaknesses, so that the power of Christ may rest upon me. 10 For the sake of Christ, then,

[1] Or *often in fasting* [2] Or *hears from me, even because of the surpassing greatness of the revelations. So to keep me from becoming conceited*

I am content with weaknesses, insults,
hardships, persecutions, and calamities.
For when I am weak, then I am strong.

Concern for the Corinthian Church

11 I have been a fool! You forced me to it,
for I ought to have been commended by
you. For I was not at all inferior to these
super-apostles, even though I am noth-
ing. 12 The signs of a true apostle were per-
formed among you with utmost patience,
with signs and wonders and mighty
works. 13 For in what were you less favored
than the rest of the churches, except that
I myself did not burden you? Forgive me
this wrong!

14 Here for the third time I am ready to
come to you. And I will not be a burden,
for I seek not what is yours but you. For
children are not obligated to save up for
their parents, but parents for their chil-
dren. 15 I will most gladly spend and be
spent for your souls. If I love you more,
am I to be loved less? 16 But granting that
I myself did not burden you, I was crafty,
you say, and got the better of you by de-
ceit. 17 Did I take advantage of you through
any of those whom I sent to you? 18 I urged
Titus to go, and sent the brother with him.
Did Titus take advantage of you? Did we
not act in the same spirit? Did we not take
the same steps?

19 Have you been thinking all along that
we have been defending ourselves to you?
It is in the sight of God that we have been
speaking in Christ, and all for your upbuild-
ing, beloved. 20 For I fear that perhaps when
I come I may find you not as I wish, and
that you may find me not as you wish—
that perhaps there may be quarreling,
jealousy, anger, hostility, slander, gossip,
conceit, and disorder. 21 I fear that when I
come again my God may humble me before
you, and I may have to mourn over many
of those who sinned earlier and have not
repented of the impurity, sexual immoral-
ity, and sensuality that they have practiced.

Final Warnings

13 This is the third time I am com-
ing to you. Every charge must be
established by the evidence of two or three
witnesses. 2 I warned those who sinned
before and all the others, and I warn them
now while absent, as I did when present
on my second visit, that if I come again
I will not spare them— 3 since you seek
proof that Christ is speaking in me. He is
not weak in dealing with you, but is pow-
erful among you. 4 For he was crucified in
weakness, but lives by the power of God.
For we also are weak in him, but in deal-
ing with you we will live with him by the
power of God.

5 Examine yourselves, to see whether
you are in the faith. Test yourselves. Or
do you not realize this about yourselves,
that Jesus Christ is in you?—unless in-
deed you fail to meet the test! 6 I hope you
will find out that we have not failed the
test. 7 But we pray to God that you may
not do wrong—not that we may appear
to have met the test, but that you may
do what is right, though we may seem to
have failed. 8 For we cannot do anything
against the truth, but only for the truth.
9 For we are glad when we are weak and
you are strong. Your restoration is what
we pray for. 10 For this reason I write these
things while I am away from you, that
when I come I may not have to be severe
in my use of the authority that the Lord
has given me for building up and not for
tearing down.

Final Greetings

11 Finally, brothers,[1] rejoice. Aim for
restoration, comfort one another,[2] agree
with one another, live in peace; and the
God of love and peace will be with you.
12 Greet one another with a holy kiss. 13 All
the saints greet you.

14 The grace of the Lord Jesus Christ and
the love of God and the fellowship of the
Holy Spirit be with you all.

[1] *Or brothers and sisters* [2] *Or listen to my appeal*

Introduction to

Galatians

Author
Paul the apostle

Date
About A.D. 48–51

Key People
Paul; Cephas (Peter); James, the Lord's brother; false teachers

Purpose
The purpose of Galatians is to show that people are justified (counted righteous by God) through faith alone, and not by faith plus obedience, as some false teachers were saying.

Central Themes
Paul's authority as an apostle was given to him by God; we receive salvation by faith, not by a mixture of faith plus works of the law; to count on works of the law for salvation contradicts grace; Christ's death has begun the new age that was longed for in the Old Testament; the Holy Spirit enables believers to bear the fruit of godliness.

Memory Verses
Only one gospel (Galatians 1:6–9); justification through faith, not works (Galatians 2:16); life in Christ (Galatians 2:19–20); the law and the gospel promise (Galatians 3:23–29); freedom (Galatians 5:1, 13–14); fruit of the Spirit (Galatians 5:16–24); boasting in the cross (Galatians 6:14)

Introduction

Paul had brought the gospel to the Galatians who had eagerly accepted it. Now false teachers had come, questioning Paul's authority and teaching and saying Paul's gospel wasn't enough. They taught that the Galatians must also obey Jewish laws. The Galatians eagerly accepted this teaching, too! Paul rebukes the Galatians for listening to these false teachers. Paul tells them there is no other gospel (Galatians 1:6–9). He describes how God had called him to be an apostle and had revealed the gospel to him. He shows how it was the same gospel all the apostles preached (Galatians 1:11–2:10). Paul insists that justification—being counted righteous by God—comes only through faith in Jesus and what He did on the cross. If the Galatians trust in how well they keep Jewish laws, they will only make their situation before God worse (Galatians 2:11–5:12). Paul urges the Galatians to resist the false teachers, guarding their freedom in Christ and using it to serve others (Galatians 5:13–15). If believers will be led by the Holy Spirit, Paul writes, they will produce fruit that honors God and will live with love for each other (Galatians 5:16–6:10). Paul ends by saying that we should boast only in the cross of Christ (Galatians 6:11–18).

About A.D. 33/34	About A.D. 48/49–51	About A.D. 64–67
Conversion of Paul	Paul visits, writes to Galatians	Paul martyred in Rome

The Letter of Paul to the

Galatians

Greeting

1 Paul, an apostle—not from men nor through man, but through Jesus Christ and God the Father, who raised him from the dead— 2 and all the brothers[1] who are with me,

To the churches of Galatia:

3 Grace to you and peace from God our Father and the Lord Jesus Christ, 4 who gave himself for our sins to deliver us from the present evil age, according to the will of our God and Father, 5 to whom be the glory forever and ever. Amen.

No Other Gospel

6 I am astonished that you are so quickly deserting him who called you in the grace of Christ and are turning to a different gospel— 7 not that there is another one, but there are some who trouble you and want to distort the gospel of Christ. 8 But even if we or an angel from heaven should preach to you a gospel contrary to the one we preached to you, let him be accursed. 9 As we have said before, so now I say again: If anyone is preaching to you a gospel contrary to the one you received, let him be accursed.

10 For am I now seeking the approval of man, or of God? Or am I trying to please man? If I were still trying to please man, I would not be a servant[2] of Christ.

Paul Called by God

11 For I would have you know, brothers, that the gospel that was preached by me is not man's gospel.[3] 12 For I did not receive it from any man, nor was I taught it, but I received it through a revelation of Jesus Christ. 13 For you have heard of my former life in Judaism, how I persecuted the church of God violently and tried to destroy it. 14 And I was advancing in Judaism beyond many of my own age among my people, so extremely zealous was I for the traditions of my fathers. 15 But when he who had set me apart before I was born,[4] and who called

1669

me by his grace, 16 was pleased to reveal his Son to[5] me, in order that I might preach him among the Gentiles, I did not immediately consult with anyone;[6] 17 nor did I go up to Jerusalem to those who were apostles before me, but I went away into Arabia, and returned again to Damascus.

18 Then after three years I went up to Jerusalem to visit Cephas and remained with him fifteen days. 19 But I saw none of the other apostles except James the Lord's brother. 20 (In what I am writing to you, before God, I do not lie!) 21 Then I went into the regions of Syria and Cilicia. 22 And I was still unknown in person to the churches of Judea that are in Christ. 23 They only were hearing it said, "He who used to persecute us is now preaching the faith he once tried to destroy." 24 And they glorified God because of me.

Paul Accepted by the Apostles

2 Then after fourteen years I went up again to Jerusalem with Barnabas, taking Titus along with me. 2 I went up because of a revelation and set before them (though privately before those who seemed influential) the gospel that I proclaim among the Gentiles, in order to make sure I was not running or had not run in vain. 3 But even Titus, who was with me, was not forced to be circumcised, though he was a Greek. 4 Yet because of false brothers secretly brought in—who slipped in

[1] Or *brothers and sisters*. The plural Greek word *adelphoi* (translated "brothers") refers to siblings in a family. In New Testament usage, depending on the context, *adelphoi* may refer either to men or to both men and women who are siblings (brothers and sisters) in God's family, the church; also verse 11 [2] Or *slave*; Greek *bondservant* [3] Greek *not according to man* [4] Greek *set me apart from my mother's womb* [5] Greek *in* [6] Greek *with flesh and blood*

to spy out our freedom that we have in Christ Jesus, so that they might bring us into slavery— 5 to them we did not yield in submission even for a moment, so that the truth of the gospel might be preserved for you. 6 And from those who seemed to be influential (what they were makes no difference to me; God shows no partiality)—those, I say, who seemed influential added nothing to me. 7 On the contrary, when they saw that I had been entrusted with the gospel to the uncircumcised, just as Peter had been entrusted with the gospel to the circumcised 8 (for he who worked through Peter for his apostolic ministry to the circumcised worked also through me for mine to the Gentiles), 9 and when James and Cephas and John, who seemed to be pillars, perceived the grace that was given to me, they gave the right hand of fellowship to Barnabas and me, that we should go to the Gentiles and they to the circumcised. 10 Only, they asked us to remember the poor, the very thing I was eager to do.

Paul Opposes Peter

11 But when Cephas came to Antioch, I opposed him to his face, because he stood condemned. 12 For before certain men came from James, he was eating with the Gentiles; but when they came he drew back and separated himself, fearing the circumcision party. 13 And the rest of the Jews acted hypocritically along with him, so that even Barnabas was led astray by their hypocrisy. 14 But when I saw that their conduct was not in step with the truth of the gospel, I said to Cephas before them all, "If you, though a Jew, live like a Gentile and not like a Jew, how can you force the Gentiles to live like Jews?"

Justified by Faith

15 We ourselves are Jews by birth
and not Gentile sinners; 16 yet we
1663 know that a person is not justified[1] by works of the law but through faith in Jesus Christ, so we also have believed in Christ Jesus, in order to be justified by faith in Christ and not by works of the law, because by works of the law no one will be justified.

17 But if, in our endeavor to be justified in Christ, we too were found to be sinners, is Christ then a servant of sin? Certainly not! 18 For if I rebuild what I tore down, I prove myself to be a transgressor. 19 For through the law I died to the law, so that I might live to God. 20 I have been crucified with Christ. It is no longer I who live, but Christ who lives in me. And the life I now live in the flesh I live by faith in the Son of God, who loved me and gave himself for me. 21 I do not nullify the grace of God, for if righteousness[2] were through the law, then Christ died for no purpose.

By Faith, or by Works of the Law?

3 O foolish Galatians! Who has bewitched you? It was before your eyes that Jesus Christ was publicly portrayed as crucified. 2 Let me ask you only this: Did you receive the Spirit by works of the law or by hearing with faith? 3 Are you so foolish? Having begun by the Spirit, are you now being perfected by[3] the flesh? 4 Did you suffer[4] so many things in vain—if indeed it was in vain? 5 Does he who supplies the Spirit to you and works miracles among you do so by works of the law, or by hearing with faith— 6 just as Abraham "believed God, and it was counted to him as righteousness"?

7 Know then that it is those of faith
who are the sons of Abraham.
33 8 And the Scripture, foreseeing that
God would justify[5] the Gentiles by
faith, preached the gospel before-
33 hand to Abraham, saying, "In you shall all the nations be blessed." 9 So then, those who are of faith are blessed along with Abraham, the man of faith.

The Righteous Shall Live by Faith

10 For all who rely on works of the law are under a curse; for it is written, "Cursed

[1] Or *counted righteous* (three times in verse 16); also verse 17 [2] Or *justification* [3] Or *now ending with* [4] Or *experience* [5] Or *count righteous*; also verses 11, 24

be everyone who does not abide by all things written in the Book of the Law, and do them." 11 Now it is evident that no one is justified before God by the law, for "The righteous shall live by faith."[1] 12 But the law is not of faith, rather "The one who does them shall live by them." 13 Christ redeemed us from the curse of the law by becoming a curse for us—for it is written, "Cursed is everyone who is hanged on a tree"— 14 so that in Christ Jesus the blessing of Abraham might come to the Gentiles, so that we might receive the promised Spirit[2] through faith.

The Law and the Promise

15 To give a human example, brothers:[3] even with a man-made covenant, no one annuls it or adds to it once it has been ratified. 16 Now the promises were made to Abraham and to his offspring. It does not say, "And to offsprings," referring to many, but referring to one, "And to your offspring," who is Christ. 17 This is what I mean: the law, which came 430 years afterward, does not annul a covenant previously ratified by God, so as to make the promise void. 18 For if the inheritance comes by the law, it no longer comes by promise; but God gave it to Abraham by a promise.

19 Why then the law? It was added because of transgressions, until the offspring should come to whom the promise had been made, and it was put in place through angels by an intermediary. 20 Now an intermediary implies more than one, but God is one.

21 Is the law then contrary to the promises of God? Certainly not! For if a law had been given that could give life, then righteousness would indeed be by the law. 22 But the Scripture imprisoned everything under sin, so that the promise by faith in Jesus Christ might be given to those who believe.

23 Now before faith came, we were held captive under the law, imprisoned until the coming faith would be revealed. 24 So then, the law was our guardian until Christ came, in order that we might be justified by faith. 25 But now that faith has come, we are no longer under a guardian, 26 for in Christ Jesus you are all sons of God, through faith. 27 For as many of you as were baptized into Christ have put on Christ. 28 There is neither Jew nor Greek, there is neither slave[4] nor free, there is no male and female, for you are all one in Christ Jesus. 29 And if you are Christ's, then you are Abraham's offspring, heirs according to promise.

Sons and Heirs

4 I mean that the heir, as long as he is a child, is no different from a slave,[5] though he is the owner of everything, 2 but he is under guardians and managers until the date set by his father. 3 In the same way we also, when we were children, were enslaved to the elementary principles[6] of the world. 4 But when the fullness of time had come, God sent forth his Son, born of woman, born under the law, 5 to redeem those who were under the law, so that we might receive adoption as sons. 6 And because you are sons, God has sent the Spirit of his Son into our hearts, crying, "Abba! Father!" 7 So you are no longer a slave, but a son, and if a son, then an heir through God.

Paul's Concern for the Galatians

8 Formerly, when you did not know God, you were enslaved to those that by nature are not gods. 9 But now that you have come to know God, or rather to be known by God, how can you turn back again to the weak and worthless elementary principles of the world, whose slaves you want to be once more? 10 You observe days and months and seasons and years! 11 I am afraid I may have labored over you in vain.

12 Brothers,[7] I entreat you, become as

[1] Or *The one who by faith is righteous will live* [2] Greek *receive the promise of the Spirit* [3] Or *brothers and sisters* [4] Greek *bondservant* [5] Greek *bondservant*; also verse 7 [6] Or *elemental spirits*; also verse 9 [7] Or *Brothers and sisters*; also verses 28, 31

I am, for I also have become as you are. You did me no wrong. 13 You know it was because of a bodily ailment that I preached the gospel to you at first, 14 and though my condition was a trial to you, you did not scorn or despise me, but received me as an angel of God, as Christ Jesus. 15 What then has become of the blessing you felt? For I testify to you that, if possible, you would have gouged out your eyes and given them to me. 16 Have I then become your enemy by telling you the truth?[1] 17 They make much of you, but for no good purpose. They want to shut you out, that you may make much of them. 18 It is always good to be made much of for a good purpose, and not only when I am present with you, 19 my little children, for whom I am again in the anguish of childbirth until Christ is formed in you! 20 I wish I could be present with you now and change my tone, for I am perplexed about you.

Example of Hagar and Sarah

21 Tell me, you who desire to be
under the law, do you not listen to
53 the law? 22 For it is written that
Abraham had two sons, one by a slave woman and one by a free woman. 23 But the son of the slave was born according to the flesh, while the son of the free woman was born through promise. 24 Now this may be interpreted allegorically: these women are two covenants. One is from Mount Sinai, bearing children for slavery; she is Hagar. 25 Now Hagar is Mount Sinai in Arabia;[2] she corresponds to the present Jerusalem, for she is in slavery with her children. 26 But the Jerusalem above is free, and she is our mother. 27 For it is written,

"Rejoice, O barren one who does not
bear;
break forth and cry aloud, you
who are not in labor!
For the children of the desolate one
will be more
than those of the one who has a
husband."

28 Now you,[3] brothers, like Isaac, are children of promise. 29 But just as at that time he who was born according to the flesh persecuted him who was born according to the Spirit, so also it is now. 30 But what does the Scripture say? "Cast out the slave woman and her son, for the son of the slave woman shall not inherit with the son of the free woman." 31 So, brothers, we are not children of the slave but of the free woman.

Christ Has Set Us Free

5 For freedom Christ has set us free; stand firm therefore, and do not submit again to a yoke of slavery.

2 Look: I, Paul, say to you that if you accept circumcision, Christ will be of no advantage to you. 3 I testify again to every man who accepts circumcision that he is obligated to keep the whole law. 4 You are severed from Christ, you who would be justified[4] by the law; you have fallen away from grace. 5 For through the Spirit, by faith, we ourselves eagerly wait for the hope of righteousness. 6 For in Christ Jesus neither circumcision nor uncircumcision counts for anything, but only faith working through love.

7 You were running well. Who hindered you from obeying the truth? 8 This persuasion is not from him who calls you. 9 A little leaven leavens the whole lump. 10 I have confidence in the Lord that you will take no other view than mine, and the one who is troubling you will bear the penalty, whoever he is. 11 But if I, brothers,[5] still preach[6] circumcision, why am I still being persecuted? In that case the offense of the cross has been removed. 12 I wish those who unsettle you would emasculate themselves!

[1] Or *by dealing truthfully with you* [2] Some manuscripts *For Sinai is a mountain in Arabia* [3] Some manuscripts *we* [4] Or *counted righteous* [5] Or *brothers and sisters*; also verse 13 [6] Greek *proclaim*

13 For you were called to freedom, broth-
ers. Only do not use your freedom as an
opportunity for the flesh, but through love
serve one another. **14** For the whole law is
fulfilled in one word: "You shall love your
neighbor as yourself." **15** But if you bite and
devour one another, watch out that you
are not consumed by one another.

Walk by the Spirit

16 But I say, walk by the Spirit, and you
will not gratify the desires of the flesh.
17 For the desires of the flesh are against
the Spirit, and the desires of the Spirit are
against the flesh, for these are opposed
to each other, to keep you from doing the
things you want to do. **18** But if you are led
by the Spirit, you are not under the law.
19 Now the works of the flesh are evident:
sexual immorality, impurity, sensuality,
20 idolatry, sorcery, enmity, strife, jealousy,
fits of anger, rivalries, dissensions, divi-
sions, **21** envy,[1] drunkenness, orgies, and
things like these. I warn you, as I warned
you before, that those who do such things
will not inherit the kingdom of God. **22** But
the fruit of the Spirit is love, joy, peace,
patience, kindness, goodness, faithful-
ness, **23** gentleness, self-control; against
such things there is no law. **24** And those
who belong to Christ Jesus have crucified
the flesh with its passions and desires.

25 If we live by the Spirit, let us also walk
by the Spirit. **26** Let us not become con-
ceited, provoking one another, envying
one another.

Bear One Another's Burdens

6 Brothers,[2] if anyone is caught in any
transgression, you who are spiritual
should restore him in a spirit of gentle-
ness. Keep watch on yourself, lest you too
be tempted. **2** Bear one another's burdens,
and so fulfill the law of Christ. **3** For if any-
one thinks he is something, when he is
nothing, he deceives himself. **4** But let
each one test his own work, and then his
reason to boast will be in himself alone
and not in his neighbor. **5** For each will
have to bear his own load.

6 One who is taught the word must
share all good things with the one who
teaches. **7** Do not be deceived: God is not
mocked, for whatever one sows, that will
he also reap. **8** For the one who sows to his
own flesh will from the flesh reap corrup-
tion, but the one who sows to the Spirit
will from the Spirit reap eternal life. **9** And
let us not grow weary of doing good, for in
due season we will reap, if we do not give
up. **10** So then, as we have opportunity, let
us do good to everyone, and especially to
those who are of the household of faith.

Final Warning and Benediction

11 See with what large letters I am writ-
ing to you with my own hand. **12** It is those
who want to make a good showing in the
flesh who would force you to be circum-
cised, and only in order that they may not
be persecuted for the cross of Christ. **13** For
even those who are circumcised do not
themselves keep the law, but they desire
to have you circumcised that they may
boast in your flesh. **14** But far be it from
me to boast except in the cross of our Lord
Jesus Christ, by which[3] the world has been
crucified to me, and I to the world. **15** For
neither circumcision counts for anything,
nor uncircumcision, but a new creation.
16 And as for all who walk by this rule,
peace and mercy be upon them, and upon
the Israel of God.

17 From now on let no one cause me
trouble, for I bear on my body the marks
of Jesus.

18 The grace of our Lord Jesus Christ be
with your spirit, brothers. Amen.

[1] Some manuscripts add *murder* [2] Or *Brothers and sisters*; also verse 18 [3] Or *through whom*

Introduction to

Ephesians

Author
Paul the apostle

Date
About A.D. 62

Purpose
The purpose of Ephesians is to show the great salvation that the Father, Son, and Holy Spirit have accomplished for the church and how its members are free to live as a result.

Central Themes
All people are spiritually dead; God predestined His people to spiritual life; salvation is through Jesus' life and death on the cross; salvation is a free gift of God's grace; all who believe are united in one body, the Church; members of this body are to love and serve each other and live lives of holiness and obedience to God.

Memory Verses
Election in Christ (Ephesians 1:3–10); saved by grace (Ephesians 2:8–10); unity through service (Ephesians 4:11–16); Bridegroom and Bride (Ephesians 5:22–33)

Introduction

Paul begins this letter by praising God the Father, God the Son, and God the Holy Spirit for what each has done in our salvation (Ephesians 1). Paul describes our desperate need, and then tells how God saves sinners by grace because of His mercy, not because of anything they have done (Ephesians 2:1–10). God joins saved sinners who are Jews and saved sinners who are Gentiles into one body, the Church. He then gives them all spiritual blessings to show His wisdom, mercy, and glory (Ephesians 2:11–3:21). Then Paul describes the response Christians should have to all this wonderful goodness of God toward them. Paul says Christians should serve each other, helping each other grow in Christ. They should not live the sinful lives they used to live, but should imitate the Lord Jesus, especially in loving and forgiving each other (Ephesians 4:1–5:21). Paul tells how Christians should act toward members of their families and how masters and slaves should treat each other (Ephesians 5:22–6:9). He describes the "armor" Christians have for defending themselves against Satan's attacks. He urges them to resist temptation by using this armor and praying diligently (Ephesians 6:10–24).

About A.D. 33/34	About A.D. 52–57	About A.D. 62
Conversion of Paul	Paul's third missionary journey	Paul arrested, writes Ephesians

The Letter of Paul to the

Ephesians

Greeting

1 Paul, an apostle of Christ Jesus by the
will of God,
To the saints who are in Ephesus, and
are faithful[1] in Christ Jesus:
2 Grace to you and peace from God our
Father and the Lord Jesus Christ.

Spiritual Blessings in Christ

3 Blessed be the God and Father of our
Lord Jesus Christ, who has blessed us in
Christ with every spiritual blessing in the
heavenly places, **4** even as he chose us in
him before the foundation of the world,
that we should be holy and blameless
before him. In love **5** he predestined us[2]
for adoption as sons through Jesus Christ,
according to the purpose of his will, **6** to
the praise of his glorious grace, with
which he has blessed us in the Beloved.
7 In him we have redemption through his
blood, the forgiveness of our trespasses,
according to the riches of his grace,
8 which he lavished upon us, in all wis-
dom and insight **9** making known[3] to us
the mystery of his will, according to his
purpose, which he set forth in Christ **10** as
a plan for the fullness of time, to unite all
things in him, things in heaven and things
on earth.
11 In him we have obtained an
inheritance, having been predes-
747 tined according to the purpose of
him who works all things according to
the counsel of his will, **12** so that we who
were the first to hope in Christ might be
to the praise of his glory. **13** In him you
also, when you heard the word of truth,
the gospel of your salvation, and believed
in him, were sealed with the promised
Holy Spirit, **14** who is the guarantee[4] of
our inheritance until we acquire posses-
sion of it,[5] to the praise of his glory.

Thanksgiving and Prayer

15 For this reason, because I have heard
of your faith in the Lord Jesus and your
love[6] toward all the saints, **16** I do not cease
to give thanks for you, remembering you
in my prayers, **17** that the God of our Lord
Jesus Christ, the Father of glory, may give
you a spirit of wisdom and of revelation in
the knowledge of him, **18** having the eyes of
your hearts enlightened, that you may
know what is the hope to which he has
called you, what are the riches of his glori-
ous inheritance in the saints, **19** and what
is the immeasurable greatness of
his power toward us who believe,
1611 according to the working of his
great might **20** that he worked in Christ
when he raised him from the dead and
seated him at his right hand in the
heavenly places, **21** far above all rule
1611 and authority and power and
dominion, and above every name that is
named, not only in this age but also in the
one to come. **22** And he put all things under
his feet and gave him as head over all
things to the church, **23** which is his body,
the fullness of him who fills all in all.

By Grace Through Faith

2 And you were dead in the trespasses
and sins **2** in which you once walked,
following the course of this world, follow-
ing the prince of the power of the air, the
spirit that is now at work in the sons of
disobedience— **3** among whom we all
once lived in the passions of our flesh,
carrying out the desires of the body[7] and
the mind, and were by nature children of

[1] Some manuscripts *saints who are also faithful* (omitting *in Ephesus*) [2] Or *before him in love, having predestined us* [3] Or *he lavished upon us in all wisdom and insight, making known . . .* [4] Or *down payment* [5] Or *until God redeems his possession* [6] Some manuscripts omit *your love* [7] Greek *flesh*

wrath, like the rest of mankind. 4 But[1]
God, being rich in mercy, because
of the great love with which he
75 loved us, 5 even when we were
dead in our trespasses, made us alive
together with Christ—by grace you have
been saved— 6 and raised us up with him
and seated us with him in the heavenly
places in Christ Jesus, 7 so that in the com-
ing ages he might show the immeasurable
riches of his grace in kindness toward us
in Christ Jesus. 8 For by grace you have
been saved through faith. And this is not
your own doing; it is the gift of God, 9 not
a result of works, so that no one may
boast. 10 For we are his workmanship, cre-
ated in Christ Jesus for good works, which
God prepared beforehand, that we should
walk in them.

One in Christ

11 Therefore remember that at one
time you Gentiles in the flesh,
1645 called "the uncircumcision" by
what is called the circumcision, which is
made in the flesh by hands— 12 remember
that you were at that time separated from
Christ, alienated from the commonwealth
of Israel and strangers to the covenants of
promise, having no hope and without God
in the world. 13 But now in Christ
Jesus you who once were far off
1421 have been brought near by the
blood of Christ. 14 For he himself is our
peace, who has made us both one and has
broken down in his flesh the dividing wall
of hostility 15 by abolishing the law of
commandments expressed in ordinances,
that he might create in himself one new
man in place of the two, so making peace,
16 and might reconcile us both to God in
one body through the cross, thereby kill-
ing the hostility. 17 And he came and
preached peace to you who were far off
and peace to those who were near. 18 For
through him we both have access in one
Spirit to the Father. 19 So then you are no
longer strangers and aliens,[2] but you are
fellow citizens with the saints and mem-
bers of the household of God, 20 built on
the foundation of the apostles and proph-
ets, Christ Jesus himself being the corner-
stone, 21 in whom the whole structure,
being joined together, grows into a holy
temple in the Lord. 22 In him you also are
being built together into a dwelling place
for God by[3] the Spirit.

The Mystery of the Gospel Revealed

3 For this reason I, Paul, a prisoner
for Christ Jesus on behalf of you
Gentiles— 2 assuming that you have heard
of the stewardship of God's grace that was
given to me for you, 3 how the mystery
was made known to me by revelation,
as I have written briefly. 4 When you read
this, you can perceive my insight into the
mystery of Christ, 5 which was not made
known to the sons of men in other gen-
erations as it has now been revealed to his
holy apostles and prophets by the Spirit.
6 This mystery is[4] that the Gentiles are fel-
low heirs, members of the same body, and
partakers of the promise in Christ Jesus
through the gospel.

7 Of this gospel I was made a minister
according to the gift of God's grace, which
was given me by the working of his power.
8 To me, though I am the very least of all
the saints, this grace was given, to preach
to the Gentiles the unsearchable riches of
Christ, 9 and to bring to light for everyone
what is the plan of the mystery hidden for
ages in[5] God who created all things, 10 so
that through the church the manifold wis-
dom of God might now be made known to
the rulers and authorities in the heavenly
places. 11 This was according to the eter-
nal purpose that he has realized in Christ
Jesus our Lord, 12 in whom we have bold-
ness and access with confidence through
our faith in him. 13 So I ask you not to lose
heart over what I am suffering for you,
which is your glory.

[1] Or *And* [2] Or *sojourners* [3] Or *in* [4] The words *This mystery is* are inferred from verse 4 [5] Or *by*

Prayer for Spiritual Strength

14 For this reason I bow my knees before
the Father, 15 from whom every family[1]
in heaven and on earth is named, 16 that
according to the riches of his glory he may
grant you to be strengthened with power
through his Spirit in your inner being,
17 so that Christ may dwell in your hearts
through faith—that you, being rooted and
grounded in love, 18 may have strength to
comprehend with all the saints what is
the breadth and length and height and
depth, 19 and to know the love of Christ
that surpasses knowledge, that you may
be filled with all the fullness of God.

20 Now to him who is able to do far more
abundantly than all that we ask or think,
according to the power at work within
us, 21 to him be glory in the church and in
Christ Jesus throughout all generations,
forever and ever. Amen.

Unity in the Body of Christ

4 I therefore, a prisoner for the Lord,
urge you to walk in a manner wor-
thy of the calling to which you have been
called, 2 with all humility and gentleness,
with patience, bearing with one another
in love, 3 eager to maintain the unity of
the Spirit in the bond of peace. 4 There is
one body and one Spirit—just as you were
called to the one hope that belongs to your
call— 5 one Lord, one faith, one baptism,
6 one God and Father of all, who is over all
and through all and in all. 7 But grace was
given to each one of us according to the
measure of Christ's gift. 8 Therefore it says,

> "When he ascended on high he led a
> host of captives,
> and he gave gifts to men."

9 (In saying, "He ascended," what does it
mean but that he had also descended into
the lower regions, the earth?[2] 10 He who
descended is the one who also ascended
far above all the heavens, that he might fill
all things.) 11 And he gave the apostles, the
prophets, the evangelists, the shepherds[3]
and teachers,[4] 12 to equip the saints for
the work of ministry, for building up the
body of Christ, 13 until we all attain to the
unity of the faith and of the knowledge of
the Son of God, to mature manhood,[5] to
the measure of the stature of the fullness
of Christ, 14 so that we may no longer be
children, tossed to and fro by the waves
and carried about by every wind of doc-
trine, by human cunning, by craftiness in
deceitful schemes. 15 Rather, speaking the
truth in love, we are to grow up in every
way into him who is the head, into Christ,
16 from whom the whole body, joined and
held together by every joint with which it
is equipped, when each part is working
properly, makes the body grow so that it
builds itself up in love.

The New Life

17 Now this I say and testify in the Lord,
that you must no longer walk as the
Gentiles do, in the futility of their minds.
18 They are darkened in their understand-
ing, alienated from the life of God because
of the ignorance that is in them, due to
their hardness of heart. 19 They have
become callous and have given them-
selves up to sensuality, greedy to practice
every kind of impurity. 20 But that is not
the way you learned Christ!— 21 assuming
that you have heard about him and were
taught in him, as the truth is in Jesus,
22 to put off your old self,[6] which belongs
to your former manner of life and is cor-
rupt through deceitful desires, 23 and to
be renewed in the spirit of your minds,
24 and to put on the new self, created after
the likeness of God in true righteousness
and holiness.

25 Therefore, having put away falsehood,
let each one of you speak the truth with
his neighbor, for we are members one of
another. 26 Be angry and do not sin; do not
let the sun go down on your anger, 27 and
give no opportunity to the devil. 28 Let the

[1] Or *fatherhood*; the Greek word *patria* is closely related to the word for *Father* in verse 14 [2] Or *the lower parts of the earth?* [3] Or *pastors* [4] Or *the shepherd-teachers*
[5] Greek *to a full-grown man* [6] Greek *man*; also verse 24

thief no longer steal, but rather let him
labor, doing honest work with his own
hands, so that he may have something to
share with anyone in need. 29 Let no cor-
rupting talk come out of your mouths, but
only such as is good for building up, as fits
the occasion, that it may give grace to
those who hear. 30 And do not grieve the
Holy Spirit of God, by whom you were
sealed for the day of redemption. 31 Let all
bitterness and wrath and anger and
clamor and slander be put away from you,
along with all malice. 32 Be kind to
one another, tenderhearted, for-
1783 giving one another, as God in
Christ forgave you.

Walk in Love

5 Therefore be imitators of God, as
beloved children. 2 And walk in love,
as Christ loved us and gave himself up for
us, a fragrant offering and sacrifice to God.
3 But sexual immorality and all impurity
or covetousness must not even be named
among you, as is proper among saints.
4 Let there be no filthiness nor foolish talk
nor crude joking, which are out of place,
but instead let there be thanksgiving.
5 For you may be sure of this, that every-
one who is sexually immoral or impure,
or who is covetous (that is, an idolater),
has no inheritance in the kingdom of
Christ and God. 6 Let no one deceive you
with empty words, for because of these
things the wrath of God comes upon the
sons of disobedience. 7 Therefore do not
become partners with them; 8 for at one
time you were darkness, but now you are
light in the Lord. Walk as children of light
9 (for the fruit of light is found in all that is
good and right and true), 10 and try to dis-
cern what is pleasing to the Lord. 11 Take
no part in the unfruitful works of dark-
ness, but instead expose them. 12 For it is
shameful even to speak of the things that
they do in secret. 13 But when anything is
exposed by the light, it becomes visible,
14 for anything that becomes visible is
light. Therefore it says,

"Awake, O sleeper,
and arise from the dead,
and Christ will shine on you."

15 Look carefully then how you walk,
not as unwise but as wise, 16 making the
best use of the time, because the days are
evil. 17 Therefore do not be foolish, but
understand what the will of the Lord is.
18 And do not get drunk with wine, for
that is debauchery, but be filled with the
Spirit, 19 addressing one another in psalms
and hymns and spiritual songs, singing
and making melody to the Lord with your
heart, 20 giving thanks always and for
everything to God the Father in the name
of our Lord Jesus Christ, 21 submitting to
one another out of reverence for Christ.

Wives and Husbands

22 Wives, submit to your own husbands,
as to the Lord. 23 For the husband is the
head of the wife even as Christ is the head
of the church, his body, and is himself its
Savior. 24 Now as the church submits to
Christ, so also wives should submit in
everything to their husbands.
25 Husbands, love your wives, as Christ
loved the church and gave himself up for
her, 26 that he might sanctify her, having
cleansed her by the washing of water with
the word, 27 so that he might present the
church to himself in splendor, without
spot or wrinkle or any such thing, that
she might be holy and without blemish.[1]
28 In the same way husbands should love
their wives as their own bodies. He who
loves his wife loves himself. 29 For no one
ever hated his own flesh, but nourishes
and cherishes it, just as Christ does the
church, 30 because we are members of his
body. 31 "Therefore a man shall leave
his father and mother and hold fast to
his wife, and the two shall become one
flesh." 32 This mystery is profound, and

[1] Or *holy and blameless*

I am saying that it refers to Christ and the church. 33 However, let each one of you love his wife as himself, and let the wife see that she respects her husband.

Children and Parents

6 Children, obey your parents in
the Lord, for this is right.
1453 2 "Honor your father and mother"
(this is the first commandment with a promise), 3 "that it may go well with you and that you may live long in the land." 4 Fathers, do not provoke your children to anger, but bring them up in the discipline and instruction of the Lord.

Slaves and Masters

5 Slaves,[1] obey your earthly masters[2]
with fear and trembling, with a sin-
1783 cere heart, as you would Christ,
6 not by the way of eye-service, as people-pleasers, but as servants[3] of Christ, doing the will of God from the heart, 7 rendering service with a good will as to the Lord and not to man, 8 knowing that whatever good anyone does, this he will receive back from the Lord, whether he is a slave or free. 9 Masters, do the same to them, and stop your threatening, knowing that he who is both their Master[4] and yours is in heaven, and that there is no partiality with him.

The Whole Armor of God

10 Finally, be strong in the Lord and in the strength of his might. 11 Put on the whole armor of God, that you may be able to stand against the schemes of the devil. 12 For we do not wrestle against flesh and blood, but against the rulers, against the authorities, against the cosmic powers over this present darkness, against the spiritual forces of evil in the heavenly places. 13 Therefore take up the whole armor of God, that you may be able to withstand in the evil day, and having done all, to stand firm. 14 Stand therefore, having fastened on the belt of truth, and having put on the breastplate of righteousness, 15 and, as shoes for your feet, having put on the readiness given by the gospel of peace. 16 In all circumstances take up the shield of faith, with which you can extinguish all the flaming darts of the evil one; 17 and take the helmet of salvation, and the sword of the Spirit, which is the
word of God, 18 praying at all times in the
Spirit, with all prayer and supplica-
tion. To that end keep alert with all
1651 perseverance, making supplication
for all the saints, 19 and also for me, that words may be given to me in opening my mouth boldly to proclaim the mystery of the gospel, 20 for which I am an ambassador in chains, that I may declare it boldly, as I ought to speak.

Final Greetings

21 So that you also may know how I am and what I am doing, Tychicus the beloved brother and faithful minister in the Lord will tell you everything. 22 I have sent him to you for this very purpose, that you may know how we are, and that he may encourage your hearts.

23 Peace be to the brothers,[5] and love with faith, from God the Father and the Lord Jesus Christ. 24 Grace be with all who love our Lord Jesus Christ with love incorruptible.

[1] Or *servants*; Greek *bondservants*; similarly verse 8 [2] Or *your masters according to the flesh* [3] Or *slaves*; Greek *bondservants* [4] Greek *Lord* [5] Or *brothers and sisters*

Introduction to

Philippians

Author

Paul the apostle

Date

About A.D. 62

Key People

Paul; Timothy; Epaphroditus; Euodia and Syntyche

Purpose

The purpose of Philippians is to encourage the Philippians to continue to grow in Christ, to let them know that Paul and Epaphroditus were well, and to thank them for the gift of money they had sent.

Central Themes

Joy is found in Christ alone; we should be eager to serve others; Christ's humility and exaltation accomplished our salvation and are also a model for us; to know Christ is better than anything else; Christians should give generously for the advance of the gospel.

Memory Verses

To live is Christ (Philippians 1:21–26); Christ's humility and exaltation (Philippians 2:5–11); righteous through faith (Philippians 3:7–11); press on (Philippians 3:12–14); citizenship in heaven (Philippians 3:20–21)

Introduction

Paul wrote this letter from prison. Even so, he assures the Philippians he is well and the gospel is advancing. Paul doesn't know whether he'll be set free or sentenced to death, but either way he rejoices. Living means serving Christ, while dying means being with Christ (Philippians 1:1–26). Paul urges Christians to live worthy of the gospel: living for others, not themselves. He reminds them that Jesus lived in this way. He was God, but He became a man and suffered the death of a criminal to serve others. Now God has raised Him to the highest place of all (Philippians 1:27–2:16). Paul reminds the Philippians of his own example and of the examples of Timothy and their friend, Epaphroditus. These men had risked their lives to take the gospel to others (Philippians 2:17–30). Paul writes that knowing Christ and having His righteousness is better than anything else. Christians should press on for the goal of being like Christ, as Paul himself does (Philippians 3). Paul urges two women with a disagreement to get along, and he thanks the Philippians for sending gifts of money to help him spread the gospel (Philippians 4). Throughout his letter, Paul calls Christians to rejoice, whatever their circumstances.

About A.D. 33/34
Conversion of Paul

About A.D. 48/49–51
Paul plants Philippian church

About A.D. 62
Paul arrested, writes Philippians

The Letter of Paul to the

Philippians

Greeting

1 Paul and Timothy, servants[1] of Christ Jesus,

To all the saints in Christ Jesus who are at Philippi, with the overseers[2] and deacons:[3]

2 Grace to you and peace from God our Father and the Lord Jesus Christ.

Thanksgiving and Prayer

3 I thank my God in all my remembrance of you, **4** always in every prayer of mine for you all making my prayer with joy, **5** because of your partnership in the gospel from the first day until now. **6** And I am sure of this, that he who began a good work in you will bring it to completion at the day of Jesus Christ. **7** It is right for me to feel this way about you all, because I hold you in my heart, for you are all partakers with me of grace,[4] both in my imprisonment and in the defense and confirmation of the gospel. **8** For God is my witness, how I yearn for you all with the affection of Christ Jesus. **9** And it is my prayer that your love may abound more and more, with knowledge and all discernment, **10** so that you may approve what is excellent, and so be pure and blameless for the day of Christ, **11** filled with the fruit of righteousness that comes through Jesus Christ, to the glory and praise of God.

The Advance of the Gospel

12 I want you to know, brothers,[5] that what has happened to me has really served to advance the gospel, **13** so that it has become known throughout the whole imperial guard[6] and to all the rest that my imprisonment is for Christ. **14** And most of the brothers, having become confident in the Lord by my imprisonment, are much more bold to speak the word[7] without fear. **15** Some indeed preach Christ from envy and rivalry, but others from good will. **16** The latter do it out of love, knowing that I am put here for the defense of the gospel. **17** The former proclaim Christ out of rivalry, not sincerely but thinking to afflict me in my imprisonment. **18** What then? Only that in every way, whether in pretense or in truth, Christ is proclaimed, and in that I rejoice.

To Live Is Christ

Yes, and I will rejoice, **19** for I know that through your prayers and the help of the Spirit of Jesus Christ this will turn out for my deliverance, **20** as it is my eager expectation and hope that I will not be at all ashamed, but that with full courage now as always Christ will be honored in my body, whether by life or by death. **21** For to me to live is Christ, and to die is gain. **22** If I am to live in the flesh, that means fruitful labor for me. Yet which I shall choose I cannot tell. **23** I am hard pressed between the two. My desire is to depart and be with Christ, for that is far better. **24** But to remain in the flesh is more necessary on your account. **25** Convinced of this, I know that I will remain and continue with you all, for your progress and joy in the faith, **26** so that in me you may have ample cause to glory in Christ Jesus, because of my coming to you again.

27 Only let your manner of life be worthy[8] of the gospel of Christ, so that whether I come and see you or am absent, I may hear of you that you are standing firm in one spirit, with one mind striving side by

[1] Or *slaves*; Greek *bondservants* [2] Or *bishops*; Greek *episkopoi* [3] Or *servants, or ministers*; Greek *diakonoi* [4] Or *you all have fellowship with me in grace* [5] Or *brothers and sisters*. The plural Greek word *adelphoi* (translated "brothers") refers to siblings in a family. In New Testament usage, depending on the context, *adelphoi* may refer either to men or to both men and women who are siblings (brothers and sisters) in God's family, the church; also verse 14 [6] Greek *in the whole praetorium* [7] Some manuscripts add *of God* [8] Greek *Only behave as citizens worthy*

side for the faith of the gospel, 28 and not
frightened in anything by your opponents.
This is a clear sign to them of their destruc-
tion, but of your salvation, and that from
God. 29 For it has been granted to you that
for the sake of Christ you should not only
believe in him but also suffer for his sake,
30 engaged in the same conflict that you
saw I had and now hear that I still have.

Christ's Example of Humility

2 So if there is any encouragement in
Christ, any comfort from love, any
participation in the Spirit, any affection
and sympathy, 2 complete my joy by being
of the same mind, having the same love,
being in full accord and of one mind.
3 Do nothing from rivalry or conceit, but
in humility count others more signifi-
cant than yourselves. 4 Let each of you
look not only to his own interests, but
also to the interests of others. 5 Have this
mind among yourselves, which is yours
in Christ Jesus,[1] 6 who, though he was
in the form of God, did not count equal-
ity with God a thing to be grasped, 7 but
made himself nothing, taking the form
of a servant,[2] being born in the likeness of
men. 8 And being found in human form,
he humbled himself by becoming obedi-
ent to the point of death, even death on a
cross. 9 Therefore God has highly exalted
him and bestowed on him the name that
is above every name, 10 so that at the name
of Jesus every knee should bow, in heaven
and on earth and under the earth, 11 and
every tongue confess that Jesus Christ is
Lord, to the glory of God the Father.

Lights in the World

12 Therefore, my beloved, as you have
always obeyed, so now, not only as in my
presence but much more in my absence,
work out your own salvation with fear and
trembling, 13 for it is God who works in
you, both to will and to work for his good
pleasure.

14 Do all things without grumbling or
questioning, 15 that you may be blameless
and innocent, children of God without
blemish in the midst of a crooked and
twisted generation, among whom you
shine as lights in the world, 16 holding
fast to the word of life, so that in the day
of Christ I may be proud that I did not run
in vain or labor in vain. 17 Even if I am to
be poured out as a drink offering upon the
sacrificial offering of your faith, I am glad
and rejoice with you all. 18 Likewise you
also should be glad and rejoice with me.

Timothy and Epaphroditus

19 I hope in the Lord Jesus to send
Timothy to you soon, so that I too may
be cheered by news of you. 20 For I have
no one like him, who will be genuinely
concerned for your welfare. 21 For they all
seek their own interests, not those of Jesus
Christ. 22 But you know Timothy's[3] proven
worth, how as a son[4] with a father he has
served with me in the gospel. 23 I hope
therefore to send him just as soon as I see
how it will go with me, 24 and I trust in the
Lord that shortly I myself will come also.

25 I have thought it necessary to send to
you Epaphroditus my brother and fellow
worker and fellow soldier, and your mes-
senger and minister to my need, 26 for he
has been longing for you all and has been
distressed because you heard that he was
ill. 27 Indeed he was ill, near to death. But
God had mercy on him, and not only on
him but on me also, lest I should have sor-
row upon sorrow. 28 I am the more eager to
send him, therefore, that you may rejoice
at seeing him again, and that I may be
less anxious. 29 So receive him in the Lord
with all joy, and honor such men, 30 for he
nearly died for the work of Christ, risking
his life to complete what was lacking in
your service to me.

Righteousness Through Faith in Christ

3 Finally, my brothers,[5] rejoice in the
Lord. To write the same things to you
is no trouble to me and is safe for you.

[1] Or *which was also in Christ Jesus* [2] Greek *bondservant* [3] Greek *his* [4] Greek *child* [5] Or *brothers and sisters*; also verses 13, 17

[2]Look out for the dogs, look out for the
evildoers, look out for those who mutilate
the flesh. [3]For we are the circumcision,
who worship by the Spirit of God[1] and
glory in Christ Jesus and put no confidence
in the flesh— [4]though I myself have reason
for confidence in the flesh also. If
anyone else thinks he has reason
1637 for confidence in the flesh, I have
more: [5]circumcised on the eighth day, of
the people of Israel, of the tribe of
Benjamin, a Hebrew of Hebrews; as to the
law, a Pharisee; [6]as to zeal, a persecutor of
the church; as to righteousness under the
law,[2] blameless. [7]But whatever gain I had,
I counted as loss for the sake of Christ.
[8]Indeed, I count everything as loss because
of the surpassing worth of knowing Christ
Jesus my Lord. For his sake I have suffered
the loss of all things and count them as
rubbish, in order that I may gain Christ
[9]and be found in him, not having a righ-
teousness of my own that comes from the
law, but that which comes through faith in
Christ, the righteousness from God that
depends on faith— [10]that I may know him
and the power of his resurrection, and may
share his sufferings, becoming like him in
his death, [11]that by any means possible I
may attain the resurrection from the dead.

Straining Toward the Goal

[12]Not that I have already obtained this or
am already perfect, but I press on to make
it my own, because Christ Jesus has made
me his own. [13]Brothers, I do not consider
that I have made it my own. But one thing I
do: forgetting what lies behind and strain-
ing forward to what lies ahead, [14]I press on
toward the goal for the prize of the upward
call of God in Christ Jesus. [15]Let those of
us who are mature think this way, and if
in anything you think otherwise, God will
reveal *that also* to you. [16]Only let us hold
true to what we have attained.

[17]Brothers, join in imitating me, and
keep your eyes on those who walk accord-
ing to the example you have in us. [18]For
many, of whom I have often told you and
now tell you even with tears, walk as ene-
mies of the cross of Christ. [19]Their end is
destruction, their god is their belly, and
they glory in their shame, with minds set
on earthly things. [20]But our citizenship is
in heaven, and from it we await a Savior,
the Lord Jesus Christ, [21]who will trans-
form our lowly body to be like his glorious
body, by the power that enables him even
to subject all things to himself.

4 Therefore, my brothers,[3] whom I love
and long for, my joy and crown, stand
firm thus in the Lord, my beloved.

Exhortation, Encouragement, and Prayer

[2]I entreat Euodia and I entreat Syntyche
to agree in the Lord. [3]Yes, I ask you also,
true companion,[4] help these women, who
have labored side by side with me in the
gospel together with Clement and the rest
of my fellow workers, whose names are in
the book of life.

[4]Rejoice in the Lord always; again I will
say, Rejoice. [5]Let your reasonableness be
known to everyone. The Lord is at hand;
[6]do not be anxious about anything, but
in everything by prayer and sup-
plication with thanksgiving let
435 your requests be made known to
God. [7]And the peace of God, which sur-
passes all understanding, will guard your
hearts and your minds in Christ Jesus.

[8]Finally, brothers, whatever is true,
whatever is honorable, whatever is just,
whatever is pure, whatever is lovely, what-
ever is commendable, if there is any excel-
lence, if there is anything worthy of praise,
think about these things. [9]What you have
learned and received and heard and seen
in me—practice these things, and the God
of peace will be with you.

God's Provision

[10]I rejoiced in the Lord greatly that now
at length you have revived your concern
for me. You were indeed concerned for

[1] Some manuscripts *God in spirit* [2] Greek *in the law* [3] Or *brothers and sisters*; also verses 8, 21 [4] Or *loyal Syzygus*; Greek *true yokefellow*

me, but you had no opportunity. 11 Not that I am speaking of being in need, for I have learned in whatever situation I am to be content. 12 I know how to be brought low, and I know how to abound. In any and every circumstance, I have learned the secret of facing plenty and hunger, abundance and need. 13 I can do all things through him who strengthens me.

14 Yet it was kind of you to share[1] my trouble. 15 And you Philippians yourselves know that in the beginning of the gospel, when I left Macedonia, no church entered into partnership with me in giving and receiving, except you only. 16 Even in Thessalonica you sent me help for my needs once and again. 17 Not that I seek the gift, but I seek the fruit that increases to your credit.[2] 18 I have received full payment, and more. I am well supplied, having received from Epaphroditus the gifts you sent, a fragrant offering, a sacrifice acceptable and pleasing to God. 19 And my God will supply every need of yours according to his riches in glory in Christ Jesus. 20 To our God and Father be glory forever and ever. Amen.

Final Greetings

21 Greet every saint in Christ Jesus. The brothers who are with me greet you. 22 All the saints greet you, especially those of Caesar's household.

23 The grace of the Lord Jesus Christ be with your spirit.

[1] *Or have fellowship in* [2] *Or I seek the profit that accrues to your account*

Introduction to

Colossians

Author
Paul the apostle

Date
About A.D. 62

Key People
Paul; Epaphras; Tychicus; Onesimus

Purpose
The purpose of Colossians is to remind the Colossian believers that Jesus Christ alone is Lord and supreme over the Church and over the world, and that those who stay rooted in the gospel are transformed to live new lives of faith and obedience.

Central Themes
Christ is Creator; Christ is Lord of all; Christ has saved His people completely; Christ has all wisdom and knowledge; Christians have all they need in Christ; Christians are to live in such a way that they demonstrate that they are in Christ.

Memory Verses
Transferred to God's kingdom (Colossians 1:11–14); hymn of Christ (Colossians 1:15–20); the new circumcision (Colossians 2:11–14); shadow and substance (Colossians 2:16–17); glory above (Colossians 3:1–4)

Introduction

Paul was in prison in Rome when Epaphras brought him news of the Colossian church, which was being threatened by false teaching. This teaching said Christians needed to follow certain rules, get deeper knowledge than they had, and seek help from angels. Paul writes to tell the Colossians that the Lord Jesus Christ was all they needed. Paul reminded the Colossians that Jesus created and rules over all things (Colossians 1:15–20); that He reconciles believers to God through His death on the cross (Colossians 1:21–23); and that all the wisdom and knowledge they would ever need were found in Him (Colossians 2:1–4). He calls on the Colossians not to pay attention to the false teaching that had come. Instead they should hold firm to Christ because He is enough, and they should live to please Him only (Colossians 2:5–23). Paul tells the Colossians that, since they are united to Christ now and will one day share His glory, they must live holy lives (Colossians 3:1–11). Paul urges the Colossians to love, forgive, and build each other up, living with the members of their households as God would want them to (Colossians 3:12–4:5).

About A.D. 52–57
Paul evangelizes Colossae

About A.D. 62
Paul in Rome, writes Colossians

About A.D. 64–67
Paul martyred in Rome

The Letter of Paul to the

Colossians

Greeting

1 Paul, an apostle of Christ Jesus by the
will of God, and Timothy our brother,
2 To the saints and faithful brothers[1] in
Christ at Colossae:

Grace to you and peace from God our
Father.

Thanksgiving and Prayer

3 We always thank God, the Father of our
Lord Jesus Christ, when we pray for you,
4 since we heard of your faith in Christ
Jesus and of the love that you have for all
the saints, **5** because of the hope laid up
for you in heaven. Of this you have heard
before in the word of the truth, the gos-
pel, **6** which has come to you, as indeed
in the whole world it is bearing fruit and
growing—as it also does among you, since
the day you heard it and understood the
grace of God in truth, **7** just as you learned
it from Epaphras our beloved fellow ser-
vant.[2] He is a faithful minister of Christ
on your[3] behalf **8** and has made known to
us your love in the Spirit.

9 And so, from the day we heard, we
have not ceased to pray for you, asking
that you may be filled with the knowledge
of his will in all spiritual wisdom and
understanding, **10** so as to walk in a man-
ner worthy of the Lord, fully pleasing to
him, bearing fruit in every good work and
increasing in the knowledge of God.
11 May you be strengthened with all
power, according to his glorious might,
for all endurance and patience with joy,
12 giving thanks[4] to the Father, who
has qualified you[5] to share in the
1507 inheritance of the saints in light.
13 He has delivered us from the domain of
darkness and transferred us to the king-
dom of his beloved Son, **14** in whom we
have redemption, the forgiveness of sins.

The Preeminence of Christ

15 He is the image of the invisible
God, the firstborn of all creation.
5 **16** For by[6] him all things were cre-
ated, in heaven and on earth, visible and
invisible, whether thrones or dominions
or rulers or authorities—all things were
created through him and for him. **17** And he
is before all things, and in him all things
hold together. **18** And he is the head of the
body, the church. He is the beginning, the
firstborn from the dead, that in everything
he might be preeminent. **19** For in him all
the fullness of God was pleased to dwell,
20 and through him to reconcile to himself
all things, whether on earth or in heaven,
making peace by the blood of his cross.

21 And you, who once were alienated
and hostile in mind, doing evil deeds,
22 he has now reconciled in his body of
flesh by his death, in order to present you
holy and blameless and above reproach
before him, **23** if indeed you continue in
the faith, stable and steadfast, not shift-
ing from the hope of the gospel that you
heard, which has been proclaimed in all
creation[7] under heaven, and of which I,
Paul, became a minister.

Paul's Ministry to the Church

24 Now I rejoice in my sufferings for
your sake, and in my flesh I am filling up
what is lacking in Christ's afflictions for
the sake of his body, that is, the church,
25 of which I became a minister accord-
ing to the stewardship from God that was
given to me for you, to make the word

[1] Or *brothers and sisters*. The plural Greek word *adelphoi* (translated "brothers") refers to siblings in a family. In New Testament usage, depending on the context, *adelphoi* may refer either to men or to both men and women who are siblings (brothers and sisters) in God's family, the church [2] Greek *fellow bondservant* [3] Some manuscripts *our* [4] Or *patience, with joy giving thanks* [5] Some manuscripts *us* [6] That is, by means of; or *in* [7] Or *to every creature*

of God fully known, **26**the mystery hid-
den for ages and generations but now
revealed to his saints. **27**To them God
chose to make known how great among
the Gentiles are the riches of the glory of
this mystery, which is Christ in you, the
hope of glory. **28**Him we proclaim, warn-
ing everyone and teaching everyone with
all wisdom, that we may present everyone
mature in Christ. **29**For this I toil, strug-
gling with all his energy that he power-
fully works within me.

2 For I want you to know how great a
struggle I have for you and for those
at Laodicea and for all who have not seen
me face to face, **2**that their hearts may be
encouraged, being knit together in love,
to reach all the riches of full assurance
of understanding and the knowledge of
God's mystery, which is Christ, **3**in whom
are hidden all the treasures of wisdom
and knowledge. **4**I say this in order that no
one may delude you with plausible argu-
ments. **5**For though I am absent in body,
yet I am with you in spirit, rejoicing to see
your good order and the firmness of your
faith in Christ.

Alive in Christ

6Therefore, as you received Christ Jesus
the Lord, so walk in him, **7**rooted and built
up in him and established in the faith,
just as you were taught, abounding in
thanksgiving.

8See to it that no one takes you captive
by philosophy and empty deceit, accord-
ing to human tradition, according to the
elemental spirits[1] of the world, and not
according to Christ. **9**For in him the whole
fullness of deity dwells bodily, **10**and you
have been filled in him, who is the head of
all rule and authority. **11**In him also you
were circumcised with a circumcision
made without hands, by putting off the
body of the flesh, by the circumcision of
Christ, **12**having been buried with him in
baptism, in which you were also raised
with him through faith in the powerful
working of God, who raised him from the
dead. **13**And you, who were dead in your
trespasses and the uncircumcision of
your flesh, God made alive together with
him, having forgiven us all our trespasses,
14by canceling the record of debt that
stood against us with its legal demands.
This he set aside, nailing it to the cross.
15He disarmed the rulers and
authorities[2] and put them to open
411 shame, by triumphing over them
in him.[3]

Let No One Disqualify You

16Therefore let no one pass judgment
on you in questions of food and drink, or
with regard to a festival or a new moon
or a Sabbath. **17**These are a shadow of the
things to come, but the substance belongs
to Christ. **18**Let no one disqualify you,
insisting on asceticism and worship of
angels, going on in detail about visions,[4]
puffed up without reason by his sensuous
mind, **19**and not holding fast to the Head,
from whom the whole body, nourished
and knit together through its joints and
ligaments, grows with a growth that is
from God.

20If with Christ you died to the elemen-
tal spirits of the world, why, as if you were
still alive in the world, do you submit to
regulations— **21**"Do not handle, Do not
taste, Do not touch" **22**(referring to things
that all perish as they are used)—accord-
ing to human precepts and teachings?
23These have indeed an appearance of
wisdom in promoting self-made religion
and asceticism and severity to the body,
but they are of no value in stopping the
indulgence of the flesh.

Put On the New Self

3 If then you have been raised with
Christ, seek the things that are above,
where Christ is, seated at the right hand
of God. **2**Set your minds on things that
are above, not on things that are on earth.

[1] Or *elementary principles*; also verse 20 [2] Probably demonic rulers and authorities [3] Or *in it* (that is, the cross) [4] Or *about the things he has seen*

3 For you have died, and your life is hidden with Christ in God. 4 When Christ who is your[1] life appears, then you also will appear with him in glory.

5 Put to death therefore what is earthly in you:[2] sexual immorality, impurity, passion, evil desire, and covetousness, which is idolatry. 6 On account of these the wrath of God is coming.[3] 7 In these you too once walked, when you were living in them. 8 But now you must put them all away: anger, wrath, malice, slander, and obscene talk from your mouth. 9 Do not lie to one another, seeing that you have put off the old self[4] with its practices 10 and have put on the new self, which is being renewed in knowledge after the image of its creator. 11 Here there is not Greek and Jew, circumcised and uncircumcised, barbarian, Scythian, slave,[5] free; but Christ is all, and in all.

12 Put on then, as God's chosen ones, holy and beloved, compassionate hearts, kindness, humility, meekness, and patience, 13 bearing with one another and, if one has a complaint against another, forgiving each other; as the Lord has forgiven you, so you also must forgive. 14 And above all these put on love, which binds everything together in perfect harmony. 15 And let the peace of Christ rule in your hearts, to which indeed you were called in one body. And be thankful. 16 Let the word of Christ dwell in you richly, teaching and admonishing one another in all wisdom, singing psalms and hymns and spiritual songs, with thankfulness in your hearts to God. 17 And whatever you do, in word or deed, do everything in the name of the Lord Jesus, giving thanks to God the Father through him.

Rules for Christian Households

18 Wives, submit to your husbands, as is fitting in the Lord. 19 Husbands, love your wives, and do not be harsh with them. 20 Children, obey your parents in everything, for this pleases the Lord. 21 Fathers, do not provoke your children, lest they become discouraged. 22 Slaves,[6] obey in everything those who are your earthly masters,[7] not by way of eye-service, as people-pleasers, but with sincerity of heart, fearing the Lord. 23 Whatever you do, work heartily, as for the Lord and not for men, 24 knowing that from the Lord you will receive the inheritance as your reward. You are serving the Lord Christ. 25 For the wrongdoer will be paid back for the wrong he has done, and there is no partiality.

1783

4 Masters, treat your slaves[8] justly and fairly, knowing that you also have a Master in heaven.

Further Instructions

2 Continue steadfastly in prayer, being watchful in it with thanksgiving. 3 At the same time, pray also for us, that God may open to us a door for the word, to declare the mystery of Christ, on account of which I am in prison— 4 that I may make it clear, which is how I ought to speak.

5 Walk in wisdom toward outsiders, making the best use of the time. 6 Let your speech always be gracious, seasoned with salt, so that you may know how you ought to answer each person.

Final Greetings

7 Tychicus will tell you all about my activities. He is a beloved brother and faithful minister and fellow servant[9] in the Lord. 8 I have sent him to you for this very purpose, that you may know how we are and that he may encourage your hearts, 9 and with him Onesimus, our faithful and beloved brother, who is one of you. They will tell you of everything that has taken place here.

10 Aristarchus my fellow prisoner greets you, and Mark the cousin of Barnabas (concerning whom you have received instructions—if he comes to you, wel-

[1] Some manuscripts *our* [2] Greek *therefore your members that are on the earth* [3] Some manuscripts add *upon the sons of disobedience* [4] Greek *man*; also as supplied in verse 10 [5] Greek *bondservant* [6] Or *Servants*; Greek *Bondservants* [7] Or *your masters according to the flesh* [8] Or *servants*; Greek *bondservants* [9] Greek *fellow bondservant*; also verse 12

come him), [11] and Jesus who is called
Justus. These are the only men of the cir-
cumcision among my fellow workers for
the kingdom of God, and they have been a
comfort to me. [12] Epaphras, who is one of
you, a servant of Christ Jesus, greets you,
always struggling on your behalf in his
prayers, that you may stand mature and
fully assured in all the will of God. [13] For I
bear him witness that he has worked hard
for you and for those in Laodicea and in
Hierapolis. [14] Luke the beloved physician
greets you, as does Demas. [15] Give my
greetings to the brothers[1] at Laodicea, and
to Nympha and the church in her house.
[16] And when this letter has been read
among you, have it also read in the church
of the Laodiceans; and see that you also
read the letter from Laodicea. [17] And say
to Archippus, "See that you fulfill the min-
istry that you have received in the Lord."

[18] I, Paul, write this greeting with my
own hand. Remember my chains. Grace
be with you.

[1] Or *brothers and sisters*

Introduction to

1 Thessalonians

Author
Paul the apostle

Date
About A.D. 49–51

Purpose
The purpose of 1 Thessalonians is to address Jesus' second coming, to encourage the persecuted Thessalonian believers, and to spur them on to live holy lives.

Central Themes
Jesus will come again; suffering for Christ is part of the Christian life; ministers of the gospel must labor diligently in love; those who reject the gospel will be judged; believers will be resurrected to glory; Christians must pursue holiness.

Memory Verses
The resurrection of the dead (1 Thessalonians 4:16–18); blameless in Christ (1 Thessalonians 5:23–24)

Introduction

Paul had taken the gospel to the Thessalonians. He had only been with them a short time when persecution had broken out against Christians and especially against the apostles, so Paul had been forced to leave. He was troubled about this, since this had left little time to teach the new Thessalonian Christians. Paul had sent Timothy back to Thessalonica to see how they were doing. When Timothy returned, he said they were strong in the Lord in spite of the persecution they endured. Paul writes to commend the Thessalonians for this (1 Thessalonians 1:1–10; 2:13–17). He tells them not to be surprised when people persecute them for their faith, but to continue standing firm (1 Thessalonians 3:3–4). The Thessalonian believers were worried that their Christian friends who had died would miss the Lord's return, so Paul tells them that the Lord would raise their friends from the dead and bring them with Him when He returned (1 Thessalonians 4:13–18). Since the Lord was coming again, Paul encourages the Thessalonians to live holy lives as they wait for Him (1 Thessalonians 4:1–12; 5:1–22). He promises them that God will make them completely holy and blameless when Jesus returns (1 Thessalonians 5:23–24).

About A.D. 33/34	About A.D. 49–51	About A.D. 64–67
Conversion of Paul	Paul writes 1 Thessalonians	Paul martyred in Rome

The First Letter of Paul to the Thessalonians

1 Thessalonians

Greeting

1 Paul, Silvanus, and Timothy,
To the church of the Thessalonians in God the Father and the Lord Jesus Christ:

Grace to you and peace.

The Thessalonians' Faith and Example

2 We give thanks to God always for all of you, constantly[1] mentioning you in our prayers, 3 remembering before our God and Father your work of faith and labor of love and steadfastness of hope in our Lord Jesus Christ. 4 For we know, brothers[2] loved by God, that he has chosen you, 5 because our gospel came to you not only in word, but also in power and in the Holy Spirit and with full conviction. You know what kind of men we proved to be among you for your sake. 6 And you became imitators of us and of the Lord, for you received the word in much affliction, with the joy of the Holy Spirit, 7 so that you became an example to all the believers in Macedonia and in Achaia. 8 For not only has the word of the Lord sounded forth from you in Macedonia and Achaia, but your faith in God has gone forth everywhere, so that we need not say anything. 9 For they themselves report concerning us the kind of reception we had among you, and how you turned to God from idols to serve the living and true God, 10 and to wait for his Son from heaven, whom he raised from the dead, Jesus who delivers us from the wrath to come.

Paul's Ministry to the Thessalonians

2 For you yourselves know, brothers,[3] that our coming to you was not in vain. 2 But though we had already suffered and been shamefully treated at Philippi, as you know, we had boldness in our God to declare to you the gospel of God in the midst of much conflict. 3 For our appeal does not spring from error or impurity or any attempt to deceive, 4 but just as we have been approved by God to be entrusted with the gospel, so we speak, not to please man, but to please God who tests our hearts. 5 For we never came with words of flattery,[4] as you know, nor with a pretext for greed—God is witness. 6 Nor did we seek glory from people, whether from you or from others, though we could have made demands as apostles of Christ. 7 But we were gentle[5] among you, like a nursing mother taking care of her own children. 8 So, being affectionately desirous of you, we were ready to share with you not only the gospel of God but also our own selves, because you had become very dear to us.

9 For you remember, brothers, our labor and toil: we worked night and day, that we might not be a burden to any of you, while we proclaimed to you the gospel of God. 10 You are witnesses, and God also, how holy and righteous and blameless was our conduct toward you believers. 11 For you know how, like a father with his children, 12 we exhorted each one of you and encouraged you and charged you to walk in a manner worthy of God, who calls you into his own kingdom and glory.

13 And we also thank God constantly[6] for this, that when you received the word of God, which you heard from us, you accepted it not as the word of men but as what it really is, the word of God, which is at work in you believers. 14 For you, brothers, became imitators of the churches of

[1] Or *without ceasing* [2] Or *brothers and sisters*. The plural Greek word *adelphoi* (translated "brothers") refers to siblings in a family. In New Testament usage, depending on the context, *adelphoi* may refer either to men or to both men and women who are siblings (brothers and sisters) in God's family, the church [3] Or *brothers and sisters*; also verses 9, 14, 17 [4] Or *with a flattering speech* [5] Some manuscripts *infants* [6] Or *without ceasing*

God in Christ Jesus that are in Judea. For
you suffered the same things from your
own countrymen as they did from the
Jews, **15** who killed both the Lord Jesus and
the prophets, and drove us out, and dis-
please God and oppose all mankind **16** by
hindering us from speaking to the Gentiles
that they might be saved—so as always to
fill up the measure of their sins. But God's
wrath has come upon them at last![1]

Paul's Longing to See Them Again

17 But since we were torn away from
you, brothers, for a short time, in person
not in heart, we endeavored the more
eagerly and with great desire to see you
face to face, **18** because we wanted to
come to you—I, Paul, again and again—
but Satan hindered us. **19** For what is our
hope or joy or crown of boasting before
our Lord Jesus at his coming? Is it not you?
20 For you are our glory and joy.

3 Therefore when we could bear it no
longer, we were willing to be left
behind at Athens alone, **2** and we sent
Timothy, our brother and God's coworker[2]
in the gospel of Christ, to establish and
exhort you in your faith, **3** that no one be
moved by these afflictions. For you your-
selves know that we are destined for this.
4 For when we were with you, we kept tell-
ing you beforehand that we were to suffer
affliction, just as it has come to pass, and
just as you know. **5** For this reason, when
I could bear it no longer, I sent to learn
about your faith, for fear that somehow
the tempter had tempted you and our
labor would be in vain.

Timothy's Encouraging Report

6 But now that Timothy has come to us
from you, and has brought us the good
news of your faith and love and reported
that you always remember us kindly and
long to see us, as we long to see you— **7** for
this reason, brothers,[3] in all our distress
and affliction we have been comforted
about you through your faith. **8** For now
we live, if you are standing fast in the Lord.
9 For what thanksgiving can we return to
God for you, for all the joy that we feel for
your sake before our God, **10** as we pray
most earnestly night and day that we may
see you face to face and supply what is
lacking in your faith?

11 Now may our God and Father himself,
and our Lord Jesus, direct our way to you,
12 and may the Lord make you increase and
abound in love for one another and for all,
as we do for you, **13** so that he may estab-
lish your hearts blameless in holiness
before our God and Father, at the coming
of our Lord Jesus with all his saints.

A Life Pleasing to God

4 Finally, then, brothers,[4] we ask and
urge you in the Lord Jesus, that as
you received from us how you ought to
walk and to please God, just as you are
doing, that you do so more and more.
2 For you know what instructions we gave
you through the Lord Jesus. **3** For this is
the will of God, your sanctification:[5] that
you abstain from sexual immorality; **4** that
each one of you know how to control his
own body[6] in holiness and honor, **5** not in
the passion of lust like the Gentiles who
do not know God; **6** that no one trans-
gress and wrong his brother in this mat-
ter, because the Lord is an avenger in all
these things, as we told you beforehand
and solemnly warned you. **7** For God has
not called us for impurity, but in holiness.
8 Therefore whoever disregards this, dis-
regards not man but God, who gives his
Holy Spirit to you.

9 Now concerning brotherly love you
have no need for anyone to write to you,
for you yourselves have been taught by
God to love one another, **10** for that indeed
is what you are doing to all the brothers
throughout Macedonia. But we urge you,
brothers, to do this more and more, **11** and
to aspire to live quietly, and to mind your

[1] Or *completely*, or *forever* [2] Some manuscripts *servant* [3] Or *brothers and sisters* [4] Or *brothers and sisters*; also verses 10, 13 [5] Or *your holiness* [6] Or *how to take a wife for himself*; Greek *how to possess his own vessel*

own affairs, and to work with your hands,
as we instructed you, 12 so that you may
walk properly before outsiders and be
dependent on no one.

The Coming of the Lord

13 But we do not want you to be unin-
formed, brothers, about those who are
asleep, that you may not grieve as others
do who have no hope. 14 For since we
believe that Jesus died and rose again,
even so, through Jesus, God will bring with
him those who have fallen asleep. 15 For
this we declare to you by a word from the
Lord,[1] that we who are alive, who are left
until the coming of the Lord, will not pre-
cede those who have fallen asleep. 16 For
the Lord himself will descend from
heaven with a cry of command,
1847 with the voice of an archangel, and
with the sound of the trumpet of God. And
the dead in Christ will rise first. 17 Then we
who are alive, who are left, will be caught
up together with them in the clouds to
meet the Lord in the air, and so we will
always be with the Lord. 18 Therefore
encourage one another with these words.

The Day of the Lord

5 Now concerning the times and the
seasons, brothers,[2] you have no need
to have anything written to you. 2 For you
yourselves are fully aware that the day of
the Lord will come like a thief in the night.
3 While people are saying, "There is peace
and security," then sudden destruction
will come upon them as labor pains come
upon a pregnant woman, and they will
not escape. 4 But you are not in darkness,
brothers, for that day to surprise you like
a thief. 5 For you are all children[3] of light,
children of the day. We are not of the night
or of the darkness. 6 So then let us not
sleep, as others do, but let us keep awake
and be sober. 7 For those who sleep, sleep at
night, and those who get drunk, are drunk
at night. 8 But since we belong to the day,
let us be sober, having put on the breast-
plate of faith and love, and for a helmet
the hope of salvation. 9 For God has not
destined us for wrath, but to obtain salva-
tion through our Lord Jesus Christ, 10 who
died for us so that whether we are awake or
asleep we might live with him. 11 Therefore
encourage one another and build one
another up, just as you are doing.

Final Instructions and Benediction

12 We ask you, brothers, to respect those
who labor among you and are over you in
the Lord and admonish you, 13 and to
esteem them very highly in love because
of their work. Be at peace among your-
selves. 14 And we urge you, brothers,
admonish the idle,[4] encourage the faint-
hearted, help the weak, be patient with
them all. 15 See that no one repays anyone
evil for evil, but always seek to do good to
one another and to everyone. 16 Rejoice
always, 17 pray without ceasing, 18 give
thanks in all circumstances; for
this is the will of God in Christ
1507 Jesus for you. 19 Do not quench the
Spirit. 20 Do not despise prophecies, 21 but
test everything; hold fast what is good.
22 Abstain from every form of evil.

23 Now may the God of peace himself
sanctify you completely, and may your
whole spirit and soul and body be kept
blameless at the coming of our Lord Jesus
Christ. 24 He who calls you is faithful; he
will surely do it.

25 Brothers, pray for us.

26 Greet all the brothers with a holy kiss.

27 I put you under oath before the Lord
to have this letter read to all the brothers.

28 The grace of our Lord Jesus Christ be
with you.

[1] Or *by the word of the Lord* [2] Or *brothers and sisters*; also verses 4, 12, 14, 25, 26, 27 [3] Or *sons*; twice in this verse [4] Or *disorderly*, or *undisciplined*

Introduction to

2 Thessalonians

Author
Paul the apostle

Date
About A.D. 49–51

Purpose
The purpose of 2 Thessalonians is to give clearer teaching to the young believers in Thessalonica about the second coming of the Lord Jesus and to rebuke some who had stopped working and were living off other Christians.

Central Themes
When Jesus returns God will show wrath to unbelievers and show His glory to believers; before Jesus returns there will be a time of rebellion and the "man of lawlessness" will appear; Christians are called to faithful, holy living; idleness is rebuked.

Memory Verses
Grow in faith and love (2 Thessalonians 1:3); stand firm (2 Thessalonians 2:15)

Introduction

Someone had told the Thessalonian believers that the day of the Lord had already come and that they had missed it! Some people in the Thessalonian church had therefore quit working, content to let other Christians provide what they needed. Paul writes the church a letter to commend the Thessalonians again for their faith and their love for each other, even in the midst of continued persecution (2 Thessalonians 1:1–4). He tells them that when the Lord returns, their persecutors would be judged by God while the church would share in Christ's glory (2 Thessalonians 1:5–12). Paul writes that the Thessalonians must not think that the day of the Lord had already come. It had not. Before Christ returns there will be a time of rebellion on earth. An enemy of God's, the "man of lawlessness," will rise up. Since those two things had not yet happened, the Thessalonians did not need to worry that they had missed the Lord's return (2 Thessalonians 2:1–12). Then Paul told the believers not to support people who would not work to earn their food. If anyone was not willing to work, he should not be allowed to eat (2 Thessalonians 3:6–15)!

About A.D. 33/34 — Conversion of Paul

About A.D. 49–51 — Paul writes 2 Thessalonians

About A.D. 64–67 — Paul martyred in Rome

The Second Letter of Paul to the Thessalonians

2 Thessalonians

Greeting

1 Paul, Silvanus, and Timothy,
To the church of the Thessalonians in
God our Father and the Lord Jesus Christ:
2Grace to you and peace from God our
Father and the Lord Jesus Christ.

Thanksgiving

3We ought always to give thanks to God
for you, brothers,[1] as is right, because your
faith is growing abundantly, and the love of
every one of you for one another is increas-
ing. **4**Therefore we ourselves boast about
you in the churches of God for your stead-
fastness and faith in all your persecutions
and in the afflictions that you are enduring.

The Judgment at Christ's Coming

5This is evidence of the righteous judg-
ment of God, that you may be considered
worthy of the kingdom of God, for which
you are also suffering— **6**since indeed
God considers it just to repay with afflic-
tion those who afflict you, **7**and to grant
relief to you who are afflicted as well as to
us, when the Lord Jesus is revealed from
heaven with his mighty angels **8**in flaming
fire, inflicting vengeance on those who do
not know God and on those who do not
obey the gospel of our Lord Jesus. **9**They
will suffer the punishment of eternal
destruction, away from[2] the presence of
the Lord and from the glory of his might,
10when he comes on that day to be glori-
fied in his saints, and to be marveled at
among all who have believed, because our
testimony to you was believed. **11**To this
end we always pray for you, that our God
may make you worthy of his calling and
may fulfill every resolve for good and every
work of faith by his power, **12**so that the
name of our Lord Jesus may be glorified
in you, and you in him, according to the
grace of our God and the Lord Jesus Christ.

The Man of Lawlessness

2 Now concerning the coming of our
Lord Jesus Christ and our being gath-
ered together to him, we ask you, broth-
ers,[3] **2**not to be quickly shaken in mind
or alarmed, either by a spirit or a spoken
word, or a letter seeming to be from us,
to the effect that the day of the Lord has
come. **3**Let no one deceive you in any
way. For that day will not come, unless
the rebellion comes first, and the man
of lawlessness[4] is revealed, the son of
destruction,[5] **4**who opposes and exalts
himself against every so-called god or
object of worship, so that he takes his seat
in the temple of God, proclaiming him-
self to be God. **5**Do you not remember that
when I was still with you I told you these
things? **6**And you know what is restrain-
ing him now so that he may be revealed
in his time. **7**For the mystery of lawless-
ness is already at work. Only he who now
restrains it will do so until he is out of
the way. **8**And then the lawless one will
be revealed, whom the Lord Jesus will kill
with the breath of his mouth and bring to
nothing by the appearance of his coming.
9The coming of the lawless one is by the
activity of Satan with all power and false
signs and wonders, **10**and with all wicked
deception for those who are perishing,
because they refused to love the truth and
so be saved. **11**Therefore God sends them
a strong delusion, so that they may believe
what is false, **12**in order that all may be
condemned who did not believe the truth
but had pleasure in unrighteousness.

[1] Or *brothers and sisters*. The plural Greek word *adelphoi* (translated "brothers") refers to siblings in a family. In New Testament usage, depending on the context, *adelphoi* may refer either to men or to both men and women who are siblings (brothers and sisters) in God's family, the church [2] Or *destruction that comes from* [3] Or *brothers and sisters*; also verses 13, 15 [4] Some manuscripts *sin* [5] Greek *the son of perdition* (a Hebrew idiom)

Stand Firm

13 But we ought always to give thanks to God for you, brothers beloved by the Lord, because God chose you as the firstfruits[1] to be saved, through sanctification by the Spirit and belief in the truth. **14** To this he called you through our gospel, so that you may obtain the glory of our Lord Jesus Christ. **15** So then, brothers, stand firm and hold to the traditions that you were taught by us, either by our spoken word or by our letter.

16 Now may our Lord Jesus Christ himself, and God our Father, who loved us and gave us eternal comfort and good hope through grace, **17** comfort your hearts and establish them in every good work and word.

Pray for Us

3 Finally, brothers,[2] pray for us, that the word of the Lord may speed ahead and be honored,[3] as happened among you, **2** and that we may be delivered from wicked and evil men. For not all have faith. **3** But the Lord is faithful. He will establish you and guard you against the evil one.[4] **4** And we have confidence in the Lord about you, that you are doing and will do the things that we command. **5** May the Lord direct your hearts to the love of God and to the steadfastness of Christ.

Warning Against Idleness

6 Now we command you, brothers, in the name of our Lord Jesus Christ, that you keep away from any brother who is walking in idleness and not in accord with the tradition that you received from us. **7** For you yourselves know how you ought to imitate us, because we were not idle when we were with you, **8** nor did we eat anyone's bread without paying for it, but with toil and labor we worked night and day, that we might not be a burden to any of you. **9** It was not because we do not have that right, but to give you in ourselves an example to imitate. **10** For even when we were with you, we would give you this command: If anyone is not willing to work, let him not eat. **11** For we hear that some among you walk in idleness, not busy at work, but busybodies. **12** Now such persons we command and encourage in the Lord Jesus Christ to do their work quietly and to earn their own living.[5]

13 As for you, brothers, do not grow weary in doing good. **14** If anyone does not obey what we say in this letter, take note of that person, and have nothing to do with him, that he may be ashamed. **15** Do not regard him as an enemy, but warn him as a brother.

Benediction

16 Now may the Lord of peace himself give you peace at all times in every way. The Lord be with you all.

17 I, Paul, write this greeting with my own hand. This is the sign of genuineness in every letter of mine; it is the way I write. **18** The grace of our Lord Jesus Christ be with you all.

[1] Some manuscripts *chose you from the beginning* [2] Or *brothers and sisters;* also verses 6, 13 [3] Or *glorified* [4] Or *evil* [5] Greek *eat their own bread*

The First Letter of Paul to Timothy

1 Timothy

l, an apostle of Christ Jesus by
mmand of God our Savior and of
t Jesus our hope,
o Timothy, my true child in the faith:
Grace, mercy, and peace from God the
ather and Christ Jesus our Lord.

Warning Against False Teachers

[3] As I urged you when I was going to Macedonia, remain at Ephesus so that you may charge certain persons not to teach any different doctrine, [4] nor to devote themselves to myths and endless genealogies, which promote speculations rather than the stewardship[1] from God that is by faith. [5] The aim of our charge is love that issues from a pure heart and a good conscience and a sincere faith. [6] Certain persons, by swerving from these, have wandered away into vain discussion, [7] desiring to be teachers of the law, without understanding either what they are saying or the things about which they make confident assertions.

[8] Now we know that the law is good, if one uses it lawfully, [9] understanding this, that the law is not laid down for the just but for the lawless and disobedient, for the ungodly and sinners, for the unholy and profane, for those who strike their fathers and mothers, for murderers, [10] the sexually immoral, men who practice homosexuality, enslavers,[2] liars, perjurers, and whatever else is contrary to sound[3] doctrine, [11] in accordance with the gospel of the glory of the blessed God with which I have been entrusted.

Christ Jesus Came to Save Sinners

[12] I thank him who has given me
strength, Christ Jesus our Lord,
1637 because he judged me faithful,
appointing me to his service, [13] though
formerly I was a blasphemer, persecutor,
and insolent opponent. But I received
mercy because I had acted ignorantly in
unbelief, [14] and the grace of our Lord over-
flowed for me with the faith and love that
are in Christ Jesus. [15] The saying is
trustworthy and deserving of full
1637 acceptance, that Christ Jesus came
into the world to save sinners, of whom I am the foremost. [16] But I received mercy for this reason, that in me, as the foremost, Jesus Christ might display his perfect patience as an example to those who were to believe in him for eternal life. [17] To the King of ages, immortal, invisible, the only God, be honor and glory forever and ever.[4] Amen.

[18] This charge I entrust to you, Timothy, my child, in accordance with the prophecies previously made about you, that by them you may wage the good warfare, [19] holding faith and a good conscience. By rejecting this, some have made shipwreck of their faith, [20] among whom are Hymenaeus and Alexander, whom I have handed over to Satan that they may learn not to blaspheme.

Pray for All People

2 First of all, then, I urge that
supplications, prayers, inter-
1651 cessions, and thanksgivings be
made for all people, [2] for kings and all who are in high positions, that we may lead a peaceful and quiet life, godly and dignified in every way. [3] This is good, and it is pleasing in the sight of God our Savior, [4] who desires all people to be saved and to come to the knowledge of the truth. [5] For there is one God, and there is one mediator between God and men, the

[1] Or *good order* [2] That is, those who take someone captive in order to sell him into slavery [3] Or *healthy* [4] Greek *to the ages of ages*

Introduction to

1 Timothy

Author
Paul the apostle

Date
About A.D. 62–64

Key People
Paul; Timothy; overseers; deacons

Purpose
The purpose of 1 Timothy is to encourage and guide Timothy as he helps establish and lead the young church in Ephesus.

Central Themes
False teaching must be resisted and sound doctrine promoted; the gospel leads to authentic godliness; prayer should be ongoing and for all people; elders and deacons must meet certain requirements; relationships among believers should be gospel-centered; believers are called to exercise faithfulness in ministry.

Memory Verses
Chief of sinners (1 Timothy 1:15–16); one Mediator (1 Timothy 2:5–6); the mystery of godliness (1 Timothy 3:16); contentment (1 Timothy 6:6–8)

Introduction

When Paul left Ephesus, teachers of a "different doctrine" were troubling the church, so Paul had left there his young helper, Timothy, to teach truth and to combat falsehood. In this letter Paul encourages Timothy in his ministry. When people believe the gospel and the doctrine that flows from the gospel, Paul writes, it will be seen in their godly, loving lifestyle (1 Timothy 1:1–11). Christians should pray for people of all kinds and should submit to authority (1 Timothy 2). He describes the character qualities Timothy should look for as he chose men to be elders and deacons (1 Timothy 3:1–13). Paul tells Timothy to be disciplined, both in living a godly life and in teaching truth to others (1 Timothy 4:1–16; 6:11–16, 20–21). He gives Timothy guidance concerning relationships between church members and tells him that the rich should not trust in their riches, but should share them with others (1 Timothy 5:1–6:10, 17–19). Paul says he hopes to join Timothy soon but, in case he is delayed, he wants him to know how people ought to behave in the church, which is the household of God (1 Timothy 3:15).

About A.D. 48/49–51	About A.D. 62–64	About A.D. 64–67
Timothy on Paul's second journey	Paul arrested, writes 1 Timothy	Paul martyred in Rome

The First Letter of Paul to Timothy

1 Timothy

Greeting

1 Paul, an apostle of Christ Jesus by command of God our Savior and of Christ Jesus our hope,

2 To Timothy, my true child in the faith:

Grace, mercy, and peace from God the Father and Christ Jesus our Lord.

Warning Against False Teachers

3 As I urged you when I was going to Macedonia, remain at Ephesus so that you may charge certain persons not to teach any different doctrine, 4 nor to devote themselves to myths and endless genealogies, which promote speculations rather than the stewardship[1] from God that is by faith. 5 The aim of our charge is love that issues from a pure heart and a good conscience and a sincere faith. 6 Certain persons, by swerving from these, have wandered away into vain discussion, 7 desiring to be teachers of the law, without understanding either what they are saying or the things about which they make confident assertions.

8 Now we know that the law is good, if one uses it lawfully, 9 understanding this, that the law is not laid down for the just but for the lawless and disobedient, for the ungodly and sinners, for the unholy and profane, for those who strike their fathers and mothers, for murderers, 10 the sexually immoral, men who practice homosexuality, enslavers,[2] liars, perjurers, and whatever else is contrary to sound[3] doctrine, 11 in accordance with the gospel of the glory of the blessed God with which I have been entrusted.

Christ Jesus Came to Save Sinners

12 I thank him who has given me
strength, Christ Jesus our Lord,
1637 because he judged me faithful,
appointing me to his service, 13 though formerly I was a blasphemer, persecutor, and insolent opponent. But I received mercy because I had acted ignorantly in unbelief, 14 and the grace of our Lord overflowed for me with the faith and love that
are in Christ Jesus. 15 The saying is
trustworthy and deserving of full
1637 acceptance, that Christ Jesus came
into the world to save sinners, of whom I am the foremost. 16 But I received mercy for this reason, that in me, as the foremost, Jesus Christ might display his perfect patience as an example to those who were to believe in him for eternal life. 17 To the King of ages, immortal, invisible, the only God, be honor and glory forever and ever.[4] Amen.

18 This charge I entrust to you, Timothy, my child, in accordance with the prophecies previously made about you, that by them you may wage the good warfare, 19 holding faith and a good conscience. By rejecting this, some have made shipwreck of their faith, 20 among whom are Hymenaeus and Alexander, whom I have handed over to Satan that they may learn not to blaspheme.

Pray for All People

2 First of all, then, I urge that
supplications, prayers, inter-
1651 cessions, and thanksgivings be
made for all people, 2 for kings and all who are in high positions, that we may lead a peaceful and quiet life, godly and dignified in every way. 3 This is good, and it is pleasing in the sight of God our Savior, 4 who desires all people to be saved and to come to the knowledge of the truth. 5 For there is one God, and there is one mediator between God and men, the

[1] Or *good order* [2] That is, those who take someone captive in order to sell him into slavery [3] Or *healthy* [4] Greek *to the ages of ages*

man[1] Christ Jesus, 6 who gave himself as a
ransom for all, which is the testimony
given at the proper time. 7 For this I was
appointed a preacher and an apostle (I am
telling the truth, I am not lying), a teacher
of the Gentiles in faith and truth.

8 I desire then that in every place the
men should pray, lifting holy hands with-
out anger or quarreling; 9 likewise also
that women should adorn themselves
in respectable apparel, with modesty
and self-control, not with braided hair
and gold or pearls or costly attire, 10 but
with what is proper for women who pro-
fess godliness—with good works. 11 Let
a woman learn quietly with all submis-
siveness. 12 I do not permit a woman to
teach or to exercise authority over a man;
rather, she is to remain quiet. 13 For Adam
was formed first, then Eve; 14 and Adam
was not deceived, but the woman was
deceived and became a transgressor. 15 Yet
she will be saved through childbearing—if
they continue in faith and love and holi-
ness, with self-control.

CHARACTER PROFILE

TIMOTHY

Timothy was blessed all his life because his mother and grandmother loved and believed in God. These godly women taught Timothy to love God's Word, so Timothy eagerly believed in Jesus when he heard the Gospel. Soon the apostle Paul asked him to be one of his helpers. Later, Paul left Timothy behind at a new church to teach and to appoint elders while Paul traveled on to other towns. Even though Timothy was young, he had wisdom for leadership.

1663

Qualifications for Overseers

3 The saying is trustworthy: If any-
one aspires to the office of overseer,
he desires a noble task. 2 Therefore an
overseer[2] must be above reproach, the
husband of one wife,[3] sober-minded,
self-controlled, respectable, hospitable,
able to teach, 3 not a drunkard, not violent
but gentle, not quarrelsome, not a lover
of money. 4 He must manage his own
household well, with all dignity keeping
his children submissive, 5 for if someone
does not know how to manage his own
household, how will he care for God's
church? 6 He must not be a recent convert,
or he may become puffed up with con-
ceit and fall into the condemnation of the
devil. 7 Moreover, he must be well thought
of by outsiders, so that he may not fall into
disgrace, into a snare of the devil.

Qualifications for Deacons

8 Deacons likewise must be digni-
fied, not double-tongued,[4] not addicted
to much wine, not greedy for dishonest
gain. 9 They must hold the mystery of the
faith with a clear conscience. 10 And let
them also be tested first; then let them
serve as deacons if they prove themselves
blameless. 11 Their wives likewise must[5]
be dignified, not slanderers, but sober-
minded, faithful in all things. 12 Let dea-
cons each be the husband of one wife,
managing their children and their own
households well. 13 For those who serve

[1] *men* and *man* render the same Greek word that is translated *people* in verses 1 and 4 [2] Or *bishop*; Greek *episkopos*; a similar term occurs in verse 1 [3] Or *a man of one woman*; also verse 12 [4] Or *devious in speech* [5] Or *Wives, likewise, must*, or *Women, likewise, must*

well as deacons gain a good standing for themselves and also great confidence in the faith that is in Christ Jesus.

The Mystery of Godliness

14 I hope to come to you soon, but I am writing these things to you so that, 15 if I delay, you may know how one ought to behave in the household of God, which is the church of the living God, a pillar and buttress of the truth. 16 Great indeed, we confess, is the mystery of godliness:

He[1] was manifested in the flesh,
  vindicated[2] by the Spirit,[3]
    seen by angels,
proclaimed among the nations,
  believed on in the world,
    taken up in glory.

Some Will Depart from the Faith

4 Now the Spirit expressly says that in later times some will depart from the faith by devoting themselves to deceitful spirits and teachings of demons, 2 through the insincerity of liars whose consciences are seared, 3 who forbid marriage and require abstinence from foods that God created to be received with thanksgiving by those who believe and know the truth. 4 For everything created by God is good, and nothing is to be rejected if it is received with thanksgiving, 5 for it is made holy by the word of God and prayer.

A Good Servant of Christ Jesus

6 If you put these things before the brothers,[4] you will be a good servant of Christ Jesus, being trained in the words of the faith and of the good doctrine that you have followed. 7 Have nothing to do with irreverent, silly myths. Rather train yourself for godliness; 8 for while bodily training is of some value, godliness is of value in every way, as it holds promise for the present life and also for the life to come. 9 The saying is trustworthy and deserving of full acceptance. 10 For to this end we toil and strive,[5] because we have our hope set on the living God, who is the Savior of all people, especially of those who believe.

11 Command and teach these things. 12 Let no one despise you for your youth, but set the believers an example in speech, in conduct, in love, in faith, in purity. 13 Until I come, devote yourself to the public reading of Scripture, to exhortation, to teaching. 14 Do not neglect the gift you have, which was given you by prophecy when the council of elders laid their hands on you. 15 Practice these things, immerse yourself in them,[6] so that all may see your progress. 16 Keep a close watch on yourself and on the teaching. Persist in this, for by so doing you will save both yourself and your hearers.

Instructions for the Church

5 Do not rebuke an older man but encourage him as you would a father, younger men as brothers, 2 older women as mothers, younger women as sisters, in all purity.

1641
3 Honor widows who are truly widows. 4 But if a widow has children or grandchildren, let them first learn to show godliness to their own household and to make some return to their parents, for this is pleasing in the sight of God. 5 She who is truly a widow, left all alone, has set her hope on God and continues in supplications and prayers night and day, 6 but she who is self-indulgent is dead even while she lives. 7 Command these things as well, so that they may be without reproach. 8 But if anyone does not provide for his relatives, and especially for members of his household, he has denied the faith and is worse than an unbeliever.

1641
9 Let a widow be enrolled if she is not less than sixty years of age, having been the wife of one husband,[7]

[1] Greek *Who*; some manuscripts *God*; others *Which* [2] Or *justified* [3] Or *vindicated in spirit* [4] Or *brothers and sisters*. The plural Greek word *adelphoi* (translated "brothers") refers to siblings in a family. In New Testament usage, depending on the context, *adelphoi* may refer either to men or to both men and women who are siblings (brothers and sisters) in God's family, the church [5] Some manuscripts *and suffer reproach* [6] Greek *be in them* [7] Or *a woman of one man*

10 and having a reputation for good works: if she has brought up children, has shown hospitality, has washed the feet of the saints, has cared for the afflicted, and has devoted herself to every good work. 11 But refuse to enroll younger widows, for when their passions draw them away from Christ, they desire to marry 12 and so incur condemnation for having abandoned their former faith. 13 Besides that, they learn to be idlers, going about from house to house, and not only idlers, but also gossips and busybodies, saying what they should not. 14 So I would have younger widows marry, bear children, manage their households, and give the adversary no occasion for slander. 15 For some have already strayed after Satan. 16 If any believing woman has relatives who are widows, let her care for them. Let the church not be burdened, so that it may care for those who are truly widows.

1641

17 Let the elders who rule well be considered worthy of double honor, especially those who labor in preaching and teaching. 18 For the Scripture says, "You shall not muzzle an ox when it treads out the grain," and, "The laborer deserves his wages." 19 Do not admit a charge against an elder except on the evidence of two or three witnesses. 20 As for those who persist in sin, rebuke them in the presence of all, so that the rest may stand in fear. 21 In the presence of God and of Christ Jesus and of the elect angels I charge you to keep these rules without prejudging, doing nothing from partiality. 22 Do not be hasty in the laying on of hands, nor take part in the sins of others; keep yourself pure. 23 (No longer drink only water, but use a little wine for the sake of your stomach and your frequent ailments.) 24 The sins of some men are conspicuous, going before them to judgment, but the sins of others appear later. 25 So also good works are conspicuous, and even those that are not cannot remain hidden.

6 Let all who are under a yoke as slaves[1] regard their own masters as worthy of all honor, so that the name of God and the teaching may not be reviled. 2 Those who have believing masters must not be disrespectful on the ground that they are brothers; rather they must serve all the better since those who benefit by their good service are believers and beloved.

False Teachers and True Contentment

Teach and urge these things. 3 If anyone teaches a different doctrine and does not agree with the sound[2] words of our Lord Jesus Christ and the teaching that accords with godliness, 4 he is puffed up with conceit and understands nothing. He has an unhealthy craving for controversy and for quarrels about words, which produce envy, dissension, slander, evil suspicions, 5 and constant friction among people who are depraved in mind and deprived of the truth, imagining that godliness is a means of gain. 6 Now there is great gain in godliness with contentment, 7 for we brought nothing into the world, and[3] we cannot take anything out of the world. 8 But if we have food and clothing, with these we will be content. 9 But those who desire to be rich fall into temptation, into a snare, into many senseless and harmful desires that plunge people into ruin and destruction. 10 For the love of money is a root of all kinds of evils. It is through this craving that some have wandered away from the faith and pierced themselves with many pangs.

Fight the Good Fight of Faith

11 But as for you, O man of God, flee these things. Pursue righteousness, godliness, faith, love, steadfastness, gentleness. 12 Fight the good fight of the faith. Take hold of the eternal life to which you were called and about which you made the good confession in the presence of many witnesses. 13 I charge you in the presence of God, who gives life to all things, and of

[1] Greek *bondservants* [2] Or *healthy* [3] Greek *for;* some manuscripts insert [it is] *certain* [that]

Christ Jesus, who in his testimony before[1]
Pontius Pilate made the good confession,
14 to keep the commandment unstained
and free from reproach until the appear-
ing of our Lord Jesus Christ, **15** which he
will display at the proper time—he who is
the blessed and only Sovereign, the King
of kings and Lord of lords, **16** who alone
has immortality, who dwells in unap-
proachable light, whom no one has ever
seen or can see. To him be honor and eter-
nal dominion. Amen.

17 As for the rich in this present age,
charge them not to be haughty, nor to set
their hopes on the uncertainty of riches,
but on God, who richly provides us with
everything to enjoy. **18** They are to do good,
to be rich in good works, to be generous
and ready to share, **19** thus storing up trea-
sure for themselves as a good foundation
for the future, so that they may take hold
of that which is truly life.

20 O Timothy, guard the deposit en-
trusted to you. Avoid the irreverent bab-
ble and contradictions of what is falsely
called "knowledge," **21** for by professing it
some have swerved from the faith.

Grace be with you.[2]

[1] Or *in the time of* [2] The Greek for *you* is plural

Introduction to

2 Timothy

Author
Paul the apostle

Date
About A.D. 62–64

Key People
Paul; Timothy; Timothy's mother Eunice; Timothy's grandmother Lois

Purpose
The purpose of 2 Timothy is to encourage Timothy to be strong and faithful to the gospel in the face of persecution and to ask him to come visit Paul in prison.

Central Themes
Suffering is a normal part of the Christian life; Christians are to depend on God's power and keep trusting God through suffering; the good news of the gospel is our reason for enduring; Scripture is God's very Word to His people; false teaching must be firmly resisted.

Memory Verses
God's purpose and grace (2 Timothy 1:8–9); the value of sacred Scripture (2 Timothy 3:16–17)

Introduction

Paul writes 2 Timothy from prison, where he waited to be put to death for preaching the gospel. Paul's death might discourage Timothy, so Paul tells him not to give in to fear. Timothy must not be ashamed of the gospel or of suffering for it; the gospel brings life and salvation. Instead, Timothy must hold to and teach the truth Paul had passed on to him (2 Timothy 1:1–14). Paul reminds Timothy of God's goodness, which should make us willing to suffer like good soldiers of Christ (2 Timothy 2:1–13). As a pastor, Timothy must teach truth constantly, live truth as an example to his hearers, and resist false teachers and evildoers (2 Timothy 2:14–3:9). In suffering and persecution, he must continue in the scriptural teaching he had learned as a child. It would make him wise for salvation and equip him as a man of God (2 Timothy 3:10–17). Paul knows that he will soon die but that the Lord will be with him and will bring him safely to heaven, where a crown of righteousness waited. Paul asks Timothy to come see him in prison and to bring him some extra clothes, along with certain books (2 Timothy 4:6–22).

About A.D. 48/49–51	About A.D. 62–64	About A.D. 64–67
Timothy on Paul's second journey	Paul arrested, writes 2 Timothy	Paul martyred in Rome

The Second Letter of Paul to Timothy

2 Timothy

Greeting

1 Paul, an apostle of Christ Jesus by the
will of God according to the promise
of the life that is in Christ Jesus,
2 To Timothy, my beloved child:
Grace, mercy, and peace from God the
Father and Christ Jesus our Lord.

Guard the Deposit Entrusted to You

3 I thank God whom I serve, as did my
ancestors, with a clear conscience, as I
remember you constantly in my prayers
night and day. 4 As I remember your tears,
I long to see you, that I may be filled with
joy. 5 I am reminded of your sincere
faith, a faith that dwelt first in your
1663 grandmother Lois and your mother
Eunice and now, I am sure, dwells in you
as well. 6 For this reason I remind you to
fan into flame the gift of God, which is in
you through the laying on of my hands,
7 for God gave us a spirit not of fear but of
power and love and self-control.
8 Therefore do not be ashamed of the
testimony about our Lord, nor of me his
prisoner, but share in suffering for the
gospel by the power of God, 9 who saved
us and called us to[1] a holy calling, not
because of our works but because of his
own purpose and grace, which he gave
us in Christ Jesus before the ages began,[2]
10 and which now has been manifested
through the appearing of our Savior Christ
Jesus, who abolished death and brought
life and immortality to light through
the gospel, 11 for which I was appointed
a preacher and apostle and teacher,
12 which is why I suffer as I do. But I am
not ashamed, for I know whom I have
believed, and I am convinced that he is
able to guard until that Day what has been
entrusted to me.[3] 13 Follow the pattern
of the sound[4] words that you have heard
from me, in the faith and love that are
in Christ Jesus. 14 By the Holy Spirit who
dwells within us, guard the good deposit
entrusted to you.
15 You are aware that all who are in Asia
turned away from me, among whom are
Phygelus and Hermogenes. 16 May the
Lord grant mercy to the household of
Onesiphorus, for he often refreshed me
and was not ashamed of my chains, 17 but
when he arrived in Rome he searched for
me earnestly and found me— 18 may the
Lord grant him to find mercy from the
Lord on that Day!—and you well know all
the service he rendered at Ephesus.

A Good Soldier of Christ Jesus

2 You then, my child, be strengthened
by the grace that is in Christ Jesus,
2 and what you have heard from me in
the presence of many witnesses entrust
to faithful men who will be able to teach
others also. 3 Share in suffering as a good
soldier of Christ Jesus. 4 No soldier gets
entangled in civilian pursuits, since his
aim is to please the one who enlisted
him. 5 An athlete is not crowned unless
he competes according to the rules. 6 It is
the hard-working farmer who ought to
have the first share of the crops. 7 Think
over what I say, for the Lord will give you
understanding in everything.
8 Remember Jesus Christ, risen from the
dead, the offspring of David, as preached
in my gospel, 9 for which I am suffering,
bound with chains as a criminal. But the
word of God is not bound! 10 Therefore
I endure everything for the sake of the
elect, that they also may obtain the sal-
vation that is in Christ Jesus with eternal
glory. 11 The saying is trustworthy, for:

[1] Or *with* [2] Greek *before times eternal* [3] Or *what I have entrusted to him;* Greek *my deposit* [4] Or *healthy*

If we have died with him, we will
also live with him;
12 if we endure, we will also reign with
him;
if we deny him, he also will deny us;
13 if we are faithless, he remains
faithful—

for he cannot deny himself.

A Worker Approved by God

14 Remind them of these things, and charge them before God[1] not to quarrel about words, which does no good, but only ruins the hearers. 15 Do your best to present yourself to God as one approved,[2] a worker who has no need to be ashamed, rightly handling the word of truth. 16 But avoid irreverent babble, for it will lead people into more and more ungodliness, 17 and their talk will spread like gangrene. Among them are Hymenaeus and Philetus, 18 who have swerved from the truth, saying that the resurrection has already happened. They are upsetting the faith of some. 19 But God's firm foundation stands, bearing this seal: "The Lord knows those who are his," and, "Let everyone who names the name of the Lord depart from iniquity."

20 Now in a great house there are not only vessels of gold and silver but also of wood and clay, some for honorable use, some for dishonorable. 21 Therefore, if anyone cleanses himself from what is dishonorable,[3] he will be a vessel for honorable use, set apart as holy, useful to the master of the house, ready for every good work.

22 So flee youthful passions and pursue righteousness, faith, love, and peace, along with those who call on the Lord from a pure heart. 23 Have nothing to do with foolish, ignorant controversies; you know that they breed quarrels. 24 And the Lord's servant[4] must not be quarrelsome but kind to everyone, able to teach, patiently enduring evil, 25 correcting his opponents with gentleness. God may perhaps grant them repentance leading to a knowledge of the truth, 26 and they may come to their senses and escape from the snare of the devil, after being captured by him to do his will.

Godlessness in the Last Days

3 But understand this, that in the last days there will come times of difficulty. 2 For people will be lovers of self, lovers of money, proud, arrogant, abusive, disobedient to their parents, ungrateful, unholy, 3 heartless, unappeasable, slanderous, without self-control, brutal, not loving good, 4 treacherous, reckless, swollen with conceit, lovers of pleasure rather than lovers of God, 5 having the appearance of godliness, but denying its power. Avoid such people. 6 For among them are those who creep into households and capture weak women, burdened with sins and led astray by various passions, 7 always learning and never able to arrive at a knowledge of the truth. 8 Just as Jannes and Jambres opposed Moses, so these men also oppose the truth, men corrupted in mind and disqualified regarding the faith. 9 But they will not get very far, for their folly will be plain to all, as was that of those two men.

All Scripture Is Breathed Out by God

10 You, however, have followed my teaching, my conduct, my aim in life, my faith, my patience, my love, my steadfastness, 11 my persecutions and sufferings that happened to me at Antioch, at Iconium, and at Lystra—which persecutions I endured; yet from them all the Lord rescued me. 12 Indeed, all who desire to live a godly life in Christ Jesus will be persecuted, 13 while evil people and impostors will go on from bad to worse, deceiving and being deceived. 14 But as for you, continue in what you have learned and have

1629

[1] Some manuscripts *the Lord* [2] That is, one approved after being tested [3] Greek *from these things* [4] Greek *bondservant*

firmly believed, knowing from whom[1]
you learned it 15 and how from childhood
you have been acquainted with
the sacred writings, which are
1663 able to make you wise for salva-
tion through faith in Christ Jesus. 16 All
Scripture is breathed out by God and
profitable for teaching, for reproof, for
correction, and for training in righteous-
ness, 17 that the man of God[2] may be com-
petent, equipped for every good work.

Preach the Word

4 I charge you in the presence of God and of Christ Jesus, who is to judge the living and the dead, and by his appearing and his kingdom: 2 preach the word; be ready in season and out of season; reprove, rebuke, and exhort, with complete patience and teaching. 3 For the time is coming when people will not endure sound[3] teaching, but having itching ears they will accumulate for themselves teachers to suit their own passions, 4 and will turn away from listening to the truth and wander off into myths. 5 As for you, always be sober-minded, endure suffering, do the work of an evangelist, fulfill your ministry.

6 For I am already being poured out as a drink offering, and the time of my departure has come. 7 I have fought the good fight, I have finished the race, I have kept the faith. 8 Henceforth there is laid up for me the crown of righteousness, which the Lord, the righteous judge, will award to me on that Day, and not only to me but also to all who have loved his appearing.

Personal Instructions

9 Do your best to come to me soon. 10 For Demas, in love with this present world, has deserted me and gone to Thessalonica. Crescens has gone to Galatia,[4] Titus to Dalmatia. 11 Luke alone is with me. Get Mark and bring him with you, for he is very useful to me for ministry. 12 Tychicus I have sent to Ephesus. 13 When you come, bring the cloak that I left with Carpus at Troas, also the books, and above all the parchments. 14 Alexander the coppersmith did me great harm; the Lord will repay him according to his deeds. 15 Beware of him yourself, for he strongly opposed our message. 16 At my first defense no one came to stand by me, but all deserted me. May it not be charged against them! 17 But the Lord stood by me and strengthened me, so that through me the message might be fully proclaimed and all the Gentiles might hear it. So I was rescued from the lion's mouth. 18 The Lord will rescue me from every evil deed and bring me safely into his heavenly kingdom. To him be the glory forever and ever. Amen.

Final Greetings

19 Greet Prisca and Aquila, and the household of Onesiphorus. 20 Erastus remained at Corinth, and I left Trophimus, who was ill, at Miletus. 21 Do your best to come before winter. Eubulus sends greetings to you, as do Pudens and Linus and Claudia and all the brothers.[5]

22 The Lord be with your spirit. Grace be with you.[6]

[1] The Greek for *whom* is plural [2] That is, a messenger of God (the phrase echoes a common Old Testament expression) [3] Or *healthy* [4] Some manuscripts *Gaul* [5] Or *brothers and sisters*. The plural Greek word *adelphoi* (translated "brothers") refers to siblings in a family. In New Testament usage, depending on the context, *adelphoi* may refer either to men or to both men and women who are siblings (brothers and sisters) in God's family, the church [6] The Greek for *you* is plural

Introduction to

Titus

Author
Paul the apostle

Date
About A.D. 62–64

Key People
Paul; Titus; elders

Purpose
The purpose of Titus is to guide Titus as he taught and appointed elders in new churches in Crete.

Central Themes
Sound doctrine is important; doctrine and godliness go together; godly elders should be appointed; salvation comes by God's grace.

Memory Verses
Redeemed and purified (Titus 2:14); renewal by the Holy Spirit (Titus 3:4–7)

Introduction

When Paul had preached the gospel in Crete, people believed it and churches had begun. When Paul went on to preach in other places, he left Titus behind to give more teaching in these churches and to help them get off to a good start. Paul's letter begins with a reminder of the character qualities Titus should look for when appointing elders (Titus 1:5–9). There were false teachers among the churches in Crete whose ungodly lives showed that their teaching was false; these men must be rebuked and silenced (Titus 1:10–16). Paul describes godly behaviors for men and women, both young and old, and explains that believing right doctrine results in holy living. This is because the salvation God gives by His grace is for the purpose of making people holy (Titus 2). Paul tells Timothy to remind Christians to submit to authority and to be ready for every good work. We have been saved by grace, not by works, but we have been saved so that we can devote ourselves to good works (Titus 3).

About A.D. 52–57	About A.D. 62–64	About A.D. 64–67
Titus ministers with Paul	Paul writes Titus	Paul martyred in Rome

The Letter of Paul to

Titus

Greeting

1 Paul, a servant[1] of God and an apostle of Jesus Christ, for the sake of the faith of God's elect and their knowledge of the truth, which accords with godliness, **2** in hope of eternal life, which God, who never lies, promised before the ages began[2] **3** and at the proper time manifested in his word through the preaching with which I have been entrusted by the command of God our Savior;

4 To Titus, my true child in a common faith:

Grace and peace from God the Father and Christ Jesus our Savior.

Qualifications for Elders

5 This is why I left you in Crete, so that you might put what remained into order, and appoint elders in every town as I directed you— **6** if anyone is above reproach, the husband of one wife,[3] and his children are believers and not open to the charge of debauchery or insubordination. **7** For an overseer,[4] as God's steward, must be above reproach. He must not be arrogant or quick-tempered or a drunkard or violent or greedy for gain, **8** but hospitable, a lover of good, self-controlled, upright, holy, and disciplined. **9** He must hold firm to the trustworthy word as taught, so that he may be able to give instruction in sound[5] doctrine and also to rebuke those who contradict it.

10 For there are many who are insubordinate, empty talkers and deceivers, especially those of the circumcision party. **11** They must be silenced, since they are upsetting whole families by teaching for shameful gain what they ought not to teach. **12** One of the Cretans,[6] a prophet of their own, said, "Cretans are always liars, evil beasts, lazy gluttons."[7] **13** This testimony is true. Therefore rebuke them sharply, that they may be sound in the faith, **14** not devoting themselves to Jewish myths and the commands of people who turn away from the truth. **15** To the pure, all things are pure, but to the defiled and unbelieving, nothing is pure; but both their minds and their consciences are defiled. **16** They profess to know God, but they deny him by their works. They are detestable, disobedient, unfit for any good work.

Teach Sound Doctrine

2 But as for you, teach what accords with sound[8] doctrine. **2** Older men are to be sober-minded, dignified, self-controlled, sound in faith, in love, and in steadfastness. **3** Older women likewise are to be reverent in behavior, not slanderers or slaves to much wine. They are to teach what is good, **4** and so train the young women to love their husbands and children, **5** to be self-controlled, pure, working at home, kind, and submissive to their own husbands, that the word of God may not be reviled. **6** Likewise, urge the younger men to be self-controlled. **7** Show yourself in all respects to be a model of good works, and in your teaching show integrity, dignity, **8** and sound speech that cannot be condemned, so that an opponent may be put to shame, having nothing evil to say about us. **9** Slaves[9] are to be submissive to their own masters in everything; they are to be well-pleasing, not argumentative, **10** not pilfering, but showing all good faith, so that in everything they may adorn the doctrine of God our Savior.

[1] Or *slave*; Greek *bondservant* [2] Greek *before times eternal* [3] Or *a man of one woman* [4] Or *bishop*; Greek *episkopos* [5] Or *healthy*; also verse 13 [6] Greek *One of them* [7] Probably from Epimenides of Crete [8] Or *healthy*; also verses 2, 8 [9] Or *servants*; Greek *bondservants*

[11] For the grace of God has appeared, bringing salvation for all people, [12] training us to renounce ungodliness and worldly passions, and to live self-controlled, upright, and godly lives in the present age, [13] waiting for our blessed hope, the appearing of the glory of our great God and Savior Jesus Christ, [14] who gave himself for us to redeem us from all lawlessness and to purify for himself a people for his own possession who are zealous for good works.

[15] Declare these things; exhort and rebuke with all authority. Let no one disregard you.

Be Ready for Every Good Work

3 Remind them to be submissive to rulers and authorities, to be obedient, to be ready for every good work, [2] to speak evil of no one, to avoid quarreling, to be gentle, and to show perfect courtesy toward all people. [3] For we ourselves were once foolish, disobedient, led astray, slaves to various passions and pleasures, passing our days in malice and envy, hated by others and hating one another. [4] But when the goodness and loving kindness of God our Savior appeared, [5] he saved us, not because of works done by us in righteousness, but according to his own mercy, by the washing of regeneration and renewal of the Holy Spirit, [6] whom he poured out on us richly through Jesus Christ our Savior, [7] so that being justified by his grace we might become heirs according to the hope of eternal life. [8] The saying is trustworthy, and I want you to insist on these things, so that those who have believed in God may be careful to devote themselves to good works. These things are excellent and profitable for people. [9] But avoid foolish controversies, genealogies, dissensions, and quarrels about the law, for they are unprofitable and worthless. [10] As for a person who stirs up division, after warning him once and then twice, have nothing more to do with him, [11] knowing that such a person is warped and sinful; he is self-condemned.

1549

Final Instructions and Greetings

[12] When I send Artemas or Tychicus to you, do your best to come to me at Nicopolis, for I have decided to spend the winter there. [13] Do your best to speed Zenas the lawyer and Apollos on their way; see that they lack nothing. [14] And let our people learn to devote themselves to good works, so as to help cases of urgent need, and not be unfruitful.

[15] All who are with me send greetings to you. Greet those who love us in the faith.

Grace be with you all.

Introduction to

Philemon

Author
Paul the apostle

Date
About A.D. 62

Key People
Paul; Onesimus; Philemon

Purpose
Paul's purpose in this letter is to ask Philemon to receive back and forgive his runaway slave, Onesimus, who had become a Christian.

Central Themes
The greatest reconciliation is between God and man; there should be reconciliation between Christians; Christians must show love and forgiveness; debts can be both repaid and forgiven.

Memory Verses
Receive your brother (Philemon 17–18)

Introduction

Onesimus was a slave who had run away from his master, Philemon, perhaps stealing from him too. Onesimus fled to Rome, where he met Paul in prison and became a Christian. Now Paul was sending him back to his master along with this short letter. Paul's letter begins with thanksgiving for the love Philemon had shown to Paul and other Christians in the past (Philemon 1–7). Paul would have liked to have kept Onesimus with him because he loved him, and Onesimus was helpful to him, but Paul didn't want to do that without Philemon's permission (Philemon 8–14). Onesimus was coming back as a much better servant than he had been—and as a beloved brother in the Lord (Philemon 15–16). Paul urges Philemon to receive Onesimus just as he would have received Paul. If Onesimus owed him anything, Philemon should charge it to Paul—but Philemon should remember the debt he himself owed, because Paul had shared the gospel with Philemon, leading him to the Lord (Philemon 17–18). Paul says he knows Philemon will do even more than he is asking, and Paul requests that a guest room is prepared for him, since he hopes to visit Philemon once he is freed from prison (Philemon 19–22).

About A.D. 48/49–51	About A.D. 62	About A.D. 64–67
Paul in Ephesus (with Philemon?)	Paul writes Philemon	Paul martyred in Rome

Onesimus Runs Away

Philemon was a wealthy Christian man, who opened his home in the city of Colossae as a place for believers to worship and be together. Philemon had a slave named Onesimus, but Onesimus ran away from him, and stole something that belonged to Philemon.

Onesimus went all the way to Rome. When he got to Rome, Onesimus met Paul and became a Christian. Even though Paul was being held as a prisoner, nothing could stop Paul from sharing the Good News about the Savior. Onesimus joined the group of Christians there in Rome. As a follower of Jesus, Onesimus's life was completely changed, and he became a kind and helpful friend to Paul.

Paul would have liked his new friend Onesimus to stay with him in Rome. But Paul knew it was important for Onesimus to go back to the city of Colossae and to make right what he had done wrong. So Paul sent Onesimus back to Philemon, with a personal letter that Paul had written.

In the letter, Paul told Philemon about the change in Onesimus. Paul encouraged Philemon to forgive Onesimus. Paul knew that both Onesimus and Philemon were Christians now. That meant they now had a new relationship—they were brothers in God's family. Paul wanted the two men to be restored in their relationship with each other.

Paul even offered to pay any debt that Onesimus owed to Philemon.

Paul reminded Philemon that every person who trusts in Jesus has been forgiven for all his sins. Jesus paid the debt for our sins through His perfect life and His death on the cross. Paul hoped that Philemon would want to forgive Onesimus, because God had already forgiven both of them!

God loves us and forgives our sins because of Jesus. Through the Holy Spirit, God gives us power to love and forgive others too.

SEEK and FIND

WHERE TO FIND THE STORY

Philemon

KEY BIBLE VERSE

"Be kind to one another, tenderhearted, forgiving one another, as God in Christ forgave you." (Ephesians 4:32)

THREE KEY QUESTIONS

- Why did Paul send Onesimus back to Philemon?
- What new relationship did Philemon and Onesimus have?
- What is the debt that Jesus paid for us?

RELATED BIBLE READINGS

Matthew 6:9–15; 18:21–35; Ephesians 6:5–9; Colossians 3:22–4:1

The Letter of Paul to

Philemon

Greeting

1 Paul, a prisoner for Christ Jesus,
and Timothy our brother,
1783 To Philemon our beloved fel-
low worker 2 and Apphia our sister and
Archippus our fellow soldier, and the
church in your house:

3 Grace to you and peace from God our
Father and the Lord Jesus Christ.

Philemon's Love and Faith

4 I thank my God always when I
remember you in my prayers, 5 because
I hear of your love and of the faith that
you have toward the Lord Jesus and for
all the saints, 6 and I pray that the sharing
of your faith may become effective for
the full knowledge of every good thing
that is in us for the sake of Christ.[1] 7 For
I have derived much joy and comfort
from your love, my brother, because the
hearts of the saints have been refreshed
through you.

Paul's Plea for Onesimus

8 Accordingly, though I am bold enough
in Christ to command you to do what is
required, 9 yet for love's sake I prefer to
appeal to you—I, Paul, an old man and
now a prisoner also for Christ Jesus— 10 I
appeal to you for my child, Onesimus,[2]
whose father I became in my imprison-
ment. 11 (Formerly he was useless to you,
but now he is indeed useful to you and
to me.) 12 I am sending him back to you,
sending my very heart. 13 I would have
been glad to keep him with me, in order
that he might serve me on your behalf
during my imprisonment for the gospel,
14 but I preferred to do nothing without
your consent in order that your goodness
might not be by compulsion but of your
own accord. 15 For this perhaps is why
he was parted from you for a while, that
you might have him back forever, 16 no
longer as a slave[3] but more than a slave,
as a beloved brother—especially to me, but
how much more to you, both in the flesh
and in the Lord.

17 So if you consider me your partner,
receive him as you would receive me. 18 If
he has wronged you at all, or owes you
anything, charge that to my account. 19 I,
Paul, write this with my own hand: I will
repay it—to say nothing of your owing
me even your own self. 20 Yes, brother, I
want some benefit from you in the Lord.
Refresh my heart in Christ.

21 Confident of your obedience, I write
to you, knowing that you will do even
more than I say. 22 At the same time, pre-
pare a guest room for me, for I am hoping
that through your prayers I will be gra-
ciously given to you.

Final Greetings

23 Epaphras, my fellow prisoner in
Christ Jesus, sends greetings to you, 24 and
so do Mark, Aristarchus, Demas, and Luke,
my fellow workers.

25 The grace of the Lord Jesus Christ be
with your spirit.

[1] Or *for Christ's service* [2] *Onesimus* means *useful* (see verse 11) or *beneficial* (see verse 20) [3] Greek *bondservant*; twice in this verse

Introduction to

Hebrews

Author

Unknown

Date

Before A.D. 70

Key People

Christians raised as Jews; Moses; famous Old Testament heroes of faith

Purpose

The purpose of Hebrews is to show how Jesus is better than Moses, the priests, and the sacrifices of the old covenant, and to encourage Jewish Christians to stay true to Him through persecution and hardship.

Central Themes

God speaks most fully in His Son; Jesus is superior to angels and to Moses; Jesus is our great high priest; Jesus is the perfect sacrifice all other sacrifices pointed to; Christians must hold to Jesus in faith and not turn back; faith is defined using Old Testament examples.

Memory Verses

God spoke through His Son (Hebrews 1:1–4); God's living Word (Hebrews 4:12–13); Christ's blood purifies us (Hebrews 9:13–14); faith defined (Hebrews 11:1–3); run with endurance (Hebrews 12:1–2)

Introduction

This book was written to Christians who had grown up as Jews and therefore knew the Old Testament and the Jewish faith very well. They had grown weary in their faith because of persecution and hardship. They may have been tempted to turn back to keeping Jewish laws instead of going on with Christ. The book gives several reasons why that would be foolish. God's fullest revelation came, not by Old Testament prophets, but by God's Son (Hebrews 1:1–3). Jesus is greater than Moses, who gave the old covenant, and greater than Joshua, who gave the Israelites rest in the Promised Land (Hebrews 3:1–4:14). Jesus is a better priest of a better covenant (Hebrews 7:11–9:14). Jesus' sacrifice of His own blood is better than the old sacrifices of sheep and goats (Hebrews 9:15–10:18). The writer warns these Christians that if they turn back, abandoning Christ, they have nothing to look forward to but God's judgment (Hebrews 10:26–31). The author encourages his readers to remember Old Testament believers who persevered in faith through hardship (Hebrews 11) and especially to remember Jesus' example and God's promises so that they won't be discouraged (Hebrews 12–13).

About A.D. 28–33	?	A.D. 70
Jesus' ministry, death, resurrection	Hebrews written	Temple destroyed

The Letter to the

Hebrews

The Supremacy of God's Son

1 Long ago, at many times and in
many ways, God spoke to our
587 fathers by the prophets, [2]but in
these last days he has spoken to us
by his Son, whom he appointed the
441, heir of all things, through whom
587 also he created the world. [3]He is
the radiance of the glory of God and the
exact imprint of his nature, and he
upholds the universe by the word of his
power. After making purification for sins,
he sat down at the right hand of the
Majesty on high, [4]having become as much
superior to angels as the name he
has inherited is more excellent
1611 than theirs.

[5]For to which of the angels did God ever
say,

"You are my Son,
today I have begotten you"?

Or again,

"I will be to him a father,
and he shall be to me a son"?

[6]And again, when he brings the firstborn
into the world, he says,

"Let all God's angels worship him."

[7]Of the angels he says,

"He makes his angels winds,
and his ministers a flame of fire."

[8]But of the Son he says,

"Your throne, O God, is forever and
ever,
the scepter of uprightness is the
scepter of your kingdom.
9 You have loved righteousness and
hated wickedness;
therefore God, your God, has
anointed you
with the oil of gladness beyond
your companions."

[10]And,

"You, Lord, laid the foundation of the
earth in the beginning,
and the heavens are the work of
your hands;
11 they will perish, but you remain;
they will all wear out like a
garment,
12 like a robe you will roll them up,
like a garment they will be
changed.[1]
But you are the same,
and your years will have no end."

[13]And to which of the angels has he ever
said,

"Sit at my right hand
until I make your enemies a
footstool for your feet"?

[14]Are they not all ministering spirits sent
out to serve for the sake of those who are
to inherit salvation?

Warning Against Neglecting Salvation

2 Therefore we must pay much closer
attention to what we have heard,
lest we drift away from it. [2]For since the
message declared by angels proved to be
reliable, and every transgression or dis-
obedience received a just retribution,
[3]how shall we escape if we neglect such
a great salvation? It was declared at first
by the Lord, and it was attested to us by
those who heard, [4]while God also bore
witness by signs and wonders and vari-

[1] Some manuscripts omit *like a garment*

ous miracles and by gifts of the Holy Spirit distributed according to his will.

The Founder of Salvation

5 Now it was not to angels that God subjected the world to come, of which we are speaking. **6** It has been testified somewhere,

"What is man, that you are mindful
of him,
or the son of man, that you care
for him?
7 You made him for a little while
lower than the angels;
you have crowned him with glory
and honor,[1]
8 putting everything in subjection
under his feet."

Now in putting everything in subjection to him, he left nothing outside his control. At present, we do not yet see everything in subjection to him. **9** But we see him who for a little while was made lower than the angels, namely Jesus, crowned with glory and honor because of the suffering of death, so that by the grace of God he might taste death for everyone.

10 For it was fitting that he, for whom and by whom all things exist, in bringing many sons to glory, should make the founder of their salvation perfect through suffering. **11** For he who sanctifies and those who are sanctified all have one source.[2] That is why he is not ashamed to call them brothers,[3] **12** saying,

"I will tell of your name to my
brothers;
in the midst of the congregation I
will sing your praise."

13 And again,

"I will put my trust in him."

And again,

"Behold, I and the children God has
given me."

14 Since therefore the children
share in flesh and blood, he him-
1309, self likewise partook of the same
1373 things, that through death he
might destroy the one who has the power of death, that is, the devil, **15** and deliver all those who through fear of death were subject to lifelong slavery. **16** For surely it is not angels that he helps, but he helps the offspring of Abraham. **17** Therefore he had to be made like his brothers in every respect, so that he might become a merciful and faithful high priest in the service of God, to make propitiation for the sins of the people. **18** For because he himself has suffered when tempted, he is able to help those who are being tempted.

Jesus Greater Than Moses

3 Therefore, holy brothers,[4] you who share in a heavenly calling, consider Jesus, the apostle and high priest of our confession, **2** who was faithful to him who appointed him, just as Moses also was faithful in all God's[5] house. **3** For Jesus has been counted worthy of more glory than Moses—as much more glory as the builder of a house has more honor than the house itself. **4** (For every house is built by someone, but the builder of all things is God.) **5** Now Moses was faithful in all God's house as a servant, to testify to the things that were to be spoken later, **6** but Christ is faithful over God's house as a son. And we are his house if indeed we hold fast our confidence and our boasting in our hope.[6]

A Rest for the People of God

7 Therefore, as the Holy Spirit says,

"Today, if you hear his voice,
8 do not harden your hearts as in the
rebellion,

[1] Some manuscripts insert *and set him over the works of your hands* [2] Greek *all are of one* [3] Or *brothers and sisters*. The plural Greek word *adelphoi* (translated "brothers") refers to siblings in a family. In New Testament usage, depending on the context, *adelphoi* may refer either to men or to both men and women who are siblings (brothers and sisters) in God's family, the church; also verse 12 [4] Or *brothers and sisters*; also verse 12 [5] Greek *his*; also verses 5, 6 [6] Some manuscripts insert *firm to the end*

on the day of testing in the
wilderness,
9 where your fathers put me to the test
and saw my works for forty years.
10 Therefore I was provoked with that
generation,
and said, 'They always go astray in
their heart;
they have not known my ways.'
11 As I swore in my wrath,
'They shall not enter my rest.'"

12 Take care, brothers, lest there be
in any of you an evil, unbelieving
265 heart, leading you to fall away
from the living God. 13 But exhort one another every day, as long as it is called "today," that none of you may be hardened by the deceitfulness of sin. 14 For we have come to share in Christ, if indeed we hold our original confidence firm to the end. 15 As it is said,

"Today, if you hear his voice,
do not harden your hearts as in the
rebellion."

16 For who were those who heard and yet rebelled? Was it not all those who left Egypt led by Moses? 17 And with whom was he provoked for forty years? Was it not with those who sinned, whose bodies fell in the wilderness? 18 And to whom did he swear that they would not enter his rest, but to those who were disobedient? 19 So we see that they were unable to enter because of unbelief.

4 Therefore, while the promise of entering his rest still stands, let us fear lest any of you should seem to have failed to reach it. 2 For good news came to us just as to them, but the message they heard did not benefit them, because they were not united by faith with those who listened.[1] 3 For we who have believed enter that rest, as he has said,

"As I swore in my wrath,
'They shall not enter my rest,'"

although his works were finished from the foundation of the world. 4 For he has somewhere spoken of the seventh day in this way: "And God rested on the seventh day from all his works." 5 And again in this passage he said,

"They shall not enter my rest."

6 Since therefore it remains for some to enter it, and those who formerly received the good news failed to enter because of disobedience, 7 again he appoints a certain day, "Today," saying through David so long afterward, in the words already quoted,

"Today, if you hear his voice,
do not harden your hearts."

8 For if Joshua had given them rest,
God[2] would not have spoken of
351, another day later on. 9 So then,
357 there remains a Sabbath rest for
the people of God, 10 for whoever has entered God's rest has also rested from his works as God did from his.

11 Let us therefore strive to enter that rest, so that no one may fall by the same sort of disobedience. 12 For the word of God is living and active, sharper than any two-edged sword, piercing to the division of soul and of spirit, of joints and of marrow, and discerning the thoughts and intentions of the heart. 13 And no creature is hidden from his sight, but all are naked and exposed to the eyes of him to whom we must give account.

Jesus the Great High Priest

14 Since then we have a great high
priest who has passed through the
1309, heavens, Jesus, the Son of God, let
1373 us hold fast our confession. 15 For
we do not have a high priest who is
unable to sympathize with our
1309 weaknesses, but one who in every
respect has been tempted as we are, yet without sin. 16 Let us then with confidence draw near to the throne of grace, that we

[1] Some manuscripts *it did not meet with faith in the hearers* [2] Greek *he*

may receive mercy and find grace to help in time of need.

5 For every high priest chosen from among men is appointed to act on behalf of men in relation to God, to offer gifts and sacrifices for sins. 2 He can deal gently with the ignorant and wayward, since he himself is beset with weakness. 3 Because of this he is obligated to offer sacrifice for his own sins just as he does for those of the people. 4 And no one takes this honor for himself, but only when called by God, just as Aaron was.

5 So also Christ did not exalt himself to be made a high priest, but was appointed by him who said to him,

"You are my Son,
today I have begotten you";

6 as he says also in another place,

"You are a priest forever,
after the order of Melchizedek."

7 In the days of his flesh, Jesus[1] offered up prayers and supplications, with loud cries and tears, to him who was able to save him from death, and he was heard because of his reverence. 8 Although he was a son, he learned obedience through what he suffered. 9 And being made perfect, he became the source of eternal salvation to all who obey him, 10 being designated by God a high priest after the order of Melchizedek.

Warning Against Apostasy

11 About this we have much to say, and it is hard to explain, since you have become dull of hearing. 12 For though by this time you ought to be teachers, you need someone to teach you again the basic principles of the oracles of God. You need milk, not solid food, 13 for everyone who lives on milk is unskilled in the word of righteousness, since he is a child. 14 But solid food is for the mature, for those who have their powers of discernment trained by constant practice to distinguish good from evil.

6 Therefore let us leave the elementary doctrine of Christ and go on to maturity, not laying again a foundation of repentance from dead works and of faith toward God, 2 and of instruction about washings,[2] the laying on of hands, the resurrection of the dead, and eternal judgment. 3 And this we will do if God permits. 4 For it is impossible, in the case of those who have once been enlightened, who have tasted the heavenly gift, and have shared in the Holy Spirit, 5 and have tasted the goodness of the word of God and the powers of the age to come, 6 and then have fallen away, to restore them again to repentance, since they are crucifying once again the Son of God to their own harm and holding him up to contempt. 7 For land that has drunk the rain that often falls on it, and produces a crop useful to those for whose sake it is cultivated, receives a blessing from God. 8 But if it bears thorns and thistles, it is worthless and near to being cursed, and its end is to be burned.

9 Though we speak in this way, yet in your case, beloved, we feel sure of better things—things that belong to salvation. 10 For God is not unjust so as to overlook your work and the love that you have shown for his name in serving the saints, as you still do. 11 And we desire each one of you to show the same earnestness to have the full assurance of hope until the end, 12 so that you may not be sluggish, but imitators of those who through faith and patience inherit the promises.

The Certainty of God's Promise

13 For when God made a promise to Abraham, since he had no one greater by whom to swear, he swore by himself, 14 saying, "Surely I will bless you and multiply you." 15 And thus Abraham,[3] having patiently waited, obtained the promise. 16 For people swear by something greater than themselves, and in all their disputes an oath is final for confirmation. 17 So when

[1] Greek *he* [2] Or *baptisms* (that is, cleansing rites) [3] Greek *he*

God desired to show more convincingly to
the heirs of the promise the unchangeable
character of his purpose, he guaranteed it
with an oath, 18 so that by two unchange-
able things, in which it is impossible for
God to lie, we who have fled for refuge
might have strong encouragement to hold
fast to the hope set before us. 19 We have
this as a sure and steadfast anchor
of the soul, a hope that enters into
37 the inner place behind the curtain,
20 where Jesus has gone as a forerunner on
our behalf, having become a high priest for-
ever after the order of Melchizedek.

The Priestly Order of Melchizedek

7 For this Melchizedek, king of Salem,
priest of the Most High God, met
Abraham returning from the slaughter of
the kings and blessed him, 2 and to him
Abraham apportioned a tenth part of
everything. He is first, by translation of his
name, king of righteousness, and then he
is also king of Salem, that is, king of peace.
3 He is without father or mother or geneal-
ogy, having neither beginning of days nor
end of life, but resembling the Son of God
he continues a priest forever.

4 See how great this man was to whom
Abraham the patriarch gave a tenth of
the spoils! 5 And those descendants of
Levi who receive the priestly office have
a commandment in the law to take tithes
from the people, that is, from their broth-
ers,[1] though these also are descended
from Abraham. 6 But this man who does
not have his descent from them received
tithes from Abraham and blessed him who
had the promises. 7 It is beyond dispute
that the inferior is blessed by the supe-
rior. 8 In the one case tithes are received
by mortal men, but in the other case, by
one of whom it is testified that he lives.
9 One might even say that Levi himself,
who receives tithes, paid tithes through
Abraham, 10 for he was still in the loins of
his ancestor when Melchizedek met him.

Jesus Compared to Melchizedek

11 Now if perfection had been attain-
able through the Levitical priesthood (for
under it the people received the law), what
further need would there have been for
another priest to arise after the order of
Melchizedek, rather than one named after
the order of Aaron? 12 For when there is a
change in the priesthood, there is neces-
sarily a change in the law as well. 13 For
the one of whom these things are spoken
belonged to another tribe, from which no
one has ever served at the altar. 14 For it is
evident that our Lord was descended from
Judah, and in connection with that tribe
Moses said nothing about priests.

15 This becomes even more evident
when another priest arises in the like-
ness of Melchizedek, 16 who has become a
priest, not on the basis of a legal require-
ment concerning bodily descent, but by
the power of an indestructible life. 17 For
it is witnessed of him,

"You are a priest forever,
after the order of Melchizedek."

18 For on the one hand, a former com-
mandment is set aside because of its
weakness and uselessness 19 (for the law
made nothing perfect); but on the other
hand, a better hope is introduced, through
which we draw near to God.

20 And it was not without an oath. For
those who formerly became priests were
made such without an oath, 21 but this one
was made a priest with an oath by the one
who said to him:

"The Lord has sworn
and will not change his mind,
'You are a priest forever.'"

22 This makes Jesus the guarantor of a bet-
ter covenant.

23 The former priests were many in num-
ber, because they were prevented by death
from continuing in office, 24 but he holds
his priesthood permanently, because he

[1] Or *brothers and sisters*

continues forever. 25 Consequently, he is
able to save to the uttermost[1] those who
draw near to God through him, since he
always lives to make intercession for them.
26 For it was indeed fitting that we
should have such a high priest,
1373 holy, innocent, unstained, sepa-
rated from sinners, and exalted
above the heavens. 27 He has no
1309 need, like those high priests, to
offer sacrifices daily, first for his own sins
and then for those of the people, since he
did this once for all when he offered up
himself. 28 For the law appoints men in
their weakness as high priests, but the
word of the oath, which came later than
the law, appoints a Son who has been
made perfect forever.

Jesus, High Priest of a Better Covenant

8 Now the point in what we are
saying is this: we have such a
205 high priest, one who is seated at
the right hand of the throne of the Majesty
in heaven, 2 a minister in the holy places,
in the true tent[2] that the Lord set up, not
man. 3 For every high priest is appointed
to offer gifts and sacrifices; thus it is nec-
essary for this priest also to have some-
thing to offer. 4 Now if he were on earth, he
would not be a priest at all, since there are
priests who offer gifts according to the
law. 5 They serve a copy and shadow of the
heavenly things. For when Moses was
about to erect the tent, he was instructed
by God, saying, "See that you make every-
thing according to the pattern that was
shown you on the mountain." 6 But
as it is, Christ[3] has obtained a min-
1033 istry that is as much more excel-
lent than the old as the covenant he medi-
ates is better, since it is enacted on better
promises. 7 For if that first covenant had
been faultless, there would have been no
occasion to look for a second.
8 For he finds fault with them when he
says:[4]

"Behold, the days are coming,
declares the Lord,
when I will establish a new
covenant with the house of
Israel
and with the house of Judah,
9 not like the covenant that I made
with their fathers
on the day when I took them by
the hand to bring them out of
the land of Egypt.
For they did not continue in my
covenant,
and so I showed no concern for
them, declares the Lord.
10 For this is the covenant that I will
make with the house of Israel
after those days, declares the Lord:
I will put my laws into their minds,
and write them on their hearts,
and I will be their God,
and they shall be my people.
11 And they shall not teach, each one
his neighbor
and each one his brother, saying,
'Know the Lord,'
for they shall all know me,
from the least of them to the
greatest.
12 For I will be merciful toward their
iniquities,
and I will remember their sins no
more."

13 In speaking of a new covenant, he
makes the first one obsolete. And what
is becoming obsolete and growing old is
ready to vanish away.

The Earthly Holy Place

9 Now even the first covenant
had regulations for worship
205 and an earthly place of holiness.
2 For a tent[5] was prepared, the first section,
in which were the lampstand and the table
and the bread of the Presence.[6] It is called
the Holy Place. 3 Behind the second curtain

[1] That is, completely; or *at all times* [2] Or *tabernacle*; also verse 5 [3] Greek *he* [4] Some manuscripts *For finding fault with it he says to them* [5] Or *tabernacle*; also verses 11, 21 [6] Greek *the presentation of the loaves*

was a second section[1] called the Most Holy Place, 4 having the golden altar of incense and the ark of the covenant covered on all sides with gold, in which was a golden urn holding the manna, and Aaron's staff that budded, and the tablets of the covenant. 5 Above it were the cherubim of glory overshadowing the mercy seat. Of these things we cannot now speak in detail.

6 These preparations having thus been made, the priests go regularly into the first section, performing their ritual duties, 7 but into the second only the high priest goes, and he but once a year, and not without taking blood, which he offers for himself and for the unintentional sins of the people. 8 By this the Holy Spirit indicates that the way into the holy places is not yet opened as long as the first section is still standing 9 (which is symbolic for the present age).[2] According to this arrangement, gifts and sacrifices are offered that cannot perfect the conscience of the worshiper, 10 but deal only with food and drink and various washings, regulations for the body imposed until the time of reformation.

Redemption Through the Blood of Christ

11 But when Christ appeared as a high priest of the good things that have come,[3] then through the greater and more perfect tent (not made with hands, that is, not of this creation) 12 he entered once for all into the holy places, not by means of the blood of goats and calves but by means of his own blood, thus securing an eternal redemption. 13 For if the blood of goats and bulls, and the sprinkling of defiled persons with the ashes of a heifer, sanctify[4] for the purification of the flesh, 14 how much more will the blood of Christ, who through the eternal Spirit offered himself without blemish to God, purify our[5] conscience from dead works to serve the living God.

15 Therefore he is the mediator of a new covenant, so that those who are called may receive the promised eternal inheritance, since a death has occurred that redeems them from the transgressions committed under the first covenant.[6] 16 For where a will is involved, the death of the one who made it must be established. 17 For a will takes effect only at death, since it is not in force as long as the one who made it is alive. 18 Therefore not even the first covenant was inaugurated without blood. 19 For when every commandment of the law had been declared by Moses to all the people, he took the blood of calves and goats, with water and scarlet wool and hyssop, and sprinkled both the book itself and all the people, 20 saying, "This is the blood of the covenant that God commanded for you." 21 And in the same way he sprinkled with the blood both the tent and all the vessels used in worship. 22 Indeed, under the law almost everything is purified with blood, and without the shedding of blood there is no forgiveness of sins.

23 Thus it was necessary for the copies of the heavenly things to be purified with these rites, but the heavenly things themselves with better sacrifices than these. 24 For Christ has entered, not into holy places made with hands, which are copies of the true things, but into heaven itself, now to appear in the presence of God on our behalf. 25 Nor was it to offer himself repeatedly, as the high priest enters the holy places every year with blood not his own, 26 for then he would have had to suffer repeatedly since the foundation of the world. But as it is, he has appeared once for all at the end of the ages to put away sin by the sacrifice of himself. 27 And just as it is appointed for man to die once, and after that comes judgment, 28 so Christ, having been offered once to bear the sins of many, will appear a second time, not to deal with sin but to save those who are eagerly waiting for him.

[1] Greek *tent*; also verses 6, 8 [2] Or *which is symbolic for the age then present* [3] Some manuscripts *good things to come* [4] Or *For if the blood of goats and bulls, and the sprinkling of defiled persons with the ashes of a heifer, sanctifies* [5] Some manuscripts *your* [6] The Greek word means both *covenant* and *will*; also verses 16, 17

Christ's Sacrifice Once for All

10 For since the law has but a shadow
of the good things to come instead
of the true form of these realities, it can
never, by the same sacrifices that are
continually offered every year, make per-
fect those who draw near. 2 Otherwise,
would they not have ceased to be offered,
since the worshipers, having once been
cleansed, would no longer have any con-
sciousness of sins? 3 But in these sacrifices
there is a reminder of sins every year. 4 For
it is impossible for the blood of bulls and
goats to take away sins.

5 Consequently, when Christ[1] came into
the world, he said,

> "Sacrifices and offerings you have
> not desired,
> but a body have you prepared
> for me;
> 6 in burnt offerings and sin offerings
> you have taken no pleasure.
> 7 Then I said, 'Behold, I have come to
> do your will, O God,
> as it is written of me in the scroll
> of the book.'"

8 When he said above, "You have neither
desired nor taken pleasure in sacrifices
and offerings and burnt offerings and sin
offerings" (these are offered according to
the law), 9 then he added, "Behold, I have
come to do your will." He does away with
the first in order to establish the second.
10 And by that will we have been sanctified
through the offering of the body of Jesus
Christ once for all.

11 And every priest stands daily at his
service, offering repeatedly the same sac-
rifices, which can never take away sins.
12 But when Christ[2] had offered for all time
a single sacrifice for sins, he sat down at
the right hand of God, 13 waiting from that
time until his enemies should be made
a footstool for his feet. 14 For by a single
offering he has perfected for all time those
who are being sanctified.

15 And the Holy Spirit also bears witness
to us; for after saying,

> 16 "This is the covenant that I will make
> with them
> after those days, declares the Lord:
> I will put my laws on their hearts,
> and write them on their minds,"

17 then he adds,

> "I will remember their sins and their
> lawless deeds no more."

18 Where there is forgiveness of these,
there is no longer any offering for sin.

The Full Assurance of Faith

19 Therefore, brothers,[3] since we have
confidence to enter the holy places by
the blood of Jesus, 20 by the new and liv-
ing way that he opened for us through the
curtain, that is, through his flesh, 21 and
since we have a great priest over the house
of God, 22 let us draw near with a true heart
in full assurance of faith, with our hearts
sprinkled clean from an evil conscience
and our bodies washed with pure water.
23 Let us hold fast the confession of our
hope without wavering, for he who prom-
ised is faithful. 24 And let us consider how
to stir up one another to love and good
works, 25 not neglecting to meet together,
as is the habit of some, but encouraging
one another, and all the more as you see
the Day drawing near.

26 For if we go on sinning deliberately
after receiving the knowledge of the truth,
there no longer remains a sacrifice for
sins, 27 but a fearful expectation of judg-
ment, and a fury of fire that will consume
the adversaries. 28 Anyone who has set
aside the law of Moses dies without mercy
on the evidence of two or three witnesses.
29 How much worse punishment, do you
think, will be deserved by the one who has
spurned the Son of God, and has profaned
the blood of the covenant by which he was
sanctified, and has outraged the Spirit

[1] Greek *he* [2] Greek *this one* [3] Or *brothers and sisters*

of grace? 30 For we know him who said,
"Vengeance is mine; I will repay." And
again, "The Lord will judge his people."
31 It is a fearful thing to fall into the hands
of the living God.

32 But recall the former days when,
after you were enlightened, you endured
a hard struggle with sufferings, 33 some-
times being publicly exposed to reproach
and affliction, and sometimes being part-
ners with those so treated. 34 For you had
compassion on those in prison, and you
joyfully accepted the plundering of your
property, since you knew that you your-
selves had a better possession and an
abiding one. 35 Therefore do not throw
away your confidence, which has a great
reward. 36 For you have need of endur-
ance, so that when you have done the will
of God you may receive what is promised.
37 For,

> "Yet a little while,
> and the coming one will come
> and will not delay;
> 38 but my righteous one shall live by faith,
> and if he shrinks back,
> my soul has no pleasure in him."

39 But we are not of those who shrink back
and are destroyed, but of those who have
faith and preserve their souls.

By Faith

11 Now faith is the assurance
of things hoped for, the con-
137 viction of things not seen. 2 For by
it the people of old received their com-
mendation. 3 By faith we understand that
the universe was created by the word of
God, so that what is seen was not made out
of things that are visible.

4 By faith Abel offered to God a more
acceptable sacrifice than Cain, through
which he was commended as righteous,
God commending him by accepting his
gifts. And through his faith, though he
died, he still speaks. 5 By faith Enoch was
taken up so that he should not see death,
and he was not found, because God had
taken him. Now before he was taken he
was commended as having pleased God.
6 And without faith it is impossible to
please him, for whoever would draw near
to God must believe that he exists and that
he rewards those who seek him. 7 By faith
Noah, being warned by God concerning
events as yet unseen, in reverent fear con-
structed an ark for the saving of his house-
hold. By this he condemned the world and
became an heir of the righteousness that
comes by faith.

8 By faith Abraham obeyed when he was
called to go out to a place that he was to
receive as an inheritance. And he went
out, not knowing where he was going.
9 By faith he went to live in the land of
promise, as in a foreign land, living in
tents with Isaac and Jacob, heirs with him
of the same promise. 10 For he was look-
ing forward to the city that has founda-
tions, whose designer and builder is God.
11 By faith Sarah herself received power
to conceive, even when she was past the
age, since she considered him faithful
who had promised. 12 Therefore from
one man, and him as good as dead, were
born descendants as many as the stars of
heaven and as many as the innumerable
grains of sand by the seashore.

13 These all died in faith, not having
received the things promised, but having
seen them and greeted them from afar,
and having acknowledged that they were
strangers and exiles on the earth. 14 For
people who speak thus make it clear that
they are seeking a homeland. 15 If they had
been thinking of that land from which
they had gone out, they would have had
opportunity to return. 16 But as it is, they
desire a better country, that is, a heavenly
one. Therefore God is not ashamed to be
called their God, for he has prepared for
them a city.

17 By faith Abraham, when he was tested, offered up Isaac, and he who had received the promises was in the act of offering up his only son, 18 of whom it was said, "Through Isaac shall your offspring be named." 19 He considered that God was able even to raise him from the dead, from which, figuratively speaking, he did receive him back. 20 By faith Isaac invoked future blessings on Jacob and Esau. 21 By faith Jacob, when dying, blessed each of the sons of Joseph, bowing in worship over the head of his staff. 22 By faith Joseph, at the end of his life, made mention of the exodus of the Israelites and gave directions concerning his bones.

23 By faith Moses, when he was born, was hidden for three months
131 by his parents, because they saw that the child was beautiful, and they were not afraid of the king's edict. 24 By faith Moses, when he was grown up, refused to be called the son of Pharaoh's daughter, 25 choosing rather to be mistreated with the people of God than to enjoy the fleeting pleasures of sin. 26 He considered the reproach of Christ greater wealth than the treasures of Egypt, for he was looking to the reward. 27 By faith he left Egypt, not being afraid of the anger of the king, for he endured as seeing him who is invisible. 28 By faith he kept the Passover and sprinkled the blood, so that

Hebrews 11—Roll Call of the Faithful

In this chapter, the author of Hebrews reminds us of the stories of several Old Testaments saints. Even during various trials and temptations, they looked forward to the coming Savior and remained faithful to God. Instead of trusting in what they could see, they lived "by faith" and believed in God. To read the stories in detail, go to the following pages.

the Destroyer of the firstborn might not
touch them.
29 By faith the people crossed the Red
Sea as on dry land, but the Egyptians,
when they attempted to do the same, were
drowned. 30 By faith the walls of Jericho
fell down after they had been encircled for
seven days. 31 By faith Rahab the prostitute
did not perish with those who were dis-
obedient, because she had given a friendly
welcome to the spies.

32 And what more shall I say? For time
would fail me to tell of Gideon, Barak,
Samson, Jephthah, of David and Samuel
and the prophets— 33 who through faith
conquered kingdoms, enforced justice,
obtained promises, stopped the mouths
of lions, 34 quenched the power of fire,
escaped the edge of the sword, were made
strong out of weakness, became mighty
in war, put foreign armies to flight.
35 Women received back their dead by res-
urrection. Some were tortured, refusing
to accept release, so that they might rise
again to a better life. 36 Others suffered
mocking and flogging, and even chains
and imprisonment. 37 They were stoned,
they were sawn in two,[1] they were killed
with the sword. They went about in skins
of sheep and goats, destitute, afflicted,
mistreated— 38 of whom the world was
not worthy—wandering about in deserts
and mountains, and in dens and caves of
the earth.

39 And all these, though commended
through their faith, did not receive what
was promised, 40 since God had provided
something better for us, that apart from us
they should not be made perfect.

Jesus, Founder and Perfecter of Our Faith

12 Therefore, since we are sur-
rounded by so great a cloud
of witnesses, let us also lay aside every
weight, and sin which clings so closely,
and let us run with endurance the race
that is set before us, 2 looking to Jesus,
the founder and perfecter of our faith,
who for the joy that was set before him
endured the cross, despising the shame,
and is seated at the right hand of the
throne of God.

Do Not Grow Weary

3 Consider him who endured from sin-
ners such hostility against himself, so
that you may not grow weary or faint-
hearted. 4 In your struggle against sin
you have not yet resisted to the point of
shedding your blood. 5 And have you for-
gotten the exhortation that addresses you
as sons?

> "My son, do not regard lightly the
> discipline of the Lord,
> nor be weary when reproved by
> him.
> 6 For the Lord disciplines the one he
> loves,
> and chastises every son whom he
> receives."

7 It is for discipline that you have to endure.
God is treating you as sons. For what son is
there whom his father does not discipline?
8 If you are left without discipline, in which
all have participated, then you are illegiti-
mate children and not sons. 9 Besides this,
we have had earthly fathers who disci-
plined us and we respected them. Shall we
not much more be subject to the Father of
spirits and live? 10 For they disciplined us
for a short time as it seemed best to them,
but he disciplines us for our good, that we
may share his holiness. 11 For the moment
all discipline seems painful rather than
pleasant, but later it yields the peaceful
fruit of righteousness to those who have
been trained by it.

12 Therefore lift your drooping hands
and strengthen your weak knees, 13 and
make straight paths for your feet, so that
what is lame may not be put out of joint
but rather be healed. 14 Strive for peace
with everyone, and for the holiness with-

[1] Some manuscripts add *they were tempted*

out which no one will see the Lord. 15 See
to it that no one fails to obtain the
grace of God; that no "root of bit-
69 terness" springs up and causes
trouble, and by it many become defiled;
16 that no one is sexually immoral or
unholy like Esau, who sold his birthright
for a single meal. 17 For you know that
afterward, when he desired to inherit the
blessing, he was rejected, for he found no
chance to repent, though he sought it
with tears.

A Kingdom That Cannot Be Shaken

18 For you have not come to what may
be touched, a blazing fire and darkness
and gloom and a tempest 19 and the
sound of a trumpet and a voice whose
words made the hearers beg that no fur-
ther messages be spoken to them. 20 For
they could not endure the order that was
given, "If even a beast touches the moun-
tain, it shall be stoned." 21 Indeed, so ter-
rifying was the sight that Moses said, "I
tremble with fear." 22 But you have
come to Mount Zion and to the
19 city of the living God, the heav-
enly Jerusalem, and to innumerable
angels in festal gathering, 23 and to the
assembly[1] of the firstborn who are
enrolled in heaven, and to God, the judge
of all, and to the spirits of the righteous
made perfect, 24 and to Jesus, the media-
tor of a new covenant, and to the sprin-
kled blood that speaks a better word than
the blood of Abel.

25 See that you do not refuse him who is
speaking. For if they did not escape when
they refused him who warned them on
earth, much less will we escape if we
reject him who warns from heaven. 26 At
that time his voice shook the earth, but
now he has promised, "Yet once more I
will shake not only the earth but also the
heavens." 27 This phrase, "Yet once more,"
indicates the removal of things that are
shaken—that is, things that have been
made—in order that the things that can-
not be shaken may remain. 28 Therefore let
us be grateful for receiving a kingdom that
cannot be shaken, and thus let us
offer to God acceptable worship,
1545 with reverence and awe, 29 for our
God is a consuming fire.

Sacrifices Pleasing to God

13 Let brotherly love continue. 2 Do
not neglect to show hospitality to
strangers, for thereby some have enter-
tained angels unawares. 3 Remember
those who are in prison, as though in
prison with them, and those who are mis-
treated, since you also are in the body.
4 Let marriage be held in honor among all,
and let the marriage bed be undefiled, for
God will judge the sexually immoral and
adulterous. 5 Keep your life free from love
of money, and be content with what you
have, for he has said, "I will never leave
you nor forsake you." 6 So we can confi-
dently say,

"The Lord is my helper;
  I will not fear;
what can man do to me?"

7 Remember your leaders, those who
spoke to you the word of God. Consider
the outcome of their way of life, and imi-
tate their faith. 8 Jesus Christ is the same
yesterday and today and forever. 9 Do not
be led away by diverse and strange teach-
ings, for it is good for the heart to be
strengthened by grace, not by foods,
which have not benefited those devoted
to them. 10 We have an altar from which
those who serve the tent have no right to
eat. 11 For the bodies of those animals
whose blood is brought into the holy
places by the high priest as a sacrifice for
sin are burned outside the camp. 12 So
Jesus also suffered outside the gate in
order to sanctify the people through his
own blood. 13 Therefore let us go to him
outside the camp and bear the reproach

[1] Or *church*

he endured. [14]For here we have no last-
ing city, but we seek the city that
is to come. [15]Through him then
33 let us continually offer up a sacri-
fice of praise to God, that is, the fruit of
lips that acknowledge his name. [16]Do not
neglect to do good and to share what you
have, for such sacrifices are pleasing to
God.

[17]Obey your leaders and submit to
them, for they are keeping watch over
your souls, as those who will have to give
an account. Let them do this with joy and
not with groaning, for that would be of no
advantage to you.

[18]Pray for us, for we are sure that we
have a clear conscience, desiring to act
honorably in all things. [19]I urge you the
more earnestly to do this in order that I
may be restored to you the sooner.

Benediction

[20]Now may the God of peace who
brought again from the dead our
1601 Lord Jesus, the great shepherd of
the sheep, by the blood of the eternal cov-
enant, [21]equip you with everything good
that you may do his will, working in us[1]
that which is pleasing in his sight, through
Jesus Christ, to whom be glory forever and
ever. Amen.

Final Greetings

[22]I appeal to you, brothers,[2] bear with
my word of exhortation, for I have writ-
ten to you briefly. [23]You should know that
our brother Timothy has been released,
with whom I shall see you if he comes
soon. [24]Greet all your leaders and all the
saints. Those who come from Italy send
you greetings. [25]Grace be with all of you.

[1] Some manuscripts *you* [2] Or *brothers and sisters*

Introduction to

James

Author
James, brother of Jesus

Date
About A.D. 40s?

Purpose
The purpose of James is to pass on God's wisdom to Jewish Christians and to call them to live out the faith they say they have.

Central Themes
Joy and patience are required during suffering; true wisdom comes from God; believers should turn to God in prayer and faith; the Church should have a right attitude toward riches, including sharing with the needy; the tongue must be guarded; good deeds show real faith; loving the world is sin.

Memory Verses
The crown of life (James 1:12); the Father of lights (James 1:16–17); the tongue (James 3:2–3); fervent prayer (James 5:13–18)

Introduction

James was a leader in the Jerusalem church. He sent this letter to Jewish Christians scattered among the Gentile nations to encourage them and call them to live out the faith they claim to have. Knowing they are poor and persecuted, he tells them to rejoice in their trials because of how they would grow through these difficulties (James 1:2–4; 5:1–11). He encourages them to pray for what they need (James 1:5–8; 5:13–18). They must love each other, especially helping the poor among them (James 1:26–2:16; 4:11–12; 5:19–20). James warns these believers not merely to hear God's Word but also to do what it says. Anyone can believe that God exists, but true saving faith is seen in the good deeds of a person's life (James 1:21–25; 2:14–26). James warns his readers to be careful with their tongues, since a person's words can do so much damage (James 3:1–12). He reminds them that God wants their whole hearts; God does not want to share their love with the things of this world (James 4:1–10). All through his letter, James describes what God is like: generous, holy, good, sovereign, compassionate, merciful, and faithful to answer prayer.

About A.D. 28–33	About A.D. 40s?	About A.D. 62
Jesus' ministry, death, resurrection	James writes his letter	James martyred

The Letter of

James

Greeting

1 James, a servant[1] of God and of the Lord Jesus Christ,

To the twelve tribes in the Dispersion:

Greetings.

Testing of Your Faith

2 Count it all joy, my brothers,[2] when you meet trials of various kinds, 3 for you know that the testing of your faith produces steadfastness. 4 And let steadfastness have its full effect, that you may be perfect and complete, lacking in nothing.

5 If any of you lacks wisdom, let
him ask God, who gives generously
535 to all without reproach, and it will
be given him. 6 But let him ask in
faith, with no doubting, for the
535 one who doubts is like a wave of
the sea that is driven and tossed by the wind. 7 For that person must not suppose that he will receive anything from the Lord; 8 he is a double-minded man, unstable in all his ways.

9 Let the lowly brother boast in his exaltation, 10 and the rich in his humiliation, because like a flower of the grass[3] he will pass away. 11 For the sun rises with its scorching heat and withers the grass; its flower falls, and its beauty perishes. So also will the rich man fade away in the midst of his pursuits.

12 Blessed is the man who remains steadfast under trial, for when he has stood the test he will receive the crown of life, which God has promised to those who love him. 13 Let no one say when he is tempted, "I am being tempted by God," for God cannot be tempted with evil, and he himself tempts no one. 14 But each person is tempted when he is lured and enticed by his own desire. 15 Then desire when it has conceived gives birth to sin, and sin when it is fully grown brings forth death.

16 Do not be deceived, my beloved brothers. 17 Every good gift and every perfect gift is from above, coming down from the Father of lights with whom there is no variation or shadow due to change.[4] 18 Of his own will he brought us forth by the word of truth, that we should be a kind of firstfruits of his creatures.

Hearing and Doing the Word

19 Know this, my beloved brothers: let every person be quick to hear, slow to speak, slow to anger; 20 for the anger of man does not produce the righteousness of God. 21 Therefore put away all filthiness and rampant wickedness and receive with meekness the implanted word, which is able to save your souls.

22 But be doers of the word, and not hearers only, deceiving yourselves. 23 For if anyone is a hearer of the word and not a doer, he is like a man who looks intently at his natural face in a mirror. 24 For he looks at himself and goes away and at once forgets what he was like. 25 But the one who looks into the perfect law, the law of liberty, and perseveres, being no hearer who forgets but a doer who acts, he will be blessed in his doing.

26 If anyone thinks he is religious and does not bridle his tongue but deceives his heart, this person's religion is worthless. 27 Religion that is pure and undefiled before God, the Father, is this: to visit orphans and widows in their affliction, and to keep oneself unstained from the world.

[1] Or *slave*; Greek *bondservant* [2] Or *brothers and sisters*. The plural Greek word *adelphoi* (translated "brothers") refers to siblings in a family. In New Testament usage, depending on the context, *adelphoi* may refer either to men or to both men and women who are siblings (brothers and sisters) in God's family, the church; also verses 16, 19 [3] Or *a wild flower* [4] Some manuscripts *variation due to a shadow of turning*

The Sin of Partiality

2 My brothers,[1] show no partiality as
you hold the faith in our Lord Jesus
Christ, the Lord of glory. 2 For if a man
wearing a gold ring and fine clothing
comes into your assembly, and a poor
man in shabby clothing also comes in,
3 and if you pay attention to the one who
wears the fine clothing and say, "You sit
here in a good place," while you say to
the poor man, "You stand over there," or,
"Sit down at my feet," 4 have you not then
made distinctions among yourselves and
become judges with evil thoughts? 5 Listen,
my beloved brothers, has not God chosen
those who are poor in the world to be rich
in faith and heirs of the kingdom, which
he has promised to those who love him?
6 But you have dishonored the poor man.
Are not the rich the ones who oppress you,
and the ones who drag you into court? 7 Are
they not the ones who blaspheme the hon-
orable name by which you were called?
8 If you really fulfill the royal law
according to the Scripture, "You
175 shall love your neighbor as your-
self," you are doing well. 9 But if you show
partiality, you are committing sin and are
convicted by the law as transgressors.
10 For whoever keeps the whole law but
fails in one point has become accountable
for all of it. 11 For he who said, "Do not
commit adultery," also said, "Do not mur-
der." If you do not commit adultery but do
murder, you have become a transgressor
of the law. 12 So speak and so act as those
who are to be judged under the law of lib-
erty. 13 For judgment is without mercy to
one who has shown no mercy. Mercy tri-
umphs over judgment.

Faith Without Works Is Dead

14 What good is it, my brothers, if
someone says he has faith but does not
have works? Can that faith save him? 15 If
a brother or sister is poorly clothed and
lacking in daily food, 16 and one of you
says to them, "Go in peace, be warmed
and filled," without giving them the things
needed for the body, what good[2] is that?
17 So also faith by itself, if it does not have
works, is dead.

18 But someone will say, "You have faith
and I have works." Show me your faith
apart from your works, and I will show
you my faith by my works. 19 You believe
that God is one; you do well. Even the
demons believe—and shudder! 20 Do you
want to be shown, you foolish person,
that faith apart from works is useless?
21 Was not Abraham our father jus-
tified by works when he offered up
57 his son Isaac on the altar? 22 You
see that faith was active along with his
works, and faith was completed by his
works; 23 and the Scripture was fulfilled
that says, "Abraham believed God, and it
was counted to him as righteousness"—
and he was called a friend of God. 24 You
see that a person is justified by works and
not by faith alone. 25 And in the
same way was not also Rahab the
345 prostitute justified by works when
she received the messengers and sent
them out by another way? 26 For as the
body apart from the spirit is dead, so also
faith apart from works is dead.

Taming the Tongue

3 Not many of you should become
teachers, my brothers, for you know
that we who teach will be judged with
greater strictness. 2 For we all stumble
in many ways. And if anyone does not
stumble in what he says, he is a perfect
man, able also to bridle his whole body.
3 If we put bits into the mouths of horses
so that they obey us, we guide their whole
bodies as well. 4 Look at the ships also:
though they are so large and are driven
by strong winds, they are guided by a very
small rudder wherever the will of the pilot
directs. 5 So also the tongue is a small
member, yet it boasts of great things.

[1] Or *brothers and sisters*; also verses 5, 14 [2] Or *benefit*

How great a forest is set ablaze by such
a small fire! 6 And the tongue is a fire, a
world of unrighteousness. The tongue is
set among our members, staining the
whole body, setting on fire the entire
course of life,[1] and set on fire by hell.[2] 7 For
every kind of beast and bird, of reptile and
sea creature, can be tamed and has been
tamed by mankind, 8 but no
human being can tame the tongue.
9 It is a restless evil, full of deadly
poison. 9 With it we bless our Lord and
Father, and with it we curse people who
are made in the likeness of God. 10 From
the same mouth come blessing and curs-
ing. My brothers,[3] these things ought not
to be so. 11 Does a spring pour forth from
the same opening both fresh and salt
water? 12 Can a fig tree, my brothers, bear
olives, or a grapevine produce figs?
Neither can a salt pond yield fresh water.

Wisdom from Above

13 Who is wise and understanding
among you? By his good conduct let him
show his works in the meekness of wis-
dom. 14 But if you have bitter jealousy
and selfish ambition in your hearts, do
not boast and be false to the truth. 15 This
is not the wisdom that comes down
from above, but is earthly, unspiritual,
demonic. 16 For where jealousy and self-
ish ambition exist, there will be disorder
and every vile practice. 17 But the wisdom
from above is first pure, then peaceable,
gentle, open to reason, full of mercy and
good fruits, impartial and sincere. 18 And a
harvest of righteousness is sown in peace
by those who make peace.

Warning Against Worldliness

4 What causes quarrels and what
causes fights among you? Is it not
this, that your passions[4] are at war within
you?[5] 2 You desire and do not have, so you
murder. You covet and cannot obtain, so
you fight and quarrel. You do not have,
because you do not ask. 3 You ask and do
not receive, because you ask wrongly, to
spend it on your passions. 4 You adul-
terous people![6] Do you not know that
friendship with the world is enmity
with God? Therefore whoever wishes to
be a friend of the world makes himself
an enemy of God. 5 Or do you suppose it
is to no purpose that the Scripture says,
"He yearns jealously over the spirit that
he has made to dwell in us"? 6 But he
gives more grace. Therefore it says, "God
opposes the proud, but gives grace to the
humble." 7 Submit yourselves therefore
to God. Resist the devil, and he will flee
from you. 8 Draw near to God, and he will
draw near to you. Cleanse your hands,
you sinners, and purify your hearts,
you double-minded. 9 Be wretched and
mourn and weep. Let your laughter
be turned to mourning and your joy to
gloom. 10 Humble yourselves before the
Lord, and he will exalt you.

11 Do not speak evil against one another,
brothers.[7] The one who speaks against a
brother or judges his brother, speaks evil
against the law and judges the law. But if
you judge the law, you are not a doer of
the law but a judge. 12 There is only one
lawgiver and judge, he who is able to save
and to destroy. But who are you to judge
your neighbor?

Boasting About Tomorrow

13 Come now, you who say, "Today or
tomorrow we will go into such and such
a town and spend a year there and trade
and make a profit"— 14 yet you do not
know what tomorrow will bring. What is
your life? For you are a mist that appears
for a little time and then vanishes.
15 Instead you ought to say, "If the Lord
wills, we will live and do this or that."
16 As it is, you boast in your arrogance. All
such boasting is evil. 17 So whoever knows
the right thing to do and fails to do it, for
him it is sin.

[1] Or *wheel of birth* [2] Greek *Gehenna* [3] Or *brothers and sisters*; also verse 12 [4] Greek *pleasures*; also verse 3 [5] Greek *in your members* [6] Greek *You adulteresses!* [7] Or *brothers and sisters*

Warning to the Rich

5 Come now, you rich, weep and howl
for the miseries that are coming upon
you. 2 Your riches have rotted and your
garments are moth-eaten. 3 Your gold and
silver have corroded, and their corrosion
will be evidence against you and will eat
your flesh like fire. You have laid up trea-
sure in the last days. 4 Behold, the wages
of the laborers who mowed your fields,
which you kept back by fraud, are crying
out against you, and the cries of the har-
vesters have reached the ears of the Lord
of hosts. 5 You have lived on the earth in
luxury and in self-indulgence. You have
fattened your hearts in a day of slaughter.
6 You have condemned and murdered the
righteous person. He does not resist you.

Patience in Suffering

7 Be patient, therefore, brothers,[1] until
the coming of the Lord. See how the farmer
waits for the precious fruit of the earth,
being patient about it, until it receives
the early and the late rains. 8 You also, be
patient. Establish your hearts, for the com-
ing of the Lord is at hand. 9 Do not grumble
against one another, brothers, so that you
may not be judged; behold, the Judge is
standing at the door. 10 As an example of
suffering and patience, brothers, take the
prophets who spoke in the name of the
Lord. 11 Behold, we consider those blessed
who remained steadfast. You have heard
of the steadfastness of Job, and you have
seen the purpose of the Lord, how the Lord
is compassionate and merciful.

12 But above all, my brothers, do not
swear, either by heaven or by earth or by
any other oath, but let your "yes" be yes
and your "no" be no, so that you may not
fall under condemnation.

The Prayer of Faith

13 Is anyone among you suffering?
Let him pray. Is anyone cheerful?
435 Let him sing praise. 14 Is anyone
among you sick? Let him call for the elders
of the church, and let them pray over him,
anointing him with oil in the name of the
Lord. 15 And the prayer of faith will save
the one who is sick, and the Lord will raise
him up. And if he has committed sins, he
will be forgiven. 16 Therefore, confess your
sins to one another and pray for one
another, that you may be healed. The
prayer of a righteous person has great
power as it is working.[2] 17 Elijah
was a man with a nature like ours,
567 and he prayed fervently that it
might not rain, and for three years and six
months it did not rain on the earth.
18 Then he prayed again, and heaven gave
rain, and the earth bore its fruit.

19 My brothers, if anyone among you
wanders from the truth and someone
brings him back, 20 let him know that
whoever brings back a sinner from his
wandering will save his soul from death
and will cover a multitude of sins.

[1] Or *brothers and sisters*; also verses 9, 10, 12, 19 [2] Or *The effective prayer of a righteous person has great power*

Introduction to

1 Peter

Author
Simon Peter the apostle

Date
About A.D. 62–63

Purpose
The purpose of 1 Peter is to encourage God's people when they suffer, especially when they suffer because they are Christians.

Central Themes
Believers have great hope in Christ; there can be joy even in suffering; believers are called to live as a holy people for God; Jesus died to take the punishment of our sins; Christ's example is a model for suffering well; believers should submit to authority, even unjust authority; God gives grace, strength, and blessing in suffering.

Memory Verses
Ransomed by Christ's blood (1 Peter 1:17–19); the chosen people (1 Peter 2:9–10); healed by Christ (1 Peter 2:24–25)

Introduction

Peter writes to encourage suffering Christians. He begins by reminding them of the great hope they have, both for now and for the future, because of the death and resurrection of the Lord Jesus Christ (1 Peter 1:3–12). He tells them this should cause them to be holy, since the One who had saved them was holy. This holy living must include sincere love for each other (1 Peter 1:13–2:12). For the Lord's sake, they should submit to anyone who held authority over them, even if the one in authority was unjust instead of good. Jesus Himself modeled such submission: He suffered though He had never done anything to deserve it (1 Peter 2:13–3:7). If believers suffer for righteousness' sake, they will be blessed and be witnesses for Christ. Christ also had to suffer, the just for the unjust, and now is exalted at God's right hand (1 Peter 3:8–22). Persecuted Christians should not be surprised by their suffering, but should trust God, who always does what is right (1 Peter 4:12–19). Other Christians suffer too, and, in the end, God will raise up and exalt all His suffering servants to share in Christ's glory (1 Peter 5:6–11).

About A.D. 41–44	About A.D. 62–63	About A.D. 64–67
Peter jailed in Jerusalem	Peter writes first letter	Peter martyred in Rome

The First Letter of Peter

1 Peter

Greeting

1 Peter, an apostle of Jesus Christ,
To those who are elect exiles of
the dispersion in Pontus, Galatia, Cap-
padocia, Asia, and Bithynia, 2 according
to the foreknowledge of God the Father,
in the sanctification of the Spirit, for obe-
dience to Jesus Christ and for sprinkling
with his blood:

May grace and peace be multiplied to
you.

Born Again to a Living Hope

3 Blessed be the God and Father of
our Lord Jesus Christ! According to
1549 his great mercy, he has caused us
to be born again to a living hope through
the resurrection of Jesus Christ from the
dead, 4 to an inheritance that is imperish-
able, undefiled, and unfading, kept in
heaven for you, 5 who by God's power are
being guarded through faith for a salva-
tion ready to be revealed in the last time.
6 In this you rejoice, though now for a little
while, if necessary, you have been grieved
by various trials, 7 so that the tested genu-
ineness of your faith—more precious than
gold that perishes though it is tested by
fire—may be found to result in praise and
glory and honor at the revelation of Jesus
Christ. 8 Though you have not seen
him, you love him. Though you do
1597 not now see him, you believe in
him and rejoice with joy that is inexpress-
ible and filled with glory, 9 obtaining the
outcome of your faith, the salvation of
your souls.

10 Concerning this salvation, the
prophets who prophesied about
1529 the grace that was to be yours
searched and inquired carefully, 11 inquir-
ing what person or time the Spirit of
Christ in them was indicating when he
predicted the sufferings of Christ and the
subsequent glories. 12 It was revealed to
them that they were serving not them-
selves but you, in the things that have
now been announced to you through
those who preached the good news to you
by the Holy Spirit sent from heaven,
things into which angels long to look.

Called to Be Holy

13 Therefore, preparing your minds
for action,[1] and being sober-minded, set
your hope fully on the grace that will be
brought to you at the revelation of Jesus
Christ. 14 As obedient children, do not be
conformed to the passions of your for-
mer ignorance, 15 but as he who called
you is holy, you also be holy in all your
conduct, 16 since it is written, "You shall
be holy, for I am holy." 17 And if you call
on him as Father who judges impartially
according to each one's deeds, conduct
yourselves with fear throughout the time
of your exile, 18 knowing that you were
ransomed from the futile ways inherited
from your forefathers, not with perishable
things such as silver or gold, 19 but with
the precious blood of Christ, like that of a
lamb without blemish or spot. 20 He was
foreknown before the foundation of the
world but was made manifest in the last
times for the sake of you 21 who through
him are believers in God, who raised him
from the dead and gave him glory, so that
your faith and hope are in God.

22 Having purified your souls by your
obedience to the truth for a sincere broth-
erly love, love one another earnestly from
a pure heart, 23 since you have been born
again, not of perishable seed but of imper-

[1] Greek *girding up the loins of your mind*

ishable, through the living and abiding word of God; 24 for

"All flesh is like grass
and all its glory like the flower of grass.
The grass withers,
and the flower falls,
25 but the word of the Lord remains forever."

And this word is the good news that was preached to you.

A Living Stone and a Holy People

2 So put away all malice and all deceit and hypocrisy and envy and all slander. 2 Like newborn infants, long for the pure spiritual milk, that by it you may grow up into salvation— 3 if indeed you have tasted that the Lord is good.

4 As you come to him, a living stone rejected by men but in the sight of God chosen and precious, 5 you yourselves like living stones are being built up as a spiritual house, to be a holy priesthood, to offer spiritual sacrifices acceptable to God through Jesus Christ. 6 For it stands in Scripture:

"Behold, I am laying in Zion a stone,
a cornerstone chosen and precious,
and whoever believes in him will not be put to shame."

7 So the honor is for you who believe, but for those who do not believe,

"The stone that the builders rejected
has become the cornerstone,"[1]

8 and

"A stone of stumbling,
and a rock of offense."

They stumble because they disobey the word, as they were destined to do.

9 But you are a chosen race, a royal priesthood, a holy nation, a people for his own possession, that you may proclaim the excellencies of him who called you out of darkness into his marvelous light. 10 Once you were not a people, but now you are God's people; once you had not received mercy, but now you have received mercy.

11 Beloved, I urge you as sojourners and exiles to abstain from the passions of the flesh, which wage war against your soul. 12 Keep your conduct among the Gentiles honorable, so that when they speak against you as evildoers, they may see your good deeds and glorify God on the day of visitation.

Submission to Authority

13 Be subject for the Lord's sake to every human institution,[2] whether it be to the emperor[3] as supreme, 14 or to governors as sent by him to punish those who do evil and to praise those who do good. 15 For this is the will of God, that by doing good you should put to silence the ignorance of foolish people. 16 Live as people who are free, not using your freedom as a cover-up for evil, but living as servants[4] of God. 17 Honor everyone. Love the brotherhood. Fear God. Honor the emperor.

18 Servants, be subject to your masters with all respect, not only to the good and gentle but also to the unjust. 19 For this is a gracious thing, when, mindful of God, one endures sorrows while suffering unjustly. 20 For what credit is it if, when you sin and are beaten for it, you endure? But if when you do good and suffer for it you endure, this is a gracious thing in the sight of God. 21 For to this you have been called, because Christ also suffered for you, leaving you an example, so that you might follow in his steps. 22 He committed no sin, neither was deceit found in his mouth. 23 When he was reviled, he did not revile in return; when he suffered, he did not threaten, but continued entrusting himself to him who

117

1181

[1] Greek *the head of the corner* [2] Or *every institution ordained for people* [3] Or *king*; also verse 17 [4] Greek *bondservants*

judges justly. 24 He himself bore our sins
in his body on the tree, that we
might die to sin and live to righ-
1501, teousness. By his wounds you
1571 have been healed. 25 For you were
straying like sheep, but have now
returned to the Shepherd and
1605 Overseer of your souls.

Wives and Husbands

3 Likewise, wives, be subject to your
own husbands, so that even if some
do not obey the word, they may be won
without a word by the conduct of their
wives, 2 when they see your respectful
and pure conduct. 3 Do not let your adorn-
ing be external—the braiding of hair and
the putting on of gold jewelry, or the
clothing you wear— 4 but let your adorn-
ing be the hidden person of the heart
with the imperishable beauty of a gentle
and quiet spirit, which in God's sight is
very precious. 5 For this is how the holy
women who hoped in God used to adorn
themselves, by submitting to their own
husbands, 6 as Sarah obeyed Abraham,
calling him lord. And you are her chil-
dren, if you do good and do not fear any-
thing that is frightening.

7 Likewise, husbands, live with your
wives in an understanding way, showing
honor to the woman as the weaker ves-
sel, since they are heirs with you[1] of the
grace of life, so that your prayers may not
be hindered.

Suffering for Righteousness' Sake

8 Finally, all of you, have unity of mind,
sympathy, brotherly love, a tender heart,
and a humble mind. 9 Do not repay evil
for evil or reviling for reviling, but on the
contrary, bless, for to this you were called,
that you may obtain a blessing. 10 For

"Whoever desires to love life
and see good days,
let him keep his tongue from evil
and his lips from speaking deceit;
11 let him turn away from evil and do
good;
let him seek peace and pursue it.
12 For the eyes of the Lord are on the
righteous,
and his ears are open to their
prayer.
But the face of the Lord is against
those who do evil."

13 Now who is there to harm you if
you are zealous for what is good?
117 14 But even if you should suffer for
righteousness' sake, you will be blessed.
Have no fear of them, nor be troubled,
15 but in your hearts honor Christ the Lord
as holy, always being prepared to make a
defense to anyone who asks you for a rea-
son for the hope that is in you; yet do it
with gentleness and respect, 16 having a
good conscience, so that, when you are
slandered, those who revile your good be-
havior in Christ may be put to shame. 17 For
it is better to suffer for doing good, if that
should be God's will, than for doing evil.

18 For Christ also suffered[2] once for sins,
the righteous for the unrighteous, that he
might bring us to God, being put to death
in the flesh but made alive in the spirit,
19 in which[3] he went and proclaimed[4] to
the spirits in prison, 20 because[5] they for-
merly did not obey, when God's patience
waited in the days of Noah, while the ark
was being prepared, in which a few, that
is, eight persons, were brought safely
through water. 21 Baptism, which cor-
responds to this, now saves you, not as
a removal of dirt from the body but as
an appeal to God for a good conscience,
through the resurrection of Jesus Christ,
22 who has gone into heaven and is at the
right hand of God, with angels, authorities,
and powers having been subjected to him.

Stewards of God's Grace

4 Since therefore Christ suffered in the
flesh,[6] arm yourselves with the same
way of thinking, for whoever has suffered

[1] Some manuscripts *since you are joint heirs* [2] Some manuscripts *died* [3] Or *the Spirit, in whom* [4] Or *preached* [5] Or *when* [6] Some manuscripts add *for us*; some *for you*

in the flesh has ceased from sin, **2** so as to
live for the rest of the time in the flesh no
longer for human passions but for the will
of God. **3** For the time that is past suffices
for doing what the Gentiles want to do, liv-
ing in sensuality, passions, drunkenness,
orgies, drinking parties, and lawless idola-
try. **4** With respect to this they are surprised
when you do not join them in the same
flood of debauchery, and they malign you;
5 but they will give account to him who is
ready to judge the living and the dead. **6** For
this is why the gospel was preached even
to those who are dead, that though judged
in the flesh the way people are, they might
live in the spirit the way God does.

7 The end of all things is at hand; there-
fore be self-controlled and sober-minded
for the sake of your prayers. **8** Above all,
keep loving one another earnestly, since
love covers a multitude of sins. **9** Show
hospitality to one another without grum-
bling. **10** As each has received a gift, use it
to serve one another, as good stewards of
God's varied grace: **11** whoever speaks, as
one who speaks oracles of God; whoever
serves, as one who serves by the strength
that God supplies—in order that in every-
thing God may be glorified through Jesus
Christ. To him belong glory and dominion
forever and ever. Amen.

Suffering as a Christian

12 Beloved, do not be surprised at the
fiery trial when it comes upon you to test
you, as though something strange were
happening to you. **13** But rejoice insofar as
you share Christ's sufferings, that you may
also rejoice and be glad when his glory
is revealed. **14** If you are insulted for the
name of Christ, you are blessed, because
the Spirit of glory[1] and of God rests upon
you. **15** But let none of you suffer as a mur-
derer or a thief or an evildoer or as a med-
dler. **16** Yet if anyone suffers as a Christian,
let him not be ashamed, but let him glo-
rify God in that name. **17** For it is time for
judgment to begin at the household of
God; and if it begins with us, what will be
the outcome for those who do not obey
the gospel of God? **18** And

"If the righteous is scarcely saved,
what will become of the ungodly
and the sinner?"[2]

19 Therefore let those who suffer
according to God's will entrust
117 their souls to a faithful Creator
while doing good.

Shepherd the Flock of God

5 So I exhort the elders among
you, as a fellow elder and a
1605 witness of the sufferings of Christ,
as well as a partaker in the glory that is
going to be revealed: **2** shepherd the flock
of God that is among you, exercising over-
sight,[3] not under compulsion, but will-
ingly, as God would have you;[4] not for
shameful gain, but eagerly; **3** not domi-
neering over those in your charge, but
being examples to the flock. **4** And when
the chief Shepherd appears, you
will receive the unfading crown of
1571 glory. **5** Likewise, you who are
younger, be subject to the elders. Clothe
yourselves, all of you, with humility
toward one another, for "God opposes the
proud but gives grace to the humble."

6 Humble yourselves, therefore,
under the mighty hand of God so
435, that at the proper time he may
1181 exalt you, **7** casting all your anxiet-
ies on him, because he cares for you. **8** Be
sober-minded; be watchful. Your
adversary the devil prowls around
13 like a roaring lion, seeking some-
one to devour. **9** Resist him, firm in your
faith, knowing that the same kinds of suf-
fering are being experienced by your
brotherhood throughout the world. **10** And
after you have suffered a little while, the
God of all grace, who has called you to his
eternal glory in Christ, will himself

[1] Some manuscripts insert *and of power* [2] Greek *where will the ungodly and sinner appear?* [3] Some manuscripts omit *exercising oversight* [4] Some manuscripts omit *as God would have you*

restore, confirm, strengthen, and estab-
lish you. 11 To him be the dominion for-
ever and ever. Amen.

Final Greetings

12 By Silvanus, a faithful brother as I
regard him, I have written briefly to you,
exhorting and declaring that this is the true
grace of God. Stand firm in it. 13 She who is
at Babylon, who is likewise chosen, sends
you greetings, and so does Mark, my son.
14 Greet one another with the kiss of love.

Peace to all of you who are in Christ.

Introduction to

2 Peter

Author

Simon Peter the apostle

Date

About A.D. 64–67

Purpose

The purpose of 2 Peter is to teach that, in Christ, God has given Christians everything they need for eternal life and godly living, and to warn them against the wickedness of false teachers.

Central Themes

God's promises and gifts are all we need; believers must grow in Christian character; God's Word is certain; there are false teachers in the church with wicked lifestyles; Christ's return to judge the wicked is certain; Christians must wait for Jesus' return with holy living.

Memory Verses

A sure prophetic word (2 Peter 1:19–21); new heavens and a new earth (2 Peter 3:13)

Introduction

Peter writes to remind Christians to live by God's grace, making use of all God has given them for living holy lives (2 Peter 1:1–15). Peter saw the glory of the Lord Jesus Christ when he was with Him and saw Him transfigured. Even more trustworthy than Peter's experience is Scripture, which all believers have, even if they haven't seen Jesus in the same way that Peter had. Christians must pay attention to Scripture and be guided by it, since it is the very Word of God (2 Peter 1:16–21). One important reason for paying attention to God's Word is that there are false teachers, who live ungodly lives and try to trick Christians into joining them (2 Peter 2). Christians must also watch out for those who mock the idea of Jesus returning to judge people for their sin. Jesus will indeed return. Now he is patiently giving people time to repent and turn to Him. Knowing Jesus will come again to judge the world, Christians should live godly lives as they wait for His return (2 Peter 3).

About A.D. 41–44	About A.D. 54	About A.D. 64–67
Peter jailed in Jerusalem	Nero begins reign in Rome	Peter's second letter, martyrdom

The Second Letter of Peter

2 Peter

Greeting

1 Simeon[1] Peter, a servant[2] and apostle
of Jesus Christ,
To those who have obtained a faith of
equal standing with ours by the righteous-
ness of our God and Savior Jesus Christ:
2 May grace and peace be multiplied to
you in the knowledge of God and of Jesus
our Lord.

Make Your Calling and Election Sure

3 His divine power has granted to us all
things that pertain to life and godliness,
through the knowledge of him who called
us to[3] his own glory and excellence,[4] 4 by
which he has granted to us his precious
and very great promises, so that through
them you may become partakers of the
divine nature, having escaped from the
corruption that is in the world because of
sinful desire. 5 For this very reason, make
every effort to supplement your faith with
virtue,[5] and virtue with knowledge, 6 and
knowledge with self-control, and self-
control with steadfastness, and stead-
fastness with godliness, 7 and godliness
with brotherly affection, and brotherly
affection with love. 8 For if these qualities[6]
are yours and are increasing, they keep
you from being ineffective or unfruit-
ful in the knowledge of our Lord Jesus
Christ. 9 For whoever lacks these qualities
is so nearsighted that he is blind, having
forgotten that he was cleansed from his
former sins. 10 Therefore, brothers,[7] be all
the more diligent to make your calling
and election sure, for if you practice these
qualities you will never fall. 11 For in this
way there will be richly provided for you
an entrance into the eternal kingdom of
our Lord and Savior Jesus Christ.

12 Therefore I intend always to remind
you of these qualities, though you know
them and are established in the truth that
you have. 13 I think it right, as long as I
am in this body,[8] to stir you up by way of
reminder, 14 since I know that the putting
off of my body will be soon, as our Lord
Jesus Christ made clear to me. 15 And I will
make every effort so that after my depar-
ture you may be able at any time to recall
these things.

Christ's Glory and the Prophetic Word

16 For we did not follow cleverly
devised myths when we made
1339 known to you the power and com-
ing of our Lord Jesus Christ, but we
were eyewitnesses of his majesty.
1397 17 For when he received honor and
glory from God the Father, and the voice
was borne to him by the Majestic Glory,
"This is my beloved Son,[9] with whom I am
well pleased," 18 we ourselves heard this
very voice borne from heaven, for we were
with him on the holy mountain. 19 And we
have something more sure, the prophetic
word, to which you will do well to pay
attention as to a lamp shining in a dark
place, until the day dawns and the morn-
ing star rises in your hearts, 20 knowing
this first of all, that no prophecy of
Scripture comes from someone's own
interpretation. 21 For no prophecy was
ever produced by the will of man, but men
spoke from God as they were carried along
by the Holy Spirit.

False Prophets and Teachers

2 But false prophets also arose among
the people, just as there will be false
teachers among you, who will secretly

[1] Some manuscripts *Simon* [2] Or *slave*; Greek *bondservant* [3] Or *by* [4] Or *virtue* [5] Or *excellence*; twice in this verse [6] Greek *these things*; also verses 9, 10, 12 [7] Or *brothers and sisters*. The plural Greek word *adelphoi* (translated "brothers") refers to siblings in a family. In New Testament usage, depending on the context, *adelphoi* may refer either to men or to both men and women who are siblings (brothers and sisters) in God's family, the church [8] Greek *tent*; also verse 14 [9] Or *my Son, my* (or *the*) *Beloved*

bring in destructive heresies, even denying the Master who bought them, bringing upon themselves swift destruction. 2 And many will follow their sensuality, and because of them the way of truth will be blasphemed. 3 And in their greed they will exploit you with false words. Their condemnation from long ago is not idle, and their destruction is not asleep.

4 For if God did not spare angels when they sinned, but cast them into hell[1] and committed them to chains[2] of gloomy darkness to be kept until the judgment; 5 if he did not spare the ancient world, but preserved Noah, a her-
25 ald of righteousness, with seven
others, when he brought a flood upon the world of the ungodly; 6 if by turning the cities of Sodom and Gomorrah to ashes he condemned them to extinction, making them an example of what is going to happen to the ungodly;[3] 7 and if he rescued righteous Lot, greatly distressed by the sensual conduct of the wicked 8 (for as that righteous man lived among them day after day, he was tormenting his righteous soul over their lawless deeds that he saw and heard); 9 then the Lord knows how to rescue the godly from tri-
25 als,[4] and to keep the unrighteous
under punishment until the day of judgment, 10 and especially those who indulge in the lust of defiling passion and despise authority.

Bold and willful, they do not tremble as they blaspheme the glorious ones, 11 whereas angels, though greater in might and power, do not pronounce a blasphemous judgment against them before the Lord. 12 But these, like irrational animals, creatures of instinct, born to be caught and destroyed, blaspheming about matters of which they are ignorant, will also be destroyed in their destruction, 13 suffering wrong as the wage for their wrongdoing. They count it pleasure to revel in the daytime. They are blots and blemishes, reveling in their deceptions,[5] while they feast with you. 14 They have eyes full of adultery, insatiable for sin. They entice unsteady souls. They have hearts trained in greed. Accursed children! 15 Forsaking the right way, they have gone astray. They have followed the way of Balaam, the son of Beor, who loved gain from wrongdoing, 16 but was rebuked for his own transgression; a speechless donkey spoke with human voice and restrained the prophet's madness.

17 These are waterless springs and mists driven by a storm. For them the gloom of utter darkness has been reserved. 18 For, speaking loud boasts of folly, they entice by sensual passions of the flesh those who are barely escaping from those who live in error. 19 They promise them freedom, but they themselves are slaves[6] of corruption. For whatever overcomes a person, to that he is enslaved. 20 For if, after they have escaped the defilements of the world through the knowledge of our Lord and Savior Jesus Christ, they are again entangled in them and overcome, the last state has become worse for them than the first. 21 For it would have been better for them never to have known the way of righteousness than after knowing it to turn back from the holy commandment delivered to them. 22 What the true proverb says has happened to them: "The dog returns to its own vomit, and the sow, after washing herself, returns to wallow in the mire."

The Day of the Lord Will Come

3 This is now the second letter that I am writing to you, beloved. In both of them I am stirring up your sincere mind by way of reminder, 2 that you should remember the predictions of the holy prophets and the commandment of the Lord and Savior through your apostles, 3 knowing this first of all, that scoffers will come in the last days with scoffing, following their own sinful desires. 4 They will

[1] Greek *Tartarus* [2] Some manuscripts *pits* [3] Some manuscripts *an example to those who were to be ungodly* [4] Or *temptations* [5] Some manuscripts *love feasts* [6] Greek *bondservants*

say, "Where is the promise of his coming? For ever since the fathers fell asleep, all things are continuing as they were from the beginning of creation." 5 For they deliberately overlook this fact, that the heavens existed long ago, and the earth was formed out of water and through water by the word of God, 6 and that by means of these the world that then existed was deluged with water and perished. 7 But by the same word the heavens and earth that now exist are stored up for fire, being kept until the day of judgment and destruction of the ungodly.

8 But do not overlook this one fact, beloved, that with the Lord one day is as a thousand years, and a thousand years as one day. 9 The Lord is not slow to fulfill his promise as some count slowness, but is patient toward you,[1] not wishing that any should perish, but that all should reach repentance. 10 But the day of the Lord will come like a thief, and then the heavens will pass away with a roar, and the heavenly bodies[2] will be burned up and dissolved, and the earth and the works that are done on it will be exposed.[3]

1847 11 Since all these things are thus to be dissolved, what sort of people ought you to be in lives of holiness and godliness, 12 waiting for and hastening the coming of the day of God, because of which the heavens will be set on fire and dissolved, and the heavenly bodies will melt as they burn! 13 But according to his promise we are waiting for new heavens and a new earth in which righteousness dwells.

Final Words

14 Therefore, beloved, since you are waiting for these, be diligent to be found by him without spot or blemish, and at peace. 15 And count the patience of our Lord as salvation, just as our beloved brother Paul also wrote to you according to the wisdom given him, 16 as he does in all his letters when he speaks in them of these matters. There are some things in them that are hard to understand, which the ignorant and unstable twist to their own destruction, as they do the other Scriptures. 17 You therefore, beloved, knowing this beforehand, take care that you are not carried away with the error of lawless people and lose your own stability. 18 But grow in the grace and knowledge of our Lord and Savior Jesus Christ. To him be the glory both now and to the day of eternity. Amen.

[1] Some manuscripts *on your account* [2] Or *elements*; also verse 12 [3] Greek *found*; some manuscripts *will be burned up*

Introduction to

1–3 John

Author
John the apostle (called "the elder")

Date
About A.D. 85–95

Key People
John; the elect lady and her children; Gaius; Diotrephes

Purpose
The purpose of 1, 2, and 3 John is to remind Christians of the truth about Jesus and the salvation He brings, to encourage Christians to live in obedience to that truth, and to warn Christians against teachers who distort the truth.

Central Themes
Jesus is truly God and truly man; Jesus' death for our sin brings us God's forgiveness; forgiven Christians have fellowship with God; true Christians love each other, turn from sin, and obey God's commands; there are many false teachers who must be resisted; the Church should discipline its members who sin.

Memory Verses
Confession of sins (1 John 1:7–9); Jesus our advocate (1 John 2:1–2); the Son destroys the devil's work (1 John 3:8); God is love (1 John 4:7–12); true God and eternal life (1 John 5:20): beware of false teachers (2 John 9–11)

Introduction

In John's first letter, he writes that Jesus is truly God who became man to die for the sins of His people (1 John 1:1–4; 4:10–14). Christians therefore have forgiveness in Him (1 John 1:7–2:2). All this is because God is light (1 John 1:5) and God is love (1 John 4:16b). Since God is light, His children will turn away from sin and live holy lives of obedience to God (1 John 2:3–6; 3:1–10). Since God is love, His children, having been loved so wonderfully by God, will also love. They will love God more than anything else (1 John 2:15–17), and they will love each other (1 John 3:11–18; 4:7–12). John warns these believers against antichrists: people who seem good and true at first, but who really are out to deceive people and turn them from the true faith (1 John 2:18–27). John's second letter, addressed to a "lady" and her children (probably a church), also warns against false teachers and encourages Christians to love each other and obey the truth. John's third letter, written to a man named Gaius, praises him for helping traveling teachers and tells how John will discipline an unruly church member when he comes.

About A.D. 28–33	**A.D. 70**	**About A.D. 85–95**
Jesus' ministry, death, resurrection	Temple destroyed	John writes Gospel, letters

The First Letter of John

1 John

The Word of Life

1 That which was from the beginning,
which we have heard, which we have
seen with our eyes, which we looked upon
and have touched with our hands, con-
cerning the word of life— 2 the life was
made manifest, and we have seen it, and
testify to it and proclaim to you the eter-
nal life, which was with the Father and
was made manifest to us— 3 that which
we have seen and heard we proclaim also
to you, so that you too may have fellow-
ship with us; and indeed our fellowship
is with the Father and with his Son Jesus
Christ. 4 And we are writing these things
so that our[1] joy may be complete.

Walking in the Light

5 This is the message we have heard
from him and proclaim to you, that
507 God is light, and in him is no dark-
ness at all. 6 If we say we have fellowship
with him while we walk in darkness, we lie
and do not practice the truth. 7 But if we
walk in the light, as he is in the light, we
have fellowship with one another, and the
blood of Jesus his Son cleanses us from all
sin. 8 If we say we have no sin, we deceive
ourselves, and the truth is not in us. 9 If we
confess our sins, he is faithful and
just to forgive us our sins and to
507 cleanse us from all unrighteous-
ness. 10 If we say we have not
sinned, we make him a liar, and
1605 his word is not in us.

Christ Our Advocate

2 My little children, I am writing these
things to you so that you may not sin.
But if anyone does sin, we have an
advocate with the Father, Jesus
1415 Christ the righteous. 2 He is the
propitiation for our sins, and not for ours
only but also for the sins of the whole
world. 3 And by this we know that we have
come to know him, if we keep his com-
mandments. 4 Whoever says "I know him"
but does not keep his commandments is
a liar, and the truth is not in him, 5 but
whoever keeps his word, in him truly the
love of God is perfected. By this we may
know that we are in him: 6 whoever says
he abides in him ought to walk in the
same way in which he walked.

The New Commandment

7 Beloved, I am writing you no new
commandment, but an old command-
ment that you had from the beginning.
The old commandment is the word that
you have heard. 8 At the same time, it is
a new commandment that I am writing
to you, which is true in him and in you,
because[2] the darkness is passing away and
the true light is already shining. 9 Whoever
says he is in the light and hates his brother
is still in darkness. 10 Whoever loves his
brother abides in the light, and in him[3]
there is no cause for stumbling. 11 But
whoever hates his brother is in the dark-
ness and walks in the darkness, and does
not know where he is going, because the
darkness has blinded his eyes.

12 I am writing to you, little children,
because your sins are forgiven for
his name's sake.
13 I am writing to you, fathers,
because you know him who is
from the beginning.
I am writing to you, young men,
because you have overcome the
evil one.
I write to you, children,
because you know the Father.

[1] Some manuscripts *your* [2] Or *that* [3] Or *it*

14 I write to you, fathers,
because you know him who is
from the beginning.
I write to you, young men,
because you are strong,
and the word of God abides in you,
and you have overcome the evil
one.

Do Not Love the World

15 Do not love the world or the things
in the world. If anyone loves the world,
the love of the Father is not in him. 16 For
all that is in the world—the desires of the
flesh and the desires of the eyes and pride
in possessions—is not from the Father but
is from the world. 17 And the world is pass-
ing away along with its desires, but who-
ever does the will of God abides forever.

Warning Concerning Antichrists

18 Children, it is the last hour, and as
you have heard that antichrist is com-
ing, so now many antichrists have come.
Therefore we know that it is the last hour.
19 They went out from us, but they were
not of us; for if they had been of us, they
would have continued with us. But they
went out, that it might become plain
that they all are not of us. 20 But you have
been anointed by the Holy One, and you
all have knowledge.[1] 21 I write to you, not
because you do not know the truth, but
because you know it, and because no lie is
of the truth. 22 Who is the liar but he who
denies that Jesus is the Christ? This is the
antichrist, he who denies the Father and
the Son. 23 No one who denies the Son has
the Father. Whoever confesses the Son
has the Father also. 24 Let what you heard
from the beginning abide in you. If what
you heard from the beginning abides in
you, then you too will abide in the Son
and in the Father. 25 And this is the prom-
ise that he made to us[2]—eternal life.

26 I write these things to you about those
who are trying to deceive you. 27 But the
anointing that you received from him
abides in you, and you have no need
that anyone should teach you. But as his
anointing teaches you about everything,
and is true, and is no lie—just as it has
taught you, abide in him.

Children of God

28 And now, little children, abide in him,
so that when he appears we may have
confidence and not shrink from him in
shame at his coming. 29 If you know that
he is righteous, you may be sure that
everyone who practices righteousness has
been born of him.

3 See what kind of love the Father has
given to us, that we should be called
children of God; and so we are. The reason
why the world does not know us is that it
did not know him. 2 Beloved, we are God's
children now, and what we will be has not
yet appeared; but we know that when he
appears[3] we shall be like him, because we
shall see him as he is. 3 And everyone who
thus hopes in him purifies himself as he
is pure.

4 Everyone who makes a practice of
sinning also practices lawlessness; sin is
lawlessness. 5 You know that he appeared
to take away sins, and in him there is no
sin. 6 No one who abides in him keeps on
sinning; no one who keeps on sinning
has either seen him or known him. 7 Little
children, let no one deceive you. Whoever
practices righteousness is righteous, as he
is righteous. 8 Whoever makes a practice
of sinning is of the devil, for the devil has
been sinning from the beginning. The
reason the Son of God appeared was to
destroy the works of the devil. 9 No one
born of God makes a practice of sinning,
for God's[4] seed abides in him, and he can-
not keep on sinning because he has been
born of God. 10 By this it is evident who
are the children of God, and who are the
children of the devil: whoever does not
practice righteousness is not of God, nor
is the one who does not love his brother.

[1] Some manuscripts *you know everything* [2] Some manuscripts *you* [3] Or *when it appears* [4] Greek *his*

Love One Another

11 For this is the message that you
have heard from the beginning,
19 that we should love one another.
12 We should not be like Cain, who
was of the evil one and murdered
19 his brother. And why did he mur-
der him? Because his own deeds were evil
and his brother's righteous. 13 Do not be
surprised, brothers,[1] that the world hates
you. 14 We know that we have passed out
of death into life, because we love the
brothers. Whoever does not love abides in
death. 15 Everyone who hates his brother
is a murderer, and you know that no mur-
derer has eternal life abiding in him.

16 By this we know love, that he laid
down his life for us, and we ought to lay
down our lives for the brothers. 17 But if
anyone has the world's goods and
sees his brother in need, yet closes
1487 his heart against him, how does
God's love abide in him? 18 Little children,
let us not love in word or talk but in deed
and in truth.

19 By this we shall know that we are of
the truth and reassure our heart before
him; 20 for whenever our heart condemns
us, God is greater than our heart, and he
knows everything. 21 Beloved, if our heart
does not condemn us, we have confi-
dence before God; 22 and whatever we ask
we receive from him, because we keep
his commandments and do what pleases
him. 23 And this is his commandment,
that we believe in the name of his Son
Jesus Christ and love one another, just as
he has commanded us. 24 Whoever keeps
his commandments abides in God,[2] and
God[3] in him. And by this we know that he
abides in us, by the Spirit whom he has
given us.

Test the Spirits

4 Beloved, do not believe every spirit,
but test the spirits to see whether
they are from God, for many false proph-
ets have gone out into the world. 2 By this
you know the Spirit of God: every spirit
that confesses that Jesus Christ has come
in the flesh is from God, 3 and every spirit
that does not confess Jesus is not from
God. This is the spirit of the antichrist,
which you heard was coming and now is
in the world already. 4 Little children, you
are from God and have overcome them,
for he who is in you is greater than he who
is in the world. 5 They are from the world;
therefore they speak from the world, and
the world listens to them. 6 We are from
God. Whoever knows God listens to us;
whoever is not from God does not listen
to us. By this we know the Spirit of truth
and the spirit of error.

God Is Love

7 Beloved, let us love one another, for
love is from God, and whoever loves has
been born of God and knows God. 8 Any-
one who does not love does not know
God, because God is love. 9 In this
the love of God was made manifest
57 among us, that God sent his only
Son into the world, so that we might live
through him. 10 In this is love, not that we
have loved God but that he loved us and
sent his Son to be the propitiation for our
sins. 11 Beloved, if God so loved us, we also
ought to love one another. 12 No one has
ever seen God; if we love one another, God
abides in us and his love is perfected in us.

13 By this we know that we abide in him
and he in us, because he has given us of
his Spirit. 14 And we have seen and testify
that the Father has sent his Son to be the
Savior of the world. 15 Whoever confesses
that Jesus is the Son of God, God abides in
him, and he in God. 16 So we have come
to know and to believe the love that God
has for us. God is love, and whoever abides
in love abides in God, and God abides in
him. 17 By this is love perfected with us, so
that we may have confidence for the day
of judgment, because as he is so also are

[1] Or *brothers and sisters*. The plural Greek word *adelphoi* (translated "brothers") refers to siblings in a family. In New Testament usage, depending on the context, *adelphoi* may refer either to men or to both men and women who are siblings (brothers and sisters) in God's family, the church; also verses 14, 16 [2] Greek *him* [3] Greek *he*

we in this world. 18 There is no fear in love,
but perfect love casts out fear. For fear has
to do with punishment, and whoever
fears has not been perfected in love. 19 We
love because he first loved us. 20 If anyone
says, "I love God," and hates his brother,
he is a liar; for he who does not love his
brother whom he has seen cannot[1] love
God whom he has not seen. 21 And this
commandment we have from him: who-
ever loves God must also love his brother.

Overcoming the World

5 Everyone who believes that
Jesus is the Christ has been
1549 born of God, and everyone who
loves the Father loves whoever has been
born of him. 2 By this we know that we
love the children of God, when we love
God and obey his commandments. 3 For
this is the love of God, that we keep his
commandments. And his command-
ments are not burdensome. 4 For
everyone who has been born of
1549 God overcomes the world. And this
is the victory that has overcome the
world—our faith. 5 Who is it that over-
comes the world except the one who
believes that Jesus is the Son of God?

Testimony Concerning the Son of God

6 This is he who came by water and
blood—Jesus Christ; not by the water only
but by the water and the blood. And the
Spirit is the one who testifies, because the
Spirit is the truth. 7 For there are three that
testify: 8 the Spirit and the water and the
blood; and these three agree. 9 If we receive
the testimony of men, the testimony of
God is greater, for this is the testimony
of God that he has borne concerning his
Son. 10 Whoever believes in the Son of God
has the testimony in himself. Whoever
does not believe God has made him a liar,
because he has not believed in the testi-
mony that God has borne concerning his
Son. 11 And this is the testimony, that God
gave us eternal life, and this life is in his
Son. 12 Whoever has the Son has life; who-
ever does not have the Son of God does
not have life.

That You May Know

13 I write these things to you who
believe in the name of the Son of God
that you may know that you have eternal
life. 14 And this is the confidence
that we have toward him, that if
435 we ask anything according to his
will he hears us. 15 And if we know that he
hears us in whatever we ask, we know
that we have the requests that we have
asked of him.

16 If anyone sees his brother commit-
ting a sin not leading to death, he shall
ask, and God[2] will give him life—to those
who commit sins that do not lead to
death. There is sin that leads to death; I
do not say that one should pray for that.
17 All wrongdoing is sin, but there is sin
that does not lead to death.

18 We know that everyone who has
been born of God does not keep on
1549 sinning, but he who was born of
God protects him, and the evil one does
not touch him.

19 We know that we are from God, and
the whole world lies in the power of the
evil one.

20 And we know that the Son of God has
come and has given us understanding, so
that we may know him who is true; and
we are in him who is true, in his Son Jesus
Christ. He is the true God and
eternal life. 21 Little children, keep
573 yourselves from idols.

[1] Some manuscripts *how can he* [2] Greek *he*

The Second Letter of John

2 John

For the introduction, see the introduction to 1 John (p. 1817)

Greeting

1 The elder to the elect lady and her chil-
dren, whom I love in truth, and not only I,
but also all who know the truth, 2 because
of the truth that abides in us and will be
with us forever:

3 Grace, mercy, and peace will be with
us, from God the Father and from Jesus
Christ the Father's Son, in truth and love.

Walking in Truth and Love

4 I rejoiced greatly to find some of your
children walking in the truth, just as we
were commanded by the Father. 5 And now
I ask you, dear lady—not as though I were
writing you a new commandment, but the
one we have had from the beginning—that
we love one another. 6 And this is love, that
we walk according to his commandments;
this is the commandment, just as you
have heard from the beginning, so that
you should walk in it. 7 For many deceivers
have gone out into the world, those who
do not confess the coming of Jesus Christ
in the flesh. Such a one is the deceiver and
the antichrist. 8 Watch yourselves, so that
you may not lose what we[1] have worked
for, but may win a full reward. 9 Everyone
who goes on ahead and does not abide in
the teaching of Christ, does not have God.
Whoever abides in the teaching has both
the Father and the Son. 10 If anyone comes
to you and does not bring this teaching,
do not receive him into your house or give
him any greeting, 11 for whoever greets
him takes part in his wicked works.

Final Greetings

12 Though I have much to write to you,
I would rather not use paper and ink.
Instead I hope to come to you and talk face
to face, so that our joy may be complete.

13 The children of your elect sister greet
you.

[1] Some manuscripts *you*

The Third Letter of John

3 John

For the introduction, see the introduction to 1 John (p. 1817)

Greeting

1 The elder to the beloved Gaius, whom I love in truth.

2 Beloved, I pray that all may go well with you and that you may be in good health, as it goes well with your soul. 3 For I rejoiced greatly when the brothers[1] came and testified to your truth, as indeed you are walking in the truth. 4 I have no greater joy than to hear that my children are walking in the truth.

Support and Opposition

5 Beloved, it is a faithful thing you do in all your efforts for these brothers, strangers as they are, 6 who testified to your love before the church. You will do well to send them on their journey in a manner worthy of God. 7 For they have gone out for the sake of the name, accepting nothing from the Gentiles. 8 Therefore we ought to support people like these, that we may be fellow workers for the truth.

9 I have written something to the church, but Diotrephes, who likes to put himself first, does not acknowledge our authority. 10 So if I come, I will bring up what he is doing, talking wicked nonsense against us. And not content with that, he refuses to welcome the brothers, and also stops those who want to and puts them out of the church.

11 Beloved, do not imitate evil but imitate good. Whoever does good is from God; whoever does evil has not seen God. 12 Demetrius has received a good testimony from everyone, and from the truth itself. We also add our testimony, and you know that our testimony is true.

Final Greetings

13 I had much to write to you, but I would rather not write with pen and ink. 14 I hope to see you soon, and we will talk face to face.

15 Peace be to you. The friends greet you. Greet the friends, every one of them.

[1] Or *brothers and sisters*. The plural Greek word *adelphoi* (translated "brothers") refers to siblings in a family. In New Testament usage, depending on the context, *adelphoi* may refer either to men or to both men and women who are siblings (brothers and sisters) in God's family, the church; also verses 5, 10

Introduction to

Jude

Author

Jude

Date

About A.D. mid-60s

Key People

Jude; angels; the archangel Michael; Moses; Cain; Balaam; Korah; Enoch

Purpose

The purpose of Jude is to urge Christians to stand up for the truth of the Christian faith by living in obedience to it and by resisting those who twist its teachings.

Central Themes

Believers need to defend Christian truth; the false teachers are immoral; God's judgment is on false teachers; believers need to persevere; God preserves His people.

Memory Verse

Built up in the faith (Jude 20–23)

Introduction

Jude wrote his letter because people were being welcomed and accepted into the church and then teaching what was evil and false. These teachers twisted the teaching of God's grace and forgiveness to say that Christians can commit any sin they want to. By teaching and living this way, they denied Jesus as Lord and Master (Jude 4). Jude reminds his readers of immoral people in Old Testament times whom God destroyed in judgment. God will do the same in the future to those who do not repent (Jude 5–7). Jude described these sinful false teachers in the church with very strong words, wanting his readers to realize how dangerous they were (Jude 8–16). He called upon the Christians to do the following things in response to these men: contend for the true faith (Jude 3), grow in the faith themselves, pray in the Holy Spirit (Jude 20), keep themselves in the love of God while they waited for Jesus to return (Jude 21), and show mercy to any they could possibly help (Jude 22–23). Jude ended by promising that God would keep His people from stumbling and present them blameless at last in His presence (Jude 24–25).

About A.D. 28–33	About A.D. mid-60s	A.D. 70
Jesus' ministry, death, resurrection	Jude writes his letter	Temple destroyed

The Letter of

Jude

Greeting

1 Jude, a servant[1] of Jesus Christ and brother of James,

To those who are called, beloved in God the Father and kept for[2] Jesus Christ:

2 May mercy, peace, and love be multiplied to you.

Judgment on False Teachers

3 Beloved, although I was very eager to write to you about our common salvation, I found it necessary to write appealing to you to contend for the faith that was once for all delivered to the saints. 4 For certain people have crept in unnoticed who long ago were designated for this condemnation, ungodly people, who pervert the grace of our God into sensuality and deny our only Master and Lord, Jesus Christ.

5 Now I want to remind you, although you once fully knew it, that Jesus, who saved[3] a people out of the land of Egypt, afterward destroyed those who did not believe. 6 And the angels who did not stay within their own position of authority, but left their proper dwelling, he has kept in eternal chains under gloomy darkness until the judgment of the great day— 7 just as Sodom and Gomorrah and the surrounding cities, which likewise indulged in sexual immorality and pursued unnatural desire,[4] serve as an example by undergoing a punishment of eternal fire.

8 Yet in like manner these people also, relying on their dreams, defile the flesh, reject authority, and blaspheme the glorious ones. 9 But when the archangel Michael, contending with the devil, was disputing about the body of Moses, he did not presume to pronounce a blasphemous judgment, but said, "The Lord rebuke you." 10 But these people blaspheme all that they do not understand, and they are destroyed by all that they, like unreasoning animals, understand instinctively. 11 Woe to them! For they walked in the way of Cain and abandoned themselves for the sake of gain to Balaam's error and perished in Korah's rebellion. 12 These are hidden reefs[5] at your love feasts, as they feast with you without fear, shepherds feeding themselves; waterless clouds, swept along by winds; fruitless trees in late autumn, twice dead, uprooted; 13 wild waves of the sea, casting up the foam of their own shame; wandering stars, for whom the gloom of utter darkness has been reserved forever.

14 It was also about these that Enoch, the seventh from Adam, prophesied, saying, "Behold, the Lord comes with ten thousands of his holy ones, 15 to execute judgment on all and to convict all the ungodly of all their deeds of ungodliness that they have committed in such an ungodly way, and of all the harsh things that ungodly sinners have spoken against him." 16 These are grumblers, malcontents, following their own sinful desires; they are loud-mouthed boasters, showing favoritism to gain advantage.

A Call to Persevere

17 But you must remember, beloved, the predictions of the apostles of our Lord Jesus Christ. 18 They[6] said to you, "In the last time there will be scoffers, following their own ungodly passions." 19 It is these who cause divisions, worldly people, devoid of the Spirit. 20 But you, beloved, building yourselves up in your most holy

[1] Or *slave;* Greek *bondservant* [2] Or *by* [3] Some manuscripts *although you fully knew it, that the Lord who once saved* [4] Greek *other flesh* [5] Or *are blemishes* [6] Or *Christ, because they*

faith and praying in the Holy Spirit, 21 keep
yourselves in the love of God, waiting for
the mercy of our Lord Jesus Christ that
leads to eternal life. 22 And have mercy on
those who doubt; 23 save others by snatch-
ing them out of the fire; to others show
mercy with fear, hating even the garment[1]
stained by the flesh.

Doxology

24 Now to him who is able to keep you
from stumbling and to present you blame-
less before the presence of his glory with
great joy, 25 to the only God, our Savior,
through Jesus Christ our Lord, be glory,
majesty, dominion, and authority, before
all time and now and forever. Amen.

[1] Greek *chiton*, a long garment worn under the cloak next to the skin

Introduction to

Revelation

Author

John the apostle

Date

About A.D. 95–96

Key People

John; the seven churches in Asia

Purpose

The purpose of Revelation is to comfort persecuted Christians by showing them God's victory over all enemies and to provide a preview of the new Jerusalem where believers will dwell with Him forever.

Central Themes

The risen Jesus will be victorious; the Lord is with His churches; Christian churches must be holy and faithful; Satan's hatred of Jesus is behind the persecution of Christians; Satan and God's enemies can do no more than God allows; praise to God will abound forever in heaven; those who do not repent will be judged; a new heaven and a new earth will have no pain, death, or sadness.

Memory Verses

Be faithful (Revelation 2:10); Jesus at the door (Revelation 3:19–20); the song and new song (Revelation 4:11; 5:9–10); heaven's bliss (Revelation 7:15–17); conquering Satan (Revelation 12:10–11); marriage of the Lamb (Revelation 19:6–9)

Introduction

When Revelation was written, Christians faced false teaching, temptation, and persecution. John himself had been banished to an island for preaching the gospel. While he was there, the Lord gave him a vision to write down and share with struggling churches for their encouragement. What he wrote is the book we call "Revelation." It begins with a vision of Christ in His resurrection glory (Revelation 1). He gives John seven messages for seven churches in Asia, showing that He knows each church's struggles, failures, and victories (Revelation 2–3). Then John sees many different and strange visions. Some of them show the sufferings of persecuted believers; some show God's judgments upon the earth and upon His enemies; some show scenes of praise and joy in heaven. All these things demonstrate that Jesus sees what happens to His people, is with them in their sufferings, and will accomplish all His good purposes for them. John sees Jesus as a slain lamb who conquers (Revelation 5) and as a conquering warrior who destroys all His enemies (Revelation 19:11–21). The final visions show a new heaven and a new earth where God's people live with Him forever with no enemies, sadness, sin, or death (Revelation 21–22).

About A.D. 28–33	A.D. 70	About A.D. 95–96
Jesus' ministry, death, resurrection	Temple destroyed	John writes Revelation

The Revelation to John

Prologue

1 The revelation of Jesus Christ, which God gave him to show to his servants[1] the things that must soon take place. He made it known by sending his angel to his servant[2] John, 2 who bore witness to the word of God and to the testimony of Jesus Christ, even to all that he saw. 3 Blessed is the one who reads aloud the words of this prophecy, and blessed are those who hear, and who keep what is written in it, for the time is near.

Greeting to the Seven Churches

4 John to the seven churches that are in Asia:

Grace to you and peace from him who is and who was and who is to come, and from the seven spirits who are before his throne, 5 and from Jesus Christ the faithful witness, the firstborn of the dead, and the ruler of kings on earth.

To him who loves us and has freed us from our sins by his blood 6 and made us a kingdom, priests to his God and Father, to him be glory and dominion forever and ever. Amen. 7 Behold, he is coming with the clouds, and every eye will see him, even those who pierced him, and all tribes of the earth will wail[3] on account of him. Even so. Amen.

8 "I am the Alpha and the Omega," says the Lord God, "who is and who was and who is to come, the Almighty."

Vision of the Son of Man

9 I, John, your brother and partner in the tribulation and the kingdom and the patient endurance that are in Jesus, was on the island called Patmos on account of the word of God and the testimony of Jesus. 10 I was in the Spirit on the Lord's day, and I heard behind me a loud voice like a trumpet 11 saying, "Write what you see in a book and send it to the seven churches, to Ephesus and to Smyrna and to Pergamum and to Thyatira and to Sardis and to Philadelphia and to Laodicea."

12 Then I turned to see the voice that was speaking to me, and on turning I saw seven golden lampstands, 13 and in the midst of the lampstands one like a son of man, clothed with a long robe and with a golden sash around his chest. 14 The hairs of his head were white, like white wool, like snow. His eyes were like a flame of fire, 15 his feet were like burnished bronze, refined in a furnace, and his voice was like the roar of many waters. 16 In his right hand he held seven stars, from his mouth came a sharp two-edged sword, and his face was like the sun shining in full strength.

17 When I saw him, I fell at his feet as though dead. But he laid his right hand on me, saying, "Fear not, I am the first and the last, 18 and the living one. I died, and behold I am alive forevermore, and I have the keys of Death and Hades. 19 Write therefore the things that you have seen, those that are and those that are to take place after this. 20 As for the mystery of the seven stars that you saw in my right hand, and the seven golden lampstands, the seven stars are the angels of the seven churches, and the seven lampstands are the seven churches.

To the Church in Ephesus

2 "To the angel of the church in Ephesus write: 'The words of him who holds the seven stars in his right hand, who walks among the seven golden lampstands.

[1] Greek *bondservants* [2] Greek *bondservant* [3] Or *mourn*

2 "'I know your works, your toil and
your patient endurance, and how you can-
not bear with those who are evil, but have
tested those who call themselves apostles
and are not, and found them to be false.
3 I know you are enduring patiently and
bearing up for my name's sake, and you
have not grown weary. 4 But I have this
against you, that you have abandoned the
love you had at first. 5 Remember there-
fore from where you have fallen; repent,
and do the works you did at first. If not, I
will come to you and remove your lamp-
stand from its place, unless you repent.
6 Yet this you have: you hate the works of
the Nicolaitans, which I also hate. 7 He
who has an ear, let him hear what the
Spirit says to the churches. To the one who
conquers I will grant to eat of the tree of
life, which is in the paradise of God.'

To the Church in Smyrna

8 "And to the angel of the church in
Smyrna write: 'The words of the first and
the last, who died and came to life.
9 "'I know your tribulation and your
poverty (but you are rich) and the slander[1]
of those who say that they are Jews and are
not, but are a synagogue of Satan. 10 Do not
fear what you are about to suffer. Behold,
the devil is about to throw some of you
into prison, that you may be tested, and
for ten days you will have tribulation. Be
faithful unto death, and I will give you the
crown of life. 11 He who has an ear, let him
hear what the Spirit says to the churches.
The one who conquers will not be hurt by
the second death.'

To the Church in Pergamum

12 "And to the angel of the church in
Pergamum write: 'The words of him who
has the sharp two-edged sword.
13 "'I know where you dwell, where
Satan's throne is. Yet you hold fast my
name, and you did not deny my faith[2]
even in the days of Antipas my faith-
ful witness, who was killed among you,
where Satan dwells. 14 But I have a few
things against you: you have some there
who hold the teaching of Balaam, who
taught Balak to put a stumbling block
before the sons of Israel, so that they
might eat food sacrificed to idols and
practice sexual immorality. 15 So also you
have some who hold the teaching of the
Nicolaitans. 16 Therefore repent. If not,
I will come to you soon and war against
them with the sword of my mouth. 17 He
who has an ear, let him hear what the
Spirit says to the churches. To the one
who conquers I will give some of the hid-
den manna, and I will give him a white
stone, with a new name written on the
stone that no one knows except the one
who receives it.'

To the Church in Thyatira

18 "And to the angel of the church in
Thyatira write: 'The words of the Son of
God, who has eyes like a flame of fire, and
whose feet are like burnished bronze.
19 "'I know your works, your love and
faith and service and patient endurance,
and that your latter works exceed the first.
20 But I have this against you, that you
tolerate that woman Jezebel, who calls
herself a prophetess and is teaching and
seducing my servants[3] to practice sexual
immorality and to eat food sacrificed to
idols. 21 I gave her time to repent, but she
refuses to repent of her sexual immoral-
ity. 22 Behold, I will throw her onto a sick-
bed, and those who commit adultery with
her I will throw into great tribulation,
unless they repent of her works, 23 and I
will strike her children dead. And all the
churches will know that I am he who
searches mind and heart, and I will give to
each of you according to your works. 24 But
to the rest of you in Thyatira, who do not
hold this teaching, who have not learned
what some call the deep things of Satan,
to you I say, I do not lay on you any other
burden. 25 Only hold fast what you have

[1] Greek *blasphemy* [2] Or *your faith in me* [3] Greek *bondservants*

until I come. 26 The one who conquers
and who keeps my works until the end, to
him I will give authority over the nations,
27 and he will rule them with a rod of iron,
as when earthen pots are broken in pieces,
even as I myself have received authority
from my Father. 28 And I will give him the
morning star. 29 He who has an ear, let him
hear what the Spirit says to the churches.'

To the Church in Sardis

3 "And to the angel of the church in
Sardis write: 'The words of him
who has the seven spirits of God and the
seven stars.

"'I know your works. You have the
reputation of being alive, but you are
dead. 2 Wake up, and strengthen what
remains and is about to die, for I have not
found your works complete in the sight
of my God. 3 Remember, then, what you
received and heard. Keep it, and repent.
If you will not wake up, I will come like a
thief, and you will not know at what hour
I will come against you. 4 Yet you have
still a few names in Sardis, people who
have not soiled their garments, and they
will walk with me in white, for they are
worthy. 5 The one who conquers will be
clothed thus in white garments, and I will
never blot his name out of the book of life.
I will confess his name before my Father
and before his angels. 6 He who has an ear,
let him hear what the Spirit says to the
churches.'

To the Church in Philadelphia

7 "And to the angel of the church in
Philadelphia write: 'The words of the
holy one, the true one, who has the key of
David, who opens and no one will shut,
who shuts and no one opens.

8 "'I know your works. Behold, I have set
before you an open door, which no one is
able to shut. I know that you have but lit-
tle power, and yet you have kept my word
and have not denied my name. 9 Behold, I
will make those of the synagogue of Satan
who say that they are Jews and are not, but
lie—behold, I will make them come and
bow down before your feet and they will
learn that I have loved you. 10 Because you
have kept my word about patient endur-
ance, I will keep you from the hour of trial
that is coming on the whole world, to try
those who dwell on the earth. 11 I am com-
ing soon. Hold fast what you have, so that
no one may seize your crown. 12 The one
who conquers, I will make him a pillar
in the temple of my God. Never shall he
go out of it, and I will write on him the
name of my God, and the name of the
city of my God, the new Jerusalem, which
comes down from my God out of heaven,
and my own new name. 13 He who has an
ear, let him hear what the Spirit says to the
churches.'

To the Church in Laodicea

14 "And to the angel of the church in
Laodicea write: 'The words of the Amen,
the faithful and true witness, the begin-
ning of God's creation.

15 "'I know your works: you are neither
cold nor hot. Would that you were either
cold or hot! 16 So, because you are luke-
warm, and neither hot nor cold, I will spit
you out of my mouth. 17 For you say, I am
rich, I have prospered, and I need noth-
ing, not realizing that you are wretched,
pitiable, poor, blind, and naked. 18 I coun-
sel you to buy from me gold refined by
fire, so that you may be rich, and white
garments so that you may clothe yourself
and the shame of your nakedness may not
be seen, and salve to anoint your eyes, so
that you may see. 19 Those whom I love,
I reprove and discipline, so be zealous
and repent. 20 Behold, I stand at the door
and knock. If anyone hears my voice and
opens the door, I will come in to him and
eat with him, and he with me. 21 The one
who conquers, I will grant him to sit with
me on my throne, as I also conquered and
sat down with my Father on his throne.

22 He who has an ear, let him hear what the
Spirit says to the churches.'"

The Throne in Heaven

4 After this I looked, and behold, a door
standing open in heaven! And the
first voice, which I had heard speaking to
me like a trumpet, said, "Come up here,
and I will show you what must take place
after this." 2 At once I was in the Spirit,
and behold, a throne stood in heaven,
with one seated on the throne. 3 And he
who sat there had the appearance of jas-
per and carnelian, and around the throne
was a rainbow that had the appearance
of an emerald. 4 Around the throne were
twenty-four thrones, and seated on the
thrones were twenty-four elders, clothed
in white garments, with golden crowns
on their heads. 5 From the throne came
flashes of lightning, and rumblings[1] and
peals of thunder, and before the throne
were burning seven torches of fire, which
are the seven spirits of God, 6 and before
the throne there was as it were a sea of
glass, like crystal.

And around the throne, on each side of
the throne, are four living creatures, full
of eyes in front and behind: 7 the first liv-
ing creature like a lion, the second living
creature like an ox, the third living crea-
ture with the face of a man, and the fourth
living creature like an eagle in flight. 8 And
the four living creatures, each of them
with six wings, are full of eyes all around
and within, and day and night they never
cease to say,

"Holy, holy, holy, is the Lord God
Almighty,
who was and is and is to come!"

9 And whenever the living creatures give
glory and honor and thanks to him who
is seated on the throne, who lives forever
and ever, 10 the twenty-four elders fall
down before him who is seated on the
throne and worship him who lives forever
and ever. They cast their crowns before
the throne, saying,

11 "Worthy are you, our Lord and God,
to receive glory and honor and
power,
for you created all things,
and by your will they existed and
were created."

The Scroll and the Lamb

5 Then I saw in the right hand of him
who was seated on the throne a scroll
written within and on the back, sealed with
seven seals. 2 And I saw a strong angel pro-
claiming with a loud voice, "Who is wor-
thy to open the scroll and break its seals?"
3 And no one in heaven or on earth or under
the earth was able to open the scroll or to
look into it, 4 and I began to weep loudly
because no one was found worthy to open
the scroll or to look into it. 5 And one of the
elders said to me, "Weep no more; behold,
the Lion of the tribe of Judah, the Root of
David, has conquered, so that he can open
the scroll and its seven seals."

6 And between the throne and the four
living creatures and among the elders I saw
a Lamb standing, as though it had been
slain, with seven horns and with seven
eyes, which are the seven spirits of God
sent out into all the earth. 7 And he
went and took the scroll from the
57 right hand of him who was seated
on the throne. 8 And when he had taken
the scroll, the four living creatures and
the twenty-four elders fell down before
the Lamb, each holding a harp, and golden
bowls full of incense, which are the prayers
of the saints. 9 And they sang a new song,
saying,

"Worthy are you to take the scroll
and to open its seals,
for you were slain, and by your blood
you ransomed people for God
from every tribe and language
and people and nation,

[1] Or *voices*, or *sounds*

10 and you have made them a kingdom
and priests to our God,
and they shall reign on the earth."

11 Then I looked, and I heard around the
throne and the living creatures and the
elders the voice of many angels, number-
ing myriads of myriads and thousands
of thousands, 12 saying with a loud voice,
"Worthy is the Lamb who was slain, to
receive power and wealth and wisdom
and might and honor and glory and
blessing!" 13 And I heard every creature in
heaven and on earth and under the earth
and in the sea, and all that is in them, say-
ing, "To him who sits on the throne and to
the Lamb be blessing and honor and glory
and might forever and ever!" 14 And the
four living creatures said, "Amen!" and the
elders fell down and worshiped.

The Seven Seals

6 Now I watched when the Lamb
opened one of the seven seals, and I
heard one of the four living creatures say
with a voice like thunder, "Come!" 2 And
I looked, and behold, a white horse! And
its rider had a bow, and a crown was given
to him, and he came out conquering, and
to conquer.

3 When he opened the second seal,
I heard the second living creature say,
"Come!" 4 And out came another horse,
bright red. Its rider was permitted to
take peace from the earth, so that people
should slay one another, and he was given
a great sword.

5 When he opened the third seal, I heard
the third living creature say, "Come!" And
I looked, and behold, a black horse! And
its rider had a pair of scales in his hand.
6 And I heard what seemed to be a voice
in the midst of the four living creatures,
saying, "A quart[1] of wheat for a denarius,[2]
and three quarts of barley for a denarius,
and do not harm the oil and wine!"

7 When he opened the fourth seal, I
heard the voice of the fourth living crea-
ture say, "Come!" 8 And I looked, and
behold, a pale horse! And its rider's name
was Death, and Hades followed him. And
they were given authority over a fourth
of the earth, to kill with sword and with
famine and with pestilence and by wild
beasts of the earth.

9 When he opened the fifth seal, I saw
under the altar the souls of those who had
been slain for the word of God and for the
witness they had borne. 10 They cried out
with a loud voice, "O Sovereign Lord, holy
and true, how long before you will judge
and avenge our blood on those who dwell
on the earth?" 11 Then they were each
given a white robe and told to rest a little
longer, until the number of their fellow
servants[3] and their brothers[4] should be
complete, who were to be killed as they
themselves had been.

12 When he opened the sixth seal, I
looked, and behold, there was a great
earthquake, and the sun became black
as sackcloth, the full moon became like
blood, 13 and the stars of the sky fell to
the earth as the fig tree sheds its winter
fruit when shaken by a gale. 14 The sky
vanished like a scroll that is being rolled
up, and every mountain and island was
removed from its place. 15 Then the kings
of the earth and the great ones and the
generals and the rich and the powerful,
and everyone, slave[5] and free, hid them-
selves in the caves and among the rocks
of the mountains, 16 calling to the moun-
tains and rocks, "Fall on us and hide us
from the face of him who is seated on the
throne, and from the wrath of the Lamb,
17 for the great day of their wrath has
come, and who can stand?"

The 144,000 of Israel Sealed

7 After this I saw four angels stand-
ing at the four corners of the earth,
holding back the four winds of the earth,

[1] Greek *choinix*, a dry measure equal to about a quart [2] A *denarius* was a day's wage for a laborer [3] Greek *fellow bondservants* [4] Or *brothers and sisters*. The plural Greek word *adelphoi* (translated "brothers") refers to siblings in a family. In New Testament usage, depending on the context, *adelphoi* may refer either to men or to both men and women who are siblings (brothers and sisters) in God's family, the church [5] Or *servant*; Greek *bondservant*

that no wind might blow on earth or sea
or against any tree. 2 Then I saw another
angel ascending from the rising of the
sun, with the seal of the living God, and he
called with a loud voice to the four angels
who had been given power to harm earth
and sea, 3 saying, "Do not harm the earth
or the sea or the trees, until we have sealed
the servants[1] of our God on their fore-
heads." 4 And I heard the number of the
sealed, 144,000, sealed from every tribe of
the sons of Israel:

5 12,000 from the tribe of Judah were sealed,
12,000 from the tribe of Reuben,
12,000 from the tribe of Gad,
6 12,000 from the tribe of Asher,
12,000 from the tribe of Naphtali,
12,000 from the tribe of Manasseh,
7 12,000 from the tribe of Simeon,
12,000 from the tribe of Levi,
12,000 from the tribe of Issachar,
8 12,000 from the tribe of Zebulun,
12,000 from the tribe of Joseph,
12,000 from the tribe of Benjamin were sealed.

A Great Multitude from Every Nation

9 After this I looked, and behold, a
great multitude that no one could
1645 number, from every nation, from
all tribes and peoples and languages,
standing before the throne and before the
Lamb, clothed in white robes, with palm
branches in their hands, 10 and crying out
with a loud voice, "Salvation belongs to
our God who sits on the throne, and to the
Lamb!" 11 And all the angels were standing
around the throne and around the elders
and the four living creatures, and they fell
on their faces before the throne and wor-
shiped God, 12 saying, "Amen! Blessing and
glory and wisdom and thanksgiving and
honor and power and might be to our God
forever and ever! Amen."

13 Then one of the elders addressed me,
saying, "Who are these, clothed in white
robes, and from where have they come?"
14 I said to him, "Sir, you know." And he
said to me, "These are the ones coming
out of the great tribulation. They have
washed their robes and made them white
in the blood of the Lamb.

15 "Therefore they are before the throne of God,
and serve him day and night in his temple;
and he who sits on the throne will shelter them with his presence.
16 They shall hunger no more, neither thirst anymore;
1553 the sun shall not strike them, nor any scorching heat.
17 For the Lamb in the midst of the throne will be their shepherd,
and he will guide them to springs of living water,
and God will wipe away every tear from their eyes."

The Seventh Seal and the Golden Censer

8 When the Lamb opened the seventh
seal, there was silence in heaven
for about half an hour. 2 Then I saw the
seven angels who stand before God, and
seven trumpets were given to them. 3 And
another angel came and stood at the altar
with a golden censer, and he was given
much incense to offer with the prayers of
all the saints on the golden altar before
the throne, 4 and the smoke of the incense,
with the prayers of the saints, rose before
God from the hand of the angel. 5 Then
the angel took the censer and filled it
with fire from the altar and threw it on
the earth, and there were peals of thunder,
rumblings,[2] flashes of lightning, and an
earthquake.

The Seven Trumpets

6 Now the seven angels who had the
seven trumpets prepared to blow them.
7 The first angel blew his trumpet, and
there followed hail and fire, mixed with

[1] Greek *bondservants* [2] Or *voices*, or *sounds*

blood, and these were thrown upon the earth. And a third of the earth was burned up, and a third of the trees were burned up, and all green grass was burned up.

8 The second angel blew his trumpet, and something like a great mountain, burning with fire, was thrown into the sea, and a third of the sea became blood. **9** A third of the living creatures in the sea died, and a third of the ships were destroyed.

10 The third angel blew his trumpet, and a great star fell from heaven, blazing like a torch, and it fell on a third of the rivers and on the springs of water. **11** The name of the star is Wormwood.[1] A third of the waters became wormwood, and many people died from the water, because it had been made bitter.

12 The fourth angel blew his trumpet, and a third of the sun was struck, and a third of the moon, and a third of the stars, so that a third of their light might be darkened, and a third of the day might be kept from shining, and likewise a third of the night.

13 Then I looked, and I heard an eagle crying with a loud voice as it flew directly overhead, "Woe, woe, woe to those who dwell on the earth, at the blasts of the other trumpets that the three angels are about to blow!"

9 And the fifth angel blew his trumpet, and I saw a star fallen from heaven to earth, and he was given the key to the shaft of the bottomless pit.[2] **2** He opened the shaft of the bottomless pit, and from the shaft rose smoke like the smoke of a great furnace, and the sun and the air were darkened with the smoke from the shaft. **3** Then from the smoke came locusts on the earth, and they were given power like the power of scorpions of the earth. **4** *They were told not to* harm the grass of the earth or any green plant or any tree, but only those people who do not have the seal of God on their foreheads. **5** They were allowed to torment them for five months, but not to kill them, and their torment was like the torment of a scorpion when it stings someone. **6** And in those days people will seek death and will not find it. They will long to die, but death will flee from them.

7 In appearance the locusts were like horses prepared for battle: on their heads were what looked like crowns of gold; their faces were like human faces, **8** their hair like women's hair, and their teeth like lions' teeth; **9** they had breastplates like breastplates of iron, and the noise of their wings was like the noise of many chariots with horses rushing into battle. **10** They have tails and stings like scorpions, and their power to hurt people for five months is in their tails. **11** They have as king over them the angel of the bottomless pit. His name in Hebrew is Abaddon, and in Greek he is called Apollyon.[3]

12 The first woe has passed; behold, two woes are still to come.

13 Then the sixth angel blew his trumpet, and I heard a voice from the four horns of the golden altar before God, **14** saying to the sixth angel who had the trumpet, "Release the four angels who are bound at the great river Euphrates." **15** So the four angels, who had been prepared for the hour, the day, the month, and the year, were released to kill a third of mankind. **16** The number of mounted troops was twice ten thousand times ten thousand; I heard their number. **17** And this is how I saw the horses in my vision and those who rode them: they wore breastplates the color of fire and of sapphire[4] and of sulfur, and the heads of the horses were like lions' heads, and fire and smoke and sulfur came out of their mouths. **18** By these three plagues a third of mankind was killed, by the fire and smoke and sulfur coming out of their mouths. **19** For the power of the horses is in their mouths and in their tails, for their tails are like ser-

[1] *Wormwood* is the name of a plant and of the bitter-tasting extract derived from it [2] Greek *the abyss*; also verses 2, 11 [3] *Abaddon* means *destruction*; *Apollyon* means *destroyer* [4] Greek *hyacinth*

pents with heads, and by means of them
they wound.
20 The rest of mankind, who were not
killed by these plagues, did not repent
of the works of their hands nor give up
worshiping demons and idols of gold and
silver and bronze and stone and wood,
which cannot see or hear or walk, 21 nor
did they repent of their murders or their
sorceries or their sexual immorality or
their thefts.

The Angel and the Little Scroll

10 Then I saw another mighty angel
coming down from heaven,
wrapped in a cloud, with a rainbow over
his head, and his face was like the sun,
and his legs like pillars of fire. 2 He had a
little scroll open in his hand. And he set
his right foot on the sea, and his left foot
on the land, 3 and called out with a loud
voice, like a lion roaring. When he called
out, the seven thunders sounded. 4 And
when the seven thunders had sounded,
I was about to write, but I heard a voice
from heaven saying, "Seal up what the
seven thunders have said, and do not
write it down." 5 And the angel whom I saw
standing on the sea and on the land raised
his right hand to heaven 6 and swore by
him who lives forever and ever, who cre-
ated heaven and what is in it, the earth
and what is in it, and the sea and what is
in it, that there would be no more delay,
7 but that in the days of the trumpet call to
be sounded by the seventh angel, the mys-
tery of God would be fulfilled, just as he
announced to his servants[1] the prophets.
8 Then the voice that I had heard from
heaven spoke to me again, saying, "Go, take
the scroll that is open in the hand of the
angel who is standing on the sea and on
the land." 9 So I went to the angel and told
him to give me the little scroll. And he said
to me, "Take and eat it; it will make your
stomach bitter, but in your mouth it will
be sweet as honey." 10 And I took the little
scroll from the hand of the angel and ate
it. It was sweet as honey in my mouth,
but when I had eaten it my stomach was
made bitter. 11 And I was told, "You must
again prophesy about many peoples and
nations and languages and kings."

The Two Witnesses

11 Then I was given a measuring rod
like a staff, and I was told, "Rise
and measure the temple of God and the
altar and those who worship there, 2 but
do not measure the court outside the
temple; leave that out, for it is given over
to the nations, and they will trample the
holy city for forty-two months. 3 And I will
grant authority to my two witnesses, and
they will prophesy for 1,260 days, clothed
in sackcloth."
4 These are the two olive trees and the
two lampstands that stand before the
Lord of the earth. 5 And if anyone would
harm them, fire pours from their mouth
and consumes their foes. If anyone would
harm them, this is how he is doomed to
be killed. 6 They have the power to shut
the sky, that no rain may fall during the
days of their prophesying, and they have
power over the waters to turn them into
blood and to strike the earth with every
kind of plague, as often as they desire.
7 And when they have finished their tes-
timony, the beast that rises from the
bottomless pit[2] will make war on them
and conquer them and kill them, 8 and
their dead bodies will lie in the street of
the great city that symbolically[3] is called
Sodom and Egypt, where their Lord was
crucified. 9 For three and a half days some
from the peoples and tribes and lan-
guages and nations will gaze at their dead
bodies and refuse to let them be placed
in a tomb, 10 and those who dwell on the
earth will rejoice over them and make
merry and exchange presents, because
these two prophets had been a torment
to those who dwell on the earth. 11 But

[1] Greek *bondservants* [2] Or *the abyss* [3] Greek *spiritually*

after the three and a half days a breath of life from God entered them, and they stood up on their feet, and great fear fell on those who saw them. 12 Then they heard a loud voice from heaven saying to them, "Come up here!" And they went up to heaven in a cloud, and their enemies watched them. 13 And at that hour there was a great earthquake, and a tenth of the city fell. Seven thousand people were killed in the earthquake, and the rest were terrified and gave glory to the God of heaven.

14 The second woe has passed; behold, the third woe is soon to come.

The Seventh Trumpet

15 Then the seventh angel blew his trumpet, and there were loud voices in heaven, saying, "The kingdom of the world has become the kingdom of our Lord and of his Christ, and he shall reign forever and ever." 16 And the twenty-four elders who sit on their thrones before God fell on their faces and worshiped God, 17 saying,

"We give thanks to you, Lord God
    Almighty,
  who is and who was,
for you have taken your great power
  and begun to reign.
18 The nations raged,
  but your wrath came,
  and the time for the dead to be
    judged,
and for rewarding your servants,[1]
    the prophets and saints,
  and those who fear your name,
  both small and great,
and for destroying the destroyers of
    the earth."

19 Then God's temple in heaven was opened, and the ark of his covenant was seen within his temple. There were flashes of lightning, rumblings,[2] peals of thunder, an earthquake, and heavy hail.

The Woman and the Dragon

12 And a great sign appeared in heaven: a woman clothed with the sun, with the moon under her feet, and on her head a crown of twelve stars. 2 She was pregnant and was crying out in birth pains and the agony of giving birth. 3 And another sign appeared in heaven: behold, a great red dragon, with seven heads and ten horns, and on his heads seven diadems. 4 His tail swept down a third of the stars of heaven and cast them to the earth. And the dragon stood before the woman who was about to give birth, so that when she bore her child he might devour it. 5 She gave birth to a male child, one who is to rule all the nations with a rod of iron, but her child was caught up to God and to his throne, 6 and the woman fled into the wilderness, where she has a place prepared by God, in which she is to be nourished for 1,260 days.

Satan Thrown Down to Earth

7 Now war arose in heaven, Michael and his angels fighting against the dragon. And the dragon and his angels fought back, 8 but he was defeated, and there was no longer any place for them in heaven. 9 And the great dragon was thrown down, that ancient serpent, who is called the devil and Satan, the deceiver of the whole world—he was thrown down to the earth, and his angels were thrown down with him. 10 And I heard a loud voice in heaven, saying, "Now the salvation and the power and the kingdom of our God and the authority of his Christ have come, for the accuser of our brothers[3] has been thrown down, who accuses them day and night before our God. 11 And they have conquered him by the blood of the Lamb and by the word of their testimony, for they loved not their lives even unto death. 12 Therefore, rejoice, O heavens and you who dwell in them! But woe to you, O earth and sea, for the devil has come

[1] Greek *bondservants* [2] Or *voices*, or *sounds* [3] Or *brothers and sisters*

down to you in great wrath, because he
knows that his time is short!"
13 And when the dragon saw that he had
been thrown down to the earth, he pur-
sued the woman who had given birth to
the male child. 14 But the woman was given
the two wings of the great eagle so that she
might fly from the serpent into the wil-
derness, to the place where she is to be
nourished for a time, and times, and half
a time. 15 The serpent poured water like a
river out of his mouth after the woman,
to sweep her away with a flood. 16 But the
earth came to the help of the woman, and
the earth opened its mouth and swallowed
the river that the dragon had poured from
his mouth. 17 Then the dragon became
furious with the woman and went off to
make war on the rest of her offspring, on
those who keep the commandments of
God and hold to the testimony of Jesus.
And he stood[1] on the sand of the sea.

The First Beast

13 And I saw a beast rising out of
the sea, with ten horns and seven
heads, with ten diadems on its horns and
blasphemous names on its heads. 2 And
the beast that I saw was like a leopard; its
feet were like a bear's, and its mouth was
like a lion's mouth. And to it the dragon
gave his power and his throne and great
authority. 3 One of its heads seemed to
have a mortal wound, but its mortal
wound was healed, and the whole earth
marveled as they followed the beast. 4 And
they worshiped the dragon, for he had
given his authority to the beast, and they
worshiped the beast, saying, "Who is like
the beast, and who can fight against it?"
5 And the beast was given a mouth utter-
ing haughty and blasphemous words, and
it was allowed to exercise authority for
forty-two months. 6 It opened its mouth to
utter blasphemies against God, blasphem-
ing his name and his dwelling,[2] that is,
those who dwell in heaven. 7 Also it was
allowed to make war on the saints and to
conquer them.[3] And authority was given it
over every tribe and people and language
and nation, 8 and all who dwell on earth
will worship it, everyone whose name has
not been written before the foundation of
the world in the book of life of the Lamb
who was slain. 9 If anyone has an ear, let
him hear:

10 If anyone is to be taken captive,
  to captivity he goes;
if anyone is to be slain with the
    sword,
  with the sword must he be slain.

Here is a call for the endurance and faith
of the saints.

The Second Beast

11 Then I saw another beast rising out of
the earth. It had two horns like a lamb and
it spoke like a dragon. 12 It exercises all the
authority of the first beast in its presence,[4]
and makes the earth and its inhabitants
worship the first beast, whose mortal
wound was healed. 13 It performs great
signs, even making fire come down from
heaven to earth in front of people, 14 and
by the signs that it is allowed to work in
the presence of[5] the beast it deceives those
who dwell on earth, telling them to make
an image for the beast that was wounded
by the sword and yet lived. 15 And it was
allowed to give breath to the image of
the beast, so that the image of the beast
might even speak and might cause those
who would not worship the image of the
beast to be slain. 16 Also it causes all, both
small and great, both rich and poor, both
free and slave,[6] to be marked on the right
hand or the forehead, 17 so that no one can
buy or sell unless he has the mark, that is,
the name of the beast or the number of
its name. 18 This calls for wisdom: let the
one who has understanding calculate the
number of the beast, for it is the number
of a man, and his number is 666.[7]

[1] Some manuscripts *And I stood*, connecting the sentence with 13:1 [2] Or *tabernacle* [3] Some manuscripts omit this sentence [4] Or *on its behalf* [5] Or *on behalf of* [6] Greek *bondservant* [7] Some manuscripts *616*

The Lamb and the 144,000

14 Then I looked, and behold, on
Mount Zion stood the Lamb, and
with him 144,000 who had his name and
his Father's name written on their fore-
heads. 2 And I heard a voice from heaven
like the roar of many waters and like
the sound of loud thunder. The voice I
heard was like the sound of harpists
playing on their harps, 3 and they were
singing a new song before the throne
and before the four living creatures and
before the elders. No one could learn that
song except the 144,000 who had been
redeemed from the earth. 4 It is these
who have not defiled themselves with
women, for they are virgins. It is these
who follow the Lamb wherever he goes.
These have been redeemed from man-
kind as firstfruits for God and the Lamb,
5 and in their mouth no lie was found, for
they are blameless.

The Messages of the Three Angels

6 Then I saw another angel flying
directly overhead, with an eternal gospel
to proclaim to those who dwell on earth,
to every nation and tribe and language and
people. 7 And he said with a loud voice,
"Fear God and give him glory, because the
hour of his judgment has come, and wor-
ship him who made heaven and earth, the
sea and the springs of water."
8 Another angel, a second, followed,
saying, "Fallen, fallen is Babylon the great,
she who made all nations drink the wine
of the passion[1] of her sexual immorality."
9 And another angel, a third, followed
them, saying with a loud voice, "If any-
one worships the beast and its image and
receives a mark on his forehead or on his
hand, 10 he also will drink the wine of
God's wrath, poured full strength into the
cup of his anger, and he will be tormented
with fire and sulfur in the presence of the
holy angels and in the presence of the
Lamb. 11 And the smoke of their torment
goes up forever and ever, and they have no
rest, day or night, these worshipers of the
beast and its image, and whoever receives
the mark of its name."
12 Here is a call for the endurance of the
saints, those who keep the command-
ments of God and their faith in Jesus.[2]
13 And I heard a voice from heaven say-
ing, "Write this: Blessed are the dead who
die in the Lord from now on." "Blessed
indeed," says the Spirit, "that they may
rest from their labors, for their deeds fol-
low them!"

The Harvest of the Earth

14 Then I looked, and behold, a white
cloud, and seated on the cloud one like
a son of man, with a golden crown on
his head, and a sharp sickle in his hand.
15 And another angel came out of the tem-
ple, calling with a loud voice to him who
sat on the cloud, "Put in your sickle, and
reap, for the hour to reap has come, for
the harvest of the earth is fully ripe." 16 So
he who sat on the cloud swung his sickle
across the earth, and the earth was reaped.
17 Then another angel came out of the
temple in heaven, and he too had a sharp
sickle. 18 And another angel came out
from the altar, the angel who has author-
ity over the fire, and he called with a
loud voice to the one who had the sharp
sickle, "Put in your sickle and gather the
clusters from the vine of the earth, for its
grapes are ripe." 19 So the angel swung his
sickle across the earth and gathered the
grape harvest of the earth and threw it
into the great winepress of the wrath of
God. 20 And the winepress was trodden
outside the city, and blood flowed from
the winepress, as high as a horse's bridle,
for 1,600 stadia.[3]

The Seven Angels with Seven Plagues

15 Then I saw another sign in heaven,
great and amazing, seven angels
with seven plagues, which are the last, for
with them the wrath of God is finished.

[1] Or *wrath* [2] Greek *and the faith of Jesus* [3] About 184 miles; a *stadion* was about 607 feet or 185 meters

2 And I saw what appeared to be a sea of glass mingled with fire—and also those who had conquered the beast and its image and the number of its name, standing beside the sea of glass with harps of God in their hands. 3 And they sing the song of Moses, the servant[1] of God, and the song of the Lamb, saying,

"Great and amazing are your deeds,
O Lord God the Almighty!
Just and true are your ways,
O King of the nations![2]
4 Who will not fear, O Lord,
and glorify your name?
For you alone are holy.
All nations will come
and worship you,
for your righteous acts have been revealed."

5 After this I looked, and the sanctuary of the tent[3] of witness in heaven was opened, 6 and out of the sanctuary came the seven angels with the seven plagues, clothed in pure, bright linen, with golden sashes around their chests. 7 And one of the four living creatures gave to the seven angels seven golden bowls full of the wrath of God who lives forever and ever, 8 and the sanctuary was filled with smoke from the glory of God and from his power, and no one could enter the sanctuary until the seven plagues of the seven angels were finished.

The Seven Bowls of God's Wrath

16 Then I heard a loud voice from the temple telling the seven angels, "Go and pour out on the earth the seven bowls of the wrath of God."

2 So the first angel went and poured out his bowl on the earth, and harmful and painful sores came upon the people who bore the mark of the beast and worshiped its image.

3 The second angel poured out his bowl into the sea, and it became like the blood of a corpse, and every living thing died that was in the sea.

4 The third angel poured out his bowl into the rivers and the springs of water, and they became blood. 5 And I heard the angel in charge of the waters[4] say,

"Just are you, O Holy One, who is and who was,
for you brought these judgments.
6 For they have shed the blood of saints and prophets,
and you have given them blood to drink.
It is what they deserve!"

7 And I heard the altar saying,

"Yes, Lord God the Almighty,
true and just are your judgments!"

8 The fourth angel poured out his bowl on the sun, and it was allowed to scorch people with fire. 9 They were scorched by the fierce heat, and they cursed[5] the name of God who had power over these plagues. They did not repent and give him glory.

10 The fifth angel poured out his bowl on the throne of the beast, and its kingdom was plunged into darkness. People gnawed their tongues in anguish 11 and cursed the God of heaven for their pain and sores. They did not repent of their deeds.

12 The sixth angel poured out his bowl on the great river Euphrates, and its water was dried up, to prepare the way for the kings from the east. 13 And I saw, coming out of the mouth of the dragon and out of the mouth of the beast and out of the mouth of the false prophet, three unclean spirits like frogs. 14 For they are demonic spirits, performing signs, who go abroad to the kings of the whole world, to assemble them for battle on the great day of God the Almighty. 15 ("Behold, I am coming like a thief! Blessed is the one who stays awake, keeping his garments on, that he may not go about naked and be seen exposed!") 16 And they assembled

[1] Greek *bondservant* [2] Some manuscripts *the ages* [3] Or *tabernacle* [4] Greek *angel of the waters* [5] Greek *blasphemed*; also verses 11, 21

them at the place that in Hebrew is called Armageddon.

The Seventh Bowl

17 The seventh angel poured out his bowl into the air, and a loud voice came out of the temple, from the throne, saying, "It is done!" 18 And there were flashes of lightning, rumblings,[1] peals of thunder, and a great earthquake such as there had never been since man was on the earth, so great was that earthquake. 19 The great city was split into three parts, and the cities of the nations fell, and God remembered Babylon the great, to make her drain the cup of the wine of the fury of his wrath. 20 And every island fled away, and no mountains were to be found. 21 And great hailstones, about one hundred pounds[2] each, fell from heaven on people; and they cursed God for the plague of the hail, because the plague was so severe.

The Great Prostitute and the Beast

17 Then one of the seven angels who had the seven bowls came and said to me, "Come, I will show you the judgment of the great prostitute who is seated on many waters, 2 with whom the kings of the earth have committed sexual immorality, and with the wine of whose sexual immorality the dwellers on earth have become drunk." 3 And he carried me away in the Spirit into a wilderness, and I saw a woman sitting on a scarlet beast that was full of blasphemous names, and it had seven heads and ten horns. 4 The woman was arrayed in purple and scarlet, and adorned with gold and jewels and pearls, holding in her hand a golden cup full of abominations and the impurities of her sexual immorality. 5 And on her forehead was written a name of mystery: "Babylon the great, mother of prostitutes and of earth's abominations." 6 And I saw the woman, drunk with the blood of the saints, the blood of the martyrs of Jesus.[3]

When I saw her, I marveled greatly. 7 But the angel said to me, "Why do you marvel? I will tell you the mystery of the woman, and of the beast with seven heads and ten horns that carries her. 8 The beast that you saw was, and is not, and is about to rise from the bottomless pit[4] and go to destruction. And the dwellers on earth whose names have not been written in the book of life from the foundation of the world will marvel to see the beast, because it was and is not and is to come. 9 This calls for a mind with wisdom: the seven heads are seven mountains on which the woman is seated; 10 they are also seven kings, five of whom have fallen, one is, the other has not yet come, and when he does come he must remain only a little while. 11 As for the beast that was and is not, it is an eighth but it belongs to the seven, and it goes to destruction. 12 And the ten horns that you saw are ten kings who have not yet received royal power, but they are to receive authority as kings for one hour, together with the beast. 13 These are of one mind, and they hand over their power and authority to the beast. 14 They will make war on the Lamb, and the Lamb will conquer them, for he is Lord of lords and King of kings, and those with him are called and chosen and faithful."

15 And the angel[5] said to me, "The waters that you saw, where the prostitute is seated, are peoples and multitudes and nations and languages. 16 And the ten horns that you saw, they and the beast will hate the prostitute. They will make her desolate and naked, and devour her flesh and burn her up with fire, 17 for God has put it into their hearts to carry out his purpose by being of one mind and handing over their royal power to the beast, until the words of God are fulfilled. 18 And the woman that you saw is the great city that has dominion over the kings of the earth."

[1] Or *voices*, or *sounds* [2] Greek *a talent in weight* [3] Greek *the witnesses to Jesus* [4] Greek *the abyss* [5] Greek *he*

The Fall of Babylon

18 After this I saw another angel
coming down from heaven, hav-
ing great authority, and the earth was
made bright with his glory. 2 And he called
out with a mighty voice,

"Fallen, fallen is Babylon the great!
She has become a dwelling place
for demons,
a haunt for every unclean spirit,
a haunt for every unclean bird,
a haunt for every unclean and
detestable beast.
3 For all nations have drunk[1]
the wine of the passion of her
sexual immorality,
and the kings of the earth have
committed immorality with
her,
and the merchants of the earth
have grown rich from the
power of her luxurious living."

4 Then I heard another voice from heaven
saying,

"Come out of her, my people,
lest you take part in her sins,
lest you share in her plagues;
5 for her sins are heaped high as
heaven,
and God has remembered her
iniquities.
6 Pay her back as she herself has paid
back others,
and repay her double for her
deeds;
mix a double portion for her in
the cup she mixed.
7 As she glorified herself and lived in
luxury,
so give her a like measure of
torment and mourning,
since in her heart she says,
'I sit as a queen,
I am no widow,
and mourning I shall never see.'
8 For this reason her plagues will
come in a single day,
death and mourning and famine,
and she will be burned up with fire;
for mighty is the Lord God who
has judged her."

9 And the kings of the earth, who com-
mitted sexual immorality and lived in
luxury with her, will weep and wail over
her when they see the smoke of her burn-
ing. 10 They will stand far off, in fear of her
torment, and say,

"Alas! Alas! You great city,
you mighty city, Babylon!
For in a single hour your judgment
has come."

11 And the merchants of the earth weep
and mourn for her, since no one buys their
cargo anymore, 12 cargo of gold, silver, jew-
els, pearls, fine linen, purple cloth, silk,
scarlet cloth, all kinds of scented wood, all
kinds of articles of ivory, all kinds of arti-
cles of costly wood, bronze, iron and mar-
ble, 13 cinnamon, spice, incense, myrrh,
frankincense, wine, oil, fine flour, wheat,
cattle and sheep, horses and chariots, and
slaves, that is, human souls.[2]

14 "The fruit for which your soul longed
has gone from you,
and all your delicacies and your
splendors
are lost to you,
never to be found again!"

15 The merchants of these wares, who
gained wealth from her, will stand far
off, in fear of her torment, weeping and
mourning aloud,

16 "Alas, alas, for the great city
that was clothed in fine linen,
in purple and scarlet,
adorned with gold,
with jewels, and with pearls!
17 For in a single hour all this wealth
has been laid waste."

[1] Some manuscripts *fallen by* [2] Or *and slaves, and human lives*

And all shipmasters and seafaring men, sailors and all whose trade is on the sea, stood far off
18 and cried out as they saw
the smoke of her burning,

"What city was like the great city?"

19 And they threw dust on their heads as they wept and mourned, crying out,

"Alas, alas, for the great city
where all who had ships at sea
grew rich by her wealth!
For in a single hour she has been
laid waste.
20 Rejoice over her, O heaven,
and you saints and apostles and
prophets,
for God has given judgment for you
against her!"

21 Then a mighty angel took up a stone
like a great millstone and threw it into the
sea, saying,

"So will Babylon the great city be
thrown down with violence,
and will be found no more;
22 and the sound of harpists and
musicians, of flute players
and trumpeters,
will be heard in you no more,
and a craftsman of any craft
will be found in you no more,
and the sound of the mill
will be heard in you no more,
23 and the light of a lamp
will shine in you no more,
and the voice of bridegroom and
bride
will be heard in you no more,
for your merchants were the great
ones of the earth,
and all nations were deceived by
your sorcery.
24 And in her was found the blood of
prophets and of saints,
and of all who have been slain on
earth."

Rejoicing in Heaven

19 After this I heard what seemed to
be the loud voice of a great multitude in heaven, crying out,

"Hallelujah!
Salvation and glory and power
belong to our God,
2 for his judgments are true and
just;
for he has judged the great prostitute
who corrupted the earth with her
immorality,
and has avenged on her the blood of
his servants."[1]

3 Once more they cried out,

"Hallelujah!
The smoke from her goes up forever
and ever."

4 And the twenty-four elders and the four
living creatures fell down and worshiped
God who was seated on the throne, saying,
"Amen. Hallelujah!" 5 And from the throne
came a voice saying,

"Praise our God,
all you his servants,
you who fear him,
small and great."

The Marriage Supper of the Lamb

6 Then I heard what seemed to be the voice
of a great multitude, like the roar of many
waters and like the sound of mighty peals
of thunder, crying out,

"Hallelujah!
For the Lord our God
the Almighty reigns.
7 Let us rejoice and exult
and give him the glory,
for the marriage of the Lamb has
come,
and his Bride has made herself
ready;
8 it was granted her to clothe herself
with fine linen, bright and pure"—

[1] Greek *bondservants*; also verse 5

for the fine linen is the righteous deeds
of the saints.
9 And the angel said[1] to me, "Write this:
Blessed are those who are invited to the
marriage supper of the Lamb." And he said
to me, "These are the true words of God."
10 Then I fell down at his feet to worship
him, but he said to me, "You must not do
that! I am a fellow servant[2] with you and
your brothers who hold to the testimony
of Jesus. Worship God." For the testimony
of Jesus is the spirit of prophecy.

The Rider on a White Horse

11 Then I saw heaven opened, and
behold, a white horse! The one sitting
on it is called Faithful and True, and in
righteousness he judges and makes war.
12 His eyes are like a flame of fire, and on
his head are many diadems, and he has a
name written that no one knows but him-
self. 13 He is clothed in a robe dipped in[3]
blood, and the name by which he is called
is The Word of God. 14 And the armies of
heaven, arrayed in fine linen, white and
pure, were following him on white horses.
15 From his mouth comes a sharp sword
with which to strike down the nations,
and he will rule them with a rod of iron.
He will tread the winepress of the fury of
the wrath of God the Almighty. 16 On his
robe and on his thigh he has a name writ-
ten, King of kings and Lord of lords.
17 Then I saw an angel standing in the
sun, and with a loud voice he called to
all the birds that fly directly overhead,
"Come, gather for the great supper of God,
18 to eat the flesh of kings, the flesh of cap-
tains, the flesh of mighty men, the flesh
of horses and their riders, and the flesh of
all men, both free and slave,[4] both small
and great." 19 And I saw the beast and the
kings of the earth with their armies gath-
ered to make war against him who was
sitting on the horse and against his army.
20 And the beast was captured, and with
it the false prophet who in its presence[5]
had done the signs by which he deceived
those who had received the mark of the
beast and those who worshiped its image.
These two were thrown alive into the lake
of fire that burns with sulfur. 21 And the
rest were slain by the sword that came
from the mouth of him who was sitting
on the horse, and all the birds were gorged
with their flesh.

The Thousand Years

20 Then I saw an angel coming
down from heaven, holding in
his hand the key to the bottomless pit[6]
and a great chain. 2 And he seized the
dragon, that ancient serpent, who is
the devil and Satan, and bound him for
a thousand years, 3 and threw him into
the pit, and shut it and sealed it over him,
so that he might not deceive the nations
any longer, until the thousand years were
ended. After that he must be released for
a little while.
4 Then I saw thrones, and seated on
them were those to whom the authority
to judge was committed. Also I saw the
souls of those who had been beheaded
for the testimony of Jesus and for the
word of God, and those who had not wor-
shiped the beast or its image and had not
received its mark on their foreheads or
their hands. They came to life and reigned
with Christ for a thousand years. 5 The rest
of the dead did not come to life until the
thousand years were ended. This is the
first resurrection. 6 Blessed and holy is
the one who shares in the first resurrec-
tion! Over such the second death has no
power, but they will be priests of God and
of Christ, and they will reign with him for
a thousand years.

The Defeat of Satan

7 And when the thousand years are
ended, Satan will be released from his
prison 8 and will come out to deceive the
nations that are at the four corners of the
earth, Gog and Magog, to gather them for

[1] Greek *he said* [2] Greek *fellow bondservant* [3] Some manuscripts *sprinkled with* [4] Greek *bondservant* [5] Or *on its behalf* [6] Greek *the abyss*; also verse 3

The Amazing Vision that Jesus Gave to John

God gave John an amazing vision, which is written down in the book of Revelation. The vision was like a dream, but John was awake and he knew the pictures and ideas were given to him from God.

The vision showed John what is going to happen in the future—the things that would happen when Jesus comes back to take us home with Him. John wrote down everything he saw and heard, so that we could look forward to our new life with Jesus when He comes back.

In the vision, John saw that the old earth—the one we live on now—no longer existed. Everything had been completely changed and had been made new. All the sin and sadness and death of this earth were gone!

John saw the new Holy City, the new Jerusalem, in all its magnificent splendor and beauty. John heard a voice from God's throne saying that God would live in this City with His people forever. "He will dwell with them," the voice said, "and they will be His people, and God Himself will be with them as their God. He will wipe away every tear from their eyes, and death shall be no more, neither shall there be crying, nor pain anymore."

Then an angel showed John how the Holy City would come down from God in heaven. It looked like a bright jewel, shining with the glory of God! In the wall around the City there were 12 gates of pearl, with an angel standing guard at each gate.

The new Jerusalem had no temple building, because Jesus, the Lamb of God Himself, was the center of worship. There the people of God will dwell with Him forever and ever.

And the city did not need the sun or moon for light, because the glory of God shown everywhere.

And nothing evil or bad or wrong could ever come into the City. The only people inside would be Christians—people from every nation, whose names were written in the Lamb's Book of Life.

The angel showed John the river of the water of life, as bright as crystal. The river flowed from the throne of God through the middle of the City. And on both sides of the river was the tree of life.

Jesus told John that all the words John had heard were trustworthy and true. Then Jesus promised, "Surely I am coming soon."

John wrote, "Amen. Come, Lord Jesus!" Now we look forward to that day when Jesus will come again in power and great glory. And we join with John in saying, "Come soon, Lord Jesus!"

SEEK and FIND

WHERE TO FIND THE STORY

Revelation 21–22

KEY BIBLE VERSE

"And I heard a loud voice from the throne saying, 'Behold, the dwelling place of God is with man. He will dwell with them, and they will be his people, and God himself will be with them as their God.'" (Revelation 21:3)

THREE KEY QUESTIONS

- Can you describe the amazing vision that Jesus gave to John?
- Why will there be no need for the sun or the moon in the new Jerusalem?
- Why do we look forward to the day when Jesus will return?

RELATED BIBLE READINGS

Isaiah 25:6–9; 60:17–22; 65:17–19; 1 Corinthians 15:24–26; 1 Thessalonians 4:16–18; 2 Peter 3:11–13

battle; their number is like the sand of the sea. 9 And they marched up over the broad plain of the earth and surrounded the camp of the saints and the beloved city, but fire came down from heaven[1] and consumed them, 10 and the devil who had deceived them was thrown into the lake of fire and sulfur where the beast and the false prophet were, and they will be tormented day and night forever and ever.

Judgment Before the Great White Throne

11 Then I saw a great white throne and him who was seated on it. From his presence earth and sky fled away, and no place was found for them. 12 And I saw the dead, great and small, standing before the throne, and books were opened. Then another book was opened, which is the book of life. And the dead were judged by what was written in the books, according to what they had done. 13 And the sea gave up the dead who were in it, Death and Hades gave up the dead who were in them, and they were judged, each one of them, according to what they had done. 14 Then Death and Hades were thrown into the lake of fire. This is the second death, the lake of fire. 15 And if anyone's name was not found written in the book of life, he was thrown into the lake of fire.

The New Heaven and the New Earth

21 Then I saw a new heaven
and a new earth, for the
1847 first heaven and the first earth had
passed away, and the sea was no
more. 2 And I saw the holy city, new
205, Jerusalem, coming down out of
545 heaven from God, prepared as a
bride adorned for her husband.
3 And I heard a loud voice from the
1847 throne saying, "Behold, the dwell-
ing place[2] of God is with man. He will
dwell with them, and they will be his peo-
ple,[3] and God himself will be with them as
their God.[4] 4 He will wipe away every tear
from their eyes, and death shall be no
more, neither shall there be mourning,
nor crying, nor pain anymore, for the for-
mer things have passed away."
5 And he who was seated on the throne
said, "Behold, I am making all things
new." Also he said, "Write this down, for
these words are trustworthy and true."
6 And he said to me, "It is done! I am the

[1] Some manuscripts *from God, out of heaven,* or *out of heaven from God* [2] Or *tabernacle* [3] Some manuscripts *peoples* [4] Some manuscripts omit *as their God*

Alpha and the Omega, the beginning and the end. To the thirsty I will give from the spring of the water of life without payment. 7 The one who conquers will have this heritage, and I will be his God and he will be my son. 8 But as for the cowardly, the faithless, the detestable, as for murderers, the sexually immoral, sorcerers, idolaters, and all liars, their portion will be in the lake that burns with fire and sulfur, which is the second death."

The New Jerusalem

9 Then came one of the seven angels who had the seven bowls full of the seven last plagues and spoke to me, saying, "Come, I will show you the Bride, the wife of the Lamb." 10 And he carried me away in the Spirit to a great, high mountain, and showed me the holy city Jerusalem coming down out of heaven from God, 11 having the glory of God, its radiance like a most rare jewel, like a jasper, clear as crystal. 12 It had a great, high wall, with twelve gates, and at the gates twelve angels, and on the gates the names of the twelve tribes of the sons of Israel were inscribed— 13 on the east three gates, on the north three gates, on the south three gates, and on the west three gates. 14 And the wall of the city had twelve foundations, and on them were the twelve names of the twelve apostles of the Lamb.

15 And the one who spoke with me had a measuring rod of gold to measure the city and its gates and walls. 16 The city lies foursquare, its length the same as its width. And he measured the city with his rod, 12,000 stadia.[1] Its length and width and height are equal. 17 He also measured its wall, 144 cubits[2] by human measurement, which is also an angel's measurement. 18 The wall was built of jasper, while the city was pure gold, clear as glass. 19 The foundations of the wall of the city were adorned with every kind of jewel. The first was jasper, the second sapphire, the third agate, the fourth emerald, 20 the fifth onyx, the sixth carnelian, the seventh chrysolite, the eighth beryl, the ninth topaz, the tenth chrysoprase, the eleventh jacinth, the twelfth amethyst. 21 And the twelve gates were twelve pearls, each of the gates made of a single pearl, and the street of the city was pure gold, transparent as glass.

22 And I saw no temple in the city,
for its temple is the Lord God the
545 Almighty and the Lamb. 23 And the city has no need of sun or moon to shine on it, for the glory of God gives it light, and its lamp is the Lamb. 24 By its light will the nations walk, and the kings of the earth will bring their glory into it, 25 and its gates will never be shut by day—and there will be no night there. 26 They will bring into it the glory and the honor of the nations. 27 But nothing unclean will ever enter it, nor anyone who does what is detestable or false, but only those who are written in the Lamb's book of life.

The River of Life

22 Then the angel[3] showed me the river of the water of life, bright as crystal, flowing from the throne of God and of the Lamb 2 through the middle of the street of the city; also, on either side of the river, the tree of life[4] with its twelve kinds of fruit, yielding its fruit each month. The leaves of the tree were for the healing of the nations. 3 No longer will there be anything accursed, but the throne of God and of the Lamb will be in it, and his servants[5] will worship him. 4 They will see his face, and his name will be on their foreheads. 5 And night will be no more. They will need no light of lamp or sun, for the Lord God will be their light, and they will reign forever and ever.

Jesus Is Coming

6 And he said to me, "These words are trustworthy and true. And the Lord, the God of the spirits of the prophets, has sent

[1] About 1,380 miles; a *stadion* was about 607 feet or 185 meters [2] A *cubit* was about 18 inches or 45 centimeters [3] Greek *he* [4] Or *the Lamb. In the midst of the street of the city, and on either side of the river, was the tree of life* [5] Greek *bondservants*; also verse 6

his angel to show his servants what must
soon take place."

7 "And behold, I am coming soon.
Blessed is the one who keeps the words of
the prophecy of this book."

8 I, John, am the one who heard and
saw these things. And when I heard and
saw them, I fell down to worship at the
feet of the angel who showed them to
me, 9 but he said to me, "You must not
do that! I am a fellow servant[1] with you
and your brothers the prophets, and with
those who keep the words of this book.
Worship God."

10 And he said to me, "Do not seal up the
words of the prophecy of this book, for
the time is near. 11 Let the evildoer still do
evil, and the filthy still be filthy, and the
righteous still do right, and the holy still
be holy."

12 "Behold, I am coming soon, bring-
ing my recompense with me, to repay
everyone for what he has done. 13 I am the
Alpha and the Omega, the first and the
last, the beginning and the end."

14 Blessed are those who wash their
robes,[2] so that they may have the right to
the tree of life and that they may enter the
city by the gates. 15 Outside are the dogs
and sorcerers and the sexually immoral
and murderers and idolaters, and every-
one who loves and practices falsehood.

16 "I, Jesus, have sent my angel to tes-
tify to you about these things for the
churches. I am the root and the descen-
dant of David, the bright morning star."

17 The Spirit and the Bride say, "Come."
And let the one who hears say, "Come."
And let the one who is thirsty come; let
the one who desires take the water of life
without price.

18 I warn everyone who hears the words
of the prophecy of this book: if anyone
adds to them, God will add to him the
plagues described in this book, 19 and if
anyone takes away from the words of the
book of this prophecy, God will take away
his share in the tree of life and in the holy
city, which are described in this book.

20 He who testifies to these things says,
"Surely I am coming soon." Amen. Come,
Lord Jesus!

21 The grace of the Lord Jesus be with
all.[3] Amen.

[1] Greek *fellow bondservant* [2] Some manuscripts *do his commandments* [3] Some manuscripts *all the saints*

Index of Stories

Index of Profiles and Illustrations

Dictionary

A

abide - To live in a place. Jesus commands us to **abide** in him. This means that we are to trust and depend on Jesus. Psalm 91:1; John 15:4; 1 John 4:13

abound - To be great in number or amount; to be fully filled. A faithful person's life will **abound** with good things from God. In thankfulness, that person can then **abound** in love, prayer, and service. Deuteronomy 28:11; Romans 6:1; 2 Corinthians 9:8

abstain - To choose not to do something. God wants us to **abstain** from every form of evil by a definite choice. 1 Thessalonians 5:22; 1 Peter 2:11

accord - Agreement; a choice to take a certain action. Christians should be in full **accord** that Jesus is Lord. Why? He died for us of his own **accord**. Zephaniah 3:9; John 10:18; Philippians 2:2

accursed - Under a curse, doomed. The apostle Paul wrote that enemies of God are asking for a bad end: they are **accursed**. Galatians 1:8; Revelation 22:3

acknowledge - To say that something or someone is real or true. We can **acknowledge** that Jesus is Lord because we have knowledge of who he truly is. Proverbs 3:6; Matthew 10:32; Hebrews 13:15

admonish - To point out something; to warn, to correct wrong attitudes or behavior. The church leaders **admonish** the people so that they will have a change of heart. Psalm 81:8; 1 Thessalonians 5:14

adultery - An improper relationship between a married person and someone to whom he or she is not married. God wants husbands and wives to love only each other and never commit **adultery**. Exodus 20:14; Proverbs 6:32; Mark 7:21

adversary - Enemy, opponent. The devil is definitely your **adversary** for he wants you to sin against God. Isaiah 50:8; 1 Timothy 5:14; 1 Peter 5:8

advocate - A supporter or defender, one who speaks up for someone else. Jesus is a Christian's **advocate**, taking your side before God the Father. 1 John 2:1

affliction - A sickness or hardship that causes continuing pain or suffering. Whatever trouble or **affliction** we have, God understands and will either remove it or help us endure it. Genesis 16:11; Matthew 4:23; 2 Corinthians 4:17

alien - Someone who comes from another country or society, a foreigner. When a person trusts in Jesus, he is no longer an **alien**. He is in God's family. Jeremiah 22:3; Ephesians 2:19

altar - A place of sacrifice or worship. In Old Testament times, sacrifices were laid on the **altar**. Genesis 8:20; Exodus 27:1; Matthew 5:23

amen - Word to show agreement, an expression that means "So be it," often said at the end of a prayer. To say **amen** is much like saying, "Yes, God, I agree!" Psalm 41:13; 2 Corinthians 1:20; Revelation 22:21

anoint - To apply or pour special oil on a person or thing and set that person or thing apart as holy. God told Samuel to **anoint** David's head with oil because he would be king. 1 Samuel 16:3; Psalm 23:5; Luke 7:46

apostle - Men chosen by God to lead the early church, such as Peter, James, John, and Paul. An **apostle** was especially called by Jesus to serve him. Luke 6:13; Romans 1:1; Ephesians 4:11

appoint - To select for a special job. God **appointed** a large fish to swallow Jonah. Deuteronomy 16:18; Jonah 1:17; Acts 6:3

ark of the covenant - A special gold-covered wooden box God commanded the Israelites to build to hold the Ten Commandments and other holy objects. The Israelites built the **ark of the covenant** exactly as God directed. It is also called the ark of the testimony. Exodus 25:10; 1 Samuel 4:11; Revelation 11:19

ascribe - To point out what someone is like. "**Ascribe** to God glory!" said the psalmist. Deuteronomy 32:3; Psalm 29:2

atone, atonement - To pay for a sin; payment for a sin. Jesus died for us and became the **atonement** for our sin. Exodus 30:10; Leviticus 23:27; Psalm 79:9

B

baptism - A sacrament using water. Paul explained that Christian **baptism** is a washing of regeneration. Matthew 21:25; Ephesians 4:5; Titus 3:5–8; 1 Peter 3:21

barren - Not able to have children. Elizabeth was **barren**, but God took away her barrenness and chose her to be the mother of John the Baptist. Genesis 11:30; Luke 1:7; Luke 23:29

betrothed - Engaged to be married. Mary, Jesus' mother, was **betrothed** to Joseph. Matthew 1:18; 1 Corinthians 7:28

birthright - Special privilege or gift given to the firstborn of a family. Esau sold his **birthright** to his younger brother, Jacob. Genesis 25:31; Genesis 43:33; Hebrews 12:16

blasphemy - Strong words or actions to show disrespect to God. It is **blasphemy** to call God anything but who he is. Matthew 12:31

blemish - A stain or mark. God is pleased with sacrifices that are perfect and have no **blemish**. Exodus 12:5; 1 Peter 1:19

bless - To give good things to; to honor as holy. God continues to **bless** you, so **bless** his holy name. Numbers 6:24; Psalm 103:1; Luke 6:28

blessing - Special favor or good things from God. The **blessing** of joy is ours as God's children. Nehemiah 13:2; Ephesians 1:3

bondage - The condition of being a slave to something or someone. Jesus sets free from the **bondage** of sin. Jeremiah 34:13; Romans 8:21

breastplate - A piece of armor covering the chest. Paul tells us to put on the **breastplate** of righteousness so that we can stand against the devil. Isaiah 59:17; Ephesians 6:14; 1 Thessalonians 5:8

burden - A heavy weight; a serious problem. Jesus can help us with any **burden** we have to carry. Psalm 55:22; Matthew 11:30

C

census - An official count of people. The title of the book of Numbers comes from the two times the Israelites took a **census**. Numbers 1:2; Numbers 26:2

centurion - In the Roman army, a man in charge of 100 soldiers. The **centurion** Cornelius was the first non-Jewish believer. Mark 15:39; Acts 10:1

chaff - Worthless outer husk of wheat and other grains. John the Baptist compared true believers in Jesus to wheat; others who did not believe he called **chaff**. Psalm 1:4; Matthew 3:12

cherubim - Mysterious winged, angel-like creatures who worship God. On the top of the ark of the covenant were golden statues of **cherubim**. Genesis 3:24; Psalm 99:1; Hebrews 9:5

circumcised, circumcision - A special kind of surgery done on a Jewish man as a sign that he belongs to God. God made a promise to Abraham through the ceremony of **circumcision**. Genesis 17:10; Romans 4:11; Philippians 3:3

commit - To do or perform; to entrust something. Do not **commit** a sin. Instead, **commit** your life to God. Exodus 20:14; Psalm 37:5; Luke 23:46

compassion - A deep feeling of sympathy for another's suffering, with the desire to relieve it. Jesus has great **compassion** for those who are suffering. Lamentations 3:32; Mark 6:34; Colossians 3:12

conceive - To become pregnant. The prophet Isaiah said that a virgin would **conceive** and give birth to the Savior, and Mary did! Isaiah 7:14; Matthew 1:23

condemn - To judge as wrong or guilty. Jesus did not come to **condemn** the world but to save it. Job 40:8; John 3:17; John 8:11

condemnation - Strong disapproval; final, negative judgment. If we depend on Jesus, we have no fear of **condemnation** from God the Father. Romans 5:18; Romans 8:1

confess - To admit you have done wrong; to announce belief or faith in someone. A disciple will **confess** sins and **confess** that Jesus is Lord. Leviticus 26:40; Philippians 2:11; 1 John 1:9

confession - The act of admitting guilt; the announcement of belief. **Confession** of sin can lead to a **confession** of faith. Ezra 10:11; 2 Corinthians 9:13

conformed - Behaving or thinking like someone else or something else. If you are **conformed** to the world around you, it's impossible to be **conformed** to Christ. Romans 8:29; Romans 12:2

conscience - Sense of knowing right from wrong. God gave us a **conscience** to help us make good choices. Romans 2:15; 1 Peter 3:21

consecrate - To set apart. God told Moses to **consecrate** the Israelites before receiving the Ten Commandments. Exodus 13:2; Exodus 19:10; Leviticus 20:7

contrite - Sorry for wrong words or actions. God accepts the person who has a **contrite** heart and is truly sorry about sin. Psalm 51:17; Isaiah 57:15

cornerstone - A very important stone because of its size and placement at the top or bottom corner of a building. In the Bible, Jesus is called the **cornerstone** of the Christian's faith. Psalm 118:22; Ephesians 2:20; 1 Peter 2:6

covenant - A special agreement that God made with his people. God made a **covenant** with us through Noah, and the rainbow is its symbol. God made a **covenant** with Abraham, to bless the world through Christ. Genesis 9:9; Genesis 15:18; Matthew 26:28; 1 Corinthians 11:25

covet - To want something belonging to someone else. Often we quarrel and fight because we **covet** what we do not have. Exodus 20:17; James 4:2

crucify - To kill by nailing a person's wrists and feet to a cross. When Pilate offered to free Jesus, the crowd wanted to **crucify** him. Matthew 23:34; Luke 23:21

curse - Evil or misfortune coming to someone; to wish or pray for evil or misfortune to come to someone. "Bless your enemies. Don't **curse** them," commanded Jesus. Deuteronomy 11:26; Luke 6:28

D

debts - Things that are owed to another person, especially money; harm caused to someone else; sins. In the Lord's Prayer, Jesus teaches us to pray that our **debts** or our sins would be forgiven. Matthew 6:12

deceive - To trick or mislead into believing something. Don't let anyone **deceive** you into thinking that the Gospel is not true. Ephesians 5:6; 1 John 1:8

defile - To make unclean. Bad words and thoughts **defile** us. Daniel 1:8; Matthew 15:20

demon - An evil being or spirit. Jesus removed the **demon** from inside the man and changed his life. Luke 4:33; John 8:49

denarius - An ancient Roman silver coin. Jesus asked to see the coin called a **denarius**. Mark 12:15

descendant - Person coming from a family line. Jesus was the **descendant** of King David's family line. 1 Chronicles 27:3; Romans 11:1; Revelation 22:16

despise - To hate or to have strong negative feelings. **Despise** what is evil, and love what is good. Job 42:6; Proverbs 3:11; 1 Timothy 4:12

discern - To understand; to figure out. The Holy Spirit will help you **discern** the right path. Psalm 139:2; Ephesians 5:10

disciple - A loyal follower, especially of Jesus; a student, learner. Jesus called twelve **disciples** to be his closest followers. Luke 14:26; Acts 11:26

discipline - Training, correction, or practice leading to self-control. God's disciples learn from his **discipline**. Proverbs 12:1; 1 Corinthians 9:27; Hebrews 12:11

doctrine - An *official* set of beliefs. Paul tells us not to be fooled by untrue **doctrine**. Ephesians 4:14; Titus 1:9

dominion - Power or rule; territory or area of rule. God's **dominion** is over all people and all places. Genesis 1:28; Daniel 4:34; 1 Peter 4:11

E

elect - Those chosen by God and saved, through Christ. The **elect** can be sure they will go to heaven. Matthew 24:22; Romans 8:33; 1 Peter 1:1

endure - To keep going; to suffer patiently without giving up. Life can sometimes be hard. God helps us **endure** painful times. Psalm 72:17; Malachi 3:2; 2 Corinthians 1:6

enmity - Strong hatred. If we love God, we have **enmity** with the things he hates. Genesis 3:15; James 4:4

eternal - Without beginning or end; forever. God alone is **eternal** and he gives **eternal** life to everyone who trusts in Jesus. Deuteronomy 33:27; Mark 10:17; Jude 21

everlasting - Continuing forever. An **everlasting** covenant is a promise that lasts forever. Psalm 106:48; Isaiah 9:6; Ezekiel 37:26

exalt - To glorify, to praise; to raise up. We praise and **exalt** God's name. Isaiah 25:1; Hebrews 5:5; James 4:10

exile, exiles - The state of being sent away; to send away; one who is sent away or lives far from his or her home country. God's people were sent away into **exile** far from their Promised Land. 1 Chronicles 6:15; Hebrews 11:13; 1 Peter 2:11

extol - To praise, to glorify. A worship leader calls us to **extol** the name of the Lord. Psalm 145:1; Romans 15:11

F

faith - Belief and trust in God. A person is saved by grace through **faith** in Christ. Matthew 17:20; Ephesians 1:15; Ephesians 2:8-9; Hebrews 11:1

famine - Period of time without enough food. After years of little rainfall, a **famine** begins. Genesis 41:30; Amos 8:11; Romans 8:35

fast - To choose not to eat; securely, tightly. If you **fast** for religious reasons, you must hold **fast** to your beliefs. Matthew 6:16; 1 Thessalonians 5:21

firstfruits - The first harvested fruit, offered to God with thanks. The **firstfruits** are the best of what is gathered. Romans 8:23; James 1:18

flesh - The physical body with all of its natural desires; the sinful way of thinking and acting which puts those desires first. Jesus had a real body of **flesh** like us, but he did not give in to the sinful desires of the **flesh**. John 1:14; Romans 13:14; Philippians 3:3

forgive - To pardon a wrong or sin. God calls us to **forgive** one another just as he has **forgiven** us through faith in Jesus. 2 Chronicles 7:14; Luke 23:34; Ephesians 4:32; Colossians 3:13

forgiveness - The act of pardoning. Through Jesus we receive **forgiveness** of our sins. Psalm 130:4; Matthew 26:28; Ephesians 1:7

forsake - To leave or abandon. God will never **forsake** his children. Joshua 1:5; Psalm 94:14; Hebrews 13:5

fulfill - To carry out; to complete. God will **fulfill** his promises because he is trustworthy. Psalm 138:8; Matthew 5:17; 2 Peter 3:9

G

genealogy - Family tree. The **genealogy** of Jesus tells who his relatives were going back many generations. Nehemiah 7:5; Matthew 1:1

generation - A group of people born and living about the same time. A **generation** of Israelites died in the wilderness because of their disobedience. Numbers 32:13; Psalm 22:30; Joel 1:3: Matthew 16:4

Gentiles - People who are not Jewish. The Jewish Christians were amazed that Jesus' good news was for the **Gentiles** too. Matthew 10:5; Acts 10:45; 1 Peter 2:12

glory - Wonderful beauty and majesty; praise, honor. God's **glory** deserves our worship. Give him **glory**! Exodus 33:18; Luke 2:14; Revelation 21:23

gods - Images or figures that are worshiped but are not the one true God. The first commandment says we are to have no **gods** other than the one true God. Exodus 20:3; Acts 19:26

gospel - The good news that Jesus died to pay for our sins and that through faith in him, we have eternal life; written record of good news. The **gospel** of Jesus is told in the **Gospels** of Matthew, Mark, Luke, and John. Matthew 4:23; Mark 1:1; Ephesians 1:13

grace - The undeserved and overflowing gift of God's love and good favor to people. God is full of **grace**, always showing that he is a loving Father. Psalm 45:2; John 1:14; Ephesians 2:5

H

hallowed - Holy, sacred. Moses stood on **hallowed** ground before the burning bush. Matthew 6:9; Luke 11:2

heir - A person who receives the blessing or the property of someone who dies. Abram was promised that his own son would be his **heir**. Genesis 15:4; Hebrews 1:2

heresy, heresies - A belief or teaching that does not agree with God's Word. False teachers would spread **heresies** about Jesus in the early church. 2 Peter 2:1

high place, high places - A place, usually set on a hill, where people built altars and worshiped. God instructed the Israelites to destroy the idols in the **high places**. Numbers 33:52, 1 Samuel 9:12-13; 2 Kings 12:3

high priest - The most important worship leader in Jewish worship in Bible times. The **high priest** was the only one able to enter the Most Holy Place in the temple. Acts 23:2; Hebrews 3:1

holy - Set apart; sacred; perfect, pure, worthy of being worshiped. Worship God, for he is **holy**. His **Holy** Spirit will help you do this. Genesis 2:3; Isaiah 6:3; 1 Peter 1:15

hosanna - A shout of praise, which means "Save us, Lord!" The people shouted "**Hosanna**!" as Jesus entered Jerusalem. Matthew 21:9

hospitality - Welcoming others; caring for the needs of guests. The warm **hospitality** given to Paul made him feel welcome in a strange city. Romans 12:13; 1 Peter 4:9

host - A very large number. A **host** of angels told the shepherds that Jesus was born. Genesis 2:1; Jeremiah 33:22; Luke 2:13

hypocrite, hypocrites - One who pretends, a phony person. Jesus had very harsh words for **hypocrites** who pretended to be good. Psalm 26:4; Matthew 7:5

I

idol, idols - A false god; an object, such as a statue, that is worshiped. You must not worship **idols**. They are not God. Leviticus 19:4; 1 Corinthians 10:19; 1 Thessalonians 1:9

image - Something made to be like something else; a copy. God made people in his own **image** to be like him in many ways. An idol. God commands us not to worship a carved **image**. Genesis 1:26; Exodus 20:4; Psalm 106:20; Colossians 1:15

immortal - Able to live forever. Our **immortal** God will never die. Romans 1:23; 1 Timothy 1:17

imperishable - Never-ending; never spoiling, lasting forever. Although our present bodies are perishable, in Jesus our souls are **imperishable**. 1 Corinthians 15:53; 1 Peter 1:23

inheritance - A gift, such as money or property, often given from a family member after that person has died. God gave his children the **inheritance** of eternal life because of Jesus' death for us. Proverbs 13:22; Ephesians 1:18; Hebrews 9:15

iniquity - Anything that breaks God's righteous law; sin, wickedness. Jesus had no sin, but he took our **iniquity** on himself. Psalm 51:2; Isaiah 53:6

intercession, intercessions - Speaking up for someone else; prayer to God for the needs of another person. Jesus made **intercession** for us before God the Father. We pray **intercessions** for the sick. Isaiah 53:12; 1 Timothy 2:1; Hebrews 7:25

J

judge - One who decides who is right or wrong; to blame, to condemn. We are not to **judge** anyone because God is judge of the whole earth, and one day Jesus will **judge** everyone. Psalm 7:11; Matthew 7:1; Acts 17:31

Judgment Day - The final day in the future when God will punish unbelieving sinners once and for all. On **Judgment Day**, God's children can trust God's complete forgiveness because of Jesus' death on the cross. Matthew 10:15; 2 Peter 2:9; Jude 6

justice - Treating everybody according to God's good and right standards; doing what is right to all people. God commands us to show **justice** and love. Deuteronomy 10:18; Amos 5:24; Micah 6:8; Matthew 23:23

justified - To be made right with God by grace through faith in Jesus. We are **justified** because Jesus died to take our guilt away. Romans 3:24; Galatians 2:16; Titus 3:7

K

kingdom of God - God's rule over his people and his creation. Only those who trust in Jesus will enter the **kingdom of God**. Matthew 6:33; Luke 17:21; John 3:3; Romans 14:17

L

Lamb - A name or title for Jesus, who became a sacrifice for us. (See also sacrifice, Passover.) Jesus was the **Lamb** of God, killed for us. John 1:29; 1 Corinthians 5:7; Revelation 5:12

law, Law - All the rules given by God to his people, the Israelites, through Moses. God's written **Law** is given in the first five books of the Old Testament. Jesus perfectly kept God's **law**. Joshua 1:7; Psalm 19:7; Matthew 5:17; Galatians 5:4

leaven - Yeast; something that changes something else, often for the worse. Just like a little bit of **leaven** makes bread rise, a wrong idea or belief can affect your whole life. Matthew 13:33; Matthew 16:11

legion, legions - A large number; major unit of the Roman army. The man was named **Legion** because many demons lived inside him. Matthew 26:53; Mark 5:9, 15

leper, leprosy, leprous - A person with a bad skin disease, making him an outcast. Jesus healed the **leper**, making his **leprous** skin smooth and whole again. Leviticus 13:44; Numbers 12:10; Luke 5:12

Levites, sons of Levi, tribe of Levi - The family coming from Levi, Jacob's son; appointed to be priests. The **Levites** carried the ark of the covenant and led the people in worship. Exodus 6:25; Numbers 1:50; Joshua 21:3

locusts - Insects like the grasshopper, able to eat crops. God sent a plague of **locusts**, which destroyed the fields of the Egyptians who were oppressing God's people. Exodus 10:14; Matthew 3:4

LORD - (with small capital letters) Yahweh, God's Hebrew name. God said that he is the **LORD**, the great "I AM." Exodus 3:14-15; Deuteronomy 6:5; Psalm 96:1

M

malice - Meanness; intending to act on angry, bitter feelings toward another. Be kind to others, and do not hold **malice** in your heart. Romans 1:29; Colossians 3:8; 1 Peter 2:1

manna - Food that God provided each morning for the Israelites on their journey from Egypt to the Promised Land; Hebrew word meaning "What is it?" Exodus 16:31; John 6:31

mediator - One who makes peace between two or more people. Jesus is the one true **mediator** between God and sinful people like us. 1 Timothy 2:5; Hebrews 9:15; Hebrews 12:24

meditate - To think calmly and prayerfully; to ponder, reflect on. The psalmist loved to **meditate** on God's Word. Joshua 1:8; Psalm 119:15; Psalm 143:5

mercy seat - The solid gold covering or lid of the ark of the covenant; where the high priest sprinkled the blood on the Day of Atonement. The **mercy seat** was a symbol of God's kindness to his sinful people. Exodus 25:17; Leviticus 16:14; Hebrews 9:5

Messiah - The anointed one; the Savior of Israel. Jesus was the long-expected **Messiah** to save all who will believe in him. "Christ" is the Greek word for **Messiah**. John 1:41; John 4:25

miracle - An event that cannot be explained by the laws of nature; a direct work of God, such as a healing. When Jesus healed a blind man, people called the **miracle** a sign that he was the Christ. Psalm 105:5; 1 Corinthians 12:10; Hebrews 2:4

money-changers - Those who traded one country's money into that of another, often charging too much for this service. Jesus drove the **money-changers** out of the temple. Matthew 21:12

Most Holy Place - Innermost room of the tabernacle and the temple where the ark of the covenant was kept. Only the high priest could go into the **Most Holy Place**, alone and once a year. Exodus 26:33; 1 Chronicles 6:49; Hebrews 9:3

mute - Unable to speak. Jesus healed the man who was **mute**. Then he could speak! Exodus 4:11; Matthew 9:32

O

offspring - One's children, including one's grandchildren. Abraham and Sarah did not think they could have children, but God gave them many children, or **offspring**. Genesis 3:15; Psalm 89:36; Galatians 3:29

P

pagans - Those who do not worship the one true God. **Pagans** are without hope because they are without belief in God. 1 Corinthians 5:1; 1 Corinthians 12:2

parable - A story that teaches a truth. The **parable** of the Good Samaritan is one of Jesus' best-known lessons about loving and caring for your neighbor. Psalm 78:2; Matthew 13:34

paralytic - A person who cannot walk; a paralyzed person. After Jesus healed the **paralytic**, he could walk for the first time. Mark 2:3

pardon - To forgive. God **pardons** sinners and removes their guilt because of Jesus' death on the cross. Exodus 34:9; Psalm 25:11; Isaiah 55:7

Passover - God's saving of the Israelites in Egypt, when he "passed over" their homes protected by the blood of a lamb; the meal remembering this event. Jesus became our **Passover** Lamb when he died for us. Exodus 12:11; Matthew 26:19; 1 Corinthians 5:7

persecute - To treat someone cruelly because of his or her beliefs. Non-believers began to **persecute** the early Christians, even putting some to death. Matthew 5:44; John 15:20; Romans 12:14

persevere, perseverance - To continue on through a difficult task or hard time without complaining or quitting; endurance. A Christian has faith and **perseveres** through difficulties. Ephesians 6:18; James 1:25

Pharisees - Jewish leaders known for their strict attention to rules they had added to God's law and for their opposition to Jesus. Jesus told the **Pharisees** that they should value justice instead of unimportant food laws. Matthew 5:20; Matthew 23:27; Philippians 3:5

plague - A terrible disaster such as a disease or attack by things like insects. God sent one **plague** after another because Pharaoh wouldn't let the Israelites leave Egypt. Exodus 11:1; 2 Chronicles 6:28; Revelation 11:6

precepts - Commands, laws, directions. God's **precepts** are found in Scripture. They show us how to live. Psalm 19:8; Psalm 119:15; Proverbs 4:2

predestined - Planned beforehand by God. God **predestined** which people would be part of his family. Romans 8:30; Ephesians 1:5

priest - A Jewish worship leader who represents the people before God. The **priest** offered sacrifices inside the tabernacle and temple. Psalm 110:4; Hebrews 4:15

prophecy - A message from God, given through a person; often called a word from God in the Old Testament. A **prophecy** is a message of truth. Sometimes it is about the future and sometimes about the present. 1 Corinthians 14:6; 2 Peter 1:20

prophet - One who brings a message from God. Isaiah, Jeremiah, Ezekiel, Amos, and others were **prophets** speaking God's truth. Deuteronomy 18:18; Habakkuk 1:1; Mark 6:4

propitiation - Payment for sin. A sacrifice that removes God's wrath and replaces it with his favor. Jesus paid the price for our sin by giving himself as a **propitiation**. Romans 3:25; Hebrews 2:17; 1 John 2:2

proverb - Short, wise saying that teaches an important truth. Each **proverb** of King Solomon tells a truth or gives a lesson. Psalm 49:4; Proverbs 1:6; 2 Peter 2:22

psalms - Songs or prayers used in worshiping God. The **psalms** of David and other Israelites are recorded in the book of **Psalms**. Ephesians 5:19; Colossians 3:16

R

rabbi - A Jewish teacher of the law. The word "**rabbi**" means "my great one." Jesus' followers were amazed at his teaching, so they called him **Rabbi**. Matthew 23:8; John 1:38

ransom - The price needed to free a prisoner; the payment of that price. Christ gave himself as a **ransom**, which paid the price for our sin so that we could be free. Psalm 49:15; Matthew 20:28; 1 Timothy 2:6

reap - To collect; to bring in a harvest. If you plant seeds of unhappiness, you will **reap** trouble. Job 4:8; 2 Corinthians 9:6; Galatians 6:7

rebuke - To correct, to criticize; to speak sharply to someone doing wrong. Paul cared about his Christian friends, so he chose to **rebuke** them for their ungodly talk. Proverbs 27:5; Luke 17:3; Titus 2:15

reconcile, reconciliation - To bring back together, to become friends again; the fixing of a relationship. Jesus made a way for us to **reconcile** with God. He commands us to tell others that **reconciliation** with God is possible. Romans 5:11; 2 Corinthians 5:18; Ephesians 2:16

redeem, redemption - To save, to rescue, especially through an exchange; the act of saving or rescuing. Jesus took our place so that he could **redeem** us and give us new life. Through **redemption** in Jesus, we are given eternal life. 2 Samuel 7:23; Luke 21:28; Colossians 1:14; Titus 2:14

remnant - A small part that is left. Many times, only a **remnant** of Israelites were faithful to God. Genesis 45:7; Ezra 9:15; Mic. 2:12

repent - To change; to turn away from sin. God tells us to **repent** so that our sins will be removed. Job 42:6; Matthew 3:2; Acts 3:19; Acts 17:30

repentance - Change; a turning from sin. Godly sorrow brings about **repentance**, which leads to salvation. Luke 24:47; 2 Corinthians 7:10; 2 Peter 3:9

resurrection - Coming to life after being dead. Jesus' **resurrection** proves that he won the victory over death. John 11:25; Philippians 3:10; 1 Peter 1:3

revelation - The revealing or making known of truth. The book of **Revelation** reveals how God and his church will win the battle against evil. Romans 16:25; Revelation 1:1

revile - To speak against, with hatred. If your enemies **revile** you, remember that people also said terrible things to Jesus. Matthew 5:11

S

Sabbath - Day of rest; the seventh day of the week (Saturday). God rested from his work of creation on the seventh day. He told his people to make it a **Sabbath**, a holy day to rest and to worship. Exodus 20:8; Jeremiah 17:24; Matthew 12:8

sacred - Holy; blessed by God. The sanctuary was a **sacred** place, filled with God's Spirit. Acts 19:35; 2 Timothy 3:15

sacrifice - Something given up for someone else's benefit, usually as an act of worship. Jesus offered his own life as a **sacrifice** for us. Exodus 12:27; 1 Samuel 15:22; Hebrews 9:26

Sadducees - Jewish religious leaders who did not believe in resurrection. The **Sadducees** and Pharisees were enemies, but they both hated Jesus and tried to defeat him. Matthew 16:6; Matthew 22:23

saints - Believers, Christians. People who have been sanctified by God. **Saints** are not perfect people. They are people who believe in a perfect God. Psalm 97:10; Acts 9:13; Colossians 1:26

salvation - Deliverance from the power of sin and death. God's free gift of eternal life through faith in Jesus Christ. **Salvation** comes to all who believe in Jesus. Exodus 15:2; Luke 19:9; Acts 4:12; Ephesians 1:13

Samaritans - People from Samaria, said to be a lower class in Bible times. The **Samaritans** were looked down on by the Jews and others. Luke 10:33; John 4:9; Acts 8:25

sanctify, sanctification - To make holy; the process of becoming holy. **Sanctification** takes a lifetime as God works in his children to make them more like Jesus. Leviticus 21:8; John 17:17; 2 Thessalonians 2:13

scribes - Jewish leaders who wrote and copied important documents, especially the Scriptures; another word for teacher of the law. Jesus told the **scribes** and Pharisees that they were hypocrites. Esther 3:12; Matthew 16:21; Matthew 23:2

Scripture, Scriptures - Written words of God. All **Scripture** is "breathed out," or inspired, by God. Matthew 26:54; Acts 17:11; 1 Corinthians 15:3; 2 Timothy 3:16

seal - A wax mark to make a paper official; God's "mark." God the Father set his **seal** on Jesus to show he truly is God the Son. 1 Kings 21:8; 2 Corinthians 1:22; Revelation 8:1

Sheol - Invisible world where the dead live. The Israelites believed that the soul went to **Sheol** after death. Genesis 37:35; Psalm 16:10; Isaiah 7:11

slander - To speak about another person in a bad way; talk that hurts another person's reputation. Even Christians can be tempted to **slander** others in their talk. Proverbs 10:18; 2 Corinthians 12:20; 1 Peter 2:1

slothful - Lazy. Do not be **slothful** and sleep. Do your share of the work. Proverbs 12:24; Matthew 25:26; Romans 12:11

sluggard - A lazy person. The **sluggard** finds ways to get out of doing chores. Proverbs 6:6; Proverbs 26:14

soul - A person's spiritual nature, which lives forever. God tells us to love him with all our heart and **soul**. Deuteronomy 6:5; Joshua 22:5; Psalm 23:3; Matthew 10:28

spiritual - Having to do with the spirit and soul. God gives his people **spiritual** gifts so that they can serve him and help each other. Romans 12:1; 1 Corinthians 12:1; 1 Peter 2:2

steadfast - Not changing, steady; loyal. The **steadfast** love of God will never fail you. Deuteronomy 5:10; Lamentations 3:22; James 1:12

stewards - Those who take care of something. Be good **stewards** of the gifts God has given you. 1 Corinthians 4:1; 1 Peter 4:10

subject - Under the authority or power of another. Be **subject** to each other, out of respect for God. Romans 13:1; 1 Peter 2:18

submit - To surrender; to commit oneself to another. Christians are to **submit** to God because he has the right to rule over us, and his ways are good and right. Romans 10:3; Ephesians 5:22; James 4:7

supplications - Prayers that ask for something. We make **supplications** to God when we want him to help someone. 1 Timothy 2:1; Hebrews 5:7

sustain - To keep someone or something whole or safe. The strength and love of God **sustain** us in difficult times. Psalm 55:22; 1 Corinthians 1:8

swaddling cloths - Strips of cloth wrapped around a newborn baby; some translations say **swaddling clothes**. The shepherds found baby Jesus wrapped in **swaddling cloths**. Ezekiel 16:4; Luke 2:7

synagogue - Building for Jewish worship and religious study; group of Jewish worshipers, congregation. Paul entered the **synagogue** and began to teach. Matthew 13:54; Luke 4:16; Acts 18:8

T

tabernacle - A movable, tent-like place of worship which the Jews later replaced with the temple. The priest entered the **tabernacle** to make an offering to God. Exodus 25:9; Leviticus 8:10; Numbers 1:50

talent - A unit of money in the ancient world; one **talent** was considered a huge sum of money. In the parable of the **talents**, a servant was given one **talent** to manage. Exodus 25:39; 1 Kings 20:39; Matthew 25:15

temple - A building for worship. The **temple** replaced the tabernacle after Israel became firmly established in the Promised Land. 2 Chronicles 2:1; Habakkuk 2:20; 1 Corinthians 6:19

tempt - To encourage a person to sin. Satan tries to **tempt** us to do wrong. 1 Corinthians 7:5

temptation - A strong feeling to do something wrong; any test or trial. **Temptation** comes to everyone, but giving in to it is wrong. Matthew 6:13; Matthew 26:41; 1 Corinthians 10:13

testimony - A message, with or without words, in support of something; telling the truth on behalf of someone else. We give **testimony** to the good news when we tell people who Jesus is and what he has done. Matthew 24:14; 2 Timothy 1:8; 1 John 5:11

tithe - An offering to God, originally one-tenth of something; to make an offering. We should offer up our **tithe** with thanks, for everything really belongs to God. Leviticus 27:32; Nehemiah 10:38; Luke 11:42

transgression - A wrongdoing or sin; something that breaks a rule or law. God will forgive the **transgression** of those who repent. Psalm 32:1; Isaiah 53:8; Galatians 6:1

trespass - Stepping over a boundary; a serious wrongdoing, sin. Because of Adam's **trespass** we all became sinners. 1 Samuel 25:28; Romans 5:15

tribe - Group of people who trace their roots to the same person. The sons of Jacob formed the twelve **tribes** of Israel. Numbers 1:4; 1 Samuel 10:20; Revelation 13:7

V

vain - With no godly purpose; producing nothing. God commanded that his name not be spoken in **vain**. Exodus 20:7; Isaiah 65:23; Philippians 2:16

vengeance - God's just punishment for a wrongdoing; doing harm to get even with someone. Let God worry about **vengeance** when someone hurts you. Leviticus 19:18; Isaiah 34:8; Hebrews 10:30

virgin - A person who has never had sex; one who is pure. Mary became pregnant with Jesus, even though she was a **virgin**, because God was his father, not Joseph. Isaiah 7:14; Luke 1:27; 2 Corinthians 11:2

vow - A promise given to God to serve him in some specific way. Hannah made a **vow** to God and would not break this promise. Genesis 28:20; 1 Samuel 1:11; Ecclesiastes 5:4; Acts 21:23

W

witness - A telling of what someone has seen. Everything in all creation bears **witness** that Jesus is the Christ. Exodus 20:16; Joshua 22:34; John 5:39

worship - To show praise, honor, and devotion to God; a ceremony of praise and honor. **Worship** the Lord, for he is holy and worth all your praise! 1 Chronicles 16:29; Daniel 3:28; John 4:24

Y

yoke - A wooden frame put on oxen and other animals so that they can work together to do heavy work; a burden put on someone. Jesus promises that his **yoke** is easy. 1 Kings 19:19; Matthew 11:29; 1 Timothy 6:1

Z

zeal - Great excitement and devotion; a strong feeling of eagerness to work for a special purpose. Saul had much **zeal** to persecute the first Christians; but as Paul, he became zealous for Jesus. Isaiah 9:7; John 2:17; Philippians 3:6

About the ESV

The Bible

The words of the Bible are the very words of God our Creator speaking to us. They are completely truthful;[1] they are pure;[2] they are powerful;[3] and they are wise and righteous.[4] We should read these words with reverence and awe,[5] and with joy and delight.[6] Through these words God gives us eternal life,[7] and daily nourishes our spiritual lives.[8]

The ESV Translation

The English Standard Version® (ESV®) stands in the classic stream of English Bible translations that goes back nearly five centuries. In this stream, accurate faithfulness to the original text is combined with simplicity, beauty, and dignity of expression. Our goal has been to carry forward this legacy for a new century.

The ESV is an "essentially literal" translation that seeks as far as possible to capture the meaning and structure of the original text and the personal style of each Bible writer. We have sought to be "as literal as possible" while maintaining clear expression and literary excellence. Therefore the ESV is well suited for both personal reading and church ministry, for devotional reflection and serious study, and for Scripture memorization.

The ESV Publishing Team

The ESV publishing team includes more than a hundred people. The fourteen-member Translation Oversight Committee has benefited from the work of fifty biblical experts serving as Translation Review Scholars and from the comments of the more than fifty members of the Advisory Council. This international team from many denominations shares a common commitment to the truth of God's Word and to historic Christian orthodoxy.

To God's Honor and Praise

We know that no Bible translation is perfect or final; but we also know that God uses imperfect and inadequate things to his honor and praise. So to God the Father, Son, and Holy Spirit—and to his people—we offer what we have done, with our prayers that it may prove useful, with gratitude for much help given, and with ongoing wonder that our God should ever have entrusted to us so momentous a task.

To God alone be the glory!

The Translation Oversight Committee*

*Adapted from the complete Preface of the ESV Bible for this edition of the *Seek and Find* Bible. A complete list of the Translation Oversight Committee, the Translation Review Scholars, and the Advisory Council, is available upon request from Crossway.

[1] Ps. 119:160; Prov. 30:5; Titus 1:2; Heb. 6:18 [2] Ps. 12:6 [3] Jer. 23:29; Heb. 4:12; 1 Pet. 1:23 [4] Ps. 19:7–11 [5] Deut. 28:58; Ps. 119:74; Isa. 66:2 [6] Ps. 19:7–11; 119:14, 97, 103; Jer. 15:16 [7] John 6:68; 1 Pet. 1:23 [8] Deut. 32:46; Matt. 4:4

Maps

The Lands of the Patriarchs

The Exodus from Egypt

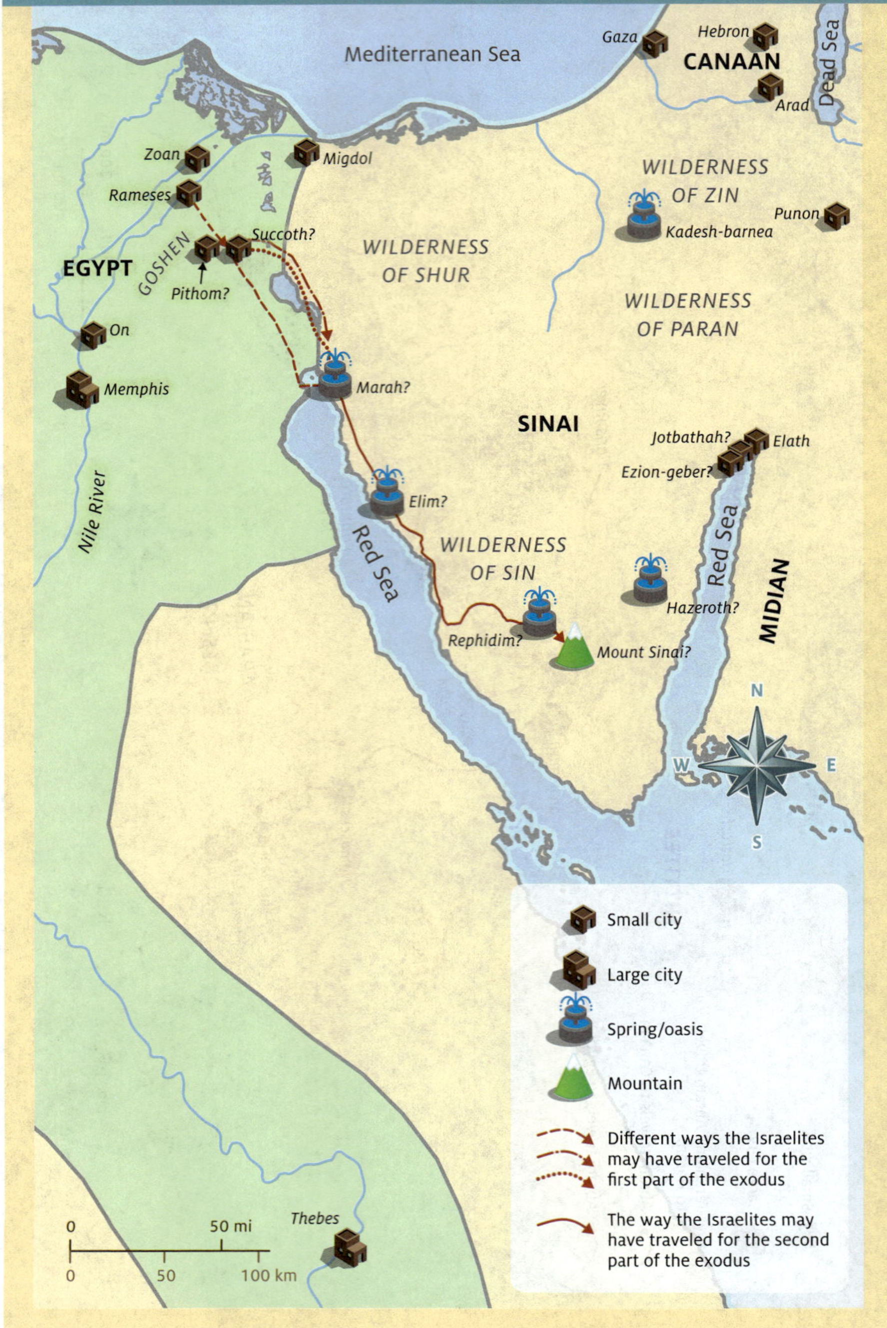

The Lands Assigned to the Tribes of Israel

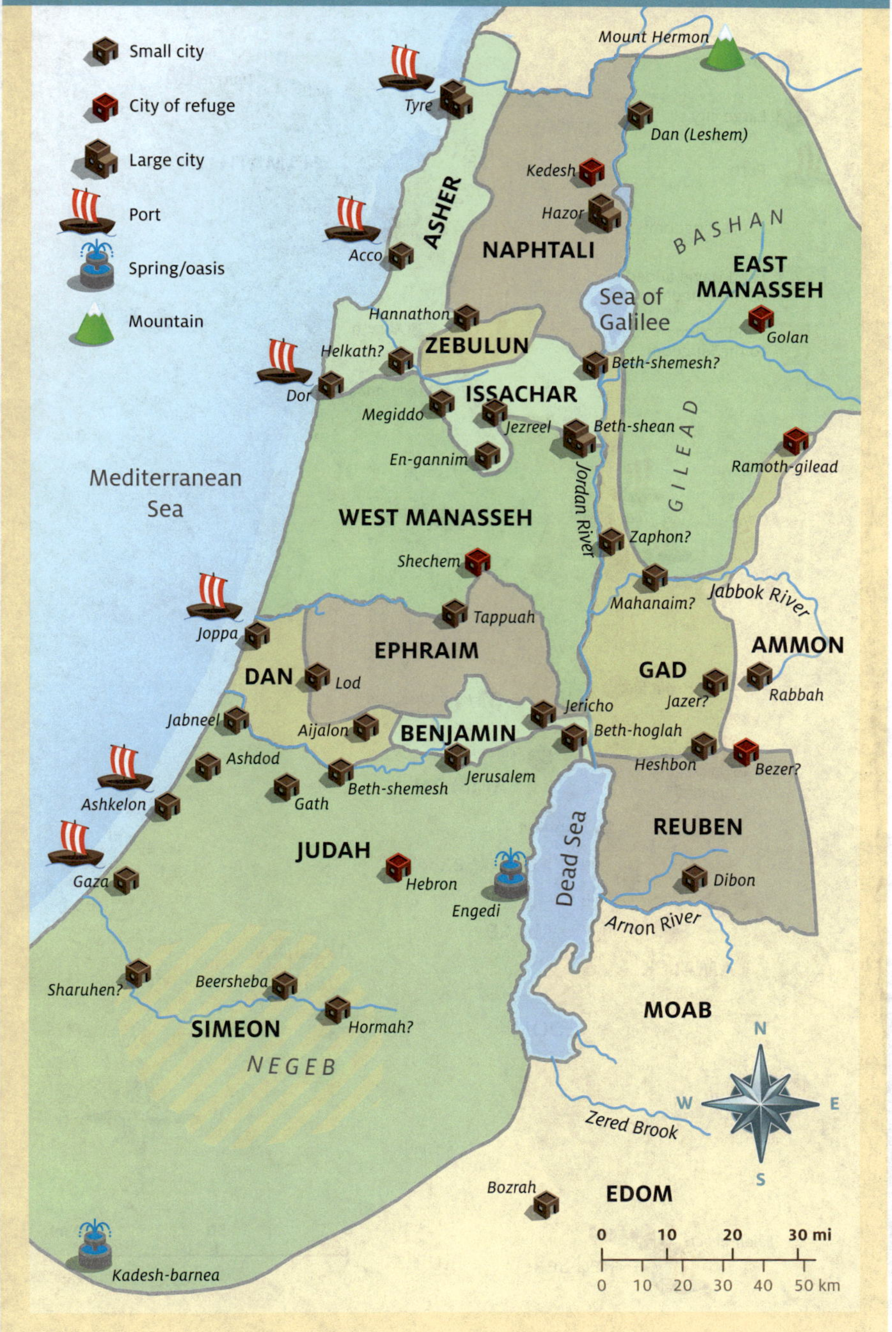

The Kingdom of Saul, David, and Solomon

The Divided Kingdom of Israel and Judah

The City of Jerusalem

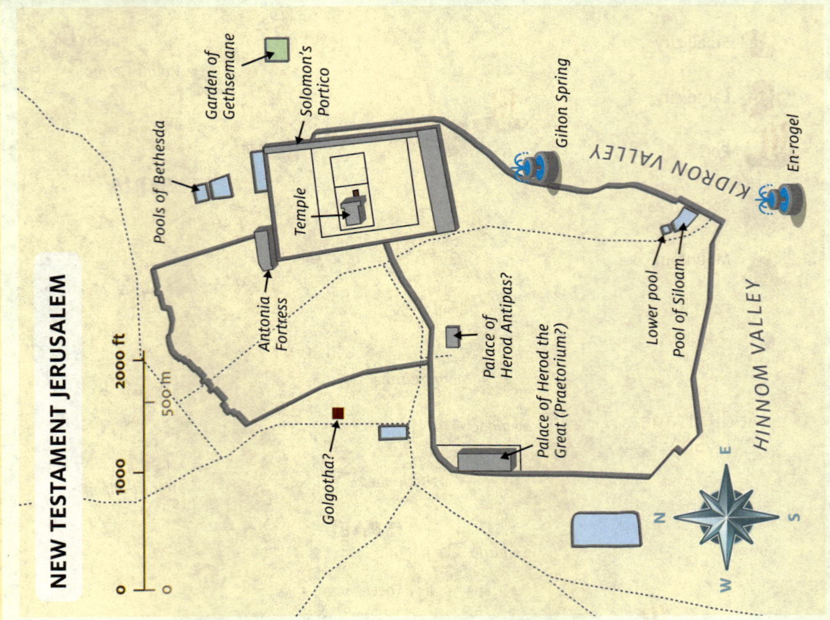

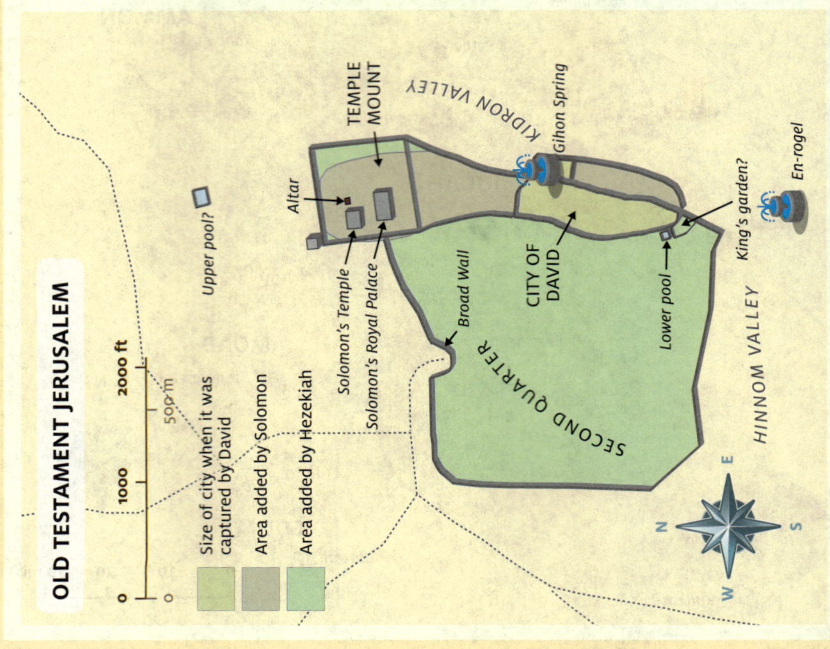

The Land of Israel during the New Testament

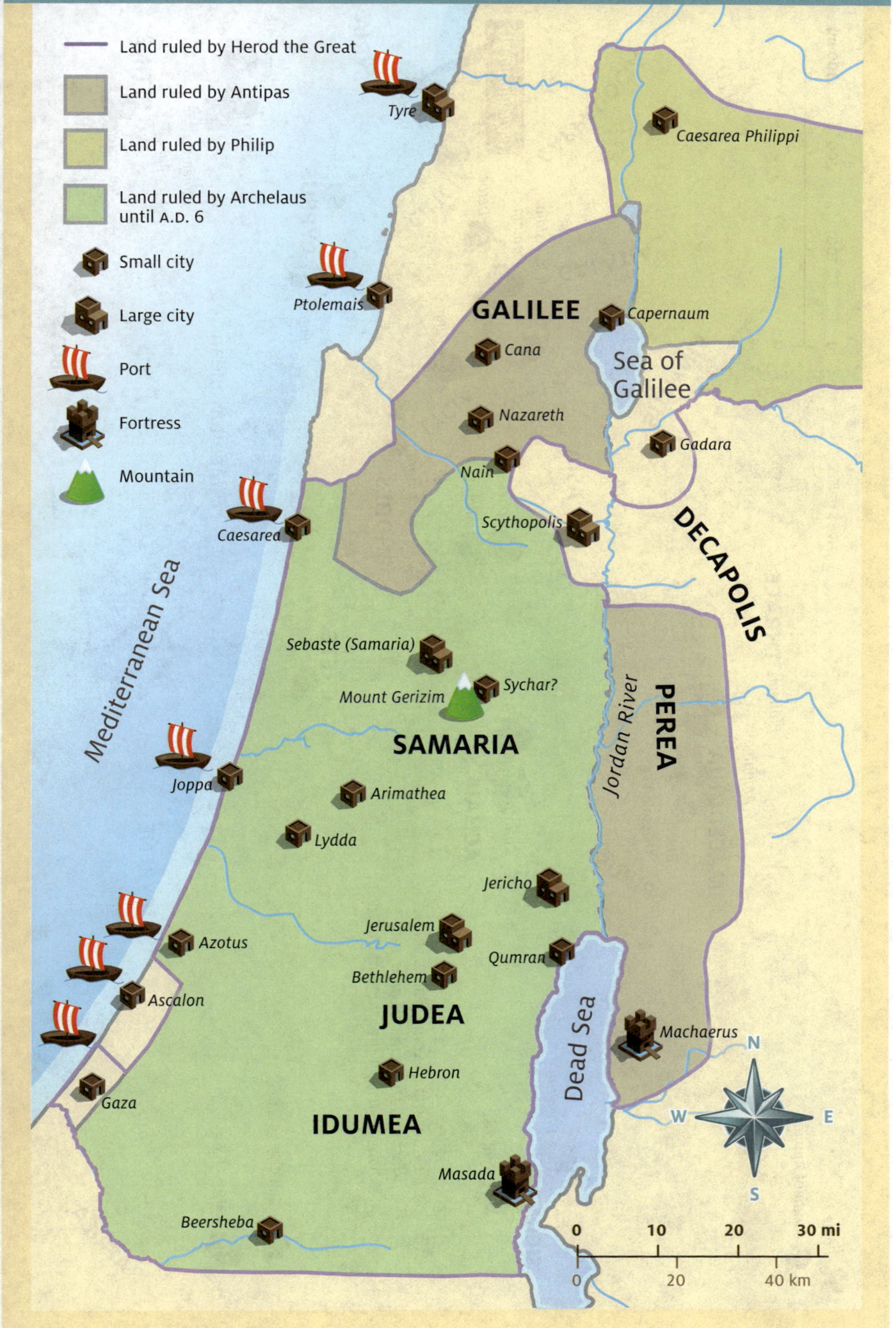

Places Paul Visited

Old Testament
CHRONOLOGY

Creation
Fall
Flood
Babel
Genesis 1–11

LINES TO TIME LINE DENOTE END OF JOURNEY OR REIGN

LINES DENOTE LAST YEAR OF REIGN OR LIFE, CO-REGENCIES AND SHORT REIGNS OMITTED.

(2300 BC – 1700 BC)

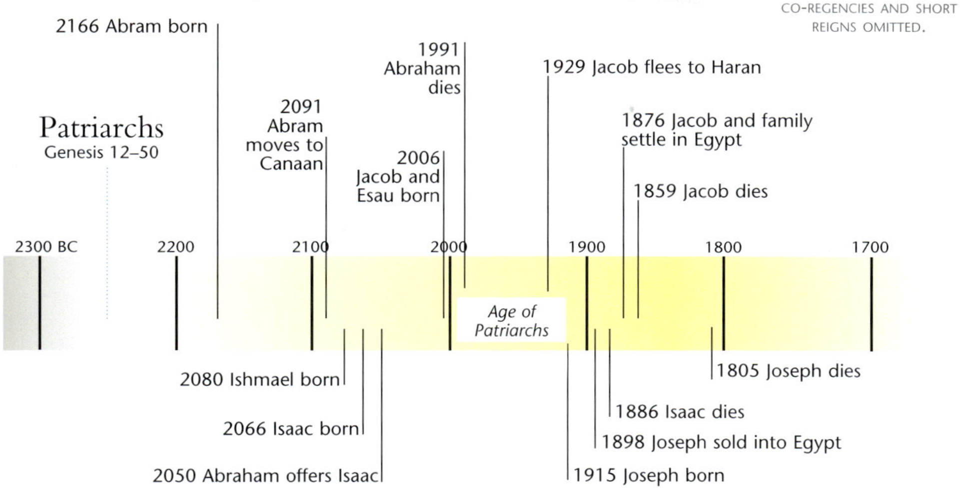

(1600 BC – 900 BC)

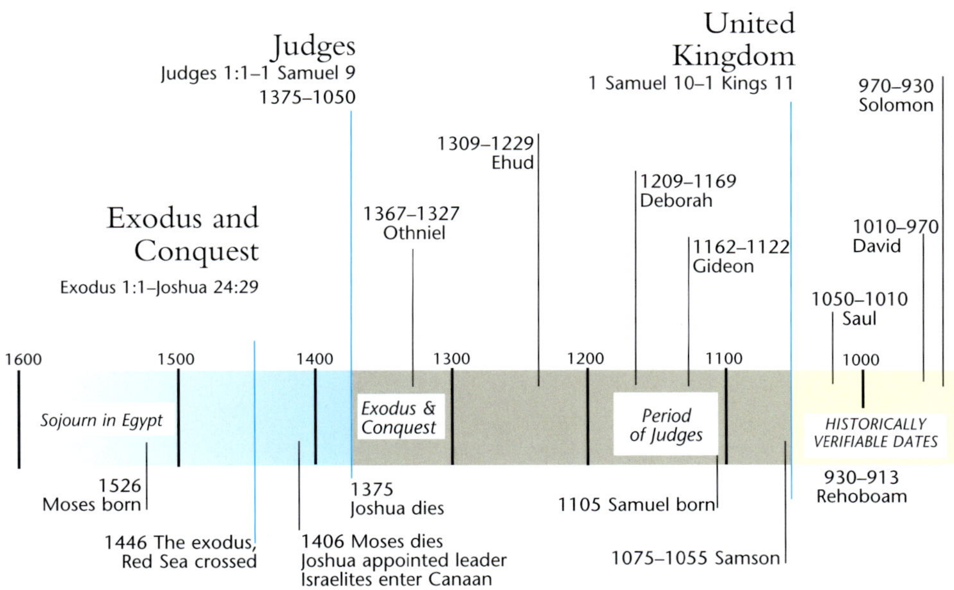

Old Testament
CHRONOLOGY

(900 BC – 400 BC)

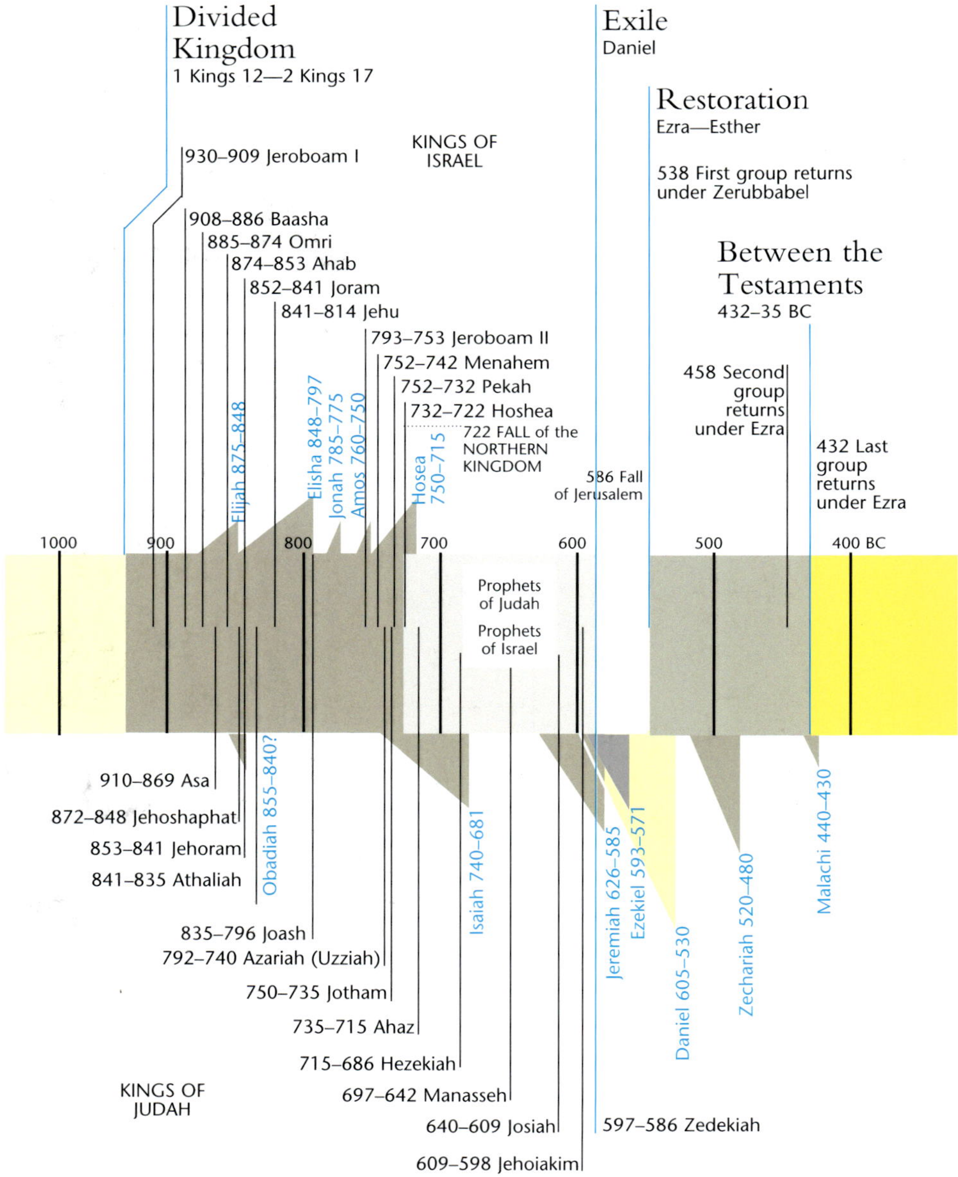

New Testament CHRONOLOGY

LINES TO TIME LINE DENOTE END OF JOURNEY OR REIGN

LINES DENOTE LAST YEAR OF REIGN OR LIFE, CO-REGENCIES AND SHORT REIGNS OMITTED.

(30 BC – AD 30)

Christ's Ministry
(Matthew 3–28; Mark; Luke 3–24; John)

30 Christ crucified
The ascension

29 Christ at Feast of Tabernacles
Christ at Feast of Dedication

28/29 John the Baptist dies

27/28 John the Baptist imprisoned

26 Christ baptized

26 Christ begins ministry

26 John the Baptist begins ministry

Christ's Early Life
(Matthew 1–2; Luke 1–2)

6/5 BC Christ born

AD 5 Christ in temple at age 12

30 BC — 20 — 10 — BC AD — 10 — 20 — 30

AD 6–15 Annas I

(AD 30 – AD 100)

The Early Church
(Acts–Revelation)

30 Christ crucified

The ascension

30 Pentecost

35 Paul converted to Christianity

44 James martyred

44 Peter imprisoned

46–48 Paul's first missionary journey

47–59 Ananias

49/50 Jerusalem Council

50–52 Paul's second missionary journey

51/52 1 & 2 Thessalonians written

53–57 Paul's third missionary journey

57 Romans written

59–61/62 Paul imprisoned in Rome

66/67 2 Timothy written

67/68 Paul dies

90–95 John exiled on Patmos

95 Revelation written

30 — 40 — 50 — 60 — 70 — 90 — AD 100

About the Commandments

Love the Lord your God with all your heart and with all your soul and with all your mind. (Matthew 22:37)

Call upon me in the day of trouble; I will deliver you, and you shall glorify me. (Psalm 50:15)

I was glad when they said to me, "Let us go to the house of the LORD!" (Psalm 122:1)

Blessed rather are those who hear the word of God and keep it. (Luke 11:28)

Let us consider how to stir up one another to love and good works, not neglecting to meet together, as is the habit of some, but encouraging one another, and all the more as you see the Day drawing near. (Hebrews 10:24–25)

Love your neighbor as yourself. (Matthew 22:39)

Blessed are the meek, for they shall inherit the earth. . . . Blessed are the merciful, for they shall receive mercy. . . . Blessed are the peacemakers, for they shall be called sons of God. (Matthew 5:5, 7, 9)

They are no longer two but one flesh. What therefore God has joined together, let not man separate. (Matthew 19:6)

I say to you: whoever divorces his wife, except for sexual immorality, and marries another, commits adultery. (Matthew 19:9)

So whatever you wish that others would do to you, do also to them, for this is the Law and the Prophets. (Matthew 7:12)

WORDS TO REMEMBER

Salvation Outline

The following seven points summarize basic information about the human condition and God's saving grace. Memorize these points so that you may share them with someone who does not yet believe in Jesus as his or her Savior.

The whole Bible is really about JESUS

"These are written so that you may believe that Jesus is the Christ, the Son of God, and that by believing you may have life in his name." (John 20:31)

1 GOD LOVES YOU! "For God so loved the world, that he gave his only Son, that whoever believes in him should not perish but have eternal life." (John 3:16)

2 You are a sinner. "For all have sinned and fall short of the glory of God." (Romans 3:23)

3 God punishes sin. "For the wages of sin is death, but the free gift of God is eternal life in Christ Jesus our Lord." (Romans 6:23)

4 Jesus took our punishment. He died for you. "But God shows his love for us in that while we were still sinners, Christ died for us." (Romans 5:8)

5 Jesus rose from the dead. "For I delivered to you as of first importance what I also received: that Christ died for our sins in accordance with the Scriptures, that he was buried, that he was raised on the third day in accordance with the Scriptures." (1 Corinthians 15:3–4)

6 Jesus offers forgiveness of sins and eternal life to those who believe in him. "Then he brought them out and said, 'Sirs, what must I do to be saved?' And they said, 'Believe in the Lord Jesus, and you will be saved, you and your household.'" (Acts 16:30–31)

7 Salvation is free—a gift from God. "For by grace you have been saved through faith. And this is not your own doing; it is the gift of God, not a result of works, so that no one may boast." (Ephesians 2:8–9)

HE IS True God

- Who has always been—John 1:1–3
- Who never changes—Hebrews 13:8
- Who has all power—Matthew 28:18
- Who knows all things—John 21:17
- Who is everywhere—Matthew 28:20

HE IS True Man

- Who became human flesh—John 1:14
- Who cried—John 11:35
- Who was hungry and tempted—Luke 4:1–13
- But who never sinned—Hebrews 4:15
- Who died—Mark 15:21–39

HE IS My Prophet

- Who is the Word of God—John 1:1, 14
- Who preached the Word—Matthew 5:1–7:29
- Who still preaches through those he has sent—Mark 16:15

HE IS My Priest

- Who kept the law for me—Galatians 4:4–5
- Who sacrificed himself—Hebrews 7:26–27
- Who prays for me—John 17:20–26

WHO *is* JESUS ?

AND WHAT HAS HE DONE FOR ME?

HE IS My King

- Who rules all things—1 Corinthians 15:25–27
- Who guards his people—Revelation 17:14
- Who will take me to heaven—John 14:1–3

HE IS My Savior

- Who saved me from sin, death, and the devil—Hebrews 2:14–15, 17
- Who bought me with his blood—1 Peter 1:18–19
- Who became poor to make me rich—2 Corinthians 8:9
- And the Savior of the World!—1 John 2:1–2

Which, after all,
is what it's all about!!!

The Six Chief Parts of Christian Doctrine as Derived from God's Word

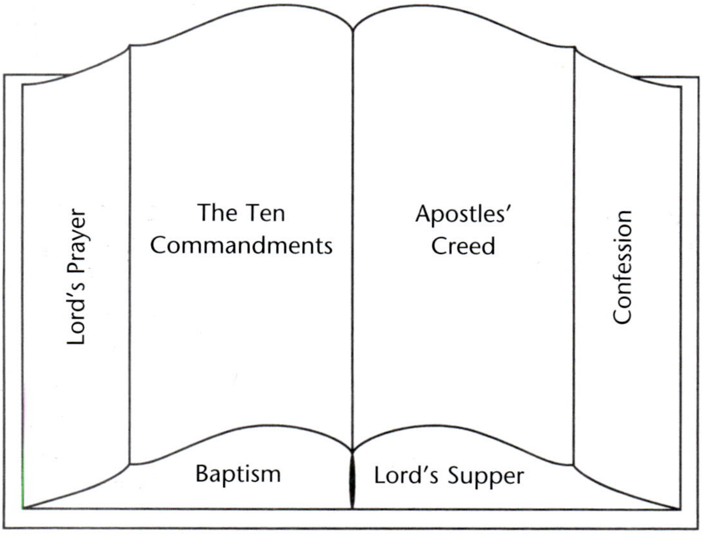

Ten Commandments
Apostles' Creed
Lord's Prayer

Baptism
Confession
Lord's Supper

The Six Chief parts of Christian doctrine may be taught and reviewed as a summary of what God's people believe and teach. These six chief parts were compiled by Martin Luther in 1529 in a catechism, a book of religious information organized in question-and- answer form. Dr. Luther organized the six chief parts in the catechism, "As the head of the family should teach them in a simple way to his household."

the TEN Commandments

If ever anything has been etched in stone, it's the Ten Commandments. After first writing them on human hearts, God then gave the commandments to Moses on two tablets of real stone. The Bible says God wrote them down with his own finger (Exodus 31:18)! Clearly, God is serious about these commandments! He expects us to keep them perfectly! And they haven't changed over all these thousands of years.

We often speak of the commandments as being "two tables." The first table, which includes the first three commandments, tells us how we are to love God. The second table, the last seven commandments, describes how we can love other people. In other words, all Ten Commandments really boil down to one word: love.

Think about each of these commandments. As Christians, we want to love God and other people (and remember, the commandments are etched in stone). But in truth, only one person has ever done that perfectly. After you've read through the commandments, read about him—and why he kept them—in 1 Timothy 1:12–17 and John 15:9–13.

You shall have no other gods before me.

I The one true God, the Father, Son, and Holy Spirit, is to be more important to us than anyone or anything else. We are to respect him, love him and count on him to provide everything we need. (Exodus 20:1–6)

You shall not take the name of the LORD your God in vain.

II Because we respect and love God, we are to speak his name only in prayer and in ways that worship and honor him, never carelessly, angrily, or dishonestly. We must also never play with activities like fortune-telling, séances, Ouija boards, and horoscopes. (Exodus 20:7)

Remember the Sabbath day, to keep it holy.

III Also because we respect and love God, we are always to be eager to hear and study his Word in church, at home, and wherever we have the chance. (Exodus 20:8–11)

Honor your father and your mother.

IV Our respect and love for God is now to move us to love other people: first of all, everyone placed over us. Parents, teachers, government leaders, and such are all representatives of God Himself. (Exodus 20:12)

You shall not murder.

V Of course, we must not kill, but we must also not hurt, hate, or be sinfully angry. We need to remember, too, that abortion and euthanasia and suicide are sins. (Exodus 20:13)

You shall not commit adultery.

VI Marriage can only be as wonderful as God intends if it is kept pure and lifelong. Therefore, sex is to be only between a husband and wife. (Exodus 20:14)

You shall not steal.

VII Not only are we never to take something that does not belong to us, we also are to share with others and actively help them get what they need. (Exodus 20:15)

You shall not bear false witness against your neighbor.

VIII Reputation is important! God asks us to speak up for everyone, especially when others gossip. We are always to speak the truth and assume the best. (Exodus 20:16)

You shall not covet your neighbor's house.

IX Coveting means being jealous of what others have instead of being happy for them and satisfied with what God has given us. (Exodus 20:17)

You shall not covet your neighbor's wife, or his male servant, or his female servant, or his ox, or his donkey, or anything that is to your neighbor's.

X Coveting is just a thought, but thoughts matter! Pure thoughts lead to loving actions; sinful thoughts lead to sins against all the other commandments. (Exodus 20:17)

Where did we get the Apostles' Creed?

Good question! And the answer may not be what you think. It's doubtful that Peter, James, John, and company sat down one day and wrote it. We really don't know who did. But from the very earliest years after Christ—even in New Testament times—Christians have expressed their faith in creeds (see Romans 10:9; 1 Corinthians 15:3–5).

Creeds help to summarize what we believe (and what the apostles themselves believed) and help us to share our faith. They also make clear what Christians do not believe.

There is a simple answer as to where we got the Apostles' Creed. It comes from the Bible! Every portion of the creed is drawn from the teachings of God's Word. As you learn the creed, you might want to read some of the passages in which God Himself teaches these truths.

	I believe in God	Romans 10:10
Malachi 2:10	**the Father Almighty**	Luke 1:37
	maker of heaven and earth	Genesis 1:1
	And in Jesus Christ, his only Son	Matthew 16:16
	our Lord	John 20:28
Matthew 1:20	**who was conceived by the Holy Spirit**	
	born of the virgin Mary	Luke 1:30–35
	suffered under Pontius Pilate	Matthew 27:11–31
	was crucified	John 19:6–30
Luke 23:44–49	**died and was buried**	Matthew 27:57–66
	He descended into hell	1 Peter 3:18–19
Matthew 28:1–10	**The third day he rose again from the dead**	
	He ascended into heaven	Luke 24:50–53
	And sits at the right hand	
	of God the Father Almighty	Ephesians 1:20–23
	From thence he will come	
	to judge the living and the dead	Matthew 25:31–32
	I believe in the Holy Spirit	John 14:26
1 Peter 2:4–10	the holy Christian church	
	the communion of saints	Ephesians 1:18
	the forgiveness of sins	2 Corinthians 5:19
	the resurrection of the body	1 Thessalonians 4:16
	and the life everlasting	Daniel 12:2–3

AMEN

What are we **really** saying in the Lord's Prayer

{ THE INTRODUCTION }

Our Father who art in heaven.

"You really want us to call you Father, don't you, God. You're just as eager to answer as my dad would be if he were perfect!" **(Romans 8:15–16)**

{ THE FIRST PETITION }

Hallowed be Thy name.

"Father, help us to keep your name holy in the pure preaching of your Word, and help us obey it, because we know it's your Word that proclaims your holy name." **(Romans 10:1–15)**

{ THE SECOND PETITION }

Thy kingdom come.

"Since we come into your kingdom, Father, by believing in Jesus, send the Holy Spirit so people will believe the Word when it's preached to them." **(Mark 1:14–15)**

{ THE THIRD PETITION }

Thy will be done
on earth as it is in heaven.

"O God, do everything you want to do—like having your Word preached and believed—even though sin and the devil oppose it." **(Romans 8:28–39)**

{ THE FOURTH PETITION }

Give us this day
our daily bread.

"Father, please give us not just bread, but every earthly thing we need." **(Psalm 145:15–16)**

{ THE FIFTH PETITION }

And forgive us our trespasses,
as we forgive those who
trespass against us.

"Forgive us, God, and help us forgive others. It's your gracious love that has brought us the forgiveness Jesus earned, and it's your power that moves us gladly and sincerely to forgive others." **(Psalm 32:1–7)**

{ THE SIXTH PETITION }

And lead us not
into temptation.

"And keep us from losing our faith when the devil and his allies tempt us." **(Ephesians 6:10–18)**

{ THE SEVENTH PETITION }

But deliver us from evil.

"Above all, Father, protect us from everything bad in this life, and then someday take us to heaven—the best deliverance of all!" **(2 Timothy 4:18)**

{ THE CONCLUSION }

For thine is the kingdom
and the power and the glory
forever and ever. Amen.

"Amen means 'truly it will be!' And we know our prayer truly will be answered, Father, because you want us to pray these things and you've got the power to make them happen!" **(Ephesians 3:20–21)**

Baptism

Who instituted Holy Baptism? Who is to be baptized? In whose name are the waters of Baptism to be applied?

- Jesus came and said to them, "All authority in heaven and on earth has been given to me. Go therefore and make disciples of all nations, baptizing them in the name of the Father and of the Son and of the Holy Spirit, teaching them to observe all that I have commanded you." (Matthew 28:19–20)

What does God give us in Baptism?

- Repent and be baptized every one of you in the name of Jesus Christ for the forgiveness of your sins, and you will receive the gift of the Holy Spirit. For the promise is for you and for your children. (Acts 2:38–39)

- Do you not know that all of us who have been baptized into Christ Jesus were baptized into his death? We were buried therefore with him by baptism into death, in order that, just as Christ was raised from the dead by the glory of the Father, we too might walk in newness of life. For if we have been united with him in a death like his, we shall certainly be united with him in a resurrection like his. (Romans 6:3–5)

- In Christ Jesus you are all sons of God, through faith. For as many of you as were baptized into Christ have put on Christ. (Galatians 3:26–27)

- He saved us, not because of works done by us in righteousness, but according to his own mercy, by the washing of regeneration and renewal of the Holy Spirit, whom he poured out on us richly through Jesus Christ our Savior, so that being justified by his grace we might become heirs according to the hope of eternal life. (Titus 3:5–7)

Confession

The Bible teaches that confession has two parts: Confession . . .

- Whoever conceals his transgressions will not prosper, but he who confesses and forsakes them will obtain mercy. (Proverbs 28:13)
- I acknowledged my sin to you, and I did not cover my iniquity; I said, "I will confess my transgressions to the LORD," and you forgave the iniquity of my sin. (Psalm 32:5)
- If we say we have no sin, we deceive ourselves, and the truth is not in us. If we confess our sins, he is faithful and just to forgive us our sins and to cleanse us from all unrighteousness. (1 John 1:8–9).

. . . and Absolution

- If you forgive the sins of any, they are forgiven them. (John 20:23)
- Come now, let us reason together, says the LORD: though your sins are like scarlet, they shall be as white as snow; though they are red like crimson, they shall become like wool. (Isaiah 1:18)
- As far as the east is from the west, so far does he remove our transgressions from us. (Psalm 103:12)
- Repent therefore, and turn again, that your sins may be blotted out, that times of refreshing may come from the presence of the Lord. (Acts 3:19–20)

What is the special authority Christ has given his church on earth called the Office of the Keys?

- [Jesus] breathed on them and said to them, "Receive the Holy Spirit. If you forgive the sins of any, they are forgiven them; if you withhold forgiveness from any, it is withheld." (John 20:22–23)
- Truly, I say to you, whatever you bind on earth shall be bound in heaven, and whatever you loose on earth shall be loosed in heaven. (Matthew 18:18)
- I will give you the keys of the kingdom of heaven. (Matthew 16:19)
- What I have forgiven . . . has been for your sake in the presence of Christ. (2 Corinthians 2:10)
- If he refuses to listen to them, tell it to the church. And if he refuses to listen even to the church, let him be to you as a Gentile and a tax collector. (Matthew 18:17)

Who instituted the Sacrament of the Altar (the Lord's Supper)?

- For I received from the Lord what I also delivered to you, that the Lord Jesus on the night when he was betrayed took bread, and when he had given thanks, he broke it, and said, "This is my body which is for you. Do this in remembrance of me." (1 Corinthians 11:23–24)

What does God's Word teach about the bread and wine received at the Lord's Table?

- The cup of blessing that we bless, is it not a participation in the blood of Christ? The bread that we break, is it not a participation in the body of Christ? (1 Corinthians 10:16)

What did Jesus mean when he said, "This do in remembrance of me"?

- For as often as you eat this bread and drink the cup, you proclaim the Lord's death until he comes. (1 Corinthians 11:26)

What blessings does God give us through this Sacrament?

- This is my blood of the covenant, which is poured out for many for the forgiveness of sins. (Matthew 26:28)
- The blood of Jesus his Son cleanses us from all sin. (1 John 1:7)
- He has now reconciled in his body of flesh by his death, in order to present you holy and blameless and above reproach before him. (Colossians 1:22)
- If Christ is in you, although the body is dead because of sin, the Spirit is life because of righteousness. (Romans 8:10)
- Because there is one bread, we who are many are one body, for we all partake of the one bread. (1 Corinthians 10:17)

the Lord's Supper

The Pericopes and the Church Year

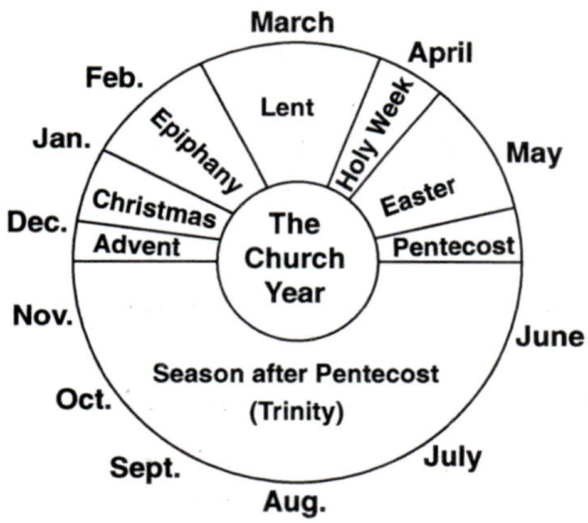

Many churches follow the same schedule of Scripture readings throughout the Church Year. We call these Scripture readings "pericopes" (puh-RIH-kuh-peez). The pericopes follow the Church Year calendar, and the chosen Scriptures provide focus for each festival and season. You will find a list of the pericopes in your hymnal.

God's people use the Church Year calendar to help them in their worship life. The Church Year calendar has two halves. The festival half extends from Advent through the Day of Pentecost, and the non-festival half extends from Trinity Sunday through the Last Sunday of the Church Year. In all, there are six seasons of the Church Year: Advent, Christmas, Epiphany, Lent, Easter, and the Season after Pentecost.

Martin Luther's Seal

Martin Luther designed the following seal to summarize his Christian faith.

The black cross in the center reminds us of our sins, for which Jesus took our place to die upon a cruel wooden cross. The red heart reminds us of the love God has for us in sending Jesus to be our Savior. The red of the heart is the color of the blood of Christ, shed for us and for our salvation. The white rose helps us remember the work of the Holy Spirit who makes us pure and holy in God's sight by bringing us to faith in Jesus and by helping us to live our lives for him. The sky blue background pictures the joy of the new life God gives to all who believe and trust in him. Finally, the golden ring outlining the seal reminds us of our eternal inheritance—a home in heaven where we will enjoy complete joy and happiness in our Savior's presence.